Next Time
DiYanni setting (66)
"Shiloh" 68-M.7

Literature
Reading Fiction, Poetry, Drama, and the Essay

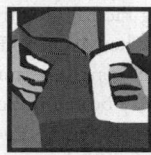

FOURTH EDITION

Robert DiYanni
Pace University, Pleasantville

McGraw Hill

Boston, Massachusetts   Burr Ridge, Illinois   Dubuque, Iowa
Madison, Wisconsin   New York, New York   San Francisco, California
St. Louis, Missouri

McGraw-Hill

A Division of The McGraw·Hill Companies

Acknowledgments appear beginning on page 2005, and on this page by reference.

1 2 3 4 5 6 7 8 9 0 KPH KPH 2 0 1 0 9 9 8 7

ISBN 0-07-017037-1

This book was set in Bembo by ComCom, Inc.
The editors were Sarah Moyers, Laura Lynch, and David A. Damstra.
The production supervisor was Elizabeth J. Strange.
The photo editor/photo researcher was Elsa Peterson.
The cover was designed by Christopher Brady.
Quebecor-Hawkins Company was printer and binder.

Cover painting: Margaret Peterson, *Three Women,* 1938. Egg tempera on wood.
The Oakland Museum of California, gift of friends of the artist.

Library of Congress Cataloging-in-Publication Data

DiYanni, Robert.
Literature : reading fiction, poetry, drama, and the essay / Robert DiYanni. — 4th ed.
   p.   cm.
   Includes index.
ISBN 0-07-017037-1 (cloth)
1. Literature. 2. Literature—Collections. I. Title.
PN49.D52   1997
808—dc21   96-54711

http://www.mhhe.com

About the Author

Robert DiYanni is Professor of English at Pace University, Pleasantville, New York, where he teaches courses in literature, writing, and humanities. He has also taught at Queens College of the City University of New York, at New York University in the Graduate Rhetoric Program, and most recently in the Expository Writing Program at Harvard University. He received his B.A. from Rutgers University (1968) and his Ph.D. from the City University of New York (1976).

Professor DiYanni has written articles and reviews on various aspects of literature, composition, and pedagogy. His books include *The McGraw-Hill Book of Poetry; Women's Voices; Like Season'd Timber: New Essays on George Herbert;* and *Modern American Poets: Their Voices and Visions* (a text to accompany the Public Broadcasting Television series that aired in 1988). With Kraft Rompf, he edited *The McGraw-Hill Book of Poetry,* (1993) and *The McGraw-Hill Book of Fiction* (1995).

For Mary
now and always

Brief Contents

PREFACE   xxix
*INTRODUCTION Reading (and Writing About)
Literature   1

PART ONE   FICTION   25

1. **Reading Stories**   27
2. **Types of Short Fiction**   43
3. **The Elements of Fiction**   49
4. **Approaching a Story: Guides for Reading and Writing**   109
*5. **Writing About Fiction**   118
*6. **Two Fiction Writers in Context**   130
7. **The Short Novel**   214
8. **A Collection of Short Fiction**   272

PART TWO   POETRY   459

9. **Reading Poems**   461
10. **Types of Poetry**   475
11. **Elements of Poetry**   479

*Chapters new to this edition

12. Approaching a Poem: Guides for Reading
    and Writing   554
13. Transformations   561
★14. Writing About Poetry   617
★15. Two Poets in Context   629
16. A Collection of Poems   682

PART THREE   DRAMA   813

17. Reading Plays   815
18. Types of Drama   837
19. Elements of Drama   841
20. Approaching a Play: Guides for Reading
    and Writing   849
★21. Writing About Drama   863
22. The Greek Theater: Sophocles in Context   877
23. The Elizabethan Theater: Shakespeare in
    Context   982
24. The Neoclassical French Theater: Molière   1182
25. The Modern Realistic Theater: Ibsen   1238
26. The Theater of the Absurd: Ionesco   1338
27. A Collection of Twentieth-Century Plays   1363
28. A Collection of Contemporary Drama   1522

PART FOUR   THE ESSAY   1709

29. Reading Essays   1711
30. Types of Essays   1735
31. Elements of the Essay   1738
32. Approaching an Essay: Guides to Reading and
    Writing   1755
★33. Writing About Essays   1764
★34. Two Essayists in Context   1784
35. A Collection of Essays   1817

PART FIVE   CRITICAL PERSPECTIVES AND
           RESEARCH   1883

★36. Critical Theory: Approaches to Literary Analysis
    and Interpretation   1885
★37. Writing with Sources   1927
38. Critical Comments About Literature   1958

★Chapters new to this edition

Contents

BRIEF TABLE OF CONTENTS   ix
PREFACE   xxix

INTRODUCTION   READING (AND WRITING ABOUT) LITERATURE   1

Reading Literature   2
  The Pleasures of Reading Literature   2
  The Pleasures of Fiction   2
  The Pleasures of Poetry   3
  The Pleasures of Drama   5
  The Pleasures of the Essay   7
  Considering Values   9
Writing About Literature   11
  Reasons for Writing About Literature   11
  Ways of Writing About Literature   11
Writing the Paper   15

PART ONE   FICTION   25

CHAPTER ONE   *Reading Stories*   27
   Luke *The Prodigal Son*   27
   The Experience of Fiction   28
   The Interpretation of Fiction   29
   The Evaluation of Fiction   31
   John Updike *A&P*   33
   The Act of Reading Fiction   38
   Kate Chopin *The Story of an Hour*   38

CHAPTER TWO   *Types of Short Fiction*   43
   Early Forms: Parable, Fable, and Tale   43
   Aesop *The Wolf and the Mastiff*   44
   Petronius *The Widow of Ephesus*   45
   The Short Story   47
   The Nonrealistic Story   48

CHAPTER THREE   *The Elements of Fiction*   49
   Plot and Structure   49
   Frank O'Connor *Guests of the Nation*   52
   Character   60
   Kay Boyle *Astronomer's Wife*   62
   Setting   66
   Bobbie Ann Mason *Shiloh*   68
   Point of View   77
   William Faulkner *A Rose for Emily*   80
   Language and Style   86
   James Joyce *Araby*   88
   Theme   92
   Eudora Welty *A Worn Path*   93
   Irony and Symbol   99
   Edgar Allan Poe *The Black Cat*   102

CHAPTER FOUR   *Approaching a Story: Guides for Reading and Writing*   109
   Guidelines for Reading   109
   Luigi Pirandello *War*   110
   Suggestions for Writing   115

CHAPTER FIVE   *Writing About Fiction*   118
   Reasons for Writing About Fiction   118
   Informal Ways of Writing About Fiction   118
   Katherine Anne Porter *Magic*   119
   Formal Ways of Writing About Fiction   123

Student Papers on Fiction 124
Questions for Writing About Fiction 128

CHAPTER **Two Fiction Writers in Context** 130
SIX **Reading D. H. Lawrence and Flannery
O'Connor in Depth** 130
Questions for In-Depth Reading 131
Introduction to D. H. Lawrence 132
Critical Comments by Lawrence 134
Critics on Lawrence 135
D. H. Lawrence: Stories 139
The Blind Man 139
The Horse Dealer's Daughter 151
The Rocking-Horse Winner 162
Introduction to Flannery O'Connor 172
Critical Comments by O'Connor 175
Critics on O'Connor 177
Flannery O'Connor: Stories 180
Good Country People 180
A Good Man Is Hard to Find 193
Everything That Rises Must Converge 203

CHAPTER **The Short Novel** 214
SEVEN Franz Kafka *The Metamorphosis* 215
James Joyce *The Dead* 245

CHAPTER **A Collection of Short Fiction** 272
EIGHT Nathaniel Hawthorne *Young Goodman Brown* 272
Anton Chekhov *The Lady with the Dog*
TRANSLATED BY CONSTANCE GARNETT 281
Charlotte Perkins Gilman *The Yellow Wallpaper* 291
Stephen Crane *The Open Boat* 302
James Joyce *The Boarding House* 318
Katherine Mansfield *Bliss* 322
Katherine Anne Porter *The Jilting of Granny Weatherall* 331
Ernest Hemingway *The Short Happy Life of Francis Macomber* 337
Jorge Luis Borges *The Garden of Forking Paths*
TRANSLATED BY DONALD YATES 357
Isaac Bashevis Singer *Gimpel the Fool*
TRANSLATED BY SAUL BELLOW 363
Tillie Olsen *I Stand Here Ironing* 373
Ralph Ellison *Battle Royal* 378
Gabriel Garcia Marquez *A Very Old Man with Enormous
Wings*
TRANSLATED BY GREGORY RABASSA 388

Margaret Atwood *Rape Fantasies*   392
Raymond Carver *Cathedral*   398
Alice Walker *Everyday Use*   408
Lee K. Abbott *The View of Me from Mars*   414
Tim O'Brien *The Things They Carried*   418
Jamaica Kincaid *Girl*   430
Leslie Marmon Silko *Yellow Woman*   431
Amy Tan *Rules of the Game*   438
Louise Erdrich *American Horse*   445
Mary Hood *How Far She Went*   453

PART TWO   POETRY   459

CHAPTER NINE **Reading Poems**   461
The Experience of Poetry   462
Robert Hayden *Those Winter Sundays*   462
The Interpretation of Poetry   464
Robert Frost *Stopping by Woods on a Snowy Evening*   466
The Evaluation of Poetry   468
Adrienne Rich *Aunt Jennifer's Tigers*   471
The Act of Reading Poetry   472
Theodore Roethke *My Papa's Waltz*   473

CHAPTER TEN **Types of Poetry**   475
Narrative Poetry   475
Lyric Poetry   477

CHAPTER ELEVEN **Elements of Poetry**   479
Voice: Speaker and Tone   479
Stephen Crane *War Is Kind*   480
Robert Browning *My Last Duchess*   481
Muriel Stuart *In the Orchard*   484
Gerard Manley Hopkins *Thou art indeed just, Lord*   485
Anonymous *Western Wind*   486
Henry Reed *Naming of Parts*   486
Jacques Prévert *Family Portrait*   487
Diction   488
William Wordsworth *I wandered lonely as a cloud*   490
Edwin Arlington Robinson *Miniver Cheevy*   492
William Wordsworth *It is a beauteous evening*   493
Robert Herrick *Delight in Disorder*   494
Adrienne Rich *Rape*   495
Imagery   496

Elizabeth Bishop *First Death in Nova Scotia*   497
William Butler Yeats *The Lake Isle of Innisfree*   499
Robert Browning *Meeting at Night*   500
H. D. (Hilda Doolittle) *Heat*   501
Thomas Hardy *Neutral Tones*   501

Figures of Speech: Simile and Metaphor   502
William Shakespeare *That time of year thou may'st in me
    behold*   503
John Donne *Hymn to God the Father*   505
Robert Wallace *The Double-Play*   506
Louis Simpson *The Battle*   507
Judith Wright *Woman to Child*   508

Symbolism and Allegory   509
Peter Meinke *Advice to My Son*   510
Christina Rossetti *Up-Hill*   511
William Blake *A Poison Tree*   512
Robert Frost *The Road Not Taken*   513
George Herbert *Virtue*   514
Emily Dickinson *Because I could not stop for Death*   515

Syntax   516
John Donne *The Sun Rising*   517
Thomas Hardy *The Man He Killed*   519
William Butler Yeats *An Irish Airman Foresees His Death*   520
Robert Frost *The Silken Tent*   521
E. E. Cummings *"Me up at does"*   522
Stevie Smith *Mother Among the Dustbins*   522

Sound: Rhyme, Alliteration, Assonance   523
Gerard Manley Hopkins *In the Valley of the Elwy*   526
Thomas Hardy *During Wind and Rain*   527
Alexander Pope *Sound and Sense*   528
Bob McKenty *Adam's Song*   529
May Swenson *The Universe*   530
Helen Chasin *The Word Plum*   531

Rhythm and Meter   531
Robert Frost *The Span of Life*   533
George Gordon, Lord Byron *The Destruction of Sennacherib*   538
Anne Sexton *Her Kind*   539
Richard Wilbur *Junk*   540
William Carlos Williams *The Red Wheelbarrow*   542

Structure: Closed Form and Open Form   542
John Keats *On First Looking into Chapman's Homer*   544
Walt Whitman *When I heard the learn'd astronomer*   545
E. E. Cummings *l(a*   546

E. E. Cummings *[Buffalo Bill's]*   547
William Carlos Williams *The Dance*   548
Denise Levertov *O Taste and See*   549
Theodore Roethke *The Waking*   550
C. P. Cavafy *The City*
  TRANSLATED BY EDMUND KEELEY AND PHILIP
    SHERRARD   551

CHAPTER   **Approaching a Poem: Guides for Reading and**
TWELVE   **Writing**   554
          Guidelines for Reading   554
          Gerard Manley Hopkins *Spring and Fall: To a Young Child*   555
          Suggestions for Writing   558

CHAPTER   **Transformations**   561
THIRTEEN **Revisions**   561
          William Blake *London*   562
          William Butler Yeats *A Dream of Death*   565
          Emily Dickinson *The Wind begun to knead the Grass*   566
          D. H. Lawrence *The Piano*   568
          Parodies   569
          William Carlos Williams *This Is Just to Say*   569
          Kenneth Koch *Variations on a Theme by William Carlos
            Williams*   570
          Gerard Manley Hopkins *Carrion Comfort*   571
          Gary Layne Hatch *Terrier Torment; or, Mr. Hopkins and His
            Dog*   571
          William Shakespeare *Shall I compare thee to a summer's day*   572
          Howard Moss *Shall I Compare Thee to a Summer's Day*   573
          Robert Frost *Dust of Snow*   573
          Bob McKenty   *Snow on Frost*   574
          Translations   574
          Rainer Maria Rilke *Der Panther [The Panther]*
            TRANSLATED BY STEPHEN MITCHELL AND C. F.
              MCINTYRE   575
          Guillaume Apollinaire *Le Pont Mirabeau [Mirabeau Bridge]*
            TRANSLATED BY RICHARD WILBUR AND W.S. MERWIN   576
          Juan Ramón Jiménez *Nocturno Soñado [Dream Nocturne]*
            TRANSLATED BY ELEANOR L. TURNBULL AND THOMAS
              MCGREEVY   579
          Poems and Paintings   580
          Vincent Van Gogh *Starry Night*   584
          Anne Sexton *The Starry Night*   585

Robert Fagles *The Starry Night* 586
Francesco de Goya *The Third of May, 1808* 586
David Gewanter *Goya's The Third of May, 1808* 586
Pieter Breughel the Elder *Landscape with the Fall of Icarus* 587
W. H. Auden *Musée des Beaux Arts* 587
Joseph Langland *Hunters in the Snow* 588
Pieter Breughel the Elder *Hunters in the Snow* 589
Edward Hopper *Sunday* 590
E. Ward Herlands *When Edward Hopper Was Painting* 590
William Blake *The Sick Rose* (watercolor) 591
William Blake *The Sick Rose* (poem) 591
Sandro Botticelli *Adoration of the Magi* 592
T. S. Eliot *Journey of the Magi* 592
Giotto di Bondone *Adoration of the Magi* 593
William Butler Yeats *The Magi* 593
Henri Matisse *Dance* 594
Natalie Safir *Matisse's Dance* 594
Pablo Picasso *Girl with a Mandolin* 595
Vinnie-Marie D'Ambrosio *If I Were a Maker I'd* 595
Pablo Picasso *Still Life with Pitcher, Bowl, & Fruit* 596
Gustav Klimt *The Kiss* 597
Lawrence Ferlinghetti *Short Story on a Painting of Gustav Klimt* 597

Adaptations (Poetry and Song) 600
Ecclesiastes *To Everything there is a Season* 600
Pete Seeger *Turn! Turn! Turn!* 600
Edwin Arlington Robinson *Richard Cory* 601
Paul Simon *Richard Cory* 602
Langston Hughes *Dream Deferred* 603
Langston Hughes *Same in Blues* 603
Woody Guthrie *This Land Is Your Land* 605
Don Maclean *Vincent* 606
John Lennon and Paul McCartney *Yesterday* 607
Lonnelle Johnson *No Mo' Blues* 608

Responses (Point-Counterpoint) 609
Christopher Marlowe *The Passionate Shepherd to His Love* 609
Sir Walter Raleigh *The Nymph's Reply to the Shepherd* 610
William Shakespeare *Not marble, nor the gilded monuments* 611
Archibald MacLeish *Not Marble Nor the Gilded Monuments* 612
Matthew Arnold *Dover Beach* 613
Anthony Hecht *The Dover Bitch: A Criticism of Life* 614
William Carlos Williams *Queen-Ann's-Lace* 615
Anne C. Coon *Queen-Ann's-Lace* 615

CHAPTER   *Writing About Poetry*   617
FOURTEEN **Reasons for Writing About Poetry**   617
          Informal Ways of Writing About Poetry   617
            Robert Hayden *Those Winter Sundays*   618
            Robert Graves *Symptoms of Love*   619
          Formal Ways of Writing About Poetry   620
          Student Papers on Poetry   622
          Questions for Writing About Poetry   627

CHAPTER   *Two Poets in Context*   629
FIFTEEN   **Reading Emily Dickinson and Robert Frost in
          Depth**   629
          Questions for In-Depth Reading   630
          Introduction to Emily Dickinson   631
            Emily Dickinson *I cannot dance upon my Toes*   633
            Emily Dickinson *The Soul selects her own Society*   634
          Emily Dickinson on Herself and Her First Poems   634
          Critics on Dickinson   635
          **Three Poems by Dickinson with Altered
          Punctuation**   640
          Emily Dickinson: Poems   641
            199 *I'm "wife"—I've finished that*   641
            214 *I taste a liquor never brewed*   642
            241 *I like a look of Agony*   642
            249 *Wild Nights—Wild Nights!*   643
            258 *There's a certain Slant of light*   643
            280 *I felt a Funeral, in my Brain*   644
            328 *Some keep the Sabbath going to Church*   644
            341 *After great pain, a formal feeling comes*   645
            348 *I dreaded that first Robin, so*   645
            419 *We grow accustomed to the Dark*   646
            435 *Much Madness is divinest Sense*   646
            449 *I died for Beauty—but was scarce*   647
            465 *I heard a Fly buzz—when I died*   647
            536 *The Heart asks Pleasure—first*   648
            585 *I like to see it lap the Miles*   648
            599 *There is a pain—so utter*   649
            650 *Pain—has an element of Blank*   649
            744 *Remorse—is Memory—awake*   649
            754 *My Life had stood—a Loaded Gun*   650
            986 *A narrow Fellow in the Grass*   650
            1068 *Further in Summer than the Birds*   651
            1078 *The Bustle in a House*   652
            1100 *The last Night that She lived*   652

1129 *Tell all the Truth but tell it slant*   653
1463 *A Route of Evanescence*   653
1624 *Apparently with no surprise*   653
1732 *My life closed twice before its close*   654
Introduction to Robert Frost   654
Critical Comments by Frost   658
Critics on Frost   661
Robert Frost: Poems   666
  Mowing   666
  The Tuft of Flowers   667
  Mending Wall   668
  Birches   669
  Home Burial   670
  Hyla Brook   673
  Putting in the Seed   674
  Fire and Ice   674
  For Once, Then, Something   675
  Two Look at Two   675
  Once by the Pacific   676
  Acquainted with the Night   677
  Tree at my Window   677
  Departmental   678
  Desert Places   679
  Design   679
  Provide, Provide   680
  The Most of It   680

CHAPTER *A Collection of Poems*   682
SIXTEEN Sappho *To me he seems like a god*   682
  Anonymous *Barbara Allan*   683
  Anonymous *Edward, Edward*   684
  Thomas Wyatt *They flee from me*   686
  Edmund Spenser *One day I wrote her name upon the strand*   687
  William Shakespeare *When in disgrace with fortune and men's eyes*   687
  William Shakespeare *Let me not to the marriage of true minds*   688
  William Shakespeare *Th' expense of spirit in a waste of shame*   688
  William Shakespeare *My mistress' eyes are nothing like the sun*   689
  John Donne *Song*   689
  John Donne *The Canonization*   690
  John Donne *A Valediction: Forbidding Mourning*   691
  John Donne *The Flea*   692
  John Donne *Death, be not proud*   693
  John Donne *Batter my heart, three-personed God*   694

Ben Jonson *On My First Son*   694

Ben Jonson *Song: To Celia*   695

Robert Herrick *Upon Julia's Clothes*   695

Robert Herrick *To the Virgins, to Make Much of Time*   696

George Herbert *The Altar*   696

John Milton *When I consider how my light is spent*   697

John Milton *On the Late Massacre in Piedmont*   697

Anne Bradstreet *To My Dear and Loving Husband*   698

Andrew Marvell *To His Coy Mistress*   698

Alexander Pope from *An Essay on Man*   700

William Blake *The Clod & the Pebble*   700

William Blake *The Lamb*   701

William Blake *The Tyger*   701

William Blake *The Garden of Love*   702

Robert Burns *A Red, Red Rose*   703

William Wordsworth *The world is too much with us*   703

William Wordsworth *The Solitary Reaper*   704

William Wordsworth *Composed upon Westminster Bridge,
    September 3, 1802*   705

William Wordsworth *Lines Composed a Few Miles Above Tintern
    Abbey*   705

Samuel Taylor Coleridge *Kubla Khan*   709

George Gordon, Lord Byron *She walks in beauty*   711

Percy Bysshe Shelley *Ozymandias*   711

Percy Bysshe Shelley *Ode to the West Wind*   712

John Keats *When I have fears that I may cease to be*   714

John Keats *La Belle Dame sans Merci*   715

John Keats *Ode to a Nightingale*   716

John Keats *Ode on a Grecian Urn*   719

Elizabeth Barrett Browning *How do I love thee?*   720

Edgar Allan Poe *To Helen*   721

Edgar Allen Poe *The Raven*   721

Alfred, Lord Tennyson *Ulysses*   724

Alfred, Lord Tennyson *The Eagle*   726

Robert Browning *Soliloquy of the Spanish Cloister*   726

Walt Whitman *A noiseless patient spider*   729

Walt Whitman *Crossing Brooklyn Ferry*   729

Lewis Carroll *Jabberwocky*   733

Thomas Hardy *The Ruined Maid*   734

Thomas Hardy *Channel Firing*   735

Thomas Hardy *Afterwards*   736

Gerard Manley Hopkins *God's Grandeur*   737

Gerard Manley Hopkins *The Windhover*   737

Gerard Manley Hopkins *Pied Beauty*   738

A. E. Housman *When I was one-and-twenty* 738
A. E. Housman *To an Athlete Dying Young* 739
William Butler Yeats *The Second Coming* 740
William Butler Yeats *The Wild Swans at Coole* 741
William Butler Yeats *Leda and the Swan* 741
William Butler Yeats *Sailing to Byzantium* 742
Paul Laurence Dunbar *We wear the mask* 743
Wallace Stevens *Thirteen Ways of Looking at a Blackbird* 744
William Carlos Williams *Spring and All* 746
William Carlos Williams *Dance Russe* 746
Ezra Pound *The River-Merchant's Wife: A Letter* 747
Marianne Moore *Poetry* 748
T. S. Eliot *The Love Song of J. Alfred Prufrock* 749
John Crowe Ransom *Piazza Piece* 753
Vicente Huidobro *Ars Poetica* 753
Archibald MacLeish *Ars Poetica* 754
Wilfred Owen *Dulce et Decorum Est* 755
E. E. Cummings *anyone lived in a pretty how town* 756
E. E. Cummings *i thank You God for this most amazing* 757
Jean Toomer *Reapers* 758
Countee Cullen *Incident* 758
Wislawa Szymborska *Nothing Twice* 759
Wislawa Szymborska *Cat in an Empty Apartment* 760
Pablo Neruda *The Word*
    TRANSLATED BY ALASTAIR REID 761
W. H. Auden *The Unknown Citizen* 763
W. H. Auden *In Memory of W. B. Yeats* 764
Theodore Roethke *Elegy for Jane* 766
Elizabeth Bishop *The Fish* 767
Elizabeth Bishop *Sestina* 768
May Swenson *Women* 770
William Stafford *Traveling Through the Dark* 771
Dylan Thomas *Fern Hill* 771
Dylan Thomas *Do not go gentle into that good night* 773
Gwendolyn Brooks *the mother* 774
Gwendolyn Brooks *First fight. Then fiddle* 775
Lawrence Ferlinghetti *Constantly Risking Absurdity* 775
Richard Wilbur *The Death of a Toad* 776
Philip Larkin *A Study of Reading Habits* 777
Rosario Castellanos *Chess*
    TRANSLATED BY MAUREEN AHERN 777
Galway Kinnell *Saint Francis and the Sow* 778
James Wright *Lying in a Hammock at William Duffy's Farm in Pine Island, Minnesota* 779

James Wright *A Blessing*   779
Anne Sexton *Two Hands*   780

A Selection of Contemporary Poetry   781
Donald Hall *My son, my executioner*   781
X. J. Kennedy *In a prominent bar in Secaucus one day*   781
Adrienne Rich *Diving into the Wreck*   783
Gregory Corso *Marriage*   785
Linda Pastan *Ethics*   788
Audre Lorde *Hanging Fire*   789
Lucille Clifton *Homage to My Hips*   790
Lucille Clifton *The Lost Baby Poem*   790
Marge Piercy *A Work of Artifice*   791
Marge Piercy *To Be of Use*   792
Bella Akhmadulina *The Bride*
    TRANSLATED BY STEPHAN STEPANCHEV   793
Margaret Atwood *This Is a Photograph of Me*   794
Raymond Carver *Photograph of My Father*   795
Seamus Heaney *Mid-Term Break*   795
Seamus Heaney *Digging*   796
Barbara Holder *Ballet Class at the Hotel Ansonia*   797
Robert Hass *Meditation at Lagunitas*   798
Nikki Giovanni *Ego Tripping*   799
Sharon Olds *Size and Sheer Will*   800
Tom Molito *Cosmic Simplicities*   801
Christopher Jane Corkery *Divorce*   801
Jane Kenyon *Otherwise*   803
Jane Kenyon *Notes from The Other Side*   803
Yusef Komunyakaa *Facing It*   804
Neal Bowers *Driving Lessons*   805
Kraft Rompf *Waiting Table*   806
Jimmy Santiago Baca from *Meditations on the South Valley
    XVII*   807
Rita Dove *Canary*   808
Judith Ortiz Cofer *The Idea of Islands*   809
Alberto Rios *A Dream of Husbands*   810
Gertrude Schnackenberg *Signs*   811
Gary Soto *Behind Grandma's House*   811
Louise Erdrich *Indian Boarding School: The Runaways*   812

PART THREE   DRAMA   813

CHAPTER   *Reading Plays*   815
SEVENTEEN   **The Experience of Drama**   815
Henrik Ibsen *A Doll House* (I,i)   816

The Interpretation of Drama 822
  Bernard Shaw *Arms and the Man* (scene II)   823
The Evaluation of Drama   827
  Sophocles *Antigonê* (scene II)   829
The Act of Reading Drama 834
  Isabella Augusta Persse, Lady Gregory *The Rising of
    the Moon* 834

CHAPTER   *Types of Drama* 837
EIGHTEEN   **Tragedy** 837
           Comedy 839
           Tragicomedy 840

CHAPTER   *Elements of Drama* 841
NINETEEN   **Plot** 841
           Character 843
           Dialogue 843
           Staging 846
           Theme 847

CHAPTER   *Approaching a Play: Guides for Reading and
TWENTY   Writing* 849
           Guidelines for Reading 849
             Isabella Augusta Persse, Lady Gregory *The Rising of the
               Moon* 850
           Suggestions for Writing 860

CHAPTER   *Writing About Drama* 863
TWENTY-   **Reasons for Writing About Drama** 863
   ONE   **Informal Ways of Writing About Drama** 863
           Formal Ways of Writing About Drama 867
           Student Papers on Drama 868
           Questions for Writing About Drama 874

CHAPTER   *The Greek Theater: Sophocles in Context* 877
TWENTY-   **Introduction to Sophocles** 880
   TWO   Sophocles *Oedipus Rex*
             TRANSLATED BY DUDLEY FITTS AND ROBERT
               FITZGERALD 880
           Sophocles *Antigonê*
             TRANSLATED BY DUDLEY FITTS AND ROBERT
               FITZGERALD 922
           Critics on Sophocles 952
           Works Inspired by Sophocles 961
             Muriel Rukeyser *Myth* 961

Ruth F. Eisenberg *Jocasta* 962
Ruth F. Eisenberg *Drafts of Part One of Jocasta* 970
Ruth F. Eisenberg *On Writing Jocasta* 972
William Butler Yeats *Purgatory* 976

CHAPTER   **The Elizabethan Theater: Shakespeare in Context** 982
TWENTY-   **Stagecraft in the Elizabethan Age** 983
THREE   **Introduction to Shakespeare** 983
              William Shakespeare *The Tragedy of Othello* 985
              William Shakespeare *Hamlet, Prince of Denmark* 1072
              Critics on Shakespeare 1174

CHAPTER   **The Neoclassical French Theater** 1182
TWENTY-   Molière (Jean-Baptiste Poquelin) *Tartuffe*
FOUR   TRANSLATED BY RICHARD WILBUR 1184

CHAPTER   **The Modern Realistic Theater** 1238
TWENTY-   Henrik Ibsen *A Doll House*
FIVE   TRANSLATED BY ROLF FJELDE 1239
              Bernard Shaw *Arms and the Man* 1292

CHAPTER   **The Theater of the Absurd** 1338
TWENTY-   Eugène Ionesco *The Lesson*
SIX   TRANSLATED BY DONALD M. ALLEN 1340

CHAPTER   **A Collection of Twentieth-Century Plays** 1363
TWENTY-   John Millington Synge *Riders to the Sea* 1364
SEVEN   Susan Glaspell *Trifles* 1373
              Arthur Miller *Death of a Salesman* 1385
              Lorraine Hansberry *A Raisin in the Sun* 1455

CHAPTER   **A Collection of Contemporary Drama** 1522
TWENTY-   Terence McNally *Andre's Mother* 1523
EIGHT   Tina Howe *Painting Churches* 1526
              August Wilson *Fences* 1570
              David Mamet *Oleanna* 1622
              Wendy Wasserstein *Tender Offer* 1652
              Martin Dockery *Oh, That Wily Snake!* 1658
              Josefina López *Simply María* 1685

              PART FOUR   THE ESSAY 1709

CHAPTER   **Reading Essays** 1711
TWENTY-   **The Experience of the Essay** 1711
NINE   Mark Twain from *"Cub" Wants to Be a Pilot* 1712

Loren Eiseley from *The Judgement of the Birds* 1712
Alice Walker from *In Search of Our Mothers' Gardens* 1714
E. B. White *The Ring of Time* 1715
The Interpretation of the Essay 1718
George Orwell *Marrakech* 1719
The Evaluation of the Essay 1725
Richard Selzer *The Masked Marvel's Last Toehold* 1727
The Act of Reading the Essay 1730
Gretel Ehrlich *About Men* 1731

CHAPTER **Types of Essay** 1735
THIRTY **Speculative Essays** 1735
Argumentative Essays 1736
Narrative Essays 1736
Expository Essays 1736

CHAPTER **Elements of the Essay** 1738
THIRTY- **Voice** 1738
ONE Joan Didion *Los Angeles Notebook* 1739
Style 1741
Henry David Thoreau *The Battle of the Ants* 1746
Structure 1748
Virginia Woolf *The Death of the Moth* 1749
Thought 1751
Francis Bacon *Of Revenge* 1753

CHAPTER **Approaching an Essay: Guides to Reading and**
THIRTY- **Writing** 1755
TWO **Guidelines for Reading** 1755
Annie Dillard *Living Like Weasels* 1756
Suggestions for Writing 1762

CHAPTER **Writing About Essays** 1764
THIRTY- **Reasons for Writing About Essays** 1764
THREE **Informal Ways of Writing About Essays** 1764
Formal Ways of Writing About Essays 1765
Writing to Interpret an Essay 1765
Zora Neale Hurston *How It Feels to Be Colored Me* 1766
Three Student Essays 1772
Questions for Writing About Essays 1783

CHAPTER **Two Essayists in Context** 1784
THIRTY- **Reading E. B. White and Maxine Hong Kingston in**
FOUR **Depth** 1784
Questions for In-Depth Reading 1785

Introduction to E. B. White 1786
White on Writing 1788
Critics on White 1789
E. B. White: Essays 1791
  Once More to the Lake 1791
  The Geese 1795
Introduction to Maxine Hong Kingston 1800
Kingston on Writing 1801
Critics on Kingston 1803
Maxine Hong Kingston: Prose 1805
  No Name Woman 1805
  Silence 1813
  On Discovery 1815

CHAPTER   *A Collection of Essays* 1817
THIRTY-   Michel de Montaigne *Of smells*
     FIVE   Translated by Donald Frame 1817
              Francis Bacon *Of Love* 1819
              John Donne *Meditation XVII: For Whom the Bell Tolls* 1820
              Jonathan Swift *A Modest Proposal* 1822
              Mark Twain *"Cub" Wants to Be a Pilot* 1827
              E. M. Forster *Our Graves in Gallipoli* 1832
              Virginia Woolf *Old Mrs. Grey* 1834
              George Orwell *Shooting an Elephant* 1835
              Loren Eiseley *The Judgment of the Birds* 1840
              James Baldwin *Notes of a Native Son* 1846
              A Sampling of Contemporary Essays 1859
              Tom Wolfe *The Right Stuff* 1859
              Alice Walker *In Search of Our Mothers' Gardens* 1869
              Bernard Cooper *Burl's* 1876

PART FIVE   CRITICAL PERSPECTIVES
                AND RESEARCH 1883

CHAPTER   *Critical Theory: Approaches to the Analysis and*
THIRTY-   *Interpretation of Literature* 1885
     SIX   **Readings for Analysis** 1886
              William Carlos Williams *The Use of Force* 1886
              Emily Dickinson *I'm 'wife'* 1888
              The Canon and the Curriculum 1889
              Formalist Perspectives 1893
              Biographical Perspectives 1896
              Historical Perspectives 1898

Psychological Perspectives 1901
Sociological Perspectives 1904
Reader-Response Perspectives 1909
Mythological Perspectives 1913
Structuralist Perspectives 1915
Deconstructive Perspectives 1919
Cultural Studies Perspectives 1922
Using Critical Perspectives as Heuristics 1924

CHAPTER **Writing with Sources** 1927
THIRTY- **Why Do Research About Literature** 1927
SEVEN **Clarifying the Assignment** 1928
Selecting a Topic 1928
Finding and Using Sources 1929
Using Computerized Databases 1930
Developing a Critical Perspectve 1931
Developing a Thesis 1932
Drafting and Revising 1933
Conventions 1934
Documenting Sources 1936
Three Student Essays Incorporating Research 1940
A Research Paper on a Single Work Using Multiple Sources 1945
A Research Paper Using Multiple Works and Multiple Sources 1951

CHAPTER **Critical Comments About Literature** 1958
THIRTY- Plato *Poetry and Inspiration*
EIGHT   TRANSLATED BY BENJAMIN JOWETT 1959
Aristotle *On Tragedy*
   TRANSLATED BY GERALD F. ELSE 1960
Sir Philip Sidney *An Apology for Poetry* 1962
Samuel Johnson *The Metaphysical Poets* 1963
William Blake *Art and Imagination* 1964
William Wordsworth *Poetry and Feeling* 1964
John Keats *The Authenticity of the Imagination* 1965
Percy Bysshe Shelley *Poets and Language* 1967
Edgar Allan Poe *True Poetry* 1968
Edgar Allan Poe *The Single Effect* 1968
Anton Chekhov *Technique in Writing the Short Story*
   TRANSLATED BY CONSTANCE GARNETT 1970
Henrik Ibsen *Notes for the Modern Tragedy*
   TRANSLATED BY A. G. CHATER 1971

Gerard Manley Hopkins *Sprung Rhythm* 1972
August Strindberg *The Scene*
 Translated by Borge Gedso Madsen 1973
Bernard Shaw *The Interpreter of Life* 1973
Robert Frost *Poetry, Delight, and Wisdom* 1974
Wallace Stevens *Observations on Poetry* 1975
T. S. Eliot *The Poet and the Tradition* 1976
Bertolt Brecht *Brecht on Theatre*
 Translated by John Willett 1977
George Seferis *Poetry and Human Living*
 Translated by A. Gagnostopoulos 1978
Frank O'Connor *Lyric Poetry and the Short Story* 1979
Pablo Neruda *"The Word"*
 Translated by Hardi St. Martin 1980
Eudora Welty *The Origin of a Story* 1981
Ralph Ellison *Folklore and Fiction* 1982
Octavio Paz *The Power of Poetry*
 Translated by Helen Lane 1983
Arthur Miller *Tragedy and the Common Man* 1984
Eric Bentley *On Drama as Literature and Performance* 1986
Martin Esslin *The Theater of the Absurd* 1987
Wendell Berry *Poetry and Song* 1988
Audre Lorde *Poems Are Not Luxuries* 1989
Mark Strand *Poetry, Language, and Meaning* 1989
Margaret Atwood *Our First Stories* 1990
Seamus Heaney *Feelings into Words* 1991
John Edgar Widemen *Stories Are Letters (To Robby)* 1993
Diane Ackerman *What a Poem Knows* 1993
Annie Dillard *What Essays Can Do* 1994
Tim O'Brien *On the Importance of Mystery in Plot* 1995
Alice Fulton *On the Validity of Free Verse* 1996

Glossary 1998
Acknowledgments 2005
Index 2019

Preface

Literature presents an approach to literary works that emphasizes reading as an active enterprise involving thought and feeling. It encourages students to value their emotional reactions and their previous experience with life and with language. Students are introduced to interpretation through illustrated discussions of the elements of literature. They are also invited to consider why they respond as they do and how their responses change during subsequent readings of a work; they are asked, in short, to relate their experience in reading literature to their experience in living. They are encouraged to see literature as a significant reflection of life and an imaginative extension of its possibilities.

From first page to last, *Literature* is designed to involve students in the twin acts of reading and analysis. Each of the four genres is introduced by a three-part explanatory overview of the reading process. The introductions are organized around the approach to texts outlined in Robert Scholes's *Textual Power* (Yale University Press, 1985), modified and adapted to my own approach to teaching literature. Scholes identifies three aspects of literary response: reading, interpretation, and criticism. The three-part structure of the introductions breaks down as follows:

- the experience of literature
- the interpretation of literature
- the evaluation of literature

Our *experience* of literature concerns our impressions of a work, especially our subjective impressions and emotional responses. Interpretation involves more intellectual and analytical thinking. And the *evaluation* of literature involves an assessment of aesthetic distinction along with a consideration of a work's social, moral, and cultural values.

Paralleling this schema for the introductory genre discussions is a similarly organized introduction to writing about literature. This chapter describes how to apply and adapt the approaches presented in the genre introductions. The writing chapters include examples of student writing, sample topics, documentation procedures, and a general review of the writing process. Additional writing topics (more than a hundred of them) appear in the four chapters devoted to approaching literary works, subtitled "Guides for Reading and Suggestions for Writing."

For each of the genre introductions, I have also provided a separate illustration of "the act of reading." The fiction section includes an interpolated reading of Kate Chopin's "The Story of an Hour." The poetry section offers a set of annotations for Theodore Roethke's "My Papa's Waltz." The drama section provides a set of questions in response to the opening scene of Lady Gregory's *The Rising of the Moon.* And the essay section presents an imaginary dialogue with Gretel Ehrlich, the author of "About Men." Taken together, the four demonstrations suggest specific strategies for the critical reading of literary works.

In addition to emphasizing the subjective, analytical, and evaluative aspects of reading literature, *Literature* introduces the traditional elements through discussions tied to works in each of the four genres: fiction, poetry, drama, and essay. Throughout these discussions, students are asked to return to certain works and reconsider them from different perspectives. In Chapter 11, Elements of Poetry, for example, students are encouraged to reread particular poems as they study a different element or technique. The repetition reinforces the recursive aspect of reading described in the opening chapters on each genre and demonstrates the need to reread literary works for the fullest possible intellectual, emotional, and aesthetic enjoyment.

The poetry section of *Literature* attempts to broaden the study of the genre with two special features: a substantial number of poems in translation and a special selection of poetic transformations. In addition to more than three hundred English and American poems, this edition of *Literature* includes more than thirty-five poems translated from eight languages. Goethe and Rilke, Borges and Lorca, Mandelstam and Akhmatova are among the poets represented. Included in Chapter 13, Poetic Transformations, are alternative translations of poems by Rilke, Jiminez, and Apollinaire. Also included in this chapter are ways in which poets have modified their own and other artists' work by means of revision, parody, and adaptation. Of particular interest are the transformations from one genre to another: poems recast as songs and poems inspired by paintings.

Finally, a word about the choice of works. The classic and contemporary selections presented reflect a wide range of styles, voices, subjects, and points of view. Complex and challenging works appear alongside more readily approachable and accessible ones. *Literature,* moreover, contains both types of works in sufficient variety for instructors to assign the more accessible ones for students to read and write about on their own, while reserving the more ambitious selections for class discussion.

Changes in This Edition

This fourth edition of *Literature* retains the previously described features of the first three editions. New selections grace the collections of fiction, poetry, drama, and essay. New fiction selections include Joyce's "The Dead," Porter's "The Jilting of Granny Weatherall," as well as stories by Tim O'Brien, Amy Tan, Louise Erdrich, and Mary Hood. The poetry anthology now includes selections by Audre Lorde, Rosario Castellanos, Barbara Holder, Robert Hass, Jimmy Santiago Baca, Judith Ortiz Cofer, Alberta Rios, Gertrude Schnackenberg, Gary Soto, and Louise Erdrich. Lonnell E. Johnson's "No Mo' Blues" and E. Wards Herlands' "When Edward Hopper Was Painting" have been included in the Music and Painting section of the Transformations chapter. Montaigne's "Of Smells" and Bernard Cooper's "Burl's" provide a new frame for the book's collection of essays. Finally, the Drama anthology has undergone a dramatic transformation, with the inclusion of eight new plays. Six of the new dramas—plays by Tina Howe, David Mamet, Wendy Wasserstein, Terence McNally, Martin Dockery, and Josefina López—are contemporary works. Instructors now also have the choice of teaching either *Othello* or *Hamlet*.

Besides freshening the selections in *Literature* the following major changes have been implemented:

• A new introduction provides an overview of the pleasures of reading literature and an approach to writing about it.

• Writing instruction has been greatly amplified with new chapters on Writing About Fiction, Poetry, Drama, and the Essay. Writing with Sources supplements the new genre-specific writing chapters.

• All works are now provided with dates of publication, performance, or composition.

• For each genre the works of two writers are highlighted and contextualized. Multiple selections are included for D. H. Lawrence and Flannery O'Connor, Emily Dickinson and Robert Frost, Sophocles and Shakespeare, E. B. White and Maxine Hong Kingston. Each of these writer's works is prefaced by an extensive biocritical introduction and by critical perspectives written by the writers themselves and by literary scholars.

• An extensive chapter on Critical Perspectives has been added in which the major schools of literary theory are described and illustrated. Guiding questions and brief bibliographies augment the application of a dozen critical approaches.

Literature represents the cooperative efforts of many people. Steve Pensinger—publisher, editor, and friend—encouraged me to develop the book and supported my work generously and graciously. His associates initially at Random House and afterward at McGraw-Hill brought intelligence and enthusiasm to their work on the project.

For the fourth edition I have had the pleasure of working with McGraw-Hill colleagues Sarah Moyers, English editor; Laura Lynch, associate editor, Alexis Walker, editorial assistant, Sylvia Warren, copy editor, and David Damstra, editing supervisor. I have also benefited from the suggestions of many colleagues who responded to a survey about the third edition. In addition, the following reviewers provided thoughtful suggestions for revision:

Thomas Tuggle, Gainesville College
Richard La Manna, St. Petersburg Junior College
Gary Grassinger, Community College of Allegheny County
Hephzibah Roskelly, University of N. Carolina at Greensboro
Lawrence Milbourn, El Paso Community College
Barbara Thompson, Columbus State Community College
Irene Fairley, Northeastern University
W. David Winsper, Springfield Technical Community College
William Provost, University of Georgia

Reviewers of previous editions gave me much good advice. For their third edition suggestions thanks to the following:

Stephen Behrendt, Barbara Belson, Jon Burton, Cornelius Cronin, Charles Crow, Lois Cuddy, Robert Dell, Alan Ehmann, Ruth Eisenberg, Peter Evarts, Chris Farris, Paula Feldman, Elizabeth Flynn, Robert Fraser, Susan Gannon, Frank Garratt, Harold Gleason, John Hanes, Jacqueline Hartwich, J. G. Janssen, Michael Johnson, Leonard Leff, Barry Maid, William McIntosh, George Miller, Hugh Ruppersburg, Robert Sayre, Thomas Watson, A. K. Weatherhead, Joseph Zavadil, and Karl Zender.

For the second edition I received lively and thoughtful advice from William McIntosh of the United States Military Academy, and also from: Bertha N. Booker, Virginia State University; Carl Brucker, Arkansas Tech University; Terre Burton, Laramie County Community College, Wyoming; James Bynum, Georgia Institute of Technology; Charles Dean, Middle Tennessee State University; William J. Everts, Jr., St. Michael's College, Vermont; John Hoey, SUNY—Genesee; Ted Johnston, El Paso Community College; Larry G. Mapp, Middle Tennessee State University; Sara M. Putzell, Georgia Institute of Technology; and Sharon Sellers, Clayton State College, Georgia.

Four reviewers of the first edition deserve acknowledgment for their perceptive comments on the entire manuscript: Richard F. Dietrich, University of South Florida; Kelley Griffith, University of North Carolina; Frank Hodgins, University of Illinois; and Richard Larson, Lehman College of the City University of New York. In addition, I benefited enormously on that edition from the expert assistance of Donald McQuade, University of California at Berkeley, and Robert B. Lyons, Queens College, City University of New York, who served as consultants.

In addition, many instructors who used the third edition of *Literature* responded to a questionnaire on the book. For their valuable comments and advice I am grateful to: Debbie A. Hanson (Augustana College); John Lux (Baruch College); Richard Stimac (Campbell University); Duncan McClinton (Central Washington University); Woodrow Holbein (The Citadel); Gary B. Cohen, Frederick Goldberg (Clayton State College); Laurie Temple (Clinton Community College); C. K. Farr (College of St. Catherine); Susan M. Marsala (Cuesta College); J. Steven Beauchamp, Rosemary D. Cox, L. A. Nardone, Mark Nunes (DeKalb College, Central Campus); Deborah Preston, Jack Riggs (DeKalb College, Gwinnett); Joanne Burgess, Marsha M. Harper, Barbara Nipp (DeKalb College, North Campus); Carole Creekmore (DeKalb College,

Rochdale); Theodore Wadley, Sally Wheeler (DeKalb College, South Campus); Barbara Dodd Galloway (Draughons Junior College); Julienne Empric (Eckerd College); David Owens (Friends University); Colleen Richmond (George Fox College); Edith Blicksilver (Georgia Institute of Technology); James Zoller (Houghton College); Margaret Corgan (King's College); Peter A. Edmunds, Silvija Meija (Lansing Community College); James Childs (Middlesex Community Technical College); Ken Huggins (Monroe Community College); Ted Brown (Murray State University); Nelvin Jager (Muskegon Community College); Zorka Milich (Nassau Community College); William Foster, Sandra Newton, Lisa Schuchter (Naugatuck Valley Community Technical College); Elaine Brown, Diane Levy (New York Institute of Technology); Sheila Wood (North Idaho College); Jean Hodgin (North Shore Community College); J. P. Wysong (Northern Essex Community College); Martin R. Trapp (Northwestern Michigan College); Marie M. Garrett (Patrick Henry Community College); Margaret Payne (Pierce Community College); David Zucker (Quinnipiac College); Emmett H. Carroll (Seattle University); Steven Beck, Robert Carter, Raymond Mize (Southeastern Community College); Michael C. White (Springfield College); Mark Jones (St. Louis University); Thomas M. Kitts, Joseph Marotta (St. Vincent's College–St. John's University); Mark W. Bourdeau, Elaine Preston (Suffolk County Community College); Rosemary Baker, Roxanna Pisiak (SUNY, Morrisville); Linda Ford, Tamara Kuzmenkov, Richard Wakefield (Tacoma Community College); Lea Williamson (Texas A & M University); Joseph Zaitchick (University of Massachusetts, Lowell); James E. Ford (University of Nebraska); Libby Bernardin University of South Carolina); Bruce G. Nims (University of South Carolina at Lancaster); Grace S. Kehrer (Valencia Community College); Marilyn Roberts (Waynesburg College); and Thomas L. Pier (Yakima Valley Community College).

I have had the additional pleasure of working with Professor Tom Kitts of St. John's University. Professor Kitts has written a practical and graceful instructor's manual, which serves as a rich and rewarding source of practical and provocative classroom applications.

Finally, I want to thank my wife, Mary, whose loving assistance enabled me to complete this revision on schedule.

ROBERT DIYANNI

INTRODUCTION

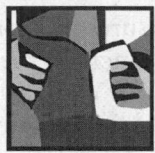

Reading (and Writing About) Literature

Many people read literature for pleasure. Many others read literary works to satisfy academic requirements in university general education programs. For them it is, initially at least, a duty. Duty and pleasure, however, are not mutually exclusive. If you are reading literature for a college course, largely as a duty, this does not prohibit you from enjoying what you read. One of the purposes of this chapter is to introduce you to some of the many pleasures literature offers.

Writing about literature is another matter. But not entirely. Most of those who write about literature typically do so for professional reasons—as book reviewers, as scholars and teachers. As a student in a university literature or writing course, you are one among many thousands around the country—indeed, around the world—who will write about literary works, partly to improve your writing ability, partly to increase your understanding of what you read. Another purpose of this chapter is to introduce you to some ways of writing about literature that you may find helpful.

The chapter is divided into two parts. First, we consider the pleasures of reading fiction, poetry, drama, and the essay—the four literary genres included in this book. Second, we consider some ways of writing about literary works. Both of these preliminary discussions are further developed in the chapters devoted to the specific genres and in the book's final part, "Critical Perspectives and Research."

READING LITERATURE

The Pleasures of Fiction

We read stories largely for the pleasures they bring us. These pleasures are emotional as well as intellectual. They include the pleasure of being surprised by a turn of events, being satisfied as our expectations are met, disturbed or confused as they are not. Well-told stories can involve us emotionally in the lives of their characters. They can also provide us with pleasures of recognition— in the worlds they portray and in the behavior of the characters who inhabit them.

But stories do more than entertain. They also instruct by showing us things about our world we had not known before reading them. Some stories make instruction, or teaching, their primary purpose, though we may enjoy other things about them besides their didactic intention. Consider this example of a fable by the ancient Greek storyteller, Aesop.

The Dog and the Shadow

One day a dog stole a piece of meat out of a butcher shop, and on his way to a safe place where he could eat it without interruption, he had to cross a footbridge over a clear stream. Looking down he saw his own reflection in the water.

Thinking that the reflection was another dog with another piece of meat, and being a greedy dog, he made up his mind to have that also. So he snarled and made a grab for the other dog's meat.

As he opened his mouth his meat dropped into the stream and was swept away.

Moral: Grasp at the shadow and lose the substance.

This story's didactic purpose is apparent in its explicit moral, though this moral invites us to put it into our own words. This, Aesop's fable says, is how you should—or rather should not—act. Don't be greedy. Don't grasp at the elusive false image of something, however attractive it appears. Be satisfied with what you have.

But why do we prefer the story to these morals? One reason is simply that stories are enjoyable in both the reading and the telling. Another reason is that stories are easy to remember. In remembering what happens to Aesop's dog, we remember the moral, or point, of the writer's fable.

Consider now another brief didactic story, this one a parable, a story with an implied moral teaching. This parable comes from the Asian tradition of religious teaching known as Zen.

Learning to Be Silent

The pupils of the Tendai school used to study meditation before Zen entered Japan. Four of them who were intimate friends promised one another to observe seven days of silence.

On the first day all were silent. Their meditation had begun auspiciously, but when night came and the oil lamps were growing dim one of the pupils could not help exclaiming to a servant: "Fix those lamps."

The second pupil was surprised to hear the first one talk: "We are not supposed to say a word," he remarked.

"You two are stupid. Why did you talk?" asked the third.

"I am the only one who has not talked," concluded the fourth pupil.

Unlike the moral of Aesop's fable, the point of "Learning to Be Silent" may not be clear right away. Perhaps you understood its point on first reading, perhaps after a second or third. Perhaps it made sense later, after you had time to think about it or talk about it with a classmate. Even then, you and your classmates may disagree about how to interpret the parable. Some may see it as being about the need for self-control; others may interpret it as being about the impossibility of achieving it. Others may understand it in still other ways—as being about pride or vanity, for example.

Although part of our pleasure in reading and hearing such stories comes from making sense of them, part derives from watching their unfolding action and their display of character. We may enjoy the crispness and directness of the dialogue. Each speaker in "Learning to be Silent" says something different. Each directs his comment to a different character, yet each does essentially the same thing. All break the rule of silence they had vowed to observe. Ironically, moreover, three of them break the rule because they try to show themselves worthier than the others, who have already broken the rule of silence. Part of our pleasure in "Learning to be Silent," thus, results from the skilled control of its telling.

In reading fiction we share the imaginative vision of another, adopting, however briefly, his or her way of perceiving the world. Through reading a wide variety of stories we can enter many different imaginative worlds, in the process enlarging and deepening our own perception of the world.

The Pleasures of Poetry

We read poetry for the many pleasures it offers—pleasures of sound and meaning, of image and symbol, of speech and feeling and thought. Some of the pleasures of poetry are intellectual, as when we enjoy a poet's witty wordplay or understand a poem's central idea. Others are emotional, as when a poem evokes sorrow or pity, fear or joy. Still others are physical, as when our skin tingles or we feel the impulse to tap our feet or nod in time to a poem's rhythmic beat. Emily Dickinson once suggested that she could tell she was reading poetry when she felt as if the top of her head was coming off. Although our own ways of acknowledging the power of poetry may not be as extravagant as Dickinson's, each of us experiences the pleasures of poetry in a meaningful way.

Poems may, at times, seem puzzling or mysterious. Yet mystery and confusion are not essential attributes of poetry. Nor is poetry simply dressed up prose, statements that have been made to look good (by being organized in stanzas) and sound good (by being arranged in patterns of rhythm and rhyme). And even though we can discuss the ideas in poems, poems can never be reduced to their intellectual content. Poems present experiences in language, experiences the poet creates for the reader to recreate. In reading poetry our experience involves more than considering the meanings of words. It includes our apprehension of a poem's form, our appreciation of its patterns of sound, and our understanding of its thought. The meaning of any poem involves our total experience of reading it, an experience that includes intellectual understanding but which is not restricted to it.

Poetry sharpens our perception of the world around us since it draws its energy from the fresh observation of life. Poetry can reveal to us things we didn't know or knew only vaguely. It can excite our capacity for wonder, and it can enlarge our appreciation of beauty. It can make us feel more acutely and deeply, and also make us more receptive to imaginative experience. Reading poetry also improves our ability to use and understand language since poems are made of words—at their best, the most carefully chosen words in the best order. Consider the following short poem.

ROBERT FROST

Dust of Snow

The way a crow
Shook down on me
The dust of snow
From a hemlock tree

Has given my heart
A change of mood
And saved some part
Of a day I had rued.

Part of our enjoyment of this poem comes from its brevity. It captures an experience and recreates it for us in just a few words. The poem's action may engage us, very likely sending us back almost immediately for a second look. We may be struck by the nature of the poem's action—a crow's jouncing a tree limb, which unloads its snow on a man beneath it. We may smile, considering that the crow's action may have been intentional. And we may reflect on the man's response—not anger or frustration, but a shift in his feelings, "a change of mood" (presumably from sorrow to something more joyous, elation perhaps).

Our pleasure in "Dust of Snow" may include a consideration of our own experience—whether or not that experience duplicates either the poem's external action or the speaker's internal change. We may find ourselves thinking about how our moods change and about what prompts those changes. We may enjoy the surprising reversal of our expectations in reading how Frost's speaker responds to the situation, perhaps comparing what our own imagined response might be.

These experiential or imaginative pleasures, moreover, might very well be supplemented by the pleasure we take in the poem's sounds—especially its rhythm and rhyme. And they may extend to other details we observe about its structure and language. We may enjoy noticing, for example, that though "Dust of Snow" is a single sentence, it is cast as two separate nearly symmetrical stanzas. And we might ask ourselves how it would differ if arranged as one stanza or constructed of two sentences. Furthermore, we might enjoy Frost's use of "rued," which stands out in a context of more common and familiar language.

Perhaps, "Dust of Snow" may lead us to speculate not only about the narrative incident it recounts, but about the event's larger significance. We might think about the relationship between human beings and the natural world that "Dust of Snow" implies—that nature can affect human beings in beneficial ways, that it can make people feel better about their experience. We may derive additional pleasure from considering other poems we have read by Frost or by other poets in relation to this one. We may find ourselves considering the larger implications of "Dust of Snow," along with a set of attitudes toward and values about the natural world and its relationship to the human world. This too may provide us with a kind of pleasure.

The Pleasures of Drama

Unlike the other literary genres, drama is meant to be performed on a stage. Much of the pleasure drama brings us comes in the way the language of the play's script comes alive in the speech of living actors who represent fictional or imaginary characters. We enjoy watching actors dramatically enact the "lives" of the characters they portray. We appreciate the way actors walk and talk, the way they interact with other characters, even their facial expressions and bodily gestures. The smallest gesture, such as the lowering of a hand, or the slightest facial movement, such as the raising of an eyebrow, contributes to our sense of the play's human experience.

When we read or view drama we are aware, if only implicitly, of its major characteristics or features. The first of these is its representational quality. Drama is a *mimetic* art, one that imitates or represents human life and experience. A large part of the pleasure drama brings us reflects its ability to show us aspects of human life meaningfully enacted. Drama is also an *active* art in which actors portraying characters say and do things to one another. Actors are agents, doers, who make things happen through speech and bodily action. In addition, drama is an *immediate* art, one that represents action that occurs in the play's present. This is so even when a play's subject is historical, that is, even when its dramatic action concerns the past. The important point about drama's immediacy is that plays bring the past into the present. Our experience of drama is thus one of watching events *as* they occur. We are first-hand witnesses of present-tense actions rather than auditors who simply hear about them later from a narrator at second hand.

One additional and critically important feature of drama derives from its mimetic, active, and immediate qualities: its *interactive nature*. The representation of human action displayed in drama is largely attributable to the interaction of its characters. The action of plays is based on *interaction,* for dramatic characters respond and relate to one another. They engage one another in dialogue and action, in speech and visual displays. Such character interaction is the heart of drama: it is the catalyst of plot, the source of meaning, and a central reason for our pleasure in dramatic experience.

Drama is interactive in still another way. Unlike fiction and poetry, which are largely verbal arts (though poetry is also allied with music or song) drama is a *composite* art—one that makes use of many of the other arts. Drama makes use of painting and architecture in the design and creation of stage sets and in the way stage and actors are lighted or kept in shadow. Drama may also use music and other sound effects to suggest feelings, to build tension, or to create mood and atmosphere. Sculpture and dance are suggested by the way characters are positioned on stage and by their movements around it. The point, however, is not so much that stationary characters can be compared with sculpture or moving ones with dancers, but rather that drama is a complex art that involves a dynamic interplay of visual and aural elements. In viewing drama and in reading it we need to be as alert as possible, keeping open our eyes, ears, and minds.

Our pleasure in drama arises from the cumulative impact of a multitude of impressions both visual and aural. Makeup and costume, lighting and sound, speech and action, posture and gesture, movement and expression—all work together to bring plays to life, to imbue them with meaning and feeling, and most importantly, to create a distinctive theatrical experience for the audience. It is this experience we attempt to capture when we read drama, knowing all the while that reading a play is not the same as sitting in a theater watching it enacted on a stage. To compensate for this fact we try to read drama *imaginatively,* as if we were watching it. We attempt to read drama *theatrically*.

But what does it mean to read a play theatrically? How do we imaginatively reconstruct a play in our minds? Essentially by translating the script we read into a mental performance that we imagine. By attending to the performative implications of the words on the page, we see imaginatively how they might be dramatized on the stage. We learn to look not only at what a play's words mean, but also at what they suggest about characters' behavior, movements, gestures, and feelings. We learn to listen for the effect their words have on one another. We try to imagine how those words might be uttered—gently or threateningly, sarcastically or sweetly, loudly or softly, swiftly or slowly—to suggest a few possibilities.

We also imagine where the characters are positioned relative to one another, how close or far apart. We imagine the manner of their walk, the style of their physical gestures, and the subtlest alteration of their voices and facial expressions. These details, coupled with changes in characters' body postures, their characteristic manner of delivering their lines, their costumes, the scenery of the play, the sounds of voices and of sound effects—all these things contribute to the richness of our imaginative reenactment of a play. The better we can imagine such elements, the better we will absorb the atmosphere and feeling of the play, and the more complete and theatrical will be our reading experience.

How do we learn to do this? By reading drama patiently and deliberately. By reading with care and attentiveness not only for the literal meanings of dialogue but for its implications and its sound and accent and rhythm as well. By reading aloud. By reading with other students in small groups. By talking with others about our mental reconstructions of scenes. In the process of learning to read plays theatrically we will also attend to the fullest expression of their literary meaning. Drama is literature as well as theater, for like poetry and fiction, drama is an art of language. While drama entertains us with its representation of life, it offers provocative ideas about the life it portrays, and it provides an imaginative extension of its possibilities.

The Pleasures of the Essay

The pleasures of the essay are not radically different from those of the other literary genres. Like the pleasures of poetry, drama, and fiction, those of the essay involve language and idea. And even though the essay's pleasures do not typically involve the imaginative transformation of reality, they do include essayists' artistry in shaping their materials. Sometimes, this shaping may result in our pleasure in seeing an idea unfold and ramify. We may admire the way a writer complicates a simple idea, enriches that idea, or applies it to everyday experience.

Besides the pleasure they afford in conveying ideas and in explaining their relevance to experience, essays also offer the pleasure of seeing writers support their ideas with evidence. In reading essays we enter the world of the writer's mind. We watch essayists build coherent and persuasive arguments about their beliefs, attitudes, and convictions. Part of our pleasure may come from being persuaded; part may come from resisting essayists' arguments and from demurring from their conclusions, even when we admire their thinking and writing.

Like the other literary genres, essays provide readers with the pleasures of hearing a writer's voice and of sharing his or her vision and perspective on life. Like the other genres, essays provide the pleasure of making us more aware of our world and ourselves. They help us make sense of our lives and our world by explaining relationships and making connections. Essays also provoke us to think by challenging our assumptions, as the following passage suggests.

BERNARD COOPER

from *Burl's*

Like most children, I once thought it possible to divide the world into male and female columns. Blue/Pink. Rooster/Hens. Trousers/Skirts. Such divisions were easy, not to mention comforting, for they simplified matter into compatible pairs. But there also existed a vast range of things that didn't fit neatly into either camp: clocks, milk, telephones, grass. There were nights I fell into a fitful sleep while trying to sex the world correctly.

Nothing typified the realms of male and female as clearly as my parents' walk-in closets. Home alone for any length of time, I always found my way inside them. I could stare at my parents' clothes for hours, grateful for the stillness and silence, haunting the very heart of their privacy.

The overhead light in my father's closet was a bare bulb. Whenever I groped for the chain in the dark, it wagged back and forth and resisted my grasp. Once the light clicked on, I saw dozens of ties hanging like stalactites. A monogrammed silk bathrobe sagged from a hook, a gift my father had received on a long-ago birthday and, thinking it fussy, rarely wore. Shirts were cramped together along the length of an aluminum pole, their starched sleeves sticking out as if in a halfhearted gesture of greeting. The medicinal odor of mothballs permeated the boxer shorts that were folded and stacked in a built-in drawer. Immaculate underwear was proof of a tenderness my mother couldn't otherwise express; she may not have touched my father often, but she laundered his boxers with infinite care. Even back then, I suspected that a sense of duty was the final erotic link between them.

Sitting in a neat row on the closet floor were my father's boots and slippers and dress shoes. I'd try on his wingtips and clomp around, slipping out of them with every step. My wary, unnatural stride made me all the more desperate to effect some authority. I'd whisper orders to imagined lackeys and take my invisible wife in my arms. But no matter how much I wanted them to fit, those shoes were as cold and hard as marble.

My mother's shoes were just as uncomfortable, but a lot more fun. From a brightly colored array of pumps and slingbacks, I'd pick a pair with the glee and deliberation of someone choosing a chocolate. Whatever embarrassment I felt was overwhelmed by the exhilaration of being taller in a pair of high heels. Things will look like this someday, I said to myself, gazing out from my new and improved vantage point as if from a crow's nest. Calves elongated, arms akimbo, I gauged each step so that I didn't fall over and moved with what might have passed for grace had someone seen me, a possibility I scrupulously avoided by locking the door.

Back and forth I went. The longer I wore a pair of heels, the better my balance. In the periphery of my vision, the shelf of wigs looked like a throng of kindly bystanders. Light streamed down from a high window, causing crystal bottles to glitter, the air ripe with perfume. A makeup mirror above the dressing table invited my self-absorption. Sound was muffled. Time slowed. It seemed as if nothing bad could happen as long as I stayed within those walls.

Though I'd never been discovered in my mother's closet, my parents knew that I was drawn toward girlish things—dolls and jump rope and jewelry—as well as to the games and preoccupations that were expected of a boy. I'm not sure now if it was my effeminacy itself that bothered them as much as my ability to slide back and forth, without the slightest warning, between male and female mannerisms. After I'd finished building the model of an F-17 bomber, say, I'd sit back to examine my handiwork, pursing my lips in concentration and crossing my legs at the knee.

One of the pleasures of this excerpt from Cooper's essay (see Chapter 35) is the way the writer undermines the clearcut conventional gender distinctions he presents. We recognize the divisions he cites—"Blue/Pink. Roosters/Hens. Trousers/Skirts"—while simultaneously perhaps questioning them. With his comments about building an F-17 bomber model, the writer eliminates the slash dividing gender categories, at least for himself, as he examines his handiwork, "pursing [his] lips in concentration and crossing [his] legs at the knee."

Those last details complicate Cooper's description of his parents' closets, and of how he feels when he tries on their shoes. That description both elaborates and undermines the gender divisions Cooper begins with in this passage. It also reveals something about the writer, thus making his essay both a personal revelation and a general discussion of gender identity.

Another pleasure of Cooper's essay is its language. In his attempt, as he puts it, "to sex the world correctly," Cooper chooses his verbs carefully to convey precise visual details—a light bulb "wagged back and forth" and a light "clicked" on. He conveys his feelings through images and carefully selected details, as when he describes how his father's shoes "were as cold and hard as marble." In addition, he conveys a sense of his parents and their relationship through describing their clothes.

Cooper's essay repays rereading. Like a good poem, story, novel, or play, a good essay rewards repeated readings. In subsequent readings we admire something previously discovered while appreciating something new we had previously overlooked.

Considering Values

Critical evaluation involves making judgments about literary works. When we evaluate a literary work, we consider and assess the values (social, moral, cultural) expressed in it. To engage in this kind of evaluation, however, we must interpret the work and be satisfied with our understanding of it. Evaluation is grounded in interpretation; our conclusions about what texts mean affect how we evaluate them.

Consider the following brief fictional text, a sketch from *In Our Time*, by Ernest Hemingway. This early modern work strongly embodies cultural dispositions and moral values.*

*For the Hemingway example I am indebted to Robert Scholes's discussion in *Textual Power* (New Haven: Yale University Press, 1985).

> While the bombardment was knocking the trench to pieces at Fossalta, he lay very flat and sweated and prayed oh jesus christ get me out of here. Dear jesus please get me out. Christ please please please christ. If you'll only keep me from getting killed I'll do anything you say. I believe in you and I'll tell every one in the world that you are the only one that matters. Please please dear jesus. The shelling moved further up the line. We went to work on the trench and in the morning the sun came up and the day was hot and muggy, and cheerful and quiet. The next night back at Mestre he did not tell the girl he went upstairs with at the Villa Rossa about Jesus. And he never told anybody.

This text, though brief, is rich in cultural and moral implications. It assumes a modest knowledge of war as it was fought in the early twentieth century. It assumes, for example, that we know what trenches are, what shelling is, and also that we can make sense of the soldier's behavior. It also assumes some familiarity with a soldier going "upstairs" with a "girl" at a place like the "Villa Rossa."

The piece, however, is reticent about these and other matters. It says little directly. It's close-mouthed and tight-lipped about what it expects from us as readers—somewhat like the soldier who "never told anybody" about his experience. But it makes a strong statement by implication, nonetheless, about its three central subjects, love, war, and religion, largely by playing off conventional expectations about these subjects. The soldier, for example, does not acquit himself heroically. Instead he cringes in the trenches to avoid being hit by enemy shells (though we may wonder what else he could do). And he prays to a God he probably ignores under normal circumstances. Moreover, his approach to prayer is to bargain with God: If you'll do this for me, I'll do something else for you. But it's a bargain he doesn't keep. Our response to this soldier's language and behavior is influenced by the cultural values we share and the moral dispositions we bring to both our reading and our living.

Our evaluation of him turns on considerations such as whether he really believes in Jesus, and what such a belief may mean. It turns on whether you think the soldier's prayer is "answered" by God in a providential intervention to move the shelling "farther up the line," or whether you see that as a coincidence, attributable purely to luck. It turns also on whether his going to a house of prostitution is something you can understand, sympathize with, and approve of—or not; and whether his not telling the girl or anybody else about Jesus is a serious violation of a solemn vow, or an excusable, perfectly understandable response.

Besides evaluating the behavior of the soldier, we also make a judgment about the values we think the text espouses. Does the author seem to display sympathy for the soldier? Does he judge him harshly? The narrative voice is noncommittal, concerned more with portraying a situation than with commenting on it. This stance of objectivity is itself a "value," an attitude or disposition we must eventually assess, as we must also respond to the fact that the world depicted is a man's world, a world of war and violence, in which women (or *girls* as the text stipulates them) figure only marginally, and then only as they can be used by men. (We know, for example, what the man feels and fears, but we are told nothing about the girl's thoughts and emotions.) Our sexual identity along with our religious disposition and our general cultural awareness and values will strongly influence what we make of and take from this text.

WRITING ABOUT LITERATURE

Reasons for Writing About Literature

Why write about literature? For many reasons. First, writing about a literary work encourages us to read it attentively and notice things we might miss during a more casual reading. Second, writing stimulates thinking, and enables us to discover what we think about literary works, how we feel about them, and why. Third, writing provides opportunities for us to state our views about the ideas and values expressed in literary works. Finally, through writing about literary works we enhance our enjoyment of the many pleasures they offer and deepen our appreciation of their artistic achievement.

Whatever our reasons for writing may be, a truly active engagement with literature intellectually and emotionally will broaden our understanding of life and language and will refine our aesthetic sensibilities. The literary works we read carefully will become a meaningful part of our lives, absorbed into our storehouse of knowledge and experience to become part of who we are, how we know, and what we feel.

Ways of Writing About Literature

Just as there are many reasons for writing about literature, there are many ways to write about it. In this section we will introduce a few common ways to write about literary works. Our approach is divided into three parts: Explicating, summarizing, and comparing and contrasting.

Explicating

A type of analysis frequently used to explain literary works is *explication,* a careful line-by-line or word-by-word examination of a passage in a poem, story, play, or essay. Explication involves a scrupulously close reading to unfold the layers of meaning in a text. It provides a close-up look at the language of a passage with a view to explaining its significance. Because explication involves such careful attention to detail, it is usually reserved for specific sections or parts of longer works, and sometimes even for parts of short works as well. As with any type of analysis, however, explication is most effective when it is used to illuminate the meaning of the work as a whole.

Explication is particularly useful for unraveling the meaning of a complex passage, something as long as a section, paragraph, stanza, or scene, or as brief as a bit of dialogue, a sentence, a line of poetry, or even a phrase. Our analysis of the ironic quality of the opening sentences of *Pride and Prejudice* (page 100) is one example. Others include the analysis of the final paragraph of Pirandello's "War" (page 113) and the final couplet of Hopkins's "Spring and Fall" (page 557).

Beginnings and endings of literary works, whether they are as long as Jane Austen's novel or as short as a brief lyric poem, offer promising sections of text to explicate. These strategic locations afford opportunities for the writer to make a lasting impression on the reader.

Summarizing

A *summary* is a succinct account of a work. As a condensation or compression of its thought, a summary is shorter than the work summarized. Writing a summary requires careful reading, in part to assure that you understand a text well. Writing a summary helps you respond to a text by requiring you to analyze and consider its details. Your goal in summarizing a text is to render a writer's ideas accurately and fairly.

A *paraphrase,* which is similar to a summary, tends to be nearly as long as the text paraphrased. When you paraphrase a poem, for example, you explain its meaning in your own words, line by line or stanza by stanza. Unlike a summary, a paraphrase follows the order of ideas, images, and details in the original text.

Writing a summary requires essentially two kinds of skills: identifying the idea of the text you are summarizing, and recognizing the evidence that supports that idea. One strategy for writing a summary is to find the key points that support the main idea. You can do this by looking for clusters of sentences or groups of paragraphs that convey the writer's meaning. Because paragraphs work together you cannot simply summarize each paragraph independently. You may need to summarize a cluster of paragraphs to best convey the idea of a text.

Read the following passage from an essay by Katherine Anne Porter.

St. Augustine and the Bullfight

W. B. Yeats remarked—I cannot find the passage now, so must say it in other words— that the unhappy man (unfortunate?) was one whose adventures outran his capacity for experience, capacity for experience being, I should say, roughly equal to the faculty for understanding what has happened to one. The difference then between mere adventure and a real experience might be this: That adventure is something you seek for pleasure, or even for profit, like a gold rush or invading a country; for the illusion of being more alive than ordinarily, the thing you will to occur; but experience is what really happens to you in the long run; the truth that finally overtakes you.

Adventure is sometimes fun, but not too often. Not if you can remember what really happened; all of it. It passes, seems to lead nowhere much, is something to tell friends to amuse them, maybe. "Once upon a time," I can hear myself saying, for I once said it, "I scaled a cliff in Boulder, Colorado, with my bare hands, and in Indian moccasins, bare-legged. And at nearly the top, after six hours of feeling for toe- and fingerholds, and the gayest feeling in the world that when I got to the top I should see something wonderful, something that sounded awfully like a bear growled out of a cave, and I scuttled down out of there in a hurry." This is a fact. I had never climbed a mountain in my life, never had the least wish to climb one. But there I was, for perfectly good reasons, in a hut on a mountainside in heavenly sunny though sometimes stormy weather, so I went out one morning and scaled a very minor cliff; alone, unsuitably clad, in the season when rattlesnakes are casting their skins; and if it was not a bear in that cave, it was some kind of unfriendly animal who growls at people; and this ridiculous escapade, which was nearly six hours of the hardest work I ever did in my life, toeholds and fingerholds on a cliff, put me to bed for just nine days with a complaint the local people called "muscle poisoning." I don't know exactly what they meant, but I do remember clearly that I could not turn over in bed without help and in great agony. And did it teach me anything? I think not, for three years later I was climbing a volcano in Mexico, that celebrated unpronounceably named volcano, Popocatepetl, which everybody who comes near it climbs sooner or later; but was that any reason for me to climb it? No. And I was knocked out for weeks, and that finally did teach me: I am not supposed to go climbing things. Why did I not know in the first place? For me, this sort of thing must come under the head of Adventure.

I think it is pastime of rather an inferior sort; yet I have heard men tell yarns like this only a very little better: their mountains were higher, or their sea was wider, or their bear was bigger and noisier, or their cliff was steeper and taller, yet there was no point whatever to any of it except that it had happened. This is not enough. May it not be, perhaps, that experience, that is, the thing that happens to a person living from day to day, is anything at all that sinks in? is, without making any claims, a part of your growing and changing life? what it is that happens in your mind, your heart?

Here are some notes based on Porter's paragraphs. The first three notes consider what Porter seems to say in each paragraph. The last three attempt to make sense of the passage overall.

Notes Toward a Summary

1. Porter begins by paraphrasing Yeats's observation that people whose adventure or experience outruns their capacity for understanding it are either unhappy or unfortunate. Porter can't seem to remember which.
2. Her second paragraph continues the indictment of adventure made in the first. She says that adventure isn't fun—not very much of it, anyway, and not very much of the time. Porter diminishes her adventure of mountain climbing by saying that she didn't learn anything from it and by noting how it caused her physical pain.
3. In her third paragraph she suggests that many people's adventures are not really different from hers. She further condemns adventure by referring to it as "climbing things"—a put-down of sorts.
4. Porter's overall evaluation of adventure is that such experiences are not enough in themselves to be meaningful or valuable. Adventure, Porter says, is *what* happens, not what the experience means, and it is the meaning that matters.
5. Porter also sees adventure as merely *external* experience. She contrasts this with *internal* experience, which occurs after the adventure is over. This internal experience is emotional and intellectual, not merely external and physical.

6. Finally, Porter defines real experience as that which changes the mind and the heart, in contrast to adventure, which she asserts, changes nothing. Yet, ironically, Porter seems to have made something of her experience having "adventures," by reflecting on them, analyzing them, and writing about them in this essay.

Here now is a summary, a compressed version of Porter's essay excerpt and a reduced version of the ideas elaborated in the Notes above.

> Porter offers both a meditation on and a definition of what she means by *experience*. She begins by recalling Yeats's idea that experiences must be understood and not merely undergone. For Porter, having "adventures" or "experiences" without reflecting on them is fruitless. Some experiences or adventures, she suggests, may be valueless not only because no meaning can be gleaned from them, but also because they are dangerous or unpleasant. *Real experience,* Porter contends, is something radically different. Real experience affects us both intellectually and emotionally, making an indelible impression on the mind and heart.

This summary recounts the gist of Porter's argument. It does not attempt to make a judgment about it. Typically, although a summary of a text requires some thought about its meaning, it usually does not include an evaluation of its accuracy, usefulness, or general worthiness. A summary, however, does more than catalog the contents of a work or describe what happens in it; a summary must also explain the point of the work as the reader sees and understands that point.

Comparing and Contrasting

One of the most common approaches to writing interpretive papers is comparison and contrast, which can be applied in numerous ways. You might compare and contrast elements in a single work, or you might compare and contrast a particular aspect of two different works. You could compare and contrast, for example, the differing perspectives on knowledge and learning of the astronomer and the speaker in Whitman's "When I heard the learn'd astronomer" (page 545). Or you might compare the uses of irony in Crane's "War is Kind" (page 480) with Hardy's "Channel Firing" (page 735). You might compare and contrast the speech and actions of the two male characters in Boyle's "Astronomer's Wife" (pages 62–66). Or you could compare the central character in Boyle's story with the protagonist of Silko's "Yellow Woman" or Gilman's "The Yellow Wallpaper." Topics that reflect such a comparative approach would include these: "Active and Passive Learning in Whitman's 'When I heard the learn'd Astronomer' "; "Two Uses of Irony: Satire and Humor in Poems by Stephen Crane and Thomas Hardy"; "Enchantment and Disenchantment: The Two Men in the Life of Kay Boyle's 'Astronomer's Wife' "; "Sanity or Madness: Women Protagonists in 'Astronomer's Wife' and 'The Yellow Wallpaper' (or 'Yellow Woman')."

Such comparative analyses can sharpen your perception of the works under consideration. By looking at two works together or at two aspects of a single work, you see their differences more clearly. In comparing two poems, you might notice, for example, that one includes rhyme and the other does not; that the action is external in one poem or story and internal in the other; that one story includes much dialogue and the other little; that the settings, tone, or points of the works differ in significant and interesting ways. Such comparative observations will lead you to ask why those differences exist and why the writers developed their works as they did.

When you write comparative papers, keep the following guidelines in mind:

1. Compare two things that seem worth the trouble, that will reward your effort. By attending carefully to a work's details you will often find significant parallels and contrasts. Follow the leads the work provides.
2. Compare works that have a significant feature in common, such as authorship, style, genre, historical period, subject, situation, or an aspect of technique like meter or point of view.
3. Make a point. Use comparison and contrast in the service of an idea, an argument, an interpretation. Your comparative analysis should lead you to a conclusion, perhaps to an evaluation, not merely to a set of parallels.
4. Decide whether to organize your comparative discussion according to the "block" method in which you discuss each subject separately; or according to the "alternating" method in which you discuss the two central subjects in point-by-point comparisons of specific characteristics. If you are comparing two characters, according to the block method, for example, you would devote the first half of your paper to one and the second half to the other character. If you followed the alternating structure, you would consider each side by side as you focused on such characteristics as their physical appearance, their interactions with other characters, their behavior at critical moments of the action, and so on.

Writing the Paper

Drafting

Once you have arrived at a tentative subject and an angle of approach, you are ready to write a rough draft of your paper. The purpose of this draft is simply to write down your ideas and to see how they can be developed and supported. Think of the rough draft as an opportunity to discover what you think about the subject and to test and refine your ideas. Don't worry about having a clearly defined thesis or main idea for your paper before beginning to write it. Instead, use your initial draft to discover an idea, to find a thesis and sharpen it so that your idea-thesis becomes clear, first to you and then to your readers.

In drafting your paper, consider your purpose. Are you writing to provide information and make observations about the work? Are you writing to argue for a particular way to interpret it? Ultimately, of course, all explanations of literary works are interpretations, and all interpretations are forms of argument. That is, they are persuasive attempts to see the literary text one way rather than in other ways. When you write about a literary work you will often attempt to convince others that what you see and say about it makes sense. In doing so, you will be arguing for the validity of your way of seeing, not necessarily to the exclusion of all other ways, but to demonstrate that your understanding of the work is reasonable and valuable. Moreover, since your readers will respond as much to how you support your arguments as to your ideas themselves, you will need to concentrate on providing evidence for your ideas carefully and thoroughly. Most often this evidence will come in the form of textual support—details of action, dialogue, imagery, description, language, and structure. Additional evidence may come from secondary sources, from the comments of experienced readers whose observations and interpretations may influence and support your own thinking. In marshalling evidence for your ideas from the work itself and from secondary sources, however, keep the following guidelines in mind:

1. Be fair-minded. Avoid oversimplifying or distorting either the work or what others have written about it.
2. Be cautious. Qualify your claims. Limit your discussion to what you feel confident you can reasonably demonstrate.
3. Be logical. See that the various elements of your argument fit together and that one part of your approach doesn't contradict another.
4. Be accurate. If you present facts, details, or quotations, present them accurately.
5. Be confident. You should believe in your ideas and present them with conviction.

After writing the first draft, try to forget it for a while—for at least a day or two, longer if possible. When you return to it, assess whether what you are saying makes sense, whether you have provided enough examples to clarify your ideas and presented sufficient evidence to make them persuasive. Read the draft critically, asking yourself what is convincing and what is not, what makes sense and what does not. Consider whether the draft centers on a single idea and stays on track. If the first draft accomplishes these things, you can begin thinking about how to tighten the paper's organization and polish its style. If, on the other hand, the draft contains frequent changes of direction and a number of different and unrelated ideas, then you will need to decide what to salvage and how to focus the paper more sharply. (This second scenario, by the way, is not uncommon in writing. It simply represents the way first efforts often begin: in some degree of confusion that eventually is dispelled with the emergence of a focus and the development of form.)

When you have written an acceptable draft, you are ready to view its organization more critically. A general organizational framework usually reveals an introductory section that clarifies your purpose and intention; a set of successive paragraphs that develop, explore, and explain your ideas; and a conclusion that rounds off the discussion. Within that framework, consider whether your ideas and examples have been arranged in a coherent and logical manner. Ask yourself whether the structure of your paper will be clear to readers. Consider also whether sufficient space (or perhaps too much space) has been allotted to clarifying and supporting your views. Ask someone to read your paper with an eye to its organization and structure.

Perhaps the most important aspect of organization is that you have a clear sense yourself of just how you are setting up the paper. You should be able to identify each part and explain how the parts are related. You should also be able to explain why you put them in the order you did. Consider the following example.

STEPHEN CRANE
[1871–1900]

War Is Kind

Do not weep, maiden, for war is kind.
Because your lover threw wild hands toward the sky
And the affrighted steed ran on alone,
Do not weep.
War is kind.   5

       Hoarse, booming drums of the regiment,
       Little souls who thirst for fight,
       These men were born to drill and die.
       The unexplained glory flies above them,
       Great is the battle god, great, and his kingdom   10
       A field where a thousand corpses lie.

Do not weep, babe, for war is kind.
Because your father tumbled in the yellow trenches,
Raged at his breast, gulped and died,
Do not weep.   15
War is kind.

       Swift blazing flag of the regiment,
       Eagle with crest of red and gold,
       These men were born to drill and die.
       Point for them the virtue of slaughter,   20
       Make plain to them the excellence of killing
       And a field where a thousand corpses lie.

Mother whose heart hung humble as a button
On the bright splendid shroud of your son,
Do not weep.   25
War is kind.

In discussing the ironic tone of "War Is Kind" you might focus on three or four details. You might decide to discuss first the ironic quality of the title. The word *kind* is not usually associated with war; war is associated instead with suffering, waste, death, and destruction. The title, then, cannot be taken literally. Next you might decide to include the speaker's advice to the lover, child, and mother of a slain soldier not to cry, since war is "kind." (These examples too will have to be arranged in a sequence that makes sense to you.) You will probably want to comment on how details such as the "field where a thousand corpses lie" and the soldier who "tumbled in the yellow trenches" can stand alongside the more seemingly patriotic images of regimental flag and thundering drums.

Whatever details you ultimately select, and however many you include, you will need to decide on a particular order in which to present them. Ask yourself how the ironic aspects of the poem can be related. Consider what these details contribute to the poem. Some details will seem more important than others; you may thus be able to subdivide and pair your examples, and perhaps contrast them. Or you may decide to consider them in order of increasing complexity, emotion, or importance. It is necessary, though, to devise an organizational plan that makes sense to you and that will seem sensible to your readers. If you write a comparative paper, your outline might look like this:

Ironic Contrasts in Crane's "War Is Kind"

I. Advice to maiden
   A. Expectation: Sympathy for loss
   B. Reality: Command not to weep
      1. details horrible—not comforting
         a. "wild hands"
         b. "affrighted steed"
      2. repetition of "war is kind"
         a. emphasizes irony
         b. leads to stanza two, details of war
II. Advice to babe
   A. Expectation: Commentary on sorrow
   B. Reality: Command not to weep
      1. details ugly—not noble
         a. "yellow trenches"
         b. "raged . . . gulped and died"
      2. repetition of "war is kind"
         a. emphasizes irony
         b. leads to stanza three, details of war
III. Advice to mother
   A. Expectation: Empathy with bereavement
   B. Reality: Command not to weep
      1. details highlight ironic contrast
         a. mother's love is "humble as a button"
         b. son's shroud (furnished by military) is "bright" and "splendid"

　　　　2. repetition of "war is kind"
　　　　　a. emphasizes irony
　　　　　b. ties together the three civilians who have suffered
　　　　　　deep losses from "kind" war

On the other hand, you might want to examine the relationship of stanzas 1, 3, and 5 to stanzas 2 and 4. In that case, your outline might look like this:

War at Home and on the Battlefield
　　I. Repetition
　　　　A. Stanzas 1, 3, 5 repeat "war is kind"
　　　　　1. represents the politic lies told to keep survivors quiet
　　　　　2. provides ironic contrast with details
　　　　B. Stanzas 2, 4 repeat "A field where a thousand corpses lie"
　　　　　1. emphasizes the enormous losses of war
　　　　　2. contrasts with the "war is kind" lie told to those at home
　　　　　3. suggests that for everyone of the thousand corpses a
　　　　　　"maiden," "babe," or "mother" mourns
　　II. Images: Effects of War
　　　　A. Stanzas 1, 3, 5 show the sorrow of those left behind
　　　　　1. images suggest reality of death in war "threw wild
　　　　　　hands"; "tumbled in the yellow trenches" which those
　　　　　　at home must picture
　　　　　2. images suggest all that is left to those at home are empty
　　　　　　symbols: "bright splendid shroud"
　　　　B. Stanzas 2, 4 images show how the propaganda of war con-
　　　　　trasts with its reality
　　　　　1. propaganda: "unexplained glory flies above them";
　　　　　　"Great is the battle god"; "Swift blazing flag of the
　　　　　　regiment"
　　　　　2. reality: "drill and die"; "a thousand corpses lie"

Besides deciding on the order of ideas and examples in the paper and the amount of space allotted to each, you must consider how to move from one example to another. You will need to link the sections of your discussion so that the writing flows smoothly. Generally, you can create transitions with phrases and sentences at the beginnings of paragraphs. (Examples include such words and phrases as "first, . . . second, . . ."; "on the other hand, . . ."; "in addition to . . ."; "another way in which . . ."). Sometimes, however, such explicit marks of transition from one point to another will not be necessary: careful ordering of the details that support your argument will be evidence enough of how one paragraph follows from and is related to another.

Revising

Revision is not something that occurs only once, at the end of the writing process. Redrafting your paper to consider the ordering of paragraphs and the use of examples is itself a significant act of revision. So too is rereading the work and thinking about it a second or third time. Revision occurs throughout the entire span of reading and writing. It requires you to reconsider your writing and your thinking not once, but several times. This reconsideration is made on three levels: conceptual, organizational, and stylistic.

Conceptual revision involves reconsidering your ideas. As you write a first or second draft, your understanding of the work and what you plan to say about it may change. While accumulating textual evidence in support of one interpretation of the work, you may discover stronger evidence for a contrasting view. When this happens, you may need to go back to the note-taking stage to explore your revised vision of the work. You will then need to make major changes in the original draft. You may end up discarding much of it and beginning again with a stronger conviction about a different approach or a revised idea. In writing about Crane's "War Is Kind," for example, you may have started out with a literal interpretation, arguing that the poem is patriotic rather than ironic. Developing your idea, however, you may have become uneasy with certain details that run counter to your interpretation and that prompt you to change your mind about what the poem means. In that case, you revise your idea and begin again.

Organizational or structural revision involves asking yourself whether the arrangement best presents your line of thinking. Is the organizational framework readily discernible? Does it make sense? Have you written an introduction that clarifies your topic and intention? Have you organized your supporting details in a sensible and logical manner? Does your conclusion follow logically from your discussion and bring it to a satisfying close? Again, taking Crane's poem as an example, you might begin by identifying its general subject—war—and move toward suggesting that even though the poem contains some language that idealizes war, its details and its tone undermine a romanticized conception. From there you would move to the body of your argument, in which you would present details that appear supportive of war's glory and show how other details of incident and language contradict them. Capping your argument/interpretation would be a precise analysis of the poem's ironies. In your conclusion, you would repeat your main point, perhaps responding personally to the poem as you understand it. You could also relate the poem to some other work you've read (by Crane or by another writer), and perhaps include an apt quotation that sums up your sense of the work's significance.

However you choose to end your paper, remember that your conclusion should answer the question: "So what?" for your reader. Even though you have presented details, reasons, and examples to support your views, your reader will still expect you to explain their significance.

Stylistic revision concerns smaller-scale details, such as matters of syntax (word order), diction (word choice), tone, imagery, and rhythm. Even though you may think about these things in early drafts, it is better to defer critical attention to them until after writing a final draft, largely because such stylistic considerations may undergo significant alteration as you rethink and reorganize your paper.

To help you focus on aspects of style that may require revision, use the following questions as a guide.

1. Are your sentences concise and clear?
2. Can you eliminate words that are not doing their job?
3. Are your tone and voice consistent? (For example, you should eliminate shifts from a formal to an informal, even colloquial, style.)
4. Is your level of language appropriate for the subject of your paper?
5. Do your words and sentences say what you want them to? Do they say anything you don't want them to?
6. Are there any grammatical errors: inconsistencies in verb tenses, problems with subject–verb agreement, run-on sentences, fragments, and the like?
7. Are there any errors in spelling and punctuation?

As a final step, proofread the paper, and make sure it conforms to your instructor's guidelines on manuscript form.

Conventions

In writing about literary works you need to observe a number of conventions, including quotations, verb tenses, and manuscript form.

Using Quotations

In writing about literature you will need to quote lines from poems, dialogue from plays and stories, and descriptive and explanatory passages from prose fiction and nonfiction. For quoted prose passages that exceed four typed lines in your paper, begin a new line and indent ten spaces from the left margin for each line of the quotation. This format, called block quotation, does not require quotation marks because the blocked passage is set off visually from the rest of your text.

Michelle Carerra uses two block quotations in her research paper on Joyce's "The Dead" (p. 1947), both from the text of the short novel. In her research essay on E. B. White (p. 1952), Radhika Jones uses three block quotations, two from White's works—an essay and a novel—and one from a secondary source. (Carerra's and Jones's papers appear in Chapter 37.)

When quoting poetry, separate the lines of poetry with slashes. Include a space before and after each slash.

> Lorraine Hansberry derived the title of her best-known play,
> *A Raisin in the Sun,* from a poem by Langston Hughes. In "Dream
> Deferred," the speaker asks, "What happens to a dream de-
> ferred? / Does it dry up / like a raisin in the sun?"

Chapter 14 contains example of student writers quoting from the poems they write about. See their papers at the end of the chapter for additional examples of how to quote poetry when writing about it. For additional examples of students introducing quotations from stories, plays, and essays into their analytical essays, see Chapters 5 (Fiction), 21 (Drama), and 33 (Essay).

Verb Tense Conventions in Literary Papers

In writing about literature, you will often need to describe a story, novel, poem, play, or essay. In doing so you will use present tense, past tense, or both. In most instances, it is conventional to use present tense when describing what happens in a literary work. Consider the following examples:

- In Robert Hayden's "Those Winter Sundays," the speaker *reflects* on his father and *realizes* how much his father *loved* the family. [Present tense is used to describe the speaker's actions of reflecting and realizing. Past tense is used to describe the father's action, which occurred in the past, well before the speaker's present acts of reflecting and realizing.]
- Ibsen's *A Doll House portrays* a conventional middle-class environment and a conventional middle-class family. In displaying a strong concern for money and for authority, Ibsen's characters *reveal* their middle class values. Ibsen often *portrayed* characters with everyday problems of the middle class. [The verbs describing what the play does are in present tense. Those describing what the dramatist does are in past tense.]

Manuscript Form

In preparing your paper for submission, observe the following guidelines:

1. Type your essay double-spaced on 8 1/2-inch by 11-inch paper.
2. Leave 1-inch margins at top, bottom, and both sides.
3. On the first page beginning in the upper-left corner 1 inch below the top and 1 inch from the left side, type the following on separate lines:
   a. your name
   b. your instructor's name
   c. course title, number, and section
   d. date
4. Double-space below the date and center your title. It is not necessary to put quotation marks around your title or to underline or italicize it. It is necessary to underline titles of books and plays used in your title. It is also necessary to put quotation marks around the titles of short stories, poems, and essays.
5. Be sure your printer's ink supply or your typewriter ribbon is adequate for clear, readable copy.
6. If your printer feeds connected sheets of paper, be sure to separate them before submitting your essay.
7. Number each page consecutively beginning with the second page, one-half inch from the upper-right corner.
8. Clip or staple the paper, being sure the pages are right side up and in correct number order.

Plagiarism

Plagiarism is the act of using someone else's words, ideas, or organizational patterns without crediting the source. Plagiarism can result from careless note taking or from deliberate misuse of someone else's work. To avoid plagiarism, it is necessary to make clear what you borrow so that your reader can distinguish your own language and ideas from those of your sources.

Research essays and papers written with little original thought and containing many long passages of quoted and summarized material strung together may include plagiarized words and ideas. Be sure to credit each source you use at the point of borrowing, even in the middle of a paragraph or the middle of a sentence. Be sure not only to acknowledge using the source but also, if you have used language from the source, to put quotation marks around the borrowed words and phrases—even if you have separated some of the borrowed material and interspersed your own language.

Plagiarism is a serious offense. A form of academic theft, plagiarism is not tolerated in colleges and universities. Some have stringent policies, including failure for the course in which the plagiarism occurs and even expulsion from school.

To avoid plagiarism observe the following guidelines in writing your research essays and papers.

- Develop your own ideas about the works you read. Keep notes of your ideas separate from the notes you take from sources.
- Jot the title, author, and page number of sources on the page or note card you use for your notes.
- Put quotation marks around quoted material you copy from sources into your notes.
- When you summarize and paraphrase a source, be sure to use your own words. Avoid having the source open before you when you summarize and paraphrase.
- If you introduce any quotations from a source into your summaries and paraphrases of sources, put quotation marks around the quoted words and phrases.
- Make sure that your ideas and your voice are the controlling centers in your research essays and papers. Use your sources to support, illustrate, and amplify your own thinking presented in your own words.
- Observe the conventions for documentation provided on page 1936 of this book, in your college handbook, and in the *MLA Handbook for Writers of Research Papers,* 4th ed. (1995).

Fiction

PART ONE

CHAPTER ONE

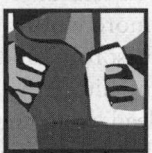

Reading Stories

We read stories for pleasure; they entertain us. And we read them for profit; they enlighten us. Stories draw us into their imaginative worlds and engage us with the power of their invention. They provide us with more than the immediate interest of narrative—of something happening—and more than the pleasures of imagination: they enlarge our understanding of ourselves and deepen our appreciation of life.

Consider this famous early story about a father and his two sons:

The Prodigal Son

A certain man had two sons: and the younger of them said to his father, "Father, give me the portion of goods that falleth to me." And he divided unto them his living. And not many days after, the younger son gathered all together, and took his journey into a far country, and there wasted his substance with riotous living. And when he had spent all, there arose a mighty famine in that land, and he began to be in want. And he went and joined himself to a citizen of that country, and he sent him into his fields to feed swine. And he would fain have filled his belly with the husks that the swine did eat: and no man gave unto him. And when he came to himself, he said, "How many hired servants of my father's have bread enough and to spare, and I perish with hunger? I will arise and go to my father, and will say unto him, 'Father, I have sinned against heaven, and before thee. And am no more worthy to be called thy son: make me as one of thy hired servants.' " And he arose, and came to his father. But when he was yet a great way off, his father saw him, and had compassion, and ran, and fell on his neck, and kissed him. And the son said unto him, "Father, I have sinned against heaven, and in thy sight, and am no more worthy to be called thy son." But the father said to his servants, "Bring forth the best robe, and put it on him, and put a ring on his hand, and shoes on his feet. And bring hither the fatted calf, and kill it, and let us eat, and be merry. For this my son was dead, and is alive again; he was lost, and is found." And they began to be merry. Now his elder son was in the field, and as he came and drew nigh to the house, he heard music and dancing. And he called one of the servants, and asked what these things meant. And he said unto him, "Thy brother is come, and thy father hath killed the fatted calf, because he hath received him safe and sound." And he was angry, and would not go in: therefore came his father out, and entreated him. And he answering said to his father, "Lo, these many years do I serve thee, neither transgressed I at any time thy commandment, and yet thou never gavest me a kid, that I might make merry with my friends: but as soon as this thy son was come, which hath devoured thy living with harlots, thou hast killed for him the fatted calf." And he said unto him, "Son, thou art ever with me, and all that I have is thine. It was meet that we should make merry, and be glad: for this thy brother was dead, and is alive again: and was lost, and is found."

When we read the story of "The Prodigal Son," we do essentially three things: (1) we take in its surface features, and form impressions of character and action; (2) we observe details, make connections among them, and draw inferences and conclusions from those connections; (3) we evaluate the story, measuring its moral, political, and cultural values against our own. We can call these three aspects of the reading process: "experience," "interpretation," and "evaluation."

THE EXPERIENCE OF FICTION

Our "experience" of fiction concerns our feelings about the characters, our sense of involvement in the story's developing action, our pleasure or confusion in its language, our joy or sorrow at its outcome. We are concerned, in short, with what the story does to us, how it affects us—and why.

How did you react to "The Prodigal Son"? What feelings did the story evoke? Did you feel sorry for the prodigal son? Did you feel anger or resentment at his behavior? At his father's or brother's behavior? Did your feelings about any of the characters change during the course of your reading or afterward? How does the story relate to your experiences as a member of a family? How does it reflect what you have observed of family relations generally?

It is important to remember that readers respond to stories in different ways. When you compare the reactions of your classmates and teacher to "The Prodigal Son," you will discover different perceptions, attitudes, and feelings about it. Why is this so? Essentially, because we bring to our reading a wide range of personal experience, social attitudes, religious beliefs, and cultural dispositions that influence our responses. We do not read a story in a vacuum: our reading is always affected by who we are, what we believe, and how we think. Christians, for example, experience "The Prodigal Son" differently from Muslims, Buddhists, or atheists. Women experience the story differently from men. Practiced readers experience the story differently from inexperienced ones. But it is not only our religious beliefs, family background, and literary sophistication that create divergent reactions. We ourselves change: we grow older; we learn more. We shift our allegiances and develop new ideas, attitudes, and beliefs. We may become parents ourselves. And in making any or all of these changes, our ways of understanding life and literature change too.

In sorting out our thoughts and feelings about "The Prodigal Son," we have been emphasizing our subjective impressions of the story—how it affects us. But while we experience a story subjectively, we are also interpreting and evaluating it. This is inevitable, since the three parts of reading are interrelated.

THE INTERPRETATION OF FICTION

When we interpret a story we explain it to ourselves and try to make sense of it. We form subjective impressions as we experience fiction, but we have relatively objective considerations in mind when we interpret it. We say "relatively" objective because no reading of a story is entirely objective: every interpretation is one way of understanding the text among many; every interpretation is influenced by our particular language, culture, and experience. What then do we mean by *interpretation?* Understanding, essentially. An interpretation is an argument about a story's meaning as we understand it. It's our way of stating and supporting, with arguments based on analysis, what the story *means,* what it says or suggests, rather than how it affects us. Interpretation, in short, relies on our intellectual comprehension rather than on our emotional response to the literary work.

Interpretation involves four related intellectual acts: observing, connecting, inferring, and concluding. To understand a fictional work, we first observe its details. We notice, for example, descriptive details about the time and place of its action; we listen carefully to what the characters say and to their manner of saying it; we note how the characters interact. As we observe, we make connections among the details and begin to formulate a sense of the story's emphasis and point. On the basis of these connections we develop inferences or interpretive hypotheses about their significance. Finally, we come to some conclusion about the story's meaning based on our observations, connections, and inferences.

The four interpretive actions of observing, connecting, inferring, and concluding often occur simultaneously, and not in neatly segregated sequential stages. We don't delay making inferences, for example, until after we have registered and related all our observations. Instead, we develop tentative conclusions *as* we read and observe, *while* we relate our observations and develop our inferences. We may change and adjust our inferences and provisional conclusions both *during* our reading of a story and *afterward* as we think back over its details. This analytical process, however, is not something we keep separate from our subjective reactions and emotional responses as we read.

In "The Prodigal Son," for example, we notice that the father sees his younger son coming from far off, that he runs to him, falls on his neck, and kisses him. Such details imply that the father has been watching for his son and hoping for his return. The father's actions speak eloquently of his unreserved acceptance of his son and deep joy at his return. Reflecting on these actions, we may connect them with the father's behavior toward his elder son and wonder what is responsible for the difference. In the process of noticing and wondering, we may also respond emotionally, thinking perhaps of our own experience or of the situation of someone we know. And we may evaluate the father's behavior according to standards we adhere to either consciously or unconsciously. The point, then, is simply that even in performing the rational, analytical act of interpretation, we cannot entirely escape a tendency to respond emotionally or to evaluate.

But our approach to interpreting stories involves something else as well: that we see a story as a story, and even more important as a particular *kind* of story. We know, for example, that "The Prodigal Son" is not a factual account of the actions of a particular father and son. A journalistic account would have included their names, perhaps their ages and address, and details about the son's behavior in the foreign land, which would have been identified. But the story gives none of this information. In fact, the details included are not those we would typically expect to find in a newspaper. It's not just that "The Prodigal Son" is short on information, but that it goes out of its way to include the kind of repetitions, for example, that would be considered unnecessary in a factual account.

It is helpful to know that "The Prodigal Son" is *fiction,* an imagined story that is not based on historical fact, and to know the conventions or implicit rules of fiction. For this story is also more than fiction to be distinguished from fact; it is a particular kind of fiction—a *parable* or brief story that teaches a lesson, often religious or spiritual in nature. As someone once cleverly put it, a parable is "an earthly story with a heavenly meaning." Parables point toward spiritual beliefs or truths and should be read symbolically, with emphasis on their spiritual meaning.

But we must go further. "The Prodigal Son" is a Christian parable—not a Hebrew or Zen parable. It was spoken by Jesus roughly two thousand years ago and recorded by the evangelist Luke in his New Testament Gospel. Thus, we look to the parable for a religious idea consistent with Jesus's teaching. It has a religious meaning that may be paraphrased like this: God (the father) is willing to forgive man (the prodigal son) any sin man commits, no matter how grievous, if only he repents and asks God's forgiveness. Alternatively: God is eager to welcome the sinner back, and in fact is happier at his return than with the fidelity of those in no spiritual danger. We can read the parable, thus, as an example of God's love, as an illustration of man's need for repentance, as a description of the relationship between God and man—or as all three.

Whatever we decide about its religious meaning, we should realize that "The Prodigal Son" means more than any interpretive comments we can make about it. This is so because the full meaning of any literary work includes our experience in reading it as well as our understanding of it—our *emotional apprehension* as well as our *intellectual comprehension*. And it includes, further, our perceptions of what is valuable, important, significant about it, for these perceptions reflect our own social, political, moral, and cultural values.

THE EVALUATION OF FICTION

The third part of our approach to reading fiction is evaluation. When we evaluate a story we do two different things. First, we assess its literary quality; we make a judgment about how good it is, how successfully it realizes its intentions, how effectively it pleases us. Second, we consider the values the story endorses—or refutes.

An evaluation is essentially a judgment, an opinion about a work formulated as a conclusion. We may agree or disagree with the father's forgiveness or the elder brother's complaint in "The Prodigal Son." We may confirm or deny the models of behavior illustrated in this or any other story. However we evaluate them, though, we invariably measure the story's values against our own.

Although evaluation is partly an unconscious process, we can make it more deliberate and more fully conscious. We simply need to ask ourselves how we respond to the values a work supports, and why. In doing so we should be able to consider our own values more clearly and perhaps discuss more sensibly and fairly why we agree or disagree with the values a story displays.

When we evaluate a story, we appraise it according to our own special combination of cultural, moral, and aesthetic values. Our cultural values derive from our lives as members of families and societies. These values are affected by our race and gender and by the language we speak. Our moral values reflect our ethical norms—what we consider to be good and evil, right and wrong. These values are influenced by our religious beliefs and sometimes by our political convictions. Our aesthetic values determine what we see as beautiful or ugly, well or ill made. Over time, with education and experience, our values often change. Through contact with other languages and cultures, we may come to understand the limiting perspectives of our own. When we live with people other than our immediate families, we may be persuaded to different ways of seeing many things we previously took for granted. Some of our beliefs, assumptions, and attitudes about religion, family, marriage, sex, love, school, work, money, and other aspects of life are almost sure to change.

As our lives and outlooks change, we may change the way we view particular literary works. A story that we once admired for what it reveals about human behavior or one whose moral perspective impressed us may come to seem trivial or unimportant. Conversely, we may find that a work we once disliked later seems engaging. Just as individual tastes in literature change over time, so do collective literary tastes. Culture evolves; moral beliefs, aesthetic values, and social attitudes change. Literary works, like musical compositions and political ideas, go in and out of fashion.

Our evaluation of a story depends upon interpretation; our judgment of a story depends on how we understand it. Our evaluation may also be linked to our first experience of the story, to first impressions based on unconsidered reactions. If our initial reaction to a story or a character is unsympathetic, we may be reluctant to change our interpretation later, even if we discover convincing evidence to warrant such a change.

Of the kinds of evaluations we make in reading fiction, those about a story's aesthetic qualities are hardest to discuss. Aesthetic responses are difficult to describe because they involve our memories and sensations, our feelings and perceptions, our subjective impressions. They also involve our expectations, which are further affected by our prior experience of reading fiction. And they are additionally complicated by our tendency to react quickly and decisively to what we like and dislike, often without knowing why. Consider the aesthetic value of "The Prodigal Son." Is it a "beautiful" story? Does it seem to be a good example of its kind—the religious parable which teaches lessons about divine forgiveness? (Or should we emphasize its human dimension, especially the relationships between people?) As we mentioned in the discussion of interpretation, understanding what kind of work we are reading affects how we interpret it. Similarly, our perception of its genre or kind also affects our evaluation. Our preference for one kind of fiction over another complicates matters still further. (We may dislike ironic stories, for example, or we may love melodrama and adventure.) When we evaluate a story, we should judge it against what it attempts to do, what it is, rather than against something it is not.

How we arrive at an aesthetic evaluation is no easy matter. We develop our aesthetic responses to fiction by letting the informed responses of other experienced readers enrich our own perceptions, by determining the criteria for what makes a story "good," and by gradually developing our sense of literary tact—the kind of balanced judgment that comes with experience in reading and living coupled with thoughtful reflection on both. There are no shortcuts or simple formulas for this development; it comes only with practice and patience.

Admittedly, without a good deal of experience in reading fiction, judgments about the values supported in a story and about its aesthetic worth need to be made cautiously. But we must begin somewhere, since evaluation is inevitable. We cannot really avoid judging the stories we read any more than we can avoid judging the people we meet. The process is natural. What we should strive for in evaluating fiction is to understand the different kinds of values it presents, and to clarify our own attitudes, dispositions, and values in responding to them.

Consider the values in John Updike's "A & P." Evaluate the behavior of each of the major characters, particularly Sammy and Lengel. Consider their attitudes toward the three girls in the story and what those attitudes reveal about each of the males. Try to assess what part your experiences and personal values play in your assessment of the story, both as an embodiment of cultural values and as an object of aesthetic value.

Interpretation
A. observe details
B. make connections
C. Influences
D Draw conclusion.

JOHN UPDIKE

[*b. 1932*]

A & P

About a Typical horny Teenager. Story about him trying to associate himself with a different type of people.

In walks these three girls in nothing but bathing suits. I'm in the third check-out slot, with my back to the door, so I don't see them until they're over by the bread. The one that caught my eye first was the one in the plaid green two-piece. She was a chunky kid, with a good tan and a sweet broad soft-looking can with those two crescents of white just under it, where the sun never seems to hit, at the top of the backs of her legs. I stood there with my hand on a box of HiHo crackers trying to remember if I rang it up or not. I ring it up again and the customer starts giving me hell. She's one of these cash-register-watchers, a witch about fifty with rouge on her cheekbones and no eyebrows, and I know it made her day to trip me up. She'd been watching cash registers for fifty years and probably never seen a mistake before.

By the time I got her feathers smoothed and her goodies into a bag—she gives me a little snort in passing, if she'd been born at the right time they would have burned her over in Salem—by the time I get her on her way the girls had circled around the bread and were coming back, without a pushcart, back my way along the counters, in the aisle between the check-outs and the Special bins. They didn't even have shoes on. There was this chunky one, with the two-piece—it was bright green and the seams on the bra were still sharp and her belly was still pretty pale so I guessed she just got it (the suit)—there was this one, with one of those chubby berry-faces, the lips all bunched together under her nose, this one, and a tall one, with black hair that hadn't quite frizzed right, and one of these sunburns right across under the eyes, and a chin that was too long—you know, the kind of girl other girls think is very "striking" and "attractive" but never quite makes it, as they very well know, which is why they like her so much—and then the third one, that wasn't quite so tall. She was the queen. She kind of led them, the other two peeking around and making their shoulders round. She didn't look around, not this queen, she just walked straight on slowly, on these long white prima donna legs. She came down a little hard on her heels, as if she didn't walk in her bare feet that much, putting down her heels and then letting the weight move along to her toes as if she was testing the floor with every step, putting a little deliberate extra action into it. You never know for sure how girls' minds work (do you really think it's a mind in there or just a little buzz like a bee in a glass jar?) but you got the idea she had talked the other two into coming in here with her, and now she was showing them how to do it, walk slow and hold yourself straight.

Topic - young men -> real general

She had on a kind of dirty-pink—beige maybe, I don't know—bathing suit with a little nubble all over it and, what got me, the straps were down. They were off her shoulders looped loose around the cool tops of her arms, and I guess as a result the suit had slipped a little on her, so all around the top of the cloth there was this shining rim. If it hadn't been there you wouldn't have known there could have been anything whiter than those shoulders. With the straps pushed off, there was nothing between the top of the suit and the top of her head except just *her,* this clean bare plane of the top of her chest down from the shoulder bones like a dented sheet of metal tilted in the light. I mean, it was more than pretty. |

She had sort of oaky hair that the sun and salt had bleached, done up in a bun that was unravelling, and a kind of prim face. Walking into the A & P with your straps down, I suppose it's the only kind of face you *can* have. She held her head so high her neck, coming up out of those white shoulders, looked kind of stretched, but I didn't mind. The longer her neck was, the more of her there was.

She must have felt in the corner of her eye me and over my shoulder Stokesie in the second slot watching, but she didn't tip. Not this queen. She kept her eyes moving across the racks, and stopped, and turned so slow it made my stomach rub the inside of my apron, and buzzed to the other two, who kind of huddled against her for relief, and they all three of them went up the cat-and-dog-food-breakfast-cereal-macaroni-rice-raisins-seasonings-spreads-spaghetti-soft-drinks-crackers-and-cookies aisle. From the third slot I look straight up this aisle to the meat counter, and I watched them all the way. The fat one with the tan sort of fumbled with the cookies, but on second thought she put the packages back. The sheep pushing their carts down the aisle—the girls were walking against the usual traffic (not that we have one-way signs or any-thing)—were pretty hilarious. You could see them, when Queenie's white shoulders dawned on them, kind of jerk, or hop, or hiccup, but their eyes snapped back to their own baskets and on they pushed. I bet you could set off dynamite in an A & P and the people would by and large keep reaching and checking oatmeal off their lists and mut-tering "Let me see, there was a third thing, began with A, asparagus, no, ah, yes, ap-plesauce!" or whatever it is they do mutter. But there was no doubt, this jiggled them. A few houseslaves in pin curlers even looked around after pushing their carts past to make sure what they had seen was correct.

You know, it's one thing to have a girl in a bathing suit down on the beach, where what with the glare nobody can look at each other much anyway, and another thing in the cool of the A & P, under the fluorescent lights, against all those stacked pack-ages, with her feet paddling along naked over our checkerboard green-and-cream rubber-tile floor.

"Oh Daddy," Stokesie said beside me. "I feel so faint."

"Darling," I said. "Hold me tight." Stokesie's married, with two babies chalked up on his fuselage already, but as far as I can tell that's the only difference. He's twenty-two, and I was nineteen this April.

"Is it done?" he asks, the responsible married man finding his voice. I forgot to say he thinks he's going to be manager some sunny day, maybe in 1990 when it's called the Great Alexandrov and Petrooshki Tea Company or something.

What he meant was, our town is five miles from a beach, with a big summer colony out on the Point, but we're right in the middle of town, and the women generally put on a shirt or shorts or something before they get out of the car into the street. And anyway these are usually women with six children and varicose veins mapping their legs and nobody, including them, could care less. As I say, we're right in the middle of town, and if you stand at our front doors you can see two banks and the Congregational church and the newspaper store and three real-estate offices and about twenty-seven old freeloaders tearing up Central Street because the sewer broke again. It's not as if we're on the Cape; we're north of Boston and there's people in this town haven't seen the ocean for twenty years.

The girls had reached the meat counter and were asking McMahon something. He pointed, they pointed, and they shuffled out of sight behind a pyramid of Diet Delight peaches. All that was left for us to see was old McMahon patting his mouth and looking after them sizing up their joints. Poor kids, I began to feel sorry for them, they couldn't help it.

Now here comes the sad part of the story, at least my family says it's sad but I don't think it's sad myself. The store's pretty empty, it being Thursday afternoon, so there was nothing much to do except lean on the register and wait for the girls to show up again. The whole store was like a pinball machine and I didn't know which tunnel they'd come out of. After a while they come around out of the far aisle, around the light bulbs, records at discount of the Caribbean Six or Tony Martin Sings or some such gunk you wonder they waste the wax on, sixpacks of candy bars, and plastic toys done up in cellophane that fall apart when a kid looks at them anyway. Around they come, Queenie still leading the way, and holding a little gray jar in her hand. Slots Three through Seven are unmanned and I could see her wondering between Stokes and me, but Stokesie with his usual luck draws an old party in baggy gray pants who stumbles up with four giant cans of pineapple juice (what do these bums *do* with all that pineapple juice? I've often asked myself) so the girls come to me. Queenie puts down the jar and I take it into my fingers icy cold. Kingfish Fancy Herring Snacks in Pure Sour Cream: 49¢. Now her hands are empty, not a ring or a bracelet, bare as God made them, and I wonder where the money's coming from. Still with that prim look she lifts a folded dollar bill out of the hollow at the center of her nubbled pink top. The jar went heavy in my hand. Really, I thought that was so cute.

Then everybody's luck begins to run out. Lengel comes in from haggling with a truck full of cabbages on the lot and is about to scuttle into that door marked MAN-AGER behind which he hides all day when the girls touch his eye. Lengel's pretty dreary, teaches Sunday school and the rest, but he doesn't miss that much. He comes over and says, "Girls, this isn't the beach."

Queenie blushes, though maybe it's just a brush of sunburn I was noticing for the first time, now that she was so close. "My mother asked me to pick up a jar of herring snacks." Her voice kind of startled me, the way voices do when you see the people first, coming out so flat and dumb yet kind of tony, too, the way it ticked over "pick up" and "snacks." All of a sudden I slid right down her voice into her living room. Her father and the other men were standing around in ice-cream coats and bow ties and the women were in sandals picking up herring snacks on toothpicks off a big plate and they were all holding drinks the color of water with olives and sprigs of mint in them. When my parents have somebody over they get lemonade and if it's a real racy affair Schlitz in tall glasses with "They'll Do It Every Time" cartoons stenciled on.

"That's all right," Lengel said. "But this isn't the beach." His repeating this struck me as funny, as if it had just occurred to him, and he had been thinking all these years the A & P was a great big dune and he was the head lifeguard. He didn't like my smiling—as I say he doesn't miss much—but he concentrates on giving the girls that sad Sunday-school-superintendent stare.

Queenie's blush is no sunburn now, and the plump one in plaid, that I liked better from the back—a really sweet can—pipes up, "We weren't doing any shopping. We just came in for the one thing."

"That makes no difference," Lengel tells her, and I could see from the way his eyes went that he hadn't noticed she was wearing a two-piece before. "We want you decently dressed when you come in here."

"We *are* decent," Queenie says suddenly, her lower lip pushing, getting sore now that she remembers her place, a place from which the crowd that runs the A & P must look pretty crummy. Fancy Herring Snacks flashed in her very blue eyes.

"Girls, I don't want to argue with you. After this come in here with your shoulders covered. It's our policy." He turns his back. That's policy for you. Policy is what the kingpins want. What the others want is juvenile delinquency.

All this while, the customers had been showing up with their carts but, you know, sheep, seeing a scene, they had all bunched up on Stokesie, who shook open a paper bag as gently as peeling a peach, not wanting to miss a word. I could feel in the silence everybody getting nervous, most of all Lengel, who asks me, "Sammy, have you rung up this purchase?"

I thought and said "No" but it wasn't about that I was thinking. I go through the punches, 4, 9, GROC, TOT—it's more complicated than you think, and after you do it often enough, it begins to make a little song, that you hear words to, in my case "Hello *(bing)* there, you *(gung)* hap-py pee-pul *(splat)!*"—the *splat* being the drawer flying out. I uncrease the bill, tenderly as you may imagine, it just having come from between the two smoothest scoops of vanilla I had ever known were there, and pass a half and a penny into her narrow pink palm, and nestle the herrings in a bag and twist its neck and hand it over, all the time thinking.

The girls, and who'd blame them, are in a hurry to get out, so I say "I quit" to Lengel quick enough for them to hear, hoping they'll stop and watch me, their unsuspected hero. They keep right on going, into the electric eye; the door flies open and they flicker across the lot to their car, Queenie and Plaid and Big Tall Goony-Goony (not that as raw material she was so bad), leaving me with Lengel and a kink in his eyebrow.

"Did you say something, Sammy?"

"I said I quit."

"I thought you did."

"You didn't have to embarrass them."

"It was they who were embarrassing us."

I started to say something that came out "Fiddle-de-doo." It's a saying of my grandmother's, and I know she would have been pleased.

"I don't think you know what you're saying," Lengel said.

"I know you don't," I said. "But I do." I pull the bow at the back of my apron and start shrugging it off my shoulders. A couple customers that had been heading for my slot begin to knock against each other, like scared pigs in a chute.

Lengel sighs and begins to look very patient and old and gray. He's been a friend of my parents for years. "Sammy, you don't want to do this to your Mom and Dad," he tells me. It's true, I don't. But it seems to me that once you begin a gesture it's fatal not to go through with it. I fold the apron, "Sammy" stitched in red on the pocket, and put it on the counter, and drop the bow tie on top of it. The bow tie is theirs, if you've ever wondered. "You'll feel this for the rest of your life," Lengel says, and I know that's true, too, but remembering how he made that pretty girl blush makes me so scrunchy inside I punch the No Sale tab and the machine whirs "pee-pul" and the drawer splats out. One advantage to this scene taking place in summer, I can follow this up with a clean exit, there's no fumbling around getting your coat and galoshes, I just saunter into the electric eye in my white shirt that my mother ironed the night before, and the door heaves itself open, and outside the sunshine is skating around on the asphalt.

I look around for my girls, but they're gone, of course. There wasn't anybody but some young married screaming with her children about some candy they didn't get by the door of a powder-blue Falcon station wagon. Looking back in the big windows, over the bags of peat moss and aluminum lawn furniture stacked on the pavement, I could see Lengel in my place in the slot, checking the sheep through. His face was dark gray and his back stiff, as if he'd just had an injection of iron, and my stomach kind of fell as I felt how hard the world was going to be to me hereafter.

(1961)

Use the following questions about "A & P" as a way of reviewing the three aspects of reading fiction we have discussed: experience, interpretation, and evaluation. *1. Because I wanted to see what would happen next. Its details and characters led me to read more.*

QUESTIONS *2. Sammys, to he's on the edge & does what he believes in. The only rules are is RULES.*

Experience *3. No*

1. Describe your experience in reading "A & P." Did the story surprise you, entertain you, annoy you? Why? Did the story engage you and hold your interest? Why or why not?
2. Consider the attitude expressed toward the girls by both Sammy and Lengel. Whose attitude do you find more appealing? Why? Do you object to Sammy's (and perhaps Updike's) language in describing Queenie—her name, her "white prima donna legs," her "two scoops of vanilla"?
3. Did your feelings about either Lengel or Sammy change in the course of reading? If so, explain where the shift occurred and why. Did they change later, on additional reflection? *4. Good, he's young and he's immature.*

Interpretation *5. He explains how he hates the register and is kind of sick of them.*

4. Characterize Sammy's style of telling his story. What do you learn about him from the kind of language he uses? From the details he includes? From the comparisons he employs to describe the store, the girls, and the other shoppers?
5. Look back to the story's climactic point, in which Sammy says, "I quit." Are there other passages of description, dialogue, or action that you see as closely related to this one?
6. How do you interpret Sammy's own response to his action? What does he mean by saying that he "felt how hard the world was going to be" for him afterwards?

Evaluation

7. Whose values does the story seem to endorse? Whose values are criticized? How do you know? How do you see Sammy's decisive action? As heroic? As silly? Something else? Why?
8. Do you find the story meaningful? Can you relate it in any significant way to your own life?
9. Do you think it is a good story, a successful example of realistic fiction? Do you find anything in it to admire from the standpoint of its language or structure?
10. Compare "A & P" to another realistic short story you have read. Which is more valuable for you? Why? Which is the more artistically wrought work? Why?

THE ACT OF READING FICTION

When we move through a text we look forward and backward at the same time: we anticipate what is to come based on our memory of what has gone before. And even though we may read stories line by line, sentence by sentence, page by page, this linearity belies what happens mentally as we read. Our mental action is cyclical rather than linear. We project ahead and we glance back; we remember and we predict. By doing so, we are able to follow and understand a story in the first place, and to see more in it on subsequent readings.

Kate Chopin's "The Story of an Hour" and interpolated comments follow. The comments do not so much interpret the story as illustrate the act of reading; they represent the kinds of observations, inferences, and judgments we make as we move toward an understanding of the story—toward some ways of seeing and thinking about it.

KATE CHOPIN

[1851–1904]

The Story of an Hour

Knowing that Mrs. Mallard was afflicted with a heart trouble, great care was taken to break to her as gently as possible the news of her husband's death.

It was her sister Josephine who told her, in broken sentences, veiled hints that revealed in half concealing. Her husband's friend Richards was there, too, near her. It was he who had been in the newspaper office when intelligence of the railroad disaster was received, with Brently Mallard's name leading the list of "killed." He had only taken the time to assure himself of its truth by a second telegram, and had hastened to forestall any less careful, less tender friend in bearing the sad message.

She did not hear the story as many women have heard the same, with a paralyzed inability to accept its significance. She wept at once, with sudden, wild abandonment, in her sister's arms. When the storm of grief had spent itself she went away to her room alone. She would have no one follow her.

Comment   The opening action is presented quickly and economically. We are not given Mrs. Mallard's first name. And we might wonder if there is any significance in the name "Mallard." Do we hear something odd in the description of Mrs. Mallard's ailment as a "heart trouble"? More important than these details is the announcement of her husband's death. Mrs. Mallard is contrasted with other women who sit paralyzed by such news—women who refuse, initially at least, to accept the significance of such an announcement. Is there a difference between accepting the significance of a husband's death and accepting the simple fact of his death? We notice, finally, that Mrs. Mallard weeps with "sudden wild abandonment."

There stood, facing the open window, a comfortable, roomy armchair. Into this she sank, pressed down by a physical exhaustion that haunted her body and seemed to reach into her soul.

She could see in the open square before her house the tops of trees that were all aquiver with the new spring life. The delicious breath of rain was in the air. In the street below a peddler was crying his wares. The notes of a distant song which some one was singing reached her faintly, and countless sparrows were twittering in the eaves.

There were patches of blue sky showing here and there through the clouds that had met and piled above the other in the west facing her window.

She sat with her head thrown back upon the cushion of the chair quite motionless, except when a sob came up into her throat and shook her, as a child who has cried itself to sleep continues to sob in its dreams.

Comment   The setting for the middle section of the story is Mrs. Mallard's room. Is the open window through which she looks of any significance? Do the details that follow—trees, birds, rain, patches of blue sky, peddler, and song—have anything in common? We notice also that Mrs. Mallard is compared to a child who sobs in its dreams and may wonder about the implications of this comparison.

She was young, with a fair, calm face, whose lines bespoke repression and even a certain strength. But now there was a dull stare in her eyes, whose gaze was fixed away off yonder on one of those patches of blue sky. It was not a glance of reflection, but rather indicated a suspension of intelligent thought.

There was something coming to her and she was waiting for it, fearfully. What was it? She did not know; it was too subtle and elusive to name. But she felt it, creeping out of the sky, reaching toward her through the sounds, the scents, the color that filled the air.

Now her bosom rose and fell tumultuously. She was beginning to recognize this thing that was approaching to possess her, and she was striving to beat it back with her will— as powerless as her two white slender hands would have been.

Comment   These paragraphs alter slightly the tone and pace of the story. We are not told what Mrs. Mallard is waiting for. Whatever it is, however, she *feels* it; she senses it coming as she looks out the window. And we see her resisting it—powerlessly. Do we perhaps also hear sexual overtones in the description of what is "approaching to possess" her? Or do we wish to assign religious or psychological significance to this imminent possession and her ambivalent feelings about it? We notice, in addition, that Mrs. Mallard is described as not conscious of what is happening to her. Chopin says that there is "a suspension of intelligent thought." She seems to *feel* rather than think.

When she abandoned herself a little whispered word escaped her slightly parted lips. She said it over and over under her breath: "Free, free, free!" The vacant stare and the look of terror that had followed it went from her eyes. They stayed keen and bright. Her pulse beat fast, and the coursing blood warmed and relaxed every inch of her body.

Comment   In the first sentence the word "abandoned" echoes the earlier description of Mrs. Mallard's "wild abandonment." But she now seems in control of herself. Her repetition of "free" signals her excitement and perhaps convinces her of its truth. Her emotional excitement is rendered in physical imagery: her pulse beats fast, and her blood courses through her body—both signs of reawakened feeling.

She did not stop to ask if it were not a monstrous joy that held her. A clear and exalted perception enabled her to dismiss the suggestion as trivial.

She knew that she would weep again when she saw the kind, tender hands folded in death; the face that had never looked save with love upon her, fixed and gray and dead. But she saw beyond that bitter moment a long procession of years to come that would belong to her absolutely. And she opened and spread her arms out to them in welcome.

There would be no one to live for during those coming years; she would live for herself. There would be no powerful will bending her in that blind persistence with which men and women believe they have a right to impose a private will upon a fellow-creature. A kind intention or a cruel intention made the act seem no less a crime as she looked upon it in that brief moment of illumination.

And yet she had loved him—sometimes. Often she had not. What did it matter! What could love, the unsolved mystery, count for in face of this possession of self-assertion which she suddenly recognized as the strongest impulse of her being!

Comment   We pause over the words "monstrous joy." Clearly Mrs. Mallard is overjoyed. And from one perspective her joy, however honestly felt, is monstrous. She is happy—exultantly happy—that her husband is dead. But the author makes clear that Mrs. Mallard does not think about what she is feeling.

The first paragraph underscores Mrs. Mallard's control and clear-sightedness. Her sense of confidence, anticipated earlier, becomes explicit and strong. We wonder if her husband treated her cruelly, but the text answers that he has been kind, which makes Mrs. Mallard's open-armed welcome of the coming years indeed monstrous. In the next paragraph Chopin does not exactly condemn Mr. Mallard but does suggest that Mrs. Mallard had to bend her will to his. Kind or not, he controlled her; loving wife or not, she resented it. Chopin here seems to move beyond the case of a particularly unhappy wife to the larger issue of the bonds of marriage, using language that strongly condemns the husband's dominance. We hear it in such words and phrases as "powerful will bending hers," "blind persistence," "impose," and "crime." This language is balanced by a lyrical evocation of Mrs. Mallard, in the years to come, living for herself rather than for her husband. The moment is described as "that brief moment of illumination." This description builds on the earlier description of her eyes as "keen and bright." Mrs. Mallard is possessed by a new sense of herself and a new self-confidence as she envisions her future life. This is the turning point of her life, a moment of recognition, insight, and enlightenment that makes her previous life with her husband pale into insignificance.

The next paragraphs could end the story:

"Free! Body and soul free!" she kept whispering.

Josephine was kneeling before the closed door with her lips to the keyhole, imploring for admission. "Louise, open the door! I beg; open the door—you will make yourself ill. What are you doing, Louise? For heaven's sake open the door."

"Go away. I am not making myself ill." No; she was drinking in a very elixir of life through that open window.

Her fancy was running riot along those days ahead of her. Spring days, and summer days, and all sorts of days that would be her own. She breathed a quick prayer that life might be long. It was only yesterday she had thought with a shudder that life might be long.

She arose at length and opened the door to her sister's importunities. There was a feverish triumph in her eyes, and she carried herself unwittingly like a goddess of Victory. She clasped her sister's waist, and together they descended the stairs. Richards stood waiting for them at the bottom.

Comment The discrepancy between what Josephine thinks is Mrs. Mallard's reason for keeping herself locked in her room and our knowledge of the real reason is ironic.★ There is irony, also, in Mrs. Mallard's praying for a long life, as only the day before she had shuddered at the thought of a long life with Brently Mallard. The language of these paragraphs is charged with feeling—somewhat overcharged perhaps—but it is in keeping with extending and intensifying Mrs. Mallard's emotion. She drinks in the "elixir of life," has a "feverish triumph in her eyes," and comports herself like a "goddess of Victory." These paragraphs could end the story, but they don't. Instead Chopin has a surprise:

Some one was opening the front door with a latchkey. It was Brently Mallard who entered, a little travel-stained, composedly carrying his grip-sack and umbrella. He had been far from the scene of accident, and did not even know there had been one. He stood amazed at Josephine's piercing cry; at Richards's quick motion to screen him from the view of his wife.

★Irony involves some kind of opposition, usually between what appears to be and what is or between what is said and what is meant. See page 99.

But Richards was too late.

When the doctors came they said she had died of heart disease—of joy that kills.

(1894)

Comment   The surprise, of course, is too much for Mrs. Mallard. Does she die of shock, of despair, of joy that kills? We are left with the impression that Josephine, Richards, and the doctor do not understand that Mrs. Mallard dies not of shock at seeing her husband alive, not out of joy, but out of something like despair. Why does the narrator suggest that none of them realize the truth?

Some interesting questions are left unresolved by this ending. Is Mrs. Mallard being punished for harboring a desire to be free of her husband? Or, is Mrs. Mallard a symbol of repressed womanhood yearning to be free of male bondage? Does the story transcend the sexual identity of its protagonist? Could we imagine a man in Mrs. Mallard's position?

Our emphasis in this interrupted reading of "The Story of an Hour" has been to illustrate the active process of thinking while you read. We have focused largely on issues of response and interpretation. But we should also consider a few additional questions about the story's values.

QUESTIONS

1. What personal and social values influence your reading of the story?
2. What values animate Mrs. Mallard's behavior and feelings?
3. What values underlie her husband's treatment of her?
4. To what extent do their values reflect or depart from society's values at the time the story was written?
5. To what extent do their values reflect or depart from today's cultural values?
6. And how are any or all of these values measured against your own?

CHAPTER TWO

Types of Short Fiction

In our discussion of reading stories in Chapter One, we considered three stories—a parable and two modern realistic short stories. But short fiction comes in more than these two varieties. Other popular forms we might know include fairy tales and mystery stories, science fiction stories, and popular romance. While we need not rehearse all of short fiction's various guises, it will nonetheless be useful to describe its more common and enduring types. We begin with some ancient forms.

EARLY FORMS: PARABLE, FABLE, AND TALE

In our discussion of "The Prodigal Son" (page 27), we defined a parable as a brief story that teaches a lesson, often of a religious or spiritual nature. Another early story form is the fable, a relative of the parable.

Like parables, *fables* are brief stories that point to a moral. The moral of the fable is stated explicitly, whereas the moral of the parable is implied. The two forms also differ in subject and tone. Fables highlight features of human nature and character, especially human failings. They frequently include animals as characters, and their tone is satirical. As we have stated, parables are stories about common life through which a religious or spiritual point is made. Their purpose is instructive, their tone serious. Although we can distinguish conveniently between fable and parable in these ways, there are stories in which such distinctions are blurred, as in George Orwell's *Animal Farm,* which includes characteristics of both. Here is a fable attributed to Aesop, whose name has become synonymous with the form.

AESOP

[*c. 620–560 B.C.*]

The Wolf and the Mastiff

A Wolf, who was almost skin and bone—so well did the dogs of the neighborhood keep guard—met, one moonshiny night, a sleek Mastiff, who was, moreover, as strong as he was fat. Bidding the Dog good-night very humbly, he praised his good looks. "It would be easy for you," replied the Mastiff, "to get as fat as I am if you liked." "What shall I have to do?" asked the Wolf. "Almost nothing," answered the Dog. They trotted off together, but, as they went along, the Wolf noticed a bare spot on the Dog's neck. "What is that mark?" said he. "Oh, the merest trifle," answered the Dog; "the collar which I wear when I am tied up is the cause of it." "Tied up!" exclaimed the Wolf, with a sudden stop; "tied up? Can you not always then run where you please?" "Well, not quite always," said the Mastiff; "but what can that matter?" "It matters much to me," rejoined the Wolf, and, leaping away, he ran once more to his native forest.

Moral: Better starve free, than be a fat slave.

Both the fable and the parable represent early forms of fiction. Another early form, one without the strong instructive intent of fable and parable, is the tale. A *tale* is a story that narrates strange or fabulous happenings in a direct manner, without detailed descriptions of character. A tale does not necessarily point to a moral as a fable or parable does, but it is almost as generalized in its depiction of character and setting. While we may read fable and parable to understand their meaning, to get the point so to speak, our interest in tales will generally incline more toward what happens. Our interest, that is, lies in action and its outcome. Additionally, it may reside in the emotions we experience in reading tales rather than in generalizations we can make about them. The following tale, written in the first century, is from the *Satyricon* of Petronius.

PETRONIUS

[*d. A.D. 66?*]

The Widow of Ephesus

Once upon a time there was a certain married woman in the city of Ephesus whose fidelity to her husband was so famous that the women from all the neighboring towns and villages used to troop into Ephesus merely to stare at this prodigy. It happened, however, that her husband one day died. Finding the normal custom of following the cortege with hair unbound and beating her breast in public quite inadequate to express her grief, the lady insisted on following the corpse right into the tomb, an underground vault of the Greek type, and there set herself to guard the body, weeping and wailing night and day. Although in her extremes of grief she was clearly courting death from starvation, her parents were utterly unable to persuade her to leave, and even the magistrates, after one last supreme attempt, were rebuffed and driven away. In short, all Ephesus had gone into mourning for this extraordinary woman, all the more since the lady was now passing her fifth consecutive day without once tasting food. Beside the failing woman sat her devoted maid, sharing her mistress' grief and relighting the lamp whenever it flickered out. The whole city could speak, in fact, of nothing else: here at last, all classes alike agreed, was the one true example of conjugal fidelity and love.

In the meantime, however, the governor of the province gave orders that several thieves should be crucified in a spot close by the vault where the lady was mourning her dead husband's corpse. So, on the following night, the soldier who had been assigned to keep watch on the crosses so that nobody could remove the thieves' bodies for burial suddenly noticed a light blazing among the tombs and heard the sounds of groaning. And prompted by a natural human curiosity to know who or what was making those sounds, he descended into the vault.

But at the sight of a strikingly beautiful woman, he stopped short in terror, thinking he must be seeing some ghostly apparition out of hell. Then, observing the corpse and seeing the tears on the lady's face and the scratches her fingernails had gashed in her cheeks, he realized what it was: a widow, in inconsolable grief. Promptly fetching his little supper back down to the tomb, he implored the lady not to persist in her sorrow or break her heart with useless mourning. All men alike, he reminded her, have the same end; the same resting place awaits us all. He used, in short, all those platitudes we use to comfort the suffering and bring them back to life. His consolations, being unwelcome, only exasperated the widow more; more violently than ever she beat her breast, and tearing out her hair by the roots, scattered it over the dead man's body. Undismayed, the soldier repeated his arguments and pressed her to take some food, until the little maid, quite overcome by the smell of the wine, succumbed and stretched out her hand to her tempter. Then, restored by the food and wine, she began herself to assail her mistress' obstinate refusal.

"How will it help you," she asked the lady, "if you faint from hunger? Why should you bury yourself alive, and go down to death before the Fates have called you? What does Vergil say?—

Do you suppose the shades and ashes of the dead are by such sorrow touched?

No, begin your life afresh. Shake off these woman's scruples; enjoy the light while you can. Look at that corpse of your poor husband: doesn't it tell you more eloquently than any words that you should live?"

None of us, of course, really dislikes being told that we must eat, that life is to be lived. And the lady was no exception. Weakened by her long days of fasting, her resistance crumbled at last, and she ate the food the soldier offered her as hungrily as the little maid had eaten earlier.

Well, you know what temptations are normally aroused in a man on a full stomach. So the soldier, mustering all those blandishments by means of which he had persuaded the lady to live, now laid determined siege to her virtue. And chaste though she was, the lady found him singularly attractive and his arguments persuasive. As for the maid, she did all she could to help the soldier's cause, repeating like a refrain the appropriate line of Vergil:

If love is pleasing, lady, yield yourself to love.

To make the matter short, the lady's body soon gave up the struggle; she yielded and our happy warrior enjoyed a total triumph on both counts. That very night their marriage was consummated, and they slept together the second and the third night too, carefully shutting the door of the tomb so that any passing friend or stranger would have thought the lady of famous chastity had at last expired over her dead husband's body.

As you can perhaps imagine, our soldier was a very happy man, utterly delighted with his lady's ample beauty and that special charm that a secret love confers. Every night, as soon as the sun had set, he bought what few provisions his slender pay permitted and smuggled them down to the tomb. One night, however, the parents of one of the crucified thieves, noticing that the watch was being badly kept, took advantage of our hero's absence to remove their son's body and bury it. The next morning, of course, the soldier was horror-struck to discover one of the bodies missing from its cross, and ran to tell his mistress of the horrible punishment which awaited him for neglecting his duty. In the circumstances, he told her, he would not wait to be tried and sentenced, but would punish himself then and there with his own sword. All he asked of her was that she make room for another corpse and allow the same gloomy tomb to enclose husband and lover together.

Our lady's heart, however, was no less tender than pure. "God forbid," she cried, "that I should have to see at one and the same time the dead bodies of the only two men I have ever loved. No, better far, I say, to hang the dead than kill the living." With these words, she gave orders that her husband's body should be taken from its bier and strung up on the empty cross. The soldier followed this good advice, and the next morning the whole city wondered by what miracle the dead man had climbed up on the cross.

(1st century A.D.)

In responding to "The Widow of Ephesus" we look less to a moral than to its action. Much of the pleasure we take in a story like this resides in its series of surprises. We may be amazed at the way the lady expresses her sorrow, surprised at her capitulation to the soldier, and amused (or appalled) at where they make love. But before we can become absorbed in these events, Petronius surprises us with another series of actions culminating in the lady's still more amazing solution to the soldier's dilemma: putting the corpse of her dead husband up on the cross.

Our admiration for the inventiveness and economy of the tale's action, however, may not eliminate our desire to look for a moral of some sort. But in such a tale, we should search cautiously. Does the story's hypothetical moral have to do with the fickleness of women? Is the story told to illustrate that all women can be tempted and seduced? Does it suggest that life is to be lived and enjoyed? Or does it imply that people are credulous, that, rather than believe the widow capable of anything but unaltered devotion to her dead husband, they believe in the miraculous ascent of a dead body onto the cross?

Whatever our sense of the tale's point and purpose, whatever meaning we finally take from it, "The Widow of Ephesus" is not as clear-cut as Aesop's fable or the parable of the Prodigal Son. And in that respect this tale more closely resembles the modern short story, whose meaning is often ambiguous or open to a variety of interpretations.

THE SHORT STORY

The *short story* as a form of short fiction developed and became popular in the nineteenth century. During this period, fiction was channeled in the direction of realism or a detailed representation of everyday life, typically the lives and experiences familiar to middle-class individuals. Besides its realistic impulse, the modern short story differs from the ancient forms of short fiction in still another way: in the ratio between summary and scene. Parables, fables, and tales tend to summarize action, to tell what happens in a general overview of the action. Short stories, on the other hand, typically reveal character in dramatic scenes, in moments of action, and in exchanges of dialogue detailed enough to represent the surface of life. In addition, the short story has traditionally been more concerned with the revelation of character through flashes of insight and shocks of recognition than the early fictional forms.

Typical features of the modern realistic short story include the following:

1. Its plot is based on probability, illustrating a sequence of causally related incidents.
2. Its characters are recognizably human, and they are motivated by identifiable social and psychological forces.
3. Its time and place are clearly established, with realistic rather than fantastic settings.
4. Its elements—plot, character, setting, style, point of view, irony, symbol and theme—work toward a single effect, unifying the story.

THE NONREALISTIC STORY

In an effort to break away from the prevailing conventions of the realistic short story, some modern storytellers have mixed features of the early story forms— elements of the supernatural, for example—with realistic conventions. I. B. Singer's "Gimpel the Fool" (page 363) includes supernatural elements, though they function in quite different ways. Such writers as Leslie Marmon Silko in "Yellow Woman" (page 431) and Gabriel Garcia Marquez in "A Very Old Man with Enormous Wings" (page 388) employ legendary materials in their stories. Shifting back and forth between the realistic and fantastic worlds, these modern storytellers have discovered and explored ways to represent human experience powerfully and incisively.

Occasionally modern writers of short fiction employ nonrealistic detail so heavily that readers are disoriented and unsettled. When we read a story like Jorge Luis Borges's "The Garden of the Forking Paths" (page 357), we may be uncertain about what exactly is happening. Part of the reason for our initial confusion is attributable to the author's use of surrealistic action or of mystery and riddle. Our confusion may also derive from our expectations: we expect the conventions of realism to operate, and when they do not we need to readjust our sense of what we are reading.

The important thing, however, about nonrealistic stories is to accept them on their own terms. In accepting their break from realistic fictional convention we increase our chances of responding fully to the pleasures they offer. We also enlarge our understanding of what a short story can be.

CHAPTER THREE

The Elements
of Fiction

In learning to read fiction well, we must understand something about its technique. One useful way to approach the techniques of fiction is to describe its basic elements or characteristics: plot and structure, character, setting, point of view, style and language, symbol, irony, and theme. We will discuss each element separately to highlight its special features. Be aware, however, that all the elements of a story work together to convey feeling and embody meaning. Thus, our analysis of any one fictional element—plot or character, for example—is related to the other elements and to the work as a whole.

PLOT AND STRUCTURE

Plot, the action element in fiction, is the arrangement of events that make up a story. A story's plot keeps us turning pages: we read to find out what will happen next. But for a plot to be effective, it must include a sequence of incidents that bear a significant causal relationship to each other. Causality is an important feature of realistic fictional plots: it simply means that one thing happens because of—as a result of—something else. The following example from E. M. Forster's *Aspects of the Novel* clarifies this point. Forster notes that "The king died and then the queen died" promises a story, but not a plot. Why? Because there is no causal connection between the two deaths. But if the sentence

read: "The king died and then the queen died of grief," we have such a connection and hence a plot.*

Many fictional plots turn on a *conflict,* or struggle between opposing forces,
that is usually resolved by the end of the story. Typical fictional plots begin with
an *exposition* that provides background information we need to make sense of
the action, describes the setting, and introduces the major characters; these plots
develop a series of *complications* or intensifications of the conflict that lead to a
crisis or moment of great tension. The conflict may reach a *climax* or turning
point, a moment of greatest tension that fixes the outcome; then, the action
falls off as the plot's complications are sorted out and resolved (the *resolution* or
denouement). The plot of a typical realistic short story can be diagrammed in the
following manner:

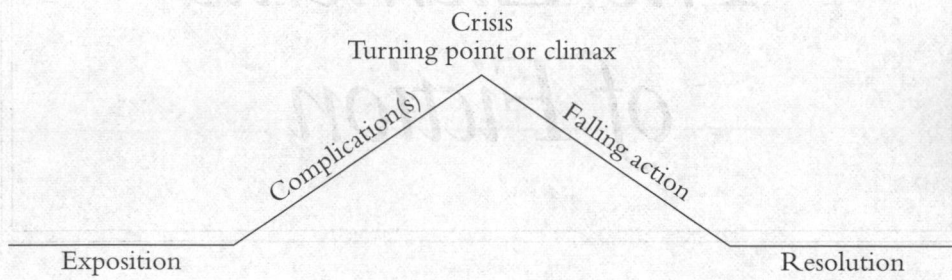

This diagram, however, is useful only as a point of departure for describing the
plot of a particular story. Most stories do not exhibit such strict formality of design. A story's climactic moment, for example, may occur simultaneously with
its ending, with little or no formal resolution. Or its action may rise and fall repeatedly in a jagged and uneven pattern rather than according to the neat symmetry of this diagram.

The action of a realistic story is usually composed of a sequence of causally
related actions or events that are not necessarily presented in chronological order.
For example, flashbacks that disrupt the linear movement of the plot to present
an earlier action are employed in many stories. To distill the plot from William
Faulkner's "A Rose for Emily" or Ernest Hemingway's "The Short Happy Life
of Francis Macomber," we must untangle a set of events that shift between past
and present. In doing so we can clarify our sense of what happened, how it happened, and why.

Whatever the plot of a story may be, the writer has ordered the events with
a view both to the overall meaning and to the responses of readers. To appreciate fictional plot, therefore, we should think about our experience in
reading a story and remember what we thought and felt at different points.
This subjective dimension of our reading experience should prompt us to investigate why the writer has chosen one arrangement of incidents over an-

*E. M. Forster, *Aspects of the Novel* (New York: Harcourt, Brace and World, Inc., 1927), p. 130.

other. And it should lead us to see how writers control our emotional responses, how they vary the tempo of the action, and how they prepare for reversals and surprises.

Consider the plot of Chopin's "The Story of an Hour," with its surprises and dramatic reversals. It begins with a reference to the accident in which Brently Mallard is purportedly killed, then shows its effect on his wife. The tempo then slows down as we watch Mrs. Mallard's reactions, particularly her behavior in her room. The plot includes an ironic twist in this descriptive section as Mrs. Mallard's shock evolves into joyful self-assertion, and then produces a stronger and more abrupt and climactic ironic reversal with its final action: the arrival of a very much alive Brently Mallard and the collapse and death of Mrs. Mallard. Returning to the beginning of the story, we can see how Chopin prepared for these shifts, how she shaped our expectations only to surprise us.

A story's structure can be examined in relation to its plot. If plot is the sequence of unfolding action, *structure* is the *design* or form of the completed action. In examining plot, we are concerned with causality, with how one action leads into or ties in with another. In examining structure, we look for patterns, for the shape of content that the story as a whole possesses. Plot directs us to the story in motion, structure to the story at rest. Plot and structure together reveal aspects of the story's artistic design.

Structure is important in fiction for a number of reasons. It satisfies our need for order, for proportion, for arrangement. A story's symmetry or balance of details may please us, as may its alternation of moments of tension and relaxation. Consider the structure of "The Prodigal Son" with its various balances and parallels. It begins and ends with a father together with his sons, it includes repeated statements by both father and prodigal son, and it substitutes the discontent of one son for the discontent of the other. Such balances make the story's form aesthetically pleasing. But structure is important for another reason: it provides a clue to a story's meaning.

We can be alert for a story's structure even as we read it for the first time, primarily by paying attention to repeated elements and recurrent details—of action and gesture, of dialogue and description—and to shifts in direction and changes of focus. Repetition signals important connections and relationships in the story, relationships between characters, connections between ideas. Shifts in direction are often signalled by such visual or aural clues as a change of scene, a new voice, blank space in the text. They may also include changes in the time and place of the action or alterations in characters' entrances and exits or in their behavior, or they may appear as changes in the pace of the story, and in its texture or language.

Keep these considerations about plot and structure in mind as you read Frank O'Connor's "Guests of the Nation," which follows. See how its plot, for example, both follows and deviates from the diagram on page 50. Note especially any shifts of emphasis and changes of tempo in the story's action. And once you have finished reading, look back and describe your expectations about the developing action.

FRANK O'CONNOR

[1903–1966]

Guests of the Nation

1

At dusk the big Englishman, Belcher, would shift his long legs out of the ashes and say "Well, chums, what about it?" and Noble or me would say "All right, chum" (for we had picked up some of their curious expressions), and the little Englishman, Hawkins, would light the lamp and bring out the cards. Sometimes Jeremiah Donovan would come up and supervise the game and get excited over Hawkins's cards, which he always played badly, and shout at him as if he was one of our own, "Ah, you divil, you, why didn't you play the tray?"

But ordinarily Jeremiah was a sober and contented poor devil like the big Englishman, Belcher, and was looked up to only because he was a fair hand at documents, though he was slow enough even with them. He wore a small cloth hat and big gaiters over his long pants, and you seldom saw him with his hands out of his pockets. He reddened when you talked to him, tilting from toe to heel and back, and looking down all the time at his big farmer's feet. Noble and me used to make fun of his broad accent, because we were from the town.

I couldn't at the time see the point of me and Noble guarding Belcher and Hawkins at all, for it was my belief that you could have planted that pair down anywhere from this to Claregalway and they'd have taken root there like a native weed. I never in my short experience seen two men to take to the country as they did.

They were handed on to us by the Second Battalion when the search for them became too hot, and Noble and myself, being young, took over with a natural feeling of responsibility, but Hawkins made us look like fools when he showed that he knew the country better than we did.

"You're the bloke they calls Bonaparte," he says to me. "Mary Brigid O'Connell told me to ask you what you done with the pair of her brother's socks you borrowed."

For it seemed, as they explained it, that the Second used to have little evenings, and some of the girls of the neighborhood turned in, and, seeing they were such decent chaps, our fellows couldn't leave the two Englishmen out of them. Hawkins learned to dance "The Walls of Limerick," "The Siege of Ennis," and "The Waves of Tory" as well as any of them, though, naturally, we couldn't return the compliment, because our lads at that time did not dance foreign dances on principle.

So whatever privileges Belcher and Hawkins had with the Second they just naturally took with us, and after the first day or two we gave up all pretense of keeping a close eye on them. Not that they could have got far, for they had accents you could cut with a knife and wore khaki tunics and overcoats with civilian pants and boots. But it's my belief that they never had any idea of escaping and were quite content to be where they were.

It was a treat to see how Belcher got off with the old woman of the house where we were staying. She was a great warrant to scold, and cranky even with us, but before ever she had a chance of giving our guests, as I may call them, a lick of her tongue, Belcher had made her his friend for life. She was breaking sticks, and Belcher, who hadn't been more than ten minutes in the house, jumped up from his seat and went over to her.

"Allow me, madam," he says, smiling his queer little smile, "please allow me"; and he takes the bloody hatchet. She was struck too paralytic to speak, and after that, Belcher would be at her heels, carrying a bucket, a basket, or a load of turf, as the case might be. As Noble said, he got into looking before she leapt, and hot water, or any little thing she wanted, Belcher would have it ready for her. For such a huge man (and though I am five foot ten myself I had to look up at him) he had an uncommon shortness— or should I say lack?—of speech. It took us some time to get used to him, walking in and out, like a ghost, without a word. Especially because Hawkins talked enough for a platoon, it was strange to hear big Belcher with his toes in the ashes come out with a solitary "Excuse me, chum," or "That's right, chum." His one and only passion was cards, and I will say for him that he was a good cardplayer. He could have fleeced myself and Noble, but whatever we lost to him Hawkins lost to us, and Hawkins played with the money Belcher gave him.

Hawkins lost to us because he had too much old gab, and we probably lost to Belcher for the same reason. Hawkins and Noble would spit at one another about religion into the early hours of the morning, and Hawkins worried the soul out of Noble, whose brother was a priest, with a string of questions that would puzzle a cardinal. To make it worse, even in treating of holy subjects, Hawkins had a deplorable tongue. I never in all my career met a man who could mix such a variety of cursing and bad language into an argument. He was a terrible man, and a fright to argue. He never did a stroke of work, and when he had no one else to talk to, he got stuck in the old woman.

He met his match in her, for one day when he tried to get her to complain profanely of the drought, she gave him a great come-down by blaming it entirely on Jupiter Pluvius (a deity neither Hawkins nor I had ever heard of, though Noble said that among the pagans it was believed that he had something to do with the rain). Another day he was swearing at the capitalists for starting the German war when the old lady laid down her iron, puckered up her little crab's mouth, and said: "Mr. Hawkins, you can say what you like about the war, and think you'll deceive me because I'm only a simple poor countrywoman, but I know what started the war. It was the Italian Count that stole the heathen divinity out of the temple in Japan. Believe me, Mr. Hawkins, nothing but sorrow and want can follow the people that disturb the hidden powers."

A queer old girl, all right.

2

We had our tea one evening, and Hawkins lit the lamp and we all sat into cards. Jeremiah Donovan came in too, and sat down and watched us for a while, and it suddenly struck me that he had no great love for the two Englishmen. It came as a great surprise to me, because I hadn't noticed anything about him before.

Late in the evening a really terrible argument blew up between Hawkins and Noble, about capitalists and priests and love of your country.

"The capitalists," says Hawkins with an angry gulp, "pays the priests to tell you about the next world so as you won't notice what the bastards are up to in this."

"Nonsense, man!" says Noble, losing his temper. "Before ever a capitalist was thought of, people believed in the next world."

Hawkins stood up as though he was preaching a sermon.

"Oh, they did, did they?" he says with a sneer. "They believed all the things you believe, isn't that what you mean? And you believe that God created Adam, and Adam created Shem, and Shem created Jehoshaphat. You believe all that silly old fairytale about Eve and Eden and the apple. Well, listen to me, chum. If you're entitled to hold a silly belief like that, I'm entitled to hold my silly belief—which is that the first thing your God created was a bleeding capitalist, with morality and Rolls-Royce complete. Am I right, chum?" he says to Belcher.

"You're right, chum," says Belcher with his amused smile, and got up from the table to stretch his long legs into the fire and stroke his moustache. So, seeing that Jeremiah Donovan was going, and that there was no knowing when the argument about religion would be over, I went out with him. We strolled down to the village together, and then he stopped and started blushing and mumbling and saying I ought to be behind, keeping guard on the prisoners. I didn't like the tone he took with me, and anyway I was bored with life in the cottage, so I replied by asking him what the hell we wanted guarding them at all for. I told him I'd talked it over with Noble, and that we'd both rather be out with a fighting column.

"What use are those fellows to us?" says I.

He looked at me in surprise and said: "I thought you knew we were keeping them as hostages."

"Hostages?" I said.

"The enemy have prisoners belonging to us," he says, "and now they're talking of shooting them. If they shoot our prisoners, we'll shoot theirs."

"Shoot them?" I said.

"What else did you think we were keeping them for?" he says.

"Wasn't it very unforeseen of you not to warn Noble and myself of that in the beginning?" I said.

"How was it?" says he. "You might have known it."

"We couldn't know it, Jeremiah Donovan," says I. "How could we when they were on our hands so long?"

"The enemy have our prisoners as long and longer," says he.

"That's not the same thing at all," says I.

"What difference is there?" says he.

I couldn't tell him, because I knew he wouldn't understand. If it was only an old dog that was going to the vet's, you'd try and not get too fond of him, but Jeremiah Donovan wasn't a man that would ever be in danger of that.

"And when is this thing going to be decided?" says I.

"We might hear tonight," he says. "Or tomorrow or the next day at latest. So if it's only hanging round here that's a trouble to you, you'll be free soon enough."

It wasn't the hanging round that was a trouble to me at all by this time. I had worse things to worry about. When I got back to the cottage the argument was still on. Hawkins was holding forth in his best style, maintaining that there was no next world, and Noble was maintaining that there was; but I could see that Hawkins had had the best of it.

"Do you know what, chum?" he was saying with a saucy smile. "I think you're just as big a bleeding unbeliever as I am. You say you believe in the next world, and you know just as much about the next world as I do, which is sweet damn-all. What's heaven? You don't know. Where's heaven? You don't know. You know sweet damn-all! I ask you again, do they wear wings?"

"Very well, then," says Noble, "they do. Is that enough for you? They do wear wings."

"Where do they get them, then? Who makes them? Have they a factory for wings? Have they a sort of store where you hands in your chit and takes your bleeding wings?"

"You're an impossible man to argue with," says Noble. "Now, listen to me—" And they were off again.

It was long after midnight when we locked up and went to bed. As I blew out the candle I told Noble what Jeremiah Donovan was after telling me. Noble took it very quietly. When we'd been in bed about an hour he asked me did I think we ought to tell the Englishmen. I didn't think we should, because it was more than likely that the English wouldn't shoot our men, and even if they did, the brigade officers, who were always up and down with the Second Battalion and knew the Englishmen well, wouldn't be likely to want them plugged. "I think so too," says Noble. "It would be great cruelty to put the wind up them now."

"It was very unforeseen of Jeremiah Donovan anyhow," says I.

It was next morning that we found it so hard to face Belcher and Hawkins. We went about the house all day scarcely saying a word. Belcher didn't seem to notice; he was stretched into the ashes as usual, with his usual look of waiting in quietness for something unforeseen to happen, but Hawkins noticed and put it down to Noble's being beaten in the argument of the night before.

"Why can't you take a discussion in the proper spirit?" he says severely. "You and your Adam and Eve! I'm a Communist, that's what I am. Communist or anarchist, it all comes to much the same thing." And for hours he went round the house, muttering when the fit took him. "Adam and Eve! Adam and Eve! Nothing better to do with their time than picking bleeding apples!"

3

I don't know how we got through that day, but I was very glad when it was over, the tea things were cleared away, and Belcher said in his peaceable way: "Well, chums, what about it?" We sat round the table and Hawkins took out the cards, and just then I heard Jeremiah Donovan's footstep on the path and a dark presentiment crossed my mind. I rose from the table and caught him before he reached the door.

"What do you want?" I asked.

"I want those two soldier friends of yours," he says, getting red.

"Is that the way, Jeremiah Donovan?" I asked.

"That's the way. There were four of our lads shot this morning, one of them a boy of sixteen."

"That's bad," I said.

At that moment Noble followed me out, and the three of us walked down the path together, talking in whispers. Feeney, the local intelligence officer, was standing by the gate.

"What are you going to do about it?" I asked Jeremiah Donovan.

"I want you and Noble to get them out; tell them they're being shifted again; that'll be the quietest way."

"Leave me out of that," says Noble under his breath.

Jeremiah Donovan looks at him hard.

"All right," he says. "You and Feeney get a few tools from the shed and dig a hole by the far end of the bog. Bonaparte and myself will be after you. Don't let anyone see you with the tools. I wouldn't like it to go beyond ourselves."

We saw Feeney and Noble go round to the shed and went in ourselves. I left Jeremiah Donovan to do the explanations. He told them that he had orders to send them back to the Second Battalion. Hawkins let out a mouthful of curses, and you could see that though Belcher didn't say anything, he was a bit upset too. The old woman was for having them stay in spite of us, and she didn't stop advising them until Jeremiah Donovan lost his temper and turned on her. He had a nasty temper, I noticed. It was pitch-dark in the cottage by this time, but no one thought of lighting the lamp, and in the darkness the two Englishmen fetched their topcoats and said good-bye to the old woman.

"Just as a man makes a home of a bleeding place, some bastard at headquarters thinks you're too cushy and shunts you off," says Hawkins, shaking her hand.

"A thousand thanks, madam," says Belcher. "A thousand thanks for everything"— as though he'd made it up.

We went round to the back of the house and down towards the bog. It was only then that Jeremiah Donovan told them. He was shaking with excitement.

"There were four of our fellows shot in Cork this morning and now you're to be shot as a reprisal."

"What are you talking about?" snaps Hawkins. "It's bad enough being mucked about as we are without having to put up with your funny jokes."

"It isn't a joke," says Donovan. "I'm sorry, Hawkins, but it's true," and begins on the usual rigmarole about duty and how unpleasant it is.

I never noticed that people who talk a lot about duty find it much of a trouble to them.

"Oh, cut it out!" says Hawkins.

"Ask Bonaparte," says Donovan, seeing that Hawkins isn't taking him seriously. "Isn't it true, Bonaparte?"

"It is," I say, and Hawkins stops.

"Ah, for Christ's sake, chum."

"I mean it, chum," I say.

"You don't sound as if you meant it."

"If he doesn't mean it, I do," says Donovan, working himself up.

"What have you against me, Jeremiah Donovan?"

"I never said I had anything against you. But why did your people take out four of our prisoners and shoot them in cold blood?"

He took Hawkins by the arm and dragged him on, but it was impossible to make him understand that we were in earnest. I had the Smith and Wesson° in my pocket and I kept fingering it and wondering what I'd do if they put up a fight for it or ran, and wishing to God they'd do one or the other. I knew if they did run for it, that I'd never fire on them. Hawkins wanted to know was Noble in it, and when we said yes, he asked us why Noble wanted to plug him. Why did any of us want to plug him? What had he done to us? Weren't we all chums? Didn't we understand him and didn't he understand us? Did we imagine for an instant that he'd shoot us for all the so-and-so officers in the so-and-so British Army?

Smith and Wesson　*pistol, like the Webley later*

By this time we'd reached the bog, and I was so sick I couldn't even answer him. We walked along the edge of it in the darkness, and every now and then Hawkins would call a halt and begin all over again, as if he was wound up, about our being chums, and I knew that nothing but the sight of the grave would convince him that we had to do it. And all the time I was hoping that something would happen; that they'd run for it or that Noble would take over the responsibility from me. I had the feeling that it was worse on Noble than on me.

4

At last we saw the lantern in the distance and made towards it. Noble was carrying it, and Feeney was standing somewhere in the darkness behind him, and the picture of them so still and silent in the bogland brought it home to me that we were in earnest, and banished the last bit of hope I had.

Belcher, on recognizing Noble, said: "Hallo, chum," in his quiet way, but Hawkins flew at him at once, and the argument began all over again, only this time Noble had nothing to say for himself and stood with his head down, holding the lantern between his legs.

It was Jeremiah Donovan who did the answering. For the twentieth time, as though it was haunting his mind, Hawkins asked if anybody thought he'd shoot Noble.

"Yes, you would," says Jeremiah Donovan.

"No, I wouldn't, damn you!"

"You would, because you'd know you'd be shot for not doing it."

"I wouldn't, not if I was to be shot twenty times over. I wouldn't shoot a pal. And Belcher wouldn't—isn't that right, Belcher?"

"That's right, chum," Belcher said, but more by way of answering the question than of joining in the argument. Belcher sounded as though whatever unforeseen thing he'd always been waiting for had come at last.

"Anyway, who says Noble would be shot if I wasn't? What do you think I'd do if I was in his place, out in the middle of a blasted bog?"

"What would you do?" asks Donovan.

"I'd go with him wherever he was going, of course. Share my last bob with him and stick by him through thick and thin. No one can ever say of me that I let down a pal."

"We had enough of this," says Jeremiah Donovan, cocking his revolver. "Is there any message you want to send?"

"No, there isn't."

"Do you want to say your prayers?"

Hawkins came out with a cold-blooded remark that even shocked me and turned on Noble again.

"Listen to me, Noble," he says. "You and me are chums. You can't come over to my side, so I'll come over to your side. That show you I mean what I say? Give me a rifle and I'll go along with you and the other lads."

Nobody answered him. We knew that was no way out.

"Hear what I'm saying?" he says. "I'm through with it. I'm a deserter or anything else you like. I don't believe in your stuff, but it's no worse than mine. That satisfy you?"

Noble raised his head, but Donovan began to speak and he lowered it again without replying.

"For the last time, have you any messages to send?" says Donovan in a cold, excited sort of voice.

"Shut up, Donovan! You don't understand me, but these lads do. They're not the sort to make a pal and kill a pal. They're not the tools of any capitalist."

I alone of the crowd saw Donovan raise his Webley to the back of Hawkins's neck, and as he did so I shut my eyes and tried to pray. Hawkins had begun to say something else when Donovan fired, and as I opened my eyes at the bang, I saw Hawkins stagger at the knees and lie out flat at Noble's feet, slowly and as quiet as a kid falling asleep, with the lantern-light on his lean legs and bright farmer's boots. We all stood very still, watching him settle out in the last agony.

Then Belcher took out a handkerchief and began to tie it about his own eyes (in our excitement we'd forgotten to do the same for Hawkins), and, seeing it wasn't big enough, turned and asked for the loan of mine. I gave it to him and he knotted the two together and pointed with his foot at Hawkins.

"He's not quite dead," he says. "Better give him another."

Sure enough, Hawkins's left knee is beginning to rise. I bend down and put my gun to his head; then, recollecting myself, I get up again. Belcher understands what's in my mind.

"Give him his first," he says. "I don't mind. Poor bastard, we don't know what's happening to him now."

I knelt and fired. By this time I didn't seem to know what I was doing. Belcher, who was fumbling a bit awkwardly with the handkerchiefs, came out with a laugh as he heard the shot. It was the first time I heard him laugh and it sent a shudder down my back; it sounded so unnatural.

"Poor bugger!" he said quietly. "And last night he was so curious about it all. It's very queer, chums, I always think. Now he knows as much about it as they'll ever let him know, and last night he was all in the dark."

Donovan helped him to tie the handkerchiefs about his eyes. "Thanks, chum," he said. Donovan asked if there were any messages he wanted sent.

"No, chum," he says. "Not for me. If any of you would like to write to Hawkins's mother, you'll find a letter from her in his pocket. He and his mother were great chums. But my missus left me eight years ago. Went away with another fellow and took the kid with her. I like the feeling of a home, as you may have noticed, but I couldn't start again after that."

It was an extraordinary thing, but in those few minutes Belcher said more than in all the weeks before. It was just as if the sound of the shot had started a flood of talk in him and he could go on the whole night like that, quite happily, talking about himself. We stood round like fools now that he couldn't see us any longer. Donovan looked at Noble, and Noble shook his head. Then Donovan raised his Webley, and at that moment Belcher gives his queer laugh again. He may have thought we were talking about him, or perhaps he noticed the same thing I'd noticed and couldn't understand it.

"Excuse me, chums," he says. "I feel I'm talking the hell of a lot, and so silly, about my being so handy about a house and things like that. But this thing came on me suddenly. You'll forgive me, I'm sure."

"You don't want to say a prayer?" asked Donovan.

"No, chum," he says. "I don't think it would help. I'm ready, and you boys want to get it over."

"You understand that we're only doing our duty?" says Donovan.

Belcher's head was raised like a blind man's, so that you could only see his chin and the tip of his nose in the lantern–light.

"I never could make out what duty was myself," he said. "I think you're all good lads, if that's what you mean. I'm not complaining."

Noble, just as if he couldn't bear any more of it, raised his fist at Donovan, and in a flash Donovan raised his gun and fired. The big man went over like a sack of meal, and this time there was no need of a second shot.

I don't remember much about the burying, but that it was worse than all the rest because we had to carry them to the grave. It was all mad lonely with nothing but a patch of lantern–light between ourselves and the dark, and birds hooting and screeching all round, disturbed by the guns. Noble went through Hawkins's belongings to find the letter from his mother, and then joined his hands together. He did the same with Belcher. Then, when we'd filled in the grave, we separated from Jeremiah Donovan and Feeney and took our tools back to the shed. All the way we didn't speak a word. The kitchen was dark and cold as we'd left it, and the old woman was sitting over the hearth, saying her beads. We walked past her into the room, and Noble struck a match to light the lamp. She rose quietly and came to the doorway with all her cantankerousness gone.

"What did ye do with them?" she asked in a whisper, and Noble started so that the match went out in his hand.

"What's that?" he asked without turning round.

"I heard ye," she said.

"What did you hear?" asked Noble.

"I heard ye. Do ye think I didn't hear ye, putting the spade back in the houseen?"

Noble struck another match and this time the lamp lit for him.

"Was that what ye did to them?" she asked.

Then, by God, in the very doorway, she fell on her knees and began praying, and after looking at her for a minute or two Noble did the same by the fireplace. I pushed my way out past her and left them at it. I stood at the door, watching the stars and listening to the shrieking of the birds dying out over the bogs. It is so strange what you feel at times like that you can't describe it. Noble says he saw everything ten times the size, as though there were nothing in the whole world but that little patch of bog with the two Englishmen stiffening into it, but with me it was as if the patch of bog where the Englishmen were was a million miles away, and even Noble and the old woman, mumbling behind me, and the birds and the bloody stars were all far away, and I was somehow very small and very lost and lonely like a child astray in the snow. And anything that happened me afterwards, I never felt the same about again.

(1931)

QUESTIONS

1. "Guests of the Nation" is constructed in four parts. Identify the central action of each part, and explain how the parts are related.
2. Analyze the plot in terms of its exposition, complication, crisis, falling action, and denouement.

CHARACTER

As readers, we come to care about fictional *characters,* the imaginary people that writers create, sometimes identifying with them, sometimes judging them. Indeed, if one reason we read stories is to find out what happens (to see how the plot works out), an equally compelling reason is to follow the fortunes of the characters. Plot and character, in fact, are inseparable; we are often less concerned with "what happened" than with "what happened to him or her." We want to know not just "how did it work out," but "how did it work out for them?"

Well-wrought fictional characters come alive for us while we read. And they are real enough to live in our memories long after their stories have ended. We might say that fictional characters possess the kind of reality that dreams have, a reality no less intense for being imagined. Although fictional characters cannot step out of the pages of their stories, we grant them a kind of reality equivalent to if not identical with our own. In doing so we make an implied contract with the writer to suspend our disbelief that his or her story is "just a story," and instead take what happens as if it were real. When we grant fiction this kind of reality, we permit ourselves to be caught up in the life of the story and its characters, perhaps to the point of allowing our own lives to be affected by them.

In short, we approach fictional characters with the same concerns with which we approach people. We need to be alert for how we are to take them, for what we are to make of them, and we need to see how they may reflect our own experience. We need to observe their actions, to listen to *what* they say and *how they say it,* to notice how they relate to other characters and how other characters respond to them, especially to what they say about each other. To make inferences about characters, we look for connections, for links and clues to their function and significance in the story. In analyzing a character or characters' relationships (and fictional characters almost always exist in relation to one another) we relate one act, one speech, one physical detail to another until we understand the character.

Characters in fiction can be conveniently classified as major and minor, static and dynamic. A *major character* is an important figure at the center of the story's action or theme. Usually a character's status as major or minor is clear. On occasion, however, not one but two characters may dominate a story, their relationship being what matters most. In Luigi Pirandello's "War," for example, no single character dominates the story the way Emily Grierson dominates Faulkner's "A Rose for Emily" or the narrator of "Araby" dominates James Joyce's story.

The major character is sometimes called a *protagonist* whose conflict with an *antagonist* may spark the story's conflict. Supporting the major character are one or more secondary or *minor characters* whose function is partly to illuminate the major characters. Minor characters are often *static* or unchanging: they remain the same from the beginning of a work to the end. *Dynamic characters,* on the other hand, exhibit some kind of change—of attitude, of purpose, of behavior—as the story progresses. We should be careful not to automatically equate major characters with dynamic ones or minor characters with static ones. For example, Emily Grierson, the major character in "A Rose for Emily," is as static as the minor characters Richards and Brently Mallard in Chopin's "The Story of an Hour," whose major character, Mrs. Mallard, undergoes significant changes as the story unfolds.

Characterization is the means by which writers present and reveal character. We look first at the way James Joyce characterizes Mrs. Mooney, a major character, in "The Boarding House" (page 318):

> Mrs. Mooney was a butcher's daughter. She was a woman who was quite able to keep things to herself: a determined woman. She had married her father's foreman and opened a butcher's shop near Spring Gardens.

The method of characterization is narrative description with explicit judgment. We are given facts (she was a butcher's daughter) and interpretive comment (she was . . . a determined woman). From both fact and comment we derive an impression of a strong woman, one who can take care of herself. As a butcher's daughter, she does not stand high on the social ladder. This initial impression is confirmed when we later discover that after her husband had become an alcoholic, had ruined his business, and had gone after Mrs. Mooney with a meat cleaver, she left him and opened a boarding house to support herself and her two children. When the narrator informs us that "she governed the house cunningly and firmly," and when he calls her "a shrewd judge," we come to share his respect for Mrs. Mooney's abilities.

The narrator's view of Mrs. Mooney, however, is not one of unqualified admiration. We learn, for example, that "all the resident young men spoke of her as *The Madam*"—a title suggestive of authority coupled with moral disrepute. And though Mrs. Mooney does not run a house of prostitution, we can't help but be aware of the moral dubiety that this title implies, for Mrs. Mooney allows her nineteen-year-old daughter, Polly, to flirt with the male residents of the boarding house. The following comment of the narrator clearly indicates that Mrs. Mooney was serious about finding Polly a husband: "Mrs. Mooney, who was a shrewd judge, knew that the young men were only passing the time away: none of them meant business." And for Mrs. Mooney, *business* means marriage to a serious and socially suitable man such as Bob Doran, a thirty-four-year-old clerk to a wine merchant.

Throughout "The Boarding House," Joyce characterizes Mrs. Mooney by means of narrative description with explicit judgment. In introducing Polly he varies the technique:

> Polly Mooney, the Madam's daughter, would also sing. She sang:

— APPEARANCE
mANNERISM
— Speech
— what others SAy
— Action

> I'm a . . . naughty girl.
> You needn't sham.
> You know I am.

Polly sings this seductive verse, presumably with her mother's approval. The implications of the song coupled with other descriptive details about Polly serve to characterize her. Unlike her mother, whose character is presented directly through narrative description with explicit judgment, Polly is characterized initially by means of narrative description with implied judgment: "Polly was a slim girl of nineteen; she had light soft hair and a small full mouth." The crucial detail is the full mouth, which suggests sensuality. Moreover, Joyce's narrator further embellishes Polly's description with the information that "her eyes . . . had a habit of glancing upwards when she spoke with anyone, which made her look like a little perverse "madonna." "Madonna," of course, is a word that sounds like *madam,* but is quite different in connotation. Polly is associated with innocence and holiness while also being called "perverse," a contradiction of the madonna image.

Joyce uses two additional devices of characterization in this story: he reveals a character's state of mind through surface details (the fogging of Bob Doran's glasses and the shaking of his hand while he attempts unsuccessfully to shave); he also reveals characters by letting us enter their consciousness, telling us what they think and feel.

We can generalize from these techniques to list the following major methods of revealing character in fiction:

1. Narrative summary without judgment
2. Narrative description with implied or explicit judgment
3. Surface details of dress and physical appearance
4. Characters' actions—what they do
5. Characters' speech—what they say (and how they say it)
6. Characters' consciousness—what they think and feel

Keep the devices of characterization in mind as you read Kay Boyle's "Astronomer's Wife." Examine the relationships among the three characters—the astronomer, his wife, and the plumber—noting especially details of speech, gesture, and behavior that reveal the nature of each. Account for what you think and feel about each character.

KAY BOYLE

[b. 1903]

Astronomer's Wife

There is an evil moment on awakening when all things seem to pause. But for women, they only falter and may be set in action by a single move: a lifted hand and the pendulum will swing, or the voice raised and through every room the pulse takes up its beating. The astronomer's wife felt the interval gaping and at once filled it to the brim. She fetched up her gentle voice and sent it warily down the stairs for coffee, swung her feet out upon the oval mat, and hailed the morning with her bare arms' quivering flesh drawn taut in rhythmic exercise: left, left, left my wife and fourteen children, right, right, right in the middle of the dusty road.

The day would proceed from this, beat by beat, without reflection, like every other day. The astronomer was still asleep, or feigning it, and she, once out of bed, had come into her own possession. Although scarcely ever out of sight of the impenetrable silence of his brow, she would be absent from him all the day in being clean, busy, kind. He was a man of other things, a dreamer. At times he lay still for hours, at others he sat upon the roof behind his telescope, or wandered down the pathway to the road and out across the mountains. This day, like any other, would go on from the removal of the spot left there from dinner on the astronomer's vest to the severe thrashing of the mayonnaise for lunch. That man might be each time the new arching wave, and woman the undertow that sucked him back, were things she had been told by his silence were so.

In spite of the earliness of the hour, the girl had heard her mistress's voice and was coming up the stairs. At the threshold of the bedroom she paused, and said: "Madame, the plumber is here."

The astronomer's wife put on her white and scarlet smock very quickly and buttoned it at the neck. Then she stepped carefully around the motionless spread of water in the hall.

"Tell him to come right up," she said. She laid her hands on the bannisters and stood looking down the wooden stairway. "Ah, I am Mrs. Ames," she said softly as she saw him mounting. "I am Mrs. Ames," she said softly, softly down the flight of stairs. "I am Mrs. Ames," spoken soft as a willow weeping. "The professor is still sleeping. Just step this way."

The plumber himself looked up and saw Mrs. Ames with her voice hushed, speaking to him. She was a youngish woman, but this she had forgotten. The mystery and silence of her husband's mind lay like a chiding finger on her lips. Her eyes were gray, for the light had been extinguished in them. The strange dim halo of her yellow hair was still uncombed and sideways on her head.

For all of his heavy boots, the plumber quieted the sound of his feet, and together they went down the hall, picking their way around the still lake of water that spread as far as the landing and lay docile there. The plumber was a tough, hardy man; but he took off his hat when he spoke to her and looked her fully, almost insolently in the eye.

"Does it come from the wash-basin," he said, "or from the other . . . ?"

"Oh, from the other," said Mrs. Ames without hesitation.

In this place the villas were scattered out few and primitive, and although beauty lay without there was no reflection of her face within. Here all was awkward and unfit; a sense of wrestling with uncouth forces gave everything an austere countenance. Even the plumber, dealing as does a woman with matters under hand, was grave and stately. The mountains round about seemed to have cast them into the shadow of great dignity.

Mrs. Ames began speaking of their arrival that summer in the little villa, mourning each event as it followed on the other.

"Then, just before going to bed last night," she said, "I noticed something was unusual."

The plumber cast down a folded square of sack-cloth on the brimming floor and laid his leather apron on it. Then he stepped boldly onto the heart of the island it shaped and looked long into the overflowing bowl.

"The water should be stopped from the meter in the garden," he said at last.

"Oh, I did that," said Mrs. Ames, "the very first thing last night. I turned it off at once, in my nightgown, as soon as I saw what was happening. But all this had already run in."

The plumber looked for a moment at her red kid slippers. She was standing just at the edge of the clear, pure-seeming tide.

"It's no doubt the soil lines," he said severely. "It may be that something has stopped them, but my opinion is that the water seals aren't working. That's the trouble often enough in such cases. If you had a valve you wouldn't be caught like this."

Mrs. Ames did not know how to meet this rebuke. She stood, swaying a little, looking into the plumber's blue relentless eye.

"I'm sorry—I'm sorry that my husband," she said, "is still—resting and cannot go into this with you. I'm sure it must be very interesting. . . ."

"You'll probably have to have the traps sealed," said the plumber grimly, and at the sound of this Mrs. Ames' hand flew in dismay to the side of her face. The plumber made no move, but the set of his mouth as he looked at her seemed to soften. "Anyway, I'll have a look from the garden end," he said.

"Oh, do," said the astronomer's wife in relief. Here was a man who spoke of action and object as simply as women did! But however hushed her voice had been, it carried clearly to Professor Ames who lay, dreaming and solitary, upon his bed. He heard their footsteps come down the hall, pause, and skip across the pool of overflow.

"Katherine!" said the astronomer in a ringing tone. "There's a problem worthy of your mettle!"

Mrs. Ames did not turn her head, but led the plumber swiftly down the stairs. When the sun in the garden struck her face, he saw there was a wave of color in it, but this may have been anything but shame.

"You see how it is," said the plumber, as if leading her mind away. "The drains run from these houses right down the hill, big enough for a man to stand upright in them, and clean as a whistle too." There they stood in the garden with the vegetation flowering in disorder all about. The plumber looked at the astronomer's wife. "They come out at the torrent on the other side of the forest beyond there," he said.

But the words the astronomer had spoken still sounded in her in despair. The mind of man, she knew, made steep and sprightly flights, pursued illusion, took foothold in the nameless things that cannot pass between the thumb and finger. But whenever the astronomer gave voice to the thoughts that soared within him, she returned in gratitude to the long expanses of his silence. Desert-like they stretched behind and before the articulation of his scorn.

Life, life is an open sea, she sought to explain it in sorrow, and to survive women cling to the floating debris on the tide. But the plumber had suddenly fallen upon his knees in the grass and had crooked his fingers through the ring of the drains' trap-door. When she looked down she saw that he was looking up into her face, and she saw too that his hair was as light as gold.

"Perhaps Mr. Ames," he said rather bitterly, "would like to come down with me and have a look around?"

"Down?" said Mrs. Ames in wonder.

"Into the drains," said the plumber brutally. "They're a study for a man who likes to know what's what."

"Oh, Mr. Ames," said Mrs. Ames in confusion. "He's still—still in bed, you see."

The plumber lifted his strong, weathered face and looked curiously at her. Surely it seemed to him strange for a man to linger in bed, with the sun pouring yellow as wine all over the place. The astronomer's wife saw his lean cheeks, his high, rugged bones, and the deep seams in his brow. His flesh was as firm and clean as wood, stained richly tan with the climate's rigor. His fingers were blunt, but comprehensible to her, gripped in the ring and holding the iron door wide. The backs of his hands were bound round and round with ripe blue veins of blood.

"At any rate," said the astronomer's wife, and the thought of it moved her lips to smile a little, "Mr. Ames would never go down there alive. He likes going up," she said. And she, in her turn, pointed, but impudently, towards the heavens. "On the roof. Or on the mountains. He's been up on the tops of them many times."

"It's a matter of habit," said the plumber, and suddenly he went down the trap. Mrs. Ames saw a bright little piece of his hair still shining, like a star, long after the rest of him had gone. Out of the depths, his voice, hollow and dark with foreboding, returned to her. "I think something has stopped the elbow," was what he said.

This was speech that touched her flesh and bone and made her wonder. When her husband spoke of height, having no sense of it, she could not picture it nor hear. Depth or magic passed her by unless a name were given. But madness in a daily shape, as elbow stopped, she saw clearly and well. She sat down on the grasses, bewildered that it should be a man who had spoken to her so.

She saw the weeds springing up, and she did not move to tear them up from life. She sat powerless, her senses veiled, with no action taking shape beneath her hands. In this way some men sat for hours on end, she knew, tracking a single thought back to its origin. The mind of man could balance and divide, weed out, destroy. She sat on the full, burdened grasses, seeking to think, and dimly waiting for the plumber to return.

Whereas her husband had always gone up, as the dead go, she knew now that there were others who went down, like the corporeal being of the dead. That men were then divided into two bodies now seemed clear to Mrs. Ames. This knowledge stunned her with its simplicity and took the uneasy motion from her limbs. She could not stir, but sat facing the mountains' rocky flanks, and harking in silence to lucidity. Her husband was the mind, this other man the meat, of all mankind.

After a little, the plumber emerged from the earth: first the light top of his head, then the burnt brow, and then the blue eyes fringed with whitest lash. He braced his thick hands flat on the pavings of the garden-path and swung himself completely from the pit.

"It's the soil lines," he said pleasantly. "The gases," he said as he looked down upon her lifted face, "are backing up the drains."

"What in the world are we going to do?" said the astronomer's wife softly. There was a young and strange delight in putting questions to which true answers would be given. Everything the astronomer had ever said to her was a continuous query to which there could be no response.

"Ah, come, now," said the plumber, looking down and smiling. "There's a remedy for every ill, you know. Sometimes it may be that," he said as if speaking to a child, "or sometimes the other thing. But there's always a help for everything amiss."

Things come out of herbs and make you young again, he might have been saying to her; or the first good rain will quench any drought; or time of itself will put a broken bone together.

"I'm going to follow the ground pipe out right to the torrent," the plumber was saying. "The trouble's between here and there and I'll find it on the way. There's nothing at all that can't be done over for the caring," he was saying, and his eyes were fastened on her face in insolence, or gentleness, or love.

The astronomer's wife stood up, fixed a pin in her hair, and turned around towards the kitchen. Even while she was calling the servant's name, the plumber began speaking again.

"I once had a cow that lost her cud," the plumber was saying. The girl came out on the kitchen-step and Mrs. Ames stood smiling at her in the sun.

"The trouble is very serious, very serious," she said across the garden. "When Mr. Ames gets up, please tell him I've gone down."

She pointed briefly to the open door in the pathway, and the plumber hoisted his kit on his arm and put out his hand to help her down.

"But I made her another in no time," he was saying, "out of flowers and things and what-not."

"Oh," said the astronomer's wife in wonder as she stepped into the heart of the earth. She took his arm, knowing that what he said was true.

Character point of view

(1936)

QUESTIONS

1. "Astronomer's Wife" is built on two sets of character contrasts: wife versus husband; astronomer versus plumber. Explain how the characters differ. Consider physical descriptions as well as actions, words, and gestures.
2. Describe the wife's relationship with her husband.

SETTING

Writers describe the world they know, its sights and sounds, its colors, textures, and accents. Stories come to life, are imagined as occurring in a place, rooted in the soil of a writer's memories. This place or location of a story's action along with the time in which it occurs is its *setting*. For writers like James Joyce and William Faulkner, setting is essential to meaning. Functioning as more than a simple backdrop for action, it provides a historical and cultural context that enhances our understanding of the characters. In Joyce's "The Boarding House," for example, Bob Doran's Irish Catholicism powerfully influences his decision to marry Polly, to make "reparation" for his sexual sin. In Faulkner's "A Rose for Emily," Emily Grierson's stubborn resistance to change is both a product of the decay of Jefferson (a fictional town in Mississippi) and the post-Civil War South and also a reflection of its shabby gentility. Moreover, Faulkner intensifies the images of decline of both Emily and the South by his careful description of the Grierson house:

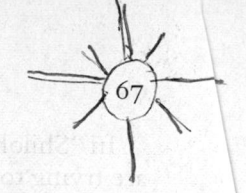

> It was a big, squarish frame house that had once been white, dec-
> orated with cupolas and spires and scrolled balconies in the heav-
> ily lightsome style of the seventies, set on what had once been
> our most select street. But garages and cotton gins had encroached
> and obliterated even the august names of that neighborhood;
> only Miss Emily's house was left, lifting its stubborn and coquet-
> tish decay above the cotton wagons and the gasoline pumps—an
> eyesore among eyesores.

Later we are taken inside the house, and finally inside one very unusual room. In each case, the physical details of setting are associated with the values, ideals, and attitudes of that place in different times. Setting in "A Rose for Emily" (and in fiction in general) is an important dimension of meaning since it reflects character and embodies theme.

Setting is important for an additional reason: it symbolizes the emotional state of the characters. In Chopin's "The Story of an Hour," for example, Mrs. Mallard looks out the window and observes life going on—birds singing, a peddler working, trees blooming. The contrast between the enclosed space of her room and the world outside implies a tension between Mrs. Mallard's subjugation and her desire for freedom. This contrast underscores a significant difference between the natural and the human worlds: nature is free of social restrictions, of conventions, and of such obligations as marriage.

Writers know that they must root stories in a reality their readers can experience, whether it is one readers actually know or one they must imagine. They realize further that the way to general truths is through concreteness and particularity. Both Joyce's Dublin and Faulkner's Jefferson are highly specified places. Yet both cities transcend their particular locale to become symbolic, representative places. It is a stunning paradox that works of such imaginative splendor as Chekhov's "The Lady with the Dog" and Faulkner's "A Rose for Emily" also display careful representations of reality. Stories like these are both realistic and symbolic; they are concrete representations of actual life that illustrate general truths about human experience, applicable not just in Yalta or Dublin or Jefferson, but in many places human beings live.

One of our finest American storytellers, Eudora Welty, has spoken eloquently about the importance of one aspect of setting—place in fiction. She suggests that "fiction depends for its life on place." Relating place to character and plot, Miss Welty writes that place is "the crossroads of circumstance, the proving ground of "What happened? Who's here? Who's coming?" But it is even more important than this. For as she suggests, place is the "conductor of all the currents of emotion and belief and moral conviction that charge out from the story." Moreover, when the world of experience is within reach of the world of appearance, place both makes and keeps the characters real; it animates them, so much so that, as Miss Welty observes, "every story would be another story, and unrecognizable as art, if it took up its characters and plot and happened somewhere else."★

★See Miss Welty's essay "Place in Fiction" in her book *The Eye of the Story* (New York: Random House, 1979), pp. 116–133.

In "Shiloh" by Bobbie Ann Mason you will read about a married couple who are trying to identify what they want from their lives both individually and together. Consider what the historical resonance of the title contributes to our view of character relationships in the story and how it relates to the setting.

BOBBIE ANN MASON
[b. 1940]

Shiloh

Leroy Moffitt's wife, Norma Jean, is working on her pectorals. She lifts three-pound dumbbells to warm up, then progresses to a twenty-pound barbell. Standing with her legs apart, she reminds Leroy of Wonder Woman.

"I'd give anything if I could just get these muscles to where they're real hard," says Norma Jean. "Feel this arm. It's not as hard as the other one."

"That's 'cause you're right-handed," says Leroy, dodging as she swings the barbell in an arc.

"Do you think so?"

"Sure."

Leroy is a truckdriver. He injured his leg in a highway accident four months ago, and his physical therapy, which involves weights and a pulley, prompted Norma Jean to try building herself up. Now she is attending a body-building class. Leroy has been collecting temporary disability since his tractor-trailer jackknifed in Missouri, badly twisting his left leg in its socket. He has a steel pin in his hip. He will probably not be able to drive his rig again. It sits in the backyard, like a gigantic bird that has flown home to roost. Leroy has been home in Kentucky for three months, and his leg is almost healed, but the accident frightened him and he does not want to drive any more long hauls. He is not sure what to do next. In the meantime, he makes things from craft kits. He started by building a miniature log cabin from notched Popsicle sticks. He varnished it and placed it on the TV set, where it remains. It reminds him of a rustic Nativity scene. Then he tried string art (sailing ships on black velvet), a macramé owl kit, a snap-together B-17 Flying Fortress, and a lamp made out of a model truck, with a light fixture screwed in the top of the cab. At first the kits were diversions, something to kill time, but now he is thinking about building a full-scale log house from a kit. It would be considerably cheaper than building a regular house, and besides, Leroy has grown to appreciate how things are put together. He has begun to realize that in all the years he was on the road he never took time to examine anything. He was always flying past scenery.

"They won't let you build a log cabin in any of the new subdivisions," Norma Jean tells him.

"They will if I tell them it's for you," he says, teasing her. Ever since they were married, he has promised Norma Jean he would build her a new home one day. They have always rented, and the house they live in is small and nondescript. It does not even feel like a home, Leroy realizes now.

Norma Jean works at the Rexall drugstore, and she has acquired an amazing amount of information about cosmetics. When she explains to Leroy the three stages of complexion care, involving creams, toners, and moisturizers, he thinks happily of other petroleum products—axle grease, diesel fuel. This is a connection between him and Norma Jean. Since he has been home, he has felt unusually tender about his wife and guilty over his long absences. But he can't tell what she feels about him. Norma Jean has never complained about his traveling; she has never made hurt remarks, like calling his truck a "widow-maker." He is reasonably certain she has been faithful to him, but he wishes she would celebrate his permanent homecoming more happily. Norma Jean is often startled to find Leroy at home, and he thinks she seems a little disappointed about it. Perhaps he reminds her too much of the early days of their marriage, before he went on the road. They had a child who died as an infant, years ago. They never speak about their memories of Randy, which have almost faded, but now that Leroy is home all the time, they sometimes feel awkward around each other, and Leroy wonders if one of them should mention the child. He has the feeling that they are waking up out of a dream together—that they must create a new marriage, start afresh. They are lucky they are still married. Leroy has read that for most people losing a child destroys the marriage—or else he heard this on *Donahue*. He can't always remember where he learns things anymore.

At Christmas, Leroy bought an electric organ for Norma Jean. She used to play the piano when she was in high school. "It don't leave you," she told him once. "It's like riding a bicycle."

The new instrument had so many keys and buttons that she was bewildered by it at first. She touched the keys tentatively, pushed some buttons, then pecked out "Chopsticks." It came out in an amplified fox-trot rhythm, with marimba sounds.

"It's an orchestra!" she cried.

The organ had a pecan-look finish and eighteen preset chords, with optional flute, violin, trumpet, clarinet, and banjo accompaniments. Norma Jean mastered the organ almost immediately. At first she played Christmas songs. Then she bought *The Sixties Songbook* and learned every tune in it, adding variations to each with the rows of brightly colored buttons.

"I didn't like these old songs back then," she said. "But I have this crazy feeling I missed something."

"You didn't miss a thing," said Leroy.

Leroy likes to lie on the couch and smoke a joint and listen to Norma Jean play "Can't Take My Eyes Off You" and "I'll Be Back." He is back again. After fifteen years on the road, he is finally settling down with the woman he loves. She is still pretty. Her skin is flawless. Her frosted curls resemble pencil trimmings.

Now that Leroy has come home to stay, he notices how much the town has changed. Subdivisions are spreading across western Kentucky like an oil slick. The sign at the edge of town says "Pop: 11,500"—only seven hundred more than it said twenty years before. Leroy can't figure out who is living in all the new houses. The farmers who used to gather around the courthouse square on Saturday afternoons to play checkers and spit tobacco juice have gone. It has been years since Leroy has thought about the farmers, and they have disappeared without his noticing.

Leroy meets a kid named Stevie Hamilton in the parking lot at the new shopping center. While they pretend to be strangers meeting over a stalled car, Stevie tosses an ounce of marijuana under the front seat of Leroy's car. Stevie is wearing orange jogging shoes and a T-shirt that says CHATTAHOOCHEE SUPER-RAT. His father is a prominent doctor who lives in one of the expensive subdivisions in a new white-columned brick house that looks like a funeral parlor. In the phone book under his name there is a separate number, with the listing "Teenagers."

"Where do you get this stuff?" asks Leroy. "From your pappy?"

"That's for me to know and you to find out," Stevie says. He is slit-eyed and skinny.

"What else you got?"

"What you interested in?"

"Nothing special. Just wondered."

Leroy used to take speed on the road. Now he has to go slowly. He needs to be mellow. He leans back against the car and says, "I'm aiming to build me a log house, soon as I get time. My wife, though, I don't think she likes the idea."

"Well, let me know when you want me again," Stevie says. He has a cigarette in his cupped palm, as though sheltering it from the wind. He takes a long drag, then stomps it on the asphalt and slouches away.

Stevie's father was two years ahead of Leroy in high school. Leroy is thirty-four. He married Norma Jean when they were both eighteen, and their child Randy was born a few months later, but he died at the age of four months and three days. He would be about Stevie's age now. Norma Jean and Leroy were at the drive-in, watching a double feature (*Dr. Strangelove* and *Lover Come Back*), and the baby was sleeping in the back seat. When the first movie ended, the baby was dead. It was the sudden infant death syndrome. Leroy remembers handing Randy to a nurse at the emergency room, as though he were offering her a large doll as a present. A dead baby feels like a sack of flour. "It just happens sometimes," said the doctor, in what Leroy always recalls as a nonchalant tone. Leroy can hardly remember the child anymore, but he still sees vividly a scene from *Dr. Strangelove* in which the President of the United States was talking in a folksy voice on the hot line to the Soviet premier about the bomber accidentally headed toward Russia. He was in the War Room, and the world map was lit up. Leroy remembers Norma Jean standing catatonically beside him in the hospital and himself thinking: Who is this strange girl? He had forgotten who she was. Now scientists are saying that crib death is caused by a virus. Nobody knows anything, Leroy thinks. The answers are always changing.

When Leroy gets home from the shopping center, Norma Jean's mother, Mabel Beasley, is there. Until this year, Leroy has not realized how much time she spends with Norma Jean. When she visits, she inspects the closets and then the plants, informing Norma Jean when a plant is droopy or yellow. Mabel calls the plants "flowers," although there are never any blooms. She always notices if Norma Jean's laundry is piling up. Mabel is a short, overweight woman whose tight, brown-dyed curls look more like a wig than the actual wig she sometimes wears. Today she has brought Norma Jean an off-white dust ruffle she made for the bed; Mabel works in a custom-upholstery shop.

"This is the tenth one I made this year," Mabel says. "I got started and couldn't stop."

"It's real pretty," says Norma Jean.

"Now we can hide things under the bed," says Leroy, who gets along with his mother-in-law primarily by joking with her. Mabel has never really forgiven him for disgracing her by getting Norma Jean pregnant. When the baby died, she said that fate was mocking her.

"What's that thing?" Mabel says to Leroy in a loud voice, pointing to a tangle of yarn on a piece of canvas.

Leroy holds it up for Mabel to see. "It's my needlepoint," he explains. "This is a *Star Trek* pillow cover."

"That's what a woman would do," says Mabel. "Great day in the morning!"

"All the big football players on TV do it," he says.

"Why, Leroy, you're always trying to fool me. I don't believe you for one minute. You don't know what to do with yourself—that's the whole trouble. Sewing!"

"I'm aiming to build us a log house," says Leroy. "Soon as my plans come."

"Like *heck* you are," says Norma Jean. She takes Leroy's needlepoint and shoves it into a drawer. "You have to find a job first. Nobody can afford to build now anyway."

Mabel straightens her girdle and says, "I still think before you get tied down y'all ought to take a little run to Shiloh."

"One of these days, Mama," Norma Jean says impatiently.

Mabel is talking about Shiloh, Tennessee. For the past few years, she has been urging Leroy and Norma Jean to visit the Civil War battleground there. Mabel went there on her honeymoon—the only real trip she ever took. Her husband died of a perforated ulcer when Norma Jean was ten, but Mabel, who was accepted into the United Daughters of the Confederacy in 1975, is still preoccupied with going back to Shiloh.

"I've been to kingdom come and back in that truck out yonder," Leroy says to Mabel, "but we never yet set foot in that battleground. Ain't that something? How did I miss it?"

"It's not even that far," Mabel says.

After Mabel leaves, Norma Jean reads to Leroy from a list she has made. "Things you could do," she announces. "You could get a job as a guard at Union Carbide, where they'd let you set on a stool. You could get on at the lumberyard. You could do a little carpenter work, if you want to build so bad. You could—"

"I can't do something where I'd have to stand up all day."

"You ought to try standing up all day behind a cosmetics counter. It's amazing that I have strong feet, coming from two parents that never had strong feet at all." At the moment Norma Jean is holding on to the kitchen counter, raising her knees one at a time as she talks. She is wearing two-pound ankle weights.

"Don't worry," says Leroy. "I'll do something."

"You could truck calves to slaughter for somebody. You wouldn't have to drive any big old truck for that."

"I'm going to build you this house," says Leroy. "I want to make you a real home."

"I don't want to live in any log cabin."

"It's not a cabin. It's a house."

"I don't care. It looks like a cabin."

"You and me together could lift those logs. It's just like lifting weights."

Norma Jean doesn't answer. Under her breath, she is counting. Now she is marching through the kitchen. She is doing goose steps.

Before his accident, when Leroy came home he used to stay in the house with Norma Jean, watching TV in bed and playing cards. She would cook fried chicken, picnic ham, chocolate pie—all his favorites. Now he is home alone much of the time. In the mornings, Norma Jean disappears, leaving a cooling place in the bed. She eats a cereal called Body Buddies, and she leaves the bowl on the table, with the soggy tan balls floating in a milk puddle. He sees things about Norma Jean that he never realized before. When she chops onions, she stares off into a corner, as if she can't bear to look. She puts on her house slippers almost precisely at nine o'clock every evening and nudges her jogging shoes under the couch. She saves bread heels for the birds. Leroy watches the birds at the feeder. He notices the peculiar way goldfinches fly past the window. They close their wings, then fall, then spread their wings to catch and lift themselves. He wonders if they close their eyes when they fall. Norma Jean closes her eyes when they are in bed. She wants the lights turned out. Even then, he is sure she closes her eyes.

He goes for long drives around town. He tends to drive a car rather carelessly. Power steering and an automatic shift make a car feel so small and inconsequential that his body is hardly involved in the driving process. His injured leg stretches out comfortably. Once or twice he has almost hit something, but even the prospect of an accident seems minor in a car. He cruises the new subdivisions, feeling like a criminal rehearsing for a robbery. Norma Jean is probably right about a log house being inappropriate here in the new subdivisions. All the houses look grand and complicated. They depress him.

One day when Leroy comes home from a drive he finds Norma Jean in tears. She is in the kitchen making a potato and mushroom-soup casserole, with grated-cheese topping. She is crying because her mother caught her smoking.

"I didn't hear her coming. I was standing here puffing away pretty as you please," Norma Jean says, wiping her eyes.

"I knew it would happen sooner or later," says Leroy, putting his arm around her.

"She don't know the meaning of the word 'knock,' " says Norma Jean. "It's a wonder she hadn't caught me years ago."

"Think of it this way," Leroy says. "What if she caught me with a joint?"

"You better not let her!" Norma Jean shrieks. "I'm warning you, Leroy Moffitt!"

"I'm just kidding. Here, play me a tune. That'll help you relax."

Norma Jean puts the casserole in the oven and sets the timer. Then she plays a ragtime tune, with horns and banjo, as Leroy lights up a joint and lies on the couch, laughing to himself about Mabel's catching him at it. He thinks of Stevie Hamilton—a doctor's son pushing grass. Everything is funny. The whole town seems crazy and small. He is reminded of Virgil Mathis, a boastful policeman Leroy used to shoot pool with. Virgil recently led a drug bust in a back room at a bowling alley, where he seized ten thousand dollars' worth of marijuana. The newspaper had a picture of him holding up the bags of grass and grinning widely. Right now, Leroy can imagine Virgil breaking down the door and arresting him with a lungful of smoke. Virgil would probably have been alerted to the scene because of all the racket Norma Jean is making. Now she sounds like a hard-rock band. Norma Jean is terrific. When she switches to a Latin-rhythm version of "Sunshine Superman," Leroy hums along. Norma Jean's foot goes up and down, up and down.

"Well, what do you think?" Leroy says, when Norma Jean pauses to search through her music.

"What do I think about what?"

His mind has gone blank. Then he says, "I'll sell my rig and build us a house." That wasn't what he wanted to say. He wanted to know what she thought—what she *really* thought—about them.

"Don't start in on that again," says Norma Jean. She begins playing "Who'll Be the Next in Line?"

Leroy used to tell hitchhikers his whole life story—about his travels, his hometown, the baby. He would end with a question: "Well, what do you think?" It was just a rhetorical question. In time, he had the feeling that he'd been telling the same story over and over to the same hitchhikers. He quit talking to hitchhikers when he realized how his voice sounded—whining and self-pitying, like some teenage-tragedy song. Now Leroy has the sudden impulse to tell Norma Jean about himself, as if he had just met her. They have known each other so long they have forgotten a lot about each other. They could become reacquainted. But when the oven timer goes off and she runs to the kitchen, he forgets why he wants to do this.

The next day, Mabel drops by. It is Saturday and Norma Jean is cleaning. Leroy is studying the plans of his log house, which have finally come in the mail. He has them spread out on the table—big sheets of stiff blue paper, with diagrams and numbers printed in white. While Norma Jean runs the vacuum, Mabel drinks coffee. She sets her coffee cup on a blueprint.

"I'm just waiting for time to pass," she says to Leroy, drumming her fingers on the table.

As soon as Norma Jean switches off the vacuum, Mabel says in a loud voice, "Did you hear about the datsun dog that killed the baby?"

Norma Jean says, "The word is 'dachshund.' "

"They put the dog on trial. It chewed the baby's legs off. The mother was in the next room all the time." She raises her voice. "They thought it was neglect."

Norma Jean is holding her ears. Leroy manages to open the refrigerator and get some Diet Pepsi to offer Mabel. Mabel still has some coffee and she waves away the Pepsi.

"Datsuns are like that," Mabel says. "They're jealous dogs. They'll tear a place to pieces if you don't keep an eye on them."

"You better watch out what you're saying, Mabel," says Leroy.

"Well, facts is facts."

Leroy looks out the window at his rig. It is like a huge piece of furniture gathering dust in the backyard. Pretty soon it will be an antique. He hears the vacuum cleaner. Norma Jean seems to be cleaning the living room rug again.

Later, she says to Leroy, "She just said that about the baby because she caught me smoking. She's trying to pay me back."

"What are you talking about?" Leroy says, nervously shuffling blueprints.

"You know good and well," Norma Jean says. She is sitting in a kitchen chair with her feet up and her arms wrapped around her knees. She looks small and helpless. She says, "The very idea, her bringing up a subject like that! Saying it was neglect."

"She didn't mean that," Leroy says.

"She might not have *thought* she meant it. She always says things like that. You don't know how she goes on."

"But she didn't really mean it. She was just talking."

Leroy opens a king-sized bottle of beer and pours it into two glasses, dividing it carefully. He hands a glass to Norma Jean and she takes it from him mechanically. For a long time, they sit by the kitchen window watching the birds at the feeder.

Something is happening. Norma Jean is going to night school. She has graduated from her six-week body-building course and now she is taking an adult-education course in composition at Paducah Community College. She spends her evenings outlining paragraphs.

"First you have a topic sentence," she explains to Leroy. "Then you divide it up. Your secondary topic has to be connected to your primary topic."

To Leroy, this sounds intimidating. "I never was any good in English," he says.

"It makes a lot of sense."

"What are you doing this for, anyhow?"

She shrugs. "It's something to do." She stands up and lifts her dumbbells a few times.

"Driving a rig, nobody cared about my English."

"I'm not criticizing your English."

Norma Jean used to say, "If I lose ten minutes' sleep, I just drag all day." Now she stays up late, writing compositions. She got a B on her first paper—a how-to theme on soup-based casseroles. Recently Norma Jean has been cooking unusual foods—tacos, lasagna, Bombay chicken. She doesn't play the organ anymore, though her second paper was called "Why Music Is Important to Me." She sits at the kitchen table, concentrating on her outlines, while Leroy plays with his log house plans, practicing with a set of Lincoln Logs. The thought of getting a truckload of notched, numbered logs scares him, and he wants to be prepared. As he and Norma Jean work together at the kitchen table, Leroy has the hopeful thought that they are sharing something, but he knows he is a fool to think this. Norma Jean is miles away. He knows he is going to lose her. Like Mabel, he is just waiting for time to pass.

One day, Mabel is there before Norma Jean gets home from work, and Leroy finds himself confiding in her. Mabel, he realizes, must know Norma Jean better than he does.

"I don't know what's got into that girl," Mabel says. "She used to go to bed with the chickens. Now you say she's up all hours. Plus her a-smoking. I like to died."

"I want to make her this beautiful home," Leroy says, indicating the Lincoln Logs. "I don't think she even wants it. Maybe she was happier with me gone."

"She don't know what to make of you, coming home like this."

"Is that it?"

Mabel takes the roof off his Lincoln Log cabin. "You couldn't get *me* in a log cabin," she says. "I was raised in one. It's no picnic, let me tell you."

"They're different now," says Leroy.

"I tell you what," Mabel says, smiling oddly at Leroy.

"What?"

"Take her on down to Shiloh. Y'all need to get out together, stir a little. Her brain's all balled up over them books."

Leroy can see traces of Norma Jean's features in her mother's face. Mabel's worn face has the texture of crinkled cotton, but suddenly she looks pretty. It occurs to Leroy that Mabel has been hinting all along that she wants them to take her with them to Shiloh.

"Let's all go to Shiloh," he says. "You and me and her. Come Sunday."

Mabel throws up her hands in protest. "Oh, no, not me. Young folks want to be by theirselves."

When Norma Jean comes in with groceries, Leroy says excitedly, "Your mama here's been dying to go to Shiloh for thirty-five years. It's about time we went, don't you think?"

"I'm not going to butt in on anybody's second honeymoon," Mabel says.

"Who's going on a honeymoon, for Christ's sake?" Norma Jean says loudly.

"I never raised no daughter of mine to talk that-a-way," Mabel says.

"You ain't seen nothing yet," says Norma Jean. She starts putting away boxes and cans, slamming cabinet doors.

"There's a log cabin at Shiloh," Mabel says. "It was there during the battle. There's bullet holes in it."

"When are you going to *shut up* about Shiloh, Mama?" asks Norma Jean.

"I always thought Shiloh was the prettiest place, so full of history," Mabel goes on. "I just hoped y'all could see it once before I die, so you could tell me about it." Later, she whispers to Leroy, "You do what I said. A little change is what she needs."

"Your name means 'the king,' " Norma Jean says to Leroy that evening. He is trying to get her to go to Shiloh, and she is reading a book about another century.

"Well, I reckon I ought to be right proud."

"I guess so."

"Am I still king around here?"

Norma Jean flexes her biceps and feels them for hardness. "I'm not fooling around with anybody, if that's what you mean," she says.

"Would you tell me if you were?"

"I don't know."

"What does *your* name mean?"

"It was Marilyn Monroe's real name."

"No kidding!"

"Norma comes from the Normans. They were invaders," she says. She closes her book and looks hard at Leroy. "I'll go to Shiloh with you if you'll stop staring at me."

On Sunday, Norma Jean packs a picnic and they go to Shiloh. To Leroy's relief, Mabel says she does not want to come with them. Norma Jean drives, and Leroy, sitting beside her, feels like some boring hitchhiker she has picked up. He tries some conversation, but she answers him in monosyllables. At Shiloh, she drives aimlessly through the park, past bluffs and trails and steep ravines. Shiloh is an immense place, and Leroy cannot see it as a battleground. It is not what he expected. He thought it would look like a golf course. Monuments are everywhere, showing through the thick clusters of trees. Norma Jean passes the log cabin Mabel mentioned. It is surrounded by tourists looking for bullet holes.

"That's not the kind of log house I've got in mind," says Leroy apologetically.

"I know *that*."

"This is a pretty place. Your mama was right."

"It's O.K.," says Norma Jean. "Well, we've seen it. I hope she's satisfied."

They burst out laughing together.

At the park museum, a movie on Shiloh is shown every half hour, but they decide that they don't want to see it. They buy a souvenir Confederate flag for Mabel, and then they find a picnic spot near the cemetery. Norma Jean has brought a picnic cooler, with pimiento sandwiches, soft drinks, and Yodels. Leroy eats a sandwich and then smokes a joint, hiding it behind the picnic cooler. Norma Jean has quit smoking altogether. She is picking cake crumbs from the cellophane wrapper, like a fussy bird.

Leroy says, "So the boys in gray ended up in Corinth. The Union soldiers zapped 'em finally. April 7, 1862."

They both know that he doesn't know any history. He is just talking about some of the historical plaques they have read. He feels awkward, like a boy on a date with an older girl. They are still just making conversation.

"Corinth is where Mama eloped to," says Norma Jean.

They sit in silence and stare at the cemetery for the Union dead and, beyond, at a tall cluster of trees. Campers are parked nearby, bumper to bumper, and small children in bright clothing are cavorting and squealing. Norma Jean wads up the cake wrapper and squeezes it tightly in her hand. Without looking at Leroy, she says, "I want to leave you."

Leroy takes a bottle of Coke out of the cooler and flips off the cap. He holds the bottle poised near his mouth but cannot remember to take a drink. Finally he says, "No, you don't."

"Yes, I do."

"I won't let you."

"You can't stop me."

"Don't do me that way."

Leroy knows Norma Jean will have her own way. "Didn't I promise to be home from now on?" he says.

"In some ways, a woman prefers a man who wanders," says Norma Jean. "That sounds crazy, I know."

"You're not crazy."

Leroy remembers to drink from his Coke. Then he says, "Yes, you *are* crazy. You and me could start all over again. Right back at the beginning."

"We *have* started all over again," says Norma Jean. "And this is how it turned out."

"What did I do wrong?"

"Nothing."

"Is this one of those women's lib things?" Leroy asks.

"Don't be funny."

The cemetery, a green slope dotted with white markers, looks like a subdivision site. Leroy is trying to comprehend that his marriage is breaking up, but for some reason he is wondering about white slabs in a graveyard.

"Everything was fine till Mama caught me smoking," says Norma Jean, standing up. "That set something off."

"What are you talking about?"

"She won't leave me alone—*you* won't leave me alone." Norma Jean seems to be crying, but she is looking away from him. "I feel eighteen again. I can't face that all over again." She starts walking away. "No, it *wasn't* fine. I don't know what I'm saying. Forget it."

Leroy takes a lungful of smoke and closes his eyes as Norma Jean's words sink in. He tries to focus on the fact that thirty-five hundred soldiers died on the grounds around him. He can only think of that war as a board game with plastic soldiers. Leroy almost smiles, as he compares the Confederates' daring attack on the Union camps and Virgil Mathis's raid on the bowling alley. General Grant, drunk and furious, shoved the Southerners back to Corinth, where Mabel and Jet Beasley were married years later, when Mabel was still thin and good-looking. The next day, Mabel and Jet visited the battleground, and then Norma Jean was born, and then she married Leroy and they had a baby, which they lost, and now Leroy and Norma Jean are here at the same battleground. Leroy knows he is leaving out a lot. He is leaving out the insides of history. History was always just names and dates to him. It occurs to him that building a house out of logs is similarly empty—too simple. And the real inner workings of a marriage, like most of history, have escaped him. Now he sees that building a log house is the dumbest idea he could have had. It was clumsy of him to think Norma Jean would want a log house. It was a crazy idea: He'll have to think of something else, quickly. He will wad the blueprints into tight balls and fling them into the lake. Then he'll get moving again. He opens his eyes. Norma Jean has moved away and is walking through the cemetery, following a serpentine brick path.

Leroy gets up to follow his wife, but his good leg is asleep and his bad leg still hurts him. Norma Jean is far away, walking rapidly toward the bluff by the river, and he tries to hobble toward her. Some children run past him, screaming noisily. Norma Jean has reached the bluff, and she is looking out over the Tennessee River. Now she turns toward Leroy and waves her arms. Is she beckoning to him? She seems to be doing an exercise for her chest muscles. The sky is unusually pale—the color of the dust ruffle Mabel made for their bed.

(1982)

QUESTIONS

1. What does the following information contribute to your understanding of the story? Shiloh was the location of a famous Civil War battle in which Union soldiers under the leadership of General Ulysses S. Grant soundly defeated the Confederate forces.
2. Look at the story's closing scene, which occurs at the famous battle site. How might that scene be related to what happened there during the Civil War? What other kinds of battlefields does the story describe?

POINT OF VIEW

An author's decisions about who is to tell the story and how it is to be told are among the most important he or she makes. In a story with an *objective point of view,* the writer shows what happens without directly stating more than can be inferred from its action and dialogue. The narrator, in short, does not tell us anything about what the characters think or feel. He remains a detached observer. The narrator of Chopin's "The Story of an Hour" does not participate in the action as a character. Kate Chopin employs a third-person point of view, letting us know directly what Mrs. Mallard feels. We learn about the characters from an outside source; in Chopin's case, it is an authority. Imagine the story told from a detached, objective point of view in which we were not let into Mrs. Mallard's consciousness. The tone and feel of the story would be radically altered.

Although third-person point of view may take us inside a character's consciousness or remain objective, it does not assume the perspective of any character. Stories with narrators who participate in the action are presented from a *first-person point of view*. Narrators of such fictions tell their stories in their own voices with their particular limitations of knowledge and vision. The limitations of a first-person narrator offer writers the opportunity to exploit the discrepancy between the writer's vision and the narrator's. In both Edgar Allan Poe's "The Black Cat" and Ralph Ellison's "Battle Royal," for example, we encounter narrators who perceive and present themselves one way, but whom we see in different ways. Reading stories narrated in the first person, we need to question the narrator's trustworthiness and remain alert for textual signals that either ensure or undermine it.

Whether a writer uses a first- or a third-person narrator, he or she must also decide how much to let the narrator know about the characters. Narrators who know everything about all the characters are "omniscient" (all-knowing) as is the narrator of Joyce's "The Boarding House" who enters the minds of each of the characters and reveals what they think and feel. Stories with such narrators are written from an *omniscient point of view.* If, however, the narrator's knowledge is limited to only one character, major or minor, rather than to all, the narrator possesses *limited omniscience,* as in Chopin's "The Story of an Hour." We can readily see the difference between limited and unlimited omniscience by comparing the following passages. First the limited omniscient narration of Katherine Mansfield's "Bliss":

> Although Bertha Young was thirty she still had moments like this when she wanted to run instead of walk, to take dancing steps on and off the pavement, to bowl a hoop, to throw something up in the air and catch it again, or to stand still and laugh at—nothing—at nothing, simply.
>
> What can you do if you are thirty and, turning the corner of your own street, you are overcome, suddenly, by a feeling of bliss—absolute bliss!—as though you'd suddenly swallowed a bright piece of that late afternoon sun and it burned in your bosom, sending out a little shower of sparks into every particle, into every finger and toe? . . .
>
> Oh, is there no way you can express it without being "drunk and disorderly"? How idiotic civilization is! Why be given a body if you have to keep it shut up in a case like a rare, rare fiddle?
>
> "No, that about the fiddle is not quite what I mean," she thought, running up the steps and feeling in her bag for the key—she'd forgotten it, as usual—and rattling the letter-box. "It's not what I mean, because—Thank you, Mary"—she went into the hall. "Is nurse back?"
>
> "Yes, M'm."
>
> "And has the fruit come?"
>
> "Yes, M'm. Everything's come."
>
> "Bring the fruit up to the dining-room, will you? I'll arrange it before I go upstairs."
>
> It was dusky in the dining-room and quite chilly. But all the same Bertha threw off her coat; she could not bear the tight clasp of it another moment, and the cold air fell on her arms.
>
> But in her bosom there was still that bright glowing place—that shower of little sparks coming from it. It was almost un-

bearable. She hardly dared to breathe for fear of fanning it higher, and yet she breathed deeply, deeply. She hardly dared to look into the cold mirror—but she did look, and it gave her back a woman, radiant, with smiling, trembling lips, with big, dark eyes and an air of listening, waiting for something . . . divine to happen . . . that she knew must happen- . . . infallibly.

Katherine Mansfield has restricted the narrator to the consciousness of Bertha, never allowing us to see anything that Bertha herself wouldn't notice or understand. Our knowledge of the other characters is filtered through Bertha's observations and inferences about them. James Joyce imposes no such limitations on his narrator in "The Boarding House." Here is the narrator revealing the thoughts of Mrs. Mooney:

She was sure she would win. To begin with she had all the weight of social opinion on her side: she was an outraged mother. She had allowed him to live beneath her roof, assuming that he was a man of honour, and he had simply abused her hospitality. . . . youth could not be pleaded as his excuse; nor could ignorance be his excuse. . . . He had simply taken advantage of Polly's youth and inexperience: that was evident. The question was: What reparation would he make?

And here is the same narrator granting us an inside view of Mr. Doran:

He had a notion that he was being had. He could imagine his friends talking of the affair and laughing. She *was* a little vulgar; sometimes she said *I seen* and *If I had've known*. But what would grammar matter if he really loved her? He could not make up his mind whether to like her or despise her for what she had done. Of course, he had done it too. His instinct urged him to remain free, not to marry. Once you are married you are done for, it said.

Giving us an inside view of each character (Polly receives the same treatment), Joyce's omniscient narrator makes us aware of multiple perspectives. That is, he lets us see what each character experiences; he shows us their differing perceptions of the same situation. In doing so Joyce shifts our sympathies from one character to another as we come to understand their different needs and desires.

The omniscient point of view that Joyce employed in his twentieth-century story "The Boarding House" was a popular choice of eighteenth- and nineteenth-century novelists. But fashions in point of view change: the limited omniscient and first-person points of view are currently popular with contemporary writers. We have described some of the narrative points of view available to writers, but there are others. As we read stories with point of view in mind, we should remember:

1. That it is important to consider *how* point of view affects our responses to the characters and how it collaborates with the other elements of fiction to convey feeling and embody meaning

2. That our response to a fictional narrator is influenced by the degree of the narrator's knowledge, the objectivity of a narrator's responses, and the degree of his or her participation in the action
3. That a first-person narrator is not always a trustworthy guide; in fact, a large part of our work as readers is to determine a narrator's reliability, to estimate the truth of that narrator's disclosures.

With these considerations in mind, read the following story, William Faulkner's "A Rose for Emily." How objective is the narrator's view of Miss Emily? How does the perception we gain of her through observing her in dialogue and with other characters in action compare with the narrator's view? Where and with what effect does the narrator's focus shift from presenting Miss Emily objectively to presenting her subjectively?

WILLIAM FAULKNER

[1897–1962]

A Rose for Emily

1

When Miss Emily Grierson died, our whole town went to her funeral: the men through a sort of respectful affection for a fallen monument, the women mostly out of curiosity to see the inside of her house, which no one save an old manservant—a combined gardener and cook—had seen in at least ten years.

It was a big, squarish frame house that had once been white, decorated with cupolas and spires and scrolled balconies in the heavily lightsome style of the seventies, set on what had once been our most select street. But garages and cotton gins had encroached and obliterated even the august names of that neighborhood; only Miss Emily's house was left, lifting its stubborn and coquettish decay above the cotton wagons and the gasoline pumps—an eyesore among eyesores. And now Miss Emily had gone to join the representatives of those august names where they lay in the cedar-bemused cemetery among the ranked and anonymous graves of Union and Confederate soldiers who fell at the battle of Jefferson.

Alive, Miss Emily had been a tradition, a duty, and a care; a sort of hereditary obligation upon the town, dating from that day in 1894 when Colonel Sartoris, the mayor—he who fathered the edict that no Negro woman should appear on the streets without an apron—remitted her taxes, the dispensation dating from the death of her father on into perpetuity. Not that Miss Emily would have accepted charity. Colonel Sartoris invented an involved tale to the effect that Miss Emily's father had loaned money to the town, which the town, as a matter of business, preferred this way of repaying. Only a man of Colonel Sartoris' generation and thought could have invented it, and only a woman could have believed it.

Wouldn't deal w/ little people

When the next generation, with its more modern ideas, became mayors and alder-men, this arrangement created some little dissatisfaction. On the first of the year they mailed her a tax notice. February came, and there was no reply. They wrote her a for-mal letter, asking her to call at the sheriff's office at her convenience. A week later the mayor wrote her himself, offering to call or to send his car for her, and received in reply a note on paper of an archaic shape, in a thin, flowing calligraphy in faded ink, to the effect that she no longer went out at all. The tax notice was also enclosed, with-out comment.

well schooled penmanship

Stubborn, "I'm the boss"

They called a special meeting of the Board of Aldermen. A deputation waited upon her, knocked at the door through which no visitor had passed since she ceased giving china-painting lessons eight or ten years earlier. They were admitted by the old Negro into a dim hall from which a stairway mounted into still more shadow. It smelled of dust and disuse—a close, dank smell. The Negro led them into the parlor. It was fur-nished in heavy, leather-covered furniture. When the Negro opened the blinds of one window, they could see that the leather was cracked; and when they sat down, a faint dust rose sluggishly about their thighs, spinning with slow motes in the single sun-ray. On a tarnished gilt easel before the fireplace stood a crayon portrait of Miss Emily's father.

hospitable rich dark seldom used parlor

They rose when she entered—a small, fat woman in black, with a thin gold chain descending to her waist and vanishing into her belt, leaning on an ebony cane with a tarnished gold head. Her skeleton was small and spare; perhaps that was why what would have been merely plumpness in another was obesity in her. She looked bloated, like a body long submerged in motionless water, and of that pallid hue. Her eyes, lost in the fatty ridges of her face, looked like two small pieces of coal pressed into a lump of dough as they moved from one face to another while the visitors stated their errand.

liked gold. expensive

unhealthy physical description

—She did not ask them to sit. She just stood in the door and listened quietly until the spokesman came to a stumbling halt. Then they could hear the invisible watch ticking at the end of the gold chain.

rude?

Her voice was dry and cold. "I have no taxes in Jefferson. Colonel Sartoris explained it to me. Perhaps one of you can gain access to the city records and satisfy yourselves."

"But we have. We are the city authorities, Miss Emily. Didn't you get a notice from the sheriff, signed by him?"

"I received a paper, yes," Miss Emily said. "Perhaps he considers himself the sher-iff. . . . I have no taxes in Jefferson."

her World dg nd her

"But there is nothing on the books to show that, you see. We must go by the—"

3rd→ "See Colonel Sartoris. I have no taxes in Jefferson."

"But, Miss Emily—"

why didn't she know?

"See Colonel Sartoris." (Colonel Sartoris had been dead almost ten years.) "I have no taxes in Jefferson. Tobe!" The Negro appeared. "Show these gentlemen out."

2

So she vanquished them, horse and foot, just as she had vanquished their fathers thirty years before about the smell. That was two years after her father's death and a short time after her sweetheart—the one we believed would marry her—had deserted her. After her father's death she went out very little; after her sweetheart went away, people hardly saw her at all. A few of the ladies had the temerity to call, but were not received, and the only sign of life about the place was the Negro man—a young man then—going in and out with a market basket.

"Just as if a man—any man—could keep a kitchen properly," the ladies said; so they were not surprised when the smell developed. It was another link between the gross, teeming world and the high and mighty Griersons.

A neighbor, a woman, complained to the mayor, Judge Stevens, eighty years old.

"But what will you have me do about it, madam?" he said.

"Why, send her word to stop it," the woman said. "Isn't there a law?"

"I'm sure that won't be necessary," Judge Stevens said. "It's probably just a snake or a rat that nigger of hers killed in the yard. I'll speak to him about it."

The next day he received two more complaints, one from a man who came in diffident deprecation. "We really must do something about it, Judge. I'd be the last one in the world to bother Miss Emily, but we've got to do something." That night the Board of Aldermen met—three graybeards and one younger man, a member of the rising generation.

"It's simple enough," he said. "Send her word to have her place cleaned up. Give her a certain time to do it in, and if she don't. . . ."

"Dammit, sir," Judge Stevens said, "will you accuse a lady to her face of smelling bad?"

So the next night, after midnight, four men crossed Miss Emily's lawn and slunk about the house like burglars, sniffing along the base of the brickwork and at the cellar openings while one of them performed a regular sowing motion with his hand out of a sack slung from his shoulder. They broke open the cellar door and sprinkled lime there, and in all the outbuildings. As they recrossed the lawn, a window that had been dark was lighted and Miss Emily sat in it, the light behind her, and her upright torso motionless as that of an idol. They crept quietly across the lawn and into the shadow of the locusts that lined the street. After a week or two the smell went away.

That was when people had begun to feel really sorry for her. People in our town, remembering how old lady Wyatt, her great-aunt, had gone completely crazy at last, believed that the Griersons held themselves a little too high for what they really were. None of the young men were quite good enough for Miss Emily and such. We had long thought of them as a tableau, Miss Emily a slender figure in white in the background, her father a spraddled silhouette in the foreground, his back to her and clutching a horsewhip, the two of them framed by the backflung front door. So when she got to be thirty and was still single, we were not pleased exactly, but vindicated; even with insanity in the family she wouldn't have turned down all of her chances if they had really materialized.

When her father died, it got about that the house was all that was left to her; and in a way, people were glad. At last they could pity Miss Emily. Being left alone, and a pauper, she had become humanized. Now she too would know the old thrill and the old despair of a penny more or less.

The day after his death all the ladies prepared to call at the house and offer condolence and aid, as is our custom. Miss Emily met them at the door, dressed as usual and with no trace of grief on her face. She told them that her father was not dead. She did that for three days, with the ministers calling on her, and the doctors, trying to persuade her to let them dispose of the body. Just as they were about to resort to law and force, she broke down, and they buried her father quickly.

We did not say she was crazy then. We believed she had to do that. We remembered all the young men her father had driven away, and we knew that with nothing left, she would have to cling to that which had robbed her, as people will.

3

She was sick for a long time. When we saw her again, her hair was cut short, making her look like a girl, with a vague resemblance to those angels in colored church windows—sort of tragic and serene.

The town had just let the contracts for paving the sidewalks, and in the summer after her father's death they began the work. The construction company came with niggers and mules and machinery, and a foreman named Homer Barron, a Yankee—a big, dark, ready man, with a big voice and eyes lighter than his face. The little boys would follow in groups to hear him cuss the niggers, and the niggers singing in time to the rise and fall of picks. Pretty soon he knew everybody in town. Whenever you heard a lot of laughing anywhere about the square, Homer Barron would be in the center of the group. Presently, we began to see him and Miss Emily on Sunday afternoons driving in the yellow-wheeled buggy and the matched team of bays from the livery stable.

At first we were glad that Miss Emily would have an interest, because the ladies all said, "Of course a Grierson would not think seriously of a Northerner, a day laborer." But there were still others, older people, who said that even grief could not cause a real lady to forget *noblesse oblige*—without calling it *noblesse oblige*. They just said, "Poor Emily. Her kinsfolk should come to her." She had some kin in Alabama; but years ago her father had fallen out with them over the estate of old lady Wyatt, the crazy woman, and there was no communication between the two families. They had not even been represented at the funeral.

And as soon as the old people said, "Poor Emily," the whispering began. "Do you suppose it's really so?" they said to one another. "Of course it is. What else could. . . ." This behind their hands; rustling of craned silk and satin behind jalousies closed upon the sun of Sunday afternoon as the thin, swift clop-clop-clop of the matched team passed: "Poor Emily."

She carried her head high enough—even when we believed that she was fallen. It was as if she demanded more than ever the recognition of her dignity as the last Grierson; as if it had wanted that touch of earthiness to reaffirm her imperviousness. Like when she bought the rat poison, the arsenic. That was over a year after they had begun to say "Poor Emily," and while the two female cousins were visiting her.

"I want some poison," she said to the druggist. She was over thirty then, still a slight woman, though thinner than usual, with cold, haughty black eyes in a face the flesh of which was strained across the temples and about the eyesockets as you imagine a lighthouse-keeper's face ought to look. "I want some poison," she said.

"Yes, Miss Emily. What kind? For rats and such? I'd recom——"

"I want the best you have. I don't care what kind."

The druggist named several. "They'll kill anything up to an elephant. But what you want is——"

"Arsenic," Miss Emily said. "Is that a good one?"

"Is . . . arsenic? Yes, ma'am. But what you want——"

"I want arsenic."

The druggist looked down at her. She looked back at him, erect, her face like a strained flag. "Why, of course," the druggist said. "If that's what you want. But the law requires you to tell what you are going to use it for."

Miss Emily just stared at him, her head tilted back in order to look him eye for eye, until he looked away and went and got the arsenic and wrapped it up. The Negro delivery boy brought her the package; the druggist didn't come back. When she opened the package at home there was written on the box, under the skull and bones: "For rats."

4

So the next day we all said, "She will kill herself"; and we said it would be the best thing. When she had first begun to be seen with Homer Barron, we had said, "She will marry him." Then we said, "She will persuade him yet," because Homer himself had remarked—he liked men, and it was known that he drank with the younger men in the Elks' Club—that he was not a marrying man. Later we said, "Poor Emily" behind the jalousies as they passed on Sunday afternoon in the glittering buggy, Miss Emily with her head high and Homer Barron with his hat cocked and a cigar in his teeth, reins and whip in a yellow glove.

Then some of the ladies began to say that it was a disgrace to the town and a bad example to the young people. The men did not want to interfere, but at last the ladies forced the Baptist minister—Miss Emily's people were Episcopal—to call upon her. He would never divulge what happened during that interview, but he refused to go back again. The next Sunday they again drove about the streets, and the following day the minister's wife wrote to Miss Emily's relations in Alabama.

So she had blood-kin under her roof again and we sat back to watch developments. At first nothing happened. Then we were sure that they were to be married. We learned that Miss Emily had been to the jeweler's and ordered a man's toilet set in silver, with the letters H.B. on each piece. Two days later we learned that she had bought a complete outfit of men's clothing, including a nightshirt, and we said, "They are married." We were really glad. We were glad because the two female cousins were even more Grierson than Miss Emily had ever been.

So we were not surprised when Homer Barron—the streets had been finished some time since—was gone. We were a little disappointed that there was not a public blowing-off, but we believed that he had gone on to prepare for Miss Emily's coming, or to give her a chance to get rid of the cousins. (By that time it was a cabal, and we were all Miss Emily's allies to help circumvent the cousins.) Sure enough, after another week they departed. And, as we had expected all along, within three days Homer Barron was back in town. A neighbor saw the Negro man admit him at the kitchen door at dusk one evening.

And that was the last we saw of Homer Barron. And of Miss Emily for some time. The Negro man went in and out with the market basket, but the front door remained closed. Now and then we would see her at the window for a moment, as the men did that night when they sprinkled the lime, but for almost six months she did not appear on the streets. Then we knew that this was to be expected too; as if that quality of her father which had thwarted her woman's life so many times had been too virulent and too furious to die.

When we next saw Miss Emily, she had grown fat and her hair was turning gray. During the next few years it grew grayer and grayer until it attained an even pepper-and-salt iron-gray, when it ceased turning. Up to the day of her death at seventy-four it was still that vigorous iron-gray, like the hair of an active man.

From that time on her front door remained closed, save during a period of six or seven years, when she was about forty, during which she gave lessons in china-painting. She fitted up a studio in one of the downstairs rooms, where the daughters and grand-daughters of Colonel Sartoris' contemporaries were sent to her with the same regularity and in the same spirit that they were sent to church on Sundays with a twenty-five-cent piece for the collection plate. Meanwhile her taxes had been remitted.

Then the newer generation became the backbone and the spirit of the town, and the painting pupils grew up and fell away and did not send their children to her with boxes of color and tedious brushes and pictures cut from the ladies' magazines. The front door closed upon the last one and remained closed for good. When the town got free postal delivery, Miss Emily alone refused to let them fasten the metal numbers above her door and attach a mailbox to it. She would not listen to them.

did not like change or being provacutive

Daily, monthly, yearly we watched the Negro grow grayer and more stooped, going in and out with the market basket. Each December we sent her a tax notice, which would be returned by the post office a week later, unclaimed. Now and then we would see her in one of the downstairs windows—she had evidently shut up the top floor of the house—like the carven torso of an idol in a niche, looking or not looking at us, we could never tell which. Thus she passed from generation to generation—dear, inescapable, impervious, tranquil, and perverse.

And so she died. Fell ill in the house filled with dust and shadows, with only a doddering Negro man to wait on her. We did not even know she was sick; we had long since given up trying to get any information from the Negro. He talked to no one, probably not even to her, for his voice had grown harsh and rusty, as if from disuse.

She died in one of the downstairs rooms, in a heavy walnut bed with a curtain, her gray head propped on a pillow yellow and moldy with age and lack of sunlight.

5

The Negro met the first of the ladies at the front door and let them in, with their hushed, sibilant voices and their quick, curious glances, and then he disappeared. He walked right through the house and out the back and was not seen again.

The two female cousins came at once. They held the funeral on the second day, with the town coming to look at Miss Emily beneath a mass of bought flowers, with the crayon face of her father musing profoundly above the bier and the ladies sibilant and macabre; and the very old men—some in their brushed Confederate uniforms—on the porch and the lawn, talking of Miss Emily as if she had been a contemporary of theirs, believing that they had danced with her and courted her perhaps, confusing time with its mathematical progression, as the old do, to whom all the past is not a diminishing road but, instead, a huge meadow which no winter ever quite touches, divided from them now by the narrow bottleneck of the most recent decade of years.

Already we knew that there was one room in that region above stairs which no one had seen in forty years, and which would have to be forced. They waited until Miss Emily was decently in the ground before they opened it.

The violence of breaking down the door seemed to fill this room with pervading dust. A thin, acrid pall as of the tomb seemed to lie everywhere upon this room decked and furnished as for a bridal: upon the valance curtains of faded rose color, upon the rose-shaded lights, upon the dressing table, upon the delicate array of crystal and the man's toilet things backed with tarnished silver, silver so tarnished that the monogram was obscured. Among them lay a collar and tie, as if they had just been removed, which, lifted, left upon the surface a pale crescent in the dust. Upon a chair hung the suit, carefully folded; beneath it the two mute shoes and the discarded socks.

The man himself lay in the bed.

For a long while we just stood there, looking down at the profound and fleshless grin. The body had apparently once lain in the attitude of an embrace, but now the long sleep that outlasts love, that conquers even the grimace of love, had cuckolded him. What was left of him, rotted beneath what was left of the nightshirt, had become inextricable from the bed in which he lay; and upon him and upon the pillow beside him lay that even coating of the patient and biding dust.

Then we noticed that in the second pillow was the indentation of a head. One of us lifted something from it, and leaning forward, that faint and invisible dust dry and acrid in the nostrils, we saw a long strand of iron-gray hair.

(1930)

QUESTION

Although "A Rose for Emily" is narrated in the first person, the narrator is not "I" but "we." The narrator thus represents a communal rather than an individual point of view. How does the narrator (and the town) view Miss Emily? Find passages that represent more than one view of her, and explain their significance.

LANGUAGE AND STYLE

The way a writer chooses words, arranges them in sentences and longer units of discourse, and exploits their significance determines his or her *style.* Style is the verbal identity of a writer, as unmistakable as his or her face or voice. Reflecting their individuality, writers' styles convey their unique ways of seeing the world.

In the discussion of the language and style of fiction, we will concentrate on *diction,* the kind of word choices a writer makes; *syntax,* the order those words assume in sentences; and the presence or absence of figurative language, especially figures of comparison (simile and metaphor).*

Here is a paragraph from William Faulkner's "A Rose for Emily."

> Alive, Miss Emily had been a tradition, a duty, and a care; a
> sort of hereditary obligation upon the town, dating from that day
> in 1894 when Colonel Sartoris, the mayor—he who fathered the
> edict that no Negro woman should appear on the streets with-
> out an apron—remitted her taxes, the dispensation dating from
> the death of her father on into perpetuity. Not that Miss Emily
> would have accepted charity. Colonel Sartoris invented an in-
> volved tale to the effect that Miss Emily's father had loaned

*For an extensive discussion of figurative language, see Chapter 11.

money to the town, which the town, as a matter of business, preferred this way of repaying. Only a man of Colonel Sartoris' generation and thought could have invented it, and only a woman
could have believed it.

In this passage from the beginning of the story, Faulkner introduces his central character, Miss Emily Grierson. He does so in a style both elegant and formal. This is equally apparent in the triple description of Miss Emily in the first
sentence ("a tradition, a duty, and a care") and in the carefully balanced phrases
of the final sentence ("only a man" . . . "only a woman"; and "could have invented it" . . . "could have believed it"). The sentences, with their artfully controlled rhythms, create an effect of eloquence. This eloquence is achieved partly
by the balanced phrasing we have already noted, and partly by the studied formality of the long sentences, especially the first. Constructions like "he who fathered the edict" and "the dispensation dating from" create a tone more elevated than that of everyday speech. Also contributing to this tone is the
repetition of words ("had loaned money to the town, which the town") and
the heavy reliance on pauses within the first and third sentences. Finally, there
is the play of sound, alliteration and assonance especially, in "*da*ting from that
*da*y" and "*d*ispensation *da*ting from the *d*eath."

Faulkner's dense, richly textured prose contrasts with Hemingway's sparse,
taut style in the following passage from "The Short Happy Life of Francis Macomber." Francis Macomber, who at an earlier point in the action had shown
himself a coward by dropping his gun and running from a lion, has redeemed
himself in the eyes of the professional hunter, Robert Wilson. After Macomber
demonstrates courage in hunting wild buffalo (reputedly more dangerous than
hunting lion), Wilson has these thoughts:

> It had taken a strange chance of hunting, a sudden precipita-
> tion into action without opportunity for worrying beforehand,
> to bring this about with Macomber, but regardless of how it had
> happened it had most certainly happened. Look at the beggar
> now, Wilson thought. It's that some of them stay little boys so
> long, Wilson thought. Sometimes all their lives. Their figures stay
> boyish when they're fifty. The great American boy-men. Damned
> strange people. But he liked this Macomber now. Damned strange
> fellow. Probably meant the end of cuckoldry too. Well, that
> would be a damned good thing. Damned good thing. Beggar had
> probably been afraid all his life. Don't know what started it. But
> over now. Hadn't had time to be afraid with the buff. That and
> being angry too. Motor car too. Motor cars made it familiar. Be
> a damn fire eater now. He'd seen it in the war work the same
> way. More of a change than any loss of virginity. Fear gone like
> an operation. Something else grew in its place. Main thing a man
> had. Made him into a man. Women knew it too. No bloody fear.

Hemingway's paragraph reads and sounds differently from Faulkner's. Although both writers repeat words and phrases, Hemingway's syntax, unlike
Faulkner's, creates a sense of abruptness and fragmentation, whereas Faulkner's

prose flows in a stately progression and expansion of phrases, gathering force as a sentence concludes. Hemingway's emphatic tone is more like the broken, halting movement of speech. That, in fact, is what it is: the inner speech of Robert Wilson. In contrast, Faulkner's style is more formal, more "written" than spoken—or if spoken, more eloquent and exalted.

Hemingway's abrupt, staccato style is also reflected in his diction. Unlike Faulkner's wide curve of language with an emphasis on polysyllabic words of Latin derivation ("obligation," "dispensation," "perpetuity") Hemingway chooses short words, often monosyllables, of Anglo-Saxon rather than foreign derivation. In Robert Wilson's description of Macomber, moreover, Hemingway uses a vocabulary appropriate to the big-game hunter: words like "beggar" with its pitying affection for Macomber, and "buff" with its fond respect for the big-game adversary.

Like Faulkner, Hemingway employs comparisons to convey Wilson's assessment of Macomber. Macomber is first compared to a boy, one of many American "boy-men" Wilson has encountered. But Wilson later sees him as a "fire-eater," that is, as a man who encounters danger fearlessly, eagerly; this term conveys Wilson's admiration for Macomber's newly found courage. The most important comparisons, however, indicate the change Macomber has undergone. His fear is described as being "gone like an operation," as if a tumor were removed by surgery. This excision makes him a man. Finally, Wilson implicitly compares Macomber's passage to manhood favorably with that of soldiers who established their manhood under fire.

Thus, the comparisons that Hemingway, Faulkner, and other writers use enrich their prose and impart a unique and personal view of the world. They are simultaneously indelible stamps of each writer's style and keys to understanding their works.

The language of the following story, "Araby" by James Joyce, reveals both the narrator's conception of himself as a boy and his adult understanding of his boyhood. Note carefully the descriptions of Mangan's sister, especially their mixture of erotic and religious details. Consider also the connotations of the first and last paragraphs and the implications of the religious imagery throughout.

JAMES JOYCE

[1882–1941]

Araby

North Richmond Street, being blind, was a quiet street except at the hour when the Christian Brothers' School set the boys free. An uninhabited house of two storeys stood at the blind end, detached from its neighbours in a square ground. The other houses of the street, conscious of decent lives within them, gazed at one another with brown imperturbable faces.

The former tenant of our house, a priest, had died in the back drawing-room. Air, musty from having been long enclosed, hung in all the rooms, and the waste room behind the kitchen was littered with old useless papers. Among these I found a few paper-covered books, the pages of which were curled and damp: *The Abbot,* by Walter Scott, *The Devout Communicant* and *The Memoirs of Vidocq*. I liked the last best because its leaves were yellow. The wild garden behind the house contained a central apple-tree and a few straggling bushes under one of which I found the late tenant's rusty bicycle-pump. He had been a very charitable priest; in his will he had left all his money to institutions and the furniture of his house to his sister.

When the short days of winter came dusk fell before we had well eaten our dinners. When we met in the street the houses had grown sombre. The space of sky above us was the colour of ever-changing violet and towards it the lamps of the street lifted their feeble lanterns. The cold air stung us and we played till our bodies glowed. Our shouts echoed in the silent street. The career of our play brought us through the dark muddy lanes behind the houses where we ran the gantlet of the rough tribes from the cottages, to the back doors of the dark dripping gardens where odours arose from the ashpits, to the dark odorous stables where a coachman smoothed and combed the horse or shook music from the buckled harness. When we returned to the street light from the kitchen windows had filled the areas. If my uncle was seen turning the corner we hid in the shadow until we had seen him safely housed. Or if Mangan's sister came out on the doorstep to call her brother in to his tea we watched her from our shadow peer up and down the street. We waited to see whether she would remain or go in and, if she remained, we left our shadow and walked up to Mangan's steps resignedly. She was waiting for us, her figure defined by the light from the half-opened door. Her brother always teased her before he obeyed and I stood by the railings looking at her. Her dress swung as she moved her body and the soft rope of her hair tossed from side to side.

Every morning I lay on the floor in the front parlour watching her door. The blind was pulled down to within an inch of the sash so that I could not be seen. When she came out on the doorstep my heart leaped. I ran to the hall, seized my books and followed her. I kept her brown figure always in my eye and, when we came near the point at which our ways diverged, I quickened my pace and passed her. This happened morning after morning. I had never spoken to her, except for a few casual words, and yet her name was like a summons to all my foolish blood.

Her image accompanied me even in places the most hostile to romance. On Saturday evenings when my aunt went marketing I had to go to carry some of the parcels. We walked through the flaring streets, jostled by drunken men and bargaining women, amid the curses of labourers, the shrill litanies of shop-boys who stood on guard by the barrels of pigs' cheeks, the nasal chanting of street-singers, who sang a *come-all-you* about O'Donovan Rossa, or a ballad about the troubles in our native land. These noises converged in a single sensation of life for me: I imagined that I bore my chalice safely through a throng of foes. Her name sprang to my lips at moments in strange prayers and praises which I myself did not understand. My eyes were often full of tears (I could not tell why) and at times a flood from my heart seemed to pour itself out into my bosom. I thought little of the future. I did not know whether I would ever speak to her or not or, if I spoke to her, how I could tell her of my confused adoration. But my body was like a harp and her words and gestures were like fingers running upon the wires.

One evening I went into the back drawing-room in which the priest had died. It was a dark rainy evening and there was no sound in the house. Through one of the broken panes I heard the rain impinge upon the earth, the fine incessant needles of water playing in the sodden beds. Some distant lamp or lighted window gleamed below me. I was thankful that I could see so little. All my senses seemed to desire to veil themselves and, feeling that I was about to slip from them, I pressed the palms of my hands together until they trembled, murmuring: *O love! O love!* many times.

At last she spoke to me. When she addressed the first words to me I was so confused that I did not know what to answer. She asked me was I going to *Araby*. I forget whether I answered yes or no. It would be a splendid bazaar, she said; she would love to go.

—And why can't you? I asked.

While she spoke she turned a silver bracelet round and round her wrist. She could not go, she said, because there would be a retreat that week in her convent. Her brother and two other boys were fighting for their caps and I was alone at the railings. She held one of the spikes, bowing her head towards me. The light from the lamp opposite our door caught the white curve of her neck, lit up her hair that rested there and, falling, lit up the hand upon the railing. It fell over one side of her dress and caught the white border of a petticoat, just visible as she stood at ease.

—It's well for you, she said.

—If I go, I said, I will bring you something.

What innumerable follies laid waste my waking and sleeping thoughts after that evening! I wished to annihilate the tedious intervening days. I chafed against the work of school. At night in my bedroom and by day in the classroom her image came between me and the page I strove to read. The syllables of the word *Araby* were called to me through the silence in which my soul luxuriated and cast an Eastern enchantment over me. I asked for leave to go to the bazaar Saturday night. My aunt was surprised and hoped it was not some Freemason affair. I answered few questions in class. I watched my master's face pass from amiability to sternness; he hoped I was not beginning to idle. I could not call my wandering thoughts together. I had hardly any patience with the serious work of life which, now that it stood between me and my desire, seemed to me child's play, ugly monotonous child's play.

On Saturday morning I reminded my uncle that I wished to go to the bazaar in the evening. He was fussing at the hallstand, looking for the hat-brush, and answered me curtly:

—Yes, boy, I know.

As he was in the hall I could not go into the front parlour and lie at the window. I left the house in bad humour and walked slowly towards the school. The air was pitilessly raw and already my heart misgave me.

When I came home to dinner my uncle had not yet been home. Still it was early. I sat staring at the clock for some time and, when its ticking began to irritate me, I left the room. I mounted the staircase and gained the upper part of the house. The high cold empty gloomy rooms liberated me and I went from room to room singing. From the front window I saw my companions playing below in the street. Their cries reached me weakened and indistinct and, leaning my forehead against the cool glass, I looked over at the dark house where she lived. I may have stood there for an hour, seeing nothing but the brown-clad figure cast by my imagination, touched discreetly by the lamplight at the curved neck, at the hand upon the railings and at the border below the dress.

When I came downstairs again I found Mrs Mercer sitting at the fire. She was an old garrulous woman, a pawnbroker's widow, who collected used stamps for some pious purpose. I had to endure the gossip of the tea-table. The meal was prolonged beyond an hour and still my uncle did not come. Mrs Mercer stood up to go: she was sorry she couldn't wait any longer, but it was after eight o'clock and she did not like to be out late, as the night air was bad for her. When she had gone I began to walk up and down the room, clenching my fists. My aunt said:

—I'm afraid you may put off your bazaar for this night of Our Lord.

At nine o'clock I heard my uncle's latchkey in the halldoor. I heard him talking to himself and heard the hallstand rocking when it had received the weight of his over-coat. I could interpret these signs. When he was midway through his dinner I asked him to give me the money to go to the bazaar. He had forgotten.

—The people are in bed and after their first sleep now, he said.

I did not smile. My aunt said to him energetically:

—Can't you give him the money and let him go? You've kept him late enough as it is.

My uncle said he was very sorry he had forgotten. He said he believed in the old say-ing: *All work and no play makes Jack a dull boy*. He asked me where I was going and, when I had told him a second time he asked me did I know *The Arab's Farewell to his Steed*. When I left the kitchen he was about to recite the opening lines of the piece to my aunt.

I held a florin tightly in my hand as I strode down Buckingham Street towards the station. The sight of the streets thronged with buyers and glaring with gas recalled to me the purpose of my journey. I took my seat in a third-class carriage of a deserted train. After an intolerable delay the train moved out of the station slowly. It crept on-ward among ruinous houses and over the twinkling river. At Westland Row Station a crowd of people pressed to the carriage doors; but the porters moved them back, say-ing that it was a special train for the bazaar. I remained alone in the bare carriage. In a few minutes the train drew up beside an improvised wooden platform. I passed out on to the road and saw by the lighted dial of a clock that it was ten minutes to ten. In front of me was a large building which displayed the magical name.

I could not find any sixpenny entrance and, fearing that the bazaar would be closed, I passed in quickly through a turnstile, handing a shilling to a weary-looking man. I found myself in a big hall girdled at half its height by a gallery. Nearly all the stalls were closed and the greater part of the hall was in darkness. I recognised a silence like that which pervades a church after a service. I walked into the centre of the bazaar timidly. A few people were gathered about the stalls which were still open. Before a curtain, over which the words *Café Chantant* were written in coloured lamps, two men were counting money on a salver. I listened to the fall of the coins.

Remembering with difficulty why I had come I went over to one of the stalls and examined porcelain vases and flowered tea-sets. At the door of the stall a young lady was talking and laughing with two young gentlemen. I remarked their English accents and listened vaguely to their conversation.

—O, I never said such a thing!

—O, but you did!

—O, but I didn't!

—Didn't she say that?

—Yes. I heard her.

—O, there's a . . . fib!

Observing me the young lady came over and asked me did I wish to buy anything. The tone of her voice was not encouraging; she seemed to have spoken to me out of a sense of duty. I looked humbly at the great jars that stood like eastern guards at either side of the dark entrance to the stall and murmured:

—No, thank you.

The young lady changed the position of one of the vases and went back to the two young men. They began to talk of the same subject. Once or twice the young lady glanced at me over her shoulder.

I lingered before her stall, though I knew my stay was useless, to make my interest in her wares seem the more real. Then I turned away slowly and walked down the middle of the bazaar. I allowed the two pennies to fall against the sixpence in my pocket. I heard a voice call from one end of the gallery that the light was out. The upper part of the hall was now completely dark.

Gazing up into the darkness I saw myself as a creature driven and derided by vanity; and my eyes burned with anguish and anger.

(1914)

QUESTIONS

1. Note the religious language of the fifth paragraph, especially the words "litanies," "chalice," "prayers and praises," and "confused adoration." What does this language reveal about the boy, about how he sees himself, about how he envisions what he is doing and thinking? Explain how the following sentence from this paragraph is related to the image invoked by his religious language: "But my body was like a harp and her words and gestures were like fingers running upon the wires."
2. Read the dialogue near the end of the story aloud, if possible with a friend. What do you hear? How can you characterize the conversation? What effect does it have on the boy? Why?
3. Reread the first and last paragraphs. Note repetitions and similarities in the language. Relate the use of the word "blind" for a dead-end street to the boy's situation as expressed at the end of the story. Why do the boy's "eyes" burn with "anguish" and "anger"?

THEME

In Chapter 1, Reading (and Writing About) Literature, we noted that the meaning of a literary work is more than any statement that can be made about it, that its meaning consists of both our experience in reading it and the ideas we may extract from it. With that in mind, let us clarify what we mean by the theme of a story. Simply put, a story's *theme* is its idea or point formulated as a generalization. The theme of a fable is its moral; the theme of a parable is its teaching; the theme of a short story is its implied view of life and conduct. Unlike the fable and parable, however, most fiction is not designed primarily to teach or preach. Its theme, thus, is more obliquely presented. In fact theme in fiction is rarely *presented* at all; it is abstracted from the details of character and action that compose the story.

To be clear about theme, we should distinguish it from plot, the story's sequence of action, and from *subject,* what the story is generally about. In explaining a story's theme we do more than state its subject or summarize its plot. To say, for example, that Pirandello's "War" is about parents and children is more a statement of subject than of theme. To pinpoint its theme we would have to explain what the story implies about parents and children, what it suggests about parents' love for their children, and even more specifically, what it values in the attitudes toward the loss of children expressed by the two major characters.

Theme is related to the other elements of fiction more as consequence than as a parallel element that can be separately identified. A story's theme, that is, grows out of the relationship of the other elements. To formulate a story's theme, we try to explain what these elements collectively suggest. Since the theme of a story derives from its details of character, plot, setting, structure, language, and point of view, any statement of theme is valid and valuable to the extent that it accounts for these details. To explain the theme of "The Prodigal Son," for example, without accounting for the father's speech to the elder son would be to distort the meaning of the story.

Perhaps the most important thing to remember about theme is that it is an abstraction from a story's complex uses of language to describe and chart action, depict setting, and portray character. A statement of theme derives from the particulars embodied in language and action. The very concreteness and particularity of fiction should make us cautious in searching out theme. In fact, it would be more useful to avoid thinking of theme as hidden somehow beneath the surface of the story and instead to see theme as the implied significance of the story's details. There are a multiplicity of ways to state a story's theme, but any such statement involves a necessary simplification of the story. In clarifying our sense of a story's idea, we also inevitably exclude some dimensions of the story and include others. We should be aware that the themes we abstract from stories are provisional understandings that never completely explain the stories.

With these considerations in mind, read Eudora Welty's "A Worn Path," with an eye to explaining its theme.

EUDORA WELTY

[b. 1909]

A Worn Path

It was December—a bright frozen day in the early morning. Far out in the country there was an old Negro woman with her head tied in a red rag, coming along a path through the pinewoods. Her name was Phoenix Jackson. She was very old and small and she walked slowly in the dark pine shadows, moving a little from side to side in her steps, with the balanced heaviness and lightness of a pendulum in a grandfather clock.

She carried a thin, small cane made from an umbrella, and with this she kept tapping the frozen earth in front of her. This made a grave and persistent noise in the still air, that seemed meditative like the chirping of a solitary little bird.

She wore a dark striped dress reaching down to her shoe tops, and an equally long apron of bleached sugar sacks, with a full pocket: all neat and tidy, but every time she took a step she might have fallen over her shoelaces, which dragged from her unlaced shoes. She looked straight ahead. Her eyes were blue with age. Her skin had a pattern all its own of numberless branching wrinkles and as though a whole little tree stood in the middle of her forehead, but a golden color ran underneath, and the two knobs of her cheeks were illumined by a yellow burning under the dark. Under the red rag her hair came down on her neck in the frailest of ringlets, still black, and with an odor like copper.

Now and then there was a quivering in the thicket. Old Phoenix said, "Out of my way, all you foxes, owls, beetles, jack rabbits, coons and wild animals! . . . Keep out from under these feet, little bob-whites. . . . Keep the big wild hogs out of my path. Don't let none of those come running my direction. I got a long way." Under her small black-freckled hand her cane, limber as a buggy whip, would switch at the brush as if to rouse up any hiding things.

On she went. The woods were deep and still. The sun made the pine needles almost too bright to look at, up where the wind rocked. The cones dropped as light as feathers. Down in the hollow was the mourning dove—it was not too late for him.

The path ran up a hill. "Seem like there is chains about my feet, time I get this far," she said, in the voice of argument old people keep to use with themselves. "Something always take a hold of me on this hill—pleads I should stay."

After she got to the top she turned and gave a full, severe look behind her where she had come. "Up through pines," she said at length. "Now down through oaks."

Her eyes opened their widest, and she started down gently. But before she got to the bottom of the hill a bush caught her dress.

Her fingers were busy and intent, but her skirts were full and long, so that before she could pull them free in one place they were caught in another. It was not possible to allow the dress to tear. "I in the thorny bush," she said. "Thorns, you doing your appointed work. Never want to let folks pass, no sir. Old eyes thought you was a pretty little *green* bush."

Finally, trembling all over, she stood free, and after a moment dared to stoop for her cane.

"Sun so high!" she cried, leaning back and looking, while the thick tears went over her eyes. "The time getting all gone here."

At the foot of this hill was a place where a log was laid across the creek.

"Now comes the trial," said Phoenix.

Putting her right foot out, she mounted the log and shut her eyes. Lifting her skirt, leveling her cane fiercely before her, like a festival figure in some parade, she began to march across. Then she opened her eyes and she was safe on the other side.

"I wasn't as old as I thought," she said.

But she sat down to rest. She spread her skirts on the bank around her and folded her hands over her knees. Up above her was a tree in a pearly cloud of mistletoe. She did not dare to close her eyes, and when a little boy brought her a plate with a slice of marble-cake on it she spoke to him. "That would be acceptable," she said. But when she went to take it there was just her own hand in the air.

So she left that tree, and had to go through a barbed-wire fence. There she had to creep and crawl, spreading her knees and stretching her fingers like a baby trying to climb the steps. But she talked loudly to herself: she could not let her dress be torn now, so late in the day, and she could not pay for having her arm or her leg sawed off if she got caught fast where she was.

At last she was safe through the fence and risen up out in the clearing. Big dead trees, like black men with one arm, were standing in the purple stalks of the withered cotton field. There sat a buzzard.

"Who you watching?"

In the furrow she made her way along.

"Glad this not the season for bulls," she said, looking sideways, "and the good Lord made his snakes to curl up and sleep in the winter. A pleasure I don't see no two-headed snake coming around that tree, where it come once. It took a while to get by him, back in the summer."

She passed through the old cotton and went into a field of dead corn. It whispered and shook and was taller than her head. "Through the maze now," she said, for there was no path.

Then there was something tall, black, and skinny there, moving before her.

At first she took it for a man. It could have been a man dancing in the field. But she stood still and listened, and it did not make a sound. It was as silent as a ghost.

"Ghost," she said sharply, "who be you the ghost of? For I have heard of nary death close by."

But there was no answer—only the ragged dancing in the wind.

She shut her eyes, reached out her hand, and touched a sleeve. She found a coat and inside that an emptiness, cold as ice.

"You scarecrow," she said. Her face lighted. "I ought to be shut up for good," she said with laughter. "My senses is gone. I too old. I the oldest people I ever know. Dance, old scarecrow," she said, "while I dancing with you."

She kicked her foot over the furrow, and with mouth drawn down, shook her head once or twice in a little strutting way. Some husks blew down and whirled in streamers about her skirts.

Then she went on, parting her way from side to side with the cane, through the whispering field. At last she came to the end, to a wagon track where the silver grass blew between the red ruts. The quail were walking around like pullets, seeming all dainty and unseen.

"Walk pretty," she said. "This the easy place. This the easy going."

She followed the track, swaying through the quiet bare fields, through the little strings of trees silver in their dead leaves, past cabins silver from weather, with the doors and windows boarded shut, all like old women under a spell sitting there. "I walking in their sleep," she said, nodding her head vigorously.

In a ravine she went where a spring was silently flowing through a hollow log. Old Phoenix bent and drank. "Sweet-gum makes the water sweet," she said, and drank more. "Nobody know who made this well, for it was here when I was born."

The track crossed a swampy part where the moss hung as white as lace from every limb. "Sleep on, alligators, and blow your bubbles." Then the track went into the road.

Deep, deep the road went down between the high green-colored banks. Overhead the live-oaks met, and it was as dark as a cave.

A black dog with a lolling tongue came up out of the weeds by the ditch. She was meditating, and not ready, and when he came at her she only hit him a little with her cane. Over she went in the ditch, like a little puff of milkweed.

Down there, her senses drifted away. A dream visited her, and she reached her hand up, but nothing reached down and gave her a pull. So she lay there and presently went to talking. "Old woman," she said to herself, "that black dog come up out of the weeds to stall you off, and now there he sitting on his fine tail, smiling at you."

A white man finally came along and found her—a hunter, a young man, with his dog on a chain.

"Well, Granny!" he laughed. "What are you doing there?"

"Lying on my back like a June-bug waiting to be turned over, mister," she said, reaching up her hand.

He lifted her up, gave her a swing in the air, and set her down. "Anything broken, Granny?"

"No, sir, them old dead weeds is springy enough," said Phoenix, when she had got her breath. "I thank you for your trouble."

"Where do you live, Granny?" he asked, while the two dogs were growling at each other.

"Away back yonder, sir, behind the ridge. You can't even see it from here."

"On your way home?"

"No sir, I going to town."

"Why, that's too far! That's as far as I walk when I come out myself, and I get something for my trouble." He patted the stuffed bag he carried, and there hung down a little closed claw. It was one of the bob-whites, with its beak hooked bitterly to show it was dead. "Now you go home, Granny!"

"I bound to go to town, mister," said Phoenix. "The time come around."

He gave another laugh, filling the whole landscape. "I know you old colored people! Wouldn't miss going to town to see Santa Claus!"

But something held old Phoenix very still. The deep lines in her face went into a fierce and different radiation. Without warning, she had seen with her own eyes a flashing nickel fall out of the man's pocket onto the ground.

"How old are you, Granny?" he was saying.

"There is no telling, mister," she said, "no telling."

Then she gave a little cry and clapped her hands and said, "Git on away from here, dog! Look! Look at that dog!" She laughed as if in admiration. "He ain't scared of nobody. He a big black dog." She whispered, "Sic him!"

"Watch me get rid of that cur," said the man. "Sic him, Pete! Sic him!"

Phoenix heard the dogs fighting, and heard the man running and throwing sticks. She even heard a gunshot. But she was slowly bending forward by that time, further and further forward, the lids stretched down over her eyes, as if she were doing this in her sleep. Her chin was lowered almost to her knees. The yellow palm of her hand came out from the fold of her apron. Her fingers slid down and along the ground under the piece of money with the grace and care they would have in lifting an egg from under a setting hen. Then she slowly straightened up, she stood erect, and the nickel was in her apron pocket. A bird flew by. Her lips moved. "God watching me the whole time. I come to stealing."

The man came back, and his own dog panted about them. "Well, I scared him off that time," he said, and then he laughed and lifted his gun and pointed it at Phoenix.

She stood straight and faced him.

"Doesn't the gun scare you?" he said, still pointing it.

"No, sir, I seen plenty go off closer by, in my day, and for less than what I done," she said, holding utterly still.

He smiled, and shouldered the gun. "Well, Granny," he said, "you must be a hundred years old, and scared of nothing. I'd give you a dime if I had any money with me. But you take my advice and stay home, and nothing will happen to you."

"I bound to go on my way, mister," said Phoenix. She inclined her head in the red rag. Then they went in different directions, but she could hear the gun shooting again and again over the hill.

She walked on. The shadows hung from the oak trees to the road like curtains. Then she smelled wood-smoke, and smelled the river, and she saw a steeple and the cabins on their steep steps. Dozens of little black children whirled around her. There ahead was Natchez shining. Bells were ringing. She walked on.

In the paved city it was Christmas time. There were red and green electric lights strung and criss-crossed everywhere, and all turned on in the daytime. Old Phoenix would have been lost if she had not distrusted her eyesight and depended on her feet to know where to take her.

She paused quietly on the sidewalk where people were passing by. A lady came along in the crowd, carrying an armful of red-, green- and silver-wrapped presents; she gave off perfume like the red roses in hot summer, and Phoenix stopped her.

"Please, missy, will you lace up my shoe?" She held up her foot.

"What do you want, Grandma?"

"See my shoe," said Phoenix. "Do all right for out in the country, but wouldn't look right to go in a big building."

"Stand still then, Grandma," said the lady. She put her packages down on the sidewalk beside her and laced and tied both shoes tightly.

"Can't lace 'em with a cane," said Phoenix. "Thank you, missy. I doesn't mind asking a nice lady to tie up my shoe, when I gets out on the street."

Moving slowly and from side to side, she went into the big building, and into a tower of steps, where she walked up and around and around until her feet knew to stop.

She entered a door, and there she saw nailed up on the wall the document that had been stamped with the gold seal and framed in the gold frame, which matched the dream that was hung up in her head.

"Here I be," she said. There was a fixed and ceremonial stiffness over her body.

"A charity case, I suppose," said an attendant who sat at the desk before her.

But Phoenix only looked above her head. There was sweat on her face, the wrinkles in her skin shone like a bright net.

"Speak up, Grandma," the woman said. "What's your name? We must have your history, you know. Have you been here before? What seems to be the trouble with you?"

Old Phoenix only gave a twitch to her face as if a fly were bothering her.

"Are you deaf?" cried the attendant.

But then the nurse came in.

"Oh, that's just old Aunt Phoenix," she said. "She doesn't come for herself—she has a little grandson. She makes these trips just as regular as clockwork. She lives away back off the Old Natchez Trace." She bent down. "Well, Aunt Phoenix, why don't you just take a seat? We won't keep you standing after your long trip." She pointed.

The old woman sat down, bolt upright in the chair.

"Now, how is the boy?" asked the nurse.

Old Phoenix did not speak.

"I said, how is the boy?"

But Phoenix only waited and stared straight ahead, her face very solemn and withdrawn into rigidity.

"Is his throat any better?" asked the nurse. "Aunt Phoenix, don't you hear me? Is your grandson's throat any better since the last time you came for the medicine?"

With her hands on her knees, the old woman waited, silent, erect and motionless, just as if she were in armor.

"You mustn't take up our time this way, Aunt Phoenix," the nurse said. "Tell us quickly about your grandson, and get it over. He isn't dead, is he?"

At last there came a flicker and then a flame of comprehension across her face, and she spoke.

"My grandson. It was my memory had left me. There I sat and forgot why I made my long trip."

"Forgot?" The nurse frowned. "After you came so far?"

Then Phoenix was like an old woman begging a dignified forgiveness for waking up frightened in the night. "I never did go to school, I was too old at the Surrender," she said in a soft voice. "I'm an old woman without an education. It was my memory fail me. My little grandson, he is just the same, and I forgot it in the coming."

"Throat never heals, does it?" said the nurse, speaking in a loud, sure voice to old Phoenix. By now she had a card with something written on it, a little list. "Yes. Swallowed lye. When was it?—January—two-three years ago—"

Phoenix spoke unasked now. "No, missy, he not dead, he just the same. Every little while his throat begin to close up again, and he not able to swallow. He not get his breath. He not able to help himself. So the time come around, and I go on another trip for the soothing medicine."

"All right. The doctor said as long as you came to get it, you could have it," said the nurse. "But it's an obstinate case."

"My little grandson, he sit up there in the house all wrapped up, waiting by himself," Phoenix went on. "We is the only two left in the world. He suffer and it don't seem to put him back at all. He got a sweet look. He going to last. He wear a little patch quilt and peep out holding his mouth open like a little bird. I remembers so plain now. I not going to forget him again, no, the whole enduring time. I could tell him from all the others in creation."

"All right." The nurse was trying to hush her now. She brought her a bottle of medicine. "Charity," she said, making a check mark in a book.

Old Phoenix held the bottle close to her eyes, and then carefully put it into her pocket.

"I thank you," she said.

"It's Christmas time, Grandma," said the attendant. "Could I give you a few pennies out of my purse?"

"Five pennies is a nickel," said Phoenix stiffly.

"Here's a nickel," said the attendant.

Phoenix rose carefully and held out her hand. She received the nickel and then fished the other nickel out of her pocket and laid it beside the new one. She stared at her palm closely, with her head on one side.

Then she gave a tap with her cane on the floor.

"This is what come to me to do," she said. "I going to the store and buy my child a little windmill they sells, made out of paper. He going to find it hard to believe there such a thing in the world. I'll march myself back where he waiting, holding it straight up in this hand."

She lifted her free hand, gave a little nod, turned around, and walked out of the doctor's office. Then her slow step began on the stairs, going down.

(1941)

QUESTIONS

1. State in a sentence or two the idea of "A Worn Path." What point does the story seem to make?
2. Develop your understanding of the story's theme in a paragraph or a brief conversation. To support your views, cite details of plot, character, setting, and language.

IRONY AND SYMBOL

Two additional facets of fictional works are irony and symbol. While not as pervasive as elements such as plot and character, irony and symbol are tremendously important. Both aspects of fiction allow writers to compress a great deal of meaning into a brief space. Both require deliberation and tact if we are to appreciate and enjoy their full range of significance. And both require us to be alert to their existence if we are to understand the works in which they occur. If we do not perceive a writer's ironic intentions, we may not just misconstrue a particular story; we may interpret it as suggesting the opposite of what it actually is intended to mean. And if we overlook a story's symbols, we may underestimate its achievement and oversimplify its significance.

Irony

Irony is not so much an element of fiction as a pervasive quality in it. It may appear in fiction (and in the other literary genres as well) in three ways: in a work's language, in its incidents, or in its point of view. But in whatever forms it emerges, *irony* always involves a contrast or discrepancy between one thing and another. The contrast may be between what is said and what is meant or between what happens and what is expected to happen.

In *verbal irony,* for example, we say the opposite of what we mean. When someone says "That was a brilliant remark" and we know that it was anything but brilliant, we understand the speaker's ironic intention. In such relatively simple instances there is usually no problem in perceiving irony. In more complex instances, however, the designation of an action or a remark as ironic can be much more complicated. At the end of O'Connor's "Good Country People," Mrs. Freeman says: "Some can't be that simple." "I know I never could." Should we take her literally? Or do we detect irony?

Besides verbal irony—in which we understand the opposite of what a speaker says—fiction makes use of *irony of circumstance* (sometimes called *irony of situation*). Writers sometimes create discrepancies between what seems to be and what is. In Chopin's "The Story of an Hour," for example, Mrs. Mallard appears to be grieving over the news of her husband's death. At least that's how her action is perceived by other characters. But we soon realize that rather than grief, her tears celebrate the joy of her new-found freedom. Her tears are ironic because they indicate the opposite of what we expect them to. Another ironic situation prevails as Mrs. Mallard "prays" for long life, presumably so she can enjoy freedom from her husband: what she is praying for and why she prays for it are out of keeping with the expected reasons for prayer on such an occasion.

Irony of circumstance or situation also refers to occasions when an individual expects one thing to occur only to discover that the opposite happens. This indeed is what Mrs. Mallard experiences when she discovers her husband had not been killed in the train crash as she had thought. The final irony, of course, is that *she* dies when she sees him walk in the door.

Although verbal irony and irony of circumstance or situation are the prevalent forms irony assumes in fiction, two others deserve mention: dramatic irony and ironic vision. More typical of plays than stories, *dramatic irony* is the discrepancy between what characters know and what readers know. Writers sometimes direct our responses by letting us see things that their characters do not. At the conclusion of Flannery O'Connor's "Good Country People," for example, the reader has quite a different view of the Bible salesman's character than either Mrs. Freeman or Mrs. Hopewell does.

Some writers exploit the discrepancy between what readers and characters know to establish an ironic vision in a work. An *ironic vision* is established in a work as an overall tone that suggests how a writer views his or her characters and subject. It is more characteristic of longer fictional works such as the novels *Pride and Prejudice* by Jane Austen or *The Adventures of Huckleberry Finn* by Mark Twain than of short stories. We can find an ironic vision, nonetheless, in O'Connor's "Good Country People." For the moment, however, consider how an ironic vision informs the opening of Jane Austen's *Pride and Prejudice:*

> It is a truth universally acknowledged, that a single man in possession of a good fortune, must be in want of a wife.
> However little known the feelings or views of such a man may be on his first entering a neighborhood, this truth is so well fixed in the minds of the surrounding families, that he is considered as the rightful property of some one or other of their daughters.

Is it a truth—that is, do we accept as fact what the opening sentence seems to assert: that a single man of means must be looking for a wife? Do we believe that this search for a wife is a phenomenon universally acknowledged, that it is recognized around the world, not merely in nineteenth-century England or twentieth-century America? It is very likely that Jane Austen's sentence presents the opposite of what we believe: that single men of means more often than not are not in search of wives. The converse is probably closer to what we have seen: single women seek out single men of means as prospective husbands. This discrepancy between what the sentence says and what we know accounts in part for its ironic quality. We are not to take it literally; we do not accept it at face value.

We can feel more confident about the ironic quality of Austen's first sentence when we examine it in relation to the sentence that follows it. We are told there that the feelings or views of the eligible bachelor mean little. But they should mean much in such an important issue. That they do not is the opposite of what we expect and hence is ironic. An additional irony is that characteristics of marriageable eligibility are limited to bachelorhood and wealth. Nothing else is mentioned as important—not character, not intelligence, not wisdom or virtue.

Portraying characters whose view of marriage is so mercenary and limited, Austen distances herself from them and from their values. This ironic distance is enforced when Austen describes their misconceptions about single men. But there is a further irony in the fact that those misconceptions do not matter. All that matters is the final outcome: the single man's loss of his bachelorhood and his entrance into the ranks of the family. Moreover, their view represents a reversal of a traditional and familiar notion: that a wife is a man's property. This idea is given an additional twist when Austen indicates that it hardly matters which girl of which family captures the prize.

For these reasons and for others that emerge as the novel develops, Austen's tone can be described as ironic. When such an ironic tone is established strongly from the beginning of a work and when it is sustained consistently throughout, we say that it is informed by an ironic vision. The ironic vision of *Pride and Prejudice* infuses the novel: it informs the plot, it controls the dialogue, and it surfaces repeatedly in the tone of the narrator's comments.

Symbol

Symbols in fiction are simply objects, actions, or events that convey meaning. The meaning they convey extends beyond their literal significance, beyond their more obvious actual reason for being included in the story. In Kate Chopin's "The Story of an Hour," for example, the room in which Mrs. Mallard sits symbolizes her domestic, homebound life. She looks out a window into a world that has previously been closed to her. With the supposed death of her husband, she sees the outside world in a fresh and invigorating way. What she observes (the trees, for example) and how she now understands those things (in this case as emblems of life, hope, and possibility) signal, for us, that symbolism is at work in the story.

How do we know if a particular detail is symbolic? How do we decide whether we should look beyond the literal meaning of a dialogue or the literal value of an object or action? The simple answer to this question is that there is no way to be certain about the symbolic value of any particular details. But we can alert ourselves to the possible symbolic overtones of such details through the following questions.

QUESTIONS

1. How important to the story is the object, action, gesture, or dialogue that we suspect is symbolic? Does it appear more than once? Does it occur at a climactic moment? Is it described in detail?
2. Does the story seem to warrant our granting its details more significance than their immediate literal value? Why?
3. Does a symbolic interpretation make sense? Does it fit in with a literal or commonsense explanation? Or does our symbolic reading contradict or otherwise distort the literal surface of the story?
4. What objections might be raised against our symbolic interpretation?

Even if we consider such questions carefully, we may still not be sure that a particular detail is symbolic. Sometimes we will be confident *that* such a detail is symbolic without being able to say just *what* it represents. This kind of uncertainty is natural, largely because symbols by their very nature resist easy and definitive explanation.

Read the following story, Edgar Allan Poe's "The Black Cat," with an eye to its ironies. Be alert for verbal irony, irony of situation, and dramatic irony. Consider whether the tone is sufficiently ironic to display an ironic vision. Identify and explain any symbols.

EDGAR ALLAN POE
[1809–1849]

The Black Cat

For the most wild yet most homely narrative which I am about to pen, I neither expect nor solicit belief. Mad indeed would I be to expect it, in a case where my very senses reject their own evidence. Yet, mad am I not—and very surely do I not dream. But to-morrow I die, and to-day I would unburden my soul. My immediate purpose is to place before the world, plainly, succinctly, and without comment, a series of mere household events. In their consequences, these events have terrified—have tortured—have destroyed me. Yet I will not attempt to expound them. To me, they have presented little but horror—to many they will seem less terrible than *baroques*. Hereafter, perhaps, some intellect may be found which will reduce my phantasm to the commonplace—some intellect more calm, more logical, and far less excitable than my own, which will perceive, in the circumstances I detail with awe, nothing more than an ordinary succession of very natural causes and effects.

From my infancy I was noted for the docility and humanity of my disposition. My tenderness of heart was even so conspicuous as to make me the jest of my companions.

I was especially fond of animals, and was indulged by my parents with a great variety of pets. With these I spent most of my time, and never was so happy as when feeding and caressing them. This peculiarity of character grew with my growth, and, in my manhood, I derived from it one of my principal sources of pleasure. To those who have cherished an affection for a faithful and sagacious dog, I need hardly be at the trouble of explaining the nature or the intensity of the gratification thus derivable. There is something in the unselfish and self-sacrificing love of a brute, which goes directly to the heart of him who has had frequent occasion to test the paltry friendship and gossamer fidelity of mere *Man*.

I married early, and was happy to find in my wife a disposition not uncongenial with my own. Observing my partiality for domestic pets, she lost no opportunity of procuring those of the most agreeable kind. We had birds, gold-fish, a fine dog, rabbits, a small monkey, and a *cat*.

This latter was a remarkably large and beautiful animal, entirely black, and sagacious to an astonishing degree. In speaking of his intelligence, my wife, who at heart was not a little tinctured with superstition, made frequent allusion to the ancient popular notion, which regarded all black cats as witches in disguise. Not that she was ever *serious* upon this point—and I mention the matter at all for no better reason than that it happens, just now, to be remembered.

Pluto—this was the cat's name—was my favorite pet and playmate. I alone fed him, and he attended me wherever I went about the house. It was even with difficulty that I could prevent him from following me through the streets.

Our friendship lasted, in this manner, for several years, during which my general temperament and character—through the instrumentality of the Fiend Intemperance—had (I blush to confess it) experienced a radical alteration for the worse. I grew, day by day, more moody, more irritable, more regardless of the feelings of others. I suffered myself to use intemperate language to my wife. At length, I even offered her personal violence. My pets, of course, were made to feel the change in my disposition. I not only neglected, but ill-used them. For Pluto, however, I still retained sufficient regard to restrain me from maltreating him, as I made no scruple of maltreating the rabbits, the monkey, or even the dog, when, by accident, or through affection, they came in my way. But my disease grew upon me—for what disease is like Alcohol!—and at length even Pluto, who was now becoming old, and consequently somewhat peevish— even Pluto began to experience the effects of my ill temper.

One night, returning home, much intoxicated, from one of my haunts about town, I fancied that the cat avoided my presence. I seized him; when, in his fright at my violence, he inflicted a slight wound upon my hand with his teeth. The fury of a demon instantly possessed me. I knew myself no longer. My original soul seemed, at once, to take its flight from my body; and a more than fiendish malevolence, gin-nurtured, thrilled every fibre of my frame. I took from my waistcoat-pocket a penknife, opened it, grasped the poor beast by the throat, and deliberately cut one of its eyes from the socket! I blush, I burn, I shudder, while I pen the damnable atrocity.

When reason returned with the morning—when I had slept off the fumes of the night's debauch—I experienced a sentiment half of horror, half of remorse, for the crime of which I had been guilty; but it was, at best, a feeble and equivocal feeling, and the soul remained untouched. I again plunged into excess, and soon drowned in wine all memory of the deed.

In the meantime the cat slowly recovered. The socket of the lost eye presented, it is true, a frightful appearance, but he no longer appeared to suffer any pain. He went about the house as usual, but, as might be expected, fled in extreme terror at my approach. I had so much of my old heart left, as to be at first grieved by this evident dislike on the part of a creature which had once so loved me. But this feeling soon gave place to irritation. And then came, as if to my final and irrevocable overthrow, the spirit of Perverseness. Of this spirit philosophy takes no account. Yet I am not more sure that my soul lives, than I am that perverseness is one of the primitive impulses of the human heart—one of the indivisible primary faculties, or sentiments, which give direction to the character of Man. Who has not, a hundred times, found himself committing a vile or stupid action, for no other reason than because he knows he should *not?* Have we not a perpetual inclination, in the teeth of our best judgment, to violate that which is *Law,* merely because we understand it to be such? This spirit of perverseness, I say, came to my final overthrow. It was this unfathomable longing of the soul *to vex itself*—to offer violence to its own nature—to do wrong for the wrong's sake only—that urged me to continue and finally to consummate the injury I had inflicted upon the unoffending brute. One morning, in cold blood, I slipped a noose about its neck and hung it to the limb of a tree;—hung it with the tears streaming from my eyes, and with the bitterest remorse at my heart;—hung it *because* I knew that it had loved me, and *because* I felt it had given me no reason of offence;—hung it *because* I knew that in so doing I was committing a sin—a deadly sin that would so jeopardize my immortal soul as to place it—if such a thing were possible—even beyond the reach of the infinite mercy of the Most Merciful and Most Terrible God.

On the night of the day on which this most cruel deed was done, I was aroused from sleep by the cry of fire. The curtains of my bed were in flames. The whole house was blazing. It was with great difficulty that my wife, a servant, and myself, made our escape from the conflagration. The destruction was complete. My entire worldly wealth was swallowed up, and I resigned myself thenceforward to despair.

I am above the weakness of seeking to establish a sequence of cause and effect, between the disaster and the atrocity. But I am detailing a chain of facts—and wish not to leave even a possible link imperfect. On the day succeeding the fire, I visited the ruins. The walls, with one exception, had fallen in. This exception was found in a compartment wall, not very thick, which stood about the middle of the house, and against which had rested the head of my bed. The plastering had here, in great measure, resisted the action of the fire—a fact which I attributed to its having been recently spread. About this wall a dense crowd were collected, and many persons seemed to be examining a particular portion of it with very minute and eager attention. The words "strange!" "singular!" and other similar expressions, excited my curiosity. I approached and saw, as if graven in *bas-relief* upon the white surface, the figure of a gigantic *cat.* The impression was given with an accuracy truly marvelous. There was a rope about the animal's neck.

When I first beheld this apparition—for I could scarcely regard it as less—my wonder and my terror were extreme. But at length reflection came to my aid. The cat, I remembered, had been hung in a garden adjacent to the house. Upon the alarm of fire, this garden had been immediately filled by the crowd—by some one of whom the animal must have been cut from the tree and thrown, through an open window, into my chamber. This had probably been done with the view of arousing me from sleep. The falling of other walls had compressed the victim of my cruelty into the substance of the freshly-spread plaster, the lime of which, with the flames, and the *ammonia* from the carcass, had then accomplished the portraiture as I saw it.

Although I thus readily accounted to my reason, if not altogether to my conscience, for the startling fact just detailed, it did not the less fail to make a deep impression upon my fancy. For months I could not rid myself of the phantasm of the cat; and, during this period, there came back into my spirit a half-sentiment that seemed, but was not, remorse. I went so far as to regret the loss of the animal, and to look about me, among the vile haunts which I now habitually frequented, for another pet of the same species, and of somewhat similar appearance, with which to supply its place.

One night as I sat, half stupefied, in a den of more than infamy, my attention was suddenly drawn to some black object, reposing upon the head of one of the immense hogsheads of gin, or of rum, which constituted the chief furniture of the apartment. I had been looking steadily at the top of this hogshead for some minutes, and what now caused me surprise was the fact that I had not sooner perceived the object thereupon. I approached it, and touched it with my hand. It was a black cat—a very large one— fully as large as Pluto, and closely resembling him in every respect but one. Pluto had not a white hair upon any portion of his body; but this cat had a large, although in- definite splotch of white, covering nearly the whole region of the breast.

Upon my touching him, he immediately arose, purred loudly, rubbed against my hand, and appeared delighted with my notice. This, then, was the very creature of which I was in search. I at once offered to purchase it of the landlord; but this person made no claim to it—knew nothing of it—had never seen it before.

I continued my caresses, and when I prepared to go home, the animal evinced a dis- position to accompany me. I permitted it to do so; occasionally stooping and patting it as I proceeded. When it reached the house it domesticated itself at once, and became immediately a great favorite with my wife.

For my own part, I soon found a dislike to it arising within me. This was just the re- verse of what I had anticipated; but—I know not how or why it was—its evident fond- ness for myself rather disgusted and annoyed me. By slow degrees these feelings of dis- gust and annoyance rose into the bitterness of hatred. I avoided the creature; a certain sense of shame, and the remembrance of my former deed of cruelty, preventing me from physically abusing it. I did not, for some weeks, strike, or otherwise violently ill use it; but gradually—very gradually—I came to look upon it with unutterable loathing, and to flee silently from its odious presence, as from the breath of a pestilence.

What added, no doubt, to my hatred of the beast, was the discovery on the morn- ing after I brought it home, that like Pluto, it also had been deprived of one of its eyes. This circumstance, however, only endeared it to my wife, who, as I have already said, possessed, in a high degree, that humanity of feeling which had once been my distin- guishing trait, and the source of many of my simplest and purest pleasures.

With my aversion to this cat, however, its partiality for myself seemed to increase. It followed my footsteps with a pertinacity which it would be difficult to make the reader comprehend. Whenever I sat, it would crouch beneath my chair, or spring upon my knees, covering me with its loathsome caresses. If I arose to walk it would get be- tween my feet and thus nearly throw me down, or, fastening its long and sharp claws in my dress, clamber, in this manner, to my breast. At such times, although I longed to destroy it with a blow, I was yet withheld from so doing, partly by a memory of my former crime, but chiefly—let me confess it at once—by absolute dread of the beast.

This dread was not exactly a dread of physical evil—and yet I should be at a loss how otherwise to define it. I am almost ashamed to own—yes, even in this felon's cell, I am almost ashamed to own—that the terror and horror with which the animal inspired me, had been heightened by one of the merest chimeras it would be possible to conceive. My wife had called my attention, more than once, to the character of the mark of white hair, of which I have spoken, and which constituted the sole visible difference between the strange beast and the one I had destroyed. The reader will remember that this mark, although large, had been originally very indefinite; but, by slow degrees—degrees nearly imperceptible, and which for a long time my reason struggled to reject as fanciful—it had, at length, assumed a rigorous distinctness of outline. It was now the representation of an object that I shudder to name—and for this, above all, I loathed, and dreaded, and would have rid myself of the monster *had I dared*—it was now, I say, the image of a hideous—of a ghastly thing—of the Gallows!—oh, mournful and terrible engine of Horror and of Crime—of Agony and of Death!

And now was I indeed wretched beyond the wretchedness of mere Humanity. And *a brute beast*—whose fellow I had contemptuously destroyed—*a brute beast* to work out for *me*—for me, a man fashioned in the image of the High God—so much of insufferable woe! Alas! neither by day nor by night knew I the blessing of rest any more! During the former the creature left me no moment alone, and in the latter I started hourly from dreams of unutterable fear to find the hot breath of *the thing* upon my face, and its vast weight—an incarnate nightmare that I had not power to shake off—incumbent eternally upon my *heart!*

Beneath the pressure of torments such as these the feeble remnant of the good within me succumbed. Evil thoughts became my sole intimates—the darkest and most evil of thoughts. The moodiness of my usual temper increased to hatred of all things and of all mankind; while from the sudden, frequent, and ungovernable outbursts of a fury to which I now blindly abandoned myself, my uncomplaining wife, alas, was the most usual and the most patient of sufferers.

One day she accompanied me, upon some household errand, into the cellar of the old building which our poverty compelled us to inhabit. The cat followed me down the steep stairs, and, nearly throwing me headlong, exasperated me to madness. Uplifting an axe, and forgetting in my wrath the childish dread which had hitherto stayed my hand, I aimed a blow at the animal, which, of course, would have proved instantly fatal had it descended as I wished. But this blow was arrested by the hand of my wife. Goaded by the interference into a rage more than demoniacal, I withdrew my arm from her grasp and buried the axe in her brain. She fell dead upon the spot without a groan.

This hideous murder accomplished, I set myself forthwith, and with entire deliberation, to the task of concealing the body. I knew that I could not remove it from the house, either by day or by night, without the risk of being observed by the neighbors. Many projects entered my mind. At one period I thought of cutting the corpse into minute fragments, and destroying them by fire. At another, I resolved to dig a grave for it in the floor of the cellar. Again, I deliberated about casting it in the well in the yard—about packing it in a box, as if merchandise, with the usual arrangements, and so getting a porter to take it from the house. Finally I hit upon what I considered a far better expedient than either of these. I determined to wall it up in the cellar, as the monks of the Middle Ages are recorded to have walled up their victims.

For a purpose such as this the cellar was well adapted. Its walls were loosely constructed, and had lately been plastered throughout with a rough plaster, which the dampness of the atmosphere had prevented from hardening. Moreover, in one of the walls was a projection, caused by a false chimney, or fireplace, that had been filled up and made to resemble the rest of the cellar. I made no doubt that I could readily displace the bricks at this point, insert the corpse, and wall the whole up as before, so that no eye could detect anything suspicious.

And in this calculation I was not deceived. By means of a crowbar I easily dislodged the bricks, and, having carefully deposited the body against the inner wall, I propped it in that position, while with little trouble I relaid the whole structure as it originally stood. Having procured mortar, sand, and hair, with every possible precaution, I prepared a plaster which could not be distinguished from the old, and with this, I very carefully went over the new brick-work. When I had finished, I felt satisfied that all was right. The wall did not present the slightest appearance of having been disturbed. The rubbish on the floor was picked up with the minutest care. I looked around triumphantly, and said to myself: "Here at least, then, my labor has not been in vain."

My next step was to look for the beast which had been the cause of so much wretchedness; for I had, at length, firmly resolved to put it to death. Had I been able to meet with it at the moment, there could have been no doubt of its fate; but it appeared that the crafty animal had been alarmed at the violence of my previous anger, and forbore to present itself in my present mood. It is impossible to describe or to imagine the deep, blissful sense of relief which the absence of the detested creature occasioned in my bosom. It did not make its appearance during the night; and thus for one night, at least, since its introduction into the house, I soundly and tranquilly slept; aye, slept even with the burden of murder upon my soul.

The second and the third day passed, and still my tormentor came not. Once again I breathed as a freeman. The monster, in terror, had fled the premises for ever! I should behold it no more! My happiness was supreme! The guilt of my dark deed disturbed me but little. Some few inquiries had been made, but these had been readily answered. Even a search had been instituted—but of course nothing was to be discovered. I looked upon my future felicity as secured.

Upon the fourth day of the assassination, a party of the police came, very unexpectedly, into the house, and proceeded again to make a rigorous investigation of the premises. Secure, however, in the inscrutability of my place of concealment, I felt no embarrassment whatever. The officers bade me accompany them in their search. They left no nook or corner unexplored. At length, for the third or fourth time, they descended into the cellar. I quivered not in a muscle. My heart beat calmly as that of one who slumbers in innocence. I walked the cellar from end to end. I folded my arms upon my bosom, and roamed easily to and fro. The police were thoroughly satisfied and prepared to depart. The glee at my heart was too strong to be restrained. I burned to say if but one word, by way of triumph, and to render doubly sure their assurance of my guiltlessness.

"Gentlemen," I said at last, as the party ascended the steps, "I delight to have allayed your suspicions. I wish you all health and a little more courtesy. By the bye, gentlemen, this—this is a very well-constructed house," (in the rabid desire to say something easily, I scarcely knew what I uttered at all),—"I may say an excellently well-constructed house. These walls—are you going, gentlemen?—these walls are solidly put together"; and here, through the mere frenzy of bravado, I rapped heavily with a cane which I held in my hand, upon that very portion of the brick-work behind which stood the corpse of the wife of my bosom.

But may God shield and deliver me from the fangs of the Arch-Fiend! No sooner had the reverberation of my blows sunk into silence, than I was answered by a voice from within the tomb!—by a cry, at first muffled and broken, like the sobbing of a child, and then quickly swelling into one long, loud, and continuous scream, utterly anomalous and inhuman—a howl—a wailing shriek, half of horror and half of triumph, such as might have arisen only out of hell, conjointly from the throats of the damned in their agony and of the demons that exult in the damnation.

Of my own thoughts it is folly to speak. Swooning, I staggered to the opposite wall. For one instant the party on the stairs remained motionless, through extremity of terror and awe. In the next a dozen stout arms were toiling at the wall. It fell bodily. The corpse, already greatly decayed and clotted with gore, stood erect before the eyes of the spectators. Upon its head, with red extended mouth and solitary eye of fire, sat the hideous beast whose craft had seduced me into murder, and whose informing voice had consigned me to the hangman. I had walled the monster up within the tomb.

(1845)

QUESTIONS

1. Identify the story's central and most important irony. Explain why it is important and how it affects our interpretation of the story and our evaluation of the narrator.
2. Consider whether the story may include other examples of irony besides that of its concluding action. Are there ironic aspects that include verbal, situational, or dramatic ironies? If so, identify a few of these and explain their significance.
3. Can the black cat be considered a symbol? Why or why not?

One of the most effective ways to improve your understanding of fiction is to read with a clear set of goals. Focus, for example, on the three aspects of the reading process explained in Chapter 1. Consider the various elements of fiction described in this chapter. And, where the opportunity arises, write about the works of fiction you read either formally or informally—to suit your own needs as a reader or to meet the requirements of a class assignment.

CHAPTER FOUR

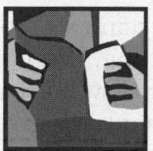

Approaching a Story: Guides for Reading and Writing

The following guidelines for reading stories derive from our discussions of the process of reading fiction, the types of fiction, and the elements of fiction. They highlight essential approaches, offering advice about how to read stories, and suggest both a method and a context for reading fiction. Use the guidelines to direct your reading of Luigi Pirandello's "War" and the stories in Chapter 8.

Guidelines for Reading

1. Read through the story for enjoyment. Savor its suspense, its humor, its language—whatever engages you, whatever distinguishes the work. If you have time, jot down a few responses to what you've read, perhaps a couple of questions. Think about your experience of the story, of how it affected you as you read it.
2. Establish the fictional type of the story. Consider how the story's typical features guide your reading and direct your understanding.
3. Read the story a second time. During this reading concentrate on its plot and characters. Evaluate the characters, and examine how the writer cre-

109

ates whatever impression of them you have. Consider the techniques of characterization that he or she employs. During this reading also, center on the subject and tentative theme of the work, thinking about its ideas and values.

4. Consider the story from the standpoint of the elements of fiction: plot and character, structure and setting, language and style, theme, symbolism, irony, and point of view. Be aware that certain elements may be more noticeable and more important in a given story. Also remember that the story is an integral work—that any analysis you make of its elements should be done with a view of the whole in mind.

5. Throughout your readings, try to be open to the work, however strange, different, or difficult it may at first seem. Relate it to your knowledge of literature and language and to your experience of life.

6. Consider the story's values as reflected in the dialogue of its major characters. Measure their values against your own.

LUIGI PIRANDELLO

[1867–1936]

War

The passengers who had left Rome by the night express had to stop until dawn at the small station of Fabriano in order to continue their journey by the small old-fashioned local joining the main line with Sulmona.

At dawn, in a stuffy and smoky second-class carriage in which five people had already spent the night, a bulky woman in deep mourning was hoisted in—almost like a shapeless bundle. Behind her, puffing and moaning, followed her husband—a tiny man, thin and weakly, his face death-white, his eyes small and bright and looking shy and uneasy.

Having at last taken a seat he politely thanked the passengers who had helped his wife and who had made room for her; then he turned round to the woman trying to pull down the collar of her coat, and politely inquired:

"Are you all right, dear?"

The wife, instead of answering, pulled up her collar again to her eyes, so as to hide her face.

"Nasty world," muttered the husband with a sad smile.

And he felt it his duty to explain to his traveling companions that the poor woman was to be pitied, for the war was taking away from her her only son, a boy of twenty to whom both had devoted their entire life, even breaking up their home at Sulmona to follow him to Rome, where he had to go as a student, then allowing him to volunteer for war with an assurance, however, that at least for six months he would not be sent to the front and now, all of a sudden, receiving a wire saying that he was due to leave in three days' time and asking them to go and see him off.

The woman under the big coat was twisting and wriggling, at times growling like a wild animal, feeling certain that all those explanations would not have aroused even a shadow of sympathy from those people who—most likely—were in the same plight as herself. One of them, who had been listening with particular attention, said: "You should thank God that your son is only leaving now for the front. Mine has been sent there the first day of the war. He has already come back twice wounded and been sent back again to the front."

"What about me? I have two sons and three nephews at the front," said another passenger.

"Maybe, but in our case it is our *only* son," ventured the husband.

"What difference can it make? You may spoil your only son with excessive attentions, but you cannot love him more than you would all your other children if you had any. Paternal love is not like bread that can be broken into pieces and split amongst the children in equal shares. A father gives *all* his love to each one of his children without discrimination, whether it be one or ten, and if I am suffering now for my two sons, I am not suffering half for each of them but double . . . ."

"True . . . true . . . ," sighed the embarrassed husband, "but suppose (of course we all hope it will never be your case) a father has two sons at the front and he loses one of them, there is still one left to console him . . . while . . . ."

"Yes," answered the other, getting cross, "a son left to console him but also a son left for whom he must survive, while in the case of the father of an only son if the son dies the father can die too and put an end to his distress. Which of the two positions is the worse? Don't you see how my case would be worse than yours?"

"Nonsense," interrupted another traveler, a fat, red-faced man with bloodshot eyes of the palest gray.

He was panting. From his bulging eyes seemed to spurt inner violence of an uncontrolled vitality which his weakened body could hardly contain.

"Nonsense," he repeated, trying to cover his mouth with his hand so as to hide the two missing front teeth. "Nonsense. Do we give life to our children for our own benefit?"

The other travelers stared at him in distress. The one who had his son at the front since the first day of the war sighed: "You are right. Our children do not belong to us, they belong to the Country. . . ."

"Bosh," retorted the fat traveler. "Do we think of the Country when we give life to our children? Our sons are born because . . . well, because they must be born and when they come to life they take our own life with them. This is the truth. We belong to them but they can never belong to us. And when they reach twenty they are exactly what we were at their age. We too had a father and mother, but there were so many other things as well . . . girls, cigarettes, illusions, new ties . . . and the Country, of course, whose call we would have answered—when we were twenty—even if father and mother had said no. Now at our age, the love of our Country is still great, of course, but stronger than it is the love for our children. Is there any one of us here who wouldn't gladly take his son's place at the front if he could?"

There was a silence all round, everybody nodding as to approve.

"Why then," continued the fat man, "shouldn't we consider the feelings of our chil-

dren when they are twenty? Isn't it natural that at their age they should consider the
love for their Country (I am speaking of decent boys, of course) even greater than the
love for us? Isn't it natural that it should be so, as after all they must look upon us as
upon old boys who cannot move any more and must stay at home? If Country exists,
if Country is a natural necessity, like bread, of which each of us must eat in order not
to die of hunger, somebody must go to defend it. And our sons go, when they are
twenty, and they don't want tears, because if they die, they die inflamed and happy (I
am speaking, of course, of decent boys). Now, if one dies young and happy, without
having the ugly sides of life, the boredom of it, the pettiness, the bitterness of disillusion . . . what more can we ask for him? Everyone should stop crying; everyone should
laugh as I do . . . or at least thank God—as I do—because my son, before dying sent
me a message saying that he was dying satisfied at having ended his life in the best way
he could have wished. That is why, as you see, I do not even wear mourning. . . ."

He shook his light fawn coat as to show it; his livid lip over his missing teeth was
trembling, his eyes were watery and motionless, and soon after he ended with a shrill
laugh which might well have been a sob.

"Quite so . . . quite so . . ." agreed the others.

The woman who, bundled in a corner under her coat, had been sitting and listening had—for the last three months—tried to find in the words of her husband and her
friends something to console her in her deep sorrow, something that might show her
how a mother should resign herself to send her son not even to death but to a probably dangerous life. Yet not a word had she found amongst the many which had been
said . . . and her grief had been greater in seeing that nobody—as she thought—could
share her feelings.

But now the words of the traveler amazed and almost stunned her. She suddenly realized that it wasn't the others who were wrong and could not understand her but herself who could not rise up to the same height of those fathers and mothers willing to
resign themselves, without crying, not only to the departure of their sons but even to
their death.

She lifted her head, she bent over from her corner trying to listen with great attention to the details which the fat man was giving to his companions about the way his
son had fallen as a hero, for his King and his Country, happy and without regrets. It
seemed to her that she had stumbled into a world she had never dreamt of, a world so
far unknown to her and she was so pleased to hear everyone joining in congratulating
that brave father who could so stoically speak of his child's death.

Then suddenly, just as if she had heard nothing of what had been said and almost as
if waking up from a dream, she turned to the old man, asking him:

"Then . . . is your son really dead?"

Everybody stared at her. The old man, too, turned to look at her, fixing his great,
bulging, horribly watery light gray eyes, deep in her face. For some little time he tried
to answer, but words failed him. He looked at her, almost as if only then—at that silly,
incongruous question—he had suddenly realized at last that his son was really dead—
gone for ever—for ever. His face contracted, became horribly distorted, then he
snatched in haste a handkerchief from his pocket and, to the amazement of everyone,
broke into harrowing, heart-rending, uncontrollable sobs.

(1939)

Comment   Pirandello's "War" seems to be less about the action or experience of war than about its consequences. It is indeed about war, but from the perspective of the soldiers' parents, whose involvement is no less intense for not being directly participatory. Or we can see the story as not one about war at all, but rather about parents' love for their children. Or, to shift our attention a bit, we might think of "War" as a story about grief and the ways people come to terms with it.

The characters are not highly individualized, though they are described with brief particularity. They exist as types rather than as fully developed characters. They seem to represent alternative ways of responding to grief, and also to typify opposing views of parents' relationship to their children. As we observe their dialogue and behavior we come to understand them. We need especially to determine whether any one of them speaks for the author or whether one view prevails.

"War" is structured as a conversation or debate that occurs between the husband of the grief-stricken woman and the man whose two sons are at the front. A third passenger who has two sons and three nephews fighting also enters this discussion, which focuses on the question of whether a parent, particularly a father, whose only son is at the front, suffers more or less than a father who has two or more sons there. It is an argument about the quantification of love. But it is one that Pirandello does not resolve—at least not directly. Instead he uses this dialogue to prepare for the entrance of the red-faced man with bloodshot eyes, who interrupts the debate by saying: "Nonsense, do we give life to our children for our own benefit?" This man's speech is much longer than the remarks of the other characters. Following his long speech, Pirandello does not devote the next part of the story to more dialogue, but describes the state of mind of the woman who has been previously inconsolable at the thought of her son's danger. These shifts—from dialogue to description, from one character to another, from external action to internal feeling, slow the story down, inviting us to pause and reflect, as they highlight places where something important is being said.

Pirandello has set us up for the surprise that follows swiftly upon the woman's question (itself a surprise since she seemed to be burying herself in her grief when she blurts it out): "Then . . . is your son really dead?" Of interest here is that Pirandello not only shows us the effect of the woman's words—they stun everyone on the train including the red-faced man—but he also explains why the man breaks into "harrowing, heart-rending, uncontrollable sobs." It is a powerful ending. And understandable, given Pirandello's indication that the man had not really allowed the fact of his son's death to reach him fully until the woman asks her question.

"War," thus, seems to show how camouflaging or repressing grief is unnatural, and how, at the moment a person fully realizes the tragedy and confronts the loss, he or she breaks down. Yet this explanation omits an important element of the story: the woman's change of attitude, the apparent shift in her feelings. Her change is as great as the man's. Perhaps this suggests that her view of the matter, which was previously his view, is as valid as his grief, which parallels her previous grief. Perhaps Pirandello indicates that the debate is not won by either side, that both views reflect deep feeling, and that both experiences are valid. And perhaps he suggests further that an individual who experiences tragedy and loss can expect to oscillate between moments when one attitude gains ascendancy only to give way to an opposite view and a counter experience. Remember also that in "War" we are not given a history of the reactions of the characters, but a close-up, a snapshot of a moment. There is nothing to deny the possibility that the man or the woman may revert to their earlier positions and states of mind.

Thus, we might view the ending of the story as balancing the views of the man and the grief-stricken woman. But another way of taking the story's ending is to notice that the man's experience occurs last. His fall into grief is given the last word. In addition, a good deal of the story can be seen as leading up to the climactic moment when he comprehends the reality and depth of his loss. Structurally, then, the story seems to deny the idea that the two perspectives are equal in weight. Depending on how heavily we lean on the final details of the story, we may see "War" as an illustration of the power of grief and the inevitability of its expression. Then we might say that the man's grief at his loss prevails and his previous attempt to find something positive in his son's death is a falsification of experience.

We find additional evidence for this interpretation in the details Pirandello provides about the man. After the man's long opening speech, which ends: "That is why, as you see, I do not even wear mourning," this description follows: "his livid lip over his missing teeth was trembling, his eyes were watery and motionless, and soon after he ended with a shrill laugh which might have been a sob." Pirandello places this paragraph between the man's long speech and the agreeing response of his listeners (their "Quite so . . . quite so"). But the *shrill* laugh is unnatural; it is as much a "sob" as a laugh. Moreover, there is a good deal of tension and urgency in his insistence that what had been said before was "nonsense." In fact, he says, "Nonsense" three times, not once, perhaps in an attempt to convince himself of what he is saying.

Finally, a word about point of view. The story is told in the third person by a narrator who does not participate in the action. Pirandello limits the omniscience of the narrator to the feelings of the grief-stricken woman. We enter her consciousness and are shown what she thinks and feels. Focusing on her, the story follows her perception of what is said and done. But when she says, "then . . . is your son really dead?" the narrative focus shifts. We are not told the effect of the man's sobs on the woman as we had previously been shown how his earlier speech had affected her. Instead, we are given a more objective, detached, and dramatic view. This shift in point of view at a climactic moment reinforces the idea that the story is more about the man than the woman, that only in confronting his grief does he realize the extent of his loss. This seems to be the story's central concern.

The following suggestions for writing emerge from the discussions of reading and interpreting fiction found in Chapters 1 and 3.

Suggestions for Writing

The Experience of Fiction

1. Write a paper in which you recount your experience of reading a particular story or series of stories by the same author. You may want to compare your initial experience with your experience when you reread the story or stories.
2. Compare the experience of reading a story with that of watching a film based on it.
3. Relate the action or situation of a story to your own experience. Explain how the story is relevant to your situation. Comment on how reading and thinking about it may have helped you view your own circumstances more clearly.

The Interpretation of Fiction

4. Describe a character who has an important decision to make. Identify the character's situation, explain the reasons for his or her decision, and speculate about the possible consequences.
5. Explicate the opening sentences or paragraph of any story. Explain the significance of the opening section in establishing the story's tone, announcing its theme, or otherwise preparing the reader for what follows.
6. Explicate the closing sentences or paragraph of any story. Explain the significance of the conclusion, commenting on its effectiveness as an ending.
7. Select two or three brief passages from a story and explain their significance. Consider how the passages may be related.
8. Analyze the plot of a story. Comment on its organization or structure. How is the plot designed to affect readers' responses? Notice whether the incidents are presented in chronological order or whether chronology is violated and, if so, for what purpose.
9. Analyze the setting of a story. Consider both the time and place of its action. Also consider small-scale aspects of setting such as whether the action takes place indoors or out. If indoors, which room does the action occur in—and why? Notice any significant changes of setting.
10. Analyze a character from a story. Evaluate the character's behavior, offering reasons and evidence for your views. Consider what the character does, says, does not say or do—and why. Identify any significant changes the character undergoes. What do other characters say about him or her, and how do they respond in action?

11. Discuss the relationship of two characters. Consider how the characters affect each other, and explain the nature and significance of their relationship.
12. Analyze the symbolism of a story. Identify its major symbols and explain their significance. Some possibilities: Faulkner's "A Rose for Emily"; Hawthorne's forest in "Young Goodman Brown"; Gilman's "Wallpaper"; Kafka's beetle in "The Metamorphosis"; Olsen's iron in "I Stand Here Ironing"; Walker's "Everyday Use"; Poe's "Black Cat."
13. Analyze the ironic dimensions of a story. Identify examples of irony, and explain their importance in the story. Some possibilities: Poe's "Black Cat"; Joyce's "Araby" and "The Boarding House"; Ellison's "Battle Royal"; Singer's "Gimpel the Fool"; O'Connor's "Guests of the Nation."
14. Analyze the point of view of a story. How would the story be different if it were narrated from a different point of view? Consider whether the narrator is believable or is somehow limited and/or perhaps unworthy of our trust.
15. Explain the theme of any story. Identify its overriding idea. Establish the grounds for your interpretation, and explain why the idea is important.
16. Analyze the use of figurative language in any story. Identify the major types of figurative language used and explain their function, effect, and significance. What would be gained or lost without them? Some possibilities: Hemingway's "Macomber"; Faulkner's "A Rose for Emily"; O'Connor's "Good Country People"; Walker's "Everyday Use"; Atwood's "Rape Fantasies."

The Evaluation of Fiction

17. Discuss the values exemplified in any story. Identify those values, relate them to your own, and comment on their significance.
18. Do a comparative evaluation of the distinctive merits of any two stories. Explain what they have in common, how they differ, and why one is more interesting, impressive, or effective than the other.
19. Evaluate a story from the standpoint of its merit or literary excellence—or lack thereof. Explain why you consider it to be a successful or unsuccessful story.

To Research or Imagine

20. Develop an alternative ending for a story, changing the outcome in whatever way you like. Be prepared to defend your revised ending. Consider why the author chose to end the story as he or she did.
21. Read some letters or essays by a fiction writer you know and enjoy. Consider how they aid your understanding or increase your pleasure in reading the writer's stories.
22. Read a full-scale biography of a fiction writer. Write a paper explaining how the writer's life is or is not reflected in the work.

23. Read a novel by a writer whose short fiction you enjoy. Write a paper explaining how the novel is related to the shorter fiction.
24. Consider a writer of fiction in his or her historical context. Read a few of the writer's stories as reflections of or denunciations of the social, moral, and cultural dispositions of his or her time.
25. Read a critical study of a fiction writer. Explain how reading the book enhanced your understanding or appreciation of the writer's fiction.

CHAPTER FIVE

Writing About Fiction

REASONS FOR WRITING ABOUT FICTION

Why write about fiction? One reason is to find out what you think about a story or novel. Another is to induce yourself to read it more carefully. You may write about a work of fiction because it engages you, and you may wish to celebrate it or to argue with its implied ideas and values. A fourth reason is that you may simply be required to do so as a course assignment.

Whatever your reasons for writing about fiction, a number of things happen when you do. First, in writing about a novel or story you tend to read it more attentively, noticing things you might overlook in a more casual reading. Second, since writing stimulates thinking, when you write about fiction you find yourself thinking more about what a particular work means and why you respond to it as you do. And third, you begin to acquire power over the works you write about, making them more meaningful to you.

INFORMAL WAYS OF WRITING ABOUT FICTION

When you write about a novel or short story, you may write for yourself or you may write for others. Writing for yourself, writing to discover what you think, often takes casual forms such as annotation and freewriting. These less formal kinds of writing are useful for helping you focus on your reading of fiction. They are helpful in studying for tests about fiction. They can serve also as preliminary forms of writing when you write more formal essays and papers about fiction.

Annotation

When you annotate a text, you make notes about it, usually in the margins or at the top and bottom of pages—or both. Annotations can also be made within the text, as underlined words, circled phrases, and bracketed sentences or paragraphs. Annotations may also assume the form of arrows, question marks, and various other marks.

Annotating a literary work offers a convenient and relatively painless way to begin writing about it. Annotating can get you started zeroing in on what you think interesting or important. You can also annotate to flag details that puzzle or disconcert you.

Your markings serve to focus your attention and clarify your understanding of a story or novel. Your annotations can save you time in rereading or studying a work. And they can also be used when you write a more formal paper.

Annotations for the following story illustrate the process.

KATHERINE ANNE PORTER

[1890–1980]

Magic

And, Madame Blanchard, believe that I am happy to be here with you and your family because it is so serene, everything, and before this I worked for a long time in a fancy house— maybe you don't know what is a fancy house? Naturally . . . everyone must have heard sometime or other. Well, Madame, I work always where there is work to be had, and so in this place I worked very hard all hours, and saw too many things, things you wouldn't believe, and I wouldn't think of telling you, only maybe it will rest you while I brush your hair. You'll excuse me too but I could not help hearing you say to the laundress maybe someone had bewitched your linens, they fall away so fast in the wash. Well, there was a girl there in that house, a poor thing, thin, but well-liked by all the men who called, and you understand she could not get along with the woman who ran the house. They quarreled, the madam cheated her on her checks: you know, the girl got a check, a brass one, every time, and at the week's end she gave those back to the madam, yes, that

line 1: We enter into a monologue that has already begun.

line 8: Does she really not want to tell Madame B. what kind of work it is?

line 11: Bewitched linens? Magic?

was the way, and got her percentage, a very small little of her earnings: it is a business, you see, like any other—and the madam used to pretend the girl had given back only so many checks, you see, and really she had given many more, but after they were out of her hands, what could she do? So she would say, I will get out of this place, and curse and cry. Then the madam would hit her over the head. She always hit people over the head with bottles, it was the way she fought. My good heavens, Madame Blanchard, what confusion there would be sometimes with a girl running raving downstairs, and the madam pulling her back by the hair and smashing a bottle on her forehead.

It was nearly always about the money, the girls got in debt so, and if they wished to go they could not without paying every sou marqué. The madam had full understanding with the police; the girls must come back with them or go to the jails. Well, they always came back with the policemen or with another kind of man friend of the madam: she could make men work for her too, but she paid them very well for all, let me tell you: and so the girls stayed on unless they were sick; if so, if they got too sick, she sent them away again.

Madame Blanchard said, 'You are pulling a little here,' and eased a strand of hair: 'and then what?'

Pardon—but this girl, there was a true hatred between her and the madam. She would say many times, I make more money than anybody else in the house, and every week were scenes. So at last she said one morning, Now I will leave this place, and she took out forty dollars from under her pillow and said, Here's your money! The madam began to shout, Where did you get all that, you—? and accused her of robbing the men who came to visit her. The girl said, Keep your hands off or I'll brain you: and at that the madam took hold of her shoulders, and began to lift her knee and kick this girl most terribly in the stomach, and even in her most secret place, Madame Blanchard, and then she beat her in the face with a bottle, and the girl fell back again into her room where I was making clean. I helped her to the bed, and she sat there holding her sides with her head hanging down, and when she got up again there was blood everywhere she had sat. So then the madam came in once more and screamed, Now you can get out, you are no good for me any more: I don't repeat all, you understand it is too much. But she took all the money she could find, and at the door she gave the girl a great push in the back with her knee, so that she fell again in the street, and then got up and went away with the dress barely on her.

After this the men who knew this girl kept saying, 'Where

is Ninette? And they kept asking this in the next days, so that the madam could not say any longer, I put her out because she is a thief. No, she began to see she was wrong to send this Ninette away, and then she said, She will be back in a few days, don't trouble yourself.

And now, Madame Blanchard, if you wish to hear, I come to the strange part, the thing recalled to me when you said your linens were bewitched. For the cook in that place was a woman, colored like myself, like myself with much French blood just the same, like myself living always among people who worked spells. But she had a very hard heart, she helped the madam in everything, she liked to watch all that happened, and she gave away tales on the girls. The madam trusted her above everything, and she said, Well, where can I find that slut? because she had gone altogether out of Basin Street before the madam began to ask the police to bring her again. Well, the cook said, I know a charm that works here in New Orleans, colored women do it to bring back their men: in seven days they come again very happy to stay and they cannot say why: even your enemy will come back to you believing you are his friend. It is a New Orleans charm for sure, for certain, they say it does not work even across the river. . . . And then they did it just as the cook said. They took the chamber pot of this girl from under her bed, and in it they mixed with water and milk all the relics of her they found there: the hair from her brush, and the face powder from the puff, and even little bits of her nails they found about the edges of the carpet where she sat by habit to cut her finger- and toe-nails; and they dipped the sheets with her blood into the water, and all the time the cook said something over it in a low voice; I could not hear all, but at last she said to the madam, Now spit in it: and the madam spat, the the cook said, When she comes back she will be dirt under your feet.

Madame Blanchard closed her perfume bottle with a thin click: 'Yes, and then?'

Then in seven nights the girl came back and she looked very sick, the same clothes and all, but happy to be there. One of the men said, Welcome home, Ninette! and when she started to speak to the madam, the madam said, Shut up and get upstairs and dress yourself. So Ninette, this girl, she said, I'll be down in just a minute. And after that she lived there quietly.

(1930)

[margin note: P 8: Magic again—this time the cook. Technique: Porter makes us curious.]

[margin note: Voodoo? Witchcraft? More magic?]

[margin note: It's the madam's psychological magic that brings her back. Why does it work?]

Freewriting

Freewriting is a kind of informal writing you do for yourself. In freewriting you explore a text to find out what you think about it and how you respond to it. When you freewrite you do not know ahead of time what your idea or your response to the work will be. Instead you write about the work to see where your thinking leads you.

Freewriting leads you to explore your memories and experience as well as aspects of the text itself. You sometimes wander from the details of the story or novel you are writing about. In the process you may discover thoughts and feelings you didn't know you had or were only dimly aware of. You can use freewriting to explore these responses. You can also use the technique to see where it leads you in thinking about the work itself.

Here is a group of responses written after students had read Kate Chopin's "The Story of an Hour" (pages 38–42). If you have not read the story, this will be a good time to do so. If you have read it, you can add your own freewriting response.

Before you read the interpolated comments printed between sections of the story, read just the story itself. Then write down four or five sentences giving your reactions to it. Compare your response with the student responses that follow. Then read the story again, this time paying attention to the interpolated comments. What is your reaction to your own first response? To the student responses?

COLLEGE FRESHMAN: My first reaction was that Brently Mallard must have been an abusing husband. Maybe verbal or maybe physical abuse. But I noticed that Mrs. Mallard said his hands were "kind and tender" and she said his face "never looked on her save with love." Then I began to think that maybe Louise Mallard was an ungrateful wife who didn't appreciate what she had. Still, she obviously felt that she had to submit to everything he wanted. She talks about his "powerful will." So she really did feel abused in some ways and maybe that's what's important. I was confused and want to read the story again.

COLLEGE SOPHOMORE: Did Louise Mallard die at the end because she was shocked or because she was so upset at losing her freedom? I don't think she died of joy, even though she did have some love for her husband, so I think the doctor was wrong. She may have died of heart trouble, but maybe it was not a physical illness of the heart. Maybe what was wrong was that Louise had never had a chance to know her own heart. So when she did begin to feel some freedom and then lost it, she was sick in her spirit (what some people would call her heart). I think her death was finding a kind of freedom that she couldn't have in life. So maybe the whole incident came out for the best for Louise.

COLLEGE FRESHMAN: I thought maybe Brently's friend Richards had something going with Louise. That was why he rushed right over to tell her about his death. And at the end he tries to protect her. But on the other hand, I couldn't figure out why Louise wouldn't have some thoughts about Richards while she was imagining her freedom. If they really were having an affair. So maybe they weren't. But why would Louise be so glad to be free if she didn't have a reason?

COLLEGE FRESHMAN: I liked all the metaphors and descriptions which really made you feel like you could understand how Louise's feelings changed. When she first heard the news she had a "storm of grief" but then she looks out the window and sees "patches of blue" so you get the idea that the storm is passing and that maybe Louise is not going to be so unhappy after all. When you read about her "two white slender hands" that are "powerless" they seem sort of like gentle swans, and you can imagine that Louise was sort of a household pet or a decoration for her husband. And that she did not have any way—or did not know any way—to oppose his "powerful will."

The focused freewriting on Kate Chopin's story and Robert Graves's poem (Chapter 14, page 619) is very much like journal entries. In fact, keeping an informal log or journal of your responses to the literary works you read is a useful and fairly easy way to prepare for class discussion of them.

FORMAL WAYS OF WRITING ABOUT FICTION

Among the more common formal ways of writing about fiction is analysis. In writing an analytical essay about a short story or a novel, your goal is to explain how one or more particular aspects or issues in the work contribute to its overall meaning. You might analyze the dialogue in Boyle's "Astronomer's Wife" or Pirandello's "War," for example, in explaining what the verbal exchanges between characters contribute to the story's meaning. You might analyze the ironic qualities of Chopin's "The Story of an Hour" or O'Connor's "Good Country People." Or you might analyze the characters in Carver's "Cathedral" or Lawrence's "The Blind Man" to explain how the relationships between the characters reveal each story's theme.

In addition to analyzing these and other fictional elements in a single story, you might also compare two stories, perhaps by focusing on their symbolism, style, tone, setting, or point of view. Or, instead of focusing on literary elements per se, you might write to see how a particular critical perspective (see Chapter 36) illumines a story. For example, you might consider the feminist implications of Updike's "A & P" or what a psychological approach to Hawthorne's "Young Goodman Brown" contributes to your understanding.

The following brief analysis focuses on the characters in Pirandello's "War." The writer considers how the dialogue and descriptions of the characters lead to a metaphorical interpretation of the story's title.

Student Papers on Fiction

Carol Holt

DEFINING WAR

Luigi Pirandello calls his short story about grieving and worried parents, "War." At first reading, the title seems a bit misleading because the setting is a railroad car rather than a battlefield, and the characters are people who have sent their sons off to the front but who are not directly involved themselves. Further reading, however, shows that each mother and father is going through a personal struggle within his or her mind. In addition, the characters fight among themselves about what view they should take of their sons' military service. In a sense, the railroad car becomes a battlefield as the characters engage in war both within themselves and with others.

The dialogue between the bulky woman's husband and the man who has two sons at the front seems like a war in several ways. They engage in conflict and each tries to outdo the other, bringing out more and more verbal weapons in an attempt to be the victor. The arguments are as empty and meaningless as are many real-life physical battles. One father argues that losing an only son is the worst fate. The other counters that the death of one son while the other lives prevents the grieving parent from the "remedy" of suicide. This war is certainly futile and cannot be resolved in a logical or satisfactory way. Each side is convinced of the truth of its own argument. Each looks only at its own point of view. Just as with real warring factions, there seems to be no way to bring the two sides together.

When the fat, red-faced man speaks, he seems to be making a statement with which all the passengers can agree. They all shake their heads as if to approve when he speaks of love of country and patriotism. Nevertheless, he, too is involved in a war. As he continues to speak and as the bulky woman starts to listen, he becomes more and more emotional. For example, his eyes are watery and he ends one of his speeches "with a shrill laugh which might well have been a sob." The bulky woman tries to resolve the conflict—the war—within herself, but as she states the one fact most frightening to her, the red-faced man reveals his own painful battle. When she says, "Then . . . is your son really dead?" the red-faced man bursts into tears. He has not resolved the fight that is going on between his sense of patriotism and his love for his fallen son.

Pirandello has extended the definition of war. Conflicts, struggles, and exchange of ammunition occur not just on the actual battlefields but also in the lives of those connected to members of fighting forces. As the title of Pirandello's story suggests, wars may be fought on metaphoric battlefields and may produce casualties who never stop a bullet.

In the next sample paper, a student describes Mark Twain's use of satire in *The Adventures of Huckleberry Finn*. The writer's focus on Twain's use of satire to criticize greed, conformity, and slavery makes the paper's purpose clear. The use of specific examples with quotations from the novel illustrates Twain's satiric technique. And the choice of three objects of Twain's satire enables the writer to organize her essay clearly and effectively.

Karen Elizabeth
Professor Hogan
English 102
October 10, 1996

                    Mark Twain's Satire in
              The Adventures of Huckleberry Finn

The Adventures of Huckleberry Finn, one of the great American novels,
tells a story of a young boy's journey down the Mississippi River. The
author, Mark Twain, uses many literary techniques to enhance the mood
and alert the reader to various themes. One major literary technique he
commonly uses in his novel is satire. Satire is a method of taking a
serious subject and presenting it in a humorous way. The object of
satire is to ridicule the subject satirized. By using satire, Twain can
dramatize the weaknesses and failings of people and society. In the
novel, Twain's satire enables the reader to view the flaws in American
society while enjoying the exciting adventures of Huckleberry Finn.

    While Huck journeys down the Mississippi River, he meets the notorious
"rapscallions" the king and the duke. They board Huck's raft, hoping the
river will be a channel to promote their work. The king and duke
represent people who honor money and success above all things. Since
they are both humorous characters who are nothing "but just low down
humbugs and frauds," the reader laughs at their ridiculous behavior. But
they are more than just silly and harmless old men. They are dangerous
and destructive, causing many individuals to suffer. What motivates them
is greed. Through them Twain shows how greed can lead to trouble and
unhappiness.

    A second social fault Twain satirizes in *Huckleberry Finn* is
conformity. Twain demonstrates the psychological need of an individual
to conform to the ideas of a group rather than to follow his own mind.
The most important example of this dangerous habit of conformity is the
ridiculous feud between the Grangerfords and the Shepherdsons. In his
portrayal of the feuding families, Twain creates a satire on the
irrationality of love and hate. Perhaps the best example of the
irrationality occurs during Huck's conversation with Buck Grangerford.
When Huck asks the young man what a feud is, he replies:

                    a feud is this way. A man has a quarrel with
                    another man, and kills him; then that other man's
                    brother kills *him;* then the other brothers, on
                    both sides, goes for one another, then the *cousins*
                    chip in—and by-and-by everybody's killed off, and
                    there ain't no more feud. But it's kind of slow,
                    and takes a long time.

As the conversation continues Twain shows that the two feuding families kill each other's members without even knowing why. Nobody seems to remember what started the feud or why the two families hate each other.

Throughout the chapters that describe the feud, Twain uses satire to show how nonsensical and irrational people can be. For example the Grangerfords and the Shepherdsons go to church on Sundays and listen to the minister preach "all about brotherly love and such like tiresomeness." Meanwhile their guns are lined up against the wall ready for use. The members of neither family ever stop to think about what they are doing and why they do it.

Finally and most importantly, the novel satirizes slavery, which Twain attacks as the greatest flaw in American society. Jim, the runaway slave, is a warm-hearted individual seeking freedom by escaping down the river with Huck. Twain shows how society's treatment of Jim is cruel, heartless, and irrational. Twain shows that Jim deserves a better fate than to be separated from the wife and children he loves and be forced to work for people who humiliate him.

Perhaps the most important way Twain reveals the absolute evil of slavery is to show how difficult it is for Huck not to turn Jim in even though Jim loves Huck dearly and has only done things to help him. Through his portrayal of Huck's crisis of conscience over what to do about Jim, Twain shows how society's values during that time were the opposite of what they should be.

Because Huck was taught at home and in school that slavery was right, it is difficult for him to go against that belief. Deep in his heart, however, he knows that Jim should be free, that he is a good man, and that to enslave and humiliate him is wrong. Society's values, however, affect Huck so strongly that he goes along with Tom Sawyer's ridiculous plans for Jim that result in Jim's further humiliation. Huck does, however, realize that Jim is not inferior to him, even though as he describes the time he apologized for his unkind treatment of Jim, he reveals that "it was fifteen minutes before I could work myself up to go and humble myself to a nigger." The important thing for Huck is that he does ask Jim's forgiveness. The important thing for Twain's readers is that they realize that in doing what society has told Huck is wrong, he ends up doing what is right and good.

Throughout the *Adventures of Huckleberry Finn,* Mark Twain treats serious matters in a humorous way. By ridiculing the weakness and faults in society, he entertains his readers while at the same time instructing them in how they should live. Through his use of satire, Twain illustrates the major themes of the novel. He gives his readers a clear perspective on the dangers of greed, the destructive consequences of conformity, and the evils of slavery.

QUESTIONS FOR WRITING ABOUT FICTION

In writing about the elements of fiction, the following questions can help you focus your thinking and prepare yourself for writing analytical essays and papers. Use the questions as a checklist to guide you to important aspects of any story or novel you read.

Plot and Structure

1. What incidents constitute the building blocks of the story's plot?
2. How are these incidents arranged? Chronologically? With flashbacks of action? With foreshadowing?
3. To what extent is the plot unified? How are its incidents related?
4. How is the story shaped, organized, or designed?
5. What patterns can you discern in the story's action? To what extent are repetition, balance, and contrast important? Why?

Character and Characterization

6. To what extent do you identify with any of the characters? To what extent do you sympathize with them or judge them harshly? Why?
7. To what extent does your response to the characters change? If your response does change, identify where that change occurs and why.
8. Are the characters dynamic or static? In the context of the story, are their actions believable? Why or why not? Do their names convey anything about them?
9. What is the function of any minor characters in the story?
10. How does the author characterize or reveal the characters? What do the characters' speech and behavior reveal about them? What do the author's description and point of view contribute to your understanding of the characters?

Setting

11. Where and when is the action of the story set?
12. To what extent are aspects of the setting symbolic? How do you know?
13. Can you imagine the story set in another place or time? Why or why not?

Point of View

14. Who narrates the story's action? Is the point of view first person or third? Does the point of view shift during the course of the story? If so, where, why, and with what implications for meaning?
15. How much does the narrator know about the characters? Is the narrator completely omniscient? Does the narrator possess limited omniscience? Or does the narrator know only as much as the reader?
16. Is the narrator a participant in the story's action or merely an observer?
17. How trustworthy is the narrator? Is the narrator a reliable witness or commenta-

tor on the action and behavior of the story's characters? Why or why not?

Symbolism

18. Do you think any objects or events in the story are symbolic? Why or why not?
19. Are there other symbolic elements—elements of character, setting, language, for example?
20. What do the symbols contribute to the meaning of the story?

Language, Style, Tone

21. How would you characterize the style of the story? The style of the characters' dialogue? Does the style shift at any point?
22. How carefully do you have to read the text? Does the language seem particularly compelling or especially complicated at any point? If so, what makes it compelling or complicated?
23. What is the author's tone or attitude toward the story's characters and action? What aspects of language in particular—diction, imagery, syntax—create that tone?
24. Is the author's tone ironic? If so, how can you tell?

Theme

25. How would you characterize the theme of the story? Is there more than a single theme?
26. Does the author convey the theme(s) directly or indirectly? That is, can you identify a key passage in which the theme is made explicit? Or do you have to infer the theme from the the story's action, dialogue, and details?
27. How does your analysis of the elements of fiction help you understand a story's theme(s)?

Critical Perspectives

28. Among the critical perspectives you might bring to bear on the story, which one(s) seem(s) particularly useful for interpreting it? Why?
29. To what extent can you base your interpretation of the story on its language and details alone? To what extent is outside information about historical and biographical context necessary or helpful in understanding it?
30. To what extent does the story mesh with your personal beliefs and values? To what extent is it antagonistic to your personal beliefs and values?

CHAPTER SIX

Two Fiction Writers in Context

READING D. H. LAWRENCE AND FLANNERY O'CONNOR IN DEPTH

When you read a fiction writer in even moderate depth, it is useful to look for connections among the works you read. At the same time, however, you should also look for differences. You might read Lawrence's "The Horse Dealer's Daughter," for example, in light of what he himself says about fiction in his essays, "The Bright Book of Life" and "Why the Novel Matters." You might also read this story in relation to others Lawrence has written. Although "The Blind Man" is not a love story in the same way as "The Horse Dealer's Daughter," you can nonetheless find shared emphases and values reflected in both stories.

In addition to looking for shared thematic preoccupations and common values espoused by different stories, you can also be alert for artistic links. At first glance, "The Rocking-Horse Winner" seems quite different from "The Blind Man" and "The Horse Dealer's Daughter." Yet all three stories have stylistic traits in common with the other stories, and all three reflect characteristics of Lawrence's writerly temperament.

As you read for connections among Lawrence's work, be careful not to pour every story into the same mold. Recognize what links the stories, but remain alert for the distinctive and individual presence of each. Consider how each work manifests its individuality at the same time that it reveals shared thematic concerns and corresponding aesthetic qualities of other works by the writer.

What is said here of Lawrence's fiction applies with equal force to the works of Flannery O'Connor. O'Connor's fiction is often read in light of her religious faith. As a strong adherent of Roman Catholicism who has written about her faith, O'Connor seems to invite readers to bring a strong Christian perspective to their reading of her work. This invitation is strengthened by the explicit Christian references in the stories themselves.

Nonetheless, when reading O'Connor's stories, readers need to maintain a balance between interpretations based on the stories' explicit use of Christian iconography and the quirky individuality of each particular fictional creation. Such balance allows readers to develop a sense of the spiritual principles in which O'Connor's fiction is grounded while respecting the particular surprises each story manifests.

As with reading multiple works by Lawrence, in reading a few of O'Connor's stories, enjoy the unique pleasures each story provides while constructing a sense of each writer's fictional world. Also, while attending to what both writers have said about their fiction, attend even more to the individual fictional works themselves. "Trust the tale," as Lawrence himself advises, not the teller. Or rather, trust the tale as the teller relates it rather than as the teller describes or otherwise explains it.

You can use the following questions as a general guide for in-depth reading of fiction.

QUESTIONS FOR IN-DEPTH READING

1. What general or overall thematic connections can you make between different works?
2. What stylistic similarities do you notice between and among different works?
3. How do the works differ in emphasis, tone, and style?
4. Once you have identified a writer's major preoccupations, place each work on a spectrum or a grid that represents the range of the writer's concerns.
5. What connections and disjunctions do you find between the following literary elements as they are embodied in different stories by the same writer?
   a. plot and structure
   b. character and characterization
   c. setting and symbolism
   d. language, style, and tone
   e. theme and thought
6. To what extent are your responses to and perceptions of different works by the same writer shared by others—by critics, by classmates, and by the writers themselves?
7. What relationships and differences do you see between the work of one writer and that of another who shares similar thematic interests, stylistic proclivities, or cultural, religious, or social values?
8. Which of the critical perspectives (pages 1893–1922) seem most useful as analytical tools for approaching the body of work of particular writers?

INTRODUCTION TO D. H. LAWRENCE

[1885–1930]

David Herbert Lawrence is best known for his novels, whose titles reveal their center of interest: *Sons and Lovers* (1913), *Women in Love* (1920), *Lady Chatterly's Lover* (1928), and *The Virgin and the Gypsy* (1930), among many others. Of these, *Lady Chatterly's Lover* achieved the greatest notoriety, if not the highest critical acclaim, when it became the occasion of a court obscenity battle. Like much of Lawrence's work, this novel explores the relations between the sexes, contrasting a debilitating relationship between Lady Chatterly and her impotent husband with a vital one between Lady Chatterly and the gamekeeper. The novel is also a compendium of Lawrence's major thematic preoccupations: the importance of instinctual life, the celebration of the natural world, the condemnation of the mechanical and the conventionally artificial, and the powerful effects of sexual surrender.

Lawrence derived a penchant for learning and an impulse to write partly from his mother, who was better educated than his father, an uneducated miner. She encouraged her son's intellectual pursuits, recognizing that his frail constitution made him unsuitable for the physical rigors of a miner's life. Affecting a somewhat self-conscious gentility, she was the intellectual superior of her husband, whose semiliteracy and working-class habits contrasted sharply with her sense of refinement. Lawrence himself, early in life, favored his mother but later came to see his father's virtues, especially his vitality, warmth, and love of the natural world.

D. H. Lawrence was born in Nottinghamshire, an English mining town. He was educated there, taking a teaching certificate from Nottingham College. He taught school from 1902 to 1912, with a one-year hiatus, before becoming a full-time writer. Between 1911, when he published his first novel, *The White Peacock,* and 1930, when he died of tuberculosis, Lawrence published more than sixty volumes, including novels, stories, poems, essays, plays, travel books, social criticism, and translations of Russian and Italian literature.

Lawrence's life was a tissue of unconventional choices. One of the most important was his love affair with Frieda von Richthofen, the German wife of a professor of French at Nottingham, whom Lawrence married after her divorce. With Frieda, Lawrence lived at various times in Germany, England, Italy, Australia, Mexico, and France, where he died. His unconventionality found its fiercest expression in his books, which repeatedly displayed the stultifying constraints and enervating hypocrisies that pervaded modern life, vestiges from Victorian pieties and the mindless conventionalism of an earlier time. Rebelling against constraints of all kinds—intellectual, emotional, sexual—Lawrence raised his voice in protest, the most effective form of which was expressed in his art.

Lawrence waged his most intense battles against an overintellectual approach to living, especially to sexual experience, an exaggerated intellectualism he described as "sex in the head." In its place Lawrence celebrated the liberation of the body, urging that human beings need to express their emotion with physical passion uncontaminated by puritanical attitudes and unrestrained by conventional moralistic tendencies. Lawrence saw sexuality as the source of a badly needed restoration of vitality and joy. He considered the primacy of erotic love an elemental force that was linked fundamentally with the physical energy of the natural world. In both his fiction and his poetry, Lawrence frequently employed elements of the natural world as emblems of human passions and impulses. Lawrence, moreover, was a careful and loving observer of nature, which he repeatedly demonstrated by his convincing depictions of animals and the natural landscape. Allied with his celebration of the natural world was his condemnation of the evils of industrialism, which he considered responsible for nearly destroying the English landscape and for its dehumanizing effects.

Lawrence was spiritual kin to the English Romantic poet William Blake and the American transcendentalist poet Walt Whitman. Like Blake, Lawrence was something of a visionary. Like Whitman, he was literarily unconventional, developing a style and voice to suit his unique vision of experience.

Lawrence's respect for instinct and his celebration of sexual love are eminently displayed in "The Horse Dealer's Daughter." This story offers a fine example of complex feelings and intense psychological drama in the developing erotic relationship between a young man and woman who, each very much alone, simultaneously desire and fear the sexual attraction that develops between them. Lawrence's patience in describing this encounter, his slowing of the narrative tempo to accommodate their conflicted feelings, and the insistence with which he describes its ultimately inevitable consequences vividly dramatize the power of sexual attraction.

The tensions in "The Blind Man" and "The Rocking-Horse Winner" are different though not unrelated to those displayed in "The Horse Dealer's Daughter." Like Dr. Fergusson in "The Horse Dealer's Daughter," the barrister Bertie in "The Blind Man" is afraid of physical contact. Lawrence sets him in opposition to the story's protagonist and places the blind man's wife squarely between the two men. She experiences a different kind of attraction toward each, the two men displaying an actual repulsion for one another. Part of our pleasure in reading this story derives from Lawrence's careful set of characterizations. Part comes also from the surprising sequence of developing action and the characters' varied understandings of its significance. Especially effective is the climactic scene in the dark barn where the blind man, alone with the barrister, attempts to breach the gulf that divides them.

"The Rocking-Horse Winner" takes us into another world—that of money and its power to affect our lives. The story can be read as an attack on materialist values, which Lawrence railed against throughout his life. But it also invites consideration of the relationship between a young boy and his mother, a subject Lawrence began exploring with his first important novel, *Sons and Lovers,* based largely on his experience.

Throughout his writing life Lawrence persisted in condeming societal attitudes that conflicted with his belief that human beings must become instinctive and intuitive, deeply in touch with their physical being and with the primal rhythms of nature. He repeatedly strove to depict not only the instinctually repressed and sexually inhibited world that he rejected, but also an alternative world in which men and women were in tune with their physical selves and could relate to one another passionately and openly. And all this would be in harmony with nature, at once source and sustenance, image and ideal of personal and social wholeness.

Lawrence rendered his romanticist vision with passionate intensity. Putting his passion in the service of art, Lawrence crafted stories at once wonderful and dangerous. Their language and incidents frequently surprise; their voice and vision repeatedly reveal Lawrence's astonishing energy and love of life.

CRITICAL COMMENTS BY LAWRENCE

from *The Bright Book of Life*

The novel is the one bright book of life. Books are not life. They are only tremulations on the ether. But the novel as a tremulation can make the whole man alive tremble. Which is more than poetry, philosophy, science, or any other book-tremulation can do.

The novel is the book of life. In this sense, the Bible is a great confused novel. You may say, it is about God. But it is really about man alive. Adam, Eve, Sarai, Abraham, Isaac, Jacob, Samuel, David, Bath-Sheba, Ruth, Esther, Solomon, Job, Isaiah, Jesus, Mark, Judas, Paul, Peter: what is it but man alive, from start to finish? Man alive, not mere bits. Even the Lord is another man alive, in a burning bush, throwing the tablets of stone at Moses's head.

I do hope you begin to get my idea, why the novel is supremely important, as a tremulation on the ether. Plato makes the perfect ideal being tremble in me. But that's only a bit of me. Perfection is only a bit, in the strange make-up of man alive. The Sermon on the Mount makes the selfless spirit of me quiver. But that, too, is only a bit of me. The Ten Commandments set the old Adam shivering in me, warning me that I am a thief and a murderer, unless I watch it. But even the old Adam is only a bit of me.

I very much like all these bits of me to be set trembling with life and the wisdom of life. But I do ask that the whole of me shall tremble in its wholeness, some time or other. . . .

To be alive, to be man alive, to be whole man alive: that is the point. And at its best, the novel, and the novel supremely, can help you. It can help you not to be dead man in life. So much of a man walks about dead and a carcass in the street and house, today: so much of women is merely dead. Like a pianoforte with half the notes mute.

But in the novel you can see, plainly, when the man goes dead, the woman goes inert. You can develop an instinct for life, if you will, instead of a theory of right and wrong, good and bad.

In life, there is right and wrong, good and bad, all the time. But what is right in one case is wrong in another. And in the novel you see one man becoming a corpse, because of his so-called goodness, another going dead because of his so-called wickedness. Right and wrong is an instinct: but an instinct of the whole consciousness in a man, bodily, mental, spiritual at once. And only in the novel are *all* things given full play, or at least, they may be given full play, when we realize that life itself, and not inert safety, is the reason for living. For out of the full play of all things emerges the only thing that is anything, the wholeness of a man, the wholeness of a woman, man alive, and live woman.

Man and Woman

from *Morality and the Novel*

The great relationship, for humanity, will always be the relation between man and woman. The relation between man and man, woman and woman, parent and child, will always be subsidiary.

And the relation between man and woman will change for ever, and will for ever be the new central clue to human life. It is the *relation itself* which is the quick and the central clue to life, not the man, nor the woman, nor the children that result from the relationship, as a contingency.

It is no use thinking you can put a stamp on the relation between man and woman, to keep it in the *status quo*. You can't. You might as well try to put a stamp on the rainbow or the rain.

As for the bond of love, better put it off when it galls. It is an absurdity, to say that men and women *must love*. Men and women will be for ever subtly and changingly related to one another; no need to yoke them with any "bond" at all. The only morality is to have man true to his manhood, woman to her womanhood, and let the relationship form of itself, in all honour. For it is, to each, *life itself*.

CRITICS ON LAWRENCE

MARK SPILKA

Ritual Form in "The Blind Man"

from *The Ethic of Love*

> . . . He lifted his hand, and laid the fingers on the scar, on the scarred eyes. Maurice suddenly covered them with his own hand, pressed the fingers of the other man upon his disfigured eye-sockets, trembling in every fibre, and rocking slightly, slowly, from side to side. He remained thus for a minute or more, whilst Bertie stood as if in a swoon, unconscious, imprisoned.

Then suddenly Maurice removed the hand of the other man
from his brow, and stood holding it in his own.
"Oh, my God," he said, "we shall know each other now,
shan't we? We shall know each other now."

A writer like James Joyce might see an "epiphany" in such an experience—a static, timeless manifestation of some spiritual essence; but Lawrence sees instead a kinetic transformation of being, in both Pervin and Reid: for when the two return to Isabel, Maurice stands "with his feet apart, like a strange colossus," while Bertie is now "like a mollusc whose shell is broken." Through the friendship rite, one man moves toward greater fullness of being; his blindness is transcended, his unresolved blood-intimacy released, and the limited circle of marriage itself is broken by "the new delicate fulfillment of mortal friendship"; but the other man is destroyed by the experience; his outer bulwark against life is smashed, his inner vacuum thoroughly exposed. Thus the ritual pattern of the story is complete. There are ironies, of course, and resonant implications, as in more static and symbolic forms. The path, the way out of darkness which opens for the Pervins is quickly closed by Bertie's fear of passionate friendship. Yet the change of being in Maurice, as in Bertie, is real and valid. The ritual form conveys a new life-possibility: a step beyond marriage which makes marriage possible, a breakthrough to that fuller life which Lawrence tried to project in all his work, in strongly dramatic terms, and with a strong *dramatic* sense of the odds against it.

W. D. SNODGRASS

A Rocking-Horse: Symbol, Pattern, Way to Live

from *The Hudson Review*

As several critics have noted, the story resembles many well-known fairy tales or magical stories in which the hero bargains with evil powers for personal advantages or forbidden knowledge. These bargains are always "rigged" so that the hero, after his apparent triumphs, will lose in the end—this being, in itself, the standard "moral." Gordon and Tate sum up their interpretation: "the boy, Paul, has invoked strange gods and pays the penalty with his death." Robert Gorham Davis goes on to point out that many witches supposedly rode hobby-horses of one sort or another (e.g., the witch's broom) to rock themselves into a magical and prophetic trance. When he rides, Paul's eyes glare blue and strange, he will speak to no one, his sisters fear him. He stares into the horse's wooden face: "Its red mouth was slightly open, its big eye was wide and glassy-bright." More and more engrossed in his doom as the story progresses, he becomes "wild-eyed and strange . . . his big blue eyes blazing with a sort of madness." We hear again and again of the uncanny blaze of his eyes until finally, at his collapse, they are "like blue stones." Clearly enough, he is held in some self-induced prophetic frenzy, a line of meaning carefully developed by the story. When Paul first asserts to his mother that he is "lucky," he claims that God told him so. This seems pure invention, yet may well be a kind of *hubris,* considering the conversation that had just passed with his mother:

> "Nobody ever knows why one person is lucky and another unlucky."
> "Don't they? Nobody at all? Does nobody know?"
> "Perhaps God. But He never tells."

Whether Paul really believes that God told him so, he certainly does become lucky. And others come to believe that superhuman powers are involved. Bassett thinks of "Master Paul" as a seer and takes an explicitly worshipful tone towards him. He grows "serious as a church" and twice tells Uncle Oscar in a "secret, religious voice. . . . 'It's as if he had it from heaven.' " These hints of occultism culminate in Uncle Oscar's benediction:

> "My God, Hester, you're eighty-odd thousand to the good, and a poor devil of a son to the bad. But poor devil, poor devil, he's best gone out of a life where he rides his rocking-horse to find a winner."

So, in some sense, Paul *is* demonic, yet a poor devil; though he has compacted with evil, his intentions were good and he has destroyed only himself. At first metaphorically, in the end literally, he has committed suicide. But that may be, finally, the essence of evil.

It is clear, then, that the story is talking about some sort of religious perversion. But *what* sort? Who are the strange gods: how does Paul serve them and receive their information? We must return here, I think, to the problem of knowledge and intellection. Paul is destroyed, we have said, by his desire to "know." It is not only that he has chosen wrong ways of knowing or wrong things to know. The evil is that he *has* chosen to know, to live by intellection. Lawrence wrote, in a letter to Ernest Collings:

> My great religion is a belief in the blood, the flesh, as being wiser than the intellect. We can go wrong in our minds. But what our blood feels and believes and says, is always true. *The intellect is only a bit and bridle.* What do I care about knowledge. . . . I conceive a man's body as a kind of flame . . . and the intellect is just the light that is shed on to the things around. . . . A flame isn't a flame because it lights up two, or twenty objects on a table. It's a flame because it is itself. And we have forgotten ourselves. . . . The real way of living is to answer to one's wants. Not "I want to light up with my intelligence as many things as possible" but ". . . I want that liberty, I want that woman, I want that pound of peaches, I want to go to sleep, I want to go to the pub and have a good time, I want to look a beastly swell today, I want to kiss that girl, I want to insult that man."

(I have italicized the bit and bridle metaphor to underscore an immediate relationship to the rocking-horse of the story.)

Not one member of this family really knows his wants. Like most idealists, they have ignored the most important part of the command *Know thyself,* and so cannot deal with their most important problem, their own needs. To know one's needs is really to know one's own limits, hence one's definition. Lawrence's notion of living by "feeling" or "blood" (as opposed to "knowledge," "mind" or "personality") may be most easily understood, perhaps, as living according to what you *are,* not what you think you should be made over into; knowing yourself, not external standards. Thus, what Lawrence calls "feeling" could well be glossed as "knowing one's wants." Paul's family, lacking true knowledge of themselves, have turned their light, their intellect, outward, hoping to control the external world. The mother, refusing to clarify what her emotions really *are,* hopes to control herself and her world by acting "gentle and anxious for her children." She tries to be or act what she thinks she should be, not taking adequate notice of what she is and needs. She acts from precepts about motherhood, not from recognition of her own will, self-respect for her own motherhood. Thus, the apparent contradiction between Hester's coldness, the "hard . . . center of her heart," and, on the other hand, "all her tormented motherhood flooding upon her" when Paul collapses near the end of the story. Some deep source of affection has apparently lain hidden (and so tormented) in her, all along; it was her business to find and release it sooner. Similarly, Paul has a need for affection which he does not, and perhaps cannot, understand or manage.

KINGSLEY WIDMER

On "The Horse Dealer's Daughter"

from *D. H. Lawrence: The Art of Perversity*

Originally entitled by Lawrence "The Miracle,"[20] *The Horse Dealer's Daughter* may be viewed as one of a series of Lawrence's tales turning about a moment of regenerative baptism. The young man, "spell-bound," "mesmerized," by something deeper than his consciousness, "felt delivered from his own fretted, daily self." The courageous breakthrough at the moment of despair and death brings out the new agony of desire. The man sees the "terrible shining joy in her eyes, which really terrified him, and yet which he wanted to see, because he feared the look of doubt still more." The necessary faith in life takes the form of erotic confrontation. Having been carried home, undressed, and warmed back to life by the doctor, Mabel regains consciousness to find herself on the desperate edge between life and death, love and despair. Lawrence has carefully created a figure of profound naiveté, and so, naked before the man, she simply draws the conclusion of need: either he loves her, or she is dead. By the very nakedness of her self and her need, she forces him to recognize desire—"he had crossed the gulf over to her." The story ends with the man's agonized assent to desire: " 'No, I want you, I want you,' " was all he answered to her question of love, "blindly, with that terrible intonation which frightened her almost more than her horror lest he should not *want* her." Such elemental courtship is not only a choice of love over death but of love as itself a kind of death—the most characteristic mark of passion.

D. H. LAWRENCE: STORIES

The Blind Man

Isabel Pervin was listening for two sounds—for the sound of wheels on the drive outside and for the noise of her husband's footsteps in the hall. Her dearest and oldest friend, a man who seemed almost indispensable to her living, would drive up in the rainy dusk of the closing November day. The trap had gone to fetch him from the station. And her husband, who had been blinded in Flanders, and who had a disfiguring mark on his brow, would be coming in from the outhouses.

He had been home for a year now. He was totally blind. Yet they had been very happy. The Grange was Maurice's own place. The back was a farmstead, and the Wernhams, who occupied the rear premises, acted as farmers. Isabel lived with her husband in the handsome rooms in front. She and he had been almost entirely alone together since he was wounded. They talked and sang and read together in a wonderful and unspeakable intimacy. Then she reviewed books for a Scottish newspaper, carrying on her old interest, and he occupied himself a good deal with the farm. Sightless, he could still discuss everything with Wernham, and he could also do a good deal of work about the place—menial work, it is true, but it gave him satisfaction. He milked the cows, carried in the pails, turned the separator, attended to the pigs and horses. Life was still very full and strangely serene for the blind man, peaceful with the almost incomprehensible peace of immediate contact in darkness. With his wife he had a whole world, rich and real and invisible.

They were newly and remotely happy. He did not even regret the loss of his sight in these times of dark, palpable joy. A certain exultance swelled his soul.

But as time wore on, sometimes the rich glamour would leave them. Sometimes, after months of this intensity, a sense of burden overcame Isabel, a weariness, a terrible ennui, in that silent house approached between a colonnade of tall-shafted pines. Then she felt she would go mad, for she could not bear it. And sometimes he had devastating fits of depression, which seemed to lay waste his whole being. It was worse than depression—a black misery, when his own life was a torture to him, and when his presence was unbearable to his wife. The dread went down to the roots of her soul as these black days recurred. In a kind of panic she tried to wrap herself up still further in her husband. She forced the old spontaneous cheerfulness and joy to continue. But the effort it cost her was almost too much. She knew she could not keep it up. She felt she would scream with the strain, and would give anything, anything, to escape. She longed to possess her husband utterly; it gave her inordinate joy to have him entirely to herself. And yet, when again he was gone in a black and massive misery, she could not bear him, she could not bear herself; she wished she could be snatched away off the earth altogether, anything rather than live at this cost.

Dazed, she schemed for a way out. She invited friends, she tried to give him some further connection with the outer world. But it was no good. After all their joy and suffering, after their dark, great year of blindness and solitude and unspeakable nearness, other people seemed to them both shallow, rattling, rather impertinent. Shallow prattle seemed presumptuous. He became impatient and irritated, she was wearied. And so they lapsed into their solitude again. For they preferred it.

But now, in a few weeks' time, her second baby would be born. The first had died, an infant, when her husband first went out to France. She looked with joy and relief to the coming of the second. It would be her salvation. But also she felt some anxiety. She was thirty years old, her husband was a year younger. They both wanted the child very much. Yet she could not help feeling afraid. She had her husband on her hands, a terrible joy to her, and a terrifying burden. The child would occupy her love and attention. And then, what of Maurice? What would he do? If only she could feel that he, too, would be at peace and happy when the child came! She did so want to luxuriate in a rich, physical satisfaction of maternity. But the man, what would he do? How could she provide for him, how avert those shattering black moods of his, which destroyed them both?

She sighed with fear. But at this time Bertie Reid wrote to Isabel. He was her old friend, a second or third cousin, a Scotchman, as she was a Scotchwoman. They had been brought up near to one another, and all her life he had been her friend, like a brother, but better than her own brothers. She loved him—though not in the marrying sense. There was a sort of kinship between them, an affinity. They understood one another instinctively. But Isabel would never have thought of marrying Bertie. It would have seemed like marrying in her own family.

Bertie was a barrister and a man of letters, a Scotchman of the intellectual type, quick, ironical, sentimental, and on his knees before the woman he adored but did not want to marry. Maurice Pervin was different. He came of a good old country family—the Grange was not a very great distance from Oxford. He was passionate, sensitive, perhaps over-sensitive, wincing—a big fellow with heavy limbs and a forehead that flushed painfully. For his mind was slow, as if drugged by the strong provincial blood that beat in his veins. He was very sensitive to his own mental slowness, his feelings being quick and acute. So that he was just the opposite to Bertie, whose mind was much quicker than his emotions, which were not so very fine.

From the first the two men did not like each other. Isabel felt that they ought to get on together. But they did not. She felt that if only each could have the clue to the other there would be such a rare understanding between them. It did not come off, however. Bertie adopted a slightly ironical attitude, very offensive to Maurice, who returned the Scotch irony with English resentment, a resentment which deepened sometimes into stupid hatred.

This was a little puzzling to Isabel. However, she accepted it in the course of things. Men were made freakish and unreasonable. Therefore, when Maurice was going out to France for the second time, she felt that, for her husband's sake, she must discontinue her friendship with Bertie. She wrote to the barrister to this effect. Bertram Reid simply replied that in this, as in all other matters, he must obey her wishes, if these were indeed her wishes.

For nearly two years nothing had passed between the two friends. Isabel rather gloried in the fact; she had no compunction. She had one great article of faith, which was, that husband and wife should be so important to one another, that the rest of the world simply did not count. She and Maurice were husband and wife. They loved one another. They would have children. Then let everybody and everything else fade into insignificance outside this connubial felicity. She professed herself quite happy and ready to receive Maurice's friends. She was happy and ready: the happy wife, the ready woman in possession. Without knowing why, the friends retired abashed, and came no more. Maurice, of course, took as much satisfaction in this connubial absorption as Isabel did.

He shared in Isabel's literary activities, she cultivated a real interest in agriculture and cattle-raising. For she, being at heart perhaps an emotional enthusiast, always cultivated the practical side of life and prided herself on her mastery of practical affairs. Thus the husband and wife had spent the five years of their married life. The last had been one of blindness and unspeakable intimacy. And now Isabel felt a great indifference coming over her, a sort of lethargy. She wanted to be allowed to bear her child in peace, to nod by the fire and drift vaguely, physically, from day to day. Maurice was like an ominous thunder-cloud. She had to keep waking up to remember him.

When a little note came from Bertie, asking if he were to put up a tombstone to their dead friendship, and speaking of the real pain he felt on account of her husband's loss of sight, she felt a pang, a fluttering agitation of reawakening. And she read the letter to Maurice.

"Ask him to come down," he said.

"Ask Bertie to come here!" she re-echoed.

"Yes—if he wants to."

Isabel paused for a few moments.

"I know he wants to—he'd only be too glad," she replied. "But what about you, Maurice? How should you like it?"

"I should like it."

"Well—in that case—But I thought you didn't care for him—"

"Oh, I don't know. I might think differently of him now," the blind man replied. It was rather abstruse to Isabel.

"Well, dear," she said, "if you're quite sure—"

"I'm sure enough. Let him come," said Maurice.

So Bertie was coming, coming this evening, in the November rain and darkness. Isabel was agitated, racked with her old restlessness and indecision. She had always suffered from this pain of doubt, just an agonizing sense of uncertainty. It had begun to pass off, in the lethargy of maternity. Now it returned, and she resented it. She struggled as usual to maintain her calm, composed, friendly bearing, a sort of mask she wore over all her body.

A woman had lighted a tall lamp beside the table and spread the cloth. The long dining-room was dim, with its elegant but rather severe pieces of old furniture. Only the round table glowed softly under the light. It had a rich, beautiful effect. The white cloth glistened and dropped its heavy, pointed lace corners almost to the carpet, the china was old and handsome, creamy-yellow, with a blotched pattern of harsh red and deep blue, the cups large and bell-shaped, the teapot gallant. Isabel looked at it with superficial appreciation.

Her nerves were hurting her. She looked automatically again at the high, uncurtained windows. In the last dusk she could just perceive outside a huge fir-tree swaying its boughs: it was as if she thought it rather than saw it. The rain came flying on the window panes. Ah, why had she no peace? These two men, why did they tear at her? Why did they not come—why was there this suspense?

She sat in a lassitude that was really suspense and irritation. Maurice, at least, might come in—there was nothing to keep him out. She rose to her feet. Catching sight of her reflection in a mirror, she glanced at herself with a slight smile of recognition, as if she were an old friend to herself. Her face was oval and calm, her nose a little arched. Her neck made a beautiful line down to her shoulder. With hair knotted loosely behind, she had something of a warm, maternal look. Thinking this of herself, she arched her eyebrows and her rather heavy eyelids, with a little flicker of a smile, and for a moment her gray eyes looked amused and wicked, a little sardonic, out of her transfigured Madonna face.

Then, resuming her air of womanly patience—she was really fatally self-determined—she went with a little jerk towards the door. Her eyes were slightly reddened.

She passed down the wide hall and through a door at the end. Then she was in the farm premises. The scent of dairy, and of farm-kitchen, and of farm-yard and of leather almost overcame her: but particularly the scent of dairy. They had been scalding out the pans. The flagged passage in front of her was dark, puddled, and wet. Light came out from the open kitchen door. She went forward and stood in the doorway. The farm-people were at tea, seated at a little distance from her, round a long, narrow table, in the centre of which stood a white lamp. Ruddy faces, ruddy hands holding food, red mouths working, heads bent over the tea-cups: men, landgirls, boys: it was tea-time, feeding-time. Some faces caught sight of her. Mrs. Wernham, going round behind the chairs with a large black teapot, halting slightly in her walk, was not aware of her for a moment. Then she turned suddenly.

"Oh, it is Madam!" she exclaimed. "Come in, then, come in! We're at tea." And she dragged forward a chair.

"No, I won't come in," said Isabel. "I'm afraid I interrupt your meal."

"No—no—not likely, Madam, not likely."

"Hasn't Mr. Pervin come in, do you know?"

"I'm sure I couldn't say! Missed him, have you, Madam?"

"No, I only wanted him to come in," laughed Isabel, as if shyly.

"Wanted him, did ye? Get up, boy—get up, now——"

Mrs. Wernham knocked one of the boys on the shoulder. He began to scrape to his feet, chewing largely.

"I believe he's in top stable," said another face from the table.

"Ah! No, don't get up. I'm going myself," said Isabel.

"Don't you go out on a dirty night like this. Let the lad go. Get along wi' ye, boy," said Mrs. Wernham.

"No, no," said Isabel, with a decision that was always obeyed. "Go on with your tea, Tom. I'd like to go across to the stable, Mrs. Wernham."

"Did ever you hear tell!" exclaimed the woman.

"Isn't the trap late?" asked Isabel.

"Why, no," said Mrs. Wernham, peering into the distance at the tall, dim clock.

"No, Madam—we can give it another quarter or twenty minutes yet, good—yes, every bit of a quarter."

"Ah! It seems late when darkness falls so early," said Isabel.

"It do, that it do. Bother the days, that they draw in so," answered Mrs. Wernham. "Proper miserable!"

"They are," said Isabel, withdrawing.

She pulled on her overshoes, wrapped a large tartan shawl around her, put on a man's felt hat, and ventured out along the causeways of the first yard. It was very dark. The wind was roaring in the great elms behind the outhouses. When she came to the second yard the darkness seemed deeper. She was unsure of her footing. She wished she had brought a lantern. Rain blew against her. Half she liked it, half she felt unwilling to battle.

She reached at last the just visible door of the stable. There was no sign of a light anywhere. Opening the upper half, she looked in: into a simple well of darkness. The smell of horses and ammonia, and of warmth was startling to her, in that full night. She listened with all her ears but could hear nothing save the night, and the stirring of a horse.

"Maurice!" she called, softly and musically, though she was afraid. "Maurice—are you there?"

Nothing came from the darkness. She knew the rain and wind blew in upon the horses, the hot animal life. Feeling it wrong, she entered the stable and drew the lower half of the door shut, holding the upper part close. She did not stir, because she was aware of the presence of the dark hind-quarters of the horses, though she could not see them, and she was afraid. Something wild stirred in her heart.

She listened intensely. Then she heard a small noise in the distance—far away, it seemed—the chink of a pan, and a man's voice speaking a brief word. It would be Maurice, in the other part of the stable. She stood motionless, waiting for him to come through the partition door. The horses were so terrifyingly near to her, in the invisible.

The loud jarring of the inner door-latch made her start; the door was opened. She could hear and feel her husband entering and invisibly passing among the horses near to her, darkness as they were, actively intermingled. The rather low sound of his voice as he spoke to the horses came velvety to her nerves. How near he was, and how invisible! The darkness seemed to be in a strange swirl of violent life, just upon her. She turned giddy.

Her presence of mind made her call quietly and musically:

"Maurice! Maurice—dear-ar!"

"Yes," he answered. "Isabel?"

She saw nothing, and the sound of his voice seemed to touch her.

"Hello!" she answered cheerfully, straining her eyes to see him. He was still busy, attending to the horses near her, but she saw only darkness. It made her almost desperate.

"Won't you come in, dear?" she said.

"Yes, I'm coming. Just half a minute. Stand over—now! Trap's not come, has it?"

"Not yet," said Isabel.

His voice was pleasant and ordinary, but it had a slight suggestion of the stable to her. She wished he would come away. Whilst he was so utterly invisible, she was afraid of him.

"How's the time?" he asked.

"Not yet six," she replied. She disliked to answer into the dark. Presently he came very near to her, and she retreated out of doors.

"The weather blows in here," he said, coming steadily forward, feeling for the doors. She shrank away. At last she could dimly see him.

"Bertie won't have much of a drive," he said, as he closed the doors.

"He won't indeed!" said Isabel calmly, watching the dark shape at the door.

"Give me your arm, dear," she said.

She pressed his arm close to her, as she went. But she longed to see him, to look at him. She was nervous. He walked erect, with face rather lifted, but with a curious tentative movement of his powerful, muscular legs. She could feel the clever, careful, strong contact of his feet with the earth, as she balanced against him. For a moment he was a tower of darkness to her, as if he rose out of the earth.

In the house-passage he wavered and went cautiously, with a curious look of silence about him as he felt for the bench. Then he sat down heavily. He was a man with rather sloping shoulders, but with heavy limbs, powerful legs that seemed to know the earth. His head was small, usually carried high and light. As he bent down to unfasten his gaiters and boots he did not look blind. His hair was brown and crisp, his hands were large, reddish, intelligent, the veins stood out in the wrists; and his thighs and knees seemed massive. When he stood up his face and neck were surcharged with blood, the veins stood out on his temples. She did not look at his blindness.

Isabel was always glad when they had passed through the dividing door into their own regions of repose and beauty. She was a little afraid of him, out there in the animal grossness of the back. His bearings also changed, as he smelt the familiar indefinable odour that pervaded his wife's surroundings, a delicate, refined scent, very faintly spicy. Perhaps it came from the potpourri bowls.

He stood at the foot of the stairs, arrested, listening. She watched him, and her heart sickened. He seemed to be listening to fate.

"He's not here yet," he said. "I'll go up and change."

"Maurice," she said, "you're not wishing he wouldn't come, are you?"

"I couldn't quite say," he answered. "I feel myself rather on the qui vive."

"I can see you are," she answered. And she reached up and kissed his cheek. She saw his mouth relax into a slow smile.

"What are you laughing at?" she said roguishly.

"You consoling me," he answered.

"Nay," she answered. "Why should I console you? You know we love each other— you know how married we are! What does anything else matter?"

"Nothing at all, my dear."

He felt for her face and touched it, smiling.

"You're all right, aren't you?" he asked anxiously.

"I'm wonderfully all right, love," she answered. "It's you I am a little troubled about, at times."

"Why me?" he said, touching her cheeks delicately with the tips of his fingers. The touch had an almost hypnotizing effect on her.

He went away upstairs. She saw him mount into the darkness, unseeing and unchanging. He did not know that the lamps on the upper corridor were unlighted. He went on into the darkness with unchanging step. She heard him in the bath-room.

Pervin moved about almost unconsciously in his familiar surroundings, dark though everything was. He seemed to know the presence of objects before he touched them. It was a pleasure to him to rock thus through a world of things, carried on the flood in a sort of blood-prescience. He did not think much or trouble much. So long as he kept this sheer immediacy of blood-contact with the substantial world he was happy, he wanted no intervention of visual consciousness. In this state there was a certain rich positivity, bordering sometimes on rapture. Life seemed to move in him like a tide lapping, lapping, and advancing, enveloping all things darkly. It was a pleasure to stretch forth the hand and meet the unseen object, clasp it, and possess it in pure contact. He did not try to remember, to visualize. He did not want to. The new way of consciousness substituted itself in him.

The rich suffusion of this state generally kept him happy, reaching its culmination in the consuming passion for his wife. But at times the flow would seem to be checked and thrown back. Then it would beat inside him like a tangled sea, and he was tortured in the shattered chaos of his own blood. He grew to dread this arrest, this throwback, this chaos inside himself, when he seemed merely at the mercy of his own powerful and conflicting elements. How to get some measure of control or surety, this was the question. And when the question rose maddening in him, he would clench his fists as if he would compel the whole universe to submit to him. But it was in vain. He could not even compel himself.

Tonight, however, he was still serene, though little tremors of unreasonable exasperation ran through him. He had to handle the razor very carefully, as he shaved, for it was not at one with him, he was afraid of it. His hearing also was too much sharpened. He heard the woman lighting the lamps on the corridor, and attending to the fire in the visitors' room. And then, as he went to his room, he heard the trap arrive. Then came Isabel's voice, lifted and calling, like a bell ringing:

"Is it you, Bertie? Have you come?"

And a man's voice answered out of the wind:

"Hello, Isabel! There you are."

"Have you had a miserable drive? I'm so sorry we couldn't send a closed carriage. I can't see you at all, you know."

"I'm coming. No, I liked the drive—it was like Perthshire. Well, how are you? You're looking fit as ever, as far as I can see."

"Oh, yes," said Isabel. "I'm wonderfully well. How are you? Rather thin, I think—"

"Worked to death—everybody's old cry. But I'm all right, Ciss. How's Pervin?— isn't he here?"

"Oh, yes, he's upstairs changing. Yes, he's awfully well. Take off your wet things; I'll send them to be dried."

"And how are you both, in spirits? He doesn't fret?"

"No—no, not at all. No, on the contrary, really. We've been wonderfully happy, incredibly. It's more than I can understand—so wonderful: the nearness, and the peace—"

"Ah! Well, that's awfully good news—"

They moved away. Pervin heard no more. But a childish sense of desolation had come over him, as he heard their brisk voices. He seemed shut out—like a child that is left out. He was aimless and excluded, he did not know what to do with himself. The helpless desolation came over him. He fumbled nervously as he dressed himself, in a state almost of childishness. He disliked the Scotch accent in Bertie's speech, and the slight response it found on Isabel's tongue. He disliked the slight purr of complacency in the Scottish speech. He disliked intensely the glib way in which Isabel spoke of their happiness and nearness. It made him recoil. He was fretful and beside himself like a child, he had almost a childish nostalgia to be included in the life circle. And at the same time he was a man, dark and powerful and infuriated by his own weakness. By some fatal flaw, he could not be by himself, he had to depend on the support of another. And this very dependence enraged him. He hated Bertie Reid, and at the same time he knew the hatred was nonsense, he knew it was the outcome of his own weakness.

He went downstairs. Isabel was alone in the dining-room. She watched him enter, head erect, his feet tentative. He looked so strong-blooded and healthy and, at the same time, cancelled. Cancelled—that was the word that flew across her mind. Perhaps it was his scar suggested it.

"You heard Bertie come, Maurice?" she said.

"Yes—isn't he here?"

"He's in his room. He looks very thin and worn."

"I suppose he works himself to death."

A woman came in with a tray—and after a few minutes Bertie came down. He was a little dark man, with a very big forehead, thin, wispy hair, and sad, large eyes. His expression was inordinately sad—almost funny. He had odd, short legs.

Isabel watched him hesitate under the door, and glance nervously at her husband. Pervin heard him and turned.

"Here you are, now," said Isabel. "Come, let us eat."

Bertie went across to Maurice.

"How are you, Pervin?" he said, as he advanced.

The blind man stuck his hand out into space, and Bertie took it.

"Very fit. Glad you've come," said Maurice.

Isabel glanced at them, and glanced away, as if she could not bear to see them.

"Come," she said. "Come to table. Aren't you both awfully hungry? I am, tremendously."

"I'm afraid you waited for me," said Bertie, as they sat down.

Maurice had a curious monolithic way of sitting in a chair, erect and distant. Isabel's heart always beat when she caught sight of him thus.

"No," she replied to Bertie. "We're very little later than usual. We're having a sort of high tea, not dinner. Do you mind? It gives us such a nice long evening, uninterrupted."

"I like it," said Bertie.

Maurice was feeling, with curious little movements, almost like a cat kneading her bed, for his plate, his knife and fork, his napkin. He was getting the whole geography of his cover into his consciousness. He sat erect and inscrutable, remote-seeming. Bertie watched the static figure of the blind man, the delicate tactile discernment of the large, ruddy hands, and the curious mindless silence of the brow, above the scar. With difficulty he looked away, and without knowing what he did, picked up a little crystal bowl of violets from the table, and held them to his nose.

"They are sweet-scented," he said. "Where do they come from?"

"From the garden—under the windows," said Isabel.

"So late in the year—and so fragrant! Do you remember the violets under Aunt Bell's south wall?"

The two friends looked at each other and exchanged a smile, Isabel's eyes lighting up.

"Don't I?" she replied. "Wasn't she queer!"

"A curious old girl," laughed Bertie. "There's a streak of freakishness in the family, Isabel."

"Ah—but not in you and me, Bertie," said Isabel. "Give them to Maurice, will you?" she added, as Bertie was putting down the flowers. "Have you smelled the violets, dear? Do!—they are so scented."

Maurice held out his hand, and Bertie placed the tiny bowl against his large, warm-looking fingers. Maurice's hand closed over the thin white fingers of the barrister. Bertie carefully extricated himself. Then the two watched the blind man smelling the violets. He bent his head and seemed to be thinking. Isabel waited.

"Aren't they sweet, Maurice?" she said at last, anxiously.

"Very," he said. And he held out the bowl. Bertie took it. Both he and Isabel were a little afraid, and deeply disturbed.

The meal continued. Isabel and Bertie chatted spasmodically. The blind man was silent. He touched his food repeatedly, with quick, delicate touches of his knife-point, then cut irregular bits. He could not bear to be helped. Both Isabel and Bertie suffered: Isabel wondered why. She did not suffer when she was alone with Maurice. Bertie made her conscious of a strangeness.

After the meal the three drew their chairs to the fire, and sat down to talk. The decanters were put on a table near at hand. Isabel knocked the logs on the fire, and clouds of brilliant sparks went up the chimney. Bertie noticed a slight weariness in her bearing.

"You will be glad when your child comes now, Isabel?" he said.

She looked up to him with a quick wan smile.

"Yes, I shall be glad," she answered. "It begins to seem long. Yes, I shall be very glad. So will you, Maurice, won't you?" she added.

"Yes, I shall," replied her husband.

"We are both looking forward so much to having it," she said.

"Yes, of course," said Bertie.

He was a bachelor, three or four years older than Isabel. He lived in beautiful rooms overlooking the river, guarded by a faithful Scottish manservant. And he had his friends among the fair sex—not lovers, friends. So long as he could avoid any danger of courtship or marriage, he adored a few good women with constant and unfailing homage, and he was chivalrously fond of quite a number. But if they seemed to encroach on him, he withdrew and detested them.

Isabel knew him very well, knew his beautiful constancy, and kindness, also his incurable weakness, which made him unable ever to enter into close contact of any sort. He was ashamed of himself because he could not marry, could not approach women physically. He wanted to do so. But he could not. At the centre of him he was afraid, helplessly and even brutally afraid. He had given up hope, had ceased to expect any more that he could escape his own weakness. Hence he was a brilliant and successful barrister, also a litterateur of high repute, a rich man, and a great social success. At the centre he felt himself neuter, nothing.

Isabel knew him well. She despised him even while she admired him. She looked at his sad face, his little short legs, and felt contempt of him. She looked at his dark grey eyes, with their uncanny, almost childlike, intuition, and she loved him. He understood amazingly—but she had no fear of his understanding. As a man she patronized him.

And she turned to the impassive, silent figure of her husband. He sat leaning back, with folded arms, and face a little uptilted. His knees were straight and massive. She sighed, picked up the poker, and again began to prod the fire, to rouse the clouds of soft brilliant sparks.

"Isabel tells me," Bertie began suddenly, "that you have not suffered unbearably from the loss of sight."

Maurice straightened himself to attend but kept his arms folded.

"No," he said, "not unbearably. Now and again one struggles against it, you know. But there are compensations."

"They say it is much worse to be stone deaf," said Isabel.

"I believe it is," said Bertie. "Are there compensations?" he added to Maurice.

"Yes. You cease to bother about a great many things." Again Maurice stretched his figure, stretched the strong muscles of his back, and leaned backwards, with uplifted face.

"And that is a relief," said Bertie. "But what is there in place of the bothering? What replaces the activity?"

There was a pause. At length the blind man replied, as out of a negligent, unattentive thinking:

"Oh, I don't know. There's a good deal when you're not active."

"Is there?" said Bertie. "What exactly? It always seems to me that when there is no thought and no action, there is nothing."

Again Maurice was slow in replying.

"There is something," he replied. "I couldn't tell you what it is."

And the talk lapsed once more, Isabel and Bertie chatting gossip and reminiscence, the blind man silent.

At length Maurice rose restlessly, a big obtrusive figure. He felt tight and hampered. He wanted to go away.

"Do you mind," he said, "if I go and speak to Wernham?"

"No—go along, dear," said Isabel.

And he went out. A silence came over the two friends. At length Bertie said:

"Nevertheless, it is a great deprivation, Cissie."

"It is, Bertie. I know it is."

"Something lacking all the time," said Bertie.

"Yes, I know. And yet—and yet—Maurice is right. There is something else, something there, which you never knew was there, and which you can't express."

"What is there?" asked Bertie.

"I don't know—it's awfully hard to define it—but something strong and immediate. There's something strange in Maurice's presence—indefinable—but I couldn't do without it. I agree that it seems to put one's mind to sleep. But when we're alone I miss nothing; it seems awfully rich, almost splendid, you know."

"I'm afraid I don't follow," said Bertie.

They talked desultorily. The wind blew loudly outside, rain chattered on the window-panes, making a sharp drum-sound because of the closed, mellow-golden shutters inside. The logs burned slowly, with hot, almost invisible small flames. Bertie seemed uneasy, there were dark circles round his eyes. Isabel, rich with her approaching maternity, leaned looking into the fire. Her hair curled in odd, loose strands, very pleasing to the man. But she had a curious feeling of old woe in her heart, old timeless night-woe.

"I suppose we're all deficient somewhere," said Bertie.

"I suppose so," said Isabel wearily.

"Damned, sooner or later."

"I don't know," she said, rousing herself. "I feel quite all right, you know. The child coming seems to make me indifferent to everything, just placid. I can't feel that there's anything to trouble about, you know."

"A good thing, I should say," he replied slowly.

"Well, there it is. I suppose it's just Nature. If only I felt I needn't trouble about Maurice, I should be perfectly content—"

"But you feel you must trouble about him?"

"Well—I don't know—" She even resented this much effort.

The night passed slowly. Isabel looked at the clock. "I say," she said. "It's nearly ten o'clock. Where can Maurice be? I'm sure they're all in bed at the back. Excuse me a moment."

She went out, returning almost immediately.

"It's all shut up and in darkness," she said. "I wonder where he is. He must have gone out to the farm—"

Bertie looked at her.

"I suppose he'll come in," he said.

"I suppose so," she said. "But it's unusual for him to be out now."

"Would you like me to go out and see?"

"Well—if you wouldn't mind. I'd go, but—" She did not want to make the physical effort.

Bertie put on an old overcoat and took a lantern. He went out from the side door. He shrank from the wet and roaring night. Such weather had a nervous effect on him: too much moisture everywhere made him feel almost imbecile. Unwilling, he went through it all. A dog barked violently at him. He peered in all the buildings. At last, as he opened the upper door of a sort of intermediate barn, he heard a grinding noise, and looking in, holding up his lantern, saw Maurice, in his shirtsleeves, standing listening, holding the handle of a turnip-pulper. He had been pulping sweet roots, a pile of which lay dimly heaped in a corner behind him.

"That you, Wernham?" said Maurice, listening.

"No, it's me," said Bertie.

A large, half-wild grey cat was rubbing at Maurice's leg. The blind man stooped to rub its sides. Bertie watched the scene, then unconsciously entered and shut the door behind him. He was in a high sort of barn-place, from which, right and left, ran off the corridors in front of the stalled cattle. He watched the slow, stooping motion of the other man, as he caressed the great cat.

Maurice straightened himself.

"You came to look for me?" he said.

"Isabel was a little uneasy," said Bertie.

"I'll come in. I like messing about doing these jobs."

The cat had reared her sinister, feline length against his leg, clawing at his thigh affectionately. He lifted her claws out of his flesh.

"I hope I'm not in your way at all at the Grange here," said Bertie, rather shy and stiff.

"My way? No, not a bit. I'm glad Isabel has somebody to talk to. I'm afraid it's I who am in the way. I know I'm not very lively company. Isabel's all right, don't you think? She's not unhappy, is she?"

"I don't think so."

"What does she say?"

"She says she's very content—only a little troubled about you."

"Why me?"

"Perhaps afraid that you might brood," said Bertie, cautiously.

"She needn't be afraid of that." He continued to caress the flattened grey head of the cat with his fingers. "What I am a bit afraid of," he resumed, "is that she'll find me a dead weight, always alone with me down here."

"I don't think you need think that," said Bertie, though this was what he feared himself.

"I don't know," said Maurice. "Sometimes I feel it isn't fair that she's saddled with me." Then he dropped his voice curiously. "I say," he asked, secretly struggling, "is my face much disfigured? Do you mind telling me?"

"There is the scar," said Bertie, wondering. "Yes, it is a disfigurement. But more pitiable than shocking."

"A pretty bad scar, though," said Maurice.

"Oh, yes."

There was a pause.

"Sometimes I feel I am horrible," said Maurice, in a low voice, talking as if to himself. And Bertie actually felt a quiver of horror.

"That's nonsense," he said.

Maurice again straightened himself, leaving the cat.

"There's no telling," he said. Then again, in an odd tone, he added: "I don't really know you, do I?"

"Probably not," said Bertie.

"Do you mind if I touch you?"

The lawyer shrank away instinctively. And yet, out of very philanthropy, he said, in a small voice: "Not at all."

But he suffered as the blind man stretched out a strong, naked hand to him. Maurice accidentally knocked off Bertie's hat.

"I thought you were taller," he said, starting. Then he laid his hand on Bertie Reid's head, closing the dome of the skull in a soft, firm grasp, gathering it, as it were; then, shifting his grasp and softly closing again, with a fine, close pressure, till he had covered the skull and the face of the smaller man, tracing the brows, and touching the full, closed eyes, touching the small nose and the nostrils, the rough, short moustache, the mouth, the rather strong chin. The hand of the blind man grasped the shoulder, the arm, the hand of the other man. He seemed to take him, in the soft, travelling grasp.

"You seem young," he said quietly, at last.

The lawyer stood almost annihilated, unable to answer.

"Your head seems tender, as if you were young," Maurice repeated. "So do your hands. Touch my eyes, will you?—touch my scar."

Now Bertie quivered with revulsion. Yet he was under the power of the blind man, as if hypnotized. He lifted his hand, and laid the fingers on the scar, on the scarred eyes. Maurice suddenly covered them with his own hand, pressed the fingers of the other man upon his disfigured eye-sockets, trembling in every fibre, and rocking slightly, slowly, from side to side. He remained thus for a minute or more, whilst Bertie stood as if in a swoon, unconscious, imprisoned.

Then suddenly Maurice removed the hand of the other man from his brow, and stood holding it in his own.

"Oh, my God," he said, "we shall know each other now, shan't we? We shall know each other now."

Bertie could not answer. He gazed mute and terrorstruck, overcome by his own weakness. He knew he could not answer. He had an unreasonable fear lest the other man should suddenly destroy him. Whereas Maurice was actually filled with hot, poignant love, the passion of friendship. Perhaps it was this very passion of friendship which Bertie shrank from most.

"We're all right together now, aren't we?" said Maurice. "It's all right now, as long as we live, so far as we're concerned?"

"Yes," said Bertie, trying by any means to escape.

Maurice stood with head lifted, as if listening. The new delicate fulfilment of mortal friendship had come as a revelation and surprise to him, something exquisite and unhoped-for. He seemed to be listening to hear if it were real.

Then he turned for his coat.

"Come," he said, "we'll go to Isabel."

Bertie took the lantern and opened the door. The cat disappeared. The two men went in silence along the causeways. Isabel, as they came, thought their footsteps sounded strange. She looked up pathetically and anxiously for their entrance. There seemed a curious elation about Maurice. Bertie was haggard, with sunken eyes.

"What is it?" she asked.

"We've become friends," said Maurice, standing with his feet apart, like a strange colossus.

"Friends!" re-echoed Isabel. And she looked again at Bertie. He met her eyes with a furtive, haggard look; his eyes were as if glazed with misery.

"I'm so glad," she said, in sheer perplexity.

"Yes," said Maurice.

He was indeed so glad. Isabel took his hand with both hers, and held it fast.

"You'll be happier now, dear," she said.

But she was watching Bertie. She knew that he had one desire—to escape from this intimacy, this friendship, which had been thrust upon him. He could not bear it that he had been touched by the blind man, his insane reserve broken in. He was like a mollusc whose shell is broken.

(1922)

The Horse Dealer's Daughter

"Well, Mabel, and what are you going to do with yourself?" asked Joe, with foolish flippancy. He felt quite safe himself. Without listening for an answer, he turned aside, worked a grain of tobacco to the tip of his tongue, and spat it out. He did not care about anything, since he felt safe himself.

The three brothers and the sister sat round the desolate breakfast-table, attempting some sort of desultory consultation. The morning's post had given the final tap to the family fortunes, and all was over. The dreary dining-room itself, with its heavy mahogany furniture, looked as if it were waiting to be done away with.

But the consultation amounted to nothing. There was a strange air of ineffectuality about the three men, as they sprawled at table, smoking and reflecting vaguely on their own condition. The girl was alone, a rather short, sullen-looking young woman of twenty-seven. She did not share the same life as her brothers. She would have been good-looking, save for the impressive fixity of her face, "bull-dog," as her brothers called it.

There was a confused tramping of horses' feet outside. The three men all sprawled round in their chairs to watch. Beyond the dark holly bushes that separated the strip of lawn from the high-road, they could see a cavalcade of shire horses swinging out of their own yard, being taken for exercise. This was the last time. These were the last horses that would go through their hands. The young men watched with critical, callous look. They were all frightened at the collapse of their lives, and the sense of disaster in which they were involved left them no inner freedom.

Yet they were three fine, well-set fellows enough. Joe, the eldest, was a man of thirty-three, broad and handsome in a hot, flushed way. His face was red, he twisted his black mustache over a thick finger, his eyes were shallow and restless. He had a sensual way of uncovering his teeth when he laughed, and his bearing was stupid. Now he watched the horses with a glazed look of helplessness in his eyes, a certain stupor of downfall.

The great draft-horses swung past. They were tied head to tail, four of them, and they heaved along to where a lane branched off from the high-road, planting their great hoofs floutingly in the fine black mud, swinging their great rounded haunches sumptuously, and trotting a few sudden steps as they were led into the lane, round the corner. Every movement showed a massive, slumbrous strength, and a stupidity which held them in subjection. The groom at the head looked back, jerking the leading rope. And the cavalcade moved out of sight up the lane, the tail of the last horse, bobbed up tight and stiff, held out taut from the swinging great haunches as they rocked behind the hedges in a motionlike sleep.

Joe watched with glazed hopeless eyes. The horses were almost like his own body to him. He felt he was done for now. Luckily he was engaged to a woman as old as himself, and therefore her father, who was steward of a neighboring estate, would provide him with a job. He would marry and go into harness. His life was over, he would be a subject animal now.

He turned uneasily aside, the retreating steps of the horses echoing in his ears. Then, with foolish restlessness, he reached for the scraps of bacon-rind from the plates, and making a faint whistling sound, flung them to the terrier that lay against the fender. He watched the dog swallow them, and waited till the creature looked into his eyes. Then a faint grin came on his face, and in a high, foolish voice he said:

"You won't get much more bacon, shall you, you little b——?"

The dog faintly and dismally wagged its tail, then lowered its haunches, circled round, and lay down again.

There was another helpless silence at the table. Joe sprawled uneasily in his seat, not willing to go till the family conclave was dissolved. Fred Henry, the second brother, was erect, clean-limbed, alert. He had watched the passing of the horses with more *sang-froid.*° If he was an animal, like Joe, he was an animal which controls, not one which is controlled. He was master of any horse, and he carried himself with a well-tempered air of mastery. But he was not master of the situations of life. He pushed his coarse brown mustache upwards, off his lip, and glanced irritably at his sister, who sat impassive and inscrutable.

"You'll go and stop with Lucy for a bit, shan't you?" he asked. The girl did not answer.

"I don't see what else you can do," persisted Fred Henry.

"Go as a skivvy,"° Joe interpolated laconically.

The girl did not move a muscle.

"If I was her, I should go in for training for a nurse," said Malcolm, the youngest of them all. He was the baby of the family, a young man of twenty-two, with a fresh, jaunty *museau.*°

But Mabel did not take any notice of him. They had talked at her and round her for so many years, that she hardly heard them at all.

The marble clock on the mantelpiece softly chimed the half-hour, the dog rose uneasily from the hearth-rug and looked at the party at the breakfast-table. But still they sat on in ineffectual conclave.

"Oh, all right," said Joe suddenly, apropos of nothing. "I'll get a move on."

He pushed back his chair, straddled his knees with a downward jerk, to get them free, in horsey fashion, and went to the fire. Still he did not go out of the room; he was curious to know what the others would do or say. He began to charge his pipe, looking down at the dog and saying in a high, affected voice:

"Going wi' me? Going wi' me are ter? Tha'rt goin' further than tha counts on just now, dost hear?"

The dog faintly wagged its tail, the man stuck out his jaw and covered his pipe with his hands, and puffed intently, losing himself in the tobacco, looking down all the while at the dog with an absent brown eye. The dog looked up at him in mournful distrust. Joe stood with his knees stuck out, in real horsey fashion.

"Have you had a letter from Lucy?" Fred Henry asked of his sister.

"Last week," came the neutral reply.

"And what does she say?"

There was no answer.

"Does she *ask* you to go and stop there?" persisted Fred Henry.

"She says I can if I like."

"Well, then, you'd better. Tell her you'll come on Monday."

This was received in silence.

"That's what you'll do then, is it?" said Fred Henry, in some exasperation.

But she made no answer. There was a silence of futility and irritation in the room. Malcolm grinned fatuously.

"You'll have to make up your mind between now and next Wednesday," said Joe loudly, "or else find yourself lodgings on the curbstone."

The face of the young woman darkened, but she sat on immutable.

"Here's Jack Fergusson!" exclaimed Malcolm, who was looking aimlessly out of the window.

sang-froid *coolness, composure*   **skivvy** *domestic worker*   **museau** *slang for face*

"Where?" exclaimed Joe loudly.

"Just gone past."

"Coming in?"

Malcolm craned his neck to see the gate.

"Yes," he said.

There was a silence. Mabel sat on like one condemned, at the head of the table. Then a whistle was heard from the kitchen. The dog got up and barked sharply. Joe opened the door and shouted:

"Come on."

After a moment a young man entered. He was muffled up in overcoat and a purple woolen scarf, and his tweed cap, which he did not remove, was pulled down on his head. He was of medium height, his face was rather long and pale, his eyes looked tired.

"Hello, Jack! Well, Jack!" exclaimed Malcolm and Joe. Fred Henry merely said: "Jack."

"What's doing?" asked the newcomer, evidently addressing Fred Henry.

"Same. We've got to be out by Wednesday. Got a cold?"

"I have—got it bad, too."

"Why don't you stop in?"

"*Me* stop in? When I can't stand on my legs, perhaps I shall have a chance," the young man spoke huskily. He had a slight Scotch accent.

"It's a knock-out, isn't it," said Joe, boisterously, "if a doctor goes round croaking with a cold. Looks bad for the patients, doesn't it?"

The young doctor looked at him slowly.

"Anything the matter with *you,* then?" he asked sarcastically.

"Not as I know of. Damn your eyes, hope not. Why?"

"I thought you were very concerned about the patients, wondered if you might be one yourself."

"Damn it, no, I've never been patient to no flaming doctor, and hope I never shall be," returned Joe.

At this point Mabel rose from the table, and they all seemed to become aware of her existence. She began putting the dishes together. The young doctor looked at her, but did not address her. He had not greeted her. She went out of the room with the tray, her face impassive and unchanged.

"When are you off then, all of you?" asked the doctor.

"I'm catching the eleven-forty," replied Malcolm. "Are you goin' down wi' th' trap,° Joe?"

"Yes, I've told you I'm going down wi' th' trap, haven't I?"

"We'd better be getting her in then. So long, Jack, if I don't see you before I go," said Malcolm, shaking hands.

He went out, followed by Joe, who seemed to have his tail between his legs.

"Well, this is the devil's own," exclaimed the doctor, when he was left alone with Fred Henry. "Going before Wednesday, are you?"

"That's the orders," replied the other.

"Where, to Northampton?"

"That's it."

trap   *a light two-wheeled carriage*

"The devil!" exclaimed Fergusson, with quiet chagrin.

And there was silence between the two.

"All settled up, are you?" asked Fergusson.

"About."

There was another pause.

"Well, I shall miss yer, Freddy, boy," said the young doctor.

"And I shall miss thee, Jack," returned the other.

"Miss you like hell," mused the doctor.

Fred Henry turned aside. There was nothing to say. Mabel came in again, to finish clearing the table.

"What are *you* going to do, then, Miss Pervin?" asked Fergusson. "Going to your sister's, are you?"

Mabel looked at him with her steady, dangerous eyes, that always made him uncomfortable, unsettling his superficial ease.

"No," she said.

"Well, what in the name of fortune *are* you going to do? Say what you mean to do," cried Fred Henry, with futile intensity.

But she only averted her head, and continued her work. She folded the white tablecloth, and put on the chenille cloth.

"The sulkiest bitch that ever trod!" muttered her brother.

But she finished her task with perfectly impassive face, the young doctor watching her interestedly all the while. Then she went out.

Fred Henry stared after her, clenching his lips, his blue eyes fixing in sharp antagonism, as he made a grimace of sour exasperation.

"You could bray her into bits, and that's all you'd get out of her," he said, in a small, narrowed tone.

The doctor smiled faintly.

"What's she *going* to do, then?" he asked.

"Strike me if *I* know!" returned the other.

There was a pause. Then the doctor stirred.

"I'll be seeing you tonight, shall I?" he said to his friend.

"Ay—where's it to be? Are we going over to Jessdale?"

"I don't know. I've got such a cold on me. I'll come round to the 'Moon and Stars,' anyway."

"Let Lizzie and May miss their night for once, eh?"

"That's it—if I feel as I do now."

"All's one ——"

The two young men went through the passage and down to the back door together. The house was large, but it was servantless now, and desolate. At the back was a small bricked houseyard and beyond that a big square, graveled fine and red, and having stables on two sides. Sloping, dank, winter-dark fields stretched away on the open sides.

But the stables were empty. Joseph Pervin, the father of the family, had been a man of no education, who had become a fairly large horse dealer. The stables had been full of horses, there was a great turmoil and come-and-go of horses and of dealers and grooms. Then the kitchen was full of servants. But of late things had declined. The old man had married a second time, to retrieve his fortunes. Now he was dead and everything was gone to the dogs, there was nothing but debt and threatening.

For months, Mabel had been servantless in the big house, keeping the home together in penury for her ineffectual brothers. She had kept house for ten years. But previously it was with unstinted means. Then, however brutal and coarse everything was, the sense of money had kept her proud, confident. The men might be foul-mouthed, the women in the kitchen might have bad reputations, her brothers might have illegitimate children. But so long as there was money, the girl felt herself established, and brutally proud, reserved.

No company came to the house, save dealers and coarse men. Mabel had no associates of her own sex, after her sister went away. But she did not mind. She went regularly to church, she attended to her father. And she lived in the memory of her mother, who had died when she was fourteen, and whom she had loved. She had loved her father, too, in a different way, depending upon him, and feeling secure in him, until at the age of fifty-four he married again. And then she had set hard against him. Now he had died and left them all hopelessly in debt.

She had suffered badly during the period of poverty. Nothing, however, could shake the curious, sullen, animal pride that dominated each member of the family. Now, for Mabel, the end had come. Still she would not cast about her. She would follow her own way just the same. She would always hold the keys of her own situation. Mindless and persistent, she endured from day to day. Why should she think? Why should she answer anybody? It was enough that this was the end, and there was no way out. She need not pass any more darkly along the main street of the small town, avoiding every eye. She need not demean herself any more, going into the shops and buying the cheapest food. This was at an end. She thought of nobody, not even of herself. Mindless and persistent, she seemed in a sort of ecstasy to be coming nearer to her fulfillment, her own glorification, approaching her dead mother, who was glorified.

In the afternoon she took a little bag, with shears and sponge and a small scrubbing-brush, and went out. It was a gray, wintry day, with saddened, dark green fields and an atmosphere blackened by the smoke of foundries not far off. She went quickly, darkly along the causeway, heeding nobody, through the town to the churchyard.

There she always felt secure, as if no one could see her, although as a matter of fact she was exposed to the stare of everyone who passed along under the churchyard wall. Nevertheless, once under the shadow of the great looming church, among the graves, she felt immune from the world, reserved within the thick churchyard wall as in another country.

Carefully she clipped the grass from the grave, and arranged the pinky white, small chrysanthemums in the tin cross. When this was done, she took an empty jar from a neighboring grave, brought water, and carefully, most scrupulously sponged the marble headstone and the coping-stone.

It gave her sincere satisfaction to do this. She felt in immediate contact with the world of her mother. She took minute pains, went through the park in a state bordering on pure happiness, as if in performing this task she came into a subtle, intimate connection with her mother. For the life she followed here in the world was far less real than the world of death she inherited from her mother.

The doctor's house was just by the church. Fergusson, being a mere hired assistant, was slave to the countryside. As he hurried now to attend to the outpatients in the surgery, glancing across the graveyard with his quick eye, he saw the girl at her task at the grave. She seemed so intent and remote, it was like looking into another world.

Some mystical element was touching in him. He slowed down as he walked, watching her as if spellbound.

She lifted her eyes, feeling him looking. Their eyes met. And each looked again at once, each feeling, in some way, found out by the other. He lifted his cap and passed on down the road. There remained distinct in his consciousness, like a vision, the memory of her face, lifted from the tombstone in the churchyard, and looking at him with slow, large, portentous eyes. It *was* portentous, her face. It seemed to mesmerize him. There was a heavy power in her eyes which laid hold of his whole being, as if he had drunk some powerful drug. He had been feeling weak and done before. Now the life came back into him, he felt delivered from his own fretted, daily self.

He finished his duties at the surgery as quickly as might be, hastily filling up the bottles of the waiting people with cheap drugs. Then, in perpetual haste, he set off again to visit several cases in another part of his round, before teatime. At all times he preferred to walk if he could, but particularly when he was not well. He fancied the motion restored him.

The afternoon was falling. It was gray, deadened, and wintry, with a slow, moist, heavy coldness sinking in and deadening all the faculties. But why should he think or notice? He hastily climbed the hill and turned across the dark green fields, following the black cinder-track. In the distance, across a shallow dip in the country, the small town was clustered like smoldering ash, a tower, a spire, a heap of low, raw, extinct houses. And on the nearest fringe of the town, sloping into the dip, was Oldmeadow, the Pervins' house. He could see the stables and the outbuildings distinctly, as they lay towards him on the slope. Well, he would not go there many more times! Another resource would be lost to him, another place gone: the only company he cared for in the alien, ugly little town he was losing. Nothing but work, drudgery, constant hastening from dwelling to dwelling among the colliers and the iron-workers. It wore him out, but at the same time he had a craving for it. It was a stimulant to him to be in the homes of the working people, moving, as it were, through the innermost body of their life. His nerves were excited and gratified. He could come so near, into the very lives of the rough, inarticulate, powerful emotional men and women: He grumbled, he said he hated the hellish hole. But as a matter of fact it excited him, the contact with the rough, strongly-feeling people was a stimulant applied direct to his nerves.

Below Oldmeadow, in the green, shallow, soddened hollow of fields, lay a square, deep pond. Roving across the landscape, the doctor's quick eye detected a figure in black passing through the gate of the field, down towards the pond. He looked again. It would be Mabel Pervin. His mind suddenly became alive and attentive.

Why was she going down there? He pulled up on the path on the slope above, and stood staring. He could just make sure of the small black figure moving in the hollow of the failing day. He seemed to see her in the midst of such obscurity, that he was like a clairvoyant, seeing rather with the mind's eye than with ordinary sight. Yet he could see her positively enough, whilst he kept his eye attentive. He felt, if he looked away from her, in the thick, ugly falling dusk, he would lose her altogether.

He followed her minutely as she moved, direct and intent, like something transmitted rather than stirring in voluntary activity, straight down from the field towards the pond. There she stood on the bank for a moment. She never raised her head. Then she waded slowly into the water.

He stood motionless as the small black figure walked slowly and deliberately towards the center of the pond, very slowly, gradually moving deeper into the motionless water, and still moving forward as the water got up to her breast. Then he could see her no more in the dusk of the dead afternoon.

"There!" he exclaimed. "Would you believe it?"

And he hastened straight down, running over the wet, soddened fields, pushing through the hedges, down into the depression of callous wintry obscurity. It took him several minutes to come to the pond. He stood on the bank, breathing heavily. He could see nothing. His eyes seemed to penetrate the dead water. Yes, perhaps that was the dark shadow of her black clothing beneath the surface of the water.

He slowly ventured into the pond. The bottom was deep, soft clay, he sank in, and the water clasped dead cold round his legs. As he stirred he could smell the cold, rotten clay that fouled up into the water. It was objectionable in his lungs. Still, repelled and yet not heeding, he moved deeper into the pond. The cold water rose over his thighs, over his loins, upon his abdomen. The lower part of his body was all sunk in the hideous cold element. And the bottom was so deeply soft and uncertain, he was afraid of pitching with his mouth underneath. He could not swim, and was afraid.

He crouched a little, spreading his hands under the water and moving them round, trying to feel for her. The dead cold pond swayed upon his chest. He moved again, a little deeper, and again, with his hands underneath, he felt all around under the water. And he touched her clothing. But it evaded his fingers. He made a desperate effort to grasp it.

And so doing he lost his balance and went under, horribly, suffocating in the foul earthy water, struggling madly for a few moments. At last, after what seemed an eternity, he got his footing, rose again into the air, and looked around. He gasped, and knew he was in the world. Then he looked at the water. She had risen near him. He grasped her clothing, and drawing her nearer, turned to take his way to land again.

He went very slowly, carefully, absorbed in the slow progress. He rose higher, climbing out of the pond. The water was now only about his legs; he was thankful, full of relief to be out of the clutches of the pond. He lifted her and staggered on to the bank, out of the horror of wet, gray clay.

He laid her down on the bank. She was quite unconscious and running with water. He made the water come from her mouth, he worked to restore her. He did not have to work very long before he could feel the breathing begin again in her; she was breathing naturally. He worked a little longer. He could feel her live beneath his hands; she was coming back. He wiped her face, wrapped her in his overcoat, looked round into the dim, dark gray world, then lifted her and staggered down the bank and across the fields.

It seemed an unthinkably long way, and his burden so heavy he felt he would never get to the house. But at last he was in the stable-yard, and then in the house-yard. He opened the door and went into the house. In the kitchen he laid her down on the hearth-rug and called. The house was empty. But the fire was burning in the grate.

Then again he kneeled to attend to her. She was breathing regularly, her eyes were wide open and as if conscious, but there seemed something missing in her look. She was conscious in herself, but unconscious of her surroundings.

He ran upstairs, took blankets from a bed, and put them before the fire to warm. Then he removed her saturated, earthy-smelling clothing, rubbed her dry with a towel, and wrapped her naked in the blankets. Then he went into the dining-room, to look for spirits. There was a little whiskey. He drank a gulp himself, and put some into her mouth.

The effect was instantaneous. She looked full into his face, as if she had been seeing him for some time, and yet had only just become conscious of him.

"Dr. Fergusson?" she said.

"What?" he answered.

He was divesting himself of his coat, intending to find some dry clothing upstairs. He could not bear the smell of the dead, clayey water, and he was mortally afraid for his own health.

"What did I do?" she asked.

"Walked into the pond," he replied. He had begun to shudder like one sick, and could hardly attend to her. Her eyes remained full on him, he seemed to be going dark in his mind, looking back at her helplessly. The shuddering became quieter in him, his life came back to him, dark and unknowing, but strong again.

"Was I out of my mind?" she asked, while her eyes were fixed on him all the time.

"Maybe, for the moment," he replied. He felt quiet, because his strength had come back. The strange fretful strain had left him.

"Am I out of my mind now?" she asked.

"Are you?" he reflected a moment. "No," he answered truthfully, "I don't see that you are." He turned his face aside. He was afraid now, because he felt dazed, and felt dimly that her power was stronger than his, in this issue. And she continued to look at him fixedly all the time. "Can you tell me where I shall find some dry things to put on?" he asked.

"Did you dive into the pond for me?" she asked.

"No," he answered. "I walked in. But I went in overhead as well."

There was silence for a moment. He hesitated. He very much wanted to go upstairs to get into dry clothing. But there was another desire in him. And she seemed to hold him. His will seemed to have gone to sleep, and left him, standing there slack before her. But he felt warm inside himself. He did not shudder at all, though his clothes were sodden on him.

"Why did you?" she asked.

"Because I didn't want you to do such a foolish thing," he said.

"It wasn't foolish," she said, still gazing at him as she lay on the floor, with a sofa cushion under her head. "It was the right thing to do. *I* knew best, then."

"I'll go and shift these wet things," he said. But still he had not the power to move out of her presence, until she sent him. It was as if she had the life of his body in her hands, and he could not extricate himself. Or perhaps he did not want to.

Suddenly she sat up. Then she became aware of her own immediate condition. She felt the blankets about her, she knew her own limbs. For a moment it seemed as if her reason were going. She looked round, with wild eye, as if seeking something. He stood still with fear. She saw her clothing lying scattered.

"Who undressed me?" she asked, her eyes resting full and inevitable on his face.

"I did," he replied, "to bring you round."

For some moments she sat and gazed at him, awfully, her lips parted.

"Do you love me, then?" she asked.

He only stood and stared at her, fascinated. His soul seemed to melt.

She shuffled forward on her knees, and put her arms round him, round his legs, as he stood there, pressing her breasts against his knees and thighs, clutching him with strange, convulsive certainty, pressing his thighs against her, drawing him to her face, her throat, as she looked up at him with flaring, humble eyes of transfiguration, triumphant in first possession.

"You love me," she murmured, in strange transport, yearning and triumphant and confident. "You love me. I know you love me, I know."

And she was passionately kissing his knees, through the wet clothing, passionately and indiscriminately kissing his knees, his legs, as if unaware of everything.

He looked down at the tangled wet hair, the wild, bare, animal shoulders. He was amazed, bewildered, and afraid. He had never thought of loving her. He had never wanted to love her. When he rescued her and restored her, he was a doctor, and she was a patient. He had had no single personal thought of her. Nay, this introduction of the personal element was very distasteful to him, a violation of his professional honor. It was horrible to have her there embracing his knees. It was horrible. He revolted from it, violently. And yet—and yet—he had not the power to break away.

She looked at him again, with the same supplication of powerful love, and that same transcendent, frightening light of triumph. In view of the delicate flame which seemed to come from her face like a light, he was powerless. And yet he had never intended to love her. He had never intended. And something stubborn in him could not give way.

"You love me," she repeated, in a murmur of deep, rhapsodic assurance. "You love me."

Her hands were drawing him, drawing him down to her. He was afraid, even a little horrified. For he had, really, no intention of loving her. Yet her hands were drawing him towards her. He put out his hand quickly to steady himself, and grasped her bare shoulder. A flame seemed to burn the hand that grasped her soft shoulder. He had no intention of loving her: his whole will was against his yielding. It was horrible. And yet wonderful was the touch of her shoulders, beautiful the shining of her face. Was she perhaps mad? He had a horror of yielding to her. Yet something in him ached also.

He had been staring away at the door, away from her. But his hand remained on her shoulder. She had gone suddenly very still. He looked down at her. Her eyes were now wide with fear, with doubt, the light was dying from her face, a shadow of terrible grayness was returning. He could not bear the touch of her eyes' question upon him, and the look of death behind the question.

With an inward groan he gave way, and let his heart yield towards her. A sudden gentle smile came on his face. And her eyes, which never left his face, slowly, slowly filled with tears. He watched the strange water rise in her eyes, like some slow fountain coming up. And his heart seemed to burn and melt away in his breast.

He could not bear to look at her any more. He dropped on his knees and caught her head with his arms and pressed her face against his throat. She was very still. His heart, which seemed to have broken, was burning with a kind of agony in his breast. And he felt her slow, hot tears wetting his throat. But he could not move.

He felt the hot tears wet his neck and the hollows of his neck, and he remained motionless, suspended through one of man's eternities. Only now it had become indispensable to him to have her face pressed close to him; he could never let her go again. He could never let her head go away from the close clutch of his arm. He wanted to remain like that for ever, with his heart hurting him in a pain that was also life to him. Without knowing, he was looking down on her damp, soft brown hair.

Then, as it were suddenly, he smelt the horrid stagnant smell of that water. And at the same moment she drew away from him and looked at him. Her eyes were wistful and unfathomable. He was afraid of them, and he fell to kissing her, not knowing what he was doing. He wanted her eyes not to have that terrible, wistful, unfathomable look.

When she turned her face to him again, a faint delicate flush was glowing, and there was again dawning that terrible shining of joy in her eyes, which really terrified him, and yet which he now wanted to see, because he feared the look of doubt still more.

"You love me?" she said, rather faltering.

"Yes." The word cost him a painful effort. Not because it wasn't true. But because it was too newly true, the *saying* seemed to tear open again his newly-torn heart. And he hardly wanted it to be true, even now.

She lifted her face to him, and he bent forward and kissed her on the mouth, gently, with the one kiss that is an eternal pledge. And as he kissed her his heart strained again in his breast. He never intended to love her. But now it was over. He had crossed over the gulf to her, and all that he had left behind had shriveled and become void.

After the kiss, her eyes again slowly filled with tears. She sat still, away from him, with her face drooped aside, and her hands folded in her lap. The tears fell very slowly. There was complete silence. He too sat there motionless and silent on the hearth-rug. The strange pain of his heart that was broken seemed to consume him. That he should love her? That this was love! That he should be ripped open in this way! Him, a doctor! How they would all jeer if they knew! It was agony to him to think they might know.

In the curious naked pain of the thought he looked again to her. She was still sitting there drooped into a muse. He saw a tear fall, and his heart flared hot. He saw for the first time that one of her shoulders was quite uncovered, one arm bare, he could see one of her small breasts; dimly, because it had become almost dark in the room.

"Why are you crying?" he asked, in an altered voice.

She looked up at him, and behind her tears the consciousness of her situation for the first time brought a dark look of shame to her eyes.

"I'm not crying, really," she said, watching him, half frightened.

He reached his hand, and softly closed it on her bare arm.

"I love you! I love you!" he said in a soft, low vibrating voice, unlike himself.

She shrank, and dropped her head. The soft, penetrating grip of his hand on her arm distressed her. She looked up at him.

"I want to go," she said. "I want to go and get you some dry things."

"Why?" he said. "I'm all right."

"But I want to go," she said. "And I want you to change your things."

He released her arm, and she wrapped herself in the blanket, looking at him rather frightened. And still she did not rise.

"Kiss me," she said wistfully.

He kissed her, but briefly, half in anger.

Then, after a second, she rose nervously, all mixed up in the blanket. He watched her in her confusion as she tried to extricate herself and wrap herself up so that she could walk. He watched her relentlessly, as she knew. And as she went, the blanket trailing, and as he saw a glimpse of her feet and her white leg, he tried to remember her as she was when he had wrapped her in the blanket. But then he didn't want to remember, because she had been nothing to him then, and his nature revolted from remembering her as she was when she was nothing to him.

A tumbling, muffled noise from within the dark house startled him. Then he heard her voice: "There are clothes." He rose and went to the foot of the stairs, and gathered up the garments she had thrown down. Then he came back to the fire, to rub himself down and dress. He grinned at his own appearance when he had finished.

The fire was sinking, so he put on coal. The house was now quite dark, save for the light of a street-lamp that shone in faintly from beyond the holly trees. He lit the gas with matches he found on the mantelpiece. Then he emptied the pockets of his own clothes, and threw all his wet things in a heap into the scullery. After which he gathered up her sodden clothes, gently, and put them in a separate heap on the copper-top in the scullery.

It was six o'clock on the clock. His own watch had stopped. He ought to go back to the surgery. He waited, and still she did not come down. So he went to the foot of the stairs and called:

"I shall have to go."

Almost immediately he heard her coming down. She had on her best dress of black voile, and her hair was tidy, but still damp. She looked at him—and in spite of herself, smiled.

"I don't like you in those clothes," she said.

"Do I look a sight?" he answered.

They were shy of one another.

"I'll make you some tea," she said.

"No, I must go."

"Must you?" And she looked at him again with the wide, strained, doubtful eyes. And again, from the pain of his breast, he knew how he loved her. He went and bent to kiss her, gently, passionately, with his heart's painful kiss.

"And my hair smells so horrible," she murmured in distraction. "And I'm so awful, I'm so awful! Oh, no, I'm too awful." And she broke into bitter, heartbroken sobbing. "You can't want to love me, I'm horrible."

"Don't be silly, don't be silly," he said, trying to comfort her, kissing her, holding her in his arms. "I want you, I want to marry you, we're going to be married, quickly, quickly—tomorrow if I can."

But she only sobbed terribly, and cried:

"I feel awful. I feel awful. I feel I'm horrible to you."

"No, I want you, I want you," was all he answered, blindly, with that terrible intonation which frightened her almost more than her horror lest he should *not* want her.

(1922)

The Rocking-Horse Winner

There was a woman who was beautiful, who started with all the advantages, yet she had no luck. She married for love, and the love turned to dust. She had bonny children, yet she felt they had been thrust upon her, and she could not love them. They looked at her coldly, as if they were finding fault with her. And hurriedly she felt she must cover up some fault in herself. Yet what it was that she must cover up she never knew. Nevertheless, when her children were present, she always felt the center of her heart go hard. This troubled her, and in her manner she was all the more gentle and anxious for her children, as if she loved them very much. Only she herself knew that at the center of her heart was a hard little place that could not feel love, no, not for anybody. Everybody else said of her: "She is such a good mother. She adores her children." Only she herself, and her children themselves, knew it was not so. They read it in each other's eyes.

There were a boy and two little girls. They lived in a pleasant house, with a garden, and they had discreet servants, and felt themselves superior to anyone in the neighborhood.

Although they lived in style, they felt always an anxiety in the house. There was never enough money. The mother had a small income, and the father had a small income, but not nearly enough for the social position which they had to keep up. The father went into town to some office. But though he had good prospects, these prospects never materialized. There was always the grinding sense of the shortage of money, though the style was always kept up.

At last the mother said: "I will see if I can't make something." But she did not know where to begin. She racked her brains, and tried this thing and the other, but could not find anything successful. The failure made deep lines come into her face. Her children were growing up, they would have to go to school. There must be more money, there must be more money. The father, who was always very handsome and expensive in his tastes, seemed as if he never *would* be able to do anything worth doing. And the mother, who had a great belief in herself, did not succeed any better, and her tastes were just as expensive.

And so the house came to be haunted by the unspoken phrase: *There must be more money! There must be more money!* The children could hear it all the time though nobody said it aloud. They heard it at Christmas, when the expensive and splendid toys filled the nursery. Behind the shining modern rocking horse, behind the smart doll's house, a voice would start whispering: "There *must* be more money! There *must* be more money!" And the children would stop playing, to listen for a moment. They would look into each other's eyes, to see if they had all heard. And each one saw in the eyes of the other two that they too had heard. "There *must* be more money! There *must* be more money!"

It came whispering from the springs of the still-swaying rocking horse, and even the horse, bending his wooden, champing head, heard it. The big doll, sitting so pink and smirking in her new pram, could hear it quite plainly, and seemed to be smirking all the more self-consciously because of it. The foolish puppy, too, that took the place of the teddy bear, he was looking so extraordinarily foolish for no other reason but that he heard the secret whisper all over the house: "There *must* be more money!"

Yet nobody ever said it aloud. The whisper was everywhere, and therefore no one spoke it. Just as no one ever says: "We are breathing!" in spite of the fact that breath is coming and going all the time.

"Mother," said the boy Paul one day, "why don't we keep a car of our own? Why do we always use Uncle's, or else a taxi?"

"Because we're the poor members of the family," said the mother.

"But why *are* we, Mother?"

"Well—I suppose," she said slowly and bitterly, "it's because your father has no luck."

The boy was silent for some time.

"Is luck money, Mother?" he asked rather timidly.

"No, Paul. Not quite. It's what causes you to have money."

"Oh!" said Paul vaguely. "I thought when Uncle Oscar said *filthy lucker,* it meant money."

"*Filthy lucre* does mean money," said the mother. "But it's lucre, not luck."

"Oh!" said the boy. "Then what *is* luck, Mother?"

"It's what causes you to have money. If you're lucky you have money. That's why it's better to be born lucky than rich. If you're rich, you may lose your money. But if you're lucky, you will always get more money."

"Oh! Will you? And is Father not lucky?"

"Very unlucky, I should say," she said bitterly.

The boy watched her with unsure eyes.

"Why?" he asked.

"I don't know. Nobody ever knows why one person is lucky and another unlucky."

"Don't they? Nobody at all? Does *nobody* know?"

"Perhaps God. But He never tells."

"He ought to, then. And aren't you lucky either, Mother?"

"I can't be, if I married an unlucky husband."

"But by yourself, aren't you?"

"I used to think I was, before I married. Now I think I am very unlucky indeed."

"Why?"

"Well—never mind! Perhaps I'm not really," she said.

The child looked at her, to see if she meant it. But he saw, by the lines of her mouth, that she was only trying to hide something from him.

"Well, anyhow," he said stoutly, "I'm a lucky person."

"Why?" said his mother, with a sudden laugh.

He stared at her. He didn't even know why he had said it.

"God told me," he asserted, brazening it out.

"I hope He did, dear!" she said, again with a laugh, but rather bitter.

"He did, Mother!"

"Excellent!" said the mother.

The boy saw she did not believe him; or, rather, that she paid no attention to his assertion. This angered him somewhat, and made him want to compel her attention.

He went off by himself, vaguely, in a childish way, seeking for the clue to "luck." Absorbed, taking no heed of other people, he went about with a sort of stealth, seeking inwardly for luck. He wanted luck, he wanted it, he wanted it. When the two girls were playing dolls in the nursery, he would sit on his big rocking horse, charging madly into space, with a frenzy that made the little girls peer at him uneasily. Wildly the horse careered, the waving dark hair of the boy tossed, his eyes had a strange glare in them. The little girls dared not speak to him.

When he had ridden to the end of his mad little journey, he climbed down and stood in front of his rocking horse, staring fixedly into its lowered face. Its red mouth was slightly open, its big eye was wide and glassy-bright.

Now! he could silently command the snorting steed. Now, take me to where there is luck! Now take me!

And he would slash the horse on the neck with the little whip he had asked Uncle

Oscar for. He *knew* the horse could take him to where there was luck, if only he forced it. So he would mount again, and start on his furious ride, hoping at last to get there. He knew he could get there.

"You'll break your horse, Paul!" said the nurse.

"He's always riding like that! I wish he'd leave off!" said his elder sister Joan.

But he only glared down on them in silence. Nurse gave him up. She could make nothing of him. Anyhow he was growing beyond her.

One day his mother and his uncle Oscar came in when he was on one of his furious rides. He did not speak to them.

"Hallo, you young jockey! Riding a winner?" said his uncle.

"Aren't you growing too big for a rocking horse? You're not a very little boy any longer, you know," said his mother.

But Paul only gave a blue glare from his big, rather close-set eyes. He would speak to nobody when he was in full tilt. His mother watched him with an anxious expression on her face.

At last he suddenly stopped forcing his horse into the mechanical gallop, and slid down.

"Well, I got there!" he announced fiercely, his blue eyes still flaring, and his sturdy long legs straddling apart.

"Where did you get to?" asked his mother.

"Where I wanted to go," he flared back at her.

"That's right, son!" said Uncle Oscar. "Don't you stop till you get there. What's the horse's name?"

"He doesn't have a name," said the boy.

"Gets on without all right?" asked the uncle.

"Well, he has different names. He was called Sansovino last week."

"Sansovino, eh? Won the Ascot. How did you know his name?"

"He always talks about horse races with Bassett," said Joan.

The uncle was delighted to find that his small nephew was posted with all the racing news. Bassett, the young gardener, who had been wounded in the left foot in the war and had got his present job through Oscar Cresswell, whose batman he had been, was a perfect blade of the "turf." He lived in the racing events, and the small boy lived with him.

Oscar Cresswell got it all from Bassett.

"Master Paul comes and asks me, so I can't do more than tell him, sir," said Bassett, his face terribly serious, as if he were speaking of religious matters.

"And does he ever put anything on a horse he fancies?"

"Well—I don't want to give him away—he's a young sport, a fine sport, sir. Would you mind asking him himself? He sort of takes a pleasure in it, and perhaps he'd feel I was giving him away, sir, if you don't mind."

Bassett was serious as a church.

The uncle went back to his nephew and took him off for a ride in the car.

"Say, Paul, old man, do you ever put anything on a horse?" the uncle asked.

The boy watched the handsome man closely.

"Why, do you think I oughtn't to?" he parried.

"Not a bit of it! I thought perhaps you might give me a tip for the Lincoln."

The car sped on into the country, going down to Uncle Oscar's place in Hampshire.

"Honor bright?" said the nephew.

"Honor bright, son!" said the uncle.

"Well, then, Daffodil."

"Daffodil! I doubt it, sonny. What about Mirza?"

"I only know the winner," said the boy. "That's Daffodil."

"Daffodil, eh?"

There was a pause. Daffodil was an obscure horse comparatively.

"Uncle!"

"Yes, son?"

"You won't let it go any further, will you? I promised Bassett."

"Bassett be damned, old man! What's he got to do with it?"

"We're partners. We've been partners from the first. Uncle, he lent me my first five shillings, which I lost. I promised him, honor bright, it was only between me and him; only you gave me that ten-shilling note I started winning with, so I thought you were lucky. You won't let it go any further, will you?"

The boy gazed at his uncle from those big, hot, blue eyes, set rather close together. The uncle stirred and laughed uneasily.

"Right you are, son! I'll keep your tip private. Daffodil, eh? How much are you putting on him?"

"All except twenty pounds," said the boy. "I keep that in reserve."

The uncle thought it a good joke.

"You keep twenty pounds in reserve, do you, you young romancer? What are you betting, then?"

"I'm betting three hundred," said the boy gravely. "But it's between you and me, Uncle Oscar! Honor bright?"

The uncle burst into a roar of laughter.

"It's between you and me all right, you young Nat Gould," he said, laughing. "But where's your three hundred?"

"Bassett keeps it for me. We're partners."

"You are, are you! And what is Bassett putting on Daffodil?"

"He won't go quite as high as I do, I expect. Perhaps he'll go a hundred and fifty."

"What, pennies?" laughed the uncle.

"Pounds," said the child, with a surprised look at his uncle. "Bassett keeps a bigger reserve than I do."

Between wonder and amusement Uncle Oscar was silent. He pursued the matter no further, but he determined to take his nephew with him to the Lincoln races.

"Now, son," he said, "I'm putting twenty on Mirza, and I'll put five for you on any horse you fancy. What's your pick?"

"Daffodil, Uncle."

No, not the fiver on Daffodil!"

"I should if it was my own fiver," said the child.

"Good! Good! Right you are! A fiver for me and a fiver for you on Daffodil."

The child had never been to a race meeting before, and his eyes were blue fire. He pursed his mouth tight, and watched. A Frenchman just in front had put his money on Lancelot. Wild with excitement, he flailed his arms up and down, yelling *Lancelot! Lancelot!* in his French accent.

Daffodil came in first, Lancelot second, Mirza third. The child, flushed and with eyes blazing, was curiously serene. His uncle brought him four five-pound notes, four to one.

"What am I to do with these?" he cried, waving them before the boy's eyes.

"I suppose we'll talk to Bassett," said the boy. "I expect I have fifteen hundred now; and twenty in reserve; and this twenty."

His uncle studied him for some moments.

"Look here, son!" he said. "You're not serious about Bassett and that fifteen hundred, are you?"

"Yes, I am. But it's between you and me, Uncle. Honor bright!"

"Honor bright all right, son! But I must talk to Bassett."

"If you'd like to be a partner, Uncle, with Bassett and me, we could all be partners. Only, you'd have to promise, honor bright, Uncle, not to let it go beyond us three. Bassett and I are lucky, and you must be lucky, because it was your ten shillings I started winning with. . . ."

Uncle Oscar took both Bassett and Paul into Richmond Park for an afternoon, and there they talked.

"It's like this, you see, sir," Bassett said. "Master Paul would get me talking about racing events, spinning yarns, you know, sir. And he was always keen on knowing if I'd made or if I'd lost. It's about a year since, now, that I put five shillings on Blush of Dawn for him—and we lost. Then the luck turned, with that ten shillings he had from you, that we put on Singhalese. And since then, it's been pretty steady, all things considering. What do you say, Master Paul?"

"We're all right when we're sure," said Paul. "It's when we're not quite sure that we go down."

"Oh, but we're careful then," said Bassett.

"But when are you *sure?*" Uncle Oscar smiled.

"It's Master Paul, sir," said Bassett, in a secret, religious voice. "It's as if he had it from heaven. Like Daffodil, now, for the Lincoln. That was as sure as eggs."

"Did you put anything on Daffodil?" asked Oscar Cresswell.

"Yes, sir. I made my bit."

"And my nephew?"

Bassett was obstinately silent, looking at Paul.

"I made twelve hundred, didn't I, Bassett? I told Uncle I was putting three hundred on Daffodil."

"That's right," said Bassett, nodding.

"But where's the money?" asked the uncle.

"I keep it safe locked up, sir. Master Paul he can have it any minute he likes to ask for it."

"What, fifteen hundred pounds?"

"And twenty! And *forty,* that is, with the twenty he made on the course."

"It's amazing!" said the uncle.

"If Master Paul offers you to be partners, sir, I would, if I were you; if you'll excuse me," said Bassett.

Oscar Cresswell thought about it.

"I'll see the money," he said.

They drove home again, and sure enough, Bassett came round to the garden house with fifteen hundred pounds in notes. The twenty pounds reserve was left with Joe Glee, in the Turf Commission deposit.

"You see, it's all right, Uncle, when I'm *sure!* Then we go strong, for all we're worth. Don't we, Bassett?"

"We do that, Master Paul."

"And when are you sure?" said the uncle, laughing.

"Oh, well, sometimes I'm *absolutely* sure, like about Daffodil," said the boy; "and sometimes I have an idea; and sometimes I haven't even an idea, have I, Bassett? Then we're careful, because we mostly go down."

"You do, do you! And when you're sure, like about Daffodil, what makes you sure, sonny?"

"Oh, well, I don't know," said the boy uneasily. "I'm sure, you know, Uncle; that's all."

"It's as if he had it from heaven, sir," Bassett reiterated.

"I should say so!" said the uncle.

But he became a partner. And when the Leger was coming on, Paul was "sure" about Lively Spark, which was a quite inconsiderable horse. The boy insisted on putting a thousand on the horse, Bassett went for five hundred, and Oscar Cresswell two hundred. Lively Spark came in first, and the betting had been ten to one against him. Paul had made ten thousand.

"You see," he said, "I was absolutely sure of him."

Even Oscar Cresswell had cleared two thousand.

"Look here, son," he said, "this sort of thing makes me nervous."

"It needn't, Uncle! Perhaps I shan't be sure again for a long time."

"But what are you going to do with your money?" asked the uncle.

"Of course," said the boy. "I started it for Mother. She said she had no luck, because Father is unlucky, so I thought if *I* was lucky, it might stop whispering."

"What might stop whispering?"

"Our house. I *hate* our house for whispering."

"What does it whisper?"

"Why—why"—the boy fidgeted—"why, I don't know. But it's always short of money, you know, Uncle."

"I know it, son, I know it."

"You know people send Mother writs, don't you, Uncle?"

"I'm afraid I do," said the uncle.

"And then the house whispers, like people laughing at you behind your back. It's awful, that is! I thought if I was lucky. . . ."

"You might stop it," added the uncle.

The boy watched him with big blue eyes, that had an uncanny cold fire in them, and he said never a word.

"Well, then!" said the uncle. "What are we doing?"

"I shouldn't like Mother to know I was lucky," said the boy.

"Why not, son?"

"She'd stop me."

"I don't think she would."

"Oh!"—and the boy writhed in an odd way—"I *don't* want her to know, Uncle."

"All right, son! We'll manage it without her knowing."

They managed it very easily. Paul, at the other's suggestion, handed over five thousand pounds to his uncle, who deposited it with the family lawyer, who was then to inform Paul's mother that a relative had put five thousand pounds into his hands, which sum was to be paid out a thousand pounds at a time, on the mother's birthday, for the next five years.

"So she'll have a birthday present of a thousand pounds for five successive years," said Uncle Oscar. "I hope it won't make it all the harder for her later."

Paul's mother had her birthday in November. The house had been "whispering" worse than ever lately, and, even in spite of his luck, Paul could not bear up against it. He was very anxious to see the effect of the birthday letter, telling his mother about the thousand pounds.

When there were no visitors, Paul now took his meals with his parents, as he was beyond the nursery control. His mother went into town nearly every day. She had discovered that she had an odd knack of sketching furs and dress materials, so she worked secretly in the studio of a friend who was the chief artist for the leading drapers. She drew the figures of ladies in furs and ladies in silk and sequins for the newspaper advertisements. This young woman artist earned several thousand pounds a year, but Paul's mother only made several hundreds, and she was again dissatisfied. She so wanted to be first in something, and she did not succeed, even in making sketches for drapery advertisements.

She was down to breakfast on the morning of her birthday. Paul watched her face as she read her letters. He knew the lawyer's letter. As his mother read it, her face hardened and became more expressionless. Then a cold, determined look came on her mouth. She hid the letter under the pile of others, and said not a word about it.

"Didn't you have anything nice in the post for your birthday, Mother?" said Paul.

"Quite moderately nice," she said, her voice cold and absent.

She went away to town without saying more.

But in the afternoon Uncle Oscar appeared. He said Paul's mother had had a long interview with the lawyer, asking if the whole five thousand could not be advanced at once, as she was in debt.

"What do you think, Uncle?" said the boy.

"I leave it to you, son."

"Oh, let her have it, then! We can get some more with the other," said the boy.

"A bird in the hand is worth two in the bush, laddie!" said Uncle Oscar.

"But I'm sure to *know* for the Grand National; or the Lincolnshire; or else the Derby. I'm sure to know for *one* of them," said Paul.

So Uncle Oscar signed the agreement, and Paul's mother touched the whole five thousand. Then something very curious happened. The voices in the house suddenly went mad, like a chorus of frogs on a spring evening. There were certain new furnishings, and Paul had a tutor. He was *really* going to Eton, his father's school, in the following autumn. There were flowers in the winter, and a blossoming of the luxury Paul's mother had been used to. And yet the voices in the house, behind the sprays of mimosa and almond blossom, and from under the piles of iridescent cushions, simply trilled and screamed in a sort of ecstasy: "There *must* be more money! Oh-h-h; there *must* be more money. Oh, now, now-w! Now-w-w—there *must* be more money!— more than ever! More than ever!"

It frightened Paul terribly. He studied away at his Latin and Greek. But his intense hours were spent with Bassett. The Grand National had gone by; he had not "known," and had lost a hundred pounds. Summer was at hand. He was in agony for the Lincoln. But even for the Lincoln he didn't "know," and he lost fifty pounds. He became wild-eyed and strange, as if something were going to explode in him.

"Let it alone, son! Don't you bother about it!" urged Uncle Oscar. But it was as if the boy couldn't really hear what his uncle was saying.

"I've got to know for the Derby! I've got to know for the Derby!" the child reiterated, his big blue eyes blazing with a sort of madness.

His mother noticed how overwrought he was.

"You'd better go to the seaside. Wouldn't you like to go now to the seaside, instead of waiting? I think you'd better," she said, looking down at him anxiously, her heart curiously heavy because of him.

But the child lifted his uncanny blue eyes. "I couldn't possibly go before the Derby, Mother!" he said. "I couldn't possibly!"

"Why not?" she said, her voice becoming heavy when she was opposed. "Why not? You can still go from the seaside to see the Derby with your uncle Oscar, if that's what you wish. No need for you to wait here. Besides, I think you care too much about these races. It's a bad sign. My family has been a gambling family, and you won't know till you grow up how much damage it has done. But it has done damage. I shall have to send Bassett away, and ask Uncle Oscar not to talk racing to you, unless you promise to be reasonable about it; go away to the seaside and forget it. You're all nerves!"

"I'll do what you like, Mother, so long as you don't send me away till after the Derby," the boy said.

"Send you away from where? Just from this house?"

"Yes," he said, gazing at her.

"Why, you curious child, what makes you care about this house so much, suddenly? I never knew you loved it."

He gazed at her without speaking. He had a secret within a secret, something he had not divulged, even to Bassett or to his uncle Oscar.

But his mother, after standing undecided and a little bit sullen for some moments, said:

"Very well, then! Don't go to the seaside till after the Derby, if you don't wish it. But promise me you won't let your nerves go to pieces. Promise you won't think so much about horse racing and *events,* as you call them!"

"Oh, no," said the boy casually. "I won't think much about them, Mother. You needn't worry. I wouldn't worry, Mother, if I were you."

"If you were me and I were you," said his mother, "I wonder what we *should* do!"

"But you know you needn't worry, Mother, don't you?" the boy repeated.

"I should be awfully glad to know it," she said wearily.

"Oh, well you *can,* you know. I mean, you *ought* to know you needn't worry," he insisted.

"Ought I? Then I'll see about it," she said.

Paul's secret of secrets was his wooden horse, that which had no name. Since he was emancipated from a nurse and a nursery governess, he had had his rocking horse removed to his own bedroom at the top of the house.

"Surely, you're too big for a rocking horse!" his mother had remonstrated.

"Well, you see, Mother, till I can have a *real* horse, I like to have *some* sort of animal about," had been his quaint answer.

"Do you feel he keeps you company?" She laughed.

"Oh, yes! He's very good, he always keeps me company, when I'm there," said Paul.

So the horse, rather shabby, stood in an arrested prance in the boy's bedroom.

The Derby was drawing near, and the boy grew more and more tense. He hardly heard what was spoken to him, he was very frail, and his eyes were really uncanny. His mother had sudden strange seizures of uneasiness about him. Sometimes, for half an hour, she would feel a sudden anxiety about him that was almost anguish. She wanted to rush to him at once, and know he was safe.

Two nights before the Derby, she was at a big party in town, when one of her rushes of anxiety about her boy, her firstborn, gripped her heart till she could hardly speak. She fought with the feeling, might and main, for she believed in common sense. But it was too strong. She had to leave the dance and go downstairs to telephone to the country. The children's nursery governess was terribly surprised and startled at being rung up in the night.

"Are the children all right, Miss Wilmot?"

"Oh, yes, they are quite all right."

"Master Paul? Is he all right?"

"He went to bed as right as a trivet. Shall I run up and look at him?"

"No," said Paul's mother reluctantly. "No! Don't trouble. It's all right. Don't sit up. We shall be home fairly soon." She did not want her son's privacy intruded upon.

"Very good," said the governess.

It was about one o'clock when Paul's mother and father drove up to their house. All was still. Paul's mother went to her room and slipped off her white fur cloak. She had told her maid not to wait up for her. She heard her husband downstairs, mixing a whisky and soda.

And then, because of the strange anxiety at her heart, she stole upstairs to her son's room. Noiselessly she went along the upper corridor. Was there a faint noise? What was it?

She stood, with arrested muscles, outside his door, listening. There was a strange, heavy, and yet not loud noise. Her heart stood still. It was a soundless noise, yet rushing and powerful. Something huge, in violent, hushed motion. What was it? What in God's name was it? She ought to know. She felt that she knew the noise. She knew what it was.

Yet she could not place it. She couldn't say what it was. And on and on it went, like a madness.

Softly, frozen with anxiety and fear, she turned the door handle.

The room was dark. Yet in the space near the window, she heard and saw something plunging to and fro. She gazed in fear and amazement.

Then suddenly she switched on the light, and saw her son, in his green pajamas, madly surging on the rocking horse. The blaze of light suddenly lit him up, as he urged the wooden horse, and lit her up, as she stood, blonde, in her dress of pale green and crystal, in the doorway.

"Paul!" she cried. "Whatever are you doing?"

"It's Malabar!" he screamed, in a powerful, strange voice. "It's Malabar!"

His eyes blazed at her for one strange and senseless second, as he ceased urging his wooden horse. Then he fell with a crash to the ground, and she, all her tormented motherhood flooding upon her, rushed to gather him up.

But he was unconscious, and unconscious he remained, with some brain fever. He talked and tossed, and his mother sat stonily by his side.

"Malabar! It's Malabar! Bassett, Bassett, I *know*! It's Malabar!"

So the child cried, trying to get up and urge the rocking horse that gave him his inspiration.

"What does he mean by Malabar?" asked the heart-frozen mother.

"I don't know," said the father stonily.

"What does he mean by Malabar?" she asked her brother Oscar.

"It's one of the horses running for the Derby," was the answer.

And, in spite of himself, Oscar Cresswell spoke to Bassett, and himself put a thousand on Malabar: at fourteen to one.

The third day of the illness was critical: they were waiting for a change. The boy, with his rather long, curly hair, was tossing ceaselessly on the pillow. He never slept nor regained consciousness, and his eyes were like blue stones. His mother sat, feeling her heart had gone, turned actually into a stone.

In the evening, Oscar Cresswell did not come, but Bassett sent a message, saying could he come up for one moment, just one moment? Paul's mother was very angry at the intrusion, but on second thought she agreed. The boy was the same. Perhaps Bassett might bring him to consciousness.

The gardener, a shortish fellow with a little brown mustache, and sharp little brown eyes, tiptoed into the room, touched his imaginary cap to Paul's mother, and stole to the bedside, staring with glittering, smallish eyes at the tossing, dying child.

"Master Paul!" he whispered. "Master Paul! Malabar came in first all right, a clean win. I did as you told me. You've made over seventy thousand pounds, you have; you've got over eighty thousand. Malabar came in all right, Master Paul."

"Malabar! Malabar! Did I say Malabar, Mother? Did I say Malabar? Do you think I'm lucky, Mother? I knew Malabar, didn't I? Over eighty thousand pounds! I call that lucky, don't you, Mother? Over eighty thousand pounds! I knew, didn't I know I knew? Malabar came in all right. If I ride my horse till I'm sure, then I tell you, Bassett, you can go as high as you like. Did you go for all you were worth, Bassett?"

"I went a thousand on it, Master Paul."

"I never told you, Mother, that if I can ride my horse, and *get there,* then I'm absolutely sure—oh, absolutely! Mother, did I ever tell you? I *am* lucky!"

"No, you never did," said the mother.

But the boy died in the night.

And even as he lay dead, his mother heard her brother's voice saying to her: "My God, Hester, you're eighty-odd thousand to the good, and a poor devil of a son to the bad. But, poor devil, poor devil, he's best gone out of a life where he rides his rocking horse to find a winner."

(1926)

INTRODUCTION TO FLANNERY O'CONNOR

[1925–1964]

Flannery O'Connor is considered one of the unique voices to emerge from the 1950s. Her widely anthologized short stories often employ humor, irony, and paradox within a system of Christian belief in evil and redemption. And because she is a social satirist as well as a religious thinker, O'Connor's images often highlight current American cultural challenges, as she delineates such timely issues as random violence, race relations, and class discrimination.

O'Connor's stories are also suggestive of the southern tradition of folktales and storytelling in which engaging, violent, and frequently grotesque characters are often treated with colloquial humor. Other writers identified with this tradition and often considered influential on O'Connor's fiction include Mark Twain, William Faulkner, and Katherine Anne Porter. Like O'Connor, these writers often point to the comic in calamity. O'Connor's forerunners would also have to include such American romance writers as Nathaniel Hawthorne, Herman Melville, Edgar Allan Poe, and Henry James who explored questions of morality while presenting experience in a highly imaginative and symbolic way.

O'Connor herself suggested that there were two strong influences on her writing: her sense of herself as a southerner and her Roman Catholic roots. A southerner all her life, O'Connor was born in Savannah, Georgia, in 1925. In 1938 she moved to Milledgeville, Georgia, the city which had been Georgia's capital before the Civil War and where she would spend most of her life. She graduated from Women's College of Georgia in 1945 where she earned a reputation as a cartoonist, contributing weekly sketches to the campus newspaper. O'Connor then went on to earn an M.F.A. in writing from the State University of Iowa in 1947. At the age of twenty-five she was struck with a debilitating illness, disseminated lupus, which forced her to return to Milledgeville in 1950, where she lived and published her fiction until her death in 1964. O'Connor felt that her identity as a southerner provided her with many of the raw materials she needed to fabricate the settings and finely detailed characters of her stories. "The things we see, hear, smell, and touch," O'Connor wrote, "affect us long before we believe anything at all. The South impresses its image on the Southerner—be he Catholic or not—from the moment he is able to distinguish one sound from another."

Though the South served as the setting for O'Connor's fiction, Roman Catholicism allowed her to transcend the confines of regionalism to make a universal statement. "The woods are full of regional writers," she once stated, "and it is the great horror of every serious Southern writer that he will become one of them." Identifying her bearing as a fiction writer, O'Connor wrote: "I see from the standpoint of Christian orthodoxy. This means that for me the meaning of life is centered in our Redemption by Christ and what I see in the world I see in its relation to that." Understanding O'Connor's religious beliefs helps to interpret her fiction, but we need not share her faith to enjoy her work. Her genius as a writer eclipsed any religious devotion. Responding to a student who once queried her as to "just what enlightenment" a student might be expected to glean from an O'Connor narrative, the author suggested that the young reader "forget about the enlightenment" and just enjoy the story.

The typical O'Connor story often begins with a comic protagonist who indulges in fantasies of moral or social superiority or has a false sense of the certainty of things. The protagonist then has an ironic and traumatic (if not fatal) encounter with other characters or a situation that suggests the disturbing possibility of an incomprehensible and frequently terrifying universe. In "Everything That Rises Must Converge," for example, both Julian and his mother are ironic figures convinced of their personal superiority as well as the correctness of their respective world views. Julian's mother fortifies herself against disappointing circumstances by assuming aristocratic airs. Ironically, she proclaims that "if you know who you are you can go anywhere." When she climbs into the mass transit bus she enters the aisle "with a little smile, as if she were going into a drawing room where everyone had been waiting for her." From her perspective she and her son are the descendants of Godhighs and Chestny's, who count plantation owners and a former governor in their bloodline. Julian, on the other hand, insists that he has a truer sense of his mother's and his place in the changing world, and

> in spite of her, he had turned out so well . . . he had, on his own
> initiative, come out with a first-rate education; in spite of grow-
> ing up dominated by a small mind, he had ended up with a large
> one; in spite of all her foolish views, he was free of prejudice and
> unafraid to face facts.

The narrator, however, implies that Julian is himself an ironic figure, as affected as his mother and only slightly more subtle in his racism. Rather than insist that black people ride in the back of the bus, he tries "to strike up an acquaintance . . . with some of the better types."

The title, "Everything That Rises Must Converge," is also ironic, alluding to the works of Teilhard de Chardin, who explains that the future will focus on an "omega point" where everything and everyone will be joined at the end of geologic time. As the story concludes, however, the characters do not so much converge as they collide, and from this collision the unimagined and terrifying universe is made apparent.

Though brief and tragically curtailed by illness, Flannery O'Connor's writing career was nevertheless recognized during her lifetime. She was awarded a *Kenyon Review* fellowship in fiction in 1953; a National Institute of Arts and Letters grant in literature in 1957; an O. Henry Award in 1957; a Ford Foundation grant in 1959; and an honorary doctor of literature from St. Mary's College in 1962 and another from Smith College in 1963. She was also awarded a Henry H. Bellaman Foundation special award in 1964. In 1971, her posthumous collection, *The Complete Stories of Flannery O'Connor,* won the National Book Award. In addition to her short-story collections [*A Good Man Is Hard to Find and Other Stories* (1955); *Everything That Rises Must Converge* (1965); *The Complete Stories of Flannery O'Connor* (1971)], Flannery O'Connor published two novels, *Wise Blood* (1952) and *The Violent Bear It Away* (1960). Also significant are her essays and ideas on literature collected in *Mystery and Manners* (1969), *The Habit of Being: Selected Letters of Flannery O'Connor* (1979), and *The Correspondence of Flannery O'Connor and the Brainard Cheneys* (1986).

The novelist and critic V. S. Pritchett has suggested that the characters in O'Connor's stories are "plain human beings in whose fractured lives the writer has discovered an uncouth relationship with the lasting myths and the violent passions of human life." For O'Connor, truth was of the greatest importance— even when it revealed itself as fractured, uncouth, or violent.

CRITICAL COMMENTS BY O'CONNOR

On Symbol and Theme

from *"The Nature and Aim of Fiction" (Mystery and Manners)*

Now the word *symbol* scares a good many people off, just as the word *art* does. They seem to feel that a symbol is some mysterious thing put in arbitrarily by the writer to frighten the common reader—sort of a literary Masonic grip that is only for the initiated. They seem to think that it is a way of saying something that you aren't actually saying, and so if they can be got to read a reputedly symbolic work at all, they approach it as if it were a problem in algebra. Find *x*. And when they do find or think they find this abstraction, *x,* then they go off with an elaborate sense of satisfaction and the notion that they have "understood" the story. Many students confuse the *process* of understanding a thing with understanding it.

I think that for the fiction writer himself, symbols are something he uses simply as a matter of course. You might say that these are details that, while having their essential place in the literal level of the story, operate in depth as well as on the surface, increasing the story in every direction. . . .

People have a habit of saying, "What is the theme of your story?" and they expect you to give them a statement: "The theme of my story is the economic pressure of the machine on the middle class"—or some such absurdity. And when they've got a statement like that, they go off happy and feel it is no longer necessary to read the story.

Some people have the notion that you read the story and then climb out of it into the meaning, but for the fiction writer himself the whole story is the meaning, because it is an experience, not an abstraction. . . .

When you can state the theme of a story, when you can separate it from the story itself, then you can be sure the story is not a very good one. The meaning of a story has to be embodied in it, has to be made concrete in it. A story is a way to say something that can't be said any other way, and it takes every word in the story to say what the meaning is. You tell a story because a statement would be inadequate. When anybody asks what a story is about, the only proper thing is to tell him to read the story.

On "A Good Man Is Hard to Find"

from *The Habit of Being: Selected Letters of Flannery O'Connor*

Week before last I went to Wesleyan and read "A Good Man Is Hard to Find." After it I went to one of the classes where I was asked questions. There were a couple of young teachers there and one of them, an earnest type, started asking the questions. "Miss O'Connor," he said, "why was the Misfit's hat *black*?" I said most countrymen in Georgia wore black hats. He looked pretty disappointed. Then he said, "Miss O'Connor, the Misfit represents Christ, does he not?" "He does not," I said. He looked crushed. "Well, Miss O'Connor," he said, "what is the significance of the Misfit's hat?" I said it was to cover his head; and after that he left me alone. . . .

There is a change of tension from the first part of the story to the second where the Misfit enters, but this is no lessening of reality. This story is, of course, not meant to be realistic in the sense that it portrays the everyday doings of people in Georgia. It is stylized and its conventions are comic even though its meaning is serious.

Bailey's only importance is as the Grandmother's boy and the driver of the car. It is the Grandmother who first recognizes the Misfit and who is most concerned with him throughout. The story is a duel of sorts between the Grandmother and her superficial beliefs and the Misfit's more profoundly felt involvement with Christ's action which set the world off balance for him.

The meaning of a story should go on expanding for the reader the more he thinks about it, but meaning cannot be captured in an interpretation. If teachers are in the habit of approaching a story as if it were a research problem for which any answer is believable so long as it is not obvious, then I think students will never learn to enjoy fiction. Too much interpretation is certainly worse than too little, and where feeling for a story is absent, theory will not supply it.

On "Good Country People"

from "Writing Short Stories" (Mystery and Manners)

In good fiction, certain of the details will tend to accumulate meaning from the action of the story itself, and when this happens they become symbolic in the way they work. I once wrote a story called "Good Country People," in which a lady Ph.D. has her wooden leg stolen by a Bible salesman whom she has tried to seduce. Now I'll admit that, paraphrased in this way, the situation is simply a low joke. The average reader is pleased to observe anybody's wooden leg being stolen. But without ceasing to appeal to him and without making any statements of high intention, this story does manage to operate at another level of experience, by letting the wooden leg accumulate meaning. Early in the story, we're presented with the fact that the Ph.D. is spiritually as well as physically crippled. She believes in nothing but her own belief in nothing, and we perceive that there is a wooden part of her soul that corresponds to her wooden leg. Now of course this is never stated. The fiction writer states as little as possible. The reader makes this connection from things he is shown. He may not even know that he makes the connection, but the connection is there nevertheless and it has its effect on him. As the story goes on, the wooden leg continues to accumulate meaning. The reader learns how the girl feels about her leg, how her mother feels about it, and how the country woman on the place feels about it; and finally, by the time the Bible sales-man comes along, the leg has accumulated so much meaning that it is, as the saying goes, loaded. And when the Bible salesman steals it, the reader realizes that he has taken away part of the girl's personality and has revealed her deeper affliction to her for the first time.

If you want to say that the wooden leg is a symbol, you can say that. But it is a wooden leg first, and as a wooden leg it is absolutely necessary to the story. It has its place on the literal level of the story, but it operates in depth as well as on the surface. It increases the story in every direction, and this is essentially the way a story escapes being short.

Now a little might be said about the way in which this happens. I wouldn't want you to think that in that story I sat down and said, "I am now going to write a story about a Ph.D. with a wooden leg, using the wooden leg as a symbol for another kind of affliction." I doubt myself if many writers know what they are going to do when they start out. When I started writing that story, I didn't know there was going to be a Ph.D. with a wooden leg in it. I merely found myself one morning writing a description of two women that I knew something about, and before I realized it, I had equipped one of them with a daughter with a wooden leg. As the story progressed, I brought in the Bible salesman, but I had no idea what I was going to do with him. I didn't know he was going to steal that wooden leg until ten or twelve lines before he did it, but when I found out that this was what was going to happen, I realized that it was inevitable. This is a story that produces a shock for the reader, and I think one reason for this is that it produced a shock for the writer.

CRITICS ON O'CONNOR

FREDERICK ASALS

On "A Good Man Is Hard to Find"

from *Flannery O'Connor: The Imagination of Extremity*

"A Good Man Is Hard to Find" continues to be O'Connor's best-known work, the story most often chosen to represent her in anthologies now as during her lifetime. Yet, fine as it is, it is not self-evidently her best story: something more than quality must account for its repeated selection by textbook editors. One reason for its popularity may well be precisely that "A Good Man Is Hard to Find" writes large the representative O'Connor themes and methods—comedy, violence, theological concern—and thus makes them quickly and unmistakably available. But another, surely, is the primordial appeal of the story, for "A Good Man Is Hard to Find" captures a very old truth, that in the midst of life we are in death, in its most compelling modern form. The characteristic contemporary nightmare of the sudden onslaught of violent death, a death that chooses its victims without warning, impersonally, apparently at random, without either motivation or remorse, the victims helpless either to escape or to defend themselves—this scenario for some of our deepest, most instinctual fears is the very basis of the story and the source of its immediate hold on our imaginations.

Interestingly enough, O'Connor's own public remarks on the story dismiss this level almost entirely. Stressing its spiritual implications, she emphasizes the grandmother's final action while brushing aside everything that leads up to it, saying, "If I took out this gesture and what she says with it, I would have no story. What was left would not be worth your attention." Her advice to readers of "A Good Man Is Hard to Find" is, "You should be on the lookout for such things as the action of grace in the Grandmother's soul, and not for the dead bodies" *(Mystery and Manners)*.

This is all very high-minded, but it would seem a little difficult for the unprejudiced reader of "A Good Man Is Hard to Find" to ignore the dead bodies; and while one may agree with O'Connor that the story is "something more than an account of a family murdered on the way to Florida" *(Mystery and Manners),* it surely is, most immediately, just that "account." Any full discussion of the story must deal with both the grandmother's soul and the dead bodies, and indeed with the tension between the two levels implied here, for that tension is at the very heart of the story.

KATHLEEN FEELEY

On *"Good Country People"*

from *Flannery O'Connor: Voice of the Peacock*

Perhaps it was her utter truthfulness which, paradoxically, allowed her to imagine and create characters who have destroyed their own integrity to pursue a false good. In a catalog of her freaks, characters who re-create themselves according to a chosen image would mark an extreme position. They are farthest away from grace because they lack the truthful appraisal of reality which grace demands. They have set up a false god—education, or art, or economic security, or comfort—and they falsify their very being in order to pay it homage. A number of Flannery O'Connor's short stories show her imagination working on the idea of falseness in a character. Some of the protagonists in these stories look perfectly normal; others have a physical deformity which is symbolic of a spiritual one. In the course of the action, all are given an opportunity to recognize their self-deception. In the author's vision, this recognition is the first step toward truth, which is, in turn, the necessary condition of Redemption. Conversion—a change of direction—is possible only after one recognizes his perversion.

Comic perversion is a key concept in "Good Country People." Both the girl Joy-Hulga and the Bible salesman have perverted their true selves, and each is revealed in his falsity after the word of God is perverted during a seduction scene—itself a perversion of love. Even the structure of the story appears to be a perversion of a traditional short-story form. Two-thirds of the story elapses before the initial meeting of Joy-Hulga and Manley Pointer, the Bible salesman, occurs. In the first section, Flannery O'Connor sets up a relationship between Mrs. Freeman, the hired man's wife, and Mrs. Hopewell, her employer, and between each of these women and the one-legged protagonist, Joy-Hulga. These relationships structure the story. The opening section also sketches Joy through the eyes of her mother: the hunting accident which destroyed her leg, her immersion in atheistic philosophy, and her attempt, at the age of twenty-one, to rename herself and to redirect her life. With relationships demonstrated, background sketched, and tone established, the first personal encounter of Hulga and her "saviour" takes place. From Manley Pointer's opening question ("You ever ate a chicken that was two days old?") to his final assertion ("I been believing in nothing since I was born") the story moves "like the advance of a heavy truck" to its moment of truth.

That the salesman is peddling Bibles is the central perversion of the story. Flannery O'Connor believed in the power of the word of God. The Bible was for her, as it is for Jews and for Scripture-oriented Christians, the power of God and the wisdom of God. God's scriptural word is not a dead letter; it is a living presence. Reading it does more than enlighten the intellect; it unleashes power that moves the spirit. As a perversion of Christianity has driven Joy to become Hulga, so a perversion of the meaning of Scripture jolts her into self-recognition.

DOROTHY TUCK MCFARLAND

On "Everything That Rises Must Converge"

from *Flannery O'Connor*

The stories in O'Connor's second collection reflect her concern with questions implicitly raised by the rather gnomic title "Everything That Rises Must Converge." The phrase comes from the work of Pierre Teilhard de Chardin, a Jesuit paleontologist-philosopher. Teilhard hypothesized that evolution, far from stopping with the emergence of *homo sapiens,* continues to progress toward higher levels of consciousness, and that its ultimate goal is pure consciousness, which is Being itself, or God.

Teilhard's concept of the progress of evolution, actual and predicted, can best be visualized as a globe. At the base of the globe—the beginning of the evolutionary process—lines radiate outward and upward, representing the diversification of many forms of life which are moving upward toward greater levels of biological complexity. At the mid-point of the globe the diversification stops and one species—man—comes to dominate the earth. Moving from the mid-point of the globe upward, the lines begin to converge as they approach the topmost pole, the evolutionary destination that Teilhard called the Omega point. The converging lines now represent individual human consciousnesses which, as they rise, grow closer and closer together.

One aspect of this convergence can be seen in the increased intercommunication and interdependence of men in modern mass society. The increasingly complex interaction of men, Teilhard believed, tends to generate fresh bursts of evolutionary energy that produce still higher levels of consciousness, and these increases in consciousness find material expression in new technological breakthroughs. Teilhard, however, did not equate rising in consciousness solely with social or intellectual or scientific advances; he saw these achievements as manifestations of an increase in consciousness that was primarily a growing toward the fullness of Being—God—that is the source of all life.

O'Connor certainly regarded an increase in consciousness—which in her stories is signified by an increase in vision—to be a growing toward Being. However, her characters typically resist this kind of rising and the spiritual convergence with others that accompanies it. This has led some commentators to conclude that O'Connor's use of the title "Everything That Rises Must Converge" is largely, if not completely, ironic. (According to one critic, nothing rises in the title story but Julian's mother's blood pressure.[1]) It is true that O'Connor deliberately plays off the meaning of the title against numerous metaphors of non-convergent rising, and especially against her characters' desire to rise without convergence; for instance, the "rising" of Negroes is acceptable to Julian's mother only as long as there is no convergence: "they should rise, yes, but on their own side of the fence." The thrust of most of the stories, however, is to bring the protagonist to a vision of himself as he really is, and thus to make possible a true rising toward Being. That this rising is inevitably painful does not discredit its validity; rather, it emphasizes (as Teilhard's conception does not) the tension between the evolutionary thrust toward Being and the human warp that resists it—the warp which O'Connor would have called original sin.

FLANNERY O'CONNOR: STORIES

Good Country People

Description of Mrs. Freeman

Besides the neutral expression that she wore when she was alone, Mrs. Freeman had two others, forward and reverse, that she used for all her human dealings. Her forward expression was steady and driving like the advance of a heavy truck. Her eyes never swerved to left or right but turned as the story turned as if they followed a yellow line down the center of it. She seldom used the other expression because it was not often necessary for her to retract a statement, but when she did, her face came to a complete stop, there was an almost imperceptible movement of her black eyes, during which they seemed to be receding, and then the observer would see that Mrs. Freeman, though she might stand there as real as several grain sacks thrown on top of each other, was no longer there in spirit. As for getting anything across to her when this was the case, Mrs. Hopewell had given it up. She might talk her head off. Mrs. Freeman could never be brought to admit herself wrong on any point. She would stand there and if she could be brought to say anything, it was something like, "Well, I wouldn't of said it was and I wouldn't of said it wasn't," or letting her gaze range over the top kitchen shelf where there was an assortment of dusty bottles, she might remark, "I see you ain't ate many of them figs you put up last summer."

They carried on their most important business in the kitchen at breakfast. Every morning Mrs. Hopewell got up at seven o'clock and lit her gas heater and Joy's. Joy *topics of conversation suggest simple mindedness*

was her daughter, a large blonde girl who had an artificial leg. Mrs. Hopewell thought of her as a child though she was thirty-two years old and highly educated. Joy would get up while her mother was eating and lumber into the bathroom and slam the door, and before long, Mrs. Freeman would arrive at the back door. Joy would hear her mother call, "Come on in," and then they would talk for a while in low voices that were indistinguishable in the bathroom. By the time Joy came in, they had usually finished the weather report and were on one or the other of Mrs. Freeman's daughters, Glynese or Carramae. Joy called them Glycerin and Caramel. Glynese, a redhead, was eighteen and had many admirers; Carramae, a blonde, was only fifteen but already married and pregnant. She could not keep anything on her stomach. Every morning Mrs. Freeman told Mrs. Hopewell how many times she had vomited since the last report.

Mrs. Hopewell liked to tell people that Glynese and Carramae were two of the finest girls she knew and that Mrs. Freeman was a *lady* and that she was never ashamed to take her anywhere or introduce her to anybody they might meet. Then she would tell how she had happened to hire the Freemans in the first place and how they were a godsend to her and how she had had them four years. The reason for her keeping them so long was that they were not trash. They were good country people. She had telephoned the man whose name they had given as a reference and he had told her that Mr. Freeman was a good farmer but that his wife was the nosiest woman ever to walk the earth. "She's got to be into everything," the man said. "If she don't get there before the dust settles, you can bet she's dead, that's all. She'll want to know all your business. I can stand him real good," he had said, "but me nor my wife neither could have stood that woman one more minute on this place." That had put Mrs. Hopewell off for a few days.

why they are "good country people"

She had hired them in the end because there were no other applicants but she had made up her mind beforehand exactly how she would handle the woman. Since she was the type who had to be into everything, then, Mrs. Hopewell had decided, she would not only let her be into everything, she would *see to it* that she was into everything—she would give her the responsibility of everything, she would put her in charge. Mrs. Hopewell had no bad qualities of her own but she was able to use other people's in such a constructive way that she never felt the lack. She had hired the Freemans and she had kept them four years.

simple mindedness

Nothing is perfect. This was one of Mrs. Hopewell's favorite sayings. Another was: that is life! And still another, the most important, was: well, other people have their opinions too. She would make these statements, usually at the table, in a tone of gentle insistence as if no one held them but her, and the large hulking Joy, whose constant outrage had obliterated every expression from her face, would stare just a little to the side of her, her eyes icy blue, with the look of someone who has achieved blindness by an act of will and means to keep it. *— description of Joy*

When Mrs. Hopewell said to Mrs. Freeman that life was like that, Mrs. Freeman would say, "I always said so myself." Nothing had been arrived at by anyone that had not first been arrived at by her. She was quicker than Mr. Freeman. When Mrs. Hopewell said to her after they had been on the place a while, "You know, you're the wheel behind the wheel," and winked, Mrs. Freeman had said, "I know it. I've always been quick. It's some that are quicker than others."

"Everybody is different," Mrs. Hopewell said.

"Yes, most people is," Mrs. Freeman said.

"It takes all kinds to make the world."

Suggests stupidity or ignorance

"I always said it did myself."

The girl was used to this kind of dialogue for breakfast and more of it for dinner; sometimes they had it for supper too. When they had no guest they ate in the kitchen because that was easier. Mrs. Freeman always managed to arrive at some point during the meal and to watch them finish it. She would stand in the doorway if it were summer but in the winter she would stand with one elbow on top of the refrigerator and look down on them, or she would stand by the gas heater, lifting the back of her skirt slightly. Occasionally she would stand against the wall and roll her head from side to side. At no time was she in any hurry to leave. All this was very trying on Mrs. Hopewell but she was a woman of great patience. She realized that nothing is perfect and that in the Freemans she had good country people and that if, in this day and age, you get good country people, you had better hang onto them. *rarity?*

She had had plenty of experience with trash. Before the Freemans she had averaged one tenant family a year. The wives of these farmers were not the kind you would want to be around you for very long. Mrs. Hopewell, who had divorced her husband long ago, needed someone to walk over the fields with her; and when Joy had to be impressed for these services, her remarks were usually so ugly and her face so glum that Mrs. Hopewell would say, "If you can't come pleasantly, I don't want you at all," to which the girl, standing square and rigid-shouldered with her neck thrust slightly forward, would reply, "If you want me, here I am—LIKE I AM." *very bitter*

Mrs. Hopewell excused this attitude because of the leg (which had been shot off in a hunting accident when Joy was ten). It was hard for Mrs. Hopewell to realize that her child was thirty-two now and that for more than twenty years she had had only one leg. She thought of her still as a child because it tore her heart to think instead of the poor stout girl in her thirties who had never danced a step or had any *normal* good times. Her name was really Joy but as soon as she was twenty-one and away from home, she had had it legally changed. Mrs. Hopewell was certain that she had thought and thought until she had hit upon the ugliest name in any language. Then she had gone and had the beautiful name, Joy, changed without telling her mother until after she had done it. Her legal name was Hulga.

When Mrs. Hopewell thought the name, Hulga, she thought of the broad blank hull of a battleship. She would not use it. She continued to call her Joy to which the girl responded but in a purely mechanical way.

Hulga had learned to tolerate Mrs. Freeman, who saved her from taking walks with her mother. Even Glynese and Carramae were useful when they occupied attention that might otherwise have been directed at her. At first she had thought she could not stand Mrs. Freeman for she had found that it was not possible to be rude to her. Mrs. Freeman would take on strange resentments and for days together she would be sullen but the source of her displeasure was always obscure; a direct attack, a positive leer, blatant ugliness to her face—these never touched her. And without warning one day, she began calling her Hulga. (*Good Country People*)

She did not call her that in front of Mrs. Hopewell who would have been incensed but when she and the girl happened to be out of the house together, she would say something and add the name Hulga to the end of it, and the big spectacled Joy-Hulga would scowl and redden as if her privacy had been intruded upon. She considered the name her personal affair. She had arrived at it first purely on the basis of its ugly sound and then the full genius of its fitness had struck her. She had a vision of the name work-

① *trying?*

② *trying!*

she really didn't want the name

ing like the ugly sweating Vulcan who stayed in the furnace and to whom, presumably, the goddess had to come when called. She saw it as the name of her highest creative act. One of her major triumphs was that her mother had not been able to turn her dust into Joy, but the greater one was that she had been able to turn it herself into Hulga. However, Mrs. Freeman's relish for using the name only irritated her. It was as if Mrs. Freeman's beady steel-pointed eyes had penetrated far enough behind her face to reach some secret fact. Something about her seemed to fascinate Mrs. Freeman and then one day Hulga realized that it was the artificial leg. Mrs. Freeman had a special fondness for the details of secret infections, hidden deformities, assaults upon children. Of diseases, she preferred the lingering or incurable. Hulga had heard Mrs. Hopewell give her the details of the hunting accident, how the leg had been literally blasted off, how she had never lost consciousness. Mrs. Freeman could listen to it any time as if it had happened an hour ago.

Control?

When Hulga stumped into the kitchen in the morning (she could walk without making the awful noise but she made it——Mrs. Hopewell was certain——because it was ugly-sounding), she glanced at them and did not speak. Mrs. Hopewell would be in her red kimono with her hair tied around her head in rags. She would be sitting at the table, finishing her breakfast and Mrs. Freeman would be hanging by her elbow outward from the refrigerator, looking down at the table. Hulga always put her eggs on the stove to boil and then stood over them with her arms folded, and Mrs. Hopewell would look at her——a kind of indirect gaze divided between her and Mrs. Freeman——and would think that if she would only keep herself up a little, she wouldn't be so bad looking. There was nothing wrong with her face that a pleasant expression wouldn't help. Mrs. Hopewell said that people who looked on the bright side of things would be beautiful even if they were not.

possibly pushed her further into bitterness

Whenever she looked at Joy this way, she could not help but feel that it would have been better if the child had not taken the Ph.D. It had certainly not brought her out any and now that she had it, there was no more excuse for her to go to school again. Mrs. Hopewell thought it was nice for girls to go to school to have a good time but Joy had "gone through." Anyhow, she would not have been strong enough to go again. The doctors had told Mrs. Hopewell that with the best of care, Joy might see forty-five. She had a weak heart. Joy had made it plain that if it had not been for this condition, she would be far from these red hills and good country people. She would be in a university lecturing to people who knew what she was talking about. And Mrs. Hopewell could very well picture her there, looking like a scarecrow and lecturing to more of the same. Here she went about all day in a six-year-old skirt and a yellow sweat shirt with a faded cowboy on a horse embossed on it. She thought this was funny; Mrs. Hopewell thought it was idiotic and showed simply that she was still a child. She was brilliant but she didn't have a grain of sense. It seemed to Mrs. Hopewell that every year she grew less like other people and more like herself——bloated, rude, and squint-eyed. And she said such strange things! To her own mother she had said——without warning, without excuse, standing up in the middle of a meal with her face purple and her mouth half full——"Woman! do you ever look inside? Do you ever look inside and see what you are *not*? God!" she had cried sinking down again and staring at her plate, "Malebranche was right: we are not our own light. We are not our own light!" Mrs. Hopewell had no idea to this day what brought that on. She had only made the remark, hoping Joy would take it in, that a smile never hurt anyone.

The girl had taken the Ph.D. in philosophy and this left Mrs. Hopewell at a complete loss. You could say, "My daughter is a nurse," or "My daughter is a school teacher," or even, "My daughter is a chemical engineer." You could not say, "My daughter is a philosopher." That was something that had ended with the Greeks and Romans. All day Joy sat on her neck in a deep chair, reading. Sometimes she went for walks but she didn't like dogs or cats or birds or flowers or nature or nice young men. She looked at nice young men as if she could smell their stupidity.

One day Mrs. Hopewell had picked up one of the books the girl had just put down and opening it at random, she read, "Science, on the other hand, has to assert its soberness and seriousness afresh and declare that it is concerned solely with what-is. Nothing—how can it be for science anything but a horror and a phantasm? If science is right, then one thing stands firm: science wishes to know nothing of nothing. Such is after all the strictly scientific approach to Nothing. We know it by wishing to know nothing of Nothing." These words had been underlined with a blue pencil and they worked on Mrs. Hopewell like some evil incantation in gibberish. She shut the book quickly and went out of the room as if she were having a chill.

This morning when the girl came in, Mrs. Freeman was on Carramae. "She thrown up four times after supper," she said, "and was up twict in the night after three o'clock. Yesterday she didn't do nothing but ramble in the bureau drawer. All she did. Stand up there and see what she could run up on."

"She's got to eat," Mrs. Hopewell muttered, sipping her coffee, while she watched Joy's back at the stove. She was wondering what the child had said to the Bible salesman. She could not imagine what kind of a conversation she could possibly have had with him.

He was a tall gaunt hatless youth who had called yesterday to sell them a Bible. He had appeared at the door, carrying a large black suitcase that weighted him so heavily on one side that he had to brace himself against the door facing. He seemed on the point of collapse but he said in a cheerful voice, "Good morning, Mrs. Cedars!" and set the suitcase down on the mat. He was not a bad-looking young man though he had on a bright blue suit and yellow socks that were not pulled up far enough. He had prominent face bones and a streak of sticky-looking brown hair falling across his forehead.

"I'm Mrs. Hopewell," she said.

"Oh!" he said, pretending to look puzzled but with his eyes sparkling, "I saw it said 'The Cedars,' on the mailbox so I thought you was Mrs. Cedars!" and he burst out in a pleasant laugh. He picked up the satchel and under cover of a pant, he fell forward into her hall. It was rather as if the suitcase had moved first, jerking him after it. "Mrs. Hopewell!" he said and grabbed her hand. "I hope you are well!" and he laughed again and then all at once his face sobered completely. He paused and gave her a straight earnest look and said, "Lady, I've come to speak of serious things."

"Well, come in," she muttered, none too pleased because her dinner was almost ready. He came into the parlor and sat down on the edge of a straight chair and put the suitcase between his feet and glanced around the room as if he were sizing her up by it. Her silver gleamed on the two sideboards; she decided he had never been in a room as elegant as this.

"Mrs. Hopewell," he began, using her name in a way that sounded almost intimate, "I know you believe in Chrustian service."

"Well yes," she murmured.

"I know," he said and paused, looking very wise with his head cocked on one side, "that you're a good woman. Friends have told me."

Mrs. Hopewell never liked to be taken for a fool. "What are you selling?" she asked.

"Bibles," the young man said and his eye raced around the room before he added, "I see you have no family Bible in your parlor, I see that is the one lack you got!"

Mrs. Hopewell could not say, "My daughter is an atheist and won't let me keep the Bible in the parlor." She said, stiffening slightly, "I keep my Bible by my bedside." This was not the truth. It was in the attic somewhere.

"Lady," he said, "the word of God ought to be in the parlor."

"Well, I think that's a matter of taste," she began. "I think . . . ."

"Lady," he said, "for a Chrustian, the word of God ought to be in every room in the house besides in his heart. I know you're a Chrustian because I can see it in every line of your face."

She stood up and said, "Well, young man, I don't want to buy a Bible and I smell my dinner burning."

He didn't get up. He began to twist his hands and looking down at them, he said softly, "Well lady, I'll tell you the truth—not many people want to buy one nowadays and besides, I know I'm real simple. I don't know how to say a thing but to say it. I'm just a country boy." He glanced up into her unfriendly face. "People like you don't like to fool with country people like me!"

"Why!" she cried, "good country people are the salt of the earth! Besides, we all have different ways of doing, it takes all kinds to make the world go 'round. That's life!"

"You said a mouthful," he said.

"Why, I think there aren't enough good country people in the world!" she said, stirred. "I think that's what's wrong with it!"

His face had brightened. "I didn't inraduce myself," he said. "I'm Manley Pointer from out in the country around Willohobie, not even from a place, just from near a place."

"You wait a minute," she said. "I have to see about my dinner." She went out to the kitchen and found Joy standing near the door where she had been listening.

"Get rid of the salt of the earth," she said, "and let's eat."

Mrs. Hopewell gave her a pained look and turned the heat down under the vegetables. *"I can't be rude to anybody,"* she murmured and went back into the parlor.

He had opened the suitcase and was sitting with a Bible on each knee.

"You might as well put those up," she told him. "I don't want one."

"I appreciate your honesty," he said. "You don't see any more real honest people unless you go way out in the country."

"I know," she said, "real genuine folks!" Through the crack in the door she heard a groan.

"I guess a lot of boys come telling you they're working their way through college," he said, "but I'm not going to tell you that. Somehow," he said, "I don't want to go to college. I want to devote my life to Chrustian service. See," he said, lowering his voice, "I got this heart condition. I may not live long. When you know it's something wrong with you and you may not live long, well then, lady . . ." He paused, with his mouth open, and stared at her.

He and Joy had the same condition! She knew that her eyes were filling with tears but she collected herself quickly and murmured, "Won't you stay for dinner? We'd love to have you!" and was sorry the instant she heard herself say it.

"Yes mam," he said in an abashed voice, "I would sher love to do that!"

Joy had given him one look on being introduced to him and then throughout the meal had not glanced at him again. He had addressed several remarks to her, which she had pretended not to hear. Mrs. Hopewell could not understand deliberate rudeness, although she lived with it, and she felt she had always to overflow with hospitality to make up for Joy's lack of courtesy. She urged him to talk about himself and he did. He said he was the seventh child of twelve and that his father had been crushed under a tree when he himself was eight year old. He had been crushed very badly, in fact, almost cut in two and was practically not recognizable. His mother had got along the best she could by hard working and she had always seen that her children went to Sunday School and that they read the Bible every evening. He was now nineteen year old and he had been selling Bibles for four months. In that time he had sold seventy-seven Bibles and had the promise of two more sales. He wanted to become a missionary because he thought that was the way you could do most for people. "He who losest his life shall find it," he said simply and he was so sincere, so genuine and earnest that Mrs. Hopewell would not for the world have smiled. He prevented his peas from sliding onto the table by blocking them with a piece of bread which he later cleaned his plate with. She could see Joy observing sidewise how he handled his knife and fork and she saw too that every few minutes, the boy would dart a keen appraising glance at the girl as if he were trying to attract her attention.

After dinner Joy cleared the dishes off the table and disappeared and Mrs. Hopewell was left to talk with him. He told her again about his childhood and his father's accident and about various things that had happened to him. Every five minutes or so she would stifle a yawn. He sat for two hours until finally she told him she must go because she had an appointment in town. He packed his Bibles and thanked her and prepared to leave, but in the doorway he stopped and wrung her hand and said that not on any of his trips had he met a lady as nice as her and he asked if he could come again. She had said she would always be happy to see him.

Joy had been standing in the road, apparently looking at something in the distance, when he came down the steps toward her, bent to the side with his heavy valise. He stopped where she was standing and confronted her directly. Mrs. Hopewell could not hear what he said but she trembled to think what Joy would say to him. She could see that after a minute Joy said something and that then the boy began to speak again, making an excited gesture with his free hand. After a minute Joy said something else at which the boy began to speak once more. Then to her amazement, Mrs. Hopewell saw the two of them walk off together, toward the gate. Joy had walked all the way to the gate with him and Mrs. Hopewell could not imagine what they had said to each other, and she had not yet dared to ask.

Mrs. Freeman was insisting upon her attention. She had moved from the refrigerator to the heater so that Mrs. Hopewell had to turn and face her in order to seem to be listening. "Glynese gone out with Harvey Hill again last night," she said. "She had this sty."

"Hill," Mrs. Hopewell said absently, "is that the one who works in the garage?"

"Nome, he's the one that goes to chiropracter school," Mrs. Freeman said. "She had this sty. Been had it two days. So she says when he brought her in the other night he says, 'Lemme get rid of that sty for you,' and she says, 'How?' and he says, 'You just lay yourself down acrost the seat of that car and I'll show you.' So she done it and he popped her neck. Kept on a-popping it several times until she made him quit. This morning," Mrs. Freeman said, "she ain't got no sty. She ain't got no traces of a sty."

"I never heard of that before," Mrs. Hopewell said.

"He ast her to marry him before the Ordinary," Mrs. Freeman went on, "and she told him she wasn't going to be married in no *office.*"

"Well, Glynese is a fine girl," Mrs. Hopewell said, "Glynese and Carramae are both fine girls."

"Carramae said when her and Lyman was married Lyman said it sure felt sacred to him. She said he said he wouldn't take five hundred dollars for being married by a preacher."

"How much would he take?" the girl asked from the stove.

"He said he wouldn't take five hundred dollars," Mrs. Freeman repeated.

"Well we all have work to do," Mrs. Hopewell said.

"Lyman said it just felt more sacred to him," Mrs. Freeman said. "The doctor wants Carramae to eat prunes. Says instead of medicine. Says them cramps is coming from pressure. You know where I think it is?"

"She'll be better in a few weeks," Mrs. Hopewell said.

"In the tube," Mrs. Freeman said. "Else she wouldn't be as sick as she is."

Hulga had cracked her two eggs into a saucer and was bringing them to the table along with a cup of coffee that she had filled too full. She sat down carefully and began to eat, meaning to keep Mrs. Freeman there by questions if for any reason she showed an inclination to leave. She could perceive her mother's eye on her. The first round-about question would be about the Bible salesman and she did not wish to bring it on. "How did he pop her neck?" she asked.

Mrs. Freeman went into a description of how he had popped her neck. She said he owned a '55 Mercury but that Glynese said she would rather marry a man with only a '36 Plymouth who would be married by a preacher. The girl asked what if he had a '32 Plymouth and Mrs. Freeman said what Glynese had said was a '36 Plymouth.

Mrs. Hopewell said there were not many girls with Glynese's common sense. She said what she admired in those girls was their common sense. She said that reminded her that they had a nice visitor yesterday, a young man selling Bibles. "Lord," she said, "he bored me to death but he was so sincere and genuine I couldn't be rude to him. He was just good country people, you know," she said, "—just the salt of the earth."

"I seen him walk up," Mrs. Freeman said, "and then later—I seen him walk off," and Hulga could feel the slight shift in her voice, the slight insinuation, that he had not walked off alone, had he? Her face remained expressionless but the color rose into her neck and she seemed to swallow it down with the next spoonful of egg. Mrs. Freeman was looking at her as if they had a secret together.

"Well, it takes all kinds of people to make the world go 'round," Mrs. Hopewell said. "It's very good we aren't all alike."

"Some people are more alike than others," Mrs. Freeman said.

Hulga got up and stumped, with about twice the noise that was necessary, into her room and locked the door. She was to meet the Bible salesman at ten o'clock at the gate. She had thought about it half the night. She had started thinking of it as a great joke and then she had begun to see profound implications in it. She had lain in bed imagining dialogues for them that were insane on the surface but that reached below to depths that no Bible salesman would be aware of. Their conversation yesterday had been of this kind.

He had stopped in front of her and had simply stood there. His face was bony and sweaty and bright, with a little pointed nose in the center of it, and his look was different from what it had been at the dinner table. He was gazing at her with open curiosity, with fascination, like a child watching a new fantastic animal at the zoo, and he was breathing as if he had run a great distance to reach her. His gaze seemed somehow familiar but she could not think where she had been regarded with it before. For almost a minute he didn't say anything. Then on what seemed an insuck of breath, he whispered, "You ever ate a chicken that was two days old?"

The girl looked at him stonily. He might have just put this question up for consideration at the meeting of a philosophical association. "Yes," she presently replied as if she had considered it from all angles.

"It must have been mighty small!" he said triumphantly and shook all over with little nervous giggles, getting very red in the face, and subsiding finally into his gaze of complete admiration, while the girl's expression remained exactly the same.

"How old are you?" he asked softly.

She waited some time before she answered. Then in a flat voice she said, "Seventeen."

His smiles came in succession like waves breaking on the surface of a little lake. "I see you got a wooden leg," he said. "I think you're real brave. I think you're real sweet."

The girl stood blank and solid and silent.

"Walk to the gate with me," he said. "You're a brave sweet little thing and I liked you the minute I seen you walk in the door."

Hulga began to move forward.

"What's your name?" he asked, smiling down on the top of her head.

"Hulga," she said.

"Hulga," he murmured, "Hulga. Hulga. I never heard of anybody name Hulga before. You're shy, aren't you, Hulga?" he asked.

She nodded, watching his large red hand on the handle of the giant valise.

"I like girls that wear glasses," he said. "I think a lot. I'm not like these people that a serious thought don't ever enter their heads. It's because I may die."

"I may die too," she said suddenly and looked up at him. His eyes were very small and brown, glittering feverishly.

"Listen," he said, "don't you think some people was meant to meet on account of what all they got in common and all? Like they both think serious thoughts and all?" He shifted the valise to his other hand so that the hand nearest her was free. He caught hold of her elbow and shook it a little. "I don't work on Saturday," he said. "I like to walk in the woods and see what Mother Nature is wearing. O'er the hills and far away. Pic-nics and things. Couldn't we go on a pic-nic tomorrow? Say yes, Hulga," he said and gave her a dying look as if he felt his insides about to drop out of him. He had even seemed to sway slightly toward her.

During the night she had imagined that she seduced him. She imagined that the two of them walked on the place until they came to the storage barn beyond the two back fields and there, she imagined, that things came to such a pass that she very easily seduced him and that then, of course, she had to reckon with his remorse. True genius can get an idea across even to an inferior mind. She imagined that she took his remorse in hand and changed it into a deeper understanding of life. She took all his shame away and turned it into something useful.

She set off for the gate at exactly ten o'clock, escaping without drawing Mrs. Hopewell's attention. She didn't take anything to eat, forgetting that food is usually taken on a picnic. She wore a pair of slacks and a dirty white shirt, and as an afterthought, she had put some Vapex on the collar of it since she did not own any perfume. When she reached the gate no one was there.

She looked up and down the empty highway and had the furious feeling that she had been tricked, that he had only meant to make her walk to the gate after the idea of him. Then suddenly he stood up, very tall, from behind a bush on the opposite embankment. Smiling, he lifted his hat which was new and wide-brimmed. He had not worn it yesterday and she wondered if he had bought it for the occasion. It was toast-colored with a red and white band around it and was slightly too large for him. He stepped from behind the bush still carrying the black valise. He had on the same suit and the same yellow socks sucked down in his shoes from walking. He crossed the highway and said, "I knew you'd come!"

The girl wondered acidly how he had known this. She pointed to the valise and asked, "Why did you bring your Bibles?"

He took her elbow, smiling down on her as if he could not stop. "You can never tell when you'll need the word of God, Hulga," he said. She had a moment in which she doubted that this was actually happening and then they began to climb the embankment. They went down into the pasture toward the woods. The boy walked lightly by her side, bouncing on his toes. The valise did not seem to be heavy today; he even swung it. They crossed half the pasture without saying anything and then, putting his hand easily on the small of her back, he asked softly, "Where does your wooden leg join on?"

She turned an ugly red and glared at him and for an instant the boy looked abashed. "I didn't mean you no harm," he said. "I only meant you're so brave and all. I guess God takes care of you."

"No," she said, looking forward and walking fast, "I don't even believe in God."

At this he stopped and whistled. "No!" he exclaimed as if he were too astonished to say anything else.

She walked on and in a second he was bouncing at her side, fanning with his hat. "That's very unusual for a girl," he remarked, watching her out of the corner of his eye. When they reached the edge of the wood, he put his hand on her back again and drew her against him without a word and kissed her heavily.

The kiss, which had more pressure than feeling behind it, produced that extra surge of adrenalin in the girl that enables one to carry a packed trunk out of a burning house, but in her, the power went at once to the brain. Even before he released her, her mind, clear and detached and ironic anyway, was regarding him from a great distance, with amusement but with pity. She had never been kissed before and she was pleased to discover that it was an unexceptional experience and all a matter of the mind's control. Some people might enjoy drain water if they were told it was vodka. When the boy, looking expectant but uncertain, pushed her gently away, she turned and walked on, saying nothing as if such business, for her, were common enough.

He came along panting at her side, trying to help her when he saw a root that she might trip over. He caught and held back the long swaying blades of thorn vine until she had passed beyond them. She led the way and he came breathing heavily behind her. Then they came out on a sunlit hillside, sloping softly into another one a little smaller. Beyond, they could see the rusted top of the old barn where the extra hay was stored.

The hill was sprinkled with small pink weeds. "Then you ain't saved?" he asked suddenly, stopping.

The girl smiled. It was the first time she had smiled at him at all. "In my economy," she said, "I'm saved and you are damned but I told you I didn't believe in God."

Nothing seemed to destroy the boy's look of admiration. He gazed at her now as if the fantastic animal at the zoo had put its paw through the bars and given him a loving poke. She thought he looked as if he wanted to kiss her again and she walked on before he had the chance.

"Ain't there somewheres we can sit down sometime?" he murmured, his voice softening toward the end of the sentence.

"In that barn," she said.

They made for it rapidly as if it might slide away like a train. It was a large two-story barn, cool and dark inside. The boy pointed up the ladder that led into the loft and said, "It's too bad we can't go up there."

"Why can't we?" she asked.

"Yer leg," he said reverently.

The girl gave him a contemptuous look and putting both hands on the ladder, she climbed it while he stood below, apparently awestruck. She pulled herself expertly through the opening and then looked down at him and said, "Well, come on if you're coming," and he began to climb the ladder, awkwardly bringing the suitcase with him.

"We won't need the Bible," she observed.

"You never can tell," he said, panting. After he had got into the loft, he was a few seconds catching his breath. She had sat down in a pile of straw. A wide sheath of sunlight, filled with dust particles, slanted over her. She lay back against a bale, her face turned away, looking out the front opening of the barn where hay was thrown from a wagon into the loft. The two pink-speckled hillsides lay back against a dark ridge of woods. The sky was cloudless and cold blue. The boy dropped down by her side and put one arm under her and the other over her and began methodically kissing her face, making little noises like a fish. He did not remove his hat but it was pushed far enough back not to interfere. When her glasses got in his way, he took them off of her and slipped them into his pocket.

The girl at first did not return any of the kisses but presently she began to and after she had put several on his cheek, she reached his lips and remained there, kissing him again and again as if she were trying to draw all the breath out of him. His breath was clear and sweet like a child's and the kisses were sticky like a child's. He mumbled about loving her and about knowing when he first seen her that he loved her, but the mumbling was like the sleepy fretting of a child being put to sleep by his mother. Her mind, throughout this, never stopped or lost itself for a second to her feelings. "You ain't said you love me none," he whispered finally, pulling back from her. "You got to say that."

She looked away from him off into the hollow sky and then down at a black ridge and then down farther into what appeared to be two green swelling lakes. She didn't realize he had taken her glasses but this landscape could not seem exceptional to her for she seldom paid any close attention to her surroundings.

"You got to say it," he repeated. "You got to say you love me."

She was always careful how she committed herself. "In a sense," she began, "if you use the word loosely, you might say that. But it's not a word I use. I don't have illusions. I'm one of those people who see *through* to nothing."

The boy was frowning. "You got to say it. I said it and you got to say it," he said.

The girl looked at him almost tenderly. "You poor baby," she murmured. "It's just as well you don't understand," and she pulled him by the neck, face-down, against her. "We are all damned," she said, "but some of us have taken off our blindfolds and see that there's nothing to see. It's a kind of salvation."

The boy's astonished eyes looked blankly through the ends of her hair. "Okay," he almost whined, "but do you love me or don'tcher?"

"Yes," she said and added, "in a sense. But I must tell you something. There mustn't be anything dishonest between us." She lifted his head and looked him in the eye. "I am thirty years old," she said. "I have a number of degrees."

The boy's look was irritated but dogged. "I don't care," he said. "I don't care a thing about what all you done. I just want to know if you love me or don'tcher?" and he caught her to him and wildly planted her face with kisses until she said, "Yes, yes."

"Okay then," he said, letting her go. "Prove it."

She smiled, looking dreamily out on the shifty landscape. She had seduced him without even making up her mind to try. "How?" she asked, feeling that he should be delayed a little.

He leaned over and put his lips to her ear. "Show me where your wooden leg joins on," he whispered.

The girl uttered a sharp little cry and her face instantly drained of color. The obscenity of the suggestion was not what shocked her. As a child she had sometimes been subject to feelings of shame but education had removed the last traces of that as a good surgeon scrapes for cancer; she would no more have felt it over what he was asking than she would have believed in his Bible. But she was as sensitive about the artificial leg as a peacock about his tail. No one ever touched it but her. She took care of it as someone else would his soul, in private and almost with her own eyes turned away. "No," she said.

"I known it," he muttered, sitting up. "You're just playing me for a sucker."

"Oh no no!" she cried. "It joins on at the knee. Only at the knee. Why do you want to see it?"

The boy gave her a long penetrating look. "Because," he said, "it's what makes you different. You ain't like anybody else."

She sat staring at him. There was nothing about her face or her round freezing-blue eyes to indicate that this had moved her; but she felt as if her heart had stopped and left her mind to pump her blood. She decided that for the first time in her life she was face to face with real innocence. This boy, with an instinct that came from beyond wisdom, had touched the truth about her. When after a minute, she said in a hoarse high voice, "All right," it was like surrendering to him completely. It was like losing her own life and finding it again, miraculously, in his.

Very gently he began to roll the slack leg up. The artificial limb, in a white sock and brown flat shoe, was bound in a heavy material like canvas and ended in an ugly jointure where it was attached to the stump. The boy's face and his voice were entirely reverent as he uncovered it and said, "Now show me how to take it off and on."

She took it off for him and put it back on again and then he took it off himself, handling it as tenderly as if it were a real one. "See!" he said with a delighted child's face. "Now I can do it myself!"

"Put it back on," she said. She was thinking that she would run away with him and that every night he would take the leg off and every morning put it back on again. "Put it back on," she said.

"Not yet," he murmured, setting it on its foot out of her reach. "Leave it off for a while. You got me instead."

She gave a little cry of alarm but he pushed her down and began to kiss her again. Without the leg she felt entirely dependent on him. Her brain seemed to have stopped thinking altogether and to be about some other function that it was not very good at. Different expressions raced back and forth over her face. Every now and then the boy, his eyes like two steel spikes, would glance behind him where the leg stood. Finally she pushed him off and said, "Put it back on me now."

"Wait," he said. He leaned the other way and pulled the valise toward him and opened it. It had a pale blue spotted lining and there were only two Bibles in it. He took one of these out and opened the cover of it. It was hollow and contained a pocket flask of whiskey, a pack of cards, and a small blue box with printing on it. He laid these out in front of her one at a time in an evenly spaced row, like one presenting offerings at the shrine of a goddess. He put the blue box in her hand. THIS PRODUCT TO BE USED ONLY FOR THE PREVENTION OF DISEASE, she read, and dropped it. The boy was unscrewing the top of the flask. He stopped and pointed, with a smile, to the deck of cards. It was not an ordinary deck but one with an obscene picture on the back of each card. "Take a swig," he said, offering her the bottle first. He held it in front of her, but like one mesmerized, she did not move.

Her voice when she spoke had an almost pleading sound. "Aren't you," she murmured, "aren't you just good country people?"

The boy cocked his head. He looked as if he were just beginning to understand that she might be trying to insult him. "Yeah," he said, curling his lip slightly, "but it ain't held me back none. I'm as good as you any day in the week."

"Give me my leg," she said.

He pushed it farther away with his foot. "Come on now, let's begin to have us a good time," he said coaxingly. "We ain't got to know one another good yet."

"Give me my leg!" she screamed and tried to lunge for it but he pushed her down easily.

"What's the matter with you all of a sudden?" he asked, frowning as he screwed the top on the flask and put it quickly back inside the Bible. "You just a while ago said you didn't believe in nothing. I thought you was some girl!"

Her face was almost purple. "You're a Christian!" she hissed. "You're a fine Christian! You're just like them all—say one thing and do another. You're a perfect Christian, you're . . ."

The boy's mouth was set angrily. "I hope you don't think," he said in a lofty indignant tone, "that I believe in that crap! I may sell Bibles but I know which end is up and I wasn't born yesterday and I know where I'm going!"

"Give me my leg!" she screeched. He jumped up so quickly that she barely saw him sweep the cards and the blue box back into the Bible and throw the Bible into the valise. She saw him grab the leg and then she saw it for an instant slanted forlornly across the inside of the suitcase with a Bible at either side of its opposite ends. He slammed the lid shut and snatched up the valise and swung it down the hole and then stepped through himself.

When all of him had passed but his head, he turned and regarded her with a look that no longer had any admiration in it. "I've gotten a lot of interesting things," he said. "One time I got a woman's glass eye this way. And you needn't to think you'll catch me because Pointer ain't really my name. I use a different name at every house I call at and don't stay nowhere long. And I'll tell you another thing, Hulga," he said, using the name as if he didn't think much of it, "you ain't so smart. I been believing in nothing ever since I was born!" and then the toast-colored hat disappeared down the hole and the girl was left, sitting on the straw in the dusty sunlight. When she turned her churning face toward the opening, she saw his blue figure struggling successfully over the green speckled lake.

Mrs. Hopewell and Mrs. Freeman, who were in the back pasture, digging up onions, saw him emerge a little later from the woods and head across the meadow toward the highway. "Why, that looks like that nice dull young man that tried to sell me a Bible yesterday," Mrs. Hopewell said, squinting. "He must have been selling them to the Negroes back in there. He was so simple," she said, "but I guess the world would be better off if we were all that simple."

Mrs. Freeman's gaze drove forward and just touched him before he disappeared under the hill. Then she returned her attention to the evil-smelling onion shoot she was lifting from the ground. "Some can't be that simple," she said. "I know I never could."

onions represent evil people hiding underground that will emerge and be found out

(1955)

A Good Man Is Hard to Find

The grandmother didn't want to go to Florida. She wanted to visit some of her connections in east Tennessee and she was seizing at every chance to change Bailey's mind. Bailey was the son she lived with, her only boy. He was sitting on the edge of his chair at the table, bent over the orange sports section of the *Journal*. "Now look here, Bailey," she said, "see here, read this," and she stood with one hand on her thin hip and the other rattling the newspaper at his bald head. "Here this fellow that calls himself The Misfit is aloose from the Federal Pen and headed toward Florida and you read here what it says he did to these people. Just you read it. I wouldn't take my children in any direction with a criminal like that aloose in it. I couldn't answer to my conscience if I did."

Bailey didn't look up from his reading so she wheeled around then and faced the children's mother, a young woman in slacks, whose face was as broad and innocent as a cabbage and was tied around with a green head-kerchief that had two points on the top like a rabbit's ears. She was sitting on the sofa, feeding the baby his apricots out of a jar. "The children have been to Florida before," the old lady said. "You all ought to take them somewhere else for a change so they would see different parts of the world and be broad. They never have been to east Tennessee."

The children's mother didn't seem to hear her but the eight-year-old boy, John Wesley, a stocky child with glasses, said, "If you don't want to go to Florida, why dontcha stay at home?" He and the little girl, June Star, were reading the funny papers on the floor.

"She wouldn't stay at home to be queen for a day," June Star said without raising her yellow head.

"Yes and what would you do if this fellow, The Misfit, caught you?" the grandmother asked.

"I'd smack his face," John Wesley said.

"She wouldn't stay at home for a million bucks," June Star said. "Afraid she'd miss something. She has to go everywhere we go."

"All right, Miss," the grandmother said. "Just remember that the next time you want me to curl your hair."

June Star said her hair was naturally curly.

The next morning the grandmother was the first one in the car, ready to go. She had her big black valise that looked like the head of a hippopotamus in one corner, and underneath it she was hiding a basket with Pity Sing, the cat, in it. She didn't intend for the cat to be left alone in the house for three days because he would miss her too much and she was afraid he might brush against one of the gas burners and accidentally asphyxiate himself. Her son, Bailey, didn't like to arrive at a motel with a cat.

She sat in the middle of the back seat with John Wesley and June Star on either side of her. Bailey and the children's mother and the baby sat in front and they left Atlanta at eight forty-five with the mileage on the car at 55890. The grandmother wrote this down because she thought it would be interesting to say how many miles they had been when they got back. It took them twenty minutes to reach the outskirts of the city.

The old lady settled herself comfortably, removing her white cotton gloves and putting them up with her purse on the shelf in front of the back window. The children's mother still had on slacks and still had her head tied up in a green kerchief, but the grandmother had on a navy blue straw sailor hat with a bunch of white violets on the brim and a navy blue dress with a small white dot in the print. Her collars and cuffs were white organdy trimmed with lace and at her neckline she had pinned a purple spray of cloth violets containing a sachet. In case of an accident, anyone seeing her dead on the highway would know at once that she was a lady.

She said she thought it was going to be a good day for driving, neither too hot nor too cold, and she cautioned Bailey that the speed limit was fifty-five miles an hour and that the patrolmen hid themselves behind billboards and small clumps of trees and sped out after you before you had a chance to slow down. She pointed out interesting details of the scenery: Stone Mountain; the blue granite that in some places came up to both sides of the highway; the brilliant red clay banks slightly streaked with purple; and the various crops that made rows of green lace-work on the ground. The trees were full of silver-white sunlight and the meanest of them sparkled. The children were reading comic magazines and their mother had gone back to sleep.

"Let's go through Georgia fast so we won't have to look at it much," John Wesley said.

"If I were a little boy," said the grandmother, "I wouldn't talk about my native state that way. Tennessee has the mountains and Georgia has the hills."

"Tennessee is just a hillbilly dumping ground," John Wesley said, "and Georgia is a lousy state too."

"You said it," June Star said.

"In my time," said the grandmother, folding her thin veined fingers, "children were more respectful of their native states and their parents and everything else. People did right then. Oh look at the cute little pickaninny!" she said and pointed to a Negro child standing in the door of a shack. "Wouldn't that make a picture, now?" she asked and they all turned and looked at the little Negro out of the back window. He waved.

"He didn't have any britches on," June Star said.

"He probably didn't have any," the grandmother explained. "Little niggers in the country don't have things like we do. If I could paint, I'd paint that picture," she said.

The children exchanged comic books.

The grandmother offered to hold the baby and the children's mother passed him over the front seat to her. She set him on her knee and bounced him and told him about the things they were passing. She rolled her eyes and screwed up her mouth and stuck her leathery thin face into his smooth bland one. Occasionally he gave her a far-away smile. They passed a large cotton field with five or six graves fenced in the middle of it, like a small island. "Look at the graveyard!" the grandmother said, pointing it out. "That was the old family burying ground. That belonged to the plantation."

"Where's the plantation?" John Wesley asked.

"Gone With the Wind," said the grandmother. "Ha. Ha."

When the children finished all the comic books they had brought, they opened the lunch and ate it. The grandmother ate a peanut butter sandwich and an olive and would not let the children throw the box and the paper napkins out the window. When there was nothing else to do they played a game by choosing a cloud and making the other two guess what shape it suggested. John Wesley took one of the shape of a cow and June Star guessed a cow and John Wesley said, no, an automobile, and June Star said he didn't play fair, and they began to slap each other over the grandmother.

The grandmother said she would tell them a story if they would keep quiet. When she told a story, she rolled her eyes and waved her head and was very dramatic. She said once when she was a maiden lady she had been courted by a Mr. Edgar Atkins Teagarden from Jasper, Georgia. She said he was a very good-looking man and a gentleman and that he brought her a watermelon every Saturday afternoon with his initials cut in it, E. A. T. Well, one Saturday, she said, Mr. Teagarden brought the watermelon and there was nobody at home and he left it on the front porch and returned in his buggy to Jasper, but she never got the watermelon, she said, because a nigger boy ate it when he saw the initials, E. A. T.! This story tickled John Wesley's funny bone and he giggled and giggled but June Star didn't think it was any good. She said she wouldn't marry a man that just brought her a watermelon on Saturday. The grandmother said she would have done well to marry Mr. Teagarden because he was a gentleman and had bought Coca-Cola stock when it first came out and that he had died only a few years ago, a very wealthy man.

They stopped at The Tower for barbecued sandwiches. The Tower was a part stucco and part wood filling station and dance hall set in a clearing outside of Timothy. A fat man named Red Sammy Butts ran it and there were signs stuck here and there on the building and for miles up and down the highway saying, TRY RED SAMMY'S FAMOUS BARBECUE. NONE LIKE FAMOUS RED SAMMY'S! RED SAM!

THE FAT BOY WITH THE HAPPY LAUGH! A VETERAN! RED SAMMY'S YOUR MAN!

Red Sammy was lying on the bare ground outside The Tower with his head under a truck while a gray monkey about a foot high, chained to a small chinaberry tree, chattered nearby. The monkey sprang back into the tree and got on the highest limb as soon as he saw the children jump out of the car and run toward him.

Inside, The Tower was a long dark room with a counter at one end and tables at the other and dancing space in the middle. They sat down at a board table next to the nickelodeon and Red Sam's wife, a tall burnt-brown woman with hair and eyes lighter than her skin, came and took their order. The children's mother put a dime in the machine and played "The Tennessee Waltz," and the grandmother said that tune always made her want to dance. She asked Bailey if he would like to dance but he only glared at her. He didn't have a naturally sunny disposition like she did and trips made him nervous. The grandmother's brown eyes were very bright. She swayed her head from side to side and pretended she was dancing in her chair. June Star said play something she could tap to so the children's mother put in another dime and played a fast number and June Star stepped out onto the dance floor and did her tap routine.

"Ain't she cute?" Red Sam's wife said, leaning over the counter. "Would you like to come be my little girl?"

"No I certainly wouldn't," June Star said. "I wouldn't live in a broken-down place like this for a million bucks!" and she ran back to the table.

"Ain't she cute?" the woman repeated, stretching her mouth politely.

"Aren't you ashamed?" hissed the grandmother.

Red Sam came in and told his wife to quit lounging on the counter and hurry up with these people's order. His khaki trousers reached just to his hip bones and his stomach hung over them like a sack of meal swaying under his shirt. He came over and sat down at a table nearby and let out a combination sigh and yodel. "You can't win," he said. "You can't win," and he wiped his sweating red face off with a gray handkerchief. "These days you don't know who to trust," he said. "Ain't that the truth?"

"People are certainly not nice like they used to be," said the grandmother.

"Two fellers come in here last week," Red Sammy said, "driving a Chrysler. It was a old beat-up car but it was a good one and these boys looked all right to me. Said they worked at the mill and you know I let them fellers charge the gas they bought? Now why did I do that?"

"Because you're a good man!" the grandmother said at once.

"Yes'm, I suppose so," Red Sam said as if he were struck with this answer.

His wife brought the orders, carrying the five plates all at once without a tray, two in each hand and one balanced on her arm. "It isn't a soul in this green world of God's that you can trust," she said. "And I don't count nobody out of that, not nobody," she repeated, looking at Red Sammy.

"Did you read about that criminal, The Misfit, that's escaped?" asked the grandmother.

"I wouldn't be a bit surprised if he didn't attact this place right here," said the woman. "If he hears about it being here, I wouldn't be none surprised to see him. If he hears it's two cent in the cash register, I wouldn't be a tall surprised if he . . ."

"That'll do," Red Sam said. "Go bring these people their Co'-Colas," and the woman went off to get the rest of the order.

"A good man is hard to find," Red Sammy said. "Everything is getting terrible. I remember the day you could go off and leave your screen door unlatched. Not no more."

He and the grandmother discussed better times. The old lady said that in her opinion Europe was entirely to blame for the way things were now. She said the way Europe acted you would think we were made of money and Red Sam said it was no use talking about it, she was exactly right. The children ran outside into the white sunlight and looked at the monkey in the lacy chinaberry tree. He was busy catching fleas on himself and biting each one carefully between his teeth as if it were a delicacy.

They drove off again into the hot afternoon. The grandmother took cat naps and woke up every few minutes with her own snoring. Outside of Toombsboro she woke up and recalled an old plantation that she had visited in this neighborhood once when she was a young lady. She said the house had six white columns across the front and that there was an avenue of oaks leading up to it and two little wooden trellis arbors on either side in front where you sat down with your suitor after a stroll in the garden. She recalled exactly which road to turn off to get to it. She knew that Bailey would not be willing to lose any time looking at an old house, but the more she talked about it, the more she wanted to see it once again and find out if the little twin arbors were still standing. "There was a secret panel in this house," she said craftily, not telling the truth but wishing that she were, "and the story went that all the family silver was hidden in it when Sherman came through but it was never found . . ."

"Hey!" John Wesley said. "Let's go see it! We'll find it! We'll poke all the woodwork and find it! Who lives there? Where do you turn off at? Hey Pop, can't we turn off there?"

"We never have seen a house with a secret panel!" June Star shrieked. "Let's go to the house with the secret panel! Hey Pop, can't we go see the house with the secret panel!"

"It's not far from here, I know," the grandmother said. "It wouldn't take over twenty minutes."

Bailey was looking straight ahead. His jaw was as rigid as a horseshoe. "No," he said.

The children began to yell and scream that they wanted to see the house with the secret panel. John Wesley kicked the back of the front seat and June Star hung over her mother's shoulder and whined desperately into her ear that they never had any fun even on their vacation, that they could never do what THEY wanted to do. The baby began to scream and John Wesley kicked the back of the seat so hard that his father could feel the blows in his kidney.

"All right!" he shouted and drew the car to a stop at the side of the road. "Will you all shut up? Will you all just shut up for one second? If you don't shut up, we won't go anywhere."

"It would be very educational for them," the grandmother murmured.

"All right," Bailey said, "but get this: this is the only time we're going to stop for anything like this. This is the one and only time."

"The dirt road that you have to turn down is about a mile back," the grandmother directed. "I marked it when we passed."

"A dirt road," Bailey groaned.

After they had turned around and were headed toward the dirt road, the grandmother recalled other points about the house, the beautiful glass over the front doorway and the candle-lamp in the hall. John Wesley said that the secret panel was probably in the fireplace.

"You can't go inside this house," Bailey said. "You don't know who lives there."

"While you all talk to the people in front, I'll run around behind and get in a window," John Wesley suggested.

"We'll all stay in the car," his mother said.

They turned onto the dirt road and the car raced roughly along in a swirl of pink dust. The grandmother recalled the times when there were no paved roads and thirty miles was a day's journey. The dirt road was hilly and there were sudden washes in it and sharp curves on dangerous embankments. All at once they would be on a hill, looking down over the blue tops of trees for miles around, then the next minute, they would be in a red depression with the dust-coated trees looking down on them.

"This place had better turn up in a minute," Bailey said, "or I'm going to turn around."

The road looked as if no one had traveled on it in months.

"It's not much farther," the grandmother said and just as she said it, a horrible thought came to her. The thought was so embarrassing that she turned red in the face and her eyes dilated and her feet jumped up, upsetting her valise in the corner. The instant the valise moved, the newspaper top she had over the basket under it rose with a snarl and Pitty Sing, the cat, sprang onto Bailey's shoulder.

The children were thrown to the floor and their mother, clutching the baby, was thrown out the door onto the ground; the old lady was thrown into the front seat. The car turned over once and landed right-side-up in a gulch off the side of the road. Bailey remained in the driver's seat with the cat—gray-striped with a broad white face and an orange nose—clinging to his neck like a caterpillar.

As soon as the children saw they could move their arms and legs, they scrambled out of the car, shouting, "We've had an ACCIDENT!" The grandmother was curled up under the dashboard, hoping she was injured so that Bailey's wrath would not come down on her all at once. The horrible thought she had had before the accident was that the house she had remembered so vividly was not in Georgia but in Tennessee.

Bailey removed the cat from his neck with both hands and flung it out the window against the side of a pine tree. Then he got out of the car and started looking for the children's mother. She was sitting against the side of the red gutted ditch, holding the screaming baby, but she only had a cut down her face and a broken shoulder. "We've had an ACCIDENT!" the children screamed in a frenzy of delight.

"But nobody's killed," June Star said with disappointment as the grandmother limped out of the car, her hat still pinned to her head but the broken front brim standing up at a jaunty angle and the violet spray hanging off the side. They all sat down in the ditch, except the children, to recover from the shock. They were all shaking.

"Maybe a car will come along," said the children's mother hoarsely.

"I believe I have injured an organ," said the grandmother, pressing her side, but no one answered her. Bailey's teeth were clattering. He had on a yellow sport shirt with bright blue parrots designed in it and his face was as yellow as the shirt. The grandmother decided that she would not mention that the house was in Tennessee.

The road was about ten feet above and they could see only the tops of the trees on the other side of it. Behind the ditch they were sitting in there were more woods, tall and dark and deep. In a few minutes they saw a car some distance away on top of a hill, coming slowly as if the occupants were watching them. The grandmother stood up and waved both arms dramatically to attract their attention. The car continued to come on slowly, disappeared around a bend and appeared again, moving even slower, on top of the hill they had gone over. It was a big black battered hearse-like automobile. There were three men in it.

It came to a stop just over them and for some minutes, the driver looked down with a steady expressionless gaze to where they were sitting, and didn't speak. Then he turned his head and muttered something to the other two and they got out. One was a fat boy in black trousers and a red sweat shirt with a silver stallion embossed on the front of it. He moved around on the right side of them and stood staring, his mouth partly open in a kind of loose grin. The other had on khaki pants and a blue striped coat and a gray hat pulled down very low, hiding most of his face. He came around slowly on the left side. Neither spoke.

The driver got out of the car and stood by the side of it, looking down at them. He was an older man than the other two. His hair was just beginning to gray and he wore silver-rimmed spectacles that gave him a scholarly look. He had a long creased face and didn't have on any shirt or undershirt. He had on blue jeans that were too tight for him and was holding a black hat and a gun. The two boys also had guns.

"We've had an ACCIDENT!" the children screamed.

The grandmother had the peculiar feeling that the bespectacled man was someone she knew. His face was as familiar to her as if she had known him all her life but she could not recall who he was. He moved away from the car and began to come down the embankment, placing his feet carefully so that he wouldn't slip. He had on tan and white shoes and no socks, and his ankles were red and thin. "Good afternoon," he said. "I see you all had you a little spill."

"We turned over twice!" said the grandmother.

"Oncet," he corrected. "We seen it happen. Try their car and see will it run, Hiram," he said quietly to the boy with the gray hat.

"What you got that gun for?" John Wesley asked. "Whatcha gonna do with that gun?"

"Lady," the man said to the children's mother, "would you mind calling them children to sit down by you? Children make me nervous. I want all you to sit down right together there where you're at."

"What are you telling US what to do for?" June Star asked.

Behind them the line of woods gaped like a dark open mouth. "Come here," said their mother.

"Look here now," Bailey began suddenly, "we're in a predicament! We're in . . ."

The grandmother shrieked. She scrambled to her feet and stood staring. "You're The Misfit!" she said. "I recognized you at once!"

"Yes'm," the man said, smiling slightly as if he were pleased in spite of himself to be known, "but it would have been better for all of you, lady, if you hadn't of reckernized me."

Bailey turned his head sharply and said something to his mother that shocked even the children. The old lady began to cry and The Misfit reddened.

"Lady," he said, "don't you get upset. Sometimes a man says things he don't mean. I don't reckon he meant to talk to you thataway."

"You wouldn't shoot a lady, would you?" the grandmother said and removed a clean handkerchief from her cuff and began to slap at her eyes with it.

The Misfit pointed the toe of his shoe into the ground and made a little hole and then covered it up again. "I would hate to have to," he said.

"Listen," the grandmother almost screamed, "I know you're a good man. You don't look a bit like you have common blood. I know you must come from nice people!"

"Yes mam," he said, "finest people in the world." When he smiled he showed a row of strong white teeth. "God never made a finer woman than my mother and my daddy's heart was pure gold," he said. The boy with the red sweat shirt had come around behind them and was standing with his gun at his hip. The Misfit squatted down on the ground. "Watch them children, Bobby Lee," he said. "You know they make me nervous." He looked at the six of them huddled together in front of him and he seemed to be embarrassed as if he couldn't think of anything to say. "Ain't a cloud in the sky," he remarked, looking up at it. "Don't see no sun but don't see no cloud neither."

"Yes, it's a beautiful day," said the grandmother. "Listen," she said, "you shouldn't call yourself The Misfit because I know you're a good man at heart. I can just look at you and tell."

"Hush!" Bailey yelled. "Hush! Everybody shut up and let me handle this! He was squatting in the position of a runner about to sprint forward but he didn't move.

"I pre-chate that, lady," The Misfit said and drew a little circle in the ground with the butt of his gun.

"It'll take a half a hour to fix this here car," Hiram called, looking over the raised hood of it.

"Well, first you and Bobby Lee get him and that little boy to step over yonder with you," The Misfit said, pointing to Bailey and John Wesley. "The boys want to ast you something," he said to Bailey. "Would you mind stepping back in them woods there with them?"

"Listen," Bailey began, "we're in a terrible predicament! Nobody realizes what this is," his voice cracked. His eyes were as blue and intense as the parrots in his shirt and he remained perfectly still.

The grandmother reached up to adjust her hat brim as if she were going to the woods with him but it came off in her hand. She stood staring at it and after a second she let it fall on the ground. Hiram pulled Bailey up by the arm as if he were assisting an old man. John Wesley caught hold of his father's hand and Bobby Lee followed. They went off toward the woods and just as they reached the dark edge, Bailey turned and supporting himself against a gray naked pine trunk, he shouted, "I'll be back in a minute, Mamma, wait on me!"

"Come back this instant!" his mother shrilled but they all disappeared into the woods.

"Bailey Boy!" the grandmother called in a tragic voice but she found she was looking at The Misfit squatting on the ground in front of her. "I just know you're a good man," she said desperately. "You're not a bit common!"

"Nome, I ain't a good man," The Misfit said after a second as if he had considered her statement carefully, "but I ain't the worst in the world neither. My daddy said I was a different breed of dog from my brothers and sisters. 'You know,' Daddy said, 'it's some that can live their whole life out without asking about it and it's others has to know why it is, and this boy is one of the latters. He's going to be into everything!'" He put on his black hat and looked up suddenly and then away deep into the woods as if he were embarrassed again. "I'm sorry I don't have on a shirt before you ladies," he said, hunching his shoulders slightly. "We buried our clothes that we had on when we escaped and we're just making do until we can get better. We borrowed these from some folks we met," he explained.

"That's perfectly all right," the grandmother said. "Maybe Bailey has an extra shirt in his suitcase."

"I'll look and see terrectly," The Misfit said.

"Where are they taking him?" the children's mother screamed.

"Daddy was a card himself," The Misfit said. "You couldn't put anything over on him. He never got in trouble with the Authorities though. Just had the knack of handling them."

"You could be honest too if you'd only try," said the grandmother. "Think how wonderful it would be to settle down and live a comfortable life and not have to think about somebody chasing you all the time."

The Misfit kept scratching in the ground with the butt of his gun as if he were thinking about it. "Yes'm, somebody is always after you," he murmured.

The grandmother noticed how thin his shoulder blades were just behind his hat because she was standing up looking down on him. "Do you ever pray?" she asked.

He shook his head. All she saw was the black hat wiggle between his shoulder blades. "Nome," he said.

There was a pistol shot from the woods, followed closely by another. Then silence. The old lady's head jerked around. She could hear the wind move through the tree tops like a long satisfied insuck of breath. "Bailey Boy!" she called.

"I was a gospel singer for a while," The Misfit said. "I been most everything. Been in the arm service, both land and sea, at home and abroad, been twice married, been an undertaker, been with the railroads, plowed Mother Earth, been in a tornado, seen a man burnt alive oncet," and looked up at the children's mother and the little girl who were sitting close together, their faces white and their eyes glassy; "I even seen a woman flogged," he said.

"Pray, pray," the grandmother began, "pray, pray . . ."

"I never was a bad boy that I remember of," The Misfit said in an almost dreamy voice, "but somewheres along the line I done something wrong and got sent to the penitentiary. I was buried alive," and he looked up and held her attention to him by a steady stare.

"That's when you should have started to pray," she said. "What did you do to get sent to the penitentiary that first time?"

"Turn to the right, it was a wall," The Misfit said, looking up again at the cloudless sky. "Turn to the left, it was a wall. Look up it was a ceiling, look down it was a floor. I forget what I done, lady. I set there and set there, trying to remember what it was I done and I ain't recalled it to this day. Oncet in a while, I would think it was coming to me, but it never come."

"Maybe they put you in by mistake," the old lady said vaguely.

"Nome," he said. "It wasn't no mistake. They had the papers on me."

"You must have stolen something," she said.

The Misfit sneered slightly. "Nobody had nothing I wanted," he said. "It was a head-doctor at the penitentiary said what I had done was kill my daddy but I know that for a lie. My daddy died in nineteen ought nineteen of the epidemic flu and I never had a thing to do with it. He was buried in the Mount Hopewell Baptist churchyard and you can go there and see for yourself."

"If you would pray," the old lady said, "Jesus would help you."

"That's right," The Misfit said.

"Well then, why don't you pray?" she asked trembling with delight suddenly.

"I don't want no hep," he said. "I'm doing all right by myself."

Bobby Lee and Hiram came ambling back from the woods. Bobby Lee was dragging a yellow shirt with bright blue parrots in it.

"Throw me that shirt, Bobby Lee," The Misfit said. The shirt came flying at him and landed on his shoulder and he put it on. The grandmother couldn't name what the shirt reminded her of. "No, lady," The Misfit said while he was buttoning it up, "I found out the crime don't matter. You can do one thing or you can do another, kill a man or take a tire off his car, because sooner or later you're going to forget what it was you done and just be punished for it."

The children's mother had begun to make heaving noises as if she couldn't get her breath. "Lady," he asked, "would you and that little girl like to step off yonder with Bobby Lee and Hiram and join your husband?"

"Yes, thank you," the mother said faintly. Her left arm dangled helplessly and she was holding the baby, who had gone to sleep, in the other. "Hep that lady up, Hiram," The Misfit said as she struggled to climb out of the ditch, "and Bobby Lee, you hold onto that little girl's hand."

"I don't want to hold hands with him," June Star said. "He reminds me of a pig."

The fat boy blushed and laughed and caught her by the arm and pulled her off into the woods after Hiram and her mother.

Alone with The Misfit, the grandmother found that she had lost her voice. There was not a cloud in the sky nor any sun. There was nothing around her but woods. She wanted to tell him that he must pray. She opened and closed her mouth several times before anything came out. Finally she found herself saying, "Jesus, Jesus," meaning, Jesus will help you, but the way she was saying it, it sounded as if she might be cursing.

"Yes'm," The Misfit said as if he agreed. "Jesus thrown everything off balance. It was the same case with Him as with me except He hadn't committed any crime and they could prove I had committed one because they had the papers on me. Of course," he said, "they never shown me my papers. That's why I sign myself now. I said long ago, you get you a signature and sign everything you do and keep a copy of it. Then you'll know what you done and you can hold up the crime to the punishment and see do they match and in the end you'll have something to prove you ain't been treated right. I call myself The Misfit," he said, "because I can't make what all I done wrong fit what all I gone through in punishment."

There was a piercing scream from the woods, followed closely by a pistol report. "Does it seem right to you, lady, that one is punished a heap and another ain't punished at all?"

"Jesus!" the old lady cried. "You've got good blood! I know you wouldn't shoot a lady! I know you come from nice people! Pray! Jesus, you ought not to shoot a lady. I'll give you all the money I've got!"

"Lady," The Misfit said, looking beyond her far into the woods, "there never was a body that give the undertaker a tip."

There were two more pistol reports and the grandmother raised her head like a parched old turkey hen crying for water and called, "Bailey Boy, Bailey Boy!" as if her heart would break.

"Jesus was the only One that ever raised the dead." The Misfit continued, "and He shouldn't have done it. He thrown everything off balance. If He did what He said, then it's nothing for you to do but throw away everything and follow him, and if He didn't, then it's nothing for you to do but enjoy the few minutes you got left the best way you can—by killing somebody or burning down his house or doing some other meanness to him. No pleasure but meanness," he said and his voice had become almost a snarl.

"Maybe He didn't raise the dead," the old lady mumbled, not knowing what she was saying and feeling so dizzy that she sank down in the ditch with her legs twisted under her.

"I wasn't there so I can't say He didn't," The Misfit said. "I wisht I had of been there," he said, hitting the ground with his fist. "It ain't right I wasn't there because if I had of been there I would of known. Listen lady," he said in a high voice, "if I had of been there I would of known and I wouldn't be like I am now." His voice seemed about to crack and the grandmother's head cleared for an instant. She saw the man's face twisted close to her own as if he were going to cry and she murmured, "Why you're one of my babies. You're one of my own children!" She reached out and touched him on the shoulder. The Misfit sprang back as if a snake had bitten him and shot her three times through the chest. Then he put his gun down on the ground and took off his glasses and began to clean them.

Hiram and Bobby Lee returned from the woods and stood over the ditch, looking down at the grandmother who half sat and half lay in a puddle of blood with her legs crossed under her like a child's and her face smiling up at the cloudless sky.

Without his glasses, The Misfit's eyes were red-rimmed and pale and defenseless-looking. "Take her off and throw her where you thrown the others," he said, picking up the cat that was rubbing itself against his leg.

"She was a talker, wasn't she?" Bobby Lee said, sliding down the ditch with a yodel.

"She would have been a good woman," The Misfit said, "if it had been somebody there to shoot her every minute of her life."

"Some fun!" Bobby Lee said.

"Shut up, Bobby Lee," The Misfit said. "It's no real pleasure in life."

(1955)

Everything That Rises Must Converge

Her doctor had told Julian's mother that she must lose twenty pounds on account of her blood pressure, so on Wednesday nights Julian had to take her downtown on the bus for a reducing class at the Y. The reducing class was designed for working girls over fifty, who weighed from 165 to 200 pounds. His mother was one of the slimmer ones, but she said ladies did not tell their age or weight. She would not ride the buses by herself at night since they had been integrated, and because the reducing class was one of her few pleasures, necessary for her health, and *free,* she said Julian could at least put himself out to take her, considering all she did for him. Julian did not like to consider all she did for him, but every Wednesday night he braced himself and took her.

She was almost ready to go, standing before the hall mirror, putting on her hat, while he, his hands behind him, appeared pinned to the door frame, waiting like Saint Sebastian for the arrows to begin piercing him. The hat was new and had cost her seven dollars and a half. She kept saying, "Maybe I shouldn't have paid that for it. No, I shouldn't have. I'll take it off and return it tomorrow. I shouldn't have bought it."

Julian raised his eyes to heaven. "Yes, you should have bought it," he said. "Put it on and let's go." It was a hideous hat. A purple velvet flap came down on one side of it and stood up on the other; the rest of it was green and looked like a cushion with the stuffing out. He decided it was less comical than jaunty and pathetic. Everything that gave her pleasure was small and depressed him.

She lifted the hat one more time and set it down slowly on top of her head. Two wings of gray hair protruded on either side of her florid face, but her eyes, sky-blue, were as innocent and untouched by experience as they must have been when she was ten. Were it not that she was a widow who had struggled fiercely to feed and clothe and put him through school and who was supporting him still, "until he got on his feet," she might have been a little girl that he had to take to town.

"It's all right, it's all right," he said. "Let's go." He opened the door himself and started down the walk to get her going. The sky was a dying violet and the houses stood out darkly against it, bulbous liver-colored monstrosities of a uniform ugliness though no two were alike. Since this had been a fashionable neighborhood forty years ago, his mother persisted in thinking they did well to have an apartment in it. Each house had a narrow collar of dirt around it in which sat, usually, a grubby child. Julian walked with his hands in his pockets, his head down and thrust forward and his eyes glazed with the determination to make himself completely numb during the time he would be sacrificed to her pleasure.

The door closed and he turned to find the dumpy figure, surmounted by the atrocious hat, coming toward him. "Well," she said, "you only live once and paying a little more for it, I at least won't meet myself coming and going."

"Some day I'll start making money," Julian said gloomily—he knew he never would—"and you can have one of those jokes whenever you take the fit." But first they would move. He visualized a place where the nearest neighbors would be three miles away on either side.

"I think you're doing fine," she said, drawing on her gloves. "You've only been out of school a year. Rome wasn't built in a day."

She was one of the few members of the Y reducing class who arrived in hat and gloves and who had a son who had been to college. "It takes time," she said, "and the world is in such a mess. This hat looked better on me than any of the others, though when she brought it out I said, 'Take that thing back. I wouldn't have it on my head,' and she said, 'Now wait till you see it on,' and when she put it on me, I said, 'we-ull,' and she said, 'If you ask me, that hat does something for you and you do something for that hat, and besides,' she said, 'with that hat, you won't meet yourself coming and going.'"

Julian thought he could have stood his lot better if she had been selfish, if she had been an old hag who drank and screamed at him. He walked along, saturated in depression, as if in the midst of his martyrdom he had lost his faith. Catching sight of his long, hopeless, irritated face, she stopped suddenly with a grief-stricken look, and pulled back on his arm. "Wait on me," she said. "I'm going back to the house and take this thing off and tomorrow I'm going to return it. I was out of my head. I can pay the gas bill with the seven-fifty."

He caught her arm in a vicious grip. "You are not going to take it back," he said. "I like it."

"Well," she said, "I don't think I ought . . ."

"Shut up and enjoy it," he muttered, more depressed than ever.

"With the world in the mess it's in," she said, "it's a wonder we can enjoy anything. I tell you, the bottom rail is on the top."

Julian sighed.

"Of course," she said, "if you know who you are, you can go anywhere." She said this every time he took her to the reducing class. "Most of them in it are not our kind of people," she said, "but I can be gracious to anybody. I know who I am."

"They don't give a damn for your graciousness," Julian said savagely. "Knowing who you are is good for one generation only. You haven't the foggiest idea where you stand now or who you are."

She stopped and allowed her eyes to flash at him. "I most certainly do know who I am," she said, "and if you don't know who you are, I'm ashamed of you."

"Oh hell," Julian said.

"Your great-grandfather was a former governor of this state," she said. "Your grandfather was a prosperous landowner. Your grandmother was a Godhigh."

"Will you look around you," he said tensely, "and see where you are now?" and he swept his arm jerkily out to indicate the neighborhood, which the growing darkness at least made less dingy.

"You remain what you are," she said. "Your great-grandfather had a plantation and two hundred slaves."

"There are no more slaves," he said irritably.

"They were better off when they were," she said. He groaned to see that she was off on that topic. She rolled onto it every few days like a train on an open track. He knew every stop, every junction, every swamp along the way, and knew the exact point at which her conclusion would roll majestically into the station: "It's ridiculous. It's simply not realistic. They should rise, yes, but on their own side of the fence."

"Let's skip it," Julian said.

"The ones I feel sorry for," she said, "are the ones that are half white. They're tragic."

"Will you skip it?"

"Suppose we were half white. We would certainly have mixed feelings."

"I have mixed feelings now," he groaned.

"Well let's talk about something pleasant," she said. "I remember going to Grandpa's when I was a little girl. Then the house had double stairways that went up to what was really the second floor—all the cooking was done on the first. I used to like to stay down in the kitchen on account of the way the walls smelled. I would sit with my nose pressed against the plaster and take deep breaths. Actually the place belonged to the Godhighs but your grandfather Chestny paid the mortgage and saved it for them. They were in reduced circumstances," she said, "but reduced or not, they never forgot who they were."

"Doubtless that decayed mansion reminded them," Julian muttered. He never spoke of it without contempt or thought of it without longing. He had seen it once when he was a child before it had been sold. The double stairways had rotted and been torn down. Negroes were living in it. But it remained in his mind as his mother had known it. It appeared in his dreams regularly. He would stand on the wide porch, listening to the rustle of oak leaves, then wander through the high-ceilinged hall into the parlor that opened onto it and gaze at the worn rugs and faded draperies. It occurred to him that it was he, not she, who could have appreciated it. He preferred its threadbare elegance to anything he could name and it was because of it that all the neighborhoods they had lived in had been a torment to him—whereas she had hardly known the difference. She called her insensitivity "being adjustable."

"And I remember the old darky who was my nurse, Caroline. There was no better person in the world. I've always had a great respect for my colored friends," she said. "I'd do anything in the world for them and they'd . . ."

"Will you for God's sake get off that subject?" Julian said. When he got on a bus by himself, he made it a point to sit down beside a Negro, in reparation as it were for his mother's sins.

"You're mighty touchy tonight," she said. "Do you feel all right?"

"Yes I feel all right," he said. "Now lay off."

She pursed her lips. "Well, you certainly are in a vile humor," she observed. "I just won't speak to you at all."

They had reached the bus stop. There was no bus in sight and Julian, his hands still jammed in his pockets and his head thrust forward, scowled down the empty street. The frustration of having to wait on the bus as well as ride on it began to creep up his neck like a hot hand. The presence of his mother was borne in upon him as she gave a pained sigh. He looked at her bleakly. She was holding herself very erect under the preposterous hat, wearing it like a banner of her imaginary dignity. There was in him an evil urge to break her spirit. He suddenly unloosened his tie and pulled it off and put it in his pocket.

She stiffened. "Why must you look like *that* when you take me to town?" she said. "Why must you deliberately embarrass me?"

"If you'll never learn where you are," he said, "you can at least learn where I am."

"You look like a—thug," she said.

"Then I must be one," he murmured.

"I'll just go home," she said. "I will not bother you. If you can't do a little thing like that for me . . ."

Rolling his eyes upward, he put his tie back on. "Restored to my class," he muttered. He thrust his face toward her and hissed, "True culture is in the mind, the *mind,*" he said, and tapped his head, "the mind."

"It's in the heart," she said, "and in how you do things and how you do things is because of who you *are.*"

"Nobody in the damn bus cares who you are."

"I care who I am," she said icily.

The lighted bus appeared on top of the next hill and as it approached, they moved out into the street to meet it. He put his hand under her elbow and hoisted her up on the creaking step. She entered with a little smile, as if she were going into a drawing room where everyone had been waiting for her. While he put in the tokens, she sat down on one of the broad front seats for three which faced the aisle. A thin woman with protruding teeth and long yellow hair was sitting on the end of it. His mother moved up beside her and left room for Julian beside herself. He sat down and looked at the floor across the aisle where a pair of thin feet in red and white canvas sandals were planted.

His mother immediately began a general conversation meant to attract anyone who felt like talking. "Can it get any hotter?" she said and removed from her purse a folding fan, black with a Japanese scene on it, which she began to flutter before her.

"I reckon it might could," the woman with the protruding teeth said, "but I know for a fact my apartment couldn't get no hotter."

"It must get the afternoon sun," his mother said. She sat forward and looked up and down the bus. It was half filled. Everybody was white. "I see we have the bus to ourselves," she said. Julian cringed.

"For a change," said the woman across the aisle, the owner of the red and white canvas sandals. "I come on one the other day and they were thick as fleas—up front and all through."

"The world is in a mess everywhere," his mother said. "I don't know how we've let it get in this fix."

"What gets my goat is all those boys from good families stealing automobile tires," the woman with the protruding teeth said. "I told my boy, I said you may not be rich but you been raised right and if I ever catch you in any such mess, they can send you on to the reformatory. Be exactly where you belong."

"Training tells," his mother said. "Is your boy in high school?"

"Ninth grade," the woman said.

"My son just finished college last year. He wants to write but he's selling typewriters until he gets started," his mother said.

The woman leaned forward and peered at Julian. He threw her such a malevolent look that she subsided against the seat. On the floor across the aisle there was an abandoned newspaper. He got up and got it and opened it out in front of him. His mother discreetly continued the conversation in a lower tone but the woman across the aisle said in a loud voice, "Well that's nice. Selling typewriters is close to writing. He can go right from one to the other."

"I tell him," his mother said, "that Rome wasn't built in a day."

Behind the newspaper Julian was withdrawing into the inner compartment of his mind where he spent most of his time. This was a kind of mental bubble in which he established himself when he could not bear to be a part of what was going on around him. From it he could see out and judge but in it he was safe from any kind of penetration from without. It was the only place where he felt free of the general idiocy of his fellows. His mother had never entered it but from it he could see her with absolute clarity.

The old lady was clever enough and he thought that if she had started from any of the right premises, more might have been expected of her. She lived according to the laws of her own fantasy world, outside of which he had never seen her set foot. The law of it was to sacrifice herself for him after she had first created the necessity to do so by making a mess of things. If he had permitted her sacrifices, it was only because her lack of foresight had made them necessary. All of her life had been a struggle to act like a Chestny without the Chestny goods, and to give him everything she thought a Chestny ought to have; but since, said she, it was fun to struggle, why complain? And when you had won, as she had won, what fun to look back on the hard times! He could not forgive her that she had enjoyed the struggle and that she thought *she* had won.

What she meant when she said she had won was that she had brought him up successfully and had sent him to college and that he had turned out so well—good looking (her teeth had gone unfilled so that his could be straightened), intelligent (he realized he was too intelligent to be a success), and with a future ahead of him (there was of course no future ahead of him). She excused his gloominess on the grounds that he was still growing up and his radical ideas on his lack of practical experience. She said he didn't yet know a thing about "life," that he hadn't even entered the real world—when already he was as disenchanted with it as a man of fifty.

The further irony of all this was that in spite of her, he had turned out so well. In spite of going to only a third-rate college, he had, on his own initiative, come out with a first-rate education; in spite of growing up dominated by a small mind, he had ended up with a large one; in spite of all her foolish views, he was free of prejudice and unafraid to face facts. Most miraculous of all, instead of being blinded by love for her as she was for him, he had cut himself emotionally free of her and could see her with complete objectivity. He was not dominated by his mother.

The bus stopped with a sudden jerk and shook him from his meditation. A woman from the back lurched forward with little steps and barely escaped falling in his newspaper as she righted herself. She got off and a large Negro got on. Julian kept his paper lowered to watch. It gave him a certain satisfaction to see injustice in daily operation. It confirmed his view that with a few exceptions there was no one worth knowing within a radius of three hundred miles. The Negro was well dressed and carried a briefcase. He looked around and then sat down on the other end of the seat where the woman with the red and white canvas sandals was sitting. He immediately unfolded a newspaper and obscured himself behind it. Julian's mother's elbow at once prodded insistently into his ribs. "Now you see why I won't ride on these buses by myself," she whispered.

The woman with the red and white canvas sandals had risen at the same time the Negro sat down and had gone further back in the bus and taken the seat of the woman who had got off. His mother leaned forward and cast her an approving look.

Julian rose, crossed the aisle, and sat down in the place of the woman with the canvas sandals. From this position, he looked serenely across at his mother. Her face had turned an angry red. He stared at her, making his eyes the eyes of a stranger. He felt his tension suddenly lift as if he had openly declared war on her.

He would have liked to get in conversation with the Negro and to talk with him about art or politics or any subject that would be above the comprehension of those around them, but the man remained entrenched behind his paper. He was either ignoring the change of seating or had never noticed it. There was no way for Julian to convey his sympathy.

His mother kept her eyes fixed reproachfully on his face. The woman with the protruding teeth was looking at him avidly as if he were a type of monster new to her.

"Do you have a light?" he asked the Negro.

Without looking away from his paper, the man reached in his pocket and handed him a packet of matches.

"Thanks," Julian said. For a moment he held the matches foolishly. A NO SMOKING sign looked down upon him from over the door. This alone would not have deterred him; he had no cigarettes. He had quit smoking some months before because he could not afford it. "Sorry," he muttered and handed back the matches. The Negro lowered the paper and gave him an annoyed look. He took the matches and raised the paper again.

His mother continued to gaze at him but she did not take advantage of his momentary discomfort. Her eyes retained their battered look. Her face seemed to be unnaturally red, as if her blood pressure had risen. Julian allowed no glimmer of sympathy to show on his face. Having got the advantage, he wanted desperately to keep it and carry it through. He would have liked to teach her a lesson that would last her a while, but there seemed no way to continue the point. The Negro refused to come out from behind his paper.

Julian folded his arms and looked stolidly before him, facing her but as if he did not see her, as if he had ceased to recognize her existence. He visualized a scene in which, the bus having reached their stop, he would remain in his seat and when she said, "Aren't you going to get off?" he would look at her as at a stranger who had rashly addressed him. The corner they got off on was usually deserted, but it was well lighted and it would not hurt her to walk by herself the four blocks to the Y. He decided to wait until the time came and then decide whether or not he would let her get off by herself. He would have to be at the Y at ten to bring her back, but he could leave her wondering if he was going to show up. There was no reason for her to think she could always depend on him.

He retired again into the high-ceilinged room sparsely settled with large pieces of antique furniture. His soul expanded momentarily but then he became aware of his mother across from him and the vision shriveled. He studied her coldly. Her feet in little pumps dangled like a child's and did not quite reach the floor. She was training on him an exaggerated look of reproach. He felt completely detached from her. At that moment he could with pleasure have slapped her as he would have slapped a particularly obnoxious child in his charge.

He began to imagine various unlikely ways by which he could teach her a lesson. He might make friends with some distinguished Negro professor or lawyer and bring him home to spend the evening. He would be entirely justified but her blood pressure would rise to 300. He could not push her to the extent of making her have a stroke, and moreover, he had never been successful at making any Negro friends. He had tried to strike up an acquaintance on the bus with some of the better types, with ones that looked like professors or ministers or lawyers. One morning he had sat down next to a distinguished-looking dark brown man who had answered his questions with a sonorous solemnity but who had turned out to be an undertaker. Another day he had sat down beside a cigar-smoking Negro with a diamond ring on his finger, but after a few stilted pleasantries, the Negro had rung the buzzer and risen, slipping two lottery tickets into Julian's hand as he climbed over him to leave.

He imagined his mother lying desperately ill and his being able to secure only a Negro doctor for her. He toyed with that idea for a few minutes and then dropped it for a momentary vision of himself participating as a sympathizer in a sit-in demonstration. This was possible but he did not linger with it. Instead, he approached the ultimate horror. He brought home a beautiful suspiciously Negroid woman. Prepare yourself, he said. There is nothing you can do about it. This is the woman I've chosen. She's intelligent, dignified, even good, and she's suffered and she hasn't thought it *fun*. Now persecute us, go ahead and persecute us. Drive her out of here, but remember, you're driving me too. His eyes were narrowed and through the indignation he had generated, he saw his mother across the aisle, purple-faced, shrunken to the dwarf-like proportions of her moral nature, sitting like a mummy beneath the ridiculous banner of her hat.

He was tilted out of his fantasy again as the bus stopped. The door opened with a sucking hiss and out of the dark a large, gaily dressed, sullen-looking colored woman got on with a little boy. The child, who might have been four, had on a short plaid suit and a Tyrolean hat with a blue feather in it. Julian hoped that he would sit down beside him and that the woman would push in beside his mother. He could think of no better arrangement.

As she waited for her tokens, the woman was surveying the seating possibilities—he hoped with the idea of sitting where she was least wanted. There was something familiar-looking about her but Julian could not place what it was. She was a giant of a woman. Her face was set not only to meet opposition but to seek it out. The downward tilt of her large lower lip was like a warning sign: DON'T TAMPER WITH ME. Her bulging figure was encased in a green crepe dress and her feet overflowed in red shoes. She had on a hideous hat. A purple velvet flap came down on one side of it and stood up on the other; the rest of it was green and looked like a cushion with the stuffing out. She carried a mammoth red pocketbook that bulged throughout as if it were stuffed with rocks.

To Julian's disappointment, the little boy climbed up on the empty seat beside his mother. His mother lumped all children, black and white, into the common category, "cute," and she thought little Negroes were on the whole cuter than little white children. She smiled at the little boy as he climbed on the seat.

Meanwhile the woman was bearing down upon the empty seat beside Julian. To his annoyance, she squeezed herself into it. He saw his mother's face change as the woman settled herself next to him and he realized with satisfaction that this was more objectionable to her than it was to him. Her face seemed almost gray and there was a look of dull recognition in her eyes, as if suddenly she had sickened at some awful confrontation. Julian saw that it was because she and the woman had, in a sense, swapped sons. Though his mother would not realize the symbolic significance of this, she would feel it. His amusement showed plainly on his face.

The woman next to him muttered something unintelligible to herself. He was conscious of a kind of bristling next to him, muted growling like that of an angry cat. He could not see anything but the red pocketbook upright on the bulging green thighs. He visualized the woman as she had stood waiting for her tokens—the ponderous figure, rising from the red shoes upward over the solid hips, the mammoth bosom, the haughty face, to the green and purple hat.

His eyes widened.

The vision of the two hats, identical, broke upon him with the radiance of a brilliant sunrise. His face was suddenly lit with joy. He could not believe that Fate had thrust upon his mother such a lesson. He gave a loud chuckle so that she would look at him and see that he saw. She turned her eyes on him slowly. The blue in them seemed to have turned a bruised purple. For a moment he had an uncomfortable sense of her innocence, but it lasted only a second before principle rescued him. Justice entitled him to laugh. His grin hardened until it said to her as plainly as if he were saying aloud: Your punishment exactly fits your pettiness. This should teach you a permanent lesson.

Her eyes shifted to the woman. She seemed unable to bear looking at him and to find the woman preferable. He became conscious again of the bristling presence at his side. The woman was rumbling like a volcano about to become active. His mother's mouth began to twitch slightly at one corner. With a sinking heart, he saw incipient signs of recovery on her face and realized that this was going to strike her suddenly as funny and was going to be no lesson at all. She kept her eyes on the woman and an amused smile came over her face as if the woman were a monkey that had stolen her hat. The little Negro was looking up at her with large fascinated eyes. He had been trying to attract her attention for some time.

"Carver!" the woman said suddenly. "Come heah!"

When he saw that the spotlight was on him at last, Carver drew his feet up and turned himself toward Julian's mother and giggled.

"Carver!" the woman said. "You heah me? Come heah!"

Carver slid down from the seat but remained squatting with his back against the base of it, his head turned slyly around toward Julian's mother, who was smiling at him. The woman reached a hand across the aisle and snatched him to her. He righted himself and hung backwards on her knees, grinning at Julian's mother. "Isn't he cute?" Julian's mother said to the woman with the protruding teeth.

"I reckon he is," the woman said without conviction.

The Negress yanked him upright but he eased out of her grip and shot across the aisle and scrambled, giggling wildly, onto the seat beside his love.

"I think he likes me," Julian's mother said, and smiled at the woman. It was the smile she used when she was being particularly gracious to an inferior. Julian saw everything lost. The lesson had rolled off her like rain on a roof.

The woman stood up and yanked the little boy off the seat as if she were snatching him from contagion. Julian could feel the rage in her at having no weapon like his mother's smile. She gave the child a sharp slap across his leg. He howled once and then thrust his head into her stomach and kicked his feet against her shins. "Behave," she said vehemently.

The bus stopped and the Negro who had been reading the newspaper got off. The woman moved over and set the little boy down with a thump between herself and Julian. She held him firmly by the knee. In a moment he put his hands in front of his face and peeped at Julian's mother through his fingers.

"I see yoooooooo!" she said and put her hand in front of her face and peeped at him.

The woman slapped his hand down. "Quit yo' foolishness," she said, "before I knock the living Jesus out of you!"

Julian was thankful that the next stop was theirs. He reached up and pulled the cord. The woman reached up and pulled it at the same time. Oh my God, he thought. He had the terrible intuition that when they got off the bus together, his mother would open her purse and give the little boy a nickel. The gesture would be as natural to her as breathing. The bus stopped and the woman got up and lunged to the front, dragging the child, who wished to stay on, after her. Julian and his mother got up and followed. As they neared the door, Julian tried to relieve her of her pocketbook.

"No," she murmured, "I want to give the little boy a nickel."

"No!" Julian hissed. "No!"

She smiled down at the child and opened her bag. The bus door opened and the woman picked him up by the arm and descended with him, hanging at her hip. Once in the street she set him down and shook him.

Julian's mother had to close her purse while she got down the bus step but as soon as her feet were on the ground, she opened it again and began to rummage inside. "I can't find but a penny," she whispered, "but it looks like a new one."

"Don't do it!" Julian said fiercely between his teeth. There was a streetlight on the corner and she hurried to get under it so that she could better see into her pocketbook. The woman was heading off rapidly down the street with the child still hanging backward on her hand.

"Oh little boy!" Julian's mother called and took a few quick steps and caught up with them just beyond the lamppost. "Here's a bright new penny for you," and she held out the coin, which shone bronze in the dim light.

The huge woman turned and for a moment stood, her shoulders lifted and her face frozen with frustrated rage, and stared at Julian's mother. Then all at once she seemed to explode like a piece of machinery that had been given one ounce of pressure too much. Julian saw the black fist swing out with the red pocketbook. He shut his eyes and cringed as he heard the woman shout, "He don't take nobody's pennies!" When he opened his eyes, the woman was disappearing down the street with the little boy staring wide-eyed over her shoulder. Julian's mother was sitting on the sidewalk.

"I told you not to do that," Julian said angrily. "I told you not to do that!"

He stood over her for a minute, gritting his teeth. Her legs were stretched out in front of her and her hat was on her lap. He squatted down and looked her in the face. It was totally expressionless. "You got exactly what you deserved," he said. "Now get up."

He picked up her pocketbook and put what had fallen out back in it. He picked the hat up off her lap. The penny caught his eye on the sidewalk and he picked that up and let it drop before her eyes into the purse. Then he stood up and leaned over and held his hands out to pull her up. She remained immobile. He sighed. Rising above them on either side were black apartment buildings, marked with irregular rectangles of light. At the end of the block a man came out of a door and walked off in the opposite direction. "All right," he said, "suppose somebody happens by and wants to know why you're sitting on the sidewalk?"

She took the hand and, breathing hard, pulled heavily up on it and then stood for a moment, swaying slightly as if the spots of light in the darkness were circling around her. Her eyes, shadowed and confused, finally settled on his face. He did not try to conceal his irritation. "I hope this teaches you a lesson," he said. She leaned forward and her eyes raked his face. She seemed trying to determine his identity. Then, as if she found nothing familiar about him, she started off with a headlong movement in the wrong direction.

"Aren't you going on to the Y?" he asked.

"Home," she muttered.

"Well, are we walking?"

For answer she kept going. Julian followed along, his hands behind him. He saw no reason to let the lesson she had had go without backing it up with an explanation of its meaning. She might as well be made to understand what had happened to her. "Don't think that was just an uppity Negro woman," he said. "That was the whole colored race which will no longer take your condescending pennies. That was your black double. She can wear the same hat as you, and to be sure," he added gratuitously (because he thought it was funny), "it looked better on her than it did on you. What all this means," he said, "is that the old world is gone. The old manners are obsolete and your graciousness is not worth a damn." He thought bitterly of the house that had been lost for him. "You aren't who you think you are," he said.

She continued to plow ahead, paying no attention to him. Her hair had come undone on one side. She dropped her pocketbook and took no notice. He stooped and picked it up and handed it to her but she did not take it.

"You needn't act as if the world had come to an end," he said, "because it hasn't. From now on you've got to live in a new world and face a few realities for a change. Buck up," he said, "it won't kill you."

She was breathing fast.

"Let's wait on the bus," he said.

"Home," she said thickly.

"I hate to see you behave like this," he said. "Just like a child. I should be able to expect more of you." He decided to stop where he was and make her stop and wait for a bus. "I'm not going any farther," he said, stopping. "We're going on the bus."

She continued to go on as if she had not heard him. He took a few steps and caught her arm and stopped her. He looked into her face and caught his breath. He was looking into a face he had never seen before. "Tell Grandpa to come get me," she said.

He stared, stricken.

"Tell Caroline to come get me," she said.

Stunned, he let her go and she lurched forward again, walking as if one leg were shorter than the other. A tide of darkness seemed to be sweeping her from him. "Mother!" he cried. "Darling, sweetheart, wait!" Crumpling, she fell to the pavement. He dashed forward and fell at her side, crying, "Mamma, Mamma!" He turned her over. Her face was fiercely distorted. One eye, large and staring, moved slightly to the left as if it had become unmoored. The other remained fixed on him, raked his face again, found nothing and closed.

"Wait here, wait here!" he cried and jumped up and began to run for help toward a cluster of lights he saw in the distance ahead of him. "Help, help!" he shouted, but his voice was thin, scarcely a thread of sound. The lights drifted farther away the faster he ran and his feet moved numbly as if they carried him nowhere. The tide of darkness seemed to sweep him back to her, postponing from moment to moment his entry into the world of guilt and sorrow.

(1950)

CHAPTER SEVEN

The Short Novel

The short novel, sometimes called the *novella,* shares characteristics with both the novel and short story. Like the longer novel the *short novel* accumulates incidents and illustrates character over time in ways the short story cannot because of its more limited scope. Yet like the short story, the short novel relies on glimpses of understanding, flashes of insight, quick turns of action to solidify theme or reveal character. And while in the short novel such moments are both more frequent and of longer duration than in the typical short story, they are rarely rendered with the leisure or richness of detail characteristic of most long novels.

Unlike the short story, which must make its mark quickly, the short novel can allow a slower unfolding of character, incident, idea. The short story's brevity demands a single snapshot of time rather than the collage or mosaic that can be created in a novel, long or short. What distinguishes the short novel from its longer counterpart in this respect is its greater efficiency and sharper focus. Lacking time and space to accumulate incident, develop character, and amplify theme, the short novel works within a narrow compass, disavowing the novel's panoramic sweep. The result is a consistency of style and focus and a concentration and compression of effect that are the hallmarks of the short novel form.

Henry James, an American master of the short novel, called it a "blessed" form. And the novelist Vladimir Nabokov suggested that "by diminishing large things and enlarging small ones," the short novel is "intrinsically artistic." Finally, Irving Howe, a contemporary critic and editor of a fine collection of modern short novels, has noted that "in masterpieces of the genre, the action forms a harmonious equivalent to the motivating idea."

Two short novels worthy of such high praise are Franz Kafka's *The Metamorphosis* and James Joyce's *The Dead*.

FRANZ KAFKA

[1883–1924]

The Metamorphosis

TRANSLATED FROM THE GERMAN BY EDWIN AND WILLA MUIR

1

As Gregor Samsa awoke one morning from uneasy dreams he found himself transformed in his bed into a gigantic insect. He was lying on his hard, as it were armor-plated, back and when he lifted his head a little he could see his dome-like brown belly divided into stiff arched segments on top of which the bed quilt could hardly keep in position and was about to slide off completely. His numerous legs, which were pitifully thin compared to the rest of his bulk, waved helplessly before his eyes.

What has happened to me? he thought. It was no dream. His room, a regular human bedroom, only rather too small, lay quiet between the four familiar walls. Above the table on which a collection of cloth samples was unpacked and spread out—Samsa was a commercial traveler—hung the picture which he had recently cut out of an illustrated magazine and put into a pretty gilt frame. It showed a lady, with a fur cap on and a fur stole, sitting upright and holding out to the spectator a huge fur muff into which the whole of her forearm had vanished!

Gregor's eyes turned next to the window, and the overcast sky—one could hear rain drops beating on the window gutter—made him quite melancholy. What about sleeping a little longer and forgetting all this nonsense, he thought, but it could not be done, for he was accustomed to sleep on his right side and in his present condition he could not turn himself over. However violently he forced himself towards his right side he always rolled on to his back again. He tried it at least a hundred times, shutting his eyes to keep from seeing his struggling legs, and only desisted when he began to feel in his side a faint dull ache he had never experienced before.

Oh God, he thought, what an exhausting job I've picked on! Traveling about day in, day out. It's much more irritating work than doing the actual business in the office, and on top of that there's the trouble of constant traveling, of worrying about train connections, the bed and irregular meals, casual acquaintances that are always new and never become intimate friends. The devil take it all! He felt a slight itching up on his belly; slowly pushed himself on his back nearer to the top of the bed so that he could lift his head more easily; identified the itching place which was surrounded by many small white spots the nature of which he could not understand and made to touch it with a leg, but drew the leg back immediately, for the contact made a cold shiver run through him.

He slid down again into his former position. This getting up early, he thought, makes one quite stupid. A man needs his sleep. Other commercials live like harem women. For instance, when I come back to the hotel of a morning to write up the orders I've got, these others are only sitting down to breakfast. Let me just try that with my chief; I'd be sacked on the spot. Anyhow, that might be quite a good thing for me, who can tell? If I didn't have to hold my hand because of my parents I'd have given notice long ago, I'd have gone to the chief and told him exactly what I think of him. That would knock him endways from his desk! It's a queer way of doing, too, this sitting on high at a desk and talking down to employees, especially when they have to come quite near because the chief is hard of hearing. Well, there's still hope; once I've saved enough money to pay back my parents' debts to him—that should take another five or six years—I'll do it without fail. I'll cut myself completely loose then. For the moment, though, I'd better get up, since my train goes at five.

He looked at the alarm clock ticking on the chest. Heavenly Father! he thought. It was half-past six o'clock and the hands were quietly moving on, it was even past the half-hour, it was getting on toward a quarter to seven. Had the alarm clock not gone off? From the bed one could see that it had been properly set for four o'clock; of course it must have gone off. Yes, but was it possible to sleep quietly through that ear-splitting noise? Well, he had not slept quietly, yet apparently all the more soundly for that. But what was he to do now? The next train went at seven o'clock; to catch that he would need to hurry like mad and his samples weren't even packed up, and he himself wasn't feeling particularly fresh and active. And even if he did catch the train he wouldn't avoid a row with the chief, since the firm's porter would have been waiting for the five o'clock train and would have long since reported his failure to turn up. The porter was a creature of the chief's, spineless and stupid. Well, supposing he were to say he was sick? But that would be most unpleasant and would look suspicious, since during his five years' employment he had not been ill once. The chief himself would be sure to come with the sick-insurance doctor, would reproach his parents with their son's laziness and would cut all excuses short by referring to the insurance doctor, who of course regarded all mankind as perfectly healthy malingerers. And would he be so far wrong on this occasion? Gregor really felt quite well, apart from a drowsiness that was utterly superfluous after such a long sleep, and he was even unusually hungry.

As all this was running through his mind at top speed without his being able to decide to leave his bed—the alarm clock had just struck a quarter to seven—there came a cautious tap at the door behind the head of his bed. "Gregor," said a voice—it was his mother's—"it's a quarter to seven. Hadn't you a train to catch?" That gentle voice! Gregor had a shock as he heard his own voice answering hers, unmistakably his own voice, it was true, but with a persistent horrible twittering squeak behind it like an undertone, that left the words in their clear shape only for the first moment and then rose up reverberating round them to destroy their sense, so that one could not be sure one had heard them rightly. Gregor wanted to answer at length and explain everything, but in the circumstances he confined himself to saying: "Yes, yes, thank you, Mother, I'm getting up now." The wooden door between them must have kept the change in his voice from being noticeable outside, for his mother contented herself with this statement and shuffled away. Yet this brief exchange of words had made the other members of the family aware that Gregor was still in the house, as they had not expected, and at one of the side doors his father was already knocking, gently, yet with his fist. "Gregor, Gregor," he called, "what's the matter with you?" And after a little while he called again in a deeper voice: "Gregor! Gregor!" At the other side door his sister was saying in a low, plaintive tone: "Gregor? Aren't you well? Are you needing anything?" He answered them both at once: "I'm just ready," and did his best to make his voice sound as normal as possible by enunciating the words very clearly and leaving long pauses between them. So his father went back to his breakfast, but his sister whispered: "Gregor, open the door, do." However, he was not thinking of opening the door, and felt thankful for the prudent habit he had acquired in traveling of locking all doors during the night, even at home.

His immediate intention was to get up quietly without being disturbed, to put on his clothes and above all eat his breakfast, and only then to consider what else was to be done, since in bed, he was well aware, his meditations would come to no sensible conclusion. He remembered that often enough in bed he had felt small aches and pains, probably caused by awkward postures, which had proved purely imaginary once he got up, and he looked forward eagerly to seeing this morning's delusions gradually fall away. That the change in his voice was nothing but the precursor of a severe chill, a standing ailment of commercial travelers, he had not the least possible doubt.

To get rid of the quilt was quite easy; he had only to inflate himself a little and it fell off by itself. But the next move was difficult, especially because he was so uncommonly broad. He would have needed arms and hands to hoist himself up; instead he had only the numerous little legs which never stopped waving in all directions and which he could not control in the least. When he tried to bend one of them it was the first to stretch itself straight; and did he succeed at last in making it do what he wanted, all the other legs meanwhile waved the more wildly in a high degree of unpleasant agitation. "But what's the use of lying idle in bed," said Gregor to himself.

He thought that he might get out of bed with the lower part of his body first, but this lower part, which he had not yet seen and of which he could form no clear conception, proved too difficult to move; it shifted so slowly; and when finally, almost wild with annoyance, he gathered his forces together and thrust out recklessly, he had miscalculated the direction and bumped heavily against the lower end of the bed, and the stinging pain he felt informed him that precisely this lower part of his body was at the moment probably the most sensitive.

So he tried to get the top part of himself out first, and cautiously moved his head towards the edge of the bed. That proved easy enough, and despite its breadth and mass the bulk of his body at last slowly followed the movement of his head. Still, when he finally got his head free over the edge of the bed he felt too scared to go on advancing, for after all if he let himself fall in this way it would take a miracle to keep his head from being injured. And at all costs he must not lose consciousness now, precisely now; he would rather stay in bed.

But when after a repetition of the same efforts he lay in his former position again, sighing, and watched his little legs struggling against each other more wildly than ever, if that were possible, and saw no way of bringing any order into this arbitrary confusion, he told himself again that it was impossible to stay in bed and that the most sensible course was to risk everything for the smallest hope of getting away from it. At the same time he did not forget meanwhile to remind himself that cool reflection, the coolest possible, was much better than desperate resolves. In such moments he focused his eyes as sharply as possible on the window, but, unfortunately, the prospect of the morning fog, which muffled even the other side of the narrow street, brought him little encouragement and comfort. "Seven o'clock already," he said to himself when the alarm clock chimed again, "seven o'clock already and still such a thick fog." And for a little while he lay quiet, breathing lightly, as if perhaps expecting such complete repose to restore all things to their real and normal condition.

But then he said to himself: "Before it strikes a quarter past seven I must be quite out of this bed, without fail. Anyhow, by that time someone will have come from the office to ask for me, since it opens before seven." And he set himself to rocking his whole body at once in a regular rhythm, with the idea of swinging it out of the bed. If he tipped himself out in that way he could keep his head from injury by lifting it at an acute angle when he fell. His back seemed to be hard and was not likely to suffer from a fall on the carpet. His biggest worry was the loud crash he would not be able to help making, which would probably cause anxiety, if not terror, behind all the doors. Still, he must take the risk.

When he was already half out of the bed—the new method was more a game than an effort, for he needed only to hitch himself across by rocking to and fro—it struck him how simple it would be if he could get help. Two strong people—he thought of his father and the servant girl—would be amply sufficient; they would only have to thrust their arms under his convex back, lever him out of the bed, bend down with their burden and then be patient enough to let him turn himself right over on to the floor, where it was to be hoped his legs would then find their proper function. Well, ignoring the fact that the doors were all locked, ought he really to call for help? In spite of his misery he could not suppress a smile at the very idea of it.

He had got so far that he could barely keep his equilibrium when he rocked himself strongly, and he would have to nerve himself very soon for the final decision since in five minutes' time it would be a quarter past seven—when the front door bell rang. "That's someone from the office," he said to himself, and grew almost rigid, while his little legs only jigged about all the faster. For a moment everything stayed quiet. "They're not going to open the door," said Gregor to himself, catching at some kind of irrational hope. But then of course the servant girl went as usual to the door with her heavy tread and opened it. Gregor needed only to hear the first good morning of the visitor to know immediately who it was—the chief clerk himself. What a fate, to be condemned to work for a firm where the smallest omission at once gave rise to the gravest suspicion! Were all employees in a body nothing but scoundrels, was there not among them one single loyal devoted man who, had he wasted only an hour or so of the firm's time in a morning, was so tormented by conscience as to be driven out of his mind and actually incapable of leaving his bed? Wouldn't it really have been sufficient to send an apprentice to inquire—if any inquiry were necessary at all—did the chief clerk himself have to come and thus indicate to the entire family, an innocent family, that this suspicious circumstance could be investigated by no one less versed in affairs than himself? And more through the agitation caused by these reflections than through any act of will Gregor swung himself out of bed with all his strength. There was a loud thump, but it was not really a crash. His fall was broken to some extent by the carpet, his back, too, was less stiff than he thought, and so there was merely a dull thud, not so very startling. Only he had not lifted his head carefully enough and had hit it; he turned it and rubbed it on the carpet in pain and irritation.

"That was something falling down in there," said the chief clerk in the next room to the left. Gregor tried to suppose to himself that something like what had happened to him today might some day happen to the chief clerk; one really could not deny that it was possible. But as if in brusque reply to this supposition the chief clerk took a couple of firm steps in the next-door room and his patent leather boots creaked. From the right-hand room his sister was whispering to inform him of the situation: "Gregor, the chief clerk's here." "I know," muttered Gregor to himself; but he didn't dare to make his voice loud enough for his sister to hear it.

"Gregor," said his father now from the left-hand room, "the chief clerk has come and wants to know why you didn't catch the early train. We don't know what to say to him. Besides, he wants to talk to you in person. So open the door, please. He will be good enough to excuse the untidiness of your room." "Good morning, Mr. Samsa," the chief clerk was calling amiably meanwhile. "He's not well," said his mother to the visitor, while his father was still speaking through the door, "He's not well, sir, believe me. What else would make him miss a train! The boy thinks about nothing but his work. It makes me almost cross the way he never goes out in the evenings; he's been here the last eight days and has stayed at home every single evening. He just sits there quietly at the table reading a newspaper or looking through railway timetables. The only amusement he gets is doing fretwork. For instance, he spent two or three evenings cutting out a little picture frame; you would be surprised to see how pretty it is; it's hanging in his room; you'll see it in a minute when Gregor opens the door. I must say I'm glad you've come, sir; we should never have got him to unlock the door by ourselves; he's so obstinate; and I'm sure he's unwell, though he wouldn't have it to be so this morning." "I'm just coming," said Gregor slowly and carefully, not moving an inch for fear of losing one word of the conversation. "I can't think of any other explanation, madam," said the chief clerk. "I hope it's nothing serious. Although on the other hand I must say that we men of business—fortunately or unfortunately—very often simply have to ignore any slight indisposition, since business must be attended to." "Well, can the chief clerk come in now?" asked Gregor's father impatiently, again knocking on the door. "No," said Gregor. In the left-hand room a painful silence followed this refusal, in the right-hand room his sister began to sob.

Why didn't his sister join the others? She was probably newly out of bed and hadn't even begun to put on her clothes yet. Well, why was she crying? Because he wouldn't get up and let the chief clerk in, because he was in danger of losing his job, and because the chief would begin dunning his parents again for the old debts? Surely these were things one didn't need to worry about for the present. Gregor was still at home and not in the least thinking of deserting the family. At the moment, true, he was lying on the carpet and no one who knew the condition he was in could seriously expect him to admit the chief clerk. But for such a small discourtesy, which could plausibly be explained away somehow later on, Gregor could hardly be dismissed on the spot. And it seemed to Gregor that it would be much more sensible to leave him in peace for the present than to trouble him with tears and entreaties. Still, of course, their uncertainty bewildered them all and excused their behavior.

"Mr. Samsa," the chief clerk called now in a louder voice, "what's the matter with you? Here you are, barricading yourself in your room, giving only 'yes' and 'no' for answers, causing your parents a lot of unnecessary trouble and neglecting—I mention this only in passing—neglecting your business duties in an incredible fashion. I am speaking here in the name of your parents and of your chief, and I beg you quite seriously to give me an immediate and precise explanation. You amaze me, you amaze me. I thought you were a quiet, dependable person, and now all at once you seem bent on making a disgraceful exhibition of yourself. The chief did hint to me early this morning a possible explanation for your disappearance—with reference to the cash payments that were entrusted to you recently—but I almost pledged my solemn word of honor that this could not be so. But now that I see how incredibly obstinate you are, I no longer have the slightest desire to take your part at all. And your position in the firm is not so unassailable. I came with the intention of telling you all this in private, but since you are wasting my time so needlessly I don't see why your parents shouldn't hear it too. For some time past your work has been most unsatisfactory; this is not the season of the year for a business boom, of course, we admit that, but a season of the year for doing no business at all, that does not exist, Mr. Samsa, must not exist."

"But, sir," cried Gregor, beside himself and in his agitation forgetting everything else, "I'm just going to open the door this very minute. A slight illness, an attack of giddiness, has kept me from getting up. I'm still lying in bed. But I feel all right again. I'm getting out of bed now. Just give me a moment or two longer! I'm not quite so well as I thought. But I'm all right, really. How a thing like that can suddenly strike one down! Only last night I was quite well, my parents can tell you, or rather I did have a slight presentiment. I must have showed some sign of it. Why didn't I report it at the office! But one always thinks that an indisposition can be got over without staying in the house. Oh sir, do spare my parents! All that you're reproaching me with now has no foundation; no one has ever said a word to me about it. Perhaps you haven't looked at the last orders I sent in. Anyhow, I can still catch the eight o'clock train, I'm much the better for my few hours' rest. Don't let me detain you here, sir; I'll be attending to business very soon, and do be good enough to tell the chief so and to make my excuses to him!"

And while all this was tumbling out pell-mell and Gregor hardly knew what he was saying, he had reached the chest quite easily, perhaps because of the practice he had had in bed, and was now trying to lever himself upright by means of it. He meant actually to open the door, actually to show himself and speak to the chief clerk; he was eager to find out what the others, after all their insistence, would say at the sight of him. If they were horrified then the responsibility was no longer his and he could stay quiet. But if they took it calmly, then he had no reason either to be upset, and could really get to the station for the eight o'clock train if he hurried. At first he slipped down a few times from the polished surface of the chest, but at length with a last heave he stood upright; he paid no more attention to the pains in the lower part of his body, however they smarted. Then he let himself fall against the back of a near-by chair, and clung with his little legs to the edges of it. That brought him into control of himself again and he stopped speaking, for now he could listen to what the chief clerk was saying.

"Did you understand a word of it?" the chief clerk was asking; "surely he can't be trying to make fools of us?" "Oh dear," cried his mother, in tears, "perhaps he's terribly ill and we're tormenting him. Grete! Grete!" she called out then. "Yes Mother?" called his sister from the other side. They were calling to each other across Gregor's room. "You must go this minute for the doctor. Gregor is ill. Go for the doctor, quick.

Did you hear how he was speaking?" "That was no human voice," said the chief clerk in a voice noticeably low beside the shrillness of the mother's. "Anna! Anna!" his father was calling through the hall to the kitchen, clapping his hands, "get a locksmith at once!" And the two girls were already running through the hall with a swish of skirts—how could his sister have got dressed so quickly?—and were tearing the front door open. There was no sound of its closing again; they had evidently left it open, as one does in houses where some great misfortune has happened.

But Gregor was now much calmer. The words he uttered were no longer understandable, apparently, although they seemed clear enough to him, even clearer than before, perhaps because his ear had grown accustomed to the sound of them. Yet at any rate people now believed that something was wrong with him, and were ready to help him. The positive certainty with which these first measures had been taken comforted him. He felt himself drawn once more into the human circle and hoped for great and remarkable results from both the doctor and the locksmith, without really distinguishing precisely between them. To make his voice as clear as possible for the decisive conversation that was now imminent he coughed a little, as quietly as he could, of course, since this noise too might not sound like a human cough for all he was able to judge. In the next room meanwhile there was complete silence. Perhaps his parents were sitting at the table with the chief clerk, whispering, perhaps they were all leaning against the door and listening.

Slowly Gregor pushed the chair towards the door, then let go of it, caught hold of the door for support—the soles at the end of his little legs were somewhat sticky—and rested against it for a moment after his efforts. Then he set himself to turning the key in the lock with his mouth. It seemed, unhappily, that he hadn't really any teeth—what could he grip the key with?—but on the other hand his jaws were certainly very strong; with their help he did manage to set the key in motion, heedless of the fact that he was undoubtedly damaging them somewhere, since a brown fluid issued from his mouth, flowed over the key and dripped on the floor. "Just listen to that," said the chief clerk next door; "he's turning the key." That was a great encouragement to Gregor; but they should all have shouted encouragement to him, his father and mother too: "Go on, Gregor," they should have called out, "keep going, hold on to that key!" And in the belief that they were all following his efforts intently, he clenched his jaws recklessly on the key with all the force at his command. As the turning of the key progressed he circled round the lock, holding on now only with his mouth, pushing on the key, as required, or pulling it down again with all the weight of his body. The louder click of the finally yielding lock literally quickened Gregor. With a deep breath of relief he said to himself: "So I didn't need the locksmith," and laid his head on the handle to open the door wide.

Since he had to pull the door towards him, he was still invisible when it was really wide open. He had to edge himself slowly round the near half of the double door, and to do it very carefully if he was not to fall plump upon his back just on the threshold. He was still carrying out this difficult manoeuvre, with no time to observe anything else, when he heard the chief clerk utter a loud "Oh!"—it sounded like a gust of wind—and now he could see the man, standing as he was nearest to the door, clapping one hand before his open mouth and slowly backing away as if driven by some invisible steady pressure. His mother—in spite of the chief clerk's being there her hair was still undone and sticking up in all directions—first clasped her hands and looked at his father, then took two steps towards Gregor and fell on the floor among her out-spread skirts, her face quite hidden on her breast. His father knotted his fist with a fierce expression on his face as if he meant to knock Gregor back into his room, then looked uncertainly round the living room, covered his eyes with his hands and wept till his great chest heaved.

Gregor did not go now into the living room, but leaned against the inside of the firmly shut wing of the door, so that only half his body was visible and his head above it bending sideways to look at the others. The light had meanwhile strengthened; on the other side of the street one could see clearly a section of the endlessly long, dark gray building opposite—it was a hospital—abruptly punctuated by its row of regular windows; the rain was still falling, but only in large singly discernible and literally singly splashing drops. The breakfast dishes were set out on the table lavishly, for breakfast was the most important meal of the day to Gregor's father, who lingered it out for hours over various newspapers. Right opposite Gregor on the wall hung a photograph of himself on military service, as a lieutenant, hand on sword, a carefree smile on his face, inviting one to respect his uniform and military bearing. The door leading to the hall was open, and one could see that the front door stood open too, showing the landing beyond and the beginning of the stairs going down.

"Well," said Gregor, knowing perfectly that he was the only one who had retained any composure, "I'll put my clothes on at once, pack up my samples and start off. Will you only let me go? You see, sir, I'm not obstinate, and I'm willing to work; traveling is a hard life, but I couldn't live without it. Where are you going, sir? To the office? Yes? Will you give a true account of all this? One can be temporarily incapacitated, but that's just the moment for remembering former services and bearing in mind that later on, when the incapacity has been got over, one will certainly work with all the more industry and concentration. I'm loyally bound to serve the chief, you know that very well. Besides, I have to provide for my parents and my sister. I'm in great difficulties, but I'll get out of them again. Don't make things any worse for me than they are. Stand up for me in the firm. Travelers are not popular there, I know. People think they earn sacks of money and just have a good time. A prejudice there's no particular reason for revising. But you, sir, have a more comprehensive view of affairs than the rest of the staff, yes, let me tell you in confidence, a more comprehensive view than the chief him-self, who, being the owner, lets his judgment easily be swayed against one of his em-ployees. And you know very well that the traveler, who is never seen in the office al-most the whole year round, can so easily fall a victim to gossip and ill luck and unfounded complaints, which he mostly knows nothing about, except when he comes back ex-hausted from his rounds, and only then suffers in person from their evil consequences, which he can no longer trace back to the original causes. Sir, sir, don't go away with-out a word to me to show that you think me in the right at least to some extent!"

But at Gregor's very first words the chief clerk had already backed away and only stared at him with parted lips over one twitching shoulder. And while Gregor was speak-ing he did not stand still one moment but stole away towards the door, without tak-ing his eyes off Gregor, yet only an inch at a time, as if obeying some secret injunc-tion to leave the room. He was already at the hall, and the suddenness with which he took his last step out of the living room would have made one believe he had burned the sole of his foot. Once in the hall he stretched his right arm before him towards the staircase, as if some supernatural power were waiting there to deliver him.

Gregor perceived that the chief clerk must on no account be allowed to go away in this frame of mind if his position in the firm were not to be endangered to the utmost. His parents did not understand this so well; they had convinced themselves in the course of years that Gregor was settled for life in this firm, and besides they were so occupied with their immediate troubles that all foresight had forsaken them. Yet Gregor had this foresight. The chief clerk must be detained, soothed, persuaded and finally won over; the whole future of Gregor and his family depended on it! If only his sister had been there! She was intelligent; she had begun to cry while Gregor was still lying quietly on his back. And no doubt the chief clerk, so partial to ladies, would have been guided by her; she would have shut the door of the flat and in the hall talked him out of his horror. But she was not there, and Gregor would have to handle the situation himself. And without remembering that he was still unaware what powers of movement he possessed, without even remembering that his words in all possibility, indeed in all likelihood, would again be unintelligible, he let go the wing of the door, pushed himself through the opening, started to walk towards the chief clerk, who was already ridiculously clinging with both hands to the railing on the landing; but immediately, as he was feeling for a support, he fell down with a little cry upon all his numerous legs. Hardly was he down when he experienced for the first time this morning a sense of physical comfort; his legs had firm ground under them; they were completely obedient, as he noted with joy; they even strove to carry him forward in whatever direction he chose; and he was inclined to believe that a final relief from all his sufferings was at hand. But in the same moment as he found himself on the floor, rocking with suppressed eagerness to move, not far from his mother, indeed just in front of her, she, who had seemed so completely crushed, sprang all at once to her feet, her arms and fingers outspread, cried: "Help, for God's sake, help!" bent her head down as if to see Gregor better, yet on the contrary kept backing senselessly away; had quite forgotten that the laden table stood behind her; sat upon it hastily, as if in absence of mind, when she bumped into it; and seemed altogether unaware that the big coffee pot beside her was upset and pouring coffee in a flood over the carpet.

"Mother, Mother," said Gregor in a low voice, and looked up at her. The chief clerk, for the moment, had quite slipped from his mind; instead, he could not resist snapping his jaws together at the sight of the streaming coffee. That made his mother scream again, she fled from the table and fell into the arms of his father, who hastened to catch her. But Gregor had now no time to spare for his parents; the chief clerk was already on the stairs; with his chin on the banisters he was taking one last backward look. Gregor made a spring, to be as sure as possible of overtaking him; the chief clerk must have divined his intention, for he leaped down several steps and vanished; he was still yelling "Ugh!" and it echoed through the whole staircase.

Unfortunately, the flight of the chief clerk seemed completely to upset Gregor's father, who had remained relatively calm until now, for instead of running after the man himself, or at least not hindering Gregor in his pursuit, he seized in his right hand the walking stick which the chief clerk had left behind on a chair, together with a hat and greatcoat, snatched in his left hand a large newspaper from the table and began stamping his feet and flourishing the stick and the newspaper to drive Gregor back into his room. No entreaty of Gregor's availed, indeed no entreaty was even understood, however humbly he bent his head his father only stamped on the floor the more loudly. Behind his father his mother had torn open a window, despite the cold weather, and was leaning far out of it with her face in her hands. A strong draught set in from the street to the staircase, the window curtains blew in, the newspapers on the table fluttered, stray pages whisked over the floor. Pitilessly Gregor's father drove him back, hissing and crying "Shoo!" like a savage. But Gregor was quite unpracticed in walking backwards, it really was a slow business. If he only had a chance to turn round he could get back to his room at once, but he was afraid of exasperating his father by the slowness of such a rotation and at any moment the stick in his father's hand might hit him a fatal blow on the back or on the head. In the end, however, nothing else was left for him to do since to his horror he observed that in moving backwards he could not even control the direction he took; and so, keeping an anxious eye on his father all the time over his shoulder, he began to turn round as quickly as he could, which was in reality very slowly. Perhaps his father noted his good intentions, for he did not interfere except every now and then to help him in the manoeuvre from a distance with the point of the stick. If only he would have stopped making that unbearable hissing noise! It made Gregor quite lose his head. He had turned almost completely round when the hissing noise so distracted him that he even turned a little the wrong way again. But when at last his head was fortunately right in front of the doorway, it appeared that his body was too broad simply to get through the opening. His father, of course, in his present mood was far from thinking of such a thing as opening the other half of the door, to let Gregor have enough space. He had merely the fixed idea of driving Gregor back into his room as quickly as possible. He would never have suffered Gregor to make the circumstantial preparations for standing up on end and perhaps slipping his way through the door. Maybe he was now making more noise than ever to urge Gregor forward, as if no obstacle impeded him; to Gregor, anyhow, the noise in his rear sounded no longer like the voice of one single father; this was really no joke, and Gregor thrust himself—come what might—into the doorway. One side of his body rose up, he was tilted at an angle in the doorway, his flank was quite bruised, horrid blotches stained the white door, soon he was stuck fast and, left to himself, could not have moved at all, his legs on one side fluttered trembling to the air, those on the other were crushed painfully to the floor—when from behind his father gave him a strong push which was literally a deliverance and he flew far into the room, bleeding freely. The door was slammed behind him with the stick, and then at last there was silence.

2

Not until it was twilight did Gregor awake out of a deep sleep, more like a swoon than a sleep. He would certainly have waked up of his own accord not much later, for he felt himself sufficiently rested and well-slept, but it seemed to him as if a fleeting step and a cautious shutting of the door leading into the hall had aroused him. The electric lights in the street cast a pale sheen here and there on the ceiling and the upper surfaces of the furniture, but down below, where he lay, it was dark. Slowly, awkwardly trying out his feelers, which he now first learned to appreciate, he pushed his way to the door to see what had been happening there. His left side felt like one single long, unpleasantly tense scar, and he had actually to limp on his two rows of legs. One little leg, moreover, had been severely damaged in the course of that morning's events—it was almost a miracle that only one had been damaged—and trailed uselessly behind him.

He had reached the door before he discovered what had really drawn him to it: the smell of food. For there stood a basin filled with fresh milk in which floated little sops of white bread. He could almost have laughed with joy, since he was now still hungrier than in the morning, and he dipped his head almost over the eyes straight into the milk. But soon in disappointment he withdrew it again; not only did he find it difficult to feed because of his tender left side—and he could only feed with the palpitating collaboration of his whole body—he did not like the milk either, although milk had been his favorite drink and that was certainly why his sister had set it there for him, indeed it was almost with repulsion that he turned away from the basin and crawled back to the middle of the room.

He could see through the crack of the door that the gas was turned on in the living room, but while usually at this time his father made a habit of reading the afternoon newspaper in a loud voice to his mother and occasionally to his sister as well, not a sound was now to be heard. Well, perhaps his father had recently given up this habit of reading aloud, which his sister had mentioned so often in conversation and in her letters. But there was the same silence all around, although the flat was certainly not empty of occupants. "What a quiet life our family has been leading," said Gregor to himself, and as he sat there motionless staring into the darkness he felt great pride in the fact that he had been able to provide such a life for his parents and sister in such a fine flat. But what if all the quiet, the comfort, the contentment were now to end in horror? To keep himself from being lost in such thoughts Gregor took refuge in movement and crawled up and down the room.

Once during the long evening one of the side doors was opened a little and quickly shut again, later the other side door too; someone had apparently wanted to come in and then thought better of it. Gregor now stationed himself immediately before the living room door, determined to persuade any hesitating visitor to come in or at least to discover who it might be; but the door was not opened again and he waited in vain. In the early morning, when the doors were locked, they had all wanted to come in, now that he had opened one door and the other had apparently been opened during the day, no one came in and even the keys were on the other side of the doors.

It was late at night before the gas went out in the living room, and Gregor could easily tell that his parents and his sister had all stayed awake until then, for he could clearly hear the three of them stealing away on tiptoe. No one was likely to visit him, not until the morning, that was certain; so he had plenty of time to meditate at his leisure on how he was to arrange his life afresh. But the lofty, empty room in which he had to lie flat on the floor filled him with an apprehension he could not account for, since it had been his very own room for the past five years—and with a half-unconscious action, not without a slight feeling of shame, he scuttled under the sofa, where he felt comfortable at once, although his back was a little cramped and he could not lift his head up, and his only regret was that his body was too broad to get the whole of it under the sofa.

He stayed there all night, spending the time partly in a light slumber, from which his hunger kept waking him up with a start, and partly in worrying and sketching vague hopes, which all led to the same conclusion, that he must lie low for the present and, by exercising patience and the utmost consideration, help the family to bear the inconvenience he was bound to cause them in his present condition.

Very early in the morning, it was still almost night, Gregor had the chance to test the strength of his new resolutions, for his sister, nearly fully dressed, opened the door from the hall and peered in. She did not see him at once, yet when she caught sight of him under the sofa—well, he had to be somewhere, he couldn't have flown away, could he?—she was so startled that without being able to help it she slammed the door shut again. But as if regretting her behavior she opened the door again immediately and came in on tiptoe, as if she were visiting an invalid or even a stranger. Gregor had pushed his head forward to the very edge of the sofa and watched her. Would she notice that he had left the milk standing, and not for lack of hunger, and would she bring in some other kind of food more to his taste? If she did not do it of her own accord, he would rather starve than draw her attention to the fact, although he felt a wild impulse to dart out from under the sofa, throw himself at her feet and beg her for something to eat. But his sister at once noticed, with surprise, that the basin was still full, except for a little milk that had been spilt all around it, she lifted it immediately, not with her bare hands, true, but with a cloth and carried it away. Gregor was wildly curious to know what she would bring instead, and made various speculations about it. Yet what she actually did next, in the goodness of her heart, he could never have guessed at. To find out what he liked she brought him a whole selection of food, all set out on an old newspaper. There were old, half-decayed vegetables, bones from last night's supper covered with a white sauce that had thickened; some raisins and almonds; a piece of cheese that Gregor would have called uneatable two days ago; a dry roll of bread, a buttered roll, and a roll both buttered and salted. Besides all that, she set down again the same basin, into which she had poured some water, and which was apparently to be reserved for his exclusive use. And with fine tact, knowing that Gregor would not eat in her presence, she withdrew quickly and even turned the key, to let him understand that he could take his ease as much as he liked. Gregor's legs all whizzed towards the food. His wounds must have healed completely, moreover, for he felt no disability, which amazed him and made him reflect how more than a month ago he had cut one finger a little with a knife and had still suffered pain from the wound only the day before yesterday. Am I less sensitive now? he thought, and sucked greedily at the cheese, which above all the other edibles attracted him at once and strongly. One after another and with tears of satisfaction in his eyes he quickly devoured the cheese, the vegetables and the sauce; the fresh food, on the other hand, had no charms for him, he could not even stand the smell of it and actually dragged away to some little distance the things he could eat. He had long finished his meal and was only lying lazily on the same spot when his sister turned the key slowly as a sign for him to retreat. That roused him at once, although he was nearly asleep, and he hurried under the sofa again. But it took considerable self-control for him to stay under the sofa, even for the short time his sister was in the room, since the large meal had swollen his body somewhat and he was so cramped he could hardly breathe. Slight attacks of breathlessness afflicted him and his eyes were staring a little out of his head as he watched his unsuspecting sister sweeping together with a broom not only the remains of what he had eaten but even the things he had not touched, as if these were now of no use to anyone, and hastily shoveling it all into a bucket, which she covered with a wooden lid and carried away. Hardly had she turned her back when Gregor came from under the sofa and stretched and puffed himself out.

    In this manner Gregor was fed, once in the early morning while his parents and the servant girl were still asleep, and a second time after they had all had their midday dinner, for then his parents took a short nap and the servant girl could be sent out on some errand or other by his sister. Not that they would have wanted him to starve, of course, but perhaps they could not have borne to know more about his feeding than from hearsay, perhaps too his sister wanted to spare them such little anxieties wherever possible, since they had quite enough to bear as it was.

Under what pretext the doctor and the locksmith had been got rid of on that first morning Gregor could not discover, for since what he said was not understood by the others it never struck any of them, not even his sister, that he could understand what they said, and so whenever his sister came into his room he had to content himself with hearing her utter only a sigh now and then and an occasional appeal to the saints. Later on, when she had got a little used to the situation—of course she could never get completely used to it—she sometimes threw out a remark which was kindly meant or could be so interpreted. "Well, he liked his dinner today," she would say when Gregor had made a good clearance of his food; and when he had not eaten, which gradually happened more and more often, she would say almost sadly: "Everything's been left standing again."

But although Gregor could get no news directly, he overheard a lot from the neighboring rooms, and as soon as voices were audible, he would run to the door of the room concerned and press his whole body against it. In the first few days especially there was no conversation that did not refer to him somehow, even if only indirectly. For two whole days there were family consultations at every mealtime about what should be done; but also between meals the same subject was discussed, for there were always at least two members of the family at home, since no one wanted to be alone in the flat and to leave it quite empty was unthinkable. And on the very first of these days the household cook—it was not quite clear what and how much she knew of the situation—went down on her knees to his mother and begged leave to go, and when she departed, a quarter of an hour later, gave thanks for her dismissal with tears in her eyes as if for the greatest benefit that could have been conferred on her, and without any prompting swore a solemn oath that she would never say a single word to anyone about what had happened.

Now Gregor's sister had to cook too, helping her mother; true, the cooking did not amount to much, for they ate scarcely anything. Gregor was always hearing one of the family vainly urging another to eat and getting no answer but: "Thanks, I've had all I want," or something similar. Perhaps they drank nothing either. Time and again his sister kept asking her father if he wouldn't like some beer and offered kindly to go and fetch it herself, and when he made no answer suggested that she could ask the concierge to fetch it, so that he need feel no sense of obligation, but then a round "No" came from his father and no more was said about it.

In the course of that very first day Gregor's father explained the family's financial position and prospects to both his mother and his sister. Now and then he rose from the table to get some voucher or memorandum out of the small safe he had rescued from the collapse of his business five years earlier. One could hear him opening the complicated lock and rustling papers out and shutting it again. This statement made by his father was the first cheerful information Gregor had heard since his imprisonment. He had been of the opinion that nothing at all was left over from his father's business, at least his father had never said anything to the contrary, and of course he had not asked him directly. At that time Gregor's sole desire was to do his utmost to help the family to forget as soon as possible the catastrophe which had overwhelmed the business and thrown them all into a state of complete despair. And so he had set to work with unusual ardor and almost overnight had become a commercial traveler instead of a little clerk, with of course much greater chances of earning money, and his success was immediately translated into good round coin which he could lay on the table for his amazed and happy family. These had been fine times, and they had never recurred, at least not with the same sense of glory, although later on Gregor had earned so much money that he was able to meet the expenses of the whole household and did so. They had simply got used to it, both the family and Gregor; the money was gratefully accepted and gladly given, but there was no special uprush of warm feeling. With his sister alone had he remained intimate, and it was a secret plan of his that she, who loved music, unlike himself, and could play movingly on the violin, should be sent next year to study at the Conservatorium, despite the great expense that would entail, which must be made up in some other way. During his brief visits home the Conservatorium was often mentioned in the talks he had with his sister, but always merely as a beautiful dream which could never come true, and his parents discouraged even these innocent references to it; yet Gregor had made up his mind firmly about it and meant to announce the fact with due solemnity on Christmas Day.

Such were the thoughts, completely futile in his present condition, that went through his head as he stood clinging upright to the door and listening. Sometimes out of sheer weariness he had to give up listening and let his head fall negligently against the door, but he always had to pull himself together again at once, for even the slight sound his head made was audible next door and brought all conversation to a stop. "What can he be doing now?" his father would say after a while, obviously turning towards the door, and only then would the interrupted conversation gradually be set going again.

Gregor was now informed as amply as he could wish—for his father tended to repeat himself in his explanations, partly because it was a long time since he had handled such matters and partly because his mother could not always grasp things at once—that a certain amount of investments, a very small amount it was true, had survived the wreck of their fortunes and had even increased a little because the dividends had not been touched meanwhile. And besides that, the money Gregor brought home every month—he had kept only a few dollars for himself—had never been quite used up and now amounted to a small capital sum. Behind the door Gregor nodded his head eagerly, rejoiced at this evidence of unexpected thrift and foresight. True, he could really have paid off some more of his father's debts to the chief with his extra money, and so brought much nearer the day on which he could quit his job, but doubtless it was better the way his father had arranged it.

Yet this capital was by no means sufficient to let the family live on the interest of it; for one year, perhaps, or at the most two, they could live on the principal, that was all. It was simply a sum that ought not to be touched and should be kept for a rainy day; money for living expenses would have to be earned. Now his father was still hale enough but an old man, and he had done no work for the past five years and could not be expected to do much; during these five years, the first years of leisure in his laborious though unsuccessful life, he had grown rather fat and become sluggish. And Gregor's old mother, how was she to earn a living with her asthma, which troubled her even when she walked through the flat and kept her lying on a sofa every other day panting for breath beside an open window? And was his sister to earn her bread, she who was still a child of seventeen and whose life hitherto had been so pleasant, consisting as it did in dressing herself nicely, sleeping long, helping in the housekeeping, going out to a few modest entertainments and above all playing the violin? At first whenever the need for earning money was mentioned Gregor let go his hold on the door and threw himself down on the cool leather sofa beside it, he felt so hot with shame and grief.

Often he just lay there the long nights through without sleeping at all, scrabbling for hours on the leather. Or he nerved himself to the great effort of pushing an armchair to the window, then crawled up over the window sill and, braced against the chair, leaned against the window panes, obviously in some recollection of the sense of freedom that looking out of a window always used to give him. For in reality day by day things that were even a little way off were growing dimmer to his sight; the hospital across the street, which he used to execrate for being all too often before his eyes, was now quite beyond his range of vision, and if he had not known that he lived in Charlotte Street, a quiet street but still a city street, he might have believed that his window gave on a desert waste where gray sky and gray land blended indistinguishably into each other. His quick-witted sister only needed to observe twice that the armchair stood by the window; after that whenever she had tidied the room she always pushed the chair back to the same place at the window and even left the inner casements open.

If he could have spoken to her and thanked her for all she had to do for him, he could have borne her ministrations better; as it was, they oppressed him. She certainly tried to make as light as possible of whatever was disagreeable in her task, and as time went on she succeeded, of course, more and more, but time brought more enlightenment to Gregor too. The very way she came in distressed him. Hardly was she in the room when she rushed to the window, without even taking time to shut the door, careful as she was usually to shield the sight of Gregor's room from the others, and as if she were almost suffocating tore the casements open with hasty fingers, standing then in the open draught for a while even in the bitterest cold and drawing deep breaths. This noisy scurry of hers upset Gregor twice a day; he would crouch trembling under the sofa all the time, knowing quite well that she would certainly have spared him such a disturbance had she found it at all possible to stay in his presence without opening a window.

On one occasion, about a month after Gregor's metamorphosis, when there was surely no reason for her to be still startled at his appearance, she came a little earlier than usual and found him gazing out of the window, quite motionless, and thus well placed to look like a bogey. Gregor would not have been surprised had she not come in at all, for she could not immediately open the window while he was there, but not only did she retreat, she jumped back as if in alarm and banged the door shut; a stranger might well have thought that he had been lying in wait for her there meaning to bite her. Of course he hid himself under the sofa at once, but he had to wait until midday before she came again, and she seemed more ill at ease than usual. This made him realize how repulsive the sight of him still was to her, and that it was bound to go on being repulsive, and what an effort it must cost her not to run away even from the sight of the small portion of his body that stuck out from under the sofa. In order to spare her that, therefore, one day he carried a sheet on his back to the sofa—it cost him four hours' labor—and arranged it there in such a way as to hide him completely, so that even if she were to bend down she could not see him. Had she considered the sheet unnecessary, she would certainly have stripped it off the sofa again, for it was clear enough that this curtaining and confining of himself was not likely to conduce Gregor's comfort, but she left it where it was, and Gregor even fancied that he caught a thankful glance from her eye when he lifted the sheet carefully a very little with his head to see how she was taking the new arrangement.

For the first fortnight his parents could not bring themselves to the point of entering his room, and he often heard them expressing their appreciation of his sister's activities, whereas formerly they had frequently scolded her for being as they thought a somewhat useless daughter. But now, both of them often waited outside the door, his father and his mother, while his sister tidied his room, and as soon as she came out she had to tell them exactly how things were in the room, what Gregor had eaten, how he had conducted himself this time and whether there was not perhaps some slight improvement in his condition. His mother, moreover, began relatively soon to want to visit him, but his father and sister dissuaded her at first with arguments which Gregor listened to very attentively and altogether approved. Later, however, she had to be held back by main force, and when she cried out: "Do let me in to Gregor, he is my unfortunate son! Can't you understand that I must go to him?" Gregor thought that it might be well to have her come in, not every day, of course, but perhaps once a week; she understood things, after all, much better than his sister, who was only a child despite the efforts she was making and had perhaps taken on so difficult a task merely out of childish thoughtlessness.

Gregor's desire to see his mother was soon fulfilled. During the daytime he did not want to show himself at the window, out of consideration for his parents, but he could not crawl very far around the few square yards of floor space he had, nor could he bear lying quietly at rest all during the night, while he was fast losing any interest he had ever taken in food, so that for mere recreation he had formed the habit of crawling crisscross over the walls and ceiling. He especially enjoyed hanging suspended from the ceiling; it was much better than lying on the floor; one could breathe more freely; one's body swung and rocked lightly; and in the almost blissful absorption induced by this suspension it could happen to his own surprise that he let go and fell plump on the floor. Yet he now had his body much better under control than formerly, and even such a big fall did him no harm. His sister at once remarked the new distraction Gregor had found for himself—he left traces behind him of the sticky stuff on his soles wherever he crawled—and she got the idea in her head of giving him as wide a field as possible to crawl in and of removing the pieces of furniture that hindered him, above all the chest of drawers and the writing desk. But that was more than she could manage all by herself; she did not dare ask her father to help her; and as for the servant girl, a young creature of sixteen who had had the courage to stay on after the cook's departure, she could not be asked to help, for she had begged as an especial favor that she might keep the kitchen door locked and open it only on a definite summons; so there was nothing left but to apply to her mother at an hour when her father was out. And the old lady did come, with exclamations of joyful eagerness, which, however, died away at the door of Gregor's room. Gregor's sister, of course, went in first, to see that everything was in order before letting his mother enter. In great haste Gregor pulled the sheet lower and rucked it more in folds so that it really looked as if it had been thrown accidentally over the sofa. And this time he did not peer out from under it; he renounced the pleasure of seeing his mother on this occasion and was only glad that she had come at all. "Come in, he's out of sight," said his sister, obviously leading her mother in by the hand. Gregor could now hear the two women struggling to shift the heavy old chest from its place, and his sister claiming the greater part of the labor for herself, without listening to the admonitions of her mother who feared she might over-strain herself. It took a long time. After at least a quarter of an hour's tugging his mother objected that the chest had better be left where it was, for in the first place it was too heavy and could never be got out before his father came home, and standing in the middle of the room like that it would only hamper Gregor's movements, while in the second place it was not at all certain that removing the furniture would be doing a ser-vice to Gregor. She was inclined to think to the contrary; the sight of the naked walls made her own heart heavy, and why shouldn't Gregor have the same feeling, consid-ering that he had been used to his furniture for so long and might feel forlorn without it. "And doesn't it look," she concluded in a low voice—in fact she had been almost whispering all the time as if to avoid letting Gregor, whose exact whereabouts she did not know, hear even the tones of her voice, for she was convinced that he could not understand her words—"doesn't it look as if we were showing him, by taking away his furniture, that we have given up hope of his ever getting better and are just leav-ing him coldly to himself? I think it would be best to keep his room exactly as it has always been, so that when he comes back to us he will find everything unchanged and be able all the more easily to forget what has happened in between."

On hearing these words from his mother Gregor realized that the lack of all direct human speech for the past two months together with the monotony of family life must have confused his mind, otherwise he could not account for the fact that he had quite earnestly looked forward to having his room emptied of furnishing. Did he really want his warm room, so comfortably fitted with old family furniture, to be turned into a naked den in which he would certainly be able to crawl unhampered in all directions but at the price of shedding simultaneously all recollection of his human background? He had indeed been so near the brink of forgetfulness that only the voice of his mother, which he had not heard for so long, had drawn him back from it. Nothing should be taken out of his room; everything must stay as it was; he could not dispense with the good influence of the furniture on his state of mind; and even if the furniture did ham-per him in his senseless crawling round and round, that was no drawback but a great advantage.

Unfortunately his sister was of the contrary opinion; she had grown accustomed, and not without reason, to consider herself an expert in Gregor's affairs as against her par-ents, and so her mother's advice was now enough to make her determined on the re-moval not only of the chest and the writing desk, which had been her first intention, but of all the furniture except the indispensable sofa. This determination was not, of course, merely the outcome of childish recalcitrance and of the self-confidence she had recently developed so unexpectedly and at such cost; she had in fact perceived that Gre-gor needed a lot of space to crawl about in, while on the other hand he never used the furniture at all, so far as could be seen. Another factor might have been also the en-thusiastic temperament of an adolescent girl, which seeks to indulge itself on every op-portunity and which now tempted Grete to exaggerate the horror of her brother's cir-cumstances in order that she might do all the more for him. In a room where Gregor lorded it all alone over empty walls no one save herself was likely ever to set foot.

And so she was not to be moved from her resolve by her mother who seemed more-

over to be ill at ease in Gregor's room and therefore unsure of herself, was soon reduced to silence and helped her daughter as best she could to push the chest outside.
Now, Gregor could do without the chest, if need be, but the writing desk he must retain. As soon as the two women had got the chest out of his room, groaning as they
pushed it, Gregor stuck his head out from under the sofa to see how he might intervene as kindly and cautiously as possible. But as bad luck would have it, his mother
was the first to return, leaving Grete clasping the chest in the room next door where
she was trying to shift it all by herself, without of course moving it from the spot. His
mother however was not accustomed to the sight of him, it might sicken her and so
in alarm Gregor backed quickly to the other end of the sofa, yet could not prevent the
sheet from swaying a little in front. That was enough to put her on the alert. She paused,
stood still for a moment and then went back to Grete.

   Although Gregor kept reassuring himself that nothing out of the way was happening, but only a few bits of furniture were being changed round, he soon had to admit
that all this trotting to and fro of the two women, their little ejaculations and the scraping of furniture along the floor affected him like a vast disturbance coming from all
sides at once, and however much he tucked in his head and legs and cowered to the
very floor he was bound to confess that he would not be able to stand it for long. They
were clearing his room out; taking away everything he loved; the chest in which he
kept his fret saw and other tools was already dragged off; they were now loosening the
writing desk which had almost sunk into the floor, the desk at which he had done all
his homework when he was at the commercial academy, at the grammar school before that, and, yes, even at the primary school—he had no more time to waste in weighing the good intentions of the two women, whose existence he had by now almost
forgotten, for they were so exhausted that they were laboring in silence and nothing
could be heard but the heavy scuffling of their feet.

   And so he rushed out—the women were just leaning against the writing desk in the
next room to give themselves a breather—and four times changed his direction, since
he really did not know what to rescue first, then on the wall opposite, which was already otherwise cleared, he was struck by the picture of the lady muffled in so much
fur and quickly crawled up to it and pressed himself to the glass, which was a good surface to hold on to and comforted his hot belly. This picture at least, which was entirely hidden beneath him, was going to be removed by nobody. He turned his head
towards the door of the living room so as to observe the women when they came back.

   They had not allowed themselves much of a rest and were already coming; Grete
had twined her arm round her mother and was almost supporting her. "Well, what
shall we take now?" said Grete, looking round. Her eyes met Gregor's from the wall.
She kept her composure, presumably because of her mother, bent her head down to
her mother, to keep her from looking up, and said, although in a fluttering, un-
premeditated voice: "Come, hadn't we better go back to the living room for a moment?" Her intentions were clear enough to Gregor, she wanted to bestow her mother
in safety and then chase him down from the wall. Well, just let her try it! He clung to
his picture and would not give it up. He would rather fly in Grete's face.

   But Grete's words had succeeded in disquieting her mother, who took a step to one
side, caught sight of the huge brown mass on the flowered wallpaper, and before she
was really conscious that what she saw was Gregor screamed in a loud, hoarse voice:
"Oh God, oh God!" fell with outspread arms over the sofa as if giving up and did not

move. "Gregor!" cried his sister, shaking her fist and glaring at him. This was the first time she had directly addressed him since his metamorphosis. She ran into the next room for some aromatic essence with which to rouse her mother from her fainting fit. Gregor wanted to help too—there was still time to rescue the picture—but he was stuck fast to the glass and had to tear himself loose; he then ran after his sister into the next room as if he could advise her, as he used to do; but then had to stand helplessly behind her; she meanwhile searched among various small bottles and when she turned round started in alarm at the sight of him; one bottle fell on the floor and broke; a splinter of glass cut Gregor's face and some kind of corrosive medicine splashed him; without pausing a moment longer Grete gathered up all the bottles she could carry and ran to her mother with them; she banged the door shut with her foot. Gregor was now cut off from his mother, who was perhaps nearly dying because of him; he dared not open the door for fear of frightening away his sister, who had to stay with her mother; there was nothing he could do but wait; and harassed by self-reproach and worry he began now to crawl to and fro, over everything, walls, furniture and ceiling, and finally in his despair, when the whole room seemed to be reeling round him, fell down on to the middle of the big table.

A little while elapsed, Gregor was still lying there feebly and all around was quiet, perhaps that was a good omen. Then the doorbell rang. The servant girl was of course locked in her kitchen, and Grete would have to open the door. It was his father. "What's been happening?" were his first words; Grete's face must have told him everything. Grete answered in a muffled voice, apparently hiding her head on his breast: "Mother has been fainting, but she's better now. Gregor's broken loose." "Just what I expected," said his father, "just what I've been telling you, but you women would never listen." It was clear to Gregor that his father had taken the worst interpretation of Grete's all too brief statement and was assuming that Gregor had been guilty of some violent act. Therefore Gregor must now try to propitiate his father, since he had neither time nor means for an explanation. And so he fled to the door of his own room and crouched against it, to let his father see as soon as he came in from the hall that his son had the good intention of getting back into his room immediately and that it was not necessary to drive him there, but that if only the door were opened he would disappear at once.

Yet his father was not in the mood to perceive such fine distinctions. "Ah!" he cried as soon as he appeared, in a tone which sounded at once angry and exultant. Gregor drew his head back from the door and lifted it to look at his father. Truly, this was not the father he had imagined to himself; admittedly he had been too absorbed of late in his new recreation of crawling over the ceiling to take the same interest as before in what was happening elsewhere in the flat, and he ought really to be prepared for some changes. And yet, and yet, could that be his father? The man who used to lie wearily sunk in bed whenever Gregor set out on a business journey; who welcomed him back of an evening lying in a long chair in a dressing gown; who could not really rise to his feet but only lifted his arms in greeting, and on the rare occasions when he did go out with his family, on one or two Sundays a year and on high holidays, walked between Gregor and his mother, who were slow walkers anyhow, even more slowly than they did, muffled in his old great-coat, shuffling laboriously forward with the help of his crook-handled stick which he set down most cautiously at every step and, whenever he wanted to say anything, nearly always came to a full stop and gathered his escort around him? Now he was standing there in fine shape; dressed in a smart blue uniform with gold buttons, such as bank messengers wear; his strong double chin bulged over the stiff high collar of his jacket; from under his bushy eyebrows his black eyes darted fresh and penetrating glances; his onetime tangled white hair had been combed flat on either side of a shining and carefully exact parting. He pitched his cap, which bore a gold monogram, probably the badge of some bank, in a wide sweep across the whole room on to a sofa and with the tail-ends of his jacket thrown back, his hands in his trouser pockets, advanced with a grim visage towards Gregor. Likely enough he did not himself know what he meant to do; at any rate he lifted his feet uncommonly high, and Gregor was dumbfounded at the enormous size of his shoe soles. But Gregor could not risk standing up to him, aware as he had been from the very first day of his new life that his father believed only the severest measures suitable for dealing with him. And so he ran before his father, stopping when he stopped and scuttling forward again when his father made any kind of move. In this way they circled the room several times without anything decisive happening; indeed the whole operation did not even look like a pursuit because it was carried out so slowly. And so Gregor did not leave the floor, for he feared that his father might take as a piece of peculiar wickedness any excursion of his over the walls or the ceiling. All the same, he could not stay this course much longer, for while his father took one step he had to carry out a whole series of movements. He was already beginning to feel breathless, just as in his former life his lungs had not been very dependable. As he was staggering along, trying to concentrate his energy on running, hardly keeping his eyes open; in his dazed state never even thinking of any other escape than simply going forward; and having almost forgotten that the walls were free to him, which in this room were well provided with finely carved pieces of furniture full of knobs and crevices—suddenly something lightly flung landed close behind him and rolled before him. It was an apple; a second apple followed immediately; Gregor came to a stop in alarm; there was no point in running on, for his father was determined to bombard him. He had filled his pockets with fruit from the dish on the sideboard and was now shying apple after apple, without taking particularly good aim for the moment. The small red apples rolled about the floor as if magnetized and cannoned into each other. An apple thrown without much force grazed Gregor's back and glanced off harmlessly. But another following immediately landed right on his back and sank in; Gregor wanted to drag himself forward, as if this startling, incredible pain could be left behind him: but he felt as if nailed to the spot and flattened himself out in a complete derangement of all his senses. With his last conscious look he saw the door of his room being torn open and his mother rushing out ahead of his screaming sister, in her underbodice, for her daughter had loosened her clothing to let her breathe more freely and recover from her swoon, he saw his mother rushing towards his father, leaving one after another behind her on the floor her loosened petticoats, stumbling over her petticoats straight to his father and embracing him, in complete union with him—but here Gregor's sight began to fail—with her hands clasped round his father's neck as she begged for her son's life.

3

The serious injury done to Gregor, which disabled him for more than a month—the apple went on sticking in his body as a visible reminder, since no one ventured to remove it—seemed to have made even his father recollect that Gregor was a member of the family, despite his present unfortunate and repulsive shape, and ought not to be treated as an enemy, that, on the contrary, family duty required the suppression of disgust and the exercise of patience, nothing but patience.

And although his injury had impaired, probably for ever, his power of movement, and for the time being it took him long, long minutes to creep across his room like an old invalid—there was no question now of crawling up the wall—yet in his own opinion he was sufficiently compensated for this worsening of his condition by the fact that towards evening the living-room door, which he used to watch intently for an hour or two beforehand, was always thrown open, so that lying in the darkness of his room, invisible to the family, he could see them all at the lamp-lit table and listen to their talk, by general consent as it were, very different from his earlier eavesdropping.

True, their intercourse lacked the lively character of former times, which he had always called to mind with a certain wistfulness in the small hotel bedrooms where he had been wont to throw himself down, tired out, on damp bedding. They were now mostly very silent. Soon after supper his father would fall asleep in his armchair; his mother and sister would admonish each other to be silent; his mother, bending low over the lamp, stitched at fine sewing for an underwear firm; his sister, who had taken a job as a salesgirl, was learning shorthand and French in the evenings on the chance of bettering herself. Sometimes his father woke up, and as if quite unaware that he had been sleeping said to his mother: "What a lot of sewing you're doing today!" and at once fell asleep again, while the two women exchanged a tired smile.

With a kind of mulishness his father persisted in keeping his uniform on even in the house; his dressing gown hung uselessly on its peg and he slept fully dressed where he sat, as if he were ready for service at any moment and even here only at the beck and call of his superior. As a result, his uniform, which was not brand-new to start with, began to look dirty, despite all the loving care of the mother and sister to keep it clean, and Gregor often spent whole evenings gazing at the many greasy spots on the garment, gleaming with gold buttons always in a high state of polish, in which the old man sat sleeping in extreme discomfort and yet quite peacefully.

As soon as the clock struck ten his mother tried to rouse his father with gentle words and to persuade him after that to get into bed, for sitting there he could not have a proper sleep and that was what he needed most, since he had to go to duty at six. But with the mulishness that had obsessed him since he became a bank messenger he always insisted on staying longer at the table, although he regularly fell asleep again and in the end only with the greatest trouble could be got out of his armchair and into his bed. However insistently Gregor's mother and sister kept urging him with gentle reminders, he would go on slowly shaking his head for a quarter of an hour, keeping his eyes shut, and refuse to get to his feet. The mother plucked at his sleeve, whispering endearments in his ear, the sister left her lessons to come to her mother's help, but Gregor's father was not to be caught. He would only sink down deeper in his chair. Not until the two women hoisted him up by the armpits did he open his eyes and look at them both, one after the other, usually with the remark: "This is a life. This is the peace and quiet of my old age." And leaning on the two of them he would heave himself up, with difficulty, as if he were a great burden to himself, suffer them to lead him as far as the door and then wave them off and go on alone, while the mother abandoned her needlework and the sister her pen in order to run after him and help him farther.

Who could find time, in this overworked and tired-out family, to bother about Gregor more than was absolutely needful? The household was reduced more and more; the servant girl was turned off; a gigantic bony charwoman with white hair flying round her head came in morning and evening to do the rough work; everything else was done by Gregor's mother, as well as great piles of sewing. Even various family ornaments, which his mother and sister used to wear with pride at parties and celebrations, had to be sold, as Gregor discovered of an evening from hearing them all discuss the prices obtained. But what they lamented most was the fact that they could not leave the flat which was much too big for their present circumstances, because they could not think of any way to shift Gregor. Yet Gregor saw well enough that consideration for him was not the main difficulty preventing the removal, for they could have easily shifted him in some suitable box with a few air holes in it; what really kept them from moving into another flat was rather their own complete hopelessness and the belief that they had been singled out for a misfortune such as had never happened to any of their relations or acquaintances. They fulfilled to the uttermost all that the world demands of poor people, the father fetched breakfast for the small clerks in the bank, the mother devoted her energy to making underwear for strangers, the sister trotted to and fro behind the counter at the behest of customers, but more than this they had not the strength to do. And the wound in Gregor's back began to nag at him afresh when his mother and sister, after getting his father into bed, came back again, left their work lying, drew close to each other and sat cheek by cheek; when his mother, pointing towards his room, said: "Shut that door now, Grete," and he was left again in darkness, while next door the women mingled their tears or perhaps sat dry-eyed staring at the table.

Gregor hardly slept at all by night or by day. He was often haunted by the idea that next time the door opened he would take the family's affairs in hand again just as he used to do; once more, after this long interval, there appeared in his thoughts the figures of the chief and the chief clerk, the commercial travelers and the apprentices, the porter who was so dull-witted, two or three friends in other firms, a chambermaid in one of the rural hotels, a sweet and fleeting memory, a cashier in a milliner's shop, whom he had wooed earnestly but too slowly—they all appeared, together with strangers or people he had quite forgotten, but instead of helping him and his family they were one and all unapproachable and he was glad when they vanished. At other times he would not be in the mood to bother about his family, he was only filled with rage at the way they were neglecting him, and although he had no clear idea of what he might care to eat he would make plans for getting into the larder to take the food that was after all his due, even if he were not hungry. His sister no longer took thought to bring him what might especially please him, but in the morning and at noon before she went to business hurriedly pushed into his room with her foot any food that was available, and in the evening cleared it out again with one sweep of the broom, heedless of whether it had been merely tasted, or—as most frequently happened—left untouched. The cleaning of his room, which she now did always in the evenings, could not have been more hastily done. Streaks of dirt stretched along the walls, here and there lay balls of dust and filth. At first Gregor used to station himself in some particularly filthy corner when his sister arrived, in order to reproach her with it, so to speak. But he could have sat there for weeks without getting her to make any improvements; she could see the dirt as well as he did, but she had simply made up her mind to leave it alone. And yet, with a touchiness that was new to her, which seemed anyhow to have infected the whole family, she jealously guarded her claim to be the sole caretaker of Gregor's room.

His mother once subjected his room to a thorough cleaning, which was achieved only by means of several buckets of water—all this dampness of course upset Gregor too and he lay widespread, sulky and motionless on the sofa—but she was well punished for it. Hardly had his sister noticed the changed aspect of his room that evening than she rushed in high dudgeon into the living room and, despite the imploringly raised hands of her mother, burst into a storm of weeping, while her parents—her father had of course been startled out of his chair—looked on at first in helpless amazement; then they too began to go into action; the father reproached the mother on his right for not having left the cleaning of Gregor's room to his sister; shrieked at the sister on his left that never again was she to be allowed to clean Gregor's room; while the mother tried to pull the father into his bedroom, since he was beyond himself with agitation; the sister, shaken with sobs, then beat upon the table with her small fists; and Gregor hissed loudly with rage because not one of them thought of shutting the door to spare him such a spectacle and so much noise.

Still, even if the sister, exhausted by her daily work, had grown tired of looking after Gregor as she did formerly, there was no need for his mother's intervention or for Gregor's being neglected at all. The charwoman was there. This old widow, whose strong bony frame had enabled her to survive the worst a long life could offer, by no means recoiled from Gregor. Without being in the least curious she had once by chance opened the door of his room and at the sight of Gregor, who, taken by surprise, began to rush to and fro although no one was chasing him, merely stood there with her arms folded. From that time she never failed to open his door a little for a moment, morning and evening, to have a look at him. At first she even used to call him to her, with words which apparently she took to be friendly, such as: "Come along, then, you old dung beetle!" or "Look at the old dung beetle, then!" To such allocutions Gregor made no answer, but stayed motionless where he was, as if the door had never been opened. Instead of being allowed to disturb him so senselessly whenever the whim took her, she should rather have been ordered to clean out his room daily, that charwoman! Once, early in the morning—heavy rain was lashing on the windowpanes, perhaps a sign that spring was on the way—Gregor was so exasperated when she began addressing him again that he ran at her, as if to attack her, although slowly and feebly enough. But the charwoman instead of showing fright merely lifted high a chair that happened to be beside the door, and as she stood there with her mouth wide open it was clear that she meant to shut it only when she brought the chair down on Gregor's back. "So you're not coming any nearer?" she asked, as Gregor turned away again, and quietly put the chair back into the corner.

Gregor was now eating hardly anything. Only when he happened to pass the food laid out for him did he take a bit of something in his mouth as a pastime, kept it there for an hour at a time and usually spat it out again. At first he thought it was chagrin over the state of his room that prevented him from eating, yet he soon got used to the various changes in his room. It had become a habit in the family to push into his room things there was no room for elsewhere, and there were plenty of these now, since one of the rooms had been let to three lodgers. These serious gentlemen—all three of them with full beards, as Gregor once observed through a crack in the door—had a passion for order, not only in their own room but, since they were now members of the household, in all its arrangements, especially in the kitchen. Superfluous, not to say dirty, objects they could not bear. Besides, they had brought with them most of the furnishings they needed. For this reason many things could be dispensed with that it was no use trying to sell but that should not be thrown away either. All of them found their way into Gregor's room. The ash can likewise and the kitchen garbage can. Anything that was not needed for the moment was simply flung into Gregor's room by the charwoman, who did everything in a hurry; fortunately Gregor usually saw only the object, whatever it was, and the hand that held it. Perhaps she intended to take the things away again as time and opportunity offered, or to collect them until she could throw them all out in a heap, but in fact they just lay wherever she happened to throw them, except when Gregor pushed his way through the junk heap and shifted it somewhat, at first out of necessity, because he had not room enough to crawl, but later with increasing enjoyment, although after such excursions, being sad and weary to death, he would lie motionless for hours. And since the lodgers often ate their supper at home in the common living room, the living-room door stayed shut many an evening, yet Gregor reconciled himself quite easily to the shutting of the door, for often enough on evenings when it was opened he had disregarded it entirely and lain in the darkest corner of his room, quite unnoticed by the family. But on one occasion the charwoman left the door open a little and it stayed ajar even when the lodgers came in for supper and the lamp was lit. They set themselves at the top end of the table where formerly Gregor and his father and mother had eaten their meals, unfolded their napkins and took knife and fork in hand. At once his mother appeared in the other doorway with a dish of meat and close behind her his sister with a dish of potatoes piled high. The food steamed with a thick vapor. The lodgers bent over the food set before them as if to scrutinize it before eating, in fact the man in the middle, who seemed to pass for an authority with the other two, cut a piece of meat as it lay on the dish, obviously to discover if it were tender or should be sent back to the kitchen. He showed satisfaction, and Gregor's mother and sister, who had been watching anxiously, breathed freely and began to smile.

The family itself took its meals in the kitchen. Nonetheless, Gregor's father came into the living room before going into the kitchen and with one prolonged bow, cap in hand, made a round of the table. The lodgers all stood up and murmured something in their beards. When they were alone again they ate their food in almost complete silence. It seemed remarkable to Gregor that among the various noises coming from the table he could always distinguish the sound of their masticating teeth, as if this were a sign to Gregor that one needed teeth in order to eat, and that with toothless jaws even of the finest make one could do nothing. "I'm hungry enough," said Gregor sadly to himself, "But not for that kind of food. How these lodgers are stuffing themselves, and here am I dying of starvation!"

On that very evening—during the whole of his time there Gregor could not remember ever having heard the violin—the sound of violin-playing came from the kitchen. The lodgers had already finished their supper, the one in the middle had brought out a newspaper and given the other two a page apiece, and now they were leaning back at ease reading and smoking. When the violin began to play they pricked up their ears, got to their feet, and went on tiptoe to the hall door where they stood huddled together. Their movements must have been heard in the kitchen, for Gregor's father called out: "Is the violin-playing disturbing you, gentlemen? It can be stopped at once." "On the contrary," said the middle lodger, "could not Fräulein Samsa come and play in this room, beside us, where it is much more convenient and comfortable?" "Oh certainly," cried Gregor's father, as if he were the violin-player. The lodgers came back into the living room and waited. Presently Gregor's father arrived with the music stand, his mother carrying the music and his sister with the violin. His sister quietly made everything ready to start playing; his parents, who had never let rooms before and so had an exaggerated idea of the courtesy due to lodgers, did not venture to sit down on their own chairs; his father leaned against the door, the right hand thrust between two buttons of his livery coat, which was formally buttoned up; but his mother was offered a chair by one of the lodgers and, since she left the chair just where he had happened to put it, sat down in a corner to one side.

Gregor's sister began to play; the father and mother, from either side, intently watched the movements of her hands. Gregor, attracted by the playing, ventured to move forward a little until his head was actually inside the living room. He felt hardly any surprise at his growing lack of consideration for the others; there had been a time when he prided himself on being considerate. And yet just on this occasion he had more reason than ever to hide himself, since owing to the amount of dust which lay thick in his room and rose into the air at the slightest movement, he too was covered with dust; fluff and hair and remnants of food trailed with him, caught on his back and along his sides; his indifference to everything was much too great for him to turn on his back and scrape himself clean on the carpet, as once he had done several times a day. And in spite of his condition, no shame deterred him from advancing a little over the spotless floor of the living room.

To be sure, no one was aware of him. The family was entirely absorbed in the violin-playing; the lodgers, however, who first of all had stationed themselves, hands in pockets, much too close behind the music stand so that they could all have read the music, which must have bothered his sister, had soon retreated to the window, half-whispering with downbent heads, and stayed there while his father turned an anxious eye on them. Indeed, they were making it more than obvious that they had been disappointed in their expectation of hearing good or enjoyable violin-playing, that they had had more than enough of the performance and only out of courtesy suffered a continued disturbance of their peace. From the way they all kept blowing the smoke of their cigars high in the air through nose and mouth one could divine their irritation. And yet Gregor's sister was playing so beautifully. Her face leaned sideways, intently and sadly her eyes followed the notes of music. Gregor crawled a little farther forward and lowered his head to the ground so that it might be possible for his eyes to meet hers. Was he an animal, that music had such an effect upon him? He felt as if the way were opening before him to the unknown nourishment he craved. He was determined to push forward till he reached his sister, to pull at her skirt and so let her know that she was to come into his room with her violin, for no one here appreciated her playing as he would appreciate it. He would never let her out of his room, at least, not so long as he lived; his frightful appearance would become, for the first time, useful to him; he would watch all the doors of his room at once and spit at intruders; but his sister should need no constraint, she should stay with him of her own free will; she should sit beside him on the sofa, bend down her ear to him and hear him confide that he had had the firm intention of sending her to the Conservatorium, and that, but for his mishap, last Christmas—surely Christmas was long past?—he would have announced it to everybody without allowing a single objection. After this confession his sister would be so touched that she would burst into tears, and Gregor would then raise himself to her shoulder and kiss her on the neck, which, now that she went to business, she kept free of any ribbon or collar.

"Mr. Samsa!" cried the middle lodger, to Gregor's father, and pointed, without wasting any more words, at Gregor, now working himself slowly forwards. The violin fell silent, the middle lodger first smiled to his friends with a shake of the head and then looked at Gregor again. Instead of driving Gregor out, his father seemed to think it more needful to begin by soothing down the lodgers, although they were not at all agitated and apparently found Gregor more entertaining than the violin-playing. He hurried toward them and, spreading out his arms, tried to urge them back into their own room and at the same time to block their view of Gregor. They now began to be really a little angry, one could not tell whether because of the old man's behavior or because it had just dawned on them that all unwittingly they had such a neighbor as Gregor next door. They demanded explanations of his father, they waved their arms like him, tugged uneasily at their beards, and only with reluctance backed towards their room. Meanwhile Gregor's sister, who stood there as if lost when her playing was so abruptly broken off, came to life again, pulled herself together all at once after standing for a while holding violin and bow in nervelessly hanging hands and staring at her music, pushed her violin into the lap of her mother, who was still sitting in her chair fighting asthmatically for breath, and ran into the lodgers' room to which they were now being shepherded by her father rather more quickly than before. One could see the pillows and blankets on the beds flying under her accustomed fingers and being laid in order. Before the lodgers had actually reached their room she had finished making the beds and slipped out.

The old man seemed once more to be so possessed by his mulish self-assertiveness that he was forgetting all the respect he should show to his lodgers. He kept driving them on and driving them on until in the very door of the bedroom the middle lodger stamped his foot loudly on the floor and so brought him to a halt. "I beg to announce," said the lodger, lifting one hand and looking also at Gregor's mother and sister, "that because of the disgusting conditions prevailing in this household and family"—here he spat on the floor with emphatic brevity—"I give you notice on the spot. Naturally I won't pay you a penny for the days I have lived here, on the contrary I shall consider bringing an action for damages against you, based on claims—believe me—that will be easily susceptible of proof." He ceased and stared straight in front of him, as if he expected something. In fact his two friends at once rushed into the breach with these words: "And we too give notice on the spot." On that he seized the door-handle and shut the door with a slam.

Gregor's father, groping with his hands, staggered forward and fell into his chair; it looked as if he were stretching himself there for his ordinary evening nap, but the marked jerkings of his head, which was as if uncontrollable, showed that he was far from asleep. Gregor had simply stayed quietly all the time on the spot where the lodgers had espied him. Disappointment at the failure of his plan, perhaps also the weakness arising from extreme hunger, made it impossible for him to move. He feared, with a fair degree of certainty, that at any moment the general tension would discharge itself in a combined attack upon him, and he lay waiting. He did not react even to the noise made by the violin as it fell off his mother's lap from under her trembling fingers and gave out a resonant note.

"My dear parents," said his sister, slapping her hand on the table by way of introduction, "things can't go on like this. Perhaps you don't realize that, but I do. I won't utter my brother's name in the presence of this creature, and so all I say is: we must try to get rid of it. We've tried to look after it and to put up with it as far as is humanly possible, and I don't think anyone could reproach us in the slightest."

"She is more than right," said Gregor's father to himself. His mother, who was still choking for lack of breath, began to cough hollowly into her hand with a wild look in her eyes.

His sister rushed over to her and held her forehead. His father's thoughts seemed to have lost their vagueness at Grete's words, he sat more upright, fingering his service cap that lay among the plates still lying on the table from the lodgers' supper, and from time to time looked at the still form of Gregor.

"We must try to get rid of it," his sister now said explicitly to her father, since her mother was coughing too much to hear a word, "it will be the death of both of you, I can see that coming. When one has to work as hard as we do, all of us, one can't stand this continual torment at home on top of it. At least I can't stand it any longer." And she burst into such a passion of sobbing that her tears dropped on her mother's face, where she wiped them off mechanically.

"My dear," said the old man sympathetically, and with evident understanding, "but what can we do?"

Gregor's sister merely shrugged her shoulders to indicate the feeling of helplessness that had now overmastered her during her weeping fit, in contrast to her former confidence.

"If he could understand us," said her father, half questioningly; Grete, still sobbing, vehemently waved a hand to show how unthinkable that was.

"If he could understand us," repeated the old man, shutting his eyes to consider his daughter's conviction that understanding was impossible, "then perhaps we might come to some agreement with him. But as it is—"

"He must go," cried Gregor's sister, "That's the only solution, Father. You must just try to get rid of the idea that this is Gregor. The fact that we've believed it for so long is the root of all our trouble. But how can it be Gregor? If this were Gregor, he would have realized long ago that human beings can't live with such a creature, and he'd have gone away on his own accord. Then we wouldn't have any brother, but we'd be able to go on living and keep his memory in honor. As it is, this creature persecutes us, drives away our lodgers, obviously wants the whole apartment to himself and would have us all sleep in the gutter. Just look, Father," she shrieked all at once, "he's at it again!" And in an access of panic that was quite incomprehensible to Gregor she even quitted her mother, literally thrusting the chair from her as if she would rather sacrifice her mother than stay so near to Gregor, and rushed behind her father, who also rose up, being simply upset by her agitation, and half-spread his arms out as if to protect her.

Yet Gregor had not the slightest intention of frightening anyone, far less his sister. He had only begun to turn round in order to crawl back to his room, but it was certainly a startling operation to watch, since because of his disabled condition he could not execute the difficult turning movements except by lifting his head and then bracing it against the floor over and over again. He paused and looked round. His good intentions seemed to have been recognized; the alarm had only been momentary. Now they were all watching him in melancholy silence. His mother lay in her chair, her legs stiffly outstretched and pressed together, her eyes almost closing for sheer weariness; his father and his sister were sitting beside each other, his sister's arm around the old man's neck.

Perhaps I can go on turning round now, thought Gregor, and began his labors again. He could not stop himself from panting with the effort, and had to pause now and then to take breath. Nor did anyone harass him, he was left entirely to himself. When he had completed the turnround he began at once to crawl straight back. He was amazed at the distance separating him from his room and could not understand how in his weak state he had managed to accomplish the same journey so recently, almost without remarking it. Intent on crawling as fast as possible, he barely noticed that not a single word, not an ejaculation from his family, interfered with his progress. Only when he was already in the doorway did he turn his head round, not completely, for his neck muscles were getting stiff, but enough to see that nothing had changed behind him except that his sister had risen to her feet. His last glance fell on his mother, who was not quite overcome by sleep.

Hardly was he well inside his room when the door was hastily pushed shut, bolted and locked. The sudden noise in his rear startled him so much that his little legs gave beneath him. It was his sister who had shown such haste. She had been standing ready waiting and had made a light spring forward, Gregor had not even heard her coming, and she cried "At last!" to her parents as she turned the key in the lock.

"And what now?" said Gregor to himself, looking round in the darkness. Soon he made the discovery that he was now unable to stir a limb. This did not surprise him, rather it seemed unnatural that he should ever actually have been able to move on these feeble little legs. Otherwise he felt relatively comfortable. True, his whole body was aching, but it seemed that the pain was gradually growing less and would finally pass away. The rotting apple in his back and the inflamed area around it, all covered with soft dust, already hardly troubled him. He thought of his family with tenderness and love. The decision that he must disappear was one that he held to even more strongly than his sister, if that were possible. In this state of vacant and peaceful meditation he remained until the tower clock struck three in the morning. The first broadening of light in the world outside the window entered his consciousness once more. Then his head sank to the floor of its own accord and from his nostrils came the last faint flicker of his breath.

When the charwoman arrived early in the morning—what between her strength and her impatience she slammed all the doors so loudly, never mind how often she had been begged not to do so, that no one in the whole apartment could enjoy any quiet sleep after her arrival—she noticed nothing unusual as she took her customary peep into Gregor's room. She thought he was lying motionless on purpose, pretending to be in the sulks; she credited him with every kind of intelligence. Since she happened to have the long-handled broom in her hand she tried to tickle him up with it from the doorway. When that too produced no reaction she felt provoked and poked at him a little harder, and only when she had pushed him along the floor without meeting any resistance was her attention aroused. It did not take her long to establish the truth of the matter, and her eyes widened, she let out a whistle, yet did not waste much time over it but tore open the door of the Samsas' bedroom and yelled into the darkness at the top of her voice: "Just look at this, it's dead; it's lying here dead and done for!"

Mr. and Mrs. Samsa started up in their double bed and before they realized the nature of the charwoman's announcement had some difficulty in overcoming the shock of it. But then they got out of bed quickly, one on either side, Mr. Samsa throwing a blanket over his shoulders, Mrs. Samsa in nothing but her nightgown; in this array they entered Gregor's room. Meanwhile the door of the living room opened, too, where Grete had been sleeping since the advent of the lodgers; she was completely dressed as if she had not been to bed, which seemed to be confirmed also by the paleness of her face. "Dead?" said Mrs. Samsa, looking questioningly at the charwoman, although she could have investigated for herself, and the fact was obvious enough without investigation. "I should say so," said the charwoman, proving her words by pushing Gregor's corpse a long way to one side with her broomstick. Mrs. Samsa made a movement as if to stop her, but checked it. "Well," said Mr. Samsa, "now thanks be to God." He crossed himself, and the three women followed his example. Grete, whose eyes never left the corpse, said: "Just see how thin he was. It's such a long time since he's eaten anything. The food came out again just as it went in." Indeed, Gregor's body was completely flat and dry, as could only now be seen when it was no longer supported by the legs and nothing prevented one from looking closely at it.

"Come in beside us, Grete, for a little while," said Mrs. Samsa with a tremulous smile, and Grete, not without looking back at the corpse, followed her parents into their bedroom. The charwoman shut the door and opened the window wide. Although it was so early in the morning a certain softness was perceptible in the fresh air. After all, it was already the end of March.

The three lodgers emerged from their room and were surprised to see no breakfast; they had been forgotten. "Where's our breakfast?" said the middle lodger peevishly to the charwoman. But she put her finger to her lips and hastily, without a word, indicated by gestures that they should go into Gregor's room. They did so and stood, their hands in the pockets of their somewhat shabby coats, around Gregor's corpse in the room where it was now fully light.

At that the door of the Samsas' bedroom opened and Mr. Samsa appeared in his uniform, his wife on one arm, his daughter on the other. They all looked a little as if they had been crying; from time to time Grete hid her face on her father's arm.

"Leave my house at once!" said Mr. Samsa, and pointed to the door without disengaging himself from the women. "What do you mean by that?" said the middle lodger, taken somewhat aback, with a feeble smile. The two others put their hands behind them and kept rubbing them together, as if in gleeful expectation of a fine set-to in which they were bound to come off the winners. "I mean just what I say," answered Mr. Samsa, and advanced in a straight line with his two companions towards the lodger. He stood his ground at first quietly, looking at the floor as if his thoughts were taking a new pattern in his head. "Then let us go, by all means," he said, and looked up at Mr. Samsa as if in a sudden access of humility he were expecting some renewed sanction for this decision. Mr. Samsa merely nodded briefly once or twice with meaning eyes. Upon that the lodger really did go with long strides into the hall, his two friends had been listening and had quite stopped rubbing their hands for some moments and now went scuttling after him as if afraid that Mr. Samsa might get into the hall before them and cut them off from their leader. In the hall they all three took their hats from the rack, their sticks from the umbrella stand, bowed in silence and quitted the apartment. With a suspiciousness which proved quite unfounded Mr. Samsa and the two women followed them out to the landing; leaning over the banister they watched the three figures slowly but surely going down the long stairs, vanishing from sight at a certain turn of the staircase on every floor and coming into view again after a moment or so; the more they dwindled, the more the Samsa family's interest in them dwindled, and when a butcher's boy met them and passed them on the stairs coming up proudly with a tray on his head, Mr. Samsa and the two women soon left the landing and as if a burden had been lifted from them went back into their apartment.

They decided to spend this day in resting and going for a stroll; they had not only deserved such a respite from work, but absolutely needed it. And so they sat down at the table and wrote three notes of excuse, Mr. Samsa to his board of management, Mrs. Samsa to her employer and Grete to the head of her firm. While they were writing, the charwoman came in to say that she was going now, since her morning's work was finished. At first they only nodded without looking up, but as she kept hovering there they eyed her irritably. "Well?" said Mr. Samsa. The charwoman stood grinning in the doorway as if she had good news to impart to the family but meant not to say a word unless properly questioned. The small ostrich feather standing upright on her hat, which had annoyed Mr. Samsa ever since she was engaged, was waving gaily in all directions. "Well, what is it then?" asked Mrs. Samsa, who obtained more respect from the charwoman than the others. "Oh," said the charwoman, giggling so amiably that she could not at once continue, "just this, you don't need to bother about how to get rid of the thing next door. It's been seen to already." Mrs. Samsa and Grete bent over their letters again, as if preoccupied; Mr. Samsa, who perceived that she was eager to begin describing it all in detail, stopped her with a decisive hand. But since she was not allowed to tell her story, she remembered the great hurry she was in, being obviously deeply huffed: "Bye, everybody," she said, whirling off violently, and departed with a frightful slamming of doors.

"She'll be given notice tonight," said Mr. Samsa, but neither from his wife nor his daughter did he get any answer, for the charwoman seemed to have shattered again the composure they had barely achieved. They rose, went to the window and stayed there, clasping each other tight. Mr. Samsa turned to his chair to look at them and quietly observed them for a little. Then he called out: "Come along, now, do. Let bygones be bygones. And you might have some consideration for me." The two of them complied at once, hastened to him, caressed him and quickly finished their letters.

Then they all three left the apartment together, which was more than they had done for months, and went by tram into the open country outside the town. The tram, in which they were the only passengers, was filled with warm sunshine. Leaning comfortably back in their seats they canvassed their prospects for the future, and it appeared on closer inspection that these were not at all bad, for the jobs they had got, which so far they had never really discussed with each other, were all three admirable and likely to lead to better things later on. The greatest immediate improvement in their condition would of course arise from moving to another house; they wanted to take a smaller and cheaper but also better situated and more easily run apartment than the one they had, which Gregor had selected. While they were thus conversing, it struck both Mr. and Mrs. Samsa, almost at the same moment, as they became aware of their daughter's increasing vivacity, that in spite of all the sorrow of recent times, which had made her cheeks pale, she had bloomed into a pretty girl with a good figure. They grew quieter and half unconsciously exchanged glances of complete agreement, having come to the conclusion that it would soon be time to find a good husband for her. And it was like a confirmation of their new dreams and excellent intentions that at the end of their journey their daughter sprang to her feet first and stretched her young body.

(1915)

JAMES JOYCE
[1882–1941]

The Dead

Lily, the caretaker's daughter, was literally run off her feet. Hardly had she brought one gentleman into the little pantry behind the office on the ground floor and helped him off with his overcoat than the wheezy hall-door bell clanged again and she had to scamper along the bare hallway to let in another guest. It was well for her she had not to attend to the ladies also. But Miss Kate and Miss Julia had thought of that and had converted the bathroom upstairs into a ladies' dressing-room. Miss Kate and Miss Julia were there, gossiping and laughing and fussing, walking after each other to the head of the stairs, peering down over the banisters and calling down to Lily to ask her who had come.

It was always a great affair, the Misses Morkan's annual dance. Everybody who knew them came to it, members of the family, old friends of the family, the members of Julia's choir, any of Kate's pupils that were grown up enough and even some of Mary Jane's pupils too. Never once had it fallen flat. For years and years it had gone off in splendid style as long as anyone could remember; ever since Kate and Julia, after the death of their brother Pat, had left the house in Stoney Batter and taken Mary Jane, their only niece, to live with them in the dark gaunt house on Usher's Island, the upper part of which they had rented from Mr. Fulham, the cornfactor on the ground floor. That was a good thirty years ago if it was a day. Mary Jane, who was then a little girl in short clothes, was now the main prop of the household for she had the organ in Haddington Road. She had been through the Academy and gave a pupils' concert every year in the upper room of the Antient Concert Rooms. Many of her pupils belonged to better-class families on the Kingstown and Dalkey line. Old as they were, her aunts also did their share. Julia, though she was quite grey, was still the leading soprano in Adam and Eve's, and Kate, being too feeble to go about much, gave music lessons to beginners on the old square piano in the back room. Lily, the caretaker's daughter, did housemaid's work for them. Though their life was modest they believed in eating well; the best of everything: diamond-bone sirloins, three-shilling tea and the best bottled stout. But Lily seldom made a mistake in the orders so that she got on well with her three mistresses. They were fussy, that was all. But the only thing they would not stand was back answers.

Of course they had good reason to be fussy on such a night. And then it was long after ten o'clock and yet there was no sign of Gabriel and his wife. Besides they were dreadfully afraid that Freddy Malins might turn up screwed. They would not wish for worlds that any of Mary Jane's pupils should see him under the influence; and when he was like that it was sometimes very hard to manage him. Freddy Malins always came late but they wondered what could be keeping Gabriel: and that was what brought them every two minutes to the banisters to ask Lily had Gabriel or Freddy come.

—O, Mr. Conroy, said Lily to Gabriel when she opened the door for him, Miss Kate and Miss Julia thought you were never coming. Good-night, Mrs. Conroy.

—I'll engage they did, said Gabriel, but they forgot that my wife here takes three mortal hours to dress herself.

He stood on the mat, scraping the snow from his goloshes, while Lily led his wife to the foot of the stairs and called out:

—Miss Kate, here's Mrs. Conroy.

Kate and Julia came toddling down the dark stairs at once. Both of them kissed Gabriel's wife, said she must be perished alive and asked was Gabriel with her.

—Here I am as right as the mail, Aunt Kate! Go on up. I'll follow, called out Gabriel from the dark.

He continued scraping his feet vigorously while the three women went upstairs, laughing, to the ladies' dressing-room. A light fringe of snow lay like a cape on the shoulders of his overcoat and like toecaps on the toes of his goloshes; and, as the buttons of his overcoat slipped with a squeaking noise through the snow-stiffened frieze, a cold fragrant air from out-of-doors escaped from crevices and folds.

—Is it snowing again, Mr. Conroy? asked Lily.

She had preceded him into the pantry to help him off with his overcoat. Gabriel smiled at the three syllables she had given his surname and glanced at her. She was a slim, growing girl, pale in complexion and with hay-coloured hair. The gas in the pantry made her look still paler. Gabriel had known her when she was a child and used to sit on the lowest step nursing a rag doll.

—Yes, Lily, he answered, and I think we're in for a night of it.

He looked up at the pantry ceiling, which was shaking with the stamping and shuffling of feet on the floor above, listened for a moment to the piano and then glanced at the girl, who was folding his overcoat carefully at the end of a shelf.

—Tell me, Lily, he said in a friendly tone, do you still go to school?

—O no, sir, she answered. I'm done schooling this year and more.

—O, then, said Gabriel gaily, I suppose we'll be going to your wedding one of these fine days with your young man, eh?

The girl glanced back at him over her shoulder and said with great bitterness:

—The men that is now is only all palaver and what they can get out of you.

Gabriel coloured as if he felt he had made a mistake and, without looking at her, kicked off his goloshes and flicked actively with his muffler at his patent-leather shoes.

He was a stout tallish young man. The high colour of his cheeks pushed upwards even to his forehead where it scattered itself in a few formless patches of pale red; and on his hairless face there scintillated restlessly the polished lenses and the bright gilt rims of the glasses which screened his delicate and restless eyes. His glossy black hair was parted in the middle and brushed in a long curve behind his ears where it curled slightly beneath the groove left by his hat.

When he had flicked lustre into his shoes he stood up and pulled his waistcoat down more tightly on his plump body. Then he took a coin rapidly from his pocket.

—O Lily, he said, thrusting it into her hands, it's Christmastime, isn't it? Just . . . here's a little. . . .

He walked rapidly towards the door.

—Oh no, sir! cried the girl, following him. Really, sir, I wouldn't take it.

—Christmas-time! Christmas-time! said Gabriel, almost trotting to the stairs and waving his hand to her in deprecation.

The girl, seeing that he had gained the stairs, called out after him:

—Well, thank you, sir.

He waited outside the drawing-room door until the waltz should finish, listening to the skirts that swept against it and to the shuffling of feet. He was still discomposed by the girl's bitter and sudden retort. It had cast a gloom over him which he tried to dispel by arranging his cuffs and the bows of his tie. Then he took from his waist-coat pocket a little paper and glanced at the headings he had made for his speech. He was undecided about the lines from Robert Browning for he feared they would be above the heads of his hearers. Some quotation that they could recognise from Shakespeare or from the Melodies would be better. The indelicate clacking of the men's heels and the shuffling of their soles reminded him that their grade of culture differed from his. He would only make himself ridiculous by quoting poetry to them which they could not understand. They would think that he was airing his superior education. He would fail with them just as he had failed with the girl in the pantry. He had taken up a wrong tone. His whole speech was a mistake from first to last, an utter failure.

Just then his aunts and his wife came out of the ladies' dressing-room. His aunts were two small plainly dressed old women. Aunt Julia was an inch or so the taller. Her hair, drawn low over the tops of her ears, was grey; and grey also, with darker shadows, was her large flaccid face. Though she was stout in build and stood erect her slow eyes and parted lips gave her the appearance of a woman who did not know where she was or where she was going. Aunt Kate was more vivacious. Her face, healthier than her sister's, was all puckers and creases, like a shrivelled red apple, and her hair, braided in the same old-fashioned way, had not lost its ripe nut colour.

They both kissed Gabriel frankly. He was their favorite nephew, the son of their dead elder sister, Ellen, who had married T.J. Conroy of the Port and Docks.

—Gretta tells me you're not going to take a cab back to Monkstown to-night, Gabriel, said Aunt Kate.

—No, said Gabriel, turning to his wife, we had quite enough of that last year, hadn't we? Don't you remember, Aunt Kate, what a cold Gretta got out of it? Cab windows rattling all the way, and the east wind blowing in after we passed Merrion. Very jolly it was. Gretta caught a dreadful cold.

Aunt Kate frowned severely and nodded her head at every word.

—Quite right, Gabriel, quite right, she said. You can't be too careful.

—But as for Gretta there, said Gabriel, she'd walk home in the snow if she were let.

Mrs. Conroy laughed.

—Don't mind him, Aunt Kate, she said. He's really an awful bother, what with green shades for Tom's eyes at night and making him do the dumb-bells, and forcing Eva to eat the stirabout. The poor child! And she simply hates the sight of it! . . . O, but you'll never guess what he makes me wear now!

She broke out into a peal of laughter and glanced at her husband, whose admiring and happy eyes had been wandering from her dress to her face and hair. The two aunts laughed heartily too, for Gabriel's solicitude was a standing joke with them.

—Goloshes! said Mrs. Conroy. That's the latest. Whenever it's wet underfoot I must put on my goloshes. To-night even he wanted me to put them on, but I wouldn't. The next thing he'll buy me will be a diving suit.

Gabriel laughed nervously and patted his tie reassuringly while Aunt Kate nearly doubled herself, so heartily did she enjoy the joke. The smile soon faded from Aunt Julia's face and her mirthless eyes were directed towards her nephew's face. After a pause she asked:

—And what are goloshes, Gabriel?

—Goloshes, Julia! exclaimed her sister. Goodness me, don't you know what goloshes are? You wear them over your . . . over your boots, Gretta, isn't it?

—Yes, said Mrs. Conroy. Guttapercha things. We both have a pair now. Gabriel says everyone wears them on the continent.

—O, on the continent, murmured Aunt Julia, nodding her head slowly.

Gabriel knitted his brows and said, as if he were slightly angered:

—It's nothing very wonderful but Gretta thinks it very funny because she says the world reminds her of Christy Minstrels.

—But tell me, Gabriel, said Aunt Kate, with brisk tact. Of course, you've seen about the room. Gretta was saying . . .

—O, the room is all right, replied Gabriel. I've taken one in the Gresham.

—To be sure, said Aunt Kate, by far the best thing to do. And the children, Gretta, you're not anxious about them?

—O, for one night, said Mrs. Conroy. Besides, Bessie will look after them.

—To be sure, said Aunt Kate again. What a comfort it is to have a girl like that, one you can depend on! There's that Lily, I'm sure I don't know what has come over her lately. She's not the girl she was at all.

Gabriel was about to ask his aunt some questions on this point but she broke off suddenly to gaze after her sister who had wandered down the stairs and was craning her neck over the banisters.

—Now, I ask you, she said, almost testily, where is Julia going? Julia! Julia! Where are you going?

Julia, who had gone halfway down one flight, came back and announced blandly:

—Here's Freddy.

At the same moment a clapping of hands and a final flourish of the pianist told that the waltz had ended. The drawing-room door was opened from within and some couples came out. Aunt Kate drew Gabriel aside hurriedly and whispered into his ear:

—Slip down, Gabriel, like a good fellow and see if he's all right, and don't let him up if he's screwed. I'm sure he's screwed. I'm sure he is.

Gabriel went to the stairs and listened over the banisters. He could hear two persons talking in the pantry. Then he recognized Freddy Malins' laugh. He went down the stairs noisily.

—It's such a relief, said Aunt Kate to Mrs. Conroy, that Gabriel is here. I always feel easier in my mind when he's here. . . . . Julia, there's Miss Daly and Miss Power will take some refreshment. Thanks for your beautiful waltz, Miss Daly. It made lovely time.

A tall wizen-faced man, with a stiff grizzled moustache and swarthy skin, who was passing out with his partner said:

—And may we have some refreshment, too, Miss Morkan?

—Julia, said Aunt Kate summarily, and here's Mr. Browne and Miss Furlong. Take them in, Julia, with Miss Daly and Miss Power.

—I'm the man for the ladies, said Mr. Browne, pursing his lips until his moustache bristled and smiling in all his wrinkles. You know, Miss Morkan, the reason they are so fond of me is—

He did not finish his sentence, but, seeing that Aunt Kate was out of earshot, at once led the three young ladies into the back room. The middle of the room was occupied by two square tables placed end to end, and on these Aunt Julia and the caretaker were straightening and smoothing a large cloth. On the sideboard were arrayed dishes and plates, and glasses and bundles of knives and forks and spoons. The top of the closed square piano served also as a sideboard for viands and sweets. At a smaller sideboard in one corner two young men were standing, drinking hop-bitters.

Mr. Browne led his charges thither and invited them all, in jest, to some ladies' punch, hot, strong and sweet. As they said they never took anything strong he opened three bottles of lemonade for them. Then he asked one of the young men to move aside, and, taking hold of the decanter, filled out for himself a goodly measure of whisky. The young men eyed him respectfully while he took a trial sip.

—God help me, he said, smiling, it's the doctor's orders.

His wizened face broke into a broader smile, and the three young ladies laughed in musical echo to his pleasantry, swaying their bodies to and for, with nervous jerks of their shoulders. The boldest said:

—O, now, Mr. Browne, I'm sure the doctor never ordered anything of the kind.

Mr. Browne took another sip of his whiskey and said, with sidling mimicry:

—Well, you see, I'm like the famous Mrs. Cassidy, who is reported to have said: *Now, Mary Grimes, if I don't take it, make me take it, for I feel I want it.*

His hot face had leaned forward a little too confidentially and he had assumed a very low Dublin accent so that the young ladies, with one instinct, received his speech in silence. Miss Furlong, who was one of Mary Jane's pupils, asked Miss Daly what was the name of the pretty waltz she had just played; and Mr. Browne, seeing that he was ignored, turned promptly to the two young men who were more appreciative.

A red-faced young woman, dressed in pansy, came into the room, excitedly clapping her hands and crying:

—Quadrilles! Quadrilles!

Close on her heels came Aunt Kate, crying:

—Two gentlemen and three ladies, Mary Jane!

—Oh, here's Mr. Bergin and Mr. Kerrigan, said Mary Jane. Mr. Kerrigan, will you take Miss Power? Miss Furlong, may I get you a partner, Mr. Bergin. O, that'll just do now.

—Three ladies, Mary Jane, said Aunt Kate.

The two young gentlemen asked the ladies if they might have the pleasure, and Mary Jane turned to Miss Daly.

—O, Miss Daly, you're really awfully good, after playing for the last two dances, but really we're so short of ladies to-night.

—I don't mind in the least, Miss Morkan.

—But I've a nice partner for you, Mr. Bartell D'Arcy, the tenor. I'll get him to sing later on. All Dublin is raving about him.

—Lovely voice, lovely voice! said Aunt Kate.

As the piano had twice begun the prelude to the first figure Mary Jane led her re-
cruits quickly from the room. They had hardly gone when Aunt Julia wandered slowly
into the room, looking behind her at something.

—What is the matter, Julia? asked Aunt Kate anxiously. Who is it?

Julia, who was carrying in a column of table-napkins turned to her sister and said,
simply, as if the question had surprised her:

—It's only Freddy, Kate, and Gabriel with him.

In fact right behind her Gabriel could be seen piloting Freddy Malins across the landing. The latter, a young man of forty, was of Gabriel's size and build, with very round
shoulders. His face was fleshy and pallid, touched with colour only at the thick hanging lobes of his ears and at the wide wings of his nose. He had coarse features, a blunt
nose, a convex and receding brow, tumid and protruded lips. His heavy-lidded eyes
and the disorder of his scanty hair made him look sleepy. He was laughing heartily in
a high key at a story which he had been telling Gabriel on the stairs and at the same
time rubbing the knuckles of his left fist backwards and forwards into his left eye.

—Good-evening, Freddy, said Aunt Julia.

Freddy Malins bade the Misses Morkan good-evening in what seemed an offhand
fashion by reason of the habitual catch in his voice and then, seeing that Mr. Browne
was grinning at him from the sideboard, crossed the room on rather shaky legs and
began to repeat in an undertone the story he had just told to Gabriel.

—He's not so bad, is he? said Aunt Kate to Gabriel.

Gabriel's brows were dark but he raised them quickly and answered:

—O no, hardly noticeable.

—Now, isn't he a terrible fellow! she said. And his poor mother made him take the
pledge on New Year's Eve. But come on, Gabriel, into the drawing-room.

Before leaving the room with Gabriel she signalled to Mr. Browne by frowning and
shaking her forefinger in warning to and fro. Mr. Browne nodded in answer and, when
she had gone, said to Freddy Malins:

—Now, then, Teddy, I'm going to fill you out a good glass of lemonade just to
buck you up.

Freddy Malins, who was nearing the climax of his story, waved the offer aside impatiently but Mr. Browne, having first called Freddy Malins' attention to a disarray in
his dress, filled out and handed him a full glass of lemonade. Freddy Malins' left hand
accepted the glass mechanically, his right hand being engaged in the mechanical read-
justment of his dress. Mr. Browne, whose face was once more wrinkling with mirth,
poured out for himself a glass of whisky while Freddy Malins exploded, before he had
well reached the climax of his story, in a kink of high-pitched bronchitic laughter and,
setting down his untasted and overflowing glass, began to rub the knuckles of his left
fist backwards and forwards into his left eye, repeating words of his last phrase as well
as his fit of laughter would allow him.

Gabriel could not listen while Mary Jane was playing her Academy piece, full of runs
and difficult passages, to the hushed drawing-room. He liked music but the piece she
was playing had no melody for him and he doubted whether it had any melody for the
other listeners, though they had begged Mary Jane to play something. Four young men,
who had come from the refreshment-room to stand in the doorway at the sound of

the piano, had gone away quietly in couples after a few minutes. The only persons who seemed to follow the music were Mary Jane herself, her hands racing along the keyboard or lifted from it at the pauses like those of a priestess in momentary imprecation, and Aunt Kate standing at her elbow to turn the page.

Gabriel's eyes, irritated by the floor, which glittered with beeswax under the heavy chandelier, wandered to the wall above the piano. A picture of the balcony scene in *Romeo and Juliet* hung there and beside it was a picture of the two murdered princes in the Tower which Aunt Julia had worked in red, blue and brown wools when she was a girl. Probably in the school they had gone to as girls that kind of work had been taught, for one year his mother had worked for him as a birthday present a waistcoat of purple tabinet, with little foxes' heads upon it, lined with brown satin and having round mulberry buttons. It was strange that his mother had had no musical talent though Aunt Kate used to call her the brains carrier of the Morkan family. Both she and Julia had always seemed a little proud of their serious and matronly sister. Her photograph stood before the pierglass. She held an open book on her knees and was pointing out something in it to Constantine who, dressed in a man-o'-war suit, lay at her feet. It was she who had chosen the names for her sons for she was very sensible of the dignity of family life. Thanks to her, Constantine was now senior curate in Balbriggan and, thanks to her, Gabriel himself had taken his degree in the Royal University. A shadow passed over his face as he remembered her sullen opposition to his marriage. Some slighting phrases she had used still rankled in his memory; she had once spoken of Gretta as being country cute and that was not true of Gretta at all. It was Gretta who had nursed her during all her last long illness in their house at Monkstown.

He knew that Mary Jane must be near the end of her piece for she was playing again the opening melody with runs of scales after every bar and while he waited for the end the resentment died down in his heart. The piece ended with a trill of octaves in the treble and a final deep octave in the bass. Great applause greeted Mary Jane as, blushing and rolling up her music nervously, she escaped from the room. The most vigorous clapping came from the four young men in the doorway who had gone away to the refreshment-room at the beginning of the piece but had come back when the piano had stopped.

Lancers were arranged. Gabriel found himself partnered with Miss Ivors. She was a frank-mannered talkative young lady, with a freckled face and prominent brown eyes. She did not wear a low-cut bodice and the large brooch which was fixed in the front of her collar bore on it an Irish device.

When they had taken their places she said abruptly:

—I have a crow to pluck with you.

—With me? said Gabriel.

She nodded her head gravely.

—What is it? asked Gabriel, smiling at her solemn manner.

—Who is G. C.? answered Miss Ivors, turning her eyes upon him.

Gabriel coloured and was about to knit his brows, as if he did not understand, when she said bluntly:

—O, innocent Amy! I have found out that you write for *The Daily Express*. Now, aren't you ashamed of yourself?

—Why should I be ashamed of myself? asked Gabriel, blinking his eyes and trying to smile.

—Well, I'm ashamed of you, said Miss Ivors frankly. To say you'd write for a rag like that. I didn't think you were a West Briton.

A look of perplexity appeared on Gabriel's face. It was true that he wrote a literary column every Wednesday in *The Daily Express,* for which he was paid fifteen shillings. But that did not make him a West Briton surely. The books he received for review were almost more welcome than the paltry cheque. He loved to feel the covers and turn over the pages of newly printed books. Nearly every day when his teaching in the college was ended he used to wander down the quays to the second-hall booksellers, to Hickey's on Bachelor's Walk, to Webb's or Massey's on Aston's Quay, or to O'Clohissey's in the by-street. He did not know how to meet her charge. He wanted to say that literature was above politics. But they were friends of many years' standing and their careers had been parallel, first at the University and then as teachers: he could not risk a grandiose phrase with her. He continued blinking his eyes and trying to smile and murmured lamely that he saw nothing political in writing reviews of books.

When their turn to cross had come he was still perplexed and inattentive. Miss Ivors promptly took his hand in a warm grasp and said in a soft friendly tone:

—Of course, I was only joking. Come, we cross now.

When they were together again she spoke of the University question, and Gabriel felt more at east. A friend of hers had shown her his review of Browning's poems. That was how she had found out the secret: but she liked the review immensely. Then she said suddenly:

—O, Mr. Conroy, will you come for an excursion to the Aran Isles this summer? We're going to stay there a whole month. It will be splendid out in the Atlantic. You ought to come. Mr. Clancy is coming, and Mr. Kilkelly and Kathleen Kearney. It would be splendid for Gretta too if she'd come. She's from Connacht, isn't she?

—Her people are, said Gabriel shortly.

—But you will come, won't you? said Miss Ivors, laying her warm hand eagerly on his arm.

—The fact is, said Gabriel, I have already arranged to go—

—Go where? asked Miss Ivors.

—Well, you know, every year I go for a cycling tour with some fellows and so—

—But where? asked Miss Ivors.

—Well, we usually go to France or Belgium or perhaps Germany, said Gabriel awkwardly.

—And why do you go to France and Belgium, said Miss Ivors, instead of visiting your own land?

—Well, said Gabriel, it's partly to keep in touch with the languages and partly for a change.

—And haven't you your own language to keep in touch with—Irish? asked Miss Ivors.

—Well, said Gabriel, if it comes to that, you know, Irish is not my language.

Their neighbours had turned to listen to the cross-examination. Gabriel glanced right and left nervously and tried to keep his good humour under the ordeal which was making a blush invade his forehead.

—And haven't you your own land to visit, continued Miss Ivors, that you know nothing of, your own people, and your own country?

—O, to tell you the truth, retorted Gabriel suddenly, I'm sick of my own country, sick of it!

—Why? asked Miss Ivors.

Gabriel did not answer for his retort had heated him.

—Why? repeated Miss Ivors.

They had to go visiting together and, as he had not answered her, Miss Ivors said warmly:

—Of course, you've no answer.

Gabriel tried to cover his agitation by taking part in the dance with great energy. He avoided her eyes for he had seen a sour expression on her face. But when they met in the long chain he was surprised to feel his hand firmly pressed. She looked at him from under her brows for a moment quizzically until he smiled. Then, just as the chain was about to start again, she stood on tiptoe and whispered into his ear:

—West Briton!

When the lancers were over Gabriel went away to a remote corner of the room where Freddy Malins' mother was sitting. She was a stout feeble old woman with white hair. Her voice had a catch in it like her son's and she stuttered slightly. She had been told that Freddy had come and that he was nearly all right. Gabriel asked her whether she had had a good crossing. She lived with her married daughter in Glasgow and came to Dublin on a visit once a year. She answered placidly that she had had a beautiful crossing and that the captain had been most attentive to her. She spoke also of the beautiful house her daughter kept in Glasgow, and of all the nice friends they had there. While her tongue rambled on Gabriel tried to banish from his mind all memory of the unpleasant incident with Miss Ivors. Of course the girl or woman, or whatever she was, was an enthusiast but there was a time for all things. Perhaps he ought not to have answered her like that. But she had no right to call him a West Briton before people, even in joke. She had tried to make him ridiculous before people, heckling him and staring at him with her rabbit's eyes.

He saw his wife making her way towards him through the waltzing couples. When she reached him she said into his ear:

—Gabriel, Aunt Kate wants to know won't you carve the goose as usual. Miss Daly will carve the ham and I'll do the pudding.

—All right, said Gabriel.

—She's sending in the younger ones first as soon as this waltz is over so that we'll have the table to ourselves.

—Were you dancing? asked Gabriel.

—Of course I was. Didn't you see me? What words had you with Molly Ivors?

—No words. Why? Did she say so?

—Something like that. I'm trying to get that Mr. D'Arcy to sing. He's full of conceit, I think.

—There were no words, said Gabriel moodily, only she wanted me to go for a trip to the west of Ireland and I said I wouldn't.

His wife clasped her hands excitedly and gave a little jump.

—O, do go, Gabriel, she cried. I'd love to see Galway again.

—You can go if you like, said Gabriel coldly.

She looked at him for a moment, then turned to Mrs. Malins and said:

—There's a nice husband for you, Mrs. Malins.

While she was threading her way back across the room Mrs. Malins, without adverting to the interruption, went on to tell Gabriel what beautiful places there were in Scotland and beautiful scenery. Her son-in-law brought them every year to the lakes and they used to go fishing. Her son-in-law was a splendid fisher. One day he caught a fish, a beautiful big big fish, and the man in the hotel boiled it for their dinner.

Gabriel hardly heard what she said. Now that supper was coming near he began to think again about his speech and about the quotation. When he saw Freddy Malins coming across the room to visit his mother Gabriel left the chair free for him and retired into the embrasure of the window. The room had already cleared and from the back room came the clatter of plates and knives. Those who still remained in the drawing-room seemed tired of dancing and were conversing quietly in little groups. Gabriel's warm trembling fingers tapped the cold pane of the window. How cool it must be outside! How pleasant it would be to walk out alone, first along by the river and then through the park! The snow would be lying on the branches of the trees and forming a bright cap on the top of the Wellington Monument. How much more pleasant it would be there than at the supper-table!

He ran over the headings of his speech: Irish hospitality, sad memories, the Three Graces, Paris, the quotation from Browning. He repeated to himself a phrase he had written in his review: *One feels that one is listening to a thought-tormented music.* Miss Ivors had praised the review. Was she sincere? Had she really any life of her own behind all her propagandism? There had never been any ill-feeling between them until that night. It unnerved him to think that she would be at the supper-table, looking up at him while he spoke with her critical quizzing eyes. Perhaps she would not be sorry to see him fail in his speech. An idea came into his mind and gave him courage. He would say, alluding to Aunt Kate and Aunt Julia: *Ladies and Gentlemen, the generation which is now on the wane among us may have had its faults but for my part I think it had certain qualities of hospitality, of humour, of humanity, which the new and very serious and hypereducated generation that is growing up around us seems to me to lack.* Very good: that was one for Miss Ivors. What did he care that his aunts were only two ignorant old women?

A murmur in the room attracted his attention. Mr. Browne was advancing from the door, gallantly escorting Aunt Julia, who leaned upon his arm, smiling and hanging her head. An irregular musketry of applause escorted her also as far as the piano and then, as Mary Jane seated herself on the stool, and Aunt Julia, no longer smiling, half turned so as to pitch her voice fairly into the room, gradually ceased. Gabriel recognized the prelude. It was that of an old song of Aunt Julia's—*Arrayed for the Bridal.* Her voice, strong and clear in tone, attacked with great spirit the runs which embellish the air and though she sang very rapidly she did not miss even the smallest of the grace notes. To follow the voice, without looking at the singer's face, was to feel and share the excitement of swift and secure flight. Gabriel applauded loudly with all the others at the close of the song and loud applause was borne in from the invisible supper-table. It sounded so genuine that a little colour struggled into Aunt Julia's face as she bent to replace in the music-stand the old leather-bound song-book that had her initials on the cover. Freddy Malins, who had listened with his head perched sideways to hear her better, was still applauding when everyone else had ceased and talking animatedly to his mother who nodded her head gravely and slowly in acquiescence. At last, when he could clap no more, he stood up suddenly and hurried across the room to Aunt Julia whose hand he seized and held in both his hands, shaking it when words failed him or the catch in his voice proved too much for him.

—I was just telling my mother, he said, I never heard you sing so well, never. No, I never heard your voice so good as it is to-night. Now! Would you believe that now? That's the truth. Upon my word and honour that's the truth. I never heard your voice sound so fresh and so . . . so clear and fresh, never.

Aunt Julia smiled broadly and murmured something about compliments as she released her hand from his grasp. Mr. Browne extended his open hand towards her and said to those who were near in the manner of a showman introducing a prodigy to an audience:

—Miss Julia Morkan, my latest discovery!

He was laughing very heartily at this himself when Freddy Malins turned to him and said:

—Well, Browne, if you're serious you might make a worse discovery. All I can say is I never heard her sing half so well as long as I am coming here. And that's the honest truth.

—Neither did I, said Mr. Browne. I think her voice has greatly improved.

Aunt Julia shrugged her shoulders and said with meek pride:

—Thirty years ago I hadn't a bad voice as voices go.

—I often told Julia, said Aunt Kate emphatically, that she was simply thrown away in that choir. But she never would be said by me.

She turned as if to appeal to the good sense of the others against a refractory child while Aunt Julia gazed in front of her, a vague smile of reminiscence playing on her face.

—No, continued Aunt Kate, she wouldn't be said or led by anyone, slaving there in that choir night and day, night and day. Six o'clock on Christmas morning! And all for what?

—Well, isn't it for the honour of God, Aunt Kate? asked Mary Jane, twisting round on the piano-stool and smiling.

Aunt Kate turned fiercely on her niece and said:

—I know all about the honour of God, Mary Jane, but I think it's not at all honourable for the pope to turn out the women out of the choirs that have slaved there all their lives and put little whipper-snappers of boys over their heads. I suppose it is for the good of the Church if the pope does it. But it's not just, Mary Jane, and it's not right.

She had worked herself into a passion and would have continued in defence of her sister for it was a sore subject with her but Mary Jane, seeing that all the dancers had come back, intervened pacifically:

—Now, Aunt Kate, you're giving scandal to Mr. Browne who is of the other persuasion.

Aunt Kate turned to Mr. Browne, who was grinning at this allusion to his religion, and said hastily:

—O, I don't question the pope's being right. I'm only a stupid old woman and I wouldn't presume to do such a thing. But there's such a thing as common everyday politeness and gratitude. And if I were in Julia's place I'd tell that Father Healy straight up to his face . . .

—And besides, Aunt Kate, said Mary Jane, we really are all hungry and when we are hungry we are all very quarrelsome.

—And when we are thirsty we are also quarrelsome, added Mr. Browne.

—So that we had better go to supper, said Mary Jane, and finish the discussion afterwards.

On the landing outside the drawing-room Gabriel found his wife and Mary Jane trying to persuade Miss Ivors to stay for supper. But Miss Ivors, who had put on her hat and was buttoning her cloak, would not stay. She did not feel in the least hungry and she had already overstayed her time.

—But only for ten minutes, Molly, said Mrs. Conroy. That won't delay you.

—To take a pick itself, said Mary Jane, after all your dancing.

—I really couldn't, said Miss Ivors.

—I am afraid you didn't enjoy yourself at all, said Mary Jane hopelessly.

—Ever so much, I assure you, said Miss Ivors, but you really must let me run off now.

—But how can you get home? asked Mrs. Conroy.

—O, it's only two steps up the quay.

Gabriel hesitated a moment and said:

—If you will allow me, Miss Ivors, I'll see you home if you really are obliged to go.

But Miss Ivors broke away from them.

—I won't hear of it, she cried. For goodness sake go in to your suppers and don't mind me. I'm quite well able to take care of myself.

—Well, you're the comical girl, Molly, said Mrs. Conroy frankly.

—*Beannacht libh,* cried Miss Ivors, with a laugh, as she ran down the staircase.

Mary Jane gazed after her, a moody puzzled expression on her face, while Mrs. Conroy leaned over the banisters to listen for the hall-door. Gabriel asked himself was he the cause of her abrupt departure. But she did not seem to be in ill humour: she had gone away laughing. He stared blankly down the staircase.

At that moment Aunt Kate came toddling out of the supper-room, almost wringing her hands in despair.

—Where is Gabriel? she cried. Where on earth is Gabriel? There's everyone waiting in there, stage to let, and nobody to carve the goose!

—Here I am, Aunt Kate! cried Gabriel, with sudden animation, ready to carve a flock of geese, if necessary.

A fat brown goose lay at one end of the table and at the other end, on a bed of creased paper strewn with sprigs of parsley, lay a great ham, stripped of its outer skin and peppered over with crust crumbs, a neat paper frill round its shin and beside this was a round of spiced beef. Between these rival ends ran parallel lines of side-dishes: two little ministers of jelly, red and yellow; a shallow dish full of blocks of blancmange and red jam, a large green leaf-shaped dish with a stalk-shaped handle, on which lay bunches of purple raisins and peeled almonds, a companion dish on which lay a solid rectangle of Smyrna figs, a dish of custard topped with grated nutmeg, a small bowl full of chocolates and sweets wrapped in gold and silver papers and a glass vase in which stood some tall celery stalks. In the centre of the table there stood, as sentries to a fruit-stand which upheld a pyramid of oranges and American apples, two squat old-fashioned decanters of cut glass, one containing port and the other dark sherry. On the closed square piano a pudding in a huge yellow dish lay in waiting and behind it were three squads of bottles of stout and ale and minerals, drawn up according to the colours of their uniforms, the first two black, with brown and red labels, the third and smallest squad white, with transverse green sashes.

Gabriel took his seat boldly at the head of the table and, having looked to the edge of the carver, plunged his fork firmly into the goose. He felt quite at ease now for he was an expert carver and liked nothing better than to find himself at the head of a well-laden table.

—Miss Furlong, what shall I send you? he asked. A wing or a slice of the breast?

—Just a small slice of the breast.

—Miss Higgins, what for you?

—O, anything at all, Mr. Conroy.

While Gabriel and Miss Daly exchanged plates of goose and plates of ham and spiced beef Lily went from guest to guest with a dish of hot floury potatoes wrapped in a white napkin. This was Mary Jane's idea and she had also suggested apple sauce for the goose but Aunt Kate had said that plain roast goose without apple sauce had always been good enough for her and she hoped she might never eat worse. Mary Jane waited on her pupils and saw that they got the best slices and Aunt Kate and Aunt Julia opened and carried across from the piano bottles of stout and ale for the gentlemen and bottles of minerals for the ladies. There was a great deal of confusion and laughter and noise, the noise of orders and counter-orders, of knives and forks, of corks and glass-stoppers. Gabriel began to carve second helpings as soon as he had finished the first round without serving himself. Everyone protested loudly so that he compromised by taking a long draught of stout for he had found the carving hot work. Mary Jane settled down quietly to her supper but Aunt Kate and Aunt Julia were still toddling round the table, walking on each other's heels, getting in each other's way and giving each other unheeded orders. Mr. Browne begged of them to sit down and eat their suppers and so did Gabriel but they said there was time enough so that, at last, Freddy Malins stood up and, capturing Aunt Kate, plumped her down on her chair amid general laughter.

When everyone had been well served Gabriel said, smiling:

—Now, if anyone wants a little more of what vulgar people call stuffing let him or her speak.

A chorus of voices invited him to begin his own supper and Lily came forward with three potatoes which she had reserved for him.

—Very well, said Gabriel amiably, as he took another preparatory draught, kindly forget my existence, ladies and gentlemen, for a few minutes.

He set to his supper and took no part in the conversation with which the table covered Lily's removal of the plates. The subject of talk was the opera company which was then at the Theatre Royal. Mr. Bartell D'Arcy, the tenor, a dark-complexioned young man with a smart moustache, praised very highly the leading contralto of the company but Miss Furlong thought she had a rather vulgar style of production. Freddy Malins said there was a negro chieftain singing in the second part of the Gaiety pantomime who had one of the finest tenor voices he had ever heard.

—Have you heard him? he asked Mr. Bartell D'Arcy across the table.

—No, answered Mr. Bartell D'Arcy carelessly.

—Because, Freddy Malins explained, now I'd be curious to hear your opinion of him. I think he has a grand voice.

—It takes Teddy to find out the really good things, said Mr. Browne familiarly to the table.

—And why couldn't he have a voice too? asked Freddy Malins sharply. Is it because he's only a black?

Nobody answered this question and Mary Jane led the table back to the legitimate opera. One of her pupils had given her a pass for *Mignon*. Of course it was very fine, she said, but it made her think of poor Georgina Burns. Mr. Browne could go back farther still, to the old Italian companies that used to come to Dublin—Tietjens, Ilma de Murzka, Campanini, the great Trebelli, Giuglini, Ravelli, Aramburo. Those were the days, he said, when there was something like singing to be heard in Dublin. He told too of how the top gallery of the old Royal used to be packed night after night, of how one night an Italian tenor had sung five encores to *Let Me Like a Soldier Fall,* introducing a high C every time, and of how the gallery boys would sometimes in their enthusiasm unyoke the horses from the carriage of some great *prima donna* and pull her themselves through the streets to her hotel. Why did they never play the grand old operas now, he asked, *Dinorah, Lucrezia Borgia?* Because they could not get the voices to sing them: that was why.

—O, well, said Mr. Bartell D'Arcy, I presume there are as good singers to-day as there were then.

—Where are they? asked Mr. Browne defiantly.

—In London, Paris, Milan, said Mr. Bartell D'Arcy warmly. I suppose Caruso, for example, is quite as good, if not better than any of the men you have mentioned.

—Maybe so, said Mr. Browne. But I may tell you I doubt it strongly.

—O, I'd give anything to hear Caruso sing, said Mary Jane.

—For me, said Aunt Kate, who had been picking a bone, there was only one tenor. To please me, I mean. But I suppose none of you ever heard of him.

—Who was he, Miss Morkan? asked Mr. Bartell D'Arcy politely.

—His name, said Aunt Kate, was Parkinson. I heard him when he was in his prime and I think he had then the purest tenor voice that was ever put into a man's throat.

—Strange, said Mr. Bartell D'Arcy. I never even heard of him.

—Yes, yes, Miss Morkan is right, said Mr. Browne. I remember hearing of old Parkinson but he's too far back for me.

—A beautiful pure sweet mellow English tenor, said Aunt Kate with enthusiasm.

Gabriel having finished, the huge pudding was transferred to the table. The clatter of forks and spoons began again. Gabriel's wife served out spoonfuls of the pudding and passed the plates down the table. Midway down they were held up by Mary Jane, who replenished them with raspberry or orange jelly or with blancmange and jam. The pudding was of Aunt Julia's making and she received praises for it from all quarters. She herself said that it was not quite brown enough.

—Well, I hope, Miss Morkan, said Mr. Browne, that I'm brown enough for you because, you know, I'm all brown.

All the gentlemen, except Gabriel, ate some of the pudding out of compliment to Aunt Julia. As Gabriel never ate sweets the celery had been left for him. Freddy Malins also took a stalk of celery and ate it with his pudding. He had been told that celery was a capital thing for the blood and he was just then under doctor's care. Mrs. Malins, who had been silent all through the supper, said that her son was going down to Mount Melleray in a week or so. The table then spoke of Mount Melleray, how bracing the air was down there, how hospitable the monks were and how they never asked for a penny-piece from their guests.

—And do you mean to say, asked Mr. Browne incredulously, that a chap can go down there and put up there as if it were a hotel and live on the fat of the land and then come away without paying a farthing?

—O, most people give some donation to the monastery when they leave, said Mary Jane.

—I wish we had an institution like that in our Church, said Mr. Browne candidly.

He was astonished to hear that the monks never spoke, got up at two in the morning and slept in their coffins. He asked what they did it for.

—That's the rule of the order, said Aunt Kate firmly.

—Yes, but why? asked Mr. Browne.

Aunt Kate repeated that it was the rule, that was all. Mr. Browne still seemed not to understand. Freddy Malins explained to him, as best he could, that the monks were trying to make up for the sins committed by all the sinners in the outside world. The explanation was not very clear for Mr. Browne grinned and said:

—I like that idea very much but wouldn't a comfortable spring bed do them as well as a coffin?

—The coffin, said Mary Jane, is to remind them of their last end.

As the subject had grown lugubrious it was buried in a silence of the table during which Mrs. Malins could be heard saying to her neighbour in an indistinct undertone:

—They are very good men, the monks, very pious men.

The raisins and almonds and figs and apples and oranges and chocolates and sweets were now passed about the table and Aunt Julia invited all the guests to have either port or sherry. At first Mr. Bartell D'Arcy refused to take either but one of his neighbours nudged him and whispered something to him upon which he allowed his glass to be filled. Gradually as the last glasses were being filled the conversation ceased. A pause followed, broken only by the noise of the wine and by unsettlings of chairs. The Misses Morkan, all three, looked down at the tablecloth. Someone coughed once or twice and then a few gentlemen patted the table gently as a signal for silence. The silence came and Gabriel pushed back his chair and stood up.

The patting at once grew louder in encouragement and then ceased altogether. Gabriel leaned his ten trembling fingers on the tablecloth and smiled nervously at the company. Meeting a row of upturned faces he raised his eyes to the chandelier. The piano was playing a waltz tune and he could hear the skirts sweeping against the drawing-room door. People, perhaps, were standing in the snow on the quay outside, gazing up at the lighted windows and listening to the waltz music. The air was pure there. In the distance lay the park where the trees were weighted with snow. The Wellington Monument wore a gleaming cap of snow that flashed westward over the white field of Fifteen Acres.

He began:

—Ladies and Gentlemen.

—It has fallen to my lot this evening, as in years past, to perform a very pleasing task but a task for which I am afraid my poor powers as a speaker are all too inadequate.

—No, no! said Mr. Browne.

—But, however that may be, I can only ask you to-night to take the will for the deed and to lend me your attention for a few moments while I endeavour to express to you in words what my feelings are on this occasion.

—Ladies and Gentlemen. It is not the first time that we have gathered together under this hospitable roof, around this hospitable board. It is not the first time that we have been the recipients—or perhaps, I had better say, the victims—of the hospitality of certain good ladies.

He made a circle in the air with his arm and paused. Everyone laughed or smiled at Aunt Kate and Aunt Julia and Mary Jane who all turned crimson with pleasure. Gabriel went on more boldly:

—I feel more strongly with every recurring year that our country has no tradition which does it so much honour and which it should guard so jealously as that of its hospitality. It is a tradition that is unique as far as my experience goes (and I have visited not a few places abroad) among the modern nations. Some would say, perhaps, that with us it is rather a failing than anything to be boasted of. But granted even that, it is, to my mind, a princely failing, and one that I trust will long be cultivated among us. Of one thing, at least, I am sure. As long as this one roof shelters the good ladies aforesaid—and I wish from my heart it may do so for many and many a long year to come— the tradition of genuine warm-hearted courteous Irish hospitality, which our forefathers have handed down to us and which we in turn must hand down to our descendants, is still alive among us.

A hearty murmur of assent ran round the table. It shot through Gabriel's mind that Miss Ivors was not there and that she had gone away discourteously: and he said with confidence in himself:

—Ladies and Gentlemen.

—A new generation is growing up in our midst, a generation actuated by new ideas and new principles. It is serious and enthusiastic for these new ideas and its enthusiasm, even when it is misdirected, is, I believe, in the main sincere. But we are living in a sceptical and, if I may use the phrase, a thought-tormented age: and sometimes I fear that this new generation, educated or hypereducated as it is, will lack those qualities of humanity, of hospitality, of kindly humour which belonged to an older day. Listening to-night to the names of all those great singers of the past it seemed to me, I must confess, that we were living in a less spacious age. Those days might, without exaggeration, be called spacious days: and if they are gone beyond recall let us hope, at least, that in gatherings such as this we shall still speak of them with pride and affection, still cherish in our hearts the memory of those dead and gone great ones whose fame the world will not willingly let die.

—Hear, hear! said Mr. Browne loudly.

—But yet, continued Gabriel, his voice falling into a softer inflection, there are always in gatherings such as this sadder thoughts that will recur to our minds: thoughts of the past, of youth, of changes, of absent faces that we miss here tonight. Our path through life is strewn with many such sad memories: and were we to brood upon them always we could not find the heart to go on bravely with our work among the living. We have all of us living duties and living affections which claim, and rightly claim, our strenuous endeavours.

—Therefore, I will not linger on the past. I will not let any gloomy moralising intrude upon us here to-night. Here we are gathered together for a brief moment from the bustle and rush of our everyday routine. We are met here as friends, in the spirit of good-fellowship, as colleagues, also to a certain extent, in the true spirit of *camaraderie,* and as the guests of—what shall I call them?—the Three Graces of the Dublin musical world.

The table burst into applause and laughter at this sally. Aunt Julia vainly asked each of her neighbours in turn to tell her what Gabriel had said.

—He says we are the Three Graces, Aunt Julia, said Mary Jane.

Aunt Julia did not understand but she looked up, smiling, at Gabriel, who continued in the same vein:

—Ladies and Gentlemen.

—I will not attempt to play to-night the part that Paris played on another occasion. I will not attempt to choose between them. The task would be an invidious one and one beyond my poor powers. For when I view them in turn, whether it be our chief hostess herself, whose good heart, whose too good heart, has become a byword with all who know her, or her sister, who seems to be gifted with perennial youth and whose singing must have been a surprise and a revelation to us all to-night, or, last but not least, when I consider our youngest hostess, talented, cheerful, hard-working and the best of nieces, I confess, Ladies and Gentlemen, that I do not know to which of them I should award the prize.

Gabriel glanced down at his aunts and, seeing the large smile on Aunt Julia's face and the tears which had risen to Aunt Kate's eyes, hastened to his close. He raised his glass of port gallantly, while every member of the company fingered a glass expectantly, and said loudly:

—Let us toast them all three together. Let us drink to their health, wealth, long life, happiness and prosperity and may they long continue to hold the proud and self-won position which they hold in their profession and the position of honour and affection which they hold in our hearts.

All the guests stood up, glass in hand, and, turning towards the three seated ladies, sang in unison, with Mr. Browne as leader:

> For they are jolly gay fellows,
> For they are jolly gay fellows,
> For they are jolly gay fellows,
> Which nobody can deny.

Aunt Kate was making frank use of her handkerchief and even Aunt Julia seemed moved. Freddy Malins beat time with his pudding-fork and the singers turned towards one another, as if in melodious conference, while they sang, with emphasis:

> Unless he tells a lie,
> Unless he tells a lie.

Then, turning once more towards their hostesses, they sang:

> For they are jolly gay fellows,
> For they are jolly gay fellows,
> For they are jolly gay fellows,
> Which nobody can deny.

The acclamation which followed was taken up beyond the door of the supper-room by many of the other guests and renewed time after time, Freddy Malins acting as officer with his fork on high.

The piercing morning air came into the hall where they were standing so that Aunt Kate said:

—Close the door, somebody. Mrs. Malins will get her death of cold.

—Browne is out there, Aunt Kate, said Mary Jane.

—Browne is everywhere, said Aunt Kate, lowering her voice.

Mary Jane laughed at her tone.

—Really, she said archly, he is very attentive.

—He has been laid on here like the gas, said Aunt Kate in the same tone, all during the Christmas.

She laughed herself this time good-humouredly and then added quickly:

—But tell him to come in, Mary Jane, and close the door. I hope to goodness he didn't hear me.

At that moment the hall-door was opened and Mr. Browne came in from the doorstep, laughing as if his heart would break. He was dressed in a long green overcoat with mock astrakhan cuffs and collar and wore on his head an oval fur cap. He pointed down the snow-covered quay from where the sound of shrill prolonged whistling was borne in.

—Teddy will have all the cabs in Dublin out, he said.

Gabriel advanced from the little pantry behind the office, struggling into his overcoat and, looking round the hall, said:

—Gretta not down yet?

—She's getting on her things, Gabriel, said Aunt Kate.

—Who's playing up there? asked Gabriel.

—Nobody. They're all gone.

—O no, Aunt Kate, said Mary Jane. Bartell D'Arcy and Miss O'Callaghan aren't gone yet.

—Someone is strumming at the piano, anyhow, said Gabriel.

Mary Jane glanced at Gabriel and Mr. Browne and said with a shiver:

—It makes me feel cold to look at you two gentlemen muffled up like that. I wouldn't like to face your journey home at this hour.

—I'd like nothing better this minute, said Mr. Browne stoutly, than a rattling fine walk in the country or a fast drive with a good spanking goer between the shafts.

—We used to have a very good horse and trap at home, said Aunt Julia sadly.

—The never-to-be-forgotten Johnny, said Mary Jane, laughing.

Aunt Kate and Gabriel laughed too.

—Why, what was wonderful about Johnny? asked Mr. Browne.

—The late lamented Patrick Morkan, our grandfather, that is, explained Gabriel, commonly known in his later years as the old gentleman, was a glue-boiler.

—O, now, Gabriel, said Aunt Kate, laughing, he had a starch mill.

—Well, glue or starch, said Gabriel, the old gentleman had a horse by the name of Johnny. And Johnny used to work in the old gentleman's mill, walking round and round in order to drive the mill. That was all very well; but now comes the tragic part about Johnny. One fine day the old gentleman thought he'd like to drive out with the quality to a military review in the park.

—The Lord have mercy on his soul, said Aunt Kate compassionately.

—Amen, said Gabriel. So the old gentleman, as I said, harnessed Johnny and put on his very best tall hat and his very best stock collar and drove out in grand style from his ancestral mansion somewhere near Back Lane, I think.

Everyone laughed, even Mrs. Malins, at Gabriel's manner and Aunt Kate said:

—O now, Gabriel, he didn't live in Back Lane, really. Only the mill was there.

—Out from the mansion of his forefathers, continued Gabriel, he drove with Johnny. And everything went on beautifully until Johnny came in sight of King Billy's statue: and whether he fell in love with the horse King Billy sits on or whether he thought he was back again in the mill, anyhow he began to walk round the statue.

Gabriel paced in a circle round the hall in his goloshes amid the laughter of the others.

—Round and round he went, said Gabriel, and the old gentleman, who was a very pompous old gentleman, was highly indignant. *Go on, sir! What do you mean, sir? Johnny! Johnny! Most extraordinary conduct! Can't understand the horse!*

The peals of laughter which followed Gabriel's imitation of the incident were interrupted by a resounding knock at the hall-door. Mary Jane ran to open it and let in Freddy Malins. Freddy Malins, with his hat well back on his head and his shoulders humped with cold, was puffing and steaming after his exertions.

—I could only get one cab, he said.

—O, we'll find another along the quay, said Gabriel.

—Yes, said Aunt Kate. Better not keep Mrs. Malins standing in the draught.

Mrs. Malins was helped down the front steps by her son and Mr. Browne and, after many manœuvres, hoisted into the cab. Freddy Malins clambered in after her and spent a long time settling her on the seat, Mr. Browne helping him with advice. At last she was settled comfortably and Freddy Malins invited Mr. Browne into the cab. There was a good deal of confused talk, and then Mr. Browne got into the cab. The cabman settled his rug over his knees, and bent down for the address. The confusion grew greater and the cabman was directed differently by Freddy Malins and Mr. Browne, each of whom had his head out through a window of the cab. The difficulty was to know where to drop Mr. Browne along the route and Aunt Kate, Aunt Julia and Mary Jane helped the discussion from the doorstep with cross-directions and contradictions and abundance of laughter. As for Freddy Malins he was speechless with laughter. He popped his head in and out of the window every moment, to the great danger of his hat, and told his mother how the discussion was progressing till at last Mr. Browne shouted to the bewildered cabman above the din of everybody's laughter:

—Do you know Trinity College?

—Yes, sir, said the cabman.

—Well, drive bang up against Trinity College gates, said Mr. Browne, and then we'll tell you where to go. You understand now?

—Yes, sir, said the cabman.

—Make like a bird for Trinity College.

—Right, sir, cried the cabman.

The horse was whipped up and the cab rattled off along the quay amid a chorus of laughter and adieus.

Gabriel had not gone to the door with the others. He was in a dark part of the hall gazing up the staircase. A woman was standing near the top of the first flight, in the shadow also. He could not see her face but he could see the terracotta and salmonpink panels of her skirt which the shadow made appear black and white. It was his wife. She was leaning on the banisters, listening to something. Gabriel was surprised at her stillness and strained his ear to listen also. But he could hear little save the noise of laughter and dispute on the front steps, a few chords struck on the piano and a few notes of a man's voice singing.

He stood still in the gloom of the hall, trying to catch the air that the voice was singing and gazing up at his wife. There was grace and mystery in her attitude as if she were a symbol of something. He asked himself what is a woman standing on the stairs in the shadow, listening to distant music, a symbol of. If he were a painter he would paint her in that attitude. Her blue felt hat would show off the bronze of her hair against the darkness and the dark panels of her skirt would show off the light ones. *Distant Music* he would call the picture if he were a painter.

The hall-door was closed; and Aunt Kate, Aunt Julia and Mary Jane came down the hall, still laughing.

—Well, isn't Freddy terrible? said Mary Jane. He's really terrible.

Gabriel said nothing but pointed up the stairs towards where his wife was standing. Now that the hall-door was closed the voice and the piano could be heard more clearly. Gabriel held up his hand for them to be silent. The song seemed to be in the old Irish tonality and the singer seemed uncertain both of his words and of his voice. The voice, made plaintive by distance and by the singer's hoarseness, faintly illuminated the cadence of the air with words expressing grief:

> O, the rain falls on my heavy locks
> And the dew wets my skin,
> My babe lies cold . . .

—O, exclaimed Mary Jane. It's Bartell D'Arcy singing and he wouldn't sing all the night. O, I'll get him to sing a song before he goes.

—O do, Mary Jane, said Aunt Kate.

Mary Jane brushed past the others and ran to the staircase but before she reached it the singing stopped and the piano was closed abruptly.

—O, what a pity! she cried. Is he coming down, Gretta?

Gabriel heard his wife answer yes and saw her come down towards them. A few steps behind her were Mr. Bartell D'Arcy and Miss O'Callaghan.

—O, Mr. D'Arcy, cried Mary Jane, it's downright mean of you to break off like that when we were all in raptures listening to you.

—I have been at him all the evening, said Miss O'Callaghan, and Mrs. Conroy too and he told us he had a dreadful cold and couldn't sing.

—O, Mr. D'Arcy, said Aunt Kate, now that was a great fib to tell.

—Can't you see that I'm as hoarse as a crow? said Mr. D'Arcy roughly.

He went into the pantry hastily and put on his overcoat. The others, taken aback by his rude speech, could find nothing to say. Aunt Kate wrinkled her brows and made signs to the others to drop the subject. Mr. D'Arcy stood swathing his neck carefully and frowning.

—It's the weather, said Aunt Julia, after a pause.

—Yes, everybody has colds, said Aunt Kate readily, everybody.

—They say, said Mary Jane, we haven't had snow like it for thirty years; and I read this morning in the newspapers that the snow is general all over Ireland.

—I love the look of snow, said Aunt Julia sadly.

—So do I, said Miss O'Callaghan. I think Christmas is never really Christmas unless we have the snow on the ground.

—But poor Mr. D'Arcy doesn't like the snow, said Aunt Kate, smiling.

Mr. D'Arcy came from the pantry, fully swathed and buttoned, and in a repentant tone told them the history of his cold. Everyone gave him advice and said it was a great pity and urged him to be very careful of his throat in the night air. Gabriel watched his wife who did not join in the conversation. She was standing right under the dusty fanlight and the flame of the gas lit up the rich bronze of her hair which he had seen her drying at the fire a few days before. She was in the same attitude and seemed unaware of the talk about her. At last she turned towards them and Gabriel saw that there was colour on her cheeks and that her eyes were shining. A sudden tide of joy went leaping out of his heart.

—Mr. D'Arcy, she said, what is the name of that song you were singing?

—It's called *The Lass of Aughrim,* said Mr. D'Arcy, but I couldn't remember it properly. Why? Do you know it?

—*The Lass of Aughrim,* she repeated. I couldn't think of the name.

—It's a very nice air, said Mary Jane. I'm sorry you were not in voice to-night.

—Now, Mary Jane, said Aunt Kate, don't annoy Mr. D'Arcy. I won't have him annoyed.

Seeing that all were ready to start she shepherded them to the door where good-night was said:

—Well, good-night, Aunt Kate, and thanks for the pleasant evening.

—Good-night, Gabriel. Good-night, Gretta!

—Good-night, Aunt Kate, and thanks ever so much. Good-night, Aunt Julia.

—O, good-night, Gretta, I didn't see you.

—Good-night, Mr. D'Arcy. Good-night, Miss O'Callaghan.

—Good-night, Miss Morkan.

Good-night, again.

—Good-night, all. Safe home.

—Good-night. Good-night.

The morning was still dark. A dull yellow light brooded over the houses and the river; and the sky seemed to be descending. It was slushy underfoot; and only streaks and patches of snow lay on the roofs, on the parapets of the quay and on the area railings. The lamps were still burning redly in the murky air and, across the river, the palace of the Four Courts stood out menacingly against the heavy sky.

She was walking on before him with Mr. Bartell D'Arcy, her shoes in a brown parcel tucked under one arm and her hands holding her skirt up from the slush. She had no longer any grace of attitude but Gabriel's eyes were still bright with happiness. The blood went bounding along his veins; and the thoughts went rioting through his brain, proud, joyful, tender, valorous.

She was walking on before him so lightly and so erect that he longed to run after her noiselessly, catch her by the shoulders and say something foolish and affectionate into her ear. She seemed to him so frail that he longed to defend her against something and then to be alone with her. Moments of their secret life together burst like stars upon his memory. A heliotrope envelope was lying beside his breakfast-cup and he was caressing it with his hand. Birds were twittering in the ivy and the sunny web of the curtain was shimmering along the floor: he could not eat for happiness. They were standing on the crowded platform and he was placing a ticket inside the warm palm of her glove. He was standing with her in the cold, looking in through a grated window at a man making bottles in a roaring furnace. It was very cold. Her face, fragrant in the cold air, was quite close to his; and suddenly she called out to the man at the furnace:

—Is the fire hot, sir?

But the man could not hear her with the noise of the furnace. It was just as well. He might have answered rudely.

A wave of yet more tender joy escaped from his heart and went coursing in warm flood along his arteries. Like the tender fires of stars moments of their life together, that no one knew of or would ever know of, broke upon and illumined his memory. He longed to recall to her those moments, to make her forget the years of their dull existence together and remember only their moments of ecstasy. For the years, he felt, had not quenched his soul or hers. Their children, his writing, her household cares had not quenched all their souls' tender fire. In one letter that he had written to her then he had said: *Why is it that words like these seem to me so dull and cold? Is it because there is no word tender enough to be your name?*

Like distant music these words that he had written years before were borne towards him from the past. He longed to be alone with her. When the others had gone away, when he and she were in their room in the hotel, then they would be alone together. He would call her softly:

—Gretta!

Perhaps she would not hear at once: she would be undressing. Then something in his voice would strike her. She would turn and look at him.

At the corner of Winetavern Street they met a cab. He was glad of its rattling noise as it saved him from conversation. She was looking out of the window and seemed tired. The others spoke only a few words, pointing out some building or street. The horse galloped along wearily under the murky morning sky, dragging his old rattling box after his heels, and Gabriel was again in a cab with her, galloping to catch the boat, galloping to their honeymoon.

As the cab drove across O'Connell Bridge Miss O'Callaghan said:

—They say you never cross O'Connell Bridge without seeing a white horse.

—I see a white man this time, said Gabriel.

—Where? asked Mr. Bartell D'Arcy.

Gabriel pointed to the statue, on which lay patches of snow. Then he nodded familiarly to it and waved his hand.

—Good-night, Dan, he said gaily.

When the cab drew up before the hotel Gabriel jumped out and, in spite of Mr. Bartell D'Arcy's protest, paid the driver. He gave the man a shilling over his fare. The man saluted and said:

—A prosperous New Year to you, sir.

—The same to you, said Gabriel cordially.

She leaned for a moment on his arm in getting out of the cab and while standing at the curbstone, bidding the others good-night. She leaned lightly on his arm, as lightly as when she had danced with him a few hours before. He had felt proud and happy then, happy that she was his, proud of her grace and wifely carriage. But now, after the kindling again of so many memories, the first touch of her body, musical and strange and perfumed, sent through him a keen pang of lust. Under cover of her silence he pressed her arm closely to his side; and, as they stood at the hotel door, he felt that they had escaped from their lives and duties, escaped from home and friends and run away together with wild and radiant hearts to a new adventure.

An old man was dozing in a great hooded chair in the hall. He lit a candle in the office and went before them to the stairs. They followed him in silence, their feet falling in soft thuds on the thickly carpeted stairs. She mounted the stairs behind the porter, her head bowed in the ascent, her frail shoulders curved as with a burden, her skirt girt tightly about her. He could have flung his arms about her hips and held her still for his arms were trembling with desire to seize her and only the stress of his nails against the palms of his hands held the wild impulse of his body in check. The porter halted on the stairs to settle his guttering candle. They halted too on the steps below him. In the silence Gabriel could hear the falling of the molten wax into the tray and the thumping of his own heart against his ribs.

The porter led them along a corridor and opened a door. Then he set his unstable candle down on a toilet-table and asked at what hour they were to be called in the morning.

—Eight, said Gabriel.

The porter pointed to the tap of the electric-light and began a muttered apology but Gabriel cut him short.

—We don't want any light. We have light enough from the street. And I say, he added, pointing to the candle, you might remove that handsome article, like a good man.

The porter took up his candle again, but slowly for he was surprised by such a novel idea. Then he mumbled good-night and went out. Gabriel shot the lock to.

A ghostly light from the street lamp lay in a long shaft from one window to the door. Gabriel threw his overcoat and hat on a couch and crossed the room towards the window. He looked down into the street in order that his emotion might calm a little. Then he turned and leaned against a chest of drawers with his back to the light. She had taken off her hat and cloak and was standing before a large swinging mirror, unhooking her waist. Gabriel paused for a few moments, watching her, and then said:

—Gretta!

She turned away from the mirror slowly and walked along the shaft of light towards him. Her face looked so serious and weary that the words would not pass Gabriel's lips. No, it was not the moment yet.

—You looked tired, he said.

—I am a little, she answered.

—You don't feel ill or weak?

—No, tired: that's all.

She went on to the window and stood there, looking out. Gabriel waited again and then, fearing that diffidence was about to conquer him, he said abruptly:

—By the way, Gretta!

—What is it?

—You know that poor fellow Malins? he said quickly.

—Yes. What about him?

—Well, poor fellow, he's a decent sort of chap after all, continued Gabriel in a false voice. He gave me back that sovereign I lent him and I didn't expect it really. It's a pity he wouldn't keep away from that Browne, because he's not a bad fellow at heart.

He was trembling now with annoyance. Why did she seem so abstracted? He did not know how he could begin. Was she annoyed, too, about something? If she would only turn to him or come to him of her own accord! To take her as she was would be brutal. No, he must see some ardour in her eyes first. He longed to be master of her strange mood.

—When did you lend him the pound? she asked, after a pause.

Gabriel strove to restrain himself from breaking out into brutal language about the sottish Malins and his pound. He longed to cry to her from his soul, to crush her body against his, to overmaster her. But he said:

—O, at Christmas, when he opened that little Christmas-card shop in Henry Street.

He was in such a fever of rage and desire that he did not hear her come from the window. She stood before him for an instant, looking at him strangely. Then, suddenly raising herself on tiptoe and resting her hands lightly on his shoulders, she kissed him.

—You are a very generous person, Gabriel, she said.

Gabriel, trembling with delight at her sudden kiss and at the quaintness of her phrase, put his hands on her hair and began smoothing it back, scarcely touching it with his fingers. The washing had made it fine and brilliant. His heart was brimming over with happiness. Just when he was wishing for it she had come to him of her own accord. Perhaps her thoughts had been running with his. Perhaps she had felt the impetuous desire that was in him and then the yielding mood had come upon her. Now that she had fallen to him so easily he wondered why he had been so diffident.

He stood, holding her head between his hands. Then, slipping one arm swiftly about her body and drawing her towards him, he said softly:

—Gretta dear, what are you thinking about?

She did not answer nor yield wholly to his arm. He said again, softly:

—Tell me what it is, Gretta. I think I know what is the matter. Do I know?

She did not answer at once. Then she said in an outburst of tears:

—O, I am thinking about that song, *The Lass of Aughrim*.

She broke loose from him and ran to the bed and, throwing her arms across the bed-rail, hid her face. Gabriel stood stock-still for a moment in astonishment and then followed her. As he passed in the way of the cheval-glass he caught sight of himself in full length, his broad, well-filled shirt-front, the face whose expression always puzzled him when he saw it in a mirror and his glimmering gilt-rimmed eyeglasses. He halted a few paces from her and said:

—What about the song? Why does that make you cry?

She raised her head from her arms and dried her eyes with the back of her hand like a child. A kinder note than he had intended went into his voice.

—Why, Gretta? he asked.

—I am thinking about a person long ago who used to sing that song.

—And who was the person long ago? asked Gabriel, smiling.

—It was a person I used to know in Galway when I was living with my grandmother, she said.

The smile passed away from Gabriel's face. A dull anger began to gather again at the back of his mind and the dull fires of his lust began to glow angrily in his veins.

—Someone you were in love with? he asked ironically.

—It was a young boy I used to know, she answered, named Michael Furey. He used to sing that song, *The Lass of Aughrim*. He was very delicate.

Gabriel was silent. He did not wish her to think that he was interested in this delicate boy.

—I can see him so plainly, she said after a moment. Such eyes as he had: big dark eyes! And such an expression in them—an expression!

—O then, you were in love with him? said Gabriel.

—I used to go out walking with him, she said, when I was in Galway.

A thought flew across Gabriel's mind.

—Perhaps that was why you wanted to go to Galway with that Ivors girl? he said coldly.

She looked at him and asked in surprise:

—What for?

Her eyes made Gabriel feel awkward. He shrugged his shoulders and said:

—How do I know? To see him perhaps.

She looked away from him along the shaft of light towards the window in silence.

—He is dead, she said at length. He died when he was only seventeen. Isn't it a terrible thing to die so young as that?

—What was he? asked Gabriel, still ironically.

—He was in the gasworks, she said.

Gabriel felt humiliated by the failure of his irony and by the evocation of this figure from the dead, a boy in the gasworks. While he had been full of memories of their secret life together, full of tenderness and joy and desire, she had been comparing him in her mind with another. A shameful consciousness of his own person assailed him. He saw himself as a ludicrous figure, acting as a pennyboy for his aunts, a nervous, well-meaning sentimentalist, orating to vulgarians and idealising his own clownish lusts, the pitiable fatuous fellow he had caught a glimpse of in the mirror. Instinctively he turned his back more to the light lest she might see the shame that burned upon his forehead.

He tried to keep up his tone of cold interrogation but his voice when he spoke was humble and indifferent.

—I suppose you were in love with this Michael Furey, Gretta, he said.

—I was great with him at that time, she said.

Her voice was veiled and sad. Gabriel, feeling now how vain it would be to try to lead her whither he had purposed, caressed one of her hands and said, also sadly:

—And what did he die of so young, Gretta? Consumption, was it?

—I think he died for me, she answered.

A vague terror seized Gabriel at this answer as if, at that hour when he had hoped to triumph, some impalpable and vindictive being was coming against him, gathering forces against him in its vague world. But he shook himself free of it with an effort of reason and continued to caress her hand. He did not question her again for he felt that she would tell him of herself. Her hand was warm and moist: it did not respond to his touch but he continued to caress it just as he had caressed her first letter to him that spring morning.

—It was in the winter, she said, about the beginning of the winter when I was going to leave my grandmother's and come up here to the convent. And he was ill at the time in his lodgings in Galway and wouldn't be let out and his people in Oughterard were written to. He was in decline, they said, or something like that. I never knew rightly.

She paused for a moment and sighed.

—Poor fellow, she said. He was very fond of me and he was such a gentle boy. We used to go out together, walking, you know, Gabriel, like the way they do in the country. He was going to study singing only for his health. He had a very good voice, poor Michael Furey.

—Well; and then? asked Gabriel.

—And then when it came to the time for me to leave Galway and come up to the convent he was much worse and I wouldn't be let see him so I wrote a letter saying I was going up to Dublin and would be back in the summer and hoping he would be better then.

She paused for a moment to get her voice under control and then went on:

—Then the night before I left I was in my grandmother's house in Nun's Island, packing up, and I heard gravel thrown up against the window. The window was so wet I couldn't see so I ran downstairs as I was and slipped out the back into the garden and there was the poor fellow at the end of the garden, shivering.

—And did you not tell him to go back? asked Gabriel.

—I implored of him to go home at once and told him he would get his death in the rain. But he said he did not want to live. I can see his eyes as well as well! He was standing at the end of the wall where there was a tree.

—And did he go home? asked Gabriel.

—Yes, he went home. And when I was only a week in the convent he died and he was buried in Oughterard where his people came from. O, the day I heard that, that he was dead!

She stopped, choking with sobs, and, overcome by emotion, flung herself face downward on the bed, sobbing in the quilt. Gabriel held her hand for a moment longer, irresolutely, and then, shy of intruding on her grief, let it fall gently and walked quietly to the window.

She was fast asleep.

Gabriel, leaning on his elbow, looked for a few moments unresentfully on her tangled hair and half-open mouth, listening to her deep-drawn breath. So she had had that romance in her life: a man had died for her sake. It hardly pained him now to think how poor a part he, her husband, had played in her life. He watched her while she slept as though he and she had never lived together as man and wife. His curious eyes rested long upon her face and on her hair: and, as he thought of what she must have been then, in that time of her first girlish beauty, a strange friendly pity for her entered his soul. He did not like to say even to himself that her face was no longer beautiful but he knew that it was no longer the face for which Michael Furey had braved death.

Perhaps she had not told him all the story. His eyes moved to the chair over which she had thrown some of her clothes. A petticoat string dangled to the floor. One boot stood upright, its limp upper fallen down: the fellow of it lay upon its side. He wondered at his riot of emotions of an hour before. From what had it proceeded? From his aunt's supper, from his own foolish speech, from the wine and dancing, the merrymaking when saying good-night in the hall, the pleasure of the walk along the river in the snow. Poor Aunt Julia! She, too, would soon be a shade with the shade of Patrick Morkan and his horse. He had caught that haggard look upon her face for a moment when she was singing *Arrayed for the Bridal*. Soon, perhaps, he would be sitting in that same drawing-room, dressed in black, his silk hat on his knees. The blinds would be drawn down and Aunt Kate would be sitting beside him, crying and blowing her nose and telling him how Julia had died. He would cast about in his mind for some words that might console her, and would find only lame and useless ones. Yes, yes: that would happen very soon.

The air of the room chilled his shoulders. He stretched himself cautiously along under the sheets and lay down beside his wife. One by one they were all becoming shades. Better pass boldly into that other world, in the full glory of some passion, than fade and wither dismally with age. He thought of how she who lay beside him had locked in her heart for so many years that image of her lover's eyes when he had told her that he did not wish to live.

Generous tears filled Gabriel's eyes. He had never felt like that himself towards any woman but he knew that such a feeling must be love. The tears gathered more thickly in his eyes and in the partial darkness he imagined he saw the form of a young man standing under a dripping tree. Other forms were near. His soul had approached that region where dwell the vast hosts of the dead. He was conscious of, but could not apprehend, their wayward and flickering existence. His own identity was fading out into a grey impalpable world: the solid world itself which these dead had one time reared and lived in was dissolving and dwindling.

A few light taps upon the pane made him turn to the window. It had begun to snow again. He watched sleepily the flakes, silver and dark, falling obliquely against the lamplight. The time had come for him to set out on his journey westward. Yes, the newspapers were right: snow was general all over Ireland. It was falling on every part of the dark central plain, on the treeless hills, falling softly upon the Bog of Allen and, farther westward, softly falling into the dark mutinous Shannon waves. It was falling, too, upon every part of the lonely churchyard on the hill where Michael Furey lay buried. It lay thickly drifted on the crooked crosses and headstones, on the spears of the little gate, on the barren thorns. His soul swooned slowly as he heard the snow falling faintly through the universe and faintly falling, like the descent of their last end, upon all the living and the dead.

(1914)

CHAPTER EIGHT

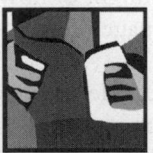

A Collection of Short Fiction

Fiction is not dream. Nor is it guess work. It is imagining based on facts. . . .
MARGARET BANNING

Fiction is like a spider's web, attached ever so slightly perhaps, but still attached to life at all four corners.
VIRGINIA WOOLF

NATHANIEL HAWTHORNE

[1804–1864]

Young Goodman Brown

Young Goodman Brown came forth at sunset, into the street of Salem village, but put his head back, after crossing the threshold, to exchange a parting kiss with his young wife. And Faith, as the wife was aptly named, thrust her own pretty head into the street, letting the wind play with the pink ribbons of her cap, while she called to Goodman Brown.

"Dearest heart," whispered she, softly and rather sadly, when her lips were close to

272

his ear, "prithee, put off your journey until sunrise, and sleep in your own bed to-night. A lone woman is troubled with such dreams and such thoughts, that she's afeard of herself, sometimes. Pray, tarry with me this night, dear husband, of all nights in the year!"

"My love and my Faith," replied young Goodman Brown, "of all nights in the year, this one night must I tarry away from thee. My journey, as thou callest it, forth and back again, must needs be done 'twixt now and sunrise. What, my sweet, pretty wife, dost thou doubt me already, and we but three months married!"

"Then God bless you!" said Faith with the pink ribbons, "and may you find all well, when you come back."

"Amen!" cried Goodman Brown. "Say thy prayers, dear Faith, and go to bed at dusk, and no harm will come to thee."

So they parted; and the young man pursued his way, until, being about to turn the corner by the meeting-house, he looked back and saw the head of Faith still peeping after him, with a melancholy air, in spite of her pink ribbons.

"Poor little Faith!" thought he, for his heart smote him. "What a wretch am I, to leave her on such an errand! She talks of dreams, too. Methought, as she spoke, there was trouble in her face, as if a dream had warned her what work is to be done to-night. But no, no! 't would kill her to think it. Well; she's a blessed angel on earth; and after this one night, I'll cling to her skirts and follow her to Heaven."

With this excellent resolve for the future, Goodman Brown felt himself justified in making more haste on his present evil purpose. He had taken a dreary road, darkened by all the gloomiest trees of the forest, which barely stood aside to let the narrow path creep through, and closed immediately behind. It was as lonely as could be; and there is this peculiarity in such a solitude, that the traveller knows not who may be concealed by the innumerable trunks and the thick boughs overhead; so that, with lonely footsteps, he may yet be, passing through an unseen multitude.

"There may be a devilish Indian behind every tree," said Goodman Brown to himself; and he glanced fearfully behind him, as he added, "What if the devil himself should be at my very elbow!"

His head being turned back, he passed a crook of the road, and looking forward again, beheld the figure of a man, in grave and decent attire, seated at the foot of an old tree. He arose at Goodman Brown's approach, and walked onward, side by side with him.

"You are late, Goodman Brown," said he. "The clock of the Old South was striking, as I came through Boston; and that is full fifteen minutes agone."

"Faith kept me back awhile," replied the young man, with a tremor in his voice, caused by the sudden appearance of his companion, though not wholly unexpected.

It was now deep dusk in the forest, and deepest in that part of it where these two were journeying. As nearly as could be discerned, the second traveller was about fifty years old, apparently in the same rank of life as Goodman Brown, and bearing a considerable resemblance to him, though perhaps more in expression than features. Still, they might have been taken for father and son. And yet, though the elder person was as simply clad as the younger, and as simple in manner too, he had an indescribable air of one who knew the world, and would not have felt abashed at the governor's dinner-table, or in King William's court, were it possible that his affairs should call him thither. But the only thing about him that could be fixed upon as remarkable, was his staff, which bore the likeness of a great black snake, so curiously wrought, that it might almost be seen to twist and wriggle itself like a living serpent. This, of course, must have been an ocular deception, assisted by the uncertain light.

"Come, Goodman Brown!" cried his fellow-traveller, "this is a dull pace for the beginning of a journey. Take my staff, if you are so soon weary."

"Friend," said the other, exchanging his slow pace for a full stop, "having kept covenant by meeting thee here, it is my purpose now to return whence I came. I have scruples, touching the matter thou wot'st of."

"Sayest thou so?" replied he of the serpent, smiling apart. "Let us walk on, nevertheless, reasoning as we go, and if I convince thee not, thou shalt turn back. We are but a little way in the forest, yet."

"Too far, too far!" exclaimed the goodman, unconsciously resuming his walk. "My father never went into the woods on such an errand, nor his father before him. We have been a race of honest men and good Christians, since the days of the martyrs. And shall I be the first of the name of Brown that ever took this path and kept—"

"Such company, thou wouldst say," observed the elder person, interrupting his pause. "Well said, Goodman Brown! I have been as well acquainted with your family as with ever a one among the Puritans; and that's no trifle to say. I helped your grandfather, the constable, when he lashed the Quaker woman so smartly through the streets of Salem. And it was I that brought your father a pitch-pine knot, kindled at my own hearth, to set fire to an Indian village, in King Philip's war. They were my good friends, both; and many a pleasant walk have we had along this path, and returned merrily after midnight. I would fain be friends with you, for their sake."

"If it be as thou sayest," replied Goodman Brown, "I marvel they never spoke of these matters. Or, verily, I marvel not, seeing that the least rumor of the sort would have driven them from New England. We are a people of prayer and good works to boot, and abide no such wickedness."

"Wickedness or not," said the traveller with the twisted staff, "I have a very general acquaintance here in New England. The deacons of many a church have drunk the communion wine with me; the selectmen, of divers towns, make me their chairman; and a majority of the Great and General Court are firm supporters of my interest. The governor and I, too—but these are state secrets."

"Can this be so!" cried Goodman Brown, with a stare of amazement at his undisturbed companion. "Howbeit, I have nothing to do with the governor and council; they have their own ways, and are no rule for a simple husbandman like me. But, were I to go on with thee, how should I meet the eye of that good old man, our minister, at Salem village? Oh, his voice would make me tremble, both Sabbath-day and lecture-day!"

Thus far, the elder traveller had listened with due gravity, but now burst into a fit of irrepressible mirth, shaking himself so violently, that his snakelike staff actually seemed to wriggle in sympathy.

"Ha, ha, ha!" shouted he, again and again; then composing himself, "Well, go on, Goodman Brown, go on; but, prithee, don't kill me with laughing!"

"Well, then, to end the matter at once," said Goodman Brown, considerably nettled, "there is my wife, Faith. It would break her dear little heart; and I'd rather break my own!"

"Nay, if that be the case," answered the other, "e'en go thy ways, Goodman Brown. I would not, for twenty old women like the one hobbling before us, that Faith should come to any harm."

As he spoke, he pointed his staff at a female figure on the path, in whom Goodman Brown recognized a very pious and exemplary dame, who had taught him his catechism in youth, and was still his moral and spiritual adviser, jointly with the minister and Deacon Gookin.

"A marvel, truly, that Goody Cloyse should be so far in the wilderness, at nightfall!" said he. "But, with your leave, friend, I shall take a cut through the woods, until we have left this Christian woman behind. Being a stranger to you, she might ask whom I was consorting with, and whither I was going."

"Be it so," said his fellow-traveller. "Betake you to the woods, and let me keep the path."

Accordingly, the young man turned aside, but took care to watch his companion, who advanced softly along the road, until he had come within a staff's length of the old dame. She, meanwhile, was making the best of her way, with singular speed for so aged a woman, and mumbling some indistinct words, a prayer, doubtless, as she went. The traveller put forth his staff, and touched her withered neck with what seemed the serpent's tail.

"The devil!" screamed the pious old lady.

"Then Goody Cloyse knows her old friend?" observed the traveller, confronting her, and leaning on his writhing stick.

"Ah, forsooth, and is it your worship, indeed?" cried the good dame. "Yea, truly is it, and in the very image of my old gossip, Goodman Brown, the grandfather of the silly fellow that now is. But, would your worship believe it? my broomstick hath strangely disappeared, stolen, as I suspect, by that unhanged witch, Goody Cory, and that, too, when I was all anointed with the juice of smallage and cinque-foil and wolf's-bane—"

"Mingled with fine wheat and the fat of a new-born babe," said the shape of old Goodman Brown.

"Ah, your worship knows the recipe," cried the old lady, cackling aloud. "So, as I was saying, being all ready for the meeting, and no horse to ride on, I made up my mind to foot it; for they tell me there is a nice young man to be taken into communion to-night. But now your good worship will lend me your arm, and we shall be there in a twinkling."

"That can hardly be," answered her friend. "I may not spare you my arm, Goody Cloyse, but here is my staff, if you will."

So saying, he threw it down at her feet, where, perhaps, it assumed life, being one of the rods which its owner had formerly lent to the Egyptian Magi. Of this fact, however, Goodman Brown could not take cognizance. He had cast his eyes in astonishment, and looking down again, beheld neither Goody Cloyse nor the serpentine staff, but his fellow-traveller alone, who waited for him as calmly as if nothing had happened.

"That old woman taught me my catechism!" said the young man; and there was a world of meaning in this simple comment.

They continued to walk onward, while the elder traveller exhorted his companion to make good speed and persevere in the path, discoursing so aptly, that his arguments seemed rather to spring up in the bosom of his auditor, than to be suggested by himself. As they went he plucked a branch of maple, to serve for a walking-stick, and began to strip it of the twigs and little boughs, which were wet with evening dew. The moment his fingers touched them, they became strangely withered and dried up, as with a week's sunshine. Thus the pair proceeded, at a good free pace, until suddenly, in a gloomy hollow of the road, Goodman Brown sat himself down on the stump of a tree, and refused to go any farther.

"Friend," said he, stubbornly, "my mind is made up. Not another step will I budge on this errand. What if a wretched old woman do choose to go to the devil, when I thought she was going to Heaven! Is that any reason why I should quit my dear Faith, and go after her?"

"You will think better of this by and by," said his acquaintance, composedly. "Sit here and rest yourself awhile; and when you feel like moving again, there is my staff to help you along."

Without more words, he threw his companion the maple stick, and was as speedily out of sight as if he had vanished into the deepening gloom. The young man sat a few moments by the roadside, applauding himself greatly, and thinking with how clear a conscience he should meet the minister, in his morning walk, nor shrink from the eye of good old Deacon Gookin. And what calm sleep would be his, that very night, which was to have been spent so wickedly, but purely and sweetly now, in the arms of Faith! Amidst these pleasant and praiseworthy meditations, Goodman Brown heard the tramp of horses along the road, and deemed it advisable to conceal himself within the verge of the forest, conscious of the guilty purpose that had brought him thither, though now so happily turned from it.

On came the hoof-tramps and the voices of the riders, two grave old voices, conversing soberly, as they drew near. These mingled sounds appeared to pass along the road, within a few yards of the young man's hiding-place; but owing, doubtless, to the depth of the gloom, at that particular spot, neither the travellers nor their steeds were visible. Though their figures brushed the small boughs by the wayside, it could not be seen that they intercepted, even for a moment, the faint gleam from the strip of bright sky, athwart which they must have passed. Goodman Brown alternately crouched and stood on tiptoe, pulling aside the branches, and thrusting forth his head as far as he durst, without discerning so much as a shadow. It vexed him the more, because he could have sworn, were such a thing possible, that he recognized the voices of the minister and Deacon Gookin, jogging along quietly, as they were wont to do, when bound to some ordination or ecclesiastical council. While yet within hearing, one of the riders stopped to pluck a switch.

"Of the two, reverend Sir," said the voice like the deacon's, "I had rather miss an ordination dinner than to-night's meeting. They tell me that some of our community are to be here from Falmouth and beyond, and others from Connecticut and Rhode Island; besides several of the Indian powwows, who, after their fashion, know almost as much deviltry as the best of us. Moreover, there is a goodly young woman to be taken into communion."

"Mighty well, Deacon Gookin!" replied the solemn old tones of the minister. "Spur up, or we shall be late. Nothing can be done, you know, until I get on the ground."

The hoofs clattered again, and the voices, talking so strangely in the empty air, passed on through the forest, where no church had ever been gathered, nor solitary Christian prayed. Whither, then, could these holy men be journeying, so deep into the heathen wilderness? Young Goodman Brown caught hold of a tree, for support, being ready to sink down on the ground, faint and over-burthened with the heavy sickness of his heart. He looked up to the sky, doubting whether there really was a Heaven above him. Yet, there was the blue arch, and the stars brightening in it.

"With Heaven above, and Faith below, I will yet stand firm against the devil!" cried Goodman Brown.

While he still gazed upward, into the deep arch of the firmament, and had lifted his hands to pray, a cloud, though no wind was stirring, hurried across the zenith, and hid the brightening stars. The blue sky was still visible, except directly overhead, where this black mass of cloud was sweeping swiftly northward. Aloft in the air, as if from the depths of the cloud, came a confused and doubtful sound of voices. Once, the listener fancied that he could distinguish the accents of townspeople of his own, men and women, both pious and ungodly, many of whom he had met at the communion-table, and had seen others rioting at the tavern. The next moment, so indistinct were the sounds, he doubted whether he had heard aught but the murmur of the old forest, whispering without a wind. Then came a stronger swell of those familiar tones, heard daily in the sunshine, at Salem village, but never, until now, from a cloud at night. There was one voice, of a young woman, tittering lamentations, yet with an uncertain sorrow, and entreating for some favor, which, perhaps, it would grieve her to obtain. And all the unseen multitude, both saints and sinners, seemed to encourage her onward.

"Faith!" shouted Goodman Brown, in a voice of agony and desperation; and the echoes of the forest mocked him, crying—"Faith! Faith!" as if bewildered wretches were seeking her, all through the wilderness.

The cry of grief, rage, and terror was yet piercing the night, when the unhappy husband held his breath for a response. There was a scream, drowned immediately in a louder murmur of voices fading into far-off laughter, as the dark cloud swept away, leaving the clear and silent sky above Goodman Brown. But something fluttered lightly down through the air, and caught on the branch of a tree. The young man seized it and beheld a pink ribbon.

"My Faith is gone!" cried he, after one stupefied moment. "There is no good on earth, and sin is but a name. Come, devil! for to thee is this world given."

And maddened with despair, so that he laughed loud and long, did Goodman Brown grasp his staff and set forth again, at such a rate, that he seemed to fly along the forest path, rather than to walk or run. The road grew wilder and drearier, and more faintly traced, and vanished at length, leaving him in the heart of the dark wilderness, still rushing onward, with the instinct that guides mortal man to evil. The whole forest was peopled with frightful sounds: the creaking of the trees, the howling of wild beasts, and the yell of Indians; while, sometimes, the wind tolled like a distant church bell, and sometimes gave a broad roar around the traveller, as if all Nature was laughing him to scorn. But he was himself the chief horror of the scene, and shrank not from its other horrors.

"Ha! ha! ha!" roared Goodman Brown, when the wind laughed at him. "Let us hear which will laugh loudest! Think not to frighten me with your deviltry! Come witch, come wizard, come Indian powwow, come devil himself! and here comes Goodman Brown. You may as well fear him as he fear you!"

In truth, all through the haunted forest, there could be nothing more frightful than the figure of Goodman Brown. On he flew, among the black pines, brandishing his staff with frenzied gestures, now giving vent to an inspiration of horrid blasphemy, and now shouting forth such laughter, as set all the echoes of the forest laughing like demons around him. The fiend in his own shape is less hideous, than when he rages in the breast of man. Thus sped the demoniac on his course, until, quivering among the trees, he saw a red light before him, as when the felled trunks and branches of a clearing have been set on fire, and throw up their lurid blaze against the sky, at the hour of midnight. He paused, in a lull of the tempest that had driven him onward, and heard the swell of what seemed a hymn, rolling solemnly from a distance, with the weight of many voices. He knew the tune. It was a familiar one in the choir of the village meeting-house. The verse died heavily away, and was lengthened by a chorus, not of human voices, but of all the sounds of the benighted wilderness, pealing in awful harmony together. Goodman Brown cried out; and his cry was lost to his own ear, by its unison with the cry of the desert.

In the interval of silence, he stole forward, until the light glared full upon his eyes. At one extremity of an open space, hemmed in by the dark wall of the forest, arose a rock, bearing some rude, natural resemblance either to an altar or a pulpit, and surrounded by four blazing pines, their tops aflame, their stems untouched, like candles at an evening meeting. The mass of foliage, that had overgrown the summit of the rock, was all on fire, blazing high into the night, and fitfully illuminating the whole field. Each pendent twig and leafy festoon was in a blaze. As the red light arose and fell, a numerous congregation alternately shone forth, then disappeared in shadow, and again grew, as it were, out of the darkness, peopling the heart of the solitary woods at once.

"A grave and dark-clad company!" quoth Goodman Brown.

In truth, they were such. Among them, quivering to-and-fro, between gloom and splendor, appeared faces that would be seen, next day, at the council-board of the province, and others which, Sabbath after Sabbath, looked devoutly heavenward, and benignantly over the crowded pews, from the holiest pulpits in the land. Some affirm, that the lady of the governor was there. At least, there were high dames well known to her, and wives of honored husbands, and widows a great multitude, and ancient maidens, all of excellent repute, and fair young girls, who trembled lest their mothers should espy them. Either the sudden gleams of light, flashing over the obscure field, bedazzled Goodman Brown, or he recognized a score of the church members of Salem village, famous for their especial sanctity. Good old Deacon Gookin had arrived, and waited at the skirts of that venerable saint, his reverend pastor. But, irreverently consorting with these grave, reputable, and pious people, these elders of the church, these chaste dames and dewy virgins, there were men of dissolute lives and women of spotted fame, wretches given over to all mean and filthy vice, and suspected even of horrid crimes. It was strange to see, that the good shrank not from the wicked, nor were the sinners abashed by the saints. Scattered, also, among their pale-faced enemies, were the Indian priests, or powwows, who had often scared their native forest with more hideous incantations than any known to English witchcraft.

"But, where is Faith?" thought Goodman Brown; and, as hope came into his heart, he trembled.

Another verse of the hymn arose, a slow and mournful strain, such as the pious love, but joined to words which expressed all that our nature can conceive of sin, and darkly hinted at far more. Unfathomable to mere mortals is the lore of fiends. Verse after verse was sung, and still the chorus of the desert swelled between, like the deepest tone of a mighty omen. And, with the final peal of that dreadful anthem, there came a sound, as if the roaring wind, the rushing streams, the howling beasts, and every other voice of the unconverted wilderness were mingling and according with the voice of guilty man, in homage to the prince of all. The four blazing pines threw up a loftier flame, and obscurely discovered shapes and visages of horror on the smoke-wreaths, above the impious assembly. At the same moment, the fire on the rock shot redly forth, and formed a glowing arch above its base, where now appeared a figure. With reverence be it spoken, the apparition bore no slight similitude, both in garb and manner, to some grave divine of the New England churches.

"Bring forth the converts!" cried a voice, that echoed through the field and rolled into the forest.

At the word, Goodman Brown stepped forth from the shadow of the trees, and approached the congregation, with whom he felt a loathful brotherhood, by the sympathy of all that was wicked in his heart. He could have well-nigh sworn, that the shape of his own dead father beckoned him to advance, looking downward from a smoke-wreath, while a woman, with dim features of despair, threw out her hand to warn him back. Was it his mother? But he had no power to retreat one step, nor to resist, even in thought, when the minister and good old Deacon Gookin seized his arms, and led him to the blazing rock. Thither came also the slender form of a veiled female, led between Goody Cloyse, that pious teacher of the catechism, and Martha Carrier, who had received the devil's promise to be queen of hell. A rampant hag was she! And there stood the proselytes, beneath the canopy of fire.

"Welcome, my children," said the dark figure, "to the communion of your race! Ye have found, thus young, your nature and your destiny. My children, look behind you!"

They turned; and flashing forth, as it were, in a sheet of flame, the fiend-worshippers were seen; the smile of welcome gleamed darkly on every visage.

"There," resumed the sable form, "are all whom ye have reverenced from youth. Ye deemed them holier than yourselves, and shrank from your own sin, contrasting it with their lives of righteousness and prayerful aspirations heavenward. Yet, here are they all, in my worshipping assembly! This night it shall be granted you to know their secret deeds; how hoary-bearded elders of the church have whispered wanton words to the young maids of their households; how many a woman, eager for widow's weeds, has given her husband a drink at bedtime, and let him sleep his last sleep in her bosom; how beardless youths have made haste to inherit their father's wealth; and how fair damsels—blush not, sweet ones!—have dug little graves in the garden, and bidden me, the sole guest, to an infant's funeral. By the sympathy of your human hearts for sin, ye shall scent out all the places—whether in church, bed-chamber, street, field, or forest—where crime has been committed, and shall exult to behold the whole earth one stain of guilt, one mighty blood-spot. Far more than this! It shall be yours to penetrate, in every bosom, the deep mystery of sin, the fountain of all wicked arts, and which inexhaustibly supplies more evil impulses than human power—than my power, at its utmost!—can make manifest in deeds. And now, my children, look upon each other."

They did so; and, by the blaze of the hell-kindled torches, the wretched man beheld his Faith, and the wife her husband, trembling before that unhallowed altar.

"Lo! there ye stand, my children," said the figure, in a deep and solemn tone, almost sad, with its despairing awfulness, as if his once angelic nature could yet mourn for our miserable race. "Depending upon one another's hearts, ye had still hoped that virtue were not all a dream! Now are ye undeceived!—Evil is the nature of mankind. Evil must be your only happiness. Welcome, again, my children, to the communion of your race!"

"Welcome!" repeated the fiend-worshippers, in one cry of despair and triumph.

And there they stood, the only pair, as it seemed, who were yet hesitating on the verge of wickedness, in this dark world. A basin was hollowed, naturally, in the rock. Did it contain water, reddened by the lurid light? or was it blood? or, perchance, a liquid flame? Herein did the Shape of Evil dip his hand, and prepare to lay the mark of baptism upon their foreheads, that they might be partakers of the mystery of sin, more conscious of the secret guilt of others, both in deed and thought, than they could now be of their own. The husband cast one look at his pale wife, and Faith at him. What polluted wretches would the next glance show them to each other, shuddering alike at what they disclosed and what they saw!

"Faith! Faith!" cried the husband. "Look up to Heaven, and resist the Wicked One!"

Whether Faith obeyed, he knew not. Hardly had he spoken, when he found himself amid calm night and solitude, listening to a roar of the wind, which died heavily away through the forest. He staggered against the rock, and felt it chill and damp, while a hanging twig, that had been all on fire, besprinkled his cheek with the coldest dew.

The next morning, young Goodman Brown came slowly into the street of Salem village staring around him like a bewildered man. The good old minister was taking a walk along the grave-yard, to get an appetite for breakfast and meditate his sermon, and bestowed a blessing, as he passed, on Goodman Brown. He shrank from the venerable saint, as if to avoid an anathema. Old Deacon Gookin was at domestic worship, and the holy words of his prayer were heard through the open window. "What God doth the wizard pray to?" quoth Goodman Brown. Goody Cloyse, that excellent old Christian, stood in the early sunshine, at her own lattice, catechizing a little girl, who had brought her a pint of morning's milk. Goodman Brown snatched away the child, as from the grasp of the fiend himself. Turning the corner by the meeting-house, he spied the head of Faith, with the pink ribbons, gazing anxiously forth, and bursting into such joy at sight of him that she skipt along the street, and almost kissed her husband before the whole village. But Goodman Brown looked sternly and sadly into her face, and passed on without a greeting.

Had Goodman Brown fallen asleep in the forest, and only dreamed a wild dream of a witch-meeting?

Be it so, if you will. But, alas! it was a dream of evil omen for young Goodman Brown. A stern, a sad, a darkly meditative, a distrustful, if not a desperate man did he become, from the night of that fearful dream. On the Sabbath day, when the congregation were singing a holy psalm, he could not listen, because an anthem of sin rushed loudly upon his ear, and drowned all the blessed strain. When the minister spoke from the pulpit, with power and fervid eloquence, and with his hand on the open Bible, of the sacred truths of our religion, and of saint-like lives and triumphant deaths, and of future bliss or misery unutterable, then did Goodman Brown turn pale, dreading lest the roof should thunder down upon the gray blasphemer and his hearers. Often, awaking suddenly at midnight, he shrank from the bosom of Faith, and at morning or eventide, when the family knelt down at prayer, he scowled, and muttered to himself, and gazed sternly at his wife, and turned away. And when he had lived long, and was borne to his grave, a hoary corpse, followed by Faith, an aged woman, and children and grand-children, a goodly procession, besides neighbors not a few, they carved no hopeful verse upon his tombstone; for his dying hour was gloom.

(1828)

ANTON CHEKHOV

[1860–1904]

The Lady with the Dog

TRANSLATED BY CONSTANCE GARNETT

1

It was said that a new person had appeared on the sea-front: a lady with a little dog. Dmitri Dmitritch Gurov, who had by then been a fortnight at Yalta, and so was fairly at home there, had begun to take an interest in new arrivals. Sitting in Verney's pavilion, he saw, walking on the sea-front, a fair-haired young lady of medium height, wearing a *béret;* a white Pomeranian dog was running behind her.

And afterwards he met her in the public gardens and in the square several times a day. She was walking alone, always wearing the same *béret,* and always with the same white dog; no one knew who she was, and every one called her simply "the lady with the dog."

"If she is here alone without a husband or friends, it wouldn't be amiss to make her acquaintance," Gurov reflected.

He was under forty, but he had a daughter already twelve years old, and two sons at school. He had been married young, when he was a student in his second year, and by now his wife seemed half as old again as he. She was a tall, erect woman with dark eyebrows, staid and dignified, and, as she said of herself, intellectual. She read a great deal, used phonetic spelling, called her husband, not Dmitri, but Dimitri, and he secretly considered her unintelligent, narrow, inelegant, was afraid of her, and did not like to be at home. He had begun being unfaithful to her long ago—had been unfaithful to her often, and, probably on that account, almost always spoke ill of women, and when they were talked about in his presence, used to call them "the lower race."

It seemed to him that he had been so schooled by bitter experience that he might call them what he liked, and yet he could not get on for two days together without "the lower race." In the society of men he was bored and not himself, with them he was cold and uncommunicative; but when he was in the company of women he felt free, and knew what to say to them and how to behave; and he was at ease with them even when he was silent. In his appearance, in his character, in his whole nature, there was something attractive and elusive which allured women and disposed them in his favour; he knew that, and some force seemed to draw him, too, to them.

Experience often repeated, truly bitter experience, had taught him long ago that with decent people, especially Moscow people—always slow to move and irresolute—every intimacy, which at first so agreeably diversifies life and appears a light and charming adventure, inevitably grows into a regular problem of extreme intricacy, and in the long run the situation becomes unbearable. But at every fresh meeting with an interesting woman this experience seemed to slip out of his memory, and he was eager for life, and everything seemed simple and amusing.

One evening he was dining in the gardens, and the lady in the *béret* came up slowly to take the next table. Her expression, her gait, her dress, and the way she did her hair told him that she was a lady, that she was married, that she was in Yalta for the first time and alone, and that she was dull there. . . . The stories told of the immorality in such places as Yalta are to a great extent untrue; he despised them, and knew that such stories were for the most part made up by persons who would themselves have been glad to sin if they had been able; but when the lady sat down at the next table three paces from him, he remembered these tales of easy conquests, of trips to the mountains, and the tempting thought of a swift, fleeting love affair, a romance with an unknown woman, whose name he did not know, suddenly took possession of him.

He beckoned coaxingly to the Pomeranian, and when the dog came up to him he shook his finger at it. The Pomeranian growled: Gurov shook his finger at it again.

The lady looked at him and at once dropped her eyes.

"He doesn't bite," she said, and blushed.

"May I give him a bone?" he asked; and when she nodded he asked courteously, "Have you been long in Yalta?"

"Five days."

"And I have already dragged out a fortnight here."

There was a brief silence.

"Time goes fast, and yet it is so dull here!" she said, not looking at him.

"That's only the fashion to say it is dull here. A provincial will live in Belyov or Zhidra and not be dull, and when he comes here it's 'Oh, the dullness! Oh, the dust!' One would think he came from Grenada."

She laughed. Then both continued eating in silence, like strangers, but after dinner they walked side by side; and there sprang up between them the light jesting conversation of people who are free and satisfied, to whom it does not matter where they go or what they talk about. They walked and talked of the strange light on the sea: the water was of a soft warm lilac hue, and there was a golden streak from the moon upon it. They talked of how sultry it was after a hot day. Gurov told her that he came from Moscow, that he had taken his degree in Arts, but had a post in a bank; that he had trained as an opera-singer, but had given it up, that he owned two houses in Moscow. . . . And from her he learnt that she had grown up in Petersburg, but had lived in S—— since her marriage two years before, that she was staying another month in Yalta, and that her husband, who needed a holiday too, might perhaps come and fetch her. She was not sure whether her husband had a post in a Crown Department or under the Provincial Council—and was amused by her own ignorance. And Gurov learnt, too, that she was called Anna Sergeyevna.

Afterwards he thought about her in his room at the hotel—thought she would certainly meet him next day; it would be sure to happen. As he got into bed he thought how lately she had been a girl at school, doing lessons like his own daughter; he recalled the diffidence, the angularity, that was still manifest in her laugh and her manner of talking with a stranger. This must have been the first time in her life she had been alone in surroundings in which she was followed, looked at, and spoken to merely from a secret motive which she could hardly fail to guess. He recalled her slender, delicate neck, her lovely grey eyes.

"There's something pathetic about her, anyway," he thought, and fell asleep.

2

A week had passed since they had made acquaintance. It was a holiday. It was sultry indoors, while in the street the wind whirled the dust round and round, and blew people's hats off. It was a thirsty day, and Gurov often went into the pavilion, and pressed Anna Sergeyevna to have syrup and water or an ice. One did not know what to do with oneself.

In the evening when the wind had dropped a little, they went out on the groyne to see the steamer come in. There were a great many people walking about the harbour; they had gathered to welcome some one, bringing bouquets. And two peculiarities of a well-dressed Yalta crowd were very conspicuous: the elderly ladies were dressed like young ones, and there were great numbers of generals.

Owing to the roughness of the sea, the steamer arrived late, after the sun had set, and it was a long time turning about before it reached the groyne. Anna Sergeyevna looked through her lorgnette at the steamer and the passengers as though looking for acquaintances, and when she turned to Gurov her eyes were shining. She talked a great deal and asked disconnected questions, forgetting next moment what she had asked; then she dropped her lorgnette in the crush.

The festive crowd began to disperse; it was too dark to see people's faces. The wind had completely dropped, but Gurov and Anna Sergeyevna still stood as though waiting to see some one else come from the steamer. Anna Sergeyevna was silent now, and sniffed the flowers without looking at Gurov.

"The weather is better this evening," he said. "Where shall we go now? Shall we drive somewhere?"

She made no answer.

Then he looked at her intently, and all at once put his arm round her and kissed her on the lips, and breathed in the moisture and the fragrance of the flowers; and he immediately looked round him, anxiously wondering whether any one had seen them.

"Let us go to your hotel," he said softly. And both walked quickly.

The room was close and smelt of the scent she had bought at the Japanese shop. Gurov looked at her and thought: "What different people one meets in the world!" From the past he preserved memories of careless, good-natured women, who loved cheerfully and were grateful to him for the happiness he gave them, however brief it might be; and of women like his wife who loved without any genuine feeling, with superfluous phrases, affectedly, hysterically, with an expression that suggested that it was not love nor passion, but something more significant; and of two or three others, very beautiful, cold women, on whose faces he had caught a glimpse of a rapacious expression—an obstinate desire to snatch from life more than it could give, and these were capricious, unreflecting, domineering, unintelligent women not in their first youth, and when Gurov grew cold to them their beauty excited his hatred, and the lace on their linen seemed to him like scales.

But in this case there was still the diffidence, the angularity of inexperienced youth, an awkward feeling; and there was a sense of consternation as though some one had suddenly knocked at the door. The attitude of Anna Sergeyevna—"the lady with the dog"—to what had happened was somehow peculiar, very grave, as though it were her fall—so it seemed, and it was strange and inappropriate. Her face dropped and faded, and on both sides of it her long hair hung down mournfully; she mused in a dejected attitude like "the woman who was a sinner" in an old-fashioned picture.

"It's wrong," she said. "You will be the first to despise me now."

There was a water-melon on the table. Gurov cut himself a slice and began eating it without haste. There followed at least half an hour of silence.

Anna Sergeyevna was touching; there was about her the purity of a good, simple woman who had seen little of life. The solitary candle burning on the table threw a faint light on her face, yet it was clear that she was very unhappy.

"How could I despise you?" asked Gurov. "You don't know what you are saying."

"God forgive me," she said, and her eyes filled with tears. "It's awful."

"You seem to feel you need to be forgiven."

"Forgiven? No. I am a bad, low woman; I despise myself and don't attempt to justify myself. It's not my husband but myself I have deceived. And not only just now; I have been deceiving myself for a long time. My husband may be a good, honest man, but he is a flunkey! I don't know what he does there, what his work is, but I know he is a flunkey! I was twenty when I was married to him. I have been tormented by curiosity; I wanted something better. 'There must be a different sort of life,' I said to myself. I wanted to live! To live, to live! . . . I was fired by curiosity . . . you don't understand it, but, I swear to God, I could not control myself; something happened to me: I could not be restrained. I told my husband I was ill, and came here. . . . And here I have been walking about as though I were dazed, like a mad creature; . . . and now I have become a vulgar, contemptible woman whom any one may despise."

Gurov felt bored already, listening to her. He was irritated by the naïve tone, by this remorse, so unexpected and inopportune; but for the tears in her eyes, he might have thought she was jesting or playing a part.

"I don't understand," he said softly. "What is it you want?"

She hid her face on his breast and pressed close to him.

"Believe me, believe me, I beseech you . . ." she said. "I love a pure, honest life, and sin is loathsome to me. I don't know what I am doing. Simple people say: 'The Evil One has beguiled me.' And I may say of myself now that the Evil One has beguiled me."

"Hush, hush! . . ." he muttered.

He looked at her fixed, scared eyes, kissed her, talked softly and affectionately, and by degrees she was comforted, and her gaiety returned; they both began laughing.

Afterwards when they went out there was not a soul on the sea-front. The town with its cypresses had quite a deathlike air, but the sea still broke noisily on the shore; a single barge was rocking on the waves, and a lantern was blinking sleepily on it.

They found a cab and drove to Oreanda.

"I found out your surname in the hall just now: it was written on the board—Von Diderits," said Gurov. "Is your husband a German?"

"No; I believe his grandfather was a German, but he is an Orthodox Russian himself."

At Oreanda they sat on a seat not far from the church, looked down at the sea, and were silent. Yalta was hardly visible through the morning mist; white clouds stood motionless on the mountain-tops. The leaves did not stir on the trees, grasshoppers chirruped, and the monotonous hollow sound of the sea rising up from below, spoke of the peace, of the eternal sleep awaiting us. So it must have sounded when there was no Yalta, no Oreanda here; so it sounds now, and it will sound as indifferently and

monotonously when we are all no more. And in this constancy, in this complete indifference to the life and death of each of us, there lies hid, perhaps, a pledge of our
eternal salvation, of the unceasing movement of life upon earth, of unceasing progress
towards perfection. Sitting beside a young woman who in the dawn seemed so lovely,
soothed and spellbound in these magical surroundings—the sea, mountains, clouds,
the open sky—Gurov thought how in reality everything is beautiful in this world when
one reflects: everything except what we think or do ourselves when we forget our
human dignity and the higher aims of our existence.

A man walked up to them—probably a keeper—looked at them and walked away.
And this detail seemed mysterious and beautiful, too. They saw a steamer come from
Theodosia, with its lights out in the glow of dawn.

"There is dew on the grass," said Anna Sergeyevna, after a silence.

"Yes. It's time to go home."

They went back to the town.

Then they met every day at twelve o'clock on the sea-front, lunched and dined together, went for walks, admired the sea. She complained that she slept badly, that her
heart throbbed violently; asked the same questions, troubled now by jealousy and now
by the fear that he did not respect her sufficiently. And often in the square or gardens,
when there was no one near them, he suddenly drew her to him and kissed her passionately. Complete idleness, these kisses in broad daylight while he looked round in
dread of some one's seeing them, the heat, the smell of the sea, and the continual passing to and fro before him of idle, well-dressed, well-fed people, made a new man of
him; he told Anna Sergeyevna how beautiful she was, how fascinating. He was impatiently passionate, he would not move a step away from her, while she was often pensive and continually urged him to confess that he did not respect her, did not love her
in the least, and thought of her as nothing but a common woman. Rather late almost
every evening they drove somewhere out of town, to Oreanda or to the waterfall; and
the expedition was always a success, the scenery invariably impressed them as grand
and beautiful.

They were expecting her husband to come, but a letter came from him, saying that
there was something wrong with his eyes, and he entreated his wife to come home as
quickly as possible. Anna Sergeyevna made haste to go.

"It's a good thing I am going away," she said to Gurov. "It's the finger of destiny!"

She went by coach and he went with her. They were driving the whole day. When
she had got into a compartment of the express, and when the second bell had rung,
she said:

"Let me look at you once more . . . look at you once again. That's right."

She did not shed tears, but was so sad that she seemed ill, and her face was quivering.

"I shall remember you . . . think of you," she said. "God be with you; be happy.
Don't remember evil against me. We are parting forever—it must be so, for we ought
never to have met. Well, God be with you."

The train moved off rapidly, its lights soon vanished from sight, and a minute later
there was no sound of it, as though everything had conspired together to end as quickly
as possible that sweet delirium, that madness. Left alone on the platform, and gazing
into the dark distance, Gurov listened to the chirrup of the grasshoppers and the hum
of the telegraph wires, feeling as though he had only just waked up. And he thought,
musing, that there had been another episode or adventure in his life, and it, too, was

at an end, and nothing was left of it but a memory. . . . He was moved, sad, and conscious of a slight remorse. This young woman whom he would never meet again had not been happy with him; he was genuinely warm and affectionate with her, but yet in his manner, his tone, and his caresses there had been a shade of light irony, the coarse condescension of a happy man who was, besides, almost twice her age. All the time she had called him kind, exceptional, lofty; obviously he had seemed to her different from what he really was, so he had unintentionally deceived her. . . .

Here at the station was already a scent of autumn; it was a cold evening.

"It's time for me to go north," thought Gurov as he left the platform. "High time!"

3

At home in Moscow everything was in its winter routine; the stoves were heated, and in the morning it was still dark when the children were having breakfast and getting ready for school, and the nurse would light the lamp for a short time. The frost had begun already. When the first snow has fallen, on the first day of sledge-driving it is pleasant to see the white earth, the white roofs, to draw soft, delicious breath, and the season brings back the days of one's youth. The old limes and birches, white with hoarfrost, have a good-natured expression; they are nearer to one's heart than cypresses and palms, and near them one doesn't want to be thinking of the sea and the mountains.

Gurov was Moscow born; he arrived in Moscow on a fine frosty day, and when he put on his fur coat and warm gloves, and walked along Petrovka, and when on Saturday evening he heard the ringing of the bells, his recent trip and the places he had seen lost all charm for him. Little by little he became absorbed in Moscow life, greedily read three newspapers a day, and declared he did not read the Moscow papers on principle! He already felt a longing to go to restaurants, clubs, dinner-parties, anniversary celebrations and he felt flattered at entertaining distinguished lawyers and artists, and at playing cards with a professor at the doctors' club. He could already eat a whole plateful of salt fish and cabbage. . . .

In another month, he fancied, the image of Anna Sergeyevna would be shrouded in a mist in his memory, and only from time to time would visit him in his dreams with a touching smile as others did. But more than a month passed, real winter had come, and everything was still clear in his memory as though he had parted with Anna Sergeyevna only the day before. And his memories glowed more and more vividly. When in the evening stillness he heard from his study the voices of his children, preparing their lessons, or when he listened to a song or the organ at the restaurant, or the storm howled in the chimney, suddenly everything would rise up in his memory: what had happened on the groyne, and the early morning with the mist on the mountains, and the steamer coming from Theodosia and the kisses. He would pace a long time about his room, remembering it all and smiling; then his memories passed into dreams, and in his fancy the past was mingled with what was to come. Anne Sergeyevna did not visit him in dreams, but followed him about everywhere like a shadow and haunted him. When he shut his eyes he saw her as though she were living before him, and she seemed to him lovelier, younger, tenderer than she was; and he imagined himself finer than he had been in Yalta. In the evenings she peeped out at him from the bookcase, from the fireplace, from the corner—he heard her breathing, the caressing rustle of her dress. In the street he watched the women, looking for some one like her.

He was tormented by an intense desire to confide his memories to some one. But in his home it was impossible to talk of his love, and he had no one outside; he could not talk to his tenants nor to any one at the bank. And what had he to talk of? Had he been in love, then? Had there been anything beautiful, poetical, or edifying or simply interesting in his relations with Anna Sergeyevna? And there was nothing for him but to talk vaguely of love, of woman, and no one guessed what it meant; only his wife twitched her black eyebrows, and said: "The part of a lady-killer does not suit you at all, Dimitri."

One evening, coming out of the doctors' club with an official with whom he had been playing cards, he could not resist saying:

"If only you knew what a fascinating woman I made the acquaintance of in Yalta!"

The official got into his sledge and was driving away, but turned suddenly and shouted:

"Dmitri Dmitritch!"

"What?"

"You were right this evening: the sturgeon was a bit too strong!"

These words, so ordinary, for some reason moved Gurov to indignation, and struck him as degrading and unclean. What savage manners, what people! What senseless nights, what uninteresting, uneventful days! The rage for card-playing, the gluttony, the drunkenness, the continual talk always about the same thing. Useless pursuits and conversations always about the same things absorb the better part of one's time, the better part of one's strength, and in the end there is left a life grovelling and curtailed, worthless and trivial, and there is no escaping or getting away from it—just as though one were in a madhouse or a prison.

Gurov did not sleep all night, and was filled with indignation. And he had a headache all next day. And the next night he slept badly; he sat up in bed, thinking, or paced up and down his room. He was sick of his children, sick of the bank; he had no desire to go anywhere or to talk of anything.

In the holidays in December he prepared for a journey, and told his wife he was going to Petersburg to do something in the interests of a young friend—and he set off for S———. What for? He did not very well know himself. He wanted to see Anna Sergeyevna and to talk with her—to arrange a meeting, if possible.

He reached S——— in the morning, and took the best room at the hotel, in which the floor was covered with grey army cloth, and on the table was an inkstand, grey with dust and adorned with a figure on horseback, with its hat in its hand and its head broken off. The hotel porter gave him the necessary information; Von Diderits lived in a house of his own in Old Gontcharny Street—it was not far from the hotel: he was rich and lived in good style, and had his own horses; every one in the town knew him. The porter pronounced the name "Dridirits."

Gurov went without haste to Old Gontcharny Street and found the house. Just opposite the house stretched a long grey fence adorned with nails.

"One would run away from a fence like that," thought Gurov, looking from the fence to the windows of the house and back again.

He considered: to-day was a holiday, and the husband would probably be at home. And in any case it would be tactless to go into the house and upset her. If he were to send her a note it might fall into her husband's hands, and then it might ruin everything. The best thing was to trust to chance. And he kept walking up and down the street by the fence, waiting for the chance. He saw a beggar go in at the gate and dogs fly at him; then an hour later he heard a piano, and the sounds were faint and indistinct. Probably it was Anna Sergeyevna playing. The front door suddenly opened, and an old woman came out, followed by the familiar white Pomeranian. Gurov was on the point of calling to the dog, but his heart began beating violently, and in his excitement he could not remember the dog's name.

He walked up and down, and loathed the grey fence more and more, and by now he thought irritably that Anna Sergeyevna had forgotten him, and was perhaps already amusing herself with some one else, and that that was very natural in a young woman who had nothing to look at from morning till night but that confounded fence. He went back to his hotel room and sat for a long while on the sofa, not knowing what to do, then he had dinner and a long nap.

"How stupid and worrying it is!" he thought when he woke and looked at the dark windows: it was already evening. "Here I've had a good sleep for some reason. What shall I do in the night?"

He sat on the bed, which was covered by a cheap grey blanket, such as one sees in hospitals, and he taunted himself in his vexation:

"So much for the lady with the dog . . . so much for the adventure. . . . You're in a nice fix. . . ."

That morning at the station a poster in large letters had caught his eye. "The Geisha" was to be performed for the first time. He thought of this and went to the theatre.

"It's quite possible she may go to the first performance," he thought.

The theatre was full. As in all provincial theatres, there was a fog above the chandelier, the gallery was noisy and restless; in the front row the local dandies were standing up before the beginning of the performance, with their hands behind them; in the Governor's box the Governor's daughter, wearing a boa, was sitting in the front seat, while the Governor himself lurked modestly behind the curtain with only his hands visible; the orchestra was a long time tuning up; the stage curtain swayed. All the time the audience were coming in and taking their seats Gurov looked at them eagerly.

Anna Sergeyevna, too, came in. She sat down in the third row, and when Gurov looked at her his heart contracted, and he understood clearly that for him there was in the whole world no creature so near, so precious, and so important to him; she, this little woman, in no way remarkable, lost in a provincial crowd, with a vulgar lorgnette in her hand, filled his whole life now, was his sorrow and his joy, the one happiness that he now desired for himself, and to the sounds of the inferior orchestra, of the wretched provincial violins, he thought how lovely she was. He thought and dreamed.

A young man with small side-whiskers, tall and stooping, came in with Anna Sergeyevna, and sat down beside her; he bent his head at every step and seemed to be continually bowing. Most likely this was the husband whom at Yalta, in a rush of bitter feeling, she had called a flunkey. And there really was in his long figure, his side-whiskers, and the small bald patch on his head, something of the flunkey's obsequiousness; his smile was sugary, and in his buttonhole there was some badge of distinction like the number on a waiter.

During the first interval the husband went away to smoke; she remained alone in her stall. Gurov, who was sitting in the stalls, too, went up to her and said in a trembling voice, with a forced smile:

"Good-evening."

She glanced at him and turned pale, then glanced again with horror, unable to believe her eyes, and tightly gripped her fan and the lorgnette in her hands, evidently struggling with herself not to faint. Both were silent. She was sitting, he was standing, frightened by her confusion and not venturing to sit down beside her. The violins and the flute began tuning up. He felt suddenly frightened; it seemed as though all the people in the boxes were looking at them. She got up and went quickly to the door; he followed her, and both walked senselessly along passages, and up and down stairs, and figures in legal, scholastic, and civil service uniforms, all wearing badges, flitted before their eyes. They caught glimpses of ladies, of fur coats hanging on pegs; the draughts blew on them, bringing a smell of stale tobacco. And Gurov, whose heart was beating violently, thought:

"Oh, heavens! Why are these people here and this orchestra! . . ."

And at that instant he recalled how when he had seen Anna Sergeyevna off at the station he had thought that everything was over and they would never meet again. But how far they were still from the end!

On the narrow, gloomy staircase over which was written "To the Amphitheatre," she stopped.

"How you have frightened me!" she said, breathing hard, still pale and overwhelmed. "Oh, how you have frightened me! I am half dead. Why have you come? Why?"

"But do understand, Anna, do understand . . ." he said hastily in a low voice. "I entreat you to understand. . . ."

She looked at him with dread, with entreaty, with love; she looked at him intently, to keep his features more distinctly in her memory.

"I am so unhappy," she went on, not heeding him. "I have thought of nothing but you all the time; I live only in the thought of you. And I wanted to forget, to forget you; but why, oh, why, have you come?"

On the landing above them two schoolboys were smoking and looking down, but that was nothing to Gurov; he drew Anna Sergeyevna to him, and began kissing her face, her cheeks, and her hands.

"What are you doing, what are you doing!" she cried in horror, pushing him away. "We are mad. Go away to-day; go away at once. . . . I beseech you by all that is sacred, I implore you. . . . There are people coming this way!"

Some one was coming up the stairs.

"You must go away," Anna Sergeyevna went on in a whisper. "Do you hear, Dmitri Dmitritch? I will come and see you in Moscow. I have never been happy; I am miserable now, and I never, never shall be happy, never! Don't make me suffer still more! I swear I'll come to Moscow. But now let us part. My precious, good, dear one, we must part!"

She pressed his hand and began rapidly going downstairs, looking round at him, and from her eyes he could see that she really was unhappy. Gurov stood for a little while, listened, then, when all sound had died away, he found his coat and left the theatre.

4

And Anna Sergeyevna began coming to see him in Moscow. Once in two or three months she left S———, telling her husband that she was going to consult a doctor about an internal complaint—and her husband believed her, and did not believe her. In Moscow she stayed at the Slaviansky Bazaar hotel, and at once sent a man in a red cap to Gurov. Gurov went to see her, and no one in Moscow knew of it.

Once he was going to see her in this way on a winter morning (the messenger had come the evening before when he was out). With him walked his daughter, whom he wanted to take to school: it was on the way. Snow was falling in big wet flakes.

"It's three degrees above freezing-point, and yet it is snowing," said Gurov to his daughter. "The thaw is only on the surface of the earth; there is quite a different temperature at a greater height in the atmosphere."

"And why are there no thunderstorms in the winter, father?"

He explained that, too. He talked, thinking all the while that he was going to see *her,* and no living soul knew of it, and probably never would know. He had two lives: one, open, seen and known by all who cared to know, full of relative truth and of relative falsehood, exactly like the lives of his friends and acquaintances; and another life running its course in secret. And through some strange, perhaps accidental, conjunction of circumstances, everything that was essential, of interest and of value to him, everything in which he was sincere and did not deceive himself, everything that made the kernel of his life, was hidden from other people; and all that was false in him, the sheath in which he hid himself to conceal the truth—such, for instance, as his work in the bank, his discussions at the club, his "lower race," his presence with his wife at anniversary festivities—all that was open. And he judged of others by himself, not believing in what he saw, and always believing that every man had his real, most interesting life under the cover of secrecy and under the cover of night. All personal life rested on secrecy, and possibly it was partly on that account that civilised man was so nervously anxious that personal privacy should be respected.

After leaving his daughter at school, Gurov went on to the Slaviansky Bazaar. He took off his fur coat below, went upstairs, and softly knocked at the door. Anna Sergeyevna, wearing his favourite grey dress, exhausted by the journey and the suspense, had been expecting him since the evening before. She was pale; she looked at him, and did not smile, and he had hardly come in when she fell on his breast. Their kiss was slow and prolonged, as though they had not met for two years.

"Well, how are you getting on there?" he asked. "What news?"

"Wait; I'll tell you directly. . . . I can't talk."

She could not speak; she was crying. She turned away from him, and pressed her handkerchief to her eyes.

"Let her have her cry out. I'll sit down and wait," he thought, and he sat down in an arm-chair.

Then he rang and asked for tea to be brought him, and while he drank his tea she remained standing at the window with her back to him. She was crying from emotion, from the miserable consciousness that their life was so hard for them; they could only meet in secret, hiding themselves from people, like thieves! Was not their life shattered?

"Come, do stop!" he said.

It was evident to him that this love of theirs would not soon be over, that he could not see the end of it. Anna Sergeyevna grew more and more attached to him. She adored him, and it was unthinkable to say to her that it was bound to have an end some day; besides, she would not have believed it!

He went up to her and took her by the shoulders to say something affectionate and cheering, and at that moment he saw himself in the looking-glass.

His hair was already beginning to turn grey. And it seemed strange to him that he had grown so much older, so much plainer during the last few years. The shoulders on which his hands rested were warm and quivering. He felt compassion for this life, still so warm and lovely, but probably already not far from beginning to fade and wither like his own. Why did she love him so much? He always seemed to women different from what he was, and they loved in him not himself, but the man created by their imagination, whom they had been eagerly seeking all their lives; and afterwards, when they noticed their mistake, they loved him all the same. And not one of them had been happy with him. Time passed, he had made their acquaintance, got on with them, parted, but he had never once loved; it was anything you like, but not love.

And only now when his head was grey he had fallen properly, really in love—for the first time in his life.

Anna Sergeyevna and he loved each other like people very close and akin, like husband and wife, like tender friends; it seemed to them that fate itself had meant them for one another, and they could not understand why he had a wife and she a husband; and it was as though they were a pair of birds of passage, caught and forced to live in different cages. They forgave each other for what they were ashamed of in their past, they forgave everything in the present, and felt that this love of theirs had changed them both.

In moments of depression in the past he had comforted himself with any arguments that came into his mind, but now he no longer cared for arguments; he felt profound compassion, he wanted to be sincere and tender. . . .

"Don't cry, my darling," he said. "You've had your cry; that's enough. . . . Let us talk now, let us think of some plan."

Then they spent a long while taking counsel together, talked of how to avoid the necessity for secrecy, for deception, for living in different towns and not seeing each other for long at a time. How could they be free from this intolerable bondage?

"How? How?" he asked, clutching his head. "How?"

And it seemed as though in a little while the solution would be found, and then a new and splendid life would begin; and it was clear to both of them that they had still a long, long road before them, and that the most complicated and difficult part of it was only just beginning.

(1899)

CHARLOTTE PERKINS GILMAN
[1860–1935]
The Yellow Wallpaper

It is very seldom that mere ordinary people like John and myself secure ancestral halls for the summer.

A colonial mansion, a hereditary estate, I would say a haunted house and reach the height of romantic felicity—but that would be asking too much of fate!

Still I will proudly declare that there is something queer about it.

Else, why should it be let so cheaply? And why have stood so long untenanted?

John laughs at me, of course, but one expects that.

John is practical in the extreme. He has no patience with faith, an intense horror of superstition, and he scoffs openly at any talk of things not to be felt and seen and put down in figures.

John is a physician, and *perhaps*—(I would not say it to a living soul, of course, but this is dead paper and a great relief to my mind)—*perhaps* that is one reason I do not get well faster.

You see, he does not believe I am sick! And what can one do?

If a physician of high standing, and one's own husband, assures friends and relatives that there is really nothing the matter with one but temporary nervous depression—a slight hysterical tendency—what is one to do?

My brother is also a physician, and also of high standing, and he says the same thing.

So I take phosphates or phosphites—whichever it is—and tonics, and air and exercise, and journeys, and am absolutely forbidden to "work" until I am well again.

Personally, I disagree with their ideas.

Personally, I believe that congenial work, with excitement and change, would do me good.

But what is one to do?

I did write for a while in spite of them; but it *does* exhaust me a good deal—having to be so sly about it, or else meet with heavy opposition.

I sometimes fancy that in my condition, if I had less opposition and more society and stimulus—but John says the very worst thing I can do is to think about my condition, and I confess it always makes me feel bad.

So I will let it alone and talk about the house.

The most beautiful place! It is quite alone, standing well back from the road, quite three miles from the village. It makes me think of English places that you read about, for there are hedges and walls and gates that lock, and lots of separate little houses for the gardeners and people.

There is a *delicious* garden! I never saw such a garden—large and shady, full of box-bordered paths, and lined with long grape-covered arbors with seats under them.

There were greenhouses, but they are all broken now.

There was some legal trouble, I believe, something about the heirs and co-heirs; anyhow, the place has been empty for years.

That spoils my ghostliness, I am afraid, but I don't care—there is something strange about the house—I can feel it.

I even said so to John one moonlight evening, but he said what I felt was a draught, and shut the window.

I get unreasonably angry with John sometimes. I'm sure I never used to be so sensitive. I think it is due to this nervous condition.

But John says if I feel so I shall neglect proper self-control; so I take pains to control myself—before him, at least, and that makes me very tired.

I don't like our room a bit. I wanted one downstairs that opened onto the piazza and had roses all over the window, and such pretty old-fashioned chintz hangings! But John would not hear of it.

He said there was only one window and not room for two beds, and no near room for him if he took another.

He is very careful and loving, and hardly lets me stir without special direction.

I have a schedule prescription for each hour in the day; he takes all care from me, and so I feel basely ungrateful not to value it more.

He said he came here solely on my account, that I was to have perfect rest and all the air I could get. "Your exercise depends on your strength, my dear," said he, "and your food somewhat on your appetite; but air you can absorb all the time." So we took the nursery at the top of the house.

It is a big, airy room, the whole floor nearly, with windows that look all ways, and air and sunshine galore. It was nursery first, and then playroom and gymnasium, I should judge, for the windows are barred for little children, and there are rings and things in the walls.

The paint and paper look as if a boys' school had used it. It is stripped off—the paper—in great patches all around the head of my bed, about as far as I can reach, and in a great place on the other side of the room low down. I never saw a worse paper in my life. One of those sprawling, flamboyant patterns committing every artistic sin.

It is dull enough to confuse the eye in following, pronounced enough constantly to irritate and provoke study, and when you follow the lame uncertain curves for a little distance they suddenly commit suicide—plunge off at outrageous angles, destroy themselves in unheard-of contradictions.

The color is repellent, almost revolting: a smouldering unclean yellow, strangely faded by the slow-turning sunlight. It is a dull yet lurid orange in some places, a sickly sulphur tint in others.

No wonder the children hated it! I should hate it myself if I had to live in this room long.

There comes John, and I must put this away—he hates to have me write a word.

We have been here two weeks, and I haven't felt like writing before, since that first day.

I am sitting by the window now, up in this atrocious nursery, and there is nothing to hinder my writing as much as I please, save lack of strength.

John is away all day, and even some nights when his cases are serious.

I am glad my case is not serious!

But these nervous troubles are dreadfully depressing.

John does not know how much I really suffer. He knows there is no reason to suffer, and that satisfies him.

Of course it is only nervousness. It does weigh on me so not to do my duty in any way!

I meant to be such a help to John, such a real rest and comfort, and here I am a comparative burden already!

Nobody would believe what an effort it is to do what little I am able—to dress and entertain, and order things.

It is fortunate Mary is so good with the baby. Such a dear baby!

And yet I *cannot* be with him, it makes me so nervous.

I suppose John never was nervous in his life. He laughs at me so about this wallpaper!

At first he meant to repaper the room, but afterward he said that I was letting it get the better of me, and that nothing was worse for a nervous patient than to give way to such fancies.

He said that after the wallpaper was changed it would be the heavy bedstead, and then the barred windows, and then that gate at the head of the stairs, and so on.

"You know the place is doing you good," he said, "and really, dear, I don't care to renovate the house just for a three months' rental."

"Then do let us go downstairs," I said. "There are such pretty rooms there."

Then he took me in his arms and called me a blessed little goose, and said he would go down cellar, if I wished, and have it whitewashed into the bargain.

But he is right enough about the beds and windows and things.

It is as as airy and comfortable a room as anyone need wish, and, of course, I would not be so silly as to make him uncomfortable just for a whim.

I'm really getting quite fond of the big room, all but that horrid paper.

Out of one window I can see the garden—those mysterious deep-shaded arbors, the riotous old-fashioned flowers, and bushes and gnarly trees.

Out of another I get a lovely view of the bay and a little private wharf belonging to the estate. There is a beautiful shaded lane that runs down there from the house. I always fancy I see people walking in these numerous paths and arbors, but John has cautioned me not to give way to fancy in the least. He says that with my imaginative power and habit of story-making, a nervous weakness like mine is sure to lead to all manner of excited fancies, and that I ought to use my will and good sense to check the tendency. So I try.

I think sometimes that if I were only well enough to write a little it would relieve the press of ideas and rest me.

But I find I get pretty tired when I try.

It is so discouraging not to have any advice and companionship about my work. When I get really well, John says we will ask Cousin Henry and Julia down for a long visit; but he says he would as soon put fireworks in my pillow-case as to let me have those stimulating people about now.

I wish I could get well faster.

But I must not think about that. This paper looks to me as if it *knew* what a vicious influence it had!

There is a recurrent spot where the pattern lolls like a broken neck and two bulbous eyes stare at you upside down.

I get positively angry with the impertinence of it and the everlastingness. Up and down and sideways they crawl, and those absurd unblinking eyes are everywhere. There is one place where two breadths didn't match, and the eyes go all up and down the line, one a little higher than the other.

I never saw so much expression in an inanimate thing before, and we all know how much expression they have! I used to lie awake as a child and get more entertainment and terror out of blank walls and plain furniture than most children could find in a toy-store.

I remember what a kindly wink the knobs of our big old bureau used to have, and there was one chair that always seemed like a strong friend.

I used to feel that if any of the other things looked too fierce I could always hop into that chair and be safe.

The furniture in this room is no worse than inharmonious, however, for we had to bring it all from downstairs. I suppose when this was used as a playroom they had to take the nursery things out, and no wonder! I never saw such ravages as the children have made here.

The wallpaper, as I said before, is torn off in spots, and it sticketh closer than a brother—they must have had perseverance as well as hatred.

Then the floor is scratched and gouged and splintered, the plaster itself is dug out here and there, and this great heavy bed, which is all we found in the room, looks as if it had been through the wars.

But I don't mind it a bit—only the paper.

There comes John's sister. Such a dear girl as she is, and so careful of me! I must not let her find me writing.

She is a perfect and enthusiastic housekeeper, and hopes for no better profession. I verily believe she thinks it is the writing which made me sick!

But I can write when she is out, and see her a long way off from these windows.

There is one that commands the road, a lovely shaded winding road, and one that just looks off over the country. A lovely country, too, full of great elms and velvet meadows.

This wallpaper has a kind of sub-pattern in a different shade, a particularly irritating one, for you can only see it in certain lights, and not clearly then.

But in the places where it isn't faded and where the sun is just so—I can see a strange, provoking, formless sort of figure that seems to skulk about behind that silly and conspicuous front design.

There's sister on the stairs!

Well, the Fourth of July is over! The people are all gone, and I am tired out. John thought it might do me good to see a little company, so we just had Mother and Nellie and the children down for a week.

Of course I didn't do a thing. Jennie sees to everything now.

But it tired me all the same.

John says if I don't pick up faster he shall send me to Weir Mitchell° in the fall.

But I don't want to go there at all. I had a friend who was in his hands once, and she says he is just like John and my brother, only more so!

Besides, it is such an undertaking to go so far.

I don't feel as if it was worthwhile to turn my hand over for anything, and I'm getting dreadfully fretful and querulous.

I cry at nothing, and cry most of the time.

Of course I don't when John is here, or anybody else, but when I am alone.

And I am alone a good deal just now. John is kept in town very often by serious cases, and Jennie is good and lets me alone when I want her to.

So I walk a little in the garden or down that lovely lane, sit on the porch under the roses, and lie down up here a good deal.

I'm getting really fond of the room in spite of the wallpaper. Perhaps *because* of the wallpaper.

It dwells in my mind so!

I lie here on this great immovable bed—it is nailed down, I believe—and follow that pattern about by the hour. It is as good as gymnastics, I assure you. I start, we'll say, at the bottom, down in the corner over there where it has not been touched, and I determine for the thousandth time that I *will* follow that pointless pattern to some sort of a conclusion.

Weir Mitchell   Silas Weir Mitchell (1829–1914), neurologist who introduced the "rest cure" for psychoneurotics.

I know a little of the principle of design, and I know this thing was not arranged on any laws of radiation, or alternation, or repetition, or symmetry, or anything else that I ever heard of.

It is repeated, of course, by the breadths, but not otherwise.

Looked at in one way, each breadth stands alone; the bloated curves and flourishes—a kind of "debased Romanesque" with delirium tremens go waddling up and down in isolated columns of fatuity.

But, on the other hand, they connect diagonally, and the sprawling outlines run off in great slanting waves of optic horror, like a lot of wallowing sea-weeds in full chase.

The whole thing goes horizontally, too, at least it seems so, and I exhaust myself trying to distinguish the order of its going in that direction.

They have used a horizontal breadth for a frieze, and that adds wonderfully to the confusion.

There is one end of the room where it is almost intact, and there, when the crosslights fade and the low sun shines directly upon it, I can almost fancy radiation after all—the interminable grotesque seems to form around a common center and rush off in head-long plunges of equal distraction.

It makes me tired to follow it. I will take a nap, I guess.

I don't know why I should write this.

I don't want to.

I don't feel able.

And I know John would think it absurd. But I *must* say what I feel and think in some way—it is such a relief!

But the effort is getting to be greater than the relief.

Half the time now I am awfully lazy, and lie down ever so much. John says I mustn't lose my strength, and has me take cod liver oil and lots of tonics and things, to say nothing of ale and wine and rare meat.

Dear John! He loves me very dearly, and hates to have me sick. I tried to have a real earnest reasonable talk with him the other day, and tell him how I wish he would let me go and make a visit to Cousin Henry and Julia.

But he said I wasn't able to go, nor able to stand it after I got there; and I did not make out a very good case for myself, for I was crying before I had finished.

It is getting to be a great effort for me to think straight. Just this nervous weakness, I suppose.

And dear John gathered me up in his arms, and just carried me upstairs and laid me on the bed, and sat by me and read to me till it tired my head.

He said I was his darling and his comfort and all he had, and that I must take care of myself for his sake, and keep well.

He says no one but myself can help me out of it, that I must use my will and self-control and not let any silly fancies run away with me.

There's one comfort—the baby is well and happy, and does not have to occupy this nursery with the horrid wallpaper.

If we had not used it, that blessed child would have! What a fortunate escape! Why, I wouldn't have a child of mine, an impressionable little thing, live in such a room for worlds.

I never thought of it before, but it is lucky that John kept me here after all; I can stand it so much easier than a baby, you see.

Of course I never mention it to them any more—I am too wise—but I keep watch for it all the same.

There are things in that wallpaper that nobody knows about but me, or ever will.

Behind that outside pattern the dim shapes get clearer every day.

It is always the same shape, only very numerous.

And it is like a woman stooping down and creeping about behind that pattern. I don't like it a bit. I wonder—I begin to think—I wish John would take me away from here!

It is so hard to talk with John about my case, because he is so wise, and because he loves me so.

But I tried it last night.

It was moonlight. The moon shines in all around just as the sun does.

I hate to see it sometimes, it creeps so slowly, and always comes in by one window or another.

John was asleep and I hated to waken him, so I kept still and watched the moonlight on that undulating wallpaper till I felt creepy.

The faint figure behind seemed to shake the pattern, just as if she wanted to get out.

I got up softly and went to feel and see if the paper *did* move, and when I came back John was awake.

"What is it, little girl?" he said. "Don't go walking about like that—you'll get cold."

I thought it was a good time to talk, so I told him that I really was not gaining here, and that I wished he would take me away.

"Why, darling!" said he. "Our lease will be up in three weeks, and I can't see how to leave before.

"The repairs are not done at home, and I cannot possibly leave town just now. Of course, if you were in any danger, I could and would, but you really are better, dear, whether you can see it or not. I am a doctor, dear, and I know. You are gaining flesh and color, your appetite is better, I feel really much easier about you."

"I don't weigh a bit more," said I, "nor as much; and my appetite may be better in the evening when you are here but it is worse in the morning when you are away!"

"Bless her little heart!" said he with a big hug. "She shall be as sick as she pleases! But now let's improve the shining hours by going to sleep, and talk about it in the morning!"

"And you won't go away?" I asked gloomily.

"Why, how can I, dear? It is only three weeks more and then we will take a nice little trip of a few days while Jennie is getting the house ready. Really, dear, you are better!"

"Better in body perhaps—" I began, and stopped short, for he sat up straight and looked at me with such a stern, reproachful look that I could not say another word.

"My darling," said he, "I beg of you, for my sake and for our child's sake, as well as for your own, that you will never for one instant let that idea enter your mind! There is nothing so dangerous, so fascinating, to a temperament like yours. It is a false and foolish fancy. Can you not trust me as a physician when I tell you so?"

So of course I said no more on that score, and we went to sleep before long. He thought I was asleep first, but I wasn't, and lay there for hours trying to decide whether that front pattern and the back pattern really did move together or separately.

On a pattern like this, by daylight, there is a lack of sequence, a defiance of law, that is a constant irritant to a normal mind.

The color is hideous enough, and unreliable enough, and infuriating enough, but the pattern is torturing.

You think you have mastered it, but just as you get well under way in following, it turns a back-somersault and there you are. It slaps you in the face, knocks you down, and tramples upon you. It is like a bad dream.

The outside pattern is a florid arabesque, reminding one of a fungus. If you can imagine a toadstool in joints, an interminable string of toadstools, budding and sprouting in endless convolutions—why, that is something like it.

That is, sometimes!

There is one marked peculiarity about this paper, a thing nobody seems to notice but myself, and that is that it changes as the light changes.

When the sun shoots in through the east window—I always watch for that first long, straight ray—it changes so quickly that I never can quite believe it.

That is why I watch it always.

By moonlight—the moon shines in all night when there is a moon—I wouldn't know it was the same paper.

At night in any kind of light, in twilight, candlelight, lamplight, and worst of all by moonlight, it becomes bars! The outside pattern, I mean, and the woman behind it is as plain as can be.

I didn't realize for a long time what the thing was that showed behind, that dim sub-pattern, but now I am quite sure it is a woman.

By daylight she is subdued, quiet. I fancy it is the pattern that keeps her so still. It is so puzzling. It keeps me quiet by the hour.

I lie down ever so much now. John says it is good for me, and to sleep all I can.

Indeed he started the habit by making me lie down for an hour after each meal.

It is a very bad habit, I am convinced, for you see, I don't sleep.

And that cultivates deceit, for I don't tell them I'm awake—oh, no!

The fact is I am getting a little afraid of John.

He seems very queer sometimes, and even Jennie has an inexplicable look.

It strikes me occasionally, just as a scientific hypothesis, that perhaps it is the paper!

I have watched John when he did not know I was looking, and come into the room suddenly on the most innocent excuses, and I've caught him several times *looking at the paper!* And Jennie too. I caught Jennie with her hand on it once.

She didn't know I was in the room, and when I asked her in a quiet, a very quiet voice, with the most restrained manner possible, what she was doing with the paper, she turned around as if she had been caught stealing, and looked quite angry—asked me why I should frighten her so!

Then she said that the paper stained everything it touched, that she had found yellow smooches on all my clothes and John's and she wished we would be more careful!

Did not that sound innocent? But I know she was studying that pattern, and I am determined that nobody shall find it out but myself!

Life is very much more exciting now than it used to be. You see, I have something more to expect, to look forward to, to watch. I really do eat better, and am more quiet than I was.

John is so pleased to see me improve! He laughed a little the other day, and said I seemed to be flourishing in spite of my wallpaper.

I turned it off with a laugh. I had no intention of telling him it was *because* of the wallpaper—he would make fun of me. He might even want to take me away.

I don't want to leave now until I have found it out. There is a week more, and I think that will be enough.

I'm feeling so much better!

I don't sleep much at night, for it is so interesting to watch developments; but I sleep a good deal during the daytime.

In the daytime it is tiresome and perplexing.

There are always new shoots on the fungus, and new shades of yellow all over it. I cannot keep count of them, though I have tried conscientiously.

It is the strangest yellow, that wallpaper! It makes me think of all the yellow things I ever saw—not beautiful ones like buttercups, but old, foul, bad yellow things.

But there is something else about that paper—the smell! I noticed it the moment we came into the room, but with so much air and sun it was not bad. Now we have had a week of fog and rain, and whether the windows are open or not, the smell is here.

It creeps all over the house.

I find it hovering in the dining-room, skulking in the parlor, hiding in the hall, lying in wait for me on the stairs.

It gets into my hair.

Even when I go to ride, if I turn my head suddenly and surprise it—there is that smell!

Such a peculiar odor, too! I have spent hours in trying to analyze it, to find what it smelled like.

It is not bad—at first—and very gentle, but quite the subtlest, most enduring odor I ever met.

In this damp weather it is awful. I wake up in the night and find it hanging over me.

It used to disturb me at first. I thought seriously of burning the house—to reach the smell.

But now I am used to it. The only thing I can think of that it is like is the *color* of the paper! A yellow smell.

There is a very funny mark on this wall, low down, near the mopboard. A streak that runs round the room. It goes behind every piece of furniture, except the bed, a long, straight, even *smooch,* as if it had been rubbed over and over.

I wonder how it was done and who did it, and what they did it for. Round and round and round—round and round and round—it makes me dizzy!

I really have discovered something at last.

Through watching so much at night, when it changes so, I have finally found out. The front pattern *does* move—and no wonder! The woman behind shakes it!

Sometimes I think there are a great many women behind, and sometimes only one, and she crawls around fast, and her crawling shakes it all over.

Then in the very bright spots she keeps still, and in the very shady spots she just takes hold of the bars and shakes them hard.

And she is all the time trying to climb through. But nobody could climb through that pattern—it strangles so; I think that is why it has so many heads.

They get through and then the pattern strangles them off and turns them upside down, and makes their eyes white!

If those heads were covered or taken off it would not be half so bad.

I think that woman gets out in the daytime!

And I'll tell you why—privately—I've seen her!

I can see her out of every one of my windows!

It is the same woman, I know, for she is always creeping, and most women do not creep by daylight.

✳ I see her in that long shaded lane, creeping up and down. I see her in those dark grape arbors, creeping all around the garden.

✳ I see her on that long road under the trees, creeping along, and when a carriage comes she hides under the blackberry vines.

I don't blame her a bit. It must be very humiliating to be caught creeping by daylight!

I always lock the door when I creep by daylight. I can't do it at night, for I know John would suspect something at once.

And John is so queer now that I don't want to irritate him. I wish he would take another room! Besides, I don't want anybody to get that woman out at night but myself.

I often wonder if I could see her out of all the windows at once.

But, turn as fast as I can, I can only see out of one at one time.

And though I always see her, she *may* be able to creep faster than I can turn! I have watched her sometimes away off in the open country, creeping as fast as a cloud shadow in a wind.

If only that top pattern could be gotten off from the under one! I mean to try it, little by little.

I have found out another funny thing, but I shan't tell it this time! It does not do to trust people too much.

There are only two more days to get this paper off, and I believe John is beginning to notice. I don't like the look in his eyes.

And I heard him ask Jennie a lot of professional questions about me. She had a very good report to give.

She said I slept a good deal in the daytime.

John knows I don't sleep very well at night, for all I'm so quiet!

He asked me all sorts of questions, too, and pretended to be very loving and kind.

As if I couldn't see through him!

Still, I don't wonder he acts so, sleeping under this paper for three months.

It only interests me, but I feel sure John and Jennie are affected by it.

Hurrah! This is the last day, but it is enough. John is to stay in town over night, and won't be out until this evening.

Jennie wanted to sleep with me—the sly thing; but I told her I should undoubtedly rest better for a night all alone.

That was clever, for really I wasn't alone a bit! As soon as it was moonlight and that poor thing began to crawl and shake the pattern, I got up and ran to help her.

I pulled and she shook. I shook and she pulled, and before morning we had peeled off yards of that paper.

A strip about as high as my head and half around the room.

And then when the sun came and that awful pattern began to laugh at me, I declared I would finish it today!

We go away tomorrow, and they are moving all my furniture down again to leave things as they were before.

Jennie looked at the wall in amazement, but I told her merrily that I did it out of pure spite at the vicious thing.

She laughed and said she wouldn't mind doing it herself, but I must not get tired. How she betrayed herself that time!

But I am here, and no person touches this paper but Me—not *alive!*

She tried to get me out of the room—it was too patent! But I said it was so quiet and empty and clean now that I believed I would lie down again and sleep all I could, and not to wake me even for dinner—I would call when I woke.

So now she is gone, and the servants are gone, and the things are gone, and there is nothing left but that great bedstead nailed down, with the canvas mattress we found on it.

We shall sleep downstairs tonight, and take the boat home tomorrow.

I quite enjoy the room, now it is bare again.

How those children did tear about here!

This bedstead is fairly gnawed!

But I must get to work.

I have locked the door and thrown the key down into the front path.

I don't want to go out, and I don't want to have anybody come in, till John comes. I want to astonish him.

I've got a rope up here that even Jennie did not find. If that woman does get out, and tries to get away, I can tie her!

But I forgot I could not reach far without anything to stand on!

This bed will *not* move!

I tried to lift and push it until I was lame, and then I got so angry I bit off a little piece at one corner—but it hurt my teeth.

Then I peeled off all the paper I could reach standing on the floor. It sticks horribly and the pattern just enjoys it! All those strangled heads and bulbous eyes and waddling fungus growths just shriek with derision!

I am getting angry enough to do something desperate. To jump out of the window would be admirable exercise, but the bars are too strong even to try.

Besides I wouldn't do it. Of course not. I know well enough that a step like that is improper and might be misconstrued.

I don't like to *look* out of the windows even—there are so many of those creeping women, and they creep so fast.

I wonder if they all come out of that wallpaper as I did?

But I am securely fastened now by my well-hidden rope—you don't get *me* out in the road there!

I suppose I shall have to get back behind the pattern when it comes night, and that is hard!

It is so pleasant to be out in this great room and creep around as I please!

I don't want to go outside. I won't, even if Jennie asks me to.

For outside you have to creep on the ground, and everything is green instead of yellow.

But here I can creep smoothly on the floor, and my shoulder just fits in that long smooch around the wall, so I cannot lose my way.

Why, there's John at the door!

It is no use, young man, you can't open it!

How he does call and pound!

Now he's crying to Jennie for an axe.

It would be a shame to break down that beautiful door!

"John, dear!" said I in the gentlest voice. "The key is down by the front steps, under a plantain leaf!"

That silenced him for a few moments.

Then he said, very quietly indeed, "Open the door, my darling!"

"I can't," said I. "The key is down by the front door under a plantain leaf!" And then I said it again, several times, very gently and slowly, and said it so often that he had to go and see, and he got it of course, and came in. He stopped short by the door.

"What is the matter?" he cried. "For God's sake, what are you doing!"

I kept on creeping just the same, but I looked at him over my shoulder.

"I've got out at last," said I, "in spite of you and Jane. And I've pulled off most of the paper, so you can't put me back!"

Now why should that man have fainted? But he did, and right across my path by the wall, so that I had to creep over him every time!

(1892)

STEPHEN CRANE

[1871–1900]

The Open Boat

A TALE INTENDED TO BE AFTER THE FACT. BEING THE EXPERIENCE OF FOUR MEN FROM THE SUNK STEAMER "COMMODORE"

1

None of them knew the color of the sky. Their eyes glanced level, and were fastened upon the waves that swept toward them. These waves were of the hue of slate, save for the tops, which were of foaming white, and all of the men knew the colors of the sea. The horizon narrowed and widened, and dipped and rose, and at all times its edge was jagged with waves that seemed thrust up in points like rocks.

Many a man ought to have a bath-tub larger than the boat which here rode upon the sea. These waves were most wrongfully and barbarously abrupt and tall, and each froth-top was a problem in small boat navigation.

The cook squatted in the bottom and looked with both eyes at the six inches of gunwale which separated him from the ocean. His sleeves were rolled over his fat forearms, and the two flaps of his unbuttoned vest dangled as he bent to bail out the boat. Often he said: "Gawd! That was a narrow clip." As he remarked it he invariably gazed eastward over the broken sea.

The oiler, steering with one of the two oars in the boat, sometimes raised himself suddenly to keep clear of water that swirled in over the stern. It was a thin little oar and it seemed often ready to snap.

The correspondent, pulling at the other oar, watched the waves and wondered why he was there.

The injured captain, lying in the bow, was at this time buried in that profound dejection and indifference which comes, temporarily at least, to even the bravest and most enduring when, willy nilly, the firm fails, the army loses, the ship goes down. The mind of the master of a vessel is rooted deep in the timbers of her, though he command for a day or a decade, and this captain had on him the stern impression of a scene in the grays of dawn of seven turned faces, and later a stump of a top-mast with a white ball on it that slashed to and fro at the waves, went low and lower, and down. Thereafter there was something strange in his voice. Although steady, it was deep with mourning, and of a quality beyond oration or tears.

"Keep 'er a little more south, Billie," said he.

"'A little more south,' sir," said the oiler in the stern.

A seat in this boat was not unlike a seat upon a bucking broncho, and, by the same token, a broncho is not much smaller. The craft pranced and reared, and plunged like an animal. As each wave came, and she rose for it, she seemed like a horse making at a fence outrageously high. The manner of her scramble over these walls of water is a mystic thing, and, moreover, at the top of them were ordinarily these problems in white water, the foam racing down from the summit of each wave, requiring a new leap, and a leap from the air. Then, after scornfully bumping a crest, she would slide, and race, and splash down a long incline, and arrive bobbing and nodding in front of the next menace.

A singular disadvantage of the sea lies in the fact that after successfully surmounting one wave you discover that there is another behind it just as important and just as nervously anxious to do something effective in the way of swamping boats. In a ten-foot dingey one can get an idea of the resources of the sea in the line of waves that is not probable to the average experience which is never at sea in a dingey. As each slaty wall of water approached, it shut all else from the view of the men in the boat, and it was not difficult to imagine that this particular wave was the final outburst of the ocean, the last effort of the grim water. There was a terrible grace in the move of the waves, and they came in silence, save for the snarling of the crests.

In the wan light, the faces of the men must have been gray. Their eyes must have glinted in strange ways as they gazed steadily astern. Viewed from a balcony, the whole thing would doubtless have been weirdly picturesque. But the men in the boat had no time to see it, and if they had had leisure there were other things to occupy their minds. The sun swung steadily up the sky, and they knew it was broad day because the color of the sea changed from slate to emerald-green, streaked with amber lights, and the foam was like tumbling snow. The process of the breaking day was unknown to them. They were aware only of this effect upon the color of the waves that rolled toward them.

In disjointed sentences the cook and the correspondent argued as to the difference between a life-saving station and a house of refuge. The cook had said: "There's a house of refuge just north of the Mosquito Inlet Light, and as soon as they see us, they'll come off in their boat and pick us up."

"As soon as who see us?" said the correspondent.

"The crew," said the cook.

"Houses of refuge don't have crews," said the correspondent. "As I understand them, they are only places where clothes and grub are stored for the benefit of shipwrecked people. They don't carry crews."

"Oh, yes, they do," said the cook.

"No, they don't," said the correspondent.

"Well, we're not there yet, anyhow," said the oiler, in the stern.

"Well," said the cook, "perhaps it's not a house of refuge that I'm thinking of as being near Mosquito Inlet Light. Perhaps it's a life-saving station."

"We're not there yet," said the oiler, in the stern.

2

As the boat bounced from the top of each wave, the wind tore through the hair of the hatless men, and as the craft plopped her stern down again the spray slashed past them. The crest of each of these waves was a hill, from the top of which the men surveyed, for a moment, a broad tumultuous expanse, shining and wind-riven. It was probably splendid. It was probably glorious, this play of the free sea, wild with lights of emerald and white and amber.

"Bully good thing it's an on-shore wind," said the cook. "If not, where would we be? Wouldn't have a show."

"That's right," said the correspondent.

The busy oiler nodded his assent.

Then the captain, in the bow, chuckled in a way that expressed humor, contempt, tragedy, all in one. "Do you think we've got much of a show now, boys?" said he.

Whereupon the three were silent, save for a trifle of hemming and hawing. To express any particular optimism at this time they felt to be childish and stupid, but they all doubtless possessed this sense of the situation in their mind. A young man thinks doggedly at such times. On the other hand, the ethics of their condition was decidedly against any open suggestion of hopelessness. So they were silent.

"Oh, well," said the captain, soothing his children, "we'll get ashore all right."

But there was that in his tone which made them think, so the oiler quoth: "Yes! If this wind holds!"

The cook was bailing: "Yes! If we don't catch hell in the surf."

Canton flannel gulls flew near and far. Sometimes they sat down on the sea, near patches of brown seaweed that rolled over the waves with a movement like carpets on a line in a gale. The birds sat comfortably in groups, and they were envied by some in the dingey, for the wrath of the sea was no more to them than it was to a covey of prairie chickens a thousand miles inland. Often they came very close and stared at the men with black bead-like eyes. At these times they were uncanny and sinister in their unblinking scrutiny, and the men hooted angrily at them, telling them to be gone. One came, and evidently decided to alight on the top of the captain's head. The bird flew parallel to the boat and did not circle, but made short sidelong jumps in the air in chicken-fashion. His black eyes were wistfully fixed upon the captain's head. "Ugly brute," said the oiler to the bird. "You look as if you were made with a jack-knife." The cook and the correspondent swore darkly at the creature. The captain naturally wished to knock it away with the end of the heavy painter; but he did not dare do it, because anything resembling an emphatic gesture would have capsized this freighted boat, and so with his open hand, the captain gently and carefully waved the gull away. After it had been discouraged from the pursuit the captain breathed easier on account of his hair, and others breathed easier because the bird struck their minds at this time as being somehow gruesome and ominous.

In the meantime the oiler and the correspondent rowed. And also they rowed.

They sat together in the same seat, and each rowed an oar. Then the oiler took both oars; then the correspondent took both oars; then the oiler; then the correspondent. They rowed and they rowed. The very ticklish part of the business was when the time came for the reclining one in the stern to take his turn at the oars. By the very last star of truth, it is easier to steal eggs from under a hen than it was to change seats in the dingey. First the man in the stern slid his hand along the thwart and moved with care, as if he were of Sèvres. Then the man in the rowing seat slid his hand along the other thwart. It was all done with the most extraordinary care. As the two sidled past each other, the whole party kept watchful eyes on the coming wave, and the captain cried: "Look out now! Steady there!"

The brown mats of seaweed that appeared from time to time were like islands, bits of earth. They were travelling, apparently, neither one way nor the other. They were, to all intents, stationary. They informed the men in the boat that it was making progress slowly toward the land.

The captain, rearing cautiously in the bow, after the dingey soared on a great swell, said that he had seen the lighthouse at Mosquito Inlet. Presently the cook remarked that he had seen it. The correspondent was at the oars then, and for some reason he too wished to look at the lighthouse, but his back was toward the far shore and the waves were important, and for some time he could not seize an opportunity to turn his head. But at last there came a wave more gentle than the others, and when at the crest of it he swiftly scoured the western horizon.

"See it?" said the captain.

"No," said the correspondent slowly. "I didn't see anything."

"Look again," said the captain. He pointed. "It's exactly in that direction."

At the top of another wave, the correspondent did as he was bid, and this time his eyes chanced on a small still thing on the edge of the swaying horizon. It was precisely like the point of a pin. It took an anxious eye to find a lighthouse so tiny.

"Think we'll make it, captain?"

"If this wind holds and the boat don't swamp, we can't do much else," said the captain.

The little boat, lifted by each towering sea, and splashed viciously by the crests, made progress that in the absence of seaweed was not apparent to those in her. She seemed just a wee thing wallowing, miraculously top up, at the mercy of five oceans. Occasionally, a great spread of water, like white flames, swarmed into her.

"Bail her, cook," said the captain serenely.

"All right, captain," said the cheerful cook.

3

It would be difficult to describe the subtle brotherhood of men that was here established on the seas. No one said that it was so. No one mentioned it. But it dwelt in the boat, and each man felt it warm him. They were a captain, an oiler, a cook, and a correspondent, and they were friends, friends in a more curiously iron-bound degree than may be common. The hurt captain, lying against the water-jar in the bow, spoke always in a low voice and calmly, but he could never command a more ready and swiftly obedient crew than the motley three of the dingey. It was more than a mere recognition of what was best for the common safety. There was surely in it a quality that was personal and heartfelt. And after this devotion to the commander of the boat there was this comradeship that the correspondent, for instance, who had been taught to be cynical of men, knew even at the time was the best experience of his life. But no one said that it was so. No one mentioned it.

"I wish we had a sail," remarked the captain. "We might try my overcoat on the end of an oar and give you two boys a chance to rest." So the cook and the correspondent held the mast and spread wide the overcoat. The oiler steered, and the little boat made good way with her new rig. Sometimes the oiler had to scull sharply to keep a sea from breaking into the boat, but otherwise sailing was a success.

Meanwhile the lighthouse had been growing slowly larger. It had now almost assumed color, and appeared like a little gray shadow on the sky. The man at the oars could not be prevented from turning his head rather often to try for a glimpse of this little gray shadow.

At last, from the top of each wave the men in the tossing boat could see land. Even as the lighthouse was an upright shadow on the sky, this land seemed but a long black shadow on the sea. It certainly was thinner than paper. "We must be about opposite New Smyrna," said the cook, who had coasted this shore often in schooners. "Captain, by the way, I believe they abandoned that life-saving station there about a year ago."

"Did they?" said the captain.

The wind slowly died away. The cook and the correspondent were not now obliged to slave in order to hold high the oar. But the waves continued their old impetuous swooping at the dingey, and the little craft, no longer under way, struggled woundily over them. The oiler or the correspondent took the oars again.

Shipwrecks are apropos of nothing. If men could only train for them and have them occur when the men had reached pink condition, there would be less drowning at sea. Of the four in the dingey none had slept any time worth mentioning for two days and two nights previous to embarking in the dingey, and in the excitement of clambering about the deck of a foundering ship they had also forgotten to eat heartily.

For these reasons, and for others, neither the oiler nor the correspondent was fond of rowing at this time. The correspondent wondered ingenuously how in the name of all that was sane could there be people who thought it amusing to row a boat. It was not an amusement; it was a diabolical punishment, and even a genius of mental aberrations could never conclude that it was anything but a horror to the muscles and a crime against the back. He mentioned to the boat in general how the amusement of rowing struck him, and the weary-faced oiler smiled in full sympathy. Previously to the foundering, by the way, the oiler had worked double-watch in the engine-room of the ship.

"Take her easy, now, boys," said the captain. "Don't spend yourselves. If we have to run a surf you'll need all your strength, because we'll sure have to swim for it. Take your time."

Slowly the land arose from the sea. From a black line it became a line of black and a line of white, trees and sand. Finally, the captain said that he could make out a house on the shore. "That's the house of refuge, sure," said the cook. "They'll see us before long, and come out after us."

The distant lighthouse reared high. "The keeper ought to be able to make us out now, if he's looking through a glass," said the captain. "He'll notify the life-saving people."

"None of those other boats could have got ashore to give word of the wreck," said the oiler, in a low voice. "Else the life-boat would be out hunting us."

Slowly and beautifully the land loomed out of the sea. The wind came again. It had veered from the north-east to the south-east. Finally, a new sound struck the ears of the men in the boat. It was the low thunder of the surf on the shore. "We'll never be able to make the lighthouse now," said the captain. "Swing her head a little more north, Billie."

"'A little more north,' sir," said the oiler.

Whereupon the little boat turned her nose once more down the wind, and all but the oarsman watched the shore grow. Under the influence of this expansion doubt and direful apprehension was leaving the minds of the men. The management of the boat was still most absorbing, but it could not prevent a quiet cheerfulness. In an hour, perhaps, they would be ashore.

Their backbones had become thoroughly used to balancing in the boat, and they now rode this wild colt of a dingey like circus men. The correspondent thought that he had been drenched to the skin, but happening to feel in the top pocket of his coat, he found therein eight cigars. Four of them were soaked with sea-water; four were perfectly scatheless. After a search, somebody produced three dry matches, and thereupon the four waifs rode in their little boat, and with an assurance of an impending rescue shining in their eyes, puffed at the big cigars and judged well and ill of all men. Everybody took a drink of water.

4

"Cook," remarked the captain, "there don't seem to be any signs of life about your house of refuge."

"No," replied the cook. "Funny they don't see us!"

A broad stretch of lowly coast lay before the eyes of the men. It was of low dunes topped with dark vegetation. The roar of the surf was plain, and sometimes they could see the white lip of a wave as it spun up the beach. A tiny house was blocked out black upon the sky. Southward, the slim lighthouse lifted its little gray length.

Tide, wind, and waves were swinging the dingey northward. "Funny they don't see us," said the men.

The surf's roar was here dulled, but its tone was, nevertheless, thunderous and mighty. As the boat swam over the great rollers, the men sat listening to this roar. "We'll swamp sure," said everybody.

It is fair to say here that there was not a life-saving station within twenty miles in either direction, but the men did not know this fact, and in consequence they made dark and opprobrious remarks concerning the eyesight of the nation's life-savers. Four scowling men sat in the dingey and surpassed records in the invention of epithets.

"Funny they don't see us."

The light-heartedness of a former time had completely faded. To their sharpened minds it was easy to conjure pictures of all kinds of incompetency and blindness and, indeed, cowardice. There was the shore of the populous land, and it was bitter and bitter to them that from it came no sign.

"Well," said the captain, ultimately, "I suppose we'll have to make a try for ourselves. If we stay out here too long, we'll none of us have strength left to swim after the boat swamps."

And so the oiler, who was at the oars, turned the boat straight for the shore. There was a sudden tightening of muscles. There was some thinking.

"If we don't all get ashore—" said the captain. "If we don't all get ashore, I suppose you fellows know where to send news of my finish?"

They then briefly exchanged some addresses and admonitions. As for the reflections of the men, there was a great deal of rage in them. Perchance they might be formulated thus: "If I am going to be drowned—if I am going to be drowned—if I am going to be drowned, why, in the name of the seven mad gods who rule the sea, was I allowed to come thus far and contemplate sand and trees? Was I brought here merely to have my nose dragged away as I was about to nibble the sacred cheese of life? It is preposterous. If this old ninny-woman, Fate, cannot do better than this, she should be deprived of the management of men's fortunes. She is an old hen who knows not her intention. If she has decided to drown me, why did she not do it in the beginning and save me all this trouble? The whole affair is absurd. . . . But no, she cannot mean to drown me. She dare not drown me. She cannot drown me. Not after all this work." Afterward the man might have had an impulse to shake his fist at the clouds: "Just you drown me, now, and then hear what I call you!"

The billows that came at this time were more formidable. They seemed always just about to break and roll over the little boat in a turmoil of foam. There was a preparatory and long growl in the speech of them. No mind unused to the sea would have concluded that the dingey could ascend these sheer heights in time. The shore was still afar. The oiler was a wily surfman. "Boys," he said swiftly, "she won't live three minutes more, and we're too far out to swim. Shall I take her to sea again, captain?"

"Yes! Go ahead!" said the captain.

This oiler, by a series of quick miracles, and fast and steady oarsmanship, turned the boat in the middle of the surf and took her safely to sea again.

There was a considerable silence as the boat bumped over the furrowed sea to deeper water. Then somebody in gloom spoke. "Well, anyhow, they must have seen us from the shore by now."

The gulls went in slanting flight up the wind toward the gray desolate east. A squall, marked by dingy clouds, and clouds brick-red, like smoke from a burning building, appeared from the south-east.

"What do you think of those life-saving people? Ain't they peaches?"

"Funny they haven't seen us."

"Maybe they think we're out here for sport! Maybe they think we're fishin'. Maybe they think we're damned fools."

It was a long afternoon. A changed tide tried to force them southward, but wind and wave said northward. Far ahead, where coastline, sea, and sky formed their mighty angle, there were little dots which seemed to indicate a city on the shore.

"St. Augustine?"

The captain shook his head. "Too near Mosquito Inlet."

And the oiler rowed, and then the correspondent rowed. Then the oiler rowed. It was a weary business. The human back can become the seat of more aches and pains than are registered in books for the composite anatomy of a regiment. It is a limited area, but it can become the theater of innumerable muscular conflicts, tangles, wrenches, knots, and other comforts.

"Did you ever like to row, Billie?" asked the correspondent.

"No," said the oiler. "Hang it!"

When one exchanged the rowing-seat for a place in the bottom of the boat, he suffered a bodily depression that caused him to be careless of everything save an obligation to wiggle one finger. There was cold sea-water swashing to and fro in the boat, and he lay in it. His head, pillowed on a thwart, was within an inch of the swirl of a wave crest, and sometimes a particularly obstreperous sea came inboard and drenched him once more. But these matters did not annoy him. It is almost certain that if the boat had capsized he would have tumbled comfortably out upon the ocean as if he felt sure that it was a great soft mattress.

"Look! There's a man on the shore!"

"Where?"

"There! See 'im? See 'im?"

"Yes, sure! He's walking along."

"Now he's stopped. Look! He's facing us!"

"He's waving at us!"

"So he is! By thunder!"

"Ah, now we're all right! Now we're all right! There'll be a boat out here for us in half an hour."

"He's going on. He's running. He's going up to that house there."

The remote beach seemed lower than the sea, and it required a searching glance to discern the little black figure. The captain saw a floating stick and they rowed to it. A bath-towel was by some weird chance in the boat, and tying this on the stick, the captain waved it. The oarsman did not dare turn his head, so he was obliged to ask questions.

"What's he doing now?"

"He's standing still again. He's looking, I think. . . . There he goes again. Toward the house. . . . Now he's stopped again."

"Is he waving at us?"

"No, not now! he was, though."

"Look! There comes another man!"

"He's running."

"Look at him go, would you."

"Why, he's on a bicycle. Now he's met the other man. They're both waving at us. Look!"

"There comes something up the beach."

"What the devil is that thing?"

"Why, it looks like a boat."

"Why, certainly it's a boat."

"No, it's on wheels."

"Yes, so it is. Well, that must be the life-boat. They drag them along shore on a wagon."

"That's the life-boat, sure."

"No, by—, it's—it's an omnibus."

"I tell you it's a life-boat."

"It is not! It's an omnibus. I can see it plain. See? One of these big hotel omnibuses."

"By thunder, you're right. It's an omnibus, sure as fate. What do you suppose they are doing with an omnibus? Maybe they are going around collecting the life-crew, hey?"

"That's it, likely. Look! There's a fellow waving a little black flag. He's standing on the steps of the omnibus. There come those other two fellows. Now they're all talking together. Look at the fellow with the flag. Maybe he ain't waving it."

"That ain't a flag, is it? That's his coat. Why, certainly, that's his coat."

"So it is. It's his coat. He's taken it off and is waving it around his head. But would you look at him swing it."

"Oh, say, there isn't any life-saving station there. That's just a winter resort hotel omnibus that has brought over some of the boarders to see us drown."

"What's that idiot with the coat mean? What's he signaling, anyhow?"

"It looks as if he were trying to tell us to go north. There must be a life-saving station up there."

"No! He thinks we're fishing. Just giving us a merry hand. See? Ah, there, Willie."

"Well, I wish I could make something out of those signals. What do you suppose he means?"

"He don't mean anything. He's just playing."

"Well, if he'd just signal us to try the surf again, or to go to sea and wait, or go north, or go south, or go to hell—there would be some reason in it. But look at him. He just stands there and keeps his coat revolving like a wheel. The ass!"

"There come more people."

"Now there's quite a mob. Look! Isn't that a boat."

"Where? Oh, I see where you mean. No, that's no boat."

"That fellow is still waving his coat."

"He must think we like to see him do that. Why don't he quit it? It don't mean anything."

"I don't know. I think he is trying to make us go north. It must be that there's a life-saving station there somewhere."

"Say, he ain't tired yet. Look at 'im wave."

"Wonder how long he can keep that up. He's been revolving his coat ever since he caught sight of us. He's an idiot. Why aren't they getting men to bring a boat out? A fishing boat—one of those big yawls—could come out here all right. Why don't he do something?"

"Oh, it's all right, now."

"They'll have a boat out here for us in less than no time, now that they've seen us."

A faint yellow tone came into the sky over the low land. The shadows on the sea slowly deepened. The wind bore coldness with it, and the men began to shiver.

"Holy smoke!" said one, allowing his voice to express his impious mood, "if we keep on monkeying out here! If we've got to flounder out here all night!"

"Oh, we'll never have to stay here all night! Don't you worry. They've seen us now, and it won't be long before they'll come chasing out after us."

The shore grew dusky. The man waving a coat blended gradually into this gloom, and it swallowed in the same manner the omnibus and the group of people. The spray, when it dashed uproariously over the side, made the voyagers shrink and swear like men who were being branded.

"I'd like to catch the chump who waved the coat. I feel like soaking him one, just for luck."

"Why? What did he do?"

"Oh, nothing, but then he seemed so damned cheerful."

In the meantime the oiler rowed, and then the correspondent rowed, and then the oiler rowed. Gray-faced and bowed forward, they mechanically, turn by turn, plied the leaden oars. The form of the lighthouse had vanished from the southern horizon, but finally a pale star appeared, just lifting from the sea. The streaked saffron in the west passed before the all-merging darkness, and the sea to the east was black. The land had vanished, and was expressed only by the low and drear thunder of the surf.

"If I am going to be drowned—if I am going to be drowned—if I am going to be drowned, why, in the name of the seven mad gods who rule the sea, was I allowed to come thus far and contemplate sand and trees? Was I brought here merely to have my nose dragged away as I was about to nibble the sacred cheese of life?"

The patient captain, drooped over the water-jar, was sometimes obliged to speak to the oarsman.

"Keep her head up! Keep her head up!"

"'Keep her head up,' sir." The voices were weary and low.

This was surely a quiet evening. All save the oarsman lay heavily and listlessly in the boat's bottom. As for him, his eyes were just capable of noting the tall black waves that swept forward in a most sinister silence, save for an occasional subdued growl of a crest.

The cook's head was on a thwart, and he looked without interest at the water under his nose. He was deep in other scenes. Finally he spoke. "Billie," he murmured, dreamfully, "what kind of pie do you like best?"

5

"Pie," said the oiler and the correspondent, agitatedly. "Don't talk about those things, blast you!"

"Well," said the cook, "I was just thinking about ham sandwiches, and—"

A night on the sea in an open boat is a long night. As darkness settled finally, the shine of the light, lifting from the sea in the south, changed to full gold. On the northern horizon a new light appeared, a small bluish gleam on the edge of the waters. These two lights were the furniture of the world. Otherwise there was nothing but waves.

Two men huddled in the stern, and distances were so magnificent in the dingey that the rower was enabled to keep his feet partly warmed by thrusting them under his companions. Their legs indeed extended far under the rowing-seat until they touched the feet of the captain forward. Sometimes, despite the efforts of the tired oarsman, a wave came piling into the boat, an icy wave of the night, and the chilling water soaked them anew. They would twist their bodies for a moment and groan, and sleep the dead sleep once more, while the water in the boat gurgled about them as the craft rocked.

The plan of the oiler and the correspondent was for one to row until he lost the ability, and then arouse the other from his sea-water couch in the bottom of the boat.

The oiler plied the oars until his head drooped forward, and the overpowering sleep blinded him. And he rowed yet afterward. Then he touched a man in the bottom of the boat, and called his name. "Will you spell me for a little while?" he said, meekly.

"Sure, Billie," said the correspondent, awakening and dragging himself to a sitting position. They exchanged places carefully, and the oiler, cuddling down in the sea-water at the cook's side, seemed to go to sleep instantly.

The particular violence of the sea had ceased. The waves came without snarling. The obligation of the man at the oars was to keep the boat headed so that the tilt of the rollers would not capsize her, and to preserve her from filling when the crests rushed past. The black waves were silent and hard to be seen in the darkness. Often one was almost upon the boat before the oarsman was aware.

In a low voice the correspondent addressed the captain. He was not sure that the captain was awake, although this iron man seemed to be always awake. "Captain, shall I keep her making for that light north, sir?"

The same steady voice answered him. "Yes. Keep it about two points off the port bow."

The cook had tied a life-belt around himself in order to get even the warmth which this clumsy cork contrivance could donate, and he seemed almost stove-like when a rower, whose teeth invariably chattered wildly as soon as he ceased his labor, dropped down to sleep.

The correspondent, as he rowed, looked down at the two men sleeping underfoot. The cook's arm was around the oiler's shoulders, and, with their fragmentary clothing and haggard faces, they were the babes of the sea, a grotesque rendering of the old babes in the wood.

Later he must have grown stupid at his work, for suddenly there was a growling of water, and a crest came with a roar and a swash into the boat, and it was a wonder that it did not set the cook afloat in his life-belt. The cook continued to sleep, but the oiler sat up, blinking his eyes and shaking with the new cold.

"Oh, I'm awful sorry, Billie," said the correspondent, contritely.

"That's all right, old boy," said the oiler, and lay down again and was asleep.

Presently it seemed that even the captain dozed, and the correspondent thought that he was the one man afloat on all the oceans. The wind had a voice as it came over the waves, and it was sadder than the end.

There was a long, loud swishing astern of the boat, and a gleaming trail of phosphorescence, like blue flame, was furrowed on the black waters. It might have been made by a monstrous knife.

Then there came a stillness, while the correspondent breathed with the open mouth and looked at the sea.

Suddenly there was another swish and another long flash of bluish light, and this time it was alongside the boat, and might almost have been reached with an oar. The correspondent saw an enormous fin speed like a shadow through the water, hurling the crystalline spray and leaving the long glowing trail.

The correspondent looked over his shoulder at the captain. His face was hidden, and he seemed to be asleep. He looked at the babes of the sea. They certainly were asleep. So, being bereft of sympathy, he leaned a little way to one side and swore softly into the sea.

But the thing did not then leave the vicinity of the boat. Ahead or astern, on one side or the other, at intervals long or short, fled the long sparkling streak, and there was to be heard the whiroo of the dark fin. The speed and power of the thing was greatly to be admired. It cut the water like a gigantic and keen projectile.

The presence of this biding thing did not affect the man with the same horror that it would if he had been a picnicker. He simply looked at the sea dully and swore in an undertone.

Nevertheless, it is true that he did not wish to be alone. He wished one of his companions to awaken by chance and keep him company with it. But the captain hung motionless over the water-jar, and the oiler and the cook in the bottom of the boat were plunged in slumber.

6

"If I am going to be drowned—if I am going to be drowned—if I am going to be drowned, why, in the name of the seven mad gods who rule the sea, was I allowed to come thus far and contemplate sand and trees?"

During this dismal night, it may be remarked that a man would conclude that it was really the intention of the seven mad gods to drown him, despite the abominable injustice of it. For it was certainly an abominable injustice to drown a man who had worked so hard, so hard. The man felt it would be a crime most unnatural. Other people had drowned at sea since galleys swarmed with painted sails, but still—

When it occurs to a man that nature does not regard him as important, and that she feels she would not maim the universe by disposing of him, he at first wishes to throw bricks at the temple, and he hates deeply the fact that there are no bricks and no temples. Any visible expression of nature would surely be pelleted with his jeers.

Then, if there be no tangible thing to hoot he feels, perhaps, the desire to confront a personification and indulge in pleas, bowed to one knee, and with hands supplicant, saying: "Yes, but I love myself."

A high cold star on a winter's night is the word he feels that she says to him. Thereafter he knows the pathos of his situation.

The men in the dingey had not discussed these matters, but each had, no doubt, reflected upon them in silence and according to his mind. There was seldom any expression upon their faces save the general one of complete weariness. Speech was devoted to the business of the boat.

To chime the notes of his emotion, a verse mysteriously entered the correspondent's head. He had even forgotten that he had forgotten this verse, but it suddenly was in his mind.

> A soldier of the Legion lay dying in Algiers,
> There was lack of woman's nursing, there was dearth of woman's tears;
> But a comrade stood beside him, and he took that comrade's hand,
> And he said: "I shall never see my own, my native land."

In his childhood, the correspondent had been made acquainted with the fact that a soldier of the Legion lay dying in Algiers, but he had never regarded the fact as important. Myriads of his school-fellows had informed him of the soldier's plight, but the dinning had naturally ended by making him perfectly indifferent. He had never considered it his affair that a soldier of the Legion lay dying in Algiers, nor had it appeared to him as a matter for sorrow. It was less to him than the breaking of a pencil's point.

Now, however, it quaintly came to him as a human, living thing. It was no longer merely a picture of a few throes in the breast of a poet, meanwhile drinking tea and warming his feet at the grate; it was an actuality—stern, mournful, and fine.

The correspondent plainly saw the soldier. He lay on the sand with his feet out straight and still. While his pale left hand was upon his chest in an attempt to thwart the going of his life, the blood came between his fingers. In the far Algerian distance, a city of low square forms was set against a sky that was faint with the last sunset hues. The correspondent, plying the oars and dreaming of the slow and slower movements of the lips of the soldier, was moved by a profound and perfectly impersonal comprehension. He was sorry for the soldier of the Legion who lay dying in Algiers.

The thing which had followed the boat and waited had evidently grown bored at the delay. There was no longer to be heard the slash of the cut water, and there was no longer the flame of the long trail. The light in the north still glimmered, but it was apparently no nearer to the boat. Sometimes the boom of the surf rang in the correspondent's ears, and he turned the craft seaward then and rowed harder. Southward, someone had evidently built a watch-fire on the beach. It was too low and too far to be seen, but it made a shimmering, roseate reflection upon the bluff back of it, and this could be discerned from the boat. The wind came stronger, and sometimes a wave suddenly raged out like a mountain-cat, and there was to be seen the sheen and sparkle of a broken crest.

The captain, in the bow, moved on his water-jar and sat erect. "Pretty long night," he observed to the correspondent. He looked at the shore. "Those life-saving people take their time."

"Did you see that shark playing around?"

"Yes, I saw him. He was a big fellow, all right."

"Wish I had known you were awake."

Later the correspondent spoke into the bottom of the boat.

"Billie!" There was a slow and gradual disentanglement. "Billie, will you spell me?"

"Sure," said the oiler.

As soon as the correspondent touched the cold comfortable seater in the bottom of the boat, and had huddled close to the cook's life-belt he was deep in sleep, despite the fact that his teeth played all the popular airs. This sleep was so good to him that it was but a moment before he heard a voice call his name in a tone that demonstrated the last stages of exhaustion. "Will you spell me?"

"Sure, Billie."

The light in the north had mysteriously vanished, but the correspondent took his course from the wide-awake captain.

Later in the night they took the boat farther out to sea, and the captain directed the cook to take one oar at the stern and keep the boat facing the seas. He was to call out if he should hear the thunder of the surf. This plan enabled the oiler and the correspondent to get respite together. "We'll give those boys a chance to get into shape again," said the captain. They curled down and, after a few preliminary chatterings and trembles, slept once more the dead sleep. Neither knew they had bequeathed to the cook the company of another shark, or perhaps the same shark.

As the boat caroused on the waves, spray occasionally bumped over the side and gave them a fresh soaking, but this had no power to break their repose. The ominous slash of the wind and the water affected them as it would have affected mummies.

"Boys," said the cook, with the notes of every reluctance in his voice, "she's drifted in pretty close. I guess one of you had better take her to sea again." The correspondent, aroused, heard the crash of the toppled crests.

As he was rowing, the captain gave him some whiskey-and-water, and this steadied the chills out of him. "If I ever get ashore and anybody shows me even a photograph of an oar—"

At last there was a short conversation.

"Billie . . . Billie, will you spell me?"

"Sure," said the oiler.

7

When the correspondent again opened his eyes, the sea and the sky were each of the gray hue of the dawning. Later, carmine and gold was painted upon the waters. The morning appeared finally, in its splendor, with a sky of pure blue, and the sunlight flamed on the tips of the waves.

On the distant dunes were set many little black cottages, and a tall white windmill reared above them. No man, nor dog, nor bicycle appeared on the beach. The cottages might have formed a deserted village.

The voyagers scanned the shore. A conference was held in the boat. "Well," said the captain, "if no help is coming, we might better try a run through the surf right away. If we stay out here much longer we will be too weak to do anything for ourselves at all." The others silently acquiesced in this reasoning. The boat was headed for the beach. The correspondent wondered if none ever ascended the tall wind-tower, and if then they never looked seaward. This tower was a giant, standing with its back to the plight of the ants. It represented in a degree, to the correspondent, the serenity of nature amid the struggles of the individual—nature in the wind, and nature in the vision of men. She did not seem cruel to him then, nor beneficent, nor treacherous, nor wise. But she was indifferent, flatly indifferent. It is, perhaps, plausible that a man in this situation, impressed with the unconcern of the universe, should see the innumerable flaws of his life, and have them taste wickedly in his mind and wish for another chance. A distinction between right and wrong seems absurdly clear to him, then, in this new ignorance of the grave-edge, and he understands that if he were given another opportunity he would mend his conduct and his words, and be better and brighter during an introduction or at a tea.

"Now, boys," said the captain, "she is going to swamp sure. All we can do is to work her in as far as possible, and then when she swamps, pile out and scramble for the beach. Keep cool now, and don't jump until she swamps sure."

The oiler took the oars. Over his shoulders he scanned the surf. "Captain," he said, "I think I'd better bring her about, and keep her head-on to the seas and back her in."

"All right, Billie," said the captain. "Back her in." The oiler swung the boat then and, seated in the stern, the cook and the correspondent were obliged to look over their shoulders to contemplate the lonely and indifferent shore.

The monstrous in-shore rollers heaved the boat high until the men were again enabled to see the white sheets of water scudding up the slanted beach. "We won't get in very close," said the captain. Each time a man could wrest his attention from the rollers, he turned his glance toward the shore, and in the expression of the eyes during this contemplation there was a singular quality. The correspondent, observing the others, knew that they were not afraid, but the full meaning of their glances was shrouded.

As for himself, he was too tired to grapple fundamentally with the fact. He tried to coerce his mind into thinking of it, but the mind was dominated at this time by the muscles, and the muscles said they did not care. It merely occurred to him that if he should drown it would be a shame.

There were no hurried words, no pallor, no plain agitation. The men simply looked at the shore. "Now, remember to get well clear of the boat when you jump," said the captain.

Seaward the crest of a roller suddenly fell with a thunderous crash, and the long white comber came roaring down upon the boat.

"Steady now," said the captain. The men were silent. They turned their eyes from the shore to the comber and waited. The boat slid up the incline, leaped at the furious top, bounced over it, and swung down the long back of the waves. Some water had been shipped and the cook bailed it out.

But the next crest crashed also. The tumbling, boiling flood of white water caught the boat and whirled it almost perpendicular. Water swarmed in from all sides. The correspondent had his hands on the gunwale at this time, and when the water entered at that place he swiftly withdrew his fingers, as if he objected to wetting them.

The little boat, drunken with this weight of water, reeled and snuggled deeper into the sea.

"Bail her out, cook! Bail her out," said the captain.

"All right, captain," said the cook.

"Now, boys, the next one will do for us, sure," said the oiler. "Mind to jump clear of the boat."

The third wave moved forward, huge, furious, implacable. It fairly swallowed the dingey, and almost simultaneously the men tumbled into the sea. A piece of life-belt had lain in the bottom of the boat, and as the correspondent went overboard he held this to his chest with his left hand.

The January water was icy, and he reflected immediately that it was colder than he had expected to find it off the coast of Florida. This appeared to his dazed mind as a fact important enough to be noted at the time. The coldness of the water was sad; it was tragic. This fact was somehow so mixed and confused with his opinion of his own situation that it seemed almost a proper reason for tears. The water was cold.

When he came to the surface he was conscious of little but the noisy water. Afterward he saw his companions in the sea. The oiler was ahead in the race. He was swimming strongly and rapidly. Off to the correspondent's left, the cook's great white and corked back bulged out of the water, and in the rear the captain was hanging with his one good hand to the keel of the overturned dingey.

There is a certain immovable quality to a shore, and the correspondent wondered at it amid the confusion of the sea.

It seemed also very attractive, but the correspondent knew that it was a long journey, and he paddled leisurely. The piece of life-preserver lay under him, and sometimes he whirled down the incline of a wave as if he were on a hand-sled.

But finally he arrived at a place in the sea where travel was beset with difficulty. He did not pause swimming to inquire what manner of current had caught him, but there his progress ceased. The shore was set before him like a bit of scenery on a stage, and he looked at it and understood with his eyes each detail of it.

As the cook passed, much farther to the left, the captain was calling to him, "Turn over on your back, cook! Turn over on your back and use the oar."

"All right, sir." The cook turned on his back, and, paddling with an oar, went ahead as if he were a canoe.

Presently the boat also passed to the left of the correspondent with the captain clinging with one hand to the keel. He would have appeared like a man raising himself to look over a board fence, if it were not for the extraordinary gymnastics of the boat. The correspondent marvelled that the captain could still hold to it.

They passed on, nearer to shore—the oiler, the cook, the captain—and following them went the water-jar, bouncing gaily over the seas.

The correspondent remained in the grip of this strange new enemy—a current. The shore, with its white slope of sand and its green bluff, topped with little silent cottages, was spread like a picture before him. It was very near to him then, but he was impressed as one who in a gallery looks at a scene from Brittany or Algiers.

He thought: "I am going to drown? Can it be possible? Can it be possible? Can it be possible?" Perhaps an individual must consider his own death to be the final phenomenon of nature.

But later a wave perhaps whirled him out of this small deadly current, for he found suddenly that he could again make progress toward the shore. Later still, he was aware that the captain, clinging with one hand to the keel of the dingey, had his face turned away from the shore and toward him, and was calling his name. "Come to the boat! Come to the boat!"

In his struggle to reach the captain and the boat, he reflected that when one gets properly wearied, drowning must really be a comfortable arrangement, a cessation of hostilities accompanied by a large degree of relief, and he was glad of it, for the main thing in his mind for some moments had been horror of the temporary agony. He did not wish to be hurt.

Presently he saw a man running along the shore. He was undressing with most remarkable speed. Coat, trousers, shirt, everything flew magically off him.

"Come to the boat," called the captain.

"All right, captain." As the correspondent paddled, he saw the captain let himself down to bottom and leave the boat. Then the correspondent performed his one little marvel of the voyage. A large wave caught him and flung him with ease and supreme speed completely over the boat and far beyond it. It struck him even then as an event in gymnastics, and a true miracle of the sea. An overturned boat in the surf is not a plaything to a swimming man.

The correspondent arrived in water that reached only to his waist but his condition did not enable him to stand for more than a moment. Each wave knocked him into a heap, and the under-tow pulled at him.

Then he saw the man who had been running and undressing, and undressing and running, come bounding into the water. He dragged ashore the cook, and then waded toward the captain, but the captain waved him away, and sent him to the correspondent. He was naked, naked as a tree in winter, but a halo was about his head, and he shone like a saint. He gave a strong pull, and a long drag, and a bully heave at the correspondent's hand. The correspondent schooled in the minor formulae, said: "Thanks, old man." But suddenly the man cried: "What's that?" He pointed a swift finger. The correspondent said: "Go."

In the shallows, face downward, lay the oiler. His forehead touched sand that was periodically, between each wave, clear of the sea.

The correspondent did not know all that transpired afterward. When he achieved safe ground he fell, striking the sand with each particular part of his body. It was as if he had dropped from a roof but the thud was grateful to him.

It seems that instantly the beach was populated with men, with blankets, clothes, and flasks, and women with coffee-pots and all the remedies sacred to their minds. The welcome of the land to the men from the sea was warm and generous, but a still and dripping shape was carried slowly up the beach, and the land's welcome for it could only be the different and sinister hospitality of the grave.

When it came night, the white waves paced to and fro in the moonlight, and the wind brought the sound of the great sea's voice to the men on shore, and they felt that they could then be interpreters.

(1897)

JAMES JOYCE
[1882–1941]

The Boarding House

Mrs. Mooney was a butcher's daughter. She was a woman who was quite able to keep things to herself: a determined woman. She had married her father's foreman and opened a butcher's shop near Spring Gardens. But as soon as his father-in-law was dead Mr. Mooney began to go to the devil. He drank, plundered the till, ran headlong into debt. It was no use making him take the pledge: he was sure to break out again a few days after. By fighting his wife in the presence of customers and by buying bad meat he ruined his business. One night he went for his wife with the cleaver and she had to sleep in a neighbour's house.

After that they lived apart. She went to the priest and got a separation from him with care of the children. She would give him neither money nor food nor house-room; and so he was obliged to enlist himself as a sheriff's man. He was a shabby stooped little drunkard with a white face and a white moustache and white eyebrows, pencilled above his little eyes, which were pink-veined and raw; and all day long he sat in the bailiff's room, waiting to be put on a job. Mrs. Mooney, who had taken what remained of her money out of the butcher business and set up a boarding house in Hardwicke Street, was a big imposing woman. Her house had a floating population made up of tourists from Liverpool and the Isle of Man and, occasionally, *artistes* from the music halls. Its resident population was made up of clerks from the city. She governed her house cunningly and firmly, knew when to give credit, when to be stern and when to let things pass. All the resident young men spoke of her as *The Madam*.

Mrs. Mooney's young men paid fifteen shillings a week for board and lodgings (beer or stout at dinner excluded). They shared in common tastes and occupations and for this reason they were very chummy with one another. They discussed with one another the chances of favourites and outsiders. Jack Mooney, the Madam's son, who was clerk to a commission agent in Fleet Street, had the reputation of being a hard case. He was fond of using soldiers' obscenities: usually he came home in the small hours.

When he met his friends he had always a good one to tell them and he was always sure to be on to a good thing—that is to say, a likely horse or a likely *artiste*. He was also handy with the mitts and sang comic songs. On Sunday nights there would often be a reunion in Mrs. Mooney's front drawing room. The music-hall *artistes* would oblige; and Sheridan played waltzes and polkas and vamped accompaniments. Polly Mooney, the Madam's daughter, would also sing. She sang:

> *I'm a . . . naughty girl.*
> *You needn't sham:*
> *You know I am.*

Polly was a slim girl of nineteen, she had light soft hair and a small full mouth. Her eyes, which were grey with a shade of green through them, had a habit of glancing upwards when she spoke with anyone, which made her look like a little perverse madonna. Mrs. Mooney had first sent her daughter to be a typist in a corn-factor's office but, as a disreputable sheriff's man used to come every other day to the office, asking to be allowed to say a word to his daughter, she had taken her daughter home again and set her to do housework. As Polly was very lively the intention was to give her the run of the young men. Besides, young men like to feel that there is a young woman not very far away. Polly, of course, flirted with the young men but Mrs. Mooney, who was a shrewd judge, knew that the young men were only passing the time away: none of them meant business. Things went on so for a long time and Mrs. Mooney began to think of sending Polly back to typewriting when she noticed that something was going on between Polly and one of the young men. She watched the pair and kept her own counsel.

Polly knew that she was being watched, but still her mother's persistent silence could not be misunderstood. There had been no open complicity between mother and daughter, no open understanding but, though people in the house began to talk of the affair, still Mrs. Mooney did not intervene. Polly began to grow a little strange in her manner and the young man was evidently perturbed. At last, when she judged it to be the right moment, Mrs. Mooney intervened. She dealt with moral problems as a cleaver deals with meat: and in this case she had made up her mind.

It was a bright Sunday morning of early summer, promising heat, but with a fresh breeze blowing. All the windows of the boarding house were open and the lace curtains ballooned gently towards the street beneath the raised sashes. The belfry of George's Church sent out constant peals and worshippers, singly or in groups, traversed the little circus before the church, revealing their purpose by their self-contained demeanor no less than by the little volumes in their gloved hands. Breakfast was over in the boarding house and the table of the breakfast-room was covered with plates on which lay yellow streaks of eggs with morsels of bacon-fat and bacon-rind. Mrs. Mooney sat in the straw arm-chair and watched the servant Mary remove the breakfast things. She made Mary collect the crusts and pieces of broken bread to help to make Tuesday's bread-pudding. When the table was cleared, the broken bread collected, the sugar and butter safe under lock and key, she began to reconstruct the interview which she had had the night before with Polly. Things were as she had suspected: she had been frank in her questions and Polly had been frank in her answers. Both had been somewhat awkward, of course. She had been made awkward by her not wishing to receive the news in too cavalier a fashion or to seem to have connived and Polly had been made awkward not merely because allusions of that kind always made her awkward but also because she did not wish it to be thought that in her wise innocence she had divined the intention behind her mother's tolerance.

Mrs. Mooney glanced instinctively at the little gilt clock on the mantelpiece as soon as she had become aware through her revery that the bells of George's Church had stopped ringing. It was seventeen minutes past eleven: she would have lots of time to have the matter out with Mr. Doran and then catch short twelve at Marlborough Street. She was sure she would win. To begin with she had all the weight of social opinion on her side: she was an outraged mother. She had allowed him to live beneath her roof, assuming that he was a man of honour, and he had simply abused her hospitality. He was thirty-four or thirty-five years of age, so that youth could not be pleaded as his excuse; nor could ignorance be his excuse since he was a man who had seen something of the world. He had simply taken advantage of Polly's youth and inexperience: that was evident. The question was: What reparation would he make?

There must be reparation made in such cases. It is all very well for the man: he can go his ways as if nothing had happened, having had his moment of pleasure, but the girl has to bear the brunt. Some mothers would be content to patch up such an affair for a sum of money; she had known cases of it. But she would not do so. For her only one reparation could make up for the loss of her daughter's honour: marriage.

She counted all her cards again before sending Mary up to Mr. Doran's room to say that she wished to speak with him. She felt sure she would win. He was a serious young man, not rakish or loud-voiced like the others. If it had been Mr. Sheridan or Mr. Meade or Bantam Lyons her task would have been much harder. She did not think he would face publicity. All the lodgers in the house knew something of the affair; details had been invented by some. Besides, he had been employed for thirteen years in a great Catholic wine-merchant's office and publicity would mean for him, perhaps, the loss of his sit. Whereas if he agreed all might be well. She knew he had a good screw for one thing and she suspected he had a bit of stuff put by.

Nearly the half-hour! She stood up and surveyed herself in the pierglass. The decisive expression of her great florid face satisfied her and she thought of some mothers she knew who could not get their daughters off their hands.

Mr. Doran was very anxious indeed this Sunday morning. He had made two attempts to shave but his hand had been so unsteady that he had been obliged to desist. Three days' reddish beard fringed his jaws and every two or three minutes a mist gathered on his glasses so that he had to take them off and polish them with his pocket-handkerchief. The recollection of his confession of the night before was a cause of acute pain to him; the priest had drawn out every ridiculous detail of the affair and in the end had so magnified his sin that he was almost thankful at being afforded a loophole of reparation. The harm was done. What could he do now but marry her or run away? He could not brazen it out. The affair would be sure to be talked of and his employer would be certain to hear of it. Dublin is such a small city: everyone knows everyone else's business. He felt his heart leap warmly in his throat as he heard in his excited imagination old Mr. Leonard calling out in his rasping voice: *Send Mr Doran here, please.*

All his long years of service gone for nothing! All his industry and diligence thrown away! As a young man he had sown his wild oats, of course; he had boasted of his free-thinking and denied the existence of God to his companions in public-houses. But that was all passed and done with . . . nearly. He still bought a copy of *Reynold's Newspaper* every week but he attended to his religious duties and for nine-tenths of the year lived a regular life. He had money enough to settle down on; it was not that. But the family would look down on her. First of all there was her disreputable father and then her mother's boarding house was beginning to get a certain fame. He had a notion that he was being had. He could imagine his friends talking of the affair and laughing. She *was* a little vulgar; sometimes she said *I seen* and *If I had've known*. But what would grammar matter if he really loved her? He could not make up his mind whether to like her or despise her for what she had done. Of course, he had done it too. His instinct urged him to remain free, not to marry. Once you are married you are done for, it said.

While he was sitting helplessly on the side of the bed in shirt and trousers she tapped lightly at his door and entered. She told him all, that she had made a clean breast of it to her mother and that her mother would speak with him that morning. She cried and threw her arms round his neck, saying:

—O, Bob! Bob! What am I to do! What am I to do at all?

She would put an end to herself, she said.

He comforted her feebly, telling her not to cry, that it would be all right, never fear. He felt against his shirt the agitation of her bosom.

It was not altogether his fault that it had happened. He remembered well, with the curious patient memory of the celibate, the first casual caresses her dress, her breath, her fingers had given him. Then late one night as he was undressing for bed she had tapped at his door, timidly. She wanted to relight her candle at his for hers had been blown out by a gust. It was her bath night. She wore a loose open combing-jacket of printed flannel. Her white instep shone in the opening of her furry slippers and the blood glowed warmly behind her perfumed skin. From her hands and wrists too as she lit and steadied her candle a faint perfume arose.

On nights when he came in very late it was she who warmed up his dinner. He scarcely knew what he was eating, feeling her beside him alone, at night, in the sleeping house. And her thoughtfulness! If the night was anyway cold or wet or windy there was sure to be a little tumbler of punch ready for him. Perhaps they could be happy together. . . .

They used to go upstairs together on tiptoe, each with a candle, and on the third landing exchange reluctant good-nights. They used to kiss. He remembered well her eyes, the touch of her hand and his delirium. . . .

But delirium passes. He echoed her phrase, applying it to himself: *What am I to do?* The instinct of the celibate warned him to hold back. But the sin was there; even his sense of honour told him that reparation must be made for such a sin.

While he was sitting with her on the side of the bed Mary came to the door and said that the missus wanted to see him in the parlour. He stood up to put on his coat and waistcoat, more helpless than ever. When he was dressed he went over to her to comfort her. It would be all right, never fear. He left her crying on the bed and moaning softly: *O my God!*

Going down the stairs his glasses became so dimmed with moisture that he had to take them off and polish them. He longed to ascend through the roof and fly away to another country where he would never hear again of his trouble, and yet a force pushed him downstairs step by step. The implacable faces of his employer and of the Madam stared upon his discomfiture. On the last flight of stairs he passed Jack Mooney who was coming up from the pantry nursing two bottles of *Bass*. They saluted coldly; and the lover's eyes rested for a second or two on a thick bulldog face and a pair of thick short arms. When he reached the foot of the staircase he glanced up and saw Jack regarding him from the door of the return room.

Suddenly he remembered the night when one of the music-hall *artistes,* a little blond Londoner, had made a rather free allusion to Polly. The reunion had been almost broken up on account of Jack's violence. Everyone tried to quiet him. The music-hall *artiste,* a little paler than usual, kept smiling and saying that there was no harm meant: but Jack kept shouting at him that if any fellow tried that sort of a game on with *his* sister he'd bloody well put his teeth down his throat, so he would.

Polly sat for a little time on the side of the bed, crying. Then she dried her eyes and went over to the looking-glass. She dipped the end of the towel in the water-jug and refreshed her eyes with the cool water. She looked at herself in profile and readjusted a hairpin above her ear. Then she went back to the bed again and sat at the foot. She regarded the pillows for a long time and the sight of them awakened in her mind secret amiable memories. She rested the nape of her neck against the cool iron bed-rail and fell into a revery. There was no longer any perturbation visible on her face.

She waited on patiently, almost cheerfully, without alarm, her memories gradually giving place to hopes and visions of the future. Her hopes and visions were so intricate that she no longer saw the white pillows on which her gaze was fixed or remembered that she was waiting for anything.

At last she heard her mother calling. She started to her feet and ran to the banisters.

—Polly! Polly!

—Yes, mamma?

Come down, dear. Mr. Doran wants to speak to you. Then she remembered what she had been waiting for.

(1914)

KATHERINE MANSFIELD

[1888–1923]

Bliss

Although Bertha Young was thirty she still had moments like this when she wanted to run instead of walk, to take dancing steps on and off the pavement, to bowl a hoop, to throw something up in the air and catch it again, or to stand still and laugh at—nothing—at nothing, simply.

What can you do if you are thirty and, turning the corner of your own street, you are overcome, suddenly, by a feeling of bliss—absolute bliss!—as though you'd suddenly swallowed a bright piece of that late afternoon sun and it burned in your bosom, sending out a little shower of sparks into every particle, into every finger and toe? . . .

Oh, is there no way you can express it without being "drunk and disorderly"? How idiotic civilization is! Why be given a body if you have to keep it shut up in a case like a rare, rare fiddle?

"No, that about the fiddle is not quite what I mean," she thought, running up the steps and feeling in her bag for the key—she'd forgotten it, as usual—and rattling the letter-box. "It's not what I mean, because—Thank you, Mary"—she went into the hall. "Is nurse back?"

"Yes, M'm."

"And has the fruit come?"

"Yes. M'm. Everything's come."

"Bring the fruit up to the dining-room, will you? I'll arrange it before I go upstairs."

It was dusky in the dining-room and quite chilly. But all the same Bertha threw off her coat; she could not bear the tight clasp of it another moment, and the cold air fell on her arms.

But in her bosom there was still that bright glowing place—that shower of little sparks coming from it. It was almost unbearable. She hardly dared to breathe for fear of fanning it higher, and yet she breathed deeply, deeply. She hardly dared to look into the cold mirror—but she did look, and it gave her back a woman, radiant, with smiling, trembling lips, with big, dark eyes and an air of listening, waiting for something . . . divine to happen . . . that she knew must happen . . . infallibly.

Mary brought in the fruit on a tray and with it a glass bowl, and a blue dish, very lovely, with a strange sheen on it as though it had been dipped in milk.

"Shall I turn on the light, M'm?"

"No, thank you. I can see quite well."

There were tangerines and apples stained with strawberry pink. Some yellow pears, smooth as silk, some white grapes covered with a silver bloom and a big cluster of purple ones. These last she had bought to tone in with the new dining-room carpet. Yes, that did sound rather far-fetched and absurd, but it was really why she had bought them. She had thought in the shop: "I must have some purples ones to bring the carpet up to the table." And it had seemed quite sense at the time.

When she had finished with them and had made two pyramids of these bright round shapes, she stood away from the table to get the effect—and it really was most curious. For the dark table seemed to melt into the dusky light and the glass dish and the blue bowl to float in the air. This, of course in her present mood, was so incredibly beautiful. . . . She began to laugh.

"No, no. I'm getting hysterical." And she seized her bag and coat and ran upstairs to the nursery.

Nurse sat at a low table giving Little B her supper after her bath. The baby had on a white flannel gown and a blue woollen jacket, and her dark, fine hair was brushed up into a funny little peak. She looked up when she saw her mother and began to jump.

"Now, my lovely, eat it up like a good girl," said Nurse, setting her lips in a way that Bertha knew, and that meant she had come into the nursery at another wrong moment.

"Has she been good, Nanny?"

"She's been a little sweet all the afternoon," whispered Nanny. "We went to the park and I sat down on a chair and took her out of the pram and a big dog came along and put its head on my knee and she clutched its ear, tugged it. Oh, you should have seen her."

Bertha wanted to ask if it wasn't rather dangerous to let her clutch at a strange dog's ear. But she did not dare to. She stood watching them, her hands by her side, like the poor little girl in front of the rich little girl with the doll.

The baby looked up at her again, stared, and then smiled so charmingly that Bertha couldn't help crying:

"Oh, Nanny, do let me finish giving her her supper while you put the bath things away."

"Well, M'm, she oughtn't to be changed hands while she's eating," said Nanny, still whispering. "It unsettles her; it's very likely to upset her."

How absurd it was. Why have a baby if it has to be kept—not in a case like a rare, rare fiddle—but in another woman's arms?

"Oh, I must!" said she.

Very offended, Nanny handed her over.

"Now, don't excite her after her supper. You know you do, M'm. And I have such a time with her after!"

Thank heaven! Nanny went out of the room with the bath towels.

"Now I've got you to myself, my little precious," said Bertha, as the baby leaned against her.

She ate delightfully, holding up her lips for the spoon and then waving her hands. Sometimes she wouldn't let the spoon go; and sometimes, just as Bertha had filled it, she waved it away to the four winds.

When the soup was finished Bertha turned round to the fire.

"You're nice—you're very nice!" said she, kissing her warm baby. "I'm fond of you. I like you."

And, indeed, she loved Little B so much—her neck as she bent forward, her exquisite toes as they shone transparent in the firelight—that all her feeling of bliss came back again, and again she didn't know how to express it—what to do with it.

"You're wanted on the telephone," said Nanny, coming back in triumph and seizing *her* Little B.

Down she flew. It was Harry.

"Oh, is that you, Ber? Look here. I'll be late. I'll take a taxi and come along as quickly as I can, but get dinner put back ten minutes—will you? All right?"

"Yes, perfectly. Oh, Harry!"

"Yes?"

What had she to say? She'd nothing to say. She only wanted to get in touch with him for a moment. She couldn't absurdly cry: "Hasn't it been a divine day!"

"What is it?" rapped out the little voice.

"Nothing. *Entendu,*" said Bertha, and hung up the receiver, thinking how more than idiotic civilization was.

They had people coming to dinner. The Norman Knights—a very sound couple—he was about to start a theatre, and she was awfully keen on interior decoration, a young man, Eddie Warren, who had just published a little book of poems and whom everybody was asking to dine, and a "find" of Bertha's called Pearl Fulton. What Miss Fulton did, Bertha didn't know. They had met at the club and Bertha had fallen in love with her, as she always did fall in love with beautiful women who had something strange about them.

The provoking thing was that, though they had been about together and met a number of times and really talked, Bertha couldn't yet make her out. Up to a certain point Miss Fulton was rarely, wonderfully frank, but the certain point was there, and beyond that she would not go.

Was there anything beyond it? Harry said "No." Voted her dullish, and "cold like all blond women, with a touch, perhaps, of anaemia of the brain." But Bertha wouldn't agree with him; not yet, at any rate.

"No, the way she has of sitting with her head a little on one side, and smiling, has something behind it, Harry, and I must find out what that something is."

"Most likely it's a good stomach," answered Harry.

He made a point of catching Bertha's heels with replies of that kind . . . "liver frozen, my dear girl," or "pure flatulence," or "kidney disease," . . . and so on. For some strange reason Bertha liked this, and almost admired it in him very much.

She went into the drawing-room and lighted the fire; then, picking up the cushions, one by one, that Mary had disposed so carefully, she threw them back on to the chairs and the couches. That made all the difference; the room came alive at once. As she was about to throw the last one she surprised herself by suddenly hugging it to her, passionately, passionately. But it did not put out the fire in her bosom. Oh, on the contrary!

The windows of the drawing-room opened on to a balcony overlooking the garden. At the far end, against the wall, there was a tall, slender pear tree in fullest, richest bloom; it stood perfect, as though becalmed against the jade-green sky. Bertha couldn't help feeling, even from this distance, that it had not a single bud or a faded petal. Down below, in the garden beds, the red and yellow tulips, heavy with flowers, seemed to lean upon the dusk. A grey cat, dragging its belly, crept across the lawn, and a black one, its shadow, trailed after. The sight of them, so intent and so quick, gave Bertha a curious shiver.

"What creepy things cats are!" she stammered, and she turned away from the window and began walking up and down. . . .

How strong the jonquils smelled in the warm room. Too strong? Oh, no. And yet, as though overcome, she flung down on a couch and pressed her hands to her eyes.

"I'm too happy—too happy!" she murmured.

And she seemed to see on her eyelids the lovely pear tree with its wide open blossoms as a symbol of her own life.

Really—really—she had everything. She was young. Harry and she were as much in love as ever, and they got on together splendidly and were really good pals. She had an adorable baby. They didn't have to worry about money. They had this absolutely satisfactory house and garden. And friends—modern, thrilling friends, writers and painters and poets or people keen on social questions—just the kind of friends they wanted. And then there were books, and there was music, and she had found a wonderful little dressmaker, and they were going abroad in the summer, and their new cook made the most superb omelettes. . . .

"I'm absurd. Absurd!" She sat up; but she felt quite dizzy, quite drunk. It must have been the spring.

Yes, it was the spring. Now she was so tired she could not drag herself upstairs to dress.

A white dress, a string of jade beads, green shoes and stockings. It wasn't intentional. She had thought of this scheme hours before she stood at the drawing-room window.

Her petals rustled softly into the hall, and she kissed Mrs. Norman Knight, who was taking off the most amusing orange coat with a procession of black monkeys round the hem and up the fronts.

". . . Why! Why! Why is the middle-class so stodgy—so utterly without a sense of humour! My dear, it's only by a fluke that I am here at all—Norman being the protective fluke. For my darling monkeys so upset the train that it rose to a man and simply ate me with its eyes. Didn't laugh—wasn't amused—that I should have loved. No, just stared—and bored me through and through."

"But the cream of it was," said Norman, pressing a large tortoiseshell-rimmed monocle into his eye, "you don't mind me telling this, Face, do you?" (In their home and among their friends they called each other Face and Mug.) "The cream of it was when she, being full fed, turned to the woman beside her and said: 'Haven't you ever seen a monkey before?'"

"Oh, yes!" Mrs. Norman Knight joined in the laughter. "Wasn't that too absolutely creamy?"

And a funnier thing still was that now her coat was off she did look like a very intelligent monkey—who had even made that yellow silk dress out of scraped banana skins. And her amber ear-rings; they were like little dangling nuts.

"This is a sad, sad fall!" said Mug, pausing in front of Little B's perambulator. "When the perambulator comes into the hall—" and he waved the rest of the quotation away.

The bell rang. It was lean, pale Eddie Warren (as usual) in a state of acute distress.

"It *is* the right house, *isn't* it?" he pleaded.

"Oh, I think so—I hope so," said Bertha brightly.

"I have had such a *dreadful* experience with a taxi-man; he was *most* sinister. I couldn't get him to *stop*. The *more* I knocked and called the *faster* he went. And *in* the moonlight this *bizarre* figure with the *flattened* head *crouching* over the *lit-tle* wheel. . . ."

He shuddered, taking off an immense white silk scarf. Bertha noticed that his socks were white, too—most charming.

"But how dreadful!" she cried.

"Yes, it really was," said Eddie, following her into the drawing-room. "I saw myself *driving* through Eternity in a *timeless* taxi."

He knew the Norman Knights. In fact, he was going to write a play for N. K. when the theatre scheme came off.

"Well, Warren, how's the play?" said Norman Knight, dropping his monocle and giving his eye a moment in which to rise to the surface before it was screwed down again.

And Mrs. Norman Knight: "Oh, Mr. Warren, what happy socks!"

"I *am* so glad you like them," said he, staring at his feet. "They seem to have got so *much* whiter since the moon rose." And he turned his lean sorrowful young face to Bertha. "There *is* a moon, you know."

She wanted to cry: "I am sure there is—often—often!"

He really was a most attractive person. But so was Face, crouched before the fire in her banana skins, and so was Mug, smoking a cigarette and saying as he flicked the ash: "Why doth the bridegroom tarry?"

"There he is, now."

Bang went the front door open and shut. Harry shouted: "Hullo, you people. Down in five minutes." And they heard him swarm up the stairs. Bertha couldn't help smiling; she knew how he loved doing things at high pressure. What, after all, did an extra five minutes matter? But he would pretend to himself that they mattered beyond measure. And then he would make a great point of coming into the drawing-room, extravagantly cool and collected.

Harry had such a zest for life. Oh, how she appreciated it in him. And his passion for fighting—for seeking in everything that came up against him another test of his power and of his courage—that, too, she understood. Even when it made him just occasionally, to other people, who didn't know him well, a little ridiculous perhaps. . . . For there were moments when he rushed into battle where no battle was. . . . She talked and laughed and positively forgot until he had come in (just as she had imagined) that Pearl Fulton had not turned up.

"I wonder if Miss Fulton has forgotten?"

"I expect so," said Harry. "Is she on the 'phone?"

"Ah! There's a taxi, now." And Bertha smiled with that little air of proprietorship that she always assumed while her women finds were new and mysterious. "She lives in taxis."

"She'll run to fat if she does," said Harry coolly, ringing the bell for dinner. "Frightful danger for blond women."

"Harry—don't," warned Bertha, laughing up at him.

Came another tiny moment, while they waited, laughing and talking, just a trifle too much at their ease, a trifle too unaware. And then Miss Fulton, all in silver, with a silver fillet binding her pale blond hair, came in smiling, her head a little on one side.

"Am I late?"

"No, not at all," said Bertha. "Come along." And she took her arm and they moved into the dining-room.

What was there in the touch of that cool arm that could fan—fan—start blazing—blazing—the fire of bliss that Bertha did not know what to do with?

Miss Fulton did not look at her; but then she seldom did look at people directly. Her heavy eyelids lay upon her eyes and the strange half smile came and went upon her lips as though she lived by listening rather than seeing. But Bertha knew, suddenly, as if the longest, most intimate look had passed between them—as if they had said to each other: "You too?"—that Pearl Fulton, stirring the beautiful red soup in the grey plate, was feeling just what she was feeling.

And the others? Face and Mug, Eddie and Harry, their spoons rising and falling—dabbing their lips with their napkins, crumbling bread, fiddling with the forks and glasses and talking.

"I met her at the Alpha show—the weirdest little person. She'd not only cut off her hair, but she seemed to have taken a dreadfully good snip off her legs and arms and her neck and her poor little nose as well."

"Isn't she very *liée* with Michael Oat?"

"The man who wrote *Love in False Teeth*?"

"He wants to write a play for me. One act. One man. Decides to commit suicide. Gives all the reasons why he should and why he shouldn't. And just as he has made up his mind either to do it or not to do it—curtain. Not half a bad idea."

"What's he going to call it—'Stomach Trouble'?"

"I *think* I've come across the *same* idea in a lit-tle French review, *quite* unknown in England."

No, they didn't share it. They were dears—dears—and she loved having them there, at her table, and giving them delicious food and wine. In fact, she longed to tell them how delightful they were, and what a decorative group they made, how they seemed to set one another off and how they reminded her of a play by Tchekof!

Harry was enjoying his dinner. It was part of his—well, not his nature, exactly, and certainly not his pose—his—something or other—to talk about food and to glory in his "shameless passion for the white flesh of the lobster" and "the green of pistachio ices—green and cold like the eyelids of Egyptian dancers."

When he looked up at her and said: "Bertha, this is a very admirable *soufflé!*" she almost could have wept with child-like pleasure.

Oh, why did she feel so tender towards the whole world tonight? Everything was good—was right. All that happened seemed to fill again her brimming cup of bliss.

And still, in the back of her mind, there was the pear tree. It would be silver now, in the light of poor dear Eddie's moon, silver as Miss Fulton, who sat there turning a tangerine in her slender fingers that were so pale a light seemed to come from them.

What she simply couldn't make out—what was miraculous—was how she should have guessed Miss Fulton's mood so exactly and so instantly. For she never doubted for a moment that she was right, and yet what had she to go on? Less than nothing.

"I believe this does happen very, very rarely between women. Never between men," thought Bertha. "But while I am making the coffee in the drawing-room perhaps she will 'give a sign.'"

What she meant by that she did not know, and what would happen after that she could not imagine.

While she thought like this she saw herself talking and laughing. She had to talk because of her desire to laugh.

"I must laugh or die."

But when she noticed Face's funny little habit of tucking something down the front of her bodice—as if she kept a tiny, secret hoard of nuts there, too—Bertha had to dig her nails into her hands—so as not to laugh too much.

It was over at last. And: "Come and see my new coffee machine," said Bertha.

"We only have a new coffee machine once a fortnight," said Harry. Face took her arm this time; Miss Fulton bent her head and followed after.

The fire had died down in the drawing-room to a red, flickering "nest of baby phoenixes," said Face.

"Don't turn up the light for a moment. It is so lovely." And down she crouched by the fire again. She was always cold . . . "without her little red flannel jacket, of course," thought Bertha.

At that moment Miss Fulton "gave the sign."

"Have you a garden?" said the cool, sleepy voice.

This was so exquisite on her part that all Bertha could do was to obey. She crossed the room, pulled the curtains apart, and opened those long windows.

"There!" she breathed.

And the two women stood side by side looking at the slender, flowering tree. Although it was so still it seemed, like the flame of a candle, to stretch up, to point, to quiver in the bright air, to grow taller and taller as they gazed—almost to touch the rim of the round, silver moon.

How long did they stand there? Both, as it were, caught in that circle of unearthly light, understanding each other perfectly, creatures of another world, and wondering what they were to do in this one with all this blissful treasure that burned in their bosoms and dropped, in silver flowers, from their hair and hands?

For ever—for a moment? And did Miss Fulton murmur: "Yes. Just *that*." Or did Bertha dream it?

Then the light was snapped on and Face made the coffee and Harry said: "My dear Mrs. Knight, don't ask me about my baby. I never see her. I shan't feel the slightest interest in her until she has a lover," and Mug took his eye out of the conservatory for a moment and then put it under glass again and Eddie Warren drank his coffee and set down the cup with a face of anguish as though he had drunk and seen the spider.

"What I want to do is to give the young men a show. I believe London is simply teeming with first-chop, unwritten plays. What I want to say to 'em is: 'Here's the theatre. Fire ahead.'"

"You know, my dear, I am going to decorate a room for the Jacob Nathans. Oh, I am so tempted to do a fried-fish scheme, with the backs of the chairs shaped like frying pans and lovely chip potatoes embroidered all over the curtains."

"The trouble with our young writing men is that they are still too romantic. You can't put out to sea without being seasick and wanting a basin. Well, why won't they have the courage of those basins?"

"A *dreadful* poem about a *girl* who was *violated* by a beggar *without* a nose in a little wood. . . ."

Miss Fulton sank into the lowest, deepest chair and Harry handed round the cigarettes.

From the way he stood in front of her shaking the silver box and saying abruptly: "Egyptian? Turkish? Virginian? They're all mixed up," Bertha realized that she not only bored him; he really disliked her. And she decided from the way Miss Fulton said: "No, thank you, I won't smoke," that she felt it, too, and was hurt.

"Oh, Harry, don't dislike her. You are quite wrong about her. She's wonderful, wonderful. And, besides, how can you feel so differently about someone who means so much to me. I shall try to tell you when we are in bed to-night what has been happening. What she and I have shared."

At those last words something strange and almost terrifying darted into Bertha's mind. And this something blind and smiling whispered to her: "Soon these people will go. The house will be quiet—quiet. The lights will be out. And you and he will be alone together in the dark room—the warm bed. . . ."

She jumped up from her chair and ran over to the piano.

"What a pity someone does not play!" she cried. "What a pity somebody does not play."

For the first time in her life Bertha Young desired her husband.

Oh, she'd loved him—she'd been in love with him, of course, in every other way, but just not in that way. And, equally, of course, she'd understood that he was different. They'd discussed it so often. It had worried her dreadfully at first to find that she was so cold, but after a time it had not seemed to matter. They were so frank with each other—such good pals. That was the best of being modern.

But now—ardently! ardently! The word ached in her ardent body! Was this what that feeling of bliss had been leading up to? But then then—

"My dear," said Mrs. Norman Knight, "you know our shame. We are the victims of time and train. We live in Hampstead. It's been so nice."

"I'll come with you into the hall," said Bertha. "I loved having you. But you must not miss the last train. That's so awful, isn't it?"

"Have a whisky, Knight, before you go?" called Harry.

"No, thanks, old chap."

Bertha squeezed his hand for that as she shook it.

"Good night, good-bye," she cried from the top step, feeling that this self of hers was taking leave of them for ever.

When she got back into the drawing-room the others were on the move.

". . . Then you can come part of the way in my taxi."

"I shall be so thankful not to have to face another drive alone after my dreadful experience."

"You can get a taxi at the rank just at the end of the street. You won't have to walk more than a few yards."

"That's a comfort. I'll go and put on my coat."

Miss Fulton moved towards the hall and Bertha was following when Harry almost pushed past.

"Let me help you."

Bertha knew that he was repenting his rudeness—she let him go. What a boy he was in some ways—so impulsive—so—simple.

And Eddie and she were left by the fire.

"I wonder if you have seen Bilks' new poem called Table d'Hôte," said Eddie softly. "It's so wonderful. In the last Anthology. Have you got a copy? I'd so like to show it to you. It begins with an incredibly beautiful line: 'Why Must it Always be Tomato Soup?' "

"Yes," said Bertha. And she moved noiselessly to a table opposite the drawing-room door and Eddie glided noiselessly after her. She picked up the little book and gave it to him; they had not made a sound.

While he looked it up she turned her head towards the hall. And she saw . . . Harry with Miss Fulton's coat in his arms and Miss Fulton with her back turned to him and her head bent. He tossed the coat away, put his hands on her shoulders and turned her violently to him. His lips said: "I adore you," and Miss Fulton laid her moonbeam fingers on his cheeks and smiled her sleepy smile. Harry's nostrils quivered; his lips curled back in a hideous grin while he whispered: "To-morrow," and with her eyelids Miss Fulton said: "Yes."

"Here it is," said Eddie. "'Why Must it Always be Tomato Soup?' It's so deeply true, don't you feel? Tomato soup is so dreadfully eternal."

"If you prefer," said Harry's voice, very loud, from the hall, "I can phone you a cab to come to the door."

"Oh, no. It's not necessary," said Miss Fulton, and she came up to Bertha and gave her the slender fingers to hold.

"Good-bye. Thank you so much."

"Good-bye," said Bertha.

Miss Fulton held her hand a moment longer.

"Your lovely pear tree!" she murmured.

And then she was gone, with Eddie following, like the black cat following the grey cat.

"I'll shut up shop," said Harry, extravagantly cool and collected.

"Your lovely pear tree—pear tree—pear tree!"

Bertha simply ran over to the long windows.

"Oh, what is going to happen now?" she cried.

But the pear tree was as lovely as ever and as full of flower and as still.

(1920)

KATHERINE ANNE PORTER
[1890–1980]

The Jilting of Granny Weatherall

She flicked her wrist neatly out of Doctor Harry's pudgy careful fingers and pulled the sheet up to her chin. The brat ought to be in knee breeches. Doctoring around the country with spectacles on his nose! "Get along now, take your schoolbooks and go. There's nothing wrong with me."

Doctor Harry spread a warm paw like a cushion on her forehead where the forked green vein danced and made her eyelids twitch. "Now, now, be a good girl, and we'll have you up in no time."

"That's no way to speak to a woman nearly eighty years old just because she's down. I'd have you respect your elders, young man."

"Well, Missy, excuse me." Doctor Harry patted her cheek. "But I've got to warn you, haven't I? You're a marvel, but you must be careful or you're going to be good and sorry."

"Don't tell me what I'm going to be. I'm on my feet now, morally speaking. It's Cornelia. I had to go to bed to get rid of her."

Her bones felt loose, and floated around in her skin, and Doctor Harry floated like a balloon around the foot of the bed. He floated and pulled down his waistcoat and swung his glasses on a cord. "Well, stay where you are, it certainly can't hurt you."

"Get along and doctor your sick," said Granny Weatherall. "Leave a well woman alone. I'll call for you when I want you. . . . Where were you forty years ago when I pulled through milkleg and double pneumonia? You weren't even born. Don't let Cornelia lead you on," she shouted, because Doctor Harry appeared to float up to the ceiling and out. "I pay my own bills, and I don't throw my money away on nonsense!"

She meant to wave goodby, but it was too much trouble. Her eyes closed of themselves, it was like a dark curtain drawn around the bed. The pillow rose and floated under her, pleasant as a hammock in a light wind. She listened to the leaves rustling outside the window. No, somebody was swishing newspapers: no, Cornelia and Doctor Harry were whispering together. She leaped broad awake, thinking they whispered in her ear.

"She was never like this, *never* like this!" "Well, what can we expect?" "Yes, eighty years old. . . ."

Well, and what if she was? She still had ears. It was like Cornelia to whisper around doors. She always kept things secret in such a public way. She was always being tactful and kind. Cornelia was dutiful; that was the trouble with her. Dutiful and good: "So good and dutiful," said Granny, "that I'd like to spank her." She saw herself spanking Cornelia and making a fine job of it.

"What'd you say, Mother?"

Granny felt her face tying up in hard knots.

"Can't a body think, I'd like to know?"

"I thought you might want something."

"I do. I want a lot of things. First off, go away and don't whisper."

She lay and drowsed, hoping in her sleep that the children would keep out and let her rest a minute. It had been a long day. Not that she was tired. It was always pleasant to snatch a minute now and then. There was always so much to be done, let me see: tomorrow.

Tomorrow was far away and there was nothing to trouble about. Things were finished somehow when the time came; thank God there was always a little margin over for peace: then a person could spread out the plan of life and tuck in the edges orderly. It was good to have everything clean and folded away, with the hair brushes and tonic bottles sitting straight on the white embroidered linen: the day started without fuss and the pantry shelves laid out with rows of jelly glasses and brown jugs and white stonechina jars with blue whirligigs and words painted on them: coffee, tea, sugar, ginger, cinnamon, allspice: and the bronze clock with the lion on top nicely dusted off. The dust that lion could collect in twenty-four hours! The box in the attic with all those letters tied up, well, she'd have to go through that tomorrow. All those letters—George's letters and John's letters and her letters to them both—lying around for the children to find afterward made her uneasy. Yes, that would be tomorrow's business. No use to let them know how silly she had been once.

While she was rummaging around she found death in her mind and it felt clammy and unfamiliar. She had spent so much time preparing for death there was no need for bringing it up again. Let it take care of itself now. When she was sixty she had felt very old, finished, and went around making farewell trips to see her children and grandchildren, with a secret in her mind: This is the very last of your mother, children! Then she made her will and came down with a long fever. That was all just a notion like a lot of other things, but it was lucky too, for she had once and for all got over the idea of dying for a long time. Now she couldn't be worried. She hoped she had better sense now. Her father had lived to be one hundred and two years old and had drunk a noggin of strong hot toddy on his last birthday. He told the reporters it was his daily habit, and he owed his long life to that. He had made quite a scandal and was very pleased about it. She believed she'd just plague Cornelia a little.

"Cornelia! Cornelia!" No footsteps, but a sudden hand on her cheek. "Bless you, where have you been?"

"Here, Mother."

"Well, Cornelia, I want a noggin of hot toddy."

"Are you cold, darling?"

"I'm chilly, Cornelia. Lying in bed stops the circulation. I must have told you that a thousand times."

Well, she could just hear Cornelia telling her husband that Mother was getting a little childish and they'd have to humor her. The thing that most annoyed her was that Cornelia thought she was deaf, dumb, and blind. Little hasty glances and tiny gestures tossed around her and over her head saying, "Don't cross her, let her have her way, she's eighty years old," and she sitting there as if she lived in a thin glass cage. Sometimes Granny almost made up her mind to pack up and move back to her own house where nobody could remind her every minute that she was old. Wait, wait, Cornelia, till your own children whisper behind your back!

In her day she had kept a better house and had got more work done. She wasn't too old yet for Lydia to be driving eighty miles for advice when one of the children jumped the track, and Jimmy still dropped in and talked things over: "Now, Mammy, you've a good business head, I want to know what you think of this? . . ." Old. Cornelia couldn't change the furniture around without asking. Little things, little things! They had been so sweet when they were little. Granny wished the old days were back again with the children young and everything to be done over. It had been a hard pull, but not too much for her. When she thought of all the food she had cooked, and all the clothes she had cut and sewed, and all the gardens she had made—well, the children showed it. There they were, made out of her, and they couldn't get away from that. Sometimes she wanted to see John again and point to them and say, Well, I didn't do so badly, did I? But that would have to wait. That was for tomorrow. She used to think of him as a man, but now all the children were older than their father, and he would be a child beside her if she saw him now. It seemed strange and there was something wrong in the idea. Why, he couldn't possibly recognize her. She had fenced in a hundred acres once, digging the postholes herself and clamping the wires with just a Negro boy to help. That changed a woman. John would be looking for a young woman with the peaked Spanish comb in her hair and the painted fan. Digging postholes changed a woman. Riding country roads in the winter when women had their babies was another thing: sitting up nights with sick horses and sick Negroes and sick children and hardly ever losing one. John, I hardly ever lost one of them! John would see that in a minute, that would be something he could understand, she wouldn't have to explain anything!

It made her feel like rolling up her sleeves and putting the whole place to rights again. No matter if Cornelia was determined to be everywhere at once, there were a great many things left undone on this place. She would start tomorrow and do them. It was good to be strong enough for everything, even if all you made melted and changed and slipped under your hands, so that by the time you finished you almost forgot what you were working for. What was it I set out to do? she asked herself intently, but she could not remember. A fog rose over the valley, she saw it marching across the creek swallowing the trees and moving up the hill like an army of ghosts. Soon it would be at the near edge of the orchard, and then it was time to go in and light the lamps. Come in, children, don't stay out in the night air.

Lighting the lamps had been beautiful. The children huddled up to her and breathed like little calves waiting at the bars in the twilight. Their eyes followed the match and watched the flame rise and settle in a blue curve, then they moved away from her. The lamp was lit, they didn't have to be scared and hang on to mother any more. Never, never, never more. God, for all my life I thank Thee. Without Thee, my God, I could never have done it. Hail, Mary, full of grace.

I want you to pick all the fruit this year and see that nothing is wasted. There's always someone who can use it. Don't let good things rot for want of using. You waste life when you waste good food. Don't let things get lost. It's bitter to lose things. Now, don't let me get to thinking, not when I am tired and taking a little nap before supper. . . .

The pillow rose about her shoulders and pressed against her heart and the memory was being squeezed out of it: oh, push down the pillow, somebody: it would smother her if she tried to hold it. Such a fresh breeze blowing and such a green day with no threats in it. But he had not come, just the same. What does a woman do when she has put on the white veil and set out the white cake for a man and he doesn't come? She tried to remember. No, I swear he never harmed me but in that. He never harmed me but in that . . . and what if he did? There was the day, the day, but a whirl of dark smoke rose and covered it, crept up and over into the bright field where everything was planted so carefully in orderly rows. That was hell, she knew hell when she saw it. For sixty years she had prayed against remembering him and against losing her soul in the deep pit of hell, and now the two things were mingled in one and the thought of him was a smoky cloud from hell that moved and crept in her head when she had just got rid of Doctor Harry and was trying to rest a minute. Wounded vanity, Ellen, said a sharp voice in the top of her mind. Don't let your wounded vanity get the upper hand of you. Plenty of girls get jilted. You were jilted, weren't you? Then stand up to it. Her eyelids wavered and let in streamers of blue-gray light like tissue paper over her eyes. She must get up and pull the shades down or she'd never sleep. She was in bed again and the shades were not down. How could that happen? Better turn over, hide from the light, sleeping in the light gave you nightmares. "Mother, how do you feel now?" and a stinging wetness on her forehead. But I don't like having my face washed in cold water!

Hapsy? George? Lydia? Jimmy? No, Cornelia, and her features were swollen and full of little puddles. "They're coming, darling, they'll all be here soon." Go wash your face, child, you look funny.

Instead of obeying, Cornelia knelt down and put her head on the pillow. She seemed to be talking but there was no sound. "Well, are you tongue-tied? Whose birthday is it? Are you going to give a party?"

Cornelia's mouth moved urgently in strange shapes. "Don't do that, you bother me, daughter."

"Oh, no, Mother. Oh, no. . . ."

Nonsense. It was strange about children. They disputed your every word. "No what, Cornelia?"

"Here's Doctor Harry."

"I won't see that boy again. He just left five minutes ago."

"That was this morning, Mother. It's night now. Here's the nurse."

"This is Doctor Harry, Mrs. Weatherall. I never saw you look so young and happy!"

"Ah, I'll never be young again—but I'd be happy if they'd let me lie in peace and get rested."

She thought she spoke up loudly, but no one answered. A warm weight on her forehead, a warm bracelet on her wrist, and a breeze went on whispering, trying to tell her something. A shuffle of leaves in the everlasting hand of God, He blew on them and they danced and rattled. "Mother, don't mind, we're going to give you a little hypodermic." "Look here, daughter, how do ants get in this bed? I saw sugar ants yesterday." Did you send for Hapsy too?

It was Hapsy she really wanted. She had to go a long way back through a great many rooms to find Hapsy standing with a baby on her arm. She seemed to herself to be Hapsy also, and the baby on Hapsy's arm was Hapsy and himself and herself, all at once, and there was no surprise in the meeting. Then Hapsy melted from within and turned flimsy as gray gauze and the baby was a gauzy shadow, and Hapsy came up close and said, "I thought you'd never come," and looked at her very searchingly and said, "You haven't changed a bit!" They leaned forward to kiss, when Cornelia began whispering from a long way off, "Oh, is there anything you want to tell me? Is there anything I can do for you?"

Yes, she had changed her mind after sixty years and she would like to see George. I want you to find George. Find him and be sure to tell him I forgot him. I want him to know I had my husband just the same and my children and my house like any other woman. A good house too and a good husband that I loved and fine children out of him. Better than I hoped for even. Tell him I was given back everything he took away and more. Oh, no, oh, God, no, there was something else besides the house and the man and the children. Oh, surely they were not all? What was it? Something not given back. . . . Her breath crowded down under her ribs and grew into a monstrous frightening shape with cutting edges; it bored up into her head, and the agony was unbelievable: Yes, John, get the Doctor now, no more talk, my time has come.

When this one was born it should be the last. The last. It should have been born first, for it was the one she had truly wanted. Everything came in good time. Nothing left out, left over. She was strong, in three days she would be as well as ever. Better. A woman needed milk in her to have her full health.

"Mother, do you hear me?"

"I've been telling you—"

"Mother, Father Connolly's here."

"I went to Holy Communion only last week. Tell him I'm not so sinful as all that."

"Father just wants to speak to you."

He could speak as much as he pleased. It was like him to drop in and inquire about her soul as if it were a teething baby, and then stay on for a cup of tea and a round of cards and gossip. He always had a funny story of some sort, usually about an Irishman who made his little mistakes and confessed them, and the point lay in some absurd thing he would blurt out in the confessional showing his struggles between native piety and original sin. Granny felt easy about her soul. Cornelia, where are your manners? Give Father Connolly a chair. She had her secret comfortable understanding with a few favorite saints who cleared a straight road to God for her. All as surely signed and sealed as the papers for the new Forty Acres. Forever . . . heirs and assigns forever. Since the day the wedding cake was not cut, but thrown out and wasted. The whole bottom dropped out of the world, and there she was blind and sweating with nothing under her feet and the walls falling away. His hand had caught her under the breast, she had not fallen, there was the freshly polished floor with the green rug on it, just as before. He had cursed like a sailor's parrot and said, "I'll kill him for you." Don't lay a hand on him, for my sake leave something to God. "Now, Ellen, you must believe what I tell you. . . ."

So there was nothing, nothing to worry about any more, except sometimes in the night one of the children screamed in a nightmare, and they both hustled out shaking and hunting for the matches and calling, "There, wait a minute, here we are!" John, get the doctor now, Hapsy's time has come. But there was Hapsy standing by the bed in a white cap. "Cornelia, tell Hapsy to take off her cap. I can't see her plain."

Her eyes opened very wide and the room stood out like a picture she had seen somewhere. Dark colors with the shadows rising toward the ceiling in long angles. The tall black dresser gleamed with nothing on it but John's picture, enlarged from a little one, with John's eyes very black when they should have been blue. You never saw him, so how do you know how he looked? But the man insisted the copy was perfect, it was very rich and handsome. For a picture, yes, but it's not my husband. The table by the bed had a linen cover and a candle and a crucifix. The light was blue from Cornelia's silk lampshades. No sort of light at all, just frippery. You had to live forty years with kerosene lamps to appreciate honest electricity. She felt very strong and she saw Doctor Harry with a rosy nimbus around him.

"You look like a saint, Doctor Harry, and I vow that's as near as you'll ever come to it."

"She's saying something."

"I heard you, Cornelia. What's all this carrying-on?"

"Father Connolly's saying—"

Cornelia's voice staggered and bumped like a cart in a bad road. It rounded corners and turned back again and arrived nowhere. Granny stepped up in the cart very lightly and reached for the reins, but a man sat beside her and she knew him by his hands, driving the cart. She did not look in his face, for she knew without seeing, but looked instead down the road where the trees leaned over and bowed to each other and a thousand birds were singing a Mass. She felt like singing too, but she put her hand in the bosom of her dress and pulled out a rosary, and Father Connolly murmured Latin in a very solemn voice and tickled her feet. My God, will you stop that nonsense? I'm a married woman. What if he did run away and leave me to face the priest by myself? I found another a whole world better. I wouldn't have exchanged my husband for anybody except St. Michael himself, and you may tell him that for me with a thank you in the bargain.

Light flashed on her closed eyelids, and a deep roaring shook her. Cornelia, is that lightning? I hear thunder. There's going to be a storm. Close all the windows. Call the children in. . . . "Mother, here we are, all of us." "Is that you, Hapsy?" "Oh, no, I'm Lydia. We drove as fast as we could." Their faces drifted above her, drifted away. The rosary fell out of her hands and Lydia put it back. Jimmy tried to help, their hands fumbled together, and Granny closed two fingers around Jimmy's thumb. Beads wouldn't do; it must be something alive. She was so amazed her thoughts ran round and round. So, my dear Lord, this is my death and I wasn't even thinking about it. My children have come to see me die. But I can't, it's not time. Oh, I always hated surprises. I wanted to give Cornelia the amethyst set—Cornelia, you're to have the amethyst set, but Hapsy's to wear it when she wants, and, Doctor Harry, do shut up. Nobody sent for you. Oh, my dear Lord, do wait a minute. I meant to do something about the Forty Acres, Jimmy doesn't need it and Lydia will later on, with that worthless husband of hers. I meant to finish the altar cloth and send six bottles of wine to Sister Borgia for her dyspepsia. I want to send six bottles of wine to Sister Borgia, Father Connolly, now don't let me forget.

Cornelia's voice made short turns and tilted over and crashed. "Oh, Mother, oh, Mother, oh, Mother. . . ."

"I'm not going, Cornelia. I'm taken by surprise. I can't go."

You'll see Hapsy again. What about her? "I thought you'd never come." Granny made a long journey outward, looking for Hapsy. What if I don't find her? What then? Her heart sank down and down, there was no bottom to death, she couldn't come to the end of it. The blue light from Cornelia's lampshade drew into a tiny point in the center of her brain, it flickered and winked like an eye, quietly it fluttered and dwindled. Granny lay curled down within herself, amazed and watchful, staring at the point of light that was herself; her body was now only a deeper mass of shadow in an endless darkness and this darkness would curl around the light and swallow it up. God, give a sign!

For the second time there was no sign. Again no bridegroom and the priest in the house. She could not remember any other sorrow because this grief wiped them all away. Oh, no, there's nothing more cruel than this—I'll never forgive it. She stretched herself with a deep breath and blew out the light.

(1930)

ERNEST HEMINGWAY

[1898–1961]

The Short Happy Life of Francis Macomber

It was now lunch time and they were all sitting under the double green fly of the dining tent pretending that nothing had happened.

"Will you have lime juice or lemon squash?" Macomber asked.

"I'll have a gimlet," Robert Wilson told him.

"I'll have a gimlet too. I need something," Macomber's wife said.

"I suppose it's the thing to do," Macomber agreed. "Tell him to make three gimlets."

The mess boy had started them already, lifting the bottles out of the canvas cooling bags that sweated wet in the wind that blew through the trees that shaded the tents.

"What had I ought to give them?" Macomber asked.

"A quid would be plenty," Wilson told him. "You don't want to spoil them."

"Will the headman distribute it?"

"Absolutely."

Francis Macomber had, half an hour before, been carried to his tent from the edge of the camp in triumph on the arms and shoulders of the cook, the personal boys, the skinner and the porters. The gun-bearers had taken no part in the demonstration. When the native boys put him down at the door of his tent, he had shaken all their hands, received their congratulations, and then gone into the tent and sat on the bed until his wife came in. She did not speak to him when she came in and he left the tent at once to wash his face and hands in the portable wash basin outside and go over to the dining tent to sit in a comfortable canvas chair in the breeze and the shade.

"You've got your lion," Robert Wilson said to him, "and a damned fine one too."

Mrs. Macomber looked at Wilson quickly. She was an extremely handsome and well-kept woman of the beauty and social position which had, five years before, commanded five thousand dollars as the price of endorsing, with photographs, a beauty product which she had never used. She had been married to Francis Macomber for eleven years.

"He is a good lion, isn't he?" Macomber said. His wife looked at him now. She looked at both these men as though she had never seen them before.

One, Wilson, the white hunter, she knew she had never truly seen before. He was about middle height with sandy hair, a stubby mustache, a very red face and extremely cold blue eyes with faint white wrinkles at the corners that grooved merrily when he smiled. He smiled at her now and she looked away from his face at the way his shoulders sloped in the loose tunic he wore with the four big cartridges held in loops where the left breast pocket should have been, at his big brown hands, his old slacks, his very dirty boots and back to his red face again. She noticed where the baked red of his face stopped in a white line that marked the circle left by his Stetson hat that hung now from one of the pegs of the tent pole.

"Well, here's to the lion," Robert Wilson said. He smiled at her again and, not smiling, she looked curiously at her husband.

Francis Macomber was very tall, very well built if you did not mind that length of bone, dark, his hair cropped like an oarsman, rather thin-lipped, and was considered handsome. He was dressed in the same sort of safari clothes that Wilson wore except that his were new, he was thirty-five years old, kept himself very fit, was good at court games, had a number of big-game fishing records, and had just shown himself, very publicly, to be a coward.

"Here's to the lion," he said. "I can't ever thank you for what you did."

Margaret, his wife, looked away from him and back to Wilson.

"Let's not talk about the lion," she said.

Wilson looked over at her without smiling and now she smiled at him.

"It's been a very strange day," she said. "Hadn't you ought to put your hat on even under the canvas at noon? You told me that, you know."

"Might put it on," said Wilson.

"You know you have a very red face, Mr. Wilson," she told him and smiled again.

"Drink," said Wilson.

"I don't think so," she said. "Francis drinks a great deal, but his face is never red."

"It's red today," Macomber tried a joke.

"No," said Margaret. "It's mine that's red today. But Mr. Wilson's is always red."

"Must be racial," said Wilson. "I say, you wouldn't like to drop my beauty as a topic, would you?"

"I've just started on it."

"Let's chuck it," said Wilson.

"Conversation is going to be so difficult," Margaret said.

"Don't be silly, Margot," her husband said.

"No difficulty," Wilson said. "Got a damn fine lion."

Margot looked at them both and they both saw that she was going to cry. Wilson had seen it coming for a long time and he dreaded it. Macomber was past dreading it.

"I wish it hadn't happened. Oh, I wish it hadn't happened," she said and started for her tent. She made no noise of crying but they could see that her shoulders were shaking under the rose-colored, sun-proofed shirt she wore.

"Women upset," said Wilson to the tall man. "Amounts to nothing. Strain on the nerves and one thing'n another."

"No," said Macomber. "I suppose that I rate that for the rest of my life now."

"Nonsense. Let's have a spot of the giant killer," said Wilson. "Forget the whole thing. Nothing to it anyway."

"We might try," said Macomber. "I won't forget what you did for me though."

"Nothing," said Wilson. "All nonsense."

So they sat there in the shade where the camp was pitched under some wide-topped acacia trees with a boulder-strewn cliff behind them, and a stretch of grass that ran to the bank of a boulder-filled stream in front with forest beyond it, and drank their just-cool lime drinks and avoided one another's eyes while the boys set the table for lunch. Wilson could tell that the boys all knew about it now and when he saw Macomber's personal boy looking curiously at his master while he was putting dishes on the table he snapped at him in Swahili. The boy turned away with his face blank.

"What were you telling him?" Macomber asked.

"Nothing. Told him to look alive or I'd see he got about fifteen of the best."

"What's that? Lashes?"

"It's quite illegal," Wilson said. "You're supposed to fine them."

"Do you still have them whipped?"

"Oh, yes. They could raise a row if they chose to complain. But they don't. They prefer it to the fines."

"How strange!" said Macomber.

"Not strange, really," Wilson said. "Which would you rather do? Take a good birching or lose your pay?"

Then he felt embarrassed at asking it and before Macomber could answer he went on, "We all take a beating every day, you know, one way or another."

This was no better. "Good God," he thought. "I am a diplomat, aren't I?"

"Yes, we take a beating," said Macomber, still not looking at him. "I'm awfully sorry about that lion business. It doesn't have to go any further, does it? I mean no one will hear about it, will they?"

"You mean will I tell it at the Mathaiga Club?" Wilson looked at him now coldly. He had not expected this. So he's a bloody four-letter man as well as a bloody coward, he thought. I rather liked him too until today. But how is one to know about an American?

"No," said Wilson. "I'm a professional hunter. We never talk about our clients. You can be quite easy on that. It's supposed to be bad form to ask us not to talk though."

He had decided now that to break would be much easier. He would eat, then, by himself and could read a book with his meals. They would eat by themselves. He would see them through the safari on a very formal basis—what was it the French called it? Distinguished consideration—and it would be a damn sight easier than having to go through this emotional trash. He'd insult him and make a good clean break. Then he could read a book with his meals and he'd still be drinking their whisky. That was the phrase for it when a safari went bad. You ran into another white hunter and you asked, "How is everything going?" and he answered, "Oh, I'm still drinking their whisky," and you knew everything had gone to pot.

"I'm sorry," Macomber said and looked at him with his American face that would stay adolescent until it became middle-aged, and Wilson noted his crew-cropped hair, fine eyes only faintly shifty, good nose, thin lips and handsome jaw. "I'm sorry I didn't realize that. There are lots of things I don't know."

So what could he do, Wilson thought. He was all ready to break it off quickly and neatly and here the beggar was apologizing after he had just insulted him. He made one more attempt. "Don't worry about me talking," he said. "I have a living to make. You know in Africa no woman ever misses her lion and no white man ever bolts."

"I bolted like a rabbit," Macomber said.

Now what in hell were you going to do about a man who talked like that, Wilson wondered.

Wilson looked at Macomber with his flat, blue, machine-gunner's eyes and the other smiled back at him. He had a pleasant smile if you did not notice how his eyes showed when he was hurt.

"Maybe I can fix it up on buffalo," he said. "We're after them next, aren't we?"

"In the morning if you like," Wilson told him. Perhaps he had been wrong. This was certainly the way to take it. You most certainly could not tell a damned thing about an American. He was all for Macomber again. If you could forget the morning. But, of course, you couldn't. The morning had been about as bad as they come.

"Here comes the Memsahib," he said. She was walking over from her tent looking refreshed and cheerful and quite lovely. She had a very perfect oval face, so perfect that you expected her to be stupid. But she wasn't stupid, Wilson thought, no, not stupid.

"How is the beautiful red-faced Mr. Wilson? Are you feeling better, Francis, my pearl?"

"Oh, much," said Macomber.

"I've dropped the whole thing," she said, sitting down at the table. "What importance is there to whether Francis is any good at killing lions? That's not his trade. That's Mr. Wilson's trade. Mr. Wilson is really very impressive killing anything. You do kill anything, don't you?"

"Oh, anything," said Wilson. "Simply anything." They are, he thought, the hardest in the world; the hardest, the cruelest, the most predatory and the most attractive and their men have softened or gone to pieces nervously as they have hardened. Or is it that they pick men they can handle? They can't know that much at the age they marry, he thought. He was grateful that he had gone through his education on American women before now because this was a very attractive one.

"We're going after buff in the morning," he told her.

"I'm coming," she said.

"No, you're not."

"Oh, yes, I am. Mayn't I, Francis?"

"Why not stay in camp?"

"Not for anything," she said. "I wouldn't miss something like today for anything."

When she left, Wilson was thinking, when she went off to cry, she seemed a hell of a fine woman. She seemed to understand, to realize, to be hurt for him and for herself and to know how things really stood. She is away for twenty minutes and now she is back, simply enamelled in that American female cruelty. They are the damnedest women. Really the damnedest.

"We'll put on another show for you tomorrow," Francis Macomber said.

"You're not coming," Wilson said.

"You're very mistaken," she told him. "And I want *so* to see you perform again. You were lovely this morning. That is if blowing things' heads off is lovely."

"Here's the lunch," said Wilson. "You're very merry, aren't you?"

"Why not? I didn't come out here to be dull."

"Well, it hasn't been dull," Wilson said. He could see the boulders in the river and the high bank beyond with the trees and he remembered the morning.

"Oh, no," she said. "It's been charming. And tomorrow. You don't know how I look forward to tomorrow."

"That's eland he's offering you," Wilson said.

"They're the big cowy things that jump like hares, aren't they?"

"I suppose that describes them," Wilson said.

"It's very good meat," Macomber said.

"Didn't you shoot it, Francis?" she asked.

"Yes."

"They're not dangerous, are they?"

"Only if they fall on you," Wilson told her.

"I'm so glad."

"Why not let up on the bitchery just a little, Margot," Macomber said, cutting the eland steak and putting some mashed potato, gravy and carrot on the down-turned fork that tined through the piece of meat.

"I suppose I could," she said, "since you put it so prettily."

"Tonight we'll have champagne for the lion," Wilson said. "It's a bit too hot at noon."

"Oh, the lion," Margot said. "I'd forgotten the lion!"

So, Robert Wilson thought to himself, she *is* giving him a ride, isn't she? Or do you suppose that's her idea of putting up a good show? How should a woman act when she discovers her husband is a bloody coward? She's damn cruel but they're all cruel. They govern, of course, and to govern one has to be cruel sometimes. Still, I've seen enough of their damn terrorism.

"Have some more eland," he said to her politely.

That afternoon, late, Wilson and Macomber went out in the motor car with the native driver and the two gun-bearers. Mrs. Macomber stayed in the camp. It was too hot to go out, she said, and she was going with them in the early morning. As they drove off Wilson saw her standing under the big tree, looking pretty rather than beautiful in her faintly rosy khaki, her dark hair drawn back off her forehead and gathered in a knot low on her neck, her face as fresh, he thought, as though she were in England. She waved to them as the car went off through the swale of high grass and curved around through the trees into the small hills of orchard bush.

In the orchard bush they found a herd of impala, and leaving the car they stalked one old ram with long, wide-spread horns and Macomber killed it with a very creditable shot that knocked the buck down at a good two hundred yards and sent the herd off bounding wildly and leaping over one another's backs in long, leg-drawn-up leaps as unbelievable and as floating as those one makes sometimes in dreams.

"That was a good shot," Wilson said. "They're a small target."

"Is it a worthwhile head?" Macomber asked.

"It's excellent," Wilson told him. "You shoot like that and you'll have no trouble."

"Do you think we'll find buffalo tomorrow?"

"There's a good chance of it. They feed out early in the morning and with luck we may catch them in the open."

"I'd like to clear away that lion business," Macomber said. "It's not very pleasant to have your wife see you do something like that."

I should think it would be even more unpleasant to do it, Wilson thought, wife or no wife, or to talk about it having done it. But he said, "I wouldn't think about that any more. Anyone could be upset by his first lion. That's all over."

But that night after dinner and a whisky and soda by the fire before going to bed, as Francis Macomber lay on his cot with his mosquito bar over him and listened to the night noises, it was not all over. It was neither all over nor was it beginning. It was there exactly as it happened with some parts of it indelibly emphasized and he was miserably ashamed at it. But more than shame he felt cold, hollow fear in him. The fear was still there like a cold slimy hollow in all the emptiness where once his confidence had been and it made him feel sick. It was still there with him now.

It had started the night before when he had wakened and heard the lion roaring somewhere up along the river. It was a deep sound and at the end there were sort of coughing grunts that made him seem just outside the tent, and when Francis Macomber woke in the night to hear it he was afraid. He could hear his wife breathing quietly, asleep. There was no one to tell he was afraid, nor to be afraid with him, and, lying alone, he did not know the Somali proverb that says a brave man is always frightened three times by a lion; when he first sees his track, when he first hears him roar and when he first confronts him. Then while they were eating breakfast by lantern light out in the dining tent, before the sun was up, the lion roared again and Francis thought he was just at the edge of camp.

"Sounds like an old-timer," Robert Wilson said, looking up from his kippers and coffee. "Listen to him cough."

"Is he very close?"

"A mile or so up the stream."

"Will we see him?"

"We'll have a look."

"Does his roaring carry that far? It sounds as though he were right in camp."

"Carries a hell of a long way," said Robert Wilson. "It's strange the way it carries. Hope he's a shootable cat. The boys said there was a very big one about here."

"If I get a shot, where should I hit him," Macomber asked, "to stop him?"

"In the shoulders," Wilson said. "In the neck if you can make it. Shoot for bone. Break him down."

"I hope I can place it properly," Macomber said.

"You shoot very well," Wilson told him. "Take your time. Make sure of him. The first one in is the one that counts."

"What range will it be?"

"Can't tell. Lion has something to say about that. Won't shoot unless it's close enough so you can make sure."

"At under a hundred yards?" Macomber asked.

Wilson looked at him quickly.

"Hundred's about right. Might have to take him a bit under. Shouldn't chance a shot at much over that. A hundred's a decent range. You can hit him wherever you want at that. Here comes the Memsahib."

"Good morning," she said. "Are we going after that lion?"

"As soon as you deal with your breakfast," Wilson said. "How are you feeling?"

"Marvellous," she said. "I'm very excited."

"I'll just go and see that everything is ready," Wilson went off. As he left the lion roared again.

"Noisy beggar," Wilson said. "We'll put a stop to that."

"What's the matter, Francis?" his wife asked him.

"Nothing," Macomber said.

"Yes, there is," she said. "What are you upset about?"

"Nothing," he said.

"Tell me," she looked at him. "Don't you feel well?"

"It's that damned roaring," he said. "It's been going on all night, you know."

"Why didn't you wake me," she said. "I'd love to have heard it."

"I've got to kill the damned thing," Macomber said, miserably.

"Well, that's what you're out here for, isn't it?"

"Yes. But I'm nervous. Hearing the thing roar gets on my nerves."

"Well then, as Wilson said, kill him and stop his roaring."

"Yes, darling," said Francis Macomber. "It sounds easy, doesn't it?"

"You're not afraid, are you?"

"Of course not. But I'm nervous from hearing him roar all night."

"You'll kill him marvellously," she said. "I know you will. I'm awfully anxious to see it."

"Finish your breakfast and we'll be starting."

"It's not light yet," she said. "This is a ridiculous hour."

Just then the lion roared in a deep-chested moaning, suddenly guttural, ascending vibration that seemed to shake the air and ended in a sigh and a heavy, deep-chested grunt.

"He sounds almost here," Macomber's wife said.

"My God," said Macomber. "I hate that damned noise."

"It's very impressive."

"Impressive. It's frightful."

Robert Wilson came up then carrying his short, ugly, shockingly big-bored .505 Gibbs and grinning.

"Come on," he said. "Your gun-bearer has your Springfield and the big gun. Everything's in the car. Have you solids?"

"Yes."

"I'm ready," Mrs. Macomber said.

"Must make him stop that racket," Wilson said. "You get in front. The Memsahib can sit back here with me."

They climbed into the motor car and, in the gray first daylight, moved off up the river through the trees. Macomber opened the breech of his rifle and saw he had metal-cased bullets, shut the bolt and put the rifle on safety. He saw his hand was trembling. He felt in his pocket for more cartridges and moved his fingers over the cartridges in the loops of his tunic front. He turned back to where Wilson sat in the rear seat of the doorless, box-bodied motor car beside his wife, them both grinning with excitement, and Wilson leaned forward and whispered,

"See the birds dropping. Means the old boy has left his kill."

On the far bank of the stream Macomber could see, above the trees, vultures circling and plummeting down.

"Chances are he'll come to drink along here," Wilson whispered. "Before he goes to lay up. Keep an eye out."

They were driving slowly along the high bank of the stream which here cut deeply to its boulder-filled bed, and they wound in and out through big trees as they drove. Macomber was watching the opposite bank when he felt Wilson take hold of his arm. The car stopped.

"There he is," he heard the whisper. "Ahead and to the right. Get out and take him. He's a marvellous lion."

Macomber saw the lion now. He was standing almost broadside, his great head up and turned toward them. The early morning breeze that blew toward them was just stirring his dark mane, and the lion looked huge, silhouetted on the rise of bank in the gray morning light, his shoulders heavy, his barrel of a body bulking smoothly.

"How far is he?" asked Macomber, raising his rifle.

"About seventy-five. Get out and take him."

"Why not shoot from where I am?"

"You don't shoot them from cars," he heard Wilson saying in his ear. "Get out. He's not going to stay there all day."

Macomber stepped out of the curved opening at the side of the front seat, onto the step and down onto the ground. The lion still stood looking majestically and coolly toward this object that his eyes only showed in silhouette, bulking like some super-rhino. There was no man smell carried toward him and he watched the object, moving his great head a little from side to side. Then watching the object, not afraid, but hesitating before going down the bank to drink with such a thing opposite him, he saw a man figure detach itself from it and he turned his heavy head and swung away toward the cover of the trees as he heard a cracking crash and felt the slam of a .30–06 220-grain solid bullet that bit his flank and ripped in sudden hot scalding nausea through his stomach. He trotted, heavy, big-footed, swinging wounded full-bellied, through the trees toward the tall grass and cover, and the crash came again to go past him ripping the air apart. Then it crashed again and he felt the blow as it hit his lower ribs and ripped on through, blood sudden hot and frothy in his mouth, and he galloped toward the high grass where he could crouch and not be seen and make them bring the crashing thing close enough so he could make a rush and get the man that held it.

Macomber had not thought how the lion felt as he got out of the car. He only knew his hands were shaking and as he walked away from the car it was almost impossible for him to make his legs move. They were stiff in the thighs, but he could feel the muscles fluttering. He raised the rifle, sighted on the junction of the lion's head and shoulders and pulled the trigger. Nothing happened though he pulled until he thought his finger would break. Then he knew he had the safety on and as he lowered the rifle to move the safety over he moved another frozen pace forward, and the lion seeing his silhouette now clear of the silhouette of the car, turned and started off at a trot, and, as Macomber fired, he heard a whunk that meant that the bullet was home; but the lion kept on going. Macomber shot again and everyone saw the bullet throw a spout of dirt beyond the trotting lion. He shot again, remembering to lower his aim, and they all heard the bullet hit, and the lion went into a gallop and was in the tall grass before he had the bolt pushed forward.

Macomber stood there feeling sick at his stomach, his hands that held the Springfield still cocked, shaking, and his wife and Robert Wilson were standing by him. Beside him too were the two gun-bearers chattering in Wakamba.

"I hit him," Macomber said. "I hit him twice."

"You gut-shot him and you hit him somewhere forward," Wilson said without enthusiasm. The gun-bearers looked very grave. They were silent now.

"You may have killed him," Wilson went on. "We'll have to wait a while before we go in to find out."

"What do you mean?"

"Let him get sick before we follow him up."

"Oh," said Macomber.

"He's a hell of a fine lion," Wilson said cheerfully. "He's gotten into a bad place though."

"Why is it bad?"

"Can't see him until you're on him."

"Oh," said Macomber.

"Come on," said Wilson. "The Memsahib can stay here in the car. We'll go to have a look at the blood spoor."

"Stay here, Margot," Macomber said to his wife. His mouth was very dry and it was hard for him to talk.

"Why?" she asked.

"Wilson says to."

"We're going to have a look," Wilson said. "You stay here. You can see even better from here."

"All right."

Wilson spoke in Swahili to the driver. He nodded and said, "Yes, Bwana."

Then they went down the steep bank and across the stream, climbing over and around the boulders and up the other bank, pulling up by some projecting roots, and along it until they found where the lion had been trotting when Macomber first shot. There was dark blood on the short grass that the gun-bearers pointed out with grass stems, and that ran away behind the river bank trees.

"What do we do?" asked Macomber.

"Not much choice," said Wilson. "We can't bring the car over. Bank's too steep. We'll let him stiffen up a bit and then you and I'll go in and have a look for him."

"Can't we set the grass on fire?" Macomber asked.

"Too green."

"Can't we send beaters?"

Wilson looked at him appraisingly. "Of course we can," he said. "But it's just a touch murderous. You see we know the lion's wounded. You can drive an unwounded lion—he'll move on ahead of a noise—but a wounded lion's going to charge. You can't see him until you're right on him. He'll make himself perfectly flat in cover you wouldn't think would hide a hare. You can't very well send boys in there to that sort of a show. Somebody bound to get mauled."

"What about the gun-bearers?"

"Oh, they'll go with us. It's their *shauri*. You see, they signed on for it. They don't look too happy though, do they?"

"I don't want to go in there," said Macomber. It was out before he knew he'd said it.

"Neither do I," said Wilson very cheerily. "Really no choice though." Then, as an afterthought, he glanced at Macomber and saw suddenly how he was trembling and the pitiful look on his face.

"You don't have to go in, of course," he said. "That's what I'm hired for, you know. That's why I'm so expensive."

"You mean you'd go in by yourself? Why not leave him there?"

Robert Wilson, whose entire occupation had been with the lion and the problem he presented, and who had not been thinking about Macomber except to note that he was rather windy, suddenly felt as though he had opened the wrong door in a hotel and seen something shameful.

"What do you mean?"

"Why not just leave him?"

"You mean pretend to ourselves he hasn't been hit?"

"No. Just drop it."

"It isn't done."

"Why not?"

"For one thing, he's certain to be suffering. For another, some one else might run onto him."

"I see."

"But you don't have to have anything to do with it."

"I'd like to," Macomber said. "I'm just scared, you know."

"I'll go ahead when we go in," Wilson said, "with Kongoni tracking. You keep behind me and a little to one side. Chances are we'll hear him growl. If we see him we'll both shoot. Don't worry about anything. I'll keep you backed up. As a matter of fact, you know, perhaps you'd better not go. It might be much better. Why don't you go over and join the Memsahib while I just get it over with?"

"No, I want to go."

"All right," said Wilson. "But don't go in if you don't want to. This is my *shauri* now, you know."

"I want to go," said Macomber.

They sat under a tree and smoked.

"Want to go back and speak to the Memsahib while we're waiting?" Wilson asked.

"No."

"I'll just step back and tell her to be patient."

"Good," said Macomber. He sat there, sweating under his arms, his mouth dry, his stomach hollow feeling, wanting to find courage to tell Wilson to go on and finish off the lion without him. He could not know that Wilson was furious because he had not noticed the state he was in earlier and sent him back to his wife. While he sat there Wilson came up. "I have your big gun," he said. "Take it. We've given him time, I think. Come on."

Macomber took the big gun and Wilson said:

"Keep behind me and about five yards to the right and do exactly as I tell you." Then he spoke in Swahili to the two gun-bearers, who looked the picture of gloom.

"Let's go," he said.

"Could I have a drink of water?" Macomber asked. Wilson spoke to the older gun-bearer, who wore a canteen on his belt, and the man unbuckled it, unscrewed the top and handed it to Macomber, who took it noticing how heavy it seemed and how hairy and shoddy the felt covering was in his hand. He raised it to drink and looked ahead at the high grass with the flat-topped trees behind it. A breeze was blowing toward them and the grass rippled gently in the wind. He looked at the gun-bearer and he could see the gun-bearer was suffering too with fear.

Thirty-five yards into the grass the big lion lay flattened out along the ground. His ears were back and his only movement was a slight twitching up and down of his long, black-tufted tail. He had turned at bay as soon as he had reached this cover and he was sick with the wound through his full belly, and weakening with the wound through his lungs that brought a thin foamy red to his mouth each time he breathed. His flanks were wet and hot and flies were on the little openings the solid bullets had made in his tawny hide, and his big yellow eyes, narrowed with hate, looked straight ahead, only blinking when the pain came as he breathed, and his claws dug in the soft baked earth. All of him, pain, sickness, hatred and all of his remaining strength, was tightening into an absolute concentration for a rush. He could hear the men talking and he waited, gathering all of himself into this preparation for a charge as soon as the men would come into the grass. As he heard their voices his tail stiffened to twitch up and down, and, as they came into the edge of the grass, he made a coughing grunt and charged.

Kongoni, the old gun-bearer, in the lead watching the blood spoor, Wilson watching the grass for any movement, his big gun ready, the second gun-bearer looking ahead and listening, Macomber close to Wilson, his rifle cocked, they had just moved into the grass when Macomber heard the blood-choked coughing grunt, and saw the swishing rush in the grass. The next thing he knew he was running; running wildly, in panic in the open, running toward the stream.

He heard the *ca-ra-wong!* of Wilson's big rifle, and again in a second crashing *carawong!* and turning saw the lion, horrible-looking now, with half his head seeming to be gone, crawling toward Wilson in the edge of the tall grass while the red-faced man worked the bolt on the short ugly rifle and aimed carefully as another blasting *carawong!* came from the muzzle, and the crawling, heavy, yellow bulk of the lion stiffened and the huge, mutilated head slid forward and Macomber, standing by himself in the clearing where he had run, holding a loaded rifle, while two black men and a white man looked back at him in contempt, knew the lion was dead. He came toward Wilson, his tallness all seeming a naked reproach, and Wilson looked at him and said:

"Want to take pictures?"

"No," he said.

That was all any one had said until they reached the motor car. Then Wilson had said:

"Hell of a fine lion. Boys will skin him out. We might as well stay here in the shade."

Macomber's wife had not looked at him nor he at her and he had sat by her in the back seat with Wilson sitting in the front seat. Once he had reached over and taken his wife's hand without looking at her and she had removed her hand from his. Looking across the stream to where the gun-bearers were skinning out the lion he could see that she had been able to see the whole thing. While they sat there his wife had reached forward and put her hand on Wilson's shoulder. He turned and she had leaned forward over the low seat and kissed him on the mouth.

"Oh, I say," said Wilson, going redder than his natural baked color.

"Mr. Robert Wilson," she said. "The beautiful red-faced Mr. Robert Wilson."

Then she sat down beside Macomber again and looked away across the stream to where the lion lay, with uplifted, white-muscled, tendon-marked naked forearms, and white bloating belly, as the black men fleshed away the skin. Finally the gun-bearers brought the skin over, wet and heavy, and climbed in behind with it, rolling it up before they got in, and the motor car started. No one had said anything more until they were back in camp.

That was the story of the lion. Macomber did not know how the lion had felt before he started his rush, nor during it when the unbelievable smash of the .505 with a muzzle velocity of two tons had hit him in the mouth, nor what kept him coming after that, when the second ripping crash had smashed his hind quarters and he had come crawling on toward the crashing, blasting thing that had destroyed him. Wilson knew something about it and only expressed it by saying, "Damned fine lion," but Macomber did not know how Wilson felt about things either. He did not know how his wife felt except that she was through with him.

His wife had been through with him before but it never lasted. He was very wealthy, and would be much wealthier, and he knew she would not leave him ever now. That was one of the few things that he really knew. He knew about that, about motorcycles—that was earliest—about motor cars, about duck-shooting, about fishing, trout, salmon and big-sea, about sex in books, many books, too many books, about all court games, about dogs, not much about horses, about hanging on to his money, about most of the other things his world dealt in, and about his wife not leaving him. His wife had been a great beauty and she was still a great beauty in Africa, but she was not a great enough beauty any more at home to be able to leave him and better herself and she knew it and he knew it. She had missed the chance to leave him and he knew it. If he had been better with women she would probably have started to worry about him getting another new, beautiful wife; but she knew too much about him to worry about him either. Also, he had always had a great tolerance which seemed the nicest thing about him if it were not the most sinister.

All in all they were known as a comparatively happily married couple, one of those whose disruption is often rumored but never occurs, and as the society columnist put it, they were adding more than a spice of *adventure* to their much envied and ever-enduring *Romance* by a *Safari* in what was known as *Darkest Africa* until the Martin Johnsons lighted it on so many silver screens where they were pursuing *Old Simba* the lion, the buffalo, *Tembo* the elephant and as well collecting specimens for the Museum of Natural History. This same columnist had reported them *on the verge* as least three times in the past and they had been. But they always made it up. They had a sound basis of union. Margot was too beautiful for Macomber to divorce her and Macomber had too much money for Margot ever to leave him.

It was now about three o'clock in the morning and Francis Macomber, who had been asleep a little while after he had stopped thinking about the lion, wakened and then slept again, woke suddenly, frightened in a dream of the bloody-headed lion standing over him, and listening while his heart pounded, he realized that his wife was not in the other cot in the tent. He lay awake with that knowledge for two hours.

At the end of that time his wife came into the tent, lifted her mosquito bar and crawled cozily into bed.

"Where have you been?" Macomber asked in the darkness.

"Hello," she said. "Are you awake?"

"Where have you been?"

"I just went out to get a breath of air."

"You did, like hell."

"What do you want me to say, darling?"

"Where have you been?"

"Out to get a breath of air."

"That's a new name for it. You *are* a bitch."

"Well, you're a coward."

"All right," he said. "What of it?"

"Nothing as far as I'm concerned. But please let's not talk, darling, because I'm very sleepy."

"You think that I'll take anything."

"I know you will, sweet."

"Well, I won't."

"Please, darling, let's not talk. I'm so very sleepy."

"There wasn't going to be any of that. You promised there wouldn't be."

"Well, there is now," she said sweetly.

"You said if we made this trip that there would be none of that. You promised."

"Yes, darling. That's the way I meant it to be. But the trip was spoiled yesterday. We don't have to talk about it, do we?"

"You don't wait long when you have an advantage, do you?"

"Please let's not talk. I'm so sleepy, darling."

"I'm going to talk."

"Don't mind me then, because I'm going to sleep." And she did.

At breakfast they were all three at the table before daylight and Francis Macomber found that, of all the many men that he had hated, he hated Robert Wilson the most.

"Sleep well?" Wilson asked in his throaty voice, filling a pipe.

"Did you?"

"Topping," the white hunter told him.

You bastard, thought Macomber, you insolent bastard.

So she woke him when she came in, Wilson thought, looking at them both with his flat, cold eyes. Well, why doesn't he keep his wife where she belongs? What does he think I am, a bloody plaster saint? Let him keep her where she belongs. It's his own fault.

"Do you think we'll find buffalo?" Margot asked, pushing away a dish of apricots.

"Chance of it," Wilson said and smiled at her. "Why don't you stay in camp?"

"Not for anything," she told him.

"Why not order her to stay in camp?" Wilson said to Macomber.

"You order her," said Macomber coldly.

"Let's not have any ordering, nor," turning to Macomber, "any silliness, Francis," Margot said quite pleasantly.

"Are you ready to start?" Macomber asked.

"Any time," Wilson told him. "Do you want the Memsahib to go?"

"Does it make any difference whether I do or not?"

The hell with it, thought Robert Wilson. The utter complete hell with it. So this is what it's going to be like. Well, this is what it's going to be like, then.

"Makes no difference," he said.

"You're sure you wouldn't like to stay in camp with her yourself and let me go out and hunt the buffalo?" Macomber asked.

"Can't do that," said Wilson. "Wouldn't talk rot if I were you."

"I'm not talking rot. I'm disgusted."

"Bad word, disgusted."

"Francis, will you please try to speak sensibly?" his wife said.

"I speak too damned sensibly," Macomber said. "Did you ever eat such filthy food?"

"Something wrong with the food?" asked Wilson quietly.

"No more than with everything else."

"I'd pull yourself together, laddybuck," Wilson said very quietly. "There's a boy waits at table that understands a little English."

"The hell with him."

Wilson stood up and puffing on his pipe strolled away, speaking a few words in Swahili to one of the gun-bearers who was standing waiting for him. Macomber and his wife sat on at the table. He was staring at his coffee cup.

"If you make a scene I'll leave you, darling," Margot said quietly.

"No, you won't."

"You can try it and see."

"You won't leave me."

"No," she said. "I won't leave you and you'll behave yourself."

"Behave myself? That's a way to talk. Behave myself."

"Yes. Behave yourself."

"Why don't *you* try behaving?"

"I've tried it so long. So very long."

"I hate that red-faced swine," Macomber said. "I loathe the sight of him."

"He's really *very* nice."

"Oh, *shut up*," Macomber almost shouted. Just then the car came up and stopped in front of the dining tent and the driver and the two gun-bearers got out. Wilson walked over and looked at the husband and wife sitting there at the table.

"Going shooting?" he asked.

"Yes," said Macomber, standing up. "Yes."

"Better bring a woolly. It will be cool in the car," Wilson said.

"I'll get my leather jacket," Margot said.

"The boy has it," Wilson told her. He climbed into the front with the driver and Francis Macomber and his wife sat, not speaking, in the back seat.

Hope the silly beggar doesn't take a notion to blow the back of my head off, Wilson thought to himself. Women *are* a nuisance on safari.

The car was grinding down to cross the river at a pebbly ford in the gray daylight and then climbed, angling up the steep bank, where Wilson had ordered a way shovelled out the day before so they could reach the parklike wooded rolling country on the far side.

It was a good morning, Wilson thought. There was a heavy dew and as the wheels went through the grass and low bushes he could smell the odor of the crushed fronds. It was an odor like verbena and he liked this early morning smell of the dew, the crushed bracken and the look of the tree trunks showing black through the early morning mist, as the car made its way through the untracked, parklike country. He had put the two in the back seat out of his mind now and was thinking about buffalo. The buffalo that he was after stayed in the daytime in a thick swamp where it was impossible to get a shot, but in the night they fed out into an open stretch of country and if he could come between them and their swamp with the car, Macomber would have a good chance at them in the open. He did not want to hunt buff with Macomber in thick cover. He did not want to hunt buff or anything else with Macomber at all, but he was a professional hunter and he had hunted with some rare ones in his time. If they got buff today there would only be rhino to come and the poor man would have gone through his dangerous game and things might pick up. He'd have nothing more to do with the woman and Macomber would get over that too. He must have gone through plenty of that before by the look of things. Poor beggar. He must have a way of getting over it. Well, it was the poor sod's own bloody fault.

He, Robert Wilson, carried a double size cot on safari to accommodate any windfalls he might receive. He had hunted for a certain clientele, the international, fast, sporting set, where the women did not feel they were getting their money's worth unless they had shared that cot with the white hunter. He despised them when he was away from them although he liked some of them well enough at the time, but he made his living by them; and their standards were his standards as long as they were hiring him.

They were his standards in all except the shooting. He had his own standards about the killing and they could live up to them or get some one else to hunt them. He knew, too, that they all respected him for this. This Macomber was an odd one though. Damned if he wasn't. Now the wife. Well, the wife. Yes, the wife. Hm, the wife. Well he'd dropped all that. He looked around at them. Macomber sat grim and furious. Margot smiled at him. She looked younger today, more innocent and fresher and not so professionally beautiful. What's in her heart God knows, Wilson thought. She hadn't talked much last night. At that it was a pleasure to see her.

The motor car climbed up a slight rise and went on through the trees and then out into a grassy prairie-like opening and kept in the shelter of the trees along the edge, the driver going slowly and Wilson looking carefully out across the prairie and all along its far side. He stopped the car and studied the opening with his field glasses. Then he motioned to the driver to go on and the car moved slowly along, the driver avoiding wart-hog holes and driving around the mud castles ants had built. Then, looking across the opening, Wilson suddenly turned and said,

"By God, there they are!"

And looking where he pointed, while the car jumped forward and Wilson spoke in rapid Swahili to the driver, Macomber saw three huge, black animals looking almost cylindrical in their long heaviness, like big black tank cars, moving at a gallop across the far edge of the open prairie. They moved at a stiff-necked, stiff bodied gallop and he could see the upswept wide black horns on their heads as they galloped heads out; the heads not moving.

"They're three old bulls," Wilson said. "We'll cut them off before they get to the swamp."

The car was going a wild forty-five miles an hour across the open and as Macomber watched, the buffalo got bigger and bigger until he could see the gray, hairless, scabby look of one huge bull and how his neck was a part of his shoulders and the shiny black of his horns as he galloped a little behind the others that were strung out in that steady plunging gait; and then, the car swaying as though it had just jumped a road, they drew up close and he could see the plunging hugeness of the bull, and the dust in his sparsely haired hide, the side boss of horn and his outstretched, wide-nostrilled muzzle, and he was raising his rifle when Wilson shouted, "Not from the car, you fool!" and he had no fear, only hatred of Wilson, while the brakes clamped on and the car skidded, plowing sideways to an almost stop and Wilson was out on one side and he on the other, stumbling as his feet hit the still speeding-by of the earth, and then he was shooting at the bull as he moved away, hearing the bullets whunk into him, emptying his rifle at him as he moved steadily away, finally remembering to get his shots forward into the shoulder, and as he fumbled to re-load, he saw the bull was down. Down on his knees, his big head tossing, and seeing the other two still galloping he shot at the leader and hit him. He shot again and missed and he heard the *carawonging* roar as Wilson shot and saw the leading bull slide forward onto his nose.

"Get that other," Wilson said. "Now you're shooting!"

But the other bull was moving steadily at the same gallop and he missed, throwing a spout of dirt, and Wilson missed and the dust rose in a cloud and Wilson shouted, "Come on. He's too far!" and grabbed his arm and they were in the car again, Macomber and Wilson hanging on the sides and rocketing swayingly over the uneven ground, drawing up on the steady, plunging, heavy-necked, straight-moving gallop of the bull.

They were behind him and Macomber was filling his rifle, dropping shells onto the ground, jamming it, clearing the jam, then they were almost up with the bull when Wilson yelled "Stop," and the car skidded so that it almost swung over and Macomber fell forward onto his feet, slammed his bolt forward and fired as far forward as he could aim into the galloping, rounded black back, aimed and shot again, then again, then again, and the bullets, all of them hitting, had no effect on the buffalo that he could see. Then Wilson shot, the roar deafening him, and he could see the bull stagger. Macomber shot again, aiming carefully, and down he came, onto his knees.

"All right," Wilson said. "Nice work. That's the three."

Macomber felt a drunken elation.

"How many times did you shoot?" he asked.

"Just three," Wilson said. "You killed the first bull. The biggest one. I helped you finish the other two. Afraid they might have got into cover. You had them killed. I was just mopping up a little. You shot damn well."

"Let's go to the car," said Macomber. "I want a drink."

"Got to finish off that buff first," Wilson told him. The buffalo was on his knees and he jerked his head furiously and bellowed in pig-eyed, roaring rage as they came toward him.

"Watch he doesn't get up," Wilson said. Then, "Get a little broadside and take him in the neck just behind the ear."

Macomber aimed carefully at the center of the huge, jerking, rage-driven neck and shot. At the shot the head dropped forward.

"That does it," said Wilson. "Got the spine. They're a hell of a looking thing, aren't they?"

"Let's get the drink," said Macomber. In his life he had never felt so good.

In the car Macomber's wife sat very white faced. "You were marvellous, darling," she said to Macomber. "What a ride."

"Was it rough?" Wilson asked.

"It was frightful. I've never been more frightened in my life."

"Let's all have a drink," Macomber said.

"By all means," said Wilson. "Give it to the Memsahib." She drank the neat whisky from the flask and shuddered a little when she swallowed. She handed the flask to Macomber who handed it to Wilson.

"It was frightfully exciting," she said. "It's given me a dreadful headache. I didn't know you were allowed to shoot them from cars though."

"No one shot from cars," said Wilson coldly.

"I mean chase them from cars."

"Wouldn't ordinarily," Wilson said. "Seemed sporting enough to me though while we were doing it. Taking more chance driving that way across the plain full of holes and one thing and another than hunting on foot. Buffalo could have charged us each time we shot if he liked. Gave him every chance. Wouldn't mention it to any one though. It's illegal if that's what you mean."

"It seemed very unfair to me," Margot said, "chasing those big helpless things in a motor car."

"Did it?" said Wilson.

"What would happen if they heard about it in Nairobi?"

"I'd lose my license for one thing. Other unpleasantnesses," Wilson said, taking a drink from the flask. "I'd be out of business."

"Really?"

"Yes, really."

"Well," said Macomber, and he smiled for the first time all day. "Now she has something on you."

"You have such a pretty way of putting things, Francis," Margot Macomber said. Wilson looked at them both. If a four-letter man marries a five-letter woman, he was thinking, what number of letters would their children be? What he said was, "We lost a gun-bearer. Did you notice it?"

"My God, no," Macomber said.

"Here he comes," Wilson said. "He's all right. He must have fallen off when we left the first bull."

Approaching them was the middle-aged gun-bearer, limping along in his knitted cap, khaki tunic, shorts and rubber sandals, gloomy-faced and disgusted looking. As he came up he called out to Wilson in Swahili and they all saw the change in the white hunter's face.

"What does he say?" asked Margot.

"He says the first bull got up and went into the bush," Wilson said with no expression in his voice.

"Oh," said Macomber blankly.

"Then it's going to be just like the lion," said Margot, full of anticipation.

"It's not going to be a damned bit like the lion," Wilson told her. "Did you want another drink, Macomber?"

"Thanks, yes," Macomber said. He expected the feeling he had had about the lion to come back but it did not. For the first time in his life he really felt wholly without fear. Instead of fear he had a feeling of definite elation.

"We'll go and have a look at the second bull," Wilson said. "I'll tell the driver to put the car in the shade."

"What are you going to do?" asked Margaret Macomber.

"Take a look at the buff," Wilson said.

"I'll come."

"Come along."

The three of them walked over to where the second buffalo bulked blackly in the open, head forward on the grass, the massive horns swung wide.

"He's a very good head," Wilson said. "That's close to a fifty-inch spread."

Macomber was looking at him with delight.

"He's hateful looking," said Margot. "Can't we go into the shade?"

"Of course," Wilson said. "Look," he said to Macomber, and pointed. "See that patch of bush?"

"Yes."

"That's where the first bull went in. The gun-bearer said when he fell off the bull was down. He was watching us helling along and the other two buff galloping. When he looked up there was the bull up and looking at him. Gun-bearer ran like hell and the bull went off slowly into that bush."

"Can we go in after him now?" asked Macomber eagerly.

Wilson looked at him appraisingly. Damned if this isn't a strange one, he thought. Yesterday he's scared sick and today he's a ruddy fire eater.

"No, we'll give him a while."

"Let's please go into the shade," Margot said. Her face was white and she looked ill.

They made their way to the car where it stood under a single, wide-spreading tree and all climbed in.

"Chances are he's dead in there," Wilson remarked. "After a little we'll have a look."

Macomber felt a wild unreasonable happiness that he had never known before.

"By God, that was a chase," he said. "I've never felt any such feeling. Wasn't it marvellous, Margot?"

"I hated it."

"Why?"

"I hated it," she said bitterly. "I loathed it."

"You know I don't think I'd ever be afraid of anything again," Macomber said to Wilson. "Something happened in me after we first saw the buff and started after him. Like a dam bursting. It was pure excitement."

"Cleans out your liver," said Wilson. "Damn funny things happen to people."

Macomber's face was shining. "You know something did happen to me," he said. "I feel absolutely different."

His wife said nothing and eyed him strangely. She was sitting far back in the seat and Macomber was sitting forward talking to Wilson who turned sideways talking over the back of the front seat.

"You know, I'd like to try another lion," Macomber said. "I'm really not afraid of them now. After all, what can they do to you?"

"That's it," said Wilson. "Worst one can do is kill you. How does it go? Shakespeare. Damned good. See if I can remember. Oh, damned good. Used to quote it to myself at one time. Let's see. 'By my troth, I care not; a man can die but once; we owe God a death and let it go which way it will he that dies this year is quit for the next.' Damned fine, eh?"

He was very embarrassed, having brought out this thing he had lived by, but he had seen men come of age before and it always moved him. It was not a matter of their twenty-first birthday.

It had taken a strange chance of hunting, a sudden precipitation into action without opportunity for worrying beforehand, to bring this about with Macomber, but regardless of how it had happened it had most certainly happened. Look at the beggar now, Wilson thought. It's that some of them stay little boys so long, Wilson thought. Sometimes all their lives. Their figures stay boyish when they're fifty. The great American boy-men. Damned strange people. But he liked this Macomber now. Damned strange fellow. Probably meant the end of cuckoldry too. Well, that would be a damned good thing. Damned good thing. Beggar had probably been afraid all his life. Don't know what started it. But over now. Hadn't had time to be afraid with the buff. That and being angry too. Motor car too. Motor cars made it familiar. Be a damn fire eater now. He'd seen it in the war work the same way. More of a change than any loss of virginity. Fear gone like an operation. Something else grew in its place. Main thing a man had. Made him into a man. Women knew it too. No bloody fear.

From the far corner of the seat Margaret Macomber looked at the two of them. There was no change in Wilson. She saw Wilson as she had seen him the day before when she had first realized what his great talent was. But she saw the change in Francis Macomber now.

"Do you have that feeling of happiness about what's going to happen?" Macomber asked, still exploring his new wealth.

"You're not supposed to mention it," Wilson said, looking in the other's face. "Much more fashionable to say you're scared. Mind you, you'll be scared too, plenty of times."

"But you *have* a feeling of happiness about action to come?"

"Yes," said Wilson. "There's that. Doesn't do to talk too much about all this. Talk the whole thing away. No pleasure in anything if you mouth it up too much."

"You're both talking rot," said Margot. "Just because you've chased some helpless animals in a motor car you talk like heroes."

"Sorry," said Wilson. "I have been gassing too much." She's worried about it already, he thought.

"If you don't know what we're talking about why not keep out of it?" Macomber asked his wife.

"You've gotten awfully brave, awfully suddenly," his wife said contemptuously, but her contempt was not secure. She was very afraid of something.

Macomber laughed, a very natural hearty laugh. "You know I *have*," he said. "I really have."

"Isn't it sort of late?" Margot said bitterly. Because she had done the best she could for many years back and the way they were together now was no one person's fault.

"Not for me," said Macomber.

Margot said nothing but sat back in the corner of the seat.

"Do you think we've given him time enough?" Macomber asked Wilson cheerfully.

"We might have a look," Wilson said. "Have you any solids left?"

"The gun-bearer has some."

Wilson called in Swahili and the older gun-bearer, who was skinning out one of the heads, straightened up, pulled a box of solids out of his pocket and brought them over to Macomber, who filled his magazine and put the remaining shells in his pocket.

"You might as well shoot the Springfield," Wilson said. "You're used to it. We'll leave the Mannlicher in the car with the Memsahib. Your gun-bearer can carry your heavy gun. I've this damned cannon. Now let me tell you about them." He had saved this until the last because he did not want to worry Macomber. "When a buff comes he comes with his head high and thrust straight out. The boss of the horns covers any sort of a brain shot. The only shot is straight into the nose. The only other shot is into his chest or, if you're to one side, into the neck or the shoulders. After they've been hit once they take a hell of a lot of killing. Don't try anything fancy. Take the easiest shot there is. They've finished skinning out that head now. Should we get started?"

He called to the gun-bearers, who came up wiping their hands, and the older one got into the back.

"I'll only take Kongoni," Wilson said. "The other can watch to keep the birds away."

As the car moved slowly across the open space toward the island of brushy trees that ran in a tongue of foliage along a dry water course that cut the open swale, Macomber felt his heart pounding and his mouth was dry again, but it was excitement, not fear.

"Here's where he went in," Wilson said. Then to the gun-bearer in Swahili, "Take the blood spoor."

The car was parallel to the patch of bush. Macomber, Wilson and the gun-bearer got down. Macomber, looking back, saw his wife, with the rifle by her side, looking at him. He waved to her and she did not wave back.

The brush was very thick ahead and the ground was dry. The middle-aged gun-bearer was sweating heavily and Wilson had his hat down over his eyes and his red neck showed just ahead of Macomber. Suddenly the gun-bearer said something in Swahili to Wilson and ran forward.

"He's dead in there," Wilson said. "Good work," and he turned to grip Macomber's hand and as they shook hands, grinning at each other, the gun-bearer shouted wildly and they saw him coming out of the brush sideways, fast as a crab, and the bull coming, nose out, mouth tight closed, blood dripping, massive head straight out, coming in a charge, his little pig eyes bloodshot as he looked at them. Wilson, who was ahead was kneeling shooting, and Macomber, as he fired, unhearing his shot in the roaring of Wilson's gun, saw fragments like slate burst from the huge boss of the horns, and the head jerked, he shot again at the wide nostrils and saw the horns jolt again and fragments fly, and he did not see Wilson now and, aiming carefully, shot again with the buffalo's huge bulk almost on him and his rifle almost level with the on-coming head, nose out, and he could see the little wicked eyes and the head started to lower and he felt a sudden white-hot, blinding flash explode inside his head and that was all he ever felt.

Wilson had ducked to one side to get in a shoulder shot. Macomber had stood solid and shot for the nose, shooting a touch high each time and hitting the heavy horns, splintering and chipping them like hitting a slate roof, and Mrs. Macomber, in the car, had shot at the buffalo with the 6.5 Mannlicher as it seemed about to gore Macomber and had hit her husband about two inches up and a little to one side of the base of his skull.

Francis Macomber lay now, face down, not two yards from where the buffalo lay on his side and his wife knelt over him with Wilson beside her.

"I wouldn't turn him over," Wilson said.

The woman was crying hysterically.

"I'd get back in the car," Wilson said. "Where's the rifle?"

She shook her head, her face contorted. The gun-bearer picked up the rifle.

"Leave it as it is," said Wilson. Then, "Go get Abdulla so that he may witness the manner of the accident."

He knelt down, took a handkerchief from his pocket, and spread it over Francis Macomber's crew-cropped head where it lay. The blood sank into the dry, loose earth.

Wilson stood up and saw the buffalo on his side, his legs out, his thinly-haired belly crawling with ticks. "Hell of a good bull," his brain registered automatically. "A good fifty inches, or better. Better." He called to the driver and told him to spread a blanket over the body and stay by it. Then he walked over to the motor car where the woman sat crying in the corner.

"That was a pretty thing to do," he said in a toneless voice. "He *would* have left you too."

"Stop it," she said.

"Of course it's an accident," he said. "I know that."

"Stop it," she said.

"Don't worry," he said. "There will be a certain amount of unpleasantness but I will have some photographs taken that will be very useful at the inquest. There's the testimony of the gun-bearers and the driver too. You're perfectly all right."

"Stop it," she said.

"There's a hell of a lot to be done," he said. "And I'll have to send a truck off to the lake to wireless for a plane to take the three of us into Nairobi. Why didn't you poison him? That's what they do in England."

"Stop it. Stop it. Stop it," the woman cried.

Wilson looked at her with his flat blue eyes.

"I'm through now," he said. "I was a little angry. I'd begun to like your husband."

"Oh, please stop it," she said. "Please, please stop it."

"That's better," Wilson said. "Please is much better. Now I'll stop."

(1938)

JORGE LUIS BORGES
[1899–1986]

The Garden of Forking Paths

TRANSLATED BY DONALD YATES

On page 22 of Liddell Hart's *History of World War I* you will read that an attack against the Serre-Montauban line by thirteen British divisions (supported by 1,400 artillery pieces), planned for the 24th of July, 1916, had to be postponed until the morning of the 29th. The torrential rains, Captain Liddell Hart comments, caused this delay, an insignificant one, to be sure.

The following statement, dictated, reread and signed by Dr. Yu Tsun, former professor of English at the *Hochschule* at Tsingtao, throws an unsuspected light over the whole affair. The first two pages of the document are missing.

". . . and I hung up the receiver. Immediately afterwards, I recognized the voice that had answered in German. It was that of Captain Richard Madden. Madden's presence in Viktor Runeberg's apartment meant the end of our anxieties and—but this seemed, *or should have seemed,* very secondary to me—also the end of our lives. It meant that Runeberg had been arrested or murdered. Before the sun set on that day, I would encounter the same fate. Madden was implacable. Or rather, he was obliged to be so. An Irishman at the service of England, a man accused of laxity and perhaps of treason, how could he fail to seize and be thankful for such a miraculous opportunity: the discovery, capture, maybe even the death of two agents of the German Reich? I went up to my room; absurdly I locked the door and threw myself on my back on the narrow iron cot. Through the window I saw the familiar roofs and the cloud-shaded six o'clock sun. It seemed incredible to me that that day without premonitions or symbols should be the one of my inexorable death. In spite of my dead father, in spite of having been a child in a symmetrical garden of Hai Feng, was I—now—going to die? Then I reflected that everything happens to a man precisely, precisely *now*. Centuries of centuries and only in the present do things happen; countless men in the air, on the face of the earth and the sea, and all that really is happening is happening to me . . . The almost intolerable recollection of Madden's horselike face banished these wanderings. In the midst of my hatred and terror (it means nothing to me now to speak of terror, now that I have mocked Richard Madden, now that my throat yearns for the noose) it occurred to me that the tumultuous and doubtless happy warrior did not suspect that I possessed the Secret. The name of the exact location of the new British artillery park on the River Ancre. A bird streaked across the gray sky and blindly I translated it into an airplane and that airplane into many (against the French sky) annihilating the artillery station with vertical bombs. If only my mouth, before a bullet shattered it, could cry out that secret name so it could be heard in Germany . . . My human voice was very weak. How might I make it carry to the ear of the Chief? To the ear of that sick and hateful man who knew nothing of Runeberg and me save that we were in Staffordshire and who was waiting in vain for our report in his arid office in Berlin, endlessly examining newspapers . . . I said out loud: *I must flee*. I sat up noiselessly, in a useless perfection of silence, as if Madden were already lying in wait for me. Something—perhaps the mere vain ostentation of proving my resources were nil—made me look through my pockets. I found what I knew I would find. The American watch, the nickel chain and the square coin, the key ring with the incriminating useless keys to Runeberg's apartment, the notebook, a letter which I resolved to destroy immediately (and which I did not destroy), a crown, two shillings and a few pence, the red and blue pencil, the handkerchief, the revolver with one bullet. Absurdly, I took it in my hand and weighed it in order to inspire courage within myself. Vaguely I thought that a pistol report can be heard at a great distance. In ten minutes my plan was perfected. The telephone book listed the name of the only person capable of transmitting the message; he lived in a suburb of Fenton, less than a half hour's train ride away.

I am a cowardly man. I say it now, now that I have carried to its end a plan whose perilous nature no one can deny. I know its execution was terrible. I didn't do it for Germany, no. I care nothing for a barbarous country which imposed upon me the abjection of being a spy. Besides, I know of a man from England—a modest man—who for me is no less great than Goethe. I talked with him for scarcely an hour, but during that hour he was Goethe . . . I did it because I sensed that the Chief somehow feared people of my race—for the innumerable ancestors who merge within me. I wanted to prove to him that a yellow man could save his armies. Besides, I had to flee from Captain Madden. His hands and his voice could call at my door at any moment. I dressed silently, bade farewell to myself in the mirror, went downstairs, scrutinized the peaceful street and went out. The station was not far from my home, but I judged it wise to take a cab. I argued that in this way I ran less risk of being recognized; the fact is that in the deserted street I felt myself visible and vulnerable, infinitely so. I remember that I told the cab driver to stop a short distance before the main entrance. I got out with voluntary, almost painful slowness; I was going to the village of Ashgrove but I bought a ticket for a more distant station. The train left within a very few minutes, at eight-fifty. I hurried; the next one would leave at nine-thirty. There was hardly a soul on the platform. I went through the coaches; I remember a few farmers, a woman dressed in mourning, a young boy who was reading with fervor the *Annals* of Tacitus, a wounded and happy soldier. The coaches jerked forward at last. A man whom I recognized ran in vain to the end of the platform. It was Captain Richard Madden. Shattered, trembling, I shrank into the far corner of the seat, away from the dreaded window.

From this broken state I passed into an almost abject felicity. I told myself that the duel had already begun and that I had won the first encounter by frustrating, even if for forty minutes, even if by a stroke of fate, the attack of my adversary. I argued that this slightest of victories foreshadowed a total victory. I argued (no less fallaciously) that my cowardly felicity proved that I was a man capable of carrying out the adventure successfully. From this weakness I took strength that did not abandon me. I foresee that man will resign himself each day to more atrocious undertakings; soon there will be no one but warriors and brigands; I give them this counsel: *The author of an atrocious undertaking ought to imagine that he has already accomplished it, ought to impose upon himself a future as irrevocable as the past.* Thus I proceeded as my eyes of a man already dead registered the elapsing of that day, which was perhaps the last, and the diffusion of the night. The train ran gently along, amid ash trees. It stopped, almost in the middle of the fields. No one announced the name of the station. "Ashgrove?" I asked a few lads on the platform. "Ashgrove," they replied. I got off.

A lamp enlightened the platform but the faces of the boys were in shadow. One questioned me, "Are you going to Dr. Stephen Albert's house?" Without waiting for my answer, another said, "The house is a long way from here, but you won't get lost if you take this road to the left and at every crossroads turn again to your left." I tossed them a coin (my last), descended a few stone steps and started down the solitary road. It went downhill, slowly. It was of elemental earth; overhead the branches were tangled; the low, full moon seemed to accompany me.

For an instant, I thought that Richard Madden in some way had penetrated my desperate plan. Very quickly, I understood that that was impossible. The instructions to turn always to the left reminded me that such was the common procedure for discovering the central point of certain labyrinths. I have some understanding of labyrinths: not for nothing am I the great grandson of that Ts'ui Pên who was governor of Yunnan and who renounced worldly power in order to write a novel that might be even more populous than the *Hung Lu Meng* and to construct a labyrinth in which all men would become lost. Thirteen years he dedicated to these heterogeneous tasks, but the hand of a stranger murdered him—and his novel was incoherent and no one found the labyrinth. Beneath English trees I meditated on that lost maze; I imagined it inviolate and perfect at the secret crest of a mountain; I imagined it erased by rice fields or beneath the water; I imagined it infinite, no longer composed of octagonal kiosks and returning paths, but of rivers and provinces and kingdoms . . . I thought of a labyrinth of labyrinths, of one sinuous spreading labyrinth that would encompass the past and the future and in some way involve the stars. Absorbed in these illusory images, I forgot my destiny of one pursued. I felt myself to be, for an unknown period of time, an abstract perceiver of the world. The vague, living countryside, the moon, the remains of the day worked on me, as well as the slope of the road which eliminated any possibility of weariness. The afternoon was intimate, infinite. The road descended and forked among the now confused meadows. A high-pitched, almost syllabic music approached and receded in the shifting of the wind, dimmed by leaves and distance. I thought that a man can be an enemy of other men, of the moments of other men, but not of a country: not of fireflies, woods, gardens, streams of water, sunsets. Thus I arrived before a tall, rusty gate. Between the iron bars I made out a poplar grove and a pavilion. I understood suddenly two things, the first trivial, the second almost unbelievable: the music came from the pavilion, and the music was Chinese. For precisely that reason I had openly accepted it without paying it any heed. I do not remember whether there was a bell or whether I knocked with my hand. The sparkling of the music continued.

From the rear of the house within a lantern approached: a lantern that the trees sometimes striped and sometimes eclipsed, a paper lantern that had the form of a drum and the color of the moon. A tall man bore it. I didn't see his face for the light blinded me. He opened the door and said slowly, in my own language: "I see that the pious Hsi P'êng persists in correcting my solitude. You no doubt wish to see the garden?"

I recognized the name of one of our consuls and I replied, disconcerted, "The garden?"

"The garden of forking paths."

Something stirred in my memory and I uttered with incomprehensible certainty, "The garden of my ancestor Ts'ui Pên."

"Your ancestor? Your illustrious ancestor? Come in."

The damp path zigzagged like those of my childhood. We came to a library of Eastern and Western books. I recognized bound in yellow silk several volumes of the Lost Encyclopedia, edited by the Third Emperor of the Luminous Dynasty but never printed. The record on the phonograph revolved next to a bronze phoenix. I also recall a *famille rose* vase and another, many centuries older, of that shade of blue which our craftsmen copied from the potters of Persia . . .

Stephen Albert observed me with a smile. He was, as I have said, very tall, sharp-featured, with gray eyes and a gray beard. He told me that he had been a missionary in Tientsin "before aspiring to become a Sinologist."

We sat down—I on a long, low divan, he with his back to the window and a tall circular clock. I calculated that my pursuer, Richard Madden, could not arrive for at least an hour. My irrevocable determination could wait.

"An astounding fate, that of Ts'ui Pên," Stephen Albert said. "Governor of his native province, learned in astronomy, in astrology and in the tireless interpretation of the canonical books, chess player, famous poet and calligrapher—he abandoned all this in order to compose a book and a maze. He renounced the pleasures of both tyranny and justice, of his populous couch, of his banquets and even of erudition—all to close himself up for thirteen years in the Pavilion of the Limpid Solitude. When he died, his heirs found nothing save chaotic manuscripts. His family, as you may be aware, wished to condemn them to the fire; but his executor—a Taoist or Buddhist monk—insisted on their publication."

"We descendants of Ts'ui Pên," I replied, "continue to curse that monk. Their publication was senseless. The book is an indeterminate heap of contradictory drafts. I examined it once: in the third chapter the hero dies, in the fourth he is alive. As for the other undertaking of Ts'ui Pên, his labyrinth . . ."

"Here is Ts'ui Pên's labyrinth," he said, indicating a tall lacquered desk.

"An ivory labyrinth!" I exclaimed. "A minimum labyrinth."

"A labyrinth of symbols," he corrected. "An invisible labyrinth of time. To me, a barbarous Englishman, has been entrusted the revelation of this diaphanous mystery. After more than a hundred years, the details are irretrievable; but it is not hard to conjecture what happened. Ts'ui Pên must have said once: *I am withdrawing to write a book.* And another time: *I am withdrawing to construct a labyrinth.* Every one imagined two works; to no one did it occur that the book and the maze were one and the same thing. The Pavilion of the Limpid Solitude stood in the center of a garden that was perhaps intricate; that circumstance could have suggested to the heirs a physical labyrinth. Ts'ui Pên died; no one in the vast territories that were his came upon the labyrinth; the confusion of the novel suggested to me that *it* was the maze. Two circumstances gave me the correct solution of the problem. One: the curious legend that Ts'ui Pên had planned to create a labyrinth which would be strictly infinite. The other: a fragment of a letter I discovered."

Albert rose. He turned his back on me for a moment; he opened a drawer of the black and gold desk. He faced me and in his hands he held a sheet of paper that had once been crimson, but was now pink and tenuous and cross-sectioned. The fame of Ts'ui Pên as a calligrapher had been justly won. I read, uncomprehendingly and with fervor, these words written with a minute brush by a man of my blood: *I leave to the various futures (not to all) my garden of forking paths.* Wordlessly, I returned the sheet. Albert continued:

"Before unearthing this letter, I had questioned myself about the ways in which a book can be infinite. I could think of nothing other than a cyclic volume, a circular one. A book whose last page was identical with the first, a book which had the possibility of continuing indefinitely. I remembered too that night which is at the middle of the Thousand and One Nights when Schehcrazade (through a magical oversight of the copyist) begins to relate word for word the story of the Thousand and One Nights, establishing the risk of coming once again to the night when she must repeat it, and thus on to infinity. I imagined as well a Platonic, hereditary work, transmitted from father to son, in which each new individual adds a chapter or corrects with pious care the pages of his elders. These conjectures diverted me; but none seemed to correspond, not even remotely, to the contradictory chapters of Ts'ui Pên. In the midst of this perplexity, I received from Oxford the manuscript you have examined. I lingered, naturally, on the sentence: *I leave to the various futures (not to all) my garden of forking paths.* Almost instantly, I understood: 'the garden of forking paths' was the chaotic novel; the phrase 'the various futures (not to all)' suggested to me the forking in time, not in space. A broad rereading of the work confirmed the theory. In all fictional works, each time a man is confronted with several alternatives, he chooses one and eliminates the others; in the fiction of Ts'ui Pên, he chooses—simultaneously—all of them. *He creates,* in this way, diverse futures, diverse times which themselves also proliferate and fork. Here, then, is the explanation of the novel's contradictions. Fang, let us say, has a secret; a stranger calls at his door; Fang resolves to kill him. Naturally, there are several possible outcomes: Fang can kill the intruder, the intruder can kill Fang, they both can escape, they both can die, and so forth. In the work of Ts'ui Pên, all possible outcomes occur; each one is the point of departure for other forkings. Sometimes, the paths of this labyrinth converge: for example, you arrive at this house, but in one of the possible pasts you are my enemy, in another, my friend. If you will resign yourself to my incurable pronunciation, we shall read a few pages."

His face, within the vivid circle of the lamplight, was unquestionably that of an old man, but with something unalterable about it, even immortal. He read with slow precision two versions of the same epic chapter. In the first, an army marches to a battle across a lonely mountain; the horror of the rocks and shadows makes the men undervalue their lives and they gain an easy victory. In the second, the same army traverses a palace where a great festival is taking place; the resplendent battle seems to them a continuation of the celebration and they win the victory. I listened with proper veneration to these ancient narratives, perhaps less admirable in themselves than the fact that they had been created by my blood and were being restored to me by a man of a remote empire, in the course of a desperate adventure, on a Western isle. I remember the last words, repeated in each version like a secret commandment: *Thus fought the heroes, tranquil their admirable hearts, violent their swords, resigned to kill and to die.*

From that moment on, I felt about me and within my dark body an invisible, intangible swarming. Not the swarming of the divergent, parallel and finally coalescent armies, but a more inaccessible, more intimate agitation that they in some manner prefigured. Stephen Albert continued:

"I don't believe that your illustrious ancestor played idly with these variations. I don't consider it credible that he would sacrifice thirteen years to the infinite execution of a rhetorical experiment. In your country, the novel is a subsidiary form of literature; in Ts'ui Pên's time it was a despicable form. Ts'ui Pên was a brilliant novelist, but he was also a man of letters who doubtless did not consider himself a mere novelist. The testimony of his contemporaries proclaims—and his life fully confirms—his metaphysical and mystical interests. Philosophic controversy usurps a good part of the novel. I know that of all problems, none disturbed him so greatly nor worked upon him so much as the abysmal problem of time. Now then, the latter is the only problem that does not figure in the pages of the *Garden*. He does not even use the word that signifies *time*. How do you explain this voluntary omission?"

I proposed several solutions—all unsatisfactory. We discussed them. Finally, Stephen Albert said to me:

"In a riddle whose answer is chess, what is the only prohibited word?"

I thought a moment and replied, "The word *chess.*"

"Precisely," said Albert. "*The Garden of Forking Paths* is an enormous riddle, or parable, whose theme is time; this recondite cause prohibits its mention. To omit a word always, to resort to inept metaphors and obvious periphrases, is perhaps the most emphatic way of stressing it. That is the tortuous method preferred, in each of the meanderings of his indefatigable novel, by the oblique Ts'ui Pên. I have compared hundreds of manuscripts, I have corrected the errors that the negligence of the copyists has introduced. I have guessed the plan of this chaos, I have re-established—I believe I have re-established—the primordial organization, I have translated the entire work: it is clear to me that not once does he employ the word 'time.' The explanation is obvious: *The Garden of Forking Paths* is an incomplete, but not false, image of the universe as Ts'ui Pên conceived it. In contrast to Newton and Schopenhauer, your ancestor did not believe in a uniform, absolute time. He believed in an infinite series of times, in a growing, dizzying net of divergent, convergent and parallel times. This network of times which approached one another, forked, broke off, or were unaware of one another for centuries, embraces *all* possibilities of time. We do not exist in the majority of these times; in some you exist, and not I; in others I, and not you; in others, both of us. In the present one, which a favorable fate has granted me, you have arrived at my house; in another, while crossing the garden, you found me dead; in still another, I utter these same words, but I am a mistake, a ghost."

"In every one," I pronounced, not without a tremble to my voice, "I am grateful to you and revere you for your re-creation of the garden of Ts'ui Pên."

"Not in all," he murmured with a smile. "Time forks perpetually toward innumerable futures. In one of them I am your enemy."

Once again I felt the swarming sensation of which I have spoken. It seemed to me that the humid garden that surrounded the house was infinitely saturated with invisible persons. Those persons were Albert and I, secret, busy and multiform in other dimensions of time. I raised my eyes and the tenuous nightmare dissolved. In the yellow and black garden there was only one man; but this man was as strong as a statue . . . this man was approaching along the path and he was Captain Richard Madden.

"The future already exists," I replied, "but I am your friend. Could I see the letter again?"

Albert rose. Standing tall, he opened the drawer of the tall desk; for the moment his back was to me. I had readied the revolver. I fired with extreme caution. Albert fell uncomplainingly, immediately. I swear his death was instantaneous—a lightning stroke.

The rest is unreal, insignificant. Madden broke in, arrested me. I have been condemned to the gallows. I have won out abominably; I have communicated to Berlin the secret name of the city they must attack. They bombed it yesterday; I read it in the same papers that offered to England the mystery of the learned Sinologist Stephen Albert who was murdered by a stranger, one Yu Tsun. The Chief had deciphered this mystery. He knew my problem was to indicate (through the uproar of the war) the city called Albert, and that I had found no other means to do so than to kill a man of that name. He does not know (no one can know) my innumerable contrition and weariness.

(1941)

ISAAC BASHEVIS SINGER

[1904–1991]

Gimpel the Fool

TRANSLATED BY SAUL BELLOW

1

I am Gimpel the fool. I don't think myself a fool. On the contrary. But that's what folks call me. They gave me the name while I was still in school. I had seven names in all: imbecile, donkey, flax-head, dope, glump, ninny, and fool. The last name stuck. What did my foolishness consist of? I was easy to take in. They said, "Gimpel, you know the rabbi's wife has been brought to childbed?" So I skipped school. Well, it turned out to be a lie. How was I supposed to know? She hadn't had a big belly. But I never looked at her belly. Was that really so foolish? The gang laughed and hee-hawed, stomped and danced and chanted a good-night prayer. And instead of the raisins they give when a woman's lying in, they stuffed my hand full of goat turds. I was no weakling. If I slapped someone he'd see all the way to Cracow. But I'm really not a slugger by nature. I think to myself: Let it pass. So they take advantage of me.

I was coming home from school and heard a dog barking. I'm not afraid of dogs, but of course I never want to start up with them. One of them may be mad, and if he bites there's not a Tartar in the world who can help you. So I made tracks. Then I looked around and saw the whole market place wild with laughter. It was no dog at all but Wolf-Leib the Thief. How was I supposed to know it was he? It sounded like a howling bitch.

When the pranksters and leg-pullers found that I was easy to fool, every one of them tried his luck with me. "Gimpel, the Czar is coming to Frampol; Gimpel, the moon fell down in Turbeen; Gimpel, little Hodel Furpiece found a treasure behind the bathhouse." And I like a golem° believed everyone. In the first place, everything is possible, as it is written in the Wisdom of the Fathers. I've forgotten just how. Second, I had to believe when the whole town came down on me! If I ever dared to say, "Ah, you're kidding!" there was trouble. People got angry. "What do you mean! You want to call everyone a liar?" What was I to do? I believed them, and I hope at least that did them some good.

I was an orphan. My grandfather who brought me up was already bent toward the grave. So they turned me over to a baker, and what a time they gave me there! Every woman or girl who came to bake a batch of noodles had to fool me at least once. "Gimpel, there's a fair in heaven; Gimpel, the rabbi gave birth to a calf in the seventh month; Gimpel, a cow flew over the roof and laid brass eggs." A student from the yeshiva came once to buy a roll, and he said, "You, Gimpel, while you stand here scraping with your baker's shovel the Messiah has come. The dead have arisen." "What do you mean?" I said. "I heard no one blowing the ram's horn!" He said, "Are you deaf?" And all began to cry, "We heard it, we heard!" Then in came Rietze the Candle-dipper and called out in her hoarse voice, "Gimpel, your father and mother have stood up from the grave. They're looking for you."

To tell the truth, I knew very well that nothing of the sort had happened, but all the same, as folks were talking, I threw on my wool vest and went out. Maybe something had happened. What did I stand to lose by looking? Well, what a cat music went up! And then I took a vow to believe nothing more. But that was no go either. They confused me so that I didn't know the big end from the small.

I went to the rabbi to get some advice. He said, "It is written, better to be a fool all your days than for one hour to be evil. You are not a fool. They are the fools. For he who causes his neighbor to feel shame loses Paradise himself." Nevertheless the rabbi's daughter took me in. As I left the rabbinical court she said, "Have you kissed the wall yet?" I said, "No; what for?" She answered, "It's the law; you've got to do it after every visit." Well, there didn't seem to be any harm in it. And she burst out laughing. It was a fine trick. She put one over on me, all right.

golem simpleton

I wanted to go off to another town, but then everyone got busy matchmaking, and they were after me so they nearly tore my coat tails off. They talked at me and talked until I got water on the ear. She was no chaste maiden, but they told me she was virgin pure. She had a limp, and they said it was deliberate, from coyness. She had a bastard, and they told me the child was her little brother. I cried, "You're wasting your time. I'll never marry that whore." But they said indignantly, "What a way to talk! Aren't you ashamed of yourself? We can take you to the rabbi and have you fined for giving her a bad name." I saw then that I wouldn't escape them so easily and I thought: They're set on making me their butt. But when you're married the husband's the master, and if that's all right with her it's agreeable to me too. Besides, you can't pass through life unscathed, nor expect to.

I went to her clay house, which was built on the sand, and the whole gang, hollering and chorusing, came after me. They acted like bear-baiters. When we came to the well they stopped all the same. They were afraid to start anything with Elka. Her mouth would open as if it were on a hinge, and she had a fierce tongue. I entered the house. Lines were strung from wall to wall and clothes were drying. Barefoot she stood by the tub, doing the wash. She was dressed in a worn hand-me-down gown of plush. She had her hair put up in braids and pinned across her head. It took my breath away, almost, the reek of it all.

Evidently she knew who I was. She took a look at me and said, "Look who's here! He's come, the drip. Grab a seat."

I told her all; I denied nothing. "Tell me the truth," I said, "are you really a virgin, and is that mischievous Yechiel actually your little brother? Don't be deceitful with me, for I'm an orphan."

"I'm an orphan myself," she answered, "and whoever tries to twist you up, may the end of his nose take a twist. But don't let them think they can take advantage of me. I want a dowry of fifty guilders, and let them take up a collection besides. Otherwise they can kiss my you-know-what." She was very plainspoken. I said, "It's the bride and not the groom who gives a dowry." Then she said, "Don't bargain with me. Either a flat 'yes' or a flat 'no'—Go back where you came from."

I thought: No bread will ever be baked from *this* dough. But ours is not a poor town. They consented to everything and proceeded with the wedding. It so happened that there was a dysentery epidemic at the time. The ceremony was held at the cemetery gates, near the little corpse-washing hut. The fellows got drunk. While the marriage contract was being drawn up I heard the most pious high rabbi ask, "Is the bride a widow or a divorced woman?" And the sexton's wife answered for her, "Both a widow and divorced." It was a black moment for me. But what was I to do, run away from under the marriage canopy?

There was singing and dancing. An old granny danced opposite me, hugging a braided white *chalah*. The master of revels made a "God 'a mercy" in memory of the bride's parents. The schoolboys threw burrs, as on Tishe b'Av fast day. There were a lot of gifts after the sermon: a noodle board, a kneading trough, a bucket, brooms, ladles, household articles galore. Then I took a look and saw two strapping young men carrying a crib. "What do we need this for?" I asked. So they said, "Don't rack your brains about it. It's all right, it'll come in handy." I realized I was going to be rooked. Take it another way though, what did I stand to lose? I reflected: I'll see what comes of it. A whole town can't go altogether crazy.

2

At night I came where my wife lay, but she wouldn't let me in. "Say, look here, is this what they married us for?" I said. And she said, "My monthly has come." "But yesterday they took you to the ritual bath, and that's afterward, isn't it supposed to be?" "Today isn't yesterday," said she, "and yesterday's not today. You can beat it if you don't like it." In short, I waited.

Not four months later she was in childbed. The townsfolk hid their laughter with their knuckles. But what could I do? She suffered intolerable pains and clawed at the walls. "Gimpel," she cried, "I'm going. Forgive me!" The house filled with women. They were boiling pans of water. The screams rose to the welkin.°

The thing to do was to go to the House of Prayer to repeat Psalms, and that was what I did.

The townsfolk liked that, all right. I stood in a corner saying Psalms and prayers, and they shook their heads at me. "Pray, pray!" they told me. "Prayer never made any woman pregnant." One of the congregation put a straw to my mouth and said, "Hay for the cows." There was something to that too, by God!

She gave birth to a boy. Friday at the synagogue the sexton stood up before the Ark, pounded on the reading table, and announced, "The wealthy Reb Gimpel invites the congregation to a feast in honor of the birth of a son." The whole House of Prayer rang with laughter. My face was flaming. But there was nothing I could do. After all, I *was* the one responsible for the circumcision honors and rituals.

Half the town came running. You couldn't wedge another soul in. Women brought peppered chick-peas, and there was a keg of beer from the tavern. I ate and drank as much as anyone, and they all congratulated me. Then there was a circumcision, and I named the boy after my father, may he rest in peace. When all were gone and I was left with my wife alone, she thrust her head through the bed-curtain and called me to her.

"Gimpel," said she, "why are you silent? Has your ship gone and sunk?"

"What shall I say?" I answered. "A fine thing you've done to me! If my mother had known of it she'd have died a second time."

She said, "Are you crazy, or what?"

"How can you make such a fool," I said, "of one who should be the lord and master?"

"What's the matter with you?" she said. "What have you taken it into your head to imagine?"

I saw that I must speak bluntly and openly. "Do you think this is the way to use an orphan?" I said. "You have borne a bastard."

She answered, "Drive this foolishness out of your head. The child is yours."

"How can he be mine?" I argued. "He was born seventeen weeks after the wedding."

She told me then that he was premature. I said, "Isn't he a little too premature?" She said, she had had a grandmother who carried just as short a time and she resembled this grandmother of hers as one drop of water does another. She swore to it with such oaths that you would have believed a peasant at the fair if he had used them. To

welkin   the sky

tell the plain truth, I didn't believe her; but when I talked it over next day with the schoolmaster he told me that the very same thing had happened to Adam and Eve. Two they went up to bed, and four they descended.

"There isn't a woman in the world who is not the granddaughter of Eve," he said.

That was how it was; they argued me dumb. But then, who really knows how such things are?

I began to forget my sorrow. I loved the child madly, and he loved me too. As soon as he saw me he'd wave his little hands and want me to pick him up, and when he was colicky I was the only one who could pacify him. I bought him a little bone teething ring and a little gilded cap. He was forever catching the evil eye from someone, and then I had to run to get one of those abracadabras for him that would get him out of it. I worked like an ox. You know how expenses go up when there's an infant in the house. I don't want to lie about it; I didn't dislike Elka either, for that matter. She swore at me and cursed, and I couldn't get enough of her. What strength she had! One of her looks could rob you of the power of speech. And her orations! Pitch and sulphur, that's what they were full of, and yet somehow also full of charm. I adored her every word. She gave me bloody wounds though.

In the evening I brought her a white loaf as well as a dark one, and also poppyseed rolls I baked myself. I thieved because of her and swiped everything I could lay my hands on: macaroons, raisins, almonds, cakes. I hope I may be forgiven for stealing from the Saturday pots the women left to warm in the baker's oven. I would take out scraps of meat, a chunk of pudding, a chicken leg or head, a piece of tripe, whatever I could nip quickly. She ate and became fat and handsome.

I had to sleep away from home all during the week, at the bakery. On Friday nights when I got home she always made an excuse of some sort. Either she had heartburn, or a stitch in the side, or hiccups, or headaches. You know what women's excuses are. I had a bitter time of it. It was rough. To add to it, this little brother of hers, the bastard, was growing bigger. He'd put lumps on me, and when I wanted to hit back she'd open her mouth and curse so powerfully I saw a green haze floating before my eyes. Ten times a day she threatened to divorce me. Another man in my place would have taken French leave and disappeared. But I'm the type that bears it and says nothing. What's one to do? Shoulders are from God, and burdens too.

One night there was a calamity in the bakery; the oven burst, and we almost had a fire. There was nothing to do but go home, so I went home. Let me, I thought, also taste the joy of sleeping in bed in mid-week. I didn't want to wake the sleeping mite and tiptoed into the house. Coming in, it seemed to me that I heard not the snoring of one but, as it were, a double snore, one a thin enough snore and the other like the snoring of a slaughtered ox. Oh, I didn't like that! I didn't like it at all. I went up to the bed, and things suddenly turned black. Next to Elka lay a man's form. Another in my place would have made an uproar, and enough noise to rouse the whole town, but the thought occurred to me that I might wake the child. A little thing like that—why frighten a little swallow, I thought. All right then, I went back to the bakery and stretched out on a sack of flour and till morning I never shut an eye. I shivered as if I had had malaria. "Enough of being a donkey," I said to myself. "Gimpel isn't going to be a sucker all his life. There's a limit even to the foolishness of a fool like Gimpel."

In the morning I went to the rabbi to get advice, and it made a great commotion in the town. They sent the beadle for Elka right away. She came, carrying the child. And what do you think she did? She denied it, denied everything, bone and stone! "He's out of his head," she said. "I know nothing of dreams or divinations." They yelled at her, warned her, hammered on the table, but she stuck to her guns: it was a false accusation, she said.

The butchers and the horse-traders took her part. One of the lads from the slaughterhouse came by and said to me, "We've got our eye on you, you're a marked man." Meanwhile the child started to bear down and soiled itself. In the rabbinical court there was an Ark of the Covenant, and they couldn't allow that, so they sent Elka away.

I said to the rabbi, "What shall I do?"

"You must divorce her at once," said he.

"And what if she refuses?" I asked.

He said, "You must serve the divorce. That's all you'll have to do."

I said, "Well, all right, Rabbi. Let me think about it."

"There's nothing to think about," said he. "You mustn't remain under the same roof with her."

"And if I want to see the child?" I asked.

"Let her go, the harlot," said he, "and her brood of bastards with her."

The verdict he gave was that I mustn't even cross her threshold—never again, as long as I should live.

During the day it didn't bother me so much. I thought: It was bound to happen, the abscess had to burst. But at night when I stretched out upon the sacks I felt it all very bitterly. A longing took me, for her and for the child. I wanted to be angry, but that's my misfortune exactly, I don't have it in me to be really angry. In the first place—this was how my thoughts went—there's bound to be a slip sometimes. You can't live without errors. Probably that lad who was with her led her on and gave her presents and what not, and women are often long on hair and short on sense, and so he got around her. And then since she denies it so, maybe I was only seeing things? Hallucinations do happen. You see a figure or a mannikin or something, but when you come up closer it's nothing, there's not a thing there. And if that's so, I'm doing her an injustice. And when I got so far in my thoughts I started to weep. I sobbed so that I wet the flour where I lay. In the morning I went to the rabbi and told him that I had made a mistake. The rabbi wrote on with his quill, and he said that if that were so he would have to reconsider the whole case. Until he had finished I wasn't to go near my wife, but I might send her bread and money by messenger.

3

Nine months passed before all the rabbis could come to an agreement. Letters went back and forth. I hadn't realized that there could be so much erudition about a matter like this.

Meanwhile Elka gave birth to still another child, a girl this time. On the Sabbath I went to the synagogue and invoked a blessing on her. They called me up to the Torah, and I named the child for my mother-in-law—may she rest in peace. The louts and loudmouths of the town who came into the bakery gave me a going over. All Frampol refreshed its spirits because of my trouble and grief. However, I resolved that I would always believe what I was told. What's the good of *not* believing? Today it's your wife you don't believe; tomorrow it's God Himself you won't take stock in.

By an apprentice who was her neighbor I sent her daily a corn or a wheat loaf, or a piece of pastry, rolls or bagels, or, when I got the chance, a slab of pudding, a slice of honeycake, or wedding strudel—whatever came my way. The apprentice was a goodhearted lad, and more than once he added something on his own. He had formerly annoyed me a lot, plucking my nose and digging me in the ribs, but when he started to be a visitor to my house he became kind and friendly. "Hey, you, Gimpel," he said to me, "you have a very decent little wife and two fine kids. You don't deserve them."

"But the things people say about her," I said.

"Well, they have long tongues," he said, "and nothing to do with them but babble. Ignore it as you ignore the cold of last winter."

One day the rabbi sent for me and said, "Are you certain, Gimpel, that you were wrong about your wife?"

I said, "I'm certain."

"Why, but look here! You yourself saw it."

"It must have been a shadow," I said.

"The shadow of what?"

"Just one of the beams, I think."

"You can go home then. You owe thanks to the Yanover rabbi. He found an obscure reference in Maimonides that favored you."

I seized the rabbi's hand and kissed it.

I wanted to run home immediately. It's no small thing to be separated for so long a time from wife and child. Then I reflected: I'd better go back to work now, and go home in the evening. I said nothing to anyone, although as far as my heart was concerned it was like one of the Holy Days. The women teased and twitted me as they did every day, but my thought was: Go on, with your loose talk. The truth is out, like the oil upon the water. Maimonides says it's right, and therefore it is right!

At night, when I had covered the dough to let it rise, I took my share of bread and a little sack of flour and started homeward. The moon was full and the stars were glistening, something to terrify the soul. I hurried onward, and before me darted a long shadow. It was winter, and a fresh snow had fallen. I had a mind to sing, but it was growing late and I didn't want to wake the householders. Then I felt like whistling, but I remembered that you don't whistle at night because it brings the demons out. So I was silent and walked as fast as I could.

Dogs in the Christian yards barked at me when I passed, but I thought: Bark your teeth out! What are you but mere dogs? Whereas I am a man, the husband of a fine wife, the father of promising children.

As I approached the house my heart started to pound as though it were the heart of a criminal. I felt no fear, but my heart went thump! thump! Well, no drawing back. I quietly lifted the latch and went in. Elka was asleep. I looked at the infant's cradle. The shutter was closed, but the moon forced its way through the cracks. I saw the newborn child's face and loved it as soon as I saw it—immediately—each tiny bone.

Then I came nearer to the bed. And what did I see but the apprentice lying there beside Elka. The moon went out all at once. It was utterly black, and I trembled. My teeth chattered. The bread fell from my hands, and my wife waked and said, "Who is that, ah?"

I muttered, "It's me."

"Gimpel?" she asked. "How come you're here? I thought it was forbidden."

"The rabbi said," I answered and shook as with a fever.

"Listen to me, Gimpel," she said, "go out to the shed and see if the goat's all right. It seems she's been sick." I have forgotten to say that we had a goat. When I heard she was unwell I went into the yard. The nannygoat was a good little creature. I had a nearly human feeling for her.

With hesitant steps I went up to the shed and opened the door. The goat stood there on her four feet. I felt her everywhere, drew her by the horns, examined her udders, and found nothing wrong. She had probably eaten too much bark. "Good night, little goat," I said. "Keep well." And the little beast answered with a "Maa" as though to thank me for the good will.

I went back. The apprentice had vanished.

"Where," I asked, "is the lad?"

"What lad?" my wife answered.

"What do you mean?" I said. "The apprentice. You were sleeping with him."

"The things I have dreamed this night and the night before," she said, "may they come true and lay you low, body and soul! An evil spirit has taken root in you and dazzles your sight." She screamed out, "You hateful creature! You moon calf! You spook! You uncouth man! Get out, or I'll scream all Frampol out of bed!"

Before I could move, her brother sprang out from behind the oven and struck me a blow on the back of the head. I thought he had broken my neck. I felt that something about me was deeply wrong, and I said, "Don't make a scandal. All that's needed now is that people should accuse me of raising spooks and *dybbuks*.°" For that was what she had meant. "No one will touch bread of my baking."

In short, I somehow calmed her.

"Well," she said, "that's enough. Lie down, and be shattered by wheels."

Next morning I called the apprentice aside. "Listen here, brother!" I said. And so on and so forth. "What do you say?" He stared at me as though I had dropped from the roof or something.

"I swear," he said, "you'd better go to an herb doctor or some healer. I'm afraid you have a screw loose, but I'll hush it up for you." And that's how the thing stood.

To make a long story short, I lived twenty years with my wife. She bore me six children, four daughters and two sons. All kinds of things happened, but I neither saw nor heard. I believed, and that's all. The rabbi recently said to me, "Belief in itself is beneficial. It is written that a good man lives by his faith."

Suddenly my wife took sick. It began with a trifle, a little growth upon the breast. But she evidently was not destined to live long; she had no years. I spent a fortune on her. I have forgotten to say that by this time I had a bakery of my own and in Frampol was considered to be something of a rich man. Daily the healer came, and every witch doctor in the neighborhood was brought. They decided to use leeches, and after that to try cupping. They even called a doctor from Lublin, but it was too late. Before she died she called me to her bed and said, "Forgive me, Gimpel."

I said, "What is there to forgive? You have been a good and faithful wife."

"Woe, Gimpel!" she said. "It was ugly how I deceived you all these years. I want to go clean to my Maker, and so I have to tell you that the children are not yours."

dybbuks   *demons or souls of the dead that enter the bodies of the living to take possession of them*

If I had been clouted on the head with a piece of wood it couldn't have bewildered me more.

"Whose are they?" I asked.

"I don't know," she said. "There were a lot . . . but they're not yours." And as she spoke she tossed her head to the side, her eyes turned glassy, and it was all up with Elka. On her whitened lips there remained a smile.

I imagined that, dead as she was, she was saying, "I deceived Gimpel. That was the meaning of my brief life."

4

One night, when the period of mourning was done, as I lay dreaming on the flour sacks, there came the Spirit of Evil himself and said to me, "Gimpel, why do you sleep?"

I said, "What should I be doing? Eating *kreplach?*"

"The whole world deceives you," he said, "and you ought to deceive the world in your turn."

"How can I deceive the world?" I asked him.

He answered, "You might accumulate a bucket of urine every day and at night pour it into the dough. Let the sages of Frampol eat filth."

"What about the judgment in the world to come?" I said.

"There is no world to come," he said. "They've sold you a bill of goods and talked you into believing you carried a cat in your belly. What nonsense!"

"Well, then," I said, "and is there a God?"

He answered, "There is no God either."

"What," I said, *"is* there, then?"

"A thick mire."

He stood before my eyes with a goatish beard and horn, long-toothed, and with a tail. Hearing such words, I wanted to snatch him by the tail, but I tumbled from the flour sacks and nearly broke a rib. Then it happened that I had to answer the call of nature, and, passing, I saw the risen dough, which seemed to say to me, "Do it!" In brief, I let myself be persuaded.

At dawn the apprentice came. We kneaded the bread, scattered caraway seeds on it, and set it to bake. Then the apprentice went away, and I was left sitting in the little trench by the oven, on a pile of rags. Well, Gimpel, I thought, you've revenged yourself on them for all the shame they've put on you. Outside the frost glittered, but it was warm beside the oven. The flames heated my face. I bent my head and fell into a doze.

I saw in a dream, at once, Elka in her shroud. She called to me, "What have you done, Gimpel?"

I said to her, "It's all your fault," and started to cry.

"You fool!" she said. "You fool! Because I was false is everything false too? I never deceived anyone but myself. I'm paying for it all, Gimpel. They spare you nothing here."

I looked at her face. It was black; I was startled and waked, and remained sitting dumb. I sensed that everything hung in the balance. A false step now and I'd lose Eternal Life. But God gave me His help. I seized the long shovel and took out the loaves, carried them into the yard, and started to dig a hole in the frozen earth.

My apprentice came back as I was doing it. "What are you doing, boss?" he said, and grew pale as a corpse.

"I know what I'm doing," I said, and I buried it all before his very eyes.

Then I went home, took my hoard from its hiding place, and divided it among the children. "I saw your mother tonight," I said. "She's turning black, poor thing."

They were so astounded they couldn't speak a word.

"Be well," I said, "and forget that such a one as Gimpel ever existed." I put on my short coat, a pair of boots, took the bag that held my prayer shawl in one hand, my stock in the other, and kissed the *mezzuzah*. When people saw me in the street they were greatly surprised.

"Where are you going?" they said.

I answered, "Into the world." And so I departed from Frampol.

I wandered over the land, and good people did not neglect me. After many years I became old and white; I heard a great deal, many lies and falsehoods, but the longer I lived the more I understood that there were really no lies. Whatever doesn't really happen is dreamed at night. It happens to one if it doesn't happen to another, tomorrow if not today, or a century hence if not next year. What difference can it make? Often I heard tales of which I said, "Now this is a thing that cannot happen." But before a year had elapsed I heard that it actually had come to pass somewhere.

Going from place to place, eating at strange tables, it often happens that I spin yarns— improbable things that could never have happened—about devils, magicians, wind- mills, and the like. The children run after me, calling, "Grandfather, tell us a story." Sometimes they ask for particular stories, and I try to please them. A fat young boy once said to me, "Grandfather, it's the same story you told us before." The little rogue, he was right.

So it is with dreams too. It is many years since I left Frampol, but as soon as I shut my eyes I am there again. And whom do you think I see? Elka. She is standing by the washtub, as at our first encounter, but her face is shining and her eyes are as radiant as the eyes of a saint, and she speaks outlandish words to me, strange things. When I wake I have forgotten it all. But while the dream lasts I am comforted. She answers all my queries, and what comes out is that all is right. I weep and implore, "Let me be with you." And she consoles me and tells me to be patient. The time is nearer than it is far. Sometimes she strokes and kisses me and weeps upon my face. When I awaken I feel her lips and taste the salt of her tears.

No doubt the world is entirely an imaginary world, but it is only once removed from the true world. At the door of the hovel where I lie, there stands the plank on which the dead are taken away. The gravedigger Jew has his spade ready. The grave waits and the worms are hungry; the shrouds are prepared—I carry them in my beg- gar's sack. Another *shnorrer*° is waiting to inherit my bed of straw. When the time comes I will go joyfully. Whatever may be there, it will be real, without complica- tion, without ridicule, without deception. God be praised: there even Gimpel can- not be deceived.

(1953)

shnorrer   *a beggar; sponger*

TILLIE OLSEN

[b. 1913]

I Stand Here Ironing

I stand here ironing, and what you asked me moves tormented back and forth with the iron.

"I wish you would manage the time to come in and talk with me about your daughter. I'm sure you can help me understand her. She's a youngster who needs help and whom I'm deeply interested in helping."

"Who needs help." . . . Even if I came, what good would it do? You think because I am her mother I have a key, or that in some way you could use me as a key? She has lived for nineteen years. There is all that life that has happened outside of me, beyond me.

And when is there time to remember, to sift, to weigh, to estimate, to total? I will start and there will be an interruption and I will have to gather it all together again. Or I will become engulfed with all I did or did not do, with what should have been and what cannot be helped.

She was a beautiful baby. The first and only one of our five that was beautiful at birth. You do not guess how new and uneasy her tenancy in her now-loveliness. You did not know her all those years she was thought homely, or see her poring over her baby pictures, making me tell her over and over how beautiful she had been—and would be, I would tell her—and was now, to the seeing eye. But the seeing eyes were few or non-existent. Including mine.

I nursed her. They feel that's important nowadays. I nursed all the children, but with her, with all the fierce rigidity of first motherhood, I did like the books then said. Though her cries battered me to trembling and my breasts ached with swollenness, I waited till the clock decreed.

Why do I put that first? I do not even know if it matters, or if it explains anything.

She was a beautiful baby. She blew shining bubbles of sound. She loved motion, loved light, loved color and music and textures. She would lie on the floor in her blue overalls patting the surface so hard in ecstasy her hands and feet would blur. She was a miracle to me, but when she was eight months old I had to leave her daytimes with the woman downstairs to whom she was no miracle at all, for I worked or looked for work and for Emily's father, who "could no longer endure" (he wrote in his good-bye note) "sharing want with us."

I was nineteen. It was the pre-relief, pre-WPA world of the depression. I would start running as soon as I got off the streetcar, running up the stairs, the place smelling sour, and awake or asleep to startle awake, when she saw me she would break into a clogged weeping that could not be comforted, a weeping I can hear yet.

After a while I found a job hashing at night so I could be with her days, and it was better. But it came to where I had to bring her to his family and leave her.

It took a long time to raise the money for her fare back. Then she got chicken pox and I had to wait longer. When she finally came, I hardly knew her, walking quick and nervous like her father, looking like her father, thin, and dressed in a shoddy red that yellowed her skin and glared at the pockmarks. All the baby loveliness gone.

She was two. Old enough for nursery school they said, and I did not know then what I know now—the fatigue of the long day, and the lacerations of group life in the kinds of nurseries that are only parking places for children.

Except that it would have made no difference if I had known. It was the only place there was. It was the only way we could be together, the only way I could hold a job.

And even without knowing, I knew. I knew the teacher that was evil because all these years it has curdled into my memory, the little boy hunched in the corner, her rasp, "why aren't you outside, because Alvin hits you? that's no reason, go out, scaredy." I knew Emily hated it even if she did not clutch and implore "don't go Mommy" like the other children, mornings.

She always had a reason why we should stay home. Momma, you look sick, Momma. I feel sick. Momma, the teachers aren't there today, they're sick. Momma, we can't go, there was a fire there last night. Momma, it's a holiday today, no school, they told me.

But never a direct protest, never rebellion. I think of our others in their three-, four-year-oldness—the explosions, the tempers, the denunciations, the demands—and I feel suddenly ill. I put the iron down. What in me demanded that goodness in her? And what was the cost, the cost to her of such goodness?

The old man living in the back once said in his gentle way: "You should smile at Emily more when you look at her." What *was* in my face when I looked at her? I loved her. There were all the acts of love.

It was only with the others I remembered what he said, and it was the face of joy, and not of care or tightness or worry I turned to them—too late for Emily. She does not smile easily, let alone almost always as her brothers and sisters do. Her face is closed and sombre, but when she wants, how fluid. You must have seen it in her pantomimes, you spoke of her rare gift for comedy on the stage that rouses a laughter out of the audience so dear they applaud and applaud and do not want to let her go.

Where does it come from, that comedy? There was none of it in her when she came back to me that second time, after I had had to send her away again. She had a new daddy now to learn to love, and I think perhaps it was a better time.

Except when we left her alone nights, telling ourselves she was old enough.

"Can't you go some other time, Mommy, like tomorrow?" she would ask. "Will it be just a little while you'll be gone? Do you promise?"

The time we came back, the front door open, the clock on the floor in the hall. She rigid awake. "It wasn't just a little while. I didn't cry. Three times I called you, just three times, and then I ran downstairs to open the door so you could come faster. The clock talked loud. I threw it away, it scared me what it talked."

She said the clock talked loud again that night I went to the hospital to have Susan. She was delirious with the fever that comes before red measles, but she was fully conscious all the week I was gone and the week after we were home when she could not come near the new baby or me.

She did not get well. She stayed skeleton thin, not wanting to eat, and night after night she had nightmares. She would call for me, and I would rouse from exhaustion to sleepily call back: "You're all right, darling, go to sleep, it's just a dream," and if she still called, in a sterner voice, "now go to sleep, Emily, there's nothing to hurt you." Twice, only twice, when I had to get up for Susan anyhow, I went in to sit with her.

Now when it is too late (as if she would let me hold and comfort her like I do the others) I get up and go to her at once at her moan or restless stirring. "Are you awake, Emily? Can I get you something?" And the answer is always the same: "No, I'm all right, go back to sleep, Mother."

They persuaded me at the clinic to send her away to a convalescent home in the country where "she can have the kind of food and care you can't manage for her, and you'll be free to concentrate on the new baby." They still send children to that place. I see pictures on the society page of sleek young women planning affairs to raise money for it, or dancing at the affairs, or decorating Easter eggs or filling Christmas stockings for the children.

They never have a picture of the children so I do not know if the girls still wear those gigantic red bows and the ravaged looks on the every other Sunday when parents can come to visit "unless otherwise notified"—as we were notified the first six weeks.

Oh it is a handsome place, green lawns and tall trees and fluted flower beds. High up on the balconies of each cottage the children stand, the girls in their red bows and white dresses, the boys in white suits and giant red ties. The parents stand below shrieking up to be heard and the children shriek down to be heard, and between them the invisible wall "Not To Be Contaminated by Parental Germs or Physical Affection."

There was a tiny girl who always stood hand in hand with Emily. Her parents never came. One visit she was gone. "They moved her to Rose Cottage," Emily shouted in explanation. "They don't like you to love anybody here."

She wrote once a week, the labored writing of a seven-year-old. "I am fine. How is the baby. If I write my letter nicly I will have a star. Love." There never was a star. We wrote every other day, letters she could never hold or keep but only hear read—once. "We simply do not have room for children to keep any personal possessions," they patiently explained when we pieced one Sunday's shrieking together to plead how much it would mean to Emily, who loved so to keep things, to be allowed to keep her letters and cards.

Each visit she looked frailer. "She isn't eating," they told us.

(They had runny eggs for breakfast or mush with lumps, Emily said later, I'd hold it in my mouth and not swallow. Nothing ever tasted good, just when they had chicken.)

It took us eight months to get her released home, and only the fact that she gained back so little of her seven lost pounds convinced the social worker.

I used to try to hold and love her after she came back, but her body would stay stiff, and after a while she'd push away. She ate little. Food sickened her, and I think much of life too. Oh she had physical lightness and brightness, twinkling by on skates, bouncing like a ball up and down up and down over the jump rope, skimming over the hill; but these were momentary.

She fretted about her appearance, thin and dark and foreign-looking at a time when every little girl was supposed to look or thought she should look a chubby blonde replica of Shirley Temple. The doorbell sometimes rang for her, but no one seemed to come and play in the house or be a best friend. Maybe because we moved so much.

There was a boy she loved painfully through two school semesters. Months later she told me how she had taken pennies from my purse to buy him candy. "Licorice was his favorite and I brought him some every day, but he still liked Jennifer better'n me. Why, Mommy?" The kind of question for which there is no answer.

School was a worry to her. She was not glib or quick in a world where glibness and quickness were easily confused with ability to learn. To her overworked and exasperated teachers she was an overconscientious "slow learner" who kept trying to catch up and was absent entirely too often.

I let her be absent, though sometimes the illness was imaginary. How different from my now-strictness about attendance with the others. I wasn't working. We had a new baby, I was home anyhow. Sometimes, after Susan grew old enough, I would keep her home from school, too, to have them all together.

Mostly Emily had asthma, and her breathing, harsh and labored, would fill the house with a curiously tranquil sound. I would bring the two old dresser mirrors and her boxes of collections to her bed. She would select beads and single earrings, bottle tops and shells, dried flowers and pebbles, old postcards and scraps, all sorts of oddments; then she and Susan would play Kingdom, setting up landscapes and furniture, peopling them with action.

Those were the only times of peaceful companionship between her and Susan. I have edged away from it, that poisonous feeling between them, that terrible balancing of hurts and needs I had to do between the two, and did so badly, those earlier years.

Oh there are conflicts between the others too, each one human, needing, demanding, hurting, taking—but only between Emily and Susan, no, Emily toward Susan that corroding resentment. It seems so obvious on the surface, yet it is not obvious. Susan, the second child, Susan, golden- and curly-haired and chubby, quick and articulate and assured, everything in appearance and manner Emily was not; Susan, not able to resist Emily's precious things, losing or sometimes clumsily breaking them; Susan telling jokes and riddles to company for applause while Emily sat silent (to say to me later: that was *my* riddle, Mother, I told it to Susan); Susan, who for all the five years' difference in age was just a year behind Emily in developing physically.

I am glad for that slow physical development that widened the difference between her and her contemporaries, though she suffered over it. She was too vulnerable for that terrible world of youthful competition, of preening and parading, of constant measuring of yourself against every other, of envy, "If I had that copper hair," "If I had that skin. . . ." She tormented herself enough about not looking like the others, there was enough of the unsureness, the having to be conscious of words before you speak, the constant caring—what are they thinking of me? without having it all magnified by the merciless physical drives.

Ronnie is calling. He is wet and I change him. It is rare there is such a cry now. That time of motherhood is almost behind me when the ear is not one's own but must always be racked and listening for the child cry, the child call. We sit for a while and I hold him, looking out over the city spread in charcoal with its soft aisles of light. "Shoogily," he breathes and curls closer. I carry him back to bed, asleep. *Shoogily*. A funny word, a family word, inherited from Emily, invented by her to say: *comfort*.

In this and other ways she leaves her seal, I say aloud. And startle at my saying it. What do I mean? What did I start to gather together, to try and make coherent? I was at the terrible, growing years. War years. I do not remember them well. I was working, there were four smaller ones now, there was not time for her. She had to help be a mother, and housekeeper, and shopper. She had to set her seal. Mornings of crisis and near hysteria trying to get lunches packed, hair combed, coats and shoes found, everyone to school or Child Care on time, the baby ready for transportation. And always the paper scribbled on by a smaller one, the book looked at by Susan then mislaid, the homework not done. Running out to that huge school where she was one, she was lost, she was a drop; suffering over the unpreparedness, stammering and unsure in her classes.

There was so little time left at night after the kids were bedded down. She would struggle over books, always eating (it was in those years she developed her enormous appetite that is legendary in our family) and I would be ironing, or preparing food for the next day, or writing V-mail to Bill, or tending the baby. Sometimes, to make me laugh, or out of her despair, she would imitate happenings or types at school.

I think I said once: "Why don't you do something like this in the school amateur show?" One morning she phoned me at work, hardly understandable through the weeping: "Mother, I did it. I won, I won; they gave me first prize; they clapped and clapped and wouldn't let me go."

Now suddenly she was Somebody, and as imprisoned in her difference as she had been in anonymity.

She began to be asked to perform at other high schools, even in colleges, then at city and statewide affairs. The first one we went to, I only recognized her that first moment when thin, shy, she almost drowned herself into the curtains. Then: Was this Emily? The control, the command, the convulsing and deadly clowning, the spell, then the roaring, stamping audience, unwilling to let this rare and precious laughter out of their lives.

Afterwards: You ought to do something about her with a gift like that—but without money or knowing how, what does one do? We have left it all to her, and the gift has as often eddied inside, clogged and clotted, as been used and growing.

She is coming. She runs up the stairs two at a time with her light graceful step, and I know she is happy tonight. Whatever it was that occasioned your call did not happen today.

"Aren't you ever going to finish the ironing, Mother? Whistler painted his mother in a rocker. I'd have to paint mine standing over an ironing board." This is one of her communicative nights and she tells me everything and nothing as she fixes herself a plate of food out of the icebox.

She is so lovely. Why did you want me to come in at all? Why were you concerned? She will find her way.

She starts up the stairs to bed. "Don't get me up with the rest in the morning." "But I thought you were having midterms." "Oh, those," she comes back in, kisses me, and says lightly, "in a couple of years when we'll all be atom-dead they won't matter a bit."

She has said it before. She *believes* it. But because I have been dredging the past, and all that compounds a human being is so heavy and meaningful in me, I cannot endure it tonight.

I will never total it all. I will never come in to say: She was a child seldom smiled at. Her father left me before she was a year old. I had to work her first six years when there was work, or I sent her home and to his relatives. There were years she had care she hated. She was dark and thin and foreign-looking in a world where the prestige went to blondeness and curly hair and dimples, she was slow where glibness was prized. She was a child of anxious, not proud, love. We were poor and could not afford for her the soil of easy growth. I was a young mother, I was a distracted mother. There were the other children pushing up, demanding. Her younger sister seemed all that she was not. There were years she did not want me to touch her. She kept too much in herself, her life was such she had to keep too much in herself. My wisdom came too late. She has much to her and probably little will come of it. She is a child of her age, of depression, of war, of fear.

Let her be. So all that is in her will not bloom—but in how many does it? There is still enough left to live by. Only help her to know—help make it so there is cause for her to know—that she is more than this dress on the ironing board, helpless before the iron.

(1961)

RALPH ELLISON
[1914–1994]

Battle Royal

It goes a long way back, some twenty years. All my life I had been looking for something, and everywhere I turned someone tried to tell me what it was. I accepted their answers too, though they were often in contradiction and even self-contradictory. I was naïve. I was looking for myself and asking everyone except myself questions which I, and only I, could answer. It took me a long time and much painful boomeranging of my expectations to achieve a realization everyone else appears to have been born with: That I am nobody but myself. But first I had to discover that I am an invisible man!

And yet I am no freak of nature, nor of history. I was in the cards, other things having been equal (or unequal) eighty-five years ago. I am not ashamed of my grandparents for having been slaves. I am only ashamed of myself for having at one time been ashamed. About eighty-five years ago they were told that they were free, united with others of our country in everything pertaining to the common good, and, in everything social, separate like the fingers of the hand. And they believed it. They exulted in it. They stayed in their place, worked hard, and brought up my father to do the same. But my grandfather is the one. He was an odd old guy, my grandfather, and I am told I take after him. It was he who caused the trouble. On his deathbed he called my father to him and said, "Son, after I'm gone I want you to keep up the good fight. I never told you, but our life is a war and I have been a traitor all my born days, a spy in the enemy's country ever since I give up my gun back in the Reconstruction. Live with your head in the lion's mouth. I want you to overcome 'em with yeses, undermine 'em with grins, agree 'em to death and destruction, let 'em swoller you till they vomit or bust wide open." They thought the old man had gone out of his mind. He had been the meekest of men. The younger children were rushed from the room, the shades drawn and the flame of the lamp turned so low that it sputtered on the wick like the old man's breathing. "Learn it to the younguns," he whispered fiercely; then he died.

But my folks were more alarmed over his last words than over his dying. It was as though he had not died at all, his words caused so much anxiety. I was warned emphatically to forget what he had said and, indeed, this is the first time it has been mentioned outside the family circle. It had a tremendous effect upon me, however. I could never be sure of what he meant. Grandfather had been a quiet old man who never made any trouble, yet on his deathbed he had called himself a traitor and a spy, and he had spoken of his meekness as a dangerous activity. It became a constant puzzle which lay unanswered in the back of my mind. And whenever things went well for me I remembered my grandfather and felt guilty and uncomfortable. It was as though I was carrying out his advice in spite of myself. And to make it worse, everyone loved me for it. I was praised by the most lily-white men of the town. I was considered an example of desirable conduct—just as my grandfather had been. And what puzzled me was that the old man had defined it as *treachery*. When I was praised for my conduct I felt a guilt that in some way I was doing something that was really against the wishes of the white folks, that if they had understood they would have desired me to act just the opposite, that I should have been sulky and mean, and that that really would have been what they wanted, even though they were fooled and thought they wanted me to act as I did. It made me afraid that some day they would look upon me as a traitor and I would be lost. Still I was more afraid to act any other way because they didn't like that at all. The old man's words were like a curse. On my graduation day I delivered an oration in which I showed that humility was the secret, indeed, the very essence of progress. (Not that I believed this—how could I, remembering my grandfather?— I only believed that it worked.) It was a great success. Everyone praised me and I was invited to give the speech at a gathering of the town's leading white citizens. It was a triumph for our whole community.

It was in the main ballroom of the leading hotel. When I got there I discovered that it was on the occasion of a smoker, and I was told that since I was to be there anyway I might as well take part in the battle royal to be fought by some of my schoolmates as part of the entertainment. The battle royal came first.

All of the town's big shots were there in their tuxedoes, wolfing down the buffet foods, drinking beer and whiskey and smoking black cigars. It was a large room with a high ceiling. Chairs were arranged in neat rows around three sides of a portable boxing ring. The fourth side was clear, revealing a gleaming space of polished floor. I had some misgivings over the battle royal, by the way. Not from a distaste for fighting, but because I didn't care too much for the other fellows who were to take part. They were tough guys who seemed to have no grandfather's curse worrying their minds. No one could mistake their toughness. And besides, I suspected that fighting a battle royal might detract from the dignity of my speech. In those pre-invisible days I visualized myself as a potential Booker T. Washington. But the other fellows didn't care too much for me either, and there were nine of them. I felt superior to them in my way, and I didn't like the manner in which we were all crowded together into the servants' elevator. Nor did they like my being there. In fact, as the warmly lighted floors flashed past the elevator we had words over the fact that I, by taking part in the fight, had knocked one of their friends out of a night's work.

We were led out of the elevator through a rococo hall into an anteroom and told to get into our fighting togs. Each of us was issued a pair of boxing gloves and ushered out into the big mirrored hall, which we entered looking cautiously about us and whispering, lest we might accidentally be heard above the noise of the room. It was foggy with cigar smoke. And already the whiskey was taking effect. I was shocked to see some of the most important men of the town quite tipsy. They were all there—bankers, lawyers, judges, doctors, fire chiefs, teachers, merchants. Even one of the more fashionable pastors. Something we could not see was going on up front. A clarinet was vibrating sensuously and the men were standing up and moving eagerly forward. We were a small tight group, clustered together, our bare upper bodies touching and shining with anticipatory sweat; while up front the big shots were becoming increasingly excited over something we still could not see. Suddenly I heard the school superintendent, who had told me to come, yell, "Bring up the shines gentlemen! Bring up the little shines!"

We were rushed up to the front of the ballroom, where it smelled even more strongly of tobacco and whiskey. Then we were pushed into place. I almost wet my pants. A sea of faces, some hostile, some amused, ringed around us, and in the center, facing us, stood a magnificent blonde—stark naked. There was dead silence. I felt a blast of cold air chill me. I tried to back away, but they were behind me and around me. Some of the boys stood with lowered heads, trembling. I felt a wave of irrational guilt and fear. My teeth chattered, my skin turned to goose flesh, my knees knocked. Yet I was strongly attracted and looked in spite of myself. Had the price of looking been blindness, I would have looked. The hair was yellow like that of a circus kewpie doll, the face heavily powdered and rouged, as though to form an abstract mask, the eyes hollow and smeared a cool blue, the color of a baboon's butt. I felt a desire to spit upon her as my eyes brushed slowly over her body. Her breasts were firm and round as the domes of East Indian temples, and I stood so close as to see the fine skin texture and beads of pearly perspiration glistening like dew around the pink and erected buds of her nipples. I wanted at one and the same time to run from the room, to sink through the floor, or go to her and cover her from my eyes and the eyes of the others with my body; to feel the soft thighs, to caress her and destroy her, to love her and murder her, to hide from her, and yet to stroke where below the small American flag tattooed upon her belly her thighs formed a capital V. I had a notion that of all in the room she saw only me with her impersonal eyes.

And then she began to dance, a slow sensuous movement; the smoke of a hundred cigars clinging to her like the thinnest of veils. She seemed like a fair bird-girl girdled in veils calling to me from the angry surface of some gray and threatening sea. I was transported. Then I became aware of the clarinet playing and the big shots yelling at us. Some threatened us if we looked and others if we did not. On my right I saw one boy faint. And now a man grabbed a silver pitcher from a table and stepped close as he dashed ice water upon him and stood him up and forced two of us to support him as his head hung and moans issued from his thick bluish lips. Another boy began to plead to go home. He was the largest of the group, wearing dark red fighting trunks much too small to conceal the erection which projected from him as though in answer to the insinuating low-registered moaning of the clarinet. He tried to hide himself with his boxing gloves.

And all the while the blonde continued dancing, smiling faintly at the big shots who watched her with fascination, and faintly smiling at our fear. I noticed a certain merchant who followed her hungrily, his lips loose and drooling. He was a large man who wore diamond studs in a shirtfront which swelled with the ample paunch underneath, and each time the blonde swayed her undulating hips he ran his hand through the thin hair of his bald head and, with his arms upheld, his posture clumsy like that of an intoxicated panda, wound his belly in a slow and obscene grind. This creature was completely hypnotized. The music had quickened. As the dancer flung herself about with a detached expression on her face, the men began reaching out to touch her. I could see their beefy fingers sink into her soft flesh. Some of the others tried to stop them and she began to move around the floor in graceful circles, as they gave chase, slipping and sliding over the polished floor. It was mad. Chairs went crashing, drinks were spilt, as they ran laughing and howling after her. They caught her just as she reached a door, raised her from the floor, and tossed her as college boys are tossed at a hazing, and above her red, fixed-smiling lips I saw the terror and disgust in her eyes, almost like my own terror and that which I saw in some of the other boys. As I watched, they tossed her twice and her soft breasts seemed to flatten against the air and her legs flung wildly as she spun. Some of the more sober ones helped her to escape. And I started off the floor, heading for the anteroom with the rest of the boys.

Some were still crying and in hysteria. But as we tried to leave we were stopped and ordered to get into the ring. There was nothing to do but what we were told. All ten of us climbed under the ropes and allowed ourselves to be blindfolded with broad bands of white cloth. One of the men seemed to feel a bit sympathetic and tried to cheer us up as we stood with our backs against the ropes. Some of us tried to grin. "See that boy over there?" one of the men said. "I want you to run across at the bell and give it to him right in the belly. If you don't get him, I'm going to get you. I don't like his looks." Each of us was told the same. The blindfolds were put on. Yet even then I had been going over my speech. In my mind each word was as bright as flame. I felt the cloth pressed into place, and frowned so that it would be loosened when I relaxed.

But now I felt a sudden fit of blind terror. I was unused to darkness. It was as though I had suddenly found myself in a dark room filled with poisonous cottonmouths. I could hear the bleary voices yelling insistently for the battle royal to begin.

"Get going in there!"

"Let me at that big nigger!"

I strained to pick up the school superintendent's voice, as though to squeeze some security out of that slightly more familiar sound.

"Let me at those black sonsabitches!" someone yelled.

"No, Jackson, no!" another voice yelled. "Here, somebody, help me hold Jack."

"I want to get at that ginger-colored nigger. Tear him limb from limb," the first voice yelled.

I stood against the ropes trembling. For in those days I was what they called ginger-colored, and he sounded as though he might crunch me between his teeth like a crisp ginger cookie.

Quite a struggle was going on. Chairs were being kicked about and I could hear voices grunting as with a terrific effort. I wanted to see, to see more desperately than ever before. But the blindfold was as tight as a thick skin-puckering scab and when I raised my gloved hands to push the layers of white aside a voice yelled, "Oh, no you don't, black bastard! Leave that alone!"

"Ring the bell before Jackson kills him a coon!" someone boomed in the sudden silence. And I heard the bell clang and the sound of the feet scuffling forward.

A glove smacked against my head. I pivoted, striking out stiffly as someone went past, and felt the jar ripple along the length of my arm to my shoulder. Then it seemed as though all nine of the boys had turned upon me at once. Blows pounded me from all sides while I struck out as best I could. So many blows landed upon me that I wondered if I were not the only blindfolded fighter in the ring, or if the man called Jackson hadn't succeeded in getting me after all.

Blindfolded, I could no longer control my motions. I had no dignity. I stumbled about like a baby or a drunken man. The smoke had become thicker and with each new blow it seemed to sear and further restrict my lungs. My saliva became like hot bitter glue. A glove connected with my head, filling my mouth with warm blood. It was everywhere. I could not tell if the moisture I felt upon my body was sweat or blood. A blow landed hard against the nape of my neck. I felt myself going over, my head hitting the floor. Streaks of blue light filled the black world behind the blindfold. I lay prone, pretending that I was knocked out, but felt myself seized by hands and yanked to my feet. "Get going, black boy! Mix it up!" My arms were like lead, my head smarting from blows. I managed to feel my way to the ropes and held on, trying to catch my breath. A glove landed in my midsection and I went over again, feeling as though the smoke had become a knife jabbed into my guts. Pushed this way and that by the legs milling around me, I finally pulled erect and discovered that I could see the black, sweat-washed forms weaving in the smoky-blue atmosphere like drunken dancers weaving to the rapid drum-like thuds of blows.

Everyone fought hysterically. It was complete anarchy. Everybody fought everybody else. No group fought together for long. Two, three, four, fought one, then turned to fight each other, were themselves attacked. Blows landed below the belt and in the kidney, with the gloves open as well as closed, and with my eye partly opened now there was not so much terror. I moved carefully, avoiding blows, although not too many to attract attention, fighting from group to group. The boys groped about like blind, cautious crabs crouching to protect their mid-sections, their heads pulled in short against their shoulders, their arms stretched nervously before them, with their fists testing the smoke-filled air like the knobbed feelers of hypersensitive snails. In one corner I glimpsed a boy violently punching the air and heard him scream in pain as he smashed his hand against a ring post. For a second I saw him bent over holding his hand, then going down as a blow caught his unprotected head. I played one group against the other, slipping in and throwing a punch then stepping out of range while pushing the others into the melee to take the blows blindly aimed at me. The smoke was agonizing and there were no rounds, no bells at three minute intervals to relieve our exhaustion. The room spun round me, a swirl of lights, smoke, sweating bodies surrounded by tense white faces. I bled from both nose and mouth, the blood spattering upon my chest.

The men kept yelling, "Slug him, black boy! Knock his guts out!"

"Uppercut him! Kill him! Kill that big boy!"

Taking a fake fall, I saw a boy going down heavily beside me as though we were felled by a single blow, saw a sneaker-clad foot shoot into his groin as the two who had knocked him down stumbled upon him. I rolled out of range, feeling a twinge of nausea.

The harder we fought the more threatening the men became. And yet, I had begun to worry about my speech again. How would it go? Would they recognize my ability? What would they give me?

I was fighting automatically and suddenly I noticed that one after another of the boys was leaving the ring. I was surprised, filled with panic, as though I had been left alone with an unknown danger. Then I understood. The boys had arranged it among themselves. It was the custom for the two men left in the ring to slug it out for the winner's prize. I discovered this too late. When the bell sounded two men in tuxedoes leaped into the ring and removed the blindfold. I found myself facing Tatlock, the biggest of the gang. I felt sick at my stomach. Hardly had the bell stopped ringing in my ears than it clanged again and I saw him moving swiftly toward me. Thinking of nothing else to do I hit him smash on the nose. He kept coming, bringing the rank sharp violence of stale sweat. His face was a black blank of a face, only his eyes alive—with hate of me and aglow with a feverish terror from what had happened to us all. I became anxious. I wanted to deliver my speech and he came at me as though he meant to beat it out of me. I smashed him again and again, taking his blows as they came. Then on a sudden impulse I struck him lightly and as we clinched, I whispered, "Fake like I knocked you out, you can have the prize."

"I'll break your behind," he whispered hoarsely.

"For *them?*"

"For *me,* sonofabitch!"

They were yelling for us to break it up and Tatlock spun me half around with a blow, and as a joggled camera sweeps in a reeling scene, I saw the howling red faces crouching tense beneath the cloud of blue-gray smoke. For a moment the world wavered, unraveled, flowed, then my head cleared and Tatlock bounced before me. That fluttering shadow before my eyes was his jabbing left hand. Then falling forward, my head against his damp shoulder, I whispered, "I'll make it five dollars more."

"Go to hell!"

But his muscles relaxed a trifle beneath my pressure and I breathed, "Seven!"

"Give it to your ma," he said, ripping me beneath the heart.

And while I still held him I butted him and moved away. I felt myself bombarded with punches. I fought back with hopeless desperation. I wanted to deliver my speech more than anything else in the world, because I felt that only these men could judge truly my ability, and now this stupid clown was ruining my chances. I began fighting carefully now, moving in to punch him and out again with my greater speed. A lucky blow to his chin and I had him going too—until I heard a loud voice yell, "I got my money on the big boy."

Hearing this, I almost dropped my guard. I was confused: Should I try to win against the voice out there? Would not this go against my speech, and was not this a moment for humility, for nonresistance? A blow to my head as I danced about sent my right eye popping like a jack-in-the-box and settled my dilemma. The room went red as I fell. It was a dream fall, my body languid and fastidious as to where to land, until the floor became impatient and smashed up to meet me. A moment later I came to. An hypnotic voice said FIVE emphatically. And I lay there, hazily watching a dark red spot of my own blood shaping itself into a butterfly, glistening and soaking into the soiled gray world of the canvas.

When the voice drawled TEN I was lifted up and dragged to a chair. I sat dazed. My eye pained and swelled with each throb of my pounding heart and I wondered if now I would be allowed to speak. I was wringing wet, my mouth still bleeding. We were grouped along the wall now. The other boys ignored me as they congratulated Tatlock and speculated as to how much they would be paid. One boy whimpered over his smashed hand. Looking up front, I saw attendants in white jackets rolling the portable ring away and placing a small square rug in the vacant space surrounded by chairs. Perhaps, I thought, I will stand on the rug to deliver my speech.

Then the M.C. called to us, "Come on up here boys and get your money."

We ran forward to where the men laughed and talked in their chairs, waiting. Everyone seemed friendly now.

"There it is on the rug," the man said. I saw the rug covered with coins of all dimensions and a few crumpled bills. But what excited me, scattered here and there, were the gold pieces.

"Boys, it's all yours," the man said. "You get all you grab."

"That's right, Sambo," a blond man said, winking at me confidentially.

I trembled with excitement, forgetting my pain. I would get the gold and the bills, I thought. I would use both hands. I would throw my body against the boys nearest me to block them from the gold.

"Get down around the rug now," the man commanded, "and don't anyone touch it until I give the signal."

"This ought to be good," I heard.

As told, we got around the square rug on our knees. Slowly the man raised his freckled hand as we followed it upward with our eyes.

I heard, "These niggers look like they're about to pray!"

Then, "Ready," the man said. "Go!"

I lunged for a yellow coin lying on the blue design of the carpet, touching it and sending a surprised shriek to join those rising around me. I tried frantically to remove my hand but could not let go. A hot, violent force tore through my body, shaking me like a wet rat. The rug was electrified. The hair bristled up on my head as I shook myself free. My muscles jumped, my nerves jangled, writhed. But I saw that this was not stopping the other boys. Laughing in fear and embarrassment, some were holding back and scooping up the coins knocked off by the painful contortions of the others. The men roared above us as we struggled.

"Pick it up, goddamnit, pick it up!" someone called like a bass-voiced parrot. "Go on, get it!"

I crawled rapidly around the floor, picking up the coins, trying to avoid the coppers and to get greenbacks and the gold. Ignoring the shock by laughing, as I brushed the coins off quickly, I discovered that I could contain the electricity—a contradiction, but it works. Then the men began to push us onto the rug. Laughing embarrassedly, we struggled out of their hands and kept after the coins. We were all wet and slippery and hard to hold. Suddenly I saw a boy lifted into the air, glistening with sweat like a circus seal, and dropped, his wet back landing flush upon the charged rug, heard him yell and saw him literally dance upon his back, his elbows beating a frenzied tattoo upon the floor, his muscles twitching like the flesh of a horse stung by many flies. When he finally rolled off, his face was gray and no one stopped him when he ran from the floor amid booming laughter.

"Get the money," the M.C. called. "That's good hard American cash!"

And we snatched and grabbed, snatched and grabbed. I was careful not to come too close to the rug now, and when I felt the hot whiskey breath descend upon me like a cloud of foul air I reached out and grabbed the leg of a chair. It was occupied and I held on desperately.

"Leggo, nigger! Leggo!"

The huge face wavered down to mine as he tried to push me free. But my body was slippery and he was too drunk. It was Mr. Colcord, who owned a chain of movie houses and "entertainment palaces." Each time he grabbed me I slipped out of his hands. It became a real struggle. I feared the rug more than I did the drunk, so I held on, surprising myself for a moment by trying to topple *him* upon the rug. It was such an enormous idea that I found myself actually carrying it out. I tried not to be obvious, yet when I grabbed his leg, trying to tumble him out of the chair, he raised up roaring with laughter, and, looking at me with soberness dead in the eye, kicked me viciously in the chest. The chair leg flew out of my hand. I felt myself going and rolled. It was as though I had rolled through a bed of hot coals. It seemed a whole century would pass before I would roll free, a century in which I was seared through the deepest levels of my body to the fearful breath within me and the breath seared and heated to the point of explosion. It'll all be over in a flash, I thought as I rolled clear. It'll all be over in a flash.

But not yet, the men on the other side were waiting, red faces swollen as though from apoplexy as they bent forward in their chairs. Seeing their fingers coming toward me I rolled away as a fumbled football rolls off the receiver's fingertips, back into the coals. That time I luckily sent the rug sliding out of place and heard the coins ringing against the floor and the boys scuffling to pick them up and the M.C. calling, "All right, boys, that's all. Go get dressed and get your money."

I was limp as a dish rag. My back felt as though it had been beaten with wires.

When we had dressed the M.C. came in and gave us each five dollars, except Tatlock, who got ten for being last in the ring. Then he told us to leave. I was not to get a chance to deliver my speech, I thought. I was going out into the dim alley in despair when I was stopped and told to go back. I returned to the ballroom, where the men were pushing back their chairs and gathering in groups to talk.

The M.C. knocked on a table for quiet. "Gentlemen," he said, "we almost forgot an important part of the program. A most serious part, gentlemen. This boy was brought here to deliver a speech which he made at his graduation yesterday. . . ."

"Bravo!"

"I'm told that he is the smartest boy we've got out there in Greenwood. I'm told that he knows more big words than a pocket-sized dictionary."

Much applause and laughter.

"So now, gentlemen, I want you to give him your attention."

There was still laughter as I faced them, my mouth dry, my eye throbbing. I began slowly, but evidently my throat was tense, because they began shouting, "Louder! Louder!"

"We of the younger generation extol the wisdom of that great leader and educator," I shouted, "who first spoke these flaming words of wisdom: 'A ship lost at sea for many days suddenly sighted a friendly vessel. From the mast of the unfortunate vessel was seen a signal: "Water, water; we die of thirst!" The answer from the friendly vessel came back: "Cast down your bucket where you are." The captain of the distressed vessel, at last heeding the injunction, cast down his bucket, and it came up full of fresh sparkling water from the mouth of the Amazon River.' And like him I say, and in his words, 'To those of my race who depend upon bettering their condition in a foreign land, or who underestimate the importance of cultivating friendly relations with the Southern white man, who is his next-door neighbor, I would say: "Cast down your bucket where you are"—cast it down in making friends in every manly way of the people of all races by whom we are surrounded. . . ."'

I spoke automatically and with such fervor that I did not realize that the men were still talking and laughing until my dry mouth, filling up with blood from the cut, almost strangled me. I coughed, wanting to stop and go to one of the tall brass, sand-filled spittoons to relieve myself, but a few of the men, especially the superintendent, were listening and I was afraid. So I gulped it down, blood, saliva and all, and continued. (What powers of endurance I had during those days! What enthusiasm! What a belief in the rightness of things!) I spoke even louder in spite of the pain. But still they talked and still they laughed, as though deaf with cotton in dirty ears. So I spoke with greater emotional emphasis. I closed my ears and swallowed blood until I was nauseated. The speech seemed a hundred times as long as before, but I could not leave out a single word. All had to be said, each memorized nuance considered, rendered. Nor was that all. Whenever I uttered a word of three or more syllables a group of voices would yell for me to repeat it. I used the phrase "social responsibility" and they yelled:

"What's the word you say, boy?"

"Social responsibility," I said.

"What?"

"Social . . ."

"Louder."

". . . responsibility."

"More!"

"Respon—"

"Repeat!"

"—sibility."

The room filled with the uproar of laughter until, no doubt, distracted by having to gulp down my blood, I made a mistake and yelled a phrase I had often seen denounced in newspaper editorials, heard debated in private.

"Social . . ."

"What?" they yelled.

". . . equality—"

The laughter hung smokelike in the sudden stillness. I opened my eyes, puzzled. Sounds of displeasure filled the room. The M.C. rushed forward. They shouted hostile phrases at me. But I did not understand.

A small dry mustached man in the front row blared out, "Say that slowly, son!"

"What sir?"

"What you just said!"

"Social responsibility, sir," I said.

"You weren't being smart, were you, boy?" he said, not unkindly.

"No, sir!"

"You sure that about 'equality' was a mistake?"

"Oh, yes, sir," I said. "I was swallowing blood."

"Well, you had better speak more slowly so we can understand. We mean to do right by you, but you've got to know your place at all times. All right, now, go on with your speech."

I was afraid. I wanted to leave but I wanted also to speak and I was afraid they'd snatch me down.

"Thank you, sir," I said, beginning where I had left off, and having them ignore me as before.

Yet when I finished there was a thunderous applause. I was surprised to see the superintendent come forth with a package wrapped in white tissue paper, and, gesturing for quiet, address the men.

"Gentlemen, you see that I did not overpraise this boy. He makes a good speech and some day he'll lead his people in the proper paths. And I don't have to tell you that that is important in these days and times. This is a good, smart boy, and so to encourage him in the right direction, in the name of the Board of Education I wish to present him a prize in the form of this . . . ."

He paused, removing the tissue paper and revealing a gleaming calfskin brief case.

". . . in the form of this first-class article from Shad Whitmore's shop."

"Boy," he said, addressing me, "take this prize and keep it well. Consider it a badge of office. Prize it. Keep developing as you are and some day it will be filled with important papers that will help shape the destiny of your people."

I was so moved that I could hardly express my thanks. A rope of bloody saliva forming a shape like an undiscovered continent drooled upon the leather and I wiped it quickly away. I felt an importance that I had never dreamed.

"Open it and see what's inside," I was told.

My fingers a-tremble, I complied, smelling the fresh leather and finding an official-looking document inside. It was a scholarship to the state college for Negroes. My eyes filled with tears and I ran awkwardly off the floor.

I was overjoyed; I did not even mind when I discovered that the gold pieces I had scrambled for were brass pocket tokens advertising a certain make of automobile.

When I reached home everyone was excited. Next day the neighbors came to congratulate me. I even felt safe from grandfather, whose deathbed curse usually spoiled my triumphs. I stood beneath his photograph with my brief case in hand and smiled triumphantly into his stolid black peasant's face. It was a face that fascinated me. The eyes seemed to follow everywhere I went.

That night I dreamed I was at a circus with him and that he refused to laugh at the clowns no matter what they did. Then later he told me to open my brief case and read what was inside and I did, finding an official envelope stamped with the state seal; and inside the envelope I found another and another, endlessly, and I thought I would fall of weariness. "Them's years," he said. "Now open that one." And I did and in it I found an engraved document containing a short message in letters of gold. "Read it," my grandfather said. "Out loud."

"To Whom It May Concern," I intoned. "Keep This Nigger-Boy Running."

I awoke with the old man's laughter ringing in my ears.

(It was a dream I was to remember and dream again for many years after. But at the time I had no insight into its meaning. First I had to attend college.)

(1952)

GABRIEL GARCIA MARQUEZ
[b. 1928]

A Very Old Man with Enormous Wings
A TALE FOR CHILDREN

TRANSLATED BY GREGORY RABASSA

On the third day of rain they had killed so many crabs inside the house that Pelayo had to cross his drenched courtyard and throw them into the sea, because the newborn child had a temperature all night and they thought it was due to the stench. The world had been sad since Tuesday. Sea and sky were a single ash-gray thing and the sands of the beach, which on March nights glimmered like powdered light, had become a stew of mud and rotten shellfish. The light was so weak at noon that when Pelayo was coming back to the house after throwing away the crabs, it was hard for him to see what it was that was moving and groaning in the rear of the courtyard. He had to go very close to see that it was an old man, a very old man, lying face down in the mud, who, in spite of his tremendous efforts, couldn't get up, impeded by his enormous wings.

Frightened by that nightmare, Pelayo ran to get Elisenda, his wife, who was putting compresses on the sick child, and he took her to the rear of the courtyard. They both looked at the fallen body with mute stupor. He was dressed like a ragpicker. There were only a few faded hairs left on his bald skull and very few teeth in his mouth, and his pitiful condition of a drenched great-grandfather had taken away any sense of grandeur he might have had. His huge buzzard wings, dirty and half-plucked, were forever entangled in the mud. They looked at him so long and so closely that Pelayo and Elisenda very soon overcame their surprise and in the end found him familiar. Then they dared speak to him, and he answered in an incomprehensible dialect with a strong sailor's voice. That was how they skipped over the inconvenience of the wings and quite intelligently concluded that he was a lonely castaway from some foreign ship wrecked by the storm. And yet, they called in a neighbor woman who knew everything about life and death to see him, and all she needed was one look to show them their mistake.

"He's an angel," she told them. "He must have been coming for the child, but the poor fellow is so old that the rain knocked him down."

On the following day everyone knew that a flesh-and-blood angel was held captive in Pelayo's house. Against the judgment of the wise neighbor woman, for whom angels in those times were the fugitive survivors of a celestial conspiracy, they did not have the heart to club him to death. Pelayo watched over him all afternoon from the kitchen, armed with his bailiff's club, and before going to bed he dragged him out of the mud and locked him up with the hens in the wire chicken coop. In the middle of the night, when the rain stopped, Pelayo and Elisenda were still killing crabs. A short time afterward the child woke up without a fever and with a desire to eat. Then they felt magnanimous and decided to put the angel on a raft with fresh water and provisions for three days and leave him to his fate on the high seas. But when they went out into the courtyard with the first light of dawn, they found the whole neighborhood in front of the chicken coop having fun with the angel, without the slightest reverence, tossing him things to eat through the openings in the wire as if he weren't a supernatural creature but a circus animal.

Father Gonzaga arrived before seven o'clock, alarmed at the strange news. By that time onlookers less frivolous than those at dawn had already arrived and they were making all kinds of conjectures concerning the captive's future. The simplest among them thought that he should be named mayor of the world. Others of sterner mind felt that he should be promoted to the rank of five-star general in order to win all wars. Some visionaries hoped that he could be put to stud in order to implant on earth a race of winged wise men who could take charge of the universe. But Father Gonzaga, before becoming a priest, had been a robust woodcutter. Standing by the wire, he reviewed his catechism in an instant and asked them to open the door so that he could take a close look at that pitiful man who looked more like a huge decrepit hen among the fascinated chickens. He was lying in a corner drying his open wings in the sunlight among the fruit peels and breakfast leftovers that the early risers had thrown him. Alien to the impertinences of the world, he only lifted his antiquarian eyes and murmured something in his dialect when Father Gonzaga went into the chicken coop and said good morning to him in Latin. The parish priest had his first suspicion of an imposter when he saw that he did not understand the language of God or know how to greet His ministers. Then he noticed that seen close up he was much too human: he had an unbearable smell of the outdoors, the back side of his wings was strewn with parasites and his main feathers had been mistreated by terrestrial winds, and nothing about him measured up to the proud dignity of angels. Then he came out of the chicken coop and in a brief sermon warned the curious against the risks of being ingenuous. He reminded them that the devil had the bad habit of making use of carnival tricks in order to confuse the unwary. He argued that if wings were not the essential element in determining the difference between a hawk and an airplane, they were even less so in the recognition of angels. Nevertheless, he promised to write a letter to his bishop so that the latter would write to his primate so that the latter would write to the Supreme Pontiff in order to get the final verdict from the highest courts.

His prudence fell on sterile hearts. The news of the captive angel spread with such rapidity that after a few hours the courtyard had the bustle of a marketplace and they had to call in troops with fixed bayonets to disperse the mob that was about to knock the house down. Elisenda, her spine all twisted from sweeping up so much marketplace trash, then got the idea of fencing in the yard and charging five cents admission to see the angel.

The curious came from far away. A traveling carnival arrived with a flying acrobat who buzzed over the crowd several times, but no one paid any attention to him because his wings were not those of an angel but, rather, those of a sidereal bat. The most unfortunate invalids on earth came in search of health: a poor woman who since childhood had been counting her heartbeats and had run out of numbers; a Portuguese man who couldn't sleep because the noise of the stars disturbed him; a sleepwalker who got up at night to undo the things he had done while awake; and many others with less serious ailments. In the midst of that shipwreck disorder that made the earth tremble,

Pelayo and Elisenda were happy with fatigue, for in less than a week they had crammed their rooms with money and the line of pilgrims waiting their turn to enter still reached beyond the horizon.

The angel was the only one who took no part in his own act. He spent his time try-ing to get comfortable in his borrowed nest, befuddled by the hellish heat of the oil lamps and sacramental candles that had been placed along the wire. At first they tried to make him eat some mothballs, which, according to the wisdom of the wise neigh-bor woman, were the food prescribed for angels. But he turned them down, just as he turned down the papal lunches that the penitents brought him, and they never found out whether it was because he was an angel or because he was an old man that in the end he ate nothing but eggplant mush. His only supernatural virtue seemed to be pa-tience. Especially during the first days, when the hens pecked at him, searching for the stellar parasites that proliferated in his wings, and the cripples pulled out feathers to touch their defective parts with, and even the most merciful threw stones at him, trying to get him to rise so they could see him standing. The only time they succeeded in arous-ing him was when they burned his side with an iron for branding steers, for he had been motionless for so many hours that they thought he was dead. He awoke with a start, ranting in his hermetic language and with tears in his eyes, and he flapped his wings a couple of times, which brought on a whirlwind of chicken dung and lunar dust and a gale of panic that did not seem to be of this world. Although many thought that his reaction had been one not of rage but of pain, from then on they were care-ful not to annoy him, because the majority understood that his passivity was not that of a hero taking his ease but that of a cataclysm in repose.

Father Gonzaga held back the crowd's frivolity with formulas of maidservant inspi-ration while awaiting the arrival of a final judgment on the nature of the captive. But the mail from Rome showed no sense of urgency. They spent their time finding out if the prisoner had a navel, if his dialect had any connection with Aramaic, how many times he could fit on the head of a pin, or whether he wasn't just a Norwegian with wings. Those meager letters might have come and gone until the end of time if a prov-idential event had not put an end to the priest's tribulations.

It so happened that during those days, among so many other carnival attractions, there arrived in town the traveling show of the woman who had been changed into a spi-der for having disobeyed her parents. The admission to see her was not only less than the admission to see the angel, but people were permitted to ask her all manner of ques-tions about her absurd state and to examine her up and down so that no one would ever doubt the truth of her horror. She was a frightful tarantula the size of a ram and with the head of a sad maiden. What was most heart-rending, however, was not her outlandish shape but the sincere affliction with which she recounted the details of her misfortune. While still practically a child she had sneaked out of her parents' house to go to a dance, and while she was coming back through the woods after having danced all night without permission, a fearful thunderclap rent the sky in two and through the crack came the lightning bolt of brimstone that changed her into a spider. Her only nourishment came from the meatballs that charitable souls chose to toss into her mouth. A spectacle like that, full of so much human truth and with such a fearful lesson, was bound to defeat without even trying that of a haughty angel who scarcely deigned to look at mortals. Besides, the few miracles attributed to the angel showed a certain men-tal disorder, like the blind man who didn't recover his sight but grew three new teeth, or the paralytic who didn't get to walk but almost won the lottery, and the leper whose sores sprouted sunflowers. Those consolation miracles, which were more like mocking fun, had already ruined the angel's reputation when the woman who had been changed into a spider finally crushed him completely. That was how Father Gonzaga was cured forever of his insomnia and Pelayo's courtyard went back to being as empty as during the time it had rained for three days and crabs walked through the bedrooms.

The owners of the house had no reason to lament. With the money they saved they built a two-story mansion with balconies and gardens and high netting so that crabs wouldn't get in during the winter, and with iron bars on the windows so that angels wouldn't get in. Pelayo also set up a rabbit warren close to town and gave up his job as bailiff for good, and Elisenda bought some satin pumps with high heels and many dresses of iridescent silk, the kind worn on Sunday by the most desirable women in those times. The chicken coop was the only thing that didn't receive any attention. If they washed it down with creolin and burned tears of myrrh inside it every so often, it was not in homage to the angel but to drive away the dungheap stench that still hung everywhere like a ghost and was turning the new house into an old one. At first, when the child learned to walk, they were careful that he not get too close to the chicken coop. But then they began to lose their fears and got used to the smell, and before the child got his second teeth he'd gone inside the chicken coop to play, where the wires were falling apart. The angel was no less standoffish with him than with other mortals, but he tolerated the most ingenious infamies with the patience of a dog who had no illusions. They both came down with chicken pox at the same time. The doctor who took care of the child couldn't resist the temptation to listen to the angel's heart, and he found so much whistling in the heart and so many sounds in his kidneys that it seemed impossible for him to be alive. What surprised him most, however, was the logic of his wings. They seemed so natural on that completely human organism that he couldn't understand why other men didn't have them too.

When the child began school it had been some time since the sun and rain had caused the collapse of the chicken coop. The angel went dragging himself about here and there like a stray dying man. They would drive him out of the bedroom with a broom and a moment later find him in the kitchen. He seemed to be in so many places at the same time that they grew to think that he'd been duplicated, that he was reproducing himself all through the house, and the exasperated and unhinged Elisenda shouted that it was awful living in that hell full of angels. He could scarcely eat and his antiquarian eyes had also become so foggy that he went about bumping into posts. All he had left were the bare cannulae of his last feathers. Pelayo threw a blanket over him and extended him the charity of letting him sleep in the shed, and only then did they notice that he had a temperature at night, and was delirious with the tongue twisters of an old Norwegian. That was one of the few times they became alarmed, for they thought he was going to die and not even the wise neighbor woman had been able to tell them what to do with dead angels.

And yet he not only survived his worst winter, but seemed improved with the first sunny days. He remained motionless for several days in the farthest corner of the courtyard, where no one would see him, and at the beginning of December some large, stiff feathers began to grow on his wings, the feathers of a scarecrow, which looked more like another misfortune of decrepitude. But he must have known the reason for those changes, for he was quite careful that no one should notice them, that no one should hear the sea chanteys that he sometimes sang under the stars. One morning Elisenda was cutting some bunches of onions for lunch when a wind that seemed to come from the high seas blew into the kitchen. Then she went to the window and caught the angel in his first attempts at flight. They were so clumsy that his fingernails opened a furrow in the vegetable patch and he was on the point of knocking the shed down with the ungainly flapping that slipped on the light and couldn't get a grip on the air. But he did manage to gain altitude. Elisenda let out a sigh of relief, for herself and for him, when she saw him pass over the last houses, holding himself up in some way with the risky flapping of a senile vulture. She kept watching him even when she was through cutting the onions and she kept on watching until it was no longer possible for her to see him, because then he was no longer an annoyance in her life but an imaginary dot on the horizon of the sea.

(1955)

MARGARET ATWOOD

[b. 1939]

Rape Fantasies

The way they're going on about it in the magazines you'd think it was just invented, and not only that but it's something terrific, like a vaccine for cancer. They put it in capital letters on the front cover, and inside they have these questionnaires like the ones they used to have about whether you were a good enough wife or an endomorph or an ectomorph, remember that? with the scoring upside down on page 73, and then these numbered do-it-yourself dealies, you know? RAPE, TEN THINGS TO DO ABOUT IT, like it was ten new hairdos or something. I mean, what's so new about it?

So at work they all have to talk about it because no matter what magazine you open, there it is, staring you right between the eyes, and they're beginning to have it on the television, too. Personally I'd prefer a June Allyson movie anytime but they don't make them anymore and they don't even have them that much on the Late Show. For instance, day before yesterday, that would be Wednesday, thank god it's Friday as they say, we were sitting around in the women's lunch room—the *lunch* room, I mean you'd think you could get some peace and quiet in there—and Chrissy closes up the magazine she's been reading and says, "How about it, girls, do you have rape fantasies?"

The four of us were having our game of bridge the way we always do, and I had a bare twelve points counting the singleton with not that much of a bid in anything. So I said one club, hoping Sondra would remember about the one club convention, because the time before when I used that she thought I really meant clubs and she bid us up to three, and all I had was four little ones with nothing higher than a six, and we went down two and on top of that we were vulnerable. She is not the world's best bridge player. I mean, neither am I but there's a limit.

Darlene passed but the damage was done, Sondra's head went round like it was on ball bearings and she said, "*What* fantasies?"

"Rape fantasies," Chrissy said. She's a receptionist and she looks like one; she's pretty but cool as a cucumber, like she's been painted all over with nail polish, if you know what I mean. Varnished. "It says here all women have rape fantasies."

"For Chrissake, I'm eating an egg sandwich," I said, "and I bid one club and Darlene passed."

"You mean, like some guy jumping you in an alley or something," Sondra said. She was eating her lunch, we all eat our lunches during the game, and she bit into a piece of that celery she always brings and started to chew away on it with this thoughtful expression in her eyes and I knew we might as well pack it in as far as the game was concerned.

"Yeah, sort of like that," Chrissy said. She was blushing a little, you could see it even under her makeup.

"I don't think you should go out alone at night," Darlene said, "you put yourself in a position," and I may have been mistaken but she was looking at me. She's the oldest, she's forty-one though you wouldn't know it and neither does she, but I looked it up in the employees' file. I like to guess a person's age and then look it up to see if I'm right. I let myself have an extra pack of cigarettes if I am, though I'm trying to cut down. I figure it's harmless as long as you don't tell. I mean, not everyone has access to that file, it's more or less confidential. But it's all right if I tell you, I don't expect you'll ever meet her, though you never know, it's a small world. Anyway.

"For *heaven's* sake, it's only *Toronto,*" Greta said. She worked in Detroit for three years and she never lets you forget it, it's like she thinks she's a war hero or something, we should all admire her just for the fact that she's still walking this earth, though she was really living in Windsor the whole time, she just worked in Detroit. Which for me doesn't really count. It's where you sleep, right?

"Well, do you?" Chrissy said. She was obviously trying to tell us about hers but she wasn't about to go first, she's cautious, that one.

"I certainly don't," Darlene said, and she wrinkled up her nose, like this, and I had to laugh. "I think it's disgusting." She's divorced, I read that in the file too, she never talks about it. It must've been years ago anyway. She got up and went over to the coffee machine and turned her back on us as though she wasn't going to have anything more to do with it.

"Well," Greta said. I could see it was going to be between her and Chrissy. They're both blondes, I don't mean that in a bitchy way but they do try to outdress each other. Greta would like to get out of Filing, she'd like to be a receptionist too so she could meet more people. You don't meet much of anyone in Filing except other people in Filing. Me, I don't mind it so much, I have outside interests.

"Well," Greta said, "I sometimes think about, you know my apartment? It's got this little balcony, I like to sit out there in the summer and I have a few plants out there. I never bother that much about locking the door to the balcony, it's one of those sliding glass ones, I'm on the eighteenth floor for heaven's sake, I've got a good view of the lake and the CN Tower and all. But I'm sitting around one night in my housecoat, watching TV with my shoes off, you know how you do, and I see this guy's feet, coming down past the window, and the next thing you know he's standing on the balcony, he's let himself down by a rope with a hook on the end of it from the floor above, that's the nineteenth, and before I can even get up off the chesterfield he's inside the apartment. He's all dressed in black with black gloves on"—I knew right away what show she got the black gloves off because I saw the same one—"and then he, well, you know."

"You know what?" Chrissy said, but Greta said, "And afterwards he tells me that he goes all over the outside of the apartment building like that, from one floor to another, with his rope and his hook . . . and then he goes out to the balcony and tosses his rope, and he climbs up it and disappears."

"Just like Tarzan," I said, but nobody laughed.

"Is that all?" Chrissy said. "Don't you ever think about, well, I think about being in the bathtub, with no clothes on . . ."

"So who takes a bath in their clothes?" I said, you have to admit it's stupid when you come to think of it, but she just went on, ". . . with lots of bubbles, what I use is Vitabath, it's more expensive but it's so relaxing, and my hair pinned up, and the door opens and this fellow's standing there . . ."

"How'd he get in?" Greta said.

"Oh, I don't know, through a window or something. Well, I can't very well get out of the bathtub, the bathroom's too small and besides he's blocking the doorway, so I just lie there, and he starts to very slowly take his own clothes off, and then he gets into the bathtub with me."

"Don't you scream or anything?" said Darlene. She'd come back with her cup of coffee, she was getting really interested. "I'd scream like bloody murder."

"Who'd hear me?" Chrissy said. "Besides, all the articles say it's better not to resist, that way you don't get hurt."

"Anyway you might get bubbles up your nose," I said, "from the deep breathing," and I swear all four of them looked at me like I was in bad taste, like I'd insulted the Virgin Mary or something. I mean, I don't see what's wrong with a little joke now and then. Life's too short, right?

"Listen," I said, "those aren't *rape* fantasies. I mean, you aren't getting *raped,* it's just some guy you haven't met formally who happens to be more attractive than Derek Cummins"—he's the Assistant Manager, he wears elevator shoes or at any rate they have these thick soles and he has this funny way of talking, we call him Derek Duck—"and you have a good time. Rape is when they've got a knife or something and you don't want to."

"So what about you, Estelle," Chrissy said, she was miffed because I laughed at her fantasy, she thought I was putting her down. Sondra was miffed too, by this time she'd finished her celery and she wanted to tell about hers, but she hadn't got in fast enough.

"All right, let me tell you one," I said. "I'm walking down this dark street at night and this fellow comes up and grabs my arm. Now it so happens that I have a plastic lemon in my purse, you know how it always says you should carry a plastic lemon in your purse? I don't really do it, I tried it once but the darn thing leaked all over my checkbook, but in this fantasy I have one, and I say to him, 'You're intending to rape me, right?' and he nods, so I open my purse to get the plastic lemon, and I can't find it! My purse is full of all this junk, Kleenex and cigarettes and my change purse and my lipstick and my driver's license, you know the kind of stuff; so I ask him to hold out his hands, like this, and I pile all this junk into them and down at the bottom there's the plastic lemon, and I can't get the top off. So I hand it to him and he's very obliging, he twists the top off and hands it back to me, and I squirt him in the eye."

I hope you don't think that's too vicious. Come to think of it, it is a bit mean, especially when he was so polite and all.

"*That's* your rape fantasy?" Chrissy says. "I don't believe it."

"She's a card," Darlene says, she and I are the ones that've been here the longest and she never will forget the time I got drunk at the office party and insisted I was going to dance under the table instead of on top of it, I did a sort of Cossack number but then I hit my head on the bottom of the table—actually it was a desk—when I went to get up, and I knocked myself out cold. She's decided that's the mark of an original mind and she tells everyone new about it and I'm not sure that's fair. Though I did do it.

"I'm being totally honest," I say. I always am and they know it. There's no point in being anything else, is the way I look at it, and sooner or later the truth will come out so you might as well not waste the time, right? "You should hear the one about the Easy-Off Oven Cleaner."

But that was the end of the lunch hour, with one bridge game shot to hell, and the next day we spent most of the time arguing over whether to start a new game or play out the hands we had left over from the day before, so Sondra never did get a chance to tell about her rape fantasy.

It started me thinking though, about my own rape fantasies. Maybe I'm abnormal or something, I mean I have fantasies about handsome strangers coming in through the window too, like Mr. Clean, I wish one would, please god somebody without flat feet and big sweat marks on his shirt, and over five feet five, believe me being tall is a handicap though it's getting better, tall guys are starting to like someone whose nose reaches higher than their belly button. But if you're being totally honest you can't count those as rape fantasies. In a real rape fantasy, what you should feel is this anxiety, like when you think about your apartment building catching on fire and whether you should use the elevator or the stairs or maybe just stick your head under a wet towel, and you try to remember everything you've read about what to do but you can't decide.

For instance, I'm walking along this dark street at night and this short, ugly fellow comes up and grabs my arm, and not only is he ugly, you know, with a sort of puffy nothing face, like those fellows you have to talk to in the bank when your account's overdrawn—of course I don't mean they're all like that—but he's absolutely covered in pimples. So he gets me pinned against the wall, he's short but he's heavy, and he starts to undo himself and the zipper gets stuck. I mean, one of the most significant moments in a girl's life, it's almost like getting married or having a baby or something, and he sticks the zipper.

So I say, kind of disgusted, "Oh for Chrissake," and he starts to cry. He tells me he's never been able to get anything right in his entire life, and this is the last straw, he's going to go jump off a bridge.

"Look," I say, I feel so sorry for him, in my rape fantasies I always end up feeling sorry for the guy, I mean there has to be something *wrong* with them, if it was Clint Eastwood it'd be different but worse luck it never is. I was the kind of little girl who buried dead robins, know what I mean? It used to drive my mother nuts, she didn't like me touching them, because of the germs I guess. So I say, "Listen, I know how you feel. You really should do something about those pimples, if you got rid of them you'd be quite good looking, honest; then you wouldn't have to go around doing stuff like this. I had them myself once," I say, to comfort him, but in fact I did, and it ends up I give him the name of my old dermatologist, the one I had in high school, that was back in Leamington, except I used to go to St. Catharines for the dermatologist. I'm telling you, I was really lonely when I first came here; I thought it was going to be such a big adventure and all, but it's a lot harder to meet people in a city. But I guess it's different for a guy.

Or I'm lying in bed with this terrible cold, my face is all swollen up, my eyes are red and my nose is dripping like a leaky tap, and this fellow comes in through the window and *he* has a terrible cold too, it's a new kind of flu that's been going around. So he says, "I'b goig do rabe you"—I hope you don't mind me holding my nose like this but that's the way I imagine it—and he lets out this terrific sneeze, which slows him down a bit, also I'm no object of beauty myself, you'd have to be some kind of pervert to want to rape someone with a cold like mine, it'd be like raping a bottle of LePages mucilage the way my nose is running. He's looking wildly around the room, and I realize it's because he doesn't have a piece of Kleenex! "Id's ride here," I say, and I pass him the Kleenex, god knows why he even bothered to get out of bed, you'd think if you were going to go around climbing in windows you'd wait till you were healthier, right? I mean, that takes a certain amount of energy. So I ask him why doesn't he let me fix him a Neo-Citran and scotch, that's what I always take, you still have the cold but you don't feel it, so I do and we end up watching the Late Show together. I mean, they aren't all sex maniacs, the rest of the time they must lead a normal life. I figure they enjoy watching the Late Show just like anybody else.

I do have a scarier one though . . . where the fellow says he's hearing angel voices that're telling him he's got to kill me, you know, you read about things like that all the time in the papers. In this one I'm not in the apartment where I live now, I'm back in my mother's house in Leamington and the fellow's been hiding in the cellar, he grabs my arm when I go downstairs to get a jar of jam and he's got hold of the axe too, out of the garage, that one is really scary. I mean, what do you say to a nut like that?

So I start to shake but after a minute I get control of myself and I say, is he sure the angel voices have got the right person, because I hear the same angel voices and they've been telling me for some time that I'm going to give birth to the reincarnation of St. Anne who in turn has the Virgin Mary and right after that comes Jesus Christ and the end of the world, and he wouldn't want to interfere with that, would he? So he gets confused and listens some more, and then he asks for a sign and I show him my vaccination mark, you can see it's sort of an odd-shaped one, it got infected because I scratched the top off, and that does it, he apologizes and climbs out the coal chute again, which is how he got in in the first place, and I say to myself there's some advantage in having been brought up a Catholic even though I haven't been to church since they changed the service into English, it just isn't the same, you might as well be a Protestant. I must write to Mother and tell her to nail up that coal chute, it always has bothered me. Funny, I couldn't tell you at all what this man looks like but I know exactly what kind of shoes he's wearing, because that's the last I see of him, his shoes going up the coal chute, and they're the old-fashioned kind that lace up the ankles, even though he's a young fellow. That's strange, isn't it?

Let me tell you though I really sweat until I see him safely out of there and I go upstairs right away and make myself a cup of tea. I don't think about that one much. My mother always said you shouldn't dwell on unpleasant things and I generally agree with that, I mean, dwelling on them doesn't make them go away. Though not dwelling on them doesn't make them go away either, when you come to think of it.

Sometimes I have these short ones where the fellow grabs my arm but I'm really a Kung-Fu expert, can you believe it, in real life I'm sure it would just be a conk on the head and that's that, like getting your tonsils out, you'd wake up and it would be all over except for the sore places, and you'd be lucky if your neck wasn't broken or something, I could never even hit the volleyball in gym and a volleyball is fairly large, you know?—and I just go *zap* with my fingers into his eyes and that's it, he falls over, or I flip him against a wall or something. But I could never really stick my fingers in anyone's eyes, could you? It would feel like hot jello and I don't even like cold jello, just thinking about it gives me the creeps. I feel a bit guilty about that one, I mean how would you like walking around knowing someone's been blinded for life because of you?

But maybe it's different for a guy.

The most touching one I have is when the fellow grabs my arm and I say, sad and kind of dignified, "You'd be raping a corpse." That pulls him up short and I explain that I've just found out I have leukemia and the doctors have only given me a few months to live. That's why I'm out pacing the streets alone at night, I need to think, you know, come to terms with myself. I don't really have leukemia but in the fantasy I do, I guess I chose that particular disease because a girl in my grade four class died of it, the whole class sent her flowers when she was in the hospital. I didn't understand then that she was going to die and I wanted to have leukemia too so I could get flowers. Kids are funny, aren't they? Well, it turns out that he has leukemia himself, and *he* only has a few months to live, that's why he's going around raping people, he's very bitter because he's so young and his life is being taken from him before he's really lived it. So we walk along gently under the street lights, it's spring and sort of misty, and we end up going for coffee, we're happy we've found the only other person in the world who can understand what we're going through, it's almost like fate, and after a while we just sort of look at each other and our hands touch, and he comes back with me and moves into my apartment and we spend our last months together before we die, we just sort of don't wake up in the morning, though I've never decided which one of us gets to die first. If it's him I have to go on and fantasize about the funeral, if it's me I don't have to worry about that, so it just about depends on how tired I am at the time. You may not believe this but sometimes I even start crying. I cry at the ends of movies, even the ones that aren't all that sad, so I guess it's the same thing. My mother's like that too.

The funny thing about these fantasies is that the man is always someone I don't know, and the statistics in the magazines, well, most of them anyway, they say it's often someone you do know, at least a little bit, like your boss or something—I mean, it wouldn't be *my* boss, he's over sixty and I'm sure he couldn't rape his way out of a paper bag, poor old thing, but it might be someone like Derek Duck, in his elevator shoes, perish the thought—or someone you just met, who invites you up for a drink, it's getting so you can hardly be sociable anymore, and how are you supposed to meet people if you can't trust them even that basic amount? You can't spend your whole life in the Filing Department or cooped up in your own apartment with all the doors and windows locked and the shades down. I'm not what you would call a drinker but I like to go out now and then for a drink or two in a nice place, even if I am by myself, I'm with Women's Lib on that even though I can't agree with a lot of other things they say. Like here for instance, the waiters all know me and if anyone, you know, bothers me. . . . I don't know why I'm telling you all this, except I think it helps you get to know a person, especially at first, hearing some of the things they think about. At work they call me the office worry wart, but it isn't so much like worrying, it's more like figuring out what you should do in an emergency, like I said before.

Anyway, another thing about it is that there's a lot of conversation, in fact I spend most of my time, in the fantasy that is, wondering what I'm going to say and what he's going to say, I think it would be better if you could get a conversation going. Like, how could a fellow do that to a person he's just had a long conversation with, once you let them know you're human, you have a life too, I don't see how they could go ahead with it, right? I mean, I know it happens but I just don't understand it, that's the part I really don't understand.

(1977)

R A Y M O N D C A R V E R
[1939–1989]
Cathedral

This blind man, an old friend of my wife's, he was on his way to spend the night. His wife had died. So he was visiting the dead wife's relatives in Connecticut. He called my wife from his in-laws'. Arrangements were made. He would come by train, a five-hour trip, and my wife would meet him at the station. She hadn't seen him since she worked for him one summer in Seattle ten years ago. But she and the blind man had kept in touch. They made tapes and mailed them back and forth. I wasn't enthusiastic about his visit. He was no one I knew. And his being blind bothered me. My idea of blindness came from the movies. In the movies, the blind moved slowly and never laughed. Sometimes they were led by seeing-eye dogs. A blind man in my house was not something I looked forward to.

That summer in Seattle she had needed a job. She didn't have any money. The man she was going to marry at the end of the summer was in officers' training school. He didn't have any money, either. But she was in love with the guy, and he was in love with her, etc. She'd seen something in the paper: HELP WANTED—*Reading to Blind Man,* and a telephone number. She phoned and went over, was hired on the spot. She'd worked with this blind man all summer. She read stuff to him, case studies, reports, that sort of thing. She helped him organize his little office in the county social-service department. They'd become good friends, my wife and the blind man. How do I know these things? She told me. And she told me something else. On her last day in the office, the blind man asked if he could touch her face. She agreed to this. She told me he touched his fingers to every part of her face, her nose—even her neck! She never forgot it. She even tried to write a poem about it. She was always trying to write a poem. She wrote a poem or two every year, usually after something really important had happened to her.

When we first started going out together, she showed me the poem. In the poem, she recalled his fingers and the way they had moved around over her face. In the poem, she talked about what she had felt at the time, about what went through her mind when the blind man touched her nose and lips. I can remember I didn't think much of the poem. Of course, I didn't tell her that. Maybe I just don't understand poetry. I admit it's not the first thing I reach for when I pick up something to read.

Anyway, this man who'd first enjoyed her favors, the officer-to-be, he'd been her childhood sweetheart. So okay. I'm saying that at the end of the summer she let the blind man run his hands over her face, said goodbye to him, married her childhood etc., who was now a commissioned officer, and she moved away from Seattle. But they'd kept in touch, she and the blind man. She made the first contact after a year or so. She called him up one night from an Air Force base in Alabama. She wanted to talk. They talked. He asked her to send him a tape and tell him about her life. She did this. She sent the tape. On the tape, she told the blind man about her husband and about their life together in the military. She told the blind man she loved her husband but she didn't like it where they lived and she didn't like it that he was a part of the military-industrial thing. She told the blind man she'd written a poem and he was in it. She told him that she was writing a poem about what it was like to be an Air Force officer's wife. The poem wasn't finished yet. She was still writing it. The blind man made a tape. He sent her the tape. She made a tape. This went on for years. My wife's officer was posted to one base and then another. She sent tapes from Moody AFB, McGuire, McConnell, and finally Travis, near Sacramento, where one night she got to feeling lonely and cut off from people she kept losing in that moving-around life. She got to feeling she couldn't go it another step. She went in and swallowed all the pills and capsules in the medicine chest and washed them down with a bottle of gin. Then she got into a hot bath and passed out.

But instead of dying, she got sick. She threw up. Her officer—why should he have a name? he was the childhood sweetheart, and what more does he want?—came home from somewhere, found her, and called the ambulance. In time, she put it all on a tape and sent the tape to the blind man. Over the years, she put all kinds of stuff on tapes and sent the tapes off lickety-split. Next to writing a poem every year, I think it was her chief means of recreation. On one tape, she told the blind man she'd decided to live away from her officer for a time. On another tape, she told him about her divorce. She and I began going out, and of course she told her blind man about it. She told him everything, or so it seemed to me. Once she asked me if I'd like to hear the latest tape from the blind man. This was a year ago. I was on the tape, she said. So I said okay, I'd listen to it. I got us drinks and we settled down in the living room. We made ready to listen. First she inserted the tape into the player and adjusted a couple of dials. Then she pushed a lever. The tape squeaked and someone began to talk in this loud voice. She lowered the volume. After a few minutes of harmless chitchat, I heard my own name in the mouth of this stranger, this blind man I didn't even know! And then this: "From all you've said about him, I can only conclude—" But we were interrupted, a knock at the door, something, and we didn't ever get back to the tape. Maybe it was just as well. I'd heard all I wanted to.

Now this same blind man was coming to sleep in my house.

"Maybe I could take him bowling," I said to my wife. She was at the draining board doing scalloped potatoes. She put down the knife she was using and turned around.

"If you love me," she said, "you can do this for me. If you don't love me, okay. But if you had a friend, any friend, and the friend came to visit, I'd make him feel comfortable." She wiped her hands with the dish towel.

"I don't have any blind friends," I said.

"You don't have *any* friends," she said. "Period. Besides," she said, "goddamn it, his wife's just died! Don't you understand that? The man's lost his wife!"

I didn't answer. She'd told me a little about the blind man's wife. Her name was Beulah. Beulah! That's a name for a colored woman.

"Was his wife a Negro?" I asked.

"Are you crazy?" my wife said. "Have you just flipped or something?" She picked up a potato. I saw it hit the floor, then roll under the stove. "What's wrong with you?" she said. "Are you drunk?"

"I'm just asking," I said.

Right then my wife filled me in with more detail than I cared to know. I made a drink and sat at the kitchen table to listen. Pieces of the story began to fall into place.

Beulah had gone to work for the blind man the summer after my wife had stopped working for him. Pretty soon Beulah and the blind man had themselves a church wedding. It was a little wedding—who'd want to go to such a wedding in the first place?—just the two of them, plus the minister and the minister's wife. But it was a church wedding just the same. It was what Beulah had wanted, he'd said. But even then Beulah must have been carrying the cancer in her glands. After they had been inseparable for eight years—my wife's word, *inseparable*—Beulah's health went into a rapid decline. She died in a Seattle hospital room, the blind man sitting beside the bed and holding on to her hand. They'd married, lived and worked together, slept together—had sex, sure—and then the blind man had to bury her. All this without his having ever seen what the goddamned woman looked like. It was beyond my understanding. Hearing this, I felt sorry for the blind man for a little bit. And then I found myself thinking what a pitiful life this woman must have led. Imagine a woman who could never see herself as she was seen in the eyes of her loved one. A woman who could go on day after day and never receive the smallest compliment from her beloved. A woman whose husband could never read the expression on her face, be it misery or something better. Someone who could wear makeup or not—what difference to him? She could, if she wanted, wear green eye-shadow around one eye, a straight pin in her nostril, yellow slacks and purple shoes, no matter. And then to slip off into death, the blind man's hand on her hand, his blind eyes streaming tears—I'm imagining now—her last thought maybe this: that he never even knew what she looked like, and she on an express to the grave. Robert was left with a small insurance policy and half of a twenty-peso Mexican coin. The other half of the coin went into the box with her. Pathetic.

So when the time rolled around, my wife went to the depot to pick him up. With nothing to do but wait—sure, I blamed him for that—I was having a drink and watching the TV when I heard the car pull into the drive. I got up from the sofa with my drink and went to the window to have a look.

I saw my wife laughing as she parked the car. I saw her get out of the car and shut the door. She was still wearing a smile. Just amazing. She went around to the other side of the car to where the blind man was already starting to get out. This blind man, feature this, he was wearing a full beard! A beard on a blind man! Too much, I say. The blind man reached into the back seat and dragged out a suitcase. My wife took his arm, shut the car door, and, talking all the way, moved him down the drive and then up the steps to the front porch. I turned off the TV. I finished my drink, rinsed the glass, dried my hands. Then I went to the door.

My wife said, "I want you to meet Robert. Robert, this is my husband. I've told you all about him." She was beaming. She had this blind man by his coat sleeve.

The blind man let go of his suitcase and up came his hand.

I took it. He squeezed hard, held my hand, and then he let it go.

"I feel like we've already met," he boomed.

"Likewise," I said. I didn't know what else to say. Then I said, "Welcome. I've heard a lot about you." We began to move then, a little group, from the porch into the living room, my wife guiding him by the arm. The blind man was carrying his suitcase in his other hand. My wife said things like, "To your left here, Robert. That's right. Now watch it, there's a chair. That's it. Sit down right here. This is the sofa. We just bought this sofa two weeks ago."

I started to say something about the old sofa. I'd liked that old sofa. But I didn't say anything. Then I wanted to say something else, small-talk, about the scenic ride along the Hudson. How going *to* New York, you should sit on the right-hand side of the train, and coming *from* New York, the left-hand side.

"Did you have a good train ride?" I said. "Which side of the train did you sit on, by the way?"

"What a question, which side!" my wife said. "What's it matter which side?" she said.

"I just asked," I said.

"Right side," the blind man said. "I hadn't been on a train in nearly forty years. Not since I was a kid. With my folks. That's been a long time. I'd nearly forgotten the sensation. I have winter in my beard now," he said. "So I've been told, anyway. Do I look distinguished, my dear?" the blind man said to my wife.

"You look distinguished, Robert," she said. "Robert," she said. "Robert, it's just so good to see you."

My wife finally took her eyes off the blind man and looked at me. I had the feeling she didn't like what she saw. I shrugged.

I've never met, or personally known, anyone who was blind. This blind man was late forties, a heavy-set, balding man with stooped shoulders, as if he carried a great weight there. He wore brown slacks, brown shoes, a light-brown shirt, a tie, a sports coat. Spiffy. He also had this full beard. But he didn't use a cane and he didn't wear dark glasses. I'd always thought dark glasses were a must for the blind. Fact was, I wished he had a pair. At first glance, his eyes looked like anyone else's eyes. But if you looked close, there was something different about them. Too much white in the iris, for one thing, and the pupils seemed to move around in the sockets without his knowing it or being able to stop it. Creepy. As I stared at his face, I saw the left pupil turn in toward his nose while the other made an effort to keep in one place. But it was only an effort, for that eye was on the roam without his knowing it or wanting it to be.

I said, "Let me get you a drink. What's your pleasure? We have a little of everything. It's one of our pastimes."

"Bub, I'm a Scotch man myself," he said fast enough in this big voice.

"Right," I said. Bub! "Sure you are. I knew it."

He let his fingers touch his suitcase, which was sitting alongside the sofa. He was taking his bearings. I didn't blame him for that.

"I'll move that up to your room," my wife said.

"No, that's fine," the blind man said loudly. "It can go up when I go up."

"A little water with the Scotch?" I said.

"Very little," he said.

"I knew it," I said.

He said, "Just a tad. The Irish actor, Barry Fitzgerald? I'm like that fellow. When I drink water, Fitzgerald said, I drink water. When I drink whiskey, I drink whiskey." My wife laughed. The blind man brought his hand up under his beard. He lifted his beard slowly and let it drop.

I did the drinks, three big glasses of Scotch with a splash of water in each. Then we made ourselves comfortable and talked about Robert's travels. First the long flight from the West Coast to Connecticut, we covered that. Then from Connecticut up here by train. We had another drink concerning that leg of the trip.

I remembered having read somewhere that the blind didn't smoke because, as speculation had it, they couldn't see the smoke they exhaled. I thought I knew that much and that much only about blind people. But this blind man smoked his cigarette down to the nubbin and then lit another one. This blind man filled his ashtray and my wife emptied it.

When we sat down at the table for dinner, we had another drink. My wife heaped Robert's plate with cube steak, scalloped potatoes, green beans. I buttered him up two slices of bread. I said, "Here's bread and butter for you." I swallowed some of my drink. "Now let us pray," I said, and the blind man lowered his head. My wife looked at me, her mouth agape. "Pray the phone won't ring and the food doesn't get cold," I said.

We dug in. We ate everything there was to eat on the table. We ate like there was no tomorrow. We didn't talk. We ate. We scarfed. We grazed that table. We were into serious eating. The blind man had right away located his foods, he knew just where everything was on his plate. I watched with admiration as he used his knife and fork on the meat. He'd cut two pieces of meat, fork the meat into his mouth, and then go all out for the scalloped potatoes, the beans next, and then he'd tear off a hunk of buttered bread and eat that. He'd follow this up with a big drink of milk. It didn't seem to bother him to use his fingers once in a while, either.

We finished everything, including half a strawberry pie. For a few moments, we sat as if stunned. Sweat beaded on our faces. Finally, we got up from the table and left the dirty plates. We didn't look back. We took ourselves into the living room and sank into our places again. Robert and my wife sat on the sofa. I took the big chair. We had us two or three more drinks while they talked about the major things that had come to pass for them in the past ten years. For the most part, I just listened. Now and then I joined in. I didn't want him to think I'd left the room, and I didn't want her to think I was feeling left out. They talked of things that had happened to them—to them!— these past ten years. I waited in vain to hear my name on my wife's sweet lips: "And then my dear husband came into my life"—something like that. But I heard nothing of the sort. More talk of Robert. Robert had done a little of everything, it seemed, a regular blind jack-of-all-trades. But most recently he and his wife had had an Amway distributorship, from which, I gathered, they'd earned their living, such as it was. The blind man was also a ham radio operator. He talked in his loud voice about conversations he'd had with fellow operators in Guam, in the Philippines, in Alaska, and even in Tahiti. He said he'd have a lot of friends there if he ever wanted to go visit those places. From time to time, he'd turn his blind face toward me, put his hand under his beard, ask me something. How long had I been in my present position? (Three years.) Did I like my work? (I didn't.) Was I going to stay with it? (What were the options?) Finally, when I thought he was beginning to run down, I got up and turned on the TV.

My wife looked at me with irritation. She was heading toward a boil. Then she looked at the blind man and said, "Robert, do you have a TV?"

The blind man said, "My dear, I have two TVs. I have a color set and a black-and-white thing, an old relic. It's funny, but if I turn the TV on, and I'm always turning it on, I turn on the color set. It's funny, don't you think?"

I didn't know what to say to that. I had absolutely nothing to say to that. No opinion. So I watched the news program and tried to listen to what the announcer was saying.

"This is a color TV," the blind man said. "Don't ask me how, but I can tell."

"We traded up a while ago," I said.

The blind man had another taste of his drink. He lifted his beard, sniffed it, and let it fall. He leaned forward on the sofa. He positioned his ashtray on the coffee table, then put the lighter to his cigarette. He leaned back on the sofa and crossed his legs at the ankles.

My wife covered her mouth, and then she yawned. She stretched. She said, "I think I'll go upstairs and put on my robe. I think I'll change into something else. Robert, you make yourself comfortable," she said.

"I'm comfortable," the blind man said.

"I want you to feel comfortable in this house," she said.

"I am comfortable," the blind man said.

After she'd left the room, he and I listened to the weather report and then to the sports roundup. By that time, she'd been gone so long I didn't know if she was going to come back. I thought she might have gone to bed. I wished she'd come back downstairs. I didn't want to be left alone with a blind man. I asked him if he wanted another drink, and he said sure. Then I asked if he wanted to smoke some dope with me. I said I'd just rolled a number. I hadn't, but I planned to do so in about two shakes.

"I'll try some with you," he said.

"Damn right," I said. "That's the stuff."

I got our drinks and sat down on the sofa with him. Then I rolled us two fat numbers. I lit one and passed it. I brought it to his fingers. He took it and inhaled.

"Hold it as long as you can," I said. I could tell he didn't know the first thing.

My wife came back downstairs wearing her pink robe and her pink slippers.

"What do I smell?" she said.

"We thought we'd have us some cannabis," I said.

My wife gave me a savage look. Then she looked at the blind man and said, "Robert, I didn't know you smoked."

He said, "I do now, my dear. There's a first time for everything. But I don't feel anything yet."

"This stuff is pretty mellow," I said. "This stuff is mild. It's dope you can reason with," I said. "It doesn't mess you up."

"Not much it doesn't, bub," he said, and laughed.

My wife sat on the sofa between the blind man and me. I passed her the number. She took it and toked and then passed it back to me. "Which way is this going?" she said. Then she said, "I shouldn't be smoking this. I can hardly keep my eyes open as it is. That dinner did me in. I shouldn't have eaten so much."

"It was the strawberry pie," the blind man said. "That's what did it," he said, and he laughed his big laugh. Then he shook his head.

"There's more strawberry pie," I said.

"Do you want some more, Robert?" my wife said.

"Maybe in a little while," he said.

We gave our attention to the TV. My wife yawned again. She said, "Your bed is made up when you feel like going to bed, Robert. I know you must have had a long day. When you're ready to go to bed, say so." She pulled his arm. "Robert?"

He came to and said, "I've had a real nice time. This beats tapes, doesn't it?"

I said, "Coming at you," and I put the number between his fingers. He inhaled, held the smoke, and then let it go. It was like he'd been doing it since he was nine years old.

"Thanks, bub," he said. "But I think this is all for me. I think I'm beginning to feel it," he said. He held the burning roach out for my wife.

"Same here," she said. "Ditto. Me, too." She took the roach and passed it to me. "I may just sit here for a while between you two guys with my eyes closed. But don't let me bother you, okay? Either one of you. If it bothers you, say so. Otherwise, I may just sit here with my eyes closed until you're ready to go to bed," she said. "Your bed's made up, Robert, when you're ready. It's right next to our room at the top of the stairs. We'll show you up when you're ready. You wake me up now, you guys, if I fall asleep." She said that and then she closed her eyes and went to sleep.

The news program ended. I got up and changed the channel. I sat back down on the sofa. I wished my wife hadn't pooped out. Her head lay across the back of the sofa, her mouth open. She'd turned so that her robe had slipped away from her legs, exposing a juicy thigh. I reached to draw her robe back over her, and it was then that I glanced at the blind man. What the hell! I flipped the robe open again.

"You say when you want some strawberry pie," I said.

"I will," he said.

I said, "Are you tired? Do you want me to take you up to your bed? Are you ready to hit the hay?"

"Not yet," he said. "No, I'll stay up with you, bub. If that's all right. I'll stay up until you're ready to turn in. We haven't had a chance to talk. Know what I mean? I feel like me and her monopolized the evening." He lifted his beard and he let it fall. He picked up his cigarettes and his lighter.

"That's all right," I said. Then I said, "I'm glad for the company."

And I guess I was. Every night I smoked dope and stayed up as long as I could before I fell asleep. My wife and I hardly ever went to bed at the same time. When I did go to sleep, I had these dreams. Sometimes I'd wake up from one of them, my heart going crazy.

Something about the church and the Middle Ages was on the TV. Not your run-of-the-mill TV fare. I wanted to watch something else. I turned to the other channels. But there was nothing on them, either. So I turned back to the first channel and apologized.

"Bub, it's all right," the blind man said. "It's fine with me. Whatever you want to watch is okay. I'm always learning something. Learning never ends. It won't hurt me to learn something tonight. I got ears," he said.

We didn't say anything for a time. He was leaning forward with his head turned at me, his right ear aimed in the direction of the set. Very disconcerting. Now and then his eyelids drooped and then they snapped open again. Now and then he put his fingers into his beard and tugged, like he was thinking about something he was hearing on the television.

On the screen, a group of men wearing cowls was being set upon and tormented by men dressed in skeleton costumes and men dressed as devils. The men dressed as devils wore devil masks, horns, and long tails. This pageant was part of a procession. The Englishman who was narrating the thing said it took place in Spain once a year. I tried to explain to the blind man what was happening.

"Skeletons," he said. "I know about skeletons," he said, and he nodded.

The TV showed this one cathedral. Then there was a long, slow look at another one. Finally, the picture switched to the famous one in Paris, with its flying buttresses and its spires reaching up to the clouds. The camera pulled away to show the whole of the cathedral rising above the skyline.

There were times when the Englishman who was telling the thing would shut up, would simply let the camera move around over the cathedrals. Or else the camera would tour the countryside, men in fields walking behind oxen. I waited as long as I could. Then I felt I had to say something. I said, "They're showing the outside of this cathedral now. Gargoyles. Little statues carved to look like monsters. Now I guess they're in Italy. Yeah, they're in Italy. There's paintings on the walls of this one church."

"Are those fresco paintings, bub?" he asked, and he sipped from his drink.

I reached for my glass. But it was empty. I tried to remember what I could remember. "You're asking me are those frescoes?" I said. "That's a good question. I don't know."

The camera moved to a cathedral outside Lisbon. The differences in the Portuguese cathedral compared with the French and Italian were not that great. But they were there. Mostly the interior stuff. Then something occurred to me, and I said, "Something has occurred to me. Do you have any idea what a cathedral is? What they look like, that is? Do you follow me? If somebody says cathedral to you, do you have any notion what they're talking about? Do you know the difference between that and a Baptist church, say?"

He let the smoke dribble from his mouth. "I know they took hundreds of workers fifty or a hundred years to build," he said. "I just heard the man say that, of course. I know generations of the same families worked on a cathedral. I heard him say that, too. The men who began their life's work on them, they never lived to see the completion of their work. In that wise, bub, they're no different from the rest of us, right?" He laughed. Then his eyelids drooped again. His head nodded. He seemed to be snoozing. Maybe he was imagining himself in Portugal. The TV was showing another cathedral now. This one was in Germany. The Englishman's voice droned on. "Cathedrals," the blind man said. He sat up and rolled his head back and forth. "If you want the truth, bub, that's about all I know. What I just said. What I heard him say. But maybe you could describe one to me? I wish you'd do it. I'd like that. If you want to know, I really don't have a good idea."

I stared hard at the shot of the cathedral on the TV. How could I even begin to describe it? But say my life depended on it. Say my life was being threatened by an insane guy who said I had to do it or else.

I stared some more at the cathedral before the picture flipped off into the countryside. There was no use. I turned to the blind man and said, "To begin with, they're very tall." I was looking around the room for clues. "They reach way up. Up and up.

Toward the sky. They're so big, some of them, they have to have these supports. To help hold them up, so to speak. These supports are called buttresses. They remind me of viaducts, for some reason. But maybe you don't know viaducts, either? Sometimes the cathedrals have devils and such carved into the front. Sometimes lords and ladies. Don't ask me why this is," I said.

He was nodding. The whole upper part of his body seemed to be moving back and forth.

"I'm not doing so good, am I?" I said.

He stopped nodding and leaned forward on the edge of the sofa. As he listened to me, he was running his fingers through his beard. I wasn't getting through to him, I could see that. But he waited for me to go on just the same. He nodded, like he was trying to encourage me. I tried to think what else to say. "They're really big," I said. "They're massive. They're built of stone. Marble, too, sometimes. In those olden days, when they built cathedrals, men wanted to be close to God. In those olden days, God was an important part of everyone's life. You could tell this from their cathedral-building. I'm sorry," I said, "but it looks like that's the best I can do for you. I'm just no good at it."

"That's all right, bub," the blind man said. "Hey, listen. I hope you don't mind my asking you. Can I ask you something? Let me ask you a simple question, yes or no. I'm just curious and there's no offense. You're my host. But let me ask if you are in any way religious? You don't mind my asking?"

I shook my head. He couldn't see that, though. A wink is the same as a nod to a blind man. "I guess I don't believe in it. In anything. Sometimes it's hard. You know what I'm saying?"

"Sure, I do," he said.

"Right," I said.

The Englishman was still holding forth. My wife sighed in her sleep. She drew a long breath and went on with her sleeping.

"You'll have to forgive me," I said. "But I can't tell you what a cathedral looks like. It just isn't in me to do it. I can't do any more than I've done."

The blind man sat very still, his head down, as he listened to me.

I said, "The truth is, cathedrals don't mean anything special to me. Nothing. Cathedrals. They're something to look at on late-night TV. That's all they are."

It was then that the blind man cleared his throat. He brought something up. He took a handkerchief from his back pocket. Then he said, "I get it, bub. It's okay. It happens. Don't worry about it," he said. "Hey, listen to me. Will you do me a favor? I got an idea. Why don't you find us some heavy paper? And a pen. We'll do something. We'll draw one together. Get us a pen and some heavy paper. Go on, bub, get the stuff," he said.

So I went upstairs. My legs felt like they didn't have any strength in them. They felt like they did after I'd done some running. In my wife's room, I looked around. I found some ballpoints in a little basket on her table. And then I tried to think where to look for the kind of paper he was talking about.

Downstairs, in the kitchen, I found a shopping bag with onion skins in the bottom of the bag. I emptied the bag and shook it. I brought it into the living room and sat down with it near his legs. I moved some things, smoothed the wrinkles from the bag, spread it out on the coffee table.

The blind man got down from the sofa and sat next to me on the carpet.

He ran his fingers over the paper. He went up and down the sides of the paper. The edges, even the edges. He fingered the corners.

"All right," he said. "All right, let's do her."

He found my hand, the hand with the pen. He closed his hand over my hand. "Go ahead, bub, draw," he said. "Draw. You'll see. I'll follow along with you. It'll be okay. Just begin now like I'm telling you. You'll see. Draw," the blind man said.

So I began. First I drew a box that looked like a house. It could have been the house I lived in. Then I put a roof on it. At either end of the roof, I drew spires. Crazy.

"Swell," he said. "Terrific. You're doing fine," he said. "Never thought anything like this could happen in your lifetime, did you, bub? Well, it's a strange life, we all know that. Go on now. Keep it up."

I put in windows with arches. I drew flying buttresses. I hung great doors. I couldn't stop. The TV station went off the air. I put down the pen and closed and opened my fingers. The blind man felt around over the paper. He moved the tips of his fingers over the paper, all over what I had drawn, and he nodded.

"Doing fine," the blind man said.

I took up the pen again, and he found my hand. I kept at it. I'm no artist. But I kept drawing just the same.

My wife opened up her eyes and gazed at us. She sat up on the sofa, her robe hanging open. She said, "What are you doing? Tell me, I want to know."

I didn't answer her.

The blind man said, "We're drawing a cathedral. Me and him are working on it. Press hard," he said to me. "That's right. That's good," he said. "Sure. You got it, bub. I can tell. You didn't think you could. But you can, can't you? You're cooking with gas now. You know what I'm saying? We're going to really have us something here in a minute. How's the old arm?" he said. "Put some people in there now. What's a cathedral without people?"

My wife said, "What's going on? Robert, what are you doing? What's going on?"

"It's all right," he said to her. "Close your eyes now," the blind man said to me.

I did it. I closed them just like he said.

"Are they closed?" he said. "Don't fudge."

"They're closed," I said.

"Keep them that way," he said. He said, "Don't stop now. Draw."

So we kept on with it. His fingers rode my fingers as my hand went over the paper. It was like nothing else in my life up to now.

Then he said, "I think that's it. I think you got it," he said. "Take a look. What do you think?"

But I had my eyes closed. I thought I'd keep them that way for a little longer. I thought it was something I ought to do.

"Well?" he said. "Are you looking?"

My eyes were still closed. I was in my house. I knew that. But I didn't feel like I was inside anything.

"It's really something," I said.

(1983)

ALICE WALKER

[b. 1944]

Everyday Use

FOR YOUR GRANDMAMA

I will wait for her in the yard that Maggie and I made so clean and wavy yesterday afternoon. A yard like this is more comfortable than most people know. It is not just a yard. It is like an extended living room. When the hard clay is swept clean as a floor and the fine sand around the edges lined with tiny, irregular grooves anyone can come and sit and look up into the elm tree and wait for the breezes that never come inside the house.

Maggie will be nervous until after her sister goes: she will stand hopelessly in corners homely and ashamed of the burn scars down her arms and legs, eyeing her sister with a mixture of envy and awe. She thinks her sister has held life always in the palm of one hand, that "no" is a word the world never learned to say to her.

You've no doubt seen those TV shows where the child who has "made it" is confronted, as a surprise, by her own mother and father, tottering in weakly from backstage. (A pleasant surprise, of course: What would they do if parent and child came on the show only to curse out and insult each other?) On TV mother and child embrace and smile into each other's faces. Sometimes the mother and father weep, the child wraps them in her arms and leans across the table to tell how she would not have made it without their help. I have seen these programs.

Sometimes I dream a dream in which Dee and I are suddenly brought together on a TV program of this sort. Out of a dark and soft-seated limousine I am ushered into a bright room filled with many people. There I meet a smiling, gray, sporty man like Johnny Carson who shakes my hand and tells me what a fine girl I have. Then we are on the stage and Dee is embracing me with tears in her eyes. She pins on my dress a large orchid, even though she has told me once that she thinks orchids are tacky flowers.

In real life I am a large, big-boned woman with rough, man-working hands. In the winter I wear flannel nightgowns to bed and overalls during the day. I can kill and clean a hog as mercilessly as a man. My fat keeps me hot in zero weather. I can work outside all day, breaking ice to get water for washing; I can eat pork liver cooked over the open fire minutes after it comes steaming from the hog. One winter I knocked a bull calf straight in the brain between the eyes with a sledge hammer and had the meat hung up to chill before nightfall. But of course all this does not show on television. I am the way my daughter would want me to be: a hundred pounds lighter, my skin like an uncooked barley pancake. My hair glistens in the hot bright lights. Johnny Carson has much to do to keep up with my quick and witty tongue.

But that is a mistake. I know even before I wake up. Who ever knew a Johnson with a quick tongue? Who can even imagine me looking a strange white man in the eye? It seems to me I have talked to them always with one foot raised in flight, with my head turned in whichever way is farthest from them. Dee, though. She would always look anyone in the eye. Hesitation was no part of her nature.

"How do I look, Mama?" Maggie says, showing just enough of her thin body enveloped in pink skirt and red blouse for me to know she's there, almost hidden by the door.

"Come out into the yard," I say.

Have you ever seen a lame animal, perhaps a dog run over by some careless person rich enough to own a car, sidle up to someone who is ignorant enough to be kind to him? That is the way my Maggie walks. She has been like this, chin on chest, eyes on ground, feet in shuffle, ever since the fire that burned the other house to the ground.

Dee is lighter than Maggie, with nicer hair and a fuller figure. She's a woman now, though sometimes I forget. How long ago was it that the other house burned? Ten, twelve years? Sometimes I can still hear the flames and feel Maggie's arms sticking to me, her hair smoking and her dress falling off her in little black papery flakes. Her eyes seemed stretched open, blazed open by the flames reflected in them. And Dee. I see her standing off under the sweet gum tree she used to dig gum out of; a look of concentration on her face as she watched the last dingy gray board of the house fall in toward the red-hot brick chimney. Why don't you do a dance around the ashes? I'd wanted to ask her. She had hated the house that much.

I used to think she hated Maggie, too. But that was before we raised the money, the church and me, to send her to Augusta to school. She used to read to us without pity; forcing words, lies, other folks' habits, whole lives upon us two, sitting trapped and ignorant underneath her voice. She washed us in a river of make-believe, burned us with a lot of knowledge we didn't necessarily need to know. Pressed us to her with the serious way she read, to shove us away at just the moment, like dimwits, we seemed about to understand.

Dee wanted nice things. A yellow organdy dress to wear to her graduation from high school; black pumps to match a green suit she'd made from an old suit somebody gave me. She was determined to stare down any disaster in her efforts. Her eyelids would not flicker for minutes at a time. Often I fought off the temptation to shake her. At sixteen she had a style of her own: and knew what style was.

I never had an education myself. After second grade the school was closed down. Don't ask me why: in 1927 colored asked fewer questions than they do now. Sometimes Maggie reads to me. She stumbles along good-naturedly but can't see well. She knows she is not bright. Like good looks and money, quickness passed her by. She will marry John Thomas (who has mossy teeth in an earnest face) and then I'll be free to sit here and I guess just sing church songs to myself. Although I never was a good singer. Never could carry a tune. I was always better at a man's job. I used to love to milk till I was hooked in the side in '49. Cows are soothing and slow and don't bother you, unless you try to milk them the wrong way.

I have deliberately turned my back on the house. It is three rooms, just like the one that burned, except the roof is tin; they don't make shingle roofs any more. There are no real windows, just some holes cut in the sides, like the portholes in a ship, but not round and not square, with rawhide holding the shutters up on the outside. This house is in a pasture, too, like the other one. No doubt when Dee sees it she will want to tear it down. She wrote me once that no matter where we "choose" to live, she will manage to come see us. But she will never bring her friends. Maggie and I thought about this and Maggie asked me, "Mama, when did Dee ever *have* any friends?"

She had a few. Furtive boys in pink shirts hanging about on washday after school. Nervous girls who never laughed. Impressed with her they worshiped the well-turned phrase, the cute shape, the scalding humor that erupted like bubbles in lye. She read to them.

When she was courting Jimmy T she didn't have much time to pay to us, but turned all her faultfinding power on him. He *flew* to marry a cheap gal from a family of ignorant flashy people. She hardly had time to recompose herself.

When she comes I will meet—but there they are!

Maggie attempts to make a dash for the house, in her shuffling way, but I stay her with my hand. "Come back here," I say. And she stops and tries to dig a well in the sand with her toe.

It is hard to see them clearly through the strong sun. But even the first glimpse of leg out of the car tells me it is Dee. Her feet were always neat-looking, as if God himself had shaped them with a certain style. From the other side of the car comes a short, stocky man. Hair is all over his head a foot long and hanging from his chin like a kinky mule tail. I hear Maggie suck in her breath. "Uhnnnh," is what it sounds like. Like when you see the wriggling end of a snake just in front of your foot on the road. "Uhnnnh."

Dee next. A dress down to the ground, in this hot weather. A dress so loud it hurts my eyes. There are yellows and oranges enough to throw back the light of the sun. I feel my whole face warming from the heat waves it throws out. Earrings gold, too, and hanging down to her shoulders. Bracelets dangling and making noises when she moves her arm up to shake the folds of the dress out of her armpits. The dress is loose and flows, and as she walks closer, I like it. I hear Maggie go "Uhnnnh" again. It is her sister's hair. It stands straight up like the wool on a sheep. It is black as night and around the edges are two long pigtails that rope about like small lizards disappearing behind her ears.

"Wa-su-zo-Tean-o!" she says, coming on in that gliding way the dress makes her move. The short stocky fellow with the hair to his navel is all grinning and he follows up with "Asalamalakim, my mother and sister!" He moves to hug Maggie but she falls back, right up against the back of my chair. I feel her trembling there and when I look up I see the perspiration falling off her chin.

"Don't get up," says Dee. Since I am stout it takes something of a push. You can see me trying to move a second or two before I make it. She turns, showing white heels through her sandals, and goes back to the car. Out she peeks next with a Polaroid. She stoops down quickly and lines up picture after picture of me sitting there in front of the house with Maggie cowering behind me. She never takes a shot without making sure the house is included. When a cow comes nibbling around the edge of the yard she snaps it and me and Maggie *and* the house. Then she puts the Polaroid in the back seat of the car, and comes up and kisses me on the forehead.

Meanwhile Asalamalakim is going through the motions with Maggie's hand. Maggie's hand is as limp as a fish, and probably as cold, despite the sweat, and she keeps trying to pull it back. It looks like Asalamalakim wants to shake hands but wants to do it fancy. Or maybe he don't know how people shake hands. Anyhow, he soon gives up on Maggie.

"Well," I say. "Dee."

"No, Mama," she says. "Not 'Dee,' Wangero Leewanika Kemanjo!"

"What happened to 'Dee'?" I wanted to know.

"She's dead," Wangero said. "I couldn't bear it any longer being named after the people who oppress me."

"You know as well as me you was named after your aunt Dicie," I said. Dicie is my sister. She named Dee. We called her "Big Dee" after Dee was born.

"But who was *she* named after?" asked Wangero.

"I guess after Grandma Dee," I said.

"And who was she named after?" asked Wangero.

"Her mother," I said, and saw Wangero was getting tired. "That's about as far back as I can trace it," I said. Though, in fact, I probably could have carried it back beyond the Civil War through the branches.

"Well," said Asalamalakim, "there you are."

"Uhnnnh," I heard Maggie say.

"There I was not," I said, "before 'Dicie' cropped up in our family, so why should I try to trace it that far back?"

He just stood there grinning, looking down on me like somebody inspecting a Model A car. Every once in a while he and Wangero sent eye signals over my head.

"How do you pronounce this name?" I asked.

"You don't have to call me by it if you don't want to," said Wangero.

"Why shouldn't I?" I asked. "If that's what you want us to call you, we'll call you."

"I know it might sound awkward at first," said Wangero.

"I'll get used to it," I said. "Ream it out again."

Well, soon we got the name out of the way. Asalamalakim had a name twice as long and three times as hard. After I tripped over it two or three times he told me to just call him Hakim-a-barber. I wanted to ask him was he a barber, but I didn't really think he was, so I didn't ask.

"You must belong to those beef-cattle peoples down the road," I said. They said "Asalamalakim" when they met you, too, but they didn't shake hands. Always too busy: feeding the cattle, fixing the fences, putting up salt-lick shelters, throwing down hay. When the white folks poisoned some of the herd the men stayed up all night with rifles in their hands. I walked a mile and a half just to see the sight.

Hakim-a-barber said, "I accept some of their doctrines, but farming and raising cattle is not my style." (They didn't tell me, and I didn't ask, whether Wangero [Dee] had really gone and married him.)

We sat down to eat and right away he said he didn't eat collards and pork was unclean. Wangero, though, went on through the chitlins and corn bread, the greens and everything else. She talked a blue streak over the sweet potatoes. Everything delighted her. Even the fact that we still used the benches her daddy made for the table when we couldn't afford to buy chairs.

"Oh, Mama!" she cried. Then turned to Hakim-a-barber. "I never knew how lovely these benches are. You can feel the rump prints," she said, running her hands underneath her and along the bench. Then she gave a sigh and her hand closed over

Grandma Dee's butter dish. "That's it!" she said. "I knew there was something I wanted to ask you if I could have." She jumped up from the table and went over in the corner where the churn stood, the milk in it clabber by now. She looked at the churn and looked at it.

"This churn top is what I need," she said. "Didn't Uncle Buddy whittle it out of a tree you all used to have?"

"Yes," I said.

"Uh huh," she said happily. "And I want the dasher, too."

"Uncle Buddy whittle that, too?" asked the barber.

Dee (Wangero) looked up at me.

"Aunt Dee's first husband whittled the dash," said Maggie so low you almost couldn't hear her. "His name was Henry, but they called him Stash."

"Maggie's brain is like an elephant's," Wangero said, laughing. "I can use the churn top as a centerpiece for the alcove table," she said, sliding a plate over the churn, "and I'll think of something artistic to do with the dasher."

When she finished wrapping the dasher the handle stuck out. I took it for a moment in my hands. You didn't even have to look close to see where hands pushing the dasher up and down to make butter had left a kind of sink in the wood. In fact, there were a lot of small sinks; you could see where thumbs and fingers had sunk into the wood. It was beautiful light yellow wood, from a tree that grew in the yard where Big Dee and Stash had lived.

After dinner Dee (Wangero) went to the trunk at the foot of my bed and started rifling through it. Maggie hung back in the kitchen over the dishpan. Out came Wangero with two quilts. They had been pieced by Grandma Dee and then Big Dee and me had hung them on the quilt frames on the front porch and quilted them. One was in the Lone Star pattern. The other was Walk Around the Mountain. In both of them were scraps of dresses Grandma Dee had worn fifty and more years ago. Bits and pieces of Grandpa Jarrell's Paisley shirts. And one teeny faded blue piece, about the size of a penny matchbox, that was from Great Grandpa Ezra's uniform that he wore in the Civil War.

"Mama," Wangero said sweet as a bird. "Can I have these old quilts?"

I heard something fall in the kitchen, and a minute later the kitchen door slammed.

"Why don't you take one or two of the others?" I asked. "These old things was just done by me and Big Dee from some tops your grandma pieced before she died."

"No," said Wangero. "I don't want those. They are stitched around the borders by machine."

"That'll make them last better," I said.

"That's not the point," said Wangero. "These are all pieces of dresses Grandma used to wear. She did all this stitching by hand. Imagine!" She held the quilts securely in her arms, stroking them.

"Some of the pieces, like those lavender ones, come from old clothes her mother handed down to her," I said, moving up to touch the quilts. Dee (Wangero) moved back just enough so that I couldn't reach the quilts. They already belonged to her.

"Imagine!" she breathed again, clutching them closely to her bosom.

"The truth is," I said, "I promised to give them quilts to Maggie, for when she marries John Thomas."

She gasped like a bee had stung her.

"Maggie can't appreciate these quilts!" she said. "She'd probably be backward enough to put them to everyday use."

"I reckon she would," I said. "God knows I been saving 'em for long enough with nobody using 'em. I hope she will!" I didn't want to bring up how I had offered Dee (Wangero) a quilt when she went away to college. Then she had told me they were old-fashioned, out of style.

"But they're *priceless!*" she was saying now, furiously; for she has a temper. "Maggie would put them on the bed and in five years they'd be in rags. Less than that!"

"She can always make some more," I said. "Maggie knows how to quilt."

Dee (Wangero) looked at me with hatred. "You just will not understand. The point is these quilts, *these* quilts!"

"Well," I said, stumped. "What would *you* do with them?"

"Hang them," she said. As if that was the only thing you *could* do with quilts.

Maggie by now was standing in the door. I could almost hear the sound her feet made as they scraped over each other.

"She can have them, Mama," she said, like somebody used to never winning anything, or having anything reserved for her. "I can 'member Grandma Dee without the quilts."

I looked at her hard. She had filled her bottom lip with checkerberry snuff and it gave her face a kind of dopey, hangdog look. It was Grandma Dee and Big Dee who taught her how to quilt herself. She stood there with her scarred hands hidden in the folds of her skirt. She looked at her sister with something like fear but she wasn't mad at her. This was Maggie's portion. This was the way she knew God to work.

When I looked at her like that something hit me in the top of my head and ran down to the soles of my feet. Just like when I'm in church and the spirit of God touches me and I get happy and shout. I did something I never had done before: hugged Maggie to me, then dragged her on into the room, snatched the quilts out of Miss Wangero's hands and dumped them into Maggie's lap. Maggie just sat there on my bed with her mouth open.

"Take one or two of the others," I said to Dee.

But she turned without a word and went out to Hakim-a-barber.

"You just don't understand," she said, as Maggie and I came out to the car.

"What don't I understand?" I wanted to know.

"Your heritage," she said. And then she turned to Maggie, kissed her, and said, "You ought to try to make something of yourself, too, Maggie. It's really a new day for us. But from the way you and Mama still live you'd never know it."

She put on some sunglasses that hid everything above the tip of her nose and her chin.

Maggie smiled; maybe at the sunglasses. But a real smile, not scared. After we watched the car dust settle I asked Maggie to bring me a dip of snuff. And then the two of us sat there just enjoying, until it was time to go in the house and go to bed.

(1973)

LEE K. ABBOTT

[b. 1947]

The View of Me from Mars

A week before I became a father, which now seems like the long ago and far away fairy tales happen in, I read a father-child story that went straight at the surprise one truth between children and parents is. It was called "Mirrors," and had an end, to the twenty-three-year-old would-be know-it-all I was, that literally threw me back in my chair—an end, sad somehow and wise, which held that it is now and then necessary for the child, in ways mysterious with love, to forgive the parent.

In "Mirrors" the child was a girl, though it could have been a boy just as easily, whose father—a decent man, we have to believe—takes her to the sideshow tent at a one-horse and one-elephant circus in the flatlands of Iowa or Nebraska or Kansas. She's seven or eight at this time, and—as we have all begged for toys or experiences it can be, I see now, our misfortune to receive—she begs and begs to see the snake charmer and the tattooed lady, the giant and the dwarf. He gives in, the girl decides much later, because of his decency; or he gives in, as my own father might say, because he's too much a milk-and-cookies sort of fool to understand that in that smelly, ill-lit tent is knowledge it is a parent's duty often to deny or to avoid. It is a good moment, I tell you, this moment when they pay their quarters and go in, one person full of pride, the other sucking on cotton candy, the sad end of them still pages and pages away.

In that tent—a whole hour, I think—walking from little stage to little stage, the girl is awestruck and puzzled and, well, breath-taken, full of questions about where these people, these creatures, live and what they do when they're not standing in front of a bunch of hayseeds and would it be possible to get a face, a tattoo, printed on her knee. "Can I touch?" she asks. "Do they talk?" A spotlight comes on, blue and harsh, and nearby, in a swirl of cigarette smoke and field dust, are two little people, Mr. and Mrs. Tiny, gussied up like a commodore and his society bride; another light snaps on, yellow this time and ten paces away, and there stands a man—"A boy," the barker tells us, "only eighteen and still growing!"—who's already nine feet tall, his arms long as shovels, nothing in his face about his own parents or what he wants to be at twenty-five. These are clichés, my smart wife, Ellen Kay, tells me ("Sounds too artsy-fartsy," her exact words were when I read the thing to her), but in the story I remember, these are the exhibitions girl and man pass by—the girl Christmas Eve impatient, the man nervous—before they come to the main display, which is, in "Mirrors," a young woman, beautiful and smooth as china, who has no arms and no legs.

The father, complaining that he's grubby-feeling and hot, wants to get out, but his daughter, her heart hammering in her ears, can't move. As never before, she's conscious of her own hands and feet, the wonders they are. She's aware of smells—breath and oil and two-dollar cologne—and of sounds—a gasp here, a whisper there, exclamations that have in them ache and horror and fear. "C'mon," the father says, taking her elbow. But onstage, businesslike as a banker, the woman—"The Human Torso," the barker announces, "smart like the dickens"—is drinking water, the glass clamped against her neck by her shoulder; is putting on lipstick; is writing her name with a brush between her teeth; is, Lordy, about to type—with her chin maybe—a letter to a Spec 4 with the Army in Korea, her boyfriend.

Outside, the midway glittering and crowded with Iowans going crosswise, the girl, more fascinated than frightened (though the fright is coming), asks how that was done. The father has a Lucky Strike out now, and the narrator—seven or eight but on the verge of learning that will stay with her until seventy or eighty—realizes he's stalling. He's embarrassed, maybe sick. He says "Howdy" to a deadbeat he'd never otherwise talk to. He says he's hungry, how about a hot dog, some buttered popcorn? He's cold, he says, too cold for September. "How?" she says again, pulling at his sleeve a little and watching his face go stiff and loose in a way that has her saying to herself, "I am not scared. No, I am not." And then he says what the narrator realizes will be his answer— sometimes comic, often not—for all thereafter that astounds or baffles and will not be known: "Mirrors, it's done with mirrors."

There's a pause here, I remember, six sentences that tell what the weather is like and how, here and there, light bulbs are missing and what the girl's favorite subjects are in school. "What?" she thinks to ask, but doesn't. "It's an illusion," he says, his voice squeaky the way it gets when he talks about money they don't have much of. "A trick, like magic." Part of her—the part that can say the sum of two plus two, and that A is for Apple, B is for Boy—knows that mirrors have nothing to do with what she's seen; another part—this the half of her that will remember this incident forever and ever— knows that her father, now as strange to her as the giant and the dwarf, is lying.

His hand is working up and down, and his expression says, as lips and eyes and cheeks will, that he's sorry, he didn't mean for her to see that, she's so young. Something is trembling inside her, a muscle or a bone. One-Mississippi, she says to herself. Two-Mississippi. Over there sits a hound dog wearing a hat and somewhere a shout is going up that says somebody won a Kewpie doll or a stuffed monkey, and up ahead, creaking and clanking, the Tilt-A-Whirl is full of people spinning round and round goggle-eyed. Her father has a smile not connected to his eyes—another lie—and his hand out to be held, and going by them is a fat lady who lives on Jefferson Street and a man with a limp who lives on Spruce. Her father seems too hairy to her now, and maybe not sharp-minded enough, with a nose too long and knobby. She tells herself what she is, which is a good dancer and smart about which side the fork goes on and who gets introduced first when strangers meet; and what she is not, which is strong enough to do pull-ups and watch-ful about who goes where and why. She is learning something, she thinks. There is being good, she thinks. And there is not. There is the truth, she thinks. And there is not.

And so, in the climax of what I read years and years ago, she says, her hands sticky and her dress white as Hollywood daylight, "Yes, mirrors, I thought so"—words that, years and years ago, said all I thought possible about lies and love and how forgiveness works.

In this story, which is true and only two days old and also about forgiveness, I am the father to be read about and the child is my son, Stuart Eliot Polk, Jr. (called "Pudge" in and out of the family); he's a semifat golfer—"linksman," he insists the proper term is—and honor student who will at the end of this summer go off to college and so cease to be a citizen in the sideshow tent my big house here in El Paso now clearly is.

Yes, forgiveness—particularly ironic in that, since my graduation years ago from Perkins Seminary at SMU, it has been my job to say, day after day after day, the noises that are "It will get better" and "We all make mistakes" to a thousand Methodists who aim to be themselves forgiven and sent home happy. There is no "freak" here, except the ordinary one I am, and no storybook midway, except my modern kitchen and its odd come and go.

I am an adulterer—an old-fashioned word, sure, but the only one appropriate to the ancient sin it names; and my lover—a modern word not so full of terror and guilt and judgment as another—was, until two days ago, Terri Ann Mackey, a rich, three-times-married former Zeta Tau Alpha Texas girl who might one day make headlines for the dramatic hair she has or the way she can sing Conway Twitty tunes. In every way likable and loud and free-minded, she has, in the last four years, met me anywhere and everywhere—in the Marriott and Hilton hotels, in the Cavern of Music in Juarez, even at a preachers' retreat at the Inn of the Mountain Gods near Ruidoso in southern New Mexico's piney forests. Dressed up in this or that outfit she sent away for or got on a trip to Dallas, she has, to my delight and education, pretended to be naughty as what we imagine the Swedish are or nice as Snow White; she has pretended, in a hundred rented rooms, to be everything I thought my wife was not—daring and wicked, heedless as a tyrant. Shameful to say, it seems we have always been here, in this bright desert cowtown, now far-flung and fifty percent ticky-tacky, drinking wine and fornicating and then hustling home to deceive people we were wed to. Shameful to say, it seems we have always been playing the eyes' version of footsy—her in pink and cactus yellow in a pew in the middle of St. Paul's, me in the pulpit sermonizing about parables and Jesus and what welfare we owe the lost and poor and beaten down.

"Yes," my wife, Ellen Kay, would answer when I told her I was at the Stanton Street Racquet Club playing handball with a UTEP management professor named Red Walker. "Go change," she'd say, herself lovely and schoolgirl trim as that woman I'd collapsed atop a half-hour before. "I phoned," she'd say, "Mrs. Denbo said you were out." Yes, I'd tell her. I was in the choir room, hunting organ music that would inspire and not be hokey; I was in the library, looking up what the Puritan Mathers had written about witchcraft and gobbledygook we are better off without; I was taking a drive in my Volvo, the better to clear my head so I could get to the drafting of a speech for the Rotarians, or the LULAC Club of Ysleta, or the Downtown Optimists. "You work too hard," she'd say, "let's go to Acapulco this year." And I'd head to my big bedroom, the men I am, the public one amazed by his private self—the first absolutely in love with a blonde continental-history major he'd courted at the University of Texas in 1967; the second still frazzled by what, in the afternoon, is made from deceit and bednoise and indecency. And until two days ago, it was possible to believe that I knew which was which, what what.

"Where were you?" Ellen Kay said, making (though too violently, I think now) the tuna casserole I like enough to eat twice a year. "I called everywhere," she said. "It was as if you didn't exist." Upset, her hair spilling out of the French roll she prefers, she said more, two or three paragraphs whose theme was my peculiar behavior and the sly way I had lately and what time I was supposed to be somewhere and was not; and suddenly, taking note of the thump-thump my heart made and how one cloud in the east looked like a bell, I stood at the sink, steadily drinking glass after glass of water, trying to put some miles between me and her suspicions. Terri Ann Mackey Cruz Robinson Cross was all over me, my hands and my thighs and my face; and, a giant step away, my wife was asking where I'd been. "You were going to call," Ellen Kay said. "You had an appointment, a meeting." I had one thought, which was about the bricked-up middle of me, and another, which was about how like TV this situation was. "I talked to Bill Watson at the bank," she said. "He hasn't seen you for a week, ten days. I called—" And her wayward husband had a moment then, familiar to all cheaters and sorry folks, when he thought he'd tell the truth; a moment, before fear hit him and he got a 3-D vision of the cheap world he'd have to live in, when he thought to make plain the creature he was and the no-account stage he stood upon.

"I was at the golf course," I said, "watching Pudge. They have a match tomorrow." The oven was closed, the refrigerator opened. "Which course?" she said. Forks and knives had been brought out, made a pile of. "Coronado Hills," I said. "Pudge is hitting the ball pretty good." She went past me a dozen times, carrying the plates and the bread and the fruit bowl, and I tried to meet her eyes and so not give away the corrupt inside of me. I thought of several Latin words—*bellum* and *verus* and *fatum*—and the Highland Park classroom I learned them in. "All right," she said, though by the dark notes in her voice it was clear she was going to ask Pudge if he'd seen me there, by the green I'd claimed to have stood next to, applauding the expert wedge shot I'd seen with my very own eyes.

As in the former story of illusions and the mess they make crashing down, there is a pause here, one of two; and you are to imagine now how herky-jerky time moved in our house when Pudge drove up and came in and said howdy and washed his hands as he'd been a million times told. You are to imagine, too, the dinner we picked at and our small talk about school and American government and what money does. While time went up and down, I thought about Pudge the way evil comic-book Martians are said to think about us: I was curious to know how I'd be affected by what, in a minute or an hour, would come from the mouth of an earthling who, so far as I knew, had never looked much beyond himself to see the insignificant dust-ball he stood upon. I saw him as his own girlfriend, Traci Dixon, must: polite, fussy as a nun, soft-spoken about everything except golf and how it is, truly, a full-fledged sport.

Part of me—that eye and ear which would make an excellent witness at an auto wreck or similar calamity—flew up to one high corner of the room, like a ghost or an angel, and wondered what could be said about these three people who sat there and there and there. They were Democrats who, in a blue moon, liked what Reagan did; they had Allstate insurance and bank books and stacks of paper that said where they were in the world and what business they conducted with it; they played Scrabble and Clue and chose to watch the news Dan Rather read. The wife, who once upon a time could run fast enough to be useful in flag football, now used all her energy to keep mostly white-collar rednecks from using the words "nigger" and "spic" in her company; the son, who had once wanted to be an astronaut or a Houston brain surgeon, now aimed to be the only Ph.D. in computer science to win the Masters at Augusta, Georgia; and the father—well, what was there to say about a supposedly learned man for whom the spitting image of God, Who was up and yonder and everywhere, was his own father, a bent-over and gin-soaked cattle rancher in Midland, Texas? I hovered in that corner, distant and disinterested, and then Ellen Kay spoke to Pudge, and I came rushing back, dumb and helpless as anything human that falls from a great height.

"Daddy says you had a good round this afternoon," Ellen Kay began. "You had an especially nice wedge shot, he says." She was being sneaky, which my own sneaky self admired; and Pudge quit the work his chewing was, a little confusion in his round, smart face. He was processing, that machine between his ears crunching data that in no way could ever be, and for the fifteen seconds we made eye contact I wanted him to put aside reason and logic and algebra and see me with his guts and heart. On his lip he had a crumb that, if you didn't tell him, would stay until kingdom come; I wanted him to stop blinking and wrinkling his forehead like a first-year theater student. The air was heavy in that room, the light coming from eight directions at once, and I wanted to remind him of our trip last January to the Phoenix Open and that too-scholarly talk we'd had about the often mixed-up relations between men and women. I had a picture of me throwing a ball to him, and of him catching it. I had a picture of him learning to drive a stick shift, and of him so carefully mowing our lawn. Oddly, I thought about fishing, which I hate, and bowling, which I am silly at, and then Ellen Kay, putting detergent in the dishwasher, asked him again about events that never happened, and I took a deep breath I expected to hold until the horror stopped.

Here is that second pause I spoke of—that moment, before time lurches forward again, when the eye needs to look elsewhere to see what is ruined, what not. Pudge now knew I was lying. His eyes went here and there, to the clock above my shoulder, to his mother's overwatered geranium on the windowsill, to his mostly empty plate. He was learning something about me—and about himself too. Like his made-up counterpart in "Mirrors," he was seeing that I, his father, was afraid and weak and damaged; and like the invented daddy in that story I read, a daddy whose interior life we were not permitted to see, I wanted my own child, however numbed or shocked, to forgive me for the tilt the world now stood at, to say I was not responsible for the sad magic trick our common back-and-forth really is. "Tell her," I said. I had in mind a story he could confirm—the Coke we shared in the clubhouse, a corny joke that was heard, and the help I tried to be with his short game—a story that had nowhere in it, two days ago, a father cold and alone and small.

He seeks to find something in his son but find something in himself.

(1991)

TIM O'BRIEN
[b. 1947]

The Things They Carried

First Lieutenant Jimmy Cross carried letters from a girl named Martha, a junior at Mount Sebastian College in New Jersey. They were not love letters, but Lieutenant Cross was hoping, so he kept them folded in plastic at the bottom of his rucksack. In the late afternoon, after a day's march, he would dig his foxhole, wash his hands under a canteen, unwrap the letters, hold them with the tips of his fingers, and spend the last hour of light pretending. He would imagine romantic camping trips into the White Mountains in New Hampshire. He would sometimes taste the envelope flaps, knowing her tongue had been there. More than anything, he wanted Martha to love him as he loved her, but the letters were mostly chatty, elusive on the matter of love. She was a virgin, he was almost sure. She was an English major at Mount Sebastian, and she wrote beautifully about her professors and roommates and midterm exams, about her respect for Chaucer and her great affection for Virginia Woolf. She often quoted lines of poetry; she never mentioned the war, except to say, Jimmy, take care of yourself. The letters weighed ten ounces. They were signed "Love, Martha," but Lieutenant Cross understood that "Love" was only a way of signing and did not mean what he sometimes pretended it meant. At dusk, he would carefully return the letters to his rucksack. Slowly, a bit distracted, he would get up and move among his men, checking the perimeter, then at full dark he would return to his hole and watch the night and wonder if Martha was a virgin.

The things they carried were largely determined by necessity. Among the necessities or near necessities were P-38 can openers, pocket knives, heat tabs, wrist watches, dog tags, mosquito repellant, chewing gum, candy, cigarettes, salt tablets, packets of Kool-Aid, lighters, matches, sewing kits, Military Payment Certificates, C rations, and two or three canteens of water. Together, these items weighed between fifteen and twenty pounds, depending upon a man's habits or rate of metabolism. Henry Dobbins, who was a big man, carried extra rations; he was especially fond of canned peaches in heavy syrup over pound cake. Dave Jensen, who practiced field hygiene, carried a toothbrush, dental floss, and several hotel-size bars of soap he'd stolen on R&R in Sydney, Australia. Ted Lavender, who was scared, carried tranquilizers until he was shot in the head outside the village of Than Khe in mid-April. By necessity, and because it was SOP,° they all carried steel helmets that weighed five pounds including the liner and camouflage cover. They carried the standard fatigue jackets and trousers. Very few carried underwear. On their feet they carried jungle boots—2.1 pounds—and Dave Jensen carried three pairs of socks and a can of Dr. Scholl's foot powder as a precaution against trench foot. Until he was shot, Ted Lavender carried six or seven ounces of premium dope, which for him was a necessity. Mitchell Sanders, the RTO,° carried condoms. Norman Bowker carried a diary. Rat Kiley carried comic books. Kiowa, a devout Baptist, carried an illustrated New Testament that had been presented to him by his father, who taught Sunday school in Oklahoma City, Oklahoma. As a hedge against bad times, however, Kiowa also carried his grandmother's distrust of the white man, his grandfather's old hunting hatchet. Necessity dictated. Because the land was mined and booby-trapped, it was SOP for each man to carry a steel-centered, nylon-covered flak jacket, which weighed 6.7 pounds, but which on hot days seemed much heavier. Because you could die so quickly, each man carried at least one large compress bandage, usually in the helmet band for easy access. Because the nights were cold, and because the monsoons were wet, each carried a green plastic poncho that could be used as a raincoat or ground sheet or makeshift tent. With its quilted liner, the poncho weighed almost two pounds, but it was worth every ounce. In April, for instance, when Ted Lavender was shot, they used his poncho to wrap him up, then to carry him across the paddy, then to lift him into the chopper that took him away.

They were called legs or grunts.

To carry something was to "hump" it, as when Lieutenant Jimmy Cross humped his love for Martha up the hills and through the swamps. In its intransitive form, "to

---

SOP *Standard operating procedure.*   **RTO** *Radiotelephone operator.*

hump" meant "to walk," or "to march," but it implied burdens far beyond the intransitive.

Almost everyone humped photographs. In his wallet, Lieutenant Cross carried two photographs of Martha. The first was a Kodachrome snapshot signed "Love," though he knew better. She stood against a brick wall. Her eyes were gray and neutral, her lips slightly open as she stared straight-on at the camera. At night, sometimes, Lieutenant Cross wondered who had taken the picture, because he knew she had boyfriends, because he loved her so much, and because he could see the shadow of the picture taker spreading out against the brick wall. The second photograph had been clipped from the 1968 Mount Sebastian yearbook. It was an action shot—women's volleyball—and Martha was bent horizontal to the floor, reaching, the palms of her hands in sharp focus, the tongue taut, the expression frank and competitive. There was no visible sweat. She wore white gym shorts. Her legs, he thought, were almost certainly the legs of a virgin, dry and without hair, the left knee cocked and carrying her entire weight, which was just over one hundred pounds. Lieutenant Cross remembered touching that left knee. A dark theater, he remembered, and the movie was *Bonnie and Clyde,* and Martha wore a tweed skirt, and during the final scene, when he touched her knee, she turned and looked at him in a sad, sober way that made him pull his hand back, but he would always remember the feel of the tweed skirt and the knee beneath it and the sound of the gunfire that killed Bonnie and Clyde, how embarrassing it was, how slow and oppressive. He remembered kissing her good night at the dorm door. Right then, he thought, he should've done something brave. He should've carried her up the stairs to her room and tied her to the bed and touched that left knee all night long. He should've risked it. Whenever he looked at the photographs, he thought of new things he should've done.

What they carried was partly a function of rank, partly of field specialty.

As a first lieutenant and platoon leader, Jimmy Cross carried a compass, maps, code books, binoculars, and a .45-caliber pistol that weighed 2.9 pounds fully loaded. He carried a strobe light and the responsibility for the lives of his men.

As an RTO, Mitchell Sanders carried the PRC-25 radio, a killer, twenty-six pounds with its battery.

As a medic, Rat Kiley carried a canvas satchel filled with morphine and plasma and malaria tablets and surgical tape and comic books and all the things a medic must carry, including M&M's for especially bad wounds, for a total weight of nearly twenty pounds.

As a big man, therefore a machine gunner, Henry Dobbins carried the M-60, which weighed twenty-three pounds unloaded, but which was almost always loaded. In addition, Dobbins carried between ten and fifteen pounds of ammunition draped in belts across his chest and shoulders.

As PFCs or Spec 4s, most of them were common grunts and carried the standard M-16 gas-operated assault rifle. The weapon weighed 7.5 pounds unloaded, 8.2 pounds with its full twenty-round magazine. Depending on numerous factors, such as topography and psychology, the riflemen carried anywhere from twelve to twenty magazines, usually in cloth bandoliers, adding on another 8.4 pounds at minimum, fourteen pounds at maximum. When it was available, they also carried M-16 maintenance gear—rods and steel brushes and swabs and tubes of LSA oil—all of which weighed about a pound. Among the grunts, some carried the M-79 grenade launcher, 5.9 pounds unloaded, a reasonably light weapon except for the ammunition, which was heavy. A single round weighed ten ounces. The typical load was twenty-five rounds. But Ted Lavender, who was scared, carried thirty-four rounds when he was shot and killed outside Than Khe, and he went down under an exceptional burden, more than twenty pounds of ammunition, plus the flak jacket and helmet and rations and water and toilet paper and tranquilizers and all the rest, plus the unweighed fear. He was dead weight. There was no twitching or flopping. Kiowa, who saw it happen, said it was like watching a rock fall, or a big sandbag or something—just boom, then down— not like the movies where the dead guy rolls around and does fancy spins and goes ass over teakettle—not like that, Kiowa said, the poor bastard just flat-fuck fell. Boom. Down. Nothing else. It was a bright morning in mid-April. Lieutenant Cross felt the pain. He blamed himself. They stripped off Lavender's canteens and ammo, all the heavy things, and Rat Kiley said the obvious, the guy's dead, and Mitchell Sanders used his radio to report one U.S. KIA° and to request a chopper. Then they wrapped Lavender in his poncho. They carried him out to a dry paddy, established security, and sat smoking the dead man's dope until the chopper came. Lieutenant Cross kept to himself. He pictured Martha's smooth young face, thinking he loved her more than anything, more than his men, and now Ted Lavender was dead because he loved her so much and could not stop thinking about her. When the dust-off arrived, they carried Lavender aboard. Afterward they burned Than Khe. They marched until dusk, then dug their holes, and that night Kiowa kept explaining how you had to be there, how fast it was, how the poor guy just dropped like so much concrete. Boom-down, he said. Like cement.

In addition to the three standard weapons—the M-60, M-16, and M-79—they carried whatever presented itself, or whatever seemed appropriate as a means of killing or staying alive. They carried catch-as-catch-can. At various times, in various situations, they carried M-14s and CAR-15s and Swedish Ks and grease guns and captured AK-47s and Chi-Coms and RPGs and Simonov carbines and black-market Uzis and .38-caliber Smith & Wesson handguns and 66 mm LAWs and shotguns and silencers and blackjacks and bayonets and C-4 plastic explosives. Lee Strunk carried a slingshot; a weapon of last resort, he called it. Mitchell Sanders carried brass knuckles. Kiowa carried his grandfather's feathered hatchet. Every third or fourth man carried a Claymore antipersonnel mine—3.5 pounds with its firing device. They all carried fragmentation grenades—fourteen ounces each. They all carried at least one M-18 colored smoke grenade—twenty-four ounces. Some carried CS or tear-gas grenades. Some carried white-phosphorus grenades. They carried all they could bear, and then some, including a silent awe for the terrible power of the things they carried.

In the first week of April, before Lavender died, Lieutenant Jimmy Cross received a good-luck charm from Martha. It was a simple pebble, an ounce at most. Smooth to the touch, it was a milky-white color with flecks of orange and violet, oval-shaped, like a miniature egg. In the accompanying letter, Martha wrote that she had found the pebble on the Jersey shoreline, precisely where the land touched water at high tide, where things came together but also separated. It was this separate-but-together quality, she

KIA   *Killed in action.*

wrote, that had inspired her to pick up the pebble and to carry it in her breast pocket for several days, where it seemed weightless, and then to send it through the mail, by air, as a token of her truest feelings for him. Lieutenant Cross found this romantic. But he wondered what her truest feelings were, exactly, and what she meant by separate-but-together. He wondered how the tides and waves had come into play on that afternoon along the Jersey shoreline when Martha saw the pebble and bent down to rescue it from geology. He imagined bare feet. Martha was a poet, with the poet's sensibilities, and her feet would be brown and bare, the toenails unpainted, the eyes chilly and somber like the ocean in March, and though it was painful, he wondered who had been with her that afternoon. He imagined a pair of shadows moving along the strip of sand where things came together but also separated. It was phantom jealousy, he knew, but he couldn't help himself. He loved her so much. On the march, through the hot days of early April, he carried the pebble in his mouth, turning it with his tongue, tasting sea salts and moisture. His mind wandered. He had difficulty keeping his attention on the war. On occasion he would yell at his men to spread out the column, to keep their eyes open, but then he would slip away into daydreams, just pretending, walking barefoot along the Jersey shore, with Martha, carrying nothing. He would feel himself rising. Sun and waves and gentle winds, all love and lightness.

What they carried varied by mission.

When a mission took them to the mountains, they carried mosquito netting, machetes, canvas tarps, and extra bug juice.

If a mission seemed especially hazardous, or if it involved a place they knew to be bad, they carried everything they could. In certain heavily mined AOs,° where the land was dense with Toe Poppers and Bouncing Betties, they took turns humping a twenty-eight-pound mine detector. With its headphones and big sensing plate, the equipment was a stress on the lower back and shoulders, awkward to handle, often useless because of the shrapnel in the earth, but they carried it anyway, partly for safety, partly for the illusion of safety.

On ambush, or other night missions, they carried peculiar little odds and ends. Kiowa always took along his New Testament and a pair of moccasins for silence. Dave Jensen carried night-sight vitamins high in carotin. Lee Strunk carried his slingshot; ammo, he claimed, would never be a problem. Rat Kiley carried brandy and M&M's. Until he was shot, Ted Lavender carried the starlight scope, which weighed 6.3 pounds with its aluminum carrying case. Henry Dobbins carried his girlfriend's pantyhose wrapped around his neck as a comforter. They all carried ghosts. When dark came, they would move out single file across the meadows and paddies to their ambush coordinates, where they would quietly set up the Claymores and lie down and spend the night waiting.

Other missions were more complicated and required special equipment. In mid-April, it was their mission to search out and destroy the elaborate tunnel complexes in the Than Khe area south of Chu Lai. To blow the tunnels, they carried one-pound blocks of pentrite high explosives, four blocks to a man, sixty-eight pounds in all. They carried wiring, detonators, and battery-powered clackers. Dave Jensen carried earplugs. Most often, before blowing the tunnels, they were ordered by higher command to search them, which was considered bad news, but by and large they just shrugged and

AOs   *Areas of operations.*

carried out orders. Because he was a big man, Henry Dobbins was excused from tunnel duty. The others would draw numbers. Before Lavender died there were seventeen men in the platoon, and whoever drew the number seventeen would strip off his gear and crawl in head first with a flashlight and Lieutenant Cross's .45-caliber pistol. The rest of them would fan out as security. They would sit down or kneel, not facing the hole, listening to the ground beneath them, imagining cobwebs and ghosts, whatever was down there—the tunnel walls squeezing in—how the flashlight seemed impossibly heavy in the hand and how it was tunnel vision in the very strictest sense, compression in all ways, even time, and how you had to wiggle in—ass and elbows—a swallowed-up feeling—and how you found yourself worrying about odd things—will your flashlight go dead? Do rats carry rabies? If you screamed, how far would the sound carry? Would your buddies hear it? Would they have the courage to drag you out? In some respects, though not many, the waiting was worse than the tunnel itself. Imagination was a killer.

On April 16, when Lee Strunk drew the number seventeen, he laughed and muttered something and went down quickly. The morning was hot and very still. Not good, Kiowa said. He looked at the tunnel opening, then out across a dry paddy toward the village of Than Khe. Nothing moved. No clouds or birds or people. As they waited, the men smoked and drank Kool-Aid, not taking much, feeling sympathy for Lee Strunk but also feeling the luck of the draw. You win some, you lose some, said Mitchell Sanders, and sometimes you settle for a rain check. It was a tired line and no one laughed.

Henry Dobbins ate a tropical chocolate bar. Ted Lavender popped a tranquilizer and went off to pee.

After five minutes, Lieutenant Jimmy Cross moved to the tunnel, leaned down, and examined the darkness. Trouble, he thought—a cave-in maybe. And then suddenly, without willing it, he was thinking about Martha. The stresses and fractures, the quick collapse, the two of them buried alive under all that weight. Dense, crushing love. Kneeling, watching the hole, he tried to concentrate on Lee Strunk and the war, all the dangers, but his love was too much for him, he felt paralyzed, he wanted to sleep inside her lungs and breathe her blood and be smothered. He wanted her to be a virgin and not a virgin, all at once. He wanted to know her. Intimate secrets—why poetry? Why so sad? Why the grayness in her eyes? Why so alone? Not lonely, just alone— riding her bike across campus or sitting off by herself in the cafeteria. Even dancing, she danced alone—and it was the aloneness that filled him with love. He remembered telling her that one evening. How she nodded and looked away. And how, later, when he kissed her, she received the kiss without returning it, her eyes wide open, not afraid, not a virgin's eyes, just flat and uninvolved.

Lieutenant Cross gazed at the tunnel. But he was not there. He was buried with Martha under the white sand at the Jersey shore. They were pressed together, and the pebble in his mouth was her tongue. He was smiling. Vaguely, he was aware of how quiet the day was, the sullen paddies, yet he could not bring himself to worry about matters of security. He was beyond that. He was just a kid at war, in love. He was twenty-two years old. He couldn't help it.

A few moments later Lee Strunk crawled out of the tunnel. He came up grinning, filthy but alive. Lieutenant Cross nodded and closed his eyes while the others clapped Strunk on the back and made jokes about rising from the dead.

Worms, Rat Kiley said. Right out of the grave. Fuckin' zombie.

The men laughed. They all felt great relief.

Spook City, said Mitchell Sanders.

Lee Strunk made a funny ghost sound, a kind of moaning, yet very happy, and right then, when Strunk made that high happy moaning sound, when he went *Ahhooooo,* right then Ted Lavender was shot in the head on his way back from peeing. He lay with his mouth open. The teeth were broken. There was a swollen black bruise under his left eye. The cheekbone was gone. Oh shit, Rat Kiley said, the guy's dead. The guy's dead, he kept saying, which seemed profound—the guy's dead. I mean really.

The things they carried were determined to some extent by superstition. Lieutenant Cross carried his good-luck pebble. Dave Jensen carried a rabbit's foot. Norman Bowker, otherwise a very gentle person, carried a thumb that had been presented to him as a gift by Mitchell Sanders. The thumb was dark brown, rubbery to the touch, and weighed four ounces at most. It had been cut from a VC corpse, a boy of fifteen or sixteen. They'd found him at the bottom of an irrigation ditch, badly burned, flies in his mouth and eyes. The boy wore black shorts and sandals. At the time of his death he had been carrying a pouch of rice, a rifle, and three magazines of ammunition.

You want my opinion, Mitchell Sanders said, there's a definite moral here.

He put his hand on the dead boy's wrist. He was quiet for a time, as if counting a pulse, then he patted the stomach, almost affectionately, and used Kiowa's hunting hatchet to remove the thumb.

Henry Dobbins asked what the moral was.

Moral?

You know. *Moral.*

Sanders wrapped the thumb in toilet paper and handed it across to Norman Bowker. There was no blood. Smiling, he kicked the boy's head, watched the flies scatter, and said, It's like with that old TV show—Paladin. Have gun, will travel.

Henry Dobbins thought about it.

Yeah, well, he finally said. I don't see no moral.

There it *is,* man.

Fuck off.

They carried USO stationery and pencils and pens. They carried Sterno, safety pins, trip flares, signal flares, spools of wire, razor blades, chewing tobacco, liberated joss sticks and statuettes of the smiling Buddha, candles, grease pencils, *The Stars and Stripes,* fingernail clippers, Psy Ops° leaflets, bush hats, bolos, and much more. Twice a week, when the resupply choppers came in, they carried hot chow in green Mermite cans and large canvas bags filled with iced beer and soda pop. They carried plastic water containers, each with a two-gallon capacity. Mitchell Sanders carried a set of starched tiger fatigues for special occasions. Henry Dobbins carried Black Flag insecticide. Dave Jensen carried empty sandbags that could be filled at night for added protection. Lee Strunk carried tanning lotion. Some things they carried in common. Taking turns, they carried the big PRC-77 scrambler radio, which weighed thirty pounds with its battery. They shared the weight of memory. They took up what others could no longer bear. Often, they carried each other, the wounded or weak. They carried infections. They

Psy Ops *Psychological operations.*

carried chess sets, basketballs, Vietnamese-English dictionaries, insignia of rank, Bronze Stars and Purple Hearts, plastic cards imprinted with the Code of Conduct. They carried diseases, among them malaria and dysentery. They carried lice and ringworm and leeches and paddy algae and various rots and molds. They carried the land itself—Vietnam, the place, the soil—a powdery orange-red dust that covered their boots and fatigues and faces. They carried the sky. The whole atmosphere, they carried it, the humidity, the monsoons, the stink of fungus and decay, all of it, they carried gravity. They moved like mules. By daylight they took sniper fire, at night they were mortared, but it was not battle, it was just the endless march, village to village, without purpose, nothing won or lost. They marched for the sake of the march. They plodded along slowly, dumbly, leaning forward against the heat, unthinking, all blood and bone, simple grunts, soldiering with their legs, toiling up the hills and down into the paddies and across the rivers and up again and down, just humping, one step and then the next and then another, but no volition, no will, because it was automatic, it was anatomy, and the war was entirely a matter of posture and carriage, the hump was everything, a kind of inertia, a kind of emptiness, a dullness of desire and intellect and conscience and hope and human sensibility. Their principles were in their feet. Their calculations were biological. They had no sense of strategy or mission. They searched the villages without knowing what to look for, not caring, kicking over jars of rice, frisking children and old men, blowing tunnels, sometimes setting fires and sometimes not, then forming up and moving on to the next village, then other villages, where it would always be the same. They carried their own lives. The pressures were enormous. In the heat of early afternoon, they would remove their helmets and flak jackets, walking bare, which was dangerous but which helped ease the strain. They would often discard things along the route of march. Purely for comfort, they would throw away rations, blow their Claymores and grenades, no matter, because by nightfall the resupply choppers would arrive with more of the same, then a day or two later still more, fresh watermelons and crates of ammunition and sunglasses and woolen sweaters—the resources were stunning—sparklers for the Fourth of July, colored eggs for Easter. It was the great American war chest—the fruits of science, the smokestacks, the canneries, the arsenals at Hartford, the Minnesota forests, the machine shops, the vast fields of corn and wheat—they carried like freight trains; they carried it on their backs and shoulders—and for all the ambiguities of Vietnam, all the mysteries and unknowns, there was at least the single abiding certainty that they would never be at a loss for things to carry.

After the chopper took Lavender away, Lieutenant Jimmy Cross led his men into the village of Than Khe. They burned everything. They shot chickens and dogs, they trashed the village well, they called in artillery and watched the wreckage, then they marched for several hours through the hot afternoon, and then at dusk, while Kiowa explained how Lavender died, Lieutenant Cross found himself trembling.

He tried not to cry. With his entrenching tool, which weighed five pounds, he began digging a hole in the earth.

He felt shame. He hated himself. He had loved Martha more than his men, and as a consequence Lavender was now dead, and this was something he would have to carry like a stone in his stomach for the rest of the war.

All he could do was dig. He used his entrenching tool like an ax, slashing, feeling both love and hate, and then later, when it was full dark, he sat at the bottom of his foxhole and wept. It went on for a long while. In part, he was grieving for Ted Lavender, but mostly it was for Martha, and for himself, because she belonged to another world, which was not quite real, and because she was a junior at Mount Sebastian College in New Jersey, a poet and a virgin and uninvolved, and because he realized she did not love him and never would.

Like cement, Kiowa whispered in the dark. I swear to God—boom-down. Not a word.
    I've heard this, said Norman Bowker.
    A pisser, you know? Still zipping himself up. Zapped while zipping.
    All right, fine. That's enough.
    Yeah, but you had to see it, the guy just—
    I *heard,* man. Cement. So why not shut the fuck *up?*
    Kiowa shook his head sadly and glanced over at the hole where Lieutenant Jimmy Cross sat watching the night. The air was thick and wet. A warm, dense fog had settled over the paddies and there was the stillness that precedes rain.
    After a time Kiowa sighed.
    One thing for sure, he said. The Lieutenant's in some deep hurt. I mean that crying jag—the way he was carrying on—it wasn't fake or anything, it was real heavy-duty hurt. The man cares.
    Sure, Norman Bowker said.
    Say what you want, the man does care.
    We all got problems.
    Not Lavender.
    No, I guess not, Bowker said. Do me a favor, though.
    Shut up?
    That's a smart Indian. Shut up.
    Shrugging, Kiowa pulled off his boots. He wanted to say more, just to lighten up his sleep, but instead he opened his New Testament and arranged it beneath his head as a pillow. The fog made things seem hollow and unattached. He tried not to think about Ted Lavender, but then he was thinking how fast it was, no drama, down and dead, and how it was hard to feel anything except surprise. It seemed un-Christian. He wished he could find some great sadness, or even anger, but the emotion wasn't there and he couldn't make it happen. Mostly he felt pleased to be alive. He liked the smell of the New Testament under his cheek, the leather and ink and paper and glue, whatever the chemicals were. He liked hearing the sounds of night. Even his fatigue, it felt fine, the stiff muscles and the prickly awareness of his own body, a floating feeling. He enjoyed not being dead. Lying there, Kiowa admired Lieutenant Jimmy Cross's capacity for grief. He wanted to share the man's pain, he wanted to care as Jimmy Cross cared. And yet when he closed his eyes, all he could think was Boom-down, and all he could feel was the pleasure of having his boots off and the fog curling in around him and the damp soil and the Bible smells and the plush comfort of night.
    After a moment Norman Bowker sat up in the dark.
    What the hell, he said. You want to talk, *talk.* Tell it to me.
    Forget it.
    No, man, go on. One thing I hate, it's a silent Indian.

For the most part they carried themselves with poise, a kind of dignity. Now and then, however, there were times of panic, when they squealed or wanted to squeal but couldn't, when they twitched and made moaning sounds and covered their heads and said Dear Jesus and flopped around on the earth and fired their weapons blindly and cringed and sobbed and begged for the noise to stop and went wild and made stupid promises to themselves and to God and to their mothers and fathers, hoping not to die. In different ways, it happened to all of them. Afterward, when the firing ended, they would blink and peek up. They would touch their bodies, feeling shame, then quickly hiding it. They would force themselves to stand. As if in slow motion, frame by frame, the world would take on the old logic—absolute silence, then the wind, then sunlight, then voices. It was the burden of being alive. Awkwardly, the men would reassemble themselves, first in private, then in groups, becoming soldiers again. They would repair the leaks in their eyes. They would check for casualties, call in dust-offs, light cigarettes, try to smile, clear their throats and spit and begin cleaning their weapons. After a time someone would shake his head and say, No lie, I almost shit my pants, and someone else would laugh, which meant it was bad, yes, but the guy had obviously not shit his pants, it wasn't that bad, and in any case nobody would ever do such a thing and then go ahead and talk about it. They would squint into the dense, oppressive sunlight. For a few moments, perhaps, they would fall silent, lighting a joint and tracking its passage from man to man, inhaling, holding in the humiliation. Scary stuff, one of them might say. But then someone else would grin or flick his eyebrows and say, Roger-dodger, almost cut me a new asshole, *almost.*

There were numerous such poses. Some carried themselves with a sort of wistful resignation, others with pride or stiff soldierly discipline or good humor or macho zeal. They were afraid of dying but they were even more afraid to show it.

They found jokes to tell.

They used a hard vocabulary to contain the terrible softness. *Greased,* they'd say. *Offed, lit up, zapped while zipping.* It wasn't cruelty, just stage presence. They were actors and the war came at them in 3-D. When someone died, it wasn't quite dying, because in a curious way it seemed scripted, and because they had their lines mostly memorized, irony mixed with tragedy, and because they called it by other names, as if to encyst and destroy the reality of death itself. They kicked corpses. They cut off thumbs. They talked grunt lingo. They told stories about Ted Lavender's supply of tranquilizers, how the poor guy didn't feel a thing, how incredibly tranquil he was.

There's a moral here, said Mitchell Sanders.

They were waiting for Lavender's chopper, smoking the dead man's dope.

The moral's pretty obvious, Sanders said, and winked. Stay away from drugs. No joke, they'll ruin your day every time.

Cute, said Henry Dobbins.

Mind-blower, get it? Talk about wiggy—nothing left, just blood and brains.

They made themselves laugh.

There it is, they'd say, over and over, as if the repetition itself were an act of poise, a balance between crazy and almost crazy, knowing without going. There it is, which meant be cool, let it ride, because oh yeah, man, you can't change what can't be changed, there it is, there it absolutely and positively and fucking well *is.*

They were tough.

They carried all the emotional baggage of men who might die. Grief, terror, love, longing—these were intangibles, but the intangibles had their own mass and specific gravity, they had tangible weight. They carried shameful memories. They carried the common secret of cowardice barely restrained, the instinct to run or freeze or hide, and in many respects this was the heaviest burden of all, for it could never be put down, it required perfect balance and perfect posture. They carried their reputations. They carried the soldier's greatest fear, which was the fear of blushing. Men killed, and died, because they were embarrassed not to. It was what had brought them to the war in the first place, nothing positive, no dreams of glory or honor, just to avoid the blush of dishonor. They died so as not to die of embarrassment. They crawled into tunnels and walked point and advanced under fire. Each morning, despite the unknowns, they made their legs move. They endured. They kept humming. They did not submit to the obvious alternative, which was simply to close the eyes and fall. So easy, really. Go limp and tumble to the ground and let the muscles unwind and not speak and not budge until your buddies picked you up and lifted you into the chopper that would roar and dip its nose and carry you off to the world. A mere matter of falling, yet no one ever fell. It was not courage, exactly; the object was not valor. Rather, they were too frightened to be cowards.

By and large they carried these things inside, maintaining the masks of composure. They sneered at sick call. They spoke bitterly about guys who had found release by shooting off their own toes or fingers. Pussies, they'd say. Candyasses. It was fierce, mocking talk, with only a trace of envy or awe, but even so, the image played itself out behind their eyes.

They imagined the muzzle against flesh. They imagined the quick, sweet pain, then the evacuation to Japan, then a hospital with warm beds and cute geisha nurses.

They dreamed of freedom birds.

At night, on guard, staring into the dark, they were carried away by jumbo jets. They felt the rush of takeoff. *Gone!* they yelled. And then velocity, wings and engines, a smiling stewardess—but it was more than a plane, it was a real bird, a big sleek silver bird with feathers and talons and high screeching. They were flying. The weights fell off, there was nothing to bear. They laughed and held on tight, feeling the cold slap of wind and altitude, soaring, thinking *It's over, I'm gone!*—they were naked, they were light and free—it was all lightness, bright and fast and buoyant, light as light, a helium buzz in the brain, a giddy bubbling in the lungs as they were taken up over the clouds and the war, beyond duty, beyond gravity and mortification and global entanglements—*Sin loi!°* they yelled, *I'm sorry, motherfuckers, but I'm out of it, I'm goofed, I'm on a space cruise, I'm gone!*—and it was a restful, disencumbered sensation, just riding the light waves, sailing that big silver freedom bird over the mountains and oceans, over America, over the farms and great sleeping cities and cemeteries and highways and the golden arches of McDonald's. It was flight, a kind of fleeing, a kind of falling, falling higher and higher, spinning off the edge of the earth and beyond the sun and through the vast, silent vacuum where there were no burdens and where everything weighed exactly nothing. *Gone!* they screamed, *I'm sorry but I'm gone!* And so at night, not quite dreaming, they gave themselves over to lightness, they were carried, they were purely borne.

On the morning after Ted Lavender died, First Lieutenant Jimmy Cross crouched at the bottom of his foxhole and burned Martha's letters. Then he burned the two photographs. There was a steady rain falling, which made it difficult, but he used heat tabs

Sin loi *"Sorry about that!"*

and Sterno to build a small fire, screening it with his body, holding the photographs over the tight blue flame with the tips of his fingers.

He realized it was only a gesture. Stupid, he thought. Sentimental, too, but mostly just stupid.

Lavender was dead. You couldn't burn the blame.

Besides, the letters were in his head. And even now, without photographs, Lieutenant Cross could see Martha playing volleyball in her white gym shorts and yellow T-shirt. He could see her moving in the rain.

When the fire died out, Lieutenant Cross pulled his poncho over his shoulders and ate breakfast from a can.

There was no great mystery, he decided.

In those burned letters Martha had never mentioned the war, except to say, Jimmy, take care of yourself. She wasn't involved. She signed the letters "Love," but it wasn't love, and all the fine lines and technicalities did not matter.

The morning came up wet and blurry. Everything seemed part of everything else, the fog and Martha and the deepening rain.

It was a war, after all.

Half smiling, Lieutenant Jimmy Cross took out his maps. He shook his head hard, as if to clear it, then bent forward and began planning the day's march. In ten minutes, or maybe twenty, he would rouse the men and they would pack up and head west, where the maps showed the country to be green and inviting. They would do what they had always done. The rain might add some weight, but otherwise it would be one more day layered upon all the other days.

He was realistic about it. There was that new hardness in his stomach.

No more fantasies, he told himself.

Henceforth, when he thought about Martha, it would be only to think that she belonged elsewhere. He would shut down the daydreams. This was not Mount Sebastian, it was another world, where there were no pretty poems or midterm exams, a place where men died because of carelessness and gross stupidity. Kiowa was right. Boom-down, and you were dead, never partly dead.

Briefly, in the rain, Lieutenant Cross saw Martha's gray eyes gazing back at him.

He understood.

It was very sad, he thought. The things men carried inside. The things men did or felt they had to do.

He almost nodded at her, but didn't.

Instead he went back to his maps. He was now determined to perform his duties firmly and without negligence. It wouldn't help Lavender, he knew that, but from this point on he would comport himself as a soldier. He would dispose of his good-luck pebble. Swallow it, maybe, or use Lee Strunk's slingshot, or just drop it along the trail. On the march he would impose strict field discipline. He would be careful to send out flank security, to prevent straggling or bunching up, to keep his troops moving at the proper pace and at the proper interval. He would insist on clean weapons. He would confiscate the remainder of Lavender's dope. Later in the day, perhaps, he would call the men together and speak to them plainly. He would accept the blame for what had happened to Ted Lavender. He would be a man about it. He would look them in the eyes, keeping his chin level, and he would issue the new SOPs in a calm, impersonal tone of voice, an officer's voice, leaving no room for argument or discussion. Commencing immediately, he'd tell them, they would no longer abandon equipment along the route of march. They would police up their acts. They would get their shit together, and keep it together, and maintain it neatly and in good working order.

He would not tolerate laxity. He would show strength, distancing himself.

Among the men there would be grumbling, of course, and maybe worse, because their days would seem longer and their loads heavier, but Lieutenant Cross reminded himself that his obligation was not to be loved but to lead. He would dispense with love; it was not now a factor. And if anyone quarreled or complained, he would simply tighten his lips and arrange his shoulders in the correct command posture. He might give a curt little nod. Or he might not. He might just shrug and say Carry on, then they would saddle up and form into a column and move out toward the villages of Than Khe.

(1986)

JAMAICA KINCAID
[*b. 1949*]

Girl

Wash the white clothes on Monday and put them on the stone heap; wash the color clothes on Tuesday and put them on the clothesline to dry; don't walk barehead in the hot sun; cook pumpkin fritters in very hot sweet oil; soak your little cloths right after you take them off; when buying cotton to make yourself a nice blouse, be sure that it doesn't have gum on it, because that way it won't hold up well after a wash; soak salt fish overnight before you cook it; is it true that you sing benna in Sunday school?; always eat your food in such a way that it won't turn someone else's stomach; on Sundays try to walk like a lady and not like the slut you are so bent on becoming; don't sing benna in Sunday school; you mustn't speak to wharf-rat boys, not even to give directions; don't eat fruits on the street—flies will follow you; *but I don't sing benna on Sundays at all and never in Sunday school;* this is how to sew on a button; this is how to make a buttonhole for the button you have just sewed on; this is how to hem a dress when you see the hem coming down and so to prevent yourself from looking like the slut I know you are so bent on becoming; this is how you iron your father's khaki shirt so that it doesn't have a crease; this is how you iron your father's khaki pants so that they don't have a crease; this is how you grow okra—far from the house, because okra tree harbors red ants; when you are growing dasheen, make sure it gets plenty of water or else it makes your throat itch when you are eating it; this is how you sweep a corner; this is how you sweep a whole house; this is how you sweep a yard; this is how you smile to someone you don't like too much; this is how you smile to someone you don't like at all; this is how you smile to someone you like completely; this is how you set a table for tea; this is how you set a table for dinner; this is how you set a table for dinner with an important guest; this is how you set a table for lunch; this is how you set a table for breakfast; this is how to behave in the presence of men who don't know you very well, and this way they won't recognize immediately the slut I have warned you against becoming; be sure to wash every day, even if it is with your own spit; don't squat down to play marbles—you are not a boy, you know; don't pick people's flowers—you might catch something; don't throw stones at blackbirds, because it might not be a blackbird at all; this is how to make a bread pudding; this is how to make doukona; this is how to make pepper pot; this is how to make a good medicine for a cold; this is how to make a good medicine to throw away a child before it even becomes a child; this is how to catch a fish; this is how to throw back a fish you don't like, and that way something bad won't fall on you; this is how to bully a man; this is how a man bullies you; this is how to love a man, and if this doesn't work there are other ways, and if they don't work don't feel too bad about giving up; this is how to spit up in the air if you feel like it, and this is how to move quick so that it doesn't fall on you; this is how to make ends meet; always squeeze bread to make sure it's fresh; *but what if the baker won't let me feel the bread?;* you mean to say that after all you are really going to be the kind of woman who the baker won't let near the bread?

(1984)

LESLIE SILKO

[b. 1948]

Yellow Woman

1

My thigh clung to his with dampness, and I watched the sun rising up through the tamaracks and willows. The small brown water birds came to the river and hopped across the mud, leaving brown scratches in the alkali-white crust. They bathed in the river silently. I could hear the water, almost at our feet where the narrow fast channel bubbled and washed green ragged moss and fern leaves. I looked at him beside me, rolled in the red blanket on the white river sand. I cleaned the sand out of the cracks between my toes, squinting because the sun was above the willow trees. I looked at him for the last time, sleeping on the white river sand.

I felt hungry and followed the river south the way we had come the afternoon before, following our footprints that were already blurred by lizard tracks and bug trails. The horses were still lying down, and the black one whinnied when he saw me but he did not get up—maybe it was because the corral was made out of thick cedar branches and the horses had not yet felt the sun like I had. I tried to look beyond the pale red mesas to the pueblo. I knew it was there, even if I could not see it, on the sandrock hill above the river, the same river that moved past me now and had reflected the moon last night.

The horse felt warm underneath me. He shook his head and pawed the sand. The bay whinnied and leaned against the gate trying to follow, and I remembered him asleep in the red blanket beside the river. I slid off the horse and tied him close to the other horse. I walked north with the river again, and the white sand broke loose in footprints over footprints.

"Wake up."

He moved in the blanket and turned his face to me with his eyes still closed. I knelt down to touch him.

"I'm leaving."

He smiled now, eyes still closed. "You are coming with me, remember?" He sat up now with his bare dark chest and belly in the sun.

"Where?"

"To my place."

"And will I come back?"

He pulled his pants on. I walked away from him, feeling him behind me and smelling the willows.

"Yellow Woman," he said.

I turned to face him. "Who are you?" I asked.

He laughed and knelt on the low, sandy bank, washing his face in the river. "Last night you guessed my name, and you knew why I had come."

I stared past him at the shallow moving water and tried to remember the night, but I could only see the moon in the water and remember his warmth around me.

"But I only said that you were him and that I was Yellow Woman—I'm not really her—I have my own name and I come from the pueblo on the other side of the mesa. Your name is Silva and you are a stranger I met by the river yesterday afternoon."

He laughed softly. "What happened yesterday has nothing to do with what you will do today, Yellow Woman."

"I know—that's what I'm saying—the old stories about the ka'tsina spirit and Yellow Woman can't mean us."

My old grandpa liked to tell those stories best. There is one about Badger and Coyote who went hunting and were gone all day, and when the sun was going down they found a house. There was a girl living there alone, and she had light hair and eyes and she told them that they could sleep with her. Coyote wanted to be with her all night so he sent Badger into a prairie-dog hole, telling him he thought he saw something in it. As soon as Badger crawled in, Coyote blocked up the entrance with rocks and hurried back to Yellow Woman.

"Come here," he said gently.

He touched my neck and I moved close to him to feel his breathing and to hear his heart. I was wondering if Yellow Woman had known who she was—if she knew that she would become part of the stories. Maybe she'd had another name that her husband and relatives called her so that only the ka'tsina from the north and the storytellers would know her as Yellow Woman. But I didn't go on; I felt him all around me, pushing me down into the white river sand.

Yellow Woman went away with the spirit from the north and lived with him and his relatives. She was gone for a long time, but then one day she came back and she brought twin boys.

"Do you know the story?"

"What story?" He smiled and pulled me close to him as he said this. I was afraid lying there on the red blanket. All I could know was the way he felt, warm, damp, his body beside me. This is the way it happens in the stories, I was thinking, with no thought beyond the moment she meets the ka'tsina spirit and they go.

"I don't have to go. What they tell in stories was real only then, back in time immemorial, like they say."

He stood up and pointed at my clothes tangled in the blanket. "Let's go," he said.

I walked beside him, breathing hard because he walked fast, his hand around my wrist. I had stopped trying to pull away from him, because his hand felt cool and the sun was high, drying the river bed into alkali. I will see someone, eventually I will see someone, and then I will be certain that he is only a man—some man from nearby— and I will be sure that I am not Yellow Woman. Because she is from out of time past and I live now and I've been to school and there are highways and pickup trucks that Yellow Woman never saw.

It was an easy ride north on horseback. I watched the change from the cottonwood trees along the river to the junipers that brushed past us in the foothills, and finally there were only piñons, and when I looked up at the rim of the mountain plateau I could see pine trees growing on the edge. Once I stopped to look down, but the pale sandstone had disappeared and the river was gone and the dark lava hills were all around. He touched my hand, not speaking, but always singing softly a mountain song and looking into my eyes.

I felt hungry and wondered what they were doing at home now—my mother, my grandmother, my husband, and the baby. Cooking breakfast, saying, "Where did she go?—maybe kidnapped," and Al going to the tribal police with the details: "She went walking along the river."

The house was made with black lava rock and red mud. It was high above the spreading miles of arroyos and long mesas. I smelled a mountain smell of pitch and buck brush. I stood there beside the black horse, looking down on the small, dim country we had passed, and I shivered.

"Yellow Woman, come inside where it's warm."

2

He lit a fire in the stove. It was an old stove with a round belly and an enamel coffeepot on top. There was only the stove, some faded Navajo blankets, and a bedroll and cardboard box. The floor was made of smooth adobe plaster, and there was one small window facing east. He pointed at the box.

"There's some potatoes and the frying pan." He sat on the floor with his arms around his knees pulling them close to his chest and he watched me fry the potatoes. I didn't mind him watching me because he was always watching me—he had been watching me since I came upon him sitting on the river bank trimming leaves from a willow twig with his knife. We ate from the pan and he wiped the grease from his fingers on his Levis.

"Have you brought women here before?" He smiled and kept chewing, so I said, "Do you always use the same tricks?"

"What tricks?" He looked at me like he didn't understand.

"The story about being a ka'tsina from the mountains. The story about Yellow Woman."

Silva was silent; his face was calm.

"I don't believe it. Those stories couldn't happen now," I said.

He shook his head and said softly, "But someday they will talk about is, and they will say, 'Those two lived long ago when things like that happened.'"

He stood up and went out. I ate the rest of the potatoes and thought about things—about the noise the stove was making and the sound of the mountain wind outside. I remembered yesterday and the day before, and then I went outside.

I walked past the corral to the edge where the narrow trail cut through the black rim rock. I was standing in the sky with nothing around me but the wind that came down from the blue mountain peak behind me. I could see faint mountain images in the distance, miles across the vast spread of mesas and valleys and plains. I wondered who was over there to feel the mountain wind on those sheer blue edges—who walks on the pine needles in those blue mountains.

"Can you see the pueblo?" Silva was standing behind me.

I shook my head. "We're too far away."

"From here I can see the world." He stepped out on the edge. "The Navajo reservation begins over there." He pointed to the east. "The Pueblo boundaries are over here." He looked below us to the south, where the narrow trail seemed to come from. "The Texans have their ranches over there, starting with that valley, the Concho Valley. The Mexicans run some cattle over there too."

"Do you ever work for them?"

"I steal from them," Silva answered. The sun was dropping behind us and shadows were filling the land below. I turned away from the edge that dropped forever into the valleys below.

"I'm cold," I said; "I'm going inside." I started wondering about this man who could speak the Pueblo language so well but who lived on a mountain and rustled cattle. I decided that this man Silva must be Navajo, because Pueblo men didn't do things like that.

"You must be a Navajo."

Silva shook his head gently. "Little Yellow Woman," he said, "you never give up, do you? I have told you who I am. The Navajo people know me, too." He knelt down and unrolled the bedroll and spread the extra blankets out on a piece of canvas. The sun was down, and the only light in the house came from outside—the dim orange light from sundown.

I stood there and waited for him to crawl under the blankets.

"What are you waiting for?" he said, and I lay down beside him. He undressed me slowly like the night before beside the river—kissing my face gently and running his hands up and down my belly and legs. He took off my pants and then he laughed.

"Why are you laughing?"

"You are breathing so hard."

I pulled away from him and turned my back to him.

He pulled me around and pinned me down with his arms and chest. "You don't understand, do you, little Yellow Woman? You will do what I want."

And again he was all around me with his skin slippery against mine, and I was afraid because I understood that his strength could hurt me. I lay underneath him and I knew that he could destroy me. But later, while he slept beside me, I touched his face and I had a feeling—the kind of feeling for him that overcame me that morning along the river. I kissed him on the forehead and he reached out for me.

When I woke up in the morning he was gone. It gave me a strange feeling because for a long time I sat there on the blankets and looked around the little house for some object of his—some proof that he had been there or maybe that he was coming back. Only the blankets and the cardboard box remained. The .30–30 that had been leaning in the corner was gone, and so was the knife I had used the night before. He was gone, and I had my chance to go now. But first I had to eat, because I knew it would be a long walk home.

I found some dried apricots in the cardboard box, and I sat down on a rock at the edge of the plateau rim. There was no wind and the sun warmed me. I was surrounded by silence. I drowsed with apricots in my mouth, and I didn't believe that there were highways or railroads or cattle to steal.

When I woke up, I stared down at my feet in the black mountain dirt. Little black ants were swarming over the pine needles around my foot. They must have smelled the apricots. I thought about my family far below me. They would be wondering about me, because this had never happened to me before. The tribal police would file a report. But if old Grandpa weren't dead he would tell them what happened—he would laugh and say, "Stolen by a ka'tsina, a mountain spirit. She'll come home—they usually do." There are enough of them to handle things. My mother and grandmother will raise the baby like they raised me. Al will find someone else, and they will go on like before, except that there will be a story about the day I disappeared while I was walking along the river. Silva had come for me, he said he had. I did not decide to go. I just went. Moonflowers blossom in the sand hills before dawn, just as I followed him. That's what I was thinking as I wandered along the trail through the pine trees.

It was noon when I got back. When I saw the stone house I remembered that I had meant to go home. But that didn't seem important any more, maybe because there were little blue flowers growing in the meadow behind the stone house and the gray squirrels were playing in the pines next to the house. The horses were standing in the corral, and there was a beef carcass hanging on the shady side of a big pine in front of the house. Flies buzzed around the clotted blood that hung from the carcass. Silva was washing his hands in a bucket full of water. He must have heard me coming because he spoke to me without turning to face me.

"I've been waiting for you."

"I went walking in the big pine trees."

I looked into the bucket full of bloody water with brown-and-white animal hairs floating in it. Silva stood there letting his hands drip, examining me intently.

"Are you coming with me?"

"Where?" I asked him.

"To sell the meat in Marquez."

"If you're sure it's O.K."

"I wouldn't ask you if it wasn't," he answered.

He sloshed the water around in the bucket before he dumped it out and set the bucket upside down near the door. I followed him to the corral and watched him saddle the horses. Even beside the horses he looked tall, and I asked him again if he wasn't Navajo. He didn't say anything; he just shook his head and kept cinching up the saddle.

"But Navajos are tall."

"Get on the horse," he said, "and let's go."

The last thing he did before we started down the steep trail was to grab the .30–30 from the corner. He slid the rifle into the scabbard that hung from his saddle.

"Do they ever try to catch you?" I asked.

"They don't know who I am."

"Then why did you bring the rifle?"

"Because we are going to Marquez where the Mexicans live."

3

The trail leveled out on a narrow ridge that was steep on both sides like an animal spine. On one side I could see where the trail went around the rocky gray hills and disappeared into the southeast where the pale sandrock mesas stood in the distance near my home. On the other side was a trail that went west, and as I looked far into the distance I thought I saw the little town. But Silva said no, that I was looking in the wrong place, that I just thought I saw houses. After that I quit looking off into the distance; it was hot and the wildflowers were closing up their deep-yellow petals. Only the waxy cactus flowers bloomed in the bright sun, and I saw every color that a cactus blossom can be; the white ones and the red ones were still buds, but the purple and the yellow were blossoms, open full and the most beautiful of all.

Silva saw him before I did. The white man was riding a big gray horse, coming up the trail toward us. He was traveling fast and the gray horse's feet sent rocks rolling off the trail into the dry tumbleweeds. Silva motioned for me to stop and we watched the white man. He didn't see us right away, but finally his horse whinnied at our horses and he stopped. He looked at us briefly before he loped the gray horse across the three hundred yards that separated us. He stopped his horse in front of Silva, and his young fat face was shadowed by the brim of his hat. He didn't look mad, but his small, pale eyes moved from the blood-soaked gunny sacks hanging from my saddle to Silva's face and then back to my face.

"Where did you get the fresh meat?" the white man asked.

"I've been hunting," Silva said, and when he shifted his weight in the saddle the leather creaked.

"The hell you have, Indian. You've been rustling cattle. We've been looking for the thief for a long time."

The rancher was fat, and sweat began to soak through his white cowboy shirt and the wet cloth stuck to the thick rolls of belly fat. He almost seemed to be panting from the exertion of talking, and he smelled rancid, maybe because Silva scared him.

Silva turned to me and smiled. "Go back up the mountain, Yellow Woman."

The white man got angry when he heard Silva speak in a language he couldn't understand. "Don't try anything, Indian. Just keep riding to Marquez. We'll call the state police from there."

The rancher must have been unarmed because he was very frightened and if he had a gun he would have pulled it out then. I turned my horse around and the rancher yelled, "Stop!" I looked at Silva for an instant and there was something ancient and dark—something I could feel in my stomach—in his eyes, and when I glanced at his hand I saw his finger on the trigger of the .30–30 that was still in the saddle scabbard. I slapped my horse across the flank and the sacks of raw meat swung against my knees as the horse leaped up the trail. It was hard to keep my balance, and once I thought I felt the saddle slipping backward; it was because of this that I could not look back.

I didn't stop until I reached the ridge where the trail forked. The horse was breathing deep gasps and there was a dark film of sweat on its neck. I looked down in the direction I had come from, but I couldn't see the place. I waited. The wind came up and pushed warm air past me. I looked up at the sky, pale blue and full of thin clouds and fading vapor trails left by jets.

I think four shots were fired—I remember hearing four hollow explosions that reminded me of deer hunting. There could have been more shots after that, but I couldn't have heard them because my horse was running again and the loose rocks were making too much noise as they scattered around his feet.

Horses have a hard time running downhill, but I went that way instead of uphill to the mountain because I thought it was safer. I felt better with the horse running southeast past the round gray hills that were covered with cedar trees and black lava rock. When I got to the plain in the distance I could see the dark green patches of tamaracks that grew along the river; and beyond the river I could see the beginning of the pale sandrock mesas. I stopped the horse and looked back to see if anyone was coming; then I got off the horse and turned the horse around, wondering if it would go back to its corral under the pines on the mountain. It looked back at me for a moment and then plucked a mouthful of green tumbleweeds before it trotted back up the trail with its ears pointed forward, carrying its head daintily to one side to avoid stepping on the dragging reins. When the horse disappeared over the last hill, the gunny sacks full of meat were still swinging and bouncing.

4

I walked toward the river on a wood-hauler's road that I knew would eventually lead to the paved road. I was thinking about waiting beside the road for someone to drive by, but by the time I got to the pavement I had decided it wasn't very far to walk if I followed the river back the way Silva and I had come.

The river water tasted good, and I sat in the shade under a cluster of silvery willows. I thought about Silva, and I felt sad at leaving him; still, there was something strange about him, and I tried to figure it out all the way back home.

I came back to the place on the river bank where he had been sitting the first time I saw him. The green willow leaves that he had trimmed from the branch were still lying there, wilted in the sand. I saw the leaves and I wanted to go back to him—to kiss him and to touch him—but the mountains were too far away now. And I told myself, because I believe it, he will come back sometime and be waiting again by the river.

I followed the path up from the river into the village. The sun was getting low, and I could smell supper cooking when I got to the screen door of my house. I could hear their voices inside—my mother was telling my grandmother how to fix the Jell-O and my husband, Al, was playing with the baby. I decided to tell them that some Navajo had kidnaped me, but I was sorry that old Grandpa wasn't alive to hear my story because it was the Yellow Woman stories he liked to tell best.

(1973)

AMY TAN

[b. 1952]

Rules of the Game

I was six when my mother taught me the art of invisible strength. It was a strategy for winning arguments, respect from others, and eventually, though neither of us knew it at the time, chess games.

"Bite back your tongue," scolded my mother when I cried loudly, yanking her hand toward the store that sold bags of salted plums. At home, she said, "Wise guy, he not go against wind. In Chinese we say, Come from South, blow with wind—poom!— North will follow. Strongest wind cannot be seen."

The next week I bit back my tongue as we entered the store with the forbidden candies. When my mother finished her shopping, she quietly plucked a small bag of plums from the rack and put it on the counter with the rest of the items.

My mother imparted her daily truths so she could help my older brothers and me rise above our circumstances. We lived in San Francisco's Chinatown. Like most of the other Chinese children who played in the back alleys of restaurants and curio shops, I didn't think we were poor. My bowl was always full, three five-course meals every day, beginning with a soup full of mysterious things I didn't want to know the names of.

We lived on Waverly Place, in a warm, clean, two-bedroom flat that sat above a small Chinese bakery specializing in steamed pastries and dim sum. In the early morning, when the alley was still quiet, I could smell fragrant red beans as they were cooked down to a pasty sweetness. By daybreak, our flat was heavy with the odor of fried sesame balls and sweet curried chicken crescents. From my bed, I would listen as my father got ready for work, then locked the door behind him, one-two-three clicks.

At the end of our two-block alley was a small sandlot playground with swings and slides well-shined down the middle with use. The play area was bordered by wood-slat benches where old-country people sat cracking roasted watermelon seeds with their golden teeth and scattering the husks to an impatient gathering of gurgling pigeons. The best playground, however, was the dark alley itself. It was crammed with daily mysteries and adventures. My brothers and I would peer into the medicinal herb shop, watching old Li dole out onto a stiff sheet of white paper the right amount of insect shells, saffron-colored seeds, and pungent leaves for his ailing customers. It was said that he once cured a woman dying of an ancestral curse that had eluded the best of American doctors. Next to the pharmacy was a printer who specialized in gold-embossed wedding invitations and festive red banners.

Farther down the street was Ping Yuen Fish Market. The front window displayed a tank crowded with doomed fish and turtles struggling to gain footing on the slimy green-tiled sides. A hand-written sign informed tourists, "Within this store, is all for food, not for pet." Inside, the butchers with their bloodstained white smocks deftly gutted the fish while customers cried out their orders and shouted, "Give me your freshest," to which the butchers always protested, "All are freshest." On less crowded market days, we would inspect the crates of live frogs and crabs which we were warned not to poke, boxes of dried cuttlefish, and row upon row of iced prawns, squid, and slippery fish. The sanddabs made me shiver each time; their eyes lay on one flattened side and reminded me of my mother's story of a careless girl who ran into a crowded street and was crushed by a cab. "Was smash flat," reported my mother.

At the corner of the alley was Hong Sing's, a four-table café with a recessed stairwell in front that led to a door marked "Tradesmen." My brothers and I believed the bad people emerged from this door at night. Tourists never went to Hong Sing's, since the menu was printed only in Chinese. A Caucasian man with a big camera once posed me and my playmates in front of the restaurant. He had us move to the side of the picture window so the photo would capture the roasted duck with its head dangling from a juice-covered rope. After he took the picture, I told him he should go into Hong Sing's and eat dinner. When he smiled and asked me what they served, I shouted, "Guts and duck's feet and octopus gizzards!" Then I ran off with my friends, shrieking with laughter as we scampered across the alley and hid in the entryway grotto of the China Gem Company, my heart pounding with hope that he would chase us.

My mother named me after the street that we lived on: Waverly Place Jong, my official name for important American documents. But my family called me Meimei, "Little Sister." I was the youngest, the only daughter. Each morning before school, my mother would twist and yank on my thick black hair until she had formed two tightly wound pigtails. One day, as she struggled to weave a hard-toothed comb through my disobedient hair, I had a sly thought.

I asked her, "Ma, what is Chinese torture?" My mother shook her head. A bobby pin was wedged between her lips. She wetted her palm and smoothed the hair above my ear, then pushed the pin in so that it nicked sharply against my scalp.

"Who say this word?" she asked without a trace of knowing how wicked I was being. I shrugged my shoulders and said, "Some boy in my class said Chinese people do Chinese torture."

"Chinese people do many things," she said simply. "Chinese people do business, do medicine, do painting. Not lazy like American people. We do torture. Best torture."

My older brother Vincent was the one who actually got the chess set. We had gone to the annual Christmas party held at the First Chinese Baptist Church at the end of the alley. The missionary ladies had put together a Santa bag of gifts donated by members of another church. None of the gifts had names on them. There were separate sacks for boys and girls of different ages.

One of the Chinese parishioners had donned a Santa Claus costume and a stiff paper beard with cotton balls glued to it. I think the only children who thought he was the real thing were too young to know that Santa Claus was not Chinese. When my turn came up, the Santa man asked me how old I was. I thought it was a trick question; I was seven according to the American formula and eight by the Chinese calendar. I said I was born on March 17, 1951. That seemed to satisfy him. He then solemnly asked if I had been a very, very good girl this year and did I believe in Jesus Christ and obey my parents. I knew the only answer to that. I nodded back with equal solemnity.

Having watched the other children opening their gifts, I already knew that the big gifts were not necessarily the nicest ones. One girl my age got a large coloring book of biblical characters, while a less greedy girl who selected a smaller box received a glass vial of lavender toilet water. The sound of the box was also important. A ten-year-old boy had chosen a box that jangled when he shook it. It was a tin globe of the world with a slit for inserting money. He must have thought it was full of dimes and nickels, because when he saw that it had just ten pennies, his face fell with such undisguised disappointment that his mother slapped the side of his head and led him out of the church hall, apologizing to the crowd for her son who had such bad manners he couldn't appreciate such a fine gift.

As I peered into the sack, I quickly fingered the remaining presents, testing their weight, imagining what they contained. I chose a heavy, compact one that was wrapped in shiny silver foil and a red satin ribbon. It was a twelve-pack of Life Savers and I spent the rest of the party arranging and rearranging the candy tubes in the order of my favorites. My brother Winston chose wisely as well. His present turned out to be a box of intricate plastic parts; the instructions on the box proclaimed that when they were properly assembled he would have an authentic miniature replica of a World War II submarine.

Vincent got the chess set, which would have been a very decent present to get at a church Christmas party, except it was obviously used and, as we discovered later, it was missing a black pawn and a white knight. My mother graciously thanked the unknown benefactor, saying, "Too good. Cost too much." At which point, an old lady with fine white, wispy hair nodded toward our family and said with a whistling whisper, "Merry, merry Christmas."

When we got home, my mother told Vincent to throw the chess set away. "She not want it. We not want it," she said, tossing her head stiffly to the side with a tight, proud smile. My brothers had deaf ears. They were already lining up the chess pieces and reading from the dog-eared instruction book.

I watched Vincent and Winston play during Christmas week. The chessboard seemed to hold elaborate secrets waiting to be untangled. The chessmen were more powerful than old Li's magic herbs that cured ancestral curses. And my brothers wore such serious faces that I was sure something was at stake that was greater than avoiding the tradesmen's door to Hong Sing's.

"Let me! Let me!" I begged between games when one brother or the other would sit back with a deep sigh of relief and victory, the other annoyed, unable to let go of the outcome. Vincent at first refused to let me play, but when I offered my Life Savers as replacements for the buttons that filled in for the missing pieces, he relented. He chose the flavors: wild cherry for the black pawn and peppermint for the white knight. Winner could eat both.

As our mother sprinkled flour and rolled out small doughy circles for the steamed dumplings that would be our dinner that night, Vincent explained the rules, pointing to each piece. "You have sixteen pieces and so do I. One king and queen, two bishops, two knights, two castles, and eight pawns. The pawns can only move forward one step, except on the first move. Then they can move two. But they can only take men by moving crossways like this, except in the beginning, when you can move ahead and take another pawn."

"Why?" I asked as I moved my pawn. "Why can't they move more steps?"

"Because they're pawns," he said.

"But why do they go crossways to take other men? Why aren't there any women and children?"

"Why is the sky blue? Why must you always ask stupid questions?" asked Vincent. "This is a game. These are the rules. I didn't make them up. See. Here. In the book." He jabbed a page with a pawn in his hand. "Pawn. P-A-W-N. Pawn. Read it yourself."

My mother patted the flour off her hands. "Let me see book," she said quietly. She scanned the pages quickly, not reading the foreign English symbols, seeming to search deliberately for nothing in particular.

"This American rules," she concluded at last. "Every time people come out from foreign country, must know rules. You not know, judge say, Too bad, go back. They not telling you why so you can use their way go forward. They say, Don't know why, you find out yourself. But they knowing all the time. Better you take it, find out why yourself." She tossed her head back with a satisfied smile.

I found out about all the whys later. I read the rules and looked up all the big words in a dictionary. I borrowed books from the Chinatown library. I studied each chess piece, trying to absorb the power each contained.

I learned about opening moves and why it's important to control the center early on; the shortest distance between two points is straight down the middle. I learned about the middle game and why tactics between two adversaries are like clashing ideas; the one who plays better has the clearest plans for both attacking and getting out of traps. I learned why it is essential in the endgame to have foresight, a mathematical understanding of all possible moves, and patience; all weaknesses and advantages become evident to a strong adversary and are obscured to a tiring opponent. I discovered that for the whole game one must gather invisible strengths and see the endgame before the game begins.

I also found out why I should never reveal "why" to others. A little knowledge withheld is a great advantage one should store for future use. That is the power of chess. It is a game of secrets in which one must show and never tell.

I loved the secrets I found within the sixty-four black and white squares. I carefully drew a handmade chessboard and pinned it to the wall next to my bed, where at night I would stare for hours at imaginary battles. Soon I no longer lost any games or Life Savers, but I lost my adversaries. Winston and Vincent decided they were more interested in roaming the streets after school in their Hopalong Cassidy cowboy hats.

On a cold spring afternoon, while walking home from school, I detoured through the playground at the end of our alley. I saw a group of old men, two seated across a folding table playing a game of chess, others smoking pipes, eating peanuts, and watching. I ran home and grabbed Vincent's chess set, which was bound in a cardboard box with rubber bands. I also carefully selected two prized rolls of Life Savers. I came back to the park and approached a man who was observing the game.

"Want to play?" I asked him. His face widened with surprise and he grinned as he looked at the box under my arm.

"Little sister, been a long time since I play with dolls," he said, smiling benevolently. I quickly put the box down next to him on the bench and displayed my retort.

Lau Po, as he allowed me to call him, turned out to be a much better player than my brothers. I lost many games and many Life Savers. But over the weeks, with each diminishing roll of candies, I added new secrets. Lau Po gave me the names. The

Double Attack from the East and West Shores. Throwing Stones on the Drowning Man. The Sudden Meeting of the Clan. The Surprise from the Sleeping Guard. The Humble Servant Who Kills the King. Sand in the Eyes of Advancing Forces. A Double Killing Without Blood.

There were also the fine points of chess etiquette. Keep captured men in neat rows, as well-tended prisoners. Never announce "Check" with vanity, lest someone with an unseen sword slit your throat. Never hurl pieces into the sandbox after you have lost a game, because then you must find them again, by yourself, after apologizing to all around you. By the end of the summer, Lau Po had taught me all he knew, and I had become a better chess player.

A small weekend crowd of Chinese people and tourists would gather as I played and defeated my opponents one by one. My mother would join the crowds during these outdoor exhibition games. She sat proudly on the bench, telling my admirers with proper Chinese humility, "Is luck."

A man who watched me play in the park suggested that my mother allow me to play in local chess tournaments. My mother smiled graciously, an answer that meant nothing. I desperately wanted to go, but I bit back my tongue. I knew she would not let me play among strangers. So as we walked home I said in a small voice that I didn't want to play in the local tournament. They would have American rules. If I lost, I would bring shame on my family.

"Is shame you fall down nobody push you," said my mother.

During my first tournament, my mother sat with me in the front row as I waited for my turn. I frequently bounced my legs to unstick them from the cold metal seat of the folding chair. When my name was called, I leapt up. My mother unwrapped something in her lap. It was her *chang,* a small tablet of red jade which held the sun's fire. "Is luck," she whispered, and tucked it into my dress pocket. I turned to my opponent, a fifteen-year-old boy from Oakland. He looked at me, wrinkling his nose.

As I began to play, the boy disappeared, the color ran out of the room, and I saw only my white pieces and his black ones waiting on the other side. A light wind began blowing past my ears. It whispered secrets only I could hear.

"Blow from the South," it murmured. "The wind leaves no trail." I saw a clear path, the traps to avoid. The crowd rustled. "Shhh! Shhh!" said the corners of the room. The wind blew stronger. "Throw sand from the East to distract him." The knight came forward ready for the sacrifice. The wind hissed, louder and louder. "Blow, blow, blow. He cannot see. He is blind now. Make him lean away from the wind so he is easier to knock down."

"Check," I said, as the wind roared with laughter. The wind died down to little puffs, my own breath.

My mother placed my first trophy next to a new plastic chess set that the neighborhood Tao society had given to me. As she wiped each piece with a soft cloth, she said, "Next time win more, lose less."

"Ma, it's not how many pieces you lose," I said. "Sometimes you need to lose pieces to get ahead."

"Better to lose less, see if you really need."

At the next tournament, I won again, but it was my mother who wore the triumphant grin.

"Lost eight piece this time. Last time was eleven. What I tell you? Better off lose less!" I was annoyed, but I couldn't say anything.

I attended more tournaments, each one farther away from home. I won all games, in all divisions. The Chinese bakery downstairs from our flat displayed my growing collection of trophies in its window, amidst the dust-covered cakes that were never picked up. The day after I won an important regional tournament, the window encased a fresh sheet cake with whipped-cream frosting and red script saying "Congratulations, Waverly Jong, Chinatown Chess Champion." Soon after that, a flower shop, headstone engraver, and funeral parlor offered to sponsor me in national tournaments. That's when my mother decided I no longer had to do the dishes. Winston and Vincent had to do my chores.

"Why does she get to play and we do all the work," complained Vincent.

"Is new American rules," said my mother. "Meimei play, squeeze all her brains out for win chess. You play, worth squeeze towel."

By my ninth birthday, I was a national chess champion. I was still some 429 points away from grand-master status, but I was touted as the Great American Hope, a child prodigy and a girl to boot. They ran a photo of me in *Life* magazine next to a quote in which Bobby Fischer said, "There will never be a woman grand master." "Your move, Bobby," said the caption.

The day they took the magazine picture I wore neatly plaited braids clipped with plastic barrettes trimmed with rhinestones. I was playing in a large high school auditorium that echoed with phlegmy coughs and the squeaky rubber knobs of chair legs sliding across freshly waxed wooden floors. Seated across from me was an American man, about the same age as Lau Po, maybe fifty. I remember that his sweaty brow seemed to weep at my every move. He wore a dark, malodorous suit. One of his pockets was stuffed with a great white kerchief on which he wiped his palm before sweeping his hand over the chosen chess piece with great flourish.

In my crisp pink-and-white dress with scratchy lace at the neck, one of two my mother had sewn for these special occasions, I would clasp my hands under my chin, the delicate points of my elbows poised lightly on the table in the manner my mother had shown me for posing for the press. I would swing my patent leather shoes back and forth like an impatient child riding on a school bus. Then I would pause, suck in my lips, twirl my chosen piece in midair as if undecided, and then firmly plant it in its new threatening place, with a triumphant smile thrown back at my opponent for good measure.

I no longer played in the alley of Waverly Place. I never visited the playground where the pigeons and old men gathered. I went to school, then directly home to learn new chess secrets, cleverly concealed advantages, more escape routes.

But I found it difficult to concentrate at home. My mother had a habit of standing over me while I plotted out my games. I think she thought of herself as my protective ally. Her lips would be sealed tight, and after each move I made, a soft "Hmmmmph" would escape from her nose.

"Ma, I can't practice when you stand there like that," I said one day. She retreated to the kitchen and made loud noises with the pots and pans. When the crashing stopped, I could see out of the corner of my eye that she was standing in the doorway. "Hmmmmph!" Only this one came out of her tight throat.

My parents made many concessions to allow me to practice. One time I complained that the bedroom I shared was so noisy that I couldn't think. Thereafter, my brothers slept in a bed in the living room facing the street. I said I couldn't finish my rice; my head didn't work right when my stomach was too full. I left the table with half-finished bowls and nobody complained. But there was one duty I couldn't avoid. I had to accompany my mother on Saturday market days when I had no tournament to play. My mother would proudly walk with me, visiting many shops, buying very little. "This my daughter Wave-ly Jong," she said to whoever looked her way.

One day after we left a shop I said under my breath, "I wish you wouldn't do that, telling everybody I'm your daughter." My mother stopped walking. Crowds of people with heavy bags pushed past us on the sidewalk, bumping into first one shoulder, then another.

"Aiii-ya. So shame be with mother?" She grasped my hand even tighter as she glared at me.

I looked down. "It's not that, it's just so obvious. It's just so embarrassing."

"Embarrass you be my daughter?" Her voice was cracking with anger.

"That's not what I meant. That's not what I said."

"What you say?"

I knew it was a mistake to say anything more, but I heard my voice speaking, "Why do you have to use me to show off? If you want to show off, then why don't you learn to play chess."

My mother's eyes turned into dangerous black slits. She had no words for me, just sharp silence.

I felt the wind rushing around my hot ears. I jerked my hand out of my mother's tight grasp and spun around, knocking into an old woman. Her bag of groceries spilled to the ground.

"Aii-ya! Stupid girl!" my mother and the woman cried. Oranges and tin cans careened down the sidewalk. As my mother stooped to help the old woman pick up the escaping food, I took off.

I raced down the street, dashing between people, not looking back as my mother screamed shrilly, "Meimei! Meimei!" I fled down an alley, past dark curtained shops and merchants washing the grime off their windows. I sped into the sunlight, into a large street crowded with tourists examining trinkets and souvenirs. I ducked into another dark alley, down another street, up another alley. I ran until it hurt and I realized I had nowhere to go, that I was not running from anything. The alleys contained no escape routes.

My breath came out like angry smoke. It was cold. I sat down on an upturned plastic pail next to a stack of empty boxes, cupping my chin with my hands, thinking hard. I imagined my mother, first walking briskly down one street or another looking for me, then giving up and returning home to await my arrival. After two hours, I stood up on creaking legs and slowly walked home.

The alley was quiet and I could see the yellow lights shining from our flat like two tiger's eyes in the night. I climbed the sixteen steps to the door, advancing quietly up each so as not to make any warning sounds. I turned the knob; the door was locked. I heard a chair moving, quick steps, the locks turning—click! click! click!—and then the door opened.

"About time you got home," said Vincent. "Boy, are you in trouble."

He slid back to the dinner table. On a platter were the remains of a large fish, its fleshy head still connected to bones swimming upstream in vain escape. Standing there waiting for my punishment, I heard my mother speak in a dry voice.

"We not concerning this girl. This girl not have concerning for us."

Nobody looked at me. Bone chopsticks clinked against the inside of bowls being emptied into hungry mouths.

I walked into my room, closed the door, and lay down on my bed. The room was dark, the ceiling filled with shadows from the dinnertime lights of neighboring flats.

In my head, I saw a chessboard with sixty-four black and white squares. Opposite me was my opponent, two angry black slits. She wore a triumphant smile. "Strongest wind cannot be seen," she said.

Her black men advanced across the plane, slowly marching to each successive level as a single unit. My white pieces screamed as they scurried and fell off the board one by one. As her men drew closer to my edge, I felt myself growing light. I rose up into the air and flew out the window. Higher and higher, above the alley, over the tops of tiled roofs, where I was gathered up by the wind and pushed up toward the night sky until everything below me disappeared and I was alone.

I closed my eyes and pondered my next move.

(1989)

LOUISE ERDRICH
[b. 1954]

American Horse

The woman sleeping on the cot in the woodshed was Albertine American Horse. The name was left over from her mother's short marriage. The boy was the son of the man she had loved and let go. Buddy was on the cot too, sitting on the edge because he'd been awake three hours watching out for his mother and besides, she took up the whole cot. Her feet hung over the edge, limp and brown as two trout. Her long arms reached out and slapped at things she saw in her dreams.

Buddy had been knocked awake out of hiding in a washing machine while herds of policemen with dogs searched through a large building with many tiny rooms. When the arm came down, Buddy screamed because it had a blue cuff and sharp silver buttons. "Tss," his mother mumbled, half awake, "wasn't nothing." But Buddy sat up after her breathing went deep again, and he watched.

There was something coming and he knew it.

It was coming from very far off but he had a picture of it in his mind. It was a large thing made of metal with many barbed hooks, points, and drag chains on it, something like a giant potato peeler that rolled out of the sky, scraping clouds down with it and jabbing or crushing everything that lay in its path on the ground.

Buddy watched his mother. If he woke her up, she would know what to do about the thing, but he thought he'd wait until he saw it for sure before he shook her. She was pretty, sleeping, and he liked knowing he could look at her as long and close up as he wanted. He took a strand of her hair and held it in his hands as if it was the rein to a delicate beast. She was strong enough and could pull him along like the horse their name was.

Buddy had his mother's and his grandmother's name because his father had been a big mistake.

"They're all mistakes, even your father. But *you* are the best thing that ever happened to me."

That was what she said when he asked.

Even Kadie, the boyfriend crippled from being in a car wreck, was not as good a thing that had happened to his mother as Buddy was. "He was a medium-sized mistake," she said. "He's hurt and I shouldn't even say that, but it's the truth." At the moment, Buddy knew that being the best thing in his mother's life, he was also the reason they were hiding from the cops.

He wanted to touch the satin roses sewed on her pink T-shirt, but he knew he shouldn't do that even in her sleep. If she woke up and found him touching the roses, she would say, "Quit that, Buddy." Sometimes she told him to stop hugging her like a gorilla. She never said that in the mean voice she used when he oppressed her, but when she said that he loosened up anyway.

There were times he felt like hugging her so hard and in such a special way that she would say to him, "Let's get married." There were also times he closed his eyes and wished that she would die, only a few times, but still it haunted him that his wish might come true. He and Uncle Lawrence would be left alone. Buddy wasn't worried, though, about his mother getting married to somebody else. She had said to her friend, Madonna, "All men suck," when she thought Buddy wasn't listening. He had made an uncertain sound, and when they heard him they took him in their arms.

"Except for you, Buddy," his mother said. "All except for you and maybe Uncle Lawrence, although he's pushing it."

"The cops suck the worst, though," Buddy whispered to his mother's sleeping face, "because they're after us." He felt tired again, slumped down, and put his legs beneath the blanket. He closed his eyes and got the feeling that the cot was lifting up beneath him, that it was arching its canvas back and then traveling, traveling very fast and in the wrong direction for when he looked up he saw the three of them were advancing to meet the great metal thing with hooks and barbs and all sorts of sharp equipment to catch their bodies and draw their blood. He heard its insides as it rushed toward them, purring softly like a powerful motor and then they were right in its shadow. He pulled the reins as hard as he could and the beast reared, lifting him. His mother clapped her hand across his mouth.

"Okay," she said. "Lay low. They're outside and they're gonna hunt."

She touched his shoulder and Buddy leaned over with her to look through a crack in the boards.

They were out there all right, Albertine saw them. Two officers and that social worker woman. Vicki Koob. There had been no whistle, no dream, no voice to warn her that they were coming. There was only the crunching sound of cinders in the yard, the engine purring, the dust sifting off their car in a fine light brownish cloud and settling around them.

The three people came to a halt in their husk of metal—the car emblazoned with the North Dakota State Highway Patrol emblem which is the glowing profile of the Sioux policeman, Red Tomahawk, the one who killed Sitting Bull. Albertine gave Buddy the blanket and told him that he might have to wrap it around him and hide underneath the cot.

"We're gonna wait and see what they do." She took him in her lap and hunched her arms around him. "Don't you worry," she whispered against his ear. "Lawrence knows how to fool them."

Buddy didn't want to look at the car and the people. He felt his mother's heart beating beneath his ear so fast it seemed to push the satin roses in and out. He put his face to them carefully and breathed the deep, soft powdery woman smell of her. That smell was also in her little face cream bottles, in her brushes, and around the washbowl after she used it. The satin felt so unbearably smooth against his cheek that he had to press closer. She didn't push him away, like he expected, but hugged him still tighter until he felt as close as he had ever been to back inside her again where she said he came from. Within the smells of her things, her soft skin, and the satin of her roses, he closed his eyes then, and took his breaths softly and quickly with her heart.

They were out there, but they didn't dare get out of the car yet because of Lawrence's big, ragged dogs. Three of these dogs had loped up the dirt driveway with the car. They were rangy, alert, and bounced up and down on their cushioned paws like wolves. They didn't waste their energy barking, but positioned themselves quietly, one at either car door and the third in front of the bellied-out screen door to Uncle Lawrence's house. It was six in the morning but the wind was up already, blowing dust, ruffling their short moth-eaten coats. The big brown one on Vicki Koob's side had unusual black and white markings, stripes almost, like a hyena and he grinned at her, tongue out and teeth showing.

"Shoo!" Miss Koob opened her door with a quick jerk.

The brown dog sidestepped the door and jumped before her, tiptoeing. Its dirty white muzzle curled and its eyes crossed suddenly as if it was zeroing its cross-hair sights in on the exact place it would bite her. She ducked back and slammed the door.

"It's mean," she told Officer Brackett. He was printing out some type of form. The other officer, Harmony, a slow man, had not yet reacted to the car's halt. He had been sitting quietly in the back seat, but now he rolled down his window and with no change in expression unsnapped his holster and drew his pistol out and pointed it at the dog on his side. The dog smacked down on its belly, wiggled under the car and was out and around the back of the house before Harmony drew his gun back. The other dogs vanished with him. From wherever they had disappeared to they began to yap and howl, and the door to the low shoebox-style house fell open.

"Heya, what's going on?"

Uncle Lawrence put his head out the door and opened wide the one eye he had in working order. The eye bulged impossibly wider in outrage when he saw the police car. But the eyes of the two officers and Miss Vicki Koob were wide open too because they had never seen Uncle Lawrence in his sleeping get-up or, indeed, witnessed anything like it. For his ribs, which were cracked from a bad fall and still mending, Uncle

Lawrence wore a thick white corset laced up the front with a striped sneakers' lace. His glass eye and his set of dentures were still out for the night so his face puckered here and there, around its absences and scars, like a damaged but fierce little cake. Although he had a few gray streaks now, Uncle Lawrence's hair was still thick, and because he wore a special contraption of elastic straps around his head every night, two oiled waves always crested on either side of his middle part. All of this would have been sufficient to astonish, even without the most striking part of his outfit—the smoking jacket. It was made of black satin and hung open around his corset, dragging a tasseled belt. Gold thread dragons struggled up the lapels and blasted their furry red breath around his neck. As Lawrence walked down the steps, he put his arms up in surrender and the gold tassels in the inner seams of his sleeves dropped into view.

"My heavens, what a sight." Vicki Koob was impressed.

"A character," apologized Officer Harmony.

As a tribal police officer who could be counted on to help out the State Patrol, Harmony thought he always had to explain about Indians or get twice as tough to show he did not favor them. He was slow-moving and shy but two jumps ahead of other people all the same, and now, as he watched Uncle Lawrence's splendid approach, he gazed speculatively at the torn and bulging pocket of the smoking jacket. Harmony had been inside Uncle Lawrence's house before and knew that above his draped orange-crate shelf of war medals a blue-black German luger was hung carefully in a net of flat-headed nails and fishing line. Thinking of this deadly exhibition, he got out of the car and shambled toward Lawrence with a dreamy little smile of welcome on his face. But when he searched Lawrence, he found that the bulging pocket held only the lonesome-looking dentures from Lawrence's empty jaw. They were still dripping denture polish.

"I had been cleaning them when you arrived," Uncle Lawrence explained with acid dignity.

He took the toothbrush from his other pocket and aimed it like a rifle.

"Quit that, you old idiot." Harmony tossed the toothbrush away. "For once you ain't done nothing. We came for your nephew."

Lawrence looked at Harmony with a faint air of puzzlement.

"Ma Frere, listen," threatened Harmony amiably, "those two white people in the car came to get him for the welfare. They got papers on your nephew that give them the right to take him."

"Papers?" Uncle Lawrence puffed out his deeply pitted cheeks. "Let me see them papers."

The two of them walked over to Vicki's side of the car and she pulled a copy of the court order from her purse. Lawrence put his teeth back in and adjusted them with busy workings of his jaw.

"Just a minute," he reached into his breast pocket as he bent close to Miss Vicki Koob. "I can't read these without I have in my eye."

He took the eye from his breast pocket delicately, and as he popped it into his face the social worker's mouth fell open in a consternated O.

"What is this," she cried in a little voice.

Uncle Lawrence looked at her mildly. The white glass of the eye was cold as lard. The black iris was strangely charged and menacing.

"He's nuts," Brackett huffed along the side of Vicki's neck. "Never mind him."

Vicki's hair had sweated down her nape in tiny corkscrews and some of the hairs were so long and dangly now that they disappeared into the zippered back of her dress. Brackett noticed this as he spoke into her ear. His face grew red and the backs of his hands prickled. He slid under the steering wheel and got out of the car. He walked around the hood to stand with Leo Harmony.

"We could take you in too," said Brackett roughly. Lawrence eyed the officers in what was taken as defiance. "If you don't cooperate, we'll get out the handcuffs," they warned.

One of Lawrence's arms was stiff and would not move until he'd rubbed it with witch hazel in the morning. His other arm worked fine though, and he stuck it out in front of Brackett.

"Get them handcuffs," he urged them. "Put me in a welfare home."

Brackett snapped one side of the handcuffs on Lawrence's good arm and the other to the handle of the police car.

"That's to hold you," he said. "We're wasting our time. Harmony, you search that little shed over by the tall grass and Miss Koob and myself will search the house."

"My rights is violated!" Lawrence shrieked suddenly. They ignored him. He tugged at the handcuff and thought of the good heavy file he kept in his tool box and the German luger oiled and ready but never loaded, because of Buddy, over his shelf. He should have used it on these bad ones, even Harmony in his big-time white man job. He wouldn't last long in that job anyway before somebody gave him what for.

"It's a damn scheme," said Uncle Lawrence, rattling his chains against the car. He looked over at the shed and thought maybe Albertine and Buddy had sneaked away before the car pulled into the yard. But he sagged, seeing Albertine move like a shadow within the boards. "Oh, it's all a damn scheme," he muttered again.

"I want to find that boy and salvage him," Vicki Koob explained to Officer Brackett as they walked into the house. "Look at his family life—the old man crazy as a bed-bug, the mother intoxicated somewhere."

Brackett nodded, energetic, eager. He was a short hopeful redhead who failed consistently to win the hearts of women. Vicki Koob intrigued him. Now, as he watched, she pulled a tiny pen out of an ornamental clip on her blouse. It was attached to a retractable line that would suck the pen back, like a child eating one strand of spaghetti. Something about the pen on its line excited Brackett to the point of discomfort. His hand shook as he opened the screendoor and stepped in, beckoning Miss Koob to follow.

They could see the house was empty at first glance. It was only one rectangular room with whitewashed walls and a little gas stove in the middle. They had already come through the cooking lean-to with the other stove and washstand and rusty old refrigerator. That refrigerator had nothing in it but some wrinkled potatoes and a package of turkey necks. Vicki Koob noted that in her perfect-bound notebook. The beds along the walls of the big room were covered with quilts that Albertine's mother, Sophie, had made from bits of old wool coats and pants that the Sisters sold in bundles at the mission. There was no one hiding beneath the beds. No one was under the little aluminum dinette table covered with a green oilcloth, or the soft brown wood chairs tucked up to it. One wall of the big room was filled with neatly stacked crates of things—old tools and springs and small half-dismantled appliances. Five or six television sets were stacked against the wall. Their control panels spewed colored wires and at least one was cracked all the way across. Only the topmost set, with coathanger antenna angled sensitively to catch the bounding signals around Little Shell, looked like it could possibly work.

Not one thing escaped Vicki Koob's trained and cataloguing gaze. She made note of the cupboard that held only commodity flour and coffee. The unsanitary tin oil drum beneath the kitchen window, full of empty surplus pork cans and beer bottles, caught her eye as did Uncle Lawrence's physical and mental deteriorations. She quickly described these "benchmarks of alcoholic dependency within the extended family of Woodrow (Buddy) American Horse" as she walked around the room with the little notebook open, pushed against her belly to steady it. Although Vicki had been there before, Albertine's presence had always made it difficult for her to take notes.

"Twice the maximum allowable space between door and threshold," she wrote now. "Probably no insulation. Two three-inch cracks in walls inadequately sealed with whitewashed mud." She made a mental note but could see no point in describing Lawrence's stuffed reclining chair that only reclined, the shadeless lamp with its plastic orchid in the bubble glass base, or the three-dimensional picture of Jesus that Lawrence had once demonstrated to her. When plugged in, lights rolled behind the water the Lord stood on so that he seemed to be strolling although he never actually went forward, of course, but only pushed the glowing waves behind him forever like a poor tame rat in a treadmill.

Brackett cleared his throat with a nervous rasp and touched Vicki's shoulder.

"What are you writing?"

She moved away and continued to scribble as if thoroughly absorbed in her work. "Officer Brackett displays an undue amount of interest in my person," she wrote. "Perhaps?"

He snatched playfully at the book, but she hugged it to her chest and moved off smiling. More curls had fallen, wetted to the base of her neck. Looking out the window, she sighed long and loud.

"All night on brush rollers for this. What a joke."

Brackett shoved his hands in his pockets. His mouth opened slightly, then shut with a small throttled cluck.

When Albertine saw Harmony ambling across the yard with his big brown thumbs in his belt, his placid smile, and his tiny black eyes moving back and forth, she put Buddy under the cot. Harmony stopped at the shed and stood quietly. He spread his arms to show her he hadn't drawn his big police gun.

"Ma Cousin," he said in the Michif dialect that people used if they were relatives or sometimes if they needed gas or a couple of dollars, "why don't you come out here and stop this foolishness?"

"I ain't your cousin," Albertine said. Anger boiled up in her suddenly. "I ain't related to no pigs."

She bit her lip and watched him through the cracks, circling, a big tan punching dummy with his boots full of sand so he never stayed down once he fell. He was empty inside, all stale air. But he knew how to get to her so much better than a white cop could. And now he was circling because he wasn't sure she didn't have a weapon, maybe a knife or the German luger that was the only thing that her father, Albert American

Horse, had left his wife and daughter besides his name. Harmony knew that Albertine was a tall strong woman who took two big men to subdue when she didn't want to go in the drunk tank. She had hard hips, broad shoulders, and stood tall like her Sioux father, the American Horse who was killed threshing in Belle Prairie.

"I feel bad to have to do this," Harmony said to Albertine. "But for godsakes, let's nobody get hurt. Come on out with the boy, why don't you? I know you got him in there."

Albertine did not give herself away this time. She let him wonder. Slowly and quietly she pulled her belt through its loops and wrapped it around and around her hand until only the big oval buckle with turquoise chunks shaped into a butterfly stuck out over her knuckles. Harmony was talking but she wasn't listening to what he said. She was listening to the pitch of his voice, the tone of it that would tighten or tremble at a certain moment when he decided to rush the shed. He kept talking slowly and reasonably, flexing the dialect from time to time, even mentioning her father.

"He was a damn good man. I don't care what they say, Albertine, I knew him."

Albertine looked at the stone butterfly that spread its wings across her fist. The wings looked light and cool, not heavy. It almost looked like it was ready to fly. Harmony wanted to get to Albertine through her father but she would not think about American Horse. She concentrated on the sky blue stone.

Yet the shape of the stone, the color, betrayed her.

She saw her father suddenly, bending at the grille of their old gray car. She was small then. The memory came from so long ago it seemed like a dream—narrowly focused, snapshot-clear. He was bending by the grille in the sun. It was hot summer. Wings of sweat, dark blue, spread across the back of his work shirt. He always wore soft blue shirts, the color of shade cloudier than this stone. His stiff hair had grown out of its short haircut and flopped over his forehead. When he stood up and turned away from the car, Albertine saw that he had a butterfly.

"It's dead," he told her. "Broke its wings and died on the grille."

She must have been five, maybe six, wearing one of the boy's T-shirts Mama bleached in Hilex-water. American Horse took the butterfly, a black and yellow one, and rubbed it on Albertine's collarbone and chest and arms until the color and the powder of it were blended into her skin.

"For grace," he said.

And Albertine had felt a strange lightening in her arms, in her chest, when he did this and said, "For grace." The way he said it, grace meant everything the butterfly was. The sharp delicate wings. The way it floated over grass. The way its wings seemed to breathe fanning in the sun. The wisdom of the way it blended into flowers or changed into a leaf. In herself she felt the same kind of possibilities and closed her eyes almost in shock or pain, she felt so light and powerful at that moment.

Then her father had caught her and thrown her high into the air. She could not remember landing in his arms or landing at all. She only remembered the sun filling her eyes and the world tipping crazily behind her, out of sight.

"He was a damn good man," Harmony said again.

Albertine heard his starched uniform gathering before his boots hit the ground. Once, twice, three times. It took him four solid jumps to get right where she wanted him. She kicked the plank door open when he reached for the handle and the corner caught him on the jaw. He faltered, and Albertine hit him flat on the chin with the butterfly.

She hit him so hard the shock of it went up her arm like a string pulled taut. Her fist opened, numb, and she let the belt unloop before she closed her hand on the tip end of it and sent the stone butterfly swooping out in a wide circle around her as if it was on the end of a leash. Harmony reeled backward as she walked toward him swinging the belt. She expected him to fall but he just stumbled. And then he took the gun from his hip.

Albertine let the belt go limp. She and Harmony stood within feet of each other, breathing. Each heard the human sound of air going in and out of the other person's lungs. Each read the face of the other as if deciphering letters carved into softly eroding veins of stone. Albertine saw the pattern of tiny arteries that age, drink, and hard living had blown to the surface of the man's face. She saw the spoked wheels of his iris and the arteries like tangled threads that sewed him up. She saw the living net of springs and tissue that held him together, and trapped him. She saw the random, intimate plan of his person.

She took a quick shallow breath and her face went strange and tight. She saw the black veins in the wings of the butterfly, roads burnt into a map, and then she was located somewhere in the net of veins and sinew that was the tragic complexity of the world so she did not see Officer Brackett and Vicki Koob rushing toward her, but felt them instead like flies caught in the same web, rocking it.

"Albertine!" Vicki Koob had stopped in the grass. Her voice was shrill and tight. "It's better this way, Albertine. We're going to help you."

Albertine straightened, threw her shoulders back. Her father's hand was on her chest and shoulders lightening her wonderfully. Then on wings of her father's hands, on dead butterfly wings, Albertine lifted into the air and flew toward the others. The light powerful feeling swept her up the way she had floated higher, seeing the grass below. It was her father throwing her up into the air and out of danger. Her arms opened for bullets but no bullets came. Harmony did not shoot. Instead, he raised his fist and brought it down hard on her head.

Albertine did not fall immediately, but stood in his arms a moment. Perhaps she gazed still farther back behind the covering of his face. Perhaps she was completely stunned and did not think as she sagged and fell. Her face rolled forward and hair covered her features, so it was impossible for Harmony to see with just what particular expression she gazed into the head-splitting wheel of light, or blackness, that overcame her.

Harmony turned the vehicle onto the gravel road that led back to town. He had convinced the other two that Albertine was more trouble than she was worth, and so they left her behind, and Lawrence too. He stood swearing in his cinder driveway as the car rolled out of sight. Buddy sat between the social worker and Officer Brackett. Vicki tried to hold Buddy fast and keep her arm down at the same time, for the words she'd screamed at Albertine had broken the seal of antiperspirant beneath her arms. She was sweating now as though she'd stored up an ocean inside of her. Sweat rolled down her back in a shallow river and pooled at her waist and between her breasts. A thin sheen of water came out on her forearms, her face. Vicki gave an irritated moan but Brackett seemed not to take notice, or take offense at least. Air-conditioned breezes were sweeping over the seat anyway, and very soon they would be comfortable. She smiled at Brackett over Buddy's head. The man grinned back. Buddy stirred. Vicki remembered the emergency chocolate bar she kept in her purse, fished it out, and offered it to Buddy. He did not react, so she closed his fingers over the package and peeled the paper off one end.

The car accelerated. Buddy felt the road and wheels pummeling each other and the rush of the heavy motor purring in high gear. Buddy knew that what he'd seen in his mind that morning, the thing coming out of the sky with barbs and chains, had hooked him. Somehow he was caught and held in the sour tin smell of the pale woman's armpit. Somehow he was pinned between their pounds of breathless flesh. He looked at the chocolate in his hand. He was squeezing the bar so hard that a thin brown trickle had melted down his arm. Automatically he put the bar in his mouth.

As he bit down he saw his mother very clearly, just as she had been when she carried him from the shed. She was stretched flat on the ground, on her stomach, and her arms were curled around her head as if in sleep. One leg was drawn up and it looked for all the world like she was running full tilt into the ground, as though she had been trying to pass into the earth, to bury herself, but at the last moment something had stopped her.

There was no blood on Albertine, but Buddy tasted blood now at the sight of her, for he bit down hard and cut his own lip. He ate the chocolate, every bit of it, tasting his mother's blood. And when he had the chocolate down inside him and all licked off his hands, he opened his mouth to say thank you to the woman, as his mother had taught him. But instead of a thank you coming out he was astonished to hear a great rattling scream, and then another, rip out of him like pieces of his own body and whirl onto the sharp things all around him.

(1983)

MARY HOOD
[b. 1946]

How Far She Went

They had quarreled all morning, squalled all summer about the incidentals: how tight the girl's cut-off jeans were, the "Every Inch a Woman" T-shirt, her choice of music and how loud she played it, her practiced inattention, her sullen look. Her granny wrung out the last boiled dishcloth, pinched it to the line, giving the basin a sling and a slap, the water flying out in a scalding arc onto the Queen Anne's lace by the path, never mind if it bloomed, that didn't make it worth anything except to chiggers, but the girl would cut it by the everlasting armload and cherish it in the old churn, going to that much trouble for a weed but not bending once—unbegged—to pick the nearest bean; she was sulking now. Bored. Displaced.

"And what do you think happens to a chigger if nobody ever walks by his weed?" her granny asked, heading for the house with that sidelong uneager unanswered glance, hoping for what? The surprise gift of a smile? Nothing. The woman shook her head and said it. "Nothing." The door slammed behind her. Let it.

"I hate it here!" the girl yelled then. She picked up a stick and broke it and threw the pieces—one from each hand—at the laundry drying in the noon. Missed. Missed.

Then she turned on her bare, haughty heel and set off high-shouldered into the heat, quick but not far, not far enough—no road was *that* long—only as far as she dared. At the gate, a rusty chain swinging between two lichened posts, she stopped, then backed up the raw drive to make a run at the barrier, lofting, clearing it clean, her long hair wild in the sun. Triumphant, she looked back at the house where she caught at the dark window her granny's face in its perpetual eclipse of disappointment, old at fifty. She stepped back, but the girl saw her.

"You don't know me!" the girl shouted, chin high, and ran till her ribs ached.

As she rested in the rattling shade of the willows, the little dog found her. He could be counted on. He barked all the way, and squealed when she pulled the burr from his ear. They started back to the house for lunch. By then the mailman had long come and gone in the old ruts, leaving the one letter folded now to fit the woman's apron pocket.

If bad news darkened her granny's face, the girl ignored it. Didn't talk at all, another of her distancings, her defiances. So it was as they ate that the woman summarized, "Your daddy wants you to cash in the plane ticket and buy you something. School clothes. For here."

Pale, the girl stared, defenseless only an instant before blurting out, "You're lying."

The woman had to stretch across the table to leave her handprint on that blank cheek. She said, not caring if it stung or not, "He's been planning it since he sent you here."

"I could turn this whole house over, dump it! Leave you slobbering over that stinking jealous dog in the dust!" The girl trembled with the vision, with the strength it gave her. It made her laugh. "Scatter the Holy Bible like confetti and ravel the crochet into miles of stupid string! I could! I will! I won't stay here!" But she didn't move, not until her tears rose to meet her color, and then to escape the shame of minding so much she fled. Just headed away, blind. It didn't matter, this time, how far she went.

The woman set her thoughts against fretting over their bickering, just went on unalarmed with chores, clearing off after the uneaten meal, bringing in the laundry, scattering corn for the chickens, ladling manure tea onto the porch flowers. She listened though. She always had been a listener. It gave her a cocked look. She forgot why she had gone into the girl's empty room, that ungirlish, tenuous lodging place with its bleak order, its ready suitcases never unpacked, the narrow bed, the contested radio on the windowsill. The woman drew the cracked shade down between the radio and the August sun. There wasn't anything else to do.

It was after six when she tied on her rough oxfords and walked down the drive and dropped the gate chain and headed back to the creosoted shed where she kept her tools. She took a hoe for snakes, a rake, shears to trim the grass where it grew, and seed in her pocket to scatter where it never had grown at all. She put the tools and her gloves and the bucket in the trunk of the old Chevy, its prime and rust like an Appaloosa's spots through the chalky white finish. She left the trunk open and the tool handles sticking out. She wasn't going far.

The heat of the day had broken, but the air was thick, sultry, weighted with honeysuckle in second bloom and the Nu-Grape scent of kudzu. The maple and poplar leaves turned over, quaking, silver. There wouldn't be any rain. She told the dog to stay, but he knew a trick. He stowed away when she turned her back, leaped right into the trunk with the tools, then gave himself away with exultant barks. Hearing him, her court jester, she stopped the car and welcomed him into the front seat beside her. Then they went on. Not a mile from her gate she turned onto the blue gravel of the cemetery lane, hauled the gearshift into reverse to whoa them, and got out to take the idle walk down to her buried hopes, bending all along to rout out a handful of weeds from between the markers of old acquaintance. She stood there and read, slow. The dog whined at her hem; she picked him up and rested her chin on his head, then he wriggled and whined to run free, contrary and restless as a child.

The crows called strong and bold MOM! MOM! A trick of the ear to hear it like that. She knew it was the crows, but still she looked around. No one called her that now. She was done with that. And what was it worth anyway? It all came to this: solitary weeding. The sinful fumble of flesh, the fear, the listening for a return that never came, the shamed waiting, the unanswered prayers, the perjury on the certificate—hadn't she lain there weary of the whole lie and it only beginning? and a voice telling her, "Here's your baby, here's your girl," and the swaddled package meaning no more to her than an extra anything, something store-bought, something she could take back for a refund.

"Tie her to the fence and give her a bale of hay," she had murmured, drugged, and they teased her, excused her for such a welcoming, blaming the anesthesia, but it went deeper than that; *she* knew, and the *baby* knew: there was no love in the begetting. That was the secret, unforgivable, that not another good thing could ever make up for, where all the bad had come from, like a visitation, a punishment. She knew that was why Sylvie had been wild, had gone to earth so early, and before dying had made this child in sudden wedlock, a child who would be just like her, would carry the hurting on into another generation. A matter of time. No use raising her hand. But she *had* raised her hand. Still wore on its palm the memory of the sting of the collision with the girl's cheek; had she broken her jaw? Her heart? Of course not. She said it aloud: "Takes more than that."

She went to work then, doing what she could with her old tools. She pecked the clay on Sylvie's grave, new-looking, unhealed after years. She tried again, scattering seeds from her pocket, every last possible one of them. Off in the west she could hear the pulpwood cutters sawing through another acre across the lake. Nearer, there was the racket of motorcycles laboring cross-country, insect-like, distracting.

She took her bucket to the well and hung it on the pump. She had half filled it when the bikers roared up, right down the blue gravel, straight at her. She let the bucket overflow, staring. On the back of one of the machines was the girl. Sylvie's girl! Her bare arms wrapped around the shirtless man riding between her thighs. They were first. The second biker rode alone. She studied their strangers' faces as they circled her. They were the enemy, all of them. Laughing. The girl was laughing too, laughing like her mama did. Out in the middle of nowhere the girl had found these two men, some moth-musk about her drawing them (too soon!) to what? She shouted it: "What in God's—" They roared off without answering her, and the bucket of water tipped over, spilling its stain blood-dark on the red dust.

The dog went wild barking, leaping after them, snapping at the tires, and there was no calling him down. The bikers made a wide circuit of the churchyard, then roared straight across the graves, leaping the ditch and landing upright on the road again, heading off toward the reservoir.

Furious, she ran to her car, past the barking dog, this time leaving him behind, driving after them, horn blowing nonstop, to get back what was not theirs. She drove after them knowing what they did not know, that all the roads beyond that point deadended. She surprised them, swinging the Impala across their path, cutting them off; let them hit it! They stopped. She got out, breathing hard, and said, when she could, "She's underage." Just that. And put out her claiming hand with an authority that made the girl's arms drop from the man's insolent waist and her legs tremble.

"I was just riding," the girl said, not looking up.

Behind them the sun was heading on toward down. The long shadows of the pines drifted back and forth in the same breeze that puffed the distant sails on the lake. Dead limbs creaked and clashed overhead like the antlers of locked and furious beasts.

"Sheeeut," the lone rider said. "I told you." He braced with his muddy boot and leaned out from his machine to spit. The man the girl had been riding with had the invading sort of eyes the woman had spent her lifetime bolting doors against. She met him now, face to face.

"Right there, missy," her granny said, pointing behind her to the car.

The girl slid off the motorcycle and stood halfway between her choices. She started slightly at the poosh! as he popped another top and chugged the beer in one uptilting of his head. His eyes never left the woman's. When he was through, he tossed the can high, flipping it end over end. Before it hit the ground he had his pistol out and, firing once, winged it into the lake.

"Freaking lucky shot," the other one grudged.

"I don't need luck," he said. He sighted down the barrel of the gun at the woman's head. "POW!" he yelled, and when she recoiled, he laughed. He swung around to the girl; he kept aiming the gun, here, there, high, low, all around. "Y'all settle it," he said, with a shrug.

The girl had to understand him then, had to know him, had to know better. But still she hesitated. He kept looking at her, then away.

"She's fifteen," her granny said. "You can go to jail."

"You can go to hell," he said.

"Probably will," her granny told him. "I'll save you a seat by the fire." She took the girl by the arm and drew her to the car; she backed up, swung around, and headed out the road toward the churchyard for her tools and dog. The whole way the girl said nothing, just hunched against the far door, staring hard-eyed out at the pines going past.

The woman finished watering the seed in, and collected her tools. As she worked, she muttered, "It's your own kin buried here, you might have the decency to glance this way one time . . ." The girl was finger-tweezing her eyebrows in the side mirror. She didn't look around as the dog and the woman got in. Her granny shifted hard, sending the tools clattering in the trunk.

When they came to the main road, there were the men. Watching for them. Waiting for them. They kicked their machines into life and followed, close, bumping them, slapping the old fenders, yelling. The girl gave a wild glance around at the one by her door and said, "Gran'ma?" and as he drew his pistol, "Gran'ma!" just as the gun nosed into the open window. She frantically cranked the glass up between her and the weapon, and her granny, seeing, spat, "Fool!" She never had been one to pray for peace or rain. She stamped the accelerator right to the floor.

The motorcycles caught up. Now she braked, hard, and swerved off the road into an alley between the pines, not even wide enough for the school bus, just a fire scrape that came out a quarter mile from her own house, if she could get that far. She slewed on the pine straw, then righted, tearing along the dark tunnel through the woods. She had for the time being bested them; they were left behind. She was winning. Then she hit the wallow where the tadpoles were already five weeks old. The Chevy plowed in and stalled. When she got it cranked again, they were stuck. The tires spattered mud three feet up the near trunks as she tried to spin them out, to rock them out. Useless. "Get out and run!" she cried, but the trees were too close on the passenger side. The girl couldn't open her door. She wasted precious time having to crawl out under the steering wheel. The woman waited but the dog ran on.

They struggled through the dusky woods, their pace slowed by the thick straw and vines. Overhead, in the last light, the martins were reeling free and sure after their prey.

"Why? Why?" the girl gasped, as they lunged down the old deer trail. Behind them they could hear shots, and glass breaking as the men came to the bogged car. The woman kept on running, swatting their way clear through the shoulder-high weeds. They could see the Greer cottage, and made for it. But it was ivied-over, padlocked, the woodpile dry-rotting under its tarp, the electric meterbox empty on the pole. No help there.

The dog, excited, trotted on, yelping, his lips white-flecked. He scented the lake and headed that way, urging them on with thirsty yips. On the clay shore, treeless, deserted, at the utter limit of land, they stood defenseless, listening to the men coming on, between them and home. The woman pressed her hands to her mouth, stifling her cough. She was exhausted. She couldn't think.

"We can get under!" the girl cried suddenly, and pointed toward the Greers' dock, gap-planked, its walkway grounded on the mud. They splashed out to it, wading in, the woman grabbing up the telltale, tattletale dog in her arms. They waded out to the far end and ducked under. There was room between the foam floats for them to crouch neck-deep.

The dog wouldn't hush, even then; never had yet, and there wasn't time to teach him. When the woman realized that, she did what she had to do. She grabbed him whimpering; held him; held him under till the struggle ceased and the bubbles rose silver from his fur. They crouched there then, the two of them, submerged to the shoulders, feet unsteady on the slimed lake bed. They listened. The sky went from rose to ocher to violet in the cracks over their heads. The motorcycles had stopped now. In the silence there was the glissando of locusts, the dry crunch of boots on the flinty beach, their low man-talk drifting as they prowled back and forth. One of them struck a match.

"—they in these woods we could burn 'em out."

The wind carried their voices away into the pines. Some few words eddied back.

"—lippy old smartass do a little work on her knees besides praying—"

Laughter. It echoed off the deserted house. They were getting closer.

One of them strode directly out to the dock, walked on the planks over their heads. They could look up and see his boot soles. He was the one with the gun. He slapped a mosquito on his bare back and cursed. The carp, roused by the troubling of the waters, came nosing around the dock, guzzling and snorting. The girl and her granny held still, so still. The man fired his pistol into the shadows, and a wounded fish thrashed, dying. The man knelt and reached for it, chuffing out his beery breath. He belched. He pawed the lake for the dead fish, cursing as it floated out of reach. He shot it again, firing at it till it sank and the gun was empty. Cursed that too. He stood then and unzipped and relieved himself of some of the beer. They had to listen to that. To know that about him. To endure that, unprotesting.

Back and forth on shore the other one ranged, restless. He lit another cigarette. He coughed. He called, "Hey! They got away, man, that's all. Don't get your shorts in a wad. Let's go."

"Yeah." He finished. He zipped. He stumped back across the planks and leaped to shore, leaving the dock tilting amid widening ripples. Underneath, they waited.

The bike cranked. The other ratcheted, ratcheted, then coughed, caught, roared. They circled, cut deep ruts, slung gravel, and went. Their roaring died away and away. Crickets resumed and a near frog bic-bic-bicked.

Under the dock, they waited a little longer to be sure. Then they ducked below the water, scraped out from under the pontoon, and came up into free air, slogging toward shore. It had seemed warm enough in the water. Now they shivered. It was almost night. One streak of light still stood reflected on the darkening lake, drew itself thinner, narrowing into a final cancellation of day. A plane winked its way west.

The girl was trembling. She ran her hands down her arms and legs, shedding water like a garment. She sighed, almost a sob. The woman held the dog in her arms; she dropped to her knees upon the random stones and murmured, private, haggard, "Oh, honey," three times, maybe all three times for the dog, maybe once for each of them. The girl waited, watching. Her granny rocked the dog like a baby, like a dead child, rocked slower and slower and was still.

"I'm sorry," the girl said then, avoiding the dog's inert, empty eye.

"It was him or you," her granny said, finally, looking up. Looking her over. "Did they mess with you? With your britches? Did they?"

"No!" Then, quieter, "No, ma'am."

When the woman tried to stand up she staggered, lightheaded, clumsy with the freight of the dog. "No, ma'am," she echoed, fending off the girl's "Let me." And she said again, "It was him or you. I know that. I'm not going to rub your face in it." They saw each other as well as they could in that failing light, in any light.

The woman started toward home, saying, "Around here, we bear our own burdens." She led the way along the weedy shortcuts. The twilight bleached the dead limbs of the pines to bone. Insects sang in the thickets, silencing at their oncoming.

"We'll see about the car in the morning," the woman said. She bore her armful toward her own moth-ridden dusk-to-dawn security light with that country grace she had always had when the earth was reliably progressing underfoot. The girl walked close behind her, exactly where *she* walked, matching her pace, matching her stride, close enough to put her hand forth (if the need arose) and touch her granny's back where the faded voile was clinging damp, the merest gauze between their wounds.

(1984)

Poetry

PART TWO

Poetry

PART TWO

CHAPTER NINE

Reading Poems

In some ways reading poetry is much like reading fiction, drama, and the essay: we observe details of action and language, make connections and inferences, and draw conclusions. We also bring to poetry the same intellectual and emotional dispositions, the same general experience with life and literature that we draw on in reading drama, fiction, and essay. And yet there is something different about reading poems. The difference, admittedly more one of degree than of kind, involves our being more attentive to the connotations of words, more receptive to the expressive qualities of sound and rhythm in line and stanza, more discerning about details of syntax and punctuation. This increased attention to linguistic detail is necessary because of the density and compression characteristic of poetry. More than fiction, drama, and essay, poetry is an art of condensation and implication; poems concentrate meaning and distill feeling.

Learning to read poetry well and to savor its pleasures involves learning to ask questions about how we experience poems, how we interpret them, and how we evaluate them. Such questions include the following:

1. What feelings does the poem evoke? What sensations, associations, and memories does it give rise to?
2. What ideas does the poem express, either directly or indirectly? What sense does it make? What do we understand it to say and suggest?

3. What view of the world does the poet present? Does it agree with your view? What do you think of the poet's view? What value does the poem hold for you as a work of art and as an influence on your way of understanding yourself and others?

Our discussion is divided into three parts: the experience of poetry, the interpretation of poetry, and the evaluation of poetry. In the experience section we will be concerned primarily with subjective responses, with personal reactions. We will reflect on how the poem may be related to our lives. In the interpretation section our concern will be the intellectual processes that we engage in as we develop an understanding of poetry. Here the focus will be analytical rather than impressionistic, rational rather than emotional. And in the evaluation of poetry, we will be concerned with the ways we bring our sense of who we are and what we believe into our consideration of any poem's significance, and with how poems are evaluated aesthetically.

THE EXPERIENCE OF POETRY

We begin by considering the following poem, first from the standpoint of our experience.

ROBERT HAYDEN

[1913–1980]

Those Winter Sundays

Sundays too my father got up early
and put his clothes on in the blueblack cold,
then with cracked hands that ached
from labor in the weekday weather made
banked fires blaze. No one ever thanked him.   5

I'd wake and hear the cold splintering, breaking.
When the rooms were warm, he'd call,
and slowly I would rise and dress,
fearing the chronic angers of that house,

Speaking indifferently to him,   10
who had driven out the cold
and polished my good shoes as well.
What did I know, what did I know
of love's austere and lonely offices?

Even from a single reading we see that the speaker of "Those Winter Sundays," now an adult, is remembering how his father used to get up on cold Sunday mornings and light the fires that would warm the house for his sleeping family. We sense that he regrets how unappreciative of his father he was as a child. We may wonder what prompts these memories and feelings. Our initial reading may also call up a memory much like the one described in Hayden's poem. But even if our experience does not echo the speaker's or if our feelings differ from his, we may respond to the description of waking up on a cold day in a warm house. Such personal responses, whatever their precise nature, are important to our reading of poetry, for in arriving at a sense of a poem's meaning and value, we often begin with them.

Here is a sampling of one reader's responses to the poem: a set of notes that describe both memories and feelings. Notice how the responses, subjective and impressionistic as they are, nonetheless reveal the reader beginning to reflect on the poem's meaning and values.

> I remember how my father used to wake up at five A.M. to light the furnace so the house would be warm when the rest of the family got up. My strongest memories of this come from my early adolescence, perhaps because it was then that I began to assume this responsibility. I would never have thought to describe the cold as "blue-black" but I like how that makes me remember what the cold felt like at that merciless hour. I also remember the way my father would come and wake us up around 6:30 to get ready for school. By then the floor was warm and the radiators crackled with steam.
>
> Like the rest of my brothers and sisters, I took my father's early morning efforts for granted. We never thought of thanking him. Perhaps we should have. He always knew that we loved him. That wasn't a problem. But as I think back, I don't remember thanking him for much of anything. I guess we were all guilty of speaking indifferently to him, or of not speaking much at all.
>
> A couple of other things about the poem strike me. One is the shoes the father polished for his son. A nice touch, those shoes. I wonder when a boy begins to be responsible for polishing his own shoes. I can't remember when I started polishing mine— high school perhaps—but I do remember often polishing my father's as well—especially on Sundays when he would rush around to get ready for church. A more confusing item is the line about "fearing the chronic angers" of the house. How can a house be angry? Perhaps the writer is referring to the father's anger? I remember my own father becoming angry. He blew his top, as he used to say, pretty regularly, one time punching a hole in the dining room wall, another time ripping the phone off the kitchen wall. I wasn't the target of his anger often, but it was unsettling to see him lose his temper.
>
> The last couple of lines with the repeated question, "What did I know, what did I know," hit me the hardest. I hear regret in them, regret for lost opportunities, regret for understanding too

late the motive behind the attentions of the speaker's father. Perhaps there is also regret for the distance that separated father and son. I know a little about that. But I also hear in these lines how love involves sacrifice and that such quiet expressions of love don't always or even often receive the recognition they deserve. For people whose fathers are still alive there is time perhaps to compensate. For me, it's too late.

THE INTERPRETATION OF POETRY

When we interpret a poem, we explain it to ourselves in order to understand it. We makes sense of it, in short. If one of our initial acts is to somehow appropriate the poem personally by relating it to our experience, another is to consider its meaning. When we interpret a poem, we concern ourselves less with how it affects us than with what it means or suggests. Interpretation relies on our intellectual comprehension and rational understanding rather than on our emotional apprehension and response.

The act of interpretation involves essentially four things: observing, connecting, inferring, and concluding. We observe details of description and action, of language and form. We look for connections among these details and begin to establish a sense of the poem's coherence (the way its details fit together in meaningful relationships). On the basis of these connections we make inferences or interpretive guesses about their significance. And finally, we come to a provisional conclusion about the poem's meaning based on our observations, connections, and inferences.

As we continue our discussion of "Those Winter Sundays," we will offer additional observations, inferences, and conclusions, pretty much in that order. This description of the interpretive process makes it seem as if we perform each of these analytical acts in succession. That's not the way it happens. Just as our personal responses and subjective impressions, our memories, sensations, and associations are stirred up *while* we read and *after,* so too all four aspects of interpretation occur simultaneously.

To see what Hayden's poem implies, let's give it a second look. We might notice, for example, that the first words, "Sundays too," indicate that the speaker's father performed his housewarming chores every day, including Sundays. We might notice also that the poem contrasts cold and warmth, with the cold dissipated as the warmth of the fires the father has started suffuses the house. And we might note further that the poem shifts from father to son, from "him" to "I." The first stanza, for example, describes the father's act, the second the boy's awakening to a warm house, while the third records a different kind of awakening—the speaker's realization of his earlier indifference and of his father's love. It is in this third and final stanza that we feel most strongly the contrast between the speaker's past and present, between the then and the now of the poem, between the love that the speaker neither noticed nor acknowledged and the love he later acknowledges and understands.

So far we have centered on the poem's speaker and its subject. (The *speaker*

refers to the voice of the character we hear in the poem; the *subject* indicates
what the poem is about.) Our first readings of a poem will usually focus on who
is speaking about what, and why. In considering speaker and subject, we solidify our sense of what the poem implies, whether its implications concern,
primarily, ideas or feelings. When the speaker notes that he feared "the chronic
angers of that house," we may sense that he points toward something important. Presumably he feared his father's anger, which on occasion may have been
directed at him. But by using the plural form of the word rather than the singular ("angers" rather than "anger") the speaker may be suggesting that there
was discord between the father and other members of the family as well. Whatever the specific nature of his fear, the speaker intimates that his fear was the
source of his own wariness and indifference toward his father.

   The lines that convey the speaker's feeling most intensely, however, are those
that end the poem:

> What did I know, what did I know
> of love's austere and lonely offices?

In these lines we sense the speaker's remorse and regret for not being aware of
all his father did for him; we sense further that even though he didn't understand and feel the extent of his father's devotion, he certainly does later. Moreover, we sense the intensity of his feelings both in his repetition of the phrase
"what did I know," and in the words that describe his father's actions: "love's
austere and lonely offices." "Austere" suggests both the rigor and self-discipline
of the father's acts and perhaps the stern severity with which he may have performed them. "Lonely" indicates that the father performed his early morning
labors alone, without help from the other members of the family. It also suggests that the father was emotionally isolated from the speaker and perhaps from
other members of the family.

   But the word "offices" conveys other ideas as well. It implies both the duties the father fulfills and the corresponding authority he possesses. In addition,
it suggests something done for another, as in the good offices of a friend. Beyond these related meanings, "offices" also refers to the daily prayers recited by
clerics. Thus, the words "austere" and "offices" convey the speaker's understanding of his father's sacrifices for him. Moreover, the highly abstract language
of the conclusion—so different from the concrete details of the preceding stanzas—may also indicate the speaker's inability to express affection directly (an
inadequacy he intimates his father suffered from as well).

   To read poetry well we need to slow down enough to observe details of language, form, and sound. By reading slowly and deliberately, we give ourselves
a chance to form connections among the poem's details. Read the following
poem twice, once straight through without stopping, then again with the interpolated commentary.

ROBERT FROST

[1874–1963]

Stopping by Woods on a Snowy Evening

Whose woods these are I think I know.
His house is in the village though;
He will not see me stopping here
To watch his woods fill up with snow.

My little horse must think it queer   5
To stop without a farmhouse near
Between the woods and frozen lake
The darkest evening of the year.

He gives his harness bells a shake
To ask if there is some mistake.   10
The only other sound's the sweep
Of easy wind and downy flake.

The woods are lovely, dark and deep,
But I have promises to keep,
And miles to go before I sleep,   15
And miles to go before I sleep.

Read the poem once more, this time along with the comments that follow each stanza. Attend to the way you make sense of the poem during this reading, particularly in light of the suggestions made in the commentary.

Whose woods these are I think I know.
His house is in the village though;
He will not see me stopping here
To watch his woods fill up with snow.

Comment   Frost's poem opens with a speaker who seems concerned momentarily about who owns the woods. The speaker seems reassured that the owner can't see him. We might wonder why the speaker should be concerned and why he bothers to mention it. Does he feel that he is doing something wrong? The poem doesn't say; instead it paints a picture of man, of woods and snow. And it raises questions: Why does he stop? What attracts him? Again, the poem doesn't provide explicit answers.

> My little horse must think it queer
> To stop without a farmhouse near
> Between the woods and frozen lake
> The darkest evening of the year.

Comment   In the first stanza the speaker describes the scene and his own action. In this stanza, although he further describes this scene and action, he begins by mentioning that his horse is unaccustomed to stopping without a reason. The first line says that the horse "must" think it queer to stop this way, indicating that the horse can't really look at the man's action any other way. Accustomed to stops for food and rest, the horse couldn't possibly understand the man's impractical reason for stopping. And though the horse is said to "think," we realize that the horse's thoughts are really the speaker's—that the speaker projects his thoughts onto the horse because a part of him sees the impracticality of his action.

> He gives his harness bells a shake
> To ask if there is some mistake.
> The only other sound's the sweep
> Of easy wind and downy flake.

Comment   The third stanza continues the emphasis of the second. The speaker interprets the horse's shaking of his harness bells as a signal to move on, as a sign that stopping there serves no useful purpose. We might notice that the poet here emphasizes the stillness of the night, the isolation and privacy of the moment, which is broken only by the sound of the horse's bell. Tension builds in the mind of the speaker: even though he seems to enjoy the stillness of the night and takes pleasure in the "easy wind" and the "downy flake," he also experiences some doubt about what he is doing.

Stanza four:

> The woods are lovely, dark and deep,
> But I have promises to keep,
> And miles to go before I sleep,
> And miles to go before I sleep.

Comment   The opening line summarizes the implications of the details in the preceding stanzas. It's as if the speaker here answers the question why he stopped by the woods. He stopped because he was attracted by their dark beauty. He nevertheless feels a pressure to move on, to return to his responsibilities and obligations.

The final stanza is solemn and serious: Frost slows its pace by including pauses (indicated by punctuation) and by repeating the third line, "And miles to go before I sleep," which he uses to end the poem. In repeating this line, the poet lifts it beyond its literal meaning, inviting us to read "sleep" as the final sleep of death. Once we make this interpretive leap, we can consider "Miles to go" as perhaps the time the speaker has left to live, and "promises" as the obligations and responsibilities he must fulfill before he dies. His stopping to look at the falling snow can be seen as a temporary reprieve from such responsibilities; it might also be seen as a desire to escape them. The essential point, however, seems to be the tug of war going on in the speaker's mind between the two possibilities—stopping to contemplate the beauty of nature, and moving on to return to the active world of work and responsibility.

We have been reading and interpreting the poem one stanza at a time to suggest the way interpretation builds cumulatively as we move through a poem. The process, however, is not simply linear or sequential. For although we interpret later details in light of earlier ones, we also make sense of earlier ones after having interpreted later ones. The act of interpretation, like the experience of reading generally, is recursive. We move back and forth through a text, remembering what we read and anticipating what is to come. The process of interpretation does not end with reading the poem; it continues as we reflect on it afterward. New ideas may come to us, particularly after we have discussed the work with a teacher and classmates or after we have read other works that we can relate to it.

One final point about the interpretation of poetry (and of literature generally): interpretation never really ends. When we interpret a work, we should be concerned less with finding the single right way of understanding it than with arriving at a satisfying explanation, one that makes sense to us, and one whose logic and good sense will appeal to others. Some interpretations, nonetheless, will be more satisfying than others. They will be more convincing, largely because they take into account more of the poem's details, more of its language and form and action. Other interpretations, while perhaps not as convincing, may be valuable for the intellectual stimulation they provide and for the pleasure they afford. Because we invariably bring different experiences of life and of literature to our reading of poems, we will see different things in them and will make different kinds of sense of them. The varying interpretations we make of poems depend largely on what matters to us, what *we* consider vital. It is to this subject, values in poetry, that we turn now.

THE EVALUATION OF POETRY

When we evaluate a poem, we do two different kinds of things. First, we assess its literary quality and make a judgment about how good it is and how successfully it realizes its poetic intentions. We examine its language and structure, for example, and consider how well they work together to embody meaning and convey feeling. Second, we consider how much significance the poem has for us personally, and what significance it may have for other readers—both those who are like us and those who differ in age, race, gender, culture, and ideology. We also consider the significance the poem may have had for the poet, both its general value as part of a body of writing and its particular expression of feelings, attitudes, ideas, and values—its perspective on experience.

Our consideration of a poem's value is a measure of its involvement with our lives, with our way of thinking and being in the actual world. Some poems "speak" to us more than others; some poems mean more to us on some days than on others; and some poems mean both more and less to us at different periods of our lives. In evaluating poems, we explore the how and why of such differences. In doing so, we turn inevitably to a consideration of the various cultural assumptions, moral attitudes, and political convictions that animate particular poems. We consider the perspective from which they were written. Our consideration may involve an investigation into the circumstances of its composition, the external facts and internal experiences of the poet's life, the attitudes and beliefs he or she may have expressed in letters or other comments, the audience and occasion for which a particular poem was written, its publication history and reception by readers past and present.

From even this brief list, we can see how complex literary evaluation can be. Complicating matters even further is how we encounter the poems we evaluate. We come to the poems in this book after many preliminary acts of evaluation by others. The poets who wrote them decided they were valuable enough to preserve. The publishers who put them in print valued them, perhaps more for their potential profit than for the feelings, attitudes, or ideas they express. The editor/author of this book values them, some for how they affect him as a reader, others for their use as illustrations of particular aspects or elements of poetry. Other readers, including the teachers who use them in their courses, also value these poems. But not all readers and teachers value them the same way, and not all for the same reasons.

Does this mean then that we cannot make definitive, final, and absolute evaluations of poems? Probably, since change and variety are the hallmarks of literary evaluation. Our valuing of any poem is therefore subject to change (though not necessarily a radical reevaluation) because the way we see and understand any poem changes as we change. We will find merit in poems whose meaning we understand and whose values are like our own. We will come to value poems whose content we have lived. And we will appreciate poems in relation to other literary works that have had an impact on our lives and our thinking. To put this another way: we can't *not* evaluate the poems we read because we inevitably and automatically measure them against other works we already value. Our evaluation of any poem, moreover, depends not only upon how we understand it (that is, upon how we interpret its meaning), but also upon how we see its relation to our lives at the time we read it.

With these considerations in mind, we can suggest a few general principles upon which to ground preliminary evaluations. First is the realization that an evaluation is essentially a judgment, a set of opinions about a literary work based on a thoughtful consideration of it. We may agree or disagree with the speaker's response to the woods in Frost's "Stopping by Woods." We may confirm or deny the models of experience illustrated in Hayden's "Those Winter Sundays." Invariably, however, we measure the sentiments of a poem against our own. We may or may not appreciate responsibility as much as Frost's speaker seems to. We may or may not cherish our memories of our fathers as Hayden's speaker seems to. And depending on these and other factors, we may arrive at very different assessments of either poem's worth for us as individual readers.

It is important to realize that in evaluating any poem, we appraise it according to our own special combination of cultural, moral, and aesthetic values which derive from our place in family and society. These values are affected by race, gender, and language. Our moral values reflect our ethical norms—what we consider good and evil, right and wrong. They are influenced by our religious beliefs and perhaps by our political convictions as well. Our aesthetic values concern what we see as beautiful or ugly, well or poorly made.

Our response to any poem's outlook (and our opinion of it) is closely related to our interpretation of it. Evaluation depends upon interpretation, for our judgment of a poem depends on how we understand it. That evaluation may be linked to our initial experience of the work, with first impressions conditioning a later response. This is not always the case, fortunately. In fact, one of the benefits of interpretation is its ability to free us from enslavement to our initial responses by enabling us to move beyond them. By bringing our intellect to bear on a work, we may discover meanings in it that were not apparent on initial reading. And while making such interpretive discoveries we may come to feel differently about a poem and derive considerable pleasure from it.

Of the kinds of evaluations we make in reading poetry, those about a poem's aesthetic merit are hardest to discuss. Aesthetic responses are difficult to describe because they involve subjective reactions about what is beautiful or not, what is pleasing or not, what is well-made or not. Our occasional unwillingness to move beyond our initial impressions, our tendency to settle into comfortable judgments and well-worn opinions, further complicates our responses. We may think that as long as we know what we like, that's enough. It's not enough if we are truly interested in developing our capacity for aesthetic appreciation.

Is Frost's "Stopping by Woods" or Hayden's "Those Winter Sundays" a beautiful poem? Does either seem to be a good example of its type—in this case, the lyric poem? What criteria will you use to make a judgment? To answer these questions, you will need to know more about poetry than you are likely to at this point. It would be helpful to have read and absorbed much of the material in Chapter 11, Elements of Poetry. Measuring a poem's achievement requires some knowledge of how poets exploit diction, imagery, syntax, and sound; how they establish form and control tone; how they work within or against a literary tradition.

Admittedly, without a good deal of knowledge about poetry and without considerable practice in reading it, judgments about the aesthetic worth of particular poems need to be made with caution. But we cannot really avoid judging the poems we read any more than we avoid judging the people we meet; the process is natural. What we should strive for in evaluating poems is to understand the merits of different kinds of poems, to judge them fairly against what they were meant to be rather than something we think they should be. Our goal should be, ultimately, to develop a sense of literary tact, the kind of informed and balanced judgment that comes with experience in reading and living, coupled with continued thoughtful reflection on both.

Your evaluation of poetry may very well change as you change. What you consider important criteria now (narrative action, perhaps, or rhymed stanzas) may not be important after you have read many more poems. Poems you dismiss now as irrelevant or uninteresting may mean much more to you if your life changes so that the concerns of those poems become your concerns. As with literary interpretation, so with literary evaluation; it does not remain constant. In the same way that our understanding of literature changes, and in the same way we acknowledge more than one absolute, definitive, and correct interpretation of literary works, so too do we recognize the many ways they may be evaluated.

We can put these ideas to the test by reading Adrienne Rich's "Aunt Jennifer's Tigers" from the standpoint of evaluation. The questions that follow the poem invite you to consider your experience and interpretation, as well as your evaluation of it. To get started, keep these questions in mind during your first couple of readings: What do each of the characters stand for? How would you describe the relationship between the uncle and his wife, Jennifer? Between the men and the tigers? Between Aunt Jennifer and the speaker? And between Aunt Jennifer and the tigers?

ADRIENNE RICH
[b. 1929]

Aunt Jennifer's Tigers

Aunt Jennifer's tigers prance across a screen,
Bright topaz denizens of a world of green.
They do not fear the men beneath the tree;
They pace in sleek chivalric certainty.

Aunt Jennifer's fingers fluttering through her wool   5
Find even the ivory needle hard to pull.
The massive weight of Uncle's wedding band
Sits heavily upon Aunt Jennifer's hand.

When Aunt is dead, her terrified hands will lie
Still ringed with ordeals she was mastered by.   10
The tigers in the panel that she made
Will go on prancing, proud and unafraid.

QUESTIONS

Experience

1. What feelings surfaced as you read this poem?
2. What words, phrases, and details triggered your strongest responses?

3. What associations about your own aunts and uncles do you bring to the poem?
4. Can the situation described here apply to your parents rather than to your aunts and uncles? To both? To neither? Why or why not?

Interpretation

5. What words, phrases, lines, and details may have confused or baffled you? Why?
6. What observations can you make about the poem's details?
7. What words and phrases recur? How? Where? Why?
8. What connections can you establish among the details of action and language?
9. What inferences can you draw from these connections?
10. How, for now at least, do you understand "Aunt Jennifer's Tigers"?

Evaluation

11. What values are associated with Aunt Jennifer? With her husband, the speaker's uncle? With the tigers? With the men who hunt them?
12. What is the relationship among the values associated with these figures?
13. What is the speaker's attitude toward her aunt, her uncle, and the tigers? To what extent do you think the speaker's attitudes are those of the author? On what do you base your view?
14. How do your own ideas and standards influence your experience, interpretation, and evaluation of the poem? Describe how the poem affects you as a reader. Do you like it? Comment on the poem's aesthetic accomplishment.
15. Return to this poem later in the term, after you have had the opportunity to read many more poems, or after you have discussed the poem with teacher(s) and class-mates. (Perhaps you can learn something about the life and work of the poet by reading her own poetry and prose or by reading critical studies of her work—or both.) Discuss your initial evaluation and your later evaluation, how they may have changed, and why.

THE ACT OF READING POETRY

Thus far we have read two poems, each followed by comments and questions emphasizing the experience and interpretation of poetry. Next we illustrate active reading—what we actually do when we read and reread a poem. Some of the marginal annotations record observations, others raise questions; all are abbreviated notes that reflect a reading that embodies both thought and feeling. In making notes about a poem in this manner, we become actively engaged in seeing and thinking. Our observations lead us to notice details of language and to think about the poem's implications. As we formulate answers to our questions, however provisional, we find ourselves exploring both its meaning and its value.

The annotations for Theodore Roethke's "My Papa's Waltz" are not concerned with technical matters such as form, rhyme scheme, and meter, or with what such technical features contribute to meaning and feeling. Another set of annotations could be made highlighting these features. In fact, some technical consideration of Roethke's poem appears later in discussions in Chapter 11 (pages 479–480, 488–489). For now, however, we focus on the poem's situation and subject. Here is the poem without annotation:

THEODORE ROETHKE
[1908–1963]

My Papa's Waltz

The whiskey on your breath
Could make a small boy dizzy;
But I hung on like death:
Such waltzing was not easy.

We romped until the pans   5
Slid from the kitchen shelf;
My mother's countenance
Could not unfrown itself.

The hand that held my wrist
Was battered on one knuckle;   10
At every step you missed
My right ear scraped a buckle.

You beat time on my head
With a palm caked hard by dirt,
Then waltzed me off to bed   15
Still clinging to your shirt.

And here it is again with annotations:

My Papa's Waltz

	An affectionate term for his father—papa
The whiskey on your breath	What kind of waltzing
Could make a small boy dizzy;	and who instigated it?
But I hung on like death:	
Such waltzing was not easy.	"Waltzed" or "danced" for "romped"?
We romped until the pans	"Face" or "expression"
Slid from the kitchen shelf;	for "countenance"?

My mother's countenance
Could not unfrown itself.

> The mother—angry?
> disapproving? mother
> as audience—as
> non-participant—

The hand that held my wrist
Was battered on one knuckle;
At every step you missed
My right ear scraped a buckle.

> The father misses steps
> but he can dance—not
> drunk.

You beat time on my head
With a palm caked hard by dirt,
Then waltzed me off to bed
Still clinging to your shirt.

> Clinging—how?
> Fearfully? Joyfully? Both?

The boy's father, a manual laborer, is clearly not literally "waltzing" with his son. His "dance" is more a romp through the house with a stop in the kitchen and another at the boy's bedroom, where presumably he is unceremoniously dumped into bed. The mother watches, her frown indicating disapproval, perhaps even anger.

The dance is somewhat rough because the boy's father has been drinking. It is also rough because he scrapes the child's ear on his belt buckle as he keeps a steady rhythm by beating time on the boy's head. The boy is described as "clinging" to his father's shirt, but the language doesn't clarify whether that clinging is purely out of terror—or whether it is part of the game father and son enjoy together. Presumably this bedtime romp is a regular ritual rather than a one-time occurrence.

The tone of the poem seems nostalgic, though not sentimentally so. The boy, now a man, remembers his father as "papa," clearly an affectionate term. The high-spirited bouncing rhythm of the poem seems to counter any indication that the father's drinking or the son's fear are its central concerns.

CHAPTER TEN

Types of Poetry

Poetry can be classified as narrative or lyric. Narrative poems stress action, and lyrics song. Each of these types has numerous subdivisions: narrative poetry includes the epic, romance, and ballad; lyric poetry includes the elegy and epigraph, sonnet and sestina, aubade and villanelle. Moreover, each major type of poetry adheres to different conventions. *Narrative poems,* for example, tell stories and describe actions; *lyric poems* combine speech and song to express feeling in varying degrees of verbal music.

NARRATIVE POETRY

The grandest of narratives is the epic. *Epics* are long narrative poems that record the adventures of a hero whose exploits are important to the history of a nation. Typically they chronicle the origins of a civilization and embody its central beliefs and values. Epics tend to be larger than life as they recount valorous deeds enacted in vast landscapes. The epic style is as grand as the action; the conventions require that the epic be formal, complex, and serious—suitable to its important subjects.

Among the more famous epics in Western literature are Homer's *Iliad* (about the Greek and Trojan war), Virgil's *Aeneid* (about the founding of Rome), Dante's *Divine Comedy* (a journey through hell, purgatory, and heaven), and Milton's *Paradise Lost* (about the revolt of the angels, and man's creation and fall). For a hint of the epic's subjects and language listen to these opening lines from *The Aeneid* and from *Paradise Lost*. First Virgil:

> I sing of warfare and a man at war.
> From the sea-coast of Troy in early days
> He came to Italy by destiny,
> To our Lavinian western shore,
> A fugitive, this captain, buffeted   5
> Cruelly on land as on the sea
> By blows from powers of the air—behind them
> Baleful Juno in her sleepless rage.
> And cruel losses were his lot in war,
> Till he could found a city and bring home   10
> His gods to Latium, land of the Latin race,
> The Alban lords, and the high walls of Rome.
> Tell me the causes now, O Muse, how galled
> In her divine pride, and how sore at heart
> From her old wound, the queen of gods compelled him—   15
> A man apart, devoted to his mission—
> To undergo so many perilous days
> And enter on so many trials.

And now Milton:

> Of man's first disobedience, and the fruit
> Of that forbidden tree whose mortal taste
> Brought death into the world, and all our woe,
> With loss of Eden, till one greater Man
> Restore us, and regain the blissful seat,   5
> Sing, Heavenly Muse, that, on the secret top
> Of Oreb, or of Sinai, didst inspire
> That shepherd who first taught the chosen seed
> In the beginning how the Heavens and Earth
> Rose out of Chaos: or, if Sion hill   10
> Delight thee more, and Siloa's brook that flowed
> Fast by the oracle of God, I thence
> Invoke thy aid to my adventurous song,
> That with no middle flight intends to soar
> Above th' Aonian mount, while it pursues   15
> Things unattempted yet in prose or rhyme.
> And chiefly thou, O Spirit, that dost prefer
> Before all temples th' upright heart and pure,
> Instruct me, for thou know'st; thou from the first
> Wast present, and, with mighty wings outspread,   20
> Dovelike sat'st brooding on the vast abyss,
> And mad'st it pregnant: what in me is dark
> Illumine; what is low, raise and support;
> That, to the height of this great argument,
> I may assert Eternal Providence,   25
> And justify the ways of God to men.

Far less ambitious than epics, *ballads* are perhaps the most popular form of narrative poetry. Originally ballads were meant to be sung or recited. Folk ballads (or popular ballads as they are sometimes called) were passed on orally, only to be written down much later. This accounts for the different versions of many ballads such as "Barbara Allan" and "Edward, Edward" (pages 683 and 684).

In addition to folk ballads of unknown (and sometimes multiple) authorship, there are also literary ballads (of known authorship). One example is "La Belle Dame sans Merci" by John Keats (pages 715–716). Literary ballads imitate the folk ballad by adhering to its basic conventions—repeated lines and stanzas in a refrain, swift action with occasional surprise endings, extraordinary events evoked in direct, simple language, and scant characterization—but are more polished stylistically and more self-conscious in their use of poetic techniques.

Another type of narrative poem is the *romance,* in which adventure is a central feature. The plots of romances tend to be complex, with surprising and even magical actions common. The chief characters are human beings, though they often confront monsters, dragons, and disguised animals in a world that does not adhere consistently to the laws of nature as we know them. Romance in short deals with the marvelous—with, for example, St. George slaying a dragon in a magical forest. Popular during the Middle Ages and Renaissance, the romance as a poetic genre has fallen from favor. Nevertheless, some of its chief characteristics have found expression in popular fictional types such as the western, the adventure story, and the romantic love story.

LYRIC POETRY

Although narrative poems, especially literary ballads, combine story with song, action with emotion, story and action predominate. In lyric poetry, however, story is subordinated to song, and action to emotion. We can define *lyrics* as subjective poems, often brief, that express the feelings and thoughts of a single speaker (who may or may not represent the poet). The lyric is more a poetic manner than a form; it is more variable and less subject to strict convention than narrative poetry.

Lyric poetry is typically characterized by brevity, melody, and emotional intensity. The music of lyrics makes them memorable, and their brevity contributes to the intensity of their emotional expression. Originally designed to be sung to a musical accompaniment (the word *lyric* derives from the Greek *lyre*), lyrics have been the predominant type of poetry in the West for several hundred years.

Forms of lyric poetry range from the *epigram,* a brief witty poem that is often satirical, such as Alexander Pope's "On the Collar of a Dog" to the *elegy,* a lament for the dead, such as Seamus Heaney's "Mid-Term Break" (page 795). Lyric forms also include the *ode,* a long stately poem in stanzas of varied length, meter, and form; and the *aubade,* a love lyric expressing complaint that dawn means the speaker must part from his lover. An example of the ode is John

Keats's "Ode to a Nightingale" (pages 716–718); the aubade is represented by John Donne's "The Sun Rising" (pages 517–518).

The tones, moods, and voices of lyric poems are as variable and as complexly intertwined as human feeling, thought, and imagination allow. Generally considered the most compressed poetic type, the lyric poem typically expresses much in little. The *sonnet,* for example, condenses into fourteen lines an expression of emotion or an articulation of idea according to one of two basic patterns: the *Italian* (or *Petrarchan*) and the *English* (or *Shakespearean*). An Italian sonnet is composed of an eight-line octave and a six-line sestet. A Shakespearean sonnet is composed of three four-line quatrains and a concluding two-line couplet (see pages 542–543). The thought and feeling expressed in each sonnet form typically follow the divisions suggested by their structural patterns. Thus an Italian sonnet may state a problem in the octave and present a solution in its sestet. A Shakespearean sonnet will usually introduce a subject in the first quatrain, expand and develop it in the second and third quatrains, and conclude something about it in its final couplet.

Although sonnets reached the height of their popularity during the Renaissance, later writers have continued to be attracted to the form. Some sonnet writers, in fact, like Gerard Manley Hopkins, William Butler Yeats, Robert Frost, and E. E. Cummings have combined the two basic patterns to suit their poetic needs. Occasionally these and other poets have modified the form itself. Robert Frost's "Acquainted with the Night" (page 677), for example, is composed of four tercets and a couplet rather than the familiar three quatrains and a couplet. Frost, moreover, has been known to write fifteen-line sonnets as well.

Less important historically than the sonnet but no less intricate and musical are two other lyric forms, sestina and villanelle, both deriving from French poetry. The *sestina* consists of six stanzas of six lines each followed by a three-line conclusion or *envoy*. The sestina requires a strict pattern of repetition of six key words that end the lines of the first stanza. Elizabeth Bishop's "Sestina" (pages 768–769) is an example.

The *villanelle,* which also relies heavily on repetition, is composed of five three-line tercets and a final four-line quatrain. Its singular feature is the way its first and third lines repeat throughout the poem. The entire first line reappears as the final line of the second and fourth tercets, and again as the third line of the third and fifth tercets and as the concluding line of the poem. Examples include Theodore Roethke's "The Waking" (page 550) and Dylan Thomas's "Do Not Go Gentle into That Good Night" (page 773).

CHAPTER ELEVEN

Elements of Poetry

We can learn to interpret and appreciate poems by understanding their basic elements. The elements of a poem include a *speaker* whose voice we hear in it; its *diction* or selection of words; its *syntax* or the order of those words; its *imagery* or details of sight, sound, taste, smell, and touch; its *figures of speech* or nonliteral ways of expressing one thing in terms of another, such as symbol and metaphor; its *sound effects,* especially rhyme, assonance, and alliteration; its *rhythm and meter* or the pattern of accents we hear in the poem's words, phrases, lines, and sentences; and its *structure* or formal pattern of organization. All the elements of a poem work together harmoniously to convey feeling and embody meaning.

VOICE: SPEAKER AND TONE

When we read or hear a poem, we hear a speaker's voice. It is this voice that conveys the poem's *tone,* its implied attitude toward its subject. Tone is an abstraction we make from the details of a poem's language: the use of meter and rhyme (or lack of them); the inclusion of certain kinds of details and exclusion of other kinds; particular choices of words and sentence pattern, of imagery and figurative language. When we listen to a poem's language and hear the voice of its speaker, we catch its tone and feeling and ultimately its meaning.

In listening to the speaker's voice, for example, in Roethke's "My Papa's Waltz," (page 473) we hear a tone different from that of the speaker in Hayden's

"Those Winter Sundays" (page 462). Roethke's speaker remembers his father fondly and addresses him ("your breath," "you missed"). He remembers and celebrates their spirited cavorting as a "romp" and a "waltz" and includes such comic details as the mother frowning while pans slide off the kitchen shelves and the father keeping time by steadily patting the boy's head. The poem's complex tone comes from its contrasted details: the boy's hanging on "like death," his ear scraping his father's belt buckle, and his "clinging" to his father's shirt.

The speaker of Hayden's "Those Winter Sundays" admires his father and perhaps feared him as a child. His attitude is suggested by the details he remembers and by the way he meticulously describes his father's attentive labors. But his tone conveys more than admiration; it conveys also a sense of regret, disappointment, and perhaps anguish at having been indifferent toward him as a child. The tone of Hayden's poem has none of the ease and playfulness of Roethke's; it is serious in its portrayal of the speaker's father and solemn in its account of the speaker's subsequent feelings.

The range of tones we find in poems is as various and complex as the range of voices and attitudes we discern in everyday experience. One of the more important and persistent is the *ironic tone* of voice. We have previously defined irony as a way of speaking that implies a discrepancy or opposition between what is said and what is meant (see pages 99–101). The following poem by Stephen Crane illustrates this ironic tone of voice.

STEPHEN CRANE

[1871–1900]

War Is Kind

Do not weep, maiden, for war is kind.
Because your lover threw wild hands toward the sky
And the affrighted steed ran on alone,
Do not weep.
War is kind.   5

       Hoarse, booming drums of the regiment,
       Little souls who thirst for fight,
       These men were born to drill and die.
       The unexplained glory flies above them,
       Great is the battle god, great, and his kingdom   10
       A field where a thousand corpses lie.

Do not weep, babe, for war is kind.
Because your father tumbled in the yellow trenches,
Raged at his breast, gulped and died,
Do not weep.   15
War is kind.

Swift blazing flag of the regiment,
Eagle with crest of red and gold,
These men were born to drill and die.
Point for them the virtue of slaughter, 20
Make plain to them the excellence of killing
And a field where a thousand corpses lie.

Mother whose heart hung humble as a button
On the bright splendid shroud of your son,
Do not weep. 25
War is kind.

How do we know that the speaker's attitude towards war is not what his words indicate, that his words are ironic? We know because the details of death in battle are antithetical to the consoling refrain of stanzas 1, 3, and 5: "Do not weep. War is kind." Moreover the details of stanzas 2 and 4 also work toward the same ironic end, but in a different way. Instead of the ironic consoling voice of stanzas 1, 3, and 5 (which of course offers no real consolation given the brutality described), stanzas 2 and 4 sound more supportive of military glory: Crane uses a march-like rhythm along with words connoting military glory in a context that makes them sound hollow and false. The view that war is glorious and that death in battle is honorable is countered with images of slaughter. Compare Crane's poem to another treating the glory of dying for one's country ironically, Wilfred Owen's "Dulce et Decorum Est" (page 755).

Unlike the poems we have been considering in which the speaker is alone, the next poem we will examine contains a speaker who is addressing someone present. A poem in which a speaker addresses a silent listener is called a *dramatic monologue*. As we listen to the speaker's monologue, we usually gain a vivid sense of his character and personality. The following poem, Robert Browning's "My Last Duchess," is a striking example of this form.

ROBERT BROWNING

[*1812–1889*]

My Last Duchess

FERRARA

That's my last Duchess painted on the wall,
Looking as if she were alive. I call
That piece a wonder, now; Frà Pandolf's hands
Worked busily a day, and there she stands.
Will 't please you sit and look at her? I said 5
"Frà Pandolf" by design, for never read

Strangers like you that pictured countenance,
The depth and passion of its earnest glance,
But to myself they turned (since none puts by
The curtain I have drawn for you, but I)   10
And seemed as they would ask me, if they durst,
How such a glance came there; so, not the first
Are you to turn and ask thus. Sir, 'twas not
Her husband's presence only, called that spot
Of joy into the Duchess' cheek; perhaps   15
Frà Pandolf chanced to say, "Her mantle laps
Over my lady's wrist too much," or "Paint
Must never hope to reproduce the faint
Half-flush that dies along her throat." Such stuff
Was courtesy, she thought, and cause enough   20
For calling up that spot of joy. She had
A heart—how shall I say?—too soon made glad,
Too easily impressed; she liked whate'er
She looked on, and her looks went everywhere.
Sir, 'twas all one! My favor at her breast,   25
The dropping of the daylight in the West,
The bough of cherries some officious fool
Broke in the orchard for her, the white mule
She rode with round the terrace—all and each
Would draw from her alike the approving speech,   30
Or blush, at least. She thanked men,—good! but thanked
Somehow—I know not how—as if she ranked
My gift of a nine-hundred-years-old name
With anybody's gift. Who'd stoop to blame
This sort of trifling? Even had you skill   35
In speech—which I have not—to make your will
Quite clear to such an one, and say "Just this
Or that in you disgusts me; here you miss,
Or there exceed the mark"—and if she let
Herself be lessoned so, nor plainly set   40
Her wits to yours, forsooth, and made excuse—
E'en then would be some stooping; and I choose
Never to stoop. Oh sir, she smiled, no doubt,
Whene'er I passed her; but who passed without
Much the same smile? This grew; I gave commands;   45
Then all smiles stopped together. There she stands
As if alive. Will 't please you rise? We'll meet
The company below, then. I repeat,
The Count your master's known munificence
Is ample warrant that no just pretense   50
Of mine for dowry will be disallowed;
Though his fair daughter's self, as I avowed
At starting, is my object. Nay, we'll go

Together down, sir. Notice Neptune, though,
Taming a sea-horse, thought a rarity,   55
Which Claus of Innsbruck cast in bronze for me!

The situation of the poem is this: the Duke of Ferrara, a city-state in Renaissance Italy, is addressing an ambassador who represents a count, the father of a marriageable aristocratic daughter. Although we hear only the duke's voice, we are aware of the ambassador's presence. We probably wonder how the ambassador reacts to what the duke tells him—especially to what he says in lines 45–46. But while the poet hints at the ambassador's actions (lines 12–13; 47–48, e.g.) he doesn't reveal his thoughts. Instead he centers our attention on the duke, whose manner, language, gestures, and concerns all reveal the kind of man he is and how he conducted himself in his relations with his last duchess.

The duke reveals himself as a monumental egotist—proud, shrewd, arrogant, and murderous. He shows himself to be a man who will not allow his will to be thwarted or his honor ignored. Intolerant of his former duchess's joy in things other than those he provided, and unwilling to "stoop" to telling her how her behavior insulted him, the duke has her killed: "I gave commands," he says. "Then all smiles stopped together."

But what has the duchess done to deserve her fate? She expressed joy in compliments given her; she took pleasure in simple things—riding her white mule, watching the sun set, accepting a gift of fruit. Her crime in the duke's eyes was in not recognizing the value of his aristocratic heritage: his name, rank, and pride did not mean enough to her.

Part of our shock in realizing what the duke has done comes from his certainty that he has behaved properly. What else could I do, he seems to say. And part derives perhaps also from the matter-of-fact manner in which the duke turns the conversation from his last duchess to the business at hand, the negotiations about the impending marriage and the dowry. But revealing as these things are, an even stronger index of the duke's egoistic pride is the way he refers to his last duchess as an object, as a possession that has been appropriately added to his prized collection. As a portrait on the wall, the duchess is fully and finally under the duke's control. (He even keeps her portrait behind a curtain so no one can see her without his authority.) The duke's pride in his wife's portrait is equal to his pride in his prized statue of Neptune taming a sea horse.

A few poems notable for their speakers and tones of voice follow. For each identify the speaker and situation. Describe the tone(s) of voice you hear, and consider what the speaker's tone contributes to the ideas and feelings that the poems convey.

MURIEL STUART
[*b. 1889–?*]

In the Orchard

'I thought you loved me.' 'No, it was only fun.'
'When we stood there, closer than all?' 'Well, the harvest moon
Was shining and queer in your hair, and it turned my head.'
'That made you?' 'Yes.' 'Just the moon and the light it made
Under the tree?' 'Well, your mouth, too.' 'Yes, my mouth?'   5
'And the quiet there that sang like the drum in the booth.
You shouldn't have danced like that.' 'Like what?' 'So close,
With your head turned up, and the flower in your hair, a rose
That smelt all warm.' 'I loved you. I thought you knew
I wouldn't have danced like that with any but you.'   10
'I didn't know. I thought you knew it was fun.'
'I thought it was love you meant.' 'Well, it's done.' 'Yes, it's done.
I've seen boys stone a blackbird, and watched them drown
A kitten . . . it clawed at the reeds, and they pushed it down
Into the pool while it screamed. Is that fun, too?'   15
'Well, boys are like that . . . Your brothers . . .' 'Yes, I know.
But you, so lovely and strong! Not you! Not you!'
'They don't understand it's cruel. It's only a game.'
'And are girls fun, too?' 'No, still in a way it's the same.
It's queer and lovely to have a girl . . .' 'Go on.'   20
'It makes you mad for a bit to feel she's your own,
And you laugh and kiss her, and maybe you give her a ring,
But it's only in fun.' 'But I gave you everything.'
'Well, you shouldn't have done it. You know what a fellow thinks
When a girl does that.' 'Yes, he talks of her over his drinks   25
And calls her a—' 'Stop that now. I thought you knew.'
'But it wasn't with anyone else. It was only you.'
'How did I know? I thought you wanted it too.
I thought you were like the rest. Well, what's to be done?'
'To be done?' 'Is it all right?' 'Yes.' 'Sure?' 'Yes, but why?'   30
'I don't know. I thought you were going to cry.
You said you had something to tell me.' 'Yes, I know.
It wasn't anything really . . . I think I'll go.'
'Yes, it's late. There's thunder about, a drop of rain
Fell on my hand in the dark. I'll see you again   35
At the dance next week. You're sure that everything's right?'
'Yes,' 'Well, I'll be going.' 'Kiss me . . .' 'Good night.' . . . 'Good night.'

QUESTIONS

1. What differences exist in the dialogue of the two speakers? How do those differences characterize the tone of each speaker's voice?
2. What do the questions, ellipses, and repeated words contribute to the poem's tone?

GERARD MANLEY HOPKINS

[1844–1889]

Thou art indeed just, Lord

Justus quidem tu es, Domine, si disputem tecum: verumtamen
justa loquar ad te: Quare via impiorum prosperatur?°

Thou art indeed just, Lord, if I contend
With thee; but, sir, so what I plead is just.
Why do sinners' ways prosper? and why must
Disappointment all I endeavour end?
Wert thou my enemy, O thou my friend,   5
How wouldst thou worse, I wonder, than thou dost
Defeat, thwart me? Oh, the sots and thralls of lust
Do in spare hours more thrive than I that spend,

Sir, life upon thy cause. See, banks and brakes
Now, leavèd how thick! lacèd they are again   10
With fretty chervil, look, and fresh wind shakes

Them; birds build—but not I build; no, but strain,
Time's eunuch, and not breed one work that wakes.
Mine, O thou lord of life, send my roots rain.

QUESTIONS

1. How do the words the speaker uses to address God help establish the tone of the first four lines? What is his attitude toward God here?
2. Lines 5–7 might be paraphrased according to the familiar saying: with friends like you, who needs enemies. What tone of voice do you hear in those lines? In lines 9–13? In the final line?

"Thou art indeed just, Lord" **Justus quidem tu es, Domine, si disputem tecum: verumtamen justa loquar ad te: Quare via impiorum prosperatur** *Epigraph. The first three lines (up to* prosper) *translate the Latin.*

ANONYMOUS

Western Wind

Western wind, when will thou blow,
  The small rain down can rain?
Christ, if my love were in my arms
And I in my bed again!

QUESTION

What tone bursts through the final couplet? What feeling does the speaker convey? How does the tone of the following alteration compare with the poem's final two lines as written?

> Oh God I wish I were in bed
> With my lover again.

HENRY REED

[b. 1914]

Naming of Parts

Today we have naming of parts. Yesterday,
We had daily cleaning. And tomorrow morning,
We shall have what to do after firing. But today,
Today we have naming of parts. Japonica
Glistens like coral in all of the neighboring gardens,   5
    And today we have naming of parts.

This is the lower sling swivel. And this
Is the upper sling swivel, whose use you will see,
When you are given your slings. And this is the piling swivel,
Which in your case you have not got. The branches   10
Hold in the gardens their silent, eloquent gestures,
    Which in our case we have not got.

This is the safety-catch, which is always released
With an easy flick of the thumb. And please do not let me

See anyone using his finger. You can do it quite easy   15
If you have any strength in your thumb. The blossoms
Are fragile and motionless, never letting anyone see
    Any of them using their finger.

And this you can see is the bolt. The purpose of this
Is to open the breech, as you see. We can slide it   20
Rapidly backwards and forwards: we call this
Easing the spring. And rapidly backwards and forwards
The early bees are assaulting and fumbling the flowers:
    They call it easing the Spring.

They call it easing the Spring: it is perfectly easy   25
If you have any strength in your thumb: like the bolt,
And the breech, and the cocking-piece, and the point of balance,
Which in our case we have not got; and the almond-blossom
Silent in all of the gardens and the bees going backwards and forwards,
    For today we have naming of parts.   30

QUESTIONS

1. Each stanza of "Naming of Parts" contains two distinct voices. Where does the first voice end and the second begin? Describe and characterize each voice.
2. Pinpoint the place where the two voices converge. What is the effect of their convergence?

JACQUES PRÉVERT
[1900–1977]

Family Portrait

    The mother knits
    The son goes to war
    She finds it all perfectly natural, Mama
    And the father, what is he doing? Papa?
    He is making little deals   5
    His wife knits
    His son goes to war
    He is making little deals
    He finds it all perfectly natural, Papa
    And the son, the son   10

What does the son find?
The son finds absolutely nothing, the son
For the son the war his Mama the knitting his Papa little deals for him the war
When it is all over, that war
He will make little deals, he and his Papa   15
The war continues Mama continues she knits
Papa continues he carries on his activity
The son is killed he no longer carries on
Papa and Mama go to the cemetery
They find it all perfectly natural, Papa and Mama   20
Life continues life with knitting war little deals
Deals war knitting war
Deals deals activity
Life along with the cemetery.

TRANSLATED BY HARRIET ZINNES

QUESTION

Characterize the tone of the first three lines. How is this tone reinforced or altered as the poem develops? What do the repeated words and phrases contribute to the tone?

DICTION

At their most successful, poems include "the best words in the best order," as Samuel Taylor Coleridge has said. In reading any poem it is necessary to know what the words mean, but it is equally important to understand what the words imply or suggest. The *denotation* or dictionary meaning of *dictator,* for example, is "a person exercising absolute power, especially one who assumes absolute control without the free consent of the people." But *dictator* also carries additional *connotations* or associations both personal and public. Beyond its dictionary meaning, *dictator* may suggest repressive force and tyrannical oppression; it may call up images of bloodbaths, purges, executions; it may trigger associations that prompt us to think of Hitler, for example, or Mussolini. The same kind of associative resonance occurs with a word like *vacation,* the connotations of which far outstrip its dictionary definition: "a period of suspension of work, study, or other activity."

Because poets often hint indirectly at more than their words directly state, it is necessary to develop the habit of considering the connotations of words as well as their denotations. Often for both poets and readers the "best words" are those that do the most work; they convey feelings and indirectly imply ideas rather than state them outright. Poets choose a particular word because it suggests what they want to suggest. Its appropriateness is a function of both its denotation and its connotation. Consider, for example, the second stanza of Roethke's "My Papa's Waltz":

We romped until the pans
Slid from the kitchen shelf;
My mother's countenance
Could not unfrown itself.

"Romped" could be replaced by *danced* since the poet is describing a dance, specifically a waltz. Why "romped" then? For one thing, it means something different from *danced*. That is, its denotation provides a different meaning, indicating play or frolic of a boisterous nature. Although "romped" is not really a dance word at all, here it suggests a kind of rough, crude dancing, far less elegant and systematic than waltzing. But it also connotes the kind of vigorous roughhousing that fathers and sons occasionally engage in and from which many mothers are excluded—though here, of course, the romp is occasioned by the father's having had too much to drink. "Romped" then both describes more precisely the kind of dance and suggests the speaker's attitude toward the experience.

Perhaps the most unusual words in the stanza, however, are "countenance" and "unfrown." "Countenance" is less familiar and more surprising than face. This is also true of "unfrown," a word you won't find in the dictionary. What makes these words noticeable is not just their uncommonness but their strangeness in the context of the stanza. "Countenance," a formal word, contrasts with the informal language of the two lines before it, lines that describe the informal romp of a dance; it suggests the mother's formality as she watches the informal play of her husband and son. Although her frown indicates disapproval, perhaps annoyance that her pans are falling, the disapproval and annoyance may be put on, part of an act. It is possible that she is responding as she is expected to respond.

If we look up *countenance* in the *Random House College Dictionary*, here is what we find:

> noun 1. appearance, esp. the expression of the face . . .
> 2. the face; visage
> 3. calm facial expression; composure
> 4. (obsolete) bearing; behavior
> trans. verb 6. to permit or tolerate
> 7. to approve, support, or encourage. . . .

Let's consider briefly the implications of these multiple denotations. The second meaning is more general than the first. It is this first meaning to which we gave priority in the discussion above. We determined our sense of the kind of expression on the mother's face from the line, "Could not unfrown itself." But in looking at definitions 3 and 4, we encounter a problem, or at least a complication. Isn't the mother's "frown" a sign of *discomposure* rather than one of the "composure" suggested by a "calm facial expression"? Or is it possible that Roethke has used *countenance* with two meanings in mind: the meaning of "facial expression" on one hand; the meanings of "tolerate and permit, approve and encourage" on the other? This double sense of *countenance* thus parallels the double sense of the experience for the child as both pleasurable and frightening.

Let us look closely at the language of the following poem.

WILLIAM WORDSWORTH
[1770–1850]

I wandered lonely as a cloud

I wandered lonely as a cloud
That floats on high o'er vales and hills,
When all at once I saw a crowd,
A host, of golden daffodils;
Beside the lake, beneath the trees,   5
Fluttering and dancing in the breeze.

Continuous as the stars that shine
And twinkle on the milky way,
They stretched in never-ending line
Along the margin of a bay: 10
Ten thousand saw I at a glance,
Tossing their heads in sprightly dance.

The waves beside them danced; but they
Outdid the sparkling waves in glee:
A poet could not but be gay,   15
In such a jocund company:
I gazed—and gazed—but little thought
What wealth the show to me had brought:

For oft, when on my couch I lie
In vacant or in pensive mood,   20
They flash upon that inward eye
Which is the bliss of solitude;
And then my heart with pleasure fills,
And dances with the daffodils.

The words of the poem are familiar; their meanings should pose no problems.
We might mention that "o'er" in line 2 is an *elision,* the omission of an unstressed
vowel or syllable to preserve the meter, of *over,* and that "oft" in line 19 is an
abbreviated form of *often.* The language, overall, is simple, direct, and clear.

We can assure ourselves of the rightness or appropriateness of the poem's diction by considering the connotations of a few words. We can take lines 3 and
4 as examples.

When all at once I saw a crowd,
A host, of golden daffodils;

Suppose they had been written this way:

> When all at once I spied a bunch,
> A group of yellow daffodils;

Consider the connotations of each version. "Spied" may indicate something secretive or even prying about the speaker's looking. It may also suggest that he
was looking for them. In contrast, "saw" carries less intense and fewer connotations; it merely indicates that the speaker noticed the daffodils, and its tone is
more matter-of-fact. The alternate version's "bunch" and "group" suggest, on
the one hand, a smaller number than Wordsworth's corresponding "crowd" and,
on the other, a less communal sense. "Crowd" and "host," moreover, carry connotations of a social gathering, of people congregated to share an experience or
simply enjoy one another's company. This implicit humanizing or personify-
ing of the daffodils (identifying them with human actions and feelings) brings
the daffodils to life: they are described as dancing and as "tossing their heads"
(line 12), and they are called a "jocund company" (line 16). "Company" underscores the sociality of the daffodils and "jocund" indicates the human quality of being joyful.

    This emphasis on the happiness of the daffodils and their large number serves
to point up sharply the isolation and disspiritedness of the speaker. Their vast number is emphasized in the second stanza where they are described as "continuous"
and as stretching in a "never-ending line." (And, of course, in the count: "ten
thousand.") But this important contrast between the isolation of the speaker and
the solidarity of the daffodils, though continued into the second stanza, gives way
in stanzas 3 and 4 as the speaker imagines himself among the daffodils rather than
simply looking at them from a distance. More important, when he remembers
them later, he thinks about being "with" them, not literally but imaginatively.

    But before we look at words describing the speaker from later stanzas, we
should return to the first adjective that describes the flowers: "golden" (line 4).
Wordsworth uses "golden," not "yellow," or "amber," or "tawny" because
"golden" suggests more than a color; it connotes light (it shines and glitters)
and wealth (money and fortune). In fact the speaker uses the word "wealth" in
line 18 to indicate how important the experience of seeing the daffodils has been.
And in the last two stanzas, we notice that the speaker uses in succession five
words denoting *joy* ("glee," "gay," "jocund," "bliss," and "pleasure") in a
crescendo that suggests the intensity of the speaker's happiness.

    Although Wordsworth uses various words to indicate joy, he occasionally
repeats rather than varies his diction. The repetitions of the words for seeing
("saw," "gazed") inaugurate and sustain the imagery of vision that is central to
the poem's meaning; the forms of the verb *to dance* ("dancing," "danced,"
"dance," and "dances") suggest both that the various elements of nature are in
harmony with one another and that nature is also in harmony with man. The
poet conveys this by bringing the elements of nature together in pairs: daffodils
and wind (stanza 1); daffodils and flowers, daffodils and stars (stanza 2); water
and wind (stanza 3). Nature and man come together explicitly in stanza 4 when
the speaker says that his heart dances with the daffodils.

A different kind of repetition appears in the movement from the loneliness of line one to the solitude of line 22. Both words denote an alone-ness, but they suggest a radical difference in the solitary person's attitude to his state of being alone. The poem moves from the sadly alienated separation felt by the speaker in the beginning to his joy in reimagining the natural scene, a movement framed by the words "loneliness" and "solitude." An analogous movement is suggested within the final stanza by the words "vacant" and "fills." The emptiness of the speaker's spirit is transformed into a fullness of feeling as he remembers the daffodils.

To gain practice in discerning and appreciating diction in poetry, read the following poems with special attention to their words.

EDWIN ARLINGTON ROBINSON
[1869–1935]

Miniver Cheevy

Miniver Cheevy, child of scorn,
    Grew lean while he assailed the seasons;
He wept that he was ever born,
    And he had reasons.

Miniver loved the days of old   5
    When swords were bright and steeds were prancing;
The vision of a warrior bold
    Would set him dancing.

Miniver sighed for what was not,
    And dreamed, and rested from his labors;   10
He dreamed of Thebes° and Camelot,°
    And Priam's neighbors.°

Miniver mourned the ripe renown
    That made so many a name so fragrant;
He mourned Romance, now on the town,   15
    And Art, a vagrant.

Miniver loved the Medici,°
    Albeit he had never seen one;

"Miniver Cheevy"   [11]**Thebes**   *Greek city famous in history and legend.*   [11]**Camelot**   *the seat of King Arthur's court.*   [12]**Priam**   *King of Troy during the Trojan war.*   [17]**The Medici**   *family of powerful merchants and bankers, rulers of Florence in the fourteenth, fifteenth, and sixteenth centuries who were known for their patronage of the arts.*

He would have sinned incessantly
    Could he have been one. 20

Miniver cursed the commonplace
    And eyed a khaki suit with loathing;
He missed the mediæval grace
    Of iron clothing.

Miniver scorned the gold he sought, 25
    But sore annoyed was he without it;
Miniver thought, and thought, and thought,
    And thought about it.

Miniver Cheevy, born too late,
    Scratched his head and kept on thinking; 30
Miniver coughed, and called it fate,
    And kept on drinking.

QUESTIONS

1. List the words in the poem that illustrate what is said in line 5: that "Miniver loved the days of old." List all the verbs that describe Miniver's action or inaction. What do they reveal about him?
2. What are the connotations of "ripe"? (line 13) and "fragrant" (line 14)? What does the combination of each respectively with ideas of fame and nobility suggest about these ideas? And how do the connotations of "on the town" (to describe Romance) and "a vagrant" (to characterize Art) suggest what has happened to Art and Romance?

WILLIAM WORDSWORTH

[1770–1850]

It is a beauteous evening

It is a beauteous evening, calm and free,
The holy time is quiet as a Nun
Breathless with adoration; the broad sun
Is sinking down in its tranquility;
The gentleness of heaven broods o'er the Sea: 5
Listen! the mighty Being is awake,
And doth with his eternal motion make
A sound like thunder—everlastingly.

Dear Child! dear Girl! that walkest with me here,
If thou appear untouched by solemn thought,   10
Thy nature is not therefore less divine:
Thou liest in Abraham's bosom all the year,
And worship'st at the Temple's inner shrine,
God being with thee when we know it not.

QUESTION

What do the following words have in common: *holy, eternal, solemn, divine, nun, adoration, heaven, God?* Which words in the last four lines are congruent with these? And how does this diction reinforce the idea and feeling of the poem?

ROBERT HERRICK

[1591–1667]

Delight in Disorder

A sweet disorder in the dress
Kindles in clothes a wantonness.
A lawn° about the shoulders thrown   fine linen
Into a fine distractiön;
An erring lace, which here and there   5
Enthralls the crimson stomacher°;
A cuff neglectful, and thereby
Ribbons to flow confusedly;
A winning wave, deserving note,
In the tempestuous petticoat;   10
A careless shoestring, in whose tie
I see a wild civility;
Do more bewitch me than when art
Is too precise in every part.

QUESTIONS

1. Examine the connotations of the words suggesting disorder: *thrown, distraction, neglectful, confusedly, careless.* Consider especially the connotations and etymology (word origin) of "erring" (line 5) and "tempestuous" (line 10).

"Delight in Disorder" ⁶*stomacher* *a garment worn under the laces of the bodice.*

2. Consider the words that describe the speaker's reaction to the disordered dress he describes: *sweet, kindles, wantonness, fine, wild, bewitch*. What do the connotations of these words suggest about the speaker?

ADRIENNE RICH
[b. 1929]

Rape

There is a cop who is both prowler and father:
he comes from your block, grew up with your brothers,
had certain ideals.
You hardly know him in his boots and silver badge,
on horseback, one hand touching his gun.   5

You hardly know him but you have to get to know him:
he has access to machinery that could kill you.
He and his stallion clop like warlords among the trash,
his ideals stand in the air, a frozen cloud
from between his unsmiling lips.   10

And so, when the time comes, you have to turn to him,
the maniac's sperm still greasing your thighs,
your mind whirling like crazy. You have to confess
to him, you are guilty of the crime
of having been forced.   15

And you see his blue eyes, the blue eyes of all the family
whom you used to know, grow narrow and glisten,
his hand types out the details
and he wants them all
but the hysteria in your voice pleases him best.

You hardly know him but now he thinks he knows you:
he has taken down your worst moment   25
on a machine and filed it in a file.
He knows, or thinks he knows, how much yo
he knows, or thinks he knows, what

He has access to machinery that coul
and if, in the sickening light of the
and if, in the sickening light of
your details sound like a portrai
will you swallow, will you deny

QUESTION

The man referred to in the poem is described in line 1 as a "prowler and father," and in line 29 as a "confessor." What are the implications of each? Explain also the implications of line 8: "He and his stallion clop like warlords among the trash."

IMAGERY

Poems are grounded in the concrete and the specific—in details that stimulate our senses—for it is through our senses that we perceive the world. We see daylight break and fade; we hear dogs bark and children laugh; we feel the sting of a bitterly cold wind; we smell the heavy aroma of perfume; we taste the tartness of lemon and the sweetness of chocolate. Poems include such details which trigger our memories, stimulate our feelings, and command our response.

When such specific details appear in poems they are called images. An *image* is a concrete representation of a sense impression, feeling, or idea. Images appeal to one or more of our senses—or, more precisely, they trigger our imaginative re-enactment of sensory experience by rendering feeling and thought in concrete details related directly to our physical perception of the world. Images may be visual (something seen), aural (something heard), tactile (something felt), olfactory (something smelled), or gustatory (something tasted).

Tactile images of heat and cold inform Hayden's "Those Winter Sundays" (page 462), in which the speaker's father wakes up early "in the blueblack cold" to make "banked fires blaze." Visual and tactile images appear in Frost's "Stopping by Woods" (page 466), in which the speaker has stopped "between the woods and frozen lake" to listen to "the sweep of easy wind" and watch the fall of "downy" flakes of snow.

We sometimes use the word *imagery* to refer to a pattern of related details in a poem. Shakespeare's sonnet "That time of year thou may'st in me behold," for example (pages 503–504), includes images of darkness and light, cold and warmth, day and night. The images cluster together to describe the passing of time. When images form patterns of related details that convey an idea or feeling beyond what the images literally describe, we call them *metaphorical* or *symbolic*. Such imagistic details suggest a meaning, attitude, or idea—they suggest something in terms of another—as for example when images of light are indicative of knowledge or of life and images of darkness are suggestive of ignorance or death.

...describes specific things—daffodils, fires, and finches' wings, for example—describes such things in specific terms: the color of the daffodils, the fire, the beating of the finches' wings. From these and other details we derive both meaning and feeling.

...of how images work together to convey feelings and ideas, ...the following poem.

ELIZABETH BISHOP
[1911–1979]

First Death in Nova Scotia

In the cold, cold parlor
my mother laid out Arthur
beneath the chromographs:
Edward, Prince of Wales,
with Princess Alexandra,   5
and King George with Queen Mary.
Below them on the table
stood a stuffed loon
shot and stuffed by Uncle
Arthur, Arthur's father.   10

Since Uncle Arthur fired
a bullet into him,
he hadn't said a word.
He kept his own counsel
on his white, frozen lake,   15
the marble-topped table.
His breast was deep and white,
cold and caressable;
his eyes were red glass,
much to be desired.   20

"Come," said my mother,
"Come and say good-bye
to your little cousin Arthur."
I was lifted up and given
one lily of the valley   25
to put in Arthur's hand.
Arthur's coffin was
a little frosted cake,
and the red-eyed loon eyed it
from his white, frozen lake.   30

Arthur was very small.
He was all white, like a doll
that hadn't been painted yet.
Jack Frost had started to paint him
the way he always painted   35

the Maple Leaf (Forever).
He had just begun on his hair,
a few red strokes, and then
Jack Frost had dropped the brush
and left him white, forever.   40

The gracious royal couples
were warm in red and ermine;
their feet were well wrapped up
in the ladies' ermine trains.
They invited Arthur to be   45
the smallest page at court.
But how could Arthur go,
clutching his tiny lily,
with his eyes shut up so tight
and the roads deep in snow?   50

The poem describes a child's view of death. Through images of what the little
girl sees and hears, it renders her incomprehension and confused feelings about
her cousin Arthur's death. Bishop does this by filtering the child's perceptions
through an adult sensibility. In a similar way, the poet presents a voice childlike in its syntactic constructions and adult in its vocabulary. Through the double perspective of the adult/the child we gain a complex inner view of the
speaker's impressions and understanding of her experience, vividly rendered in
the poem's images.

Our first sense impression is tactile: we imagine "the cold, cold parlor." Immediately after, we see two things: a picture of the British royal family and a
stuffed loon, which had been shot by the dead boy's father, also named Arthur.
The second stanza describes the loon in more detail. It sits on a marble-topped
table, a detail that conveys two tactile impressions, hardness and coldness. This
imagery is emphasized in the description of the marble table as the loon's
"white, frozen lake."

These visual images are continued in the third stanza in which the speaker
sees her dead cousin in his coffin. She holds a long-stemmed white flower which
she puts in the dead boy's hand. The images of whiteness and cold (the frozen
lake, marble table top, and the dead, stuffed white loon of the previous stanzas) are continued: the speaker describes Arthur's coffin as a "frosted cake." The
birthday cake image also indicates the limited extent of the speaker's comprehension of the reality and finality of death.

With the repeated details about the loon's red eyes and its frozen posture and
base, the child unconsciously (and the poet consciously) associate the dead boy
and the dead loon. This connection is further established by the imagery of the
fourth stanza in which Arthur is described as "all white," with "a few red
strokes" for his hair. Unlike the maple leaf with its complete and thorough red-
ness, little Arthur is left "unpainted" by Jack Frost (another image of the cold)

and is thus left white "forever." On the one hand, such a description clearly indicates the child's fantastic incomprehension of Arthur's death; on the other, it suggests that she intuitively senses that Arthur has been drained of color and of life. A similar combination of intuitive understanding and conscious ignorance is echoed in the speaker's comparison of Arthur with the doll. She sees how similar they look on the surface, but she does not consciously register their similar lifelessness.

The images of the final stanzas recall those of stanza 1. The royal couples of the chromograph are described as dressed in red clothes with white fur trim, details that connect directly with the dead loon. Moreover, the lily of the third stanza (white and short-lived like the boy) reappears clutched in Arthur's hand. The final image is one of whiteness and coldness: deep snow covers the cold ground where Arthur will soon lie.

The poem's concrete details, mostly visual and tactile images, strongly evoke the coldness and lifelessness of the dead child. But they suggest other things as well. The portrait of the royal family and the stuffed loon suggest something of the family's social identity—especially its conservatism and propriety. More importantly, however, these details, along with the others noted above, reveal the limitation of the speaker's understanding. She sees the loon, for example, as quiet: "he hadn't said a word," and "he kept his own counsel." In addition, she fantasizes that the royal family (which she sees as very much alive in their warm furs) have invited little Arthur to serve as "the smallest page at court." Even though this may be the speaker's way of coping with death, the final two images of white lily and cold snow, and the tone in which she asks her final question all point toward her near acknowledgment of the truth.

It should prove useful to return at this point to a few of the poems considered in earlier sections of this introduction and examine their imagery. For further practice in responding to poetic images, read the following poems.

WILLIAM BUTLER YEATS
[1865–1939]

The Lake Isle of Innisfree

I will arise and go now, and go to Innisfree,
And a small cabin build there, of clay and wattles° made: interwoven twigs
Nine bean-rows will I have there, a hive for the honey-bee,
And live alone in the bee-loud glade.

And I shall have some peace there, for peace comes dropping slow,   5
Dropping from the veils of the morning to where the cricket sings;
There midnight's all a glimmer, and noon a purple glow,
And evening full of the linnet's wings.

I will arise and go now, for always night and day
I hear lake water lapping with low sounds by the shore;   10
While I stand on the roadway, or on the pavements gray,
I hear it in the deep heart's core.

QUESTION

Identify the images of sound and sight and explain what they contribute to the idea
and feeling of the poem.

ROBERT BROWNING
[1812–1889]

Meeting at Night

The gray sea and the long black land;
And the yellow half-moon large and low;
And the startled little waves that leap
In fiery ringlets from their sleep,
As I gain the cove with pushing prow,   5
And quench its speed i' the slushy sand.

Then a mile of warm sea-scented beach;
Three fields to cross till a farm appears;
A tap at the pane, the quick sharp scratch
And blue spurt of a lighted match,   10
And a voice less loud, through its joys and fears,
Than the two hearts beating each to each!

QUESTION

In a series of images averaging one per line, the poet describes a lover traveling to meet
his beloved. Identify each image, the specific sense it stimulates, and the feelings the
images evoke.

H. D. (HILDA DOOLITTLE)
[1886–1961]

Heat

O wind, rend open the heat,
cut apart the heat,
rend it to tatters.

Fruit cannot drop
through this thick air— 5
that presses up and blunts
the points of pears
and rounds the grapes.

Cut the heat—
plow through it, 10
turning it on either side
of your path.

QUESTION

By asking the wind to "rend open," "cut apart," and "plow through" the heat, the poet
creates an image of it. Identify this image and explain what stanza 2 contributes to it.

THOMAS HARDY
[1840–1929]

Neutral Tones

We stood by a pond that winter day,
And the sun was white, as though chidden of God,
And a few leaves lay on the starving sod;
—They had fallen from an ash, and were gray.

Your eyes on me were as eyes that rove 5
Over tedious riddles of years ago;
And some words played between us to and fro
On which lost the more by our love.

The smile on your mouth was the deadest thing
Alive enough to have strength to die;   10
And a grin of bitterness swept thereby
    Like an ominous bird a-wing. . . .

Since then, keen lessons that love deceives,
And wrings with wrong, have shaped to me
Your face, and the God-curst sun, and a tree,   15
    And a pond edged with grayish leaves.

QUESTIONS

1. Examine the images of stanza 1. What mood do they create? How do the images of stanzas 2 and 3 develop and expand those of the opening stanza?
2. What do you notice about the images of the final stanza in relation to those that come before?

FIGURES OF SPEECH: SIMILE AND METAPHOR

Language can be conveniently classified as either literal or figurative. When we speak literally, we mean exactly what each word conveys; when we use *figurative language* we mean something other than the actual meaning of the words. "Go jump in the lake," for example, if meant literally would be intended as a command to leave (go) and jump (not dive or wade) into a lake (not a pond or stream). Usually, however, such an expression is not literally meant. In telling someone to go jump in the lake we are telling them something, to be sure, but what we mean is different from the literal meaning of the words. To get lost, perhaps, which is itself a figurative expression.

Rhetoricians have catalogued more than 250 different *figures of speech,* expressions or ways of using words in a nonliteral sense. They include *hyperbole* or exaggeration ("I'll die if I miss that game"); *litotes* or understatement ("Being flayed alive is somewhat painful"); *synecdoche* or using a part to signify the whole ("Lend me a hand"); *metonymy* or substituting an attribute of a thing for the thing itself ("step on the gas"); *personification,* endowing inanimate objects or abstract concepts with animate characteristics or qualities ("the lettuce was lonely without tomatoes and cucumbers for company"). We will not go on to name and illustrate the others but instead will concentrate on two specially important for poetry (and for the other literary genres as well): simile and metaphor.

The heart of both these figures is comparison—the making of connections between normally unrelated things, seeing one thing in terms of another. More than 2300 years ago Aristotle defined *metaphor* as "an intuitive perception of the similarity in dissimilars." And he suggested further that to be a "master of metaphor" is the greatest of a poet's achievements. In our century, Robert Frost has echoed Aristotle by suggesting that metaphor is central to poetry, and that, essentially, poetry is a way of "saying one thing and meaning another, saying one thing in terms of another."

Although both figures involve comparisons between unlike things, *simile* establishes the comparison explicitly with the words *like* or *as. Metaphor,* on the other hand, employs no such explicit verbal clue. The comparison is *implied* in such a way that the figurative term is substituted for or identified with the literal one. "My daughter dances like an angel" is a simile; "my daughter is an angel" is a metaphor. In this example the difference involves more than the word *like:* the simile is more restricted in its comparative suggestion than is the metaphor. That is, the daughter's angelic attributes are more extensive in the unspecified and unrestricted metaphor. In the simile, however, she only dances like an angel. (There's no suggestion that she possesses other angelic qualities.)

Consider the opening line of Wordsworth's poem about the daffodils: "I wandered lonely as a cloud" (page 490). The simile suggests the speaker's isolation and his aimless wandering. But it doesn't indicate other ways in which cloud and speaker are related. Later the speaker uses another simile to compare the daffodils with stars. This simile specifically highlights one aspect of the connection between stars and flowers: number. It also contains an example of hyperbole in its suggestion that the daffodils stretch in "a never-ending line."

In these examples the poet provides explicit clues that direct us to the comparative connection. He also restricts their application, as we have noted. In a metaphor, Wordsworth writes that the daffodils "flash" upon the "inward eye" of the speaker. The "flash" (an image of light) implies that he sees the flowers in his mind's eye, the inward eye of memory. Moreover, when he "sees" the daffodils in his "inward eye," he realizes the "wealth" they have brought him. This "wealth" is also figurative—Wordsworth uses "wealth" as a metaphor for joy.

These examples of simile and metaphor from Wordsworth's poem are fairly straightforward and uncomplicated. For a more complex example, consider the use of metaphor in the following sonnet by William Shakespeare.

WILLIAM SHAKESPEARE

[1564–1616]

That time of year thou may'st in me behold

That time of year thou may'st in me behold
When yellow leaves, or none, or few, do hang
Upon those boughs which shake against the cold,
Bare ruined choirs where late the sweet birds sang.
In me thou see'st the twilight of such day   5
As after sunset fadeth in the west,
Which by-and-by black night doth take away,
Death's second self that seals up all in rest.

In me thou see'st the glowing of such fire
That on the ashes of his youth doth lie,   10
As the deathbed whereon it must expire,
Consumed with that which it was nourished by.
   This thou perceiv'st, which makes thy love more strong,
   To love that well which thou must leave ere long.

Perhaps the first thing to mention about the poem's metaphorical language is that its images appeal to three senses: sight, hearing, and touch. The images of the first four lines include appeals to each of these senses: we *see* the yellow leaves and bare branches; we *feel* the cold that shakes the boughs; we *hear* (in memory) the singing birds of summer.

But these concrete representations of sensory experience become more than images with emotional reverberations. They become metaphors, ways of talking about one thing in terms of something else. The first image extended into a metaphor is that of autumn, "that time of year" when leaves turn yellow and branches become bare. The fourth line extends the image by describing the tree branches as a choir loft that the birds have recently vacated. Because Shakespeare's speaker says that "you" (we) can behold autumn *in him* ("In me thou see'st the twilight of such day," line 5), we know that he is speaking of more than autumn. We realize that he is talking about one thing in terms of another—about aging in terms of the seasons.

In the next four lines the metaphor of autumn gives way to another: that of twilight ending the day. The sun has set; night is coming on. The "black" night is described as taking away the sun's light (line 7); the sun's setting is seen as a dying of its light. The implied comparison of night with death is directly stated in line 8, where night is called "death's second self"; like death, night "seals up all in rest." Night's rest is, of course, temporary; death's, however, is final. The metaphor is both consoling (death is a kind of restful sleep) and frightening (death "seals up" life in a way that suggests there will be no unsealing).

So far we have noted two extended metaphors of autumn and of evening. Each comparison highlights the way death begins with a prelude: twilight precedes night; autumn precedes winter; illness precedes death. The speaker knows that he is in the autumn of his life, the twilight of his time. This metaphor is continued in a third image: the dying of the fire, which represents the dying out of the speaker's life. This third image emphasizes the extinguishing of light and of heat. The speaker's youth is "ashes," which serve as the "deathbed" on which he will "expire" (line 11). Literally, the lines say that the fire will expire as it burns up the fuel that feeds it. As it does so, it glows with light and heat. The glowing fire is a metaphor for the speaker's life, which is presently still "glowing" but which is beginning to die out as it consumes itself. We might notice that the fire will "expire," a word which means literally to "breathe out . . . to emit the last breath," an image that suggests the termination of breathing in the dying.

The final element of this image of the dying fire is given in line 12: "Consumed with that which it was nourished by." Literally the fire consumes itself by using up its fuel, burning up logs. In its very glowing it burns toward its own extinction. Analogously, the speaker's youthful vitality consumes itself in living. His very living has been and continues to be a dying.

For a few additional examples of how poets employ figurative language, read the following poems. Attend particularly to their figures of comparison and especially to how those comparisons aid your understanding.

JOHN DONNE
[1572–1631]

Hymn to God the Father

1

Wilt thou forgive that sin where I begun,
  Which was my sin though it were done before?
Wilt thou forgive that sin through which I run,
  And do run still, though still I do deplore?
      When thou hast done, thou hast not done,   5
        For I have more.

2

Wilt thou forgive that sin by which I've won
  Others to sin, and made my sin their door?
Wilt thou forgive that sin which I did shun
  A year or two, but wallowed in a score?   10
      When thou hast done, thou hast not done,
        For I have more.

3

I have a sin of fear, that when I've spun
  My last thread, I shall perish on the shore;
But swear by thyself that at my death thy son   15
  Shall shine as he shines now, and heretofore;
      And having done that, Thou hast done;
        I fear no more.

QUESTIONS

1. Explain the images in stanza 2: the door of sin and wallowing in sin. Relate these two images from stanza 3: spinning the last thread and perishing on the shore.
2. The final stanza contains two puns or plays on words. Identify and explain each. What do they contribute to the meaning and tone of the poem?

ROBERT WALLACE
[b. 1932]

The Double-Play

In his sea lit
distance, the pitcher winding
like a clock about to chime comes down with

the ball, hit
sharply, under the artificial   5
banks of arc-lights, bounds like a vanishing string

over the green
to the shortstop magically
scoops to his right whirling above his invisible

shadows   10
in the dust redirects
its flight to the running poised second baseman

pirouettes
leaping, above the slide, to throw
from mid-air, across the colored tightened interval,   15

to the leaning-
out first baseman ends the dance
drawing it disappearing into his long brown glove

stretches. What
is too swift for deception   20
is final, lost, among the loosened figures

jogging off the field
(the pitcher walks), casual
in the space where the poem has happened.

QUESTIONS

1. As its title suggests the poem describes a double play in baseball—getting two offensive players out on a single play. Throughout the poem the double play is compared to a dance. Pinpoint the words and phrases that establish this metaphorical connection, and explain what precisely about the double play makes it like a dance.

2. Besides the central metaphor that controls the poem, the poet has introduced other comparisons to illuminate and describe aspects or details of the double play. Identify and explain these comparisons.
3. In what way has the double play occurred "in the space where the poem has happened" (line 24)? How has a double play occurred both on the page and in the poem?

LOUIS SIMPSON

[b. 1923]

The Battle

Helmet and rifle, pack and overcoat
Marched through a forest. Somewhere up ahead
Guns thudded. Like the circle of a throat
The night on every side was turning red.

They halted and they dug. They sank like moles   5
Into the clammy earth between the trees.
And soon the sentries, standing in their holes,
Felt the first snow. Their feet began to freeze.

At dawn the first shell landed with a crack.
Then shells and bullets swept the icy woods.   10
This lasted many days. The snow was black.
The corpses stiffened in their scarlet hoods.

Most clearly of that battle I remember
The tiredness in eyes, how hands looked thin
Around a cigarette, and the bright ember   15
Would pulse with all the life there was within.

QUESTION

Identify and explain the figures of speech in the first two stanzas. What impression does each create? How is the mood they establish enforced by the rest of the poem?

JUDITH WRIGHT
[*b. 1915*]

Woman to Child

You who were darkness warmed my flesh
where out of darkness rose the seed.
Then all a world I made in me;
all the world you hear and see
hung upon my dreaming blood.   5

There moved the multitudinous stars,
and coloured birds and fishes moved.
There swam the sliding continents.
All time lay rolled in me, and sense,
and love that knew not its beloved.   10

O node and focus of the world;
I hold you deep within that well
you shall escape and not escape—
that mirrors still your sleeping shape;
that nurtures still your crescent cell.   15

I wither and you break from me;
yet though you dance in living light
I am the earth, I am the root,
I am the stem that fed the fruit,
the link that joins you to the night.   20

QUESTION

Explain the following figurative expressions:
"All a world I made in me" (line 3)
"All time lay rolled in me" (line 9)
"I hold you deep within that well" (line 12)
"I am the earth, I am the root,
I am the stem that fed the fruit" (lines 18–19)

SYMBOLISM AND ALLEGORY

A *symbol* is any object or action that means more than itself, any object or action that represents something beyond itself. A rose, for example, can represent beauty or love or transience. A tree may represent a family's roots and branches. A soaring bird might stand for freedom. Light might symbolize hope or knowledge or life. These and other familiar symbols may represent different, even opposite things, depending on how they are deployed in a particular poem. Natural symbols like light and darkness, fire and water can stand for contradictory things. Water, for example, which typically symbolizes life (rain, fertility, food, life) can also stand for death (tempests, hurricanes, floods). And fire, which often indicates destruction, can represent purgation or purification. The meaning of any symbol, whether an object, an action, or a gesture, is controlled by its context.

How then do we know if a poetic detail is symbolic? How do we decide whether to leap beyond the poem's literal detail into a symbolic interpretation? There are no simple answers to these questions. Like any interpretive connections we make in reading, the decision to view something as symbolic depends partly on our skill in reading and partly on whether the poetic context invites and rewards a symbolic reading. The following questions can guide our thinking about interpreting symbols:

1. Is the object, action, gesture, or event important to the poem? Is it described in detail? Does it occur repeatedly? Does it appear at a climactic moment in the poem?
2. Does the poem seem to warrant our granting its details more significance than their immediate literal meaning?
3. Does our symbolic reading make sense? Does it account for the literal details without either ignoring or distorting them?

Even in following such guidelines, there will be occasions when we are not certain that a poem is symbolic. And there will be times when, though we are fairly confident *that* certain details are symbolic, we are not confident about *what* they symbolize. Such uncertainty is due largely to the nature of interpretation, which is an art rather than a science. But these interpretive complications are also due to the differences in complexity and variability with which poets use symbols. The most complex symbols resist definitive and final explanation. We can circle around them, but we neither exhaust their significance nor define their meaning.

As an example of how literal details assume symbolic significance observe their use in the following poem.

PETER MEINKE

[b. 1932]

Advice to My Son

The trick is, to live your days
as if each one may be your last
(for they go fast, and young men lose their lives
in strange and unimaginable ways)
but at the same time, plan long range   5
(for they go slow: if you survive
the shattered windshield and the bursting shell
you will arrive
at our approximation here below
of heaven or hell).   10

To be specific, between the peony and the rose
plant squash and spinach, turnips and tomatoes;
beauty is nectar
and nectar, in a desert, saves—
but the stomach craves stronger sustenance   15
than the honied vine.

Therefore, marry a pretty girl
after seeing her mother;
show your soul to one man,
work with another;   20
and always serve bread with your wine.

But, son,
always serve wine.

The concrete details that invite symbolic reading are these: peony and rose;
squash, spinach, turnips and tomatoes; bread and wine. If we read the poem literally and assume the advice is meant that way, we learn something about the
need to plant and enjoy these flowers and foods. But if we suspect that the
speaker is advising his son about more than food and flowers, we will look toward their symbolic implications.

What then do the various plants and the bread and wine symbolize? How is
the speaker's advice about them related to the more general advice about living? In the first stanza the general advice implies two contradictory courses of
action: (1) live each day to the fullest as if it will be the last; (2) look to the fu-

ture and plan wisely so your future will not be marred by unwise decisions. By advising his son to plant peonies and roses, the speaker urges him to see the need for beauty and luxury, implying that he needs food for the spirit as well as sustenance for the body.

The symbols of bread and wine suggest a related point. The speaker urges his son to serve both bread and wine as bread is a dietary staple, something basic and common, but wine enhances the bread, making it seem more than mere common fare. Wine symbolizes something festive; it provides a touch of celebration. Thus the speaker's advice about bread and wine parallels his earlier suggestions. In each case, he urges his son to balance and blend, to fulfill both his basic and his spiritual needs. By making his advice concrete the speaker does indeed advocate literally what he says: plant roses and peonies with your vegetables; drink wine with your bread. But by including such specific instructions in a poem that contains other more serious advice about living (live for today, live for the future) the poet invites us to see bread and wine, vegetables and flowers more than literally. If our interpretation of their symbolic dimension is congruent with other parts of the poem, and if it makes sense, then we should feel confident that we are not imposing a symbolic reading where it is not warranted.

Related to symbolism, *allegory* is a form of narrative in which people, places, and happenings have hidden or symbolic meaning; allegory is especially suitable as a vehicle for teaching. In an allegorical work there are most often two levels of meaning, the literal and the symbolic. To understand an allegorical work we must make sense of its details by interpreting their symbolic meaning.

Allegory is thus a type of symbolism. It differs from symbolism in establishing a strict system of correspondences between details of action and a pattern of meaning. Symbolic works that are not allegorical are less systematic and more open-ended in what their symbols mean.

The following allegorical poem describes a journey along an uphill road that ends with the traveler arriving at an inn. We can readily see that the uphill road represents a struggling journey through life, that day and night stand for a lifespan ending in death. The question-and-answer structure of the poem and its reassuring tone suggest that it can be read as a religious allegory, specifically a Christian one.

CHRISTINA ROSSETTI

[*1830–1894*]

Up-Hill

Does the road wind up-hill all the way?
   Yes, to the very end.
Will the day's journey take the whole long day?
   From morn to night, my friend.

But is there for the night a resting-place?   5
  A roof for when the slow dark hours begin.
May not the darkness hide it from my face?
  You cannot miss that inn.

Shall I meet other wayfarers at night?
  Those who have gone before.   10
Then must I knock, or call when just in sight?
  They will not keep you standing at that door.

Shall I find comfort, travel-sore and weak?
  Of labor you shall find the sum.
Will there be beds for me and all who seek?   15
  Yea, beds for all who come.

   For more exercise in interpreting symbol and allegory, read the following poems with attention to their symbolic and allegorical details. All the poems are symbolic, but not in the same way.

WILLIAM BLAKE
[1757–1827]

A Poison Tree

1 I was angry with my friend:
2 I told my wrath, my wrath did end.
3 I was angry with my foe:
4 I told it not, my wrath did grow.

5 And I waterd it in fears,   5
6 Night & morning with my tears;
7 And I sunnéd it with smiles,
8 And with soft deceitful wiles.

9 And it grew both day and night,
10 Till it bore an apple bright.   10
11 And my foe beheld it shine,
12 And he knew that it was mine,

13 And into my garden stole,
14 When the night had veild the pole;
15 In the morning glad I see   15
16 My foe outstretchd beneath the tree.

QUESTIONS

1. "A Poison Tree" describes a series of events—it tells a story. Explain your understanding of the story's significance.
2. What does the apple in a garden represent? What difference would it make if it were a peach in an orchard?

ROBERT FROST

[1874–1963]

The Road Not Taken

Two roads diverged in a yellow wood,
And sorry I could not travel both
And be one traveler, long I stood
And looked down one as far as I could
To where it bent in the undergrowth;   5

Then took the other, as just as fair,
And having perhaps the better claim,
Because it was grassy and wanted wear;
Though as for that, the passing there
Had worn them really about the same,   10

And both that morning equally lay
In leaves no step had trodden black.
Oh, I kept the first for another day!
Yet knowing how way leads on to way,
I doubted if I should ever come back.   15

I shall be telling this with a sigh
Somewhere ages and ages hence:
Two roads diverged in a wood, and I—
I took the one less traveled by,
And that has made all the difference.   20

QUESTIONS

1. On one level this is a poem about walking in the woods and choosing one of two paths to follow. What invites us to see the poem as something more? What is this something more?
2. Frost is careful not to specify what the two roads represent: he does not limit their

possible symbolic meanings. And yet the nature of the experience he describes does pivot the poem on a central human problem: the inescapable necessity to make choices. Specify some of the choices we all must make that could be represented by the two roads of the poem.

GEORGE HERBERT
[1593–1633]

Virtue

Sweet day, so cool, so calm, so bright,
    The bridal of the earth and sky:
The dew shall weep thy fall tonight;
        For thou must die.

Sweet rose, whose hue, angry and brave,   5
    Bids the rash gazer wipe his eye:
Thy root is ever in its grave,
        And thou must die.

Sweet spring, full of sweet days and roses,
    A box where sweets° compacted lie;   perfumes   10
My music shows ye have your closes°,   musical cadences
        And all must die.

Only a sweet and virtuous soul,
    Like seasoned timber, never gives;
But though the whole world turn to coal,   15
        Then chiefly lives.

QUESTION

The major contrast in the poem is between things that die and the one thing that does not. Identify and comment on the aptness of Herbert's symbols for transience and mortality.

EMILY DICKINSON

[1830–1886]

Because I could not stop for Death

Because I could n ot stop for Death—
He kindly stopped for me—
The Carriage held but just Ourselves—
And Immortality.

We slowly drove—He knew no haste   5
And I had put away
My labor and my leisure too,
For His Civility—

We passed the School, where Children strove
At Recess—in the Ring—   10
We passed the Fields of Gazing Grain—
We passed the Setting Sun—

Or rather—He passed Us—
The Dews drew quivering and chill—
For only Gossamer, my Gown—   15
My Tippet°—only Tulle—   scarf or stole

We paused before a House that seemed
A Swelling of the Ground—
The Roof was scarcely visible—
The Cornice—in the Ground—   20

Since then—'tis Centuries—and yet
Feels shorter than the Day
I first surmised the Horses' Heads
Were toward Eternity—

QUESTION

Is this poem generally symbolic or is it allegorical? Explain the significance of the details in lines 9–13 and lines 17–20.

SYNTAX

We have previously defined *syntax* as the order of words in sentence, phrase, or clause. From a Greek word meaning "to arrange together," *syntax* refers to the grammatical structure of words in sentences and the deployment of sentences in longer units throughout the poem. Poets use syntax as they use imagery, diction, structure, sound, and rhythm—to express meaning and convey feeling. A poem's syntax is an important element of its tone and a guide to a speaker's state of mind. Speakers who repeat themselves or who break off abruptly in the midst of a thought, for example, reveal something about how they feel.

Let us briefly consider what syntax contributes to the meaning and feeling of a few poems discussed earlier. In "Those Winter Sundays" (page 462) Robert Hayden uses normal word order for each of the poem's four sentences, but he varies their lengths radically. In the first stanza, for example, Hayden follows a long sentence with a short one. The effect is to increase the emphasis on the short sentence: "No one ever thanked him." In the last stanza, Hayden uses a question rather than a statement for the speaker's remembrance of his father's acts of love. Both the question and the repetition of the phrase "What did I know" reveal the intensity of the speaker's regret at his belated understanding.

In "Stopping by Woods on a Snowy Evening" (page 466), Robert Frost achieves emphasis differently through *inversion* or the reversal of the standard order of words in a line or sentence. The word order of the first line of the poem is inverted:

Whose woods these are I think I know.

Normal word order would be:

I think I know whose woods these are.

In the more conversational alternative, emphasis falls on what the speaker knows or thinks he knows. In Frost's line emphasis falls on "the woods," which are more important than what the speaker thinks he knows as he looks at them. Perhaps more important still is the difference in tone between the two versions. Frost's inverted syntax lifts the line, giving it a more even rhythm, slowing it down slightly. The alternate version lacks the rhythmic regularity of Frost's original and reads like a casual statement.

Another aspect of syntax worth noting in Frost's poem is the variations in tempo among the four stanzas. The sentences of the first and last stanzas are the most heavily stopped with punctuation and pauses. The opening stanza contains three pauses before it ends; stanza four includes three in its first line alone and five altogether. In contrast stanza three contains only one stop, halfway through. And stanza two is one long sentence without a single pause or break. Frost carefully controls the movement and speed, the pace and pause of his poem by using punctuation and grammatical form to heighten its expressiveness and to control its tone.

Unlike the inverted and varied syntax of Frost's "Stopping by Woods on a Snowy Evening," (page 466) William Wordsworth's syntax in "I wandered lonely as a cloud" (page 490) is simple and direct; it does not call attention to itself. The two little syntactic twists that it does contain highlight an important dimension of the poem—visual imagery. One is an inversion: "saw I" (line 11); the other is a repetition: "I gazed—and gazed" (line 17). And consider Walt Whitman's "When I heard the learn'd astronomer" (page 545), which is cast as a single expansive subordinate sentence that sweeps over the first four lines like a wave and then ebbs in the next four. The action of the last four lines is suspended over the first four: we are made to wait for the final simple and important act that Whitman renders in the most direct syntax of any line in the poem: the speaker "look'd up in perfect silence at the stars."

Consider how syntax orders thought and highlights feeling in "The Sun Rising," by John Donne.

JOHN DONNE

[1572–1631]

The Sun Rising

    Busy old fool, unruly sun,
     Why dost thou thus,
Through windows, and through curtains call on us?
Must to thy motions lovers' seasons run?
     Saucy pedantic wretch, go chide   5
     Late schoolboys, and sour prentices,
  Go tell court-huntsmen that the King will ride,
  Call country ants to harvest offices;
Love, all alike, no season knows, nor clime,
Nor hours, days, months, which are the rags of time. 10

     Thy beams, so reverend and strong
     Why shouldst thou think?
I could eclipse and cloud them with a wink,
But that I would not lose her sight so long;
     If her eyes have not blinded thine, 15
     Look, and tomorrow late, tell me
  Whether both the Indias of spice and mine
  Be where thou left'st them, or lie here with me.
Ask for those kings whom thou saw'st yesterday,
And thou shalt hear, All here in one bed lay. 20

                    She's all states, and all princes, I,
                    Nothing else is.
          Princes do but play us; compared to this,
          All's honor's mimic, all wealth alchemy.
                    Thou, sun, art half as happy as we,   25
                    In that the world's contracted thus;
          Thine age asks ease, and since thy duties be
          To warm the world, that's done in warming us.
          Shine here to us, and thou art everywhere;
          This bed thy center is, these walls, thy sphere.   30

Perhaps the first thing we notice is the dislocation of syntax in the two opening questions. The first question could be rewritten so as to approximate more
conventional discourse:

          Unruly sun, busy old fool,
          Why dost thou thus call on us
          Through windows, and through curtains?

Besides an alteration of rhythm, we notice a different emphasis in Donne's lines.
The alternate version puts the emphasis on "windows" and "curtains," far less
important words than "us," the word Donne's lines emphasize, as the poem is
about a pair of lovers.

   After another inverted sentence ("Must to thy motions lovers' seasons run")
and a short one following the longer opening sentence, we hear a series of tonal
shifts. The speed and abruptness of Donne's second question convey the
speaker's tone of impatient defiance. The two questions with their emphatic
dislocations prepare the way for the series of imperatives that increase our sense
of the speaker's authority. This tone gives way abruptly in the last two lines of
the stanza to a more leisurely verse movement ("Love, all alike, no season knows,
nor clime, / Nor hours, days, months, which are the rags of time"). The dignified and stately tone of these lines derives partly from the simple declarative
sentences, partly from the monosyllabic diction, and partly from the frequent
pauses marked by punctuation. The overall effect is a slower line and a more
exalted tone.

   In stanza two the tone shifts back to the playful exaggeration of the beginning of the poem, with similar dislocations of syntax in its opening question.
The second sentence (lines 13–18), neither question, statement, nor command,
is a statement of possibility. The tone remains playfully defiant ("tell me /
Whether both the Indias of spice and mine / Be where thou left'st them"); the
speaker continues to exaggerate. The syntax is more convoluted, the sentences
more complex than in the first stanza. Again, however, as in the opening stanza,
the final line of stanza two resolves into a direct authoritative assertion:

          "All here in one bed lay."

Unlike the first two stanzas, the last begins with the declarative syntax and simple, direct assertiveness with which the other two stanzas end. The entire stanza is composed of a series of balanced statements, some parallel, some antithetical. (Not completely, however, since there is something of the complex argument of stanza two midway through this last stanza. And there is also a brief return to the imperative voice in line 29, "Shine here to us.") But from these deviations the speaker quickly returns to the authority of direct declaration, an authority enhanced by the parallel form of the final line, by its slight dislocation of the verbs, and by the tightness of its structure (eliminating a conjunction between the clauses and omitting the implied verb of the second half of the line):

"This bed thy center is, these walls thy sphere."

There are many syntactical possibilities available to poets. For some interesting syntactical forms and their effects see T. S. Eliot's "The Love Song of J. Alfred Prufrock" for its associative syntax (syntax that reflects the mental associations of the speaker [pages 749–753]); Gerard Manley Hopkins's "Thou art indeed just, Lord" (page 485) for its use of fractured or broken syntax; John Milton's "On the Late Massacre in Piedmont" (page 697) for its Latinate syntax; and Alexander Pope's "An Essay on Man," (page 700) for its tightly formal, balanced, and antithetical syntax.

In the poems that follow Thomas Hardy uses broken syntax in "The Man He Killed"; Robert Frost uses ambiguous syntax so that multiple meanings coexist and coincide in "The Silken Tent"; and E. E. Cummings uses mimetic syntax, which imitates what it describes, in "Me up at does."

THOMAS HARDY
[1840–1928]

The Man He Killed

"Had he and I but met
By some old ancient inn,
We should have sat us down to wet
Right many a nipperkin!

"But ranged as infantry,   5
And staring face to face,
I shot at him as he at me,
And killed him in his place.

"I shot him dead because—
Because he was my foe,   10

Just so: my foe of course he was;
That's clear enough; although

"He thought he'd 'list, perhaps,
Off-hand-like—just as I—
Was out of work—had sold his traps—   15
No other reason why.

"Yes; quaint and curious war is!
You shoot a fellow down
You'd treat if met where any bar is,
Or help to half-a-crown."   20

QUESTIONS

1. The first two stanzas are each a single sentence. Explain their logical and syntactic relationship.
2. Unlike the smooth unbroken sentences of the first two stanzas, we find breaks in the syntax (indicated by dashes) in the next two stanzas. After reading the stanzas aloud, explain what the breaks suggest about the speaker's state of mind.
3. Does the speaker's fluent syntax in the last stanza suggest that he has worked through the state of mind you found evident in stanzas three and four? Explain.

WILLIAM BUTLER YEATS

[1865–1939]

An Irish Airman Foresees His Death

I know that I shall meet my fate
Somewhere among the clouds above;
Those that I fight I do not hate,
Those that I guard I do not love;°
My country is Kiltartan Cross   5
My countrymen Kiltartan's poor,
No likely end could bring them loss
Or leave them happier than before.
Nor law, nor duty bade me fight,
Nor public men, nor cheering crowds,   10

"An Irish Airman Foresees His Death"   3-4*Those that I fight . . . I do not love.*   Yeats is referring to the Germans and the English respectively; the war is World War I.

A lonely impulse of delight
Drove to this tumult in the clouds;
I balanced all, brought all to mind,
The years to come seemed waste of breath,
A waste of breath the years behind   15
In balance with this life, this death.

QUESTIONS

1. Point out the ways the syntax of this poem is balanced and controlled. How does the poem's balanced syntax reinforce its meaning?
2. Explain the connection between its syntax and its central idea: the pilot's attitude toward his country, his enemy, his fate.

ROBERT FROST

[1874–1963]

The Silken Tent

She is as in a field a silken tent
At midday when a sunny summer breeze
Has dried the dew and all its ropes relent,
So that in guys it gently sways at ease,
And its supporting central cedar pole,   5
That is its pinnacle to heavenward
And signifies the sureness of the soul,
Seems to owe naught to any single cord,
But strictly held by none, is loosely bound
By countless silken ties of love and thought   10
To everything on earth the compass round,
And only by one's going slightly taut
In the capriciousness of summer air
Is of the slightest bondage made aware.

QUESTION

Perhaps the most astonishing thing about this sonnet is that it is only a single sentence. Go through the poem again attending to the way the sentence develops. Account for all the conjunctions: *so* (line 4), *and* (line 5), *And* (line 7), *But* (line 9), *And* (line 12). How do those conjunctions help us follow the sentence?

E. E. CUMMINGS
[1894–1962]

"Me up at does"

Me up at does

out of the floor
quietly Stare

a poisoned mouse

still who alive

is asking What
have i done that

You wouldn't have

QUESTIONS

1. Rearrange the syntax of this poem to approximate the normal word order of an English sentence. Where do you have to make the heaviest adjustment?
2. How is Cummings's word order related to the situation the poem describes? What does Cummings gain by ordering his words as he does?

STEVIE SMITH
[1902–1971]

Mother, Among the Dustbins

Mother, among the dustbins and the manure
I feel the measure of my humanity, an allure
As of the presence of God. I am sure

In the dustbins, in the manure, in the cat at play,
Is the presence of God, in a sure way
He moves there. Mother, what do you say?

5

I too have felt the presence of God in the broom
I hold, in the cobwebs in the room,
But most of all in the silence of the tomb.

Ah! but that thought that informs the hope of our kind   10
Is but an empty thing, what lies behind?—
Naught but the vanity of a protesting mind

That would not die. This is the thought that bounces
Within a conceited head and trounces
Inquiry. Man is most frivolous when he pronounces.   15

Well Mother, I shall continue to think as I do,
And I think you would be wise to do so too,
Can you question the folly of man in the creation of God?
        Who are you?

QUESTION

Examine the way the poet uses balanced phrasing, primarily repeated phrases throughout the poem. Notice the play of long sentence against short, of question against statement. What do these syntactic elements contribute to the tone and attitude of the poem?

SOUND: RHYME, ALLITERATION, ASSONANCE

The most familiar element of poetry is *rhyme,* which can be defined as the matching of final vowel and consonant sounds in two or more words. When the corresponding sounds occur at the ends of lines we have *end rhyme;* when they occur
within lines we have *internal rhyme.* The opening stanza of Edgar Allan Poe's
"The Raven" illustrates both:

> Once upon a midnight dreary, while I pondered weak and weary,
> Over many a quaint and curious volume of forgotten lore—
> While I nodded nearly napping, suddenly there came a tapping,
> As of some one gently rapping, rapping at my chamber door.
> "'Tis some visitor," I muttered, "tapping at my chamber door—
>   Only this and nothing more."

For the reader rhyme is a pleasure, for the poet a challenge. Part of its pleasure for the reader is in anticipating and hearing a poem's echoing song. Part
of its challenge for the poet is in rhyming naturally, without forcing the rhythm,
the syntax, or the sense. When the challenge is met successfully, the poem is a
pleasure to listen to; it sounds natural to the ear, and its rhyme makes it easier
to remember.

Robert Frost's "Stopping by Woods on a Snowy Evening" is one such rhyming success. Reread it once more, preferably aloud, and listen to its music.

> Whose woods these are I think I know.
> His house is in the village, though;
> He will not see me stopping here
> To watch his woods fill up with snow.
>
> My little horse must think it queer
> To stop without a farmhouse near
> Between the woods and frozen lake
> The darkest evening of the year.
>
> He gives his harness bells a shake
> To ask if there is some mistake.
> The only other sound's the sweep
> Of easy wind and downy flake.
>
> The woods are lovely, dark and deep,
> But I have promises to keep,
> And miles to go before I sleep,
> And miles to go before I sleep.

Notice how in each of the first three stanzas, three of the four lines rhyme (lines 1, 2, and 4), and Frost picks up the nonrhymed sound of each stanza (the third line) and links it with the rhyming sound of the stanza that follows it, until the fourth stanza when he closes with four matching rhymes. Part of our pleasure in Frost's rhyming may derive from the pattern of departure and return it voices. Part may stem also from the way the rhyme pattern supports the poem's meaning. The speaker is caught between his desire to remain still, peacefully held by the serene beauty of the woods, and his contrasting need to leave, to return to his responsibilities. In a similar way, the poem's rhyme is caught between a surge forward toward a new sound and a return to a sound repeated earlier. The pull and counterpull of the rhyme reflect the speaker's ambivalence.

The rhymes in Frost's poem are *exact* or *perfect rhymes:* that is, the rhyming words share corresponding sounds and stresses and a similar number of syllables. While Frost's poem contains perfect rhymes ("know," "though," and "snow," for example), we sometimes hear in poems a less exact, *imperfect, approximate,* or *slant rhyme.* Emily Dickinson's "Crumbling is not an instant's Act" (page 552) includes both exact rhyme ("dust"-"rust") and slant rhyme ("slow"-"law"). Theodore Roethke's "My Papa's Waltz" (page 473) contains a slant rhyme on (*"dizzy"-"easy"*), which also exemplifies *feminine rhyme.* In feminine rhyme the final syllable of a rhymed word is unstressed; in *masculine rhyme* the final syllable is stressed—or the words rhymed are each only one syllable.

Besides rhyme, two other forms of sound play prevail in poetry: *alliteration* or the repetition of consonant sounds, especially at the beginning of words, and *assonance* or the repetition of vowel sounds. In his witty guide to poetic technique, *Rhyme's Reason,* John Hollander describes alliteration and assonance like this:

> Assonance is the spirit of a rhyme,
> A common vowel, hovering like a sigh
> After its consonantal body dies. . . .
>
> . . . .
>
> Alliteration lightly links
> Stressed syllables with common consonants.

Walt Whitman's "When I Heard the Learn'd Astronomer," (page 545) though lacking in end rhyme, possesses a high degree of assonance. The long *i*'s in lines 1, 3, and 4 accumulate and gather force as the poem glides into its last four lines: "*I,*" "t*i*red," "r*i*sing," "gl*i*ding," "*I,*" "m*y*self," "n*i*ght," "t*i*me to t*i*me," and "s*i*lence." This assonance sweetens the sound of the second part of the poem, highlighting its radical shift of action and feeling.

Both alliteration and assonance are clearly audible in "Stopping by Woods," particularly in the third stanza:

> He gives his harness bells a shake
> To ask if there is some mistake.
> The only other sound's the sweep
> Of easy wind and downy flake.

Notice that the long *e* of "sweep" is echoed in "*ea*-sy" and "down-*y,*" and that the *ow* of "d*ow*ny" echoes the same sound in "s*ow*nd's." These repetitions of sound accentuate the images the words embody, aural images (wind-blow and snow-fall), tactile images (the soft fluff of down and the feel of the gently blowing wind), and visual images (the white flakes of snow).

The alliterative *s*'s in "*s*ome," "*s*ound," and "*s*weep" are supported by the internal and terminal *s*'s: "Give*s,*" "hi*s,*" "harne*ss* bell*s,*" and "i*s,*" and also by mid-word *s*'s: "a*s*k," "mi*s*take," and "ea*s*y." Some of these sounds are heavier than others—the two similar heavy *s*'s of "easy" and "his" contrast the lighter softer "*s*" in "harness" and "mistake."

Listen to the sound effects of rhyme, alliteration, and assonance, in the following poem. Try to determine what sound contributes to its meaning.

GERARD MANLEY HOPKINS

[1844–1889]

In the Valley of the Elwy

I remember a house where all were good
  To me, God knows, deserving no such thing:
  Comforting smell breathed at very entering,
Fetched fresh, as I suppose, off some sweet wood.
That cordial air madeF those kind people a hood   5
  All over, as a bevy of eggs the mothering wing
  Will, or mild nights the new morsels of Spring:
Why, it seemed of course; seemed of right it should.

Lovely the woods, waters, meadows, combes, vales,
All the air things wear that build this world of Wales;   10
  Only the inmate does not correspond:

God, lover of souls, swaying considerate scales,
Complete thy creature dear O where it fails,
  Being mighty a master, being a father and fond.

We note first that the rhyme scheme reveals a Petrarchan sonnet: *abba, abba, ccd, ccd* (see page 543). Also we might note that its rhyme pattern corresponds to its sentence structure: the octave splits into two sentences, lines 1–4 and 5–8; the sestet, though only one sentence, splits into two equal parts, lines 9–11 and 12–14. Hopkins's use of the Italian rhyme scheme keeps similar sounds repeating throughout: *good, wood, hood, should; thing, entering, wing, Spring; vales, Wales, scales, fails; correspond, fond.* (The rhyme pattern of the Shakespearean or English sonnet, by contrast, as heard in "That time of year," [page 543] contains fewer rhyming repetitions, as it uses a greater number of different sounds.)

Besides extensive rhyme, Hopkins uses alliteration and assonance—lightly in the octave and more heavily in the sestet. Lines 3–6, for example, collect short *e*'s in "sm*e*ll," "v*e*ry," "*e*ntering," "f*e*tched" and "fr*e*sh," "b*e*vy" and "*e*ggs." Lines 4–8 begin an alliterative use of *w*, which is more elaborately sounded in lines 9–10 of the sestet; in lines 4–8 we hear: "*sw*eet *w*ood," "*w*ing *W*ill," and "*w*hy." In addition, in line 7 "m*i*ld n*i*ghts" picks up the long *i* of "*Wh*y," which finds an echo in the rhyme on "right." This seventh line also contains what we might call a reversed or crisscrossed alliteration in "*m*ild *n*ights" and "*n*ew *m*orsels."

But these sound effects are only a pale indication of what we hear in the sestet. Perhaps the most musical lines of the entire poem are the opening lines of the sestet (lines 9–10). *L*'s frame both of these lines: "*L*ovely . . . va*l*es" and "A*ll* . . . Wa*l*es." *L*'s are further sounded in "bui*l*d this wor*l*d." The *w*, which as we noted ended the octave, is carried into the sestet in *"w*oods," *"w*aters," *"w*eadows," *"w*ear," *"w*orld," and *"W*ales." The sestet also includes a variety of vowels: lovely, w*o*ods, w*a*ter, m*ea*dows, c*o*mbes, v*a*les, *a*ll, *a*ir, w*ea*r, th*a*t, b*ui*ld, th*i*s, w*o*rld, W*a*les.

Hopkins sounds a similarly varied vowel music in the last line, where he also uses alliteration and repetition to call attention to important attributes of God:

"Being mighty a master, being a father and fond."

One line, however, especially lacks music: line 11. Coming amidst such splendid sounds, it stands out even more sharply:

"Only the inmate does not correspond."

This expressive use of sound variation supports the idea that the line conveys: that in this beautiful natural world, the "inmate," the speaker in the guise of prisoner, does not fit. He feels out of place, out of harmony with his environment. In the lines that follow (12–14), he asks God to "complete" him, to make him whole, to integrate him into the world. And he prays in language that immediately picks up the sound play of assonance and alliteration that had been momentarily suspended in line 11. The speaker's harmony and wholeness are thus restored in the poem's beauty of sound.

To further develop your ear for sound in poetry, listen to the poems that follow:

THOMAS HARDY

[1840–1928]

During Wind and Rain

They sing their dearest songs—
He, she, all of them—yea,
Treble and tenor and bass,
   And one to play;
With the candles mooning each face. . . .   5
   Ah, no; the years O!
How the sick leaves reel down in throngs!

They clear the creeping moss—
Elders and juniors—aye,
Making the pathway neat   10
   And the garden gay;
And they build a shady seat. . . .
   Ah, no; the years, the years;
See, the white stormbirds wing across!

They are blithely breakfasting all—   15
Men and maidens—yea,
Under the summer tree,
    With a glimpse of the bay,
While pet fowl come to the knee. . . .
    Ah, no; the years O!   20
And the rotten rose is ripped from the wall.

They change to a high new house,
He, she, all of them—aye,
Clocks and carpets, and chairs
    On the lawn all day,   25
And brightest things that are theirs. . . .
    Ah, no; the years, the years;
Down their carved names the rain drop ploughs.

QUESTIONS

1. Chart the poem's rhyme scheme. Note the repetitions of lines ("Ah no: the years")
   and of words ("O," "aye," and "yea"). What do these repetitions contribute to the
   idea and feeling of the poem?
2. Identify examples of alliteration and comment on their effect.

ALEXANDER POPE

[1688–1744]

Sound and Sense

True ease in writing comes from art, not chance,
As those move easiest who have learned to dance.
'Tis not enough no harshness gives offense,
The sound must seem an echo to the sense:
Soft is the strain when Zephyr° gently blows,   5
And the smooth stream in smoother numbers flows;
But when loud surges lash the sounding shore,
The hoarse, rough verse should like the torrent roar.
When Ajax° strives, some rock's vast weight to throw,
The line too labors, and the words move slow;   10
Not so, when swift Camilla° scours the plain,

"Sound And Sense"   ⁵*Zephyr*   *the west wind.*   ⁹*Ajax*   *a strong Greek warrior in the Trojan War.*
¹¹*Camilla*   *an ancient Volcian queen noted for her speed and lightness of step.*

Flies o'er th' unbending corn, and skims along the main.
Hear how Timotheus'° varied lays surprise,
And bid alternate passions fall and rise!
While, at each change, the son of Libyan Jove°,   15
Now burns with glory, and then melts with love;
Now his fierce eyes with sparkling fury glow,
Now sighs steal out, and tears begin to flow;
Persians and Greeks like turns of nature found,
And the world's victor stood subdued by sound!   20
The pow'r of music all our hearts allow,
And what Timotheus was, is DRYDEN now.

QUESTIONS

1. How does the poet enact verbally what he asserts in line 4, that "the sound must seem an echo to the sense"?
2. What contrast is described and imitated in sound effects in lines 5–6 and 7–8? Between lines 9–10 and lines 11–12?

BOB MCKENTY

[b. 1935]

Adam's Song

Come live with me and be my love.
Come romp with me in Eden's grove
In unabated joy, not shy
But unabashed by nudity,
Where you can bare—sans shame—your breast   5
Until the fell Forbidden Feast.
Thereafter I shall toil and sweat
To earn whatever bread we eat
And you, in bearing children, shall
Know pain and suffering. The Fall   10
Will bring us sickness, death, and fear,
Embarrassment and underwear
(For which the Fig donates its leaf)
And poets who are surely deaf.

"Sound And Sense"   [13] **Timotheus**   *a musician in John Dryden's poem "Alexander's Feast."*   [15] *the son of* **Libyan Jove**   *Alexander the Great (356–323 B.C.), king of Macedonia and military conqueror who spread Greek culture throughout the ancient world.*

QUESTION

Identify the sound effects at play in "Adam's Song." Consider especially the poem's rhymes.

MAY SWENSON
[1919–1989]

The Universe

What
       is it about,
the universe,
the universe about us stretching out?
We, within our brains,   5
    within it,
        think
we must unspin
the laws that spin it.
    We think *why*   10
because we think
because.
Because we think,
  we think
    the universe about us.   15

But does it think,
  the universe?
    Then what about?
        About us?
      If not,   20
must there be cause
    in the universe?
Must it have laws?
    And what
  if the universe   25
      is not about us?
  Then what?
    What
      is it about?
  And what   30
       about *us?*

QUESTION

Is this poem merely a witty game of repeating words or does it employ sound effects to sound effect? Consider especially lines 10–15 and 24–31.

HELEN CHASIN

[*b. 1938*]

The Word *Plum*

The word *plum* is delicious

pout and push, luxury of
self-love, and savoring murmur

full in the mouth and falling   5
like fruit

taut skin
pierced, bitten, provoked into
juice, and tart flesh

question   10
and reply, lip and tongue
of pleasure.

QUESTIONS

1. How is the word *p-l-u-m* sounded and resounded in the poem? Look at and listen to lines 2–3 in particular.
2. Map out the poem's patterns of alliteration and vowel repetition.

RHYTHM AND METER

Rhythm refers to the regular recurrence of the accent or stress in poem or song. It is the pulse or beat we feel in a phrase of music or a line of poetry. We derive our sense of rhythm from everyday life and from our experience with language and music. We experience the rhythm of day and night, the seasonal rhythms of the year, the beat of our hearts, and the rise and fall of our chests as we breathe in and out.

Perhaps our earliest memories of rhythm in language are associated with nursery rhymes like

> JACK and JILL went UP the HILL★
> to FETCH a PAIL of WAter.

Later we probably learned songs like "America," whose rhythm we might indicate like this:

> MY COUN-TRY 'tis of THEE
> SWEET LAND of LIberTY
> Of THEE i SING.

Since then we have developed an ear for the rhythm of language in everyday speech:

> I THINK I'll HIT the HAY
> Did you SEE that?
> Or: Did you see THAT?
> or: GO and DON'T come BACK.

   Poets rely heavily on rhythm to express meaning and convey feeling. In "The Sun Rising" John Donne puts words together in a pattern of stressed and unstressed syllables:

> BUsy old FOOL, unRULy SUN
> WHY DOST THOU THUS
> Through WINdows, and through CURtains, CALL on US?

Donne uses four accents per line—even in the second more slowly paced short line. Later in the stanza, he retards the tempo further. Listen to the accents in the following lines:

> LOVE, all aLIKE, no SEAson knows, nor CLIME,
> Nor HOURS, DAYS, MONTHS, which ARE the RAGS of TIME.

The accents result partly from Donne's use of monosyllabic words and partly from pauses within the line (indicated by commas). Such pauses are called *caesuras* and are represented by a double slash (//). The final couplet of Donne's poem illustrates a common use of caesura—to split a line near its midpoint:

> Shine here to us, // and thou art everywhere;
> This bed thy center is, // these walls thy sphere.

Marking the accents as well, we get this:

> SHINE HERE to US, // and THOU art EVeryWHERE;
> THIS BED thy CENter IS, // THESE WALLS thy SPHERE.

★Capitalization indicates stressed syllables, lower case letters unstressed ones.

Notice again how the monosyllabic diction and the balanced phrasing combine with the caesuras to slow the lines down. The stately rhythm enforces the speaker's dignified tone and serious point: "Here is everywhere; this room is a world in itself; it is all that matters to us."

In the following brief poem by Robert Frost, you can readily hear and feel the contrasting pace and rhythms of its two lines:

The Span of Life

The OLD DOG BARKS BACKward withOUT GETting UP.
I can reMEMber when HE was a PUP.

The first line is slower than the second. It is harder to pronounce and takes longer to say because Frost clusters the hard consonants, *d, k* and *g* sounds, in the first line, and because the first line contains seven stresses to the four accents of the second. Three of the seven stresses fall at the beginning of the line, which gets it off to a slow start, whereas the accents of the second line are evenly spaced. The contrasting rhythms of the lines reinforce their contrasting images and sound effects. More importantly, however, the differences in the sounds and rhythms in the two lines echo their contrast of youth and age.

But we cannot proceed any further in this discussion of rhythm without introducing more precise terms to refer to the patterns of accents we hear in a poem. If rhythm is the pulse or beat we hear in the line, then we can define *meter* as the measure or patterned count of a poetic line. Meter is a count of the stresses we feel in the poem's rhythm. By convention the unit of poetic meter in English is the *foot,* a unit of measure consisting of stressed and unstressed syllables. A poetic foot may be either *iambic* or *trochaic, anapestic* or *dactylic.* An iambic line is composed primarily of *iambs,* an *iamb* being defined as an unaccented syllable followed by an accented one as in the word "preVENT" or "conTAIN." Reversing the order of accented and unaccented syllables we get a *trochee,* which is an accented syllable followed by an unaccented one, as in "FOOTball" or "LIquor." We can represent an accented syllable by a ´ and an unaccented syllable by a ˇ: thus, prevént (ˇ ´), an iamb, and líquŏr (´ˇ), a trochee. Because both iambic and trochaic feet contain two syllables per foot, they are called *duple* (or double) meters. These duple meters can be distinguished from *triple* meters (three-syllable meters) like anapestic and dactylic meters. An *anapest* (ˇˇ ´) consists of two unaccented syllables followed by an accented one as in comprĕHEND or intĕrVENE. A *dactyl* reverses the anapest, beginning with an accented syllable followed by two unaccented ones. DÁNgĕroŭs and CHEERfŭllŷ are examples. So is the word ANăpĕst.

Three additional points must be noted about poetic meter. First, anapestic (ˇˇ ´) and iambic (ˇ ´) meters move from an unstressed syllable to a stressed one. For this reason they are called *rising* meters. (They "rise" to the stressed syllable.) Lines in anapestic or iambic meter frequently end with a stressed syllable. Trochaic (´ˇ) and dactylic (´ˇˇ) meters, on the other hand, are said to be *falling* meters because they begin with a stressed syllable and decline in pitch and emphasis. (Syllables at the ends of trochaic and dactylic lines are generally unstressed.)

Second, the regularity of a poem's meter is not inflexible. In a predominantly iambic poem (Shakespeare's sonnet "That time of year thou may'st in me behold," for example, or Frost's "Stopping by Woods"), every line will not usually conform exactly to the strict metrical pattern. Frost's poem is much more regular in its iambic meter than is Shakespeare's, but Frost avoids metrical monotony by subtly altering his rhythm. And in one important instance Frost departs from the pattern slightly. We can divide the last stanza of Frost's poem into metrical feet and mark the accents in this manner, separating the feet with slashes.

> The woods / are love / ly, dark / and deep. /
> But I' / have pro / mises / to keep,
> And miles / to go /before / I sleep,
> And miles / to go /before / I sleep,

If we regard the pattern of this stanza and the pattern of the poem as a whole as regularly, even insistently, iambic, then the second line of this final stanza marks a slight deviation from that norm. The second and third feet of the line can be read as two accented syllables followed by two unaccented syllables, a spondaic foot followed by a pyrrhic. That's the way I've marked them. Two accented syllables together is called a *spondee* (KNICK-KNACK); two unaccented ones, a *pyrrhic* (ŏf thĕ). Both spondaic and pyrrhic feet serve as substitute feet for iambic and trochaic feet. Neither can serve as the metrical norm of an English poem.

Third, we give names to lines of poetry based on the number of feet they contain. You may have noticed in looking back at "Stopping by Woods on a Snowy Evening" that it consists of eight-syllable or *octosyllabic* lines. Since the meter is iambic (˘ ´) with two syllables per foot, the line contains four iambic feet and is hence called a *tetrameter* line (from the Greek word for *four*). Thus Frost's poem is written in *iambic tetrameter*, unlike Shakespeare's sonnet "That time of year thou may'st in me behold," for example, which contains ten-syllable lines, also predominantly iambic. Such five-foot lines are named *pentameters* (from the Greek "penta" for five), making the sonnet a poem in *iambic pentameter*.

Here is a chart of the various meters and poetic feet.

	Foot	Meter	Example
Rising or Ascending Feet	iamb	iambic	prevent
	anapest	anapestic	comprehend
Falling or Descending Feet	trochee	trochaic	football
	dactyl	dactylic	cheerfully
Substitute Feet	spondee	spondaic	knick-knack
	pyrrhic	pyrrhic	(light) of the (world)

Duple Meters: two syllables per foot: iambic and trochaic

Triple Meters: three syllables per foot: anapestic and dactylic

Number of feet per line

one foot	monometer
two feet	dimeter
three feet	trimeter
four feet	tetrameter
five feet	pentameter
six feet	hexameter
seven feet	heptameter
eight feet	octameter

You should now be better able to discern the meter and rhythm of a poem. You can make an instructive comparison for yourself by taking the measure of two poems in the same meter: Shakespeare's sonnet "That time of year thou may'st in me behold" (page 543) and Hopkins's "In the Valley of the Elwy," (page 526) both written in iambic pentameter. In Hopkins's sonnet, see if you can account for the speed of the octave and the slower pace of the sestet: look to changes in the basic iambic pattern; look for caesuras; and watch for *enjambed* or run-on lines, whose sense and grammar runs over and into the next line. You should be alert in both poems for how parallel sentence structure and the sound play of alliteration and assonance collaborate with rhythm and meter to support each poem's feeling and meaning. Listen carefully, especially to the last line of the octave and sestet of Hopkins's sonnet and to Shakespeare's concluding couplet.

Metrical Variation

We noted earlier that Frost's "Stopping by Woods" is written in strict iambic pentameter with only one slight variation in line 14. How then does Frost manage to avoid the monotony of fifteen lines of ta TUM / ta TUM / ta TUM / ta TUM / ? One way is by varying the reader's focus on different details: woods, snow, and speaker (stanza 1); horse and darkness (stanza 2); horse and snow (stanza 3); woods and darkness and speaker (stanza 4). Another is to vary the syntax, as he does with the inversion of the opening line. A third is simply to use a familiar diction in a normal speaking voice. Fourth and perhaps most important is Frost's masterful control of tempo. Of the four stanzas none carry the same pattern of end stopping. Stanza 1 is end-stopped at the first, second, and fourth lines, with line 3 enjambed. Stanza 3 is the closest to the second stanza, with two end-stopped lines and two enjambed lines. Stanza 4 is heavily stopped with two caesuras in its initial line and with end stops at every line. (It is here that we are slowed down to feel the seductive beauty of the woods; it is here that the symbolic weight of the poem is heaviest.) But we should not overlook the contrasting second stanza, which is cast as a single flowing sentence. The iambic pattern inhabits this stanza as it beats in the others. But as a result of the variety of technical resources Frost displays in the poem, we hear the iambic beat but are not overwhelmed by it.

Frost's rhythmical variations can be compared with Whitman's expressive use of metrical variation in "When I heard the learn'd astronomer," (page 545) a poem in *free verse,* verse without a fixed metrical pattern. Whitman's poem is characteristic of much free verse in its varying line lengths and accents per line, and in its imitation of the cadences of speech. The poem's final line ("Look'd up in perfect silence at the stars"), however, differs from the others, as Paul Fussell has pointed out in *Poetic Meter and Poetic Form.*★ It is written in strict iambic pentameter, a variation which carries considerable expressive power, coming after the seemingly casual metrical organization of the previous lines. Because Whitman's line must be read in the context of the whole poem for its expressive impact to be felt, you should turn to it, preferably to read it aloud. Consider whether, as some readers have suggested, the poem is not really in free verse at all, but rather in *blank verse,* unrhymed iambic pentameter.

Besides this expressive use of metrical variation, Whitman's poem exhibits additional elements of rhythmic control: in its consistency of end-stopped lines; in its flexible use of caesura (lines 2, 3, and 7); in its absence of caesura from the shorter lines (1, and 4–8). We can perhaps gain a greater appreciation of Whitman's rhythmical accomplishment by recasting his lines like this:

> When I heard the learn'd astronomer,
> When the proofs, the figures
> Were ranged in columns before me,
> When I was shown the charts and diagrams
> To add, divide, and measure them,
> When I sitting heard the astronomer
> Where he lectured to much applause
> In the lecture-room. . . .

Or like this:

> When I heard
> The learn'd astronomer,
> When the proofs,
> The figures were ranged
> In columns
> Before me,
> When I was shown
> The charts and diagrams
> To add, divide and
> Measure them. . . .

Both versions destroy the poem: they eliminate the sweep of its long lines, destroying its cadences and rhythm, and ultimately inhibiting its expressiveness.

Before leaving the poem, we should note that Whitman's rhythmic effects work together with other devices of sound, structure, and diction. In the same way, for example, that the strict iambic pentameter of the last line varies the

★Paul Fussell, *Poetic Meter and Poetic Form* (New York: Random House, 1979), p. 85.

prevailing meter expressively, so too does its assonance (the long *i*'s) deviate expressively from the poem's previously established avoidance of vowel music. In addition, the meter of the final line stresses *si'leñce* and *sta'rs,* both of which the speaker values. Finally, the iambic rhythm of the line has us looking U'P and A'T the stars, an unusual metrical effect since prepositions are almost always unstressed.

Throughout these comments on the rhythm and meter of the poems by Whitman and Frost, we have been engaged in the act of *scansion,* measuring verse, identifying its prevailing meter and rhythm, and accounting for deviations from the metrical pattern. In scanning a poem, we try to determine its dominant rhythm and meter, and to account for variations from the norm. The pattern we hear as dominant will influence how we read lines that do not conform metrically, and also how we interpret and respond to those lines. Consider, for example, the words "at a glance" abstracted from their place in a line of Wordsworth's "I wandered lonely as a cloud." Do you hear them as anapestic: ǎt ǎ gla'nce? This is a likely way to hear the words outside the context of the poem. But when we return them to the poem, we may hear them another way:

> Těn th'ousǎnd sa'w Ǐ a't ǎ gla'nce.

In such a case we will probably hear both the rhythmic pattern of the normal speaking voice (ǎt ǎ gla'nce) and the metrical pattern of iambic pentameter (a't ǎ gla'nce). Our experience of rhythm thus will often involve a tension between the two patterns as we hear one superimposed on the other.

One last note about rhythm and meter. Without the turn of the poetic line, without the division of words into lines, we have no poem. For what distinguishes poetry from prose is the line; it is the line that makes verse what it is (from the Latin *versus,* to turn). And as the poet Wendell Berry has pointed out, it is the line of verse that "checks the merely impulsive flow of speech, subjects it to another pulse, to measure."★ Without the measure of meter, without the turn of the line, there is no music and no poem. Meter and rhythm are not merely technical elements, no more than diction and imagery, syntax and structure and sound. All of these interrelated elements of poetry have effects on readers, do things to readers. We sense them and feel them and thereby understand a poem, not just with our minds, but also with our eyes and ears.

Here are a few additional poems for rhythmic and metrical consideration.

★Wendell Berry, *Standing By Words* (San Francisco: North Point Press, 1983), p. 28.

GEORGE GORDON, LORD BYRON

[1788–1824]

The Destruction of Sennacherib°

The Assyrian came down like the wolf on the fold,
And his cohorts were gleaming in purple and gold;
And the sheen of their spears was like stars on the sea,
When the blue wave rolls nightly on deep Galilee.

Like the leaves of the forest when summer is green,   5
That host with their banners at sunset were seen:
Like the leaves of the forest when autumn hath blown,
That host on the morrow lay withered and strown.

For the Angel of Death spread his wings on the blast,
And breathed in the face of the foe as he passed;   10
And the eyes of the sleepers waxed deadly and chill,
And their hearts but once heaved—and for ever grew still!

And there lay the steed with his nostril all wide,
But through it there rolled not the breath of his pride;
And the foam of his gasping lay white on the turf,   15
And cold as the spray of the rock-beating surf.

And there lay the rider distorted and pale,
With the dew on his brow, and the rust on his mail;
And the tents were all silent, the banners alone,
The lances unlifted, the trumpet unblown.   20

And the widows of Ashur are loud in their wail,
And the idols are broke in the temple of Baal;
And the might of the Gentile, unsmote by the sword,
Hath melted like snow in the glance of the Lord!

QUESTIONS

1. Identify the poem's meter. What kind of movement and rhythm does the meter
   create?
2. How is it appropriate to the action and idea of the poem?

"The Destruction of Sennacherib"   *The poem is based on the biblical account (II Kings 19:35) of the Assyrian
king, Sennacherib, whose army was destroyed by the angel of the Lord in an invasion of Jerusalem.*

ANNE SEXTON —committed suicide
[1928–1974]

Her Kind

I have gone out, a possessed witch,
haunting the black air, braver at night;
dreaming evil, I have done my hitch
over the plain houses, light by light:
lonely thing, twelve-fingered, out of mind.   5
A woman like that is not a woman, quite.
I have been her kind.

I have found the warm caves in the woods,
filled them with skillets, carvings, shelves,
closets, silks, innumerable goods;   10
fixed the suppers for the worms and the elves:
whining, rearranging the disaligned.
A woman like that is misunderstood.
I have been her kind.

I have ridden in your cart, driver,   15
waved my nude arms at villages going by,
learning the last bright routes, survivor
where your flames still bite my thigh
and my ribs crack where your wheels wind.
A woman like that is not ashamed to die.   20
I have been her kind.

QUESTIONS

1. Identify the prevailing meter of the poem. How does Sexton keep the poem moving?
2. Examine her uses of caesura and enjambment, and comment on their effect on the
   poem's rhythm.

RICHARD WILBUR
[b. 1921]

Junk

Huru Welandes
                    worc ne geswiceð
monna ænigum
                    ðara ðe Mimming can
heardne gehealdan.
                              WALDERE°

An axe angles
                    from my neighbor's ashcan;
It is hell's handiwork,
                    the wood not hickory,
The flow of the grain
                    not faithfully followed.
The shivered shaft
                    rises from a shellheap
Of plastic playthings,
                    paper plates,   5
And the sheer shards
                    of shattered tumblers
That were not annealed
                    for the time needful.
At the same curbside,
                    a cast-off cabinet
Of wavily-warped
                    unseasoned wood
Waits to be trundled
                    in the trash-man's truck.   10
Haul them off! Hide them!
                    The heart winces
For junk and gimcrack,
                    for jerrybuilt things
And the men who make them
                    for a little money,
Bartering pride
                    like the bought boxer

"Junk" **Huru Welandes . . . heardne gehealdan** *The epigraph, from* Waldere, *I, 2–4, can be translated: "Indeed Weland's handiwork does not fail any man who hard Mimming can hold." Waldere, a long Anglo-Saxon epic poem, survives only as a fragment. Weland is a lengendary Germanic smith, and Mimming is the name of a sword he made. The letter ð is called "eth" and is roughly equivalent to the modern "th."*

Who pulls his punches,
                              or the paid-off jockey   15
Who in the home stretch
                              holds in his horse.
Yet the things themselves
                              in thoughtless honor
Have kept composure,
                              like captives who would not
Talk under torture.
                    Tossed from a tailgate
Where the dump displays
                              its random dolmens,   20
Its black barrows
                    and blazing valleys,
They shall waste in the weather
                                    and toward what they were.
The sun shall glory
                         in the glitter of glass-chips,
Foreseeing the salvage
                              of the prisoned sand,
And the blistering paint
                              peel off in patches,   25
That the good grain
                         be discovered again.
Then burnt, bulldozed,
                              they shall all be buried
To the depth of diamonds,
                              in the making dark
Where halt Hephaestus
                         keeps his hammer
And Wayland's work
                         is worn away.   30

QUESTION

How does the rhythm and meter of "Junk" differ from the meters and rhythms of the
other poems in this section?

WILLIAM CARLOS WILLIAMS
[1883–1963]

The Red Wheelbarrow

so much depends
upon

a red wheel
barrow

glazed with rain
water

beside the white
chickens

QUESTIONS

1. Mark the poem's meter. Which lines match each other metrically?
2. What is the effect of the breaks between lines 3–4 and lines 5–6?

STRUCTURE: CLOSED FORM AND OPEN FORM

When we analyze a poem's structure, we focus on its patterns of organization. *Form* exists in poems on many levels from patterns of sound and image to structures of syntax and of thought; it is as much a matter of phrase and line as of stanza and whole poem.

Among the most popular forms of poetry has been the *sonnet*, a fourteen-line poem usually written in iambic pentameter (see pages 531–535). Because the form of the sonnet is strictly constrained, it is considered a *closed* or *fixed form*. We can recognize poems in fixed forms such as the sonnet, sestina, and villanelle by their patterns of rhyme, meter, and repetition; they reveal their structural patterns both aurally and visually. We see the shapes of their stanzas and the patterns of their line lengths; we feel their metrical beat, and we hear their play of sound.

The *Shakespearean* or *English sonnet* falls into three *quatrains* or four-line sections with the rhyme pattern *abab cdcd efef* followed by a *couplet* or pair of rhymed lines with the pattern *gg*. Let us reread Shakespeare's sonnet, "That time of year thou may'st in me behold."

That time of year thou may'st in me behold	*a*
When yellow leaves, or none, or few, do hang	*b*
Upon those boughs which shake against the cold,	*a*
Bare ruined choirs, where late the sweet birds sang.	*b*
In me thou see'st the twilight of such day	*c*
As after sunset fadeth in the west;	*d*
Which by-and-by black night doth take away,	*c*
Death's second self that seals up all in rest.	*d*
In me thou see'st the glowing of such fire	*e*
That on the ashes of his youth doth lie,	*f*
As the deathbed whereon it must expire,	*e*
Consumed with that which it was nourished by.	*f*
This thou perceiv'st, which makes thy love more strong,	*g*
To love that well which thou must leave ere long.	*g*

Each of the three quatrains of the poem is a single sentence, as is the couplet. This organization of the poem's sentences corresponds to its rhyme and images, which are also arranged in three quatrains and a final couplet. The pattern is reinforced, moreover, by the use of repeated words in the three quatrains: "In me behold"; "In me thou see'st"; "In me thou see'st."

There is a progression in the imagery in the sonnet: daylight becomes twilight; twilight turns into night. And there is a countermovement from images of longer duration to those of shorter: from the dying of a season to the dying of a day to the dying of a fire. In addition, within each image there is a movement from optimism to pessimism. Each image begins more hopefully than it ends: the yellow leaves become "bare ruined choirs" (lines 1–4); the twilight gives way to "Death's second self" (lines 5–8); the "glowing . . . fire" becomes "ashes" on a "deathbed" (lines 9–12).

The couplet is both a logical and an emotional response to the three quatrains that precede it. In the couplet is an implied *therefore* or *because* that can be heard by reversing the word order of its first line: Since you perceive this, it makes your love more strong. The last line is both a plea and a command to "love that well which thou must leave ere long," with "which" carrying the force of *because*.

Not every sonnet Shakespeare wrote is structured as tightly as this one. Look at the sonnets on pages 687–689 to see how Shakespeare varies this pattern, how, for example, he uses the couplet not only to respond to the quatrains, but to summarize their point or extend their implications as well.

An alternative to the Shakespearean sonnet is the *Petrarchan* or *Italian sonnet,* which falls into two parts: an *octave* of eight lines and a *sestet* of six. The octave rhyme pattern is *abba abba* (two sets of four lines); the sestet's lines are more variable: *cde cde;* or *ced ced;* or *cd cd cd.* The following is an example of the Italian form:

JOHN KEATS
[1795–1821]

On First Looking into Chapman's Homer

Much have I traveled in the realms of gold	*a*
And many goodly states and kingdoms seen;	*b*
Round many western islands have I been	*b*
Which bards in fealty° to Apollo° hold.	*a* allegiance
Oft of one wide expanse had I been told	*a* 5
That deep-browed Homer ruled as his demesne;°	*b* domain
Yet never did I breathe its pure serene°	*b* atmosphere
Till I heard Chapman speak out loud and bold:	*a*
Then felt I like some watcher of the skies	*c*
When a new planet swims into his ken;	*d* 10
Or like stout Cortez° when with eagle eyes	*c*
He stared at the Pacific—and all his men	*d*
Looked at each other with a wild surmise—	*c*
Silent, upon a peak in Darien.	*d*

Perhaps the most notable structural feature of the Italian sonnet is the way it turns on the ninth line. The first eight lines of Keats's sonnet describe the speaker's wide reading and compare reading with traveling. Lines 9–14 dramatically convey the speaker's feelings upon first reading Chapman's translation of Homer's great epic poems, *The Iliad* and *The Odyssey*. The speaker's excitement appears in lines 12 and 13, whose broken syntax contrasts with the smooth fluency of the first part of the sonnet. In addition, the octave and sestet differ in diction as well. The diction of the octave is elevated and formal, employing archaic words like "goodly" and "bards," and roundabout expressions like "realms of gold." Such words and phrases create an impression of the remoteness of the past, of its grandeur and dignity. In the sestet the diction is simpler and more direct. Keats's use of figures of comparison in the sestet contributes to the striking change in diction. The two major comparisons, both similes, convey the excitement of discovery. By means of descriptions of action (they "looked" and "stared") and reaction (their "wild surmise" and stunned silence) Keats conveys vividly the speaker's feeling of elation and excitement. Keats capitalizes on the structural possibilities of the Italian sonnet by reserving this elation for the sestet and by varying the diction of octave and sestet.

"On First Looking Into Chapman's Homer"   *Title: Translation of Homer's* Odyssey *by George Chapman, a contemporary of Shakespeare.*   [4]**Apollo**   *god of the sun and poetic inspiration.*   [11–14]**Cortez . . . Darien** *Spanish conqueror of Mexico. Balboa, not Cortez, however, was the first European to see the Pacific from Darien in Panama.*

But not all poems are written in fixed forms. Many poets have resisted the limitations inherent in using a consistent and specific metrical pattern or in rhyming lines in a prescribed manner. As an alternative to the strictness of fixed form, they developed and discovered looser, more *open* and *free forms. Open* or *free form* does not imply formlessness. It suggests, instead, that poets capitalize on the freedom either to create their own forms or to use the traditional fixed forms in more flexible ways. An example of a poem in open form by Walt Whitman follows.

WALT WHITMAN

[*1819–1892*]

When I heard the learn'd astronomer

When I heard the learn'd astronomer,
When the proofs, the figures, were ranged in columns before me,
When I was shown the charts and diagrams, to add, divide, and measure them,
When I sitting heard the astronomer where he lectured with much applause in the
　　lecture-room,
How soon unaccountable I became tired and sick,
Till rising and gliding out I wander'd off by myself,
In the mystical moist night-air, and from time to time,
Look'd up in perfect silence at the stars.

Although Whitman's poem is arranged as a single sentence, it can be divided into two parts, each of four lines. The two-part division accumulates a set of contrasts: the speaker with other people and the speaker alone; the speaker sitting inside and the speaker standing outside looking at the stars; the noise inside and the silence outside; the lecturer's activity and the speaker's passivity; the clutter of details in lines 1–4 and the spareness of details in lines 5–8.

These contrasts reflect the poem's movement from one kind of learning about nature to another: from passive listening to active observation; from indirect factual knowledge to direct mystical apprehension. Whether the poet rejects the first form of knowledge for the second, or whether he suggests that both are needed is not directly stated. The emphasis, nevertheless, is on the speaker's need to be alone and to experience nature directly.

More elaborate departures from fixed form include poems such as this unusual configuration of E. E. Cummings:

E. E. CUMMINGS

[1894–1962]

l (a

l(a

le
af
fa

ll

s)
one
l

iness

Perhaps the first things to notice are the lack of capital letters and the absence of punctuation (except for the parentheses). What we don't see is as important as what we do. We don't see any recognizable words or sentences, to say nothing of traditional stanzas or lines of poetry. The poem strikes the eye as a series of letters that stream down the page, for the most part two to a line. Rearranging the letters horizontally we find these words: *(a leaf falls) loneliness.* (The first *l* of *loneliness* appears before the parenthesis, like this: *l (a leaf falls) oneliness;* to get *loneliness* you have to move the *l* in front of *oneliness.*

A single falling leaf is a traditional symbol of loneliness; this image is not new. What is new, however, is the way Cummings has coupled the concept with the image, the way he has formed and shaped them into a nontraditional poem. But what has the poet gained by arranging his poem this way? By breaking the horizontal line of verse into a series of fragments (from the horizontal viewpoint), Cummings illustrates visually the separation that is the primary cause of loneliness. Both the word *loneliness* and the image described in *a leaf falls* are broken apart, separated in this way. In addition, by splitting the initial letter from *loneliness,* the poet has revealed the hidden *one* in the word. It's as if he is saying: loneliness is *one*-liness. This idea is further corroborated in the visual ambiguity of "l." Initially we are not sure whether this symbol "l" is a number—*one*—or the letter *l.* By shaping and arranging his poem this way, Cummings unites form and content, structure and idea. He also invites us to play the poetry game with him by remaking the poem as we put its pieces

together. In doing so we step back and see in the design of the poem a leaf
falling

> d
> o
> w
> n

the page. By positioning the letters as he does; Cummings pictures a
leaf fall:

> le
> af
> fa
> ll
> s.

If "l(a" is a poem for the eye, the following poem, also by Cummings, is
arranged for voice. From the standpoint of traditional poetic form, it too exhibits peculiarities of sound and structure, line and stanza.

E. E. CUMMINGS
[1894–1962]

[Buffalo Bill's]

> Buffalo Bill's
> defunct
>   who used to
>   ride a watersmooth-silver
>   stallion
> and break onetwothreefourfive pigeons justlikethat
>   Jesus
> he was a handsome man
>   and what i want to know is
> how do you like your blueeyed boy
> Mister Death

5

10

Before we listen closely to the voice of the poem, let's glance at how it hits
the eye. "Buffalo Bill's," "stallion," "defunct," "Jesus," and "Mister Death" are
all set on separate lines *as* complete lines. "Buffalo Bill's," "Mister Death," and
"Jesus" are the only words capitalized. "Buffalo Bill" and "Mister Death" frame
the poem; "Jesus" is set off on its own as far to the right as the line will go.
Other words also receive a visual stress. At two points in line 6, Cummings

buncheswordstogetherlikethis. Both of these visual effects are translated from eye to voice to ear so that we read the poem acknowledging the stress in each case. Cummings has used typography as a formal way of laying out language on the page to direct our reading. To see and hear what he has accomplished in this respect, read aloud the following rearranged version, which deliberately flattens the special effects Cummings highlights.

> Buffalo Bill's defunct,
> Who used to ride
> a water-smooth silver stallion
> and break one, two, three, four, five
> pigeons just like that
> Jesus he was a handsome man
> And what I would like to know is
> how do you like your
> blueeyed boy, Mister Death?

Let us, finally, summarize our remarks about structure and form. By discerning a poem's structure, we gain a clue to its meaning. We can increase our ability to apprehend a poem's organization by doing the following:

1. Looking and listening for changes of diction and imagery, tone and mood, rhythm and rhyme, time and place and circumstance.
2. Watching for repeated elements: words, images, patterns of syntax, rhythm and rhyme.
3. Remembering that structure is an aspect of meaning. It is not something independent of meaning, but works with other poetic elements to embody meaning, to formulate it. A poem's structure, its form, is part of what the poem says, part of how it means what it does.

Test out these ideas by analyzing the form of the following poems.

WILLIAM CARLOS WILLIAMS
[1883–1963]

The Dance

In Breughel's° great picture, The Kermess,
the dancers go round, they go round and
around, the squeal and the blare and the
tweedle of bagpipes, a bugle and fiddles

"The Dance"   [1]**Breughel**   *Pieter Breughel the Elder (1525–1569), Flemish painter of peasant life. The Kermess is a painting of a peasant wedding dance. See pp. 587 and 589 for reproductions of two of Breughel's paintings and the poems they inspired.*

tipping their bellies (round as the thick-
sided glasses whose wash they impound)
their hips and their bellies off balance
to turn them. Kicking and rolling about   5
the Fair Grounds, swinging their butts, those
shanks must be sound to bear up under such   10
rollicking measures, prance as they dance
in Breughel's great picture, The Kermess.

QUESTIONS

1. What kind of dance does the poem describe? What kind of action does the first long
   sentence imitate (lines 1–8)?
2. Comment on the relationship between the first and last lines.

DENISE LEVERTOV

[b. 1923]

O Taste and See

The world is
not with us enough.
O taste and see

the subway Bible poster said,
meaning The Lord, meaning   5
if anything all that lives
to the imagination's tongue,

grief, mercy, language,
tangerine, weather, to
breathe them, bite,   10
savor, chew, swallow, transform

into our flesh our
deaths, crossing the street, plum, quince,
living in the orchard and being

hungry, and plucking   15
the fruit.

QUESTION

Imagine this poem written as a single stanza. What is the advantage of the poet's having structured it as she has?

THEODORE ROETHKE

[1908–1963]

The Waking

I wake to sleep, and take my waking slow.
I feel my fate in what I cannot fear.
I learn by going where I have to go.

We think by feeling. What is there to know?
I hear my being dance from ear to ear.   5
I wake to sleep, and take my waking slow.

Of those so close beside me, which are you?
God bless the Ground! I shall walk softly there,
And learn by going where I have to go.

Light takes the Tree; but who can tell us how?   10
The lowly worm climbs up a winding stair;
I wake to sleep, and take my waking slow.

Great Nature has another thing to do
To you and me; so take the lively air,
And, lovely, learn by going where to go.   15

This shaking keeps me steady. I should know.
What falls away is always. And is near.
I wake to sleep, and take my waking slow.
I learn by going where I have to go.

QUESTION

Describe the patterns of repetition that prevail in the poem. Consider repeated rhyme and repeated lines. What is their effect on the poem's tone and feeling?

C. P. CAVAFY

[1863–1933]

The City

You said: "I'll go to another country, go to another shore,
find another city better than this one.
Whatever I try to do is fated to turn out wrong
and my heart lies buried as though it were something dead.
How long can I let my mind moulder in this place?   5
Wherever I turn, wherever I happen to look,
I see the black ruins of my life, here,
where I've spent so many years, wasted them, destroyed
   them totally."

You won't find a new country, won't find another shore.   10
This city will always pursue you. You will walk
the same streets, grow old in the same neighborhoods,
will turn gray in these same houses.
You will always end up in this city. Don't hope for things
   elsewhere: 15
there is no ship for you, there is no road.
As you've wasted your life here, in this small corner,
you've destroyed it everywhere else in the world.

TRANSLATED BY EDMUND KEELEY AND PHILIP SHERRARD

QUESTION

Why is the poem divided the way it is?

THEME

We have previously defined theme as an abstraction or generalization drawn from the details of a literary work and stated that theme refers to an idea or intellectually apprehensible meaning inherent and implicit in a work (see pages 92–93). In determining a poem's theme we should be careful neither to oversimplify the poem nor to distort its meaning. To suggest that the theme of Hayden's "Those Winter Sundays," for example, is a father's loving concern for his family is to highlight only part of the poem's meaning, for it does not take into account the speaker's remorse about his indifference to his father. Analogously, if we see Roethke's "My Papa's Waltz" as a statement about a child's terror at his father's horseplay, we misrepresent the complexity of the speaker's response to his memories of his father and their bedtime ritual.

We should also recognize that poems can have multiple themes: poems can be interpreted from more than one perspective and there is more than one way to state or explain a poem's meaning. Let us briefly reconsider Frost's "Stopping by Woods on a Snowy Evening" (page 466).

We can say, for example, that the theme of Frost's poem is the necessity to face the responsibilities inherent in adult life. We can go on to say that the poem centers on a tension in our lives between our desire for rest and peace and our need to fulfill responsibilities and meet obligations. But we shouldn't remain satisfied with this explanation. For, as we have previously stated, the speaker's "miles to go" before he "sleeps" metaphorically describes all he must accomplish before he dies. The final stanza reveals a tension between the speaker's desire to continue and an impulse to stay at rest, to ease himself into the peace of death. We might further interpret the seductiveness of death as an attractive way of escaping the pressures of circumstance and the weight of responsibility.

We can abstract yet another theme: the ability of man to appreciate beauty, particularly the beauty of nature. We might argue, for example, that Frost contrasts man's capacity for taking pleasure in watching the snow fall in a dark wood with an animal's inability to enjoy either the spectacular beauty of the scene or its serenity. Animals, unlike men, do not possess an aesthetic faculty, the ability to appreciate beauty.

Consider the subject and theme of the following poem.

EMILY DICKINSON
[1830–1886]

Crumbling is not an instant's Act

> Crumbling is not an instant's Act,
> A fundamental pause
> Dilapidation's processes
> Are organized Decays.
>
> 'Tis first a Cobweb on the Soul,   5
> A Cuticle of Dust,
> A Borer in the Axis,
> An Elemental Rust—
>
> Ruin is formal—Devil's work,
> Consecutive and slow—   10
> Fail in an instant, no man did
> Slipping—is Crash's law.

The central idea of the poem is expressed in its opening line. We might para-phrase it this way: crumbling does not happen instantaneously; it is a gradual process, occurring slowly, cumulatively over time. The remainder of the first stanza further establishes this idea by accenting how "crumbling" is a conse-quence of dilapidation, which is a result of "decay." The deterioration that re-sults is progressive; it is an organized, systematic process: one stage of decay leads to the next until destruction inevitably follows.

The gradual nature of decay is further emphasized with the statement that no one ever failed in an "instant," that the catastrophe occurs after, and as a consequence of, a series of failures. We can thus read the poem as a statement about the process of ruin (personal, emotional, financial) as well as a descrip-tion of the process of decay. And we can summarize its theme thus: failure and destruction can be traced to small-scale elements that precede and cause them.

This theme is further extended in the second stanza, which contains four im-ages of decay: cobweb, rust, dust, and the borer in the axis. These images are all accompanied by bits of specifying detail. The dust is a "cuticle," an image with suggestions of something at the "edges," of something on the outside and also of something human; the "cobweb on the soul" suggests spiritual deterio-ration ("cobwebs" suggest neglect); the "elemental" rust puts decay at the heart of things, at the center and vital core where the "borer" is operating. The poet applies each of these images of decay to a person, particularly to his or her soul: the dust encircling it, the cobweb netting it, the borer eating into it, and the rust corrupting it. Such an emphasis on spiritual decay seems further warranted by the first line of the third stanza: "Ruin is formal—devil's work." Ruin is perhaps the word most strongly suggestive of human and spiritual collapse; "devil's work" speaks for itself. Thus, a statement of the poem's theme must accommodate the idea of spiritual decay.

Centering on a poem's theme then, we work toward understanding a poem's significance—what it says, what it implies, what it means.

CHAPTER TWELVE

Approaching a Poem: Guides for Reading and Writing

The following guidelines for reading poems will help you focus on both what a poem expresses and how it expresses it. The guidelines are applied to Gerard Manley Hopkins's "Spring and Fall" and may be kept in mind as you read the poems in Chapter 16.

Guidelines for Reading

1. Read the poem a few times slowly and deliberately. If possible read it aloud. Identify the speaker, subject, situation, and tone.
2. Make sure you understand the grammar of each sentence so that you can follow what each sentence literally says. Note any deviations from normal syntax and consider the reasons for them.
3. Test the poem against your own experience. Consider how your experience with life and language can be related to the poem.
4. Attend to the words of the poem, both their denotations and their connotations. Use a dictionary to acquaint yourself with unfamiliar words and to enrich your sense of those you already know. Look for connections

among the words and images. Think about the implications of any metaphors, similes, images, or symbols you discover.

5. Listen to the poem's sound and rhythm. Identify places where music and rhythm are most expressive and try to explain why. Notice where the tempo of the poem changes or where its language is heightened or otherwise altered. Listen for changes of rhythm and rhyme and relate the poem's sound to its meaning.

6. Consider the poem's form and how its structure shapes its thought and its emotion.

7. Identify the social, cultural, and moral values that emerge in the poem. Consider how your own values influence your interpretation and evaluation of its worth.

8. Consider the poem's aesthetic merit.

GERARD MANLEY HOPKINS

[1844–1889]

Spring and Fall:
to a Young Child

Márgarét, áre you grieving
Over Goldengrove unleaving?
Leáves, like the things of man, you
With your fresh thoughts care for, can you?
Áh! ás the heart grows older   5
It will come to such sights colder
By and by, nor spare a sigh
Though worlds of wanwood leafmeal lie;
And yet you *will* weep and know why.
Now no matter, child, the name: 10
Sórrow's spríngs áre the same.
Nor mouth had, no nor mind, expressed
What heart heard of, ghost guessed:
It ís the blight man was born for,
It is Margaret you mourn for.   15

Speaker and Tone   An adult speaks to a child. The time: autumn; the place: a grove of trees where falling leaves have turned yellow. The child cries over the scene and also over something she is only dimly aware of. The speaker's tone mixes gentle consolation with mild reproof.

Diction   Line two stops us first with "Goldengrove," a combination of the word *grove* (a small woods) and the color of their leaves. We are confronted by another unusual word in "unleaving," a word the poet invented to describe the leaves falling from their branches. In line 8 we have "wanwood," and "leafmeal." On the order of *piecemeal, leafmeal* suggests that the fallen leaves have begun to be ground up into mealy fragments on the ground and "wanwood" suggests pale or dead wood. Together they also suggest natural decay.

"Ghost" (line 13) means spirit or soul. Consider the connotation of "Spring and Fall" (title) and the denotation and connotations of "blight" in line 14. Try substituting *cry* or *weep* for "mourn" (line 15). Which word works best? Why?

Syntax   The poem is composed of five sentences; two are questions and three are statements. Once clear about the words in line two, the first sentence should give no trouble, but the second is a bit more difficult. Reorder the words to clarify its sense. Here is one possibility: Can you with your fresh thoughts care for leaves as you care for the things of man? Or in slightly altered form: Can you in your innocence be sad over falling leaves with the same sorrow you feel for human loss? And should you? The couplet in lines 12–13 may be paraphrased like this: "You have never said outright and have never really been consciously aware of what you have known in your heart, what your spirit has sensed." (The colon that ends line 13 tells us that what the heart and soul has sensed will follow. Lines 14–15 complete the sense of lines 12–13. In fact line 15 completes the sense of line 14 the way line 14 explains the paraphrase of lines 12–13 above.)

Other observations about syntax: The first two interrogative sentences are couplets. The third sentence (line 5) involves a change of tone introduced by "Ah!" This third sentence is expansive, covering five lines, with a break between the fourth and fifth lines. Make sure you understand the logical connection between the assertion made in line 9 and that made in lines 5–8. Consider also how the two parts of the poem's third and fourth sentences are linked.

Imagery   Visual images inhere in the following words: "goldengrove," "wanwood," "unleaving," "leafmeal," "blight," and "springs." In addition to understanding their denotations and connotations, be alert for the sensory impression each word creates. Is "colder" (line 6) used in a tactile way? "Weep" suggests tears, of course, which are wet, thus conveying a tactile image, though more important for each is the feeling the word expresses. What implied comparisons exist in lines 5–6?

Sound   We should note that the triple rhyme on long *i* (sigh-lie-why) is framed by assonance of the same vowel sound in the lines before and after: line 6: "sights" and line 10: "child." Locate the two additional rhymes in lines 6–10. Then pick up the following alliterations: *g*'s in lines 1 and 2; *l* and *v* in lines 2 and 3; *c*'s in lines 3 and 4; *s*'s in lines 6 and 7; *w*'s and *l*'s in lines eight and nine with *y*'s in line nine; *n*'s in line 10; *s*'s in line eleven; *m*'s and *n*'s in a crisscross pattern in line 12; *h*'s and *g*'s in line 13; *b*'s in line 14; *m*'s in line 15.

Line 5, the only line not alliterated, contains an assonance on long *o* ("grows older") that introduces the rhyme in lines 5–6: "older"-"colder." This rhyme encapsulates the movement of the poem from youth to age, from caring to indifference.

And finally consider how alliteration highlights the important ideas suggested in the final lines: "*b*light . . . *b*orn"; "*M*argaret . . . *m*ourn." Notice also how the rhyme on "born"-"mourn" collaborates with that on "older"-"colder" to establish a connection between what the words literally say. The rhymes seem to suggest an inevitability, a predetermined relationship between birth and sorrow, experience and loss.

Rhythm Four things should be noted relating to the poem's rhythm. First, the rhythm is slowed down by the displaced syntax of lines 3 and 4. It is also slowed both by the alliteration in the second half of the poem and by rhyme and assonance throughout. Second, the repeated vowels and the slower pace contribute to the solemnity of the tone. Third, the parallel syntax of the final couplet and its alliteration return to the feminine rhyme used in the first six lines; the middle section of the poem (lines 7–13) departs from this feminine rhyme. Fourth, there is skillful use of caesura and enjambment to vary the poem's tempo and tone.

Meter The meter is basically trochaic, moving from accented to unaccented syllables. We can scan the first two lines to follow Hopkins's accentual markings:

Már / ğaret are yóu / grievĭng
Ovĕr / Goldĕn / grove ŭn / leavĭng?

The first line poses a slight problem since it contains an odd number of syllables. Since the trochaic pattern is clear from line 2, we adapt our scansion of line 1 to correspond. Hence the first foot of line 1 is irregular as it lacks one syllable. The remainder of the line then reads easily as trochaic, which is the poem's prevailing meter. The length of the lines is also irregular, varying from six syllables to eight. Regardless of this variation, however, we always hear four stresses per line.

Structure The pattern of rhyme in the poem includes six couplets with a triple rhyme (three rhymed lines in succession) splitting the couplets. The poem is divided into five sentences, two before and two after the long five-line sentence that includes the triple rhyme.

The poem *turns* on the triplet. The lines assert that as Margaret grows older she will learn not to weep over such a scene but for another reason. Margaret's grief frames the poem, with the first line containing an implied question (Margaret *why* are you grieving) and the last line answering it. Moreover, the speaker's answer corrects Margaret's sense of why she grieves.

Theme What then can we say about the theme of "Spring and Fall"? The last couplet suggests that Margaret is mourning the loss of innocence she now possesses as a child and the loss of life that awaits her. Sorrow, suffering, grief, loss—these are inevitable, inescapable. As we grow from childhood to adulthood, from innocence to experience, we experience a loss as well as a gain.

The "blight" of the last couplet is the blight of original sin, the blight of failure, weakness, death. "Blight" is linked to the "Fall" of the title, which suggests the fall into experience, into sin, the fall from grace, perfection, and happiness; the "Spring" of the title suggests youth, vitality, innocence, life. Overall, the poem suggests that the values and virtues of innocence don't last, and it conveys a sadness at the inevitable end of all living things.

Suggestions for Writing
The Experience of Poetry

1. Write a paper in which you recount your experience of reading a particular poem or a series of poems by the same author. You may want to compare your initial experience of reading the poem(s) with your subsequent experience.
2. Relate the action or situation of a poem to your experience. Explain how the poem is relevant to your situation, and comment on how reading and thinking about it may have helped you view your own situation and experience more clearly.

The Interpretation of Poetry

3. Characterize the speaker of any poem. Present a sketch of the speaker's character by referring to the language of the poem. Consider not only what the speaker says but the manner in which it is said and what it reveals about the speaker.
4. Describe the narrative element in any poem. Consider how important its "story" or narrative material is, and what would be gained or lost without it. Consider also how the narrative dimension of the poem would work as a story, play, or essay.
5. Explicate the opening lines of a poem. Explain the significance of the lines in the context of the poem overall.
6. Explicate the closing lines of a poem. Consider how they can be related to earlier lines.
7. Select two or more key lines from a short poem (or groups of lines from longer ones). Explain their significance and consider their relationship to one another.
8. Read five or more poems by the same poet and discuss the features they have in common.
9. Analyze a single poem that is representative of a poet's work. Explain what makes the poem representative.
10. Analyze the diction or word choices of a poem. Consider other words the poet could have chosen. Examine the denotations and connotations

of the words the poet chose. Use your analysis of the diction to develop an interpretation of the poem.

11. Analyze the imagery of a poem. List the poem's significant details (if a long poem) or all the details if it's short. Discuss what the images contribute to the poem's tone, feeling, and/or meaning.

12. Analyze the figurative language of a poem. Identify and explain each figure of speech and discuss its function in the poem overall.

13. Discuss the ironic dimensions of a poem. Identify examples of irony, and explain their significance and effect.

14. Identify the allusions in a poem and explain what they contribute to your understanding of it.

15. Analyze the structure of a poem. Consider both its overall structure and its small-scale structure—how the individual parts themselves are organized. Identify the main parts of the poem and comment on their relationship to each other.

16. Analyze the sound effects of a poem. Explain how sound contributes to its sense and spirit.

17. Analyze the rhythm and meter of a poem. Identify its prevailing metrical pattern. Acknowledge any deviations from this meter and comment on the significance of these deviations. Consider what the poem's rhythm and meter contribute to its overall meaning and feeling.

The Evaluation of Poetry

18. Discuss the values exemplified in one or more poems. Consider, that is, the cultural, moral, social, or ethical norms that either appear explicitly in the poem(s) or are implied by it. Identify those values, relate them to your own, and comment on their significance.

19. Compare two poems, evaluating their literary and linguistic merit. Explain what the two poems have in common, how they differ, and why one is superior to the other.

20. Evaluate a poem from the standpoint of its literary excellence. Explain why you consider it to be an effective or ineffective poem.

To Research or Imagine

21. Develop an alternative ending for a poem, changing the outcome of its action, altering its pattern of rhythm or rhyme, or making other changes. Be prepared to defend your alternative version as a reasonable possibility. Consider why the poet chose to end the poem as he or she did.

22. Read some letters or essays by a poet whose poetry you know and enjoy. Consider how your reading of the poet's prose aids your understanding or increases your enjoyment.

23. Read a full-scale biography of a poet whose work you admire. Write a paper explaining how the poet's life is or is not reflected in the poetic work.

24. Write a paper in which you examine how a particular poet worked within and/or against the prevailing social attitudes, moral beliefs, or cultural dispositions of his or her time.

25. Read a critical study of any poet you would like to learn more about. Write a paper explaining how reading the book has increased your understanding and/or appreciation of the poetry.

CHAPTER THIRTEEN

Transformations

REVISIONS

Unlike the goddess Athena, who sprang full-grown from the head of Zeus, poems rarely emerge fully formed from poets' heads. When they do, however, it is often because the poet worked on them both consciously and subconsciously before putting a word on paper. The product of labor as well as inspiration, good poems are the result of considerable care, of repeated efforts to find the right words and put them in the right order.

And yet for all the effort involved, the words and lines of a poem should seem natural, even inevitable. The great modern Irish poet William Butler Yeats put it this way:

> . . . A line will take us hours maybe;
> Yet if it does not seem a moment's thought,
> Our stitching and unstitching has been nought.

We suspect that these lines and the complete poem from which they are taken, "Adam's Curse," took more than a few moments to compose. So too did the following lines in which John Keats describes a woman preparing for bed. Keats's notebook reveals his struggle to bring them to the point where he felt satisfied with them. Here are the lines as published in his "The Eve of St. Agnes":

561

> . . . her vespers done,
> Of all its wreathed pearls her hair she frees
> Unclasps her warmed jewels one by one;
> Loosens her fragrant bodice; by degrees
> Her rich attire creeps rustling to her knees . . .

Other less successful renderings, however, preceded this final version of the description. Previously, for example, Keats had written "her praying done" rather than "her vespers done." And before that he had written: "her prayers said." Both of these versions are less precise and less musical than the final one. "Vespers," which means evening prayers, is more precise than "prayers"; it is also more musical, echoing the *e* of "her." For "frees" Keats had previously written "strips," a word with quite different connotations and sound. For "warmed" he had written "bosom," and for "rich," "sweet." Of her dress he had also written that it "falls light" instead of "creeps rustling" to her knees. In each case Keats worked toward phrases that possess greater sensuousness and that were richer in sound and imagistic effects. But it is in the fourth line that we can see Keats struggle hardest before he settles on "Loosens her fragrant bodice; by degrees." Here are the earlier attempts:

1. Loosens her bursting, her bodice from her
2. Loosens her bodice lace string
3. Loosens her bodice and her bosom bare
4. Loosens her fragrant bodice and doth bare/Her
5. Loosens her fragrant bodice: and down slips

We have only to consider the images and connotations of "bursting bodice" and "bosom bare" to see how different an effect is achieved with "fragrant bodice." Keats deliberately avoids the stronger sexual overtones of the earlier versions, replacing words suggesting physical sensuality with others of a sensuous rather than a sensual nature.

We can see the process of revision at work more fully in the following poem by William Blake, reprinted in two versions.

WILLIAM BLAKE

[1757–1827]

London

I wander thro' each dirty street,
Near where the dirty Thames does flow,
And [see] mark in every face I meet
Marks of weakness, marks of woe.

In every cry of every man   5
In [every voice of every child] every infant's cry of fear
In every voice, in every ban
The [german] mind forg'd [links I hear] manacles I hear.

[But most] How the chimney sweeper's cry
[Blackens o'er the churches' walls]
Every black'ning church appalls,   10
And the hapless soldier's sigh
Runs in blood down palace walls.

[But most the midnight harlot's curse
From every dismal street I hear,
Weaves around the marriage hearse   15
And blasts the new born infant's tear.]

[Alternate fourth stanza]
But most [from every] thro' wintry streets I hear
How the midnight harlot's curse
Blasts the new born infant's tear,   20
And [hangs] smites with plagues the marriage hearse.

London

I wander thro' each charter'd street,
Near where the charter'd Thames does flow,
And mark in every face I meet
Marks of weakness, marks of woe.

In every cry of every Man,   5
In every Infant's cry of fear,
In every voice, in every ban,
The mind-forg'd manacles I hear.

How the Chimney-sweeper's cry
Every black'ning Church appalls;   10
And the hapless Soldier's sigh
Runs in blood down Palace walls.

But most thro' midnight streets I hear
How the youthful Harlot's curse
Blasts the new born Infant's tear,   15
And blights with plagues the Marriage hearse.

Let's consider the changes in "London" stanza by stanza to determine the implications of each alteration and to estimate how the accumulated changes affect the tone and meaning of the poem as Blake published it.

Stanza 1   In line 1 "charter'd" replaces "dirty." Although both words are trochaic, the sound of "charter'd" echoes "wander." More important than this use of assonance are the meanings of "charter'd." It denotes something for lease or hire, something established by a charter (a written certificate defining the legal conditions under which a corporate body is organized). The applicable meaning seems to be "hired out." The word's connotations include something defined, planned, laid out, bounded, limited by law, perhaps fixed or determined by decree. Both the street and the river Thames are described as "charter'd," as hired out and bound.

The second alteration in this stanza is Blake's substitution of "mark" for "see." "Mark" means "to take notice of; to give attention; to consider." But it also suggests a more emotionally moving seeing, a more intense noticing than "see." This use of *mark* as a verb in line 3 is further intensified with its appearance as a noun in the next line. Two denotations of the word there seem applicable: "something appearing distinctly on a surface, as a line, spot, scar, or dent" and "something indicative of one's condition, feelings."

Stanza 2   "Man" replaces "man" and "Infant's" replaces "infant's." How important, in each case, is the difference? The early version of the second line has "voice" of a "child." Why do you think Blake changed these words to the "cry" of an infant, and a "cry of fear" at that? "German" in the fourth line means "germane," suggesting something closely related or akin. This word gives way in the later version to "mind-forg'd." "Links" is replaced by "manacles." Consider the denotations and connotations of the words of the later version. How does the meaning of "manacles" support the meanings of "charter'd" and "marks"? How can "manacles" be "mind-forg'd"? And why "forg'd" and not some other word like "made"?

Stanza 3   Consider the implications of the second line in both versions. In the early version the blackening is attributed to the chimney sweeper's cry. In the revised version Blake makes "black'ning" an adjective modifying Church. How can the church's walls be blackened by the cry of a chimney sweeper? And, why does Blake use the adjective "black'ning" to modify "Church"? Reflect on the connotations of "black," "blacken," and "black'ning," and consider the denotations and connotations of "appalls."

Stanza 4   Here we have more than revisions of words or lines. Though many details from the early version are carried over to the later one, they are rearranged, recombined, and rethought. In addition, some details disappear and others emerge. The rhymes, though the same, are reversed, with "hear-tear" ending the early version and "curse-hearse" concluding the final one. In the later version "the midnight harlot" has become "the youthful Harlot"—the word *youthful* a detail that intensifies our emotional response. The "curse" of the second line is both the curse that the harlot passes on to her infant, blinding it at birth with the effects of venereal disease, and the curse of the harlot's own life. Her position echoes the implications of "charter'd" and "wandered" of stanza one. She wanders the streets, but she is hardly free. She is bound, fixed, a body for hire. The final line of the stanza is the most heavily altered. "Blights" and "plagues" suggest not only the ruin of the harlot and her child, but also the destruction of the social order: marriage is cursed, innocent children suffer, soldiers die senselessly, and in general the London populace exhibits signs of desperate suffering.

Blake's revisions intensify his indictment of the institutions—moral, military, and legal—responsible for the human squalor and the misery suffered by innocent people. His revisions increase the emotional intensity of the poem as they darken its view of the lives of the people of London and, by extension, the lives of other urban inhabitants.

Below you will find two versions of three different poems. For each pair examine changes in diction, imagery, syntax, structure, sound, rhythm, meter, and meaning. Explain the significance of the changes and indicate which version of each pair you prefer and why.

WILLIAM BUTLER YEATS

[1865–1939]

A Dream of Death

I dreamed that one had died in a strange place
Near no accustomed hand,
And they had nailed the boards above her face
The peasants of that land,

And wondering planted by her solitude   5
A cypress and a yew.
I came and wrote upon a cross of wood—
Man had no more to do—

'She was more beautiful than thy first love,
This lady by the trees';   10
And gazed upon the mournful stars above,
And heard the mournful breeze.

A Dream of Death

I dreamed that one had died in a strange place
Near no accustomed hand;
And they had nailed the boards above her face,
The peasants of that land,
Wondering to lay her in that solitude,   5
And raised above her mound
A cross they had made out of two bits of wood,
And planted cypress round;
And left her to the indifferent stars above
Until I carved these words: 10
She was more beautiful than thy first love,
But now lies under boards.

QUESTIONS

1. Compare the tone of the last four lines of each version. Consider especially the difference between "mournful stars" and "indifferent stars."
2. What details have disappeared in the second version and what has been added? To what effect?

EMILY DICKINSON
[1830–1886]

The Wind begun to knead the Grass

The Wind begun to knead the Grass—
As Women do a Dough—
He flung a Hand full at the Plain—
A Hand full at the Sky—
The Leaves unhooked themselves from Trees—   5
And started all abroad—
The Dust did scoop itself like Hands—
And throw away the Road—
The Wagons quickened on the Street—
The Thunders gossiped low—   10
The Lightning showed a Yellow Head—
And then a livid Toe—
The Birds put up the Bars to Nests—
The Cattle flung to Barns—

Then came one drop of Giant Rain—
And then, as if the Hands
That held the Dams—had parted hold—
The Waters Wrecked the Sky—
But overlooked my Father's House—
Just Quartering a Tree—

The Wind begun to rock the Grass

The Wind begun to rock the Grass
With threatening Tunes and low—
He threw a Menace at the Earth—
A Menace at the Sky.

The Leaves unhooked themselves from Trees—
And started all abroad
The Dust did scoop itself like Hands
And threw away the Road.

The Wagons quickened on the Streets
The Thunder hurried slow—
The Lightning showed a Yellow Beak
And then a livid Claw.

The Birds put up the Bars to Nests—
The Cattle fled to Barns—
There came one drop of Giant Rain
And then as if the Hands

That held the Dams had parted hold
The Waters Wrecked the Sky,
But overlooked my Father's House—
Just quartering a Tree—

5

10

15

20

QUESTIONS

1. Comment on the change in the organization. Does the poem's appearance in stanzas make it easier or more difficult to read?
2. Compare the tone of the first four lines of each version.
3. In lines 11–12 of each version, which image is more consistent and more vivid?

D. H. LAWRENCE
[1885–1930]

The Piano

Somewhere beneath that piano's superb sleek black
Must hide my mother's piano, little and brown, with the back
That stood close to the wall, and the front's faded silk both torn,
And the keys with little hollows, that my mother's fingers had worn.

Softly, in the shadows, a woman is singing to me   5
Quietly, through the years I have crept back to see
A child sitting under the piano, in the boom of the shaking strings
Pressing the little poised feet of the mother who smiles as she sings.

The full throated woman has chosen a winning, living song
And surely the heart that is in me must belong   10
To the old Sunday evenings, when darkness wandered outside
And hymns gleamed on our warm lips, as we watched mother's fingers glide.

Or this is my sister at home in the old front room
Singing love's first surprised gladness, alone in the gloom.
She will start when she sees me, and blushing, spread out her hands   15
To cover my mouth's raillery, till I'm bound in her shame's heart-spun bands

A woman is singing me a wild Hungarian air
And her arms, and her bosom, and the whole of her soul is bare,
And the great black piano is clamouring as my mother's never could clamour
And my mother's tunes are devoured of this music's ravaging glamour.   20

Piano

Softly, in the dusk, a woman is singing to me;
Taking me back down the vista of years, till I see
A child sitting under the piano, in the boom of the tingling strings
And pressing the small, poised feet of a mother who smiles as she sings.

In spite of myself, the insidious mastery of song   5
Betrays me back, till the heart of me weeps to belong
To the old Sunday evenings at home, with winter outside
And hymns in the cosy parlour, the tinkling piano our guide.

So now it is vain for the singer to burst into clamour
With the great black piano appassionato. The glamour   10
Of childish days is upon me, my manhood is cast
Down in the flood of remembrance, I weep like a child for the past.

QUESTIONS

1. Which details have been eliminated from the second version? Which have been added?
2. Discuss the difference in tone and idea between the two versions of the poem.

PARODIES

A *parody* is a humorous, mocking imitation of another work. A parodic poem ridicules by distorting and exaggerating aspects of the poem it imitates. There may be distortions of the tone and purpose of the original poem or exaggerations of its stylistic mannerisms. The best parodists respect the works they parody, for to write parody well writers must understand and appreciate what they poke fun at. Good parodies catch the special manner and flavor of the originals. In them we hear echoes of the voice of the earlier poem. By extending the original beyond its limits, a parodist can point to the virtues of the poem he or she parodies. The following parody of William Carlos Williams's "This Is Just to Say" seems to do this. First, Williams's poem.

WILLIAM CARLOS WILLIAMS
[1883–1963]

This Is Just to Say

I have eaten
the plums
that were in
the icebox

and which   5
you were probably
saving
for breakfast

Forgive me
they were delicious   10

so sweet
and so cold

Now Kenneth Koch's parody:

KENNETH KOCH

[b. 1925]

Variations on a Theme by William Carlos Williams

1

I chopped down the house that you had been saving to live in next summer.
I am sorry, but it was morning, and I had nothing to do
and its wooden beams were so inviting.

2

We laughed at the hollyhocks together
And then I sprayed them with lye.
Forgive me. I simply do not know what I am doing.

3

I gave away the money that you had been saving to live on for the next ten years.
The man who asked for it was shabby
and the firm March wind on the porch was so juicy and cold.

4

Last evening we went dancing and I broke your leg.
Forgive me. I was clumsy, and
I wanted you here in the wards, where I am the doctor!

QUESTIONS

1. Explain Koch's title.
2. Would his parody be as effective if he cut it down to one or two stanzas? If the four stanzas were rearranged? How long, in comparison, is Williams's poem, and why do you think Koch made his parody four times as long?
3. What do the four variations have in common?
4. Does the parody seem fair to Williams? Is it a coherent and engaging poem in its own right?

The following poem and its parodic counterpart are sonnets. Gary Hatch follows G. M. Hopkins closely as he parodies "Carrion Comfort," imitating the earlier poet's syntax strictly in some lines and more loosely in others.

GERARD MANLEY HOPKINS

[1844–1889]

Carrion Comfort

Not, I'll not, carrion comfort, Despair, not feast on thee;
Not untwist—slack they may be—these last strands of man
In me ór, most weary, cry *I can no more.* I can;
Can something, hope, wish day come, not choose not to be.

But ah, but O thou terrible, why wouldst thou rude on me   5
Thy wring-world right foot rock? lay a lionlimb against me? scan
With darksome devouring eyes my bruisèd bones? and fan,
O in turns of tempest, me heaped there; me frantic to avoid thee and flee?

Why? That my chaff might fly; my grain lie, sheer and clear.
Nay in all that toil, that coil, since (seems) I kissed the rod,   10
Hand rather, my heart lo! lapped strength, stole joy, would laugh, chéer.
Cheer whom though? The hero whose heaven-handling flung me, fóot tród
Me? or me that fought him? O which one? is it each one? That night, that year
Of now done darkness I wretch lay wrestling with (my God!) my God.

GARY LAYNE HATCH

[b. 1964]

Terrier Torment; or, Mr. Hopkins and his Dog

(FROM THE LESSER-KNOWN TERRIER SONNETS)

Put, stay put, Terrier Torment, Heel! I'll put on thee—
Quick though thou be—this leash. And,
Most wary, try to hold you still. I can;
Plan something—hold, wash dog, (come!) not choose to let you flee.

But ow! but oh thou terrier, why wouldst thou, wet on me,   5
Thy bark-loud-mutt-mouth munch? put a puppy paw against me? You plan
With funsome, frolicking eyes to dodge my dives and land
(Ow!) in squalls of squiggling—dog-piled there—wiggling to get free.

Why? That thy hair might dry, thy fur lie sheen and clean.
In all that toil, that soil, since (seems) I washed the dog,   10
(Dried rather) his hide (oh!) gobbed grime, caked crud.
I could wash, clean. Clean whom though? Him whose water-wiggling soused me, sud
Soaked me? or me that caught him? O which one? is it each one? That hour, that day
That soap-sick Saturday when I (drench) lay wrestling with my doggone dog.

                                                                              (1995)

In the next pair of poems you hear two very different voices. Account for
the difference in tone between them. Explain how Howard Moss's poem parodies Shakespeare's sonnet. Consider, finally, the sense the later poem makes
on its own, unrelated to the sonnet.

WILLIAM SHAKESPEARE

[1564–1616]

Shall I compare thee to a summer's day

Shall I compare thee to a summer's day?
Thou art more lovely and more temperate:
Rough winds do shake the darling buds of May,
And summer's lease hath all too short a date;
Sometime too hot the eye of heaven shines,   5
And often is his gold complexion dimm'd;
And every fair from fair sometime declines,
By chance or nature's changing course untrimm'd:
But thy eternal summer shall not fade
Nor lose possession of that fair thou ow'st;   10
Nor shall Death brag thou wand'rest in his shade,
When in eternal lines to time thou grow'st;
So long as men can breathe or eyes can see,
So long lives this, and this gives life to thee.

HOWARD MOSS
[*b. 1922*]

Shall I Compare Thee to a Summer's Day?

Who says you're like one of the dog days?
You're nicer. And better.
Even in May, the weather can be gray,
And a summer sub-let doesn't last forever.
Sometimes the sun's too hot;   5
Sometimes it is not.
Who can stay young forever?
People break their necks or just drop dead!
But you? Never!
If there's just one condensed reader left   10
Who can figure out the abridged alphabet
    After you're dead and gone,
    In this poem you'll live on!

Finally, consider the following brief poem by Robert Frost and an equally
brief parody by Bob McKenty.

ROBERT FROST
[*1874–1963*]

Dust of Snow

The way a crow
Shook down on me
The dust of snow
From a hemlock tree

Has given my heart   5
A change of mood
And saved some part
Of a day I had rued.

BOB MCKENTY

[b. 1935]

Snow on Frost

A wayward crow
Shook down on him
The dust of snow
From a hemlock limb.

Amused (I recall)   5
The poet stopped,
Delighted that's all
The black bird dropped.

QUESTION

In what ways does McKenty's parody mimic Frost's poem? In what ways does the
parody depart from the original?

TRANSLATIONS

Robert Frost once described poetry as "what gets lost in translation." He
meant, of course, that it is impossible to carry over from one language into another the special qualities of a poem—its sound and rhythm, its meter, syntax,
and connotations. Some critics have felt that in translating poems, translators
betray them, inevitably turning the translation into something which at best
may approximate, but which invariably distorts, the original. This point of view,
however, has not prevented translators from continuing their difficult but important work. (To appreciate the difficulties translators encounter, try translating a short poem such as Frost's "The Span of Life," page 533, if you know a
second language.)

    Read the following poems in their original languages if you know them.
There are two translations for three of the poems. Compare the translations as
poems in their own right. What differences do you notice in the choices translators have made in diction and imagery, in line length and rhythm, in syntax
and rhyme? Which of the paired translations do you prefer as a translation?
Which as a poem in itself?

RAINER MARIA RILKE
[1875–1926]

Der Panther

IM JARDIN DES PLANTES, PARIS

Sein Blick ist vom Vorübergehn der Stäbe
so müd geworden, daß er nichts mehr hält.
Ihm ist, als ob es tausend Stäbe gäbe
und hinter tausend Stäben keine Welt.

Der weiche Gang geschmeidig starker Schritte,   5
der sich im allerkleinsten Kreise dreht,
ist wie ein Tanz von Kraft um eine Mitte,
in der betäubt ein großer Wille steht.

Nur manchmal schiebt der Vorhang der Pupille
sich lautlos auf—. Dann geht ein Bild hinein,   10
geht durch der Glieder angespannte Stille—
und hört im Herzen auf zu sein.

The Panther

IN THE JARDIN DES PLANTES, PARIS

His vision, from the constantly passing bars
has grown so weary that it cannot hold
anything else. It seems to him there are
a thousand bars; and behind the bars, no world.

As he paces in cramped circles, over and over,   5
the movement of his powerful soft strides
is like a ritual dance around a center
in which a mighty will stands paralyzed.

Only at times, the curtain of the pupils
lifts, quietly—. An image enters in,   10
rushes down through the tensed, arrested muscles,
plunges into the heart and is gone.

TRANSLATED BY STEPHEN MITCHELL

The Panther

JARDIN DES PLANTES, PARIS

His sight from ever gazing through the bars
has grown so blunt that it sees nothing more.
It seems to him that thousands of bars are
before him, and behind them nothing merely.

The easy motion of his supple stride,   5
which turns about the very smallest circle,
is like a dance of strength about a center
in which a mighty will stands stupefied.

Only sometimes when the pupil's film
soundlessly opens . . . then one image fills   10
and glides through the quiet tension of the limbs
into the heart and ceases and is still.

TRANSLATED BY C. F. MACINTYRE

GUILLAUME APOLLINAIRE

[1880–1918]

Le Pont Mirabeau

Sous le pont Mirabeau coule la Seine
    Et nos amours
    Faut-il qu'il m'en souvienne
La joie venait toujours après la peine

    Vienne la nuit sonne l'heure   5
    Les jours s'en vont je demeure

Les mains dans les mains restons face à face
    Tandis que sous
    Le pont de nos bras passe
Des éternels regards l'onde si lasse   10

    Vienne la nuit sonne l'heure
    Les jours s'en vont je demeure

L'amour s'en va comme cette eau courante
L'amour s'en va
Comme la vie est lente   15
Et comme l'Espérance est violente

Vienne la nuit sonne l'heure
Les jours s'en vont je demeure

Passent les jours et passent les semaines
Ni temps passé   20
Ni les amours reviennent
Sous le pont Mirabeau coule la Seine

Vienne la nuit sonne l'heure
Les jours s'en vont je demeure

Mirabeau Bridge

Under the Mirabeau Bridge there flows the Seine
Must I recall
Our loves recall how then
After each sorrow joy came back again

Let night come on bells end the day   5
The days go by me still I stay

Hands joined and face to face let's stay just so
While underneath
The bridge of our arms shall go
Weary of endless looks the river's flow   10

Let night come on bells end the day
The days go by me still I stay

All love goes by as water to the sea
All love goes by
How slow life seems to me   15
How violent the hope of love can be

Let night come on bells end the day
The days go by me still I stay

The days the weeks pass by beyond our ken
Neither time past   20

Nor love comes back again
Under the Mirabeau Bridge there flows the Seine

Let night come on bells end the day
The days go by me still I stay

TRANSLATED BY RICHARD WILBUR

The Mirabeau Bridge

LE PONT MIRABEAU

Under the Mirabeau Bridge the Seine
Flows and our love
Must I be reminded again
How joy came always after pain

Night comes the hour is rung   5
The days go I remain

Hands within hands we stand face to face
While underneath
The bridge of our arms passes
The loose waves of our gazing which is endless   10

Night comes the hour is rung
The days go I remain

Love slips away like this water flowing
Love slips away
How slow life is in its going   15
And hope is so violent a thing

Night comes the hour is rung
The days go I remain

The days pass the weeks pass and are gone
Neither time that is gone   20
Nor love ever returns again
Under the Mirabeau Bridge flows the Seine

Night comes the hour is rung
The days go I remain

TRANSLATED BY W. S. MERWIN

JUAN RAMÓN JIMÉNEZ
[1881–1958]

Nocturno Soñado

La tierra lleva por la tierra;
mas tú, mar,
llevas por el cielo.
   ¡Con qué seguridad de luz de plata y oro,
nos marcan las estrellas   5
la ruta!—Se diría
que es la tierra el camino
del cuerpo,
que el mar es el camino
del alma—.   10
   Sí, parece
que es el alma la sola viajera
del mar, que el cuerpo, solo,
se quedó allá en las playas,
sin ella, despidiéndola,   15
pesado, frío, igual que muerto.
   ¡Qué semejante
el viaje del mar al de la muerte,
al de la eterna vida!

Dream Nocturne

The earth leads through the earth;
but you, sea,
lead through heaven.
   With what a steady light of gold and silver
do the stars show us   5
the way!—One would say
that the earth is the way
of the flesh,
that the sea is the way
of the soul—.   10
   Yes, it seems
that the soul is the only traveler
of the sea, that the flesh, alone,
remained there on the shore
without her, saying farewell,   15

heavy and cold, like unto death.
   A voyage on the ocean,
how it resembles the voyage to death,
voyage to life eternal!

TRANSLATED BY ELEANOR L. TURNBULL

Dream Nocturne

The earth leads by the earth.
But, sea,
You lead by the heavens.
With what security of gold and silver light
Do the stars mark the road for us!   5
One would think
That the earth was the road
Of the body,
That the sea was the road
Of the soul.   10
Yes. It seems
That the soul is the only traveler
Of the sea; that the body, alone,
Remains behind, on the beach,
Without her, saying goodbye,   15
Heavy, cold, as though dead.
How like
Is a journey by sea
To death,
To eternal life!

TRANSLATED BY THOMAS MCGREEVY

POEMS AND PAINTINGS

In Roman times and again during the Renaissance, poems were characterized as speaking pictures and painting as silent poetry. A poem, that is, was seen as a visual image given speech, a painting as a silent visual poem. Earlier, in our discussion of structure, we noted that the shape of a poem, its arrangement on the page, is an important dimension of its effect.

Here, however, we will consider another dimension of the relationship between words and visual images. On the pages that follow you will find poems paired with the paintings that inspired them. Three of the paintings are accompanied by more than one poem so you will have a chance to compare different interpretations and "translations" of a painting into a poem. As you consider each pair, spend some time looking carefully at the painting. Take an inventory of its details; observe its color and texture, its organization and perspective, its line, and its form. Think about the implications of its title; examine the action or scene it depicts. Then read the poem(s) as interpretation(s) and translation(s) of the painting. Notice what the poets include, what they omit, what they alter.

Even though you will be comparing poem with painting and poem with poem, remember that each poem is a separate and individual work. Read each the way you would read any other poem, giving careful attention to its formal elements. Consider whether the poems can stand alone without their corresponding paintings. And finally, observe how each poet has transformed the painting to create a new work, one which conveys its own feelings and bears its own implications.

QUESTIONS

Vincent Van Gogh, *The Starry Night*

1. About the series of poems he wrote based on Van Gogh's paintings, Robert Fagles has written: "I wanted to try my hand at a kind of translation I hadn't done before, not from a foreign language, but from a group of paintings." What has Fagles translated from the painting into the poem?
2. Does either Fagles's poem or Sexton's help you to see things in the painting that you had overlooked? Why or why not?
3. Does either poem seem to emphasize the painting more than the painter? Does it present a neutral description of the work? Does it imply or state a judgment about either the artist or his painting?
4. Compare Fagles's poem with Anne Sexton's "The Starry Night" (page 584). Consider tone, imagery, structure, and feeling.

Francesco Goya y Lucientes, *The Third of May*

1. Compare Gewanter's use of Goya with Fagles's use of Van Gogh. How does each poet convey the sense of the art he describes? How does each use that art for his own purposes?
2. Is Gewanter's poem comprehensible without the *painting*? Why or why not? How does the poem help you to see and understand Goya's art better?

Pieter Breughel the Elder, *Landscape with the Fall of Icarus*

1. Where is Icarus mentioned in Auden's poem? What does Auden end with and what does that ending imply?
2. How does Auden's poem offer us a clue to its intentions from the beginning? Would it matter if Auden's stanzas were reversed? Why or why not?
3. "Museé des Beaux Arts" can be divided into two parts. What is their relationship?
4. How does the title of Auden's poem reflect its author's preoccupations with the painting?

Pieter Breughel the Elder, *Hunters in the Snow*

1. How does Langland's poem better help you to see the details of the painting? How does the poem help you to better understand its symbolic implications?
2. Where does the poem depart from the details of the painting? In what ways and for what purposes?
3. What is emphasized in the opening stanza and the ending?
4. Langland's poem neither rhymes nor uses a consistent metrical pattern, yet it does exhibit formal organization. What devices of form, sound, and rhythm does it include? What do they contribute to the meaning and feeling of the work?

Edward Hopper, *Sunday*

1. How would you characterize the mood of Hopper's painting? What details contribute to or help establish that mood?
2. What does the poet E. Ward Herlands do with Hopper's painting? How does her treatment differ from the other poets inspired by paintings?
3. What is different about the form of Herlands's piece, a "prose poem"? What qualities make it poetic, and what qualities make it prosaic?

William Blake, *The Sick Rose*

1. How does Blake's art help you to understand his poem? How does it enable you to see something about the poem you may have overlooked, or to make connections you may have missed?
2. To what extent, if any, does Blake's illustration channel your reading of the poem, limiting the way you interpret it? Is it possible that the poem was written to illustrate the painting, or do you think the painting was designed to parallel the poem?

Sandro Botticelli, Giotto di Bondone, *The Adoration of the Magi*

1. Compare the two paintings as stories. What does Botticelli emphasize? What does Giotto focus on? Identify figures common to both paintings and explain their significance.
2. Compare Eliot's and Yeats's poems as treatments of the general subject of the Magi. What is Yeats's concern and what is Eliot's? Do you think either poem was inspired by a painting? Why or why not?
3. Consider the poetic styles of Eliot and Yeats. Characterize each by focusing on the poet's uses of language and detail, rhythm and structure.
4. Who is the speaker in Eliot's poem? In Yeats's? Which line or lines in each poem best reveal the speaker's attitude toward what he describes?

Henri Matisse, *Dance*

1. How would you characterize the mood and spirit of the painting? What elements contribute most to these?
2. What is the significance of the ring of dancers and of the space between two of them?

3. Describe the relationship between Matisse's painting and Natalie Safir's poem. To what extent do the two works share a common theme and tone?

4. Why do you think Matisse used large patches of bold simple colors against which to set his human figures? How detailed is his rendering of the human figures? What is the effect of that rendering?

Pablo Picasso, *Girl with Mandolin*

1. What do you see when you look at Picasso's painting? What is the effect of the painter's transforming and combining objects in the manner he has done here?

2. What is the relation of Vinnie D'Ambrosio's poem to Picasso's painting?

3. Consider the language D'Ambrosio employs, especially the sounds of the words she uses. Why does she choose the sounds she does?

4. Do you prefer this painting of Picasso or the next one? Why?

Pablo Picasso, *Still Life with Pitcher, Bowl, & Fruit*

1. What elements of Picasso's painting are echoed in the poem?

2. To what extent does D'Ambrosio's poem suggest Picasso's style of painting?

3. If you could devise an alternative title for this painting, what would it be? Why?

4. Identify elements of sound play in Vinnie D'Ambrosio's poem. What do they contribute to the tone of the poem? What feeling do you come away with from reading "If I Were a Maker I'd"?

Gustav Klimt, *The Kiss*

1. What is your initial impression upon looking at Klimt's painting? How would you characterize the painting's style? its emphasis?

2. What effect does Ferlinghetti's poem have on your subsequent viewing of the painting? Why?

3. To what extent is Ferlinghetti's poem a description of Klimt's painting? To what extent is his poem an interpretation of the painting? Where is this interpretive inclination strongest?

4. Do you think the title of the poem and that of the painting are aptly chosen? Why or why not?

Vincent van Gogh, The Starry Night (1889). OIL ON CANVAS, 29 × 36 1/4″.
COLLECTION, THE MUSEUM OF MODERN ART, NEW YORK.
ACQUIRED THROUGH THE LILLIE P. BLISS BEQUEST.

ANNE SEXTON

[1928–1975]

The Starry Night

That does not keep me from having a terrible need of—shall I say the word—religion.
Then I go out at night to paint the stars.

VINCENT VAN GOGH in a letter to his brother

The town does not exist
except where one black-haired tree slips
up like a drowned woman into the hot sky.
The town is silent. The night boils with eleven stars
Oh starry starry night! This is how   5
I want to die.

It moves. They are all alive.
Even the moon bulges in its orange irons
to push children, like a god, from its eye.
The old unseen serpent swallows up the stars.   10
Oh starry starry night! This is how
I want to die:

into that rushing beast of the night,
sucked up by that great dragon, to split
from my life with no flag,   15
no belly,
no cry.

584

ROBERT FAGLES

[*b. 1933*]

The Starry Night

Long as I paint
I feel myself
less mad
the brush in my hand
a lightning rod to madness   5

But never ground that madness
execute it ride the lightning up
from these benighted streets and steeple up
with the cypress look its black is burning green

I am that I am it cries   10
it lifts me up the nightfall up
the cloudrack coiling like a dragon's flanks
a third of the stars of heaven wheeling in its wake
wheels in wheels around the moon that cradles round the sun

and if I can only trail these whirling eternal stars   15
with one sweep of the brush like Michael's sword if I can
cut the life out of the beast—safeguard the mother and the son
all heaven will hymn in conflagration blazing down
          the night the mountain ranges down
the claustrophobic valleys of the mad   20

                    Madness
          is what I have instead of heaven
          God deliver me—help me now deliver
          all this frenzy back into your hands
          our brushstrokes burning clearer into dawn   25

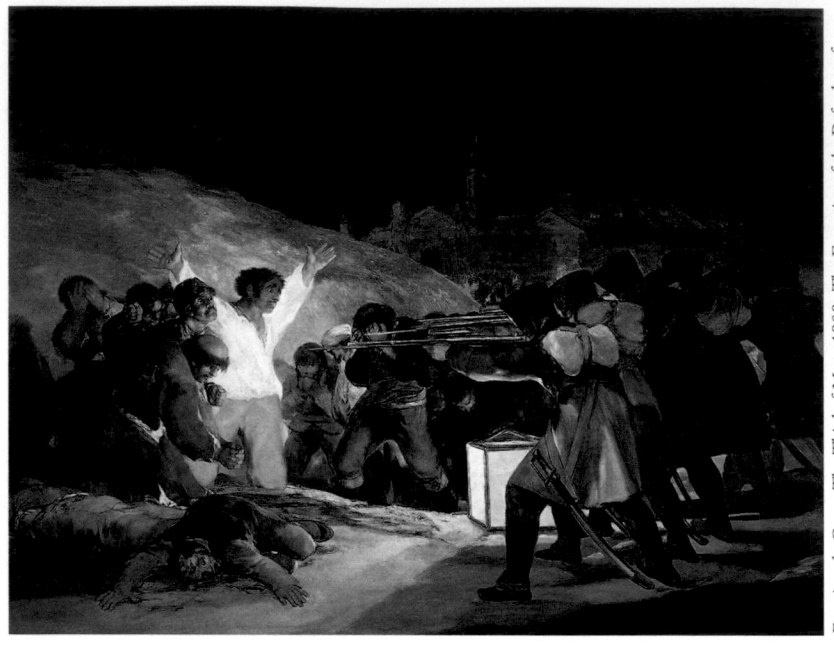

Francisco de Goya, The Third of May, 1808: The Execution of the Defenders of Madrid (1814). PRADO MUSEUM, MADRID. SCALA/ART RESOURCE.

DAVID GEWANTER
[b. 1954]

Goya's "The Third of May, 1808"

I'll show you:
onto the dirt-grey
canvas he's smeared—
jam on bread—
a sticky red for blood   5
oozed from the broken
heads and shot-up bodies
heaped near the cowering group
agape at soldiers hunched above
their knived rifles.   10
The air is oil-black,
smokeless, the whole scene
painted right before the guns
report, and more killed;
see the soldiers bend   15
in careful aim, bent
like mothers nursing—
one geometry of care:
exact angle for Madonna,
for men aiming murder—   20
and yet suspended,
the crisis held up for us

to observe at leisure—
in "The Resurrection" by
Grünewald, think how Christ   25
has bolted from his tomb,
rising, splendid,
while blinded soldiers
hurl themselves down,
never landing—   30
all are trapped in place:
one can't reach heaven,
the others never fall—
and here, before the dull wedge
representing *hill*,   35
one of Goya's victims
raises his arms up,
waiting always—
you know him, his shirt
blank as a page—   40
here, hand me a butterknife
to scrape with, I'll show you how
he painted bullets
inside the painted guns.

586

Pieter Breughel the Elder, Landscape with the Fall of Icarus (c. 1558).
MUSÉES ROYAUX DES BEAUX-ARTS, BRUSSELS. SCALA/ART RESOURCE, NY.

W. H. AUDEN
[1907–1973]

Musée des Beaux Arts

About suffering they were never wrong,
The old Masters: how well they understood
Its human position: how it takes place
While someone else is eating or opening a window or just walking dully along;
How, when the aged are reverently, passionately waiting   5
For the miraculous birth, there always must be
Children who did not specially want it to happen, skating
On a pond at the edge of the wood:
They never forgot
That even the dreadful martyrdom must run its course   10
Anyhow in a corner, some untidy spot
Where the dogs go on with their doggy life and the torturer's horse
Scratches its innocent behind on a tree.

In Breughel's *Icarus,* for instance: how everything turns away
Quite leisurely from the disaster; the ploughman may   15
Have heard the splash, the forsaken cry,
But for him it was not an important failure; the sun shone
As it had to on the white legs disappearing into the green
Water, and the expensive delicate ship that must have seen
Something amazing, a boy falling out of the sky,   20
Had somewhere to get to and sailed calmly on.

587

[b. 1917]

Hunters in the Snow: Breughel

Quail and rabbit hunters with tawny hounds,
Shadowless, out of late afternoon
Trudge toward the neutral evening of indeterminate form.
Done with their blood-annunciated day
Public dogs and all the passionless mongrels   5
Through deep snow
Trail their deliberate masters
Descending from the upper village home in lowering light.
Sooty lamps
Glow in the stone-carved kitchens.   10

This is the fabulous hour of shape and form
When Flemish children are gray-black-olive
And green-dark-brown
Scattered and skating informal figures
On the mill ice pond.   15
Moving in stillness
A hunched dame struggles with her bundled sticks,
Letting her evening's comfort cudgel her
While she, like jug or wheel, like a wagon cart
Walked by lazy oxen along the old snowlanes,   20
Creeps and crunches down the dusky street.
High in the fire-red dooryard
Half unhitched the sign of the Inn
Hangs in wind
Tipped to the pitch of the roof.   25
Near it anonymous parents and peasant girl,
Living like proverbs carved in the alehouse walls,
Gather the country evening into their arms
And lean to the glowing flames.

Now in the dimming distance fades   30
The other village; across the valley
Imperturbable Flemish cliffs and crags
Vaguely advance, close in loom
Lost in nearness. Now
The night-black raven perched in branching boughs   35
Opens its early wing and slipping out
Above the gray-green valley
Weaves a net of slumber over the snow-capped homes.
And now the church, and then the walls and roofs
Of all the little houses are become   40

Close kin to shadow with small lantern eyes.
And now the bird of evening
With shadows streaming down from its gliding wings
Circles the neighboring hills
Of Hertogenbosch, Brabant.   45

Darkness stalks the hunters,
Slowly sliding down,
Falling in beating rings and soft diagonals.
Lodged in the vague vast valley the village sleeps.

Pieter Breughel the Elder, Hunters in the Snow (1565). KUNSTHISTORISCHES MUSEUM, VIENNA. ART RESOURCE, NY.

Edward Hopper, Sunday, (1926). OIL ON CANVAS, 29 × 36 1/4″. THE MUSEUM OF MODERN ART, NEW YORK. ACQUIRED THROUGH THE LILLIE P. BLISS BEQUEST.

E. WARD HERLANDS

[b. 1925]

When Edward Hopper Was Painting

I like to think that on a Sunday afternoon when Edward Hopper was painting his lone man seated on a street curb, with shaft of light warming that man's right arm & right cheek, I like to think that on that very same day I was there, somewhere round that corner, dressed in a Wedgewood-blue velvet-collared English wool coat, (incongruous elegance for a workingman's child) offspring of a proud Austro-Hungarian immigrant & a first generation American. I like to believe that in the minutes just after the seated man arose from his head-bowed position, that my father came strolling down the very same street pushing me in my gray straw perambulator & when his path & ours were parallel & as that man approached, I like to think that the lone man in the Hopper painting looked down at me, smiled & said, Nice kid you've got there, Dad.

William Blake, The Sick Rose from *Songs of Experience* (1794).
THE HUNTINGTON LIBRARY, SAN MARINO, CALIFORNIA.

WILLIAM BLAKE
[1757–1827]

The Sick Rose

O Rose, thou art sick!
The invisible worm
That flies in the night,
In the howling storm,

Has found out thy bed
Of crimson joy,
And his dark secret love
Does thy life destroy.

Sandro Botticelli, Adoration of the Magi (c. 1475).
UFFIZI GALLERY, FLORENCE. SCALA/ART RESOURCE, NY.

T. S. ELIOT
[1888–1965]

Journey of the Magi

'A cold coming we had of it,
Just the worst time of the year
For a journey, and such a long journey:
The ways deep and the weather sharp,
The very dead of winter.'   5
And the camels galled, sore-footed, refractory,
Lying down in the melting snow.
There were times we regretted
The summer palaces on slopes, the terraces,
And the silken girls bringing sherbet.   10
Then the camel men cursing and grumbling
And running away, and wanting their liquor and women,
And the night-fires going out, and the lack of shelters,
And the cities hostile and the towns unfriendly
And the villages dirty and charging high prices: 15
A hard time we had of it.
At the end we preferred to travel all night,
Sleeping in snatches,
With the voices singing in our ears, saying
That this was all folly.   20

Then at dawn we came down to a temperate valley,
Wet, below the snow line, smelling of vegetation;
With a running stream and a water-mill beating the darkness,
And three trees on the low sky,

And an old white horse galloped away in the meadow.   25
Then we came to a tavern with vine-leaves over the lintel,
Six hands at an open door dicing for pieces of silver,
And feet kicking the empty wine-skins.
But there was no information, and so we continued
And arrived at evening, not a moment too soon   30
Finding the place; it was (you may say) satisfactory.

All this was a long time ago, I remember,
And I would do it again, but set down
This set down
This: were we led all that way for   35
Birth or Death? There was a Birth, certainly,
We had evidence and no doubt. I had seen birth and death,
But had thought they were different; this Birth was
Hard and bitter agony for us, like Death, our death.
We returned to our places, these Kingdoms,   40
But no longer at ease here, in the old dispensation,
With an alien people clutching their gods.
I should be glad of another death.

Giotto di Bondone, Adoration of the Magi (1313).
SCROVEGNI CHAPEL, PADUA. SCALA/ART RESOURCE.

WILLIAM   BUTLER   YEATS
[1865–1939]

The Magi

Now as at all times I can see in the mind's eye,
In their stiff, painted clothes, the pale unsatisfied ones
Appear and disappear in the blue depth of the sky
With all their ancient faces like rain-beaten stones,
And all their helms of silver hovering side by side,   5
And all their eyes still fixed, hoping to find once more,
Being by Calvary's turbulence unsatisfied,
The uncontrollable mystery on the bestial floor.

Henri Matisse, Dance (first version). Paris. (March 1909). OIL ON CANVAS, 8′ 6 1/2″ × 12′ 9 1/2″. MUSEUM OF MODERN ART, NEW YORK. GIFT OF NELSON A. ROCKEFELLER IN HONOR OF ALFRED H. BARR, JR.

NATALIE SAFIR

[*b. 1935*]

Matisse's Dance

A break in the circle dance of naked women,
dropped stitch between the hands
of the slender figure stretching too hard
to reach her joyful sisters.

Spirals of glee sail from the arms   5
of the tallest woman. She pulls the circle
around with her fire. What has she found
that she doesn't keep losing,
her torso a green-burning torch?

Grass mounds curve ripely beneath   10
two others who dance beyond the blue.
Breasts swell and multiply and
rhythms rise to a gallop.

Hurry, frightened one, and grab on—before
the stitch is forever lost, before the dance   15
unravels and a black sun swirls from that space.

Pablo Picasso, Girl with a Mandolin (Fanny Tellier). Paris (late spring 1910). OIL ON CANVAS 39 1/2″ × 29″. THE MUSEUM OF MODERN ART, NEW YORK NELSON A. ROCKEFELLER BEQUEST.

VINNIE-MARIE D'AMBROSIO
[b. 1928]

If I Were a Maker I'd

make a melon
            orange in yellow
add a rod
fret it   and string it

and trim a pick   5
from a suppleplump pit.

My tools would burgeon
bunches of grapes and

            then ghosts in motley
            no–shaped and graced
            would pin the grapes

to their pointed shoes   and ring-a-ling them.

One shade would dandle my banjo gently—
and soon

you'd see a melon roll through air!
you'd see grapes leaping and lighting!

and you'd hear my mooncurled song!

Pablo Picasso, Still Life with Pitcher, Bowl, & Fruit (1931). PRIVATE COLLECTION.
GIRAUDON/ART RESOURCE, NY.

Gustav Klimt, The Kiss (1907–1908). KUNSTHISTORICHES
MUSEUM, VIENNA. ERICK LESSING/ART RESOURCE, NY.

LAWRENCE FERLINGHETTI
[b. 1919]

Short Story on a Painting of Gustav Klimt

They are kneeling upright on a flowered bed
  He
     has just caught her there
             and holds her still
    Her gown   5
       has slipped down
              off her shoulder
  He has an urgent hunger
        His dark head
            bends to hers   10
              hungrily
And the woman the woman
  turns her tangerine lips from his
     one hand like the head of a dead swan
        draped down over   15
               his heavy neck
       the fingers
        strangely crimped
           tightly together
  her other arm doubled up   20
      against her tight breast

597

                    her hand a languid claw
                                    clutching his hand
                        which would turn her mouth
                                                to his   25
                her long dress made
                            of multicolored blossoms
                                    quilted on gold
                    her Titian hair
                            with blue stars in it   30
                And his gold
                            harlequin robe
                                        checkered with
                                                dark squares
                                                                                 35
                Gold garlands
                        stream down over
                                        her bare calves &
                                            tensed feet
        Nearby there must be
                    a jeweled tree   40
                        with glass leaves aglitter
                            in the gold air
        It must be
                    morning
                            in a faraway place somewhere   45
        They
                are silent together
                                as in a flowered field
                    upon the summer couch
                                which must be hers   50
            And he holds her still
                            so passionately
                holds her head to his
                            so gently so insistently
                    to make her turn   55
                            her lips to his
        Her eyes are closed
                        like folded petals
        She
                will not open   60
                    He
                        is not the One

598

ADAPTATIONS (POETRY AND SONG)

Adaptations go beyond translations; they alter literary works by bringing them into a different medium. Novels and plays, for example, are frequently adapted as films; poems are often adapted as songs. For thousands of years, in fact, poetry has been closely allied with song. Below you will find a number of songs, three of which are adaptations that transform the poem into song. Examine each pair and explain how the adapter has transformed the original. Consider what has been added, what deleted, and what altered. For the others, simply consider their merits as songlike poems or poemlike songs.

From Ecclesiastes: 3.1–8.

To every *thing there is* a season, and a time to every
purpose under the heaven:
2 A time to be born, and a time to die; a time to plant,
and a time to pluck up *that which is* planted;
3 A time to kill, and a time to heal; a time to break
down, and a time to build up;
4 A time to weep, and a time to laugh; a time to mourn,
and a time to dance;
5 A time to cast away stones, and a time to gather stones
together; a time to embrace, and a time to refrain from
embracing;
6 A time to get, and a time to lose; a time to keep, and a
time to cast away;
7 A time to rend, and a time to sew; a time to keep
silence, and a time to speak;
8 A time to love, and a time to hate; a time of war, and a
time of peace.

PETE SEEGER

[*b. 1919*]

Turn! Turn! Turn!

To everything,
Turn, turn, turn,
There is a season,
Turn, turn, turn,
And a time to every purpose under heaven.

A time to be born, a time to die,
A time to plant, a time to reap,
A time to kill, a time to heal,
A time to laugh, a time to weep.

To everything,
Turn, turn, turn,
There is a season,
Turn, turn, turn,
And a time to every purpose under heaven.

A time to build up, a time to break down,
A time to get, a time to want,
A time to cast away stones, a time to gather stones together.

To everything,
Turn, turn, turn,
There is a season,
Turn, turn, turn,
And a time to every purpose under heaven.

A time of love, a time of hate,
A time of war, a time of peace,
A time you may embrace, a time to refrain from embracing.

To everything,
Turn, turn, turn,
There is a season,
Turn, turn, turn,
And a time to every purpose under heaven.

A time to gain, a time to lose,
A time to rend, a time to sew,
A time for love, a time for hate,
A time for peace, I swear it's not too late.

EDWIN ARLINGTON ROBINSON

[*1869–1935*]

Richard Cory

Whenever Richard Cory went down town,
We people on the pavement looked at him:
He was a gentleman from sole to crown,
Clean favored and imperially slim.

And he was always quietly arrayed,   5
And he was always human when he talked;
But still he fluttered pulses when he said,
"Good-morning," and he glittered when he walked.

And he was rich—yes, richer than a king—
And admirably schooled in every grace: 10
In fine, we thought that he was everything
To make us wish that we were in his place.

So on we worked, and waited for the light,
And went without the meat and cursed the bread;
And Richard Cory, one calm summer night,   15
Went home and put a bullet through his head.

PAUL SIMON

[*b. 1942*]

Richard Cory

They say that Richard Cory owns one-half of this whole town,
With political connections to spread his wealth around.
Born into society, a banker's only child,
He had everything a man could want: power, grace and style.

But I work in his factory,
And I curse the life I'm living,
And I curse my poverty
And I wish that I could be
Richard Cory.

The papers print his picture almost everywhere he goes,
Richard Cory at the opera, Richard Cory at the show,
And the rumor of his parties, and the orgies on his yacht;
Oh, he surely must be happy with everything he's got.

But I work in his factory,
And I curse the life I'm living,
And I curse my poverty
And I wish that I could be
Richard Cory.

He freely gave to charity, he had the common touch,
And they were grateful for his patronage, and they thanked him very much.
So my mind is filled with wonder, when the evening headlines read:
"Richard Cory went home last night and put a bullet through his head."

But I work in his factory,
And I curse the life I'm living,
And I curse my poverty
And I wish that I could be
Richard Cory.

LANGSTON HUGHES
[1902–1967]

Dream Deferred

What happens to a dream deferred?

Does it dry up
like a raisin in the sun?
Or fester like a sore—
And then run?   5
Does it stink like rotten meat?
Or crust and sugar over—
like a syrupy sweet?

Maybe it just sags
like a heavy load.   10

Or does it explode?

Same in Blues

I said to my baby,
Baby, take it slow.
I can't, she said, I can't!
I got to go!

> There's a certain
> amount of traveling
> in a dream deferred.

Lulu said to Leonard,
I want a diamond ring.
Leonard said to Lulu,
You won't get a goddamn thing!

> A certain
> amount of nothing
> in a dream deferred.

Daddy, daddy, daddy,
All I want is you.
You can have me, baby—
but my lovin' days is through.

> A certain
> amount of impotence
> in a dream deferred.

Three parties
On my party line—
But that third party,
Lord, ain't mine!

> There's liable
> to be confusion
> in a dream deferred.

From river to river
Uptown and down,
There's liable to be confusion
when a dream gets kicked around.

> You talk like
> they don't kick
> dreams around
> Downtown.

I expect they do—
But I'm talking about
Harlem to you!
Harlem to you!
Harlem to you!
Harlem to you!

WOODY GUTHRIE

[1912–1967]

This Land Is Your Land

This land is your land, this land is my land,
From California to the New York island;
from the redwood forest, to the Gulf Stream waters
This land was made for you and me.

As I was walking that ribbon of highway
I saw above me the endless skyway:
I saw below me that golden valley:
This land was made for you and me.

I've roamed and rambled and I followed my footsteps
To the sparkling sands of her diamond deserts;
And all around me a voice was sounding:
This land was made for you and me.

When the sun came shining, and I was strolling,
And the wheat fields waving and the dust clouds rolling,
As the fog was lifting a voice was chanting:
This land was made for you and me.

As I went walking, I saw a sign there,
And on the sign it said "No Trespassing."
But on the other side it didn't say nothing,
That side was made for you and me.

In the shadow of the steeple I saw my people,
By the relief office I seen my people;

As they stood there hungry, I stood there asking
Is this land made for you and me?

Nobody living can ever stop me,
As I go walking that freedom highway;
Nobody living can ever make me turn back,
This land was made for you and me.

DON MACLEAN

[*b. 1945*]

Vincent

Starry, starry night
Paint your palette blue and gray.
Look out on a summer's day
With eyes that know the darkness in my soul.

Shadows on the hills
Sketch the trees and the daffodils,
Catch the breeze and the winterchills,
In colors on the snowy linen land.

Now I understand
What you tried to say to me,
How you suffered for your sanity,
And how you tried to set them free.

They would not listen.
They did not know how.
Perhaps they'll listen now.

Starry, starry night,
Flaming flowers that brightly blaze,
Swirling clouds in violet haze
Reflect in Vincent's eyes of china blue.

Colors changing hue
Morning fields of amber gray,
Weathered faces lined in pain
Are soothed beneath the artist's loving hand.

Now I understand
What you tried to say to me,
And how you suffered for your sanity
And how you tried to set them free.

They would not listen.
They did not know how.
Perhaps they'll listen now.

For they could not love you,
But still your love was true.
And when no hope was left inside
On that starry, starry night,
You took your life as lovers often do.

But I could have told you, Vincent,
This world was never meant
For one as beautiful as you.

Starry, starry night
Portraits hung in empty halls,
Frameless heads on nameless walls,
With eyes that watch the world and can't forget.

Like the strangers that you've met
The ragged men in ragged clothes,
The silver thorn and bloody rose
Lie crushed and broken on the virgin snow.

Now I think I know
What you tried to say to me,
And how you suffered for your sanity
And how you tried to set them free.

They would not listen.
They're not listening still.
Perhaps they never will.

JOHN LENNON AND PAUL MCCARTNEY
[*1940–1980; b. 1942*]

Yesterday

Yesterday, all my troubles seemed so far away,
Now it looks as though they're here to stay,
Oh I believe in yesterday.

Suddenly, I'm not half the man I used to be,
There's a shadow hanging over me,
Oh yesterday came suddenly.

Why she had to go I don't know,
She wouldn't say.
I said something wrong
Now I long for yesterday.

Yesterday, love was such an easy game to play.
Now I need a place to hide away,
Oh I believe in yesterday.

LONNELLE JOHNSON
[*b. 1942*]

No Mo Blues

I use to be a big-time blues singer
In the union for singers of the blues.
I use to be a big-time blues singer
In the union for singers of the blues,
But I turnt in my union card,
Ain't gonna pay no mo union dues.

When I was a full-time blues singer,
Doin whatsonever I choose—
When I was a full-time blues singer,
Doin whatsonever I choose—
Drinkin and smokin and screwin round
I was payin my blues singer's dues.

When I use to sing the low down blues,
I could show nuff cry and croon.
When I use to sing the low down blues,
I could show nuff cry and croon,
Then I met my pretty baby,
Now I'm hummin a brand new tune.

I gotta go find my agent
And tell him, "Say, Man, you been fired!"
I gotta go find my agent
And tell him, "Say, Man, you been fired!"
Since I met my pretty baby,
This old blues singer done retired.

I'm gonna tell everybody,
I want the whole wide world to see.
I'm gonna tell everybody,
I want the whole world to see
I just gotta testify
What my pretty baby done for me.

The day she stepped into my heart,
The sun shined in my front door.
The day she stepped into my heart
The sun shined in my front door,
And since I met my pretty baby,
I ain't gonna sing the blues no mo.

RESPONSES (POINT–COUNTERPOINT)

Throughout literary history poets have written poems that respond to works by earlier poets. Sometimes the later poem imitates the earlier one by adapting its poetic conventions. One famous example is Sir Walter Raleigh's reply to Christopher Marlowe's "The Passionate Shepherd to His Love." Sometimes a poet simply alludes to the title or most famous line of an earlier poem to develop a counterstatement to it. One of many such poetic counterpoints is Archibald MacLeish's "Not Marble Nor the Gilded Monuments," which offers a counterperspective to Shakespeare's sonnet of the same title. Some poets may refer specifically and by name to an earlier poet and his work as Anthony Hecht did in "The Dover Bitch," his response to Mathew Arnold's "Dover Beach."

As you read the following pairs of poems, consider how the later poet responds to the earlier. Consider what each poet seems to be saying and suggesting, and consider how the later poem modifies the view or perspective of its predecessor.

CHRISTOPHER MARLOWE
[*1564–1593*]

The Passionate Shepherd to His Love

Come live with me and be my love,
And we will all the pleasures prove°   try
That valleys, groves, hills, and fields,
Woods, or steepy mountain yields.

And we will sit upon the rocks,   5
Seeing the shepherds feed their flocks,
By shallow rivers to whose falls
Melodious birds sing madrigals.

And I will make thee beds of roses
And a thousand fragrant posies,   10
A cap of flowers, and a kirtle°   a long dress
Embroidered all with leaves of myrtle;

A gown made of the finest wool
Which from our pretty lambs we pull;
Fair lined slippers for the cold,   15
With buckles of the purest gold;

A belt of straw and ivy buds,
With coral clasps and amber studs:
And if these pleasures may thee move,
Come live with me, and be my love.   20

The shepherds' swains shall dance and sing
For thy delight each May morning:
If these delights thy mind may move,
Then live with me and be my love.

SIR WALTER RALEIGH
[*c. 1552–1618*]

The Nymph's Reply to the Shepherd

If all the world and love were young,
And truth in every shepherd's tongue,
These pretty pleasures might me move
To live with thee and be thy love.

Time drives the flocks from field to fold   5
When rivers rage and rocks grow cold,
And Philomel° becometh dumb;
The rest complains of cares to come.

The flowers do fade, and wanton fields
To wayward winter reckoning yields;   10
A honey tongue, a heart of gall,
Is fancy's spring, but sorrow's fall.

Thy gowns, thy shoes, thy beds of roses,
Thy cap, thy kirtle,° and thy posies   long dress
Soon break, soon wither, soon forgotten—   15
In folly ripe, in reason rotten.

Thy belt of straw and ivy buds,
Thy coral clasps and amber studs,
All these in me no means can move
To come to thee and be thy love.   20

But could youth last and love still breed,
Had joys no date° nor age no need,   end
Then these delights my mind might move
To live with thee and be thy love.

"The Nymph's Reply to the Shepherd"   [7]***Philomel***   *the nightingale. According to Ovid's* Metamorphoses,
Philomel's brother-in-law Tereus had her tongue cut out to prevent her from revealing that he had raped her. See also
Bob McKenty's "Adam's Song," page 529.

WILLIAM SHAKESPEARE
[1564–1616]

Not marble, nor the gilded monuments

Not marble, nor the gilded monuments
Of princes, shall outlive this powerful rhyme;
But you shall shine more bright in these conténts
Than unswept stone, besmeared with sluttish time.
When wasteful war shall statues overturn,   5
And broils root out the work of masonry,
Nor Mars his sword nor war's quick fire shall burn
The living record of your memory.
'Gainst death and all-oblivious enmity
Shall you pace forth; your praise shall still find room.   10
Even in the eyes of all posterity
That wear this world out to the ending doom°.   judgment day
So, till the judgment that yourself arise,
You live in this, and dwell in lovers' eyes.

ARCHIBALD MACLEISH
[1892–1982]

"Not Marble Nor the Gilded Monuments"

The praisers of women in their proud and beautiful poems
Naming the grave mouth and the hair and the eyes
Boasted those they loved should be forever remembered
These were lies

The words sound but the face in the Istrian sun is forgotten   5
The poet speaks but to her dead ears no more
The sleek throat is gone—and the breast that was troubled to listen
Shadow from door

Therefore I will not praise your knees nor your fine walking
Telling you men shall remember your name as long   10
As lips move or breath is spent or the iron of English
Rings from a tongue

I shall say you were young and your arms straight and your mouth scarlet
I shall say you will die and none will remember you
Your arms change and none remember the swish of your garments   15
Nor the click of your shoe

Not with my hand's strength not with difficult labor
Springing the obstinate words to the bones of your breast
And the stubborn line to your young stride and the breath to your breathing
And the beat to your haste   20
Shall I prevail on the hearts of unborn men to remember

(What is a dead girl but a shadowy ghost
Or a dead man's voice but a distant and vain affirmation
Like dream words most)

Therefore I will not speak of the undying glory of women   25
I will say you were young and straight and your skin fair
And you stood in the door and the sun was a shadow of leaves on your shoulders
And a leaf on your hair

I will not speak of the famous beauty of dead women
I will say the shape of a leaf lay once on your hair   30
Till the world ends and the eyes are out and the mouths broken
Look! It is there!

MATTHEW ARNOLD

[1822–1888]

Dover Beach

The sea is calm tonight.
The tide is full, the moon lies fair
Upon the straits; on the French coast the light
Gleams and is gone; the cliffs of England stand,
Glimmering and vast, out in the tranquil bay.   5
Come to the window, sweet is the night-air!
Only, from the long line of spray
Where the sea meets the moon-blanched land,
Listen! you hear the grating roar
Of pebbles which the waves draw back, and fling,   10
At their return, up the high strand,
Begin, and cease, and then again begin,
With tremulous cadence slow, and bring
The eternal note of sadness in.

Sophocles long ago   15
Heard it on the Aegean,° and it brought
Into his mind the turbid ebb and flow
Of human misery; we
Find also in the sound a thought,
Hearing it by this distant northern sea.   20

The Sea of Faith
Was once, too, at the full, and round earth's shore
Lay like the folds of a bright girdle furled.
But now I only hear
Its melancholy, long, withdrawing roar,   25
Retreating, to the breath
Of the night-wind, down the vast edges drear
And naked shingles of the world.

Ah, love, let us be true
To one another! for the world, which seems   30
To lie before us like a land of dreams,
So various, so beautiful, so new,
Hath really neither joy, nor love, nor light,
Nor certitude, nor peace, nor help for pain;
And we are here as on a darkling plain   35
Swept with confused alarms of struggle and flight,
Where ignorant armies clash by night.

ANTHONY HECHT

[b. 1923]

The Dover Bitch: A Criticism of Life

FOR ANDREWS WANNING

So there stood Matthew Arnold and this girl
With the cliffs of England crumbling away behind them,
And he said to her, "Try to be true to me,
And I'll do the same for you, for things are bad
All over, etc., etc."   5
Well now, I knew this girl. It's true she had read
Sophocles in a fairly good translation
And caught that bitter allusion to the sea,
But all the time he was talking she had in mind

---

[16] **Aegean**   See Sophocles, *Antigone, ll. 583–591* (chapter 22 in this text).

The notion of what his whiskers would feel like   10
On the back of her neck. She told me later on
That after a while she got to looking out
At the lights across the channel, and really felt sad,
Thinking of all the wine and enormous beds
And blandishments in French and the perfumes.   15
And then she got really angry. To have been brought
All the way down from London, and then be addressed
As a sort of mournful cosmic last resort
Is really tough on a girl, and she was pretty.
Anyway, she watched him pace the room   20
And finger his watch-chain and seem to sweat a bit,
And then she said one or two unprintable things.
But you mustn't judge her by that. What I mean to say is,
She's really all right. I still see her once in a while
And she always treats me right. We have a drink   25
And I give her a good time, and perhaps it's a year
Before I see her again, but there she is,
Running to fat, but dependable as they come.
And sometimes I bring her a bottle of *Nuit d'Amour.*°

WILLIAM CARLOS WILLIAMS

[1883–1963]

Queen-Ann's-Lace

Her body is not so white as
anemone petals nor so smooth—nor
so remote a thing. It is a field
of the wild carrot taking
the field by force; the grass   5
does not raise above it.
Here is no question of whiteness,
white as can be, with a purple mole
at the center of each flower.
Each flower is a hand's span   10
of her whiteness. Wherever
his hand has lain there is
a tiny purple blemish. Each part
is a blossom under his touch
to which the fibres of her being   15

---

²⁹*Nuit d'Amour*   brand of perfume. The French words mean "night of love."

stem one by one, each to its end,
until the whole field is a
white desire, empty, a single stem,
a cluster, flower by flower,
a pious wish to whiteness gone over— 20
or nothing.

(1921)

ANNE C. COON

[*b. 1952*]

Queen-Ann's-Lace

We argued about the dot
   blood-red garnet
   in a field of diamonds.
That was the spot where the queen
   pricked her finger as she worked. 5
I'd been told the story as a child
   when hundreds, thousands, more
   of the lacy heads
   brushed together
   along the road to school and lake. 10
And always, in private confirmation, I sought
   each flower's
   secret pricklet of blood,
   shed by the queen who shared my name,
   the flaw that made each blossom perfect. 15

At eighteen I met a boy
   born and bred where chicory
   Indian paintbrushes
   fat-headed clover
   burdock 20
   butter-cup
   and milkweed
   never ever grew there
      was no such thing, he said.
   No red dot. 25

I stopped the car,
   and with a lover's hand

led him
to a top-heavy clump—
starry umbrellas   30
and a miracle of fine bulwark
nodding on thin, tough stalks.

And, of course, each blossom
    bore the mark—
    black-crimson dot of pain   35
        on the queen's whitest lacework—
        soft antimacassar perfectly stained.

He broke away, slipping—
    running now—among
    the stands of flowers   40
    grabbing soft heads
    thrusting them aside
    incredulous not to find
    just one
    for him   45
    unblemished.

CHAPTER FOURTEEN

Writing About Poetry

REASONS FOR WRITING ABOUT POETRY

Why write about poetry? One reason is to find out what you think about a poem. Another is to induce yourself to read it more carefully. You may write about a work of poetry because it engages you, and you may wish to celebrate it or to argue with its implied ideas and values. Still another reason is that you may simply be required to do so as a course assignment.

Whatever your reasons for writing about poetry, a number of things happen when you do. First, in writing about a poem you tend to read it more attentively, noticing things you might overlook in a more casual reading. Second, since writing stimulates thinking, when you write about poetry you find yourself thinking more about what a particular work means and why you respond to it as you do. And third, you begin to acquire power over the works you write about, making them more meaningful to you.

INFORMAL WAYS OF WRITING ABOUT POETRY

When you write about a poem, you may write for yourself or you may write for others. Writing for yourself, writing to discover what you think, often takes casual forms such as annotation and freewriting. These less formal kinds of writing are useful for helping you focus on your reading of fiction. They are helpful in studying for tests about poetry. They can also serve as preliminary forms of writing when you write more formal essays and papers about poetry.

617

Annotation

When you annotate a text, you make notes about it, usually in the margins or at the top and bottom of pages—or both. Annotations can also be made within the text, as underlined words, circled phrases, and bracketed sentences or paragraphs. Annotations may also assume the form of arrows, question marks, and various other marks.

Annotating a literary work offers a convenient and relatively painless way to begin writing about it. Annotating can get you started zeroing in on what you think interesting or important. You can also annotate to signal details that puzzle or disconcert you.

Your markings serve to focus your attention and clarify your understanding of a poem. Your annotations can save you time in rereading or studying a work. And they can also be used when you write a more formal paper.

Annotations for the following poem illustrate the process.

ROBERT HAYDEN

Those Winter Sundays

Sundays <u>too my father</u> got up early
and put <u>his</u> clothes on in the <u>blueblack</u>
    cold,
then with cracked hands that ached
from labor in the weekday weather made
banked fires blaze. <u>No one ever thanked</u>
<u>him.</u>

I'd wake and hear the cold splintering,
    breaking,
When the rooms were warm, <u>he'd</u> call,
and slowly <u>I</u> would rise and dress,
<u>fearing</u> the chronic angers of that house,

Speaking <u>indifferently</u> to him,
who had driven out the <u>cold</u>
and polished my good shoes as well.
<u>What did I know, what did I know</u> of
    <u>love's</u> austere and <u>lonely</u> offices?

Margin annotations:

This father gets up early *every* day—*even* on Sundays.

How can cold be "blueblack"?

No one? Not other family members? Not the speaker?

Stanza 1 emphasizes the speaker's father; stanza 2 shifts emphasis to the speaker himself.

Speaker remembers his *fear*. Fear of what? His father's anger? Was it directed at him?

Father drives out the cold—warms the house, literally. Is the father himself a "warm" person, or "cold"?

Repeats the question. Tone? Feeling? Speaker knows *now* what he did not know then.

Father's loneliness/father's love.

Freewriting

Freewriting is a kind of informal writing you do for yourself. In freewriting you explore a text to find out what you think about it and how you respond to it. When you freewrite, you do not know ahead of time what your ideas about the work will be. Freewriting leads you to explore your memories and experience as well as aspects of the text itself. You sometimes wander from the details of the poem you are writing about. In the process you may discover thoughts and feelings you didn't know you had or were only dimly aware of. You can use freewriting to explore all your responses to a work. You can also use the technique to see where it leads you in thinking about the work itself.

First read Robert Graves's "Symptoms of Love," then look at some sample responses written by students who had heard Graves's poem read aloud and then read it once to themselves.

ROBERT GRAVES
[1895–1985]

Symptoms of Love

Love is a universal migraine,
A bright stain on the vision
Blotting out reason.

Symptoms of true love
Are leanness, jealousy,
Laggard dawns;

Are omens and nightmares—
Listening for a knock,
Waiting for a sign:

For a touch of her fingers
In a darkened room,
For a searching look.

Take courage, lover!
Could you endure such pain
At any hand but hers?

COLLEGE FRESHMAN: This lover is really bitter. He thinks love is a headache (migraine) and sees love mainly as negative and frightening. I noticed he talked about "omens and nightmares." He could have said "promises and dreams" or something like that, but he didn't. So as far as I am concerned, this speaker is a person who does not see any hope or possibility of growing better because of love. This is all pessimistic.

COLLEGE SOPHOMORE: Not that I haven't seen many failed relationships, but as a "thirty-something" male, I think the speaker in this poem (who also seems to be male) is very young. He sees "true love" as something that "blots out reason" and is always jealously waiting for a sign that the lady returns his feelings. I think as most people get older, they do not spend so much time thinking about "how is she (or he, in the case of a woman) going to react to me?" Instead they are looking for someone who will not cause them pain, someone who will be on the same wavelength.

COLLEGE JUNIOR: The first thing I thought when I was listening to the poem being read was that it was a terrible way to look at love. Like a migraine headache. Then when I read it myself, it made me smile some at the end. It was a sad smile—or maybe an ironic smile is what I mean. Because at the end, the speaker advises other lovers to "Take courage," so I thought that showed that he was at least willing to try again. He seemed to be saying that, yes, love is painful but it is a pain that can be worth it if you get rewarded with that "searching look" while the two of you are "in a darkened room." What he is talking about is that "chemistry" between two people who are really attracted to each other, but maybe they aren't meant for each other because of their opposing personalities. But the physical attraction is something that you just can't always push away.

COLLEGE FRESHMAN: A man wrote this poem and the character in the poem is a man, but the feelings are something I can really understand. I think more of women or girls being the ones who wait around for signs or who stay up all night or lose weight because they are in love with someone who isn't responding. I can certainly understand watching for every look and trying to figure out what it might mean and whether it might be saying that this person likes you. I've had plenty of headaches waiting for the phone to ring. Graves is right on target when he says "Love is a universal migraine."

The responses show the wide variety of reactions readers have when they encounter the same text. Note that the second reader and the fourth reader, particularly, include thoughts and feelings related to their own circumstances.

FORMAL WAYS OF WRITING ABOUT POETRY

Among the more common formal ways of writing about poetry is analysis. In writing an analytical essay about a poem, your goal is to explain how one or more particular aspects or issues in the work contribute to its overall meaning.

You might analyze the dialogue in Stewart's "In the Orchard" or the voices in Reed's "Naming of Parts," for example, in explaining what the verbal exchanges between characters or the difference in voices contributes to each poem's meaning. You might analyze the imagery of H. D.'s "Heat" or Hardy's "Neutral Tones" to see what that imagery suggests about the speaker's perspective or the author's attitude. Or you might analyze the syntax of Frost's "The Silken Tent" or Cummings's "Me up at does" for what that syntax reveals about each poem's theme.

In addition to analyzing these and other poetic elements in a single poem, you might also write to compare two poems, perhaps by focusing on their symbolism, sound effects, rhythm and meter, structure, or figures of speech. Or, instead of focusing on literary elements per se, you might write to see how a particular critical perspective (see Chapter 36) illuminates a poem. For example, you might consider the ways reader response criticism contributes to your understanding of Piercy's "To Be of Use" or new historicism contributes to your understanding of Poe's "To Helen."

The following brief analysis of Plath's "The Mirror" focuses on the poem's imagery and its structure. The writer considers how Plath's language and organization convey an implied idea about women.

STUDENT PAPERS ON POETRY

Jennifer Stepkowski
Professor O'Leary

Reflections on Sylvia Plath's "Mirror"

   Sylvia Plath's poem, "Mirror," presents a portrayal of womanhood
that is both accurate and upsetting. The mirror in Plath's poem
reflects honestly both inanimate objects and the faces of those who
peer into it. To convey the mirror's uncompromising accuracy in
reflecting what shows in its glass surface, Plath uses such words
as "exact," "truthful," "really," and "faithfully." Plath
personifies her mirror and makes it the poem's speaker. "I am
silver and exact," the speaker begins. "I have no preconceptions"
(1.1). This exactness of the mirror's reflection of reality coupled
with Plath's precise diction present a harsh reality in which women
grow old inexorably. Women have old age to look forward to, and old
age in which the young girls they once were have been "drowned"
(1.17).

   The image of drowning follows logically from the opening of the
poem's second stanza in which the mirror is compared to a lake. It
is in this lake (or mirror as lake) that a woman searches for her
self, reaching, as Plath writes, "for what she really is" (1.10).
What the woman finds, however, so disconcerts her that she responds
with "an agitation of hands" (1.14), which calls up a vision of the
woman's hands in flurried motion around her face. Yet even though
she is upset by what she sees in the mirror, the woman returns
repeatedly, for as the mirror says, "I am important to her" (1.15).

   Plath is uncompromising in portraying women's need to see
themselves, a need fed by a powerful concern with their appearance.
She also conveys without compromise the inevitable process of
aging, rendered powerfully in the simile that concludes the poem.
Plath conveys a sense of the woman at three stages of life: as she
is now, growing older in the poem's present; as she was once as a
young girl; and as she will be as an old woman who "rises toward
her day after day, like a terrible fish" (1.18).

   The images of the second stanza—of lake and tears and agitated
hands of a drowning girl and old woman rising like a fish—reflect
concretely the first stanza's general statements. There Plath
describes the mirror as having "no preconceptions" (1.1), as
"swallow[ing] immediately just as
it is," whatever it sees, "unmisted by love or dislike." Soon the
woman will be swallowed by the mirror as it has swallowed the young
girl she once was. Only the old woman remains, coming and going

from the mirror, staring into it and looking for the middle-aged woman and the young girl who will have long since vanished.

A Paper That Compares Two Versions of a Poem

In the following paper Amanda Gates compares an early version of Blake's "London" (pages 562–563) with the published version. The writer carefully analyzes Blake's diction and selection of detail to arrive at an interpretation of the later version. Seeing what words Blake rejected and changed helped her understand what Blake's published poem emphasizes.

→ THESIS = specific idea around which essay revolves

very important

Ackerman, Amanda
DiYanni
8/3/92
Third Essay

              The Sad World of "London"

   In William Blake's "London," the speaker takes a midnight walk
through London's dismal streets. As the speaker travels, he remarks
on the depravity, the weakness, and the sad restrictions which
abound in the London society. However, due to Blake's affinity for
perfection in his poetry, the speaker's footsteps are thoughtfully
planned. In fact, it was necessary for Blake to make several
revisions within his first draft of "London" before he was
satisfied with the final version. Each change that Blake makes
bears significance, whether it is as subtle as the capitalization
of one letter, or as dramatic as the complete revision of an entire
stanza. With each change, the poem becomes richer with connotations
of restraint, with imagery far more vivid and alarming, and with an
expression of a devastation ultimately more heart-felt.

   The majority of the changes that Blake makes within the first
three stanzas of the poem are deceptively minute, yet their impact
is anything but insignificant. For example, by simply replacing
three words within the first stanza of the original version, Blake
allows the second version of "London" to immediately take on an
altogether different feeling. In the earlier version of the poem,
Blake expresses his discontent by describing the Thames and the
London streets as "dirty." By sharp contrast, in the later version
Blake describes the same scene as "charter'd," a word that denotes
boundaries and restrictions: "I wander through each charter'd
street, Near where the charter'd Thames does flow . . ." (lines 1-
2). Instead of providing the reader with a vague and somewhat
cryptic idea of London's decay, Blake instantly alerts the reader
to the sad reality of London's restrictions. London is a world so
devastated by repression, that even the "free flowing" Thames and
the city streets themselves are weakened. Nothing and no one is
left untouched by London's all-consuming restrictions, for the
reader "sees in every face [he] meets, Marks of weakness, marks of
woe." This image, although disturbing, cannot compare to the deeper
despair expressed in the second version, for in this version the
speaker "marks in every face [he] meets, Marks of weakness, marks
of woe . . ." The grief of those that the speaker sees becomes much
more terrifying, for their faces are so miserable and weak that
they are able to leave a permanent impression on those who see
them. This is a much more powerful image than that of a person

despondently "seeing" the sad faces of those around him. Also, by changing "see" to "mark," Blake creates a haunting repetition which not only enhances the fluidity of the poem, but more importantly "marks" the reader himself by echoing the dismal truth.

Again, Blake makes revisions in the second stanza which appear small, but nonetheless which add tremendously to the impact of the poem. To begin with, Blake makes what appears to be a simple grammatical change; he capitalizes words such as "Man" and "Infant" in the second version. By doing this, Blake makes those unknown people that he describes seem much more frighteningly human, for he capitalizes their names just as we would capitalize the name of an individual person. Also, the striking image of a grown man crying becomes much more devastating when that "man" becomes "Man"—a universal representation for all mankind. In addition, the capitalized letters of these words allow them to stand out, and thus magnify their impact. Blake also makes another significantly effective change within the second stanza; he changes "In every voice of every child" to "In every Infant's cry of fear," a line much richer in impact and feeling. The first line gives a somewhat vague picture of the sadness in the lives of many faceless children, whereas the second line evokes a much more specific and alarming image, for it is the purest and most innocent of all human beings—the newborn baby—which even in its naivete feels the pain of repression so intensely that it "cries out."

As frightening as that image is, Blake affects the reader even more deeply by revealing the two terrifying sources of London's restricted freedom—one being the human mind. The already unnerving image of the human mind being its own means of imprisonment is made much more vivid when Blake changes the "mind forg'd links" described in the first version, to the "mind-forg'd manacles" of the second. The word "manacles" is a word so rich with connotations of restraint and imprisonment, that the reader is given a both alarming and sickening image of the mind itself—the only possession of man thought to be truly incapable of being barred or restricted—eating away at its own freedom. Blake also reveals the other source of London's grief and repressed freedom in a bold protest against the leadership of his time—Blake identifies the leaders themselves as the source of London's anguish. Again, by capitalizing certain words and by changing one line in the third stanza, Blake makes his attack on the leadership of his time all the more forceful and justifiable. In the second version, Blake capitalizes words such as "Chimney-sweeper's," "Church," "Soldier's," and "Palace" in order to display his discontent much more emphatically. The reader ultimately takes much more notice of the young Chimney-sweeper's cry, and of the unfortunate Soldier whose own lifeblood is "running down the walls" of the buildings where the incompetent leaders reside.

Blake further stresses the heartlessness of London's leaders
through another significant revision; he changes the line
"Blacken's o'er the church walls" to "Every black'ning Church
appalls." In the second version, the Church of England—thought to
be a sacred place of sanctuary and of guidance—instead of
providing its people with any kind of relief, is actively
"appalling" or denunciating the efforts of its impoverished
people, particularly the poor child-laborers who must sweep
chimneys in order to survive. This is a much more horrifying image
than that of the first.

However, in the last stanza Blake provides the reader with
perhaps the most alarming imagery of all, as London has been reduced
to a state where nothing at all is sacred. In the last stanza, Blake
brings about a marked difference in the impact of the poem through
several dramatic changes. The earlier version of the poem uses
imagery which vaguely connotes the sadness and the depravity found
in the London society. However, Blake expresses this detestable
human condition much more forcefully in the final version. Instead
of the "midnight harlot," "dismal street," and "curses weaving and
blasting," Blake uses much more powerful words and imagery. A strong
image such as a "midnight street" brings a much darker and ominous
feeling to the poem. Also, in an astonishing paradox, Blake refers
to the harlot as "youthful." By doing this, Blake brings about a
much more alarming image of the corrupted and devastated innocence
of a child. Also, the "curses" of the harlot appear to be much more
cruel and hurtful as they "blight with plagues" rather than "weave"
around a marriage hearse. In this second image a youthful mother is
trying to destroy her own infant's tears—no sooner has the infant
experienced its first moments of life in the world, than it is
feeling the sickness of repression. Nothing is sacred any longer in
the dismal world of London, certainly not the bond between mother
and child, and not even marriage. Blake ends the final version of
his poem with the lasting impression of a "Marriage Hearse." This
last image leaves the reader devastated, as it is marriage—probably
considered the most sacred and beautiful institution of man—which
itself is dead and on its way to being buried.

Although the reader encounters feelings of deep sadness,
corruption, and repression within the lines of Blake's first
version of "London," the walk that the reader takes through
London's dreary streets in the final version of the poem provides
the reader with a much more heart-felt insight into London's
miserable reality. Regardless of the size of each revision, each
change that Blake makes within his poem produces a more powerful
understanding and a more profound idea. Specifically the idea of
restriction, the idea that mankind himself has created a world in
which he has stifled his own expression and put boundaries on his

growth—in the sad world of London.

QUESTIONS FOR WRITING ABOUT POETRY

In writing about the elements of poetry, the following questions can help you focus your thinking and prepare yourself for writing analytical essays and papers. Use the questions as a checklist to guide you to important aspects of any poem you read.

Voice: Speaker and Situation

1. Who is the speaker of the poem? How would you characterize this speaker?
2. Where does the speaker reveal his or her attitude toward the poem's subject? Do the speaker's attitude or feelings change at any point? If so, where and with what implications?
3. What is the speaker's situation? What is happening in the poem?

Diction and Imagery

4. Do you understand the denotations of all the words used in the poem? Look up any words you are not completely sure of.
5. Which words convey the richest connotations? What do these connotations contribute to your understanding of the poem?
6. What kinds of imagery does the poem include? Do you detect any patterns among the images? What do the images collectively suggest?

Figures of Speech

7. What kinds of figures of speech occur in the poem? How important are figures of comparison—simile and metaphor?
8. How do the poem's figures of speech contribute to the poem's vividness and concreteness? What do they contribute to its feeling and meaning?

Symbolism and Allegory

9. What details of language and action carry symbolic implications? How do you know?
10. Does the poem exhibit a pattern of linked allegorical details?

Syntax and Structure

11. What kinds of sentences does the poet use? What kinds of structure and pattern do

the poem's sentences exhibit?

12. What does the poem's syntax reveal about the state of mind of its speaker?
13. How is the poem organized? How do its stanzas or major sections develop?
14. How are the stanzas or major sections of the poem related?

Sound, Rhythm, and Meter

15. Does the poem rhyme? Does it employ assonance, alliteration, onomatopoeia, or other forms of sound play? With what effects?
16. What kinds of rhythm and meter does the poem include? Does the rhythm change or is the meter varied at any point? With what effects?

Theme

17. How do the poetic elements create and convey the poem's meaning(s)?
18. Do you think there is more than one theme? Why or why not?
19. Is the theme of the poem explicit or implicit? Is it conveyed more clearly in one part of the poem than another?

Critical Perspectives

20. Which of the critical perspectives (pages 1893–1922) best helps you make sense of the poem? Why?
21. To what extent do the poem's language and details convey its meaning? To what extent do you need to go outside the poem for an understanding of its allusions, its historical or biographical implications, or other kinds of information?
22. To what extent does the poem confirm or support, confute or contradict your personal values, beliefs, attitudes, or dispositions? Why?

CHAPTER FIFTEEN

Two Poets in Context

READING EMILY DICKINSON AND ROBERT FROST IN DEPTH

The primary context for reading any single poem is other poems by the same poet. Additional contexts include other poems by contemporary poets and by poets with similar thematic preoccupations or stylistic inclinations. Emily Dickinson's poems, for example, can be read in relation to those of her contemporary Walt Whitman. Dickinson's poems can also be read in relation to seventeenth-century metaphysical poetry, especially the poems of George Herbert and John Donne, with whom Dickinson shared religious interests and some stylistic traits.

Additional contexts for reading Dickinson's poetry include her letters and her life. To some extent at least, a poet's work reflects his or her life. Knowing at least the broad outlines of poets' lives can be helpful in gaining additional perspectives on their poetry.

The context of poets' lives is naturally extended by their culture and environment. Knowing something of mid- to late-nineteenth-century New England social and literary culture enhances a reader's understanding of Dickinson's poetry. Similarly, knowing something about the development of literary modernism and about Robert Frost's relationship to that movement situates Frost's poetry in the context of his time and delineates it sharply against that backdrop.

Moreover, what is true for the life of Dickinson is also true for the life of Frost. Knowing the facts of Frost's life enhances our reading of his poetry. This having been said, however, it is the inner lives of both poets rather than their external lives that are most manifest and of most interest in their poems. Thus, primary emphasis in reading Dickinson and Frost should be on their artistry, on how they deploy language to create art, rather than on how their poems manifest aspects of their lives.

Still another context for reading both Dickinson and Frost is provided by their comments on the art and craft of poetry. Dickinson discusses poetry in her letters, Frost in both letters and essays. Neither poet provides interpretations of their poems. Frost, in fact, often had fun with audiences who asked about the meanings of particular poems, frequently teasing them with irrelevant information (only occasionally accurate) about how his poems were composed. Nonetheless poets' comments on the art of poetry generally and on their particular poetic intentions can be helpful in approaching their work. Frost's interest in how a poem can convey the intonational qualities of the spoken voice is a case in point. Since Frost takes this issue up repeatedly in his letters and essays, it is something readers should attend to, along with other, less technical matters that interest them.

Dickinson and Frost have both attracted a wide range of critical interpretation, providing still another context for their work. A sample of that criticism is included in this chapter.

QUESTIONS FOR IN-DEPTH READING

1. What general or overall thematic connections can you make between different works?
2. What stylistic similarities do you notice between and among different works?
3. How do the works differ in emphasis, tone, and style?
4. Once you have identified a writer's major preoccupations, place each work on a spectrum or a grid that represents the range of the writer's concerns.
5. What connections and disjunctions do you find between the following literary elements as they are embodied in different poems by the same writer?
   a. speaker and situation
   b. diction and imagery
   c. figures of speech
   d. symbolism and allegory
   e. syntax and structure
   f. sound and sense
   g. rhythm and meter
   h. theme and thought
6. To what extent are your responses to and perceptions of different works by the same writer shared by others—by critics, by classmates, and by the writers themselves?
7. What relationships and differences do you see between the work of one writer and that of another who shares similar thematic interests, stylistic proclivities, or cultural, religious, or social values?

8. Which of the critical perspectives (p. 000–000) seem most useful as analytical tools for approaching the body of work of particular writers?

INTRODUCTION TO EMILY DICKINSON

[1830–1886]

Emily Dickinson's external life was remarkably circumscribed. Born in 1830 in Amherst, Massachusetts, and educated at Amherst Academy, she lived there her entire life, except for a brief stay at what was later to become Mount Holyoke College. She lived a life of seclusion, leaving Massachusetts only once and rarely leaving her father's house during the last fifteen years of her life. She died in the house where she was born.

If Dickinson's external life was unadventurous, her interior life was not. Her mind was anything but provincial. She read widely in English literature and thought deeply about what she read. She expressed a particular fondness for the poetry of John Keats and Robert Browning, the prose of John Ruskin and Sir Thomas Browne, and the novels of George Eliot and Charlotte and Emily Brontë. And although she disclaimed knowledge of Whitman's work, she treasured a book that significantly influenced both Whitman's poetry and her own: the King James translation of the Bible. She especially liked the Book of Revelation.

Dickinson is often bracketed with Whitman as a cofounder of modern American poetry. Each brought to poetry something new, fresh, and strikingly original. But their poems, however prototypically modern, could not be more different. A mere glance at the page reveals a significant visual difference. Whitman's poems are large and expansive. The lines are long and the poems are typically ample and open. Dickinson's poems, by contrast, are highly compressed. They squeeze moments of intensely felt life and thought into tight four-line stanzas that compress feeling and condense thought.

The openness of Whitman's form is paralleled by the openness of his stance, his public outgoing manner. Dickinson's poetry is much more private, tending toward inwardness. Hers is a more meditative poetry than Whitman's, a poetry rooted partly in the metaphysical poetry of such seventeenth-century writers as John Donne and George Herbert. More directly influential on Dickinson's poetry than the metaphysical poets, however, was the tradition of Protestant hymnology. Her poems frequently employ the meter of hymns and follow their typical stanzaic pattern. Here, for example, is the opening verse of "Our God, Our Help in Ages Past," its accented syllables marked with ´.

> Our God, our help in ages past,
> Our hope for years to come,
> Our shelter from the stormy blast,
> And our eternal home.

The hymn's meter and formal structure are highly regular. The first and third lines are in iambic tetrameter, the second and fourth in iambic trimeter. The lack of metrical variation results in a steady, predictable rhythm, essential for singing. Dickinson varies this standard pattern to suit her poetic purpose. Her numerous variations amply testify to the ingenious and stunning uses to which she put this familiar meter. Consider, for example, "I felt a Funeral, in my Brain," "I like a look of Agony," "I died for Beauty—but was scarce," and "I heard a Fly buzz—when I died."

Dickinson's adaptation of hymn meter accords with her adaptation of the traditional religious doctrines of orthodox Christianity. For although her poems reflect a Calvinist heritage—particularly in their probing self-analysis, in which an intensely religious disposition intersects with profound psychological experience—she was not an orthodox Christian. Her religious ideas, like her life and poetry, were distinctive and individual. And even when her views tend toward orthodox teaching, as in her attitude toward immortality, her literary expression of such a belief is strikingly original. In addition, Dickinson's mischievous wit contrasts sharply with the brooding solemnity characteristic of much Calvinist-inspired religious writing. Finally, her love for nature separates her from her Puritan precursors, allying her instead with such transcendentalist contemporaries as Emerson, Whitman, and Thoreau, though her vision of life is starker than theirs.

Dickinson's poetry requires repeated and careful readings. Her diction is frequently surprising. Her elliptical syntax occasionally departs from the normal pattern. Readers must consequently fill in the gaps her language creates. Her taut lines need to be loosened; her tight poems need to be opened up. Words, phrases, lines cry out for the expansion of interpretive paraphrase.

Though a dictionary is necessary to identify the meanings of many of the words in Dickinson's poems, we need to attend to their richness of connotation as well. In "A narrow Fellow in the Grass," for example, we can explore the connotations of "Fellow," "transport," "cordiality," and "Zero at the Bone," considering how they fuse thought and feeling. In "The Bustle in a House," we can be alert for the fresh treatment of metaphor in the second stanza and attentive to the connotations of "industries," "Morning," and "Enacted" from the opening lines. And in "Tell all the Truth but tell it slant," we can discover the general idea implied by the poem and then apply it to specific areas of our experience. In doing so we will discover how Dickinson treats both nature and human experience obliquely and indirectly. To read her poems requires, in addition, a willingness to wait for the poem's possibilities of meaning to reveal themselves. Since many of her poems are cast as riddles, we must be willing to accept uncertainty, ambiguity, and partial understanding in interpreting them.

We also have to extend our notion of what constitutes acceptable poetic technique—something her contemporaries found nearly impossible. Dickinson was criticized for using inexact rhymes, rough rhythms, and colloquial diction, and for taking liberties with grammar. Her odd punctuation—heavy on dashes—and her peculiar use of capitalization were also unappreciated. But Dickinson exploited these and other poetic resources to convey complex states of mind and feeling. She employed these and other poetic idiosyncrasies not for their own sake, but for emotional and psychological impact.

In his extensive biography of Dickinson, Richard B. Sewall describes her resolve to portray the state of her mind and being in all their unorthodox complexity. He also describes Dickinson's early and futile hopes for publication and appreciation as well as her resignation to what she termed her "barefoot rank: of anonymity." Sewall also reveals her determination to pursue truth and to make poems her way. When Thomas Wentworth Higginson, an influential contemporary critic, advised her to write a more polite poetry, less indirect and metaphoric, smoother in rhythm and rhyme, simpler in thought, and less colloquial in idiom, she replied with a poem. Her answer is that although she could have written otherwise, she chose to write as she did.

326

I cannot dance upon my Toes—
No Man instructed me—
But oftentimes, among my mind,
A Glee possesseth me,

That had I Ballet knowledge—
Would put itself abroad
In Pirouette to blanch a Troupe—
Or lay a Prima, mad,

And though I had no Gown of Gauze
No ringlet, to my Hair,
Nor hopped to Audiences—like Birds,
One claw upon the Air,

Nor tossed my shape in Eider Balls,
Nor rolled on wheels of snow
Till I was out of sight, in sound,
The House encore me so—

Nor any know I know the Art
I mention—easy—Here—
Nor any Placard boast me—
It's full as Opera

Sewall describes how Dickinson's poems reflect her poetic vocation. He demonstrates how basic religious texts such as the Bible and Thomas à Kempis's *The Imitation of Christ* sustained her both spiritually and poetically. Though allowing that Dickinson's decision to cloister herself in her chamber could have had its roots in neurosis, he argues that her firm resolve was motivated by a commitment to the art of poetry akin to the ascetic discipline of religious devotion. In fact, he suggests that one of her more famous poems—one usually interpreted as a love poem—can be read as a dedication to the spiritual or poetic life. It can also be read as a celebration of individual choice.

303

The Soul selects her own Society—
Then—shuts the Door—
To her divine Majority—
Present no more—

Unmoved—she notes the Chariots—pausing—   5
At her low Gate—
Unmoved—an Emperor be kneeling
Upon her Mat—

I've known her—from an ample nation—
Choose One—   10
Then—close the Valves of her attention—
Like Stone—

Sewall's central point about the relationship between Dickinson's life and art is that although we may not be certain which interpretation to favor when considering this and many other poems, we can remain satisfied with our uncertainty because such ambiguity is central to her art. She writes metaphorically, concealing as much as she reveals. As readers we share in apprehending the nature of the experience she describes—in the poem above, the experience of making a decisive choice involving commitment and renunciation. In doing so, however, we also supply specific details from our own lives to render the decision specific and significant. Dickinson's poetry, in other words, conveys the essence of an experience, its heart and core. Her poems, as Sewall aptly notes, do not tell us so much how to live as what it feels like to be alive.

Emily Dickinson's poems do not encompass a wide range of experience; instead they probe deeply into a few of life's major experiences—love, death, doubt, and faith. In examining her experience, Dickinson makes a scrupulous effort to tell the truth, but she tells it "slant." Part of her originality and artistry includes the way she invites us to share in her search for truth. The qualified assertions we frequently find in her poems, their riddles and uncertainties, and their questioning stance demand our participation and response. In considering her representation of intensely felt moments of consciousness, we experience for ourselves her explosive power. And in learning to share Dickinson's acute perceptions and feelings, we also come to understand our own.

EMILY DICKINSON ON HERSELF & HER FIRST POEMS

Mr Higginson,
    Your kindness claimed earlier gratitude—but I was ill—and write today, from my pillow.

Thank you for the surgery—it was not so painful as I supposed. I bring you others—as you ask—though they might not differ—

While my thought is undressed—I can make the distinction, but when I put them in the Gown—they look alike, and numb.

You asked how old I was? I made no verse—but one or two—until this winter—Sir—

I had a terror—since September—I could tell to none—and so I sing, as the Boy does by the Burying Ground—because I am afraid—You inquire my Books—For Poets—I have Keats—and Mr and Mrs Browning. For Prose—Mr Ruskin—Sir Thomas Browne—and the Revelations. I went to school—but in your manner of the phrase—had no education. When a little Girl, I had a friend, who taught me Immortality—but venturing too near, himself—he never returned—Soon after, my Tutor, died—and for several years, my Lexicon—was my only companion—Then I found one more—but he was not contented I be his scholar—so he left the Land.

You ask of my Companions Hills—Sir—and the Sundown—and a Dog—large as myself, that my Father bought me—They are better than Beings—because they know—but do not tell—and the noise in the Pool, at Noon—excels my Piano. I have a Brother and Sister—My Mother does not care for thought—and Father, too busy with his Briefs—to notice what we do—He buys me many Books—but begs me not to read them—because he fears they joggle the Mind. They are religious—except me—and address an Eclipse, every morning—whom they call their "Father." But I fear my story fatigues you—I would like to learn—Could you tell me how to grow—or is it unconveyed—like Melody—or Witchcraft?

From a letter to Thomas Wentworth Higginson, April 25, 1862

CRITICS ON DICKINSON

ALLEN TATE

Dickinson and Knowledge

Dickinson pursues that knowledge wherever it is to be found, no matter how it makes her feel. She reports her pursuit, seemingly as it occurs, with such profound attention that her poems offer exhilaration, no matter how sombre their topic.

To see Dickinson as an epistemological poet, a poet who advances a theory of knowledge in her work, doesn't mean that she is exclusively, or even primarily, an intellectual poet. She was brilliant, well educated, and confident in her use of conceptual, scientific, legal and linguistic terminology, but the truly remarkable quality of mind in her poetry comes from her refusal to separate this mind from the body and emotions which temper it. Dickinson writes close to the traditions of post-Romantic poetry and women's poetry in that her poetry expresses strong emotion. She stands to the side of it to the extent that the drive for knowledge dominates, and the affairs of the heart are seen as part of that knowledge, not separate. Hers is an epistemology of feeling. It is actually quite difficult to locate Dickinson's refusal to sublimate in literary-historical terms, because it is so alien to our usual structuring of dualism. Dickinson has the direct access to emotion which is thought to be—and is—a characteristic of much women's poetry. She doesn't, however, soften those emotions into acceptability or use poetry as an escape, either for herself or for her reader. Perhaps her knowledge has gone unrecognized for just this reason: she doesn't present it as a solution to human loss and pain. Rather, it is a way of experiencing fully and with utmost clarity whatever must be experienced.

Emily Dickinson's poetry runs the full emotive range from ecstatic celebration to numb despair. Huge shifts of perspective, imagery of thresholds, gems, open and closed space, stars, planets and firmaments mark Dickinson's sublime. In a few, very striking, poems she sees both human and writerly desires as capable of fulfilment. Imagery of plentitude—wine, feasting, nectar, flood and luxury—accompanies Dickinson's joyous knowledge. In these poems, her tone is often highly erotic:

> Wild Nights—Wild Nights!
> Were I with thee
> Wild Nights should be
> Our luxury!

As Dickinson would have known, the Latin word *luxus,* from which 'luxury' stems, means sensual excess or debauchery. Her declaration is actually redundant, further emphasizing its ecstatic triumph by the repetition of 'Wild Nights'. It is as if sensuous bliss is a state in which everything means the same thing, which is itself. The second stanza of 'Wild Nights—Wild Nights!' develops this oceanic emotion into a nautical metaphor as Dickinson, somewhat more conventionally, declares that 'Winds' are 'futile' 'To a Heart in port—'. Nor will this mariner need 'Compass' or 'Chart' to guide herself.

The poem's last stanza takes off from this hint of exultant freedom. The sexual beat of the rower's oars gives way to sheer exclamation:

> Rowing in Eden—
> Ah, the Sea!
> Might I but moor—Tonight—
> In Thee!

The last image may look like gender reversal, with the speaker seeing herself as the active partner, but Dickinson isn't concerned with whether or not her ecstasy fits Victorian convention. The image is one of choosing to be contained by the lover. Mooring tonight is a way of remaining eternally in the oceanic paradise of Eros.

From "Emily Dickinson," in Collected Essays

JUDITH FARR

On *"Wild Nights"*

"Wild Nights," its theatrical opening spondees worthy of turbulence and storm, justifies Dickinson's heritage as an admirer of Emily Brontë and *Wuthering Heights*. The seas
that separate or unite Charlotte Brontë's heroines and their "masters" also come to mind.
Here is a scene reminiscent not only of the intensity of the Brontës' world but also of
hundreds of dark canvases by the Hudson River and Luminist painters. Cole's *Tornado
in an American Forest* (1835), like his *Expulsion from Eden,* had made the frenzy of storm
synonymous with *passio*—distress or love—while seascapes like Fitz Hugh Lane's *Ships
and an Approaching Storm off Owl's Head, Maine* (1860) or Heade's *Approaching Storm:
Beach Near Newport* (1860) made angry seas expressive of the sea of feeling. Furthermore, Dickinson's image of the rowboat was conceived during the 1860s, when the
idea of the lone boat in contest with high seas was particularly popular. There were
many studies like Church's *An Old Boat* (1850), in which failure and loss were described
by an abandoned rowboat at the edge of brimming, light-filled waters. Whistler expressed *The Sea* (1865) of defeat by picturing a rowboat stranded at the edge of sullen
tides. Dickinson's lyrics about the "Edifice of Ocean" with its "tumultuous Rooms"
(1217) would find analogues in the vehement seascapes of Winslow Homer, for whom
the ocean could also be a metaphor of grandeur and grief. As a favorite nineteenth-
century sport, however, rowing on smooth water was described by Thomas Eakins'
Luminist paintings: for example, the famous *Max Schmitt in a Single Scull* (1871), which
has a serene if rather triste formality.

Having said all this, it is equally important to say that "Wild Nights" is among the
most Dickinsonian of the lyrics: ironic, paradoxical, voluptuous, and terse all at once.
At first it projects a tumultuous nocturnal seascape, the wildness Nature's. But the next
three lines of the first quatrain propose this as a luxury: that is, a rare experience to be
enjoyed. Thus the imagined wildness is also human, internal, joyous. The next quatrain,
spoken from the vantage point of one who has felt winds, declares how futile they would
be in port, at rest, where neither they nor a compass or chart—the scientific instruments
of explorers—are needed. By the closing quatrain, the speaker is "Rowing in Eden,"
her visionary desire having triumphed over the course of a life's voyage. Dickinson may
have been remembering Bowles's rowing in Eden and all those betrothed nineteenth-
century lovers so often depicted rowing together as one stroke in the same boat. (Thus
in chapter 41 of *Little Women,* to give a popular example, Amy and Laurie row their
boat "smoothly through the water" opposite Chillon, then decide to marry.) In Eden
Dickinson finds a sea of love that is pleasurable, not frightening, and a Thee in which
she might safely moor or harbor. Dickinson's inclusion of a sea in Eden, a garden, reminds us that the book of Genesis provides a river in Eden that waters the garden (2:10).
(Other poems, such as "My River runs to thee" [162], may be related to her imagery

of primal—sexual—waters. That poem was sent in a letter to Mary Bowles in August 1861; but like most of her words to Mary, it was probably intended for her husband.) In *Expulsion from Eden* Cole included a placid lake and a gentle waterfall in his Eden. When Dickinson's first quatrain is taken together with the last in poem 249, however, the reader realizes that she means to "moor" in passion, to luxuriate in wildness. For though hers is a boat that rows rather than rides the waters, her satisfaction in "Wild Nights" comes from strong delight. Even in Eden, she hears the sea. To moor is still to be wild for this prohibited voice that prays "Might I . . .".

From The Passion of Emily Dickinson

ALLEN TATE

On "Because I Could Not Stop for Death"

If the word "great" means anything in poetry, this poem is one of the greatest in the English language. The rhythm charges with movement the pattern of suspended action back of the poem. Every image is precise and, moreover, not merely beautiful, but fused with the central idea. Every image extends and intensifies every other. The third stanza especially shows Miss Dickinson's power to fuse, into a single order of perception, a heterogeneous series: the children, the grain, and the setting sun (time) have the same degree of credibility; the first subtly preparing for the last. The sharp *gazing* before *grain* instills into nature a cold vitality of which the qualitative richness has infinite depth. The content of death in the poem eludes explicit definition. He is a gentleman taking a lady out for a drive. But note the restraint that keeps the poet from carrying this so far that it becomes ludicrous and incredible; and note the subtly interfused erotic motive, which the idea of death has presented to most romantic poets, love being a symbol interchangeable with death. The terror of death is objectified through this figure of the genteel driver, who is made ironically to serve the end of Immortality. This is the heart of the poem: she has presented a typical Christian theme in its final irresolution, without making any final statements about it. There is no solution to the problem; there can be only a presentation of it in the full context of intellect and feeling. A construction of the human will, elaborated with all the abstracting powers of the mind, is put to the concrete test of experience: the idea of immortality is confronted with the fact of physical disintegration. We are not told what to think; we are told to look at the situation.

The framework of the poem is, in fact, the two abstractions, mortality and eternity, which are made to associate in equality with the images: she sees the ideas, and thinks the perceptions. She did, of course, nothing of the sort; but we must use the logical distinctions, even to the extent of paradox, if we are to form any notion of this rare quality of mind. She could not in the proper sense think at all, and unless we prefer the feeble poetry of moral ideas that flourished in New England in the eighties, we must conclude that her intellectual deficiency contributed at least negatively to her great distinction. Miss Dickinson is probably the only Anglo-American poet of her century whose work exhibits the perfect literary situation—in which is possible the fusion of sensibility and thought. Unlike her contemporaries, she never succumbed to her ideas, to easy solutions, to her private desires. . . .

Neither the feeling nor the style of Miss Dickinson belongs to the seventeenth century; yet between her and Donne there are remarkable ties. Their religious ideas, their abstractions, are momently toppling from the rational plane to the level of perception. The ideas, in fact, are no longer the impersonal religious symbols created anew in the heat of emotion, that we find in poets like Herbert and Vaughan. They have become, for Donne, the terms of personality; they are mingled with the miscellany of sensation. In Miss Dickinson, as in Donne, we may detect a singularly morbid concern, not for religious truth, but for personal revelation. The modern word is self-exploitation. It is egoism grown irresponsible in religion and decadent in morals. In religion it is blasphemy; in society it means usually that culture is not self-contained and sufficient, that the spiritual community is breaking up. This is, along with some other features that do not concern us here, the perfect literary situation.

From "Emily Dickinson," in Collected Essays

HELEN MCNEIL

Dickinson's Method

Many Victorian poems describe unexamined abstractions, as if society agreed about what constituted sorrow or love. These could be personified, and their attributes could be listed and elaborated metaphorically. Dickinson takes on a frightening abstraction and evolves its attributes from experience, not tradition. In poetry and philosophy, the subject—the experiencing person—may wonder about the existence of other minds. Dickinson wrote many poems on this problem. In 'Pain—has an Element of Blank', she contemplates the possibility that there may be circumstances in which the perceiving consciousness also does not exist, erased by its own emotion. 'The Soul has Bandaged moments—' she begins another poem; the abstract soul is a bandaged body, in a metaphor which denies dualism. Time is also represented physically, bound up by pain. As Dickinson concludes at the end of 'The Soul has Bandaged moments—', such recognitions 'are not brayed of Tongue—' in the public discourse of her society, or, for that matter, our society either.

Dickinson wrote about feeling, but out of feeling she constructed a theory of knowledge—not *beyond* feeling, or free from it, or in any way separate, but using it as a kind of knowing. In effect—though not in conventional terms—she is an epistemological poet, a poet who advances a theory of knowledge. Dickinson made this concern explicit. After the forms of the verb 'to be', 'know' is the most frequently used verb in Dickinson's poetry, appearing 230 times, more even than any noun except 'day'.

Dickinson's constant pressure towards knowing means that she can treat even the most tormented situations with great calm. She can begin by writing 'I felt a Funeral, in my Brain', or 'Pain—has an Element of Blank—' or 'I felt my life with both my hands—' and then proceed to delineate that state with a commanding accuracy. In a manner more resembling the Metaphysical poets than her Victorian contemporaries, male or female, she uses emotionally heightened states as occasions for clarity.

American poetry characteristically embodies acts of process: the Dickinsonian 'process' is passionate investigation. Her investigative process often implies narrative by taking speaker and reader through a sequence of rapidly changing images, even when all the action is interior. These investigations structure Dickinson's poetry; I suspect that the flexibility of her investigative movement is the major reason why Dickinson generally was contented with common metre. She may even have enjoyed the way her condensed discoveries press against the limits of a small form.

From Emily Dickinson

THREE POEMS BY EMILY DICKINSON WITH ALTERED PUNCTUATION

After her death, Emily Dickinson's poems were published with their punctuation changed to conform to conventional usage of the time. Compare these versions with Dickinson's originals.

650

Pain has an element of blank;
It cannot recollect
When it began, or if there were
A day when it was not.

It has no future but itself,
Its infinite realms contain
Its past, enlightened to perceive
New periods of pain.

632

The brain is wider than the sky,
For, put them side by side,
The one the other will include
With ease, and you beside.

The brain is deeper than the sea,
For, hold them, blue to blue,
The one the other will absorb,
As sponges, buckets do.

The brain is just the weight of God,
For, lift them, pound for pound,
And they will differ, if they do,
As syllable from sound.

303

The soul selects her own society,
Then shuts the door;
On her divine majority
Obtrude no more.

Unmoved, she notes the chariot's pausing
At her low gate;
Unmoved, an emperor is kneeling
Upon her mat.

I've known her from an ample nation
Choose one;
Then close the valves of her attention
Like stone.

EMILY DICKINSON: POEMS

I'm "wife"—I've finished that

I'm "wife"—I've finished that—
That other state—
I'm Czar—I'm "Woman" now—
It's safer so—

How odd the Girl's life looks   5
Behind this soft Eclipse—
I think that Earth feels so
To folks in Heaven—now—

This being comfort—then
That other kind—was pain—   10

But why compare?
I'm "Wife"! Stop there!

(#199, 1860, 1890)

I taste a liquor never brewed

I taste a liquor never brewed—
From Tankards scooped in Pearl—
Not all the Vats upon the Rhine
Yield such an Alcohol!

Inebriate of Air—am I—   5
And Debauchee of Dew—
Reeling—thro endless summer days—
From inns of Molten Blue—

When "Landlords" turn the drunken Bee
Out of the Foxglove's door—   10
When Butterflies—renounce their "drams"—
I shall but drink the more!

Till Seraphs swing their snowy Hats—
And Saints—to windows run—
To see the little Tippler   15
Leaning against the—Sun—

(#214, 1860, 1861)

I like a look of Agony

I like a look of Agony,
Because I know it's true—
Men do not sham Convulsion,
Nor simulate, a Throe—

The Eyes glaze once—and that is Death—   5
Impossible to feign
The Beads upon the Forehead
By homely Anguish strung.

(#241, 1861, 1890)

Wild Nights—Wild Nights

Wild Nights—Wild Nights!
Were I with thee
Wild Nights should be
Our luxury!

Futile—the Winds—　　　　　　　　　　　5
To a Heart in port—
Done with the Compass—
Done with the Chart!

Rowing in Eden—
Ah, the Sea!　　　　　　　　　　　　10
Might I but moor—Tonight—
In Thee!

　　　　　　　　　　　　　　(#249, 1861, 1891)

There's a certain Slant of light

There's a certain Slant of light,
Winter Afternoons—
That oppresses, like the Heft
Of Cathedral Tunes—

Heavenly Hurt, it gives us—　　　　　　　5
We can find no scar,
But internal difference,
Where the Meanings, are—

None may teach it—Any—
'Tis the Sea Despair—　　　　　　　　　10
An imperial affliction
Sent us of the Air—

When it comes, the Landscape listens—
Shadows—hold their breath—
When it goes, 'tis like the Distance　　　　15
On the look of Death—

　　　　　　　　　　　　　　(#258, 1861, 1890)

I felt a Funeral, in my Brain

I felt a Funeral, in my Brain,
And Mourners to and fro
Kept treading—treading—till it seemed
That Sense was breaking through—

And when they all were seated,   5
A Service, like a Drum—
Kept beating—beating—till I thought
My Mind was going numb—

And I heard them lift a Box
And creak across my Soul   10
With those same Boots of Lead, again,
Then Space—began to toll,

As all the Heavens were a Bell,
And Being, but an Ear,
And I, and Silence, some strange Race   15
Wrecked, solitary, here—

And then a Plank in Reason, broke,
And I dropped down, and down—
And hit a World, at every plunge,
And Finished knowing—then—   20

(#280, 1861, 1896)

Some keep the Sabbath going to Church

Some keep the Sabbath going to Church—
I keep it, staying at Home—
With a Bobolink for a Chorister—
And an Orchard, for a Dome—

Some keep the Sabbath in Surplice—   5
I just wear my Wings—
And instead of tolling the Bell, for Church,
Our little Sexton—sings.

God preaches, a noted Clergyman—
And the sermon is never long,   10
So instead of getting to Heaven, at last—
I'm going, all along.

(#328, 1862, 1891)

After great pain, a formal feeling comes

After great pain, a formal feeling comes—
The Nerves sit ceremonious, like Tombs—
The stiff Heart questions was it He, that bore,
And Yesterday, or Centuries before?

The Feet, mechanical, go round— 5
Of Ground, or Air, or Ought—
A Wooden way
Regardless grown,
A Quartz contentment, like a stone—

This is the Hour of Lead— 10
Remembered, if outlived,
As Freezing persons, recollect the Snow—
First—Chill—then Stupor—then the letting go—

(#341, 1862, 1929)

I dreaded that first Robin, so

I dreaded that first Robin, so,
But He is mastered, now,
I'm some accustomed to Him grown,
He hurts a little, though—

I thought if I could only live 5
Till that first Shout got by—
Not all Pianos in the Woods
Had power to mangle me—

I dared not meet the Daffodils—
For fear their Yellow Gown 10
Would pierce me with a fashion
So foreign to my own—

I wished the Grass would hurry—
So—when 'twas time to see—
He'd be too tall, the tallest one 15
Could stretch—to look at me—

I could not bear the Bees should come,
I wished they'd stay away
In those dim countries where they go,
What word had they, for me? 20

They're here, though; not a creature failed—
No Blossom stayed away
In gentle deference to me—
The Queen of Calvary—

Each one salutes me, as he goes,   25
And I, my childish Plumes,
Lift, in bereaved acknowledgment
Of their unthinking Drums—

                                              (#348, 1862, 1891)

We grow accustomed to the Dark

We grow accustomed to the Dark—
When Light is put away—
As when the Neighbor holds the Lamp
To witness her Goodbye—

A Moment—We uncertain step   5
For newness of the night—
Then—fit our Vision to the Dark—
And meet the Road—erect—

And so of larger—Darknesses—
Those Evenings of the Brain—   10
When not a Moon disclose a sign—
Or Star—come out—within—

The Bravest—grope a little—
And sometimes hit a Tree
Directly in the Forehead—   15
But as they learn to see—

Either the Darkness alters—
Or something in the sight
Adjusts itself to Midnight—
And Life steps almost straight.   20

                                              (#419, 1862, 1935)

Much Madness is divinest Sense

Much Madness is divinest Sense—
To a discerning Eye—

Much Sense—the starkest Madness—
'Tis the Majority
In this, as All, prevail—   5
Assent—and you are sane—
Demur—you're straightway dangerous—
And handled with a Chain—

(#435, 1862, 1935)

I died for Beauty—but was scarce

I died for Beauty—but was scarce
Adjusted in the Tomb
When One who died for Truth, was lain
In an adjoining Room—

He questioned softly "Why I failed?"   5
"For Beauty," I replied—
"And I—for Truth—Themself are One—
We Brethren, are," He said—

And so, as Kinsmen, met a Night—
We talked between the Rooms—   10
Until the Moss had reached our lips—
And covered up—our names—

(#449, 1862, 1890)

I heard a Fly buzz—when I died

I heard a Fly buzz—when I died—
The Stillness in the Room
Was like the Stillness in the Air—
Between the Heaves of Storm—

The Eyes around—had wrung them dry—   5
And Breaths were gathering firm
For that last Onset—when the King
Be witnessed—in the Room—

I willed my Keepsakes—Signed away
What portion of me be   10
Assignable—and then it was
There interposed a Fly—

With Blue—uncertain stumbling Buzz—
Between the light—and me—
And then the Windows failed—and then   15
I could not see to see—

                                  (#465, 1862, 1896)

The Heart asks Pleasure—first

The Heart asks Pleasure—first—
And then—Excuse from Pain—
And then—those little Anodynes
That deaden suffering—

And then—to go to sleep—   5
And then—if it should be
The will of its Inquisition
The privilege to die—

                                  (#536, 1862, 1890)

I like to see it lap the Miles

I like to see it lap the Miles—
And lick the Valleys up—
And stop to feed itself at Tanks—
And then—prodigious step

Around a Pile of Mountains—   5
And supercilious peer
In Shanties—by the sides of Roads—
And then a Quarry pare

To fit its Ribs
And crawl between   10
Complaining all the while
In horrid—hooting stanza—
Then chase itself down Hill—

And neigh like Boanerges—
Then—punctual as a Star   15
Stop—docile and omnipotent
At its own stable door—

                                  (#585, 1862, 1891)

There is a pain—so utter

There is a pain—so utter—
It swallows substance up—
Then covers the Abyss with Trance—
So Memory can step
Around—across—upon it—   5
As one within a Swoon—
Goes safely—where an open eye—
Would drop Him—Bone by Bone.

(#599, 1862, 1929)

Pain—has an Element of Blank

Pain—has an Element of Blank—
It cannot recollect
When it begun—or if there were
A time when it was not—

It has no Future—but itself—   5
Its Infinite contain
Its Past—enlightened to perceive
New Periods—of Pain.

(#650, 1862, 1890)

Remorse—is Memory—awake

Remorse—is Memory—awake—
Her Parties all astir—
A Presence of Departed Acts—
At window—and at Door—

Its Past—set down before the Soul   5
And lighted with a Match—
Perusal—to facilitate—
And help Belief to stretch—

Remorse is cureless—the Disease
Not even God—can heal—   10
For 'tis His institution—and
The Adequate of Hell—

(#744, 1863, 1891)

My Life had stood—a Loaded Gun

My Life had stood—a Loaded Gun—
In Corners—till a Day
The Owner passed—identified—
And carried Me away—

And now We roam in Sovereign Woods—   5
And now We hunt the Doe—
And every time I speak for Him—
The Mountains straight reply—

And do I smile, such cordial light
Upon the Valley glow—   10
It is as a Vesuvian face
Had let its pleasure through—

And when at Night—Our good Day done—
I guard My Master's Head—
'Tis better than the Eider-Duck's   15
Deep Pillow—to have shared—

To foe of His—I'm deadly foe—
None stir the second time—
On whom I lay a Yellow Eye—
Or an emphatic Thumb—   20

Though I than He—may longer live
He longer must—than I—
For I have but the power to kill,
Without—the power to die—

(#754, 1863, 1929)

A narrow Fellow in the Grass

A narrow Fellow in the Grass
Occasionally rides—
You may have met Him—did you not
His notice sudden is—

The Grass divides as with a Comb—   5
A spotted shaft is seen—
And then it closes at your feet
And opens further on—

He likes a Boggy Acre
A floor too cool for Corn—
Yet when a Boy, and Barefoot—
I more than once at Noon
Have passed, I thought, a Whip lash
Unbraiding in the Sun
When stooping to secure it
It wrinkled, and was gone—

Several of Nature's People
I know, and they know me—
I feel for them a transport
Of cordiality—

But never met this Fellow
Attended, or alone
Without a tighter breathing
And Zero at the Bone—

(#986, 1865, 1866)

Further in Summer than the Birds

Further in Summer than the Birds
Pathetic from the Grass
A minor Nation celebrates
Its unobtrusive Mass.

No Ordinance be seen
So gradual the Grace
A pensive Custom it becomes
Enlarging Loneliness.

Antiquest felt at Noon
When August burning low
Arise this spectral Canticle
Repose to typify

Remit as yet no Grace
No Furrow on the Glow
Yet a Druidic Difference
Enhances Nature now

(#1068, 1866, 1891)

The Bustle in a House

The Bustle in a House
The Morning after Death
Is solemnest of industries
Enacted upon Earth—

The Sweeping up the Heart   5
And putting Love away
We shall not want to use again
Until Eternity.

                                                    (#1078, 1866, 1890)

The last Night that She lived

The last Night that She lived
It was a Common Night
Except the Dying—this to Us
Made Nature different

We noticed smallest things—   5
Things overlooked before
By this great light upon our Minds
Italicized—as 'twere.

As We went out and in
Between Her final Room   10
And Rooms where Those to be alive
Tomorrow were, a Blame

That Others could exist
While She must finish quite
A Jealousy for Her arose   15
So nearly infinite—

We waited while She passed—
It was a narrow time—
Too jostled were Our Souls to speak
At length the notice came.   20

She mentioned, and forgot—
Then lightly as a Reed
Bent to the Water, struggled scarce—
Consented, and was dead—

And We—We placed the Hair— 25
And drew the Head erect—
And then an awful leisure was
Belief to regulate—

(#1100, 1866, 1890)

Tell all the Truth but tell it slant

Tell all the Truth but tell it slant—
Success in Circuit lies
Too bright for our infirm Delight
The Truth's superb surprise

As Lightning to the Children eased 5
With explanation kind
The Truth must dazzle gradually
Or every man be blind—

(#1129, 1868, 1945)

A Route of Evanescence

A Route of Evanescence
With a revolving Wheel—
A Resonance of Emerald—
A Rush of Cochineal—
And every Blossom on the Bush 5
Adjusts its tumbled Head—
The mail from Tunis, probably,
An easy Morning's Ride—

(#1463, 1879, 1891)

Apparently with no surprise

Apparently with no surprise
To any happy Flower
The Frost beheads it at its play—
In accidental power—
The blonde Assassin passes on— 5
The Sun proceeds unmoved
To measure off another Day
For an Approving God.

(#1624, 1884, 1890)

My life closed twice before its close

My life closed twice before its close—
It yet remains to see
If Immortality unveil
A third event to me

So huge, so hopeless to conceive   5
As these that twice befell.
Parting is all we know of heaven,
And all we need of hell.

(#1732, 1896)

INTRODUCTION TO ROBERT FROST

[1874–1963]

Like Walt Whitman before him, Robert Frost yearned to become America's foremost poet. Aiming for both critical and popular acclaim, Frost hoped to achieve recognition as a major poet and to reach the widest possible audience. And although he did succeed in becoming a popular poet (perhaps the most popular in America's history), in the minds of some readers his very popularity diminished his critical stature. Frost himself, however, was partly responsible for this. The image he projected—folksy, lovable, homespun—undercut his reputation as a major poet. Even today, with Frost's poetic stature widely acknowledged, he is occasionally seen as a less serious, less impressive, less demanding, and hence less important poet than his contemporaries Ezra Pound, T. S. Eliot, and Wallace Stevens.

There is a measure of truth in this assessment, perhaps, but only a small measure. Frost's poems are easier to read than those of Pound, Eliot, or Stevens: his familiar vocabulary and traditional forms enhance their accessibility. But his poems are neither simple nor easy to understand. Their diction is more richly allusive and connotative than at first may appear. Their paraphrasable thought is subtler and more profound than an initial reading might suggest. Moreover, their form, though traditional, is more intricately wrought and more decisively experimental than is generally recognized. Before turning to consider these claims, we should be aware of the course of Frost's poetic career, particularly of his popularity as an honored national poet, who, ironically, was first recognized abroad rather than at home.

Although Robert Frost is considered a New England farmer-poet who captures in his verse the tang of Yankee speech, he was born in San Francisco and lived there until the age of eleven, when his family moved to Lawrence, Massachusetts. He attended high school in Lawrence and was covaledictorian of his graduating class with Elinor White, whom he later married. Frost continued his education at Dartmouth College, where he remained for only one term, and later at Harvard University, where he studied for two years without taking a degree. After working at a succession of odd jobs including farming and factory work, Frost taught at Pinkerton Academy, where from 1906 to 1910 he reformed the English syllabus, directed theatrical productions, and wrote many of the poems later included in his first book, *A Boy's Will.*

In 1911, in an attempt to attract the attention of prominent and influential members in the literary world, he sold his farm in Derry, New Hampshire, and moved with his family to England. There he met and received the support of Ezra Pound, who helped secure publication of his first two volumes of poems, and of Edward Thomas, who reviewed them perceptively. Having launched his career, Frost returned to America in 1915 and quickly secured an American publisher—Henry Holt and Co.—for the two books published in England, *A Boy's Will* (1913) and *North of Boston* (1914), and for subsequent volumes as well. With the publication in 1916 of *Mountain Interval,* Frost's fame grew. In 1917, and periodically thereafter, he was poet in residence at Amherst College and served in a similar capacity at various other colleges and universities including Dartmouth, Wesleyan, Michigan, Harvard, and Yale. Frost received awards and prizes, among them the Bollingen Poetry Prize (1963) and four Pulitzer Prizes (1924, 1931, 1937, and 1943). In addition many honorary degrees, including ones from Oxford and Cambridge universities, were conferred on him. Although Frost was fond of joking that he could make a blanket of the many academic hoods he had acquired, he valued them, particularly those from the British institutions. Later in his life Frost was appointed goodwill emissary to South America and the Soviet Union. At the time he was also the only American poet honored with an invitation to read his work at a presidential inauguration. In January 1961, at the inauguration of John F. Kennedy, Frost read "The Gift Outright" and another poem he had composed for the occasion.

This brief summary of Frost's career, however, oversimplifies what was in reality a more complex and arduous process. Initially an obscure writer, Frost experienced difficulty in breaking into print in a significant way. He later struggled with the decline of his poetic powers, most of his best work being produced when he was younger. And more tragically, he suffered the deaths of his wife and three of his children, one of whom committed suicide. He also saw his sister and one of his daughters succumb to mental illness. And finally, despite his many prizes and awards, Frost was bitter that he never won a Nobel Prize. He died in 1963, two weeks short of his eighty-ninth birthday.

What accounts for Frost's fame and popularity? Three things, at least: his shrewd management of his career, including the cultivation of his poetic image; his use of familiar subjects, especially the natural world and people engaged in recognizable activities; and his accessible language and apparent simplicity of thought. From the beginning, Frost skillfully managed his poetic career, going abroad to England to win the approval of the prominent poets and critics of his day. Frost, of course, did not plan every step of his rise to fame; rather he trusted to his highly developed instinct for sizing up opportunities and capitalizing on them. As William Pritchard explains in *Robert Frost: A Literary Life Reconsidered,* Frost retrospectively structured his literary life as one of adversity overcome.

The most important aspect of this biographical semifictionalizing was Frost's portrayal of himself as a literary exile unappreciated in his home country. Allied with this biographical mythmaking was Frost's control over his public image. He refused, for example, to read his darker, more skeptical poems in public, preferring instead to reveal his more congenial, folksy side. And he carefully masked from public exposure his hunger for fame and an occasional nasty denigration of those poets he considered his strongest rivals.

More important to his popularity than his masterly manipulation of his public persona, however, is the readability of his poetry. Frost avoids obscure language, preferring the familiar word and the idiomatic phrase. He also shuns foreign words and shies away from all but the scantiest of references to economic, literary, and political history. And instead of the structural openness, fragmentation, and discontinuity favored by some of his contemporaries, Frost used traditional poetic forms characterized by coherence and continuity.

That Frost's poems are relatively easy to read does not mean that they are necessarily easy to understand. Frost is a master of concealment, of saying one thing in terms of another, and especially of saying two or more things simultaneously. Even his most accessible poems such as "Birches," "Mending Wall," and "The Road Not Taken" contain clear invitations to consider their symbolic ramifications. The symbolic nature of these poems doesn't manifest itself immediately. To appreciate the fullness of Frost's achievement, we need to read with attention to their symbolic detail, whether we are reading the meditative blank verse of "Birches" or "Mending Wall" or the lyrical descriptions of "Desert Places" or "Stopping by Woods on a Snowy Evening."

It is also a mistake to assume, on the basis of a familiarity with a few of Frost's more famous lyrics, that his poetry lacks either drama or humor. "Departmental" reveals Frost's humorous side, while "Home Burial" shows him at work in a longer, more dramatic form. Though his poems are certainly serious, they are not solemn. This is as true of "Stopping by Woods" and "The Road Not Taken" as it is for "The Silken Tent," a witty extended comparison between a woman and a pitched tent; "Provide, Provide," a pragmatic set of admonitions about how to get on in the world; and "A Considerable Speck," a satirical jab at human limitations, particularly the performances of writers. Moreover, Frost himself warned us against taking him too seriously. Although we cannot completely trust him in such matters since he enjoyed teasing his audiences, we can at least regard his work as a mixture of playfulness and seriousness. "If it is with outer seriousness," he once remarked, "it must with inner humor; if with inner seriousness, then with outer humor."

Complicating matters further is Frost's view of nature. More often than not, nature appears as a powerful, dangerous, and cruel force, its purpose and design not immediately apparent. Frost avoids a simple representation of the relationship between the natural and human worlds. He does not share Emerson's belief in nature as a moral teacher. He does not believe, for example, that in reading nature we discover moral and spiritual truths. That romantic view is questioned in poems like "Desert Places" and "The Most of It," where nature seems to express "nothing" to the human observer. Yet other poems, such as "The Tuft of Flowers" and "Two Look at Two," are entirely compatible with

Emersonian and Whitmanesque transcendentalist ideas, in which nature and man form part of a harmonious whole.

Frost's response to nature is, essentially, to wonder skeptically just how much "meaning" in nature there really is for human beings. A poem like "Tree at My Window" explores this issue. In the first part of the poem, there seems to be a definite connection between nature (trees) and people; the human and the natural worlds intersect. But the last stanza suggests that there are radical differences between the two worlds, differences that separate them more than their similarities bind them.

The complexity and richness of Frost's vision of nature are paralleled by the subtlety of his technical achievement. Though he worked in traditional forms— sonnet, heroic couplet, blank verse, four-line stanza—the effects he wrought in them are remarkable for their range and versatility. To take just one example, consider his sonnets, which include poems in both of the traditional forms, Shakespearean and Petrarchan. "Putting in the Seed" is constructed according to the Shakespearean, or English, pattern with three quatrains and a concluding couplet (though Frost alters the rhyme pattern slightly). "Design" follows the Petrarchan model: an octave of eight lines followed by a sestet of six. The octave of "Design" describes a natural scene (a white spider finding on a white flower a white moth that it kills and devours). The sestet explores the significance of the event. Though conventional in logical organization, "Design" exhibits a variation from the Petrarchan rhyme scheme: *abba abba cde cde* (or *cd cd cd*). Frost's poem uses only three rhymes throughout both octave and sestet: *abba abba acc caa*.

Frost's sonnets often diverge in some way from the traditional sonnet and thus make something new and fresh of the form. "Mowing," for example, while composed according to the Petrarchan structure, contains a strong concluding couplet more characteristic of the Shakespearean sonnet. It also varies from the rhyme scheme of both traditional patterns, though using the same number of different sounds as the Shakespearean form: *abca bdec dfeg fg*. The poem displays a curious use of overlapping sound effects that Frost worked out more elaborately and systematically in other lyrics. Other sonnet variations appear in "The Silken Tent," which is constructed as a single sentence spun out over the fourteen lines in a Shakespearean pattern. Working against that rhyme scheme, however, is a logical structure more characteristic of the Petrarchan division into two major sections, with a turn at the ninth line. Such hybrid sonnets are accompanied by other sonnet experiments such as "Once by the Pacific," in seven couplets rhyming *aa bb cc dd ee ff gg,* and "Acquainted with the Night," composed in the interlocking rhymes of *terza rima: aba bcb cdc ded ee.*

Frost was a skilled wordsmith who cared about the sounds of his sentences. He noted more than once how "the sentence sound says more than the words"; how "tones of voice" can "mean more than words." In such voice tones Frost heard the sounds of sense and captured them in his verse, heightening their expressiveness by combining the inflections of ordinary speech with the measured regularity of meter. Because Frost's achievement in this regard surpasses that of most other modern American poets, we should be particularly attentive to the way he makes poetry out of the spoken word. His poems often mask the most elegant and subtle of his technical accomplishments. Perhaps the best way to read Frost's poems is to approach them as performances, as poetic acts of skill-ful daring, of risks taken, of technical dangers overcome. In doing so we may share the pleasure Frost took in poetic performance. In addition, we can see how Frost's poetry often "begins in delight and ends in wisdom," offering along the way what he called "a momentary stay against confusion."

CRITICAL COMMENTS BY FROST

ROBERT FROST

The figure a poem makes. It begins in delight and ends in wisdom. The figure is the same as for love. No one can really hold that the ecstasy should be static and stand still in one place. It begins in delight, it inclines to the impulse, it assumes direction with the first line laid down, it runs a course of lucky events, and ends in a clarification of life—not necessarily a great clarification, such as sects and cults are founded on, but in a momentary stay against confusion. It has denouement. It has an outcome that though unforeseen was predestined from the first image of the original mood—and indeed from the very mood. It is but a trick poem and no poem at all if the best of it was thought of first and saved for the last. It finds its own name as it goes and discovers the best waiting for it in some final phrase at once wise and sad—the happy-sad blend of the drinking song.

No tears in the writer, no tears in the reader. No surprise for the writer, no surprise for the reader. For me the initial delight is in the surprise of remembering something I didn't know I knew. I am in a place, in a situation, as if I had materialized from cloud or risen out of the ground. There is a glad recognition of the long lost and the rest fol-lows. Step by step the wonder of unexpected supply keeps growing. The impressions most useful to my purpose seem always those I was unaware of and so made no note of at the time when taken, and the conclusion is come to that like giants we are always hurling experience ahead of us to pave the future with against the day when we may want to strike a line of purpose across it for somewhere. The line will have the more charm for not being mechanically straight. We enjoy the straight crookedness of a good walking stick. Modern instruments of precision are being used to make things crooked as if by eye and hand in the old days. . . .

More than once I should have lost my soul to radicalism if it had been the original-ity it was mistaken for by its young converts. Originality and initiative are what I ask for my country. For myself the originality need be no more than the freshness of a poem run in the way I have described: from delight to wisdom. The figure is the same as for love. Like a piece of ice on a hot stove the poem must ride on its own melting. A poem may be worked over once it is in being, but may not be worried into being. Its most previous quality will remain its having run itself and carried away the poet with it. Read it a hundred times: it will forever keep its freshness as a metal keeps its fragrance. It can never lose its sense of a meaning that once unfolded by surprise as it went.

From The Figure a Poem Makes

I give you a new definition of a sentence:

A sentence is a sound in itself on which other sounds called words may be strung.

You may string words together without a sentence-sound to string them on just as you may tie clothes together by the sleeves and stretch them without a clothes line between two trees, but—it is bad for the clothes.

The number of words you may string on one sentence-sound is not fixed but there is always danger of over loading.

The sentence-sounds are very definite entities. (This is no literary mysticism I am preaching.) They are as definite as words. It is not impossible that they could be collected in a book though I don't at present see on what system they would be catalogued.

They are apprehended by the ear. They are gathered by the ear from the vernacular and brought into books. Many of them are already familiar to us in books. I think no writer invents them. The most original writer only catches them fresh from talk, where they grow spontaneously.

A man is all a writer if *all* his words are strung on definite recognizable sentence sounds. The voice of the imagination, the speaking voice must know certainly how to behave how to posture in every sentence he offers.

A man is a marked writer if his words are largely strung on the more striking sentence sounds.

A word about recognition: In literature it is our business to give people the thing that will make them say, "Oh yes I know what you mean." It is never to tell them something they dont know, but something they know and hadnt thought of saying. It must be something they recognize. . . .

The sentence as a sound in itself apart from the word sounds is no mere figure of speech. I shall show the sentence sound saying all that the sentence conveys with little or no help from the meaning of the words. I shall show the sentence sound opposing the sense of the words as in irony. And so till I establish the distinction between the grammatical sentence and the vital sentence. The grammatical sentence is merely accessory to the other and chiefly valuable as furnishing a clue to the other. You recognize the sentence sound in this: *You,* you—! It is so strong that if you hear it as I do you have to pronounce the two you's differently. Just so many sentence sounds belong to man as just so many vocal runs belong to one kind of bird. We come into the world with them and create none of them.

There are many other things I have found myself saying about poetry, but the chiefest of these is that it is metaphor, saying one thing and meaning another, saying one thing in terms of another, the pleasure of ulteriority. Poetry is simply made of metaphor. So also is philosophy—and science, too, for that matter, if it will take the soft impeachment from a friend. Every poem is a new metaphor inside or it is nothing. And there is a sense in which all poems are the same old metaphor always.

From "The Constant Symbol"

There are two kinds of language: the spoken language and the written language—our everyday speech which we call the vernacular; and a more literary, sophisticated, artificial, elegant language that belongs to books. We often hear it said that a man talks like a book in this second way. We object to anybody's talking in this literary, artificial English; we don't object to anybody's writing in it; we rather expect people to write in a literary, somewhat artificial style. I, myself, could get along very well without this bookish language altogether. I agree with the poet who visited this country not long ago when he said that all our literature has got to come down, sooner or later, to the talk of everyday life. William Butler Yeats says that all our words, phrases, and idioms to be effective must be in the manner of everyday speech.

We've got to come down to this speech of everyday, to begin with—the hard everyday word of the street, business, trades, work in summer—to begin with; but there is some sort of obligation laid on us, to lift the words of every day, to give them a metaphorical turn. No, you don't want to use that term—give the words a poetic touch. I'll show you what I mean by an example: take for example the word "lemon," that's a good practical word with no literary associations—a word that you use with the grocer and in the kitchen; it has no literary associations at all; "Peach" is another one; but you boys have taken these two words and given them a poetic twist.

From "The Unmade Word, Or Fetching and Far-Fetching"

CRITICS ON FROST

NORMAN HOLLAND

Reading Frost

We can explore the workings of Frost's brain—or mind—through one of his better-known poems, "Once by the Pacific" (see page 676). I think this poem had at the core of its creation a widespread and well-known childhood fear. I find it of particular interest therefore, because it allows us to see how Frost defended himself against fears we may well have experienced ourselves. As I put the poem together for myself, I respond most immediately to its violence, to words like "rage," "din," or the menacing phrase, "dark intent." The first substantial word I hear is "shattered" and the final rhyme is "broken," although, to be sure, it is only "water" that is shattered and broken, a water that is (ironically) "Pacific"—peaceful.

This night is unique: the waves "thought of doing something to the shore / That water never did to land before." And immense. I imagine huge dimensions from phrases like "great waves," "ocean-water," or words like "land," "continent," or (in time) "an age." I find these sizes made still bigger by a pattern of buttressing, doubling, and increasing. The shore is backed by cliff, and the cliff is backed by continent. "There would be *more* than ocean-water broken." Waves looked over *other* waves. This was not just a night, but an age. And finally, the poem, having begun with the storm, ends with God and the Last Judgment, a final doubling, a bigness bigger than even waves and continent, an immensity of words called forth by words. In reciting this poem, one of the critics recalls, Frost would drop into a deep voice for God's words at the end.

I hear about a "misty din," and waves think of "doing something." "Someone had better be prepared." I get a feeling of indefiniteness from these phrases. "You could not tell" exactly, but you surmise a "dark intent." "More than ocean-water" would be broken—but what? "Something," Stanley Burnshaw points out, is "the most significant single word in the poems." It occurs 137 times in the Frost canon, "someone" 77 times, and "somehow" 8 times. They are all part of what Frost called in an essay of his, "Extravagance," the going beyond domestic boundaries to find something wild and, here, ominous.

"Someone" is going to be a victim, and in "some*one*," I find yet another tendency, one that works along with the vagueness, namely, personification. Frost gives the whole scene human attributes. The sea "looked" and "thought." The night has an "intent," and the land is "lucky" because it is backed by other land. One critic, Judith P. Saunders, is "amused to see waves and clouds endowed with the motives and appearance of stock villains in a Grade B movie." Most see it as beginning ominously and becoming still more ominous.

One would think that personification would counter the sense of indefiniteness, but somehow, in my mind, at any rate, it makes it still more ominous: the people are huge and vague and therefore all the more menacing. Intimations of warring personalities reach a height for me in lines 6 and 7, when the poem pivots from "the gleam of eyes" associated with the skies to a direct "you." It is as if the interpersonal conflict comes about precisely because *you looked*. Finally, at the end of the poem, there is God who seems to be both the instigator of violence and the one who puts an end to it. Possibly, C. Hines Edwards suggests, Blake's picture of God inspired Frost's imagining here. . . .

Here, it seems to me, we are coming very close to the nature of Frost's creativity as a poet, perhaps the creativity of all poets. Language occupies a special, pivotal place in Frost's psychic economy. He can use words two ways: to call up the kind of thing he most fears (being overpowered, unmanned, unselved, fused into another) and to manage that same fantasy. He can use words both to evoke a fantasy that feels particularly dangerous to him and to limit that same fantasy. To the extent we can re-create in our own terms our equivalent for that fearful fantasy and manage it using *his* words (because we share Frost's language), we say his poem succeeds. We award its author the accolade of "creativity."

In effect, language serves Frost as an agent both of fantasy and of mastery. In "Once by the Pacific," he uses a poetic form that resembles a familiar defense mechanism: projection. He starts with a storm, but it turns out to be more than a storm. In this poem, he starts with a wall but it turns out not to be "just a wall." In both instances, his language enables him and us to build a process of projection: "something" doesn't like the wall; its gaps have a mysterious quality ("No one has seen them made or heard them made"); it seems to be engaged in a struggle between human beings (as the high waves by the Pacific were). In effect, Frost's language projects (in a paranoid way that probably accounts for the faint *frisson* I feel at this poem) human attributes onto the inanimate world. His words put the dangerous wishes and fears within himself out into the world around him. Then his poem explores those mental states in the guise of physically dealing with the actualities of a New England farm or the San Francisco coast.

From The Brain of Robert Frost

WILLIAM PRITCHARD

On "Stopping By Woods"

With respect to his most anthologized poem, "Stopping By Woods . . ." which he called "my best bid for remembrance," such "feats" are seen in its rhyme scheme, with the third unrhyming line in each of the first three stanzas becoming the rhyme word of each succeeding stanza until the last one, all of whose end words rhyme and whose final couplet consists of a repeated "And miles to go before I sleep." Or they can be heard in the movement of the last two lines of stanza three:

> He gives his harness bells a shake
> To ask if there is some mistake.
> The only other sound's the sweep
> Of easy wind and downy flake.

As with "Her early leaf's a flower," the contraction effortlessly carries us along into "the sweep / Of easy wind" so that we arrive at the end almost without knowing it.

Discussion of this poem has usually concerned itself with matters of "content" or meaning (What do the woods represent? Is this a poem in which suicide is contemplated?). Frost, accordingly, as he continued to read it in public made fun of efforts to draw out or fix its meaning as something large and impressive, something to do with man's existential loneliness or other ultimate matters. Perhaps because of these efforts, and on at least one occasion—his last appearance in 1962 at the Ford Forum in Boston—he told his audience that the thing which had given him most pleasure in composing the poem was the effortless sound of that couplet about the horse and what it does when stopped by the woods: "He gives his harness bells a shake / To ask if there is some mistake." We might guess that he held these lines up for admiration because they are probably the hardest ones in the poem out of which to make anything significant: regular in their iambic rhythm and suggesting nothing more than they assert, they establish a sound against which the "other sound" of the following lines can, by contrast, make itself heard. Frost's fondness for this couplet suggests that however much he cared about the "larger" issues or questions which "Stopping By Woods . . ." raises and provokes, he wanted to direct his readers away from solemnly debating them; instead he invited them simply to be pleased with how he had put it. He was to say later on about Edwin Arlington Robinson something which could more naturally have been said about himself—that his life as a poet was "a revel in the felicities of language." "Stopping By Woods . . ." can be appreciated only by removing it from its pedestal and noting how it is a miniature revel in such felicities.

From Robert Frost: A Literary Life Reconsidered

RICHARD POIRIER

On "Stopping by Woods on a Snowy Evening"

As its opening words suggest—"Whose woods these are I think I know"—["Stopping by Woods on a Snowy Evening"] is a poem concerned with ownership and also

with someone who cannot be or does not choose to be very emphatic even about own-
ing himself. He does not want or expect to be seen. And his reason, aside from being
on someone else's property, is that it would apparently be out of character for him to
be there, communing alone with a woods fast filling up with snow. He is, after all, a
man of business who has promised his time, his future to other people. It would appear that he is not only a scheduled man but a fairly convivial one. He knows who
owns which parcels of land, or thinks he does, and his language has a sort of pleasant
neighborliness, as in the phrase "stopping by." It is no wonder that his little horse would
think his actions "queer" or that he would let the horse, instead of himself, take responsibility for the judgment. He is in danger of losing himself; and his language by
the end of the third stanza begins to carry hints of a seductive luxuriousness unlike anything preceding it—"Easy wind and downy flake . . . lovely, dark and deep." Even
before the somnolent repetition of the last two lines, he is ready to drop off. His opening question about who owns the woods becomes, because of the very absence from
the poem of any man "too exactly himself," a question of whether the woods are to
"own" him. With the drowsy repetitiousness of rhymes in the last stanza, four in a row,
it takes some optimism to be sure that (thanks mostly to his little horse, who makes the
only assertive sound in the poem) he will be able to keep his promises. At issue, of
course, is really whether or not he will be able to "keep" his life.

From Robert Frost: The Work of Knowing

RICHARD POIRIER

On "Mending Wall"

The limits, boundaries, or customs which define a "home," a personal property, are
often taken, that is, as an occasion for freedom rather than for confinement. The real
significance of the famous poem "Mending Wall" is that it suggests how much for Frost
freedom is contingent upon some degree of restriction. More specifically, it can be said
that restrictions, or forms, are a precondition for expression. Without them, even nature ceases to offer itself up for a reading. Forms of any sort have been so overwhelmed
in "Desert Places," for example, that the prospect is for "a blanker whiteness of benighted snow / With no expression, nothing to express," the world as a blank sheet of
paper enveloped in darkness.

Natural forces in "Mending Wall," having each year to encounter the human imposition of a freshly repaired wall, tend to become expressive in a quite selective way. Whatever it is "that doesn't love a wall," "*sends* the frozen-ground-swell under it / And *spills*
the upper boulders in the sun, / And *makes* gaps even two can pass abreast" (my italics).
More important, this active response to human structurings prompts a counterresponse

and activity from people who are committed to the making and remaking of those structures. And who are such people? The point usually missed, along with most other things
importantly at work in this poem, is that it is not the neighbor, described as "an old-
stone savage armed," a man who can only dully repeat, "Good fences make good
neighbors"—that it is not he who initiates the fence-making. Rather it is the far more
spirited, lively, and "mischievous" speaker of the poem. While admitting that they do
not need the wall, it is he who each year "lets my neighbor know beyond the hill" that
it is time to do the job anyway, and who will go out alone to fill the gaps made in the
wall by hunters: "I have come after them and made repairs / When they have left not
one stone on a stone." Though the speaker may or may not think that good neighbors
are made by good fences, it is abundantly clear that he likes the yearly ritual, the yearly
"outdoor game" by which fences are made. Because if fences do not "make good neighbors" the *"making"* of fences can. More is "made" in this "outdoor game" than fences.
The two men also "make" talk, or at least that is what the speaker tries to do as against
the reiterated assertions of his companion, which are as heavy and limited as the wall itself. So hopeless is this speaker of any response, that all his talk may be only to himself.
He is looking for some acknowledgment of those forces at work which are impatient
of convention and of merely repeated forms; but he is looking in vain.

From Robert Frost: The Work of Knowing

YVOR WINTERS

Robert Frost: Or, the Spiritual Drifter as Poet

Frost writes of rural subjects, and the American reader of our time has an affection for
rural subjects which is partly the product of the Romantic sentimentalization of "nature," but which is partly also a nostalgic looking back to the rural life which pre-
dominated in this nation a generation or two ago; the rural life is somehow regarded
as the truly American life. I have no objection to the poet's employing rural settings;
but we should remember that it is the poet's business to evaluate human experience,
and the rural setting is no more valuable for this purpose than any other or than no
particular setting, and one could argue with some plausibility that an exclusive concentration on it may be limiting.

Frost early began his endeavor to make his style approximate as closely as possible
the style of conversation, and this endeavor has added to his reputation: it has helped
to make him seem "natural." But poetry is not conversation, and I see no reason why
poetry should be called upon to imitate conversation. Conversation is the most careless and formless of human utterance; it is spontaneous and unrevised, and its vocabulary is commonly limited. Poetry is the most difficult form of human utterance; we re-

vise poems carefully in order to make them more nearly perfect. The two forms of expression are extremes, they are not close to each other. We do not praise a violinist for playing as if he were improvising; we praise him for playing well. And when a man plays well or writes well, his audience must have intelligence, training, and patience in order to appreciate him. We do not understand difficult matters "naturally." . . .

Frost, as far as we have examined him, then, is a poet who holds the following views: he believes that impulse is trustworthy and reason contemptible, that formative decisions should be made casually and passively, that the individual should retreat from cooperative action with his kind should retreat not to engage in intellectual activity but in order to protect himself from the contamination of outside influence, that affairs manage themselves for the best if left alone, that ideas of good and evil need not be taken very seriously. These views are sure to be a hindrance to self-development, and they effectually cut Frost off from any really profound understanding of human experience, whether political, moral, metaphysical, or religious. The result in the didactic poems is the perversity and incoherence of thought; the result in the narrative poems is either slightness of subject or a flat and uninteresting apprehension of the subject; the result in the symbolic lyrics is a disturbing dislocation between the descriptive surface, which is frequently lovely, and the ultimate meaning, which is usually sentimental and unacceptable. The result in nearly all the poems is a measure of carelessness in the style, sometimes small and sometimes great, but usually evident: the conversational manner will naturally suit a poet who takes all experience so casually, and it is only natural that the conversational manner should often become very conversational indeed.

From The Function of Criticism

ROBERT FROST: POEMS

Mowing

There was never a sound beside the wood but one,
And that was my long scythe whispering to the ground.
What was it it whispered? I knew not well myself;
Perhaps it was something about the heat of the sun,
Something, perhaps, about the lack of sound—　　　　　5
And that was why it whispered and did not speak.
It was no dream of the gift of idle hours,
Or easy gold at the hand of fay or elf:
Anything more than the truth would have seemed too weak
To the earnest love that laid the swale in rows,　　　　　10
Not without feeble-pointed spikes of flowers
(Pale orchises), and scared a bright green snake.
The fact is the sweetest dream that labor knows.
My long scythe whispered and left the hay to make.

(1913)

The Tuft of Flowers

I went to turn the grass once after one
Who mowed it in the dew before the sun.

The dew was gone that made his blade so keen
Before I came to view the leveled scene.

I looked for him behind an isle of trees;   5
I listened for his whetstone in the breeze.

But he had gone his way, the grass all mown,
And I must be, as he had been,—alone,

"As all must be," I said within my heart,
"Whether they work together or apart."   10

But as I said it, swift there passed me by
On noiseless wing a bewildered butterfly,

Seeking with memories grown dim o'er night
Some resting flower of yesterday's delight.

And once I marked his flight go round and round,   15
As where some flower lay withering on the ground.

And then he flew as far as eye could see,
And then on tremulous wing came back to me.

I thought of questions that have no reply,
And would have turned to toss the grass to dry;   20

But he turned first, and led my eye to look
At a tall tuft of flowers beside a brook,

A leaping tongue of bloom the scythe had spared
Beside a reedy brook the scythe had bared.

The mower in the dew had loved them thus,   25
By leaving them to flourish, not for us,

Nor yet to draw one thought of ours to him,
But from sheer morning gladness at the brim.

The butterfly and I had lit upon,
Nevertheless, a message from the dawn,   30

That made me hear the wakening birds around,
And hear his long scythe whispering to the ground,

And feel a spirit kindred to my own;
So that henceforth I worked no more alone;

But glad with him, I worked as with his aid,   35
And weary, sought at noon with him the shade;

And dreaming, as it were, held brotherly speech
With one whose thought I had not hoped to reach.

"Men work together," I told him from the heart,
"Whether they work together or apart."   40

                                                    (1913)

Mending Wall

Something there is that doesn't love a wall,
That sends the frozen-ground-swell under it,
And spills the upper boulders in the sun;
And makes gaps even two can pass abreast.
The work of hunters is another thing: 5
I have come after them and made repair
Where they have left not one stone on a stone,
But they would have the rabbit out of hiding,
To please the yelping dogs. The gaps I mean,
No one has seen them made or heard them made,   10
But at spring mending-time we find them there.
I let my neighbor know beyond the hill;
And on a day we meet to walk the line
And set the wall between us once again.
We keep the wall between us as we go.   15
To each the boulders that have fallen to each.
And some are loaves and some so nearly balls
We have to use a spell to make them balance:
"Stay where you are until our backs are turned!"
We wear our fingers rough with handling them.   20
Oh, just another kind of outdoor game,
One on a side. It comes to little more:
There where it is we do not need the wall:
He is all pine and I am apple orchard.
My apple trees will never get across   25
And eat the cones under his pines, I tell him.
He only says, "Good fences make good neighbors."

Spring is the mischief in me, and I wonder
If I could put a notion in his head:
"*Why* do they make good neighbors? Isn't it   30
Where there are cows? But here there are no cows.
Before I built a wall I'd ask to know
What I was walling in or walling out,
And to whom I was like to give offense.
Something there is that doesn't love a wall,   35
That wants it down." I could say "Elves" to him,
But it's not elves exactly, and I'd rather
He said it for himself. I see him there
Bringing a stone grasped firmly by the top
In each hand, like an old-stone savage armed.   40
He moves in darkness as it seems to me,
Not of woods only and the shade of trees.
He will not go behind his father's saying,
And he likes having thought of it so well
He says again, "Good fences make good neighbors."   45

(1914)

Birches

When I see birches bend to left and right
Across the lines of straighter darker trees,
I like to think some boy's been swinging them.
But swinging doesn't bend them down to stay
As ice-storms do. Often you must have seen them   5
Loaded with ice a sunny winter morning
After a rain. They click upon themselves
As the breeze rises, and turn many-colored
As the stir cracks and crazes their enamel.
Soon the sun's warmth makes them shed crystal shells   10
Shattering and avalanching on the snow-crust—
Such heaps of broken glass to sweep away
You'd think the inner dome of heaven had fallen.
They are dragged to the withered bracken by the load,
And they seem not to break; though once they are bowed   15
So low for long, they never right themselves:
You may see their trunks arching in the woods
Years afterwards, trailing their leaves on the ground
Like girls on hands and knees that throw their hair
Before them over their heads to dry in the sun.   20
But I was going to say when Truth broke in
With all her matter-of-fact about the ice-storm,
I should prefer to have some boy bend them

As he went out and in to fetch the cows—
Some boy too far from town to learn baseball,   25
Whose only play was what he found himself,
Summer or winter, and could play alone.
One by one he subdued his father's trees
By riding them down over and over again
Until he took the stiffness out of them,   30
And not one but hung limp, not one was left
For him to conquer. He learned all there was
To learn about not launching out too soon
And so not carrying the tree away
Clear to the ground. He always kept his poise   35
To the top branches, climbing carefully
With the same pains you use to fill a cup
Up to the brim, and even above the brim.
Then he flung outward, feet first, with a swish,
Kicking his way down through the air to the ground.   40
So was I once myself a swinger of birches.
And so I dream of going back to be.
It's when I'm weary of considerations,
And life is too much like a pathless wood
Where your face burns and tickles with the cobwebs   45
Broken across it, and one eye is weeping
From a twig's having lashed across it open.
I'd like to get away from earth awhile
And then come back to it and begin over.
May no fate willfully misunderstand me   50
And half grant what I wish and snatch me away
Not to return. Earth's the right place for love:
I don't know where it's likely to go better.
I'd like to go by climbing a birch tree,
And climb black branches up a snow-white trunk   55
Toward heaven, till the tree could bear no more,
But dipped its top and set me down again.
That would be good both going and coming back.
One could do worse than be a swinger of birches.

                                                        (1916)

Home Burial

He saw her from the bottom of the stairs
Before she saw him. She was starting down,
Looking back over her shoulder at some fear.
She took a doubtful step and then undid it
To raise herself and look again. He spoke   5

Advancing toward her: "What is it you see
From up there always—for I want to know."
She turned and sank upon her skirts at that,
And her face changed from terrified to dull.
He said to gain time: "What is it you see"   10
Mounting until she cowered under him.
"I will find out now—you must tell me, dear."
She, in her place, refused him any help
With the least stiffening of her neck and silence.
She let him look, sure that he wouldn't see,   15
Blind creature; and awhile he didn't see.
But at last he murmured, "Oh," and again, "Oh."

"What is it—what?" she said.
                                "Just that I see."

"You don't," she challenged. "Tell me what it is."

"The wonder is I didn't see at once.   20
I never noticed it from here before.
I must be wonted to it—that's the reason.
The little graveyard where my people are!
So small the window frames the whole of it.
Not so much larger than a bedroom, is it?   25
There are three stones of slate and one of marble,
Broad-shouldered little slabs there in the sunlight
On the sidehill. We haven't to mind *those*.
But I understand: it is not the stones,
But the child's mound—"
                    "Don't, don't, don't,
        don't," she cried.   30

She withdrew shrinking from beneath his arm
That rested on the banister, and slid downstairs;
And turned on him with such a daunting look,
He said twice over before he knew himself:
"Can't a man speak of his own child he's lost?"   35

"Not you! Oh, where's my hat? Oh, I don't need it!
I must get out of here. I must get air.
I don't know rightly whether any man can."

"Amy! Don't go to someone else this time.
Listen to me. I won't come down the stairs."   40
He sat and fixed his chin between his fists.
"There's something I should like to ask you, dear."

"You don't know how to ask it."
                              "Help me, then."

Her fingers moved the latch for all reply.

"My words are nearly always an offense.   45
I don't know how to speak of anything
So as to please you. But I might be taught
I should suppose. I can't say I see how.
A man must partly give up being a man
With women-folk. We could have some arrangement   50
By which I'd bind myself to keep hands off
Anything special you're a-mind to name.
Though I don't like such things 'twixt those that love.
Two that don't love can't live together without them.
But two that do can't live together with them."   55
She moved the latch a little. "Don't—don't go.
Don't carry it to someone else this time.
Tell me about it if it's something human.
Let me into your grief. I'm not so much
Unlike other folks as your standing there   60
Apart would make me out. Give me my chance.
I do think, though, you overdo it a little.
What was it brought you up to think it the thing
To take your mother-loss of a first child
So inconsolably—in the face of love.   65
You'd think his memory might be satisfied—"

"There you go sneering now!"
                          "I'm not, I'm not!
You make me angry. I'll come down to you.
God, what a woman! And it's come to this,
A man can't speak of his own child that's dead."   70

"You can't because you don't know how to speak.
If you had any feelings, you that dug
With your own hand—how could you?—his little grave;
I saw you from that very window there,
Making the gravel leap and leap in air,   75
Leap up, like that, like that, and land so lightly
And roll back down the mound beside the hole.
I thought, Who is that man? I didn't know you.
And I crept down the stairs and up the stairs
To look again, and still your spade kept lifting.   80
Then you came in. I heard your rumbling voice
Out in the kitchen, and I don't know why,
But I went near to see with my own eyes.

You could sit there with the stains on your shoes
Of the fresh earth from your own baby's grave   85
And talk about your everyday concerns.
You had stood the spade up against the wall
Outside there in the entry, for I saw it."

"I shall laugh the worst laugh I ever laughed.
I'm cursed. God, if I don't believe I'm cursed."   90

"I can repeat the very words you were saying.
'Three foggy mornings and one rainy day
Will rot the best birch fence a man can build.'
Think of it, talk like that at such a time!
What had how long it takes a birch to rot   95
To do with what was in the darkened parlor?
You *couldn't* care! The nearest friends can go
With anyone to death, comes so far short
They might as well not try to go at all.
No, from the time when one is sick to death,   100
One is alone, and he dies more alone.
Friends make pretense of following to the grave,
But before one is in it, their minds are turned
And making the best of their way back to life
And living people, and things they understand.   105
But the world's evil. I won't have grief so
If I can change it. Oh, I won't, I won't!"

"There, you have said it all and you feel better.
You won't go now. You're crying. Close the door.
The heart's gone out of it: why keep it up.   110
Amy! There's someone coming down the road!"

"You—oh, you think the talk is all. I must go—
Somewhere out of this house. How can I make you—"

"If—you—do!" She was opening the door wider.
"Where do you mean to go? First tell me that.   115
I'll follow and bring you back by force. I *will!*—"

                                                              (1914)

Hyla Brook

By June our brook's run out of song and speed.
Sought for much after that, it will be found
Either to have gone groping underground
(And taken with it all the Hyla breed

That shouted in the mist a month ago,   5
Like ghost of sleigh bells in a ghost of snow)—
Or flourished and come up in jewelweed,
Weak foliage that is blown upon and bent
Even against the way its waters went.
Its bed is left a faded paper sheet   10
Of dead leaves stuck together by the heat—
A brook to none but who remember long.
This as it will be seen is other far
Than with brooks taken otherwhere in song.
We love the things we love for what they are.   15

(1916)

Putting in the Seed

You come to fetch me from my work tonight
When supper's on the table, and we'll see
If I can leave off burying the white
Soft petals fallen from the apple tree
(Soft petals, yes, but not so barren quite,   5
Mingled with these, smooth bean and wrinkled pea),
And go along with you ere you lose sight
Of what you came for and become like me,
Slave to a springtime passion for the earth.
How Love burns through the Putting in the Seed   10
On through the watching for that early birth
When, just as the soil tarnishes with weed,
The sturdy seedling with arched body comes
Shouldering its way and shedding the earth crumbs.

(1916)

Fire and Ice

Some say the world will end in fire,
Some say in ice.
From what I've tasted of desire
I hold with those who favor fire.
But if it had to perish twice,   5
I think I know enough of hate
To say that for destruction ice
Is also great
And would suffice.

(1923)

For Once, Then, Something

Others taunt me with having knelt at well-curbs
Always wrong to the light, so never seeing
Deeper down in the well than where the water
Gives me back in a shining surface picture
Me myself in the summer heaven godlike   5
Looking out of a wreath of fern and cloud puffs.
Once, when trying with chin against a well-curb,
I discerned, as I thought, beyond the picture,
Through the picture, a something white, uncertain,
Something more of the depths—and then I lost it.   10
Water came to rebuke the too clear water.
One drop fell from a fern, and lo, a ripple
Shook whatever it was lay there at bottom,
Blurred it, blotted it out. What was that whiteness?
Truth? A pebble of quartz? For once, then, something.   15

(1923)

Two Look at Two

Love and forgetting might have carried them
A little further up the mountainside
With night so near, but not much further up.
They must have halted soon in any case
With thoughts of the path back, how rough it was   5
With rock and washout, and unsafe in darkness;
When they were halted by a tumbled wall
With barbed-wire binding. They stood facing this,
Spending what onward impulse they still had
In one last look the way they must not go,   10
On up the failing path, where, if a stone
On earthside moved at night, it moved itself;
No footstep moved it. "This is all," they sighed,
"Good-night to woods." But not so; there was more.
A doe from round a spruce stood looking at them   15
Across the wall, as near the wall as they.
She saw them in their field, they her in hers.
The difficulty of seeing what stood still,
Like some up-ended boulder split in two,
Was in her clouded eyes: they saw no fear there.   20
She seemed to think that two thus they were safe.
Then, as if they were something that, though strange,
She could not trouble her mind with too long,
She sighed and passed unscared along the wall.

"*This*, then, is all. What more is there to ask?"   25
But no, not yet. A snort to bid them wait.
A buck from round the spruce stood looking at them
Across the wall, as near the wall as they.
This was an antlered buck of lusty nostril,   30
Not the same doe come back into her place.
He viewed them quizzically with jerks of head,
As if to ask, "Why don't you make some motion?
Or give some sign of life? Because you can't.
I doubt if you're as living as you look."
Thus till he had them almost feeling dared   35
To stretch a proffering hand—and a spell-breaking.
Then he too passed unscared along the wall.
Two had seen two, whichever side you spoke from.
"This *must* be all." It was all. Still they stood,
A great wave from it going over them,   40
As if the earth in one unlooked-for favor
Had made them certain earth returned their love.

                                                                   (1923)

Once by the Pacific

The shattered water made a misty din.
Great waves looked over others coming in,
And thought of doing something to the shore
That water never did to land before.
The clouds were low and hairy in the skies,   5
Like locks blown forward in the gleam of eyes.
You could not tell, and yet it looked as if
The shore was lucky in being backed by cliff,
The cliff in being backed by continent;
It looked as if a night of dark intent   10
Was coming, and not only a night, an age.
Someone had better be prepared for rage.
There would be more than ocean-water broken
Before God's last *Put out the Light* was spoken.

                                                                   (1928)

Acquainted with the night

I have been one acquainted with the night.
I have walked out in rain—and back in rain.
I have outwalked the furthest city light.

I have looked down the saddest city lane.
I have passed by the watchman on his beat   5
And dropped my eyes, unwilling to explain.

I have stood still and stopped the sound of feet
When far away an interrupted cry
Came over houses from another street,

But not to call me back or say good-by;   10
And further still at an unearthly height
One luminary clock against the sky

Proclaimed the time was neither wrong nor right.
I have been one acquainted with the night.

(1928)

Tree at my window

Tree at my window, window tree,
My sash is lowered when night comes on;
But let there never be curtain drawn
Between you and me.

Vague dream-head lifted out of the ground,   5
And thing next most diffuse to cloud,
Not all your light tongues talking aloud
Could be profound.

But, tree, I have seen you taken and tossed,
And if you have seen me when I slept,   10
You have seen me when I was taken and swept
And all but lost.

That day she put our heads together,
Fate had her imagination about her,
Your head so much concerned with outer,   15
Mine with inner, weather.

(1928)

Departmental

An ant on the tablecloth
Ran into a dormant moth
Of many times his size.
He showed not the least surprise.
His business wasn't with such.   5
He gave it scarcely a touch,
And was off on his duty run.
Yet if he encountered one
Of the hive's enquiry squad
Whose work is to find out God   10
And the nature of time and space,
He would put him onto the case.
Ants are a curious race;
One crossing with hurried tread
The body of one of their dead   15
Isn't given a moment's arrest—
Seems not even impressed.
But he no doubt reports to any
With whom he crosses antennae,
And they no doubt report   20
To the higher up at court.
Then word goes forth in Formic:
"Death's come to Jerry McCormic,
Our selfless forager Jerry.
Will the special Janizary   25
Whose office it is to bury
The dead of the commissary
Go bring him home to his people.
Lay him in state on a sepal.
Wrap him for shroud in a petal.   30
Embalm him with ichor of nettle.
This is the word of your Queen."
And presently on the scene
Appears a solemn mortician:
And taking formal position   35
With feelers calmly atwiddle,
Seizes the dead by the middle,
And heaving him high in the air,
Carries him out of there.
No one stands round to stare.   40
It is nobody else's affair.

It couldn't be called ungentle.
But how thoroughly departmental.

                                                    (1936)

Desert Places

Snow falling and night falling fast, oh, fast
In a field I looked into going past,
And the ground almost covered smooth in snow,
But a few weeds and stubble showing last.

The woods around it have it—it is theirs. 5
All animals are smothered in their lairs.
I am too absent-spirited to count;
The loneliness includes me unawares.

And lonely as it is, that loneliness
Will be more lonely ere it will be less— 10
A blanker whiteness of benighted snow
With no expression, nothing to express.

They cannot scare me with their empty spaces
Between stars—on stars where no human race is.
I have it in me so much nearer home 15
To scare myself with my own desert places.

(1936)

Design

I found a dimpled spider, fat and white,
On a white heal-all, holding up a moth
Like a white piece of rigid satin cloth—
Assorted characters of death and blight
Mixed ready to begin the morning right, 5
Like the ingredients of a witches' broth—
A snow-drop spider, a flower like a froth,
And dead wings carried like a paper kite.

What had that flower to do with being white,
The wayside blue and innocent heal-all? 10
What brought the kindred spider to that height,
Then steered the white moth thither in the night?
What but design of darkness to appall?—
If design govern in a thing so small.

(1936)

Provide, Provide

The witch that came (the withered hag)
To wash the steps with pail and rag,
Was once the beauty Abishag,

The picture pride of Hollywood.
Too many fall from great and good   5
For you to doubt the likelihood.

Die early and avoid the fate.
Or if predestined to die late,
Make up your mind to die in state.

Make the whole stock exchange your own!   10
If need be occupy a throne,
Where nobody can call *you* crone.

Some have relied on what they knew;
Others on being simply true.
What worked for them might work for you.   15

No memory of having starred
Atones for later disregard
Or keeps the end from being hard.

Better to go down dignified
With boughten friendship at your side   20
Than none at all. Provide, provide!

(1936)

The Most of It

He thought he kept the universe alone;
For all the voice in answer he could wake
Was but the mocking echo of his own
From some tree-hidden cliff across the lake.
Some morning from the boulder-broken beach   5
He would cry out on life, that what it wants
Is not its own love back in copy speech,
But counter-love, original response.
And nothing ever came of what he cried
Unless it was the embodiment that crashed   10
In the cliff's talus on the other side,
And then in the far-distant water splashed,

But after a time allowed for it to swim,
Instead of proving human when it neared
And someone else additional to him,   15
As a great buck it powerfully appeared,
Pushing the crumpled water up ahead,
And landed pouring like a waterfall,
And stumbled through the rocks with horny tread,
And forced the underbrush—and that was all.   20

(1942)

CHAPTER SIXTEEN

A Collection of Poems

The forms of things unknown, the poet's pen / Turns them to shapes, and gives to airy nothing / A local habitation and a name.

WILLIAM SHAKESPEARE

A good poem is a contribution to reality. The world is never the same once a good poem has been added to it.

DYLAN THOMAS

SAPPHO

[*7th–6th century B.C.*]

To me he seems like a god

To me he seems like a god
as he sits facing you and
hears you near as you speak
softly and laugh
in a sweet echo that jolts
the heart in my ribs. For now
as I look at you my voice
is empty and

5

can say nothing as my tongue
cracks and slender fire is quick   10
under my skin. My eyes are dead
to light, my ears

pound, and sweat pours over me.
I convulse, paler than grass,
and feel my mind slip as I   15
go close to death

[but must suffer all, being poor.]

TRANSLATED BY WILLIS BARNSTONE

(c. 6th century B.C.*)*

ANONYMOUS

Barbara Allan

1

It was in and about the Martinmas time,
   When the green leaves were a falling,
That Sir John Græme, in the West Country,
   Fell in love with Barbara Allan.

2

He sent his man down through the town,   5
   To the place where she was dwelling:
"O haste and come to my master dear,
   Gin° ye be Barbara Allan."   if

3

O hooly,° hooly rose she up,   gently
   To the place where he was lying,   10
And when she drew the curtain by:
   "Young man, I think you're dying."

4

"O it's I'm sick, and very, very sick,
   And 'tis a' for Barbara Allan."

"Barbara Allan"   [1]*Martinmas*   *Mass (or feast) of St. Martin (d. 655) on November 11.*

"O the better for me ye s'° never be,   shall   15
    Though your heart's blood were a-spilling.

5

"O dinna ye mind, young man," said she,
    "When ye was in the tavern a drinking,
That ye made the healths gae° round and round,   go
    And slighted Barbara Allan?"   20

6

He turned his face unto the wall,
    And death was with him dealing:
"Adieu, adieu, my dear friends all,
    And be kind to Barbara Allan."

7

And slowly, slowly raise she up,   25
    And slowly, slowly left him,
And sighing said, she could not stay,
    Since death of life had reft° him.   deprived

8

She had not gane° a mile but twa,°   gone/two
    When she heard the dead-bell ringing,   30
And every jow° that the dead-bell geid,°   beat/gave
    It cried, "Woe to Barbara Allan!"

9

"O mother, mother, make my bed!
    O make it saft and narrow!
Since my love died for me to-day,   35
    I'll die for him to-morrow."

(c. 14th century)

ANONYMOUS

Edward, Edward

1

"Why does your brand° sae° drap wi' bluid,   sword/so
    Edward, Edward,

---

[17]**dinna ye mind**   *don't you remember.*

Why does your brand sae drap wi' bluid,
    And why sae sad gang° ye, O?"   go
"O I ha'e killed my hawk sae guid,   5
    Mither, mither,
O I ha'e killed my hawk sae guid,
    And I had nae mair but he, O."

2

"Your hawk's bluid was never sae reid,°   red
    Edward, Edward,   10
Your hawk's bluid was never sae reid,
    My dear son, I tell thee, O."
"O I ha'e killed my reid-roan steed,
    Mither, mither,
O I ha'e killed my reid-roan steed,   15
    That erst was sae fair and free, O."

3

"Your steed was auld, and ye ha'e gat mair,
    Edward, Edward,
Your steed was auld, and ye ha'e gat mair,
    Some other dule° ye drie°, O."   grief/suffer   20
"O I ha'e killed my fader dear,
    Mither, mither,
O I ha'e killed my fader dear,
    Alas, and wae° is me, O!"   woe

4

"And whatten° penance wul ye dree for that,   what kind of   25
    Edward, Edward?
And whatten penance wul ye dree for that,
    My dear son, now tell me O?"
"I'll set my feet in yonder boat,
    Mither, mither,   30
I'll set my feet in yonder boat,
    And I'll fare over the sea, O."

5

"And what wul ye do wi' your towers and your ha',
    Edward, Edward?
And what wul ye do wi' your towers and your ha',   35
    That were sae fair to see, O?"
"I'll let them stand tul they down fa',
    Mither, mither,
I'll let them stand tul they down fa',
    For here never mair maun° I be, O."   must   40

6

"And what wul ye leave to your bairns° and your wife,   *children*
     Edward, Edward?
And what wul ye leave to your bairns and your wife,
     Whan ye gang over the sea, O?"
"The warlde's room, let them beg thrae° life,   *through*   45
     Mither, mither,
The warlde's room, let them beg thrae life,
     For them never mair wul I see, O."

7

"And what wul ye leave to your ain mither dear,
     Edward, Edward?   50
And what wul ye leave to your ain mither dear,
     My dear son, now tell me, O?"
"The curse of hell frae° me sall° ye bear,   *from/shall*
     Mither, mither,
The curse of hell frae me sall ye bear,   55
     Sic° counsels ye gave to me, O."   *such*

(c. 14th century)

THOMAS WYATT

[1503–1542]

They flee from me

They flee from me, that sometime did me seek,
With naked foot stalking in my chamber.
I have seen them, gentle, tame, and meek,
That now are wild, and do not remember
That sometime they put themselves in danger   5
To take bread at my hand; and now they range,
Busily seeking with a continual change.

Thanked be Fortune it hath been otherwise,
Twenty times better; but once in special,
In thin array, after a pleasant guise,   10
When her loose gown from her shoulders did fall,
And she me caught in her arms long and small,°   *thin*
And therewith all sweetly did me kiss
And softly said, "Dear heart, how like you this?"

It was no dream, I lay broad waking.   15
But all is turned, thorough° my gentleness,   through
Into a strange fashion of forsaking;
And I have leave to go, of her goodness,
And she also to use newfangleness.
But since that I so kindely am served,   20
I fain would know what she hath deserved.

       (1557)

EDMUND SPENSER
[1552–1599]

One day I wrote her name upon the strand

One day I wrote her name upon the strand°,   beach
But came the waves and washéd it away:
Agayne I wrote it with a second hand,
But came the tyde, and made my paynes his pray.
"Vayne man," sayd she, "that doest in vaine assay,   5
A mortall thing so to immortalize,
For I my selve shall lyke to this decay,
And eek° my name bee wypéd out lykewize."   also
"Not so," quod° I, "let baser things devize°   said/devise
To dy in dust, but you shall live by fame: 10
My verse your vertues rare shall eternize,
And in the hevens wryte your glorious name.
Where whenas death shall all the world subdew,
Our love shall live, and later life renew."

      (1595)

WILLIAM SHAKESPEARE
[1564–1616]

When in disgrace with fortune and men's eyes

When, in disgrace with fortune and men's eyes,
I all alone beweep my outcast state,
And trouble deaf heaven with my bootless° cries,   useless
And look upon myself, and curse my fate,

Wishing me like to one more rich in hope,   5
Featured like him, like him with friends possessed,
Desiring this man's art and that man's scope,
With what I most enjoy contented least;
Yet in these thoughts myself almost despising,
Haply I think on thee—and then my state,   10
Like to the lark at break of day arising
From sullen earth, sings hymns at heaven's gate;
For thy sweet love remembered such wealth brings
That then I scorn to change my state with kings.

                                                                              (1609)

Let me not to the marriage of true minds

Let me not to the marriage of true minds
Admit impediments°. Love is not love   hindrances
Which alters when it alteration finds,
Or bends with the remover to remove:
Oh, no! it is an ever-fixéd mark,   5
That looks on tempests and is never shaken;
It is the star to every wandering bark,°   ship
Whose worth's unknown, although his height be taken.
Love's not Time's fool, though rosy lips and cheeks
Within his bending sickle's compass come;   10
Love alters not with his brief hours and weeks,
But bears° it out even to the edge of doom.°   lasts/judgment day
If this be error and upon me proved,
I never writ, nor no man ever loved.

                                                                              (1609)

Th' expense of spirit in a waste of shame

Th' expense of spirit in a waste of shame
Is lust in action; and till action, lust
Is perjured, murderous, bloody, full of blame,
Savage, extreme, rude, cruel, not to trust;
Enjoyed no sooner but despiséd straight: 5
Past reason hunted; and no sooner had,
Past reason hated, as a swallowed bait,
On purpose laid to make the taker mad:
Mad in pursuit, and in possession so;

"Let Me Not to the Marraige of True Minds"   [8]*height be taken*   *its elevation be measured.*

Had, having, and in quest to have, extreme;   10
A bliss in proof,° and proved, a very woe;   in the experience
Before, a joy proposed; behind, a dream.
All this the world well knows; yet none knows well
To shun the heaven that leads men to this hell.

(1609)

My mistress' eyes are nothing like the sun

My mistress' eyes are nothing like the sun;
Coral is far more red than her lips' red;
If snow be white, why then her breasts are dun;
If hairs be wires, black wires grow on her head.
I have seen roses damasked,° red and white,   variegated   5
But no such roses see I in her cheeks;
And in some perfumes is there more delight
Than in the breath that from my mistress reeks.
I love to hear her speak, yet well I know
That music hath a far more pleasing sound;   10
I grant I never saw a goddess go°;   walk
My mistress, when she walks, treads on the ground.
And yet, by heaven, I think my love as rare
As any she belied with false compare.

(1609)

JOHN DONNE
[1572–1631]

Song

Go, and catch a falling star,
    Get with child a mandrake root,
Tell me, where all past years are,
    Or who cleft the devil's foot,
Teach me to hear mermaids singing   5
Or to keep off envy's stinging,
        And find
        What wind
Serves to advance an honest mind.

"Song"   [2]**mandrake root**   *Resembling a human body, the forked root of the mandrake was used as a medicine to induce conception.*

If thou beest born to strange sights,   10
    Things invisible to see,
Ride ten thousand days and nights,
    Till age snow white hairs on thee;
Thou, when thou return'st, wilt tell me
All strange wonders that befell thee,   15
       And swear,
       No where
Lives a woman true, and fair.

If thou find'st one, let me know:
    Such a pilgrimage were sweet.   20
Yet do not, I would not go,
    Though at next door we might meet:
Though she were true when you met her,
And last till you write your letter,
       Yet she   25
       Will be
False, ere I come, to two, or three.

                     (1633)

The Canonization

For God's sake hold your tongue, and let me love,
    Or chide my palsy, or my gout,
My five gray hairs, or ruined fortune, flout,
    With wealth your state, your mind with arts improve,
      Take you a course,° get you a place,°   direction/appointment 5
      Observe His Honor, or His Grace,
Or the King's real, or his stampéd face°   on a coin
      Contémplate; what you will, approve°,   try
      So you will let me love.

Alas, alas, who's injured by my love?   10
    What merchant's ships have my sighs drowned?
Who says my tears have overflowed his ground?
    When did my colds a forward spring remove?
      When did the heats which my veins fill
      Add one more to the plaguy bill?°   list of victims 15
Soldiers find wars, and lawyers find out still
    Litigious men, which quarrels move,
    Though she and I do love.

Call us what you will, we're made such by love;
    Call her one, me another fly,   20

We're tapers too, and at our own cost die,
    And we in us find th' eagle and the dove
       The phoenix riddle hath more wit°   sense
       By us: we two being one, are it.
So, to one neutral thing both sexes fit.   25
    We die and rise the same, and prove
    Mysterious by this love.

We can die by it, if not live by love,
    And if unfit for tombs and hearse
Our legend be, it will be fit for verse;   30
    And if no piece of chronicle we prove,
       We'll build in sonnets pretty rooms;
       As well a well-wrought urn becomes
The greatest ashes, as half-acre tombs;
    And by these hymns, all shall approve   35
    Us canonized for love:

And thus invoke us: You whom reverend love
    Made one another's hermitage;
You, to whom love was peace, that now is rage;
    Who did the whole world's soul contract, and drove   40
       Into the glasses of your eyes
       (So made such mirrors, and such spies,
That they did all to you epitomize)
    Countries, towns, courts: Beg from above
    A pattern of your love!

                                                            (1633)

A Valediction: Forbidding Mourning

As virtuous men pass mildly away,
    And whisper to their souls to go,
Whilst some of their sad friends do say,
    "The breath goes now," and some say, "No,"

So let us melt, and make no noise,   5
    No tear-floods, nor sigh-tempests move;
    'Twere profanation of our joys
       To tell the laity our love.

"The Canonization" ²¹**at our own cost die** *Death was a metaphor for sexual intercourse; each act of sexual congress supposedly shortened one's life by a day.* ²³**the phoenix riddle** *a legendary, mythological bird, the only one of its kind. It is consumed in fire and then resurrected from the ashes to begin life anew.*

Moving of the earth° brings harms and fears,   earthquakes
    Men reckon what it did and meant;   10
But trepidation of the spheres,
    Though greater far, is innocent.

Dull sublunary° lovers' love   earthly
    (Whose soul is sense) cannot admit
Absence, because it doth remove   15
    Those things which elemented° it.   composed

But we, by a love so much refined
    That our selves know not what it is,
Inter-assured of the mind,
    Care less, eyes, lips, and hands to miss.   20

Our two souls therefore, which are one,
    Though I must go, endure not yet
A breach, but an expansion,
    Like gold to airy thinness beat.

If they be two, they are two so   25
    As stiff twin compasses are two:
Thy soul, the fixed foot, makes no show
    To move, but doth, if the other do;

And though it in the center sit,
    Yet when the other far doth roam,   30
It leans, and hearkens after it,
    And grows erect, as that comes home.

Such wilt thou be to me, who must,
    Like the other foot, obliquely run;
Thy firmness makes my circle just,   35
    And makes me end where I begun.

                                              (1633)

The Flea

Mark but this flea, and mark in this
How little that which thou deny'st me is;
It sucked me first, and now sucks thee,
And in this flea our two bloods mingled be;

"A Valediction"   [11] **trepidation of the spheres**   *movement in the outermost of the heavenly spheres. In Ptolemy's astronomy these outer spheres caused others to vary from their orbits.*   [26] **twin compasses**   *the two feet of a mathematical compass used for drawing circles.*

Thou know'st that this cannot be said   5
A sin, nor shame, nor loss of maidenhead;
    Yet this enjoys before it woo,
    And pampered swells with one blood made of two,
    And this, alas, is more than we would do.

Oh stay, three lives in one flea spare,   10
Where we almost, yea, more than married are.
This flea is you and I, and this
Our marriage bed and marriage temple is;
Though parents grudge, and you, we are met
And cloistered in these living walls of jet.   15
    Though use° make you apt to kill me,   custom
    Let not to that, self-murder added be,
    And sacrilege, three sins in killing three.

Cruel and sudden, hast thou since
Purpled thy nail in blood of innocence?   20
Wherein could this flea guilty be,
Except in that drop which it sucked from thee?
Yet thou triumph'st and say'st that thou
Find'st not thyself, nor me the weaker now.
    'Tis true. Then learn how false fears be: 25
    Just so much honor, when thou yield'st to me,
    Will waste, as this flea's death took life from thee.

(1633)

Death, be not proud

Death, be not proud, though some have callèd thee
Mighty and dreadful, for thou are not so;
For those whom thou think'st thou dost overthrow
Die not, poor Death, nor yet canst thou kill me.
From rest and sleep, which but thy pictures be,   5
Much pleasure; then from thee much more must flow,
And soonest our best men with thee do go,
Rest of their bones, and soul's delivery.
Thou art slave to fate, chance, kings, and desperate men,
And dost with poison, war, and sickness dwell,   10
And poppy or charms can make us sleep as well
And better than thy stroke; why swell'st thou then?
One short sleep past, we wake eternally
And death shall be no more; Death, thou shalt die.

(1633)

Batter my heart, three-personed God

Batter my heart, three-personed God; for You
As yet but knock, breathe, shine, and seek to mend;
That I may rise and stand, o'erthrow me, and bend
Your force to break, blow, burn, and make me new.
I, like an usurped town, to another due,   5
Labor to admit You, but O, to no end;
Reason, Your viceroy in me, me should defend,
But is captíved, and proves weak or untrue.
Yet dearly I love You, and would be lovéd fain°,   gladly
But am betrothed unto Your enemy.   10
Divorce me, untie or break that knot again;
Take me to You, imprison me, for I,
Except You enthrall me, never shall be free,
Nor ever chaste, except You ravish me.

                                                         (1633)

BEN JONSON
[1573?–1637]

On My First Son

Farewell, thou child of my right hand, and joy;
My sin was too much hope of thee, loved boy:
Seven years thou wert lent to me, and I thee pay,
Exacted by thy fate, on the just day.
O could I lose all father now! for why   5
Will man lament the state he should envý,
To have so soon 'scaped world's and flesh's rage,
And, if no other misery, yet age?
Rest in soft peace, and asked, say, "Here doth lie
Ben Jonson his best piece of poetry."   10
For whose sake henceforth all his vows be such
As what he loves may never like too much.

                                                         (1616)

"On My First Son" ¹*child of my right hand* the literal meaning, in Hebrew, of Benjamin, the boy's name.
⁴*the just day* Jonson's son died on his seventh birthday.

Song: To Celia

Drink to me only with thine eyes,
And I will pledge with mine;
Or leave a kiss but in the cup,
And I'll not look for wine.
The thirst that from the soul doth rise,   5
Doth ask a drink divine:
But might I of Jove's nectar sup,
I would not change for thine.

I sent thee late a rosy wreath,
Not so much honoring thee,   10
As giving it a hope, that there
It could not withered be.
But thou thereon did'st only breathe,
And sent'st it back to me;
Since when it grows and smells, I swear,   15
Not of itself, but thee.

                                                        (1606)

ROBERT HERRICK
[1591–1667]

Upon Julia's Clothes

Whenas in silks my Julia goes,
Then, then, methinks, how sweetly flows
That liquefaction of her clothes.

Next, when I cast mine eyes and see
That brave vibration each way free,   5
O how that glittering taketh me!

                                                        (1648)

To the Virgins, to Make Much of Time

Gather ye rosebuds while ye may:
    Old Time is still a-flying;
And this same flower that smiles today,
    Tomorrow will be dying.

The glorious lamp of heaven, the sun,
     The higher he's a-getting,
The sooner will his race be run,
     And nearer he's to setting.   5

That age is best which is the first,
     When youth and blood are warmer;   10
But being spent, the worse, and worst
     Times, still succeed the former.

Then be not coy, but use your time;
     And while ye may, go marry:
For, having lost but once your prime,   15
     You may for ever tarry.

                                                          (1648)

GEORGE HERBERT

[1593–1633]

The Altar

A   broken   altar,   Lord,   Thy   servant   rears,
Made   of   a   heart   and   cemented   with   tears;
  Whose   parts   are   as   Thy   hand   did   frame;
  No   workman's   tool   hath   touched   the   same.
                    A   heart   alone   5
                    Is   such   a   stone,
                    As   nothing   but
                    Thy   power   doth   cut.
                    Wherefore   each   part
                    Of   my   hard   heart   10
                    Meets   in   this   frame
                    To   praise   Thy   name,
That   if   I   chance   to   hold   my   peace,
These   stones   to   praise   Thee   may   not   cease.
Oh,   let   Thy   blessed   sacrifice   be   mine,   15
And sanctify this altar to be Thine.

                                                          (1633)

JOHN MILTON
[1608–1674]

When I consider how my light is spent

When I consider how my light is spent
   Ere half my days, in this dark world and wide,
   And that one talent which is death to hide
   Lodged with me useless, though my soul more bent
To serve therewith my Maker, and present   5
   My true account, lest he returning chide;
   "Doth God exact day-labor, light denied?"
   I fondly° ask; but Patience to prevent   *foolishly*
That murmur, soon replies, "God doth not need
   Either man's work or his own gifts; who best   10
   Bear his mild yoke, they serve him best. His state
Is kingly. Thousands at his bidding speed
   And post o'er land and ocean without rest:
   They also serve who only stand and wait."

(1673)

On the Late Massacre in Piedmont

Avenge, O Lord, thy slaughtered saints, whose bones
   Lie scattered on the Alpine mountains cold,
   Even them who kept thy truth so pure of old
   When all our fathers worshiped stocks° and stones   *idols*
Forget not: in thy book record their groans   5
   Who were thy sheep and in their ancient fold
   Slain by the bloody Piedmontese that rolled
   Mother with infant down the rocks. Their moans
The vales redoubled to the hills, and they
   To Heaven. Their martyred blood and ashes sow   10
   O'er all th' Italian fields where still doth sway
The triple tyrant: that from these may grow
   A hundredfold, who having learnt thy way
   Early may fly the Babylonian woe.

(1673)

"When I Consider How My Light Is Spent" *Milton went blind in 1651.* ³**one talent** *an allusion to Jesus's parable of the talents, in which the servant who buried the talent given him by his master was cast into the darkness (Matthew 25:14–30).* "On the Late Massacre" *The Duke of Savoy in 1655 massacred 1,700 Waldensians, members of a Protestant sect.* ¹²**The triple tyrant** *the pope, whose tiara contains three crowns.*

ANNE BRADSTREET
[1612–1672]

To My Dear and Loving Husband

If ever two were one, then surely we.
If ever man were loved by wife, then thee;
If ever wife was happy in a man,
Compare with me, ye women, if you can.
I prize thy love more than whole mines of gold   5
Or all the riches that the East doth hold.
My love is such that rivers cannot quench,
Nor aught but love from thee give recompense.
Thy love is such I can no way repay,
The heavens reward thee manifold, I pray.   10
Then while we live, in love let's so perséver
That when we live no more, we may live ever.

(1678)

ANDREW MARVELL
[1621–1678]

To His Coy Mistress

Had we but world enough, and time,
This coyness, lady, were no crime.
We would sit down, and think which way
To walk, and pass our long love's day.
Thou by the Indian Ganges' side   5
Shoudst rubies find; I by the tide
Of Humber would complain. I would
Love you ten years before the flood,
And you should, if you please, refuse
Till the conversion of the Jews.   10
My vegetable love should grow
Vaster than empires and more slow;

"To His Coy Mistress"   6*rubies*   *associated with virginity.*   7***Humber***   *the river that runs through Marvell's native town, Hull.*   10***the conversion of the Jews***   *supposedly to occur at the end of time.*   11***vegetable love*** *a reference to the idea that vegetables have the power to grow but lack consciousness.*

An hundred years should go to praise
Thine eyes, and on thy forehead gaze;
Two hundred to adore each breast,   15
But thirty thousand to the rest;
An age at least to every part,
And the last age should show your heart.
For, lady, you deserve this state,
Nor would I love at lower rate.   20
    But at my back I always hear
Time's wingéd chariot hurrying near;
And yonder all before us lie
Deserts of vast eternity.
Thy beauty shall no more be found;   25
Nor, in thy marble vault, shall sound
My echoing song; then worms shall try
That long-preserved virginity,
And your quaint° honor turn to dust,   overscrupulous
And into ashes all my lust: 30
The grave's a fine and private place,
But none, I think, do there embrace.
    Now therefore, while the youthful hue
Sits on thy skin like morning dew
And while thy willing soul transpires°   breathes forth 35
At every pore with instant fires,
Now let us sport us while we may,
And now, like amorous birds of prey,
Rather at once our time devour
Than languish in his slow-chapped° power.   slow-jawed 40
Let us roll all our strength and all
Our sweetness up into one ball,
And tear our pleasures with rough strife
Thorough the iron gates of life:
Thus, though we cannot make our sun   45
Stand still, yet we will make him run.

                                   (1681)

ALEXANDER POPE

[1688–1744]

from *An Essay on Man*

from *Epistle II*

I. Know then thyself, presume not God to scan°;   scrutinize
The proper study of mankind is Man.
Placed on this isthmus of a middle state,
A being darkly wise, and rudely° great;   crudely
With too much knowledge for the Sceptic side,   5
With too much weakness for the Stoic's pride,
He hangs between; in doubt to act, or rest,
In doubt to deem himself a god, or beast;
In doubt his mind or body to prefer,
Born but to die, and reasoning but to err;   10
Alike in ignorance, his reason such,
Whether he thinks too little, or too much:
Chaos of thought and passion, all confused;
Still by himself abused, or disabused;
Created half to rise, and half to fall;   15
Great lord of all things, yet a prey to all;
Sole judge of truth, in endless error hurled:
The glory, jest, and riddle of the world!

                                                                      (1711)

WILLIAM BLAKE

[1757–1827]

The Clod & the Pebble

"Love seeketh not Itself to please,
Nor for itself hath any care;
But for another gives its ease,
And builds a Heaven in Hell's despair."

So sang a little Clod of Clay,   5
Trodden with the cattle's feet;
But a Pebble of the brook,
Warbled out these metres meet:

"Love seeketh only Self to please,
To bind another to its delight,   10
Joys in another's loss of ease,
And builds a Hell in Heaven's despite."

(1794)

The Lamb

Little Lamb, who made thee?
    Dost thou know who made thee?
Gave thee life & bid thee feed,
By the stream & o'er the mead;
Gave thee clothing of delight,   5
Softest clothing wooly bright;
Gave thee such a tender voice,
Making all the vales rejoice!
    Little Lamb who made thee?
    Dost thou know who made thee?   10

Little Lamb I'll tell thee,
    Little Lamb I'll tell thee!
He is callèd by thy name,
For he calls himself a Lamb:
He is meek & he is mild,   15
He became a little child:
I a child & thou a lamb,
We are callèd by his name.
    Little Lamb God bless thee.
    Little Lamb God bless thee.   20

(1789)

The Tyger

Tyger! Tyger! burning bright
In the forests of the night,
What immortal hand or eye
Could frame thy fearful symmetry?

In what distant deeps or skies   5
Burnt the fire of thine eyes?
On what wings dare he aspire?
What the hand, dare seize the fire?

And what shoulder, & what art,
Could twist the sinews of thy heart?   10
And when thy heart began to beat,
What dread hand? & what dread feet?

What the hammer? what the chain?
In what furnace was thy brain?
What the anvil? what dread grasp   15
Dare its deadly terrors clasp?

When the stars threw down their spears,
And water'd heaven with their tears,
Did he smile his work to see?
Did he who made the Lamb make thee?   20

Tyger! Tyger! burning bright
In the forests of the night,
What immortal hand or eye
Dare frame thy fearful symmetry?

(1794)

The Garden of Love

I went to the Garden of Love,
And saw what I never had seen:
A Chapel was built in the midst,
Where I used to play on the green.

And the gates of this Chapel were shut,   5
And "Thou shalt not" writ over the door;
So I turn'd to the Garden of Love,
That so many sweet flowers bore,

And I saw it was filled with graves,
And tomb-stones where flowers should be: 10
And Priests in black gowns were walking their rounds,
And binding with briars my joys & desires.

(1794)

ROBERT BURNS
[1759–1796]

A Red, Red Rose

O my luve's like a red, red rose,
  That's newly sprung in June;
O my luve's like the melodie
  That's sweetly played in tune.

As fair art thou, my bonnie lass,   5
  So deep in luve am I;
And I will luve thee still, my dear,
  Till a' the seas gang dry.

Till a' the seas gang dry, my dear,
  And the rocks melt wi' the sun: 10
O I will love thee still, my dear,
  While the sands o' life shall run.

And fare thee weel, my only luve,
  And fare thee weel awhile!
And I will come again, my luve,   15
  Though it were ten thousand mile.

                                        (1796)

WILLIAM WORDSWORTH
[1770–1850]

The world is too much with us

The world is too much with us; late and soon,
Getting and spending, we lay waste our powers;
Little we see in Nature that is ours;
We have given our hearts away, a sordid boon°!   gift
This Sea that bares her bosom to the moon,   5
The winds that will be howling at all hours,

And are up-gathered now like sleeping flowers,
For this, for everything, we are out of tune;
It moves us not.—Great God! I'd rather be   10
A Pagan suckled in a creed outworn;
So might I, standing on this pleasant lea,
Have glimpses that would make me less forlorn;
Have sight of Proteus rising from the sea;
Or hear old Triton blow his wreathèd horn.

                                                                        (1807)

The Solitary Reaper

Behold her, single in the field,
Yon solitary Highland Lass!
Reaping and singing by herself;
Stop here, or gently pass!
Alone she cuts and binds the grain,   5
And sings a melancholy strain;
O listen! for the Vale profound
Is overflowing with the sound.

No Nightingale did ever chaunt
More welcome notes to weary bands   10
Of travelers in some shady haunt,
Among Arabian sands;
A voice so thrilling ne'er was heard
In springtime from the Cuckoo bird,
Breaking the silence of the seas   15
Among the farthest Hebrides.

Will no one tell me what she sings?—
Perhaps the plaintive numbers flow
For old, unhappy, far-off things,
And battles long ago;   20
Or is it some more humble lay,
Familiar matter of today?

Some natural sorrow, loss, or pain,
That has been, and may be again?
Whate'er the theme, the Maiden sang   25
As if her song could have no ending;
I saw her singing at her work,

"The World Is Too Much with Us"   13-14*Proteus . . . Triton*   *classical sea gods. Triton's conch-shell horn calmed the waves.*

And o'er the sickle bending—
I listened, motionless and still;
And, as I mounted up the hill,   30
The music in my heart I bore,
Long after it was heard no more.

(1807)

Composed upon Westminster Bridge, September 3, 1802

Earth has not anything to show more fair:
Dull would he be of soul who could pass by
A sight so touching in its majesty;
This City now doth, like a garment, wear
The beauty of the morning; silent, bare,   5
Ships, towers, domes, theaters, and temples lie
Open unto the fields, and to the sky;
All bright and glittering in the smokeless air.
Never did sun more beautifully steep
In his first splendor, valley, rock, or hill;   10
Ne'er saw I, never felt, a calm so deep!
The river glideth at his own sweet will:
Dear God! the very houses seem asleep;
And all that mighty heart is lying still!

(1807)

Lines

COMPOSED A FEW MILES ABOVE TINTERN ABBEY ON REVISITING THE BANKS OF THE WYE
DURING A TOUR. JULY 13, 1798

Five years have passed; five summers, with the length
Of five long winters! and again I hear
These waters, rolling from their mountain-springs
With a soft inland murmur. Once again
Do I behold these steep and lofty cliffs,   5
That on a wild secluded scene impress
Thoughts of more deep seclusion; and connect
The landscape with the quiet of the sky.
The day is come when I again repose
Here, under this dark sycamore, and view   10
These plots of cottage ground, these orchard tufts,
Which at this season, with their unripe fruits,
Are clad in one green hue, and lose themselves
Mid groves and copses°. Once again I see   thickets
These hedgerows, hardly hedgerows, little lines   15
Of sportive wood run wild; these pastoral farms,

Green to the very door; and wreaths of smoke
Sent up, in silence, from among the trees!
With some uncertain notice, as might seem
Of vagrant dwellers in the houseless woods,   20
Or of some Hermit's cave, where by his fire
The Hermit sits alone.

                    These beauteous forms,
Through a long absence, have not been to me
As is a landscape to a blind man's eye;
But oft, in lonely rooms, and 'mid the din   25
Of towns and cities, I have owed to them,
In hours of weariness, sensations sweet,
Felt in the blood, and felt along the heart;
And passing even into my purer mind
With tranquil restoration—feelings too   30
Of unremembered pleasure; such, perhaps,
As have no slight or trivial influence
On that best portion of a good man's life,
His little, nameless, unremembered, acts
Of kindness and of love. Nor less, I trust,   35
To them I may have owed another gift,
Of aspect more sublime; that blessed mood,
In which the burthen of the mystery,
In which the heavy and the weary weight
Of all this unintelligible world,   40
Is lightened—that serene and blessed mood,
In which the affections gently lead us on—
Until, the breath of this corporeal frame
And even the motion of our human blood
Almost suspended, we are laid asleep   45
In body, and become a living soul;
While with an eye made quiet by the power
Of harmony, and the deep power of joy,
We see into the life of things.

                        If this
Be but a vain belief, yet, oh! how oft—   50
In darkness and amid the many shapes
Of joyless daylight; when the fretful stir
Unprofitable, and the fever of the world,
Have hung upon the beatings of my heart—
How oft, in spirit, have I turned to thee,   55
O sylvan Wye! thou wanderer through the woods,
How often has my spirit turned to thee!

    And now, with gleams of half-extinguished thought,
With many recognitions dim and faint,

And somewhat of a sad perplexity, 60
The picture of the mind revives again;
While here I stand, not only with the sense
Of present pleasure, but with pleasing thoughts
That in this moment there is life and food
For future years. And so I dare to hope, 65
Though changed, no doubt, from what I was when first
I came among these hills; when like a roe
I bounded o'er the mountains, by the sides
Of the deep rivers, and the lonely streams,
Wherever nature led—more like a man 70
Flying from something that he dreads than one
Who sought the thing he loved. For nature then
(The coarser pleasures of my boyish days,
And their glad animal movements all gone by)
To me was all in all.—I cannot paint 75
What then I was. The sounding cataract
Haunted me like a passion; the tall rock,
The mountain, and the deep and gloomy wood,
Their colors and their forms, were then to me
An appetite; a feeling and a love, 80
That had no need of a remoter charm,
By thought supplied, nor any interest
Unborrowed from the eye.—That time is past,
And all its aching joys are now no more,
And all its dizzy raptures. Not for this 85
Faint I, nor mourn nor murmur; other gifts
Have followed; for such loss, I would believe,
Abundant recompense. For I have learned
To look on nature, not as in the hour
Of thoughtless youth, but hearing oftentimes 90
The still, sad music of humanity,
Nor harsh nor grating, though of ample power
To chasten and subdue. And I have felt
A presence that disturbs me with the joy
Of elevated thoughts; a sense sublime 95
Of something far more deeply interfused,
Whose dwelling is the light of setting suns,
And the round ocean and the living air,
And the blue sky, and in the mind of man:
A motion and a spirit, that impels 100
All thinking things, all objects of all thought,
And rolls through all things. Therefore am I still
A lover of the meadows and the woods,
And mountains; and of all that we behold
From this green earth; of all the mighty world 105
Of eye, and ear—both what they half create,
And what perceive; well pleased to recognize

In nature and the language of the sense
The anchor of my purest thoughts, the nurse,
The guide, the guardian of my heart, and soul   110
Of all my moral being.

                    Nor perchance,
If I were not thus taught, should I the more
Suffer my genial spirits° to decay: powers
For thou art with me here upon the banks
Of this fair river; thou my dearest Friend,   115
My dear, dear Friend; and in thy voice I catch
The language of my former heart, and read
My former pleasures in the shooting lights
Of thy wild eyes. Oh! yet a little while
May I behold in thee what I was once,   120
My dear, dear Sister! and this prayer I make,
Knowing that Nature never did betray
The heart that loved her; 'tis her privilege,
Through all the years of this our life, to lead
From joy to joy: for she can so inform°   give form to 125
The mind that is within us, so impress
With quietness and beauty, and so feed
With lofty thoughts, that neither evil tongues,
Rash judgments, nor the sneers of selfish men,
Nor greetings where no kindness is, nor all   130
The dreary intercourse of daily life,
Shall e'er prevail against us, or disturb
Our cheerful faith, that all which we behold
Is full of blessings. Therefore let the moon
Shine on thee in thy solitary walk;   135
And let the misty mountain winds be free
To blow against thee: and, in after years,
When these wild ecstasies shall be matured
Into a sober pleasure; when thy mind
Shall be a mansion for all lovely forms,   140
Thy memory be as a dwelling place
For all sweet sounds and harmonies; oh! then,
If solitude, or fear, or pain, or grief
Should be thy portion, with what healing thoughts
Of tender joy wilt thou remember me,   145
And these my exhortations! Nor, perchance—
If I should be where I no more can hear
Thy voice, nor catch from thy wild eyes these gleams
Of past existence—wilt thou then forget
That on the banks of this delightful stream   150

"Lines Composed a Few Miles Above Tintern Abbey"   115 **Friend**   *Wordsworth's sister, Dorothy.*

We stood together; and that I, so long
A worshiper of Nature, hither came
Unwearied in that service; rather say
With warmer love—oh! with far deeper zeal
Of holier love. Nor wilt thou then forget,   155
That after many wanderings, many years
Of absence, these steep woods and lofty cliffs,
And this green pastoral landscape, were to me
More dear, both for themselves and for thy sake!

                                                            (1798)

SAMUEL TAYLOR COLERIDGE
[1772–1834]

Kubla Khan

OR A VISION IN A DREAM. A FRAGMENT

In Xanadu did Kubla Khan
A stately pleasure dome decree:
Where Alph, the sacred river, ran
Through caverns measureless to man
  Down to a sunless sea.   5

So twice five miles of fertile ground
With walls and towers were girdled round:
And there were gardens bright with sinuous rills,
Where blossomed many an incense-bearing tree;
And here were forests ancient as the hills,   10
Enfolding sunny spots of greenery.

But oh! that deep romantic chasm which slanted
Down the green hill athwart a cedarn cover!
A savage place! as holy and enchanted
As e'er beneath a waning moon was haunted   15
By woman wailing for her demon lover!
And from this chasm, with ceaseless turmoil seething,
As if this earth in fast thick pants were breathing,
A mighty fountain momently was forced:
Amid whose swift half-intermitted burst   20

"Kubla Khan"   *the first ruler of the Mongol dynasty in thirteenth-century China. Coleridge's topography and place names are imaginary.*

Huge fragments vaulted like rebounding hail,
Or chaffy grain beneath the thresher's flail:
And 'mid these dancing rocks at once and ever
It flung up momently the sacred river.
Five miles meandering with a mazy motion   25
Through wood and dale the sacred river ran,
Then reached the caverns measureless to man,
And sank in tumult to a lifeless ocean:
And 'mid this tumult Kubla heard from far
Ancestral voices prophesying war!   30

    The shadow of the dome of pleasure
    Floated midway on the waves;
    Where was heard the mingled measure
    From the fountain and the caves.
It was a miracle of rare device,   35
A sunny pleasure dome with caves of ice!

    A damsel with a dulcimer
    In a vision once I saw:
    It was an Abyssinian maid,
    And on her dulcimer she played,   40
    Singing of Mount Abora.
    Could I revive within me
    Her symphony and song,
    To such a deep delight 'twould win me,
That with music loud and long,   45
I would build that dome in air,
That sunny dome! those caves of ice!
And all who heard should see them there,
And all should cry, Beware! Beware!
His flashing eyes, his floating hair!   50
Weave a circle round him thrice,
And close your eyes with holy dread,
For he on honey-dew hath fed,
And drunk the milk of Paradise.

(1798)

GEORGE GORDON, LORD BYRON
[1788–1824]

She walks in beauty

1

She walks in beauty, like the night
   Of cloudless climes and starry skies;
And all that's best of dark and bright
   Meet in her aspect and her eyes:
Thus mellowed to that tender light   5
   Which heaven to gaudy day denies.

2

One shade the more, one ray the less,
   Had half impaired the nameless grace
Which waves in every raven tress,
   Or softly lightens o'er her face;   10
Where thoughts serenely sweet express
   How pure, how dear their dwelling place.

3

And on that cheek, and o'er that brow,
   So soft, so calm, yet eloquent,
The smiles that win, the tints that glow,   15
   But tell of days in goodness spent,
A mind at peace with all below,
   A heart whose love is innocent!

(1815)

PERCY BYSSHE SHELLEY
[1792–1822]

Ozymandias

I met a traveler from an antique land
Who said: Two vast and trunkless legs of stone

"Ozymandias"   *Greek name for the Egyptian ruler Rameses II, who erected a huge statue in his own likeness, among numerous other monuments.*

Stand in the desert . . . Near them, on the sand,
Half sunk, a shattered visage lies, whose frown,
And wrinkled lip, and sneer of cold command,   5
Tell that its sculptor well those passions read
Which yet survive, stamped on these lifeless things,
The hand that mocked them, and the heart that fed:
And on the pedestal these words appear:
"My name is Ozymandias, king of kings: 10
Look on my works, ye Mighty, and despair!"
Nothing beside remains. Round the decay
Of that colossal wreck, boundless and bare
The lone and level sands stretch far away.

(1818)

Ode to the West Wind

1

O wild West Wind, thou breath of Autumn's being,
Thou, from whose unseen presence the leaves dead
Are driven, like ghosts from an enchanter fleeing,

Yellow, and black, and pale, and hectic red,
Pestilence-stricken multitudes: O thou,   5
Who chariotest to their dark wintry bed

The wingéd seeds, where they lie cold and low,
Each like a corpse within its grave, until
Thine azure sister of the Spring shall blow

Her clarion° o'er the dreaming earth, and fill   trumpet call   10
(Driving sweet buds like flocks to feed in air)
With living hues and odors plain and hill:

Wild Spirit, which art moving everywhere;
Destroyer and preserver; hear, oh, hear!

2

Thou on whose stream, mid the steep sky's commotion,   15
Loose clouds like earth's decaying leaves are shed,
Shook from the tangled boughs of Heaven and Ocean,

Angels° of rain and lightning: there are spread   messengers
On the blue surface of thine aëry surge,
Like the bright hair uplifted from the head   20

Of some fierce Maenad, even from the dim verge
Of the horizon to the zenith's height,
The locks of the approaching storm. Thou dirge

Of the dying year, to which this closing night
Will be the dome of a vast sepulcher,
Vaulted with all thy congregated might   25

Of vapors, from whose solid atmosphere
Black rain, and fire, and hail will burst: oh, hear!

3

Thou who didst waken from his summer dreams
The blue Mediterranean, where he lay,   30
Lulled by the coil of his crystálline streams,

Beside a pumice isle in Baiae's bay,
And saw in sleep old palaces and towers
Quivering within the wave's intenser day,

All overgrown with azure moss and flowers   35
So sweet, the sense faints picturing them! Thou
For whose path the Atlantic's level powers

Cleave themselves into chasms, while far below
The sea-blooms and the oozy woods which wear
The sapless foliage of the ocean, know   40

Thy voice, and suddenly grow gray with fear,
And tremble and despoil themselves: oh, hear!

4

If I were a dead leaf thou mightest bear;
If I were a swift cloud to fly with thee;
A wave to pant beneath thy power, and share   45

The impulse of thy strength, only less free
Than thou, O uncontrollable! If even
I were as in my boyhood, and could be

The comrade of thy wanderings over Heaven,
As then, when to outstrip thy skyey speed   50
Scarce seemed a vision; I would ne'er have striven

"Ode to the West Wind"   [21]**Maenad**   *frenzied female worshipper of Dionysus, god of wine and fertility.*

As thus with thee in prayer in my sore need.
Oh, lift me as a wave, a leaf, a cloud!
I fall upon the thorns of life! I bleed!

A heavy weight of hours has chained and bowed   55
One too like thee: tameless, and swift, and proud.

5

Make me thy lyre°, even as the forest is: small harp
What if my leaves are falling like its own!
The tumult of thy mighty harmonies

Will take from both a deep, autumnal tone,   60
Sweet though in sadness. Be thou, Spirit fierce,
My spirit! Be thou me, impetuous one!

Drive my dead thoughts over the universe
Like withered leaves to quicken a new birth!
And, by the incantation of this verse,   65

Scatter, as from an unextinguished hearth
Ashes and sparks, my words among mankind!
Be through my lips to unawakened earth

The trumpet of a prophecy! O Wind,
If Winter comes, can Spring be far behind?   70

(1820)

JOHN KEATS

[1795–1821]

When I have fears

When I have fears that I may cease to be
  Before my pen has gleaned my teeming brain,
Before high-pilèd books, in charact'ry°,   written symbols
  Hold like rich garners the full-ripened grain;
When I behold, upon the night's starred face,   5
  Huge cloudy symbols of a high romance,
And think that I may never live to trace
  Their shadows, with the magic hand of chance;
And when I feel, fair creature of an hour,
  That I shall never look upon thee more,   10

Never have relish in the faery° power   magical
     Of unreflecting love!—then on the shore
Of the wide world I stand alone, and think
Till Love and Fame to nothingness do sink.

                                (1818, 1848)

La Belle Dame sans Merci

O what can ail thee, Knight at arms,
     Alone and palely loitering?
The sedge has withered from the Lake
     And no birds sing!

O what can ail thee, Knight at arms,   5
     So haggard, and so woebegone?
The squirrel's granary is full
     And the harvest's done.

I see a lily on thy brow
     With anguish moist and fever dew,   10
And on thy cheeks a fading rose
     Fast withereth too.

"I met a Lady in the Meads°,   meadows
     Full beautiful, a faery's child,
Her hair was long, her foot was light   15
     And her eyes were wild.

"I made a Garland for her head,
     And bracelets too, and fragrant Zone°;   girdle
She looked at me as she did love
     And made sweet moan.   20

"I set her on my pacing steed
     And nothing else saw all day long,
For sidelong would she bend and sing
     A faery's song.

                                      25
"She found me roots of relish sweet,
     And honey wild, and manna dew,
And sure in language strange she said
     'I love thee true.'

"La Belle Dame sans Merci"   *the beautiful lady without mercy.*

"She took me to her elfin grot
 And there she wept and sighed full sore,   30
And there I shut her wild wild eyes
 With kisses four.

"And there she lulléd me asleep,
 And there I dreamed, Ah Woe betide!
The latest dream I ever dreamt   35
 On the cold hill side.

"I saw pale Kings, and Princes too,
 Pale warriors, death-pale were they all;
They cried, 'La belle dame sans merci
 Hath thee in thrall!'   40

"I saw their starved lips in the gloam
 With horrid warning gapéd wide,
And I awoke, and found me here
 On the cold hill's side.

"And this is why I sojourn here,   45
 Alone and palely loitering;
Though the sedge is withered from the Lake
 And no birds sing."

                (1819, 1888)

Ode to a Nightingale

1

My heart aches, and a drowsy numbness pains
 My sense, as though of hemlock I had drunk,
Or emptied some dull opiate to the drains°   dregs
 One minute past, and Lethe-wards had sunk:
'Tis not through envy of thy happy lot,   5
 But being too happy in thine happiness—
  That thou, light-wingéd Dryad° of the trees,   tree nymph
   In some melodious plot
 Of beechen green, and shadows numberless,
  Singest of summer in full-throated ease.   10

2

O, for a draught of vintage! that hath been
 Cooled a long age in the deep-delvéd earth,

"Ode to a Nightingale" ²**hemlock** *opiate; poisonous in large quantities.* ⁴**Lethe-wards** *towards Lethe, the river of forgetfulness.*

Tasting of Flora and the country green,
    Dance, and Provençal song, and sunburnt mirth!
O for a beaker full of the warm South,   15
    Full of the true, the blushful Hippocrene,
        With beaded bubbles winking at the brim,
            And purple-stainéd mouth;
    That I might drink, and leave the world unseen,
    And with thee fade away into the forest dim: 20

3

Fade far away, dissolve, and quite forget
    What thou among the leaves hast never known,
The weariness, the fever, and the fret
    Here, where men sit and hear each other groan;
Where palsy shakes a few, sad, last gray hairs,   25
    Where youth grows pale, and specter-thin, and dies,
        Where but to think is to be full of sorrow
            And leaden-eyed despairs,
    Where Beauty cannot keep her lustrous eyes,
    Or new Love pine at them beyond tomorrow.   30

4

Away! away! for I will fly to thee,
    Not charioted by Bacchus and his pards,
But on the viewless° wings of Poesy,   invisible
    Though the dull brain perplexes and retards:
Already with thee! tender is the night,   35
    And haply° the Queen-Moon is on her throne,   perhaps
        Clustered around by all her starry Fays°;   fairies
            But here there is no light,
Save what from heaven is with the breezes blown
    Through verdurous glooms and winding mossy ways.   40

5

I cannot see what flowers are at my feet,
    Nor what soft incense hangs upon the boughs,
But, in embalméd° darkness, guess each sweet   scented
    Wherewith the seasonable month endows
The grass, the thicket, and the fruit tree wild;   45
    White hawthorn, and the pastoral eglantine°;   sweetbriar
        Fast fading violets covered up in leaves;
            And mid-May's eldest child,

---

[13]**Flora** *goddess of the flowers.*   [14]**Provençal song** *Provence, in southern France, home of the troubadours.*
[16]**true . . . Hippocrene** *wine. A fountain on Mount Helicon in Greece, whose waters reputedly stimulated poetic imagination.*   [32]**Bacchus . . . pards** *the god of wine and revelry and the leopards who drew his chariot.*

The coming musk-rose, full of dewy wine,
   The murmurous haunt of flies on summer eves.   50

6

Darkling° I listen; and for many a time   *in darkness*
   I have been half in love with easeful Death,
Called him soft names in many a muséd rhyme,
   To take into the air my quiet breath;
Now more than ever seems it rich to die,   55
   To cease upon the midnight with no pain,
      While thou art pouring forth thy soul abroad
         In such an ecstasy!
   Still wouldst thou sing, and I have ears in vain—
      To thy high requiem become a sod.   60

7

Thou wast not born for death, immortal Bird!
   No hungry generations tread thee down;
The voice I hear this passing night was heard
   In ancient days by emperor and clown:
Perhaps the selfsame song that found a path   65
   Through the sad heart of Ruth, when, sick for home,
      She stood in tears amid the alien corn;
         The same that ofttimes hath
   Charmed magic casements, opening on the foam
      Of perilous seas, in faery lands forlorn.   70

8

Forlorn! the very word is like a bell
   To toll me back from thee to my sole self!
Adieu! the fancy cannot cheat so well
   As she is famed to do, deceiving elf.
Adieu! adieu! thy plaintive anthem fades   75
   Past the near meadows, over the still stream,
      Up the hill side; and now 'tis buried deep
         In the next valley-glades:
   Was it a vision, or a waking dream?
      Fled is that music:—Do I wake or sleep?   80

                                     (1819, 1820)

66–67 **Ruth . . . corn** *a Biblical heroine who worked in the harvest fields in a foreign land.*

Ode on a Grecian Urn

1

Thou still unravished bride of quietness,
    Thou foster child of silence and slow time,
Sylvan° historian, who canst thus express   woodland
    A flowery tale more sweetly than our rhyme:
What leaf-fringed legend haunts about thy shape   5
    Of deities or mortals, or of both,
        In Tempe or the dales of Arcady?
    What men or gods are these? What maidens loath?
What mad pursuit? What struggle to escape?
    What pipes and timbrels? What wild ecstasy?   10

2

Heard melodies are sweet, but those unheard
    Are sweeter; therefore, ye soft pipes, play on;
Not to the sensual ear, but, more endeared,
    Pipe to the spirit ditties of no tone:
Fair youth, beneath the trees, thou canst not leave   15
    Thy song, nor ever can those trees be bare;
        Bold Lover, never, never canst thou kiss,
Though winning near the goal—yet, do not grieve;
        She cannot fade, though thou hast not thy bliss,
    Forever wilt thou love, and she be fair!   20

3

Ah, happy, happy boughs! that cannot shed
    Your leaves, nor ever bid the Spring adieu;
And, happy melodist, unweariéd,
    Forever piping songs forever new;
More happy love! more happy, happy love!   25
    Forever warm and still to be enjoyed,
        Forever panting, and forever young;
All breathing human passion far above,
    That leaves a heart high-sorrowful and cloyed,
        A burning forehead, and a parching tongue.   30

4

Who are these coming to the sacrifice?
    To what green altar, O mysterious priest,
Lead'st thou that heifer lowing at the skies,
    And all her silken flanks with garlands dressed?

"Ode on a Grecian Urn" [7]*Tempe . . . Arcady*   *in Greece, beautiful rural regions.*

What little town by river or sea shore,   35
    Or mountain-built with peaceful citadel,
        Is emptied of this folk, this pious morn?
And, little town, thy streets forevermore
    Will silent be; and not a soul to tell
        Why thou art desolate, can e'er return.   40

5

O Attic shape! Fair attitude! with brede°   woven pattern
    Of marble men and maidens overwrought°,   ornamented
With forest branches and the trodden weed;
    Thou, silent form, dost tease us out of thought
As doth eternity: Cold Pastoral!   45
    When old age shall this generation waste,
        Thou shalt remain, in midst of other woe
        Than ours, a friend to man, to whom thou say'st,
"Beauty is truth, truth beauty,"—that is all
    Ye know on earth, and all ye need to know.

                                                  (1819, 1820)

ELIZABETH BARRETT BROWNING
[1806–1861]

How do I love thee? Let me count the ways

How do I love thee? Let me count the ways.
I love thee to the depth and breadth and height
My soul can reach, when feeling out of sight
For the ends of Being and ideal Grace.
I love thee to the level of everyday's   5
Most quiet need, by sun and candle-light.
I love thee freely, as men strive for Right;
I love thee purely, as they turn from Praise.
I love thee with the passion put to use
In my old griefs, and with my childhood's faith.   10
I love thee with a love I seemed to lose
With my lost saints—I love thee with the breath,
Smiles, tears, of all my life!—and, if God choose,
I shall but love thee better after death.

                                                  (1850)

EDGAR ALLAN POE

[1809–1849]

To Helen

Helen, thy beauty is to me
   Like those Nicean barks° of yore,   ships
That gently, o'er a perfumed sea,
   The weary, way-worn wanderer bore
   To his own native shore.   5

On desperate seas long wont to roam,
   Thy hyacinth hair, thy classic face,
Thy Naiad airs have brought me home
   To the glory that was Greece
And the grandeur that was Rome.   10

Lo! in yon brilliant window-niche
   How statue-like I see thee stand!
   The agate lamp within thy hand,
Ah! Psyche from the regions which
   Are Holy Land!   15

(1831, 1845)

The Raven

Once upon a midnight dreary, while I pondered, weak and weary,
Over many a quaint and curious volume of forgotten lore—
While I nodded, nearly napping, suddenly there came a tapping,
As of some one gently rapping, rapping at my chamber door—
"'Tis some visiter," I muttered, "tapping at my chamber door—   5
   Only this and nothing more."

Ah, distinctly I remember it was in the bleak December;
And each separate dying ember wrought its ghost upon the floor.
Eagerly I wished the morrow;—vainly I had sought to borrow
From my books surcease of sorrow—sorrow for the lost Lenore—   10
For the rare and radiant maiden whom the angels name Lenore—
   Nameless *here* for evermore.

"To Helen" ⁷**hyacinth hair** *allusion to the curled hair of the slain youth Hyacinthus, beloved of Apollo.*
⁸**Naiad** *water nymph.*

And the silken, sad, uncertain rustling of each purple curtain
Thrilled me—filled me with fantastic terrors never felt before;
So that now, to still the beating of my heart, I stood repeating 15
"'Tis some visiter entreating entrance at my chamber door—
Some late visiter entreating entrance at my chamber door;—
  This it is and nothing more."

Presently my soul grew stronger; hesitating then no longer,
"Sir," said I, "or Madam, truly your forgiveness I implore; 20
But the fact is I was napping, and so gently you came rapping,
And so faintly you came tapping, tapping at my chamber door,
  That I scarce was sure I heard you"—here I opened wide the door;—
  Darkness there and nothing more.

Deep into that darkness peering, long I stood there wondering,
  fearing, 25
Doubting, dreaming dreams no mortal ever dared to dream before;
But the silence was unbroken, and the stillness gave no token,
And the only word there spoken was the whispered word, "Lenore!"
This I whispered, and an echo murmured back the word, "Lenore!"
  Merely this and nothing more. 30

Back into the chamber turning, all my soul within me burning,
Soon again I heard a tapping somewhat louder than before.
"Surely," said I, "surely that is something at my window lattice;
Let me see, then, what thereat is, and this mystery explore—
Let my heart be still a moment and this mystery explore;— 35
  'Tis the wind and nothing more!"

Open here I flung the shutter, when, with many a flirt and flutter,
In there stepped a stately Raven of the saintly days of yore;
Not the least obeisance made he; not a minute stopped or stayed he;
But, with mien of lord or lady, perched above my chamber door— 40
Perched upon a bust of Pallas just above my chamber door—
  Perched, and sat, and nothing more.

Then this ebony bird beguiling my sad fancy into smiling,
By the grave and stern decorum of the countenance it wore,
"Though thy crest be shorn and shaven, thou," I said, "art sure no craven, 45
Ghastly grim and ancient Raven wandering from the Nightly shore—
Tell me what thy lordly name is on the Night's Plutonian shore!"
  Quoth the Raven "Nevermore."

Much I marvelled this ungainly fowl to hear discourse so plainly,
Though its answer little meaning—little relevancy bore; 50
For we cannot help agreeing that no living human being

"The Raven" [41]*Pallas* *Pallas Athene, patron goddess of Athens.* [47]*Plutonian* *Pluto, god of the underworld.*

Ever yet was blessed with seeing bird above his chamber door—
Bird or beast upon the sculptured bust above his chamber door,
    With such name as "Nevermore."

But the Raven, sitting lonely on the placid bust, spoke only   55
That one word, as if his soul in that one word he did outpour.
Nothing farther then he uttered—not a feather then he fluttered—
Till I scarcely more than muttered "Other friends have flown before—
On the morrow *he* will leave me, as my Hopes have flown before."
    Then the bird said "Nevermore."   60

Startled at the stillness broken by reply so aptly spoken,
"Doubtless," said I, "what it utters is its only stock and store
Caught from some unhappy master whom unmerciful Disaster
Followed fast and followed faster till his songs one burden bore—
Till the dirges of his Hope that melancholy burden bore   65
    Of 'Never—nevermore.'"

But the Raven still beguiling my sad fancy into smiling,
Straight I wheeled a cushioned seat in front of bird, and bust and door;
Then, upon the velvet sinking, I betook myself to linking
Fancy unto fancy, thinking what this ominous bird of yore—   70
What this grim, ungainly, ghastly, gaunt, and ominous bird of yore
    Meant in croaking "Nevermore."

Thus I sat engaged in guessing, but no syllable expressing
To the fowl whose fiery eyes now burned into my bosom's core;
This and more I sat divining, with my head at ease reclining   75
On the cushion's velvet lining that the lamp-light gloated o'er,
But whose velvet-violet lining with the lamp-light gloating o'er,
    She shall press, ah, nevermore!

Then, methought, the air grew denser, perfumed from an unseen censer
Swung by seraphim whose foot-falls tinkled on the tufted floor.   80
"Wretch," I cried, "thy God hath lent thee—by these angels he hath sent thee
Respite—respite and nepenthe from thy memories of Lenore;
Quaff, oh quaff this kind nepenthe and forget this lost Lenore!"
    Quoth the Raven "Nevermore."

"Prophet!" said I, "thing of evil!—prophet still, if bird or devil!—   85
Whether Tempter sent, or whether tempest tossed thee here ashore,
Desolate yet all undaunted, on this desert land enchanted—
Oh this home by Horror haunted—tell me truly, I implore—
Is there—*is* there balm in Gilead?—tell me—tell me, I implore!"
    Quoth the Raven "Nevermore."   90

"Prophet!" said I, "thing of evil!—prophet still, if bird or devil!
By that Heaven that bends above us—by that God we both adore—

Tell this soul with sorrow laden if, within the distant Aidenn,
It shall clasp a sainted maiden whom the angels name Lenore—
Clasp a rare and radiant maiden whom the angels name Lenore." 95
    Quoth the Raven "Nevermore."

"Be that word our sign of parting, bird or fiend!" I shrieked, upstarting—
"Get thee back into the tempest and the Night's Plutonian shore!
Leave no black plume as a token of that lie thy soul hath spoken!
Leave my loneliness unbroken!—quit the bust above my door! 100
Take thy beak from out my heart, and take thy form from off my door!"
    Quoth the Raven "Nevermore."

And the Raven, never flitting, still is sitting, *still* is sitting
On the pallid bust of Pallas just above my chamber door;
And his eyes have all the seeming of a demon's that is dreaming, 105
And the lamp-light o'er him streaming throws his shadow on the floor;
And my soul from out that shadow that lies floating on the floor
    Shall be lifted—nevermore!

(1845)

ALFRED, LORD TENNYSON
[1809–1892]

Ulysses

It little profits that an idle king,
By this still hearth, among these barren crags,
Matched with an aged wife, I mete and dole
Unequal laws unto a savage race,
That hoard, and sleep, and feed, and know not me. 5
I cannot rest from travel; I will drink
Life to the lees. All times I have enjoyed
Greatly, have suffered greatly, both with those
That loved me, and alone; on shore, and when
Through scudding drifts the rainy Hyades 10
Vext the dim sea. I am become a name;
For always roaming with a hungry heart
Much have I seen and known—cities of men
And manners°, climates, councils, governments,   customs

"Ulysses" *According to Dante (in* The Inferno, Canto 26) *Ulysses, having been away for ten years during the Trojan War, is restless upon returning to his island kingdom of Ithaca, and he persuades a band of followers to accompany him on a journey.* [10]*Hyades a constellation of stars whose rising with the sun forecasts rain.*

Myself not least, but honored of them all,—   15
And drunk delight of battle with my peers,
Far on the ringing plains of windy Troy.
I am a part of all that I have met;
Yet all experience is an arch wherethrough
Gleams that untraveled world whose margin fades   20
For ever and for ever when I move.
How dull it is to pause, to make an end,
To rust unburnished, not to shine in use!
As though to breathe were life! Life piled on life
Were all too little, and of one to me   25
Little remains; but every hour is saved
From that eternal silence, something more,
A bringer of new things; and vile it were
For some three suns to store and hoard myself,
And this gray spirit yearning in desire   30
To follow knowledge like a sinking star,
Beyond the utmost bound of human thought.

    This is my son, mine own Telemachus,
To whom I leave the scepter and the isle,
Well-loved of me, discerning to fulfill   35
This labor, by slow prudence to make mild
A rugged people, and through soft degrees
Subdue them to the useful and the good.
Most blameless is he, centered in the sphere
Of common duties, decent° not to fail   proper   40
In offices° of tenderness, and pay   duties
Meet° adoration to my household gods,   appropriate
When I am gone. He works his work, I mine.

    There lies the port; the vessel puffs her sail;
There gloom the dark, broad seas. My mariners,   45
Souls that have toiled, and wrought, and thought with me,
That ever with a frolic welcome took
The thunder and the sunshine, and opposed
Free hearts, free foreheads—you and I are old;
Old age hath yet his honor and his toil.   50
Death closes all; but something ere the end,
Some work of noble note, may yet be done,
Not unbecoming men that strove with gods.
The lights begin to twinkle from the rocks;
The long day wanes; the slow moon climbs; the deep   55
Moans round with many voices. Come, my friends,
'Tis not too late to seek a newer world.
Push off, and sitting well in order smite
The sounding furrows; for my purpose holds
To sail beyond the sunset, and the baths   60
Of all the western stars, until I die.

It may be that the gulfs will wash us down;
It may be we shall touch the Happy Isles,
And see the great Achilles, whom we knew.
Though much is taken, much abides; and though   65
We are not now that strength which in old days
Moved earth and heaven, that which we are, we are,
One equal temper of heroic hearts,
Made weak by time and fate, but strong in will
To strive, to seek, to find, and not to yield.   70

                                        (1842)

The Eagle

FRAGMENT

He clasps the crag with crooked hands;
Close to the sun in lonely lands,
Ringed with the azure world, he stands.

The wrinkled sea beneath him crawls;
He watches from his mountain walls,   5
And like a thunderbolt he falls.

                                        (1851)

R O B E R T   B R O W N I N G
[1812–1889]

Soliloquy of the Spanish Cloister

1

Gr-r-r—there go, my heart's abhorrence!
    Water your damned flower-pots, do!
If hate killed men, Brother Lawrence,
    God's blood, would not mine kill you!
What? your myrtle-bush wants trimming?   5
    Oh, that rose has prior claims—
Needs its leaden vase filled brimming?
    Hell dry you up with its flames!

---

[63] **Happy Isles**   *the abode after death of those favored by the gods.*   "Soliloquy of the Spanish Cloister"
[4] **God's blood**   *an oath.*

2

At the meal we sit together:
   Salve tibi! I must hear   10
Wise talk of the kind of weather,
   Sort of season, time of year:
Not a plenteous cork-crop: scarcely
   Dare we hope oak-galls, I doubt:
What's the Latin name for "parsley"?   15
   What's the Greek name for Swine's Snout?

3

Whew! We'll have our platter burnished,
   Laid with care on our own shelf!
With a fire-new spoon we're furnished,
   And a goblet for ourself,   20
Rinsed like something sacrificial
   Ere 'tis fit to touch our chaps—
Marked with L for our initial!
   (He-he! There his lily snaps!)

4

Saint, forsooth! While brown Dolores   25
   Squats outside the Convent bank
With Sanchicha, telling stories,
   Steeping tresses in the tank,
Blue-black, lustrous, thick like horsehairs,
   —Can't I see his dead eye glow,   30
Bright as 'twere a Barbary corsair's?
   (That is, if he'd let it show!)

5

When he finishes refection°,   dinner
   Knife and fork he never lays
Cross-wise, to my recollection,   35
   As do I, in Jesu's praise.
I the Trinity illustrate,
   Drinking watered orange-pulp—
In three sips the Arian frustrate;
   While he drains his at one gulp.   40

6

Oh, those melons? If he's able
   We're to have a feast! so nice!

---

[10] **Salve tibi** *Hail to thee!* [14] **oak-galls** *growths produced on oak leaves by gallflies.* [31] **Barbary corsair's** *pirate's.* [39] **Arian** *Arius, a fourth-century heretic, denied the doctrine of the Trinity.*

One goes to the Abbot's table,
    All of us get each a slice.
How go on your flowers? None double?   45
    Not one fruit-sort can you spy?
Strange! And I, too, at such trouble,
    Keep them close-nipped on the sly!

7

There's a great text in Galatians,
    Once you trip on it, entails   50
Twenty-nine distinct damnations,
    One sure, if another fails:
If I trip him just a-dying,
    Sure of heaven as sure can be,
Spin him around and send him flying   55
    Off to hell, a Manichee?

8

Or, my scrofulous French novel
    On grey paper with blunt type!
Simply glance at it, you grovel
    Hand and foot in Belial's gripe: 60
If I double down its pages
    At the woeful sixteenth print,
When he gathers his greengages,
    Ope a sieve and slip it in't?

9

Or, there's Satan! one might venture   65
    Pledge one's soul to him, yet leave
Such a flaw in the indenture
    As he'd miss till, past retrieve,
Blasted lay that rose-acacia
    We're so proud of! *Hy, Zy, Hine* . . .   70
'St, there's vespers! *Plena gratiâ*
    Ave, Virgo! Gr-r-r—you swine!

                                        (1842)

---

[49]**Galatians** *a New Testament epistle of St. Paul; see Chapter 5, 14–15 and 16–24.*   [56]**Manichee** *The Manichean heresy divided the world into two equally powerful forces of darkness (evil) and light (good).*   [60]**Belial's gripe** *in the devil's grip.*   [70]**Hy, Zy, Hine** *an incantation.*   [71]**Plena gratiâ** *Full of grace.*   [72]**Ave, Virgo** *Hail Virgin (reverses the opening words of the Ave Maria).*

WALT WHITMAN

[1819–1892]

A noiseless patient spider

A noiseless patient spider,
I mark'd where on a little promontory it stood isolated,
Mark'd how to explore the vacant vast surrounding,
It launch'd forth filament, filament, filament, out of itself,
Ever unreeling them, ever tirelessly speeding them. 5

And you O my soul where you stand,
Surrounded, detached, in measureless oceans of space,
Ceaselessly musing, venturing, throwing, seeking the spheres to connect them,
Till the bridge you will need be form'd, till the ductile anchor hold,
Till the gossamer thread you fling catch somewhere, O my soul. 10

(1881)

Crossing Brooklyn Ferry

1

Flood-tide below me! I see you face to face!
Clouds of the west—sun there half an hour high—I see you also face to face.
Crowds of men and women attired in the usual costumes, how curious you are to me!
On the ferry-boats the hundreds and hundreds that cross, returning home, are more
    curious to me than you suppose,
And you that shall cross from shore to shore years hence are more to me, and more
    in my meditations, than you might suppose. 5

2

The impalpable sustenance of me from all things at all hours of the day,
The simple, compact, well-join'd scheme, myself disintegrated, every one disintegrated
    yet part of the scheme,
The similitudes of the past and those of the future,
The glories strung like beads on my smallest sights and hearings, on the walk in the
    street and the passage over the river,
The current rushing so swiftly and swimming with me far away, 10
The others that are to follow me, the ties between me and them,
The certainty of others, the life, love, sight, hearing of others.

Others will enter the gates of the ferry and cross from shore to shore,
Others will watch the run of the flood-tide,
Others will see the shipping of Manhattan north and west, and the heights of Brooklyn
    to the south and east,   15
Others will see the islands large and small;
Fifty years hence, others will see them as they cross, the sun half an hour high,
A hundred years hence, or ever so many hundred years hence, others will see them,
Will enjoy the sunset, the pouring-in of the flood-tide, the falling-back to the sea of
    the ebb-tide.

3

It avails not, time nor place—distance avails not,   20
I am with you, you men and women of a generation, or ever so many generations
hence,
Just as you feel when you look on the river and sky, so I felt,
Just as any of you is one of a living crowd, I was one of a crowd,
Just as you are refresh'd by the gladness of the river and the bright flow, I was refresh'd,
Just as you stand and lean on the rail, yet hurry with the swift current, I stood yet was
    hurried,   25
Just as you look on the numberless masts of ships and the thick-stemm'd pipes of
    steamboats, I look'd.

I too many and many a time cross'd the river of old,
Watched the Twelfth-month° sea-gulls, saw them high in the air floating   December
    with motionless wings, oscillating their bodies,
Saw how the glistening yellow lit up parts of their bodies and left the rest in strong
    shadow,
Saw the slow-wheeling circles and the gradual edging toward the south,   30
Saw the reflection of the summer sky in the water,
Had my eyes dazzled by the shimmering track of beams,
Look'd at the fine centrifugal spokes of light round the shape of my head in the sunlit
    water,
Look'd on the haze on the hills southward and south-westward,
Look'd on the vapor as it flew in fleeces tinged with violet,   35
Look'd toward the lower bay to notice the vessels arriving,
Saw their approach, saw aboard those that were near me,
Saw the white sails of schooners and sloops, saw the ships at anchor,
The sailors at work in the rigging or out astride the spars,
The round masts, the swinging motion of the hulls, the slender serpentine   40
    pennants,
The large and small steamers in motion, the pilots in their pilot-houses,
The white wake left by the passage, the quick tremulous whirl of the wheels,
The flags of all nations, the falling of them at sunset,
The scallop-edged waves in the twilight, the ladled cups, the frolicsome crests and
    glistening,
The stretch afar growing dimmer and dimmer, the gray walls of the granite storehouses
    by the docks,   45

On the river the shadowy group, the big steam-tug closely flank'd on each side by the
    barges, the hay-boat, the belated lighter,
On the neighboring shore the fires from the foundry chimneys burning high and
    glaringly into the night,
Casting their flicker of black contrasted with wild red and yellow light over the tops
    of houses, and down into the clefts of streets.

4

These and all else were to me the same as they are to you,
I loved well those cities, loved well the stately and rapid river,   50
The men and women I saw were all near to me,
Others the same—others who look back on me because I look'd forward to them,
(The time will come, though I stop° here to-day and to-night.)   stay

5

What is it then between us?
What is the count of the scores or hundreds of years between us?   55

Whatever it is, it avails not—distance avails not, and place avails not,
I too lived, Brooklyn of ample hills was mine,
I too walk'd the streets of Manhattan island, and bathed in the waters around it,
I too felt the curious abrupt questionings stir within me,
In the day among crowds of people sometimes they came upon me,   60
In my walks home late at night or as I lay in my bed they came upon me,
I too had been struck from the float forever held in solution,
I too had receiv'd identity by my body,
That I was I knew was of my body, and what I should be I knew I should be of my
    body.

6

It is not upon you alone the dark patches fall,   65
The dark threw its patches down upon me also,
The best I had done seem'd to me blank and suspicious,
My great thoughts as I supposed them, were they not in reality meager?
Nor is it you alone who know what it is to be evil,
I am he who knew what it was to be evil,   70
I too knitted the old knot of contrariety,
Blabb'd, blush'd, resented, lied, stole, grudg'd,
Had guile, anger, lust, hot wishes I dared not speak,
Was wayward, vain, greedy, shallow, sly, cowardly, malignant,
The wolf, the snake, the hog, not wanting in me,   75
The cheating look, the frivolous word, the adulterous wish, not wanting,
Refusals, hates, postponements, meanness, laziness, none of these wanting,
Was one with the rest, the days and haps of the rest,
Was call'd by my nighest name by clear loud voices of young men as they saw me
    approaching or passing,

Felt their arms on my neck as I stood, or the negligent leaning of their flesh against
  me as I sat,   80
Saw many I loved in the street or ferry-boat or public assembly, yet never told them
  a word,
Lived the same life with the rest, the same old laughing, gnawing, sleeping,
Play'd the part that still looks back on the actor or actress,
The same old role, the role that is what we make it, as great as we like,
Or as small as we like, or both great and small.   85

7

Closer yet I approach you,
What thought you have of me now, I had as much of you—I laid in my stores in
  advance,
I consider'd long and seriously of you before you were born.

Who was to know what should come home to me?
Who knows but I am enjoying this?   90
Who knows, for all the distance, but I am as good as looking at you now, for all you
  cannot see me?

8

Ah, what can ever be more stately and admirable to me than mast-hemm'd Manhattan?
River and sunset and scallop-edg'd waves of flood-tide?
The sea-gulls oscillating their bodies, the hay-boat in the twilight, and the belated
  lighter?
What gods can exceed these that clasp me by the hand, and with voices I love call me
  promptly and loudly by my nighest name as I approach?   95
What is more subtle than this which ties me to the woman or man that looks in my
  face?
Which fuses me into you now, and pours my meaning into you?

We understand then do we not?
What I promis'd without mentioning it, have you not accepted?
What the study could not teach—what the preaching could not accomplish is accom-
  plish'd, is it not?   100

9

Flow on, river! flow with the flood-tide, and ebb with the ebb-tide!
Frolic on, crested and scallop-edg'd waves!
Gorgeous clouds of the sunset! drench with your splendor me, or the men and women
  generations after me!
Cross from shore to shore, countless crowds of passengers!
Stand up, tall masts of Mannahatta! stand up, beautiful hills of Brooklyn! 105
Throb, baffled and curious brain! throw out questions and answers!
Suspend here and everywhere, eternal float of solution!
Gaze, loving and thirsting eyes, in the house or street or public assembly!

Sound out, voices of young men! loudly and musically call me by my nighest name!
Live, old life! play the part that looks back on the actor or actress! 110
Play the old role, the role that is great or small according as one makes it!
Consider, you who peruse me, whether I may not in unknown ways be looking upon
    you;
Be firm, rail over the river, to support those who lean idly, yet haste with the hasting
    current;
Fly on, sea birds! fly sideways, or wheel in large circles high in the air;
Receive the summer sky, you water, and faithfully hold it till all downcast eyes have
    time to take it from you! 115
Diverge, fine spokes of light, from the shape of my head, or any one's head, in the sunlit
    water!
Come on, ships from the lower bay! pass up or down, white-sail'd schooners, sloops,
    lighters!
Flaunt away, flags of all nations! be duly lower'd at sunset!
Burn high your fires, foundry chimneys! cast black shadows at nightfall! cast red and
    yellow light over the tops of the houses!
Appearances, now or henceforth, indicate what you are, 120
You necessary film, continue to envelop the soul,
About my body for me, and your body for you, be hung our divinest aromas,
Thrive, cities—bring your freight, bring your shows, ample and sufficient rivers,
Expand, being than which none else is perhaps more spiritual,
Keep your places, objects than which none else is more lasting. 125

You have waited, you always wait, you dumb, beautiful ministers,
We receive you with free sense at last, and are insatiate henceforward,
Not you any more shall be able to foil us, or withhold yourselves from us,
We use you, and do not cast you aside—we plant you permanently within us,
We fathom you not—we love you—there is perfection in you also, 130
You furnish your parts toward eternity,
Great or small, you furnish your parts toward the soul.

(1856)

LEWIS CARROLL (CHARLES LUTWIDGE DODGSON)

[1832–1898]

Jabberwocky

'Twas brillig, and the slithy toves
   Did gyre and gimble in the wabe:
All mimsy were the borogoves,
   And the mome raths outgrabe.

"Beware the Jabberwock, my son!   5
 The jaws that bite, the claws that catch!
Beware the Jubjub bird, and shun
 The frumious Bandersnatch!"

He took his vorpal sword in hand:
 Long time the manxome foe he sought—   10
So rested he by the Tumtum tree,
 And stood awhile in thought.

And, as in uffish thought he stood,
 The Jabberwock, with eyes of flame,
Came whiffling through the tulgey wood,   15
 And burbled as it came!

One, two! One, two! And through and through
 The vorpal blade went snicker-snack!
He left it dead, and with its head
 He went galumphing back.   20

"And hast thou slain the Jabberwock?
 Come to my arms, my beamish boy!
O frabjous day! Callooh! Callay!"
 He chortled in his joy.

'Twas brillig, and the slithy toves   25
 Did gyre and gimble in the wabe:
All mimsy were the borogoves,
 And the mome raths outgrabe.

(1871)

THOMAS HARDY

[1840–1928]

The Ruined Maid

"O'Melia, my dear, this does everything crown!
Who could have supposed I should meet you in Town?
And whence such fair garments, such prosperi-ty?"
"O didn't you know I'd been ruined?" said she.

"You left us in tatters, without shoes or socks,   5
Tired of digging potatoes, and spudding up docks;

And now you've gay bracelets and bright feathers three!"
"Yes: that's how we dress when we're ruined," said she.

"At home in the barton° you said 'thee' and 'thou,'   farm
And 'thik oon,' and 'theäs oon,' and 't'other'; but now   10
Your talking quite fits 'ee for high compa-ny!"
"Some polish is gained with one's ruin," said she.

"Your hands were like paws then, your face blue and bleak
But now I'm bewitched by your delicate cheek,
And your little gloves fit as on any la-dy!"   15
"We never do work when we're ruined," said she.

"You used to call home-life a hag-ridden dream,
And you'd sigh, and you'd sock; but at present you seem
To know not of megrims° or melancho-ly!"   low spirits
"True. One's pretty lively when ruined," said she.   20

"I wish I had feathers, a fine sweeping gown,
And a delicate face, and could strut about Town!"
"My dear—a raw country girl, such as you be,
Cannot quite expect that. You ain't ruined," said she.

                                              (1898)

Channel Firing

That night your great guns, unawares,
Shook all our coffins as we lay,
And broke the chancel window-squares,
We thought it was the Judgment-day

And sat upright. While drearisome   5
Arose the howl of wakened hounds:
The mouse let fall the altar-crumb,
The worms drew back into the mounds,

The glebe° cow drooled. Till God called, "No;   small field
It's gunnery practice out at sea   10
Just as before you went below;
The world is as it used to be:

"All nations striving strong to make
Red war yet redder. Mad as hatters
They do no more for Christés sake   15
Than you who are helpless in such matters.

"That this is not the judgment-hour
For some of them's a blessed thing,
For if it were they'd have to scour
Hell's floor for so much threatening. . . .   20

"Ha, ha. It will be warmer when
I blow the trumpet (if indeed
I ever do; for you are men,
And rest eternal sorely need)."

So down we lay again. "I wonder,   25
Will the world ever saner be,"
Said one, "than when He sent us under
In our indifferent century!"

And many a skeleton shook his head.
"Instead of preaching forty year,"   30
My neighbor Parson Thirdly said,
"I wish I had stuck to pipes and beer."

Again the guns disturbed the hour,
Roaring their readiness to avenge,
As far inland as Stourton Tower,   35
And Camelot, and starlit Stonehenge.

(1914)

Afterwards

When the Present has latched its postern behind my tremulous stay,
    And the May month flaps its glad green leaves like wings,
Delicate-filmed as new-spun silk, will the neighbours say,
    "He was a man who used to notice such things"?

If it be in the dusk when, like an eyelid's soundless blink,   5
    The dewfall-hawk comes crossing the shades to alight
Upon the wind-warped upland thorn, a gazer may think,
    "To him this must have been a familiar sight."

If I pass during some nocturnal blackness, mothy, and warm,
    When the hedgehog travels furtively over the lawn,   10
One may say, "He strove that such innocent creatures should come to no harm,
    But he could do little for them; and now he is gone."

"Channel Firing"   [36] **Stonehenge**   *a circular grouping of stone monuments near Salisbury, England, dating back*
to the Bronze Age.   "Afterwards"   [1] **postern**   *gate.*

If, when hearing that I have been stilled at last, they stand at the door,
    Watching the full-starred heavens that winter sees,
Will this thought rise on those who will meet my face no more,   15
    "He was one who had an eye for such mysteries"?

And will any say when my bell of quittance is heard in the gloom
    And a crossing breeze cuts a pause in its outrollings,
Till they rise again, as they were a new bell's boom,
    "He hears it not now, but used to notice such things"?   20

(1928)

GERARD MANLEY HOPKINS
[1844–1889]

God's Grandeur

The world is charged with the grandeur of God.
    It will flame out, like shining from shook foil;
    It gathers to a greatness, like the ooze of oil
Crushed. Why do men then now not reck his rod?
Generations have trod, have trod, have trod;   5
    And all is seared with trade; bleared, smeared with toil;
    And wears man's smudge and shares man's smell: the soil
Is bare now, nor can foot feel, being shod.

And for all this, nature is never spent;
    There lives the dearest freshness deep down things;   10
And though the last lights off the black West went
    Oh, morning, at the brown brink eastward, springs—
Because the Holy Ghost over the bent
    World broods with warm breast and with ah! bright wings.

(1877, 1895)

The Windhover

TO CHRIST OUR LORD

I caught this morning morning's minion°, king-   darling
    dom of daylight's dauphin°, dapple-dawn-drawn Falcon, in his   prince
    riding

---

[17] **bell of quittance** *death bell.*   "God's Grandeur" [2] ***foil*** *gold or tinsel foil.*   [4] **Crushed** *as when olives are crushed for their oil.*   "The Windover" *a kestrel, a kind of falcon.*

Of the rolling level underneath him steady air, and striding
High there, how he rung upon the rein of a wimpling° wing   rippling
In his ecstasy! then off, off forth on swing,   5
   As a skate's heel sweeps smooth on a bow-bend: the hurl and gliding
   Rebuffed the big wind. My heart in hiding
Stirred for a bird,—the achieve of, the mastery of the thing!

Brute beauty and valour and act, oh, air, pride, plume, here
   Buckle! AND the fire that breaks from thee then, a billion
Times told lovelier, more dangerous, O my chevalier°!   knight 10

   No wonder of it: shéer plód makes plough down sillion°   furrow
Shine, and blue-bleak embers, ah my dear,
   Fall, gall themselves, and gash gold-vermilion.

                                                  (1877, 1918)

Pied° Beauty   variegated

Glory be to God for dappled things—
   For skies of couple-colour as a brinded° cow;   brindled, streaked
      For rose-moles all in stipple upon trout that swim;
Fresh-firecoal chestnut-falls; finches' wings;
   Landscape plotted and pieced—fold, fallow, and plough;   5
      And áll trádes, their gear and tackle and trim°.   equipment
All things counter, original, spare°, strange;   unusual
   Whatever is fickle, freckled (who knows how?)
      With swift, slow; sweet, sour; adazzle, dim;
He fathers-forth whose beauty is past change: 10
                  Praise him.

                                                (1877, 1918)

A. E. HOUSMAN

[1859–1936]

When I was one-and-twenty

When I was one-and-twenty
   I heard a wise man say,
'Give crowns and pounds and guineas

"Pied Beauty"   **⁴chestnut-falls**   *roasted chestnuts stripped of their husks.*

    But not your heart away;
  Give pearls away and rubies   5
      But keep your fancy free.'
  But I was one-and-twenty,
      No use to talk to me.

  When I was one-and-twenty
      I heard him say again,   10
  'The heart out of the bosom
      Was never given in vain;
  'Tis paid with sighs a plenty
      And sold for endless rue.'
  And I am two-and-twenty,   15
      And oh, 'tis true, 'tis true.

                                                     (1896)

To an Athlete Dying Young

The time you won your town the race
We chaired you through the market-place;
Man and boy stood cheering by,
And home we brought you shoulder-high.

To-day, the road all runners come,   5
Shoulder-high we bring you home,
And set you at your threshold down,
Townsman of a stiller town.

Smart lad, to slip betimes away
From fields where glory does not stay   10
And early though the laurel grows
It withers quicker than the rose.

Eyes the shady night has shut
Cannot see the record cut,
And silence sounds no worse than cheers   15
After earth has stopped the ears:

Now you will not swell the rout
Of lads that wore their honours out,
Runners whom renown outran
And the name died before the man.   20

So set, before its echoes fade,
The fleet foot on the sill of shade,

And hold to the low lintel up
The still-defended challenge-cup.

And round that early-laurelled head   25
Will flock to gaze the strengthless dead
And find unwithered on its curls
The garland briefer than a girl's.

                                                                      (1896)

WILLIAM BUTLER YEATS
[1865–1939]

The Second Coming

Turning and turning in the widening gyre°   spiral
The falcon cannot hear the falconer;
Things fall apart; the center cannot hold;
Mere anarchy is loosed upon the world,
The blood-dimmed tide is loosed, and everywhere   5
The ceremony of innocence is drowned;
The best lack all conviction, while the worst
Are full of passionate intensity.

Surely some revelation is at hand;
Surely the Second Coming is at hand;   10
The Second Coming! Hardly are those words out
When a vast image out of *Spiritus Mundi*
Troubles my sight: somewhere in sands of the desert
A shape with lion body and the head of a man,
A gaze blank and pitiless as the sun,   15
Is moving its slow thighs, while all about it
Reel shadows of the indignant desert birds.
The darkness drops again; but now I know
That twenty centuries of stony sleep
Were vexed to nightmare by a rocking cradle,   20
And what rough beast, its hour come round at last,
Slouches towards Bethlehem to be born?

                                                                      (1921)

"The Second Coming"   *The title alludes to the prophesized return of Jesus Christ and also to the beast of the Apocalypse. See Matthew 24 and Revelation.*   [12]***Spiritus Mundi***   *for Yeats, a common storehouse of images, a communal human memory.*

The Wild Swans at Coole

The trees are in their autumn beauty,
The woodland paths are dry,
Under the October twilight the water
Mirrors a still sky;
Upon the brimming water among the stones   5
Are nine-and-fifty swans.

The nineteenth autumn has come upon me
Since I first made my count;
I saw, before I had well finished,
All suddenly mount   10
And scatter wheeling in great broken rings
Upon their clamorous wings.

I have looked upon those brilliant creatures,
And now my heart is sore.
All's changed since I, hearing at twilight,   15
The first time on this shore,
The bell-beat of their wings above my head,
Trod with a lighter tread.

Unwearied still, lover by lover,
They paddle in the cold   20
Companionable streams or climb the air;
Their hearts have not grown old;
Passion or conquest, wander where they will,
Attend upon them still.

But now they drift on the still water,   25
Mysterious, beautiful;
Among what rushes will they build,
By what lake's edge or pool
Delight men's eyes when I awake some day
To find they have flown away?   30

                                                        (1917)

Leda and the Swan

A sudden blow: the great wings beating still
Above the staggering girl, her thighs caressed

"Leda and the Swan" *Zeus, in the guise of a swan, raped Leda, Queen of Sparta. Helen, their daughter, married Menelaus, King of Sparta, but ran off with Paris, son of Priam, King of Troy. A ten-year siege of Troy by the Greeks ensued to bring Helen back.*

By the dark webs, her nape caught in his bill,
He holds her helpless breast upon his breast.

How can those terrified vague fingers push   5
The feathered glory from her loosening thighs?
And how can body, laid in that white rush,
But feel the strange heart beating where it lies?

A shudder in the loins engenders there
The broken wall, the burning roof and tower   10
And Agamemnon dead.
                    Being so caught up,
So mastered by the brute blood of the air,
Did she put on his knowledge with his power
Before the indifferent beak could let her drop?   15

(1928)

Sailing to Byzantium

1

That is no country for old men. The young
In one another's arms, birds in the trees
—Those dying generations—at their song,
The salmon-falls, the mackerel-crowded seas,
Fish, flesh, or fowl, commend all summer long   5
Whatever is begotten, born, and dies.
Caught in that sensual music all neglect
Monuments of unaging intellect.

2

An aged man is but a paltry thing,
A tattered coat upon a stick, unless   10
Soul clap its hands and sing, and louder sing
For every tatter in its mortal dress,
Nor is there singing school but studying
Monuments of its own magnificence;
And therefore I have sailed the seas and come   15
To the holy city of Byzantium.

3

O sages standing in God's holy fire
As in the gold mosaic of a wall,

"Sailing to Byzantium"   *Byzantium was the capital of the eastern Roman Empire and an important center of art and architecture.*

Come from the holy fire, perne° in a gyre°,   descend/spiral
And be the singing-masters of my soul.   20
Consume my heart away; sick with desire
And fastened to a dying animal
It knows not what it is; and gather me
Into the artifice of eternity.

4

Once out of nature I shall never take   25
My bodily form from any natural thing,
But such a form as Grecian goldsmiths make
Of hammered gold and gold enameling
To keep a drowsy Emperor awake;
Or set upon a golden bough to sing   30
To lords and ladies of Byzantium
Of what is past, or passing, or to come.

                                                              (1927)

PAUL LAURENCE DUNBAR
[1872–1906]

We wear the mask

We wear the mask that grins and lies,
It hides our cheeks and shades our eyes—
This debt we pay to human guile;
With torn and bleeding hearts we smile,
And mouth with myriad subtleties.   5

Why should the world be over-wise,
In counting all our tears and sighs?
Nay, let them only see us, while
        We wear the mask.

We smile, but, O great Christ, our cries
To thee from tortured souls arise.   10
We sing, but oh the clay is vile
Beneath our feet, and long the mile;
But let the world dream otherwise,
        We wear the mask!

                                                              (1896)

WALLACE STEVENS
[1879–1955]

Thirteen Ways of Looking at a Blackbird

1

Among twenty snowy mountains,
The only moving thing
Was the eye of the blackbird.

2

I was of three minds,
Like a tree
In which there are three blackbirds.   5

3

The blackbird whirled in the autumn winds.
It was a small part of the pantomime.

4

A man and a woman
Are one.   10
A man and a woman and a blackbird
Are one.

5

I do not know which to prefer,
The beauty of inflections
Or the beauty of innuendoes,   15
The blackbird whistling
Or just after.

6

Icicles filled the long window
With barbaric glass.
The shadow of the blackbird   20
Crossed it to and fro.
The mood
Traced in the shadow
An indecipherable cause.

7

O thin men of Haddam,   25
Why do you imagine golden birds?
Do you not see how the blackbird
Walks around the feet
Of the women about you?

8

I know noble accents   30
And lucid, inescapable rhythms;
But I know, too,
That the blackbird is involved
In what I know.

9

When the blackbird flew out of sight,   35
It marked the edge
Of one of many circles.

10

At the sight of blackbirds
Flying in a green light,
Even the bawds of euphony   40
Would cry out sharply.

11

He rode over Connecticut
In a glass coach.
Once, a fear pierced him,
In that he mistook   45
The shadow of his equipage
For blackbirds.

12

The river is moving.
The blackbird must be flying.

13

It was evening all afternoon.   50
It was snowing
And it was going to snow.
The blackbird sat
In the cedar-limbs.

(1923)

WILLIAM CARLOS WILLIAMS
[1883–1963]

Spring and All

By the road to the contagious hospital
under the surge of the blue
mottled clouds driven from the
northeast—a cold wind. Beyond, the
waste of broad, muddy fields   5
brown with dried weeds, standing and fallen

patches of standing water
the scattering of tall trees

All along the road the reddish
purplish, forked, upstanding, twiggy   10
stuff of bushes and small trees
with dead, brown leaves under them
leafless vines—

Lifeless in appearance, sluggish
dazed spring approaches—   15

They enter the new world naked,
cold, uncertain of all
save that they enter. All about them
the cold, familiar wind—

Now the grass, tomorrow   20
the stiff curl of wildcarrot leaf
One by one objects are defined—
It quickens: clarity, outline of leaf

But now the stark dignity of
entrance—Still, the profound change   25
has come upon them: rooted, they
grip down and begin to awaken

(1923)

Danse Russe

If when my wife is sleeping
and the baby and Kathleen

are sleeping
and the sun is a flame-white disc
in silken mists
above shining trees,—
if I in my north room
dance naked, grotesquely
before my mirror
waving my shirt round my head
and singing softly to myself:
"I am lonely, lonely.
I was born to be lonely,
I am best so!"
If I admire my arms, my face,
my shoulders, flanks, buttocks
against the yellow drawn shades,—

Who shall say I am not
the happy genius of my household?

(1917)

E Z R A   P O U N D

[1885–1972]

The River-Merchant's Wife: A Letter

While my hair was still cut straight across my forehead
Played I about the front gate, pulling flowers.
You came by on bamboo stilts, playing horse,
You walked about my seat, playing with blue plums.
And we went on living in the village of Chōkan:
Two small people, without dislike or suspicion.

At fourteen I married My Lord you.
I never laughed, being bashful.
Lowering my head, I looked at the wall.
Called to, a thousand times, I never looked back.

At fifteen I stopped scowling,
I desired my dust to be mingled with yours
Forever and forever and forever.
Why should I climb the look out?

"The River-Merchant's Wife"   *Pound translated and adapted this poem from the Chinese. Rihaku is the Japanese name for the Chinese poet, Li Bai, formerly known as Li Po, who wrote the poem that Pound adapted.*

At sixteen you departed,   15
You went into far Ku-tō-en, by the river of swirling eddies,
And you have been gone five months.
The monkeys make sorrowful noise overhead.

You dragged your feet when you went out.
By the gate now, the moss is grown, the different mosses,   20
Too deep to clear them away!
The leaves fall early this autumn, in wind.
The paired butterflies are already yellow with August

Over the grass in the West garden;
They hurt me. I grow older.   25
If you are coming down through the narrows of the river Kiang,
Please let me know before hand,
And I will come out to meet you
                As far as Chō-fū-Sa.   30

        By Rihaku

                              (1916)

MARIANNE MOORE
[1887–1972]

Poetry

I, too, dislike it: there are things that are important beyond all this fiddle.
  Reading it, however, with a perfect contempt for it, one discovers in
  it after all, a place for the genuine.
    Hands that can grasp, eyes
    that can dilate, hair that can rise   5
      if it must, these things are important not because a

high-sounding interpretation can be put upon them but because they are
  useful. When they become so derivative as to become unintelligible,
  the same thing may be said for all of us, that we
    do not admire what   10
    we cannot understand: the bat
      holding on upside down or in quest of something to

eat, elephants pushing, a wild horse taking a roll, a tireless wolf under
  a tree, the immovable critic twitching his skin like a horse that feels
    a flea, the base-

ball fan, the statistician—
    nor is it valid
        to discriminate against "business documents and

15

school-books"; all these phenomena are important. One must make a distinction
    however: when dragged into prominence by half poets, the result is not poetry,
    nor till the poets among us can be
        "literalists of
        the imagination"—above
        insolence and triviality and can present

20

for inspection, "imaginary gardens with real toads in them," shall we have
    it. In the meantime, if you demand on the one hand,
    the raw material of poetry in
        all its rawness and
        that which is on the other hand
        genuine, you are interested in poetry.

25

(1921)

T. S. ELIOT

[*1888 1965*]

The Love Song of J. Alfred Prufrock

    S'io credesse che mia risposta fosse
    A persona che mai tornasse al mondo,
    Questa fiamma staria senza più scosse.
    Ma perciocche giammai di questo fondo
    Non tornò vivo alcun, s'i'odo il vero,
    Senza tema d'infamia ti rispondo.°

    Let us go then, you and I,
    When the evening is spread out against the sky
    Like a patient etherized upon a table;
    Let us go, through certain half-deserted streets,
    The muttering retreats
    Of restless nights in one-night cheap hotels
    And sawdust restaurants with oyster-shells:
    Streets that follow like a tedious argument
    Of insidious intent

5

"The Love Song of J. Alfred Prufrock"   *Epigraph from Dante's* Inferno, *canto XXVII, 61–66. The words are spoken by Guido da Montefeltro when asked to identify himself: "If I thought my answer were given to anyone who could ever return to the world, this flame would shake no more; but since none ever did return above from this depth, if what I hear is true, without fear of infamy I answer thee."*

To lead you to an overwhelming question . . .   10
Oh, do not ask, "What is it?"
Let us go and make our visit.

In the room the women come and go
Talking of Michelangelo.

The yellow fog that rubs its back upon the window-panes   15
The yellow smoke that rubs its muzzle on the window-panes
Licked its tongue into the corners of the evening,
Lingered upon the pools that stand in drains,
Let fall upon its back the soot that falls from chimneys,
Slipped by the terrace, made a sudden leap,   20
And seeing that it was a soft October night,
Curled once about the house, and fell asleep.

And indeed there will be time
For the yellow smoke that slides along the street,
Rubbing its back upon the window-panes;   25
There will be time, there will be time
To prepare a face to meet the faces that you meet;
There will be time to murder and create,
And time for all the works and days of hands
That lift and drop a question on your plate;   30
Time for you and time for me,
And time yet for a hundred indecisions,
And for a hundred visions and revisions,
Before the taking of a toast and tea.

In the room the women come and go   35
Talking of Michelangelo.

And indeed there will be time
To wonder, "Do I dare?" and, "Do I dare?"
Time to turn back and descend the stair,
With a bald spot in the middle of my hair—   40
[They will say: "How his hair is growing thin!"]
My morning coat, my collar mounting firmly to the chin,
My necktie rich and modest, but asserted by a simple pin—
[They will say: "But how his arms and legs are thin!"]
Do I dare   45
Disturb the universe?
In a minute there is time
For decisions and revisions which a minute will reverse.

For I have known them all already, known them all:
Have known the evenings, mornings, afternoons,   50
I have measured out my life with coffee spoons;

I know the voices dying with a dying fall
Beneath the music from a farther room.
　　So how should I presume?

And I have known the eyes already, known them all—   55
The eyes that fix you in a formulated phrase,
And when I am formulated, sprawling on a pin,
When I am pinned and wriggling on the wall,
Then how should I begin
To spit out all the butt-ends of my days and ways?   60
　　And how should I presume?

And I have known the arms already, known them all—
Arms that are braceleted and white and bare
[But in the lamplight, downed with light brown hair!]
Is it perfume from a dress   65
That makes me so digress?
Arms that lie along a table, or wrap about a shawl.
　　And should I then presume?
　　And how should I begin?

Shall I say, I have gone at dusk through narrow streets   70
And watched the smoke that rises from the pipes
Of lonely men in shirt-sleeves, leaning out of windows? . . .

I should have been a pair of ragged claws
Scuttling across the floors of silent seas.

And the afternoon, the evening, sleeps so peacefully!   75
Smoothed by long fingers,
Asleep . . . tired . . . or it malingers,
Stretched on the floor, here beside you and me.
Should I, after tea and cakes and ices,
Have the strength to force the moment to its crisis?   80
But though I have wept and fasted, wept and prayed,
Though I have seen my head [grown slightly bald] brought in upon a platter,
I am no prophet—and here's no great matter;
I have seen the moment of my greatness flicker,
And I have seen the eternal Footman hold my coat, and snicker,   85
And in short, I was afraid.

And would it have been worth it, after all,
After the cups, the marmalade, the tea,
Among the porcelain, among some talk of you and me,
Would it have been worth while,   90

---

[82]**head . . . platter**　*John the Baptist was beheaded at the order of King Herod to please his wife and daughter. See Matthew 14:1–11.*

To have bitten off the matter with a smile,
To have squeezed the universe into a ball
To roll it toward some overwhelming question,
To say: "I am Lazarus, come from the dead,
Come back to tell you all, I shall tell you all"—   95
If one, settling a pillow by her head,
      Should say: "That is not what I meant at all.
      That is not it, at all."

And would it have been worth it, after all,
Would it have been worth while,   100
After the sunsets and the dooryards and the sprinkled streets,
After the novels, after the teacups, after the skirts that trail along the floor—
And this, and so much more?—
It is impossible to say just what I mean!
But as if a magic lantern threw the nerves in patterns on a screen: 105
Would it have been worth while
If one, settling a pillow or throwing off a shawl,
And turning toward the window, should say:
      "That is not it at all,
      That is not what I meant, at all."   110
                    . . . . .

No! I am not Prince Hamlet, nor was meant to be;
Am an attendant lord, one that will do
To swell a progress, start a scene or two,
Advise the prince; no doubt, an easy tool,
Deferential, glad to be of use,   115
Politic, cautious, and meticulous;
Full of high sentence°, but a bit obtuse;   sententiousness
At times, indeed, almost ridiculous—
Almost, at times, the Fool.

I grow old . . . I grow old . . .   120
I shall wear the bottoms of my trousers rolled.

Shall I part my hair behind? Do I dare to eat a peach?
I shall wear white flannel trousers, and walk upon the beach.
I have heard the mermaids singing, each to each.

I do not think that they will sing to me.   125

I have seen them riding seaward on the waves
Combing the white hair of the waves blown back
When the wind blows the water white and black.

---

⁹⁴**Lazarus** *Jesus raised him from the dead. See John 11:1–44.*

We have lingered in the chambers of the sea
By sea-girls wreathed with seaweed red and brown   130
Till human voices wake us, and we drown.

(1917)

JOHN CROWE RANSOM
[1888–1974]

Piazza Piece

—I am a gentleman in a dustcoat trying
To make you hear. Your ears are soft and small
And listen to an old man not at all,
They want the young men's whispering and sighing.
But see the roses on your trellis dying   5
And hear the spectral singing of the moon;
For I must have my lovely lady soon,
I am a gentleman in a dustcoat trying.

—I am a lady young in beauty waiting
Until my truelove comes, and then we kiss.   10
But what grey man among the vines is this
Whose words are dry and faint as in a dream?
Back from my trellis, Sir, before I scream!
I am a lady young in beauty waiting.

(1927)

VICENTE HUIDOBRO
[1892–1948]

Ars Poetica   The art of poetry

Let poetry be like a key
Opening a thousand doors.
A leaf falls; something flies by;
Let all the eye sees be created
And the soul of the listener tremble.   5

Invent new worlds and watch your word;
The adjective, when it doesn't give life, kills it.

We are in the age of nerves.
The muscle hangs,
Like a memory, in museums;   10
But we are not the weaker for it:
True vigor
Resides in the head.

Oh Poets, why sing of roses!
Let them flower in your poems;   15

For us alone
Do all things live beneath the Sun.

The poet is a little God.

TRANSLATED BY DAVID M. GUSS

(1932)

ARCHIBALD MACLEISH
[1892–1982]

Ars Poetica

A poem should be palpable and mute
As a globed fruit,

Dumb
As old medallions to the thumb,

Silent as the sleeve-worn stone   5
Of casement ledges where the moss has grown—

A poem should be wordless
As the flight of birds.

A poem should be motionless in time
As the moon climbs,   10

Leaving, as the moon releases
Twig by twig the night-entangled trees,

Leaving, as the moon behind the winter leaves,
Memory by memory the mind—

A poem should be motionless in time   15
As the moon climbs.

A poem should be equal to:
Not true.

For all the history of grief
An empty doorway and a maple leaf.   20

For love
The leaning grasses and two lights above the sea—

A poem should not mean
But be.

                                        (1926)

WILFRED OWEN

[1893–1918]

Dulce et Decorum Est°

Bent double, like old beggars under sacks,
Knock-kneed, coughing like hags, we cursed through sludge,
Till on the haunting flares we turned our backs
And towards our distant rest began to trudge.
Men marched asleep. Many had lost their boots   5
But limped on, blood-shod. All went lame; all blind;
Drunk with fatigue; deaf even to the hoots
Of tired, outstripped Five-Nines that dropped behind.

Gas! GAS! Quick, boys!—An ecstasy of fumbling,
Fitting the clumsy helmets just in time;   10
But someone still was yelling out and stumbling
And flound'ring like a man in fire or lime . . .
Dim, through the misty panes and thick green light,
As under a green sea, I saw him drowning.

In all my dreams, before my helpless sight,   15
He plunges at me, guttering, choking, drowning.

"Dulce et Decorum Est"   *"It is sweet and fitting to die for one's country." See the last two lines, which are from*
Horace, Odes, III, ii.13.

If in some smothering dreams you too could pace
Behind the wagon that we flung him in,
And watch the white eyes writhing in his face,
His hanging face, like a devil's sick of sin;   20
If you could hear, at every jolt, the blood
Come gargling from the froth-corrupted lungs,
Obscene as cancer, bitter as the cud
Of vile, incurable sores on innocent tongues,—
My friend, you would not tell with such high zest   25
To children ardent for some desperate glory,
The old Lie: *Dulce et decorum est*
Pro patria mori.

(1920)

E. E. CUMMINGS

[1894–1962]

anyone lived in a pretty how town

anyone lived in a pretty how town
(with up so floating many bells down)
spring summer autumn winter
he sang his didn't he danced his did.

Women and men(both little and small)   5
cared for anyone not at all
they sowed their isn't they reaped their same
sun moon stars rain

children guessed(but only a few
and down they forgot as up they grew   10
autumn winter spring summer)
that noone loved him more by more

when by now and tree by leaf
she laughed his joy she cried his grief
bird by snow and stir by still   15
anyone's any was all to her

someones married their everyones
laughed their cryings and did their dance
(sleep wake hope and then)they
said their nevers they slept their dream   20

stars rain sun moon
(and only the snow can begin to explain
how children are apt to forget to remember
with up so floating many bells down)

one day anyone died i guess   25
(and noone stooped to kiss his face)
busy folk buried them side by side
little by little and was by was

all by all and deep by deep
and more by more they dream their sleep   30
noone and anyone earth by april
wish by spirit and if by yes.

Women and men(both dong and ding)
summer autumn winter spring
reaped their sowing and went their came   35
sun moon stars rain

(1940)

i thank You God for most this amazing

i thank You God for most this amazing
day:for the leaping greenly spirits of trees
and a blue true dream of sky; and for everything
which is natural which is infinite which is yes

(i who have died am alive again today,   5
and this is the sun's birthday; this is the birth
day of life and of love and wings:and of the gay
great happening illimitably earth)

how should tasting touching hearing seeing
breathing any—lifted from the no   10
of all nothing—human merely being
doubt unimaginable You?

(now the ears of my ears awake and
now the eyes of my eyes are opened)

(1950)

JEAN TOOMER
[1894–1967]

Reapers

Black reapers with the sound of steel on stones
Are sharpening scythes. I see them place the hones
In their hip-pockets as a thing that's done,
And start their silent swinging, one by one.
Black horses drive a mower through the weeds,   5
And there, a field rat, startled, squealing bleeds,
His belly close to ground. I see the blade,
Blood-stained, continue cutting weeds and shade.

                                                        (1923)

COUNTEE CULLEN
[1903–1946]

Incident

Once riding in old Baltimore,
        Heart-filled, head-filled with glee,
I saw a Baltimorean
        Keep looking straight at me.

Now I was eight and very small,   5
        And he was no whit bigger,
And so I smiled, but he poked out
        His tongue and called me, "Nigger."

I saw the whole of Baltimore
        From May until December: 10
Of all the things that happened there
        That's all that I remember.

                                                        (1925)

WISLOWA SZYMBORSKA
[b. 1923]

Nothing Twice

Nothing can ever happen twice.
In consequence, the sorry fact is
that we arrive here improvised
and leave without the chance to practice.

Even if there is no one dumber,   5
if you're the planet's biggest dunce,
you can't repeat the class in summer:
this course is only offered once.

No day copies yesterday,
no two nights will teach what bliss is   10
in precisely the same way,
with exactly the same kisses.

One day, perhaps, some idle tongue
mentions your name by accident:
I feel as if a rose were flung   15
into the room, all hue and scent.

The next day, though you're here with me,
I can't help looking at the clock:
A rose? A rose? What could that be?
Is it a flower or a rock?   20

Why do we treat the fleeting day
with so much needless fear and sorrow?
It's in its nature not to stay:
Today is always gone tomorrow.

With smiles and kisses, we prefer   25
to seek accord beneath our star,
although we're different (we concur)
just as two drops of water are.

(1957)

Cat in an Empty Apartment

Die—you can't do that to a cat.
Since what can a cat do
in an empty apartment?
Climb the walls?
Rub up against the furniture?   5
Nothing seems different here,
but nothing is the same.
Nothing has been moved,
but there's more space.
And at nighttime no lamps are lit.   10

Footsteps on the staircase,
but they're new ones.
The hand that puts fish on the saucer
has changed, too.

Something doesn't start   15
at its usual time.
Something doesn't happen
as it should.
Someone was always, always here,
then suddenly disappeared   20
and stubbornly stays disappeared.

Every closet has been examined.
Every shelf has been explored.
Excavations under the carpet turned up nothing.
A commandment was even broken,   25
papers scattered everywhere.
What remains to be done.
Just sleep and wait.

Just wait till he turns up,
just let him show his face.   30
Will he ever get a lesson
on what not to do to a cat.
Sidle toward him
as if unwilling
and ever so slow   35
on visibly offended paws,
and no leaps or squeals at least to start.

(1993)

PABLO NERUDA

[*b. 1904*]

The Word

The word
was born in the blood,
grew in the dark body, beating,
and took flight through the lips and the mouth.

Farther away and nearer   5
still, still it came
from dead fathers and from wandering races,
from lands which had turned to stone,
lands weary of their poor tribes,
for when grief took to the roads   10
the people set out and arrived
and married new land and water
to grow their words again.
And so this is the inheritance;
this is the wavelength which connects us   15
with dead men and the dawning
of new beings not yet come to light.

Still the atmosphere quivers
with the first word uttered
dressed up   20
in terror and sighing.
It emerged
from the darkness
and until now there is no thunder
that ever rumbles with the iron voice   25
of that word,
the first
word uttered—
perhaps it was only a ripple, a single drop,
and yet its great cataract falls and falls.   30

Later on, the word fills with meaning.
Always with child, it filled up with lives.
Everything was births and sounds—
affirmation, clarity, strength,
negation, destruction, death—   35
the verb took over all the power

and blended existence with essence
in the electricity of its grace.

Human word, syllable, flank
of extending light and solid silverwork,   40
hereditary goblet which receives
the communications of the blood—
here is where silence came together with
the wholeness of the human word,
and, for human beings, not to speak is to die—   45
language extends even to the hair,
the mouth speaks without the lips moving,
all of a sudden, the eyes are words.

I take the word and pass it through my senses
as though it were no more than a human shape;   50
its arrangements awe me and I find my way
through each resonance of the spoken word—
I utter and I am and, speechless, I approach
across the edge of words silence itself.

I drink to the word, raising   55
a word or a shining cup;
in it I drink

the pure wine of language
or inexhaustible water,
maternal source of words,   60
and cup and water and wine
give rise to my song
because the verb is the source
and vivid life—it is blood,
blood which expresses its substance   65
and so ordains its own unwinding.
Words give glass quality to glass, blood to blood,
and life to life itself.

TRANSLATED BY ALASTAIR REID

(1939)

W. H. AUDEN
[1907–1973]

The Unknown Citizen

(To JS/07/M/378 This Marble Monument Is Erected by the State)

He was found by the Bureau of Statistics to be
One against whom there was no official complaint,
And all the reports on his conduct agree
That, in the modern sense of an old-fashioned word, he was a saint,
For in everything he did he served the Greater Community.   5
Except for the War till the day he retired
He worked in a factory and never got fired
But satisfied his employers, Fudge Motors Inc.
Yet he wasn't a scab or odd in his views,
For his Union reports that he paid his dues,   10
(Our report on his Union shows it was sound)
And our Social Psychology workers found
That he was popular with his mates and liked a drink.
The Press are convinced that he bought a paper every day
And that his reactions to advertisements were normal in every way.   15
Policies taken out in his name prove that he was fully insured,
And his Health-card shows he was once in hospital but left it cured.
Both Producers Research and High-Grade Living declare
He was fully sensible to the advantages of the Installment Plan
And had everything necessary to the Modern Man,   20
A phonograph, a radio, a car and a frigidaire.
Our researchers into Public Opinion are content
That he held the proper opinions for the time of year;
When there was peace, he was for peace; when there was war, he went.
He was married and added five children to the population,   25
Which our Eugenist says was the right number for a parent of his generation.
And our teachers report that he never interfered with their education.

Was he free? Was he happy? The question is absurd:
Had anything been wrong, we should certainly have heard.

(1940)

In Memory of W. B. Yeats

[d. January 1939]

1

He disappeared in the dead of winter:
The brooks were frozen, the air-ports almost deserted,
And snow disfigured the public statues;
The mercury sank in the mouth of the dying day.
O all the instruments agree   5
The day of his death was a dark cold day.

Far from his illness
The wolves ran on through the evergreen forests,
The peasant river was untempted by the fashionable quays;
By mourning tongues   10
The death of the poet was kept from his poems.

But for him it was his last afternoon as himself,
An afternoon of nurses and rumours;
The provinces of his body revolted,
The squares of his mind were empty,   15
Silence invaded the suburbs,
The current of his feeling failed: he became his admirers.

Now he is scattered among a hundred cities
And wholly given over to unfamiliar affections;
To find his happiness in another kind of wood   20
And be punished under a foreign code of conscience.
The words of a dead man
Are modified in the guts of the living.

But in the importance and noise of to-morrow
When the brokers are roaring like beasts on the floor of
    the Bourse°,   stock exchange 25
And the poor have the sufferings to which they are fairly accustomed,
And each in the cell of himself is almost convinced of his freedom;
A few thousand will think of this day
As one thinks of a day when one did something slightly unusual.

O all the instruments agree   30
The day of his death was a dark cold day.

2

You were silly like us: your gift survived it all;
The parish of rich women, physical decay,

Yourself; mad Ireland hurt you into poetry.
Now Ireland has her madness and her weather still,
For poetry makes nothing happen: it survives
In the valley of its saying where executives
Would never want to tamper; it flows south
From ranches of isolation and the busy griefs,
Raw towns that we believe and die in; it survives,
A way of happening, a mouth.

3

Earth, receive an honoured guest;
William Yeats is laid to rest:
Let the Irish vessel lie
Emptied of its poetry.

Time that is intolerant
Of the brave and innocent,
And indifferent in a week
To a beautiful physique,

Worships language and forgives
Everyone by whom it lives;
Pardons cowardice, conceit,
Lays its honours at their feet.

Time that with this strange excuse
Pardoned Kipling and his views,
And will pardon Paul Claudel,
Pardons him for writing well.

In the nightmare of the dark
All the dogs of Europe bark,
And the living nations wait,
Each sequestered in its hate;

Intellectual disgrace
Stares from every human face,
And the seas of pity lie
Locked and frozen in each eye.

Follow, poet, follow right
To the bottom of the night,
With your unconstraining Voice
Still persuade us to rejoice;

35
40
45
50
55
60
65

"In Memory of W. B. Yeats" [55]*Kipling* *Rudyard Kipling (1865–1936), English writer with imperialistic views.* [56]*Paul Claudel French Catholic writer (1868–1955) of extreme political conservatism.* [58]*the dark World War II broke out a few months after Auden wrote this poem.*

With the farming of a verse   70
Make a vineyard of the curse,
Sing of human unsuccess
In a rapture of distress;

In the deserts of the heart
Let the healing fountain start,   75
In the prison of his days
Teach the free man how to praise.

                                                    (1940)

THEODORE ROETHKE

[1908–1963]

Elegy for Jane

MY STUDENT, THROWN BY A HORSE

I remember the neckcurls, limp and damp as tendrils;
And her quick look, a sidelong pickerel smile;
And how, once startled into talk, the light syllables leaped for her,
And she balanced in the delight of her thought,
A wren, happy, tail into the wind,   5
Her song trembling the twigs and small branches.
The shade sang with her;
The leaves, their whispers turned to kissing;
And the mold sang in the bleached valleys under the rose.

Oh, when she was sad, she cast herself down into such a pure depth,   10
Even a father could not find her:
Scraping her cheek against straw;
Stirring the clearest water.

My sparrow, you are not here,
Waiting like a fern, making a spiny shadow.   15
The sides of wet stones cannot console me,
Nor the moss, wound with the last light.

If only I could nudge you from this sleep,
My maimed darling, my skittery pigeon.
Over this damp grave I speak the words of my love: 20
I, with no rights in this matter,
Neither father nor lover.

                                                    (1953)

ELIZABETH BISHOP
[1911–1979]

The Fish

I caught a tremendous fish
and held him beside the boat
half out of water, with my hook
fast in a corner of his mouth.
He didn't fight.   5
He hadn't fought at all.
He hung a grunting weight,
battered and venerable
and homely. Here and there
his brown skin hung in strips   10
like ancient wallpaper,
and its pattern of darker brown
was like wallpaper:
shapes like full-blown roses
stained and lost through age.   15
He was speckled with barnacles,
fine rosettes of lime,
and infested
with tiny white sea lice,
and underneath two or three   20
rags of green weed hung down.
While his gills were breathing in
the terrible oxygen
—the frightening gills,
fresh and crisp with blood,   25
that can cut so badly—
I thought of the coarse white flesh
packed in like feathers,
the big bones and the little bones,
the dramatic reds and blacks   30
of his shiny entrails,
and the pink swim-bladder
like a big peony.
I looked into his eyes
which were far larger than mine   35
but shallower, and yellowed,
the irises backed and packed
with tarnished tinfoil
seen through the lenses
of old scratched isinglass°.   mica   40

They shifted a little, but not
to return my stare.
—It was more like the tipping
of an object toward the light.
I admired his sullen face,   45
the mechanism of his jaw,
and then I saw
that from his lower lip
—if you could call it a lip—
grim, wet, and weaponlike,   50
hung five old pieces of fish-line,
or four and a wire leader
with the swivel still attached,
with all their five big hooks
grown firmly in his mouth.   55
A green line, frayed at the end
where he broke it, two heavier lines,
and a fine black thread
still crimped from the strain and snap
when it broke and he got away.   60
Like medals with their ribbons
frayed and wavering,
a five-haired beard of wisdom
trailing from his aching jaw.
I stared and stared   65
and victory filled up
the little rented boat,
from the pool of bilge
where oil had spread a rainbow
around the rusted engine   70
to the bailer rusted orange,
the sun-cracked thwarts,
the oarlocks on their strings,
the gunnels—until everything
was rainbow, rainbow, rainbow!   75
And I let the fish go.

                                                    (1946)

Sestina

September rain falls on the house.
In the failing light, the old grandmother
sits in the kitchen with the child
beside the Little Marvel Stove,
reading the jokes from the almanac,   5
laughing and talking to hide her tears.

She thinks that her equinoctial tears
and the rain that beats on the roof of the house
were both foretold by the almanac,
but only known to a grandmother.
The iron kettle sings on the stove.
She cuts some bread and says to the child,

It's time for tea now; but the child
is watching the teakettle's small hard tears
dance like mad on the hot black stove,
the way the rain must dance on the house.
Tidying up, the old grandmother
hangs up the clever almanac

on its string. Birdlike, the almanac
hovers half open above the child,
hovers above the old grandmother
and her teacup full of dark brown tears.
She shivers and says she thinks the house
feels chilly, and puts more wood in the stove.

It was to be, says the Marvel Stove.
I know what I know, says the almanac.
With crayons the child draws a rigid house
and a winding pathway. Then the child
puts in a man with buttons like tears
and shows it proudly to the grandmother.

But secretly, while the grandmother
busies herself about the stove,
the little moons fall down like tears
from between the pages of the almanac
into the flower bed the child
has carefully placed in the front of the house.

Time to plant tears, says the almanac.
The grandmother sings to the marvelous stove
and the child draws another inscrutable house.

(1965)

MAY SWENSON

[1913–1989]

Women

Woman   Or they
should be   should be
pedestals   little horses
moving   those wooden
pedestals   sweet
moving   oldfashioned
to the   painted
motions   rocking
of men   horses

the gladdest things in the toyroom.

the   feelingly
pegs   and then
of their   unfeelingly
ears   To be
so familiar joyfully
and dear   ridden
to the trusting rockingly
fists   ridden until
To be chafed the restored

egos dismount and the legs stride away

Immobile   willing
sweetlipped to be set
sturdy   into motion
and smiling Women
women   should be
should always pedestals
be waiting   to men

(1970)

WILLIAM STAFFORD

[*b. 1914*]

Traveling through the dark

Traveling through the dark I found a deer
dead on the edge of the Wilson River road.
It is usually best to roll them into the canyon:
that road is narrow; to swerve might make more dead.

By glow of the tail-light I stumbled back of the car   5
and stood by the heap, a doe, a recent killing;
she had stiffened already, almost cold.
I dragged her off; she was large in the belly.

My fingers touching her side brought me the reason—
her side was warm; her fawn lay there waiting,   10
alive, still, never to be born.
Beside that mountain road I hesitated.

The car aimed ahead its lowered parking lights;
under the hood purred the steady engine.
I stood in the glare of the warm exhaust turning red;   15
around our group I could hear the wilderness listen.

I thought hard for us all—my only swerving—,
then pushed her over the edge into the river.

(1957)

DYLAN THOMAS

[*1914–1953*]

Fern Hill

Now as I was young and easy under the apple boughs
About the lilting house and happy as the grass was green,
   The night above the dingle starry,
     Time let me hail and climb
    Golden in the heydays of his eyes,   5
And honored among wagons I was prince of the apple towns

And once below a time I lordly had the trees and leaves
　　　Trail with daisies and barley
　　Down the rivers of the windfall light.

And as I was green and carefree, famous among the barns   10
About the happy yard and singing as the farm was home,
　　　In the sun that is young once only,
　　　　Time let me play and be
　　　Golden in the mercy of his means,
And green and golden I was huntsman and herdsman, the calves   15
Sang to my horn, the foxes on the hills barked clear and cold,
　　　And the sabbath rang slowly
　　In the pebbles of the holy streams.

All the sun long it was running, it was lovely, the hay
Fields high as the house, the tunes from the chimneys, it was air   20
　　　And playing, lovely and watery
　　　　And fire green as grass.
　　And nightly under the simple stars
As I rode to sleep the owls were bearing the farm away,
All the moon long I heard, blessed among stables, the night-jars   25
　　　Flying with the ricks, and the horses
　　　　Flashing into the dark.

And then to awake, and the farm, like a wanderer white
With the dew, come back, the cock on his shoulder: it was all
　　　Shining, it was Adam and maiden,   30
　　　　The sky gathered again
　　And the sun grew round that very day.
So it must have been after the birth of the simple light
In the first, spinning place, the spellbound horses walking warm
　　　Out of the whinnying green stable   35
　　　　On to the fields of praise.

And honored among foxes and pheasants by the gay house
Under the new made clouds and happy as the heart was long,
　　　In the sun born over and over,
　　　　I ran my heedless ways,   40
　　　My wishes raced through the house high hay
And nothing I cared, at my sky blue trades, that time allows
In all his tuneful turning so few and such morning songs
　　　Before the children green and golden
　　　　Follow him out of grace,   45

Nothing I cared, in the lamb white days, that time would take me
Up to the swallow thronged loft by the shadow of my hand,
　　　In the moon that is always rising,

        Nor that riding to sleep
      I should hear him fly with the high fields   50
And wake to the farm forever fled from the childless land.
Oh as I was young and easy in the mercy of his means,
          Time held me green and dying
       Though I sang in my chains like the sea.

                                            (1946)

Do not go gentle into that good night

    Do not go gentle into that good night,
    Old age should burn and rave at close of day;
    Rage, rage against the dying of the light.

    Though wise men at their end know dark is right,
    Because their words had forked no lightning they   5
    Do not go gentle into that good night.

    Good men, the last wave by, crying how bright
    Their frail deeds might have danced in a green bay,
    Rage, rage against the dying of the light.

    Wild men who caught and sang the sun in flight,   10
    And learn, too late, they grieved it on its way,
    Do not go gentle into that good night.

    Grave men, near death, who see with blinding sight
    Blind eyes could blaze like meteors and be gay,
    Rage, rage against the dying of the light.   15

    And you, my father, there on the sad height,
    Curse, bless, me now with your fierce tears, I pray.
    Do not go gentle into that good night.
    Rage, rage against the dying of the light.

                                             (1952)

GWENDOLYN BROOKS
[b. 1917]

the mother

Abortions will not let you forget.
You remember the children you got that you did not get,
The damp small pulps with a little or with no hair,
The singers and workers that never handled the air.
You will never neglect or beat   5
Them, or silence or buy with a sweet.
You will never wind up the sucking-thumb
Or scuttle off ghosts that come.
You will never leave them, controlling your luscious sigh,
Return for a snack of them, with gobbling mother-eye.   10

I have heard in the voices of the wind the voices of my dim killed children.
I have contracted. I have eased
My dim dears at the breasts they could never suck.
I have said, Sweets, if I sinned, if I seized
Your luck   15
And your lives from your unfinished reach,
If I stole your births and your names,
Your straight baby tears and your games,
Your stilted or lovely loves, your tumults, your marriages, aches, and your deaths,
If I poisoned the beginnings of your breaths,
Believe that even in my deliberateness I was not deliberate.   20
Though why should I whine,
Whine that the crime was other than mine?—
Since anyhow you are dead.
Or rather, or instead,
You were never made.   25

But that too, I am afraid,
Is faulty: oh, what shall I say, how is the truth to be said?
You were born, you had body, you died.
It is just that you never giggled or planned or cried.
Believe me, I loved you all.   30
Believe me, I knew you, though faintly, and I loved, I loved you
All.

(1945)

First fight. Then fiddle

First fight. Then fiddle. Ply the slipping string
With feathery sorcery; muzzle the note
With hurting love; the music that they wrote
Bewitch, bewilder. Qualify to sing
Threadwise. Devise no salt, no hempen thing   5
For the dear instrument to bear. Devote
The bow to silks and honey. Be remote
A while from malice and from murdering.
But first to arms, to armor. Carry hate
In front of you and harmony behind.   10
Be deaf to music and to beauty blind.
Win war. Rise bloody, maybe not too late
For having first to civilize a space
Wherein to play your violin with grace.

(1945)

LAWRENCE FERLINGHETTI
[b. 1919]

Constantly Risking Absurdity

Constantly risking absurdity
                    and death
        whenever he performs
                    above the heads
                        of his audience   5

    the poet like an acrobat
                climbs on rime
                    to a high wire of his own making
and balancing on eyebeams
                    above a sea of faces   10
        paces his way
                to the other side of day
    performing entrechats

                    and sleight-of-foot tricks
and other high theatrics   15

                    and all without mistaking
        any thing
                for what it may not be

For he's the super realist
                    who must perforce perceive   20
          taut truth
                    before the taking of each stance or step
     in his supposed advance
                    toward that still higher perch
where Beauty stands and waits   25
               with gravity
                         to start her death-defying leap

     And he
          a little charleychaplin man
                    who may or may not catch   30
          her fair eternal form
                    spreadeagled in the empty air
          of existence

                                                              (1958)

RICHARD WILBUR

[b. 1921]

The Death of a Toad

     A toad the power mower caught,
Chewed and clipped of a leg, with a hobbling hop has got
     To the garden verge, and sanctuaried him
     Under the cineraria leaves, in the shade
          Of the ashen heartshaped leaves, in a dim,   5
               Low, and a final glade.

     The rare original heartsblood goes,
Spends on the earthen hide, in the folds and wizenings, flows
     In the gutters of the banked and staring eyes. He lies
     As still as if he would return to stone,   10
          And soundlessly attending, dies
               Toward some deep monotone,

     Toward misted and ebullient seas
And cooling shores, toward lost Amphibia's emperies.
     Day dwindles, drowning, and at length is gone   15
     In the wide and antique eyes, which still appear
          To watch, across the castrate lawn,
               The haggard daylight steer.

                                                              (1956)

PHILIP LARKIN

[*b. 1922*]

A Study of Reading Habits

When getting my nose in a book
Cured most things short of school,
It was worth ruining my eyes
To know I could still keep cool,
And deal out the old right hook   5
To dirty dogs twice my size.

Later, with inch-thick specs,
Evil was just my lark:
Me and my cloak and fangs
Had ripping times in the dark.   10
The women I clubbed with sex!
I broke them up like meringues.

Don't read much now: the dude
Who lets the girl down before
The hero arrives, the chap   15
Who's yellow and keeps the store,
Seem far too familiar. Get stewed:
Books are a load of crap.

(1964)

ROSARIO CASTELLANOS

[*1925–1974*]

Chess

Because we were friends and sometimes loved each other,
perhaps to add one more tie
to the many that already bound us,
we decided to play games of the mind.

We set up a board between us;   5
equally divided into pieces, values,
and possible moves.
We learned the rules, we swore to respect them,
and the match began.

We've been sitting here for centuries, meditating   10
ferociously
how to deal the one last blow that will finally
annihilate the other one forever.

TRANSLATED BY MAUREEN AHERN

(1988)

GALWAY KINNELL
[b. 1927]

Saint Francis and the Sow

The bud
stands for all things,
even for those things that don't flower,
for everything flowers, from within, of self-blessing;
though sometimes it is necessary   5
to reteach a thing its loveliness,
to put a hand on its brow
of the flower
and retell it in words and in touch
it is lovely   10
until it flowers again from within, of self-blessing;
as Saint Francis
put his hand on the creased forehead
of the sow, and told her in words and in touch
blessings of earth on the sow, and the sow   15
began remembering all down her thick length,
from the earthen snout all the way
through the fodder and slops to the spiritual curl of the tail,
from the hard spininess spiked out from the spine
down through the great broken heart   20
to the sheer blue milken dreaminess spurting and shuddering
from the fourteen teats into the fourteen mouths sucking and
    blowing beneath them:
the long, perfect loveliness of sow.

(1980)

"Saint Francis and the Sow"   [12] *Saint Francis*   *Saint Francis of Assisi (1182–1226) was famed for his love of all creation, especially animals.*

JAMES WRIGHT

[b. 1927]

Lying in a Hammock at William Duffy's Farm in Pine Island, Minnesota

Over my head, I see the bronze butterfly,
Asleep on the black trunk,
Blowing like a leaf in green shadow.
Down the ravine behind the empty house,
The cowbells follow one another   5
Into the distances of the afternoon.
To my right,
In a field of sunlight between two pines,
The droppings of last year's horses
Blaze up into golden stones.   10
I lean back, as the evening darkens and comes on.
A chicken hawk floats over, looking for home.
I have wasted my life.

(1963)

A Blessing

Just off the highway to Rochester, Minnesota,
Twilight bounds softly forth on the grass.
And the eyes of those two Indian ponies
Darken with kindness.
They have come gladly out of the willows   5
To welcome my friend and me.
We step over the barbed wire into the pasture
Where they have been grazing all day, alone.
They ripple tensely, they can hardly contain their happiness
That we have come.   10
They bow shyly as wet swans. They love each other.
There is no loneliness like theirs.
At home once more,
They begin munching the young tufts of spring in the darkness.
I would like to hold the slenderer one in my arms,   15
For she has walked over to me
And nuzzled my left hand.
She is black and white,
Her mane falls wild on her forehead,

And the light breeze moves me to caress her long ear   20
That is delicate as the skin over a girl's wrist.
Suddenly I realize
That if I stepped out of my body I would break
Into blossom.

                                                                      (1963)

ANNE SEXTON

[1928–1975]

Two Hands

From the sea came a hand,
ignorant as a penny,
troubled with the salt of its mother,
mute with the silence of the fishes,
quick with the altars of the tides,   5
and God reached out of His mouth
and called it man.
Up came the other hand
and God called it woman.
The hands applauded.   10
And this was no sin.
It was as it was meant to be.

I see them roaming the streets:
Levi complaining about his mattress,
Sarah studying a beetle,   15
Mandrake holding his coffee mug,
Sally playing the drum at a football game,
John closing the eyes of the dying woman,
and some who are in prison,
even the prison of their bodies,   20
as Christ was prisoned in His body
until the triumph came.

Unwind, hands,
you angel webs,
unwind like the coil of a jumping jack,   25
cup together and let yourselves fill up with sun
and applaud, world,
applaud.

                                                                      (1969)

A SELECTION OF CONTEMPORARY POEMS

DONALD HALL

[*b. 1928*]

My son, my executioner

My son, my executioner,
    I take you in my arms,
Quiet and small and just astir,
    And whom my body warms.

Sweet death, small son, our instrument   5
    Of immortality,
Your cries and hungers document
    Our bodily decay.

We twenty-five and twenty-two,
    Who seemed to live forever,   10
Observe enduring life in you
    And start to die together.

                                         (1955)

X. J. KENNEDY

[*b. 1929*]

In a prominent bar in Secaucus one day

To the tune of "The Old Orange Flute" or
the tune of "Sweet Betsy from Pike"

In a prominent bar in Secaucus one day
Rose a lady in skunk with a topheavy sway,
Raised a knobby red finger—all turned from their beer—
While with eyes bright as snowcrust she sang high and clear:

"Now who of you'd think from an eyeload of me   5
That I once was a lady as proud as could be?
Oh I'd never sit down by a tumbledown drunk
If it wasn't, my dears, for the high cost of junk.

"All the gents used to swear that the white of my calf
Beat the down of the swan by a length and a half.   10
In the kerchief of linen I caught to my nose
Ah, there never fell snot, but a little gold rose.

"I had seven gold teeth and a toothpick of gold,
My Virginia cheroot° was a leaf of it rolled   cigar
And I'd light it each time with a thousand in cash—   15
Why the bums used to fight if I flicked them an ash.

"Once the toast of the Biltmore, the belle of the Taft,
I would drink bottle beer at the Drake, never draft,
And dine at the Astor on Salisbury steak
With a clean tablecloth for each bite I did take.   20

"In a car like the Roxy I'd roll to the track,
A steel-guitar trio, a bar in the back,
And the wheels made no noise, they turned over so fast,
Still it took you ten minutes to see me go past.

"When the horses bowed down to me that I might choose,   25
I bet on them all, for I hated to lose.
Now I'm saddled each night for my butter and eggs
And the broken threads race down the backs of my legs.

"Let you hold in mind, girls, that your beauty must pass
Like a lovely white clover that rusts with its grass.   30
Keep your bottoms off barstools and marry you young
Or be left—an old barrel with many a bung.

"For when time takes you out for a spin in his car
You'll be hard-pressed to stop him from going too far
And be left by the roadside, for all your good deeds,   35
Two toadstools for tits and a face full of weeds."

All the house raised a cheer, but the man at the bar
Made a phonecall and up pulled a red patrol car
And she blew us a kiss as they copped her away
From that prominent bar in Secaucus, N.J.   40

                                                    (1985)

"In a Prominent Bar in Secaucus One Day"   17–19 *Biltmore . . . Astor*   *once-fine hotels in New York City.*
21 **Roxy**   *a large, garish movie theater.*

ADRIENNE RICH
[b. 1929]

Diving into the Wreck

First having read the book of myths,
and loaded the camera,
and checked the edge of the knife-blade,
I put on
the body-armor of black rubber   5
the absurd flippers
the grave and awkward mask.
I am having to do this
not like Cousteau with his
assiduous team   10
aboard the sun-flooded schooner
but here alone.

There is a ladder.
The ladder is always there
hanging innocently   15
close to the side of the schooner.
We know what it is for,
we who have used it.
Otherwise
it's a piece of maritime floss   20
some sundry equipment.

I go down.
Rung after rung and still
the oxygen immerses me
the blue light   25
the clear atoms
of our human air.

I go down.
My flippers cripple me,
I crawl like an insect down the ladder   30
and there is no one
to tell me when the ocean
will begin.

First the air is blue and then
it is bluer and then green and then   35

black I am blacking out and yet
my mask is powerful
it pumps my blood with power
the sea is another story
the sea is not a question of power   40
I have to learn alone
to turn my body without force
in the deep element.

And now: it is easy to forget
what I came for   45
among so many who have always
lived here
swaying their crenellated fans
between the reefs
and besides   50
you breathe differently down here.

I came to explore the wreck.
The words are purposes.
The words are maps.
I came to see the damage that was done   55
and the treasures that prevail.
I stroke the beam of my lamp
slowly along the flank
of something more permanent
than fish or weed   60

the thing I came for:
the wreck and not the story of the wreck
the thing itself and not the myth
the drowned face always staring
toward the sun   65
the evidence of damage
worn by salt and sway into this threadbare beauty
the ribs of the disaster
curving their assertion
among the tentative haunters.   70

This is the place.
And I am here, the mermaid whose dark hair
streams black, the merman in his armored body
We circle silently
about the wreck   75
we dive into the hold.
I am she: I am he

whose drowned face sleeps with open eyes
whose breasts still bear the stress
whose silver, copper, vermeil cargo lies   80
obscurely inside barrels
half-wedged and left to rot
we are the half-destroyed instruments
that once held to a course
the water-eaten log   85
the fouled compass

We are, I am, you are
by cowardice or courage
the one who find our way
back to this scene   90
carrying a knife, a camera
a book of myths
in which
our names do not appear.

                                                                  (1973)

GREGORY CORSO

[b. 1930]

Marriage

Should I get married? Should I be good?
Astound the girl next door with my velvet suit and faustus hood?
Don't take her to movies but to cemeteries
tell all about werewolf bathtubs and forked clarinets
then desire her and kiss her and all the preliminaries   5
and she going just so far and I understanding why
not getting angry saying You must feel! It's beautiful to feel!
Instead take her in my arms lean against an old crooked tombstone
and woo her the entire night the constellations in the sky—

When she introduces me to her parents   10
back straightened, hair finally combed, strangled by a tie,
should I sit knees together on their 3rd degree sofa
and not ask Where's the bathroom?
How else to feel other than I am,

"Marraige"   ²*faustus hood*   *Dr. Faustus, German magician and astrologer (ca. 1480–1538) was reputed to have sold his soul to the Devil in exchange for knowledge and power.*

often thinking Flash Gordon soap—   15
O how terrible it must be for a young man
seated before a family and the family thinking
We never saw him before! He wants our Mary Lou!
After tea and homemade cookies they ask What do you do for a living?

Should I tell them? Would they like me then?   20
Say All right get married, we're losing a daughter
but we're gaining a son—
And should I then ask Where's the bathroom?

O God, and the wedding! All her family and her friends
and only a handful of mine all scroungy and bearded   25
just wait to get at the drinks and food—
And the priest! he looking at me as if I masturbated
asking me Do you take this woman for your lawful wedded wife?
And I trembling what to say say Pie Glue!
I kiss the bride all those corny men slapping me on the back   30
She's all yours, boy! Ha-ha-ha!
And in their eyes you could see some obscene honeymoon going on—
Then all that absurd rice and clanky cans and shoes
Niagara Falls! Hordes of us! Husbands! Wives! Flowers! Chocolates!
All streaming into cozy hotels   35
All going to do the same thing tonight

The indifferent clerk he knowing what was going to happen
The lobby zombies they knowing what
The whistling elevator man he knowing
The winking bellboy knowing   40
Everybody knowing! I'd be almost inclined not to do anything!
Stay up all night! Stare that hotel clerk in the eye!
Screaming: I deny honeymoon! I deny honeymoon!
running rampant into those almost climactic suites
yelling Radio belly! Cat shovel!   45
O I'd live in Niagara forever! in a dark cave beneath the Falls
I'd sit there the Mad Honeymooner
devising ways to break marriages, a scourge of bigamy
a saint of divorce—

But I should get married I should be good   50
How nice it'd be to come home to her
and sit by the fireplace and she in the kitchen
aproned young and lovely wanting my baby
and so happy about me she burns the roast beef
and comes crying to me and I get up from my big papa chair   55
saying Christmas teeth! Radiant brains! Apple deaf!
God what a husband I'd make! Yes, I should get married!

So much to do! like sneaking into Mr Jones' house late at night
and cover his golf clubs with 1920 Norwegian books
Like hanging a picture of Rimbaud on the lawnmower
like pasting Tannu Tuva postage stamps all over the picket fence
like when Mrs Kindhead comes to collect for the Community Chest
grab her and tell her There are unfavorable omens in the sky!
And when the mayor comes to get my vote tell him
When are you going to stop people killing whales!
And when the milkman comes leave him a note in the bottle
Penguin dust, bring me penguin dust, I want penguin dust—

Yet if I should get married and it's Connecticut and snow
and she gives birth to a child and I am sleepless, worn,
up for nights, head bowed against a quiet window, the past behind me,
finding myself in the most common of situations a trembling man
knowledged with responsibility not twig-smear nor Roman coin soup—
O what would that be like!
Surely I'd give it for a nipple a rubber Tacitus
For a rattle a bag of broken Bach records
Tack Della Francesca all over its crib
Sew the Greek alphabet on its bib
And build for its playpen a roofless Parthenon

No, I doubt I'd be that kind of father
Not rural not snow no quiet window
but hot smelly tight New York City
seven flights up, roaches and rats in the walls
a fat Reichian wife screeching over potatoes Get a job!
And five nose running brats in love with Batman
And the neighbors all toothless and dry haired
like those hag masses of the 18th century
all wanting to come in and watch TV

The landlord wants his rent
Grocery store Blue Cross Gas & Electric Knights of Columbus
Impossible to lie back and dream Telephone snow, ghost parking—
No! I should not get married I should never get married!
But—imagine if I were married to a beautiful sophisticated woman
tall and pale wearing an elegant black dress and long black gloves
holding a cigarette holder in one hand and a highball in the other
and we lived high up in a penthouse with a huge window
from which we could see all of New York and ever farther on clearer days
No, can't imagine myself married to that pleasant prison dream—

60 **Rimbaud** *Arthur Rimbaud (1854–1891), French poet.* 61 **Tannu Tuva** *a republic in Siberia, part of the* USSR. 74 **Tacitus** *Roman historian (A.D. 55–117).* 76 **Della Francesca** *Italian Renaissance painter (1420–1492).* 83 **Reichian** *follower of psychoanalyst Wilhelm Reich (1897–1957).*

O but what about love? I forget love
not that I am incapable of love
it's just that I see love as odd as wearing shoes—   100
I never wanted to marry a girl who was like my mother
And Ingrid Bergman was always impossible
And there's maybe a girl now but she's already married
And I don't like men and—
but there's got to be somebody!   105
Because what if I'm 60 years old and not married,
all alone in a furnished room with pee stains on my underwear
and everybody else is married! All the universe married but me!

Ah, yet well I know that were a woman possible as I am possible
then marriage would be possible—   110
Like SHE in her lonely alien gaud waiting her Egyptian lover
so I wait—bereft of 2,000 years and the bath of life.

(1960)

LINDA PASTAN

[*b. 1932*]

Ethics

In ethics class so many years ago
our teacher asked this question every fall:
if there were a fire in a museum
which would you save, a Rembrandt painting
or an old woman who hadn't many   5
years left anyhow? Restless on hard chairs
caring little for pictures or old age
we'd opt one year for life, the next for art
and always half-heartedly. Sometimes
the woman borrowed my grandmother's face   10
leaving her usual kitchen to wander
some drafty, half imagined museum.
One year, feeling clever, I replied
why not let the woman decide herself?
Linda, the teacher would report, eschews   15
the burdens of responsibility.
This fall in a real museum I stand
before a real Rembrandt, old woman,

"Marraige"   [111]**SHE**   *the heroine of H. Rider Haggard's novel* She *(1887) who gains eternal youth by bathing in fire and who waits thousands of years for her lover's return.*

or nearly so, myself. The colors
within this frame are darker than autumn,   20
darker even than winter—the browns of earth,
though earth's most radiant elements burn
through the canvas. I know now that woman
and painting and season are almost one   25
and all beyond saving by children.

(1981)

AUDRE LORDE
[1934–1992]

Hanging Fire

I am fourteen
and my skin has betrayed me
the boy I cannot live without
still sucks his thumb
in secret   5
how come my knees are
always so ashy
what if I die
before morning
and mamma's in the bedroom   10
with the door closed.

I have to learn how to dance
in time for the next party
my room is too small for me
suppose I die before graduation   15
they will sing sad melodies
but finally
tell the truth about me
There is nothing I want to do
and too much   20
that has to be done
and momma's in the bedroom
with the door closed.

Nobody even stops to think
about my side of it   25
I should have been on Math Team
my marks were better than his

why do I have to be
the one
wearing braces   30
I have nothing to wear tomorrow
will I live long enough
to grow up
and momma's in the bedroom
with the door closed.   35

(1978)

LUCILLE CLIFTON

[b. 1936]

Homage to My Hips

these hips are big hips.
they need space to
move around in.
they don't fit into little
petty places. these hips   5
are free hips.
they don't like to be held back.
these hips have never been enslaved,
they go where they want to go
they do what they want to do.   10
these hips are mighty hips.
these hips are magic hips.
i have known them
to put a spell on a man and
spin him like a top!   15

(1972)

The Lost Baby Poem

the time i dropped your almost body down
down to meet the waters under the city
and run one with the sewage to the sea
what did i know about waters rushing back
what did i know about drowning   5
or being drowned

you would have been born into winter
in the year of the disconnected gas
and no car   we would have made the thin
walk over Genesee hill into the Canada wind 10
to watch you slip like ice into strangers' hands
you would have fallen naked as snow into winter
if you were here i could tell you these
and some other things

if i am ever less than a mountain 15
for your definite brothers and sisters
let the rivers pour over my head
let the sea take me for a spiller
of seas   let black men call me stranger
always   for your never named sake 20

(1972)

MARGE PIERCY

[b. 1936]

A Work of Artifice

The bonsai tree
in the attractive pot
could have grown eighty feet tall
on the side of a mountain
till split by lightning. 5
But a gardener
carefully pruned it.
It is nine inches high.
Every day as he
whittles back the branches 10
the gardener croons,
It is your nature
to be small and cozy,
domestic and weak;
how lucky, little tree, 15
to have a pot to grow in.
With living creatures
one must begin very early
to dwarf their growth:
the bound feet, 20

                    the crippled brain,
                    the hair in curlers,
                    the hands you
                    love to touch.

                                                        (1973)

To Be of Use

The people I love the best
jump into work head first
without dallying in the shallows
and swim off with sure strokes almost out of sight.
They seem to become natives of that element,   5
the black sleek heads of seals
bouncing like half-submerged balls.

I love people who harness themselves, an ox to a heavy cart,
who pull like water buffalo, with massive patience,
who strain in the mud and the muck to move things forward,   10
who do what has to be done, again and again.

I want to be with people who submerge
in the task, who go into the fields to harvest
and work in a row and pass the bags along,
who are not parlor generals and field deserters   15
but move in a common rhythm
when the food must come in or the fire be put out.

The work of the world is common as mud.
Botched, it smears the hands, crumbles to dust.
But the thing worth doing well done   20
has a shape that satisfies, clean and evident.
Greek amphoras for wine or oil,
Hopi vases that held corn, are put in museums
but you know they were made to be used.
The pitcher cries for water to carry   25
and a person for work that is real.

                                                        (1973)

BELLA AKHMADULINA

[b. 1937]

The Bride

Oh to be a bride
Brilliant in my curls
Under the white canopy
Of a modest veil!

How my hands tremble,   5
Bound by my icy rings!
The glasses gather, brimming
With red compliments.

At last the world says yes;
It wishes me roses and sons.   10
My friends stand shyly at the door,
Carrying love gifts.

Chemises in cellophane,
Plates, flowers, lace . . .
They kiss my cheeks, they marvel   15
I'm to be a wife.

Soon my white gown
Is stained with wine like blood;
I feel both lucky and poor
As I sit, listening, at the table.   20

Terror and desire
Loom in the forward hours.
My mother, the darling, weeps—
Mama is like the weather.

. . . My rich, royal attire   25
I lay aside on the bed.
I find I am afraid
To look at you, to kiss you.

Loudly the chairs are set
Against the wall, eternity . . .   30

My love, what more can happen
To you and to me?

TRANSLATED BY STEPHAN STEPANCHEV

(1967)

MARGARET ATWOOD
[*b. 1939*]

This Is a Photograph of Me

It was taken some time ago.
At first it seems to be
a smeared
print: blurred lines and grey flecks
blended with the paper;   5
then, as you scan
it, you see in the left-hand corner
a thing that is like a branch: part of a tree
(balsam or spruce) emerging
and, to the right, halfway up   10
what ought to be a gentle
slope, a small frame house.

In the background there is a lake,
and beyond that, some low hills.

(The photograph was taken   15
the day after I drowned.

I am in the lake, in the center
of the picture, just under the surface.

It is difficult to say where
precisely, or to say   20
how large or small I am:
the effect of water
on light is a distortion

but if you look long enough,
eventually   25
you will be able to see me.)

(1966)

RAYMOND CARVER

[*1939–1988*]

Photograph of My Father in His Twenty-second Year

October. Here in this dank, unfamiliar kitchen
I study my father's embarrassed young man's face.
Sheepish grin, he holds in one hand a string
of spiny yellow perch, in the other
a bottle of Carlsbad beer.   5

In jeans and denim shirt, he leans
against the front fender of a 1934 Ford.
He would like to pose bluff and hearty for his posterity,
wear his old hat cocked over his ear.
All his life my father wanted to be bold.   10

But the eyes give him away, and the hands
that limply offer the string of dead perch
and the bottle of beer. Father, I love you,
yet how can I say thank you, I who can't hold my liquor either,
and don't even know the places to fish?   15

(*1988*)

SEAMUS HEANEY

[*b. 1939*]

Mid-Term Break

I sat all morning in the college sick bay
Counting bells knelling classes to a close.
At two o'clock our neighbors drove me home.

In the porch I met my father crying—
He had always taken funerals in his stride—   5
And Big Jim Evans saying it was a hard blow.

The baby cooed and laughed and rocked the pram
When I came in, and I was embarrassed
By old men standing up to shake my hand

And tell me they were "sorry for my trouble,"   10
Whispers informed strangers I was the eldest,
Away at school, as my mother held my hand

In hers and coughed out angry tearless sighs.
At ten o'clock the ambulance arrived   15
With the corpse, stanched and bandaged by the nurses.

Next morning I went up into the room. Snowdrops
And candles soothed the bedside; I saw him
For the first time in six weeks. Paler now,

Wearing a poppy bruise on his left temple,
He lay in the four foot box as in his cot.   20
No gaudy scars, the bumper knocked him clear.

A four foot box, a foot for every year.

                                        (1966)

Digging

Between my finger and my thumb
The squat pen rests; snug as a gun.

Under my window, a clean rasping sound
When the spade sinks into gravelly ground:
My father, digging. I look down   5

Till his straining rump among the flowerbeds
Bends low, comes up twenty years away
Stooping in rhythm through potato drills
Where he was digging.

The coarse boot nestled on the lug, the shaft   10
Against the inside knee was levered firmly.
He rooted out tall tops, buried the bright edge deep
To scatter new potatoes that we picked
Loving their cool hardness in our hands.

By God, the old man could handle a spade.   15
Just like his old man.

My grandfather cut more turf in a day
Than any other man on Toner's bog.
Once I carried him milk in a bottle

Corked sloppily with paper. He straightened up   20
To drink it, then fell to right away

Nicking and slicing neatly, heaving sods
Over his shoulder, going down and down
For the good turf. Digging.

The cold smell of potato mould, the squelch and slap   25
Of soggy peat, the curt cuts of an edge
Through living roots awaken in my head.
But I've no spade to follow men like them.

Between my finger and my thumb
The squat pen rests.   30
I'll dig with it.

(1966)

BARBARA HOLDER
[*b. 1939*]

Ballet Class at the Hotel Ansonia: For Vera Nemtchinova

Through rear windows, the dark slit
of old crowded buildings, pigeons bobbing
on tarred roofs, their feces the city's
white sludge.

Inside, Madame, hair drawn back, demonstrates   5
the slow incantation of adagio, long neck
muscled under an elegant head, her creased face
flecked powder white, onyx eyes and bow mouth
making her a live Coppelia

Or White Swan just four feet away, her still agile   10
body with the trace of Nijinsky's hands, as we
witness, sweat pouring down us like baptismal water.
We had come for grace.

(1998)

ROBERT HASS

[b. 1941]

Meditation at Lagunitas

All the new thinking is about loss.
In this it resembles all the old thinking.
The idea, for example, that each particular erases
the luminous clarity of a general idea. That the clown-
faced woodpecker probing the dead sculpted trunk   5
of that black birch is, by his presence,
some tragic falling off from a first world
of undivided light. Or the other notion that,
because there is in this world no one thing
to which the bramble of *blackberry* corresponds,   10
a word is elegy to what it signifies.
We talked about it late last night and in the voice
of my friend, there was a thin wire of grief, a tone
almost querulous. After a while I understood that,
talking this way, everything dissolves: *justice,*   15
pine, hair, woman, you and *I.* There was a woman
I made love to and I remembered how, holding
her small shoulders in my hands sometimes,
I felt a violent wonder at her presence
like a thirst for salt, for my childhood river   20
with its island willows, silly music from the pleasure boat,
muddy places where we caught the little orange-silver fish
called *pumpkinseed.* It hardly had to do with her.
Longing, we say, because desire is full
of endless distances. I must have been the same to her.   25
But I remember so much, the way her hands dismantled bread,
the thing her father said that hurt her, what
she dreamed. There are moments when the body is as numinous
as words, days that are the good flesh continuing.
Such tenderness, those afternoons and evenings,   30
saying *blackberry, blackberry, blackberry.*

                                                                    (1979)

NIKKI GIOVANNI
[b. 1943]

Ego Tripping
(THERE MAY BE A REASON WHY)

I was born in the congo
I walked to the fertile crescent and built
    the sphinx
I designed a pyramid so tough that a star
    that only glows every one hundred years falls   5
    into the center giving divine perfect light
I am bad

I sat on the throne
    drinking nectar with allah
I got hot and sent an ice age to europe   10
    to cool my thirst
My oldest daughter is nefertiti
    the tears from my birth pains
    created the nile
I am a beautiful woman   15

I gazed on the forest and burned
    out the sahara desert
    with a packet of goat's meat
    and a change of clothes
I crossed it in two hours   20
I am a gazelle so swift
    so swift you can't catch me

    For a birthday present when he was three
I gave my son hannibal an elephant
    He gave me rome for mother's day   25
My strength flows ever on

My son noah built new/ark and
I stood proudly at the helm
    as we sailed on a soft summer day
I turned myself into myself and was   30
    jesus
    men intone my loving name

All praises All praises
I am the one who would save

I sowed diamonds in my back yard   35
My bowels deliver uranium
        the filings from my fingernails are
        semi-precious jewels
        On a trip north
I caught a cold and blew   40
My nose giving oil to the arab world
I am so hip even my errors are correct
I sailed west to reach east and had to round off
        the earth as I went
        The hair from my head thinned and gold was laid   45
        across three continents
I am so perfect so divine so ethereal so surreal
I cannot be comprehended
        except by my permission

I mean . . . I . . . can fly   50
        like a bird in the sky . . . .

                                                                  (1970)

SHARON OLDS

[b. 1942]

Size and Sheer Will

The fine, green pajama cotton,
washed so often it is paper-thin and
iridescent, has split like a sheath
and the glossy white naked bulbs of
Gabriel's toes thrust forth like crocus   5
this early Spring. The boy is growing
as fast as he can, elongated
wrists dangling, lean meat
showing between the shirt and the belt.
If there were a rack to stretch himself, he would   10
strap his slight body to it.
If there were a machine to enter,
skip the next ten years and be
sixteen immediately, this boy would

15

do it. All day long he cranes his
neck, like a plant in the dark with a single
light above it, or a sailor under
tons of green water, longing
for the surface, for his rightful life.

(1975)

TOM MOLITO
[*b. 1944*]

Cosmic Simplicities

We basically don't know where we
came from before birth—

We basically don't know where we go
after death—

Now, tell me how to live my life if you
dare—

The truth probably lies somewhere
between Plato and Pluto.

5

(1998)

CHRISTOPHER JANE CORKERY
[*b. 1946*]

Divorce

A small girl on a porch
left by her mother
while Mother drives Father
to the 8:02 train.

Father always goes
when the sun hits the porch.
It is June, those are lilacs,
she does not know the word

5

for what is hers,
what is his.   10
What is the thing
between them?

But she does feel something
pressing against her
as the Plymouths and Fords   15
bump along the road.

It is flying inside her,
trying to get out.
It is rising through her body,
beating in her hands.   20

She feels tears in her eyes
but they are not hers.
They belong to those stupid
girls in the stories.

Her legs are crossed   25
at the ankles. Her feet swing
above the grey boards
where six ants are running.

She knows that the birds
in the lilacs are warblers.   30
Her father told her that
but flicker is her favorite

word for a bird.
The white on his back
when he flies away   35
is how she remembers.

Flicker. Flicker.

The red on his head
means love forever.
He's a good bird, she says,   40
And he loves to fly.

(1985)

JANE KENYON

[1947–1995]

Otherwise

I got out of bed
on two strong legs.
It might have been
otherwise. I ate
cereal, sweet   5
milk, ripe, flawless
peach. It might
have been otherwise.
I took the dog uphill
to the birch wood.   10
All morning I did
the work I love.

At noon I lay down
with my mate. It might
have been otherwise.   15
We ate dinner together
at a table with silver
candlesticks. It might
have been otherwise.
I slept in a bed   20
in a room with paintings
on the walls, and
planned another day
just like this day.
But one day, I know,   25
it will be otherwise.

(1990)

Notes from the Other Side

I divested myself of despair
and fear when I came here.

Now there is no more catching
one's own eye in the mirror,

there are no bad books, no plastic,
no insurance premiums, and of course   5

no illness. Contrition
does not exist, nor gnashing

of teeth. No one howls as the first
clod of earth hits the casket.   10

The poor we no longer have with us.
Our calm hearts strike only the hour,

and God, as promised, proves
to be mercy clothed in light.

(1990)

YUSEF KOMUNYAKAA
[b. 1947]

Facing It

My black face fades,
hiding inside the black granite.
I said I wouldn't,
dammit: No tears.
I'm stone. I'm flesh.   5
My clouded reflection eyes me
like a bird of prey, the profile of night
slanted against morning. I turn
this way—the stone lets me go.
I turn that way—I'm inside   10
the Vietnam Veterans Memorial
again, depending on the light
to make a difference.
I go down the 58,022 names,
half-expecting to find   15
my own in letters like smoke.
I touch the name Andrew Johnson;
I see the booby trap's white flash.
Names shimmer on a woman's blouse
but when she walks away   20
the names stay on the wall.

Brushstrokes flash, a red bird's
wings cutting across my stare.
The sky. A plane in the sky.
A white vet's image floats   25
closer to me, then his pale eyes
look through mine. I'm a window.
He's lost his right arm
inside the stone. In the black mirror
a woman's trying to erase names: 30
No, she's brushing a boy's hair.

(1988)

NEAL BOWERS

[b. 1948]

Driving Lessons

I learned to drive in a parking lot
on Sundays, when the stores were closed—
slow maneuvers out beyond the light-poles,
no destination, just the ritual of clutch and gas,
my father clenching with the grinding gears,   5
finally giving up and leaving my mother
to buck and plunge with me and say,
repeatedly, "Once more. Try just once more."

She walked out on him once
when I was six or seven, my father   10
driving beside her, slow as a beginner,
pleading, my baby brother and I
crying out the windows, "Mama, don't go!"
It was a scene to break your heart
or make you laugh—those wailing kids,   15
a woman walking briskly with a suitcase,
the slow car following like a faithful dog.

I don't know why she finally got in
and let us take her back
to whatever she had made up her mind to leave;   20
but the old world swallowed her up
as soon as she opened that door,
and the other life she might have lived
lay down forever in its dark infancy.

Sometimes, when I'm home, driving   25
through the old neighborhoods, stopping
in front of each little house we rented,
my stillborn other life gets in,
the boy I would have been if
my mother had kept on walking.   30
He wants to be just like her,
far away and gone forever, wants
me to press down on the gas;
but however fast I squeal away,
the shaggy past keeps loping behind,   35
sniffing every turn.

When I stop in the weedy parking lot,
the failed stores of the old mall
make a dark wall straight ahead;
and I'm alone again, until my parents get in,   40
unchanged after all these years,
my father, impatient, my mother
trying hard to smile, waiting for me
to steer my way across this emptiness.

                                                   (1992)

KRAFT ROMPF

[b. 1948]

Waiting Table

To serve, I wait and pluck
the rose, brush crumbs, carry

madly trays of oysters and
Bloody Marys. Swinging through

doors, I hear them: mouths   5
open, eyes bugging, choking;

they beat a white clothed
table for caffeine piping

hot and sweet, sweet sugar.
Oh, I should pour it in   10

their eyes! And set their
tongues afire. How the chef

understands when I order
tartare and shout, "Let them

eat it raw!" Oh I would stuff   15
their noses with garlic

and the house pianist
could play the Hammer March

on their toes. But for a
tip—for a tip, for a tip   20

I would work so very, very
hard, and so gladly let

them shine into my soul,
and bow to them and laugh

with them and sing. I would   25
gladly give them everything.

                                                    (1978)

JIMMY SANTIAGO BACA
[b. 1952]

from *Meditations on the South Valley*

XVII

I love the wind
when it blows through my barrio.
It hisses its snake love
down calles de polvo,
and cracks egg-shell skins   5
of abandoned homes.
Stray dogs find shelter
along the river,
where great cottonwoods rattle
like old covered wagons,   10
stuck in stagnant waterholes.

Days when the wind blows
full of sand and grit,
men and women make decisions
that change their whole lives.   15
Windy days in the barrio
give birth to divorce papers
and squalling separation. The wind tells us
what others refuse to tell us,
informing men and women of a secret,   20
that they move away to hide from.

(1979)

RITA DOVE

[b. 1952]

Canary

FOR MICHAEL S. HARPER

Billie Holiday's burned voice
had as many shadows as lights,
a mournful candelabra against a sleek piano,
the gardenia her signature under that ruined face.

(Now you're cooking, drummer to bass,   5
magic spoon, magic needle.
Take all day if you have to
with your mirror and your bracelet of song.)

Fact is, the invention of women under siege
has been to sharpen love in the service of myth.   10

If you can't be free, be a mystery.

(1989)

JUDITH ORTIZ COFER
[b. 1952]

The Idea of Islands

The place where I was born,
that mote in a cartographer's eye,
interests you?
Today Atlanta is like a port city
enveloped in mist. The temperature   5
is plunging with the abandon
of a woman rushing to a rendezvous.
Since you ask, things were simpler
on the island. Food and shelter
were never the problem. Most days,   10
a hat and a watchful eye were all
one needed for protection, the climate being
rarely inclement. Fruit could be plucked
from trees languishing under the weight
of their own fecundity. The thick sea   15
spewed out fish that crawled into the pots
of women whose main occupation was to dress
each other's manes with scarlet hibiscus,
which as you may know, blooms
without restraint in the tropics.   20
I was always the ambitious one, overdressed
by my neighbors' standards, and unwilling
to eat mangoes three times a day.
In truth, I confess to spending my youth
guarding the fire by the beach, waiting   25
to be rescued from the futile round
of paradisial life.
How do I like the big city?
City lights are just as bright
as the stars that enticed me then;   30
the traffic ebbs and rises like the tides
and in a crowd,
everyone is an island.

(1989)

ALBERTO RIOS
[b. 1952]

A Dream of Husbands

Though we thought it, Doña Carolina did not die.
She was too old for that nonsense, and too set.
That morning she walked off just a little farther
into her favorite dream, favorite but not nice
so much, not nice and not bad, so it was not death.   5
She dreamed the dream of husbands
and over there she found him after all the years.
Cabrón, she called him, *animal,* very loud
so we could hear it, for us it was a loud truck
passing, or thunder, or too many cats, very loud   10
for having left her for so long and so far. Days now
her voice is the squeak of the rocking chair
as she complains, we hear it, it will not go
not with oils or sanding or shouts back at her.
But it becomes too the sound a spoon makes, her old   15
very large wooden spoon as it stirs a pot of soup.
Dinnertimes, we think of her, the good parts, of her
cooking, we like her best then, even the smell of her.
But then, *cabrones* she calls us, *animales,* irritated,
from over there, from the dream, they come, her words   20
they are the worst sounds of the street in the night
so that we will not get so comfortable about her,
so comfortable with her having left us
we thinking that her husband and her long dream
are so perfect, because no, they are not, not so much,   25
she is not so happy this way, not in this dream,
this is not heaven, don't think it. She tells us this,
sadness too is hers, a half measure, sadness at having
no time for the old things, for rice, for chairs.

(1985)

GERTRUDE SCHNACKENBERG
[b. 1952]

Signs

Threading the palm, a web of little lines
Spells out the lost money, the heart, the head,
The wagging tongues, the sudden deaths, in signs
We would smooth out, like imprints on a bed,

In signs that can't be helped, geese heading south,   5
In signs read anxiously, like breath that clouds
A mirror held to a barely open mouth,
Like telegrams, the gathering of crowds—

The plane's X in the sky, spelling disaster:
Before the whistle and hit, a tracer flare;   10
Before rubble, a hairline crack in plaster
And a housefly's panicked scribbling on the air.

           (1982)

GARY SOTO
[b. 1952]

Behind Grandma's House

At ten I wanted fame. I had a comb
And two Coke bottles, a tube of Bryl-creem.
I borrowed a dog, one with
Mismatched eyes and a happy tongue,
And wanted to prove I was tough   5
In the alley, kicking over trash cans,
A dull chime of tuna cans falling.
I hurled light bulbs like grenades
And men teachers held their heads,
Fingers of blood lengthening   10
On the ground. I flicked rocks at cats,
Their goofy faces spurred with foxtails.
I kicked fences. I shooed pigeons.
I broke a branch from a flowering peach

And frightened ants with a stream of spit.   15
I said *"Chale,"* "In your face," and "No way
Daddy-O" to an imaginary priest
Until grandma came into the alley,
Her apron flapping in a breeze,
Her hair mussed, and said, "Let me help you,"   20
And punched me between the eyes.

(1985)

LOUISE ERDRICH

[*b. 1954*]

Indian Boarding School: The Runaways

Home's the place we head for in our sleep.
Boxcars stumbling north in dreams
don't wait for us. We catch them on the run.
The rails, old lacerations that we love,
shoot parallel across the face and break   5
just under Turtle Mountains. Riding scars
you can't get lost. Home is the place they cross.

The lame guard strikes a match and makes the dark
less tolerant. We watch through cracks in boards
as the land starts rolling, rolling till it hurts   10
to be here, cold in regulation clothes.
We know the sheriff's waiting at midrun
to take us back. His car is dumb and warm.
The highway doesn't rock, it only hums
like a wing of long insults. The worn-down welts   15
of ancient punishments lead back and forth.

All runaways wear dresses, long green ones,
the color you would think shame was. We scrub
the sidewalks down because it's shameful work.
Our brushes cut the stone in watered arcs   20
and in the soak frail outlines shiver clear
a moment, things us kids pressed on the dark
face before it hardened, place, remembering
delicate old injuries, the spines of names and leaves.

(1984)

Drama

PART THREE

CHAPTER SEVENTEEN

Reading Plays

Drama, unlike the other literary genres, is a staged art. Plays are written to be performed by actors before an audience. But the plays we wish to see are not always performed. We might have to wait years, for example, to see a production of Sophocles' *Antigonê* or Arthur Miller's *Death of a Salesman*. We simply might never have an opportunity to see certain plays. A reasonable alternative is to read them with attention to both their theatrical and literary dimensions.

THE EXPERIENCE OF DRAMA

As a literary genre, drama has affinities with fiction, poetry, and the essay. Like fiction, drama possesses a narrative dimension: a play often narrates a story in the form of a plot. Like fiction, drama relies on dialogue and description, which takes the form of *stage directions,* lines describing characters, scenes, or actions with clues to production. Unlike fiction, however, in which a narrator often mediates between us and the story, there is no such authorial presence in drama. Instead, we hear the words of the characters directly.

Although drama is most like fiction, it shares features with poetry as well. Plays may, in fact, be written in verse: Shakespeare wrote in *blank verse* (un-rhymed iambic pentameter), Molière in rhymed couplets. Plays, like lyric poems, are also overheard: we listen to characters expressing their concerns as if there were no audience present. Poems also contain dramatic elements. The dramatic lyrics and monologues of Robert Browning and some of the poems of John Donne portray characters speaking and listening to one another.

Plays, like essays, may be vehicles of persuasion. The playwrights Henrik Ibsen and Bernard Shaw frequently used the stage to dramatize ideas and issues. And for most of his plays Shaw wrote essay prefaces in which he discussed their dominant ideas. In both essay and drama, ideas possess more primacy than they do in poetry and fiction, something to which critics of the genre testify. Aristotle, for example, made *thought* one of his six elements of drama; Eric Bentley, a modern critic, entitled one of his books *The Playwright as Thinker.*

But if we look exclusively to the literary aspects of drama, to its poetic and fictional elements, and to its dramatization of ideas, we may fail to appreciate its uniquely theatrical idiom. To gain this appreciation we should read drama with special attention to its performance elements. We can try to hear the voices of characters, and imagine tones and inflections. We can try to see mentally how characters look, where they stand in relation to one another, how they move and gesture. We can read, in short, as armchair directors and as aspiring actors and actresses considering the physical and practical realities of performance.

In doing so we will enrich our experience of the plays we read. Our experience of drama includes more than an intellectual understanding of the ideas particular plays may dramatize. It also includes our emotional reactions to plots and our responses to the interaction of the characters. It encompasses our vision of their dramatic worlds, and it is affected by our changing perceptions and feelings as we read. Our experience of reading drama involves more than a rational and analytic understanding of the text. More inclusive, more integrated, and more imaginative, that experience includes feelings as well as thought, emotional apprehension as well as intellectual comprehension.

As active readers of drama we will bring a special awareness of the ways the written text of a play (its *script*) suggests possibilities for performance. To suggest how we might do this, we include excerpts from three plays, each accompanied by notes and comments. As you read the first excerpt, the opening scene of Henrik Ibsen's *A Doll House,* consider what the stage directions and cast of characters reveal about the world of the play.

CHARACTERS

TORVALD HELMER, *a lawyer*
NORA, *his wife*
DR. RANK
MRS. LINDE
NILS KROGSTAD, *a bank clerk*
THE HELMERS' THREE SMALL CHILDREN
ANNE-MARIE, *their nurse*
HELENE, *a maid*
A DELIVERY BOY

The action takes place in HELMER'S *residence.*

ACT I

A comfortable room, tastefully but not expensively furnished. A door to the right in the back wall leads to the entryway, another to the left leads to HELMER'S *study. Between these doors, a piano. Midway in the left-hand wall a door, and further back a window. Near the window a round table with an armchair and a small sofa. In the right-hand wall, toward the rear a door, and nearer the foreground a porcelain stove with two armchairs and a rocking chair beside it. Between the stove and the side door, a small table. Engravings on the walls. An etagére with china figures and other small art objects; a small bookcase with richly bound books; the floor carpeted; a fire burning in the stove. It is a winter day.*

A bell rings in the entryway; shortly after we hear the door being unlocked. NORA *comes into the room, humming happily to herself; she is wearing street clothes and carries an armload of packages, which she puts down on the table to the right. She has left the hall door open; and through it a* DELIVERY BOY *is seen, holding a Christmas tree and a basket which he gives to the* MAID *who let them in.*

NORA   Hide the tree well, Helene. The children mustn't get a glimpse of it till this evening, after it's trimmed. *(To the* DELIVERY BOY, *taking out her purse)* How much?

DELIVERY BOY   Fifty, ma'am.

NORA   There's a crown. No, keep the change. *(The* BOY *thanks her and leaves.* NORA *shuts the door. She laughs softly to herself while taking off her street things. Drawing a bag of macaroons from her pocket, she eats a couple, then steals over and listens at her husband's study door.)* Yes, he's home. *(Hums again as she moves to the table, right.)*

HELMER   *(from the study)* Is that my little lark twittering out there?

NORA   *(busy opening some packages)* Yes, it is.

HELMER   Is that my squirrel rummaging around?

NORA   Yes!

HELMER   When did my squirrel get in?

NORA   Just now. *(Putting the macaroon bag in her pocket and wiping her mouth)* Do come in, Torvald, and see what I've bought.

HELMER   Can't be disturbed. *(After a moment he opens the door and peers in, pen in hand.)* Bought, you say? All that there? Has the little spendthrift been out throwing money around again?

NORA   Oh, but Torvald, this year we really should let ourselves go a bit. It's the first Christmas we haven't had to economize.

HELMER   But you know we can't go squandering.

NORA   Oh yes, Torvald, we can squander a little now. Can't we? Just a tiny, wee bit. Now that you've got a big salary and are going to make piles and piles of money.

HELMER   Yes—starting New Year's. But then it's a full three months till the raise comes through.

NORA   Pooh! We can borrow that long.

HELMER   Nora! *(Goes over and playfully takes her by the ear)* Are your scatter-brains off again? What if today I borrowed a thousand crowns, and you squandered them over Christmas week, and then on New Year's Eve a roof tile fell on my head, and I lay there—

NORA   *(putting her hand on his mouth)* Oh! Don't say such things!

HELMER   Yes, but what if it happened—then what?

NORA   If anything so awful happened, then it just wouldn't matter if I had debts or not.

HELMER   Well, but the people I'd borrowed from?

NORA   Them? Who cares about them! They're strangers.

HELMER   Nora, Nora, how like a woman! No, but seriously, Nora, you know what I think about that. No debts! Never borrow! Something of freedom's lost—and something of beauty, too—from a home that's founded on borrowing and debt. We've made a brave stand up to now, the two of us; and we'll go right on like that the little while we have to.

NORA   *(going toward the stove)* Yes, whatever you say, Torvald.

HELMER   *(following her)* Now, now, the little lark's wings mustn't droop. Come on, don't be a sulky squirrel. *(Taking out his wallet)* Nora, guess what I have here.

NORA   *(turning quickly)* Money!

HELMER   There, see. *(Hands her some notes)* Good grief, I know how costs go up in a house at Christmastime.

NORA   Ten—twenty—thirty—forty. Oh, thank you. Torvald; I can manage no end on this.

HELMER   You really will have to.

NORA   Oh yes, I promise I will! But come here so I can show you everything I bought. And so cheap! Look, new clothes for Ivar here—and a sword. Here a horse and a trumpet for Bob. And a doll and a doll's bed here for Emmy; they're nothing much, but she'll tear them to bits in no time anyway. And here I have dress material and handkerchiefs for the maids. Old Anne-Marie really deserves something more.

HELMER   And what's in that package there?

NORA   *(with a cry)* Torvald, no! You can't see that till tonight!

HELMER   I see. But tell me now, you little prodigal, what have you thought of for yourself?

NORA   For myself? Oh, I don't want anything at all.

HELMER   Of course you do. Tell me just what—within reason—you'd most like to have.

NORA   I honestly don't know. Oh, listen, Torvald—

HELMER   Well?

NORA   *(fumbling at his coat buttons, without looking at him)* If you want to give me something, then maybe you could—you could—

HELMER   Come on, out with it.

NORA   *(hurriedly)* You could give me money, Torvald. No more than you think you can spare, then one of these days I'll buy something with it.

HELMER   But Nora—

NORA   Oh, please, Torvald darling, do that! I beg you, please. Then I could hang the bills in pretty gilt paper on the Christmas tree. Wouldn't that be fun?

HELMER   What are those little birds called that always fly through their fortunes?

NORA   Oh yes, spendthrifts; I know all that. But let's do as I say, Torvald; then I'll have time to decide what I really need most. That's very sensible, isn't it?

HELMER   *(smiling)* Yes, very—that is, if you actually hung onto the money I give you, and you actually used it to buy yourself something, But it goes for the house and for all sorts of foolish things, and then I only have to lay out some more.

NORA   Oh, but Torvald—

HELMER   Don't deny it, my dear little Nora. *(Putting his arm around her waist)* Spendthrifts are sweet, but they use up a frightful amount of money. It's incredible what it costs a man to feed such birds.

NORA   Oh, how can you say that! Really, I save everything I can.

HELMER   *(laughing)* Yes, that's the truth. Everything you can. But that's nothing at all.

NORA   *(humming, with a smile of quiet satisfaction)* Hm, if you only knew what expenses we larks and squirrels have, Torvald.

HELMER   You're an odd little one. Exactly the way your father was. You're never at a loss for scaring up money; but the moment you have it, it runs right out through your fingers; you never know what you've done with it. Well, one takes you as you are. It's deep in your blood. Yes, these things are hereditary, Nora.

NORA   Ah, I could wish I'd inherited many of Papa's qualities.

HELMER   And I couldn't wish you anything but just what you are, my sweet little lark. But wait; it seems to me you have a very—what should I call it?— a very suspicious look today—

NORA   I do?

HELMER   You certainly do. Look me straight in the eye.

NORA   *(looking at him)* Well?

HELMER   *(shaking an admonitory finger)* Surely my sweet tooth hasn't been running riot in town today, has she?

NORA   No. Why do you imagine that?

HELMER   My sweet tooth really didn't make a little detour through the confectioner's?

NORA   No, I assure you, Torvald—

HELMER   Hasn't nibbled some pastry?

NORA   No, not at all.

HELMER   Not even munched a macaroon or two?

NORA   No, Torvald, I assure you, really—

HELMER   There, there now. Of course I'm only joking.

NORA   *(going to the table, right)* You know I could never think of going against you.

HELMER   No, I understand that; and you *have* given me your word. *(Going over to her)* Well, you keep your little Christmas secrets to yourself, Nora darling. I expect they'll come to light this evening, when the tree is lit.

NORA   Did you remember to ask Dr. Rank?

HELMER   No. But there's no need for that; it's assumed he'll be dining with us. All the same, I'll ask him when he stops by here this morning. I've ordered some fine wine. Nora, you can't imagine how I'm looking forward to this evening.

NORA   So am I. And what fun for the children, Torvald!

HELMER   Ah, it's so gratifying to know that one's gotten a safe, secure job, and with a comfortable salary. It's a great satisfaction, isn't it?

NORA   Oh, its wonderful!

HELMER   Remember last Christmas? Three whole weeks before, you shut yourself in every evening till long after midnight, making flowers for the Christmas tree, and all the other decorations to surprise us. Ugh, that was the dullest time I've ever lived through.

NORA   It wasn't at all dull for me.

HELMER   *(smiling)* But the outcome *was* pretty sorry, Nora.

NORA   Oh, don't tease me with that again. How could I help it that the cat came in and tore everything to shreds.

HELMER   No, poor thing, you certainly couldn't. You wanted so much to please us all, and that's what counts. But it's just as well that the hard times are past.

NORA   Yes, it's really wonderful.

HELMER   Now I don't have to sit here alone, boring myself, and you don't have to tire your precious eyes and your fair little delicate hands—

NORA   *(clapping her hands)* No, is it really true, Torvald, I don't have to? Oh, how wonderfully lovely to hear! *(Taking his arm)* Now I'll tell you just how I've thought we should plan things. Right after Christmas—*(The doorbell rings.)* Oh, the bell. *(Straightening the room up a bit)* Somebody would have to come. What a bore!

HELMER   I'm not at home to visitors, don't forget.

MAID   *(from the hall doorway)* Ma'am, a lady to see you—

NORA   All right, let her come in.

MAID   *(to* HELMER*)* And the doctor's just come too.

HELMER   Did he go right to my study?

MAID   Yes, he did.

The first thing we notice is the title: *A Doll House.* Does Ibsen alert us to a central concern of the play with this provocative title? Is it literal or symbolic? As we read the opening scene we test our preliminary sense of the title's implications. As we watch the relationship between Nora and Torvald unfold, we consider what the title suggests about their marriage.

Beneath the title is a list of characters. It's worth pausing over, for a playwright may signal important relationships there. Although only the husband-and-wife relationship of Torvald and Nora is signaled in Ibsen's list, we gain a sense of the play's social milieu from it. We notice that Torvald Helmer is a lawyer and Nils Krogstad a bank clerk, and that another woman and a doctor appear (in addition to minor figures such as a nurse and delivery boy).

We may pass quickly over these details before getting to the script. The first sentences set the scene we must keep in our mind's eye. The italicized words are stage directions (notes to the reader that establish the play's social context). Ibsen's opening stage directions describe the living room of a middle-class family with its piano, books, and pictures. The room represents a familiar world for many readers both in its realistic detail and its bourgeois domesticity.

The manner of Nora's arrival with her packages, the Christmas tree, and basket create an impression of the gaiety typically associated with the Christmas season. The playful quality of Nora's first words—about hiding the Christmas tree—reinforce our sense of this lightheartedness.

As we watch the inital incidents unfold, we begin making inferences and drawing tentative conclusions about the characters. We may wonder, for example, about the large tip Nora gives the delivery boy. Is it a sign of generosity or of extravagance? Does it reflect her state of mind? Does it reveal an inadequate attentiveness to money? Such questions occur almost unconsciously as we read, and the provisional answers we arrive at will be modified, strengthened, or abandoned as we read further.

After the exchange with the delivery boy, Nora hums softly to herself. Eating a few macaroons, she tiptoes stealthily to the closed door of her husband's study. Whatever our sense of these opening moments, the brief series of actions forms a prologue to the first major action of the play, Nora's conversation with Torvald. It is here that we gain our sense of Torvald, particularly of his concern for Nora's spending habits, which may unsettle our previous expectations about Nora's tip as an instance of generosity. We become alert.

Perhaps even stronger is our response to Torvald's pet names for Nora. He calls her "little lark" and "my squirrel," and repeatedly uses diminutives and possessives in addressing her. He also teases her, calling her "the little spendthrift," then gives her the money she wants. In a few swift strokes of dialogue and action, Ibsen shows us how seriously Torvald takes himself and how patronizingly he treats his wife.

Nora seems to accept the role Torvald assigns her. She submits to his teasing, accepts his explanations, and responds with childlike enthusiasm. Their gestures bear out the implications of the dialogue: Torvald pulls her ear, Nora clamps her hand over his mouth, plays flirtatiously with Torvald's coat buttons, claps her hands, and twice walks away from him—presumably knowing that he will follow. Torvald seems to enjoy the game as much as Nora. He follows her, probably not realizing that she is leading him and that he is responding as she wants him to.

When we see Torvald wag his finger at Nora and accuse her of eating sweets, we may sense that he doesn't really believe his accusation; he says as much almost immediately. But we, of course, know something that he does not: that Nora has indeed been eating macaroons. And we may suspect that there are other things about her that Torvald does not know from her previous remark, "Hm. If you only knew what expenses we larks and squirrels have, Torvald."

This dialogue is worth considering a bit further. Essentially, Ibsen has Torvald repeat his suspicious question and Nora deny that she has eaten sweets four times. The game that they make of this suggests that it is a familiar ritual. The action seems humorous partly because Torvald's accusations become increasingly accurate while he seems to remain unaware of their truth. Ibsen treats him ironically; there is a discrepancy between his view of himself and our view of him. How do we respond to his presumption and complacency? How do we evaluate his position as master of his house? And how might we sum up Torvald's attitude toward women?

As we read the opening scene of *A Doll House,* observing the action and listening in on the dialogue, we have been drawing tentative conclusions about the characters and their relationship. Our curiosity has been aroused by dialogue, by action, and by the arrival of additional characters. Subsequent dialogue and action will either confirm our initial impressions or dispel them. We are left at the end of this first scene with a sense of uncertainty. While we don't know that this is not a happy household, neither do we know that it is. We have become alerted to possible problems involving matters of money and of secrecy. And we have been prepared to attend to the developing action as the scene changes and new characters appear. When we read the entire play (page 1239), we will discover if our inferences are accurate and our suspicions justified.

Ibsen's opening scene draws us into the world of the play—into the lives of Nora and Torvald Helmer. Our perspective on their speech and behavior and our general attitude toward them depends in part on our own experience of living in the world. (It depends, that is, on what we have seen of, heard about, or directly experienced of marital relationships.) It also depends on our prior experience with drama in performance or as literature. And it depends finally on our opinions, beliefs, and attitudes about men, women, and the ways they relate to one another.

THE INTERPRETATION OF DRAMA

In our discussion of the opening scene of *A Doll House,* we have focused on our experience of the developing action, on our impression of its two central characters, and on our attitudes toward them. Implicit in this discussion, however, was also an inevitable movement in the direction of interpretation. The questions we raised, the details we observed, and the hypotheses we entertained are all aspects of interpretation.

Interpretation is a series of intellectual and analytical mental acts that lead to a conclusion about the play's meaning and significance. We can isolate four aspects of interpretation that we perform almost automatically. First, we observe details of speech, setting, and action. Second, we connect these details into patterns; we relate them so they begin to make sense to us. Third, we draw inferences—educated guesses or hypotheses—based on these connections. Finally, we formulate from our inferences a consistent and coherent interpretation of the play.

In reading (or viewing) any play, it is important to distinguish between our experience of a play and our interpretation of it. Our experience concerns our direct apprehension of the ongoing performance either on stage or in our mind's eye; interpretation concerns our comprehension of the work after we have finished reading or seeing it performed. Our experience of a play involves our emotions and subjective impressions of the play's dramatic action. Our interpretation of a play involves our ideas and thoughts about the meaning of that action. Our experience of a play is private, personal, and subjective: we discover how it entertains, moves, pleases, frustrates, or otherwise affects us. Our interpretation, though based on our experience, moves outward from it toward a set of more public and objective considerations. In interpreting a play, we try to discover what it might mean for others as well. We ask ourselves not so much: "How do I respond to the speech and actions of the characters?" but instead "What do their speech and actions signify; what do they mean?"

Having examined the visual detail and gestures and actions of the central characters in the scene from Ibsen's *A Doll House,* we will now consider how dialogue orients us to a play. Read the following scene from Bernard Shaw's *Arms and the Man* with special attention to its language, but without losing sight of gesture and action. The language we hear in this excerpt differs from what we heard in *A Doll House.* In Shaw's play we move away from the realistic bourgeois patterns of speech of Ibsen's characters toward a more oratorical and theatrical language. The scene presents Raina, the fiancée of Sergius, alone with him for the first time since his return from a successful military battle. The commentary illustrates the cumulative way interpretation develops.

RAINA   *(placing her hands on his shoulders as she looks up at him with admiration and worship)* My hero! My king!

SERGIUS   My queen! *(He kisses her on the forehead.)*

RAINA   How I have envied you, Sergius! You have been out in the world, on the field of battle, able to prove yourself there worthy of any woman in the world; whilst I have had to sit at home inactive—dreaming—useless—doing nothing that could give me the right to call myself worthy of any man.

SERGIUS   Dearest: all my deeds have been yours. You inspired me. I have gone through the war like a knight in a tournament with his lady looking down at him!

RAINA   And you have never been absent from my thoughts for a moment. *(Very solemnly)* Sergius: I think we two have found the higher love. When I think of you, I feel that I could never do a base deed, or think an ignoble thought.

SERGIUS   My lady and my saint! *(He clasps her reverently.)*

RAINA   *(returning his embrace)* My lord and my—

SERGIUS   Sh—sh! Let me be the worshipper, dear. You little know how unworthy even the best man is of a girl's pure passion!

Comment   What are we to make of such grand language and such royal gestures? Do we see them as heroic and the characters as impressive? Or do we take the characters with less seriousness than they take themselves? Their style of speech and their manner are suitable for a certain kind of play, heroic melodrama, a type of play Shaw's nineteenth-century audience was familiar with. But it doesn't take us long to discover that the scene is comical because the actions of Raina and Sergius and the language of the other characters fail to support the seemingly heroic dialogue.

Consider Raina's elevation of Sergius to royal heights ("My hero! My king!") and Sergius's reciprocal coronation of Raina ("My queen!"). This language is exaggerated and their behavior stilted, for Shaw was satirizing the attitudes toward romantic love and military glory they represent. We also hear Raina's speech as a set of clichés: the valiant hero fights at war while the helpless female waits uselessly behind; she is the lady who inspires her knight to heights of valor. We hear Sergius's speech as a bit of heroic posturing, which we quickly come to see through.

Their talk of the "higher" love extends their idealization of each other. The exaggeration continues to the point of absurdity with their reverential language—"My lady and my saint!" . . . "My lord and my—." Poking fun at their romanticizing deification of one another, Shaw suggests that their devotion is part of an act, a game they play with and for each other. Sergius comes close to honesty, however, in his remark that a man is not worthy of his fiancée's pure passion. Sergius's remark is comical because it can be understood in two ways: 1) as passion divested of its erotic and physical elements, as spiritualized passion; 2) as pure or unadulterated passionate desire in the erotic and physical sense. And even if we ignore this ambiguity and take Sergius's remark to mean simply that he is unworthy of Raina's devoted love, we sense that he is implying something about himself and about men generally that makes them incapable of the "higher," spiritual love he and Raina have been talking about.

RAINA   I trust you. I love you. You will never disappoint me, Sergius. (LOUKA *is heard singing within the house. They quickly release each other.*) I can't pretend to talk indifferently before her: my heart is too full. (LOUKA *comes from the house with her tray. She goes to the table, and begins to clear it, with her back turned to them.*) I will get my hat; and then we can go out until lunch time. Wouldn't you like that?

SERGIUS   Be quick. If you are away five minutes, it will seem five hours. (RAINA *runs to the top of the steps, and turns there to exchange looks with him and wave him a kiss with both hands. He looks after her with emotion for a moment; then turns slowly away, his face radiant with the loftiest exaltation. The movement shifts his field of vision, into the corner of which there now comes the tail of* LOUKA'S *double apron. His attention is arrested at once. He takes a stealthy look at her, and begins to twirl his moustache mischievously, with his left hand akimbo on his hip. Finally, striking the ground with his heels in something of a cavalry swagger, he strolls over to the other side of the table, opposite her, and says*) Louka: do you know what the higher love is?

LOUKA   (*astonished*) No, sir.

SERGIUS   Very fatiguing thing to keep up for any length of time, Louka. One feels the need of some relief after it.

LOUKA   (*innocently*) Perhaps you would like some coffee, sir? (*She stretches her hand across the table for the coffee pot.*)

SERGIUS   (*taking her hand*) Thank you, Louka.

LOUKA   (*pretending to pull*) Oh, sir, you know I didn't mean that. I'm surprised at you!

SERGIUS   (*coming clear of the table and drawing her with him*) I am surprised at myself, Louka. What would Sergius, the hero of Slivnitza, say if he saw me now? What would Sergius, the apostle of the higher love, say if he saw me now? What would the half dozen Sergiuses who keep popping in and out of this handsome figure of mine say if they caught us here? (*Letting go her hand and slipping his arm dexterously round her waist*) Do you consider my figure handsome, Louka?

LOUKA   Let me go, sir. I shall be disgraced. (*She struggles: he holds her inexorably.*) Oh, will you let go?

SERGIUS   (*looking straight into her eyes*) No.

LOUKA   Then stand back where we can't be seen. Have you no common sense?

SERGIUS   Ah! that's reasonable. *(He takes her into the stable yard gateway, where they are hidden from the house.)*

Comment   Ironies emerge in Raina's comment that she can't pretend in front of the servant girl, Louka. She means, of course, that she won't be able to conceal her emotion, that the effort to engage in polite conversation with Sergius in her presence will be unbearable. And Sergius's pretense is made apparent as he approaches Louka. It is additionally ironic that neither can pretend in front of Louka, partly because Louka is too smart to be taken in by their act, and partly because her view of romance and reality differs from theirs. Notice, by the way, that Louka sings as she works, which is her way of warning the lovers that she is coming. She also keeps her back to them as she cleans the table, not wanting to embarrass them and presumably not wanting to let them see she is aware of anything going on.

The crux of this part of the scene, however, is Sergius's abrupt change of behavior. His mischievous, swaggering gestures and his dialogue with Louka quickly puncture the bubble of the "higher" love he had been blowing up moments before. Notice also Louka's gestures. She too is playing a part, especially by feigning surprise at the turn of events. Her acquiescence after a brief and cursory struggle parallels the change in Sergius's behavior.

LOUKA   *(plaintively)* I may have been seen from the windows: Miss Raina is sure to be spying about after you.

SERGIUS   *(stung: letting her go)* Take care, Louka. I may be worthless enough to betray the higher love; but do not you insult it.

LOUKA   *(demurely)* Not for the world, sir, I'm sure. May I go on with my work, please, now?

SERGIUS   *(again putting his arm round her)* You are a provoking little witch, Louka. If you were in love with me, would you spy out of windows on me?

LOUKA   Well, you see, sir, since you say you are half a dozen different gentlemen all at once, I should have a great deal to look after.

SERGIUS   *(charmed)* Witty as well as pretty. *(He tries to kiss her.)*

LOUKA   *(avoiding him)* No: I don't want your kisses. Gentlefolk are all alike: you making love to me behind Miss Raina's back; and she doing the same behind yours.

SERGIUS   *(recoiling a step)* Louka!

LOUKA   It shews how little you really care.

SERGIUS   *(dropping his familiarity, and speaking with freezing politeness)* If our conversation is to continue, Louka, you will please remember that a gentleman does not discuss the conduct of the lady he is engaged to with her maid.

LOUKA   It's so hard to know what a gentleman considers right. I thought from your trying to kiss me that you had given up being so particular.

SERGIUS   *(turning from her and striking his forehead as he comes back into the garden from the gateway)* Devil! devil!

LOUKA   Ha! ha! I expect one of the six of you is very like me, sir; though I am only Miss Raina's maid. *(She goes back to her work at the table, taking no further notice of him.)*

SERGIUS   *(speaking to himself)* Which of the six is the real man? that's the question that torments me. One of them is a hero, another a buffoon, another a humbug, another perhaps a bit of a blackguard. *(He pauses, and looks furtively at* LOUKA *as he adds, with deep bitterness)* And one, at least, is a coward: jealous, like all cowards. *(He goes to the table.)* Louka.

LOUKA   Yes?

SERGIUS   Who is my rival?

LOUKA   You shall never get that out of me, for love or money.

SERGIUS   Why?

LOUKA   Never mind why. Besides, you would tell that I told you; and I should lose my place.

SERGIUS   *(holding out his right hand in affirmation)* No! on the honor of a—*(He checks himself; and his hand drops, nerveless, as he concludes sardonically)*—of a man capable of behaving as I have been behaving for the last five minutes. Who is he?

LOUKA   I don't know. I never saw him. I only heard his voice through the door of her room.

SERGIUS   Damnation! How dare you?

LOUKA   *(retreating)* Oh, I mean no harm: you've no right to take up my words like that. The mistress knows all about it. And I tell you that if that gentleman ever comes here again, Miss Raina will marry him, whether he likes it or not. I know the difference between the sort of manner you and she put on before one another and the real manner.

Comment   Shaw keeps the surprises coming. Just as we adjust to the amorous play between Louka and Sergius, Sergius shifts ground to defend the honor of his insulted lady when Louka suggests that Raina is spying on him. (We subsequently discover that she really was spying on him, a fact that affects our response to her remark that she trusts Sergius.) Shaw continues the back and forth movement in action and dialogue as Sergius advances on Louka and then retreats, feigning offended pride. Louka comes across as shrewd, quick-witted, and capable of taking care of herself. She knows the difference between real passion and counterfeit coin, and in her suspicion of Sergius's mannered artifice, she gives voice to a realistic rather than a romantic view of love. She uses Sergius's words against him, making him look a fool, which he acknowledges by calling himself a buffoon and a humbug. By accepting Louka's accusation so readily, he assents to a view of Raina, of himself, and of the nature of love radically at variance with what he and Raina had declared earlier.

(SERGIUS shivers as if she had stabbed him. Then, setting his face like iron, he strides grimly to her, and grips her above the elbows with both hands.)

SERGIUS   Now listen you to me.

LOUKA   *(wincing)* Not so tight: you're hurting me.

SERGIUS   That doesn't matter. You have stained my honor by making me a party to your eavesdropping. And you have betrayed your mistress.

LOUKA   *(writhing)* Please—

SERGIUS   That shews that you are an abominable little clod of common clay, with the soul of a servant. *(He lets her go as if she were an unclean thing, and turns away, dusting his hands of her, to the bench by the wall, where he sits down with averted head, meditating gloomily.)*

LOUKA   *(whimpering angrily with her hands up her sleeves, feeling her bruised arms)* You know how to hurt with your tongue as well as with your hands. But I don't care, now I've found out that whatever clay I'm made of, you're made of the same. As for her, she's a liar; and her fine airs are a cheat; and I'm worth six of her. *(She shakes the pain off hardily; tosses her head; and sets to work to put the things on the tray.)*

(He looks doubtfully at her. She finishes packing the tray, and laps the cloth over the edges, so as to carry all out together. As she stoops to lift it, he rises.)

SERGIUS   Louka! *(She stops and looks defiantly at him.)* A gentleman has no right to hurt a woman under any circumstances. *(With profound humility, uncovering his head)* I beg your pardon.

LOUKA   That sort of apology may satisfy a lady. Of what use is it to a servant?

SERGIUS   *(rudely crossed in his chivalry, throws it off with a bitter laugh, and says slightingly)* Oh! you wish to be paid for the hurt! *(He puts on his shako, and takes some money from his pocket.)*

LOUKA   *(her eyes filling with tears in spite of herself)* No: I want my hurt made well.

SERGIUS   *(sobered by her tone)* How?

(She rolls up her left sleeve; clasps her arm with the thumb and fingers of her right hand; and looks down at the bruise. Then she raises her head and looks straight at him. Finally, with a superb gesture, she presents her arm to be kissed. Amazed, he looks at her; at the arm; at her again; hesitates; and then, with shuddering intensity, exclaims Never! *and gets away as far as possible from her.*

Her arm drops. Without a word, and with unaffected dignity, she takes her tray, and is approaching the house when RAINA *returns, wearing a hat and jacket in the height of the Vienna fashion of the previous year, 1885.* LOUKA *makes way proudly for her, and then goes into the house.)*

RAINA   I'm ready. What's the matter? *(Gaily)* Have you been flirting with Louka?

SERGIUS   *(hastily)* No, no. How can you think such a thing?

RAINA   *(ashamed of herself)* Forgive me, dear: it was only a jest. I am so happy today.

Comment   Louka's forthright declaration angers Sergius to the point of hurting her. But Louka insists that although she may be "clay," so is Sergius, that he and Raina are no better and no "higher" than she. The scene ends with Sergius frustrated, Louka resentful, and Raina lighthearted as she teases Sergius about his flirtation. At this point, we wonder where Shaw will take Sergius, Raina, and Louka.

In general, we can interpret the scene as a satirical portrait of both Sergius and Raina as Shaw contrasts their romantic posturing about love and honor with their actual feelings.

THE EVALUATION OF DRAMA

Our discussion of the scenes from *A Doll House* and *Arms and the Man* focused explicitly on our experience of the play and on our acts of interpretation. And although we separated these discussions to identify more precisely each aspect of reading drama, our experience and interpretation of plays actually occur simultaneously; the two aspects of reading reinforce each other. But there is a third dimension to our reading of drama—evaluation—which was implicit in our previous discussions. Our comments about *A Doll House* and *Arms and the Man* raised questions about the values displayed in the characters' speech and actions.

What do we mean by the values displayed in a play? Generally speaking, we mean such things as cultural attitudes, moral dispositions, religious beliefs, and social norms. In considering such values as they emerge from our reading of any play, we should be careful to distinguish between the attitudes and dispositions of individual characters and those of the play (those of the author). We should also be aware of how our social and cultural perspectives may differ in important ways from the social norms and cultural attitudes of earlier times. To acknowledge how our individual way of responding to a play is influenced by gender, race, and ethnicity, as well as religious and cultural identity, is important in assessing its worth both for ourselves and for others. Since the values a play's characters display typically constitute an important focus of dramatic interest, our perception of the characters' values will affect to a considerable degree our own experience, interpretion, and evaluation of the overall work.

Further complicating our evaluation of a play is the extent to which we appreciate and enjoy its literary and theatrical artistry. For example, we may admire the way playwrights structure plots, largely by dangling before us a series of temporarily unanswered questions. We may find merit in portrayals of characters or the symbolic use of costume and setting. We may be affected by the language of the play, both in long speeches and in briefer exchanges of dialogue. We may derive aesthetic pleasure from these and many other exhibitions of stagecraft. And the enjoyment we derive, coupled with our assessment of what we understand as the playwright's central values or controlling idea, constitute the basis for our evaluation.

So the evaluation of any play is tied to our interpretation of it. But our interpretation is affected by our perception of the moral and cultural values it exhibits. In identifying the play's central concerns and in deciding which values are endorsed by the playwright, we shift back and forth between interpretation and evaluation. We do not first interpret the play and then evaluate it; we perform the two acts together. We evaluate and interpret a play, moreover, in conjunction with a subjective and immediate response to our experience of it. We can say, then, that each aspect of reading (experience, interpretation, evaluation) affects the other, and that the three aspects of reading drama taken together define our "reading" of any play.

Consider for a moment the way our values shape our interpretation and evaluation. If we see Ibsen's Torvald as an admirable figure, one whose treatment of his wife is appropriate and commendable, we will regard his behavior differently than if we see him as a fool who is manipulated by his wife. Our perspective on Torvald's character and on Nora's will be influenced partly by our gender. Women may be even more affected by Nora's game playing than by Torvald's male chauvinism. Additional influences on our perceptions of *A Doll House* include our cultural backround, our experiences as a member of a family, our religious beliefs, and our ethnic traditions as they relate to marriage and the norms governing the relationship between husbands and wives.

Again, if in *Arms and the Man* we see Raina and Sergius as truly grand figures, dashing, romantic, and enviable, we will view them differently than if we see them as superficial and hypocritical. Our sense of Shaw's point of view hinges directly on our understanding of his characters. The commentary on pages 823–827 suggests that Shaw views them ironically; he satirizes Sergius and Raina by showing the discrepancy between how they think and how they act, between what they say and what they do. We see them more clearly than they see either each other or themselves. What they value—heroism, honor, loyality, and love—or at least their conceptions of these abstractions, are shown to be hollow and false. As foils, Shaw presents Louka and later Nicola, whose values are based on more immediate and practical needs—money, for example, and the desire to get what they can with as little cost as possible to themselves.

Our aesthetic evaluation of *A Doll House* and *Arms and the Man* will be based on these and similar observations about the characters and our understanding of the author's view of them. Our evaluation will be affected by how relevant we find the central concerns of the play. (And what we find relevant at one time we may find irrelevant at another—and vice versa.) Our evaluation will also be influenced by our experience in reading and seeing other plays. Aesthetic evaluation thus involves comparing the literary and theatrical artistry of one play with the stagecraft of others. Without considerable experience with drama, judgments about a play's aesthetic merit need to be made with caution. But we must begin somewhere. Evaluation is inevitable, and we cannot avoid judging the plays we read, any more than we can avoid judging the people we meet.

The scene from Sophocles' *Antigonê* that follows provides an immediate opportunity to test these ideas. In reading the entire play later, we can consider how the characters' competing values, as evidenced in the excerpt, serve as the central conflict in the play. Scene II begins at the point where Antigonê, the daughter of Oedipus, has been taken into custody for violating an edict of Creon, King of Thebes. The edict concerns Antigonê's brother, Polyneicês, who was killed in a battle while fighting against Thebes. Creon has forbidden Polyneicês' burial; Antigonê has buried him.

SCENE II

Reenter SENTRY *leading* ANTIGONÊ

CHORAGOS. What does this mean? Surely this captive woman
    Is the Princess, Antigonê. Why should she be taken?
SENTRY. Here is the one who did it! We caught her
    In the very act of burying him.—Where is Creon?
CHORAGOS. Just coming from the house.

Enter CREON, *center.*

CREON.   What has happened?   5
    Why have you come back so soon?
SENTRY *(expansively).*   O King,
    A man should never be too sure of anything:
    I would have sworn
    That you'd not see me here again: your anger
    Frightened me so, and the things you threatened me with;   10
    But how could I tell then
    That I'd be able to solve the case so soon?
    No dice-throwing this time: I was only too glad to come!

Here is this woman. She is the guilty one:
We found her trying to bury him. 15
Take her, then; question her; judge her as you will.
I am through with the whole thing now, and glad of it.
CREON. But this is Antigonê! Why have you brought her here?
SENTRY. She was burying him, I tell you!
CREON (severely).   Is this the truth?
SENTRY. I saw her with my own eyes. Can I say more? 20
CREON. The details: come, tell me quickly!
SENTRY.   It was like this:
After those terrible threats of yours, King,
We went back and brushed the dust away from the body.
The flesh was soft by now, and stinking,
So we sat on a hill to windward and kept guard. 25
No napping this time! We kept each other awake.
But nothing happened until the white round sun
Whirled in the center of the round sky over us:
Then, suddenly,
A storm of dust roared up from the earth, and the sky 30
Went out, the plain vanished with all its trees
In the stinging dark. We closed our eyes and endured it.
The whirlwind lasted a long time, but it passed;
And then we looked, and there was Antigonê!
I have seen 35
A mother bird come back to a stripped nest, heard
Her crying bitterly a broken note or two
For the young ones stolen. Just so, when this girl
Found the bare corpse, and all her love's work wasted,
She wept, and cried on heaven to damn the hands 40
That had done this thing.
                              And then she brought more dust
And sprinkled wine three times for her brother's ghost.

We ran and took her at once. She was not afraid,
Not even when we charged her with what she had done.
She denied nothing.
                              And this was a comfort to me, 45
And some uneasiness: for it is a good thing
To escape from death, but it is no great pleasure
To bring death to a friend.
                              Yet I always say
There is nothing so comfortable as your own safe skin!
CREON (slowly, dangerously). And you, Antigonê, 50
    You with your head hanging,—do you confess this thing?
ANTIGONÊ. I do. I deny nothing.
CREON (to SENTRY).   You may go.
                              (Exit SENTRY.)

(To ANTIGONÊ.*)* Tell me, tell me briefly:
Had you heard my proclamation touching this matter?
ANTIGONÊ. It was public. Could I help hearing it?   55
CREON. And yet you dared defy the law.
ANTIGONÊ.   I dared.
     It was not God's proclamation. That final Justice
     That rules the world below makes no such laws.

     Your edict, King, was strong,
     But all your strength is weakness itself against   60
     The immortal unrecorded laws of God.
     They are not merely now: they were, and shall be,
     Operative for ever, beyond man utterly.

     I knew I must die, even without your decree:
     I am only mortal. And if I must die   65
     Now, before it is my time to die,
     Surely this is no hardship: can anyone
     Living, as I live, with evil all about me,
     Think Death less than a friend? This death of mine
     Is of no importance; but if I had left my brother   70
     Lying in death unburied, I should have suffered.
     Now I do not.
             You smile at me. Ah Creon,
     Think me a fool, if you like; but it may well be
     That a fool convicts me of folly.
CHORAGOS. Like father, like daughter: both headstrong, deaf to reason!   75
     She has never learned to yield:
CREON.   She has much to learn.
     The inflexible heart breaks first, the toughest iron
     Cracks first, and the wildest horses bend their necks
     At the pull of the smallest curb.
                 Pride? In a slave?
     This girl is guilty of a double insolence,   80
     Breaking the given laws and boasting of it.
     Who is the man here,
     She or I, if this crime goes unpunished?
     Sister's child, or more than sister's child,
     Or closer yet in blood—she and her sister   85
     Win bitter death for this!
                 (To SERVANTS.*)*
                Go, some of you,
     Arrest Ismenê. I accuse her equally.
     Bring her: you will find her sniffling in the house there.

     Her mind's a traitor: crimes kept in the dark
     Cry for light, and the guardian brain shudders;   90

But how much worse than this
Is brazen boasting of barefaced anarchy!

ANTIGONÊ. Creon, what more do you want than my death?

CREON.   Nothing.
That gives me everything.

ANTIGONÊ.   Then I beg you: kill me.
This talking is a great weariness: your words   95
Are distasteful to me, and I am sure that mine
Seem so to you. And yet they should not seem so:
I should have praise and honor for what I have done.
All these men here would praise me
Were their lips not frozen shut with fear of you.   100
(Bitterly.) Ah the good fortune of kings,
Licensed to say and do whatever they please!

CREON. You are alone here in that opinion.

ANTIGONÊ. No, they are with me. But they keep their tongues in leash.

CREON. Maybe. But you are guilty, and they are not.   105

ANTIGONÊ. There is no guilt in reverence for the dead.

CREON. But Eteoclês—was he not your brother too?

ANTIGONÊ. My brother too.

CREON.   And you insult his memory?

ANTIGONÊ (softly). The dead man would not say that I insult it.

CREON. He would: for you honor a traitor as much as him.   110

ANTIGONÊ. His own brother, traitor or not, and equal in blood.

CREON. He made war on his country. Eteoclês defended it.

ANTIGONÊ. Nevertheless, there are honors due all the dead.

CREON. But not the same for the wicked as for the just.

ANTIGONÊ. Ah Creon, Creon,   115
Which of us can say what the gods hold wicked?

CREON. An enemy is an enemy, even dead.

ANTIGONÊ. It is my nature to join in love, not hate.

CREON (finally losing patience). Go join them then; if you must have your
love, Find it in hell!   120

CHORAGOS. But see, Ismenê comes:

Enter ISMENÊ, *guarded.*

Those tears are sisterly, the cloud
That shadows her eyes rains down gentle sorrow.

CREON. You too, Ismenê,
Snake in my ordered house, sucking my blood   125
Stealthily—and all the time I never knew
That these two sisters were aiming at my throne!
                                                                    Ismenê,
Do you confess your share in this crime, or deny it?
Answer me.

ISMENÊ. Yes, if she will let me say so. I am guilty.   130

ANTIGONÊ *(coldly)*. No, Ismenê. You have no right to say so.
  You would not help me, and I will not have you help me.
ISMENÊ. But now I know what you meant; and I am here
  To join you, to take my share of punishment.
ANTIGONÊ. The dead man and the gods who rule the dead   135
  Know whose act this was. Words are not friends.
ISMENÊ. Do you refuse me, Antigonê? I want to die with you:
  I too have a duty that I must discharge to the dead.
ANTIGONÊ. You shall not lessen my death by sharing it.
ISMENÊ. What do I care for life when you are dead?   140
ANTIGONÊ. Ask Creon. You're always hanging on his opinions.
ISMENÊ. You are laughing at me. Why, Antigonê?
ANTIGONÊ. It's a joyless laughter, Ismenê.
ISMENÊ.   But can I do nothing?
ANTIGONÊ. Yes. Save yourself. I shall not envy you.
  There are those who will praise you; I shall have honor, too.   145
ISMENÊ. But we are equally guilty!
ANTIGONÊ. ·   No more, Ismenê.
  You are alive, but I belong to Death.
CREON *(to the* CHORUS*)*. Gentlemen, I beg you to observe these girls:
  One has just now lost her mind; the other,
  It seems, has never had a mind at all.   150
ISMENÊ. Grief teaches the steadiest minds to waver, King.
CREON. Yours certainly did, when you assumed guilt with the guilty!
ISMENÊ. But how could I go on living without her?
CREON.   You are.
  She is already dead.
ISMENÊ.   But your own son's bride!
CREON. There are places enough for him to push his plow.   155
  I want no wicked women for my sons!
ISMENÊ. O dearest Haimon, how your father wrongs you!
CREON. I've had enough of your childish talk of marriage!
CHORAGOS. Do you really intend to steal this girl from your son?
CREON. No; Death will do that for me.
CHORAGOS.   Then she must die?   160
CREON *(ironically)*. You dazzle me.
                      —But enough of this talk!
  (To GUARDS.*)* You, there, take them away and guard them well:
  For they are but women, and even brave men run
  When they see Death coming.

                 Exeunt ISMENÊ, ANTIGONÊ, *and* GUARDS.

In this scene we witness a developing conflict between Creon and Antigonê, one that is more than a clash of two stubborn wills. Opposing views of propriety emerge, along with competing moral values and contrasting attitudes toward political authority. What are we to make of these attitudes and these arguments? How does our sense of their tone and manner affect our perception and evaluation of the substance of their speech and action? Whose values do you think should take precedence, and why? And finally, how highly do we rate the literary and theatrical qualities of the text? As a portion of a work of art, how successfully does it achieve its artistic and dramatic aims?

THE ACT OF READING DRAMA

To read drama actively, it is helpful to read with a pen in hand and to make notes in the margins. Here we illustrate a variation on that approach to active reading: asking questions of the play as we read it. Our questions will range over various concerns we have in reading, including evaluation, interpretation, and our experience of the text, as well as how to bring its theatrical and performance qualities to life in our minds.

To this end, we consider the opening scene of Lady Gregory's *The Rising of the Moon.*

The Rising of the Moon

Scene: Side of a quay in a seaport town. Some posts and chains. A large barrel. Enter three policemen. Moonlight.

SERGEANT, *who is older than the others, crosses the stage to right and looks down steps. The others put down a pastepot and unroll a bundle of placards.*

POLICEMAN B.   I think this would be a good place to put up a notice. *(He points to barrel.)*

POLICEMAN X.   Better ask him. *(Calls to* SERGEANT*)* Will this be a good place for a placard? *(No answer.)*

POLICEMAN B.   Will we put up a notice here on the barrel? *(No answer.)*

SERGEANT.   There's a flight of steps here that leads to the water. This is a place that should be minded well. If he got down here, his friends might have a boat to meet him; they might send it in here from outside.

POLICEMAN B.   Would the barrel be a good place to put a notice up?

SERGEANT.   It might; you can put it there.

(They paste the notice up.)

SERGEANT   *(reading it)*. Dark hair—dark eyes, smooth face, height five feet five—there's not much to take hold of in that—It's a pity I had no chance of seeing him before he broke out of gaol. They say he's a wonder, that it's he makes all the plans for the whole organization. There isn't another man in Ireland would have broken gaol the way he did. He must have some friends among the gaolers.

POLICEMAN B.   A hundred pounds is little enough for the Government to offer for him. You may be sure any man in the force that takes him will get promotion.

SERGEANT.   I'll mind this place myself. I wouldn't wonder at all if he came this way. He might come slipping along there *(points to side of quay),* and his friends might be waiting for him there *(points down steps),* and once he got away it's little chance we'd have of finding him; it's maybe under a load of kelp he'd be in a fishing boat, and not one to help a married man that wants it to the reward.

POLICEMAN X.   And if we get him itself, nothing but abuse on our heads for it from the people, and maybe from our own relations.

SERGEANT.   Well, we have to do our duty in the force. Haven't we the whole country depending on us to keep law and order? It's those that are down would be up and those that are up would be down, if it wasn't for us. Well, hurry on, you have plenty of other places to placard yet, and come back here then to me. You can take the lantern. Don't be too long now. It's very lonesome here with nothing but the moon.

POLICEMAN B.   It's a pity we can't stop with you. The Government should have brought more police into the town, with *him* in gaol, and at assize time too. Well, good luck to your watch. *(They go out.)*

SERGEANT   *(walks up and down once or twice and looks at placard).* A hundred pounds and promotion sure. There must be a great deal of spending in a hundred pounds. It's a pity some honest man not to be the better of that.

(A ragged man appears at left and tries to slip past. SERGEANT *suddenly turns.)*

Here is a list of questions we might generate during an active interrogation of the text.

1. What are the implications of the title, "The Rising of the Moon"? How is the title related to the suggested lighting? How important will the moon and the moonlight become?
2. Why don't the policemen have names? Of what importance are their repeated questions and the sergeant's distracted answer?
3. Why does the sergeant say that "it's a pity" he didn't see the criminal before his escape from jail? Is it simply that the sergeant would know what the man looked like and thus could recognize him more easily?
4. How does Lady Gregory draw us into the play? How does she engage our interest in these characters and their situation?
5. How important will the theme of duty become? Is it significant that the sergeant introduces this topic?
6. How effective theatrically is the sergeant's pointing to the quay and steps as he imagines the escaped man coming past where he stands?
7. Where in fact do the sergeant and his men stand on stage? How are they dressed? And where is the barrel placed?
8. As each character speaks, how does he gesture? At whom does he look? Where is he positioned in relation to the others?
9. How important to the play's action and idea are the props—the barrel, placards, and lantern? What other props will become important?
10. Of what significance is policeman X's comment about getting abuse from the people and his relatives for capturing the escaped convict?
11. How important are the sergeant's references to a reward and promotion?

His references to the escaped man's friends? Might these references be significant beyond their function in the play's action?

12. Why are certain words and phrases repeated?

13. How helpful are the italicized stage directions in letting us imagine the scene
and the action?

14. What do we expect to happen next? How well has the playwright prepared
readers/viewers for the sergeant's encounter with the "ragged man"?

15. With whom do our are sympathies lie? Why? How do our attitudes about
police officers and the concept of the "law" affect our response?

Asking questions such as these involves us actively in reading the play. Some
of these questions can be asked during an initial reading; others may arise during subsequent readings. As with writing marginal annotations or interpolated
commentary, writing out a series of questions enables us to focus on aspects of
the text we may have overlooked or perhaps noticed only vaguely. Also, in-
terrogating the text can lead us to an interpretation that is thoroughly grounded
in careful observation. The answers to our questions provide the authoritative
basis for an interpretation worthy of consideration by other readers.

CHAPTER EIGHTEEN

Types of Drama

Some plays elicit laughter, others evoke tears. Some are comic, others tragic, still others a mixture of both. The two major dramatic modes, *tragedy* and *comedy*, have been represented traditionally by contrasting masks, one sorrowful, the other joyful. The masks represent more than different types of plays: they also stand for contrasting ways of looking at the world, aptly summarized in Horace Walpole's remark, "the world is a comedy to those who think and a tragedy to those who feel."

The comic view celebrates life and affirms it; it is typically joyous and festive. The tragic view highlights life's sorrows; it is typically brooding and solemn. Tragic plays end unhappily, often with the death of the hero; comedies usually end happily, often with a celebration such as a marriage. Both comedy and tragedy contain changes of fortune, with the fortunes of comic characters turning from bad to good and those of tragic characters from good to bad.

TRAGEDY

In the *Poetics*, Aristotle described *tragedy* as "an imitation of an action that is serious, complete in itself, and of a certain magnitude." This definition suggests that tragedies are solemn plays concerned with grave human actions and their consequences. The action of a tragedy is complete—it possesses a beginning, a middle, and an end. Elsewhere in the *Poetics,* Aristotle notes that the incidents of a tragedy must be causally connected. The events have to be logically related, one growing naturally out of another, each leading to the inevitable catastrophe, usually the downfall of the hero.

Some readers of tragedy have suggested that, according to Aristotle, the catastrophe results from a flaw in the character of the hero. Others have contended that the hero's tragic flaw results from fate or coincidence, from circumstances beyond the hero's control. A third view proposes that tragedy results from an error of judgment committed by the hero, one that may or may not have as its source a weakness in character. Typically, tragic protagonists make mistakes: they misjudge other characters, they misinterpret events, and they confuse appearance with reality. Shakespeare's Othello, for example, mistakes Iago for an honest, loving friend; and he mistakes his faithful wife, Desdemona, for an adultress. Sophocles' Oedipus mistakes his own identity and misconstrues his destiny. The misfortune and catastrophes of tragedy are frequently precipitated by errors of judgment; mistaken perceptions lead to misdirected actions that eventually result in catastrophe.

Tragic heroes such as Oedipus and Othello are grand, noble characters. They are men, as Aristotle says, "of high estate," who enjoy "great reputation and prosperity." Tragic heroes, in short, are privileged, exalted personages who have earned their high repute and status by heroic exploit (Othello), by intelligence (Oedipus), or by their inherent nobility (Othello and Oedipus). Their tragedy resides in a fall from glory that crushes not only the tragic hero himself but other related characters as well. Othello's tragedy includes his wife and his faithful lieutenant, Cassio. Oedipus' tragedy extends to his entire family, including his wife-mother, his two sons, his daughters, and his brother-in-law, Creon, and his family. Greek tragedy, typically, involves the destruction and downfall of an entire house or family, reaching across generations. The catastrophe of Shakespearean tragedy is usually not as extensive.

An essential element of the tragic hero's experience is a *recognition* of what has happened to him. Frequently this takes the form of the hero discovering something previously unknown or something he knew but misconstrued. According to Aristotle, the tragic hero's recognition (or discovery) is often allied with a reversal of his expectations. Such an ironic reversal occurs in *Oedipus Rex* when the messenger's speech unsettles rather than reassures Oedipus about who he is and what he has done. Once the reversal and discovery occur, tragic plots move swiftly to their conclusions.

We may consider why, amid such suffering and catastrophe, tragedies are not depressing. Aristotle suggested that the pity and fear aroused in the audience are purged or released and the audience experiences a cleansing of those emotions and a sense of relief that the action is over. Perhaps tragedy represents for us the ultimate downfall we will all experience in death: we watch in fascination and awe a dramatic reminder of our own inevitable mortality. Or perhaps we are somehow exalted in witnessing the high human aspiration and the noble conception of human character embodied in tragic heroes like Oedipus and Othello.

COMEDY

Some of the same dramatic elements we find in tragedy occur in comedy as well. Discovery scenes and consequent reversals of fortune, for example, occur in both. So too do misperceptions and errors of judgment, exhibitions of human weakness and failure. But in comedy the reversals and errors lead not to calamity as they do in tragedy, but to prosperity and happiness. Comic heroes are usually ordinary people; they are less grand, less noble than tragic protagonists. Moreover, comic characters are frequently one-dimensional to the extent that many are stereotypes: the braggart, for example, or the hypocrite, the unfaithful wife, the cuckold, the ardent young lovers.

If comic characters are frequently predictable in their behavior, comic plots are not: they thrive on the surprise of the unexpected and on improbability. Cinderella stories like these are the staples of comedy: an impoverished student inherits a fortune; a beggar turns out to be a prince; a wife (or husband or child) presumed dead turns up alive and well; the war (between nations, classes, families, the sexes) ends, the two sides are reconciled and everybody lives happily ever after. To these large-scale improbabilities we can add smaller-scale incongruities: for example, in Shaw's *Arms and the Man,* Bluntschli carries chocolate creams rather than bullets in his cartridge belt; Sergius professes devoted love to Raina then tries to seduce the housemaid; the Petkoffs' library about which we hear so much is a mere shelf of a few odd books. But whether the incongruities of comedy exist between a character's speech and actions, between what we expect the characters to be and what they show themselves to be, or between how they think of themselves and how we see them, things work out in the end.

The happy endings of comedies are not always happy for all the characters involved. This marks one of the significant differences between the two major types of comedy: *satiric* and *romantic* comedy. Though much of what we have said so far about comedy applies to both types, it applies more extensively to romantic than to satiric comedy, or satire. *Satire* exposes human folly, criticizes human conduct, and aims to correct it. Ridiculing the weaknesses of human nature, satiric comedy shows us the low level to which human behavior can sink. Molière's *Tartuffe* is such a satiric comedy; it exposes religious hypocrisy, castigates folly, and ultimately celebrates virtue. Although things may work out well in the end for most of the characters, the play contains some harsh moments and a bitter ending for at least one character.

Romantic comedy, on the other hand, portrays characters gently, even generously; its spirit is more tolerant and its tone more genial. Whatever adversities the heroes and heroines of romantic comedy must overcome, the tone is typically devoid of rancor and bitterness. The humor of romantic comedy is more sympathetic than corrective, and it intends more to entertain than instruct, to delight than ridicule.

Because of such differences, our approaches to reading satire and romance should be different. When we read satiric comedies such as Shaw's *Arms and the Man,* we should identify the object of the dramatist's criticism and determine why the behavior of certain characters is objectionable. In reading romantic comedies, such as Shakespeare's *A Midsummer Night's Dream,* we are invited simply to enjoy the raveling and unraveling of plot as the protagonists are led to the inevitable happy ending.

These distinctions, however, are useful only as they help us gauge a play's prevailing characteristics. They should serve as guidelines to prevailing tendencies rather than as rigid descriptions of dramatic types. Frequently romantic comedies may contain elements of satire and satiric comedies elements of romance. *Tartuffe,* for example, is unmistakably a satire. But it contains, nevertheless, a staple of romantic comedy in its pair of young lovers. And *Arms and the Man* mixes romance and satire in about equal measure.

TRAGICOMEDY

Many modern plays mix not just modes of comedy, but elements of comedy and tragedy as well. Ibsen's *A Doll House,* for example, begins like a comedy but ends more like a tragedy. Eugene Ionesco's *The Lesson,* which ends with a brutal murder, has some uproariously funny moments. This and other works are not so easy to classify. In fact, it's often less important to decide whether a play is predominantly comic or tragic, romantic or satiric, than to acknowledge its mixture of modes and to respond fully to the characters or situations it dramatizes. Such plays as Anton Chekhov's *The Cherry Orchard* and Samuel Beckett's *Waiting for Godot* do not adhere strictly to tragic or comic conventions, and are often designated *tragicomedies* to identify their mode. Moreover, some twentieth-century dramatists have found that tragicomedy is more suitable for representing a complex, uncertain, and often irrational world than either tragedy or comedy alone.

CHAPTER NINETEEN

Elements of Drama

The elements of drama include plot, character, dialogue, staging, and theme. Our discussions of each of these elements individually allows us to highlight the characteristic features of drama in a convenient way. We should remember, however, that analysis of any single element of drama (plot, for example) should not blind us to its function in conjunction with such other elements as character. Ultimately any analysis we engage in must be followed by an act of synthesis in which we bring a number of elements of the play into relationship with one another.

PLOT

Plot is the structure of a play's action. Although it encompasses what happens in a play, plot is more than the sum of its incidents. Plot is the order of the incidents, their arrangement and form. Following Aristotle, we can distinguish between all the little actions or incidents that make up a play and the single *action* that unifies them. It is this unified structure of incidents (or little actions) Aristotle calls *action* and we call *plot.*

Traditional plot structure consists of an *exposition,* presentation of background information necessary for the development of the plot; *rising action,* a set of conflicts and crises; *climax,* the play's most decisive crisis; *falling action,* a follow-up that moves toward the play's resolution or *denouement* (French for the untying of a knot).

The plot of a realistic drama can be diagrammed in the following manner:

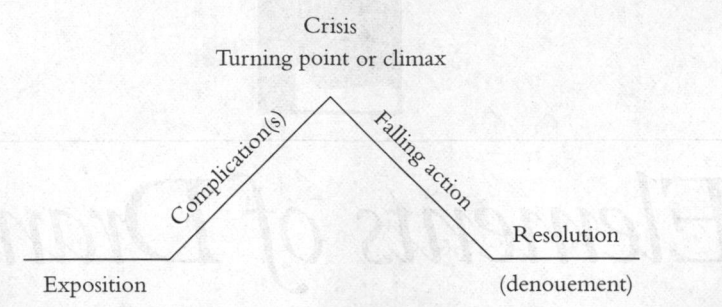

Crisis
Turning point or climax

Complication(s)

Falling action

Exposition

Resolution

(denouement)

Whether playwrights use a traditional plot structure or vary the formula, they control our expectations about what is happening through plot. They decide when to present action and information, what to reveal and what to conceal. By the arrangement of incidents, a dramatist may create suspense, evoke laughter, cause anxiety, or elicit surprise. One of our main sources of pleasure in plot is surprise, whether we are shown something we didn't expect or whether we see *how* something will happen even when we may know *what* will happen. Frequently surprise follows suspense—fulfilling our need to find out what will happen as we wait for a resolution of a play's action.

Suspense is created by conflict. Drama is essentially the development and resolution of conflicts. Each of the scenes excerpted in Chapter 17, Reading Plays, contains conflict. The conflict in Sophocles' *Antigonê* is overt and explicit. It occurs relentlessly in the play's dialogue and action. In the opening scene of Ibsen's *A Doll House* the conflict is implicit, at least initially. As the play develops, we see that Nora's conflict is less an opposition to Torvald than a conflict within herself. And in Shaw's *Arms and the Man* the conflict arises from a collision between different attitudes toward romantic love and military glory.

Besides looking at how instances of conflict are structured into plot in these scenes, we must also consider what each contributes to the plot of the play overall. What, for example, does Antigonê's debate with Creon lead up to? How does the behavior of Raina and Sergius relate to their behavior in previous and successive scenes in *Arms and the Man*? How is the opening scene of *A Doll House* related to its developing action, its concluding scene, its themes?

When we examine the plot of any play, we should be concerned with its developing action, the play in motion, and its completed action, the play at rest. By remaining attentive to what happens to us as we read and by highlighting the arrangement of scenes, we alert ourselves to the play as a performance. When we detach ourselves from the play to study its construction, the relationship among its parts, we study and appreciate the play as literature. Drama is both theater and literature. Study of plot can enrich our experience of each.

CHARACTER

If plot is the skeletal framework of a play, character is its vital center. Characters bring plays to life. First and last we become absorbed in the characters: how they look and what their appearance tells us about them; what they say and what their manner of saying expresses; what they do and how their actions reveal who they are and what they represent. We may come to know them and respond to them in ways we come to know and respond to actual people, all the while realizing that characters are literary imitations of human beings.

But even though the characters in plays are not real people, their human dimension is impossible to ignore since actors portray them, and their human qualities are perhaps their most engaging feature. It is, indeed, their *human* aspect that attracts us to the characters of drama, not their symbolic significance. When we see characters engaged in significant human action, we examine their words and deeds. We make sense of them by relying on models of human behavior and by applying standards of conduct derived from our everyday experience; we assess their motives and evaluate their behavior in accordance with psychological probability. It is nearly impossible not to.

Nonetheless, it is helpful to remain mindful of the distinction between dramatic characters and actual people so that we do not always expect them to behave realistically. Nor should we expect playwrights to tell us everything about them. They will tell us only what we need to know. If it is not important for us to know Nora's age or Raina's height, the playwrights won't bother us with such information. Dramatists like Ibsen and Shaw reveal only what is relevant to their dramatic purposes.

Drama lives in the encounter of characters, for its action is interaction. Its essence is human relationships, the things men and women say and do to each other. Dramatic characters come together and affect each other, making things happen by coming into conflict. It is in conflict that characters reveal themselves and advance the plot.

DIALOGUE

Ezra Pound, the modern American poet, once described drama as "persons moving about on a stage using words"—in short, people talking. Listening to their talk we hear identifiable, individual voices. In their presence we encounter persons, for dialogue inevitably brings us back to character, drama's human center. And though dialogue in plays typically has three major functions—to advance the plot, to establish setting (the time and place of the action), and to reveal character, its most important and consistent function is the revelation of character.

Our examples come from Act IV, Scene III of Shakespeare's *Othello*. Consider first the following conversation between Desdemona (wife of the military hero Othello) and Emilia (maid to Desdemona and wife of Othello's lieutenant, Iago). They are talking about adultery:

DESDEMONA. Dost thou in conscience think, tell me, Emilia,
      That there be women do abuse their husbands
      In such gross kind?
EMILIA.   There be some such, no question.
DESDEMONA. Wouldst thou do such a deed for all the world?
EMILIA. Why, would not you?
DESDEMONA.   No, by this heavenly light!
EMILIA. Nor I either by this heavenly light.
      I might do't as well i'the dark.
DESDEMONA. Wouldst thou do such a deed for all the world?
EMILIA. The world's a huge thing; it is a great price for a small vice.
DESDEMONA.   In troth, I think thou
  wouldst not.
EMILIA. In troth, I think I should; and undo't when I had done. Marry, I would not do such a
  thing for a joint-ring, nor for measures of lawn, nor gowns, petticoats, nor caps, nor any petty
  exhibition, but for all the whole world? Why, who would not make her husband a cuckold
  to make a monarch? I should venture purgatory for't.
DESDEMONA. Beshrew me if I would do such a wrong for the whole world.
EMILIA. Why, the wrong is but a wrong i' th'world; and having the world for your labor, 'tis a
  wrong in your own world, and you might quickly make it right.
DESDEMONA. I do not think there is any such woman.

    In this dialogue we not only see and hear evidence of a radical difference of
values, but we also observe a striking difference of character. Desdemona's innocence is underscored by her unwillingness to be unfaithful to her husband; her
naiveté, by her inability to believe in any woman's infidelity. Emilia is willing
to compromise her virtue and finds enough practical reasons to assure herself
of its correctness. Her joking tone and bluntness also contrast with Desdemona's
solemnity and inability to name directly what she is referring to: adultery.
    And now listen to Iago working on Desdemona's father, Brabantio, to tell
him about his daughter's elopement with Othello (Act I, Scene I):

          Zounds, sir y'are robbed! For shame. Put on your gown.
          Your heart is burst, you have lost half your soul.
          Even now, now, very now, an old black ram
          Is tupping your white ewe. Arise, arise!
          Awake the snorting citizens with the bell,
          Or else the devil will make a grandsire of you.
          . . . .
          I am one sir, that comes to tell you your daughter
          and the Moor are making the beast with two backs.

Iago's language reveals his coarseness; he crudely reduces sexual love to animal
copulation. It also shows his ability to make things happen: he has infuriated
Brabantio. The remainder of the scene shows the consequences of his speech,
its power to inspire action. Iago is thus revealed as both an instigator and a man
of crude sensibilities.
    His language is cast in a similar mold in Act II, Scene I, when he tries to con-
vince Roderigo, a rejected suitor of Desdemona, that Desdemona will tire of

Othello and turn to someone else for sexual satisfaction. Notice how Iago's words stress the carnality of sex and reveal his violent imagination:

> Her eye must be fed. And what delight
> shall she have to look on the devil? When the
> blood is made dull with the act of sport, there
> should be a game to inflame it and to give
> satiety a fresh appetite, loveliness in favor,
> sympathy in years, manners, and beauties; all
> which the Moor is defective in. Now for want of
> these required conveniences, her delicate tenderness will find
> itself abused, begin to heave the gorge, disrelish and
> abhor the Moor. Very nature will instruct her in it
> and compel her to some second choice. . . .

Othello's language, like Iago's, reveals his character and his decline from a courageous and confident leader to a jealous lover distracted to madness by Iago's insinuations about his wife's infidelity. The elegance and control, even the exaltation of his early speeches, give way to the crude degradation of his later remarks. Here is Othello in Act I, Scene II, responding to a search party out to find him:

> Hold your hands,
> Both you of my inclining and the rest,
> Were it my cue to fight, I should have known it
> Without a prompter. Whither will you that I go
> To answer this your charge?

The language of this speech is formal, stately, and controlled. It bespeaks a man in command of himself, one who assumes authority naturally and easily.

In Act I, Scene III, Othello speaks to the political authorities and to Brabantio, Desdemona's enraged father:

> Most potent, grave, and reverend signiors,
> My very noble and approved good masters,
> That I have ta'en away this old man's daughter,
> It is most true; true I have married her.
> The very head and front of my offending
> Hath this extent, no more. . . .

From these few lines alone we can sense Othello's stature, his dignity, his self-confidence, and his courtesy. Coupled with other passages from the first two acts of the play, we come away impressed with Othello's gravity and grandeur. His language in large part accounts for our sympathetic response to him, for our admiration, not only for his military exploits, but for his measure of control, poise, and equanimity.

By the middle of Act III, however, this view of Othello is no longer tenable. Othello is reduced by Iago to an incoherent babbler, to a man at odds with himself, one who has lost his equilibrium. In Act IV, Scene I, we see the Othello Iago has created by suggesting that Desdemona has been unchaste with Othello's lieutenant, Michael Cassio:

OTHELLO.   Lie with her? Lie on her?—We say lie on her when they belie her—Lie with her! Zounds, that's fulsome. Handkerchief—confession—handkerchief—To confess, and be hanged for his labor—first to be hanged, and then to confess! I tremble at it. . . . It is not words that shake me thus.—Pish! Noses, ears, and lips? Is't possible?—Confess?—Handkerchief?—O devil.

In the language of both Iago and Othello we see meaning enacted as well as expressed. The verbal dimension of their dialogue is reinforced by action, gesture, movement. We can observe in these brief excerpts and throughout the play not only how language reveals character, advances the action, and establishes the setting, but how it also makes things happen and in effect itself becomes action.

STAGING

By *staging* we have in mind the spectacle a play presents in performance, its visual detail. This includes such things as the positions of actors onstage (sometimes referred to as *blocking*), their nonverbal gestures and movements (also called *stage business*), the scenic background, the props and costumes, lighting, and sound effects.

Though often taken for granted, costumes can reveal the characters beneath them. It is true that costume emerges partly from historical circumstances, particularly fashion. The soldiers' costumes in Shaw's *Arms and the Man,* for example, reflect the military attire of nineteenth-century Europe. But costume also emerges from the characters themselves. Sergius's full-dress uniform, weighted with decorations, testifies to his importance—at least to his self-importance and dubious heroism. Bluntschli's simple attire contrasts dramatically with Sergius's ornate costume; it suggests his naturalness, bluntness, and lack of pretension. It is important to notice, also, that Bluntschli's change of costume during the play indicates his changing fortunes.

Like Bluntschli, whose costume change signals changing circumstances (but not, however, a change in character), Ibsen's Nora changes costumes more than once. She appears by turns in ordinary clothing, in a multicolored shawl, in a dancing costume, and in a black shawl. Each costume change expresses a change in Nora's feelings.

Besides costume, any physical object that appears in a play has the potential to become an important dramatic symbol. The Christmas tree, which stands throughout Ibsen's *A Doll House,* is an ironic visual counterpart to the play's unfolding action. More dramatic perhaps and more central to plot is the handkerchief in *Othello.* Having its own history, which we learn when Desdemona wipes Othello's brow, the handkerchief becomes a crucial dramatic object, one that offers Othello the "ocular proof" he requires to condemn Desdemona as an adulterer.

Visual tokens need not be physical objects. In *Arms and the Man* Raina's and Sergius's exaggerated gestures of loving adoration speak to us of their excessive and false sentiments. So too does Raina's superbly comic gesture of holding up Sergius's framed picture in what seems like a parody of religious devotion.

From costumes, objects, and gestures we turn to sound. Ibsen uses sound effectively in *A Doll House* when he asks for music to accompany Nora's frenzied dancing as she attempts to delay Torvald's discovery of Krogstad's letter. In this same scene Ibsen also uses sound to heighten suspense as he has Torvald open the mailbox off-stage: we hear but don't see the mailbox click open.

A playwright's stage directions will sometimes help us see and hear things like these as we read. But with or without stage directions, we have to use our aural as well as our visual imagination. An increased imaginative alertness to the sights and sounds of a play, while no substitute for direct physical apprehension, can nonetheless help us approximate the experience of a dramatic performance. It can also enhance our appreciation of the dramatist's craftsmanship and increase our understanding of the play.

THEME

From plot, character, dialogue, and staging we derive a sense of the play's meaning or significance. An abstraction of this meaning is its central idea or *theme*. It is often helpful to try to express the theme of a play in a carefully worded sentence or two, but we should be aware, however, that any summary statement of a complex work of art is bound to be limited and limiting.

Nonetheless as readers we reach for theme as a way of organizing our responses to a play. At the same time we also let the work modify and alter our notion of its theme. We work back and forth between its details (of dialogue, gesture, and movement, for example) and our conception of their significance. As we notice details and connect them, as we discover and remember, our sense of the play's theme changes. It may change in such a way that we end up, provisionally at least, seeing the play's theme as ambiguous (suggesting contradictory or opposite ideas simultaneously with a resulting uncertainty and indefiniteness about its meaning). And of course there is the very good chance that a play will include more than one theme.

Perhaps we can best approach consideration of a play's theme by noting the dialogue of its characters, who frequently represent conflicting ideals and viewpoints. Some plays, for example, Sophocles' *Antigonê,* can certainly be approached this way. Antigonê herself, for example, represents a commitment to a religious ideal ineluctably in conflict with the political idea that Creon stands for. In her debate with Creon, Antigonê appeals to higher laws, religious and spiritual principles that require burial of the dead, especially if the dead are relatives. Because Antigonê acts in violation of Creon's edict, and since Creon as king represents the supreme authority of the state, she can be seen to pit God's law against man's. Another way of saying this is to note that she values a religious obligation more than a legal code. Still another is to see it as a conflict between two kinds of duty: duty to the state and duty to one's family. Legal obligation conflicts with moral responsibility; public duty collides with private conscience.

We have stated that Antigonê and Creon represent two different positions, two conflicting ideals. We make such a generalization, confident that we are not violating the play because the speeches of both characters refer directly to the ideals that motivate them. If we elaborate, however, we will have to qualify the view of their conflict suggested so far for two reasons. This paradigm is too neat: it ignores aspects of Antigonê's and Creon's motivation and character, and it also reduces the play as a whole to this conflict of values.

Because Greek tragedy typically enacts a reconciliation of the human and divine orders, Antigonê's appeal must be seen as an attempt to make that reconciliation and Creon's refusal as a denial of it. Thus, her appeal is not only personal—based on family honor—but is much more inclusive, far more so than Creon's reasons of state. To express this as a theme we might say that in the conflict between two goods, one divinely based (Antigonê's) and one humanly based (Creon's) the higher good should prevail.

We have been using Sophocles' drama to suggest that it is both natural and necessary to generalize from a play's action and dialogue to an idea it embodies. But we have also noted that to reduce the play's thought to a satisfactorily inclusive statement of theme is no easy matter. At best such a statement offers an approximation of a play's meaning, one that clarifies and illuminates our experience. At worst it oversimplifies the play, distorting its significance and impoverishing our experience of it.

CHAPTER TWENTY

Approaching a Play: Guides for Reading and Writing

The following guidelines summarize the main ideas about reading plays in the preceding chapters. These guidelines are followed by a one-act play, Lady Gregory's *The Rising of the Moon*, and a commentary that applies to it.

Guidelines for Reading

1. Read the opening stage directions carefully. Try to set the scene mentally. If a cast of characters is listed, spend a few minutes ascertaining the characters' relationships.
2. Read the opening scene slowly, referring back to the cast of characters if you become confused about who is who. Read slowly and deliberately, noting details which may assume prominence later.
3. Note places in the action where conflicts develop most intensely. Satisfy yourself that you understand the nature of the conflict—what causes it and how it might be resolved. Pinpoint the play's crisis and consider its implications.
4. Decide what values the characters embody and believe in. Consider what

they may represent. Examine their relationships with one another, noting especially their effects on each other.

5. Listen carefully to the play's dialogue. Notice what the characters say and *how* they say things. Try to hear their tones of voice; try to imagine the pace and tempo of the dialogue. Consider what the characters' speech reveals about them.

6. Try staging parts of the play in your mind. Imagine where the actors would stand, how they would be dressed, how they would deliver their lines, and what nonverbal gestures they might make. Try to visualize the play's setting from the dialogue and stage directions. Notice the visual details of the play. Consider their dramatic function and their possible symbolic significance.

7. Consider whether the play is a tragedy, comedy, or tragicomedy. If it is a comedy, is it satiric or romantic? Also consider the play's mood and tone.

8. Try to sum up your sense of the play's central ideas. What point does it seem to make? What values emerge, what attitudes are taken toward these values, and where does the playwright seem to stand on the issues, attitudes, and ideas the play embodies?

9. Consider the play's characters and action in relation to your own experience. Assess their values in light of your own. Also consider the author's point of view in light of your own.

10. Make a provisional aesthetic judgment about the play. Consider how effective it is as a literary and theatrical work.

ISABELLA AUGUSTA PERSSE,
LADY GREGORY

[1859–1932]

The Rising of the Moon

Scene: Side of a quay in a seaport town. Some posts and chains. A large barrel. Enter three policemen. Moonlight.

SERGEANT, *who is older than the others, crosses the stage to right and looks down steps. The others put down a pastepot and unroll a bundle of placards.*

POLICEMAN B.   I think this would be a good place to put up a notice. *(He points to barrel.)*

POLICEMAN X.   Better ask him. *(Calls to* SERGEANT*)* Will this be a good place for a placard? *(No answer.)*

POLICEMAN B.   Will we put up a notice here on the barrel? *(No answer.)*

SERGEANT.   There's a flight of steps here that leads to the water. This is a place that should be minded well. If he got down here, his friends might have a boat to meet him; they might send it in here from outside.

POLICEMAN B.   Would the barrel be a good place to put a notice up?

SERGEANT.   It might; you can put it there.

(They paste the notice up.)

SERGEANT   *(reading it)*. Dark hair—dark eyes, smooth face, height five feet five—there's not much to take hold of in that—It's a pity I had no chance of seeing him before he broke out of gaol. They say he's a wonder, that it's he makes all the plans for the whole organization. There isn't another man in Ireland would have broken gaol the way he did. He must have some friends among the gaolers.

POLICEMAN B.   A hundred pounds is little enough for the Government to offer for him. You may be sure any man in the force that takes him will get promotion.

SERGEANT.   I'll mind this place myself. I wouldn't wonder at all if he came this way. He might come slipping along there *(points to side of quay)*, and his friends might be waiting for him there *(points down steps)*, and once he got away it's little chance we'd have of finding him; it's maybe under a load of kelp he'd be in a fishing boat, and not one to help a married man that wants it to the reward.

POLICEMAN X.   And if we get him itself, nothing but abuse on our heads for it from the people, and maybe from our own relations.

SERGEANT.   Well, we have to do our duty in the force. Haven't we the whole country depending on us to keep law and order? It's those that are down would be up and those that are up would be down, if it wasn't for us. Well, hurry on, you have plenty of other places to placard yet, and come back here then to me. You can take the lantern. Don't be too long now. It's very lonesome here with nothing but the moon.

POLICEMAN B.   It's a pity we can't stop with you. The Government should have brought more police into the town, with *him* in gaol, and at assize time too. Well, good luck to your watch. *(They go out.)*

SERGEANT   *(walks up and down once or twice and looks at placard)*. A hundred pounds and promotion sure. There must be a great deal of spending in a hundred pounds. It's a pity some honest man not to be the better of that.

(A ragged man appears at left and tries to slip past. SERGEANT *suddenly turns.)*

SERGEANT.   Where are you going?

MAN.   I'm a poor ballad-singer, your honor. I thought to sell some of these *(holds out bundle of ballads)* to the sailors. *(He goes on.)*

SERGEANT.   Stop! Didn't I tell you to stop? You can't go on there.

MAN.   Oh, very well. It's a hard thing to be poor. All the world's against the poor!

SERGEANT.   Who are you?

MAN.   You'd be as wise as myself if I told you, but I don't mind. I'm one Jimmy Walsh, a ballad-singer.

SERGEANT.   Jimmy Walsh? I don't know that name.

MAN.   Ah, sure, they know it well enough in Ennis. Were you ever in Ennis, Sergeant?

SERGEANT.   What brought you here?

MAN.   Sure, it's to the assizes I came, thinking I might make a few shillings here or there. It's in the one train with the judges I came.

SERGEANT.   Well, if you came so far, you may as well go farther, for you'll walk out of this.

MAN.   I will, I will; I'll just go on where I was going. *(Goes toward steps.)*

SERGEANT.   Come back from those steps; no one has leave to pass down them tonight.

MAN.   I'll just sit on the top of the steps till I see will some sailor buy a ballad off me that would give me my supper. They do be late going back to the ship. It's often I saw them in Cork carried down the quay in a hand-cart.

SERGEANT.   Move on, I tell you. I won't have any one lingering about the quay tonight.

MAN.   Well, I'll go. It's the poor have the hard life! Maybe yourself might like one, Sergeant. Here's a good sheet now. *(Turns one over)* "Content and a pipe"—that's not much. "The Peeler and the Goat"—you wouldn't like that. "Johnny Hart"—that's a lovely song.

SERGEANT.   Move on.

MAN.   Ah, wait till you hear it.

(Sings.)

> There was a rich farmer's daughter lived near the town of Ross;
> She courted a Highland soldier, his name was Johnny Hart;
> Says the mother to her daughter, "I'll go distracted mad
> If you marry that Highland soldier dressed up in Highland plaid."

SERGEANT.   Stop that noise.

(MAN wraps up his ballads and shuffles toward the steps.)

SERGEANT.   Where are you going?

MAN.   Sure you told me to be going, and I am going.

SERGEANT.   Don't be a fool. I didn't tell you to go that way; I told you to go back to the town.

MAN.   Back to the town, is it?

SERGEANT   *(taking him by the shoulder and shoving him before him).* Here, I'll show you the way. Be off with you. What are you stopping for?

MAN   *(who has been keeping his eye on the notice, points to it).* I think I know what you're waiting for, Sergeant.

SERGEANT.   What's that to you?

MAN.   And I know well the man you're waiting for—I know him well—I'll be going. *(He shuffles on.)*

SERGEANT.   You know him? Come back here. What sort is he?

MAN.   Come back is it, Sergeant? Do you want to have me killed?

SERGEANT.   Why do you say that?

MAN.   Never mind. I'm going. I wouldn't be in your shoes if the reward was ten times as much. *(Goes on off stage to left)* Not if it was ten times as much.

SERGEANT   *(rushing after him).* Come back here, come back. *(Drags him back)* What sort is he? Where did you see him?

MAN. I saw him in my own place, in the County Clare. I tell you you wouldn't like to be looking at him. You'd be afraid to be in the one place with him. There isn't a weapon he doesn't know the use of, and as to strength, his muscles are as hard as that board. *(Slaps barrel.)*

SERGEANT. Is he as bad as that?

MAN. He is then.

SERGEANT. Do you tell me so?

MAN. There was a poor man in our place, a sergeant from Ballyvaughan.— It was with a lump of stone he did it.

SERGEANT. I never heard of that.

MAN. And you wouldn't, Sergeant. It's not everything that happens gets into the papers. And there was a policeman in plain clothes, too . . . . It is in Limerick he was. . . . It was after the time of the attack on the police barrack at Kilmallock. . . . Moonlight . . . just like this . . . waterside. . . . Nothing was known for certain.

SERGEANT. Do you say so? It's a terrible county to belong to.

MAN. That's so, indeed! You might be standing there, looking out that way, thinking you saw him coming up this side of the quay *(points),* and he might be coming up this other side *(points),* and he'd be on you before you knew where you were.

SERGEANT. It's a whole troop of police they ought to put here to stop a man like that.

MAN. But if you'd like me to stop with you, I could be looking down this side. I could be sitting up here on this barrel.

SERGEANT. And you know him well, too?

MAN. I'd know him a mile off, Sergeant.

SERGEANT. But you wouldn't want to share the reward?

MAN. Is it a poor man like me, that has to be going the roads and singing in fairs, to have the name on him that he took a reward? But you don't want me. I'll be safer in the town.

SERGEANT. Well, you can stop.

MAN *(getting up on barrel).* All right, Sergeant. I wonder, now, you're not tired out, Sergeant, walking up and down the way you are.

SERGEANT. If I'm tired I'm used to it.

MAN. You might have hard work before you tonight yet. Take it easy while you can. There's plenty of room up here on the barrel, and you see farther when you're higher up.

SERGEANT. Maybe so. *(Gets up beside him on barrel, facing right. They sit back to back, looking different ways)* You made me feel a bit queer with the way you talked.

MAN. Give me a match, Sergeant *(he gives it and* MAN *lights pipe); take a draw yourself? It'll quiet you. Wait now till I give you a light, but you needn't turn round. Don't take your eye off the quay for the life of you.

SERGEANT. Never fear, I won't. *(Lights pipe. They both smoke)* Indeed it's a hard thing to be in the force, out at night and no thanks for it, for all the danger we're in. And it's little we get but abuse from the people, and no choice but to obey our orders, and never asked when a man is sent into danger, if you are a married man with a family.

MAN   *(sings).*

> *As through the hills I walked to view the hills and shamrock plain,*
> *I stood awhile where nature smiles to view the rocks and streams,*
> *On a matron fair I fixed my eyes beneath a fertile vale,*
> *As she sang her song it was on the wrong of poor old Granuaile.*

SERGEANT.   Stop that; that's no song to be singing in these times.

MAN.   Ah, Sergeant, I was only singing to keep my heart up. It sinks when I think of him. To think of us two sitting here, and he creeping up the quay, maybe, to get to us.

SERGEANT.   Are you keeping a good lookout?

MAN   I am; and for no reward too. Amn't I the foolish man? But when I saw a man in trouble, I never could help trying to get him out of it. What's that? Did something hit me? *(Rubs his heart.)*

SERGEANT   *(patting him on the shoulder).* You will get your reward in heaven.

MAN.   I know that, I know that, Sergeant, but life is precious.

SERGEANT.   Well, you can sing if it gives you more courage.

MAN   *(sings).*

> *Her head was bare, her hands and feet with iron bands were bound,*
> *Her pensive strain and plaintive wail mingles with the evening gale,*
> *And the song she sang with mournful air, I am old Granuaile.*
> *Her lips so sweet that monarchs kissed . . .*

SERGEANT.   That's not it. . . . "Her gown she wore was stained with gore." . . . That's it—you missed that.

MAN.   You're right, Sergeant, so it is; I missed it. *(Repeats line)* But to think of a man like you knowing a song like that.

SERGEANT.   There's many a thing a man might know and might not have any wish for.

MAN.   Now, I daresay, Sergeant, in your youth, you used to be sitting up on a wall, the way you are sitting up on this barrel now, and the other lads beside you, and you singing "Granuaile"? . . .

SERGEANT.   I did then.

MAN.   And the "Shan Bhean Bhocht"? . . .

SERGEANT.   I did then.

MAN.   And the "Green on the Cape"?

SERGEANT.   That was one of them.

MAN.   And maybe the man you are watching for tonight used to be sitting on the wall, when he was young, and singing those same songs. . . . It's a queer world.

SERGEANT.   Whisht! . . . I think I see something coming. . . . It's only a dog.

MAN.   And isn't it a queer world? . . . Maybe it's one of the boys you used to be singing with that time you will be arresting today or tomorrow, and sending into the dock.

SERGEANT.   That's true indeed.

MAN.   And maybe one night, after you had been singing, if the other boys had told you some plan they had, some plan to free the country, you might have joined with them . . . and maybe it is you might be in trouble now.

SERGEANT.   Well, who knows but I might? I had a great spirit in those days.

MAN. It's a queer world, Sergeant, and it's little any mother knows when she sees her child creeping on the floor what might happen to it before it has gone through its life, or who will be who in the end.

SERGEANT. That's a queer thought now, and a true thought. Wait now till I think it out. . . . If it wasn't for the sense I have, and for my wife and family, and for me joining the force the time I did, it might be myself now would be after breaking gaol and hiding in the dark, and it might be him that's hiding in the dark and that got out of gaol would be sitting up where I am on this barrel. . . . And it might be myself would be creeping up trying to make my escape from himself, and it might be himself would be keeping the law, and myself would be breaking it, and myself would be trying maybe to put a bullet in his head, or to take up a lump of a stone the way you said he did . . . no, that myself did. . . . Oh! *(Gasps. After a pause)* What's that? *(Grasps* MAN's *arm.)*

MAN *(jumps off barrel and listens, looking out over water)*. It's nothing, Sergeant.

SERGEANT. I thought it might be a boat. I had a notion there might be friends of his coming about the quays with a boat.

MAN. Sergeant, I am thinking it was with the people you were, and not with the law you were, when you were a young man.

SERGEANT. Well, if I was foolish then, that time's gone.

MAN. Maybe, Sergeant, it comes into your head sometimes, in spite of your belt and your tunic, that it might have been as well for you to have followed Granuaile.

SERGEANT. It's no business of yours what I think.

MAN. Maybe, Sergeant, you'll be on the side of the country yet.

SERGEANT *(gets off barrel)*. Don't talk to me like that. I have my duties and I know them. *(Looks round)* That was a boat; I hear the oars. *(Goes to the steps and looks down.)*

MAN *(sings)*.

> O, then, tell me, Shawn O'Farrell,
> Where the gathering is to be.
> In the old spot by the river
> Right well known to you and me!

SERGEANT. Stop that! Stop that, I tell you!

MAN *(sings louder)*.

> One word more, for signal token,
> Whistle up the marching tune,
> With your pike upon your shoulder,
> At the Rising of the Moon.

SERGEANT. If you don't stop that, I'll arrest you. *(A whistle from below answers, repeating the air.)*

SERGEANT. That's a signal. *(Stands between him and steps)* You must not pass this way. . . . Step farther back. . . . Who are you? You are no ballad-singer.

MAN. You needn't ask who I am; that placard will tell you. *(Points to placard.)*

SERGEANT. You are the man I am looking for.

MAN *(takes off hat and wig.* SERGEANT *seizes them)*. I am. There's a hundred pounds on my head. There is a friend of mine below in a boat. He knows a safe place to bring me to.

SERGEANT   *(looking still at hat and wig).* It's a pity! It's a pity. You deceived me. You deceived me well.

MAN.   I am a friend of Granuaile. There is a hundred pounds on my head.

SERGEANT.   It's a pity, it's a pity!

MAN.   Will you let me pass, or must I make you let me?

SERGEANT.   I am in the force. I will not let you pass.

MAN.   I thought to do it with my tongue. *(Puts hand in breast)* What is that? *(Voice of* POLICEMAN X *outside.)* Here, this is where we left him.

SERGEANT.   It's my comrades coming.

MAN.   You won't betray me . . . the friend of Granuaile. *(Slips behind barrel.)* *(Voice of* POLICEMAN B.*)* That was the last of the placards.

POLICEMAN X   *(as they come in).* If he makes his escape it won't be unknown he'll make it.

*(*SERGEANT *puts hat and wig behind his back.)*

POLICEMAN B.   Did any one come this way?

SERGEANT   *(after a pause).* No one.

POLICEMAN B.   No one at all?

SERGEANT.   No one at all.

POLICEMAN B.   We had no orders to go back to the station; we can stop along with you.

SERGEANT.   I don't want you. There is nothing for you to do here.

POLICEMAN B.   You bade us to come back here and keep watch with you.

SERGEANT.   I'd sooner be alone. Would any man come this way and you making all that talk? It is better the place to be quiet.

POLICEMAN B.   Well, we'll leave you the lantern anyhow. *(Hands it to him.)*

SERGEANT.   I don't want it. Bring it with you.

POLICEMAN B.   You might want it. There are clouds coming up and you have the darkness of the night before you yet. I'll leave it over here on the barrel. *(Goes to barrel.)*

SERGEANT.   Bring it with you I tell you. No more talk.

POLICEMAN B.   Well, I thought it might be a comfort to you. I often think when I have it in my hand and can be flashing it about into every dark corner *(doing so)* that it's the same as being beside the fire at home, and the bits of bog-wood blazing up now and again. *(Flashes it about, now on the barrel, now on* SERGEANT.*)*

SERGEANT   *(furious).* Be off the two of you, yourselves and your lantern! *(They go out.* MAN *comes from behind barrel. He and* SERGEANT *stand looking at one another.)*

SERGEANT.   What are you waiting for?

MAN.   For my hat, of course, and my wig. You wouldn't wish me to get my death of cold?

*(*SERGEANT *gives them.)*

MAN   *(going toward steps).* Well, good night, comrade, and thank you. You did me a good turn tonight, and I'm obliged to you. Maybe I'll be able to do as much for you when the small rise up and the big fall down . . . when we all change places at the Rising *(waves his hand and disappears)* of the Moon.

SERGEANT   *(turning his back to audience and reading placard).* A hundred pounds reward! A hundred pounds! *(Turns toward audience)* I wonder, now, am I as great a fool as I think I am?

(1907)

Plot   The play is tightly structured; the plot is unified, the action centering overtly on the appearance and disappearance of the wanted man and covertly on the Sergeant's crisis of conscience. The larger action of the play can be broken down into a series of incidents. The first comprises the discussion between the Sergeant and the police officers about putting up placards and finding the criminal. This segment ending with the appearance of "the ragged man" is the play's exposition.

A second incident begins with the conversation between the Sergeant and the ragged man. A conflict develops as the sergeant tries to move the man on and he, while pretending to acquiesce, remains where he is. This initial complication begins the play's rising action, which continues with an additional conflict, the Sergeant's internal one. The Sergeant's conflict occurs when the ballad singer tells him that he knows the wanted man. The dramatist complicates the action here as we discover that the escaped man has a reputation for being dangerous. Tension and suspense build as we watch the Sergeant become increasingly anxious about his situation. The next incident complicates the action further by introducing questions about how the Sergeant's life might have been different. These questions lead to a moment of crisis as the Sergeant realizes who the man is. At this point we wonder what the Sergeant will do. The playwright stretches this section of the play out to retain suspense, then takes the play up to and through the climax when the other policemen return and the Sergeant makes his decision. The play's falling action begins when the Sergeant reveals his decision and sends the other two policemen off. The denouement occurs with the play's final conversation.

In addition to noting the unity and economy of this plot, we should also acknowledge its reliance on irony. The action reverses itself, with the Sergeant doing the very thing he least expects to do—the opposite, in fact, of what he expected to do. This follows upon the additional reversal of his sitting, smoking, and talking with the very man he seeks to capture and imprison. These and other small-scale ironies are revealed further in the playwright's presentation of character.

Character   Policemen B and X are clearly minor characters, necessary primarily to the functioning of the plot. They also serve to reveal the character of the Sergeant. In the first scene, we note how differently the Sergeant responds to the state of affairs than they do. Policemen B and X are quite matter-of-fact about their job. They seem more concerned with details like finding a place for the placards than with the nature of their job—to capture a dangerous criminal. The Sergeant, in contrast, is visibly uneasy. His anxiety surfaces when, intent on scanning the water for signs of the criminal, he does not hear his subordinates' questions about the placards. He's also shown to be a more seasoned veteran of police work and more aware of the dangers involved than the two younger policemen.

But the most important relationship is the one that develops between the Sergeant and the man. Their relationship is fundamentally ironic because neither is what he seems to be. The Sergeant does not uphold the law and arrest the man; the man does not live up to his reputation as a dangerous killer. Both have ample opportunity to act within their respective roles, but neither does. Each surprises the other; both surprise us and probably themselves as well.

The most significant moment of character revelation occurs as the Sergeant muses about fate. He can imagine his life having turned out differently, with himself as a hunted criminal. And in a corresponding leap of imagination, he envisions the hunted criminal as an officer of the law hunting him. At this moment the Sergeant realizes the essential similarity, the connection between seemingly different and opposing individuals. It's an important moment of understanding, an illumination that leads him to a radically altered perception of his responsibility as a man. Perceiving the essential brotherhood he shares with the other man, the Sergeant realizes the injustice of the escaped man's predicament and the justness of his cause.

Dialogue   The connections between protagonist and antagonist (Sergeant and man) are underscored in the play's action and dialogue. Notice, for example, how their first exchange shows a radical difference in their speech: the Sergeant's curt, firm tone contrasts with the man's relaxed familiarity. And notice too how by the end of the play they converse naturally, casually, familiarly—like friends rather than adversaries, like brothers rather than strangers. The simple natural eloquence of the man helps turn the Sergeant's thoughts to his past, to his youthful idealism, which, presumably, has been buried under the pressures of responsibility and circumstance, and brings about their spiritual companionship. The Sergeant also turns eloquent at the man's instigation as he imagines the reversal of their fortunes.

We should note also the ambivalence of the Sergeant's final remark about what he has done. He seems to lament the loss of the one-hundred-pound reward. At the same time, however, though he sees himself as a fool, he is also happy with his decision to let the man go. His tone reveals a contented and easy mind, one radically different from the state of mind he exhibited at the beginning of the play. Yet, while he clearly is at peace with himself (his conscience is clear), he can't help thinking how close he came to the reward.

A similar ambivalence is revealed in his language at the beginning of the play. As he reads the man's description from the placard, he seems to regret not having seen the man personally, presumably because he would then know who he was looking for. At the same time, however, there's more than a note of admiration in his voice as he recounts what people say about the escapee: "They say he's a wonder, that it's he makes all the plans for the whole organization. There isn't another man in Ireland would have broken gaol the way he did."

Staging   Let us first consider sound. How do we hear the characters' voices? How much admiration, for example, might an actor convey in reading the Sergeant's speech in the preceding paragraph? None? Some? A lot? And in what tone of voice and with how much strength and feeling should the man sing his ballads?

Even in reading the ballad stanzas we can imagine, if not their tune, at least their tone—the way their sentiments could be expressed. We should note here, too, how the playwright has integrated the ballads into the dialogue, making them echo the play's thematic concerns while simultaneously advancing the action.

Besides effective use of sound, the play contains simple but significant uses of visual details and of gesture. For example, toward the end of the play as the two policemen return and the Sergeant allows the man to hide behind the barrel, he holds behind his back the man's hat and wig. The hat and wig, of course, are a disguise. By hiding them, the Sergeant effectually hides the man and protects him. Thus, the visual details underscore their collaboration. Their connection also is established by yet another set of visual details. The image created by the two of them sitting on the barrel like friends expresses simply but eloquently their fundamental brotherhood. At the same time, however, their act of sharing the barrel occurs at a moment when the Sergeant is unaware of who sits there with him. By having them sit back to back, Lady Gregory underscores the danger the Sergeant is in and increases suspense.

The other detail suggesting their connection involves a similar gesture. Both the Sergeant and the man point to the side of the quay as they imagine, in similar language, where the man or his friends might appear.

SERGEANT. [*to* POLICEMEN] I wouldn't wonder at all if he came this way. He might come slipping along there (*points to side of quay*), and his friends might be waiting for him there (*points down steps*), and once he got away it's little chance we'd have of finding him.

MAN. [*to* SERGEANT] That's so, indeed! You might be standing there, looking out that way, thinking you saw him coming up this side of the quay (*points*), and he might be coming up this other side (*points*), and he'd be on you before you knew where you were.

Theme   What, finally, does the play add up to? Without insisting on a message, we can point to a few of its central issues and speculate about what it implies.

First, it is a political play, taking as its context the turmoil of a beleaguered Irish populace. The historical details of the political situation are not explicitly rendered (because they would be familiar to Lady Gregory's audience) but they are alluded to in references to "Granuaile." Clearly, we are meant to side with the man who fights for the cause of Granuaile.

Another aspect of the play's political impulse is the way it suggests that the rich and poor will change places. A revolution is in order: there's a spirit of optimism and idealism, and a sense that things won't always remain as they are, with injustice and inequity prevailing. There's an implication and a belief that the common people eventually will triumph and that the country will be free.

This political context is closely associated with the crisis of conscience that the Sergeant undergoes. His decision to trust his instinctive sympathy for the man and his cause, and his impulse to act in accordance with his reawakened idealism rather than to capture the criminal are dramatized powerfully and economically. And though the play ends with a question, it is clearly rhetorical. When the Sergeant asks, "Am I as great a fool as I think I am," we answer "No, you're not a fool, but a decent man, and you're at one with the people from whom you sprang."

Suggestions for Writing
The Experience of Drama

1. Write a paper in which you recount your experience of reading a particular play or series of plays by the same author. You may want to compare your initial experience with your experience in later readings.

2. Write a paper comparing your experience reading a play with your experience witnessing a performance of it.

3. Discuss your changing perception or understanding of a particular play. Indicate how you felt about the play initially and what made you change your way of responding to it.

4. Relate the action or situation of a play to your own experience. Explain how the play is relevant to your situation, and comment on how reading and thinking about it may have helped you see your own life and experience more clearly.

5. Compare reading a play with watching a film of a performance or a film based on a play. For a filmed performance of a play, consider watching the videocassette of Arthur Miller's *Death of a Salesman,* starring Dustin Hoffman. For a film based on a play, consider viewing the movie version of Hansberry's *A Raisin in the Sun,* starring Sidney Poitier.

The Interpretation of Drama

6. Describe and characterize a single character from any play. Present a sketch of the character by referring to the language of his or her speeches and to the playwright's use of costume and stage directions.

7. Analyze a character at the moment he or she is making an important decision. Identify the situation, explain the reasons for the character's decision, and speculate about the possible consequences. Some possibilities: Nora in *A Doll House,* Antigonê in *Antigonê,* Raina in *Arms and the Man,* Othello in *Othello,* the Sergeant in *The Rising of the Moon.*

8. Explicate the opening dialogue of any play. Explain the significance of the opening section in setting the tone, establishing thematic preoccupations, and preparing us for what follows.

9. Select two or three brief passages that appear to be significant in their implications. They may be descriptive passages or dialogue. Establish the connections between one passage and the others, and explain their cumulative significance.

10. Analyze the closing dialogue of any play. Explain the significance of the ending and comment on its appropriateness.

11. Analyze the imagery of a play. Consider how particular kinds of language serve to advance the play's theme(s) or to reveal its characters. Some possibilities: political and natural images in Sophocles' *Antigonê;* animal imagery in *Othello;* images of dream and illusion in Arthur Miller's *Death of a Salesman.*

12. Analyze the ironic dimensions of any play. Consider how the playwright uses irony in the plot, dialogue, and/or setting. Some possibilities: *Oedipus Rex, Antigonê, Tartuffe, Arms and the Man, Trifles, M. Butterfly.*

13. Explain the symbolic implications of any props used in the play. Consider the dramatic functions of the objects and their resonance as symbols. Some possibilities: the handkerchief in *Othello;* the Christmas tree in *A Doll House;* the balloons in *Andre's Mother.*

14. Analyze the structure of any play. Consider its major parts or sections—its acts and scenes. Explain what each contributes to the whole and how the parts fit together into a unified whole.

15. Analyze the plot of a play. Comment on the way it illustrates or deviates from the classic plot structure.

16. Analyze the setting of a play. Consider both time and place. Also consider small-scale aspects of setting, such as whether the action occurs indoors or out. Notice the descriptive details about the setting, whether the setting changes, and whether the action occurs in one time or place.

17. Analyze a character from any play. Evaluate the character, offering reasons and evidence for your views. Consider what the character does, says, does not do or say—and why. Note also what other characters say about him or her, and how they respond in action. Consider whether the character changes during the course of the play and what that possible change (or lack thereof) may signify.

18. Discuss any character relationship. Consider how the characters affect each other. Explain the nature of their relationship and speculate on its probable future.

The Evaluation of Drama

19. Evaluate a play from the point of view of its merit or excellence—or lack thereof. Explain why you consider it to be a successful or unsuccessful play.

20. Do a comparative evaluation of the merit of any two plays. Explain what they share, how they differ, and why one is more impressive or effective than the other.

21. Discuss the values exemplified by the characters in any play. Identify those values, relate them to your own, and comment on their significance. You may also wish to discuss the author's point of view as you see it reflected in the play.

22. Write a review of the performance of a play. Consider the staging and

lighting of the performance, the costumes, the set design, and the sound effects.

23. Write a review of a play's performance concentrating on the acting. Consider how well the actors and actresses delivered their lines, how well they worked together and how well they communicated emotions and ideas.

24. Write a review of a film, concentrating on its theatrical characteristics and qualities.

To Research or Imagine

25. Develop an alternative ending for any play, changing the outcome in whatever way you deem appropriate. Be prepared to defend your alternative ending as a reasonable possibility. Consider why the author chose to end the play as he or she did.

26. Try your hand at writing a scene from a play. Invent a scenario, create a couple of characters, and start them talking and acting.

27. Read a few letters or essays written by a dramatist. Consider what light they shed on your reading of the play(s).

28. Read a full-scale biography of a dramatist. Write a paper explaining how the author's life is or is not reflected in his work.

29. Discuss how a particular playwright reflects or rebels against important social, political, moral, or cultural issues of his or her time.

30. Read a critical study of a writer's plays. Write a paper explaining how the book aids your understanding or enhances your enjoyment of the play(s).

CHAPTER TWENTY-ONE

Writing About Drama

REASONS FOR WRITING ABOUT DRAMA

Why write about drama? One reason is to find out what you think about a play. Another is to induce yourself to read it more carefully. You may write about a work of drama because it engages you, and you may wish to celebrate it or to argue with its implied ideas and values. Still another reason is that you may simply be required to do so as a course assignment.

Whatever your reasons for writing about drama, a number of things happen when you do. First, in writing about a play you tend to read it more attentively, noticing things you might overlook in a more casual reading. Second, since writing stimulates thinking, when you write about drama you find yourself thinking more about what a particular work means and why you respond to it as you do. And third, you begin to acquire power over the works you write about, making them more meaningful to you.

INFORMAL WAYS OF WRITING ABOUT DRAMA

When you write about a play, you may write for yourself or you may write for others. Writing for yourself, often to discover what you think, often takes casual forms such as annotation and freewriting. These less formal kinds of writing are useful for helping you focus on your reading of plays. They are helpful in studying for tests about drama. They can also serve as preliminary forms of writing when you write more formal essays and papers.

Annotation

When you annotate a text, you make notes about it, usually in the margins or at the top and bottom of pages—or both. Annotations can also be made within the text, as underlined words, circled phrases, or bracketed sentences or paragraphs. Annotations may also assume the form of arrows, question marks, and various other marks.

Annotating a literary work offers a convenient and relatively painless way to begin writing about it. Annotating can get you started zeroing on what you think interesting or important. You can also annotate to signal details that puzzle or disconcert you.

Your markings serve to focus your attention and clarify your understanding of a story or novel. Your annotations can save you time in rereading or studying a work. And they can also be used when you write a more formal paper.

Annotations for the following scene illustrate the process.

The following excerpt from *Antigonê* begins at the point where Antigonê has been taken into custody for violating an edict of Creon, king of Thebes. Creon's edict concerns Antigonê's brother, Polyneicês, who was killed in a battle while fighting against Thebes. Creon has forbidden Polyneicês' burial, but in violation of the edict Antigonê has buried him.

CREON *to* SENTRY: You may go.
Exit SENTRY.
   (To ANTIGONÊ*)* Tell me, tell me briefly:
   Had you heard my proclamation touching this matter?

> Creon can't believe that she would disobey—hence his question.

ANTIGONÊ: It was public. Could I help hearing it?
CREON: And yet you dared defy the law.
ANTIGONÊ: I dared.
   It was not God's proclamation. That final Justice
   That rules the world below makes no such laws.

> He sees himself as "the law."

   Your edict, King, was strong,
   But all your strength is weakness itself against
   The immortal unrecorded laws of God.
   They are not merely now: they were, and shall be,
   Operative for ever, beyond man utterly.

> Antigonê identifies conflict: God/man divine/human

   I knew I must die, even without your decree:
   I am only mortal. And if I must die
   Now, before it is my time to die,
   Surely this is no hardship: can anyone
   Living, as I live, with evil all about me,
   Think Death less than a friend? This death of mine
   is of no importance; but if I had left my brother

> Is she a bit too eager to die?

lying in death unburied, I should have suffered.
Now I do not.

　　　　　　You smile at me. Ah Creon,
Think me a fool, if you like; but it may well be
That a fool convicts me of folly.

CHORAGOS:　Like father, like daughter:
　　both headstrong, deaf to reason!
She has never learned to yield:

CREON:　She has much to learn.
The inflexible heart breaks first, the toughest iron
Cracks first, and the wildest horses bend their necks
At the pull of the smallest curb.

　　　　　　　　　Pride? In a slave?
This girl is guilty of a double insolence.
Breaking the given laws and boasting of it.
Who is the man here,
She or I, if this crime goes unpunished?
Sister's child, or more than sister's child,
Or closer yet in blood—she and her sister
Win bitter death for this!

　　　　(To SERVANTS.*)*
　　　　　　Go, some of you.
Arrest Ismenê. I accuse her equally.
Bring her: you will find her sniffling in the house there.
Her mind's a traitor: crimes kept in the dark
Cry for light, and the guardian brain shudders;
But how much worse than this
Is brazen boasting of barefaced anarchy!

ANTIGONÊ:　Creon, what more do you want than my death?

CREON:　　　　　　　　　　　　　Nothing.
That gives me everything.

ANTIGONÊ:　　　　　　　Then I beg you: kill me.
This talking is a great weariness: your words
Are distasteful to me, and I am sure that mine
Seem so to you. And yet they should not seem so:
I should have praise and honor for what I have done.
All these men here would praise me
Were their lips not frozen shut with fear of you.
(Bitterly.) Ah the good fortune of kings.
Licensed to say and do whatever they please!

CREON:　You are alone here in that opinion.

ANTIGONÊ:　No, they are with me. But they
　keep their tongues in leash.

CREON:　Maybe. But you are guilty, and they are not.

ANTIGONÊ:　There is no guilt in reverence for the dead.

CREON:　But Eteoclês—was he not your brother too?

ANTIGONÊ:　My brother too.

CREON:　　　　　　　And you insult his memory?

ANTIGONÊ *(softly)*:　The dead man would not say that I insult it.

CREON:　He would: for you honor a traitor as much as him.

ANTIGONÊ:　His own brother, traitor or not, and equal in blood.

Right margin annotations:

implicit stage direction: "You smile . . ."

How important is this choral comment?

images: iron, horses

conflict: man/woman age/youth

Why does Creon accuse Ismenê?

Anarchy? Is Creon a bit paranoid?

She knows how to fight back.

image: dogs on a leash held in check by fear

a complication: the other brother, Eteoclês

tempo: pace picks up here with rapid-fire dialogue exchange

CREON: He made war on his country. Eteoclês defended it.
ANTIGONÊ: Nevertheless, there are honors due all the dead.
CREON: But not the same for the wicked as for the just.   buildup of intensity
ANTIGONÊ: Ah Creon, Creon,
    Which of us can say what the gods hold wicked?
CREON: An enemy is an enemy, even dead.
ANTIGONÊ: It is my nature to join in love, not hate.
CREON (*finally losing patience*): Go join them then;
    if you must have your love. Find it in hell!

Double-Column Notebook

Another way of writing for yourself, informally, is to use the double-column notebook. To create a double-column notebook, divide a page in half vertically (or open a notebook so that you face two blank pages side by side). On one side *take* notes, summarizing the scene's situation, action, and ideas. On the other side, the responding side, *make* notes, recording your thinking about what you summarized on the opposite side. On the responding side, ask questions; speculate; make connections.

Here is an example of a double-column notebook for the excerpt from *Antigonê* annotated above. Notice how the entries in the double-column notebook are more detailed, and written in a more formal style, than the annotations shown with the excerpt.

Summary and Observations

Responses and Reactions

Creon's language is formal, even self-important. He sounds like, or tries to sound like, a king.

Part of Creon's anger stems from Antigonê's rebellion against *him,* against *his* law. Part derives from her seeming disregard for the law of the land more generally.

Antigonê's view seems to be that since Creon's law was a bad one, she shouldn't obey it. And even further, that she has a responsibility to disobey it since the gods require that family members honor their dead. She points out that her burial of her brother was necessary for her own peace of mind.

Creon is unpalatable here. He's pompous and arrogant. Yet to some extent he seems justified in being angry. What's interesting here is why Creon reacts so strongly to the violation of his edict. It probably has something to do with his recent acquisition of power. He is very likely more than a little insecure in his new position. He must feel the need to assert himself and establish his authority. Suppose he ignores Antigonê's action. What will people think of him? Won't they see him as weak?

Antigonê's point has merit. She has to do what she has to do.

Antigonê seems the more likeable of the two.

Antigonê at one point angers Creon by reminding him that he is not almighty. She attempts to put him in his place, to remind

Antigonê enjoys pulling Creon down a peg. Her tone does sound insulting. She almost seems to enjoy thinking of herself as a martyr him that his rule has limits. He doesn't like that. Nor does he like her suggestion that it is better to die than to obey an unjust law or live in a corrupt society.

for a cause. Isn't she a bit theatrical here, relishing her role and the image she projects as much as, or even more than, the idea and point of view she stands up for?

Creon, of course, sees her act of rebellion and her disrespectful attitude toward him as king as the cause of societal corruption.

Doesn't Creon overreact here in seeing Antigonê's action as an example of "anarchy"? And doesn't he also overreact in assuming that Ismenê is also guilty? He assumes things without testing them.

During the course of their dialogue (more a confrontation or debate than a conversation), they insult each other. Creon calls Antigonê stubborn; Antigonê calls Creon a fool.

As in any good fight, the antagonists really do try to hurt each other.

It's an enjoyable verbal battle—for us readers.

Creon's long speech parallels and answers Antigonê's. Once the two positions have been established, we watch and listen as the dialogue speeds up as Antigonê and Creon trade arguments and insults.

Even though the dialogue is somewhat stylized and conventional, it is beautifully arranged for maximum punch and counterpunch.

Throughout this taut scene both characters seem tense and angry. They neither like nor respect each other.

The effect overall is of tension building to the point of explosion.

FORMAL WAYS OF WRITING ABOUT DRAMA

Among the more common formal ways of writing about drama is analysis. In writing an analytical essay about a play or a scene from a play, your goal is to explain how one or more particular aspects or issues in the work or the scene contributes to its overall meaning. You might analyze the dialogue in a scene from Shaw's *Arms and the Man* or Lady Gregory's *The Rising of the Moon*. Your goal would be to explain what the verbal exchanges between characters contribute to the play's meaning and to its effect on the audience. You might analyze the imagery of Sophocles' *Oedipus the King* or Shakespeare's *Othello* to see what that imagery suggests about a character's perspective or the author's attitude toward the characters or the action. Or you might analyze the plot or staging of Glaspell's *Trifles* or Molière's *Tartuffe* to see how the playwright's manipulation of action creates tension and conflict, humor and irony.

In addition to analyzing these and other dramatic elements in a play, you might also compare two plays or scenes, perhaps by focusing on their use of stage directions, lighting, or other theatrical effects. Or, instead of focusing on literary elements per se, you might write to see how a particular critical perspective (see Chapter 36) illuminates a play. For example, you might consider the ways reader response criticism or new historicism contributes to your understanding of Hansberry's *A Raisin in the Sun* or Manet's *Oleanna,* respectively.

STUDENT PAPERS ON DRAMA

Carolyn Kaparini
Prof. Eisenstadt

Hamlet's Conflict Resolved

In Shakespearean tragedies, characters often are confronted with problems they must resolve. *The Tragedy of Hamlet, Prince of Denmark* is one tragedy that reveals a tormented hero who suffers greatly during the course of the play. Hamlet, the tragic hero, must resolve many conflicts, which include confusion and anger at his mother's hasty remarriage, horror at the ghost's request to avenge the murder of his father, and a general disgust with life as he contemplates suicide. Before he can accept the responsibility of setting his world aright, Hamlet must resolve his internal conflicts.

The first dilemma Hamlet must resolve results from the loss of his father. Hamlet is first seen dressed in black as he mourns the death of King Hamlet, his father. Hamlet cannot understand why no one besides himself and Horatio continues to grieve for Hamlet's father. What is even more upsetting to Hamlet is that the court is celebrating the coronation of Claudius and his royal marriage to Hamlet's mother, Queen Gertrude. Hamlet is especially infuriated with his mother, who he thinks has not mourned her husband's death sufficiently. In an important soliloquy in Act I, scene ii, Hamlet complains that even a beast "would have mourned longer" than his mother did. And he reveals his disgust with both her and Claudius when he calls their hasty marriage both "wicked" and "incestuous." Throughout the play, Hamlet will continue to find their marriage itself and its hasty occurrence after his father's death consistently painful to think about.

A second internal conflict with which Hamlet deals is the problem presented by the ghost. When Hamlet first encounters the ghost he asks whether the ghost is "a spirit of health or goblin damned." Before anything else, Hamlet has to resolve the problem of the ghost's good or evil nature, of whether he can trust the ghost to be honest and truthful. Once he decides that the ghost really is the spirit of his dead father, Hamlet faces an even greater problem: to act on the command the ghost gives him to avenge the foul murder committed by Claudius. Hamlet is appalled by the story the ghost of his father tells about how Claudius murdered him to acquire first his crown and then his queen. The absolute evil of Claudius's actions and Hamlet's disgust with his mother's behavior lead him to recognize that "something's rotten in the state of

Denmark." Hamlet describes his predicament in the following lines:

> The time is out of joint. O cursed spite,
> That ever I was born to set it right.

Before Hamlet can set things right, however, he has to come to
terms with the world of destructive evil that Claudius's act
typifies.

Hamlet's greatest conflict occurs as a result of his indecision
over what to do about his mother and how to avenge his father's
murder. Even though these both distress him greatly, he suffers
from a deeper and more pervasive disgust with life. Because of
Claudius's crime, he sees evil all around him, especially at court.
Because of his mother's actions, he thinks of all women as sinful,
even the innocent Ophelia. He expresses his general dissatisfaction
with life many times. On one occasion right after describing man as
"noble" and a "paragon," after comparing him with angels and gods,
Hamlet says "and yet to me, what is this quintessence of dust? Man
delights not me." Later, he considers the question of whether it is
better to live or to die:

> To be, or not to be: that is the question:
> Whether 'tis nobler in the mind to suffer
> The slings and arrows of outrageous fortune,
> Or to take arms against a sea of troubles,
> And by opposing end them.

These and many other lines in the play reveal Hamlet disappointed
with the injustice and cruelty of life. His anger and frustration
lead him to think constantly about death and to make plans to
avenge his father's death. But he does not act. Instead he thinks
and delays acting.

Hamlet perceives how difficult his task really is. Perhaps that
is why it takes him so long to act. He is also seriously depressed
by the state of affairs in Denmark. One turning point comes when
Hamlet decides to confront his mother. He unleashes his anger and
criticizes her severely for marrying Claudius. He also urges her
not to sleep with the king. Another turning point occurs, when upon
discovering Claudius's plot to have him murdered, Hamlet
substitutes another letter ensuring the deaths of Rosencrantz and
Guildenstern. In addition, during Hamlet's time away from the court
when he is captured by pirates and then released to make his way
home, he seems to have changed. When he reappears in Act V, Hamlet
is more accepting of what fate or God has in store for him. Even
though he does not yet know of the treachery that Laertes and
Claudius have planned for him, he is determined to do what is
necessary and to accept the consequences.

One important indication of this change of attitude occurs when he holds the skull of Yorick and he talks about the inevitability of death. He describes how death comes to all people, the great and important as well as the common people. All are equal when their bodies have decayed and their souls have departed. In addition, Hamlet recognizes that, as he tells Horatio, "there's a divinity that shapes our ends," regardless of what we prepare for ourselves. This recognition of a divine power governing the lives of men is acknowledged in another speech that reveals that Hamlet has learned from his suffering. It suggests that he has mentally resolved his internal conflicts. He says to Horatio:

> There is special providence in the fall of a
> sparrow. If it be now, 'tis not to come; if it
> be not to come, it will be now; if it be not
> now, yet it will come. The readiness is all.
> Since no man of aught he leaves knows, what is't
> to leave betimes? Let be.

In the play's final scene, Hamlet settles the score with Claudius by stabbing him with his sword. He has already resolved his argument with his mother, and the treacherous drink Claudius had prepared for Hamlet does the rest. After Hamlet and Laertes, Gertrude and Claudius die, Horatio is left to explain what really happened and what Hamlet himself was really like. It is left to Fortinbras to restore order to the disorder of Denmark. Even though Hamlet alone could not set his world aright, he had found his own peace and resolved his internal conflicts.

Alayna Phieffer
Dr. Kitts
12/10/96

   Antigonê: A Struggle Between Human and Divine Powers

   In *Antigonê* by Sophocles there are several ways to interpret the
conflict between Creon and Antigonê. Perhaps the most widely
accepted interpretation is that their conflict represents a
struggle between State and individual. This reading is valid but it
is also shallow; if looked into deeper, we can see that the
struggle in this play lies between earthly and divine powers.

   Creon represents a tyrannical rule that makes no allowances for
the unwritten laws, spiritual in nature, which so often guide
humans to act. He is so consumed with ruling the state and so
intoxicated with the power he possesses that he is unable to
comprehend the motives behind Antigonê's burial of her brother
Polyneicês. This can be seen in the first encounter between
Antigonê and Creon.

> *Creon:* And yet you dared defy the law.
> *Antigonê:*   I dared.
>   It was not God's proclamation. That final Justice
>   That rules the world below makes no such law.
>
>   Your edict, King, was strong,
>   But all your strength is weakness itself against
>   The immortal unrecorded laws of God.
>   They are not merely now: they were, and shall be,
>   Operative for ever, beyond man utterly.
>
>   . . . but if I had left my brother
>   Lying in death unburied, I should have suffered.
>   Now I do not.   (II, 56–70)

This conversation immediately establishes Antigonê's ideal; to her,
divine law is more powerful and right than any law decreed by the
state. Creon, to save face and maintain order, sticks to his decree
and sentences her to death.

   This conflict of harsh state laws with one's inner duty goes
still deeper, and it is clear that the gods are on Antigonê's
side. It seems best to look at what Antigonê and others say about
divine intervention and their actions concerning it. The first
evidence that the Gods are involved can be seen in the double
burial. Antigonê is apprehended when she goes to her brother's
body, but just before this we are told by the Sentry that someone

has buried the body of Polyneicês. He states that there are no signs of human involvement, no wheel tracks or any sign of animals present; the body is covered with a light dusting. We can perceive this statement to be true; otherwise why would Sophocles have included it? Why did Antigonê then go back to her brother for a second time? Perhaps the answer lies in a statement made by the chorus-leader: "I have been wondering, King: can it be that the gods have done this?" (I, 99).

The watchman's actions, upon entering the palace, are revealing. He twists and turns as though he is afraid that Creon will not believe him; after all, he cannot understand it himself. If the body had been buried deep in the ground, one could argue that this is evidence that it was done by man, but the light dusting of the body implies something more.

Another piece of evidence to support God's involvement in this play's action is apparent in the first conversation between Antigonê and Ismenê. Antigonê says "Creon is not strong enough to stand in my way" (Prologue, 35). And later after Ismenê says how dangerous it is to go against authority, Antigonê responds:

> If that is what you think,
> I should not want you, even if you asked to come.
> You have made your choice, you can be what you want to be.
> But I will bury him; and if I must die,
> I say that this crime is holy: I shall lie down
> With him in death, and I shall be as dear
> To him as he is to me.
> It is the dead,
> Not the living, who make the longest demands:
> We die for ever . . .
> You may do as you like,
> Since apparently the laws of the gods mean nothing to you.
>
> (Prologue, 52–61)

Antigonê is saying that she is acting in accordance with the will of the gods; divine law will always surpass any human laws.

Later, she tells Creon that it was not the words of the gods that she disobeyed, but it was their word that led her to act. This idea is common in Greek tragedy. When characters like Antigonê, act in ways fundamentally necessary in human life, or out of a place deep within themselves, they are said to be working with the gods, and this becomes so sacred that not even written law could stop them.

As Antigonê is about to be buried alive, she realizes that no one understands her. Still she feels that she was obeying a divine law, even though now the gods seem to have nothing to do with her and have made no attempt to save her. But still she maintains her deep belief that she had to do it, and says that she had no choice:

    Thebes, and you my fathers' gods,
    And rulers of Thebes, you see me now, the last
    Unhappy daughter of a line of kings,
    Your kings, led away to death. You will remember
    What things I suffer, and at what men's hands,
    Because I would not transgress the laws of heaven.
                                                 (IV, 75-80)

To her, the laws of heaven must guide our lives and they must
always be obeyed no matter the consequence.

Finally we see the divine hand in prophecy, most obviously in
the tragic destiny of Oedipus. His tragedy is sorrowfully left
behind to his descendants. Tragedy must fall upon Antigonê as it
fell upon her brothers. When she decides to bury Polyneicês, it is
indeed an act of freewill, but one cannot disclaim the necessity of
this action by fate—a tragic, inherited curse.

Teiresias may help Creon decide to amend his law, but he also
serves a deeper purpose. Prophecy delivered by the gods implies
law. Creon, by refusing to bury Polyneicês, has gone against the
gods. Teiresias makes Creon's offense to the gods clear. He tells
of evil omens that he has witnessed, like the fighting birds and
the fat not catching on fire. These incidents portend Creon's
tragic destiny. His conflicts are now with both upper and nether
gods.

Creon's actions lead him into a world of suffering; for although
he recognizes his mistakes and tries to correct them, he is too
late. After taking care of Polyneicês's remains, he hurries to
Antigonê's tomb only to find his son and Antigonê dead. Upon
hearing the news of her son, his wife kills herself. This leaves
Creon in a world full of despair. With his son and wife dead he is
left to suffer and remember that universal laws are more powerful
than any he may ever decree.

The idea that runs throughout this play is that there will
always be certain forces and absolutes in life that must be
respected, and essentially will be because they are divine in
nature. When individuals do not look past the apparent causes and
fail to see the divine implications, they may work against these
laws. If the laws are offended, the wrath will be felt, not
necessarily from supernatural powers, but in the actions and
reactions of people who are strong enough or desperate enough to
follow their own hearts and live by their ideals. Life on earth
produces no human laws that are unbreakable. The only way to be
sure of not wreaking this havoc upon oneself is to understand and
respect the gods. By doing so one demonstrates respect for humanity
as well.

QUESTIONS FOR WRITING ABOUT DRAMA

In writing about the elements of drama, the following questions can help you focus your thinking and prepare yourself for writing analytical essays and papers. Use the questions as a checklist to guide you to important aspects of any play you read.

Plot

1. How does the playwright order the incidents of the play? What is the effect of this arrangement of incidents?
2. What is the central conflict of the play? What subsidiary conflicts are related to it?
3. Where is the play's climax? How is that climax prepared for dramatically? With what effects?

Character

4. To what extent are the play's characters—its *dramatis personae*—similar to actual people? In what ways are the play's characters different from actual people?
5. Using the characters' actions and speech, how would you evaluate their behavior? How are the characters related to one another dramatically and in other ways?
6. What function does each of the minor characters serve? If there is a chorus, what are its functions?

Dialogue

7. How would you characterize the voices of the various characters? How do you imagine them sounding in each of their major soliloquies or exchanges with other characters?
8. How does the dialogue advance the plot of the play? How does the dialogue establish setting?
9. How does the dialogue reveal character and motivation? Which particular speeches or other verbal exchanges are especially important for revealing character? Why?

Staging

10. What information is explicitly provided or implicitly suggested about how the play's characters are costumed? Do they change costumes at any point? Why? To what extent might such costume changes signal changes in attitude, behavior, or state of mind?
11. What objects or props in the play are emphasized? Which carry symbolic weight? How do you know?
12. What kinds of stage directions are provided? How do they help you understand the action? What do they contribute to your understanding of the characters?
13. How does the setting of the play contribute to its mood and theme? What do lighting and the use of sound contribute to the play's overall effects?

Theme

14. What is the central theme of the play? What subsidiary or ancillary themes support or accompany it?
15. How does your analysis of the elements of drama help you understand a play's theme?
16. Does the playwright convey the theme directly or indirectly? Can you identify one or more key passages in which the theme is made explicit? Or do you have to infer the theme from the implications of the play's dialogue and action, setting, staging, and character relationships?

Critical Perspectives

17. Among the critical perspectives you might bring to bear on the play, which one(s) seem(s) particularly useful for interpreting it? Why?
18. To what extent can you base your interpretation of the play on its language and details alone? To what extent is outside information about historical and biographical context necessary or helpful in understanding it?
19. To what extent does the play confirm or support your personal beliefs and values? To what extent is it in conflict with those beliefs and values? To what extent do your values and personal dispositions affect or influence your interpretation?
20. How do you imagine seeing the play staged would enhance your understanding, increase your emotional response, or otherwise alter your perception of the play?

QUESTIONS FOR IN-DEPTH READING

1. What general or overall thematic connections can you make between different works?
2. What stylistic similarities do you notice between and among different works?
3. How do the works differ in emphasis, tone, and style?
4. Once you have identified a writer's major preoccupations, place each work on a spectrum or a grid that represents the range of the writer's concerns.
5. What connections and disjunctions do you find between the following literary elements as they are embodied in different plays by the same writer?
   a. plot and structure
   b. character and characterization
   c. dialogue and monologue
   d. staging and setting
   e. theme and thought
6. To what extent are your responses to and perceptions of different works by the same writer shared by others—by critics, by classmates, and by the writers themselves?
7. What relationships and differences do you see between the work of one writer and that of another who shares similar thematic interests, stylistic proclivities, or cultural, religious, or social values?
8. Which of the critical perspectives (pages 1899–1922) seem most useful as analyti-

cal tools for approaching the body of work of particular writers?

THE GREEK THEATER: SOPHOCLES IN CONTEXT

foreground, and below the stage was the orchestra or dancing place for the chorus. Sometimes voicing a communal viewpoint, the chorus engaged the
common or communal viewpoint, the chorus engaged
the chorus in dialogue with the other characters, and sometimes the choragos
engaged in dialogue with the chorus.

An important function of the chorus was to mark the divisions between the
scenes of a play, when the chorus would recite and chant poetry. Lyric rather
than dramatic in form, these choral passages sometimes commented on the
action, sometimes generalized from it. They remained in Greek drama as vestiges of its origins in religious ritual. For modern readers these choric interludes
precede the play, affording respite from the gradually intensifying action and at
the same time providing a context for it.

with the third usually an observer who occasionally commented on the
debate occurring between the other two characters. Sometimes most of a scene
was given over to a debate between two characters, as, for example, in Antigone, with the...

CHAPTER TWENTY-TWO

The Greek Theater: Sophocles in Context

Greek drama developed from celebrations honoring Dionysus, the Greek god
of wine and fertility. These celebrations included choric dancing as part of the
religious ritual. It is possible that the leader of the chorus (the *choragos*) may have
engaged the rest of the chorus in responsive chanting. Legend suggests that the
poet Thespis introduced a speaker who, detached from the chorus, engaged in
dialogue with it. At that point drama was born. A second actor was added by
Aeschylus (524–456 B.C.) and a third by Sophocles (496?–406 B.C.). In Greek
drama no more than three characters appeared onstage together at one time,
although it was common for actors to double and triple parts, changing masks
for their multiple roles.

Greek plays were performed in huge outdoor amphitheaters capable of seating upwards of fourteen thousand people. Members of the audience were seated
in tiers that sloped up hillsides where the theaters were built; the hills echoed
the sound of the actors' voices. The actors wore masks that amplified their voices
in the manner of megaphones. The masks were large, and with the elevated
shoes sometimes worn by the actors, they projected the characters as larger-than-
life figures. The masks and elevated shoes restricted what the actors could do
and what the dramatist could expect of them. Subtle nuances of voice, of facial
expression, and of gesture were impossible. The playwright's language rather
than his stage business conveyed nuances of meaning and feeling.

The plays were performed on an elevated platform. Behind the acting area
was a scene building *(skene)* that functioned both as dressing room and as scenic

background, and below the stage was the *orchestra* or dancing place for the chorus. Standing between the actors and the audience, the chorus represented the common or communal viewpoint. Its leader, the choragos, sometimes engaged the chorus in dialogue with the other characters, and sometimes the choragos engaged in dialogue with the chorus itself.

An important function of the chorus was to mark the divisions between the scenes of a play, when the chorus would dance and chant poetry. Lyric rather than dramatic in form, these choral interludes sometimes commented on the action, sometimes generalized from it. They remained in Greek drama as vestiges of its origins in religious ritual. For modern readers these choric interludes pace the play, affording respite from the gradually intensifying action, and allowing time to ponder its implications.

The scenes of Greek plays usually consist of two, sometimes three characters with the third usually acting as an observer who occasionally comments on the debate occurring between the other two characters. Sometimes most of a scene is given over to a debate between two characters, as, for example, in Scene III of *Antigonê* with Haimon challenging Creon, his father, or Scene I of *Oedipus Rex* in which Oedipus argues with Teiresias. Some scenes, such as Scene II of *Antigonê,* include debates between Creon-Antigonê, Antigonê-Ismenê, Ismenê-Creon, and Creon-Choragos. The debates typically begin with leisurely speeches in which each character sets forth a position. The speeches are followed by rapid-fire dialogue *(stichomythia)* that brings the characters' antagonisms to a climax. This pattern is repeated throughout the play in something like a theme with variations, each scene usually developing a conflict. The accumulation of conflicts advances the action, leading to the inevitable tragic catastrophe.

Brevity is a characteristic of Greek tragedy: the plays are short with most having a playing time of roughly ninety minutes. Greek dramatists based their plays on myths that were familiar to the audience, which reduced the amount of time allotted for exposition. The plays also have a musical dimension, which, combined with the dancing and chanting of the chorus, increased the emotional impact of the ancient performances.

Of the three great Greek tragic dramatists, Sophocles is perhaps the most widely read today. Unlike his forebear Aeschylus, Sophocles focused his plays on human rather than religious concerns. As theater historian Peter Arnott has noted, he wrote "for a generation whose religious faith was waning."* His most famous plays center on a crisis and portray characters under duress. *Antigonê,* which takes place in Thebes, a city prostrated by war, turns on the difficult decisions both Antigonê and Creon must make. In *Oedipus Rex,* set against a background of the plague-stricken city of Thebes, Sophocles examines the behavior of Oedipus, who has been destined to murder his father and marry his mother. Though the two tragedies differ in the way their calamities ensue, both raise questions about inescapable human problems and portray characters confronting them with dignity and courage.

The following chart clarifies the relationships among the Theban royal families:

*Peter Arnott, *The Theatre in Its Time* (Boston: Little, Brown, 1981), page 51.

Labdacus (grandson of Kadmos, founder
of Thebes, father of Laïos)

Laïos = Iocastê

Oedipus = Iocastê

Eteoclês   Polyneicês   Ismenê   Antigonê

Iocastê was Creon's sister.

Creon = Eurydicê

Haimon   Megareus

The Athenian audience that watched performances of *Oedipus Tyrannus* (the original Greek title of the play) would have been familiar with Oedipus's story from sources as early as Homer's *Odyssey*. They would have known, for example, that Oedipus was fated to kill his father and marry his mother, and that to prevent this from happening, the infant Oedipus was given up by his parents, King Laius and Queen Jocasta, and left in the wilderness to die. This plan went awry when Oedipus was taken by a shepherd to Corinth, where he was adopted by a childless couple, King Polybus and Queen Merope. The Athenian audience would also have been aware of the reason for Oedipus's clubfoot (his feet had been pinned together as an infant). They would have known too of how upon hearing the oracle pronounce his grisly fate, Oedipus had left Corinth, where he had been raised as a prince, thinking that he had to get as far away as he could from Polybus and Merope, who he assumed were his biological parents. For the Athenian audience, then, and for later audiences who know the Oedipus story, the play's power resides less in the surprising twists and turns of its plot than in its relentless tragic action.

Oedipus Rex begins at the point when Thebes is undergoing a series of catastrophes, most important of which is a devastating plague. Prior to this series of events, Oedipus had saved Thebes from the Sphinx, a winged creature with the body of a lion and the head of a woman. The Sphinx had terrorized the city by devouring anyone who crossed its path and who was unable to answer its riddle correctly: What goes on four legs in the morning, two legs in the afternoon, and three legs in the evening? Oedipus solved the riddle by answering "Man." After he slew the Sphinx, he was given in reward the kingship of Thebes and the hand of its recently widowed queen, Jocasta. Unknown to Oedipus, but known to the Athenian audience, was the fact that Jocasta was his mother and that her recently slain husband, Laius, had been killed by Oedipus himself (who of course did not know who Laius really was). All this and more Oedipus soon discovers.

INTRODUCTION TO SOPHOCLES

[*c. 496–406 B.C.*]

The ancient Greek tragic dramatist Sophocles lived during the Athenian Golden Age, when the military power, artistic glory, and philosophical achievements of Athens were at their zenith. The most generally admired of the ancient Greek dramatists, Sophocles was also acknowledged for his musical skill and his handsome appearance.

Sophocles also held political and military positions. He served, for example, as a general with the Athenian statesman Pericles and was a commissioner of the Athenian empire. He was also a priest of Asclepius, the Greek god of healing and medicine. It is for his plays, however, that Sophocles is best known and most widely admired.

Sophocles wrote more than one hundred plays, only seven of which have survived. Many of his plays were entered in competition with plays by other Greek tragic dramatists, including Aeschylus and Euripides, whose work Sophocles surpassed on at least twenty occasions. More conservative than the other Greek dramatists who were his contemporaries, Sophocles emphasized the individual's uncompromising search for truth, which is evident in both *Oedipus Rex* and *Antigonê*.

SOPHOCLES

Oedipus Rex

AN ENGLISH VERSION BY DUDLEY FITTS AND ROBERT FITZGERALD

CHARACTERS

OEDIPUS

A PRIEST

CREON

TEIRESIAS

IOCASTÊ

MESSENGER

SHEPHERD OF LAÏOS

SECOND MESSENGER

CHORUS OF THEBAN ELDERS

Scene. *Before the palace of* OEDIPUS, *King of Thebes. A central door and two lateral doors open onto a platform which runs the length of the façade. On the platform, right and left, are altars; and three steps lead down into the "orchestra," or chorus-ground. At the beginning of the action these steps are crowded by* SUPPLIANTS *who have brought branches and chaplets of olive leaves and who lie in various attitudes of despair.* OEDIPUS *enters.*

PROLOGUE

OEDIPUS. My children, generations of the living
    In the line of Kadmos,° nursed at his ancient hearth:
    Why have you strewn yourselves before these altars
    In supplication, with your boughs and garlands?
    The breath of incense rises from the city   5
    With a sound of prayer and lamentation.
                              Children,
    I would not have you speak through messengers,
    And therefore I have come myself to hear you—
    I, Oedipus, who bear the famous name.
    (To a PRIEST.*)* You, there, since you are eldest in the company,   10
    Speak for them all, tell me what preys upon you,
    Whether you come in dread, or crave some blessing:
    Tell me, and never doubt that I will help you
    In every way I can; I should be heartless
    Were I not moved to find you suppliant here.   15
PRIEST. Great Oedipus, O powerful King of Thebes!
    You see how all the ages of our people
    Cling to your altar steps: here are boys
    Who can barely stand alone, and here are priests
    By weight of age, as I am a priest of God,   20
    And young men chosen from those yet unmarried;
    As for the others, all that multitude,
    They wait with olive chaplets in the squares,
    At the two shrines of Pallas,° and where Apollo°
    Speaks in the glowing embers.
                       Your own eyes   25
    Must tell you: Thebes is in her extremity
    And cannot lift her head from the surge of death.
    A rust consumes the buds and fruits of the earth;
    The herds are sick; children die unborn,
    And labor is vain. The god of plague and pyre   30
    Raids like detestable lightning through the city,
    And all the house of Kadmos is laid waste,

---

²**Kadmos** *legendary founder of Thebes.* ²⁴**Pallas** *Athena, goddess of wisdom.* ²⁴**Apollo** *god of poetry and prophecy.*

All emptied, and all darkened: Death alone
Battens upon the misery of Thebes.
You are not one of the immortal gods, we know;   35
Yet we have come to you to make our prayer
As to the man of all men best in adversity
And wisest in the ways of God. You saved us
From the Sphinx,° that flinty singer, and the tribute
We paid to her so long; yet you were never   40
Better informed than we, nor could we teach you:
It was some god breathed in you to set us free.

Therefore, O mighty King, we turn to you:
Find us our safety, find us a remedy,
Whether by counsel of the gods or the men.   45
A king of wisdom tested in the past
Can act in a time of troubles, and act well.
Noblest of men, restore
Life to your city! Think how all men call you
Liberator for your triumph long ago;   50
Ah, when your years of kingship are remembered,
Let them not say *We rose, but later fell*—
Keep the State from going down in the storm!
Once, years ago, with happy augury,
You brought us fortune; be the same again!   55
No man questions your power to rule the land:
But rule over men, not over a dead city!
Ships are only hulls, citadels are nothing,
When no life moves in the empty passageways.
OEDIPUS. Poor children! You may be sure I know   60
All that you longed for in your coming here.
I know that you are deathly sick; and yet,
Sick as you are, not one is as sick as I.
Each of you suffers in himself alone
His anguish, not another's; but my spirit   65
Groans for the city, for myself, for you.

I was not sleeping, you are not waking me.
No, I have been in tears for a long while
And in my restless thought walked many ways.
In all my search, I found one helpful course,   70
And that I have taken: I have sent Creon,
Son of Menoikeus, brother of the Queen,
To Delphi, Apollo's place of revelation,
To learn there, if he can,
What act or pledge of mine may save the city.   75
I have counted the days, and now, this very day,

---

[39]**The Sphinx**   *a monster with a lion's body, birds' wings, and woman's face.*

I am troubled, for he has overstayed his time.
What is he doing? He has been gone too long.
Yet whenever he comes back, I should do ill
To scant whatever hint the god may give. 80
PRIEST. It is a timely promise. At this instant
They tell me Creon is here.
OEDIPUS.   O Lord Apollo!
May his news be fair as his face is radiant!
PRIEST. It could not be otherwise: he is crowned with bay,
The chaplet is thick with berries.
OEDIPUS.   We shall soon know; 85
He is near enough to hear us now.

Enter CREON.

O Prince:
Brother: son of Menoikeus:
What answer do you bring us from the god?
CREON. It is favorable. I can tell you, great afflictions
Will turn out well, if they are taken well. 90
OEDIPUS. What was the oracle? These vague words
Leave me still hanging between hope and fear.
CREON. Is it your pleasure to hear me with all these
Gathered around us? I am prepared to speak,
But should we not go in?
OEDIPUS.   Let them all hear it. 95
It is for them I suffer, more than myself.
CREON. Then I will tell you what I heard at Delphi.

In plain words
The god commands us to expel from the land of Thebes
An old defilement that it seems we shelter. 100
It is a deathly thing, beyond expiation.
We must not let it feed upon us longer.
OEDIPUS. What defilement? How shall we rid ourselves of it?
CREON. By exile or death, blood for blood. It was
Murder that brought the plague-wind on the city. 105
OEDIPUS. Murder of whom? Surely the god has named him?
CREON. My lord: long ago Laïos was our king,
Before you came to govern us.
OEDIPUS.   I know;
I learned of him from others; I never saw him.
CREON. He was murdered; and Apollo commands us now 110
To take revenge upon whoever killed him.
OEDIPUS. Upon whom? Where are they? Where shall we find a clue
To solve that crime, after so many years?
CREON. Here in this land, he said.
                          If we make enquiry,
We may touch things that otherwise escape us. 115

OEDIPUS. Tell me: Was Laïos murdered in his house,
  Or in the fields, or in some foreign country?
CREON. He said he planned to make a pilgrimage.
  He did not come home again.
OEDIPUS.   And was there no one,
  No witness, no companion, to tell what happened?   120
CREON. They were all killed but one, and he got away
  So frightened that he could remember one thing only.
OEDIPUS. What was that one thing? One may be the key
  To everything, if we resolve to use it.
CREON. He said that a band of highwaymen attacked them,   125
  Outnumbered them, and overwhelmed the King.
OEDIPUS. Strange, that a highwayman should be so daring—
  Unless some faction here bribed him to do it.
CREON. We thought of that. But after Laïos' death
  New troubles arose and we had no avenger.   130
OEDIPUS. What troubles could prevent your hunting down the killers?
CREON. The riddling Sphinx's song
  Made us deaf to all mysteries but her own.
OEDIPUS. Then once more I must bring what is dark to light.
  It is most fitting that Apollo shows,   135
  As you do, this compunction for the dead.
  You shall see how I stand by you, as I should,
  To avenge the city and the city's god,
  And not as though it were for some distant friend,
  But for my own sake, to be rid of evil.   140
  Whoever killed King Laïos might—who knows?—
  Decide at any moment to kill me as well.
  By avenging the murdered king I protect myself.
  Come, then, my children: leave the altar steps,
  Lift up your olive boughs!
                              One of you go   145
  And summon the people of Kadmos to gather here.
  I will do all that I can; you may tell them that.

                    (*Exit a* PAGE.)

  So, with the help of God,
  We shall be saved—or else indeed we are lost.
PRIEST. Let us rise, children. It was for this we came,   150
  And now the King has promised it himself.
  Phoibos° has sent us an oracle; may he descend
  Himself to save us and drive out the plague.

Exeunt OEDIPUS *and* CREON *into the palace by the central door. The* PRIEST *and the*
SUPPLIANTS *disperse right and left. After a short pause the* CHORUS *enters the orchestra.*

---

[152]**Phoibos** *Phoebus Apollo, the sun god.*

PÁRODOS°

Strophe 1

CHORUS. What is God singing in his profound
Delphi of gold and shadow?
What oracle for Thebes, the sunwhipped city?
Fear unjoints me, the roots of my heart tremble.
Now I remember, O Healer, your power, and wonder;   5
Will you send doom like a sudden cloud, or weave it
Like nightfall of the past?
Speak, speak to us, issue of holy sound:
Dearest to our expectancy: be tender!

Antistrophe 1

Let me pray to Athenê, the immortal daughter of Zeus,   10
And to Artemis her sister
Who keeps her famous throne in the market ring,
And to Apollo, bowman at the far butts of heaven—

O gods, descend! Like three streams leap against
The fires of our grief, the fires of darkness;   15
Be swift to bring us rest!

As in the old time from the brilliant house
Of air you stepped to save us, come again!

Strophe 2

Now our afflictions have no end,
Now all our stricken host lies down   20
And no man fights off death with his mind;

The noble plowland bears no grain,
And groaning mothers cannot bear—

See, how our lives like birds take wing.
Like sparks that fly when a fire soars,   25
To the shore of the god of evening.

Antistrophe 2

The plague burns on, it is pitiless,
Though pallid children laden with death

°**Párodos**   sung as the chorus enters the stage area. Presumbly they sang the strophe while dancing from right to left and the antistrophe as they reversed direction.

Lie unwept in the stony ways,
And old gray women by every path   30
Flock to the strand about the altars

There to strike their breasts and cry
Worship of Phoibos in wailing prayers:
Be kind, God's golden child!

Strophe 3

There are no swords in this attack by fire,   35
No shields, but we are ringed with cries.
Send the besieger plunging from our homes
Into the vast sea-room of the Atlantic
Or into the waves that foam eastward of Thrace—
For the day ravages what the night spares—   40

Destroy our enemy, lord of the thunder!
Let him be riven by lightning from heaven!

Antistrophe 3

Phoibos Apollo, stretch the sun's bowstring,
That golden cord, until it sing for us,
Flashing arrows in heaven!
                          Artemis,° Huntress,   45
Race with flaring lights upon our mountains!
O scarlet god, O golden-banded brow,
O Theban Bacchos° in a storm of Maenads,°

             Enter OEDIPUS, *center.*

Whirl upon Death, that all the Undying hate!
Come with blinding cressets, come in joy!   50

SCENE I

OEDIPUS. Is this your prayer? It may be answered. Come,
    Listen to me, act as the crisis demands,
    And you shall have relief from all these evils.

     Until now I was a stranger to this tale,
    As I had been a stranger to the crime.   5

---

[45]**Artemis**   *goddess of hunting and chastity.*   [48]**Bacchos . . . Maenads**   *god of wine and revelry with his attendants.*

Could I track down the murderer without a clue?
But now, friends,
As one who became a citizen after the murder,
I make this proclamation to all Thebans:
If any man knows by whose hand Laïos, son of Labdakos,   10
Met his death, I direct that man to tell me everything,
No matter what he fears for having so long withheld it.
Let it stand as promised that no further trouble
Will come to him, but he may leave the land in safety.

Moreover: If anyone knows the murderer to be foreign,   15
Let him not keep silent: he shall have his reward from me.
However, if he does conceal it; if any man
Fearing for his friend or for himself disobeys this edict,
Hear what I propose to do:

I solemnly forbid the people of this country,   20
Where power and throne are mine, ever to receive that man
Or speak to him, no matter who he is, or let him
Join in sacrifice, lustration, or in prayer.
I decree that he be driven from every house,

Being, as he is, corruption itself to us: the Delphic   25
Voice of Zeus has pronounced this revelation.
Thus I associate myself with the oracle
And take the side of the murdered king.

As for the criminal, I pray to God—
Whether it be a lurking thief, or one of a number—   30
I pray that that man's life be consumed in evil and
    wretchedness.
And as for me, this curse applies no less
If it should turn out that the culprit is my guest here,
Sharing my hearth.
                    You have heard the penalty.
I lay it on you now to attend to this   35
For my sake, for Apollo's, for the sick
Sterile city that heaven has abandoned.
Suppose the oracle had given you no command:
Should this defilement go uncleansed for ever?
You should have found the murderer: your king,   40
A noble king, had been destroyed!
                    Now I,
Having the power that he held before me,
Having his bed, begetting children there
Upon his wife, as he would have, had he lived—
Their son would have been my children's brother,   45

If Laïos had had luck in fatherhood!
(But surely ill luck rushed upon his reign)—
I say I take the son's part, just as though
I were his son, to press the fight for him
And see it won! I'll find the hand that brought   50
Death to Labdakos' and Polydoros' child,
Heir of Kadmos' and Agenor's line.
And as for those who fail me,
May the gods deny them the fruit of the earth,
Fruit of the womb, and may they rot utterly!   55
Let them be wretched as we are wretched, and worse!

For you, for loyal Thebans, and for all
Who find my actions right, I pray the favor
Of justice, and of all the immortal gods.
CHORAGOS. Since I am under oath, my lord, I swear   60
I did not do the murder, I cannot name
The murderer. Might not the oracle
That has ordained the search tell where to find him?
OEDIPUS. An honest question. But no man in the world
Can make the gods do more than the gods will.   65
CHORAGOS. There is one last expedient—
OEDIPUS.   Tell me what it is.
Though it seem slight, you must not hold it back.
CHORAGOS. A lord clairvoyant to the lord Apollo,
As we all know, is the skilled Teiresias.
One might learn much about this from him, Oedipus.   70
OEDIPUS. I am not wasting time:
Creon spoke of this, and I have sent for him—
Twice, in fact; it is strange that he is not here.
CHORAGOS. The other matter—that old report—seems useless.
OEDIPUS. Tell me. I am interested in all reports.   75
CHORAGOS. The King was said to have been killed by highwaymen.
OEDIPUS. I know. But we have no witnesses to that.
CHORAGOS. If the killer can feel a particle of dread,
Your curse will bring him out of hiding!
OEDIPUS.   No.
The man who dared that act will fear no curse.   80

Enter the blind seer TEIRESIAS, *led by a* PAGE.

CHORAGOS. But there is one man who may detect the criminal.
This is Teiresias, this is the holy prophet
In whom, alone of all men, truth was born.
OEDIPUS. Teiresias: seer: student of mysteries,
Of all that's taught and all that no man tells,   85
Secrets of Heaven and secrets of the earth:

Blind though you are, you know the city lies
Sick with plague; and from this plague, my lord,
We find that you alone can guard or save us.

Possibly you did not hear the messengers? 90
Apollo, when we sent to him,
Sent us back word that this great pestilence
Would lift, but only if we established clearly
The identity of those who murdered Laïos.
They must be killed or exiled.
                                        Can you use 95
Birdflight or any art of divination
To purify yourself, and Thebes, and me
From this contagion? We are in your hands.
There is no fairer duty
Than that of helping others in distress. 100
TEIRESIAS. How dreadful knowledge of the truth can be
   When there's no help in truth! I knew this well,
   But did not act on it: else I should not have come.
OEDIPUS. What is troubling you? Why are your eyes so cold?
TEIRESIAS. Let me go home. Bear your own fate, and I'll 105
   Bear mine. It is better so: trust what I say.
OEDIPUS. What you say is ungracious and unhelpful
   To your native country. Do not refuse to speak.
TEIRESIAS. When it comes to speech, your own is neither temperate
   Nor opportune. I wish to be more prudent. 110
OEDIPUS. In God's name, we all beg you —
TEIRESIAS.   You are all ignorant.
   No; I will never tell you what I know.
   Now it is my misery; then, it would be yours.
OEDIPUS. What! You do know something, and will not tell us?
   You would betray us all and wreck the State? 115
TEIRESIAS. I do not intend to torture myself, or you.
   Why persist in asking? You will not persuade me.
OEDIPUS. What a wicked old man you are! You'd try a stone's
   Patience! Out with it! Have you no feeling at all?
TEIRESIAS. You call me unfeeling. If you could only see 120
   The nature of your own feelings . . .
OEDIPUS.   Why,
   Who would not feel as I do? Who could endure
   Your arrogance toward the city?
TEIRESIAS.   What does it matter!
   Whether I speak or not, it is bound to come.
OEDIPUS. Then, if "it" is bound to come, you are bound
   to tell me. 125
TEIRESIAS. No, I will not go on. Rage as you please.

OEDIPUS. Rage? Why not!
                And I'll tell you what I think:
  You planned it, you had it done, you all but
  Killed him with your own hands: if you had eyes,
  I'd say the crime was yours, and yours alone.   130
TEIRESIAS. So? I charge you, then,
  Abide by the proclamation you have made:
  From this day forth
  Never speak again to these men or to me;
  You yourself are the pollution of this country.   135
OEDIPUS. You dare say that! Can you possibly think you have
  Some way of going free, after such insolence?
TEIRESIAS. I have gone free. It is the truth sustains me.
OEDIPUS. Who taught you shamelessness? It was not your craft.
TEIRESIAS. You did. You made me speak. I did not want to.   140
OEDIPUS. Speak what? Let me hear it again more clearly.
TEIRESIAS. Was it not clear before? Are you tempting me?
OEDIPUS. I did not understand it. Say it again.
TEIRESIAS. I say that you are the murderer whom you seek.
OEDIPUS. Now twice you have spat out infamy. You'll
      pay for it!   145
TEIRESIAS. Would you care for more? Do you wish to be really angry?
OEDIPUS. Say what you will. Whatever you say is worthless.
TEIRESIAS. I say you live in hideous shame with those
  Most dear to you. You cannot see the evil.
OEDIPUS. It seems you can go on mouthing like this for ever.   150
TEIRESIAS. I can, if there is power in truth.
OEDIPUS.   There is:
  But not for you, not for you,
  You sightless, witless, senseless, mad old man!
TEIRESIAS. You are the madman. There is no one here
  Who will not curse you soon, as you curse me.   155
OEDIPUS. You child of endless night! You cannot hurt me
  Or any other man who sees the sun.
TEIRESIAS. True: it is not from me your fate will come.
  That lies within Apollo's competence,
  As it is his concern.
OEDIPUS.   Tell me: 160
  Are you speaking for Creon, or for yourself?
TEIRESIAS. Creon is no threat. You weave your own doom.
OEDIPUS. Wealth, power, craft of statesmanship!
  Kingly position, everywhere admired!
  What savage envy is stored up against these,   165
  If Creon, whom I trusted, Creon my friend,
  For this great office which the city once
  Put in my hands unsought—if for this power
  Creon desires in secret to destroy me!

He has brought this decrepit fortune-teller, this 170
Collector of dirty pennies, this prophet fraud—
Why, he is no more clairvoyant than I am!

Tell us:

Has your mystic mummery ever approached the truth?
When that hellcat the Sphinx was performing here,
What help were you to these people? 175
Her magic was not for the first man who came along:
It demanded a real exorcist. Your birds—
What good were they? or the gods, for the matter of that?
But I came by,
Oedipus, the simple man, who knows nothing— 180
I thought it out for myself, no birds helped me!
And this is the man you think you can destroy,
That you may be close to Creon when he's king!
Well, you and your friend Creon, it seems to me,
Will suffer most. If you were not an old man, 185
You would have paid already for your plot.

CHORAGOS. We cannot see that his words or yours
Have been spoken except in anger, Oedipus,
And of anger we have no need. How can God's will
Be accomplished best? That is what most concerns us. 190

TEIRESIAS. You are a king. But where argument's concerned
I am your man, as much a king as you.
I am not your servant, but Apollo's.
I have no need of Creon to speak for me.

Listen to me. You mock my blindness, do you? 195
But I say that you, with both your eyes, are blind:
You cannot see the wretchedness of your life,
Nor in whose house you live, no, nor with whom.
Who are your father and mother? Can you tell me?
You do not even know the blind wrongs 200
That you have done them, on earth and in the world below.
But the double lash of your parents' curse will whip you
Out of this land some day, with only night
Upon your precious eyes.
Your cries then—where will they not be heard? 205
What fastness of Kithairon will not echo them?
And that bridal-descant of yours—you'll know it then,
The song they sang when you came here to Thebes
And found your misguided berthing.
All this, and more, that you cannot guess at now, 210
Will bring you to yourself among your children.
Be angry, then. Curse Creon. Curse my words.
I tell you, no man that walks upon the earth
Shall be rooted out more horribly than you.

OEDIPUS. Am I to bear this from him?—Damnation   215
    Take you! Out of this place! Out of my sight!
TEIRESIAS. I would not have come at all if you had not asked me.
OEDIPUS. Could I have told that you'd talk nonsense, that
    You'd come here to make a fool of yourself, and of me?
TEIRESIAS. A fool? Your parents thought me sane enough.   220
OEDIPUS. My parents again!—Wait: who were my parents?
TEIRESIAS. This day will give you a father, and break your heart.
OEDIPUS. Your infantile riddles! Your damned abracadabra!
TEIRESIAS. You were a great man once at solving riddles.
OEDIPUS. Mock me with that if you like; you will find it true.   225
TEIRESIAS. It was true enough. It brought about your ruin.
OEDIPUS. But if it saved this town?
TEIRESIAS *(to the* PAGE*)*. Boy, give me your hand.
OEDIPUS. Yes, boy; lead him away.
                              —While you are here
    We can do nothing. Go; leave us in peace.
TEIRESIAS. I will go when I have said what I have to say.   230
    How can you hurt me? And I tell you again:
    The man you have been looking for all this time,
    The damned man, the murderer of Laïos,
    That man is in Thebes. To your mind he is foreignborn,
    But it will soon be shown that he is a Theban,   235
    A revelation that will fail to please.
                              A blind man,
    Who has his eyes now; a penniless man, who is rich now;
    And he will go tapping the strange earth with his staff;
    To the children with whom he lives now he will be
    Brother and father—the very same; to her   240
    Who bore him, son and husband—the very same
    Who came to his father's bed, wet with his father's blood.

    Enough. Go think that over.
    If later you find error in what I have said,
    You may say that I have no skill in prophecy.   245

        Exit TEIRESIAS, *led by his* PAGE. OEDIPUS *goes into the palace.*

                        ODE I°

Strophe 1

CHORUS. The Delphic stone of prophecies
        Remembers ancient regicide

°**Ode**   *a poetic song sung by the chorus.*

And a still bloody hand.
That killer's hour of flight has come.
He must be stronger than riderless   5
Coursers of untiring wind,
For the son of Zeus° armed with his father's thunder
Leaps in lightning after him;
And the Furies° follow him, the sad Furies.

Antistrophe 1

Holy Parnossos' peak of snow   10
Flashes and blinds that secret man,
That all shall hunt him down:
Though he may roam the forest shade
Like a bull gone wild from pasture
To rage through glooms of stone.   15
Doom comes down on him; flight will not avail him;
For the world's heart calls him desolate,
And the immortal Furies follow, for ever follow.

Strophe 2

But now a wilder thing is heard
From the old man skilled at hearing Fate in the
    wingbeat of a bird.   20
Bewildered as a blown bird, my soul hovers and cannot find
Foothold in this debate, or any reason or rest of mind.
But no man ever brought—none can bring
Proof of strife between Thebes' royal house,
Labdakos' line,° and the son of Polybos;°   25
And never until now has any man brought word
Of Laïos' dark death staining Oedipus the King.

Antistrophe 2

Divine Zeus and Apollo hold
Perfect intelligence alone of all tales ever told;
And well though this diviner works, he works in his own night;   30
No man can judge that rough unknown or trust in second sight,
For wisdom changes hands among the wise.
Shall I believe my great lord criminal
At a raging word that a blind old man let fall?
I saw him, when the carrion woman faced him of old,   35
Prove his heroic mind! These evil words are lies.

---

[7]*son of Zeus* Apollo. [9]*the Furies* *three women spirits who punished evildoers.* [25]***Labdakos' line***
his descendants. [25]***Polybos*** *King of Corinth who adopted Oedipus as an infant.*

SCENE II

CREON. Men of Thebes:
  I am told that heavy accusations
  Have been brought against me by King Oedipus.
  I am not the kind of man to bear this tamely.

  If in these present difficulties   5
  He holds me accountable for any harm to him
  Through anything I have said or done—why, then,
  I do not value life in this dishonor.
  It is not as though this rumor touched upon
  Some private indiscretion. The matter is grave.   10
  The fact is that I am being called disloyal
  To the State, to my fellow citizens, to my friends.
CHORAGOS. He may have spoken in anger, not from his mind.
CREON. But did you not hear him say I was the one
  Who seduced the old prophet into lying?   15
CHORAGOS. The thing was said; I do not know how seriously.
CREON. But you were watching him! Were his eyes steady?
  Did he look like a man in his right mind?
CHORAGOS.   I do not know.
  I cannot judge the behavior of great men.
  But here is the King himself.

                         Enter OEDIPUS.

OEDIPUS.   So you dared come back.   20
  Why? How brazen of you to come to my house,
  You murderer!
                 Do you think I do not know
  That you plotted to kill me, plotted to steal my throne?
  Tell me, in God's name: am I coward, a fool,
  That you should dream you could accomplish this?   25
  A fool who could not see your slippery game?
  A coward, not to fight back when I saw it?
  You are the fool, Creon, are you not? hoping
  Without support or friends to get a throne?
  Thrones may be won or bought: you could do neither.   30
CREON. Now listen to me. You have talked; let me talk, too.
  You cannot judge unless you know the facts.
OEDIPUS. You speak well: there is one fact; but I find it hard
  To learn from the deadliest enemy I have.
CREON. That above all I must dispute with you.   35
OEDIPUS. That above all I will not hear you deny.
CREON. If you think there is anything good in being stubborn
  Against all reason, then I say you are wrong.

OEDIPUS. If you think a man can sin against his own kind
    And not be punished for it, I say you are mad.   40

CREON. I agree. But tell me: what have I done to you?

OEDIPUS. You advised me to send for that wizard, did you not?

CREON. I did. I should do it again.

OEDIPUS.   Very well. Now tell me:
    How long has it been since Laïos—

CREON.   What of Laïos?

OEDIPUS. Since he vanished in that onset by the road?   45

CREON. It was long ago, a long time.

OEDIPUS.   And this prophet,
    Was he practicing here then?

CREON.   He was; and with honor, as now.

OEDIPUS. Did he speak of me at that time?

CREON.   He never did;
    At least, not when I was present.

OEDIPUS.   But . . . the enquiry?
    I suppose you held one?

CREON.   We did, but we learned nothing.   50

OEDIPUS. Why did the prophet not speak against me then?

CREON. I do not know; and I am the kind of man
    Who holds his tongue when he has no facts to go on.

OEDIPUS. There's one fact that you know, and you could tell it.

CREON. What fact is that? If I know it, you shall have it.   55

OEDIPUS. If he were not involved with you, he could not say
    That it was I who murdered Laïos.

CREON. If he says that, you are the one that knows it!—
    But now it is my turn to question you.

OEDIPUS. Put your questions. I am no murderer.   60

CREON. First, then: You married my sister?

OEDIPUS.   I married your sister.

CREON. And you rule the kingdom equally with her?

OEDIPUS. Everything that she wants she has from me.

CREON. And I am the third, equal to both of you?

OEDIPUS. That is why I call you a bad friend.   65

CREON. No. Reason it out, as I have done.
    Think of this first. Would any sane man prefer
    Power, with all a king's anxieties,
    To that same power and the grace of sleep?
    Certainly not I.   70
    I have never longed for the king's power—only his rights.
    Would any wise man differ from me in this?
    As matters stand, I have my way in everything
    With your consent, and no responsibilities.
    If I were king, I should be a slave to policy.   75
    How could I desire a scepter more
    Than what is now mine—untroubled influence?

Best speech [handwritten annotation]

No, I have not gone mad; I need no honors,
Except those with the perquisites I have now.
I am welcome everywhere; every man salutes me,   80
And those who want your favor seek my ear,
Since I know how to manage what they ask.
Should I exchange this ease for that anxiety?
Besides, no sober mind is treasonable.
I hate anarchy   85
And never would deal with any man who likes it.

Test what I have said. Go to the priestess
At Delphi, ask if I quoted her correctly.
And as for this other thing: if I am found
Guilty of treason with Teiresias,   90
Then sentence me to death! You have my word
It is a sentence I should cast my vote for—
But not without evidence!

               You do wrong
When you take good men for bad, bad men for good.
A true friend thrown aside—why, life itself   95
Is not more precious!

             In time you will know this well:
For time, and time alone, will show the just man,
Though scoundrels are discovered in a day.
CHORAGOS. This is well said, and a prudent man would ponder it.
    Judgments too quickly formed are dangerous.   100
OEDIPUS. But is he not quick in his duplicity?
    And shall I not be quick to parry him?
    Would you have me stand still, hold my peace, and let
    This man win everything, through my inaction?
CREON. And you want—what is it, then? To banish me?   105
OEDIPUS. No, not exile. It is your death I want,
    So that all the world may see what treason means.
CREON. You will persist, then? You will not believe me?
OEDIPUS. How can I believe you?
CREON.   Then you are a fool.
OEDIPUS. To save myself?
CREON.   In justice, think of me.   110
OEDIPUS. You are evil incarnate.
CREON.   But suppose that you are wrong?
OEDIPUS. Still I must rule.
CREON.   But not if you rule badly.
OEDIPUS. O city, city!
CREON.   It is my city, too!
CHORAGOS. Now, my lords, be still. I see the Queen,
    Iocastê, coming from her palace chambers;   115

And it is time she came, for the sake of you both.
This dreadful quarrel can be resolved through her.

Enter IOCASTÊ.

IOCASTÊ. Poor foolish men, what wicked din is this?
With Thebes sick to death, is it not shameful
That you should rake some private quarrel up?　　　　　120

(To OEDIPUS.*)*

Come into the house.
　　　　　　　　　—And you, Creon, go now:
Let us have no more of this tumult over nothing.
CREON. Nothing? No, sister: what your husband plans for me
Is one of two great evils: exile or death.
OEDIPUS. He is right.
　　　　　　　　Why, woman, I have caught him squarely　　　　125
Plotting against my life.
CREON.　　　　　　　　No! Let me die
Accurst if ever I have wished you harm!
IOCASTÊ. Ah, believe it, Oedipus!
In the name of the gods, respect this oath of his
For my sake, for the sake of these people here!　　　　　130

Strophe 1

CHORAGOS. Open your mind to her, my lord. Be ruled by her, I beg you!
OEDIPUS. What would you have me do?
CHORAGOS. Respect Creon's word. He has never spoken like a fool,
And now he has sworn an oath.
OEDIPUS. You know what you ask?
CHORAGOS.　　　　　　　　　I do.
OEDIPUS.　　　　　　　　　　　Speak on, then.
CHORAGOS. A friend so sworn should not be baited so,　　　　　135
In blind malice, and without final proof.
OEDIPUS. You are aware, I hope, that what you say
Means death for me, or exile at the least.

Strophe 2

CHORAGOS. No, I swear by Helios, first in Heaven!
May I die friendless and accurst,　　　　　140
The worst of deaths, if ever I meant that!
　　　　It is the withering fields
　　　　　　That hurt my sick heart:
　　　　Must we bear all these ills,
　　　　　　And now your bad blood as well?　　　　　145

OEDIPUS. Then let him go. And let me die, if I must,
  Or be driven by him in shame from the land of Thebes.
  It is your unhappiness, and not his talk,
  That touches me.
                      As for him—
  Wherever he is, I will hate him as long as I live. 150
CREON. Ugly in yielding, as you were ugly in rage!
  Natures like yours chiefly torment themselves.
OEDIPUS. Can you not go? Can you not leave me?
CREON.   I can.
  You do not know me; but the city knows me,
  And in its eyes I am just, if not in yours. 155

(Exit CREON.*)*

Antistrophe 1

CHORAGOS. Lady Iocastê, did you not ask the King
  to go to his chambers?
IOCASTÊ. First tell me what has happened.
CHORAGOS. There was suspicion without evidence; yet it rankled
  As even false charges will.
IOCASTÊ.   On both sides?
CHORAGOS.   On both.
IOCASTÊ.   But what was said?
CHORAGOS. Oh let it rest, let it be done with! 160
  Have we not suffered enough?
OEDIPUS. You see to what your decency has brought you:
  You have made difficulties where my heart saw none.

Antistrophe 2

CHORAGOS. Oedipus, it is not once only I have told you—
  You must know I should count myself unwise 165
  To the point of madness, should I now forsake you—
      You, under whose hand,
        In the storm of another time,
      Our dear land sailed out free.
        But now stand fast at the helm! 170
IOCASTÊ. In God's name, Oedipus, inform your wife as well:
  Why are you so set in this hard anger?
OEDIPUS. I will tell you, for none of these men deserves
  My confidence as you do. It is Creon's work,
  His treachery, his plotting against me. 175
IOCASTÊ. Go on, if you can make this clear to me.
OEDIPUS. He charges me with the murder of Laïos.
IOCASTÊ. Has he some knowledge? Or does he speak from hearsay?
OEDIPUS. He would not commit himself to such a charge,

But he has brought in that damnable soothsayer 180
To tell his story.

IOCASTÊ.   Set your mind at rest.
If it is a question of soothsayers, I tell you
That you will find no man whose craft gives knowledge
Of the unknowable.

                    Here is my proof:

An oracle was reported to Laïos once 185
(I will not say from Phoibos himself, but from
His appointed ministers, at any rate)
That his doom would be death at the hands of his own son—
His son, born of his flesh and of mine!

Now, you remember the story: Laïos was killed 190
By marauding strangers where three highways meet;
But his child had not been three days in this world
Before the King had pierced the baby's ankles
And left him to die on a lonely mountainside.

Thus, Apollo never caused that child 195
To kill his father, and it was not Laïos' fate
To die at the hands of his son, as he had feared.
This is what prophets and prophecies are worth!
Have no dread of them.

                    It is God himself
Who can show us what he wills, in his own way. 200

OEDIPUS. How strange a shadowy memory crossed my mind,
    Just now while you were speaking; it chilled my heart.
IOCASTÊ. What do you mean? What memory do you speak of?
OEDIPUS. If I understand you, Laïos was killed
    At a place where three roads meet.
IOCASTÊ.   So it was said; 205
    We have no later story.
OEDIPUS.   Where did it happen?
IOCASTÊ. Phokis, it is called: at a place where the Theban Way
    Divides into the roads towards Delphi and Daulia.
OEDIPUS. When?
IOCASTÊ.   We had the news not long before you came
    And proved the right to your succession here. 210
OEDIPUS. Ah, what net has God been weaving for me?
IOCASTÊ. Oedipus! Why does this trouble you?
OEDIPUS.   Do not ask me yet.
    First, tell me how Laïos looked, and tell me
    How old he was.
IOCASTÊ.   He was tall, his hair just touched
    With white; his form was not unlike your own. 215

OEDIPUS. I think that I myself may be accurst
   By my own ignorant edict.
IOCASTÊ.   You speak strangely.
   It makes me tremble to look at you, my King.
OEDIPUS. I am not sure that the blind man cannot see.
   But I should know better if you were to tell me—   220
IOCASTÊ. Anything—though I dread to hear you ask it.
OEDIPUS. Was the King lightly escorted, or did he ride
   With a large company, as a ruler should?
IOCASTÊ. There were five men with him in all: one was a herald;
   And a single chariot, which he was driving.   225
OEDIPUS. Alas, that makes it plain enough!
                                   But who—
   Who told you how it happened?
IOCASTÊ.   A household servant,
   The only one to escape.
OEDIPUS.   And is he still
   A servant of ours?
IOCASTÊ.   No; for when he came back at last
   And found you enthroned in the place of the dead king,   230
   He came to me, touched my hand with his, and begged
   That I would send him away to the frontier district
   Where only the shepherds go—
   As far away from the city as I could send him.
   I granted his prayer; for although the man was a slave,   235
   He had earned more than this favor at my hands.
OEDIPUS. Can he be called back quickly?
IOCASTÊ.   Easily.
   But why?
OEDIPUS.   I have taken too much upon myself
   Without enquiry; therefore I wish to consult him.
IOCASTÊ. Then he shall come.
                       But am I not one also   240
   To whom you might confide these fears of yours!
OEDIPUS. That is your right; it will not be denied you,
   Now least of all; for I have reached a pitch
   Of wild foreboding. Is there anyone
   To whom I should sooner speak?   245
   Polybos of Corinth is my father.
   My mother is a Dorian: Meropê.
   I grew up chief among the men of Corinth
   Until a strange thing happened—
   Not worth my passion, it may be, but strange.   250

   At a feast, a drunken man maundering in his cups
   Cries out that I am not my father's son!

I contained myself that night, though I felt anger
And a sinking heart. The next day I visited
My father and mother, and questioned them. They stormed, 255
Calling it all the slanderous rant of a fool;
And this relieved me. Yet the suspicion
Remained always aching in my mind;
I knew there was talk; I could not rest;
And finally, saying nothing to my parents, 260
I went to the shrine at Delphi.
The god dismissed my question without reply;
He spoke of other things.
                         Some were clear,
Full of wretchedness, dreadful, unbearable:
As, that I should lie with my own mother, breed 265
Children from whom all men would turn their eyes;
And that I should be my father's murderer.

I heard all this, and fled. And from that day
Corinth to me was only in the stars
Descending in that quarter of the sky, 270
As I wandered farther and farther on my way
To a land where I should never see the evil
Sung by the oracle. And I came to this country
Where, so you say, King Laïos was killed.
I will tell you all that happened there, my lady. 275

There were three highways
Coming together at a place I passed;
And there a herald came towards me, and a chariot
Drawn by horses, with a man such as you describe
Seated in it. The groom leading the horses 280
Forced me off the road at his lord's command;
But as this charioteer lurched over towards me
I struck him in my rage. The old man saw me
And brought his double goad down upon my head
As I came abreast.
                   He was paid back, and more! 285
Swinging my club in this right hand I knocked him
Out of his car, and he rolled on the ground.
                                    I killed him.

I killed them all.
Now if that stranger and Laïos were—kin,
Where is a man more miserable than I?
More hated by the gods? Citizen and alien alike 290
Must never shelter me or speak to me—

I must be shunned by all.

And I myself

Pronounced this malediction upon myself!

Think of it: I have touched you with these hands,   295
These hands that killed your husband. What defilement!

Am I all evil, then? It must be so,
Since I must flee from Thebes, yet never again
See my own countrymen, my own country,
For fear of joining my mother in marriage   300
And killing Polybos, my father.

Ah,

If I was created so, born to this fate,
Who could deny the savagery of God?

O holy majesty of heavenly powers!
May I never see that day! Never!   305
Rather let me vanish from the race of men
Than know the abomination destined me!

CHORAGOS. We too, my lord, have felt dismay at this.
But there is hope: you have yet to hear the shepherd.

OEDIPUS. Indeed, I fear no other hope is left me.   310

IOCASTÊ. What do you hope from him when he comes?

OEDIPUS.   This much:
If his account of the murder tallies with yours,
Then I am cleared.

IOCASTÊ.   What was it that I said
Of such importance?

OEDIPUS.   Why, "marauders," you said,
Killed the King, according to this man's story.   315
If he maintains that still, if there were several,
Clearly the guilt is not mine: I was alone.
But if he says one man, singlehanded, did it,
Then the evidence all points to me.

IOCASTÊ. You may be sure that he said there were several;   320
And can he call back that story now? He cannot.
The whole city heard it as plainly as I.
But suppose he alters some detail of it:
He cannot ever show that Laïos' death
Fulfilled the oracle: for Apollo said   325
My child was doomed to kill him; and my child—
Poor baby!—it was my child that died first.

No. From now on, where oracles are concerned,
I would not waste a second thought on any.

OEDIPUS. You may be right.

But come: let someone go   330

For the shepherd at once. This matter must be settled.

IOCASTÊ. I will send for him.

I would not wish to cross you in anything,

And surely not in this.—Let us go in.

Exeunt into the palace.

ODE II

Strophe 1

CHORUS. Let me be reverent in the ways of right,
   Lowly the paths I journey on;
   Let all my words and actions keep
   The laws of the pure universe
   From highest Heaven handed down.   5
   For Heaven is their bright nurse,
   Those generations of the realms of light;
   Ah, never of mortal kind were they begot,
   Nor are they slaves of memory, lost in sleep:
   Their Father is greater than Time, and ages not.   10

Antistrophe 1

   The tyrant is a child of Pride = Hubris
   Who drinks from his great sickening cup
   Recklessness and vanity,
   Until from his high crest headlong
   He plummets to the dust of hope.   15
   That strong man is not strong.
   But let no fair ambition be denied;
   May God protect the wrestler for the State
   In government, in comely policy,
   Who will fear God, and on His ordinance wait.   20

Strophe 2

   Haughtiness and the high hand of disdain
   Tempt and outrage God's holy law;
   And any mortal who dares hold
   No immortal Power in awe
   Will be caught up in a net of pain: 25
   The price for which his levity is sold.

Let each man take due earnings, then,
And keep his hands from holy things,
And from blasphemy stand apart—
Else the crackling blast of heaven   30
Blows on his head, and on his desperate heart;
Though fools will honor impious men,
In their cities no tragic poet sings.

Antistrophe 2

Shall we lose faith in Delphi's obscurities,
We who have heard the world's core   35
Discredited, and the sacred wood
Of Zeus at Elis praised no more?
The deeds and the strange prophecies
Must make a pattern yet to be understood.
Zeus, if indeed you are lord of all,   40
Throned in light over night and day,
Mirror this in your endless mind:
Our masters call the oracle
Words on the wind, and the Delphic vision blind!
Their hearts no longer know Apollo,   45
And reverence for the gods has died away.

SCENE III

Enter IOCASTÊ.

IOCASTÊ. Princes of Thebes, it has occurred to me
To visit the altars of the gods, bearing
These branches as a suppliant, and this incense.
Our King is not himself: his noble soul
Is overwrought with fantasies of dread,   5
Else he would consider
The new prophecies in the light of the old.
He will listen to any voice that speaks disaster,
And my advice goes for nothing.

                              She approaches the altar, right.
                              To you, then, Apollo,
Lycean lord, since you are nearest, I turn in prayer.   10
Receive these offerings, and grant us deliverance
From defilement. Our hearts are heavy with fear
When we see our leader distracted, as helpless sailors
Are terrified by the confusion of their helmsman.

Enter MESSENGER.

MESSENGER. Friends, no doubt you can direct me: 15
   Where shall I find the house of Oedipus,
   Or, better still, where is the King himself?
CHORAGOS. It is this very place, stranger; he is inside.
   This is his wife and mother of his children.
MESSENGER. I wish her happiness in a happy house,   20
   Blest in all the fulfillment of her marriage.
IOCASTÊ. I wish as much for you: your courtesy
   Deserves a like good fortune. But now, tell me:
   Why have you come? What have you to say to us?
MESSENGER. Good news, my lady, for your house and your husband.   25
IOCASTÊ. What news? Who sent you here?
MESSENGER.   I am from Corinth.
   The news I bring ought to mean joy for you,
   Though it may be you will find some grief in it.
IOCASTÊ. What is it? How can it touch us in both ways?
MESSENGER. The people of Corinth, they say,   30
   Intend to call Oedipus to be their king.
IOCASTÊ. But old Polybos—is he not reigning still?
MESSENGER. No. Death holds him in his sepulchre.
IOCASTÊ. What are you saying? Polybos is dead?
MESSENGER. If I am not telling the truth, may I die myself.   35
IOCASTÊ (*to a* MAIDSERVANT). Go in, go quickly; tell this to your master.

   O riddlers of God's will, where are you now!
   This was the man whom Oedipus, long ago,
   Feared so, fled so, in dread of destroying him—
   But it was another fate by which he died.   40

Enter OEDIPUS, *center.*

OEDIPUS. Dearest Iocastê, why have you sent for me?
IOCASTÊ. Listen to what this man says, and then tell me
   What has become of the solemn prophecies.
OEDIPUS. Who is this man? What is his news for me?
IOCASTÊ. He has come from Corinth to announce your father's death!   45
OEDIPUS. Is it true, stranger? Tell me in your own words.
MESSENGER. I cannot say it more clearly: the King is dead.
OEDIPUS. Was it by treason? Or by an attack of illness?
MESSENGER. A little thing brings old men to their rest.
OEDIPUS. It was sickness, then?
MESSENGER.   Yes, and his many years.   50
OEDIPUS. Ah!
   Why should a man respect the Pythian hearth,° or

---

⁵²**Pythian hearth**   *Delphi, also called Pytho because a large dragon, the Python, had guarded the chasm at Delphi until Apollo killed it and established his oracle on the site.*

Give heed to the birds that jangle above his head?
They prophesied that I should kill Polybos,
Kill my own father; but he is dead and buried,   55
And I am here—I never touched him, never,
Unless he died in grief for my departure,
And thus, in a sense, through me. No. Polybos
Has packed the oracles off with him underground.
They are empty words.

IOCASTÊ.   Had I not told you so?   60
OEDIPUS. You had; it was my faint heart that betrayed me.
IOCASTÊ. From now on never think of those things again.
OEDIPUS. And yet—must I not fear my mother's bed?
IOCASTÊ. Why should anyone in this world be afraid,
   Since Fate rules us and nothing can be foreseen?   65
   A man should live only for the present day.
   Have no more fear of sleeping with your mother:
   How many men, in dreams, have lain with their mothers!
   No reasonable man is troubled by such things.
OEDIPUS. That is true; only—   70
   If only my mother were not still alive!
   But she is alive. I cannot help my dread.
IOCASTÊ. Yet this news of your father's death is wonderful.
OEDIPUS. Wonderful. But I fear the living woman.
MESSENGER. Tell me, who is this woman that you fear?   75
OEDIPUS. It is Meropê, man; the wife of King Polybos.
MESSENGER. Meropê? Why should you be afraid of her?
OEDIPUS. An oracle of the gods, a dreadful saying.
MESSENGER. Can you tell me about it or are you sworn to silence?
OEDIPUS. I can tell you, and I will.   80
   Apollo said through his prophet that I was the man
   Who should marry his own mother, shed his father's blood
   With his own hands. And so, for all these years
   I have kept clear of Corinth, and no harm has come—
   Though it would have been sweet to see my parents again.   85
MESSENGER. And is this the fear that drove you out of Corinth?
OEDIPUS. Would you have me kill my father?
MESSENGER.   As for that
   You must be reassured by the news I gave you.
OEDIPUS. If you could reassure me, I would reward you.
MESSENGER. I had that in mind, I will confess: I thought   90
   I could count on you when you returned to Corinth.
OEDIPUS. No: I will never go near my parents again.
MESSENGER. Ah, son, you still do not know what you are doing—
OEDIPUS. What do you mean? In the name of God tell me!
MESSENGER.—If these are your reasons for not going home.   95
OEDIPUS. I tell you, I fear the oracle may come true.
MESSENGER. And guilt may come upon you through your parents?

OEDIPUS. That is the dread that is always in my heart.

MESSENGER. Can you not see that all your fears are groundless?

OEDIPUS. How can you say that? They are my parents, surely?   100

MESSENGER. Polybos was not your father.

OEDIPUS.   Not my father?

MESSENGER. No more your father than the man speaking to you.

OEDIPUS. But you are nothing to me!

MESSENGER.   Neither was he.

OEDIPUS. Then why did he call me son?

MESSENGER.   I will tell you: 105

  Long ago he had you from my hands, as a gift.

OEDIPUS. Then how could he love me so, if I was not his?

MESSENGER. He had no children, and his heart turned to you.

OEDIPUS. What of you? Did you buy me? Did you find me by chance?

MESSENGER. I came upon you in the crooked pass of Kithairon.

OEDIPUS. And what were you doing there?

MESSENGER.   Tending my flocks.   110

OEDIPUS. A wandering shepherd?

MESSENGER.   But your savior, son, that day.

OEDIPUS. From what did you save me?

MESSENGER.   Your ankles should tell you that.

OEDIPUS. Ah, stranger, why do you speak of that childhood pain?

MESSENGER. I cut the bonds that tied your ankles together.

OEDIPUS. I have had the mark as long as I can remember.   115

MESSENGER. That was why you were given the name you bear.°

OEDIPUS. God! Was it my father or my mother who did it?

  Tell me!

MESSENGER. I do not know. The man who gave you to me

  Can tell you better than I.   120

OEDIPUS. It was not you that found me, but another?

MESSENGER. It was another shepherd gave you to me.

OEDIPUS. Who was he? Can you tell me who he was?

MESSENGER. I think he was said to be one of Laïos' people.

OEDIPUS. You mean the Laïos who was king here years ago?   125

MESSENGER. Yes; King Laïos; and the man was one of his herdsmen.

OEDIPUS. Is he still alive? Can I see him?

MESSENGER.   These men here

  Know best about such things.

OEDIPUS.   Does anyone here

  Know this shepherd that he is talking about?

  Have you seen him in the fields, or in the town?   130

  If you have, tell me. It is time things were made plain.

CHORAGOS. I think the man he means is that same shepherd

  You have already asked to see. Iocastê perhaps

  Could tell you something.

---

[116] **name you bear**   *"Oedipus" means "swollen-foot."*

OEDIPUS.   Do you know anything
  About him, Lady? Is he the man we have summoned?   135
  Is that the man this shepherd means?
IOCASTÊ.   Why think of him?
  Forget this herdsman. Forget it all.
  This talk is a waste of time.
OEDIPUS.   How can you say that,
  When the clues to my true birth are in my hands?
IOCASTÊ. For God's love, let us have no more questioning!   140
  Is your life nothing to you?
  My own is pain enough for me to bear.
OEDIPUS. You need not worry. Suppose my mother a slave,
  And born of slaves: no baseness can touch you.
IOCASTÊ. Listen to me, I beg you: do not do this thing!   145
OEDIPUS. I will not listen; the truth must be made known.
IOCASTÊ. Everything that I say is for your own good!
OEDIPUS.   My own good
  Snaps my patience, then: I want none of it.
IOCASTÊ. You are fatally wrong! May you never learn who you are!
OEDIPUS. Go, one of you, and bring the shepherd here.   150
  Let us leave this woman to brag of her royal name.
IOCASTÊ. Ah, miserable!
  That is the only word I have for you now.
  That is the only word I can ever have.

Exit into the palace.

CHORAGOS. Why has she left us, Oedipus? Why has she gone   155
  In such a passion of sorrow? I fear this silence:
  Something dreadful may come of it.
OEDIPUS.   Let it come!
  However base my birth, I must know about it.
  The Queen, like a woman, is perhaps ashamed
  To think of my low origin. But I   160
  Am a child of luck; I cannot be dishonored.
  Luck is my mother; the passing months, my brothers,
  Have seen me rich and poor.
                If this is so,
  How could I wish that I were someone else?
  How could I not be glad to know my birth?   165

ODE III

Strophe

CHORUS. If ever the coming time were known
  To my heart's pondering,

Kithairon, now by Heaven I see the torches
At the festival of the next full moon,
And see the dance, and hear the choir sing   5
A grace to your gentle shade:
Mountain where Oedipus was found,
O mountain guard of a noble race!
May the god who heals us lend his aid,
And let that glory come to pass   10
For our king's cradling-ground.

Antistrophe

Of the nymphs that flower beyond the years,
Who bore you, royal child,
To Pan of the hills or the timberline Apollo,
Cold in delight where the upland clears,   15
Or Hermês for whom Kyllenê's heights° are piled?
Or flushed as evening cloud,
Great Dionysos, roamer of mountains,
He—was it he who found you there,
And caught you up in his own proud   20
Arms from the sweet god-ravisher
Who laughed by the Muses' fountains?

SCENE IV

OEDIPUS. Sirs: though I do not know the man,
  I think I see him coming, this shepherd we want:
  He is old, like our friend here, and the men
  Bringing him seem to be servants of my house.
  But you can tell, if you have ever seen him.   5

Enter SHEPHERD *escorted by servants.*

CHORAGOS. I know him, he was Laïos' man. You can trust him.
OEDIPUS. Tell me first, you from Corinth: is this the shepherd
  We were discussing?
MESSENGER.   This is the very man.
OEDIPUS (*to* SHEPHERD). Come here. No, look at me. You must answer
  Everything I ask.—You belonged to Laïos?   10
SHEPHERD. Yes: born his slave, brought up in his house.
OEDIPUS. Tell me: what kind of work did you do for him?
SHEPHERD. I was a shepherd of his, most of my life.
OEDIPUS. Where mainly did you go for pasturage?

---

[16] **Kyllenê's heights**   *holy mountain, birthplace of Hermes, messenger of the gods.*

SHEPHERD. Sometimes Kithairon, sometimes the hills near-by.   15
OEDIPUS. Do you remember ever seeing this man out there?
SHEPHERD. What would he be doing there? This man?
OEDIPUS. This man standing here. Have you ever seen him before?
SHEPHERD. No. At least, not to my recollection.
MESSENGER. And that is not strange, my lord. But I'll refresh   20
   His memory: he must remember when we two
   Spent three whole seasons together, March to September,
   On Kithairon or thereabouts. He had two flocks;
   I had one. Each autumn I'd drive mine home
   And he would go back with his to Laïos' sheepfold.—   25
   Is this not true, just as I have described it?
SHEPHERD. True, yes; but it was all so long ago.
MESSENGER. Well, then: do you remember, back in those days
   That you gave me a baby boy to bring up as my own?
SHEPHERD. What if I did? What are you trying to say?   30
MESSENGER. King Oedipus was once that little child.
SHEPHERD. Damn you, hold your tongue!
OEDIPUS.   No more of that!
   It is your tongue needs watching, not this man's.
SHEPHERD. My King, my Master, what is it I have done wrong?
OEDIPUS. You have not answered his question about the boy.   35
SHEPHERD. He does not know . . . He is only making trouble . . .
OEDIPUS. Come, speak plainly, or it will go hard with you.
SHEPHERD. In God's name, do not torture an old man!
OEDIPUS. Come here, one of you; bind his arms behind him.
SHEPHERD. Unhappy king! What more do you wish to learn?   40
OEDIPUS. Did you give this man the child he speaks of?
SHEPHERD.   I did.
   And I would to God I had died that very day.
OEDIPUS. You will die now unless you speak the truth.
SHEPHERD. Yet if I speak the truth, I am worse than dead.
OEDIPUS. Very well; since you insist upon delaying—   45
SHEPHERD. No! I have told you already that I gave him the boy.
OEDIPUS. Where did you get him? From your house?
   From somewhere else?
SHEPHERD. Not from mine, no. A man gave him to me.
OEDIPUS. Is that man here? Do you know whose slave he was?
SHEPHERD. For God's love, my King, do not ask me any more!   50
OEDIPUS. You are a dead man if I have to ask you again.
SHEPHERD. Then . . . Then the child was from the palace of Laïos.
OEDIPUS. A slave child? or a child of his own line?
SHEPHERD. Ah, I am on the brink of dreadful speech!
OEDIPUS. And I of dreadful hearing. Yet I must hear.   55
SHEPHERD. If you must be told, then . . .
                        They said it was Laïos' child,
   But it is your wife who can tell you about that.

OEDIPUS. My wife!—Did she give it to you?
SHEPHERD.   My lord, she did.
OEDIPUS. Do you know why?
SHEPHERD.   I was told to get rid of it.
OEDIPUS. An unspeakable mother!
SHEPHERD.   There had been prophecies . . .   60
OEDIPUS. Tell me.
SHEPHERD.   It was said that the boy would kill his own father.
OEDIPUS. Then why did you give him over to this old man?
SHEPHERD. I pitied the baby, my King.
  And I thought that this man would take him far away
  To his own country.
                                He saved him—but for what a fate!   65
  For if you are what this man says you are,
  No man living is more wretched than Oedipus.
OEDIPUS. Ah God!
  It was true!
            All the prophecies!
                              —Now,
  O Light, may I look on you for the last time!   70
  I, Oedipus,
  Oedipus, damned in his birth, in his marriage damned,
  Damned in the blood he shed with his own hand!

                He rushes into the palace.

                      ODE IV

Strophe 1

CHORUS. Alas for the seed of men.
  What measure shall I give these generations
  That breathe on the void and are void
  And exist and do not exist?

  Who bears more weight of joy   5
  Than mass of sunlight shifting in images,
  Or who shall make his thought stay on
  That down time drifts away?

  Your splendor is all fallen.

  O naked brow of wrath and tears,   10
  O change of Oedipus!
  I who saw your days call no man blest—
  Your great days like ghósts góne.

Antistrophe 1

> That mind was a strong bow.
> Deep, how deep you drew it then, hard archer,
> At a dim fearful range,
> And brought dear glory down!

15

> You overcame the stranger—
> The virgin with her hooking lion claws—
> And though death sang, stood like a tower
> To make pale Thebes take heart.

20

> Fortress against our sorrow!

> Divine king, giver of laws,
> Majestic Oedipus!
> No prince in Thebes had ever such renown,
> No prince won such grace of power.

25

Strophe 2

> And now of all men ever known
> Most pitiful is this man's story:
> His fortunes are most changed, his state
> Fallen to a low slave's
> Ground under bitter fate.

30

> O Oedipus, most royal one!
> The great door that expelled you to the light
> Gave at night—ah, gave night to your glory:
> As to the father, to the fathering son.

35

> All understood too late.

> How could that queen whom Laïos won,
> The garden that he harrowed at his height,
> Be silent when that act was done?

Antistrophe 2

> But all eyes fail before time's eye,
> All actions come to justice there.
> Though never willed, though far down the deep past,
> Your bed, your dread sirings,
> Are brought to book at last.
> Child by Laïos doomed to die,

40

45

Then doomed to lose that fortunate little death,
Would God you never took breath in this air
That with my wailing lips I take to cry:

For I weep the world's outcast.

I was blind, and now I can tell why: 50
Asleep, for you had given ease of breath
To Thebes, while the false years went by.

EXODOS

Enter, from the palace, SECOND MESSENGER.

SECOND MESSENGER. Elders of Thebes, most honored in this land,
    What horrors are yours to see and hear, what weight
    Of sorrow to be endured, if, true to your birth,
    You venerate the line of Labdakos!
    I think neither Istros nor Phasis, those great rivers,   5
    Could purify this place of the corruption
    It shelters now, or soon must bring to light—
    Evil not done unconsciously, but willed.

The greatest griefs are those we cause ourselves.
CHORAGOS. Surely, friend, we have grief enough already;   10
    What new sorrow do you mean?
SECOND MESSENGER.   The Queen is dead.
CHORAGOS. Iocastê? Dead? But at whose hand?
SECOND MESSENGER.   Her own.
    The full horror of what happened you cannot know,
    For you did not see it; but I, who did, will tell you
    As clearly as I can how she met her death.   15

    When she had left us,
    In passionate silence, passing through the court,
    She ran to her apartment in the house,
    Her hair clutched by the fingers of both hands.
    She closed the doors behind her; then, by that bed   20
    Where long ago the fatal son was conceived—
    That son who should bring about his father's death—
    We heard her call upon Laïos, dead so many years,
    And heard her wail for the double fruit of her marriage,
    A husband by her husband, children by her child.   25

Exactly how she died I do not know:
For Oedipus burst in moaning and would not let us
Keep vigil to the end: it was by him
As he stormed about the room that our eyes were caught.
From one to another of us he went, begging a sword,   30
Cursing the wife who was not his wife, the mother
Whose womb had carried his own children and himself.
I do not know: it was none of us aided him,
But surely one of the gods was in control!
For with a dreadful cry   35
He hurled his weight, as though wrenched out of himself,
At the twin doors: the bolts gave, and he rushed in.
And there we saw her hanging, her body swaying
From the cruel cord she had noosed about her neck.
A great sob broke from him heartbreaking to hear,   40
As he loosed the rope and lowered her to the ground.

I would blot out from my mind what happened next!
For the King ripped from her gown the golden brooches
That were her ornament, and raised them, and plunged them down
Straight into his own eyeballs, crying, "No more,   45
No more shall you look on the misery about me,
The horrors of my own doing! Too long you have known
The faces of those whom I should never have seen,
Too long been blind to those for whom I was searching!
From this hour, go in darkness!" And as he spoke,   50
He struck at his eyes—not once, but many times;
And the blood spattered his beard,
Bursting from his ruined sockets like red hail.

So from the unhappiness of two this evil has sprung,
A curse on the man and woman alike. The old   55
Happiness of the house of Labdakos
Was happiness enough: where is it today?
It is all wailing and ruin, disgrace, death—all
The misery of mankind that has a name—
And it is wholly and for ever theirs.   60
CHORAGOS. Is he in agony still? Is there no rest for him?
SECOND MESSENGER. He is calling for someone to lead him to the gates
So that all the children of Kadmos may look upon
His father's murderer, his mother's—no,
I cannot say it!
                        And then he will leave Thebes,   65
Self-exiled, in order that the curse
Which he himself pronounced may depart from the house.
He is weak, and there is none to lead him,
So terrible is his suffering.

                    But you will see:
    Look, the doors are opening; in a moment   70
    You will see a thing that would crush a heart of stone.

            The central door is opened; OEDIPUS, *blinded, is led in.*

CHORAGOS. Dreadful indeed for men to see.
    Never have my own eyes
    Looked on a sight so full of fear.

    Oedipus!   75
    What madness came upon you, what daemon
    Leaped on your life with heavier
    Punishment than a mortal man can bear?
    No: I cannot even
    Look at you, poor ruined one.   80
    And I would speak, question, ponder,
    If I were able. No.
    You make me shudder.
OEDIPUS. God. God.
    Is there a sorrow greater?   85
    Where shall I find harbor in this world?
    My voice is hurled far on a dark wind.
    What has God done to me?
CHORAGOS. Too terrible to think of, or to see.

Strophe 1

OEDIPUS. O cloud of night,   90
    Never to be turned away: night coming on,
    I cannot tell how: night like a shroud!
    My fair winds brought me here.
                        Oh God. Again
    The pain of the spikes where I had sight,
    The flooding pain   95
    Of memory, never to be gouged out.
CHORAGOS. This is not strange.
    You suffer it all twice over, remorse in pain,
    Pain in remorse.

Antistrophe 1

OEDIPUS. Ah dear friend   100
    Are you faithful even yet, you alone?
    Are you still standing near me, will you stay here,
    Patient, to care for the blind?
                        The blind man!
    Yet even blind I know who it is attends me,

By the voice's tone—   105
Though my new darkness hide the comforter.
CHORAGOS. Oh fearful act!
What god was it drove you to rake black
Night across your eyes?

Strophe 2

OEDIPUS. Apollo. Apollo. Dear   110
Children, the god was Apollo.
He brought my sick, sick fate upon me.
But the blinding hand was my own!
How could I bear to see
When all my sight was horror everywhere?   115
CHORAGOS. Everywhere; that is true.
OEDIPUS. And now what is left?
Images? Love? A greeting even,
Sweet to the senses? Is there anything?
Ah, no, friends: lead me away.   120
Lead me away from Thebes.
                              Lead the great wreck
And hell of Oedipus, whom the gods hate.
CHORAGOS. Your fate is clear, you are not blind to that.
Would God you had never found it out!

Antistrophe 2

OEDIPUS. Death take the man who unbound   125
My feet on that hillside
And delivered me from death to life! What life?
If only I had died,
This weight of monstrous doom
Could not have dragged me and my darlings down.   130
CHORAGOS. I would have wished the same.
OEDIPUS. Oh never to have come here
With my father's blood upon me! Never
To have been the man they call his mother's husband!
Oh accurst! Oh child of evil,   135
To have entered that wretched bed—
                              the selfsame one!
More primal than sin itself, this fell to me.
CHORAGOS. I do not know how I can answer you.
You were better dead than alive and blind.
OEDIPUS. Do not counsel me any more. This punishment   140
That I have laid upon myself is just.
If I had eyes,

I do not know how I could bear the sight
Of my father, when I came to the house of Death,
Or my mother: for I have sinned against them both   145
So vilely that I could not make my peace
By strangling my own life.
                 Or do you think my children,
Born as they were born, would be sweet to my eyes?
Ah never, never! Nor this town with its high walls,
Nor the holy images of the gods.   150
                For I,
Thrice miserable—Oedipus, noblest of all the line
Of Kadmos, have condemned myself to enjoy
These things no more, by my own malediction
Expelling that man whom the gods declared
To be a defilement in the house of Laïos.   155
After exposing the rankness of my own guilt,
How could I look men frankly in the eyes?
No, I swear it,
If I could have stifled my hearing at its source,
I would have done it and made all this body   160
A tight cell of misery, blank to light and sound:
So I should have been safe in a dark agony
Beyond all recollection.
               Ah Kithairon!
Why did you shelter me? When I was cast upon you,
Why did I not die? Then I should never   165
Have shown the world my execrable birth.

Ah Polybos! Corinth, city that I believed
The ancient seat of my ancestors: how fair
I seemed, your child! And all the while this evil
Was cancerous within me!   170
               For I am sick
In my daily life, sick in my origin.

O three roads, dark ravine, woodland and way
Where three roads met you, drinking my father's blood,
My own blood, spilled by my own hand: can you remember
The unspeakable things I did there, and the things   175
I went on from there to do?
              O marriage, marriage!
The act that engendered me, and again the act
Performed by the son in the same bed—
                Ah, the net
Of incest, mingling fathers, brothers, sons,
With brides, wives, mothers: the last evil   180

That can be known by men: no tongue can say
How evil!
　　　　　No. For the love of God, conceal me
Somewhere far from Thebes; or kill me; or hurl me
Into the sea, away from men's eyes for ever.
Come, lead me. You need not fear to touch me.　　　185
Of all men, I alone can bear this guilt.

Enter CREON.

CHORAGOS. We are not the ones to decide; but Creon here
　　May fitly judge of what you ask. He only
　　Is left to protect the city in your place.
OEDIPUS. Alas, how can I speak to him? What right have I　　190
　　To beg his courtesy whom I have deeply wronged?
CREON. I have not come to mock you, Oedipus,
　　Or to reproach you, either.
　　　　　　　　(To ATTENDANTS.*)*
　　　　　　　—You, standing there:
　　If you have lost all respect for man's dignity,
　　At least respect the flame of Lord Helios:　　195
　　Do not allow this pollution to show itself
　　Openly here, an affront to the earth
　　And Heaven's rain and the light of day. No, take him
　　Into the house as quickly as you can.
　　For it is proper　　200
　　That only the close kindred see his grief.
OEDIPUS. I pray you in God's name, since your courtesy
　　Ignores my dark expectation, visiting
　　With mercy this man of all men most execrable:
　　Give me what I ask—for your good, not for mine.　　205
CREON. And what is it that you would have me do?
OEDIPUS. Drive me out of this country as quickly as may be
　　To a place where no human voice can ever greet me.
CREON. I should have done that before now—only,
　　God's will had not been wholly revealed to me.　　210
OEDIPUS. But his command is plain: the parricide
　　Must be destroyed. I am that evil man.
CREON. That is the sense of it, yes; but as things are,
　　We had best discover clearly what is to be done.
OEDIPUS. You would learn more about a man like me?　　215
CREON. You are ready now to listen to the god.
OEDIPUS. I will listen. But it is to you
　　That I must turn for help. I beg you, hear me.

　　The woman in there—
　　Give her whatever funeral you think proper:　　220
　　She is your sister.

—But let me go, Creon!
Let me purge my father's Thebes of the pollution
Of my living here, and go out to the wild hills,
To Kithairon, that has won such fame with me,
The tomb my mother and father appointed for me,   225
And let me die there, as they willed I should.
And yet I know
Death will not ever come to me through sickness
Or in any natural way: I have been preserved
For some unthinkable fate. But let that be.   230
As for my sons, you need not care for them.
They are men, they will find some way to live.
But my poor daughters, who have shared my table,
Who never before have been parted from their father—
Take care of them, Creon; do this for me.   235
And will you let me touch them with my hands
A last time, and let us weep together?
Be kind, my lord,
Great prince, be kind!
                    Could I but touch them,
They would be mine again, as when I had my eyes.   240

            Enter ANTIGONÊ *and* ISMENÊ, *attended.*

Ah, God!
Is it my dearest children I hear weeping?
Has Creon pitied me and sent my daughters?
CREON. Yes, Oedipus: I knew that they were dear to you
    In the old days, and know you must love them still.   245
OEDIPUS. May God bless you for this—and be a friendlier
    Guardian to you than he has been to me!

Children, where are you?
Come quickly to my hands: they are your brother's—
Hands that have brought your father's once clear eyes   250
To this way of seeing—
                    Ah dearest ones,
I had neither sight nor knowledge then, your father
By the woman who was the source of his own life!
And I weep for you—having no strength to see you—,
I weep for you when I think of the bitterness   255
That men will visit upon you all your lives.
What homes, what festivals can you attend
Without being forced to depart again in tears?
And when you come to marriageable age,
Where is the man, my daughters, who would dare   260
Risk the bane that lies on all my children?
Is there any evil wanting? Your father killed

His father; sowed the womb of her who bore him;
Engendered you at the fount of his own existence!
That is what they will say of you.
                                        Then, whom   265
Can you ever marry? There are no bridegrooms for you,
And your lives must wither away in sterile dreaming.
O Creon, son of Menoikeus!
You are the only father my daughters have,
Since we, their parents, are both of us gone for ever.   270
They are your own blood: you will not let them
Fall into beggary and loneliness;
You will keep them from the miseries that are mine!
Take pity on them; see, they are only children,
Friendless except for you. Promise me this,   275
Great Prince, and give me your hand in token of it.

          CREON *clasps his right hand.*

Children:
I could say much, if you could understand me,
But as it is, I have only this prayer for you:
Live where you can, be as happy as you can—   280
Happier, please God, than God has made your father!
CREON. Enough. You have wept enough. Now go within.
OEDIPUS. I must; but it is hard.
CREON.   Time eases all things.
OEDIPUS. But you must promise—
CREON.   Say what you desire.
OEDIPUS. Send me from Thebes!
CREON.   God grant that I may!   285
OEDIPUS. But since God hates me . . .
CREON.   No, he will grant your wish.
OEDIPUS. You promise?
CREON.   I cannot speak beyond my knowledge.
OEDIPUS. Then lead me in.
CREON.   Come now, and leave your children.
OEDIPUS. No! Do not take them from me!
CREON.   Think no longer
That you are in command here, but rather think   290
How, when you were, you served your own destruction.

Exeunt into the house all but the CHORUS; *the* CHORAGOS *chants directly to the audience.*

CHORAGOS. Men of Thebes: look upon Oedipus.
This is the king who solved the famous riddle
And towered up, most powerful of men
No mortal eyes but looked on him with envy.   295
Yet in the end ruin swept over him.

Let every man in mankind's frailty
Consider his last day; and let none
Presume on his good fortune until he find
Life, at his death, a memory without pain.   300

(*c. 430 B.C.*)

QUESTIONS

1. What makes Oedipus a tragic hero? What makes his predicament fascinating rather than merely horrifying? Account for the continued appeal of the play.
2. Evaluate Oedipus' actions. Is he to blame for what happens? Account for his change of attitude and manner by comparing his speech and behavior in the opening and closing scenes. What is your impression of Oedipus at these points?
3. Identify and explain the different types of irony in *Oedipus Rex*. (For a discussion of irony see pages 99–101.)
4. How is the imagery of light and darkness employed throughout the play? How is it related to Oedipus' blindness?
5. What roles do the chorus and choragos assume? Compare their functions in the beginning, middle, and end of the play.
6. Rather than dramatize on stage the shocking and horrible events in which the play culminates, Sophocles has them occur offstage, and we learn about them through a messenger's report. What are the limitations and advantages of such a method?
7. Iocastê appears a number of times, but she has little to say. What is she like? How much do we know about her—especially her thoughts and feelings? Read Ruth Eisenberg's poem "Jocasta" (pages 962–970) and compare Eisenberg's characterization of Iocastê with Sophocles' in *Oedipus Rex*.

Readers will be able to understand *Antigonê* more fully if they understand the background of Polyneicês' death. After Oedipus exiled himself from Thebes (see the conclusion of *Oedipus Rex*), his two sons, Eteoclês and Polyneicês, shared the rule of Thebes. Although they originally agreed to reign in alternate years, Eteoclês refused to step down when his allotted time had passed. Polyneicês, with the help of the king of Argos, attempted to remove Eteoclês from the throne. In the attack on Thebes, the brothers killed one another. Creon assumed the throne and declared that Eteoclês should be buried with full honors. Because Polyneicês had attacked his native city, his body was to be shamefully left lying where he fell.

The stage directions for *Antigonê* are simple, stating that the play begins at dawn in front of the palace in Thebes. Antigonê and Ismenê enter from the palace, engaged in a conversation that clearly establishes their relationship and the conflicts between them. Tension builds slowly; Antigonê and Creon do not come face to face until Scene II, with the clash between law (represented by Creon) and justice (represented by Antigonê) constituting one of the play's primary themes.

Antigonê

AN ENGLISH VERSION BY DUDLEY FITTS AND ROBERT FITZGERALD

CHARACTERS

ANTIGONÊ

ISMENÊ

EURYDICÊ

CREON

HAIMON

TEIRESIAS

A SENTRY

A MESSENGER

CHORUS

Scene. *Before the palace of* CREON, *King of Thebes. A central double door, and two lateral doors. A platform extends the length of the façade, and from this platform three steps lead down into the "orchestra," or chorus-ground.*

Time. *Dawn of the day after the repulse of the Argive army from the assault on Thebes.*

PROLOGUE

ANTIGONÊ *and* ISMENÊ *enter from the central door of the palace.*

ANTIGONÊ. Ismenê, dear sister,
  You would think that we had already suffered enough
  For the curse on Oedipus.°
  I cannot imagine any grief
  That you and I have not gone through. And now—   5
  Have they told you of the new decree of our King Creon?
ISMENÊ. I have heard nothing: I know
  That two sisters lost two brothers, a double death
  In a single hour; and I know that the Argive army
  Fled in the night; but beyond this, nothing.   10
ANTIGONÊ. I thought so. And that is why I wanted you
  To come out here with me. There is something we must do.

³**Oedipus** *former King of Thebes, father of Antigonê and Ismenê, and of Polyneicês and Eteoclês, their brothers. Oedipus unwittingly killed his father, Laïos, and married his mother, Iocastê. When he learned what he had done, he blinded himself and left Thebes. Eteoclês and Polyneicês quarreled; Polyneicês was defeated but returned to assault Thebes. Both brothers were killed in the battle; Creon ordered that Polyneicês remain unburied.*

ISMENÊ. Why do you speak so strangely?

ANTIGONÊ. Listen, Ismenê:

Creon buried our brother Eteoclês   15
With military honors, gave him a soldier's funeral,
And it was right that he should; but Polyneicês,
Who fought as bravely and died as miserably,—
They say that Creon has sworn
No one shall bury him, no one mourn for him,   20
But his body must lie in the fields, a sweet treasure
For carrion birds to find as they search for food.
That is what they say, and our good Creon is coming here
To announce it publicly; and the penalty—
Stoning to death in the public square!

                         There it is,   25
And now you can prove what you are:
A true sister, or a traitor to your family.

ISMENÊ. Antigonê, you are mad! What could I possibly do?

ANTIGONÊ. You must decide whether you will help me or not.

ISMENÊ. I do not understand you. Help you in what?   30

ANTIGONÊ. Ismenê, I am going to bury him. Will you come?

ISMENÊ. Bury him! You have just said the new law forbids it.

ANTIGONÊ. He is my brother. And he is your brother, too.

ISMENÊ. But think of the danger! Think what Creon will do!

ANTIGONÊ. Creon is not strong enough to stand in my way.   35

ISMENÊ. Ah sister!

Oedipus died, everyone hating him
For what his own search brought to light, his eyes
Ripped out by his own hand; and Iocastê died,
His mother and wife at once: she twisted the cords   40
That strangled her life; and our two brothers died,
Each killed by the other's sword. And we are left:
But oh, Antigonê,
Think how much more terrible than these
Our own death would be if we should go against Creon   45
And do what he has forbidden! We are only women,
We cannot fight with men, Antigonê!
The law is strong, we must give in to the law
In this thing, and in worse. I beg the Dead
To forgive me, but I am helpless: I must yield   50
To those in authority. And I think it is dangerous business
To be always meddling.

ANTIGONÊ.   If that is what you think,
I should not want you, even if you asked to come.
You have made your choice, you can be what you want to be.
But I will bury him; and if I must die,   55
I say that this crime is holy: I shall lie down
With him in death, and I shall be as dear

To him as he to me.
                    It is the dead,
Not the living, who make the longest demands:
We die for ever . . .
                              You may do as you like,   60
Since apparently the laws of the gods mean nothing to you.
ISMENÊ. They mean a great deal to me; but I have no strength
    To break laws that were made for the public good.
ANTIGONÊ. That must be your excuse, I suppose. But as for me,
    I will bury the brother I love.
ISMENÊ.   Antigonê,   65
    I am so afraid for you!
ANTIGONÊ.   You need not be:
    You have yourself to consider, after all.
ISMENÊ. But no one must hear of this, you must tell no one!
    I will keep it a secret, I promise!
ANTIGONÊ.   O tell it! Tell everyone!
    Think how they'll hate you when it all comes out   70
    If they learn that you knew about it all the time!
ISMENÊ. So fiery! You should be cold with fear.
ANTIGONÊ. Perhaps. But I am doing only what I must.
ISMENÊ. But can you do it? I say that you cannot.
ANTIGONÊ. Very well: when my strength gives out,
    I shall do no more.   75
ISMENÊ. Impossible things should not be tried at all.
ANTIGONÊ. Go away, Ismenê:
    I shall be hating you soon, and the dead will too,
    For your words are hateful. Leave me my foolish plan:
    I am not afraid of the danger; if it means death,   80
    It will not be the worst of deaths—death without honor.
ISMENÊ. Go then, if you feel that you must.
    You are unwise,
    But a loyal friend indeed to those who love you.

Exit into the palace. ANTIGONÊ *goes off, left. Enter the* CHORUS.

PÁRODOS

Strophe 1

CHORUS. Now the long blade of the sun, lying
    Level east to west, touches with glory
    Thebes of the Seven Gates. Open, unlidded
    Eye of golden day! O marching light
    Across the eddy and rush of Dircê's stream,°   5

---

[5] ***Dircê's stream***   *river near Thebes.*

Striking the white shields of the enemy
Thrown headlong backward from the blaze of morning!
CHORAGOS.° Polyneicês their commander
  Roused them with windy phrases,
  He the wild eagle screaming   10
  Insults above our land,
  His wings their shields of snow,
  His crest their marshalled helms.

Antistrophe 1

CHORUS. Against our seven gates in a yawning ring
  The famished spears came onward in the night;   15
  But before his jaws were sated with our blood,
  Or pinefire took the garland of our towers,
  He was thrown back; and as he turned, great Thebes—
  No tender victim for his noisy power—
  Rose like a dragon behind him, shouting war.   20
CHORAGOS. For God hates utterly
  The bray of bragging tongues;
  And when he beheld their smiling,
  Their swagger of golden helms,
  The frown of his thunder blasted   25
  Their first man from our walls.

Strophe 2

CHORUS. We heard his shout of triumph high in the air
  Turn to a scream; far out in a flaming arc
  He fell with his windy torch, and the earth struck him.
  And others storming in fury no less than his   30
  Found shock of death in the dusty joy of battle.
CHORAGOS. Seven captains at seven gates
  Yielded their clanging arms to the god
  That bends the battle-line and breaks it.
  These two only, brothers in blood,   35
  Face to face in matchless rage,
  Mirroring each the other's death,
  Clashed in long combat.

Antistrophe 2

CHORUS. But now in the beautiful morning of victory
  Let Thebes of the many chariots sing for joy!   40
  With hearts for dancing we'll take leave of war:
  Our temples shall be sweet with hymns of praise,
  And the long nights shall echo with our chorus.

---

[8]*Choragos*   *leader of the chorus.*

SCENE I

CHORAGOS. But now at last our new King is coming:
Creon of Thebes, Menoikeus' son.
In this auspicious dawn of his reign
What are the new complexities
That shifting Fate has woven for him?   5
What is his counsel? Why has he summoned
The old men to hear him?

Enter CREON *from the palace, center. He addresses the* CHORUS *from the top step.*

CREON. Gentlemen: I have the honor to inform you that our Ship of State,
which recent storms have threatened to destroy, has come safely to harbor   10
at last, guided by the merciful wisdom of Heaven. I have summoned you
here this morning because I know that I can depend upon you: your devotion to King Laïos was absolute; you never hesitated in your duty to
our late ruler Oedipus; and when Oedipus died, your loyalty was transferred to his children. Unfortunately, as you know, his two sons, the   15
princes Eteoclês and Polyneicês, have killed each other in battle; and I, as
the next in blood, have succeeded to the full power of the throne.

I am aware, of course, that no Ruler can expect complete loyalty from
his subjects until he has been tested in office. Nevertheless, I say to you at
the very outset that I have nothing but contempt for the kind of Governor   20
who is afraid, for whatever reason, to follow the course that he knows is
best for the State; and as for the man who sets private friendship above the
public welfare,—I have no use for him, either. I call God to witness that
if I saw my country headed for ruin, I should not be afraid to speak out
plainly; and I need hardly remind you that I would never have any dealings 25
with an enemy of the people. No one values friendship more highly than
I; but we must remember that friends made at the risk of wrecking our Ship
are not real friends at all.

These are my principles, at any rate, and that is why I have made the
following decision concerning the sons of Oedipus: Eteoclês, who died as   30
a man should die, fighting for his country, is to be buried with full military
honors, with all the ceremony that is usual when the greatest heroes die;
but his brother Polyneicês, who broke his exile to come back with fire and
sword against his native city and the shrines of his fathers' gods, whose one
idea was to spill the blood of his blood and sell his own people into slav-   35
ery—Polyneicês, I say, is to have no burial: no man is to touch him or say
the least prayer for him; he shall lie on the plain, unburied; and the birds
and the scavenging dogs can do with him whatever they like.

This is my command, and you can see the wisdom behind it. As long   40
as I am King, no traitor is going to be honored with the loyal man. But
whoever shows by word and deed that he is on the side of the State,—he
shall have my respect while he is living and my reverence when he is dead.
CHORAGOS. If that is your will, Creon son of Menoikeus,
You have the right to enforce it: we are yours.   45

CREON. That is my will. Take care that you do your part.

CHORAGOS. We are old men: let the younger ones carry it out.

CREON. I do not mean that: the sentries have been appointed.

CHORAGOS. Then what is it that you would have us do?

CREON. You will give no support to whoever breaks this law.   50

CHORAGOS. Only a crazy man is in love with death!

CREON. And death it is; yet money talks, and the wisest
    Have sometimes been known to count a few coins too many.

Enter SENTRY *from left.*

SENTRY. I'll not say that I'm out of breath from running, King, because every
    time I stopped to think about what I have to tell you, I felt like going back.   55
    And all the time a voice kept saying, "You fool, don't you know you're
    walking straight into trouble?"; and then another voice: "Yes, but if you
    let somebody else get the news to Creon first, it will be even worse than
    that for you!" But good sense won out, at least I hope it was good sense,   60
    and here I am with a story that makes no sense at all; but I'll tell it anyhow,
    because, as they say, what's going to happen's going to happen and—

CREON. Come to the point. What have you to say?

SENTRY. I did not do it. I did not see who did it. You must not punish me for
    what someone else has done.   65

CREON. A comprehensive defense! More effective, perhaps,
    If I knew its purpose. Come: what is it?

SENTRY: A dreadful thing . . . I don't know how to put it—

CREON. Out with it!

SENTRY.   Well, then;
    The dead man—
          Polyneicês—

Pause. The SENTRY *is overcome, fumbles for words.* CREON *waits impassively.*

                 out there—
                      someone,—   70
    New dust on the slimy flesh!

Pause. No sign from CREON.

    Someone has given it burial that way, and
    Gone . . .

Long pause. CREON *finally speaks with deadly control.*

CREON. And the man who dared do this?

SENTRY.   I swear I
    Do not know! You must believe me!   75
     Listen:
    The ground was dry, not a sign of digging, no,
    Not a wheeltrack in the dust, no trace of anyone.
    It was when they relieved us this morning: and one of them,
    The corporal, pointed to it.
            There it was,

The strangest—
              Look: 80
The body, just mounded over with light dust: you see?
Not buried really, but as if they'd covered it
Just enough for the ghost's peace. And no sign
Of dogs or any wild animal that had been there.
And then what a scene there was! Every man of us   85
Accusing the other: we all proved the other man did it,
We all had proof that we could not have done it.
We were ready to take hot iron in our hands,
Walk through fire, swear by all the gods,
It was not I!   90
I do not know who it was, but it was not I!

CREON's *rage has been mounting steadily, but the* SENTRY *is too intent upon his story to notice it.*

And then, when this came to nothing, someone said
A thing that silenced us and made us stare
Down at the ground: you had to be told the news,
And one of us had to do it! We threw the dice,   95
And the bad luck fell to me. So here I am,
No happier to be here than you are to have me:
Nobody likes the man who brings bad news.
CHORAGOS. I have been wondering, King: can it be that the gods have
      done this?
CREON (*furiously*). Stop!   100
Must you doddering wrecks
Go out of your heads entirely? "The gods"!
Intolerable!
The gods favor this corpse? Why? How had he served them?
Tried to loot their temples, burn their images,`   105
Yes, and the whole State, and its laws with it!
Is it your senile opinion that the gods love to honor bad men?
A pious thought!—
                            No, from the very beginning
There have been those who have whispered together,
Stiff-necked anarchists, putting their heads together,   110
Scheming against me in alleys. These are the men,
And they have bribed my own guard to do this thing.
(*Sententiously.*) Money!
There's nothing in the world so demoralizing as money.
Down go your cities,   115
Homes gone, men gone, honest hearts corrupted,
Crookedness of all kinds, and all for money!
                                 (*To* SENTRY.)
                                               But you—!

I swear by God and by the throne of God,
The man who has done this thing shall pay for it!
Find that man, bring him here to me, or your death 120
Will be the least of your problems: I'll string you up
Alive, and there will be certain ways to make you
Discover your employer before you die;
And the process may teach you a lesson you seem to have missed:
The dearest profit is sometimes all too dear: 125
That depends on the source. Do you understand me?
A fortune won is often misfortune.

SENTRY. King, may I speak?

CREON.   Your very voice distresses me.

SENTRY. Are you sure that it is my voice, and not your conscience?

CREON. By God, he wants to analyze me now! 130

SENTRY. It is not what I say, but what has been done, that hurts you.

CREON. You talk too much.

SENTRY.   Maybe; but I've done nothing.

CREON. Sold your soul for some silver: that's all you've done.

SENTRY. How dreadful it is when the right judge judges wrong!

CREON. Your figures of speech 135
May entertain you now; but unless you bring me the man,
You will get little profit from them in the end.

Exit CREON *into the palace.*

SENTRY. "Bring me the man"—!
I'd like nothing better than bringing him the man!
But bring him or not, you have seen the last of me here. 140
At any rate, I am safe!

(Exit SENTRY.*)*

ODE I

Strophe 1

CHORUS. Numberless are the world's wonders, but none
More wonderful than man; the stormgray sea
Yields to his prows, the huge crests bear him high;
Earth, holy and inexhaustible, is graven
With shining furrows where his plows have gone 5
Year after year, the timeless labor of stallions.

Antistrophe 1

The lightboned birds and beasts that cling to cover,
The lithe fish lighting their reaches of dim water,

All are taken, tamed in the net of his mind;
The lion on the hill, the wild horse windy-maned,   10
Resign to him; and his blunt yoke has broken
The sultry shoulders of the mountain bull.

Strophe 2

Words also, and thought as rapid as air,
He fashions to his good use; statecraft is his,
And his the skill that deflects the arrows of snow,   15
The spears of winter rain: from every wind
He has made himself secure—from all but one:
In the late wind of death he cannot stand.

Antistrophe 2

O clear intelligence, force beyond all measure!
O fate of man, working both good and evil!   20
When the laws are kept, how proudly his city stands!
When the laws are broken, what of his city then?
Never may the anárchic man find rest at my hearth,
Never be it said that my thoughts are his thoughts.

SCENE II

Reenter SENTRY *leading* ANTIGONÊ.

CHORAGOS. What does this mean? Surely this captive woman
    Is the Princess, Antigonê. Why should she be taken?
SENTRY. Here is the one who did it! We caught her
    In the very act of burying him.—Where is Creon?
CHORAGOS. Just coming from the house.

Enter CREON, *center.*

CREON.   What has happened?   5
    Why have you come back so soon?
SENTRY (*expansively*).   O King,
    A man should never be too sure of anything:
    I would have sworn
    That you'd not see me here again: your anger
    Frightened me so, and the things you threatened me with;   10
    But how could I tell then
    That I'd be able to solve the case so soon?
    No dice-throwing this time: I was only too glad to come!
    Here is this woman. She is the guilty one:
    We found her trying to bury him.   15

Take her, then; question her; judge her as you will.
I am through with the whole thing now, and glad of it.

CREON. But this is Antigonê! Why have you brought her here?

SENTRY. She was burying him, I tell you!

CREON (*severely*).   Is this the truth?   20

SENTRY. I saw her with my own eyes. Can I say more?

CREON. The details: come, tell me quickly!

SENTRY.   It was like this:

After those terrible threats of yours, King,
We went back and brushed the dust away from the body.
The flesh was soft by now, and stinking,
So we sat on a hill to windward and kept guard.   25
No napping this time! We kept each other awake.
But nothing happened until the white round sun
Whirled in the center of the round sky over us:
Then, suddenly,
A storm of dust roared up from the earth, and the sky   30
Went out, the plain vanished with all its trees
In the stinging dark. We closed our eyes and endured it.
The whirlwind lasted a long time, but it passed;
And then we looked, and there was Antigonê!
I have seen   35
A mother bird come back to a stripped nest, heard
Her crying bitterly a broken note or two
For the young ones stolen. Just so, when this girl
Found the bare corpse, and all her love's work wasted,
She wept, and cried on heaven to damn the hands   40
That had done this thing.
                         And then she brought more dust
And sprinkled wine three times for her brother's ghost.

We ran and took her at once. She was not afraid,
Not even when we charged her with what she had done.
She denied nothing.
                    And this was a comfort to me,   45
And some uneasiness: for it is a good thing
To escape from death, but it is no great pleasure
To bring death to a friend.
                           Yet I always say
There is nothing so comfortable as your own safe skin!

CREON (*slowly, dangerously*). And you, Antigonê,   50
You with your head hanging,—do you confess this thing?

ANTIGONÊ. I do. I deny nothing.

CREON (*to* SENTRY).   You may go.

(*Exit* SENTRY.)

(*To* ANTIGONÊ.) Tell me, tell me briefly:
Had you heard my proclamation touching this matter?

ANTIGONÊ. It was public. Could I help hearing it?   55

CREON. And yet you dared defy the law.

ANTIGONÊ.   I dared.

It was not God's proclamation. That final Justice
That rules the world below makes no such laws.

Your edict, King, was strong,
But all your strength is weakness itself against   60
The immortal unrecorded laws of God.
They are not merely now: they were, and shall be,
Operative for ever, beyond man utterly.

I knew I must die, even without your decree:
I am only mortal. And if I must die   65
Now, before it is my time to die,
Surely this is no hardship: can anyone
Living, as I live, with evil all about me,
Think Death less than a friend? This death of mine
Is of no importance; but if I had left my brother   70
Lying in death unburied, I should have suffered.
Now I do not.
             You smile at me. Ah Creon,
Think me a fool, if you like; but it may well be
That a fool convicts me of folly.

CHORAGOS. Like father, like daughter: both headstrong, deaf to reason!   75
She has never learned to yield:

CREON.   She has much to learn.
The inflexible heart breaks first, the toughest iron
Cracks first, and the wildest horses bend their necks
At the pull of the smallest curb.
                   Pride? In a slave?
This girl is guilty of a double insolence,   80
Breaking the given laws and boasting of it.
Who is the man here,
She or I, if this crime goes unpunished?
Sister's child, or more than sister's child,
Or closer yet in blood—she and her sister   85
Win bitter death for this!

               (To SERVANTS.*)*
             Go, some of you,
Arrest Ismenê. I accuse her equally.
Bring her: you will find her sniffling in the house there.

Her mind's a traitor: crimes kept in the dark
Cry for light, and the guardian brain shudders;   90
But how much worse than this
Is brazen boasting of barefaced anarchy!

ANTIGONÊ. Creon, what more do you want than my death?

CREON.   Nothing.
   That gives me everything.

ANTIGONÊ.   Then I beg you: kill me.
   This talking is a great weariness: your words   95
   Are distasteful to me, and I am sure that mine
   Seem so to you. And yet they should not seem so:
   I should have praise and honor for what I have done.
   All these men here would praise me
   Were their lips not frozen shut with fear of you.   100
   (Bitterly.) Ah the good fortune of kings,
   Licensed to say and do whatever they please!

CREON. You are alone here in that opinion.

ANTIGONÊ. No, they are with me. But they keep their tongues in leash.

CREON. Maybe. But you are guilty, and they are not.   105

ANTIGONÊ. There is no guilt in reverence for the dead.

CREON. But Eteoclês—was he not your brother too?

ANTIGONÊ. My brother too.

CREON.   And you insult his memory?

ANTIGONÊ *(softly)*. The dead man would not say that I insult it.

CREON. He would: for you honor a traitor as much as him.   110

ANTIGONÊ. His own brother, traitor or not, and equal in blood.

CREON. He made war on his country. Eteoclês defended it.

ANTIGONÊ. Nevertheless, there are honors due all the dead.

CREON. But not the same for the wicked as for the just.

ANTIGONÊ. Ah Creon, Creon,   115
   Which of us can say what the gods hold wicked?

CREON. An enemy is an enemy, even dead.

ANTIGONÊ. It is my nature to join in love, not hate.

CREON *(finally losing patience)*. Go join them then; if you must have your love,
   Find it in hell!   120

CHORAGOS. But see, Ismenê comes:

Enter ISMENÊ, *guarded.*

   Those tears are sisterly, the cloud
   That shadows her eyes rains down gentle sorrow.

CREON. You too, Ismenê,
   Snake in my ordered house, sucking my blood   125
   Stealthily—and all the time I never knew
   That these two sisters were aiming at my throne!
                                      Ismenê,
   Do you confess your share in this crime, or deny it?
   Answer me.

ISMENÊ. Yes, if she will let me say so. I am guilty.   130

ANTIGONE *(coldly)*. No, Ismenê. You have no right to say so.
   You would not help me, and I will not have you help me.

ISMENÊ. But now I know what you meant; and I am here
   To join you, to take my share of punishment.

ANTIGONÊ. The dead man and the gods who rule the dead   135
    Know whose act this was. Words are not friends.
ISMENÊ. Do you refuse me, Antigonê? I want to die with you:
    I too have a duty that I must discharge to the dead.
ANTIGONÊ. You shall not lessen my death by sharing it.
ISMENÊ. What do I care for life when you are dead?   140
ANTIGONÊ. Ask Creon. You're always hanging on his opinions.
ISMENÊ. You are laughing at me. Why, Antigonê?
ANTIGONÊ. It's a joyless laughter, Ismenê.
ISMENÊ.   But can I do nothing?
ANTIGONÊ. Yes. Save yourself. I shall not envy you.
    There are those who will praise you; I shall have honor, too.   145
ISMENÊ. But we are equally guilty!
ANTIGONÊ.   No more, Ismenê.
    You are alive, but I belong to Death.
CREON (to the CHORUS). Gentlemen, I beg you to observe these girls:
    One has just now lost her mind; the other,
    It seems, has never had a mind at all.   150
ISMENÊ. Grief teaches the steadiest minds to waver, King.
CREON. Yours certainly did, when you assumed guilt with the guilty!
ISMENÊ. But how could I go on living without her?
CREON.   You are.
    She is already dead.
ISMENÊ.   But your own son's bride!
CREON. There are places enough for him to push his plow.   155
    I want no wicked women for my sons!
ISMENÊ. O dearest Haimon, how your father wrongs you!
CREON. I've had enough of your childish talk of marriage!
CHORAGOS. Do you really intend to steal this girl from your son?
CREON. No; Death will do that for me.
CHORAGOS.   Then she must die?   160
CREON (ironically). You dazzle me.
            —But enough of this talk!
(To GUARDS.) You, there, take them away and guard them well:
For they are but women, and even brave men run
When they see Death coming.

        Exeunt ISMENÊ, ANTIGONÊ, *and* GUARDS.

ODE II

Strophe 1

CHORUS. Fortunate is the man who has never tasted God's vengeance!
    Where once the anger of heaven has struck, that house is shaken
    For ever: damnation rises behind each child

Like a wave cresting out of the black northeast,
When the long darkness under sea roars up   5
And bursts drumming death upon the windwhipped sand.

Antistrophe 1

I have seen this gathering sorrow from time long past
Loom upon Oedipus' children: generation from generation
Takes the compulsive rage of the enemy god.
So lately this last flower of Oedipus' line   10
Drank the sunlight! but now a passionate word
And a handful of dust have closed up all its beauty.

Strophe 2

    What mortal arrogance
    Transcends the wrath of Zeus?
Sleep cannot lull him nor the effortless long months   15
Of the timeless gods: but he is young for ever,
And his house is the shining day of high Olympos.
      All that is and shall be,
      And all the past, is his.
No pride on earth is free of the curse of heaven.   20

Antistrophe 2

The straying dreams of men
    May bring them ghosts of joy:
But as they drowse, the waking embers burn them;
Or they walk with fixed eyes, as blind men walk.
But the ancient wisdom speaks for our own time: 25
      Fate works most for woe
      With Folly's fairest show.
Man's little pleasure is the spring of sorrow.

SCENE III

CHORAGOS. But here is Haimon, King, the last of all your sons.
    Is it grief for Antigonê that brings him here,
    And bitterness at being robbed of his bride?

Enter HAIMON.

CREON. We shall soon see, and no need of diviners.
                    —Son,
    You have heard my final judgment on that girl: 5

Have you come here hating me, or have you come
With deference and with love, whatever I do?
HAIMON. I am your son, father. You are my guide.
You make things clear for me, and I obey you.
No marriage means more to me than your continuing wisdom.   10
CREON. Good. That is the way to behave: subordinate
Everything else, my son, to your father's will.
This is what a man prays for, that he may get
Sons attentive and dutiful in his house,
Each one hating his father's enemies,   15
Honoring his father's friends. But if his sons
Fail him, if they turn out unprofitably,
What has he fathered but trouble for himself
And amusement for the malicious?
                              So you are right
Not to lose your head over this woman.   20
Your pleasure with her would soon grow cold, Haimon,
And then you'd have a hellcat in bed and elsewhere.
Let her find her husband in Hell!
Of all the people in this city, only she
Has had contempt for my law and broken it.   25

Do you want me to show myself weak before the people?
Or to break my sworn word? No, and I will not.
The woman dies.
I suppose she'll plead "family ties." Well, let her.
If I permit my own family to rebel,   30
How shall I earn the world's obedience?
Show me the man who keeps his house in hand,
He's fit for public authority.
                              I'll have no dealings
With lawbreakers, critics of the government:
Whoever is chosen to govern should be obeyed—   35
Must be obeyed, in all things, great and small,
Just and unjust! O Haimon,
The man who knows how to obey, and that man only,
Knows how to give commands when the time comes.
You can depend on him, no matter how fast   40
The spears come: he's a good soldier, he'll stick it out.

Anarchy, anarchy! Show me a greater evil!
This is why cities tumble and the great houses rain down,
This is what scatters armies!
No, no: good lives are made so by discipline.   45
We keep the laws then, and the lawmakers,
And no woman shall seduce us. If we must lose,
Let's lose to a man, at least! Is a woman stronger than we?

CHORAGOS. Unless time has rusted my wits,
   What you say, King, is said with point and dignity.   50
HAIMON *(boyishly earnest)*. Father:
   Reason is God's crowning gift to man, and you are right
   To warn me against losing mine. I cannot say—
   I hope that I shall never want to say!—that you
   Have reasoned badly. Yet there are other men   55
   Who can reason, too; and their opinions might be helpful.
   You are not in a position to know everything
   That people say or do, or what they feel:
   Your temper terrifies—everyone
   Will tell you only what you like to hear.   60
   But I, at any rate, can listen; and I have heard them
   Muttering and whispering in the dark about this girl.
   They say no woman has ever, so unreasonably,
   Died so shameful a death for a generous act:
   "She covered her brother's body. Is this indecent?   65
   She kept him from dogs and vultures. Is this a crime?
   Death?—She should have all the honor that we can give her!"

   This is the way they talk out there in the city.

   You must believe me:
   Nothing is closer to me than your happiness.   70
   What could be closer? Must not any son
   Value his father's fortune as his father does his?
   I beg you, do not be unchangeable:
   Do not believe that you alone can be right.
   The man who thinks that,   75
   The man who maintains that only he has the power
   To reason correctly, the gift to speak, the soul—
   A man like that, when you know him, turns out empty.

   It is not reason never to yield to reason!

   In flood time you can see how some trees bend,   80
   And because they bend, even their twigs are safe,
   While stubborn trees are torn up, roots and all.
   And the same thing happens in sailing:
   Make your sheet fast, never slacken,—and over you go,
   Head over heels and under: and there's your voyage.   85
   Forget you are angry! Let yourself be moved!
   I know I am young; but please let me say this:
   The ideal condition
   Would be, I admit, that men should be right by instinct;
   But since we are all too likely to go astray,   90
   The reasonable thing is to learn from those who can teach.

CHORAGOS. You will do well to listen to him, King,
    If what he says is sensible. And you, Haimon,
    Must listen to your father.—Both speak well.
CREON. You consider it right for a man of my years and experience   95
    To go to school to a boy?
HAIMON.   It is not right
    If I am wrong. But if I am young, and right,
    What does my age matter?
CREON. You think it right to stand up for an anarchist?
HAIMON. Not at all. I pay no respect to criminals.   100
CREON. Then she is not a criminal?
HAIMON. The City would deny it, to a man.
CREON. And the City proposes to teach me how to rule?
HAIMON. Ah. Who is it that's talking like a boy now?
CREON. My voice is the one voice giving orders in this City!   105
HAIMON. It is no City if it takes orders from one voice.
CREON. The State is the King!
HAIMON.   Yes, if the State is a desert.

Pause.

CREON. This boy, it seems, has sold out to a woman.
HAIMON. If you are a woman: my concern is only for you.
CREON. So? Your "concern"! In a public brawl with your father!   110
HAIMON. How about you, in a public brawl with justice?
CREON. With justice, when all that I do is within my rights?
HAIMON. You have no right to trample on God's right.
CREON (*completely out of control*). Fool, adolescent fool! Taken in
    by a woman!
HAIMON. You'll never see me taken in by anything vile.   115
CREON. Every word you say is for her!
HAIMON (*quietly, darkly*).   And for you.
    And for me. And for the gods under the earth.
CREON. You'll never marry her while she lives.
HAIMON. Then she must die.—But her death will cause another.
CREON. Another?   120
    Have you lost your senses? Is this an open threat?
HAIMON. There is no threat in speaking to emptiness.
CREON. I swear you'll regret this superior tone of yours!
    You are the empty one!
HAIMON.   If you were not my father, I'd say you were
    perverse.   125
CREON. You girlstruck fool, don't play at words with me!
HAIMON. I am sorry. You prefer silence.
CREON.   Now, by God—!
    I swear, by all the gods in heaven above us,
    You'll watch it, I swear you shall!
                      (*To the* SERVANTS.)
                      Bring her out!

Bring the woman out! Let her die before his eyes!   130
Here, this instant, with her bridegroom beside her!
HAIMON. Not here, no; she will not die here, King.
And you will never see my face again.
Go on raving as long as you've a friend to endure you.

(Exit HAIMON.)

CHORAGOS. Gone, gone.
Creon, a young man in a rage is dangerous!   135
CREON. Let him do, or dream to do, more than a man can.
He shall not save these girls from death.
CHORAGOS.   These girls?
You have sentenced them both?
CREON.   No, you are right.
I will not kill the one whose hands are clean.   140
CHORAGOS. But Antigonê?
CREON (somberly).   I will carry her far away
Out there in the wilderness, and lock her
Living in a vault of stone. She shall have food,
As the custom is, to absolve the State of her death.
And there let her pray to the gods of hell: 145
They are her only gods:
Perhaps they will show her an escape from death,
Or she may learn,
                        though late,
That piety shown the dead is pity in vain.

(Exit CREON.)

ODE III

Strophe

CHORUS. Love, unconquerable
Waster of rich men, keeper
Of warm lights and all-night vigil
In the soft face of a girl:
Sea-wanderer, forest-visitor!   5
Even the pure Immortals cannot escape you,
And mortal man, in his one day's dusk,
Trembles before your glory.

Antistrophe

Surely you swerve upon ruin
The just man's consenting heart,   10
As here you have made bright anger

Strike between father and son—
And none has conquered but Love!
A girl's glánce wórking the will of heaven:
Pleasure to her alone who mocks us,
Merciless Aphroditê.°

15

SCENE IV

CHORAGOS *(as* ANTIGONÊ *enters guarded).* But I can no longer stand
    in awe of this,
Nor, seeing what I see, keep back my tears.
Here is Antigonê, passing to that chamber
Where all find sleep at last.

Strophe 1

ANTIGONÊ. Look upon me, friends, and pity me
    Turning back at the night's edge to say
    Good-by to the sun that shines for me no longer;
    Now sleepy Death
    Summons me down to Acheron,° that cold shore:
    There is no bridesong there, nor any music.
CHORUS. Yet not unpraised, not without a kind of honor,
    You walk at last into the underworld;
    Untouched by sickness, broken by no sword.
    What woman has ever found your way to death?

5

10

Antistrophe 1

ANTIGONÊ. How often I have heard the story of Niobê,
    Tantalos' wretched daughter, how the stone
    Clung fast about her, ivy-close: and they say
    The rain falls endlessly
    And sifting soft snow; her tears are never done.
    I feel the loneliness of her death in mine.
CHORUS. But she was born of heaven, and you
    Are woman, woman-born. If her death is yours,
    A mortal woman's, is this not for you
    Glory in our world and in the world beyond?

15

20

Strophe 2

ANTIGONÊ. You laugh at me. Ah, friends, friends,
    Can you not wait until I am dead? O Thebes,

25

---

[16]**Aphroditê** *goddess of love.*   [9]**Acheron** *a river of the underworld.*

O men many-charioted, in love with Fortune,
Dear springs of Dircê, sacred Theban grove,
Be witnesses for me, denied all pity,
Unjustly judged! and think a word of love   30
For her whose path turns
Under dark earth, where there are no more tears.
CHORUS. You have passed beyond human daring and come at last
Into a place of stone where Justice sits.
I cannot tell   35
What shape of your father's guilt appears in this.

Antistrophe 2

ANTIGONÊ. You have touched it at last: that bridal bed
Unspeakable, horror of son and mother mingling:
Their crime, infection of all our family!
O Oedipus, father and brother!   40
Your marriage strikes from the grave to murder mine.
I have been a stranger here in my own land:
All my life
The blasphemy of my birth has followed me.
CHORUS. Reverence is a virtue, but strength   45
Lives in established law: that must prevail.
You have made your choice,
Your death is the doing of your conscious hand.

Epode

ANTIGONÊ. Then let me go, since all your words are bitter,
And the very light of the sun is cold to me.   50
Lead me to my vigil, where I must have
Neither love nor lamentation; no song, but silence.

                    CREON *interrupts impatiently.*

CREON. If dirges and planned lamentations could put off death,
Men would be singing for ever.
                    (To the SERVANTS.*)*
                    Take her, go!
You know your orders: take her to the vault   55
And leave her alone there. And if she lives or dies,
That's her affair, not ours: our hands are clean.

ANTIGONÊ. O tomb, vaulted bride-bed in eternal rock,
Soon I shall be with my own again
Where Persephonê° welcomes the thin ghosts underground: 60
And I shall see my father again, and you, mother,

---

⁶⁰**Persephonê**   *queen of the underworld.*

And dearest Polyneicês—
        dearest indeed
To me, since it was my hand
That washed him clean and poured the ritual wine:
And my reward is death before my time!   65

And yet, as men's hearts know, I have done no wrong,
I have not sinned before God. Or if I have,
I shall know the truth in death. But if the guilt
Lies upon Creon who judged me, then, I pray,
May his punishment equal my own.
CHORAGOS.   O passionate heart,   70
  Unyielding, tormented still by the same winds!
CREON. Her guards shall have good cause to regret their delaying.
ANTIGONÊ. Ah! That voice is like the voice of death!
CREON. I can give you no reason to think you are mistaken.
ANTIGONÊ. Thebes, and you my fathers' gods,   75
  And rulers of Thebes, you see me now, the last
Unhappy daughter of a line of kings,
Your kings, led away to death. You will remember
What things I suffer, and at what men's hands,
Because I would not transgress the laws of heaven.   80
(To the GUARDS, *simply.)* Come: let us wait no longer.

       (Exit ANTIGONÊ, *left, guarded.)*

ODE IV

Strophe 1

CHORUS. All Danaê's beauty was locked away
  In a brazen cell where the sunlight could not come:
  A small room still as any grave, enclosed her.
  Yet she was a princess too,
  And Zeus in a rain of gold poured love upon her.   5
  O child, child,
  No power in wealth or war
  Or tough sea-blackened ships
  Can prevail against untiring Destiny!

Antistrophe 1

  And Dryas' son° also, that furious king,   10
  Bore the god's prisoning anger for his pride:

---

[10] **Dryas' son** *Lycurgus, King of Thrace.*

Sealed up by Dionysos in deaf stone,
His madness died among echoes.
So at the last he learned what dreadful power
His tongue had mocked: 15
For he had profaned the revels,
And fired the wrath of the nine
Implacable Sisters° that love the sound of the flute.

Strophe 2

And old men tell a half-remembered tale
Of horror where a dark ledge splits the sea   20
And a double surf beats on the gráy shóres:
How a king's new woman°, sick
With hatred for the queen he had imprisoned,
Ripped out his two sons' eyes with her bloody hands
While grinning Arês° watchcd the shuttle plunge   25
Four times: four blind wounds crying for revenge,

Antistrophe 2

Crying, tears and blood mingled.—Piteously born,
Those sons whose mother was of heavenly birth!
Her fathcr was the god of the North Wind
And she was cradled by gales,   30
She raced with young colts on the glittering hills
And walked untrammeled in the open light:
But in her marriage deathless Fate found means
To build a tomb like yours for all her joy.

SCENE V

Enter blind TEIRESIAS, *led by a boy. The opening speeches of* TEIRESIAS *should be in singsong contrast to the realistic lines of* CREON.

TEIRESIAS. This is the way the blind man comes, Princes, Princes,
    Lock-step, two heads lit by the eyes of one.
CREON. What new thing have you to tell us, old Tciresias?
TEIRESIAS. I have much to tell you: listen to the prophet, Creon.
CREON. I am not aware that I have ever failed to listen.   5
TEIRESIAS. Then you have done wisely, King, and ruled well.
CREON. I admit my debt to you. But what have you to say?

---

[18]*Implacable Sisters*   The Muses.   [22]*King's new woman*   Eidothea, second wife of King Phineas, blinded her stepsons after the King had imprisoned their mother in a cave.   [25]*Arês*   god of war.

TEIRESIAS. This, Creon: you stand once more on the edge of fate.
CREON. What do you mean? Your words are a kind of dread.
TEIRESIAS. Listen, Creon: 10
    I was sitting in my chair of augury, at the place
    Where the birds gather about me. They were all a-chatter,
    As is their habit, when suddenly I heard
    A strange note in their jangling, a scream, a
    Whirring fury; I knew that they were fighting,   15
    Tearing each other, dying
    In a whirlwind of wings clashing. And I was afraid.
    I began the rites of burnt-offering at the altar,
    But Hephaistos° failed me: instead of bright flame,
    There was only the sputtering slime of the fat thigh-flesh   20
    Melting: the entrails dissolved in gray smoke,
    The bare bone burst from the welter. And no blaze!
    This was a sign from heaven. My boy described it,
    Seeing for me as I see for others.

    I tell you, Creon, yourself have brought   25
    This new calamity upon us. Our hearths and altars
    Are stained with the corruption of dogs and carrion birds
    That glut themselves on the corpse of Oedipus' son.
    The gods are deaf when we pray to them, their fire
    Recoils from our offering, their birds of omen   30
    Have no cry of comfort, for they are gorged
    With the thick blood of the dead.
                           O my son,
    These are no trifles! Think: all men make mistakes,
    But a good man yields when he knows his course is wrong,
    And repairs the evil. The only crime is pride.   35

    Give in to the dead man, then: do not fight with a corpse—
    What glory is it to kill a man who is dead?
    Think, I beg you:
    It is for your own good that I speak as I do.
    You should be able to yield for your own good.   40
CREON. It seems that prophets have made me their especial province.
    All my life long
    I have been a kind of butt for the dull arrows
    Of doddering fortune-tellers!
                       No, Teiresias:
    If your birds—if the great eagles of God himself   45
    Should carry him stinking bit by bit to heaven,
    I would not yield. I am not afraid of pollution:
    No man can defile the gods.

---

[19] **Hephaistos**   *god of fire.*

Do what you will,
Go into business, make money, speculate
In India gold or that synthetic gold from Sardis,   50
Get rich otherwise than by my consent to bury him.
Teiresias, it is a sorry thing when a wise man
Sells his wisdom, lets out his words for hire!

TEIRESIAS. Ah Creon! Is there no man left in the world—
CREON. To do what?—Come, let's have the aphorism!   55
TEIRESIAS. No man who knows that wisdom outweighs any wealth?
CREON. As surely as bribes are baser than any baseness.
TEIRESIAS. You are sick, Creon! You are deathly sick!
CREON. As you say: it is not my place to challenge a prophet.
TEIRESIAS. Yet you have said my prophecy is for sale.   60
CREON. The generation of prophets has always loved gold.
TEIRESIAS. The generation of kings has always loved brass.
CREON. You forget yourself! You are speaking to your King.
TEIRESIAS. I know it. You are a king because of me.
CREON. You have a certain skill; but you have sold out.   65
TEIRESIAS. King, you will drive me to words that—
CREON.   Say them, say them!
    Only remember: I will not pay you for them.
TEIRESIAS. No, you will find them too costly.
CREON.   No doubt. Speak:
    Whatever you say, you will not change my will.
TEIRESIAS. Then take this, and take it to heart!   70
    The time is not far off when you shall pay back
    Corpse for corpse, flesh of your own flesh.
    You have thrust the child of this world into living night,
    You have kept from the gods below the child that is theirs:
    The one in a grave before her death, the other,   75
    Dead, denied the grave. This is your crime:
    And the Furies and the dark gods of Hell
    Are swift with terrible punishment for you.

    Do you want to buy me now, Creon?
    Not many days,
    And your house will be full of men and women weeping,   80
    And curses will be hurled at you from far
    Cities grieving for sons unburied, left to rot
    Before the walls of Thebes.

    These are my arrows, Creon: they are all for you.

    (To BOY.*)* But come, child: lead me home.   85
    Let him waste his fine anger upon younger men.
    Maybe he will learn at last
    To control a wiser tongue in a better head.

(Exit TEIRESIAS.*)*

CHORAGOS. The old man has gone, King, but his words
Remain to plague us. I am old, too, 90
But I cannot remember that he was ever false.
CREON. That is true. . . . It troubles me.
Oh it is hard to give in! but it is worse
To risk everything for stubborn pride.
CHORAGOS. Creon: take my advice.
CREON. What shall I do? 95
CHORAGOS. Go quickly: free Antigonê from her vault
And build a tomb for the body of Polyneicês.
CREON. You would have me do this!
CHORAGOS. Creon, yes!
And it must be done at once: God moves
Swiftly to cancel the folly of stubborn men. 100
CREON. It is hard to deny the heart! But I
Will do it: I will not fight with destiny.
CHORAGOS. You must go yourself, you cannot leave it to others.
CREON. I will go.
—Bring axes, servants:
Come with me to the tomb. I buried her. I 105
Will set her free.
Oh quickly!
My mind misgives—
The laws of the gods are mighty, and a man must serve them
To the last day of his life!

(Exit CREON.*)*

PAEAN°

Strophe 1

CHORAGOS. God of many names
CHORUS. O Iacchos°
son
of Kadmeian Sémelê°
O born of the Thunder!
Guardian of the West
Regent
of Eleusis' plain
O Prince of maenad° Thebes
and the Dragon Field by rippling Ismenós.° 5

Paean *a hymn.* [1]Iacchos *Bacchos or Dionysos, god of wine and revelry.* [2]Sémelê *mother of Iacchos, consort of Zeus.* [4]maenad *female worshipper, attendant of Iacchos.* [5]Ismenós *a river near Thebes where, according to legend, dragon's teeth were sown from which sprang the ancestors of Thebes.*

Antistrophe 1

CHORAGOS. God of many names
CHORUS.   the flame of torches
   flares on our hills
                         the nymphs of Iacchos
   dance at the spring of Castalia.°
   from the vine-close mountain
                              come ah come in ivy:
   Evohé evohé! sings through the streets of Thebes   10

Strophe 2

CHORAGOS. God of many names
CHORUS.   Iacchos of Thebes
   heavenly Child
                    of Sémelê bride of the Thunderer!
   The shadow of plague is upon us:
                                     come
   with clement feet
                       oh come from Parnasos
   down the long slopes
                         across the lamenting water   15

Antistrophe 2

CHORAGOS. Iô Fire! Chorister of the throbbing stars!
   O purest among the voices of the night!
   Thou son of God, blaze for us!
CHORUS. Come with choric rapture of circling Maenads
   Who cry *Iô Iacche!*
                         God of many names!   20

EXODOS

Enter MESSENGER *from left.*

MESSENGER. Men of the line of Kadmos,° you who live
   Near Amphion's citadel,°
                            I cannot say
   Of any condition of human life "This is fixed,
   This is clearly good, or bad." Fate raises up,
   And Fate casts down the happy and unhappy alike: 5

---

⁸**Castalia**   *a spring on Mount Parnasos.*   ¹**Kadmos**   *sowed the dragon's teeth; founded Thebes.*   ²**Amphion's citadel**   *Amphion's lyre playing charmed stones to form a wall around Thebes.*

No man can foretell his Fate.
                    Take the case of Creon:
Creon was happy once, as I count happiness:
Victorious in battle, sole governor of the land,
Fortunate father of children nobly born.
And now it has all gone from him! Who can say   10
That a man is still alive when his life's joy fails?
He is a walking dead man. Grant him rich,
Let him live like a king in his great house:
If his pleasure is gone, I would not give
So much as the shadow of smoke for all he owns.   15

CHORAGOS. Your words hint at sorrow: what is your news for us?

MESSENGER. They are dead. The living are guilty of their death.

CHORAGOS. Who is guilty? Who is dead? Speak!

MESSENGER.   Haimon.
Haimon is dead; and the hand that killed him
Is his own hand.

CHORAGOS. His father's? or his own?   20

MESSENGER. His own, driven mad by the murder his father had done.

CHORAGOS. Teiresias, Teiresias, how clearly you saw it all!

MESSENGER. This is my news: you must draw what conclusions you can
    from it.

CHORAGOS. But look: Eurydicê, our Queen:
    Has she overheard us?   25

Enter EURYDICÊ *from the palace, center.*

EURYDICÊ. I have heard something, friends:
    As I was unlocking the gate of Pallas' shrine,
    For I needed her help today, I heard a voice
    Telling of some new sorrow. And I fainted
    There at the temple with all my maidens about me.   30
    But speak again: whatever it is, I can bear it:
    Grief and I are no strangers.

MESSENGER.   Dearest Lady,
    I will tell you plainly all that I have seen.
    I shall not try to comfort you: what is the use,
    Since comfort could lie only in what is not true?   35
    The truth is always best.
                    I went with Creon
    To the outer plain where Polyneicês was lying,
    No friend to pity him, his body shredded by dogs.
    We made our prayers in that place to Hecatê
    And Pluto, that they would be merciful. And we bathed   40
    The corpse with holy water, and we brought
    Fresh-broken branches to burn what was left of it,
    And upon the urn we heaped up a towering barrow
    Of the earth of his own land.

When we were done, we ran
To the vault where Antigonê lay on her couch of stone.   45
One of the servants had gone ahead,
And while he was yet far off he heard a voice
Grieving within the chamber, and he came back
And told Creon. And as the King went closer,
The air was full of wailing, the words lost,   50
And he begged us to make all haste. "Am I a prophet?"
He said, weeping, "And must I walk this road,
The saddest of all that I have gone before?
My son's voice calls me on. Oh quickly, quickly!
Look through the crevice there, and tell me   55
If it is Haimon, or some deception of the gods!"

We obeyed; and in the cavern's farthest corner
We saw her lying:
She had made a noose of her fine linen veil
And hanged herself. Haimon lay beside her,   60
His arms about her waist, lamenting her,
His love lost under ground, crying out
That his father had stolen her away from him.

When Creon saw him the tears rushed to his eyes
And he called to him: "What have you done, child?
     Speak to me.   65
What are you thinking that makes your eyes so strange?
O my son, my son, I come to you on my knees!"
But Haimon spat in his face. He said not a word,
Staring—
          And suddenly drew his sword
And lunged. Creon shrank back, the blade missed; and the boy,   70
Desperate against himself, drove it half its length
Into his own side, and fell. And as he died
He gathered Antigonê close in his arms again,
Choking, his blood bright red on her white cheek.
And now he lies dead with the dead, and she is his   75
At last, his bride in the house of the dead.

Exit EURYDICÊ *into the palace.*

CHORAGOS. She has left us without a word. What can this mean?
MESSENGER. It troubles me, too; yet she knows what is best,
     Her grief is too great for public lamentation,
     And doubtless she has gone to her chamber to weep   80
     For her dead son, leading her maidens in his dirge.

Pause.

CHORAGOS. It may be so: but I fear this deep silence.

MESSENGER. I will see what she is doing. I will go in.

Exit MESSENGER *into the palace.*

Enter CREON *with attendants, bearing* HAIMON'S *body.*

CHORAGOS. But here is the king himself: oh look at him,
  Bearing his own damnation in his arms.   85
CREON. Nothing you say can touch me any more.
  My own blind heart has brought me
  From darkness to final darkness. Here you see
  The father murdering, the murdered son—
  And all my civic wisdom!   90

  Haimon my son, so young, so young to die,
  I was the fool, not you; and you died for me.
CHORAGOS. That is the truth; but you were late in learning it.
CREON. This truth is hard to bear. Surely a god
  Has crushed me beneath the hugest weight of heaven,   95
  And driven me headlong a barbaric way
  To trample out the thing I held most dear.

  The pains that men will take to come to pain!

Enter MESSENGER *from the palace.*

MESSENGER. The burden you carry in your hands is heavy,
  But it is not all: you will find more in your house.   100
CREON. What burden worse than this shall I find there?
MESSENGER. The Queen is dead.
CREON. O port of death, deaf world,
  Is there no pity for me? And you, Angel of evil,
  I was dead, and your words are death again.   105
  Is it true, boy? Can it be true?
  Is my wife dead? Has death bred death?
MESSENGER. You can see for yourself.

The doors are opened and the body of EURYDICÊ *is disclosed within.*

CREON. Oh pity!
  All true, all true, and more than I can bear!   110
  O my wife, my son!
MESSENGER. She stood before the altar, and her heart
  Welcomed the knife her own hand guided,
  And a great cry burst from her lips for Megareus dead,
  And for Haimon dead, her sons; and her last breath   115
  Was a curse for their father, the murderer of her sons.
  And she fell, and the dark flowed in through her closing eyes.
CREON. O God, I am sick with fear.
  Are there no swords here? Has no one a blow for me?

MESSENGER. Her curse is upon you for the deaths of both. 120

CREON. It is right that it should be. I alone am guilty.

I know it, and I say it. Lead me in,

Quickly, friends.

I have neither life nor substance. Lead me in.

CHORAGOS. You are right, if there can be right in so much wrong. 125

The briefest way is best in a world of sorrow.

CREON. Let it come,

Let death come quickly, and be kind to me.

I would not ever see the sun again.

CHORAGOS. All that will come when it will; but we, meanwhile, 130

Have much to do. Leave the future to itself.

CREON. All my heart was in that prayer!

CHORAGOS. Then do not pray any more: the sky is deaf.

CREON. Lead me away. I have been rash and foolish.

I have killed my son and my wife. 135

I look for comfort; my comfort lies here dead.

Whatever my hands have touched has come to nothing.

Fate has brought all my pride to a thought of dust.

As CREON *is being led into the house, the* CHORAGOS *advances and speaks directly to the audience.*

CHORAGOS. There is no happiness where there is no wisdom;

No wisdom but in submission to the gods. 140

Big words are always punished,

And proud men in old age learn to be wise.

(*c. 441 B.C.*)

QUESTIONS

1. Describe the central problem of the play. Whose rights should assume priority—Creon's to legislate and punish, or Antigonê's to bury her brother? Is there any way to resolve the competing claims of Creon and Antigonê?
2. How does Sophocles characterize Creon and Antigonê? Consider their speeches, actions, and gestures.
3. What is Haimon's role in the play? What does Haimon's dialogue with his father reveal about the two characters?
4. What do Ismenê and Euridycê contribute to the play? How would *Antigonê* differ if either or both were absent?
5. Describe the structure of the play. How is its plot constructed and developed? Explain the focus of each scene. What is the purpose of the poetic odes that punctuate the dramatic action of the play?
6. What is the chorus's role? Single out two important comments made by the chorus and explain their significance.

7. Compare Antigonê's tragedy with Creon's suffering. Which character do you sympathize with most? Why?

8. Compare Creon's actions at the beginning and end of the play. How does he change?

CRITICS ON SOPHOCLES

ARISTOTLE

[384–322 B.C.]

The Six Elements of Tragedy

TRANSLATED BY GERALD F. ELSE

At present let us deal with tragedy, recovering from what has been said so far the definition of its essential nature, as it was in development. Tragedy, then, is a process of imitating an action which has serious implications, is complete, and possesses magnitude; by means of language which has been made sensuously attractive, with each of its varieties found separately in the parts; enacted by the persons themselves and not presented through narrative; through a course of pity and fear completing the purification of tragic acts which have those emotional characteristics. By "language made sensuously attractive" I mean language that has rhythm and melody, and by "its varieties found separately" I mean the fact that certain parts of the play are carried on through spoken verses alone and others the other way around, through song.

Now first of all, since they perform the imitation through action (by acting it), the adornment of their visual appearance will perforce constitute some part of the making of tragedy; and song-composition and verbal expression also, for those are the media in which they perform the imitation. By "verbal expression" I mean the actual composition of the verses, and by "song-composition" something whose meaning is entirely clear.

Next, since it is an imitation of an action and is enacted by certain people who are performing the action, and since those people must necessarily have certain traits both of character and thought (for it is thanks to these two factors that we speak of people's actions also as having a defined character, and it is in accordance with their actions that all either succeed or fail); and since the imitation of the action is the plot, for by "plot" I mean here the structuring of the events, and by the "characters" that in accordance with which we say that the persons who are acting have a defined moral character, and by "thought" all the passages in which they attempt to prove some thesis or set forth an opinion—it follows of necessity, then, that tragedy as a whole has just six constituent elements, in relation to the essence that makes it a distinct species; and they are plot, characters, verbal expression, thought, visual adornment, and song-composition. For the elements by which they imitate are two (i.e., verbal expression and song-composition), the manner in which they imitate is one (visual adornment), the things they imitate are three (plot, characters, thought), and there is nothing more beyond these. These then are the constituent forms they use.

From Poetics: Tragedy

Simple and Complex Plots

Among simple plots and actions the episodic are the worst. By "episodic" plot I mean one in which there is no probability or necessity for the order in which the episodes follow one another. Such structures are composed by the bad poets because they are bad poets, but by the good poets because of the actors: in composing contest pieces for them, and stretching out the plot beyond its capacity, they are forced frequently to dislocate the sequence.

Furthermore, since the tragic imitation is not only of a complete action but also of events that are fearful and pathetic, and these come about best when they come about contrary to one's expectation yet logically, one following from the other; that way they will be more productive of wonder than if they happen merely at random, by chance—because even among chance occurrences the ones people consider most marvelous are those that seem to have come about as if on purpose: for example the way the statue of Mitys at Argos killed the man who had been the cause of Mitys's death, by falling on him while he was attending the festival; it stands to reason, people think, that such things don't happen by chance—so plots of that sort cannot fail to be artistically superior.

Some plots are simple, others are complex; indeed the actions of which the plots are imitations already fall into these two categories. By "simple" action I mean one the development of which being continuous and unified in the manner stated above, the reversal comes without peripety or recognition, and by "complex" action one in which the reversal is continuous but with recognition or peripety or both. And these developments must grow out of the very structure of the plot itself, in such a way that on the basis of what has happened previously this particular outcome follows either by necessity or in accordance with probability; for there is a great difference in whether these events happen because of those or merely after them.

"Peripety" is a shift of what is being undertaken to the opposite in the way previously stated, and that in accordance with probability or necessity as we have just been saying; as for example in the *Oedipus* the man who has come, thinking that he will reassure Oedipus, that is, relieve him of his fear with respect to his mother, by revealing who he once was, brings about the opposite; and in the *Lynceus,* as he (Lynceus) is being led away with every prospect of being executed, and Danaus pursuing him with every prospect of doing the executing, it comes about as a result of the other things that have happened in the play that *he* is executed and Lynceus is saved. And "recognition" is, as indeed the name indicates, a shift from ignorance to awareness, pointing in the direction either of close blood ties or of hostility, of people who have previously been in a clearly marked state of happiness or unhappiness.

The finest recognition is one that happens at the same time as a peripety, as is the case with the one in the *Oedipus*. Naturally, there are also other kinds of recognition: it is possible for one to take place in the prescribed manner in relation to inanimate objects and chance occurrences, and it is possible to recognize whether a person has acted or not acted. But the form that is most integrally a part of the plot, the action, is the one aforesaid; for that kind of recognition combined with peripety will excite either pity or fear (and these are the kinds of action of which tragedy is an imitation according to our definition), because both good and bad fortune will also be most likely to follow that kind of event. Since, further, the recognition is a recognition of persons, some are of one person by the other one only (when it is already known who the "other one" is), but sometimes it is necessary for both persons to go through a recognition, as for example, Iphigenia is recognized by her brother through the sending of the letter, but of him by Iphigenia another recognition is required.

These then are two elements of plot: peripety and recognition; third is the *pathos*. Of these, peripety and recognition have been discussed; a *pathos* is a destructive or painful act, such as deaths on stage, paroxysms of pain, woundings, and all that sort of thing.

From Poetics: Tragedy

SIGMUND FREUD

[1856–1939]

The Oedipus Complex

The action of the play consists in nothing other than the process of revealing, with cunning delays and ever-mounting excitement—a process that can be likened to the work of a psychoanalysis—that Oedipus himself is the murderer of Laïus, but further that he is the son of the murdered man and of Jocasta. Appalled at the abomination which he has unwittingly perpetrated, Oedipus blinds himself and forsakes his home. The oracle has been fulfilled.

Oedipus Rex is what is known as a tragedy of destiny. Its tragic effect is said to lie in the contrast between the supreme will of the gods and the vain attempts of mankind to escape the evil that threatens them. The lesson which, it is said, the deeply moved spectator should learn from the tragedy is submission to the divine will and realization of his own impotence. Modern dramatists have accordingly tried to achieve a similar tragic effect by weaving the same contrast into a plot invented by themselves. But the spectators have looked on unmoved while a curse or an oracle was fulfilled in spite of all the efforts of some innocent man: later tragedies of destiny have failed in their effect.

If *Oedipus Rex* moves a modern audience no less than it did the contemporary Greek one, the explanation can only be that its effect does not lie in the contrast between destiny and human will, but is to be looked for in the particular nature of the material on which that contrast is exemplified. There must be something which makes a voice within us ready to recognize the compelling force of destiny in the *Oedipus,* while we can dismiss as merely arbitrary such dispositions as are laid down in [Grillparzer's] *Die Ahnfrau* or other modern tragedies of destiny. And a factor of this kind is in fact involved in the story of King Oedipus. His destiny moves us only because it might have been ours—because the oracle laid the same curse upon us before our birth as upon him. It is the fate of all of us, perhaps, to direct our first sexual impulse toward our mother and our first hatred and our first murderous wish against our father. Our dreams convince us that that is so. King Oedipus, who slew his father Laïus and married his mother Jocasta, merely shows us the fulfillment of our own childhood wishes. But, more fortunate than he, we have meanwhile succeeded, in so far as we have not become psychoneurotics, in detaching our sexual impulses from our mothers and in forgetting our jealousy of our fathers. Here is one in whom these primeval wishes of our childhood have been fulfilled, and we shrink back from him with the whole force of the repression by which those wishes have since that time been held down within us. While the poet, as he unravels the past, brings to light the guilt of Oedipus, he is at the same time compelling us to recognize our own inner minds, in which those same impulses, though suppressed, are still to be found. The contrast with which the closing Chorus leaves us confronted—

> . . . Fix on Oedipus your eyes,
> Who resolved the dark enigma, noblest champion and most wise.
> Like a star his envied fortune mounted beaming far and wide:
> Now he sinks in seas of anguish, whelmed beneath a raging tide . . .[1]

—strikes as a warning at ourselves and our pride, at us who since our childhood have grown so wise and so mighty in our own eyes. Like Oedipus, we live in ignorance of these wishes, repugnant to morality, which have been forced upon us by Nature, and after their revelation we may all of us well seek to close our eyes to the scenes of our childhood.

There is an unmistakable indication in the text of Sophocles' tragedy itself that the legend of Oedipus sprang from some primeval dream material which had as its content the distressing disturbance of a child's relation to his parents owing to the first stirrings of sexuality. At a point when Oedipus, though he is not yet enlightened, has begun to feel troubled by his recollection of the oracle, Jocasta consoles him by referring to a dream which many people dream, though, as she thinks, it has no meaning:

> Many a man ere now in dreams hath lain
> With her who bare him. He hath least annoy
> Who with such omens troubleth not his mind.[2]

Today, just as then, many men dream of having sexual relations with their mothers, and speak of the fact with indignation and astonishment. It is clearly the key to the tragedy and the complement to the dream of the dreamer's father being dead. The story

---

[1]Lewis Campbell's translation, lines 1524ff (Fitts and Fitzgerald, Antistrophe 2, lines 292–96).
[2]Lewis Campbell's translation, lines 982ff (Fitts and Fitzgerald, Scene 3, lines 67–69).

of Oedipus is the reaction of the imagination to these two typical dreams. And just as these dreams, when dreamt by adults, are accompanied by feelings of repulsion, so too the legend must include horror and self-punishment. Its further modification originates once again in a misconceived secondary revision of the material, which has sought to exploit it for theological purposes. . . . The attempt to harmonize divine omnipotence with human responsibility must naturally fail in connection with this subject matter just as with any other.

From The Interpretation of Dreams

BERNARD KNOX

Sophocles' Oedipus

In an earlier Sophoclean play, *Antigone,* the chorus sings a hymn to this man the conqueror. "Many are the wonders and terrors, and nothing more wonderful and terrible than man." He has conquered the sea, "this creature goes beyond the white sea pressing forward as the swell crashes about him"; and he has conquered the land, "earth, highest of the gods . . . he wears away with the turning plough." He has mastered not only the elements, sea, and land, but the birds, beasts, and fishes; "through knowledge and technique," sings the chorus, he is yoker of the horse, tamer of the bull. "And he has taught himself speech and thought swift as the wind and attitudes which enable him to live in communities and means to shelter himself from the frost and rain. Full of resources he faces the future, nothing will find him at a loss. Death, it is true, he will not avoid, yet he has thought out ways of escape from desperate diseases. His knowledge, ingenuity and technique are beyond anything that could have been foreseen." These lyrics describe the rise to power of *anthropos tyrannos;* self-taught, he seizes control of his environment, he is master of the elements, the animals, the arts and sciences of civilization. "Full of resources he faces the future"—an apt description of Oedipus at the beginning of our play.

And it is not the only phrase of this ode which is relevant; for Oedipus is connected by the terms he uses, and which are used to and about him, with the whole range of human achievement which has raised man to his present level. All the items of this triumphant catalog recur in the *Oedipus Tyrannos;* the images of the play define him as helmsman, conqueror of the sea, and ploughman, conqueror of the land, as hunter, master of speech and thought, inventor, legislator, physician. Oedipus is faced in the play with an intellectual problem, and as he marshals his intellectual resources to solve it, the language of the play suggests a comparison between Oedipus' methods in the play and the whole range of sciences and techniques which have brought man to mastery, made him *tyrannos* of the world.

Oedipus' problem is apparently simple: "Who is the murderer of Laius?" But as he pursues the answer, the question changes shape. It becomes a different problem: "Who am I?" And the answer to this problem involves the gods as well as man. The answer to the question is not what he expected, it is in fact a reversal, that *peripeteia* which Aristotle speaks of in connection with this play. The state of Oedipus is reversed from "first of men" to "most accursed of men"; his attitude from the proud ἀρκτέον, "I must rule," to the humble πειστέον, "I must obey." "Reversal," says Aristotle, "is a change of the action into the opposite," and one meaning of this much disputed phrase is that the action produces the opposite of the actor's intentions. So Oedipus curses the murderer of Laius and it turns out that he has cursed himself. But this reversal is not confined to the action; it is also the process of all the great images of the play which identify Oedipus as the inventive, critical spirit of his century. As the images unfold, the inquirer turns into the object of inquiry, the hunter into the prey, the doctor into the patient, the investigator into the criminal, the revealer into the thing revealed, the finder into the thing found, the savior into the thing saved ("I was saved, for some dreadful destiny"), the liberator into the thing released ("I released your feet from the bonds which pierced your ankles," says the Corinthian messenger). The accuser becomes the defendant, the ruler the subject, the teacher not only the pupil but also the object lesson, the example—a change of the action into its opposite, from active to passive.

And the two opening images of the *Antigone* ode recur with hideous effect. Oedipus the helmsman, who steers the ship of state, is seen, in Tiresias' words, as one who "steers his ship into a nameless anchorage," who, in the chorus's words, "shared the same great harbour with his father." And Oedipus the ploughman—"How," asks the chorus, "how could the furrows which your father ploughed bear you in silence for so long?"

This reversal is the movement of the play, parallel in the imagery and the action: it is the overthrow of the *tyrannos,* of man who seized power and thought himself "equated to the gods." The bold metaphor of the priest introduces another of the images which parallel in their development the reversal of the hero and suggest that Oedipus is a figure symbolic of human intelligence and achievement in general. He is not only helmsman, ploughman, inventor, legislator, liberator, revealer, doctor—he is also equator, mathematician, calculator; "equated" is a mathematical term, and it is only one of a whole complex of such terms which present Oedipus in yet a fresh aspect of man *tyrannos.* One of Oedipus' favorite words is "measure," and this is of course a significant metaphor: measure, mensuration, number, calculation—these are among the most important inventions which have brought man to power. Aeschylus' Prometheus, the mythical civilizer of human life, counts number among the foremost of his gifts to man. "And number, too, I invented, outstanding among clever devices." In the river valleys of the East, generations of mensuration and calculation had brought man to an understanding of the movements of the stars and of time: in the histories of his friend Herodotus, Sophocles had read of the calculation and mensuration which had gone into the building of the pyramids. "Measure"—it is Protagoras' word: "Man is the measure of all things." In this play man's measure is taken, his true equation found. The play is full of equations, some of them incomplete, some false; the final equation shows man equated not to the gods but to himself, as Oedipus is finally equated to himself. For there are in the play not one Oedipus but two.

One is the magnificent figure set before us in the opening scenes, *tyrannos,* the man of wealth and power, first of men, the intellect and energy which drive on the search. The other is the object of the search, a shadowy figure who has violated the most fundamental human taboos, an incestuous parricide, "most accursed of men." And even before the one Oedipus finds the other, they are connected and equated in the name which they both bear, Oedipus. Oedipus—Swollen-foot; it emphasizes the physical blemish which scars the body of the splendid *tyrannos,* a defect which he tries to forget but which reminds us of the outcast child this *tyrannos* once was and the outcast man he is soon to be. The second half of the name πονζ, "foot," recurs throughout the play, as a mocking phrase which recalls this other Oedipus. "The Sphinx forced us to look at what was at our feet," says Creon. Tiresias invokes "the dread-footed curse of your father and mother." And the choral odes echo and re-echo with this word. "Let the murderer of Laius set his foot in motion in flight." "The murderer is a man alone with forlorn foot." "The laws of Zeus are high-footed." "The man of pride plunges down into doom where he cannot use his foot."

These mocking repetitions of one-half the name invoke the unknown Oedipus who will be revealed: the equally emphatic repetition of the first half emphasizes the dominant attitude of the man before us.

From Word and Action

ADRIAN POOLE

Oedipus and Athens

Oedipus is quick to decide and to act; he anticipates advice and suggestion. When the priest hints that he should send to Delphi for help, he has already done so; when the chorus suggests sending for Tiresias, the prophet has already been summoned and is on the way. This swiftness in action is a well-known Athenian quality, one their enemies are well aware of. "They are the only people," say the Corinthians, "who simultaneously hope for and have what they plan, because of their quick fulfillment of decisions." But this action is not rash, it is based on reflection; Oedipus reached the decision to apply to Delphi "groping, laboring over many paths of thought." This too is typically Athenian. "We are unique," says Pericles, "in our combination of the most courageous action and rational discussion of our plans." The Athenians also spoke with pride of the intelligence that informed such discussion: Pericles attributes the Athenian victories over the Persians "not to luck, but to intelligence." And this is the claim of Oedipus, too. "The flight of my own intelligence hit the mark," he says, as he recalls his solution of the riddle of the Sphinx. The riddle has sinister verbal connections with his fate (his name in Greek is *Oidipous,* and *dipous* is the Greek word for "two-footed" in the riddle, not to mention the later prophecy of Tiresias that he would leave Thebes as a blind man, "a stick tapping before him step by step"), but the answer he proposed to the riddle—"Man"—is appropriate for the optimistic picture of man's achievement and potential that the figure of Oedipus represents.

Above all, as we see from the priest's speech in the prologue and the prompt, energetic action Oedipus takes to rescue his subjects from the plague, he is a man dedicated to the interests and the needs of the city. It is this public spirit that drives him on to the discovery of the truth—to reject Creon's hint that the matter should be kept under wraps, to send for Tiresias, to pronounce the curse and sentence of banishment on the murderer of Laius. This spirit was the great civic virtue that Pericles preached—"I would have you fix your eyes every day on the greatness of Athens until you fall in love with her"—and that the enemies of Athens knew they had to reckon with. "In the city's service," say the Corinthians, "they use their bodies as if they did not belong to them."

All this does not necessarily mean that Sophocles' audience drew a conscious parallel between Oedipus and Athens (or even that Sophocles himself did); what is important is that they could have seen in Oedipus a man endowed with the temperament and talents they prized most highly in their own democratic leaders and in their ideal vision of themselves. Oedipus the King is a dramatic embodiment of the creative vigor and intellectual daring of the fifth-century Athenian spirit.

But there is an even greater dimension to this extraordinary dramatic figure. The fifth century in Athens saw the birth of the historical spirit. The past came to be seen no longer as a golden age from which there had been a decline if not a fall, but as a steady progress from primitive barbarism to the high civilization of the city-state. . . .

The figure of Oedipus represents not only the techniques of the transition from savagery to civilization and the political achievements of the newly settled society, but also the temper and methods of the fifth-century intellectual revolution. His speeches are full of words, phrases, and attitudes that link him with the "enlightenment" of Sophocles' own Athens. "I'll bring it all to light," he says; he is like some Protagoras or Democritus dispelling the darkness of ignorance and superstition. He is a questioner, a researcher, a discoverer—the Greek words are those of the sophistic vocabulary. Above all Oedipus is presented to the audience as a symbol of two of the greatest scientific achievements of the age—mathematics and medicine. Mathematical language recurs incessantly in the imagery of the play—such terms as "measure" *(metrein)*, "equate" *(isoun)*, "define" *(diorizein)*—and at one climactic moment Oedipus expresses as a mathematical axiom his hope that a discrepancy in the evidence will clear him of the charge of Laius's murder: "One can't equal many." This obsessive image, Oedipus the calculator, is one more means of investing the mythical figure with the salient characteristics of the fifth-century achievement, but it is also magnificently functional. For, in his search for truth, he is engaged in a great calculation to determine the measure of man, whom Protagoras called "the measure of all things."

From Tragedy: Shakespeare and the Greek Example

GEORGE STEINER

[b. 1929]

Principal Constants of Conflict in Antigone

It has, I believe, been given to only one literary text to express all the principal constants of conflict in the condition of man. These constants are fivefold: the confrontation of men and of women; of age and of youth; of society and of the individual; of the living and the dead; of men and of god(s). The conflicts which come of these five orders of confrontation are not negotiable. Men and women, old and young, the individual and the community or state, the quick and the dead, mortals and immortals, define themselves in the conflictual process of defining each other. Self-definition and the agonistic recognition of "otherness" (of *l'autre*) across the threatened boundaries of self are indissociable. The polarities of masculinity and of femininity, of aging and of youth, of private autonomy and of social collectivity, of existence and mortality, of the human and the divine, can be crystallized only in adversative terms (whatever the many shades of accommodation between them). To arrive at oneself—the primordial journey—is to come up, polemically, against "the other." The boundary-conditions of the human person are those set by gender, by age, by community, by the cut between life and death, and by the potentials of accepted or denied encounter between the existential and the transcendent.

But "collision" is, of course, a monistic and, therefore, inadequate term. Equally decisive are those categories of reciprocal perception, of grappling with "otherness," that can be defined as erotic, filial, social, ritual, and metaphysical. Men and women, old and young, individual and *communitas,* living and deceased, mortals and gods, meet and mesh in contiguities of love, of kinship, of commonality and group-communion, of caring remembrance, of worship. Sex, the honeycomb of generations and of kinship, the social unit, the presentness of the departed in the weave of the living, the practices of religion, are the modes of enactment of ultimate ontological dualities. In essence, the constants of conflict and of positive intimacy are the same. When man and woman meet, they stand against each other as they stand close. Old and young seek in each other the pain of remembrance and the matching solace of futurity. Anarchic individuation seeks interaction with the compulsions of law, of collective cohesion in the body politic. The dead inhabit the living and, in turn, await their visit. The duel between men and god(s) is the most aggressively amorous known to experience. In the physics of man's being, fission is also fusion.

It is in lines 441–581 [pages 79–82] of Sophocles' *Antigone* that each of the five fundamental categories of man's definition and self-definition through conflict is realized, and that all five are at work in a single act of confrontation. No other moment that I know of, in either sacred or secular imagining, achieves this totality. Creon and Antigone clash as man and as woman. Creon is a mature, indeed an aging, man;

Antigone's is the virginity of youth. Their fatal debate turns on the nature of the co-existence between private vision and public need, between ego and community. The imperatives of immanence, of the living in the [*polis*], πόλις, press on Creon; in Antigone, these imperatives encounter the no less exigent night-throng of the dead. No syllable spoken, no gesture made, in the dialogue of Antigone and Creon but has within it the manifold, perhaps duplicitous, nearness of the gods.

From Antigones

WORKS INSPIRED BY SOPHOCLES

The three works that follow were inspired by Sophocles' *Oedipus the King*. First, in a short poem, Muriel Rukeyser imagines Oedipus meeting the Sphinx for the second time. The poet gives the Sphinx the last word in response to a question concerning their previous meeting. Next, Ruth F. Eisenberg presents the Oedipus myth from the perspective of Jocasta. Her dramatic poem illuminates woman's role in the myth, which Sophocles' play leaves largely in shadow. And last, in a brief one-act play, William Butler Yeats recounts, describes, and dramatizes a harrowing set of events that owe part of their inspiration to the story of Oedipus.

MURIEL RUKEYSER

[1913–1980]

Myth

Long afterward, Oedipus, old and blinded, walked the
roads.   He smelled a familiar smell.   It was
the Sphinx.   Oedipus said, "I want to ask one question.
Why didn't I recognize my mother?"   "You gave the
wrong answer," said the Sphinx.   "But that was what
made everything possible," said Oedipus.   "No," she said.
"When I asked, What walks on four legs in the morning,
two at noon, and three in the evening, you answered,
Man.   You didn't say anything about woman."
"When you say Man," said Oedipus, "you include women
too. Everyone knows that."   She said, "That's what
you think."

(1973)

RUTH F. EISENBERG

[1927–1996]

Jocasta

1

When she learned the king's power,
Jocasta lost delight in being queen.
Laius was a cold, dry man. Looking at him
brought the image of her baby, his feet
pierced and bound, her baby left to die   5
on the mountain slope. They would
have no other children.

I remember Laius drunk that night, crying
for Chrysippus, the source of his curse.
Wanting his boy, he took me instead   10
and threw me on my back to have his way.
I am fifteen and afraid to resist
and tell myself it is my husband's right;
the gods decree a wife obey her spouse.

Sober, Laius recalls Apollo's threat: 15
our son will kill him, beget upon me.
Nine months drag like oxen ploughing.
With icy eyes Laius watches me swell.
I fear the gods and beg Hera for a girl,
but as foretold, I give birth to a son.   20
Laius takes the child to bind its feet.
The baby cries, and Laius turns away.
He summons a servant and orders me to hand
my baby over, threatening me when I cry.
The king will keep his own hands clean.   25

At the public altar, Laius
offered bulls and lambs in ritual
slaughter. The everburning fire raged
so the offerings charred, and Jocasta
trembled at the gods' displeasure.   30

"Jocasta"   *wife and mother of Oedipus. See Sophocles' play* Oedipus Rex, *pp. 880–921.*   [3]*Laius   father of Oedi-*
pus.   [9]*Chrysippus   Laius's male lover.*   [15]*Apollo   The sun god.*   [19]*Hera   wife of Zeus, leader of the gods.*

Upon the gates this dawn, a strange creature
appeared and woke all Thebes. In raucous voice
she cried, "A riddle. Who'll solve my riddle?"
At first our people came to gawk, then marvel.
Some trembled, children hid their heads and cried.   35
I've heard old tales the minstrels sing of her,
but never did expect to really see
a Sphinx—part woman, bird, and lion too . . .
And what she asks is strange as well: four legs,
then two, then three. What can it be? No one   40
knows the answer. No one.

   The Sphinx brought pestilence and
drought. Rivers and streams ran dry, vines
shriveled. But until her riddle was solved,
the creature would not leave. On the gates   45
she stayed, her destructive song echoing
from empty wells.

My life is a toad. All day and all night
the Sphinx. We cannot escape her song.
Song! More like wail or whine or scream.   50
Laius is useless as always. Deceitful
man, I hate him, hate his touch.

The land is parched; flocks die. Our people
haggard, starving, plead to ease their distress.
What can we do? Mortals cannot make the rain.   55
I suggest Laius seek Apollo's help.
To get away, he welcomes the idea to go
to Delphi and proclaims a pilgrimage.

   On the sunswept road to Delphi,
Laius was killed. The servant reporting   60
the death begged Jocasta to let him tend
flocks in the hills. Sending him on his way,
she shut herself in the palace.

The prophesy was false. How can that be
if gods control all things? For surely chance   65
does not . . . No, no. Yet Laius killed our son
and not the other way. That sin diseased
his soul. I bless the gods that I,
at last, am free.

I dream of my baby night after night.   70
He is dancing for the gods with bound feet.

I do not understand how he can dance so.
When he jumps, he trips, falling in a heap.
The gods just laugh and turn away to drink.
I sit ravelling knots. The knots become rope.   75
I wake shaking and muffle my tears in the sheets.

2

"Man" answered the young stranger
whose red hair caught the sun's rays,
and the riddle was solved. True to her
promise, the Sphinx dashed herself to   80
death. Thebes was free.

Hailing their hero, the people
elected Oedipus king. Gratefully,
he accepted the rule and with it the hand
of Thebes' queen, Jocasta.   85

I see young Oedipus in radiant
sunlight, Apollo blinding me to all
but young and vital strength. Deep in myself
I feel a pulsebeat, something asleep
begins to wake, as though a dormant seed   90
sends up a shoot, opens a leaf. That's how
Aphrodite touches me. I love this youth.
My sun, I rise to him and rise with him.

From a land of rock and misery, Thebes
became a bower. Brilliant poppies   95
dotted the land. The wells filled, crops
flourished, and the flocks grew fat again.

Before the people's eyes, Jocasta
became young. Her dark hair gleamed, her
eye was bright and her laughter cheered   100
the halls of the palace.

Oedipus has become my Apollo warming
my days and nights. I am eighteen again
with poppies in my hair. I am the poppies,
bright little blooms with milk in them.   105
Like them, I seem to spring from rocky ground.
Like their color and his hair, our love flames.

Sweet Aphrodite, you rush through me, a stream
until you burst like foam that crests the sea.

Your blessing washes what was once a barren
ground. I walk among the roses, feel
your blush upon my cheeks. Oh lovely goddess,
I send you swans and doves.

110

Thebes prospered these years:
the gnarled olive bent lower with fruit.
Lambs frisked in the fields and pipers'
songs rang through the hills. Jocasta had
four children. Psalms of joy were sung
and danced for the gods.

115

With four children, the hours run away.
Their hunger, games and tears take all my time.
In bed, with Oedipus, I sleep in peace.
He was at first my headstrong bull, but now
he is what a man, a king, should be.
I like to see him walking in the yard,
his funny stiff gait, his hair burnished
by Apollo's brilliant rays.

120

125

Mine turns grey but he doesn't seem to mind.
Our love has brought to me the joy I missed
when I was young and thought I'd never know.
At last, I lay to rest my little boy,
his shadow vanished now from all my dreams.

130

3

Years of plenty at an end, Thebes
was inflicted with drought. The earth
burned as crops withered, cattle and
sheep sickened.

135

While days were once too short, now each one drags
a slow furrow, the earth heavy with heat,
lament and prayer. When I go to the fields
the women clutch my gown and plead my help.
Too many children sicken. The healthy droop.
At home, the girls sit listless, my sons tangle
while Oedipus complains his ankles twinge.
He limps and growls just like a wounded pup.

140

Jocasta, very grey now, walked
with a more measured step. More than
a loving wife, she was also counsellor
to Oedipus.

145

Blaming himself because the land is parched,
Oedipus frets alarmed he's failed the gods   150
in some unknown way, searching within himself.
In turn, I pray, lighting fire after fire,
but none burn true. I call on Aphrodite
and offer her doves, but they flap their wings
and peck each others' eyes. When I ask Apollo   155
to dim his eye, his answer scalds.

    No relief at hand, Oedipus sought
aid from Delphi. The report came back
a confusing riddle about Laius' death.
Suspecting treason, Oedipus feared   160
conspiracy against his own throne.

Oedipus needs someone to blame. He calls
Creon traitor, Tiresias false seer.
I take him in my arms and stroke his hair.
He tells me what Tiresias has foreseen.   165
I laugh and tell him I too once believed
that prophesy controlled our lives, that seers
had magic vision the rest of us did not.
I tell the story of Laius, how it
was foretold he would die at his son's hand   170
and how that baby died when one week old.

As I speak I feel so strange, as though my tale
came from another life about someone else.

My words do not comfort, they flame new fears.
He relates what drove him from home, tales that he   175
would kill his father and bring rank fruit
from his mother's womb. He fears he has
been cursed. Dear gods, how can I comfort him?

4

    From Corinth, a messenger
brought news of Polybus' death,   180
the king whom Oedipus called father.

You say that Polybus is dead. Dare I
greet death with joy? Can that be blasphemy?
My heart flies into song: His father's dead—
my Oedipus lives safe. His prophesy   185
is false. Is false as Laius' was. Oh bless
your fate, dear love, you need no longer fear.

Corinth wished Oedipus to return
and rule. Fearing he would sleep with
his mother, Oedipus refused. Nothing   190
to fear, the messenger assured. Merope
was a barren woman.

Jocasta began to tremble. Her hands
rose to cover her mouth.

    What's this? What's this? What words do I hear?   195
How can I shut his silly mouth, tell him
Go. Leave. We will not heed your words.
My tongue stops, rooted in my mouth.

    I look at Oedipus. He does not see
me watching him. His face is strained, his eyes   200
are glaring blue. I try to stop the questions.
"Oedipus, I beg you, do not hear this out."

When Oedipus insisted, the
messenger told the story of the king's
infancy,—how he, a shepherd then,   205
had helped to save the king's life
when a baby, a baby with bound feet.

    Oh God. Oh cold, gold God. Apollo,
you chill me. My mind is ice, and I hear
my mouth say freezing words to Oedipus.   210
To my husband. My son. "God keep you from
the knowledge of who you are. Unhappy,
Oedipus, my poor, damned Oedipus,
that is all I can call you, and the last thing
I shall ever call you."   215

5

Her face ashen, Jocasta rushed
into the palace, her hands showing her
the way to her own quarters. She
ordered the guards to let no one in.
Ignoring all offers of help, she commanded   220
her women to leave her alone.

    I can't believe. I can't believe. Oh God.
He is my son. I've loved my son but not
as mothers should, but in my bed, in me.
All that I loved the most, his youth that made   225

our love the summer sun, wrong, all wrong.
Vile. He caressed me here and here. And I
returned his touch. Odious hands. My flesh
crawls with worms.

My God, we've had four children.   230

   In her chamber, she looked at her
bed, sat on it, then jumped up as though
stung. Covering her eyes with her hands,
she shook her head back and forth, again
and again, her body rocking.   235

      Oh, Oedipus, what good was our love if
   it comes only to shame? To children whom
   all Thebes can curse? Such children, even ours,
   are rightly damned.

      Although we could not know who we were   240
   and loved in innocence, still we are monsters
   in the eyes of god and man. Our names will mean
   disgrace and guilt forever.

   Walking to her dressing table,
she stood before it picking up small   245
objects: combs, a gold box, a pair of
brooches. Noticing a bracelet given her
by her father when she was a bride,
she let forth a dreadful groan.

      Oh Laius, Laius, you brought this on me.   250
   My fate was sealed my wedding day. Chrysippus
   was innocent as I; for you this curse
   was uttered, a curse that falls on me. Oh,
   that I must bear the shame, that I must be
   destroyed by your corruption. And our son,   255
   because you sinned, is ruined, damned.

      My marriage day . . . what choices did I have?
   As many as the night you came to me.
   The only choice a woman has is that she wed
   accepting what the gods and men decree.   260
   It is not just. It never can be right.

   Moving decisively, she walked to the
doors and bolted them, straining against
their heavy weight. The women on the other

side called to her, but again she bade them   265
go away.

    Falling on her knees, she pummeled
her stomach as though to punish her
womb. As she did, she called her children's names, one name, Oedipus, again   270
and again.

    I thought him buried, forgotten. But no,
for countless days and nights these many years
he's thrust himself on me instead. My bed
once stained with birthing blood is now forever   275
stained; what once was love become a rank
corruption.

    Rising painfully, sore, she turned
to the small altar in her chamber.
Smashing a jar which held incense, she   280
began in a voice of char to call on
Apollo and Aphrodite.

    As she raised her eyes, she raised
her fist and shook it against
the silent air.   285

    Apollo, you blinded me to his scars,
his age, any resemblance to Laius.
And you, Aphrodite, cruel sister of the sun,
set my woman's body afire, matching my
ripe years and hungers with his youth and strength.   290
Paralyzing my mind, you inflamed my heart.

The years I prayed to you and praised you
were all charade. You so enjoyed my dance.
We are your fools to trifle with, your joke.

We tremble to question what the future holds.   295
As though it matters, we think asking will spoil
our luck, but your injustice mocks all hope.

I hear a chant pounding inside my head.
Five babies. Five abominations.
As though a chorus raises call to prayer.   300
Five babies. Five abominations.

No call to prayer. It is a call to curse
the gods. No longer will I be their fool.

From her robe, she removed her
braided belt. As she looped its strands,   305
she heard, from the courtyard, a man's
voice scream in anguish. Undeflected, she
tied the necessary knots, slipping the loop
back and forth. Satisfied, she settled
the noose around her neck.   310

Five babies cursed by heavenly whim,
cursed in their lives without chance or hope.
Mothers ought not love their children so.

Gathering her skirts, she climbed
up on the stool.   315

And wives be more than merely bedside pawns.
Those who cannot shape their lives are better
dead.

She stepped onto the air.

(1986)

Drafts 1 and 2 of Eisenberg's "Jocasta," Part 1

"Jocasta" didn't spring full-blown from the author's head; it is the result of many drafts. Below are a couple of earlier versions of Part I. Although we can't determine from them what prompted the poet to revise them—exactly what went on in her thinking—we can look at the differences and do some intelligent guessing: What seem to have been Eisenberg's motives for revision? What significant changes are you able to detect between the 1st and 2nd drafts? Between the second draft and Eisenberg's published version?

RUTH F. EISENBERG

Draft #1: Jocasta Part 1

Laius was never any good after that.
She'd lie with him and imagine that baby
Tied and immobile
Cold on the mountain
Stony Cithaeron,   5
Her husband's arm a bent dry stick.

Privately she blamed him.
She knew the prophesy but
Laius, not Apollo, had come to her
Seeded in   10
That baby.
Once she felt used,
His cold root no longer filled her.

Nothing could warm them.
Together they prayed,   15
Built fires, burned incense;
The fires roared,
Their offerings charred,
Husband and wife remained cold
And Thebes barren.   20

At Laius's death
Jocasta grieved but
was angry too.
Doubt assailed her.
Was her baby killed for false prophesy?   25
Confusion reigned.

Draft #2: Jocasta Part 1

Laius was never any good after that
She'd lie with him remembering
her baby cold on the mountain
tied, immobile
Her husband's arm a bent dry stick   5
his root could not fill her

That fateful night, he comes in drunk, crying
For Chryssipus, the source of his curse.
Wanting his boy, he takes me instead
Pouring his libation into my womb.   10
Sober, he remembers Apollo's threat:
Our son will kill him, beget upon me.
My pregnancy is no joy. With eyes of ice
Laius watches me swell. I fear the gods and pray
For a daughter. In good time, I birth our son.   15
Even as I weep on my still bloody bed,
Laius takes the baby, and binds his feet,
He calls a servant to carry him away
To Kithaeron, to die on the mountain's slopes.

Publicly, they prayed   20
burned incense, sacrificed lambs.
Fires charred their offerings and
husband and wife trembled
Why were the gods displeased?
In barren Thebes   25
the land thrust rocks
Soon the Sphinx's song
echoed from empty wells
On the sun-swept road to Delphi
Laius died   30
killed by bandits, they said
Hearing the news, Jocasta shuttered herself in
Let Creon rule

The prophecy was false. He killed my child
To save his cursed life. I can not grieve.   35
He killed my boy for his own corrupt hide.
My son was never given any chance.
I dream of my baby night after night.
He is dancing for the gods with bound feet.
He dances, turns, trips, and falls. The gods laugh.
I am raveling knots. The knots become rope.   40
Feeling entangled, I wake with raw throat.

Read the poet's essay about how she came to write "Jocasta" and then revise it and revise it again. In what ways do her comments reflect your own current sense of how writers revise? How is revision different from what Eisenberg labels "a final tidying up"?

Writing "Jocasta"

I don't know when the idea first took hold of me that Jocasta had a story to tell. I'd
taught Oedipus so many times, I don't know when or why the realization first broke
through. At any rate, I do remember voicing the thought at a poetry workshop. "Some
day," I mused out loud, "someone ought to write a poem about Jocasta." Quick as a
match, Natale Safir, our workshop leader, struck, "Why don't you?" I answered with
a truly modest, who me? and dismissed the idea. I didn't know enough, I wasn't skilled
enough. Heck, I'd only been writing poetry seriously for about nine months.

Well, some kids run before they can walk properly, and six weeks later, I began.
The poem started in the middle of the night (most of my poems begin unexpectedly
and inconveniently). I had to flick the lamp on and off through the early morning hours
as bunches of lines came to me. By the time I'd finished that first handwritten draft it
ran to six and a half pages. That was December, 1978. In the course of the next three
and a half years, the poem would almost triple in length and change from free verse

and one voice into the more complex structure involving two voices. Many subtle shifts in point of view and imagery also came into being as my commitment to my character became deeper.

For that first version, I had done no research, relying on what I had learned from my many classroom preparations of *Oedipus*. But I had a clear formulation of Jocasta's relationships with Oedipus and Laius, which came from thinking of them as real people and considering their ages at the time of the critical events. I figured that if Oedipus was seventeen to nineteen when he came to Thebes, that would make Jocasta thirty-three to thirty-five. She couldn't be any older and still have four children with him. These ages put them both at their sexual prime—which is important. Looking back, I realized Jocasta would have been about sixteen when she gave birth, fifteen or so at marriage. That was reasonable for that time and place. Therefore, if Jocasta and Oedipus were loving partners (which we are led to believe from Sophocles' play), by way of contrast Jocasta and Laius would not be. So I made him cold, essentially impotent.

The images that dominated were of hot and cold. This was natural because Apollo, after all, is the dominant god of both the play and the poem. In the first version, the opening stanza had the baby "cold on the mountain" and Laius cold as a lover. Besides references to the sun god, there was lots of fire. I just kept working those images through—working them to death I might add. Much, much later I would introduce the paradoxical idea of a chilling Apollo.

In structure, the poem emerged as a narrative. I simply retold the story from Jocasta's point of view. In all the early versions, the poem opened with Laius: "Laius was never any good after that"; it closed with the focus on Oedipus: "When Oedipus bulled his way into her chamber/Her swaying body had already grown cold." This happened in the writing unconsciously; later when I realized it, I thought it made an interesting commentary of its own: as men shaped her life, they framed its retelling. Later, I would change that.

The first version on paper, I went to the library to research. But I didn't find much about Jocasta other than alternate spellings of her name and some family background. Many indexes didn't list her at all, although they always listed Oedipus and sometimes Laius. So I checked out Laius. Not only did that confirm my feeling that he was much older than she, but it also gave me fuller information on the source of the curse (which I may have once known but forgot). Laius' homoerotic relationship with Chrysippus supported handily my decision to make him a lousy husband and lover.

The research also revealed conflicting stories about the night of Oedipus' conception. One version said they were both drunk, but all the others had only Laius drunk, so of course I went with the majority. Jocasta was not just Laius' wife, she was his victim, caught in his curse, and ultimately destroyed through no fault of her own.

If the research gave me no other information, it uncovered an injustice: whether the source was myth, anthropology, or psychology, the emphasis was on the men. Jocasta, as full a player in this tragedy as the others, was ignored. Looking back now, I think this awareness fired me to do the many revisions. Consciously, I was trying to make a better poem. Unconsciously, I was righting a wrong, doing what I could to give equal importance to the female figure in this most significant of western myths.

The most significant change—the one that transformed the poem—was the decision to split it into two voices. Natale felt, rightly, that the poem was too much a narrative. Jocasta needed to speak for herself. This meant more than a change in form and structure. It meant that if I was going to deal with Jocasta's feelings, I was going to have to go deep inside myself. This was no easy task, for several reasons, one of which was an anachronism. I am a 20th-century American woman strongly influenced by existential thinking, and I was writing about a primitive Greek. While I see Jocasta as a representative figure, someone who speaks for all women of any time, I didn't want her to be out of her time. I had to think of an agricultural society but keep in mind universal feelings.

I used my own experiences as a woman in love to generate the feelings in the love passages (still among my favorite lines). I am a mother who has known what it's like to have time melt away because of household tasks and children's demands. I had to use my imagination for the fright and disgust of the rape and the horror she feels when she confronts her incest. But Jocasta is speaking for me directly in her closing lines because it is the feminist and existentialist in me that created her feelings about her dominated, if not fated, life.

As my involvement with her life grew deeper, my imagery grew richer. Hot and cold would no longer do; images of poppies would express her love, her pregnancy would drag "like oxen ploughing"; when she was depressed, her life was "a toad." Thus nature and farm images entered into the poem.

One of the more difficult tasks was in finding a verse form for Jocasta. I tried rhyme, even rhymed couplets, but they were awful. Finally, I chose blank verse, which seemed right. It's a controlled form and it has dignity. Dominated now by iambic pentameter, I sat at the typewriter counting syllables and beats. There were times that, struggling with a line, I regretted the decision, but all in all, I think it was the correct one.

The narrative voice provided other problems. At first I continued the free verse. My lines became barer and more linear as I tried to keep from telling too much. It began to have a staccato beat. I had wanted the narrative voice to be a Chorus character; not just to tell the story, but to indicate commentary as well. Casting it in prose finally gave me that freedom. I could retain a slightly ironic tone; I had room enough now for description with the narration. The prose was in the past tense, a contrast to Jocasta's voice in the present tense.

The divisions of the poem almost formed themselves. The easiest for me to write was II; the most challenging V. Later I would realize the hardest ones were III and IV because I was scared to death of Sophocles. However, dividing the poem into sections turned out to be helpful. It made revision easier; I could treat each section as an entity as well as a part of a whole concept.

Somewhat more than two years had now passed since that December night. Of course, I didn't work on the poem steadily, but in fits and starts. Sometimes I'd quit just because I couldn't stand putting the same page through the typewriter one more time (I'm a rotten typist). The poem sat waiting, and I'd come back.

About this time, I saw a dramatization of the play. The audience watched Oedipus, I watched the actress who played Jocasta. She gave me new ideas about action: Jocasta would stroke his hair, hold Oedipus in her arms, would pick up and drop her jewelry, and pummel her stomach. Some of the ideas I copied from the actress; the rest I invented.

My focus on her had deepened. Now the poem opened with "When Jocasta learned the king's power, she lost delight . . ." and ended with "She stepped onto the air." For the last line, I owe a small debt to Housman ("And dead on air will stand").

My line, I think, extends the meaning of her death. Jocasta steps into eternity and our consciousness.

By this time, I had also discovered some things about the poem. For instance, in its structure, without conscious plan, I had placed the gods in each section, thus giving the poem some of its unity. All the settings, I realized, are indoor or near the palace. When we were working on the videotape of the poem, I became more conscious that it opens and closes in the bedroom, reflecting the domestic and circumscribed life she led.

And Jocasta speaks for me often. Any moral urgency in the poem is mine. As I said earlier, her final injunctions, her final defiance of tradition and values for their own and the gods' sake is inevitably mine. The viewpoint was there from the beginning, only to be modified for diction or rhythm, not for the thought.

I needed to hear the poem. For me poetry is a spoken art, and as I write I always say the lines out loud. But to hear the poem in a voice other than mine, to hear the responses of others to the lines, would be, I knew, a great help. When it happened, interestingly enough, three women read the poem. My imaginative director friend, Joan Thorne, saw Jocasta as three women in one: the innocent, the queen, and the wife-mother. She also saw the five sections in two different ways: first as musical themes, and secondly as a progressive movement towards a woman's interior life.

The reading revealed weaknesses in Sections III and IV. They were the least dramatically alive: the most narrative, most derivative, and the least felt. At this revelation I became aware of how intimidated I was by the play. How dare I to have trespassed on sacred ground? For me Oedipus Rex is the greatest play ever written. How could I challenge Sophocles on his own turf?

Then I realized I wasn't challenging him, that my turf and his were different. He was concerned with Oedipus. Jocasta's lines were for his reaction; she was his foil, and in her recognition scene, his antagonist. Sophocles didn't even give her many lines in that scene. Therefore, anything I had added didn't challenge him; rather, I had accepted an opportunity to fill in the blanks. I added new verses in her voice. Jocasta goes through an absolute roller coaster of feeling when she hears the words of the messenger from Corinth, from a sense of false reassurance to horror. She tries to protect Oedipus from the knowledge (he, if you recall, turns on her and mistakes her motive) and stands not just awed but appalled at the work of the gods.

Readying "Jocasta" for this book meant a final tidying up. All along I was confronted with pronoun reference problems, sentence balance and variety, punctuation, working a balanced statement out from the demands of the meter. Now I had to prepare my "fair copy." However, I am reasonably sure that even when the proofs come back, the process will continue of trying to make a poem worthy of its tragic protagonist.

(1986)

W. B. YEATS

[1865–1939]

Purgatory

CHARACTERS

A BOY

AN OLD MAN

Scene: A ruined house and a bare tree in the background.

BOY: Half-door, hall door,
　Hither and thither day and night,
　Hill or hollow, shouldering his pack,
　Hearing you talk.
OLD MAN: 　　　　　Study that house.
　I think about its jokes and stories;　　　　　　　　　　　　　5
　I try to remember what the butler
　Said to a drunken gamekeeper
　In mid-October, but I cannot.
　If I cannot, none living can.
　Where are the jokes and stories of a house,　　　　　　　10
　Its threshold gone to patch a pig-sty?
BOY: So you have come this path before?
OLD MAN: The moonlight falls upon the path,
　The shadow of a cloud upon the house,
　And that's symbolical; study that tree,　　　　　　　　　15
　What is it like?
BOY: 　　　　　A silly old man.
OLD MAN: It's like—no matter what it's like.
　I saw it a year ago stripped bare as now,
　So I chose a better trade.
　I saw it fifty years ago　　　　　　　　　　　　　　　20
　Before the thunderbolt had riven it,
　Green leaves, ripe leaves, leaves thick as butter,
　Fat, greasy life. Stand there and look,
　Because there is somebody in that house.

(The BOY *puts down pack and stands in the doorway.)*

BOY: There's nobody here.

OLD MAN: There's somebody there.   25
BOY: The floor is gone, the window's gone,
  And where there should be roof there's sky,
  And here's a bit of an egg-shell thrown
  Out of a jackdaw's nest.
OLD MAN: But there are some
  That do not care what's gone, what's left: 30
  The souls of Purgatory that come back
  To habitations and familiar spots.
BOY: Your wits are out again.
OLD MAN: Re-live
  Their transgressions, and that not once
  But many times; they know at last   35
  The consequence of those transgressions
  Whether upon others or upon themselves;
  Upon others, others may bring help,
  For when the consequence is at an end
  The dream must end; if upon themselves,   40
  There is no help but in themselves
  And in the mercy of God.
BOY: I have had enough!
  Talk to the jackdaws, if talk you must.
OLD MAN: Stop! Sit there upon that stone.
  That is the house where I was born.   45
BOY: The big old house that was burnt down?
OLD MAN: My mother that was your grand-dam owned it,
  This scenery and this countryside,
  Kennel and stable, horse and hound—
  She had a horse at the Curragh, and there met   50
  My father, a groom in the training stable,
  Looked at him and married him.
  Her mother never spoke to her again,
  And she did right.
BOY: What's right and wrong?
  My grand-dad got the girl and the money.   55
OLD MAN: Looked at him and married him,
  And he squandered everything she had.
  She never knew the worst, because
  She died in giving birth to me,
  But now she knows it all, being dead.   60
  Great people lived and died in this house;
  Magistrates, colonels, members of Parliament,
  Captains and Governors, and long ago
  Men that had fought at Aughrim and the Boyne.
  Some that had gone on government work   65
  To London or to India came home to die,
  Or came from London every spring
  To look at the may-blossom in the park.

They had loved the trees that he cut down
To pay what he had lost at cards   70
Or spent on horses, drink, and women;
Had loved the house, had loved all
The intricate passages of the house,
But he killed the house; to kill a house
Where great men grew up, married, died,   75
I here declare a capital offence.
BOY: My God, but you had luck! Grand clothes,
     And maybe a grand horse to ride.
OLD MAN: That he might keep me upon his level
     He never sent me to school, but some   80
     Half-loved me for my half of her:
     A gamekeeper's wife taught me to read,
     A Catholic curate taught me Latin.
     There were old books and books made fine
     By eighteenth-century French binding, books   85
     Modern and ancient, books by the ton.
BOY: What education have you given me?
OLD MAN: I gave the education that befits
     A bastard that a pedlar got
     Upon a tinker's daughter in a ditch.   90
     When I had come to sixteen years old
     My father burned down the house when drunk.
BOY: But that is my age, sixteen years old,
     At the Puck Fair.
OLD MAN: And everything was burnt;
     Books, library, all were burnt.   95
BOY: Is what I have heard upon the road the truth,
     That you killed him in the burning house?
OLD MAN: There's nobody here but our two selves?
BOY: Nobody, Father.
OLD MAN: I stuck him with a knife,
     That knife that cuts my dinner now,   100
     And after that I left him in the fire.
     They dragged him out, somebody saw
     The knife wound but could not be certain
     Because the body was all black and charred.
     Then some that were his drunken friends   105
     Swore they would put me upon trial,
     Spoke of quarrels, a threat I had made.
     The gamekeeper gave me some old clothes,
     I ran away, worked here and there
     Till I became a pedlar on the roads,   110
     No good trade, but good enough
     Because I am my father's son,
     Because of what I did or may do.
     Listen to the hoof-beats! Listen, listen!

BOY: I cannot hear a sound.

OLD MAN: Beat! Beat!   115
  This night is the anniversary
  Of my mother's wedding night,
  Or of the night wherein I was begotten.
  My father is riding from the public-house,
  A whiskey-bottle under his arm.   120

(A window is lit showing a young girl.)

  Look at the window; she stands there
  Listening, the servants are all in bed,
  She is alone, he has stayed late
  Bragging and drinking in the public-house.

BOY: There's nothing but an empty gap in the wall.   125
  You have made it up. No, you are mad!
  You are getting madder every day.

OLD MAN: Its louder now because he rides
  Upon a gravelled avenue
  All grass today. The hoof-beat stops,   130
  He has gone to the other side of the house,
  Gone to the stable, put the horse up.
  She has gone down to open the door.
  This night she is no better than her man
  And does not mind that he is half drunk,   135
  She is mad about him. They mount the stairs,
  She brings him into her own chamber.
  And that is the marriage-chamber now.

(The window is dimly lit again.)

  Do not let him touch you! It is not true
  That drunken men cannot beget,   140
  And if he touch he must beget
  And you must bear his murderer.
  Deaf! Both deaf! If I should throw
  A stick or a stone they would not hear;
  And that's a proof my wits are out.   145
  But there's a problem: she must live
  Through everything in exact detail,
  Driven to it by remorse, and yet
  Can she renew the sexual act
  And find no pleasure in it, and if not,   150
  If pleasure and remorse must both be there,
  Which is the greater?
                    I lack schooling.
  Go fetch Tertullian; he and I
  Will ravel all that problem out
  Whilst those two lie upon the mattress   155
  Begetting me.

Come back! Come back!
And so you thought to slip away,
My bag of money between your fingers,
And that I could not talk and see!
You have been rummaging in the pack.   160

(The light in the window has faded out.)

BOY: You never gave me my right share.
OLD MAN: And had I given it, young as you are,
  You would have spent it upon drink.
BOY: What if I did? I had a right
  To get it and spend it as I chose.   165
OLD MAN: Give me that bag and no more words.
BOY: I will not.
OLD MAN: I will break your fingers.

(They struggle for the bag. In the struggle it drops, scattering the money. The OLD MAN *staggers but does not fall. They stand looking at each other. The window is lit up. A man is seen pouring whiskey into a glass.)*

BOY: What if I killed you? You killed my grand-dad,
  Because you were young and he was old.
  Now I am young and you are old.   170
OLD MAN *(staring at window):* Better-looking, those sixteen years—
BOY: What are you muttering?
OLD MAN: Younger—and yet
  She should have known he was not her kind.
BOY: What are you saying? Out with it!

*(*OLD MAN *points to window.)*

My God! The window is lit up   175
And somebody stands there, although
The floorboards are all burnt away.
OLD MAN: The window is lit up because my father
  Has come to find a glass for his whiskey.
  He leans there like some tired beast.   180
BOY: A dead, living, murdered man!
OLD MAN: "Then the bride-sleep fell upon Adam":
  Where did I read those words?
            And yet
  There's nothing leaning in the window
  But the impression upon my mother's mind;   185
  Being dead she is alone in her remorse.
BOY: A body that was a bundle of old bones
  Before I was born, Horrible! Horrible!

(He covers his eyes.)

OLD MAN: That beast there would know nothing, being nothing,

If I should kill a man under the window 190
He would not even turn his head.

(He stabs the BOY.*)*

My father and my son on the same jack-knife!
That finishes—there—there—there—

(He stabs again and again. The window grows dark.)

"Hush-a-bye baby, thy father's a knight,
Thy mother a lady, lovely and bright." 195
No, that is something that I read in a book,
And if I sing it must be to my mother,
And I lack rhyme.

(The stage has grown dark except where the tree stands in white light.)

Study that tree.
It stands there like a purified soul,
All cold, sweet, glistening light. 200
Dear mother, the window is dark again,
But you are in the light because
I finished all that consequence.
I killed that lad because had he grown up
He would have struck a woman's fancy, 205
Begot, and passed pollution on.

I am a wretched foul old man
And therefore harmless. When I have stuck
This old jack-knife into a sod
And pulled it out all bright again, 210
And picked up all the money that he dropped,
I'll to a distant place, and there
Tell my old jokes among new men.

(He cleans the knife and begins to pick up money.)

Hoof-beats! Dear God,
How quickly it returns—beat—beat—! 215

Her mind cannot hold up that dream.
Twice a murderer and all for nothing,
And she must animate that dead night
Not once but many times!
O God,
Release my mother's soul from its dream! 220
Mankind can do no more. Appease
The misery of the living and the remorse of the dead.

(1939)

CHAPTER TWENTY-THREE

The Elizabethan Theater: Shakespeare in Context

STAGECRAFT IN THE ELIZABETHAN AGE

The drama of Shakespeare's time, the Elizabethan Age (1558–1603), shares some features with Greek drama. Like the Greek dramatists, Elizabethan playwrights wrote both comedies and tragedies, but the Elizabethans extended the possibilities of each genre. They wrote domestic tragedies, tragedies of character, and revenge tragedies; they contributed comedies of manners and comedies of humors to the earlier romantic and satiric comedies. In Greek and Elizabethan theater, props were few, scenery was simple, and dialogue often indicated changes of locale and time. Elizabethan plays were also written in verse rather than prose.

An Elizabethan playhouse such as the Globe, where many of Shakespeare's plays were staged, had a much smaller seating capacity than the large Greek amphitheaters, which could seat thousands (fifteen thousand at Epidaurus). The Globe could accommodate about twenty-three hundred people, including roughly eight hundred groundlings who, exposed to the elements, stood around the stage. The stage itself projected from an inside wall into their midst. More prosperous spectators sat in one of the three stories that nearly encircled the stage. The vastly smaller size and seating capacity of the Elizabethan theater and the projection of its stage made for a greater intimacy between actors and audience. Though actors still had to project their voices and exaggerate their gestures, they could be heard and seen without the aid of large megaphonic masks and elevated shoes. Elizabethan actors could modulate their voices and vary their pitch, stress, and intonation in ways not suited to the Greek stage. They could also make greater and more subtle use of facial expression and of gesture to enforce their greater verbal and vocal flexibility.

In addition to greater intimacy, the Elizabethan stage also offered more versatility than its Greek counterpart. Although the Greek *skene* building could be used for scenes occuring above the ground, such as a god descending in a machine (*deus ex machina*),* the Greek stage was really a single-level acting area. Not so the Elizabethan stage, which contained a second-level balcony (from which Brabantio looks out in Act I, scene II of *Othello*). Besides its balcony, Shakespeare's stage had doors at the back for entrances and exits, a curtained alcove (useful for scenes of intrigue), and a stage floor trapdoor, from which the Ghost ascends in Shakespeare's *Hamlet*. Such a stage was suitable for rapidly shifting scenes and continuous action. Thus, Elizabethan stage conventions did not include divisions between scenes as in Greek drama. The act and scene divisions that appear in *Othello* and *Hamlet* were devised by modern editors.

INTRODUCTION TO SHAKESPEARE

[1564–1616]

William Shakespeare, the most famous English writer, is also among the most popular. His fame and popularity rest on his plays more than on his nondramatic poetry—though his sonnets remain perennially in fashion. What makes Shakespeare such a literary phenomenon? Why are readers so drawn to his work? Here are two simple explanations: (1) his revelation of human character, especially his exploration of complex states of mind and feeling; (2) his explosive and exuberant language, particularly the richness and variety of his metaphors. Both of these literary virtues abound in the sequence of 154 sonnets Shakespeare wrote in the 1590s. Both also consistently appear in his thirty-seven plays, particularly in the soliloquies, those inward meditative speeches of the major characters. The richness of Shakespeare's language is also apparent in the songs he wrote for the plays, especially the songs in the comedies.

Another source of Shakespeare's popularity is his immense quotability. Shakespeare's plays and poems provide a repository of familiar sayings and recognizable quotations. From *Hamlet* alone we glean the following:

> In my mind's eye
>
> To the manner born
>
> There are more things in heaven and earth
>
> Hold the mirror up to nature
>
> I must be cruel only to be kind.

---

*A god who resolves the entanglements of a play by his supernatural intervention (literally, a god from the machine) or any artificial device used to resolve a plot.

> Brevity is the soul of wit.
>
> To be or not to be, that is the question.
>
> Neither a borrower nor a lender be.
>
> Something's rotten in the state of Denmark.
>
> What a piece of work is a man.

To reduce Shakespeare's appeal to the fact that he is eminently quotable, however, is to ignore other important dimensions of his popularity. It is, moreover, to get things backward—to put the cart before the horse. Shakespeare is not a great writer because he is quotable; he is quotable because he is a great writer. It is his manipulation of language and his revelation of character that have made him both widely read and deeply revered.

Very little is known with certainty about Shakespeare's life. Scholars, however, have determined the following basic facts. He was born in Stratford-on-Avon in April of 1564. He attended the local grammar school, where he would have studied Latin and perhaps a little Greek. His formal education does not include attendance at the university—in his day either Oxford or Cambridge. Instead, at eighteen, he married Anne Hathaway, who bore three children in as many years, a daughter in 1583 and twins, a boy and girl, in 1585. Shakespeare wrote and acted in plays, for by 1592 he was known in London as both actor and playwright.

Many tributes have been paid to Shakespeare. One, however, stands above the rest: his contemporary Ben Jonson's judgment that "he is not for an age, but for all time."

Othello

Shakespeare's plays generally, and *Othello* in particular, appealed to an audience ranging from the illiterate to the educated: bawdy jokes exist alongside sublime poetry; subtle introspective moments coexist with violence and passion. Shakespeare's language is among the richest and most resourceful ever written (and spoken), and *Othello* testifies to its vitality and exuberance. Written predominantly in blank verse, *Othello* also includes prose passages (many spoken by Iago) and rhymed couplets (which punctuate the ends of some scenes). The play's language is rich in metaphor and images, puns, and other forms of wordplay.

Deriving the story of Othello from a sixteenth-century tale by Giraldi Cinthio, Shakespeare improved the plot, enriched the language, and deepened the characters. *Othello* has been among the most admired of Shakespeare's plays. Part of its attraction is its language, but its characters are perhaps even more immediately compelling: the noble Othello; his gentle and naive Venetian wife, Desdemona; the brilliant, magnetic, and inexplicable Iago; his crude and manipulated wife, Emilia. The play's central concerns—love and trust, good and evil, nobility and debasement—are also universal.

WILLIAM SHAKESPEARE

The Tragedy of Othello

THE MOOR OF VENICE

EDITED BY ALVIN KERNAN

CHARACTERS

OTHELLO, *the Moor*
BRABANTIO, *father to Desdemona*
CASSIO, *an honorable lieutenant*
IAGO, *a villain*
RODERIGO, *a gulled gentleman*
DUKE OF VENICE
SENATORS
MONTANO, *Governor of Cyprus*
GENTLEMEN OF CYPRUS
LODOVICO AND GRATIANO, *two noble Venetians*
SAILORS
CLOWN
DESDEMONA, *wife to Othello*
EMILIA, *wife to Iago*
BIANCA, *a courtesan*
(MESSENGER, HERALD, OFFICERS, GENTLEMEN, MUSICIANS, ATTENDANTS)

Scene. *Venice and Cyprus.*

ACT I

Scene I [Venice. A street.]

RODERIGO: Tush! Never tell me? I take it much unkindly
  That thou, Iago, who hast had my purse
  As if the strings were thine, shouldst know of this.
IAGO: 'Sblood°, but you'll not hear me! If ever I did dream
  Of such a matter, abhor me.

I.i.   [4] *'Sblood   by God's blood.*

RODERIGO: Thou told'st me   5
  Thou didst hold him in thy hate.
IAGO: Despise me
  If I do not. Three great ones of the city,
  In personal suit to make me his lieutenant,
  Off-capped° to him; and, by the faith of man,
  I know my price; I am worth no worse a place.   10
  But he, as loving his own pride and purposes,
  Evades them with a bombast circumstance°,
  Horribly stuffed with epithets of war;
  Nonsuits° my mediators. For, "Certes," says he,
  "I have already chose my officer." And what was he?   15
  Forsooth, a great arithmetician°,
  One Michael Cassio, a Florentine,
  (A fellow almost damned in a fair wife)°
  That never set a squadron in the field,
  Nor the division of a battle knows   20
  More than a spinster; unless the bookish theoric,
  Wherein the tonguèd° consuls can propose
  As masterly as he. Mere prattle without practice
  Is all his soldiership. But he, sir, had th' election;
  And I, of whom his eyes had seen the proof   25
  At Rhodes, at Cyprus, and on other grounds
  Christian and heathen, must be belee'd and calmed
  By debitor and creditor. This counter-caster°,
  He, in good time, must his lieutenant be,
  And I—God bless the mark!—his Moorship's ancient°.   30
RODERIGO: By heaven, I rather would have been his hangman.
IAGO: Why, there's no remedy. 'Tis the curse of service:
  Preferment goes by letter and affection°,
  And not by old gradation°, where each second
  Stood heir to th' first. Now, sir, be judge yourself,   35
  Whether I in any just term am affined°
  To love the Moor.
RODERIGO: I would not follow him then.
IAGO: O, sir, content you.
  I follow him to serve my turn upon him.
  We cannot all be masters, nor all masters   40
  Cannot be truly followed. You shall mark

---

⁹**Off-capped**   *doffed their caps—as a mark of respect.*   ¹²**bombast circumstance**   *stuffed, roundabout speech.*
¹⁴**Nonsuits**   *rejects.*   ¹⁶**arithmetician**   *theorist (rather than practical).*   ¹⁸**A . . . wife**   *(a much-disputed pas-*
sage, probably best taken as a general sneer at Cassio as a dandy and a ladies' man. But in the story from which Shake-
speare took his plot the counterpart of Cassio is married, and it may be that at the beginning of the play Shakespeare had
decided to keep him married but later changed his mind).   ²²**tonguèd**   *eloquent.*   ²⁸**counter-caster**   *i.e., a book-*
keeper who casts (reckons up) figures on a counter (abacus).   ³⁰**ancient**   *standard-bearer; an under-officer.*   ³³**let-**
ter and affection   *recommendations (from men of power) and personal preference.*   ³⁴**old gradation**   *seniority.*
³⁶**affined**   *bound.*

Many a duteous and knee-crooking° knave
That, doting on his own obsequious bondage,
Wears out his time, much like his master's ass,
For naught but provender; and when he's old, cashiered. 45
Whip me such honest knaves! Others there are
Who, trimmed in forms and visages of duty,
Keep yet their hearts attending on themselves,
And, throwing but shows of service on their lords,
Do well thrive by them, and when they have lined their coats, 50
Do themselves homage. These fellows have some soul;
And such a one do I profess myself. For, sir,
It is as sure as you are Roderigo,
Were I the Moor, I would not be Iago.
In following him, I follow but myself. 55
Heaven is my judge, not I for love and duty,
But seeming so, for my peculiar° end;
For when my outward action doth demonstrate
The native° act and figure of my heart
In complement extern°, 'tis not long after 60
But I will wear my heart upon my sleeve
For daws to peck at; I am not what I am.
RODERIGO: What a full fortune does the thick-lips owe°
    If he can carry't thus!
IAGO: Call up her father,
    Rouse him. Make after him, poison his delight, 65
    Proclaim him in the streets, incense her kinsmen,
    And though he in a fertile climate dwell,
    Plague him with flies; though that his joy be joy,
    Yet throw such chances of vexation on't
    As it may lose some color. 70
RODERIGO: Here is her father's house. I'll call aloud.
IAGO: Do, with like timorous° accent and dire yell
    As when, by night and negligence, the fire
    Is spied in populous cities.
RODERIGO: What, ho, Brabantio! Signior Brabantio, ho! 75
IAGO: Awake! What, ho, Brabantio! Thieves! Thieves!
    Look to your house, your daughter, and your bags!
    Thieves! Thieves!

        BRABANTIO *above*° [*at a window*].

BRABANTIO: What is the reason of this terrible summons?
    What is the matter there? 80

---

[42]**knee-crooking** *bowing.* [57]**peculiar** *personal.* [59]**native** *natural, innate.* [60]**complement ext-
ern** *outward appearance.* [63]**owe** *own.* [72]**timorous** *frightening.* [78]**s.d. above** *(i.e., on the small
upper stage above and to the rear of the main platform stage, which resembled the projecting upper story of an Elizabethan house).*

RODERIGO: Signior, is all your family within?

IAGO: Are your doors locked?

BRABANTIO: Why, wherefore ask you this?

IAGO: Zounds, sir, y'are robbed! For shame. Put on your gown!
   Your heart is burst, you have lost half your soul.
   Even now, now, very now, an old black ram   85
   Is tupping your white ewe. Arise, arise!
   Awake the snorting citizens with the bell,
   Or else the devil will make a grandsire of you.
   Arise, I say!

BRABANTIO: What, have you lost your wits?

RODERIGO: Most reverend signior, do you know my voice?   90

BRABANTIO: Not I. What are you?

RODERIGO: My name is Roderigo.

BRABANTIO: The worser welcome!
   I have charged thee not to haunt about my doors.
   In honest plainness thou hast heard me say
   My daughter is not for thee; and now, in madness,   95
   Being full of supper and distemp'ring draughts°,
   Upon malicious knavery dost thou come
   To start° my quiet.

RODERIGO: Sir, sir, sir—

BRABANTIO: But thou must needs be sure
   My spirits and my place° have in their power   100
   To make this bitter to thee.

RODERIGO: Patience, good sir.

BRABANTIO: What tell'st thou me of robbing? This is Venice,
   My house is not a grange°.

RODERIGO: Most grave Brabantio,
   In simple and pure soul I come to you.

IAGO: Zounds, sir, you are one of those that will not serve God if the devil   105
   bid you. Because we come to do you service and you think we are ruffi-
   ans, you'll have your daughter covered with a Barbary° horse, you'll have
   your nephews° neigh to you, you'll have coursers for cousins°, and gen-
   nets for germans°.

BRABANTIO: What profane wretch art thou?   110

IAGO: I am one, sir, that comes to tell you your daughter and the Moor are
   making the beast with two backs.

BRABANTIO: Thou art a villain.

IAGO: You are—a senator.

BRABANTIO: This thou shalt answer. I know thee, Roderigo.

RODERIGO: Sir, I will answer anything. But I beseech you,   115

---

⁹⁶***distemp'ring draughts*** *unsettling drinks.*   ⁹⁸***start*** *disrupt.*   ¹⁰⁰***place*** *rank, i.e., of senator.*
¹⁰³***grange*** *isolated house.*   ¹⁰⁷***Barbary*** *Arabian, i.e., Moorish.*   ¹⁰⁸***nephews*** *i.e., grandsons.*
¹⁰⁸***cousins*** *relations.*   ¹⁰⁹***gennets for germans*** *Spanish horses for blood relatives.*

If't be your pleasure and most wise consent,
As partly I find it is, that your fair daughter,
At this odd-even° and dull watch o' th' night,
Transported, with no worse nor better guard
But with a knave of common hire, a gondolier,   120
To the gross clasps of a lascivious Moor—
If this be known to you, and your allowance,
We then have done you bold and saucy wrongs;
But if you know not this, my manners tell me
We have your wrong rebuke. Do not believe   125
That from the sense of all civility°
I thus would play and trifle with your reverence.
Your daughter, if you have not given her leave,
I say again, hath made a gross revolt,
Tying her duty, beauty, wit, and fortunes   130
In an extravagant° and wheeling stranger
Of here and everywhere. Straight satisfy yourself.
If she be in her chamber, or your house,
Let loose on me the justice of the state
For thus deluding you.

BRABANTIO: Strike on the tinder, ho!   135
Give me a taper! Call up all my people!
This accident° is not unlike my dream.
Belief of it oppresses me already.
Light, I say! Light!   *Exit [above]*.

IAGO: Farewell, for I must leave you.
It seems not meet, nor wholesome to my place,   140
To be produced—as, if I stay, I shall—
Against the Moor. For I do know the State,
However this may gall him with some check°,
Cannot with safety cast° him; for he's embarked
With such loud reason to the Cyprus wars,   145
Which even now stands in act°, that for their souls
Another of his fathom° they have none
To lead their business; in which regard,
Though I do hate him as I do hell-pains,
Yet, for necessity of present life,   150
I must show out a flag and sign of love,
Which is indeed but sign. That you shall surely find him,
Lead to the Sagittary° that raisèd search:
And there will I be with him. So farewell.   *[Exit.]*

Enter BRABANTIO *[in his nightgown], with* SERVANTS *and torches.*

---

[118]**odd-even**   *between night and morning.*   [126]**sense of all civility**   *feeling of what is proper.*   [131]**ex-**
travagant   *vagrant, wandering (Othello is not Venetian and thus may be considered a wandering soldier of fortune).*
[137]**accident**   *happening.*   [143]**check**   *restraint.*   [144]**cast**   *dismiss.*   [146]**stands in act**   *takes place.*
[147]**fathom**   *ability.*   [153]**Sagittary**   *(probably the name of an inn).*

BRABANTIO: It is too true an evil. Gone she is;   155
   And what's to come of my despisèd time
   Is naught but bitterness. Now, Roderigo,
   Where didst thou see her?—O unhappy girl!—
   With the Moor, say'st thou?—Who would be a father?—
   How didst thou know 'twas she?—O, she deceives me   160
   Past thought!—What said she to you? Get moe° tapers!
   Raise all my kindred!—Are they married, think you?
RODERIGO: Truly I think they are.
BRABANTIO: O heaven! How got she out? O treason of the blood!
   Fathers, from hence trust not your daughters' minds   165
   By what you see them act°. Is there not charms
   By which the property° of youth and maidhood
   May be abused? Have you not read, Roderigo,
   Of some such thing?
RODERIGO: Yes, sir, I have indeed.
BRABANTIO: Call up my brother.—O, would you had had her!—   170
   Some one way, some another.—Do you know
   Where we may apprehend her and the Moor?
RODERIGO: I think I can discover him, if you please
   To get good guard and go along with me.
BRABANTIO: Pray you lead on. At every house I'll call;   175
   I may command at most.—Get weapons, ho!
   And raise some special officers of night.—
   On, good Roderigo; I will deserve your pains°.   [*Exeunt.*]

Scene II [*A street.*]

       Enter OTHELLO, IAGO, ATTENDANTS *with torches.*

IAGO: Though in the trade of war I have slain men,
   Yet do I hold it very stuff° o' th' conscience
   To do no contrived murder. I lack iniquity
   Sometime to do me service. Nine or ten times
   I had thought t' have yerked° him here, under the ribs.   5
OTHELLO: 'Tis better as it is.
IAGO: Nay, but he prated,
   And spoke such scurvy and provoking terms
   Against your honor, that with the little godliness I have
   I did full hard forbear him. But I pray you, sir,
   Are you fast married? Be assured of this,   10
   That the magnifico° is much beloved,
   And hath in his effect a voice potential

---

¹⁶¹**moe** more.   ¹⁶⁶**act** do.   ¹⁶⁷**property** true nature.   ¹⁷⁸**deserve your pains** be worthy of (and re-
ward) your efforts.   **I.ii.** ²**stuff** essence.   ⁵**yerked** stabbed.   ¹¹**magnifico** nobleman.

As double as the Duke's°. He will divorce you,
Or put upon you what restraint or grievance
The law, with all his might to enforce it on,   15
Will give him cable°.

OTHELLO: Let him do his spite.
My services which I have done the Signiory°
Shall out-tongue his complaints. 'Tis yet to know°—
Which when I know that boasting is an honor
I shall promulgate—I fetch my life and being   20
From men of royal siege°, and my demerits°
May speak unbonneted to as proud a fortune
As this that I have reached°. For know, Iago,
But that I love the gentle Desdemona,
I would not my unhousèd° free condition   25
Put into circumscription and confine
For the seas' worth. But look, what lights come yond?

Enter CASSIO, *with* [OFFICERS *and*] *torches.*

IAGO: Those are the raisèd father and his friends.
You were best go in.

OTHELLO: Not I. I must be found.
My parts, my title, and my perfect soul°   30
Shall manifest me rightly. Is it they?

IAGO: By Janus, I think no.

OTHELLO: The servants of the Duke? And my lieutenant?
The goodness of the night upon you, friends.
What is the news?

CASSIO: The Duke does greet you, general;   35
And he requires your haste-posthaste appearance
Even on the instant.

OTHELLO: What is the matter, think you?

CASSIO: Something from Cyprus, as I may divine.
It is a business of some heat. The galleys
Have sent a dozen sequent° messengers   40
This very night at one another's heels,
And many of the consuls, raised and met,
Are at the Duke's already. You have been hotly called for.
When, being not at your lodging to be found,
The Senate hath sent about three several° quests   45
To search you out.

OTHELLO: 'Tis well I am found by you.
I will but spend a word here in the house,
And go with you.   [*Exit.*]

---

¹²⁻¹³**hath . . . Duke's** *i.e., can be as effective as the Duke.*   ¹⁶**cable** *range, scope.*   ¹⁷**Signiory** *the rulers of Venice.*   ¹⁸**yet to know** *unknown as yet.*   ²¹**siege** *rank.*   ²¹**demerits** *deserts.*
²²⁻²³**May . . . reached** *i.e., are the equal of the family I have married into.*   ²⁵**unhousèd** *unconfined.*
³⁰**perfect soul** *clear, unflawed conscience.*   ⁴⁰**sequent** *successive.*   ⁴⁵**several** *separate.*

CASSIO: Ancient, what makes he here?

IAGO: Faith, he tonight hath boarded a land carack°.

  If it prove lawful prize, he's made forever.   50

CASSIO: I do not understand.

IAGO: He's married.

CASSIO: To who?

[Enter OTHELLO.]

IAGO: Marry°, to—Come captain, will you go?

OTHELLO: Have with you.

CASSIO: Here comes another troop to seek for you.

Enter BRABANTIO, RODERIGO, with OFFICERS and torches.

IAGO: It is Brabantio. General, be advised.

  He comes to bad intent.

OTHELLO: Holla! Stand there!   55

RODERIGO: Signior, it is the Moor.

BRABANTIO: Down with him, thief! *[They draw swords.]*

IAGO: You, Roderigo? Come, sir, I am for you.

OTHELLO: Keep up your bright swords, for the dew will rust them.

  Good signior, you shall more command with years

  Than with your weapons.   60

BRABANTIO: O thou foul thief, where hast thou stowed my daughter?

  Damned as thou art, thou hast enchanted her!

  For I'll refer me to all things of sense°,

  If she in chains of magic were not bound,

  Whether a maid so tender, fair, and happy,   65

  So opposite to marriage that she shunned

  The wealthy, curlèd darlings of our nation,

  Would ever have, t'incur a general mock°,

  Run from her guardage to the sooty bosom

  Of such a thing as thou—to fear, not to delight.   70

  Judge me the world if 'tis not gross in sense°

  That thou hast practiced° on her with foul charms,

  Abused her delicate youth with drugs or minerals

  That weaken motion°. I'll have't disputed on;

  'Tis probable, and palpable to thinking.   75

  I therefore apprehend and do attach° thee

  For an abuser of the world, a practicer

  Of arts inhibited and out of warrant°.

  Lay hold upon him. If he do resist,

  Subdue him at his peril.

OTHELLO: Hold your hands,   80

⁴⁹*carack*   treasure ship.   ⁵²**Marry** By Mary (an interjection).   ⁶³*refer . . . sense* i.e., base (my argument) on all ordinary understanding of nature.   ⁶⁸**general mock** public shame.   ⁷¹**gross in sense** obvious.   ⁷²**practiced** used tricks.   ⁷⁴**motion** thought, i.e., reason.   ⁷⁶**attach** arrest.   ⁷⁸**inhibited**
. . . **warrant** prohibited and illegal (black magic).

Both you of my inclining and the rest.
Were it my cue to fight, I should have known it
Without a prompter. Whither will you that I go
To answer this your charge?

BRABANTIO: To prison, till fit time
Of law and course of direct session   85
Call thee to answer.

OTHELLO: What if I do obey?
How may the Duke be therewith satisfied,
Whose messengers are here about my side
Upon some present° business of the state
To bring me to him?

OFFICER: 'Tis true, most worthy signior.   90
The Duke's in council, and your noble self
I am sure is sent for.

BRABANTIO: How? The Duke in council?
In this time of the night? Bring him away.
Mine's not an idle cause. The Duke himself,
Or any of my brothers° of the state,   95
Cannot but feel this wrong as 'twere their own;
For if such actions may have passage free,
Bondslaves and pagans shall our statesmen be.   *Exeunt.*

Scene III [*A council chamber.*]

Enter DUKE, SENATORS, *and* OFFICERS [*set at a table, with lights and* ATTENDANTS].

DUKE: There's no composition° in this news
That gives them credit°.

FIRST SENATOR: Indeed, they are disproportioned.
My letters say a hundred and seven galleys.

DUKE: And mine a hundred forty.

SECOND SENATOR: And mine two hundred.
But though they jump° not on a just accompt°—   5
As in these cases where the aim° reports
'Tis oft with difference—yet do they all confirm
A Turkish fleet, and bearing up to Cyprus.

DUKE: Nay, it is possible enough to judgment°.
I do not so secure me in the error,   10
But the main article I do approve
In fearful sense°.

SAILOR (*Within*):   What, ho! What, ho! What, ho!

---

[89]*present* immediate.   [95]*brothers* i.e., the other senators.   **I.iii.** [1]*composition* agreement.
[2]*gives them credit* makes them believable.   [5]*jump* agree.   [5]*just accompt* exact counting.   [6]*aim*
approximation.   [9]*to judgment* when carefully considered.   [10-12]*I do . . . sense* i.e., just because the
numbers disagree in the reports, I do not doubt that the principal information (that the Turkish fleet is out) is fearfully true.

Enter SAILOR.

OFFICER: A messenger from the galleys.

DUKE: Now? What's the business?

SAILOR: The Turkish preparation makes for Rhodes.
    So was I bid report here to the State   15
    By Signior Angelo.

DUKE: How say you by this change?

FIRST SENATOR: This cannot be
    By no assay of reason. 'Tis a pageant°
    To keep us in false gaze°. When we consider
    Th' importancy of Cyprus to the Turk,   20
    And let ourselves again but understand
    That, as it more concerns the Turk than Rhodes,
    So may he with more facile question° bear it,
    For that it stands not in such warlike brace°,
    But altogether lacks th' abilities   25
    That Rhodes is dressed in. If we make thought of this,
    We must not think the Turk is so unskillful
    To leave that latest which concerns him first,
    Neglecting an attempt of ease and gain
    To wake and wage a danger profitless.   30

DUKE: Nay, in all confidence he's not for Rhodes.

OFFICER: Here is more news.

Enter a MESSENGER.

MESSENGER: The Ottomites, reverend and gracious,
    Steering with due course toward the isle of Rhodes,
    Have there injointed them with an after° fleet.   35

FIRST SENATOR: Ay, so I thought. How many, as you guess?

MESSENGER: Of thirty sail; and now they do restem
    Their backward course, bearing with frank appearance
    Their purposes toward Cyprus. Signior Montano,
    Your trusty and most valiant servitor,   40
    With his free duty° recommends° you thus,
    And prays you to believe him.

DUKE: 'Tis certain then for Cyprus.
    Marcus Luccicos, is not he in town?

FIRST SENATOR: He's now in Florence.   45

DUKE: Write from us to him; post-posthaste dispatch.

FIRST SENATOR: Here comes Brabantio and the valiant Moor.

Enter BRABANTIO, OTHELLO, CASSIO, IAGO, RODERIGO, *and* OFFICERS.

---

[18] ***pageant*** show, pretense.   [19] ***in false gaze*** *looking the wrong way.*   [23] ***facile question*** *easy struggle.*   [24] ***warlike brace*** *"military posture."*   [35] ***after*** *following.*   [41] ***free duty*** *unlimited respect.*   [41] ***recommends*** *informs.*

DUKE: Valiant Othello, we must straight° employ you
    Against the general° enemy Ottoman.
    [*To* BRABANTIO] I did not see you. Welcome, gentle signior.   50
    We lacked your counsel and your help tonight.
BRABANTIO: So did I yours. Good your grace, pardon me.
    Neither my place, nor aught I heard of business,
    Hath raised me from my bed; nor doth the general care
    Take hold on me; for my particular grief   55
    Is of so floodgate and o'erbearing nature
    That it engluts and swallows other sorrows,
    And it is still itself.
DUKE: Why, what's the matter?
BRABANTIO: My daughter! O, my daughter!
SENATORS: Dead?
BRABANTIO: Ay, to me.
    She is abused, stol'n from me, and corrupted   60
    By spells and medicines bought of mountebanks;
    For nature so prepost'rously to err,
    Being not deficient, blind, or lame of sense,
    Sans° witchcraft could not.
DUKE: Whoe'er he be that in this foul proceeding   65
    Hath thus beguiled your daughter of herself,
    And you of her, the bloody book of law
    You shall yourself read in the bitter letter
    After your own sense; yea, though our proper° son
    Stood in your action°.
BRABANTIO: Humbly I thank your Grace.   70
    Here is the man—this Moor, whom now, it seems,
    Your special mandate for the state affairs
    Hath hither brought.
ALL: We are very sorry for't.
DUKE [*To* OTHELLO]: What in your own part can you say to this?
BRABANTIO: Nothing, but this is so.   75
OTHELLO: Most potent, grave, and reverend signiors,
    My very noble and approved° good masters,
    That I have ta'en away this old man's daughter,
    It is most true; true I have married her.
    The very head and front° of my offending   80
    Hath this extent, no more. Rude am I in my speech,
    And little blessed with the soft phrase of peace.
    For since these arms of mine had seven years' pith°
    Till now some nine moons wasted°, they have used

---

⁴⁸**straight** *at once.* ⁴⁹**general** *universal.* ⁶⁴**Sans** *without.* ⁶⁹**proper** *own.* ⁷⁰**Stood in your**
action *were the accused in your suit.* ⁷⁷**approved** *tested, proven by past performance.* ⁸⁰**head and front**
extreme form (front = forehead). ⁸³**pith** *strength.* ⁸⁴**wasted** *past.*

Their dearest° action in the tented field;   85
And little of this great world can I speak
More than pertains to feats of broils and battle;
And therefore little shall I grace my cause
In speaking for myself. Yet, by your gracious patience,
I will a round° unvarnished tale deliver   90
Of my whole course of love—what drugs, what charms,
What conjuration, and what mighty magic,
For such proceeding I am charged withal,
I won his daughter—

BRABANTIO: A maiden never bold,
Of spirit so still and quiet that her motion   95
Blushed at herself°, and she, in spite of nature,
Of years, of country, credit, everything,
To fall in love with what she feared to look on!
It is a judgment maimed and most imperfect
That will confess perfection so could err   100
Against all rules of nature, and must be driven
To find out practices of cunning hell
Why this should be. I therefore vouch again
That with some mixtures pow'rful o'er the blood,
Or with some dram, conjured to this effect,   105
He wrought upon her.

DUKE: To vouch this is no proof,
Without more wider and more overt test
Than these thin habits° and poor likelihoods
Of modern° seeming do prefer against him.

FIRST SENATOR: But, Othello, speak.   110
Did you by indirect and forcèd courses
Subdue and poison this young maid's affections?
Or came it by request, and such fair question°
As soul to soul affordeth?

OTHELLO: I do beseech you,
Send for the lady to the Sagittary   115
And let her speak of me before her father.
If you do find me foul in her report,
The trust, the office, I do hold of you
Not only take away, but let your sentence
Even fall upon my life.

DUKE: Fetch Desdemona hither.   120

OTHELLO: Ancient, conduct them; you best know the place.

[*Exit* IAGO, *with two or three* ATTENDANTS.]

85**dearest** *most important.*   90**round** *blunt.*   95–96**her motion/Blushed at herself** *i.e., she was so mod-
est that she blushed at every thought (and movement).*   108**habits** *clothing.*   109**modern** *trivial.*
113**question** *discussion.*

And till she come, as truly as to heaven
I do confess the vices of my blood,
So justly to your grave ears I'll present
How I did thrive in this fair lady's love,   125
And she in mine.
DUKE: Say it, Othello.
OTHELLO: Her father loved me; oft invited me;
   Still° questioned me the story of my life
From year to year, the battle, sieges, fortune
That I have passed.   130
I ran it through, even from my boyish days
To th' very moment that he bade me tell it.
Wherein I spoke of most disastrous chances,
Of moving accidents by flood and field,
Of hairbreadth scapes i' th' imminent° deadly breach,   135
Of being taken by the insolent foe
And sold to slavery, of my redemption thence
And portance° in my travel's history,
Wherein of anters° vast and deserts idle°,
Rough quarries, rocks, and hills whose heads touch heaven,   140
It was my hint to speak. Such was my process.
And of the Cannibals that each other eat,
The Anthropophagi°, and men whose heads
Grew beneath their shoulders. These things to hear
Would Desdemona seriously incline;   145
But still the house affairs would draw her thence;
Which ever as she could with haste dispatch,
She'd come again, and with a greedy ear
Devour up my discourse. Which I observing,
Took once a pliant hour, and found good means   150
To draw from her a prayer of earnest heart
That I would all my pilgrimage dilate°,
Whereof by parcels she had something heard,
But not intentively°. I did consent,
And often did beguile her of her tears   155
When I did speak of some distressful stroke
That my youth suffered. My story being done,
She gave me for my pains a world of kisses.
She swore in faith 'twas strange, 'twas passing° strange;
'Twas pitiful, 'twas wondrous pitiful.   160
She wished she had not heard it; yet she wished
That heaven had made her such a man. She thanked me,
And bade me, if I had a friend that loved her,

128*Still* regularly.   135*imminent* threatening.   138*portance* manner of acting.   139*anters* caves.
139*idle* empty, sterile.   143*Anthropophagi* maneaters.   152*dilate* relate in full.   154*intentively* at
length and in sequence.   159*passing* surpassing.

I should but teach him how to tell my story,
And that would woo her. Upon this hint I spake.   165
She loved me for the dangers I had passed,
And I loved her that she did pity them.
This only is the witchcraft I have used.
Here comes the lady. Let her witness it.

Enter DESDEMONA, IAGO, ATTENDANTS.

DUKE: I think this tale would win my daughter too.   170
  Good Brabantio, take up this mangled matter at the best°.
  Men do their broken weapons rather use
  Than their bare hands.

BRABANTIO: I pray you hear her speak.
  If she confess that she was half the wooer,
  Destruction on my head if my bad blame   175
  Light on the man. Come hither, gentle mistress.
  Do you perceive in all this noble company
  Where most you owe obedience?

DESDEMONA: My noble father,
  I do perceive here a divided duty.
  To you I am bound for life and education;   180
  My life and education both do learn me
  How to respect you. You are the lord of duty,
  I am hitherto your daughter. But here's my husband,
  And so much duty as my mother showed
  To you, preferring you before her father,   185
  So much I challenge° that I may profess
  Due to the Moor my lord.

BRABANTIO: God be with you. I have done.
  Please it your Grace, on to the state affairs.
  I had rather to adopt a child than get° it.
  Come hither, Moor.   190
  I here do give thee that with all my heart
  Which, but thou hast already, with all my heart
  I would keep from thee. For your sake°, jewel,
  I am glad at soul I have no other child,
  For thy escape would teach me tyranny,   195
  To hang clogs on them. I have done, my lord.

DUKE: Let me speak like yourself and lay a sentence°
  Which, as a grise° or step, may help these lovers.
  When remedies are past, the griefs are ended
  By seeing the worst, which late on hopes depended°.   200
  To mourn a mischief that is past and gone
  Is the next° way to draw new mischief on.

171*take . . . best* i.e., make the best of this disaster.   186*challenge* claim as right.   189*get* beget.
193*For your sake* because of you.   197*lay a sentence* provide a maxim.   198*grise* step.   200*late on
hopes depended* was supported by hope (of a better outcome) until lately.   202*next* closest, surest.

What cannot be preserved when fortune takes,
Patience her injury a mock'ry makes.
The robbed that smiles, steals something from the thief; 205
He robs himself that spends a bootless° grief.
BRABANTIO: So let the Turk of Cyprus us beguile:
We lose it not so long as we can smile.
He bears the sentence well that nothing bears
But the free comfort which from thence he hears; 210
But he bears both the sentence and the sorrow
That to pay grief must of poor patience borrow.
These sentences, to sugar, or to gall,
Being strong on both sides, are equivocal.
But words are words. I never yet did hear 215
That the bruisèd heart was piercèd° through the ear.
I humbly beseech you, proceed to th' affairs of state.
DUKE: The Turk with a most mighty preparation makes for Cyprus. Othello,
the fortitude° of the place is best known to you; and though we have there
a substitute° of most allowed sufficiency°, yet opinion, a more sovereign 220
mistress of effects, throws a more safer voice on you°. You must therefore
be content to slubber° the gloss of your new fortunes with this more
stubborn and boisterous° expedition.
OTHELLO: The tyrant Custom, most grave senators,
Hath made the flinty and steel couch of war 225
My thrice-driven° bed of down. I do agnize°
A natural and prompt alacrity
I find in hardness and do undertake
These present wars against the Ottomites.
Most humbly, therefore, bending to your state, 230
I crave fit disposition for my wife,
Due reference of place, and exhibition°,
With such accommodation and besort
As levels with° her breeding.
DUKE: Why, at her father's.
BRABANTIO: I will not have it so.
OTHELLO: Nor I. 235
DESDEMONA: Nor would I there reside,
To put my father in impatient thoughts
By being in his eye. Most gracious Duke,
To my unfolding° lend your prosperous° ear,

---

²⁰⁶*bootless valueless.*   ²¹⁶*piercèd (some editors emend to* piecèd, *i.e., "healed." But* piercèd *makes good sense: Brabantio is saying in effect that his heart cannot be further hurt [pierced] by the indignity of the useless, conventional advice the Duke offers him. Piercèd can also mean, however, "lanced" in the medical sense, and would then mean "treated").   ²¹⁹*fortitude fortification.*   ²²⁰*substitute viceroy.*   ²²⁰*most allowed suffi-ciency generally acknowledged capability.*   ²²⁰⁻²²¹*opinion . . . you i.e., the general opinion, which finally controls affairs, is that you would be the best man in this situation.*   ²²²*slubber besmear.*   ²²³*stubborn and boisterous rough and violent.*   ²²⁶*thrice–driven i.e., softest.*   ²²⁶*agnize know in myself.*   ²³²*exhibition grant of funds.*   ²³⁴*levels with is suitable to.*   ²³⁹*unfolding explana-tion.*   ²³⁹*prosperous favoring.*

And let me find a charter° in your voice,   240
  T' assist my simpleness.
DUKE: What would you, Desdemona?
DESDEMONA: That I love the Moor to live with him,
  My downright violence, and storm of fortunes,
  May trumpet to the world. My heart's subdued
  Even to the very quality of my lord.°   245
  I saw Othello's visage in his mind,
  And to his honors and his valiant parts
  Did I my soul and fortunes consecrate.
  So that, dear lords, if I be left behind,
  A moth of peace, and he go to the war,   250
  The rites° for why I love him are bereft me,
  And I a heavy interim shall support
  By his dear absence. Let me go with him.
OTHELLO: Let her have your voice°.
  Vouch with me, heaven, I therefore beg it not   255
  To please the palate of my appetite,
  Nor to comply with heat°—the young affects°
  In me defunct—and proper satisfaction°;
  But to be free and bounteous to her mind;
  And heaven defend° your good souls that you think   260
  I will your serious and great business scant
  When she is with me. No, when light-winged toys
  Of feathered Cupid seel° with wanton° dullness
  My speculative and officed instrument°,
  That my disports corrupt and taint my business,   265
  Let housewives make a skillet of my helm,
  And all indign° and base adversities
  Make head° against my estimation°!—
DUKE: Be it as you shall privately determine,
  Either for her stay or going. Th' affair cries haste,   270
  And speed must answer it.
FIRST SENATOR: You must away tonight.
OTHELLO: With all my heart.
DUKE: At nine i' th' morning here we'll meet again.
  Othello, leave some officer behind,
  And he shall our commission bring to you,   275
  And such things else of quality and respect
  As doth import you.
OTHELLO: So please your grace, my ancient;

---

²⁴⁰**charter** *permission.*   ²⁴⁴⁻²⁴⁵**My . . . lord** *i.e., I have become one in nature and being with the man I mar-*
ried (therefore, I too would go to the wars like a soldier).   ²⁵¹**rites** *(may refer either to the marriage rites or to the*
rites, formalities, of war).   ²⁵⁴**voice** *consent.*   ²⁵⁷**heat** *lust.*   ²⁵⁷**affects** *passions.*   ²⁵⁸**proper**
satisfaction *i.e., consummation of the marriage.*   ²⁶⁰**defend** *forbid.*   ²⁶³**seel** *sew up.*   ²⁶³**wanton** *lasci-*
vious.   ²⁶⁴**speculative . . . instrument** *i.e., sight (and, by extension, the mind).*   ²⁶⁷**indign** *unwor-*
thy.   ²⁶⁸**Make head** *form an army, i.e., attack.*   ²⁶⁸**estimation** *reputation.*

A man he is of honesty and trust.
To his conveyance I assign my wife,
With what else needful your good grace shall think   280
to be sent after me.

DUKE: Let it be so.
Good night to every one. [*To* BRABANTIO] And, noble signior,
If virtue no delighted° beauty lack,
Your son-in-law is far more fair than black.

FIRST SENATOR: Adieu, brave Moor. Use Desdemona well.   285

BRABANTIO: Look to her, Moor, if thou hast eyes to see:
She has deceived her father, and may thee.

              [*Exeunt* DUKE, SENATORS, OFFICERS, *& c.*]

OTHELLO: My life upon her faith! Honest Iago,
My Desdemona must I leave to thee.
I prithee let thy wife attend on her,   *love*   290
And bring them after in the best advantage°.
Come, Desdemona. I have but an hour
Of love, of worldly matter, and direction
To spend with thee. We must obey the time.

             Exit [MOOR *with* DESDEMONA].

RODERIGO: Iago?   295

IAGO: What say'st thou, noble heart?

RODERIGO: What will I do, think'st thou?

IAGO: Why, go to bed and sleep.

RODERIGO: I will incontinently° drown myself.

IAGO: If thou dost, I shall never love thee after. Why, thou silly gentleman? 300

RODERIGO: It is silliness to live when to live is torment; and then have we a
prescription to die when death is our physician.

IAGO: O villainous! I have looked upon the world for four times seven years,
and since I could distinguish betwixt a benefit and an injury, I never
found man that knew how to love himself. Ere I would say I would 305
drown myself for the love of a guinea hen, I would change my humanity
with a baboon.

RODERIGO: What should I do? I confess it is my shame to be so fond, but it is
not in my virtue° to amend it.

IAGO: Virtue? A fig! 'Tis in ourselves that we are thus, or thus. Our bodies are 310
our gardens, to the which our wills are gardeners; so that if we will plant
nettles or sow lettuce, set hyssop and weed up thyme, supply it with one
gender of herbs or distract° it with many—either to have it sterile with
idleness or manured with industry—why, the power and corrigible° authority of this lies in our wills. If the balance of our lives had not one scale 315
of reason to poise another of sensuality, the blood and baseness of our

---

²⁸³*delighted* delightful.   ²⁹¹*advantage* opportunity.   ²⁹⁹*incontinently* at once.   ³⁰⁹*virtue*
strength (Roderigo is saying that his nature controls him).   ³¹³*distract* vary.   ³¹⁴*corrigible* corrective.

natures would conduct us to most prepost'rous conclusions°. But we have reason to cool our raging motions, our carnal sting or unbitted° lusts, whereof I take this that you call love to be a sect or scion°.

RODERIGO: It cannot be.   320

IAGO: It is merely a lust of the blood and a permission of the will. Come, be a man! Drown thyself? Drown cats and blind puppies! I have professed me thy friend, and I confess me knit to thy deserving with cables of perdurable toughness. I could never better stead° thee than now. Put money in thy purse. Follow thou the wars; defeat thy favor° with an usurped° 325 beard. I say, put money in thy purse. It cannot be long that Desdemona should continue her love to the Moor. Put money in thy purse. Nor he his to her. It was a violent commencement in her and thou shalt see an answerable° sequestration—put but money in thy purse. These Moors are changeable in their wills—fill thy purse with money. The food that 330 to him now is as luscious as locusts° shall be to him shortly as bitter as coloquintida°. She must change for youth; when she is sated with his body, she will find the errors of her choice. Therefore, put money in thy purse. If thou wilt needs damn thyself, do it a more delicate way than drowning. Make all the money thou canst. If sanctimony° and a frail vow 335 betwixt an erring° barbarian and supersubtle Venetian be not too hard for my wits, and all the tribe of hell, thou shalt enjoy her. Therefore, make money. A pox of drowning thyself, it is clean out of the way. Seek thou rather to be hanged in compassing° thy joy than to be drowned and go without her.   340

RODERIGO: Wilt thou be fast to my hopes, if I depend on the issue?

IAGO: Thou art sure of me. Go, make money. I have told thee often, and I retell thee again and again, I hate the Moor. My cause is hearted°; thine hath no less reason. Let us be conjunctive° in our revenge against him. If thou canst cuckold him, thou dost thyself a pleasure, me a sport. There are 345 many events in the womb of time, which will be delivered. Traverse, go, provide thy money! We will have more of this tomorrow. Adieu.

RODERIGO: Where shall we meet i' th' morning?

IAGO: At my lodging.

RODERIGO: I'll be with thee betimes.   350

IAGO: Go to, farewell. Do you hear, Roderigo?

RODERIGO: I'll sell all my land.   *Exit.*

IAGO: Thus do I ever make my fool my purse;
    For I mine own gained knowledge° should profane
    If I would time expend with such snipe   355
    But for my sport and profit. I hate the Moor,
    And it is thought abroad that 'twixt my sheets

---

³¹⁷**conclusions** *ends.*   ³¹⁸**unbitted** *i.e., uncontrolled.*   ³¹⁹**sect or scion** *off-shoot.*   ³²⁴**stead** *serve.* ³²⁵**defeat thy favor** *disguise your face.*   ³²⁵**usurped** *assumed.*   ³²⁹**answerable** *similar.*   ³³¹**locusts** *(a sweet fruit).*   ³³²**coloquintida** *a purgative derived from a bitter apple.*   ³³⁵**sanctimony** *sacred bond (of marriage).*   ³³⁶**erring** *wandering.*   ³³⁹**compassing** *encompassing, achieving.*   ³⁴³**hearted** *deepseated in the heart.*   ³⁴⁴**conjunctive** *joined.*   ³⁵⁴**gained knowledge** *i.e., practical, worldly wisdom.*

H'as done my office. I know not if't be true,
But I, for mere suspicion in that kind,
Will do, as if for surety°. He holds me well;   360
The better shall my purpose work on him.
Cassio's a proper° man. Let me see now:
To get his place, and to plume up my will°
In double knavery. How? How? Let's see.
After some time, to abuse Othello's ears   365
That he is too familiar with his wife.
He hath a person and a smooth dispose°
To be suspected—framed° to make women false.
The Moor is of a free and open nature
That thinks men honest that but seem to be so;   370
And will as tenderly be led by th' nose
As asses are.
I have't! It is engendered! Hell and night
Must bring this monstrous birth to the world's light.   [*Exit.*]

ACT II

Scene I [*Cyprus.*]

Enter MONTANO *and two* GENTLEMEN [*one above*]°.

MONTANO: What from the cape can you discern at sea?
FIRST GENTLEMAN: Nothing at all, it is a high-wrought flood.
I cannot 'twixt the heaven and the main
Descry a sail.
MONTANO: Methinks the wind hath spoke aloud at land;   5
A fuller blast ne'er shook our battlements.
If it hath ruffianed so upon the sea,
What ribs of oak, when mountains melt on them,
Can hold the mortise? What shall we hear of this?
SECOND GENTLEMAN: A segregation° of the Turkish fleet.   10
For do but stand upon the foaming shore,
The chidden billow seems to pelt the clouds;
The wind-shaked surge, with high and monstrous main°,

---

³⁶⁰**surety** *certainty.* ³⁶²**proper** *handsome.* ³⁶³**plume up my will** *(many explanations have been offered for this crucial line, which in Q₁ reads "make up my will." The general sense is something like "to make more proud and gratify my ego").* ³⁶⁷**dispose** *manner.* ³⁶⁸**framed** *designed.* **II.i. s.d.** *(the Folio arrangement of this scene requires that the First Gentleman stand above—on the upper stage—and act as a lookout reporting sights which cannot be seen by Montano standing below on the main stage).* ¹⁰**segregation** *separation.* ¹³**main** *(both "ocean" and "strength").*

Seems to cast water on the burning Bear
And quench the guards of th' ever-fixèd pole.°   15
I never did like molestation view
On the enchafèd flood.
MONTANO: If that the Turkish fleet
Be not ensheltered and embayed, they are drowned;
It is impossible to bear it out.

Enter a [third] GENTLEMAN.

THIRD GENTLEMAN: News, lads! Our wars are done.   20
The desperate tempest hath so banged the Turks
That their designment halts. A noble ship of Venice
Hath seen a grievous wrack and sufferance°
On most part of their fleet.
MONTANO: How? Is this true?
THIRD GENTLEMAN: The ship is here put in,   25
A Veronesa; Michael Cassio,
Lieutenant to the warlike Moor Othello,
Is come on shore; the Moor himself at sea,
And is in full commission here for Cyprus.
MONTANO: I am glad on't. 'Tis a worthy governor.   30
THIRD GENTLEMAN: But this same Cassio, though he speak of comfort
Touching the Turkish loss, yet he looks sadly
And prays the Moor be safe, for they were parted
With foul and violent tempest.
montano: Pray heavens he be;
For I have served him, and the man commands   35
Like a full soldier. Let's to the seaside, ho!
As well to see the vessel that's come in
As to throw out our eyes for brave Othello,
Even till we make the main and th' aerial blue
An indistinct regard°.
THIRD GENTLEMAN: Come, let's do so;   40
For every minute is expectancy
Of more arrivancie°.

Enter CASSIO.

CASSIO: Thanks, you the valiant of the warlike isle,
That so approve° the Moor. O, let the heavens
Give him defense against the elements,   45
For I have lost him on a dangerous sea.
MONTANO: Is he well shipped?

---

¹⁴⁻¹⁵**Seems . . . pole**   *(the constellation Ursa Minor contains two stars which are the guards, or companions, of the pole, or North Star).*   ²³**sufferance**   *damage.*   ³⁹⁻⁴⁰**the main . . . regard**   *i.e., the sea and sky become indistinguishable.*   ⁴²**arrivancie**   *arrivals.*   ⁴⁴**approve**   *("honor" or, perhaps, "are as warlike and valiant as your governor").*

CASSIO: His bark is stoutly timbered, and his pilot
  Of very expert and approved allowance°;
  Therefore my hopes, not surfeited to death°,   50
  Stand in bold cure°. (*Within:* A sail, a sail, a sail!)
CASSIO: What noise?
FIRST GENTLEMAN: The town is empty; on the brow o' th' sea
  Stand ranks of people, and they cry, "A sail!"
CASSIO: My hopes do shape him for the governor.   [*A shot.*] 55
SECOND GENTLEMAN: They do discharge their shot of courtesy:
  Our friends at least.
CASSIO: I pray you, sir, go forth
  And give us truth who 'tis that is arrived.
SECOND GENTLEMAN: I shall.   [*Exit.*]
MONTANO: But, good lieutenant, is your general wived?   60
CASSIO: Most fortunately. He hath achieved a maid
  That paragons° description and wild fame°;
  One that excels the quirks of blazoning pens°,
  And in th' essential vesture of creation°
  Does tire the ingener°.

            Enter [Second] GENTLEMAN.
          How now? Who has put in?   65
SECOND GENTLEMAN: 'Tis one Iago, ancient to the general.
CASSIO: H'as had most favorable and happy speed:
  Tempests themselves, high seas, and howling winds,
  The guttered° rocks and congregated° sands,
  Traitors ensteeped° to enclog the guiltless keel,   70
  As having sense° of beauty, do omit
  Their mortal° natures, letting go safely by
  The divine Desdemona.
MONTANO: What is she?
CASSIO: She that I spake of, our great captain's captain,
  Left in the conduct of the bold Iago,   75
  Whose footing° here anticipates our thoughts
  A se'nnight's° speed. Great Jove, Othello guard,
  And swell his sail with thine own pow'rful breath,
  That he may bless this bay with his tall° ship,
  Make love's quick pants in Desdemona's arms,   80
  Give renewed fire to our extinct spirits.

      Enter DESDEMONA, IAGO, RODERIGO, *and* EMILIA.

---

[49] **approved allowance** *known and tested.*   [50] **not surfeited to death** *i.e., not so great as to be in danger.*
[51] **Stand in bold cure** *i.e., are likely to be restored.*   [62] **paragons** *exceeds.* [62] **wild fame** *extravagant report.*   [63] **quirks of blazoning pens** *ingenuities of praising pens.* [64] **essential vesture of creation** *essential human nature as given by the Creator.* [65] **tire the ingener** *a difficult line that probably means something like "outdo the human ability to imagine and picture."* [69] **guttered** *jagged.* [69] **congregated** *gathered.*
[70] **ensteeped** *submerged.* [71] **sense** *awareness.* [72] **mortal** *deadly.* [76] **footing** *landing.* [77] **se'nnight's** *week's.* [79] **tall** *brave.*

O, behold! The riches of the ship is come on shore!
You men of Cyprus, let her have your knees.   *[Kneeling.]*
Hail to thee, lady! and the grace of heaven,
Before, behind thee, and on every hand,   85
Enwheel thee round.

DESDEMONA: I thank you, valiant Cassio.
What tidings can you tell of my lord?

CASSIO: He is not yet arrived, nor know I aught
But that he's well and will be shortly here.

DESDEMONA: O but I fear. How lost you company?   90

CASSIO: The great contention of sea and skies
Parted our fellowship. (*Within:* A sail, a sail!)   *[A shot.]*
But hark. A sail!

SECOND GENTLEMAN: They give this greeting to the citadel;
This likewise is a friend.

CASSIO: See for the news.   *[Exit* GENTLEMAN.]   95
Good ancient, you are welcome. [*To* EMILIA] Welcome, mistress.
Let it not gall your patience, good Iago,
That I extend° my manners. 'Tis my breeding°
That gives me this bold show of courtesy.   *[Kisses* EMILIA.]

IAGO: Sir, would she give you so much of her lips   100
As of her tongue she oft bestows on me,
You would have enough.

DESDEMONA: Alas, she has no speech.

IAGO: In faith, too much.
I find it still when I have leave to sleep°.
Marry, before your ladyship°, I grant,   105
She puts her tongue a little in her heart
And chides with thinking.

EMILIA: You have little cause to say so.

IAGO: Come on, come on! You are pictures° out of door,
Bells in your parlors, wildcats in your kitchens,
Saints in your injuries°, devils being offended,   110
Players in your housewifery°, and housewives in your beds.

DESDEMONA: O, fie upon thee, slanderer!

IAGO: Nay, it is true, or else I am a Turk.
You rise to play, and go to bed to work.

EMILIA: You shall not write my praise.

IAGO: No, let me not.   115

DESDEMONA: What wouldst write of me, if thou shouldst praise me?

---

⁹⁸**extend** stretch.   ⁹⁸**breeding** *careful training in manners (Cassio is considerably more the polished gentle-*
man than Iago, and aware of it).   ¹⁰⁴**still . . . sleep** *i.e., even when she allows me to sleep she continues to*
scold.   ¹⁰⁵**before your ladyship** *in your presence.*   ¹⁰⁸**pictures** *models (of virtue).*   ¹¹⁰**in your in-**
juries *when you injure others.*   ¹¹¹**housewifery** *this word can mean "careful, economical household manage-*
ment," and Iago would then be accusing women of only pretending to be good housekeepers, while in bed they are ei-
ther [1] economical of their favors, or more likely [2] serious and dedicated workers.

IAGO: O gentle lady, do not put me to't.
   For I am nothing if not critical.
DESDEMONA: Come on, assay. There's one gone to the harbor?
IAGO: Ay, madam.
DESDEMONA [*Aside*]: I am not merry; but I do beguile   120
   The thing I am by seeming otherwise.—
   Come, how wouldst thou praise me?
IAGO: I am about it; but indeed my invention
   Comes from my pate as birdlime° does from frieze°—
   It plucks out brains and all. But my Muse labors,   125
   And thus she is delivered:
   If she be fair° and wise: fairness and wit,
   The one's for use, the other useth it.
DESDEMONA: Well praised. How if she be black° and witty?
IAGO: If she be black, and thereto have a wit,   130
   She'll find a white that shall her blackness fit.
DESDEMONA: Worse and worse!
EMILIA: How if fair and foolish?
IAGO: She never yet was foolish that was fair,
   For even her folly helped her to an heir.   135
DESDEMONA: Those are old fond° paradoxes to make fools laugh i' th' ale-
   house. What miserable praise hast thou for her that's foul and foolish?
IAGO: There's none so foul, and foolish thereunto,
   But does foul pranks which fair and wise ones do.

DESDEMONA: O heavy ignorance. Thou praisest the worst best. But what 140
   praise couldst thou bestow on a deserving woman indeed—one that
   in the authority of her merit did justly put on the vouch of very malice
   itself°?
IAGO: She that was ever fair, and never proud;
   Had tongue at will, and yet was never loud;   145
   Never lacked gold, and yet went never gay;
   Fled from her wish, and yet said "Now I may";
   She that being angered, her revenge being nigh,
   Bade her wrong stay, and her displeasure fly;
   She that in wisdom never was so frail   150
   To change the cod's head for the salmon's tail°;
   She that could think, and nev'r disclose her mind;
   See suitors following, and not look behind:
   She was a wight° (if ever such wights were)—
DESDEMONA: To do what?   155

124*birdlime*   *a sticky substance put on branches to catch birds.*   124*frieze*   *rough cloth.*   127*fair*   *light-complexioned.*   129*black*   *brunette.*   136*fond*   *foolish.*   141–43*one . . . itself*   *i.e., a woman so honest and deserving that even malice would be forced to approve of her.*   151*To . . . tail*   *i.e., to exchange something valuable for something useless.*   154*wight*   *person.*

IAGO: To suckle fools and chronicle small beer°.

DESDEMONA: O most lame and impotent conclusion. Do not learn of him, Emilia, though he be thy husband. How say you, Cassio? Is he not a most profane and liberal° counselor?

CASSIO: He speaks home°, madam. You may relish him more in° the soldier [160] than in the scholar. [*Takes* DESDEMONA's *hand.*]

IAGO [*Aside*]: He takes her by the palm. Ay, well said, whisper! With as little a web as this will I ensnare as great a fly as Cassio. Ay, smile upon her, do! I will gyve° thee in thine own courtship.—You say true; 'tis so, indeed!— If such tricks as these strip you out of your lieutenantry, it had been bet- [165] ter you had not kissed your three fingers so oft—which now again you are most apt to play the sir° in. Very good! Well kissed! An excellent curtsy°! 'Tis so, indeed. Yet again your fingers to your lips? Would they were clyster pipes° for your sake! [*Trumpets within.*] The Moor! I know his trumpet°. [170]

CASSIO: 'Tis truly so.

DESDEMONA: Let's meet him and receive him.

CASSIO: Lo, where he comes.

Enter OTHELLO *and* ATTENDANTS.

OTHELLO: O my fair warrior!

DESDEMONA: My dear Othello.

OTHELLO: It gives me wonder great as my content [175]
To see you here before me. O my soul's joy!
If after every tempest come such calms,
May the winds blow till they have wakened death.
And let the laboring bark climb hills of seas
Olympus-high, and duck again as low [180]
As hell's from heaven. If it were now to die,
'Twere now to be most happy; for I fear
My soul hath her content so absolute
That not another comfort like to this
Succeeds in unknown fate.

DESDEMONA: The heavens forbid [185]
But that our loves and comforts should increase
Even as our days do grow.

OTHELLO: Amen to that, sweet powers!
I cannot speak enough of this content:
It stops me here [*touches his heart*]; it is too much of joy.
And this, and this, the greatest discords be   [*They kiss.*] [190]
That e'er our hearts shall make!

IAGO [*Aside*]:   O, you are well tuned now!

---

[156]**chronicle small beer**   i.e., keep household accounts (the most trivial of occupations in Iago's opinion).   [159]**lib-eral**   licentious.   [160]**speaks home**   thrusts deeply with his speech.   [160]**relish him more in**   enjoy him more as.   [164]**gyve**   bind.   [167]**the sir**   the fashionable gentleman.   [168]**curtsy**   courtesy, i.e., bow.   [169]**clyster pipes**   enema tubes.   [170]**his trumpet**   (great men had their own distinctive calls).

But I'll set down the pegs° that make this music,
As honest as I am.
OTHELLO: Come, let us to the castle.
News, friends! Our wars are done; the Turks are drowned.
How does my old acquaintance of this isle? [195]
Honey, you shall be well desired in Cyprus;
I have found great love amongst them. O my sweet,
I prattle out of fashion, and I dote
In mine own comforts. I prithee, good Iago,
Go to the bay and disembark my coffers. [200]
Bring thou the master to the citadel;
He is a good one and his worthiness
Does challenge° much respect. Come, Desdemona,
Once more well met at Cyprus.

Exit OTHELLO *and* DESDEMONA [*and all but* IAGO *and* RODERIGO].

IAGO [*To an Attendant*]: Do thou meet me presently at the harbor. [*To* [205]
RODERIGO] Come hither. If thou be'st valiant (as they say base men being
in love have then a nobility in their natures more than is native to them),
list me. The lieutenant tonight watches on the court of guard°. First, I must
tell thee this: Desdemona is directly in love with him.
RODERIGO: With him? Why, 'tis not possible. [210]
IAGO: Lay thy finger thus [*puts his finger to his lips*], and let thy soul be instructed. Mark me with what violence she first loved the Moor but for
bragging and telling her fantastical lies. To love him still for prating? Let
not thy discreet heart think it. Her eye must be fed. And what delight shall
she have to look on the devil? When the blood is made dull with the act [215]
of sport, there should be a game° to inflame it and to give satiety a fresh
appetite, loveliness in favor°, sympathy in years°, manners, and beauties;
all which the Moor is defective in. Now for want of these required
conveniences°, her delicate tenderness will find itself abused, begin to
heave the gorge°, disrelish and abhor the Moor. Very nature will instruct [220]
her in it and compel her to some second choice. Now sir, this granted—
as it is a most pregnant° and unforced position—who stands so eminent
in the degree of this fortune as Cassio does? A knave very voluble; no further conscionable° than in putting on the mere form of civil and humane°
seeming for the better compass of his salt° and most hidden loose° affec- [225]
tion. Why, none! Why, none! A slipper° and subtle knave, a finder of occasion, that has an eye can stamp and counterfeit advantages, though true
advantage never present itself. A devilish knave. Besides, the knave is
handsome, young, and hath all those requisites in him that folly and green

---

[192]**set down the pegs** loosen the strings (to produce discord).   [203]**challenge** require, exact.   [208]**court of
guard** guardhouse.   [216]**game** sport (with the added sense of "gamey," "rank").   [217]**favor** countenance, appearance.   [217]**sympathy in years** sameness of age.   [219]**conveniences** advantages.   [220]**heave
the gorge** vomit.   [222]**pregnant** likely.   [223–24]**no further conscionable** having no more conscience.
[224]**humane** polite.   [225]**salt** lecherous.   [225]**loose** immoral.   [226]**slipper** slippery.

minds look after. A pestilent complete knave, and the woman hath found 230
him already.

RODERIGO: I cannot believe that in her; she's full of most blessed condition.

IAGO: Blessed fig's-end! The wine she drinks is made of grapes. If she had been
blessed, she would never have loved the Moor. Blessed pudding! Didst thou
not see her paddle with the palm of his hand? Didst not mark that? 235

RODERIGO: Yes, that I did; but that was but courtesy.

IAGO: Lechery, by this hand! [*Extends his index finger.*] An index° and obscure
prologue to the history of lust and foul thoughts. They met so near with
their lips that their breaths embraced together. Villainous thoughts,
Roderigo. When these mutualities so marshal the way, hard at hand comes 240
the master and main exercise, th' incorporate° conclusion: Pish! But, sir, be
you ruled by me. I have brought you from Venice. Watch you tonight; for
the command, I'll lay't upon you. Cassio knows you not. I'll not be far
from you. Do you find some occasion to anger Cassio, either by speaking
too loud, or tainting° his discipline, or from what other course you please 245
which the time shall more favorably minister.

RODERIGO: Well.

IAGO: Sir, he's rash and very sudden in choler°, and haply may strike at you.
Provoke him that he may; for even out of that will I cause these of Cyprus
to mutiny, whose qualification shall come into no true taste° again but by 250
the displanting of Cassio. So shall you have a shorter journey to your
desires by the means I shall then have to prefer them; and the impediment
most profitably removed without the which there were no expectation of
our prosperity.

RODERIGO: I will do this if you can bring it to any opportunity. 255

IAGO: I warrant thee. Meet me by and by at the citadel. I must fetch his
necessaries ashore. Farewell.

RODERIGO: Adieu.   *Exit.*

IAGO: That Cassio loves her, I do well believe't;
That she loves him, 'tis apt and of great credit. 260
The Moor, howbeit that I endure him not,
Is of a constant, loving, noble nature,
And I dare think he'll prove to Desdemona
A most dear° husband. Now I do love her too;
Not out of absolute° lust, though peradventure° 265
I stand accountant for as great a sin,
But partly led to diet° my revenge,
For that I do suspect the lusty Moor
Hath leaped into my seat; the thought whereof
Doth, like a poisonous mineral, gnaw my inwards; 270

---

²³⁷*index* pointer.   ²⁴¹*incorporate* carnal.   ²⁴⁵*tainting* discrediting.   ²⁴⁸*choler* anger.
²⁵⁰*qualification . . . taste* i.e., appeasement will not be brought about (wine was "qualified" by adding water).
²⁶⁴*dear* expensive.   ²⁶⁵*out of absolute* absolutely out of.   ²⁶⁵*peradventure* perchance.   ²⁶⁷*diet*
feed.

And nothing can or shall content my soul
Till I am evened with him, wife for wife.
Or failing so, yet that I put the Moor
At least into a jealousy so strong   275
That judgment cannot cure. Which thing to do,
If this poor trash of Venice, whom I trace°
For his quick hunting, stand the putting on,
I'll have our Michael Cassio on the hip,
Abuse him to the Moor in the right garb°   280
(For I fear Cassio with my nightcap too),
Make the Moor thank me, love me, and reward me
For making him egregiously an ass
And practicing upon° his peace and quiet,
Even to madness. 'Tis here, but yet confused:
Knavery's plain face is never seen till used.   *Exit.*   285

Scene II [*A street.*]

Enter OTHELLO'S HERALD, *with a proclamation.*

HERALD: It is Othello's pleasure, our noble and valiant general, that upon
certain tidings now arrived importing the mere perdition° of the Turkish
fleet, every man put himself into triumph. Some to dance, some to make
bonfires, each man to what sport and revels his addition° leads him. For,
besides these beneficial news, it is the celebration of his nuptial. So much   5
was his pleasure should be proclaimed. All offices° are open, and there is
full liberty of feasting from this present hour of five till the bell have told
eleven. Bless the isle of Cyprus and our noble general Othello!   *Exit.*

Scene III [*The citadel of Cyprus.*]

Enter OTHELLO, DESDEMONA, CASSIO, *and* ATTENDANTS.

OTHELLO: Good Michael, look you to the guard tonight.
Let's teach ourselves that honorable stop,
Not to outsport direction.
CASSIO: Iago hath discretion what to do;
But notwithstanding, with my personal eye   5
Will I look to't.
OTHELLO: Iago is most honest. — *deceives*
Michael, good night. Tomorrow with your earliest
Let me have speech with you. [*To* DESDEMONA] Come, my dear love,
The purchase made, the fruits are to ensue.

---

²⁷⁶**trace** (most editors emend to "trash," meaning to hang weights on a dog to slow his hunting: but "trace" clearly
means something like "put on the trace" or "set on the track").   ²⁷⁹**right garb** i.e., "proper fashion."   ²⁸³**practicing upon** scheming to destroy. **II.ii.** ²**mere perdition** absolute destruction.   ⁴**addition** rank.
⁶**offices** kitchens and storerooms of food.

That profit's yet to come 'tween me and you.   10
Good night.   *Exit* [OTHELLO *with* DESDEMONA *and* ATTENDANTS].

Enter IAGO.

CASSIO: Welcome, Iago. We must to the watch.

IAGO: Not this hour, lieutenant; 'tis not yet ten o' th' clock. Our general cast°
us thus early for the love of his Desdemona; who let us not therefore
blame.He hath not yet made wanton the night with her, and she is sport   15
for Jove.

CASSIO: She's a most exquisite lady.

IAGO: And, I'll warrant her, full of game.

CASSIO: Indeed, she's a most fresh and delicate creature.

IAGO: What an eye she has! Methinks it sounds a parley to provocation.   20

CASSIO: An inviting eye; and yet methinks right modest.

IAGO: And when she speaks, is it not an alarum° to love?

CASSIO: She is indeed perfection.

IAGO: Well, happiness to their sheets! Come, lieutenant, I have a stoup° of
wine, and here without are a brace of Cyprus gallants that would fain have   25
a measure to the health of black Othello.

CASSIO: Not tonight, good Iago. I have very poor and unhappy brains for
drinking; I could well wish courtesy would invent some other custom of
entertainment.

IAGO: O, they are our friends. But one cup! I'll drink for you.   30

CASSIO: I have drunk but one tonight, and that was craftily qualified° too; and
behold what innovation it makes here. I am unfortunate in the infirmity
and dare not task my weakness with any more.

IAGO: What, man! 'Tis a night of revels, the gallants desire it.

CASSIO: Where are they?   35

IAGO: Here, at the door. I pray you call them in.

CASSIO: I'll do't, but it dislikes me.   *Exit.*

IAGO: If I can fasten but one cup upon him
With that which he hath drunk tonight already,
He'll be as full of quarrel and offense   40
As my young mistress' dog. Now, my sick fool Roderigo,
Whom love hath turned almost the wrong side out,
To Desdemona hath tonight caroused
Potations pottle-deep°; and he's to watch.
Three else° of Cyprus, noble swelling spirits,   45
That hold their honors in a wary distance°,
The very elements of this warlike isle,
Have I tonight flustered with flowing cups,
And they watch too. Now, 'mongst this flock of drunkards

II.iii.   ¹³**cast** *dismissed.*   ²²**alarum**   *the call to action, "general quarters."*   ²⁴**stoup**   *two-quart tankard.*
³¹**qualified** *diluted.*   ⁴⁴**pottle-deep** *to the bottom of the cup.*   ⁴⁵**else** *others.*   ⁴⁶**hold . . . distance**
are scrupulous in maintaining their honor.

Am I to put our Cassio in some action   50
That may offend the isle. But here they come.

Enter CASSIO, MONTANO, *and* GENTLEMEN.

If consequence do but approve my dream,
My boat sails freely, both with wind and stream.
CASSIO: 'Fore God, they have given me a rouse° already.
MONTANO: Good faith, a little one; not past a pint, as I am a soldier.   55
IAGO: Some wine, ho!
   [*Sings*] And let me the canakin clink, clink;
                  And let me the canakin clink.
                  A soldier's a man;
                  O man's life's but a span.   60
                  Why then, let a soldier drink.
   Some wine, boys!
CASSIO: 'Fore God, an excellent song!
IAGO: I learned it in England, where indeed they are most potent in potting.
   Your Dane, your German, and your swag-bellied° Hollander—Drink,   65
   ho!—are nothing to your English.
CASSIO: Is your Englishman so exquisite° in his drinking?
IAGO: Why, he drinks you with facility your Dane dead drunk; he sweats not
   to overthrow your Almain; he gives your Hollander a vomit ere the next
   pottle can be filled.   70
CASSIO: To the health of our general!
MONTANO: I am for it, lieutenant, and I'll do you justice.
IAGO: O sweet England!
   [*Sings*] King Stephen was and a worthy peer;
                  His breeches cost him but a crown;   75
                  He held them sixpence all too dear,
                  With that he called the tailor lown°.
                  He was a wight of high renown,
                  And thou art but of low degree:
                  'Tis pride that pulls the country down;   80
                  And take thine auld cloak about thee.
   Some wine, ho!
CASSIO: 'Fore God, this is a more exquisite song than the other.
IAGO: Will you hear't again?
CASSIO: No, for I hold him to be unworthy of his place that does those things.   85
   Well, God's above all; and there be souls must be saved, and there be souls
   must not be saved.
IAGO: It's true, good lieutenant.
CASSIO: For mine own part—no offense to the general, nor any man of
   quality—I hope to be saved.   90
IAGO: And so do I too, lieutenant.

---

⁵⁴**rouse** *drink.*   ⁶⁵**swag–bellied** *pendulous-bellied.*   ⁶⁷**exquisite** *superb.*   ⁷⁷**lown** *lout.*

(marginal note: fall of Cassio to Iago)

CASSIO: Ay, but, by your leave, not before me. The lieutenant is to be saved
    before the ancient. Let's have no more of this; let's to our affairs.—God
    forgive us our sins!—Gentlemen, let's look to our business. Do not think,
    gentlemen, I am drunk. This is my ancient; this is my right hand, and this   95
    is my left. I am not drunk now. I can stand well enough, and I speak well
    enough.
GENTLEMEN: Excellent well!
CASSIO: Why, very well then. You must not think then that I am drunk.

                                                                        Exit.

MONTANO: To th' platform, masters. Come, let's set the watch.   100
IAGO: You see this fellow that is gone before.
    He's a soldier fit to stand by Caesar
    And give direction; and do but see his vice.
    'Tis to his virtue a just equinox°,
    The one as long as th' other. 'Tis pity of him.   105
    I fear the trust Othello puts him in,
    On some odd time of his infirmity,
    Will shake this island.

(marginal note: decieves Montano)

MONTANO: But is he often thus?
IAGO: 'Tis evermore his prologue to his sleep:
    He'll watch the horologe a double set°   110
    If drink rock not his cradle.
MONTANO: It were well
    The general were put in mind of it.
    Perhaps he sees it not, or his good nature
    Prizes the virtue that appears in Cassio
    And looks not on his evils. Is not this true?   115

                        Enter RODERIGO.

IAGO [*Aside*]: How now, Roderigo?
    I pray you after the lieutenant, go!   [*Exit* RODERIGO.]
MONTANO: And 'tis great pity that the noble Moor
    Should hazard such a place as his own second
    With one of an ingraft° infirmity.   120
    It were an honest action to say so
    To the Moor.
IAGO: Not I, for this fair island!
    I do love Cassio well and would do much
    To cure him of this evil.   (Help! Help! *Within.*)
    But hark! What noise?   125

                Enter CASSIO, *pursuing* RODERIGO.

CASSIO: Zounds, you rogue! You rascal!

---

[104] *just equinox* exact balance (of dark and light).   [110] *watch . . . set* stay awake twice around the clock.
[120] *ingraft* ingrained.

MONTANO: What's the matter, lieutenant?

CASSIO: A knave teach me my duty? I'll beat the knave into a twiggen°
    bottle.

RODERIGO: Beat me?   130

CASSIO: Dost thou prate, rogue?   [*Strikes him.*]

MONTANO: Nay, good lieutenant! I pray you, sir, hold your hand.

[*Stays him.*]

CASSIO: Let me go, sir, or I'll knock you o'er the mazzard°.

MONTANO: Come, come, you're drunk!

CASSIO: Drunk?   [*They fight.*] 135

IAGO [*Aside to* RODERIGO]: Away, I say! Go out and cry a mutiny!

[*Exit* RODERIGO.]

Nay, good lieutenant. God's will, gentlemen!
Help, ho! Lieutenant. Sir. Montano.
Help, masters! Here's a goodly watch indeed!   [*A bell rung.*]
Who's that which rings the bell? Diablo, ho!   140
The two will rise. God's will, lieutenant,
You'll be ashamed forever.

Enter OTHELLO *and* ATTENDANTS.

OTHELLO: What is the matter here?

MONTANO: Zounds, I bleed still. I am hurt to the death.

He dies.   [*He and* CASSIO *fight again.*]

OTHELLO: Hold for your lives!   145

IAGO: Hold, ho! Lieutenant. Sir. Montano. Gentlemen!
Have you forgot all place of sense and duty?
Hold! The general speaks to you. Hold, for shame!

OTHELLO: Why, how now, ho? From whence ariseth this?
Are we turned Turks, and to ourselves do that   150
Which heaven hath forbid the Ottomites°?
For Christian shame put by this barbarous brawl!
He that stirs next to carve for his own rage
Holds his soul light°; he dies upon his motion.
Silence that dreadful bell! It frights the isle   155
From her propriety°. What is the matter, masters?
Honest Iago, that looks dead with grieving,
Speak. Who began this? On thy love, I charge thee.

IAGO: I do not know. Friends all, but now, even now,
In quarter° and in terms like bride and groom   160
Devesting them for bed; and then, but now—
As if some planet had unwitted men—
Swords out, and tilting one at other's breasts

---

¹²⁸*twiggen*   wicker-covered.   ¹³³*mazzard*   head.   ¹⁵¹*heaven . . . Ottomites*   i.e., by sending the storm
which dispersed the Turks.   ¹⁵⁴*Holds his soul light*   values his soul lightly.   ¹⁵⁶*propriety*   proper order.
¹⁶⁰*In quarter*   on duty.

In opposition bloody. I cannot speak
Any beginning to this peevish odds°,   165
And would in action glorious I had lost
Those legs that brought me to a part of it!
OTHELLO: How comes it, Michael, you are thus forgot?
CASSIO: I pray you pardon me; I cannot speak.
OTHELLO: Worthy Montano, you were wont to be civil;   170
Thy gravity and stillness of your youth
The world hath noted, and your name is great
In mouths of wisest censure°. What's the matter
That you unlace° your reputation thus
And spend your rich opinion° for the name   175
Of a night-brawler? Give me answer to it.
MONTANO: Worthy Othello, I am hurt to danger.
Your officer, Iago, can inform you.
While I spare speech, which something now offends° me,
Of all that I do know; nor know I aught   180
By me that's said or done amiss this night,
Unless self-charity be sometimes a vice,
And to defend ourselves it be a sin
When violence assails us.
OTHELLO: Now, by heaven,
My blood begins my safer guides to rule,   185
And passion, having my best judgment collied°,
Assays to lead the way. If I once stir
Or do but lift this arm, the best of you
Shall sink in my rebuke. Give me to know
How this foul rout began, who set it on;   190
And he that is approved in this offense,
Though he had twinned with me, both at a birth,
Shall lose me. What? In a town of war
Yet wild, the people's hearts brimful of fear,
To manage° private and domestic quarrel?   195
In night, and on the court and guard of safety?
'Tis monstrous. Iago, who began't?
MONTANO: If partially affined, or leagued in office°,
Thou dost deliver more or less than truth,
Thou art no soldier.
IAGO: Touch me not so near.   200
I had rather have this tongue cut from my mouth
Than it should do offense to Michael Cassio.

---

¹⁶⁵**odds** *quarrel.*   ¹⁷³**censure** *judgment.*   ¹⁷⁴**unlace** *undo (the term refers specifically to the dressing of a wild boar killed in the hunt).*   ¹⁷⁵**opinion** *reputation.*   ¹⁷⁹**offends** *harms, hurts.*   ¹⁸⁶**collied** *darkened.*   ¹⁹⁵**manage** *conduct.*   ¹⁹⁸**If . . . office** *if you are partial because you are related ("affined") or the brother officer (of Cassio).*

Yet I persuade myself to speak the truth
Shall nothing wrong him. This it is, general.
Montano and myself being in speech,   205
There comes a fellow crying out for help,
And Cassio following him with determined sword
To execute upon him. Sir, this gentleman
Steps in to Cassio and entreats his pause.
Myself the crying fellow did pursue,   210
Lest by his clamor—as it so fell out—
The town might fall in fright. He, swift of foot,
Outran my purpose; and I returned then rather
For that I heard the clink and fall of swords,
And Cassio high in oath; which till tonight   215
I ne'er might say before. When I came back—
For this was brief—I found them close together
At blow and thrust, even as again they were
When you yourself did part them.
More of this matter cannot I report;   220
But men are men; the best sometimes forget.
Though Cassio did some little wrong to him,
As men in rage strike those that wish them best,
Yet surely Cassio I believe received
From him that fled some strange indignity,   225
Which patience could not pass°.
OTHELLO: I know, Iago,
Thy honesty and love doth mince° this matter,
Making it light to Cassio. Cassio, I love thee;
But never more be officer of mine.

           Enter DESDEMONA, *attended.*

— cast out because of Iago

Look if my gentle love be not raised up.   230
I'll make thee an example.
DESDEMONA: What is the matter, dear?
othello: All's well, sweeting; come away to bed.
  [*To* MONTANO] Sir, for your hurts, myself will be your surgeon.
Lead him off.   [MONTANO *led off.*]
Iago, look with care about the town   235
And silence those whom this vile brawl distracted.
Come, Desdemona: 'tis the soldiers' life
To have their balmy slumbers waked with strife.

       Exit [*with all but* IAGO *and* CASSIO].

IAGO: What, are you hurt, lieutenant?
CASSIO: Ay, past all surgery.   240

---

²²⁶**pass**   allow to pass.   ²²⁷**mince**   cut up (i.e., tell only part of).

IAGO: Marry, God forbid!

CASSIO: Reputation, reputation, reputation! O, I have lost my reputation! I have lost the immortal part of myself, and what remains is bestial. My reputation, Iago, my reputation.

IAGO: As I am an honest man, I had thought you had received some bodily [245] wound. There is more sense° in that than in reputation. Reputation is an idle and most false imposition°, oft got without merit and lost without deserving. You have lost no reputation at all unless you repute yourself such a loser. What, man, there are more ways to recover the general again. You are but now cast in his mood°—a punishment more in policy° than [250] in malice—even so as one would beat his offenseless dog to affright an imperious lion. Sue to him again, and he's yours.

CASSIO: I will rather sue to be despised than to deceive so good a commander with so slight, so drunken, and so indiscreet an officer. Drunk! And speak parrot°! And squabble! Swagger! Swear! and discourse fustian° with one's [255] own shadow! O thou invisible spirit of wine, if thou hast no name to be known by, let us call thee devil!

IAGO: What was he that you followed with your sword? What had he done to you?

CASSIO: I know not.

IAGO: Is't possible? [260]

CASSIO: I remember a mass of things, but nothing distinctly: a quarrel, but nothing wherefore. O God, that men should put an enemy in their mouths to steal away their brains! that we should with joy, pleasance, revel, and applause transform ourselves into beasts! [265]

IAGO: Why, but you are now well enough. How came you thus recovered?

CASSIO: It hath pleased the devil drunkenness to give place to the devil wrath. One unperfectness shows me another, to make me frankly despise myself.

IAGO: Come, you are too severe a moraler. As the time, the place, and the condition of this country stands, I could heartily wish this had not befall'n; [270] but since it is as it is, mend it for your own good.

CASSIO: I will ask him for my place again: he shall tell me I am a drunkard. Had I as many mouths as Hydra, such an answer would stop them all. To be now a sensible man, by and by a fool, and presently a beast! O strange! Every inordinate cup is unblest, and the ingredient is a devil. [275]

IAGO: Come, come, good wine is a good familiar creature if it be well used. Exclaim no more against it. And, good lieutenant, I think you think I love you.

CASSIO: I have well approved it, sir. I drunk?

IAGO: You or any man living may be drunk at a time, man. I tell you what [280] you shall do. Our general's wife is now the general. I may say so in this

---

[246] **sense** *physical feeling.*   [247] **imposition** *external thing.*   [250] **cast in his mood** *dismissed because of his anger.*   [250] **in policy** *politically necessary.*   [254–55] **speak parrot** *gabble without sense.*   [255] **discourse fustian** *speak nonsense ("fustian" was a coarse cotton cloth used for stuffing).*

respect, for all he hath devoted and given up himself to the contemplation, mark, and devotement of her parts° and graces. Confess yourself freely to her; importune her help to put you in your place again. She is of so free, so kind, so apt, so blessed a disposition she holds it a vice in her goodness not to do more than she is requested. This broken joint between you and her husband entreat her to splinter°; and my fortunes against any lay° worth naming, this crack of your love shall grow stronger than it was before. 285

[handwritten: will Desdemona to get to Othello's heart again - Yes!]

CASSIO: You advise me well.

IAGO: I protest, in the sincerity of love and honest kindness. 290

CASSIO: I think it freely; and betimes in the morning I will beseech the virtuous Desdemona to undertake for me. I am desperate of my fortunes if they check° me.

IAGO: You are in the right. Good night, lieutenant; I must to the watch.

CASSIO: Good night, honest Iago. *Exit* CASSIO. 295

IAGO: And what's he then that says I play the villain,
When this advice is free° I give, and honest,
Probal to° thinking, and indeed the course
To win the Moor again? For 'tis most easy
Th' inclining° Desdemona to subdue 300
In any honest suit; she's framed as fruitful°
As the free elements°. And then for her
To win the Moor—were't to renounce his baptism,
All seals and symbols of redeemèd sin—
His soul is so enfettered to her love 305
That she may make, unmake, do what she list,
Even as her appetite° shall play the god
With his weak function°. How am I then a villain
To counsel Cassio to this parallel course,
Directly to his good? Divinity of hell! 310
When devils will the blackest sins put on°,
They do suggest at first with heavenly shows°,
As I do now. For whiles this honest fool
Plies Desdemona to repair his fortune,
And she for him pleads strongly to the Moor, 315
I'll pour this pestilence into his ear:
That she repeals him° for her body's lust; *[handwritten: Cassio]*
And by how much she strives to do him good,
She shall undo her credit with the Moor.
So will I turn her virtue into pitch, 320
And out of her own goodness make the net
That shall enmesh them all. How now, Roderigo?

[handwritten: sin always looks good at first - disguise]

---

²⁸³**devotement of her parts** *devotion to her qualities.* ²⁸⁷**splinter** *splint.* ²⁸⁷**lay** *wager.* ²⁹³**check** *repulse.* ²⁹⁷**free** *generous and open.* ²⁹⁸**Probal to** *provable by.* ³⁰⁰**inclining** *inclined (to be helpful).* ³⁰¹**framed as fruitful** *made as generous.* ³⁰²**elements** *i.e., basic nature.* ³⁰⁷**appetite** *liking.* ³⁰⁸**function** *thought.* ³¹¹**put on** *advance, further.* ³¹²**shows** *appearances.* ³¹⁷**repeals him** *asks for (Cassio's reinstatement).*

Enter RODERIGO.

RODERIGO: I do not follow here in the chase, not like a hound that hunts, but
   one that fills up the cry°. My money is almost spent; I have been tonight
   exceedingly well cudgeled; and I think the issue will be, I shall have so °325
   much experience for my pains; and so, with no money at all, and a little
   more wit, return again to Venice.
IAGO: How poor are they that have not patience!
   What wound did ever heal but by degrees?
   Thou know'st we work by wit, and not by witchcraft;   330
   And wit depends on dilatory time.
   Does't not go well? Cassio hath beaten thee,
   And thou by that small hurt hath cashiered Cassio.
   Though other things grow fair against the sun,
   Yet fruits that blossom first will first be ripe.   335
   Content thyself awhile. By the mass, 'tis morning!
   Pleasure and action make the hours seem short.
   Retire thee, go where thou art billeted.
   Away, I say! Thou shalt know more hereafter.
   Nay, get thee gone!   *Exit* RODERIGO.
                         Two things are to be done: 340
   My wife must move° for Cassio to her mistress;
   I'll set her on;
   Myself awhile° to draw the Moor apart
   And bring him jump° when he may Cassio find
   Soliciting his wife. Ay, that's the way!   345
   Dull not device by coldness and delay.   *Exit.*

ACT III

Scene I [*A street.*]

Enter CASSIO [*and*] MUSICIANS.

CASSIO: Masters, play here. I will content your pains°.
   Something that's brief; and bid "Good morrow, general." [*They play.*]

[*Enter* CLOWN°.]

CLOWN: Why, masters, have your instruments been in Naples° that they speak
   i' th' nose thus?

---

324 **fills up the cry**   *makes up one of the hunting pack, adding to the noise but not actually tracking.*   341 **move**
petition.   343 **awhile**   *at the same time.*   344 **jump**   *at the precise moment and place.*   **III.i.**   1 **content your pains**   *reward your efforts.*   **s.d. Clown**   *fool.*   3 **Naples**   *this may refer either to the Neapolitan nasal tone, or to syphilis—rife in Naples—which breaks down the nose.*

MUSICIAN: How, sir, how?

CLOWN: Are these, I pray you, wind instruments?

MUSICIAN: Ay, marry, are they, sir.

CLOWN: O, thereby hangs a tale.

MUSICIAN: Whereby hangs a tale, sir?

CLOWN: Marry, sir, by many a wind instrument that I know. But, masters, here's money for you; and the general so likes your music that he desires you, for love's sake, to make no more noise with it.

MUSICIAN: Well, sir, we will not.

CLOWN: If you have any music that may not be heard, to't again. But, as they say, to hear music the general does not greatly care.

MUSICIAN: We have none such, sir.

CLOWN: Then put up your pipes in your bag, for I'll away. Go, vanish into air, away!   *Exit* MUSICIANS.

CASSIO: Dost thou hear me, mine honest friend?

CLOWN: No. I hear not your honest friend. I hear you.

CASSIO: Prithee keep up thy quillets°. There's a poor piece of gold for thee. If the gentlewoman that attends the general's wife be stirring, tell her there's one Cassio entreats her a little favor of speech. Wilt thou do this?

CLOWN: She is stirring, sir. If she will stir hither, I shall seem to notify unto her°.   *Exit* CLOWN.

Enter IAGO.

CASSIO: In happy time, Iago.

IAGO: You have not been abed then?

CASSIO: Why no, the day had broke before we parted.
I have made bold, Iago, to send in to your wife;
My suit to her is that she will to virtuous Desdemona
Procure me some access.

IAGO: I'll send her to you presently,
And I'll devise a mean to draw the Moor
Out of the way, that your converse and business
May be more free.

CASSIO: I humbly thank you for't.   *Exit* [IAGO].

A Florentine° more kind and honest.

Enter EMILIA.

EMILIA: Good morrow, good lieutenant. I am sorry
For your displeasure°; but all will sure be well.
The general and his wife are talking of it,
And she speaks for you stoutly. The Moor replies

---

²¹**quillets** puns.   ²⁵⁻²⁶**seem . . . her** (the Clown is mocking Cassio's overly elegant manner of speaking). ³⁷**Florentine** i.e., Iago is as kind as if he were from Cassio's home town, Florence.   ³⁹**displeasure** discomforting.

That he you hurt is of great fame in Cyprus
And great affinity°, and that in wholesome wisdom
He might not but refuse you. But he protests he loves you.
And needs no other suitor but his likings   45
To bring you in again.
CASSIO: Yet I beseech you,
If you think fit, or that it may be done,
Give me advantage of some brief discourse
With Desdemona alone.
EMILIA: Pray you come in.
I will bestow you where you shall have time   50
To speak your bosom° freely.
CASSIO: I am much bound to you.   [*Exeunt.*]

Scene II [*The citadel.*]

Enter OTHELLO, IAGO, *and* GENTLEMEN.

OTHELLO: These letters give, Iago, to the pilot
And by him do my duties to the Senate.
That done, I will be walking on the works;
Repair° there to me.
IAGO: Well, my good lord, I'll do't.
OTHELLO: This fortification, gentlemen, shall we see't?   5
GENTLEMEN: We'll wait upon your lordship.   *Exeunt.*

Scene III [*The citadel.*]

Enter DESDEMONA, CASSIO, *and* EMILIA.

DESDEMONA: Be thou assured, good Cassio, I will do
All my abilities in thy behalf.
EMILIA: Good madam, do. I warrant it grieves my husband
As if the cause were his.
DESDEMONA: O, that's an honest fellow. Do not doubt, Cassio, 5
But I will have my lord and you again
As friendly as you were.
CASSIO: Bounteous madam,
Whatever shall become of Michael Cassio,
He's never anything but your true servant.
DESDEMONA: I know't; I thank you. You do love my lord.   10
You have known him long, and be you well assured
He shall in strangeness stand no farther off
Than in a politic distance.°
CASSIO: Ay, but, lady,

---

⁴³*affinity* *family.*   ⁵¹*bosom* *inmost thoughts.*   **III.ii.** ⁴*Repair* *go.*   **III.iii.**   ¹²⁻¹³*He . . . dis-*
tance *i.e., he shall act no more distant to you than is necessary for political reasons.*

That policy may either last so long,
Or feed upon such nice° and waterish diet, 15
Or breed itself so out of circumstances°,
That, I being absent, and my place supplied°,
My general will forget my love and service.

DESDEMONA: Do not doubt° that; before Emilia here
I give thee warrant of thy place. Assure thee, 20
If I do vow a friendship, I'll perform it
To the last article. My lord shall never rest;
I'll watch him tame° and talk him out of patience;
His bed shall seem a school, his board a shrift°;
I'll intermingle everything he does 25
With Cassio's suit. Therefore be merry, Cassio,
For thy solicitor shall rather die
Than give thy cause away.

Enter OTHELLO *and* IAGO [*at a distance*].

EMILIA: Madam, here comes my lord.
CASSIO: Madam, I'll take my leave. 30
DESDEMONA: Why, stay, and hear me speak.
CASSIO: Madam, not now. I am very ill at ease,
   Unfit for mine own purposes.
DESDEMONA: Well, do your discretion.   *Exit* CASSIO.
IAGO: Ha! I like not that.
OTHELLO: What dost thou say? 35
IAGO: Nothing, my lord; or if—I know not what.
OTHELLO: Was not that Cassio parted from my wife?
IAGO: Cassio, my lord? No, sure, I cannot think it
   That he would steal away so guilty-like,
   Seeing you coming.
OTHELLO: I do believe 'twas he. 40
DESDEMONA [*Coming to them*]: How now, my lord?
   I have been talking with a suitor here,
   A man that languishes in your displeasure.
OTHELLO: Who is't you mean?
DESDEMONA: Why, your lieutenant, Cassio. Good my lord, 45
   If I have any grace or power to move you,
   His present° reconciliation take.
   For if he be not one that truly loves you,
   That errs in ignorance, and not in cunning,
   I have no judgment in an honest face. 50
   I prithee call him back.
OTHELLO: Went he hence now?

---

[15] **nice** *trivial.*   [16] **Or . . . circumstance** *i.e., or grow so on the basis of accidental happenings and political needs.*   [17] **supplied** *filled.*   [19] **doubt** *imagine.*   [23] **watch him tame** (*animals were tamed by being kept awake*)   [24] **board a shrift** *table (seem) a confessional.*   [47] **present** *immediate.*

DESDEMONA: I' sooth so humbled
   That he hath left part of his grief with me
   To suffer with him. Good love, call him back.
OTHELLO: Not now, sweet Desdemon; some other time.   55
DESDEMONA: But shall't be shortly?
OTHELLO: The sooner, sweet, for you.
DESDEMONA: Shall't be tonight at supper?
OTHELLO: No, not tonight.
DESDEMONA: Tomorrow dinner then?
OTHELLO: I shall not dine at home;
   I meet the captains at the citadel.
DESDEMONA: Why then, tomorrow night, on Tuesday morn,   60
   On Tuesday noon, or night, on Wednesday morn.
   I prithee name the time, but let it not
   Exceed three days. In faith, he's penitent;
   And yet his trespass, in our common reason
   (Save that, they say, the wars must make example   65
   Out of her best), is not almost a fault
   T' incur a private check.° When shall he come?
   Tell me, Othello. I wonder in my soul
   What you would ask me that I should deny
   Or stand so mamm'ring° on. What? Michael Cassio,   70
   That came awooing with you, and so many a time,
   When I have spoke of you dispraisingly,
   Hath ta'en your part—to have so much to do
   To bring him in? By'r Lady, I could do much—
OTHELLO: Prithee no more. Let him come when he will!   75
   I will deny thee nothing.
DESDEMONA: Why, this is not a boon;
   'Tis as I should entreat you wear your gloves,
   Or feed on nourishing dishes, or keep you warm,
   Or sue to you to do a peculiar profit°
   To your own person. Nay, when I have a suit   80
   Wherein I mean to touch your love indeed,
   It shall be full of poise° and difficult weight,
   And fearful to be granted.
OTHELLO: I will deny thee nothing!
   Whereon I do beseech thee grant me this,
   To leave me but a little to myself.   85
DESDEMONA: Shall I deny you? No. Farewell, my lord.
OTHELLO: Farewell, my Desdemona: I'll come to thee straight°.
DESDEMONA: Emilia, come. Be as your fancies teach you;
   Whate'er you be, I am obedient.   *Exit [with* EMILIA].
OTHELLO: Excellent wretch! Perdition catch my soul   90

66–67**is . . . check**   *is almost not serious enough for a private rebuke (let alone a public disgrace).*   70**mamm'ring**
hesitating.   79**peculiar profit**   *particularly personal good.*   82**poise**   *weight.*   87**straight**   *at once.*

But I do love thee! And when I love thee not,
  Chaos is come again.
IAGO: My noble lord—
OTHELLO: What dost thou say, Iago?
IAGO: Did Michael Cassio, when you wooed my lady,
  Know of your love?   95
OTHELLO: He did, from first to last. Why dost thou ask?
IAGO: But for a satisfaction of my thought,
  No further harm.
OTHELLO: Why of thy thought, Iago?
IAGO: I did not think he had been acquainted with her.
OTHELLO: O, yes, and went between us° very oft.   100
IAGO: Indeed?
OTHELLO: Indeed? Ay, indeed! Discern'st thou aught in that?
  Is he not honest?
IAGO: Honest, my lord?
OTHELLO: Honest? Ay, honest.
IAGO: My lord, for aught I know.
OTHELLO: What dost thou think?
IAGO: Think, my lord?
OTHELLO: Think, my lord?   105
  By heaven, thou echoest me,
  As if there were some monster in thy thought
  Too hideous to be shown. Thou dost mean something.
  I heard thee say even now, thou lik'st not that,
  When Cassio left my wife. What didst not like?   110
  And when I told thee he was of my counsel°
  Of my whole course of wooing, thou cried'st "Indeed?"
  And didst contract and purse thy brow together,
  As if thou then hadst shut up in thy brain
  Some horrible conceit°. If thou dost love me,   115
  Show me thy thought.
IAGO: My lord, you know I love you.
OTHELLO: I think thou dost;
  And, for I know thou'rt full of love and honesty
  And weigh'st thy words before thou giv'st them breath,
  Therefore these stops° of thine fright me the more;   120
  For such things in a false disloyal knave
  Are tricks of custom°; but in a man that's just
  They're close dilations°, working from the heart
  That passion cannot rule.
IAGO: For Michael Cassio,
  I dare be sworn, I think that he is honest.   125
OTHELLO: I think so too.

IAGO: Men should be what they seem;
   Or those that be not, would they might seem none!
OTHELLO: Certain, men should be what they seem.
IAGO: Why then, I think Cassio's an honest man.
OTHELLO: Nay, yet there's more in this?   130
   I prithee speak to me as to thy thinkings,
   As thou dost ruminate, and give thy worst of thoughts
   The worst of words.
IAGO: Good my lord, pardon me:
   Though I am bound to every act of duty,
   I am not bound to that all slaves are free to.   135
   Utter my thoughts? Why, say they are vile and false,
   As where's that palace whereinto foul things
   Sometimes intrude not? Who has that breast so pure
   But some uncleanly apprehensions
   Keep leets and law days°, and in sessions sit   140
   With meditations lawful?
OTHELLO: Thou dost conspire against thy friend, Iago,
   If thou but think'st him wronged, and mak'st his ear
   A stranger to thy thoughts.
IAGO: I do beseech you—
   Though I perchance am vicious in my guess   145
   (As I confess it is my nature's plague
   To spy into abuses, and of my jealousy
   Shape faults that are not), that your wisdom
   From one that so imperfectly conceits
   Would take no notice, nor build yourself a trouble   150
   Out of his scattering and unsure observance.
   It were not for your quiet nor your good,
   Nor for my manhood, honesty, and wisdom,
   To let you know my thoughts.
OTHELLO: What dost thou mean?
IAGO: Good name in man and woman, dear my lord,   155
   Is the immediate jewel of their souls.
   Who steals my purse steals trash; 'tis something, nothing;
   'Twas mine, 'tis his, and has been slave to thousands;
   But he that filches from me my good name
   Robs me of that which not enriches him   160
   And makes me poor indeed.
OTHELLO: By heaven, I'll know thy thoughts!
IAGO: You cannot, if my heart were in your hand;
   Nor shall not whilst 'tis in my custody.
OTHELLO: Ha!
IAGO: O, beware, my lord, of jealousy!   165
   It is the green-eyed monster, which doth mock
   The meat it feeds on. That cuckold lives in bliss

---

¹⁴⁰*leets and law days*   *meetings of local courts.*

Who, certain of his fate, loves not his wronger;
But O, what damnèd minutes tells° he o'er
Who dotes, yet doubts—suspects, yet fondly° loves!   170

OTHELLO: O misery.

IAGO: Poor and content is rich, and rich enough;
But riches fineless° is as poor as winter
To him that ever fears he shall be poor.
Good God the souls of all my tribe defend   175
From jealousy!

OTHELLO: Why? Why is this?
Think'st thou I'd make a life of jealousy,
To follow still° the changes of the moon
With fresh suspicions? No! To be once in doubt
Is to be resolved. Exchange me for a goat   180
When I shall turn the business of my soul
To such exsufflicate and blown° surmises,
Matching thy inference. 'Tis not to make me jealous
To say my wife is fair, feeds well, loves company,
Is free of speech, sings, plays, and dances;   185
Where virtue is, these are more virtuous.
Nor from mine own weak merits will I draw
The smallest fear or doubt of her revolt,
For she had eyes, and chose me. No, Iago;
I'll see before I doubt; when I doubt, prove;   190
And on the proof there is no more but this:
Away at once with love or jealousy!

IAGO: I am glad of this; for now I shall have reason
To show the love and duty that I bear you
With franker spirit. Therefore, as I am bound,   195
Receive it from me. I speak not yet of proof.
Look to your wife; observe her well with Cassio;
Wear your eyes thus: not jealous nor secure.
I would not have your free and noble nature
Out of self-bounty° be abused. Look to't.   200
I know our country disposition well:
In Venice they do let heaven see the pranks
They dare not show their husbands; their best conscience
Is not to leave't undone, but kept unknown.°

OTHELLO: Dost thou say so?   205

IAGO: She did deceive her father, marrying you;
And when she seemed to shake and fear your looks,
She loved them most.

OTHELLO: And so she did.

169*tells* counts.   170*fondly* foolishly.   173*fineless* infinite.   178**To follow still** to change always
(as the phases of the moon).   182**exsufflicate and blown** inflated and flyblown.   200**self-bounty** innate kindness (which attributes his own motives to others).   203–4**their . . . unknown** i.e., their morality does not forbid adultery, but it does forbid being found out.

IAGO: Why, go to then!
　She that so young could give out such a seeming
　To seel° her father's eyes up close as oak°—   210
　He thought 'twas witchcraft. But I am much to blame.
　I humbly do beseech you of your pardon
　For too much loving you.
OTHELLO: I am bound to thee forever.
IAGO: I see this hath a little dashed your spirits.
OTHELLO: Not a jot, not a jot.
IAGO: Trust me, I fear it has.   215
　I hope you will consider what is spoke
　Comes from my love. But I do see y' are moved.
　I am to pray you not to strain° my speech
　To grosser issues nor to larger reach°   219
　Than to suspicion.   220
OTHELLO: I will not.
IAGO: Should you do so, my lord,
　My speech should fall into such vile success
　Which my thoughts aimed not. Cassio's my worthy friend—
　My lord, I see y' are moved.
OTHELLO: No, not much moved.
　I do not think but Desdemona's honest.   225
IAGO: Long live she so. And long live you to think so.
OTHELLO: And yet, how nature erring from itself—
IAGO: Ay, there's the point, as (to be bold with you)
　Not to affect many proposèd matches
　Of her own clime, complexion, and degree°,   230
　Whereto we see in all things nature tends°—
　Foh! one may smell in such a will most rank,
　Foul disproportions, thoughts unnatural.
　But, pardon me, I do not in position°
　Distinctly° speak of her; though I may fear   235
　Her will, recoiling to her better judgment,
　May fall to match° you with her country forms°,
　And happily° repent.
OTHELLO: Farewell, farewell!
　If more thou dost perceive, let me know more.
　Set on thy wife to observe. Leave me, Iago.   240
IAGO: My lord, I take my leave.   [*Going.*]
OTHELLO: Why did I marry? This honest creature doubtless
　Sees and knows more, much more, than he unfolds.
IAGO [*Returns*]: My lord, I would I might entreat your honor

---

²¹⁰**seel** hoodwink.   ²¹⁰**oak** (a close-grained wood).   ²¹⁸**strain** enlarge the meaning.   ²¹⁹**reach** meaning.   ²³⁰**degree** social station.   ²³¹**in . . . tends** i.e., all things in nature seek out their own kind. ²³⁴**position** general argument.   ²³⁵**Distinctly** specifically.   ²³⁷**fall to match** happen to compare. ²³⁷**country forms** i.e., the familiar appearance of her countrymen.   ²³⁸**happily** by chance.

To scan this thing no farther. Leave it to time. 245
Although 'tis fit that Cassio have his place,
For sure he fills it up with great ability,
Yet, if you please to hold him off awhile,
You shall by that perceive him and his means.
Note if your lady strains his entertainment° 250
With any strong or vehement importunity;
Much will be seen in that. In the meantime
Let me be thought too busy in my fears
(As worthy cause I have to fear I am)
And hold her free, I do beseech your honor. 255

OTHELLO: Fear not my government°.

IAGO: I once more take my leave.   *Exit.*

OTHELLO: This fellow's of exceeding honesty,
And knows all qualities°, with a learnèd spirit
Of human dealings. If I do prove her haggard°,
Though that her jesses° were my dear heartstrings, 260
I'd whistle her off and let her down the wind°
To prey at fortune. Haply for° I am black
And have not those soft parts° of conversation
That chamberers° have, or for I am declined
Into the vale of years—yet that's not much— 265
She's gone. I am abused, and my relief
Must be to loathe her. O curse of marriage,
That we can call these delicate creatures ours,
And not their appetites! I had rather be a toad
And live upon the vapor of a dungeon 270
Than keep a corner in the thing I love
For others' uses. Yet 'tis the plague to great ones;
Prerogatived are they less than the base.
'Tis destiny unshunnable, like death.
Even then this forkèd° plague is fated to us 275
When we do quicken°. Look where she comes.

Enter DESDEMONA *and* EMILIA.

If she be false, heaven mocked itself!
I'll not believe't.

DESDEMONA: How now, my dear Othello?
Your dinner, and the generous islanders
By you invited, do attend° your presence. 280

OTHELLO: I am to blame.

---

²⁵⁰*strains his entertainment*   *urge strongly that he be reinstated.*   ²⁵⁶*government*   *self-control.*   ²⁵⁸*qual-*
ities   *natures, types of people.*   ²⁵⁹*haggard*   *a partly trained hawk which has gone wild again.*   ²⁶⁰*jesses*
straps which held the hawk's legs to the trainer's wrist.   ²⁶¹*I'd . . . wind*   *I would release her (like an untamable*
hawk) and let her fly free.   ²⁶²*Haply for*   *it may be because.*   ²⁶³*soft parts*   *gentle qualities and manners.*
²⁶⁴*chamberers*   *courtiers—or, perhaps, accomplished seducers.*   ²⁷⁵*forkèd*   *horned (the sign of the cuckold was*
horns).   ²⁷⁶*do quicken*   *are born.*   ²⁸⁰*attend*   *wait.*

DESDEMONA: Why do you speak so faintly?
  Are you not well?
OTHELLO: I have a pain upon my forehead, here°.
DESDEMONA: Why, that's with watching; 'twill away again,
  Let me but bind it hard, within this hour   285
  It will be well.
OTHELLO: Your napkin° is too little;

[*He pushes the handkerchief away, and it falls.*]

Let it° alone. Come, I'll go in with you.
DESDEMONA: I am very sorry that you are not well.   *Exit* [*with* OTHELLO].
EMILIA: I am glad I have found this napkin;
  This was her first remembrance from the Moor.   290
  My wayward husband hath a hundred times
  Wooed me to steal it; but she so loves the token
  (For he conjured her she should ever keep it)
  That she reserves it evermore about her
  To kiss and talk to. I'll have the work ta'en out°   295
  And give't Iago. What he will do with it,
  Heaven knows, not I; I nothing° but to please his fantasy°.

Enter IAGO.

IAGO: How now? What do you here alone?
EMILIA: Do not you chide; I have a thing for you.
IAGO: You have a thing for me? It is a common thing—   300
EMILIA: Ha?
IAGO: To have a foolish wife.
EMILIA: O, is that all? What will you give me now
  For that same handkerchief?
IAGO: What handkerchief?
EMILIA: What handkerchief!   305
  Why, that the Moor first gave to Desdemona,
  That which so often you did bid me steal.
IAGO: Hast stol'n it from her?
EMILIA: No, but she let it drop by negligence,
  And to th' advantage°, I, being here, took't up.   310
  Look, here 't is.
IAGO: A good wench. Give it me.
EMILIA: What will you do with't, that you have been so earnest
  To have me filch it?
IAGO: Why, what is that to you?   [*Takes it.*]

---

²⁸³*here* *(he points to his imaginary horns).*   ²⁸⁶*napkin* *elaborately worked handkerchief.*   ²⁸⁷*it* *(it makes a considerable difference in the interpretation of later events whether this "it" refers to Othello's forehead or to the handkerchief; nothing in the text makes the reference clear).*   ²⁹⁵*work ta'en out* *needlework copied.*   ²⁹⁷*I nothing* *I wish nothing.*   ²⁹⁷*fantasy* *fancy, whim.*   ³¹⁰*to th' advantage* *being lucky.*

EMILIA: If it be not for some purpose of import°,
    Give't me again. Poor lady, she'll run mad   315
    When she shall lack° it.
IAGO: Be not acknown on't°.
    I have use for it. Go, leave me.   *Exit* EMILIA.
    I will in Cassio's lodging lose this napkin
    And let him find it. Trifles light as air
    Are to the jealous confirmations strong   320
    As proofs of Holy Writ. This may do something.
    The Moor already changes with my poison:
    Dangerous conceits are in their natures poisons,
    Which at the first are scarce found to distaste°,
    But with a little°, act upon the blood,   325
    Burn like the mines of sulfur. I did say so.

Enter OTHELLO.

    Look where he comes! Not poppy nor mandragora°,
    Nor all the drowsy syrups of the world,
    Shall ever medicine thee to that sweet sleep
    Which thou owedst° yesterday.
OTHELLO: Ha! ha! False to me?   330
IAGO: Why, how now, general? No more of that.
OTHELLO: Avaunt! be gone! Thou hast set me on the rack.
    I swear 'tis better to be much abused
    Than but to know't a little.
IAGO: How now, my lord?
OTHELLO: What sense had I of her stol'n hours of lust?   335
    I saw't not, thought it not, it harmed not me;
    I slept the next night well, fed well, was free and merry;
    I found not Cassio's kisses on her lips.
    He that is robbed, not wanting° what is stol'n,
    Let him not know't, and he's not robbed at all.   340
IAGO: I am sorry to hear this.
OTHELLO: I had been happy if the general camp,
    Pioners° and all, had tasted her sweet body,
    So I had nothing known. O now, forever
    Farewell the tranquil mind! Farewell content!   345
    Farewell the plumèd troops, and the big wars
    That make ambition virtue! O, farewell!
    Farewell the neighing steed and the shrill trump,
    The spirit-stirring drum, th' ear-piercing fife,

314*import* importance.   316*lack* miss.   316*Be not acknown on't* forget you ever saw it.   324*are
scarce found to distaste* scarcely can be tasted.   325*with a little* in a short time.   327*poppy nor man-
dragora* soporifics.   330*owedst* possessed.   339*wanting* missing.   343*Pioners* the basest manual
laborers in the army, who dug trenches and mines.

The royal banner, and all quality,   350
Pride, pomp, and circumstance° of glorious war!
And O you mortal engines° whose rude throats
Th' immortal Jove's dread clamors° counterfeit,
Farewell! Othello's occupation's gone!

IAGO: Is't possible, my lord?   355

OTHELLO: Villain, be sure thou prove my love a whore!
    Be sure of it; give me the ocular proof;
    Or, by the worth of mine eternal soul,
    Thou hadst been better have been born a dog
    Than answer my waked wrath!

IAGO: Is't come to this?   360

OTHELLO: Make me to see't; or at the least so prove it
    That the probation° bear no hinge nor loop
    To hang a doubt on—or woe upon thy life!

IAGO: My noble lord—

OTHELLO: If thou dost slander her and torture me,   365
    Never pray more; abandon all remorse;
    On horror's head horrors accumulate;
    Do deeds to make heaven weep, all earth amazed;
    For nothing canst thou to damnation add
    Greater than that.

IAGO: O grace! O heaven forgive me!   370
    Are you a man? Have you a soul or sense?
    God b' wi' you! Take mine office. O wretched fool,
    That lov'st to make thine honesty a vice!
    O monstrous world! Take note, take note, O world,
    To be direct and honest is not safe.   375
    I thank you for this profit, and from hence
    I'll love no friend, sith° love breeds such offense.

OTHELLO: Nay, stay. Thou shouldst be honest.

IAGO: I should be wise; for honesty's a fool
    And loses that it works for.

OTHELLO: By the world,   380
    I think my wife be honest, and think she is not;
    I think that thou art just, and think thou are not.
    I'll have some proof. My name, that was as fresh
    As Dian's° visage, is now begrimed and black
    As mine own face. If there be cords, or knives,   385
    Poison, or fire, or suffocating streams,
    I'll not endure it. Would I were satisfied!

IAGO: I see you are eaten up with passion.
    I do repent me that I put it to you.
    You would be satisfied?

---

³⁵¹**circumstance** *pageantry.*   ³⁵²**mortal engines** *lethal weapons, i.e., cannon.*   ³⁵³**clamors** *i.e., thun-*
der.   ³⁶²**probation** *proof.*   ³⁷⁷**sith** *since.*   ³⁸⁴**Dian's** *Diana's (goddess of the moon and of chastity).*

OTHELLO: Would? Nay, and I will.   390

IAGO: And may; but how? How satisfied, my lord?
   Would you, the supervisor°, grossly gape on?
   Behold her topped?

OTHELLO: Death and damnation! O!

IAGO: It were a tedious° difficulty, I think,
   To bring them to that prospect°. Damn them then,   395
   If ever mortal eyes do see them bolster°
   More than their own! What then? How then?
   What shall I say? Where's satisfaction?
   It is impossible you should see this,
   Were they as prime° as goats, as hot as monkeys,   400
   As salt as wolves in pride°, and fools as gross
   As ignorance made drunk. But yet, I say,
   If imputation and strong circumstances
   Which lead directly to the door of truth
   Will give you satisfaction, you might hav't.   405

OTHELLO: Give me a living reason she's disloyal.

IAGO: I do not like the office°.
   But sith I am entered in this cause so far,
   Pricked° to't by foolish honesty and love,
   I will go on. I lay with Cassio lately,   410
   And being troubled with a raging tooth,
   I could not sleep.
   There are a kind of men so loose of soul
   That in their sleeps will mutter their affairs.
   One of this kind is Cassio.   415
   In sleep I heard him say, "Sweet Desdemona,
   Let us be wary, let us hide our loves!"
   And then, sir, would he gripe° and wring my hand,
   Cry "O sweet creature!" Then kiss me hard,
   As if he plucked up kisses by the roots   420
   That grew upon my lips; laid his leg o'er my thigh,
   And sigh, and kiss, and then cry, "Cursèd fate
   That gave thee to the Moor!"

OTHELLO: O monstrous! monstrous!

IAGO: Nay, this was but his dream.

OTHELLO: But this denoted a foregone conclusion°,   425
   'Tis a shrewd doubt°, though it be but a dream.

IAGO: And this may help to thicken other proofs
   That do demonstrate° thinly.

OTHELLO: I'll tear her all to pieces!

[handwritten note: – lie about Desdemona & Cassio]

---

392 **supervisor** *onlooker.*   394 **tedious** *hard to arrange.*   395 **prospect** *sight (where they can be seen).*   396 **bolster** *go to bed with.*   400–01 **prime, salt** *lustful.*   401 **pride** *heat.*   407 **office** *duty.*   409 **Pricked** *spurred.*   418 **gripe** *seize.*   425 **foregone conclusion** *consummated fact.*   426 **shrewd doubt** *penetrating guess.*   428 **demonstrate** *show, appear.*

IAGO: Nay, yet be wise. Yet we see nothing done;
   She may be honest yet. Tell me but this:
   Have you not sometimes seen a handkerchief
   Spotted with strawberries in your wife's hand?

OTHELLO: I gave her such a one; 'twas my first gift.

IAGO: I know not that; but such a handkerchief—
   I am sure it was your wife's—did I today
   See Cassio wipe his beard with.

OTHELLO: If it be that—

IAGO: If it be that or any that was hers,
   It speaks against her with the other proofs.

OTHELLO: O, that the slave had forty thousand lives!
   One is too poor, too weak for my revenge.
   Now do I see 'tis true. Look here, Iago:
   All my fond love thus do I blow to heaven.
   'Tis gone.
   Arise, black vengeance, from the hollow hell!
   Yield up, O love, thy crown and hearted° throne
   To tyrannous hate! Swell, bosom, with thy fraught°,
   For 'tis of aspics'° tongues.

IAGO: Yet be content°.

OTHELLO: O, blood, blood, blood!

IAGO: Patience, I say. Your mind may change.

OTHELLO: Never, Iago. Like to the Pontic Sea°,
   Whose icy current and compulsive course
   Nev'r keeps retiring ebb, but keeps due on
   To the Propontic and the Hellespont,
   Even so my bloody thoughts, with violent pace,
   Shall nev'r look back, nev'r ebb to humble love,
   Till that a capable and wide° revenge
   Swallow them up. [*He kneels.*] Now, by yond marble heaven,
   In the due reverence of a sacred vow
   I here engage my words.

IAGO: Do not rise yet.   [*IAGO kneels.*]
   Witness, you ever-burning lights above,
   You elements that clip° us round about,
   Witness that here Iago doth give up
   The execution° of his wit, hands, heart
   To wronged Othello's service! Let him command,
   And to obey shall be in me remorse°,
   What bloody business ever°.   [*They rise.*]

OTHELLO: I greet thy love,
   Not with vain thanks but with acceptance bounteous°,

430

435

440

445

450

455

460

465

445**hearted** *seated in the heart.*   446**fraught** *burden.*   447**aspics'** *asps'.*   447**content** *patient, quiet.*
450**Pontic Sea** *the Black Sea (famous for the strong and constant current with which it flows through the Bosporus into the Mediterranean, where the water level is lower).*   456**capable and wide** *sufficient and far-reaching*   461**clip** *enfold.*   463**execution** *workings, action.*   465**remorse** *pity.*   466**ever** *soever.*   467**bounteous** *absolute.*

And will upon the instant put thee to 't°
Within these three days let me hear thee say
That Cassio's not alive.   470
IAGO: My friend is dead. 'Tis done at your request.
   But let her live.
OTHELLO: Damn her, lewd minx! O, damn her! Damn her!
   Come, go with me apart. I will withdraw
   To furnish me with some swift means of death
   For the fair devil. Now art thou my lieutenant.   475
IAGO: I am your own forever.   *Exeunt.*

Scene IV [A street.]

Enter DESDEMONA, EMILIA, *and* CLOWN.

DESDEMONA: Do you know, sirrah, where Lieutenant Cassio lies°?
CLOWN: I dare not say he lies anywhere.
DESDEMONA: Why, man?
CLOWN: He's a soldier, and for me to say a soldier lies, 'tis stabbing.
DESDEMONA: Go to. Where lodges he?   5
CLOWN: To tell you where he lodges is to tell you where I lie.
DESDEMONA: Can anything be made of this?
CLOWN: I know not where he lodges, and for me to devise a lodging, and
   say he lies here or he lies there, were to lie in mine own throat°.
DESDEMONA: Can you enquire him out, and be edified° by report?   10
CLOWN: I will catechize the world for him; that is, make questions, and by
   them answer.
DESDEMONA: Seek him, bid him come hither. Tell him I have moved° my
   lord on his behalf and hope all will be well.
CLOWN: To do this is within the compass° of man's wit, and therefore I will 15
   attempt the doing it.   *Exit* CLOWN.
DESDEMONA: Where should° I lose the handkerchief, Emilia?
EMILIA: I know not, madam.
DESDEMONA: Believe me, I had rather have lost my purse
   Full of crusadoes°. And but my noble Moor   20
   Is true of mind, and made of no such baseness
   As jealous creatures are, it were enough
   To put him to ill thinking.
EMILIA: Is he not jealous?
DESDEMONA: Who? He? I think the sun where he was born
   Drew all such humors° from him.
EMILIA: Look where he comes.   25

Enter OTHELLO.

---

⁴⁶⁸***to't*** *i.e., to the work you have said you are prepared to do.* **III.iv.** ¹***lies*** *lodges.* ⁹***lie in mine own***
throat *(to lie in the throat is to lie absolutely and completely).* ¹⁰***edified*** *enlightened (Desdemona mocks the*
Clown's overly elaborate diction). ¹³***moved*** *pleaded with.* ¹⁵***compass*** *reach.* ¹⁷***should*** *might.*
²⁰***crusadoes*** *Portuguese gold coins.* ²⁵***humors*** *characteristics.*

DESDEMONA: I will not leave him now till Cassio
  Be called to him. How is't with you, my lord?
OTHELLO: Well, my good lady. [*Aside*] O, hardness to dissemble°!—
  How do you, Desdemona?
DESDEMONA: Well, my good lord.
OTHELLO: Give me your hand. This hand is moist°, my lady.   30
DESDEMONA: It hath felt no age nor known no sorrow.
OTHELLO: This argues° fruitfulness and liberal° heart.
  Hot, hot, and moist. This hand of yours requires
  A sequester° from liberty; fasting and prayer;
  Much castigation; exercise devout;   35
  For here's a young and sweating devil here
  That commonly rebels. 'Tis a good hand,
  A frank one.
DESDEMONA: You may, indeed, say so;
  For 'twas that hand that gave away my heart.
OTHELLO: A liberal hand! The hearts of old gave hands,   40
  But our new heraldry° is hands, not hearts.
DESDEMONA: I cannot speak of this. Come now, your promise!
OTHELLO: What promise, chuck?
DESDEMONA: I have sent to bid Cassio come speak with you.
OTHELLO: I have a salt and sorry rheum° offends me.   45
  Lend me thy handkerchief.
DESDEMONA: Here, my lord.
OTHELLO: That which I gave you.
DESDEMONA: I have it not about me.
OTHELLO: Not?
DESDEMONA: No, indeed, my lord.
OTHELLO: That's a fault.
  That handkerchief   50
  Did an Egyptian to my mother give.
  She was a charmer°, and could almost read
  The thoughts of people. She told her, while she kept it
  'Twould make her amiable° and subdue my father
  Entirely to her love; but if she lost it   55
  Or made a gift of it, my father's eye
  Should hold her loathèd, and his spirits should hunt
  After new fancies. She, dying, gave it me,
  And bid me, when my fate would have me wived,
  To give it her. I did so; and take heed on't;   60
  Make it a darling like your precious eye.

---

[28]**hardness to dissemble** (*Othello may refer here either to the difficulty he has in maintaining his appearance of composure, or to what he believes to be Desdemona's hardened hypocrisy*). [30]**moist** (*a moist, hot hand was taken as a sign of a lustful nature*). [32]**argues** *suggests.* [32]**liberal** *free, open (but also with a suggestion of "licentious"; from here on in this scene Othello's words bear a double meaning, seeming to be normal but accusing Desdemona of being unfaithful).* [34]**sequester** *separation.* [41]**heraldry** *heraldic symbolism.* [45]**a salt and sorry rheum** *a heavy, running head cold.* [52]**charmer** *magician.* [54]**amiable** *desirable.*

To lose't or give't away were such perdition
As nothing else could match.
DESDEMONA: Is't possible?
OTHELLO: 'Tis true. There's magic in the web° of it.
A sibyl that had numbered in the world   65
The sun to course two hundred compasses,
In her prophetic fury° sewed the work;
The worms were hallowed that did breed the silk,
And it was dyed in mummy° which the skillful
Conserved of maidens' hearts.
DESDEMONA: Indeed? Is't true?   70
OTHELLO: Most veritable. Therefore look to't well.
DESDEMONA: Then would to God that I had never seen't!
OTHELLO: Ha! Wherefore?
DESDEMONA: Why do you speak so startingly and rash?
OTHELLO: Is't lost? Is't gone? Speak, is it out o' th' way?   75
DESDEMONA: Heaven bless us!
OTHELLO: Say you?
DESDEMONA: It is not lost. But what an if it were?
OTHELLO: How?
DESDEMONA: I say it is not lost.   80
OTHELLO: Fetch't, let me see't!
DESDEMONA: Why, so I can; but I will not now.
This is a trick to put me from my suit:
Pray you let Cassio be received again.
OTHELLO: Fetch me the handkerchief! My mind misgives.   85
DESDEMONA: Come, come!
You'll never meet a more sufficient° man—
OTHELLO: The handkerchief!
DESDEMONA: A man that all his time
Hath founded his good fortunes on your love,
Shared dangers with you—   90
OTHELLO: The handkerchief!
DESDEMONA: I'faith, you are to blame.
OTHELLO: Away!   *Exit* OTHELLO.
EMILIA: Is not this man jealous?
DESDEMONA: I nev'r saw this before.   95
Sure there's some wonder in this handkerchief;
I am most unhappy in the loss of it.
EMILIA: 'Tis not a year or two shows us a man.
They are all but stomachs, and we all but food;
They eat us hungerly, and when they are full,   100
They belch us.
                    Enter IAGO *and* CASSIO.
          Look you, Cassio and my husband.

---

⁶⁴**web**   *weaving.*   ⁶⁷**prophetic fury**   *seized by the spirit and able to prophesy.*   ⁶⁹**mummy**   *liquid drained from*
embalmed bodies.   ⁸⁷**sufficient**   *complete, with all proper qualities.*

IAGO: There is no other way; 'tis she must do't.
  And lo the happiness! Go and importune her.
DESDEMONA: How now, good Cassio? What's the news with you?
CASSIO: Madam, my former suit. I do beseech you   105
  That by your virtuous means I may again
  Exist, and be a member of his love
  Whom I with all the office° of my heart
  Entirely honor. I would not be delayed.
  If my offense be of such mortal kind   110
  That nor my service past, nor present sorrows,
  Nor purposed merit in futurity,
  Can ransom me into his love again,
  But to know so must be my benefit°.
  So shall I clothe me in a forced content,   115
  And shut myself up in some other course
  To fortune's alms.
DESDEMONA: Alas, thrice-gentle Cassio,
  My advocation° is not now in tune.
  My lord is not my lord; nor should I know him
  Were he in favor° as in humor altered.   120
  So help me every spirit sanctified
  As I have spoken for you all my best
  And stood within the blank° of his displeasure
  For my free speech. You must awhile be patient.
  What I can do I will; and more I will   125
  Than for myself I dare. Let that suffice you.
IAGO: Is my lord angry?
EMILIA: He went hence but now,
  And certainly in strange unquietness.
IAGO: Can he be angry? I have seen the cannon
  When it hath blown his ranks into the air   130
  And, like the devil, from his very arm
  Puffed his own brother. And is he angry?
  Something of moment° then. I will go meet him.
  There's matter in't indeed if he be angry.
DESDEMONA: I prithee do so.   *Exit* [IAGO.]
                         Something sure of state°,   135
  Either from Venice or some unhatched practice°
  Made demonstrable here in Cyprus to him,
  Hath puddled° his clear spirit; and in such cases
  Men's natures wrangle with inferior things,
  though great ones are their object. 'Tis even so.   140
  For let our finger ache, and it endues°

---

¹⁰⁸**office** duty.   ¹¹⁴**benefit** good.   ¹¹⁸**advocation** advocacy.   ¹²⁰**favor** countenance.   ¹²³**blank** bull's-eye of a target.   ¹³³**moment** importance.   ¹³⁵**of state** state affairs.   ¹³⁶**unhatched practice** undisclosed plot.   ¹³⁸**puddled** muddied.   ¹⁴¹**endues** leads.

Our other, healthful members even to a sense
Of pain. Nay, we must think men are not gods,
Nor of them look for such observancy
As fits the bridal. Beshrew me much, Emilia,   145
I was, unhandsome warrior as I am,
Arraigning his unkindness with my soul;
But now I find I had suborned the witness,
And he's indicted falsely.

EMILIA: Pray heaven it be
State matters, as you think, and no conception   150
Nor no jealous toy° concerning you.

DESDEMONA: Alas the day! I never gave him cause.

EMILIA: But jealous souls will not be answered so;
They are not ever jealous for the cause,
But jealous for they're jealous. It is a monster   155
Begot upon itself, born on itself.

DESDEMONA: Heaven keep the monster from Othello's mind!

EMILIA: Lady, amen.

DESDEMONA: I will go seek him. Cassio, walk here about.
If I do find him fit°, I'll move your suit   160
And seek to effect it to my uttermost.

CASSIO: I humbly thank your ladyship.   *Exit* [DESDEMONA *with* EMILIA].

Enter BIANCA.

BIANCA: Save you, friend Cassio!

CASSIO: What make you from home?
How is't with you, my most fair Bianca?
I' faith, sweet love, I was coming to your house.   165

BIANCA: And I was going to your lodging, Cassio.
What, keep a week away? Seven days and nights?
Eightscore eight hours? And lovers' absent hours
More tedious than the dial eightscore times?
O weary reck'ning°.

CASSIO: Pardon me, Bianca.   170
I have this while with leaden thoughts been pressed,
But I shall in a more continuate° time
Strike off this score° of absence. Sweet Bianca,

[*Gives her* DESDEMONA's *handkerchief.*]

Take me this work out.

BIANCA: O Cassio, whence came this?
This is some token from a newer friend.   175
To the felt absence now I feel a cause.
Is't come to this? Well, well.

---

¹⁵¹**toy** trifle.   ¹⁶⁰**fit** receptive.   ¹⁷⁰**reck'ning** addition.   ¹⁷²**continuate** uninterrupted.
¹⁷³**Strike off this score** i.e., pay this bill (the score being the account of drinks kept in a tavern).

CASSIO: Go to, woman!
  Throw your vile guesses in the devil's teeth,
  From whence you have them. You are jealous now
  That this is from some mistress, some remembrance.   180
  No, by my faith, Bianca.
BIANCA: Why, whose is it?
CASSIO: I know not neither; I found it in my chamber.
  I like the work well; ere it be demanded°,
  As like enough it will, I would have it copied.
  Take it and do't, and leave me for this time.   185
BIANCA: Leave you? Wherefore?
CASSIO: I do attend here on the general
  And think it no addition, nor my wish,
  To have him see me womaned.
BIANCA: Why, I pray you?
CASSIO: Not that I love you not.
BIANCA: But that you do not love me!   190
  I pray you bring° me on the way a little,
  And say if I shall see you soon at night.
CASSIO: 'Tis but a little way that I can bring you,
  For I attend here; but I'll see you soon.
BIANCA: 'Tis very good. I must be circumstanced°.   *Exeunt omnes.* 195

ACT IV

Scene I [A street.]

Enter OTHELLO *and* IAGO.

IAGO: Will you think so?
OTHELLO: Think so, Iago?
IAGO: What,
  To kiss in private?
OTHELLO: An unauthorized° kiss?
IAGO: Or to be naked with her friend in bed
  An hour or more, not meaning any harm?
OTHELLO: Naked in bed, Iago, and not mean harm?   5
  It is hypocrisy against the devil.
  They that mean virtuously, and yet do so,
  The devil their virtue tempts, and they tempt heaven.
IAGO: If they do nothing, 'tis a venial slip.
  But if I give my wife a handkerchief—   10
OTHELLO: What then?

---

¹⁸³**demanded**   *asked for (by the person who lost it).*   ¹⁹¹**bring**   *accompany.*   ¹⁹⁵**be circumstanced**   *accept things as they are.*   **IV.i.**   ²**unauthorized**   *illicit.*

IAGO: Why, then 'tis hers, my lord; and being hers,
 She may, I think, bestow't on any man.
OTHELLO: She is protectress of her honor too.
 May she give that?   15
IAGO: Her honor is an essence that's not seen;
 They have it very oft that have it not.
 But for the handkerchief—
OTHELLO: By heaven, I would most gladly have forgot it!
 Thou said'st—O, it comes o'er my memory   20
 As doth the raven° o'er the infected house,
 Boding to all—he had my handkerchief.
IAGO: Ay, what of that?
OTHELLO: That's not so good now.
IAGO: What if I had said I had seen him do you wrong?
 Or heard him say—as knaves be such abroad°   25
 Who having, by their own importunate suit,
 Or voluntary dotage° of some mistress,
 Convincèd or supplied° them, cannot choose
 But they must blab—
OTHELLO: Hath he said anything?
IAGO: He hath, my lord; but be you well assured,   30
 No more than he'll unswear.
OTHELLO: What hath he said?
IAGO: Why, that he did—I know not what he did.
OTHELLO: What? what?
IAGO: Lie—
OTHELLO: With her?
IAGO: With her, on her; what you will.   35
OTHELLO: Lie with her? Lie on her?—We say lie on her when they belie
 her.—Lie with her! Zounds, that's fulsome°.—Handkerchief—confes-
 sions—handkerchief!—To confess, and be hanged for his labor—first to
 be hanged, and[40] then to confess! I tremble at it. Nature would not invest
 herself in such shadowing passion without some instruction°. It is not   40
 words that shakes me thus.—Pish! Noses, ears, and lips? Is't possible?—
 Confess?—Handkerchief?—O devil!   *Falls in a trance.*
IAGO: Work on.
 My med'cine works! Thus credulous fools are caught,
 And many worthy and chaste dames even thus,   45
 All guiltless, meet reproach°. What, ho! My lord!
 My lord, I say! Othello!

         Enter CASSIO.

       How now, Cassio?

---

[21]**raven** *(a harbinger of death).*   [25]**abroad** *i.e., in the world.*   [27]**voluntary dotage** *weakness of the will.*
[28]**Convincèd or supplied** *persuaded or gratified (the mistress).*   [37]**fulsome** *foul, repulsive.*   [39–40]**Nature . . .**
instruction *i.e., my mind would not become so darkened (with anger) unless there were something in this (accusation);*
(it should be remembered that Othello believes in the workings of magic and supernatural forces).   [46]**reproach** *shame.*

CASSIO: What's the matter?

IAGO: My lord is fall'n into an epilepsy.
This is his second fit; he had one yesterday. 50

CASSIO: Rub him about the temples.

IAGO: The lethargy° must have his quiet course.
If not, he foams at mouth, and by and by
Breaks out to savage madness. Look, he stirs.
Do you withdraw yourself a little while. 55
He will recover straight. When he is gone,
I would on great occasion° speak with you. [*Exit* CASSIO.]
How is it, general? Have you not hurt your head?

OTHELLO: Dost thou mock° me?

IAGO: I mock you not, by heaven.
Would you would bear your fortune like a man. 60

OTHELLO: A hornèd man's a monster and a beast.

IAGO: There's many a beast then in a populous city,
And many a civil° monster.

OTHELLO: Did he confess it?

IAGO: Good, sir, be a man.
Think every bearded fellow that's but yoked 65
May draw° with you. There's millions now alive
That nightly lie in those unproper° beds
Which they dare swear peculiar.° Your case is better.
O, 'tis the spite of hell, the fiend's arch-mock,
To lip a wanton in a secure couch, 70
And to suppose her chaste. No, let me know;
And knowing what I am, I know what she shall be.

OTHELLO: O, thou art wise! 'Tis certain.

IAGO: Stand you awhile apart;
Confine yourself but in a patient list.°
Whilst you were here, o'erwhelmèd with your grief— 75
A passion most unsuiting such a man—
Cassio came hither. I shifted him away°
And laid good 'scuses upon your ecstasy°,
Bade him anon return, and here speak with me;
The which he promised. Do but encave° yourself 80
And mark the fleers°, the gibes, and notable° scorns
That dwell in every region of his face.
For I will make him tell the tale anew:

---

⁵²**lethargy** *coma.*   ⁵⁷**great occasion** *very important matter.*   ⁵⁹**mock** *(Othello takes Iago's comment as a reference to his horns—which it is).*   ⁶³**civil** *city-dwelling.*   ⁶⁶**draw** *i.e., like the horned ox.*   ⁶⁷**unproper** *i.e., not exclusively the husband's.*   ⁶⁸**peculiar** *their own alone.*   ⁷⁴**a patient list** *the bounds of patience.*   ⁷⁷**shifted him away** *got rid of him by a strategem.*   ⁷⁸**ecstasy** *trance (the literal meaning, "outside oneself," bears on the meaning of the change Othello is undergoing).*   ⁸⁰**encave** *hide.*   ⁸¹**fleers** *mocking looks or speeches.*   ⁸¹**notable** *obvious.*

Where, how, how oft, how long ago, and when
He hath, and is again to cope your wife. 85
I say, but mark his gesture. Marry patience,
Or I shall say you're all in all in spleen°,
And nothing of a man.
OTHELLO: Dost thou hear, Iago?
I will be found most cunning in my patience;
But—dost thou hear?—most bloody.
IAGO: That's not amiss; 90
But yet keep time in all. Will you withdraw?

[OTHELLO *moves to one side, where his remarks are not audible to* CASSIO *and* IAGO.]

Now will I question Cassio of Bianca,
A huswife° that by selling her desires
Buys herself bread and cloth. It is a creature
That dotes on Cassio, as 'tis the strumpet's plague 95
To beguile many and be beguiled by one.
He, when he hears of her, cannot restrain
From the excess of laughter. Here he comes.

Enter CASSIO.

As he shall smile, Othello shall go mad:
And his unbookish° jealousy must conster° 100
Poor Cassio's smiles, gestures, and light behaviors
Quite in the wrong. How do you, lieutenant?
CASSIO: The worser that you give me the addition°
Whose want even kills me.
IAGO: Ply Desdemona well, and you are sure on't. 105
Now, if this suit lay in Bianca's power,
How quickly should you speed!
CASSIO: Alas, poor caitiff!°
OTHELLO: Look how he laughs already!
IAGO: I never knew woman love man so.
CASSIO: Alas, poor rogue! I think, i' faith, she loves me. 110
OTHELLO: Now he denies it faintly, and laughs it out.
IAGO: Do you hear, Cassio?
OTHELLO: Now he importunes him
To tell it o'er. Go to! Well said, well said!
IAGO: She gives it out that you shall marry her.
Do you intend it? 115
CASSIO: Ha, ha, ha!

---

87 *spleen* passion, particularly anger.   93 *huswife* housewife (but with the special meaning here of "prostitute").
100 *unbookish* ignorant.   100 *conster* construe.   103 *addition* title.   107 *caitiff* wretch.

OTHELLO: Do ye triumph, Roman? Do you triumph?

CASSIO: I marry? What, a customer°? Prithee bear some charity to my wit; do not think it so unwholesome. Ha, ha, ha!

OTHELLO: So, so, so, so. They laugh that win.   120

IAGO: Why, the cry goes that you marry her.

CASSIO: Prithee, say true.

IAGO: I am a very villain else.

OTHELLO: Have you scored° me? Well.

CASSIO: This is the monkey's own giving out. She is persuaded I will marry 125
her out of her own love and flattery, not out of my promise.

OTHELLO: Iago beckons me; now he begins the story.

[OTHELLO *moves close enough to hear.*]

CASSIO: She was here even now; she haunts me in every place. I was the other
day talking on the sea bank with certain Venetians, and thither comes the
bauble°, and falls me thus about my neck—   130

OTHELLO: Crying "O dear Cassio!" as it were. His gesture imports it.

CASSIO: So hangs, and lolls, and weeps upon me; so shakes and pulls me! Ha,
ha, ha!

OTHELLO: Now he tells how she plucked him to my chamber. O, I see that
nose of yours, but not that dog I shall throw it to.   135

CASSIO: Well, I must leave her company.

IAGO: Before me!° Look where she comes.

Enter BIANCA.

CASSIO: 'Tis such another fitchew!° Marry a perfumed one? What do you
mean by this haunting of me?

BIANCA: Let the devil and his dam haunt you! What did you mean by that 140
same handkerchief you gave me even now? I was a fine fool to take it. I
must take out the work? A likely piece of work that you should find it in
your chamber and know not who left it there! This is some minx's token,
and I must take out the work? There! [*She throws down the handkerchief.*]
Give it your hobbyhorse°. Wheresoever you had it, I'll take out no work 145
on't.

CASSIO: How now, my sweet Bianca? How now? how now?

OTHELLO: By heaven, that should be my handkerchief!

BIANCA: If you'll come to supper tonight, you may; if you will not, come
when you are next prepared for°.   *Exit.* 150

IAGO: After her, after her!

CASSIO: Faith, I must; she'll rail in the streets else.

---

¹¹⁸**customer** *one who sells, a merchant (here, a prostitute).*   ¹²⁴**scored** *marked, defaced.*   ¹³⁰**bauble** *play-
thing.*   ¹³⁷**Before me!** *(an exclamation of surprise).*   ¹³⁸**fitchew** *polecat, i.e., strong-smelling creature.*
¹⁴⁵**hobbyhorse** *prostitute.*   ¹⁵⁰**next prepared for** *next expected—i.e., never.*

IAGO: Will you sup there?

CASSIO: Yes, I intend so.

IAGO: Well, I may chance to see you, for I would very fain speak with you. [155]

CASSIO: Prithee come. Will you?

IAGO: Go to, say no more.   [*Exit* CASSIO.]

OTHELLO [*Comes forward*]: How shall I murder him, Iago?

IAGO: Did you perceive how he laughed at his vice?

OTHELLO: O Iago! [160]

IAGO: And did you see the handkerchief?

OTHELLO: Was that mine?

IAGO: Yours, by this hand! And to see how he prizes the foolish woman your wife! She gave it him, and he hath giv'n it his whore.

OTHELLO: I would have him nine years a-killing!—A fine woman, a fair [165] woman, a sweet woman?

IAGO: Nay, you must forget that.

OTHELLO: Ay, let her rot, and perish, and be damned tonight; for she shall not live. No, my heart is turned to stone; I strike it, and it hurts my hand. O, the world hath not a sweeter creature! She might lie by an emperor's [170] side and command him tasks.

IAGO: Nay, that's not your way°.

OTHELLO: Hang her! I do but say what she is. So delicate with her needle. An admirable musician. O, she will sing the savageness out of a bear! Of so high and plenteous wit and invention°— [175]

IAGO: She's the worse for all this.

OTHELLO: O, a thousand, a thousand times. And then, of so gentle a condition°?

IAGO: Ay, too gentle.

OTHELLO: Nay, that's certain. But yet the pity of it, Iago. O Iago, the pity [180] of it, Iago.

IAGO: If you are so fond over her iniquity, give her patent to offend; for if it touch° not you, it comes near nobody.

OTHELLO: I will chop her into messes°! Cuckold me!

IAGO: O, 'tis foul in her. [185]

OTHELLO: With mine officer!

IAGO: That's fouler.

OTHELLO: Get me some poison, Iago, this night. I'll not expostulate with her, lest her body and beauty unprovide my mind° again. This night, Iago!

IAGO: Do it not with poison. Strangle her in her bed, even the bed she hath [190] contaminated.

OTHELLO: Good, good! The justice of it pleases. Very good!

IAGO: And for Cassio, let me be his undertaker°. You shall hear more by midnight.

---

[172]*way* proper course.   [175]*invention* imagination.   [177–78]*gentle a condition* (1) well born (2) of a gentle nature.   [183]*touch* affects.   [184]*messes* bits.   [189]*unprovide my mind* undo my resolution. [193]*undertaker* (not "burier" but "one who undertakes to do something").

OTHELLO: Excellent good!   [*A trumpet.*]
                    What trumpet is that same?   195
IAGO: I warrant something from Venice.

                Enter LODOVICO, DESDEMONA, *and* ATTENDANTS.

                                        'Tis Lodovico.
    This comes from the Duke. See, your wife's with him.
LODOVICO: God save you, worthy general.
OTHELLO: With° all my heart, sir.
LODOVICO: The Duke and the senators of Venice greet you.

                                        [*Gives him a letter.*]

OTHELLO: I kiss the instrument of their pleasures.   200

                                        [*Opens the letter and reads.*]

DESDEMONA: And what's the news, good cousin Lodovico?
IAGO: I am very glad to see you, signior.
    Welcome to Cyprus.
LODOVICO: I thank you. How does Lieutenant Cassio?
IAGO: Lives, sir.
DESDEMONA: Cousin, there's fall'n between him and my lord   205
    An unkind° breach; but you shall make all well.
OTHELLO: Are you sure of that?
DESDEMONA: My lord?
OTHELLO [*Reads*]: "This fail you not to do, as you will—"
LODOVICO: He did not call; he's busy in the paper.   210
    Is there division 'twixt my lord and Cassio?
DESDEMONA: A most unhappy one. I would do much
    T' atone° them, for the love I bear to Cassio.
OTHELLO: Fire and brimstone!
DESDEMONA: My lord?
OTHELLO: Are you wise?
DESDEMONA: What, is he angry?
LODOVICO: May be th' letter moved him;   215
    For, as I think, they do command him home,
    Deputing Cassio in his government°.
DESDEMONA: Trust me, I am glad on't.
OTHELLO: Indeed?
DESDEMONA: My lord?
OTHELLO: I am glad to see you mad.
DESDEMONA: Why, sweet Othello—
OTHELLO: Devil!   [*Strikes her.*] 220
DESDEMONA: I have not deserved this.
LODOVICO: My lord, this would not be believed in Venice,

---

¹⁹⁸**With** *i.e., I greet you with.*   ²⁰⁶**unkind** *unnatural.*   ²¹³**atone** *reconcile.*   ²¹⁷**government**
office.

Though I should swear I saw't. 'Tis very much.
Make her amends; she weeps.

OTHELLO: O devil, devil!
If that the earth could teem° with woman's tears,   225
Each drop she falls° would prove a crocodile°.
Out of my sight!

DESDEMONA: I will not stay to offend you.   [*Going.*]

LODOVICO: Truly, an obedient lady.
I do beseech your lordship call her back.

OTHELLO: Mistress!

DESDEMONA: My lord?

OTHELLO: What would you with her, sir?   230

LODOVICO: Who? I, my lord?

OTHELLO: Ay! You did wish that I would make her turn.
Sir, she can turn, and turn, and yet go on
And turn again; and she can weep, sir, weep;
And she's obedient; as you say, obedient.   235
Very obedient. Proceed you in your tears.
Concerning this, sir—O well-painted passion!
I am commanded home.—Get you away;
I'll send for you anon.—Sir, I obey the mandate
And will return to Venice.—Hence, avaunt!   [*Exit* DESDEMONA.] 240
Cassio shall have my place. And, sir, tonight
I do entreat that we may sup together.
You are welcome, sir, to Cyprus.—Goats and monkeys!   *Exit.*

LODOVICO: Is this the noble Moor whom our full Senate
Call all in all sufficient? Is this the nature   245
Whom passion could not shake? whose solid virtue
The shot of accident nor dart of chance
Could neither graze nor pierce?

IAGO: He is much changed.

LODOVICO: Are his wits safe? Is he not light of brain?

IAGO: He's that he is; I may not breathe my censure.   250
What he might be (if, what he might, he is not)
I would to heaven he were!

LODOVICO: What, strike his wife?

IAGO: Faith, that was not so well; yet would I knew
That stroke would prove the worst.

LODOVICO: Is it his use?°
Or did the letters work upon his blood°   255
And new-create his fault?

IAGO: Alas, alas!
It is not honesty in me to speak
What I have seen and known. You shall observe him,

---

²²⁵*teem*   conceive.   ²²⁶*falls*   drops.   ²²⁶*crocodile*   *(the crocodile was supposed to shed false tears to lure its victims).*   ²⁵⁴*use*   habit.   ²⁵⁵*blood*   passion.

And his own courses° will denote him so
That I may save my speech. Do but go after   260
And mark how he continues.
LODOVICO: I am sorry that I am deceived in him.   *Exeunt.*

Scene II [*The citadel.*]

Enter OTHELLO *and* EMILIA.

OTHELLO: You have seen nothing then?
EMILIA: Nor ever heard, nor ever did suspect.
OTHELLO: Yes, you have seen Cassio and she together.
EMILIA: But then I saw no harm, and then I heard
    Each syllable that breath made up° between them.   5
OTHELLO: What, did they never whisper?
EMILIA: Never, my lord.
OTHELLO: Nor send you out o' th' way?
EMILIA: Never.
OTHELLO: To fetch her fan, her gloves, her mask, nor nothing?
EMILIA: Never, my lord.   10
OTHELLO: That's strange.
EMILIA: I durst, my lord, to wager she is honest,
    Lay down my soul at stake°. If you think other,
    Remove your thought. It doth abuse your bosom.
    If any wretch have put this in your head,   15
    Let heaven requite it with the serpent's curse°,
    For if she be not honest°, chaste, and true,
    There's no man happy. The purest of their wives
    Is foul as slander.
OTHELLO: Bid her come hither. Go.   *Exit* EMILIA.
    She says enough; yet she's a simple bawd°   20
    That cannot say as much. This is a subtle whore,
    A closet lock and key of villainous secrets,
    And yet she'll kneel and pray; I have seen her do't.

Enter DESDEMONA *and* EMILIA.

DESDEMONA: My lord, what is your will?
OTHELLO: Pray you, chuck, come hither.
DESDEMONA: What is your pleasure?
OTHELLO: Let me see your eyes.   25
    Look in my face.
DESDEMONA: What horrible fancy's this?
OTHELLO [*To* EMILIA]: Some of your function°, mistress:

259*courses* actions.   **IV.ii.** 5*that breath made up* spoken.   13*at stake* as the wager.   16*serpent's curse* (God's curse on the serpent after the fall in Eden).   17*honest* chaste.   20*bawd* procuress.   27*Some of your function* do your proper work (as the operator of a brothel).

Leave procreants alone and shut the door;
Cough or cry hem if anybody come.
Your mystery°, your mystery! Nay, dispatch!   *Exit* EMILIA. 30
DESDEMONA: Upon my knee, what doth your speech import?
   I understand a fury in your words°.
OTHELLO: Why, what art thou?
DESDEMONA: Your wife, my lord; your true
   And loyal wife.
OTHELLO: Come, swear it, damn thyself;
   Lest, being like one of heaven, the devils themselves   35
   Should fear to seize thee. Therefore be doubledamned:
   Swear thou art honest.
DESDEMONA: Heaven doth truly know it.
OTHELLO: Heaven truly knows that thou art false as hell.
DESDEMONA: To whom, my lord? With whom? How am I false?
OTHELLO: Ah, Desdemon! Away! Away! Away!   40
DESDEMONA: Alas the heavy day! Why do you weep?
   Am I the motive° of these tears, my lord?
   If haply° you my father do suspect
   An instrument of this your calling back,
   Lay not your blame on me. If you have lost him,   45
   I have lost him too.
OTHELLO: Had it pleased heaven
   To try me with affliction, had they rained
   All kinds of sores and shames on my bare head,
   Steeped° me in poverty to the very lips,   50
   Given to captivity me and my utmost hopes,
   I should have found in some place of my soul
   A drop of patience. But alas, to make me
   The fixèd figure for the time of scorn°
   To point his slow and moving finger at.
   Yet could I bear that too, well, very well.   55
   But there where I have garnered up my heart,
   Where either I must live or bear no life,
   The fountain from the which my current runs
   Or else dries up—to be discarded thence,
   Or keep it as a cistern for foul toads   60
   To knot and gender° in—turn thy complexion there,
   Patience, thou young and rose-lipped cherubin!
   I here look grim as hell!°
DESDEMONA: I hope my noble lord esteems me honest.
OTHELLO: O, ay, as summer flies are in the shambles°,   65

°⁰mystery trade.   ³²words (Q1 adds to this line, "But not the words").   ⁴²motive cause.
⁴³haply by chance.   ⁴⁹Steeped submerged.   ⁵³The . . . scorn the very image of scorn in our time.
⁶¹knot and gender twist in bunches and procreate.   ⁶¹⁻⁶³turn . . . hell (the rough sense would seem to be
"even Patience would grow pale, turn complexion, at Desdemona's perfidy, but that Othello looks grimly on").
⁶⁵shambles abattoirs.

That quicken even with blowing°. O thou weed,
Who art so lovely fair, and smell'st so sweet,
That the sense aches at thee, would thou hadst never been born!
DESDEMONA: Alas, what ignorant° sin have I committed?
OTHELLO: Was this fair paper, this most goodly book,   70
Made to write "whore" upon? What committed?
Committed? O thou public commoner°,
I should make very forges of my cheeks
That would to cinders burn up modesty,
Did I but speak thy deeds. What committed?   75
Heaven stops the nose at it, and the moon winks°;
The bawdy wind that kisses all it meets
Is hushed within the hollow mine of earth
And will not hear't. What committed?
DESDEMONA: By heaven, you do me wrong!   80
OTHELLO: Are not you a strumpet?
DESDEMONA: No, as I am a Christian!
If to preserve this vessel for my lord
From any other foul unlawful touch
Be not to be a strumpet, I am none.
OTHELLO: What, not a whore?
DESDEMONA: No, as I shall be saved!   85
OTHELLO: Is't possible?
DESDEMONA: O, heaven forgive us!
OTHELLO: I cry you mercy° then.
I took you for that cunning whore of Venice
That married with Othello. [*Calling*] You, mistress,

Enter EMILIA.

That have the office opposite to Saint Peter   90
And keep the gate of hell! You, you, ay, you!
We have done our course; there's money for your pains.

[*Throws her some coins.*]

I pray you turn the key and keep our counsel.   *Exit.*
EMILIA: Alas, what does this gentleman conceive?
How do you, madam? How do you, my good lady?   95
DESDEMONA: Faith, half asleep.
EMILIA: Good madam, what's the matter with my lord?
DESDEMONA: With who?
EMILIA: Why, with my lord, madam.
DESDEMONA: Who is thy lord?
EMILIA: He that is yours, sweet lady.   100
DESDEMONA: I have none. Do not talk to me, Emilia.

---

⁶⁶**quicken even with blowing**   *become impregnated as soon as they lay their eggs.*   ⁶⁹**ignorant**   *unknowing.*
⁷²**commoner**   *prostitute.*   ⁷⁶**winks**   *closes its eyes (the moon was the symbol of chastity).*   ⁸⁷**cry you mercy**
ask your pardon.

I cannot weep, nor answers have I none
But what should go by water°. Prithee tonight
Lay on my bed my wedding sheets, remember;
And call thy husband hither.
EMILIA: Here's a change indeed!   *Exit.* 105
DESDEMONA: 'Tis meet I should be used so, very meet.
How have I been behaved, that he might stick
The small'st opinion on my least misuse°?

Enter IAGO *and* EMILIA.

IAGO: What is your pleasure, madam? How is't with you?
DESDEMONA: I cannot tell. Those that do teach young babes   110
Do it with gentle means and easy tasks.
He might have chid me so; for, in good faith,
I am a child to chiding.
IAGO: What is the matter, lady?
EMILIA: Alas, Iago, my lord hath so bewhored her,
Thrown such despite° and heavy terms upon her   115
That true hearts cannot bear it.
DESDEMONA: Am I that name, Iago?
IAGO: What name, fair lady?
DESDEMONA: Such as she said my lord did say I was.
EMILIA: He called her whore. A beggar in his drink
Could not have laid such terms upon his callet°.   120
IAGO: Why did he so?
DESDEMONA: I do not know; I am sure I am none such.
IAGO: Do not weep, do not weep. Alas the day.
EMILIA: Hath she forsook so many noble matches,
Her father and her country, and her friends,   125
To be called whore? Would it not make one weep?
DESDEMONA: It is my wretched fortune.
IAGO: Beshrew° him for't!
How comes this trick upon him?
DESDEMONA: Nay, heaven doth know.
EMILIA: I will be hanged if some eternal villain,
Some busy and insinuating rogue,   130
Some cogging°, cozening slave, to get some office,
Have not devised this slander. I will be hanged else.
IAGO: Fie, there is no such man! It is impossible.
DESDEMONA: If any such there be, heaven pardon him.
EMILIA: A halter pardon him! And hell gnaw his bones!   135
Why should he call her whore? Who keeps her company?
What place? What time? What form? What likelihood?
The Moor's abused by some most villainous knave,

---

¹⁰³*water* tears.   ¹⁰⁷⁻⁰⁸*stick . . . misuse* *base any doubt on my smallest fault.*   ¹¹⁵*despite* *abuse.*
¹²⁰*callet* slut.   ¹²⁷*Beshrew* curse.   ¹³¹*cogging* cheating.

Some base notorious knave, some scurvy fellow.
O heavens, that such companions° thou'dst unfold°,   140
And put in every honest hand a whip
To lash the rascals naked through the world
Even from the east to th' west!

IAGO: Speak within door°.

EMILIA: O, fie upon them! Some such squire° he was
That turned your wit the seamy side without   145
And made you to suspect me with the Moor.

IAGO: You are a fool. Go to.

DESDEMONA: Alas, Iago,
What shall I do to win my lord again?
Good friend, go to him, for, by this light of heaven,
I know not how I lost him. Here I kneel: 150
If e'er my will did trespass 'gainst his love
Either in discourse of thought° or actual deed,
Or that mine eyes, mine ears, or any sense
Delighted them in any other form;
Or that I do not yet, and ever did,   155
And ever will (though he do shake me off
To beggarly divorcement) love him dearly,
Comfort forswear me. Unkindness may do much,
And his unkindness may defeat° my life,
But never taint my love. I cannot say "whore."   160
It does abhor me now I speak the word;
To do the act that might the addition earn
Not the world's mass of vanity could make me.

IAGO: I pray you be content. 'Tis but his humor°.
The business of the state does him offense.   165

DESDEMONA: If 'twere no other.

IAGO: It is but so, I warrant.   [*Trumpets within.*]
Hark how these instruments summon to supper.
The messengers of Venice stay the meat°.
Go in, and weep not. All things shall be well.

[*Exeunt* DESDEMONA *and* EMILIA. *Enter* RODERIGO.]

How now, Roderigo?   170

RODERIGO: I do not find that thou deal'st justly with me.

IAGO: What in the contrary?

RODERIGO: Every day thou daff'st° me with some device°, Iago, and rather,
as it seems to me now, keep'st from me all conveniency° than suppliest
me with the least advantage of hope. I will indeed no longer endure it; 175

---

nor am I yet persuaded to put up° in peace what already I have foolishly suffered.

IAGO: Will you hear me, Roderigo?

RODERIGO: I have heard too much, and your words and performances are no kin together.   180

IAGO: You charge me most unjustly.

RODERIGO: With naught but truth. I have wasted myself out of my means. The jewels you have had from me to deliver Desdemona would half have corrupted a votarist°. You have told me she hath received them, and re-turned me expectations and comforts of sudden respect° and acquaintance; 185 but I find none.

IAGO: Well, go to; very well.

RODERIGO: Very well? Go to? I cannot go to, man; nor 'tis not very well. Nay, I think it is scurvy, and begin to find myself fopped° in it.

IAGO: Very well.   190

RODERIGO: I tell you 'tis not very well. I will make myself known to Des-demona. If she will return me my jewels, I will give over my suit and re-pent my unlawful solicitation. If not, assure yourself I will seek satisfac-tion of you.

IAGO: You have said now?   195

RODERIGO: Ay, and said nothing but what I protest° intendment of doing.

IAGO: Why, now I see there's mettle° in thee, and even from this instant do build on thee a better opinion than ever before. Give me thy hand, Roderigo. Thou hast taken against me a most just exception°, but yet I protest I have dealt most directly° in thy affair.   200

RODERIGO: It hath not appeared.

IAGO: I grant indeed it hath not appeared, and your suspicion is not without wit and judgment. But, Roderigo, if thou hast that in thee indeed which I have greater reason to believe now than ever—I mean purpose, courage, and valor—this night show it. If thou the next night following enjoy not 205 Desdemona, take me from this world with treachery and devise engines for° my life.

RODERIGO: Well, what is it? Is it within reason and compass°?

IAGO: Sir, there is especial commission come from Venice to depute Cassio in Othello's place.   210

RODERIGO: Is that true? Why, then Othello and Desdemona return again to Venice.

IAGO: O, no; he goes into Mauritania and taketh away with him the fair Des-demona, unless his abode be lingered here by some accident; wherein none can be so determinate° as the removing of Cassio.   215

RODERIGO: How do you mean, removing him?

IAGO: Why, by making him uncapable of Othello's place—knocking out his brains.

---

¹⁷⁶***put up*** *accept.*   ¹⁸⁴***votarist*** *nun.*   ¹⁸⁵***sudden respect*** *immediate consideration.*   ¹⁸⁹***fopped*** *duped*   ¹⁹⁶***protest*** *aver.*   ¹⁹⁷***mettle*** *spirit.*   ¹⁹⁹***exception*** *objection.*   ²⁰⁰***directly*** *straight-forwardly.*   ^{206–207}***engines for*** *schemes against.*   ²⁰⁸***compass*** *possibility.*   ²¹⁵***determinate*** *effective.*

RODERIGO: And that you would have me to do?

IAGO: Ay, if you dare do yourself a profit and a right. He sups tonight with a ²²⁰ harlotry°, and thither will I go to him. He knows not yet of his honorable fortune. If you will watch his going thence, which I will fashion to fall out° between twelve and one, you may take him at your pleasure. I will be near to second° your attempt, and he shall fall between us. Come, stand not amazed at it, but go along with me. I will show you such a necessity ²²⁵ in his death that you shall think yourself bound to put it on him. It is now high supper time, and the night grows to waste. About it.

RODERIGO: I will hear further reason for this.

IAGO: And you shall be satisfied.   *Exeunt.*

Scene III [The citadel.]

Enter OTHELLO, LODOVICO, DESDEMONA, EMILIA, *and* ATTENDANTS.

LODOVICO: I do beseech you, sir, trouble yourself no further.

OTHELLO: O, pardon me; 'twill do me good to walk.

LODOVICO: Madam, good night. I humbly thank your ladyship.

DESDEMONA: Your honor is most welcome.

OTHELLO: Will you walk, sir? O, Desdemona.   5

DESDEMONA: My lord?

OTHELLO: Get you to bed on th' instant; I will be returned forthwith. Dismiss your attendant there. Look't be done.

DESDEMONA: I will, my lord.   *Exit* [OTHELLO, *with* LODOVICO *and* ATTENDANTS].

EMILIA: How goes it now? He looks gentler than he did.   10

DESDEMONA: He says he will return incontinent°,
     And hath commanded me to go to bed.
     And bade me to dismiss you.

EMILIA: Dismiss me?

DESDEMONA: It was his bidding; therefore, good Emilia,
     Give me my nightly wearing, and adieu.   15
     We must not now displease him.

EMILIA: I would you had never seen him!

DESDEMONA: So would not I. My love doth so approve him
     That even his stubbornness, his checks°, his frowns—
     Prithee unpin me—have grace and favor.   20

EMILIA: I have laid these sheets you bade me on the bed.

DESDEMONA: All's one°. Good Father, how foolish are our minds!
     If I do die before, prithee shroud me
     In one of these same sheets.

EMILIA: Come, come! You talk.

DESDEMONA: My mother had a maid called Barbary.   25
     She was in love; and he she loved proved mad
     And did forsake her. She had a song of "Willow";

²²¹*harlotry* female.   ²²²⁻²²³*fall out* occur.   ²²⁴*second* support.   **IV.iii.** ¹¹*incontinent* at once.
¹⁹*checks* rebukes.   ²²*All's one* no matter.

An old thing 'twas, but it expressed her fortune,
And she died singing it. That song tonight
Will not go from my mind; I have much to do   30
But to go hang my head all at one side
And sing it like poor Barbary. Prithee dispatch.
EMILIA: Shall I go fetch your nightgown?
DESDEMONA: No, unpin me here.
This Lodovico is a proper man.   35
EMILIA: A very handsome man.
DESDEMONA: He speaks well.
EMILIA: I know a lady in Venice would have walked barefoot to Palestine for
a touch of his nether lip.
DESDEMONA [*Sings*]:
"The poor soul sat singing by a sycamore tree,   40
    Sing all a green willow;
Her hand on her bosom, her head on her knee,
    Sing willow, willow, willow.
The fresh streams ran by her and murmured her moans;
    Sing willow, willow, willow;   45
Her salt tears fell from her, and soft'ned the stones—
    Sing willow, willow, willow—"
Lay by these.   [*Gives* EMILIA *her clothes.*]
    "Willow, Willow"—
Prithee hie° thee; he'll come anon°.   50
    "Sing all a green willow must be my garland
    Let nobody blame him; his scorn I approve"—
Nay, that's not next. Hark! Who is't that knocks?
EMILIA: It is the wind.
DESDEMONA [*Sings*]:
    "I called my love false love; but what said he then?   55
    Sing willow, willow, willow:
If I court moe° women, you'll couch with moe men."
So, get thee gone; good night. Mine eyes do itch.
Doth that bode weeping?
EMILIA: 'Tis neither here nor there.
DESDEMONA: I have heard it said so. O, these men, these men.   60
Dost thou in conscience think, tell me, Emilia,
That there be women do abuse their husbands
In such gross kind?
EMILIA: There be some such, no question.
DESDEMONA: Wouldst thou do such a deed for all the world?
EMILIA: Why, would not you?
DESDEMONA: No, by this heavenly light!   65
EMILIA: Nor I neither by this heavenly light.
I might do't as well i' th' dark.
DESDEMONA: Wouldst thou do such a deed for all the world?

---

⁵⁰**hie** *hurry.*   ⁵⁰**anon** *at once.*   ⁵⁷**moe** *more.*

EMILIA: The world's a huge thing; it is a great price for a small vice.

DESDEMONA: In troth, I think thou wouldst not. 70

EMILIA: In troth, I think I should; and undo't when I had done. Marry, I
would not do such a thing for a joint-ring°, nor for measures of lawn°, nor
for gowns, petticoats, nor caps, nor any petty exhibition°, but for all the
whole world? Why, who would not make her husband a cuckold to make
him a monarch? I should venture purgatory for't. 75

DESDEMONA: Beshrew me if I would do such a wrong for the whole world.

EMILIA: Why, the wrong is but a wrong i' th' world; and having the world
for your labor, 'tis a wrong in your own world, and you might quickly make
it right.

DESDEMONA: I do not think there is any such woman. 80

EMILIA: Yes, a dozen; and as many to th' vantage as would store° the world
they played for.
But I do think it is their husbands' faults
If wives do fall. Say that they slack their duties
And pour our treasures into foreign° laps; 85
Or else break out in peevish jealousies,
Throwing restraint upon us; or say they strike us,
Or scant our former having in despite°—
Why, we have galls; and though we have some grace,
Yet have we some revenge. Let husbands know 90
Their wives have sense like them. They see, and smell,
And have their palates both for sweet and sour,
As husbands have. What is it that they do
When they change° us for others? Is it sport?
I think it is. And doth affection° breed it? 95
I think it doth. Is't frailty that thus errs?
It is so too. And have not we affections?
Desires for sport? and frailty? as men have?
Then let them use us well; else let them know,
The ills we do, their ills instruct us so°. 100

DESDEMONA: Good night, good night. Heaven me such uses° send,
Not to pick bad from bad, but by bad mend.   *Exeunt.*

ACT V

Scene I [A street.]

Enter IAGO *and* RODERIGO.

IAGO: Here, stand behind this bulk°; straight will he come.
Wear thy good rapier bare, and put it home.

72*joint-ring* (a ring with two interlocking halves).   72*lawn* fine linen.   73*exhibition* payment.
81*to . . . store* in addition as would fill.   85*foreign* alien, i.e., other than the wife.   88*scant . . . despite*
reduce, in spite, our household allowance (?).   94*change* exchange.   95*affection* strong feeling, desire.
100*instruct us so* teach us to do likewise.   101*uses* practices.   **V.i.** 1*bulk* projecting stall of a shop.

Quick, quick! Fear nothing; I'll be at thy elbow.
It makes us, or it mars us, think on that,
And fix most firm thy resolution. 5

RODERIGO: Be near at hand; I may miscarry in't.

IAGO: Here, at thy hand. Be bold, and take thy stand.   [*Moves to one side.*]

RODERIGO: I have no great devotion to the deed,
And yet he hath given me satisfying reasons.
'Tis but a man gone. Forth my sword! He dies! 10

IAGO: I have rubbed this young quat° almost to the sense°,
And he grows angry. Now, whether he kill Cassio,
Or Cassio him, or each do kill the other,
Every way makes my gain. Live Roderigo,
He calls me to a restitution large 15
Of gold and jewels that I bobbed° from him
As gifts to Desdemona.
It must not be. If Cassio do remain,
He hath a daily beauty in his life
That makes me ugly; and besides, the Moor 20
May unfold me to him; there stand I in much peril.
No, he must die. But so, I hear him coming.

Enter CASSIO.

RODERIGO: I know his gait. 'Tis he. Villain, thou diest!   [*Thrusts at* CASSIO.]

CASSIO: That thrust had been mine enemy indeed
But that my coat° is better than thou know'st. 25
I will make proof of thine.   [*Fights with* RODERIGO.]

RODERIGO.   O, I am slain!°

CASSIO: I am maimed forever. Help, ho! Murder! Murder!

Enter OTHELLO [*to one side*].

OTHELLO: The voice of Cassio. Iago keeps his word.

RODERIGO: O, villain that I am!

OTHELLO: It is even so.

CASSIO: O help, ho! Light! A surgeon! 30

OTHELLO: 'Tis he. O brave Iago, honest and just,
That hast such noble sense of thy friend's wrong!
Thou teachest me. Minion°, your dear lies dead,
And your unblest° fate hies°. Strumpet, I come.
Forth of my heart those charms, thine eyes, are blotted. 35
Thy bed, lust-stained, shall with lust's blood be spotted.

---

¹¹**quat** pimple.   ¹¹**to the sense** raw.   ¹⁶**bobbed** swindled.   ²⁵**coat** i.e., a mail shirt or bullet-proof vest.   ²⁶**slain** most editors add here a stage direction that has Iago wounding Cassio in the leg from behind, but remaining unseen. However, nothing in the text requires this, and Cassio's wound can be given him in the fight with Roderigo, for presumably when Cassio attacks Roderigo the latter would not simply accept the thrust but would parry. Since Iago enters again at line 46, he must exit at some point after line 22.   ³³**Minion** hussy, i.e., Desdemona.   ³⁴**unblest** unsanctified.   ³⁴**hies** approaches swiftly.

Exit OTHELLO. *Enter* LODOVICO *and* GRATIANO.

CASSIO: What, ho? No watch? No passage°? Murder! Murder!

GRATIANO: 'Tis some mischance. The voice is very direful.

CASSIO: O, help!

LODOVICO: Hark!   40

RODERIGO: O wretched villain!

LODOVICO: Two or three groan. 'Tis heavy night.
    These may be counterfeits. Let's think't unsafe
    To come into the cry without more help.

RODERIGO: Nobody come? Then shall I bleed to death.   45

LODOVICO: Hark!

Enter IAGO [*with a light*].

GRATIANO: Here's one comes in his shirt, with light and weapons.

IAGO: Who's there? Whose noise is this that cries on murder?

LODOVICO: We do not know.

IAGO: Do not you hear a cry?

CASSIO: Here, here! For heaven's sake, help me!

IAGO: What's the matter?   50

GRATIANO: This is Othello's ancient, as I take it.

LODOVICO: The same indeed, a very valiant fellow.

IAGO: What are you here that cry so grievously?

CASSIO: Iago? O, I am spoiled, undone by villains.
    Give me some help.   55

IAGO: O me, lieutenant! What villains have done this?

CASSIO: I think that one of them is hereabout
    And cannot make away.

IAGO: O treacherous villains!
    [*To* LODOVICO *and* GRATIANO] What are you there?
    Come in, and give some help.   60

RODERIGO: O, help me here!

CASSIO: That's one of them.

IAGO: O murd'rous slave! O villain! [*Stabs* RODERIGO.]

RODERIGO: O damned Iago! O inhuman dog!

IAGO: Kill men i' th' dark?—Where be these bloody thieves?—
    How silent is this town!—Ho! Murder! Murder!—   65
    What may you be? Are you of good or evil?

LODOVICO: As you shall prove us, praise us.

IAGO: Signior Lodovico?

LODOVICO: He, sir.

IAGO: I cry you mercy. Here's Cassio hurt by villains.   70

GRATIANO: Cassio?

IAGO: How is't, brother?

³⁷ **passage** *passers-by.*

CASSIO: My leg is cut in two.
IAGO: Marry, heaven forbid!
   Light, gentlemen. I'll bind it with my shirt.

Enter BIANCA.

BIANCA: What is the matter, ho? Who is't that cried?   75
IAGO: Who is't that cried?
BIANCA: O my dear Cassio! My sweet Cassio!
   O Cassio, Cassio, Cassio!
IAGO: O notable strumpet!—Cassio, may you suspect
   Who they should be that have thus mangled you?   80
CASSIO: No.
GRATIANO: I am sorry to find you thus. I have been to seek you.
IAGO: Lend me a garter. So. O for a chair
   To bear him easily hence.
BIANCA: Alas, he faints! O Cassio, Cassio, Cassio!   85
IAGO: Gentlemen all, I do suspect this trash
   To be a party in this injury.—
   Patience awhile, good Cassio.—Come, come.
   Lend me a light. Know we this face or no?
   Alas, my friend and my dear countryman   90
   Roderigo? No.—Yes, sure.—Yes, 'tis Roderigo!
GRATIANO: What, of Venice?
IAGO: Even he, sir. Did you know him?
GRATIANO: Know him? Ay.
IAGO: Signior Gratiano? I cry your gentle pardon.   95
   These bloody accidents must excuse my manners
   That so neglected you.
GRATIANO: I am glad to see you.
IAGO: How do you, Cassio?—O, a chair, a chair!
GRATIANO: Roderigo?
IAGO: He, he, 'tis he! [*A chair brought in.*] O, that's well said°; the chair.
   Some good man bear him carefully from hence.   100
   I'll fetch the general's surgeon. [*To* BIANCA] For you, mistress,
   Save you your labor. [*To* CASSIO] He that lies slain here, Cassio,
   Was my dear friend. What malice was between you?
CASSIO: None in the world; nor do I know the man.
IAGO: What, look you pale?—O, bear him out o' th' air.   105

[CASSIO *is carried off.*]

   Stay you, good gentlemen.—Look you pale, mistress?
   Do you perceive the gastness° of her eye?
   Nay, if you stare, we shall hear more anon.
   Behold her well; I pray you look upon her.

---

[99] **well said** *well done.*   [107] **gastness** *terror.*

Do you see, gentlemen? Nay, guiltiness will speak,   110
Though tongues were out of use°.

[*Enter* EMILIA.]

EMILIA: Alas, what is the matter? What is the matter, husband?
IAGO: Cassio hath here been set on in the dark
  By Roderigo and fellows that are scaped.
  He's almost slain, and Roderigo quite dead.   115
EMILIA: Alas, good gentleman! Alas, good Cassio!
IAGO: This is the fruits of whoring. Prithee, Emilia,
  Go know of Cassio where he supped tonight.
  [*To* BIANCA] What, do you shake at that?
BIANCA: He supped at my house; but I therefore shake not.   120
IAGO: O, did he so? I charge° you go with me.
EMILIA: Oh fie upon thee, strumpet!
BIANCA: I am no strumpet, but of life as honest
  As you that thus abuse me.
EMILIA: As I? Fie upon thee!
IAGO: Kind gentlemen, let's go see poor Cassio dressed°.   125
  [*To* BIANCA] Come, mistress, you must tell's another tale.
  Emilia, run you to the citadel
  And tell my lord and lady what hath happed   [*Exit* EMILIA.]
  Will you go on afore?   *Exeunt* [*all but* IAGO].
                 This is the night
  That either makes me or fordoes me quite°.   [*Exit.*] 130

Scene II. [DESDEMONA'S *chamber*.]

Enter OTHELLO [*with a light*]; *and* DESDEMONA *in her bed*.

OTHELLO: It is the cause, it is the cause, my soul.
  Let me not name it to you, you chaste stars.
  It is the cause. Yet I'll not shed her blood,
  Nor scar that whiter skin of hers than snow
  And smooth as monumental alabaster.   5
  Yet she must die, else she'll betray more men.
  Put out the light, and then put out the light.
  If I quench thee, thou flaming minister°,
  I can again thy former light restore,
  Should I repent me; but once put out thy light,   10
  Thou cunning'st° pattern of excelling nature,
  I know not where is that Promethean heat°
  That can thy light relume°. When I have plucked the rose,

---

¹¹¹*tongues were out of use* men no longer spoke.   ¹²¹*charge* command.   ¹²⁵*dressed* bandaged.
¹³⁰*fordoes me quite* completely ruins me.   **V.ii.** ⁸*minister* worker, servant.   ¹¹*cunning'st* most intricate and skillfully wrought (by nature excelling itself).   ¹²**Promethean heat** divine fire (Prometheus is the Titan
who stole fire from heaven and gave it to man).   ¹³*relume* relight.

I cannot give it vital° growth again;
It needs must wither. I'll smell thee on the tree.   [*He kisses her.*] 15
O balmy breath, that dost almost persuade
Justice to break her sword. One more, one more!
Be thus when thou art dead, and I will kill thee,
And love thee after. One more, and that's the last!
So sweet was ne'er so fatal. I must weep,   20
But they are cruel tears. This sorrow's heavenly;
It strikes where it doth love. She wakes.

DESDEMONA: Who's there? Othello?

OTHELLO: Ay, Desdemona.

DESDEMONA: Will you come to bed, my lord?

OTHELLO: Have you prayed tonight, Desdemon?

DESDEMONA: Ay, my lord.   25

OTHELLO: If you bethink yourself of any crime
     Unreconciled as yet to heaven and grace,
     Solicit for it straight.

DESDEMONA: Alack, my lord, what may you mean by that?

OTHELLO: Well, do it, and be brief; I will walk by°.   30
     I would not kill thy unprepared spirit.
     No, heavens forfend! I would not kill thy soul.

DESDEMONA: Talk you of killing?

OTHELLO: Ay, I do.

DESDEMONA: Then heaven
     Have mercy on me!

OTHELLO: Amen, with all my heart.

DESDEMONA: If you say so, I hope you will not kill me.   35

OTHELLO: Humh.

DESDEMONA: And yet I fear you; for you're fatal then
     When your eyes roll so. Why I should fear I know not,
     Since guiltiness I know not; but yet I feel I fear.

OTHELLO: Think on thy sins.

DESDEMONA: They are loves I bear to you.   40

OTHELLO: Ay, and for that thou diest.

DESDEMONA: That death's unnatural that kills for loving.
     Alas, why gnaw you so your nether lip?
     Some bloody passion shakes your very frame.
     These are portents; but yet I hope, I hope,   45
     They do not point on me.

OTHELLO: Peace and be still.

DESDEMONA: I will so. What's the matter?

OTHELLO: That handkerchief which I so loved and gave thee,
     Thou gav'st to Cassio.

DESDEMONA: No, by my life and soul!
     Send for the man and ask him.

---

¹⁴**vital** *living.*   ³⁰**by** *nearby.*

OTHELLO: Sweet soul, take heed,   50
Take heed of perjury; thou art on thy deathbed.
DESDEMONA: Ay, but not yet to die.
OTHELLO: Presently°.
Therefore confess thee freely of thy sin,
For to deny each article° with oath
Cannot remove nor choke the strong conception   55
That I do groan withal. Thou art to die.
DESDEMONA: Then Lord have mercy on me.
OTHELLO: I say, amen.
DESDEMONA: And have you mercy too. I never did
Offend you in my life; never loved Cassio
But with such general warranty° of heaven   60
As I might love. I never gave him token.
OTHELLO: By heaven, I saw my handkerchief in's hand!
O perjured woman! thou dost stone° my heart,
And mak'st me call what I intend to do
A murder, which I thought a sacrifice.   65
I saw the handkerchief.
DESDEMONA: He found it then.
I never gave it him. Send for him hither.
Let him confess a truth.
OTHELLO: He hath confessed.
DESDEMONA: What, my lord?
OTHELLO: That he hath used thee.
DESDEMONA: How? Unlawfully?
OTHELLO: Ay.   70
DESDEMONA: He will not say so.
OTHELLO: No, his mouth is stopped.
Honest Iago hath ta'en order for't°.
DESDEMONA: O, my fear interprets. What, is he dead?
OTHELLO: Had all his hairs been lives, my great revenge
Had stomach° for them all.   75
DESDEMONA: Alas, he is betrayed, and I undone!
OTHELLO: Out, strumpet! Weep'st thou for him to my face?
DESDEMONA: O, banish me, my lord, but kill me not!
OTHELLO: Down, strumpet!
DESDEMONA: Kill me tomorrow; let me live tonight!   80
OTHELLO: Nay, if you strive—
DESDEMONA: But half an hour!
OTHELLO: Being done, there is no pause.
DESDEMONA: But while I say one prayer!
OTHELLO: It is too late.   *Smothers her.*

---

[52] ***Presently***   *immediately.*   [54] ***article***   *item (of the charge of adultery. Othello makes heavy use of legal terms in*
this scene).   [60] ***warranty***   *allowance.*   [63] ***stone***   *turn to stone.*   [72] ***ta'en order for't***   *made sure of it.*
[75] ***stomach***   *appetite.*

EMILIA *at the door.*

EMILIA [*Calls within*]: My lord, my lord! What, ho, my lord, my lord!

OTHELLO: What noise is this? Not dead? Not yet quite dead?   85
  I that am cruel am yet merciful;
  I would not have thee linger in thy pain.

EMILIA [*Within*]: What, ho! My lord, my lord!

OTHELLO: So, so. Who's there?

EMILIA [*Within*]: O, good my lord, I would speak a word with you.

OTHELLO: Yes, 'tis Emilia.—By and by.—She's dead.—   90
  'Tis like she comes to speak of Cassio's death.
  The noise was high°. Ha! No more moving?
  Still as the grave.—Shall she come in? Were't good?—
  I think she stirs again. No.—What's best to do?
  If she come in, she'll sure speak to my wife.   95
  My wife! My wife! What wife? I have no wife.
  O, insupportable! O heavy hour!
  Methinks it should be now a huge eclipse
  Of sun and moon, and that th' affrighted globe
  Should yawn° at alteration.

EMILIA [*Within*]:   I do beseech you   100
  That I may speak with you, O good my lord!

OTHELLO: I had forgot thee. O, come in, Emilia.
  Soft, by and by.—Let me the curtains draw.—

[*Draws the bed hangings and then opens the door.*]

  Where art thou?

Enter EMILIA.

                          What's the matter with thee now?

EMILIA: O my good lord, yonder's foul murders done!   105

OTHELLO: What? Now?

EMILIA: But now, my lord.

OTHELLO: It is the very error° of the moon.
  She comes more nearer earth than she was wont
  And makes men mad.   110

EMILIA: Cassio, my lord, hath killed a young Venetian
  Called Roderigo.

OTHELLO: Roderigo killed?
  And Cassio killed?

EMILIA: No, Cassio is not killed.

OTHELLO: Not Cassio killed? Then murder's out of tune,
  And sweet revenge grows harsh.   115

---

⁹²**high** *loud (Q1 reads "here").*   ⁹⁸⁻¹⁰⁰**Methinks . . . alteration** *(the Elizabethans believed that great changes in human affairs were reflected by disorders in nature).*   ¹⁰⁰**yawn** *gape open (as in an earthquake).*   ¹⁰⁸**error** *wandering out of regular course (disorders in the heavens were believed by some to cause disorders on earth, as well as vice versa).*

DESDEMONA: O, falsely, falsely murdered!

EMILIA: O Lord! What cry is that?

OTHELLO: That? What?

EMILIA: Out and alas! that was my lady's voice.
    Help! Help, ho! Help! O lady, speak again!
    Sweet Desdemona! O sweet mistress, speak!   120

DESDEMONA: A guiltless death I die.

EMILIA: O, who hath done this deed?

DESDEMONA: Nobody—I myself. Farewell.
    Commend me to my kind lord. O, farewell!   [*She dies.*]

OTHELLO: Why, how should she be murd'red?

EMILIA: Alas, who knows?   125

OTHELLO: You heard her say herself, it was not I.

EMILIA: She said so. I must needs report the truth.

OTHELLO: She's like a liar gone to burning hell!
    'Twas I that killed her.

EMILIA: O, the more angel she,
    And you the blacker devil!   130

OTHELLO: She turned to folly, and she was a whore.

EMILIA: Thou dost belie her, and thou art a devil.

OTHELLO: She was false as water.

EMILIA: Thou art rash as fire to say
    That she was false. O, she was heavenly true!

OTHELLO: Cassio did top her. Ask thy husband else.   135
    O, I were damned beneath all depth in hell
    But that I did proceed upon just grounds
    To this extremity. Thy husband knew it all.

EMILIA: My husband?

OTHELLO: Thy husband.

EMILIA: That she was false to wedlock?

OTHELLO: Ay, with Cassio. Had she been true,   140
    If heaven would make me such another world
    Of one entire and perfect chrysolite°,
    I'd not have sold her for it.

EMILIA: My husband?

OTHELLO: Ay, 'twas he that told me on her first.
    An honest man he is, and hates the slime   145
    That sticks on filthy deeds.

EMILIA: My husband?

OTHELLO: What needs this iterance? Woman, I say thy husband.

EMILIA: O mistress, villainy hath made mocks with love!
    My husband say she was false?

OTHELLO: He, woman.
    I say, thy husband. Dost understand the word?   150
    My friend, thy husband; honest, honest Iago.

---

[142] **chrysolite**   *topaz.*

EMILIA: If he say so, may his pernicious soul
    Rot half a grain a day! He lies to th' heart.
    She was too fond of her most filthy bargain.
OTHELLO: Hah?   155
EMILIA: Do thy worst.
    This deed of thine is no more worthy heaven
    Than thou wast worthy her.
OTHELLO: Peace, you were best°.
EMILIA: Thou hast not half that pow'r to do me harm
    As I have to be hurt. O gull! O dolt!   160
    As ignorant as dirt! Thou hast done a deed—

        [OTHELLO *moves to draw his sword.*]

    I care not for thy sword; I'll make thee known,
    Though I lost twenty lives. Help! Help! Ho! Help!
    The Moor hath killed my mistress! Murder! murder!

        Enter MONTANO, GRATIANO, *and* IAGO [*and Others*].

MONTANO: What is the matter? How now, general?   165
EMILIA: O, are you come, Iago? You have done well,
    That men must lay their murders on your neck.
GRATIANO: What is the matter?
EMILIA: Disprove this villain, if thou be'st a man.
    He says thou told'st him that his wife was false.   170
    I know thou didst not; thou'rt not such a villain.
    Speak, for my heart is full.
IAGO: I told him what I thought, and told no more
    Than what he found himself was apt and true.
EMILIA: But did you ever tell him she was false?   175
IAGO: I did.
EMILIA: You told a lie, an odious damnèd lie!
    Upon my soul, a lie! A wicked lie!
    She false with Cassio? Did you say with Cassio?
IAGO: With Cassio, mistress. Go to, charm° your tongue.   180
EMILIA: I will not charm my tongue; I am bound to speak:
    My mistress here lies murdered in her bed.
ALL: O heavens forfend!
EMILIA: And your reports have set the murder on.
OTHELLO: Nay, stare not, masters. It is true indeed.   185
GRATIANO: 'Tis a strange truth.
MONTANO: O monstrous act!
EMILIA: Villainy, villainy, villainy!
    I think upon't—I think I smell't!—O villainy!
    I thought so then.—I'll kill myself for grief.—
    O villainy, villainy!   190
IAGO: What, are you mad? I charge you get you home.

---

[158]*Peace, you were best*   i.e., you had better be silent.   [180]*charm*   control.

EMILIA: Good gentlemen, let me have leave to speak.
  'Tis proper I obey him, but not now.
  Perchance, Iago, I will ne'er go home.
OTHELLO: O! O! O!   *[Falls on the bed.]*
EMILIA: Nay, lay thee down and roar,   195
  For thou hast killed the sweetest innocent
  That e'er did lift up eye.
OTHELLO: O, she was foul!   *[Rises.]*
  I scarce did know you, uncle. There lies your niece,
  Whose breath, indeed, these hands have newly stopped.
  I know this act shows horrible and grim.   200
GRATIANO: Poor Desdemona! I am glad thy father's dead.
  Thy match was mortal to him, and pure grief
  Shore his old thread in twain. Did he live now,
  This sight would make him do a desperate turn;
  Yea, curse his better angel from his side,   205
  And fall to reprobation°.
OTHELLO: 'Tis pitiful; but yet Iago knows
  That she with Cassio hath the act of shame
  A thousand times committed. Cassio confessed it;
  And she did gratify his amorous works   210
  With that recognizance and pledge of love,
  Which I first gave her. I saw it in his hand.
  It was a handkerchief, an antique token
  My father gave my mother.
EMILIA: O God! O heavenly God!   215
IAGO: Zounds, hold your peace!
EMILIA: 'Twill out, 'twill out! I peace?
  No, I will speak as liberal as the north°.
  Let heaven and men and devils, let them all,
  All, all, cry shame against me, yet I'll speak.
IAGO: Be wise, and get you home.
EMILIA: I will not.   220

        [IAGO draws and threatens EMILIA.]

GRATIANO: Fie! Your sword upon a woman?
EMILIA: O thou dull Moor, that handkerchief thou speak'st of
  I found by fortune, and did give my husband;
  For often with a solemn earnestness—
  More than indeed belonged to such a trifle—   225
  He begged of me to steal't.
IAGO: Villainous whore!
EMILIA: She give it Cassio? No, alas, I found it,
  And I did give't my husband.
IAGO: Filth, thou liest!

---

²⁰⁶**reprobation** *damnation.*   ²¹⁷**liberal as the north** *freely (and bitingly) as the north wind blows.*

EMILIA: By heaven, I do not, I do not, gentlemen.
O murd'rous coxcomb! What should such a fool　　　230
Do with so good a wife?

OTHELLO:　　　　　　　Are there no stones° in heaven
But what serves for the thunder? Precious villain!

[*The* MOOR *runs at* IAGO, *but is disarmed by* MONTANO. IAGO *kills his wife.*]

GRATIANO: The woman falls. Sure he hath killed his wife.

EMILIA: Ay, ay. O, lay me by my mistress' side.　　　　　[*Exit* IAGO.]

GRATIANO: He's gone, but his wife's killed.　　　　　235

MONTANO: 'Tis a notorious° villain. Take you this weapon,
Which I have recovered from the Moor.
Come, guard the door without. Let him not pass,
But kill him rather. I'll after that same villain,
For 'tis a damnèd slave.　　　　　*Exit* [*with all but* OTHELLO *and* EMILIA].

OTHELLO:　　　　　　I am not valiant neither;　　　240
But every puny whipster° gets my sword.
But why should honor outlive honesty?
Let it go all.

EMILIA:　　　　What did thy song bode, lady?
Hark, canst thou hear me? I will play the swan,
And die in music. [*Sings*] "Willow, willow, willow."　　　245
Moor, she was chaste. She loved thee, cruel Moor,
So come my soul to bliss as I speak true.
So speaking as I think, alas, I die.　　　　　[*She dies.*]

OTHELLO: I have another weapon in this chamber;
It was a sword of Spain, the ice-brook's temper.　　　250
O, here it is.—Uncle, I must come forth.

GRATIANO [*Within*]: If thou attempt it, it will cost thee dear.
Thou hast no weapon, and perforce must suffer.

OTHELLO: Look in upon me then and speak with me,
Or, naked as I am, I will assault thee.　　　255

[*Enter* GRATIANO.]

GRATIANO: What is the matter?

OTHELLO:　　　　　　　Behold, I have a weapon;
A better never did itself sustain
Upon a soldier's thigh. I have seen the day
That with this little arm and this good sword
I have made my way through more impediments　　　260
Than twenty times your stop. But O vain boast!
Who can control his fate? 'Tis not so now.
Be not afraid, though you do see me weaponed.
Here is my journey's end, here is my butt°,

---

²³¹**stones** *thunderbolts.* ²³⁶**notorious** *out-and-out.* ²⁴¹**puny whipster** *small top-whipping boy (?).*
²⁶⁴**butt** *target, stopping place.*

And very seamark of my utmost sail°.   265
Do you go back dismayed? 'Tis a lost fear.
Man but a rush° against Othello's breast.
And he retires. Where should Othello go?
Now, how dost thou look now? O ill-starred wench!
Pale as thy smock! When we shall meet at compt°,   270
This look of thine will hurl my soul from heaven,
And fiends will snatch at it. Cold, cold, my girl?
Even like thy chastity.
O cursèd, cursèd slave! Whip me, ye devils,
From the possession of° this heavenly sight!   275
Blow me about in winds! roast me in sulfur!
Wash me in steep-down gulfs of liquid fire!
O Desdemon! Dead Desdemon; dead. O! O!

Enter LODOVICO, CASSIO, MONTANO, *and* IAGO [*as prisoner,*] *with Officers.*

LODOVICO: Where is this rash and most unfortunate man?
OTHELLO: That's he that was Othello? Here I am.   280
LODOVICO: Where is that viper? Bring the villain forth.
OTHELLO: I look down towards his feet°—but that's a fable.
    If that thou be'st a devil, I cannot kill thee.   [*Wounds* IAGO.]
LODOVICO: Wrench his sword from him.   [OTHELLO *is disarmed.*]
IAGO: I bleed, sir, but not killed.
OTHELLO: I am not sorry neither. I'd have thee live;   285
    For in my sense, 'tis happiness to die.
LODOVICO: O thou Othello that was once so good,
    Fall'n in the practice° of a cursèd slave,
    What shall be said to thee?
OTHELLO: Why, anything:
    An honorable murderer, if you will;   290
    For naught I did in hate, but all in honor.
LODOVICO: This wretch hath part confessed his villainy.
    Did you and he consent in Cassio's death?
OTHELLO: Ay.
CASSIO: Dear general, I never gave you cause.   295
OTHELLO: I do believe it, and I ask your pardon.
    Will you, I pray, demand that demi-devil
    Why he hath thus ensnared my soul and body?
IAGO: Demand me nothing. What you know, you know.
    From this time forth I never will speak word.   300
LODOVICO: What, not to pray?
GRATIANO: Torments will ope your lips.
OTHELLO: Well, thou dost best.
LODOVICO: Sir, you shall understand what hath befall'n,

---

²⁶⁵*seamark of my utmost sail*   *maker of my furthest journey.*   ²⁶⁷*Man but a rush*   *attack with only a reed.*
²⁷⁰*compt*   *Judgment Day.*   ²⁷⁵*the possession of*   *being possessed by.*   ²⁸²*towards his feet*   *i.e., for his*
cloven hoofs.   ²⁸⁸*practice*   *plotting.*

Which, as I think, you know not. Here is a letter
Found in the pocket of the slain Roderigo;   305
And here another. The one of them imports
The death of Cassio to be undertook
By Roderigo.

OTHELLO: O villain!

CASSIO: Most heathenish and most gross!

LODOVICO: Now here's another discontented paper   310
  Found in his pocket too; and this, it seems,
  Roderigo meant t' have sent this damnèd villain;
  But that, belike, Iago in the interim
  Came in and satisfied him.

OTHELLO: O thou pernicious caitiff!
  How came you, Cassio, by that handkerchief   315
  That was my wife's?

CASSIO: I found it in my chamber;
  And he himself confessed it but even now
  That there he dropped it for a special purpose
  Which wrought to his desire.

OTHELLO: O fool! Fool! Fool!

CASSIO: There is besides in Roderigo's letter,   320
  How he upbraids Iago that he made him
  Brave me upon the watch; whereon it came
  That I was cast; and even but now he spake,
  After long seeming dead—Iago hurt him,
  Iago set him on.   325

LODOVICO. You must forsake this room and go with us.
  Your power and your command is taken off,
  And Cassio rules in Cyprus. For this slave,
  If there be any cunning cruelty
  That can torment him much and hold him long,   330
  It shall be his. You shall close prisoner rest
  Till that the nature of your fault be known
  To the Venetian state. Come, bring away.

OTHELLO: Soft you, a word or two before you go.
  I have done the state some service and they know't.   335
  No more of that. I pray you, in your letters,
  When you shall these unlucky deeds relate,
  Speak of me as I am. Nothing extenuate,
  Nor set down aught in malice. Then must you speak
  Of one that loved not wisely, but too well;   340
  Of one not easily jealous, but, being wrought,
  Perplexed in the extreme; of one whose hand,
  Like the base Judean°, threw a pearl away
  Richer than all his tribe; of one whose subdued eyes,

---

³⁴³**Judean**   (most editors use the Q1 reading, "Indian," here, but F is clear: both readings point toward the infidel, the unbeliever.

Albeit unusèd to the melting mood,   345
Drops tears as fast as the Arabian trees
Their med'cinable gum. Set you down this.
And say besides that in Aleppo once,
Where a malignant and a turbaned Turk
Beat a Venetian and traduced the state,   350
I took by th' throat the circumcisèd dog
And smote him—thus.   [*He stabs himself.*]
LODOVICO: O bloody period!°
GRATIANO: All that is spoke is marred.
OTHELLO: I kissed thee ere I killed thee. No way but this,
    Killing myself, to die upon a kiss.   [*He falls over* DESDEMONA *and dies.*] 355
CASSIO: This did I fear, but thought he had no weapon;
    For he was great of heart.
LODOVICO [*To* IAGO]:   O Spartan dog,
    More fell° than anguish, hunger, or the sea!
    Look on the tragic loading of this bed.
    This is thy work. The object poisons sight;   360
    Let it be hid.   [*Bed curtains drawn.*]
                Gratiano, keep° the house,
    And seize upon the fortunes of the Moor,
    For they succeed on you. To you, lord governor,
    Remains the censure of this hellish villain,
    The time, the place, the torture. O, enforce it!   365
    Myself will straight aboard, and to the state
    This heavy act with heavy heart relate.   *Exeunt.*

QUESTIONS

1. What makes Othello a tragic figure? Is his tragedy self-inflicted or is it beyond his control? What is his tragic flaw?
2. Compare Othello's speeches from the beginning, middle, and end of the play (Acts I, III, and V). Explain the significance of their differences in style and tone.
3. Iago is a resourceful and clever character who knows how to manipulate people. Explain how he manipulates Roderigo, Cassio, and Othello.
4. What reason does Iago give for seeking Othello's destruction? Does this seem an adequate or a credible motive?
5. How does Emilia's role help us to better understand Iago? In what ways is she a *foil* (a contrasting character) to Desdemona? What other characters serve to balance each other?
6. Of what significance is Bianca's role in the play? Brabantio's?
7. *Othello* has a dual setting—Venice and Cyprus. With what values and ideas is each place associated, and how are these related to the action and themes of the play?

353*period*   end.   358*fell*   cruel.   361*keep*   remain in.

8. What ideas about love are expressed by Othello and Desdemona? What images of the sexual bond emerge in the speech and actions of Roderigo, Iago, and Emilia?
9. How does Shakespeare use Desdemona's handkerchief dramatically and symbolically? In which scenes is it most important? With what is it associated?
10. Examine the scene in which Othello kills Desdemona (Act V, Scene II). Read his speech beginning, "It is the cause" (lines 1–22). Explain how Othello sees himself at this point, and describe his state of mind.
11. Examine the scene in which Othello secretly watches Cassio talking to Bianca (Act IV, Scene I). Explain how Iago controls Othello's perception, leading him to misinterpret what he sees. In what other scenes does Iago direct other characters to misinterpret one another's actions and speech?
12. Any staging of *Othello* requires careful attention to lighting. Single out two scenes in which lighting is especially important, and explain how you would stage them.
13. Look carefully at the beginning and ending of any two acts. Consider how Shakespeare guides the audience's responses at these points. Consider also the effectiveness of each beginning and ending in relation to the development of the plot.
14. Locate two scenes in which characters' speeches shift between prose and verse. Explain the significance of these shifts.

Hamlet

Hamlet, the most famous play in English literature, continues to fascinate and challenge both readers and audiences. Interpretations of Hamlet's character and actions abound, because the play has produced so many intense and varied responses. No small indication of the tragedy's power is that actors long to play its title role.

A brief summary can suggest the movement of the plot but not the depth of Hamlet's character. After learning of his father's death, Prince Hamlet returns to the Danish court from his university studies to find Claudius, the dead king's brother, ruling Denmark and married to Hamlet's mother, Gertrude. Her remarriage within two months of his father's death has left Hamlet disillusioned, confused, and suspicious of Claudius. When his father's ghost appears before Hamlet to reveal that Claudius murdered the king, Hamlet is confronted with having to avenge his father's death.

Hamlet's efforts to carry out this obligation would have been a familiar kind of plot to Elizabethan audiences. *Revenge tragedy* was a well-established type of drama that traced its antecedents to Greek and Roman plays, particularly through the Roman playwright Seneca (c. 3 B.C.–A.D. 65), whose plays were translated and produced in English in the late sixteenth century. Shakespeare's audiences knew its conventions, particularly from Thomas Kyd's popular *Spanish Tragedy* (c. 1587). Basically, this type of play consists of a murder that has to be avenged by a relative of the victim. Typically, the victim's ghost appears to demand revenge, and invariably madness of some sort is worked into subsequent events, which ultimately result in the deaths of the murderer, the avenger, and a number of other characters. Crime, madness, ghostly anguish, poison, overheard conversations, conspiracies, and a final scene littered with corpses:

Hamlet subscribes to the basic ingredients of the formula, but it also transcends the conventions of revenge tragedy because Hamlet contemplates not merely revenge but suicide and the meaning of life itself.

Hamlet must face not only a diseased social order but also conflicts within himself when his indecisiveness becomes as agonizing as the corruption surrounding him. However, Hamlet is also a forceful and attractive character. His intelligence is repeatedly revealed in his penetrating use of language; through images and metaphors he creates a perspective on his world that is at once satiric and profoundly painful. His astonishing and sometimes shocking wit is leveled at his mother, his beloved Ophelia, and Claudius as well as himself. Nothing escapes his critical eye and divided imagination. Hamlet, no less than the people around him, is perplexed by his alienation from life.

Hamlet's limitations as well as his virtues make him one of Shakespeare's most complex characters. His keen self-awareness is both agonizing and liberating. Although he struggles throughout the play with painful issues ranging from family loyalties to matters of state, he retains his dignity as a tragic hero, whom generations of audiences have found compelling.

Hamlet, Prince of Denmark

CHARACTERS

CLAUDIUS, *King of Denmark*
HAMLET, *son to the late and nephew to the present king*
POLONIUS, *lord chamberlain*
HORATIO, *friend to Hamlet*
LAERTES, *son to Polonius*
VOLTIMAND ⎫
CORNELIUS ⎪
ROSENCRANTZ ⎬ *courtiers*
GUILDENSTERN ⎪
OSRIC ⎭
A GENTLEMAN
A PRIEST
MARCELLUS ⎫
          ⎬ *officers*
BERNARDO ⎭
FRANCISCO, *a soldier*
REYNALDO, *servant to Polonius*
PLAYERS
TWO CLOWNS, *grave-diggers*
FORTINBRAS, *Prince of Norway*
A CAPTAIN
ENGLISH AMBASSADORS

GERTRUDE, *Queen of Denmark, and mother to Hamlet*
OPHELIA, *daughter to Polonius*
GHOST *of Hamlet's Father*
(LORDS, LADIES, OFFICERS, SOLDIERS, SAILORS, MESSENGERS, AND OTHER ATTENDANTS)

Scene. *Denmark.*

ACT I

Scene I [Elsinore. A platform° before the castle.]

Enter BERNARDO *and* FRANCISCO, *two sentinels.*

BERNARDO: Who's there?
FRANCISCO: Nay, answer me:° stand, and unfold yourself.
BERNARDO: Long live the king!°
FRANCISCO: Bernardo?
BERNARDO: He.   5
FRANCISCO: You come most carefully upon your hour.
BERNARDO: 'Tis now struck twelve; get thee to bed, Francisco.
FRANCISCO: For this relief much thanks: 'tis bitter cold,
   And I am sick at heart.
BERNARDO: Have you had quiet guard?
FRANCISCO: Not a mouse stirring.   10
BERNARDO: Well, good night.
   If you do meet Horatio and Marcellus,
   The rivals° of my watch, bid them make haste.

Enter HORATIO *and* MARCELLUS.

FRANCISCO: I think I hear them. Stand, ho! Who is there?
HORATIO: Friends to this ground.
MARCELLUS: And liegemen to the Dane.   15
FRANCISCO: Give you° good night.
MARCELLUS: O, farewell, honest soldier:
   Who hath reliev'd you?
FRANCISCO: Bernardo hath my place.
   Give you good night.   *Exit* FRANCISCO.
MARCELLUS: Holla! Bernardo!
BERNARDO: Say,
   What, is Horatio there?
HORATIO: A piece of him.

I.i.   platform   *a level space on the battlements of the royal castle at Elsinore, a Danish seaport; now Helsingör.*
²**me**   *this is emphatic, since Francisco is the sentry.*   ³***Long live the king***   *either a password or greeting; Hora-tio and Marcellus use a different one in line 15.*   ¹³***rivals***   *partners.*   ¹⁶***Give you***   *God give you.*

BERNARDO: Welcome, Horatio: welcome, good Marcellus.   20
MARCELLUS: What, has this thing appear'd again to-night?
BERNARDO: I have seen nothing.
MARCELLUS: Horatio says 'tis but our fantasy,
   And will not let belief take hold of him.
   Touching this dreaded sight, twice seen of us: 25
   Therefore I have entreated him along
   With us to watch the minutes of this night;
   That if again this apparition come,
   He may approve° our eyes and speak to it.
HORATIO: Tush, tush, 'twill not appear.
BERNARDO: Sit down awhile;   30
   And let us once again assail your ears,
   That are so fortified against our story
   What we have two nights seen.
HORATIO: Well, sit we down,
   And let us hear Bernardo speak of this.
BERNARDO: Last night of all,   35
   When yond same star that's westward from the pole°
   Had made his course t' illume that part of heaven
   Where now it burns, Marcellus and myself,
   The bell then beating one,—

Enter GHOST.

MARCELLUS: Peace, break thee off; look, where it comes again!   40
BERNARDO: In the same figure, like the king that's dead.
MARCELLUS: Thou art a scholar;° speak to it, Horatio.
BERNARDO: Looks 'a not like the king? mark it, Horatio.
HORATIO: Most like: it harrows° me with fear and wonder.
BERNARDO: It would be spoke to.°
MARCELLUS: Speak to it, Horatio.   45
HORATIO: What art thou that usurp'st this time of night,
   Together with that fair and warlike form
   In which the majesty of buried Denmark°
   Did sometimes march? by heaven I charge thee, speak!
MARCELLUS: It is offended.
BERNARDO: See it stalks away!   50
HORATIO: Stay! speak, speak! I charge thee, speak!   *Exit* GHOST.
MARCELLUS: 'Tis gone, and will not answer.
BERNARDO: How now, Horatio! you tremble and look pale:
   Is not this something more than fantasy?
   What think you on 't?   55
HORATIO: Before my God, I might not this believe

---

²⁹**approve** *corroborate.*   ³⁶**pole** *polestar.*   ⁴²**scholar** *exorcisms were performed in Latin, which Horatio as an educated man would be able to speak.*   ⁴⁴**harrows** *lacerates the feelings.*   ⁴⁵**It . . . to** *a ghost could not speak until spoken to.*   ⁴⁸**buried Denmark** *the buried king of Denmark.*

Without the sensible and true avouch
Of mine own eyes.
MARCELLUS: Is it not like the king?
HORATIO: As thou art to thyself:
  Such was the very armour he had on   60
  When he the ambitious Norway combated;
  So frown'd he once, when, in an angry parle,
  He smote° the sledded Polacks° on the ice.
  'Tis strange.
MARCELLUS: Thus twice before, and jump° at this dead hour,   65
  With martial stalk hath he gone by our watch.
HORATIO: In what particular thought to work I know not;
  But in the gross and scope° of my opinion,
  This bodes some strange eruption to our state.
MARCELLUS: Good now,° sit down, and tell me, he that knows,   70
  Why this same strict and most observant watch
  So nightly toils° the subject° of the land,
  And why such daily cast° of brazen cannon,
  And foreign mart° for implements of war;
  Why such impress° of shipwrights, whose sore task   75
  Does not divide the Sunday from the week;
  What might be toward, that this sweaty haste
  Doth make the night joint-labourer with the day:
  Who is't that can inform me?
HORATIO: That can I;
  At least, the whisper goes so. Our last king,   80
  Whose image even but now appear'd to us,
  Was, as you know, by Fortinbras of Norway,
  Thereto prick'd on° by a most emulate° pride,
  Dar'd to the combat; in which our valiant Hamlet—
  For so this side of our known world esteem'd him—   85
  Did slay this Fortinbras; who, by a seal'd compact,
  Well ratified by law and heraldry,°
  Did forfeit, with his life, all those his lands
  Which he stood seiz'd° of, to the conqueror:
  Against the which, a moiety competent°   90
  Was gaged by our king; which had return'd
  To the inheritance of Fortinbras,
  Had he been vanquisher; as, by the same comart,°
  And carriage° of the article design'd,
  His fell to Hamlet. Now, sir, young Fortinbras,   95

---

[63]**smote** *defeated.*   [63]**sledded Polacks** *Polanders using sledges.*   [65]**jump** *exactly.*   [68]**gross and scope** *general drift.*   [70]**Good now** *an expression denoting entreaty or expostulation.*   [72]**toils** *causes or makes to toil.*   [72]**subject** *people, subjects.*   [73]**cast** *casting, founding.*   [74]**mart** *buying and selling, traffic.*   [75]**impress** *impressment.*   [83]**prick'd on** *incited.*   [83]**emulate** *rivaling.*   [87]**law and heraldry** *heraldic law, governing combat.*   [89]**seiz'd** *possessed.*   [90]**moiety competent** *adequate or sufficient portion.*   [93]**comart** *joint bargain.*   [94]**carriage** *import, bearing.*

Of unimproved° mettle hot and full,°
Hath in the skirts of Norway here and there
Shark'd up° a list of lawless resolutes,°
For food and diet,° to some enterprise
That hath a stomach in't; which is no other—   100
As it doth well appear unto our state—
But to recover of us, by strong hand
And terms compulsatory, those foresaid lands
So by his father lost: and this, I take it,
Is the main motive of our preparations,   105
The source of this our watch and the chief head
Of this post-haste and romage° in the land.

BERNARDO: I think it be no other but e'en so:
   Well may it sort° that this portentous figure
   Comes armed through our watch; so like the king   110
   That was and is the question of these wars.

HORATIO: A mote° it is to trouble the mind's eye.
   In the most high and palmy state° of Rome,
   A little ere the mightiest Julius fell,
   The graves stood tenantless and the sheeted dead   115
   Did squeak and gibber in the Roman streets:
   As stars with trains of fire° and dews of blood,
   Disasters° in the sun; and the moist star°
   Upon whose influence Neptune's empire° stands
   Was sick almost to doomsday with eclipse: 120
   And even the like precurse° of fear'd events,
   As harbingers preceding still the fates
   And prologue to the omen coming on,
   Have heaven and earth together demonstrated
   Unto our climatures and countrymen.—   125

Enter GHOST.

But soft, behold! lo, where it comes again!
I'll cross° it, though it blast me. Stay, illusion!
If thou hast any sound, or use of voice,
Speak to me!   *It° spreads his arms.*
If there be any good thing to be done,   130
That may to thee do ease and grace to me,
Speak to me!
If thou art privy to thy country's fate,
Which, happily, foreknowing may avoid,

---

[96]**unimproved** *not turned to account.* [96]**hot and full** *full of fight.* [98]**Shark'd up** *got together in hap-*
hazard fashion. [98]**resolutes** *desperadoes.* [99]**food and diet** *no pay but their keep.* [107]**romage**
bustle, commotion. [109]**sort** *suit.* [112]**mote** *speck of dust* [113]**palmy state** *triumphant sovereignty.*
[117]**stars . . . fire** *i.e., comets.* [118]**Disasters** *unfavorable aspects.* [118]**moist star** *the moon, governing*
tides. [119]**Neptune's empire** *the sea.* [121]**precurse** *heralding.* [127]**cross** *meet, face, thus bringing*
down the evil influence on the person who crosses it. [129]**It** *the Ghost, or perhaps Horatio.* [133–139]**If . . .**
it *Horatio recites the traditional reasons why ghosts might walk.*

O, speak!   135
Or if thou hast uphoarded in thy life
Extorted treasure in the womb of earth,
For which, they say, you spirits oft walk in death,   *The cock crows.*
Speak of it:° stay, and speak! Stop it, Marcellus.
MARCELLUS: Shall I strike at it with my partisan?°   140
HORATIO: Do, if it will not stand.
BERNARDO: 'Tis here!
HORATIO: 'Tis here!
MARCELLUS: 'Tis gone!   [*Exit* GHOST.]
   We do it wrong, being so majestical,
   To offer it the show of violence;
   For it is, as the air, invulnerable,   145
   And our vain blows malicious mockery.
BERNARDO: It was about to speak, when the cock crew.°
HORATIO: And then it started like a guilty thing
   Upon a fearful summons. I have heard,
   The cock, that is the trumpet to the morn,   150
   Doth with his lofty and shrill-sounding throat
   Awake the god of day; and, at his warning,
   Whether in sea or fire, in earth or air,
   Th' extravagant and erring° spirit hies
   To his confine:° and of the truth herein   155
   This present object made probation.°
MARCELLUS: It faded on the crowing of the cock.
   Some say that ever 'gainst° that season comes
   Wherein our Saviour's birth is celebrated,
   The bird of dawning singeth all night long: 160
   And then, they say, no spirit dare stir abroad;
   The nights are wholesome; then no planets strike,°
   No fairy takes, nor witch hath power to charm,
   So hallow'd and so gracious° is that time.
HORATIO: So have I heard and do in part believe it.   165
   But, look, the morn, in russet mantle clad,
   Walks o'er the dew of yon high eastward hill:
   Break we our watch up; and by my advice,
   Let us impart what we have seen to-night
   Unto young Hamlet; for, upon my life,   170
   This spirit, dumb to us, will speak to him.
   Do you consent we shall acquaint him with it,
   As needful in our loves, fitting our duty?
MARCELLUS: Let's do 't, I pray; and I this morning know
   Where we shall find him most conveniently.   *Exeunt.* 175

---

¹⁴⁰**partisan**   *long-handled spear with a blade having lateral projections.*   ¹⁴⁷**cock crew**   *according to tradi-*
tional ghost lore, spirits returned to their confines at cockcrow.   ¹⁵⁴**extravagant and erring**   *wandering. Both*
words mean the same thing.   ¹⁵⁵**confine**   *place of confinement.*   ¹⁵⁶**probation**   *proof, trial.*   ¹⁵⁸**'gainst**
just before.   ¹⁶²**planets strike**   *was thought that planets were malignant and might strike travelers by night.*
¹⁶⁴**gracious**   *full of goodness.*

Scene II [*A room of state in the castle.*]

Flourish. Enter CLAUDIUS, *King of Denmark,* GERTRUDE *the Queen,* COUNCILORS, POLONIUS *and his Son* LAERTES, HAMLET, *cum aliis*° [*including* VOLTIMAND *and* CORNELIUS].

KING: Though yet of Hamlet our dear brother's death
    The memory be green, and that it us befitted
    To bear our hearts in grief and our whole kingdom
    To be contracted in one brow of woe,
    Yet so far hath discretion fought with nature   5
    That we with wisest sorrow think on him,
    Together with remembrance of ourselves.
    Therefore our sometime sister, now our queen,
    Th' imperial jointress° to this warlike state,
    Have we, as 'twere with a defeated joy,—   10
    With an auspicious and a dropping eye,
    With mirth in funeral and with dirge in marriage,
    In equal scale weighing delight and dole,—
    Taken to wife: nor have we herein barr'd
    Your better wisdoms, which have freely gone   15
    With this affair along. For all, our thanks.
    Now follows, that° you know, young Fortinbras,
    Holding a weak supposal° of our worth,
    Or thinking by our late dear brother's death
    Our state to be disjoint° and out of frame,°   20
    Colleagued° with this dream of his advantage,°
    He hath not fail'd to pester us with message,
    Importing° the surrender of those lands
    Lost by his father, with all bands of law,
    To our most valiant brother. So much for him.   25
    Now for ourself and for this time of meeting:
    Thus much the business is: we have here writ
    To Norway, uncle of young Fortinbras,—
    Who, impotent and bed-rid, scarcely hears
    Of this his nephew's purpose,—to suppress   30
    His further gait° herein; in that the levies,
    The lists and full proportions, are all made
    Out of his subject:° and we here dispatch
    You, good Cornelius, and you, Voltimand,
    For bearers of this greeting to old Norway;   35
    Giving to you no further personal power
    To business with the king, more than the scope

I.ii. *cum aliis* with others. [9]*jointress* woman possessed of a jointure, or, joint tenancy of an estate. [17]*that* that which. [18]*weak supposal* low estimate. [20]*disjoint* distracted, out of joint. [20]*frame* order. [21]*Colleagued* added to. [21]*dream . . . advantage* visionary hope of success. [23]*Importing* purporting, pertaining to. [31]*gait* proceeding. [33]*Out of his subject* at the expense of Norway's subjects (collectively).

Of these delated° articles allow.
Farewell, and let your haste commend your duty.

CORNELIUS:
VOLTIMAND: } In that and all things will we show our duty.   40

KING: We doubt it nothing: heartily farewell.

[*Exeunt* VOLTIMAND *and* CORNELIUS.]

And now, Laertes, what's the news with you?
You told us of some suit; what is't, Laertes?
You cannot speak of reason to the Dane,°
And lose your voice:° what wouldst thou beg, Laertes,   45
That shall not be my offer, not thy asking?
The head is not more native° to the heart,
The hand more instrumental° to the mouth,
Than is the throne of Denmark to thy father.
What wouldst thou have, Laertes?

LAERTES: My dread lord,   50
Your leave and favour to return to France;
From whence though willingly I came to Denmark,
To show my duty in your coronation,
Yet now, I must confess, that duty done,
My thoughts and wishes bend again toward France   55
And bow them to your gracious leave and pardon.°

KING: Have you your father's leave? What says Polonius?

POLONIUS: He hath, my lord, wrung from me my slow leave
By laboursome petition, and at last
Upon his will I seal'd my hard consent: 60
I do beseech you, give him leave to go.

KING: Take thy fair hour, Laertes; time be thine,
And thy best graces spend it at thy will!
But now, my cousin° Hamlet, and my son,—

HAMLET [*aside*]: A little more than kin, and less than kind!°   65

KING: How is it that the clouds still hang on you?

HAMLET: Not so, my lord; I am too much in the sun.°

QUEEN: Good Hamlet, cast thy nighted colour off,
And let thine eye look like a friend on Denmark.
Do not for ever with thy vailed lids   70
Seek for thy noble father in the dust:
Thou know'st 'tis common; all that lives must die,
Passing through nature to eternity.

---

[38] *delated   expressly stated.*   [44] *the Dane   Danish king.*   [45] *lose your voice   speak in vain.*   [47] *native
closely connected, related.*   [48] *instrumental   serviceable.*   [56] *leave and pardon   permission to depart.*
[64] *cousin   any kin not of the immediate family.*   [65] *A little . . . kind   i.e., my relation to you has become more
than kinship warrants; it has also become unnatural.*   [67] *I am . . . sun   the senses seem to be: I am too much out
of doors, I am too much in the sun of your grace (ironical), I am too much of a son to you. Possibly an allusion to the
proverb "Out of heaven's blessing into the warm sun"; i.e., Hamlet is out of house and home in being deprived of the
kingship.*

HAMLET: Ay, madam, it is common.°

QUEEN: If it be,
  Why seems it so particular with thee?   75

HAMLET: Seems, madam! nay, it is; I know not "seems."
  'Tis not alone my inky cloak, good mother,
  Nor customary suits° of solemn black,
  Nor windy suspiration° of forc'd breath,
  No, nor the fruitful river in the eye,   80
  Nor the dejected 'haviour of the visage,
  Together with all forms, moods, shapes of grief,
  That can denote me truly: these indeed seem,
  For they are actions that a man might play:
  But I have that within which passeth show;   85
  These but the trappings and the suits of woe.

KING: 'Tis sweet and commendable in your nature, Hamlet,
  To give these mourning duties to your father:
  But, you must know, your father lost a father;
  That father lost, lost his, and the survivor bound   90
  In filial obligation for some term
  To do obsequious° sorrow: but to persever
  In obstinate condolement° is a course
  Of impious stubbornness; 'tis unmanly grief;
  It shows a will most incorrect° to heaven,   95
  A heart unfortified, a mind impatient,
  An understanding simple and unschool'd:
  For what we know must be and is as common
  As any the most vulgar thing° to sense,
  Why should we in our peevish opposition   100
  Take it to heart? Fie! 'tis a fault to heaven,
  A fault against the dead, a fault to nature,
  To reason most absurd; whose common theme
  Is death of fathers, and who still hath cried,
  From the first corse till he that died to-day,   105
  "This must be so." We pray you, throw to earth
  This unprevailing° woe, and think of us
  As of a father: for let the world take note,
  You are the most immediate° to our throne;
  And with no less nobility° of love   110
  Than that which dearest father bears his son,
  Do I impart° toward you. For your intent
  In going back to school in Wittenberg,°
  It is most retrograde° to our desire:

---

[74]*Ay . . . common* i.e., *it is common, but it hurts nevertheless; possibly a reference to the commonplace quality of the queen's remark.* [78]*customary suits* *suits prescribed by custom for mourning.* [79]*windy suspiration* *heavy sighing.* [92]*obsequious* *dutiful.* [93]*condolement* *sorrowing.* [95]*incorrect* *Untrained, uncorrected.* [99]*vulgar thing* *common experience.* [107]*unprevailing* *unavailing.* [109]*most immediate* *next in succession.* [110]*nobility* *high degree.* [112]*impart* *the object is apparently love (l.110).* [113]*Wittenberg* *famous German university founded in 1502.* [114]*retrograde* *contrary.*

And we beseech you, bend you° to remain 115
Here, in the cheer and comfort of our eye,
Our chiefest courtier, cousin, and our son.

QUEEN: Let not thy mother lose her prayers, Hamlet:
I pray thee, stay with us; go not to Wittenberg.

HAMLET: I shall in all my best obey you, madam. 120

KING: Why, 'tis a loving and a fair reply:
Be as ourself in Denmark. Madam, come;
This gentle and unforc'd accord of Hamlet
Sits smiling to my heart: in grace whereof,
No jocund health that Denmark drinks to-day, 125
But the great cannon to the clouds shall tell,
And the king's rouse° the heaven shall bruit again,°
Re-speaking earthly thunder. Come away.

Flourish. Exeunt all but HAMLET.

HAMLET: O, that this too too sullied flesh would melt,
Thaw and resolve itself into a dew! 130
Or that the Everlasting had not fix'd
His canon 'gainst self-slaughter! O God! God!
How weary, stale, flat and unprofitable,
Seem to me all the uses of this world!
Fie on 't! ah fie! 'tis an unweeded garden, 135
That grows to seed; things rank and gross in nature
Possess it merely.° That it should come to this!
But two months dead: nay, not so much, not two:
So excellent a king; that was, to this,
Hyperion° to a satyr; so loving to my mother 140
That he might not beteem° the winds of heaven
Visit her face too roughly. Heaven and earth!
Must I remember? why, she would hang on him,
As if increase of appetite had grown
By what it fed on: and yet, within a month— 145
Let me not think on 't—Frailty, thy name is woman!—
A little month, or ere those shoes were old
With which she followed my poor father's body,
Like Niobe,° all tears:—why she, even she—
O God! a beast, that wants discourse of reason,° 150
Would have mourn'd longer—married with my uncle,
My father's brother, but no more like my father
Than I to Hercules: within a month:
Ere yet the salt of most unrighteous tears
Had left the flushing in her galled° eyes, 155

---

¹¹⁵**bend you**   *incline yourself; imperative.*   ¹²⁷**rouse**   *draft of liquor.*   ¹²⁷**bruit again**   *echo.*   ¹³⁷**merely**
completely, entirely.   ¹⁴⁰**Hyperion**   *God of the sun in the older regime of ancient gods.*   ¹⁴¹**beteem**   *allow.*
¹⁴⁹**Niobe**   *Tantalus's daughter, who boasted that she had more sons and daughters than Leto; for this Apollo and
Artemis slew her children. She was turned into stone by Zeus on Mount Sipylus.*   ¹⁵⁰**discourse of reason**   *process
or faculty of reason.*   ¹⁵⁵**galled**   *irritated.*

She married. O, most wicked speed, to post
With such dexterity° to incestuous sheets!
It is not nor it cannot come to good:
But break, my heart; for I must hold my tongue.

Enter HORATIO, MARCELLUS, *and* BERNARDO.

HORATIO: Hail to your lordship!
HAMLET: I am glad to see you well: 160
   Horatio!—or I do forget myself.
HORATIO: The same, my lord, and your poor servant ever.
HAMLET: Sir, my good friend; I'll change that name with you:°
   And what make you from Wittenberg, Horatio?
   Marcellus?   165
MARCELLUS: My good lord—
HAMLET: I am very glad to see you. Good even, sir.
   But what, in faith, make you from Wittenberg?
HORATIO: A truant disposition, good my lord.
HAMLET: I would not hear your enemy say so,   170
   Nor shall you do my ear that violence,
   To make it truster of your own report
   Against yourself: I know you are no truant.
   But what is your affair in Elsinore?
   We'll teach you to drink deep ere you depart.   175
HORATIO: My lord, I came to see your father's funeral.
HAMLET: I prithee, do not mock me, fellow-student;
   I think it was to see my mother's wedding.
HORATIO: Indeed, my lord, it follow'd hard° upon.
HAMLET: Thrift, thrift, Horatio! the funeral bak'd meats°   180
   Did coldly furnish forth the marriage tables.
   Would I had met my dearest° foe in heaven
   Or ever I had seen that day, Horatio!
   My father!—methinks I see my father.
HORATIO: Where, my lord!
HAMLET: In my mind's eye, Horatio.   185
HORATIO: I saw him once; 'a° was a goodly king.
HAMLET: 'A was a man, take him for all in all,
   I shall not look upon his like again.
HORATIO: My lord, I think I saw him yesternight.
HAMLET: Saw? who?   190
HORATIO: My lord, the king your father.
HAMLET: The king my father!
HORATIO: Season your admiration° for a while
   With an attent ear, till I may deliver,

157**dexterity** *facility.*   163**I'll . . . you** *I'll be your servant, you shall be my friend; also explained as "I'll exchange the name of friend with you."*   179**hard** *close.*   180**bak'd meats** *meat pies.*   182**dearest** *direst; the adjective* dear *in Shakespeare has two different origins: O.E.* deore, *"beloved," and O.E.* deor, *"fierce." Dearest is the superlative of the second.*   186**'a** *he.*   192**Season your admiration** *restrain your astonishment.*

Upon the witness of these gentlemen,
This marvel to you.

HAMLET: For God's love, let me hear.   195

HORATIO: Two nights together had these gentlemen,
Marcellus and Bernardo, on their watch,
In the dead waste and middle of the night,
Been thus encount'red. A figure like your father,
Armed at point exactly, cap-a-pe,°   200
Appears before them, and with solemn march
Goes slow and stately by them: thrice he walk'd
By their oppress'd° and fear-surprised eyes,
Within his truncheon's° length; whilst they, distill'd°
Almost to jelly with the act° of fear,   205
Stand dumb and speak not to him. This to me
In dreadful secrecy impart they did;
And I with them the third night kept the watch:
Where, as they had deliver'd, both in time,
Form of the thing, each word made true and good,   210
The apparition comes: I knew your father;
These hands are not more like.

HAMLET: But where was this?

MARCELLUS: My lord, upon the platform where we watch'd.

HAMLET: Did you not speak to it?

HORATIO: My lord, I did;
But answer made it none: yet once methought   215
It lifted up it° head and did address
Itself to motion, like as it would speak;
But even then the morning cock crew loud,
And at the sound it shrunk in haste away,
And vanish'd from our sight.

HAMLET: 'Tis very strange.   220

HORATIO: As I do live, my honour'd lord, 'tis true;
And we did think it writ down in our duty
To let you know of it.

HAMLET: Indeed, indeed, sirs, but this troubles me.
Hold you the watch to-night?

MARCELLUS: ⎫
BERNARDO: ⎭   We do, my lord.   225

HAMLET: Arm'd, say you?

MARCELLUS: ⎫
BERNARDO: ⎭ Arm'd, my lord.

HAMLET: From top to toe?

MARCELLUS: ⎫
BERNARDO: ⎭   My lord, from head to foot.

HAMLET: Then saw you not his face?

200*cap-a-pe from head to foot.*   203*oppress'd   distressed.*   204*truncheon officer's staff.*   204*dis-*
till'd softened, weakened.   205*act action.*   216*it its.*

HORATIO: O, yes, my lord; he wore his beaver° up.　　　　　230

HAMLET: What, look'd he frowningly?

HORATIO:　　　　　　　　　　　　　A countenance more
　　In sorrow than in anger.

HAMLET:　　　　　　　　　　Pale or red?

HORATIO: Nay, very pale.

HAMLET:　　　　　　　　　And fix'd his eyes upon you?

HORATIO: Most constantly.

HAMLET:　　　　　　　　　　　I would I had been there.

HORATIO: It would have much amaz'd you.　　　　　235

HAMLET: Very like, very like. Stay'd it long?

HORATIO: While one with moderate haste might tell a hundred.

MARCELLUS: ⎫
　　　　　　　⎬ Longer, longer.
BERNARDO: ⎭

HORATIO: Not when I saw't.

HAMLET:　　　　　　　　His beard was grizzled,—no?

HORATIO: It was, as I have seen it in his life,　　　　　240
　　A sable° silver'd.

HAMLET:　　　　　　　I will watch to-night;
　　Perchance 'twill walk again.

HORATIO:　　　　　　　　　　I warr'nt it will.

HAMLET: If it assume my noble father's person,
　　I'll speak to it, though hell itself should gape
　　And bid me hold my peace. I pray you all,　　　　　245
　　If you have hitherto conceal'd this sight,
　　Let it be tenable in your silence still;
　　And whatsoever else shall hap to-night,
　　Give it an understanding, but no tongue:
　　I will requite your loves. So, fare you well:　　　　　250
　　Upon the platform, 'twixt eleven and twelve,
　　I'll visit you.

ALL:　　　　　　　　Our duty to your honour.

HAMLET: Your loves, as mine to you: farewell.　　　　*Exeunt [all but HAMLET].*
　　My father's spirit in arms! all is not well;
　　I doubt° some foul play: would the night were come!　　　　255
　　Till then sit still, my soul: foul deeds will rise,
　　Though all the earth o'erwhelm them, to men's eyes.　　　　*Exit.*

Scene III [A room in Polonius's house.]

Enter LAERTES *and* OPHELIA, *his Sister.*

LAERTES: My necessaries are embark'd: farewell:
　　And, sister, as the winds give benefit
　　And convoy is assistant,° do not sleep,
　　But let me hear from you.

---

²³⁰**beaver** *visor on the helmet.*　　²⁴¹**sable** *black color.*　　²⁵⁵**doubt** *fear.*　　**I.iii.**　　³**convoy is assistant** *means of conveyance are available.*

OPHELIA: Do you doubt that?

LAERTES: For Hamlet and the trifling of his favour,   5
   Hold it a fashion° and a toy in blood,°
   A violet in the youth of primy° nature,
   Forward,° not permanent, sweet, not lasting,
   The perfume and suppliance of a minute;°
   No more.

OPHELIA: No more but so?

LAERTES: Think it no more: 10
   For nature, crescent,° does not grow alone
   In thews° and bulk, but, as this temple° waxes,
   The inward service of the mind and soul
   Grows wide withal. Perhaps he loves you now,
   And now no soil° nor cautel° doth besmirch   15
   The virtue of his will: but you must fear,
   His greatness weigh'd,° his will is not his own;
   For he himself is subject to his birth:
   He may not, as unvalued persons do,
   Carve for himself; for on his choice depends   20
   The safety and health of this whole state;
   And therefore must his choice be circumscrib'd
   Unto the voice and yielding° of that body
   Whereof he is the head. Then if he says he loves you,
   It fits your wisdom so far to believe it   25
   As he in his particular act and place
   May give his saying deed;° which is no further
   Than the main voice of Denmark goes withal.
   Then weigh what loss your honour may sustain,
   If with too credent° ear you list his songs,   30
   Or lose your heart, or your chaste treasure open
   To his unmast'red° importunity.
   Fear it, Ophelia, fear it, my dear sister,
   And keep you in the rear of your affection,
   Out of the shot and danger of desire.   35
   The chariest° maid is prodigal enough,
   If she unmask her beauty to the moon:
   Virtue itself 'scapes not calumnious strokes:
   The canker galls the infants of the spring,°
   Too oft before their buttons° be disclos'd,°   40
   And in the morn and liquid dew° of youth
   Contagious blastments° are most imminent.

---

⁶*fashion* custom, prevailing usage.   ⁶*toy in blood* passing amorous fancy.   ⁷*primy* in its prime.   ⁸*For-*
ward precocious.   ⁹*suppliance of a minute* diversion to fill up a minute.   ¹¹*crescent* growing, waxing.
¹²*thews* bodily strength.   ¹²*temple* body.   ¹⁵*soil* blemish.   ¹⁵*cautel* crafty device.   ¹⁷*great-*
ness weigh'd high position considered.   ²³*voice and yielding* assent, approval.   ²⁷*deed* effect.
³⁰*credent* credulous.   ³²*unmast'red* unrestrained.   ³⁶*chariest* most scrupulously modest.   ³⁹*The canker*
. . . spring the cankerworm destroys the young plants of spring.   ⁴⁰*buttons* buds.   ⁴⁰*disclos'd* opened.
⁴¹*liquid dew* i.e., time when dew is fresh.   ⁴²*blastments* blights.

Be wary then; best safety lies in fear:
Youth to itself rebels, though none else near.

OPHELIA: I shall the effect of this good lesson keep,   45
As watchman to my heart. But, good my brother,
Do not, as some ungracious° pastors do,
Show me the steep and thorny way to heaven;
Whiles, like a puff'd° and reckless libertine,
Himself the primrose path of dalliance treads,   50
And recks° not his own rede.°

Enter POLONIUS.

LAERTES: O, fear me not.
I stay too long: but here my father comes.
A double° blessing is a double grace;
Occasion° smiles upon a second leave.

POLONIUS: Yet here, Laertes? aboard, aboard, for shame!   55
The wind sits in the shoulder of your sail,
And you are stay'd for. There; my blessing with thee!
And these few precepts° in thy memory
Look thou character.° Give thy thoughts no tongue,
Nor any unproportion'd° thought his act.   60
Be thou familiar, but by no means vulgar.°
Those friends thou hast, and their adoption tried,
Grapple them to thy soul with hoops of steel;
But do not dull thy palm with entertainment
Of each new-hatch'd, unfledg'd° comrade. Beware   65
Of entrance to a quarrel, but being in,
Bear't that th' opposed may beware of thee.
Give every man thy ear, but few thy voice;
Take each man's censure, but reserve thy judgement.
Costly thy habit as thy purse can buy,   70
But not express'd in fancy;° rich, not gaudy;
For the apparel oft proclaims the man,
And they in France of the best rank and station
Are of a most select and generous chief in that.°
Neither a borrower nor a lender be;   75
For loan oft loses both itself and friend,
And borrowing dulleth edge of husbandry.°
This above all: to thine own self be true,
And it must follow, as the night the day,

---

⁴⁷**ungracious** *graceless.*   ⁴⁹**puff'd** *bloated.*   ⁵¹**recks** *heeds.*   ⁵¹**rede** *counsel.*   ⁵³**double** *i.e.,*
Laertes has already bade his father good-by.   ⁵⁴**Occasion** *opportunity.*   ⁵⁸**precepts** *many parallels have*
been found to the series of maxims which follows, one of the closer being that in Lyly's Euphues.   ⁵⁹**character**
inscribe.   ⁶⁰**unproportion'd** *inordinate.*   ⁶¹**vulgar** *common.*   ⁶⁵**unfledg'd** *immature.*   ⁷¹**express'd**
in fancy *fantastical in design.*   ⁷⁴**Are . . . that** *chief is usually taken as a substantive meaning "head," "emi-*
nence."   ⁷⁷**husbandry** *thrift.*

Thou canst not then be false to any man. 80
Farewell: my blessing season° this in thee!
LAERTES: Most humbly do I take my leave, my lord.
POLONIUS: The time invites you; go; your servants tend.
LAERTES: Farewell, Ophelia; and remember well
  What I have said to you.
OPHELIA: 'Tis in my memory lock'd, 85
  And you yourself shall keep the key of it.
LAERTES: Farewell.   *Exit* LAERTES.
POLONIUS: What is 't, Ophelia, he hath said to you?
OPHELIA: So please you, something touching the Lord Hamlet.
POLONIUS: Marry, well bethought: 90
  'Tis told me, he hath very oft of late
  Given private time to you; and you yourself
  Have of your audience been most free and bounteous:
  If it be so, as so't is put on° me,
  And that in way of caution, I must tell you, 95
  You do not understand yourself so clearly
  As it behooves my daughter and your honour.
  What is between you? give me up the truth.
OPHELIA: He hath, my lord, of late made many tenders°
  Of his affection to me. 100
POLONIUS: Affection! pooh! you speak like a green girl,
  Unsifted° in such perilous circumstance.
  Do you believe his tenders, as you call them?
OPHELIA: I do not know, my lord, what I should think.
POLONIUS: Marry, I will teach you: think yourself a baby; 105
  That you have ta'en these tenders° for true pay,
  Which are not sterling.° Tender° yourself more dearly;
  Or—not to crack the wind° of the poor phrase,
  Running it thus—you'll tender me a fool.°
OPHELIA: My lord, he hath importun'd me with love 110
  In honourable fashion.
POLONIUS: Ay, fashion° you may call it; go to, go to.
OPHELIA: And hath given countenance° to his speech, my lord,
  With almost all the holy vows of heaven.
POLONIUS: Ay, springes° to catch woodcocks.° I do know, 115
  When the blood burns, how prodigal the soul
  Lends the tongue vows: these blazes, daughter,
  Giving more light than heat, extinct in both,
  Even in their promise, as it is a-making,
  You must not take for fire. From this time 120

---

⁸¹*season* mature. ⁹⁴*put on* impressed on. ⁹⁹, ¹⁰³*tenders* offers. ¹⁰²*Unsifted* untried. ¹⁰⁶*tenders* promises to pay. ¹⁰⁷*sterling* legal currency. ¹⁰⁷*Tender* hold. ¹⁰⁸*crack the wind* i.e., run it until it is broken-winded. ¹⁰⁹*tender . . . fool* show me a fool (for a daughter). ¹¹²*fashion* mere form, pretense. ¹¹³*countenance* credit, support. ¹¹⁵*springes* snares. ¹¹⁵*woodcocks* birds easily caught, type of stupidity.

Be somewhat scanter of your maiden presence;
Set your entreatments° at a higher rate
Than a command to parley.° For Lord Hamlet,
Believe so much in him,° that he is young,
And with a larger tether may he walk   125
Than may be given you: in few,° Ophelia,
Do not believe his vows; for they are brokers;°
Not of that dye° which their investments° show,
But mere implorators of° unholy suits,
Breathing° like sanctified and pious bawds,   130
The better to beguile. This is for all:
I would not, in plain terms, from this time forth,
Have you so slander° any moment leisure,
As to give words or talk with the Lord Hamlet.
Look to 't, I charge you: come your ways.   135
OPHELIA: I shall obey, my lord.   *Exeunt.*

Scene IV [The platform.]

Enter HAMLET, HORATIO, *and* MARCELLUS.

HAMLET: The air bites shrewdly; it is very cold.
HORATIO: It is a nipping and an eager air.
HAMLET: What hour now?
HORATIO: I think it lacks of twelve.
MARCELLUS: No, it is struck.
HORATIO: Indeed? I heard it not: then it draws near the season   5
  Wherein the spirit held his wont to walk.

A flourish of trumpets, and two pieces go off.

What does this mean, my lord?
HAMLET: The king doth wake° to-night and takes his rouse,°
  Keeps wassail,° and the swagg'ring up-spring° reels;°
  And, as he drains his draughts of Rhenish° down,   10
  The kettle-drum and trumpet thus bray out
  The triumph of his pledge.°
HORATIO: Is it a custom?
HAMLET: Ay, marry, is 't:
  But to my mind, though I am native here
  And to the manner born,° it is a custom   15

entreatments *conversations, interviews.* [123]command to parley *mere invitation to talk.* [124]so . . . him
this much concerning him. [126]in few *briefly.* [127]brokers *go-betweens, procurers.* [128]dye *color or*
sort. [128]investments *clothes.* [129]implorators of *solicitors of.* [130]Breathing *speaking.* [133]slan-
der *bring disgrace or reproach upon.* I.iv. [8]wake *stay awake, hold revel.* [8]rouse *carouse, drinking*
bout. [9]wassail *carousal.* [9]up-spring *last and wildest dance at German merry-makings.* [9]reels *reels*
through. [10]Rhenish *rhine wine.* [12]triumph . . . pledge *his glorious achievement as a drinker.* [15]to
. . . born *destined by birth to be subject to the custom in question.*

More honour'd in the breach than the observance.
This heavy-headed revel east and west
Makes us traduc'd and tax'd of other nations:
They clepe° us drunkards, and with swinish phrase°
Soil our addition;° and indeed it takes   20
From our achievements, though perform'd at height,
The pith and marrow of our attribute.°
So, oft it chances in particular men,
That for some vicious mole of nature° in them,
As, in their birth—wherein they are not guilty,   25
Since nature cannot choose his origin—
By the o'ergrowth of some complexion,
Oft breaking down the pales° and forts of reason,
Or by some habit that too much o'er-leavens°
The form of plausive° manners, that these men,   30
Carrying, I say, the stamp of one defect,
Being nature's livery,° or fortune's star,°—
Their virtues else—be they as pure as grace,
As infinite as man may undergo—
Shall in the general censure take corruption   35
From that particular fault: the dram of eale°
Doth all the noble substance of a doubt
To his own scandal.°

Enter GHOST.

HORATIO: Look, my lord, it comes!
HAMLET: Angels and ministers of grace° defend us!
Be thou a spirit of health or goblin damn'd,   40
Bring with thee airs from heaven or blasts from hell,
Be thy intents wicked or charitable,
Thou com'st in such a questionable° shape
That I will speak to thee: I'll call thee Hamlet,
King, father, royal Dane: O, answer me!   45
Let me not burst in ignorance; but tell
Why thy canoniz'd° bones, hearsed° in death,
Have burst their cerements;° why the sepulchre,
Wherein we saw thee quietly interr'd,
Hath op'd his ponderous and marble jaws,   50
To cast thee up again. What may this mean,

---

¹⁹*clepe* call.   ¹⁹*with swinish phrase* by calling us swine.   ²⁰*addition* reputation.   ²²*attribute* reputation.   ²⁴*mole of nature* natural blemish in one's constitution.   ²⁸*pales* palings (as of a fortification).   ²⁹*o'er-leavens* induces a change throughout (as yeast works in bread).   ³⁰*plausive* pleasing.   ³²*nature's livery* endowment from nature.   ³²*fortune's star* the position in which one is placed by fortune, a reference to astrology. The two phrases are aspects of the same thing.   ³⁶⁻³⁸*the dram . . . scandal* a famous crux.   ³⁶*dram of eale* has had various interpretations, the preferred one being probably, "a dram of evil."   ³⁹*ministers of grace* messengers of God.   ⁴³*questionable* inviting question or conversation.   ⁴⁷*canoniz'd* buried according to the canons of the church.   ⁴⁷*hearsed* coffined.   ⁴⁸*cerements* grave-clothes.

That thou, dead corse, again in complete steel
Revisits thus the glimpses of the moon,°
Making night hideous; and we fools of nature°
So horridly to shake our disposition   55
With thoughts beyond the reaches of our souls?
Say, why is this? wherefore? what should we do?

[GHOST] beckons [HAMLET].

HORATIO: It beckons you to go away with it,
   As if it some impartment° did desire
   To you alone.
MARCELLUS: Look, with what courteous action   60
   It waves you to a more removed° ground:
   But do not go with it.
HORATIO: No, by no means.
HAMLET: It will not speak; then I will follow it.
HORATIO: Do not, my lord!
HAMLET: Why, what should be the fear?
   I do not set my life at a pin's fee;   65
   And for my soul, what can it do to that,
   Being a thing immortal as itself?
   It waves me forth again: I'll follow it.
HORATIO: What if it tempt you toward the flood, my lord,
   Or to the dreadful summit of the cliff   70
   That beetles o'er° his base into the sea,
   And there assume some other horrible form,
   Which might deprive your sovereignty of reason°
   And draw you into madness? think of it:
   The very place puts toys of desperation,°   75
   Without more motive, into every brain
   That looks so many fathoms to the sea
   And hears it roar beneath.
HAMLET: It waves me still.
   Go on; I'll follow thee.
MARCELLUS: You shall not go, my lord.
HAMLET: Hold off your hands!   80
HORATIO: Be rul'd; you shall not go.
HAMLET: My fate cries out,
   And makes each petty artere° in this body
   As hardy as the Nemean lion's° nerve.°

---

[53]*glimpses of the moon*   *the earth by night.*   [54]*fools of nature*   *mere men, limited to natural knowledge.*   [59]**im-
partment**   *communication.*   [61]**removed**   *remote.*   [71]**beetles o'er**   *overhangs threateningly.*   [73]**deprive
. . . reason**   *take away the sovereignty of your reason. It was thought that evil spirits would sometimes assume the
form of departed spirits in order to work madness in a human creature.*   [75]**toys of desperation**   *freakish notions of
suicide.*   [82]**artere**   *artery.*   [83]**Nemean lion's**   *Nemean lion was one of the monsters slain by Hercules.*
[83]**nerve**   *sinew, tendon. The point is that the arteries which were carrying the spirits out into the body were functioning and were as stiff and hard as the sinews of the lion.*

Still am I call'd. Unhand me, gentlemen.
By heaven, I'll make a ghost of him that lets° me! 85
I say, away! Go on; I'll follow thee.   *Exeunt* GHOST *and* HAMLET.
HORATIO: He waxes desperate with imagination.
MARCELLUS: Let's follow; 'tis not fit thus to obey him.
HORATIO: Have after. To what issue° will this come?
MARCELLUS: Something is rotten in the state of Denmark. 90
HORATIO: Heaven will direct it.°
MARCELLUS: Nay, let's follow him.   *Exeunt.*

Scene V [Another part of the platform.]

Enter GHOST *and* HAMLET.

HAMLET: Whither wilt thou lead me? speak; I'll go no further.
GHOST: Mark me.
HAMLET: I will.
GHOST: My hour is almost come,
  When I to sulphurous and tormenting flames
  Must render up myself.
HAMLET: Alas, poor ghost!
GHOST: Pity me not, but lend thy serious hearing 5
  To what I shall unfold.
HAMLET: Speak; I am bound to hear.
GHOST: So art thou to revenge, when thou shalt hear.
HAMLET: What?
GHOST: I am thy father's spirit,
  Doom'd for a certain term to walk the night, 10
  And for the day confin'd to fast° in fires,
  Till the foul crimes done in my days of nature
  Are burnt and purg'd away. But that I am forbid
  To tell the secrets of my prison-house,
  I could a tale unfold whose lightest word 15
  Would harrow up thy soul, freeze thy young blood,
  Make thy two eyes, like stars, start from their spheres,°
  Thy knotted° and combined° locks to part
  And each particular hair to stand an end,
  Like quills upon the fretful porpentine:° 20
  But this eternal blazon° must not be
  To ears of flesh and blood. List, list, O, list!
  If thou didst ever thy dear father love—
HAMLET: O God!
GHOST: Revenge his foul and most unnatural° murder. 25

---

⁸⁵*lets* hinders.   ⁸⁹*issue* outcome.   ⁹¹*it* i.e., the outcome.   **I.v.**   ¹¹*fast* probably, do without food.
It has been sometimes taken in the sense of doing general penance.   ¹⁷*spheres* orbits.   ¹⁸*knotted* perhaps intricately arranged.   ¹⁸*combined* tied, bound.   ²⁰*porpentine* porcupine.   ²¹*eternal blazon* promul-
gation or proclamation of eternity, revelation of the hereafter.   ²⁵*unnatural* i.e., pertaining to fratricide.

HAMLET: Murder!

GHOST: Murder most foul, as in the best it is;
But this most foul, strange and unnatural.

HAMLET: Haste me to know't, that I, with wings as swift
As meditation or the thoughts of love,   30
May sweep to my revenge.

GHOST: I find thee apt;
And duller shouldst thou be than the fat weed°
That roots itself in ease on Lethe wharf,°
Wouldst thou not stir in this. Now, Hamlet, hear:
'Tis given out that, sleeping in my orchard,   35
A serpent stung me; so the whole ear of Denmark
Is by a forged process of my death
Rankly abus'd: but know, thou noble youth,
The serpent that did sting thy father's life
Now wears his crown.

HAMLET: O my prophetic soul!   40
My uncle!

GHOST: Ay, that incestuous, that adulterate° beast,
With witchcraft of his wit, with traitorous gifts,—
O wicked wit and gifts, that have the power
So to seduce!—won to his shameful lust   45
The will of my most seeming-virtuous queen:
O Hamlet, what a falling-off was there!
From me, whose love was of that dignity
That it went hand in hand even with the vow
I made to her in marriage, and to decline   50
Upon a wretch whose natural gifts were poor
To those of mine!
But virtue, as it never will be moved,
Though lewdness court it in a shape of heaven,
So lust, though to a radiant angel link'd,   55
Will sate itself in a celestial bed,
And prey on garbage.
But, soft! methinks I scent the morning air;
Brief let me be. Sleeping within my orchard,
My custom always of the afternoon,   60
Upon my secure° hour thy uncle stole,
With juice of cursed hebona° in a vial,
And in the porches of my ears did pour
The leperous° distilment; whose effect
Holds such an enmity with blood of man   65

---

³²*fat weed* *many suggestions have been offered as to the particular plant intended, including asphodel; probably a
general figure for plants growing along rotting wharves and piles.* ³³*Lethe wharf* *bank of the river of forgetfulness in Hades.* ⁴²*adulterate* *adulterous.* ⁶¹*secure* *confident, unsuspicious.* ⁶²*hebona* *generally supposed to mean henbane, conjectured hemlock; ebenus, meaning "yew."* ⁶⁴*leperous* *causing leprosy.*

That swift as quicksilver it courses through
The natural gates and alleys of the body,
And with a sudden vigour it doth posset°
And curd, like eager° droppings into milk,
The thin and wholesome blood: so did it mine;   70
And a most instant tetter bark'd about,
Most lazar-like,° with vile and loathsome crust,
All my smooth body.
Thus was I, sleeping, by a brother's hand
Of life, of crown, of queen, at once dispatch'd:°   75
Cut off even in the blossoms of my sin,
Unhous'led,° disappointed,° unanel'd,°
No reck'ning made, but sent to my account
With all my imperfections on my head:
O, horrible! O, horrible! most horrible!°   80
If thou hast nature in thee, bear it not;
Let not the royal bed of Denmark be
A couch for luxury° and damned incest.
But, howsomever thou pursues this act,
Taint not thy mind,° nor let thy soul contrive   85
Against thy mother aught: leave her to heaven
And to those thorns that in her bosom lodge,
To prick and sting her. Fare thee well at once!
The glow-worm shows the matin° to be near,
And 'gins to pale his uneffectual fire:°   90
Adieu, adieu, adieu! remember me.   [*Exit.*]
HAMLET: O all you host of heaven! O earth! what else?
And shall I couple° hell? O, fie! Hold, hold, my heart;
And you, my sinews, grow not instant old,
But bear me stiffly up. Remember thee!   95
Ay, thou poor ghost, whiles memory holds a seat
In this distracted globe.° Remember thee!
Yea, from the table of my memory
I'll wipe away all trivial fond records,
All saws° of books, all forms, all pressures° past,   100
That youth and observation copied there;
And thy commandment all alone shall live
Within the book and volume of my brain,
Unmix'd with baser matter: yes, by heaven!
O most pernicious woman!   105

---

⁶⁸***posset*** coagulate, curdle.   ⁶⁹***eager*** sour, acid.   ⁷²***lazar-like*** leperlike.   ⁷⁵***dispatch'd*** suddenly
bereft.   ⁷⁷***Unhous'led*** without having received the sacrament.   ⁷⁷***disappointed*** unready, without equipment
for the last journey.   ⁷⁷***unanel'd*** without having received extreme unction.   ⁸⁰***O . . . horrible*** many editors give this line to Hamlet; Garrick and Sir Henry Irving spoke it in that part.   ⁸³***luxury*** lechery.   ⁸⁵***Taint . . .
mind*** probably, deprave not thy character, do nothing except in the pursuit of a natural revenge.   ⁸⁹***matin*** morning.   ⁹⁰***uneffectual fire*** cold light.   ⁹³***couple*** add.   ⁹⁷***distracted globe*** confused head.   ¹⁰⁰***saws***
wise sayings.   ¹⁰⁰***pressures*** impressions stamped.

O villain, villain, smiling, damned villain!
My tables,°—meet it is I set it down,
That one may smile, and smile, and be a villain;
At least I am sure it may be so in Denmark: [*Writing.*]
So, uncle, there you are. Now to my word;°   110
It is "Adieu, adieu! remember me,"
I have sworn't.

Enter HORATIO *and* MARCELLUS.

HORATIO: My lord, my lord—
MARCELLUS: Lord Hamlet,—
HORATIO: Heavens secure him!
HAMLET: So be it!
MARCELLUS: Hillo, ho, ho,° my lord!   115
HAMLET: Hillo, ho, ho, boy! come, bird, come.
MARCELLUS: How is't, my noble lord?
HORATIO: What news, my lord?
HAMLET: O, wonderful!
HORATIO: Good my lord, tell it.
HAMLET: No; you will reveal it.
HORATIO: Not I, my lord, by heaven.
MARCELLUS: Nor I, my lord.   120
HAMLET: How say you, then; would heart of man once think it?
   But you'll be secret?
HORATIO: }
MARCELLUS: }   Ay, by heaven, my lord.
HAMLET: There's ne'er a villain dwelling in all Denmark
   But he's an arrant° knave.
HORATIO: There needs no ghost, my lord, come from the grave   125
   To tell us this.
HAMLET: Why, right; you are in the right;
   And so, without more circumstance at all,
   I hold it fit that we shake hands and part:
   You, as your business and desire shall point you;
   For every man has business and desire,   130
   Such as it is; and for my own poor part,
   Look you, I'll go pray.
HORATIO: These are but wild and whirling words, my lord.
HAMLET: I am sorry they offend you, heartily;
   Yes, 'faith, heartily.
HORATIO: There's no offence, my lord.   135
HAMLET: Yes, by Saint Patrick,° but there is, Horatio,
   And much offence too. Touching this vision here,

---

¹⁰⁷**tables** *probably a small portable writing-tablet carried at the belt.* ¹¹⁰**word** *watchword.* ¹¹⁵**Hillo, ho,**
ho *a falconer's call to a hawk in air.* ¹²⁴**arrant** *thoroughgoing.* ¹³⁶**Saint Patrick** *St. Patrick was*
keeper of Purgatory and patron saint of all blunders and confusion.

It is an honest° ghost, that let me tell you:
For your desire to know what is between us,
O'ermaster 't as you may. And now, good friends,   140
As you are friends, scholars and soldiers,
Give me one poor request.

HORATIO: What is 't, my lord? we will.

HAMLET: Never make known what you have seen to-night.

HORATIO:
MARCELLUS: } My lord, we will not.

HAMLET: Nay, but swear 't.

HORATIO: In faith,   145
My lord, not I.

MARCELLUS: Nor I, my lord, in faith.

HAMLET: Upon my sword.°

MARCELLUS: We have sworn, my lord, already.

HAMLET: Indeed, upon my sword, indeed.   *Ghost cries under the stage.*

GHOST: Swear.

HAMLET: Ah, ha, boy! say'st thou so? art thou there, truepenny?°   150
Come on—you hear this fellow in the cellarage—
Consent to swear.

HORATIO: Propose the oath, my lord.

HAMLET: Never to speak of this that you have seen,
Swear by my sword.

GHOST [*beneath*]: Swear.   155

HAMLET: Hic et ubique?° then we'll shift our ground.
Come hither, gentlemen,
And lay your hands again upon my sword:
Swear by my sword,
Never to speak of this that you have heard.   160

GHOST [*beneath*]: Swear by his sword.

HAMLET: Well said, old mole! canst work i' th' earth so fast?
A worthy pioner!° Once more remove, good friends.

HORATIO: O day and night, but this is wondrous strange!

HAMLET: And therefore as a stranger give it welcome.   165
There are more things in heaven and earth, Horatio,
Than are dreamt of in your philosophy.
But come;
Here, as before, never, so help you mercy,
How strange or odd soe'er I bear myself,   170
As I perchance hereafter shall think meet
To put an antic° disposition on,
That you, at such times seeing me, never shall,
With arms encumb'red° thus, or this head-shake,

---

¹³⁸**honest** *i.e., a real ghost and not an evil spirit.* ¹⁴⁷**sword** *i.e., the hilt in the form of a cross.* ¹⁵⁰**true-penny** *good old boy, or the like.* ¹⁵⁶**Hic et ubique?** *here and everywhere?* ¹⁶³**pioner** *digger, miner.* ¹⁷²**antic** *fantastic.* ¹⁷⁴**encumb'red** *folded or entwined.*

Or by pronouncing of some doubtful phrase,   175
As "Well, well, we know," or "We could, an if we would,"
Or "If we list to speak," or "There be, an if they might,"
Or such ambiguous giving out,° to note°
That you know aught of me: this not to do,
So grace and mercy at your most need help you,   180
Swear.
GHOST [*beneath*]: Swear.
HAMLET: Rest, rest, perturbed spirit! [*They swear.*] So, gentlemen,
With all my love I do commend me to you:
And what so poor a man as Hamlet is   185
May do, t' express his love and friending° to you,
God willing, shall not lack. Let us go in together;
And still your fingers on your lips, I pray.
The time is out of joint: O cursed spite,
That ever I was born to set it right!   190
Nay, come, let's go together.   *Exeunt.*

ACT II

Scene I [A room in Polonius's house.]

Enter old POLONIUS *with his man* [REYNALDO].

POLONIUS: Give him this money and these notes, Reynaldo.
REYNALDO: I will, my lord.
POLONIUS: You shall do marvellous wisely, good Reynaldo,
    Before you visit him, to make inquire
    Of his behaviour.
REYNALDO: My lord, I did intend it.   5
POLONIUS: Marry, well said; very well said. Look you, sir,
    Inquire me first what Danskers° are in Paris;
    And how, and who, what means, and where they keep,°
    What company, at what expense; and finding
    By this encompassment° and drift° of question   10
    That they do know my son, come you more nearer
    Than your particular demands will touch it:°
    Take° you as 'twere, some distant knowledge of him;
    As thus, "I know his father and his friends;
    And in part him": do you mark this, Reynaldo?   15
REYNALDO: Ay, very well, my lord.

---

¹⁷⁸**giving out** *profession of knowledge.*   ¹⁷⁸**to note** *to give a sign.*   ¹⁸⁶**friending** *friendliness.*   **II.i.**
⁷**Danskers** *Danke was a common variant for "Denmark"; hence "Dane."*   ⁸**keep** *dwell.*   ¹⁰**encom-**
passment *roundabout talking.*   ¹⁰**drift** *gradual approach or course.*   ^{11–12}**come . . . it** *i.e., you will find
out more this way than by asking pointed questions.*   ¹³**Take** *assume, pretend.*

POLONIUS: "And in part him; but" you may say "not well:
  But, if 't be he I mean, he's very wild;
  Addicted so and so": and there put on° him
  What forgeries° you please; marry, none so rank   20
  As may dishonour him; take heed of that;
  But, sir, such wanton,° wild and usual slips
  As are companions noted and most known
  To youth and liberty.
REYNALDO: As gaming, my lord.
POLONIUS: Ay, or drinking, fencing,° swearing, quarrelling,   25
  Drabbing;° you may go so far.
REYNALDO: My lord, that would dishonour him.
POLONIUS: 'Faith, no; as you may season it in the charge.
  You must not put another scandal on him,
  That he is open to incontinency;°   30
  That's not my meaning: but breathe his faults so quaintly°
  That they may seem the taints of liberty,°
  The flash and outbreak of a fiery mind,
  A savageness in unreclaimed° blood,
  Of general assault.°   35
REYNALDO: But, my good lord,—
POLONIUS: Wherefore should you do this?
REYNALDO: Ay, my lord,
  I would know that.
POLONIUS: Marry, sir, here's my drift;
  And, I believe, it is a fetch of wit:°
  You laying these slight sullies on my son,   40
  As 'twere a thing a little soil'd i' th' working,
  Mark you,
  Your party in converse, him you would sound,
  Having ever° seen in the prenominate° crimes
  The youth you breathe of guilty, be assur'd   45
  He closes with you in this consequence;°
  "Good sir," or so, or "friend," or "gentleman,"
  According to the phrase or the addition
  Of man and country.
REYNALDO: Very good, my lord.
POLONIUS: And then, sir, does 'a this—'a does—what was I about to say?
  By the mass, I was about to say something: where did I leave?   50
REYNALDO: At "closes in the consequence," at "friend or so," and "gentle-
  man."

---

[19]*put on* impute to.   [20]*forgeries* invented tales.   [22]*wanton* sportive, unrestrained.   [25]*fencing* indicative of the ill repute of professional fencers and fencing schools in Elizabethan times.   [26]*Drabbing* associating with immoral women.   [30]*incontinency* habitual loose behavior.   [31]*quaintly* delicately, ingeniously.   [32]*taints of liberty* blemishes due to freedom.   [34]*unreclaimed* untamed.   [36]*general assault* tendency that assails all untrained youth.   [38]*fetch of wit* clever trick.   [43]*ever* at any time.   [43]*prenominate* before-mentioned.   [45]*closes . . . consequence* agrees with you in this conclusion.

POLONIUS: At "closes in the consequence," ay, marry;
 He closes thus: "I know the gentleman;
 I saw him yesterday, or t' other day,   55
 Or then, or then; with such, or such; and, as you say,
 There was 'a gaming; there o'ertook in 's rouse;°
 There falling out at tennis": or perchance,
 "I saw him enter such a house of sale,"
 Videlicet,° a brothel, or so forth.   60
 See you now;
 Your bait of falsehood takes this carp of truth:
 And thus do we of wisdom and of reach,°
 With windlasses° and with assays of bias,°
 By indirections° find directions° out: 65
 So by my former lecture° and advice,
 Shall you my son. You have me, have you not?
REYNALDO: My lord, I have.
POLONIUS: God bye ye;° fare ye well.
REYNALDO: Good my lord!
POLONIUS: Observe his inclination in yourself.°   70
REYNALDO: I shall, my lord.
POLONIUS: And let him ply his music.°
REYNALDO: Well, my lord.
POLONIUS: Farewell!   *Exit* REYNALDO.

Enter OPHELIA.

      How now, Ophelia! what's the matter?
OPHELIA: O, my lord, my lord, I have been so affrighted!
POLONIUS: With what, i' th' name of God?   75
OPHELIA: My lord, as I was sewing in my closet,°
 Lord Hamlet, with his doublet° all unbrac'd;°
 No hat upon his head; his stockings foul'd,
 Ungart'red, and down-gyved° to his ankle;
 Pale as his shirt; his knees knocking each other;   80
 And with a look so piteous in purport
 As if he had been loosed out of hell
 To speak of horrors,—he comes before me.
POLONIUS: Mad for thy love?
OPHELIA: My lord, I do not know;
 But truly, I do fear it.
POLONIUS: What said he?   85
OPHELIA: He took me by the wrist and held me hard;

---

⁵⁷**o'ertook in 's rouse** *overcome by drink.* ⁶⁰**Videlicet** *namely.* ⁶³**reach** *capacity, ability.* ⁶⁴**wind-lasses** *i.e., circuitous paths.* ⁶⁴**assays of bias** *attempts that resemble the course of the bowl, which, being weighted on one side, has a curving motion.* ⁶⁵**indirections** *devious courses.* ⁶⁵**directions** *straight courses, i.e., the truth.* ⁶⁶**lecture** *admonition.* ⁶⁹**bye ye** *be with you.* ⁷⁰**Observe . . . yourself** *in your own person, not by spies; or conform your own conduct to his inclination; or test him by studying yourself.* ⁷²**ply his music** *probably to be taken literally.* ⁷⁶**closet** *private chamber.* ⁷⁷**doublet** *close-fitting coat.* ⁷⁷**unbrac'd** *unfastened.* ⁷⁹**down-gyved** *fallen to the ankles (like gyves or fetters).*

Then goes he to the length of all his arm;
And, with his other hand thus o'er his brow,
He falls to such perusal of my face
As 'a would draw it. Long stay'd he so;   90
At last, a little shaking of mine arm
And thrice his head thus waving up and down,
He rais'd a sigh so piteous and profound
As it did seem to shatter all his bulk°
And end his being: that done, he lets me go: 95
And, with his head over his shoulder turn'd,
He seem'd to find his way without his eyes;
For out o'doors he went without their helps,
And, to the last, bended their light on me.

POLONIUS: Come, go with me: I will go seek the king.   100
This is the very ecstasy of love,
Whose violent property° fordoes° itself
And leads the will to desperate undertakings
As oft as any passion under heaven
That does afflict our natures. I am sorry.   105
What, have you given him any hard words of late?

OPHELIA: No, my good lord, but, as you did command,
I did repel his letters and denied
His access to me.

POLONIUS: That hath made him mad.
I am sorry that with better heed and judgement   110
I had not quoted° him: I fear'd he did but trifle,
And meant to wrack thee; but, beshrew my jealousy!°
By heaven, it is as proper to our age
To cast beyond° ourselves in our opinions
As it is common for the younger sort   115
To lack discretion. Come, go we to the king:
This must be known; which, being kept close, might move
More grief to hide than hate to utter love.°
Come.   *Exeunt.*

Scene II [A room in the castle.]

Flourish. Enter KING *and* QUEEN, ROSENCRANTZ, *and* GUILDENSTERN *[with others].*

KING: Welcome, dear Rosencrantz and Guildenstern!
Moreover that° we much did long to see you,
The need we have to use you did provoke
Our hasty sending. Something have you heard
Of Hamlet's transformation; so call it,   5

---

⁹⁴**bulk** *body.*   ¹⁰²**property** *nature*   ¹⁰²**fordoes** *destroys.*   ¹¹¹**quoted** *observed.*   ¹¹²**beshrew
my jealousy** *curse my suspicions.*   ¹¹⁴**cast beyond** *overshoot, miscalculate.*   ¹¹⁷⁻¹¹⁸**might . . . love**
*i.e., I might cause more grief to others by hiding the knowledge of Hamlet's love to Ophelia than hatred to me and mine
by telling of it.*   **II.ii.**   ²**Moreover that** *besides the fact that.*

Sith° nor th' exterior nor the inward man
Resembles that it was. What it should be,
More than his father's death, that thus hath put him
So much from th' understanding of himself,
I cannot dream of: I entreat you both,   10
That, being of so young days° brought up with him,
And sith so neighbour'd to his youth and haviour,
That you vouchsafe your rest° here in our court
Some little time: so by your companies
To draw him on to pleasures, and to gather,   15
So much as from occasion you may glean,
Whether aught, to us unknown, afflicts him thus,
That, open'd, lies within our remedy.
QUEEN: Good gentlemen, he hath much talk'd of you;
And sure I am two men there are not living   20
To whom he more adheres. If it will please you
To show us so much gentry° and good will
As to expend your time with us awhile,
For the supply and profit° of our hope,
Your visitation shall receive such thanks   25
As fits a king's remembrance.
ROSENCRANTZ: Both your majesties
Might, by the sovereign power you have of us,
Put your dread pleasures more into command
Than to entreaty.
GUILDENSTERN: But we both obey,
And here give up ourselves, in the full bent°   30
To lay our service freely at your feet,
To be commanded.
KING: Thanks, Rosencrantz and gentle Guildenstern.
QUEEN: Thanks, Guildenstern and gentle Rosencrantz:
And I beseech you instantly to visit   35
My too much changed son. Go, some of you,
And bring these gentlemen where Hamlet is.
GUILDENSTERN: Heavens make our presence and our practices
Pleasant and helpful to him!
QUEEN: Ay, amen!

Exeunt ROSENCRANTZ *and* GUILDENSTERN [*with some* ATTENDANTS].

Enter POLONIUS.

POLONIUS: Th' ambassadors from Norway, my good lord,   40
Are joyfully return'd.
KING: Thou still hast been the father of good news.
POLONIUS: Have I, my lord? I assure my good liege,

---

⁶**Sith** *since.*   ¹¹**of . . . days** *from such early youth.*   ¹³**vouchsafe your rest** *please to stay.*   ²²**gentry**
courtesy.   ²⁴**supply and profit** *aid and successful outcome.*   ³⁰**in . . . bent** *to the utmost degree of our*
mental capacity.

I hold my duty, as I hold my soul,

Both to my God and to my gracious king: 45

And I do think, or else this brain of mine

Hunts not the trail of policy so sure

As it hath us'd to do, that I have found

The very cause of Hamlet's lunacy.

KING: O, speak of that; that do I long to hear. 50

POLONIUS: Give first admittance to th' ambassadors;

My news shall be the fruit to that great feast.

KING: Thyself do grace to them, and bring them in. [*Exit* POLONIUS.]

He tells me, my dear Gertrude, he hath found

The head and source of all your son's distemper. 55

QUEEN: I doubt° it is no other but the main;°

His father's death, and our o'erhasty marriage.

KING: Well, we shall sift him.

Enter AMBASSADORS [VOLTIMAND *and* CORNELIUS, *with* POLONIUS.]

Welcome, my good friends!

Say, Voltimand, what from our brother Norway?

VOLTIMAND: Most fair return of greetings and desires. 60

Upon our first, he sent out to suppress

His nephew's levies; which to him appear'd

To be a preparation 'gainst the Polack;

But, better look'd into, he truly found

It was against your highness: whereat griev'd, 65

That so his sickness, age and impotence

Was falsely borne in hand,° sends out arrests

On Fortinbras; which he, in brief, obeys;

Receives rebuke from Norway, and in fine°

Makes vow before his uncle never more 70

To give th' assay° of arms against your majesty.

Whereon old Norway, overcome with joy,

Gives him three score thousand crowns in annual fee,

And his commission to employ those soldiers,

So levied as before, against the Polack: 75

With an entreaty, herein further shown, [*giving a paper.*]

That it might please you to give quiet pass

Through your dominions for this enterprise,

On such regards of safety and allowance°

As therein are set down.

KING: It likes° us well; 80

And at our more consider'd° time we'll read,

Answer, and think upon this business.

Meantime we thank you for your well-took labour:

---

⁵⁶**doubt** *fear.*   ⁵⁶**main** *chief point, principal concern.*   ⁶⁷**borne in hand** *deluded.*   ⁶⁹**in fine** *in the end.*   ⁷¹**assay** *assault, trial (of arms).*   ⁷⁹**safety and allowance** *pledges of safety to the country and terms of permission for the troops to pass.*   ⁸⁰**likes** *pleases.*   ⁸¹**consider'd** *suitable for deliberation.*

Go to your rest; at night we'll feast together:

Most welcome home!   *Exeunt* AMBASSADORS.

POLONIUS: This business is well ended.   85

My liege, and madam, to expostulate

What majesty should be, what duty is,

Why day is day, night night, and time is time,

Were nothing but to waste night, day and time.

Therefore, since brevity is the soul of wit,°   90

And tediousness the limbs and outward flourishes,°

I will be brief: your noble son is mad:

Mad call I it; for, to define true madness

What is 't but to be nothing else but mad?

But let that go.

QUEEN: More matter, with less art.   95

POLONIUS: Madam, I swear I use no art at all.

That he is mad, 'tis true: 'tis true 'tis pity;

And pity 'tis 'tis true: a foolish figure;°

But farewell it, for I will use no art.

Mad let us grant him, then: and now remains   100

That we find out the cause of this effect,

Or rather say, the cause of this defect,

For this effect defective comes by cause:

Thus it remains, and the remainder thus.

Perpend.°   105

I have a daughter—have while she is mine—

Who, in her duty and obedience, mark,

Hath given me this: now gather, and surmise. [*Reads the letter*] "To the

celestial and my soul's idol,

the most beautified Ophelia,"—   110

That's an ill phrase, a vile phrase; "beautified" is a vile phrase: but you

shall hear. Thus: [*Reads.*]

"In her excellent white bosom, these, & c."

QUEEN: Came this from Hamlet to her?

POLONIUS: Good madam, stay awhile; I will be faithful.   [*Reads.*] 115

              "Doubt thou the stars are fire;

                  Doubt that the sun doth move;

                  Doubt truth to be a liar;

                  But never doubt I love.

"O dear Ophelia, I am ill at these numbers;° I have not art to reckon° my 120

groans: but that I love thee best, O most best, believe it. Adieu.

          "Thine evermore, most dear lady, whilst this machine° is to

him,

                                                            HAMLET."

This, in obedience, hath my daughter shown me,

---

⁹⁰*wit* *sound sense or judgment.*   ⁹¹*flourishes* *ostentation, embellishments.*   ⁹⁸*figure* *figure of speech.*
¹⁰⁵*Perpend* *consider.*   ¹²⁰*ill . . . numbers* *unskilled at writing verses.*   ¹²⁰*reckon* *number metrically, scan.*
¹²²*machine* *bodily frame.*

And more above,° hath his solicitings,   125
  As they fell out° by time, by means° and place,
  All given to mine ear.
KING: But how hath she
  Receiv'd his love?
POLONIUS: What do you think of me?
KING: As of a man faithful and honourable.
POLONIUS: I would fain prove so. But what might you think,   130
  When I had seen this hot love on the wing—
  As I perceiv'd it, I must tell you that,
  Before my daughter told me—what might you,
  Or my dear majesty your queen here, think,
  If I had play'd the desk or table-book,°   135
  Or given my heart a winking,° mute and dumb,
  Or look'd upon this love with idle sight;
  What might you think? No, I went round to work,
  And my young mistress thus I did bespeak:°
  "Lord Hamlet is a prince, out of thy star;°   140
  This must not be": and then I prescripts gave her,
  That she should lock herself from his resort,
  Admit no messengers, receive no tokens.
  Which done, she took the fruits of my advice;
  And he, repelled—a short tale to make—   145
  Fell into a sadness, then into a fast,
  Thence to a watch,° thence into a weakness,
  Thence to a lightness,° and, by this declension,°
  Into the madness wherein now he raves,
  And all we mourn for.
KING: Do you think 'tis this?   150
QUEEN: It may be, very like.
POLONIUS: Hath there been such a time—I would fain know that—
  That I have positively said " 'Tis so,"
  When it prov'd otherwise?
KING: Not that I know.
POLONIUS [*pointing to his head and shoulder*]: Take this from this, if this be
  otherwise: 155
  If circumstances lead me, I will find
  Where truth is hid, though it were hid indeed
  Within the centre.°
KING: How may we try it further?
POLONIUS: You know, sometimes he walks four hours together
  Here in the lobby.

---

¹²⁵***more above*** moreover.   ¹²⁶***fell out*** occurred.   ¹²⁶***means*** opportunities (of access).   ¹³⁵***play'd . . .***
table-book i.e., remained shut up, concealed this information.   ¹³⁶***given . . . winking*** given my heart a sig-
nal to keep silent.   ¹³⁹***bespeak*** address.   ¹⁴⁰***out . . . star*** above thee in position.   ¹⁴⁷***watch*** state of
sleeplessness.   ¹⁴⁸***lightness*** lightheadedness.   ¹⁴⁸***declension*** decline, deterioration.   ¹⁵⁸***centre*** middle
point of the earth.

QUEEN: So he does indeed.   160
POLONIUS: At such a time I'll loose my daughter to him:
  Be you and I behind an arras° then;
  Mark the encounter: if he love her not
  And be not from his reason fall'n thereon,°
  Let me be no assistant for a state,   165
  But keep a farm and carters.
KING: We will try it.

Enter HAMLET [*reading on a book*].

QUEEN: But, look, where sadly the poor wretch comes reading.
POLONIUS: Away, I do beseech you both, away:

                          Exeunt KING *and* QUEEN [*with* ATTENDANTS].

  I'll board° him presently. O, give me leave.
  How does my good Lord Hamlet?   170
HAMLET: Well, God-a-mercy.
POLONIUS: Do you know me, my lord?
HAMLET: Excellent well; you are a fishmonger.°
POLONIUS: Not I, my lord.
HAMLET: Then I would you were so honest a man.   175
POLONIUS: Honest, my lord!
HAMLET: Ay, sir; to be honest, as this world goes, is to be one man picked
  out of ten thousand.
POLONIUS: That's very true, my lord.
HAMLET: For if the sun breed maggots in a dead dog, being a good kissing   180
  carrion,°—Have you a daughter?
POLONIUS: I have, my lord.
HAMLET: Let her not walk i' the sun:° conception° is a blessing: but as your
  daughter may conceive—Friend, look to 't.
POLONIUS [*aside*]: How say you by° that? Still harping on my daughter: yet 185
  he knew me not at first; 'a said I was a fishmonger: 'a is far gone, far gone:
  and truly in my youth I suffered much extremity for love; very near this.
  I'll speak to him again. What do you read, my lord?
HAMLET: Words, words, words.
POLONIUS: What is the matter,° my lord?   190
HAMLET: Between who?°
POLONIUS: I mean, the matter that you read, my lord.
HAMLET: Slanders, sir: for the satirical rogue says here that old men have grey
  beards, that their faces are wrinkled, their eyes purging° thick amber and
  plum-tree gum and that they have a plentiful lack of wit, together with   195
  most weak hams: all which, sir, though I most powerfully and potently

believe, yet I hold it not honesty° to have it thus set down, for yourself,
sir, should be old as I am, if like a crab you could go backward.

POLONIUS [*aside*]: Though this be madness, yet there is method in 't.—Will
you walk out of the air, my lord?   200

HAMLET: Into my grave.

POLONIUS: Indeed, that's out of the air. [*Aside.*] How pregnant sometimes
his replies are! a happiness° that often madness hits on, which reason and
sanity could not so prosperously° be delivered of. I will leave him, and
suddenly contrive the means of meeting between him and my daughter.— 205
My honourable lord, I will most humbly take my leave of you.

HAMLET: You cannot, sir, take from me any thing that I will more willingly
part withal: except my life, except my life, except my life.

Enter GUILDENSTERN *and* ROSENCRANTZ.

POLONIUS: Fare you well, my lord.

HAMLET: These tedious old fools!   210

POLONIUS: You go to seek the Lord Hamlet; there he is.

ROSENCRANTZ [*to* POLONIUS]: God save you, sir!   [*Exit* POLONIUS.]

GUILDENSTERN: My honoured lord!

ROSENCRANTZ: My most dear lord!

HAMLET: My excellent good friends! How dost thou, Guildenstern? Ah, 215
Rosencrantz! Good lads, how do ye both?

ROSENCRANTZ: As the indifferent° children of the earth.

GUILDENSTERN: Happy, in that we are not over-happy;
On Fortune's cap we are not the very button.

HAMLET: Nor the soles of her shoe?   220

ROSENCRANTZ: Neither, my lord.

HAMLET: Then you live about her waist, or in the middle of her favours?

GUILDENSTERN: 'Faith, her privates° we.

HAMLET: In the secret parts of Fortune? O, most true; she is a strumpet.
What's the news?   225

ROSENCRANTZ: None, my lord, but that the world's grown honest.

HAMLET: Then is doomsday near: but your news is not true. Let me question more in particular: what have you, my good friends, deserved at the
hands of Fortune, that she sends you to prison hither?

GUILDENSTERN: Prison, my lord!   230

HAMLET: Denmark's a prison.

ROSENCRANTZ: Then is the world one.

HAMLET: A goodly one; in which there are many confines,° wards and dungeons, Denmark being one o' the worst.

ROSENCRANTZ: We think not so, my lord.   235

HAMLET: Why, then, 'tis none to you; for there is nothing either good or
bad, but thinking makes it so: to me it is a prison.

---

[197] **honesty** *decency.*   [203] **happiness** *felicity of expression.*   [204] **prosperously** *successfully.*   [217] **indifferent** *ordinary.*   [223] **privates** *i.e., ordinary men (sexual pun on private parts).*   [233] **confines** *places of confinement.*

ROSENCRANTZ: Why then, your ambition makes it one; 'tis too narrow for your mind.

HAMLET: O God, I could be bounded in a nutshell and count myself a king [240] of infinite space, were it not that I have bad dreams.

GUILDENSTERN: Which dreams indeed are ambition, for the very substance of the ambitious° is merely the shadow of a dream.

HAMLET: A dream itself is but a shadow.

ROSENCRANTZ: Truly, and I hold ambition of so airy and light a quality that [245] it is but a shadow's shadow.

HAMLET: Then are our beggars bodies, and our monarchs and outstretched heroes the beggars' shadows. Shall we to the court? for, by my fay,° I can- not reason.°

ROSENCRANTZ: ⎫
GUILDENSTERN: ⎬ We'll wait upon° you.   250

HAMLET: No such matter: I will not sort° you with the rest of my servants, for, to speak to you like an honest man, I am most dreadfully attended.° But, in the beaten way of friendship,° what make you at Elsinore?

ROSENCRANTZ: To visit you, my lord: no other occasion.

HAMLET: Beggar that I am, I am ever poor in thanks; but I thank you: and [255] sure, dear friends, my thanks are too dear a° halfpenny. Were you not sent for? Is it your own inclining? Is it a free visitation? Come, come, deal justly with me: come, come; nay, speak.

GUILDENSTERN: What should we say, my lord?

HAMLET: Why, any thing, but to the purpose. You were sent for; and there [260] is a kind of confession in your looks which your modesties have not craft enough to colour: I know the good king and queen have sent for you.

ROSENCRANTZ: To what end, my lord?

HAMLET: That you must teach me. But let me conjure° you, by the rights of our fellowship, by the consonancy of our youth,° by the obligation of [265] our ever-preserved love, and by what more dear a better proposer° could charge you withal, be even and direct with me, whether you were sent for, or no?

ROSENCRANTZ [*aside to* GUILDENSTERN]: What say you?

HAMLET [*aside*]: Nay, then, I have an eye of you.—If you love me, hold not [270] off.

GUILDENSTERN: My lord, we were sent for.

HAMLET: I will tell you why; so shall my anticipation prevent your discov- ery,° and your secrecy to the king and queen moult no feather. I have of late—but wherefore I know not—lost all my mirth, forgone all custom [275] of exercises; and indeed it goes so heavily with my disposition that this goodly frame, the earth, seems to me a sterile promontory, this most ex- cellent canopy, the air, look you, this brave o'erhanging firmament, this

---

[243]*very . . . ambitious*   *that seemingly most substantial thing which the ambitious pursue.*   [248]*fay*   *faith.*
[249]*reason*   *argue.*   [250]*wait upon*   *accompany.*   [251]*sort*   *class.*   [252]*dreadfully attended*   *poorly pro-*
vided with servants.   [253]*in the . . . friendship*   *as a matter of course among friends.*   [256]*a*   *i.e., at a.*
[264]*conjure*   *adjure, entreat.*   [265]*consonancy of our youth*   *the fact that we are of the same age.*   [266]*better*
proposer   *one more skillful in finding proposals.*   [273–274]*prevent your discovery*   *forestall your disclosure.*

majestical roof fretted° with golden fire, why, it appeareth nothing to
me but a foul and pestilent congregation of vapours. What a piece of[280]
work is a man! how noble in reason! how infinite in faculties!° in form
and moving how express° and admirable! in action how like an angel!
in apprehension° how like a god! the beauty of the world! the paragon
of animals! And yet, to me, what is this quintessence° of dust? man delights not me: no, nor woman neither, though by your smiling you seem[285]
to say so.

ROSENCRANTZ: My lord, there was no such stuff in my thoughts.

HAMLET: Why did you laugh then, when I said "man delights not me"?

ROSENCRANTZ: To think, my lord, if you delight not in man, what lenten°
entertainment the players shall receive from you: we coted° them on the[290]
way; and hither are they coming, to offer you service.

HAMLET: He that plays the king shall be welcome; his majesty shall have tribute of me; the adventurous knight shall use his foil and target;° the lover
shall not sigh gratis; the humorous man° shall end his part in peace; the
clown shall make those laugh whose lungs are tickle o' the sere;° and the[295]
lady shall say her mind freely, or the blank verse shall halt for 't.° What
players are they?

ROSENCRANTZ: Even those you were wont to take delight in, the tragedians
of the city.

HAMLET: How chances it they travel? their residence,° both in reputation[300]
and profit, was better both ways.

ROSENCRANTZ: I think their inhibition° comes by the means of the late innovation.°

HAMLET: Do they hold the same estimation they did when I was in the city?
are they so followed?[305]

ROSENCRANTZ: No, indeed, are they not.

HAMLET: How° comes it? do they grow rusty?

ROSENCRANTZ: Nay, their endeavour keeps in the wonted pace: but there is,
sir, an aery° of children, little eyases,° that cry out on the top of question,°
and are most tyrannically° clapped for 't: these are now the fashion, and[310]
so berattle° the common stages°—so they call them—that many wearing
rapiers° are afraid of goose-quills° and dare scarce come thither.

---

[279]*fretted* adorned.   [281]*faculties* capacity.   [282]*express* well-framed(?), exact(?).   [283]*apprehension*
understanding.   [284]*quintessence* the fifth essence of ancient philosophy, supposed to be the substance of the
heavenly bodies and to be latent in all things.   [289]*lenten* meager.   [290]*coted* overtook and passed beyond.   [293]*foil and target* sword and shield.   [294]*humorous man* actor who takes the part of the humor
characters.   [295]*tickle o' the sere* easy on the trigger.   [296]*the lady . . . for 't* the lady (fond of talking) shall
have opportunity to talk, blank verse or no blank verse.   [300]*residence* remaining in one place.   [302]*inhibition*
formal prohibition (from acting plays in the city or, possibly, at court).   [302–303]*innovation* the new fashion
in satirical plays performed by boy actors in the "private" theaters.   [307–325]*How . . . load too* the passage
is the famous one dealing with the War of the Theatres (1599–1602); namely, the rivalry between the children's
companies and the adult actors.   [309]*aery* nest.   [309]*eyases* young hawks.   [309]*cry . . . question*
speak in a high key dominating conversation; clamor forth the height of controversy; probably "excel" (cf. line 459);
perhaps intended to decry leaders of the dramatic profession.   [310]*tyrannically* outrageously.   [311]*berattle*
berate.   [311]*common stages* public theaters.   [311–312]*many wearing rapiers* many men of fashion, who
were afraid to patronize the common players for fear of being satirized by the poets who wrote for the children.
[312]*goose-quills* i.e., pens of satirists.

HAMLET: What, are they children? who maintains 'em? how are they escoted?° Will they pursue the quality° no longer than they can sing?° will they not say afterwards, if they should grow themselves to common° players—as it is most like, if their means are no better—their writers do them wrong, to make them exclaim against their own succession?°

ROSENCRANTZ: 'Faith, there has been much to do on both sides; and the nation holds it no sin to tarre° them to controversy: there was, for a while, no money bid for argument,° unless the poet and the players went to cuffs° in the question.°

HAMLET: Is't possible?

GUILDENSTERN: O, there has been much throwing about of brains.

HAMLET: Do the boys carry it away?°

ROSENCRANTZ: Ay, that they do, my lord; Hercules and his load° too.

HAMLET: It is not very strange; for my uncle is king of Denmark, and those that would make mows° at him while my father lived, give twenty, forty, fifty, a hundred ducats° a-piece for his picture in little.° 'Sblood, there is something in this more than natural, if philosophy could find it out.

A flourish [of trumpets within].

GUILDENSTERN: There are the players.

HAMLET: Gentlemen, you are welcome to Elsinore. Your hands, come then: the appurtenance of welcome is fashion and ceremony: let me comply° with you in this garb,° lest my extent° to the players, which, I tell you, must show fairly outwards, should more appear like entertainment than yours. You are welcome: but my uncle-father and aunt-mother are deceived.

GUILDENSTERN: In what, my dear lord?

HAMLET: I am but mad north-north-west:° when the wind is southerly I know a hawk from a handsaw.°

Enter POLONIUS.

POLONIUS: Well be with you, gentlemen!

HAMLET: Hark you, Guildenstern; and you too: at each ear a hearer: that great baby you see there is not yet out of his swaddling-clouts.°

ROSENCRANTZ: Happily he is the second time come to them; for they say an old man is twice a child.

HAMLET: I will prophesy he comes to tell me of the players; mark it.—You say right, sir: o' Monday morning;° 'twas then indeed.

---

³¹³**escoted** *maintained.* ³¹⁴**quality** *acting profession.* ³¹⁴**no longer . . . sting** *i.e., until their voices change.* ³¹⁵**common** *regular, adult.* ³¹⁷**succession** *future careers.* ³¹⁹**tarre** *set on (as dogs).* ³²⁰**argument** *probably, plot for a play.* ³²⁰**went to cuffs** *came to blows.* ³²¹**question** *controversy.* ³²⁴**carry it away** *win the day.* ³²⁵**Hercules . . . load** *regarded as an allusion to the sign of the Globe Theatre, which was Hercules bearing the world on his shoulder.* ³²⁷**mows** *grimaces.* ³²⁸**ducats** *gold coins worth 9s. 4d.* ³²⁸**in little** *in miniature.* ³³²**comply** *observe the formalities of courtesy.* ³³³**garb** *manner.* ³³³**extent** *showing of kindness.* ³³⁸**I am . . . north-north-west** *I am only partly mad, i.e., in only one point of the compass.* ³³⁹**handsaw** *a proposed reading of* hernshaw *would mean "heron"; handsaw may be an early corruption of* hernshaw. *Another view regards* hawk *as the variant of* hack, *a tool of the pickax type, and* handsaw *as a saw operated by hand.* ³⁴²**swaddling-clouts** *cloths in which to wrap a newborn baby.* ³⁴⁶**o' Monday morning** *said to mislead Polonius.*

POLONIUS: My lord, I have news to tell you.

HAMLET: My lord, I have news to tell you. When Roscius° was an actor in
Rome,—

POLONIUS: The actors are come hither, my lord. 350

HAMLET: Buz, buz!°

POLONIUS: Upon my honour,—

HAMLET: Then came each actor on his ass,—

POLONIUS: The best actors in the world, either for tragedy, comedy, history,
pastoral, pastoral-comical, historical-pastoral, tragical-historical, tragical- 355
comical-historical-pastoral, scene individable,° or poem unlimited:°
Seneca° cannot be too heavy, nor Plautus° too light. For the law of writ
and the liberty,° these are the only men.

HAMLET: O Jephthah, judge of Israel,° what a treasure hadst thou!

POLONIUS: What a treasure had he, my lord? 360

HAMLET: Why,
"One fair daughter, and no more,
The which he loved passing well."

POLONIUS [*aside*]: Still on my daughter.

HAMLET: Am I not i' the right, old Jephthah? 365

POLONIUS: If you call me Jephthah, my lord, I have a daughter that I love
passing° well.

HAMLET: Nay, that follows not.

POLONIUS: What follows, then, my lord?

HAMLET: Why, 370
"As by lot, God wot,"
and then, you know,
"It came to pass, as most like° it was,"—
the first row° of the pious chanson° will show you more; for look, where
my abridgement comes.° 375

Enter the PLAYERS.

You are welcome, masters; welcome, all. I am glad to see thee well. Welcome, good friends. O, old friend! why, thy face is valanced° since I saw
thee last: comest thou to beard me in Denmark? What, my young lady
and mistress! By'r lady, your ladyship is nearer to heaven than when I saw
you last, by the altitude of a chopine.° Pray God, your voice, like a piece 380
of uncurrent° gold, be not cracked within the ring.° Masters, you are all
welcome. We'll e'en to 't like French falconers, fly at any thing we see:

---

[348]**Roscius** *a famous Roman actor.* [351]**Buz, buz** *an interjection used at Oxford to denote stale news.* [356]**scene individable** *a play observing the unity of place.* [356]**poem unlimited** *a play disregarding the unities of time and place.* [357]**Seneca** *writer of Latin tragedies, model of early Elizabethan writers of tragedy.* [357]**Plautus** *writer of Latin comedy.* [357–358]**law . . . liberty** *pieces written according to rules and without rules, i.e., "classical" and "romantic" dramas.* [359]**Jephthah . . . Israel** *Jephthah had to sacrifice his daughter; see Judges 11.* [367]**passing** *surpassingly.* [373]**like** *probable.* [374]**row** *stanza.* [374]**chanson** *ballad.* [375]**abridgement comes** *opportunity comes for cutting short the conversation.* [377]**valanced** *fringed (with a beard).* [380]**chopine** *kind of shoe raised by the thickness of the heel; worn in Italy, particularly at Venice.* [381]**uncurrent** *not passable as lawful coinage.* [381]**cracked within the ring** *in the center of coins were rings enclosing the sovereign's head; if the coin was cracked within this ring, it was unfit for currency.*

we'll have a speech straight: come, give us a taste of your quality; come,
a passionate speech.

FIRST PLAYER: What speech, my good lord?   385

HAMLET: I heard thee speak me a speech once, but it was never acted; or, if
it was, not above once; for the play, I remember, pleased not the million;
'twas caviary to the general:° but it was—as I received it, and others,
whose judgements in such matters cried in the top of° mine—an excellent play, well digested in the scenes, set down with as much modesty as 390
cunning.° I remember, one said there were no sallets° in the lines to make
the matter savoury, nor no matter in the phrase that might indict° the
author of affectation; but called it an honest method, as wholesome as
sweet, and by very much more handsome than fine.° One speech in 't I
chiefly loved: 'twas Æneas' tale to Dido;° and thereabout of it especially, 395
where he speaks of Priam's slaughter: if it live in your memory, begin at
this line: let me see, let me see—

"The rugged Pyrrhus,° like th' Hyrcanian beast,"°—
'tis not so:—it begins with Pyrrhus:—
"The rugged Pyrrhus, he whose sable arms,   400
Black as his purpose, did the night resemble
When he lay couched in the ominous horse,°
Hath now this dread and black complexion smear'd
With heraldry more dismal; head to foot
Now is he total gules;° horridly trick'd°   405
With blood of fathers, mothers, daughters, sons,
Bak'd and impasted° with the parching streets,
That lend a tyrannous and a damned light
To their lord's murder: roasted in wrath and fire,
And thus o'er-sized° with coagulate gore,   410
With eyes like carbuncles, the hellish Pyrrhus
Old grandsire Priam seeks."
So, proceed you.

POLONIUS: 'Fore God, my lord, well spoken, with good accent and good
discretion.   415

FIRST PLAYER: "Anon he finds him
Striking too short at Greeks; his antique sword,
Rebellious to his arm, lies where it falls,
Repugnant° to command: unequal match'd,
Pyrrhus at Priam drives; in rage strikes wide;   420
But with the whiff and wind of his fell sword

388*caviary to the general*   *not relished by the multitude.*   389*cried in the top of*   *spoke with greater authority*
than.   391*cunning*   *skill.*   391*sallets*   *salads: here, spicy improprieties.*   392*indict*   *convict.*   394*as*
wholesome . . . fine   *its beauty was not that of elaborate ornament, but that of order and proportion.*   395*Æneas'*
tale to Dido   *the lines recited by the player are imitated from Marlowe and Nashe's* Dido Queen of Carthage *(II.i.214*
ff.). They are written in such a way that the conventionality of the play within a play is raised above that of ordinary
drama.   398*Pyrrhus*   *a Greek hero in the Trojan War.*   398*Hyrcanian beast*   *the tiger; see Virgil,* Aeneid,
IV.266.   402*ominous horse*   *Trojan horse.*   405*gules*   *red, a heraldic term.*   405*trick'd*   *spotted, smeared.*
407*impasted*   *made into a paste.*   410*o'er-sized*   *covered as with size or glue.*   419*Repugnant*   *disobedient.*

Th' unnerved father falls. Then senseless Ilium,°
Seeming to feel this blow, with flaming top
Stoops to his base, and with a hideous crash
Takes prisoner Pyrrhus' ear: for, lo! his sword   425
Which was declining on the milky head
Of reverend Priam, seem'd i' th' air to stick:
So, as a painted tyrant,° Pyrrhus stood,
And like a neutral to his will and matter,°
Did nothing.   430
But, as we often see, against° some storm,
A silence in the heavens, the rack° stand still,
The bold winds speechless and the orb below
As hush as death, anon the dreadful thunder
Doth rend the region,° so, after Pyrrhus' pause,   435
Aroused vengeance sets him new a-work;
And never did the Cyclops' hammers fall
On Mars's armour forg'd for proof eterne°
With less remorse than Pyrrhus' bleeding sword
Now falls on Priam.   440
Out, out, thou strumpet, Fortune! All you gods,
In general synod,° take away her power;
Break all the spokes and fellies° from her wheel,
And bowl the round nave° down the hill of heaven,
As low as to the fiends!"   445
POLONIUS: This is too long.
HAMLET: It shall to the barber's, with your beard. Prithee, say on: he's for a
    jig° or a tale of bawdry,° or he sleeps: say on: come to Hecuba.°
FIRST PLAYER: "But who, ah woe! had seen the mobled° queen—"
HAMLET: "The mobled queen?"   450
POLONIUS: That's good; "mobled queen" is good.
FIRST PLAYER: "Run barefoot up and down, threat'ning the flames
    With bisson rheum;° a clout° upon that head
    Where late the diadem stood, and for a robe,
    About her lank and all o'er-teemed° loins,   455
    A blanket, in the alarm of fear caught up;
    Who this had seen, with tongue in venom steep'd,
    'Gainst Fortune's state would treason have pronounc'd:°
    But if the gods themselves did see her then
    When she saw Pyrrhus make malicious sport   460
    In mincing with his sword her husband's limbs,
    The instant burst of clamour that she made,

422*Then senseless Ilium* insensate Troy.   428*painted tyrant* tyrant in a picture.   429*matter* task.
431*against* before.   432*rack* mass of clouds.   435*region* assembly.   438*proof eterne* external resistance to assault.   442*synod* assembly.   443*fellies* pieces of wood forming the rim of a wheel.   444*nave*
hub.   448*jig* comic performance given at the end or in an interval of a play.   448*bawdry* indecency.
448*Hecuba* wife of Priam, king of Troy.   449*mobled* muffled.   453*bisson rheum* blinding tears.   453*clout*
piece of cloth.   455*o'er-teemed* worn out with bearing children.   458*pronounc'd* proclaimed.

Unless things mortal move them not at all,
Would have made milch° the burning eyes of heaven,
And passion in the gods."   465

POLONIUS: Look, whe'r he has not turned° his colour and has tears in 's eyes.
Prithee, no more.

HAMLET: 'Tis well; I'll have thee speak out the rest soon. Good my lord, will
you see the players well bestowed? Do you hear, let them be well used;
for they are the abstract° and brief chronicles of the time: after your death   470
you were better have a bad epitaph than their ill report while you live.

POLONIUS: My lord, I will use them according to their desert.

HAMLET: God's bodykins,° man, much better: use every man after his desert,
and who shall 'scape whipping? Use them after your own honour and
dignity: the less they deserve, the more merit is in your bounty. Take   475
them in.

POLONIUS: Come, sirs.

HAMLET: Follow him, friends: we'll hear a play tomorrow. [*Aside to* FIRST
PLAYER.] Dost thou hear me, old friend; can you play the Murder of
Gonzago?   480

FIRST PLAYER: Ay, my lord.

HAMLET: We'll ha 't to-morrow night. You could, for a need, study a speech
of some dozen or sixteen lines,° which I would set down and insert in 't,
could you not?

FIRST PLAYER: Ay, my lord.   485

HAMLET: Very well. Follow that lord; and look you mock him not.—My
good friends, I'll leave you till night: you are welcome to Elsinore.

                                                Exeunt POLONIUS *and* PLAYERS.

ROSENCRANTZ: Good my lord!   *Exeunt* [ROSENCRANTZ *and* GUILDENSTERN.]

HAMLET: Ay, so, God bye to you.—Now I am alone.
O, what a rogue and peasant° slave am I!   490
Is it not monstrous that this player here,
But in a fiction, in a dream of passion,
Could force his soul so to his own conceit
That from her working all his visage wann'd,°
Tears in his eyes, distraction in 's aspect,   495
A broken voice, and his whole function suiting
With forms to his conceit?° and all for nothing!
For Hecuba!
What's Hecuba to him, or he to Hecuba,
That he should weep for her? What would he do,   500
Had he the motive and the cue for passion
That I have? He would drown the stage with tears
And cleave the general ear with horrid speech,

---

464 **milch** *moist with tears.*   466 **turned** *changed.*   470 **abstract** *summary account.*   473 **bodykins** *diminutive form of the oath "by God's body."*   483 **dozen or sixteen lines** *critics have amused themselves by trying to locate Hamlet's lines. Lucianus's speech III.ii.226–231 is the best guess.*   490 **peasant** *base.*   494 **wann'd** *grew pale.*   496–497 **his whole . . . conceit** *his whole being responded with forms to suit his thought.*

Make mad the guilty and appall the free,
Confound the ignorant, and amaze indeed 505
The very faculties of eyes and ears.
Yet I,
A dull and muddy-mettled° rascal, peak,°
Like John-a-dreams,° unpregnant of° my cause,
And can say nothing; no, not for a king. 510
Upon whose property° and most dear life
A damn'd defeat was made. Am I a coward?
Who calls me villain? breaks my pate across?
Plucks off my beard, and blows it in my face?
Tweaks me by the nose? gives me the lie i' th' throat, 515
As deep as to the lungs? who does me this?
Ha!
'Swounds, I should take it: for it cannot be
But I am pigeon-liver'd° and lack gall
To make oppression bitter, or ere this 520
I should have fatted all the region kites°
With this slave's offal: bloody, bawdy villain!
Remorseless, treacherous, lecherous, kindless° villain!
O, vengeance!
Why, what an ass am I! This is most brave, 525
That I, the son of a dear father murder'd,
Prompted to my revenge by heaven and hell,
Must, like a whore, unpack my heart with words,
And fall a-cursing, like a very drab,°
A stallion!° 530
Fie upon 't! foh! About,° my brains! Hum, I have heard
That guilty creatures sitting at a play
Have by the very cunning of the scene
Been struck so to the soul that presently
They have proclaim'd their malefactions; 535
For murder, though it have no tongue, will speak
With most miraculous organ. I'll have these players
Play something like the murder of my father
Before mine uncle: I'll observe his looks:
I'll tent° him to the quick: if 'a do blench,° 540
I know my course. The spirit that I have seen
May be the devil:° and the devil hath power
T' assume a pleasing shape; yea, and perhaps
Out of my weakness and my melancholy,

508**muddy-mettled** *dull-spirited.*　　508**peak** *mope, pine.*　　509**John-a-dreams** *an expression occurring elsewhere in Elizabethan literature to indicate a dreamer.*　　509**unpregnant of** *not quickened by.*　　511**property** *proprietorship (of crown and life).*　　519**pigeon-liver'd** *the pigeon was supposed to secrete no gall; if Hamlet, so he says, had had gall, he would have felt the bitterness of oppression, and avenged it.*　　521**region kites** *kites of the air.*　　523**kindless** *unnatural.*　　529**drab** *prostitute.*　　530**stallion** *prostitute (male or female).*　　531**About** *about it, or turn thou right about.*　　540**tent** *probe.*　　540**blench** *quail, flinch.*　　542**May be the devil** *Hamlet's suspicion is properly grounded in the belief of the time.*

As he is very potent with such spirits,°   545
Abuses me to damn me: I'll have grounds
More relative° than this:° the play's the thing
Wherein I'll catch the conscience of the king.   *Exit.*

ACT III

Scene I [A room in the castle.]

Enter KING, QUEEN, POLONIUS, OPHELIA, ROSENCRANTZ, GUILDENSTERN, LORDS.

KING: And can you, by no drift of conference,°
    Get from him why he puts on this confusion,
    Grating so harshly all his days of quiet
    With turbulent and dangerous lunacy?
ROSENCRANTZ: He does confess he feels himself distracted;   5
    But from what cause 'a will by no means speak.
GUILDENSTERN: Nor do we find him forward° to be sounded,
    But, with a crafty madness, keeps aloof,
    When we would bring him on to some confession
    Of his true state.
QUEEN: Did he receive you well?   10
ROSENCRANTZ: Most like a gentleman.
GUILDENSTERN: But with much forcing of his disposition.°
ROSENCRANTZ: Niggard of question;° but, of our demands,
    Most free in his reply.
QUEEN: Did you assay° him
    To any pastime?   15
ROSENCRANTZ: Madam, it so fell out, that certain players
    We o'er-raught° on the way: of these we told him;
    And there did seem in him a kind of joy
    To hear of it: they are here about the court,
    And, as I think, they have already order   20
    This night to play before him.
POLONIUS: 'Tis most true:
    And he beseech'd me to entreat your majesties
    To hear and see the matter.
KING: With all my heart; and it doth much content me
    To hear him so inclin'd.   25
    Good gentlemen, give him a further edge,°
    And drive his purpose into these delights.
ROSENCRANTZ: We shall, my lord.   *Exeunt* ROSENCRANTZ *and* GUILDENSTERN.
KING: Sweet Gertrude, leave us too;

545*spirits* humors.   547*relative* closely related, definite.   547*this* i.e., the ghosts' story.   **III.i.** 1*drift of conference* device of conversation.   7*forward* willing.   12*forcing of his disposition* i.e., against his will.   13*Niggard of question* sparing of conversation.   14*assay* try to win.   17*o'er-raught* overtook.   26*edge* incitement.

For we have closely° sent for Hamlet hither,
That he, as 'twere by accident, may here   30
Affront° Ophelia:
    Her father and myself, lawful espials,°
Will so bestow ourselves that, seeing, unseen,
We may of their encounter frankly judge,
And gather by him, as he is behav'd,   35
If 't be th' affliction of his love or no
That thus he suffers for.
QUEEN: I shall obey you.
    And for your part, Ophelia, I do wish
That your good beauties be the happy cause
Of Hamlet's wildness:° so shall I hope your virtues   40
Will bring him to his wonted way again,
To both your honours.
OPHELIA: Madam, I wish it may.   [*Exit* QUEEN.]
POLONIUS: Ophelia, walk you here. Gracious,° so please you,
    We will bestow ourselves. [*To* OPHELIA.] Read on this book;
That show of such an exercise° may colour°   45
Your loneliness. We are oft to blame in this,—
'Tis too much prov'd—that with devotion's visage
And pious action we do sugar o'er
The devil himself.
KING: [*aside*] O, 'tis too true!
    How smart a lash that speech doth give my conscience!   50
The harlot's cheek, beautied with plast'ring art,
Is not more ugly to° the thing° that helps it
Than is my deed to my most painted word:
O heavy burthen!
POLONIUS: I hear him coming: let's withdraw, my lord.   55

                    [*Exeunt* KING *and* POLONIUS.]

                    Enter HAMLET.

HAMLET: To be, or not to be: that is the question:
    Whether 'tis nobler in the mind to suffer
The slings and arrows of outrageous fortune,
Or to take arms against a sea° of troubles,
And by opposing end them? To die: to sleep;   60
No more; and by a sleep to say we end
The heart-ache and the thousand natural shocks
That flesh is heir to, 'tis a consummation
Devoutly to be wish'd. To die, to sleep;

---

[29]*closely* *secretly.*   [31]*Affront* *confront.*   [32]*lawful espials* *legitimate spies.*   [40]*wildness* *madness.*
[43]*Gracious* *your grace (addressed to the king).*   [45]*exercise* *act of devotion (the book she reads is one of devo-*
tion).   [45]*colour* *give a plausible appearance to.*   [52]*to* *compared to.*   [52]*thing* *i.e., the cosmetic.*
[59]*sea* *the mixed metaphor of this speech has often been commented on; a later emendation* siege *has sometimes been*
spoken on the stage.

To sleep: perchance to dream: ay, there's the rub;   65
For in that sleep of death what dreams may come
When we have shuffled° off this mortal coil,°
Must give us pause: there's the respect°
That makes calamity of so long life;°
For who would bear the whips and scorns of time,°   70
Th' oppressor's wrong, the proud man's contumely,
The pangs of despis'd° love, the law's delay,
The insolence of office° and the spurns°
That patient merit of th' unworthy takes,
When he himself might his quietus° make   75
With a bare bodkin?° who would fardels° bear,
To grunt and sweat under a weary life,
But that the dread of something after death,
The undiscover'd country from whose bourn°
No traveller returns, puzzles the will   80
And makes us rather bear those ills we have
Than fly to others that we know not of?
Thus conscience° does make cowards of us all;
And thus the native hue° of resolution
Is sicklied o'er° with the pale cast° of thought,   85
And enterprises of great pitch° and moment°
With this regard° their currents° turn awry,
And lose the name of action—Soft you now!
The fair Ophelia! Nymph, in thy orisons°
Be all my sins remem'bred.

OPHELIA: Good my lord,   90
How does your honour for this many a day?

HAMLET: I humbly thank you; well, well, well.

OPHELIA: My lord, I have remembrances of yours,
That I have longed long to re-deliver;
I pray you, now receive them.

HAMLET: No, not I;   95
I never gave you aught.

OPHELIA: My honour'd lord, you know right well you did;
And, with them, words of so sweet breath compos'd
As made the things more rich: their perfume lost,
Take these again; for to the noble mind   100
Rich gifts wax poor when givers prove unkind.
There, my lord.

---

⁶⁷*shuffled* *sloughed, cast.*   ⁶⁷*coil* *usually means "turmoil"; here, possibly "body" (conceived of as wound about the soul like rope); clay, soil, veil, have been suggested as emendations.*   ⁶⁸*respect* *consideration.*   ⁶⁹*of . . . life so long-lived.*   ⁷⁰*time* *the world.*   ⁷²*despis'd* *rejected.*   ⁷³*office* *office-holders.*   ⁷³*spurns* *insults.*   ⁷⁵*quietus* *acquittance; here, death.*   ⁷⁶*bare bodkin* *mere dagger; bare is sometimes understood as "unsheathed."*   ⁷⁶*fardels* *burdens.*   ⁷⁹*bourn* *boundary.*   ⁸³*conscience* *probably, inhibition by the faculty of reason restraining the will from doing wrong.*   ⁸⁴*native hue* *natural color; metaphor derived from the color of the face.*   ⁸⁵*sicklied o'er* *given a sickly tinge.*   ⁸⁵*cast* *shade of color.*   ⁸⁶*pitch* *height (as of a falcon's flight).*   ⁸⁶*moment* *importance.*   ⁸⁷*regard* *respect, consideration.*   ⁸⁷*currents* *courses.*   ⁸⁹*orisons* *prayers.*

HAMLET: Ha, ha! are you honest?°
OPHELIA: My lord?
HAMLET: Are you fair?   105
OPHELIA: What means your lordship?
HAMLET: That if you be honest and fair, your honesty° should admit no
　　discourse to° your beauty.
OPHELIA: Could beauty, my lord, have better commerce° than with honesty?
HAMLET: Ay, truly; for the power of beauty will sooner transform honesty 110
　　from what it is to a bawd than the force of honesty can translate beauty
　　into his likeness: this was sometime a paradox, but now the time° gives it
　　proof. I did love you once.
OPHELIA: Indeed, my lord, you made me believe so.
HAMLET: You should not have believed me; for virtue cannot so inoculate° 115
　　our old stock but we shall relish of it:° I loved you not.
OPHELIA: I was the more deceived.
HAMLET: Get thee to a nunnery: why wouldst thou be a breeder of sinners?
　　I am myself indifferent honest;° but yet I could accuse me of such things
　　that it were better my mother had not borne me: I am very proud, 120
　　revengeful, ambitious, with more offences at my beck° than I have
　　thoughts to put them in, imagination to give them shape, or time to act
　　them in. What should such fellows as I do crawling between earth and
　　heaven? We are arrant knaves, all; believe none of us. Go thy ways to a
　　nunnery. Where's your father?   125
OPHELIA: At home, my lord.
HAMLET: Let the doors be shut upon him, that he may play the fool no where
　　but in 's own house. Farewell.
OPHELIA: O, help him, you sweet heavens!
HAMLET: If thou dost marry, I'll give thee this plague for thy dowry: be thou 130
　　as chaste as ice, as pure as snow, thou shalt not escape calumny. Get thee
　　to a nunnery, go: farewell. Or, if thou wilt needs marry, marry a fool; for
　　wise men know well enough what monsters° you make of them. To a
　　nunnery, go, and quickly too. Farewell.
OPHELIA: O heavenly powers, restore him!   135
HAMLET: I have heard of your° paintings too, well enough; God hath given
　　you one face, and you make yourselves another: you jig,° you amble, and
　　you lisp; you nick-name God's creatures, and make your wantonness
　　your ignorance.° Go to, I'll no more on 't; it hath made me mad. I say,
　　we will have no more marriage: those that are married already, all but one,° 140
　　shall live; the rest shall keep as they are. To a nunnery, go.   *Exit.*

103–108*are you honest . . . beauty*　honest *meaning "truthful" and "chaste" and* fair *meaning "just, honorable"*
(line 105) and "beautiful" (line 107) are not mere quibbles; the speech has the irony of a double entendre.   107*your*
honesty　your chastity.   108*discourse to*　familiar intercourse with.   109*commerce*　intercourse.
112*the time*　the present age.   115*inoculate*　graft (metaphorical).   116*but . . . it*　i.e., that we do not
still have about us a taste of the old stock; i.e., retain our sinfulness.   119*indifferent honest*　moderately vir-
tuous.   121*beck*　command.   133*monsters*　an allusion to the horns of a cuckold.   136*your*　indefi-
nite use.   137*jig*　move with jerky motion; probably allusion to the jig, or song and dance, of the current stage.
138–139*make . . . ignorance*　i.e., excuse your wantonness on the ground of your ignorance.   140*one*　i.e.,
the king.

OPHELIA: O, what a noble mind is here o'er-thrown!
The courtier's, soldier's, scholar's, eye, tongue, sword;
Th' expectancy and rose° of the fair state,
The glass of fashion and the mould of form,°   145
Th' observ'd of all observers,° quite, quite down!
And I, of ladies most deject and wretched,
That suck'd the honey of his music vows,
Now see that noble and most sovereign reason,
Like sweet bells jangled, out of time and harsh;   150
That unmatch'd form and feature of blown° youth
Blasted with ecstasy:° O, woe is me,
T' have seen what I have seen, see what I see!

Enter KING *and* POLONIUS.

KING: Love! his affections do not that way tend;
Nor what he spake, though it lack'd form a little,   155
Was not like madness. There's something in his soul,
O'er which his melancholy sits on brood;
And I do doubt° the hatch and the disclose°
Will be some danger: which for to prevent,
I have in quick determination   160
Thus set it down: he shall with speed to England,
For the demand of our neglected tribute:
Haply the seas and countries different
With variable° objects shall expel
This something-settled° matter in his heart,   165
Whereon his brains still beating puts him thus
From fashion of himself.° What think you on 't?

POLONIUS: It shall do well: but yet do I believe
The origin and commencement of his grief
Sprung from neglected love. How now, Ophelia!   170
You need not tell us what Lord Hamlet said;
We heard it all. My lord, do as you please;
But, if you hold it fit, after the play
Let his queen mother all alone entreat him
To show his grief: let her be round° with him;   175
And I'll be plac'd, so please you, in the ear
Of all their conference. If she find him not,
To England send him, or confine him where
Your wisdom best shall think.

KING: It shall be so:
Madness in great ones must not unwatch'd go.   *Exeunt.* 180

---

¹⁴⁴**expectancy and rose** *source of hope.*   ¹⁴⁵**The glass . . . form** *the mirror of fashion and the pattern of courtly
behavior.*   ¹⁴⁶**observ'd . . . observers** *i.e., the center of attention in the court.*   ¹⁵¹**blown** *blooming.*
¹⁵²**ecstasy** *madness.*   ¹⁵⁸**doubt** *fear.*   ¹⁵⁸**disclose** *disclosure or revelation (by chipping of the shell).*
¹⁶⁴**variable** *various.*   ¹⁶⁵**something-settled** *somewhat settled.*   ¹⁶⁷**From . . . himself** *out of his nat-
ural manner.*   ¹⁷⁵**round** *blunt.*

Scene II [*A hall in the castle.*]

Enter HAMLET *and three of the* PLAYERS.

HAMLET: Speak the speech, I pray you, as I pronounced it to you, trippingly
on the tongue: but if you mouth it, as many of your° players do, I had
as lief the town-crier spoke my lines. Nor do not saw the air too much
with your hand, thus, but use all gently; for in the very torrent, tempest,
and, as I may say, whirlwind of your passion, you must acquire and beget   5
a temperance that may give it smoothness. O, it offends me to the soul
to hear a robustious° periwig-pated° fellow tear a passion to tatters, to
very rags, to split the ears of the groundlings,° who for the most part are
capable of° nothing but inexplicable dumb-shows and noise: I would
have such a fellow whipped for o'er-doing Termagant;° it out-herods   10
Herod:° pray you, avoid it.

FIRST PLAYER: I warrant your honour.

HAMLET: Be not too tame neither, but let your own discretion be your tutor:
suit the action to the word, the word to the action; with this special
observance, that you o'er-step not the modesty of nature: for any thing   15
so overdone is from the purpose of playing, whose end, both at the first
and now, was and is, to hold, as 't were, the mirror up to nature; to show
virtue her own feature, scorn her own image, and the very age and body
of the time his form and pressure.° Now this overdone, or come tardy
off,° though it make the unskilful laugh, cannot but make the judicious   20
grieve; the censure of the which one° must in your allowance o'erweigh
a whole theatre of others. O, there be players that I have seen play, and
heard others praise, and that highly, not to speak it profanely, that, neither having the accent of Christians nor the gait of Christian, pagan, nor
man, have so strutted and bellowed that I have thought some of nature's   25
journeymen° had made men and not made them well, they imitated
humanity so abominably.

FIRST PLAYER: I hope we have reformed that indifferently° with us, sir.

HAMLET: O, reform it altogether. And let those that play your clowns speak
no more than is set down for them; for there be of° them that will them-   30
selves laugh, to set on some quantity of barren° spectators to laugh too;
though, in the mean time, some necessary question of the play be then to
be considered: that's villanous, and shows a most pitiful ambition in the
fool that uses it. Go, make you ready.

[*Exeunt* PLAYERS.]

III.ii. ²*your* *indefinite use.* ⁷*robustious* *violent, boisterous.* ⁷*periwig-pated* *wearing a wig.*
⁸*groundlings* *those who stood in the yard of the theater.* ⁹*capable of* *susceptible of being influenced by.*
⁹*inexplicable* *of no significance worth explaining.* ¹⁰*Termagant* *a god of the Saracens; a character in the St.*
Nicholas play, where one of his worshipers, leaving him in charge of goods, returns to find them stolen; whereupon he
beats the god (or idol), which howls vociferously. ¹¹*Herod* *Herod of Jewry; a character in* The Slaughter of the
Innocents *and other cycle plays. The part was played with great noise and fury.* ¹⁹*pressure* *stamp, impressed*
character. ¹⁹⁻²⁰*come tardy off* *inadequately done.* ²¹*the censure . . . one* *the judgment of even one of*
whom. ²⁶*journeymen* *laborers not yet masters in their trade.* ²⁸*indifferently* *fairly, tolerably.* ³⁰*of*
i.e., some among them. ³¹*barren* *i.e., of wit.*

Enter POLONIUS, GUILDENSTERN, *and* ROSENCRANTZ.

How now, my lord! will the king hear this piece of work?   35
POLONIUS: And the queen too, and that presently.
HAMLET: Bid the players make haste.   [*Exit* POLONIUS.]
    Will you two help to hasten them?
ROSENCRANTZ: ⎫
              ⎬ We will, my lord.   *Exeunt they two.*
GUILDENSTERN: ⎭
HAMLET: What ho! Horatio!

Enter HORATIO.

HORATIO: Here, sweet lord, at your service.   40
HAMLET: Horatio, thou art e'en as just° a man
    As e'er my conversation cop'd withal.
HORATIO: O, my dear lord,—
HAMLET: Nay, do not think I flatter;
    For what advancement may I hope from thee
    That no revenue hast but thy good spirits,   45
    To feed and clothe thee? Why should the poor be flatter'd?
    No, let the candied tongue lick absurd pomp,
    And crook the pregnant° hinges of the knee
    Where thrift° may follow fawning. Dost thou hear?
    Since my dear soul was mistress of her choice   50
    And could of men distinguish her election,
    S' hath seal'd thee for herself; for thou hast been
    As one, in suff'ring all, that suffers nothing,
    A man that fortune's buffets and rewards
    Hast ta'en with equal thanks: and blest are those   55
    Whose blood and judgement are so well commeddled,
    That they are not a pipe for fortune's finger
    To sound what stop° she please. Give me that man
    That is not passion's slave, and I will wear him
    In my heart's core, ay, in my heart of heart,   60
    As I do thee.—Something too much of this.—
    There is a play to-night before the king;
    One scene of it comes near the circumstance
    Which I have told thee of my father's death:
    I prithee, when thou seest that act afoot,   65
    Even with the very comment of thy soul°
    Observe my uncle: if his occulted° guilt
    Do not itself unkennel in one speech,
    It is a damned° ghost that we have seen,
    And my imaginations are as foul   70
    As Vulcan's stithy.° Give him heedful note;

---

⁴¹**just** *honest, honorable.*   ⁴⁸**pregnant** *pliant.*   ⁴⁹**thrift** *profit.*   ⁵⁸**stop** *hole in a wind instrument for controlling the sound.*   ⁶⁶**very . . . soul** *inward and sagacious criticism.*   ⁶⁷**occulted** *hidden.*   ⁶⁹**damned** *in league with Satan.*   ⁷¹**stithy** *smithy, place of stiths (anvils).*

For I mine eyes will rivet to his face,
And after we will both our judgements join
In censure of his seeming.°
HORATIO: Well, my lord:
If 'a steal aught the whilst this play is playing,
And 'scape detecting, I will pay the theft.

75

Enter trumpets and kettledrums, KING, QUEEN, POLONIUS, OPHELIA, [ROSENCRANTZ,
GUILDENSTERN, *and others*].

HAMLET: They are coming to the play; I must be idle:° Get you a place.
KING: How fares our cousin Hamlet?
HAMLET: Excellent, i' faith; of the chameleon's dish:° I eat the air, promise-
crammed: you cannot feed capons so.
KING: I have nothing with° this answer, Hamlet; these words are not mine.°
HAMLET: No, nor mine now. [*To* POLONIUS.] My lord, you played once i'
the university, you say?
POLONIUS: That did I, my lord; and was accounted a good actor.
HAMLET: What did you enact?
POLONIUS: I did enact Julius Cæsar: I was killed i' the Capitol; Brutus killed
me.
HAMLET: It was a brute part of him to kill so capital a calf there. Be the play-
ers ready?
ROSENCRANTZ: Ay, my lord; they stay upon your patience.
QUEEN: Come hither, my dear Hamlet, sit by me.
HAMLET: No, good mother, here's metal more attractive.
POLONIUS [*to the king*]: O, ho! do you mark that?
HAMLET: Lady, shall I lie in your lap?   [*Lying down at* OPHELIA's *feet.*]
OPHELIA: No, my lord.
HAMLET: I mean, my head upon your lap?
OPHELIA: Ay, my lord.
HAMLET: Do you think I meant country° matters?
OPHELIA: I think nothing, my lord.
HAMLET: That's a fair thought to lie between maids' legs.
OPHELIA: What is, my lord?
HAMLET: Nothing.
OPHELIA: You are merry, my lord.
HAMLET: Who, I?
OPHELIA: Ay, my lord.
HAMLET: O God, your only° jig-maker.° What should a man do but be
merry? for, look you, how cheerfully my mother looks, and my father died
within's two hours.

80

85

90

95

100

105

⁷⁴*censure . . . seeming* *judgment of his appearance or behavior.*   ⁷⁷*idle* *crazy, or not attending to anything
serious.*   ⁷⁹*chameleon's dish* *chameleons were supposed to feed on air. (Hamlet deliberately misinterprets the king's
"fares" as "feeds.")*   ⁸¹*have . . . with* *make nothing of.*   ⁸¹*are not mine* *do not respond to what I
ask.*   ⁹⁸*country* *with a bawdy pun.*   ¹⁰⁶*your only* *only your.*   ¹⁰⁶*jig-maker* *composer of jigs (song
and dance).*

OPHELIA: Nay, 'tis twice two months, my lord.

HAMLET: So long? Nay then, let the devil wear black, for I'll have a suit of[110] sables.° O heavens! die two months ago, and not forgotten yet? Then there's hope a great man's memory may outlive his life half a year: but, by 'r lady, 'a must build churches, then; or else shall 'a suffer not thinking on,° with the hobbyhorse, whose epitaph is "For, O, for, O, the hobbyhorse is forgot."°
[115]

The trumpets sound. Dumb show follows.

Enter a KING *and a* QUEEN [*very lovingly*]; *the* QUEEN *embracing him, and he her.* [*She kneels, and makes show of protestation unto him.*] *He takes her up, and declines his head upon her neck: he lies him down upon a bank of flowers: she, seeing him asleep, leaves him. Anon comes in another man, takes off his crown, kisses it, pours poison in the sleeper's ears, and leaves him. The* QUEEN *returns; finds the* KING *dead, makes passionate action. The* POISONER, *with some three or four come in again, seem to condole with her. The dead body is carried away. The* POISONER *woos the* QUEEN *with gifts: she seems harsh awhile, but in the end accepts love.* [*Exeunt.*]

OPHELIA: What means this, my lord?

HAMLET: Marry, this is miching mallecho;° it means mischief.

OPHELIA: Belike this show imports the argument of the play.

Enter PROLOGUE.

HAMLET: We shall know by this fellow: the players cannot keep counsel; they'll tell all.
[120]

OPHELIA: Will 'a tell us what this show meant?

HAMLET: Ay, or any show that you'll show him: be not you ashamed to show, he'll not shame to tell you what it means.

OPHELIA: You are naught, you are naught:° I'll mark the play.

PROLOGUE: For us, and for our tragedy,
[125]
Here stooping° to your clemency,
We beg your hearing patiently.   [*Exit.*]

HAMLET: Is this a prologue, or the posy° of a ring?

OPHELIA: 'Tis brief, my lord.

HAMLET: As woman's love.
[130]

Enter [*two Players as*] KING *and* QUEEN.

PLAYER KING: Full thirty times hath Phoebus' cart gone round
Neptune's salt wash° and Tellus'° orbed ground,
And thirty dozen moons with borrowed° sheen
About the world have times twelve thirties been,

110–111 **suit of sables** *garments trimmed with the fur of the sable, with a quibble on sable meaning "black."* 113–114 **suffer . . . on** *undergo oblivion.*   114–115 **"For . . . forgot"** *verse of a song occurring also in* Love's Labour's Lost, *III.i.30; the hobbyhorse was a character in the Morris Dance.*   117 **miching mallecho** *sneaking mischief.* 124 **naught** *indecent.*   126 **stooping** *bowing.*   128 **posy** *motto.*   132 **salt wash** *the sea.*   132 **Tellus** *goddess of the earth (orbed ground).*   133 **borrowed** *i.e., reflected.*

Since love our hearts and Hymen° did our hands   135
Unite commutual° in most sacred bands.
PLAYER QUEEN: So many journeys may the sun and moon
Make us again count o'er ere love be done!
But, woe is me, you are so sick of late,
So far from cheer and from your former state,   140
That I distrust° you. Yet, though I distrust,
Discomfort you, my lord, it nothing must:
For women's fear and love holds quantity;°
In neither aught, or in extremity.
Now, what my love is, proof hath made you know;   145
And as my love is siz'd, my fear is so:
Where love is great, the littlest doubts are fear;
Where little fears grow great, great love grows there.
PLAYER KING: 'Faith, I must leave thee, love, and shortly too;
My operant° powers their functions leave° to do: 150
And thou shalt live in this fair world behind,
Honour'd, belov'd; and haply one as kind
For husband shalt thou—
PLAYER QUEEN: O, confound the rest!
Such love must needs be treason in my breast:
In second husband let me be accurst!   155
None wed the second but who kill'd the first.
HAMLET *(aside)*: Wormwood, wormwood.
PLAYER QUEEN: The instances that second marriage move
Are base respects of thrift, but none of love:
A second time I kill my husband dead,   160
When second husband kisses me in bed.
PLAYER KING: I do believe you think what now you speak;
But what we do determine oft we break.
Purpose is but the slave to memory,
Of violent birth, but poor validity: 165
Which now, like fruit unripe, sticks on the tree;
But fall, unshaken, when they mellow be.
Most necessary 'tis that we forget
To pay ourselves what to ourselves is debt:
What to ourselves in passion we propose,   170
The passion ending, doth the purpose lose.
The violence of either grief or joy
Their own enactures° with themselves destroy:
Where joy most revels, grief doth most lament;
Grief joys, joy grieves, on slender accident.   175
This world is not for aye,° nor 'tis not strange

---

¹³⁵**Hymen** *god of matrimony.*   ¹³⁶**commutual** *mutually.*   ¹⁴¹**distrust** *am anxious about.*   ¹⁴³**holds quantity** *keeps proportion between.*   ¹⁵⁰**operant** *active.*   ¹⁵⁰**leave** *cease.*   ¹⁷³**enactures** *fulfillments.*   ¹⁷⁶**aye** *ever.*

That even our loves should with our fortunes change;
For 'tis a question left us yet to prove,
Whether love lead fortune, or else fortune love.
The great man down, you mark his favourite flies;   180
The poor advanc'd makes friends of enemies.
And hitherto doth love on fortune tend;
For who° not needs shall never lack a friend,
And who in want a hollow friend doth try,
Directly seasons° him his enemy.   185
But, orderly to end where I begun,
Our wills and fates do so contrary run
That our devices still are overthrown;
Our thoughts are ours, their ends° none of our own:
So think thou wilt no second husband wed;   190
But die thy thoughts when thy first lord is dead.

PLAYER QUEEN: Nor earth to me give food, nor heaven light!
Sport and repose lock from me day and night!
To desperation turn my trust and hope!
An anchor's° cheer° in prison be my scope!   195
Each opposite° that blanks° the face of joy
Meet what I would have well and it destroy!
Both here and hence pursue me lasting strife,
If, once a widow, ever I be wife!

HAMLET: If she should break it now!   200

PLAYER KING: 'Tis deeply sworn. Sweet, leave me here awhile;
My spirits grow dull, and fain I would beguile
The tedious day with sleep.   [*Sleeps.*]

PLAYER QUEEN: Sleep rock thy brain;
And never come mischance between us twain!   *Exit.*

HAMLET: Madam, how like you this play?   205

QUEEN: The lady doth protest too much, methinks.

HAMLET: O, but she'll keep her word.

KING: Have you heard the argument? Is there no offence in 't?

HAMLET: No, no, they do but jest, poison in jest; no offence i' the world.

KING: What do you call the play?   210

HAMLET: The Mouse-trap. Marry, how? Tropically.° This play is the image
of a murder done in Vienna: Gonzago° is the duke's name; his wife, Bap-
tista: you shall see anon; 't is a knavish piece of work: but what o' that? your
majesty and we that have free souls, it touches us not: let the galled jade°
winch,° our withers° are unwrung.°   215

---

¹⁸³*who* whoever.   ¹⁸⁵*seasons* matures, ripens.   ¹⁸⁹*ends* results.   ¹⁹⁵*An anchor's* an anchorite's.
¹⁹⁵*cheer* fare; sometimes printed as chair.   ¹⁹⁶*opposite* adverse thing.   ¹⁹⁶*blanks* causes to blanch or
grow pale.   ²¹¹*Tropically* figuratively, trapically suggests a pun on trap in Mouse-trap (1.211).   ²¹²*Gon-*
zago in 1538 Luigi Gonzago murdered the Duke of Urbano by pouring poisoned lotion in his ears.   ²¹⁴*galled jade*
horse whose hide is rubbed by saddle or harness.   ²¹⁵*winch* wince.   ²¹⁵*withers* the part between the horse's
shoulder blades.   ²¹⁵*unwrung* not wrung or twisted.

Enter LUCIANUS.

This is one Lucianus, nephew to the king.

OPHELIA: You are as good as a chorus,° my lord.

HAMLET: I could interpret between you and your love, if I could see the puppets dallying.°

OPHELIA: You are keen, my lord, you are keen.   220

HAMLET: It would cost you a groaning to take off my edge.

OPHELIA: Still better, and worse.°

HAMLET: So you mistake° your husbands. Begin, murderer; pox,° leave thy damnable faces, and begin. Come: the croaking raven doth bellow for revenge.   225

LUCIANUS: Thoughts black, hands apt, drugs fit, and time agreeing;
   Confederate° season, else no creature seeing;
   Thou mixture rank, of midnight weeds collected,
   With Hecate's° ban° thrice blasted, thrice infected,
   Thy natural magic and dire property,   230
   On wholesome life usurp immediately.

[*Pours the poison into the sleeper's ears.*]

HAMLET: 'A poisons him i' the garden for his estate. His name's Gonzago: the story is extant, and written in very choice Italian: you shall see anon how the murderer gets the love of Gonzago's wife.   235

OPHELIA: The king rises.

HAMLET: What, frighted with false fire!°

QUEEN: How fares my lord?

POLONIUS: Give o'er the play.

KING: Give me some light: away!

POLONIUS: Lights, lights, lights!   *Exeunt all but* HAMLET *and* HORATIO. 240

HAMLET: Why, let the strucken deer go weep,
      The hart ungalled play;
   For some must watch, while some must sleep:
      Thus runs the world away.°
   Would not this,° sir, and a forest of feathers°—if the rest of my fortunes   245
   turn Turk with° me—with two Provincial roses° on my razed° shoes, get
   me a fellowship in a cry° of players,° sir?

HORATIO: Half a share.°

---

[217]**chorus**   *in many Elizabethan plays the action was explained by an actor known as the "chorus"; at a puppet show the actor who explained the action was known as an "interpreter," as indicated by the lines following.* [219]**dallying** *with sexual suggestion, continued in* **keen** *(sexually aroused),* **groaning** *(i.e., in pregnancy), and* **edge** *(i.e., sexual desire or impetuosity).* [222]**Still . . . worse** *more keen, less decorous.* [223]**mistake** *err in taking.* [223]**pox** *an imprecation.* [227]**Confederate** *conspiring (to assist the murderer).* [229]**Hecate** *the goddess of witchcraft.* [229]**ban** *curse.* [236]**false fire** *fireworks, or a blank discharge.* [241–244]**Why . . . away** *probably from an old ballad, with allusion to the popular belief that a wounded deer retires to weep and die. Cf. As You Like It, II.i.66.* [245]**this** *i.e., the play.* [245]**feathers** *allusion to the plumes which Elizabethan actors were fond of wearing.* [246]**turn Turk with** *go back on.* [246]**two Provincial roses** *rosettes of ribbon like the roses of Provins near Paris, or else the roses of Provence.* [246]**razed** *cut, slashed (by way of ornament).* [247]**cry** *pack (as of hounds).* [247]**fellowship . . . players** *partnership in a theatrical company.* [248]**Half a share** *allusion to the custom in dramatic companies of dividing the ownership into a number of shares among the householders.*

HAMLET: A whole one, I.
  For thou dost know, O Damon dear,   250
    This realm dismantled° was
  Of Jove himself; and now reigns here
    A very, very°—pajock.°
HORATIO: You might have rhymed.
HAMLET: O good Horatio, I'll take the ghost's word for a thousand pound. 255
  Didst perceive?
HORATIO: Very well, my lord.
HAMLET: Upon the talk of the poisoning?
HORATIO: I did very well note him.
HAMLET: Ah, ha! Come, some music! come, the recorders!°   260
  For if the king like not the comedy,
  Why then, belike, he likes it not, perdy.°
  Come, some music!

Enter ROSENCRANTZ *and* GUILDENSTERN.

GUILDENSTERN: Good my lord, vouchsafe me a word with you.
HAMLET: Sir, a whole history.   265
GUILDENSTERN: The king, sir,—
HAMLET: Ay, sir, what of him?
GUILDENSTERN: Is in his retirement marvellous distempered.
HAMLET: With drink, sir?
GUILDENSTERN: No, my lord, rather with choler.°   270
HAMLET: Your wisdom should show itself more richer to signify this to his
  doctor; for, for me to put him to his purgation would perhaps plunge him
  into far more choler.
GUILDENSTERN: Good my lord, put your discourse into some frame° and start
  not so wildly from my affair.   275
HAMLET: I am tame, sir: pronounce.
GUILDENSTERN: The queen, your mother, in most great affliction of spirit,
  hath sent me to you.
HAMLET: You are welcome.
GUILDENSTERN: Nay, good my lord, this courtesy is not of the right breed. 280
  If it shall please you to make me a wholesome° answer, I will do your
  mother's commandment; if not, your pardon and my return shall be the
  end of my business.
HAMLET: Sir, I cannot.
GUILDENSTERN: What, my lord?   285
HAMLET: Make you a wholesome answer; my wit's diseased: but, sir, such
  answer as I can make, you shall command; or, rather, as you say, my
  mother: therefore no more, but to the matter:° my mother, you say,—

---

²⁵¹**dismantled** *stripped, divested.*   ²⁵⁰⁻²⁵³**For . . . very** *probably from an old ballad having to do with*
Damon and Pythias.   ²⁵³**pajock** *peacock (a bird with a bad reputation). Possibly the word was* patchock,
diminutive of patch, *clown.*   ²⁶⁰**recorders** *wind instruments of the flute kind.*   ²⁶²**perdy** *corruption*
of par dieu.   ²⁷⁰**choler** *bilious disorder, with quibble on the sense "anger."*   ²⁷⁴**frame** *order.*   ²⁸¹**whole-**
some *sensible.*   ²⁸⁸**matter** *matter in hand.*

ROSENCRANTZ: Then thus she says; your behaviour hath struck her into amazement and admiration. 290

HAMLET: O wonderful son, that can so 'stonish a mother! But is there no sequel at the heels of this mother's admiration? Impart.

ROSENCRANTZ: She desires to speak with you in her closet, ere you go to bed.

HAMLET: We shall obey, were she ten times our mother. Have you any further trade with us? 295

ROSENCRANTZ: My lord, you once did love me.

HAMLET: And do still, by these pickers and stealers.°

ROSENCRANTZ: Good my lord, what is your cause of distemper? you do, surely, bar the door upon your own liberty, if you deny your griefs to your friend. 300

HAMLET: Sir, I lack advancement.

ROSENCRANTZ: How can that be, when you have the voice° of the king himself for your succession in Denmark?

HAMLET: Ay, sir, but "While the grass grows,"°—the proverb is something musty. 305

Enter the PLAYERS *with recorders.*

O, the recorders! let me see one. To withdraw° with you:—why do you go about to recover the wind° of me, as if you would drive me into a toil?°

GUILDENSTERN: O, my lord, if my duty be too bold, my love is too unmannerly.° 310

HAMLET: I do not well understand that. Will you play upon this pipe?

GUILDENSTERN: My lord, I cannot.

HAMLET: I pray you.

GUILDENSTERN: Believe me, I cannot.

HAMLET: I beseech you. 315

GUILDENSTERN: I know no touch of it, my lord.

HAMLET: 'Tis as easy as lying: govern these ventages° with your fingers and thumb, give it breath with your mouth, and it will discourse most eloquent music. Look you, these are the stops.

GUILDENSTERN: But these cannot I command to any utterance of harmony; 320 I have not the skill.

HAMLET: Why, look you now, how unworthy a thing you make of me! You would play upon me; you would seem to know my stops; you would pluck out the heart of my mystery; you would sound me from my lowest note to the top of my compass:° and there is much music, excellent voice, in 325 this little organ;° yet cannot you make it speak. 'Sblood, do you think I

297**pickers and stealers** *hands, so called from the catechism "to keep my hands from picking and stealing."* 302**voice** *support.* 304**"While . . . grows"** *the rest of the proverb is "the silly horse starves." Hamlet may be destroyed while he is waiting for the succession to the kingdom.* 306**withdraw** *speak in private.* 307**recover the wind** *get to the windward side.* 308**toil** *snare.* 309–310**if . . . unmannerly** *if I am using an unmannerly boldness, it is my love which occasions it.* 317**ventages** *stops of the recorders.* 325**compass** *range of voice.* 326**organ** *musical instrument, i.e., the pipe.*

am easier to be played on than a pipe? Call me what instrument you will, though you can fret° me, you cannot play upon me.

Enter POLONIUS.

God bless you, sir!

POLONIUS: My lord, the queen would speak with you, and presently.   330

HAMLET: Do you see yonder cloud that 's almost in shape of a camel?

POLONIUS: By the mass, and 'tis like a camel, indeed.

HAMLET: Methinks it is like a weasel.

POLONIUS: It is backed like a weasel.

HAMLET: Or like a whale?   335

POLONIUS: Very like a whale.

HAMLET: Then I will come to my mother by and by. [*Aside.*] They fool me
   to the top of my bent.°—I will come by and by.°

POLONIUS: I will say so.   [*Exit.*]

HAMLET: By and by is easily said.   340
   Leave me, friends.   [*Exeunt all but* HAMLET.]
   'Tis now the very witching time° of night,
   When churchyards yawn and hell itself breathes out
   Contagion to this world: now could I drink hot blood,
   And do such bitter business as the day   345
   Would quake to look on. Soft! now to my mother.
   O heart, lose not thy nature; let not ever
   The soul of Nero° enter this firm bosom:
   Let me be cruel, not unnatural:
   I will speak daggers to her, but use none;   350
   My tongue and soul in this be hypocrites;
   How in my words somever she be shent,°
   To give them seals° never, my soul, consent!   *Exit.*

Scene III [*A room in the castle.*]

Enter KING, ROSENCRANTZ, and GUILDENSTERN.

KING: I like him not, nor stands it safe with us
   To let his madness range. Therefore prepare you;
   I your commission will forthwith dispatch,°
   And he to England shall along with you:
   The terms° of our estate° may not endure   5
   Hazard so near us as doth hourly grow
   Out of his brows.°

---

³²⁸**fret** *quibble on meaning "irritate" and the piece of wood, gut, or metal which regulates the fingering.*   ³³⁸**top of my bent** *limit of endurance, i.e., extent to which a bow may be bent.*   ³³⁸**by and by** *immediately.*   ³⁴²**witching time** *i.e., time when spells are cast.*   ³⁴⁸**Nero** *murderer of his mother, Agrippina.*   ³⁵²**shent** *rebuked.*   ³⁵³**give them seals** *confirm with deeds.*   **III.iii.** ³**dispatch** *prepare.*   ⁵**terms** *condition, circumstances.*   ⁵**estate** *state.*   ⁷**brows** *effronteries.*

GUILDENSTERN: We will ourselves provide:
  Most holy and religious fear it is
  To keep those many many bodies safe
  That live and feed upon your majesty.   10
ROSENCRANTZ: The single and peculiar° life is bound,
  With all the strength and armour of the mind,
  To keep itself from noyance;° but much more
  That spirit upon whose weal depend and rest
  The lives of many. The cess° of majesty   15
  Dies not alone; but, like a gulf,° doth draw
  What's near it with it: it is a massy wheel,
  Fix'd on the summit of the highest mount,
  To whose huge spokes ten thousand lesser things
  Are mortis'd and adjoin'd; which, when it falls,   20
  Each small annexment, petty consequence,
  Attends° the boist'rous ruin. Never alone
  Did the king sigh, but with a general groan.
KING: Arm° you, I pray you, to this speedy voyage;
  For we will fetters put about this fear,   25
  Which now goes too free-footed.
ROSENCRANTZ: We will haste us.

Exeunt GENTLEMEN [ROSENCRANTZ *and* GUILDENSTERN].

Enter POLONIUS.

POLONIUS: My lord, he's going to his mother's closet:
  Behind the arras° I'll convey° myself,
  To hear the process;° I'll warrant she'll tax him home.°
  And, as you said, and wisely was it said,   30
  'Tis meet that some more audience than a mother,
  Since nature makes them partial, should o'erhear
  The speech, of vantage.° Fare you well, my liege:
  I'll call upon you ere you go to bed,
  And tell you what I know.
KING: Thanks, dear my lord.   *Exit* [POLONIUS].   35
  O, my offence is rank, it smells to heaven;
  It hath the primal eldest curse° upon't,
  A brother's murder. Pray can I not,
  Though inclination be as sharp as will:°
  My stronger guilt defeats my strong intent;   40
  And, like a man to double business bound,
  I stand in pause where I shall first begin,

---

[11] *single and peculiar* individual and private.   [13] *noyance* harm.   [15] *cess* decease.   [16] *gulf* whirlpool.
[22] *Attends* participates in.   [24] *Arm* prepare.   [28] *arras* screen of tapestry placed around the walls of
household apartments.   [28] *convey* implication of secrecy; convey was often used to mean "steal."   [29] *process*
proceedings.   [29] *tax him home* reprove him severely.   [33] *of vantage* from an advantageous place.   [37] *pri-*
mal eldest curse the curse of Cain, the first to kill his brother.   [39] *sharp as will* i.e., his desire is as strong as
his determination.

And both neglect. What if this cursed hand
Were thicker than itself with brother's blood,
Is there not rain enough in the sweet heavens
To wash it white as snow? Whereto serves mercy   45
But to confront° the visage of offence?
And what's in prayer but this two-fold force,
To be forestalled° ere we come to fall,
Or pardon'd being down? Then I'll look up;   50
My fault is past. But, O, what form of prayer
Can serve my turn? "Forgive me my foul murder"?
That cannot be: since I am still possess'd
Of those effects for which I did the murder,
My crown, mine own ambition° and my queen.   55
May one be pardon'd and retain th' offence?°
In the corrupted currents° of this world
Offence's gilded hand° may shove by justice,
And oft 'tis seen the wicked prize° itself
Buys out the law: but 'tis not so above;   60
There is no shuffling,° there the action lies°
In his true nature; and we ourselves compell'd,
Even to the teeth and forehead° of our faults,
To give in evidence. What then? what rests?°
Try what repentance can: what can it not?   65
Yet what can it when one can not repent?
O wretched state! O bosom black as death!
O limed° soul, that, struggling to be free,
Art more engag'd!° Help, angels! Make assay!°
Bow, stubborn knees; and, heart with strings of steel,   70
Be soft as sinews of the new-born babe!
All may be well.   [*He kneels.*]

Enter HAMLET.

HAMLET: Now might I do it pat,° now he is praying;
And now I'll do't. And so 'a goes to heaven;
And so am I reveng'd. That would be scann'd:°   75
A villain kills my father; and for that,
I, his sole son, do this same villain send
To heaven.
Why, this is hire and salary, not revenge.
'A took my father grossly, full of bread;°   80

---

[47] **confront** *oppose directly.*   [49] **forestalled** *prevented.*   [55] **ambition** *i.e., realization of ambition.*   [56] **offence** *benefit accruing from offense.*   [57] **currents** *courses.*   [58] **gilded hand** *hand offering gold as a bribe.*   [59] **wicked prize** *prize won by wickedness.*   [61] **shuffling** *escape by trickery.*   [61] **lies** *is sustainable.*   [63] **teeth and forehead** *very face.*   [64] **rests** *remains.*   [68] **limed** *caught as with birdlime.*   [69] **engag'd** *embedded.*   [69] **assay** *trial.*   [73] **pat** *opportunely.*   [75] **would be scann'd** *needs to be looked into.*   [80] **full of bread** *enjoying his worldly pleasures (see Ezekiel 16:49).*

With all his crimes broad blown,° as flush° as May;
And how his audit stands who knows save heaven?
But in our circumstance and course° of thought,
'Tis heavy with him: and am I then reveng'd,
To take him in the purging of his soul,   85
When he is fit and season'd for his passage?°
No!
Up, sword; and know thou a more horrid hent:°
When he is drunk asleep,° or in his rage,
Or in th' incestuous pleasure of his bed;   90
At game, a-swearing, or about some act
That has no relish of salvation in't;
Then trip him, that his heels may kick at heaven,
And that his soul may be as damn'd and black
As hell, whereto it goes. My mother stays: 95
This physic° but prolongs thy sickly days.   *Exit.*
KING: [*Rising*] My words fly up, my thoughts remain below:
Words without thoughts never to heaven go.   *Exit.*

Scene IV [*The Queen's closet.*]

Enter [QUEEN] GERTRUDE *and* POLONIUS.

POLONIUS: 'A will come straight. Look you lay° home to him:
Tell him his pranks have been too broad° to bear with,
And that your grace hath screen'd and stood between
Much heat° and him. I'll sconce° me even here.
Pray you, be round° with him.   5
HAMLET (*within*): Mother, mother, mother!
QUEEN: I'll warrant you,
Fear me not: withdraw, I hear him coming.

[POLONIUS *hides behind the arras.*]

Enter HAMLET.

HAMLET: Now, mother, what's the matter?
QUEEN: Hamlet, thou hast thy father much offended.
HAMLET: Mother, you have my father° much offended.   10
QUEEN: Come, come, you answer with an idle tongue.
HAMLET: Go, go, you question with a wicked tongue.
QUEEN: Why, how now, Hamlet!
HAMLET: What's the matter now?
QUEEN: Have you forgot me?

---

⁸¹*broad blown* in full bloom.   ⁸¹*flush* lusty.   ⁸³*in . . . course* as we see it in our mortal situation.
⁸⁶*fit . . . passage* i.e., reconciled to heaven by forgiveness of his sins.   ⁸⁸*hent* seizing; or more probably, occasion of seizure.   ⁸⁹*drunk asleep* in a drunken sleep.   ⁹⁶*physic* purging (by prayer).   **III.iv.**
¹*lay* thrust.   ²*broad* unrestrained.   ⁴*Much heat* i.e., the king's anger.   ⁴*sconce* hide.
⁵*round* blunt.   ^{9–10}*thy father, my father* i.e., Claudius, the elder Hamlet.

HAMLET: No, by the rood,° not so:
  You are the queen, your husband's brother's wife;   15
  And—would it were not so!—you are my mother.
QUEEN: Nay, then, I'll set those to you that can speak.
HAMLET: Come, come, and sit you down; you shall not budge;
  You go not till I set you up a glass
  Where you may see the inmost part of you.   20
QUEEN: What wilt thou do? thou wilt not murder me?
  Help, help, ho!
POLONIUS [*behind*]: What, ho! help, help; help!
HAMLET [*drawing*]: How now! a rat? Dead, for a ducat, dead!
                          [*Makes a pass through the arras.*]
POLONIUS [*behind*]: O, I am slain!   [*Falls and dies.*]   25
QUEEN: O me, what hast thou done?
HAMLET: Nay, I know not:
  Is it the king?
QUEEN: O, what a rash and bloody deed is this!
HAMLET: A bloody deed! almost as bad, good mother,
  As kill a king, and marry with his brother.   30
QUEEN: As kill a king!
HAMLET: Ay, lady, it was my word.
                [*Lifts up the arras and discovers* POLONIUS.]
  Thou wretched, rash, intruding fool, farewell!
  I took thee for thy better: take thy fortune;
  Thou find'st to too busy is some danger.
  Leave wringing of your hands: peace! sit you down,   35
  And let me wring your heart; for so I shall,
  If it be made of penetrable stuff,
  If damned custom have not braz'd° it so
  That it be proof and bulwark against sense.
QUEEN: What have I done, that thou dar'st wag thy tongue   40
  In noise so rude against me?
HAMLET: Such an act
  That blurs the grace and blush of modesty,
  Calls virtue hypocrite, takes off the rose
  From the fair forehead of an innocent love
  And sets a blister° there, makes marriage-vows   45
  As false as dicers' oaths: O, such a deed
  As from the body of contraction° plucks
  The very soul, and sweet religion° makes
  A rhapsody° of words: heaven's face does glow
  O'er this solidity and compound mass   50

---

¹⁴**rood** *cross.*   ³⁸**braz'd** *brazened, hardened.*   ⁴⁵**sets a blister** *brands as a harlot.*   ⁴⁷**contraction** *the marriage contract.*   ⁴⁸**religion** *religious vows.*   ⁴⁹**rhapsody** *senseless string.*

With heated visage, as against the doom
Is thought-sick at the act.°
QUEEN: Ay me, what act,
That roars so loud, and thunders in the index?°
HAMLET: Look here, upon this picture, and on this.
The counterfeit presentment° of two brothers.   55
See, what a grace was seated on this brow;
Hyperion's° curls; the front° of Jove himself;
An eye like Mars, to threaten and command;
A station° like the herald Mercury
New-lighted on a heaven-kissing hill;   60
A combination and a form indeed,
Where every god did seem to set his seal,
To give the world assurance° of a man:
This was your husband. Look you now, what follows:
Here is your husband; like a mildew'd ear,°   65
Blasting his wholesome brother. Have you eyes?
Could you on this fair mountain leave to feed,
And batten° on this moor?° Ha! have you eyes?
You cannot call it love; for at your age
The hey-day° in the blood is tame, it's humble,   70
And waits upon the judgement: and what judgement
Would step from this to this? Sense, sure, you have,
Else could you not have motion;° but sure, that sense
Is apoplex'd;° for madness would not err,
Nor sense to ecstasy was ne'er so thrall'd°   75
But it reserv'd some quantity of choice,°
To serve in such a difference. What devil was't
That thus hath cozen'd° you at hoodman-blind?°
Eyes without feeling, feeling without sight,
Ears without hands or eyes, smelling sans° all,   80
Or but a sickly part of one true sense
Could not so mope.°
O shame! where is thy blush? Rebellious hell,
If thou canst mutine° in a matron's bones,
To flaming youth let virtue be as wax,   85

---

⁴⁹⁻⁵²*heaven's . . . act* heaven's face blushes to look down upon this world, compounded of the four elements, with hot face as though the day of doom were near, and thought-sick at the deed (i.e., Gertrude's marriage). ⁵³*index* prelude or preface. ⁵⁵*counterfeit presentment* portrayed representation. ⁵⁷*Hyperion's* the sun god's. ⁵⁷*front* brow. ⁵⁹*station* manner of standing. ⁶³*assurance* pledge, guarantee. ⁶⁵*mildew'd ear* see Genesis 41:5–7. ⁶⁸*batten* grow fat. ⁶⁸*moor* barren upland. ⁷⁰*hey-day* state of excitement. ⁷²⁻⁷³*Sense . . . motion* sense and motion are functions of the middle or sensible soul, the possession of sense being the basis of motion. ⁷⁴*apoplex'd* paralyzed; mental derangement was thus of three sorts: apoplexy, ecstasy, and diabolic possession. ⁷⁵*thrall'd* enslaved. ⁷⁶*quantity of choice* fragment of the power to choose. ⁷⁸*cozen'd* tricked, cheated. ⁷⁸*hoodman-blind* blindman's buff. ⁸⁰*sans* without. ⁸²*mope* be in a depressed, spiritless state, act aimlessly. ⁸⁴*mutine* mutiny, rebel.

And melt in her own fire: proclaim no shame
When the compulsive ardour gives the charge,°
Since frost itself as actively doth burn
And reason pandars will.°

QUEEN: O Hamlet, speak no more:
Thou turn'st mine eyes into my very soul;   90
And there I see such black and grained° spots
As will not leave their tinct.

HAMLET: Nay, but to live
In the rank sweat of an enseamed° bed,
Stew'd in corruption, honeying and making love
Over the nasty sty,—

QUEEN: O, speak to me no more;   95
These words, like daggers, enter in mine ears;
No more, sweet Hamlet!

HAMLET: A murderer and a villain;
A slave that is not twentieth part the tithe
Of your precedent lord;° a vice of kings;°
A cutpurse of the empire and the rule,   100
That from a shelf the precious diadem stole,
And put it in his pocket!

QUEEN: No more!

Enter GHOST.

HAMLET: A king of shreds and patches,°—
Save me, and hover o'er me with your wings,
You heavenly guards! What would your gracious figure?   105

QUEEN: Alas, he's mad!

HAMLET: Do you not come your tardy son to chide,
That, laps'd in time and passion,° lets go by
Th' important° acting of your dread command?
O, say!   110

GHOST: Do not forget: this visitation
Is but to whet thy almost blunted purpose.
But, look, amazement° on thy mother sits:
O, step between her and her fighting soul:
Conceit in weakest bodies strongest works: 115
Speak to her, Hamlet.

HAMLET: How is it with you, lady?

---

⁸⁷*gives the charge*   *delivers the attack.*   ⁸⁹*reason pandars will*   *the normal and proper situation was one in which reason guided the will in the direction of good; here, reason is perverted and leads in the direction of evil.*   ⁹¹*grained*   *dyed in grain.*   ⁹³*enseamed*   *loaded with grease, greased.*   ⁹⁹*precedent lord*   *i.e., the elder Hamlet.*   ⁹⁹*vice of kings*   *buffoon of kings; a reference to the Vice, or clown, of the morality plays and interludes.*   ¹⁰³*shreds and patches*   *i.e., motley, the traditional costume of the Vice.*   ¹⁰⁸*laps'd . . . passion*   *having suffered time to slip and passion to cool; also explained as "engrossed in casual events and lapsed into mere fruitless passion, so that he no longer entertains a rational purpose."*   ¹⁰⁹*important*   *urgent.*   ¹¹³*amazement*   *frenzy, distraction.*

QUEEN: Alas, how is 't with you,
That you do bend your eye on vacancy
And with th' incorporal° air do hold discourse?
Forth at your eyes your spirits wildly peep;   120
And, as the sleeping soldiers in th' alarm,
Your bedded° hair, like life in excrements,°
Start up, and stand an° end. O gentle son,
Upon the heat and flame of thy distemper
Sprinkle cool patience. Whereon do you look?   125

HAMLET: On him, on him! Look you, how pale he glares!
His form and cause conjoin'd,° preaching to stones,
Would make them capable.—Do not look upon me;
Lest with this piteous action you convert
My stern effects:° then what I have to do   130
Will want true colour;° tears perchance for blood.

QUEEN: To whom do you speak this?

HAMLET: Do you see nothing there?

QUEEN: Nothing at all; yet all that is I see.

HAMLET: Nor did you nothing hear?

QUEEN: No, nothing but ourselves.

HAMLET: Why, look you there! look, how it steals away!   135
My father, in his habit as he liv'd!
Look, where he goes, even now, out at the portal!   *Exit* GHOST.

QUEEN: This is the very coinage of your brain:
This bodiless creation ecstasy
Is very cunning in.

HAMLET: Ecstasy!   140
My pulse, as yours, doth temperately keep time,
And makes as healthful music: it is not madness
That I have utt'red: bring me to the test,
And I the matter will re-word,° which madness
Would gambol° from. Mother, for love of grace,   145
Lay not that flattering unction° to your soul,
That not your trespass, but my madness speaks:
It will but skin and film the ulcerous place,
Whiles rank corruption, mining° all within,
Infects unseen. Confess yourself to heaven;   150
Repent what's past; avoid what is to come;°
And do not spread the compost° on the weeds,

---

¹¹⁹*incorporal* immaterial.   ¹²²*bedded* laid in smooth layers;.   ¹²²*excrements* the hair was considered an
excrement or voided part of the body.   ¹²³*an* on.   ¹²⁷*conjoin'd* united.   ¹²⁹⁻³⁰*convert . . . effects* di-
vert me from my stern duty. For effects, possibly affects (affections of the mind).   ¹³¹*want true colour* lack good
reason so that (with a play on the normal sense of colour) I shall shed tears instead of blood.   ¹⁴⁴*re-word* repeat
in words.   ¹⁴⁵*gambol* skip away.   ¹⁴⁶*unction* ointment used medicinally or as a rite; suggestion that forgiveness for sin may not be so easily achieved.   ¹⁴⁹*mining* working under the surface.   ¹⁵¹*what is to come* i.e.,
the sins of the future.   ¹⁵²*compost* manure.

To make them ranker. Forgive me this my virtue;°
For in the fatness° of these pursy° times
Virtue itself of vice must pardon beg,   155
Yea, curb° and woo for leave to do him good.
QUEEN: O Hamlet, thou hast cleft my heart in twain.
HAMLET: O, throw away the worser part of it,
And live the purer with the other half.
Good night: but go not to my uncle's bed;   160
Assume a virtue, if you have it not.
That monster, custom, who all sense doth eat,
Of habits devil, is angel yet in this,
That to the use of actions fair and good
He likewise gives a frock or livery,   165
That aptly is put on. Refrain to-night,
And that shall lend a kind of easiness
To the next abstinence: the next more easy;
For use almost can change the stamp of nature,
And either . . . the devil, or throw him out°   170
With wondrous potency. Once more, good night:
And when you are desirous to be bless'd,°
I'll blessing beg of you. For this same lord,   [*Pointing to* POLONIUS.]
I do repent: but heaven hath pleas'd it so,
To punish me with this and this with me,   175
That I must be their scourge and minister.
I will bestow him, and will answer well
The death I gave him. So, again, good night.
I must be cruel, only to be kind:
Thus bad begins and worse remains behind.   180
One word more, good lady.
QUEEN: What shall I do?
HAMLET: Not this, by no means, that I bid you do:
Let the bloat° king tempt you again to bed;
Pinch wanton on your cheek; call you his mouse;
And let him, for a pair of reechy° kisses,   185
Or paddling in your neck with his damn'd fingers,
Make you to ravel all this matter out,
That I essentially° am not in madness,
But mad in craft. 'Twere good you let him know;
For who, that's but a queen, fair, sober, wise,   190
Would from a paddock,° from a bat, a gib,°
Such dear concernings° hide? who would do so?
No, in despite of sense and secrecy,

153*this my virtue* my virtuous talk in reproving you.   154*fatness* grossness.   154*pursy* short-winded,
corpulent.   156*curb* bow, bend the knee.   170*defective line usually emended by inserting* master *after*
either.   172*be bless'd* become blessed, i.e., repentant.   183*bloat* bloated.   185*reechy* dirty,
filthy.   188*essentially* in my essential nature.   191*paddock* toad.   191*gib* tomcat.   192*dear con-
cernings* important affairs.

Unpeg the basket on the house's top,
Let the birds fly, and, like the famous ape,°   195
To try conclusions,° in the basket creep,
And break your own neck down.
QUEEN: Be thou assur'd, if words be made of breath,
And breath of life, I have no life to breathe
What thou hast said to me.   200
HAMLET: I must to England; you know that?
QUEEN: Alack,
I had forgot: 'tis so concluded on.
HAMLET: There's letters seal'd: and my two schoolfellows,
Whom I will trust as I will adders fang'd,
They bear the mandate; they must sweep my way,°   205
And marshal me to knavery. Let it work;
For 'tis the sport to have the enginer°
Hoist° with his own petar:° and 't shall go hard
But I will delve one yard below their mines,
And blow them at the moon: O, 'tis most sweet,   210
When in one line two crafts° directly meet.
This man shall set me packing:°
I'll lug the guts into the neighbour room.
Mother, good night. Indeed this counsellor
Is now most still, most secret and most grave,   215
Who was in life a foolish prating knave.
Come, sir, to draw° toward an end with you.
Good night, mother.

Exeunt [severally; HAMLET dragging in POLONIUS.]

ACT IV

Scene I [A room in the castle.]

Enter KING and QUEEN, with ROSENCRANTZ and GUILDENSTERN.]

KING: There's matter in these sighs, these profound heaves:
You must translate: 'tis fit we understand them.
Where is your son?

---

¹⁹⁵**the famous ape** *a letter from Sir John Suckling seems to supply other details of the story, otherwise not identi-
fied: "It is the story of the jackanapes and the partridges; thou starest after a beauty till it be lost to thee, then let'st out
another, and starest after that till it is gone too."* ¹⁹⁶**conclusions** *experiments.* ²⁰⁵**sweep my way**
clear my path. ²⁰⁷**enginer** *constructor of military works, or possibly, artilleryman.* ²⁰⁸**Hoist** *blown up.*
²⁰⁸**petar** *defined as a small engine of war used to blow in a door or make a breach, and as a case filled with ex-
plosive materials.* ²¹¹**two crafts** *two acts of guile, with quibble on the sense of "two ships."* ²¹²**set me
packing** *set me to making schemes, and set me to lugging (him), and, also, send me off in a hurry.* ²¹⁷**draw**
come, with quibble on literal sense.

QUEEN: Bestow this place on us a little while.

> [*Exeunt* ROSENCRANTZ *and* GUILDENSTERN.]

Ah, mine own lord, what have I seen to-night!   5

KING: What, Gertrude? How does Hamlet?

QUEEN: Mad as the sea and wind, when both contend
Which is the mightier: in his lawless fit,
Behind the arras hearing something stir,
Whips out his rapier, cries, "A rat, a rat!"   10
And, in this brainish° apprehension,° kills
The unseen good old man.

KING: O heavy deed!
It had been so with us, had we been there:
His liberty is full of threats to all;
To you yourself, to us, to every one.   15
Alas, how shall this bloody deed be answer'd?
It will be laid to us, whose providence°
Should have kept short,° restrain'd and out of haunt,°
This mad young man: but so much was our love,
We would not understand what was most fit;   20
But, like the owner of a foul disease,
To keep it from divulging,° let it feed
Even on the pith of life. Where is he gone?

QUEEN: To draw apart the body he hath kill'd:
O'er whom his very madness, like some ore   25
Among a mineral° of metals base,
Shows itself pure; 'a weeps for what is done.

KING: O Gertrude, come away!
The sun no sooner shall the mountains touch,
But we will ship him hence: and this vile deed   30
We must, with all our majesty and skill,
Both countenance and excuse. Ho, Guildenstern!

> *Enter* ROSENCRANTZ *and* GUILDENSTERN.

Friends both, go join you with some further aid:
Hamlet in madness hath Polonius slain,
And from his mother's closet hath he dragg'd him: 35
Go seek him out; speak fair, and bring the body
Into the chapel. I pray you, haste in this.

> [*Exeunt* ROSENCRANTZ *and* GUILDENSTERN.]

Come, Gertrude, we'll call up our wisest friends;
And let them know, both what we mean to do,
And what's untimely done . . .°   40

IV.i. ¹¹*brainish* headstrong, passionate. ¹¹*apprehension* conception, imagination. ¹⁷*providence* foresight. ¹⁸*short* i.e., on a short tether. ¹⁸*out of haunt* secluded. ²²*divulging* becoming evident. ²⁶*mineral* mine. ⁴⁰*defective line; some editors add:* so, haply, slander; *others add:* for, haply, slander; *other conjectures.*

Whose whisper o'er the world's diameter,°
As level° as the cannon to his blank,°
Transports his pois'ned shot, may miss our name,
And hit the woundless° air. O, come away!
My soul is full of discord and dismay.   *Exeunt.*   45

Scene II [Another room in the castle.]

Enter HAMLET.

HAMLET: Safely stowed.

ROSENCRANTZ: ⎫
                  ⎬ *(within)* Hamlet! Lord Hamlet!
GUILDENSTERN: ⎭

HAMLET: But soft, what noise? who calls on Hamlet? O, here they come.

Enter ROSENCRANTZ and GUILDENSTERN.

ROSENCRANTZ: What have you done, my lord, with the dead body?

HAMLET: Compounded it with dust, whereto 'tis kin.

ROSENCRANTZ: Tell us where 'tis, that we may take it thence   5
And bear it to the chapel.

HAMLET: Do not believe it.

ROSENCRANTZ: Believe what?

HAMLET: That I can keep your counsel° and not mine own. Besides, to be
demanded of a sponge! what replication° should be made by the son of a   10
king?

ROSENCRANTZ: Take you me for a sponge, my lord?

HAMLET: Ay, sir, that soaks up the king's countenance, his rewards, his authorities.° But such officers do the king best service in the end: he keeps
them, like an ape an apple, in the corner of his jaw; first mouthed, to be   15
last swallowed: when he needs what you have gleaned, it is but squeezing
you, and, sponge, you shall be dry again.

ROSENCRANTZ: I understand you not, my lord.

HAMLET: I am glad of it: a knavish speech sleeps in a foolish ear.

ROSENCRANTZ: My lord, you must tell us where the body is, and go with   20
us to the king.

HAMLET: The body is with the king, but the king is not with the body.° The
king is a thing—

GUILDENSTERN: A thing, my lord!

HAMLET: Of nothing: bring me to him. Hide fox, and all after.°   *Exeunt.*   25

---

⁴¹*diameter* extent from side to side.   ⁴²*level* straight.   ⁴²*blank* white spot in the center of a target.
⁴⁴*woundless* invulnerable.   **IV.ii.**   ⁹*keep your counsel* Hamlet is aware of their treachery but says nothing
about it.   ¹⁰*replication* reply.   ¹⁴*authorities* authoritative backing.   ²²*The body . . . body* there
are many interpretations; possibly, "The body lies in death with the king, my father; but my father walks disembod-
ied"; or "Claudius has the bodily possession of kingship, but kingliness, or justice of inheritance, is not with him."
²⁵*Hide . . . after* an old signal cry in the game of hide-and-seek.

Scene III [*Another room in the castle.*]

Enter KING, *and two or three.*

KING: I have sent to seek him, and to find the body.
How dangerous is it that this man goes loose!
Yet must not we put the strong law on him:
He's lov'd of the distracted° multitude,
Who like not in their judgement, but their eyes;   5
And where 'tis so, th' offender's scourge° is weigh'd,°
But never the offence. To bear all smooth and even,
This sudden sending him away must seem
Deliberate pause:° diseases desperate grown
By desperate appliance are reliev'd,   10
Or not at all.

Enter ROSENCRANTZ, [GUILDENSTERN,] *and all the rest.*

How now! what hath befall'n?
ROSENCRANTZ: Where the dead body is bestow'd, my lord,
We cannot get from him.
KING: But where is he?
ROSENCRANTZ: Without, my lord; guarded, to know your pleasure.
KING: Bring him before us.   15
ROSENCRANTZ: Ho! bring in the lord.

They enter [with HAMLET].

KING: Now, Hamlet, where's Polonius?
HAMLET: At supper.
KING: At supper! where?
HAMLET: Not where he eats, but where 'a is eaten: a certain convocation of   20
politic° worms° are e'en at him. Your worm is your only emperor for diet:
we fat all creatures else to fat us, and we fat ourselves for maggots: your
fat king and your lean beggar is but variable service,° two dishes, but to
one table: that's the end.
KING: Alas, alas!   25
HAMLET: A man may fish with the worm that hath eat of a king, and eat of
the fish that hath fed of that worm.
KING: What dost thou mean by this?
HAMLET: Nothing but to show you how a king may go a progress° through
the guts of a beggar.   30
KING: Where is Polonius?
HAMLET: In heaven; send thither to see: if your messenger find him not there,
seek him i' the other place yourself. But if indeed you find him not within
this month, you shall nose him as you go up the stairs into the lobby.

IV.iii.   [4]*distracted* *i.e., without power of forming logical judgments.*   [6]*scourge* *punishment.*   [6]*weigh'd*
taken into consideration.   [9]*Deliberate pause* *considered action.*   [20–21]*convocation . . . worms* *allusion to*
the Diet of Worms (1521).   [21]*politic* *crafty.*   [23]*variable service* *a variety of dishes.*   [29]*progress* *royal*
journey of state.

KING [*to some* ATTENDANTS]: Go seek him there. 35
HAMLET: 'A will stay till you come.   [*Exeunt* ATTENDANTS.]
KING: Hamlet, this deed, for thine especial safety,—
    Which we do tender,° as we dearly grieve
    For that which thou hast done,—must send thee hence
    With fiery quickness: therefore prepare thyself; 40
    The bark is ready, and the wind at help,
    Th' associates tend, and everything is bent
    For England.
HAMLET: For England!
KING: Ay, Hamlet.
HAMLET: Good.
KING: So is it, if thou knew'st our purposes.
HAMLET: I see a cherub° that sees them. But, come; for England! Farewell, 45
    dear mother.
KING: Thy loving father, Hamlet.
HAMLET: My mother: father and mother is man and wife; man and wife is
    one flesh; and so, my mother. Come, for England!   *Exit.*
KING: Follow him at foot;° tempt him with speed aboard; 50
    Delay it not; I'll have him hence to-night:
    Away! for every thing is seal'd and done
    That else leans on th' affair: pray you, make haste.
                         [*Exeunt all but the* KING.]
    And, England, if my love thou hold'st at aught—
    As my great power thereof may give thee sense, 55
    Since yet thy cicatrice° looks raw and red
    After the Danish sword, and thy free awe°
    Pays homage to us—thou mayst not coldly set
    Our sovereign process; which imports at full,
    By letters congruing to that effect, 60
    The present death of Hamlet. Do it, England;
    For like the hectic° in my blood he rages,
    And thou must cure me: till I know 'tis done,
    Howe'er my haps,° my joys were ne'er begun.   *Exit.*

Scene IV [*A plain in Denmark.*]

Enter FORTINBRAS *with his Army over the stage.*

FORTINBRAS: Go, captain, from me greet the Danish king;
    Tell him that, by his license,° Fortinbras
    Craves the conveyance° of a promis'd march
    Over his kingdom. You know the rendezvous.
    If that his majesty would aught with us, 5

---

³⁸**tender** *regard, hold dear.* ⁴⁵**cherub** *cherubim are angels of knowledge.* ⁵⁰**at foot** *close behind, at heel.*
⁵⁶**cicatrice** *scar.* ⁵⁷**free awe** *voluntary show of respect.* ⁶²**hectic** *fever.* ⁶⁴**haps** *fortunes.*
IV.iv. ²**license** *leave.* ³**conveyance** *escort, convoy.*

We shall express our duty in his eye;°
And let him know so.

CAPTAIN: I will do't, my lord.

FORTINBRAS: Go softly° on.   [*Exeunt all but* CAPTAIN.]

Enter HAMLET, ROSENCRANTZ, [GUILDENSTERN,] &c.

HAMLET: Good sir, whose powers are these?

CAPTAIN: They are of Norway, sir.   10

HAMLET: How purpos'd, sir, I pray you?

CAPTAIN: Against some part of Poland.

HAMLET: Who commands them, sir?

CAPTAIN: The nephew to old Norway, Fortinbras.

HAMLET: Goes it against the main° of Poland, sir,   15
    Or for some frontier?

CAPTAIN: Truly to speak, and with no addition,
    We go to gain a little patch of ground
    That hath in it no profit but the name.
    To pay five ducats, five, I would not farm it;°   20
    Nor will it yield to Norway or the Pole
    A ranker rate, should it be sold in fee.°

HAMLET: Why, then the Polack never will defend it.

CAPTAIN: Yes, it is already garrison'd.

HAMLET: Two thousand souls and twenty thousand ducats   25
    Will not debate the question of this straw;°
    This is th' imposthume° of much wealth and peace,
    That inward breaks, and shows no cause without
    Why the man dies. I humbly thank you, sir.

CAPTAIN: God be wi' you, sir.   [*Exit.*]

ROSENCRANTZ: Will 't please you go, my lord?   30

HAMLET: I'll be with you straight. Go a little before.

                                        [*Exeunt all except* HAMLET.]

    How all occasions° do inform against° me,
    And spur my dull revenge! What is a man,
    If his chief good and market of his time°
    Be but to sleep and feed? a beast, no more.   35
    Sure, he that made us with such large discourse,
    Looking before and after, gave us not
    That capability and god-like reason
    To fust° in us unus'd. Now, whether it be
    Bestial oblivion, or some craven scruple   40
    Of thinking too precisely on th' event,

---

⁶*in his eye* *in his presence.*   ⁸*softly* *slowly.*   ¹⁵*main* *country itself.*   ²⁰*farm it* *take a lease
of it.*   ²²*fee* *fee simple.*   ²⁶*debate . . . straw* *settle this trifling matter.*   ²⁷*imposthume* *purulent
abscess or swelling.*   ³²*occasions* *incidents, events.*   ³²*inform against* *generally defined as "show," "betray"
(i.e., his tardiness); more probably* inform *means "take shape," as in Macbeth, II.i.48.*   ³⁴*market of his time*
the best use he makes of his time, or, that for which he sells his time.   ³⁹*fust* *grow moldy.*

A thought which, quarter'd, hath but one part wisdom
And ever three parts coward, I do not know
Why yet I live to say "This thing 's to do";
Sith I have cause and will and strength and means   45
To do 't. Examples gross as earth exhort me:
Witness this army of such mass and charge
Led by a delicate and tender prince,
Whose spirit with divine ambition puff'd
Makes mouths at the invisible event,   50
Exposing what is mortal and unsure
To all that fortune, death and danger dare,
Even for an egg-shell. Rightly to be great
Is not to stir without great argument,
But greatly to find quarrel in a straw   55
When honour's at the stake. How stand I then,
That have a father kill'd, a mother stain'd,
Excitements of° my reason and my blood,
And let all sleep? while, to my shame, I see
The imminent death of twenty thousand men,   60
That, for a fantasy and trick° of fame,
Go to their graves like beds, fight for a plot°
Whereon the numbers cannot try the cause,
Which is not tomb enough and continent
To hide the slain? O, from this time forth,   65
My thoughts be bloody, or be nothing worth!   *Exit.*

Scene V [Elsinore. A room in the castle.]

Enter HORATIO, [QUEEN] GERTRUDE, *and a* GENTLEMAN.

QUEEN: I will not speak with her.
GENTLEMAN: She is importunate, indeed distract:
  Her mood will needs be pitied.
QUEEN: What would she have?
GENTLEMAN: She speaks much of her father; says she hears
  There's tricks° i' th' world; and hems, and beats her heart;°   5
  Spurns enviously at straws;° speaks things in doubt,
  That carry but half sense: her speech is nothing,
  Yet the unshaped° use of it doth move
  The hearers to collection;° they yawn° at it,
  And botch° the words up fit to their own thoughts;   10
  Which, as her winks, and nods, and gestures yield° them,

58*Excitements of* incentives to.   61*trick* toy, trifle.   62*plot* i.e., of ground.   **IV.v.** 5*tricks* deceptions.   5*heart* i.e., breast.   6*Spurns . . . straws* kicks spitefully at small objects in her path.   8*unshaped* unformed, artless.   9*collection* inference, a guess at some sort of meaning.   9*yawn* wonder.
10*botch* patch.   11*yield* deliver, bring forth (her words).

Indeed would make one think there might be thought,
Though nothing sure, yet much unhappily.°
HORATIO: 'Twere good she were spoken with: for she may strew
Dangerous conjectures in ill-breeding minds.°   15
QUEEN: Let her come in.   [*Exit* GENTLEMAN.]
[*Aside.*] To my sick soul, as sin's true nature is,
Each toy seems prologue to some great amiss:°
So full of artless jealousy is guilt,
It spills itself in fearing to be spilt.°   20

Enter OPHELIA [*distracted*].

OPHELIA: Where is the beauteous majesty of Denmark?
QUEEN: How now, Ophelia!
OPHELIA (*she sings*): How should I your true love know
     From another one?
By his cockle hat° and staff,   25
     And his sandal shoon.°
QUEEN: Alas, sweet lady, what imports this song?
OPHELIA: Say you? nay, pray you mark.
     (*Song*) He is dead and gone, lady,
          He is dead and gone;   30
     At his head a grass-green turf,
          At his heels a stone.
     O, ho!
QUEEN: Nay, but, Ophelia—
OPHELIA: Pray you, mark   35
[*Sings.*] White his shroud as the mountain snow,—

Enter KING.

QUEEN: Alas, look here, my lord.
OPHELIA (*Song*): Larded° all with flowers;
Which bewept to the grave did not go
     With true-love showers.   40
KING: How do you, pretty lady?
OPHELIA: Well, God 'ild° you! They say the owl° was a baker's daughter. Lord,
     we know what we are, but know not what we may be. God be at your table!
KING: Conceit upon her father.
OPHELIA: Pray let's have no words of this; but when they ask you what it   45
     means, say you this:

---

¹³**much unhappily** *expressive of much unhappiness.*   ¹⁵**ill-breeding minds** *minds bent on mischief.*
¹⁸**great amiss** *calamity, disaster.*   ^{19–20}**So . . . spilt** *guilt is so full of suspicion that it unskillfully betrays itself in fearing to be betrayed.*   ²⁵**cockle hat** *hat with cockleshell stuck in it as a sign that the wearer has been a pilgrim to the shrine of St. James of Compostella; the pilgrim's garb was a conventional disguise for lovers.*   ²⁶**shoon** *shoes.*   ³⁸**Larded** *decorated.*   ⁴²**God 'ild** *god yield or reward.*   ⁴²**owl** *reference to a monkish legend that a baker's daughter was turned into an owl for refusing bread to the Savior.*

(Song) To-morrow is Saint Valentine's day,
  All in the morning betime,
And I a maid at your window,
  To be your Valentine.°   50
Then up he rose, and donn'd his clothes,
  And dupp'd° the chamber-door;
Let in the maid, that out a maid
  Never departed more.

KING: Pretty Ophelia!   55
OPHELIA: Indeed, la, without an oath, I'll make an end on 't:
  [*Sings.*] By Gis° and by Saint Charity,
    Alack, and fie for shame!
  Young men will do 't, if they come to 't;
    By cock,° they are to blame.   60
  Quoth she, before you tumbled me,
    You promis'd me to wed.
  So would I ha' done, by yonder sun,
    An thou hadst not come to my bed.

KING: How long hath she been thus?   65
OPHELIA: I hope all will be well. We must be patient: but I cannot choose
  but weep, to think they would lay him i' the cold ground. My brother
  shall know of it: and so I thank you for your good counsel. Come, my
  coach! Good night, ladies; good night, sweet ladies; good night, good
  night.   [*Exit.*] 70
KING: Follow her close; give her good watch, I pray you.   [*Exit* HORATIO.]
  O, this is the poison of deep grief; it springs
  All from her father's death. O Gertrude, Gertrude,
  When sorrows come, they come not single spies,
  But in battalions. First, her father slain: 75
  Next your son gone; and he most violent author
  Of his own just remove: the people muddied,
  Thick and unwholesome in their thoughts and whispers,
  For good Polonius' death; and we have done but greenly,°
  In hugger-mugger° to inter him: poor Ophelia   80
  Divided from herself and her fair judgement,
  Without the which we are pictures, or mere beasts:
  Last, and as much containing as all these,
  Her brother is in secret come from France;
  Feeds on his wonder, keeps himself in clouds,°   85
  And wants not buzzers° to infect his ear
  With pestilent speeches of his father's death;

---

⁵⁰**Valentine** *this song alludes to the belief that the first girl seen by a man on the morning of this day was his valentine or true love.*   ⁵²**dupp'd** *opened.*   ⁵⁷**Gis** *Jesus.*   ⁶⁰**cock** *perversion of* "God" *in oaths.*   ⁷⁹**greenly** *foolishly.*   ⁸⁰**hugger-mugger** *secret haste.*   ⁸⁵**in clouds** *invisible.* ⁸⁶**buzzers** *gossipers.*

Wherein necessity, of matter beggar'd,°
Will nothing stick° our person to arraign
In ear and ear.° O my dear Gertrude, this,   90
Like to a murd'ring-piece,° in many places
Gives me superfluous death.   *A noise within.*

QUEEN: Alack, what noise is this?

KING: Where are my Switzers?° Let them guard the door.

Enter a MESSENGER.

What is the matter?

MESSENGER: Save yourself, my lord:
The ocean, overpeering° of his list,°   95
Eats not the flats with more impiteous haste
Than young Laertes, in a riotous head,
O'erbears your officers. The rabble call him lord;
And, as the world were now but to begin,
Antiquity forgot, custom not known,   100
The ratifiers and props of every word,°
They cry "Choose we: Laertes shall be king":
Caps, hands, and tongues, applaud it to the clouds:
"Laertes shall be king, Laertes king!"   *A noise within.*

QUEEN: How cheerfully on the false trail they cry!   105
O, this is counter,° you false Danish dogs!

KING: The doors are broke.

Enter LAERTES *with others.*

LAERTES: Where is this king? Sirs, stand you all without.

DANES: No, let's come in.

LAERTES: I pray you, give me leave.

DANES: We will, we will.   *[They retire without the door.]* 110

LAERTES: I thank you: keep the door. O thou vile king,
Give me my father!

QUEEN: Calmly, good Laertes.

LAERTES: That drop of blood that's calm proclaims me bastard,
Cries cuckold to my father, brands the harlot
Even here, between the chaste unsmirched brow   115
Of my true mother.

KING: What is the cause, Laertes,
That thy rebellion looks so giant-like?
Let him go, Gertrude; do not fear our person:
There's such divinity doth hedge a king,
That treason can but peep to° what it would,°   120

Acts little of his will. Tell me, Laertes,
Why thou art thus incens'd. Let him go, Gertrude.
Speak, man.

LAERTES: Where is my father?

KING: Dead.

QUEEN: But not by him.

KING: Let him demand his fill.   125

LAERTES: How came he dead? I'll not be juggled with:
To hell, allegiance! vows, to the blackest devil!
Conscience and grace, to the profoundest pit!
I dare damnation. To this point I stand,
That both the worlds I give to negligence,°   130
Let come what comes; only I'll be reveng'd
Most throughly° for my father.

KING: Who shall stay you?

LAERTES: My will,° not all the world's:
And for my means, I'll husband them so well,
They shall go far with little.

KING: Good Laertes,   135
If you desire to know the certainty
Of your dear father, is 't writ in your revenge,
That, swoopstake,° you will draw both friend and foe,
Winner and loser?

LAERTES: None but his enemies.

KING: Will you know them then?   140

LAERTES: To his good friends thus wide I'll ope my arms;
And like the kind life-rend'ring pelican,°
Repast° them with my blood.

KING: Why, now you speak
Like a good child and a true gentleman.
That I am guiltless of your father's death,   145
And am most sensibly in grief for it,
It shall as level to your judgement 'pear
As day does to your eye.

A noise within: "Let her come in."

LAERTES: How now! what noise is that?

Enter Ophelia.

O heat,° dry up my brains! tears seven times salt,   150
Burn out the sense and virtue of mine eye!
By heaven, thy madness shall be paid with weight,

---

¹³⁰**give to negligence**   *he despises both the here and the hereafter.*   ¹³²**throughly**   *thoroughly.*   ¹³³**My will**   *he will not be stopped except by his own will.*   ¹³⁸**swoopstake**   *literally, drawing the whole stake at once, i.e., indiscriminately.*   ¹⁴²**pelican**   *reference to the belief that the pelican feeds its young with its own blood.*   ¹⁴³**Repast**   *feed.*   ¹⁵⁰**heat**   *probably the heat generated by the passion of grief.*

Till our scale turn the beam. O rose of May!
Dear maid, kind sister, sweet Ophelia!
O heavens! is 't possible, a young maid's wits   155
Should be as mortal as an old man's life?
Nature is fine in love, and where 'tis fine,
It sends some precious instance of itself
After the thing it loves.

OPHELIA *(Song)*: They bore him barefac'd on the bier;   160
   Hey non nonny, nonny, hey nonny;
   And in his grave rain'd many a tear:—
Fare you well, my dove!

LAERTES: Hadst thou thy wits, and didst persuade revenge,
It could not move thus.   165

OPHELIA *[sings]*: You must sing a-down a-down,
   An you call him a-down-a.
O, how the wheel° becomes it! It is the false steward,° that stole his
master's daughter.

LAERTES: This nothing's more than matter.   170

OPHELIA: There's rosemary,° that's for remembrance; pray you, love, remember: and there is pansies,° that's for thoughts.

LAERTES: A document° in madness, thoughts and remembrance fitted.

OPHELIA: There's fennel° for you, and columbines:° there's rue° for you; and
here's some for me: we may call it herb of grace o' Sundays: O, you must 175
wear your rue with a difference. There's a daisy:° I would give you some
violets,° but they withered all when my father died: they say 'a made a
good end,—
[Sings.] For bonny sweet Robin is all my joy.°

LAERTES: Thought° and affliction, passion, hell itself,   180
She turns to favour and to prettiness.

OPHELIA *(Song)*: And will 'a not come again?°
   And will 'a not come again?
     No, no, he is dead:
     Go to thy death-bed: 185
   He never will come again.

   His beard was as white as snow,
   All flaxen was his poll:°

168*wheel* spinning wheel as accompaniment to the song refrain.   168–169*false steward . . . daughter* the
story is unknown.   171*rosemary* used as a symbol of remembrance both at weddings and at funerals.   172*pansies* emblems of love and courtship. *Cf.* French pensées.   173*document* piece of instruction or lesson.
174*fennel* emblem of flattery.   174*columbines* emblem of unchastity (?) or ingratitude (?).   174*rue*
emblem of repentance. It was usually mingled with holy water and then known as herb of grace. Ophelia is probably playing on the two meanings of *rue* "repentant" and "even for ruth (pity)"; the former signification is for the
queen, the latter for herself.   176*daisy* emblem of dissembling, faithlessness.   177*violets* emblems of
faithfulness.   179*For . . . joy* probably a line from a Robin Hood ballad.   180*Thought* melancholy
thought.   182*And . . . again* this song appeared in the songbooks as "The Merry Milkmaids' Dumps."
188*poll* head.

He is gone, he is gone,
 And we cast away° moan: 190
God ha' mercy on his soul!
And of all Christian souls, I pray God. God be wi' you.   [*Exit.*]
LAERTES: Do you see this, O God?
KING: Laertes, I must commune with your grief,
 Or you deny me right.° Go but apart,   195
 Make choice of whom your wisest friends you will,
 And they shall hear and judge 'twixt you and me:
 If by direct or by collateral° hand
 They find us touch'd,° we will our kingdom give,
 Our crown, our life, and all that we call ours,   200
 To you in satisfaction; but if not,
 Be you content to lend your patience to us,
 And we shall jointly labour with your soul
 To give it due content.
LAERTES: Let this be so;
 His means of death, his obscure funeral—   205
 No trophy, sword, nor hatchment° o'er his bones,
 No noble rite nor formal ostentation—
 Cry to be heard, as 'twere from heaven to earth,
 That I must call 't in question.
KING: So you shall;
 And where th' offence is let the great axe fall.   210
 I pray you, go with me.   *Exeunt.*

Scene VI [Another room in the castle.]

Enter HORATIO *and others.*

HORATIO: What are they that would speak with me?
GENTLEMAN: Sea-faring men, sir: they say they have letters for you.
HORATIO: Let them come in.   [*Exit* GENTLEMAN.]
 I do not know from what part of the world
 I should be greeted, if not from lord Hamlet.   5

Enter SAILORS.

FIRST SAILOR: God bless you, sir.
HORATIO: Let him bless thee too.
FIRST SAILOR: 'A shall sir, an 't please him. There's a letter for you, sir; it
 comes from the ambassador that was bound for England; if your name be
 Horatio, as I am let to know it is.   10
HORATIO [*reads*]: "Horatio, when thou shalt have overlooked this, give these
 fellows some means° to the king: they have letters for him. Ere we were

---

¹⁹⁰**cast away** *shipwrecked.*   ¹⁹⁵**right** *my rights.*   ¹⁹⁸**collateral** *indirect.*   ¹⁹⁹**touch'd** *implicated.*
²⁰⁶**hatchment** *tablet displaying the armorial bearings of a deceased person.*   **IV.vi.** ¹²**means** *means of access.*

two days old at sea, a pirate of very warlike appointment gave us chase. Finding ourselves too slow of sail, we put on a compelled valour, and in the grapple I boarded them: on the instant they got clear of our ship; so I ¹⁵ alone became their prisoner. They have dealt with me like thieves of mercy:° but they knew what they did; I am to do a good turn for them. Let the king have the letters I have sent; and repair thou to me with as much speed as thou wouldst fly death. I have words to speak in thine ear will make thee dumb; yet are they much too light for the bore° of the ²⁰ matter. These good fellows will bring thee where I am. Rosencrantz and Guildenstern hold their course for England: of them I have much to tell thee. Farewell.

"He that thou knowest thine, HAMLET."

Come, I will give you way for these your letters;   ²⁵
And do 't the speedier, that you may direct me
To him from whom you brought them.   *Exeunt.*

Scene VII [Another room in the castle.]

Enter KING *and* LAERTES.

KING: Now must your conscience° my acquittance seal,
And you must put me in your heart for friend,
Sith you have heard, and with a knowing ear,
That he which hath your noble father slain
Pursued my life.
LAERTES: It well appears: but tell me   5
Why you proceeded not against these feats,
So criminal and so capital° in nature,
As by your safety, wisdom, all things else,
You mainly° were stirr'd up.
KING: O, for two special reasons;
Which may to you, perhaps, seem much unsinew'd,°   10
But yet to me th' are strong. The queen his mother
Lives almost by his looks; and for myself—
My virtue or my plague, be it either which—
She's so conjunctive° to my life and soul,
That, as the star moves not but in his sphere,°   15
I could not but by her. The other motive,
Why to a public count° I might not go,
Is the great love the general gender° bear him;
Who, dipping all his faults in their affection,

---

¹⁶⁻¹⁷*thieves of mercy* merciful thieves.   ²⁰*bore* caliber, importance.   **IV.vi.** ¹*conscience* knowledge that this is true.   ⁷*capital* punishable by death.   ⁹*mainly* greatly.   ¹⁰*unsinew'd* weak.   ¹⁴*conjunctive* conformable (the next line suggesting planetary conjunction).   ¹⁵*sphere* the hollow sphere in which, according to Ptolemaic astronomy, the planets were supposed to move.   ¹⁷*count* account, reckoning.   ¹⁸*general gender* common people.

Would, like the spring° that turneth wood to stone,　　　　20
Convert his gyves° to graces; so that my arrows,
Too slightly timber'd° for so loud° a wind,
Would have reverted to my bow again,
And not where I had aim'd them.
LAERTES: And so have I a noble father lost;　　　　25
A sister driven into desp'rate terms,°
Whose worth, if praises may go back° again,
Stood challenger on mount° of all the age°
For her perfections: but my revenge will come.
KING: Break not your sleeps for that: you must not think　　　　30
That we are made of stuff so flat and dull
That we can let our beard be shook with danger
And think it pastime. You shortly shall hear more:
I lov'd your father, and we love ourself;
And that, I hope, will teach you to imagine—　　　　35

Enter a MESSENGER *with letters.*

How now! what news?
MESSENGER:　　　　　　Letters, my lord, from Hamlet:
These to your majesty; this to the queen.°
KING: From Hamlet! who brought them?
MESSENGER: Sailors, my lord, they say; I saw them not:
They were given me by Claudio;° he receiv'd them　　　　40
Of him that brought them.
KING:　　　　　　　　Laertes, you shall hear them.
Leave us.　　　　　　　　　　　　　　[*Exit* MESSENGER.]
[*Reads.*] "High and mighty, You shall know I am set naked° on your king-
dom. To-morrow shall I beg leave to see your kingly eyes: when I shall,　　45
first asking your pardon thereunto, recount the occasion of my sudden and
more strange return.　　　　　　　　　　　　"HAMLET."
What should this mean? Are all the rest come back?
Or is it some abuse, and no such thing?
LAERTES: Know you the hand?
KING:　　　　　　　'Tis Hamlet's character. "Naked!"
And in a postscript here, he says "alone."　　　　50
Can you devise° me?
LAERTES: I'm lost in it, my lord. But let him come;
It warms the very sickness in my heart,
That I shall live and tell him to his teeth,
"Thus didst thou."

---

²⁰*spring* i.e., one heavily charged with lime.　²¹*gyves* fetters; here, faults, or possibly, punishments inflicted (on him).　²²*slightly timber'd* light.　²²*loud* strong.　²⁶*terms* state, condition.　²⁷*go back* i.e., to Ophelia's former virtues.　²⁸*on mount* set up on high, mounted (on horseback).　²⁸*of all the age* qualifies challenger *and not* mount.　³⁷*to the queen* one hears no more of the letter to the queen.　⁴⁰*Claudio* this character does not appear in the play.　⁴³*naked* unprovided (with retinue).　⁵¹*devise* explain to.

KING: If it be so, Laertes—   55
  As how should it be so? how otherwise?°—
  Will you be rul'd by me?
LAERTES: Ay, my lord;
  So you will not o'errule me to a peace.
KING: To thine own peace. If he be now return'd,
  As checking at° his voyage, and that he means   60
  No more to undertake it, I will work him
  To an exploit, now ripe in my device,
  Under the which he shall not choose but fall:
  And for his death no wind of blame shall breathe,
  But even his mother shall uncharge the practice°   65
  And call it accident.
LAERTES: My lord, I will be rul'd;
  The rather, if you could devise it so
  That I might be the organ.°
KING: It falls right.
  You have been talk'd of since your travel much,
  And that in Hamlet's hearing, for a quality   70
  Wherein, they say, you shine: your sum of parts
  Did not together pluck such envy from him
  As did that one, and that, in my regard,
  Of the unworthiest siege.°
LAERTES: What part is that, my lord?
KING: A very riband in the cap of youth,   75
  Yet needful too; for youth no less becomes
  The light and careless livery that it wears
  Than settled age his sables° and his weeds,
  Importing health and graveness. Two months since,
  Here was a gentleman of Normandy:—   80
  I have seen myself, and serv'd against, the French,
  And they can well° on horseback: but this gallant
  Had witchcraft in 't; he grew unto his seat;
  And to such wondrous doing brought his horse,
  As had he been incorps'd and demi-natur'd°   85
  With the brave beast: so far he topp'd° my thought,
  That I, in forgery° of shapes and tricks,
  Come short of what he did.
LAERTES: A Norman was 't?
KING: A Norman.

---

[56]*As . . . otherwise?* how can this (Hamlet's return) be true? (yet) how otherwise than true (since we have the evidence of his letter)? Some editors read "How should it not be so," etc., making the words refer to Laertes's desire to meet with Hamlet.   [60]*checking at* used in falconry of a hawk's leaving the quarry to fly at a chance bird, turn aside.   [65]*uncharge the practice* acquit the stratagem of being a plot.   [68]*organ* agent, instrument.   [74]*siege* rank.   [78]*sables* rich garments.   [82]*can well* are skilled.   [85]*incorps'd and demi-natur'd* of one body and nearly of one nature (like the centaur).   [86]*topp'd* surpassed.   [87]*forgery* invention.

LAERTES: Upon my life, Lamord.°

KING: The very same.   90

LAERTES: I know him well: he is the brooch indeed
    And gem of all the nation.

KING: He made confession° of you,
    And gave you such a masterly report
    For art and exercise° in your defence°   95
    And for your rapier most especial,
    That he cried out, 'twould be a sight indeed,
    If one could match you: the scrimers° of their nation,
    He swore, had neither motion, guard, nor eye,
    If you oppos'd them. Sir, this report of his   100
    Did Hamlet so envenom with his envy
    That he could nothing do but wish and beg
    Your sudden coming o'er, to play° with you.
    Now, out of this,—

LAERTES: What out of this, my lord?

KING: Laertes, was your father dear to you?   105
    Or are you like the painting of a sorrow,
    A face without a heart?

LAERTES: Why ask you this?

KING: Not that I think you did not love your father;
    But that I know love is begun by time;
    And that I see, in passages of proof,°   110
    Time qualifies the spark and fire of it.
    There lives within the very flame of love
    A kind of wick or snuff that will abate it;
    And nothing is at a like goodness still;
    For goodness, growing to a plurisy,°   115
    Dies in his own too much:° that we would do,
    We should do when we would; for this "would" changes
    And hath abatements° and delays as many
    As there are tongues, are hands, are accidents;°
    And then this "should" is like a spendthrift° sigh,   120
    That hurts by easing. But, to the quick o' th' ulcer:°—
    Hamlet comes back: what would you undertake,
    To show yourself your father's son in deed
    More than in words?

LAERTES: To cut his throat i' th' church.

KING: No place, indeed, should murder sanctuarize;°   125

---

⁹⁰**Lamord** *this refers possibly to Pietro Monte, instructor to Louis XII's master of the horse.*   ⁹³**confession**
grudging admission of superiority.   ⁹⁵**art and exercise** *skillful exercise.*   ⁹⁵**defence** *science of defense in
sword practice.*   ⁹⁸**scrimers** *fencers.*   ¹⁰³**play** *fence.*   ¹¹⁰**passages of proof** *proved instances.*
¹¹⁵**plurisy** *excess, plethora.*   ¹¹⁶**in his own too much** *of its own excess.*   ¹¹⁸**abatements** *diminu-
tions.*   ¹¹⁹**accidents** *occurrences, incidents.*   ¹²⁰**spendthrift** *an allusion to the belief that each sigh cost
the heart a drop of blood.*   ¹²¹**quick o' th' ulcer** *heart of the difficulty.*   ¹²⁵**sanctuarize** *protect from
punishment; allusion to the right of sanctuary with which certain religious places were invested.*

Revenge should have no bounds. But, good Laertes,
Will you do this, keep close within your chamber.
Hamlet return'd shall know you are come home:
We'll put on those shall praise your excellence
And set a double varnish on the fame   130
The Frenchman gave you, bring you in fine together
And wager on your heads: he, being remiss,
Most generous and free from all contriving,
Will not peruse the foils; so that, with ease,
Or with a little shuffling, you may choose   135
A sword unbated,° and in a pass of practice°
Requite him for your father.

LAERTES: I will do 't:
And, for that purpose, I'll anoint my sword.
I bought an unction of a mountebank,°
So mortal that, but dip a knife in it,   140
Where it draws blood no cataplasm° so rare,
Collected from all simples° that have virtue
Under the moon,° can save the thing from death
That is but scratch'd withal: I'll touch my point
With this contagion, that, if I gall° him slightly,   145
It may be death.

KING: Let's further think of this;
Weigh what convenience both of time and means
May fit us to our shape:° if this should fail,
And that our drift look through our bad performance,°
'Twere better not assay'd: therefore this project   150
Should have a back or second, that might hold,
If this should blast in proof.° Soft! let me see:
We'll make a solemn wager on your cunnings:°
I ha 't:
When in your motion you are hot and dry—   155
As make your bouts more violent to that end—
And that he calls for drink, I'll have prepar'd him
A chalice° for the nonce, whereon but sipping,
If he by chance escape your venom'd stuck,°
Our purpose may hold there. But stay, what noise?   160

Enter QUEEN.

QUEEN: One woe doth tread upon another's heel,
So fast they follow: your sister's drown'd, Laertes.
LAERTES: Drown'd! O, where?

---

[136]**unbated** *not blunted, having no button.*   [136]**pass of practice** *treacherous thrust.*   [139]**mountebank** *quack doctor.*   [141]**cataplasm** *plaster or poultice.*   [142]**simples** *herbs.*   [143]**Under the moon** *i.e., when collected by moonlight to add to their medicinal value.*   [145]**gall** *graze, wound.*   [148]**shape** *part we propose to act.*   [149]**drift . . . performance** *intention be disclosed by our bungling.*   [152]**blast in proof** *burst in the test (like a cannon).*   [153]**cunnings** *skills.*   [158]**chalice** *cup.*   [159]**stuck** *thrust (from* stoccado*).*

QUEEN: There is a willow° grows askant° the brook,
 That shows his hoar° leaves in the glassy stream;   165
 There with fantastic garlands did she make
 Of crow-flowers,° nettles, daisies, and long purples°
 That liberal° shepherds give a grosser name,
 But our cold maids do dead men's fingers call them:
 There, on the pendent boughs her crownet° weeds   170
 Clamb'ring to hang, an envious sliver° broke;
 When down her weedy° trophies and herself
 Fell in the weeping brook. Her clothes spread wide;
 And, mermaid-like, awhile they bore her up:
 Which time she chanted snatches of old lauds;°   175
 As one incapable° of her own distress,
 Or like a creature native and indued°
 Upon that element: but long it could not be
 Till that her garments, heavy with their drink,
 Pull'd the poor wretch from her melodious lay   180
 To muddy death.
LAERTES: Alas, then, she is drown'd?
QUEEN: Drown'd, drown'd.
LAERTES: Too much of water hast thou, poor Ophelia,
 And therefore I forbid my tears: but yet
 It is our trick;° nature her custom holds,   185
 Let shame say what it will: when these are gone,
 The woman will be out.° Adieu, my lord:
 I have a speech of fire, that fain would blaze,
 But that this folly drowns it.   *Exit.* 190
KING: Let's follow, Gertrude.
 How much I had to do to calm his rage!
 Now fear I this will give it start again;
 Therefore let 's follow.   *Exeunt.*

ACT V

Scene I [*A churchyard.*]

Enter two CLOWNS° [*with spades, &c.*].

FIRST CLOWN: Is she to be buried in Christian burial when she wilfully seeks
 her own salvation?

---

¹⁶⁴**willow** *for its significance of forsaken love.* ¹⁶⁴**askant** *aslant.* ¹⁶⁵**hoar** *white (i.e., on the underside).*
¹⁶⁷**crow-flowers** *buttercups.* ¹⁶⁷**long purples** *early purple orchids.* ¹⁶⁸**liberal** *probably, free-spoken.*
¹⁷⁰**crownet** *coronet; made into a chaplet.* ¹⁷¹**sliver** *branch.* ¹⁷²**weedy** *i.e., of plants.* ¹⁷⁵**lauds**
hymns. ¹⁷⁶**incapable** *lacking capacity to apprehend.* ¹⁷⁷**indued** *endowed with qualities fitting her for liv-*
ing in water. ¹⁸⁵**trick** *way.* ¹⁸⁶⁻¹⁸⁷**when ... out** *when my tears are all shed, the woman in me will be*
satisfied. **V.i.** **Clowns** *the word* clown *was used to denote peasants as well as humorous characters; here ap-*
plied to the rustic type of clown.

SECOND CLOWN: I tell thee she is; therefore make her grave straight:° the crowner° hath sat on her, and finds it Christian burial.

FIRST CLOWN: How can that be, unless she drowned herself in her own de- 5
fence?

SECOND CLOWN: Why, 'tis found so.

FIRST CLOWN: It must be "se offendendo";° it cannot be else. For here lies the point: if I drown myself wittingly,° it argues an act: and an act hath three branches;° it is, to act, to do, and to perform: argal,° she drowned 10
herself wittingly.

SECOND CLOWN: Nay, but hear you, goodman delver,°—

FIRST CLOWN: Give me leave. Here lies the water; good: here stands the man; good: if the man go to this water, and drown himself, it is, will he, nill he, he goes,—mark you that; but if the water come to him and drown him, 15
he drowns not himself: argal, he that is not guilty of his own death short-ens not his own life.

SECOND CLOWN: But is this law?

FIRST CLOWN: Ay, marry, is 't; crowner's quest° law.

SECOND CLOWN: Will you ha' the truth on 't? If this had not been a gen- 20
tlewoman, she should have been buried out o' Christian burial.

FIRST CLOWN: Why, there thou say'st:° and the more pity that great folk should have countenance° in this world to drown or hang themselves, more than their even° Christian. Come, my spade. There is no ancient gentlemen but gardeners, ditchers, and grave-makers: they hold up° 25
Adam's profession.

SECOND CLOWN: Was he a gentleman?

FIRST CLOWN: 'A was the first that ever bore arms.

SECOND CLOWN: Why, he had none.

FIRST CLOWN: What, art a heathen? How dost thou understand the Scrip- 30
ture? The Scripture says "Adam digged": could he dig without arms? I'll put another question to thee: if thou answerest me not to the purpose, confess thyself°—

SECOND CLOWN: Go to.°

FIRST CLOWN: What is he that builds stronger than either the mason, the ship- 35
wright, or the carpenter?

SECOND CLOWN: The gallows-maker; for that frame outlives a thousand tenants.

FIRST CLOWN: I like thy wit well, in good faith: the gallows does well; but how does it well? it does well to those that do ill: now thou dost ill to say 40
the gallows is built stronger than the church: argal, the gallows may do well to thee. To 't again, come.

SECOND CLOWN: "Who builds stronger than a mason, a shipwright, or a car-penter?"

---

³*straight* straightway, immediately; some interpret *"from east to west in a direct line, parallel with the church."*
⁴*crowner* coroner.   ⁸*"se offendendo"* for se defendendo, *term used in verdicts of justifiable homicide.*   ⁹*wit-*
tingly intentionally.   ¹⁰*three branches* parody of legal phraseology.   ¹⁰*argal* corruption of ergo, therefore.   ¹²*delver* digger.   ¹⁹*quest* inquest.   ²²*there thou say'st* that's right.   ²³*countenance* privilege.   ²⁴*even* fellow.   ²⁵*hold up* maintain, continue.   ³³*confess thyself* "and be hanged" completes the
proverb.   ³⁴*Go to* perhaps, "begin," or some other form of concession.

FIRST CLOWN: Ay, tell me that, and unyoke.° ⁴⁵

SECOND CLOWN: Marry, now I can tell.

FIRST CLOWN: To 't.

SECOND CLOWN: Mass,° I cannot tell.

Enter HAMLET *and* HORATIO [*at a distance*].

FIRST CLOWN: Cudgel thy brains no more about it, for your dull ass will not
mend his pace with beating; and, when you are asked this question next, ⁵⁰
say "a grave-maker": the houses he makes lasts till doomsday. Go, get thee
in, and fetch me a stoup° of liquor.

[*Exit* SECOND CLOWN.] *Song.* [*He digs.*]

In youth, when I did love, did love,
    Methought it was very sweet,
To contract—O—the time, for—a—my behove,° ⁵⁵
    O, methought, there—a—was nothing—a—meet.

HAMLET: Has this fellow no feeling of his business, that 'a sings at grave-
making?

HORATIO: Custom hath made it in him a property of easiness.°

HAMLET: 'Tis e'en so: the hand of little employment hath the daintier sense. ⁶⁰

FIRST CLOWN: (*Song.*) But age, with his stealing steps,
    Hath claw'd me in his clutch,
And hath shipped me into the land
    As if I had never been such.   [*Throws up a skull.*]

HAMLET: That skull had a tongue in it, and could sing once: how the knave ⁶⁵
jowls° it to the ground, as if 'twere Cain's jaw-bone,° that did the first
murder! This might be the pate of a politician,° which this ass now o'er-
reaches;° one that would circumvent God, might it not?

HORATIO: It might, my lord.

HAMLET: Or of a courtier; which could say "Good morrow, sweet lord! How ⁷⁰
dost thou, sweet lord?" This might be my lord such-a-one, that praised
my lord such-a-one's horse, when he meant to beg it; might it not?

HORATIO: Ay, my lord.

HAMLET: Why, e'en so: and now my Lady Worm's; chapless,° and knocked
about the mazzard° with a sexton's spade: here's fine revolution, an we ⁷⁵
had the trick to see 't. Did these bones cost no more the breeding, but to
play at loggats° with 'em? mine ache to think on 't.

FIRST CLOWN: (*Song.*) A pick-axe, and a spade, a spade,
    For and° a shrouding sheet:
O, a pit of clay for to be made ⁸⁰
    For such a guest is meet.   [*Throws up another skull.*]

HAMLET: There's another: why may not that be the skull of a lawyer? Where

---

⁴⁵*unyoke*   *after this great effort you may unharness the team of your wits.*   ⁴⁸*Mass*   *by the Mass.*   ⁵²*stoup*
Two-quart measure.   ⁵⁵*behove*   *benefit.*   ⁵⁹*property of easiness*   *a peculiarity that now is easy.*
⁶⁶*jowls*   *dashes*   ⁶⁶*Cain's jaw-bone*   *allusion to the old tradition that Cain slew Abel with the jawbone of*
an ass.   ⁶⁷*politician*   *schemer, plotter.*   ⁶⁷⁻⁶⁸*o'er-reaches*   *quibble on the literal sense and the sense "cir-*
cumvent."   ⁷⁴*chapless*   *having no lower jaw.*   ⁷⁵*mazzard*   *head.*   ⁷⁷*loggats*   *a game in which six*
sticks are thrown to lie as near as possible to a stake fixed in the ground, or block of wood on a floor.   ⁷⁹*For and*
and moreover.

be his quiddities° now, his quillities,° his cases, his tenures,° and his
tricks? why does he suffer this mad knave now to knock him about the
sconce° with a dirty shovel, and will not tell him of his action of battery? 85
Hum! This fellow might be in 's time a great buyer of land, with his
statutes, his recognizances,° his fines, his double vouchers,° his recoveries:° is this the fine° of his fines, and the recovery of his recoveries, to
have his fine pate full of fine dirt? will his vouchers vouch him no more
of his purchases, and double ones too, than the length and breadth of a 90
pair of indentures?° The very conveyances of his lands will scarcely lie in
this box; and must the inheritor° himself have no more, ha?

HORATIO: Not a jot more, my lord.

HAMLET: Is not parchment made of sheep-skins?

HORATIO: Ay, my lord, and of calf-skins° too.   95

HAMLET: They are sheep and calves which seek out assurance in that.° I will
speak to this fellow. Whose grave's this, sirrah?

FIRST CLOWN: Mine, sir.

[*Sings.*] O, a pit of clay for to be made
    For such a guest is meet.   100

HAMLET: I think it be thine, indeed; for thou liest in 't.

FIRST CLOWN: You lie out on 't, sir, and therefore 't is not yours: for my
part, I do not lie in 't, yet it is mine.

HAMLET: Thou dost lie in 't, to be in 't and say it is thine: 'tis for the dead,
not for the quick; therefore thou liest.   105

FIRST CLOWN: 'Tis a quick lie, sir; 'twill away again, from me to you.

HAMLET: What man dost thou dig it for?

FIRST CLOWN: For no man, sir.

HAMLET: What woman, then?

FIRST CLOWN: For none, neither.   110

HAMLET: Who is to be buried in 't?

FIRST CLOWN: One that was a woman, sir; but, rest her soul, she's dead.

HAMLET: How absolute° the knave is! we must speak by the card,° or equiv-
ocation° will undo us. By the Lord, Horatio, these three years I have taken
note of it; the age is grown so picked° that the toe of the peasant comes 115
so near the heel of the courtier, he galls° his kibe.° How long hast thou
been a grave-maker?

FIRST CLOWN: Of all the day i' the year, I came to 't that day that our last
king Hamlet overcame Fortinbras.

HAMLET: How long is that since?   120

FIRST CLOWN: Cannot you tell that? every fool can tell that: it was the very

<hr/>

83*quiddities* subtleties, quibbles.   83*quillities* verbal niceties, subtle distinctions.   83*tenures* the holding of a piece of property or office or the conditions or period of such holding.   85*sconce* head.   87*statutes,*
recognizances legal terms connected with the transfer of land.   87*vouchers* persons called on to warrant a tenant's title.   87-88*recoveries* process for transfer of entailed estate.   88*fine* the four uses of this word are
as follows: (1) end, (2) legal process, (3) elegant, (4) small.   91*indentures* conveyances or contracts.   92*in-*
heritor possessor, owner.   95*calf-skins* parchments.   96*assurance in that* safety in legal parchments.
113*absolute* positive, decided.   113*by the card* with precision, i.e., by the mariner's card on which the points
of the compass were marked.   113-114*equivocation* ambiguity in the use of terms.   115*picked* refined, fastidious.   116*galls* chafes.   116*kibe* chilblain.

day that young Hamlet was born; he that is mad, and sent into England.

HAMLET: Ay, marry, why was he sent into England?

FIRST CLOWN: Why, because 'a was mad: 'a shall recover his wits there; or, if 'a do not, 'tis no great matter there. 125

HAMLET: Why?

FIRST CLOWN: 'Twill not be seen in him there; there the men are as mad as he.

HAMLET: How came he mad?

FIRST CLOWN: Very strangely, they say.

HAMLET: How strangely? 130

FIRST CLOWN: Faith, e'en with losing his wits.

HAMLET: Upon what ground?

FIRST CLOWN: Why, here in Denmark: I have been sexton here, man and boy, thirty years.°

HAMLET: How long will a man lie i' the earth ere he rot? 135

FIRST CLOWN: Faith, if 'a be not rotten before 'a die—as we have many pocky° corses now-a-days, that will scarce hold the laying in—'a will last you some eight year or nine year: a tanner will last you nine year.

HAMLET: Why he more than another?

FIRST CLOWN: Why, sir, his hide is so tanned with his trade, that 'a will keep 140 out water a great while; and your water is a sore decayer of your whoreson dead body. Here's a skull now hath lain you i' th' earth three and twenty years.

HAMLET: Whose was it?

FIRST CLOWN: A whoreson mad fellow's it was: whose do you think it was? 145

HAMLET: Nay, I know not.

FIRST CLOWN: A pestilence on him for a mad rogue! 'a poured a flagon of Rhenish on my head once. This same skull, sir, was Yorick's skull, the king's jester.

HAMLET: This? 150

FIRST CLOWN: E'en that.

HAMLET: Let me see. [*Takes the skull.*] Alas, poor Yorick! I knew him, Horatio: a fellow of infinite jest, of most excellent fancy: he hath borne me on his back a thousand times; and now, how abhorred in my imagination it is! my gorge rises at it. Here hung those lips that I have kissed I know 155 not how oft. Where be your gibes now? your gambols? your songs? your flashes of merriment, that were wont to set the table on a roar? Not one now, to mock your own grinning? quite chap-fallen? Now get you to my lady's chamber, and tell her, let her paint an inch thick, to this favour she must come; make her laugh at that. Prithee, Horatio, tell me one thing. 160

HORATIO: What's that, my lord?

HAMLET: Dost thou think Alexander looked o' this fashion i' the earth?

HORATIO: E'en so.

HAMLET: And smelt so? pah! [*Puts down the skull.*]

HORATIO: E'en so, my lord. 165

HAMLET: To what base uses we may return, Horatio! Why may not imagi-

---

[134]**thirty years** *this statement with that in line 122 shows Hamlet's age to be thirty years.* [137]**pocky** *rotten, diseased.*

nation trace the noble dust of Alexander, till 'a find it stopping a bung-
hole?

HORATIO: 'Twere to consider too curiously,° to consider so.

HAMLET: No, faith, not a jot; but to follow him thither with modesty enough,   170
and likelihood to lead it: as thus: Alexander died, Alexander was buried,
Alexander returneth into dust; the dust is earth; of earth we make loam;°
and why of that loam, whereto he was converted, might they not stop a
beer-barrel?

> Imperious° Cæsar, dead and turn'd to clay,   175
> Might stop a hole to keep the wind away:
> O, that that earth, which kept the world in awe,
> Should patch a wall t'expel the winter's flaw!°

But soft! but soft awhile! here comes the king,

Enter KING, QUEEN, LAERTES, *and the Corse of* [OPHELIA, *in procession, with* PRIEST,
LORDS, *etc.*].

The queen, the courtiers: who is this they follow?   180
And with such maimed rites? This doth betoken
The corse they follow did with desp'rate hand
Fordo° it° own life: 'twas of some estate.
Couch° we awhile, and mark.   [*Retiring with* HORATIO.]

LAERTES: What ceremony else?

HAMLET: That is Laertes,   185
A very noble youth: mark.

LAERTES: What ceremony else?

FIRST PRIEST: Her obsequies have been as far enlarg'd°
As we have warranty: her death was doubtful;
And, but that great command o'ersways the order,   190
She should in ground unsanctified have lodg'd
Till the last trumpet; for charitable prayers,
Shards,° flints and pebbles should be thrown on her:
Yet here she is allow'd her virgin crants,°
Her maiden strewments° and the bringing home   195
Of bell and burial.°

LAERTES: Must there no more be done?

FIRST PRIEST: No more be done:
We should profane the service of the dead
To sing a requiem and such rest to her
As to peace-parted° souls.

LAERTES: Lay her i' th' earth: 200
And from her fair and unpolluted flesh

---

¹⁶⁹**curiously** *minutely.*   ¹⁷²**loam** *clay paste for brickmaking.*   ¹⁷⁵**Imperious** *imperial.*   ¹⁷⁸**flaw**
gust of wind.   ¹⁸³**Fordo** *destroy.*   ¹⁸³**it** *its.*   ¹⁸⁴**Couch** *hide, lurk.*   ¹⁸⁸**enlarg'd** *extended, refer-*
ring to the fact that suicides are not given full burial rites.   ¹⁹³**Shards** *broken bits of pottery.*   ¹⁹⁴**crants** *gar-*
lands customarily hung upon the biers of unmarried women.   ¹⁹⁵**strewments** *traditional strewing of flowers.*
¹⁹⁵⁻¹⁹⁶**bringing . . . burial** *the laying to rest of the body, to the sound of the bell.*   ²⁰⁰**peace-parted** *allu-*
sion to the text "Lord, now lettest thou thy servant depart in peace."

May violets spring! I tell thee, churlish priest,
A minist'ring angel shall my sister be,
When thou liest howling.°

HAMLET: What, the fair Ophelia!

QUEEN: Sweets to the sweet: farewell!   [*Scattering flowers.*] 205
I hop'd thou shouldst have been my Hamlet's wife;
I thought thy bride-bed to have deck'd, sweet maid,
And not have strew'd thy grave.

LAERTES: O, treble woe
Fall ten times treble on that cursed head,
Whose wicked deed thy most ingenious sense°   210
Depriv'd thee of! Hold off the earth awhile,
Till I have caught her once more in mine arms: [*Leaps into the grave.*]
Now pile your dust upon the quick and dead,
Till of this flat a mountain you have made,
T' o'ertop old Pelion,° or the skyish head   215
Of blue Olympus.

HAMLET: [*Advancing*] What is he whose grief
Bears such an emphasis? whose phrase of sorrow
Conjures the wand'ring stars,° and makes them stand
Like wonder-wounded hearers? This is I,
Hamlet the Dane.   [*Leaps into the grave.*]

LAERTES: The devil take thy soul!   [*Grappling with him.*] 220

HAMLET: Thou pray'st not well.
I prithee, take thy fingers from my throat;
For, though I am not splenitive° and rash,
Yet have I in me something dangerous,
Which let thy wisdom fear: hold off thy hand.   225

KING: Pluck them asunder.

QUEEN: Hamlet, Hamlet!

ALL: Gentlemen,—

HORATIO: Good my lord, be quiet.

[*The* ATTENDANTS *part them, and they come out of the grave.*]

HAMLET: Why, I will fight with him upon this theme
Until my eyelids will no longer wag.°
QUEEN: O my son, what theme?   230
HAMLET: I lov'd Ophelia: forty thousand brothers
Could not, with all their quantity° of love,
Make up my sum. What wilt thou do for her?
KING: O, he is mad, Laertes.
QUEEN: For love of God, forbear° him.   235

---

²⁰⁴**howling**   *i.e., in hell.*   ²¹⁰**ingenious sense**   *mind endowed with finest qualities.*   ²¹⁵**Pelion**   *Olympus, Pelion, and Ossa are mountains in the north of Thessaly.*   ²¹⁸**wand'ring stars**   *planets.*   ²²³**splenitive**   *quick-tempered.*   ²²⁹**wag**   *move (not used ludicrously).*   ²³²**quantity**   *some suggest that the word is used in a deprecatory sense (little bits, fragments).*   ²³⁵**forbear**   *leave alone.*

HAMLET: 'Swounds,° show me what thou 'lt do:
    Woo 't° weep? woo 't fight? woo 't fast? woo 't tear thyself?
    Woo 't drink up eisel?° eat a crocodile?
    I'll do 't. Dost thou come here to whine?
    To outface me with leaping in her grave?   240
    Be buried quick with her, and so will I:
    And, if thou prate of mountains, let them throw
    Millions of acres on us, till our ground,
    Singeing his pate against the burning zone,°
    Make Ossa like a wart! Nay, an thou 'lt mouth,   245
    I'll rant as well as thou.
QUEEN: This is mere madness:
    And thus awhile the fit will work on him;
    Anon, as patient as the female dove.
    When that her golden couplets° are disclos'd,
    His silence will sit drooping.
HAMLET: Hear you, sir;   250
    What is the reason that you use me thus?
    I lov'd you ever: but it is no matter;
    Let Hercules himself do what he may,
    The cat will mew and dog will have his day.
KING: I pray thee, good Horatio, wait upon him.   *Exit* HAMLET *and* HORATIO. 255
    [*To* LAERTES.] Strengthen your patience in° our last night's speech;
    We'll put the matter to the present push.°
    Good Gertrude, set some watch over your son.
    This grave shall have a living° monument:
    An hour of quiet shortly shall we see;   260
    Till then, in patience our proceeding be.   *Exeunt.*

Scene II [*A hall in the castle.*]

Enter HAMLET *and* HORATIO.

HAMLET: So much for this, sir: now shall you see the other;
    You do remember all the circumstance?
HORATIO: Remember it, my lord!
HAMLET: Sir, in my heart there was a kind of fighting,
    That would not let me sleep: methought I lay   5
    Worse than the mutines° in the bilboes.° Rashly,°
    And prais'd be rashness for it, let us know,
    Our indiscretion sometime serves us well,
    When our deep plots do pall:° and that should learn us

---

²³⁶**'Swounds** oath, "God's wounds."   ²³⁷**Woo 't** wilt thou.   ²³⁸**eisel** vinegar. *Some editors have taken this to be the name of a river, such as the Yssel, the Weissel, and the Nile.*   ²⁴⁴**burning zone** sun's orbit. ²⁴⁹**golden couplets** *the pigeon lays two eggs; the young when hatched are covered with golden down.* ²⁵⁶**in** *by recalling.*   ²⁵⁷**present push** immediate test.   ²⁵⁹**living** lasting; *also refers (for Laertes' benefit) to the plot against Hamlet.*   **V.ii.** ⁶**mutines** mutineers.   ⁶**bilboes** shackles.   ⁶**Rashly** *goes with line 12.*   ⁹**pall** fail.

There's a divinity that shapes our ends, [10]
Rough-hew° them how we will,—

HORATIO: That is most certain.

HAMLET: Up from my cabin,
My sea-gown° scarf'd about me, in the dark
Grop'd I to find out them; had my desire,
Finger'd° their packet, and in fine° withdrew [15]
To mine own room again; making so bold,
My fears forgetting manners, to unseal
Their grand commission; where I found, Horatio,—
O royal knavery!—an exact command,
Larded° with many several sorts of reasons [20]
Importing Denmark's health and England's too,
With, ho! such bugs° and goblins in my life,°
That, on the supervise,° no leisure bated,°
No, not to stay the grinding of the axe,
My head should be struck off.

HORATIO: Is 't possible? [25]

HAMLET: Here's the commission: read it at more leisure.
But wilt thou hear me how I did proceed?

HORATIO: I beseech you.

HAMLET: Being thus be-netted round with villanies,—
Ere I could make a prologue to my brains, [30]
They had begun the play°—I sat me down,
Devis'd a new commission, wrote it fair:
I once did hold it, as our statists° do,
A baseness to write fair° and labour'd much
How to forget that learning, but, sir, now [35]
It did me yeoman's° service: wilt thou know
Th' effect of what I wrote?

HORATIO: Ay, good my lord.

HAMLET: An earnest conjuration from the king,
As England was his faithful tributary,
As love between them like the palm might flourish, [40]
As peace should still her wheaten garland° wear
And stand a comma° 'tween their amities,
And many such-like 'As'es° of great charge,°
That, on the view and knowing of these contents,
Without debatement further, more or less, [45]

---

[11]**Rough-hew** *shape roughly; it may mean "bungle."*   [13]**sea-gown** *"A sea-gown, or a corase, high-collered, and short-sleeved gowne, reaching down to the mid-leg, and used most by seamen and saylors" (Cotgrave, quoted by Singer).*   [15]**finger'd** *pilfered, filched.*   [15]**in fine** *finally.*   [20]**Larded** *enriched.*   [22]**bugs** *bugbears.*   [22]**such . . . life** *such imaginary dangers if I were allowed to live.*   [23]**supervise** *perusal.*   [23]**leisure bated** *delay allowed.*   [30-31]**prologue . . . play** *i.e., before I could begin to think, my mind had made its decision.*   [33]**statists** *statesmen.*   [34]**fair** *in a clear hand.*   [36]**yeoman's** *i.e., faithful.*   [41]**wheaten garland** *symbol of peace.*   [42]**comma** *smallest break or separation. Here amity begins and amity ends the period, and peace stands between like a dependent clause. The comma indicates continuity, link.*   [43]**'As'es** *the "whereases" of a formal document, with play on the word ass.*   [43]**charge** *import, and burden.*

He should the bearers put to sudden death,
Not shriving-time° allow'd.

HORATIO: How was this seal'd?

HAMLET: Why, even in that was heaven ordinant.°
I had my father's signet in my purse,
Which was the model of that Danish seal;   50
Folded the writ up in the form of th' other,
Subscrib'd it, gave 't th' impression, plac'd it safely,
The changeling never known. Now, the next day
Was our sea-fight; and what to this was sequent°
Thou know'st already.   55

HORATIO: So Guildenstern and Rosencrantz go to 't.

HAMLET: Why, man, they did make love to this employment;
They are not near my conscience; their defeat
Does by their own insinuation° grow:
'Tis dangerous when the baser nature comes   60
Between the pass° and fell incensed° points
Of mighty opposites.

HORATIO: Why, what a king is this!

HAMLET: Does it not, think thee, stand° me now upon—
He that hath kill'd my king and whor'd my mother,
Popp'd in between th' election° and my hopes,   65
Thrown out his angle° for my proper life,
And with such coz'nage°—is 't not perfect conscience,
To quit° him with this arm? and is 't not to be damn'd,
To let this canker° of our nature come
In further evil?   70

HORATIO: It must be shortly known to him from England
What is the issue of the business there.

HAMLET: It will be short: the interim is mine;
And a man's life's no more than to say "One."
But I am very sorry, good Horatio,   75
That to Laertes I forgot myself;
For, by the image of my cause, I see
The portraiture of his: I'll court his favours:
But, sure, the bravery° of his grief did put me
Into a tow'ring passion.

HORATIO: Peace! who comes here?   80

Enter a COURTIER [OSRIC].

OSRIC: Your lordship is right welcome back to Denmark.

HAMLET: I humbly thank you, sir. [*To* HORATIO.] Dost know this water-fly?°

---

⁴⁷*shriving-time* *time for absolution.* ⁴⁸*ordinant* *directing.* ⁵⁴*sequent* *subsequent.* ⁵⁹*insinuation* *interference.* ⁶¹*pass* *thrust.* ⁶¹*fell incensed* *fiercely angered.* ⁶³*stand* *become incumbent.*
⁶⁵*election* *the Danish throne was filled by election.* ⁶⁶*angle* *fishing line.* ⁶⁷*coz'nage* *trickery.*
⁶⁸*quit* *repay.* ⁶⁹*canker* *ulcer, or possibly the worm which destroys buds and leaves.* ⁷⁹*bravery* *bravado.*
⁸²*water-fly* *vain or busily idle person.*

HORATIO: No, my good lord.

HAMLET: Thy state is the more gracious; for 'tis a vice to know him. He hath
much land, and fertile: let a beast be lord of beasts,° and his crib shall stand [85]
at the king's mess:° 'tis a chough;° but, as I say, spacious in the possession
of dirt.

OSRIC: Sweet lord, if your lordship were at leisure, I should impart a thing
to you from his majesty.

HAMLET: I will receive it, sir, with all diligence of spirit. Put your bonnet to [90]
his right use; 'tis for the head.

OSRIC: I thank you lordship, it is very hot.

HAMLET: No, believe me, 'tis very cold; the wind is northerly.

OSRIC: It is indifferent° cold, my lord, indeed.

HAMLET: But yet methinks it is very sultry and hot for my complexion. [95]

OSRIC: Exceedingly, my lord; it is very sultry,—as 'twere,—I cannot tell
how. But, my lord, his majesty bade me signify to you that 'a has laid a
great wager on your head: sir, this is the matter,—

HAMLET: I beseech you, remember°—

[HAMLET *moves him to put on his hat.*]

OSRIC: Nay, good my lord; for mine ease,° in good faith. Sir, here is newly [100]
come to court Laertes; believe me, an absolute gentleman, full of most excellent differences, of very soft° society and great showing:° indeed, to
speak feelingly° of him, he is the card° or calendar of gentry,° for you shall
find in him the continent of what part a gentleman would see.

HAMLET: Sir, his definement° suffers no perdition° in you; though, I know, [105]
to divide him inventorially° would dozy° the arithmetic of memory, and
yet but yaw° neither, in respect of his quick sail. But, in the verity of
extolment, I take him to be a soul of great article;° and his infusion° of
such dearth and rareness,° as, to make true diction of him, his semblable°
is his mirror; and who else would trace° him, his umbrage,° nothing [110]
more.

OSRIC: Your lordship speaks most infallibly of him.

HAMLET: The concernancy,° sir? why do we wrap the gentleman in our more
rawer breath?°

OSRIC: Sir? [115]

HORATIO [*aside to* HAMLET]: Is 't not possible to understand in another
tongue?° You will do 't, sir, really.

---

[85]*lord of beasts* cf. Genesis 1:26, 28.   [85–86]*his crib . . . mess* he shall eat at the king's table, i.e., be one
of the group of persons (usually four) constituting a mess at a banquet.   [86]*chough* probably, chattering jackdaw;
also explained as chuff, provincial boor or churl.   [94]*indifferent* somewhat.   [99]*remember* i.e., remember thy courtesy; conventional phrase for "Be covered."   [100]*mine ease* conventional reply declining the invitation of
"Remember thy courtesy."   [102]*soft* gentle.   [102]*showing* distinguished appearance.   [103]*feelingly* with just
perception.   [103]*card* chart, map.   [103]*gentry* good breeding.   [105]*definement* definition.   [105]*perdition* loss, diminution.   [106]*divide him inventorially* i.e., enumerate his graces.   [106]*dozy* dizzy.
[107]*yaw* to move unsteadily (of a ship).   [108]*article* moment or importance.   [108]*infusion* infused temperament, character imparted by nature.   [109]*dearth and rareness* rarity.   [109]*semblable* true likeness.
[110]*trace* follow.   [110]*umbrage* shadow.   [113]*concernancy* import.   [114]*breath* speech.
[116–117]*Is 't . . . tongue?* i.e., can one converse with Osric only in this outlandish jargon?

HAMLET: What imports the nomination° of this gentleman?

OSRIC: Of Laertes?

HORATIO [*aside to* HAMLET]: His purse is empty already; all 's golden words [120] are spent.

HAMLET: Of him, sir.

OSRIC: I know you are not ignorant—

HAMLET: I would you did, sir; yet, in faith, if you did, it would not much approve° me. Well, sir? [125]

OSRIC: You are not ignorant of what excellence Laertes is—

HAMLET: I dare not confess that, lest I should compare with him in excellence; but, to know a man well, were to know himself.°

OSRIC: I mean, sir, for his weapon; but in the imputation° laid on him by them, in his meed° he's unfellowed. [130]

HAMLET: What's his weapon?

OSRIC: Rapier and dagger.

HAMLET: That's two of his weapons: but, well.

OSRIC: The king, sir, hath wagered with him six Barbary horses: against the which he has impawned,° as I take it, six French rapiers and poniards, with [135] their assigns, as girdle, hangers,° and so: three of the carriages, in faith, are very dear to fancy,° very responsive° to the hilts, most delicate° carriages, and of very liberal conceit.°

HAMLET: What call you the carriages?

HORATIO [*aside to* HAMLET]: I knew you must be edified by the margent° [140] ere you had done.

OSRIC: The carriages, sir, are the hangers.

HAMLET: The phrase would be more german° to the matter, if we could carry cannon by our sides: I would it might be hangers till then. But, on: six Barbary horses against six French swords, their assigns, and three liberal- [145] conceited carriages; that's the French bet against the Danish. Why is this "impawned," as you call it?

OSRIC: The king, sir, hath laid, that in a dozen passes between yourself and him, he shall not exceed you three hits: he hath laid on twelve for nine; and it would come to immediate trial, if your lordship would vouchsafe [150] the answer.

HAMLET: How if I answer "no"?

OSRIC: I mean, my lord, the opposition of your person in trial.

HAMLET: Sir, I will walk here in the hall: if it please his majesty, it is the breathing time° of day with me; let the foils be brought, the gentleman [155] willing, and the king hold his purpose, I will win for him as I can; if not, I will gain nothing but my shame and the odd hits.

OSRIC: Shall I re-deliver you e'en so?

[118]*nomination* naming. [125]*approve* command.   [128]*but . . . himself* but to know a man as excellent were to know Laertes.   [129]*imputation* reputation.   [130]*meed* merit.   [135]*he has impawned* he has wagered.   [136]*hangers* straps on the sword belt from which the sword hung.   [137]*dear to fancy* fancifully made.   [137]*responsive* probably, well balanced, corresponding closely.   [137]*delicate* i.e., in workmanship. [138]*liberal conceit* elaborate design.   [140]*margent* margin of a book, place for explanatory notes.   [143]*german* germane, appropriate.   [155]*breathing time* exercise period.

HAMLET: To this effect, sir; after what flourish your nature will.

OSRIC: I commend my duty to your lordship. 160

HAMLET: Yours, yours. [*Exit* OSRIC.] He does well to commend it himself; there are no tongues else for 's turn.

HORATIO: This lapwing° runs away with the shell on his head.

HAMLET: 'A did comply, sir, with his dug,° before 'a sucked it. Thus has hey—and many more of the same breed that I know the drossy° age dotes 165 on—only got the tune° of the time and out of an habit of encounter;° a kind of yesty° collection, which carries them through and through the most fann'd and winnowed° opinions; and do but blow them to their trial, the bubbles are out.°

Enter a LORD.

LORD: My lord, his majesty commended him to you by young Osric, who 170 brings back to him, that you attend him in the hall: he sends to know if your pleasure hold to play with Laertes, or that you will take longer time.

HAMLET: I am constant to my purposes; they follow the king's pleasure: if his fitness speaks, mine is ready; now or whensoever, provided I be so able as now. 175

LORD: The king and queen and all are coming down.

HAMLET: In happy time.°

LORD: The queen desires you to use some gentle entertainment to Laertes before you fall to play.

HAMLET: She well instructs me.   [*Exit* LORD.] 180

HORATIO: You will lose this wager, my lord.

HAMLET: I do not think so; since he went into France, I have been in continual practice; I shall win at the odds. But thou wouldst not think how ill all 's here about my heart: but it is no matter.

HORATIO: Nay, good my lord,— 185

HAMLET: It is but foolery; but it is such a kind of gain-giving,° as would perhaps trouble a woman.

HORATIO: If your mind dislike any thing, obey it: I will forestall their repair hither, and say you are not fit.

HAMLET: Not a whit, we defy augury: there's a special providence in the fall 190 of a sparrow. If it be now, 'tis not to come; if it be not to come, it will be now; if it be not now, yet it will come: the readiness is all:° since no man of aught he leaves knows, what is 't to leave betimes? Let be.

A table prepared. [*Enter*] *Trumpets, Drums, and Officers with cushions;* KING, QUEEN, [OSRIC,] *and all the State; foils, daggers,* [*and wine borne in;*] *and* LAERTES.

KING: Come, Hamlet, come, and take this hand from me.

---

[163] **lapwing**   *peewit; noted for its wiliness in drawing a visitor away from its nest and its supposed habit of running about when newly hatched with its head in the shell; possibly an allusion to Osric's hat.*   [164] **did comply . . . dug**   *paid compliments to his mother's breast.*   [165] **drossy**   *frivolous.*   [166] **tune**   *temper, mood.*   [166] **habit of encounter**   *demeanor of social intercourse.*   [167] **yesty**   *frothy.*   [168] **fann'd and winnowed**   *select and refined.*   [168–169] **blow . . . out**   *i.e., put them to the test, and their ignorance is exposed.*   [177] **in happy time**   *a phrase of courtesy.*   [186] **gain-giving**   *misgiving.*   [192] **all**   *all that matters.*

[The KING *puts* LAERTES'*s hand into* HAMLET'*s.]*

HAMLET: Give me your pardon, sir: I have done you wrong;   195
   But pardon 't as you are a gentleman.
   This presence° knows,
   And you must needs have heard, how I am punish'd
   With a sore distraction. What I have done,
   That might your nature, honour and exception°   200
   Roughly awake, I here proclaim was madness.
   Was 't Hamlet wrong'd Laertes? Never Hamlet:
   If Hamlet from himself be ta'en away,
   And when he's not himself does wrong Laertes,
   Then Hamlet does it not, Hamlet denies it.   205
   Who does it, then? His madness: if 't be so,
   Hamlet is of the faction that is wrong'd;
   His madness is poor Hamlet's enemy.
   Sir, in this audience,
   Let my disclaiming from a purpos'd evil   210
   Free me so far in your most generous thoughts,
   That I have shot mine arrow o'er the house,
   And hurt my brother.
LAERTES: I am satisfied in nature,°
   Whose motive, in this case, should stir me most
   To my revenge: but in my terms of honour   215
   I stand aloof; and will no reconcilement,
   Till by some elder masters, of known honour,
   I have a voice° and precedent of peace,
   To keep my name ungor'd. But till that time,
   I do receive your offer'd love like love,   220
   And will not wrong it.
HAMLET: I embrace it freely;
   And will this brother's wager frankly play.
   Give us the foils. Come on.
LAERTES: Come, one for me.
HAMLET: I'll be your foil,° Laertes: in mine ignorance
   Your skill shall, like a star i' th' darkest night,   225
   Stick fiery off° indeed.
LAERTES: You mock me, sir.
HAMLET: No, by this hand.
KING: Give them the foils, young Osric. Cousin Hamlet,
   You know the wager?
HAMLET: Very well, my lord;
   Your grace has laid the odds o' th' weaker side.   230

---

¹⁹⁷**presence** *royal assembly.*   ²⁰⁰**exception** *disapproval.*   ²¹³**nature** *i.e., he is personally satisfied, but his honor must be satisfied by the rules of the code of honor.*   ²¹⁸**voice** *authoritative pronouncement.*   ²²⁴**foil** *quibble on the two senses: "background which sets something off," and "blunted rapier for fencing."*   ²²⁶**Stick fiery off** *stand out brilliantly.*

KING: I do not fear it; I have seen you both:
  But since he is better'd, we have therefore odds.
LAERTES: This is too heavy, let me see another.
HAMLET: This likes me well. These foils have all a length?

[They prepare to play.]

OSRIC: Ay, my good lord.   235
KING: Set me the stoups of wine upon that table.
  If Hamlet give the first or second hit,
  Or quit in answer of the third exchange,
  Let all the battlements their ordnance fire;
  The king shall drink to Hamlet's better breath;   240
  And in the cup an union° shall he throw,
  Richer than that which four successive kings
  In Denmark's crown have worn. Give me the cups;
  And let the kettle° to the trumpet speak,
  The trumpet to the cannoneer without,   245
  The cannons to the heavens, the heavens to earth,
  "Now the king drinks to Hamlet." Come begin: *Trumpets the while.*
  And you, the judges, bear a wary eye.
HAMLET: Come on, sir.
LAERTES: Come, my lord.   *[They play.]*
HAMLET: One.
LAERTES: No.
HAMLET: Judgement.
OSRIC: A hit, a very palpable hit.

Drums, trumpets, and shot. Flourish. A piece goes off.

LAERTES: Well; again.   250
KING: Stay; give me drink. Hamlet, this pearl° is thine;
  Here's to thy health. Give him the cup.
HAMLET: I'll play this bout first; set it by awhile.
  Come. *[They play.]* Another hit; what say you?
LAERTES: A touch, a touch, I do confess 't.   255
KING: Our son shall win.
QUEEN: He's fat,° and scant of breath.
  Here, Hamlet, take my napkin, rub thy brows:
  The queen carouses° to thy fortune, Hamlet.
HAMLET: Good madam!
KING: Gertrude, do not drink.
QUEEN: I will, my lord; I pray you, pardon me. *[Drinks.]*   260
KING *[aside]*: It is the poison'd cup: it is too late.
HAMLET: I dare not drink yet, madam; by and by.

---

²⁴¹**union** *pearl.*   ²⁴⁴**kettle** *kettledrum.*   ²⁵¹**pearl** *i.e., the poison.*   ²⁵⁶**fat** *not physically fit, out of training. Some earlier editors speculated that the term applied to the corpulence of Richard Burbage, who originally played the part, but the allusion now appears unlikely. "Fat" may also suggest "sweaty."*   ²⁵⁸**carouses** *drinks a toast.*

QUEEN: Come, let me wipe thy face.

LAERTES: My lord, I'll hit him now.

KING: I do not think 't.

LAERTES [*aside*]: And yet 'tis almost 'gainst my conscience.   265

HAMLET: Come, for the third, Laertes: you but dally;
  I pray you, pass with your best violence;
  I am afeard you make a wanton° of me.

LAERTES: Say you so? come on.   [*They play.*]

OSRIC: Nothing, neither way.   270

LAERTES: Have at you now!

[LAERTES *wounds* HAMLET; *then, in scuffling, they change rapiers,*° *and* HAMLET *wounds*
LAERTES.]

KING: Part them; they are incens'd.

HAMLET: Nay, come again.   [*The* QUEEN *falls.*]

OSRIC: Look to the queen there, ho!

HORATIO: They bleed on both sides. How is it, my lord?

OSRIC: How is 't, Laertes?

LAERTES: Why, as a woodcock° to mine own springe,° Osric;   275
  I am justly kill'd with mine own treachery.

HAMLET: How does the queen?

KING: She swounds° to see them bleed.

QUEEN: No, no, the drink, the drink,—O my dear Hamlet,—
  The drink, the drink! I am poison'd.   [*Dies.*]

HAMLET: O villany! Ho! let the door be lock'd: 280
  Treachery! Seek it out.   [LAERTES *falls.*]

LAERTES: It is here, Hamlet: Hamlet, thou art slain;
  No med'cine in the world can do thee good;
  In thee there is not half an hour of life;
  The treacherous instrument is in thy hand,   285
  Unbated° and envenom'd: the foul practice
  Hath turn'd itself on me; lo, here I lie,
  Never to rise again: thy mother's poison'd:
  I can no more: the king, the king's to blame.

HAMLET: The point envenom'd too!   290
  Then, venom, to thy work.   [*Stabs the* KING.]

ALL: Treason! treason!

KING: O, yet defend me, friends; I am but hurt.

HAMLET: Here, thou incestuous, murd'rous, damned Dane.
  Drink off this potion. Is thy union here?   295
  Follow my mother.   [KING *dies.*]

---

²⁶⁸**wanton**   *spoiled child.*   ²⁷¹**in scuffling, they change rapiers**   *according to a widespread stage tradition, Hamlet receives a scratch, realizes that Laertes's sword is unbated, and accordingly forces an exchange.*   ²⁷⁵**woodcock**
as type of stupidity or as decoy.   ²⁷⁵**springe**   *trap, snare.*   ²⁷⁷**swounds**   *swoons.*   ²⁸⁶**Unbated**   *Not
blunted with a button.*

LAERTES: He is justly serv'd;
  It is a poison temper'd° by himself.
  Exchange forgiveness with me, noble Hamlet:
  Mine and my father's death come not upon thee,
  Nor thine on me!   *[Dies.]* 300

HAMLET: Heaven make thee free of it! I follow thee.
  I am dead, Horatio. Wretched queen, adieu!
  You that look pale and tremble at this chance,
  That are but mutes° or audience to this act,
  Had I but time—as this fell sergeant,° Death,   305
  Is strict in his arrest—O, I could tell you—
  But let it be. Horatio, I am dead;
  Thou livest; report me and my cause aright
  To the unsatisfied.

HORATIO: Never believe it:
  I am more an antique Roman° than a Dane: 310
  Here's yet some liquor left.

HAMLET: As th' art a man,
  Give me the cup: let go, by heaven, I'll ha 't.
  O God! Horatio, what a wounded name,
  Things standing thus unknown, shall live behind me!
  If thou didst ever hold me in thy heart,   315
  Absent thee from felicity awhile,
  And in this harsh world draw thy breath in pain,
  To tell my story.   *A march afar off.*
            What warlike noise is this?

OSRIC: Young Fortinbras, with conquest come from Poland,
  To the ambassadors of England gives   320
  This warlike volley.

HAMLET: O, I die, Horatio;
  The potent poison quite o'er-crows° my spirit:
  I cannot live to hear the news from England;
  But I do prophesy th' election lights
  On Fortinbras: he has my dying voice;   325
  So tell him, with th' occurrents,° more and less,
  Which have solicited.° The rest is silence.   *[Dies.]*

HORATIO: Now cracks a noble heart. Good night, sweet prince;
  And flights of angels sing thee to thy rest!
  Why does the drum come hither?   *[March within.]* 330

     Enter FORTINBRAS, *with the [English]* AMBASSADORS *[and others].*

FORTINBRAS: Where is this sight?

---

²⁹⁷**temper'd** *mixed.*   ³⁰⁴**mutes** *performers in a play who speak no words.*   ³⁰⁵**sergeant** *sheriff's officer.*
³¹⁰**Roman** *it was the Roman custom to follow masters in death.*   ³²²**o'er-crows** *triumphs over.*   ³²⁶**occur-**
rents *events, incidents.*   ³²⁷**solicited** *moved, urged.*

HORATIO: What is it you would see?
  If aught of woe or wonder, cease your search.
FORTINBRAS: This quarry° cries on havoc.° O proud Death,
  What feast is toward in thine eternal cell,
  That thou so many princes at a shot   335
  So bloodily hast struck?
FIRST AMBASSADOR: The sight is dismal;
  And our affairs from England come too late:
  The ears are senseless that should give us hearing,
  To tell him his commandment is fulfill'd,
  That Rosencrantz and Guildenstern are dead: 340
  Where should we have our thanks?
HORATIO: Not from his mouth,°
  Had it th' ability of life to thank you:
  He never gave commandment for their death.
  But since, so jump° upon this bloody question,°
  You from the Polack wars, and you from England,   345
  Are here arriv'd, give order that these bodies
  High on a stage° be placed to the view;
  And let me speak to th' yet unknowing world
  How these things came about: so shall you hear
  Of carnal, bloody, and unnatural acts,   350
  Of accidental judgements, casual slaughters,
  Of deaths put on by cunning and forc'd cause,
  And, in this upshot, purposes mistook
  Fall'n on th' inventors' heads: all this can I
  Truly deliver.
FORTINBRAS: Let us haste to hear it,   355
  And call the noblest to the audience.
  For me, with sorrow I embrace my fortune:
  I have some rights of memory° in this kingdom,
  Which now to claim my vantage doth invite me.
HORATIO: Of that I shall have also cause to speak,   360
  And from his mouth whose voice will draw on more:°
  But let this same be presently perform'd,
  Even while men's minds are wild; lest more mischance,
  On° plots and errors, happen.
FORTINBRAS: Let four captains
  Bear Hamlet, like a soldier, to the stage;   365
  For he was likely, had he been put on,
  To have prov'd most royal: and, for his passage,°

---

³³³*quarry* *heap of dead.*   ³³³*cries on havoc* *proclaims a general slaughter.*   ³⁴¹*his mouth* *i.e., the king's.*
³⁴⁴*jump* *precisely.*   ³⁴⁴*question* *dispute.*   ³⁴⁷*stage* *platform.*   ³⁵⁸*of memory* *traditional, re-*
membered.   ³⁶¹*voice . . . more* *vote will influence still others.*   ³⁶⁴*On* *on account of, or possibly, on top of,*
in addition to.   ³⁶⁷*passage* *death.*

The soldiers' music and the rites of war
Speak loudly for him.
Take up the bodies: such a sight as this   370
Becomes the field,° but here shows much amiss.
Go, bid the soldiers shoot.

Exeunt [marching, bearing off the dead bodies; after which a peal of ordnance is shot off].

(1600)

QUESTIONS

1. What makes Hamlet a tragic figure? To what extent is he responsible for the tragic events of the play?
2. Compare Hamlet's speeches from the beginning and end of the play. Select one of his speeches from Act I or II and compare its tone, attitude, and feeling with a speech from the last act.
3. Explain the roles of Laertes and Fortinbras in the play.
4. What reasons are suggested for Hamlet's delay in exacting revenge for his father's death? Do you find these reasons plausible? Why or why not?
5. Identify the various settings in the play. Explain how each setting contributes to the play's dramatic mood and action. Compare, for example, the settings in Act I, scene i, and Act I, scene ii.
6. What images of women are found in the play? How are Ophelia and Gertrude characterized?
7. Discuss the character of Claudius. Can he be considered a tragic figure? Why or why not?
8. Characterize Horatio. What functions does Horatio serve in the play? Which of his personal qualities does Hamlet most admire? Why?
9. Rosencrantz and Guildenstern appear briefly and then disappear from the play. Explain their purpose for the plot of the play.
10. Explain how you would direct the actor playing Polonius. How, for example, would you advise the actor to deliver Polonius's counsel? How much self-knowledge and understanding do you think Polonius possesses?
11. Compare Hamlet and Othello as tragic heroes. What qualities of character distinguish them?
12. Compare Claudius and Iago as villains who precipitate tragedy in the lives of others.
13. What does the gravedigger scene in Act V, scene i, contribute to the play's tone and themes?
14. Any staging of *Hamlet* requires careful attention to lighting. Single out any two scenes in which lighting seems important and explain how you would stage these scenes.
15. Identify two scenes in which the characters' speeches shift between verse and prose. Explain the significance of these shifts.

371**field**   i.e., of battle.

16. One of the highlights of *Hamlet* is its language. Single out two places where you
    find the language especially rich, complex, and suggestive. You may choose solil-
    oquies, dialogue exchanges, or both.

CRITICS ON SHAKESPEARE

ADRIAN POOLE

Hamlet and Oedipus

For Freud, Hamlet was always closely associated with Oedipus. Again Freud finds a
likeness solely in what the two fictional characters suffer from, the desires with which
they are supposedly cursed. But Hamlet too has a side to him that Freud ignores. What
Hamlet has in common with Oedipus and Freud is that he asks a lot of questions. Freud
sees only half of each character, the half that could play the part of patient to his own
analyst. And in extricating them from their own dramas and recasting them in his own,
Freud seizes the role of analyst for himself, displacing the Oedipus and the Hamlet who
make such courageous efforts to understand the story of their lives in the very act of
its composition.

The most significant thing that Freud has to say about Sophocles' Oedipus is to do
with the form and structure of the play rather than its hidden content: "The action of
the play consists in nothing other than the process of revelation, with cunning delays
and ever mounting excitement—a process that can be likened to the work of a psychoanalysis—that Oedipus himself is the murderer of Laius." "The work of *a* psychoanalysis": that is, the specific confrontation and intercourse between analyst and patient. This suggests that a psychoanalysis is constructed like a tragedy, or at least like
this tragedy, and that what a psychoanalysis and a tragedy have in common is something to do with their work of discovery. In each case we are moved by the products
of revelation only in so far as we are moved by the process of revelation.

When we consider the importance of Oedipus for Freud, we should therefore recall not only the image of a man who acts out our (supposedly) deepest fantasies, but
also the action of the play through which Oedipus must discover the truth. If there is
a 'compulsion' in Sophocles' play, it is much less obviously the compulsion to act out
infantile fantasies than the compulsion to know the truth. Sophocles' Oedipus and
Shakespeare's Hamlet are the two characters in tragic drama most actively engaged in
analysis and interpretation. Their importance for Freud is more to do with a passion
for knowledge than with an occult or repressed guilt. Or rather, it is with their explo-

ration of the mysterious relations between knowledge and guilt, a mystery which Freud radically simplifies by attributing guilt solely to the object of interpretation.

Oedipus and Hamlet are on their own within their worlds. Watching their efforts to interpret and understand from within the flow of their own lives, we recognize a universal predicament. Both Oedipus and Hamlet possess great powers of mind, but the questions to which they address themselves involve their whole being. The riddles they attempt to solve, the guilts discovered and incurred in the process of trying to solve them, these are written in flesh and blood, their own and others'.

from Tragedy: Shakespeare and the Greek Example

MAYNARD MACK

The Readiness Is All: Hamlet

Hamlet's world is preeminently in the interrogative mood. It reverberates with questions, anguished, meditative, alarmed. There are questions that in this play, to an extent I think unparalleled in any other, mark the phases and even the nuances of the action, helping to establish its peculiar baffled tone. There are other questions whose interrogations, innocent at first glance, are subsequently seen to have reached beyond their contexts and to point toward some pervasive inscrutability in Hamlet's world as a whole. Such is that tense series of challenges with which the tragedy begins: Bernardo's of Francisco, "Who's there?" Francisco's of Horatio and Marcellus, "Who is there?" Horatio's of the ghost, "What art thou . . . ?"

And then there are the famous questions. In them the interrogations seem to point not only beyond the context but beyond the play, out of Hamlet's predicaments into everyone's: "What a piece of work is a man! . . . And yet to me what is this quintessence of dust?" (2.2.300). "To be, or not to be—that is the question" (3.1.56). "Get thee to a nunnery. Why wouldst thou be a breeder of sinners?" (3.1.121). "I am very proud, revengeful, ambitious, with more offenses at my beck than I have thoughts to put them in, imagination to give them shape, or time to act them in. What should such fellows as I do crawling between earth and heaven?" (3.1.124). "Dost thou think Alexander looked o' this fashion i' th' earth? . . . And smelt so?" (5.1.185).

Further, Hamlet's world is a world of riddles. The hero's own language is often riddling, as the critics have pointed out. When he puns, his puns have receding depths in them, like the one which constitutes his first speech: "A little more than kin, and less than kind!" (1.2.65). His utterances in madness, even if wild and whirling, are simultaneously, as Polonius discovers, pregnant: "Do you know me, my lord?" "Excellent well. You are a fishmonger" (2.2.173). Even the madness itself is riddling: How much is real? How much is feigned? What does it mean?

Sane or mad, Hamlet's mind plays restlessly about his world, turning up one riddle upon another. The riddle of character, for example, and how it is that in a man whose virtues else are "pure as grace," some vicious mole of nature, some "dram of evil," can "all the noble substance [oft adulter]" (1.4.36). Or the riddle of the player's art, and how a man can so project himself into a fiction, a dream of passion, that he can weep for Hecuba (2.2.535). Or the riddle of action: how we may think too little—"What to ourselves in passion we propose," says the player-king. "The passion ending, doth the purpose lose" (3.2.186); and again, how we may think too much: "Thus conscience does make cowards of us all, And thus the native hue of resolution Is sicklied o'er with the pale cast of thought" (3.1.83).

There are also more immediate riddles. His mother—how could she "on this fair mountain leave to feed, And batten on this moor" (3.4.67)? The ghost—which may be a devil, for "the devil hath power T' assume a pleasing shape" (2.2.585). Ophelia—what does her behavior to him mean? Surprising her in her closet, he falls to such perusal of her face as he would draw it (2.1.90). Even the king at his prayers is a riddle. Will a revenge that takes him in the purging of his soul be vengeance, or hire and salary (3.3.79)? As for himself, Hamlet realizes, he is the greatest riddle of all—a mystery, he warns Rosencrantz and Guildenstern, from which he will not have the heart plucked out. He cannot tell why he has of late lost all his mirth, forgone all custom of exercises. Still less can he tell why he delays: "I do not know Why yet I live to say, 'This thing's to do,' Sith I have cause, and will, and strength, and means To do 't" (4.4.43).

Thus the mysteriousness of Hamlet's world is of a piece. It is not simply a matter of missing motivations, to be expunged if only we could find the perfect clue. It is built in. It is evidently an important part of what the play wishes to say to us. And it is certainly an element that the play thrusts upon us from the opening word. Everyone, I think, recalls the mysteriousness of that first scene. The cold middle of the night on the castle platform, the muffled sentries, the uneasy atmosphere of apprehension, the challenges leaping out of the dark, the questions that follow the challenges, feeling out the darkness, searching for identities, for relations, for assurance. "Bernardo?" "Have you had quiet guard?" "Who hath relieved you?" "What, is Horatio there?" "What, has this thing appeared again tonight?" "Looks 'a not like the king?" "How now, Horatio! . . . Is not this something more than fantasy? What think you on 't?" "Is it not like the King?" "Why this same strict and most observant watch . . . ?" "Shall I strike at it with my partisan?" "Do you consent we shall acquaint [young Hamlet] with it?"

We need not be surprised that critics and playgoers alike have been tempted to see in this an evocation not simply of Hamlet's world but of their own. Human beings in their aspect of bafflement, moving in darkness on a rampart between two worlds, unable to reject, or quite accept, the one that, when they face it, "to-shakes" their dispositions with thoughts beyond the reaches of their souls—comforting themselves with hints and guesses. We hear these hints and guesses whispering through the darkness as the several watchers speak. "At least, the whisper goes so" (1.1.80), says one. "I think it be no other but e'en so," says another. "I have heard" that on the crowing of the cock "Th' extravagant and erring spirit hies To his confine," says a third. "Some say" at Christmas time "This bird of dawning" sings all night, "And then, they say, no spirit dare stir abroad." "So have I heard," says the first, "and do in part believe it." However we choose to take the scene, it is clear that it creates a world where uncertainties are of the essence.

from Everybody's Shakespeare

CAROLYN HEILBRUN

The Character of Hamlet's Mother

To understand Gertrude properly, it is only necessary to examine the lines Shakespeare has chosen for her to say. She is, except for her description of Ophelia's death, concise and pithy in speech, with a talent for seeing the essence of every situation presented before her eyes. If she is not profound, she is certainly never silly. We first hear her asking Hamlet to stop wearing black, to stop walking about with his eyes downcast, and to realize that death is an inevitable part of life. She is, in short, asking him not to give way to the passion of grief, a passion of whose force and dangers the Elizabethans were aware, as Miss Campbell has shown. Claudius echoes her with a well-reasoned argument against grief which was, in its philosophy if not in its language, a piece of commonplace Elizabethan lore. After Claudius' speech, Gertrude asks Hamlet to remain in Denmark, where he is rightly loved. Her speeches have been short, however warm and loving, and conciseness of statement is not the mark of a dull and shallow woman.

We next hear her, as Queen and gracious hostess, welcoming Rosencrantz and Guildenstern to the court, hoping, with the King, that they may cheer Hamlet and discover what is depressing him. Claudius then tells Gertrude, when they are alone, that Polonius believes he knows what is upsetting Hamlet. The Queen answers:

> I doubt it is no other than the main,
> His father's death and our o'er-hasty marriage.
> (II.ii. 56–57)

This statement is concise, remarkably to the point, and not a little courageous. It is not the statement of a dull, slothful woman who can only echo her husband's words. Next, Polonius enters with his most unbrief apotheosis to brevity. The Queen interrupts him with five words: "More matter, with less art" (II. ii. 95). It would be difficult to find a phrase more applicable to Polonius. When this gentleman, in no way deterred from his loquacity, after purveying the startling news that he has a daughter, begins to read a letter, the Queen asks pointedly "Came this from Hamlet to her?" (II. ii. 114).

We see Gertrude next in Act III, asking Rosencrantz and Guildenstern, with her usual directness, if Hamlet received them well, and if they were able to tempt him to any pastime. But before leaving the room, she stops for a word of kindness to Ophelia. It is a humane gesture, for she is unwilling to leave Ophelia, the unhappy tool of the King and Polonius, without some kindly and intelligent appreciation of her help:

> And for your part, Ophelia, I do wish
> That your good beauties be the happy cause
> Of Hamlet's wildness. So shall I hope your virtues
> Will bring him to his wonted way again,
> To both your honors.   (III. i. 38–42)

[S]he dies. But before she dies she does not waste time on vituperation; she warns Hamlet that the drink is poisoned to prevent his drinking it. They are her last words. Those critics who have thought her stupid admire her death; they call it uncharacteristic.

In Act III, when Hamlet goes to his mother in her closet his nerves are pitched at the very height of tension; he is on the edge of hysteria. The possibility of murdering his mother has in fact entered his mind, and he has just met and refused an opportunity to kill Claudius. His mother, meanwhile, waiting for him, has told Polonius not to fear for her, but she knows when she sees Hamlet that he may be violently mad. Hamlet quips with her, insults her, tells her he wishes she were not his mother, and when she, still retaining dignity, attempts to end the interview, Hamlet seizes her and she cries for help. The important thing to note is that the Queen's cry "Thou wilt not murder me?" (III. iv. 22) is not foolish. She has seen from Hamlet's demeanor that he is capable of murder, as indeed in the next instant he proves himself to be.

We next learn from the Queen's startled "As kill a king?" (III. iv. 31) that she has no knowledge of the murder, though of course this is only confirmation here of what we already know. Then the Queen asks Hamlet why he is so hysterical:

> What have I done, that thou dar'st wag thy tongue
> In noise so rude against me?   (III. iv. 39–40)

Hamlet tells her: it is her lust, the need of sexual passion, which has driven her from the arms and memory of her husband to the incomparably cruder charms of his brother.

from Hamlet's Mother and Other Women

A. D. NUTTAL

Othello

Othello's tragedy indeed is strangely—and formally—introverted; it consists in the fact that he left the arena proper to tragedy, the battlefield, and entered a subtragic world for which he was not fitted. *Othello* is the story of a hero who went into a house.

Long ago A.C. Bradley observed that, if the heroes of *Hamlet* and *Othello* change places, each play ends very quickly. Hamlet would see through Iago in the first five minutes and be parodying him in the next. Othello, receiving clear instructions like "Kill that usurper" from a ghost, would simply have gone to work. Thus, as the classic problem of *Hamlet* is the hero's delay, so the classic problem of *Othello* is the hero's gullibility. The stronger our sense of Othello's incongruity in the domestic world, the less puzzling this becomes. Certainly, *Othello* is about a man who, having come from a strange and remote place, found his feet in the world of Venetian professional soldiership—and then exchanged that spacious world for a little, dim world of unimaginable horror. "War is no strife/To the dark house and the detested wife" comes not from Othello but from a comedy, but it will serve here. Its note of peculiarly masculine pain and hatred can still score the nerves. It is therefore not surprising that Shakespeare avails himself of the metaphor of the caged hawk. Desdemona says, "I'll watch him tame," at III. iii. 23. The real process of taming a hawk by keeping it awake and so breaking its spirit is described at length in T. H. White's *The Goshawk* [1953]. Othello turns the image round when he says of Desdemona,

> If I do prove her haggard,
> Though that her jesses were my dear heart-strings,
> I'd whistle her off and let her down the wind
> To prey at fortune. (III. iii. 264–7)

He speaks formally of Desdemona, but it is hard not to feel that in the last words it is his own dream of liberty which speaks.

Othello is also about insiders and outsiders. The exotic Moor finds when he leaves the public, martial sphere that he is not accepted, is not understood and cannot understand. The Venetian colour bar is sexual, not professional. Iago plays on this with his "old black ram . . . tupping your white ewe" (I. i. 89–90) and the same note is struck by Roderigo with his "gross clasps of a lascivious Moor" (I. i. 127). Othello's gullibility is not really so very strange. Coal-black among the glittering Venetians, he is visibly the outsider, and in his bewilderment he naturally looks for the man who is visibly the insider, the man who knows the ropes, the sort of man who is always around in the bar, the "good chap" or (as they said then) the "honest" man. And he finds him.

There are two schools of thought on the sort of actor who should play Iago. School A chooses a dark, waspish fellow. School B chooses a bluff, straw-haired, pink-faced sort of man, solid-looking with no nonsense about him. In production School B triumphs, for the role, cast in this way, becomes both credible and terrifying. Although Iago is everywhere spoken of as a "good chap," he has no friends, no loves, no positive desires. He, and not Othello, proves to be the true outsider of the play, for he is foreign to humanity itself. Othello comes from a remote clime, but Iago, in his simpler darkness, comes from the far side of chaos—hence the pathos of Shakespeare's best departure from his source. In Cinthio's *novella* the Ensign (that is, the Iago-figure) with a cunning affectation of reluctance, suggests that Desdemona is false and then seeing his chance, adds, "Your blackness already displeases her." In Shakespeare's play we have instead a note of bar-room masculine intimacy, in assumed complicity of sentiment. Iago says, in effect "Well, she went with black man, so what is one to think?" (III. iii. 232–7). Othello's need to be accepted and guided makes him an easy victim of this style. The hero is set for his sexual humiliation.

from A New Mimesis

MAURICE CHARNEY

Shakespeare's Villains

The malevolence of Shakespeare's villains is difficult to account for either by their past history or by their present grievances. Shakespeare wants to avoid giving them a believable background that would justify or explain their evil. The villains are generally not motivated at all—at least not by detective-story standards—but are presented to us already securely entrenched in their moral condition. Their evil is a positive and active force, and its unquestioned energy makes the villains seem diabolic. We need to accept them as they appear without probing the origins of their conduct. This requires forbearance from the audience, whose love of scandalous explanation is deliberately frustrated.

What are we to make of the reasons Iago offers for his savage revenge on Othello? Is he acting from thwarted ambition, because Cassio has the promotion Iago thinks he himself deserves? Or are the reasons more subtle and more personal? As Iago tells us,

> I hate the Moor;
> And it is thought abroad that 'twixt my
>   sheets
> 'Has done my office. I know not if 't be true;
> Yet I, for mere suspicion in that kind,
> Will do as if for surety.   (1.3.380–84)

There is a cynical coldness in "I know not if't be true," and Iago never troubles himself to find out. Personal honor means nothing to him, since in his view all women are whores and all human activity is base, coarse, gross, and disgusting. What is important is that Iago hates the Moor. That is enough, and reasons are alleged merely to satisfy public opinion.

In a much-quoted phrase, Coleridge spoke of this aspect of Iago's morality as the "motive-hunting of motiveless malignity." In other words, there are no motives and there is no cause that can account for Iago's evil. Othello never understands this, because even at the very end of the play he still wants to learn from that "demi-devil" "Why he hath thus ensnar'd my soul and body" (5.2.305). But Iago refuses any final comforts for Othello's tragic rationalism: "Demand me nothing. What you know, you know./ From this time forth I never will speak word" (306–7). Ultimately, there can be no answer to Othello's question. We have only a hint of explanation when Iago justifies the murder of Cassio: "He hath a daily beauty in his life/ That makes me ugly" (5.1.19–20). This judgment has the true satanic ring. Like Lucifer, Iago is irresistibly attracted to the beauty from which he has been excluded for all eternity, and this sense of damnation makes his revenge so monomaniacal.

Iago is Shakespeare's most brilliant villain, who dominates his play in a way no other villain can (except perhaps Macbeth, a villain-hero). He forces us to consider one of the most difficult paradoxes of tragedy: Why is the villain usually so much more intelligent, insightful, sensitive, and imaginative than his victim? The villain seems to be the surrogate for the diabolic-creative powers of the dramatist. Iago is wonderfully complex in his manipulation of the dramatic action; his plots and Shakespeare's seem to come together, so that one could speak of the stagecraft of villainy and its aesthetics. But in his moral nature Iago is wonderfully simple, if not actually simplified. The presence of both Iago and Desdemona in a single play assumes that good and evil exist as warring postulates. This is the morality play aspect of Shakespearean tragedy.

from How to Read Shakespeare

CHAPTER TWENTY - FOUR

The Neoclassical French Theater

Perhaps the first thing to say about the neoclassical French theater is that its conventions were inspired by the classical drama of Greece and Rome. Hence the term *neoclassical* to describe it. Like its ancient antecedents, the seventeenth-century French theater observed the ancient *unities:* the unity of time, a stipulation that a play's action be confined to a twenty-four-hour period; the unity of place, a single setting; and the unity of action, a single plot. Molière's *Tartuffe* honors all three. Plays that violated the unities were thought to be crude and inelegant by the educated neoclassical audience, which consisted largely of courtiers and aristocrats (*Tartuffe* was performed for the court of Louis XIV) and well-to-do merchants. French neoclassical plays sometimes reflected the ideas and upheld the values popular among these classes; sometimes they satirized them. In either case, the good manners, wit, and common sense of neoclassical comedy mirrored the aristocratic world and suited its audience.

The neoclassical stage differed from the stages of Shakespeare and Sophocles in being an indoor theater with a picture-frame stage. The proscenium arch with its curtain separated audience from actors. Neoclassical plays were enacted on a box stage, which represented a room with a missing fourth wall, allowing the audience to look in on the action. Though the scenery was not elaborate, it was painted and it served as a backdrop for the action. Candles and lanterns illuminated both the actors and the audience. Costume tended toward the elaborate and ornate as in Elizabethan drama. On both the Elizabethan and neoclassical stages actors were ordinarily costumed in contemporary dress that was appropriate to the social status of the characters. A major difference between neoclassical and earlier drama was that female actresses assumed women's roles, enabling playwrights to include more extensive, more frequent, and more realistic love scenes than had been possible previously (since boys had assumed women's roles in Shakespeare's time). As in the earlier eras of drama, however, language still did much of the work, so that even though the intimacy of the French neoclassical playhouse—with a capacity to seat perhaps four hundred spectators—allowed for refinements of facial and physical gesture, action remained subordinate to dialogue.

MOLIÈRE

[1622-1673]

Molière, like Shakespeare and Sophocles before him, was a poet and an actor as well as a playwright. Like Shakespeare, Molière also performed in his own plays, playing Orgon in *Tartuffe*. Molière's genius, unlike Shakespeare's however, was limited to comedy. And his comedies, again unlike Shakespeare's, were satiric rather than romantic. *Tartuffe* satirizes both religious hypocrisy and fraudulence. It also pokes fun at the obsessive fanaticism and the blind gullibility of those who allow themselves to be victimized by the greedy and the self-serving.

When *Tartuffe* was first staged in 1664, it stirred up those who considered it an attack on religion. Even though Molière retitled it *The Impostor* to indicate that Tartuffe's piety is fraudulent, the original version of the play was censored and banned. To defend himself and the play against charges that *Tartuffe* attacked religion, Molière wrote three prefaces and later changed his original ending. The publicity enhanced the play's popularity, and the work was returned to the stage under the protection of the King. Its three-hundred-year-plus life span, however, is due neither to royal protection nor to notoriety, but rather to the ingenuity and vitality of its plot, the profundity of its characterization, and the brilliance of its language, unerringly translated by Richard Wilbur into rhymed iambic pentameter couplets.

MOLIÈRE (JEAN-BAPTISTE POQUELIN)

Tartuffe

TRANSLATED BY RICHARD WILBUR

CHARACTERS

MADAME PERNELLE, *Orgon's mother*
ORGON, *Elmire's husband*
ELMIRE, *Orgon's wife*
DAMIS, *Orgon's son, Elmire's stepson*
MARIANE, *Orgon's daughter, Elmire's stepdaughter, in love with Valère*
VALÈRE, *in love with Mariane*
CLÉANTE, *Orgon's brother-in-law*
TARTUFFE, *a hypocrite*
DORINE, *Mariane's lady's-maid*
MONSIEUR LOYAL, *a bailiff*
A POLICE OFFICER
FLIPOTE, *Madame Pernelle's maid*

The Scene throughout: ORGON's *house in Paris.*

ACT I

Scene I

MADAME PERNELLE *and* FLIPOTE, *her maid,* ELMIRE, MARIANE, DORINE, DAMIS, CLÉANTE

MADAME PERNELLE: Come, come, Flipote; it's time I left this place.
ELMIRE: I can't keep up, you walk at such a pace.
MADAME PERNELLE: Don't trouble, child; no need to show me out.
  It's not your manners I'm concerned about.
ELMIRE: We merely pay you the respect we owe.
  But Mother, why this hurry? Must you go?
MADAME PERNELLE: I must. This house appalls me. No one in it
  Will pay attention for a single minute.

5

Children, I take my leave much vexed in spirit.
I offer good advice, but you won't hear it.   10
You all break in and chatter on and on.
It's like a madhouse with the keeper gone.
DORINE: If . . .
MADAME PERNELLE:
                Girl, you talk too much, and I'm afraid
You're far too saucy for a lady's-maid.
You push in everywhere and have your say.   15
DAMIS: But . . .
MADAME PERNELLE:
                You, boy, grow more foolish every day.
To think my grandson should be such a dunce!
I've said a hundred times, if I've said it once,
That if you keep the course on which you've started,
You'll leave your worthy father broken-hearted.   20
MARIANE: I think . . .
MADAME PERNELLE: And you, his sister, seem so pure,
So shy, so innocent, and so demure.
But you know what they say about still waters.
I pity parents with secretive daughters.
ELMIRE: Now, Mother . . .
MADAME PERNELLE: And as for you, child, let me add   25
That your behavior is extremely bad,
And a poor example for these children, too.
Their dear, dead mother did far better than you.
You're much too free with money, and I'm distressed
To see you so elaborately dressed.   30
When it's one's husband that one aims to please,
One has no need of costly fripperies.
CLÉANTE: Oh, Madam, really . . .
MADAME PERNELLE: You are her brother, Sir,
And I respect and love you; yet if I were
My son, this lady's good and pious spouse,   35
I wouldn't make you welcome in my house.
You're full of worldly counsels which, I fear,
Aren't suitable for decent folk to hear.
I've spoken bluntly, Sir; but it behooves us
Not to mince words when righteous fervor moves us.   40
DAMIS: Your man Tartuffe is full of holy speeches . . .
MADAME PERNELLE: And practices precisely what he preaches.
He's a fine man, and should be listened to.
I will not hear him mocked by fools like you.
DAMIS: Good God! Do you expect me to submit   45
To the tyranny of that carping hypocrite?
Must we forgo all joys and satisfactions
Because that bigot censures all our actions?

DORINE: To hear him talk—and he talks all the time—
  There's nothing one can do that's not a crime.   50
  He rails at everything, your dear Tartuffe.
MADAME PERNELLE: Whatever he reproves deserves reproof.
  He's out to save your souls, and all of you
  Must love him, as my son would have you do.
DAMIS: Ah no, Grandmother, I could never take   55
  To such a rascal, even for my father's sake.
  That's how I feel, and I shall not dissemble.
  His every action makes me seethe and tremble
  With helpless anger, and I have no doubt
  That he and I will shortly have it out.   60
DORINE: Surely it is a shame and a disgrace
  To see this man usurp the master's place—
  To see this beggar who, when first he came,
  Had not a shoe or shoestring to his name
  So far forget himself that he behaves   65
  As if the house were his, and we his slaves.
MADAME PERNELLE: Well, mark my words, your souls would fare far better
  If you obeyed his precepts to the letter.
DORINE: You see him as a saint. I'm far less awed;
  In fact, I see right through him. He's a fraud.   70
MADAME PERNELLE: Nonsense!
DORINE: His man Laurent's the same, or worse;
  I'd not trust either with a penny purse.
MADAME PERNELLE: I can't say what his servant's morals may be;
  His own great goodness I can guarantee.
  You all regard him with distaste and fear   75
  Because he tells you what you're loath to hear,
  Condemns your sins, points out your moral flaws,
  And humbly strives to further Heaven's cause.
dorine: If sin is all that bothers him, why is it
  He's so upset when folk drop in to visit?   80
  Is Heaven so outraged by a social call
  That he must prophesy against us all?
  I'll tell you what I think: if you ask me,
  He's jealous of my mistress' company.
MADAME PERNELLE:
  Rubbish! *(To* ELMIRE:*)* He's not alone, child, in complaining   85
  Of all of your promiscuous entertaining.
  Why, the whole neighborhood's upset, I know,
  By all these carriages that come and go,
  With crowds of guests parading in and out
  And noisy servants loitering about.   90
  In all of this, I'm sure there's nothing vicious;
  But why give people cause to be suspicious?
CLÉANTE: They need no cause; they'll talk in any case.

Madam, this world would be a joyless place
If, fearing what malicious tongues might say,   95
We locked our doors and turned our friends away.
And even if one did so dreary a thing,
D'you think those tongues would cease their chattering?
One can't fight slander; it's a losing battle;
Let us instead ignore their tittle-tattle.   100
Let's strive to live by conscience' clear decrees,
And let the gossips gossip as they please.

DORINE: If there is talk against us, I know the source:
It's Daphne and her little husband, of course.
Those who have greatest cause for guilt and shame   105
Are quickest to besmirch a neighbor's name.
When there's a chance for libel, they never miss it;
When something can be made to seem illicit
They're off at once to spread the joyous news,
Adding to fact what fantasies they choose.   110
By talking up their neighbor's indiscretions
They seek to camouflage their own transgressions,
Hoping that others' innocent affairs
Will lend a hue of innocence to theirs,
Or that their own black guilt will come to seem   115
Part of a general shady color-scheme.

MADAME PERNELLE: All that is quite irrelevant. I doubt
That anyone's more virtuous and devout
Than dear Orante; and I'm informed that she
Condemns your mode of life most vehemently.   120

DORINE: Oh, yes, she's strict, devout, and has no taint
Of worldliness; in short, she seems a saint.
But it was time which taught her that disguise;
She's thus because she can't be otherwise.
So long as her attractions could enthrall,   125
She flounced and flirted and enjoyed it all,
But now that they're no longer what they were
She quits a world which fast is quitting her,
And wears a veil of virtue to conceal
Her bankrupt beauty and her lost appeal.   130
That's what becomes of old coquettes today:
Distressed when all their lovers fall away,
They see no recourse but to play the prude,
And so confer a style on solitude.
Thereafter, they're severe with everyone,   135
Condemning all our actions, pardoning none,
And claiming to be pure, austere, and zealous
When, if the truth were known, they're merely jealous,
And cannot bear to see another know
The pleasures time has forced them to forgo.   140

MADAME PERNELLE *(initially to* ELMIRE*)*:
    That sort of talk is what you like to hear;
    Therefore you'd have us all keep still, my dear,
    While Madam rattles on the livelong day.
    Nevertheless, I mean to have my say.
    I tell you that you're blest to have Tartuffe   145
    Dwelling, as my son's guest, beneath this roof;
    That Heaven has sent him to forestall its wrath
    By leading you, once more, to the true path;
    That all he reprehends is reprehensible,
    And that you'd better heed him, and be sensible.   150
    These visits, balls, and parties in which you revel
    Are nothing but inventions of the Devil.
    One never hears a word that's edifying:
    Nothing but chaff and foolishness and lying,
    As well as vicious gossip in which one's neighbor   155
    Is cut to bits with epee, foil, and saber.
    People of sense are driven half-insane
    At such affairs, where noise and folly reign
    And reputations perish thick and fast.
    As a wise preacher said on Sunday last,   160
    Parties are Towers of Babylon, because
    The guests all babble on with never a pause;
    And then he told a story which, I think . . .

                    (To CLÉANTE:*)*

    I heard that laugh, Sir, and I saw that wink!
    Go find your silly friends and laugh some more!   165
    Enough; I'm going; don't show me to the door.
    I leave this household much dismayed and vexed;
    I cannot say when I shall see you next.

                  (Slapping FLIPOTE:*)*

    Wake up, don't stand there gaping into space!
    I'll slap some sense into that stupid face.   170
    Move, move, you slut.

Scene II

                  CLÉANTE, DORINE

CLÉANTE: I think I'll stay behind;
    I want no further pieces of her mind.
    How that old lady . . .
DORINE: Oh, what wouldn't she say
    If she could hear you speak of her that way!

She'd thank you for the *lady,* but I'm sure
She'd find the *old* a little premature.

CLÉANTE: My, what a scene she made, and what a din!
And how this man Tartuffe has taken her in!

DORINE: Yes, but her son is even worse deceived;
His folly must be seen to be believed.
In the late troubles, he played an able part
And served his king with wise and loyal heart,
But he's quite lost his senses since he fell
Beneath Tartuffe's infatuating spell.
He calls him brother, and loves him as his life,
Preferring him to mother, child, or wife.
In him and him alone will he confide;
He's made him his confessor and his guide;
He pets and pampers him with love more tender
Than any pretty maiden could engender,
Gives him the place of honor when they dine,
Delights to see him gorging like a swine,
Stuffs him with dainties till his guts distend,
And when he belches, cries "God bless you, friend!"
In short, he's mad; he worships him; he dotes;
His deeds he marvels at, his words he quotes,
Thinking each act a miracle, each word
Oracular as those that Moses heard.
Tartuffe, much pleased to find so easy a victim,
Has in a hundred ways beguiled and tricked him,
Milked him of money, and with his permission
Established here a sort of Inquisition.
Even Laurent, his lackey, dares to give
Us arrogant advice on how to live;
He sermonizes us in thundering tones
And confiscates our ribbons and colognes.
Last week he tore a kerchief into pieces
Because he found it pressed in a *Life of Jesus:*
He said it was a sin to juxtapose
Unholy vanities and holy prose.

Scene III

ELMIRE, MARIANE, DAMIS, CLÉANTE, DORINE

ELMIRE *(to* CLÉANTE*):* You did well not to follow; she stood in the door
And said *verbatim* all she'd said before.
I saw my husband coming. I think I'd best
Go upstairs now, and take a little rest.

CLÉANTE: I'll wait and greet him here; then I must go.
I've really only time to say hello.

DAMIS: Sound him about my sister's wedding, please.
   I think Tartuffe's against it, and that he's
   Been urging Father to withdraw his blessing.
   As you well know, I'd find that most distressing.   10
   Unless my sister and Valère can marry,
   My hopes to wed *his* sister will miscarry,
   And I'm determined . . .
DORINE: He's coming.

Scene IV

ORGON, CLÉANTE, DORINE

ORGON: Ah, Brother, good-day.
CLÉANTE: Well, welcome back. I'm sorry I can't stay.
   How was the country? Blooming, I trust, and green?
ORGON: Excuse me, Brother; just one moment.
                        (To DORINE:*)*

                                      Dorine . . .
                        (To CLÉANTE:*)*

   To put my mind at rest, I always learn   5
   The household news the moment I return.
                        (To DORINE:*)*

   Has all been well, these two days I've been gone?
   How are the family? What's been going on?
DORINE: Your wife, two days ago, had a bad fever,
   And a fierce headache which refused to leave her.   10
ORGON: Ah. And Tartuffe?
DORINE: Tartuffe? Why, he's round and red,
   Bursting with health, and excellently fed.
ORGON: Poor fellow!
DORINE: That night, the mistress was unable
   To take a single bite at the dinner-table.
   Her headache-pains, she said, were simply hellish.   15
ORGON: Ah. And Tartuffe?
DORINE: He ate his meal with relish,
   And zealously devoured in her presence
   A leg of mutton and a brace of pheasants.
ORGON: Poor fellow!
DORINE: Well, the pains continued strong,
   And so she tossed and tossed the whole night long,   20
   Now icy-cold, now burning like a flame.
   We sat beside her bed till morning came.
ORGON: Ah. And Tartuffe?
DORINE: Why, having eaten, he rose
   And sought his room, already in a doze,

Got into his warm bed, and snored away 25
In perfect peace until the break of day.

ORGON: Poor fellow!

DORINE: After much ado, we talked her
Into dispatching someone for the doctor.
He bled her, and the fever quickly fell.

ORGON: Ah. And Tartuffe?

DORINE: He bore it very well. 30
To keep his cheerfulness at any cost,
And make up for the blood *Madame* had lost,
He drank, at lunch, four beakers full of port.

ORGON: Poor fellow!

DORINE: Both are doing well, in short.
I'll go and tell *Madame* that you've expressed 35
Keen sympathy and anxious interest.

Scene V

ORGON, CLÉANTE

CLÉANTE: That girl was laughing in your face, and though
I've no wish to offend you, even so
I'm bound to say that she had some excuse.
How can you possibly be such a goose?
Are you so dazed by this man's hocus-pocus 5
That all the world, save him, is out of focus?
You've given him clothing, shelter, food, and care;
Why must you also . . .

ORGON: Brother, stop right there.
You do not know the man of whom you speak.

CLÉANTE: I grant you that. But my judgment's not so weak 10
That I can't tell, by his effect on others . . .

ORGON: Ah, when you meet him, you two will be like brothers!
There's been no loftier soul since time began.
He is a man who . . . a man who . . . an excellent man.
To keep his precepts is to be reborn, 15
And view this dunghill of a world with scorn.
Yes, thanks to him I'm a changed man indeed.
Under his tutelage my soul's been freed
From earthly loves, and every human tie:
My mother, children, brother, and wife could die, 20
And I'd not feel a single moment's pain.

CLÉANTE: That's a fine sentiment, Brother; most humane.

ORGON: Oh, had you seen Tartuffe as I first knew him,
Your heart, like mine, would have surrendered to him.
He used to come into our church each day 25

And humbly kneel nearby, and start to pray.
He'd draw the eyes of everybody there
By the deep fervor of his heartfelt prayer;
He'd sigh and weep, and sometimes with a sound
Of rapture he would bend and kiss the ground;   30
And when I rose to go, he'd run before
To offer me holy-water at the door.
His serving-man, no less devout than he,
Informed me of his master's poverty;
I gave him gifts, but in his humbleness   35
He'd beg me every time to give him less.
"Oh, that's too much," he'd cry, "too much by twice!
I don't deserve it. The half, Sir, would suffice."
And when I wouldn't take it back, he'd share
Half of it with the poor, right then and there.   40
At length, Heaven prompted me to take him in
To dwell with us, and free our souls from sin.
He guides our lives, and to protect my honor
Stays by my wife, and keeps an eye upon her;
He tells me whom she sees, and all she does,   45
And seems more jealous than I ever was!
And how austere he is! Why, he can detect
A mortal sin where you would least suspect;
In smallest trifles, he's extremely strict.
Last week, his conscience was severely pricked   50
Because, while praying, he had caught a flea
And killed it, so he felt, too wrathfully.
CLÉANTE: Good God, man! Have you lost your common sense—
   Or is this all some joke at my expense?
   How can you stand there and in all sobriety . . .   55
ORGON: Brother, your language savors of impiety.
   Too much free-thinking's made your faith unsteady,
   And as I've warned you many times already,
   'Twill get you into trouble before you're through.
CLÉANTE: So I've been told before by dupes like you: 60
   Being blind, you'd have all others blind as well;
   The clear-eyed man you call an infidel,
   And he who sees through humbug and pretense
   Is charged, by you, with want of reverence.
   Spare me your warnings, Brother; I have no fear   65
   Of speaking out, for you and Heaven to hear,
   Against affected zeal and pious knavery.
   There's true and false in piety, as in bravery,
   And just as those whose courage shines the most
   In battle, are the least inclined to boast,   70
   So those whose hearts are truly pure and lowly
   Don't make a flashy show of being holy.

There's a vast difference, so it seems to me,
Between true piety and hypocrisy:
How do you fail to see it, may I ask? 75
Is not a face quite different from a mask?
Cannot sincerity and cunning art,
Reality and semblance, be told apart?
Are scarecrows just like men, and do you hold
That a false coin is just as good as gold? 80
Ah, Brother, man's a strangely fashioned creature
Who seldom is content to follow Nature,
But recklessly pursues his inclination
Beyond the narrow bounds of moderation,
And often, by transgressing Reason's laws, 85
Perverts a lofty aim or noble cause.
A passing observation, but it applies.

ORGON: I see, dear Brother, that you're profoundly wise;
You harbor all the insight of the age.
You are our one clear mind, our only sage, 90
The era's oracle, its Cato too,
And all mankind are fools compared to you.

CLÉANTE: Brother, I don't pretend to be a sage,
Nor have I all the wisdom of the age.
There's just one insight I would dare to claim: 95
I know that true and false are not the same;
And just as there is nothing I more revere
Than a soul whose faith is steadfast and sincere,
Nothing that I more cherish and admire
Than honest zeal and true religious fire, 100
So there is nothing that I find more base
Than specious piety's dishonest face—
Than these bold mountebanks, these histrios
Whose impious mummeries and hollow shows
Exploit our love of Heaven, and make a jest 105
Of all that men think holiest and best;
These calculating souls who offer prayers
Not to their Maker, but as public wares,
And seek to buy respect and reputation
With lifted eyes and sighs of exaltation; 110
These charlatans, I say, whose pilgrim souls
Proceed, by way of Heaven, toward earthly goals,
Who weep and pray and swindle and extort,
Who preach the monkish life, but haunt the court,
Who make their zeal the partner of their vice— 115
Such men are vengeful, sly, and cold as ice,
And when there is an enemy to defame
They cloak their spite in fair religion's name,
Their private spleen and malice being made

To seem a high and virtuous crusade,   120
Until, to mankind's reverent applause,
They crucify their foe in Heaven's cause.
Such knaves are all too common; yet, for the wise,
True piety isn't hard to recognize,
And, happily, these present times provide us   125
With bright examples to instruct and guide us.
Consider Ariston and Périandre;
Look at Oronte, Alcidamas, Clitandre;
Their virtue is acknowledged; who could doubt it?
But you won't hear them beat the drum about it.   130
They're never ostentatious, never vain,
And their religion's moderate and humane;
It's not their way to criticize and chide:
They think censoriousness a mark of pride,
And therefore, letting others preach and rave,   135
They show, by deeds, how Christians should behave.
They think no evil of their fellow man,
But judge of him as kindly as they can.
They don't intrigue and wangle and conspire;
To lead a good life is their one desire;   140
The sinner wakes no rancorous hate in them;
It is the sin alone which they condemn;
Nor do they try to show a fiercer zeal
For Heaven's cause than Heaven itself could feel.
These men I honor, these men I advocate   145
As models for us all to emulate.
Your man is not their sort at all, I fear:
And, while your praise of him is quite sincere,
I think that you've been dreadfully deluded.
ORGON: Now then, dear Brother, is your speech concluded? 150
CLÉANTE: Why, yes.
ORGON: Your servant, Sir. *(He turns to go.)*
CLÉANTE: No, Brother; wait.
    There's one more matter. You agreed of late
    That young Valère might have your daughter's hand.
ORGON: I did.
CLÉANTE: And set the date, I understand.
ORGON: Quite so.
CLÉANTE: You've now postponed it; is that true?   155
ORGON: No doubt.
CLÉANTE: The match no longer pleases you?
ORGON: Who knows?
CLÉANTE: D'you mean to go back on your word?
ORGON: I won't say that.
CLÉANTE: Has anything occurred
    Which might entitle you to break your pledge?

ORGON: Perhaps.

CLÉANTE:　　　　Why must you hem, and haw, and hedge? 160
　　The boy asked me to sound you in this affair . . .

ORGON: It's been a pleasure.

CLÉANTE:　　　　　But what shall I tell Valère?

ORGON: Whatever you like.

CLÉANTE:　　　　　But what have you decided?
　　What are your plans?

ORGON:　　　　　I plan, Sir, to be guided
　　By Heaven's will.

CLÉANTE:　　　　Come, Brother, don't talk rot. 165
　　You've given Valère your word; will you keep it, or not?

ORGON: Good day.

CLÉANTE:　　　This looks like poor Valère's undoing;
　　I'll go and warn him that there's trouble brewing.

ACT II

Scene I

ORGON, MARIANE

ORGON: Mariane.

MARIANE:　　　Yes, Father?

ORGON:　　　　　A word with you; come here.

MARIANE: What are you looking for?

ORGON *(peering into a small closet)*: Eavesdroppers, dear.
　　I'm making sure we shan't be overheard.
　　Someone in there could catch our every word.
　　Ah, good, we're safe. Now, Mariane, my child 5
　　You're a sweet girl who's tractable and mild,
　　Whom I hold dear, and think most highly of.

MARIANE: I'm deeply grateful, Father, for your love.

ORGON: That's well said, Daughter; and you can repay me
　　If, in all things, you'll cheerfully obey me. 10

MARIANE: To please you, Sir, is what delights me best.

ORGON: Good, good. Now, what d'you think of Tartuffe, our guest?

MARIANE: I, Sir?

ORGON:　　　Yes. Weigh your answer; think it through.

MARIANE: Oh, dear. I'll say whatever you wish me to.

ORGON: That's wisely said, my Daughter. Say of him, then, 15
　　That he's the very worthiest of men,
　　And that you're fond of him, and would rejoice
　　In being his wife, if that should be my choice.
　　Well?

MARIANE: What?
ORGON: What's that?
MARIANE: I . . .
ORGON: Well?
MARIANE: Forgive me, pray.
ORGON: Did you not hear me?
MARIANE: Of *whom,* Sir, must I say   20
    That I am fond of him, and would rejoice
    In being his wife, if that should be your choice?
ORGON: Why, of Tartuffe.
MARIANE: But, Father, that's false, you know.
    Why would you have me say what isn't so?
ORGON: Because I am resolved it shall be true.   25
    That it's my wish should be enough for you.
MARIANE: You can't mean, Father . . .
ORGON: Yes, Tartuffe shall be
    Allied by marriage to this family,
    And he's to be your husband, is that clear?
    It's a father's privilege . . .   30

Scene II

DORINE, ORGON, MARIANE

ORGON *(to Dorine):*   What are you doing in here?
    Is curiosity so fierce a passion
    With you, that you must eavesdrop in this fashion?
DORINE: There's lately been a rumor going about—
    Based on some hunch or chance remark, no doubt—   5
    That you mean Mariane to wed Tartuffe.
    I've laughed it off, of course, as just a spoof.
ORGON: You find it so incredible?
DORINE: Yes, I do.
    I won't accept that story, even from you.
ORGON: Well, you'll believe it when the thing is done.   10
DORINE: Yes, yes, of course. Go on and have your fun.
ORGON: I've never been more serious in my life.
DORINE: Ha!
ORGON: Daughter, I mean it; you're to be his wife.
DORINE: No, don't believe your father; it's all a hoax.
ORGON: See here, young woman . . . .
DORINE: Come, Sir, no more jokes;   15
    You can't fool us.
ORGON: How dare you talk that way?
DORINE: All right, then; we believe you, sad to say.
    But how a man like you, who looks so wise

And wears a moustache of such splendid size,
Can be so foolish as to . . .

ORGON: Silence, please!
My girl, you take too many liberties.
I'm master here, as you must not forget.

DORINE: Do let's discuss this calmly; don't be upset.
You can't be serious, Sir, about this plan.
What should that bigot want with Mariane?
Praying and fasting ought to keep him busy.
And then, in terms of wealth and rank, what is he?
Why should a man of property like you
Pick out a beggar son-in-law?

ORGON: That will do.
Speak of his poverty with reverence.
His is a pure and saintly indigence
Which far transcends all worldly pride and pelf.
He lost his fortune, as he says himself,
Because he cared for Heaven alone, and so
Was careless of his interests here below.
I mean to get him out of his present straits
And help him to recover his estates—
Which, in his part of the world, have no small fame.
Poor though he is, he's a gentleman just the same.

DORINE: Yes, so he tells us; and, Sir, it seems to me
Such pride goes very ill with piety.
A man whose spirit spurns this dungy earth
Ought not to brag of lands and noble birth;
Such worldly arrogance will hardly square
With meek devotion and the life of prayer.
. . . But this approach, I see, has drawn a blank;
Let's speak, then, of his person, not his rank.
Doesn't it seem to you a trifle grim
To give a girl like her to a man like him?
When two are so ill-suited, can't you see
What the sad consequence is bound to be?
A young girl's virtue is imperiled, Sir,
When such a marriage is imposed on her;
For if one's bridegroom isn't to one's taste,
It's hardly an inducement to be chaste,
And many a man with horns upon his brow
Has made his wife the thing that she is now.
It's hard to be a faithful wife, in short,
To certain husbands of a certain sort,
And he who gives his daughter to a man she hates
Must answer for her sins at Heaven's gates.
Think, Sir, before you play so risky a role.

ORGON: This servant-girl presumes to save my soul!

DORINE: You would do well to ponder what I've said.
ORGON: Daughter, we'll disregard this dunderhead.   65
  Just trust your father's judgment. Oh, I'm aware
  That I once promised you to young Valère;
  But now I hear he gambles, which greatly shocks me;
  What's more, I've doubts about his orthodoxy.
  His visits to church, I note, are very few.   70
DORINE: Would you have him go at the same hours as you,
  And kneel nearby, to be sure of being seen?
ORGON: I can dispense with such remarks, Dorine.

(To MARIANE:)

Tartuffe, however, is sure of Heaven's blessing,
And that's the only treasure worth possessing.   75
This match will bring you joys beyond all measure;
Your cup will overflow with every pleasure;
You two will interchange your faithful loves
Like two sweet cherubs, or two turtle-doves.
No harsh word shall be heard, no frown be seen,   80
And he shall make you happy as a queen.
DORINE: And she'll make him a cuckold, just wait and see.
ORGON: What language!
DORINE: Oh, he's a man of destiny;
  He's *made* for horns, and what the stars demand
  Your daughter's virtue surely can't withstand.   85
ORGON: Don't interrupt me further. Why can't you learn
  That certain things are none of your concern?
DORINE: It's for your own sake that I interfere.

(She repeatedly interrupts ORGON *just as he is turning to speak to his daughter:)*

ORGON: Most kind of you. Now, hold your tongue, d'you hear?
DORINE: If I didn't love you . . .
ORGON: Spare me your affection.   90
DORINE: I'll love you, Sir, in spite of your objection.
ORGON: Blast!
DORINE: I can't bear, Sir, for your honor's sake,
  To let you make this ludicrous mistake.
ORGON: You mean to go on talking?
DORINE: If I didn't protest
  This sinful marriage, my conscience couldn't rest.   95
ORGON: If you don't hold your tongue, you little shrew . . .
DORINE: What, lost your temper? A pious man like you?
ORGON: Yes! Yes! You talk and talk. I'm maddened by it.
  Once and for all, I tell you to be quiet.
DORINE: Well, I'll be quiet. But I'll be thinking hard.   100
ORGON: Think all you like, but you had better guard
  That saucy tongue of yours, or I'll . . .

(Turning back to MARIANE:*)*

Now, child,

I've weighed this matter fully.

DORINE *(aside):*   It drives me wild

That I can't speak.

*(*ORGON *turns his head, and she is silent.)*

ORGON: Tartuffe is no young dandy,

But, still, his person . . .

DORINE *(aside):*   Is as sweet as candy.   105

ORGON: Is such that, even if you shouldn't care

For his other merits . . .

(He turns and stands facing DORINE, *arms crossed.)*

DORINE *(aside):*   They'll make a lovely pair.

If I were she, no man would marry me

Against my inclination, and go scot-free.

He'd learn, before the wedding-day was over,   110

How readily a wife can find a lover.

ORGON *(to* DORINE*):* It seems you treat my orders as a joke.

DORINE: Why, what's the matter? 'Twas not to you I spoke.

ORGON: What *were* you doing?

DORINE: Talking to myself, that's all.

ORGON: Ah! *(aside:)* One more bit of impudence and gall,   115

And I shall give her a good slap in the face.

(He puts himself in position to slap her; DORINE, *whenever he glances at her, stands immobile and silent:)*

Daughter, you shall accept, and with good grace,

The husband I've selected . . . Your wedding day . . .

(To DORINE:*)*

Why don't you talk to yourself?

DORINE: I've nothing to say.

ORGON: Come, just one word.

DORINE: No thank you, Sir. I pass.   120

ORGON: Come, speak; I'm waiting.

DORINE: I'd not be such an ass.

ORGON *(turning to Mariane):* In short, dear Daughter, I mean to be obeyed,

And you must bow to the sound choice I've made.

DORINE *(moving away):* I'd not wed such a monster, even in jest.

*(*ORGON *attempts to slap her, but misses.)*

ORGON: Daughter, that maid of yours is a thorough pest;   125

She makes me sinfully annoyed and nettled.

I can't speak further; my nerves are too unsettled.

She's so upset me by her insolent talk,

I'll calm myself by going for a walk.

Scene III

DORINE, MARIANE

DORINE *(returning):* Well, have you lost your tongue, girl? Must I play
    Your part, and say the lines you ought to say?
    Faced with a fate so hideous and absurd,
    Can you not utter one dissenting word?
MARIANE: What good would it do? A father's power is great.   5
DORINE: Resist him now, or it will be too late.
MARIANE: But . . .
DORINE: Tell him one cannot love at a father's whim;
    That you shall marry for yourself, not him;
    That since it's you who are to be the bride,
    It's you, not he, who must be satisfied;   10
    And that if his Tartuffe is so sublime,
    He's free to marry him at any time.
MARIANE: I've bowed so long to Father's strict control,
    I couldn't oppose him now, to save my soul.
DORINE: Come, come, Mariane. Do listen to reason, won't you?   15
    Valère has asked your hand. Do you love him, or don't you?
MARIANE: Oh, how unjust of you! What can you mean
    By asking such a question, dear Dorine?
    You know the depth of my affection for him;
    I've told you a hundred times how I adore him.   20
DORINE: I don't believe in everything I hear;
    Who knows if your professions were sincere?
MARIANE: They were, Dorine, and you do me wrong to doubt it;
    Heaven knows that I've been all too frank about it.
DORINE: You love him, then?
MARIANE: Oh, more than I can express.   25
DORINE: And he, I take it, cares for you no less?
MARIANE: I think so.
DORINE: And you both, with equal fire,
    Burn to be married?
MARIANE: That is our one desire.
DORINE: What of Tartuffe, then? What of your father's plan?
MARIANE: I'll kill myself, if I'm forced to wed that man.   30
DORINE: I hadn't thought of that recourse. How splendid!
    Just die, and all your troubles will be ended!
    A fine solution. Oh, it maddens me
    To hear you talk in that self-pitying key.
MARIANE: Dorine, how harsh you are! It's most unfair.   35
    You have no sympathy for my despair.
DORINE: I've none at all for people who talk drivel
    And, faced with difficulties, whine and snivel.
MARIANE: No doubt I'm timid, but it would be wrong . . .

DORINE: True love requires a heart that's firm and strong. 40

MARIANE: I'm strong in my affection for Valère,
But coping with my father is his affair.

DORINE: But if your father's brain has grown so cracked
Over his dear Tartuffe that he can retract
His blessing, though your wedding day was named, 45
It's surely not Valère who's to be blamed.

MARIANE: If I defied my father, as you suggest,
Would it not seem unmaidenly, at best?
Shall I defend my love at the expense
Of brazenness and disobedience? 50
Shall I parade my heart's desires, and flaunt . . .

DORINE: No, I ask nothing of you. Clearly you want
To be Madame Tartuffe, and I feel bound
Not to oppose a wish so very sound.
What right have I to criticize the match? 55
Indeed, my dear, the man's a brilliant catch.
Monsieur Tartuffe! Now, there's a man of weight!
Yes, yes, Monsieur Tartuffe, I'm bound to state,
Is quite a person; that's not to be denied;
'Twill be no little thing to be his bride. 60
The world already rings with his renown;
He's a great noble—in his native town;
His ears are red, he has a pink complexion,
And all in all, he'll suit you to perfection.

MARIANE: Dear God!

DORINE: Oh, how triumphant you will feel 65
At having caught a husband so ideal!

MARIANE: Oh, do stop teasing, and use your cleverness
To get me out of this appalling mess.
Advise me, and I'll do whatever you say.

DORINE: Ah no, a dutiful daughter must obey 70
Her father, even if he weds her to an ape.
You've a bright future; why struggle to escape?
Tartuffe will take you back where his family lives,
To a small town aswarm with relatives—
Uncles and cousins whom you'll be charmed to meet. 75
You'll be received at once by the elite,
Calling upon the bailiff's wife, no less—
Even, perhaps, upon the mayoress,
Who'll sit you down in the *best* kitchen chair.
Then, once a year, you'll dance at the village fair 80
To the drone of bagpipes—two of them, in fact—
And see a puppet-show, or an animal act.
Your husband . . .

MARIANE: Oh, you turn my blood to ice!
Stop torturing me, and give me your advice.

DORINE *(threatening to go):* Your servant, Madam.

MARIANE: Dorine, I beg of you . . .   85
DORINE: No, you deserve it; this marriage must go through.
MARIANE: Dorine!
DORINE: No.
MARIANE: Not Tartuffe! You know I think him . . .
DORINE: Tartuffe's your cup of tea, and you shall drink him.
MARIANE: I've always told you everything, and relied . . .
DORINE: No. You deserve to be tartuffified.   90
MARIANE: Well, since you mock me and refuse to care,
    I'll henceforth seek my solace in despair:
    Despair shall be my counsellor and friend,
    And help me bring my sorrows to an end.

(She starts to leave.)

DORINE: There, now, come back; my anger has subsided.   95
    You do deserve some pity, I've decided.
MARIANE: Dorine, if Father makes me undergo
    This dreadful martyrdom, I'll die, I know.
DORINE: Don't fret; it won't be difficult to discover
    Some plan of action . . . But here's Valère, your lover.   100

Scene IV

VALÈRE, MARIANE, DORINE

VALÈRE: Madam, I've just received some wondrous news
    Regarding which I'd like to hear your views.
MARIANE: What news?
VALÈRE: You're marrying Tartuffe.
MARIANE: I find
    That Father does have such a match in mind.
VALÈRE: Your father, Madam . . .
MARIANE: . . . has just this minute said   5
    That it's Tartuffe he wishes me to wed.
VALÈRE: Can he be serious?
MARIANE: Oh, indeed he can;
    He's clearly set his heart upon the plan.
VALÈRE: And what position do you propose to take,
    Madam?
MARIANE: Why—I don't know.
VALÈRE: For heaven's sake—   10
    You don't know?
MARIANE: No.
VALÈRE: Well, well!
MARIANE: Advise me, do.
VALÈRE: Marry the man. That's my advice to you.

MARIANE: That's your advice?

VALÈRE: Yes.

MARIANE: Truly?

VALÈRE: Oh, absolutely.

    You couldn't choose more wisely, more astutely.

MARIANE: Thanks for this counsel; I'll follow it, of course.   15

VALÈRE: Do, do; I'm sure 'twill cost you no remorse.

MARIANE: To give it didn't cause your heart to break.

VALÈRE: I gave it, Madam, only for your sake.

MARIANE: And it's for your sake that I take it, Sir.

DORINE (*withdrawing to the rear of the stage*):

    Let's see which fool will prove the stubborner.   20

VALÈRE: So! I am nothing to you, and it was flat

    Deception when you . . .

MARIANE: Please, enough of that.

    You've told me plainly that I should agree

    To wed the man my father's chosen for me,

    And since you've deigned to counsel me so wisely,   25

    I promise, Sir, to do as you advise me.

VALÈRE: Ah, no, 'twas not by me that you were swayed.

    No, your decision was already made;

    Though now, to save appearances, you protest

    That you're betraying me at my behest.   30

MARIANE: Just as you say.

VALÈRE: Quite so. And I now see

    That you were never truly in love with me.

MARIANE: Alas, you're free to think so if you choose.

VALÈRE: I choose to think so, and here's a bit of news:

    You've spurned my hand, but I know where to turn   35

    For kinder treatment, as you shall quickly learn.

MARIANE: I'm sure you do. Your noble qualities

    Inspire affection . . .

VALÈRE: Forget my qualities, please.

    They don't inspire you overmuch, I find.

    But there's another lady I have in mind   40

    Whose sweet and generous nature will not scorn

    To compensate me for the loss I've borne.

MARIANE: I'm no great loss, and I'm sure that you'll transfer

    Your heart quite painlessly from me to her.

VALÈRE: I'll do my best to take it in my stride.   45

    The pain I feel at being cast aside

    Time and forgetfulness may put an end to.

    Or if I can't forget, I shall pretend to.

    No self-respecting person is expected

    To go on loving once he's been rejected.   50

MARIANE: Now, that's a fine, high-minded sentiment.

VALÈRE: One to which any sane man would assent.

Would you prefer it if I pined away
In hopeless passion till my dying day?
Am I to yield you to a rival's arms
And not console myself with other charms?   55

MARIANE: Go then; console yourself; don't hesitate.
    I wish you to; indeed, I cannot wait.

VALÈRE: You wish me to?

MARIANE: Yes.

VALÈRE: That's the final straw.
    Madam, farewell. Your wish shall be my law.   60

(He starts to leave, and then returns: this repeatedly:)

MARIANE: Splendid.

VALÈRE *(coming back again)*:
               This breach, remember, is of your making;
    It's you who've driven me to the step I'm taking.

MARIANE: Of course.

VALÈRE *(coming back again)*:
               Remember, too, that I am merely
    Following your example.

MARIANE: I see that clearly.

VALÈRE: Enough. I'll go and do your bidding, then.   65

MARIANE: Good.

VALÈRE *(coming back again)*:
               You shall never see my face again.

MARIANE: Excellent.

VALÈRE *(walking to the door, then turning about)*:
               Yes?

MARIANE: What?

VALÈRE: What's that? What did you say?

MARIANE: Nothing. You're dreaming.

VALÈRE: Ah. Well, I'm on my way.
    Farewell, *Madame.*

(He moves slowly away.)

MARIANE: Farewell.

DORINE *(to MARIANE)*:   If you ask me,
    Both of you are as mad as mad can be.   70
    Do stop this nonsense, now. I've only let you
    Squabble so long to see where it would get you.
    Whoa there, Monsieur Valère!

(She goes and seizes VALÈRE by the arm; he makes a great show of resistance.)

VALÈRE: What's this, Dorine?

DORINE: Come here.

VALÈRE: No, no, my heart's too full of spleen.
    Don't hold me back; her wish must be obeyed.   75

DORINE: Stop!

VALÈRE: It's too late now; my decision's made.

DORINE: Oh, pooh!

MARIANE *(aside)*   He hates the sight of me, that's plain.

I'll go, and so deliver him from pain.

DORINE *(leaving* VALÈRE, *running after* MARIANE*)*:

And now *you* run away! Come back.

MARIANE: No, no.

Nothing you say will keep me here. Let go!   80

VALÈRE *(aside)*: She cannot bear my presence, I perceive.

To spare her further torment, I shall leave.

DORINE *(leaving* MARIANE, *running after* VALÈRE*)*:

Again! You'll not escape, Sir; don't you try it.

Come here, you two. Stop fussing, and be quiet.

(She takes VALÈRE *by the hand, then* MARIANE, *and draws them together.)*

VALÈRE *(to* DORINE*)*: What do you want of me?

MARIANE *(to* DORINE*)*:   What is the point of this?   85

DORINE: We're going to have a little armistice.

(To VALÈRE*:)*

Now, weren't you silly to get so overheated?

VALÈRE: Didn't you see how badly I was treated?

DORINE *(to* MARIANE*)*: Aren't you a simpleton, to have lost your head?

MARIANE: Didn't you hear the hateful things he said?   90

DORINE *(to* VALÈRE*)*: You're both great fools. Her sole desire, Valère,

Is to be yours in marriage. To that I'll swear.

(To MARIANE*:)*

He loves you only, and he wants no wife

But you, Mariane. On that I'll stake my life.

MARIANE *(to* VALÈRE*)*: Then why you advised me so, I cannot see.   95

VALÈRE *(to* MARIANE*)*: On such a question, why ask advice of *me*?

DORINE: Oh, you're impossible. Give me your hands, you two.

(To VALÈRE*:)*

Yours first.

VALÈRE *(giving* DORINE *his hand)*:

            But why?

DORINE *(to* MARIANE*)*: And now a hand from you.

MARIANE *(also giving* DORINE *her hand)*:

What are you doing?

DORINE: There: a perfect fit.

You suit each other better than you'll admit.   100

*(*VALÈRE *and* MARIANE *hold hands for some time without looking at each other.)*

VALÈRE *(turning toward* MARIANE*)*:
    Ah, come, don't be so haughty. Give a man
    A look of kindness, won't you, Mariane?

(MARIANE *turns toward* VALÈRE *and smiles.*)

DORINE: I tell you, lovers are completely mad!
VALÈRE *(to* MARIANE*)*: Now come, confess that you were very bad
    To hurt my feelings as you did just now.   105
    I have a just complaint, you must allow.
MARIANE: *You* must allow that you were most unpleasant . . .
DORINE: Let's table that discussion for the present;
    Your father has a plan which must be stopped.
MARIANE: Advise us, then; what means must we adopt?   110
DORINE: We'll use all manner of means, and all at once.

(*To* MARIANE:)

    Your father's addled; he's acting like a dunce.
    Therefore you'd better humor the old fossil.
    Pretend to yield to him, be sweet and docile,
    And then postpone, as often as necessary,   115
    The day on which you have agreed to marry.
    You'll thus gain time, and time will turn the trick.
    Sometimes, for instance, you'll be taken sick,
    And that will seem good reason for delay;
    Or some bad omen will make you change the day—   120
    You'll dream of muddy water, or you'll pass
    A dead man's hearse, or break a looking-glass.
    If all else fails, no man can marry you
    Unless you take his ring and say "I do."
    But now, let's separate. If they should find   125
    Us talking here, our plot might be divined.

(*To* VALÈRE:)

    Go to your friends, and tell them what's occurred,
    And have them urge her father to keep his word.
    Meanwhile, we'll stir her brother into action,
    And get Elmire, as well, to join our faction.   130
    Good-bye.
VALÈRE *(to* MARIANE*)*:
            Though each of us will do his best,
    It's your true heart on which my hopes shall rest.
MARIANE *(to* VALÈRE*)*: Regardless of what Father may decide,
    None but Valère shall claim me as his bride.
VALÈRE: Oh, how those words content me! Come what will . . .   135
DORINE: Oh, lovers, lovers! Their tongues are never still.
    Be off, now.

VALÈRE *(turning to go, then turning back):*
> One last word . . .

DORINE: No time to chat:
> *You* leave by this door; and *you* leave by that.

> *(Dorine pushes them, by the shoulders, toward opposing doors.)*

ACT III

Scene I

DAMIS, DORINE

DAMIS: May lightning strike me even as I speak,
> May all men call me cowardly and weak,
> If any fear or scruple holds me back
> From settling things, at once, with that great quack!

DORINE: Now, don't give way to violent emotion.   5
> Your father's merely talked about this notion,
> And words and deeds are far from being one.
> Much that is talked about is never done.

DAMIS: No, I must stop that scoundrel's machinations;
> I'll go and tell him off; I'm out of patience.   10

DORINE: Do calm down and be practical. I had rather
> My mistress dealt with him—and with your father.
> She has some influence with Tartuffe, I've noted.
> He hangs upon her words, seems most devoted,
> And may, indeed, be smitten by her charm.   15
> Pray Heaven it's true! 'Twould do our cause no harm.
> She sent for him, just now, to sound him out
> On this affair you're so incensed about;
> She'll find out where he stands, and tell him too,
> What dreadful strife and trouble will ensue   20
> If he lends countenance to your father's plan.
> I couldn't get in to see him, but his man
> Says that he's almost finished with his prayers.
> Go, now. I'll catch him when he comes downstairs.

DAMIS: I want to hear this conference, and I will.   25

DORINE: No, they must be alone.

DAMIS: Oh, I'll keep still.

DORINE: Not you. I know your temper. You'd start a brawl,
> And shout and stamp your foot and spoil it all.
> Go on.

DAMIS: I won't; I have a perfect right . . .

DORINE: Lord, you're a nuisance! He's coming; get out of sight.   30

> *(DAMIS conceals himself in a closet at the rear of the stage.)*

Scene II

TARTUFFE, DORINE

TARTUFFE (observing dorine, *and calling to his manservant offstage*):
  Hang up my hair-shirt, put my scourge in place,
  And pray, Laurent, for Heaven's perpetual grace.
  I'm going to the prison now, to share
  My last few coins with the poor wretches there.
DORINE (aside): Dear God, what affectation! What a fake!   5
TARTUFFE: You wished to see me?
DORINE: Yes . . .
TARTUFFE (taking a handkerchief from his pocket):
                                        For mercy's sake,
  Please take this handkerchief, before you speak.
DORINE: What?
TARTUFFE: Cover that bosom, girl. The flesh is weak,
  And unclean thoughts are difficult to control.
  Such sights as that can undermine the soul.   10
DORINE: Your soul, it seems, has very poor defenses,
  And flesh makes quite an impact on your senses.
  It's strange that you're so easily excited;
  My own desires are not so soon ignited,
  And if I saw you naked as a beast,   15
  Not all your hide would tempt me in the least.
TARTUFFE: Girl, speak more modestly; unless you do,
  I shall be forced to take my leave of you.
DORINE: Oh, no, it's I who must be on my way;
  I've just one little message to convey.   20
  Madame is coming down, and begs you, Sir,
  To wait and have a word or two with her.
TARTUFFE: Gladly.
DORINE (aside):
              That had a softening effect!
  I think my guess about him was correct.
TARTUFFE: Will she be long?
DORINE: No: that's her step I hear.   25
  Ah, here she is, and I shall disappear.

Scene III

ELMIRE, TARTUFFE

TARTUFFE: May Heaven, whose infinite goodness we adore,
  Preserve your body and soul forevermore,
  And bless your days, and answer thus the plea
  Of one who is its humblest votary.

ELMIRE: I thank you for that pious wish, but please,   5
  Do take a chair and let's be more at ease.

(They sit down.)

TARTUFFE: I trust that you are once more well and strong?
ELMIRE: Oh, yes: the fever didn't last for long.
TARTUFFE: My prayers are too unworthy, I am sure,
  To have gained from Heaven this most gracious cure;   10
  But lately, Madam, my every supplication
  Has had for object your recuperation.
ELMIRE: You shouldn't have troubled so. I don't deserve it.
TARTUFFE: Your health is priceless, Madam, and to preserve it
  I'd gladly give my own, in all sincerity.   15
ELMIRE: Sir, you outdo us all in Christian charity.
  You've been most kind. I count myself your debtor.
TARTUFFE: 'Twas nothing, Madam. I long to serve you better.
ELMIRE: There's a private matter I'm anxious to discuss.
  I'm glad there's no one here to hinder us.   20
TARTUFFE: I too am glad; it floods my heart with bliss
  To find myself alone with you like this.
  For just this chance I've prayed with all my power—
  But prayed in vain, until this happy hour.
ELMIRE: This won't take long, Sir, and I hope you'll be   25
  Entirely frank and unconstrained with me.
TARTUFFE: Indeed, there's nothing I had rather do
  Than bare my inmost heart and soul to you.
  First, let me say that what remarks I've made
  About the constant visits you are paid   30
  Were prompted not by any mean emotion,
  But rather by a pure and deep devotion,
  A fervent zeal . . .
ELMIRE: No need for explanation.
  Your sole concern, I'm sure, was my salvation.
TARTUFFE *(taking* ELMIRE's *hand and pressing her fingertips):*
  Quite so; and such great fervor do I feel . . .   35
ELMIRE: Ooh! Please! You're pinching!
TARTUFFE: 'Twas from excess of zeal.
  I never meant to cause you pain, I swear.
  I'd rather . . .

(He places his hand on ELMIRE's *knee.)*

ELMIRE: What can your hand be doing there?
TARTUFFE: Feeling your gown: what soft, fine-woven stuff!
ELMIRE: Please, I'm extremely ticklish. That's enough.   40

(She draws her chair away; TARTUFFE *pulls his after her.)*

TARTUFFE *(fondling the lace collar of her gown):*
  My, my, what lovely lacework on your dress!

The workmanship's miraculous, no less.
I've not seen anything to equal it.
ELMIRE: Yes, quite. But let's talk business for a bit.
    They say my husband means to break his word   45
    And give his daughter to you, Sir. Had you heard?
TARTUFFE: He did once mention it. But I confess
    I dream of quite a different happiness.
    It's elsewhere, Madam, that my eyes discern
    The promise of that bliss for which I yearn.   50
ELMIRE: I see: you care for nothing here below.
TARTUFFE: Ah, well—my heart's not made of stone, you know.
ELMIRE: All your desires mount heavenward, I'm sure,
    In scorn of all that's earthly and impure.
TARTUFFE: A love of heavenly beauty does not preclude   55
    A proper love for earthly pulchritude;
    Our senses are quite rightly captivated
    By perfect works our Maker has created.
    Some glory clings to all that Heaven has made;
    In you, all Heaven's marvels are displayed.   60
    On that fair face, such beauties have been lavished,
    The eyes are dazzled and the heart is ravished;
    How could I look on you, O flawless creature,
    And not adore the Author of all Nature,
    Feeling a love both passionate and pure
    For you, his triumph of self-portraiture?   65
    At first, I trembled lest that love should be
    A subtle snare that Hell had laid for me;
    I vowed to flee the sight of you, eschewing
    A rapture that might prove my soul's undoing;
    But soon, fair being, I became aware   70
    That my deep passion could be made to square
    With rectitude, and with my bounden duty.
    I thereupon surrendered to your beauty.
    It is, I know, presumptuous on my part
    To bring you this poor offering of my heart,   75
    And it is not my merit, Heaven knows,
    But your compassion on which my hopes repose.
    You are my peace, my solace, my salvation;
    On you depends my bliss—or desolation;
    I bide your judgment and, as you think best,   80
    I shall be either miserable or blest.
ELMIRE: Your declaration is most gallant, Sir,
    But don't you think it's out of character?
    You'd have done better to restrain your passion
    And think before you spoke in such a fashion.   85
    It ill becomes a pious man like you . . .
TARTUFFE: I may be pious, but I'm human too:

With your celestial charms before his eyes,
A man has not the power to be wise.
I know such words sound strangely, coming from me, 90
But I'm no angel, nor was meant to be,
And if you blame my passion, you must needs
Reproach as well the charms on which it feeds.
Your loveliness I had no sooner seen
Than you became my soul's unrivalled queen; 95
Before your seraph glance, divinely sweet,
My heart's defenses crumbled in defeat,
And nothing fasting, prayer, or tears might do
Could stay my spirit from adoring you.
My eyes, my sighs have told you in the past 100
What now my lips make bold to say at last,
And if, in your great goodness, you will deign
To look upon your slave, and ease his pain,—
If, in compassion for my soul's distress,
You'll stoop to comfort my unworthiness, 105
I'll raise to you, in thanks for that sweet manna,
An endless hymn, an infinite hosanna.
With me, of course, there need be no anxiety,
No fear of scandal or of notoriety.
These young court gallants, whom all the ladies fancy, 110
Are vain in speech, in action rash and chancy;
When they succeed in love, the world soon knows it;
No favor's granted them but they disclose it
And by the looseness of their tongues profane
The very altar where their hearts have lain. 115
Men of my sort, however, love discreetly,
And one may trust our reticence completely.
My keen concern for my good name insures
The absolute security of yours;
In short, I offer you, my dear Elmire, 120
Love without scandal, pleasure without fear.
ELMIRE: I've heard your well-turned speeches to the end,
And what you urge I clearly apprehend.
Aren't you afraid that I may take a notion
To tell my husband of your warm devotion, 125
And that, supposing he were duly told,
His feelings toward you might grow rather cold?
TARTUFFE: I know, dear lady, that your exceeding charity
Will lead your heart to pardon my temerity;
That you'll excuse my violent affection 130
As human weakness, human imperfection;
And that—O fairest!—you will bear in mind
That I'm but flesh and blood, and am not blind.
ELMIRE: Some women might do otherwise, perhaps,

But I shall be discreet about your lapse;   135
I'll tell my husband nothing of what's occurred
If, in return, you'll give your solemn word
To advocate as forcefully as you can
The marriage of Valère and Mariane,
Renouncing all desire to dispossess   140
Another of his rightful happiness,
And . . .

Scene IV

DAMIS, ELMIRE, TARTUFFE

DAMIS (*emerging from the closet where he has been hiding*):
                  No! We'll not hush up this vile affair;
I heard it all inside that closet there,
Where Heaven, in order to confound the pride
Of this great rascal, prompted me to hide.
Ah, now I have my long-awaited chance   5
To punish his deceit and arrogance,
And give my father clear and shocking proof
Of the black character of his dear Tartuffe.
ELMIRE: Ah no, Damis! I'll be content if he
Will study to deserve my leniency.   10
I've promised silence—don't make me break my word;
To make a scandal would be too absurd.
Good wives laugh off such trifles, and forget them;
Why should they tell their husbands, and upset them?
DAMIS: You have your reasons for taking such a course,   15
And I have reasons, too, of equal force.
To spare him now would be insanely wrong.
I've swallowed my just wrath for far too long
And watched this insolent bigot bringing strife
And bitterness into our family life.   20
Too long he's meddled in my father's affairs,
Thwarting my marriage-hopes, and poor Valère's.
It's high time that my father was undeceived,
And now I've proof that can't be disbelieved—
Proof that was furnished me by Heaven above.   25
It's too good not to take advantage of.
This is my chance, and I deserve to lose it
If, for one moment, I hesitate to use it.
ELMIRE: Damis . . .
DAMIS: No, I must do what I think right.
Madam, my heart is bursting with delight,   30
And, say whatever you will, I'll not consent

To lose the sweet revenge on which I'm bent.
I'll settle matters without more ado;
And here, most opportunely, is my cue.

Scene V

ORGON, DAMIS, TARTUFFE, ELMIRE

DAMIS: Father, I'm glad you've joined us. Let us advise you
Of some fresh news which doubtless will surprise you.
You've just now been repaid with interest
For all your loving-kindness to our guest.
He's proved his warm and grateful feelings toward you;   5
It's with a pair of horns he would reward you.
Yes, I surprised him with your wife, and heard
His whole adulterous offer, every word.
She, with her all too gentle disposition,
Would not have told you of his proposition;   10
But I shall not make terms with brazen lechery,
And feel that not to tell you would be treachery.
ELMIRE: And I hold that one's husband's peace of mind
Should not be spoilt by tattle of this kind.
One's honor doesn't require it: to be proficient   15
In keeping men at bay is quite sufficient.
These are my sentiments, and I wish, Damis,
That you had heeded me and held your peace.

Scene VI

ORGON, DAMIS, TARTUFFE

ORGON: Can it be true, this dreadful thing I hear?
TARTUFFE: Yes, Brother, I'm a wicked man, I fear:
A wretched sinner, all depraved and twisted,
The greatest villain that has ever existed.
My life's one heap of crimes, which grows each minute;   5
There's naught but foulness and corruption in it;
And I perceive that Heaven, outraged by me,
Has chosen this occasion to mortify me.
Charge me with any deed you wish to name;
I'll not defend myself, but take the blame.   10
Believe what you are told, and drive Tartuffe
Like some base criminal from beneath your roof;
Yes, drive me hence, and with a parting curse:
I shan't protest, for I deserve far worse.

ORGON (*to* DAMIS): Ah, you deceitful boy, how dare you try   15
    To stain his purity with so foul a lie?
DAMIS: What! Are you taken in by such a bluff?
    Did you not hear . . . ?
ORGON: Enough, you rogue, enough!
TARTUFFE: Ah, Brother, let him speak: you're being unjust.
    Believe his story; the boy deserves your trust.   20
    Why, after all, should you have faith in me?
    How can you know what I might do, or be?
    Is it on my good actions that you base
    Your favor? Do you trust my pious face?
    Ah, no, don't be deceived by hollow shows;   25
    I'm far, alas, from being what men suppose;
    Though the world takes me for a man of worth,
    I'm truly the most worthless man on earth.

                (*To* DAMIS:)

    Yes, my dear son, speak out now: call me the chief
    Of sinners, a wretch, a murderer, a thief;   30
    Load me with all the names men most abhor;
    I'll not complain; I've earned them all, and more;
    I'll kneel here while you pour them on my head
    As a just punishment for the life I've led.
ORGON (*to* TARTUFFE): This is too much, dear Brother.
                (*To* DAMIS:)
                                  Have you no heart?   35
DAMIS: Are you so hoodwinked by this rascal's art . . . ?
ORGON: Be still, you monster.

               (*To* TARTUFFE:)
               Brother, I pray you, rise.

               (*To* DAMIS:)

    Villain!
DAMIS: But . . .
ORGON: Silence!
DAMIS: Can't you realize . . . ?
ORGON: Just one word more, and I'll tear you limb from limb.
TARTUFFE: In God's name, Brother, don't be harsh with him.   40
    I'd rather far be tortured at the stake
    Than see him bear one scratch for my poor sake.
ORGON (*to* DAMIS): Ingrate!
TARTUFFE: If I must beg you, on bended knee,
    To pardon him . . .
ORGON (*falling to his knees, addressing* tartuffe):
                      Such goodness cannot be!

(To DAMIS:*)*

Now, there's true charity!
DAMIS: What, you . . . ?
ORGON: Villain, be still!   45
I know your motives; I know you wish him ill:
Yes, all of you—wife, children, servants, all—
Conspire against him and desire his fall,
Employing every shameful trick you can
To alienate me from this saintly man.   50
Ah, but the more you seek to drive him away,
The more I'll do to keep him. Without delay,
I'll spite this household and confound its pride
By giving him my daughter as his bride.
DAMIS: You're going to force her to accept his hand?   55
ORGON: Yes, and this very night, d'you understand?
I shall defy you all, and make it clear
That I'm the one who gives the orders here.
Come, wretch, kneel down and clasp his blessed feet,
And ask his pardon for your black deceit.   60
DAMIS: I ask that swindler's pardon? Why, I'd rather . . .
ORGON: So! You insult him, and defy your father!
A stick! A stick! *(To* TARTUFFE:*)* No, no—release me, do.

(To DAMIS.*)*

Out of my house this minute! Be off with you,
And never dare set foot in it again.   65
DAMIS: Well, I shall go, but . . .
ORGON: Well, go quickly, then.
I disinherit you; an empty purse
Is all you'll get from me—except my curse!

Scene VII

ORGON, TARTUFFE

ORGON: How he blasphemed your goodness! What a son!
TARTUFFE: Forgive him, Lord, as I've already done.

(To ORGON:*)*

You can't know how it hurts when someone tries
To blacken me in my dear Brother's eyes.
ORGON: Ahh!

TARTUFFE: The mere thought of such ingratitude
    Plunges my soul into so dark a mood . . .
    Such horror grips my heart . . . I gasp for breath,
    And cannot speak, and feel myself near death.
ORGON: *(He runs, in tears, to the door through which he has just driven his son.)*
    You blackguard! Why did I spare you? Why did I not
    Break you in little pieces on the spot?
    Compose yourself, and don't be hurt, dear friend.
TARTUFFE: These scenes, these dreadful quarrels, have got to end.
    I've much upset your household, and I perceive
    That the best thing will be for me to leave.
ORGON: What are you saying!
TARTUFFE: They're all against me here;
    They'd have you think me false and insincere.
ORGON: Ah, what of that? Have I ceased believing in you?
TARTUFFE: Their adverse talk will certainly continue,
    And charges which you now repudiate
    You may find credible at a later date.
ORGON: No, Brother, never.
TARTUFFE: Brother, a wife can sway
    Her husband's mind in many a subtle way.
ORGON: No, no.
TARTUFFE: To leave at once is the solution;
    Thus only can I end their persecution.
ORGON: No, no, I'll not allow it; you shall remain.
TARTUFFE: Ah, well; 'twill mean much martyrdom and pain,
    But if you wish it . . .
ORGON: Ah!
TARTUFFE: Enough; so be it.
    But one thing must be settled, as I see it.
    For your dear honor, and for our friendship's sake,
    There's one precaution I feel bound to take.
    I shall avoid your wife, and keep away . . .
ORGON: No, you shall not, whatever they may say.
    It pleases me to vex them, and for spite
    I'd have them see you with her day and night.
    What's more, I'm going to drive them to despair
    By making you my only son and heir;
    This very day, I'll give to you alone
    Clear deed and title to everything I own.
    A dear, good friend and son-in-law-to-be
    Is more than wife, or child, or kin to me.
    Will you accept my offer, dearest son?
TARTUFFE: In all things, let the will of Heaven be done.
ORGON: Poor fellow! Come, we'll go draw up the deed.
    Then let them burst with disappointed greed!

5

10

15

20

25

30

35

40

ACT IV

Scene I

CLÉANTE, TARTUFFE

CLÉANTE: Yes, all the town's discussing it, and truly,
   Their comments do not flatter you unduly.
   I'm glad we've met, Sir, and I'll give my view
   Of this sad matter in a word or two.
   As for who's guilty, that I shan't discuss;   5
   Let's say it was Damis who caused the fuss;
   Assuming, then, that you have been ill-used
   By young Damis, and groundlessly accused,
   Ought not a Christian to forgive, and ought
   He not to stifle every vengeful thought?   10
   Should you stand by and watch a father make
   His only son an exile for your sake?
   Again I tell you frankly, be advised:
   The whole town, high and low, is scandalized;
   This quarrel must be mended, and my advice is   15
   Not to push matters to a further crisis.
   No, sacrifice your wrath to God above,
   And help Damis regain his father's love.
TARTUFFE: Alas, for my part I should take great joy
   In doing so. I've nothing against the boy.   20
   I pardon all, I harbor no resentment;
   To serve him would afford me much contentment.
   But Heaven's interest will not have it so:
   If he comes back, then I shall have to go.
   After his conduct—so extreme, so vicious—   25
   Our further intercourse would look suspicious.
   God knows what people would think! Why, they'd describe
   My goodness to him as a sort of bribe;
   They'd say that out of guilt I made pretense
   Of loving-kindness and benevolence—   30
   That, fearing my accuser's tongue, I strove
   To buy his silence with a show of love.
CLÉANTE: Your reasoning is badly warped and stretched,
   And these excuses, Sir, are most far-fetched.
   Why put yourself in charge of Heaven's cause?   35
   Does Heaven need our help to enforce its laws?
   Leave vengeance to the Lord, Sir; while we live,
   Our duty's not to punish, but forgive;
   And what the Lord commands, we should obey
   Without regard to what the world may say.   40

What! Shall the fear of being misunderstood
Prevent our doing what is right and good?
No, no: let's simply do what Heaven ordains,
And let no other thoughts perplex our brains.

TARTUFFE: Again, Sir, let me say that I've forgiven   45
Damis, and thus obeyed the laws of Heaven;
But I am not commanded by the Bible
To live with one who smears my name with libel.

CLÉANTE: Were you commanded, Sir, to indulge the whim
Of poor Orgon, and to encourage him   50
In suddenly transferring to your name
A large estate to which you have no claim?

TARTUFFE: 'Twould never occur to those who know me best
To think I acted from self-interest.
The treasures of this world I quite despise;   55
Their specious glitter does not charm my eyes;
And if I have resigned myself to taking
The gift which my dear Brother insists on making,
I do so only, as he well understands,
Lest so much wealth fall into wicked hands,   60
Lest those to whom it might descend in time
Turn it to purposes of sin and crime,
And not, as I shall do, make use of it
For Heaven's glory and mankind's benefit.

CLÉANTE: Forget these trumped-up fears. Your argument   65
Is one the rightful heir might well resent;
It *is* a moral burden to inherit
Such wealth, but give Damis a chance to bear it.
And would it not be worse to be accused
Of swindling, than to see that wealth misused?   70
I'm shocked that you allowed Orgon to broach
This matter, and that you feel no self-reproach:
Does true religion teach that lawful heirs
May freely be deprived of what is theirs?
And if the Lord has told you in your heart   75
That you and young Damis must dwell apart,
Would it not be the decent thing to beat
A generous and honorable retreat,
Rather than let the son of the house be sent,
For your convenience, into banishment?   80
Sir, if you wish to prove the honesty
Of your intentions . . .

TARTUFFE: Sir, it is half-past three.
I've certain pious duties to attend to,
And hope my prompt departure won't offend you.

CLÉANTE (*alone*): Damn.

Scene II

ELMIRE, MARIANE, CLÉANTE, DORINE

DORINE: Stay, Sir, and help Mariane, for Heaven's sake!
    She's suffering so, I fear her heart will break.
    Her father's plan to marry her off tonight
    Has put the poor child in a desperate plight.
    I hear him coming. Let's stand together, now,   5
    And see if we can't change his mind, somehow,
    About this match we all deplore and fear.

Scene III

ORGON, ELMIRE, MARIANE, CLÉANTE, DORINE

ORGON: Hah! Glad to find you all assembled here.

        (To MARIANE:*)*

    This contract, child, contains your happiness,
    And what it says I think your heart can guess.
MARIANE *(falling to her knees):*
    Sir, by that Heaven which sees me here distressed,
    And by whatever else can move your breast,   5
    Do not employ a father's power, I pray you,
    To crush my heart and force it to obey you,
    Nor by your harsh commands oppress me so
    That I'll begrudge the duty which I owe—
    And do not so embitter and enslave me   10
    That I shall hate the very life you gave me.
    If my sweet hopes must perish, if you refuse
    To give me to the one I've dared to choose,
    Spare me at least—I beg you, I implore—
    The pain of wedding one whom I abhor;   15
    And do not, by a heartless use of force,
    Drive me to contemplate some desperate course.
ORGON *(feeling himself touched by her:)*
    Be firm, my soul. No human weakness, now.
MARIANE: I don't resent your love for him. Allow
    Your heart free rein, Sir; give him your property,   20
    And if that's not enough, take mine from me;
    He's welcome to my money; take it, do,
    But don't, I pray, include my person too.
    Spare me, I beg you; and let me end the tale
    Of my sad days behind a convent veil.   25
ORGON: A convent! Hah! When crossed in their amours,

All lovesick girls have the same thought as yours.
Get up! The more you loathe the man, and dread him,
The more ennobling it will be to wed him.
Marry Tartuffe, and mortify your flesh!
Enough; don't start that whimpering afresh.

DORINE: But why . . . ?

ORGON: Be still, there. Speak when you're spoken to.
Not one more bit of impudence out of you.

CLÉANTE: If I may offer a word of counsel here . . .

ORGON: Brother, in counselling you have no peer;
All your advice is forceful, sound, and clever;
I don't propose to follow it, however.

ELMIRE (to Orgon): I am amazed, and don't know what to say;
Your blindness simply takes my breath away.
You are indeed bewitched, to take no warning
From our account of what occurred this morning.

ORGON: Madam, I know a few plain facts, and one
Is that you're partial to my rascal son;
Hence, when he sought to make Tartuffe the victim
Of a base lie, you dared not contradict him.
Ah, but you underplayed your part, my pet;
You should have looked more angry, more upset.

ELMIRE: When men make overtures, must we reply
With righteous anger and a battle-cry?
Must we turn back their amorous advances
With sharp reproaches and with fiery glances?
Myself, I find such offers merely amusing,
And make no scenes and fusses in refusing;
My taste is for good-natured rectitude,
And I dislike the savage sort of prude
Who guards her virtue with her teeth and claws,
And tears men's eyes out for the slightest cause:
The Lord preserve me from such honor as that,
Which bites and scratches like an alley-cat!
I've found that a polite and cool rebuff
Discourages a lover quite enough.

ORGON: I know the facts, and I shall not be shaken.

ELMIRE: I marvel at your power to be mistaken.
Would it, I wonder, carry weight with you
If I could *show* you that our tale was true?

ORGON: Show me?

ELMIRE: Yes.

ORGON: Rot.

ELMIRE: Come, what if I found a way
To make you see the facts as plain as day?

ORGON: Nonsense.

ELMIRE: Do answer me; don't be absurd.

I'm not now asking you to trust our word.
Suppose that from some hiding-place in here 70
You learned the whole sad truth by eye and ear—
What would you say of your good friend, after that?
ORGON: Why, I'd say . . . nothing, by Jehoshaphat!
It can't be true.
ELMIRE: You've been too long deceived,
And I'm quite tired of being disbelieved. 75
Come now: let's put my statements to the test,
And you shall see the truth made manifest.
ORGON: I'll take that challenge. Now do your uttermost.
We'll see how you make good your empty boast.
ELMIRE (to DORINE): Send him to me.
DORINE: He's crafty; it may be hard 80
To catch the cunning scoundrel off his guard.
ELMIRE: No, amorous men are gullible. Their conceit
So blinds them that they're never hard to cheat.
Have him come down

(To CLÉANTE and MARIANE:)
Please leave us, for a bit.

Scene IV

ELMIRE, ORGON

ELMIRE: Pull up this table, and get under it.
ORGON: What?
ELMIRE: It's essential that you be well-hidden.
ORGON: Why there?
ELMIRE: Oh, Heavens! Just do as you are bidden.
I have my plans; we'll soon see how they fare.
Under the table, now; and once you're there,
Take care that you are neither seen nor heard. 5
ORGON: Well, I'll indulge you, since I gave my word
To see you through this infantile charade.
ELMIRE: Once it is over, you'll be glad we played.

(To her husband, who is now under the table:)

I'm going to act quite strangely, now, and you 10
Must not be shocked at anything I do.
Whatever I may say, you must excuse
As part of that deceit I'm forced to use.
I shall employ sweet speeches in the task
Of making that imposter drop his mask; 15
I'll give encouragement to his bold desires,
And furnish fuel to his amorous fires.
Since it's for your sake, and for his destruction,

That I shall seem to yield to his seduction,
I'll gladly stop whenever you decide   20
That all your doubts are fully satisfied.
I'll count on you, as soon as you have seen
What sort of man he is, to intervene,
And not expose me to his odious lust
One moment longer than you feel you must.   25
Remember: you're to save me from my plight
Whenever . . . He's coming! Hush! Keep out of sight!

Scene V

TARTUFFE, ELMIRE, ORGON

TARTUFFE: You wish to have a word with me, I'm told.
ELMIRE: Yes. I've a little secret to unfold.
   Before I speak, however, it would be wise
   To close that door, and look about for spies.

(TARTUFFE *goes to the door, closes it, and returns.*)

   The very last thing that must happen now   5
   Is a repetition of this morning's row.
   I've never been so badly caught off guard.
   Oh, how I feared for you! You saw how hard
   I tried to make that troublesome Damis
   Control his dreadful temper, and hold his peace.   10
   In my confusion, I didn't have the sense
   Simply to contradict his evidence;
   But as it happened, that was for the best,
   And all has worked out in our interest.
   This storm has only bettered your position;   15
   My husband doesn't have the least suspicion,
   And now, in mockery of those who do,
   He bids me be continually with you.
   And that is why, quite fearless of reproof,
   I now can be alone with my Tartuffe,   20
   And why my heart—perhaps too quick to yield—
   Feels free to let its passion be revealed.
TARTUFFE: Madam, your words confuse me. Not long ago,
   You spoke in quite a different style, you know.
ELMIRE: Ah, Sir, if that refusal made you smart,   25
   It's little that you know of woman's heart,
   Or what that heart is trying to convey
   When it resists in such a feeble way!
   Always, at first, our modesty prevents

The frank avowal of tender sentiments; 30
However high the passion which inflames us,
Still, to confess its power somehow shames us.
Thus we reluct, at first, yet in a tone
Which tells you that our heart is overthrown,
That what our lips deny, our pulse confesses, 35
And that, in time, all noes will turn to yesses.
I fear my words are all too frank and free,
And a poor proof of woman's modesty;
But since I'm started, tell me, if you will—
Would I have tried to make Damis be still, 40
Would I have listened, calm and unoffended,
Until your lengthy offer of love was ended,
And been so very mild in my reaction,
Had your sweet words not given me satisfaction?
And when I tried to force you to undo 45
The marriage-plans my husband has in view,
What did my urgent pleading signify
If not that I admired you, and that I
Deplored the thought that someone else might own
Part of a heart I wished for mine alone? 50
TARTUFFE: Madam, no happiness is so complete
As when, from lips we love, come words so sweet;
Their nectar floods my every sense, and drains
In honeyed rivulets through all my veins.
To please you is my joy, my only goal; 55
Your love is the restorer of my soul;
And yet I must beg leave, now, to confess
Some lingering doubts as to my happiness.
Might not this be a trick? Might not the catch
Be that you wish me to break off the match 60
With Mariane, and so have feigned to love me?
I shan't quite trust your fond opinion of me
Until the feelings you've expressed so sweetly
Are demonstrated somewhat more concretely,
And you have shown, by certain kind concessions, 65
That I may put my faith in your professions.
ELMIRE: *(She coughs, to warn her husband.)*
Why be in such a hurry? Must my heart
Exhaust its bounty at the very start?
To make that sweet admission cost me dear,
But you'll not be content, it would appear, 70
Unless my store of favors is disbursed
To the last farthing, and at the very first.
TARTUFFE: The less we merit, the less we dare to hope,
And with our doubts, mere words can never cope.

We trust no promised bliss till we receive it;
Not till a joy is ours can we believe it.
I, who so little merit your esteem,
Can't credit this fulfillment of my dream,
And shan't believe it, Madam, until I savor
Some palpable assurance of your favor.   80
ELMIRE: My, how tyrannical your love can be,
    And how it flusters and perplexes me!
    How furiously you take one's heart in hand,
    And make your every wish a fierce command!
    Come, must you hound and harry me to death?   85
    Will you not give me time to catch my breath?
    Can it be right to press me with such force,
    Give me no quarter, show me no remorse,
    And take advantage, by your stern insistence,
    Of the fond feelings which weaken my resistance?   90
TARTUFFE: Well, if you look with favor upon my love,
    Why, then, begrudge me some clear proof thereof?
ELMIRE: But how can I consent without offense
    To Heaven, toward which you feel such reverence?
TARTUFFE: If Heaven is all that holds you back, don't worry.   95
    I can remove that hindrance in a hurry.
    Nothing of that sort need obstruct our path.
ELMIRE: Must one not be afraid of Heaven's wrath?
TARTUFFE: Madam, forget such fears, and be my pupil,
    And I shall teach you how to conquer scruple.   100
    Some joys, it's true, are wrong in Heaven's eyes;
    Yet Heaven is not averse to compromise;
    There is a science, lately formulated,
    Whereby one's conscience may be liberated,
    And any wrongful act you care to mention   105
    May be redeemed by purity of intention.
    I'll teach you, Madam, the secrets of that science;
    Meanwhile, just place on me your full reliance.
    Assuage my keen desires, and feel no dread:
    The sin, if any, shall be on my head.   110

                (ELMIRE coughs, this time more loudly.)

    You've a bad cough.
ELMIRE: Yes, yes. It's bad indeed.
TARTUFFE *(producing a little paper bag)*:
    A bit of licorice may be what you need.
ELMIRE: No, I've a stubborn cold, it seems. I'm sure it
    Will take much more than licorice to cure it.
TARTUFFE: How aggravating.
ELMIRE: Oh, more than I can say.   115
TARTUFFE: If you're still troubled, think of things this way:

No one shall know our joys, save us alone,
And there's no evil till the act is known;
It's scandal, Madam, which makes it an offense,
And it's no sin to sin in confidence. 120
ELMIRE *(having coughed once more):* Well, clearly I must do as
   you require,
And yield to your importunate desire.
It is apparent, now, that nothing less
Will satisfy you, and so I acquiesce.
To go so far is much against my will; 125
I'm vexed that it should come to this; but still,
Since you are so determined on it, since you
Will not allow mere language to convince you,
And since you ask for concrete evidence, I
See nothing for it, now, but to comply. 130
If this is sinful, if I'm wrong to do it,
So much the worse for him who drove me to it.
The fault can surely not be charged to me.
TARTUFFE: Madam, the fault is mine, if fault there be,
And . . .
ELMIRE: Open the door a little, and peek out; 135
I wouldn't want my husband poking about.
TARTUFFE: Why worry about the man? Each day he grows
More gullible; one can lead him by the nose.
To find us here would fill him with delight,
And if he saw the worst, he'd doubt his sight. 140
ELMIRE: Nevertheless, do step out for a minute
Into the hall, and see that no one's in it.

Scene VI

ORGON, ELMIRE

ORGON *(coming out from under the table):*
That man's a perfect monster, I must admit!
I'm simply stunned. I can't get over it.
ELMIRE: What, coming out so soon? How premature!
Get back in hiding, and wait until you're sure.
Stay till the end, and be convinced completely; 5
We mustn't stop till things are proved concretely.
ORGON: Hell never harbored anything so vicious!
ELMIRE: Tut, don't be hasty. Try to be judicious.
Wait, and be certain that there's no mistake.
No jumping to conclusions, for Heaven's sake! 10
   (She places ORGON *behind her, as* TARTUFFE *re-enters.)*

Scene VII

TARTUFFE, ELMIRE, ORGON

TARTUFFE *(not seeing* ORGON*)*:
   Madam, all things have worked out to perfection;
   I've given the neighboring rooms a full inspection;
   No one's about; and now I may at last . . .
ORGON *(intercepting him)*: Hold on, my passionate fellow, not so fast!
   I should advise a little more restraint.   5
   Well, so you thought you'd fool me, my dear saint!
   How soon you wearied of the saintly life—
   Wedding my daughter, and coveting my wife!
   I've long suspected you, and had a feeling
   That soon I'd catch you at your double-dealing.   10
   Just now, you've given me evidence galore;
   It's quite enough; I have no wish for more.
ELMIRE *(to* TARTUFFE*)*: I'm sorry to have treated you so slyly,
   But circumstances forced me to be wily.
TARTUFFE: Brother, you can't think . . .
ORGON: No more talk from you;   15
   Just leave this household, without more ado.
TARTUFFE: What I intended . . .
ORGON: That seems fairly clear.
   Spare me your falsehoods and get out of here.
TARTUFFE: No, I'm the master, and you're the one to go!
   This house belongs to me, I'll have you know,   20
   And I shall show you that you can't hurt *me*
   By this contemptible conspiracy,
   That those who cross me know not what they do,
   And that I've means to expose and punish you,
   Avenge offended Heaven, and make you grieve   25
   That ever you dared order me to leave.

Scene VIII

ELMIRE, ORGON

ELMIRE: What was the point of all that angry chatter?
ORGON: Dear God, I'm worried. This is no laughing matter.
ELMIRE: How so?
ORGON: I fear I understood his drift.
   I'm much disturbed about that deed of gift.
ELMIRE: You gave him . . . ?
ORGON: Yes, it's all been drawn and signed.   5
   But one thing more is weighing on my mind.

ELMIRE: What's that?
ORGON: I'll tell you; but first let's see if there's
    A certain strong-box in his room upstairs.

ACT V

Scene I

ORGON, CLÉANTE

CLÉANTE: Where are you going so fast?
ORGON: God knows!
CLÉANTE: Then wait;
    Let's have a conference, and deliberate
    On how this situation's to be met.
ORGON: That strong-box has me utterly upset;
    This is the worst of many, many shocks.   5
CLÉANTE: Is there some fearful mystery in that box?
ORGON: My poor friend Argas brought that box to me
    With his own hands, in utmost secrecy;
    'Twas on the very morning of his flight.
    It's full of papers which, if they came to light,   10
    Would ruin him — or such is my impression.
CLÉANTE: Then why did you let it out of your possession?
ORGON: Those papers vexed my conscience, and it seemed best
    To ask the counsel of my pious guest.
    The cunning scoundrel got me to agree   15
    To leave the strong-box in his custody,
    So that, in case of an investigation,
    I could employ a slight equivocation
    And swear I didn't have it, and thereby,
    At no expense to conscience, tell a lie.   20
CLÉANTE: It looks to me as if you're out on a limb.
    Trusting him with that box, and offering him
    That deed of gift, were actions of a kind
    Which scarcely indicate a prudent mind.
    With two such weapons, he has the upper hand,   25
    And since you're vulnerable, as matters stand,
    You erred once more in bringing him to bay.
    You should have acted in some subtler way.
ORGON: Just think of it: behind that fervent face,
    A heart so wicked, and a soul so base!   30
    I took him in, a hungry beggar, and then . . .
    Enough, by God! I'm through with pious men:
    Henceforth I'll hate the whole false brotherhood,
    And persecute them worse than Satan could.

CLÉANTE: Ah, there you go—extravagant as ever!　　　　35
　　Why can you not be rational? You never
　　Manage to take the middle course, it seems,
　　But jump, instead, between absurd extremes.
　　You've recognized your recent grave mistake
　　In falling victim to a pious fake;　　　　40
　　Now, to correct that error, must you embrace
　　An even greater error in its place,
　　And judge our worthy neighbors as a whole
　　By what you've learned of one corrupted soul?
　　Come, just because one rascal made you swallow　　　　45
　　A show of zeal which turned out to be hollow,
　　Shall you conclude that all men are deceivers,
　　And that, today, there are no true believers?
　　Let atheists make that foolish inference;
　　Learn to distinguish virtue from pretense,　　　　50
　　Be cautious in bestowing admiration,
　　And cultivate a sober moderation.
　　Don't humor fraud, but also don't asperse
　　True piety; the latter fault is worse,
　　And it is best to err, if err one must,　　　　55
　　As you have done, upon the side of trust.

Scene II

DAMIS, ORGON, CLÉANTE

DAMIS: Father, I hear that scoundrel's uttered threats
　　Against you; that he pridefully forgets
　　How, in his need, he was befriended by you,
　　And means to use your gifts to crucify you.
ORGON: It's true, my boy. I'm too distressed for tears.　　　　5
DAMIS: Leave it to me, Sir; let me trim his ears.
　　Faced with such insolence, we must not waver.
　　I shall rejoice in doing you the favor
　　Of cutting short his life, and your distress.
CLÉANTE: What a display of young hotheadedness!　　　　10
　　Do learn to moderate your fits of rage.
　　In this just kingdom, this enlightened age,
　　One does not settle things by violence.

Scene III

MADAME PERNELLE, MARIANE, ELMIRE, DORINE, DAMIS, ORGON, CLÉANTE

MADAME PERNELLE: I hear strange tales of very strange events.
ORGON: Yes, strange events which these two eyes beheld.

The man's ingratitude is unparalleled.
I save a wretched pauper from starvation,
House him, and treat him like a blood relation, 5
Shower him every day with my largesse,
Give him my daughter, and all that I possess;
And meanwhile the unconscionable knave
Tries to induce my wife to misbehave;
And not content with such extreme rascality, 10
Now threatens me with my own liberality,
And aims, by taking base advantage of
The gifts I gave him out of Christian love,
To drive me from my house, a ruined man,
And make me end a pauper, as he began. 15

DORINE: Poor fellow!

MADAME PERNELLE: No, my son, I'll never bring
Myself to think him guilty of such a thing.

ORGON: How's that?

MADAME PERNELLE: The righteous always were maligned.

ORGON: Speak clearly, Mother. Say what's on your mind.

MADAME PERNELLE: I mean that I can smell a rat, my dear. 20
You know how everybody hates him, here.

ORGON: That has no bearing on the case at all.

MADAME PERNELLE: I told you a hundred times, when you were small,
That virtue in this world is hated ever;
Malicious men may die, but malice never. 25

ORGON: No doubt that's true, but how does it apply?

MADAME PERNELLE: They've turned you against him by a clever lie.

ORGON: I've told you, I was there and saw it done.

MADAME PERNELLE: Ah, slanderers will stop at nothing, Son.

ORGON: Mother, I'll lose my temper . . . . For the last time, 30
I tell you I was witness to the crime.

MADAME PERNELLE: The tongues of spite are busy night and noon,
And to their venom no man is immune.

ORGON: You're talking nonsense. Can't you realize
I saw it; saw it; saw it with my eyes? 35
Saw, do you understand me? Must I shout it
Into your ears before you'll cease to doubt it?

MADAME PERNELLE: Appearances can deceive, my son. Dear me,
We cannot always judge by what we see.

ORGON: Drat! Drat!

MADAME PERNELLE: One often interprets things awry; 40
Good can seem evil to a suspicious eye.

ORGON: Was I to see his pawing at Elmire
As an act of charity?

MADAME PERNELLE: Till his guilt is clear,
A man deserves the benefit of the doubt.
You should have waited, to see how things turned out. 45

ORGON: Great God in Heaven, what more proof did I need?
    Was I to sit there, watching, until he'd . . .
    You drive me to the brink of impropriety.
MADAME PERNELLE: No, no, a man of such surpassing piety   50
    Could not do such a thing. You cannot shake me.
    I don't believe it, and you shall not make me.
ORGON: You vex me so that, if you weren't my mother,
    I'd say to you . . . some dreadful thing or other.
DORINE: It's your turn now, Sir, not to be listened to;
    You'd not trust us, and now she won't trust you.   55
CLÉANTE: My friends, we're wasting time which should be spent
    In facing up to our predicament.
    I fear that scoundrel's threats weren't made in sport.
DAMIS: Do you think he'd have the nerve to go to court?
ELMIRE: I'm sure he won't; they'd find it all too crude   60
    A case of swindling and ingratitude.
CLÉANTE: Don't be too sure. He won't be at a loss
    To give his claims a high and righteous gloss;
    And clever rogues with far less valid cause
    Have trapped their victims in a web of laws.   65
    I say again that to antagonize
    A man so strongly armed was most unwise.
ORGON: I know it; but the man's appalling cheek
    Outraged me so, I couldn't control my pique.
CLÉANTE: I wish to Heaven that we could devise   70
    Some truce between you, or some compromise.
ELMIRE: If I had known what cards he held, I'd not
    Have roused his anger by my little plot.
ORGON (to DORINE, *as* M. LOYAL *enters*):
    What is that fellow looking for? Who is he?
    Go talk to him—and tell him that I'm busy.   75

Scene IV

MONSIEUR LOYAL, MADAME PERNELLE, ORGON, DAMIS, MARIANE, DORINE, ELMIRE,
CLÉANTE

MONSIEUR LOYAL: Good day, dear sister. Kindly let me see
    Your master.
DORINE: He's involved with company,
    And cannot be disturbed just now, I fear.
MONSIEUR LOYAL: I hate to intrude; but what has brought me here
    Will not disturb your master, in any event.   5
    Indeed, my news will make him most content.
DORINE: Your name?
MONSIEUR LOYAL: Just say that I bring greetings from
    Monsieur Tartuffe, on whose behalf I've come.

DORINE *(to* ORGON*)*: Sir, he's a very gracious man, and bears
  A message from Tartuffe, which, he declares,   10
  Will make you most content.
CLÉANTE: Upon my word,
  I think this man had best be seen, and heard.
ORGON: Perhaps he has some settlement to suggest.
  How shall I treat him? What manner would be best?
CLÉANTE: Control your anger, and if he should mention   15
  Some fair adjustment, give him your full attention.
MONSIEUR LOYAL: Good health to you, good Sir. May Heaven confound
  Your enemies, and may your joys abound.
ORGON *(aside, to* CLÉANTE*)*: A gentle salutation: it confirms
  My guess that he is here to offer terms.   20
MONSIEUR LOYAL: I've always held your family most dear;
  I served your father, Sir, for many a year.
ORGON: Sir, I must ask your pardon; to my shame,
  I cannot now recall your face or name.
MONSIEUR LOYAL: Loyal's my name; I come from Normandy,   25
  And I'm a bailiff, in all modesty.
  For forty years, praise God, it's been my boast
  To serve with honor in that vital post,
  And I am here, Sir, if you will permit
  The liberty, to serve you with this writ . . .   30
ORGON: To—*what?*
MONSIEUR LOYAL: Now, please, Sir, let us have no friction:
  It's nothing but an order of eviction.
  You are to move your goods and family out
  And make way for new occupants, without
  Deferment or delay, and give the keys . . .   35
ORGON: I? Leave this house?
MONSIEUR LOYAL: Why yes, Sir, if you please.
  This house, Sir, from the cellar to the roof,
  Belongs now to the good Monsieur Tartuffe,
  And he is lord and master of your estate
  By virtue of a deed of present date,   40
  Drawn in due form, with clearest legal phrasing . . .
DAMIS: Your insolence is utterly amazing!
MONSIEUR LOYAL: Young man, my business here is not with you,
  But with your wise and temperate father, who,
  Like every worthy citizen, stands in awe   45
  Of justice, and would never obstruct the law.
ORGON: But . . .
MONSIEUR LOYAL:
                Not for a million, Sir, would you rebel
  Against authority; I know that well.
  You'll not make trouble, Sir, or interfere
  With the execution of my duties here.   50

DAMIS: Someone may execute a smart tattoo
  On that black jacket of yours, before you're through.
MONSIEUR LOYAL: Sir, bid your son be silent. I'd much regret
  Having to mention such a nasty threat
  Of violence, in writing my report.   55
DORINE *(aside):* This man Loyal's a most disloyal sort!
MONSIEUR LOYAL: I love all men of upright character,
  And when I agreed to serve these papers, Sir,
  It was your feelings that I had in mind.
  I couldn't bear to see the case assigned   60
  To someone else, who might esteem you less
  And so subject you to unpleasantness.
ORGON: What's more unpleasant than telling a man to leave
  His house and home?
MONSIEUR LOYAL: You'd like a short reprieve?
  If you desire it, Sir, I shall not press you,   65
  But wait until tomorrow to dispossess you.
  Splendid. I'll come and spend the night here, then,
  Most quietly, with half a score of men.
  For form's sake, you might bring me, just before
  You go to bed, the keys to the front door.   70
  My men, I promise, will be on their best
  Behavior, and will not disturb your rest.
  But bright and early, Sir, you must be quick
  And move out all your furniture, every stick:
  The men I've chosen are both young and strong,   75
  And with their help it shouldn't take you long.
  In short, I'll make things pleasant and convenient,
  And since I'm being so extremely lenient,
  Please show me, Sir, a like consideration,
  And give me your entire cooperation.   80
ORGON *(aside):* I may be all but bankrupt, but I vow
  I'd give a hundred louis, here and now,
  Just for the pleasure of landing one good clout
  Right on the end of that complacent snout.
CLÉANTE: Careful; don't make things worse.
DAMIS: My bootsole itches   85
  To give that beggar a good kick in the breeches.
DORINE: Monsieur Loyal, I'd love to hear the whack
  Of a stout stick across your fine broad back.
MONSIEUR LOYAL: Take care: a woman too may go to jail if
  She uses threatening language to a bailiff.   90
CLÉANTE: Enough, enough, Sir. This must not go on.
  Give me that paper, please, and then begone.
MONSIEUR LOYAL: Well, *au revoir.* God give you all good cheer!
ORGON: May God confound you, and him who sent you here!

Scene V

ORGON, CLÉANTE, MARIANE, ELMIRE, MADAME PERNELLE, DORINE, DAMIS

ORGON: Now, Mother, was I right or not? This writ
　　Should change your notion of Tartuffe a bit.
　　Do you perceive his villainy at last?
MADAME PERNELLE: I'm thunderstruck. I'm utterly aghast.
DORINE: Oh, come, be fair. You mustn't take offense　　　5
　　At this new proof of his benevolence.
　　He's acting out of selfless love, I know.
　　Material things enslave the soul, and so
　　He kindly has arranged your liberation
　　From all that might endanger your salvation.　　　10
ORGON: Will you not ever hold your tongue, you dunce?
CLÉANTE: Come, you must take some action, and at once.
ELMIRE: Go tell the world of the low trick he's tried.
　　The deed of gift is surely nullified
　　By such behavior, and public rage will not　　　15
　　Permit the wretch to carry out his plot.

Scene VI

VALÈRE, ORGON, CLÉANTE, ELMIRE, MARIANE, MADAME PERNELLE, DAMIS, DORINE

VALÈRE: Sir, though I hate to bring you more bad news,
　　Such is the danger that I cannot choose.
　　A friend who is extremely close to me
　　And knows my interest in your family
　　Has, for my sake, presumed to violate　　　5
　　The secrecy that's due to things of state,
　　And sends me word that you are in a plight
　　From which your one salvation lies in flight.
　　That scoundrel who's imposed upon you so
　　Denounced you to the King an hour ago　　　10
　　And, as supporting evidence, displayed
　　The strong-box of a certain renegade
　　Whose secret papers, so he testified,
　　You had disloyally agreed to hide.
　　I don't know just what charges may be pressed,　　　15
　　But there's a warrant out for your arrest;
　　Tartuffe has been instructed, furthermore,
　　To guide the arresting officer to your door.
CLÉANTE: He's clearly done this to facilitate
　　His seizure of your house and your estate.　　　20
ORGON: That man, I must say, is a vicious beast!
VALÈRE: You can't afford to delay, Sir, in the least.

My carriage is outside, to take you hence;
This thousand louis should cover all expense.
Let's lose no time, or you shall be undone;   25
The sole defense, in this case, is to run.
I shall go with you all the way, and place you
In a safe refuge to which they'll never trace you.
ORGON: Alas, dear boy, I wish that I could show you
    My gratitude for everything I owe you.   30
    But now is not the time; I pray the Lord
    That I may live to give you your reward.
    Farewell, my dears; be careful . . .
CLÉANTE: Brother, hurry.
    We shall take care of things; you needn't worry.

Scene VII

THE OFFICER, TARTUFFE, VALÈRE, ORGON, ELMIRE, MARIANE, MADAME PERNELLE,
DORINE, CLÉANTE, DAMIS

TARTUFFE: Gently, Sir, gently; stay right where you are.
    No need for haste; your lodging isn't far.
    You're off to prison, by order of the Prince.
ORGON: This is the crowning blow, you wretch; and since
    It means my total ruin and defeat,   5
    Your villainy is now at last complete.
TARTUFFE: You needn't try to provoke me; it's no use.
    Those who serve Heaven must expect abuse.
CLÉANTE: You are indeed most patient, sweet, and blameless.
DORINE: How he exploits the name of Heaven! It's shameless.   10
TARTUFFE: Your taunts and mockeries are all for naught;
    To do my duty is my only thought.
MARIANE: Your love of duty is most meritorious,
    And what you've done is little short of glorious.
TARTUFFE: All deeds are glorious, Madam, which obey   15
    The sovereign prince who sent me here today.
ORGON: I rescued you when you were destitute;
    Have you forgotten that, you thankless brute?
TARTUFFE: No, no, I well remember everything;
    But my first duty is to serve my King.   20
    That obligation is so paramount
    That other claims, beside it, do not count;
    And for it I would sacrifice my wife,
    My family, my friend, or my own life.
ELMIRE: Hypocrite!
DORINE: All that we most revere, he uses   25
    To cloak his plots and camouflage his ruses.

CLÉANTE: If it is true that you are animated
 By pure and loyal zeal, as you have stated,
 Why was this zeal not roused until you'd sought
 To make Orgon a cuckold, and been caught?   30
 Why weren't you moved to give your evidence
 Until your outraged host had driven you hence?
 I shan't say that the gift of all his treasure
 Ought to have damped your zeal in any measure;
 But if he is a traitor, as you declare,   35
 How could you condescend to be his heir?
TARTUFFE *(to the* officer*):*
 Sir, spare me all this clamor; it's growing shrill.
 Please carry out your orders, if you will.
OFFICER: Yes, I've delayed too long, Sir. Thank you kindly.
 You're just the proper person to remind me.   40
 Come, you are off to join the other boarders
 In the King's prison, according to his orders.
TARTUFFE: Who? I, Sir?
OFFICER: Yes.
TARTUFFE: To prison? This can't be true!
OFFICER: I owe an explanation, but not to you.

(To ORGON:*)*

 Sir, all is well; rest easy, and be grateful.   45
 We serve a Prince to whom all sham is hateful,
 A Prince who sees into our inmost hearts,
 And can't be fooled by any trickster's arts.
 His royal soul, though generous and human,
 Views all things with discernment and acumen;   50
 His sovereign reason is not lightly swayed,
 And all his judgments are discreetly weighed.
 He honors righteous men of every kind,
 And yet his zeal for virtue is not blind,
 Nor does his love of piety numb his wits   55
 And make him tolerant of hypocrites.
 'Twas hardly likely that this man could cozen
 A King who's foiled such liars by the dozen.
 With one keen glance, the King perceived the whole
 Perverseness and corruption of his soul,   60
 And thus high Heaven's justice was displayed:
 Betraying you, the rogue stood self-betrayed.
 The King soon recognized Tartuffe as one
 Notorious by another name, who'd done
 So many vicious crimes that one could fill   65
 Ten volumes with them, and be writing still.
 But to be brief: our sovereign was appalled
 By this man's treachery toward you, which he called

The last, worst villainy of a vile career,
And bade me follow the imposter here   70
To see how gross his impudence could be,
And force him to restore your property.
Your private papers, by the King's command,
I hereby seize and give into your hand.
The King, by royal order, invalidates   75
The deed which gave this rascal your estates,
And pardons, furthermore, your grave offense
In harboring an exile's documents.
By these decrees, our Prince rewards you for
Your loyal deeds in the late civil war,   80
And shows how heartfelt is his satisfaction
In recompensing any worthy action,
How much he prizes merit, and how he makes
More of men's virtues than of their mistakes.

DORINE: Heaven be praised!

MADAME PERNELLE: I breathe again, at last.   85

ELMIRE: We're safe.

MARIANE: I can't believe the danger's past.

ORGON (to TARTUFFE):
  Well, traitor, now you see . . .

CLÉANTE: Ah, Brother, please,
  Let's not descend to such indignities.
  Leave the poor wretch to his unhappy fate,
  And don't say anything to aggravate   90
  His present woes; but rather hope that he
  Will soon embrace an honest piety,
  And mend his ways, and by a true repentance
  Move our just King to moderate his sentence.
  Meanwhile, go kneel before your sovereign's throne   95
  And thank him for the mercies he has shown.

ORGON: Well said: let's go at once and, gladly kneeling,
  Express the gratitude which all are feeling.
  Then, when that first great duty has been done,
  We'll turn with pleasure to a second one,   100
  And give Valère, whose love has proven so true,
  The wedded happiness which is his due.

                                                        (1664)

QUESTIONS

1. Do you find Tartuffe an appealing or an appalling character? Is it possible to condemn his behavior while simultaneously admiring his shrewdness? What makes him
   engaging, even entertaining?

2. Tartuffe does not make his appearance until Act III, Scene I. What effect does this delay have? What do we know about him by the time he enters? How well does Tartuffe fulfill the expectations we have about him?
3. Describe briefly the central role of the following characters: Orgon, Elmire, Cléante, and Dorine. Who is the most complex character? Who is the most entertaining? Can any be seen as a spokesman for Molière himself?
4. What makes *Tartuffe* a satiric rather than a romantic comedy? What elements of romance exist in the play? How would you characterize its prevailing tone?
5. Examine any scene you find particularly effective as comedy. Discuss how this scene should be staged, considering such details as the location of the characters, their relative positions, their physical gestures and facial expressions, and their tones of voice.
6. *Tartuffe* has been criticized as a play that ridicules religion and piety. Agree or disagree with this assessment.

CHAPTER TWENTY-FIVE

The Modern Realistic Theater

Realism can be defined as the representation of everyday life in literature. Concerned with the average, the commonplace, the ordinary, realism employs theatrical conventions to create the illusion of everyday life. With realistic drama came the depiction of subjects close to the lives of middle-class people: work, marriage, and family life. From this standpoint, Arthur Miller's *Death of a Salesman* and Henrik Ibsen's *A Doll House* are more realistic than Shakespeare's *Othello*, which in turn, is more realistic than Sophocles' *Oedipus the King*. Though each of these plays possesses a true-to-life quality, each operates according to different theatrical conventions. Royal personages, gods, military heroes, and exalted language are absent from Miller's and Ibsen's plays, as modern dramatists turned to an approximation of the daily life of the lower and middle classes.

One means by which realistic drama creates the illusion of everyday life is through setting. Whereas settings consist primarily of painted backdrops in Molière's plays and are often established by dialogue in Shakespeare's plays, the settings of modern realistic plays are designed to look authentic. Moreover, setting in plays such as Ibsen's *A Doll House* often functions symbolically. In *Elements of Literature 3,* Robert Scholes has noted that the elaborately detailed setting of *A Doll House* symbolizes both "the impact of the Helmers' environment on their marriage" and the "very nature of their marriage"; it also embodies "the profound pressures placed on Helmer and Nora by the material and social conditions of their world."*

*Robert Scholes, *et al., Elements of Literature 3* (New York: Oxford University Press, 1982), p. 966.

Other conventions designed to create and sustain the illusion that the audience was watching a slice of domestic life include the following: the use of a three-walled room with an open fourth wall into which the audience peers to view and overhear the action; dialogue that approximates the idiom of everyday discourse, polished to be sure, but designed especially to sound like speech rather than poetry; plots that, though highly contrived, seem to turn on a series of causally related actions; subjects not from mythology or history, but from the concerns of ordinary life.

HENRIK IBSEN

[1828–1906]

Besides accommodating himself to the conventions of realism in *A Doll House,* Ibsen also made the play a *cause célèbre* by raising questions in it about the rights of women, a subject that was beginning to receive attention in the late nineteenth century. *A Doll House,* written in 1879, performed in London (1889) and Paris (1894), attracted attention wherever it played. Nonetheless, Ibsen insisted that the play was less about the rights of women than about human rights generally, less about the particular social conditions responsible for the position of women in nineteenth-century Norway than about the need for individuals of both sexes to treat each other with mutual respect.

HENRIK IBSEN

A Doll House

TRANSLATED BY ROLF FJELDE

CHARACTERS

TORVALD HELMER, *a lawyer*
NORA, *his wife*
DR. RANK
MRS. LINDE
NILS KROGSTAD, *a bank clerk*
THE HELMERS' THREE SMALL CHILDREN
ANNE-MARIE, *their nurse*
HELENE, *a maid*
A DELIVERY BOY

The action takes place in HELMER'S *residence.*

ACT I

A comfortable room, tastefully but not expensively furnished. A door to the right in the back wall leads to the entryway, another to the left leads to HELMER'S *study. Between these doors, a piano. Midway in the left-hand wall a door, and further back a window. Near the window a round table with an armchair and a small sofa. In the right-hand wall, toward the rear a door, and nearer the foreground a porcelain stove with two armchairs and a rocking chair beside it. Between the stove and the side door, a small table. Engravings on the walls. An etagére with china figures and other small art objects; a small bookcase with richly bound books; the floor carpeted; a fire burning in the stove. It is a winter day.*

A bell rings in the entryway; shortly after we hear the door being unlocked. NORA *comes into the room, humming happily to herself; she is wearing street clothes and carries an armload of packages, which she puts down on the table to the right. She has left the hall door open; and through it a* DELIVERY BOY *is seen, holding a Christmas tree and a basket which he gives to the* MAID *who let them in.*

NORA   Hide the tree well, Helene. The children mustn't get a glimpse of it till this evening, after it's trimmed. (*To the* DELIVERY BOY, *taking out her purse*) How much?

DELIVERY BOY   Fifty, ma'am.

NORA   There's a crown. No, keep the change. (*The* BOY *thanks her and leaves.* NORA *shuts the door. She laughs softly to herself while taking off her street things. Drawing a bag of macaroons from her pocket, she eats a couple, then steals over and listens at her husband's study door.*) Yes, he's home. (*Hums again as she moves to the table, right.*)

HELMER   (*from the study*) Is that my little lark twittering out there?

NORA   (*busy opening some packages*) Yes, it is.

HELMER   Is that my squirrel rummaging around?

NORA   Yes!

HELMER   When did my squirrel get in?

NORA   Just now. (*Putting the macaroon bag in her pocket and wiping her mouth*) Do come in, Torvald, and see what I've bought.

HELMER   Can't be disturbed. (*After a moment he opens the door and peers in, pen in hand.*) Bought, you say? All that there? Has the little spendthrift been out throwing money around again?

NORA   Oh, but Torvald, this year we really should let ourselves go a bit. It's the first Christmas we haven't had to economize.

HELMER   But you know we can't go squandering.

NORA   Oh yes, Torvald, we can squander a little now. Can't we? Just a tiny, wee bit. Now that you've got a big salary and are going to make piles and piles of money.

HELMER   Yes—starting New Year's. But then it's a full three months till the raise comes through.

NORA   Pooh! We can borrow that long.

HELMER   Nora! (*Goes over and playfully takes her by the ear*) Are your scatter-brains off again? What if today I borrowed a thousand crowns, and you squandered them over Christmas week, and then on New Year's Eve a roof tile fell on my head, and I lay there—

NORA   (*putting her hand on his mouth*) Oh! Don't say such things!

HELMER   Yes, but what if it happened—then what?

NORA   If anything so awful happened, then it just wouldn't matter if I had debts or not.

HELMER   Well, but the people I'd borrowed from?

NORA   Them? Who cares about them! They're strangers.

HELMER   Nora, Nora, how like a woman! No, but seriously, Nora, you know what I think about that. No debts! Never borrow! Something of freedom's lost—and something of beauty, too—from a home that's founded on borrowing and debt. We've made a brave stand up to now, the two of us; and we'll go right on like that the little while we have to.

NORA   (*going toward the stove*) Yes, whatever you say, Torvald.

HELMER   (*following her*) Now, now, the little lark's wings mustn't droop. Come on, don't be a sulky squirrel. (*Taking out his wallet*) Nora, guess what I have here.

NORA   (*turning quickly*) Money!

HELMER   There, see. (*Hands her some notes*) Good grief, I know how costs go up in a house at Christmastime.

NORA   Ten—twenty—thirty—forty. Oh, thank you. Torvald; I can manage no end on this.

HELMER   You really will have to.

NORA   Oh yes, I promise I will! But come here so I can show you everything I bought. And so cheap! Look, new clothes for Ivar here—and a sword. Here a horse and a trumpet for Bob. And a doll and a doll's bed here for Emmy; they're nothing much, but she'll tear them to bits in no time anyway. And here I have dress material and handkerchiefs for the maids. Old Anne-Marie really deserves something more.

HELMER   And what's in that package there?

NORA   (*with a cry*) Torvald, no! You can't see that till tonight!

HELMER   I see. But tell me now, you little prodigal, what have you thought of for yourself?

NORA   For myself? Oh, I don't want anything at all.

HELMER   Of course you do. Tell me just what—within reason—you'd most like to have.

NORA   I honestly don't know. Oh, listen, Torvald—

HELMER   Well?

NORA   (*fumbling at his coat buttons, without looking at him*) If you want to give me something, then maybe you could—you could—

HELMER   Come on, out with it.

NORA   (*hurriedly*) You could give me money, Torvald. No more than you think you can spare, then one of these days I'll buy something with it.

HELMER   But Nora—

NORA   Oh, please, Torvald darling, do that! I beg you, please. Then I could hang the bills in pretty gilt paper on the Christmas tree. Wouldn't that be fun?

HELMER   What are those little birds called that always fly through their fortunes?

NORA   Oh yes, spendthrifts; I know all that. But let's do as I say, Torvald; then I'll have time to decide what I really need most. That's very sensible, isn't it?

HELMER   (*smiling*) Yes, very—that is, if you actually hung onto the money I give you, and you actually used it to buy yourself something. But it goes for the house and for all sorts of foolish things, and then I only have to lay out some more.

NORA   Oh, but Torvald—

HELMER   Don't deny it, my dear little Nora. (*Putting his arm around her waist*) Spendthrifts are sweet, but they use up a frightful amount of money. It's incredible what it costs a man to feed such birds.

NORA   Oh, how can you say that! Really, I save everything I can.

HELMER   (*laughing*) Yes, that's the truth. Everything you can. But that's nothing at all.

NORA   (*humming, with a smile of quiet satisfaction*) Hm, if you only knew what expenses we larks and squirrels have, Torvald.

HELMER   You're an odd little one. Exactly the way your father was. You're never at a loss for scaring up money; but the moment you have it, it runs right out through your fingers; you never know what you've done with it. Well, one takes you as you are. It's deep in your blood. Yes, these things are hereditary, Nora.

NORA   Ah, I could wish I'd inherited many of Papa's qualities.

HELMER   And I couldn't wish you anything but just what you are, my sweet little lark. But wait; it seems to me you have a very—what should I call it?—a very suspicious look today—

NORA   I do?

HELMER   You certainly do. Look me straight in the eye.

NORA   (*looking at him*) Well?

HELMER   (*shaking an admonitory finger*) Surely my sweet tooth hasn't been running riot in town today, has she?

NORA   No. Why do you imagine that?

HELMER   My sweet tooth really didn't make a little detour through the confectioner's?

NORA   No, I assure you, Torvald—

HELMER   Hasn't nibbled some pastry?

NORA   No, not at all.

HELMER   Nor even munched a macaroon or two?

NORA   No, Torvald, I assure you, really—

HELMER   There, there now. Of course I'm only joking.

NORA   (*going to the table, right*) You know I could never think of going against you.

HELMER   No, I understand that; and you *have* given me your word. (*Going over to her.*) Well, you keep your little Christmas secrets to yourself, Nora darling. I expect they'll come to light this evening, when the tree is lit.

NORA Did you remember to ask Dr. Rank?

HELMER No. But there's no need for that; it's assumed he'll be dining with us. All the same, I'll ask him when he stops by here this morning. I've ordered some fine wine. Nora, you can't imagine how I'm looking forward to this evening.

NORA So am I. And what fun for the children, Torvald!

HELMER Ah, it's so gratifying to know that one's gotten a safe, secure job, and with a comfortable salary. It's a great satisfaction, isn't it?

NORA Oh, it's wonderful!

HELMER Remember last Christmas? Three whole weeks before, you shut yourself in every evening till long after midnight, making flowers for the Christmas tree, and all the other decorations to surprise us. Ugh, that was the dullest time I've ever lived through.

NORA It wasn't at all dull for me.

HELMER (*smiling*) But the outcome *was* pretty sorry, Nora.

NORA Oh, don't tease me with that again. How could I help it that the cat came in and tore everything to shreds.

HELMER No, poor thing, you certainly couldn't. You wanted so much to please us all, and that's what counts. But it's just as well that the hard times are past.

NORA Yes, it's really wonderful.

HELMER Now I don't have to sit here alone, boring myself, and you don't have to tire your precious eyes and your fair little delicate hands—

NORA (*clapping her hands*) No, is it really true, Torvald, I don't have to? Oh, how wonderfully lovely to hear! (*Taking his arm.*) Now I'll tell you just how I've thought we should plan things. Right after Christmas—(*The doorbell rings.*) Oh, the bell. (*Straightening the room up a bit.*) Somebody would have to come. What a bore!

HELMER I'm not at home to visitors, don't forget.

MAID (*from the hall doorway*) Ma'am, a lady to see you—

NORA All right, let her come in.

MAID (*to Helmer*) And the doctor's just come too.

HELMER Did he go right to my study?

MAID Yes, he did.

HELMER *goes into his room. The* MAID *shows in* MRS. LINDE, *dressed in traveling clothes, and shuts the door after her.*

MRS. LINDE (*in a dispirited and somewhat hesitant voice*) Hello, Nora.

NORA (*uncertain*) Hello—

MRS. LINDE You don't recognize me.

NORA No, I don't know—but wait, I think—(*Exclaiming.*) What! Kristine! Is it really you?

MRS. LINDE Yes, it's me.

NORA Kristine! To think I didn't recognize you. But then, how could I? (*More quietly.*) How you've changed, Kristine!

MRS. LINDE   Yes, no doubt I have. In nine—ten long years.

NORA   Is it so long since we met! Yes, it's all of that. Oh, these last eight years have been a happy time, believe me. And so now you've come in to town, too. Made the long trip in the winter. That took courage.

MRS. LINDE   I just got here by ship this morning.

NORA   To enjoy yourself over Christmas, of course. Oh, how lovely! Yes, enjoy ourselves, we'll do that. But take your coat off. You're not still cold? (*Helping her.*) There now, let's get cozy here by the stove. No, the easy chair there! I'll take the rocker here. (*Seizing her hands.*) Yes, now you have your old look again; it was only in that first moment. You're a bit more pale, Kristine—and maybe a bit thinner.

MRS. LINDE   And much, much older, Nora.

NORA   Yes, perhaps, a bit older; a tiny, tiny bit; not much at all. (*Stopping short; suddenly serious*) Oh, but thoughtless me, to sit here, chattering away. Sweet, good Kristine, can you forgive me?

MRS. LINDE   What do you mean, Nora?

NORA   (*softly*) Poor Kristine, you've become a widow.

MRS. LINDE   Yes, three years ago.

NORA   Oh, I knew it, of course; I read it in the papers. Oh Kristine, you must believe me; I often thought of writing you then, but I kept postponing it, and something always interfered.

MRS. LINDE   Nora dear, I understand completely.

NORA   No, it was awful of me, Kristine. You poor thing, how much you must have gone through. And he left you nothing?

MRS. LINDE   No.

NORA   And no children?

MRS. LINDE   No.

NORA   Nothing at all, then?

MRS. LINDE   Not even a sense of loss to feed on.

NORA   (*looking incredulously at her*) But Kristine, how could that be?

MRS. LINDE   (*smiling wearily and smoothing her hair*) Oh, sometimes it happens, Nora.

NORA   So completely alone. How terribly hard that must be for you. I have three lovely children. You can't see them now; they're out with the maid. But now you must tell me everything—

MRS. LINDE   No, no, no, tell me about yourself.

NORA   No, you begin. Today I don't want to be selfish. I want to think only of you today. But there *is* something I must tell you. Did you hear of the wonderful luck we had recently?

MRS. LINDE   No, what's that?

NORA   My husband's been made manager in the bank, just think!

MRS. LINDE   Your husband? How marvelous!

NORA   Isn't it? Being a lawyer is such an uncertain living, you know, especially if one won't touch any cases that aren't clean and decent. And of course Torvald would never do that, and I'm with him completely there. Oh, we're simply delighted, believe me! He'll join the bank right after New Year's and start getting a huge salary and lots of commissions. From now on we can live quite differently—jus as we want. Oh, Kristine, I feel so light and happy! Won't it be lovely to have stacks of money and not a care in the world?

MRS. LINDE   Well, anyway, it would be lovely to have enough for necessities.

NORA   No, not just for necessities, but stacks and stacks of money!

MRS. LINDE   (*smiling*) Nora, Nora, aren't you sensible yet? Back in school you were such a free spender.

NORA   (*with a quiet laugh*) Yes, that's what Torvald still says. (*Shaking her finger*) But "Nora, Nora" isn't as silly as you all think. Really, we've been in no position for me to go squandering. We've had to work, both of us.

MRS. LINDE   You too?

NORA   Yes, at odd jobs—needlework, crocheting, embroidery, and such— (*Casually*) and other things too. You remember that Torvald left the department when we were married? There was no chance of promotion in his office, and of course he needed to earn more money. But that first year he drove himself terribly. He took on all kinds of extra work that kept him going morning and night. It wore him down, and then he fell deathly ill. The doctors said it was essential for him to travel south.

MRS. LINDE   Yes, didn't you spend a whole year in Italy?

NORA   That's right. It wasn't easy to get away, you know. Ivar had just been born. But of course we had to go. Oh, that was a beautiful trip, and it saved Torvald's life. But it cost a frightful sum, Kristine.

MRS. LINDE   I can well imagine.

NORA   Four thousand, eight hundred crowns it cost. That's really a lot of money.

MRS. LINDE   But it's lucky you had it when you needed it.

NORA   Well, as it was, we got it from Papa.

MRS. LINDE   I see. It was just about the time your father died.

NORA   Yes, just about then. And, you know, I couldn't make the trip out to nurse him. I had to stay here, expecting Ivar any moment, and with my poor sick Torvald to care for. Dearest Papa, I never saw him again, Kristine. Oh, that was the worst time I've known in all my marriage.

MRS. LINDE   I know how you loved him. And then you went off to Italy?

NORA   Yes. We had the means now, and the doctors urged us. So we left a month after.

MRS. LINDE   And your husband came back completely cured?

NORA   Sound as a drum!

MRS. LINDE   But—the doctor?

NORA   Who?

MRS. LINDE   I thought the maid said he was a doctor, the man who came in with me.

NORA   Yes, that was Dr. Rank—but he's not making a sick call. He's our closest friend, and he stops by at least once a day. No, Torvald hasn't had a sick moment since, and the children are fit and strong, and I am, too. (*Jumping up and clapping her hands*) Oh, dear God, Kristine, what a lovely thing to live and be happy! But how disgusting of me—I'm talking of nothing but my own affairs. (*Sits on a stool close by* KRISTINE, *arms resting across her knees*) Oh, don't be angry with me! Tell me, is it really true that you weren't in love with your husband? Why did you marry him, then?

MRS. LINDE   My mother was still alive, but bedridden and helpless—and I had two younger brothers to look after. In all conscience, I didn't think I could turn him down.

NORA   No, you were right there. But was he rich at the time?

MRS. LINDE   He was very well off, I'd say. But the business was shaky, Nora. When he died, it all fell apart, and nothing was left.

NORA   And then—?

MRS. LINDE   Yes, so I had to scrape up a living with a little shop and a little teaching and whatever else I could find. The last three years have been like one endless workday without a rest for me. Now it's over, Nora. My poor mother doesn't need me, for she's passed on. Nor the boys, either; they're working now and can take care of themselves.

NORA   How free you must feel—

MRS. LINDE   No—only unspeakably empty. Nothing to live for now. (*Standing up anxiously*) That's why I couldn't take it any longer out in that desolate hole. Maybe here it'll be easier to find something to do and keep my mind occupied. If I could only be lucky enough to get a steady job, some office work—

NORA   Oh, but Kristine, that's so dreadfully tiring, and you already look so tired. It would be much better for you if you could go off to a bathing resort.

MRS. LINDE   (*going toward the window*) I have no father to give me travel money, Nora.

NORA   (*rising*) Oh, don't be angry with me.

MRS. LINDE   (*going to her*) Nora dear, don't you be angry with me. The worst of my kind of situation is all the bitterness that's stored away. No one to work for, and yet you're always having to snap up your opportunities. You have to live; and so you grow selfish. When you told me the happy change in your lot, do you know I was delighted less for your sakes than for mine?

NORA   How so? Oh, I see. You think maybe Torvald could do something for you.

MRS. LINDE   Yes, that's what I thought.

NORA   And he will, Kristine! Just leave it to me; I'll bring it up so delicately—find something attractive to humor him with. Oh, I'm so eager to help you.

MRS. LINDE   How very kind of you, Nora, to be so concerned over me—doubly kind, considering you really know so little of life's burdens yourself.

NORA   I—? I know so little—?

MRS. LINDE   (*smiling*) Well, my heavens—a little needlework and such—Nora, you're just a child.

NORA   (*tossing her head and pacing the floor*) You don't have to act so superior.

MRS. LINDE   Oh?

NORA   You're just like the others. You all think I'm incapable of anything serious—

MRS. LINDE   Come now—

NORA That I've never had to face the raw world.

MRS. LINDE Nora dear, you've just been telling me all your troubles.

NORA Hm! Trivia! (*Quietly*) I haven't told you the big thing.

MRS. LINDE Big thing? What do you mean?

NORA You look down on me so, Kristine, but you shouldn't. You're proud that you worked so long and hard for your mother.

MRS. LINDE I don't look down on a soul. But it is true; I'm proud—and happy, too—to think it was given to me to make my mother's last days almost free of care.

NORA And you're also proud thinking of what you've done for your brothers.

MRS. LINDE I feel I've a right to be.

NORA I agree. But listen to this, Kristine—I've also got something to be proud and happy for.

MRS. LINDE I don't doubt it. But whatever do you mean?

NORA Not so loud. What if Torvald heard! He mustn't, not for anything in the world. Nobody must know, Kristine. No one but you.

MRS. LINDE But what is it, then?

NORA Come here. (*Drawing her down beside her on the sofa*) It's true—I've also got something to be proud and happy for. I'm the one who saved Torvald's life.

MRS. LINDE Saved—? Saved how?

NORA I told you about the trip to Italy. Torvald never would have lived if he hadn't gone south—

MRS. LINDE Of course, your father gave you the means—

NORA (*smiling*) That's what Torvald and all the rest think, but—

MRS. LINDE But—?

NORA Papa didn't give us a pin. I was the one who raised the money.

MRS. LINDE You? The whole amount?

NORA Four thousand, eight hundred crowns. What do you say to that?

MRS. LINDE But Nora, how was it possible? Did you win the lottery?

NORA (*disdainfully*) The lottery? Pooh! No art to that.

MRS. LINDE But where did you get it from then?

NORA (*humming, with a mysterious smile*) Hmm, tra-la-la-la.

MRS. LINDE Because you couldn't have borrowed it.

NORA No? Why not?

MRS. LINDE A wife can't borrow without her husband's consent.

NORA (*tossing her head*) Oh, but a wife with a little business sense, a wife who knows how to manage—

MRS. LINDE Nora, I simply don't understand—

NORA You don't have to. Whoever said I *borrowed* the money? I could have gotten it other ways. (*Throwing herself back on the sofa*) I could have gotten it from some admirer or other. After all, a girl with my ravishing appeal—

MRS. LINDE You lunatic.

NORA I'll bet you're eaten up with curiosity, Kristine.

MRS. LINDE Now listen here, Nora—you haven't done something indiscreet?

NORA *(sitting up again)* Is it indiscreet to save your husband's life?

MRS. LINDE I think it's indiscreet that without his knowledge you—

NORA But that's the point: he mustn't know! My Lord, can't you understand? He mustn't ever know the close call he had. It was to *me* the doctors came to say his life was in danger—that nothing could save him but a stay in the south. Didn't I try strategy then! I began talking about how lovely it would be for me to travel abroad like other young wives; I begged and I cried; I told him please to remember my condition, to be kind and indulge me; and then I dropped a hint that he could easily take out a loan. But at that, Kristine, he nearly exploded. He said I was frivolous, and it was his duty as man of the house not to indulge me in whims and fancies—as I think he called them. Aha, I thought, now you'll just have to be saved—and that's when I saw my chance.

MRS. LINDE And your father never told Torvald the money wasn't from him?

NORA No, never. Papa died right about then. I'd considered bringing him into my secret and begging him never to tell. But he was too sick at the time—and then, sadly, it didn't matter.

MRS. LINDE And you've never confided in your husband since?

NORA For heaven's sake, no! Are you serious? He's so strict on that subject. Besides—Torvald, with all his masculine pride—how painfully humiliating for him if he ever found out he was in debt to me. That would just ruin our relationship. Our beautiful happy home would never be the same.

MRS. LINDE Won't you ever tell him?

NORA *(thoughtfully, half smiling)* Yes—maybe sometime, years from now, when I'm no longer so attractive. Don't laugh! I only mean when Torvald loves me less than now, when he stops enjoying my dancing and dressing up and reciting for him. Then it might be wise to have something in reserve— *(Breaking off)* How ridiculous! That'll never happen—Well, Kristine, what do you think of my big secret? I'm capable of something too, hm? You can imagine, of course, how this thing hangs over me. It really hasn't been easy meeting the payments on time. In the business world there's what they call quarterly interest and what they call amortization, and these are always so terribly hard to manage. I've had to skimp a little here and there, wherever I could, you know. I could hardly spare anything from my house allowance, because Torvald has to live well. I couldn't let the children go poorly dressed; whatever I got for them, I felt I had to use up completely—the darlings!

MRS. LINDE Poor Nora, so it had to come out of your own budget, then?

NORA Yes, of course. But I was the one most responsible, too. Every time Torvald gave me money for new clothes and such, I never used more than half; always bought the simplest, cheapest outfits. It was a godsend that everything looks so well on me that Torvald never noticed. But it did weigh me down at times, Kristine. It *is* such a joy to wear fine things. You understand.

MRS. LINDE Oh, of course.

NORA And then I found other ways of making money. Last winter I was lucky enough to get a lot of copying to do. I locked myself in and sat writing every evening till late in the night. Ah, I was tired so often, dead tired. But still it was wonderful fun, sitting and working like that, earning money. It was almost like being a man.

MRS. LINDE   But how much have you paid off this way so far?

NORA   That's hard to say, exactly. These accounts, you know, aren't easy to figure. I only know that I've paid out all I could scrape together. Time and again I haven't known where to turn. (*Smiling*) Then I'd sit here dreaming of a rich old gentleman who had fallen in love with me—

MRS. LINDE   What! Who is he?

NORA   Oh, really! And that he'd died, and when his will was opened, there in big letters it said, "All my fortune shall be paid over in cash, immediately, to that enchanting Mrs. Nora Helmer."

MRS. LINDE   But Nora dear—who *was* this gentleman?

NORA   Good grief, can't you understand? The old man never existed; that was only something I'd dream up time and again whenever I was at my wits' end for money. But it makes no difference now; the old fossil can go where he pleases for all I care; I don't need him or his will—because now I'm free. (*Jumping up*) Oh, how lovely to think of that, Kristine! Carefree! To know you're carefree, utterly carefree, to be able to romp and play with the children, and to keep up a beautiful, charming home—everything just the way Torvald likes it! And think, spring is coming, with big blue skies. Maybe we can travel a little then. Maybe I'll see the ocean again. Oh yes, it *is* so marvelous to live and be happy!

(*The front doorbell rings.*)

MRS. LINDE   (*rising*) There's the bell. It's probably best that I go.

NORA   No, stay. No one's expected. It must be for Torvald.

MAID   (*from the hall doorway*) Excuse me, ma'am—there's a gentleman here to see Mr. Helmer, but I didn't know—since the doctor's with him—

NORA   Who is the gentleman?

KROGSTAD   (*from the doorway*) It's me, Mrs. Helmer.

(MRS. LINDE *starts and turns away toward the window.*)

NORA   (*stepping toward him, tense, her voice a whisper*) You? What is it? Why do you want to speak to my husband?

KROGSTAD   Bank business—after a fashion. I have a small job in the investment bank, and I hear now your husband is going to be our chief—

NORA   In other words, it's—

KROGSTAD   Just dry business, Mrs. Helmer. Nothing but that.

NORA   Yes, then please be good enough to step into the study. (*She nods indifferently, as she sees him out by the hall door, then returns and begins stirring up the stove.*)

MRS. LINDE   Nora—who was that man?

NORA   That was a Mr. Krogstad—a lawyer.

MRS. LINDE   Then it really was him.

NORA   Do you know that person?

MRS. LINDE   I did once—many years ago. For a time he was a law clerk in our town.

NORA   Yes, he's been that.

MRS. LINDE   How he's changed.

NORA   I understand he had a very unhappy marriage.

MRS. LINDE   He's a widower now.

NORA   With a number of children. There now, it's burning. (*She closes the stove door and moves the rocker a bit to one side.*)

MRS. LINDE   They say he has a hand in all kinds of business.

NORA   Oh? That may be true; I wouldn't know. But let's not think about business. It's so dull.

(DR. RANK *enters from* HELMER'S *study.*)

RANK   (*still in the doorway*) No, no, really—I don't want to intrude, I'd just as soon talk a little while with your wife. (*Shuts the door, then notices* MRS. LINDE) Oh, beg pardon, I'm intruding here too.

NORA   No, not at all. (*Introducing him*) Dr. Rank, Mrs. Linde.

RANK   Well now, that's a name much heard in this house. I believe I passed the lady on the stairs as I came.

MRS. LINDE   Yes, I take the stairs very slowly. They're rather hard on me.

RANK   Uh-hm, some touch of internal weakness?

MRS. LINDE   More overexertion, I'd say.

RANK   Nothing else? Then you're probably here in town to rest up in a round of parties?

MRS. LINDE   I'm here to look for work.

RANK   Is that the best cure for overexertion?

MRS. LINDE   One has to live, Doctor.

RANK   Yes, there's a common prejudice to that effect.

NORA   Oh, come on, Dr. Rank—you really do want to live yourself.

RANK   Yes, I really do. Wretched as I am, I'll gladly prolong my torment indefinitely. All my patients feel like that. And it's quite the same, too, with the morally sick. Right at this moment there's one of those moral invalids in there with Helmer—

MRS. LINDE   (*softly*) Ah!

NORA   Who do you mean?

RANK   Oh, it's a lawyer, Krogstad, a type you wouldn't know. His character is rotten to the root—but even he began chattering all-importantly about how he had to *live.*

NORA   Oh? What did he want to talk to Torvald about?

RANK   I really don't know. I only heard something about the bank.

NORA   I didn't know that Krog—that this man Krogstad had anything to do with the bank.

RANK   Yes, he's gotten some kind of berth down there. (*To* MRS. LINDE) I don't know if you also have, in your neck of the woods, a type of person who scuttles about breathlessly, sniffing out hints of moral corruption, and then maneuvers his victim into some sort of key position where he can keep an eye on him. It's the healthy these days that are out in the cold.

MRS. LINDE   All the same, it's the sick who most need to be taken in.

RANK   (*with a shrug*) Yes, there we have it. That's the concept that's turning society into a sanatorium.

(NORA, *lost in her thoughts, breaks out into quiet laughter and claps her hands.*)

RANK   Why do you laugh at that? Do you have any real idea of what society is?

NORA   What do I care about dreary old society? I was laughing at something quite different—something terribly funny. Tell me, Doctor—is everyone who works in the bank dependent now on Torvald?

RANK   Is that what you find so terribly funny?

NORA   (*smiling and humming*) Never mind, never mind! (*Pacing the floor*) Yes, that's really immensely amusing: that we—that Torvald has so much power now over all those people. (*Taking the bag out of her pocket*) Dr. Rank, a little macaroon on that?

RANK   See here, macaroons! I thought they were contraband here.

NORA   Yes, but these are some that Kristine gave me.

MRS. LINDE   What? I—?

NORA   Now, now, don't be afraid. You couldn't possibly know that Torvald had forbidden them. You see, he's worried they'll ruin my teeth. But hmp! Just this once! Isn't that so, Dr. Rank? Help yourself! (*Puts a macaroon in his mouth*) And you too, Kristine. And I'll also have one, only a little one—or two, at the most. (*Walking about again*) Now I'm really tremendously happy. Now there's just one last thing in the world that I have an enormous desire to do.

RANK   Well! And what's that?

NORA   It's something I have such a consuming desire to say so Torvald could hear.

RANK   And why can't you say it?

NORA   I don't dare. It's quite shocking.

MRS. LINDE   Shocking?

RANK   Well, then it isn't advisable. But in front of us you certainly can. What do you have such a desire to say so Torvald could hear?

NORA   I have such a huge desire to say—to hell and be damned!

RANK   Are you crazy?

MRS. LINDE   My goodness, Nora!

RANK   Go on, say it. Here he is.

NORA   (*hiding the macaroon bag*) Shh, shh, shh!

(HELMER *comes in from his study, hat in hand, overcoat over his arm.*)

NORA   (*going toward him*) Well, Torvald dear, are you through with him?

HELMER   Yes, he just left.

NORA   Let me introduce you—this is Kristine, who's arrived here in town.

HELMER   Kristine—? I'm sorry, but I don't know—

NORA   Mrs. Linde, Torvald dear. Mrs. Kristine Linde.

HELMER   Of course. A childhood friend of my wife's, no doubt?

MRS. LINDE   Yes, we knew each other in those days.

NORA   And just think, she made the long trip down here in order to talk with you.

HELMER   What's this?

MRS. LINDE   Well, not exactly—

NORA   You see, Kristine is remarkably clever in office work, and so she's terribly eager to come under a capable man's supervision and add more to what she already knows—

HELMER   Very wise, Mrs. Linde.

NORA   And then when she heard that you'd become a bank manager—the story was wired out to the papers—then she came in as fast as she could and—Really, Torvald, for my sake you can do a little something for Kristine, can't you?

HELMER   Yes, it's not at all impossible. Mrs. Linde, I suppose you're a widow?

MRS. LINDE   Yes.

HELMER   Any experience in office work?

MRS. LINDE   Yes, a good deal.

HELMER   Well, it's quite likely that I can make an opening for you—

NORA   (*clapping her hands*) You see, you see!

HELMER   You've come at a lucky moment, Mrs. Linde.

MRS. LINDE   Oh, how can I thank you?

HELMER   Not necessary. (*Putting his overcoat on*) But today you'll have to excuse me—

RANK   Wait, I'll go with you. (*He fetches his coat from the hall and warms it at the stove.*)

NORA   Don't stay out long, dear.

HELMER   An hour; no more.

NORA   Are you going too, Kristine?

MRS. LINDE   (*putting on her winter garments*) Yes, I have to see about a room now.

HELMER   Then perhaps we can all walk together.

NORA   (*helping her*) What a shame we're so cramped here, but it's quite impossible for us to—

MRS. LINDE   Oh, don't even think of it! Good-bye, Nora dear, and thanks for everything.

NORA   Good-bye for now. Of course you'll be back again this evening. And you too, Dr. Rank. What? If you're well enough? Oh, you've got to be! Wrap up tight now.

(*In a ripple of small talk the company moves out into the hall; children's voices are heard outside on the steps.*)

NORA   There they are! There they are! (*She runs to open the door. The children come in with their nurse,* ANNE-MARIE.) Come in, come in! (*Bends down and kisses them*) Oh, you darlings—! Look at them, Kristine. Aren't they lovely!

RANK   No loitering in the draft here.

HELMER   Come, Mrs. Linde—this place is unbearable now for anyone but mothers.

(DR. RANK, HELMER, *and* MRS. LINDE *go down the stairs.* ANNE-MARIE *goes into the living room with the children.* NORA *follows, after closing the hall door.*)

NORA   How fresh and strong you look. Oh, such red cheeks you have! Like apples and roses. (*The children interrupt her throughout the following.*) And it was so much fun? That's wonderful. Really? You pulled both Emmy and Bob on the sled? Imagine, all together! Yes, you're a clever boy, Ivar. Oh, let me hold her a bit, Anne-Marie. My sweet little doll baby! (*Takes the smallest from the nurse and dances with her*) Yes, yes, Mama will dance with Bob as well. What? Did you throw snowballs? Oh, if I'd only been there! No, don't bother, Anne-Marie—I'll undress them myself. Oh yes, let me. It's such fun. Go in and rest; you look half frozen. There's hot coffee waiting for you on the stove. (*The nurse goes into the room to the left. Nora takes the children's winter things off, throwing them about, while the children talk to her all at once.*) Is that so? A big dog chased you? But it didn't bite? No, dogs never bite little, lovely doll babies. Don't peek in the packages, Ivar! What is it? Yes, wouldn't you like to know. No, no, it's an ugly something. Well? Shall we play? What shall we play? Hide-and-seek? Yes, let's play hide-and-seek. Bob must hide first. I must? Yes, let me hide first. (*Laughing and shouting, she and the children play in and out of the living room and the adjoining room to the right. At last* NORA *hides under the table. The children come storming in, search, but cannot find her, then hear her muffled laughter, dash over to the table, lift the cloth and find her. Wild shouting. She creeps forward as if to scare them. More shouts. Meanwhile, a knock at the hall door; no one has noticed it. Now the door half opens, and* KROGSTAD *appears. He waits a moment; the game goes on.*)

KROGSTAD   Beg pardon, Mrs. Helmer—

NORA   (*with a strangled cry, turning and scrambling to her knees*) Oh! what do you want?

KROGSTAD   Excuse me. The outer door was ajar; it must be someone forgot to shut it—

NORA   (*rising*) My husband isn't home, Mr. Krogstad.

KROGSTAD   I know that.

NORA   Yes—then what do you want here?

KROGSTAD   A word with you.

NORA   With—? (*To the children, quietly*) Go in to Anne-Marie. What? No, the strange man won't hurt Mama. When he's gone, we'll play some more. (*She leads the children into the room to the left and shuts the door after them. Then, tense and nervous*) You want to speak to me?

KROGSTAD   Yes, I want to.

NORA   Today? But it's not yet the first of the month—

KROGSTAD   No, it's Christmas Eve. It's going to be up to you how merry a Christmas you have.

NORA   What is it you want? Today I absolutely can't—

KROGSTAD   We won't talk about that till later. This is something else. You do have a moment to spare, I suppose?

NORA   Oh yes, of course—I do, except—

KROGSTAD   Good. I was sitting over at Olsen's Restaurant when I saw your husband go down the street—

NORA   Yes?

KROGSTAD   With a lady.

NORA   Yes. So?

KROGSTAD   If you'll pardon my asking: wasn't that lady a Mrs. Linde?

NORA   Yes.

KROGSTAD   Just now come into town?

NORA   Yes, today.

KROGSTAD   She's a good friend of yours?

NORA   Yes, she is. But I don't see——

KROGSTAD   I also knew her once.

NORA   I'm aware of that.

KROGSTAD   Oh? You know all about it. I thought so. Well, then let me ask you short and sweet: is Mrs. Linde getting a job in the bank?

NORA   What makes you think you can cross-examine me, Mr. Krogstad—you, one of my husband's employees? But since you ask, you might as well know—yes, Mrs. Linde's going to be taken on at the bank. And I'm the one who spoke for her, Mr. Krogstad. Now you know.

KROGSTAD   So I guessed right.

NORA   (*pacing up and down*) Oh, one does have a tiny bit of influence, I should hope. Just because I am a woman, don't think it means that—When one has a subordinate position, Mr. Krogstad, one really ought to be careful about pushing somebody who—hm—

KROGSTAD   Who has influence?

NORA   That's right.

KROGSTAD   (*in a different tone*) Mrs. Helmer, would you be good enough to use your influence on my behalf?

NORA   What? What do you mean?

KROGSTAD   Would you please make sure that I keep my subordinate position in the bank?

NORA   What does that mean? Who's thinking of taking away your position?

KROGSTAD   Oh, don't play the innocent with me. I'm quite aware that your friend would hardly relish the chance of running into me again; and I'm also aware now whom I can thank for being turned out.

NORA   But I promise you——

KROGSTAD   Yes, yes, yes, to the point: there's still time, and I'm advising you to use your influence to prevent it.

NORA   But Mr. Krogstad, I have absolutely no influence.

KROGSTAD   You haven't? I thought you were just saying——

NORA   You shouldn't take me so literally. I! How can you believe that I have any such influence over my husband?

KROGSTAD   Oh, I've known your husband from our student days. I don't think the great bank manager's more steadfast than any other married man.

NORA   You speak insolently about my husband, and I'll show you the door.

KROGSTAD   The lady has spirit.

NORA   I'm not afraid of you any longer. After New Year's, I'll soon be done with the whole business.

KROGSTAD   (*restraining himself*) Now listen to me, Mrs. Helmer. If necessary, I'll fight for my little job in the bank as if it were life itself.

NORA   Yes, so it seems.

KROGSTAD   It's not just a matter of income; that's the least of it. It's something else—All right, out with it! Look, this is the thing. You know, just like all the others, of course, that once, a good many years ago, I did something rather rash.

NORA   I've heard rumors to that effect.

KROGSTAD   The case never got into court; but all the same, every door was closed in my face from then on. So I took up those various activities you know about. I had to grab hold somewhere; and I dare say I haven't been among the worst. But now I want to drop all that. My boys are growing up. For their sakes, I'll have to win back as much respect as possible here in town. That job in the bank was like the first rung in my ladder. And now your husband wants to kick me right back down in the mud again.

NORA   But for heaven's sake, Mr. Krogstad, it's simply not in my power to help you.

KROGSTAD   That's because you haven't the will to—but I have the means to make you.

NORA   You certainly won't tell my husband that I owe you money?

KROGSTAD   Hm—what if I told him that?

NORA   That would be shameful of you. (*Nearly in tears*) This secret—my joy and my pride—that he should learn it in such a crude and disgusting way— learn it from you. You'd expose me to the most horrible unpleasantness—

KROGSTAD   Only unpleasantness?

NORA   (*vehemently*) But go on and try. It'll turn out the worst for you, because then my husband will really see what a crook you are, and then you'll *never* be able to hold your job.

KROGSTAD   I asked if it was just domestic unpleasantness you were afraid of?

NORA   If my husband finds out, then of course he'll pay what I owe at once, and then we'd be through with you for good.

KROGSTAD   (*a step closer*) Listen, Mrs. Helmer—you've either got a very bad memory, or else no head at all for business. I'd better put you a little more in touch with the facts.

NORA   What do you mean?

KROGSTAD   When your husband was sick, you came to me for a loan of four thousand, eight hundred crowns.

NORA   Where else could I go?

KROGSTAD   I promised to get you that sum—

NORA   And you got it.

KROGSTAD   I promised to get you that sum, on certain conditions. You were so involved in your husband's illness, and so eager to finance your trip, that I guess you didn't think out all the details. It might just be a good idea to remind you. I promised you the money on the strength of a note I drew up.

NORA   Yes, and that I signed.

KROGSTAD   Right. But at the bottom I added some lines for your father to guarantee the loan. He was supposed to sign down there.

NORA   Supposed to? He did sign.

KROGSTAD   I left the date blank. In other words, your father would have dated his signature himself. Do you remember that?

NORA   Yes, I think—

KROGSTAD   Then I gave you the note for you to mail to your father. Isn't that so?

NORA   Yes.

KROGSTAD   And naturally you sent it at once—because only some five, six days later you brought me the note, properly signed. And with that, the money was yours.

NORA   Well, then; I've made my payments regularly, haven't I?

KROGSTAD   More or less. But—getting back to the point—those were hard times for you then, Mrs. Helmer.

NORA   Yes, they were.

KROGSTAD   Your father was very ill, I believe.

NORA   He was near the end.

KROGSTAD   He died soon after?

NORA   Yes.

KROGSTAD   Tell me, Mrs. Helmer, do you happen to recall the date of your father's death? The day of the month, I mean.

NORA   Papa died the twenty-ninth of September.

KROGSTAD   That's quite correct; I've already looked into that. And now we come to a curious thing—*(Taking out a paper)* which I simply cannot comprehend.

NORA   Curious thing? I don't know—

KROGSTAD   This is the curious thing: that your father co-signed the note for your loan three days after his death.

NORA   How—? I don't understand.

KROGSTAD   Your father died the twenty-ninth of September. But look. Here your father dated his signature October second. Isn't that curious, Mrs. Helmer? (NORA *is silent.*) Can you explain it to me? (NORA *remains silent.*) It's also remarkable that the words "October second" and the year aren't written in your father's hand, but rather in one that I think I know. Well, it's easy to understand. Your father forgot perhaps to date his signature, and then someone or other added it, a bit sloppily, before anyone knew of his death. There's nothing wrong in that. It all comes down to the signature. And there's no question about *that,* Mrs. Helmer. It really *was* your father who signed his own name here, wasn't it?

NORA   *(after a short silence, throwing her head back and looking squarely at him)* No, it wasn't. I signed Papa's name.

KROGSTAD   Wait, now—are you fully aware that this is a dangerous confession?

NORA   Why? You'll soon get your money.

KROGSTAD   Let me ask you a question—why didn't you send the paper to your father?

NORA   That was impossible. Papa was so sick. If I'd asked him for his signature, I also would have had to tell him what the money was for. But I couldn't tell him, sick as he was, that my husband's life was in danger. That was just impossible.

KROGSTAD   Then it would have been better if you'd given up the trip abroad.

NORA   I couldn't possibly. The trip was to save my husband's life. I couldn't give that up.

KROGSTAD   But didn't you ever consider that this was a fraud against me?

NORA   I couldn't let myself be bothered by that. You weren't any concern of mine. I couldn't stand you, with all those cold complications you made, even though you knew how badly off my husband was.

KROGSTAD   Mrs. Helmer, obviously you haven't the vaguest idea of what you've involved yourself in. But I can tell you this: it was nothing more and nothing worse than I once did—and it wrecked my whole reputation.

NORA   You? Do you expect me to believe that you ever acted bravely to save your wife's life?

KROGSTAD   Laws don't inquire into motives.

NORA   Then they must be very poor laws.

KROGSTAD   Poor or not—if I introduce this paper in court, you'll be judged according to law.

NORA   This I refuse to believe. A daughter hasn't a right to protect her dying father from anxiety and care? A wife hasn't a right to save her husband's life? I don't know much about laws, but I'm sure that somewhere in the books these things are allowed. And you don't know anything about it—you who practice the law? You must be an awful lawyer, Mr. Krogstad.

KROGSTAD   Could be. But business—the kind of business we two are mixed up in—don't you think I know about that? All right. Do what you want now. But I'm telling you *this:* if I get shoved down a second time, you're going to keep me company.   (*He bows and goes out through the hall.*)

NORA   (*pensive for a moment, then tossing her head*) Oh, really! Trying to frighten me! I'm not so silly as all that. (*Begins gathering up the children's clothes, but soon stops*) But   ? No, but that's impossible! I did it out of love.

THE CHILDREN   (*in the doorway, left*) Mama, that strange man's gone out the door.

NORA   Yes, yes, I know it. But don't tell anyone about the strange man. Do you hear. Not even Papa!

THE CHILDREN   No, Mama. But now will you play again?

NORA   No, not now.

THE CHILDREN   Oh, but Mama, you promised.

NORA   Yes, but I can't now. Go inside; I have too much to do. Go in, go in, my sweet darlings. (*She herds them gently back in the room and shuts the door after them. Settling on the sofa, she takes up a piece of embroidery and makes some stitches, but soon stops abruptly.*) No! (*Throws the work aside, rises, goes to the hall door and calls out*) Helene! Let me have the tree in here. (*Goes to the table, left, opens the table drawer, and stops again*) No, but that's utterly impossible!

MAID   (*with the Christmas tree*) Where should I put it, Ma'am?

NORA   There. The middle of the floor.

MAID   Should I bring anything else?

NORA   No, thanks. I have what I need.

(*The* MAID, *who has set the tree down, goes out.*)

NORA   (*absorbed in trimming the tree*) Candles here—and flowers here. That terrible creature! Talk, talk, talk! There's nothing to it at all. The tree's going to be lovely. I'll do anything to please you, Torvald. I'll sing for you, dance for you—

(HELMER *comes in from the hall, with a sheaf of papers under his arm.*)

NORA   Oh! You're back so soon?

HELMER   Yes. Has anyone been here?

NORA   Here? No.

HELMER   That's odd. I saw Krogstad leaving the front door.

NORA   So? Oh yes, that's true. Krogstad was here a moment.

HELMER   Nora, I can see by your face that he's been here, begging you to put in a good word for him.

NORA   Yes.

HELMER   And it was supposed to seem like your own idea? You were to hide it from me that he'd been here. He asked you that, too, didn't he?

NORA   Yes, Torvald, but—

HELMER   Nora, Nora, and you could fall for that? Talk with that sort of person and promise him anything? And then in the bargain, tell me an untruth.

NORA   An untruth—?

HELMER   Didn't you say that no one had been here? (*Wagging his finger*) My little songbird must never do that again. A songbird needs a clean beak to warble with. No false notes. (*Putting his arm about her waist*) That's the way it should be, isn't it? Yes, I'm sure of it. (*Releasing her*) And so, enough of that. (*Sitting by the stove*) Ah, how snug and cozy it is here. (*Leafing among his papers*)

NORA   (*busy with the tree, after a short pause*) Torvald!

HELMER   Yes.

NORA   I'm so much looking forward to the Stenborg's costume party, day after tomorrow.

HELMER   And I can't wait to see what you'll surprise me with.

NORA   Oh, that stupid business.

HELMER   What?

NORA   I can't find anything that's right. Everything seems so ridiculous, so inane.

HELMER   So my little Nora's come to *that* recognition?

NORA   (*going behind his chair, her arms resting on its back*) Are you very busy, Torvald?

HELMER   Oh—

NORA   What papers are those?

HELMER   Bank matters.

NORA   Already?

HELMER   I've gotten full authority from the retiring management to make all necessary changes in personnel and procedure. I'll need Christmas week for that. I want to have everything in order by New Year's.

NORA   So that was the reason this poor Krogstad—

HELMER   Hm.

NORA   (*still leaning on the chair and slowly stroking the nape of his neck*) If you weren't so very busy, I would have asked you an enormous favor, Torvald.

HELMER   Let's hear. What is it?

NORA   You know, there isn't anyone who has your good taste—and I want so much to look well at the costume party. Torvald, couldn't you take over and decide what I should be and plan my costume?

HELMER   Ah, is my stubborn little creature calling for a lifeguard?

NORA   Yes, Torvald, I can't get anywhere without your help.

HELMER   All right—I'll think it over. We'll hit on something.

NORA   Oh, how sweet of you. (*Goes to the tree again. Pause.*) Aren't the red flowers pretty—? But tell me, was it really such a crime that this Krogstad committed?

HELMER   Forgery. Do you have any idea what that means?

NORA   Couldn't he have done it out of need?

HELMER   Yes, or thoughtlessness, like so many others. I'm not so heartless that I'd condemn a man categorically for just one mistake.

NORA   No, of course not, Torvald!

HELMER   Plenty of men have redeemed themselves by openly confessing their crimes and taking their punishments.

NORA   Punishment—?

HELMER   But now Krogstad didn't go that way. He got himself out by sharp practices, and that's the real cause of his moral breakdown.

NORA   Do you really think that would—?

HELMER   Just imagine how a man with that sort of guilt in him has to lie and cheat and deceive on all sides, has to wear a mask even with the nearest and dearest he has, even with his own wife and children. And with the children, Nora—that's where it's most horrible.

NORA   Why?

HELMER   Because that kind of atmosphere of lies infects the whole life of a home. Every breath the children take in is filled with the terms of something degenerate.

NORA   (*coming closer behind him*) Are you sure of that?

HELMER   Oh, I've seen it often enough as a lawyer. Almost everyone who goes bad early in life has a mother who's a chronic liar.

NORA   Why just—the mother?

HELMER   It's usually the mother's influence that's dominant, but the father's works in the same way, of course. Every lawyer is quite familiar with it. And still this Krogstad's been going home year in, year out, poisoning his own children with lies and pretense; that's why I call him morally lost. (*Reaching his hands out toward her*) So my sweet little Nora must promise me never to plead his cause. Your hand on it. Come, come, what's this? Give me your hand. There, now. All settled. I can tell you it'd be impossible for me to work alongside of him. I literally feel physically revolted when I'm anywhere near such a person.

NORA   (*withdraws her hand and goes to the other side of the Christmas tree*) How hot it is here! And I've got so much to do.

HELMER   (*getting up and gathering his papers*) Yes, and I have to think about getting some of these read through before dinner. I'll think about your costume, too. And something to hang on the tree in gilt paper, I may even see about that. (*Putting his hand on her head*) Oh you, my darling little songbird.

(*He goes into his study and closes the door after him.*)

NORA   (*softly, after a silence*) Oh, really! it isn't so. It's impossible. It must be impossible.

ANNE-MARIE   (*in the doorway, left*) The children are begging so hard to come in to Mama.

NORA   No, no, no, don't let them in to me! You stay with them, Anne-Marie.

ANNE-MARIE   Of course, Ma'am. (*Closes the door*)

NORA   (*pale with terror*) Hurt my children—! Poison my home? (*A moment's pause; then she tosses her head.*) That's not true. Never. Never in all the world.

ACT II

Same room. Beside the piano the Christmas tree now stands stripped of ornament, burned-down candle stubs on its ragged branches. NORA'S *street clothes lie on the sofa.* NORA, *alone in the room, moves restlessly about; at last she stops at the sofa and picks up her coat.*

NORA   (*dropping the coat again*) Someone's coming! (*Goes toward the door, listens*) No—there's no one. Of course—nobody's coming today, Christmas Day—or tomorrow, either. But maybe—(*Opens the door and looks out*) No, nothing in the mailbox. Quite empty. (*Coming forward*) What nonsense! He won't do anything serious. Nothing terrible could happen. It's impossible. Why, I have three small children.

(ANNE-MARIE, *with a large carton, comes in from the room to the left.*)

ANNE-MARIE   Well, at last I found the box with the masquerade clothes.

NORA   Thanks. Put it on the table.

ANNE-MARIE   (*does so*) But they're all pretty much of a mess.

NORA   Ahh! I'd love to rip them in a million pieces!

ANNE-MARIE   Oh, mercy, they can be fixed right up. Just a little patience.

NORA   Yes, I'll go get Mrs. Linde to help me.

ANNE-MARIE   Out again now? In this nasty weather? Miss Nora will catch cold—get sick.

NORA   Oh, worse things could happen—How are the children?

ANNE-MARIE   The poor mites are playing with their Christmas presents, but—

NORA   Do they ask for me much?

ANNE-MARIE   They're so used to having Mama around, you know.

NORA   Yes, but Anne-Marie, I *can't* be together with them as much as I was.

ANNE-MARIE   Well, small children get used to anything.

NORA   You think so? Do you think they'd forget their mother if she was gone for good?

ANNE-MARIE   Oh, mercy—gone for good!

NORA   Wait, tell me, Anne-Marie—I've wondered so often—how could you ever have the heart to give your child over to strangers?

ANNE-MARIE   But I had to, you know, to become little Nora's nurse.

NORA   Yes, but how could you *do* it?

ANNE-MARIE   When I could get such a good place? A girl who's poor and who's gotten in trouble is glad enough for that. Because that slippery fish, he didn't do a thing for me, you know.

NORA   But your daughter's surely forgotten you.

ANNE-MARIE   Oh, she certainly has not. She's written to me, both when she was confirmed and when she was married.

NORA   (*clasping her about the neck*) You old Anne-Marie, you were a good mother for me when I was little.

ANNE-MARIE   Poor little Nora, with no other mother but me.

NORA   And if the babies didn't have one, then I know that you'd—What silly talk! (*Opening the carton*) Go in to them. Now I'll have to—Tomorrow you can see how lovely I'll look.

ANNE-MARIE   Oh, there won't be anyone at the party as lovely as Miss Nora.
(*She goes off into the room, left.*)

NORA   (*begins unpacking the box, but soon throws it aside*) Oh, if I dared to go out. If only nobody would come. If only nothing would happen here while I'm out. What craziness—nobody's coming. Just don't think. This muff—needs a brushing. Beautiful gloves, beautiful gloves. Let it go. Let it go! One, two, three, four, five, six—(*With a cry*) Oh, there they are! (*Poises to move toward the door, but remains irresolutely standing.* MRS. LINDE *enters from the hall, where she has removed her street clothes.*)

NORA   Oh, it's you, Kristine. There's no one else out there? How good that you've come.

MRS. LINDE   I hear you were up asking for me.

NORA   Yes, I just stopped by. There's something you really can help me with. Let's get settled on the sofa. Look, there's going to be a costume party tomorrow evening at the Stenborgs' right above us, and now Torvald wants me to go as a Neapolitan peasant girl and dance the tarantella that I learned in Capri.

MRS. LINDE   Really, you are giving a whole performance?

NORA   Torvald says yes, I should. See, here's the dress. Torvald had it made for me down there; but now it's all so tattered that I just don't know—

MRS. LINDE   Oh, we'll fix that up in no time. It's nothing more than the trimmings—they're a bit loose here and there. Needle and thread? Good, now we have what we need.

NORA   Oh, how sweet of you!

MRS. LINDE   (*sewing*) So you'll be in disguise tomorrow, Nora. You know what? I'll stop by then for a moment and have a look at you all dressed up. But listen, I've absolutely forgotten to thank you for that pleasant evening yesterday.

NORA   (*getting up and walking about*) I don't think it was as pleasant as usual yesterday. You should have come to town a bit sooner, Kristine—Yes, Torvald really knows how to give a home elegance and charm.

MRS. LINDE   And you do, too, if you ask me. You're not your father's daughter for nothing. But tell me, is Dr. Rank always so down in the mouth as yesterday?

NORA   No, that was quite an exception. But he goes around critically ill all the time—tuberculosis of the spine, poor man. You know, his father was a disgusting thing who kept mistresses and so on—and that's why the son's been sickly from birth.

MRS. LINDE   (*lets her sewing fall to her lap*) But my dearest Nora, how do you know about such things?

NORA   (*walking more jauntily*) Hmp! When you've had three children, then you've had a few visits from—women who know something of medicine, and they tell you this and that.

MRS. LINDE   (*resumes sewing; a short pause*) Does Dr. Rank come here every day?

NORA   Every blessed day. He's Torvald's best friend from childhood, and *my* good friend, too. Dr. Rank almost belongs to this house.

MRS. LINDE   But tell me—is he quite sincere? I mean, doesn't he rather enjoy flattering people?

NORA   Just the opposite. Why do you think that?

MRS. LINDE   When you introduced us yesterday, he was proclaiming that he'd often heard my name in this house; but later I noticed that your husband hadn't the slightest idea who I really was. So how could Dr. Rank—?

NORA   But it's all true, Kristine. You see, Torvald loves me beyond words, and, as he puts it, he'd like to keep me all to himself. For a long time he'd almost be jealous if I even mentioned any of my old friends back home. So of course I dropped that. But with Dr. Rank I talk a lot about such things, because he likes hearing about them.

MRS. LINDE   Now listen, Nora; in many ways you're still like a child. I'm a good deal older than you, with a little more experience. I'll tell you something; you ought to put an end to all this with Dr. Rank.

NORA   What should I put an end to?

MRS. LINDE   Both parts of it, I think. Yesterday you said something about a rich admirer who'd provide you with money—

NORA   Yes, one who doesn't exist—worse luck. So?

MRS. LINDE   Is Dr. Rank well off?

NORA   Yes, he is.

MRS. LINDE   With no dependents?

NORA   No, no one. But—

MRS. LINDE   And he's over here every day?

NORA   Yes, I told you that.

MRS. LINDE   How can a man of such refinement be so grasping?

NORA   I don't follow you at all.

MRS. LINDE   Now don't try to hide it, Nora. You think I can't guess who loaned you the forty-eight hundred crowns?

NORA   Are you out of your mind? How could you think of such a thing! A friend of ours, who comes here every single day. What an intolerable situation that would have been!

MRS. LINDE   Then it really wasn't him.

NORA   No, absolutely not. It never even crossed my mind for a moment— And he had nothing to lend in those days; his inheritance came later.

MRS. LINDE   Well, I think that was a stroke of luck for you, Nora dear.

NORA   No, it never would have occurred to me to ask Dr. Rank—Still, I'm quite sure that if I had asked him—

MRS. LINDE   Which you won't, of course.

NORA   No, of course not. I can't see that I'd ever need to. But I'm quite positive that if I talked to Dr. Rank—

MRS. LINDE   Behind your husband's back?

NORA   I've got to clear up this other thing; *that's* also behind his back. I've *got* to clear it all up.

MRS. LINDE   Yes, I was saying that yesterday, but—

NORA   (*pacing up and down*) A man handles these problems so much better than a woman—

MRS. LINDE   One's husband does, yes.

NORA   Nonsense. (*Stopping*) When you pay everything you owe, then you get your note back, right?

MRS. LINDE   Yes, naturally.

NORA   And can rip it into a million pieces and burn it up—that filthy scrap of paper!

MRS. LINDE   (*looking hard at her, laying her sewing aside, and rising slowly*) Nora, you're hiding something from me.

NORA   You can see it in my face?

MRS. LINDE   Something's happened to you since yesterday morning. Nora, what is it?

NORA   (*hurrying toward her*) Kristine! (*Listening*) Shh! Torvald's home. Look, go in with the children a while. Torvald can't bear all this snipping and stitching. Let Anne-Marie help you.

MRS. LINDE   (*gathering up some of the things*) All right, but I'm not leaving here until we've talked this out. (*She disappears into the room, left, as* TORVALD *enters from the hall.*)

NORA   Oh, how I've been waiting for you, Torvald dear.

HELMER   Was that the dressmaker?

NORA   No, that was Kristine. She's helping me fix up my costume. You know, it's going to be quite attractive.

HELMER   Yes, wasn't that a bright idea I had?

NORA   Brilliant! But then wasn't I good as well to give in to you?

HELMER   Good—because you give in to your husband's judgment? All right, you little goose, I know you didn't mean it like that. But I won't disturb you. You'll want to have a fitting, I suppose.

NORA   And you'll be working?

HELMER   Yes. (*Indicating a bundle of papers*) See. I've been down to the bank. (*Starts toward his study*)

NORA   Torvald.

HELMER   (*stops*) Yes.

NORA   If your little squirrel begged you, with all her heart and soul, for something—?

HELMER   What's that?

NORA   Then would you do it?

HELMER   First, naturally, I'd have to know what it was.

NORA   Your squirrel would scamper about and do tricks, if you'd only be sweet and give in.

HELMER   Out with it.

NORA   Your lark would be singing high and low in every room—

HELMER   Come on, she does that anyway.

NORA   I'd be a wood nymph and dance for you in the moonlight.

HELMER   Nora—don't tell me it's that same business from this morning?

NORA   (*coming closer*) Yes, Torvald, I beg you, please!

HELMER   And you actually have the nerve to drag that up again?

NORA   Yes, yes, you've got to give in to me; you have to let Krogstad keep his job in the bank.

HELMER   My dear Nora, I've slated his job for Mrs. Linde.

NORA   That's awfully kind of you. But you could just fire another clerk instead of Krogstad.

HELMER   This is the most incredible stubbornness! Because you go and give an impulsive promise to speak up for him, I'm expected to—

NORA   That's not the reason, Torvald. It's for your own sake. That man does writing for the worst papers; you said it yourself. He could do you any amount of harm. I'm scared to death of him—

HELMER   Ah, I understand. It's the old memories haunting you.

NORA   What do you mean by that?

HELMER   Of course, you're thinking about your father.

NORA   Yes, all right. Just remember how those nasty gossips wrote in the papers about Papa and slandered him so cruelly. I think they'd have had him dismissed if the department hadn't sent you up to investigate, and if you hadn't been so kind and open-minded toward him.

HELMER   My dear Nora, there's a notable difference between your father and me. Your father's official career was hardly above reproach. But mine is; and I hope it'll stay that way as long as I hold my position.

NORA   Oh, who can ever tell what vicious minds can invent? We could be so snug and happy now in our quiet, carefree home—you and I and the children, Torvald! That's why I'm pleading with you so—

HELMER   And just by pleading for him you make it impossible for me to keep him on. It's already known at the bank that I'm firing Krogstad. What if it's rumored around now that the new bank manager was vetoed by his wife—

NORA   Yes, what then—?

HELMER   Oh yes—as long as your little bundle of stubbornness gets her way—! I should go and make myself ridiculous in front of the whole office—give people the idea I can be swayed by all kinds of outside pressure. Oh, you can bet I'd feel the effects of that soon enough! Besides—there's something that rules Krogstad right out at the bank as long as I'm the manager.

NORA   What's that?

HELMER   His moral failings I could maybe overlook if I had to—

NORA   Yes, Torvald, why not?

HELMER   And I hear he's quite efficient on the job. But he was a crony of mine back in my teens—one of those rash friendships that crop up again and again to embarrass you later in life. Well, I might as well say it straight out: we're on a first-name basis. And that tactless fool makes no effort at all to hide it in front of others. Quite the contrary—he thinks that entitles him to take a familiar air around me, and so every other second he comes booming out with his "Yes, Torvald!" and "Sure thing, Torvald!" I tell you, it's been excruciating for me. He's out to make my place in the bank unbearable.

NORA   Torvald, you can't be serious about all this.

HELMER   Oh no? Why not?

NORA   Because these are such petty considerations.

HELMER   What are you saying? Petty? You think I'm petty!

NORA   No, just the opposite, Torvald dear. That's exactly why—

HELMER   Never mind. You call my motives petty; then I might as well be just that. Petty! All right! We'll put a stop to this for good. (*Goes to the hall door and calls*) Helene!

NORA   What do you want?

HELMER   (*searching among his papers*) A decision. (*The* MAID *comes in.*) Look here; take this letter; go out with it at once. Get hold of a messenger and have him deliver it. Quick now. It's already addressed. Wait, here's some money.

MAID   Yes, sir. (*She leaves with the letter.*)

HELMER   (*straightening his papers*) There, now, little Miss Willful.

NORA   (*breathlessly*) Torvald, what was that letter?

HELMER   Krogstad's notice.

NORA   Call it back, Torvald! There's still time. Oh, Torvald, call it back! Do it for my sake—for your sake, for the children's sake! Do you hear, Torvald; do it! You don't know how this can harm us.

HELMER   Too late.

NORA   Yes, too late.

HELMER   Nora dear, I can forgive you this panic, even though basically you're insulting me. Yes, you are! Or isn't it an insult to think that I should be afraid of a courtroom hack's revenge? But I forgive you anyway, because this shows so beautifully how much you love me. (*Takes her in his arms*) This is the way it should be, my darling Nora. Whatever comes, you'll see: when it really counts, I have strength and courage enough as a man to take on the whole weight myself.

NORA   (*terrified*) What do you mean by that?

HELMER   The whole weight, I said.

NORA   (*resolutely*) No, never in all the world.

HELMER   Good. So we'll share it, Nora, as man and wife. That's as it should be. (*Fondling her*) Are you happy now? There, there, there—not these frightened dove's eyes. It's nothing at all but empty fantasies—Now you should run through your tarantella and practice your tambourine. I'll go to the inner office and shut both doors, so I won't hear a thing; you can make all the noise you like. (*Turning in the doorway*) And when Rank comes, just tell him where he can find me. (*He nods to her and goes with his papers into the study, closing the door.*)

NORA   (*standing as though rooted, dazed with fright, in a whisper*) He really could do it. He will do it. He'll do it in spite of everything. No, not that, never, never! Anything but that! Escape! A way out—*(The doorbell rings.)* Dr. Rank! Anything but that! Anything, whatever it is! *(Her hands pass over her face, smoothing it; she pulls herself together, goes over and opens the hall door.* DR. RANK *stands outside, hanging his fur coat up. During the following scene, it begins getting dark.)*

NORA   Hello, Dr. Rank. I recognized your ring. But you mustn't go in to Torvald yet; I believe he's working.

RANK   And you?

NORA   For you, I always have an hour to spare—you know that. *(He has entered, and she shuts the door after him.)*

RANK   Many thanks. I'll make use of these hours while I can.

NORA   What do you mean by that? While you can?

RANK   Does that disturb you?

NORA   Well, it's such an odd phrase. Is anything going to happen?

RANK   What's going to happen is what I've been expecting so long—but I honestly didn't think it would come so soon.

NORA   *(gripping his arm)* What is it you've found out? Dr. Rank, you have to tell me!

RANK   *(sitting by the stove)* It's all over with me. There's nothing to be done about it.

NORA   *(breathing easier)* Is it you—then—?

RANK   Who else? There's no point in lying to one's self. I'm the most miserable of all my patients, Mrs. Helmer. These past few days I've been auditing my internal accounts. Bankrupt! Within a month I'll probably be laid out and rotting in the churchyard.

NORA   Oh, what a horrible thing to say.

RANK   The thing itself is horrible. But the worst of it is all the other horror before it's over. There's only one final examination left; when I'm finished with that, I'll know about when my disintegration will begin. There's something I want to say. Helmer with his sensitivity has such a sharp distaste for anything ugly. I don't want him near my sickroom.

NORA   Oh, but Dr. Rank—

RANK   I won't have him in there. Under no condition. I'll lock my door to him—As soon as I'm completely sure of the worst, I'll send you my calling card marked with a black cross, and you'll know then the wreck has started to come apart.

NORA   No, today you're completely unreasonable. And I wanted you so much to be in a really good humor.

RANK   With death up my sleeve? And then to suffer this way for somebody else's sins. Is there any justice in that? And in every single family, in some way or another, this inevitable retribution of nature goes on—

NORA   *(her hands pressed over her ears)* Oh, stuff! Cheer up! Please—be gay!

RANK   Yes, I'd just as soon laugh at it all. My poor, innocent spine, serving time for my father's gay army days.

NORA   *(by the table, left)* He was so infatuated with asparagus tips and *pâté de foie gras,* wasn't that it?

RANK   Yes—and with truffles.

NORA   Truffles, yes. And then with oysters, I suppose?

RANK   Yes, tons of oysters, naturally.

NORA   And then the port and champagne to go with it. It's so sad that all these delectable things have to strike at our bones.

RANK   Especially when they strike at the unhappy bones that never shared in the fun.

NORA   Ah, that's the saddest of all.

RANK   (*looks searchingly at her*) Hm.

NORA   (*after a moment*) Why did you smile?

RANK   No, it was you who laughed.

NORA   No, it was you who smiled, Dr. Rank!

RANK   (*getting up*) You're even a bigger tease than I'd thought.

NORA   I'm full of wild ideas today.

RANK   That's obvious.

NORA   (*putting both hands on his shoulders*) Dear, dear Dr. Rank, you'll never die for Torvald and me.

RANK   Oh, that loss you'll easily get over. Those who go away are soon forgotten.

NORA   (*looks fearfully at him*) You believe that?

RANK   One makes new connections, and then—

NORA   Who makes new connections?

RANK   Both you and Torvald will when I'm gone. I'd say you're well under way already. What was that Mrs. Linde doing here last evening?

NORA   Oh, come—you can't be jealous of poor Kristine?

RANK   Oh yes, I am. She'll be my successor here in the house. When I'm down under, that woman will probably—

NORA   Shh! Not so loud. She's right in there.

RANK   Today as well. So you see.

NORA   Only to sew on my dress. Good gracious, how unreasonable you are. (*Sitting on the sofa*) Be nice now, Dr. Rank. Tomorrow you'll see how beautifully I'll dance, and you can imagine then that I'm dancing only for you—yes, and of course for Torvald, too—that's understood. (*Takes various items out of the carton*) Dr. Rank, sit over here and I'll show you something.

RANK   (*sitting*) What's that?

NORA   Look here. Look.

RANK   Silk stockings.

NORA   Flesh-colored. Aren't they lovely? Now it's so dark here, but tomorrow—No, no, no, just look at the feet. Oh well, you might as well look at the rest.

RANK   I Im—

NORA   Why do you look so critical? Don't you believe they'll fit?

RANK   I've never had any chance to form an opinion on that.

NORA   (*glancing at him a moment*) Shame on you. (*Hits him lightly on the ear with the stockings*) That's for you. (*Puts them away again*)

RANK   And what other splendors am I going to see now?

NORA   Not the least bit more, because you've been naughty. (*She hums a little and rummages among her things.*)

RANK   (*after a short silence*) When I sit here together with you like this, completely easy and open, then I don't know—I simply can't imagine—whatever would have become of me if I'd never come into this house.

NORA   (*smiling*) Yes, I really think you feel completely at ease with us.

RANK   (*more quietly, staring straight ahead*) And then to have to go away from it all—

NORA   Nonsense, you're not going away.

RANK   (*his voice unchanged*)—and not even be able to leave some poor show of gratitude behind, scarcely a fleeting regret—no more than a vacant place that anyone can fill.

NORA   And if I asked you now for—? No—

RANK   For what?

NORA   For a great proof of your friendship—

RANK   Yes, yes?

NORA   No, I mean—for an exceptionally big favor—

RANK   Would you really, for once, make me so happy?

NORA   Oh, you haven't the vaguest idea what it is.

RANK   All right, then tell me.

NORA   No, but I can't, Dr. Rank—it's all out of reason. It's advice and help, too—and a favor—

RANK   So much the better. I can't fathom what you're hinting at. Just speak out. Don't you trust me?

NORA   Of course. More than anyone else. You're my best and truest friend, I'm sure. That's why I want to talk to you. All right, then, Dr. Rank: there's something you can help me prevent. You know how deeply, how inexpressibly dearly Torvald loves me; he'd never hesitate a second to give up his life for me.

RANK   (*leaning close to her*) Nora—do you think he's the only one—

NORA   (*with a slight start*) Who—?

RANK   Who'd gladly give up his life for you.

NORA   (*heavily*) I see.

RANK   I swore to myself you should know this before I'm gone. I'll never find a better chance. Yes, Nora, now you know. And also you know now that you can trust me beyond anyone else.

NORA   (*rising, natural and calm*) Let me by.

RANK   (*making room for her, but still sitting*) Nora—

NORA   (*in the hall doorway*) Helene, bring the lamp in. (*Goes over to the stove*) Ah, dear Dr. Rank, that was really mean of you.

RANK   (*getting up*) That I've loved you just as deeply as somebody else? Was *that* mean?

NORA   No, but that you came out and told me. That was quite unnecessary—

RANK   What do you mean? Have you known—?

(*The* MAID *comes in with the lamp, sets it on the table, and goes out again.*)

RANK   Nora—Mrs. Helmer—I'm asking you: have you known about it?

NORA   Oh, how can I tell what I know or don't know? Really, I don't know what to say—Why did you have to be so clumsy, Dr. Rank! Everything was so good.

RANK   Well, in any case, you now have the knowledge that my body and soul are at your command. So won't you speak out?

NORA   (*Looking at him*) After that?

RANK   Please, just let me know what it is.

NORA   You can't know anything now.

RANK   I have to. You mustn't punish me like this. Give me the chance to do whatever is humanly possible for you.

NORA   Now there's nothing you can do for me. Besides, actually, I don't need any help. You'll see—it's only my fantasies. That's what it is. Of course! (*Sits in the rocker, looks at him, and smiles*) What a nice one you are, Dr. Rank. Aren't you a little bit ashamed, now that the lamp is here?

RANK   No, not exactly. But perhaps I'd better go—for good?

NORA   No, you certainly can't do that. You must come here just as you always have. You know Torvald can't do without you.

RANK   Yes, but *you?*

NORA   You know how much I enjoy it when you're here.

RANK   That's precisely what threw me off. You're a mystery to me. So many times I've felt you'd almost rather be with me than with Helmer.

NORA   Yes—you see, there are some people that one loves most and other people that one would almost prefer being with.

RANK   Yes, there's something to that.

NORA   When I was back home, of course I loved Papa most. But I always thought it was so much fun when I could sneak down to the maids' quarters, because they never tried to improve me, and it was always so amusing, the way they talked to each other.

RANK   Aha, so it's *their* place that I've filled.

NORA   (*jumping up and going to him*) Oh, dear sweet Dr. Rank, that's not what I meant at all. But you can understand that with Torvald it's just the same as with Papa—

(*The* MAID *enters from the hall.*)

MAID   Ma'am—please! (*She whispers to* NORA *and hands her a calling card.*)

NORA   (*glancing at the card*) Ah! (*Slips in into her pocket*)

RANK   Anything wrong?

NORA   No, no, not at all. It's only some—it's my new dress—

RANK   Really? But—there's your dress.

NORA   Oh, that. But this is another one—I ordered it—Torvald mustn't know—

RANK   Ah, now we have the big secret.

NORA   That's right. Just go in with him—he's back in the inner study. Keep him there as long as—

RANK   Don't worry. He won't get away.   (*Goes into the study.*)

NORA   (*to the* MAID) And he's standing waiting in the kitchen.

MAID   Yes, he came up by the back stairs.

NORA   But didn't you tell him somebody was here?

MAID   Yes, but that didn't do any good.

NORA   He won't leave?

MAID   No, he won't go till he's talked with you, ma'am.

NORA   Let him come in, then—but quietly. Helene, don't breathe a word about this. It's a surprise for my husband.

MAID   Yes, yes, I understand—   (*Goes out.*)

NORA   This horror—it's going to happen. No, no, no, it can't happen, it mustn't. (*She goes and bolts* HELMER'S *door. The* MAID *opens the hall door for* KROGSTAD *and shuts it behind him. He is dressed for travel in a fur coat, boots and a fur cap.*)

NORA   (*going toward him*) Talk softly. My husband's home.

KROGSTAD   Well, good for him.

NORA   What do you want?

KROGSTAD   Some information.

NORA   Hurry up, then. What is it?

KROGSTAD   You know, of course, that I got my notice.

NORA   I couldn't prevent it, Mr. Krogstad. I fought for you to the bitter end, but nothing worked.

KROGSTAD   Does your husband's love for you run so thin? He knows everything I can expose you too, and all the same he dares to—

NORA   How can you imagine he knows anything about this?

KROGSTAD   Ah, no—I can't imagine it either, now. It's not at all like my fine Torvald Helmer to have so much guts—

NORA   Mr. Krogstad, I demand respect for my husband!

KROGSTAD   Why, of course—all due respect. But since the lady's keeping it so carefully hidden, may I presume to ask if you're also a bit better informed than yesterday about what you've actually done?

NORA   More than you ever could teach me.

KROGSTAD   Yes, I *am* such an awful lawyer.

NORA   What is it you want from me?

KROGSTAD   Just a glimpse of how you are, Mrs. Helmer. I've been thinking about you all day long. A cashier, a night-court scribbler, a—well, a type like me also has a little of what they call a heart, you know.

NORA   Then show it. Think of my children.

KROGSTAD   Did you or your husband ever think of mine? But never mind. I simply wanted to tell you that you don't need to take this thing too seriously. For the present, I'm not proceeding with any action.

NORA   Oh no, really! Well—I knew that.

KROGSTAD   Everything can be settled in a friendly spirit. It doesn't have to get around town at all; it can stay just among us three.

NORA   My husband may never know anything of this.

KROGSTAD   How can you manage that? Perhaps you can pay me the balance?

NORA   No, not right now.

KROGSTAD   Or you know some way of raising the money in a day or two?

NORA   No way that I'm willing to use.

KROGSTAD   Well, it wouldn't have done you any good, anyway. If you stood in front of me with a fistful of bills, you still couldn't buy your signature back.

NORA   Then tell me what you're going to do with it.

KROGSTAD   I'll just hold onto it—keep it on file. There's no outsider who'll even get wind of it. So if you've been thinking of taking some desperate step—

NORA   I have.

KROGSTAD   Been thinking of running away from home—

NORA   I have!

KROGSTAD   Or even of something worse—

NORA   How could you guess that?

KROGSTAD   You can drop those thoughts.

NORA   How could you guess I was thinking of *that?*

KROGSTAD   Most of us think about *that* at first. I thought about it too, but I discovered I hadn't the courage—

NORA   (*lifelessly*) I don't either.

KROGSTAD   (*relieved*) That's true, you haven't the courage? You too?

NORA   I don't have it—I don't have it.

KROGSTAD   It would be terribly stupid, anyway. After that first storm at home blows out, why, then—I have here in my pocket a letter for your husband—

NORA   Telling everything?

KROGSTAD   As charitably as possible.

NORA   (*quickly*) He mustn't ever get that letter. Tear it up. I'll find some way to get money.

KROGSTAD   Beg pardon, Mrs. Helmer, but I think I just told you—

NORA   Oh, I don't mean the money I owe you. Let me know how much you want from my husband, and I'll manage it.

KROGSTAD   I don't want any money from your husband.

NORA   What do you want, then?

KROGSTAD   I'll tell you what. I want to recoup, Mrs. Helmer; I want to get on in the world—and there's where your husband can help me. For a year and a half I've kept myself clean of anything disreputable—all that time struggling with the worst conditions; but I was satisfied, working my way up step by step. Now I've been written right off, and I'm just not in the mood to come crawling back. I tell you, I want to move on. I want to get back in the bank—in a better position. Your husband can set up a job for me—

NORA   He'll never do that!

KROGSTAD   He'll do it. I know him. He won't dare breathe a word of protest. And once I'm in there together with him, you just wait and see! Inside of a year, I'll be the manager's right-hand man. It'll be Nils Krogstad, not Torvald Helmer, who runs the bank.

NORA   You'll never see the day!

KROGSTAD   Maybe you think you can—

NORA   I have the courage now—for *that.*

KROGSTAD   Oh, you don't scare me. A smart, spoiled lady like you—

NORA   You'll see; you'll see!

KROGSTAD   Under the ice, maybe? Down in the freezing, coal-black water?

There, till you float up in the spring, ugly, unrecognizable, with your hair falling out—

NORA   You don't frighten me.

KROGSTAD   Nor do you frighten me. One doesn't do these things, Mrs. Helmer. Besides, what good would it be? I'd still have him safe in my pocket.

NORA   Afterwards? When I'm no longer—?

KROGSTAD   Are you forgetting that *I'll* be in control then over your final reputation? (NORA *stands speechless, staring at him.*) Good; now I've warned you. Don't do anything stupid. When Helmer's read my letter, I'll be waiting for his reply. And bear in mind that it's your husband himself who's forced me back to my old ways. I'll never forgive him for that. Good-bye, Mrs. Helmer.

(*He goes out through the hall.*)

NORA   (*goes to the hall door, opens it a crack, and listens*) He's gone. Didn't leave the letter. Oh no, no, that's impossible too! (*Opening the door more and more*) What's that? He's standing outside—not going downstairs. He's thinking it over? Maybe he'll—? (*A letter falls in the mailbox; then* KROGSTAD'S *footsteps are heard, dying away down a flight of stairs.* NORA *gives a muffled cry and runs over toward the sofa table. A short pause.*) In the mailbox. (*Slips warily over to the hall door*) It's lying there. Torvald, Torvald—now we're lost!

MRS. LINDE   (*entering with the costume from the room, left*) There now, I can't see anything else to mend. Perhaps you'd like to try—

NORA   (*in a hoarse whisper*) Kristine, come here.

MRS. LINDE   (*tossing the dress on the sofa*) What's wrong? You look upset.

NORA   Come here. See that letter? *There!* Look—through the glass in the mailbox.

MRS. LINDE   Yes, yes, I see it.

NORA   That letter's from Krogstad—

MRS. LINDE   Nora—it's Krogstad who loaned you the money!

NORA   Yes, and now Torvald will find out everything.

MRS. LINDE   Believe me, Nora, it's best for both of you.

NORA   There's more you don't know. I forged a name.

MRS. LINDE   But for heaven's sake—?

NORA   I only want to tell you that, Kristine, so that you can be my witness.

MRS. LINDE   Witness? Why should I—?

NORA   If I should go out of my mind—it could easily happen—

MRS. LINDE   Nora!

NORA   Or anything else occurred—so I couldn't be present here—

MRS. LINDE   Nora, Nora, you aren't yourself at all!

NORA   And someone should try to take on the whole weight, all of the guilt, you follow me—

MRS. LINDE   Yes, of course, but why do you think—?

NORA   Then you're the witness that it isn't true, Kristine. I'm very much myself; my mind right now is perfectly clear; and I'm telling you: nobody else has known about this; I alone did everything. Remember that.

MRS. LINDE   I will. But I don't understand all this.

NORA   Oh, how could you ever understand it? It's the miracle now that's going to take place.

MRS. LINDE   The miracle?

NORA   Yes, the miracle. But it's so awful, Kristine. It mustn't take place, not for anything in the world.

MRS. LINDE   I'm going right over and talk with Krogstad.

NORA   Don't go near him; he'll do you some terrible harm!

MRS. LINDE   There was a time once when he'd gladly have done anything for me.

NORA   He?

MRS. LINDE   Where does he live?

NORA   Oh, how do I know? Yes. (*Searches in her pocket*) Here's his card. But the letter, the letter—!

HELMER   (*from the study, knocking on the door*) Nora!

NORA   (*with a cry of fear*) Oh! What is it? What do you want?

HELMER   Now, now, don't be so frightened. We're not coming in. You locked the door—are you trying on the dress?

NORA   Yes, I'm trying it. I'll look just beautiful, Torvald.

MRS. LINDE   (*who has read the card*) He's living right around the corner.

NORA   Yes, but what's the use? We're lost. The letter's in the box.

MRS. LINDE   And your husband has the key?

NORA   Yes, always.

MRS. LINDE   Krogstad can ask for his letter back unread; he can find some excuse—

NORA   But it's just this time that Torvald usually—

MRS. LINDE   Stall him. Keep him in there. I'll be back as quick as I can. (*She hurries out through the hall entrance.*)

NORA   (*goes to* HELMER'S *door, opens it, and peers in*) Torvald!

HELMER   (*from the inner study*) Well—does one dare set foot in one's own living room at last? Come on, Rank, now we'll get a look—(*In the doorway*) But what's this?

NORA   What, Torvald dear?

HELMER   Rank had me expecting some grand masquerade.

RANK   (*in the doorway*) That was my impression, but I must have been wrong.

NORA   No one can admire me in my splendor—not until tomorrow.

HELMER   But Nora dear, you look so exhausted. Have you practiced too hard?

NORA   No, I haven't practiced at all yet.

HELMER   You know, it's necessary—

NORA   Oh, it's absolutely necessary, Torvald. But I can't get anywhere without your help. I've forgotten the whole thing completely.

HELMER   Ah, we'll soon take care of that.

NORA   Yes, take care of me, Torvald, please! Promise me that? Oh, I'm so nervous. That big party—You must give up everything this evening for me. No business—don't even touch your pen. Yes? Dear Torvald, promise?

HELMER   It's a promise. Tonight I'm totally at your service—you little help-less thing. Hm—but first there's one thing I want to—(*Goes toward the hall door*)

NORA   What are you looking for?

HELMER   Just to see if there's any mail.

NORA   No, no, don't do that, Torvald!

HELMER   Now what?

NORA   Torvald, please. There isn't any.

HELMER   Let me look, though. (*Starts out.* NORA, *at the piano, strikes the first notes of the tarantella.* HELMER, *at the door, stops.*) Aha!

NORA   I can't dance tomorrow if I don't practice with you.

HELMER   (*going over to her*) Nora dear, are you really so frightened?

NORA   Yes, so terribly frightened. Let me practice right now; there's still time before dinner. Oh, sit down and play for me, Torvald. Direct me. Teach me, the way you always have.

HELMER   Gladly, if it's what you want. (*Sits at the piano*)

NORA   (*snatches the tambourine up from the box, then a long, varicolored shawl, which she throws around herself, whereupon she springs forward and cries out*) Play for me now! Now I'll dance!

(HELMER *plays and* NORA *dances.* RANK *stands behind* HELMER *at the piano and looks on.*)

HELMER   (*as he plays*) Slower. Slow down.

NORA   Can't change it.

HELMER   Not so violent, Nora!

NORA   Has to be just like this.

HELMER   (*stopping*) No, no, that won't do at all.

NORA   (*laughing and swinging her tambourine*) Isn't that what I told you?

RANK   Let me play for her.

HELMER   (*getting up*) Yes, go on. I can teach her more easily then.

(RANK *sits at the piano and plays;* NORA *dances more and more wildly.* HELMER *has stationed himself by the stove and repeatedly gives her directions; she seems not to hear them; her hair loosens and falls over her shoulders; she does not notice, but goes on dancing.* MRS. LINDE *enters.*)

MRS. LINDE   (*standing dumbfounded at the door*) Ah—!

NORA   (*still dancing*) See what fun, Kristine!

HELMER   But Nora darling, you dance as if your life were at stake.

NORA   And it is.

HELMER   Rank, stop! This is pure madness. Stop it, I say!

(RANK *breaks off playing, and* NORA *halts abruptly.*)

HELMER   (*going over to her*) I never would have believed it. You've forgotten everything I taught you.

NORA   (*throwing away the tambourine*) You see for yourself.

HELMER   Well, there's certainly room for instruction here.

NORA   Yes, you see how important it is. You've got to teach me to the very last minute. Promise me that, Torvald?

HELMER   You can bet on it.

NORA   You mustn't, either today or tomorrow, think about anything else but me; you mustn't open any letters—or the mailbox—

HELMER   Ah, it's still the fear of that man—

NORA   Oh yes, yes, that too.

HELMER   Nora, it's written all over you—there's already a letter from him out there.

NORA   I don't know. I guess so. But you mustn't read such things now; there mustn't be anything ugly between us before it's all over.

RANK   (*quietly to* HELMER) You shouldn't deny her.

HELMER   (*putting his arm around her*) The child can have her way. But tomorrow night, after you've danced—

NORA   Then you'll be free.

MAID   (*in the doorway, right*) Ma'am, dinner is served.

NORA   We'll be wanting champagne, Helene.

MAID   Very good, ma'am.   (*Goes out*)

HELMER   So—a regular banquet, hm?

NORA   Yes, a banquet—champagne till daybreak! (*Calling out*) And some macaroons, Helene. Heaps of them—just this once.

HELMER   (*taking her hands*) Now, now, now—no hysterics. Be my own little lark again.

NORA   Oh, I will soon enough. But go on in—and you, Dr. Rank. Kristine, help me put up my hair.

RANK   (*whispering, as they go*) There's nothing wrong—really wrong, is there?

HELMER   Oh, of course not. It's nothing more than this childish anxiety I was telling you about.   (*They go out, right.*)

NORA   Well?

MRS. LINDE   Left town.

NORA   I could see by your face.

MRS. LINDE   He'll be home tomorrow evening. I wrote him a note.

NORA   You shouldn't have. Don't try to stop anything now. After all, it's a wonderful joy, this waiting here for the miracle.

MRS. LINDE   What is it you're waiting for?

NORA   Oh, you can't understand that. Go in to them, I'll be along in a moment.

(MRS. LINDE *goes into the dining room.* NORA *stands a short while as if composing herself; then she looks at her watch.*)

NORA   Five. Seven hours to midnight. Twenty-four hours to the midnight after, and then the tarantella's done. Seven and twenty-four? Thirty-one hours to live.

HELMER   (*in the doorway, right*) What's become of the little lark?

NORA   (*going toward him with open arms*) Here's your lark!

ACT III

Same scene. The table, with chairs around it, has been moved to the center of the room. A lamp on the table is lit. The hall door stands open. Dance music drifts down from the floor above. MRS. LINDE *sits at the table, absently paging through a book, trying to read, but apparently unable to focus her thoughts. Once or twice she pauses, tensely listening for a sound at the outer entrance.*

MRS. LINDE   (*glancing at her watch*) Not yet—and there's hardly any time left. If only he's not—(*Listening again*) Ah, there he is. (*She goes out in the hall and cautiously opens the outer door. Quiet footsteps are heard on the stairs. She whispers.*) Come in. Nobody's here.

KROGSTAD   (*in the doorway*) I found a note from you at home. What's back of all this?

MRS. LINDE   I just *had* to talk to you.

KROGSTAD   Oh? And it just *had* to be here in this house?

MRS. LINDE   At my place it was impossible; my room hasn't a private entrance. Come in; we're all alone. The maid's asleep, and the Helmers are at the dance upstairs.

KROGSTAD   (*entering the room*) Well, well, the Helmers are dancing tonight? Really?

MRS. LINDE   Yes, why not?

KROGSTAD   How true—why not?

MRS. LINDE   All right, Krogstad, let's talk.

KROGSTAD   Do we two have anything more to talk about?

MRS. LINDE   We have a great deal to talk about.

KROGSTAD   I wouldn't have thought so.

MRS. LINDE   No, because you've never understood me, really.

KROGSTAD   Was there anything more to understand—except what's all too common in life? A calculating woman throws over a man the moment a better catch comes by.

MRS. LINDE   You think I'm so thoroughly calculating? You think I broke it off lightly?

KROGSTAD   Didn't you?

MRS. LINDE   Nils—is that what you really thought?

KROGSTAD   If you cared, then why did you write me the way you did?

MRS. LINDE   What else could I do? If I had to break off with you, then it was my job as well to root out everything you felt for me.

KROGSTAD   (*wringing his hands*) So that was it. And this—all this, simply for money!

MRS. LINDE   Don't forget I had a helpless mother and two small brothers. We couldn't wait for you, Nils; you had such a long road ahead of you then.

KROGSTAD   That may be; but you still hadn't the right to abandon me for somebody else's sake.

MRS. LINDE   Yes—I don't know. So many, many times I've asked myself if I did have that right.

KROGSTAD   (*more softly*) When I lost you, it was as if all the solid ground dissolved from under my feet. Look at me; I'm a half-drowned man now, hanging onto a wreck.

MRS. LINDE   Help may be near.

KROGSTAD   It was near—but then you came and blocked it off.

MRS. LINDE   Without my knowing it, Nils. Today for the first time I learned that it's you I'm replacing at the bank.

KROGSTAD   All right—I believe you. But now that you know, will you step aside?

MRS. LINDE   No, because that wouldn't benefit you in the slightest.

KROGSTAD   Not "benefit" me, hm! I'd step aside anyway.

MRS. LINDE   I've learned to be realistic. Life and hard, bitter necessity have taught me that.

KROGSTAD   And life's taught me never to trust fine phrases.

MRS. LINDE   Then life's taught you a very sound thing. But you do have to trust in actions, don't you?

KROGSTAD   What does that mean?

MRS. LINDE   You said you were hanging on like a half-drowned man to a wreck.

KROGSTAD   I've good reason to say that.

MRS. LINDE   I'm also like a half-drowned woman on a wreck. No one to suffer with; no one to care for.

KROGSTAD   You made your choice.

MRS. LINDE   There wasn't any choice then.

KROGSTAD   So—what of it?

MRS. LINDE   Nils, if only we two shipwrecked people could reach across to each other.

KROGSTAD   What are you saying?

MRS. LINDE   Two on one wreck are at least better off than each on his own.

KROGSTAD   Kristine!

MRS. LINDE   Why do you think I came into town?

KROGSTAD   Did you really have some thought of me?

MRS. LINDE   I have to work to go on living. All my born days, as long as I can remember, I've worked, and it's been my best and my only joy. But now I'm completely alone in the world; it frightens me to be so empty and lost. To work for yourself—there's no joy in that. Nils, give me something—someone to work for.

KROGSTAD   I don't believe all this. It's just some hysterical feminine urge to go out and make a noble sacrifice.

MRS. LINDE   Have you ever found me to be hysterical?

KROGSTAD   Can you honestly mean this? Tell me—do you know everything about my past?

MRS. LINDE   Yes.

KROGSTAD   And you know what they think I'm worth around here.

MRS. LINDE   From what you were saying before, it would seem that with me you could have been another person.

KROGSTAD   I'm positive of that.

MRS. LINDE   Couldn't it happen still?

KROGSTAD   Kristine—you're saying this in all seriousness? Yes, you are! I can see it in you. And do you really have the courage, then—?

MRS. LINDE   I need to have someone to care for; and your children need a mother. We both need each other. Nils, I have faith that you're good at heart—I'll risk everything together with you.

KROGSTAD   (*gripping her hands*) Kristine, thank you, thank you—Now I know I can win back a place in their eyes. Yes—but I forgot—

MRS. LINDE   (*listening*) Shh! The tarantella. Go now! Go on!

KROGSTAD   Why? What is it?

MRS. LINDE   Hear the dance up there? When that's over, they'll be coming down.

KROGSTAD   Oh, then I'll go. But—it's all pointless. Of course, you don't know the move I made against the Helmers.

MRS. LINDE   Yes, Nils, I know.

KROGSTAD   And all the same, you have the courage to—?

MRS. LINDE   I know how far despair can drive a man like you.

KROGSTAD   Oh, if I only could take it all back.

MRS. LINDE   You easily could—your letter's still lying in the mailbox.

KROGSTAD   Are you sure of that?

MRS. LINDE   Positive. But—

KROGSTAD   (*looks at her searchingly*) Is that the meaning of it, then? You'll have your friend at any price. Tell me straight out. Is that it?

MRS. LINDE   Nils—anyone who's sold herself for somebody else once isn't going to do it again.

KROGSTAD   I'll demand my letter back.

MRS. LINDE   No, no.

KROGSTAD   Yes, of course. I'll stay here till Helmer comes down; I'll tell him to give me my letter again—that it only involves my dismissal—that he shouldn't read it—

MRS. LINDE   No, Nils, don't call the letter back.

KROGSTAD   But wasn't that exactly why you wrote me to come here?

MRS. LINDE   Yes, in that first panic. But it's been a whole day and night since then, and in that time I've seen such incredible things in this house. Helmer's got to learn everything; this dreadful secret has to be aired; those two have to come to a full understanding; all these lies and evasions can't go on.

KROGSTAD   Well, then, if you want to chance it. But at least there's one thing I can do, and do right away—

MRS. LINDE   (*listening*) Go now, go quick! The dance is over. We're not safe another second.

KROGSTAD   I'll wait for you downstairs.

MRS. LINDE   Yes, please do; take me home.

KROGSTAD   I can't believe it; I've never been so happy. (*He leaves by way of the outer door; the door between the room and the hall stays open.*)

MRS. LINDE   (*straightening up a bit and getting together her street clothes*) How different now! How different! Someone to work for, to live for—a home to build. Well, it is worth the try! Oh, if they'd only come! (*Listening*) Ah, there they are. Bundle up. (*She picks up her hat and coat.* NORA'S *and* HELMER'S *voices can be heard outside; a key turns in the lock, and* HELMER *brings* NORA *into the hall almost by force. She is wearing the Italian costume with a large black shawl about her; he has on evening dress, with a black domino open over it.*)

NORA   (*struggling in the doorway*) No, no, no, not inside! I'm going up again. I don't want to leave so soon.

HELMER   But Nora dear—

NORA   Oh, I beg you, please, Torvald. From the bottom of my heart, *please*—only an hour more!

HELMER   Not a single minute, Nora darling. You know our agreement. Come on, in we go; you'll catch cold out here. (*In spite of her resistance, he gently draws her into the room.*)

MRS. LINDE   Good evening.

NORA   Kristine!

HELMER   Why, Mrs. Linde—are you here so late?

MRS. LINDE   Yes, I'm sorry, but I did want to see Nora in costume.

NORA   Have you been sitting here, waiting for me?

MRS. LINDE   Yes. I didn't come early enough; you were all upstairs; and then I thought I really couldn't leave without seeing you.

HELMER   (*removing* NORA'S *shawl*) Yes, take a good look. She's worth looking at, I can tell you that, Mrs. Linde. Isn't she lovely?

MRS. LINDE   Yes, I should say—

HELMER   A dream of loveliness, isn't she? That's what everyone thought at the party, too. But she's horribly stubborn—this sweet little thing. What's to be done with her? Can you imagine, I almost had to use force to pry her away.

NORA   Oh, Torvald, you're going to regret you didn't indulge me, even for just a half hour more.

HELMER   There, you see. She danced her tarantella and got a tumultuous hand—which was well earned, although the performance may have been a bit too naturalistic—I mean it rather overstepped the proprieties of art. But never mind—what's important is, she made a success, an overwhelming success. You think I could let her stay on after that and spoil the effect? Oh no; I took my lovely little Capri girl—my capricious little Capri girl, I should say— took her under my arm; one quick tour of the ballroom, a curtsy to every side, and then—as they say in novels—the beautiful vision disappeared. An exit should always be effective, Mrs. Linde, but that's what I can't get Nora to grasp. Phew, it's hot in here. (*Flings the domino on a chair and opens the door to his room*) Why's it dark in here? Oh yes, of course. Excuse me. (*He goes in and lights a couple of candles.*)

NORA   (*in a sharp, breathless whisper*) So?

MRS. LINDE   (*quietly*) I talked with him.

NORA   And—?

MRS. LINDE   Nora—you must tell your husband everything.

NORA   (*dully*) I knew it.

MRS. LINDE   You've got nothing to fear from Krogstad, but you have to speak out.

NORA   I won't tell.

MRS. LINDE   Then the letter will.

NORA   Thanks, Kristine. I know now what's to be done. Shh!

HELMER   (*reentering*) Well, then, Mrs. Linde—have you admired her?

MRS. LINDE   Yes, and now I'll say good night.

HELMER   Oh, come, so soon? Is this yours, this knitting?

MRS. LINDE   Yes, thanks. I nearly forgot it.

HELMER   Do you knit, then?

MRS. LINDE   Oh yes.

HELMER   You know what? You should embroider instead.

MRS. LINDE   Really? Why?

HELMER   Yes, because it's a lot prettier. See here, one holds the embroidery so, in the left hand, and then one guides the needle with the right—so—in an easy, sweeping curve—right?

MRS. LINDE   Yes, I guess that's—

HELMER   But, on the other hand, knitting—it can never be anything but ugly. Look, see here, the arms tucked in, the knitting needles going up and down—there's something Chinese about it. Ah, that was really a glorious champagne they served.

MRS. LINDE   Yes, good night, Nora, and don't be stubborn anymore.

HELMER   Well put, Mrs. Linde!

MRS. LINDE   Good night, Mr. Helmer.

HELMER   (*accompanying her to the door*) Good night, good night. I hope you get home all right. I'd be very happy to—but you don't have far to go. Good night, good night. (*She leaves. He shuts the door after her and returns.*) There, now, at last we got her out the door. She's a deadly bore, that creature.

NORA   Aren't you pretty tired, Torvald?

HELMER   No, not a bit.

NORA   You're not sleepy?

HELMER   Not at all. On the contrary, I'm feeling quite exhilarated. But you? Yes, you really look tired and sleepy.

NORA   Yes, I'm very tired. Soon now I'll sleep.

HELMER   See! You see! I was right all along that we shouldn't stay longer.

NORA   Whatever you do is always right.

HELMER   (*kissing her brow*) Now my little lark talks sense. Say, did you notice what a time Rank was having tonight?

NORA   Oh, was he? I didn't get to speak with him.

HELMER   I scarcely did either, but it's a long time since I've seen him in such high spirits. (*Gazes at her a moment, then comes nearer her*) Hm— it's marvelous, though, to be back home again—to be completely alone with you. Oh, you bewitchingly lovely young woman!

NORA   Torvald, don't look at me like that!

HELMER   Can't I look at my richest treasure? At all that beauty that's mine, mine alone—completely and utterly.

NORA   (*moving around to the other side of the table*) You mustn't talk to me that way tonight.

HELMER   (*following her*) The tarantella is still in your blood, I can see—and it makes you even more enticing. Listen. The guests are beginning to go. (*Dropping his voice*) Nora—it'll soon be quiet through this whole house.

NORA   Yes, I hope so.

HELMER   You do, don't you, my love? Do you realize—when I'm out at a party like this with you—do you know why I talk to you so little, and keep such a distance away; just send you a stolen look now and then—you know why I do it? It's because I'm imagining then that you're my secret darling, my secret young bride-to-be, and that no one suspects there's anything between us.

NORA   Yes, yes; oh, yes, I know you're always thinking of me.

HELMER   And then when we leave and I place the shawl over those fine young rounded shoulders—over that wonderful curving neck—then I pretend that you're my young bride, that we're just coming from the wedding, that for the first time I'm bringing you into my house—that for the first time I'm alone with you—completely alone with you, your trembling young beauty! All this evening I've longed for nothing but you. When I saw you turn and sway in the tarantella—my blood was pounding till I couldn't stand it—that's why I brought you down here so early—

NORA   Go away, Torvald! Leave me alone. I don't want all this.

HELMER   What do you mean? Nora, you're teasing me. You will, won't you? Aren't I your husband—?

(A knock at the outside door)

NORA   *(startled)* What's that?

HELMER   *(going toward the hall)* Who is it?

RANK   *(outside)* It's me. May I come in a moment?

HELMER   *(with quiet irritation)* Oh, what does he want now? *(Aloud)* Hold on. *(Goes and opens the door)* Oh, how nice that you didn't just pass us by!

RANK   I thought I heard your voice, and then I wanted so badly to have a look in. *(Lightly glancing about)* Ah, me, these old familiar haunts. You have it snug and cozy in here, you two.

HELMER   You seemed to be having it pretty cozy upstairs, too.

RANK   Absolutely. Why shouldn't I? Why not take in everything in life? As much as you can, anyway, and as long as you can. The wine was superb—

HELMER   The champagne especially.

RANK   You noticed that too? It's amazing how much I could guzzle down.

NORA   Torvald also drank a lot of champagne this evening.

RANK   Oh?

NORA   Yes, and that always makes him so entertaining.

RANK   Well, why shouldn't one have a pleasant evening after a well-spent day?

HELMER   Well spent? I'm afraid I can't claim that.

RANK   *(slapping him on the back)* But I can, you see!

NORA   Dr. Rank, you must have done some scientific research today.

RANK   Quite so.

HELMER   Come now—little Nora talking about scientific research!

NORA   And can I congratulate you on the results?

RANK   Indeed you may.

NORA   Then they were good?

RANK   The best possible for both doctor and patient—certainty.

NORA   *(quickly and searchingly)* Certainty?

RANK   Complete certainty. So don't I owe myself a gay evening afterwards?

NORA   Yes, you're right, Dr. Rank.

HELMER   I'm with you—just so long as you don't have to suffer for it in the morning.

RANK   Well, one never gets something for nothing in life.

NORA   Dr. Rank—are you very fond of masquerade parties?

RANK   Yes, if there's a good array of odd disguises—

NORA   Tell me, what should we two go as at the next masquerade?

HELMER   You little feather head—already thinking of the next!

RANK   We two? I'll tell you what: you must go as Charmed Life—

HELMER   Yes, but find a costume for *that!*

RANK   Your wife can appear just as she looks every day.

HELMER   That was nicely put. But don't you know what you're going to be?

RANK   Yes, Helmer, I've made up my mind.

HELMER   Well?

RANK   At the next masquerade I'm going to be invisible.

HELMER   That's a funny idea.

RANK   They say there's a hat—black, huge—have you never heard of the hat that makes you invisible? You put it on, and then no one on earth can see you.

HELMER   (*suppressing a smile*) Ah, of course.

RANK   But I'm quite forgetting what I came for. Helmer, give me a cigar, one of the dark Havanas.

HELMER   With the greatest pleasure. (*Holds out his case*)

RANK   Thanks. (*Takes one and cuts off the tip*)

NORA   (*striking a match*) Let me give you a light.

RANK   Thank you. (*She holds the match for him; he lights the cigar.*) And now good-bye.

HELMER   Good-bye, good-bye, old friend.

NORA   Sleep well, Doctor.

RANK   Thanks for that wish.

NORA   Wish me the same.

RANK   You? All right, if you like—Sleep well. And thanks for the light.

(*He nods to them both and leaves.*)

HELMER   (*his voice subdued*) He's been drinking heavily.

NORA   (*absently*) Could be. (HELMER *takes his keys from his pocket and goes out in the hall.*) Torvald—what are you after?

HELMER   Got to empty the mailbox; it's nearly full. There won't be room for the morning papers.

NORA   Are you working tonight?

HELMER   You know I'm not. Why—what's this? Someone's been at the lock.

NORA   At the lock—?

HELMER   Yes, I'm positive. What do you suppose—? I can't imagine one of the maids—? Here's a broken hairpin. Nora, it's yours—

NORA   (*quickly*) Then it must be the children—

HELMER   You'd better break them of that. Hm, hm—well, opened it after all. (*Takes the contents out and calls into the kitchen*) Helene! Helene, would you put out the lamp in the hall. (*He returns to the room, shutting the hall door, then displays the handful of mail.*) Look how it's piled up. (*Sorting through them*) Now what's this?

NORA   (*at the window*) The letter! Oh, Torvald, no!

HELMER   Two calling cards—from Rank.

NORA   From Dr. Rank?

HELMER   (*examining them*) "Dr. Rank, Consulting Physician." They were on top. He must have dropped them in as he left.

NORA   Is there anything on them?

HELMER   There's a black cross over the name. See? That's a gruesome notion. He could almost be announcing his own death.

NORA   That's just what he's doing.

HELMER   What! You've heard something? Something he's told you?

NORA   Yes. That when those cards came, he'd be taking his leave of us. He'll shut himself in now and die.

HELMER   Ah, my poor friend! Of course I knew he wouldn't be here much longer. But so soon—And then to hide himself away like a wounded animal.

NORA   If it has to happen, then it's best it happens in silence—don't you think so, Torvald?

HELMER   (*pacing up and down*) He's grown right into our lives. I simply can't imagine him gone. He with his suffering and loneliness—like a dark cloud setting off our sunlit happiness. Well, maybe it's best this way. For him, at least. (*Standing still*) Any maybe for us too, Nora. Now we're thrown back on each other, completely. (*Embracing her*) Oh you, my darling wife, how can I hold you close enough? You know what, Nora—time and again I've wished you were in some terrible danger, just so I could stake my life and soul and everything, for your sake.

NORA   (*tearing herself away, her voice firm and decisive*) Now you must read your mail, Torvald.

HELMER   No, no, not tonight. I want to stay with you, dearest.

NORA   With a dying friend on your mind?

HELMER   You're right. We've both had a shock. There's ugliness between us—these thoughts of death and corruption. We'll have to get free of them first. Until then—we'll stay apart.

NORA   (*clinging about his neck*) Torvald—good night! Good night!

HELMER   (*kissing her on the cheek*) Good night, little songbird. Sleep well, Nora. I'll be reading my mail now.

(*He takes the letters into his room and shuts the door after him.*)

NORA   (*with bewildered glances, groping about, seizing* HELMER'*s domino, throwing it around her, and speaking in short, hoarse, broken whispers*) Never see him again. Never, never. (*Putting her shawl over her head*) Never see the children either—them, too. Never, never. Oh, the freezing black water! The depths—down—Oh, I wish it were over—He has it now; he's reading it—now. Oh no, no, not yet. Torvald, good-bye, you and the children— (*She starts for the hall; as she does,* HELMER *throws open his door and stands with an open letter in his hand.*)

HELMER   Nora!

NORA   (*screams*) Oh—!

HELMER   What is this? You know what's in this letter?

NORA   Yes, I know. Let me go! Let me out!

HELMER   (*holding her back*) Where are you going?

NORA   (*struggling to break loose*) You can't save me, Torvald!

HELMER   (*slumping back*) True! Then it's true what he writes? How horrible! No, no, it's impossible—it can't be true.

NORA   It *is* true. I've loved you more than all this world.

HELMER   Ah, none of your slippery tricks.

NORA   (*taking one step toward him*) Torvald—!

HELMER   What *is* this you've blundered into!

NORA   Just let me loose. You're not going to suffer for my sake. You're not going to take on my guilt.

HELMER   No more playacting. (*Locks the hall door*) You stay right here and give me a reckoning. You understand what you've done? Answer! You understand?

NORA   (*looking squarely at him, her face hardening*) Yes. I'm beginning to understand everything now.

HELMER   (*striding about*) Oh, what an awful awakening! In all these eight years—she who was my pride and joy—a hypocrite, a liar—worse, worse—a criminal! How infinitely disgusting it all is! The shame! (NORA *says nothing and goes on looking straight at him. He stops in front of her.*) I should have suspected something of the kind. I should have known. All your father's flimsy values—Be still! All your father's flimsy values have come out in you. No religion, no morals, no sense of duty—Oh, how I'm punished for letting him off! I did it for your sake, and you repay me like this.

NORA   Yes, like this.

HELMER   Now you've wrecked all my happiness—ruined my whole future. Oh, it's awful to think of. I'm in a cheap little grafter's hands; he can do anything he wants with me, ask for anything, play with me like a puppet—and I can't breathe a word. I'll be swept down miserably into the depths on account of a featherbrained woman.

NORA   When I'm gone from this world, you'll be free.

HELMER   Oh, quit posing. Your father had a mess of those speeches too. What good would that ever do me if you were gone from this world, as you say? Not the slightest. He can still make the whole thing known; and if he does, I could be falsely suspected as your accomplice. They might even think that I was behind it—that I put you up to it. And all that I can thank you for—you that I've coddled the whole of our marriage. Can you see now what you've done to me?

NORA   (*icily calm*) Yes.

HELMER   It's so incredible, I just can't grasp it. But we'll have to patch up whatever we can. Take off the shawl. I said, take it off! I've got to appease him somehow or other. The thing has to be hushed up at any cost. And as for you and me, it's got to seem like everything between us is just as it was—to the outside world, that is. You'll go right on living in this house, of course. But you can't be allowed to bring up the children; I don't dare trust you with them— Oh, to have to say this to someone I've loved so much! Well, that's done with. From now on happiness doesn't matter; all that matters is saving the bits and pieces, the appearance—(*The doorbell rings.* HELMER *starts.*) What's that? And so late. Maybe the worst—? You think he'd—? Hide, Nora! Say you're sick. (NORA *remains standing motionless.* HELMER *goes and opens the door.*)

MAID   (*half dressed, in the hall*) A letter for Mrs. Helmer.

HELMER   I'll take it. (*Snatches the letter and shuts the door*) Yes, it's from him. You don't get it; I'm reading it myself.

NORA   Then read it.

HELMER   (*by the lamp*) I hardly dare. We may be ruined, you and I. But—I've got to know. (*Rips open the letter, skims through a few lines, glances at an enclosure, then cries out joyfully*) Nora! (NORA *looks inquiringly at him.*) Nora! Wait—better check it again—Yes, yes, it's true. I'm saved. Nora, I'm saved!

NORA   And I?

HELMER   You too, of course. We're both saved, both of us. Look. He's sent back your note. He says he's sorry and ashamed—that a happy development in his life—oh, who cares what he says! Nora, we're saved! No one can hurt you. Oh, Nora, Nora—but first, this ugliness all has to go. Let me see—(*Takes a look at the note*) No, I don't want to see it; I want the whole thing to fade like a dream. (*Tears the note and both letters to pieces, throws them into the stove and watches them burn*) There—now there's nothing left—He wrote that since Christmas Eve you—Oh, they must have been three terrible days for you, Nora.

NORA   I fought a hard fight.

HELMER   And suffered pain and saw no escape but—No, we're not going to dwell on anything unpleasant. We'll just be grateful and keep on repeating; it's over now, it's over! You hear me, Nora? You don't seem to realize—it's over. What's it mean—that frozen look? Oh, poor little Nora, I understand. You can't believe I've forgiven you. But I have, Nora; I swear I have. I know that what you did, you did out of love for me.

NORA   That's true.

HELMER   You loved me the way a wife ought to love her husband. It's simply the means that you couldn't judge. But you think I love you any the less for not knowing how to handle your affairs? No, no—just lean on me: I'll guide you and teach you. I wouldn't be a man if this feminine helplessness didn't make you twice as attractive to me. You mustn't mind those sharp words I said—that was all in the first confusion of thinking my world had collapsed. I've forgiven you, Nora; I swear I've forgiven you.

NORA   My thanks for your forgiveness.   (*She goes out through the door, right.*)

HELMER   No, wait—(*Peers in*) What are you doing in there?

NORA   (*inside*) Getting out of my costume.

HELMER   (*by the open door*) Yes, do that. Try to calm yourself and collect your thoughts again, my frightened little songbird. You can rest easy now; I've got wide wings to shelter you with. (*Walking about close by the door*) How snug and nice our home is, Nora. You're safe here; I'll keep you like a hunted dove I've rescued out of a hawk's claws. I'll bring peace to your poor, shuddering heart. Gradually it'll happen, Nora; you'll see. Tomorrow all this will look different to you; then everything will be as it was. I won't have to go on repeating I forgive you; you'll feel it for yourself. How can you imagine I'd ever conceivably want to disown you—or even blame you in any way? Ah, you don't know a man's heart, Nora. For a man there's something indescribably sweet and satisfying in knowing he's forgiven his wife—and forgiven her out of a full and open heart. It's as if she belongs to him in two ways now: in a sense he's given her fresh into the world again, and she's become his wife and his child as well. From now on that's what you'll be to me—you little, bewildered, helpless thing. Don't be afraid of anything, Nora; just open your heart to me, and I'll be conscience and will to you both——(NORA *enters in her regular clothes.*) What's this? Not in bed? You've changed your dress?

NORA   Yes, Torvald, I've changed my dress.

HELMER   But why now, so late?

NORA   Tonight I'm not sleeping.

HELMER   But Nora dear——

NORA   (*looking at her watch*) It's still not so very late. Sit down, Torvald; we have a lot to talk over. (*She sits at one side of the table.*)

HELMER   Nora—what is this? That hard expression——

NORA   Sit down. This'll take some time. I have a lot to say.

HELMER   (*sitting at the table directly opposite her*) You worry me, Nora. And I don't understand you.

NORA   No, that's exactly it. You don't understand me. And I've never understood you either—until tonight. No, don't interrupt. You can just listen to what I say. We're closing out accounts, Torvald.

HELMER   How do you mean that?

NORA   (*after a short pause*) Doesn't anything strike you about our sitting here like this?

HELMER   What's that?

NORA   We've been married now eight years. Doesn't it occur to you that this is the first time we two, you and I, man and wife, have ever talked seriously together?

HELMER   What do you mean—seriously?

NORA   In eight whole years—longer even—right from our first acquaintance, we've never exchanged a serious word on any serious thing.

HELMER   You mean I should constantly go and involve you in problems you couldn't possibly help me with?

NORA   I'm not talking of problems, I'm saying that we've never sat down seriously together and tried to get to the bottom of anything.

HELMER   But dearest, what good would that ever do you?

NORA   That's the point right there: you've never understood me. I've been wronged greatly, Torvald—first by Papa, and then by you.

HELMER   What! By us—the two people who've loved you more than anyone else?

NORA   (*shaking her head*) You never loved me. You've thought it fun to be in love with me, that's all.

HELMER   Nora, what a thing to say!

NORA   Yes, it's true now, Torvald. When I lived at home with Papa, he told me all his opinions, so I had the same ones too; or if they were different I hid them, since he wouldn't have cared for that. He used to call me his doll-child, and he played with me the way I played with my dolls. Then I came into your house——

HELMER   How can you speak of our marriage like that?

NORA   (*unperturbed*) I mean, then I went from Papa's hands into yours. You arranged everything to your own taste, and so I got the same taste as you—or I pretended to; I can't remember. I guess a little of both, first one, then the other. Now when I look back, it seems as if I'd lived here like a beggar—just from hand to mouth. I've lived by doing tricks for you, Torvald. But that's the way you wanted it. It's a great sin what you and Papa did to me. You're to blame that nothing's become of me.

HELMER   Nora, how unfair and ungrateful you are! Haven't you been happy here?

NORA   No, never. I thought so—but I never have.

HELMER   Not—not happy!

NORA   No, only lighthearted. And you've always been so kind to me. But our home's been nothing but a playpen. I've been your doll-wife here, just as at home I was Papa's doll-child. And in turn the children have been my dolls. I thought it was fun when you played with me, just as they thought it fun when I played with them. That's been our marriage, Torvald.

HELMER   There's some truth in what you're saying—under all the raving exaggeration. But it'll all be different after this. Playtime's over; now for the schooling.

NORA   Whose schooling—mine or the children's?

HELMER   Both yours and the children's, dearest.

NORA   Oh, Torvald, you're not the man to teach me to be a good wife to you.

HELMER   And you can say that?

NORA   And I—how am I equipped to bring up children?

HELMER   Nora!

NORA   Didn't you say a moment ago that that was no job to trust me with?

HELMER   In a flare of temper! Why fasten on that?

NORA   Yes, but you were so very right. I'm not up to the job. There's another job I have to do first. I have to try to educate myself. You can't help me with that. I've got to do it alone. And that's why I'm leaving you now.

HELMER   (*jumping up*) What's that?

NORA   I have to stand completely alone, if I'm ever going to discover myself and the world out there. So I can't go on living with you.

HELMER   Nora, Nora!

NORA   I want to leave right away. Kristine should put me up for the night—

HELMER   You're insane! You've no right! I forbid you!

NORA   From here on, there's no use forbidding me anything. I'll take with me whatever is mine. I don't want a thing from you, either now or later.

HELMER   What kind of madness is this!

NORA   Tomorrow I'm going home—I mean, home where I came from. It'll be easier up there to find something to do.

HELMER   Oh, you blind, incompetent child!

NORA   I must learn to be competent, Torvald.

HELMER   Abandon your home, your husband, your children! And you're not even thinking what people will say.

NORA   I can't be concerned about that. I only know how essential this is.

HELMER   Oh, it's outrageous. So you'll run out like this on your most sacred vows.

NORA   What do you think are my most sacred vows?

HELMER   And I have to tell you that! Aren't they your duties to your husband and children?

NORA   I have other duties equally sacred.

HELMER   That isn't true. What duties are they?

NORA   Duties to myself.

HELMER   Before all else, you're a wife and a mother.

NORA   I don't believe in that anymore. I believe that, before all else, I'm a human being, no less than you—or anyway, I ought to try to become one. I know the majority thinks you're right, Torvald, and plenty of books agree with you, too. But I can't go on believing what the majority says, or what's written in books. I have to think over these things myself and try to understand them.

HELMER   Why can't you understand your place in your own home? On a point like that, isn't there one everlasting guide you can turn to? Where's your religion?

NORA   Oh, Torvald, I'm really not sure what religion is.

HELMER   What—?

NORA   I only know what the minister said when I was confirmed. He told me religion was this thing and that. When I get clear and away by myself, I'll go into that problem too. I'll see if what the minister said was right, or, in any case, if it's right for me.

HELMER   A young woman your age shouldn't talk like that. If religion can't move you, I can try to rouse your conscience. You do have some moral feeling? Or, tell me—has that gone too?

NORA   It's not easy to answer that, Torvald. I simply don't know. I'm all confused about these things. I just know I see them so differently from you. I find out, for one thing, that the law's not at all what I'd thought—but I can't get it through my head that the law is fair. A woman hasn't a right to protect her dying father or save her husband's life! I can't believe that.

HELMER   You talk like a child. You don't know anything of the world you live in.

NORA   No, I don't. But now I'll begin to learn for myself. I'll try to discover who's right, the world or I.

HELMER   Nora, you're sick; you've got a fever. I almost think you're out of your head.

NORA   I've never felt more clearheaded and sure in my life.

HELMER   And—clearheaded and sure—you're leaving your husband and children?

NORA   Yes.

HELMER   Then there's only one possible reason.

NORA   What?

HELMER   You no longer love me.

NORA   No. That's exactly it.

HELMER   Nora! You can't be serious!

NORA   Oh, this is so hard, Torvald—you've been so kind to me always. But I can't help it. I don't love you anymore.

HELMER   (*struggling for composure*) Are you also clearheaded and sure about that?

NORA   Yes, completely. That's why I can't go on staying here.

HELMER   Can you tell me what I did to lose your love?

NORA   Yes, I can tell you. It was this evening when the miraculous thing didn't come—then I knew you weren't the man I'd imagined.

HELMER   Be more explicit; I don't follow you.

NORA   I've waited now so patiently eight long years—for, my Lord, I know miracles don't come every day. Then this crisis broke over me, and such a certainty filled me: *now* the miraculous event would occur. While Krogstad's letter was lying out there, I never for an instant dreamed that you could give in to his terms. I was so utterly sure you'd say to him: go on, tell your tale to the whole wide world. And when he'd done that—

HELMER   Yes, what then? When I'd delivered my own wife into shame and disgrace—!

NORA   When he'd done that, I was so utterly sure that you'd step forward, take the blame on yourself and say: I am the guilty one.

HELMER   Nora—!

NORA   You're thinking I'd never accept such a sacrifice from you? No, of course not. But what good would my protests be against you? That was the miracle I was waiting for, in terror and hope. And to stave that off, I would have taken my life.

HELMER   I'd gladly work for you day and night, Nora—and take on pain and deprivation. But there's no one who gives up honor for love.

NORA   Millions of women have done just that.

HELMER   Oh, you think and talk like a silly child.

NORA   Perhaps. But you neither think nor talk like the man I could join myself to. When your big fright was over—and it wasn't from any threat against me, only for what might damage you—when all the danger was past, for you it was just as if nothing had happened. I was exactly the same, your little lark, your doll, that you'd have to handle with double care now that I'd turned out so brittle and frail. (*Gets up*) Torvald—in that instant it dawned on me that for eight years I've been living here with a stranger, and that I'd even conceived three children—oh, I can't stand the thought of it! I could tear myself to bits.

HELMER   (*heavily*) I see. There's a gulf that's opened between us—that's clear. Oh, but Nora, can't we bridge it somehow?

NORA   The way I am now, I'm no wife for you.

HELMER   I have the strength to make myself over.

NORA   Maybe—if your doll gets taken away.

HELMER   But to part! To part from you! No, Nora, no—I can't imagine it.

NORA   (*going out, right*) All the more reason why it has to be. (*She reenters with her coat and a small overnight bag, which she puts on a chair by the table.*)

HELMER   Nora, Nora, not now! Wait till tomorrow.

NORA   I can't spend the night in a strange man's room.

HELMER   But couldn't we live here like brother and sister—

NORA   You know very well how long that would last. (*Throws her shawl about her*) Good-bye, Torvald. I won't look in on the children. I know they're in better hands than mine. The way I am now, I'm no use to them.

HELMER   But someday, Nora—someday—?

NORA   How can I tell? I haven't the least idea what'll become of me.

HELMER   But you're my wife, now and wherever you go.

NORA   Listen, Torvald—I've heard that when a wife deserts her husband's house just as I'm doing, then the law frees him from all responsibility. In any case, I'm freeing you from being responsible. Don't feel yourself bound, any more than I will. There has to be absolute freedom for us both. Here, take your ring back. Give me mine.

HELMER   That too?

NORA   That too.

HELMER   There it is.

NORA   Good. Well, now it's all over. I'm putting the keys here. The maids know all about keeping up the house—better than I do. Tomorrow, after I've left town, Kristine will stop by to pack up everything that's mine from home. I'd like those things shipped to me.

HELMER   Over! All over! Nora, won't you ever think about me?

NORA   I'm sure I'll think of you often, and about the children and the house here.

HELMER   May I write you?

NORA   No—never. You're not to do that.

HELMER   Oh, but let me send you—

NORA   Nothing. Nothing.

HELMER   Or help you if you need it.

NORA   No. I accept nothing from strangers.

HELMER   Nora—can I never be more than a stranger to you?

NORA   (picking up the overnight bag) Ah, Torvald—it would take the greatest miracle of all—

HELMER   Tell me the greatest miracle!

NORA   You and I both would have to transform ourselves to the point that—Oh, Torvald, I've stopped believing in miracles.

HELMER   But I'll believe. Tell me! Transform ourselves to the point that—?

NORA   That our living together could be a true marriage.

(She goes out down the hall.)

HELMER   (sinks down on a chair by the door, face buried in his hands) Nora! Nora! (Looking about and rising) Empty. She's gone. (A sudden hope leaps in him) The greatest miracle—?

(From below, the sound of a door slamming shut)

(1879)

QUESTIONS

1. Describe Torvald Helmer. What aspects of his character are most evident in the early scenes? Does he give any evidence of having changed by the end of the play? Do you think he is capable of sharing the kind of marriage Nora describes at the end of the play?

2. Evaluate Nora's behavior. Does she make the right decision in leaving her family? Why or why not?

3. Ibsen has remarked that A Doll House is more about human rights than women's rights. What kind of rights do you think he had in mind?

4. A Doll House has been performed with an alternative ending in which Nora and Torvald are reconciled, and Nora remains with her family. Is this an artistically appropriate and theatrically effective ending? Why or why not?

5. Consider the function of the following characters: Nils Krogstad, Dr. Rank, and Kristine Linde.
6. Examine the play's plot. How does Ibsen control our responses and arouse our curiosity? Point out places where the tempo or pace of the play changes. What effects do these changes have?
7. Identify two or three visual details or objects that function as symbols, and explain their significance.
8. Choose one scene important for its revelation of character and explain how you would dramatize it.

BERNARD SHAW

[1856-1950]

Another comic realist who, like Chekhov, straddles the nineteenth and twentieth centuries is Bernard Shaw. Shaw lived considerably longer than Chekhov and wrote much more. His more than sixty plays have been collected with his letters, novels, and criticism in over thirty volumes. In whatever genre he worked, Shaw's comedy turned not just on characters and situations, but on ideas. Ideas permeate his work the way they do Ibsen's. But Shaw's use of ideas is much more various than Ibsen's and considerably more comical. Frequently Shaw turns to satire as a mode of dramatizing ideas, as he does in *Arms and the Man*.

Produced in 1894 and published in 1898, *Arms and the Man* was Shaw's first "pleasant" play, as he called a group of them, and his first to be commercially staged. In his preface to *Plays Pleasant,* Shaw explained his antipathy to "idealism, which is only a flattering name for romance in politics and morals." With such idealistic, romanticized notions of love and war in mind, Shaw wrote *Arms and the Man* to express a more realistic view of each.

Unlike Chekhov, who avoided witty repartee, curtain clinching acts, and convoluted, melodramatic plots, Shaw took full advantage of such devices. His realism and his comedy thus differ radically from Chekhov's, as does his desire to use his plays, like Ibsen did, for didactic purposes. Shaw expressed his didactic and polemical impulses in a series of long prefaces to many of his plays, prefaces in which he discoursed on issues the plays dramatized. Nor was Shaw above replying to critics of his plays, as he did to the critics of *Arms* in the essay "A Dramatic Realist to His Critics." From that essay we gain a sense of Shaw as a realist dramatist whose business is to get outside systems that classify characters ethically or morally.

Shaw was basically an iconoclast who encouraged his audience to look more critically at ideas and ideals that they had previously accepted without question. Beneath the witty surface of his comedies lie serious questions. *Arms and the Man,* whose title announces its dual subjects, love and war, and whose first line echoes Vergil's *Aeneid,* ends with an exclamation: "Is he a man!" Sergius observes this about Bluntschli, the antiheroic hero of the play. And we wonder as we read the play, "just what is a man anyway?"

BERNARD SHAW

Arms and the Man

A PLEASANT PLAY

CHARACTERS

RAINA PETKOFF, *a young Bulgarian lady*.
CATHERINE PETKOFF, *her mother*.
LOUKA, *the Petkoffs' maid*.
CAPTAIN BLUNTSCHLI, *a Swiss officer in the Serbian army*.
A RUSSIAN OFFICER *in the Bulgarian army*.
NICOLA, *the Petkoffs' butler*.
PETKOFF, *Raina's father, a major in the Bulgarian army*.
SERGIUS SARANOFF, *Raina's fiancé, a major in the Bulgarian army*.

ACT I

(*Night: A lady's bedchamber in Bulgaria, in a small town near the Dragoman Pass, late in November in the year 1885. Through an open window with a little balcony a peak of the Balkans, wonderfully white and beautiful in the starlit snow, seems quite close at hand, though it is really miles away. The interior of the room is not like anything to be seen in the west of Europe. It is half rich Bulgarian, half cheap Viennese. Above the head of the bed, which stands against a little wall cutting off the left hand corner of the room, is a painted wooden shrine, blue and gold, with an ivory image of Christ, and a light hanging before it in a pierced metal ball suspended by three chains. The principal seat, placed towards the other side of the room and opposite the window, is a Turkish ottoman. The counterpane and hangings of the bed, the window curtains, the little carpet, and all the ornamental textile fabrics in the room are oriental and gorgeous; the paper on the walls is occidental and paltry. The washstand, against the wall on the side nearest the ottoman and window, consists of an enamelled iron basin with a pail beneath it in a painted metal frame, and a single towel on the rail at the side. The dressing table, between the bed and the window, is a common pine table, covered with a cloth of many colours, with an expensive toilet mirror on it. The door is on the side nearest the bed; and there is a chest of drawers between. This chest of drawers is also covered by a variegated native cloth; and on it there is a pile of paper backed novels, a box of chocolate creams, and a miniature easel with a large photograph of an extremely handsome officer, whose lofty bearing and magnetic glance can be felt even from the portrait. The room is lighted by a candle on the chest of drawers, and another on the dressing table with a box of matches beside it.*

The window is hinged doorwise and stands wide open. Outside, a pair of wooden shutters, opening outwards, also stand open. On the balcony a young lady, intensely conscious of the romantic beauty of the night, and of the fact that her own youth and beauty are part of it, is gazing at the snowy Balkans. She is in her nightgown, well covered by a long mantle of furs, worth, on a moderate estimate, about three times the furniture of the room.

Her reverie is interrupted by her mother, CATHERINE PETKOFF, *a woman over forty, imperiously energetic, with magnificent black hair and eyes, who might be a very splendid specimen of the wife of a mountain farmer, but is determined to be a Viennese lady, and to that end wears a fashionable tea gown on all occasions.*)

CATHERINE (*entering hastily, full of good news*): Raina! (*She pronounces it Raheena, with the stress on the ee.*) Raina! (*She goes to the bed, expecting to find* RAINA *there.*) Why, where—? (RAINA *looks into the room.*) Heavens, child! are you out in the night air instead of in your bed? You'll catch your death. Louka told me you were asleep.

RAINA (*dreamily*): I sent her away. I wanted to be alone. The stars are so beautiful! What is the matter?

CATHERINE: Such news! There has been a battle.

RAINA (*her eyes dilating*): Ah! (*She comes eagerly to* CATHERINE.)

CATHERINE: A great battle at Slivnitza! A victory! And it was won by Sergius.

RAINA (*with a cry of delight*): Ah! (*They embrace rapturously.*) Oh, mother! (*Then, with sudden anxiety*) is father safe?

CATHERINE: Of course: he sends me the news. Sergius is the hero of the hour, the idol of the regiment.

RAINA: Tell me, tell me. How was it? (*Ecstatically*) Oh, mother! mother! mother! (*She pulls her mother down on the ottoman; and they kiss one another frantically.*)

CATHERINE (*with surging enthusiasm*): You can't guess how splendid it is. A cavalry charge! think of that! He defied our Russian commanders— acted without orders—led a charge on his own responsibility—headed it himself—was the first man to sweep through their guns. Can't you see it, Raina: our gallant splendid Bulgarians with their swords and eyes flashing, thundering down like an avalanche and scattering the wretched Serbs and their dandified Austrian officers like chaff. And you! you kept Sergius waiting a year before you would be betrothed to him. Oh, if you have a drop of Bulgarian blood in your veins, you will worship him when he comes back.

RAINA: What will he care for my poor little worship after the acclamations of a whole army of heroes? But no matter: I am so happy! so proud! (*She rises and walks about excitedly.*) It proves that all our ideas were real after all.

CATHERINE (*indignantly*): Our ideas real! What do you mean?

RAINA: Our ideas of what Sergius would do. Our patriotism. Our heroic ideals. I sometimes used to doubt whether they were anything but dreams. Oh, what faithless little creatures girls are! When I buckled on Sergius's sword he looked so noble: it was treason to think of disillusion or humiliation or failure. And yet—and yet—(*She sits down again suddenly.*) Promise me you'll never tell him.

CATHERINE: Don't ask me for promises until I know what I'm promising.

RAINA: Well, it came into my head just as he was holding me in his arms and looking into my eyes, that perhaps we only had our heroic ideas because we are so fond of reading Byron and Pushkin, and because we were so delighted with the opera that season at Bucharest. Real life is so seldom like that! indeed never, as far as I knew it then. (*Remorsefully*) Only think, mother: I doubted him: I wondered whether all his heroic qualities and his soldiership might not prove mere imagination when he went into a real battle. I had an uneasy fear that he might cut a poor figure there beside all those clever officers from the Tsar's court.

CATHERINE: A poor figure! Shame on you! The Serbs have Austrian officers who are just as clever as the Russians; but we have beaten them in every battle for all that.

RAINA (*laughing and snuggling against her mother*): Yes: I was only a prosaic little coward. Oh, to think that it was all true! that Sergius is just as splendid and noble as he looks! that the world is really a glorious world for women who can see its glory and men who can act its romance! What happiness! what unspeakable fulfillment!

(*They are interrupted by the entry of* LOUKA, *a handsome proud girl in a pretty Bulgarian peasant's dress with double apron, so defiant that her servility to* RAINA *is almost insolent. She is afraid of* CATHERINE, *but even with her goes as far as she dares.*)

LOUKA: If you please, madam, all the windows are to be closed and the shutters made fast. They say there may be shooting in the streets. (RAINA *and* CATHERINE *rise together, alarmed.*) The Serbs are being chased right back through the pass; and they say they may run into the town. Our cavalry will be after them; and our people will be ready for them, you may be sure, now they're running away. (*She goes out on the balcony, and pulls the outside shutters to; then steps back into the room.*)

CATHERINE (*businesslike, housekeeping instincts aroused*): I must see that everything is made safe downstairs.

RAINA: I wish our people were not so cruel. What glory is there in killing wretched fugitives?

CATHERINE: Cruel! Do you suppose they would hesitate to kill you—or worse?

RAINA (*to* LOUKA): Leave the shutters so that I can just close them if I hear any noise.

CATHERINE (*authoritatively, turning on her way to the door*): Oh no, dear: you must keep them fastened. You would be sure to drop off to sleep and leave them open. Make them fast, Louka.

LOUKA: Yes, madam. (*She fastens them.*)

RAINA: Don't be anxious about me. The moment I hear a shot, I shall blow out the candles and roll myself up in bed with my ears well covered.

CATHERINE: Quite the wisest thing you can do, my love. Goodnight.

RAINA: Goodnight. (*Her emotion comes back for a moment.*) Wish me joy. (*They kiss.*) This is the happiest night of my life—if only there are no fugitives.

CATHERINE: Go to bed, dear; and don't think of them. (*She goes out.*)

LOUKA   (*secretly to* RAINA): If you would like the shutters open, just give them a push like this (*she pushes them: they open: she pulls them to again.*) One of them ought to be bolted at the bottom; but the bolt's gone.

RAINA   (*with dignity, reproving her*): Thanks, Louka; but we must do what we are told. (LOUKA *makes a grimace.*) Goodnight.

LOUKA   (*carelessly*): Goodnight. (*She goes out, swaggering.*)

(RAINA, *left alone, takes off her fur cloak and throws it on the ottoman. Then she goes to the chest of drawers, and adores the portrait there with feelings that are beyond all expression. She does not kiss it or press it to her breast, or shew it any mark of bodily affection; but she takes it in her hands and elevates it, like a priestess.*)

RAINA   (*looking up at the picture*): Oh, I shall never be unworthy of you any more, my soul's hero: never, never, never. (*She replaces it reverently. Then she selects a novel from the little pile of books. She turns over the leaves dreamily; finds her page; turns the book inside out at it; and, with a happy sigh, gets into bed and prepares to read herself to sleep. But before abandoning herself to fiction, she raises her eyes once more, thinking of the blessed reality, and murmurs.*) My hero! my hero!

(*A distant shot breaks the quiet of the night. She starts, listening; and two more shots, much nearer, follow, startling her so that she scrambles out of bed, and hastily blows out the candle on the chest of drawers. Then, putting her fingers in her ears, she runs to the dressing table, blows out the light there, and hurries back to bed in the dark, nothing being visible but the glimmer of the light in the pierced ball before the image, and the starlight seen through the slits at the top of the shutters. The firing breaks out again: there is a startling fusillade quite close at hand. Whilst it is still echoing, the shutters disappear, pulled open from without; and for an instant the rectangle of snowy starlight flashes out with the figure of a man silhouetted in black upon it. The shutters close immediately; and the room is dark again. But the silence is now broken by the sound of panting. Then there is a scratch; and the flame of a match is seen in the middle of the room.*)

RAINA   (*crouching on the bed*): Who's there? (*The match is out instantly.*) Who's there? Who is that?

A MAN'S VOICE   (*in the darkness, subduedly, but threateningly*): Sh—sh! Don't call out; or you'll be shot. Be good; and no harm will happen to you. (*She is heard leaving her bed, and making for the door.*) Take care: it's no use trying to run away.

RAINA: But who—

THE VOICE   (*warning*): Remember: if you raise your voice my revolver will go off. (*Commandingly*) Strike a light and let me see you. Do you hear. (*Another moment of silence and darkness as she retreats to the chest of drawers. Then she lights a candle; and the mystery is at an end. He is a man of about 35, in a deplorable plight, bespattered with mud and blood and snow, his belt and the strap of his revolver case keeping together the torn ruins of the blue tunic of a Serbian artillery officer. All that the candlelight and his unwashed unkempt condition make it possible to discern is that he is of middling stature and undistinguished appearance, with strong neck and shoulders, roundish obstinate looking head covered with short crisp bronze curls, clear quick eyes and good brows and mouth, hopelessly prosaic nose like that of a strong minded baby, trim sol-*

dierlike carriage and energetic manner, and with all his wits about him in spite of his desperate predicament: even with a sense of the humor of it, without, however, the least intention of trifling with it or throwing away a chance. Reckoning up what he can guess about RAINA: *her age, her social position, her character, and the extent to which she is frightened, he continues, more politely but still most determinedly*) Excuse my disturbing you; but you recognize my uniform? Serb! If I'm caught I shall be killed. (*Menacingly*) Do you understand that?

RAINA: Yes.

THE MAN: Well, I don't intend to get killed if I can help it. (*Still more formidably*) Do you understand that? (*He locks the door quickly but quietly.*)

RAINA   (*disdainfully*): I suppose not. (*She draws herself up superbly, and looks him straight in the face, adding, with cutting emphasis*) Some soldiers, I know, are afraid to die.

THE MAN   (*with grim goodhumor*): All of them, dear lady, all of them, believe me. It is our duty to live as long as we can. Now, if you raise an alarm—

RAINA   (*cutting him short*): You will shoot me. How do you know that *I* am afraid to die?

THE MAN   (*cunningly*): Ah; but suppose I don't shoot you, what will happen then? A lot of your cavalry will burst into this pretty room of yours and slaughter me here like a pig; for I'll fight like a demon: they shan't get me into the street to amuse themselves with: I know what they are. Are you prepared to receive that sort of company in your present undress? (RAINA, *suddenly conscious of her nightgown, instinctively shrinks and gathers it more closely about her neck. He watches her and adds pitilessly*) Hardly presentable, eh? (*She turns to the ottoman. He raises his pistol instantly, and cries*) Stop! (*She stops.*) Where are you going?

RAINA   (*with dignified patience*): Only to get my cloak.

THE MAN   (*passing swiftly to the ottoman and snatching the cloak*): A good idea! I'll keep the cloak; and you'll take care that nobody comes in and sees you without it. This is a better weapon than the revolver: eh? (*He throws the pistol down on the ottoman.*)

RAINA   (*revolted*): It is not the weapon of a gentleman!

THE MAN: It's good enough for a man with only you to stand between him and death. (*As they look at one another for a moment,* RAINA *hardly able to believe that even a Serbian officer can be so cynically and selfishly unchivalrous, they are startled by a sharp fusillade in the street. The chill of imminent death hushes the man's voice as he adds*) Do you hear? If you are going to bring those blackguards in on me you shall receive them as you are.

(*Clamor and disturbance. The pursuers in the street batter at the house door, shouting,* Open the door! Open the door! Wake up, will you! *A man servant's voice calls to them angrily from within,* This is Major Petkoff's house: you can't come in here; *but a renewal of the clamor, and a torrent of blows on the door, end with his letting a chain down with a clank, followed by a rush of heavy footsteps and a din of triumphant yells, dominated at last by the voice of* CATHERINE, *indignantly addressing an officer with* What does this mean, sir? Do you know where you are? *The noise subsides suddenly.*)

LOUKA   (*outside, knocking at the bedroom door*): My lady! my lady! get up quick and open the door. If you don't they will break it down.

(*The fugitive throws up his head with the gesture of a man who sees that it is all over with him, and drops the manner he has been assuming to intimidate* RAINA.)

THE MAN   (*sincerely and kindly*): No use, dear: I'm done for. (*Flinging the cloak to her*) Quick! wrap yourself up: they're coming.

RAINA: Oh, thank you. (*She wraps herself up with intense relief.*)

THE MAN   (*between his teeth*): Don't mention it.

RAINA   (*anxiously*): What will you do?

THE MAN   (*grimly*): The first man in will find out. Keep out of the way; and don't look. It won't last long; but it will not be nice. (*He draws his sabre and faces the door, waiting.*)

RAINA   (*impulsively*): I'll help you. I'll save you.

THE MAN: You can't.

RAINA: I can. I'll hide you. (*She drags him towards the window.*) Here! behind the curtains.

THE MAN   (*yielding to her*): There's just half a chance, if you keep your head.

RAINA   (*drawing the curtain before him*): S-sh! (*She makes for the ottoman.*)

THE MAN   (*putting out his head*): Remember—

RAINA   (*running back to him*): Yes?

THE MAN:—nine soldiers out of ten are born fools.

raina: Oh! (*She draws the curtain angrily before him.*)

THE MAN   (*looking out at the other side*): If they find me, I promise you a fight: a devil of a fight.

(*She stamps at him. He disappears hastily. She takes off her cloak, and throws it across the foot of the bed. Then, with a sleepy, disturbed air, she opens the door.* LOUKA *enters excitedly.*)

LOUKA: One of those beasts of Serbs has been seen climbing up the water-pipe to your balcony. Our men want to search for him; and they are so wild and drunk and furious. (*She makes for the other side of the room to get as far from the door as possible.*) My lady says you are to dress at once and to—(*She sees the revolver lying on the ottoman, and stops, petrified.*)

RAINA   (*as if annoyed at being disturbed*): They shall not search here. Why have they been let in?

CATHERINE   (*coming in hastily*): Raina, darling, are you safe? Have you seen anyone or heard anything?

RAINA: I heard the shooting. Surely the soldiers will not dare come in here?

CATHERINE: I have found a Russian officer, thank Heaven: he knows Sergius. (*Speaking through the door to someone outside*) Sir: will you come in now. My daughter will receive you.

(*A young Russian officer, in Bulgarian uniform, enters, sword in hand.*)

OFFICER   (*with soft feline politeness and stiff military carriage*): Good evening, gracious lady. I am sorry to intrude; but there is a Serb hiding on the balcony. Will you and the gracious lady your mother please to withdraw whilst we search?

RAINA   (*petulantly*): Nonsense, sir: you can see that there is no one on the balcony. (*She throws the shutters wide open and stands with her back to the curtain where the man is hidden, pointing to the moonlit balcony. A couple of shots are fired right under the window; and a bullet shatters the glass opposite* RAINA, *who winks and gasps, but stands her ground; whilst* CATHERINE *screams, and* THE OFFICER, *with a cry of* Take care! *rushes to the balcony.*)

THE OFFICER   (*on the balcony, shouting savagely down to the street*): Cease firing there, you fools: do you hear? Cease firing, damn you! (*He glares down for a moment; then turns to* RAINA, *trying to resume his polite manner.*) Could anyone have got in without your knowledge? Were you asleep?

RAINA: No: I have not been to bed.

THE OFFICER   (*impatiently, coming back into the room*): Your neighbors have their heads so full of runaway Serbs that they see them everywhere. (*Politely*) Gracious lady: a thousand pardons. Goodnight. (*Military bow, which* RAINA *returns coldly. Another to* CATHERINE, *who follows him out.*)

(RAINA *closes the shutters. She turns and sees* LOUKA, *who has been watching the scene curiously.*)

RAINA: Don't leave my mother, Louka, until the soldiers go away.

(LOUKA *glances at* RAINA, *at the ottoman, at the curtain; then purses her lips secretively, laughs insolently, and goes out.* RAINA, *highly offended by this demonstration, follows her to the door, and shuts it behind her with a slam, locking it violently. The man immediately steps out from behind the curtain, sheathing his sabre. Then, dismissing the danger from his mind in a businesslike way, he comes affably to* RAINA.)

THE MAN: A narrow shave; but a miss is as good as a mile. Dear young lady: your servant to the death. I wish for your sake I had joined the Bulgarian army instead of the other one. I am not a native Serb.

RAINA   (*haughtily*): No: you are one of the Austrians who set the Serbs on to rob us of our national liberty, and who officer their army for them. We hate them!

THE MAN: Austrian! not I. Don't hate me, dear young lady. I am a Swiss, fighting merely as a professional soldier. I joined the Serbs because they came first on the road from Switzerland. Be generous: you've beaten us hollow.

RAINA: Have I not been generous?

THE MAN: Noble! Heroic! But I'm not saved yet. This particular rush will soon pass through; but the pursuit will go on all night by fits and starts. I must take my chance to get off in a quiet interval. (*Pleasantly*) You don't mind my waiting just a minute or two, do you?

RAINA   (*putting on her most genteel society manner*): Oh, not at all. Won't you sit down?

THE MAN: Thanks. (*He sits on the foot of the bed.*)

(RAINA *walks with studied elegance to the ottoman and sits down. Unfortunately she sits on the pistol, and jumps up with a shriek. The man, all nerves, shies like a frightened horse to the other side of the room.*)

THE MAN   (*irritably*): Don't frighten me like that. What is it?

RAINA: Your revolver! It was staring that officer in the face all the time. What an escape!

THE MAN   (*vexed at being unnecessarily terrified*): Oh, is that all?

RAINA   (*staring at him rather superciliously as she conceives a poorer and poorer opinion of him, and feels proportionately more and more at her ease*): I am sorry I frightened you. (*She takes up the pistol and hands it to him.*) Pray take it to protect yourself against me.

THE MAN   (*grinning wearily at the sarcasm as he takes the pistol*): No use, dear young lady; there's nothing in it. It's not loaded. (*He makes a grimace at it, and drops it despairingly into his revolver case.*)

RAINA: Load it by all means.

THE MAN: I've no ammunition. What use are cartridges in battle? I always carry chocolate instead; and I finished the last cake of that hours ago.

RAINA   (*outraged in her most cherished ideals of manhood*): Chocolate! Do you stuff your pockets with sweets—like a schoolboy—even in the field?

THE MAN   (*grinning*): Yes: isn't it contemptible? (*Hungrily*) I wish I had some now.

RAINA: Allow me. (*She sails away scornfully to the chest of drawers, and returns with the box of confectionery in her hand.*) I am sorry I have eaten them all except these. (*She offers him the box.*)

THE MAN   (*ravenously*): You're an angel! (*He gobbles the contents.*) Creams! Delicious! (*He looks anxiously to see whether there are any more. There are none: he can only scrape the box with his fingers and suck them. When that nourishment is exhausted he accepts the inevitable with pathetic goodhumor, and says, with grateful emotion*) Bless you, dear lady! You can always tell an old soldier by the inside of his holsters and cartridge boxes. The young ones carry pistols and cartridges: the old ones, grub. Thank you. (*He hands back the box. She snatches it contemptuously from him and throws it away. He shies again, as if she had meant to strike him.*) Ugh! Don't do things so suddenly, gracious lady. It's mean to revenge yourself because I frightened you just now.

RAINA   (*loftily*): Frighten me! Do you know, sir, that though I am only a woman, I think I am at heart as brave as you.

THE MAN: I should think so. You haven't been under fire for three days as I have. I can stand two days without shewing it much; but no man can stand three days: I'm as nervous as a mouse. (*He sits down on the ottoman, and takes his head in his hands.*) Would you like to see me cry?

RAINA   (*alarmed*): No.

THE MAN: If you would, all you have to do is to scold me just as if I were a little boy and you my nurse. If I were in camp now, they'd play all sorts of tricks on me.

RAINA   (*a little moved*): I'm sorry. I won't scold you. (*Touched by the sympathy in her tone, he raises his head and looks gratefully at her: she immediately draws back and says stiffly*): You must excuse me: our soldiers are not like that. (*She moves away from the ottoman.*)

THE MAN: Oh yes they are. There are only two sorts of soldiers: old ones and young ones. I've served fourteen years: half of your fellows never smelt powder before. Why, how is it that you've just beaten us? Sheer ignorance of the art of war, nothing else. (*Indignantly*) I never saw anything so unprofessional.

RAINA   (*ironically*): Oh! was it unprofessional to beat you?

THE MAN: Well, come! is it professional to throw a regiment of cavalry on a battery of machine guns, with the dead certainty that if the guns go off not a horse or man will ever get within fifty yards of the fire? I couldn't believe my eyes when I saw it.

RAINA   (*eagerly turning to him, as all her enthusiasm and her dreams of glory rush back on her*): Did you see the great cavalry charge? Oh, tell me about it. Describe it to me.

THE MAN: You never saw a cavalry charge, did you?

RAINA: How could I?

THE MAN: Ah, perhaps not. No: of course not! Well, it's a funny sight. It's like slinging a handful of peas against a window pane: first one comes; then two or three close behind him; and then all the rest in a lump.

RAINA   (*her eyes dilating as she raises her clasped hands ecstatically*): Yes, first One! the bravest of the brave!

THE MAN   (*prosaically*): Hm! you should see the poor devil pulling at his horse.

RAINA: Why should he pull at his horse?

THE MAN   (*impatient of so stupid a question*): It's running away with him, of course: do you suppose the fellow wants to get there before the others and be killed? Then they all come. You can tell the young ones by their wildness and their slashing. The old ones come bunched up under the number one guard: they know that they're mere projectiles, and that it's no use trying to fight. The wounds are mostly broken knees, from the horses cannoning together.

RAINA: Ugh! But I don't believe the first man is a coward. I know he is a hero!

THE MAN   (*goodhumoredly*): That's what you'd have said if you'd seen the first man in the charge today.

RAINA   (*breathless, forgiving him everything*): Ah, I knew it! Tell me. Tell me about him.

THE MAN: He did it like an operatic tenor. A regular handsome fellow, with flashing eyes and lovely moustache, shouting his war-cry and charging like Don Quixote at the windmills. We did laugh.

RAINA: You dared to laugh!

THE MAN: Yes; but when the sergeant ran up as white as a sheet, and told us they'd sent us the wrong ammunition, and that we couldn't fire a round for the next ten minutes, we laughed at the other side of our mouths. I never felt so sick in my life; though I've been in one or two very tight places. And I hadn't even a revolver cartridge: only chocolate. We'd no bayonets: nothing. Of course, they just cut us to bits. And there was Don Quixote flourishing like a drum major, thinking he'd done the cleverest thing ever known, whereas he ought to be courtmartialled for it. Of all the fools ever let loose on a field of battle, that man must be the very maddest. He and his regiment simply committed suicide; only the pistol missed fire: that's all.

RAINA   (*deeply wounded, but steadfastly loyal to her ideals*): Indeed! Would you know him again if you saw him?

THE MAN: Shall I ever forget him!

(*She again goes to the chest of drawers. He watches her with a vague hope that she may have something more for him to eat. She takes the portrait from its stand and brings it to him.*)

RAINA: That is a photograph of the gentleman—the patriot and hero—to whom I am betrothed.

THE MAN   (*recognizing it with a shock*): I'm really very sorry. (*Looking at her*) Was it fair to lead me on? (*He looks at the portrait again.*) Yes: that's Don Quixote: not a doubt of it. (*He stifles a laugh.*)

RAINA   (*quickly*): Why do you laugh?

THE MAN   (*apologetic, but still greatly tickled*): I didn't laugh, I assure you. At least I didn't mean to. But when I think of him charging the windmills and imagining he was doing the finest thing—(*He chokes with suppressed laughter.*)

RAINA   (*sternly*): Give me back the portrait, sir.

THE MAN   (*with sincere remorse*): Of course. Certainly. I'm really very sorry. (*He hands her the picture. She deliberately kisses it and looks him straight in the face before returning to the chest of drawers to replace it. He follows her, apologizing.*) Perhaps I'm quite wrong, you know: no doubt I am. Most likely he had got wind of the cartridge business somehow, and knew it was a safe job.

RAINA: That is to say, he was a pretender and a coward! You did not dare say that before.

THE MAN   (*with a comic gesture of despair*): It's no use, dear lady: I can't make you see it from the professional point of view. (*As he turns away to get back to the ottoman, a couple of distant shots threaten renewed trouble.*)

RAINA   (*sternly, as she sees him listening to the shots*): So much the better for you!

THE MAN   (*turning*): How?

RAINA: You are my enemy; and you are at my mercy. What would I do if I were a professional soldier?

THE MAN: Ah, true, dear young lady: you're always right. I know how good you've been to me: to my last hour I shall remember those three chocolate creams. It was unsoldierly; but it was angelic.

RAINA   (*coldly*): Thank you. And now I will do a soldierly thing. You cannot stay here after what you have just said about my future husband; but I will go out on the balcony and see whether it is safe for you to climb down into the street. (*She turns to the window.*)

THE MAN   (*changing countenance*): Down that waterpipe! Stop! Wait! I can't! I daren't! The very thought of it makes me giddy. I came up it fast enough with death behind me. But to face it now in cold blood—! (*He sinks on the ottoman.*) It's no use: I give up: I'm beaten. Give the alarm. (*He drops his head on his hands in the deepest dejection.*)

RAINA   (*disarmed by pity*): Come: don't be disheartened. (*She stoops over him almost maternally: he shakes his head.*) Oh, you are a very poor soldier: a chocolate cream soldier! Come, cheer up! it takes less courage to climb down than to face capture: remember that.

THE MAN   (*dreamily, lulled by her voice*): No: capture only means death; and death is sleep: oh, sleep, sleep, sleep, undisturbed sleep! Climbing down the pipe means doing something—exerting myself—thinking! Death ten times over first.

RAINA   (*softly and wonderingly, catching the rhythm of his weariness*): Are you as sleepy as that?

THE MAN: I've not had two hours undisturbed sleep since I joined. I haven't closed my eyes for forty-eight hours.

RAINA   (*at her wit's end*): But what am I to do with you?

THE MAN   (*staggering up, roused by her desperation*): Of course. I must do something. (*He shakes himself; pulls himself together; and speaks with rallied vigor and courage.*) You see, sleep or no sleep, hunger or no hunger, tired or not tired, you can always do a thing when you know it must be done. Well, that pipe must be got down: (*he hits himself on the chest*) do you hear that, you chocolate cream soldier? (*He turns to the window.*)

RAINA   (*anxiously*): But if you fall?

THE MAN: I shall sleep as if the stones were a feather bed. Goodbye. (*He makes boldly for the window; and his hand is on the shutter when there is a terrible burst of firing in the street beneath.*)

RAINA   (*rushing to him*): Stop! (*She seizes him recklessly, and pulls him quite round.*) They'll kill you.

THE MAN   (*coolly, but attentively*): Never mind: this sort of thing is all in my day's work. I'm bound to take my chance. (*Decisively*) Now do what I tell you. Put out the candle; so that they shan't see the light when I open the shutters. And keep away from the window, whatever you do. If they see me they're sure to have a shot at me.

RAINA   (*clinging to him*): They're sure to see you: it's bright moonlight. I'll save you. Oh, how can you be so indifferent! You want me to save you, don't you?

THE MAN: I really don't want to be troublesome. (*She shakes him in her impatience.*) I am not indifferent, dear young lady, I assure you. But how is it to be done?

RAINA: Come away from the window. (*She takes him firmly back to the middle of the room. The moment she releases him he turns mechanically towards the window again. She seizes him and turns him back, exclaiming*) Please! (*He becomes motionless, like a hypnotized rabbit, his fatigue gaining fast on him. She releases him, and addresses him patronizingly.*) Now listen. You must trust to our hospitality. You do not yet know in whose house you are. I am a Petkoff.

THE MAN: A pet what?

RAINA   (*rather indignantly*): I mean that I belong to the family of the Petkoffs, the richest and best known in our country.

THE MAN: Oh, yes, of course. I beg your pardon. The Petkoffs, to be sure. How stupid of me!

RAINA: You know you never heard of them until this moment. How can you stoop to pretend!

THE MAN: Forgive me: I'm too tired to think; and the change of subject was too much for me. Don't scold me.

RAINA: I forgot. It might make you cry. (*He nods, quite seriously. She pouts and then resumes her patronizing tone.*) I must tell you that my father holds the highest command of any Bulgarian in our army. He is (*proudly*) a Major.

THE MAN (*pretending to be deeply impressed*): A Major! Bless me! Think of that!

RAINA: You shewed great ignorance in thinking that it was necessary to climb up to the balcony because ours is the only private house that has two rows of windows. There is a flight of stairs inside to get up and down by.

THE MAN: Stairs! How grand! You live in great luxury indeed, dear young lady.

RAINA: Do you know what a library is?

THE MAN: A library? A roomful of books?

RAINA: Yes. We have one, the only one in Bulgaria.

THE MAN: Actually a real library! I should like to see that.

RAINA (*affectedly*): I tell you these things to shew you that you are not in the house of ignorant country folk who would kill you the moment they saw your Serbian uniform, but among civilized people. We go to Bucharest every year for the opera season; and I have spent a whole month in Vienna.

THE MAN: I saw that, dear young lady. I saw at once that you knew the world.

RAINA: Have you ever seen the opera of Ernani?

THE MAN: Is that the one with the devil in it in red velvet, and a soldiers' chorus?

RAINA (*contemptuously*): No!

THE MAN (*stifling a heavy sigh of weariness*): Then I don't know it.

RAINA: I thought you might have remembered the great scene where Ernani, flying from his foes just as you are tonight, takes refuge in the castle of his bitterest enemy, an old Castilian noble. The noble refuses to give him up. His guest is sacred to him.

THE MAN (*quickly, waking up a little*): Have your people got that notion?

RAINA (*with dignity*): My mother and I can understand that notion, as you call it. And if instead of threatening me with your pistol as you did you had simply thrown yourself as a fugitive on our hospitality, you would have been as safe as in your father's house.

THE MAN: Quite sure?

RAINA (*turning her back on him in disgust*): Oh, it is useless to try to make you understand.

THE MAN: Don't be angry: you see how awkward it would be for me if there was any mistake. My father is a very hospitable man: he keeps six hotels; but I couldn't trust him as far as that. What about your father?

RAINA: He is away at Slivnitza fighting for his country. I answer for your safety. There is my hand in pledge of it. Will that reassure you? (*She offers him her hand.*)

THE MAN (*looking dubiously at his own hand*): Better not touch my hand, dear young lady. I must have a wash first.

RAINA (*touched*): That is very nice of you. I see that you are a gentleman.

THE MAN (*puzzled*): Eh?

RAINA: You must not think I am surprised. Bulgarians of really good standing—people in our position—wash their hands nearly every day. So you see I can appreciate your delicacy. You may take my hand. (*She offers it again.*)

THE MAN   (*kissing it with his hands behind his back*): Thanks, gracious young lady: I feel safe at last. And now would you mind breaking the news to your mother? I had better not stay here secretly longer than is necessary.

RAINA: If you will be so good as to keep perfectly still whilst I am away.

THE MAN: Certainly. (*He sits down on the ottoman.*)

(RAINA *goes to the bed and wraps herself in the fur cloak. His eyes close. She goes to the door. Turning for a last look at him, she sees that he is dropping off to sleep.*)

RAINA   (*at the door*): You are not going asleep, are you?

(*He murmurs inarticulately: she runs to him and shakes him.*) Do you hear? Wake up: you are falling asleep.

THE MAN: Eh? Falling aslee—? Oh no: not the least in the world: I was only thinking. It's all right: I'm wide awake.

RAINA   (*severely*): Will you please stand up while I am away. (*He rises reluctantly.*) All the time, mind.

THE MAN   (*standing unsteadily*): Certainly. Certainly: you may depend on me.

(RAINA *looks doubtfully at him. He smiles weakly. She goes reluctantly, turning again at the door, and almost catching him in the act of yawning. She goes out.*)

THE MAN   (*drowsily*): Sleep, sleep, sleep, sleep, slee—(*The words trail off into a murmur. He wakes again with a shock on the point of falling.*) Where am I? That's what I want to know: where am I? Must keep awake. Nothing keeps me awake except danger: remember that: (*intently*) danger, danger, danger, dan—(*trailing off again: another shock*) Where's danger? Mus' find it. (*He starts off vaguely round the room in search of it.*) What am I looking for? Sleep—danger—don't know. (*He stumbles against the bed.*) Ah yes: now I know. All right now. I'm to go to bed, but not to sleep. Be sure not to sleep, because of danger. Not to lie down either, only sit down. (*He sits on the bed. A blissful expression comes into his face.*) Ah! (*With a happy sigh he sinks back at full length; lifts his boots into the bed with a final effort; and falls fast asleep instantly.*)

(CATHERINE *comes in, followed by* RAINA.)

RAINA   (*looking at the ottoman*): He's gone! I left him here.

CATHERINE: Here! Then he must have climbed down from the—

RAINA   (*seeing him*): Oh! (*She points.*)

CATHERINE   (*scandalized*): Well! (*She strides to the bed,* RAINA *following until she is opposite her on the other side.*) He's fast asleep. The brute!

RAINA   (*anxiously*): Sh!

CATHERINE   (*shaking him*): Sir! (*Shaking him again, harder*) Sir!! (*Vehemently, shaking very hard*) Sir!!!

RAINA   (*catching her arm*): Don't, mamma; the poor darling is worn out. Let him sleep.

CATHERINE   (*letting him go, and turning amazed to* RAINA): The poor darling! Raina!!! (*She looks sternly at her daughter.*)

(*The man sleeps profoundly.*)

ACT II

(*The sixth of March, 1886. In the garden of* MAJOR PETKOFF'S *house. It is a fine spring morning: the garden looks fresh and pretty. Beyond the paling the tops of a couple of minarets can be seen, shewing that there is a valley there, with the little town in it. A few miles further the Balkan mountains rise and shut in the landscape. Looking towards them from within the garden, the side of the house is seen on the left, with a garden door reached by a little flight of steps. On the right the stable yard, with its gateway, encroaches on the garden. There are fruit bushes along the paling and house, covered with washing spread out to dry. A path runs by the house, and rises by two steps at the corner, where it turns out of sight. In the middle, a small table, with two bent wood chairs at it, is laid for breakfast with Turkish coffee pot, cups, rolls, etc.; but the cups have been used and the bread broken. There is a wooden garden seat against the wall on the right.*

LOUKA, *smoking a cigaret, is standing between the table and the house, turning her back with angry disdain on a man servant who is lecturing her. He is a middle-aged man of cool temperament and low but clear and keen intelligence, with the complacency of the servant who values himself on his rank in servitude, and the imperturbability of the accurate calculator who has no illusions. He wears a white Bulgarian costume: jacket with embroidered border, sash, wide knickerbockers, and decorated gaiters. His head is shaved up to the crown, giving him a high Japanese forehead. His name is* NICOLA.)

NICOLA: Be warned in time, Louka: mend your manners. I know the mistress. She is so grand that she never dreams that any servant could dare be disrespectful to her; but if she once suspects that you are defying her, out you go.

LOUKA: I do defy her. I will defy her. What do I care for her?

NICOLA: If you quarrel with the family, I never can marry you. It's the same as if you quarrelled with me!

LOUKA: You take her part against me, do you?

NICOLA   (*sedately*): I shall always be dependent on the good will of the family. When I leave their service and start a shop in Sofia, their custom will be half my capital: their bad word would ruin me.

LOUKA: You have no spirit. I should like to catch them saying a word against me!

NICOLA   (*pityingly*): I should have expected more sense from you, Louka. But you're young: you're young!

LOUKA: Yes; and you like me the better for it, don't you? But I know some family secrets they wouldn't care to have told, young as I am. Let them quarrel with me if they dare!

NICOLA   (*with compassionate superiority*): Do you know what they would do if they heard you talk like that?

LOUKA: What could they do?

NICOLA: Discharge you for untruthfulness. Who would believe any stories you told after that? Who would give you another situation? Who in this house would dare be seen speaking to you ever again? How long would your father be left on his little farm? (*She impatiently throws away the end of her cigaret, and stamps on it.*) Child: you don't know the power such high people have over the like of you and me when we try to rise out of our poverty against them. (*He goes close to her and lowers his voice.*) Look at me, ten years in their service. Do you think I know no secrets? I know things about the mistress that she wouldn't have the master know for a thousand levas. I know things about him that she wouldn't let him hear the last of for six months if I blabbed them to her. I know things about Raina that would break off her match with Sergius if—

LOUKA   (*turning on him quickly*): How do you know? I never told you!

NICOLA   (*opening his eyes cunningly*): So that's your little secret, is it? I thought it might be something like that. Well, you take my advice and be respectful; and make the mistress feel that no matter what you know or don't know, she can depend on you to hold your tongue and serve the family faithfully. That's what they like; and that's how you'll make most out of them.

LOUKA   (*with searching scorn*): You have the soul of a servant, Nicola.

NICOLA   (*complacently*): Yes: that's the secret of success in service.

(*A loud knocking with a whip handle on a wooden door is heard from the stable yard.*)

MALE VOICE OUTSIDE: Hollo! Hollo there! Nicola!

LOUKA: Master! back from the war!

NICOLA   (*quickly*): My word for it, Louka, the war's over. Off with you and get some fresh coffee. (*He runs out into the stable yard.*)

LOUKA   (*as she collects the coffee pot and cups on the tray, and carries it into the house*): You'll never put the soul of a servant into me.

(MAJOR PETKOFF *comes from the stable yard, followed by* NICOLA. *He is a cheerful, excitable, insignificant, unpolished man of about fifty, naturally unambitious except as to his income and his importance in local society, but just now greatly pleased with the military rank which the war has thrust on him as a man of consequence in his town. The fever of plucky patriotism which the Serbian attack roused in all the Bulgarians has pulled him through the war; but he is obviously glad to be home again.*)

PETKOFF   (*pointing to the table with his whip*): Breakfast out here, eh?

NICOLA: Yes, sir. The mistress and Miss Raina have just gone in.

PETKOFF   (*sitting down and taking a roll*): Go in and say I've come; and get me some fresh coffee.

NICOLA: It's coming, sir. (*He goes to the house door.* LOUKA, *with fresh coffee, a clean cup, and a brandy bottle on her tray, meets him.*) Have you told the mistress?

LOUKA: Yes: she's coming.

(NICOLA *goes into the house.* LOUKA *brings the coffee to the table.*)

PETKOFF: Well: the Serbs haven't run away with you, have they?

LOUKA: No, sir.

PETKOFF: That's right. Have you brought me some cognac?

LOUKA   (*putting the bottle on the table*): Here, sir.

PETKOFF: That's right. (*He pours some into his coffee.*)

(CATHERINE, *who, having at this early hour made only a very perfunctory toilet, wears a Bulgarian apron over a once brilliant but now half worn-out dressing gown, and a colored hand-kerchief tied over her thick black hair, comes from the house with Turkish slippers on her bare feet, looking astonishingly handsome and stately under all the circumstances.* LOUKA *goes into the house.*)

CATHERINE: My dear Paul: what a surprise for us! (*She stoops over the back of his chair to kiss him.*) Have they brought you fresh coffee?

PETKOFF: Yes: Louka's been looking after me. The war's over. The treaty was signed three days ago at Bucharest; and the decree for our army to demobilize was issued yesterday.

CATHERINE (*springing erect, with flashing eyes*): Paul: have you let the Austrians force you to make peace?

PETKOFF (*submissively*): My dear: they didn't consult me. What could I do? (*She sits down and turns away from him.*) But of course we saw to it that the treaty was an honorable one. It declares peace—

CATHERINE (*outraged*): Peace!

PETKOFF (*appeasing her*):—but not friendly relations: remember that. They wanted to put that in; but I insisted on its being struck out. What more could I do?

CATHERINE: You could have annexed Serbia and made Prince Alexander Emperor of the Balkans. That's what I would have done.

PETKOFF: I don't doubt it in the least, my dear. But I should have had to subdue the whole Austrian Empire first; and that would have kept me too long away from you. I missed you greatly.

CATHERINE (*relenting*): Ah! (*She stretches her hand affectionately across the table to squeeze his.*)

PETKOFF: And how have you been, my dear?

CATHERINE: Oh, my usual sore throats: that's all.

PETKOFF (*with conviction*): That comes from washing your neck every day. I've often told you so.

CATHERINE: Nonsense, Paul!

PETKOFF (*over his coffee and cigaret*): I don't believe in going too far with these modern customs. All this washing can't be good for the health; it's not natural. There was an Englishman at Philippopolis who used to wet himself all over with cold water every morning when he got up. Disgusting! It all comes from the English: their climate makes them so dirty that they have to be perpetually washing themselves. Look at my father! he never had a bath in his life; and he lived to be ninety-eight, the healthiest man in Bulgaria. I don't mind a good wash once a week to keep up my position; but once a day is carrying the thing to a ridiculous extreme.

CATHERINE: You are a barbarian at heart still, Paul. I hope you behaved yourself before all those Russian officers.

PETKOFF: I did my best. I took care to let them know that we have a library.

CATHERINE: Ah; but you didn't tell them that we have an electric bell in it? I have had one put up.

PETKOFF: What's an electric bell?

CATHERINE: You touch a button; something tinkles in the kitchen; and then Nicola comes up.

PETKOFF: Why not shout for him?

CATHERINE: Civilized people never shout for their servants. I've learnt that while you were away.

PETKOFF: Well, I'll tell you something I've learnt too. Civilized people don't hang out their washing to dry where visitors can see it: so you'd better have all that (*indicating the clothes on the bushes*) put somewhere else.

CATHERINE: Oh, that's absurd, Paul: I don't believe really refined people notice such things.

SERGIUS   (*knocking at the stable gates*): Gate, Nicola!

PETKOFF: There's Sergius. (*Shouting*) Hollo, Nicola!

CATHERINE: Oh, don't shout, Paul: it really isn't nice.

PETKOFF: Bosh! (*He shouts louder than before*): Nicola!

NICOLA   (*appearing at the house door*): Yes, sir.

PETKOFF: Are you deaf? Don't you hear Major Saranoff knocking? Bring him round this way. (*He pronounces the name with the stress on the second syllable: Sarahnoff.*)

NICOLA: Yes, Major. (*He goes into the stable yard.*)

PETKOFF: You must talk to him, my dear, until Raina takes him off our hands. He bores my life out about our not promoting him. Over my head, if you please.

CATHERINE: He certainly ought to be promoted when he marries Raina. Besides, the country should insist on having at least one native general.

PETKOFF: Yes; so that he could throw away whole brigades instead of regiments. It's no use, my dear: he hasn't the slightest chance of promotion until we're quite sure that the peace will be a lasting one.

NICOLA   (*at the gate, announcing*): Major Sergius Saranoff! (*He goes into the house and returns presently with a third chair, which he places at the table. He then withdraws.*)

(MAJOR SERGIUS SARANOFF, *the original of the portrait in* RAINA'S *room, is a tall romantically handsome man, with the physical hardihood, the high spirit, and the susceptible imagination of an untamed mountaineer chieftain. But his remarkable personal distinction is of a characteristically civilized type. The ridges of his eyebrows, curving with an interrogative twist round the projections at the outer corners; his jealously observant eye; his nose, thin, keen, and apprehensive in spite of the pugnacious high bridge and large nostril; his assertive chin would not be out of place in a Parisian salon, shewing that the clever imaginative barbarian has an acute critical faculty which has been thrown into intense activity by the arrival of western civilization in the Balkans. The result is precisely what the advent of nineteenth century thought first produced in England: to wit, Byronism. By his brooding on the perpetual failure, not only of others, but of himself, to live up to his ideals; by his consequent cynical scorn for humanity; by his jejune credulity as to the absolute validity of his concepts and the unworthiness of the world in disregarding them; by his wincings and mockeries under the sting of the petty disillusions which every hour spent among men brings to his sensitive observation, he has acquired the half tragic, half ironic air, the mysterious moodiness, the suggestion of a strange and terrible history that has left nothing but undying remorse, by which Childe Harold fascinated the grandmothers of his English contemporaries. It is clear that here or nowhere is* RAINA'S *ideal hero.* CATHERINE *is hardly less enthusiastic about him than her daughter, and much less reserved in shewing her enthusiasm. As he enters from the stable gate, she rises effusively to greet him.* PETKOFF *is distinctly less disposed to make a fuss about him.*)

PETKOFF: Here already, Sergius! Glad to see you.

CATHERINE: My dear Sergius! (*She holds out both her hands.*)

SERGIUS   (*kissing them with scrupulous gallantry*): My dear mother, if I may call you so.

PETKOFF (*drily*): Mother-in-law, Sergius: mother-in-law! Sit down; and have some coffee.

SERGIUS: Thank you: none for me. (*He gets away from the table with a certain distaste for* PETKOFF'S *enjoyment of it, and posts himself with conscious dignity against the rail of the steps leading to the house.*)

CATHERINE: You look superb. The campaign has improved you, Sergius. Everybody here is mad about you. We were all wild with enthusiasm about that magnificent cavalry charge.

SERGIUS (*with grave irony*): Madam: it was the cradle and the grave of my military reputation.

CATHERINE: How so?

SERGIUS: I won the battle the wrong way when our worthy Russian generals were losing it the right way. In short, I upset their plans, and wounded their self-esteem. Two Cossack colonels had their regiments routed on the most correct principles of scientific warfare. Two major-generals got killed strictly according to military etiquette. The two colonels are now major-generals; and I am still a simple major.

CATHERINE: You shall not remain so, Sergius. The women are on your side; and they will see that justice is done you.

SERGIUS: It is too late. I have only waited for the peace to send in my resignation.

PETKOFF (*dropping his cup in his amazement*): Your resignation!

CATHERINE: Oh, you must withdraw it!

SERGIUS (*with resolute measured emphasis, folding his arms*): I never withdraw.

PETKOFF (*vexed*): Now who could have supposed you were going to do such a thing?

SERGIUS (*with fire*): Everyone that knew me. But enough of myself and my affairs. How is Raina; and where is Raina?

RAINA (*suddenly coming round the corner of the house and standing at the top of the steps in the path*): Raina is here.

(*She makes a charming picture as they turn to look at her. She wears an underdress of pale green silk, draped with an overdress of thin ecru canvas embroidered with gold. She is crowned with a dainty eastern cap of gold tinsel. Sergius goes impulsively to meet her. Posing regally, she presents her hand: he drops chivalrously on one knee and kisses it.*)

PETKOFF (*aside to* CATHERINE, *beaming with parental pride*): Pretty, isn't it? She always appears at the right moment.

CATHERINE (*impatiently*): Yes; she listens for it. It is an abominable habit.

(SERGIUS *leads* RAINA *forward with splendid gallantry. When they arrive at the table, she turns to him with a bend of the head: he bows; and thus they separate, he coming to his place and she going behind her father's chair.*)

RAINA (*stooping and kissing her father*): Dear father! Welcome home!

PETKOFF (*patting her cheek*): My little pet girl. (*He kisses her. She goes to the chair left by* NICOLA *for* SERGIUS, *and sits down.*)

CATHERINE: And so you're no longer a soldier, Sergius.

SERGIUS: I am no longer a soldier. Soldiering, my dear madam, is the coward's art of attacking mercilessly when you are strong, and keeping out of harm's way when you are weak. That is the whole secret of successful fighting. Get your enemy at a disadvantage; and never, on any account, fight him on equal terms.

PETKOFF: They wouldn't let us make a fair stand-up fight of it. However, I suppose soldiering has to be a trade like any other trade.

SERGIUS: Precisely. But I have no ambition to shine as a tradesman; so I have taken the advice of that bagman of a captain that settled the exchange of prisoners with us at Pirot, and given it up.

PETKOFF: What! that Swiss fellow? Sergius: I've often thought of that exchange since. He over-reached us about those horses.

SERGIUS: Of course he over-reached us. His father was a hotel and livery stable keeper; and he owed his first step to his knowledge of horse-dealing. (*With mock enthusiasm*) Ah, he was a soldier: every inch a soldier! If only I had bought the horses for my regiment instead of foolishly leading it into danger, I should have been a field-marshal now!

CATHERINE: A Swiss? What was he doing in the Serbian army?

PETKOFF: A volunteer, of course: keen on picking up his profession. (*Chuckling*) We shouldn't have been able to begin fighting if these foreigners hadn't shewn us how to do it: we knew nothing about it; and neither did the Serbs. Egad, there'd have been no war without them!

RAINA: Are there many Swiss officers in the Serbian Army?

PETKOFF: No. All Austrians, just as our officers were all Russians. This was the only Swiss I came across. I'll never trust a Swiss again. He humbugged us into giving him fifty ablebodied men for two hundred worn out chargers. They weren't even eatable!

SERGIUS: We were two children in the hands of that consummate soldier, Major: simply two innocent little children.

RAINA: What was he like?

CATHERINE: Oh, Raina, what a silly question!

SERGIUS: He was like a commercial traveller in uniform. Bourgeois to his boots!

PETKOFF   (*grinning*): Sergius: tell Catherine that queer story his friend told us about how he escaped after Slivnitza. You remember. About his being hid by two women.

SERGIUS   (*with bitter irony*): Oh yes: quite a romance! He was serving in the very battery I so unprofessionally charged. Being a thorough soldier, he ran away like the rest of them, with our cavalry at his heels. To escape their sabres he climbed a waterpipe and made his way into the bedroom of a young Bulgarian lady. The young lady was enchanted by his persuasive commercial traveller's manners. She very modestly entertained him for an hour or so, and then called in her mother lest her conduct should appear unmaidenly. The old lady was equally fascinated; and the fugitive was sent on his way in the morning, disguised in an old coat belonging to the master of the house, who was away at the war.

RAINA   (*rising with marked stateliness*): Your life in the camp has made you coarse, Sergius. I did not think you would have repeated such a story before me. (*She turns away coldly.*)

CATHERINE   (*also rising*): She is right, Sergius. If such women exist, we should be spared the knowledge of them.

PETKOFF: Pooh! nonsense! what does it matter?

SERGIUS   (*ashamed*): No, Petkoff: I was wrong. (*To* RAINA, *with earnest humility*): I beg your pardon. I have behaved abominably. Forgive me, Raina. (*She bows reservedly.*) And you too, madam. (CATHERINE *bows graciously and sits down. He proceeds solemnly, again addressing* RAINA.) The glimpses I have had of the seamy side of life during the last few months have made me cynical; but I should not have brought my cynicism here: least of all into your presence, Raina. I—(*Here, turning to the others, he is evidently going to begin a long speech when the Major interrupts him.*)

PETKOFF: Stuff and nonsense, Sergius! That's quite enough fuss about nothing: a soldier's daughter should be able to stand up without flinching to a little strong conversation. (*He rises.*) Come: it's time for us to get to business. We have to make up our minds how those three regiments are to get back to Philippopolis: there's no forage for them on the Sofia route. (*He goes towards the house.*) Come along. (SERGIUS *is about to follow him when* CATHERINE *rises and intervenes.*)

CATHERINE: Oh, Paul, can't you spare Sergius for a few moments? Raina has hardly seen him yet. Perhaps I can help you to settle about the regiments.

SERGIUS   (*protesting*): My dear madam, impossible: you—

CATHERINE   (*stopping him playfully*): You stay here, my dear Sergius: there's no hurry. I have a word or two to say to Paul. (SERGIUS *instantly bows and steps back.*) Now, dear (*taking* PETKOFF'S *arm*): come and see the electric bell.

PETKOFF: Oh, very well, very well.

(*They go into the house together affectionately.* SERGIUS, *left alone with* RAINA, *looks anxiously at her, fearing that she is still offended. She smiles, and stretches out her arms to him.*)

SERGIUS   (*hastening to her*): Am I forgiven?

RAINA   (*placing her hands on his shoulders as she looks up at him with admiration and worship*): My hero! My king!

SERGIUS: My queen! (*He kisses her on the forehead.*)

RAINA: How I have envied you, Sergius! You have been out in the world, on the field of battle, able to prove yourself there worthy of any woman in the world; whilst I have had to sit at home inactive—dreaming—useless—doing nothing that could give me the right to call myself worthy of any man.

SERGIUS: Dearest: all my deeds have been yours. You inspired me. I have gone through the war like a knight in a tournament with his lady looking down at him!

RAINA: And you have never been absent from my thoughts for a moment. (*Very solemnly*) Sergius: I think we two have found the higher love. When I think of you, I feel that I could never do a base deed, or think an ignoble thought.

SERGIUS: My lady and my saint! (*He clasps her reverently.*)

RAINA   (*returning his embrace*): My lord and my—

SERGIUS: Sh—sh! Let me be the worshipper, dear. You little know how unworthy even the best man is of a girl's pure passion!

RAINA: I trust you. I love you. You will never disappoint me, Sergius.

(LOUKA *is heard singing within the house. They quickly release each other.*) I can't pretend to talk indifferently before her: my heart is too full. (LOUKA *comes from the house with her tray. She goes to the table, and begins to clear it, with her back turned to them.*) I will get my hat; and then we can go out until lunch time. Wouldn't you like that?

SERGIUS: Be quick. If you are away five minutes, it will seem five hours. (RAINA *runs to the top of the steps, and turns there to exchange looks with him and wave him a kiss with both hands. He looks after her with emotion for a moment; then turns slowly away, his face radiant with the loftiest exaltation. The movement shifts his field of vision, into the corner of which there now comes the tail of* LOUKA'S *double apron. His attention is arrested at once. He takes a stealthy look at her, and begins to twirl his moustache mischievously, with his left hand akimbo on his hip. Finally, striking the ground with his heels in something of a cavalry swagger, he strolls over to the other side of the table, opposite her, and says*) Louka: do you know what the higher love is?

LOUKA   (*astonished*): No, sir.

SERGIUS: Very fatiguing thing to keep up for any length of time, Louka. One feels the need of some relief after it.

LOUKA   (*innocently*): Perhaps you would like some coffee, sir? (*She stretches her hand across the table for the coffee pot.*)

SERGIUS   (*taking her hand*): Thank you, Louka.

LOUKA   (*pretending to pull*): Oh, sir, you know I didn't mean that. I'm surprised at you!

SERGIUS   (*coming clear of the table and drawing her with him*): I am surprised at myself, Louka. What would Sergius, the hero of Slivnitza, say if he saw me now? What would Sergius, the apostle of the higher love, say if he saw me now? What would the half dozen Sergiuses who keep popping in and out of this handsome figure of mine say if they caught us here? (*Letting go her hand and slipping his arm dexterously round her waist*) Do you consider my figure handsome, Louka?

LOUKA: Let me go, sir. I shall be disgraced. (*She struggles: he holds her inexorably.*) Oh, will you let go?

SERGIUS   (*looking straight into her eyes*): No.

LOUKA: Then stand back where we can't be seen. Have you no common sense?

SERGIUS: Ah! that's reasonable. (*He takes her into the stable yard gateway, where they are hidden from the house.*)

LOUKA   (*plaintively*): I may have been seen from the windows: Miss Raina is sure to be spying about after you.

SERGIUS   (*stung: letting her go*): Take care, Louka. I may be worthless enough to betray the higher love; but do not you insult it.

LOUKA   (*demurely*): Not for the world, sir, I'm sure. May I go on with my work, please, now?

SERGIUS   (*again putting his arm round her*): You are a provoking little witch, Louka. If you were in love with me, would you spy out of windows on me?

LOUKA: Well, you see, sir, since you say you are half a dozen different gentlemen all at once, I should have a great deal to look after.

SERGIUS   (*charmed*): Witty as well as pretty. (*He tries to kiss her.*)

LOUKA   (*avoiding him*): No: I don't want your kisses. Gentlefolk are all alike:

you making love to me behind Miss Raina's back; and she doing the same behind yours.

SERGIUS   (*recoiling a step*): Louka!

LOUKA: It shews how little you really care.

SERGIUS   (*dropping his familiarity, and speaking with freezing politeness*): If our
conversation is to continue, Louka, you will please remember that a gentleman
does not discuss the conduct of the lady he is engaged to with her maid.

LOUKA: It's so hard to know what a gentleman considers right. I thought
from your trying to kiss me that you had given up being so particular.

SERGIUS   (*turning from her and striking his forehead as he comes back into the garden from the gateway*): Devil! devil!

LOUKA: Ha! ha! I expect one of the six of you is very like me, sir; though
I am only Miss Raina's maid. (*She goes back to her work at the table, taking no further notice of him.*)

SERGIUS   (*speaking to himself*): Which of the six is the real man? that's the
question that torments me. One of them is a hero, another a buffoon, another
a humbug, another perhaps a bit of a blackguard. (*He pauses, and looks furtively
at* LOUKA *as he adds, with deep bitterness*) And one, at least, is a coward: jealous,
like all cowards. (*He goes to the table.*) Louka.

LOUKA: Yes?

SERGIUS: Who is my rival?

LOUKA: You shall never get that out of me, for love or money.

SERGIUS: Why?

LOUKA: Never mind why. Besides, you would tell that I told you; and I
should lose my place.

SERGIUS   (*holding out his right hand in affirmation*): No! on the honor of a—
(*He checks himself; and his hand drops, nerveless, as he concludes sardonically*)—of a
man capable of behaving as I have been behaving for the last five minutes. Who
is he?

LOUKA: I don't know. I never saw him. I only heard his voice through the
door of her room.

SERGIUS: Damnation! How dare you?

LOUKA   (*retreating*): Oh, I mean no harm: you've no right to take up my
words like that. The mistress knows all about it. And I tell you that if that gentleman ever comes here again, Miss Raina will marry him, whether he likes it
or not. I know the difference between the sort of manner you and she put on
before one another and the real manner.

(SERGIUS *shivers as if she had stabbed him. Then, setting his face like iron, he strides grimly
to her, and grips her above the elbows with both hands.*)

SERGIUS: Now listen you to me.

LOUKA   (*wincing*): Not so tight: you're hurting me.

SERGIUS: That doesn't matter. You have stained my honor by making me
a party to your eavesdropping. And you have betrayed your mistress.

LOUKA   (*writhing*): Please—

SERGIUS: That shews that you are an abominable little clod of common clay,
with the soul of a servant. (*He lets her go as if she were an unclean thing, and turns*

away, dusting his hands of her, to the bench by the wall, where he sits down with averted head, meditating gloomily.)

LOUKA   (*whimpering angrily with her hands up her sleeves, feeling her bruised arms*): You know how to hurt with your tongue as well as with your hands. But I don't care, now I've found out that whatever clay I'm made of, you're made of the same. As for her, she's a liar; and her fine airs are a cheat; and I'm worth six of her. (*She shakes the pain off hardily; tosses her head; and sets to work to put the things on the tray.*)

(*He looks doubtfully at her. She finishes packing the tray, and laps the cloth over the edges, so as to carry all out together. As she stoops to lift it, he rises.*)

SERGIUS: Louka! (*She stops and looks defiantly at him.*) A gentleman has no right to hurt a woman under any circumstances. (*With profound humility, uncovering his head*) I beg your pardon.

LOUKA: That sort of apology may satisfy a lady. Of what use is it to a servant?

SERGIUS   (*rudely crossed in his chivalry, throws it off with a bitter laugh, and says slightingly*): Oh! you wish to be paid for the hurt! (*He puts on his shako, and takes some money from his pocket.*)

LOUKA   (*her eyes filling with tears in spite of herself*): No: I want my hurt made well.

SERGIUS   (*sobered by her tone*): How?

(*She rolls up her left sleeve; clasps her arm with the thumb and fingers of her right hand; and looks down at the bruise. Then she raises her head and looks straight at him. Finally, with a superb gesture, she presents her arm to be kissed. Amazed, he looks at her; at the arm; at her again; hesitates; and then, with shuddering intensity, exclaims* Never! *and gets away as far as possible from her.*

Her arm drops. Without a word, and with unaffected dignity, she takes her tray, and is approaching the house when RAINA *returns, wearing a hat and jacket in the height of the Vienna fashion of the previous year, 1885.* LOUKA *makes way proudly for her, and then goes into the house.*)

RAINA: I'm ready. What's the matter? (*Gaily*) Have you been flirting with Louka?

SERGIUS   (*hastily*): No, no. How can you think such a thing?

RAINA   (*ashamed of herself*): Forgive me, dear: it was only a jest. I am so happy today.

(*He goes quickly to her, and kisses her hand remorsefully.* CATHERINE *comes out and calls to them from the top of the steps.*)

CATHERINE   (*coming down to them*): I am sorry to disturb you, children; but Paul is distracted over those three regiments. He doesnt know how to send them to Philippopolis; and he objects to every suggestion of mine. You must go and help him, Sergius. He is in the library.

RAINA   (*disappointed*): But we are just going out for a walk.

SERGIUS: I shall not be long. Wait for me just five minutes. (*He runs up the steps to the door.*)

RAINA   (*following him to the foot of the steps and looking up at him with timid co-*

quetry): I shall go round and wait in full view of the library windows. Be sure you draw father's attention to me. If you are a moment longer than five minutes, I shall go in and fetch you, regiments or no regiments.

SERGIUS (*laughing*): Very well. (*He goes in.*)

(RAINA *watches him until he is out of her sight. Then, with a perceptible relaxation of manner, she begins to pace up and down the garden in a brown study.*)

CATHERINE: Imagine their meeting that Swiss and hearing the whole story! The very first thing your father asked for was the old coat we sent him off in. A nice mess you have got us into!

RAINA (*gazing thoughtfully at the gravel as she walks*): The little beast!

CATHERINE: Little beast! What little beast?

RAINA: To go and tell! Oh, if I had him here, I'd cram him with chocolate creams til he couldn't ever speak again!

CATHERINE: Don't talk such stuff. Tell me the truth, Raina. How long was he in your room before you came to me?

RAINA (*whisking round and recommencing her march in the opposite direction*): Oh, I forget.

CATHERINE: You cannot forget! Did he really climb up after the soldiers were gone: or was he there when that officer searched the room?

RAINA: No. Yes: I think he must have been there then.

CATHERINE: You think! Oh, Raina! Raina! Will anything ever make you straightforward? If Sergius finds out, it will be all over between you.

RAINA (*with cool impertinence*): Oh, I know Sergius is your pet. I sometimes wish you could marry him instead of me. You would just suit him. You would pet him, and spoil him, and mother him to perfection.

CATHERINE (*opening her eyes very widely indeed*): Well, upon my word!

RAINA (*capriciously: half to herself*): I always feel a longing to do or say something dreadful to him—to shock his propriety—to scandalize the five senses out of him. (*To* CATHERINE, *perversely*) I don't care whether he finds out about the chocolate cream soldier or not. I half hope he may. (*She again turns and strolls flippantly away up the path to the corner of the house.*)

CATHERINE: And what should I be able to say to your father, pray?

RAINA (*over her shoulder, from the top of the two steps*): Oh, poor father! As if he could help himself! (*She turns the corner and passes out of sight.*)

CATHERINE (*looking after her, her fingers itching*): Oh, if you were only ten years younger! (LOUKA *comes from the house with a salver, which she carries hanging down by her side.*) Well?

LOUKA: There's a gentleman just called, madam. A Serbian officer.

CATHERINE (*flaming*): A Serb! And how dare he—(*checking herself bitterly*): Oh, I forgot. We are at peace now. I suppose we shall have them calling every day to pay their compliments. Well: if he is an officer why don't you tell your master? He is in the library with Major Saranoff. Why do you come to me?

LOUKA: But he asks for you, madam. And I don't think he knows who you are: he said the lady of the house. He gave me this little ticket for you. (*She takes a card out of her bosom; puts it on the salver; and offers it to* CATHERINE.)

CATHERINE (*reading*): "Captain Bluntschli"? That's a German name.

LOUKA: Swiss, madam, I think.

CATHERINE   (*with a bound that makes* LOUKA *jump back*): Swiss! What is he like?

LOUKA   (*timidly*): He has a big carpet bag, madam.

CATHERINE: Oh Heavens! he's come to return the coat. Send him away: say we're not at home: ask him to leave his address and I'll write to him. Oh stop: that will never do. Wait! (*She throws herself into a chair to think it out.* LOUKA *waits.*) The master and Major Saranoff are busy in the library, aren't they?

LOUKA: Yes, madam.

CATHERINE   (*decisively*): Bring the gentleman out here at once. (*Peremptorily*): And be very polite to him. Don't delay. Here (*impatiently snatching the salver from her*): leave that here; and go straight back to him.

LOUKA: Yes, madam (*going.*)

CATHERINE: Louka!

LOUKA   (*stopping*): Yes, madam.

CATHERINE: Is the library door shut?

LOUKA: I think so, madam.

CATHERINE: If not, shut it as you pass through.

LOUKA: Yes, madam (*going*).

CATHERINE: Stop (LOUKA *stops.*) He will have to go that way (*indicating the gate of the stable yard.*) Tell Nicola to bring his bag here after him. Don't forget.

LOUKA   (*surprised*): His bag?

CATHERINE: Yes: here: as soon as possible. (*Vehemently*) Be quick! (LOUKA *runs into the house.* CATHERINE *snatches her apron off and throws it behind a bush. She then takes up the salver and uses it as a mirror, with the result that the handkerchief tied round her head follows the apron. A touch to her hair and a shake to her dressing gown make her presentable.*) Oh, how? how? how can a man be such a fool! Such a moment to select! (LOUKA *appears at the door of the house, announcing* Captain Bluntschli. *She stands aside at the top of the steps to let him pass before she goes in again. He is the man of the midnight adventure in* RAINA'S *room, clean, well brushed, smartly uniformed, and out of trouble, but still unmistakably the same man. The moment* LOUKA'S *back is turned,* CATHERINE *swoops on him with impetuous, urgent, coaxing appeal.*) Captain Bluntschli: I am very glad to see you; but you must leave this house at once. (*He raises his eyebrows.*) My husband has just returned with my future son-in-law; and they know nothing. If they did, the consequences would be terrible. You are a foreigner: you do not feel our national animosities as we do. We still hate the Serbs: the effect of the peace on my husband has been to make him feel like a lion baulked of his prey. If he discovers our secret, he will never forgive me; and my daughter's life will hardly be safe. Will you, like the chivalrous gentleman and soldier you are, leave at once before he finds you here?

BLUNTSCHLI   (*disappointed, but philosophical*): At once, gracious lady. I only came to thank you and return the coat you lent me. If you will allow me to take it out of my bag and leave it with your servant as I pass out, I need detain you no further. (*He turns to go into the house.*)

CATHERINE   (*catching him by the sleeve*): Oh, you must not think of going back that way. (*Coaxing him across to the stable gates*) This is the shortest way out. Many thanks. So glad to have been of service to you. Goodbye.

BLUNTSCHLI: But my bag?

CATHERINE: It shall be sent on. You will leave me your address.

BLUNTSCHLI: True. Allow me. (*He takes out his cardcase, and stops to write his address, keeping* CATHERINE *in an agony of impatience. As he hands her the card,* PETKOFF, *hatless, rushes from the house in a fluster of hospitality, followed by* SERGIUS.)

PETKOFF   (*as he hurries down the steps*): My dear Captain Bluntschli—

CATHERINE: Oh Heavens! (*She sinks on the seat against the wall.*)

PETKOFF   (*too preoccupied to notice her as he shakes* BLUNTSCHLI's *hand heartily*): Those stupid people of mine thought I was out here, instead of in the—haw!—library (*he cannot mention the library without betraying how proud he is of it*). I saw you through the window. I was wondering why you didn't come in. Saranoff is with me: you remember him, don't you?

SERGIUS   (*saluting humorously, and then offering his hand with great charm of manner*): Welcome, our friend the enemy!

PETKOFF: No longer the enemy, happily. (*Rather anxiously*) I hope you've called as a friend, and not about horses or prisoners.

CATHERINE: Oh, quite as a friend, Paul. I was just asking Captain Bluntschli to stay to lunch; but he declares he must go at once.

SERGIUS   (*sardonically*): Impossible, Bluntschli. We want you here badly. We have to send on three cavalry regiments to Philippopolis; and we don't in the least know how to do it.

BLUNTSCHLI   (*suddenly attentive and businesslike*): Philippopolis? The forage is the trouble, I suppose.

PETKOFF   (*eagerly*): Yes: that's it. (*To* SERGIUS) He sees the whole thing at once.

BLUNTSCHLI: I think I can shew you how to manage that.

SERGIUS: Invaluable man! Come along! (*Towering over* BLUNTSCHLI, *he puts his hand on his shoulder and takes him to the steps,* PETKOFF *following.*)

(RAINA *comes from the house as* BLUNTSCHLI *puts his foot on the first step.*)

RAINA: Oh! The chocolate cream soldier!

(BLUNTSCHLI *stands rigid.* SERGIUS, *amazed, looks at* RAINA, *then at* PETKOFF, *who looks back at him and then at his wife.*)

CATHERINE   (*with commanding presence of mind*): My dear Raina, don't you see that we have a guest here? Captain Bluntschli: one of our new Serbian friends.

(RAINA *bows:* BLUNTSCHLI *bows.*)

RAINA: How silly of me! (*She comes down into the centre of the group, between* BLUNTSCHLI *and* PETKOFF.) I made a beautiful ornament this morning for the ice pudding; and that stupid Nicola has just put down a pile of plates on it and spoilt it. (*To* BLUNTSCHLI, *winningly*) I hope you didn't think that you were the chocolate cream soldier, Captain Bluntschli.

BLUNTSCHLI   (*laughing*): I assure you I did. (*Stealing a whimsical glance at her*) Your explanation was a relief.

PETKOFF   (*suspiciously, to* RAINA): And since when, pray, have you taken to cooking?

CATHERINE: Oh, whilst you were away. It is her latest fancy.

PETKOFF   (*testily*): And has Nicola taken to drinking? He used to be careful enough. First he shews Captain Bluntschli out here when he knew quite well I was in the library; and then he goes downstairs and breaks Raina's chocolate soldier. He must—(NICOLA *appears at the top of the steps with the bag. He descends; places it respectfully before* BLUNTSCHLI; *and waits for further orders. General amazement.* NICOLA, *unconscious of the effect he is producing, looks perfectly satisfied with himself. When* PETKOFF *recovers his power of speech, he breaks out at him with*) Are you mad, Nicola?

NICOLA   (*taken aback*): Sir?

PETKOFF: What have you brought that for?

NICOLA: My lady's orders, major. Louka told me that—

CATHERINE   (*interrupting him*): My orders! Why should I order you to bring Captain Bluntschli's luggage out here? What are you thinking of, Nicola?

NICOLA   (*after a moment's bewilderment, picking up the bag as he addresses* BLUNTSCHLI *with the very perfection of servile discretion*): I beg your pardon, captain, I am sure. (*To* CATHERINE): My fault, madame: I hope you'll overlook it. (*He bows, and is going to the steps with the bag, when* PETKOFF *addresses him angrily.*)

PETKOFF: You'd better go and slam that bag, too, down on Miss Raina's ice pudding! (*This is too much for* NICOLA. *The bag drops from his hand almost on his master's toes, eliciting a roar of*) Begone, you butter-fingered donkey.

NICOLA   (*snatching up the bag, and escaping into the house*): Yes, Major.

CATHERINE: Oh, never mind. Paul: don't be angry.

PETKOFF   (*blustering*): Scoundrel! He's got out of hand while I was away. I'll teach him. Infernal blackguard! The sack next Saturday! I'll clear out the whole establishment—(*He is stifled by the caresses of his wife and daughter, who hang round his neck, petting him.*)

CATHERINE	Now, now, now, it

(*together*):

RAINA	Wow, wow, wow:

mustn't be angry. He meant
not on your first day at home.

no harm. Be good to please
I'll make another ice pudding.

me, dear. Sh-sh-sh-sh!
Tch-ch-ch!

PETKOFF   (*yielding*): Oh well, never mind. Come, Bluntschli: let's have no more nonsense about going away. You know very well you're not going back to Switzerland yet. Until you do go back you'll stay with us.

RAINA: Oh, do, Captain Bluntschli.

PETKOFF   (*to* CATHERINE): Now, Catherine: it's of you he's afraid. Press him: and he'll stay.

CATHERINE: Of course I shall be only too delighted if (*appealingly*) Captain Bluntschli really wishes to stay. He knows my wishes.

BLUNTSCHLI   (*in his driest military manner*): I am at madam's orders.

SERGIUS   (*cordially*): That settles it!

PETKOFF   (*heartily*): Of course!

RAINA: You see you must stay.

BLUNTSCHLI   (*smiling*): Well, if I must, I must. (*Gesture of despair from* CATHERINE.)

ACT III

(*In the library after lunch. It is not much of a library. Its literary equipment consists of a single fixed shelf stocked with old paper covered novels, broken backed, coffee stained, torn and thumbed; and a couple of little hanging shelves with a few gift books on them: the rest of the wall space being occupied by trophies of war and the chase. But it is a most comfortable sitting room. A row of three large windows shews a mountain panorama, just now seen in one of its friendliest aspects in the mellowing afternoon light. In the corner next the right hand window a square earthenware stove, a perfect tower of glistening pottery, rises nearly to the ceiling and guarantees plenty of warmth. The ottoman is like that in* RAINA'S *room, and similarly placed; and the window seats are luxurious with decorated cushions. There is one object, however, hopelessly out of keeping with its surroundings. This is a small kitchen table, much the worse for wear, fitted as a writing table with an old canister full of pens, an eggcup filled with ink, and a deplorable scrap of heavily used pink blotting paper.*

At the side of this table, which stands to the left of anyone facing the window, BLUNTSCHLI *is hard at work with a couple of maps before him, writing orders. At the head of it sits* SERGIUS, *who is supposed to be also at work, but is actually gnawing the feather of a pen, and contemplating* BLUNTSCHLI'S *quick, sure, businesslike progress with a mixture of envious irritation at his own incapacity and awestruck wonder at an ability which seems to him almost miraculous, though its prosaic character forbids him to esteem it.* THE MAJOR *is comfortably established on the ottoman, with a newspaper in his hand and the tube of his hookah within easy reach.* CATHERINE *sits at the stove, with her back to them, embroidering.* RAINA, *reclining on the divan, is gazing in a daydream out at the Balkan landscape, with a neglected novel in her lap.*

The door is on the same side as the stove, farther from the window. The button of the electric bell is at the opposite side, behind BLUNTSCHLI.)

PETKOFF   (*looking up from his paper to watch how they are getting on at the table*): Are you sure I can't help in any way, Bluntschli?

BLUNTSCHLI   (*without interrupting his writing or looking up*): Quite sure, thank you. Saranoff and I will manage it.

SERGIUS   (*grimly*): Yes: we'll manage it. He finds out what to do; draws up the orders; and I sign 'em. Division of labor! (BLUNTSCHLI *passes him a paper.*) Another one? Thank you. (*He plants the paper squarely before him; sets his chair carefully parallel to it; and signs with his cheek on his elbow and his protruded tongue following the movements of his pen.*) This hand is more accustomed to the sword than to the pen.

PETKOFF: It's very good of you, Bluntschli: it is indeed, to let yourself be put upon in this way. Now are you quite sure I can do nothing?

CATHERINE (*in a low warning tone*): You can stop interrupting, Paul.

PETKOFF (*starting and looking round at her*): Eh? Oh! Quite right, my love: Quite right. (*He takes his newspaper up again, but presently lets it drop.*) Ah, you haven't been campaigning, Catherine: you don't know how pleasant it is for us to sit here, after a good lunch, with nothing to do but enjoy ourselves. There's only one thing I want to make me thoroughly comfortable.

CATHERINE: What is that?

PETKOFF: My old coat. I'm not at home in this one: I feel as if I were on parade.

CATHERINE: My dear Paul, how absurd you are about that old coat! It must be hanging in the blue closet where you left it.

PETKOFF: My dear Catherine, I tell you I've looked there. Am I to believe my own eyes or not? (CATHERINE *rises and crosses the room to press the button of the electric bell.*) What are you shewing off that bell for? (*She looks at him majestically, and silently resumes her chair and her needlework.*) My dear: if you think the obstinacy of your sex can make a coat out of two old dressing gowns of Raina's, your waterproof, and my mackintosh, you're mistaken. That's exactly what the blue closet contains at present.

(NICOLA *presents himself.*)

CATHERINE: Nicola: go to the blue closet and bring your master's old coat here: the braided one he wears in the house.

NICOLA: Yes, madame. (*He goes out.*)

PETKOFF: Catherine.

CATHERINE: Yes, Paul.

PETKOFF: I bet you any piece of jewellery you like to order from Sofia against a week's housekeeping money that the coat isn't there.

CATHERINE: Done, Paul!

PETKOFF (*excited by the prospect of a gamble*): Come: here's an opportunity for some sport. Who'll bet on it? Bluntschli: I'll give you six to one.

BLUNTSCHLI (*imperturbably*): It would be robbing you, Major. Madame is sure to be right. (*Without looking up, he passes another batch of papers to* SERGIUS.)

SERGIUS (*also excited*): Bravo, Switzerland! Major: I bet my best charger against an Arab mare for Raina that Nicola finds the coat in the blue closet.

PETKOFF (*eagerly*): Your best char—

CATHERINE (*hastily interrupting him*): Don't be foolish, Paul. An Arabian mare will cost you 50,000 levas.

RAINA (*suddenly coming out of her picturesque revery*): Really, mother, if you are going to take the jewellery, I don't see why you should grudge me my Arab.

(NICOLA *comes back with the coat, and brings it to* PETKOFF, *who can hardly believe his eyes.*)

CATHERINE: Where was it, Nicola?

NICOLA: Hanging in the blue closet, madame.

PETKOFF: Well, I am d—

CATHERINE   (*stopping him*): Paul!

PETKOFF: I could have sworn it wasn't there. Age is beginning to tell on me. I'm getting hallucinations. (*To* NICOLA) Here: help me to change. Excuse me, Bluntschli. (*He begins changing coats,* NICOLA *acting as valet.*) Remember: I didn't take that bet of yours, Sergius. You'd better give Raina that Arab steed yourself, since you've roused her expectations. Eh, Raina? (*He looks round at her; but she is again rapt in the landscape. With a little gush of parental affection and pride, he points her out to them, and says*) She's dreaming, as usual.

SERGIUS: Assuredly she shall not be the loser.

PETKOFF: So much the better for her. *I* shan't come off so cheaply, I expect. (*The change is now complete.* NICOLA *goes out with the discarded coat.*) Ah, now I feel at home at last. (*He sits down and takes his newspaper with a grunt of relief.*)

BLUNTSCHLI   (*to* SERGIUS, *handing a paper*): That's the last order.

PETKOFF   (*jumping up*): What! Finished?

BLUNTSCHLI: Finished.

PETKOFF   (*with childlike envy*): Haven't you anything for me to sign?

BLUNTSCHLI: Not necessary. His signature will do.

PETKOFF   (*inflating his chest and thumping it*): Ah well, I think we've done a thundering good day's work. Can I do anything more?

BLUNTSCHLI: You had better both see the fellows that are to take these. (SERGIUS *rises.*) Pack them off at once; and shew them that I've marked on the orders the time they should hand them in by. Tell them that if they stop to drink or tell stories—if they're five minutes late, they'll have the skin taken off their backs.

SERGIUS   (*stiffening indignantly*): I'll say so. (*He strides to the door.*) And if one of them is man enough to spit in my face for insulting him, I'll buy his discharge and give him a pension. (*He goes out.*)

BLUNTSCHLI   (*confidentially*): Just see that he talks to them properly, Major, will you?

PETKOFF   (*officiously*): Quite right, Bluntschli, quite right. I'll see to it. (*He goes to the door importantly, but hesitates on the threshold.*) By the bye, Catherine, you may as well come too. They'll be far more frightened of you than of me.

CATHERINE   (*putting down her embroidery*): I daresay I had better. You would only splutter at them. (*She goes out,* PETKOFF *holding the door for her and following her.*)

BLUNTSCHLI: What an army! They make cannons out of cherry trees; and the officers send for their wives to keep discipline! (*He begins to fold and docket the papers.*)

(RAINA, *who has risen from the divan, marches slowly down the room with her hands clasped behind her, and looks mischievously at him.*)

RAINA: You look ever so much nicer than when we last met. (*He looks up, surprised.*) What have you done to yourself?

BLUNTSCHLI: Washed; brushed; good night's sleep and breakfast. That's all.

RAINA: Did you get back safely that morning?

BLUNTSCHLI: Quite, thanks.

RAINA: Were they angry with you for running away from Sergius's charge?

BLUNTSCHLI   (*grinning*): No: they were glad; because they'd all just run away themselves.

RAINA   (*going to the table, and leaning over it towards him*): It must have made a lovely story for them: all that about me and my room.

BLUNTSCHLI: Capital story. But I only told it to one of them: a particular friend.

RAINA: On whose discretion you could absolutely rely?

BLUNTSCHLI: Absolutely.

RAINA: Hm! He told it all to my father and Sergius the day you exchanged the prisoners. (*She turns away and strolls carelessly across to the other side of the room.*)

BLUNTSCHLI   (*deeply concerned, and half incredulous*): No! You don't mean that, do you?

RAINA   (*turning, with sudden earnestness*): I do indeed. But they don't know that it was in this house you took refuge. If Sergius knew, he would challenge you and kill you in a duel.

BLUNTSCHLI: Bless me! then don't tell him.

RAINA: Please be serious, Captain Bluntschli. Can you not realize what it is to me to deceive him? I want to be quite perfect with Sergius: no meanness, no smallness, no deceit. My relation to him is the one really beautiful and noble part of my life. I hope you can understand that.

BLUNTSCHLI   (*sceptically*): You mean that you wouldn't like him to find out that the story about the ice pudding was a—a—a—You know.

RAINA   (*wincing*): Ah, don't talk of it in that flippant way. I lied: I know it. But I did it to save your life. He would have killed you. That was the second time I ever uttered a falsehood. (BLUNTSCHLI *rises quickly and looks doubtfully and somewhat severely at her.*) Do you remember the first time?

BLUNTSCHLI: I! No. Was I present?

RAINA: Yes; and I told the officer who was searching for you that you were not present.

BLUNTSCHLI: True. I should have remembered it.

RAINA   (*greatly encouraged*): Ah, it is natural that you should forget it first. It cost you nothing: it cost me a lie! A lie!

(*She sits down on the ottoman, looking straight before her with her hands clasped round her knee.* BLUNTSCHLI, *quite touched, goes to the ottoman with a particularly reassuring and considerate air, and sits down beside her.*)

BLUNTSCHLI: My dear young lady, don't let this worry you. Remember: I'm a soldier. Now what are the two things that happen to a soldier so often that he comes to think nothing of them? One is hearing people tell lies (RAINA *recoils*): the other is getting his life saved in all sorts of ways by all sorts of people.

RAINA   (*rising in indignant protest*): And so he becomes a creature incapable of faith and of gratitude.

BLUNTSCHLI   (*making a wry face*): Do you like gratitude? I don't. If pity is akin to love, gratitude is akin to the other thing.

RAINA: Gratitude! (*Turning on him*) If you are incapable of gratitude you are incapable of any noble sentiment. Even animals are grateful. Oh, I see now exactly what you think of me! You were not surprised to hear me lie. To you it was something I probably did every day! every hour! That is how men think of women. (*She paces the room tragically.*)

BLUNTSCHLI   (*dubiously*): There's reason in everything. You said you'd told only two lies in your whole life. Dear young lady: isn't that rather a short allowance? I'm quite a straightforward man myself; but it wouldn't last me a whole morning.

RAINA   (*staring haughtily at him*): Do you know, sir, that you are insulting me?

BLUNTSCHLI   I can't help it. When you strike that noble attitude and speak in that thrilling voice, I admire you; but I find it impossible to believe a single word you say.

RAINA   (*superbly*): Captain Bluntschli!

BLUNTSCHLI   (*unmoved*): Yes?

RAINA   (*standing over him, as if she could not believe her senses*): Do you mean what you said just now? Do you know what you said just now?

BLUNTSCHLI: I do.

RAINA   (*gasping*): I! I!!! (*She points to herself incredulously, meaning "I, Raina Petkoff tell lies!" He meets her gaze unflinchingly. She suddenly sits down beside him, and adds, with a complete change of manner from the heroic to a babyish familiarity*) How did you find me out?

BLUNTSCHLI   (*promptly*): Instinct, dear young lady. Instinct, and experience of the world.

RAINA   (*wonderingly*): Do you know, you are the first man I ever met who did not take me seriously?

BLUNTSCHLI: You mean, don't you, that I am the first man that has ever taken you quite seriously?

RAINA: Yes: I suppose I do mean that. (*Cosily, quite at her ease with him*) How strange it is to be talked to in such a way! You know, I've always gone on like that.

BLUNTSCHLI: You mean the—?

RAINA: I mean the noble attitude and the thrilling voice. (*They laugh together.*) I did it when I was a tiny child to my nurse. She believed in it. I do it before my parents. They believe in it. I do it before Sergius. He believes in it.

BLUNTSCHLI: Yes: he's a little in that line himself, isn't he?

RAINA   (*startled*): Oh! Do you think so?

BLUNTSCHLI: You know him better than I do.

RAINA: I wonder—I wonder is he? If I thought that—! (*Discouraged*) Ah, well; what does it matter? I suppose, now you've found me out, you despise me.

BLUNTSCHLI   (*warmly, rising*): No, my dear young lady, no, no, no a thousand times. It's part of your youth: part of your charm. I'm like all the rest of them: the nurse, your parents, Sergius: I'm your infatuated admirer.

RAINA   (*pleased*): Really?

BLUNTSCHLI   (*slapping his breast smartly with his hand, German fashion*): Hand aufs Herz! Really and truly.

RAINA   (*very happy*): But what did you think of me for giving you my portrait?

BLUNTSCHLI   (*astonished*): Your portrait! You never gave me your portrait.

RAINA   (*quickly*): Do you mean to say you never got it?

BLUNTSCHLI: No. (*He sits down beside her, with renewed interest, and says, with some complacency*) When did you send it to me?

RAINA   (*indignantly*): I did not send it to you. (*She turns her head away, and adds, reluctantly*) It was in the pocket of that coat.

BLUNTSCHLI   (*pursing his lips and rounding his eyes*): Oh-o-oh! I never found it. It must be there still.

RAINA   (*springing up*): There still! for my father to find the first time he puts his hand in his pocket! Oh, how could you be so stupid?

BLUNTSCHLI   (*rising also*): It doesn't matter: I suppose it's only a photograph: how can he tell who it was intended for? Tell him he put it there himself.

RAINA   (*bitterly*): Yes: that is so clever! isn't it? (*Distractedly*) Oh! what shall I do?

BLUNTSCHLI: Ah, I see. You wrote something on it. That was rash.

RAINA   (*vexed almost to tears*): Oh, to have done such a thing for you, who care no more—except to laugh at me—oh! Are you sure nobody has touched it?

BLUNTSCHLI: Well, I can't be quite sure. You see, I couldn't carry it about with me all the time: one can't take much luggage on active service.

RAINA: What did you do with it?

BLUNTSCHLI: When I got through to Pirot I had to put it in safe keeping somehow. I thought of the railway cloak room; but that's the surest place to get looted in modern warfare. So I pawned it.

RAINA: Pawned it!!!

BLUNTSCHLI: I know it doesn't sound nice: but it was much the safest plan. I redeemed it the day before yesterday. Heaven only knows whether the pawn-broker cleared out the pockets or not.

RAINA   (*furious: throwing the words right into his face*): You have a low shop-keeping mind. You think of things that would never come into a gentleman's head.

BLUNTSCHLI   (*phlegmatically*): That's the Swiss national character, dear lady. (*He returns to the table.*)

RAINA: Oh, I wish I had never met you. (*She flounces away, and sits at the window fuming.*)

(LOUKA *comes in with a heap of letters and telegrams on her salver, and crosses, with her bold free gait, to the table. Her left sleeve is looped up to the shoulder with a brooch, shewing her naked arm, with a broad gilt bracelet covering the bruise.*)

LOUKA   (*to* BLUNTSCHLI): For you. (*She empties the salver with a fling on to the table.*) The messenger is waiting. (*She is determined not to be civil to an enemy, even if she must bring him his letters.*)

BLUNTSCHLI   (*to* RAINA): Will you excuse me: the last postal delivery that reached me was three weeks ago. These are the subsequent accumulations. Four telegrams: a week old. (*He opens one.*) Oho! Bad news!

RAINA   (*rising and advancing a little remorsefully*): Bad news?

BLUNTSCHLI: My father's dead. (*He looks at the telegram with his lips pursed, musing on the unexpected change in his arrangements.* LOUKA *crosses herself hastily.*)

RAINA: Oh, how very sad!

BLUNTSCHLI: Yes: I shall have to start for home in an hour. He has left a lot of big hotels behind him to be looked after. (*He takes up a fat letter in a long blue envelope.*) Here's a whacking letter from the family solicitor. (*He puts out the enclosures and glances over them.*) Great Heavens! Seventy! Two hundred! (*In a crescendo of dismay*) Four hundred! Four thousand!! Nine thousand six hundred!!! What on earth am I to do with them all?

RAINA (*timidly*): Nine thousand hotels?

BLUNTSCHLI: Hotels nonsense. If you only knew! Oh, it's too ridiculous! Excuse me: I must give my fellow orders about starting. (*He leaves the room hastily, with the documents in his hand.*)

LOUKA (*knowing instinctively that she can annoy* RAINA *by disparaging* BLUNTSCHLI): He has not much heart, that Swiss. He has not a word of grief for his poor father.

RAINA (*bitterly*): Grief! A man who has been doing nothing but killing people for years! What does he care? What does any soldier care? (*She goes to the door, restraining her tears with difficulty.*)

LOUKA: Major Saranoff has been fighting too; and he has plenty of heart left. (RAINA, *at the door, draws herself up haughtily and goes out.*) Aha! I thought you wouldn't get much feeling out of your soldier. (*She is following* RAINA *when* NICOLA *enters with an armful of logs for the stove.*)

NICOLA (*grinning amorously at her*): I've been trying all the afternoon to get a minute alone with you, my girl. (*His countenance changes as he notices her arm.*) Why, what fashion is that of wearing your sleeve, child?

LOUKA (*proudly*): My own fashion.

NICOLA: Indeed! If the mistress catches you, she'll talk to you. (*He puts the logs down, and seats himself comfortably on the ottoman.*)

LOUKA: Is that any reason why you should take it on yourself to talk to me?

NICOLA: Come! don't be contrary with me. I've some good news for you. (*She sits down beside him. He takes out some paper money.* LOUKA, *with an eager gleam in her eyes, tries to snatch it; but he shifts it quickly to his left hand, out of her reach.*) See! a twenty leva bill! Sergius gave me that, out of pure swagger. A fool and his money are soon parted. There's ten levas more. The Swiss gave me that for backing up the mistress' and Raina's lies about him. He's no fool, he isn't. You should have heard old Catherine downstairs as polite as you please to me, telling me not to mind the Major being a little impatient; for they knew what a good servant I was—after making a fool and a liar of me before them all! The twenty will go to our savings; and you shall have the ten to spend if you'll only talk to me so as to remind me I'm a human being. I get tired of being a servant occasionally.

LOUKA: Yes: sell your manhood for 30 levas, and buy me for 10! (*Rising scornfully*) Keep your money. You were born to be a servant. I was not. When you set up your shop you will only be everybody's servant instead of somebody's servant. (*She goes moodily to the table and seats herself regally in* SERGIUS'S *chair.*)

NICOLA (*picking up his logs, and going to the stove*): Ah, wait til you see. We shall have our evenings to ourselves; and I shall be master in my own house, I promise you. (*He throws the logs down and kneels at the stove.*)

LOUKA: You shall never be master in mine.

NICOLA　(*turning, still on his knees, and squatting down rather forlornly on his calves, daunted by her implacable disdain*): You have a great ambition in you, Louka. Remember: if any luck comes to you, it was I that made a woman of you.

LOUKA:　You!

NICOLA　(*scrambling up and going to her*): Yes, me. Who was it made you give up wearing a couple of pounds of false black hair on your head and reddening your lips and cheeks like any other Bulgarian girl! I did. Who taught you to trim your nails, and keep your hands clean, and be dainty about yourself, like a fine Russian lady! Me: do you hear that? me! (*She tosses her head defiantly; and he turns away, adding more coolly*) I've often thought that if Raina were out of the way, and you just a little less of a fool and Sergius just a little more of one, you might come to be one of my grandest customers, instead of only being my wife and costing me money.

LOUKA:　I believe you would rather be my servant than my husband. You would make more out of me. Oh, I know that soul of yours.

NICOLA　(*going closer to her for greater emphasis*): Never you mind my soul; but just listen to my advice. If you want to be a lady, your present behaviour to me won't do at all, unless when we're alone. It's too sharp and impudent; and impudence is a sort of familiarity: it shews affection for me. And don't you try being high and mighty with me, either. You're like all country girls: you think it's genteel to treat a servant the way I treat a stableboy. That's only your ignorance; and don't you forget it. And don't be so ready to defy everybody. Act as if you expected to have your own way, not as if you expected to be ordered about. The way to get on as a lady is the same as the way to get on as a servant: you've got to know your place: that's the secret of it. And you may depend on me to know my place if you get promoted. Think over it, my girl. I'll stand by you: one servant should always stand by another.

LOUKA　(*rising impatiently*): Oh, I must behave in my own way. You take all the courage out of me with your cold-blooded wisdom. Go and put those logs in the fire: that's the sort of thing you understand.

(*Before* NICOLA *can retort,* SERGIUS *comes in. He checks himself a moment on seeing* LOUKA; *then goes to the stove.*)

SERGIUS　(*to* NICOLA): I am not in the way of your work, I hope.

NICOLA　(*in a smooth, elderly manner*): Oh no, sir: thank you kindly. I was only speaking to this foolish girl about her habit of running up here to the library whenever she gets a chance, to look at the books. That's the worst of her education, sir: it gives her habits above her station. (*To* LOUKA) Make that table tidy, Louka, for the Major. (*He goes out sedately.*)

(LOUKA, *without looking at* SERGIUS, *pretends to arrange the papers on the table. He crosses slowly to her, and studies the arrangement of her sleeve reflectively.*)

SERGIUS:　Let me see: is there a mark there? (*He turns up the bracelet and sees the bruise made by his grasp. She stands motionless, not looking at him: fascinated, but on her guard*): Ffff! Does it hurt?

LOUKA:　Yes.

SERGIUS:　Shall I cure it?

LOUKA   (*instantly withdrawing herself proudly, but still not looking at him*): No. You cannot cure it now.

SERGIUS   (*masterfully*): Quite sure? (*He makes a movement as if to take her in his arms.*)

LOUKA: Don't trifle with me, please. An officer should not trifle with a servant.

SERGIUS   (*indicating the bruise with a merciless stroke of his forefinger*): That was no trifle, Louka.

LOUKA   (*flinching; then looking at him for the first time*): Are you sorry?

SERGIUS   (*with measured emphasis, folding his arms*): I am never sorry.

LOUKA   (*wistfully*): I wish I could believe a man could be as unlike a woman as that. I wonder are you really a brave man?

SERGIUS   (*unaffectedly, relaxing his attitude*): Yes: I am a brave man. My heart jumped like a woman's at the first shot; but in the charge I found that I was brave. Yes: that at least is real about me.

LOUKA: Did you find in the charge that the men whose fathers are poor like mine were any less brave than the men who are rich like you?

SERGIUS   (*with bitter levity*): Not a bit. They all slashed and cursed and yelled like heroes. Psha! the courage to rage and kill is cheap. I have an English bull terrier who has as much of that sort of courage as the whole Bulgarian nation, and the whole Russian nation at its back. But he lets my groom thrash him, all the same. That's your soldier all over! No, Louka: your poor men can cut throats; but they are afraid of their officers; they put up with insults and blows; they stand by and see one another punished like children: aye, and help to do it when they are ordered. And the officers!!! Well (*with a short harsh laugh*) I am an officer. Oh, (*fervently*) give me the man who will defy to the death any power on earth or in heaven that sets itself up against his own will and conscience: he alone is the brave man.

LOUKA: How easy it is to talk! Men never seem to me to grow up: they all have schoolboy's ideas. You don't know what true courage is.

SERGIUS   (*ironically*): Indeed! I am willing to be instructed. (*He sits on the ottoman, sprawling magnificently.*)

LOUKA: Look at me! How much am I allowed to have my own will? I have to get your room ready for you: to sweep and dust, to fetch and carry. How could that degrade me if it did not degrade you to have it done for you? But (*with subdued passion*) if I were Empress of Russia, above everyone in the world, then!! Ah then, though according to you I could shew no courage at all, you should see, you should see.

SERGIUS: What would you do, most noble Empress?

LOUKA: I would marry the man I loved, which no other queen in Europe has the courage to do. If I loved you, though you would be as far beneath me as I am beneath you, I would dare to be the equal of my inferior. Would you dare as much if you loved me? No: if you felt the beginnings of love for me you would not let it grow. You would not dare: you would marry a rich man's daughter because you would be afraid of what other people would say of you.

SERGIUS   (*bounding up*): You lie: it is not so, by all the stars! If I loved you, and I were the Tsar himself, I would set you on the throne by my side. You know that I love another woman, a woman as high above you as heaven is above earth. And you are jealous of her.

LOUKA: I have no reason to be. She will never marry you now. The man I told you of has come back. She will marry the Swiss.

SERGIUS (*recoiling*): The Swiss!

LOUKA: A man worth ten of you. Then you can come to me; and I will refuse you. You are not good enough for me. (*She turns to the door.*)

SERGIUS (*springing after her and catching her fiercely in his arms*): I will kill the Swiss; and afterwards I will do as I please with you.

LOUKA (*in his arms, passive and steadfast*): The Swiss will kill you, perhaps. He has beaten you in love. He may beat you in war.

SERGIUS (*tormentedly*): Do you think I believe that she—she! whose worst thoughts are higher than your best ones, is capable of trifling with another man behind my back?

LOUKA: Do you think she would believe the Swiss if he told her now that I am in your arms?

SERGIUS (*releasing her in despair*): Damnation! Oh, damnation! Mockery! mockery everywhere! everything I think is mocked by everything I do! (*He strikes himself frantically on the breast.*) Coward! liar! fool! Shall I kill myself like a man, or live and pretend to laugh at myself? (*She again turns to go.*) Louka! (*She stops near the door.*) Remember: you belong to me.

LOUKA (*turning*): What does that mean? An insult?

SERGIUS (*commandingly*): It means that you love me, and that I have had you here in my arms, and will perhaps have you there again. Whether that is an insult I neither know nor care: take it as you please. But (*vehemently*) I will not be a coward and a trifler. If I choose to love you, I dare marry you, in spite of all Bulgaria. If these hands ever touch you again, they shall touch my affianced bride.

LOUKA: We shall see whether you dare keep your word. And take care. I will not wait long.

SERGIUS (*again folding his arms and standing motionless in the middle of the room*): Yes: we shall see. And you shall wait my pleasure.

(BLUNTSCHLI, *much preoccupied, with his papers still in his hand, enters, leaving the door open for* LOUKA *to go out. He goes across to the table, glancing at her as he passes.* SERGIUS, *without altering his resolute attitude, watches him steadily.* LOUKA *goes out, leaving the door open.*)

BLUNTSCHLI (*absently, sitting at the table as before, and putting down his papers*): Thats a remarkable-looking young woman.

SERGIUS (*gravely, without moving*): Captain Bluntschli.

BLUNTSCHLI: Eh?

SERGIUS: You have deceived me. You are my rival. I brook no rivals. At six o'clock I shall be in the drilling-ground on the Klissoura road, alone, on horseback, with my sabre. Do you understand?

BLUNTSCHLI (*staring, but sitting quite at his ease*): Oh, thank you: that's a cavalry man's proposal. I'm in the artillery; and I have the choice of weapons. If I go, I shall take a machine gun. And there shall be no mistake about the cartridges this time.

SERGIUS (*flushing, but with deadly coldness*): Take care, sir. It is not our custom in Bulgaria to allow invitations of that kind to be trifled with.

BLUNTSCHLI (*warmly*): Pooh! don't talk to me about Bulgaria. You don't know what fighting is. But have it your own way. Bring your sabre along. I'll meet you.

SERGIUS (*fiercely delighted to find his opponent a man of spirit*): Well said, Switzer. Shall I lend you my best horse?

BLUNTSCHLI: No: damn your horse! thank you all the same, my dear fellow. (RAINA *comes in, and hears the next sentence.*) I shall fight you on foot. Horseback's too dangerous; I don't want to kill you if I can help it.

RAINA (*hurrying forward anxiously*): I have heard what Captain Bluntschli said, Sergius. You are going to fight. Why? (SERGIUS *turns away in silence, and goes to the stove, where he stands watching her as she continues, to* BLUNTSCHLI) What about?

BLUNTSCHLI: I don't know: he hasn't told me. Better not interfere, dear young lady. No harm will be done: I've often acted as sword instructor. He won't be able to touch me; and I'll not hurt him. It will save explanations. In the morning I shall be off home; and you'll never see me or hear of me again. You and he will then make it up and live happily ever after.

RAINA (*turning away deeply hurt, almost with a sob in her voice*): I never said I wanted to see you again.

SERGIUS (*striding forward*): Ha! That is a confession.

RAINA (*haughtily*): What do you mean?

SERGIUS: You love that man!

RAINA (*scandalized*): Sergius!

SERGIUS: You allow him to make love to you behind my back, just as you treat me as your affianced husband behind his. Bluntschli: you knew our relations; and you deceived me. It is for that that I call you to account, not for having received favors *I* never enjoyed.

BLUNTSCHLI (*jumping up indignantly*): Stuff! Rubbish! I have received no favors. Why, the young lady doesn't even know whether I'm married or not.

RAINA (*forgetting herself*): Oh! (*Collapsing on the ottoman*) Are you?

SERGIUS: You see the young lady's concern, Captain Bluntschli. Denial is useless. You have enjoyed the privilege of being received in her own room, late at night—

BLUNTSCHLI (*interrupting him pepperily*): Yes, you blockhead! she received me with a pistol at her head. Your cavalry were at my heels. I'd have blown out her brains if she'd uttered a cry.

SERGIUS (*taken aback*): Bluntschli! Raina: is this true?

RAINA (*rising in wrathful majesty*): Oh, how dare you, how dare you?

BLUNTSCHLI: Apologize, man: apologize. (*He resumes his seat at the table.*)

SERGIUS (*with the old measured emphasis, folding his arms*): I never apologize!

RAINA (*passionately*): This is the doing of that friend of yours, Captain Bluntschli. It is he who is spreading this horrible story about me. (*She walks about excitedly.*)

BLUNTSCHLI: No: he's dead. Burnt alive.

RAINA (*stopping, shocked*): Burnt alive!

BLUNTSCHLI: Shot in the hip in a woodyard. Couldn't drag himself out.

Your fellows' shells set the timber on fire and burnt him, with a half a dozen other poor devils in the same predicament.

RAINA: How horrible!

SERGIUS: And how ridiculous! Oh, war! war! the dream of patriots and heroes! A fraud, Bluntschli. A hollow sham, like love.

RAINA (*outraged*): Like love! You say that before me!

BLUNTSCHLI: Come, Saranoff: that matter is explained.

SERGIUS: A hollow sham, I say. Would you have come back here if nothing had passed between you except at the muzzle of your pistol? Raina is mistaken about your friend who was burnt. He was not my informant.

RAINA: Who then? (*Suddenly guessing the truth*) Ah, Louka! my maid! my servant! You were with her this morning all that time after—after—Oh, what sort of god is this I have been worshipping! (*He meets her gaze with sardonic enjoyment of her disenchantment. Angered all the more, she goes closer to him, and says, in a lower, intenser tone*) Do you know that I looked out of the window as I went upstairs, to have another sight of my hero; and I saw something I did not understand then. I know now that you were making love to her.

SERGIUS (*with grim humor*): You saw that?

RAINA: Only too well. (*She turns away, and throws herself on the divan under the centre window, quite overcome.*)

SERGIUS (*cynically*): Raina: our romance is shattered. Life's a farce.

BLUNTSCHLI (*to* RAINA, *whimsically*): You see: he's found himself out now.

SERGIUS (*going to him*): Bluntschli: I have allowed you to call me a blockhead. You may now call me a coward as well. I refuse to fight you. Do you know why?

BLUNTSCHLI: No; but it doesn't matter. I didn't ask the reason when you cried on; and I don't ask the reason now that you cry off. I'm a professional soldier! I fight when I have to, and am very glad to get out of it when I haven't to. You're only an amateur: you think fighting's an amusement.

SERGIUS (*sitting down at the table, nose to nose with him*): You shall hear the reason all the same, my professional. The reason is that it takes two men—real men—men of heart, blood and honor—to make a genuine combat. I could no more fight with you than I could make love to an ugly woman. You've no magnetism: you're not a man: you're a machine.

BLUNTSCHLI (*apologetically*): Quite true, quite true. I always was that sort of chap. I'm very sorry.

SERGIUS: Psha!

BLUNTSCHLI: But now that you've found that life isn't a farce, but something quite sensible and serious, what further obstacle is there to your happiness?

RAINA (*rising*): You are very solicitous about my happiness and his. Do you forget his new love—Louka? It is not you that he must fight now, but his rival, Nicola.

SERGIUS: Rival!! (*Bouncing half across the room.*)

RAINA: Don't you know that they're engaged?

SERGIUS: Nicola! Are fresh abysses opening? Nicola!

RAINA (*sarcastically*): A shocking sacrifice, isn't it? Such beauty! such intellect! such modesty! wasted on a middle-aged servant man. Really, Sergius, you cannot stand by and allow such a thing. It would be unworthy of your chivalry.

SERGIUS   (*losing all self-control*): Viper! Viper! (*He rushes to and fro, raging.*)

BLUNTSCHLI: Look here, Saranoff: you're getting the worst of this.

RAINA   (*getting angrier*): Do you realize what he has done, Captain Bluntschli? He has set this girl as a spy on us; and her reward is that he makes love to her.

SERGIUS: False! Monstrous!

RAINA: Monstrous! (*Confronting him*) Do you deny that she told you about Captain Bluntschli being in my room?

SERGIUS: No; but—

RAINA   (*interrupting*): Do you deny that you were making love to her when she told you?

SERGIUS: No; but I tell you—

RAINA   (*cutting him short contemptuously*): It is unnecessary to tell us anything more. That is quite enough for us. (*She turns away from him and sweeps majestically back to the window.*)

BLUNTSCHLI   (*quietly, as* SERGIUS, *in an agony of mortification, sinks on the ottoman, clutching his averted head between his fists*): I told you you were getting the worst of it, Saranoff.

SERGIUS: Tiger cat!

RAINA   (*running excitedly to* BLUNTSCHLI): You hear this man calling me names, Captain Bluntschli?

BLUNTSCHLI: What else can he do, dear lady? He must defend himself somehow. Come (*very persuasively*): don't quarrel. What good does it do?

(RAINA, *with a gasp, sits down on the ottoman, and after a vain effort to look vexedly at* BLUNTSCHLI, *falls a victim to her sense of humor, and actually leans back babyishly against the writhing shoulder of* SERGIUS.)

SERGIUS: Engaged to Nicola! Ha! ha! Ah well, Bluntschli, you are right to take this huge imposture of a world coolly.

RAINA   (*quaintly to* BLUNTSCHLI, *with an intuitive guess at his state of mind*): I daresay you think us a couple of grownup babies, don't you?

SERGIUS   (*grinning savagely*): He does: he does. Swiss civilization nursetending Bulgarian barbarism, eh?

BLUNTSCHLI   (*blushing*): Not at all, I assure you. I'm only very glad to get you two quieted. There! there! let's be pleasant and talk it over in a friendly way. Where is this other young lady?

RAINA: Listening at the door, probably.

SERGIUS   (*shivering as if a bullet had struck him, and speaking with quiet but deep indignation*): I will prove that that, at least, is a calumny. (*He goes with dignity to the door and opens it. A yell of fury bursts from him as he looks out. He darts into the passage, and returns dragging in* LOUKA, *whom he flings violently against the table, exclaiming*) Judge her, Bluntschli. You, the cool impartial one: judge the eavesdropper.

(LOUKA *stands her ground, proud and silent.*)

BLUNTSCHLI   (*shaking his head*): I mustn't judge her. I once listened myself outside a tent when there was a mutiny brewing. It's all a question of the degree of provocation. My life was at stake.

LOUKA: My love was at stake. I am not ashamed.

RAINA   (*contemptuously*): Your love! Your curiosity, you mean.

LOUKA   (*facing her and returning her contempt with interest*): My love, stronger than anything you can feel, even for your chocolate cream soldier.

SERGIUS   (*with quick suspicion, to* LOUKA): What does that mean?

LOUKA   (*fiercely*): It means—

SERGIUS   (*interrupting her slightingly*): Oh, I remember: the ice pudding. A paltry taunt, girl!

(MAJOR PETKOFF *enters, in his shirtsleeves.*)

PETKOFF: Excuse my shirtsleeves, gentlemen. Raina: somebody has been wearing that coat of mine: I'll swear it. Somebody with a differently shaped back. It's all burst open at the sleeve. Your mother is mending it. I wish she'd make haste: I shall catch cold. (*He looks more attentively at them.*) Is anything the matter?

RAINA: No. (*She sits down at the stove, with a tranquil air.*)

SERGIUS: Oh no. (*He sits down at the end of the table, as at first.*)

BLUNTSCHLI   (*who is already seated*): Nothing. Nothing.

PETKOFF   (*sitting down on the ottoman in his old place*): That's all right. (*He notices* LOUKA.) Anything the matter, Louka?

LOUKA: No, sir.

PETKOFF   (*genially*): That's all right. (*He sneezes*): Go and ask your mistress for my coat, like a good girl, will you?

(NICOLA *enters with the coat.* LOUKA *makes a pretence of having business in the room by taking the little table with the hookah away to the wall near the windows.*)

RAINA   (*rising quickly as she sees the coat on* NICOLA'S *arm*): Here it is papa. Give it to me Nicola; and do you put some more wood on the fire. (*She takes the coat, and brings it to* the major, *who stands up to put it on.* NICOLA *attends to the fire.*)

PETKOFF   (*to* RAINA, *teasing her affectionately*): Aha! Going to be very good to poor old papa just for one day after his return from the wars, eh?

RAINA   (*with solemn reproach*): Ah, how can you say that to me, father?

PETKOFF: Well, well, only a joke, little one. Come: give me a kiss. (*She kisses him.*) Now give me the coat.

RAINA: No: I am going to put it on for you. Turn your back. (*He turns his back and feels behind him with his arms for the sleeves. She dexterously takes the photograph from the pocket and throws it on the table before* BLUNTSCHLI, *who covers it with a sheet of paper under the very nose of* SERGIUS, *who looks on amazed, with his suspicions roused in the highest degree. She then helps* PETKOFF *on with his coat.*) There, dear! Now are you comfortable?

PETKOFF: Quite, little love. Thanks. (*He sits down; and* RAINA *returns to her seat near the stove.*) Oh, by the bye, I've found something funny. What's the meaning of this? (*He puts his hand into the picked pocket.*) Eh? Hallo! (*He tries the other pocket.*) Well, I could have sworn—! (*Much puzzled, he tries the breast pocket.*) I wonder—(*trying the original pocket.*) Where can it—? (*He rises, exclaiming*) Your mother's taken it!

RAINA   (*very red*): Taken what?

PETKOFF: Your photograph, with the inscription: "Raina, to her Chocolate Cream Soldier: a Souvenir." Now you know there's something more in this than meets the eye; and I'm going to find it out. (*Shouting*) Nicola!

NICOLA   (*coming to him*): Sir!

PETKOFF: Did you spoil any pastry of Miss Raina's this morning?

NICOLA: You heard Miss Raina say that I did, sir.

PETKOFF: I know that, you idiot. Was it true?

NICOLA: I am sure Miss Raina is incapable of saying anything that is not true, sir.

PETKOFF: Are you? Then I'm not. (*Turning to the others*) Come: do you think I don't see it all? (*He goes to* SERGIUS, *and slaps him on the shoulder.*) Sergius: you're the chocolate cream soldier, aren't you?

SERGIUS   (*starting up*): I! A chocolate cream soldier! Certainly not.

PETKOFF: Not! (*He looks at them. They are all very serious and very conscious.*) Do you mean to tell me that Raina sends things like that to other men?

SERGIUS   (*enigmatically*): The world is not such an innocent place as we used to think, Petkoff.

BLUNTSCHLI   (*rising*): It's all right, Major. I'm the chocolate cream soldier. (PETKOFF *and* SERGIUS *are equally astonished.*) The gracious young lady saved my life by giving me chocolate creams when I was starving: shall I ever forget their flavour! My late friend Stolz told you the story at Pirot. I was the fugitive.

PETKOFF: You! (*He gasps.*) Sergius: do you remember how those two women went on this morning when we mentioned it? (SERGIUS *smiles cynically.* PETKOFF *confronts* RAINA *severely.*) You're a nice young woman, aren't you?

RAINA   (*bitterly*): Major Saranoff has changed his mind. And when I wrote that on the photograph, I did not know that Captain Bluntschli was married.

BLUNTSCHLI   (*startled into vehement protest*): I'm not married.

RAINA   (*with deep reproach*): You said you were.

BLUNTSCHLI: I did not. I positively did not. I never was married in my life.

PETKOFF   (*exasperated*): Raina: will you kindly inform me, if I am not asking too much, which of these gentlemen you are engaged to?

RAINA: To neither of them. This young lady (*introducing* LOUKA, *who faces them all proudly*) is the object of Major Saranoff's affections at present.

PETKOFF: Louka! Are you mad, Sergius? Why, this girl's engaged to Nicola.

NICOLA: I beg your pardon, sir. There is a mistake. Louka is not engaged to me.

PETKOFF: Not engaged to you, you scoundrel! Why, you had twenty-five levas from me on the day of your betrothal; and she had that gilt bracelet from Miss Raina.

NICOLA   (*with cool unction*): We gave it out so, sir. But it was only to give Louka protection. She had a soul above her station; and I have been no more than her confidential servant. I intend, as you know, sir, to set up a shop later on in Sofia; and I look forward to her custom and recommendation should she marry into the nobility. (*He goes out with impressive discretion, leaving them all staring after him.*)

PETKOFF   (*breaking the silence*): Well, I am—hm!

SERGIUS: This is either the finest heroism or the most crawling baseness. Which is it, Bluntschli?

BLUNTSCHLI: Never mind whether it's heroism or baseness. Nicola's the ablest man I've met in Bulgaria. I'll make him manager of a hotel if he can speak French and German.

LOUKA   (*suddenly breaking out at* SERGIUS): I have been insulted by everyone here. You set them the example. You owe me an apology.

(SERGIUS, *like a repeating clock of which the spring has been touched, immediately begins to fold his arms.*)

BLUNTSCHLI   (*before he can speak*): It's no use. He never apologizes.

LOUKA: Not to you, his equal and his enemy. To me, his poor servant, he will not refuse to apologize.

SERGIUS   (*approvingly*): You are right. (*He bends his knee in his grandest manner.*) Forgive me.

LOUKA: I forgive you. (*She timidly gives him her hand, which he kisses.*) That touch makes me your affianced wife.

SERGIUS   (*springing up*): Ah! I forgot that.

LOUKA   (*coldly*): You can withdraw if you like.

SERGIUS: Withdraw! Never! You belong to me. (*He puts his arm about her.*)

(CATHERINE *comes in and finds* LOUKA *in* SERGIUS' *arms, with all the rest gazing at them in bewildered astonishment.*)

CATHERINE: What does this mean?

(SERGIUS *releases* LOUKA.)

PETKOFF: Well, my dear, it appears that Sergius is going to marry Louka instead of Raina. (*She is about to break out indignantly at him: he stops her by exclaiming testily*): Don't blame me: I've nothing to do with it. (*He retreats to the stove.*)

CATHERINE: Marry Louka! Sergius: you are bound by your word to us!

SERGIUS   (*folding his arms*) Nothing binds me.

BLUNTSCHLI   (*much pleased by this piece of common sense*): Saranoff: your hand. My congratulations. These heroics of yours have their practical side after all. (*To* LOUKA): Gracious young lady: the best wishes of a good Republican! (*He kisses her hand, to* RAINA'S *great disgust, and returns to his seat.*)

CATHERINE: Louka: you have been telling stories.

LOUKA: I have done Raina no harm.

CATHERINE   (*haughtily*): Raina!

(RAINA, *equally indignant, almost snorts at the liberty.*)

LOUKA: I have a right to call her Raina: she calls me Louka. I told Major Saranoff she would never marry him if the Swiss gentleman came back.

BLUNTSCHLI   (*rising, much surprised*): Hallo!

LOUKA   (*turning to* RAINA): I thought you were fonder of him than of Sergius. You know best whether I was right.

BLUNTSCHLI: What nonsense! I assure you, my dear Major, my dear Madame, the gracious young lady simply saved my life, nothing else. She never cared two straws for me. Why, bless my heart and soul, look at the young lady and look at me. She, rich, young, beautiful, with her imagination full of fairy princes and noble natures and cavalry charges and goodness knows what! And I, a commonplace Swiss soldier who hardly knows what a decent life is after fifteen years of barracks and battles: a vagabond, a man who has spoiled all his chances in life through an incurably romantic disposition, a man—

SERGIUS   (*starting as if a needle had pricked him and interrupting* BLUNTSCHLI *in incredulous amazement*): Excuse me, Bluntschli: what did you say had spoiled your chances in life?

BLUNTSCHLI   (*promptly*): An incurably romantic disposition. I ran away from home twice when I was a boy. I went into the army instead of into my father's business. I climbed the balcony of this house when a man of sense would have dived into the nearest cellar. I came sneaking back here to have another look at the young lady when any other man of my age would have sent the coat back—

PETKOFF: My coat!

BLUNTSCHLI:—yes: that's the coat I mean—would have sent it back and gone quietly home. Do you suppose I am the sort of fellow a young girl falls in love with? Why, look at our ages! I'm thirty-four: I don't suppose the young lady is much over seventeen. (*This estimate produces a marked sensation, all the rest turning and staring at one another. He proceeds innocently*): All that adventure which was life or death to me, was only a schoolgirl's game to her—chocolate creams and hide and seek. Here's the proof! (*He takes the photograph from the table.*) Now, I ask you, would a woman who took the affair seriously have sent me this and written on it "Raina, to her Chocolate Cream Soldier: a Souvenir"? (*He exhibits the photograph triumphantly, as if it settled the matter beyond all possibility of refutation.*)

PETKOFF: That's what I was looking for. How the deuce did it get there? (*He comes from the stove to look at it, and sits down on the ottoman.*)

BLUNTSCHLI   (*to* RAINA, *complacently*): I have put everything right, I hope, gracious young lady.

RAINA   (*going to the table to face him*): I quite agree with your account of yourself. You are a romantic idiot. (BLUNTSCHLI *is unspeakably taken back.*) Next time, I hope you will know the difference between a schoolgirl of seventeen and a woman of twenty-three.

BLUNTSCHLI   (*stupefied*): Twenty-three!

(RAINA *snaps the photograph contemptuously from his hand; tears it up; throws the pieces in his face; and sweeps back to her former place.*)

SERGIUS   (*with grim enjoyment of his rival's discomfiture*): Bluntschli: my one last belief is gone. Your sagacity is a fraud, like everything else. You have less sense than even I!

BLUNTSCHLI   (*overwhelmed*): Twenty-three! Twenty-three!! (*He considers.*) Hm! (*Swiftly making up his mind and coming to his host*) In that case, Major Petkoff, I beg to propose formally to become a suitor for your daughter's hand, in place of Major Saranoff retired.

RAINA: You dare!

BLUNTSCHLI: If you were twenty-three when you said those things to me this afternoon, I shall take them seriously.

CATHERINE (*loftily polite*): I doubt, sir, whether you quite realize either my daughter's position or that of Major Sergius Saranoff, whose place you propose to take. The Petkoffs and the Saranoffs are known as the richest and most important families in the country. Our position is almost historical: we can go back for twenty years.

PETKOFF: Oh, never mind that, Catherine. (*To* BLUNTSCHLI) We should be most happy, Bluntschli, if it were only a question of your position; but hang it, you know, Raina is accustomed to a very comfortable establishment. Sergius keeps twenty horses.

BLUNTSCHLI: But who wants twenty horses? We're not going to keep a circus.

CATHERINE (*severely*): My daughter, sir, is accustomed to a first-rate stable.

RAINA: Hush, mother: you're making me ridiculous.

BLUNTSCHLI: Oh well, if it comes to a question of an establishment, here goes! (*He darts impetuously to the table; seizes the papers in the blue envelope; and turns to* SERGIUS.) How many horses did you say?

SERGIUS: Twenty, noble Switzer.

BLUNTSCHLI: I have two hundred horses. (*They are amazed.*) How many carriages?

SERGIUS: Three.

BLUNTSCHLI: I have seventy. Twenty-four of them will hold twelve inside, besides two on the box, without counting the driver and conductor. How many tablecloths have you?

SERGIUS: How the deuce do I know?

BLUNTSCHLI: Have you four thousand?

SERGIUS: No.

BLUNTSCHLI: I have. I have nine thousand six hundred pairs of sheets and blankets, with two thousand four hundred eider-down quilts. I have ten thousand knives and forks, and the same quantity of dessert spoons. I have three hundred servants. I have six palatial establishments, besides two livery stables, a tea garden, and a private house. I have four medals for distinguished services; I have the rank of an officer and the standing of a gentleman; and I have three native languages. Shew me any man in Bulgaria that can offer as much!

PETKOFF (*with childish awe*): Are you Emperor of Switzerland?

BLUNTSCHLI: My rank is the highest known in Switzerland: I am a free citizen.

CATHERINE: Then, Captain Bluntschli, since you are my daughter's choice—

RAINA (*mutinously*): He's not.

CATHERINE (*ignoring her*):—I shall not stand in the way of her happiness. (PETKOFF *is about to speak.*) That is Major Petkoff's feeling also.

PETKOFF: Oh, I shall be only too glad. Two hundred horses! Whew!

SERGIUS: What says the lady?

RAINA (*pretending to sulk*): The lady says that he can keep his tablecloths and his omnibuses. I am not here to be sold to the highest bidder. (*She turns her back on him.*)

BLUNTSCHLI: I won't take that answer. I appealed to you as a fugitive, a beggar, and a starving man. You accepted me. You gave me your hand to kiss, your bed to sleep in, and your roof to shelter me.

RAINA: I did not give them to the Emperor of Switzerland.

BLUNTSCHLI: That's just what I say. (*He catches her by the shoulders and turns her face-to-face with him.*) Now tell us whom you did give them to.

RAINA   (*succumbing with a shy smile*): To my chocolate cream soldier.

BLUNTSCHLI   (*with a boyish laugh of delight*): That'll do. Thank you. (*He looks at his watch and suddenly becomes businesslike.*) Time's up, Major. You've managed those regiments so well that you're sure to be asked to get rid of some of the infantry of the Timok division. Send them home by way of Lom Palanka. Saranoff: don't get married until I come back: I shall be here punctually at five in the evening on Tuesday fortnight. Gracious ladies (*his heels click*) good evening. (*He makes them a military bow, and goes.*)

SERGIUS: What a man! Is he a man!

(1894)

QUESTIONS

1. Which elements of *Arms and the Man* make it a romantic play and which make it a satiric one?
2. How important are Shaw's stage directions? What functions do they serve?
3. How does the play's title reflect its subjects? What are the meanings of *arms?* What are the connotations of *man?*
4. Of what importance are Louka and Nicola to the play? What does each contribute individually, and what is their function as a couple?
5. Compare and contrast the characters of Sergius and Bluntschli. Consider how each role should be acted.
6. What do you make of the ending? How seriously are we to take Raina's and Bluntschli's changes of attitude?

CHAPTER TWENTY-SIX

The Theater of the Absurd

One of the most noteworthy developments in theater following the rise of realism has been the emergence of the Theater of the Absurd in the second half of the twentieth century. Absurdist drama, as it is called, is nonrealistic, even antirealistic. Rejecting the conventions of realism, absurdist playwrights substitute storyless action for well-contrived plots; they replace believable characters of psychological complexity with barely recognizable figures; and for witty repartee and grand speeches they offer incoherent ramblings and disconnected dialogue.

Why such an about-face, why such a rejection of realistic theatrical conventions? Primarily because ways of perceiving reality had changed so radically that realistic dramatic conventions were inadequate to the task of representing reality as dramatists of the absurd envisioned it. Absurdist dramatists reject the implications that lie behind realistic conventions; they object, for example, to the idea that characters can be understood or that plot should be ordered. For them people are not understandable, and life is disorderly and chaotic. Absurdist writers attempt to dramatize these and other conceptions in plays that depict experience as meaningless and existence as purposeless; they portray human beings as irrational, pathetic figures, helpless against life's chaos. For the absurdist, human beings are deracinated, cut off from their historical context, dispossessed of religious certainty, alienated from their social and physical environment, and unable to communicate with others.

Martin Esslin, a leading drama critic and expert on absurdist drama, has noted that the word *absurd* when used with reference to the Theater of the Absurd does not mean "ridiculous," but "out of harmony."★ Modern people are out of synch with their world—with nature, with others, and ultimately with themselves. This sense of being out of harmony, of being at odds with life, is both cause and consequence of the desperate loneliness and alienation that thwart happiness and rob life of meaning.

Esslin has also recognized that dramatists of the absurd, like Ionesco, have moved beyond arguing about the absurdity of the human condition to present it "in terms of concrete stage images." When dramatists of the absurd violate the rules of conventional dramaturgy, they do so because they see that strategy as the most effective way to dramatize the conditions they experience. Their intention is to make us experience the condition of absurdity. Hence the outrageousness that characterizes many of their plays.

Absurdist plays can be comic and horrifying simultaneously. Eugène Ionesco's *The Lesson* includes comic dialogue that rivals Molière's in *Tartuffe* or Shaw's in *Arms and the Man*. But unlike those plays, *The Lesson* serves up violence along with its humor, and its farce gives way to nightmare. Such rapid shifts in action and tone can disturb our sense of comfort and our certainty about what we are reading (or viewing) and perhaps shake us up enough to question our perceptions of reality.

Absurdist plays rely on more than abrupt changes of direction and tone to create their effects. Since a dominant theme of much absurdist drama is the inadequacy of language to serve the ends of human understanding, many absurdist plays illustrate the breakdown of language as an instrument of communication. Dialogue, for example, may be riddled with non sequiturs and disconnected remarks by different characters, or it may be absent altogether as characters mime and gesture rather than talk. In *The Lesson* Ionesco illustrates the inability of teacher and student to understand each other. Although their conversational exchanges are funny, they also frighteningly portray their inability to communicate. Language, as the dialogue of *The Lesson* suggests, is closely allied with power and dominance. As nightmarish as the action of the play becomes, perhaps it is not as illogical and random as it may at first seem. Perhaps it has something to do with the way some absurdist writers see all human communication: as a contest for control, as a conflict to determine mastery rather than an attempt to establish human connections.

★Martin Esslin, *The Theatre of the Absurd* (New York: Doubleday, 1969), pp. 5–7.

EUGÈNE IONESCO

[b. 1912]

The Lesson

TRANSLATED BY DONALD M. ALLEN

THE CHARACTERS

THE PROFESSOR, *aged 50 to 60*
THE YOUNG PUPIL, *aged 18*
THE MAID, *aged 45 to 50*

Scene. *The office of the old professor, which also serves as a dining room. To the left, a door opens onto the apartment stairs; upstage, to the right, another door opens onto a corridor of the apartment. Upstage, a little left of center, a window, not very large, with plain curtains; on the outside sill of the window are ordinary potted plants. The low buildings with red roofs of a small town can be seen in the distance. The sky is grayish-blue. On the right stands a provincial buffet. The table doubles as a desk, it stands at stage center. There are three chairs around the table, and two more stand on each side of the window. Light-colored wallpaper, some shelves with books.*

[*When the curtain rises the stage is empty, and it remains so for a few moments. Then we hear the doorbell ring.*]

VOICE OF THE MAID   [*from the corridor*]: Yes. I'm coming.

[*The* MAID *comes in, after having run down the stairs. She is stout, aged 45 to 50, red-faced, and wears a peasant woman's cap. She rushes in, slamming the door to the right behind her, and dries her hands on her apron as she runs towards the door on the left. Meanwhile we hear the doorbell ring again.*]

MAID: Just a moment, I'm coming.

[*She opens the door. A young* PUPIL, *aged 18, enters. She is wearing a gray student's smock, a small white collar, and carries a student's satchel under her arm.*]

MAID: Good morning, miss.
PUPIL: Good morning, madam. Is the Professor at home?
MAID: Have you come for the lesson?
PUPIL: Yes, I have.
MAID: He's expecting you. Sit down for a moment. I'll tell him you're here.
PUPIL: Thank you.

[*She seats herself near the table, facing the audience; the hall door is to her left; her back is to the other door, through which the* maid *hurriedly exits, calling:*]

MAID: Professor, come down please, your pupil is here.

VOICE OF THE PROFESSOR [*rather reedy*]: Thank you. I'm coming . . . in just a moment . . .

[*The* MAID *exits; the* PUPIL *draws in her legs, holds her satchel on her lap, and waits demurely. She casts a glance or two around the room, at the furniture, at the ceiling too. Then she takes a notebook out of her satchel, leafs through it, and stops to look at a page for a moment as though reviewing a lesson, as though taking a last look at her homework. She seems to be a well-brought-up girl, polite, but lively, gay, dynamic; a fresh smile is on her lips. During the course of the play she progressively loses the lively rhythm of her movement and her carriage, she becomes withdrawn. From gay and smiling she becomes progressively sad and morose; from very lively at the beginning, she becomes more and more fatigued and somnolent. Towards the end of the play her face must clearly express a nervous depression; her way of speaking shows the effects of this, her tongue becomes thick, words come to her memory with difficulty and emerge from her mouth with as much difficulty; she comes to have a manner vaguely paralyzed, the beginning of aphasia. Firm and determined at the beginning, so much so as to appear to be almost aggressive, she becomes more and more passive, until she is almost a mute and inert object, seemingly inanimate in the* PROFESSOR'*s hands, to such an extent that when he makes his final gesture, she no longer reacts. Insensible, her reflexes deadened, only her eyes in an expressionless face will show inexpressible astonishment and fear. The transition from one manner to the other must of course be made imperceptibly.*

The PROFESSOR *enters. He is a little old man with a little white beard. He wears pince-nez, a black skullcap, a long black schoolmaster's coat, trousers and shoes of black, detachable white collar, a black tie. Excessively polite, very timid, his voice deadened by his timidity, very proper, very much the teacher. He rubs his hands together constantly; occasionally a lewd gleam comes into his eyes and is quickly repressed.*

During the course of the play his timidity will disappear progressively, imperceptibly; and the lewd gleams in his eyes will become a steady devouring flame in the end. From a manner that is inoffensive at the start, the PROFESSOR *becomes more and more sure of himself, more and more nervous, aggressive, dominating, until he is able to do as he pleases with the* PUPIL, *who has become, in his hands, a pitiful creature. Of course, the voice of the* PROFESSOR *must change too, from thin and reedy, to stronger and stronger, until at the end it is extremely powerful, ringing, sonorous, while the* PUPIL'*s voice changes from the very clear and ringing tones that she has at the beginning of the play until it is almost inaudible. In these first scenes the* PROFESSOR *might stammer very slightly.*]

PROFESSOR: Good morning, young lady. You . . . I expect that you . . . that you are the new pupil?

PUPIL [*turns quickly with a lively and self-assured manner; she gets up, goes toward the* PROFESSOR, *and gives him her hand*]: Yes, Professor. Good morning, Professor. As you see, I'm on time. I didn't want to be late.

PROFESSOR: That's fine, miss. Thank you, you didn't really need to hurry. I am very sorry to have kept you waiting . . . I was just finishing up . . . well . . . I'm sorry . . . You will excuse me, won't you? . . .

PUPIL: Oh, certainly, Professor. It doesn't matter at all, Professor.

PROFESSOR: Please excuse me . . . Did you have any trouble finding the house?

PUPIL: No . . . Not at all. I just asked the way. Everybody knows you around here.

PROFESSOR: For thirty years I've lived in this town. You've not been here for long? How do you find it?

PUPIL: It's all right. The town is attractive and even agreeable, there's a nice park, a boarding school, a bishop, nice shops and streets . . .

PROFESSOR: That's very true, young lady. And yet, I'd just as soon live somewhere else. In Paris, or at least Bordeaux.

PUPIL: Do you like Bordeaux?

PROFESSOR: I don't know. I've never seen it.

PUPIL: But you know Paris?

PROFESSOR: No, I don't know it either, young lady, but if you'll permit me, can you tell me, Paris is the capital city of . . . miss?

PUPIL   [searching her memory for a moment, then, happily guessing]: Paris is the capital city of . . . France?

PROFESSOR: Yes, young lady, bravo, that's very good, that's perfect. My congratulations. You have your French geography at your finger tips. You know your chief cities.

PUPIL: Oh! I don't know them all yet, Professor, it's not quite that easy, I have trouble learning them.

PROFESSOR: Oh! it will come . . . you mustn't give up . . . young lady . . . I beg your pardon . . . have patience . . . little by little . . . You will see, it will come in time . . . What a nice day it is today . . . or rather, not so nice . . . Oh! but then yes it is nice. In short, it's not too bad a day, that's the main thing . . . ahem . . . ahem . . . it's not raining and it's not snowing either.

PUPIL: That would be most unusual, for it's summer now.

PROFESSOR: Excuse me, miss, I was just going to say so . . . but as you will learn, one must be ready for anything.

PUPIL: I guess so, Professor.

PROFESSOR: We can't be sure of anything, young lady, in this world.

PUPIL: The snow falls in the winter. Winter is one of the four seasons. The other three are . . . uh . . . spr . . .

PROFESSOR: Yes?

PUPIL: . . . ing, and then summer . . . and . . . uh . . .

PROFESSOR: It begins like "automobile," miss.

PUPIL: Ah, yes, autumn . . .

PROFESSOR: That's right, miss. That's a good answer, that's perfect. I am convinced that you will be a good pupil. You will make real progress. You are intelligent, you seem to me to be well informed, and you've a good memory.

PUPIL: I know my seasons, don't I, Professor?

PROFESSOR: Yes, indeed, miss . . . or almost. But it will come in time. In any case, you're coming along. Soon you'll know all the seasons, even with your eyes closed. Just as I do.

PUPIL: It's hard.

PROFESSOR: Oh, no. All it takes is a little effort, a little good will, miss. You will see. It will come, you may be sure of that.

PUPIL: Oh, I do hope so, Professor. I have a great thirst for knowledge. My parents also want me to get an education. They want me to specialize. They consider a little general culture, even if it is solid, is no longer enough, in these times.

PROFESSOR: Your parents, miss, are perfectly right. You must go on with your studies. Forgive me for saying so, but it is very necessary. Our contemporary life has become most complex.

PUPIL: And so very complicated too ... My parents are fairly rich, I'm lucky. They can help me in my work, help me in my very advanced studies.

PROFESSOR: And you wish to qualify for ... ?

PUPIL: Just as soon as possible, for the first doctor's orals. They're in three weeks' time.

PROFESSOR: You already have your high school diploma, if you'll pardon the question?

PUPIL: Yes, Professor, I have my science diploma and my arts diploma, too.

PROFESSOR: Ah, you're very far advanced, even perhaps too advanced for your age. And which doctorate do you wish to qualify for? In the physical sciences or in moral philosophy?

PUPIL: My parents are very much hoping—if you think it will be possible in such a short time—they very much hope that I can qualify for the total doctorate.

PROFESSOR: The total doctorate? ... You have great courage, young lady, I congratulate you sincerely. We will try, miss, to do our best. In any case, you already know quite a bit, and at so young an age too.

PUPIL: Oh, Professor.

PROFESSOR: Then, if you'll permit me, pardon me, please, I do think that we ought to get to work. We have scarcely any time to lose.

PUPIL: Oh, but certainly, Professor, I want to. I beg you to.

PROFESSOR: Then, may I ask you to sit down ... there ... Will you permit me, miss, that is if you have no objections, to sit down opposite you?

PUPIL: Oh, of course, Professor, please do.

PROFESSOR: Thank you very much, miss. [*They sit down facing each other at the table, their profiles to the audience.*] There we are. Now have you brought your books and notebooks?

PUPIL   [*taking notebooks and books out of her satchel*]: Yes, Professor. Certainly, I have brought all that we'll need.

PROFESSOR: Perfect, miss. This is perfect. Now, if this doesn't bore you ... shall we begin?

PUPIL: Yes, indeed, Professor, I am at your disposal.

PROFESSOR: At my disposal? [*A gleam comes into his eyes and is quickly extinguished; he begins to make a gesture that he suppresses at once.*] Oh, miss, it is I who am at *your* disposal. I am only your humble servant.

PUPIL: Oh, Professor ...

PROFESSOR: If you will ... now ... we ... we ... I ... I will begin by making a brief examination of your knowledge, past and present, so that we may chart our future course ... Good. How is your perception of plurality?

PUPIL: It's rather vague . . . confused.

PROFESSOR: Good. We shall see.

[*He rubs his hands together. The* MAID *enters, and this appears to irritate the* PROFESSOR. *She goes to the buffet and looks for something, lingering.*]

PROFESSOR: Now, miss, would you like to do a little arithmetic, that is if you want to . . .

PUPIL: Oh, yes, Professor. Certainly, I ask nothing better.

PROFESSOR: It is rather a new science, a modern science, properly speaking, it is more a method than a science . . . And it is also a therapy. [*To the* MAID:] Have you finished, Marie?

MAID: Yes, Professor, I've found the plate. I'm just going . . .

PROFESSOR: Hurry up then. Please go along to the kitchen, if you will.

MAID: Yes, Professor, I'm going. [*She starts to go out.*] Excuse me, Professor, but take care, I urge you to remain calm.

PROFESSOR: You're being ridiculous, Marie. Now, don't worry.

MAID: That's what you always say.

PROFESSOR: I will not stand for your insinuations. I know perfectly well how to comport myself. I am old enough for that.

MAID: Precisely, Professor. You will do better not to start the young lady on arithmetic. Arithmetic is tiring, exhausting.

PROFESSOR: Not at my age. And anyhow, what business is it of yours? This is my concern. And I know what I'm doing. This is not your department.

MAID: Very well, Professor. But you can't say that I didn't warn you.

PROFESSOR: Marie, I can get along without your advice.

MAID: As you wish, Professor. [*She exits.*]

PROFESSOR: Miss, I hope you'll pardon this absurd interruption . . . Excuse this woman . . . She is always afraid that I'll tire myself. She fusses over my health.

PUPIL: Oh, that's quite all right, Professor. It shows that she's very devoted. She loves you very much. Good servants are rare.

PROFESSOR: She exaggerates. Her fears are stupid. But let's return to our arithmetical knitting.

PUPIL: I'm following you, Professor.

PROFESSOR   [*wittily*]: Without leaving your seat!

PUPIL   [*appreciating his joke*]: Like you, Professor.

PROFESSOR: Good. Let us arithmetize a little now.

PUPIL: Yes, gladly, Professor.

PROFESSOR: It wouldn't be too tiresome for you to tell me . . .

PUPIL: Not at all, Professor, go on.

PROFESSOR: How much are one and one?

PUPIL: One and one make two.

PROFESSOR   [*marveling at the* PUPIL's *knowledge*]: Oh, but that's very good. You appear to me to be well along in your studies. You should easily achieve the total doctorate, miss.

PUPIL: I'm so glad. Especially to have someone like you tell me this.

PROFESSOR: Let's push on: how much are two and one?

PUPIL: Three.

PROFESSOR: Three and one?

PUPIL: Four.

PROFESSOR: Four and one?

PUPIL: Five.

PROFESSOR: Five and one?

PUPIL: Six.

PROFESSOR: Six and one?

PUPIL: Seven.

PROFESSOR: Seven and one?

PUPIL: Eight.

PROFESSOR: Seven and one?

PUPIL: Eight again.

PROFESSOR: Very well answered. Seven and one?

PUPIL: Eight once more.

PROFESSOR: Perfect. Excellent. Seven and one?

PUPIL: Eight again. And sometimes nine.

PROFESSOR: Magnificent. You are magnificent. You are exquisite. I congratulate you warmly, miss. There's scarcely any point in going on. At addition you are a past master. Now, let's look at subtraction. Tell me, if you are not exhausted, how many are four minus three?

PUPIL: Four minus three? . . . Four minus three?

PROFESSOR: Yes. I mean to say: subtract three from four.

PUPIL: That makes . . . seven?

PROFESSOR: I am sorry but I'm obliged to contradict you. Four minus three does not make seven. You are confused: four plus three makes seven, four minus three does not make seven . . . This is not addition anymore, we must subtract now.

PUPIL   [*trying to understand*]: Yes . . . yes . . .

PROFESSOR: Four minus three makes . . . How many? . . . How many?

PUPIL: Four?

PROFESSOR: No, miss, that's not it.

PUPIL: Three, then.

PROFESSOR: Not that either, miss . . . Pardon, I'm sorry . . . I ought to say, that's not it . . . excuse me.

PUPIL: Four minus three . . . Four minus three . . . Four minus three? . . . But now doesn't that make ten?

PROFESSOR: Oh, certainly not, miss. It's not a matter of guessing, you've got to think it out. Let's try to deduce it together. Would you like to count?

PUPIL: Yes, Professor. One . . . two . . . uh . . .

PROFESSOR: You know how to count? How far can you count up to?

PUPIL: I can count to . . . to infinity.

PROFESSOR: That's not possible, miss.

PUPIL: Well then, let's say to sixteen.

PROFESSOR: That is enough. One must know one's limits. Count then, if you will, please.

PUPIL: One . . . two . . . and after two, comes three . . . then four . . .

PROFESSOR: Stop there, miss. Which number is larger? Three or four?

PUPIL: Uh . . . three or four? Which is the larger? The larger of three or four? In what sense larger?

PROFESSOR: Some numbers are smaller and others are larger. In the larger numbers there are more units than in the small . . .

PUPIL: Than in the small numbers?

PROFESSOR: Unless the small ones have smaller units. If they are very small, then there might be more units in the small numbers than in the large . . . if it is a question of other units . . .

PUPIL: In that case, the small numbers can be larger than the large numbers?

PROFESSOR: Let's not go into that. That would take us much too far. You must realize simply that more than numbers are involved here . . . there are also magnitudes, totals, there are groups, there are heaps, heaps of such things as plums, trucks, geese, prune pits, etc. To facilitate our work, let's merely suppose that we have only equal numbers, then the bigger numbers will be those that have the most units.

PUPIL: The one that has the most is the biggest? Ah, I understand, Professor, you are identifying quality with quantity.

PROFESSOR: That is too theoretical, miss, too theoretical. You needn't concern yourself with that. Let us take an example and reason from a definite case. Let's leave the general conclusions for later. We have the number four and the number three, and each has always the same number of units. Which number will be larger, the smaller or the larger?

PUPIL: Excuse me, Professor . . . What do you mean by the larger number? Is it the one that is not so small as the other?

PROFESSOR: That's it, miss, perfect. You have understood me very well.

PUPIL: Then, it is four.

PROFESSOR: What is four—larger or smaller than three?

PUPIL: Smaller . . . no, larger.

PROFESSOR: Excellent answer. How many units are there between three and four? . . . Or between four and three, if you prefer?

PUPIL: There aren't any units, Professor, between three and four. Four comes immediately after three; there is nothing at all between three and four!

PROFESSOR: I haven't made myself very well understood. No doubt, it is my fault. I've not been sufficiently clear.

PUPIL: No, Professor, it's my fault.

PROFESSOR: Look here. Here are three matches. And here is another one, that makes four. Now watch carefully—we have four matches. I take one away, now how many are left?

[We don't see the matches, nor any of the objects that are mentioned. The PROFESSOR gets up from the table, writes on the imaginary blackboard with an imaginary piece of chalk, etc.]

PUPIL: Five. If three and one make four, four and one make five.

PROFESSOR: That's not it. That's not it at all. You always have a tendency to add. But one must be able to subtract too. It's not enough to integrate, you must also disintegrate. That's the way life is. That's philosophy. That's science. That's progress, civilization.

PUPIL: Yes, Professor.

PROFESSOR: Let's return to our matches. I have four of them. You see, there are really four. I take one away, and there remain only . . .

PUPIL: I don't know, Professor.

PROFESSOR: Come now, think. It's not easy, I admit. Nevertheless, you've had enough training to make the intellectual effort required to arrive at an understanding. So?

PUPIL: I can't get it, Professor. I don't know, Professor.

PROFESSOR: Let us take a simpler example. If you had two noses, and I pulled one of them off . . . how many would you have left?

PUPIL: None.

PROFESSOR: What do you mean, none?

PUPIL: Yes, it's because you haven't pulled off any, that's why I have one now. If you had pulled it off, I wouldn't have it anymore.

PROFESSOR: You've not understood my example. Suppose that you have only one ear.

PUPIL: Yes, and then?

PROFESSOR: If I gave you another one, how many would you have then?

PUPIL: Two.

PROFESSOR: Good. And if I gave you still another ear. How many would you have then?

PUPIL: Three ears.

PROFESSOR: Now, I take one away . . . and there remain . . . how many ears?

PUPIL: Two.

PROFESSOR: Good. I take away still another one, how many do you have left?

PUPIL: Two.

PROFESSOR: No. You have two, I take one away, I eat one up, then how many do you have left?

PUPIL: Two.

PROFESSOR: I eat one of them . . . one.

PUPIL: Two.

PROFESSOR: One.

PUPIL: Two.

PROFESSOR: One!

PUPIL: Two!

PROFESSOR: One!!!

PUPIL: Two!!!

PROFESSOR: One!!!

PUPIL: Two!!!

PROFESSOR: One!!!

PUPIL: Two!!!

PROFESSOR: No. No. That's not right. The example is not . . . it's not convincing. Listen to me.

PUPIL: Yes, Professor.

PROFESSOR: You've got . . . you've got . . . you've got . . .

PUPIL: Ten fingers!

PROFESSOR: If you wish. Perfect. Good. You have then ten fingers.

PUPIL: Yes, Professor.

PROFESSOR: How many would you have if you had only five of them?

PUPIL: Ten, Professor.

PROFESSOR: That's not right!

PUPIL: But it is, Professor.

PROFESSOR: I tell you it's not!

PUPIL: You just told me that I had ten . . .

PROFESSOR: I also said, immediately afterwards, that you had five!

PUPIL: I don't have five, I've got ten!

PROFESSOR: Let's try another approach . . . for purposes of subtraction let's limit ourselves to the numbers from one to five . . . Wait now, miss, you'll soon see. I'm going to make you understand.

[*The* PROFESSOR *begins to write on the imaginary blackboard. He moves it closer to the* PUPIL, *who turns around in order to see it.*]

PROFESSOR: Look here, miss . . . [*He pretends to draw a stick on the blackboard and the number 1 below the stick; then two sticks and the number 2 below, then three sticks and the number 3 below, then four sticks with the number 4 below.*] You see . . .

PUPIL: Yes, Professor.

PROFESSOR: These are sticks, miss, sticks. This is one stick, these are two sticks, and three sticks, then four sticks, then five sticks. One stick, two sticks, three sticks, four and five sticks, these are numbers. When we count the sticks, each stick is a unit, miss . . . What have I just said?

PUPIL: "A unit, miss! What have I just said?"

PROFESSOR: Or a figure! Or a number! One, two, three, four, five, these are the elements of numeration, miss.

PUPIL   [*hesitant*]: Yes, Professor. The elements, figures, which are sticks, units and numbers . . .

PROFESSOR: At the same time . . . that's to say, in short—the whole of arithmetic is there.

PUPIL: Yes, Professor. Good, Professor. Thanks, Professor.

PROFESSOR: Now, count, if you will please, using these elements . . . add and subtract . . .

PUPIL   [*as though trying to impress them on her memory*]: Sticks are really figures and numbers are units?

PROFESSOR: Hmm . . . so to speak. And then?

PUPIL: One could subtract two units from three units, but can one subtract two twos from three threes? And two figures from four numbers? And three numbers from one unit?

PROFESSOR: No, miss.

PUPIL: Why, Professor?

PROFESSOR: Because, miss.

PUPIL: Because why, Professor? Since one is the same as the other?

PROFESSOR: That's the way it is, miss. It can't be explained. This is only comprehensible through internal mathematical reasoning. Either you have it or you don't.

PUPIL: So much the worse for me.

PROFESSOR: Listen to me, miss, if you don't achieve a profound understanding of these principles, these arithmetical archetypes, you will never be able to perform correctly the functions of a polytechnician. Still less will you be able to teach a course in a polytechnical school . . . or the primary grades. I realize that this is not easy, it is very, very abstract . . . obviously . . . but unless you can comprehend the primary elements, how do you expect to be able to calculate mentally—and this is the least of the things that even an ordinary engineer must be able to do—how much, for example, are three billion seven hundred fifty-five million nine hundred ninety-eight thousand two hundred fifty-one, multiplied by five billion one hundred sixty-two million three hundred and three thousand five hundred and eight?

PUPIL   [*very quickly*]: That makes nineteen quintillion three hundred ninety quadrillion two trillion eight hundred forty-four billion two hundred nineteen million one hundred sixty-four thousand five hundred and eight . . .

PROFESSOR   [*astonished*]: No. I don't think so. That must make nineteen quintillion three hundred ninety quadrillion two trillion eight hundred forty-four billion two hundred nineteen million one hundred sixty-four thousand five hundred and nine . . .

PUPIL: . . . No . . . five hundred and eight . . .

PROFESSOR   [*more and more astonished, calculating mentally*]: Yes . . . you are right . . . the result is indeed . . . [*He mumbles unintelligibly:*] . . . quintillion, quadrillion, trillion, billion, million . . . [*Clearly:*] one hundred sixty-four thousand five hundred and eight . . . [*Stupefied:*] But how did you know that, if you don't know the principles of arithmetical reasoning?

PUPIL: It's easy. Not being able to rely on my reasoning, I've memorized all the products of all possible multiplications.

PROFESSOR: That's pretty good . . . However, permit me to confess to you that that doesn't satisfy me, miss, and I do not congratulate you: in mathematics and in arithmetic especially, the thing that counts—for in arithmetic it is always necessary to count—the thing that counts is, above all, understanding . . . It is by mathematical reasoning, simultaneously inductive and deductive, that you ought to arrive at this result—as well as at any other result. Mathematics is the sworn enemy of memory, which is excellent otherwise, but disastrous, arithmetically speaking! . . . That's why I'm not happy with this . . . this won't do, not at all . . .

PUPIL   [*desolated*]: No, Professor.

PROFESSOR: Let's leave it for the moment. Let's go on to another exercise . . .

PUPIL: Yes, Professor.

MAID   [*entering*]: Hmm, hmm, Professor . . .

PROFESSOR   [*who doesn't hear her*]: It is unfortunate, miss, that you aren't further along in specialized mathematics . . .

MAID   [*taking him by the sleeve*]: Professor! Professor!

PROFESSOR: I hear that you will not be able to qualify for the total doctor's orals . . .

PUPIL: Yes, Professor, it's too bad!

PROFESSOR: Unless you . . . [*To the* MAID:] Let me be, Marie . . . Look here, why are you bothering me? Go back to the kitchen! To your pots and pans! Go away! Go away! [*To the* PUPIL:] We will try to prepare you at least for the partial doctorate . . .

MAID: Professor! . . . Professor! . . . [*She pulls his sleeve.*]

PROFESSOR   [*to the* MAID]: Now leave me alone! Let me be! What's the meaning of this? . . . [*To the* PUPIL:] I must therefore teach you, if you really do insist on attempting the partial doctorate . . .

PUPIL: Yes, Professor.

PROFESSOR: . . . The elements of linguistics and of comparative philology . . .

MAID: No, Professor, no! . . . You mustn't do that! . . .

PROFESSOR: Marie, you're going too far!

MAID: Professor, especially not philology, philology leads to calamity . . .

PUPIL   [*astonished*]: To calamity? [*Smiling, a little stupidly:*] That's hard to believe.

PROFESSOR   [*to the* MAID]: That's enough now! Get out of here!

MAID: All right, Professor, all right. But you can't say that I didn't warn you! Philology leads to calamity!

PROFESSOR: I'm an adult, Marie!

PUPIL: Yes, Professor.

MAID: As you wish.

[*She exits.*]

PROFESSOR: Let's continue, miss.

PUPIL: Yes, Professor.

PROFESSOR: I want you to listen now with the greatest possible attention to a lecture I have prepared . . .

PUPIL: Yes, Professor!

PROFESSOR: . . . Thanks to which, in fifteen minutes' time, you will be able to acquire the fundamental principles of the linguistic and comparative philology of the neo-Spanish languages.

PUPIL: Yes, Professor, oh good!

[*She claps her hands.*]

PROFESSOR   [*with authority*]: Quiet! What do you mean by that?

PUPIL: I'm sorry, Professor.

[*Slowly, she replaces her hands on the table.*]

PROFESSOR: Quiet! [*He gets up, walks up and down the room, his hands behind his back; from time to time he stops at stage center or near the* pupil, *and underlines his words with a gesture of his hand; he orates, but without being too emotional. The pupil follows him with her eyes, occasionally with some difficulty, for she has to turn her head far around; once or twice, not more, she turns around completely.*] And now, miss, Spanish is truly the mother tongue which gave birth to all the neo-Spanish languages, of which Spanish, Latin, Italian, our own French, Portuguese, Romanian, Sardinian or Sardanapalian, Spanish and neo-Spanish—and also, in certain of its aspects, Turkish which is otherwise very close to Greek, which is only logical, since it is a fact that Turkey is a neighbor of Greece and Greece is even closer to Turkey than you are to me—this is only one more illustration of the very important linguistic law which states that geography and philology are twin sisters . . . You may take notes, miss.

PUPIL [*in a dull voice*]: Yes, Professor!

PROFESSOR: That which distinguishes the neo-Spanish languages from each other and their idioms from the other linguistic groups, such as the group of languages called Austrian and neo-Austrian or Hapsburgian, as well as the Esperanto, Helvetian, Monacan, Swiss, Andorran, Basque, and jai alai groups, and also the groups of diplomatic and technical languages—that which distinguishes them, I repeat, is their striking resemblance which makes it so hard to distinguish them from each other—I'm speaking of the neo-Spanish languages which one is able to distinguish from each other, however, only thanks to their distinctive characteristics, absolutely indisputable proofs of their extraordinary resemblance, which renders indisputable their common origin, and which, at the same time, differentiates them profoundly—through the continuation of the distinctive traits which I've just cited.

PUPIL: Oooh! Ye-e-e-s-s-s, Professor!

PROFESSOR: But let's not linger over generalities . . .

PUPIL [*regretfully, but won over*]: Oh, Professor . . .

PROFESSOR: This appears to interest you. All the better, all the better.

PUPIL: Oh, yes, Professor . . .

PROFESSOR: Don't worry, miss. We will come back to it later . . . That is if we come back to it at all. Who can say?

PUPIL [*enchanted in spite of everything*]: Oh, yes, Professor.

PROFESSOR: Every tongue—you must know this, miss, and remember it *until the hour of your death* . . .

PUPIL: Oh! yes, Professor, until the hour of my death . . . Yes, Professor . . .

PROFESSOR: . . . And this, too, is a fundamental principle, every tongue is at bottom nothing but language, which necessarily implies that it is composed of sounds, or . . .

PUPIL: Phonemes . . .

PROFESSOR: Just what I was going to say. Don't parade your knowledge. You'd do better to listen.

PUPIL: All right, Professor. Yes, Professor.

PROFESSOR: The sounds, miss, must be seized on the wing as they fly so that they'll not fall on deaf ears. As a result, when you set out to articulate, it is recommended, insofar as possible, that you lift up your neck and chin very high, and rise up on the tips of your toes, you see, this way . . .

PUPIL: Yes, Professor.

PROFESSOR: Keep quiet. Remain seated, don't interrupt me . . . And project the sounds very loudly with all the force of your lungs in conjunction with that of your vocal cords. Like this, look: "Butterfly," "Eureka," "Trafalgar," "Papaya." This way, the sounds become filled with a warm air that is lighter than the surrounding air so that they can fly without danger of falling on deaf ears, which are veritable voids, tombs of sonorities. If you utter several sounds at an accelerated speed, they will automatically cling to each other, constituting thus syllables, words, even sentences, that is to say groupings of various importance, purely irrational assemblages of sounds, denuded of all sense, but for that very reason the more capable of maintaining themselves without danger at a high altitude in the air. By themselves, words charged with significance will fall, weighted down by their meaning, and in the end they always collapse, fall . . .

PUPIL: . . . On deaf ears.

PROFESSOR: That's it, but don't interrupt . . . and into the worst confusion . . . Or else burst like balloons. Therefore, miss . . . [*The* PUPIL *suddenly appears to be unwell.*] What's the matter?

PUPIL: I've got a toothache, Professor.

PROFESSOR: That's not important. We're not going to stop for anything so trivial. Let us go on . . .

PUPIL   [*appearing to be in more and more pain*]: Yes, Professor.

PROFESSOR: I draw your attention in passing to the consonants that change their nature in combinations. In this case *f* becomes *v, d* becomes *t, g* becomes *k,* and vice versa, as in these examples that I will cite for you: "That's all right," "hens and chickens," "Welsh rabbit," "lots of nothing," "not at all."*

PUPIL: I've got a toothache.

PROFESSOR: Let's continue.

PUPIL: Yes.

PROFESSOR: To resume: it takes years and years to learn to pronounce. Thanks to science, we can achieve this in a few minutes. In order to project words, sounds and all the rest, you must realize that it is necessary to pitilessly expel air from the lungs, and make it pass delicately, caressingly, over the vocal cords, which, like harps or leaves in the wind, will suddenly shake, agitate, vibrate, vibrate, vibrate or uvulate, or fricate or jostle against each other, or sibilate, sibilate, placing everything in movement, the uvula, the tongue, the palate, the teeth . . .

PUPIL: I have a toothache.

PROFESSOR: . . . And the lips . . . Finally the words come out through the nose, the mouth, the ears, the pores, drawing along with them all the organs that we have named, torn up by the roots, in a powerful, majestic flight, which is none other than what is called, improperly, the voice, whether modulated in singing or transformed into a terrible symphonic storm with a whole procession . . . of garlands of all kinds of flowers, of sonorous artifices: labials, dentals, occlusives, palatals, and others, some caressing, some bitter or violent.

PUPIL: Yes, Professor, I've got a toothache.

PROFESSOR: Let's go on, go on. As for the neo-Spanish languages, they are closely related, so closely to each other, that they can be considered as true second cousins. Moreover, they have the same mother: Spanishe, with a mute *e.* That is why it is so difficult to distinguish them from one another. That is why it is so useful to pronounce carefully, and to avoid errors in pronunciation. Pronunciation itself is worth a whole language. A bad pronunciation can get you into trouble. In this connection, permit me, parenthetically, to share a personal experience with you. [*Slight pause. The* PROFESSOR *goes over his memories for a moment; his features mellow, but he recovers at once.*] I was very young, little more than a child. It was during my military service. I had a friend in the regiment, a vicomte, who suffered from a rather serious defect in his pronunciation: he

*All to be heavily elided.—Translator's note.

could not pronounce the letter *f*. Instead of *f*, he said *f*. Thus, instead of "Birds of a feather flock together," he said: "Birds of a feather flock together." He pronounced filly instead of filly, Firmin instead of Firmin, French bean instead of French bean, go frig yourself instead of go frig yourself, farrago instead of farrago, fee fi fo fum instead of fee fi fo fum, Philip instead of Philip, fictory instead of fictory, February instead of February, March-April instead of March-April, Gerard de Nerval and not as is correct—Gerard de Nerval, Mirabeau instead of Mirabeau, etc., instead of etc., and thus instead of etc., instead of etc., and thus and so forth. However, he managed to conceal his fault so effectively that, thanks to the hats he wore, no one ever noticed it.

PUPIL: Yes, I've got a toothache.

PROFESSOR   [*abruptly changing his tone, his voice hardening*]: Let's go on. We'll first consider the points of similarity in order the better to apprehend, later on, that which distinguishes all these languages from each other. The differences can scarcely be recognized by people who are not aware of them. Thus, all the words of all the languages . . .

PUPIL: Uh, yes? . . . I've got a toothache.

PROFESSOR: Let's continue . . . are always the same, just as all the suffixes, all the prefixes, all the terminations, all the roots . . .

PUPIL: Are the roots of words square?

PROFESSOR: Square or cube. That depends.

PUPIL: I've got a toothache.

PROFESSOR: Let's go on. Thus, to give you an example which is little more than an illustration, take the word "front" . . .

PUPIL: How do you want me to take it?

PROFESSOR: However you wish, so long as you take it, but above all do not interrupt.

PUPIL: I've got a toothache.

PROFESSOR: Let's continue . . . I said: Let's continue. Take now the word "front." Have you taken it?

PUPIL: Yes, yes, I've got it. My teeth, my teeth . . .

PROFESSOR: The word "front" is the root of "frontispiece." It is also to be found in "affronted." "Ispiece" is the suffix, and "af" the prefix. They are so called because they do not change. They don't want to.

PUPIL: I've got a toothache.

PROFESSOR: Let's go on. [*Rapidly:*] These prefixes are of Spanish origin. I hope you noticed that, did you?

PUPIL: Oh, how my tooth aches.

PROFESSOR: Let's continue. You've surely also noticed that they've not changed in French. And now, young lady, nothing has succeeded in changing them in Latin either, nor in Italian, nor in Portuguese, nor in Sardanapalian, nor in Sardanapali, nor in Romanian, nor in neo-Spanish, nor in Spanish, nor even in the Oriental: front, frontispiece, affronted, always the same word, invariably with the same root, the same suffix, the same prefix, in all the languages I have named. And it is always the same for all words.

PUPIL: In all languages, these words mean the same thing? I've got a toothache.

PROFESSOR: Absolutely. Moreover, it's more a notion than a word. In any case, you have always the same signification, the same composition, the same sound structure, not only for this word, but for all conceivable words, in all languages. For one single notion is expressed by one and the same word, and its synonyms, in all countries. Forget about your teeth.

PUPIL: I've got a toothache. Yes, yes, yes.

PROFESSOR: Good, let's go on. I tell you, let's go on . . . How would you say, for example, in French: the roses of my grandmother are as yellow as my grandfather who was Asiatic?

PUPIL: My teeth ache, ache, ache.

PROFESSOR: Let's go on, let's go on, go ahead and answer, anyway.

PUPIL: In French?

PROFESSOR: In French.

PUPIL: Uhh . . . I should say in French: the roses of my grandmother are . . . ?

PROFESSOR: As yellow as my grandfather who was Asiatic . . .

PUPIL: Oh well, one would say, in French, I believe, the roses . . . of my . . . how do you say "grandmother" in French?

PROFESSOR: In French? Grandmother.

PUPIL: The roses of my grandmother are as yellow—in French, is it "yellow"?

PROFESSOR: Yes, of course!

PUPIL: Are as yellow as my grandfather when he got angry.

PROFESSOR: No . . . who was A . . .

PUPIL: . . . siatic . . . I've got a toothache.

PROFESSOR: That's it.

PUPIL: I've got a tooth . . .

PROFESSOR: Ache . . . so what . . . let's continue! And now translate the same sentence into Spanish, then into neo-Spanish . . .

PUPIL: In Spanish . . . this would be: the roses of my grandmother are as yellow as my grandfather who was Asiatic.

PROFESSOR: No. That's wrong.

PUPIL: And in neo-Spanish: the roses of my grandmother are as yellow as my grandfather who was Asiatic.

PROFESSOR: That's wrong. That's wrong. That's wrong. You have inverted it, you've confused Spanish with neo-Spanish, and neo-Spanish with Spanish . . . Oh . . . no . . . it's the other way around . . .

PUPIL: I've got a toothache. You're getting mixed up.

PROFESSOR: You're the one who is mixing me up. Pay attention and take notes. I will say the sentence to you in Spanish, then in neo-Spanish, and finally, in Latin. You will repeat after me. Pay attention, for the resemblances are great. In fact, they are identical resemblances. Listen, follow carefully . . .

PUPIL: I've got a tooth . . .

PROFESSOR: . . . Ache.

PUPIL: Let us go on . . . Ah! . . .

PROFESSOR: . . . In Spanish: the roses of my grandmother are as yellow as my grandfather who was Asiatic; in Latin: the roses of my grandmother are as yellow as my grandfather who was Asiatic. Do you detect the differences? Translate this into . . . Romanian.

PUPIL: The . . . how do you say "roses" in Romanian?

PROFESSOR: But "roses," what else?

PUPIL: It's not "roses"? Oh, how my tooth aches!

PROFESSOR: Certainly not, certainly not, since "roses" is a translation in Oriental of the French word "roses," in Spanish "roses," do you get it? In Sardanapali, "roses" . . .

PUPIL: Excuse me, Professor, but . . . Oh, my toothache! . . . I don't get the difference.

PROFESSOR: But it's so simple! So simple! It's a matter of having a certain experience, a technical experience and practice in these diverse languages, which are so diverse in spite of the fact that they present wholly identical characteristics. I'm going to try to give you a key . . .

PUPIL: Toothache . . .

PROFESSOR: That which differentiates these languages, is neither the words, which are absolutely the same, nor the structure of the sentence which is everywhere the same, nor the intonation, which does not offer any differences, nor the rhythm of the language . . . that which differentiates them . . . are you listening?

PUPIL: I've got a toothache.

PROFESSOR: Are you listening to me, young lady? Aah! We're going to lose our temper.

PUPIL: You're bothering me, Professor. I've got a toothache.

PROFESSOR: Son of a cocker spaniel! Listen to me!

PUPIL: Oh well . . . yes . . . yes . . . go on . . .

PROFESSOR: That which distinguishes them from each other, on the one hand, and from their mother, Spanishe with its mute *e,* on the other hand . . . is . . .

PUPIL [*grimacing*]: Is what?

PROFESSOR: Is an intangible thing. Something intangible that one is able to perceive only after very long study, with a great deal of trouble and after the broadest experience . . .

PUPIL: Ah?

PROFESSOR: Yes, young lady. I cannot give you any rule. One must have a feeling for it, and well, that's it. But in order to have it, one must study, study, and then study some more.

PUPIL: Toothache.

PROFESSOR: All the same, there are some specific cases where words differ from one language to another . . . but we cannot base our knowledge on these cases, which arc, so to speak, exceptional.

PUPIL: Oh, yes? . . . Oh, Professor, I've got a toothache.

PROFESSOR: Don't interrupt! Don't make me lose my temper! I can't answer for what I'll do. I was saying, then . . . Ah, yes, the exceptional cases, the so-called easily distinguished . . . or facilely distinguished . . . or conveniently . . . if you prefer . . . I repeat, if you prefer, for I see that you're not listening to me . . .

PUPIL: I've got a toothache.

PROFESSOR: I say then: in certain expressions in current usage, certain words differ totally from one language to another, so much so that the language employed is, in this case, considerably easier to identify. I'll give you an example: the neo-Spanish expression, famous in Madrid: "My country is the new Spain," becomes in Italian: "My country is . . .

PUPIL: The new Spain.

PROFESSOR: No! "My country is Italy." Tell me now, by simple deduction, how do you say "Italy" in French?

PUPIL: I've got a toothache.

PROFESSOR: But it's so easy: for the word "Italy," in French we have the word "France," which is an exact translation of it. My country is France. And "France" in Oriental: "Orient!" My country is the Orient. And "Orient" in Portuguese: "Portugal!" The Oriental expression: My country is the Orient is translated then in the same fashion into Portuguese: My country is Portugal! And so on . . .

PUPIL: Oh, no more, no more. My teeth . . .

PROFESSOR: Ache! ache! ache! . . . I'm going to pull them out, I will! One more example. The word "capital"—it takes on, according to the language one speaks, a different meaning. That is to say that when a Spaniard says: "I reside in the capital," the word "capital" does not mean at all the same thing that a Portuguese means when he says: "I reside in the capital." All the more so in the case of a Frenchman, a neo-Spaniard, a Romanian, a Latin, a Sardanapali . . . Whenever you hear it, young lady—young lady, I'm saying this for you! Pooh! Whenever you hear the expression: "I reside in the capital," you will immediately and easily know whether this is Spanish or Spanish, neo-Spanish, French, Oriental, Romanian, or Latin, for it is enough to know which metropolis is referred to by the person who pronounces the sentence . . . at the very moment he pronounces it . . . But these are almost the only precise examples that I can give you . . .

PUPIL: Oh dear! My teeth . . .

PROFESSOR: Silence! Or I'll bash in your skull!

PUPIL: Just try to! Skulldugger!

[*The* PROFESSOR *seizes her wrist and twists it.*]

PUPIL: Oww!

PROFESSOR: Keep quiet now! Not a word!

PUPIL [*whimpering*]: Toothache . . .

PROFESSOR: One thing that is the most . . . how shall I say it? . . . the most paradoxical . . . yes . . . that's the word . . . the most paradoxical thing, is that a lot of people who are completely illiterate speak these different languages . . . do you understand? What did I just say?

PUPIL: . . . "Speak these different languages! What did I just say?"

PROFESSOR: You were lucky that time! . . . The common people speak a Spanish full of neo-Spanish words that they are entirely unaware of, all the while believing that they are speaking Latin . . . or they speak Latin, full of Oriental words, all the while believing that they're speaking Romanian . . . or Spanish, full of neo-Spanish, all the while believing that they're speaking Sardanapali, or Spanish . . . Do you understand?

PUPIL: Yes! yes! yes! yes! What more do you want . . . ?

PROFESSOR: No insolence, my pet, or you'll be sorry . . . [*In a rage:*] But the worst of all, young lady, is that certain people, for example, in a Latin that they suppose is Spanish, say: "Both my kidneys are of the same kidney," in addressing themselves to a Frenchman who does not know a word of Spanish, but the latter understands it as if it were his own language. For that matter he thinks it is his own language. And the Frenchman will reply, in French: "Me too, sir, mine are too," and this will be perfectly comprehensible to a Spaniard, who will feel certain that the reply is in pure Spanish and that Spanish is being spoken . . . when, in reality, it was neither Spanish nor French, but Latin in the neo-Spanish dialect . . . Sit still, young lady, don't fidget, stop tapping your feet . . .

PUPIL: I've got a toothache.

PROFESSOR: How do you account for the fact that, in speaking without knowing which language they speak, or even while each of them believes that he is speaking another, the common people understand each other at all?

PUPIL: I wonder.

PROFESSOR: It is simply one of the inexplicable curiosities of the vulgar empiricism of the common people—not to be confused with experience!—a paradox, a non-sense, one of the aberrations of human nature, it is purely and simply instinct—to put it in a nutshell . . . That's what is involved here.

PUPIL: Hah! hah!

PROFESSOR: Instead of staring at the flies while I'm going to all this trouble . . . you would do much better to try to be more attentive . . . it is not I who is going to qualify for the partial doctor's orals . . . I passed mine a long time ago . . . and I've won my total doctorate, too . . . and my supertotal diploma . . . Don't you realize that what I'm saying is for your own good?

PUPIL: Toothache!

PROFESSOR: Ill-mannered . . . It can't go on like this, it won't do, it won't do, it won't do . . .

PUPIL: I'm . . . listening . . . to you . . .

PROFESSOR: Ahah! In order to learn to distinguish all the different languages, as I've told you, there is nothing better than practice . . . Let's take them up in order. I am going to try to teach you all the translations of the word "knife."

PUPIL: Well, all right . . . if you want . . .

PROFESSOR   [*calling the* MAID]: Marie! Marie! She's not there . . . Marie! Marie! . . . Marie, where are you? [*He opens the door on the right.*] Marie! . . .

[*He exits. The* PUPIL *remains alone several minutes, staring into space, wearing a stupefied expression.*]

PROFESSOR   [*offstage, in a shrill voice*]: Marie! What are you up to? Why don't you come! When I call you, you must come! [*He re-enters, followed by Marie.*] It is I who gives the orders, do you hear? [*He points at the* pupil:] She doesn't understand anything, that girl. She doesn't understand!

MAID: Don't get into such a state, sir, you know where it'll end! You're going to go too far, you're going to go too far.

PROFESSOR: I'll be able to stop in time.

MAID: That's what you always say. I only wish I could see it.

PUPIL: I've got a toothache.

MAID: You see, it's starting, that's the symptom!

PROFESSOR: What symptom? Explain yourself? What do you mean?

PUPIL   [*in a spiritless voice*]: Yes, what do you mean? I've got a toothache.

MAID: The final symptom! The chief symptom!

PROFESSOR: Stupid! stupid! stupid! [*The* MAID *starts to exit.*] Don't go away like that! I called you to help me find the Spanish, neo-Spanish, Portuguese, French, Oriental, Romanian, Sardanapali, Latin and Spanish knives.

MAID   [*severely*]: Don't ask me. [*She exits.*]

PROFESSOR   [*makes a gesture as though to protest, then refrains, a little helpless. Suddenly, he remembers*]: Ah! [*He goes quickly to the drawer where he finds a big knife, invisible or real according to the preference of the director. He seizes it and brandishes it happily.*] Here is one, young lady, here is a knife. It's too bad that we only have this one, but we're going to try to make it serve for all the languages, anyway! It will be enough if you will pronounce the word "knife" in all the languages, while looking at the object, very closely, fixedly, and imagining that it is in the language that you are speaking.

PUPIL: I've got a toothache.

PROFESSOR   [*almost singing, chanting*]: Now, say "kni," like "kni," "fe," like "fe" . . . And look, look, look at it, watch it . . .

PUPIL: What is this one in? French, Italian or Spanish?

PROFESSOR: That doesn't matter now . . . That's not your concern. Say: "kni."

PUPIL: "Kni."

PROFESSOR: . . . "fe" . . . Look.

[*He brandishes the knife under the* PUPIL's *eyes.*]

PUPIL: "fe" . . .

PROFESSOR: Again . . . Look at it.

PUPIL: Oh, no! My God! I've had enough. And besides, I've got a toothache, my feet hurt me, I've got a headache.

PROFESSOR   [*abruptly*]: Knife . . . look . . . knife . . . look . . . knife . . . look . . .

PUPIL: You're giving me an earache, too. Oh, your voice! It's so piercing!

PROFESSOR: Say: knife . . . kni . . . fe . . .

PUPIL: No! My ears hurt, I hurt all over . . .

PROFESSOR: I'm going to tear them off, your ears, that's what I'm going to do to you, and then they won't hurt you anymore, my pet.

PUPIL: Oh . . . you're hurting me, oh, you're hurting me . . .

PROFESSOR: Look, come on, quickly, repeat after me: "kni" . . .

PUPIL: Oh, since you insist . . . knife . . . knife . . . [*In a lucid moment, ironically:*] Is that neo-Spanish . . . ?

PROFESSOR: If you like, yes, it's neo-Spanish, but hurry up . . . we haven't got time . . . And then, what do you mean by that insidious question? What are you up to?

PUPIL   [*becoming more and more exhausted, weeping, desperate, at the same time both exasperated and in a trance*]: Ah!

PROFESSOR: Repeat, watch. [*He imitates a cuckoo:*] Knife, knife . . . knife, knife . . . knife, knife . . . knife, knife . . .

PUPIL: Oh, my head . . . aches . . . [*With her hand she caressingly touches the parts of her body as she names them:*] . . . My eyes . . .

PROFESSOR   [*like a cuckoo*]: Knife, knife . . . knife, knife . . .

[*They are both standing. The* PROFESSOR *still brandishes his invisible knife, nearly beside him self, as he circles around her in a sort of scalp dance, but it is important that this not be exaggerated and that his dance steps be only suggested. The* PUPIL *stands facing the audience, then recoils in the direction of the window, sickly, languid, victimized.*]

PROFESSOR: Repeat, repeat: knife . . . knife . . . knife . . .

PUPIL: I've got a pain . . . my throat, neck . . . oh, my shoulders . . . my breast . . . knife . . .

PROFESSOR: Knife . . . knife . . . knife . . .

PUPIL: My hips . . . knife . . . my thighs . . . kni . . .

PROFESSOR: Pronounce it carefully . . . knife . . . knife . . .

PUPIL: Knife . . . my throat . . .

PROFESSOR: Knife . . . knife . . .

PUPIL: Knife . . . my shoulders . . . my arms, my breast, my hips . . . knife . . . knife . . .

PROFESSOR: That's right . . . Now, you're pronouncing it well . . .

PUPIL: Knife . . . my breast . . . my stomach . . .

PROFESSOR   [*changing his voice*]: Pay attention . . . don't break my window . . . the knife kills . . .

PUPIL   [*in a weak voice*]: Yes, yes . . . the knife kills?

PROFESSOR   [*striking the* PUPIL *with a very spectacular blow of the knife*]: Aaah! That'll teach you!

[PUPIL *also cries "Aah!" then falls, flopping in an immodest position onto a chair which, as though by chance, is near the window. The murderer and his victim shout "Aaah!" at the same moment. After the first blow of the knife, the* PUPIL *flops onto the chair, her legs spread wide and hanging over both sides of the chair. The* PROFESSOR *remains standing in front of her, his back to the audience. After the first blow, he strikes her dead with a second slash of the knife, from bottom to top. After that blow a noticeable convulsion shakes his whole body.*]

PROFESSOR   [*winded, mumbling*]: Bitch . . . Oh, that's good, that does me good . . . Ah! Ah! I'm exhausted . . . I can scarcely breathe . . . Aah! [*He breathes with difficulty; he falls—fortunately a chair is there; he mops his brow, mumbles some incomprehensible words; his breathing becomes normal. He gets up, looks at the knife in his hand, looks at the young girl, then as though he were waking up, in a panic:*] What have I done! What's going to happen to me now! What's going to happen! Oh! dear! Oh dear, I'm in trouble! Young lady, young lady, get up! [*He is agitated, still holding onto the invisible knife, which he doesn't know what to do with.*] Come now, young lady, the lesson is over . . . you may go . . . you can pay another time . . . Oh! she is dead . . . dea-ead . . . And by my knife . . . She is dea-ead . . . It's terrible. [*He calls the* MAID:] Marie! Marie! My good Marie, come here!

Ah! ah! [*The door on the right opens a little and* MARIE *appears.*] No . . . don't come in . . . I made a mistake . . . I don't need you, Marie . . . I don't need you any-more . . . do you understand? . . .

    [MAID *enters wearing a stern expression, without saying a word. She sees the corpse.*]

PROFESSOR   [*in a voice less and less assured*]: I don't need you, Marie . . .

MAID   [*sarcastic*]: Then, you're satisfied with your pupil, she's profited by your lesson?

PROFESSOR   [*holding the knife behind his back*]: Yes, the lesson is finished . . . but . . . she . . . she's still there . . . she doesn't want to leave . . .

MAID   [*very harshly*]: Is that a fact? . . .

PROFESSOR   [*trembling*]: It wasn't I . . . it wasn't I . . . Marie . . . No . . . I assure you . . . it wasn't I, my little Marie . . .

MAID: And who was it? Who was it then? Me?

PROFESSOR: I don't know . . . maybe . . .

MAID: Or the cat?

PROFESSOR: That's possible . . . I don't know . . .

MAID: And today makes it the fortieth time! . . . And every day it's the same thing! Every day! You should be ashamed, at your age . . . and you're going to make yourself sick! You won't have any pupils left. That will serve you right.

PROFESSOR   [*irritated*]: It wasn't my fault! She didn't want to learn! She was disobedient! She was a bad pupil! She didn't want to learn!

MAID: Liar! . . .

PROFESSOR   [*craftily approaching the* MAID, *holding the knife behind his back*]: It's none of your business! [*He tries to strike her with a great blow of the knife; the* MAID *seizes his wrist in mid-gesture and twists it; the* PROFESSOR *lets the knife fall to the floor*]: . . . I'm sorry!

MAID   [*gives him two loud, strong slaps; the* professor *falls onto the floor, on his prat; he sobs*]: Little murderer! bastard! You're disgusting! You wanted to do that to me? I'm not one of your pupils, not me! [*She pulls him up by the collar, picks up his skullcap and puts it on his head; he's afraid she'll slap him again and holds his arm up to protect his face, like a child.*] Put the knife back where it belongs, go on! [*The* PROFESSOR *goes and puts it back in the drawer of the buffet, then comes back to her.*] Now didn't I warn you, just a little while ago: arithmetic leads to philol-ogy, and philology leads to crime . . .

PROFESSOR: You said "to calamity"!

MAID: It's the same thing.

PROFESSOR: I didn't understand you. I thought that "calamity" was a city and that you meant that philology leads to the city of Calamity . . .

MAID: Liar! Old fox! An intellectual like you is not going to make a mis-take in the meanings of words. Don't try to pull the wool over my eyes.

PROFESSOR   [*sobbing*]: I didn't kill her on purpose!

MAID: Are you sorry at least?

PROFESSOR: Oh, yes, Marie, I swear it to you!

MAID: I can't help feeling sorry for you! Ah! you're a good boy in spite of everything! I'll try to fix this. But don't start it again . . . It could give you a heart attack . . .

PROFESSOR: Yes, Marie! What are we going to do, now?

MAID: We're going to bury her . . . along with the thirty-nine others . . . that will make forty coffins . . . I'll call the undertakers and my lover, Father Auguste . . . I'll order the wreaths . . .

PROFESSOR: Yes, Marie, thank you very much.

MAID: Well, that's that. And perhaps it won't be necessary to call Auguste, since you yourself are something of a priest at times, if one can believe the gossip.

PROFESSOR: In any case, don't spend too much on the wreaths. She didn't pay for her lesson.

MAID: Don't worry . . . The least you can do is cover her up with her smock, she's not decent that way. And then we'll carry her out . . .

PROFESSOR: Yes, Marie, yes. [*He covers up the body.*] There's a chance that we'll get pinched . . . with forty coffins . . . Don't you think . . . people will be surprised . . . Suppose they ask us what's inside them?

MAID: Don't worry so much. We'll say that they're empty. And besides, people won't ask questions, they're used to it.

PROFESSOR: Even so . . .

MAID   [*she takes out an armband with an insignia, perhaps the Nazi swastika*]: Wait, if you're afraid, wear this, then you won't have anything more to be afraid of. [*She puts the armband around his arm.*] . . . That's good politics.

PROFESSOR: Thanks, my little Marie. With this, I won't need to worry . . . You're a good girl, Marie . . . very loyal . . .

MAID: That's enough. Come on, sir. Are you all right?

PROFESSOR: Yes, my little Marie. [*The* MAID *and the* PROFESSOR *take the body of the young girl, one by the shoulders, the other by the legs, and move towards the door on the right.*] Be careful. We don't want to hurt her.

[*They exit. The stage remains empty for several moments. We hear the doorbell ring at the left.*]

VOICE OF THE MAID: Just a moment, I'm coming!

[*She appears as she was at the beginning of the play, and goes towards the door. The doorbell rings again.*]

MAID   [*aside*]: She's certainly in a hurry, this one! [*Aloud:*] Just a moment! [*She goes to the door on the left, and opens it.*] Good morning, miss! You are the new pupil? You have come for the lesson? The Professor is expecting you. I'll go tell him that you've come. He'll be right down. Come in, miss, come in!

(1958)

QUESTIONS

1. Describe your emotional response to the play. Did you find yourself responding with different feelings at different places in the action? How did you respond to the ending?

2. What comic ingredients does the play include? Single out an especially funny segment and account for its comic effects. How would you characterize the nature and purpose of the play's comedy?
3. Consider *The Lesson* as a satire. What does it ridicule? By what means?
4. What is the function of the housekeeper? Would it make any difference if her role were deleted?
5. What lesson(s) does the play teach, either directly or indirectly?
6. How would you cast and direct the play? What advice would you give the performers?

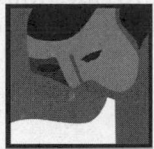

CHAPTER TWENTY-SEVEN

A Collection of Twentieth-Century Plays

All the world's a stage,
And all the men and women merely players:
They have their exits and their entrances,
And one man in his time plays many parts. . . .
—WILLIAM SHAKESPEARE, *As You Like It*, II, VII

JOHN MILLINGTON SYNGE

[1871–1909]

Like Lady Gregory and William Butler Yeats, John Millington Synge was an Irish dramatist intensely involved in the Irish literary renaissance. With Yeats and Lady Gregory, Synge served as codirector of the Abbey Theatre in Dublin. At Yeats's suggestion, Synge brought his knowledge and experience of the Irish peasantry, especially from his visits to the Aran Islands, into the language and dramatic situations of his plays. Yeats convinced Synge to abandon writing criticism and to write plays about simple people whose language reflected an intimate contact with earth, sea, and sky. In addition to *Riders to the Sea* (1904), which shows the extent to which he took Yeats's advice, Synge is best known for his masterful comedy, *The Playboy of the Western World* (1907). His journal of impressions *(The Aran Islands)* provides important information about the life of the island people and a helpful glimpse into the raw material Synge shaped into dramatic art.

JOHN MILLINGTON SYNGE

Riders to the Sea

CHARACTERS

MAURYA, *an old woman*
BARTLEY, *her son*
CATHLEEN, *her daughter*
NORA, *a younger daughter*
MEN AND WOMEN

Scene. *An island off the West of Ireland.*

Cottage kitchen, with nets, oilskins, spinning-wheel, some new boards standing by the wall, etc. CATHLEEN, *a girl of about twenty, finishes kneading cake, and puts it down in the pot-oven by the fire; then wipes her hands, and begins to spin at the wheel.* NORA, *a young girl, puts her head in at the door.*

NORA *(in a low voice):* Where is she?
CATHLEEN: She's lying down, God help her, and maybe sleeping, if she's able.

NORA *comes in softly, and takes a bundle from under her shawl.*

CATHLEEN *(spinning the wheel rapidly):* What is it you have?
NORA: The young priest is after bringing them. It's a shirt and a plain stocking were got off a drowned man in Donegal.

CATHLEEN *stops her wheel with a sudden movement, and leans out to listen.*

NORA: We're to find out if it's Michael's they are, some time herself will be down looking by the sea.
CATHLEEN: How would they be Michael's, Nora? How would he go the length of that way to the far north?

NORA: The young priest says he's known the like of it. 'If it's Michael's they are,' says he, 'you can tell herself he's got a clean burial, by the grace of God; and if they're not his, let no one say a word about them, for she'll be getting her death,' says he, 'with crying and lamenting.'

The door which NORA *half closed is blown open by a gust of wind.*

CATHLEEN (*looking out anxiously*): Did you ask him would he stop Bartley going this day with the horses to the Galway fair?

NORA: 'I won't stop him,' says he; 'but let you not be afraid. Herself does be saying prayers half through the night, and the Almighty God won't leave her destitute,' says he, 'with no son living.'

CATHLEEN: Is the sea bad by the white rocks, Nora?

NORA: Middling bad, God help us. There's a great roaring in the west, and it's worse it'll be getting when the tide's turned to the wind. (*She goes over to the table with the bundle.*) Shall I open it now?

CATHLEEN: Maybe she'd wake up on us, and come in before we'd done (*coming to the table*). It's a long time we'll be, and the two of us crying.

NORA (*goes to the inner door and listens*): She's moving about on the bed. She'll be coming in a minute.

CATHLEEN: Give me the ladder, and I'll put them up in the turf-loft, the way she won't know of them at all, and maybe when the tide turns she'll be going down to see would he be floating from the east.

They put the ladder against the gable of the chimney; CATHLEEN *goes up a few steps and hides the bundle in the turf-loft.* MAURYA *comes from the inner room.*

MAURYA (*looking up at* CATHLEEN *and speaking querulously*): Isn't it turf enough you have for this day and evening?

CATHLEEN: There's a cake baking at the fire for a short space (*throwing down the turf*), and Bartley will want it when the tide turns if he goes to Connemara.

NORA *picks up the turf and puts it round the pot-oven.*

MAURYA (*sitting down on a stool at the fire*): He won't go this day with the wind rising from the south and west. He won't go this day, for the young priest will stop him surely.

NORA: He'll not stop him, mother; and I heard Eamon Simon and Stephen Pheety and Colum Shawn saying he would go.

MAURYA: Where is he itself?

NORA: He went down to see would there be another boat sailing in the week, and I'm thinking it won't be long till he's here now, for the tide's turning at the green head, and the hooker's tacking from the east.

CATHLEEN: I hear some one passing the big stones.

NORA (*looking out*): He's coming now, and he in a hurry.

BARTLEY (*comes in and looks round the room. Speaking sadly and quietly*): Where is the bit of new rope, Cathleen, was bought in Connemara?

CATHLEEN (*coming down*): Give it to him, Nora; it's on a nail by the white boards. I hung it up this morning, for the pig with the black feet was eating it.

NORA (*giving him a rope*): Is that it, Bartley?

MAURYA: You'd do right to leave that rope, Bartley, hanging by the boards

(BARTLEY *takes the rope*). It will be wanting in this place, I'm telling you, if Michael is washed up tomorrow morning or the next morning, or any morning in the week; for it's a deep grave we'll make him, by the grace of God.

BARTLEY *(beginning to work with the rope)*:   I've no halter the way I can ride down on the mare, and I must go now quickly. This is the one boat going for two weeks or beyond it, and the fair will be a good fair for horses, I heard them saying below.

MAURYA: It's a hard thing they'll be saying below if the body is washed up and there's no man in it to make the coffin, and I after giving a big price for the finest white boards you'd find in Connemara.

She looks round at the boards.

BARTLEY: How would it be washed up, and we after looking each day for nine days, and a strong wind blowing a while back from the west and south?

MAURYA: If it isn't found itself, that wind is raising the sea, and there was a star up against the moon, and it rising in the night. If it was a hundred horses, or a thousand horses, you had itself, what is the price of a thousand horses against a son where there is one son only?

BARTLEY *(working at the halter, to* CATHLEEN*)*:   Let you go down each day, and see the sheep aren't jumping in on the rye, and if the jobber comes you can sell the pig with the black feet if there is a good price going.

MAURYA: How would the like of her get a good price for a pig?

BARTLEY *(to* CATHLEEN*)*:   If the west wind holds with the last bit of the moon let you and Nora get up weed enough for another cock for the kelp. It's hard set we'll be from this day with no one in it but one man to work.

MAURYA: It's hard set we'll be surely the day you're drowned with the rest. What way will I live and the girls with me, and I an old woman looking for the grave?

BARTLEY *lays down the halter, takes off his old coat, and puts on a newer one of the same flannel.*

BARTLEY *(to* NORA*)*:   Is she coming to the pier?

NORA *(looking out)*:   She's passing the green head and letting fall her sails.

BARTLEY *(getting his purse and tobacco)*:   I'll have half an hour to go down, and you'll see me coming again in two days, or in three days, or maybe in four days if the wind is bad.

MAURYA *(turning round to the fire, and putting her shawl over her head)*:   Isn't it a hard and cruel man won't hear a word from an old woman, and she holding him from the sea?

CATHLEEN: It's the life of a young man to be going on the sea, and who would listen to an old woman with one thing and she saying it over?

BARTLEY *(taking the halter)*:   I must go now quickly. I'll ride down on the red mare, and the grey pony 'ill run behind me. . . . . The blessing of God on you.

He goes out.

MAURYA *(crying out as he is in the door)*:   He's gone now, God spare us, and we'll not see him again. He's gone now, and when the black night is falling I'll have no son left me in the world.

CATHLEEN: Why wouldn't you give him your blessing and he looking round in the door? Isn't it sorrow enough is on every one in this house without you sending him out with an unlucky word behind him, and a hard word in his ear?

MAURYA *takes up the tongs and begins raking the fire aimlessly without looking round.*

NORA *(turning towards her)*:   You're taking away the turf from the cake.
CATHLEEN *(crying out)*:   The Son of God forgive us, Nora, we're after forgetting his bit of bread. *(She comes over to the fire.)*
NORA: And it's destroyed he'll be going till dark night, and he after eating nothing since the sun went up.
CATHLEEN *(turning the cake out of the oven)*:   It's destroyed he'll be, surely. There's no sense left on any person in a house where an old woman will be talking for ever.

MAURYA *sways herself on her stool.*

CATHLEEN *(cutting off some of the bread and rolling it in a cloth; to MAURYA)*:   Let you go down now to the spring well and give him this and he passing. You'll see him then and the dark word will be broken, and you can say 'God speed you,' the way he'll be easy in his mind.
MAURYA *(taking the bread)*:   Will I be in it as soon as himself?
CATHLEEN: If you go now quickly.
MAURYA *(standing up unsteadily)*:   It's hard set I am to walk.
CATHLEEN *(looking at her anxiously)*:   Give her the stick, Nora, or maybe she'll slip on the big stones.
NORA: What stick?
CATHLEEN: The stick Michael brought from Connemara.
MAURYA *(taking a stick NORA gives her)*.   In the big world the old people do be leaving things after them for their sons and children, but in this place it is the young men do be leaving things behind for them that do be old.

She goes out slowly. NORA *goes over to the ladder.*

CATHLEEN: Wait, Nora, maybe she'd turn back quickly. She's that sorry, God help her, you wouldn't know the thing she'd do.
NORA: Is she gone round by the bush?
CATHLEEN *(looking out)*:   She's gone now. Throw it down quickly, for the Lord knows when she'll be out of it again.
NORA *(getting the bundle from the loft)*:   The young priest said he'd be passing tomorrow, and we might go down and speak to him below if it's Michael's they are surely.
CATHLEEN *(taking the bundle)*:   Did he say what way they were found?
NORA *(coming down)*:   'There were two men,' says he, 'and they rowing round with poteen before the cocks crowed, and the oar of one of them caught the body, and they passing the black cliffs of the north.'
CATHLEEN *(trying to open the bundle)*:   Give me a knife, Nora; the string's perished with salt water, and there's a black knot on it you wouldn't loosen in a week.
NORA *(giving her a knife)*:   I've heard tell it was a long way to Donegal.

CATHLEEN *(cutting the string)*:   It is surely. There was a man in here a while ago—the man sold us that knife—and he said if you set off walking from the rocks beyond, it would be in seven days you'd be in Donegal.

NORA: And what time would a man take, and he floating?

CATHLEEN *opens the bundle and takes out a bit of a shirt and a stocking. They look at them eagerly.*

CATHLEEN *(in a low voice)*:   The Lord spare us, Nora! isn't it a queer hard thing to say if it's his they are surely?

NORA: I'll get his shirt off the hook the way we can put the one flannel on the other. *(She looks through some clothes hanging in the corner.)* It's not with them, Cathleen, and where will it be?

CATHLEEN: I'm thinking Bartley put it on him in the morning, for his own shirt was heavy with the salt in it. *(Pointing to the corner.)* There's a bit of a sleeve was of the same stuff. Give me that and it will do.

NORA *brings it to her and they compare the flannel.*

CATHLEEN: It's the same stuff, Nora; but if it is itself, aren't there great rolls of it in the shops of Galway, and isn't it many another man may have a shirt of it as well as Michael himself?

NORA *(who has taken up the stocking and counted the stitches, crying out)*:   It's Michael, Cathleen, it's Michael; God spare his soul, and what will herself say when she hears this story, and Bartley on the sea?

CATHLEEN *(taking the stocking)*:   It's a plain stocking.

NORA: It's the second one of the third pair I knitted, and I put up three-score stitches, and I dropped four of them.

CATHLEEN *(counts the stitches)*:   It's that number is in it *(crying out)*. Ah, Nora, isn't it a bitter thing to think of him floating that way to the far north, and no one to keen him but the black hags that do be flying on the sea?

NORA *(swinging herself half round, and throwing out her arms on the clothes)*:   And isn't it a pitiful thing when there is nothing left of a man who was a great rower and fisher but a bit of an old shirt and a plain stocking?

CATHLEEN *(after an instant)*:   Tell me is herself coming, Nora? I hear a little sound on the path.

NORA *(looking out)*:   She is, Cathleen. She's coming up to the door.

CATHLEEN: Put these things away before she'll come in. Maybe it's easier she'll be after giving her blessing to Bartley, and we won't let on we've heard anything the time he's on the sea.

NORA *(helping CATHLEEN to close the bundle)*:   We'll put them here in the corner.

They put them into a hole in the chimney corner. CATHLEEN *goes back to the spinning-wheel.*

NORA: Will she see it was crying I was?

CATHLEEN: Keep your back to the door the way the light'll not be on you.

NORA *sits down at the chimney corner, with her back to the door.* MAURYA *comes in very slowly, without looking at the girls, and goes over to her stool at the other side of the fire. The cloth with the bread is still in her hand. The girls look at each other, and* NORA *points to the bundle of bread.*

CATHLEEN (*after spinning for a moment*):   You didn't give him his bit of bread?

MAURYA *begins to keen softly, without turning round.*

CATHLEEN: Did you see him riding down?

MAURYA *goes on keening.*

CATHLEEN (*a little impatiently*):   God forgive you; isn't it a better thing to raise your voice and tell what you seen, than to be making lamentation for a thing that's done? Did you see Bartley, I'm saying to you?

MAURYA (*with a weak voice*):   My heart's broken from this day.

CATHLEEN (*as before*):   Did you see Bartley?

MAURYA: I seen the fearfulest thing.

CATHLEEN (*leaves her wheel and looks out*):   God forgive you; he's riding the mare now over the green head, and the grey pony behind him.

MAURYA (*Starts, so that her shawl falls back from her head and shows her white tossed hair. With a frightened voice*):   The grey pony behind him. . . .

CATHLEEN (*coming to the fire*):   What is it ails you at all?

MAURYA (*speaking very slowly*):   I've seen the fearfulest thing any person has seen since the day Bride Dara seen the dead man with the child in his arms.

CATHLEEN *and* NORA: Uah.

They crouch down in front of the old woman at the fire.

NORA: Tell us what it is you seen.

MAURYA: I went down to the spring well, and I stood there saying a prayer to myself. Then Bartley came along, and he riding on the red mare with the grey pony behind him (*she puts up her hands, as if to hide something from her eyes*). The Son of God spare us, Nora!

CATHLEEN: What is it you seen?

MAURYA: I seen Michael himself.

CATHLEEN (*speaking softly*):   You did not, mother. It wasn't Michael you seen, for his body is after being found in the far north, and he's got a clean burial, by the grace of God.

MAURYA (*a little defiantly*):   I'm after seeing him this day, and he riding and galloping. Bartley came first on the red mare, and I tried to say 'God speed you,' but something choked the words in my throat. He went by quickly; and 'the blessing of God on you,' says he, and I could say nothing. I looked up then, and I crying, at the grey pony, and there was Michael upon it—with fine clothes on him, and new shoes on his feet.

CATHLEEN (*begins to keen*):   It's destroyed we are from this day. It's destroyed, surely.

NORA: Didn't the young priest say the Almighty God won't leave her destitute with no son living?

MAURYA (*in a low voice, but clearly*):   It's little the like of him knows of the sea. . . . Bartley will be lost now, and let you call in Eamon and make me a good coffin out of the white boards, for I won't live after them. I've had a husband, and a husband's father, and six sons in this house—six fine men, though it was a hard birth I had with every one of them and they coming to the world—and some of them were found and some of them were not found, but they're gone now the lot of them. . . . There were Stephan and Shawn were lost in the great wind, and found after in the Bay of Gregory of the Golden Mouth, and carried up the two of them on one plank, and in by that door.

She pauses for a moment, the girls start as if they heard something through the door that is half open behind them.

NORA *(in a whisper)*:   Did you hear that, Cathleen? Did you hear a noise in the north-east?

CATHLEEN *(in a whisper)*:   There's someone after crying out by the seashore.

MAURYA *(continues without hearing anything)*:   There was Sheamus and his father, and his own father again, were lost in a dark night, and not a stick or sign was seen of them when the sun went up. There was Patch after was drowned out of a curagh that turned over. I was sitting here with Bartley, and he a baby lying on my two knees, and I seen two women, and three women, and four women coming in, and they crossing themselves and not saying a word. I looked out then, and there were men coming after them, and they holding a thing in the half of a red sail, and water dripping out of it—it was a dry day, Nora—and leaving a track to the door.

She pauses again with her hand stretched out towards the door. It opens softly and old women begin to come in, crossing themselves on the threshold, and kneeling down in front of the stage with red petticoats over their heads.

MAURYA *(half in a dream, to* CATHLEEN*)*:   Is it Patch, or Michael, or what is it at all?

CATHLEEN: Michael is after being found in the far north, and when he is found there how could he be here in this place?

MAURYA: There does be a power of young men floating round in the sea, and what way would they know if it was Michael they had, or another man like him, for when a man is nine days in the sea, and the wind blowing, it's hard set his own mother would be to say what man was in it.

CATHLEEN: It's Michael, God spare him, for they're after sending us a bit of his clothes from the far north.

She reaches out and hands MAURYA *the clothes that belonged to Michael.* MAURYA *stands up slowly, and takes them in her hands.* NORA *looks out.*

NORA: They're carrying a thing among them, and there's water dripping out of it and leaving a track by the big stones.

CATHLEEN *(in a whisper to the women who have come in)*:   Is it Bartley it is?

ONE OF THE WOMEN: It is, surely, God rest his soul.

Two younger women come in and pull out the table. Then men carry in the body of BARTLEY, *laid on a plank, with a bit of a sail over it, and lay it on the table.*

CATHLEEN (*to the women as they are doing so*):   What way was he drowned?

ONE OF THE WOMEN: The grey pony knocked him over into the sea, and he was washed out where there is a great surf on the white rocks.

MAURYA *has gone over and knelt down at the head of the table. The women are keening softly and swaying themselves with a slow movement.* CATHLEEN *and* NORA *kneel at the other end of the table. The men kneel near the door.*

MAURYA (*raising her head and speaking as if she did not see the people around her*): They're all gone now, and there isn't anything more the sea can do to me. . . . I'll have no call now to be up crying and praying when the wind breaks from the south, and you can hear the surf is in the east, and the surf is in the west, making a great stir with the two noises, and they hitting one on the other. I'll have no call now to be going down and getting Holy Water in the dark nights after Samhain, and I won't care what way the sea is when the other women will be keening. (*To* NORA.) Give me the Holy Water, Nora; there's a small sup still on the dresser.

NORA *gives it to her.*

MAURYA (*drops Michael's clothes across* BARTLEY'S *feet, and sprinkles the Holy Water over him*):   It isn't that I haven't prayed for you, Bartley, to the Almighty God. It isn't that I haven't said prayers in the dark night till you wouldn't know what I'd be saying; but it's a great rest I'll have now, and it's time, surely. It's a great rest I'll have now, and great sleeping in the long nights after Samhain, if it's only a bit of wet flour we do have to eat, and maybe a fish that would be stinking.

She kneels down again, crossing herself, and saying prayers under her breath.

CATHLEEN (*to an old man*):   Maybe yourself and Eamon would make a coffin when the sun rises. We have fine white boards herself bought, God help her, thinking Michael would be found, and I have a new cake you can eat while you'll be working.

THE OLD MAN (*looking at the boards*):   Are there nails with them?

CATHLEEN: There are not, Colum; we didn't think of the nails.

ANOTHER MAN: It's a great wonder she wouldn't think of the nails, and all the coffins she's seen made already.

CATHLEEN: It's getting old she is, and broken.

MAURYA *stands up again very slowly and spreads out the pieces of Michael's clothes beside the body, sprinkling them with the last of the Holy Water.*

NORA (*in a whisper to* CATHLEEN):   She's quiet now and easy; but the day Michael was drowned you could hear her crying out from this to the spring well. It's fonder she was of Michael, and would anyone have thought that?

CATHLEEN (*slowly and clearly*):   An old woman will be soon tired with anything she will do, and isn't it nine days herself is after crying and keening, and making great sorrow in the house?

MAURYA (*puts the empty cup mouth downwards on the table, and lays her hands together on Bartley's feet*):   They're all together this time, and the end is come.

May the Almighty God have mercy on Bartley's soul, and on Michael's soul, and on the souls of Sheamus and Patch, and Stephen and Shawn *(bending her head);* and may He have mercy on my soul, Nora, and on the soul of every one is left living in the world.

She pauses, and the keen rises a little more loudly from the women, then sinks away.

MAURYA *(continuing):*   Michael has a clean burial in the far north, by the grace of Almighty God. Bartley will have a fine coffin out of the white boards, and a deep grave surely. What more can we want than that? No man at all can be living for ever, and we must be satisfied.

She kneels down again and the curtain falls slowly.

(1904)

QUESTIONS

1. To what extent can *Riders to the Sea* be described as a tragedy?
2. Characterize the play's language, especially the speech style of the central characters. Of what importance is its religious dimension?
3. Distinguish between the rank and roles of Nora and Cathleen.
4. What is Maurya's role? Describe in general terms the kind of actress you imagine would be well suited to her role.
5. Identify the props used, and comment on their dramatic and symbolic significance.
6. Explain the significance of the title. How does Synge make the presence and the power of the sea felt?

SUSAN GLASPELL

[1882–1948]

Susan Glaspell, an American novelist and playwright, was one of the cofounders of the Provincetown Players, an influential theatrical company. With her husband, George Cram Cook, she collaborated on a number of plays, including her one-act satire on Freudian psychoanalysis, *Suppressed Desires,* published in 1916. In the same year Glaspell produced another fine one-act play, *Trifles,* which has continued to be her most frequently performed play.

SUSAN GLASPELL

Trifles

CHARACTERS

GEORGE HENDERSON, *County Attorney*
HENRY PETERS, *Sheriff*
LEWIS HALE, *A Neighboring Farmer*
MRS. PETERS
MRS. HALE

Scene. *The kitchen in the now abandoned farmhouse of* JOHN WRIGHT, *a gloomy kitchen, and left without having been put in order—unwashed pans under the sink, a loaf of bread outside the breadbox, a dish towel on the table—other signs of incompleted work. At the rear the outer door opens and the* SHERIFF *comes in followed by the* COUNTY ATTORNEY *and* HALE. *The* SHERIFF *and* HALE *are men in middle life, the* COUNTY ATTORNEY *is a young man; all are much bundled up and go at once to the stove. They are followed by two women—the* SHERIFF'S *wife first; she is a slight wiry woman, a thin nervous face.* MRS. HALE *is larger and would ordinarily be called more comfortable looking, but she is disturbed now and looks fearfully about as she enters. The women have come in slowly, and stand close together near the door.*

COUNTY ATTORNEY [*rubbing his hands*]:   This feels good. Come up to the fire, ladies.

MRS. PETERS [*after taking a step forward*]:   I'm not—cold.

SHERIFF [*unbuttoning his overcoat and stepping away from the stove as if to mark the beginning of official business*]:   Now, Mr. Hale, before we move things about, you explain to Mr. Henderson just what you saw when you came here yesterday morning.

COUNTY ATTORNEY: By the way, has anything been moved? Are things just as you left them yesterday?

SHERIFF [*looking about*]:   It's just the same. When it dropped below zero last night I thought I'd better send Frank out this morning to make a fire for us—no use getting pneumonia with a big case on, but I told him not to touch anything except the stove—and you know Frank.

COUNTY ATTORNEY: Somebody should have been left here yesterday.

SHERIFF: Oh—yesterday. When I had to send Frank to Morris Center for that man who went crazy—I want you to know I had my hands full yesterday,

I knew you could get back from Omaha by today and as long as I went over everything here myself—

COUNTY ATTORNEY: Well, Mr. Hale, tell just what happened when you came here yesterday morning.

HALE: Harry and I had started to town with a load of potatoes. We came along the road from my place and as I got here I said, "I'm going to see if I can't get John Wright to go in with me on a party telephone." I spoke to Wright about it once before and he put me off, saying folks talked too much anyway, and all he asked was peace and quiet—I guess you know about how much he talked himself; but I thought maybe if I went to the house and talked about it before his wife, though I said to Harry that I didn't know as what his wife wanted made much difference to John—

COUNTY ATTORNEY: Let's talk about that later, Mr. Hale. I do want to talk about that, but tell now just what happened when you got to the house.

HALE: I didn't hear or see anything; I knocked at the door, and still it was all quiet inside. I knew they must be up, it was past eight o'clock. So I knocked again, and I thought I heard somebody say, "Come in." I wasn't sure, I'm not sure yet, but I opened the door—this door [*Indicating the door by which the two women are still standing*] and there in that rocker—[*Pointing to it.*] sat Mrs. Wright.

[*They all look at the rocker.*]

COUNTY ATTORNEY: What—was she doing?

HALE: She was rockin' back and forth. She had her apron in her hand and was kind of—pleating it.

COUNTY ATTORNEY: And how did she—look?

HALE: Well, she looked queer.

COUNTY ATTORNEY: How do you mean—queer?

HALE: Well, as if she didn't know what she was going to do next. And kind of done up.

COUNTY ATTORNEY: How did she seem to feel about your coming?

HALE: Why, I don't think she minded—one way or other. She didn't pay much attention. I said, "How do, Mrs. Wright, it's cold, ain't it?" And she said, "Is it?"—and went on kind of pleating at her apron. Well, I was surprised; she didn't ask me to come up to the stove, or to set down, but just sat there, not even looking at me, so I said, "I want to see John." And then she—laughed. I guess you would call it a laugh. I thought of Harry and the team outside, so I said a little sharp: "Can't I see John?" "No," she says, kind o' dull like. "Ain't he home?" says I. "Yes," says she, "he's home." "Then why can't I see him?" I asked her, out of patience. "'Cause he's dead," says she. *"Dead?"* says I. She just nodded her head, not getting a bit excited, but rockin' back and forth. "Why—where is he?" says I, not knowing what to say. She just pointed upstairs—like that [*Himself pointing to the room above*]. I got up, with the idea of going up there. I walked from there to here—then I says, "Why, what did he die of?" "He died of a rope round his neck," says she, and just went on pleatin' at her apron. Well, I went out and called Harry. I thought I might—need help. We went upstairs and there he was lyin'—

COUNTY ATTORNEY: I think I'd rather have you go into that upstairs, where you can point it all out. Just go on now with the rest of the story.

HALE: Well, my first thought was to get that rope off. It looked . . . [*Stops, his face twitches.*] . . . but Harry, he went up to him, and he said, "No, he's dead all right, and we'd better not touch anything." So we went back down stairs. She was still sitting that same way. "Has anybody been notified?" I asked. "No," says she, unconcerned. "Who did this, Mrs. Wright?" said Harry. He said it businesslike—and she stopped pleatin' of her apron. "I don't know," she says. "You don't *know?*" says Harry. "No," says she. "Weren't you sleepin' in the bed with him?" says Harry. "Yes," says she, "but I was on the inside." "Somebody slipped a rope round his neck and strangled him and you didn't wake up?" says Harry. "I didn't wake up," she said after him. We must 'a looked as if we didn't see how that could be, for after a minute she said, "I sleep sound." Harry was going to ask her more questions but I said maybe we ought to let her tell her story first to the coroner, or the sheriff, so Harry went fast as he could to Rivers' place, where there's a telephone.

COUNTY ATTORNEY: And what did Mrs. Wright do when she knew that you had gone for the coroner?

HALE: She moved from that chair to this one over here [*Pointing to a small chair in the corner.*] and just sat there with her hands held together and looking down. I got a feeling that I ought to make some conversation, so I said I had come in to see if John wanted to put in a telephone, and at that she started to laugh, and then she stopped and looked at me—scared. [*The* COUNTY ATTORNEY, *who has had his notebook out, makes a note.*] I dunno, maybe it wasn't scared. I wouldn't like to say it was. Soon Harry got back, and then Dr. Lloyd came, and you, Mr. Peters, and so I guess that's all I know that you don't.

COUNTY ATTORNEY [*looking around*]:   I guess we'll go upstairs first—and then out to the barn and around there. [*to the* SHERIFF] You're convinced that there was nothing important here—nothing that would point to any motive.

SHERIFF: Nothing here but kitchen things.

[*The* COUNTY ATTORNEY, *after again looking around the kitchen, opens the door of a cupboard closet. He gets up on a chair and looks on a shelf. Pulls his hand away, sticky.*]

COUNTY ATTORNEY: Here's a nice mess.

[*The women draw nearer.*]

MRS. PETERS [*to the other woman*]:   Oh, her fruit; it did freeze. [*To the* COUNTY ATTORNEY] She worried about that when it turned so cold. She said the fire'd go out and her jars would break.

SHERIFF: Well, can you beat the women! Held for murder and worryin' about her preserves.

COUNTY ATTORNEY: I guess before we're through she may have something more serious than preserves to worry about.

HALE: Well, women are used to worrying over trifles.

[*The two women move a little closer together.*]

COUNTY ATTORNEY [*with the gallantry of a young politician*]: And yet, for all their worries, what would we do without the ladies? [*The women do not unbend. He goes to the sink, takes a dipperful of water from the pail and pouring it into a basin, washes his hands. Starts to wipe them on the roller towel, turns it for a cleaner place.*] Dirty towels! [*Kicks his foot against the pans under the sink.*] Not much of a house-keeper, would you say, ladies?

MRS. HALE [*stiffly*]: There's a great deal of work to be done on a farm.

COUNTY ATTORNEY: To be sure. And yet [*With a little bow to her*] I know there are some Dickson county farmhouses which do not have such roller towels.

[*He gives it a pull to expose its full length again.*]

MRS. HALE: Those towels get dirty awful quick. Men's hands aren't always as clean as they might be.

COUNTY ATTORNEY: Ah, loyal to your sex, I see. But you and Mrs. Wright were neighbors. I suppose you were friends, too.

MRS. HALE [*shaking her head*]: I've not seen much of her of late years. I've not been in this house—it's more than a year.

COUNTY ATTORNEY: And why was that? You didn't like her?

MRS. HALE: I liked her all well enough. Farmers' wives have their hands full, Mr. Henderson. And then—

COUNTY ATTORNEY: Yes—?

MRS. HALE [*looking about*]: It never seemed a very cheerful place.

COUNTY ATTORNEY: No—it's not cheerful. I shouldn't say she had the homemaking instinct.

MRS. HALE: Well, I don't know as Wright had, either.

COUNTY ATTORNEY: You mean that they didn't get on very well?

MRS. HALE: No, I don't mean anything. But I don't think a place'd be any cheerfuller for John Wright's being in it.

COUNTY ATTORNEY: I'd like to talk more of that a little later. I want to get the lay of things upstairs now.

[*He goes to the left, where three steps lead to a stair door.*]

SHERIFF: I suppose anything Mrs. Peters does'll be all right. She was to take in some clothes for her, you know, and a few little things. We left in such a hurry yesterday.

COUNTY ATTORNEY: Yes, but I would like to see what you take, Mrs. Peters, and keep an eye out for anything that might be of use to us.

MRS. PETERS: Yes, Mr. Henderson.

[*The women listen to the men's steps on the stairs, then look about the kitchen.*]

MRS. HALE: I'd hate to have men coming into my kitchen, snooping around and criticising.

[*She arranges the pans under sink which the COUNTY ATTORNEY had shoved out of place.*]

MRS. PETERS: Of course it's no more than their duty.

MRS. HALE: Duty's all right, but I guess that deputy sheriff that came out to make the fire might have got a little of this on. [*Gives the roller towel a pull.*] Wish I'd thought of that sooner. Seems mean to talk about her for not having things slicked up when she had to come away in such a hurry.

MRS. PETERS [*Who has gone to a small table in the left rear corner of the room, and lifted one end of a towel that covers a pan*]:   She had bread set.

[*Stands still.*]

MRS. HALE [*eyes fixed on a loaf of bread beside the breadbox, which is on a low shelf at the other side of the room. Moves slowly toward it*]:   She was going to put this in there. [*Picks up loaf, then abruptly drops it. In a manner of returning to familiar things.*] It's a shame about her fruit. I wonder if it's all gone. [*Gets up on the chair and looks.*] I think there's some here that's all right, Mrs. Peters. Yes—here; [*Holding it toward the window.*] this is cherries, too. [*Looking again.*] I declare I believe that's the only one. [*Gets down, bottle in her hand. Goes to the sink and wipes it off on the outside.*] She'll feel awful bad after all her hard work in the hot weather. I remember the afternoon I put up my cherries last summer.

[*She puts the bottle on the big kitchen table, center of the room. With a sigh, is about to sit down in the rocking-chair. Before she is seated realizes what chair it is; with a slow look at it, steps back. The chair which she has touched rocks back and forth.*]

MRS. PETERS: Well, I must get those things from the front room closet. [*She goes to the door at the right, but after looking into the other room, steps back.*] You coming with me, Mrs. Hale? You could help me carry them.

[*They go in the other room; reappear,* MRS. PETERS *carrying a dress and skirt,* MRS. HALE *following with a pair of shoes.*]

MRS. PETERS: My, it's cold in there.

[*She puts the clothes on the big table, and hurries to the stove.*]

MRS. HALE [*examining her skirt*]:   Wright was close. I think maybe that's why she kept so much to herself. She didn't even belong to the Ladies Aid. I suppose she felt she couldn't do her part, and then you don't enjoy things when you feel shabby. She used to wear pretty clothes and be lively, when she was Minnie Foster, one of the town girls singing in the choir. But that—oh, that was thirty years ago. This all you was to take in?

MRS. PETERS: She said she wanted an apron. Funny thing to want, for there isn't much to get you dirty in jail, goodness knows. But I suppose just to make her feel more natural. She said they was in the top drawer in this cupboard. Yes, here. And then her little shawl that always hung behind the door. [*Opens stair door and looks.*] Yes, here it is.

[*Quickly shuts door leading upstairs.*]

MRS. HALE [*abruptly moving toward her*]:   Mrs. Peters?
MRS. PETERS: Yes, Mrs. Hale?
MRS. HALE: Do you think she did it?
MRS. PETERS [*in a frightened voice*]:   Oh, I don't know.

MRS. HALE: Well, I don't think she did. Asking for an apron and her little shawl. Worrying about her fruit.

MRS. PETERS [*starts to speak, glances up, where footsteps are heard in the room above. In a low voice*]:   Mr. Peters says it looks bad for her. Mr. Henderson is awful sarcastic in a speech and he'll make fun of her sayin' she didn't wake up.

MRS. HALE: Well, I guess John Wright didn't wake when they was slipping that rope under his neck.

MRS. PETERS: No, it's strange. It must have been done awful crafty and still. They say it was such a—funny way to kill a man, rigging it all up like that.

MRS. HALE: That's just what Mr. Hale said. There was a gun in the house. He says that's what he can't understand.

MRS. PETERS: Mr. Henderson said coming out that what was needed for the case was a motive; something to show anger, or—sudden feeling.

MRS. HALE [*who is standing by the table*]:   Well, I don't see any signs of anger around here. [*She puts her hand on the dish towel which lies on the table, stands looking down at table, one half of which is clean, the other half messy.*] It's wiped to here. [*Makes a move as if to finish work, then turns and looks at loaf of bread outside the breadbox. Drops towel. In that voice of coming back to familiar things.*] Wonder how they are finding things upstairs. I hope she had it a little more red-up up there. You know, it seems kind of *sneaking*. Locking her up in town and then coming out here and trying to get her own house to turn against her!

MRS. PETERS: But Mrs. Hale, the law is the law.

MRS. HALE: I s'pose 'tis. [*Unbuttoning her coat.*] Better loosen up your things, Mrs. Peters. You won't feel them when you go out.

[MRS. PETERS *takes off her fur tippet, goes to hang it on hook at back of room, stands looking at the under part of the small corner table.*]

MRS. PETERS: She was piecing a quilt.

[*She brings the large sewing basket and they look at the bright pieces.*]

MRS. HALE: It's log cabin pattern. Pretty, isn't it? I wonder if she was goin' to quilt it or just knot it?

[*Footsteps have been heard coming down the stairs. The* SHERIFF *enters followed by* HALE *and the* COUNTY ATTORNEY.]

SHERIFF: They wonder if she was going to quilt it or just knot it!

[*The men laugh; the women look abashed.*]

COUNTY ATTORNEY [*rubbing his hands over the stove*]:   Frank's fire didn't do much up there, did it? Well, let's go out to the barn and get that cleared up.

[*The men go outside.*]

MRS. HALE [*resentfully*]:   I don't know as there's anything so strange, our takin' up our time with little things while we're waiting for them to get the evidence. [*She sits down at the big table smoothing out a block with decision.*] I don't see as it's anything to laugh about.

MRS. PETERS [*apologetically*]:   Of course they've got awful important things on their minds.

[*Pulls up a chair and joins* MRS. HALE *at the table.*]

MRS. HALE [*examining another block*]:   Mrs. Peters, look at this one. Here, this is the one she was working on, and look at the sewing! All the rest of it has been so nice and even. And look at this! It's all over the place! Why, it looks as if she didn't know what she was about!

[*After she has said this they look at each other, then start to glance back at the door. After an instant* MRS. HALE *has pulled at a knot and ripped the sewing.*]

MRS. PETERS: Oh, what are you doing, Mrs. Hale?

MRS. HALE [*mildly*]:   Just pulling out a stitch or two that's not sewed very good. [*Threading a needle.*] Bad sewing always made me fidgety.

MRS. PETERS [*nervously*]:   I don't think we ought to touch things.

MRS. HALE: I'll just finish up this end. [*Suddenly stopping and leaning forward.*] Mrs. Peters?

MRS. PETERS: Yes, Mrs. Hale?

MRS. HALE: What do you suppose she was so nervous about?

MRS. PETERS: Oh—I don't know. I don't know as she was nervous. I sometimes sew awful queer when I'm just tired. [MRS. HALE *starts to say something, looks at* MRS. PETERS, *then goes on sewing.*] Well, I must get these things wrapped up. They may be through sooner than we think. [*Putting apron and other things together.*] I wonder where I can find a piece of paper, and string.

MRS. HALE: In that cupboard, maybe.

MRS. PETERS [*looking in cupboard*]:   Why, here's a birdcage. [*Holds it up.*] Did she have a bird, Mrs. Hale?

MRS. HALE: Why, I don't know whether she did or not—I've not been here for so long. There was a man around last year selling canaries cheap, but I don't know as she took one; maybe she did. She used to sing real pretty herself.

MRS. PETERS [*glancing around*]:   Seems funny to think of a bird here. But she must have had one, or why would she have a cage? I wonder what happened to it.

MRS. HALE: I s'pose maybe the cat got it.

MRS. PETERS: No, she didn't have a cat. She's got that feeling some people have about cats—being afraid of them. My cat got in her room and she was real upset and asked me to take it out.

MRS. HALE: My sister Bessie was like that. Queer, ain't it?

MRS. PETERS [*examining the cage*]:   Why, look at this door. It's broke. One hinge is pulled apart.

MRS. HALE [*looking too*]:   Looks as if someone must have been rough with it.

MRS. PETERS: Why, yes.

[*She brings the cage forward and puts it on the table.*]

MRS. HALE: I wish if they're going to find any evidence they'd be about it. I don't like this place.

MRS. PETERS: But I'm awful glad you came with me, Mrs. Hale. It would be lonesome for me sitting here alone.

MRS. HALE: It would, wouldn't it? [*Dropping her sewing.*] But I tell you what I do wish, Mrs. Peters. I wish I had come over sometimes when *she* was here. I—[*Looking around the room.*]—wish I had.

MRS. PETERS: But of course you were awful busy, Mrs. Hale—your house and your children.

MRS. HALE: I could've come. I stayed away because it weren't cheerful—and that's why I ought to have come. I—I've never liked this place. Maybe because it's down in a hollow and you don't see the road. I dunno what it is but it's a lonesome place and always was. I wish I had come over to see Minnie Foster sometimes. I can see now—

[*Shakes her head.*]

MRS. PETERS: Well, you mustn't reproach yourself, Mrs. Hale. Somehow we just don't see how it is with other folks until—something comes up.

MRS. HALE: Not having children makes less work—but it makes a quiet house, and Wright out to work all day, and no company when he did come in. Did you know John Wright, Mrs. Peters?

MRS. PETERS: Not to know him; I've seen him in town. They say he was a good man.

MRS. HALE: Yes—good; he didn't drink, and kept his word as well as most, I guess, and paid his debts. But he was a hard man, Mrs. Peters. Just to pass the time of day with him—[*Shivers.*] Like a raw wind that gets to the bone. [*Pauses, her eye falling on the cage.*] I should think she would 'a wanted a bird. But what do you suppose went with it?

MRS. PETERS: I don't know, unless it got sick and died.

[*She reaches over and swings the broken door, swings it again. Both women watch it.*]

MRS. HALE: You weren't raised round here, were you? [MRS. PETERS *shakes her head.*] You didn't know—her?

MRS. PETERS: Not till they brought her yesterday.

MRS. HALE: She—come to think of it, she was kind of like a bird herself—real sweet and pretty, but kind of timid and—fluttery. How—she—did—change. [*Silence; then as if struck by a happy thought and relieved to get back to every day things.*] Tell you what, Mrs. Peters, why don't you take the quilt in with you? It might take up her mind.

MRS. PETERS: Why, I think that's a real nice idea, Mrs. Hale. There couldn't possibly be any objection to it, could there? Now, just what would I take? I wonder if her patches are in here—and her things.

[*They look in the sewing basket.*]

MRS. HALE: Here's some red. I expect this has got sewing things in it. [*Brings out a fancy box.*] What a pretty box. Looks like something somebody would give you. Maybe her scissors are in here. [*Opens box. Suddenly puts her hand to her nose.*] Why—[MRS. PETERS *bends nearer, then turns her face away.*] There's something wrapped up in this piece of silk.

MRS. PETERS: Why, this isn't her scissors.

MRS. HALE [*lifting the silk*]:   Oh, Mrs. Peters—it's—

[MRS. PETERS *bends closer.*]

MRS. PETERS: It's the bird.

MRS. HALE [*jumping up*]:   But, Mrs. Peters—look at it! Its neck! Look at its neck! It's all—other side *to.*

MRS. PETERS: Somebody—wrung—its—neck.

[*Their eyes meet. A look of growing comprehension, of horror. Steps are heard outside.* MRS. HALE *slips box under quilt pieces, and sinks into her chair. Enter* SHERIFF *and* COUNTY ATTORNEY. MRS. PETERS *rises.*]

COUNTY ATTORNEY [*as one turning from serious things to little pleasantries*]: Well, ladies have you decided whether she was going to quilt it or knot it?

MRS. PETERS: We think she was going to—knot it.

COUNTY ATTORNEY: Well, that's interesting, I'm sure. [*Seeing the birdcage.*] Has the bird flown?

MRS. HALE [*putting more quilt pieces over the box*]:   We think the—cat got it.

COUNTY ATTORNEY [*Preoccupied*]:   Is there a cat?

[MRS. HALE *glances in a quick covert way at* MRS. PETERS.]

MRS. PETERS: Well, not *now.* They're superstitious, you know. They leave.

COUNTY ATTORNEY [*to* SHERIFF PETERS, *continuing an interrupted conversation*]: No sign at all of anyone having come from the outside. Their own rope. Now let's go up again and go over it piece by piece. [*They start upstairs.*] It would have to have been someone who knew just the—

[MRS. PETERS *sits down. The two women sit there not looking at one another, but as if peering into something and at the same time holding back. When they talk now it is in the manner of feeling their way over strange ground, as if afraid of what they are saying, but as if they can not help saying it.*]

MRS. HALE: She liked the bird. She was going to bury it in that pretty box.

MRS. PETERS [*in a whisper*]:   When I was a girl—my kitten—there was a boy took a hatchet, and before my eyes—and before I could get there—[*Covers her face an instant.*] If they hadn't held me back I would have—[*Catches herself, looks upstairs where steps are heard, falters weakly.*]—hurt him.

MRS. HALE [*with a slow look around her*]:   I wonder how it would seem never to have had any children around. [*Pause.*] No, Wright wouldn't like the bird— a thing that sang. She used to sing. He killed that, too.

MRS. PETERS [*moving uneasily*]:   We don't know who killed the bird.

MRS. HALE: I knew John Wright.

MRS. PETERS: It was an awful thing was done in this house that night, Mrs. Hale. Killing a man while he slept, slipping a rope around his neck that choked the life out of him.

MRS. HALE: His neck. Choked the life out of him.

[*Her hand goes out and rests on the birdcage.*]

MRS. PETERS [*with rising voice*]:   We don't know who killed him. We don't *know*.

MRS. HALE [*her own feeling not interrupted*]:   If there'd been years and years of nothing, then a bird to sing to you, it would be awful—still, after the bird was still.

MRS. PETERS [*something within her speaking*]:   I know what stillness is. When we homesteaded in Dakota, and my first baby died—after he was two years old, and me with no other then—

MRS. HALE [*moving*]:   How soon do you suppose they'll be through, looking for the evidence?

MRS. PETERS: I know what stillness is. [*Pulling herself back.*] The law has got to punish crime, Mrs. Hale.

MRS. HALE [*not as if answering that*]:   I wish you'd seen Minnie Foster when she wore a white dress with blue ribbons and stood up there in the choir and sang. [*A look around the room.*] Oh, I *wish* I'd come over here once in a while! That was a crime! That was a crime! Who's going to punish that?

MRS. PETERS [*looking upstairs*]:   We mustn't—take on.

MRS. HALE: I might have known she needed help! I know how things can be—for women. I tell you, it's queer, Mrs. Peters. We live close together and we live far apart. We all go through the same things—it's all just a different kind of the same thing. [*Brushes her eyes; noticing the bottle of fruit, reaches out for it.*] If I was you I wouldn't tell her her fruit was gone. Tell her it *ain't*. Tell her it's all right. Take this in to prove it to her. She—she may never know whether it was broke or not.

MRS. PETERS [*takes the bottle, looks about for something to wrap it in; takes petticoat from the clothes brought from the other room, very nervously begins winding this around the bottle. In a false voice*]:   My, it's a good thing the men couldn't hear us. Wouldn't they just laugh! Getting all stirred up over a little thing like a— dead canary. As if that could have anything to do with—with—wouldn't they *laugh!*

[*The men are heard coming down stairs.*]

MRS. HALE [*under her breath*]:   Maybe they would—maybe they wouldn't.

COUNTY ATTORNEY: No, Peters, it's all perfectly clear except a reason for doing it. But you know juries when it comes to women. If there was some definite thing. Something to show—something to make a story about—a thing that would connect up with this strange way of doing it—

[*The women's eyes meet for an instant. Enter* HALE *from outer door.*]

HALE: Well, I've got the team around. Pretty cold out there.

COUNTY ATTORNEY: I'm going to stay here a while by myself. [*To the* SHERIFF.] You can send Frank out for me, can't you? I want to go over everything. I'm not satisfied that we can't do better.

SHERIFF: Do you want to see what Mrs. Peters is going to take in?

[*The* COUNTY ATTORNEY *goes to the table, picks up the apron, laughs.*]

COUNTY ATTORNEY: Oh, I guess they're not very dangerous things the ladies have picked out. [*Moves a few things about, disturbing the quilt pieces which cover the box. Steps back.*] No, Mrs. Peters doesn't need supervising. For that matter, a sheriff's wife is married to the law. Ever think of it that way, Mrs. Peters?

MRS. PETERS: Not—just that way.

SHERIFF [*Chuckling*]:   Married to the law. [*Moves toward the other room.*] I just want you to come in here a minute, George. We ought to take a look at these windows.

COUNTY ATTORNEY [*scoffingly*]:   Oh, windows!

SHERIFF: We'll be right out, Mr. Hale.

[HALE *goes outside. The* SHERIFF *follows the* COUNTY ATTORNEY *into the other room. Then* MRS. HALE *rises, hands tight together, looking intensely at* MRS. PETERS, *whose eyes make a slow turn, finally meeting* MRS. HALE'S. *A moment* MRS. HALE *holds her, then her own eyes point the way to where the box is concealed. Suddenly* MRS. PETERS *throws back quilt pieces and tries to put the box in the bag she is wearing. It is too big. She opens box, starts to take bird out, cannot touch it, goes to pieces, stands there helpless. Sound of a knob turning in the other room.* MRS. HALE *snatches the box and puts it in the pocket of her big coat. Enter* COUNTY ATTORNEY *and* SHERIFF.]

COUNTY ATTORNEY [*facetiously*]:   Well, Henry, at least we found out that she was not going to quilt it. She was going to—what is it you call it, ladies?

MRS. HALE [*her hand against her pocket*]:   We call it—knot it, Mr. Henderson.

Curtain

(1916)

QUESTIONS

1. Explain the significance of the title. Do you prefer this title or the one Glaspell gave her rewriting of the play as a short story, "A Jury of Her Peers"? Why?
2. How does Glaspell characterize the men in the play? The sheriff? The attorney? The neighboring farmer? What attitudes toward women do the men display?
3. How does Glaspell enlist our sympathy for the women? How do Mrs. Hale and Mrs. Peters get along with the men?
4. Which of the stage props are most important for the play's dramatic action? For its theme? Why?
5. At what point in reading *Trifles* did you realize that Mrs. Wright had murdered her husband?
6. Explain the significance of the final line of dialogue.

ARTHUR MILLER

[b. 1915]

Death of a Salesman is Arthur Miller's most famous and notable play. Produced and published in 1949, it had a long original Broadway run and has been frequently revived, most recently in 1984 with noted film actor Dustin Hoffman as the salesman Willy Loman. The play is in the tradition of social realism inaugurated by Ibsen and continued by Chekhov, Strindberg, and Shaw. The dialogue of the characters, their financial and emotional problems, and their behavior are all indicative of a typically realistic drama. Like Ibsen's *A Doll House,* Miller's *Salesman* raises questions about social values and attitudes—in this case, the pursuit of success and the American dream. Like Chekhov's tone in *The Cherry Orchard,* Miller's tone mixes sympathy and judgment, criticism and compassion. And as Shaw did in *Arms and the Man,* Miller provides extensive and detailed stage directions. Miller's directions differ, however, from Shaw's in one important way: Shaw provides elaborate descriptions of scene and setting, whereas Miller furnishes information about the lives his characters lead, giving us a better sense of their past.

These realistic touches blend, however, with other dramatic elements that are less realistic and that we will call *expressionistic.* Expressionistic playwrights attempt to dramatize a subjective picture of reality as seen by an individual consciousness. They attempt to show the inner life of a character, portraying external reality as he or she sees it. *Death of a Salesman* is expressionistic in that it dramatizes Willy Loman's subjective sense of things, rather than exhibiting a concern for a strict and exact representation of external detail. The play is particularly expressionistic in its memory scenes, in which Willy recalls events from the past in such a way that he reenacts rather than merely remembers them. In these scenes different times, places, and states of mind fluctuate and merge as Miller reveals Willy's thoughts, attitudes, and beliefs, his inflated hopes and deflated dreams. The expressionistic quality of the play is enhanced by lighting and music that signal flashbacks and contribute to its mood.

One issue readers, audiences, and critics have consistently raised about *Death of a Salesman* concerns its status as tragedy. The main question turns on whether Willy Loman is a tragic figure. Is he grand and noble enough to be a tragic hero? Is his failure tragic or merely pathetic? Over the years Miller has written about these and related questions in essays such as "On Social Drama" and "Tragedy and the Common Man." He has suggested that "the common man is as apt a subject for tragedy as kings"; and also that "the tragic feeling is evoked in us when we are in the presence of a character who is ready to lay down his life" to secure his dignity. How far these observations apply to Willy Loman is a matter for discussion.

ARTHUR MILLER

Death of a Salesman

Certain Private Conversations in Two Acts
and a Requiem

CHARACTERS

WILLY LOMAN
LINDA
BIFF
HAPPY
BERNARD
THE WOMAN
CHARLEY
UNCLE BEN
HOWARD WAGNER
JENNY
STANLEY
MISS FORSYTHE
LETTA

The action takes place in WILLY LOMAN's *house and yard and in various places he visits in the New York and Boston of today.*

Throughout the play, in the stage directions, left and right mean stage left and stage right.

ACT I

A melody is heard, played upon a flute. It is small and fine, telling of grass and trees and the horizon. The curtain rises.

Before us is the Salesman's house. We are aware of towering, angular shapes behind it, surrounding it on all sides. Only the blue light of the sky falls upon the house and forestage; the surrounding area shows an angry glow of orange. As more light appears, we see a solid vault of apartment houses around the small, fragile-seeming home. An air of the dream clings to the place, a dream rising out of reality. The kitchen at center seems actual enough, for there is a kitchen table with three chairs, and a refrigerator. But no other fixtures are seen. At the back of the kitchen there is a draped entrance, which leads to the livingroom. To the right of the kitchen, on a level raised two feet, is a bedroom furnished only with a brass bedstead and a straight chair. On a shelf over the bed a silver athletic trophy stands. A window opens onto the apartment house at the side.

Behind the kitchen, on a level raised six and a half feet, is the boys' bedroom, at present barely visible. Two beds are dimly seen, and at the back of the room a dormer window. (This bedroom is above the unseen livingroom.) At the left a stairway curves up to it from the kitchen.

The entire setting is wholly or, in some places, partially transparent. The roof-line of the house is one-dimensional; under and over it we see the apartment buildings. Before the house lies an apron, curving beyond the forestage into the orchestra. This forward area serves as the back yard as well as the locale of all WILLY'S *imaginings and of his city scenes. Whenever the action is in the present the actors observe the imaginary wall-lines, entering the house only through the door at the left. But in the scenes of the past these boundaries are broken, and characters enter or leave a room by stepping "through" a wall onto the forestage.*

From the right, WILLY LOMAN, *the Salesman, enters, carrying two large sample cases. The flute plays on. He hears but is not aware of it. He is past sixty years of age, dressed quietly. Even as he crosses the stage to the doorway of the house, his exhaustion is apparent. He unlocks the door, comes into the kitchen, and thankfully lets his burden down, feeling the soreness of his palms. A word-sigh escapes his lips—it might be "Oh, boy, oh, boy." He closes the door, then carries his cases out into the livingroom, through the draped kitchen doorway.*

LINDA, *his wife, has stirred in her bed at the right. She gets out and puts on a robe, listening. Most often jovial, she has developed an iron repression of her exceptions to* WILLY'S *behavior—she more than loves him, she admires him, as though his mercurial nature, his temper, his massive dreams and little cruelties, served her only as sharp reminders of the turbulent longings within him, longings which she shares but lacks the temperament to utter and follow to their end.*

LINDA   *(hearing* WILLY *outside the bedroom, calls with some trepidation):* Willy!

WILLY: It's all right. I came back.

LINDA: Why? What happened? *(Slight pause.)* Did something happen, Willy?

WILLY: No, nothing happened.

LINDA: You didn't smash the car, did you?

WILLY   *(with casual irritation):* I said nothing happened. Didn't you hear me?

LINDA: Don't you feel well?

WILLY: I am tired to the death. *(The flute has faded away. He sits on the bed beside her, a little numb.)* I couldn't make it. I just couldn't make it, Linda.

LINDA   *(very carefully, delicately):* Where were you all day? You look terrible.

WILLY: I got as far as a little above Yonkers. I stopped for a cup of coffee. Maybe it was the coffee.

LINDA: What?

WILLY   *(after a pause):* I suddenly couldn't drive any more. The car kept going onto the shoulder, y'know?

LINDA   *(helpfully):* Oh. Maybe it was the steering again. I don't think Angelo knows the Studebaker.

WILLY: No, it's me, it's me. Suddenly I realize I'm goin' sixty miles an hour and I don't remember the last five minutes. I'm—I can't seem to—keep my mind to it.

LINDA: Maybe it's your glasses. You never went for your new glasses.

WILLY: No, I see everything. I came back ten miles an hour. It took me nearly four hours from Yonkers.

LINDA   (*resigned*): Well, you'll just have to take a rest, Willy, you can't continue this way.

WILLY: I just got back from Florida.

LINDA: But you didn't rest your mind. Your mind is overactive, and the mind is what counts, dear.

WILLY: I'll start out in the morning. Maybe I'll feel better in the morning. (*She is taking off his shoes.*) These goddam arch supports are killing me.

LINDA: Take an aspirin. Should I get you an aspirin? It'll soothe you.

WILLY   (*with wonder*): I was driving along, you understand? And I was fine. I was even observing the scenery. You can imagine, me looking at scenery, on the road every week of my life. But it's so beautiful up there, Linda, the trees are so thick, and the sun is warm. I opened the windshield and just let the warm air bathe over me. And then all of a sudden I'm goin' off the road! I'm tellin' ya, I absolutely forgot I was driving. If I'd've gone the other way over the white line I might've killed somebody. So I went on again—and five minutes later I'm dreamin' again, and I nearly— (*He presses two fingers against his eyes.*) I have such thoughts, I have such strange thoughts.

LINDA: Willy, dear. Talk to them again. There's no reason why you can't work in New York.

WILLY: They don't need me in New York. I'm the New England man. I'm vital in New England.

LINDA: But you're sixty years old. They can't expect you to keep traveling every week.

WILLY: I'll have to send a wire to Portland. I'm supposed to see Brown and Morrison tomorrow morning at ten o'clock to show the line. Goddammit, I could sell them! (*He starts putting on his jacket.*)

LINDA   (*taking the jacket from him*): Why don't you go down to the place tomorrow and tell Howard you've simply got to work in New York? You're too accommodating, dear.

WILLY: If old man Wagner was alive I'd a been in charge of New York now! That man was a prince, he was a masterful man. But that boy of his, that Howard, he don't appreciate. When I went north the first time, the Wagner Company didn't know where New England was!

LINDA: Why don't you tell those things to Howard, dear?

WILLY   (*encouraged*): I will, I definitely will. Is there any cheese?

LINDA: I'll make you a sandwich.

WILLY: No, go to sleep. I'll take some milk. I'll be up right away. The boys in?

LINDA: They're sleeping. Happy took Biff on a date tonight.

WILLY   (*interested*): That so?

LINDA: It was so nice to see them shaving together, one behind the other, in the bathroom. And going out together. You notice? The whole house smells of shaving lotion.

WILLY: Figure it out. Work a lifetime to pay off a house. You finally own it, and there's nobody to live in it.

LINDA: Well, dear, life is a casting off. It's always that way.

WILLY: No, no, some people—some people accomplish something. Did Biff say anything after I went this morning?

LINDA: You shouldn't have criticized him, Willy, especially after he just got off the train. You mustn't lose your temper with him.

WILLY: When the hell did I lose my temper? I simply asked him if he was making any money. Is that a criticism?

LINDA: But, dear, how could he make any money?

WILLY   (*worried and angered*): There's such an undercurrent in him. He became a moody man. Did he apologize when I left this morning?

LINDA: He was crestfallen, Willy. You know how he admires you. I think if he finds himself, then you'll both be happier and not fight any more.

WILLY: How can he find himself on a farm? Is that a life? A farmhand? In the beginning, when he was young, I thought, well, a young man, it's good for him to tramp around, take a lot of different jobs. But it's more than ten years now and he has yet to make thirty-five dollars a week!

LINDA: He's finding himself, Willy.

WILLY: Not finding yourself at the age of thirty-four is a disgrace!

LINDA: Shh!

WILLY: The trouble is he's lazy, goddammit!

LINDA: Willy, please!

WILLY: Biff is a lazy bum!

LINDA: They're sleeping. Get something to eat. Go on down.

WILLY: Why did he come home? I would like to know what brought him home.

LINDA: I don't know. I think he's still lost, Willy. I think he's very lost.

WILLY: Biff Loman is lost. In the greatest country in the world a young man with such—personal attractiveness, gets lost. And such a hard worker. There's one thing about Biff—he's not lazy.

LINDA: Never.

WILLY   (*with pity and resolve*): I'll see him in the morning; I'll have a nice talk with him. I'll get him a job selling. He could be big in no time. My God! Remember how they used to follow him around in high school? When he smiled at one of them their faces lit up. When he walked down the street . . . (*He loses himself in reminiscences.*)

LINDA   (*trying to bring him out of it*): Willy, dear, I got a new kind of American-type cheese today. It's whipped.

WILLY: Why do you get American when I like Swiss?

LINDA: I just thought you'd like a change—

WILLY: I don't want a change! I want Swiss cheese. Why am I always being contradicted?

LINDA   (*with a covering laugh*): I thought it would be a surprise.

WILLY: Why don't you open a window in here, for God's sake?

LINDA   (*with infinite patience*): They're all open, dear.

WILLY: The way they boxed us in here. Bricks and windows, windows and bricks.

LINDA: We should've bought the land next door.

WILLY: The street is lined with cars. There's not a breath of fresh air in the neighborhood. The grass don't grow any more, you can't raise a carrot in the back yard. They should've had a law against apartment houses. Remember those two beautiful elm trees out there? When I and Biff hung the swing between them?

LINDA: Yeah, like being a million miles from the city.

WILLY: They should've arrested the builder for cutting those down. They massacred the neighborhood. (*Lost.*) More and more I think of those days, Linda. This time of year it was lilac and wisteria. And then the peonies would come out, and the daffodils. What fragrance in this room!

LINDA: Well, after all, people had to move somewhere.

WILLY: No, there's more people now.

LINDA: I don't think there's more people. I think—

WILLY: There's more people! That's what's ruining this country! Population is getting out of control. The competition is maddening! Smell the stink from that apartment house! And another on the other side . . . How can they whip cheese?

On WILLY's *last line,* BIFF *and* HAPPY *raise themselves up in their beds, listening.*

LINDA: Go down, try it. And be quiet.

WILLY   (*turning to* LINDA, *guiltily*): You're not worried about me, are you, sweetheart?

BIFF: What's the matter?

HAPPY: Listen!

LINDA: You've got too much on the ball to worry about.

WILLY: You're my foundation and my support, Linda.

LINDA: Just try to relax, dear. You make mountains out of molehills.

WILLY: I won't fight with him any more. If he wants to go back to Texas, let him go.

LINDA: He'll find his way.

WILLY: Sure. Certain men just don't get started till later in life. Like Thomas Edison, I think. Or B. F. Goodrich. One of them was deaf. (*He starts for the bedroom doorway.*) I'll put my money on Biff.

LINDA: And Willy—if it's warm Sunday we'll drive in the country. And we'll open the windshield, and take lunch.

WILLY: No, the windshields don't open on the new cars.

LINDA: But you opened it today.

WILLY: Me? I didn't. (*He stops.*) Now isn't that peculiar! Isn't that a remarkable— (*He breaks off in amazement and fright as the flute is heard distantly.*)

LINDA: What, darling?

WILLY: That is the most remarkable thing.

LINDA: What, dear?

WILLY: I was thinking of the Chevvy. (*Slight pause.*) Nineteen twenty-eight . . . when I had that red Chevvy— (*Breaks off.*) That funny? I coulda sworn I was driving that Chevvy today.

LINDA: Well, that's nothing. Something must've reminded you.

WILLY: Remarkable. Ts. Remember those days? The way Biff used to simonize that car? The dealer refused to believe there was eighty thousand miles on it. (*He shakes his head.*) Heh! (*To* LINDA.) Close your eyes, I'll be right up. (*He walks out of the bedroom.*)

HAPPY   (*to Biff*): Jesus, maybe he smashed up the car again!

LINDA   (*calling after* WILLY): Be careful on the stairs, dear! The cheese is on the middle shelf! (*She turns, goes over to the bed, takes his jacket, and goes out of the bedroom.*)

Light has risen on the boys' room. Unseen, WILLY *is heard talking to himself, "Eighty thousand miles," and a little laugh.* BIFF *gets out of bed, comes downstage a bit, and stands attentively.* BIFF *is two years older than his brother* HAPPY, *well built, but in these days bears a worn air and seems less self-assured. He has succeeded less, and his dreams are stronger and less acceptable than* HAPPY'S. HAPPY *is tall, powerfully made. Sexuality is like a visible color on him, or a scent that many women have discovered. He, like his brother, is lost, but in a different way, for he has never allowed himself to turn his face toward defeat and is thus more confused and hard-skinned, although seemingly more content.*

HAPPY   (*getting out of bed*): He's going to get his license taken away if he keeps that up. I'm getting nervous about him, y'know, Biff?

BIFF: His eyes are going.

HAPPY: No, I've driven with him. He sees all right. He just doesn't keep his mind on it. I drove into the city with him last week. He stops at a green light and then it turns red and he goes. (*He laughs.*)

BIFF: Maybe he's color-blind.

HAPPY: Pop? Why he's got the finest eye for color in the business. You know that.

BIFF   (*sitting down on his bed*): I'm going to sleep.

HAPPY: You're not still sour on Dad, are you, Biff?

BIFF: He's all right, I guess.

WILLY   (*underneath them, in the livingroom*): Yes, sir, eighty thousand miles—eighty-two thousand!

BIFF: You smoking?

HAPPY   (*holding out a pack of cigarettes*): Want one?

BIFF   (*taking a cigarette*): I can never sleep when I smell it.

WILLY: What a simonizing job, heh!

HAPPY   (*with deep sentiment*): Funny, Biff, y'know? Us sleeping in here again? The old beds. (*He pats his bed affectionately.*) All the talk that went across those two beds, huh? Our whole lives.

BIFF: Yeah. Lotta dreams and plans.

HAPPY   (*with a deep and masculine laugh*): About five hundred women would like to know what was said in this room.

They share a soft laugh.

BIFF: Remember that big Betsy something—what the hell was her name—over on Bushwick Avenue?

HAPPY   (*combing his hair*): With the collie dog!

BIFF: That's the one. I got you in there, remember?

HAPPY: Yeah, that was my first time—I think. Boy, there was a pig! (*They laugh, almost crudely.*) You taught me everything I know about women. Don't forget that.

BIFF: I bet you forgot how bashful you used to be. Especially with girls.

HAPPY: Oh, I still am, Biff.

BIFF: Oh, go on.

HAPPY: I just control it, that's all. I think I got less bashful and you got more so. What happened, Biff? Where's the old humor, the old confidence? (*He shakes* BIFF's *knee.* BIFF *gets up and moves restlessly about the room.*) What's the matter?

BIFF: Why does Dad mock me all the time?

HAPPY: He's not mocking you, he—

BIFF: Everything I say there's a twist of mockery on his face. I can't get near him.

HAPPY: He just wants you to make good, that's all. I wanted to talk to you about Dad for a long time, Biff. Something's—happening to him. He—talks to himself.

BIFF: I noticed that this morning. But he always mumbled.

HAPPY: But not so noticeable. It got so embarrassing I sent him to Florida. And you know something? Most of the time he's talking to you.

BIFF: What's he say about me?

HAPPY: I can't make it out.

BIFF: What's he say about me?

HAPPY: I think the fact that you're not settled, that you're still kind of up in the air . . .

BIFF: There's one or two other things depressing him, Happy.

HAPPY: What do you mean?

BIFF: Never mind. Just don't lay it all to me.

HAPPY: But I think if you just got started—I mean—is there any future for you out there?

BIFF: I tell ya, Hap, I don't know what the future is. I don't know—what I'm supposed to want.

HAPPY: What do you mean?

BIFF: Well, I spent six or seven years after high school trying to work myself up. Shipping clerk, salesman, business of one kind or another. And it's a measly manner of existence. To get on that subway on the hot mornings in summer. To devote your whole life to keeping stock, or making phone calls, or selling or buying. To suffer fifty weeks of the year for the sake of a two-week vacation, when all you really desire is to be outdoors, with your shirt off. And always to have to get ahead of the next fella. And still—that's how you build a future.

HAPPY: Well, you really enjoy it on a farm? Are you content out there?

BIFF (*with rising agitation*): Hap, I've had twenty or thirty different kinds of jobs since I left home before the war, and it always turns out the same. I just realized it lately. In Nebraska when I herded cattle, and the Dakotas, and Arizona, and now in Texas. It's why I came home now, I guess, because I realized it. This farm I work on, it's spring there now, see? And they've got about fifteen new colts. There's nothing more inspiring or—beautiful than the sight of a mare and a new colt. And it's cool there now, see? Texas is cool now, and it's spring. And whenever spring comes to where I am, I suddenly get the feeling, my God, I'm not gettin' anywhere! What the hell am I doing, playing around with horses, twenty-eight dollars a week! I'm thirty-four years old, I oughta be makin' my future. That's when I come running home. And now, I get here, and I don't know what to do with myself. (*After a pause.*) I've always made a point of not wasting my life, and everytime I come back here I know that all I've done is to waste my life.

HAPPY: You're a poet, you know that, Biff? You're a—you're an idealist!

BIFF: No, I'm mixed up very bad. Maybe I oughta get married. Maybe I oughta get stuck into something. Maybe that's my trouble. I'm like a boy. I'm not married, I'm not in business, I just—I'm like a boy. Are you content, Hap? You're a success, aren't you? Are you content?

HAPPY: Hell, no!

BIFF: Why? You're making money, aren't you?

HAPPY   (*moving about with energy, expressiveness*): All I can do now is wait for the merchandise manager to die. And suppose I get to be merchandise manager? He's a good friend of mine, and he just built a terrific estate on Long Island. And he lived there about two months and sold it, and now he's building another one. He can't enjoy it once it's finished. And I know that's just what I would do. I don't know what the hell I'm workin' for. Sometimes I sit in my apartment—all alone. And I think of the rent I'm paying. And it's crazy. But then, it's what I always wanted. My own apartment, a car, and plenty of women. And still, goddammit, I'm lonely.

BIFF   (*with enthusiasm*): Listen, why don't you come out West with me?

HAPPY: You and I, heh?

BIFF: Sure, maybe we could buy a ranch. Raise cattle, use our muscles. Men built like we are should be working out in the open.

HAPPY   (*avidly*): The Loman Brothers, heh?

BIFF   (*with vast affection*): Sure, we'd be known all over the counties!

HAPPY   (*enthralled*): That's what I dream about, Biff. Sometimes I want to just rip my clothes off in the middle of the store and outbox that goddam merchandise manager. I mean I can outbox, outrun, and outlift anybody in that store, and I have to take orders from those common, petty, sons-of-bitches till I can't stand it any more.

BIFF: I'm tellin' you, kid, if you were with me I'd be happy out there.

HAPPY   (*enthused*): See, Biff, everybody around me is so false that I'm constantly lowering my ideals . . .

BIFF: Baby, together we'd stand up for one another, we'd have someone to trust.

HAPPY: If I were around you—

BIFF: Hap, the trouble is we weren't brought up to grub for money. I don't know how to do it.

HAPPY: Neither can I!

BIFF: Then let's go!

HAPPY: The only thing is—what can you make out there?

BIFF: But look at your friend. Builds an estate and then hasn't the peace of mind to live in it.

HAPPY: Yeah, but when he walks into the store the waves part in front of him. That's fifty-two thousand dollars a year coming through the revolving door, and I got more in my pinky finger than he's got in his head.

BIFF: Yeah, but you just said—

HAPPY: I gotta show some of those pompous, self-important executives over there that Hap Loman can make the grade. I want to walk into the store the way he walks in. Then I'll go with you, Biff. We'll be together yet, I swear. But take those two we had tonight. Now weren't they gorgeous creatures?

BIFF: Yeah, yeah, most gorgeous I've had in years.

HAPPY: I get that any time I want, Biff. Whenever I feel disgusted. The only trouble is, it gets like bowling or something. I just keep knockin' them over and it doesn't mean anything. You still run around a lot?

BIFF: Naa. I'd like to find a girl—steady, somebody with substance.

HAPPY: That's what I long for.

BIFF: Go on! You'd never come home.

HAPPY: I would! Somebody with character, with resistance! Like Mom, y'-know? You're gonna call me a bastard when I tell you this. That girl Charlotte I was with tonight is engaged to be married in five weeks. (*He tries on his new hat.*)

BIFF: No kiddin'!

HAPPY: Sure, the guy's in line for the vice-presidency of the store. I don't know what gets into me, maybe I just have an overdeveloped sense of competition or something, but I went and ruined her, and furthermore I can't get rid of her. And he's the third executive I've done that to. Isn't that a crummy characteristic? And to top it all, I go to their weddings! (*Indignantly, but laughing.*) Like I'm not supposed to take bribes. Manufacturers offer me a hundred-dollar bill now and then to throw an order their way. You know how honest I am, but it's like this girl, see. I hate myself for it. Because I don't want the girl, and, still, I take it and—I love it!

BIFF: Let's go to sleep.

HAPPY: I guess we didn't settle anything, heh?

BIFF: I just got one idea that I think I'm going to try.

HAPPY: What's that?

BIFF: Remember Bill Oliver?

HAPPY: Sure, Oliver is very big now. You want to work for him again?

BIFF: No, but when I quit he said something to me. He put his arm on my shoulder, and he said, "Biff, if you ever need anything, come to me."

HAPPY: I remember that. That sounds good.

BIFF: I think I'll go to see him. If I could get ten thousand or even seven or eight thousand dollars I could buy a beautiful ranch.

HAPPY: I bet he'd back you. 'Cause he thought highly of you, Biff, I mean, they all do. You're well liked, Biff. That's why I say to come back here, and we both have the apartment. And I'm tellin' you, Biff, any babe you want . . .

BIFF: No, with a ranch I could do the work I like and still be something. I just wonder though. I wonder if Oliver still thinks I stole that carton of basketballs.

HAPPY: Oh, he probably forgot that long ago. It's almost ten years. You're too sensitive. Anyway, he didn't really fire you.

BIFF: Well, I think he was going to. I think that's why I quit. I was never sure whether he knew or not. I know he thought the world of me, though. I was the only one he'd let lock up the place.

WILLY   *(below)*: You gonna wash the engine, Biff?
HAPPY: Shh!

BIFF *looks at* HAPPY, *who is gazing down, listening.* WILLY *is mumbling in the parlor.*

HAPPY: You hear that?

They listen. WILLY *laughs warmly.*

BIFF   *(growing angry)*: Doesn't he know Mom can hear that?
WILLY: Don't get your sweater dirty, Biff!

A look of pain crosses BIFF'S *face.*

HAPPY: Isn't that terrible? Don't leave again, will you? You'll find a job here. You gotta stick around. I don't know what to do about him, it's getting embarrassing.
WILLY: What a simonizing job!
BIFF: Mom's hearing that!
WILLY: No kiddin', Biff, you got a date? Wonderful!
HAPPY: Go on to sleep. But talk to him in the morning, will you?
BIFF   *(reluctantly getting into bed)*: With her in the house. Brother!
HAPPY   *(getting into bed)*: I wish you'd have a good talk with him.

The light on their room begins to fade.

BIFF   *(to himself in bed)*: That selfish, stupid . . .
HAPPY: Sh . . . Sleep, Biff.

Their light is out. Well before they have finished speaking, WILLY'S *form is dimly seen below in the darkened kitchen. He opens the refrigerator, searches in there, and takes out a bottle of milk. The apartment houses are fading out, and the entire house and surroundings become covered with leaves. Music insinuates itself as the leaves appear.*

WILLY: Just wanna be careful with those girls, Biff, that's all. Don't make any promises. No promises of any kind. Because a girl, y'know, they always believe what you tell 'em, and you're very young, Biff, you're too young to be talking seriously to girls.

Light rises on the kitchen. WILLY, *talking, shuts the refrigerator door and comes downstage to the kitchen table. He pours milk into a glass. He is totally immersed in himself, smiling faintly.*

WILLY: Too young entirely, Biff. You want to watch your schooling first. Then when you're all set, there'll be plenty of girls for a boy like you. *(He smiles broadly at a kitchen chair.)* That so? The girls pay for you? *(He laughs.)* Boy, you must really be makin' a hit.

WILLY *is gradually addressing—physically—a point offstage, speaking through the wall of the kitchen, and his voice has been rising in volume to that of a normal conversation.*

WILLY: I been wondering why you polish the car so careful. Ha! Don't leave the hubcaps, boys. Get the chamois to the hubcaps. Happy, use newspaper on the windows, it's the easiest thing. Show him how to do it, Biff! You see,

Happy? Pad it up, use it like a pad. That's it, that's it, good work. You're doin'
all right, Hap. (*He pauses, then nods in approbation for a few seconds, then looks upward.*) Biff, first thing we gotta do when we get time is clip that big branch over
the house. Afraid it's gonna fall in a storm and hit the roof. Tell you what. We
get a rope and sling her around, and then we climb up there with a couple of
saws and take her down. Soon as you finish the car, boys, I wanna see ya. I got
a surprise for you, boys.

BIFF   (*offstage*): Whatta ya got, Dad?

WILLY: No, you finish first. Never leave a job till you're finished—remember that. (*Looking toward the "big trees."*) Biff, up in Albany I saw a beautiful hammock. I think I'll buy it next trip, and we'll hang it right between those
two elms. Wouldn't that be something? Just swingin' there under those
branches. Boy, that would be . . . .

YOUNG BIFF *and* YOUNG HAPPY *appear from the direction* WILLY *was addressing.* HAPPY *carries rags and a pail of water.* BIFF, *wearing a sweater with a block "S," carries a football.*

BIFF   (*pointing in the direction of the car offstage*): How's that, Pop, professional?

WILLY: Terrific. Terrific job, boys. Good work, Biff.

HAPPY: Where's the surprise, Pop?

WILLY: In the back seat of the car.

HAPPY: Boy! (*He runs off.*)

BIFF: What is it, Dad? Tell me, what'd you buy?

WILLY   (*laughing, cuffs him*): Never mind, something I want you to have.

BIFF   (*turns and starts off*): What is it, Hap?

HAPPY   (*offstage*): It's a punching bag!

BIFF: Oh, Pop!

WILLY: It's got Gene Tunney's signature on it!

HAPPY *runs onstage with a punching bag.*

BIFF: Gee, how'd you know we wanted a punching bag?

WILLY: Well, it's the finest thing for the timing.

HAPPY   (*lies down on his back and pedals with his feet*): I'm losing weight, you
notice, Pop?

WILLY   (*to* HAPPY): Jumping rope is good too.

BIFF: Did you see the new football I got?

WILLY   (*examining the ball*): Where'd you get a new ball?

BIFF: The coach told me to practice my passing.

WILLY: That so? And he gave you the ball, heh?

BIFF: Well, I borrowed it from the locker room. (*He laughs confidentially.*)

WILLY   (*laughing with him at the theft*): I want you to return that.

HAPPY: I told you he wouldn't like it!

BIFF   (*angrily*): Well, I'm bringing it back!

WILLY   (*stopping the incipient argument, to* HAPPY): Sure, he's gotta practice with
a regulation ball, doesn't he? (*To* BIFF.) Coach'll probably congratulate you on
your initiative!

BIFF: Oh, he keeps congratulating my initiative all the time, Pop.

WILLY: That's because he likes you. If somebody else took that ball there'd be an uproar. So what's the report, boys, what's the report?

BIFF: Where'd you go this time, Dad? Gee we were lonesome for you.

WILLY   (*pleased, puts an arm around each boy and they come down to the apron*): Lonesome, heh?

BIFF: Missed you every minute.

WILLY: Don't say? Tell you a secret, boys. Don't breathe it to a soul. Someday I'll have my own business, and I'll never have to leave home any more.

HAPPY: Like Uncle Charley, heh?

WILLY: Bigger than Uncle Charley! Because Charley is not—liked. He's liked, but he's not—well liked.

BIFF: Where'd you go this time, Dad?

WILLY: Well, I got on the road, and I went north to Providence. Met the Mayor.

BIFF: The Mayor of Providence!

WILLY: He was sitting in the hotel lobby.

BIFF: What'd he say?

WILLY: He said, "Morning!" And I said, "You've got a fine city here, Mayor." And then he had coffee with me. And then I went to Waterbury. Waterbury is a fine city. Big clock city, the famous Waterbury clock. Sold a nice bill there. And then Boston—Boston is the cradle of the Revolution. A fine city. And a couple of other towns in Mass., and on to Portland and Bangor and straight home!

BIFF: Gee, I'd love to go with you sometime, Dad.

WILLY: Soon as summer comes.

HAPPY: Promise?

WILLY: You and Hap and I, and I'll show you all the towns. America is full of beautiful towns and fine, upstanding people. And they know me, boys, they know me up and down New England. The finest people. And when I bring you fellas up, there'll be open sesame for all of us, 'cause one thing, boys: I have friends. I can park my car in any street in New England, and the cops protect it like their own. This summer, heh?

BIFF and HAPPY   (*together*): Yeah! You bet!

WILLY: We'll take our bathing suits.

HAPPY: We'll carry your bags, Pop!

WILLY: Oh, won't that be something! Me comin' into the Boston stores with you boys carryin' my bags. What a sensation!

BIFF *is prancing around, practicing passing the ball.*

WILLY: You nervous, Biff, about the game?

BIFF: Not if you're gonna be there.

WILLY: What do they say about you in school, now that they made you captain?

HAPPY: There's a crowd of girls behind him everytime the classes change.

BIFF   (*taking* WILLY'S *hand*): This Saturday, Pop, this Saturday—just for you, I'm going to break through for a touchdown.

HAPPY: You're supposed to pass.

BIFF: I'm takin' one play for Pop. You watch me, Pop, and when I take off my helmet, that means I'm breakin' out. Then you watch me crash through that line!

WILLY   (*kisses* BIFF): Oh, wait'll I tell this in Boston!

BERNARD *enters in knickers. He is younger than* BIFF, *earnest and loyal, a worried boy.*

BERNARD: Biff, where are you? You're supposed to study with me today.

WILLY: Hey, looka Bernard. What're you lookin' so anemic about, Bernard?

BERNARD: He's gotta study, Uncle Willy. He's got Regents next week.

HAPPY   (*tauntingly, spinning* BERNARD *around*): Let's box, Bernard!

BERNARD: Biff! (*He gets away from* HAPPY.) Listen, Biff, I heard Mr. Birnbaum say that if you don't start studyin' math he's gonna flunk you, and you won't graduate. I heard him!

WILLY: You better study with him, Biff. Go ahead now.

BERNARD: I heard him!

BIFF: Oh, Pop, you didn't see my sneakers! (*He holds up a foot for* WILLY *to look at.*)

WILLY: Hey, that's a beautiful job of printing!

BERNARD   (*wiping his glasses*): Just because he printed University of Virginia on his sneakers doesn't mean they've got to graduate him, Uncle Willy!

WILLY   (*angrily*): What're you talking about? With scholarships to three universities they're gonna flunk him?

BERNARD: But I heard Mr. Birnbaum say—

WILLY: Don't be a pest, Bernard! (*To his boys.*) What an anemic!

BERNARD: Okay, I'm waiting for you in my house, Biff.

BERNARD *goes off. The* LOMANS *laugh.*

WILLY: Bernard is not well liked, is he?

BIFF: He's liked, but he's not well liked.

HAPPY: That's right, Pop.

WILLY: That's just what I mean. Bernard can get the best marks in school, y'understand, but when he gets out in the business world, y'understand, you are going to be five times ahead of him. That's why I thank Almighty God you're both built like Adonises. Because the man who makes an appearance in the business world, the man who creates personal interest, is the man who gets ahead. Be liked and you will never want. You take me, for instance. I never have to wait in line to see a buyer. "Willy Loman is here!" That's all they have to know, and I go right through.

BIFF: Did you knock them dead, Pop?

WILLY: Knocked 'em cold in Providence, slaughtered 'em in Boston.

HAPPY   (*on his back, pedaling again*): I'm losing weight, you notice, Pop?

LINDA *enters, as of old, a ribbon in her hair, carrying a basket of washing.*

LINDA   (*with youthful energy*): Hello, dear!

WILLY: Sweetheart!

LINDA: How'd the Chevvy run?

WILLY: Chevrolet, Linda, is the greatest car ever built. (*To the boys.*) Since when do you let your mother carry wash up the stairs?

BIFF: Grab hold there, boy!

HAPPY: Where to, Mom?

LINDA: Hang them up on the line. And you better go down to your friends, Biff. The cellar is full of boys. They don't know what to do with themselves.

BIFF: Ah, when Pop comes home they can wait!

WILLY   (*laughs appreciatively*): You better go down and tell them what to do, Biff.

BIFF: I think I'll have them sweep out the furnace room.

WILLY: Good work, Biff.

BIFF   (*goes through wall-line of kitchen to doorway at back and calls down*): Fellas! Everybody sweep out the furnace room! I'll be right down!

VOICES: All right! Okay, Biff.

BIFF: George and Sam and Frank, come out back! We're hangin' up the wash! Come on, Hap, on the double! (*He and* HAPPY *carry out the basket.*)

LINDA: The way they obey him!

WILLY: Well, that's training, the training. I'm tellin' you, I was sellin' thousands and thousands, but I had to come home.

LINDA: Oh, the whole block'll be at that game. Did you sell anything?

WILLY: I did five hundred gross in Providence and seven hundred gross in Boston.

LINDA: No! Wait a minute, I've got a pencil. (*She pulls pencil and paper out of her apron pocket.*) That makes your commission . . . Two hundred—my God! Two hundred and twelve dollars!

WILLY: Well, I didn't figure it yet, but . . .

LINDA: How much did you do?

WILLY: Well, I—I did—about a hundred and eighty gross in Providence. Well, no—it came to—roughly two hundred gross on the whole trip.

LINDA   (*without hesitation*): Two hundred gross. That's . . . (*She figures.*)

WILLY: The trouble was that three of the stores were half closed for inventory in Boston. Otherwise I woulda broke records.

LINDA: Well, it makes seventy dollars and some pennies. That's very good.

WILLY: What do we owe?

LINDA: Well, on the first there's sixteen dollars on the refrigerator—

WILLY: Why sixteen?

LINDA: Well, the fan belt broke, so it was a dollar eighty.

WILLY: But it's brand new.

LINDA: Well, the man said that's the way it is. Till they work themselves in, y'know.

They move through the wall-line into the kitchen.

WILLY: I hope we didn't get stuck on that machine.

LINDA: They got the biggest ads of any of them!

WILLY: I know, it's a fine machine. What else?

LINDA:　Well, there's nine-sixty for the washing machine. And for the vacuum cleaner there's three and a half due on the fifteenth. Then the roof, you got twenty-one dollars remaining.

WILLY:　It don't leak, does it?

LINDA:　No, they did a wonderful job. Then you owe Frank for the carburetor.

WILLY:　I'm not going to pay that man! That goddam Chevrolet, they ought to prohibit the manufacture of that car!

LINDA:　Well, you owe him three and a half. And odds and ends, comes to around a hundred and twenty dollars by the fifteenth.

WILLY:　A hundred and twenty dollars! My God, if business don't pick up I don't know what I'm gonna do!

LINDA:　Well, next week you'll do better.

WILLY:　Oh, I'll knock them dead next week. I'll go to Hartford. I'm very well liked in Hartford. You know, the trouble is, Linda, people don't seem to take to me.

They move onto the forestage.

LINDA:　Oh, don't be foolish.

WILLY:　I know it when I walk in. They seem to laugh at me.

LINDA:　Why? Why would they laugh at you? Don't talk that way, Willy.

WILLY *moves to the edge of the stage.* LINDA *goes into the kitchen and starts to darn stockings.*

WILLY:　I don't know the reason for it, but they just pass me by. I'm not noticed.

LINDA:　But you're doing wonderful, dear. You're making seventy to a hundred dollars a week.

WILLY:　But I gotta be at it ten, twelve hours a day. Other men—I don't know—they do it easier. I don't know why—I can't stop myself—I talk too much. A man oughta come in with a few words. One thing about Charley. He's a man of few words, and they respect him.

LINDA:　You don't talk too much, you're just lively.

WILLY　(*smiling*): Well, I figure, what the hell, life is short, a couple of jokes. (*To himself.*) I joke too much! (*The smile goes.*)

LINDA:　Why? You're—

WILLY:　I'm fat. I'm very—foolish to look at, Linda. I didn't tell you, but Christmas time I happened to be calling on F. H. Stewarts, and a salesman I know, as I was going in to see the buyer I heard him say something about—walrus. And I—I cracked him right across the face. I won't take that. I simply will not take that. But they do laugh at me. I know that.

LINDA:　Darling . . .

WILLY:　I gotta overcome it. I know I gotta overcome it. I'm not dressing to advantage, maybe.

LINDA:　Willy, darling, you're the handsomest man in the world—

WILLY:　Oh, no, Linda.

LINDA:　To me you are. (*Slight pause.*) The handsomest.

From the darkness is heard the laughter of a woman. WILLY *doesn't turn to it, but it continues through* LINDA'S *lines.*

LINDA: And the boys, Willy. Few men are idolized by their children the way you are.

Music is heard as behind a scrim, to the left of the house, THE WOMAN, *dimly seen, is dressing.*

WILLY   (*with great feeling*): You're the best there is, Linda, you're a pal, you know that? On the road—on the road I want to grab you sometimes and just kiss the life outa you.

The laughter is loud now, and he moves into a brightening area at the left, where THE WOMAN *has come from behind the scrim and is standing, putting on her hat, looking into a "mirror" and laughing.*

WILLY: 'Cause I get so lonely—especially when business is bad and there's nobody to talk to. I get the feeling that I'll never sell anything again, that I won't make a living for you, or a business, a business for the boys. (*He talks through* THE WOMAN'S *subsiding laughter;* THE WOMAN *primps at the "mirror."*) There's so much I want to make for—

THE WOMAN: Me? You didn't make me, Willy. I picked you.

WILLY   (*pleased*): You picked me?

THE WOMAN   (*who is quite proper-looking,* WILLY'S *age*): I did. I've been sitting at that desk watching all the salesmen go by, day in, day out. But you've got such a sense of humor, and we do have such a good time together, don't we?

WILLY: Sure, sure. (*He takes her in his arms.*) Why do you have to go now?

THE WOMAN: It's two o'clock . . .

WILLY: No, come on in! (*He pulls her.*)

THE WOMAN: . . . my sisters'll be scandalized. When'll you be back?

WILLY: Oh, two weeks about. Will you come up again?

THE WOMAN: Sure thing. You do make me laugh. It's good for me. (*She squeezes his arm, kisses him.*) And I think you're a wonderful man.

WILLY: You picked me, heh?

THE WOMAN: Sure. Because you're so sweet. And such a kidder.

WILLY: Well, I'll see you next time I'm in Boston.

THE WOMAN: I'll put you right through to the buyers.

WILLY   (*slapping her bottom*): Right. Well, bottoms up!

THE WOMAN   (*slaps him gently and laughs*): You just kill me, Willy. (*He suddenly grabs her and kisses her roughly.*) You kill me. And thanks for the stockings. I love a lot of stockings. Well, good night.

WILLY: Good night. And keep your pores open!

THE WOMAN: Oh, Willy!

THE WOMAN *bursts out laughing, and* LINDA'S *laughter blends in.* THE WOMAN *disappears into the dark. Now the area at the kitchen table brightens.* LINDA *is sitting where she was at the kitchen table, but now is mending a pair of silk stockings.*

LINDA: You are, Willy. The handsomest man. You've got no reason to feel that—

WILLY   (*coming out of* THE WOMAN'S *dimming area and going over to* LINDA): I'll make it all up to you, Linda, I'll—

LINDA: There's nothing to make up, dear. You're doing fine, better than—

WILLY   (*noticing her mending*): What's that?

LINDA: Just mending my stockings. They're so expensive—

WILLY   (*angrily, taking them from her*): I won't have you mending stockings in this house! Now throw them out!

LINDA *puts the stockings in her pocket.*

BERNARD   (*entering on the run*): Where is he? If he doesn't study!

WILLY   (*moving to the forestage, with great agitation*): You'll give him the answers!

BERNARD: I do, but I can't on a Regents! That's a state exam! They're liable to arrest me!

WILLY: Where is he? I'll whip him, I'll whip him!

LINDA: And he'd better give back that football, Willy, it's not nice.

WILLY: Biff! Where is he? Why is he taking everything?

LINDA: He's too tough with the girls, Willy. All the mothers are afraid of him!

WILLY: I'll whip him!

BERNARD: He's driving the car without a license!

THE WOMAN's *laugh is heard.*

WILLY: Shut up!

LINDA: All the mothers—

WILLY: Shut up!

BERNARD   (*backing quietly away and out*): Mr. Birnbaum says he's stuck up.

WILLY: Get outa here!

BERNARD: If he doesn't buckle down he'll flunk math! (*He goes off.*)

LINDA: He's right, Willy, you've gotta—

WILLY   (*exploding at her*): There's nothing the matter with him! You want him to be a worm like Bernard? He's got spirit, personality . . .

As he speaks, LINDA, *almost in tears, exits into the livingroom.* WILLY *is alone in the kitchen, wilting and staring. The leaves are gone. It is night again, and the apartment houses look down from behind.*

WILLY: Loaded with it. Loaded! What is he stealing? He's giving it back, isn't he? Why is he stealing? What did I tell him? I never in my life told him anything but decent things.

HAPPY *in pajamas has come down the stairs;* WILLY *suddenly becomes aware of* HAPPY's *presence.*

HAPPY: Let's go now, come on.

WILLY   (*sitting down at the kitchen table*): Huh! Why did she have to wax the floors herself? Everytime she waxes the floors she keels over. She knows that!

HAPPY: Shh! Take it easy. What brought you back tonight?

WILLY: I got an awful scare. Nearly hit a kid in Yonkers. God! Why didn't

I go to Alaska with my brother Ben that time! Ben! That man was a genius, that man was success incarnate! What a mistake! He begged me to go.

HAPPY: Well, there's no use in—

WILLY: You guys! There was a man started with the clothes on his back and ended up with diamond mines!

HAPPY: Boy, someday I'd like to know how he did it.

WILLY: What's the mystery? The man knew what he wanted and went out and got it! Walked into a jungle, and comes out, the age of twenty-one, and he's rich! The world is an oyster, but you don't crack it open on a mattress!

HAPPY: Pop, I told you I'm gonna retire you for life.

WILLY: You'll retire me for life on seventy goddam dollars a week? And your women and your car and your apartment, and you'll retire me for life! Christ's sake, I couldn't get past Yonkers today! Where are you guys, where are you? The woods are burning! I can't drive a car!

CHARLEY *has appeared in the doorway. He is a large man, slow of speech, laconic, immovable. In all he says, despite what he says, there is pity, and, now, trepidation. He has a robe over his pajamas, slippers on his feet. He enters the kitchen.*

CHARLEY: Everything all right?

HAPPY: Yeah, Charley, everything's . . .

WILLY: What's the matter?

CHARLEY: I heard some noise. I thought something happened. Can't we do something about the walls? You sneeze in here, and in my house hats blow off.

HAPPY: Let's go to bed, Dad. Come on.

CHARLEY *signals to* HAPPY *to go.*

WILLY: You go ahead, I'm not tired at the moment.

HAPPY   (*to* WILLY): Take it easy, huh? (*He exits.*)

WILLY: What're you doin' up?

CHARLEY   (*sitting down at the kitchen table opposite* WILLY): Couldn't sleep good. I had a heartburn.

WILLY: Well, you don't know how to eat.

CHARLEY: I eat with my mouth.

WILLY: No, you're ignorant. You gotta know about vitamins and things like that.

CHARLEY: Come on, let's shoot. Tire you out a little.

WILLY   (*hesitantly*): All right. You got cards?

CHARLEY   (*taking a deck from his pocket*): Yeah, I got them. Someplace. What is it with those vitamins?

WILLY   (*dealing*): They build up your bones. Chemistry.

CHARLEY: Yeah, but there's no bones in a heartburn.

WILLY: What are you talkin' about? Do you know the first thing about it?

CHARLEY: Don't get insulted.

WILLY: Don't talk about something you don't know anything about.

They are playing. Pause.

CHARLEY: What're you doin' home?

WILLY: A little trouble with the car.

CHARLEY: Oh. (*Pause.*) I'd like to take a trip to California.

WILLY: Don't say.

CHARLEY: You want a job?

WILLY: I got a job, I told you that. (*After a slight pause.*) What the hell are you offering me a job for?

CHARLEY: Don't get insulted.

WILLY: Don't insult me.

CHARLEY: I don't see no sense in it. You don't have to go on this way.

WILLY: I got a good job. (*Slight pause.*) What do you keep comin' in here for?

CHARLEY: You want me to go?

WILLY (*after a pause, withering*): I can't understand it. He's going back to Texas again. What the hell is that?

CHARLEY: Let him go.

WILLY: I got nothin' to give him, Charley, I'm clean, I'm clean.

CHARLEY: He won't starve. None a them starve. Forget about him.

WILLY: Then what have I got to remember?

CHARLEY: You take it too hard. To hell with it. When a deposit bottle is broken you don't get your nickel back.

WILLY: That's easy enough for you to say.

CHARLEY: That ain't easy for me to say.

WILLY: Did you see the ceiling I put up in the livingroom?

CHARLEY: Yeah, that's a piece of work. To put up a ceiling is a mystery to me. How do you do it?

WILLY: What's the difference?

CHARLEY: Well, talk about it.

WILLY: You gonna put up a ceiling?

CHARLEY: How could I put up a ceiling?

WILLY: Then what the hell are you bothering me for?

CHARLEY: You're insulted again.

WILLY: A man who can't handle tools is not a man. You're disgusting.

CHARLEY: Don't call me disgusting, Willy.

UNCLE BEN, *carrying a valise and an umbrella, enters the forestage from around the right corner of the house. He is a stolid man, in his sixties, with a mustache and an authoritative air. He is utterly certain of his destiny, and there is an aura of far places about him. He enters exactly as* WILLY *speaks.*

WILLY: I'm getting awfully tired, Ben.

BEN'S *music is heard.* BEN *looks around at everything.*

CHARLEY: Good, keep playing; you'll sleep better. Did you call me Ben?

BEN *looks at his watch.*

WILLY: That's funny. For a second there you reminded me of my brother Ben.

BEN: I have only a few minutes. (*He strolls, inspecting the place.* WILLY *and* CHARLEY *continue playing.*)

CHARLEY: You never heard from him again, heh? Since that time?

WILLY: Didn't Linda tell you? Couple of weeks ago we got a letter from his wife in Africa. He died.

CHARLEY: That so.

BEN   (*chuckling*): So this is Brooklyn, eh?

CHARLEY: Maybe you're in for some of his money.

WILLY: Naa, he had seven sons. There's just one opportunity I had with that man . . .

BEN: I must make a train, William. There are several properties I'm looking at in Alaska.

WILLY: Sure, sure! If I'd gone with him to Alaska that time, everything would've been totally different.

CHARLEY: Go on, you'd froze to death up there.

WILLY: What're you talking about?

BEN: Opportunity is tremendous in Alaska, William. Surprised you're not up there.

WILLY: Sure, tremendous.

CHARLEY: Heh?

WILLY: There was the only man I ever met who knew the answers.

CHARLEY: Who?

BEN: How are you all?

WILLY   (*taking a pot, smiling*): Fine, fine.

CHARLEY: Pretty sharp tonight.

BEN: Is Mother living with you?

WILLY: No, she died a long time ago.

CHARLEY: Who?

BEN: That's too bad. Fine specimen of a lady, Mother.

WILLY   (*to* CHARLEY): Heh?

BEN: I'd hoped to see the old girl.

CHARLEY: Who died?

BEN: Heard anything from Father, have you?

WILLY   (*unnerved*): What do you mean, who died?

CHARLEY   (*taking a pot*): What're you talkin' about?

BEN   (*looking at his watch*): William, it's half-past eight!

WILLY   (*as though to dispel his confusion he angrily stops* CHARLEY's *hand*): That's my build!

CHARLEY: I put the ace—

WILLY: If you don't know how to play the game I'm not gonna throw my money away on you!

CHARLEY   (*rising*): It was my ace, for God's sake!

WILLY: I'm through, I'm through!

BEN: When did Mother die?

WILLY: Long ago. Since the beginning you never knew how to play cards.

CHARLEY   (*picks up the cards and goes to the door*): All right! Next time I'll bring a deck with five aces.

WILLY: I don't play that kind of game!

CHARLEY   (*turning to him*): You should be ashamed of yourself!

WILLY: Yeah?

CHARLEY: Yeah! (*He goes out.*)

WILLY   (*slamming the door after him*): Ignoramus!

BEN   (*as* WILLY *comes toward him through the wall-line of the kitchen*): So you're William.

WILLY   (*shaking* BEN's *hand*): Ben! I've been waiting for you so long! What's the answer? How did you do it?

BEN: Oh, there's a story in that.

LINDA *enters the forestage, as of old, carrying the wash basket.*

LINDA: Is this Ben?

BEN   (*gallantly*): How do you do, my dear.

LINDA: Where've you been all these years? Willy's always wondered why you—

WILLY   (*pulling* BEN *away from her impatiently*): Where is Dad? Didn't you follow him? How did you get started?

BEN: Well, I don't know how much you remember.

WILLY: Well, I was just a baby, of course, only three or four years old—

BEN: Three years and eleven months.

WILLY: What a memory, Ben!

BEN: I have many enterprises, William, and I have never kept books.

WILLY: I remember I was sitting under the wagon in—was it Nebraska?

BEN: It was South Dakota, and I gave you a bunch of wild flowers.

WILLY: I remember you walking away down some open road.

BEN   (*laughing*): I was going to find Father in Alaska.

WILLY: Where is he?

BEN: At that age I had a very faulty view of geography, William. I discovered after a few days that I was heading due south, so instead of Alaska, I ended up in Africa.

LINDA: Africa!

WILLY: The Gold Coast!

BEN: Principally, diamond mines.

LINDA: Diamond mines!

BEN: Yes, my dear. But I've only a few minutes—

WILLY: No! Boys! Boys! (YOUNG BIFF *and* HAPPY *appear.*) Listen to this. This is your Uncle Ben, a great man! Tell my boys, Ben!

BEN: Why, boys, when I was seventeen I walked into the jungle, and when I was twenty-one I walked out. (*He laughs.*) And by God I was rich.

WILLY   (*to the boys*): You see what I been talking about? The greatest things can happen!

BEN   (*glancing at his watch*): I have an appointment in Ketchikan Tuesday week.

WILLY: No, Ben! Please tell about Dad. I want my boys to hear. I want them to know the kind of stock they spring from. All I remember is a man with a big beard, and I was in Mamma's lap, sitting around a fire, and some kind of high music.

BEN: His flute. He played the flute.

WILLY: Sure, the flute, that's right!

New music is heard, a high, rollicking tune.

BEN: Father was a very great and a very wild-hearted man. We would start in Boston, and he'd toss the whole family into the wagon, and then he'd drive the team right across the country; through Ohio, and Indiana, Michigan, Illinois, and all the Western states. And we'd stop in the towns and sell the flutes that he'd made on the way. Great inventor, Father. With one gadget he made more in a week than a man like you could make in a lifetime.

WILLY: That's just the way I'm bringing them up, Ben—rugged, well liked, all-around.

BEN: Yeah? (*To* BIFF.) Hit that, boy—hard as you can. (*He pounds his stomach.*)

BIFF: Oh, no, sir!

BEN   (*taking boxing stance*): Come on, get to me! (*He laughs.*)

WILLY: Go to it, Biff! Go ahead, show him!

BIFF: Okay! (*He cocks his fist and starts in.*)

LINDA   (*to* WILLY): Why must he fight, dear?

BEN   (*sparring with* BIFF): Good boy! Good boy!

WILLY: How's that, Ben, heh?

HAPPY: Give him the left, Biff!

LINDA: Why are you fighting?

BEN: Good boy! (*Suddenly comes in, trips* BIFF, *and stands over him, the point of his umbrella poised over* BIFF'S *eye.*)

LINDA: Look out, Biff!

BIFF: Gee!

BEN   (*patting* BIFF'S *knee*): Never fight fair with a stranger, boy. You'll never get out of the jungle that way. (*Taking* LINDA'S *hand and bowing.*) It was an honor and a pleasure to meet you, Linda.

LINDA   (*withdrawing her hand coldly, frightened*): Have a nice—trip.

BEN   (*to* WILLY): And good luck with your—what do you do?

WILLY: Selling.

BEN: Yes. Well . . . (*He raises his hand in farewell to all.*)

WILLY: No, Ben, I don't want you to think . . . (*He takes* BEN'S *arm to show him.*) It's Brooklyn, I know, but we hunt too.

BEN: Really, now.

WILLY: Oh, sure, there's snakes and rabbits and—that's why I moved out here. Why, Biff can fell any one of these trees in no time! Boys! Go right over to where they're building the apartment house and get some sand. We're gonna rebuild the entire front stoop right now! Watch this, Ben!

BIFF: Yes, sir! On the double, Hap!

HAPPY   (*as he and* BIFF *run off*): I lost weight, Pop, you notice?

CHARLEY *enters in knickers, even before the boys are gone.*

CHARLEY: Listen, if they steal any more from that building the watchman'll put the cops on them!

LINDA   (*to* WILLY): Don't let Biff . . .

BEN *laughs lustily.*

WILLY: You shoulda seen the lumber they brought home last week. At least a dozen six-by-tens worth all kinds a money.

CHARLEY: Listen, if that watchman—

WILLY: I gave them hell, understand. But I got a couple of fearless characters there.

CHARLEY: Willy, the jails are full of fearless characters.

BEN   (*clapping* WILLY *on the back, with a laugh at* CHARLEY): And the stock exchange, friend!

WILLY   (*joining in* BEN'S *laughter*): Where are the rest of your pants?

CHARLEY: My wife bought them.

WILLY: Now all you need is a golf club and you can go upstairs and go to sleep. (*To* BEN.) Great athlete! Between him and his son Bernard they can't hammer a nail!

BERNARD   (*rushing in*): The watchman's chasing Biff!

WILLY   (*angrily*): Shut up! He's not stealing anything!

LINDA   (*alarmed, hurrying off left*): Where is he? Biff, dear! (*She exits.*)

WILLY   (*moving toward the left, away from* BEN): There's nothing wrong. What's the matter with you?

BEN: Nervy boy. Good!

WILLY   (*laughing*): Oh, nerves of iron, that Biff!

CHARLEY: Don't know what it is. My New England man comes back and he's bleedin', they murdered him up there.

WILLY: It's contacts, Charley, I got important contacts!

CHARLEY   (*sarcastically*): Glad to hear it, Willy. Come in later, we'll shoot a little casino. I'll take some of your Portland money. (*He laughs at* WILLY *and exits.*)

WILLY   (*turning to* BEN): Business is bad, it's murderous. But not for me, of course.

BEN: I'll stop by on my way back to Africa.

WILLY   (*longingly*): Can't you stay a few days? You're just what I need, Ben, because I—I have a fine position here, but I—well, Dad left when I was such a baby and I never had a chance to talk to him and I still feel—kind of temporary about myself.

BEN: I'll be late for my train.

They are at opposite ends of the stage.

WILLY: Ben, my boys—can't we talk? They'd go into the jaws of hell for me, see, but I—

BEN: William, you're being first-rate with your boys. Outstanding, manly chaps!

WILLY   (*hanging on to his words*): Oh, Ben, that's good to hear! Because sometimes I'm afraid that I'm not teaching them the right kind of— Ben, how should I teach them?

BEN   (*giving great weight to each word, and with a certain vicious audacity*): William, when I walked into the jungle, I was seventeen. When I walked out I was twenty-one. And, by God, I was rich! (*He goes off into darkness around the right corner of the house.*)

WILLY: . . . was rich! That's just the spirit I want to imbue them with! To walk into a jungle! I was right! I was right! I was right!

BEN *is gone, but* WILLY *is still speaking to him as* LINDA, *in nightgown and robe, enters the kitchen, glances around for* WILLY, *then goes to the door of the house, looks out and sees him. Comes down to his left. He looks at her.*

LINDA: Willy, dear? Willy?

WILLY: I was right!

LINDA: Did you have some cheese? (*He can't answer.*) It's very late, darling. Come to bed, heh?

WILLY (*looking straight up*): Gotta break your neck to see a star in this yard.

LINDA: You coming in?

WILLY: What ever happened to that diamond watch fob? Remember? When Ben came from Africa that time? Didn't he give me a watch fob with a diamond in it?

LINDA: You pawned it, dear. Twelve, thirteen years ago. For Biff's radio correspondence course.

WILLY: Gee, that was a beautiful thing. I'll take a walk.

LINDA: But you're in your slippers.

WILLY (*starting to go around the house at the left*): I was right! I was! (*Half to* LINDA, *as he goes, shaking his head.*) What a man! There was a man worth talking to. I was right!

LINDA (*calling after* WILLY): But in your slippers, Willy!

WILLY *is almost gone when* BIFF, *in his pajamas, comes down the stairs and enters the kitchen.*

BIFF: What is he doing out there?

LINDA: Sh!

BIFF: God Almighty, Mom, how long has he been doing this?

LINDA: Don't, he'll hear you.

BIFF: What the hell is the matter with him?

LINDA: It'll pass by morning.

BIFF: Shouldn't we do anything?

LINDA: Oh, my dear, you should do a lot of things, but there's nothing to do, so go to sleep.

HAPPY *comes down the stairs and sits on the steps.*

HAPPY: I never heard him so loud, Mom.

LINDA: Well, come around more often; you'll hear him. (*She sits down at the table and mends the lining of* WILLY's *jacket.*)

BIFF: Why didn't you ever write me about this, Mom?

LINDA: How would I write to you? For over three months you had no address.

BIFF: I was on the move. But you know I thought of you all the time. You know that, don't you, pal?

LINDA: I know, dear, I know. But he likes to have a letter. Just to know that there's still a possibility for better things.

BIFF: He's not like this all the time, is he?

LINDA: It's when you come home he's always the worst.

BIFF: When I come home?

LINDA: When you write you're coming, he's all smiles, and talks about the future, and—he's just wonderful. And then the closer you seem to come, the more shaky he gets, and then, by the time you get here, he's arguing, and he seems angry at you. I think it's just that maybe he can't bring himself to—to open up to you. Why are you so hateful to each other? Why is that?

BIFF   (*evasively*): I'm not hateful, Mom.

LINDA: But you no sooner come in the door than you're fighting!

BIFF: I don't know why. I mean to change. I'm tryin', Mom, you understand?

LINDA: Are you home to stay now?

BIFF: I don't know. I want to look around, see what's doin'.

LINDA: Biff, you can't look around all your life, can you?

BIFF: I just can't take hold, Mom. I can't take hold of some kind of a life.

LINDA: Biff, a man is not a bird, to come and go with the springtime.

BIFF: Your hair . . . (*He touches her hair.*) Your hair got so gray.

LINDA: Oh, it's been gray since you were in high school. I just stopped dyeing it, that's all.

BIFF: Dye it again, will ya? I don't want my pal looking old. (*He smiles.*)

LINDA: You're such a boy! You think you can go away for a year and . . . You've got to get it into your head now that one day you'll knock on this door and there'll be strange people here—

BIFF: What are you talking about? You're not even sixty, Mom.

LINDA: But what about your father?

BIFF   (*lamely*): Well, I meant him too.

HAPPY: He admires Pop.

LINDA: Biff, dear, if you don't have any feeling for him, then you can't have any feeling for me.

BIFF: Sure I can, Mom.

LINDA: No. You can't just come to see me, because I love him. (*With a threat, but only a threat, of tears.*) He's the dearest man in the world to me, and I won't have anyone making him feel unwanted and low and blue. You've got to make up your mind now, darling, there's no leeway any more. Either he's your father and you pay him that respect, or else you're not to come here. I know he's not easy to get along with—nobody knows that better than me—but . . .

WILLY   (*from the left, with a laugh*): Hey, hey, Biffo!

BIFF   (*starting to go out after* WILLY): What the hell is the matter with him? (HAPPY *stops him.*)

LINDA: Don't—don't go near him!

BIFF: Stop making excuses for him! He always, always wiped the floor with you. Never had an ounce of respect for you.

HAPPY: He's always had respect for—

BIFF: What the hell do you know about it?

HAPPY   (*surlily*): Just don't call him crazy!

BIFF: He's got no character—Charley wouldn't do this. Not in his own house—spewing out that vomit from his mind.

HAPPY: Charley never had to cope with what he's got to.

BIFF: People are worse off than Willy Loman. Believe me, I've seen them!

LINDA: Then make Charley your father, Biff. You can't do that, can you? I don't say he's a great man. Willy Loman never made a lot of money. His name was never in the paper. He's not the finest character that ever lived. But he's a human being, and a terrible thing is happening to him. So attention must be paid. He's not to be allowed to fall into his grave like an old dog. Attention, attention must be finally paid to such a person. You called him crazy—

BIFF: I didn't mean—

LINDA: No, a lot of people think he's lost his—balance. But you don't have to be very smart to know what his trouble is. The man is exhausted.

HAPPY: Sure!

LINDA: A small man can be just as exhausted as a great man. He works for a company thirty-six years this March, opens up unheard-of territories to their trademark, and now in his old age they take his salary away.

HAPPY   (*indignantly*): I didn't know that, Mom.

LINDA: You never asked, my dear! Now that you get your spending money someplace else you don't trouble your mind with him.

HAPPY: But I gave you money last—

LINDA: Christmas time, fifty dollars! To fix the hot water it cost ninety-seven fifty! For five weeks he's been on straight commission, like a beginner, an unknown!

BIFF: Those ungrateful bastards!

LINDA: Are they any worse than his sons? When he brought them business, when he was young, they were glad to see him. But now his old friends, the old buyers that loved him so and always found some order to hand him in a pinch—they're all dead, retired. He used to be able to make six, seven calls a day in Boston. Now he takes his valises out of the car and puts them back and takes them out again and he's exhausted. Instead of walking he talks now. He drives seven hundred miles, and when he gets there no one knows him any more, no one welcomes him. And what goes through a man's mind, driving seven hundred miles home without having earned a cent? Why shouldn't he talk to himself? Why? When he has to go to Charley and borrow fifty dollars a week and pretend to me that it's his pay? How long can that go on? How long? You see what I'm sitting here and waiting for? And you tell me he has no character? The man who never worked a day but for your benefit? When does he get the medal for that? Is this his reward—to turn around at the age of sixty-three and find his sons, who he loved better than his life, one a philandering bum—

HAPPY: Mom!

LINDA: That's all you are, my baby! (*To* BIFF.) And you! What happened to the love you had for him? You were such pals! How you used to talk to him on the phone every night! How lonely he was till he could come home to you!

BIFF: All right, Mom. I'll live here in my room, and I'll get a job. I'll keep away from him, that's all.

LINDA: No, Biff. You can't stay here and fight all the time.

BIFF: He threw me out of this house, remember that.

LINDA: Why did he do that? I never knew why.

BIFF: Because I know he's a fake and he doesn't like anybody around who knows!

LINDA: Why a fake? In what way? What do you mean?

BIFF: Just don't lay it all at my feet. It's between me and him—that's all I have to say. I'll chip in from now on. He'll settle for half my pay check. He'll be all right. I'm going to bed. (*He starts for the stairs.*)

LINDA: He won't be all right.

BIFF   (*turning on the stairs, furiously*): I hate this city and I'll stay here. Now what do you want?

LINDA: He's dying, Biff.

HAPPY *turns quickly to her, shocked.*

BIFF   (*after a pause.*): Why is he dying?

LINDA: He's been trying to kill himself.

BIFF   (*with great horror*): How?

LINDA: I live from day to day.

BIFF: What're you talking about?

LINDA: Remember I wrote you that he smashed up the car again? In February?

BIFF: Well?

LINDA: The insurance inspector came. He said that they have evidence. That all these accidents in the last year—weren't—weren't—accidents.

HAPPY: How can they tell that? That's a lie.

LINDA: It seems there's a woman . . . (*She takes a breath as—*)

BIFF   (*sharply but contained*): What woman?

LINDA   (*simultaneously*): . . . and this woman . . .

LINDA: What?

BIFF: Nothing. Go ahead.

LINDA: What did you say?

BIFF: Nothing. I just said what woman?

HAPPY: What about her?

LINDA: Well, it seems she was walking down the road and saw his car. She says that he wasn't driving fast at all, and that he didn't skid. She says he came to that little bridge, and then deliberately smashed into the railing, and it was only the shallowness of the water that saved him.

BIFF: Oh, no, he probably just fell asleep again.

LINDA: I don't think he fell asleep.

BIFF: Why not?

LINDA: Last month . . . (*With great difficulty.*) Oh, boys, it's so hard to say a thing like this! He's just a big stupid man to you, but I tell you there's more good in him than in many other people. (*She chokes, wipes her eyes.*) I was looking for a fuse. The lights blew out, and I went down the cellar. And behind the fuse box—it happened to fall out—was a length of rubber pipe—just short.

HAPPY: No kidding?

LINDA: There's a little attachment on the end of it. I knew right away. And sure enough, on the bottom of the water heater there's a new little nipple on the gas pipe.

HAPPY   (*angrily*): That—jerk.

BIFF: Did you have it taken off?

LINDA: I'm—I'm ashamed to. How can I mention it to him? Every day I go down and take away that little rubber pipe. But, when he comes home, I put it back where it was. How can I insult him that way? I don't know what to do. I live from day to day, boys. I tell you, I know every thought in his mind. It sounds so old-fashioned and silly, but I tell you he put his whole life into you and you've turned your backs on him. (*She is bent over in the chair, weeping, her face in her hands.*) Biff, I swear to God! Biff, his life is in your hands!

HAPPY   (*to* BIFF): How do you like that damned fool!

BIFF   (*kissing her*): All right, pal, all right. It's all settled now. I've been remiss. I know that, Mom. But now I'll stay, and I swear to you, I'll apply myself. (*Kneeling in front of her, in a fever of self-reproach.*) It's just—you see, Mom, I don't fit in business. Not that I won't try. I'll try, and I'll make good.

HAPPY: Sure you will. The trouble with you in business was you never tried to please people.

BIFF: I know, I—

HAPPY: Like when you worked for Harrison's. Bob Harrison said you were tops, and then you go and do some damn fool thing like whistling whole songs in the elevator like a comedian.

BIFF   (*against* HAPPY): So what? I like to whistle sometimes.

HAPPY: You don't raise a guy to a responsible job who whistles in the elevator!

LINDA: Well, don't argue about it now.

HAPPY: Like when you'd go off and swim in the middle of the day instead of taking the line around.

BIFF   (*his resentment rising*): Well, don't you run off? You take off sometimes, don't you? On a nice summer day?

HAPPY: Yeah, but I cover myself!

LINDA: Boys!

HAPPY: If I'm going to take a fade the boss can call any number where I'm supposed to be and they'll swear to him that I just left. I'll tell you something that I hate to say, Biff, but in the business world some of them think you're crazy.

BIFF   (*angered*): Screw the business world!

HAPPY: All right, screw it! Great, but cover yourself!

LINDA: Hap, Hap!

BIFF: I don't care what they think! They've laughed at Dad for years, and you know why? Because we don't belong in this nut-house of a city! We should be mixing cement on some open plain, or—or carpenters. A carpenter is allowed to whistle!

WILLY *walks in from the entrance of the house, at left.*

WILLY: Even your grandfather was better than a carpenter. (*Pause. They watch him.*) You never grew up. Bernard does not whistle in the elevator, I assure you.

BIFF   (*as though to laugh* WILLY *out of it*): Yeah, but you do, Pop.

WILLY: I never in my life whistled in an elevator! And who in the business world thinks I'm crazy?

BIFF: I didn't mean it like that, Pop. Now don't make a whole thing out of it, will ya?

WILLY: Go back to the West! Be a carpenter, a cowboy, enjoy yourself!

LINDA: Willy, he was just saying—

WILLY: I heard what he said!

HAPPY   (*trying to quiet* WILLY): Hey, Pop, come on now . . .

WILLY   (*continuing over* HAPPY'S *line*): They laugh at me, heh? Go to Filene's, go to the Hub, go to Slattery's, Boston. Call out the name Willy Loman and see what happens! Big shot!

BIFF: All right, Pop.

WILLY: Big!

BIFF: All right!

WILLY: Why do you always insult me?

BIFF: I didn't say a word. (*To* LINDA.) Did I say a word?

LINDA: He didn't say anything, Willy.

WILLY   (*going to the doorway of the livingroom*): All right, good night, good night.

LINDA: Willy, dear, he just decided . . .

WILLY   (*to* BIFF): If you get tired hanging around tomorrow, paint the ceiling I put up in the livingroom.

BIFF: I'm leaving early tomorrow.

HAPPY: He's going to see Bill Oliver, Pop.

WILLY   (*interestedly*): Oliver? For what?

BIFF   (*with reserve, but trying, trying*): He always said he'd stake me. I'd like to go into business, so maybe I can take him up on it.

LINDA: Isn't that wonderful?

WILLY: Don't interrupt. What's wonderful about it? There's fifty men in the City of New York who'd stake him. (*To* BIFF.) Sporting goods?

BIFF: I guess so. I know something about it and—

WILLY: He knows something about it! You know sporting goods better than Spalding, for God's sake! How much is he giving you?

BIFF: I don't know, I didn't even see him yet, but—

WILLY: Then what're you talkin' about?

BIFF   (*getting angry*): Well, all I said was I'm gonna see him, that's all!

WILLY   (*turning away*): Ah, you're counting your chickens again.

BIFF   (*starting left for the stairs*): Oh, Jesus, I'm going to sleep!

WILLY   (*calling after him*): Don't curse in this house!

BIFF   (*turning*): Since when did you get so clean!

HAPPY   (*trying to stop them*): Wait a . . .

WILLY: Don't use that language to me! I won't have it!

HAPPY   (*grabbing* BIFF, *shouts*): Wait a minute! I got an idea. I got a feasible idea. Come here, Biff, let's talk this over now, let's talk some sense here. When I was down in Florida last time, I thought of a great idea to sell sporting goods. It just came back to me. You and I, Biff—we have a line, the Loman Line. We train a couple of weeks, and put on a couple of exhibitions, see?

WILLY: That's an idea!

HAPPY: Wait! We form two basketball teams, see? Two water-polo teams.

We play each other. It's a million dollars' worth of publicity. Two brothers, see? The Loman Brothers. Displays in the Royal Palms—all the hotels. And banners over the ring and the basketball court: "Loman Brothers." Baby, we could sell sporting goods!

WILLY: That is a one-million-dollar idea.

LINDA: Marvelous!

BIFF: I'm in great shape as far as that's concerned.

HAPPY: And the beauty of it is, Biff, it wouldn't be like a business. We'd be out playin' ball again . . .

BIFF   (*enthused*): Yeah, that's . . .

WILLY: Million-dollar . . .

HAPPY: And you wouldn't get fed up with it, Biff. It'd be the family again. There'd be the old honor, and comradeship, and if you wanted to go off for a swim or somethin'—well, you'd do it! Without some smart cooky gettin' up ahead of you!

WILLY: Lick the world! You guys together could absolutely lick the civilized world.

BIFF: I'll see Oliver tomorrow. Hap, if we could work that out . . .

LINDA: Maybe things are beginning to—

WILLY   (*wildly enthused, to* LINDA): Stop interrupting! (*To* BIFF.) But don't wear sport jacket and slacks when you see Oliver.

BIFF: No, I'll—

WILLY: A business suit, and talk as little as possible, and don't crack any jokes.

BIFF: He did like me. Always liked me.

LINDA: He loved you!

WILLY   (*to* LINDA): Will you stop! (*To* BIFF.) Walk in very serious. You are not applying for a boy's job. Money is to pass. Be quiet, fine, and serious. Everybody likes a kidder, but nobody lends him money.

HAPPY: I'll try to get some myself, Biff. I'm sure I can.

WILLY: I can see great things for you, kids, I think your troubles are over. But remember, start big and you'll end big. Ask for fifteen. How much you gonna ask for?

BIFF: Gee, I don't know—

WILLY: And don't say "Gee." "Gee" is a boy's word. A man walking in for fifteen thousand dollars does not say "Gee!"

BIFF: Ten, I think, would be top though.

WILLY: Don't be so modest. You always started too low. Walk in with a big laugh. Don't look worried. Start off with a couple of your good stories to lighten things up. It's not what you say, it's how you say it—because personality always wins the day.

LINDA: Oliver always thought the highest of him—

WILLY: Will you let me talk?

BIFF: Don't yell at her, Pop, will ya?

WILLY   (*angrily*): I was talking, wasn't I?

BIFF: I don't like you yelling at her all the time, and I'm tellin' you, that's all.

WILLY: What're you, takin' over this house?

LINDA: Willy—

WILLY (*turning on her*): Don't take his side all the time, goddammit!

BIFF (*furiously*): Stop yelling at her!

WILLY (*suddenly pulling on his cheek, beaten down, guilt ridden*): Give my best to Bill Oliver—he may remember me. (*He exits through the livingroom doorway.*)

LINDA (*her voice subdued*): What'd you have to start that for? (BIFF *turns away.*) You see how sweet he was as soon as you talked hopefully? (*She goes over to* BIFF.) Come up and say good night to him. Don't let him go to bed that way.

HAPPY: Come on, Biff, let's buck him up.

LINDA: Please, dear. Just say good night. It takes so little to make him happy. Come. (*She goes through the livingroom doorway, calling upstairs from within the livingroom.*) Your pajamas are hanging in the bathroom. Willy!

HAPPY (*looking toward where* LINDA *went out*): What a woman! They broke the mold when they made her. You know that, Biff?

BIFF: He's off salary. My God, working on commission!

HAPPY: Well, let's face it: he's no hot-shot selling man. Except that sometimes, you have to admit, he's a sweet personality.

BIFF (*deciding*): Lend me ten bucks, will ya? I want to buy some new ties.

HAPPY: I'll take you to a place I know. Beautiful stuff. Wear one of my striped shirts tomorrow.

BIFF: She got gray. Mom got awful old. Gee, I'm gonna go in to Oliver tomorrow and knock him for a—

HAPPY: Come on up. Tell that to Dad. Let's give him a whirl. Come on.

BIFF (*steamed up*): You know, with ten thousand bucks, boy!

HAPPY (*as they go into the livingroom*): That's the talk, Biff, that's the first time I've heard the old confidence out of you! (*From within the livingroom, fading off.*) You're gonna live with me, kid, and any babe you want just say the word . . . (*The last lines are hardly heard. They are mounting the stairs to their parents' bedroom.*)

LINDA (*entering her bedroom and addressing* WILLY, *who is in the bathroom. She is straightening the bed for him*): Can you do anything about the shower? It drips.

WILLY (*from the bathroom*): All of a sudden everything falls to pieces! Goddam plumbing, oughta be sued, those people. I hardly finished putting it in and the thing . . . (*His words rumble off.*)

LINDA: I'm just wondering if Oliver will remember him. You think he might?

WILLY (*coming out of the bathroom in his pajamas*): Remember him? What's the matter with you, you crazy? If he'd've stayed with Oliver he'd be on top by now! Wait'll Oliver gets a look at him. You don't know the average caliber any more. The average young man today—(*he is getting into bed*)—is got a caliber of zero. Greatest thing in the world for him was to bum around.

BIFF *and* HAPPY *enter the bedroom. Slight pause.*

WILLY (*stops short, looking at* BIFF): Glad to hear it, boy.

HAPPY: He wanted to say good night to you, sport.

WILLY (*to* BIFF): Yeah. Knock him dead, boy. What'd you want to tell me?

BIFF: Just take it easy, Pop. Good night. (*He turns to go.*)

WILLY   (*unable to resist*): And if anything falls off the desk while you're talking to him—like a package or something—don't you pick it up. They have office boys for that.

LINDA: I'll make a big breakfast—

WILLY: Will you let me finish? (*To* BIFF.) Tell him you were in the business in the West. Not farm work.

BIFF: All right, Dad.

LINDA: I think everything—

WILLY   (*going right through her speech*): And don't undersell yourself. No less than fifteen thousand dollars.

BIFF   (*unable to bear him*): Okay. Good night, Mom. (*He starts moving.*)

WILLY: Because you got a greatness in you, Biff, remember that. You got all kinds a greatness . . . (*He lies back, exhausted.* BIFF *walks out.*)

LINDA   (*calling after* BIFF): Sleep well, darling!

HAPPY: I'm gonna get married, Mom. I wanted to tell you.

LINDA: Go to sleep, dear.

HAPPY   (*going*): I just wanted to tell you.

WILLY: Keep up the good work. (HAPPY *exits.*) God . . . remember that Ebbets Field game? The championship of the city?

LINDA: Just rest. Should I sing to you?

WILLY: Yeah. Sing to me. (LINDA *hums a soft lullaby.*) When that team came out—he was the tallest, remember?

LINDA: Oh, yes. And in gold.

BIFF *enters the darkened kitchen, takes a cigarette, and leaves the house. He comes downstage into a golden pool of light. He smokes, staring at the night.*

WILLY: Like a young god. Hercules—something like that. And the sun, the sun all around him. Remember how he waved to me? Right up from the field, with the representatives of three colleges standing by? And the buyers I brought, and the cheers when he came out—Loman, Loman, Loman! God Almighty, he'll be great yet. A star like that, magnificent, can never really fade away!

The light on WILLY *is fading. The gas heater begins to glow through the kitchen wall, near the stairs, a blue flame beneath red coils.*

LINDA   (*timidly*): Willy, dear, what has he got against you?

WILLY: I'm so tired. Don't talk any more.

BIFF *slowly returns to the kitchen. He stops, stares toward the heater.*

LINDA: Will you ask Howard to let you work in New York?

WILLY: First thing in the morning. Everything'll be all right.

BIFF *reaches behind the heater and draws out a length of rubber tubing. He is horrified and turns his head toward* WILLY'S *room, still dimly lit, from which the strains of* LINDA'S *desperate but monotonous humming rise.*

WILLY   (*staring through the window into the moonlight*): Gee, look at the moon moving between the buildings!

BIFF *wraps the tubing around his hand and quickly goes up the stairs. Curtain.*

ACT II

Music is heard, gay and bright. The curtain rises as the music fades away. WILLY, *in shirt sleeves, is sitting at the kitchen table, sipping coffee, his hat in his lap.* LINDA *is filling his cup when she can.*

WILLY: Wonderful coffee. Meal in itself.

LINDA: Can I make you some eggs?

WILLY: No. Take a breath.

LINDA: You look so rested, dear.

WILLY: I slept like a dead one. First time in months. Imagine, sleeping till ten on a Tuesday morning. Boys left nice and early, heh?

LINDA: They were out of here by eight o'clock.

WILLY: Good work!

LINDA: It was so thrilling to see them leaving together. I can't get over the shaving lotion in this house.

WILLY   (*smiling*): Mmm—

LINDA: Biff was very changed this morning. His whole attitude seemed to be hopeful. He couldn't wait to get downtown to see Oliver.

WILLY: He's heading for a change. There's no question, there simply are certain men that take longer to get—solidified. How did he dress?

LINDA: His blue suit. He's so handsome in that suit. He could be a—anything in that suit!

WILLY gets up from the table. LINDA *holds his jacket for him.*

WILLY: There's no question, no question at all. Gee, on the way home tonight I'd like to buy some seeds.

LINDA   (*laughing*): That'd be wonderful. But not enough sun gets back there. Nothing'll grow any more.

WILLY: You wait, kid, before it's all over we're gonna get a little place out in the country, and I'll raise some vegetables, a couple of chickens . . .

LINDA: You'll do it yet, dear.

WILLY walks out of his jacket. LINDA *follows him.*

WILLY: And they'll get married, and come for a weekend. I'd build a little guest house. 'Cause I got so many fine tools, all I'd need would be a little lumber and some peace of mind.

LINDA   (*joyfully*): I sewed the lining . . .

WILLY: I could build two guest houses, so they'd both come. Did he decide how much he's going to ask Oliver for?

LINDA   (*getting him into the jacket*): He didn't mention it, but I imagine ten or fifteen thousand. You going to talk to Howard today?

WILLY: Yeah. I'll put it to him straight and simple. He'll just have to take me off the road.

LINDA: And Willy, don't forget to ask for a little advance, because we've got the insurance premium. It's the grace period now.

WILLY: That's a hundred . . . ?

LINDA: A hundred and eight, sixty-eight. Because we're a little short again.

WILLY: Why are we short?

LINDA: Well, you had the motor job on the car . . .

WILLY: That goddam Studebaker!

LINDA: And you got one more payment on the refrigerator . . .

WILLY: But it just broke again!

LINDA: Well, it's old, dear.

WILLY: I told you we should've bought a well-advertised machine. Charley bought a General Electric and it's twenty years old and it's still good, that son-of-a-bitch.

LINDA: But, Willy—

WILLY: Whoever heard of a Hastings refrigerator? Once in my life I would like to own something outright before it's broken! I'm always in a race with the junkyard! I just finished paying for the car and it's on its last legs. The refrigerator consumes belts like a goddam maniac. They time those things. They time them so when you finally paid for them, they're used up.

LINDA   (*buttoning up his jacket as he unbuttons it*): All told, about two hundred dollars would carry us, dear. But that includes the last payment on the mortgage. After this payment, Willy, the house belongs to us.

WILLY: It's twenty-five years!

LINDA: Biff was nine years old when we bought it.

WILLY: Well, that's a great thing. To weather a twenty-five year mortgage is—

LINDA: It's an accomplishment.

WILLY: All the cement, the lumber, the reconstruction I put in this house! There ain't a crack to be found in it any more.

LINDA: Well, it served its purpose.

WILLY: What purpose? Some stranger'll come along, move in, and that's that. If only Biff would take this house, and raise a family . . . (*He starts to go.*) Good-by, I'm late.

LINDA   (*suddenly remembering*): Oh, I forgot! You're supposed to meet them for dinner.

WILLY: Me?

LINDA: At Frank's Chop House on Forty-eighth near Sixth Avenue.

WILLY: Is that so! How about you?

LINDA: No, just the three of you. They're gonna blow you to a big meal!

WILLY: Don't say! Who thought of that?

LINDA: Biff came to me this morning, Willy, and he said, "Tell Dad, we want to blow him to a big meal." Be there six o'clock. You and your two boys are going to have dinner.

WILLY: Gee whiz! That's really somethin'. I'm gonna knock Howard for a loop, kid. I'll get an advance, and I'll come home with a New York job. Goddammit, now I'm gonna do it!

LINDA: Oh, that's the spirit, Willy!

WILLY: I will never get behind a wheel the rest of my life!

LINDA: It's changing, Willy, I can feel it changing!

WILLY: Beyond a question. G'by, I'm late. (*He starts to go again.*)

LINDA   (*calling after him as she runs to the kitchen table for a handkerchief*): You got your glasses?

WILLY   (*feels for them, then comes back in*): Yeah, yeah, got my glasses.

LINDA   (*giving him the handkerchief*): And a handkerchief.

WILLY: Yeah, handkerchief.

LINDA: And your saccharine?

WILLY: Yeah, my saccharine.

LINDA: Be careful on the subway stairs.

She kisses him, and a silk stocking is seen hanging from her hand. WILLY *notices it.*

WILLY: Will you stop mending stockings? At least while I'm in the house. It gets me nervous. I can't tell you. Please.

LINDA *hides the stocking in her hand as she follows* WILLY *across the forestage in front of the house.*

LINDA: Remember, Frank's Chop House.

WILLY   (*passing the apron*): Maybe beets would grow out there.

LINDA   (*laughing*): But you tried so many times.

WILLY: Yeah. Well, don't work hard today. (*He disappears around the right corner of the house.*)

LINDA: Be careful!

As WILLY *vanishes,* LINDA *waves to him. Suddenly the phone rings. She runs across the stage and into the kitchen and lifts it.*

LINDA: Hello? Oh, Biff! I'm so glad you called, I just . . . Yes, sure, I just told him. Yes, he'll be there for dinner at six o'clock, I didn't forget. Listen, I was just dying to tell you. You know that little rubber pipe I told you about? That he connected to the gas heater? I finally decided to go down the cellar this morning and take it away and destroy it. But it's gone! Imagine? He took it away himself, it isn't there! (*She listens.*) When? Oh, then you took it. Oh— nothing, it's just that I'd hoped he'd taken it away himself. Oh, I'm not worried, darling, because this morning he left in such high spirits, it was like the old days! I'm not afraid any more. Did Mr. Oliver see you? . . . Well, you wait there then. And make a nice impression on him, darling. Just don't perspire too much before you see him. And have a nice time with Dad. He may have big news too! . . . That's right, a New York job. And be sweet to him tonight, dear. Be loving to him. Because he's only a little boat looking for a harbor. (*She is trembling with sorrow and joy.*) Oh, that's wonderful, Biff, you'll save his life. Thanks, darling. Just put your arm around him when he comes into the restaurant. Give him a smile. That's the boy . . . Good-by, dear. . . . You got your comb? . . . That's fine. Good-by, Biff dear.

In the middle of her speech, HOWARD *wagner, thirty-six, wheels in a small typewriter table on which is a wire-recording machine and proceeds to plug it in. This is on the left forestage. Light slowly fades on* LINDA *as it rises on* HOWARD. HOWARD *is intent on threading the machine and only glances over his shoulder as* WILLY *appears.*

WILLY: Pst! Pst!

HOWARD: Hello, Willy, come in.

WILLY: Like to have a little talk with you, Howard.

HOWARD: Sorry to keep you waiting. I'll be with you in a minute.

WILLY: What's that, Howard?

HOWARD: Didn't you ever see one of these? Wire recorder.

WILLY: Oh. Can we talk a minute?

HOWARD: Records things. Just got delivery yesterday. Been driving me crazy, the most terrific machine I ever saw in my life. I was up all night with it.

WILLY: What do you do with it?

HOWARD: I bought it for dictation, but you can do anything with it. Listen to this. I had it home last night. Listen to what I picked up. The first one is my daughter. Get this. (*He flicks the switch and "Roll out the Barrel" is heard being whistled.*) Listen to that kid whistle.

WILLY: That is lifelike, isn't it?

HOWARD: Seven years old. Get that tone.

WILLY: Ts, ts. Like to ask a little favor if you . . .

The whistling breaks off, and the voice of HOWARD'S DAUGHTER *is heard.*

HIS DAUGHTER: "Now you, Daddy."

HOWARD: She's crazy for me! (*Again the same song is whistled.*) That's me! Ha! (*He winks.*)

WILLY: You're very good!

The whistling breaks off again. The machine runs silent for a moment.

HOWARD: Sh! Get this now, this is my son.

HIS SON: "The capital of Alabama is Montgomery; the capital of Arizona is Phoenix; the capital of Arkansas is Little Rock; the capital of California is Sacramento . . ." (*And on, and on.*)

HOWARD   (*holding up five fingers*): Five years old, Willy!

WILLY: He'll make an announcer some day!

HIS SON   (*continuing*): "The capital . . ."

HOWARD: Get that—alphabetical order! (*The machine breaks off suddenly.*) Wait a minute. The maid kicked the plug out.

WILLY: It certainly is a—

HOWARD: Sh, for God's sake!

HIS SON: "It's nine o'clock, Bulova watch time. So I have to go to sleep."

WILLY: That really is—

HOWARD: Wait a minute! The next is my wife.

They wait.

HOWARD'S VOICE: "Go on, say something." (*Pause.*) "Well, you gonna talk?"

HIS WIFE: "I can't think of anything."

HOWARD'S VOICE: "Well, talk—it's turning."

HIS WIFE   (*shyly, beaten*): "Hello." (*Silence.*) "Oh, Howard, I can't talk into this . . ."

HOWARD   (*snapping the machine off*): That was my wife.

WILLY: That is a wonderful machine. Can we—

HOWARD: I tell you, Willy, I'm gonna take my camera, and my bandsaw, and all my hobbies, and out they go. This is the most fascinating relaxation I ever found.

WILLY: I think I'll get one myself.

HOWARD: Sure, they're only a hundred and a half. You can't do without it. Supposing you wanna hear Jack Benny, see? But you can't be at home at that hour. So you tell the maid to turn the radio on when Jack Benny comes on, and this automatically goes on with the radio . . .

WILLY: And when you come home you . . .

HOWARD: You can come home twelve o'clock, one o'clock, any time you like, and you get yourself a Coke and sit yourself down, throw the switch, and there's Jack Benny's program in the middle of the night!

WILLY: I'm definitely going to get one. Because lots of time I'm on the road, and I think to myself, what I must be missing on the radio!

HOWARD: Don't you have a radio in the car?

WILLY: Well, yeah, but who ever thinks of turning it on?

HOWARD: Say, aren't you supposed to be in Boston?

WILLY: That's what I want to talk to you about, Howard. You got a minute?

He draws a chair in from the wing.

HOWARD: What happened? What're you doing here?

WILLY: Well . . .

HOWARD: You didn't crack up again, did you?

WILLY: Oh, no. No . . .

HOWARD: Geez, you had me worried there for a minute. What's the trouble?

WILLY: Well, to tell you the truth, Howard, I've come to the decision that I'd rather not travel any more.

HOWARD: Not travel! Well, what'll you do?

WILLY: Remember, Christmas time, when you had the party here? You said you'd try to think of some spot for me here in town.

HOWARD: With us?

WILLY: Well, sure.

HOWARD: Oh, yeah, yeah. I remember. Well, I couldn't think of anything for you, Willy.

WILLY: I tell ya, Howard. The kids are all grown up, y'know. I don't need much any more. If I could take home—well, sixty-five dollars a week, I could swing it.

HOWARD: Yeah, but Willy, see I—

WILLY: I tell ya why, Howard. Speaking frankly and between the two of us, y'know—I'm just a little tired.

HOWARD: Oh, I could understand that, Willy. But you're a road man, Willy, and we do a road business. We've only got a half-dozen salesmen on the floor here.

WILLY: God knows, Howard, I never asked a favor of any man. But I was with the firm when your father used to carry you in here in his arms.

HOWARD: I know that, Willy, but—

WILLY: Your father came to me the day you were born and asked me what I thought of the name of Howard, may he rest in peace.

HOWARD: I appreciate that, Willy, but there just is no spot here for you. If I had a spot I'd slam you right in, but I just don't have a single, solitary spot.

He looks for his lighter. WILLY *has picked it up and gives it to him. Pause.*

WILLY   (*with increasing anger*): Howard, all I need to set my table is fifty dollars a week.

HOWARD: But where am I going to put you, kid?

WILLY: Look, it isn't a question of whether I can sell merchandise, is it?

HOWARD: No, but it's a business, kid, and everybody's gotta pull his own weight.

WILLY   (*desperately*): Just let me tell you a story, Howard—

HOWARD: 'Cause you gotta admit, business is business.

WILLY   (*angrily*): Business is definitely business, but just listen for a minute. You don't understand this. When I was a boy—eighteen, nineteen—I was already on the road. And there was a question in my mind as to whether selling had a future for me. Because in those days I had a yearning to go to Alaska. See, there were three gold strikes in one month in Alaska, and I felt like going out. Just for the ride, you might say.

HOWARD   (*barely interested*): Don't say.

WILLY: Oh, yeah, my father lived many years in Alaska. He was an adventurous man. We've got quite a little streak of self-reliance in our family. I thought I'd go out with my older brother and try to locate him, and maybe settle in the North with the old man. And I was almost decided to go, when I met a salesman in the Parker House. His name was Dave Singleman. And he was eighty-four years old, and he'd drummed merchandise in thirty-one states. And old Dave, he'd go up to his room, y'understand, put on his green velvet slippers—I'll never forget—and pick up his phone and call the buyers, and without ever leaving his room, at the age of eighty-four, he made his living. And when I saw that, I realized that selling was the greatest career a man could want. 'Cause what could be more satisfying than to be able to go, at the age of eighty-four, into twenty or thirty different cities, and pick up a phone, and be remembered and loved and helped by so many different people? Do you know? when he died—and by the way he died the death of a salesman, in his green velvet slippers in the smoker of the New York, New Haven and Hartford, going into Boston—when he died, hundreds of salesmen and buyers were at his funeral. Things were sad on a lotta trains for months after that. (*He stands up.* HOWARD *has not looked at him.*) In those days there was personality in it, Howard. There was respect, and comradeship, and gratitude in it. Today, it's all cut and dried, and there's no chance for bringing friendship to bear—or personality. You see what I mean? They don't know me any more.

HOWARD   (*moving away, to the right*): That's just the thing, Willy.

WILLY: If I had forty dollars a week—that's all I'd need. Forty dollars, Howard.

HOWARD: Kid, I can't take blood from a stone, I—

WILLY   (*desperation is on him now*): Howard, the year Al Smith was nominated, your father came to me and—

HOWARD   (*starting to go off*): I've got to see some people, kid.

WILLY   (*stopping him*): I'm talking about your father! There were promises made across this desk! You mustn't tell me you've got people to see—I put thirty-four years into this firm, Howard, and now I can't pay my insurance! You can't eat the orange and throw the peel away—a man is not a piece of fruit! (*After a pause.*) Now pay attention. Your father—in 1928 I had a big year. I averaged a hundred and seventy dollars a week in commissions.

HOWARD   (*impatiently*): Now, Willy, you never averaged—

WILLY   (*banging his hand on the desk*): I averaged a hundred and seventy dollars a week in the year of 1928! And your father came to me—or rather, I was in the office here—it was right over this desk—and he put his hand on my shoulder—

HOWARD   (*getting up*): You'll have to excuse me, Willy, I gotta see some people. Pull yourself together. (*Going out.*) I'll be back in a little while.

On HOWARD'S *exit, the light on his chair grows very bright and strange.*

WILLY: Pull myself together! What the hell did I say to him? My God, I was yelling at him! How could I! (WILLY *breaks off, staring at the light, which occupies the chair, animating it. He approaches this chair, standing across the desk from it.*) Frank, Frank, don't you remember what you told me that time? How you put your hand on my shoulder, and Frank . . . (*He leans on the desk and as he speaks the dead man's name he accidentally switches on the recorder, and instantly—*)

HOWARD'S SON: ". . . of New York is Albany. The capital of Ohio is Cincinnati, the capital of Rhode Island is . . ." (*The recitation continues.*)

WILLY   (*leaping away with fright, shouting*): Ha! Howard! Howard! Howard!

HOWARD   (*rushing in*): What happened?

WILLY   (*pointing at the machine, which continues nasally, childishly, with the capital cities*): Shut it off! Shut it off!

HOWARD   (*pulling the plug out*): Look, Willy . . .

WILLY   (*pressing his hands to his eyes*): I gotta get myself some coffee. I'll get some coffee . . .

WILLY *starts to walk out.* HOWARD *stops him.*

HOWARD   (*rolling up the cord*): Willy, look . . .

WILLY: I'll go to Boston.

HOWARD: Willy, you can't go to Boston for us.

WILLY: Why can't I go?

HOWARD: I don't want you to represent us. I've been meaning to tell you for a long time now.

WILLY: Howard, are you firing me?

HOWARD: I think you need a good long rest, Willy.

WILLY: Howard—

HOWARD: And when you feel better, come back, and we'll see if we can work something out.

WILLY: But I gotta earn money, Howard. I'm in no position—

HOWARD: Where are your sons? Why don't your sons give you a hand?

WILLY: They're working on a very big deal.

HOWARD: This is no time for false pride, Willy. You go to your sons and tell them that you're tired. You've got two great boys, haven't you?

WILLY:　Oh, no question, no question, but in the meantime . . .

HOWARD:　Then that's that, heh?

WILLY:　All right, I'll go to Boston tomorrow.

HOWARD:　No, no.

WILLY:　I can't throw myself on my sons. I'm not a cripple!

HOWARD:　Look, kid, I'm busy this morning.

WILLY　(*grasping* HOWARD's *arm*): Howard, you've got to let me go to Boston!

HOWARD　(*hard, keeping himself under control*): I've got a line of people to see this morning. Sit down, take five minutes, and pull yourself together, and then go home, will ya? I need the office, Willy. (*He starts to go, turns, remembering the recorder, starts to push off the table holding the recorder.*) Oh, yeah. Whenever you can this week, stop by and drop off the samples. You'll feel better, Willy, and then come back and we'll talk. Pull yourself together, kid, there's people outside.

HOWARD *exits, pushing the table off left.* WILLY *stares into space, exhausted. Now the music is heard—*BEN's *music—first distantly, then closer, closer. As* WILLY *speaks,* BEN *enters from the right. He carries valise and umbrella.*

WILLY:　Oh, Ben, how did you do it? What is the answer? Did you wind up the Alaska deal already?

BEN:　Doesn't take much time if you know what you're doing. Just a short business trip. Boarding ship in an hour. Wanted to say good-by.

WILLY:　Ben, I've got to talk to you.

BEN　(*glancing at his watch*): Haven't the time, William.

WILLY　(*crossing the apron to* BEN): Ben, nothing's working out. I don't know what to do.

BEN:　Now, look here, William. I've bought timberland in Alaska and I need a man to look after things for me.

WILLY:　God, timberland! Me and my boys in those grand outdoors!

BEN:　You've a new continent at your doorstep, William. Get out of these cities, they're full of talk and time payments and courts of law. Screw on your fists and you can fight for a fortune up there.

WILLY:　Yes, yes! Linda! Linda!

LINDA *enters as of old, with the wash.*

LINDA:　Oh, you're back?

BEN:　I haven't much time.

WILLY:　No, wait! Linda, he's got a proposition for me in Alaska.

LINDA:　But you've got— (*To* BEN.) He's got a beautiful job here.

WILLY:　But in Alaska, kid, I could—

LINDA:　You're doing well enough, Willy!

BEN　(*to* LINDA): Enough for what, my dear?

LINDA　(*frightened of* BEN *and angry at him*): Don't say those things to him! Enough to be happy right here, right now. (*To* WILLY, *while* BEN *laughs.*) Why must everybody conquer the world? You're well liked, and the boys love you, and someday—(*to* BEN)—why, old man Wagner told him just the other day that if he keeps it up he'll be a member of the firm, didn't he, Willy?

WILLY: Sure, sure. I am building something with this firm, Ben, and if a man is building something he must be on the right track, mustn't he?

BEN: What are you building? Lay your hand on it. Where is it?

WILLY (*hesitantly*): That's true, Linda, there's nothing.

LINDA: Why? (*To* BEN.) There's a man eighty-four years old—

WILLY: That's right, Ben, that's right. When I look at that man I say, what is there to worry about?

BEN: Bah!

WILLY: It's true, Ben. All he has to do is go into any city, pick up the phone, and he's making his living and you know why?

BEN (*picking up his valise*): I've got to go.

WILLY (*holding* BEN *back*): Look at this boy!

BIFF, *in his high school sweater, enters carrying suitcase.* HAPPY *carries* BIFF'S *shoulder guards, gold helmet, and football pants.*

WILLY: Without a penny to his name, three great universities are begging for him, and from there the sky's the limit, because it's not what you do, Ben. It's who you know and the smile on your face! It's contacts, Ben, contacts! The whole wealth of Alaska passes over the lunch table at the Commodore Hotel, and that's the wonder, the wonder of this country, that a man can end with diamonds here on the basis of being liked! (*He turns to* BIFF.) And that's why when you get out on that field today it's important. Because thousands of people will be rooting for you and loving you. (*To* BEN, *who has again begun to leave.*) And Ben! when he walks into a business office his name will sound out like a bell and all the doors will open to him! I've seen it, Ben, I've seen it a thousand times! You can't feel it with your hand like timber, but it's there!

BEN: Good-by, William.

WILLY: Ben, am I right? Don't you think I'm right? I value your advice.

BEN: There's a new continent at your doorstep, William. You could walk out rich. Rich. (*He is gone.*)

WILLY: We'll do it here, Ben! You hear me? We're gonna do it here!

Young BERNARD *rushes in. The gay music of the boys is heard.*

BERNARD: Oh, gee, I was afraid you left already!

WILLY: Why? What time is it?

BERNARD: It's half-past one!

WILLY: Well, come on, everybody! Ebbets Field next stop! Where's the pennants? (*He rushes through the wall-line of the kitchen and out into the livingroom.*)

LINDA (*to* BIFF): Did you pack fresh underwear?

BIFF (*who has been limbering up*): I want to go!

BERNARD: Biff, I'm carrying your helmet, ain't I?

HAPPY: No, I'm carrying the helmet.

BERNARD: Oh, Biff, you promised me.

HAPPY: I'm carrying the helmet.

BERNARD: How am I going to get in the locker room?

LINDA: Let him carry the shoulder guards. (*She puts her coat and hat on in the kitchen.*)

BERNARD: Can I, Biff? 'Cause I told everybody I'm going to be in the locker room.

HAPPY: In Ebbets Field it's the clubhouse.

BERNARD: I meant the clubhouse. Biff!

HAPPY: Biff!

BIFF   (*grandly, after a slight pause*): Let him carry the shoulder guards.

HAPPY   (*as he gives* BERNARD *the shoulder guards*): Stay close to us now.

WILLY *rushes in with the pennants.*

WILLY   (*handing them out*): Everybody wave when Biff comes out on the field. (HAPPY *and* BERNARD *run off.*) You set now, boy?

The music has died away.

BIFF: Ready to go, Pop. Every muscle is ready.

WILLY   (*at the edge of the apron*): You realize what this means?

BIFF: That's right, Pop.

WILLY   (*feeling* BIFF'S *muscles*): You're comin' home this afternoon captain of the All-Scholastic Championship Team of the City of New York.

BIFF: I got it, Pop. And remember, pal, when I take off my helmet, that touchdown is for you.

WILLY: Let's go! (*He is starting out, with his arm around* BIFF, *when* CHARLEY *enters, as of old, in knickers.*) I got no room for you, Charley.

CHARLEY: Room? For what?

WILLY: In the car.

CHARLEY: You goin' for a ride? I wanted to shoot some casino.

WILLY   (*furiously*): Casino! (*Incredulously*): Don't you realize what today is?

LINDA: Oh, he knows, Willy. He's just kidding you.

WILLY: That's nothing to kid about!

CHARLEY: No, Linda, what's goin' on?

LINDA: He's playing in Ebbets Field.

CHARLEY: Baseball in this weather?

WILLY: Don't talk to him. Come on, come on! (*He is pushing them out.*)

CHARLEY: Wait a minute, didn't you hear the news?

WILLY: What?

CHARLEY: Don't you listen to the radio? Ebbets Field just blew up.

WILLY: You go to hell! (CHARLEY *laughs. Pushing them out.*) Come on, come on! We're late.

CHARLEY   (*as they go*): Knock a homer, Biff, knock a homer!

WILLY   (*the last to leave, turning to* CHARLEY): I don't think that was funny, Charley. This is the greatest day of his life.

CHARLEY: Willy, when are you going to grow up?

WILLY: Yeah, heh? When this game is over, Charley, you'll be laughing out of the other side of your face. They'll be calling him another Red Grange. Twenty-five thousand a year.

CHARLEY   (*kidding*): Is that so?

WILLY: Yeah, that's so.

CHARLEY: Well, then, I'm sorry, Willy. But tell me something.

WILLY: What?

CHARLEY: Who is Red Grange?

WILLY: Put up your hands. Goddam you, put up your hands!

CHARLEY, *chuckling, shakes his head and walks away, around the left corner of the stage.* WILLY *follows him. The music rises to a mocking frenzy.*

WILLY   (*offstage*): Who the hell do you think you are, better than everybody else? You don't know everything, you big, ignorant, stupid . . . Put up your hands!

Light rises, on the right side of the forestage, on a small table in the reception room of CHARLEY'S *office. Traffic sounds are heard.* BERNARD, *now mature, sits whistling to himself. A pair of tennis rackets and an overnight bag are on the floor beside him.*

WILLY   (*offstage*): What are you walking away for? Don't walk away! If you're going to say something say it to my face! I know you laugh at me behind my back. You'll laugh out of the other side of your goddam face after this game. Touchdown! Touchdown! Eighty thousand people! Touchdown! Right between the goal posts.

BERNARD *is a quiet, earnest, but self-assured young man.* WILLY'S *voice is coming from right upstage now.* BERNARD *lowers his feet off the table and listens.* JENNY, *his father's secretary, enters.*

JENNY   (*distressed*): Say, Bernard, will you go out in the hall?

BERNARD: What is that noise? Who is it?

JENNY: Mr. Loman. He just got off the elevator.

BERNARD   (*getting up*): Who's he arguing with?

JENNY: Nobody. There's nobody with him. I can't deal with him any more, and your father gets all upset everytime he comes. I've got a lot of typing to do, and your father's waiting to sign it. Will you see him?

WILLY   (*entering*): Touchdown! Touch— (*He sees* JENNY.) Jenny, Jenny, good to see you. How're ya? Workin'? Or still honest?

JENNY: Fine. How've you been feeling?

WILLY: Not much any more, Jenny. Ha, ha! (*He is surprised to see the rackets.*)

BERNARD: Hello, Uncle Willy.

WILLY   (*almost shocked*): Bernard! Well, look who's here! (*He comes quickly, guiltily, to* BERNARD *and warmly shakes his hand.*)

BERNARD: How are you? Good to see you.

WILLY: What are you doing here?

BERNARD: Oh, just stopped by to see Pop. Get off my feet till my train leaves. I'm going to Washington in a few minutes.

WILLY: Is he in?

BERNARD: Yes, he's in his office with the accountant. Sit down.

WILLY   (*sitting down*): What're you going to do in Washington?

BERNARD: Oh, just a case I've got there, Willy.

WILLY: That so? (*indicating the rackets.*) You going to play tennis there?

BERNARD: I'm staying with a friend who's got a court.

WILLY: Don't say. His own tennis court. Must be fine people, I bet.

BERNARD: They are, very nice. Dad tells me Biff's in town.

WILLY   (*with a big smile*): Yeah, Biff's in. Working on a very big deal, Bernard.

BERNARD: What's Biff doing?

WILLY: Well, he's been doing very big things in the West. But he decided to establish himself here. Very big. We're having dinner. Did I hear your wife had a boy?

BERNARD: That's right. Our second.

WILLY: Two boys! What do you know!

BERNARD: What kind of a deal has Biff got?

WILLY: Well, Bill Oliver—very big sporting-goods man—he wants Biff very badly. Called him in from the West. Long distance, carte blanche, special deliveries. Your friends have their own private tennis court?

BERNARD: You still with the old firm, Willy?

WILLY   (*after a pause*): I'm—I'm overjoyed to see how you made the grade, Bernard, overjoyed. It's an encouraging thing to see a young man really—really— Looks very good for Biff—very— (*He breaks off, then.*) Bernard— (*He is so full of emotion, he breaks off again.*)

BERNARD: What is it, Willy?

WILLY   (*small and alone*): What—what's the secret?

BERNARD: What secret?

WILLY: How—how did you? Why didn't he ever catch on?

BERNARD: I wouldn't know that, Willy.

WILLY   (*confidentially, desperately*): You were his friend, his boyhood friend. There's something I don't understand about it. His life ended after that Ebbets Field game. From the age of seventeen nothing good ever happened to him.

BERNARD: He never trained himself for anything.

WILLY: But he did, he did. After high school he took so many correspondence courses. Radio mechanics; television; God knows what, and never made the slightest mark.

BERNARD   (*taking off his glasses*): Willy, do you want to talk candidly?

WILLY   (*rising, faces* BERNARD): I regard you as a very brilliant man, Bernard. I value your advice.

BERNARD: Oh, the hell with the advice, Willy. I couldn't advise you. There's just one thing I've always wanted to ask you. When he was supposed to graduate, and the math teacher flunked him—

WILLY: Oh, that son-of-a-bitch ruined his life.

BERNARD: Yeah, but, Willy, all he had to do was go to summer school and make up that subject.

WILLY: That's right, that's right.

BERNARD: Did you tell him not to go to summer school?

WILLY: Me? I begged him to go. I ordered him to go!

BERNARD: Then why wouldn't he go?

WILLY: Why? Why! Bernard, that question has been trailing me like a ghost for the last fifteen years. He flunked the subject, and laid down and died like a hammer hit him!

BERNARD: Take it easy, kid.

WILLY: Let me talk to you—I got nobody to talk to. Bernard, Bernard, was it my fault? Y'see? It keeps going around in my mind, maybe I did something to him. I got nothing to give him.

BERNARD: Don't take it so hard.

WILLY: Why did he lay down? What is the story there? You were his friend!

BERNARD: Willy, I remember, it was June, and our grades came out. And he'd flunked math.

WILLY: That son-of-a-bitch!

BERNARD: No, it wasn't right then. Biff just got very angry, I remember, and he was ready to enroll in summer school.

WILLY   (*surprised*): He was?

BERNARD: He wasn't beaten by it at all. But then, Willy, he disappeared from the block for almost a month. And I got the idea that he'd gone up to New England to see you. Did he have a talk with you then?

WILLY *stares in silence.*

BERNARD: Willy?

WILLY   (*with a strong edge of resentment in his voice*): Yeah, he came to Boston. What about it?

BERNARD: Well, just that when he came back—I'll never forget this, it always mystifies me. Because I'd thought so well of Biff, even though he'd always taken advantage of me. I loved him, Willy, y'know? And he came back after that month and took his sneakers—remember those sneakers with "University of Virginia" printed on them? He was so proud of those, wore them every day. And he took them down in the cellar, and burned them up in the furnace. We had a fist fight. It lasted at least half an hour. Just the two of us, punching each other down the cellar, and crying right through it. I've often thought of how strange it was that I knew he'd given up his life. What happened in Boston, Willy?

WILLY *looks at him as at an intruder.*

BERNARD: I just bring it up because you asked me.

WILLY   (*angrily*): Nothing. What do you mean, "What happened?" What's that got to do with anything?

BERNARD: Well, don't get sore.

WILLY: What are you trying to do, blame it on me? If a boy lays down is that my fault?

BERNARD: Now, Willy, don't get—

WILLY: Well, don't—don't talk to me that way! What does that mean, "What happened?"

CHARLEY *enters. He is in his vest, and he carries a bottle of bourbon.*

CHARLEY: Hey, you're going to miss that train. (*He waves the bottle.*)

BERNARD: Yeah, I'm going. (*He takes the bottle.*) Thanks, Pop. (*He picks up his rackets and bag.*) Good-by, Willy, and don't worry about it. You know, "If at first you don't succeed . . ."

WILLY: Yes, I believe in that.

BERNARD: But sometimes, Willy, it's better for a man just to walk away.

WILLY: Walk away?

BERNARD: That's right.

WILLY: But if you can't walk away?

BERNARD   (*after a slight pause*): I guess that's when it's tough. (*Extending his hand.*) Good-by, Willy.

WILLY   (*shaking* BERNARD's *hand*): Good-by, boy.

CHARLEY   (*an arm on* BERNARD's *shoulder*): How do you like this kid? Gonna argue a case in front of the Supreme Court.

BERNARD   (*protesting*): Pop!

WILLY   (*genuinely shocked, pained, and happy*): No! The Supreme Court!

BERNARD: I gotta run. 'By, Dad!

CHARLEY: Knock 'em dead, Bernard!

BERNARD *goes off.*

WILLY   (*as* CHARLEY *takes out his wallet*): The Supreme Court! And he didn't even mention it!

CHARLEY   (*counting out money on the desk*): He don't have to—he's gonna do it.

WILLY: And you never told him what to do, did you? You never took any interest in him.

CHARLEY: My salvation is that I never took any interest in anything. There's some money—fifty dollars. I got an accountant inside.

WILLY: Charley, look . . . (*With difficulty.*) I got my insurance to pay. If you can manage it—I need a hundred and ten dollars.

CHARLEY *doesn't reply for a moment; merely stops moving.*

WILLY: I'd draw it from my bank but Linda would know, and I . . .

CHARLEY: Sit down, Willy.

WILLY   (*moving toward the chair*): I'm keeping an account of everything, remember. I'll pay every penny back. (*He sits.*)

CHARLEY: Now listen to me, Willy.

WILLY: I want you to know I appreciate . . .

CHARLEY   (*sitting down on the table*): Willy, what're you doin'? What the hell is goin' on in your head?

WILLY: Why? I'm simply . . .

CHARLEY: I offered you a job. You can make fifty dollars a week. And I won't send you on the road.

WILLY: I've got a job.

CHARLEY: Without pay? What kind of a job is a job without pay? (*He rises.*) Now, look, kid, enough is enough. I'm no genius but I know when I'm being insulted.

WILLY: Insulted!

CHARLEY: Why don't you want to work for me?

WILLY: What's the matter with you? I've got a job.

CHARLEY: Then what're you walkin' in here every week for?

WILLY   (*getting up*): Well, if you don't want me to walk in here—

CHARLEY: I am offering you a job.

WILLY: I don't want your goddam job!

CHARLEY: When the hell are you going to grow up?

WILLY   (*furiously*): You big ignoramus, if you say that to me again I'll rap you one! I don't care how big you are! (*He's ready to fight.*)

Pause.

CHARLEY   (*kindly, going to him*): How much do you need, Willy?

WILLY: Charley, I'm strapped. I'm strapped. I don't know what to do. I was just fired.

CHARLEY: Howard fired you?

WILLY: That snotnose. Imagine that? I named him. I named him Howard.

CHARLEY: Willy, when're you gonna realize that them things don't mean anything? You named him Howard, but you can't sell that. The only thing you got in this world is what you can sell. And the funny thing is that you're a salesman, and you don't know that.

WILLY: I've always tried to think otherwise, I guess. I always felt that if a man was impressive, and well liked, that nothing—

CHARLEY: Why must everybody like you? Who liked J. P. Morgan? Was he impressive? In a Turkish bath he'd look like a butcher. But with his pockets on he was very well liked. Now listen, Willy, I know you don't like me, and nobody can say I'm in love with you, but I'll give you a job because—just for the hell of it, put it that way. Now what do you say?

WILLY: I—I just can't work for you, Charley.

CHARLEY: What're you, jealous of me?

WILLY: I can't work for you, that's all, don't ask me why.

CHARLEY   (*angered, takes out more bills*): You been jealous of me all your life, you damned fool! Here, pay your insurance. (*He puts the money in* WILLY'S *hand.*)

WILLY: I'm keeping strict accounts.

CHARLEY: I've got some work to do. Take care of yourself. And pay your insurance.

WILLY   (*moving to the right*): Funny, y'know? After all the highways, and the trains, and the appointments, and the years, you end up worth more dead than alive.

CHARLEY: Willy, nobody's worth nothin' dead. (*After a slight pause.*) Did you hear what I said?

WILLY *stands still, dreaming.*

CHARLEY: Willy!

WILLY: Apologize to Bernard for me when you see him. I didn't mean to argue with him. He's a fine boy. They're all fine boys, and they'll end up big— all of them. Someday they'll all play tennis together. Wish me luck, Charley. He saw Bill Oliver today.

CHARLEY: Good luck.

WILLY   (*on the verge of tears*): Charley, you're the only friend I got. Isn't that a remarkable thing? (*He goes out.*)

CHARLEY: Jesus!

CHARLEY *stares after him a moment and follows. All light blacks out. Suddenly raucous music is heard, and a red glow rises behind the screen at right.* STANLEY, *a young waiter, appears, carrying a table, followed by* HAPPY, *who is carrying two chairs.*

STANLEY   (*putting the table down*): That's all right, Mr. Loman, I can handle it myself. (*He turns and takes the chairs from* HAPPY *and places them at the table.*)

HAPPY   (*glancing around*): Oh, this is better.

STANLEY: Sure, in the front there you're in the middle of all kinds a noise. Whenever you got a party, Mr. Loman, you just tell me and I'll put you back here. Y'know, there's a lotta people they don't like it private, because when they go out they like to see a lotta action around them because they're sick and tired to stay in the house by theirself. But I know you, you ain't from Hackensack. You know what I mean?

HAPPY   (*sitting down*): So how's it coming, Stanley?

STANLEY: Ah, it's a dog's life. I only wish during the war they'd a took me in the Army. I coulda been dead by now.

HAPPY: My brother's back, Stanley.

STANLEY: Oh, he come back, heh? From the Far West.

HAPPY: Yeah, big cattle man, my brother, so treat him right. And my father's coming too.

STANLEY: Oh, your father too!

HAPPY: You got a couple of nice lobsters?

STANLEY: Hundred per cent, big.

HAPPY: I want them with the claws.

STANLEY: Don't worry, I don't give you no mice. (HAPPY *laughs.*) How about some wine? It'll put a head on the meal.

HAPPY: No. You remember, Stanley, that recipe I brought you from overseas? With the champagne in it?

STANLEY: Oh, yeah, sure. I still got it tacked up yet in the kitchen. But that'll have to cost a buck apiece anyways.

HAPPY: That's all right.

STANLEY: What'd you, hit a number or somethin'?

HAPPY: No, it's a little celebration. My brother is—I think he pulled off a big deal today. I think we're going into business together.

STANLEY: Great! That's the best for you. Because a family business, you know what I mean?—that's the best.

HAPPY: That's what I think.

STANLEY: 'Cause what's the difference? Somebody steals? It's in the family. Know what I mean? (*Sotto voce.*) Like this bartender here. The boss is goin' crazy what kinda leak he's got in the cash register. You put it in but it don't come out.

HAPPY   (*raising his head*): Sh!

STANLEY: What?

HAPPY: You notice I wasn't lookin' right or left, was I!

STANLEY: No.

HAPPY: And my eyes are closed.

STANLEY: So what's the—?

HAPPY: Strudel's comin'.

STANLEY   (*catching on, looks around*): Ah, no, there's no—

He breaks off as a furred, lavishly dressed GIRL *enters and sits at the next table. Both follow her with their eyes.*

STANLEY: Geez, how'd ya know?

HAPPY: I got radar or something. (*Staring directly at her profile.*) Oooooooo . . . Stanley.

STANLEY: I think that's for you, Mr. Loman.

HAPPY: Look at that mouth. Oh, God. And the binoculars.

STANLEY: Geez, you got a life, Mr. Loman.

HAPPY: Wait on her.

STANLEY   (*going to* THE GIRL'S *table*): Would you like a menu, ma'am?

GIRL: I'm expecting someone, but I'd like a—

HAPPY: Why don't you bring her—excuse me, miss, do you mind? I sell champagne, and I'd like you to try my brand. Bring her a champagne, Stanley.

GIRL: That's awfully nice of you.

HAPPY: Don't mention it. It's all company money. (*He laughs.*)

GIRL: That's a charming product to be selling, isn't it?

HAPPY: Oh, gets to be like everything else. Selling is selling, y'know.

GIRL: I suppose.

HAPPY: You don't happen to sell, do you?

GIRL: No, I don't sell.

HAPPY: Would you object to a compliment from a stranger? You ought to be on a magazine cover.

GIRL   (*looking at him a little archly*): I have been.

STANLEY *comes in with a glass of champagne.*

HAPPY: What'd I say before, Stanley? You see? She's a cover girl.

STANLEY: Oh, I could see, I could see.

HAPPY   (*to* THE GIRL): What magazine?

GIRL: Oh, a lot of them. (*She takes the drink.*) Thank you.

HAPPY: You know what they say in France, don't you? "Champagne is the drink of the complexion"—Hya, Biff!

BIFF *has entered and sits with* HAPPY.

BIFF: Hello, kid. Sorry I'm late.

HAPPY: I just got here. Uh, Miss—?

GIRL: Forsythe.

HAPPY: Miss Forsythe, this is my brother.

BIFF: Is Dad here?

HAPPY: His name is Biff. You might've heard of him. Great football player.

GIRL: Really? What team?

HAPPY: Are you familiar with football?

GIRL: No, I'm afraid I'm not.

HAPPY: Biff is quarterback with the New York Giants.

GIRL: Well, that is nice, isn't it? (*She drinks.*)

HAPPY: Good health.

GIRL: I'm happy to meet you.

HAPPY: That's my name. Hap. It's really Harold, but at West Point they called me Happy.

GIRL   (*now really impressed*): Oh, I see. How do you do? (*She turns her profile.*)

BIFF: Isn't Dad coming?

HAPPY: You want her?

BIFF: Oh, I could never make that.

HAPPY: I remember the time that idea would never come into your head. Where's the old confidence, Biff?

BIFF: I just saw Oliver—

HAPPY: Wait a minute. I've got to see that old confidence again. Do you want her? She's on call.

BIFF: Oh, no. (*He turns to look at* THE GIRL.)

HAPPY: I'm telling you. Watch this. (*Turning to* THE GIRL.) Honey? (*She turns to him.*) Are you busy?

GIRL: Well, I am . . . but I could make a phone call.

HAPPY: Do that, will you, honey? And see if you can get a friend. We'll be here for a while. Biff is one of the greatest football players in the country.

GIRL   (*standing up*): Well, I'm certainly happy to meet you.

HAPPY: Come back soon.

GIRL: I'll try.

HAPPY: Don't try, honey, try hard.

THE GIRL *exits.* STANLEY *follows, shaking his head in bewildered admiration.*

HAPPY: Isn't that a shame now? A beautiful girl like that? That's why I can't get married. There's not a good woman in a thousand. New York is loaded with them, kid!

BIFF: Hap, look—

HAPPY: I told you she was on call!

BIFF   (*strangely unnerved*): Cut it out, will ya? I want to say something to you.

HAPPY: Did you see Oliver?

BIFF: I saw him all right. Now look, I want to tell Dad a couple of things and I want you to help me.

HAPPY: What? Is he going to back you?

BIFF: Are you crazy? You're out of your goddam head, you know that?

HAPPY: Why? What happened?

BIFF   (*breathlessly*): I did a terrible thing today, Hap. It's been the strangest day I ever went through. I'm all numb, I swear.

HAPPY: You mean he wouldn't see you?

BIFF: Well, I waited six hours for him, see? All day. Kept sending my name in. Even tried to date his secretary so she'd get me to him, but no soap.

HAPPY: Because you're not showin' the old confidence, Biff. He remembered you, didn't he?

BIFF (*stopping* HAPPY *with a gesture*): Finally, about five o'clock, he comes out. Didn't remember who I was or anything. I felt like such an idiot, Hap.

HAPPY: Did you tell him my Florida idea?

BIFF: He walked away. I saw him for one minute. I got so mad I could've torn the walls down! How the hell did I ever get the idea I was a salesman there? I even believed myself that I'd been a salesman for him! And then he gave me one look and—I realized what a ridiculous lie my whole life has been! We've been talking in a dream for fifteen years. I was a shipping clerk.

HAPPY: What'd you do?

BIFF (*with great tension and wonder*): Well, he left, see. And the secretary went out. I was all alone in the waiting-room. I don't know what came over me, Hap. The next thing I know I'm in his office—paneled walls, everything. I can't explain it. I—Hap, I took his fountain pen.

HAPPY: Geez, did he catch you?

BIFF: I ran out. I ran down all eleven flights. I ran and ran and ran.

HAPPY: That was an awful dumb—what'd you do that for?

BIFF (*agonized*): I don't know, I just—wanted to take something, I don't know. You gotta help me, Hap. I'm gonna tell Pop.

HAPPY: You crazy? What for?

BIFF: Hap, he's got to understand that I'm not the man somebody lends that kind of money to. He thinks I've been spiting him all these years and it's eating him up.

HAPPY: That's just it. You tell him something nice.

BIFF: I can't.

HAPPY: Say you got a lunch date with Oliver tomorrow.

BIFF: So what do I do tomorrow?

HAPPY: You leave the house tomorrow and come back at night and say Oliver is thinking it over. And he thinks it over for a couple of weeks, and gradually it fades away and nobody's the worse.

BIFF: But it'll go on forever!

HAPPY: Dad is never so happy as when he's looking forward to something!

WILLY *enters.*

HAPPY: Hello, scout!

WILLY: Gee, I haven't been here in years!

STANLEY *has followed* WILLY *in and sets a chair for him.* STANLEY *starts off but* HAPPY *stops him.*

HAPPY: Stanley!

STANLEY *stands by, waiting for an order.*

BIFF (*going to* WILLY *with guilt, as to an invalid*): Sit down, Pop. You want a drink?

WILLY: Sure, I don't mind.

BIFF: Let's get a load on.

WILLY: You look worried.

BIFF: N-no. (*To* STANLEY.) Scotch all around. Make it doubles.

STANLEY: Doubles, right. (*He goes.*)

WILLY: You had a couple already, didn't you?

BIFF: Just a couple, yeah.

WILLY: Well, what happened, boy? (*Nodding affirmatively, with a smile.*) Everything go all right?

BIFF   (*takes a breath, then reaches out and grasps* WILLY'S *hand*): Pal . . . (*He is smiling bravely, and* WILLY *is smiling too.*) I had an experience today.

HAPPY: Terrific, Pop.

WILLY: That so? What happened?

BIFF   (*high, slightly alcoholic, above the earth*): I'm going to tell you everything from first to last. It's been a strange day. (*Silence. He looks around, composes himself as best he can, but his breath keeps breaking the rhythm of his voice.*) I had to wait quite a while for him, and—

WILLY: Oliver?

BIFF: Yeah, Oliver. All day, as a matter of cold fact. And a lot of—instances—facts, Pop, facts about my life came back to me. Who was it, Pop? Who ever said I was a salesman with Oliver?

WILLY: Well, you were.

BIFF: No, Dad, I was a shipping clerk.

WILLY: But you were practically—

BIFF   (*with determination*): Dad, I don't know who said it first, but I was never a salesman for Bill Oliver.

WILLY: What're you talking about?

BIFF: Let's hold on to the facts tonight, Pop. We're not going to get anywhere bullin' around. I was a shipping clerk.

WILLY   (*angrily*): All right, now listen to me—

BIFF: Why don't you let me finish?

WILLY: I'm not interested in stories about the past or any crap of that kind because the woods are burning, boys, you understand? There's a big blaze going on all around. I was fired today.

BIFF   (*shocked*): How could you be?

WILLY: I was fired, and I'm looking for a little good news to tell your mother, because the woman has waited and the woman has suffered. The gist of it is that I haven't got a story left in my head, Biff. So don't give me a lecture about facts and aspects. I am not interested. Now what've you got to say to me?

STANLEY *enters with three drinks. They wait until he leaves.*

WILLY: Did you see Oliver?

BIFF: Jesus, Dad!

WILLY: You mean you didn't go up there?

HAPPY: Sure he went up there.

BIFF: I did. I—saw him. How could they fire you?

WILLY   (*on the edge of his chair*): What kind of a welcome did he give you?

BIFF: He won't even let you work on commission?

WILLY: I'm out! (*Driving.*) So tell me, he gave you a warm welcome?

HAPPY: Sure, Pop, sure!

BIFF   (*driven*): Well, it was kind of—

WILLY: I was wondering if he'd remember you. (*To* HAPPY.) Imagine, man doesn't see him for ten, twelve years and gives him that kind of a welcome!

HAPPY: Damn right!

BIFF   (*trying to return to the offensive*): Pop, look—

WILLY: You know why he remembered you, don't you? Because you impressed him in those days.

BIFF: Let's talk quietly and get this down to the facts, huh?

WILLY   (*as though* BIFF *had been interrupting*): Well, what happened? It's great news, Biff. Did he take you into his office or'd you talk in the waitingroom?

BIFF: Well, he came in, see, and—

WILLY: (*with a big smile*): What'd he say? Betcha he threw his arm around you.

BIFF: Well, he kinda—

WILLY: He's a fine man. (*To* HAPPY.) Very hard man to see, y'know.

HAPPY   (*agreeing*): Oh, I know.

WILLY   (*to* BIFF): Is that where you had the drinks?

BIFF: Yeah, he gave me a couple of—no, no!

HAPPY   (*cutting in*): He told him my Florida idea.

WILLY: Don't interrupt. (*To* BIFF.) How'd he react to the Florida idea?

BIFF: Dad, will you give me a minute to explain?

WILLY: I've been waiting for you to explain since I sat down here! What happened? He took you into his office and what?

BIFF: Well—I talked. And—and he listened, see.

WILLY: Famous for the way he listens, y'know. What was his answer?

BIFF: His answer was— (*He breaks off, suddenly angry.*) Dad, you're not letting me tell you what I want to tell you!

WILLY   (*accusing, angered*): You didn't see him, did you?

BIFF: I did see him!

WILLY: What'd you insult him or something? You insulted him, didn't you?

BIFF: Listen, will you let me out of it, will you just let me out of it!

HAPPY: What the hell!

WILLY: Tell me what happened!

BIFF   (*to* HAPPY): I can't talk to him!

A single trumpet note jars the ear. The light of green leaves stains the house, which holds the air of night and a dream. YOUNG BERNARD *enters and knocks on the door of the house.*

YOUNG BERNARD   (*frantically*): Mrs. Loman, Mrs. Loman!

HAPPY: Tell him what happened!

BIFF   (*to* HAPPY): Shut up and leave me alone!

WILLY: No, no! You had to go and flunk math!

BIFF: What math? What're you talking about?

YOUNG BERNARD: Mrs. Loman, Mrs. Loman!

LINDA *appears in the house, as of old.*

WILLY   (*wildly*): Math, math, math!

BIFF: Take it easy, Pop!

YOUNG BERNARD: Mrs. Loman!

WILLY   (*furiously*): If you hadn't flunked you'd've been set by now!

BIFF: Now, look, I'm gonna tell you what happened, and you're going to listen to me.

YOUNG BERNARD: Mrs. Loman!

BIFF: I waited six hours—

HAPPY: What the hell are you saying?

BIFF: I kept sending in my name but he wouldn't see me. So finally he . . . (*He continues unheard as light fades low on the restaurant.*)

YOUNG BERNARD: Biff flunked math!

LINDA: No!

YOUNG BERNARD: Birnbaum flunked him! They won't graduate him!

LINDA: But they have to. He's gotta go to the university. Where is he? Biff! Biff!

YOUNG BERNARD: No, he left. He went to Grand Central.

LINDA: Grand— You mean he went to Boston!

YOUNG BERNARD: Is Uncle Willy in Boston?

LINDA: Oh, maybe Willy can talk to the teacher. Oh, the poor, poor boy!

Light on house area snaps out.

BIFF   (*at the table, now audible, holding up a gold fountain pen*): . . . so I'm washed up with Oliver, you understand? Are you listening to me?

WILLY   (*at a loss*): Yeah, sure. If you hadn't flunked—

BIFF: Flunked what? What're you talking about?

WILLY: Don't blame everything on me! I didn't flunk math—you did! What pen?

HAPPY: That was awful dumb, Biff, a pen like that is worth—

WILLY   (*seeing the pen for the first time*): You took Oliver's pen?

BIFF   (*weakening*): Dad, I just explained it to you.

WILLY: You stole Bill Oliver's fountain pen!

BIFF: I didn't exactly steal it! That's just what I've been explaining to you!

HAPPY: He had it in his hand and just then Oliver walked in, so he got nervous and stuck it in his pocket!

WILLY: My God, Biff!

BIFF: I never intended to do it, Dad!

OPERATOR'S voice: Standish Arms, good evening!

WILLY   (*shouting*): I'm not in my room!

BIFF   (*frightened*): Dad, what's the matter? (*He and* HAPPY *stand up.*)

OPERATOR: Ringing Mr. Loman for you!

WILLY: I'm not there, stop it!

BIFF   (*horrified, gets down on one knee before* WILLY): Dad, I'll make good, I'll make good. (WILLY *tries to get to his feet.* BIFF *holds him down.*) Sit down now.

WILLY: No, you're no good, you're no good for anything.

BIFF: I am, Dad, I'll find something else, you understand? Now don't worry about anything. (*He holds up* WILLY'S *face.*) Talk to me, Dad.

OPERATOR: Mr. Loman does not answer. Shall I page him?

WILLY   (*attempting to stand, as though to rush and silence the* OPERATOR): No, no, no!

HAPPY: He'll strike something, Pop.

WILLY: No, no . . .

BIFF   (*desperately, standing over* WILLY): Pop, listen! Listen to me! I'm telling you something good. Oliver talked to his partner about the Florida idea. You listening? He—he talked to his partner, and he came to me . . . I'm going to be all right, you hear? Dad, listen to me, he said it was just a question of the amount!

WILLY: Then you . . . got it?

HAPPY: He's gonna be terrific, Pop!

WILLY   (*trying to stand*): Then you got it, haven't you? You got it! You got it!

BIFF   (*agonized, holds* WILLY *down*): No, no. Look, Pop. I'm supposed to have lunch with them tomorrow. I'm just telling you this so you'll know that I can still make an impression, Pop. And I'll make good somewhere, but I can't go tomorrow, see?

WILLY: Why not? You simply—

BIFF: But the pen, Pop!

WILLY: You give it to him and tell him it was an oversight!

HAPPY: Sure, have lunch tomorrow!

BIFF: I can't say that—

WILLY: You were doing a crossword puzzle and accidentally used his pen!

BIFF: Listen, kid, I took those balls years ago, now I walk in with his fountain pen? That clinches it, don't you see? I can't face him like that! I'll try elsewhere.

PAGE'S VOICE: Paging Mr. Loman!

WILLY: Don't you want to be anything?

BIFF: Pop, how can I go back?

WILLY: You don't want to be anything, is that what's behind it?

BIFF   (*now angry at* WILLY *for not crediting his sympathy*): Don't take it that way! You think it was easy walking into that office after what I'd done to him? A team of horses couldn't have dragged me back to Bill Oliver!

WILLY: Then why'd you go?

BIFF: Why did I go? Why did I go? Look at you! Look at what's become of you!

Off left, THE WOMAN *laughs.*

WILLY: Biff, you're going to go to that lunch tomorrow, or—

BIFF: I can't go. I've got no appointment!

HAPPY: Biff, for . . . !

WILLY: Are you spiting me?

BIFF: Don't take it that way! Goddammit!

WILLY   (*strikes* BIFF *and falters away from the table*): You rotten little louse! Are you spiting me?

THE WOMAN: Someone's at the door, Willy!

BIFF: I'm no good, can't you see what I am?

HAPPY   (*separating them*): Hey, you're in a restaurant! Now cut it out, both of you! (THE girls *enter.*) Hello, girls, sit down.

THE WOMAN *laughs, off left.*

MISS FORSYTHE: I guess we might as well. This is Letta.

THE WOMAN: Willy, are you going to wake up?

BIFF (*ignoring* WILLY): How're ya, miss, sit down. What do you drink?

MISS FORSYTHE: Letta might not be able to stay long.

LETTA: I gotta get up very early tomorrow. I got jury duty. I'm so excited! Were you fellows ever on a jury?

BIFF: No, but I been in front of them! (THE GIRLS *laugh*.) This is my father.

LETTA: Isn't he cute? Sit down with us, Pop.

HAPPY: Sit him down, Biff!

BIFF (*going to him*): Come on, slugger, drink us under the table. To hell with it! Come on, sit down, pal.

On BIFF'S *last insistence,* WILLY *is about to sit.*

THE WOMAN   (*now urgently*): Willy, are you going to answer the door!

THE WOMAN'S *call pulls* WILLY *back. He starts right, befuddled.*

BIFF: Hey, where are you going?

WILLY: Open the door.

BIFF: The door?

WILLY: The washroom . . . the door . . . where's the door?

BIFF (*leading* WILLY *to the left*): Just go straight down.

WILLY *moves left.*

THE WOMAN: Willy, Willy, are you going to get up, get up, get up, get up?

WILLY *exits left.*

LETTA: I think it's sweet you bring your daddy along.

MISS FORSYTHE: Oh, he isn't really your father!

BIFF   (*at left, turning to her resentfully*): Miss Forsythe, you've just seen a prince walk by. A fine, troubled prince. A hard-working, unappreciated prince. A pal, you understand? A good companion. Always for his boys.

LETTA: That's so sweet.

HAPPY: Well, girls, what's the program? We're wasting time. Come on, Biff. Gather round. Where would you like to go?

BIFF: Why don't you do something for him?

HAPPY: Me!

BIFF: Don't you give a damn for him, Hap?

HAPPY: What're you talking about? I'm the one who—

BIFF: I sense it, you don't give a good goddam about him. (*He takes the rolled-up hose from his pocket and puts it on the table in front of* HAPPY.) Look what I found in the cellar, for Christ's sake. How can you bear to let it go on?

HAPPY: Me? Who goes away? Who runs off and—

BIFF: Yeah, but he doesn't mean anything to you. You could help him— I can't! Don't you understand what I'm talking about? He's going to kill himself, don't you know that?

HAPPY: Don't I know it! Me!

BIFF: Hap, help him! Jesus . . . help him . . . Help me, help me, I can't bear to look at his face! (*Ready to weep, he hurries out, up right.*)

HAPPY   (*starting after him*): Where are you going?

MISS FORSYTHE: What's he so mad about?

HAPPY: Come on, girls, we'll catch up with him.

MISS FORSYTHE   (*as* HAPPY *pushes her out*): Say, I don't like that temper of his!

HAPPY: He's just a little overstrung, he'll be all right!

WILLY   (*off left, as* THE WOMAN *laughs*): Don't answer! Don't answer!

LETTA: Don't you want to tell your father—

HAPPY: No, that's not my father. He's just a guy. Come on, we'll catch Biff, and, honey, we're going to paint this town! Stanley, where's the check! Hey, Stanley!

They exit. STANLEY *looks toward left.*

STANLEY   (*calling to* HAPPY *indignantly*): Mr. Loman! Mr. Loman!

STANLEY *picks up a chair and follows them off. Knocking is heard off left.* THE WOMAN *enters, laughing.* WILLY *follows her. She is in a black slip; he is buttoning his shirt. Raw, sensuous music accompanies their speech.*

WILLY: Will you stop laughing? Will you stop?

THE WOMAN: Aren't you going to answer the door? He'll wake the whole hotel.

WILLY: I'm not expecting anybody.

THE WOMAN: Whyn't you have another drink, honey, and stop being so damn self-centered?

WILLY: I'm so lonely.

THE WOMAN: You know you ruined me, Willy? From now on, whenever you come to the office, I'll see that you go right through to the buyers. No waiting at my desk any more, Willy. You ruined me.

WILLY: That's nice of you to say that.

THE WOMAN: Gee, you are self-centered! Why so sad? You are the saddest self-centeredest soul I ever did see-saw. (*She laughs. He kisses her.*) Come on inside, drummer boy. It's silly to be dressing in the middle of the night. (*As knocking is heard.*) Aren't you going to answer the door?

WILLY: They're knocking on the wrong door.

THE WOMAN: But I felt the knocking. And he heard us talking in here. Maybe the hotel's on fire!

WILLY   (*his terror rising*): It's a mistake.

THE WOMAN: Then tell him to go away!

WILLY: There's nobody there.

THE WOMAN: It's getting on my nerves, Willy. There's somebody standing out there and it's getting on my nerves!

WILLY   (*pushing her away from him*): All right, stay in the bathroom here, and don't come out. I think there's a law in Massachusetts about it, so don't come out. It may be that new room clerk. He looked very mean. So don't come out. It's a mistake, there's no fire.

The knocking is heard again. He takes a few steps away from her, and she vanishes into the wing. The light follows him, and now he is facing YOUNG BIFF, *who carries a suitcase.* BIFF *steps toward him. The music is gone.*

BIFF: Why didn't you answer?

WILLY: Biff! What are you doing in Boston?

BIFF: Why didn't you answer? I've been knocking for five minutes, I called you on the phone—

WILLY: I just heard you. I was in the bathroom and had the door shut. Did anything happen home?

BIFF: Dad—I let you down.

WILLY: What do you mean?

BIFF: Dad . . .

WILLY: Biffo, what's this about? (*Putting his arm around* BIFF.) Come on, let's go downstairs and get you a malted.

BIFF: Dad, I flunked math.

WILLY: Not for the term?

BIFF: The term. I haven't got enough credits to graduate.

WILLY: You mean to say Bernard wouldn't give you the answers?

BIFF: He did, he tried, but I only got a sixty-one.

WILLY: And they wouldn't give you four points?

BIFF: Birnbaum refused absolutely. I begged him, Pop, but he won't give me those points. You gotta talk to him before they close the school. Because if he saw the kind of man you are, and you just talked to him in your way, I'm sure he'd come through for me. The class came right before practice, see, and I didn't go enough. Would you talk to him? He'd like you, Pop. You know the way you could talk.

WILLY: You're on. We'll drive right back.

BIFF: Oh, Dad, good work! I'm sure he'll change it for you!

WILLY: Go downstairs and tell the clerk I'm checkin' out. Go right down.

BIFF: Yes, Sir! See, the reason he hates me, Pop—one day he was late for class so I got up at the blackboard and imitated him. I crossed my eyes and talked with a lithp.

WILLY   (*laughing*): You did? The kids like it?

BIFF: They nearly died laughing!

WILLY: Yeah? What'd you do?

BIFF: The thquare root of thixthy twee is . . . (WILLY *bursts out laughing;* BIFF *joins him.*) And in the middle of it he walked in!

WILLY *laughs and* THE WOMAN *joins in offstage.*

WILLY   (*without hesitating*): Hurry downstairs and—

BIFF: Somebody in there?

WILLY: No, that was next door.

THE WOMAN *laughs offstage.*

BIFF: Somebody got in your bathroom!

WILLY: No, it's the next room, there's a party—

THE WOMAN   (*enters, laughing. She lisps this*): Can I come in? There's something in the bathtub, Willy, and it's moving!

WILLY *looks at* BIFF, *who is staring open-mouthed and horrified at* THE WOMAN.

WILLY: Ah—you better go back to your room. They must be finished painting by now. They're painting her room so I let her take a shower here. Go back, go back . . . (*He pushes her.*)

THE WOMAN (*resisting*): But I've got to get dressed, Willy, I can't—

WILLY: Get out of here! Go back, go back . . . (*Suddenly striving for the ordinary.*) This is Miss Francis, Biff, she's a buyer. They're painting her room. Go back, Miss Francis, go back . . .

THE WOMAN: But my clothes, I can't go out naked in the hall!

WILLY (*pushing her offstage*): Get outa here! Go back, go back!

BIFF *slowly sits down on his suitcase as the argument continues offstage.*

THE WOMAN: Where's my stockings? You promised me stockings, Willy!

WILLY: I have no stockings here!

THE WOMAN: You had two boxes of size nine sheers for me, and I want them!

WILLY: Here, for God's sake, will you get outa here!

THE WOMAN (*enters holding a box of stockings*): I just hope there's nobody in the hall. That's all I hope. (*To* BIFF.) Are you football or baseball?

BIFF: Football.

THE WOMAN (*angry, humiliated*): That's me too. G'night. (*She snatches her clothes from* WILLY, *and walks out.*)

WILLY (*after a pause*): Well, better get going. I want to get to the school first thing in the morning. Get my suits out of the closet. I'll get my valise. (BIFF *doesn't move.*) What's the matter? (BIFF *remains motionless, tears falling.*) She's a buyer. Buys for J. H. Simmons. She lives down the hall—they're painting. You don't imagine— (*He breaks off. After a pause.*) Now listen, pal, she's just a buyer. She sees merchandise in her room and they have to keep it looking just so . . . (*Pause. Assuming command.*) All right, get my suits. (BIFF *doesn't move.*) Now stop crying and do as I say. I gave you an order. Biff, I gave you an order! Is that what you do when I give you an order? How dare you cry! (*Putting his arm around* BIFF.) Now look, Biff, when you grow up you'll understand about these things. You mustn't—you mustn't overemphasize a thing like this. I'll see Birnbaum first thing in the morning.

BIFF: Never mind.

WILLY (*getting down beside* BIFF): Never mind! He's going to give you those points. I'll see to it.

BIFF: He wouldn't listen to you.

WILLY: He certainly will listen to me. You need those points for the U. of Virginia.

BIFF: I'm not going there.

WILLY: Heh? If I can't get him to change that mark you'll make it up in summer school. You've got all summer to—

BIFF (*his weeping breaking from him*): Dad . . .

WILLY (*infected by it*): Oh, my boy . . .

BIFF: Dad . . .

WILLY: She's nothing to me, Biff. I was lonely, I was terribly lonely.

BIFF: You—you gave her Mama's stockings! (*His tears break through and he rises to go.*)

WILLY   (*grabbing for* BIFF): I gave you an order!

BIFF: Don't touch me, you—liar!

WILLY: Apologize for that!

BIFF: You fake! You phony little fake! You fake! (*Overcome, he turns quickly and weeping fully goes out with his suitcase.* WILLY *is left on the floor on his knees.*)

WILLY: I gave you an order! Biff, come back here or I'll beat you! Come back here! I'll whip you!

STANLEY *comes quickly in from the right and stands in front of* WILLY.

WILLY   (*shouts at* STANLEY): I gave you an order . . .

STANLEY: Hey, let's pick it up, pick it up, Mr. Loman. (*He helps* WILLY *to his feet.*) Your boys left with the chippies. They said they'll see you home.

A second waiter watches some distance away.

WILLY: But we were supposed to have dinner together.

Music is heard, WILLY'S *theme.*

STANLEY: Can you make it?

WILLY: I'll—sure, I can make it. (*Suddenly concerned about his clothes.*) Do I— I look all right?

STANLEY: Sure, you look all right. (*He flicks a speck off* WILLY'S *lapel.*)

WILLY: Here—here's a dollar.

STANLEY: Oh, your son paid me. It's all right.

WILLY   (*putting it in* STANLEY'S *hand*): No, take it. You're a good boy.

STANLEY: Oh, no, you don't have to . . .

WILLY: Here—here's some more, I don't need it any more. (*After a slight pause.*) Tell me—is there a seed store in the neighborhood?

STANLEY: Seeds? You mean like to plant?

As WILLY *turns,* STANLEY *slips the money back into his jacket pocket.*

WILLY: Yes. Carrots, peas . . .

STANLEY: Well, there's hardware stores on Sixth Avenue, but it may be too late now.

WILLY   (*anxiously*): Oh, I'd better hurry. I've got to get some seeds. (*He starts off to the right.*) I've got to get some seeds, right away. Nothing's planted. I don't have a thing in the ground.

WILLY *hurries out as the light goes down.* STANLEY *moves over to the right after him, watches him off. The other waiter has been staring at* WILLY.

STANLEY   (*to the waiter*): Well, whatta you looking at?

The waiter picks up the chairs and moves off right. STANLEY *takes the table and follows him. The light fades on this area. There is a long pause, the sound of the flute coming over. The light gradually rises on the kitchen, which is empty.* HAPPY *appears at the door of the house, followed by* BIFF. HAPPY *is carrying a large bunch of long-stemmed roses. He enters the kitchen, looks around for* LINDA. *Not seeing her, he turns to* BIFF, *who is just outside the house door, and makes a gesture with his hands, indicating "Not here, I guess." He looks into the livingroom and freezes. Inside,* LINDA, *unseen, is seated,* WILLY'S *coat on her lap. She rises ominously and quietly and moves toward* HAPPY, *who backs up into the kitchen, afraid.*

HAPPY: Hey, what're you doing up? (LINDA *says nothing but moves toward him implacably.*) Where's Pop? (*He keeps backing to the right, and now* LINDA *is in full view in the doorway to the livingroom.*) Is he sleeping?

LINDA: Where were you?

HAPPY   (*trying to laugh it off*): We met two girls, Mom, very fine types. Here, we brought you some flowers. (*Offering them to her.*) Put them in your room, Ma.

She knocks them to the floor at BIFF'S *feet. He has now come inside and closed the door behind him. She stares at* BIFF, *silent.*

HAPPY: Now what'd you do that for? Mom, I want you to have some flowers—

LINDA   (*cutting* HAPPY *off, violently to* BIFF): Don't you care whether he lives or dies?

HAPPY   (*going to the stairs*): Come upstairs, Biff.

BIFF   (*with a flare of disgust, to* HAPPY): Go away from me! (*To* LINDA.) What do you mean, lives or dies? Nobody's dying around here, pal.

LINDA: Get out of my sight! Get out of here!

BIFF: I wanna see the boss.

LINDA: You're not going near him!

BIFF: Where is he? (*He moves into the livingroom and* LINDA *follows.*)

LINDA   (*shouting after* BIFF): You invite him for dinner. He looks forward to it all day—(BIFF *appears in his parents' bedroom, looks around, and exits*)—and then you desert him there. There's no stranger you'd do that to!

HAPPY: Why? He had a swell time with us. Listen, when I—(LINDA *comes back into the kitchen*)—desert him I hope I don't outlive the day!

LINDA: Get out of here!

HAPPY: Now look, Mom . . .

LINDA: Did you have to go to women tonight? You and your lousy rotten whores!

BIFF re-enters the kitchen.

HAPPY: Mom, all we did was follow Biff around trying to cheer him up! (*To* BIFF.) Boy, what a night you gave me!

LINDA: Get out of here, both of you, and don't come back! I don't want you tormenting him any more. Go on now, get your things together! (*To* BIFF.) You can sleep in his apartment. (*She starts to pick up the flowers and stops herself.*) Pick up this stuff, I'm not your maid any more. Pick it up, you bum, you!

HAPPY turns his back to her in refusal. BIFF slowly moves over and gets down on his knees, picking up the flowers.

LINDA: You're a pair of animals! Not one, not another living soul would have had the cruelty to walk out on that man in a restaurant!

BIFF   (*not looking at her*): Is that what he said?

LINDA: He didn't have to say anything. He was so humiliated he nearly limped when he came in.

HAPPY: But, Mom, he had a great time with us—

BIFF   (*cutting him off violently*): Shut up!

Without another word, HAPPY *goes upstairs.*

LINDA: You! You didn't even go in to see if he was all right!

BIFF   (*still on the floor in front of* LINDA, *the flowers in his hand; with selfloathing*): No. Didn't. Didn't do a damned thing. How do you like that, heh? Left him babbling in a toilet.

LINDA: You louse. You . . .

BIFF: Now you hit it on the nose! (*He gets up, throws the flowers in the waste-basket.*) The scum of the earth, and you're looking at him!

LINDA: Get out of here!

BIFF: I gotta talk to the boss, Mom. Where is he?

LINDA: You're not going near him. Get out of this house!

BIFF   (*with absolute assurance, determination*): No. We're gonna have an abrupt conversation, him and me.

LINDA: You're not talking to him!

Hammering is heard from outside the house, off right. BIFF *turns toward the noise.*

LINDA   (*suddenly pleading*): Will you please leave him alone?

BIFF: What's he doing out there?

LINDA: He's planting the garden!

BIFF   (*quietly*): Now? Oh, my God!

BIFF *moves outside,* LINDA *following. The light dies down on them and comes up on the center of the apron as* WILLY *walks into it. He is carrying a flashlight, a hoe and a handful of seed packets. He raps the top of the hoe sharply to fix it firmly, and then moves to the left, measuring off the distance with his foot. He holds the flashlight to look at the seed packets, reading off the instructions. He is in the blue of night.*

WILLY: Carrots . . . quarter-inch apart. Rows . . . one-foot rows. (*He measures it off.*) One foot. (*He puts down a package and measures off.*) Beets. (*He puts down another package and measures again.*) Lettuce. (*He reads the package, puts it down.*) One foot— (*He breaks off as* BEN *appears at the right and moves slowly down to him.*) What a proposition, ts, ts. Terrific, terrific. 'Cause she's suffered, Ben, the woman has suffered. You understand me? A man can't go out the way he came in, Ben, a man has got to add up to something. You can't, you can't— (BEN *moves toward him as though to interrupt.*) You gotta consider, now. Don't answer so quick. Remember, it's a guaranteed twenty-thousand-dollar proposition. Now look, Ben, I want you to go through the ins and outs of this thing with me. I've got nobody to talk to, Ben, and the woman has suffered, you hear me?

BEN   (*standing still, considering*): What's the proposition?

WILLY: It's twenty thousand dollars on the barrelhead. Guaranteed, gilt-edged, you understand?

BEN: You don't want to make a fool of yourself. They might not honor the policy.

WILLY: How can they dare refuse? Didn't I work like a coolie to meet every premium on the nose? And now they don't pay off? Impossible!

BEN: It's called a cowardly thing, William.

WILLY: Why? Does it take more guts to stand here the rest of my life ringing up a zero?

BEN   (*yielding*): That's a point, William. (*He moves, thinking, turns.*) And twenty thousand—that is something one can feel with the hand, it is there.

WILLY   (*now assured, with rising power*): Oh, Ben, that's the whole beauty of it! I see it like a diamond, shining in the dark, hard and rough, that I can pick up and touch in my hand. Not like—like an appointment! This would not be another damned-fool appointment, Ben, and it changes all the aspects. Because he thinks I'm nothing, see, and so he spites me. But the funeral— (*Straightening up.*) Ben, that funeral will be massive! They'll come from Maine, Massachusetts, Vermont, New Hampshire! All the old-timers with the strange license plates—that boy will be thunder-struck, Ben, because he never realized—I am known! Rhode Island, New York, New Jersey—I am known, Ben, and he'll see it with his eyes once and for all. He'll see what I am, Ben! He's in for a shock, that boy!

BEN   (*coming down to the edge of the garden*): He'll call you a coward.

WILLY   (*suddenly fearful*): No, that would be terrible.

BEN: Yes. And a damned fool.

WILLY: No, no, he mustn't, I won't have that! (*He is broken and desperate.*)

BEN: He'll hate you, William.

The gay music of the boys is heard.

WILLY: Oh, Ben, how do we get back to all the great times? Used to be so full of light, and comradeship, the sleigh-riding in winter, and the ruddiness on his cheeks. And always some kind of good news coming up, always something nice coming up ahead. And never even let me carry the valises in the house, and simonizing, simonizing that little red car! Why, why can't I give him something and not have him hate me?

BEN: Let me think about it. (*He glances at his watch.*) I still have a little time. Remarkable proposition, but you've got to be sure you're not making a fool of yourself.

BEN *drifts off upstage and goes out of sight.* BIFF *comes down from the left.*

WILLY   (*suddenly conscious of* BIFF, *turns and looks up at him, then begins picking up the packages of seeds in confusion*): Where the hell is that seed? (*Indignantly.*) You can't see nothing out here! They boxed in the whole goddam neighborhood!

BIFF: There are people all around here. Don't you realize that?

WILLY: I'm busy. Don't bother me.

BIFF   (*taking the hoe from* WILLY): I'm saying good-by to you, Pop. (WILLY *looks at him, silent, unable to move.*) I'm not coming back any more.

WILLY: You're not going to see Oliver tomorrow?

BIFF: I've got no appointment, Dad.

WILLY: He put his arm around you, and you've got no appointment?

BIFF: Pop, get this now, will you? Everytime I've left it's been a fight that sent me out of here. Today I realized something about myself and I tried to explain it to you and I—I think I'm just not smart enough to make any sense out of it for you. To hell with whose fault it is or anything like that. (*He takes* WILLY'S *arm.*) Let's just wrap it up, heh? Come on in, we'll tell Mom. (*He gently tries to pull* WILLY *to the left.*)

WILLY   (*frozen, immobile, with guilt in his voice*): No, I don't want to see her.

BIFF: Come on! (*He pulls again, and* WILLY *tries to pull away.*)

WILLY   (*highly nervous*): No, no, I don't want to see her.

BIFF   (*tries to look into* WILLY'S *face, as if to find the answer there*): Why don't you want to see her?

WILLY   (*more harshly now*): Don't bother me, will you?

BIFF: What do you mean, you don't want to see her? You don't want them calling you yellow, do you? This isn't your fault; it's me, I'm a bum. Now come inside! (WILLY *strains to get away.*) Did you hear what I said to you?

WILLY *pulls away and quickly goes by himself into the house.* BIFF *follows.*

LINDA   (*to* WILLY): Did you plant, dear?

BIFF   (*at the door, to* LINDA): All right, we had it out. I'm going and I'm not writing any more.

LINDA   (*going to* WILLY *in the kitchen*): I think that's the best way, dear. 'Cause there's no use drawing it out, you'll just never get along.

WILLY *doesn't respond.*

BIFF: People ask where I am and what I'm doing, you don't know, and you don't care. That way it'll be off your mind and you can start brightening up again. All right? That clears it, doesn't it? (WILLY *is silent, and* BIFF *goes to him.*) You gonna wish me luck, scout? (*He extends his hand.*) What do you say?

LINDA: Shake his hand, Willy.

WILLY   (*turning to her, seething with hurt*): There's no necessity to mention the pen at all, y'know.

BIFF   (*gently*): I've got no appointment, Dad.

WILLY   (*erupting fiercely*): He put his arm around . . . ?

BIFF: Dad, you're never going to see what I am, so what's the use of arguing? If I strike oil I'll send you a check. Meantime forget I'm alive.

WILLY   (*to* LINDA): Spite, see?

BIFF: Shake hands, Dad.

WILLY: Not my hand.

BIFF: I was hoping not to go this way.

WILLY: Well, this is the way you're going. Good-by.

BIFF *looks at him a moment, then turns sharply and goes to the stairs.*

WILLY   (*stops him with*): May you rot in hell if you leave this house!

BIFF   (*turning*): Exactly what is it that you want from me?

WILLY: I want you to know, on the train, in the mountains, in the valleys, wherever you go, that you cut down your life for spite!

BIFF: No, no.

WILLY: Spite, spite, is the word of your undoing! And when you're down and out, remember what did it. When you're rotting somewhere beside the railroad tracks, remember, and don't you dare blame it on me!

BIFF: I'm not blaming it on you!

WILLY: I won't take the rap for this, you hear?

HAPPY *comes down the stairs and stands on the bottom step, watching.*

BIFF: That's just what I'm telling you!

WILLY   (*sinking into a chair at the table, with full accusation*): You're trying to put a knife in me—don't think I don't know what you're doing!

BIFF: All right, phony! Then let's lay it on the line. (*He whips the rubber tube out of his pocket and puts it on the table.*)

HAPPY: You crazy—

LINDA: Biff! (*She moves to grab the hose, but* BIFF *holds it down with his hand.*)

BIFF: Leave it there! Don't move it!

WILLY   (*not looking at it*): What is that?

BIFF: You know goddam well what that is.

WILLY   (*caged, wanting to escape*): I never saw that.

BIFF: You saw it. The mice didn't bring it into the cellar! What is this supposed to do, make a hero out of you? This supposed to make me sorry for you?

WILLY: Never heard of it.

BIFF: There'll be no pity for you, you hear it? No pity!

WILLY   (*to* LINDA): You hear the spite!

BIFF: No, you're going to hear the truth—what you are and what I am!

LINDA: Stop it!

WILLY: Spite!

HAPPY   (*coming down toward* BIFF): You cut it now!

BIFF   (*to* HAPPY): The man don't know who we are! The man is gonna know! (*To* WILLY.) We never told the truth for ten minutes in this house!

HAPPY: We always told the truth!

BIFF   (*turning on him*): You big blow, are you the assistant buyer? You're one of the two assistants to the assistant, aren't you?

HAPPY: Well, I'm practically—

BIFF: You're practically full of it! We all are! And I'm through with it. (*To* WILLY.) Now hear this, Willy, this is me.

WILLY: I know you!

BIFF: You know why I had no address for three months? I stole a suit in Kansas City and I was in jail. (*To* LINDA, *who is sobbing.*) Stop crying. I'm through with it.

LINDA *turns away from them, her hands covering her face.*

WILLY: I suppose that's my fault!

BIFF: I stole myself out of every good job since high school!

WILLY: And whose fault is that?

BIFF: And I never got anywhere because you blew me so full of hot air I could never stand taking orders from anybody! That's whose fault it is!

WILLY: I hear that!

LINDA: Don't, Biff!

BIFF: It's goddam time you heard that! I had to be boss big shot in two weeks, and I'm through with it!

WILLY: Then hang yourself! For spite, hang yourself!

BIFF: No! Nobody's hanging himself, Willy! I ran down eleven flights with a pen in my hand today. And suddenly I stopped, you hear me? And in the middle of that office building, do you hear this? I stopped in the middle of that building and I saw—the sky. I saw the things that I love in this world. The work and the food and time to sit and smoke. And I looked at the pen and said to myself, what the hell am I grabbing this for? Why am I trying to become what I don't want to be? What am I doing in an office, making a contemptuous, begging fool of myself, when all I want is out there, waiting for me the minute I say I know who I am! Why can't I say that, Willy? (*He tries to make* WILLY *face him, but* WILLY *pulls away and moves to the left.*)

WILLY   (*with hatred, threateningly*): The door of your life is wide open!

BIFF: Pop! I'm a dime a dozen, and so are you!

WILLY   (*turning on him now in an uncontrolled outburst*): I am not a dime a dozen! I am Willy Loman, and you are Biff Loman!

BIFF *starts for* WILLY, *but is blocked by* HAPPY. *In his fury,* BIFF *seems on the verge of attacking his father.*

BIFF: I am not a leader of men, Willy, and neither are you. You were never anything but a hard-working drummer who landed in the ash can like all the rest of them! I'm one dollar an hour, Willy! I tried seven states and couldn't raise it. A buck an hour! Do you gather my meaning? I'm not bringing home any prizes any more, and you're going to stop waiting for me to bring them home!

WILLY   (*directly to* BIFF): You vengeful, spiteful mutt!

BIFF *breaks from* HAPPY. WILLY, *in fright, starts up the stairs.* BIFF *grabs him.*

BIFF   (*at the peak of his fury*): Pop, I'm nothing! I'm nothing, Pop. Can't you understand that? There's no spite in it any more. I'm just what I am, that's all.

BIFF'S *fury has spent itself, and he breaks down, sobbing, holding on to* WILLY, *who dumbly fumbles for* BIFF'S *face.*

WILLY   (*astonished*): What're you doing? What're you doing? (*To* LINDA.) Why is he crying?

BIFF   (*crying, broken*): Will you let me go, for Christ's sake? Will you take that phony dream and burn it before something happens? (*Struggling to contain himself, he pulls away and moves to the stairs.*) I'll go in the morning. Put him—put him to bed. (*Exhausted,* BIFF *moves up the stairs to his room.*)

WILLY   (*after a long pause, astonished, elevated*): Isn't that remarkable? Biff—he likes me!

LINDA: He loves you, Willy!

HAPPY   (*deeply moved*): Always did, Pop.

WILLY: Oh, Biff! (*Staring wildly.*) He cried! Cried to me. (*He is choking with his love, and now cries out his promise.*) That boy—that boy is going to be magnificent!

BEN *appears in the light just outside the kitchen.*

BEN: Yes, outstanding, with twenty thousand behind him.

LINDA   (*sensing the racing of his mind, fearfully, carefully*): Now come to bed, Willy. It's all settled now.

WILLY   (*finding it difficult not to rush out of the house*): Yes, we'll sleep. Come on. Go to sleep, Hap.

BEN: And it does take a great kind of man to crack the jungle.

In accents of dread, BEN'S *idyllic music starts up.*

HAPPY   (*his arm around* LINDA): I'm getting married, Pop, don't forget it. I'm changing everything. I'm gonna run that department before the year is up. You'll see, Mom. (*He kisses her.*)

BEN: The jungle is dark but full of diamonds, Willy.

WILLY *turns, moves, listening to* BEN.

LINDA: Be good. You're both good boys, just act that way, that's all.

HAPPY: 'Night, Pop. (*He goes upstairs.*)

LINDA   (*to* WILLY): Come, dear.

BEN   (*with greater force*): One must go in to fetch a diamond out.

WILLY   (*to* LINDA, *as he moves slowly along the edge of the kitchen, toward the door*): I just want to get settled down, Linda. Let me sit alone for a little.

LINDA   (*almost uttering her fear*): I want you upstairs.

WILLY   (*taking her in his arms*): In a few minutes, Linda. I couldn't sleep right now. Go on, you look awful tired. (*He kisses her.*)

BEN: Not like an appointment at all. A diamond is rough and hard to the touch.

WILLY: Go on now. I'll be right up.

LINDA: I think this is the only way, Willy.

WILLY: Sure, it's the best thing.

BEN: Best thing!

WILLY: The only way. Everything is gonna be—go on, kid, get to bed. You look so tired.

LINDA: Come right up.

WILLY: Two minutes.

LINDA *goes into the livingroom, then reappears in her bedroom.* WILLY *moves just outside the kitchen door.*

WILLY: Loves me. (Wonderingly.) Always loved me. Isn't that a remarkable thing? Ben, he'll worship me for it!

BEN   (*with promise*): It's dark there, but full of diamonds.

WILLY: Can you imagine that magnificence with twenty thousand dollars in his pocket?

LINDA   (*calling from her room*): Willy! Come up!

WILLY   (*calling from the kitchen*): Yes! Yes. Coming! It's very smart, you realize that, don't you, sweetheart? Even Ben sees it. I gotta go, baby. 'By! By! (*Going over to* BEN, *almost dancing.*) Imagine? When the mail comes he'll be ahead of Bernard again!

BEN: A perfect proposition all around.

WILLY: Did you see how he cried to me? Oh, if I could kiss him, Ben!

BEN: Time, William, time!

WILLY: Oh, Ben, I always knew one way or another we were gonna make it, Biff and I!

BEN   (*looking at his watch*): The boat. We'll be late. (*He moves slowly off into the darkness.*)

WILLY   (*elegiacally, turning to the house*): Now when you kick off, boy, I want a seventy-yard boot, and get right down the field under the ball, and when you hit, hit low and hit hard, because it's important, boy. (*He swings around and faces the audience.*) There's all kinds of important people in the stands, and the first thing you know . . . (*Suddenly realizing he is alone.*) Ben! Ben, where do I . . . ? (*He makes a sudden movement of search.*) Ben, how do I . . . ?

LINDA   (*calling*): Willy, you coming up?

WILLY   (*uttering a gasp of fear, whirling about as if to quiet her*): Sh! (*He turns around as if to find his way; sounds, faces, voices, seem to be swarming in upon him and he flicks at them, crying.*) Sh! Sh! (*Suddenly music, faint and high, stops him. It rises in intensity, almost to an unbearable scream. He goes up and down on his toes, and rushes off around the house.*) Shhh!

LINDA: Willy?

There is no answer. LINDA *waits.* BIFF *gets up off his bed. He is still in his clothes.* HAPPY *sits up.* BIFF *stands listening.*

LINDA   (*with real fear*): Willy, answer me! Willy!

There is the sound of a car starting and moving away at full speed.

LINDA: No!

BIFF   (*rushing down the stairs*): Pop!

As the car speeds off, the music crashes down in a frenzy of sound, which becomes the soft pulsation of a single cello string. BIFF *slowly returns to his bedroom. He and* HAPPY *gravely don their jackets.* LINDA *slowly walks out of her room. The music has developed into a dead march. The leaves of day are appearing over everything.* CHARLEY *and* BERNARD, *somberly dressed, appear and knock on the kitchen door.* BIFF *and* HAPPY *slowly descend the stairs to the kitchen as* CHARLEY *and* BERNARD *enter. All stop a moment when* LINDA, *in clothes of mourning, bearing a little bunch of roses, comes through the draped doorway into the kitchen. She goes to* CHARLEY *and takes his arm. Now all move toward the audience, through the wall-line of the kitchen. At the limit of the apron,* LINDA *lays down the flowers, kneels, and sits back on her heels. All stare down at the grave.*

REQUIEM

CHARLEY: It's getting dark, Linda.

LINDA *doesn't react. She stares at the grave.*

BIFF: How about it, Mom? Better get some rest, heh? They'll be closing the gate soon.

LINDA *makes no move. Pause.*

HAPPY   (*deeply angered*): He had no right to do that! There was no necessity for it. We would've helped him.

CHARLEY   (*grunting*): Hmmm.

BIFF: Come along, Mom.

LINDA: Why didn't anybody come?

CHARLEY: It was a very nice funeral.

LINDA: But where are all the people he knew? Maybe they blame him.

CHARLEY: Naa. It's a rough world, Linda. They wouldn't blame him.

LINDA: I can't understand it. At this time especially. First time in thirty-five years we were just about free and clear. He only needed a little salary. He was even finished with the dentist.

CHARLEY: No man only needs a little salary.

LINDA: I can't understand it.

BIFF: There were a lot of nice days. When he'd come home from a trip; or on Sundays, making the stoop; finishing the cellar; putting on the new porch; when he built the extra bathroom; and put up the garage. You know something, Charley, there's more of him in that front stoop than in all the sales he ever made.

CHARLEY: Yeah. He was a happy man with a batch of cement.

LINDA: He was so wonderful with his hands.

BIFF: He had the wrong dreams. All, all, wrong.

HAPPY   (*almost ready to fight* BIFF): Don't say that!

BIFF: He never knew who he was.

CHARLEY   (*stopping* HAPPY'S *movement and reply. To* BIFF.) Nobody dast blame this man. You don't understand: Willy was a salesman. And for a salesman, there is no rock bottom to the life. He don't put a bolt to a nut, he don't tell you the law or give you medicine. He's a man out there in the blue, riding on a smile and a shoeshine. And when they start not smiling back—that's an earthquake. And then you get yourself a couple of spots on your hat, and you're finished. Nobody dast blame this man. A salesman is got to dream, boy. It comes with the territory.

BIFF: Charley, the man didn't know who he was.

HAPPY   (*infuriated*): Don't say that!

BIFF: Why don't you come with me, Happy?

HAPPY: I'm not licked that easily. I'm staying right in this city, and I'm gonna beat this racket! (*He looks at* BIFF, *his chin set.*) The Loman Brothers!

BIFF: I know who I am, kid.

HAPPY: All right, boy. I'm gonna show you and everybody else that Willy Loman did not die in vain. He had a good dream. It's the only dream you can have—to come out number-one man. He fought it out here, and this is where I'm gonna win it for him.

BIFF   (*with a hopeless glance at* HAPPY, *bends toward his mother*): Let's go, Mom.

LINDA: I'll be with you in a minute. Go on, Charley. (*He hesitates.*) I want to, just for a minute. I never had a chance to say good-by.

CHARLEY *moves away, followed by* HAPPY. BIFF *remains a slight distance up and left of* LINDA. *She sits there, summoning herself. The flute begins, not far away, playing behind her speech.*

LINDA: Forgive me, dear. I can't cry. I don't know what it is, but I can't cry. I don't understand it. Why did you ever do that? Help me, Willy, I can't cry. It seems to me that you're just on another trip. I keep expecting you. Willy, dear, I can't cry. Why did you do it? I search and search and I search, and I can't understand it, Willy. I made the last payment on the house today. Today, dear. And there'll be nobody home. (*A sob rises in her throat.*) We're free and clear. (*Sobbing more fully, released.*) We're free. (BIFF *comes slowly toward her.*) We're free . . . We're free . . .

BIFF *lifts her to her feet and moves out up right with her in his arms.* LINDA *sobs quietly.* BERNARD *and* CHARLEY *come together and follow them, followed by* HAPPY. *Only the music of the flute is left on the darkening stage as over the house the hard towers of the apartment buildings rise into sharp focus, and—*

Curtain

(1949)

QUESTIONS

1. Comment on the significance of the title. What kinds of deaths might be referred to? Explain.
2. What significance do you attach to the names of the characters?
3. Describe Biff's relationship with his father and with his brother, Happy.
4. How does Miller characterize Willy? Which of his characteristics are highlighted? What kind of man is he? To what extent and by what means is he considered a failure? Does anyone consider him a success? Why or why not?
5. What roles do women have in this play? Comment on Willy's relationships with them. Consider Biff's relationship with women as well.
6. Identify two minor characters and explain their significance for the play's action and theme(s).
7. Describe Miller's staging of the play. Consider his use of lighting and music, and the way he dramatizes dreams and memories.
8. What is typically "American" about Miller's play? What cultural attitudes and values displayed by the characters provide it with an American tone?
9. Published in 1947, *Death of a Salesman* has been among the most popular plays of the American theater. What accounts for the play's perennial appeal?
10. Read Miller's essay "Tragedy and the Common Man" and comment on the degree to which his remarks illuminate his intentions and define his achievement in the play.

LORRAINE HANSBERRY

[1930–1965]

Lorraine Hansberry was born and raised in Chicago. She studied painting at the Chicago Art Institute and the University of Wisconsin before turning to writing following a move to New York. *A Raisin in the Sun* (1959), her first Broadway play, was quickly made into a movie, starring Sidney Poitier and Claudia

McNeil. Although the play reflects Hansberry's deep concern with civil rights, it transcends its racial and urban focus. Like Arthur Miller's *Death of a Salesman*, *A Raisin in the Sun* dramatizes the powerful attractions of the American dream of success. Like Miller's play also, Hansberry's is largely concerned with family life.

LORRAINE HANSBERRY

A Raisin in the Sun

What happens to a dream deferred?
Does it dry up
Like a raisin in the sun?
Or fester like a sore—
And then run?
Does it stink like rotten meat?
Or crust and sugar over—
Like a syrupy sweet?

Maybe it just sags
Like a heavy load.

Or does it explode?

—Langston Hughes

CHARACTERS

(In order of appearance)

RUTH YOUNGER
TRAVIS YOUNGER
WALTER LEE YOUNGER (BROTHER)
BENEATHA YOUNGER
LENA YOUNGER (MAMA)
JOSEPH ASAGAI
GEORGE MURCHISON
KARL LINDNER
BOBO
MOVING MEN

The action of the play is set in Chicago's Southside, sometime between World War II and the present.

Act I

Scene One: Friday morning.

Scene Two: The following morning.

Act II

Scene One: Later, the same day.

Scene Two: Friday night, a few weeks later.

Scene Three: Moving day, one week later.

Act III

An hour later.

ACT I

Scene I

 The YOUNGER *living room would be a comfortable and well-ordered room if it were not for a number of indestructible contradictions to this state of being. Its furnishings are typical and undistinguished and their primary feature now is that they have clearly had to accommodate the living of too many people for too many years—and they are tired. Still, we can see that at some time, a time probably no longer remembered by the family (except perhaps for* MAMA*), the furnishings of this room were actually selected with care and love and even hope—and brought to this apartment and arranged with taste and pride.*

 That was a long time ago. Now the once loved pattern of the couch upholstery has to fight to show itself from under acres of crocheted doilies and couch covers which have themselves finally come to be more important than the upholstery. And here a table or a chair has been moved to disguise the worn places in the carpet; but the carpet has fought back by showing its weariness, with depressing uniformity, elsewhere on its surface.

 Weariness has, in fact, won in this room. Everything has been polished, washed, sat on, used, scrubbed too often. All pretenses but living itself have long since vanished from the very atmosphere of this room.

 Moreover, a section of this room, for it is not really a room unto itself, though the landlord's lease would make it seem so, slopes backward to provide a small kitchen area, where the family prepares the meals that are eaten in the living room proper, which must also serve as dining room. The single window that has been provided for these "two" rooms is located in this kitchen area. The sole natural light the family may enjoy in the course of a day is only that which fights its way through this little window.

 At left, a door leads to a bedroom which is shared by MAMA *and her daughter,* BENEATHA. *At right, opposite, is a second room (which in the beginning of the life of this apartment was probably a breakfast room) which serves as a bedroom for* WALTER *and his wife,* RUTH.

 Time: Sometime between World War II and the present.

 Place: Chicago's Southside.

 At Rise: It is morning dark in the living room. TRAVIS *is asleep on the make-down bed at center. An alarm clock sounds from within the bedroom at right, and presently* RUTH *enters from that room and closes the door behind her. She crosses sleepily toward the window. As she passes her sleeping son she reaches down and shakes him a little. At the window she raises the shade and a dusky Southside morning light comes in feebly. She fills a pot with water and puts it on to boil. She calls to the boy, between yawns, in a slightly muffled voice.*

RUTH *is about thirty. We can see that she was a pretty girl, even exceptionally so, but now it is apparent that life has been little that she expected, and disappointment has already begun to hang in her face. In a few years, before thirty-five even, she will be known among her people as a "settled woman."*

She crosses to her son and gives him a good, final, rousing shake.

RUTH: Come on now, boy, it's seven thirty! (*Her son sits up at last, in a stupor of sleepiness*) I say hurry up, Travis! You ain't the only person in the world got to use a bathroom! (*The child, a sturdy, handsome little boy of ten or eleven, drags himself out of the bed and almost blindly takes his towels and "today's clothes" from drawers and a closet and goes out to the bathroom, which is in an outside hall and which is shared by another family or families on the same floor.* RUTH *crosses to the bedroom door at right and opens it and calls in to her husband*) Walter Lee! . . . It's after seven thirty! Lemme see you do some waking up in there now! (*She waits*) You better get up from there, man! It's after seven thirty I tell you. (*She waits again*) All right, you just go ahead and lay there and next thing you know Travis be finished and Mr. Johnson'll be in there and you'll be fussing and cussing round here like a madman! And be late too! (*She waits, at the end of patience*) Walter Lee—it's time for you to GET UP!

(*She waits another second and then starts to go into the bedroom, but is apparently satisfied that her husband has begun to get up. She stops, pulls the door to, and returns to the kitchen area. She wipes her face with a moist cloth and runs her fingers through her sleep-disheveled hair in a vain effort and ties an apron around her housecoat. The bedroom door at right opens and her husband stands in the doorway in his pajamas, which are rumpled and mismated. He is a lean, intense young man in his middle thirties, inclined to quick nervous movements and erratic speech habits—and always in his voice there is a quality of indictment*)

WALTER: Is he out yet?

RUTH: What you mean *out*? He ain't hardly got in there good yet.

WALTER (*wandering in, still more oriented to sleep than to a new day*):   Well, what was you doing all that yelling for if I can't even get in there yet? (*Stopping and thinking*) Check coming today?

RUTH: They *said* Saturday and this is just Friday and I hopes to God you ain't going to get up here first thing this morning and start talking to me 'bout no money—'cause I 'bout don't want to hear it.

WALTER: Something the matter with you this morning?

RUTH: No—I'm just sleepy as the devil. What kind of eggs you want?

WALTER: Not scrambled. (RUTH *starts to scramble eggs*) Paper come? (RUTH *points impatiently to the rolled up* Tribune *on the table, and he gets it and spreads it out and vaguely reads the front page*) Set off another bomb yesterday.

RUTH (*maximum indifference*):   Did they?

WALTER (*looking up*):   What's the matter with you?

RUTH: Ain't nothing the matter with me. And don't keep asking me that this morning.

WALTER: Ain't nobody bothering you. (*Reading the news of the day absently again*) Say Colonel McCormick is sick.

RUTH (*affecting tea-party interest*):　Is he now? Poor thing.

WALTER (*sighing and looking at his watch*):　Oh, me. (*He waits*) Now what is that boy doing in that bathroom all this time? He just going to have to start getting up earlier. I can't be being late to work on account of him fooling around in there.

RUTH (*turning on him*):　Oh, no he ain't going to be getting up no earlier no such thing! It ain't his fault that he can't get to bed no earlier nights 'cause he got a bunch of crazy good-for-nothing clowns sitting up running their mouths in what is supposed to be his bedroom after ten o'clock at night . . .

WALTER:　That's what you mad about, ain't it? The things I want to talk about with my friends just couldn't be important in your mind, could they?

(*He rises and finds a cigarette in her handbag on the table and crosses to the little window and looks out, smoking and deeply enjoying this first one*)

RUTH (*almost matter of factly, a complaint too automatic to deserve emphasis*): Why you always got to smoke before you eat in the morning?

WALTER (*at the window*):　Just look at 'em down there . . . Running and racing to work . . . (*He turns and faces his wife and watches her a moment at the stove, and then, suddenly*) You look young this morning, baby.

RUTH (*indifferently*):　Yeah?

WALTER:　Just for a second—stirring them eggs. Just for a second it was— you looked real young again. (*He reaches for her; she crosses away. Then, drily*) It's gone now—you look like yourself again!

RUTH:　Man, if you don't shut up and leave me alone.

WALTER (*looking out to the street again*):　First thing a man ought to learn in life is not to make love to no colored woman first thing in the morning. You all some eeeevil people at eight o'clock in the morning.

(TRAVIS *appears in the hall doorway, almost fully dressed and quite wide awake now, his towels and pajamas across his shoulders. He opens the door and signals for his father to make the bathroom in a hurry*)

TRAVIS (*watching the bathroom*):　Daddy, come on!

(WALTER *gets his bathroom utensils and flies out to the bathroom*)

RUTH:　Sit down and have your breakfast, Travis.

TRAVIS:　Mama, this is Friday. (*Gleefully*) Check coming tomorrow, huh?

RUTH:　You get your mind off money and eat your breakfast.

TRAVIS (*eating*):　This is the morning we supposed to bring the fifty cents to school.

RUTH:　Well, I ain't got no fifty cents this morning.

TRAVIS:　Teacher say we have to.

RUTH:　I don't care what teacher say. I ain't got it. Eat your breakfast, Travis.

TRAVIS:　I *am* eating.

RUTH:　Hush up now and just eat!

(*The boy gives her an exasperated look for her lack of understanding, and eats grudgingly*)

TRAVIS: You think Grandmama would have it?

RUTH: No! And I want you to stop asking your grandmother for money, you hear me?

TRAVIS (*outraged*):   Gaaaleee! I don't ask her, she just gimme it sometimes!

RUTH: Travis Willard Younger—I got too much on me this morning to be—

TRAVIS: Maybe Daddy—

RUTH: *Travis!*

(*The boy hushes abruptly. They are both quiet and tense for several seconds*)

TRAVIS (*presently*):   Could I maybe go carry some groceries in front of the supermarket for a little while after school then?

RUTH: Just hush, I said. (TRAVIS *jabs his spoon into his cereal bowl viciously, and rests his head in anger upon his fists*) If you through eating, you can get over there and make up your bed.

(*The boy obeys stiffly and crosses the room, almost mechanically, to the bed and more or less folds the bedding into a heap, then angrily gets his books and cap*)

TRAVIS (*sulking and standing apart from her unnaturally*):   I'm gone.

RUTH (*looking up from the stove to inspect him automatically*):   Come here. (*He crosses to her and she studies his head*) If you don't take this comb and fix this here head, you better! (TRAVIS *puts down his books with a great sigh of oppression, and crosses to the mirror. His mother mutters under her breath about his "slubbornness"*) 'Bout to march out of here with that head looking just like chickens slept in it! I just don't know where you get your slubborn ways . . . And get your jacket, too. Looks chilly out this morning.

TRAVIS (*with conspicuously brushed hair and jacket*):   I'm gone.

RUTH: Get carfare and milk money—(*Waving one finger*)—and not a single penny for no caps, you hear me?

TRAVIS (*with sullen politeness*):   Yes'm.

(*He turns in outrage to leave. His mother watches after him as in his frustration he approaches the door almost comically. When she speaks to him, her voice has become a very gentle tease*)

RUTH (*mocking; as she thinks he would say it*):   Oh, Mama makes me so mad sometimes, I don't know what to do! (*She waits and continues to his back as he stands stock-still in front of the door*) I wouldn't kiss that woman good-bye for nothing in this world this morning! (*The boy finally turns around and rolls his eyes at her, knowing the mood has changed and he is vindicated; he does not, however, move toward her yet*) Not for nothing in this world! (*She finally laughs aloud at him and holds out her arms to him and we see that it is a way between them, very old and practiced. He crosses to her and allows her to embrace him warmly but keeps his face fixed with masculine rigidity. She holds him back from her presently and looks at him and runs her fingers over the features of his face. With utter gentleness—*) Now—whose little old angry man are you?

TRAVIS (*the masculinity and gruffness start to fade at last*):   Aw gaalee—Mama . . .

RUTH (*Mimicking*):   Aw—gaaaaalleeeee, Mama! (*She pushes him, with rough playfulness and finality, toward the door*) Get on out of here or you going to be late.

TRAVIS (*in the face of love, new aggressiveness*):   Mama, could I *please* go carry groceries?

RUTH: Honey, it's starting to get so cold evenings.

WALTER (*coming in from the bathroom and drawing a make-believe gun from a make-believe holster and shooting at his son*):   What is it he wants to do?

RUTH: Go carry groceries after school at the supermarket.

WALTER: Well, let him go . . .

TRAVIS (*quickly, to the ally*):   I have to—she won't gimme the fifty cents . . .

WALTER (*to his wife only*):   Why not?

RUTH (*simply, and with flavor*):   'Cause we don't have it.

WALTER (*to RUTH only*):   What you tell the boy things like that for? (*Reaching down into his pants with a rather important gesture*) Here, son—

(*He hands the boy the coin, but his eyes are directed to his wife's. TRAVIS takes the money happily*)

TRAVIS: Thanks, Daddy.

(*He starts out. RUTH watches both of them with murder in her eyes. WALTER stands and stares back at her with defiance, and suddenly reaches into his pocket again on an afterthought*)

WALTER (*without even looking at his son, still staring hard at his wife*):   In fact, here's another fifty cents . . . Buy yourself some fruit today—or take a taxicab to school or something!

TRAVIS: Whoopee—

(*He leaps up and clasps his father around the middle with his legs, and they face each other in mutual appreciation; slowly WALTER LEE peeks around the boy to catch the violent rays from his wife's eyes and draws his head back as if shot*)

WALTER: You better get down now—and get to school, man.

TRAVIS (*at the door*):   O.K. Good-bye.

(*He exits*)

WALTER (*after him, pointing with pride*):   That's *my* boy. (*She looks at him in disgust and turns back to her work*) You know what I was thinking 'bout in the bathroom this morning?

RUTH: No.

WALTER: How come you always try to be so pleasant!

RUTH: What is there to be pleasant 'bout!

WALTER: You want to know what I was thinking 'bout in the bathroom or not!

RUTH: I know what you thinking 'bout.

WALTER (*ignoring her*):   'Bout what me and Willy Harris was talking about last night.

RUTH (*immediately—a refrain*):   Willy Harris is a good-for-nothing loudmouth.

WALTER: Anybody who talks to me has got to be a good-for-nothing loudmouth, ain't he? And what you know about who is just a good-for-nothing loudmouth? Charlie Atkins was just a "good-for-nothing loudmouth" too, wasn't he! When he wanted me to go in the dry-cleaning business with him. And now—he's grossing a hundred thousand a year. A hundred thousand dollars a year! You still call *him* a loudmouth!

RUTH (*bitterly*):   Oh, Walter Lee . . .

(*She folds her head on her arms over the table*)

WALTER (*rising and coming to her and standing over her*):   You tired, ain't you? Tired of everything. Me, the boy, the way we live—this beat-up hole—everything. Ain't you? (*She doesn't look up, doesn't answer*) So tired—moaning and groaning all the time, but you wouldn't do nothing to help, would you? You couldn't be on my side that long for nothing, could you?

RUTH: Walter, please leave me alone.

WALTER: A man needs for a woman to back him up . . .

RUTH: Walter—

WALTER: Mama would listen to you. You know she listen to you more than she do me and Bennie. She think more of you. All you have to do is just sit down with her when you drinking your coffee one morning and talking 'bout things like you do and—(*He sits down beside her and demonstrates graphically what he thinks her methods and tone should be*)—you just sip your coffee, see, and say easy like that you been thinking 'bout that deal Walter Lee is so interested in, 'bout the store and all, and sip some more coffee, like what you saying ain't really that important to you— And the next thing you know, she be listening good and asking you questions and when I come home—I can tell her the details. This ain't no fly-by-night proposition, baby. I mean we figured it out, me and Willy and Bobo.

RUTH (*with a frown*):   Bobo?

WALTER: Yeah. You see, this little liquor store we got in mind cost seventy-five thousand and we figured the initial investment on the place be 'bout thirty thousand, see. That be ten thousand each. Course, there's a couple of hundred you got to pay so's you don't spend your life just waiting for them clowns to let your license get approved—

RUTH: You mean graft?

WALTER (*frowning impatiently*):   Don't call it that. See there, that just goes to show you what women understand about the world. Baby, don't *nothing* happen for you in this world 'less you pay *somebody* off!

RUTH: Walter, leave me alone! (*She raises her head and stares at him vigorously—then says, more quietly*) *Eat* your eggs, they gonna be cold.

WALTER (*straightening up from her and looking off*):   That's it. There you are. Man say to his woman: I got me a dream. His woman say: Eat your eggs. (*Sadly, but gaining in power*) Man say: I got to take hold of this here world, baby! And a woman will say: Eat your eggs and go to work. (*Passionately now*) Man say: I got to change my life, I'm choking to death, baby! And his woman say—(*In utter anguish as he brings his fists down on his thighs*)—Your eggs is getting cold!

RUTH (*softly*):   Walter, that ain't none of our money.

WALTER (*not listening at all or even looking at her*):   This morning, I was lookin' in the mirror and thinking about it . . . I'm thirty-five years old; I been married eleven years and I got a boy who sleeps in the living room—(*Very, very quietly*)—and all I got to give him is stories about how rich white people live . . .

RUTH: Eat your eggs, Walter.

WALTER (*slams the table and jumps up*):   —DAMN MY EGGS—DAMN ALL THE EGGS THAT EVER WAS!

RUTH: Then go to work.

WALTER (*looking up at her*):   See—I'm trying to talk to you 'bout myself— (*Shaking his head with the repetition*)—and all you can say is eat them eggs and go to work.

RUTH (*wearily*):   Honey, you never say nothing new. I listen to you every day, every night and every morning, and you never say nothing new. (*Shrugging*) So you would rather *be* Mr. Arnold than be his chauffeur. So—I would *rather* be living in Buckingham Palace.

WALTER: That is just what is wrong with the colored woman in this world . . . . Don't understand about building their men up and making 'em feel like they somebody. Like they can do something.

RUTH (*drily, but to hurt*):   There *are* colored men who do things.

WALTER: No thanks to the colored woman.

RUTH: Well, being a colored woman, I guess I can't help myself none.

(*She rises and gets the ironing board and sets it up and attacks a huge pile of rough-dried clothes, sprinkling them in preparation for the ironing and then rolling them into tight fat balls*)

WALTER (*mumbling*):   We one group of men tied to a race of women with small minds!

(*His sister* BENEATHA *enters. She is about twenty, as slim and intense as her brother. She is not as pretty as her sister-in-law, but her lean, almost intellectual face has a handsomeness of its own. She wears a bright-red flannel nightie, and her thick hair stands wildly about her head. Her speech is a mixture of many things; it is different from the rest of the family's insofar as education has permeated her sense of English—and perhaps the Midwest rather than the South has finally— at last—won out in her inflection; but not altogether, because over all of it is a soft slurring and transformed use of vowels which is the decided influence of the Southside. She passes through the room without looking at either* RUTH *or* WALTER *and goes to the outside door and looks, a little blindly, out to the bathroom. She sees that it has been lost to the Johnsons. She closes the door with a sleepy vengeance and crosses to the table and sits down a little defeated*)

BENEATHA: I am going to start timing those people.

WALTER: You should get up earlier.

BENEATHA (*her face in her hands. She is still fighting the urge to go back to bed*): Really—would you suggest dawn? Where's the paper?

WALTER (*pushing the paper across the table to her as he studies her almost clinically, as though he has never seen her before*):   You a horrible-looking chick at this hour.

BENEATHA (*drily*):   Good morning, everybody.

WALTER (*senselessly*):   How is school coming?

BENEATHA (*in the same spirit*):   Lovely. Lovely. And you know, biology is the greatest. (*Looking up at him*) I dissected something that looked just like you yesterday.

WALTER: I just wondered if you've made up your mind and everything.

BENEATHA (*gaining in sharpness and impatience*): And what did I answer yesterday morning—and the day before that?

RUTH (*from the ironing board, like someone disinterested and old*): Don't be so nasty, Bennie.

BENEATHA (*still to her brother*): And the day before that and the day before that!

WALTER (*defensively*): I'm interested in you. Something wrong with that? Ain't many girls who decide—

WALTER *and* BENEATHA (*in unison*): —"to be a doctor."

(*Silence*)

WALTER: Have we figured out yet just exactly how much medical school is going to cost?

RUTH: Walter Lee, why don't you leave that girl alone and get out of here to work?

BENEATHA (*exits to the bathroom and bangs on the door*): Come on out of there, please!

(*She comes back into the room*)

WALTER (*looking at his sister intently*): You know the check is coming tomorrow.

BENEATHA (*turning on him with a sharpness all her own*): That money belongs to Mama, Walter, and it's for her to decide how she wants to use it. I don't care if she wants to buy a house or a rocket ship or just nail it up somewhere and look at it. It's hers. Not ours—*hers.*

WALTER (*bitterly*): Now ain't that fine! You just got your mother's interest at heart, ain't you, girl? You such a nice girl—but if Mama got that money she can always take a few thousand and help you through school too—can't she?

BENEATHA: I have never asked anyone around here to do anything for me!

WALTER: No! And the line between asking and just accepting when the time comes is big and wide—ain't it!

BENEATHA (*with fury*): What do you want from me, Brother—that I quit school or just drop dead, which!

WALTER: I don't want nothing but for you to stop acting holy 'round here. Me and Ruth done made some sacrifices for you—why can't you do something for the family?

RUTH: Walter, don't be dragging me in it.

WALTER: You are in it—Don't you get up and go work in somebody's kitchen for the last three years to help put clothes on her back?

RUTH: Oh, Walter—that's not fair . . .

WALTER: It ain't that nobody expects you to get on your knees and say thank you, Brother; thank you, Ruth; thank you, Mama—and thank you, Travis, for wearing the same pair of shoes for two semesters—

BENEATHA (*dropping to her knees*): Well—I *do*—all right?—thank everybody! And forgive me for ever wanting to be anything at all! (*Pursuing him on her knees across the floor*) FORGIVE ME, FORGIVE ME, FORGIVE ME!

RUTH: Please stop it! Your mama'll hear you.

WALTER: Who the hell told you you had to be a doctor? If you so crazy 'bout messing 'round with sick people—then go be a nurse like other women— or just get married and be quiet . . .

BENEATHA: Well—you finally got it said . . . It took you three years but you finally got it said. Walter, give up; leave me alone—it's Mama's money.

WALTER: *He was my father, too!*

BENEATHA: So what? He was mine, too—and Travis' grandfather—but the insurance money belongs to Mama. Picking on me is not going to make her give it to you to invest in any liquor stores—(*Underbreath, dropping into a chair*)— and I for one say, God bless Mama for that!

WALTER (*to* RUTH):   See—did you hear? Did you hear!

RUTH: Honey, please go to work.

WALTER: Nobody in this house is ever going to understand me.

BENEATHA: Because you're a nut.

WALTER: Who's a nut?

BENEATHA: You—you are a nut. Thee is mad, boy.

WALTER (*looking at his wife and his sister from the door, very sadly*):   The world's most backward race of people, and that's a fact.

BENEATHA (*turning slowly in her chair*):   And then there are all those prophets who would lead us out of the wilderness—(WALTER *slams out of the house*)— into the swamps!

RUTH: Bennie, why you always gotta be pickin' on your brother? Can't you be a little sweeter sometimes? (*Door opens.* WALTER *walks in. He fumbles with his cap, starts to speak, clears throat, looks everywhere but at* RUTH. *Finally:*)

WALTER (*to* RUTH):   I need some money for carfare.

RUTH (*looks at him, then warms; teasing, but tenderly*):   Fifty cents? (*She goes to her bag and gets money*) Here—take a taxi!

(WALTER *exits.* MAMA *enters. She is a woman in her early sixties, full-bodied and strong. She is one of those women of a certain grace and beauty who wear it so unobtrusively that it takes a while to notice. Her dark-brown face is surrounded by the total whiteness of her hair, and, being a woman who has adjusted to many things in life and overcome many more, her face is full of strength. She has, we can see, wit and faith of a kind that keep her eyes lit and full of interest and expectancy. She is, in a word, a beautiful woman. Her bearing is perhaps most like the noble bearing of the women of the Hereros of Southwest Africa—rather as if she imagines that as she walks she still bears a basket or a vessel upon her head. Her speech, on the other hand, is as careless as her carriage is precise—she is inclined to slur everything—but her voice is perhaps not so much quiet as simply soft*)

MAMA: Who that 'round here slamming doors at this hour?

(*She crosses through the room, goes to the window, opens it, and brings in a feeble little plant growing doggedly in a small pot on the window sill. She feels the dirt and puts it back out*)

RUTH: That was Walter Lee. He and Bennie was at it again.

MAMA: My children and they tempers. Lord, if this little old plant don't get more sun than it's been getting it ain't never going to see spring again. (*She turns from the window*) What's the matter with you this morning, Ruth? You looks right peaked. You aiming to iron all them things? Leave some for me. I'll get to 'em this afternoon. Bennie honey, it's too drafty for you to be sitting 'round half dressed. Where's your robe?

BENEATHA: In the cleaners.

MAMA: Well, go get mine and put it on.

BENEATHA: I'm not cold, Mama, honest.

MAMA: I know—but you so thin . . .

BENEATHA (*irritably*): Mama, I'm not cold.

MAMA (*seeing the make-down bed as* TRAVIS *has left it*): Lord have mercy, look at that poor bed. Bless his heart—he tries, don't he?

(*She moves to the bed* TRAVIS *has sloppily made up*)

RUTH: No—he don't half try at all 'cause he knows you going to come along behind him and fix everything. That's just how come he don't know how to do nothing right now—you done spoiled that boy so.

MAMA (*folding bedding*): Well—he's a little boy. Ain't supposed to know 'bout housekeeping. My baby, that's what he is. What you fix for his breakfast this morning?

RUTH (*angrily*): I feed my son, Lena!

MAMA: I ain't meddling—(*Underbreath; busy-bodyish*) I just noticed all last week he had cold cereal, and when it starts getting this chilly in the fall a child ought to have some hot grits or something when he goes out in the cold—

RUTH (*furious*): I gave him hot oats—is that all right!

MAMA: I ain't meddling. (*Pause*) Put a lot of nice butter on it? (RUTH *shoots her an angry look and does not reply*) He likes lots of butter.

RUTH (*exasperated*): Lena—

MAMA (*to* BENEATHA. MAMA *is inclined to wander conversationally sometimes*): What was you and your brother fussing 'bout this morning?

BENEATHA: It's not important, Mama.

(*She gets up and goes to look out at the bathroom, which is apparently free, and she picks up her towels and rushes out*)

MAMA: What was they fighting about?

RUTH: Now you know as well as I do.

MAMA (*shaking her head*): Brother still worrying hisself sick about that money?

RUTH: You know he is.

MAMA: You had breakfast?

RUTH: Some coffee.

MAMA: Girl, you better start eating and looking after yourself better. You almost thin as Travis.

RUTH: Lena—

MAMA: Uh-hunh?

RUTH: What are you going to do with it?

MAMA: Now don't you start, child. It's too early in the morning to be talking about money. It ain't Christian.

RUTH: It's just that he got his heart set on that store—

MAMA: You mean that liquor store that Willy Harris want him to invest in?

RUTH: Yes—

MAMA: We ain't no business people, Ruth. We just plain working folks.

RUTH: Ain't nobody business people till they go into business. Walter Lee say colored people ain't never going to start getting ahead till they start gambling on some different kinds of things in the world—investments and things.

MAMA: What done got into you, girl? Walter Lee done finally sold you on investing.

RUTH: No. Mama, something is happening between Walter and me. I don't know what it is—but he needs something—something I can't give him any more. He needs this chance, Lena.

MAMA (*frowning deeply*): But liquor, honey—

RUTH: Well—like Walter say—I spec people going to always be drinking themselves some liquor.

RUTH: Well—whether they drinks it or not ain't none of my business. But whether I go into business selling it to 'em *is,* and I don't want that on my ledger this late in life. (*Stopping suddenly and studying her daughter-in-law*) Ruth Younger, what's the matter with you today? You look like you could fall over right there.

RUTH: I'm tired.

MAMA: Then you better stay home from work today.

RUTH: I can't stay home. She'd be calling up the agency and screaming at them, "My girl didn't come in today—send me somebody! My girl didn't come in!" Oh, she just have a fit . . .

MAMA: Well, let her have it. I'll just call her up and say you got the flu—

RUTH (*laughing*): Why the flu?

MAMA: 'Cause it sounds respectable to 'em. Something white people get, too. They know 'bout the flu. Otherwise they think you been cut up or something when you tell 'em you sick.

RUTH: I got to go in. We need the money.

MAMA: Somebody would of thought my children done all but starved to death the way they talk about money here late. Child, we got a great big old check coming tomorrow.

RUTH (*sincerely, but also self-righteously*): Now that's your money. It ain't got nothing to do with me. We all feel like that—Walter and Bennie and me—even Travis.

MAMA (*thoughtfully, and suddenly very far away*): Ten thousand dollars—

RUTH: Sure is wonderful.

MAMA: Ten thousand dollars.

RUTH: You know what you should do, Miss Lena? You should take yourself a trip somewhere. To Europe or South America or someplace—

MAMA (*throwing up her hands at the thought*): Oh, child!

RUTH: I'm serious. Just pack up and leave! Go on away and enjoy yourself some. Forget about the family and have yourself a ball for once in your life—

MAMA (*drily*): You shound like I'm just about ready to die. Who'd go with me? What I look like wandering 'round Europe by myself?

RUTH: Shoot—these here rich white women do it all the time. They don't think nothing of packing up they suitcases and piling on one of them big steamships and—swoosh!—they gone, child.

MAMA: Something always told me I wasn't no rich white woman.

RUTH: Well—what are you going to do with it then?

MAMA: I ain't rightly decided. (*Thinking. She speaks now with emphasis*) Some of it got to be put away for Beneatha and her schoolin'—and ain't nothing going to touch that part of it. Nothing. (*She waits several seconds, trying to make up her mind about something, and looks at* RUTH *a little tentatively before going on*) Been thinking that we maybe could meet the notes on a little old two-story somewhere, with a yard where Travis could play in the summertime, if we use part of the insurance for a down payment and everybody kind of pitch in. I could maybe take on a little day work again, few days a week—

RUTH (*studying her mother-in-law furtively and concentrating on her ironing, anxious to encourage without seeming to*):   Well, Lord knows, we've put enough rent into this here rat trap to pay for four houses by now . . .

MAMA (*looking up at the words "rat trap" and then looking around and leaning back and sighing—in a suddenly reflective mood—*):   "Rat trap"—yes, that's all it is. (*Smiling*) I remember just as well the day me and Big Walter moved in here. Hadn't been married but two weeks and wasn't planning on living here no more than a year. (*She shakes her head at the dissolved dream*) We was going to set away, little by little, don't you know, and buy a little place out in Morgan Park. We had even picked out the house. (*Chuckling a little*) Looks right dumpy today. But Lord, child, you should know all the dreams I had 'bout buying that house and fixing it up and making me a little garden in the back—(*She waits and stops smiling*) And didn't none of it happen.

(*Dropping her hands in a futile gesture*)

RUTH (*keeps her head down, ironing*):   Yes, life can be a barrel of disappointments, sometimes.

MAMA: Honey, Big Walter would come in here some nights back then and slump down on that couch there and just look at the rug, and look at me and look at the rug and then back at me—and I'd know he was down then . . . really down. (*After a second very long and thoughtful pause; she is seeing back to times that only she can see*) And then, Lord, when I lost that baby—little Claude—I almost thought I was going to lose Big Walter too. Oh, that man grieved hisself! He was one man to love his children.

RUTH: Ain't nothin' can tear at you like losin' your baby.

MAMA: I guess that's how come that man finally worked hisself to death like he done. Like he was fighting his own war with this here world that took his baby from him.

RUTH: He sure was a fine man, all right. I always liked Mr. Younger.

MAMA: Crazy 'bout his children! God knows there was plenty wrong with Walter Younger—hard-headed, mean, kind of wild with women—plenty wrong with him. But he sure loved his children. Always wanted them to have something—be something. That's where Brother gets all these notions, I reckon. Big Walter used to say, he'd get right wet in the eyes sometimes, lean his head back with the water standing in his eyes and say, "Seem like God didn't see fit to give the black man nothing but dreams—but He did give us children to make them dreams seem worth while." (*She smiles*) He could talk like that, don't you know.

RUTH: Yes, he sure could. He was a good man, Mr. Younger.

MAMA: Yes, a fine man—just couldn't never catch up with his dreams, that's all.

(BENEATHA *comes in, brushing her hair and looking up to the ceiling, where the sound of a vacuum cleaner has started up*)

BENEATHA: What could be so dirty on that woman's rugs that she has to vacuum them every single day?

RUTH: I wish certain young women 'round here who I could name would take inspiration about certain rugs in a certain apartment I could also mention.

BENEATHA (*shrugging*):   How much cleaning can a house need, for Christ's sakes.

MAMA (*not liking the Lord's name used thus*):   Bennie!

RUTH: Just listen to her—just listen!

BENEATHA: Oh, God!

MAMA: If you use the Lord's name just one more time—

BENEATHA (*a bit of a whine*):   Oh, Mama—

RUTH: Fresh—just fresh as salt, this girl!

BENEATHA (*drily*):   Well—if the salt loses its savor—

MAMA: Now that will do. I just ain't going to have you 'round here reciting the scriptures in vain—you hear me?

BENEATHA: How did I manage to get on everybody's wrong side by just walking into a room?

RUTH: If you weren't so fresh—

BENEATHA: Ruth, I'm twenty years old.

MAMA: What time you be home from school today?

BENEATHA: Kind of late. (*With enthusiasm*) Madeline is going to start my guitar lessons today.

(MAMA *and* RUTH *look up with the same expression*)

MAMA: Your *what* kind of lessons?

BENEATHA: Guitar.

RUTH: Oh, Father!

MAMA: How come you done taken it in your mind to learn to play the guitar?

BENEATHA: I just want to, that's all.

MAMA (*smiling*):   Lord, child, don't you know what to do with yourself? How long it going to be before you get tired of this now—like you got tired of that little play-acting group you joined last year? (*Looking at* RUTH) And what was it the year before that?

RUTH: The horseback-riding club for which she bought that fifty-five-dollar riding habit that's been hanging in the closet ever since!

MAMA (*to* BENEATHA):   Why you got to flit so from one thing to another, baby?

BENEATHA (*sharply*):   I just want to learn to play the guitar. Is there anything wrong with that?

MAMA: Ain't nobody trying to stop you. I just wonders sometimes why you

has to flit so from one thing to another all the time. You ain't never done nothing with all that camera equipment you brought home—

BENEATHA: I don't flit! I—I experiment with different forms of expression—

RUTH: Like riding a horse?

BENEATHA: —People have to express themselves one way or another.

MAMA: What is it you want to express?

BENEATHA (*angrily*):   Me! (MAMA *and* RUTH *look at each other and burst into
raucous laughter*) Don't worry—I don't expect you to understand.

MAMA (*to change the subject*):   Who you going out with tomorrow night?

BENEATHA (*with displeasure*):   George Murchison again.

MAMA (*pleased*):   Oh—you getting a little sweet on him?

RUTH: You ask me, this child ain't sweet on nobody but herself—(*Underbreath*) Express herself!

(*They laugh*)

BENEATHA: Oh—I like George all right, Mama. I mean I like him enough
to go out with him and stuff, but—

RUTH (*for devilment*):   What does *and stuff* mean?

BENEATHA: Mind your own business.

MAMA: Stop picking at her now, Ruth. (*She chuckles—then a suspicious sudden look at her daughter as she turns in her chair for emphasis*) What DOES it mean?

BENEATHA (*wearily*):   Oh, I just mean I couldn't ever really be serious about
George. He's—he's so shallow.

RUTH: Shallow—what do you mean he's shallow? He's *Rich!*

MAMA: Hush, Ruth.

BENEATHA: I know he's rich. He knows he's rich, too.

RUTH: Well   what other qualities a man got to have to satisfy you, little
girl?

BENEATHA: You wouldn't even begin to understand. Anybody who married Walter could not possibly understand.

MAMA (*outraged*):   What kind of way is that to talk about your brother?

BENEATHA: Brother is a flip—let's face it.

MAMA (TO RUTH, *helplessly*):   What's a flip?

RUTH (glad to add kindling):   She's saying he's crazy.

BENEATHA: Not crazy. Brother isn't really crazy yet—he—he's an elaborate neurotic.

MAMA: Hush your mouth!

BENEATHA: As for George. Well. George looks good—he's got a beautiful car and he takes me to nice places and, as my sister-in-law says, he is probably the richest boy I will ever get to know and I even like him sometimes—
but if the Youngers are sitting around waiting to see if their little Bennie is going
to tie up the family with the Murchisons, they are wasting their time.

RUTH: You mean you wouldn't marry George Murchison if he asked you
someday? That pretty, rich thing? Honey, I knew you was odd—

BENEATHA: No I would not marry him if all I felt for him was what I feel
now. Besides, George's family wouldn't really like it.

MAMA: Why not?

BENEATHA: Oh, Mama—The Murchisons are honest-to-God-real-*live*-rich colored people, and the only people in the world who are more snobbish than rich white people are rich colored people. I thought everybody knew that. I've met Mrs. Murchison. She's a scene!

MAMA: You must not dislike people 'cause they well off, honey.

BENEATHA: Why not? It makes just as much sense as disliking people 'cause they are poor, and lots of people do that.

RUTH (*a wisdom-of-the-ages manner. To* MAMA):   Well, she'll get over some of this—

BENEATHA: Get over it? What are you talking about, Ruth? Listen, I'm going to be a doctor. I'm not worried about who I'm going to marry yet—if I ever get married.

MAMA *and* RUTH: *If!*

MAMA: Now, Bennie—

BENEATHA: Oh, I probably will . . . but first I'm going to be a doctor, and George, for one, still thinks that's pretty funny. I couldn't be bothered with that. I am going to be a doctor and everybody around here better understand that!

MAMA (*kindly*):   'Course you going to be a doctor, honey, God willing.

BENEATHA (*drily*):   God hasn't got a thing to do with it.

MAMA: Beneatha—that just wasn't necessary.

BENEATHA: Well—neither is God. I get sick of hearing about God.

MAMA: Beneatha!

BENEATHA: I mean it! I'm just tired of hearing about God all the time. What has He got to do with anything? Does he pay tuition?

MAMA: You 'bout to get your fresh little jaw slapped!

RUTH: That's just what she needs, all right!

BENEATHA: Why? Why can't I say what I want to around here, like everybody else?

MAMA: It don't sound nice for a young girl to say things like that—you wasn't brought up that way. Me and your father went to trouble to get you and Brother to church every Sunday.

BENEATHA: Mama, you don't understand. It's all a matter of ideas, and God is just one idea I don't accept. It's not important. I am not going out and be immoral or commit crimes because I don't believe in God. I don't even think about it. It's just that I get tired of Him getting credit for all the things the human race achieves through its own stubborn effort. There simply is no blasted God— there is only man and it is *he* who makes miracles!

(MAMA *absorbs this speech, studies her daughter and rises slowly and crosses to* BENEATHA *and slaps her powerfully across the face. After, there is only silence and the daughter drops her eyes from her mother's face, and* MAMA *is very tall before her*)

MAMA: Now—you say after me, in my mother's house there is still God. (*There is a long pause and* BENEATHA *stares at the floor wordlessly.* MAMA *repeats the phrase with precision and cool emotion*) In my mother's house there is still God.

BENEATHA: In my mother's house there is still God.

(*A long pause*)

MAMA (*walking away from* BENEATHA, *too disturbed for triumphant posture. Stopping and turning back to her daughter*): There are some ideas we ain't going to have in this house. Not long as I am at the head of this family.

BENEATHA: Yes, ma'am.

(MAMA *walks out of the room*)

RUTH (*almost gently, with profound understanding*): You think you a woman, Bennie—but you still a little girl. What you did was childish—so you got treated like a child.

BENEATHA: I see. (*Quietly*) I also see that everybody thinks it's all right for Mama to be a tyrant. But all the tyranny in the world will never put a God in the heavens!

(*She picks up her books and goes out. Pause*)

RUTH (*goes to* MAMA'S *door*): She said she was sorry.

MAMA (*coming out, going to her plant*): They frightens me, Ruth. My children.

RUTH: You got good children, Lena. They just a little off sometimes—but they're good.

MAMA: No—there's something come down between me and them that don't let us understand each other and I don't know what it is. One done almost lost his mind thinking 'bout money all the time and the other done commence to talk about things I can't seem to understand in no form or fashion. What is it that's changing, Ruth.

RUTH (*soothingly, older than her years*): Now . . . you taking it all too seriously. You just got strong-willed children and it takes a strong woman like you to keep 'em in hand.

MAMA (*looking at her plant and sprinkling a little water on it*): They spirited all right, my children. Got to admit they got spirit—Bennie and Walter. Like this little old plant that ain't never had enough sunshine or nothing—and look at it . . .

(*She has her back to* RUTH, *who has had to stop ironing and lean against something and put the back of her hand to her forehead*)

RUTH (*trying to keep* MAMA *from noticing*): You . . . sure . . . loves that little old thing, don't you? . . .

MAMA: Well, I always wanted me a garden like I used to see sometimes at the back of the houses down home. This plant is close as I ever got to having one. (*She looks out of the window as she replaces the plant*) Lord, ain't nothing as dreary as the view from this window on a dreary day, is there? Why ain't you singing this morning, Ruth? Sing that "No Ways Tired." That song always lifts me up so—(*She turns at last to see that* RUTH *has slipped quietly to the floor, in a state of semiconsciousness*) Ruth! Ruth honey—what's the matter with you . . . Ruth!

Curtain

Scene II

It is the following morning; a Saturday morning, and house cleaning is in progress at the YOUNGERS. *Furniture has been shoved hither and yon and* MAMA *is giving the kitchen-area walls a washing down.* BENEATHA, *in dungarees, with a handkerchief tied around her face, is spraying insecticide into the cracks in the walls. As they work, the radio is on and a Southside disk-jockey program is inappropriately filling the house with a rather exotic saxophone blues.* TRAVIS, *the sole idle one, is leaning on his arms, looking out of the window.*

TRAVIS: Grandmama, that stuff Bennie is using smells awful. Can I go downstairs, please?

MAMA: Did you get all them chores done already? I ain't seen you doing much.

TRAVIS: Yes'm—finished early. Where did Mama go this morning?

MAMA (*looking at* BENEATHA):   She had to go on a little errand.

(*The phone rings.* BENEATHA *runs to answer it and reaches it before* WALTER, *who has entered from bedroom*)

TRAVIS: Where?

MAMA: To tend to her business.

BENEATHA: Haylo . . . (*Disappointed*) Yes, he is. (*She tosses the phone to* WALTER, *who barely catches it*) It's Willie Harris again.

WALTER (*as privately as possible under* MAMA'S *gaze*):   Hello, Willie. Did you get the papers from the lawyer? . . . No, not yet. I told you the mailman doesn't get here till ten-thirty . . . No, I'll come there . . . Yeah! Right away. (*He hangs up and goes for his coat*)

BENEATHA: Brother, where did Ruth go?

WALTER (*as he exits*):   How should I know!

TRAVIS: Aw come on, Grandma. Can I go outside?

MAMA: Oh, I guess so. You stay right in front of the house, though, and keep a good lookout for the postman.

TRAVIS: Yes'm. (*He darts into bedroom for stickball and bat, reenters, and sees* BENEATHA *on her knees spraying under sofa with behind upraised. He edges closer to the target, takes aim, and lets her have it. She screams*) Leave them poor little cockroaches alone, they ain't bothering you none! (*He runs as she swings the spraygun at him viciously and playfully*) Grandma! Grandma!

MAMA: Look out there, girl, before you be spilling some of that stuff on that child!

TRAVIS (*safely behind the bastion of* MAMA):   That's right—look out, now! (*He exits*)

BENEATHA (*drily*):   I can't imagine that it would hurt him—it has never hurt the roaches.

MAMA: Well, little boys' hides ain't as tough as Southside roaches. You better get over there behind the bureau. I seen one marching out of there like Napoleon yesterday.

BENEATHA: There's really only one way to get rid of them, Mama—

MAMA: How?

BENEATHA: Set fire to this building! Mama, where did Ruth go?

MAMA (*looking at her with meaning*):   To the doctor, I think.

BENEATHA: The doctor? What's the matter? (*They exchange glances*) You don't think—

MAMA (*with her sense of drama*):   Now I ain't saying what I think. But I ain't never been wrong 'bout a woman neither.

(*The phone rings*)

BENEATHA (*at the phone*): Hay-lo . . . (*Pause, and a moment of recognition*) Well—when did you get back! . . . And how was it? . . . Of course I've missed you—in my way . . . This morning? No . . . house cleaning and all that and Mama hates it if I let people come over when the house is like this . . . You *have?* Well, that's different . . . What is it—Oh, what the hell, come on over . . . Right, see you then. *Arrividerci.*

(*She hangs up*)

MAMA (*who has listened vigorously, as is her habit*): Who is that you inviting over here with this house looking like this? You ain't got the pride you was born with!

BENEATHA: Asagai doesn't care how houses look, Mama—he's an intellectual.

MAMA: *Who?*

BENEATHA: Asagai—Joseph Asagai. He's an African boy I met on campus. He's been studying in Canada all summer.

MAMA: What's his name?

BENEATHA: Asagai, Joseph. Ah-sah-guy . . . He's from Nigeria.

MAMA: Oh, that's the little country that was founded by slaves way back . . .

BENEATHA: No, Mama—that's Liberia.

MAMA: I don't think I never met no African before.

BENEATHA: Well, do me a favor and don't ask him a whole lot of ignorant questions about Africans. I mean, do they wear clothes and all that—

MAMA: Well, now, I guess if you think we so ignorant 'round here maybe you shouldn't bring your friends here—

BENEATHA: It's just that people ask such crazy things. All anyone seems to know about when it comes to Africa is Tarzan—

MAMA (*indignantly*): Why should I know anything about Africa?

BENEATHA: Why do you give money at church for the missionary work?

MAMA: Well, that's to help save people.

BENEATHA: You mean save them from *heathenism*—

MAMA (*innocently*): Yes.

BENEATHA: I'm afraid they need more salvation from the British and the French.

(RUTH *comes in forlornly and pulls off her coat with dejection. They both turn to look at her*)

RUTH (*dispiritedly*): Well, I guess from all the happy faces—everybody knows.

BENEATHA: You pregnant?

MAMA: Lord have mercy, I sure hope it's a little old girl. Travis ought to have a sister.

(BENEATHA *and* RUTH *give her a hopeless look for this grandmotherly enthusiasm*)

BENEATHA: How far along are you?

RUTH: Two months.

BENEATHA: Did you mean to? I mean did you plan it or was it an accident?

MAMA: What do you know about planning or not planning?

BENEATHA: Oh, Mama.

RUTH (*wearily*):   She's twenty years old, Lena.

BENEATHA: Did you plan it, Ruth?

RUTH: Mind your own business.

BENEATHA: It is my business—where is he going to live, on the *roof*? (*There is silence following the remark as the three women react to the sense of it*) Gee—I didn't mean that, Ruth, honest. Gee, I don't feel like that at all. I—I think it is wonderful.

RUTH (*dully*):   Wonderful.

BENEATHA: Yes—really.

MAMA (*looking at* RUTH, *worried*):   Doctor say everything going to be all right?

RUTH (*Far away*):   Yes—she says everything is going to be fine . . .

MAMA (*immediately suspicious*):   "She"—What doctor you went to?

(RUTH *folds over, near hysteria*)

MAMA (*worriedly hovering over* RUTH):   Ruth honey—what's the matter with you—you sick?

(RUTH *has her fists clenched on her thighs and is fighting hard to suppress a scream that seems to be rising in her*)

BENEATHA: What's the matter with her, Mama?

MAMA (*working her fingers in* RUTH'S *shoulders to relax her*):   She be all right. Women gets right depressed sometimes when they get her way. (*Speaking softly, expertly, rapidly*) Now you just relax. That's right . . . just lean back, don't think 'bout nothing at all . . . nothing at all—

RUTH: I'm all right . . .

(*The glassy-eyed look melts and then she collapses into a fit of heavy sobbing. The bell rings*)

BENEATHA: Oh, my God—that must be Asagai.

MAMA (*to* RUTH):   Come on now, honey. You need to lie down and rest awhile . . . then have some nice hot food.

(*They exit,* RUTH'S *weight on her mother-in-law.* BENEATHA, *herself profoundly disturbed, opens the door to admit a rather dramatic-looking young man with a large package*)

ASAGAI: Hello, Alaiyo—

BENEATHA (*holding the door open and regarding him with pleasure*):   Hello . . . (*Long pause*) Well—come in. And please excuse everything. My mother was very upset about my letting anyone come here with the place like this.

ASAGAI (*coming into the room*):   You look disturbed too . . . Is something wrong?

BENEATHA (*still at the door, absently*):   Yes . . . we've all got acute ghetto-itus. (*She smiles and comes toward him, finding a cigarette and sitting*) So—sit down! No! Wait! (*She whips the spraygun off sofa where she had left it and puts the cushions back. At last perches on arm of sofa. He sits*) So, how was Canada?

ASAGAI (*a sophisticate*):   Canadian.

BENEATHA (*looking at him*):   Asagai, I'm very glad you are back.

ASAGAI (*looking back at her in turn*): Are you really?

BENEATHA: Yes—very.

ASAGAI: Why?—you were quite glad when I went away. What happened?

BENEATHA: You went away.

ASAGAI: Ahhhhhhhh.

BENEATHA: Before—you wanted to be so serious before there was time.

ASAGAI: How much time must there be before one knows what one feels?

BENEATHA (*stalling this particular conversation. Her hands pressed together, in a deliberately childish gesture*): What did you bring me?

ASAGAI (*handing her the package*): Open it and see.

BENEATHA (*eagerly opening the package and drawing out some records and the colorful robes of a Nigerian woman*): Oh, Asagai! . . . You got them for me! . . . How beautiful . . . and the records too! (*She lifts out the robes and runs to the mirror with them and holds the drapery up in front of herself*)

ASAGAI (*coming to her at the mirror*): I shall have to teach you how to drape it properly. (*He flings the material about her for the moment and stands back to look at her*) Ah—Oh-pay-gay-day, oh-gbah-mu-shay. (*A Yoruba exclamation for admiration*) You wear it well . . . very well . . . mutilated hair and all.

BENEATHA (*turning suddenly*): My hair—what's wrong with my hair?

ASAGAI (*shrugging*): Were you born with it like that?

BENEATHA (*reaching up to touch it*): No . . . of course not.

(*She looks back to the mirror, disturbed*)

ASAGAI (*smiling*): How then?

BENEATHA: You know perfectly well how . . . as crinkly as yours . . . that's how.

ASAGAI: And it is ugly to you that way?

BENEATHA (*quickly*): Oh, no—not ugly . . . (*More slowly, apologetically*) But it's so hard to manage when it's, well—raw.

ASAGAI: And so to accommodate that—you mutilate it every week?

BENEATHA: It's not mutilation!

ASAGAI (*laughing aloud at her seriousness*): Oh . . . please! I am only teasing you because you are so very serious about these things. (*He stands back from her and folds his arms across his chest as he watches her pulling at her hair and frowning in the mirror*) Do you remember the first time you met me at school? . . . (*He laughs*) You came up to me and you said—and I thought you were the most serious little thing I had ever seen—you said: (*He imitates her*) "Mr. Asagai—I want very much to talk with you. About Africa. You see, Mr. Asagai, I am looking for my *identity!*"

(*He laughs*)

BENEATHA (*turning to him, not laughing*): Yes—

(*Her face is quizzical, profoundly disturbed*)

ASAGAI (*still teasing and reaching out and taking her face in his hands and turning her profile to him*): Well . . . it is true that this is not so much a profile of a Hollywood queen as perhaps a queen of the Nile—(*A mock dismissal of the impor-*

tance of the question) But what does it matter? Assimilationism is so popular in your country.

BENEATHA (*wheeling, passionately, sharply*):   I am not an assimilationist!

ASAGAI (*the protest hangs in the room for a moment and* ASAGAI *studies her, his laughter fading*):   Such a serious one. (*There is a pause*) So—you like the robes? You must take excellent care of them—they are from my sister's personal wardrobe.

BENEATHA (*with incredulity*):   You—you sent all the way home—for me?

ASAGAI (*with charm*):   For you—I would do much more . . . Well, that is what I came for. I must go.

BENEATHA: Will you call me Monday?

ASAGAI: Yes . . . We have a great deal to talk about. I mean about identity and time and all that.

BENEATHA: Time?

ASAGAI: Yes. About how much time one needs to know what one feels.

BENEATHA: You see! You never understood that there is more than one kind of feeling which can exist between a man and a woman—or, at least, there should be.

ASAGAI (*shaking his head negatively but gently*):   No. Between a man and a woman there need be only one kind of feeling. I have that for you . . . Now even . . . right this moment . . .

BENEATHA: I know—and by itself—it won't do. I can find that anywhere.

ASAGAI: For a woman it should be enough.

BENEATHA: I know—because that's what it says in all the novels that men write. But it isn't. Go ahead and laugh—but I'm not interested in being someone's little episode in America or—(*With feminine vengeance*)—one of them! (ASAGAI *has burst into laughter again*) That's funny as hell, huh!

ASAGAI: It's just that every American girl I have known has said that to me. White—black—in this you are all the same. And the same speech, too!

BENEATHA (*angrily*):   Yuk, yuk, yuk!

ASAGAI: It's how you can be sure that the world's most liberated women are not liberated at all. You all talk about it too much!

(MAMA *enters and is immediately all social charm because of the presence of a guest*)

BENEATHA: Oh—Mama—this is Mr. Asagai.

MAMA: How do you do?

ASAGAI (*total politeness to an elder*):   How do you do, Mrs. Younger. Please forgive me for coming at such an outrageous hour on a Saturday.

MAMA: Well, you are quite welcome. I just hope you understand that our house don't always look like this. (*Chatterish*) You must come again. I would love to hear all about—(*Not sure of the name*)—your country. I think it's so sad the way our American Negroes don't know nothing about Africa 'cept Tarzan and all that. And all that money they pour into these churches when they ought to be helping you people over there drive out them French and Englishmen done taken away your land.

(*The mother flashes a slightly superior look at her daughter upon completion of the recitation*)

ASAGAI (*taken aback by this sudden and acutely unrelated expression of sympathy*): Yes . . . yes . . .

MAMA (*smiling at him suddenly and relaxing and looking him over*):   How many miles is it from here to where you come from?

ASAGAI: Many thousands.

MAMA (*looking at him as she would* WALTER):   I bet you don't half look after yourself, being away from your mama either. I spec you better come 'round here from time to time to get yourself some decent home-cooked meals . . .

ASAGAI (*moved*):   Thank you. Thank you very much. (*They are all quiet, then—*) Well . . . I must go. I will call you Monday, Alaiyo.

MAMA: What's that he call you?

ASAGAI: Oh—"Alaiyo." I hope you don't mind. It is what you would call a nickname, I think. It is a Yoruba word. I am a Yoruba.

MAMA (*looking at* BENEATHA):   I—I thought he was from—(*Uncertain*)

ASAGAI (*understanding*):   Nigeria is my country. Yoruba is my tribal origin—

BENEATHA: You didn't tell us what Alaiyo means . . . for all I know, you might be calling me Little Idiot or something . . .

ASAGAI: Well . . . let me see . . . I do not know how just to explain it . . . The sense of a thing can be so different when it changes languages.

BENEATHA: You're evading.

ASAGAI: No—really it is difficult . . . (*Thinking*) It means . . . it means One for Whom Bread—Food—Is Not Enough. (*He looks at her*) Is that all right?

BENEATHA (*understanding, softly*):   Thank you.

MAMA (*looking from one to the other and not understanding any of it*):   Well . . . that's nice . . . You must come see us again—Mr.——

ASAGAI: Ah-sah-guy . . .

MAMA: Yes . . . Do come again.

ASAGAI: Good-bye.

(*He exits*)

MAMA (*after him*):   Lord, that's a pretty thing just went out here! (*Insinuatingly, to her daughter*) Yes, I guess I see why we done commence to get so interested in Africa 'round here. Missionaries my aunt Jenny!

(*She exits*)

BENEATHA: Oh, Mama! . . .

(*She picks up the Nigerian dress and holds it up to her in front of the mirror again. She sets the headdress on haphazardly and then notices her hair again and clutches at it and then replaces the headdress and frowns at herself. Then she starts to wriggle in front of the mirror as she thinks a Nigerian woman might.* TRAVIS *enters and stands regarding her*)

TRAVIS: What's the matter, girl, you cracking up?

BENEATHA: Shut up.

(*She pulls the headdress off and looks at herself in the mirror and clutches at her hair again and squinches her eyes as if trying to imagine something. Then, suddenly, she gets her raincoat and kerchief and hurriedly prepares for going out*)

MAMA (*coming back into the room*):   She's resting now. Travis, baby, run next door and ask Miss Johnson to please let me have a little kitchen cleanser. This here can is empty as Jacob's kettle.

TRAVIS: I just came in.

MAMA: Do as you told. (*He exits and she looks at her daughter*) Where you going?

BENEATHA (*halting at the door*):   To become a queen of the Nile!

(*She exits in a breathless blaze of glory.* RUTH *appears in the bedroom doorway*)

MAMA: Who told you to get up?

RUTH: Ain't nothing wrong with me to be lying in no bed for. Where did Bennie go?

MAMA (*drumming her fingers*):   Far as I could make out—to Egypt. (RUTH *just looks at her*) What time is it getting to?

RUTH: Ten twenty. And the mailman going to ring that bell this morning just like he done every morning for the last umpteen years.

(TRAVIS *comes in with the cleanser can*)

TRAVIS: She say to tell you that she don't have much.

MAMA (*angrily*):   Lord, some people I could name sure is tight-fisted! (*Directing her grandson*) Mark two cans of cleanser down on the list there. If she that hard up for kitchen cleanser, I sure don't want to forget to get her none!

RUTH: Lena—maybe the woman is just short on cleanser—

MAMA (*not listening*):   —Much baking powder as she done borrowed from me all these years, she could of done gone into the baking business!

(*The bell sounds suddenly and sharply and all three are stunned—serious and silent—mid-speech. In spite of all the other conversations and distractions of the morning, this is what they have been waiting for, even* TRAVIS, *who looks helplessly from his mother to his grandmother.* RUTH *is the first to come to life again*)

RUTH (*to* TRAVIS):   Get down them steps, boy!

(TRAVIS *snaps to life and flies out to get the mail*)

MAMA (*her eyes wide, her hand to her breast*):   You mean it done really come?

RUTH (*excited*):   Oh, Miss Lena!

MAMA (*collecting herself*):   Well . . . I don't know what we all so excited about 'round here for. We known it was coming for months.

RUTH: That's a whole lot different from having it come and being able to hold it in your hands . . . a piece of paper worth ten thousand dollars . . . (TRAVIS *bursts back into the room. He holds the envelope high above his head, like a little dancer, his face is radiant and he is breathless. He moves to his grandmother with sudden slow ceremony and puts the envelope into her hands. She accepts it, and then merely holds it and looks at it*) Come on! Open it . . . Lord have mercy, I wish Walter Lee was here!

TRAVIS: Open it, Grandmama!

MAMA (*staring at it*):   Now you all be quiet. It's just a check.

RUTH: Open it . . .

MAMA (*still staring at it*):   Now don't act silly . . . We ain't never been no people to act silly 'bout no money—

RUTH (*swiftly*):   We ain't never had none before—OPEN IT!

(MAMA *finally makes a good strong tear and pulls out the thin blue slice of paper and inspects it closely. The boy and his mother study it raptly over* MAMA'S *shoulders*)

MAMA: *Travis!* (*She is counting off with doubt*) Is that the right number of zeros.

TRAVIS: Yes'm . . . ten thousand dollars. Gaalee, Grandmama, you rich.

MAMA (*she holds the check away from her, still looking at it. Slowly her face sobers into a mask of unhappiness*): Ten thousand dollars. (*She hands it to* RUTH) Put it away somewhere, Ruth. (*She does not look at* RUTH; *her eyes seem to be seeing something somewhere very far off*) Ten thousand dollars they give you. Ten thousand dollars.

TRAVIS (*to his mother, sincerely*): What's the matter with Grandmama—don't she want to be rich?

RUTH (*distractedly*): You go on out and play now, baby. (TRAVIS *exits.* MAMA *starts wiping dishes absently, humming intently to herself.* RUTH *turns to her, with kind exasperation*) You've gone and got yourself upset.

MAMA (*not looking at her*): I spec if it wasn't for you all . . . I would just put that money away or give it to the church or something.

RUTH: Now what kind of talk is that. Mr. Younger would just be plain mad if he could hear you talking foolish like that.

MAMA (*stopping and staring off*): Yes . . . he sure would. (*Sighing*) We got enough to do with that money, all right. (*She halts then, and turns and looks at her daughter-in-law hard;* RUTH *avoids her eyes and* MAMA *wipes her hands with finality and starts to speak firmly to* RUTH) Where did you go today, girl?

RUTH: To the doctor.

MAMA (*impatiently*): Now, Ruth . . . you know better than that. Old Doctor Jones is strange enough in his way but there ain't nothing 'bout him make somebody slip and call him "she"—like you done this morning.

RUTH: Well, that's what happened—my tongue slipped.

MAMA: You went to see that woman, didn't you?

RUTH (*defensively, giving herself away*): What woman you talking about?

MAMA (*angrily*): That woman who—

(WALTER *enters in great excitement*)

WALTER: Did it come?

MAMA (*quietly*): Can't you give people a Christian greeting before you start asking about money?

WALTER (*to* RUTH): Did it come? (RUTH *unfolds the check and lays it quietly before him, watching him intently with thoughts of her own.* WALTER *sits down and grasps it close and counts off the zeros*) Ten thousand dollars—(*He turns suddenly, frantically to his mother and draws some papers out of his breast pocket*) Mama—look. Old Willy Harris put everything on paper—

MAMA: Son—I think you ought to talk to your wife . . . I'll go on out and leave you alone if you want—

WALTER: I can talk to her later—Mama, look—

MAMA: Son—

WALTER: WILL SOMEBODY PLEASE LISTEN TO ME TODAY!

MAMA (*quietly*): I don't 'low no yellin' in this house, Walter Lee, and you know it—(WALTER *stares at them in frustration and starts to speak several times*) And there ain't going to be no investing in no liquor stores.

WALTER: But, Mama, you ain't even looked at it.

MAMA: I don't aim to have to speak on that again.

(*A long pause*)

WALTER: You ain't looked at it and you don't aim to have to speak on that again? You ain't even looked at it and *you* have decided—(*Crumpling his papers*) Well, *you* tell that to my boy tonight when you put him to sleep on the living-room couch . . . (*Turning to* MAMA *and speaking directly to her*) Yeah—and tell it to my wife, Mama, tomorrow when she has to go out of here to look after somebody else's kids. And tell it to *me,* Mama, every time we need a new pair of curtains and I have to watch *you* go out and work in somebody's kitchen. Yeah, you tell me then!

(WALTER *starts out*)

RUTH: Where you going?

WALTER: I'm going out!

RUTH: Where?

WALTER: Just out of this house somewhere—

RUTH (*getting her coat*):   I'll come too.

WALTER: I don't want you to come!

RUTH: I got something to talk to you about, Walter.

WALTER: That's too bad.

MAMA (*still quietly*):   Walter Lee—(*She waits and he finally turns and looks at her*) Sit down.

WALTER: I'm a grown man, Mama.

MAMA: Ain't nobody said you wasn't grown. But you still in my house and my presence. And as long as you are—you'll talk to your wife civil. Now sit down.

RUTH (*suddenly*):   Oh, let him go on out and drink himself to death! He makes me sick to my stomach! (*She flings her coat against him and exits to bedroom*)

WALTER (*violently flinging the coat after her*):   And you turn mine too, baby! (*The door slams behind her*) That was my biggest mistake—

MAMA (*still quietly*):   Walter, what is the matter with you?

WALTER: Matter with me? Ain't nothing the matter with *me!*

MAMA: Yes there is. Something eating you up like a crazy man. Something more than me not giving you this money. The past few years I been watching it happen to you. You get all nervous acting and kind of wild in the eyes—(WALTER *jumps up impatiently at her words*) I said sit there now, I'm talking to you!

WALTER: Mama—I don't need no nagging at me today.

MAMA: Seem like you getting to a place where you always tied up in some kind of knot about something. But if anybody ask you 'bout it you just yell at 'em and bust out the house and go out and drink somewheres. Walter Lee, people can't live with that. Ruth's a good, patient girl in her way—but you getting to be too much. Boy, don't make the mistake of driving that girl away from you.

WALTER: Why—what she do for me?

MAMA: She loves you.

WALTER: Mama—I'm going out. I want to go off somewhere and be by myself for a while.

MAMA: I'm sorry 'bout your liquor store, son. It just wasn't the thing for us to do. That's what I want to tell you about—

WALTER: I got to go out, Mama—

(*He rises*)

MAMA: It's dangerous, son.

WALTER: What's dangerous?

MAMA: When a man goes outside his home to look for peace.

WALTER (*beseechingly*): Then why can't there never be no peace in this house then?

MAMA: You done found it in some other house?

WALTER: No—there ain't no woman! Why do women always think there's a woman somewhere when a man gets restless. (*Picks up the check*) Do you know what this money means to me? Do you know what this money can do for us? (*Puts it back*) Mama—Mama—I want so many things . . .

MAMA: Yes, son—

WALTER: I want so many things that they are driving me kind of crazy . . . Mama—look at me.

MAMA: I'm looking at you. You a good-looking boy. You got a job, a nice wife, a fine boy and—

WALTER: A job. (*Looks at her*) Mama, a job? I open and close car doors all day long. I drive a man around in his limousine and I say, "Yes, sir; no, sir; very good, sir; shall I take the Drive, sir?" Mama, that ain't no kind of job . . . that ain't nothing at all. (*Very quietly*) Mama, I don't know if I can make you understand.

MAMA: Understand what, baby?

WALTER (*quietly*): Sometimes it's like I can see the future stretched out in front of me—just plain as day. The future, Mama. Hanging over there at the edge of my days. Just waiting for me—a big, looming blank space—full of *nothing*. Just waiting for *me*. But it don't have to be. (*Pause. Kneeling beside her chair*) Mama—sometimes when I'm downtown and I pass them cool, quiet-looking restaurants where them white boys are sitting back and talking 'bout things . . . sitting there turning deals worth millions of dollars . . . sometimes I see guys don't look much older than me—

MAMA: Son—how come you talk so much 'bout money?

WALTER (*with immense passion*): Because it is life, Mama!

MAMA (*quietly*): Oh—(*Very quietly*) So now it's life. Money is life. Once upon a time freedom used to be life—now it's money. I guess the world really do change . . .

WALTER: No—it was always money, Mama. We just didn't know about it.

MAMA: No . . . something has changed. (*She looks at him*) You something new, boy. In my time we was worried about not being lynched and getting to the North if we could and how to stay alive and still have a pinch of dignity too . . . Now here come you and Beneatha—talking 'bout things we ain't never even thought about hardly, me and your daddy. You ain't satisfied or proud of nothing we done. I mean that you had a home; that we kept you out of trouble till you was grown; that you don't have to ride to work on the back of nobody's streetcar— You my children—but how different we done become.

WALTER (*a long beat. He pats her hand and gets up*):   You just don't understand, Mama, you just don't understand.

MAMA: Son—do you know your wife is expecting another baby? (WALTER *stands, stunned, and absorbs what his mother has said*) That's what she wanted to talk to you about. (WALTER *sinks down into a chair*) This ain't for me to be telling—but you ought to know. (*She waits*) I think Ruth is thinking 'bout getting rid of that child.

WALTER (*slowly understanding*):   —No—no—Ruth wouldn't do that.

MAMA: When the world gets ugly enough—a woman will do anything for her family. *The part that's already living.*

WALTER: You don't know Ruth, Mama, if you think she would do that.

(RUTH *opens the bedroom door and stands there a little limp*)

RUTH (*beaten*):   Yes I would too, Walter. (*Pause*) I gave her a five-dollar down payment.

(*There is total silence as the man stares at his wife and the mother stares at her son*)

MAMA (*presently*):   Well—(*Tightly*) Well—son, I'm waiting to hear you say something . . . (*She waits*) I'm waiting to hear how you be your father's son. Be the man he was . . . (*Pause. The silence shouts*) Your wife say she going to destroy your child. And I'm waiting to hear you talk like him and say we a people who give children life, not who destroys them—(*She rises*) I'm waiting to see you stand up and look like your daddy and say we done give up one baby to poverty and that we ain't going to give up nary another one . . . I'm waiting.

WALTER: Ruth—(*He can say nothing*)

MAMA: If you a son of mine, tell her! (WALTER *picks up his keys and his coat and walks out. She continues, bitterly*) You . . . you are a disgrace to your father's memory. Somebody get me my hat!

Curtain

ACT II

Scene I

Time: Later the same day.

At rise: RUTH *is ironing again. She has the radio going. Presently* BENEATHA'S *bedroom door opens and* RUTH'S *mouth falls and she puts down the iron in fascination.*

RUTH: What have we got on tonight!

BENEATHA (*emerging grandly from the doorway so that we can see her thoroughly robed in the costume Asagai brought*): You are looking at what a well-dressed Nigerian woman wears—(*She parades for* RUTH, *her hair completely hidden by the headdress; she is coquettishly fanning herself with an ornate oriental fan, mistakenly more like Butterfly than any Nigerian that ever was*) Isn't it beautiful? (*She promenades to the radio and, with an arrogant flourish, turns off the good loud blues that is playing*) Enough of this assimilationist junk! (RUTH *follows her with her eyes as she goes to the phonograph and puts on a record and turns and waits ceremoniously for the music to come up. Then, with a shout*—) OCOMOGOSIAY!

(RUTH *jumps. The music comes up, a lovely Nigerian melody.* BENEATHA *listens, enraptured, her eyes far away— "back to the past." She begins to dance.* RUTH *is dumbfounded*)

RUTH: What kind of dance is that?

BENEATHA: A folk dance.

RUTH (*Pearl Bailey*):   What kind of folks do that, honey?

BENEATHA: It's from Nigeria. It's a dance of welcome.

RUTH: Who you welcoming?

BENEATHA: The men back to the village.

RUTH: Where they been?

BENEATHA: How should I know—out hunting or something. Anyway, they are coming back now . . .

RUTH: Well, that's good.

BENEATHA (*with the record*):

    Alundi, alundi

    Alundi alunya

    Jop pu à jeepua

    Ang gu soooooooooo

    Ai yai yae . . .

    Ayehaye—alundi . . .

(WALTER *comes in during this performance; he has obviously been drinking. He leans against the door heavily and watches his sister, at first with distaste. Then his eyes look off— "back to the past"—as he lifts both his fists to the roof, screaming*)

WALTER: YEAH . . . AND ETHIOPIA STRETCH FORTH HER HANDS AGAIN! . . .

RUTH (*drily, looking at him*):   Yes—and Africa sure is claiming her own tonight. (*She gives them both up and starts ironing again*)

WALTER (*all in a drunken, dramatic shout*):   Shut up! . . . I'm digging them drums . . . them drums move me! . . . (*He makes his weaving way to his wife's face and leans in close to her*) In my *heart of hearts*—(*He thumps his chest*)—I am much warrior!

RUTH (*without even looking up*):   In your heart of hearts you are much drunkard.

WALTER (*coming away from her and starting to wander around the room, shouting*): Me and Jomo . . . (*Intently, in his sister's face. She has stopped dancing to watch him in this unknown mood*) That's my man, Kenyatta. (*Shouting and thumping his chest*) FLAMING SPEAR! HOT DAMN! (*He is suddenly in possession of an imaginary spear and actively spearing enemies all over the room*) OCOMOGOSIAY . . .

BENEATHA (*to encourage* WALTER, *thoroughly caught up with this side of him*): OCOMOGOSIAY, FLAMING SPEAR!

WALTER: THE LION IS WAKING . . . OWIMOWEH!

(*He pulls his shirt open and leaps up on the table and gestures with his spear*)

BENEATHA: OWIMOWEH!

WALTER (*on the table, very far gone, his eyes pure glass sheets. He sees what we cannot, that he is a leader of his people, a great chief, a descendant of Chaka, and that the hour to march has come*):   Listen, my black brothers—

BENEATHA: OCOMOGOSIAY!

WALTER: —Do you hear the waters rushing against the shores of the coastlands—

BENEATHA: OCOMOGOSIAY!

WALTER: —Do you hear the screeching of the cocks in yonder hills beyond where the chiefs meet in council for the coming of the mighty war—

BENEATHA: OCOMOGOSIAY!

(*And now the lighting shifts subtly to suggest the world of* WALTER'S *imagination, and the mood shifts from pure comedy. It is the inner* WALTER *speaking: the Southside chauffeur has assumed an unexpected majesty*)

WALTER: —Do you hear the beating of the wings of the birds flying low over the mountains and the low places of our land—

BENEATHA: OCOMOGOSIAY!

WALTER: —Do you hear the singing of the women, singing the war songs of our fathers to the babies in the great houses? Singing the sweet war songs! (*The doorbell rings*) OH, DO YOU HEAR, MY *BLACK* BROTHERS!

BENEATHA (*completely gone*):   We hear you, Flaming Spear—

(RUTH *shuts off the phonograph and opens the door.* GEORGE MURCHISON *enters*)

WALTER: Telling us to prepare for the GREATNESS OF THE TIME! (*Lights back to normal. He turns and sees* GEORGE) Black Brother!

(*He extends his hand for the fraternal clasp*)

GEORGE: Black Brother, hell!

RUTH (*having had enough, and embarrassed for the family*):   Beneatha, you got company—what's the matter with you? Walter Lee Younger, get down off that table and stop acting like a fool . . .

(WALTER *comes down off the table suddenly and makes a quick exit to the bathroom*)

RUTH: He's had a little to drink . . . I don't know what her excuse is.

GEORGE (*to* BENEATHA):   Look honey, we're going *to* the theatre—we're not going to be *in* it . . . so go change, huh?

(BENEATHA *looks at him and slowly, ceremoniously, lifts her hands and pulls off the headdress. Her hair is close-cropped and unstraightened.* GEORGE *freezes mid-sentence and* RUTH'S *eyes all but fall out of her head*)

GEORGE: What in the name of—

RUTH (*touching* BENEATHA'S *hair*):   Girl, you done lost your natural mind!? Look at your head!

GEORGE: What have you done to your head—I mean your hair!

BENEATHA: Nothing—except cut it off.

RUTH: Now that's the truth—it's what ain't been done to it! You expect this boy to go out with you with your head all nappy like that?

BENEATHA (*looking at* GEORGE):   That's up to George. If he's ashamed of his heritage—

GEORGE: Oh, don't be so proud of yourself, Bennie—just because you look eccentric.

BENEATHA: How can something that's natural be eccentric?

GEORGE: That's what being eccentric means—being natural. Get dressed.

BENEATHA: I don't like that, George.

RUTH: Why must you and your brother make an argument out of everything people say?

BENEATHA: Because I hate assimilationist Negroes!

RUTH: Will somebody please tell me what assimila-who-ever means!

GEORGE: Oh, it's just a college girl's way of calling people Uncle Toms—but that isn't what it means at all.

RUTH: Well, what does it mean?

BENEATHA (*cutting* GEORGE *off and staring at him as she replies to* RUTH):   It means someone who is willing to give up his own culture and submerge himself completely in the dominant, and in this case *oppressive* culture!

GEORGE: Oh, dear, dear, dear! Here we go! A lecture on the African past! On our Great West African Heritage! In one second we will hear all about the great Ashanti empires; the great Songhay civilizations; and the great sculpture of Bénin—and then some poetry in the Bantu—and the whole monologue will end with the word *heritage!* (*Nastily*) Let's face it, baby, your heritage is nothing but a bunch of raggedy-assed spirituals and some grass huts!

BENEATHA: GRASS HUTS! (RUTH *crosses to her and forcibly pushes her toward the bedroom*) See there . . . you are standing there in your splendid ignorance talking about people who were the first to smelt iron on the face of the earth! (RUTH *is pushing her through the door*) The Ashanti were performing surgical operations when the English—(RUTH *pulls the door to, with* BENEATHA *on the other side, and smiles graciously at* GEORGE. BENEATHA *opens the door and shouts the end of the sentence defiantly at* GEORGE)—were still tatooing themselves with blue dragons! (*She goes back inside*)

RUTH: Have a seat, George (*They both sit.* RUTH *folds her hands rather primly on her lap, determined to demonstrate the civilization of the family*) Warm, ain't it? I mean for September. (*Pause*) Just like they always say about Chicago weather: If it's too hot or cold for you, just wait a minute and it'll change. (*She smiles happily at this cliché of clichés*) Everybody say it's got to do with them bombs and things they keep setting off. (*Pause*) Would you like a nice cold beer?

GEORGE: No, thank you. I don't care for beer. (*He looks at his watch*) I hope she hurries up.

RUTH: What time is the show?

GEORGE: It's an eight-thirty curtain. That's just Chicago, though. In New York standard curtain time is eight forty.

(*He is rather proud of this knowledge*)

RUTH (*properly appreciating it*):   You get to New York a lot?

GEORGE (*offhand*):   Few times a year.

RUTH: Oh—that's nice. I've never been to New York.

(WALTER *enters. We feel he has relieved himself, but the edge of unreality is still with him*)

WALTER: New York ain't got nothing Chicago ain't. Just a bunch of hustling people all squeezed up together—being "Eastern."

(*He turns his face into a screw of displeasure*)

GEORGE: Oh—you've been?

WALTER: *Plenty* of times.

RUTH (*shocked at the lie*):   Walter Lee Younger!

WALTER (*staring her down*):   Plenty! (*Pause*) What we got to drink in this house? Why don't you offer this man some refreshment. (*To* GEORGE) They don't know how to entertain people in this house, man.

GEORGE: Thank you—I don't really care for anything.

WALTER (*feeling his head; sobriety coming*):   Where's Mama?

RUTH: She ain't come back yet.

WALTER (*looking* MURCHISON *over from head to toe, scrutinizing his carefully casual tweed sports jacket over cashmere V-neck sweater over soft eyelet shirt and tie, and soft slacks, finished off with white buckskin shoes*):   Why all you college boys wear them faggoty-looking white shoes?

RUTH: Walter Lee!

(GEORGE MURCHISON *ignores the remark*)

WALTER (*to* RUTH):   Well, they look crazy as hell—white shoes, cold as it is.

RUTH (*crushed*):   You have to excuse him—

WALTER: No he don't! Excuse me for what? What you always excusing me for! I'll excuse myself when I needs to be excused! (*A pause*) They look as funny as them black knee socks Beneatha wears out of here all the time.

RUTH: It's the college *style,* Walter.

WALTER: Style, hell. She looks like she got burnt legs or something!

RUTH: Oh, Walter—

WALTER (*an irritable mimic*):   Oh, Walter! Oh, Walter! (*To* MURCHISON) How's your old man making out? I understand you all going to buy that big hotel on the Drive? (*He finds a beer in the refrigerator, wanders over to* MURCHISON, *sipping and wiping his lips with the back of his hand, and straddling a choir backwards to talk to the other man*) Shrewd move. Your old man is all right, man. (*Tapping his head and half winking for emphasis*) I mean he knows how to operate. I mean he thinks *big,* you know what I mean, I mean for a *home,* you know? But I think he's kind of running out of ideas now. I'd like to talk to him. Listen, man, I got some plans that could turn this city upside down. I

mean think like he does. *Big.* Invest big, gamble big, hell, lose *big* if you have
to, you know what I mean. It's hard to find a man on this whole Southside
who understands my kind of thinking—you dig? (*He scrutinizes* MURCHISON
again, drinks his beer, squints his eyes and leans in close, confidential, man to man)
Me and you ought to sit down and talk sometimes, man. Man, I got me some
ideas . . .

MURCHISON (*with boredom*):   Yeah—sometimes we'll have to do that,
Walter.

WALTER (*understanding the indifference, and offended*):   Yeah—well, when you
get the time, man. I know you a busy little boy.

RUTH: Walter, please—

WALTER (*bitterly, hurt*):   I know ain't nothing in this world as busy as you
colored college boys with your fraternity pins and white shoes . . .

RUTH (*covering her face with humiliation*):   Oh, Walter Lee—

WALTER: I see you all all the time—with the books tucked under your
arms—going to your (*British A—a mimic*) "clahsses." And for what! What the
hell you learning over there? Filling up your heads—(*Counting off on his fingers*)—with the sociology and the psychology—but they teaching you how to
be a man? How to take over and run the world? They teaching you how to
run a rubber plantation or a steel mill? Naw—just to talk proper and read books
and wear them faggoty-looking white shoes . . .

GEORGE (*looking at him with distaste, a little above it all*):   You're all wacked
up with bitterness, man.

WALTER (*intently, almost quietly, between the teeth, glaring at the boy*):   And
you—ain't you bitter, man? Ain't you just about had it yet? Don't you see no
stars gleaming that you can't reach out and grab? You happy?—You contented
son-of-a-bitch—you happy? You got it made? Bitter? Man, I'm a volcano. Bitter? Here I am a giant—surrounded by ants! Ants who can't even understand
what it is the giant is talking about.

RUTH (*passionately and suddenly*):   Oh, Walter—ain't you with nobody!

WALTER (*violently*):   No! 'Cause ain't nobody with me! Not even my own
mother!

RUTH: Walter, that's a terrible thing to say!

(BENEATHA *enters, dressed for the evening in a cocktail dress and earrings, hair natural*)

GEORGE: Well—hey—(*Crosses to* BENEATHA; *thoughtful, with emphasis, since
this is a reversal*) You look great!

WALTER (*seeing his sister's hair for the first time*):   What's the matter with your
head?

BENEATHA (*tired of the jokes now*):   I cut it off, Brother.

WALTER (*coming close to inspect it and walking around her*):   Well, I'll be damned.
So that's what they mean by the African bush . . .

BENEATHA: Ha ha. Let's go, George.

GEORGE (*looking at her*):   You know something? I like it. It's sharp. I mean
it really is. (*Helps her into her wrap*)

RUTH: Yes—I think so, too. (*She goes to the mirror and starts to clutch at her
hair*)

WALTER: Oh no! You leave yours alone, baby. You might turn out to have a pin-shaped head or something!

BENEATHA: See you all later.

RUTH: Have a nice time.

GEORGE: Thanks. Good night. (*Half out the door, he reopens it. To* WALTER) Good night, Prometheus!

(BENEATHA *and* GEORGE *exit*)

WALTER (*to* RUTH):   Who is Prometheus?

RUTH: I don't know. Don't worry about it.

WALTER (*in fury, pointing after* GEORGE):   See there—they get to a point where they can't insult you man to man—they got to go talk about something ain't nobody never heard of!

RUTH: How do you know it was an insult? (*To humor him*) Maybe Prometheus is a nice fellow.

WALTER: Prometheus! I bet there ain't even no such thing! I bet that simple-minded clown—

RUTH: Walter—

(*She stops what she is doing and looks at him*)

WALTER (*yelling*):   Don't start!

RUTH: Start what?

WALTER: Your nagging! Where was I? Who was I with? How much money did I spend?

RUTH (*plaintively*):   Walter Lee—why don't we just try to talk about it . . .

WALTER (*not listening*):   I been out talking with people who understand me. People who care about the things I got on my mind.

RUTH (*wearily*):   I guess that means people like Willy Harris.

WALTER: Yes, people like Willy Harris.

RUTH (*with a sudden flash of impatience*):   Why don't you all just hurry up and go into the banking business and stop talking about it!

WALTER: Why? You want to know why? 'Cause we all tied up in a race of people that don't know how to do nothing but moan, pray and have babies!

(*The line is too bitter even for him and he looks at her and sits down*)

RUTH: Oh, Walter . . . (*Softly*) Honey, why can't you stop fighting me?

WALTER (*without thinking*):   Who's fighting you? Who even cares about you?

(*This line begins the retardation of his mood*)

RUTH: Well—(*She waits a long time, and then with resignation starts to put away her things*) I guess I might as well go on to bed . . . (*More or less to herself*) I don't know where we lost it . . . but we have . . . (*Then, to him*) I—I'm sorry about this new baby, Walter. I guess maybe I better go on and do what I started . . . I guess I just didn't realize how bad things was with us . . . I guess I just didn't really realize—(*She starts out to the bedroom and stops*) You want some hot milk?

WALTER: Hot milk?

RUTH: Yes—hot milk.

WALTER: Why hot milk?

RUTH: 'Cause after all that liquor you come home with you ought to have something hot in your stomach.

WALTER: I don't want no milk.

RUTH: You want some coffee then?

WALTER: No, I don't want no coffee. I don't want nothing hot to drink. (*Almost plaintively*) Why you always trying to give me something to eat?

RUTH (*standing and looking at him helplessly*):   What *else* can I give you, Walter Lee Younger?

(*She stands and looks at him and presently turns to go out again. He lifts his head and watches her going away from him in a new mood which began to emerge when he asked her "Who cares about you?"*)

WALTER: It's been rough, ain't it, baby? (*She hears and stops but does not turn around and he continues to her back*) I guess between two people there ain't never as much understood as folks generally thinks there is. I mean like between me and you—(*She turns to face him*) How we gets to the place where we scared to talk softness to each other. (*He waits, thinking hard himself*) Why you think it got to be like that? (*He is thoughtful, almost as a child would be*) Ruth, what is it gets into people ought to be close?

RUTH: I don't know, honey. I think about it a lot.

WALTER: On account of you and me, you mean? The way things are with us. The way something done come down between us.

RUTH: There ain't so much between us, Walter . . . Not when you come to me and try to talk to me. Try to be with me . . . a little even.

WALTER (*total honesty*):   Sometimes . . . sometimes . . . I don't even know how to try.

RUTH: Walter—

WALTER: Yes?

RUTH (*coming to him, gently and with misgiving, but coming to him*):   Honey . . . life don't have to be like this. I mean sometimes people can do things so that things are better . . . You remember how we used to talk when Travis was born . . . about the way we were going to live . . . the kind of house . . . (*She is stroking his head*) Well, it's all starting to slip away from us . . .

(*He turns her to him and they look at each other and kiss, tenderly and hungrily. The door opens and* MAMA *enters—*WALTER *breaks away and jumps up. A beat*)

WALTER: Mama, where have you been?

MAMA: My—them steps is longer than they used to be. Whew! (*She sits down and ignores him*) How you feeling this evening, Ruth?

(RUTH *shrugs, disturbed at having been interrupted and watching her husband knowingly*)

WALTER: Mama, where have you been all day?

MAMA (*still ignoring him and leaning on the table and changing to more comfortable shoes*):   Where's Travis?

RUTH: I let him go out earlier and he ain't come back yet. Boy, is he going to get it!

WALTER: Mama!

MAMA (*as if she has heard him for the first time*):   Yes, son?

WALTER: Where did you go this afternoon?

MAMA: I went downtown to tend to some business that I had to tend to.

WALTER: What kind of business?

MAMA: You know better than to question me like a child, Brother.

WALTER (*rising and bending over the table*):   Where were you, Mama? (*Bringing his fists down and shouting*) Mama, you didn't go do something with that insurance money, something crazy?

(*The front door opens slowly, interrupting him, and* TRAVIS *peeks his head in, less than hopefully*)

TRAVIS (*to his mother*):   Mama, I—

RUTH: "Mama I" nothing! You're going to get it, boy! Get on in that bedroom and get yourself ready!

TRAVIS: But I—

MAMA: Why don't you all never let the child explain hisself.

RUTH: Keep out of it now, Lena.

(MAMA *clamps her lips together, and* RUTH *advances toward her son menacingly*)

RUTH: A thousand times I have told you not to go off like that—

MAMA (*holding out her arms to her grandson*):   Well—at least let me tell him something. I want him to be the first one to hear . . . Come here, Travis. (*The boy obeys, gladly*) Travis—(*She takes him by the shoulder and looks into his face*)—you know that money we got in the mail this morning?

TRAVIS: Yes'm—

MAMA: Well—what you think your grandmama gone and done with that money?

TRAVIS: I don't know, Grandmama.

MAMA (*putting her finger on his nose for emphasis*):   She went out and she bought you a house! (*The explosion comes from* WALTER *at the end of the revelation and he jumps up and turns away from all of them in a fury.* MAMA *continues, to* TRAVIS) You glad about the house? It's going to be yours when you get to be a man.

TRAVIS: Yeah—I always wanted to live in a house.

MAMA: All right, gimme some sugar then—(TRAVIS *puts his arms around her neck as she watches her son over the boy's shoulder. Then, to* TRAVIS, *after the embrace*) Now when you say your prayers tonight, you thank God and your grandfather—'cause it was him who give you the house—in his way.

RUTH (*taking the boy from* MAMA *and pushing him toward the bedroom*):   Now you get out of here and get ready for your beating.

TRAVIS: Aw, Mama—

RUTH: Get on in there—(*Closing the door behind him and turning radiantly to her mother-in-law*) So you went and did it!

MAMA (*quietly, looking at her son with pain*):   Yes, I did.

RUTH (*raising both arms classically*):   PRAISE GOD! (*Looks at* WALTER *a moment, who says nothing. She crosses rapidly to her husband*) Please, honey—let me be glad . . . you be glad too. (*She has laid her hands on his shoulders, but he shakes himself free of her roughly, without turning to face her*) Oh, Walter . . . a home . . . a home. (*She comes back to* MAMA) Well—where is it? How big is it? How much it going to cost?

MAMA: Well—

RUTH: When we moving?

MAMA (*smiling at her*):   First of the month.

RUTH (*throwing back her head with jubilance*):   Praise God!

MAMA (*tentatively, still looking at her son's back turned against her and* RUTH): It's—it's a nice house too . . . (*She cannot help speaking directly to him. An imploring quality in her voice, her manner, makes her almost like a girl now*) Three bedrooms—nice big one for you and Ruth. . . . Me and Beneatha still have to share our room, but Travis have one of his own—and (*With difficulty*) I figure if the—new baby—is a boy, we could get one of them double-decker outfits . . . And there's a yard with a little patch of dirt where I could maybe get to grow me a few flowers . . . And a nice big basement . . .

RUTH: Walter honey, be glad—

MAMA (*still to his back, fingering things on the table*):   'Course I don't want to make it sound fancier than it is . . . It's just a plain little old house—but it's made good and solid—and it will be *ours*. Walter Lee—it makes a difference in a man when he can walk on floors that belong to *him* . . .

RUTH: Where is it?

MAMA (*frightened at this telling*):   Well—well—it's out there in Clybourne Park—

(RUTH'S *radiance fades abruptly, and* WALTER *finally turns slowly to face his mother with incredulity and hostility*)

RUTH: Where?

MAMA (*matter-of-factly*):   Four o six Clybourne Street, Clybourne Park.

RUTH: Clybourne Park? Mama, there ain't no colored people living in Clybourne Park.

MAMA (*almost idiotically*):   Well, I guess there's going to be some now.

WALTER (*bitterly*):   So that's the peace and comfort you went out and bought for us today!

MAMA (*raising her eyes to meet his finally*):   Son—I just tried to find the nicest place for the least amount of money for my family.

RUTH (*trying to recover from the shock*):   Well—well—'course I ain't one never been 'fraid of no crackers, mind you—but—well, wasn't there no other houses nowhere?

MAMA: Them houses they put up for colored in them areas way out all seem to cost twice as much as other houses. I did the best I could.

RUTH (*struck senseless with the news, in its various degrees of goodness and trouble, she sits a moment, her fists propping her chin in thought, and then she starts to rise, bringing her fists down with vigor, the radiance spreading from cheek to cheek again*):   Well— well!—All I can say is—if this is my time in life—MY TIME—to say goodbye—(*And she builds with momentum as she starts to circle the room with an exuberant, almost tearfully happy release*)—to these Goddamned cracking walls!—(*She pounds the walls)*—and these marching roaches!—(*She wipes at an imaginary army of march-ing roaches*)—and this cramped little closet which ain't now or never was no kitchen! . . . then I say it loud and good, HALLELUJAH! AND GOOD-BYE MISERY . . . I DON'T NEVER WANT TO SEE YOUR UGLY FACE AGAIN! (*She laughs joyously, having practically destroyed the apartment, and flings her arms up and lets them come down happily, slowly, reflectively, over her abdomen, aware for the first time perhaps that the life therein pulses with happiness and not despair*) Lena?

MAMA (*moved, watching her happiness*):   Yes, honey?

RUTH (*looking off*):   Is there—is there a whole lot of sunlight?

MAMA (*understanding*):   Yes, child, there's a whole lot of sunlight.

(*Long pause*)

RUTH (*collecting herself and going to the door of the room* TRAVIS *is in*):   Well— I guess I better see 'bout Travis. (*To* MAMA) Lord, I sure don't feel like whip-ping nobody today!

(*She exits*)

MAMA (*the mother and son are left alone now and the mother waits a long time, con-sidering deeply, before she speaks*):   Son—you—you understand what I done, don't you? (WALTER *is silent and sullen*) I—I just seen my family falling apart today . . . just falling to pieces in front of my eyes . . . We couldn't of gone on like we was today. We was going backwards 'stead of forwards—talking 'bout killing babies and wishing each other was dead . . . When it gets like that in life—you just got to do something different, push on out and do something bigger . . . (*She waits*) I wish you say something, son . . . I wish you'd say how deep inside you you think I done the right thing—

WALTER (*crossing slowly to his bedroom door and finally turning there and speaking measuredly*):   What you need me to say you done right for? *You* the head of this family. You run our lives like you want to. It was your money and you did what you wanted with it. So what you need for me to say it was all right for? (*Bitterly, to hurt her as deeply as he knows is possible*) So you butchered up a dream of mine—you—who always talking 'bout your children's dreams . . .

MAMA: Walter Lee—

(*He just closes the door behind him.* MAMA *sits alone, thinking heavily*)

Curtain

Scene II

Time: Friday night. A few weeks later.

At rise: Packing crates mark the intention of the family to move. BENEATHA *and* GEORGE *come in, presumably from an evening out again.*

GEORGE: O.K. . . . O.K., whatever you say . . . (*They both sit on the couch. He tries to kiss her. She moves away*) Look, we've had a nice evening; let's not spoil it, huh? . . .

(*He again turns her head and tries to nuzzle in and she turns away from him, not with distaste but with momentary lack of interest; in a mood to pursue what they were talking about*)

BENEATHA: I'm *trying* to talk to you.

GEORGE: We always talk.

BENEATHA: Yes—and I love to talk.

GEORGE (*exasperated; rising*):   I know it and I don't mind it sometimes . . . I want you to cut it out, see—The moody stuff, I mean. I don't like it. You're a nice-looking girl . . . all over. That's all you need, honey, forget the atmosphere. Guys aren't going to go for the atmosphere—they're going to go for what they see. Be glad for that. Drop the Garbo routine. It doesn't go with you. As for myself, I want a nice—(*Groping*)—simple (*Thoughtfully*)—sophisticated girl . . . not a poet—O.K.?

(*He starts to kiss her, she rebuffs him again and he jumps up*)

BENEATHA: Why are you angry, George?

GEORGE: Because this is stupid! I don't go out with you to discuss the nature of "quiet desperation" or to hear all about your thoughts—because the world will go on thinking what it thinks regardless—

BENEATHA: Then why read books? Why go to school?

GEORGE (*with artificial patience, counting on his fingers*):   It's simple. You read books—to learn facts—to get grades—to pass the course—to get a degree. That's all—it has nothing to do with thoughts.

(*A long pause*)

BENEATHA: I see. (*He starts to sit*) Good night, George.

(GEORGE *looks at her a little oddly, and starts to exit. He meets* MAMA *coming in*)

GEORGE: Oh—hello, Mrs. Younger.

MAMA: Hello, George, how you feeling?

GEORGE: Fine—fine, how are you?

MAMA: Oh, a little tired. You know them steps can get you after a day's work. You all have a nice time tonight?

GEORGE: Yes—a fine time. A fine time.

MAMA: Well, good night.

GEORGE: Good night. (*He exits.* MAMA *closes the door behind her*) Hello, honey. What you sitting like that for?

BENEATHA: I'm just sitting.

MAMA: Didn't you have a nice time?

BENEATHA: No.

MAMA: No? What's the matter?

BENEATHA: Mama, George is a fool—honest. (*She rises*)

MAMA (*hustling around unloading the packages she has entered with. She stops*):   Is he, baby?

BENEATHA: Yes.

(BENEATHA *makes up* TRAVIS' *bed as she talks*)

MAMA: You sure?

BENEATHA: Yes.

MAMA: Well—I guess you better not waste your time with no fools.

(BENEATHA *looks up at her mother, watching her put groceries in the refrigerator. Finally she gathers up her things and starts into the bedroom. At the door she stops and looks back at her mother*)

BENEATHA: Mama—

MAMA: Yes, baby—

BENEATHA: Thank you.

MAMA: For what?

BENEATHA: For understanding me this time.

(*She exits quickly and the mother stands, smiling a little, looking at the place where* BENEATHA *just stood.* RUTH *enters*)

RUTH: Now don't you fool with any of this stuff, Lena—

MAMA: Oh, I just thought I'd sort a few things out. Is Brother here?

RUTH: Yes.

MAMA (*with concern*): Is he—

RUTH (*reading her eyes*): Yes.

(MAMA *is silent and someone knocks on the door.* MAMA *and* RUTH *exchange weary and knowing glances and* RUTH *opens it to admit the neighbor,* MRS. JOHNSON,★ *who is a rather squeaky wide-eyed lady of no particular age, with a newspaper under her arm*)

MAMA (*changing her expression to acute delight and a ringing cheerful greeting*): Oh—hello there, Johnson.

JOHNSON (*This is a woman who decided long ago to be enthusiastic about EVERY-THING in life and she is inclined to wave her wrist vigorously at the height of her exclamatory comments*): Hello there, yourself! H'you this evening, Ruth?

RUTH (*not much of a deceptive type*): Fine, Mis' Johnson, h'you?

JOHNSON: Fine. (*Reaching out quickly, playfully, and patting* RUTH'S *stomach*) Ain't you starting to poke out none yet! (*She mugs with delight at the over-familiar remark and her eyes dart around looking at the crates and packing preparation;* MAMA'S *face is a cold sheet of endurance*) Oh, ain't we getting ready round here, though! Yessir! Lookathere! I'm telling you the Youngers is really getting ready to "move on up a little higher!"—Bless God!

MAMA (*a little drily, doubting the total sincerity of the Blesser*): Bless God.

JOHNSON: He's good, ain't He?

MAMA: Oh yes, He's good.

JOHNSON: I mean sometimes He works in mysterious ways . . . but He works, don't He!

MAMA (*the same*): Yes, he does.

JOHNSON: I'm just soooooo happy for y'all. And this here child—(*About* RUTH) looks like she could just pop open with happiness, don't she. Where's all the rest of the family?

★This character and the scene of her visit were cut from the original production and early editions of the play.

MAMA: Bennie's gone to bed—

JOHNSON: Ain't no . . . (*The implication is pregnancy*) sickness done hit you—
I hope . . . ?

MAMA: No—she just tired. She was out this evening.

JOHNSON (*all is a coo, an emphatic coo*):   Aw—ain't that lovely. She still going
out with the little Murchison boy?

MAMA (*drily*):   Ummmm huh.

JOHNSON: That's lovely. You sure got lovely children, Younger. Me and Isaiah talks all the time 'bout what fine children you was blessed with. We sure do.

MAMA: Ruth, give Mis' Johnson a piece of sweet potato pie and some milk.

JOHNSON: Oh honey, I can't stay hardly a minute—I just dropped in to
see if there was anything I could do. (*Accepting the food easily*) I guess y'all seen
the news what's all over the colored paper this week . . .

MAMA: No—didn't get mine yet this week.

JOHNSON (*lifting her head and blinking with the spirit of catastrophe*):   You mean
you ain't read 'bout them colored people that was bombed out their place out
there?

(RUTH *straightens with concern and takes the paper and reads it.* JOHNSON *notices her and feeds
commentary*)

JOHNSON: Ain't it something how bad these here white folks is getting here
in Chicago! Lord, getting so you think you right down in Mississippi! (*With a
tremendous and rather insincere sense of melodrama*) 'Course I thinks it's wonderful
how our folks keeps on pushing out. You hear some of these Negroes round
here talking 'bout how they don't go where they ain't wanted and all that—
but not me, honey! (*This is a lie*) Wilhemenia Othella Johnson goes anywhere,
any time she feels like it! (*With head movement for emphasis*) Yes I do! Why if we
left it up to these here crackers, the poor niggers wouldn't have nothing—(*She
clasps her hand over her mouth*) Oh, I always forgets you don't 'low that word in
your house.

MAMA (*quietly, looking at her*):   No—I don't 'low it.

JOHNSON (*vigorously again*):   Me neither! I was just telling Isaiah yesterday
when he come using it in front of me—I said, "Isaiah, it's just like Mis' Younger
says all the time—"

MAMA: Don't you want some more pie?

JOHNSON: No—no thank you; this was lovely. I got to get on over home
and have my midnight coffee. I hear some people say it don't let them sleep
but I finds I can't close my eyes right lessen I done had that laaaast cup of coffee . . . (*She waits. A beat. Undaunted*) My Goodnight coffee, I calls it!

MAMA (*with much eye-rolling and communication between herself and* RUTH): Ruth,
why don't you give Mis' Johnson some coffee.

(RUTH *gives* MAMA *an unpleasant look for her kindness*)

JOHNSON (*accepting the coffee*):   Where's Brother tonight?

MAMA: He's lying down.

JOHNSON: MMmmmmm, he sure gets his beauty rest, don't he? Good-
looking man. Sure is a good-looking man! (*Reaching out to pat* RUTH'S *stomach*

again) I guess that's how come we keep on having babies around here. (*She winks at* MAMA) One thing 'bout Brother, he always know how to have a *good* time. And soooooo ambitious! I bet it was his idea y'all moving out to Clybourne Park. Lord—I bet this time next month y'all's names will have been in the papers plenty—(*Holding up her hands to mark off each word of the headline she can see in front of her*) "NEGROES INVADE CLYBOURNE PARK—BOMBED!"

MAMA (*she and* RUTH *look at the woman in amazement*):   We ain't exactly moving out there to get bombed.

JOHNSON: Oh, honey—you know I'm praying to God every day that don't nothing like that happen! But you have to think of life like it is—and these here Chicago peckerwoods is some baaaad peckerwoods.

MAMA (*wearily*):   We done thought about all that Mis' Johnson.

(BEANEATHA *comes out of the bedroom in her robe and passes through to the bathroom.* MRS. JOHNSON *turns*)

JOHNSON: Hello there, Bennie!

BEANEATHA (*crisply*):   Hello, Mrs. Johnson.

JOHNSON: How is school?

BEANEATHA (*crisply*):   Fine, thank you. (*She goes out.*)

JOHNSON (*insulted*):   Getting so she don't have much to say to nobody.

MAMA: The child was on her way to the bathroom.

JOHNSON: I know—but sometimes she act like ain't got time to pass the time of day with nobody ain't been to college. Oh—I ain't criticizing her none. It's just—you know how some of our young people gets when they get a little education. (MAMA *and* RUTH *say nothing, just look at her*) Yes—well. Well, I guess I better get on home. (*Unmoving*) 'Course I can understand how she must be proud and everything—being the only one in the family to make something of herself. I know just being a chauffeur ain't never satisfied Brother none. He shouldn't feel like that, though. Ain't nothing wrong with being a chauffeur.

MAMA: There's plenty wrong with it.

JOHNSON: What?

MAMA: Plenty. My husband always said being any kind of a servant wasn't a fit thing for a man to have to be. He always said a man's hands was made to make things, or to turn the earth with—not to drive nobody's car for 'em—or—(*She looks at her own hands*) carry they slop jars. And my boy is just like him—he wasn't meant to wait on nobody.

JOHNSON (*rising, somewhat offended*):   Mmmmmmmmmm. The Youngers is too much for me! (*She looks around*) You sure one proud-acting bunch of colored folks. Well—I always thinks like Booker T. Washington said that time—"Education has spoiled many a good plow hand"—

MAMA: Is that what old Booker T. said?

JOHNSON: He sure did.

MAMA: Well, it sounds just like him. The fool.

JOHNSON (*indignantly*):   Well—he was one of our great men.

MAMA: Who said so?

JOHNSON (*nonplussed*):   You know, me and you ain't never agreed about some things, Lena Younger. I guess I better be going—

RUTH (*quickly*):   Good night.

JOHNSON: Good night. Oh—(*Thrusting it at her*) You can keep the paper! (*With a trill*) 'Night.

MAMA: Good night, Mis' Johnson.

(MRS. JOHNSON *exits*)

RUTH: If ignorance was gold . . .

MAMA: Shush. Don't talk about folks behind their backs.

RUTH: You do.

MAMA: I'm old and corrupted. (BENEATHA *enters*) You was rude to Mis' Johnson, Beneatha, and I don't like it at all.

BENEATHA (*at her door*):   Mama, if there are two things we, as a people, have got to overcome, one is the Klu Klux Klan—and the other is Mrs. Johnson. (*She exits*)

MAMA: Smart aleck.

(*The phone rings*)

RUTH: I'll get it.

MAMA: Lord, ain't this a popular place tonight.

RUTH (*at the phone*):   Hello—Just a minute. (*Goes to door*) Walter, it's Mrs. Arnold. (*Waits. Goes back to the phone. Tense*) Hello. Yes, this is his wife speaking . . . He's lying down now. Yes . . . well, he'll be in tomorrow. He's been very sick. Yes—I know we should have called, but we were so sure he'd be able to come in today. Yes—yes, I'm very sorry. Yes . . . Thank you very much. (*She hangs up.* WALTER *is standing in the doorway of the bedroom behind her*) That was Mrs. Arnold.

WALTER (*indifferently*):   Was it?

RUTH: She said if you don't come in tomorrow that they are getting a new man . . .

WALTER: Ain't that sad—ain't that crying sad.

RUTH: She said Mr. Arnold has had to take a cab for three days . . . Walter, you ain't been to work for three days! (*This is a revelation to her*) Where you been, Walter Lee Younger? (WALTER *looks at her and starts to laugh*) You're going to lose your job.

WALTER: That's right . . . (*He turns on the radio*)

RUTH: Oh, Walter, and with your mother working like a dog every day—

(*A steamy, deep blues pours into the room*)

WALTER: That's sad too—Everything is sad.

MAMA: What you been doing for these three days, son?

WALTER: Mama—you don't know all the things a man what got leisure can find to do in this city . . . What's this—Friday night? Well—Wednesday I borrowed Willy Harris' car and I went for a drive . . . just me and myself and I drove and drove . . . Way out . . . way past South Chicago, and I parked the car and I sat and looked at the steel mills all day long. I just sat in the car and looked at them big black chimneys for hours. Then I drove back and I went to the Green Hat. (*Pause*) And Thursday—Thursday I borrowed the car again and I got in it and I pointed it the other way and I drove the other way—for hours—way, way up to Wisconsin, and I looked at the farms. I just drove and looked at the farms. Then I drove back and I went to the Green Hat. (*Pause*) And today—today I didn't get the car. Today I just walked. All over the Southside. And I looked at the Negroes and they looked at me and finally I just sat down on the curb at Thirty-ninth and South Parkway and I just sat there and watched the Negroes go by. And then I went to the Green Hat. You all sad? You all depressed? And you know where I am going right now—

(RUTH *goes out quietly*)

MAMA: Oh, Big Walter, is this the harvest of our days?

WALTER: You know what I like about the Green Hat? I like this little cat they got there who blows a sax . . . He blows. He talks to me. He ain't but 'bout five feet tall and he's got a conked head and his eyes is always closed and he's all music—

MAMA (*rising and getting some papers out of her handbag*):   Walter—

WALTER: And there's this other guy who plays the piano . . . and they got a sound. I mean they can work on some music . . . They got the best little combo in the world in the Green Hat . . . You can just sit there and drink and listen to them three men play and you realize that don't nothing matter worth a damn, but just being there—

MAMA: I've helped do it to you, haven't I, son? Walter I been wrong.

WALTER: Naw—you ain't never been wrong about nothing, Mama.

MAMA: Listen to me, now. I say I been wrong, son. That I been doing to you what the rest of the world been doing to you. (*She turns off the radio*) Walter—(*She stops and he looks up slowly at her and she meets his eyes pleadingly*) What you ain't never understood is that I ain't got nothing, don't own nothing, ain't never really wanted nothing that wasn't for you. There ain't nothing as precious to me . . . There ain't nothing worth holding on to, money, dreams, nothing else—if it means—if it means it's going to destroy my boy. (*She takes an envelope out of her handbag and puts it in front of him and he watches her without speaking or moving*) I paid the man thirty-five hundred dollars down on the house. That leaves sixty-five hundred dollars. Monday morning I want you to take this money and take three thousand dollars and put it in a savings account for Beneatha's medical schooling. The rest you put in a checking account— with your name on it. And from now on any penny that come out of it or that go in it is for you to look after. For you to decide. (*She drops her hands a little helplessly*) It ain't much, but it's all I got in the world and I'm putting it in your hands. I'm telling you to be the head of this family from now on like you supposed to be.

WALTER (*stares at the money*):   You trust me like that, Mama?

MAMA: I ain't never stop trusting you. Like I ain't never stop loving you.

(*She goes out, and* WALTER *sits looking at the money on the table. Finally, in a decisive gesture, he gets up, and, in mingled joy and desperation, picks up the money. At the same moment,* TRAVIS *enters for bed*)

TRAVIS: What's the matter, Daddy? You drunk?

WALTER (*sweetly, more sweetly than we have ever known him*):   No, Daddy ain't drunk. Daddy ain't going to never be drunk again. . . .

TRAVIS: Well, good night, Daddy.

(*The* FATHER *has come from behind the couch and leans over, embracing his son*)

WALTER: Son, I feel like talking to you tonight.

TRAVIS: About what?

WALTER: Oh, about a lot of things. About you and what kind of man you going to be when you grow up. . . . Son—son, what do you want to be when you grow up?

TRAVIS: A bus driver.

WALTER (*laughing a little*):   A what? Man, that ain't nothing to want to be!

TRAVIS: Why not?

WALTER: 'Cause, man—it ain't big enough—you know what I mean.

TRAVIS: I don't know then. I can't make up my mind. Sometimes Mama asks me that too. And sometimes when I tell her I just want to be like you— she says she don't want me to be like that and sometimes she says she does. . . .

WALTER (*gathering him up in his arms*):   You know what, Travis? In seven years you going to be seventeen years old. And things is going to be very different with us in seven years, Travis. . . . One day when you are seventeen I'll come home—home from my office downtown somewhere—

TRAVIS: You don't work in no office, Daddy.

WALTER: No—but after tonight. After what your daddy gonna do tonight, there's going to be offices—a whole lot of offices. . . .

TRAVIS: What you gonna do tonight, Daddy?

WALTER: You wouldn't understand yet, son, but your daddy's gonna make a transaction . . . a business transaction that's going to change our lives. . . . That's how come one day when you 'bout seventeen years old I'll come home and I'll be pretty tired, you know what I mean, after a day of conferences and secretaries getting things wrong the way they do . . . 'cause an executive's life is hell, man—(*The more he talks the farther away he gets*) And I'll pull the car up on the driveway . . . just a plain black Chrysler, I think, with white walls—no—black tires. More elegant. Rich people don't have to be flashy . . . though I'll have to get something a little sportier for Ruth—maybe a Cadillac convertible to do her shopping in. . . . And I'll come up the steps to the house and the gardener will be clipping away at the hedges and he'll say, "Good evening, Mr. Younger." And I'll say, "Hello, Jefferson, how are you this evening?" And I'll go inside and Ruth will come downstairs and meet me at the door and we'll kiss each other and she'll take my arm and we'll go up to your room to see you sitting on the floor with the catalogues of all the great schools in America around you. . . . All the great schools in the world! And—and I'll say, all right son—it's your seventeenth birthday, what is it you've decided? . . . Just tell me where you want to go to school and you'll *go*. Just tell me, what it is you want to be—and you'll *be* it. . . . Whatever you want to be—Yessir! (*He holds his arms open for* TRAVIS) You just name it, son . . . (TRAVIS *leaps into them*) and I hand you the world!

(WALTER'S *voice has risen in pitch and hysterical promise and on the last line he lifts* TRAVIS *high*)

(*Blackout*)

Scene III

Time: Saturday, moving day, one week later.

Before the curtain rises, RUTH'S *voice, a strident, dramatic church alto, cuts through the silence.*

It is, in the darkness, a triumphant surge, a penetrating statement of expectation: "Oh, Lord, I don't feel no ways tired! Children, oh, glory hallelujah!"

As the curtain rises we see that RUTH *is alone in the living room, finishing up the family's packing. It is moving day. She is nailing crates and tying cartons.* BENEATHA *enters, carrying a guitar case, and watches her exuberant sister-in-law.*

RUTH: Hey!

BENEATHA (*putting away the case*): Hi.

RUTH (*pointing at a package*): Honey—look in that package there and see what I found on sale this morning at the South Center. (RUTH *gets up and moves to the package and draws out some curtains*) Lookahere—hand-turned hems!

BENEATHA: How do you know the window size out there?

RUTH (*who hadn't thought of that*): Oh—Well, they bound to fit something in the whole house. Anyhow, they was too good a bargain to pass up. (RUTH *slaps her head, suddenly remembering something*) Oh, Bennie—I meant to put a special note on that carton over there. That's your mama's good china and she wants 'em to be very careful with it.

BENEATHA: I'll do it.

(BENEATHA *finds a piece of paper and starts to draw large letters on it*)

RUTH: You know what I'm going to do soon as I get in that new house?

BENEATHA: What?

RUTH: Honey—I'm going to run me a tub of water up to here . . . (*With her fingers practically up to her nostrils*) And I'm going to get in it—and I am going to sit . . . and sit . . . and sit in that hot water and the first person who knocks to tell *me* to hurry up and come out—

BENEATHA: Gets shot at sunrise.

RUTH (*laughing happily*): You said it, sister! (*Noticing how large* BENEATHA *is absent-mindedly making the note*) Honey, they ain't going to read that from no airplane.

BENEATHA (*laughing herself*): I guess I always think things have more emphasis if they are big, somehow.

RUTH (*looking up at her and smiling*): You and your brother seem to have that as a philosophy of life. Lord, that man—done changed so 'round here. You know—you know what we did last night? Me and Walter Lee?

BENEATHA: What?

RUTH (*smiling to herself*): We went to the movies. (*Looking at* BENEATHA *to see if she understands*) We went to the movies. You know the last time me and Walter went to the movies together?

BENEATHA: No.

RUTH: Me neither. That's how long it been. (*Smiling again*) But we went last night. The picture wasn't much good, but that didn't seem to matter. We went—and we held hands.

BENEATHA: Oh, Lord!

RUTH: We held hands—and you know what?

BENEATHA: What?

RUTH: When we come out of the show it was late and dark and all the stores and things was closed up . . . and it was kind of chilly and there wasn't many people on the streets . . . and we was still holding hands, me and Walter.

BENEATHA: You're killing me.

(WALTER *enters with a large package. His happiness is deep in him; he cannot keep still with his new-found exuberance. He is singing and wiggling and snapping his fingers. He puts his package in a corner and puts a phonograph record, which he has brought in with him, on the record player. As the music, soulful and sensuous, comes up he dances over to* RUTH *and tries to get her to dance with him. She gives in at last to his raunchiness and in a fit of giggling allows herself to be drawn into his mood. They dip and she melts into his arms in a classic, body-melding "slow drag"*)

BENEATHA (*regarding them a long time as they dance, then drawing in her breath for a deeply exaggerated comment which she does not particularly mean*): Talk about—olddddddddddd-fashionedddddddd—Negroes!

WALTER (*stopping momentarily*): What kind of Negroes? (*He says this in fun. He is not angry with her today, nor with anyone. He starts to dance with his wife again*)

BENEATHA: Old-fashioned.

WALTER (*as he dances with* RUTH): You know, when these *New Negroes* have their convention—(*Pointing at his sister*)—that is going to be the chairman of the Committee on Unending Agitation. (*He goes on dancing, then stops*) Race, race, race! . . . Girl, I do believe you are the first person in the history of the entire human race to successfully brainwash yourself. (BENEATHA *breaks up and he goes on dancing. He stops again, enjoying his tease*) Damn, even the N double A C P takes a holiday sometimes! (BENEATHA *and* RUTH *laugh. He dances with* RUTH *some more and starts to laugh and stops and pantomimes someone over an operating table*) I can just see that chick someday looking down at some poor cat on an operating table and before she starts to slice him, she says . . . (*Pulling his sleeves back maliciously*) "By the way, what are your views on civil rights down there? . . ."

(*He laughs at her again and starts to dance happily. The bell sounds*)

BENEATHA: Sticks and stones may break my bones but . . . words will never hurt me!

(BENEATHA *goes to the door and opens it as* WALTER *and* RUTH *go on with the clowning.* BENEATHA *is somewhat surprised to see a quiet-looking middle-aged white man in a business suit holding his hat and a briefcase in his hand and consulting a small piece of paper*)

MAN: Uh—how do you do, miss. I am looking for a Mrs.—(*He looks at the slip of paper*) Mrs. Lena Younger? (*He stops short, struck dumb at the sight of the oblivious* WALTER *and* RUTH)

BENEATHA (*smoothing her hair with slight embarrassment*):   Oh—yes, that's my mother. Excuse me (*She closes the door and turns to quiet the other two*) Ruth! Brother! (*Enunciating precisely but soundlessly: "There's a white man at the door!" They stop dancing,* RUTH *cuts off the phonograph,* BENEATHA *opens the door. The man casts a curious quick glance at all of them*) Uh—come in please.

MAN (*coming in*):   Thank you.

BENEATHA: My mother isn't here just now. Is it business?

MAN: Yes . . . well, of a sort.

WALTER (*freely, the Man of the House*):   Have a seat. I'm Mrs. Younger's son. I look after most of her business matters.

(RUTH *and* BENEATHA *exchange amused glances*)

MAN (*regarding* WALTER, *and sitting*):   Well—My name is Karl Lindner . . .

WALTER (*stretching out his hand*):   Walter Younger. This is my wife—(RUTH *nods politely*)—and my sister.

LINDNER: How do you do.

WALTER (*amiably, as he sits himself easily on a chair, leaning forward on his knees with interest and looking expectantly into the newcomer's face*):   What can we do for you, Mr. Lindner!

LINDNER (*some minor shuffling of the hat and briefcase on his knees*):   Well—I am a representative of the Clybourne Park Improvement Association—

WALTER (*pointing*):   Why don't you sit your things on the floor?

LINDNER: Oh—yes. Thank you. (*He slides the briefcase and hat under the chair*) And as I was saying—I am from the Clybourne Park Improvement Association and we have had it brought to our attention at the last meeting that you people—or at least your mother—has bought a piece of residential property at—(*He digs for the slip of paper again*)—four o six Clybourne Street . . .

WALTER: That's right. Care for something to drink? Ruth, get Mr. Lindner a beer.

LINDNER (*upset for some reason*):   Oh—no, really. I mean thank you very much, but no thank you.

RUTH (*innocently*):   Some coffee?

LINDNER: Thank you, nothing at all.

(BENEATHA *is watching the man carefully*)

LINDNER: Well, I don't know how much you folks know about our organization. (*He is a gentle man; thoughtful and somewhat labored in his manner*) It is one of these community organizations set up to look after—oh, you know, things like block upkeep and special projects and we also have what we call our New Neighbors Orientation Committee . . .

BENEATHA (*drily*):   Yes—and what do they do?

LINDNER (*turning a little to her and then returning the main force to* WALTER): Well—it's what you might call a sort of welcoming committee, I guess. I mean they, we—I'm the chairman of the committee—go around and see the new people who move into the neighborhood and sort of give them the lowdown on the way we do things in Clybourne Park.

BENEATHA (*with appreciation of the two meanings, which escape* RUTH *and* WALTER): Un-huh.

LINDNER: And we also have the category of what the association calls—(*He looks elsewhere*)—uh—special community problems . . .

BENEATHA: Yes—and what are some of those?

WALTER: Girl, let the man talk.

LINDNER (*with understated relief*): Thank you. I would sort of like to explain this thing in my own way. I mean I want to explain to you in a certain way.

WALTER: Go ahead.

LINDNER: Yes. Well. I'm going to try to get right to the point. I'm sure we'll all appreciate that in the long run.

BENEATHA: Yes.

WALTER: Be still now!

LINDNER: Well—

RUTH (*still innocently*): Would you like another chair—you don't look comfortable.

LINDNER (*more frustrated than annoyed*): No, thank you very much. Please. Well—to get right to the point I—(*A great breath, and he is off at last*) I am sure you people must be aware of some of the incidents which have happened in various parts of the city when colored people have moved into certain areas—(BENEATHA *exhales heavily and starts tossing a piece of fruit up and down in the air*) Well—because we have what I think is going to be a unique type of organization in American community life—not only do we deplore that kind of thing but we are trying to do something about it. (BENEATHA *stops tossing and turns with a new and quizzical interest to the man*) We feel—(*gaining confidence in his mission because of the interest in the faces of the people he is talking to*)—we feel that most of the trouble in this world, when you come right down to it—(*He hits his knee for emphasis*)—most of the trouble exists because people just don't sit down and talk to each other.

RUTH (*nodding as she might in church, pleased with the remark*): You can say that again, mister.

LINDNER (*more encouraged by such affirmation*): That we don't try hard enough in this world to understand the other fellow's problem. The other guy's point of view.

RUTH: Now that's right.

(BENEATHA *and* WALTER *merely watch and listen with genuine interest*)

LINDNER: Yes—that's the way we feel out in Clybourne Park. And that's why I was elected to come here this afternoon and talk to you people. Friendly like, you know, the way people should talk to each other and see if we couldn't find some way to work this thing out. As I say, the whole business is a matter of *caring* about the other fellow. Anybody can see that you are a nice family of folks, hard working and honest I'm sure. (BENEATHA *frowns slightly, quizzically, her head tilted regarding him*) Today everybody knows what it means to be on the outside of *something*. And of course, there is always somebody who is out to take advantage of people who don't always understand.

WALTER: What do you mean?

LINDNER: Well—you see our community is made up of people who've worked hard as the dickens for years to build up that little community. They're not rich and fancy people; just hard-working, honest people who don't really have much but those little homes and a dream of the kind of community they want to raise their children in. Now, I don't say we are perfect and there is a lot wrong in some of the things they want. But you've got to admit that a man, right or wrong, has the right to want to have the neighborhood he lives in a certain kind of way. And at the moment the overwhelming majority of our people out there feel that people get along better, take more of a common interest in the life of the community, when they share a common background. I want you to believe me when I tell you that race prejudice simply doesn't enter into it. It is a matter of the people of Clybourne Park believing, rightly or wrongly, as I say, that for the happiness of all concerned that our Negro families are happier when they live in their *own* communities.

BENEATHA (*with a grand and bitter gesture*):   This, friends, is the Welcoming Committee!

WALTER (*dumbfounded, looking at* LINDNER):   Is this what you came marching all the way over here to tell us?

LINDNER: Well, now we've been having a fine conversation. I hope you'll hear me all the way through.

WALTER (*tightly*):   Go ahead, man.

LINDNER: You see—in the face of all the things I have said, we are prepared to make your family a very generous offer . . .

BENEATHA: Thirty pieces and not a coin less!

WALTER: Yeah?

LINDNER (*putting on his glasses and drawing a form out of the briefcase*):   Our association is prepared, through the collective effort of our people, to buy the house from you at a financial gain to your family.

RUTH: Lord have mercy, ain't this the living gall!

WALTER: All right, you through?

LINDNER: Well, I want to give you the exact terms of the financial arrangement—

WALTER: We don't want to hear no exact terms of no arrangements. I want to know if you got any more to tell us 'bout getting together?

LINDNER (*taking off his glasses*):   Well—I don't suppose that you feel . . .

WALTER: Never mind how I feel—you got any more to say 'bout how people ought to sit down and talk to each other? . . . Get out of my house, man.

(*He turns his back and walks to the door*)

LINDNER (*Looking around at the hostile faces and reaching and assembling his hat and briefcase*):   Well—I don't understand why you people are reacting this way. What do you think you are going to gain by moving into a neighborhood where you just aren't wanted and where some elements—well—people can get awful worked up when they feel that their whole way of life and everything they've ever worked for is threatened.

WALTER: Get out.

LINDNER (*at the door, holding a small card*):   Well—I'm sorry it went like this.

WALTER: Get out.

LINDNER (*almost sadly regarding* WALTER):   You just can't force people to change their hearts, son.

(*He turns and put his card on a table and exits.* WALTER *pushes the door to with stinging hatred, and stands looking at it.* RUTH *just sits and* BENEATHA *just stands. They say nothing.* MAMA *and* TRAVIS *enter*)

MAMA: Well—this all the packing got done since I left out of here this morning. I testify before God that my children got all the energy of the *dead!* What time the moving men due?

BENEATHA: Four o'clock. You had a caller, Mama.

(*She is smiling, teasingly*)

MAMA: Sure enough—who?

BENEATHA (*her arms folded saucily*):   The Welcoming Committee.

(WALTER *and* RUTH *giggle*)

MAMA (*innocently*):   Who?

BENEATHA: The Welcoming Committee. They said they're sure going to be glad to see you when you get there.

WALTER (*devilishly*):   Yeah, they said they can't hardly wait to see your face.

(*Laughter*)

MAMA (*sensing their facetiousness*):   What's the matter with you all?

WALTER: Ain't nothing the matter with us. We just telling you 'bout the gentleman who came to see you this afternoon. From the Clybourne Park Improvement Association.

MAMA: What he want?

RUTH (*in the same mood as* BENEATHA *and* WALTER):   To welcome you, honey.

WALTER: He said they can't hardly wait. He said the one thing they don't have, that they just *dying* to have out there is a fine family of fine colored people! (*To* RUTH *and* BENEATHA) Ain't that right!

RUTH (*mockingly*):   Yeah! He left his card—

BENEATHA (*handing card to* MAMA):   In case.

(MAMA *reads and throws it on the floor—understanding and looking off as she draws her chair up to the table on which she has put her plant and some sticks and some cord*)

MAMA: Father, give us strength. (*knowingly—and without fun*) Did he threaten us?

BENEATHA: Oh—Mama—they don't do it like that any more. He talked Brotherhood. He said everybody ought to learn how to sit down and hate each other with good Christian fellowship.

(*She and* WALTER *shake hands to ridicule the remark*)

MAMA (*sadly*):   Lord, protect us . . .

RUTH: You should hear the money those folks raised to buy the house from us. All we paid and then some.

BENEATHA: What they think we going to do—eat 'em?

RUTH: No, honey, marry 'em.

MAMA (*shaking her head*):   Lord, Lord, Lord . . .

RUTH: Well—that's the way the crackers crumble. (*A beat*) Joke.

BENEATHA (*laughingly noticing what her mother is doing*):   Mama, what are you doing?

MAMA: Fixing my plant so it won't get hurt none on the way . . .

BENEATHA: Mama, you going to take *that* to the new house?

MAMA: Un-huh—

BENEATHA: That raggedy-looking old thing?

MAMA (*stopping and looking at her*):   It expresses ME!

RUTH (*with delight, to* BENEATHA):   So there, Miss Thing!

(WALTER *comes to* MAMA *suddenly and bends down behind her and squeezes her in his arms with all his strength. She is overwhelmed by the suddenness of it and, though delighted, her manner is like that of* RUTH *and* TRAVIS)

MAMA: Look out now, boy! You make me mess up my thing here!

WALTER (*his face lit, he slips down on his knees beside her, his arms still about her*): Mama . . . you know what it means to climb up in the chariot?

MAMA (*gruffly, very happy*):   Get on away from me now . . .

RUTH (*near the gift-wrapped package, trying to catch* WALTER'S *eye*):   Psst—

WALTER: What the old song say, Mama . . .

RUTH: Walter—Now?

(*She is pointing at the package*)

WALTER (*speaking the lines, sweetly, playfully, in his mother's face*)
I got wings . . . you got wings . . .
All God's Children got wings . . .

MAMA: Boy—get out of my face and do some work . . .

WALTER
When I get to heaven gonna put on my wings,
Gonna fly all over God's heaven . . .

BENEATHA (*teasingly, from across the room*):   Everybody talking 'bout heaven ain't going there!

WALTER (*to* RUTH, *who is carrying the box across to them*):   I don't know, you think we ought to give her that . . . Seems to me she ain't been very appreciative around here.

MAMA (*eying the box, which is obviously a gift*):   What is that?

WALTER (*taking it from* RUTH *and putting it on the table in front of* MAMA): Well—what you all think? Should we give it to her?

RUTH: Oh—she was pretty good today.

MAMA: I'll good you—

(*She turns her eyes to the box again*)

BENEATHA: Open it, Mama.

(*She stands up, looks at it, turns and looks at all of them, and then presses her hands together and does not open the package*)

WALTER (*sweetly*):   Open it, Mama. It's for you. (MAMA *looks in his eyes. It is the first present in her life without its being Christmas. Slowly she opens her package and lifts out, one by one, a brand-new sparkling set of gardening tools.* WALTER *continues, prodding*) Ruth made up the note—read it . . .

MAMA (*picking up the card and adjusting her glasses*):   "To our own Mrs. Miniver—Love from Brother, Ruth and Beneatha." Ain't that lovely . . .

TRAVIS (*tugging at his father's sleeve*):   Daddy, can I give her mine now?

WALTER: All right, son. (TRAVIS *flies to get his gift*)

MAMA: Now I don't have to use my knives and forks no more . . .

WALTER: Travis didn't want to go in with the rest of us, Mama. He got his own. (*Somewhat amused*) We don't know what it is . . .

TRAVIS (*racing back in the room with a large hatbox and putting it in front of his grandmother*):   Here!

MAMA: Lord have mercy, baby. You done gone and bought your grandmother a hat?

TRAVIS (*very proud*):   Open it!

(*She does and lifts out an elaborate, but very elaborate, wide gardening hat, and all the adults break up at the sight of it*)

RUTH: Travis, honey, what is that?

TRAVIS (*who thinks it is beautiful and appropriate*):   It's a gardening hat! Like the ladies always have on in the magazines when they work in their gardens.

BENEATHA (*giggling fiercely*):   Travis—we were trying to make Mama Mrs. Miniver—not Scarlett O'Hara!

MAMA (*indignantly*):   What's the matter with you all! This here is a beautiful hat! (*Absurdly*) I always wanted me one just like it!

(*She pops it on her head to prove it to her grandson, and the hat is ludicrous and considerably oversized*)

RUTH: Hot dog! Go, Mama!

WALTER (*doubled over with laughter*):   I'm sorry, Mama—but you look like you ready to go out and chop you some cotton sure enough!

(*They all laugh except* MAMA, *out of deference to* TRAVIS' *feelings*)

MAMA (*gathering the boy up to her*):   Bless your heart—this is the prettiest hat I ever owned— (WALTER, RUTH *and* BENEATHA *chime in—noisily, festively and insincerely congratulating* TRAVIS *on his gift*) What are we all standing around here for? We ain't finished packin' yet. Bennie, you ain't packed one book.

(*The bell rings*)

BENEATHA: That couldn't be the movers . . . it's not hardly two good yet—

(BENEATHA *goes into her room.* MAMA *starts for door*)

WALTER (*turning, stiffening*):   Wait—wait—I'll get it.

(*He stands and looks at the door*)

MAMA: You expecting company, son?

WALTER (*just looking at the door*):   Yeah—yeah . . .

(MAMA *looks at* RUTH, *and they exchange innocent and unfrightened glances*)

MAMA (*not understanding*):   Well, let them in, son.

BENEATHA (*from her room*):   We need some more string.

MAMA: Travis—you run to the hardware and get me some string cord.

(MAMA *goes out and* WALTER *turns and looks at* RUTH. TRAVIS *goes to a dish for money*)

RUTH: Why don't you answer the door, man?

WALTER (*suddenly bounding across the floor to embrace her*):   'Cause sometimes it hard to let the future begin!

(*Stooping down in her face*)

I got wings! You got wings!
All God's children got wings!

(*He crosses to the door and throws it open. Standing there is a very slight little man in a not too prosperous business suit and with haunted frightened eyes and a hat pulled down tightly, brim up, around his forehead.* TRAVIS *passes between the men and exits.* WALTER *leans deep in the man's face, still in his jubilance*)

When I get to heaven gonna put on my wings,
Gonna fly all over God's heaven . . .

(*The little man just stares at him*)

Heaven—

(*Suddenly he stops and looks past the little man into the empty hallway*) Where's Willy, man?

BOBO: He ain't with me.

WALTER (*not disturbed*):   Oh—come on in. You know my wife.

BOBO (*dumbly, taking off his hat*):   Yes—h'you, Miss Ruth.

RUTH (*quietly, a mood apart from her husband already, seeing* BOBO):   Hello, Bobo.

WALTER: You right on time today . . . Right on time. That's the way! (*He slaps* BOBO *on his back*) Sit down . . . lemme hear.

(RUTH *stands stiffly and quietly in back of them, as though somehow she senses death, her eyes fixed on her husband*)

BOBO (*his frightened eyes on the floor, his hat in his hands*):   Could I please get a drink of water, before I tell you about it, Walter Lee?

(WALTER *does not take his eyes off the man.* RUTH *goes blindly to the tap and gets a glass of water and brings it to* BOBO)

WALTER: There ain't nothing wrong, is there?

BOBO: Lemme tell you—

WALTER: Man—didn't nothing go wrong?

BOBO: Lemme tell you—Walter Lee. (*Looking at* RUTH *and talking to her more than to* WALTER) You know how it was. I got to tell you how it was. I mean first I got to tell you how it was all the way . . . I mean about the money I put in, Walter Lee . . .

WALTER (*with taut agitation now*):   What about the money you put in?

BOBO: Well—it wasn't much as we told you—me and Willy—(*He stops*) I'm sorry, Walter. I got a bad feeling about it. I got a real bad feeling about it . . .

WALTER: Man, what you telling me about all this for? . . . Tell me what happened in Springfield . . .

BOBO: Springfield.

RUTH (*like a dead woman*):   What was supposed to happen in Springfield?

BOBO (*to her*):   This deal that me and Walter went into with Willy—Me and Willy was going to go down to Springfield and spread some money 'round so's we wouldn't have to wait so long for the liquor license . . . That's what we were going to do. Everybody said that was the way you had to do, you understand, Miss Ruth?

WALTER: Man—what happened down there?

BOBO (*a pitiful man, near tears*):   I'm trying to tell you, Walter.

WALTER (*screaming at him suddenly*):   THEN TELL ME, GODDAMMIT . . . WHAT'S THE MATTER WITH YOU?

BOBO: Man . . . I didn't go to no Springfield, yesterday.

WALTER (*halted, life hanging in the moment*):   Why not?

BOBO (*the long way, the hard way to tell*):   'Cause I didn't have no reasons to . . .

WALTER: Man, what are you talking about!

BOBO: I'm talking about the fact that when I got to the train station yesterday morning—eight o'clock like we planned . . . Man—*Willy didn't never show up*.

WALTER: Why . . . where was he . . . where is he?

BOBO: That's what I'm trying to tell you . . . I don't know . . . I waited six hours . . . I called his house . . . and I waited . . . six hours . . . I waited in that train station six hours . . . (*Breaking into tears*) That was all the extra money I had in the world . . . (*Looking up at* WALTER *with the tears running down his face*) Man, *Willy is gone*.

WALTER: Gone, what you mean Willy is gone? Gone where? You mean he went by himself. You mean he went off to Springfield by himself—to take care of getting the license—(*Turns and looks anxiously at* RUTH) You mean maybe he didn't want too many people in on the business down there? (*Looks to* RUTH *again, as before*) You know Willy got his own ways. (*Looks back to* BOBO) Maybe you was late yesterday and he just went on down there without you. Maybe—maybe—he's been callin' you at home tryin' to tell you what happened or something. Maybe—maybe—he just got sick. He's somewhere—he's got to be somewhere. We just got to find him—me and you got to find him. (*Grabs* BOBO *senselessly by the collar and starts to shake him*) We got to!

BOBO (*in sudden angry, frightened agony*):   What's the matter with you, Walter! *When a cat take off with your money he don't leave you no road maps!*

WALTER (*turning madly, as though he is looking for* WILLY *in the very room*): Willy! . . . Willy . . . don't do it . . . Please don't do it . . . Man, not with that money . . . Man, please, not with that money . . . Oh, God . . . Don't let it be true . . . (*He is wandering around, crying out for* WILLY *and looking for him or perhaps for help from God*) Man . . . I trusted you . . . Man, I put my life in your hands . . . (*He starts to crumple down on the floor as* RUTH *just covers her face in horror.* MAMA *opens the door and comes into the room, with* BENEATHA *behind her*) Man . . . (*He starts to pound the floor with his fists, sobbing wildly*) THAT MONEY IS MADE OUT OF MY FATHER'S FLESH——

BOBO (*standing over him helplessly*):   I'm sorry, Walter . . . (*Only* WALTER'S *sobs reply.* BOBO *puts on his hat*) I had my life staked on this deal, too . . .

(*He exits*)

MAMA (*to* WALTER):   Son—(*She goes to him, bends down to him, talks to his bent head*) Son . . . Is it gone? Son, I gave you sixty-five hundred dollars. Is it gone? All of it? Beneatha's money too?

WALTER (*lifting his head slowly*):   Mama . . . I never . . . went to the bank at all . . .

MAMA (*not wanting to believe him*):   You mean . . . your sister's school money . . . you used that too . . . Walter? . . .

WALTER: Yessss! All of it . . . It's all gone . . .

(*There is total silence.* RUTH *stands with her face covered with her hands;* BENEATHA *leans forlornly against a wall, fingering a piece of red ribbon from the mother's gift.* MAMA *stops and looks at her son without recognition and then, quite without thinking about it, starts to beat him senselessly in the face.* BENEATHA *goes to them and stops it*)

BENEATHA: Mama!

(MAMA *stops and looks at both of her children and rises slowly and wanders vaguely, aimlessly away from them*)

MAMA: I seen . . . him . . . night after night . . . come in . . . and look at that rug . . . and then look at me . . . the red showing in his eyes . . . the veins moving in his head . . . I seen him grow thin and old before he was forty . . . working and working and working like somebody's old horse . . . killing himself . . . and you—you give it all away in a day—(*She raises her arms to strike him again*)

BENEATHA: Mama—

MAMA: Oh, God . . . (*She looks up to Him*) Look down here—and show me the strength.

BENEATHA: Mama—

MAMA (*folding over*):   Strength . . .

BENEATHA (*plaintively*):   Mama . . .

MAMA: Strength!

Curtain

ACT III

An hour later.

At curtain, there is a sullen light of gloom in the living room, gray light not unlike that which began the first scene of Act One. At left we can see WALTER *within his room, alone with himself. He is stretched out on the bed, his shirt out and open, his arms under his head. He does not smoke, he does not cry out, he merely lies there, looking up at the ceiling, much as if he were alone in the world.*

In the living room BENEATHA *sits at the table, still surrounded by the now almost ominous packing crates. She sits looking off. We feel that this is a mood struck perhaps an hour before, and it lingers now, full of the empty sound of profound disappointment. We see on a line from her brother's bedroom the sameness of their attitudes. Presently the bell rings and* BENEATHA *rises without ambition or interest in answering. It is* ASAGAI, *smiling broadly, striding into the room with energy and happy expectation and conversation.*

ASAGAI: I came over . . . I had some free time. I thought I might help with the packing. Ah, I like the look of packing crates! A household in preparation for a journey! It depresses some people . . . but for me . . . it is another feeling. Something full of the flow of life, do you understand? Movement, progress . . . It makes me think of Africa.

BENEATHA: Africa!

ASAGAI: What kind of a mood is this? Have I told you how deeply you move me?

BENEATHA: He gave away the money, Asagai . . .

ASAGAI: Who gave away what money?

BENEATHA: The insurance money. My brother gave it away.

ASAGAI: Gave it away?

BENEATHA: He made an investment! With a man even Travis wouldn't have trusted with his most worn-out marbles.

ASAGAI: And it's gone?

BENEATHA: Gone!

ASAGAI: I'm very sorry . . . And you, now?

BENEATHA: Me? . . . Me? . . . Me, I'm nothing . . . Me. When I was very small . . . we used to take our sleds out in the wintertime and the only hills we had were the ice-covered stone steps of some houses down the street. And we used to fill them in with snow and make them smooth and slide down them all day . . . and it was very dangerous, you know . . . far too steep . . . and sure enough one day a kid named Rufus came down too fast and hit the sidewalk and we saw his face just split open right there in front of us . . . And I remember standing there looking at his bloody open face thinking that was the end of Rufus. But the ambulance came and they took him to the hospital and they fixed the broken bones and they sewed it all up . . . and the next time I saw Rufus he just had a little line down the middle of his face . . . I never got over that . . .

ASAGAI: What?

BENEATHA: That that was what one person could do for another, fix him up—sew up the problem, make him all right again. That was the most marvelous thing in the world . . . I wanted to do that. I always thought it was the one concrete thing in the world that a human being could do. Fix up the sick, you know—and make them whole again. This was truly being God . . .

ASAGAI: You wanted to be God?

BENEATHA: No—I wanted to cure. It used to be so important to me. I wanted to cure. It used to matter. I used to care. I mean about people and how their bodies hurt . . .

ASAGAI: And you've stopped caring?

BENEATHA: Yes—I think so.

ASAGAI: Why?

BENEATHA (*bitterly*):   Because it doesn't seem deep enough, close enough to what ails mankind! It was a child's way of seeing things—or an idealist's.

ASAGAI: Children see things very well sometimes—and idealists even better.

BENEATHA: I know that's what you think. Because you are still where I left off. You with all your talk and dreams about Africa! You still think you can patch up the world. Cure the Great Sore of Colonialism—(*Loftily, mocking it*) with the Penicillin of Independence—!

ASAGAI: Yes!

BENEATHA: Independence *and then what?* What about all the crooks and thieves and just plain idiots who will come into power and steal and plunder the same as before—only now they will be black and do it in the name of the new Independence—WHAT ABOUT THEM?!

ASAGAI: That will be the problem for another time. First we must get there.

BENEATHA: And where does it end?

ASAGAI: End? Who even spoke of an end? To life? To living?

BENEATHA: An end to misery! To stupidity! Don't you see there isn't any real progress, Asagai, there is only one large circle that we march in, around and around, each of us with our own little picture in front of us—our own little mirage that we think is the future.

ASAGAI: That is the mistake.

BENEATHA: What?

ASAGAI: What you just said—about the circle. It isn't a circle—it is simply a long line—as in geometry, you know, one that reaches into infinity. And because we cannot see the end—we also cannot see how it changes. And it is very odd but those who see the changes—who dream, who will not give up—are called idealists . . . and those who see only the circle—we call *them* the "realists"!

BENEATHA: Asagai, while I was sleeping in that bed in there, people went out and took the future right out of my hands! And nobody asked me, nobody consulted me—they just went out and changed my life!

ASAGAI: Was it your money?

BENEATHA: What?

ASAGAI: Was it your money he gave away?

BENEATHA: It belonged to all of us.

ASAGAI: But did you earn it? Would you have had it at all if your father had not died?

BENEATHA: No.

ASAGAI: Then isn't there something wrong in a house—in a world—where all dreams, good or bad, must depend on the death of a man? I never thought

to see *you* like this, Alaiyo. You! Your brother made a mistake and you are grateful to him so that now you can give up the ailing human race on account of it!
You talk about what good is struggle, what good is anything! Where are we all
going and why are we bothering!

BENEATHA: AND YOU CANNOT ANSWER IT!

ASAGAI (*shouting over her*): *I LIVE THE ANSWER!* (*Pause*) In my village at
home it is the exceptional man who can even read a newspaper . . . or who
ever sees a book at all. I will go home and much of what I will have to say will
seem strange to the people of my village. But I will teach and work and things
will happen, slowly and swiftly. At times it will seem that nothing changes at
all . . . and then again the sudden dramatic events which make history leap into
the future. And then quiet again. Retrogression even. Guns, murder, revolution. And I even will have moments when I wonder if the quiet was not better than all that death and hatred. But I will look about my village at the illit-
eracy and disease and ignorance and I will not wonder long. And perhaps . . .
perhaps I will be a great man . . . I mean perhaps I will hold on to the substance
of truth and find my way always with the right course . . . and perhaps for it I
will be butchered in my bed some night by the servants of empire . . .

BENEATHA: *The martyr!*

ASAGAI (*he smiles*): . . . or perhaps I shall live to be a very old man, respected
and esteemed in my new nation . . . And perhaps I shall hold office and this is
what I'm trying to tell you, Alaiyo: Perhaps the things I believe now for my
country will be wrong and outmoded, and I will not understand and do terrible things to have things my way or merely to keep my power. Don't you see
that there will be young men and women—not British soldiers then, but my
own black countrymen—to step out of the shadows some evening and slit my
then useless throat? Don't you see they have always been there . . . that they
always will be. And that such a thing as my own death will be an advance? They
who might kill me even . . . actually replenish all that I was.

BENEATHA: Oh, Asagai, I know all that.

ASAGAI: Good! Then stop moaning and groaning and tell me what you plan
to do.

BENEATHA: Do?

ASAGAI: I have a bit of a suggestion.

BENEATHA: What?

ASAGAI (*rather quietly for him*): That when it is all over—that you come home
with me—

BENEATHA (*staring at him and crossing away with exasperation*): Oh—Asagai—
at this moment you decide to be romantic!

ASAGAI (*quickly understanding the misunderstanding*): My dear, young creature
of the New World—I do not mean across the city—I mean across the ocean:
home—to Africa.

BENEATHA (*slowly understanding and turning to him with murmured amazement*):
To Africa?

ASAGAI: Yes! . . . (*Smiling and lifting his arms playfully*) Three hundred years
later the African Prince rose up out of the seas and swept the maiden back across
the middle passage over which her ancestors had come—

BENEATHA (*unable to play*): To—to Nigeria?

ASAGAI: Nigeria. Home. (*Coming to her with genuine romantic flippancy*) I will show you our mountains and our stars; and give you cool drinks from gourds and teach you the old songs and the ways of our people—and, in time, we will pretend that—(*Very Softly*)—you have only been away for a day. Say that you'll come—(*He swings her around and takes her full in his arms in a kiss which proceeds to passion*)

BENEATHA (*pulling away suddenly*):   You're getting me all mixed up—

ASAGAI: Why?

BENEATHA: Too many things—too many things have happened today. I must sit down and think. I don't know what I feel about anything right this minute.

(*She promptly sits down and props her chin on her fist*)

ASAGAI (*charmed*):   All right, I shall leave you. No—don't get up. (*Touching her, gently, sweetly*) Just sit awhile and think . . . Never be afraid to sit awhile and think. (*He goes to door and looks at her*) How often I have looked at you and said, "Ah—so this is what the New World hath finally wrought . . ."

(*He exits.* BENEATHA *sits on alone. Presently* WALTER *enters from his room and starts to rummage through things, feverishly looking for something. She looks up and turns in her seat*)

BENEATHA (*hissingly*):   Yes—just look at what the New World hath wrought! . . . Just look! (*She gestures with bitter disgust*) There he is! *Monsieur le petit bourgeois noir*—himself! There he is—Symbol of a Rising Class! Entrepreneur! Titan of the system! (WALTER *ignores her completely and continues frantically and destructively looking for something and hurling things to floor and tearing things out of their place in his search.* BENEATHA *ignores the eccentricity of his actions and goes on with the monologue of insult*) Did you dream of yachts on Lake Michigan, Brother? Did you see yourself on that Great Day sitting down at the Conference Table, surrounded by all the mighty bald-headed men in America? All halted, waiting, breathless, waiting for your pronouncements on industry? Waiting for you—Chairman of the Board! (WALTER *finds what he is looking for—a small piece of white paper—and pushes it in his pocket and puts on his coat and rushes out without ever having looked at her. She shouts after him*) I look at you and I see the final triumph of stupidity in the world!

(*The door slams and she returns to just sitting again.* RUTH *comes quickly out of* MAMA'S *room*)

RUTH: Who was that?

BENEATHA: Your husband.

RUTH: Where did he go?

BENEATHA: Who knows—maybe he has an appointment at U.S. Steel.

RUTH (*anxiously, with frightened eyes*):   You didn't say nothing bad to him, did you?

BENEATHA: Bad? Say anything bad to him? No—I told him he was a sweet boy and full of dreams and everything is strictly peachy keen, as the ofay kids say!

(MAMA *enters from her bedroom. She is lost, vague, trying to catch hold, to make some sense of her former command of the world, but it still eludes her. A sense of waste overwhelms her gait; a measure of apology rides on her shoulders. She goes to her plant, which has remained on the table, looks at it, picks it up and takes it to the window sill and sits it outside, and she stands and looks at it a long moment. Then she closes the window, straightens her body with effort and turns around to her children)*

MAMA: Well—ain't it a mess in here, though? *(A false cheerfulness, a beginning of something)* I guess we all better stop moping around and get some work done. All this unpacking and everything we got to do. (RUTH *raises her head slowly in response to the sense of the line; and* BENEATHA *in similar manner turns very slowly to look at her mother)* One of you all better call the moving people and tell 'em not to come.

RUTH: Tell 'em not to come?

MAMA: Of course, baby. Ain't no need in 'em coming all the way here and having to go back. They charges for that too. *(She sits down, fingers to her brow, thinking)* Lord, ever since I was a little girl, I always remembers people saying, "Lena—Lena Eggleston, you aims too high all the time. You needs to slow down and see life a little more like it is. Just slow down some." That's what they always used to say down home—"Lord, that Lena Eggleston is a high-minded thing. She'll get her due one day!"

RUTH: No, Lena . . .

MAMA: Me and Big Walter just didn't never learn right.

RUTH: Lena, no! We gotta go. Bennie—tell her . . . *(She rises and crosses to* BENEATHA *with her arms outstretched.* BENEATHA *doesn't respond)* Tell her we can still move . . . the notes ain't but a hundred and twenty-five a month. We got four grown people in this house—we can work . . .

MAMA *(to herself)*: Just aimed too high all the time—

RUTH *(turning and going to* MAMA *fast—the words pouring out with urgency and desperation)*. Lena—I'll work . . . I'll work twenty hours a day in all the kitchens in Chicago . . . I'll strap my baby on my back if I have to and scrub all the floors in America and wash all the sheets in America if I have to—but we got to MOVE! We got to get OUT OF HERE!!

*(*MAMA *reaches out absently and pats* RUTH'S *hand)*

MAMA: No—I sees things differently now. Been thinking 'bout some of the things we could do to fix this place up some. I seen a second-hand bureau over on Maxwell Street just the other day that could fit right there. *(She points to where the new furniture might go.* RUTH *wanders away from her)* Would need some new handles on it and then a little varnish and it look like something brand-new. And—we can put up them new curtains in the kitchen . . . Why this place be looking fine. Cheer us all up so that we forget trouble ever come . . . *(To* RUTH*)* And you could get some nice screens to put up in your room round the baby's bassinet . . . *(She looks at both of them, pleadingly)* Sometimes you just got to know when to give up some things . . . and hold on to what you got. . . .

*(*WALTER *enters from the outside, looking spent and leaning against the door, his coat hanging from him)*

MAMA: Where you been, son?

WALTER *(breathing hard)*: Made a call.

MAMA: To who, son?

WALTER: To The Man. (*He heads for his room*)

MAMA: What man, baby?

WALTER (*stops in the door*):   The Man, Mama. Don't you know who The Man is?

RUTH: Walter Lee?

WALTER: *The Man*. Like the guys in the streets say—The Man. Captain Boss—Mistuh Charley . . . Old Cap'n Please Mr. Bossman . . .

BENEATHA (*suddenly*):   Lindner!

WALTER: That's right! That's good. I told him to come right over.

BENEATHA (*fiercely, understanding*):   For what? What do you want to see him for!

WALTER (*looking at his sister*):   We going to do business with him.

MAMA: What you talking 'bout, son?

WALTER: Talking 'bout life, Mama. You all always telling me to see life like it is. Well—I laid in there on my back today . . . and I figured it out. Life just like it is. Who gets and who don't get. (*He sits down with his coat on and laughs*) Mama, you know it's all divided up. Life is. Sure enough. Between the takers and the "tooken." (*He laughs*) I've figured it out finally. (*He looks around at them*) Yeah. Some of us always getting "tooken." (*He laughs*) People like Willy Harris, they don't never get "tooken." And you know why the rest of us do? 'Cause we all mixed up. Mixed up bad. We get to looking 'round for the right and the wrong; and we worry about it and cry about it and stay up nights trying to figure out 'bout the wrong and the right of things all the time . . . And all the time, man, them takers is out there operating, just taking and taking. Willy Harris? Shoot—Willy Harris don't even count. He don't even count in the big scheme of things. But I'll say one thing for old Willy Harris . . . he's taught me something. He's taught me to keep my eye on what counts in this world. Yeah—(*Shouting out a little*) Thanks, Willy!

RUTH: What did you call that man for, Walter Lee?

WALTER: Called him to tell him to come on over to the show. Gonna put on a show for the man. Just what he wants to see. You see, Mama, the man came here today and he told us that them people out there where you want us to move—well they so upset they willing to pay us *not* to move! (*Ha laughs again*) And—and oh, Mama—you would of been proud of the way me and Ruth and Bennie acted. We told him to get out . . . Lord have mercy! We told the man to get out! Oh, we was some proud folks this afternoon, yeah. (*He lights a cigarette*) We were still full of that old-time stuff . . .

RUTH (*coming toward him slowly*):   You talking 'bout taking them people's money to keep us from moving in that house?

WALTER: I ain't just talking 'bout it, baby—I'm telling you that's what's going to happen!

BENEATHA: Oh, God! Where is the bottom! Where is the real honest-to-God bottom so he can't go any farther!

WALTER: See—that's the old stuff. You and that boy that was here today. You all want everybody to carry a flag and a spear and sing some marching songs, huh? You wanna spend your life looking into things and trying to find the right and the wrong part, huh? Yeah. You know what's going to happen to that boy someday—he'll find himself sitting in a dungeon, locked in forever—and the takers will have the key! Forget it, baby! There ain't no causes—there ain't nothing but taking in this world, and he who takes most is smartest—and it don't make a damn bit of difference *how*.

MAMA: You making something inside me cry, son. Some awful pain inside me.

WALTER: Don't cry, Mama. Understand. That white man is going to walk in that door able to write checks for more money than we ever had. It's important to him and I'm going to help him . . . I'm going to put on the show, Mama.

MAMA: Son—I come from five generations of people who was slaves and sharecroppers—but ain't nobody in my family never let nobody pay 'em no money that was a way of telling us we wasn't fit to walk the earth. We ain't never been that poor. (*Raising her eyes and looking at him*) We ain't never been that—dead inside.

BENEATHA: Well—we are dead now. All the talk about dreams and sunlight that goes on in this house. It's all dead now.

WALTER: What's the matter with you all! I didn't make this world! It was give to me this way! Hell, yes, I want me some yachts someday! Yes, I want to hang some real pearls 'round my wife's neck. Ain't she supposed to wear no pearls? Somebody tell me—tell me, who decides which women is suppose to wear pearls in this world. I tell you I am a *man*—and I think my wife should wear some pearls in this world!

(*This last line hangs a good while and* WALTER *begins to move about the room. The word "Man" has penetrated his consciousness; he mumbles it to himself repeatedly between strange agitated pauses as he moves about*)

MAMA: Baby, how you going to feel on the inside?

WALTER: Fine! . . . Going to feel fine . . . a man . . .

MAMA: You won't have nothing left then, Walter Lee.

WALTER (*coming to her*): I'm going to feel fine, Mama. I'm going to look that son-of-a-bitch in the eyes and say—(*He falters*)—and say, "All right, Mr. Lindner—(*He falters even more*)—that's *your* neighborhood out there! You got the right to keep it like you want! You got the right to have it like you want! Just write the check and—the house is yours." And—and I am going to say— (*His voice almost breaks*) "And you—you people just put the money in my hand and you won't have to live next to this bunch of stinking niggers! . . ." (*He straightens up and moves away from his mother, walking around the room*) And maybe—maybe I'll just get down on my black knees . . . (*He does so;* RUTH *and* BENNIE *and* MAMA *watch him in frozen horror*) "Captain, Mistuh, Bossman—(*Groveling and grinning and wringing his hands in profoundly anguished imitation of the slow-witted movie stereotype*) A-hee-hee-hee! Oh, yassuh boss! Yasssssuh! Great white—(*Voice breaking, he forces himself to go on*)—Father, just gi' ussen de money, fo' God's sake, and we's—we's ain't gwine come out deh and dirty up yo' white folks neighborhood . . ." (*He breaks down completely*) And I'll feel fine! Fine! FINE! (*He gets up and goes into the bedroom*)

BENEATHA: That is not a man. That is nothing but a toothless rat.

MAMA: Yes—death done come in this here house. (*She is nodding, slowly, reflectively*) Done come walking in my house on the lips of my children. You what supposed to be my beginning again. You—what supposed to be my harvest. (*To* BENEATHA) You—you mourning your brother?

BENEATHA: He's no brother of mine.

MAMA: What you say?

BENEATHA: I said that that individual in that room is no brother of mine.

MAMA: That's what I thought you said. You feeling like you better than he is today? (BENEATHA *does not answer*) Yes? What you tell him a minute ago? That he wasn't a man? Yes? You give him up for me? You done wrote his epitaph too—like the rest of the world? Well, who give you the privilege?

BENEATHA: Be on my side for once! You saw what he just did, Mama! You saw him—down on his knees. Wasn't it you who taught me to despise any man who would do that? Do what he's going to do?

MAMA: Yes—I taught you that. Me and your daddy. But I thought I taught you something else too . . . I thought I taught you to love him.

BENEATHA: Love him? There is nothing left to love.

MAMA: There is *always* something left to love. And if you ain't learned that, you ain't learned nothing. (*Looking at her*) Have you cried for that boy today? I don't mean for yourself and for the family 'cause we lost the money. I mean for him: what he been through and what it done to him. Child, when do you think is the time to love somebody the most? When they done good and made things easy for everybody? Well then, you ain't through learning—because that ain't the time at all. It's when he's at his lowest and can't believe in hisself 'cause the world done whipped him so! When you starts measuring somebody, measure him right, child, measure him right. Make sure you done taken into account what hills and valleys he come through before he got to wherever he is.

(TRAVIS *bursts into the room at the end of the speech, leaving the door open*)

TRAVIS: Grandmama—the moving men are downstairs! The truck just pulled up.

MAMA (*turning and looking at him*):   Are they, baby? They downstairs?

(*She sighs and sits.* LINDNER *appears in the doorway. He peers in and knocks lightly, to gain attention, and comes in. All turn to look at him*)

LINDNER (*hat and briefcase in hand*):   Uh—hello . . .

(RUTH *crosses mechanically to the bedroom door and opens it and lets it swing open freely and slowly as the lights come up on* WALTER *within, still in his coat, sitting at the far corner of the room. He looks up and out through the room to* LINDNER)

RUTH: He's here.

(*A long minute passes and* WALTER *slowly gets up*)

LINDNER (*coming to the table with efficiency, putting his briefcase on the table and starting to unfold papers and unscrew fountain pens*):   Well, I certainly was glad to hear from you people. (WALTER *has begun the trek out of the room, slowly and awkwardly, rather like a small boy, passing the back of his sleeve across his mouth from time to time*) Life can really be so much simpler than people let it be most of the time.

Well—with whom do I negotiate? You, Mrs. Younger, or your son here? (MAMA *sits with her hands folded on her lap and her eyes closed as* WALTER *advances.* TRAVIS *goes closer to* LINDNER *and looks at the papers curiously*) Just some official papers, sonny.

RUTH: Travis, you go downstairs—

MAMA (*opening her eyes and looking into* WALTER'S):   No. Travis, you stay right here. And you make him understand what you doing, Walter Lee. You teach him good. Like Willy Harris taught you. You show where our five generations done come to. (WALTER *looks from her to the boy, who grins at him innocently*) Go ahead, son—(*She folds her hands and closes her eyes*) Go ahead.

WALTER (*at last crosses to* LINDNER, *who is reviewing the contract*):   Well, Mr. Lindner. (BENEATHA *turns away*) We called you—(*There is a profound, simple groping quality in his speech*)—because, well, me and my family (*He looks around and shifts from one foot to the other*) Well—we are very plain people . . .

LINDNER: Yes—

WALTER: I mean—I have worked as a chauffeur most of my life—and my wife here, she does domestic work in people's kitchens. So does my mother. I mean—we are plain people . . .

LINDNER: Yes, Mr. Younger—

WALTER (*really like a small boy, looking down at his shoes and then up at the man*): And—uh—well, my father, well, he was a laborer most of his life. . . .

LINDNER (*absolutely confused*):   Uh, yes—yes, I understand. (*He turns back to the contract*)

WALTER (*a beat; staring at him*):   And my father—(*With sudden intensity*) My father almost *beat a man to death* once because this man called him a bad name or something, you know what I mean?

LINDNER (*looking up, frozen*):   No, no, I'm afraid I don't—

WALTER (*a beat. The tension hangs; then* WALTER *steps back from it*):   Yeah. Well—what I mean is that we come from people who had a lot of *pride.* I mean—we are very proud people. And that's my sister over there and she's going to be a doctor—and we are very proud—

LINDNER: Well—I am sure that is very nice, but—

WALTER: What I am telling you is that we called you over here to tell you that we are very proud and that this—(*Signaling to* TRAVIS) Travis, come here. (TRAVIS *crosses and* WALTER *draws him before him facing the man*) This is my son, and he makes the sixth generation our family in this country. And we have all thought about your offer—

LINDNER: Well, good . . . good—

WALTER: And we have decided to move into our house because my father—my father—he earned it for us brick by brick. (MAMA *has her eyes closed and is rocking back and forth as though she were in church, with her head nodding the Amen yes*) We don't want to make no trouble for nobody or fight no causes, and we will try to be good neighbors. And that's *all* we got to say about that. (*He looks the man absolutely in the eyes*) We don't want your money. (*He turns and walks away*)

LINDNER (*looking around at all of them*):   I take it then—that you have decided to occupy . . .

BENEATHA: That's what the man said.

LINDNER (*to* MAMA *in her reverie*):   Then I would like to appeal to you, Mrs. Younger. You are older and wiser and understand things better, I am sure . . .

MAMA: I am afraid you don't understand. My son said we was going to move and there ain't nothing left for me to say. (*Briskly*) You know how these young folks is nowadays, mister. Can't do a thing with 'em! (*As he opens his mouth, she rises*) Good-bye.

LINDNER (*folding up his materials*):   Well—if you are that final about it . . . there is nothing left for me to say. (*He finishes, almost ignored by the family, who are concentrating on* WALTER LEE. *At the door* LINDNER *halts and looks around*) I sure hope you people know what you're getting into.

(*He shakes his head and exits*)

RUTH (*looking around and coming to life*):   Well, for God's sake—if the moving men are here—LET'S GET THE HELL OUT OF HERE!

MAMA (*into action*):   Ain't it the truth! Look at all this here mess. Ruth, put Travis' good jacket on him . . . Walter Lee, fix your tie and tuck your shirt in, you look like somebody's hoodlum! Lord have mercy, where is my plant? (*She flies to get it amid the general bustling of the family, who are deliberately trying to ignore the nobility of the past moment*) You all start on down . . . Travis child, don't go empty-handed . . . Ruth, where did I put that box with my skillets in it? I want to be in charge of it myself . . . I'm going to make us the biggest dinner we ever ate tonight . . . Beneatha, what's the matter with them stockings? Pull them things up, girl . . .

(*The family starts to file out as two moving men appear and begin to carry out the heavier pieces of furniture, bumping into the family as they move about*)

BENEATHA: Mama, Asagai asked me to marry him today and go to Africa—

MAMA (*in the middle of her getting-ready activity*):   He did? You ain't old enough to marry nobody—(*Seeing the moving men lifting one of her chairs precariously*) Darling, that ain't no bale of cotton, please handle it so we can sit in it again! I had that chair twenty-five years . . .

(*The movers sigh with exasperation and go on with their work*)

BENEATHA (*girlishly and unreasonably trying to pursue the conversation*):   To go to Africa, Mama—be a doctor in Africa . . .

MAMA (*distracted*):   Yes, baby—

WALTER: *Africa!* What he want you to go to Africa for?

BENEATHA: To practice there . . .

WALTER: Girl, if you don't get all them silly ideas out your head! You better marry yourself a man with some loot . . .

BENEATHA (*angrily, precisely as in the first scene of the play*):   What have you got to do with who I marry!

WALTER: Plenty. Now I think George Murchison—

BENEATHA: *George Murchison!* I wouldn't marry him if he was Adam and I was Eve!

(WALTER *and* BENEATHA *go out yelling at each other vigorously and the anger is loud and real till their voices diminish.* RUTH *stands at the door and turns to* MAMA *and smiles knowingly*)

MAMA (*fixing her hat at last*): Yeah—they something all right, my children . . .

RUTH: Yeah—they're something. Let's go, Lena.

MAMA (*stalling, starting to look around at the house*): Yes—I'm coming. Ruth—

RUTH: Yes?

MAMA (*quietly, woman to woman*): He finally come into his manhood today, didn't he? Kind of like a rainbow after the rain . . .

RUTH (*biting her lip lest her own pride explode in front of* MAMA): Yes, Lena.

(WALTER'S *voice calls for them raucously*)

WALTER (*off stage*): Y'all come on! These people charges by the hour, you know!

MAMA (*waving* RUTH *out vaguely*): All right, honey—go on down. I be down directly.

(RUTH *hesitates, then exits.* MAMA *stands, at last alone in the living room, her plant on the table before her as the lights start to come down. She looks around at all the walls and ceilings and suddenly, despite herself, while the children call below, a great heaving thing rises in her and she puts her fist to her mouth to stifle it, takes a final desperate look, pulls her coat about her, pats her hat and goes out. The lights dim down. The door opens and she comes back in, grabs her plant, and goes out for the last time*)

Curtain

(1959)

QUESTIONS

1. Did you find this play engaging or interesting? Why or why not? What makes it specifically an urban play? A "minority" play? In what ways does it transcend these categories?

2. Describe the relationship of Mama (Lena) with her daughter, Beneatha, and with her son, Walter. What expectations does she have for the future of each? Why?

3. Give two explanations for the primary conflicts of the play. What precipitates the various arguments and battles the characters wage with one another?

4. Explain the roles of Joseph Asagai and George Murchison. Does either character have thematic significance? Explain.

5. Identify and discuss a major theme of the play. Support your ideas with references to specific events and speeches.

6. Identify two important stage props and comment on their role in the play. Discuss whether either or both may be symbolic, and why.

7. Select a scene you find compelling and describe how to stage it.

8. Are you satisfied with the play's ending? Why or why not? How do you envision the future of the family, particularly of Ruth and Walter and of Beneatha?

9. Some readers consider this play a modern American classic. What do you think may have led them to such an assessment?

10. How is Hansberry's play a comment on the Langston Hughes poem that she uses as her epigraph?

A Collection of Contemporary Drama

TERENCE MCNALLY

[b. 1939]

Terence McNally has long been a fixture on and off-Broadway. His plays have won wide acclaim for their wit, wisdom, and humanity. Among his numerous plays are *A Perfect Ganesh; Lips Together, Teeth Apart; Whisky; The Ritz;* and *Things That Go Bump in the Night*. McNally has also written screenplays, scripts for television, and the book for the musical adaptation of Manuel Puig's *The Kiss of the Spiderwoman*.

    Andre's Mother was written as a script for television. It won the 1990 Emmy Award for Best Writing in a Miniseries or Special.

TERENCE MCNALLY

Andre's Mother

CHARACTERS

CAL
ARTHUR
PENNY
ANDRE'S MOTHER

Four people enter. They are nicely dressed and carry white helium-filled balloons on a string. They are CAL, *a young man;* ARTHUR, *his father;* PENNY, *his sister; and* ANDRE'S MOTHER.

CAL: You know what's really terrible? I can't think of anything terrific to say. Goodbye. I love you. I'll miss you. And I'm supposed to be so great with words!

PENNY: What's that over there?

ARTHUR: Ask your brother.

CAL: It's a theatre. An outdoor theatre. They do plays there in the summer. Shakespeare's plays. (*To* ANDRE'S MOTHER.) God, how much he wanted to play Hamlet. It was his greatest dream. I think he would have sold his soul to play it. He would have gone to Timbuktu to have another go at that part. The summer he did it in Boston, he was so happy!

PENNY: Cal, I don't think she . . . ! It's not the time. Later.

ARTHUR: Your son was a . . . the Jews have a word for it . . .

PENNY: (*Quietly appalled.*) Oh my God!

ARTHUR: Mensch, I believe it is and I think I'm using it right. It means warm, solid, the real thing. Correct me if I'm wrong.

PENNY: Fine, dad, fine. Just quit while you're ahead.

ARTHUR: I won't say he was like a son to me. Even my son isn't always like a son to me. I mean . . . ! In my clumsy way, I'm trying to say how much I liked Andre. And how much he helped me to know my own boy. Cal was always two hands full but Andre and I could talk about anything under the sun. My wife was very fond of him, too.

PENNY: Cal, I don't understand about the balloons.

CAL: They represent the soul. When you let go, it means you're letting his soul ascend to Heaven. That you're willing to let go. Breaking the last earthly ties.

PENNY: Does the Pope know about this?

ARTHUR: Penny!

PENNY: Andre loved my sense of humor. Listen, you can hear him laughing. (*She lets go of her white balloon.*) So long, you glorious, wonderful, I-know-
what-Cal-means-about-words . . . *man!* God forgive me for wishing you were
straight every time I laid eyes on you. But if any man was going to have you,
I'm glad it was my brother! Look how fast it went up. I bet that means something. Something terrific.

ARTHUR: (ARTHUR *lets his balloon go.*) Goodbye. God speed.

PENNY: Cal?

CAL: I'm not ready yet.

PENNY: Okay. We'll be over there. Come on, pop, you can buy your little girl a Good Humor.

ARTHUR: They still make Good Humor?

PENNY: Only now they're called Dove Bars and they cost 12 dollars.

(PENNY *takes* ARTHUR *off.* CAL *and* ANDRE'S MOTHER *stand with their balloons.*)

CAL: I wish I knew what you were thinking. I think it would help me.
You know almost nothing about me and I only know what Andre told me
about you. I'd always had it in my mind that one day we would be friends,
you and me. But if you didn't know about Andre and me . . . If this hadn't
happened, I wonder if he would have ever told you. When he was so sick, if
I asked him once I asked him a thousand times, tell her. She's your mother.
She won't mind. But he was so afraid of hurting you and of your disapproval.
I don't know which was worse. (*No response. He sighs.*) God, how many of us
live in this city because we don't want to hurt our mothers and live in mortal
terror of their disapproval. We lose ourselves here. Our lives aren't furtive, just
our feelings toward people like you are! A city of fugitives from our parent's
scorn or heartbreak. Sometimes he'd seem a little down and I'd say, "What's
the matter, babe?" and this funny sweet, sad smile would cross his face and he'd
say, "Just a little homesick, Cal, just a little bit." I always accused him of being
a country boy just playing at being a hot shot, sophisticated New Yorker. (*He
sighs.*) It's bullshit. It's all bullshit. (*Still no response.*) Do you remember the comic
strip Little Lulu? Her mother had no name, she was so remote, so formidable
to all the children. She was just Lulu's mother. "Hello, Lulu's Mother," Lulu's
friends would say. She was almost anonymous in her remoteness. You remind
me of her. Andre's Mother. Let me answer the questions you can't ask and then
I'll leave you alone and you won't ever have to see me again. Andre died of
AIDS. I don't know how he got it. I tested negative. He died bravely. You
would have been proud of him. The only thing that frightened him was you.
I'll have everything that was his sent to you. I'll pay for it. There isn't much.
You should have come up the summer he played Hamlet. He was magnificent. Yes, I'm bitter. I'm bitter I've lost him. I'm bitter what's happening. I'm
bitter even now, after all this, I can't reach you. I'm beginning to feel your disapproval and it's making me ill. (*He looks at his balloon.*) Sorry, old friend. I blew
it. (*He lets go of the balloon.*) Good night, sweet prince, and flights of angels sing
thee to thy rest! (*Beat.*) Goodbye, Andre's Mother. (*He goes.* ANDRE'S MOTHER

stands alone holding her white balloon. Her lip trembles. She looks on the verge of break-ing down. She is about to let go of the balloon when she pulls it down to her. She looks at it a while before she gently kisses it. She lets go of the balloon. She follows it with her eyes as it rises and rises. The lights are beginning to fade. ANDRE'S MOTHER's *eyes are still on the balloon. Blackout.*)

(1988)

QUESTIONS

1. Why is the play entitled "Andre's Mother"? What effect does the playwright achieve by making the mother's part silent?
2. What is the significance of Cal's allusion to Lulu's mother?
3. What is the effect of Cal's references to *Hamlet*? What is conveyed through Cal's quoting from Shakespeare's play?
4. What is the significance of the helium balloons and of what the characters do with them?
5. What is the significance of the final stage direction?
6. What is the overall theme of *Andre's Mother*?

TINA HOWE

[b. 1937]

Tina Howe was born in New York City and raised in New England. She grad-uated from Sarah Lawrence College, where she wrote her first play. After liv-ing in Paris she returned to the East Coast, where she established her play-wrighting career with plays such as *The Nest, Birth and After Birth, Museum,* and *Coastal Disturbances.*

Painting Churches was first produced in New York's Theater Row in 1983. Televised in 1986 on *American Playhouse,* the play has won a number of awards, including an Outer Critics Circle Award. Its blend of stark realism with zany humor, along with its shifts in emotional register make for compelling theater.

TINA HOWE

Painting Churches

ACT ONE

Scene 1

The living room of the Churches' townhouse on Beacon Hill one week before everything will be moved to Cape Cod. Empty packing cartons line the room and all the furniture has been tagged with brightly colored markers. At first glance it looks like any discreet Boston interior, but on closer scrutiny one notices a certain flamboyance. Oddities from secondhand stores are mixed in with the fine old furniture, and exotic handmade curios vie with tasteful family objets d'art. What makes the room remarkable, though, is the play of light that pours through three soaring arched windows. At one hour it's hard edged and brilliant; the next, it's dappled and yielding. It transforms whatever it touches, giving the room a distinct feeling of unreality. It's several years ago, a bright spring morning.

FANNY *is sitting on the sofa, wrapping a valuable old silver coffee service. She's wearing a worn bathrobe and fashionable hat. As she works, she makes a list of everything on a yellow legal pad.* GARDNER *can be heard typing in his study down the hall.*

FANNY *(Picks up a coffee pot):*   God, this is good-looking! I'd forgotten how handsome Mama's old silver was! It's probably worth a fortune. It certainly weighs   enough!   *(Calling)*   GARRRRRRRRRRRRRRRRRRRRRD-NERRRRRRRRRRRR?... Well, it should bring us a pretty penny, that's for sure. *(Wraps it, places it in a carton, and then picks up the tray that goes with it. She holds it up like a mirror and adjusts her hat. Louder in another register)* OH, GARRRRRRRRRRRRRRRRRRRRRDNERRRRR?

*(*GARDNER *continues typing. She then reaches for a small box and opens it with reverence)* Grandma's Paul Revere teaspoons!... *(She takes out several and fondles them)* I don't care how desperate things get, these will never go! One has to maintain some standards! *(She writes on her list)* Grandma's Paul Revere teaspoons, Cotuit! ... WASN'T IT THE AMERICAN WING OF THE METROPOLITAN MUSEUM OF ART THAT WANTED GRANDMA'S PAUL REVERE TEASPOONS SO BADLY?... *(She looks at her reflection in the tray again)* This is a very good-looking hat, if I do say so. I was awfully smart to grab it up. *(Silence)* DON'T YOU REMEMBER A DISTINGUISHED-LOOKING MAN COMING TO THE HOUSE AND OFFERING US FIFTY THOUSAND DOLLARS FOR GRANDMA'S PAUL REVERE TEASPOONS?... HE HAD ON THESE MARVELOUS SHOES! THEY WERE SO POINTED AT THE ENDS WE COULDN'T IMAGINE HOW HE EVER GOT THEM ON AND THEY WERE SHINED TO WITHIN AN INCH OF

THEIR LIVES AND I REMEMBER HIM SAYING HE CAME FROM THE . . . AMERICAN WING OF THE METROPOLITAN MUSEUM OF ART! . . . HELLO? . . . GARDNER? . . . ARE YOU THERE! *(The typing stops)* YOO-HOOOOOOO . . . *(Like a foghorn)* GARRRRRRRRRRRD-NERRRRRRR?

GARDNER *(Offstage; from his study):* YES, DEAR . . . IS THAT YOU?

FANNY: OF COURSE IT'S ME! WHO ELSE COULD IT POSSIBLY BE? . . . DARLING, PLEASE COME HERE FOR A MINUTE. *(The typing resumes)* FOR GOD'S SAKE, WILL YOU STOP THAT DREADFUL TYPING BEFORE YOU SEND ME STRAIGHT TO THE NUT HOUSE? . . . *(In a new register)* GARRRRRRRRRRRRRRDNERRRRRR?

He stops.

GARDNER *(Offstage):* WHAT'S THAT? MAGS IS BACK FROM THE NUT HOUSE?

FANNY: I SAID . . . Lord, I hate this yelling. . . . PLEASE . . . COME . . . HERE!

Brief silence.

GARDNER *(Offstage):* I'LL BE WITH YOU IN A MOMENT, I DIDN'T HEAR HER RING. *(Starts singing)* "Nothing could be finer than to be in Carolina."

FANNY: It's a wonder I'm not in a straitjacket already. Actually, it might be rather nice for a change . . . peaceful. DARLING . . . I WANT TO SHOW YOU MY NEW HAT!

Silence. GARDNER *enters, still singing. He's wearing mismatched tweeds and is holding a stack of papers which keep drifting to the floor.*

GARDNER: Oh, don't you look nice! Very attractive, very attractive!

FANNY: But I'm still in my bathrobe.

GARDNER *(Looking around the room, leaking more papers):* Well, where's Mags?

FANNY: Darling, you're dropping your papers all over the floor.

GARDNER *(Spies the silver tray):* I remember this! Aunt Alice gave it to us, didn't she? *(He picks it up)* Good Lord, it's heavy. What's it made of? Lead?!

FANNY: No, Aunt Alice did *not* give it to us. It was Mama's.

GARDNER: Oh, yes . . . *(He starts to exit with it)*

FANNY: Could I have it back, please?

GARDNER *(Hands it to her, dropping more papers):* Oh, sure thing. . . . Where's Mags? I thought you said she was here.

FANNY: I didn't say Mags was here, I asked *you* to come here.

GARDNER *(Papers spilling):* Damned papers keep falling . . .

FANNY: I wanted to show you my new hat. I bought it in honor of Mags' visit. Isn't it marvelous?

GARDNER *(Picking up the papers as more drop):* Yes, yes, very nice . . .

FANNY: Gardner, you're not even looking at it!

GARDNER: Very becoming . . .

FANNY: You don't think it's too bright, do you? I don't want to look like a traffic light. Guess how much it cost?

GARDNER *(A whole sheaf of papers slides to the floor; he dives for them):* OH,

SHIT!

FANNY *(Gets to them first)*:   It's all right, I've got them, I've got them. *(She hands them to him)*

GARDNER: You'd think they had wings on them . . .

FANNY: Here you go . . .

GARDNER: . . . damned things won't

FANNY: Gar . . . ?

hold still!

GARDNER *(Engrossed in one of the pages)*:   Mmmmm?

FANNY: HELLO?

GARDNER *(Startled)*:   What's that?

FANNY *(In a whisper)*:   My hat. Guess how much it cost.

GARDNER: Oh, yes. Let's see . . . ten dollars?

FANNY: Ten dollars . . . IS THAT ALL?

GARDNER: Twenty?

FANNY: GARDNER, THIS HAPPENS TO BE A DESIGNER HAT! DESIGNER HATS START AT FIFTY DOLLARS . . . SEVENTY-FIVE!

GARDNER *(Jumps)*:   Was that the door bell?

FANNY: No, it wasn't the door bell. Though it's high time Mags were here. She was probably in a train wreck!

GARDNER *(Looking through his papers)*:   I'm beginning to get fond of Wallace Stevens again.

FANNY: This damned move is going to kill me! Send me straight to my grave!

GARDNER *(Reading from a page)*:
"The mules that angels ride come slowly down
The blazing passes, from beyond the sun.
Descensions of their tinkling bells arrive.
These muleteers are dainty of their way . . ."
(Pause) Don't you love that! "These muleteers are *dainty* of their way"!?

FANNY: Gar, the hat. How much? *(GARDNER sighs)* Darling . . . ?

GARDNER: Oh, yes. Let's see . . . fifty dollars? Seventy-five?

FANNY: It's French.

GARDNER: Three hundred!

FANNY *(Triumphant)*:   No, eighty-five cents.

GARDNER: Eighty-five cents! . . . I thought you said . . .

FANNY: That's right . . . eighty . . . five . . . *cents!*

GARDNER: Well, you sure had me fooled!

FANNY: I found it at the thrift shop.

GARDNER: I thought it cost at least fifty dollars or seventy-five. You know, designer hats are very expensive!

FANNY: It was on the markdown table. *(She takes it off and shows him the label)* See that? Lily Daché! When I saw that label, I nearly keeled over right into the fur coats!

GARDNER *(Handling it)*:   Well, what do you know, that's the same label that's in my bathrobe.

FANNY: Darling, Lily Daché designed hats, not men's bathrobes!

GARDNER: Yup . . . Lily Daché . . . same name . . .

FANNY: If you look again, I'm sure you'll see . . .

GARDNER: . . . same script, same color, same size. I'll show you. *(He exits)*

FANNY: Poor lamb can't keep anything straight anymore. *(Looks at herself in the tray again)* God, this is a good-looking hat!

GARDNER *(Returns with a nondescript plaid bathrobe. He points to the label)*: See that? . . . What does it say?

FANNY *(Refusing to look at it)*: Lily Daché was a *hat* designer! She designed ladies' *hats!*

GARDNER: What . . . does . . . it . . . say?

FANNY: Gardner, you're being ridiculous.

GARDNER *(Forcing it on her)*: Read . . . the label!

FANNY: Lily Daché did *not* design this bathrobe, I don't care what the label says!

GARDNER: READ! *(FANNY reads it)* ALL RIGHT, NOW WHAT DOES IT SAY?

FANNY *(Chagrined)*: Lily Daché.

GARDNER: I told you!

FANNY: Wait a minute, let me look at that again. *(She does; then throws the robe at him in disgust)* Gar, Lily Daché never designed a bathrobe in her life! Someone obviously ripped the label off one of her hats and then sewed it into the robe.

GARDNER *(Puts it on over his jacket)*: It's damned good-looking. I've always loved this robe. I think you gave it to me. . . . Well, I've got to get back to work. *(He abruptly exits)*

FANNY: Where did you get that robe anyway? . . . I didn't give it to you, did I . . . ?

Silence. GARDNER *resumes typing.*

FANNY *(Holding the tray up again and admiring herself)*: You know, I think I *did* give it to him. I remember how excited I was when I found it at the thrift shop . . . fifty cents and never worn! *I* couldn't have sewn that label in to impress him, could I? . . . I can't be that far gone! . . . The poor lamb wouldn't even notice it, let alone understand its cachet. . . . Uuuuuuh, this damned tray is even heavier than the coffee pot. They must have been amazons in the old days! *(Writes on her pad)* "Empire tray, Parke-Bernet Galleries," and good riddance! *(She wraps it and drops it into the carton with the coffee pot)* Where *is* that wretched Mags? It would be just like her to get into a train wreck! She was supposed to be here hours ago. Well, if she doesn't show up soon, I'm going to drop dead of exhaustion. God, wouldn't that be wonderful? . . . Then they could just cart me off into storage with all the old chandeliers and china . . .

The doorbell rings.

FANNY: IT'S MAGS, IT'S MAGS! *(A pause. Dashing out of the room, colliding into GARDNER)* GOOD GOD, LOOK AT ME! I'M STILL IN MY BATHROBE!

GARDNER *(Offstage)*: COMING, COMING . . . I'VE GOT IT . . . COMING! *(Dashing into the room, colliding into FANNY)* I'VE GOT IT . . . HOLD ON . . . COMING . . . COMING . . .

FANNY *(Offstage)*:   MAGS IS HERE! IT'S MAGS. . . . SHE'S FINALLY HERE!

GARDNER *exits to open the front door.* MAGS *come staggering in carrying a suitcase and an enormous duffel bag. She wears wonderfully distinctive clothes and has very much her own look. She's extremely out of breath and too wrought up to drop her heavy bags.*

MAGS: I'm sorry . . . I'm sorry I'm so late. . . . Everything went wrong! A passenger had a heart attack outside of New London and we had to stop. . . . It was terrifying! All these medics and policemen came swarming onto the train and the conductor kept running up and down the aisles telling everyone not to leave their seats under any circumstances. . . . Then the New London fire department came screeching down to the tracks, sirens blaring, lights whirling, and all these men in black rubber suits started pouring through the doors. . . . *That* took two hours . . .

FANNY *(Offstage)*:   DARLING . . . DARLING . . . WHERE ARE YOU?

MAGS: *Then,* I couldn't get a cab at the station. There just weren't any! I must have circled the block fifteen times. Finally I just stepped out into the traffic with my thumb out, but no one would pick me up . . . so I walked . . .

FANNY *(Offstage)*:   Damned zipper's stuck . . .

GARDNER: You walked all the way from the South Station?

MAGS: Well actually, I ran . . .

GARDNER: You had poor Mum scared to death.

MAGS *(Finally puts the bags down with a deep sigh)*:   I'm sorry. . . . I'm really sorry. It was a nightmare.

FANNY *reenters the room, her dress over her head. The zipper's stuck; she staggers around blindly.*

FANNY: Damned zipper! Gar, will you please help me with this?

MAGS: I sprinted all the way up Beacon Hill.

GARDNER *(Opening his arms wide)*:   Well come here and let's get a look at you. *(He hugs her)* Mags!

MAGS *(Squeezing him tight)*:   Oh, Daddy . . . Daddy!

GARDNER: My Mags!

MAGS: I never thought I'd get here! . . . Oh, you look wonderful!

GARDNER: Well, you don't look so bad yourself!

MAGS: I love your hair. It's gotten so . . . white!

FANNY *(Still lost in her dress, struggling with the zipper)*:   This is *so* typical . . . just as Mags arrives, my zipper has to break! *(She grunts and struggles)*

MAGS *(Waves at her)*:   Hi, Mum . . .

FANNY: Just a minute, dear, my zipper's . . .

GARDNER *(Picks up MAGS' bags)*:   Well, sit down and take a load off your feet . . .

MAGS: I was so afraid I'd never make it . . .

GARDNER *(Staggering under the weight of the bags)*:   What have you got in here? Lead weights?

MAGS: I can't believe you're finally letting me do you.

FANNY *flings her arms around* MAGS, *practically knocking her over.*

FANNY: OH, DARLING ... MY PRECIOUS MAGS, YOU'RE HERE AT LAST.

GARDNER *(Lurching around in circles)*: Now let's see ... where should I put these ... ?

FANNY: I was sure your train had derailed and you were lying dead in some ditch!

MAGS *(Pulls away from FANNY to come to GARDNER's rescue)*: Daddy, please, let me ... these are much too heavy.

FANNY *(Finally noticing MAGS)*: GOOD LORD, WHAT HAVE YOU DONE TO YOUR HAIR?!

MAGS *(Struggling to take the bags from GARDNER)*: Come on, give them to me ... please? *(She sets them down by the sofa)*

FANNY *(As her dress starts to slide off one shoulder)*: Oh, not again! ... Gar, would you give me a hand and see what's wrong with this zipper. One minute it's stuck, the next it's falling to pieces.

GARDNER *goes to her and starts fussing with it.*

MAGS *(Pacing)*: I don't know, it's been crazy all week. Monday, I forgot to keep an appointment I'd made with a new model. ... Tuesday, I overslept and stood up my advanced painting students. ... Wednesday, the day of my meeting with Max Zoll, I forgot to put on my underpants ...

FANNY: GODDAMMIT, GAR, CAN'T YOU DO ANYTHING ABOUT THIS ZIPPER?!

MAGS: I mean, there I was, racing down Broome Street in this gauzy Tibetan skirt when I tripped and fell right at his feet ... SPLATTT! My skirt goes flying over my head and there I am ... everything staring him in the face ...

FANNY: COME ON, GAR, USE A LITTLE MUSCLE!

MAGS *(Laughing)*: Oh, well, all that matters is that I finally got here. ... I mean ... there you are ...

GARDNER *(Struggling with the zipper)*: I can't see it, it's too small!

FANNY *(Whirls away from GARDNER, pulling her dress off altogether)*: OH, FORGET IT! JUST FORGET IT! The trolley's probably missing half its teeth, just like someone else I know. *(To MAGS)* I grind my teeth in my sleep now, I've worn them all down to stubs. Look at that! *(She flings open her mouth and points)* Nothing left but the gums!

GARDNER: I never hear you grind your teeth ...

FANNY: That's because I'm snoring so loud. How could you hear anything through all that racket? It even wakes me up. It's no wonder poor Daddy has to sleep downstairs.

MAGS *(Looking around)*: Jeez, look at the place! So, you're finally doing it ... selling the house and moving to Cotuit year round. I don't believe it. I just don't believe it!

GARDNER: Well, how about a drink to celebrate Mags' arrival?

MAGS: You've been here so long. Why move now?

FANNY: Gardner, what are you wearing that bathrobe for?

MAGS: You can't move. I won't let you!

FANNY *(Softly to* GARDNER*)*:   Really, darling, you ought to pay more attention to your appearance.

MAGS: You love this house. *I* love this house . . . the room . . . the light.

GARDNER: So, Mags, how about a little . . . *(He drinks from an imaginary glass)* to wet your whistle?

FANNY: We can't start drinking now, it isn't even noon yet!

MAGS: I'm starving. I've got to get something to eat before I collapse! *(She exits towards the kitchen)*

FANNY: What *have* you done to your hair, dear? The color's so queer and all your nice curl is gone.

GARDNER: It looks to me as if she dyed it.

FANNY: Yes, that's it. You're absolutely right! It's a completely different color. She dyed it bright red!

MAGS *can be heard thumping and thudding through the icebox.*

FANNY: NOW, MAGS, I DON'T WANT YOU FILLING UP ON SNACKS. . . . I'VE MADE A PERFECTLY BEAUTIFUL LEG OF LAMB FOR LUNCH! . . . HELLO? . . . DO YOU HEAR ME? . . . *(To* GARDNER*)* No one in our family has *ever* had red hair, it's so common looking.

GARDNER: I like it. It brings out her eyes.

FANNY: WHY ON EARTH DID YOU DYE YOUR HAIR *RED*, OF ALL COLORS?!

MAGS *(Returns, eating Saltines out of the box)*:   I didn't dye my hair, I just added some highlight.

FANNY: I suppose that's what your arty friends in New York do . . . dye their hair all the colors of the rainbow!

GARDNER: Well, it's damned attractive if you ask me . . . damned attractive!

MAGS *unzips her duffel bag and rummages around in it while eating the Saltines.*

FANNY: Darling, I told you not to bring a lot of stuff with you. We're trying to get rid of things.

MAGS *(Pulls out a folding easel and starts setting it up)*:   AAAAAHHHHHH, here it is. Isn't it a beauty? I bought it just for you!

FANNY: Please don't get crumbs all over the floor. Crystal was just here yesterday. It was her last time before we move.

MAGS *(At her easel)*:   God, I can hardly wait! I can't believe you're finally letting me do you.

FANNY: *Do* us? . . . What *are* you talking about?

GARDNER *(Reaching for the Saltines)*:   Hey, Mags, could I have a couple of those?

MAGS *(Tosses him the box)*:   Sure! *(To* FANNY*)* Your portrait.

GARDNER: Thanks. *(He starts munching on a handful)*

FANNY: You're planning to paint our portrait now? While we're trying to move . . . ?

GARDNER *(Sputtering Saltines)*:   Mmmmm, I'd forgotten just how delicious Saltines are!

MAGS: It's a perfect opportunity. There'll be no distractions; you'll be completely at my mercy. Also, you promised.

FANNY: I did?

MAGS: Yes, you did.

FANNY: Well, I must have been off my rocker.

MAGS: No, you said, "You can paint us, you can dip us in concrete, you can do anything you want with us just so long as you help us get out of here!"

GARDNER *(Offering the box of Saltines to* FANNY*)*:   You really ought to try some of these, Fan, they're absolutely delicious!

FANNY *(Taking a few)*:   Why, thank you.

MAGS: I figure we'll pack in the morning and you'll pose in the afternoons. It'll be a nice diversion.

FANNY: These *are* good!

GARDNER: Here, dig in . . . take some more.

MAGS: I have some wonderful news . . . amazing news! I wanted to wait till I got here to tell you.

GARDNER *and* FANNY *eat their Saltines, passing the box back and forth as* MAGS *speaks.*

MAGS: You'll die! Just fall over into the packing cartons and die! Are you ready? . . . BRACE YOURSELVES. . . . OKAY, HERE GOES. . . . I'm being given a one-woman show at one of the most important galleries in New York this fall. Me, Margaret Church, exhibited at Castelli's, 420 West Broadway. . . . Can you believe it?! . . . MY PORTRAITS HANGING IN THE SAME ROOMS THAT HAVE SHOWN RAUSCHENBERG, JOHNS, WAR-HOL, KELLY, LICHTENSTEIN, STELLA, SERRA, ALL THE HEAVIES. . . . It's incredible, beyond belief . . . I mean, at my age. . . . Do you know how good you have to be to get in there? It's a miracle . . . an honest-to-God, star-spangled miracle!

Pause.

FANNY *(Mouth full)*:   Oh, darling, that's wonderful. We're so happy for you!

GARDNER *(Mouth full)*:   No one deserves it more, no one deserves it more!

MAGS: Through some fluke, some of Castelli's people showed up at our last faculty show at Pratt and were knocked out . . .

FANNY *(Reaching for the box of Saltines)*:   More, more . . .

MAGS: They said they hadn't seen anyone handle light like me since the French Impressionists. They said I was this weird blend of Pierre Bonnard, Mary Cassatt and David Hockney . . .

GARDNER *(Swallowing his mouthful)*:   I told you they were good.

MAGS: Also, no one's doing portraits these days. They're considered passé. I'm so out of it, I'm in.

GARDNER: Well, you're loaded with talent and always have been.

FANNY: She gets it all from Mama, you know. Her miniature of Henry James is still one of the main attractions at the Atheneum. Of course no woman of breeding could be a professional artist in her day. It simply wasn't done. But talk about talent . . . that woman had talent to burn!

MAGS: I want to do one of you for the show.

FANNY: Oh, do Daddy, he's the famous one.

MAGS: No, I want to do you both. I've always wanted to do you and now I've finally got a good excuse.

FANNY: It's high time somebody painted Daddy again! I'm sick to death of that dreadful portrait of him in the National Gallery they keep reproducing. He looks like an undertaker!

GARDNER: Well, I think you should just do Mum. She's never looked handsomer.

FANNY: Oh, come on, I'm a perfect fright and you know it.

MAGS: I want to do you both. Side by side. In this room. Something really classy. You look so great. Mum with her crazy hats and everything and you with that face. If I could just get you to hold still long enough and actually pose.

GARDNER *(Walking around, distracted)*:   Where are those papers I just had? Goddammit, Fanny . . .

MAGS: I have the feeling it's either now or never.

GARDNER: I can't hold on to anything around here. *(He exits to his study)*

MAGS: I've always wanted to do you. It would be such a challenge.

FANNY *(Pulling MAGS onto the sofa next to her)*:   I'm so glad you're finally here, Mags. I'm very worried about Daddy.

MAGS: Mummy, please. I just got here.

FANNY: He's getting quite gaga.

MAGS: Mummy . . . !

FANNY: You haven't seen him in almost a year. Two weeks ago he walked through the front door of the Codman's house, kissed Emily on the cheek and settled down in the maid's room, thinking he was home!

MAGS: Oh, come on, you're exaggerating.

FANNY: He's as mad as a hatter and getting worse every day! It's this damned new book of his. He works on it around the clock. I've read some of it, and it doesn't make one word of sense, it's all at sixes and sevens . . .

GARDNER *(Pokes his head back in the room, spies some of his papers on a table and grabs them)*:   Ahhh, here they are. *(He exits)*

FANNY *(Voice lowered)*:   Ever since this dry spell with his poetry, he's been frantic, absolutely . . . frantic!

MAGS: I hate it when you do this.

FANNY: I'm just trying to get you to face the facts around here.

MAGS: There's nothing wrong with him! He's just as sane as the next man. Even saner, if you ask me.

FANNY: You know what he's doing now? You couldn't guess in a million years! . . . He's writing criticism! Daddy! *(She laughs)* Can you believe it? The man doesn't have one analytic bone in his body. His mind is a complete jumble and always has been!

There's a loud crash from GARDNER's study.

GARDNER *(Offstage)*:   SHIT!

MAGS: He's abstracted. . . . That's the way he is.

FANNY: He doesn't spend any time with me anymore. He just holes up in that filthy study with Toots. God, I hate that bird! Though actually they're quite cunning together. Daddy's teaching him Gray's *Elegy*. You ought to see them in there, Toots perched on top of Daddy's head, spouting out verse after verse . . . Daddy, tap-tap-tapping away on his typewriter. They're quite a pair.

GARDNER *(Pokes his head back in)*: Have you seen that Stevens' poem I was reading before?

FANNY *(Long-suffering)*: NO, I HAVEN'T SEEN THAT STEVENS' POEM YOU WERE READING BEFORE! . . . Things are getting very tight around here, in case you haven't noticed. Daddy's last Pulitzer didn't even cover our real estate tax, and now that he's too doddery to give readings anymore, that income is gone . . . *(Suddenly handing MAGS the sugar bowl she'd been wrapping)* Mags, do take this sugar bowl. You can use it to serve tea to your students at that wretched art school of yours . . .

MAGS: It's called Pratt! The Pratt Institute.

FANNY: Pratt, Splatt, whatever . . .

MAGS: And I don't serve tea to my students, I teach them how to paint.

FANNY: Well, I'm sure none of them has ever seen a sugar bowl as handsome as this before.

GARDNER *(Reappearing again)*: You're sure you haven't seen it?

FANNY *(Loud and angry)*: YES, I'M SURE I HAVEN'T SEEN IT! I JUST TOLD YOU I HAVEN'T SEEN IT!

GARDNER *(Retreating)*: Right you are, right you are. *(He exits)*

FANNY: God!

Silence.

MAGS: What do you have to yell at him like that for?

FANNY: Because the poor thing's as deaf as an adder!

MAGS sighs deeply; silence. FANNY, suddenly exuberant, leads her over to a lamp.

FANNY: Come, I want to show you something.

MAGS *(Looking at it)*: What is it?

FANNY: Something I made. *(MAGS is about to turn it on)* WAIT, DON'T TURN IT ON YET! It's got to be dark to get the full effect. *(She rushes to the windows and pulls down the shades)*

MAGS: What *are* you doing?

FANNY: Hold your horses a minute. You'll see . . . *(As the room gets darker and darker)* Poor me, you wouldn't believe the lengths I go to to amuse myself these days . . .

MAGS *(Touching the lampshade)*: What is this? It looks like a scene of some sort.

FANNY: It's an invention I made . . . a kind of magic lantern.

MAGS: Gee . . . it's amazing . . .

FANNY: What I did was buy an old engraving of the Grand Canal . . .

MAGS: You *made* this?

FANNY: . . . and then color it in with crayons. Next, I got out my sewing scissors and cut out all the street lamps and windows . . . anything that light would shine through. Then I pasted it over a plain lampshade, put the shade on this old horror of a lamp, turned on the switch and . . . *(She turns it on)* VOILÀ . . . VENICE TWINKLING AT DUSK! It's quite effective, don't you think . . . ?

MAGS *(Walking around it)*:   Jeeez . . .

FANNY: And see, I poked out all the little lights on the gondolas with a straight pin.

MAGS: Where on earth did you get the idea?

FANNY: Well you know, idle minds . . . *(She spins the shade, making the lights whirl)*

MAGS: It's really amazing. I mean, you could sell this in a store!

GARDNER *(Enters)*:   HERE IT IS. IT WAS RIGHT ON TOP OF MY DESK THE WHOLE TIME. *(He crashes into a table)* OOOOOWW- WWW!

FANNY: LOOK OUT, LOOK OUT!

MAGS *(Rushes over to* GARDNER*)*: Oh, Daddy, are you all right?

FANNY: WATCH WHERE YOU'RE GOING, WATCH WHERE YOU'RE GOING!

GARDNER *(Hopping up and down on one leg)*:   GODDAMMIT! . . . I HIT MY SHIN.

FANNY: I was just showing Mags my lamp . . .

GARDNER *(Limping over to it)*:   Oh, yes, isn't that something? Mum is awfully clever with that kind of thing. . . . It was all her idea. Buying the engraving, coloring it in, cutting out all those little dots.

FANNY: Not "dots". . . lights and windows, lights and windows!

GARDNER: Right, right . . . lights and windows.

FANNY: Well, we'd better get some light back in here before someone breaks their neck. *(She zaps the shades back up)*

GARDNER *(Puts his arm around* MAGS*)*:   Gee, it's good to have you back.

MAGS: It's good to be back.

GARDNER: And I like that new red hair of yours. It's very becoming.

MAGS: But I told you, I hardly touched it . . .

GARDNER: Well, something's different. You've got a glow. So . . . how do you want us to pose for this grand portrait of yours . . . ? *(He poses self-consciously)*

MAGS: Oh, Daddy, setting up a portrait takes a lot of time and thought. You've got to figure out the background, the lighting, what to wear, the sort of mood you want to—

FANNY: OOOOH, LET'S DRESS UP, LET'S DRESS UP! *(She grabs a packing blanket, drapes it around herself and links arms with* GARDNER*, striking an elegant pose)* This *is* going to be fun. She was absolutely right! Come on, Gar, look distinguished!

MAGS: Mummy, please, it's not a game!

FANNY *(More and more excited)*:   You still have your tuxedo, don't you? And I'll wear my marvelous long black dress that makes me look like that fascinating woman in the Sargent painting! *(She strikes the famous profile pose)*

MAGS: MUMMY?!

FANNY: I'm sorry, we'll behave, just tell us what to do.

FANNY *and* GARDNER *settle down next to each other.*

GARDNER: That's right, you're the boss.

FANNY: Yes, you're the boss.

MAGS: But I'm not ready yet; I haven't set anything up.

FANNY: Relax, darling, we just want to get the hang of it . . .

FANNY *and* GARDNER *stare straight ahead, trying to look like suitable subjects, but they can't hold still. They keep making faces, lifting an eyebrow, wriggling a nose, twitching a lip. Nothing big and grotesque, just flickering changes; a half-smile here, a self-important frown there. They steal glances at each other every so often.*

GARDNER: How am I doing, Fan?

FANNY: Brilliantly, absolutely brilliantly!

MAGS: But you're making faces.

FANNY: *I'm* not making faces. *(Turning to* GARDNER *and making a face)* Are *you* making faces, Gar?

GARDNER *(Instantly making one):* Certainly not! I'm the picture of restraint!

Without meaning to, FANNY *and* GARDNER *get sillier and sillier. They start giggling, then laughing.*

MAGS *(Can't help but join in):* You two are impossible . . . completely impossible! I was crazy to think I could ever pull this off! *(Laughing away)* Look at you . . . just . . . look at you!

Blackout.

Scene 2

Two days later, around five in the afternoon. Half of the Church household has been dragged into the living room for packing. Overflowing cartons are everywhere. They're filled with pots and pans, dishes and glasses, and the entire contents of two linen closets. MAGS *has placed a stepladder under one of the windows. A pile of tablecloths and curtains is flung beneath it. Two side chairs are in readiness for the eventual pose.*

MAGS *has just pulled a large crimson tablecloth out of a carton. She unfurls it with one shimmering toss.*

MAGS: PERFECT . . . PERFECT!

FANNY *(Seated on the sofa, clutches an old pair of galoshes to her chest):* Look at these old horrors; half the rubber is rotted away and the fasteners are falling to pieces. . . . GARDNER? . . . OH, GARRRRRRRRRRDNERRRRR?

MAGS *(Rippling out the tablecloth with shorter snapping motions):* Have you ever seen such a color?

FANNY: I'VE FOUND YOUR OLD SLEDDING GALOSHES IN WITH THE POTS AND PANS. DO YOU STILL WANT THEM?

MAGS: It's like something out of a Rubens!

MAGS *slings the tablecloth over a chair and then sits on a footstool to finish the Sara Lee banana cake she started. As she eats, she looks at the tablecloth, making happy grunting sounds.* FANNY *lovingly puts the galoshes on over her shoes and wiggles her feet.*

FANNY: God, these bring back memories! There were real snowstorms in the old days. Not these pathetic little two-inch droppings we have now. After a particularly heavy one, Daddy and I used to go sledding on the Common. This was way before you were born. . . . God, it was a hundred years ago! . . . Daddy would stop writing early, put on these galoshes and come looking for me, jingling the fasteners like castanets. It was a kind of mating call, almost . . . *(She jingles them)* The Common was always deserted after a storm; we had the whole place to ourselves. It was so romantic. . . . We'd haul the sled up Beacon Street, stop under the State House, and aim it straight down to the Park Street Church, which was much further away in those days. . . . Then Daddy would lie down on the sled, I'd lower myself on top of him, we'd rock back and forth a few times to gain momentum and then . . . WHOOOOOOOOOSSSSSSSHHHHH . . . down we'd plunge like a pair of eagles locked in a spasm of lovemaking. God, it was wonderful! . . . The city whizzing past us at ninety miles an hour . . . the cold . . . the darkness . . . Daddy's hair in my mouth . . . GAR . . . REMEMBER HOW WE USED TO GO SLEDDING IN THE OLD DAYS? . . . Sometimes he'd lie on top of me. That was fun. I liked that even more. *(In her foghorn voice)* GARRRRRRRRRDNERRRRR?

MAGS: Didn't he say he was going out this afternoon?

FANNY: Why, so he did! I completely forgot. *(She takes off the galoshes)* I'm getting just as bad as him. *(She drops them into a different carton—wistful)* Gar's galoshes, Cotuit.

A pause. MAGS *picks up the tablecloth again, holds it high over her head.*

MAGS: Isn't this fabulous? . . . *(She then wraps* FANNY *in it)* It's the perfect backdrop. Look what it does to your skin.

FANNY: Mags, what *are* you doing?

MAGS: It makes you glow like a pomegranate . . . *(She whips it off her)* Now all I need is a hammer and nails . . . *(She finds them)* YES! *(She climbs up the stepladder and starts hammering a corner of the cloth into the molding of one of the windows)* This is going to look so great! . . . I've never seen such color!

FANNY: Darling, what is going on . . . ?

MAGS: Rembrandt, eat your heart out! You seventeenth-century Dutch has-been, you. *(She hammers more furiously)*

FANNY: MARGARET, THIS IS NOT A CONSTRUCTION SITE. . . . PLEASE . . . STOP IT. . . . YOO-HOOOOO . . . DO YOU HEAR ME?

GARDNER *suddenly appears, dressed in a raincoat.*

GARDNER: YES, DEAR, HERE I AM. I JUST STEPPED OUT FOR A WALK DOWN CHESTNUT STREET. BEAUTIFUL AFTERNOON, ABSOLUTELY BEAUTIFUL! . . . WHY, THAT LOOKS VERY NICE, MAGS, very nice indeed . . .

FANNY *(To* MAGS*)*:   YOU'RE GOING TO RUIN THE WALLS TO SAY NOTHING OF MAMA'S BEST TABLECLOTH. . . . MAGS, DO YOU HEAR ME? . . . YOO-HOO! . . . DARLING, I MUST INSIST you stop that dreadful . . .

MAGS (*Steps down; stands back and looks at the tablecloth*):   That's it. That's *IT!*

FANNY (*To* GARDNER, *worried*):   Where have *you* been?

MAGS *kisses her fingers at the backdrop and settles back into her banana cake.*

GARDNER (*To* FANNY):   You'll never guess who I ran into on Chestnut Street . . . Pate Baldwin!

GARDNER *takes his coat off and drops it on the floor. He sits in one of the posing chairs.*

MAGS (*Mouth full of cake*):   Oh, Daddy, I'm nowhere near ready for you yet.

FANNY (*Picks up* GARDNER*'s coat and hands it to him*):   Darling, coats do *not* go on the floor.

GARDNER (*Rises, but forgets where he's supposed to go*):   He was in terrible shape. I hardly recognized him. Well, it's the Parkinson's disease . . .

FANNY: You mean, Hodgkin's disease . . .

GARDNER: Hodgkin's disease . . . ?

MAGS (*Leaves her cake and returns to the tablecloth*):   Now to figure out exactly how to use this gorgeous light . . .

FANNY: Yes, Pate has Hodgkin's disease, not Parkinson's disease. Sammy Bishop has Parkinson's disease. In the closet . . . your coat goes . . . in the closet!

GARDNER: You're absolutely right! Pate has Hodgkin's disease. (*He stands motionless, the coat over his arm*)

FANNY: And Goat Davis has Addison's disease.

GARDNER: I always get them confused.

FANNY (*Pointing towards the closet*):   That way . . .

GARDNER *exits to the closet;* FANNY *calls after him.*

FANNY: Grace Phelps has it too, I think. Or, it might be Hodgkin's, like Pate. I can't remember.

GARDNER (*Returns with a hanger*):   Doesn't The Goat have Parkinson's disease?

FANNY: No, that's Sammy Bishop.

GARDNER: God, I haven't seen The Goat in ages! (*The coat still over his arm, he hands* FANNY *the hanger*)

FANNY: He hasn't been well.

GARDNER: Didn't Heppy . . . *die?!*

FANNY: What are you giving me this for? . . . Oh, Heppy's been dead for years. She died on the same day as Luster Bright, don't you remember?

GARDNER: I always liked her.

FANNY (*Gives* GARDNER *back the hanger*):   Here, I don't want this.

GARDNER: She was awfully attractive.

FANNY: Who?

GARDNER: Heppy!

FANNY: Oh, yes, Heppy had real charm.

MAGS (*Keeps adjusting the tablecloth*):   Better . . . better . . .

GARDNER: Which is something The Goat is short on, if you ask me. He has Hodgkin's disease, doesn't he? (*Puts his raincoat back on and sits down*)

FANNY: Darling, what *are* you doing? I thought you wanted to hang up your coat!

GARDNER *(After a pause)*:   OH, YES, THAT'S RIGHT!

GARDNER goes back to the closet; a pause.

FANNY: Where were we?

GARDNER *(Returns with yet another hanger)*:   Let's see . . .

FANNY *(Takes both hangers from him)*:   FOR GOD'S SAKE, GAR, PAY ATTENTION!

GARDNER: It was something about The Goat . . .

FANNY *(Takes the coat from GARDNER)*:   HERE, LET ME DO IT! . . . *(Under her breath to MAGS)* See what I mean about him? You don't know the half of it!

FANNY hangs the raincoat up in the closet.

FANNY: Not the half.

MAGS *(Still tinkering with the backdrop)*:   Almost . . . almost . . .

GARDNER *(Sitting back down in one of the posing chairs)*:   Oh, Fan, did I tell you, I ran into Pate Baldwin just now. I'm afraid he's not long for this world.

FANNY *(Returning)*:   Well, it's that Hodgkin's disease . . . *(She sits on the posing chair next to him)*

GARDNER: God, I'd hate to see him go. He's one of the great editors of our times. I couldn't have done it without him. He gave me everything, everything!

MAGS *(Makes a final adjustment)*:   Yes, that's it! *(She stands back and gazes at them)* You look wonderful!

FANNY: Isn't it getting to be . . . *(She taps at an imaginary watch on her wrist and drains an imaginary glass)* cocktail time?!

GARDNER *(Looks at his watch)*:   On the button, on the button! *(He rises)*

FANNY: I'll have the usual, please. Do join us, Mags! Daddy bought some Dubonnet especially for you!

MAGS: Hey. I was just getting some ideas.

GARDNER *(To MAGS, as he exits for the bar)*:   How about a little . . . *Dubonnet* to wet your whistle?

FANNY: Oh, Mags, it's like old times having you back with us like this!

GARDNER *(Offstage)*:   THE USUAL FOR YOU, FAN?

FANNY: I wish we saw more of you. . . . PLEASE! . . . Isn't he darling? Have you ever known anyone more darling than Daddy?

GARDNER *(Offstage; hums Jolson's "You Made Me Love You")*:   MAGS, HOW ABOUT YOU? . . . A LITTLE . . . DUBONNET?

FANNY: Oh, *do* join us!   MAGS *(To GARDNER)*:   No, nothing, thanks.

FANNY: Well, what do you think of your aged parents picking up and moving to Cotuit year round? Pretty crazy, eh what? . . . Nothing but the gulls, oysters and us!

GARDNER *(Returns with FANNY's drink)*:   Here you go . . .

FANNY: Why thank you, Gar. *(To MAGS)* You sure you won't join us?

GARDNER *(Lifts his glass towards FANNY and MAGS)*:   Cheers!

GARDNER *and* FANNY *take that first lifesaving gulp.*

FANNY: Aaaaahhhhh!   GARDNER: Hits the spot, hits the spot!

MAGS: Well, I certainly can't do you like that!

FANNY: Why not? I think we look very . . . *comme il faut!*

FANNY *slouches into a rummy pose;* GARDNER *joins her.*

FANNY: WAIT . . . I'VE GOT IT! I'VE GOT IT! *(She whispers excitedly to* GARDNER*)*

MAGS: Come on, let's not start this again!

GARDNER: What's that? . . . Oh, yes . . . yes, yes . . . I know the one you mean. Yes, right, right . . . of course.

A pause.

FANNY: How's . . . *this?!*

FANNY *grabs a large serving fork and she and* GARDNER *fly into an imitation of Grant Wood's* American Gothic.

MAGS: And I wonder why it's taken me all these years to get you to pose for me. You just don't take me seriously! Poor old Mags and her ridiculous portraits . . .

FANNY: Oh, darling, your portraits aren't *ridiculous!* They may not be all that one *hopes* for, but they're certainly not—

MAGS: Remember how you behaved at my first group show in Soho? . . . Oh, come on, you remember. It was a real circus! Think back. . . . It was about six years ago. . . . Daddy had just been awarded some presidential medal of achievement and you insisted he wear it around his neck on a bright red ribbon, and you wore this . . . *huge* feathered hat to match! I'll never forget it! It was the size of a giant pizza with twenty-inch red turkey feathers shooting straight up into the air. . . . Oh, come on, you remember, don't you?

FANNY *(Leaping to her feet):* HOLD EVERYTHING! THIS IS IT! THIS IS REALLY IT! Forgive me for interrupting, Mags darling, it'll just take a minute. *(She whispers excitedly to* GARDNER*)*

MAGS: I had about eight portraits in the show, mostly of friends of mine, except for this old one I'd done of Mrs. Crowninshield.

GARDNER: All right, all right . . . let's give it a whirl.

A pause; then they mime Michelangelo's Pietà *with* GARDNER *lying across* FANNY*'s lap as the dead Christ.*

MAGS *(Depressed):* The *Pietà.* Terrific!

FANNY *(Jabbing* GARDNER *in the ribs):* Hey, we're getting good at this.

GARDNER: Of course it would help if we didn't have all these modern clothes on.

MAGS: AS I WAS SAYING . . .

FANNY: Sorry, Mags . . . sorry . . .

Huffing and creaking with the physical exertion of it all, FANNY *and* GARDNER *return to their seats.*

MAGS: As soon as you stepped foot in the gallery you spotted it and cried out, "MY GOD, WHAT'S MILLICENT CROWNINSHIELD DOING HERE?" Everyone looked up, what with Daddy's clanking medal and your amazing hat which I was sure would take off and start flying around the room. A crowd gathered. . . . Through some utter fluke, you latched on to *the* most important critic in the city, I mean . . . Mr. Modern Art himself, and you hauled him over to the painting, trumpeting out for all to hear, "THAT'S MILLI-CENT CROWNINSHIELD! I GREW UP WITH HER. SHE LIVES RIGHT DOWN THE STREET FROM US IN BOSTON. BUT IT'S A VERY POOR LIKENESS, IF YOU ASK ME! HER NOSE ISN'T NEARLY THAT LARGE AND SHE DOESN'T HAVE SOMETHING QUEER GROWING OUT OF HER CHIN! THE CROWNINSHIELDS ARE REALLY QUITE GOOD-LOOKING, STUFFY, BUT GOOD-LOOKING NONETHELESS!"

GARDNER *(Suddenly jumps up, ablaze)*:   WAIT, WAIT . . . IF IT'S MICHELANGELO YOU WANT . . . I'm sorry, Mags. . . . One more . . . just one more . . . please?

MAGS: Sure, why not? Be my guest.

GARDNER: FANNY, *prepare yourself!*

More whispering.

FANNY: But I think *you* should be God.

GARDNER: Me? . . . Really?

FANNY: Yes, it's much more appropriate.

GARDNER: Well, if you say so . . .

FANNY *and* GARDNER *ease down to the floor with some difficulty and lie on their sides,* FANNY *as Adam,* GARDNER *as God, their fingers inching closer and closer in the attitude of Michelangelo's* The Creation. *Finally they touch.* MAGS *cheers, whistles, applauds.*

MAGS: THREE CHEERS . . . VERY GOOD . . . NICELY DONE, NICELY DONE!

FANNY *and* GARDNER *hold the pose a moment more, flushed with pleasure; then rise, dust themselves off and grope back to their chairs.*

MAGS: So, there we were . . .

FANNY: Yes, *do* go on!

MAGS: . . . huddled around Millicent Crowninshield, when you whipped into your pocketbook and suddenly announced, "HOLD EVERYTHING! I'VE GOT A PHOTOGRAPH OF HER RIGHT HERE, THEN YOU CAN SEE WHAT SHE REALLY LOOKS LIKE!". . . You then proceeded to crouch down to the floor and dump everything out of your bag, and I mean . . . *every-thing!* . . . leaking packets of sequins and gummed stars, seashells, odd pieces of fur, crochet hooks, a monarch butterfly embedded in plastic, dental floss, antique glass buttons, small jingling bells, lace . . . I thought I'd die! Just sink to the floor and quietly die! . . . You couldn't find it, you see. I mean, you spent the rest of the afternoon on your hands and knees crawling through this ocean of junk, muttering, "It's *got* to be here somewhere; I know I had it with me!". . . Then Daddy pulled me into the thick of it all and said, "By the way, have you met our daughter Mags yet? She's the one who did all these pictures . . . paintings . . . portraits . . . whatever you call them." *(She drops to her hands and knees and begins crawling out of the room)* By this time, Mum had somehow crawled out of the gallery and was lost on another floor. She began calling for me . . ."YOO-HOO, MAGS . . . WHERE ARE YOU? . . . OH, MAGS, DARLING . . . HELLO? . . . ARE YOU THERE?" *(She reenters and faces them)* This was at my *first* show.

Blackout.

Scene 3

Twenty-four hours later. The impact of the impending move has struck with hurricane force. FANNY *has lugged all their clothing into the room and dumped it in various cartons. There are coats, jackets, shoes, skirts, suits, hats, sweaters, dresses, the works. She and* GARDNER *are seated on the sofa, going through it all.* FANNY, *wearing a different hat and dress, holds up a ratty overcoat.*

FANNY: What about this gruesome old thing?

GARDNER *is wearing several sweaters and vests, a Hawaiian holiday shirt, and a variety of scarves and ties around his neck. He holds up a pair of shoes.*

GARDNER: God . . . remember these shoes? Pound gave them to me when he came back from Italy. I remember it vividly.

FANNY: *Do* let me give it to the thrift shop! *(She stuffs the coat into the appropriate carton)*

GARDNER: He bought them for me in Rome. Said he couldn't resist; bought himself a pair too since we both wore the same size. God, I miss him! *(Pause)* HEY, WHAT ARE YOU DOING WITH MY OVERCOAT?!

FANNY: Darling, it's threadbare!

GARDNER: But that's my overcoat! *(He grabs it out of the carton)* I've been wearing it every day for the past thirty-five years!

FANNY: That's just my point: it's had it.

GARDNER *(Puts it on over everything else)*:   There's nothing wrong with this coat!

FANNY: I trust you remember that the cottage is an eighth the size of this place and you simply won't have room for half this stuff! *(She holds up a sports jacket)* This dreary old jacket, for instance. You've had it since Hector was a pup!

GARDNER *(Grabs the jacket and puts it on over his coat)*:   Oh, no, you don't . . .

FANNY: And this God-awful hat . . .

GARDNER: Let me see that.

GARDNER *stands next to* FANNY *and they fall into a lovely tableau.* MAGS *suddenly pops out from behind a wardrobe carton with a flash camera and takes a picture of them.*

MAGS: PERFECT!

FANNY *(Hands flying to her face)*:   GARDNER *(Hands flying to his heart)*:
GOOD GOD, WHAT WAS   JESUS CHRIST, I'VE BEEN
THAT . . . ?   SHOT!

MAGS *(Walks to the center of the room, advancing the film)*:   That was terrific. See if you can do it again.

FANNY: What *are* you doing . . . ?

GARDNER *(Feeling his chest)*:   Is there blood?

FANNY: I see lace everywhere . . .

MAGS: It's all right, I was just taking a picture of you. I often use a Polaroid at this stage.

FANNY *(Rubbing her eyes)*:   Really, Mags, you might have given us some warning!

MAGS: But that's the whole point: to catch you unawares!

GARDNER *(Rubbing his eyes)*:   It's the damndest thing. . . . I see lace everywhere.

FANNY: Yes, so do I . . .

GARDNER: It's rather nice, actually. It looks as if you're wearing a veil.

FANNY: I *am* wearing a veil!

The camera spits out the photograph.

MAGS: OH GOODY, HERE COMES THE PICTURE!

FANNY *(Grabs the partially developed print out of her hands)*:   Let me see, let me see . . .

GARDNER: Yes, let's have a look.

GARDNER *and* FANNY *have another quiet moment together looking at the photograph.* MAGS *tiptoes away from them and takes another picture.*

MAGS: YES!

FANNY: NOT AGAIN! PLEASE,   GARDNER: WHAT WAS THAT?
DARLING!   . . . WHAT HAPPENED?

FANNY *and* GARDNER *stagger towards each other.*

MAGS: I'm sorry, I just couldn't resist. You looked so—

FANNY: WHAT ARE YOU TRYING TO DO . . . *BLIND* US?!

GARDNER: Really, Mags, enough is enough . . .

GARDNER *and* FANNY *keep stumbling about kiddingly.*

FANNY: Are you still there, Gar?

GARDNER: Right as rain, right as rain!

MAGS: I'm sorry; I didn't mean to scare you. It's just a photograph can show you things you weren't aware of. Here, have a look. *(She gives them to* FANNY*)* Well, I'm going out to the kitchen to get something to eat. Anybody want anything? *(She exits)*

FANNY *(Looking at the photos, half-amused, half-horrified)*:   Oh, Gardner, have you ever . . . ?

GARDNER *(Looks at the photos and laughs)*:   Good grief . . .

MAGS *(Offstage; from the kitchen)*:   IS IT ALL RIGHT IF I TAKE THE REST OF THIS TAPIOCA FROM LAST NIGHT?

FANNY: IT'S ALL RIGHT WITH ME. How about you, Gar?

GARDNER: Sure, go right ahead. I've never been that crazy about tapioca.

FANNY: What are you talking about, tapioca is one of your favorites.

MAGS *(Enters, slurping from a large bowl)*:   Mmmmmmmm . . .

FANNY: Really, Mags, I've never seen anyone eat as much as you.

MAGS *(Takes the photos back)*:   It's strange. I only do this when I come home.

FANNY: What's the matter, don't I feed you enough?

GARDNER: Gee, it's hot in here! *(Starts taking off his coat)*

FANNY: God knows, you didn't eat anything as a child! I've never seen such a fussy eater. Gar, what *are* you doing?

GARDNER *(Shedding clothes to the floor)*:   Taking off some of these clothes. It's hotter than Tophet in here!

MAGS *(Looking at her photos)*:   Yes, I like you looking at each other like that . . .

FANNY *(To GARDNER)*:   Please watch where you're dropping things; I'm trying to keep some order around here.

GARDNER *(Picks up what he dropped, dropping even more in the process)*:   Right, right . . .

MAGS: Now all I've got to do is figure out what you should wear.

FANNY: Well, I'm going to wear my long black dress, and you'd be a fool not to do Daddy in his tuxedo. He looks so distinguished in it, just like a banker!

MAGS: I haven't really decided yet.

FANNY: Just because you walk around looking like something the cat dragged in, doesn't mean Daddy and I want to, do we Gar?

GARDNER *is making a worse and worse tangle of his clothes.*

FANNY: HELLO . . . ?

GARDNER *(Looks up at FANNY)*:   Oh, yes, awfully attractive, awfully attractive!

FANNY *(To MAGS)*:   If you don't mind me saying so, I've never seen you looking so forlorn. You'll never catch a husband looking that way. Those peculiar clothes, that God-awful hair . . . really, Mags, it's very distressing!

MAGS: I don't think my hair's so bad, not that it's terrific or anything . . .

FANNY: Well, I don't see other girls walking around like you. I mean, girls from your background. What would Lyman Wigglesworth think if he saw you in the street?

MAGS: Lyman Wigglesworth?! . . . Uuuuuuughhhhhhh! *(She shudders)*

FANNY: All right then, that brilliant Cabot boy . . . what *is* his name?

GARDNER: Sammy.

FANNY: No, not Sammy . . .

GARDNER: Stephen . . . Stanley . . . Stuart . . . Sheldon . . . Sherlock . . . Sherlock! It's *Sherlock!*

MAGS: Spence!

FANNY: SPENCE, THAT'S IT!   GARDNER: THAT'S IT . . . HIS NAME IS SPENCE!   SPENCE! SPENCE CABOT!

FANNY: Spence Cabot was first in his class at Harvard.

MAGS: Mum, he has no facial hair.

FANNY: He has his own law firm on Arlington Street.

MAGS: Spence Cabot has six fingers on his right hand!

FANNY: So, he isn't the best-looking thing in the world. Looks isn't every-thing. He can't help it if he has extra fingers. Have a little sympathy!

MAGS: But the extra one has this weird nail on it that looks like a talon. . . . It's long and black and . . . *(She shudders)*

FANNY: No one's perfect, darling. He has lovely handwriting and an ab-solutely saintly mother. Also, he's as rich as Croesus! He's a lot more promising than some of those creatures you've dragged home. What was the name of that dreadful Frenchman who smelled like sweaty socks? . . . Jean Duke of Scripto?

MAGS *(Laughing)*:   Jean-Luc Zichot!

FANNY: And that peculiar little Oriental fellow with all the teeth! Really, Mags, he could have been put on display at the circus!

MAGS: Oh, yes, Tsu Chin. He was strange, but very sexy . . .

FANNY *(Shudders)*:   He had such tiny . . . feet! Really, Mags, you've got to bear down. You're not getting any younger. Before you know it, all the nice young men will be taken and then where will you be? . . . All by yourself in that grim little apartment of yours with those peculiar clothes and that bright red hair . . .

MAGS: MY HAIR IS NOT BRIGHT RED!

FANNY: I only want what's best for you, you know that. You seem to go out of your way to look wanting. I don't understand it. . . . Gar, what *are* you putting your coat on for? . . . You look like some derelict out on the street. We don't wear coats in the house. *(She helps him out of it)* That's the way. . . . I'll just put this in the carton along with everything else . . . *(She drops it into the carton, then pauses)* Isn't it about time for . . . *cocktails!*

GARDNER: What's that?

FANNY *taps her wrist and mimes drinking.*

GARDNER *(Looks at his watch)*:   Right you are, right you are! *(Exits to the bar)* THE USUAL . . . ?

FANNY: *Please!*

GARDNER *(Offstage)*:   HOW ABOUT SOMETHING FOR YOU, MAGS?

MAGS: SURE, WHY NOT? . . . LET 'ER RIP!

GARDNER *(Offstage)*:   WHAT'S THAT . . . ?

FANNY: SHE SAID YES. SHE   MAGS: I'LL HAVE SOME DU-
SAID YES!   BONNET!

GARDNER *(Poking his head back in)*:   How about a little Dubonnet?

FANNY: That's just what she said. . . . She'd like some . . . Dubonnet!

GARDNER *(Goes back to the bar and hums another Jolson tune)*:   GEE, IT'S GREAT HAVING YOU BACK LIKE THIS, MAGS . . . IT'S JUST GREAT! *(More singing)*

FANNY *(Leaning closer to MAGS)*:   You have such *potential,* darling! It breaks my heart to see how you've let yourself go. If Lyman Wigglesworth . . .

MAGS: Amazing as it may seem, I don't *care* about Lyman Wigglesworth!

FANNY: From what I've heard, he's quite a lady killer!

MAGS: But with whom? . . . Don't think I haven't heard about his fling with . . . Hopie Stonewall!

FANNY *(Begins to laugh)*:   Oh, God, let's not get started on Hopie Stonewall again . . . ten feet tall with spots on her neck . . . *(To* GARDNER*)* OH, DAR-LING, DO HURRY BACK! WE'RE TALKING ABOUT PATHETIC HOPIE STONEWALL!

MAGS: It's not so much her incredible height and spotted skin; it's those tiny pointed teeth and the size eleven shoes!

FANNY: I love it when you're like this!

MAGS *starts clomping around the room making tiny pointed-teeth nibbling sounds.*

FANNY: GARDNER . . . YOU'RE MISSING EVERYTHING! *(Still laughing)* Why is it Boston girls are always so . . . tall?

MAGS: Hopie Stonewall isn't a Boston girl; she's a giraffe. *(She prances around the room with an imaginary dwarf-sized Lyman)* She's perfect for Lyman Wigglesworth!

GARDNER *(Returns with* FANNY*'s drink, which he hands her)*:   Now, where were we . . . ?

FANNY *(Trying not to laugh)*:   HOPIE STONEWALL . . . !

GARDNER: Oh, yes, she's the very tall one, isn't she?

FANNY *and* MAGS *burst into gales.*

MAGS: The only hope for us . . . "Boston girls" is to get as far away from our kind as possible.

FANNY: She always asks after you, darling. She's very fond of you, you know.

MAGS: Please, I don't want to hear!

FANNY: Your old friends are *always* asking after you.

MAGS: It's not so much how creepy they all are, as how much they remind me of myself!

FANNY: But you're not "creepy," darling . . . just . . . shabby!

MAGS: I mean, give me a few more inches and some brown splotches here and there, and Hopie and I could be sisters!

FANNY *(In a whisper to* GARDNER*)*:   Don't you love it when Mags is like this? I could listen to her forever!

MAGS: I mean . . . look at me!

FANNY *(Gasping)*:   Don't stop, don't stop!

MAGS: Awkward . . . plain . . . I don't know how to dress, I don't know how to talk. When people find out Daddy's my father, they're always amazed. . . . "Gardner Church is YOUR father?! Aw, come on, you're kidding?!"

FANNY *(In a whisper)*:   Isn't she divine . . . ?

MAGS: Sometimes I don't even tell them. I pretend I grew up in the Midwest somewhere . . . farming people . . . we work with our hands.

GARDNER *(To* MAGS*)*:   Well, how about a little refill . . . ?

MAGS: No, no more thanks.

Pause.

FANNY: What did you have to go and interrupt her for? She was just getting up a head of steam . . .

MAGS *(Walking over to her easel):*   The great thing about being a portrait painter, you see, is it's the *other* guy that's exposed; you're safely hidden behind the canvas and easel. *(Standing behind it)* You can be as plain as a pitchfork, as inarticulate as mud, but it doesn't matter because you're completely concealed: your body, your face, your intentions. Just as you make your most intimate move, throw open your soul . . . they stretch and yawn, remembering the dog has to be let out at five. . . . To be so invisible while so enthralled . . . it takes your breath away!

GARDNER: Well put, Mags. Awfully well put!

MAGS: That's why I've always wanted to paint you, to see if I'm up to it. It's quite a risk. Remember what I went through as a child with my great masterpiece . . . ?

FANNY: You painted a masterpiece when you were a child . . . ?

MAGS: Well, it was a masterpiece to me.

FANNY: I had no idea you were precocious as a child. Gardner, do you remember Mags painting a masterpiece as a child?

MAGS: I didn't paint it. It was something I made!

FANNY: Well, this is all news to me! Gar, *do* get me another drink! I haven't had this much fun in years! *(She hands him her glass and reaches for MAGS's)* Come on, darling, join me . . .

MAGS: No, no more, thanks. I don't really like the taste.

FANNY: Oh, come on, kick up your heels for once!

MAGS: No, nothing . . . really.

FANNY: Please? Pretty please? . . . To keep me company?!

MAGS *(Hands GARDNER her glass):*   Oh, all right, what the hell . . .

FANNY: That's a good girl!   GARDNER *(Exiting):*   Coming right
                                                   up, coming right up!

FANNY *(Yelling after GARDNER):*   DON'T GIVE ME TOO MUCH NOW. THE LAST ONE WAS AWFULLY STRONG . . . AND HURRY BACK SO YOU DON'T MISS ANYTHING! . . . Daddy's so cunning, I don't know what I'd do without him. If anything should happen to him, I'd just . . .

MAGS: Mummy, nothing's going to happen to him . . . !

FANNY: Well, wait till you're our age, it's no garden party. Now . . . where were we . . . ?

MAGS: My first masterpiece . . .

FANNY: Oh, yes, but *do* wait till Daddy gets back so he can hear it too. . . . YOO-HOO . . . GARRRRRRDNERRRRRR? . . . ARE YOU COMING? *(Silence)* Go and check on him, will you?

GARDNER enters with both drinks. He's very shaken.

GARDNER: I couldn't find the ice.

FANNY: Well, *finally!*

GARDNER: It just up and disappeared . . . *(Hands FANNY her drink)* There you go. *(FANNY kisses her fingers and takes a hefty swig)* Mags. *(He hands MAGS her drink)*

MAGS: Thanks, Daddy.

GARDNER: Sorry about the ice.

MAGS: No problem, no problem.

GARDNER *sits down; silence.*

FANNY *(To* MAGS*):*   Well, drink up, drink up! *(*MAGS *downs it in one gulp)* GOOD GIRL! . . . Now, what's all this about a masterpiece . . . ?

MAGS: I did it during that winter you sent me away from the dinner table. I was about nine years old.

FANNY: We sent you from the dinner table?

MAGS: I was banished for six months.

FANNY: You *were?* . . . How extraordinary!

MAGS: Yes, it *was* rather extraordinary!

FANNY: But why?

MAGS: Because I played with my food.

FANNY: You did?

MAGS: I used to squirt it out between my front teeth.

FANNY: Oh, I remember that! God, it used to drive me crazy, absolutely . . . crazy! *(Pause)* "MARGARET, STOP THAT OOZING RIGHT THIS MINUTE, YOU ARE *NOT* A TUBE OF TOOTHPASTE!"

GARDNER: Oh, yes . . .

FANNY: It was perfectly disgusting!

GARDNER: I remember. She used to lean over her plate and squirt it out in long runny ribbons . . .

FANNY: That's enough, dear.

GARDNER: They were quite colorful, actually; decorative almost. She made the most intricate designs. They looked rather like small, moist Oriental rugs . . .

FANNY *(To* MAGS*):*   But why, darling? What on earth possessed you to do it?

MAGS: I couldn't swallow anything. My throat just closed up. I don't know, I must have been afraid of choking or something.

GARDNER: I remember one in particular. We'd had chicken fricassee and spinach. . . . She made the most extraordinary—

FANNY *(To* GARDNER*):*   WILL YOU PLEASE SHUT UP?! *(Pause)* Mags, what *are* you talking about? You never choked in your entire life! This is the most distressing conversation I've ever had. Don't you think it's distressing, Gar?

GARDNER: Well, that's not quite the word I'd use.

FANNY: What word *would* you use, then?

GARDNER: I don't know right off the bat, I'd have to think about it.

FANNY: THEN, THINK ABOUT IT!

Silence.

MAGS: I guess I was afraid of making a mess. I don't know; you were awfully strict about table manners. I was always afraid of losing control. What if I started to choke and began spitting up over everything . . . ?

FANNY: All right, dear, that's enough.

MAGS: No, I was really terrified about making a mess; you always got so

mad whenever I spilled. If I just got rid of everything in neat little curlicues beforehand, you see . . .

FANNY: I SAID: THAT'S ENOUGH!

Silence.

MAGS: *I* thought it was quite ingenious, but you didn't see it that way. You
finally sent me from the table with, "When you're ready to eat like a human
being, you can come back and join us!" . . . So, it was off to my room with a
tray. But I couldn't seem to eat there either. I mean, it was so strange settling
down to dinner in my *bedroom*. . . . So I just flushed everything down the toilet and sat on my bed listening to you: clinkity-clink, clatter clatter, slurp, slurp
. . . but that got pretty boring after a while, so I looked around for something
to do. It was wintertime, because I noticed I'd left some crayons on top of my
radiator and they'd melted down into these beautiful shimmering globs, like
spilled jello, trembling and pulsing . . .

GARDNER *(Overlapping; eyes closed)*:
"This luscious and impeccable fruit of life
Falls, it appears, of its own weight to earth . . ."

MAGS: Naturally, I wanted to try it myself, so I grabbed a red one and pressed
it down against the hissing lid. It oozed and bubbled like raspberry jam!

GARDNER:
"When you were Eve, its acrid juice was sweet,
Untasted, in its heavenly, orchard air . . ."

MAGS: I mean, that radiator was really hot! It took incredible will power
not to let go, but I held on, whispering, "Mags, if you let go of this crayon,
you'll be run over by a truck on Newberry Street, so help you God!" . . . So I
pressed down harder, my fingers steaming and blistering . . .

FANNY: I had no idea about any of this, did you, Gar?

MAGS: Once I'd melted one, I was hooked! I finished off my entire supply
in one night, mixing color over color until my head swam! . . . The heat, the
smell, the brilliance that sank and rose . . . I'd never felt such exhilaration! . . .
Every week I spent my allowance on crayons. I must have cleared out every
box of Crayolas in the city!

GARDNER *(Gazing at MAGS)*:   You know, I don't think I've ever seen you
looking prettier! You're awfully attractive when you get going!

FANNY: Why, what a lovely thing to say.

MAGS: AFTER THREE MONTHS THAT RADIATOR WAS . . . SPEC-
TACULAR! I MEAN, IT LOOKED LIKE SOME COLOSSAL FRUIT-
CAKE, FIVE FEET TALL . . . !

FANNY: It sounds perfectly hideous.

MAGS: It was a knockout; shimmering with pinks and blues, lavenders and
maroons, turquoise and golds, oranges and creams. . . . For every color, I imagined a taste . . . YELLOW: lemon curls dipped in sugar . . . RED: glazed
cherries laced with rum . . . GREEN: tiny peppermint leaves veined with
chocolate . . . PURPLE:—

FANNY: That's quite enough!

MAGS: And then the frosting . . . ahhhh, the frosting! A satiny mix of white and silver . . . I kept it hidden under blankets during the day. . . . My huge . . . *(She starts laughing)* looming . . . teetering sweet—

FANNY: I ASKED YOU TO STOP! GARDNER, WILL YOU PLEASE GET HER TO STOP!

GARDNER: See here, Mags, Mum asked you to—

MAGS: I was so . . . *hungry* . . . losing weight every week. I looked like a scarecrow what with the bags under my eyes and bits of crayon wrapper leaking out of my clothes. It's a wonder you didn't notice. But finally you came to my rescue . . . if you could call what happened a rescue. It was more like a rout!

FANNY: Darling . . . *please!*   GARDNER: Now, look, young
                                                                    lady—

MAGS: The winter was almost over. . . . It was very late at night. . . . I must have been having a nightmare because suddenly you and Daddy were at my bed, shaking me. . . . I quickly glanced towards the radiator to see if it was covered. . . . *It wasn't!* It glittered and towered in the moonlight like some . . . gigantic Viennese pastry! You followed my gaze and saw it. Mummy screamed . . . "WHAT HAVE YOU GOT IN HERE? . . . MAGS, WHAT HAVE YOU BEEN DOING?" . . . She crept forward and touched it, and then jumped back. "IT'S FOOD!" she cried . . . "IT'S ALL THE FOOD SHE'S BEEN SPITTING OUT! OH, GARDNER, IT'S A MOUNTAIN OF ROTTING GARBAGE!"

FANNY *(Softly)*:   Yes . . . it's coming back . . . it's coming back . . .

MAGS: Daddy exited as usual; left the premises. He fainted, just keeled over onto the floor . . .

GARDNER: Gosh, I don't remember any of this . . .

MAGS: My heart stopped! I mean, I knew it was all over. My lovely creation didn't have a chance. Sure enough . . . out came the blowtorch. Well, it couldn't have *really* been a blowtorch, I mean, where would you have ever gotten a blowtorch? . . . I just have this very strong memory of you standing over my bed, your hair streaming around your face, aiming this . . . flamethrower at my confection . . . my cake . . . my tart . . . my strudel. . . . "IT'S GOT TO BE DESTROYED IMMEDIATELY! THE THING'S ALIVE WITH VERMIN! . . . JUST LOOK AT IT! . . . IT'S PRACTICALLY CRAWLING ACROSS THE ROOM!" . . . Of course in a sense you were right. It *was* a monument of my castoff dinners, only I hadn't built it with food. . . . I found my own materials. I was languishing with hunger, but oh, dear Mother . . . I FOUND MY OWN MATERIALS . . . !

FANNY: Darling . . . *please?!*

MAGS: I tried to stop you, but you wouldn't listen. . . . OUT SHOT THE FLAME! . . . I remember these waves of wax rolling across the room and Daddy coming to, wondering what on earth was going on. . . . Well, what did you know about my abilities? . . . You see, I had . . . I mean, I *have* abilities . . . *(Struggling to say it)* I have abilities. I have . . . strong abilities. I have . . . very strong abilities. They are very strong . . . very, very strong . . .

MAGS *rises and runs out of the room overcome as* FANNY *and* GARDNER *watch, speechless. The curtain falls.*

ACT TWO

Scene 1

Three days later. Miracles have been accomplished. Almost all of the Churches' furniture has been moved out, and the cartons of dishes and clothing are gone. All that remains are odds and ends. MAGS's *tableau looms, impregnable.* FANNY *and* GARDNER *are dressed in their formal evening clothes, frozen in their pose. They hold absolutely still.* MAGS *stands at her easel, her hands covering her eyes.*

FANNY: All right, you can look now.

MAGS *(Removes her hands)*:   Yes! . . . I told you you could trust me on the pose.

FANNY: Well, thank God you let us dress up. It makes all the difference. Now we really look like something.

MAGS *(Starts to sketch them)*:   I'll say . . .

A silence as she sketches.

GARDNER *(Recites Yeats's "The Song of Wandering Aengus" in a wonderfully resonant voice as they pose)*:
"I went out to the hazel wood,
Because a fire was in my head,
And cut and peeled a hazel wand,
And hooked a berry to a thread,
And when white moths were on the wing,
And moth-like stars were flickering out,
I dropped the berry in a stream
And caught a little silver trout.

When I had laid it on the floor
I went to blow the fire a-flame,
But something rustled on the floor,
And someone called me by my name:
It had become a glimmering girl
With apple blossoms in her hair
Who called me by my name and ran
And faded through the brightening air.

Though I am old with wandering
Through hollow lands and hilly lands,
I will find out where she has gone,
And kiss her lips and take her hands;
And walk among long dappled grass,
And pluck till time and times are done,
The silver apples of the moon,
The golden apples of the sun."

FANNY: That's lovely, dear. Just lovely. Is it one of yours?

GARDNER: No, no, it's Yeats. I'm using it in my book.

FANNY: Well, you recited it beautifully, but then you've always recited beautifully. That's how you wooed me, in case you've forgotten. . . . You must have memorized every love poem in the English language! There was no stopping you when you got going . . . your Shakespeare, Byron, and Shelley . . . you were shameless . . . *shameless!*

GARDNER *(Eyes closed)*:
"I will find out where she has gone,
And kiss her lips and take her hands . . ."

FANNY: And then there was your own poetry to do battle with; your sonnets and quatrains. When you got going with them, there was nothing left of me! You could have had your pick of any girl in Boston! Why you chose me, I'll never understand. I had no looks to speak of and nothing much in the brains department. . . . Well, what did you know about women and the world? . . . What did any of us know . . . ?

Silence.

FANNY: GOD, MAGS, HOW LONG ARE WE SUPPOSED TO SIT LIKE THIS? . . . IT'S AGONY!

MAGS *(Working away)*:   You're doing fine . . . just fine . . .

FANNY *(Breaking her pose)*:   It's so . . . boring!

MAGS: Come on, don't move. You can have a break soon.

FANNY: I had no idea it would be so boring!

GARDNER: Gee, I'm enjoying it.

FANNY: You would . . . !

A pause.

GARDNER *(Begins reciting more Yeats, almost singing it)*:
"He stood among a crowd at Drumahair;
His heart hung all upon a silken dress,
And he had known at last some tenderness,
Before earth made of him her sleepy care;
But when a man poured fish into a pile,
It seemed they raised their little silver heads . . ."

FANNY: Gar . . . PLEASE! *(She lurches out of her seat)* God, I can't take this anymore!

MAGS *(Keeps sketching GARDNER)*:   I know it's tedious at first, but it gets easier . . .

FANNY: It's like a Chinese water torture! *(Crosses to MAGS and looks at GARDNER posing)* Oh, darling, you look marvelous, absolutely marvelous! Why don't you just do Daddy!?

MAGS: Because you look marvelous too. I want to do you both!

FANNY: Please! . . . I have one foot in the grave and you know it! Also, we're way behind in our packing. There's still one room left which everyone seems to have forgotten about!

GARDNER: Which one is that?

FANNY: You know perfectly well which one it is!

GARDNER: I do . . . ?

FANNY: Yes, you do!

GARDNER: Well, it's news to me.

FANNY: I'll give you a hint. It's in . . . *that* direction. *(She points)*

GARDNER: The dining room?

FANNY: No.

GARDNER: The bedroom?

FANNY: No.

GARDNER: Mags' room?

FANNY: No.

GARDNER: The kitchen?

FANNY: *Gar?!*

GARDNER: The guest room?

FANNY: Your God-awful study!

GARDNER: Oh, shit!

FANNY: That's right, "Oh, shit!" It's books and papers up to the ceiling! If you ask me, we should just forget it's there and quietly tiptoe away . . .

GARDNER: My study . . . !

FANNY: Let the new owners dispose of everything . . .

GARDNER *(Gets out of his posing chair)*: Now, just one minute . . .

FANNY: You never look at half the stuff in there!

GARDNER: I don't want you touching those books! They're mine!

FANNY: Darling, we're moving to a cottage the size of a handkerchief! Where, pray tell, is there room for all your books?

GARDNER: I don't know. We'll just have to make room!

MAGS *(Sketching away)*: RATS!

FANNY: I don't know what we're doing fooling around with Mags like this when there's still so much to do . . .

GARDNER *(Sits back down, overwhelmed)*: My study . . . !

FANNY: You can stay with her if you'd like, but one of us has got to tackle those books! *(She exits to his study)*

GARDNER: I'm not up to this.

MAGS: Oh, good, you're staying!

GARDNER: There's a lifetime of work in there . . .

MAGS: Don't worry, I'll help. Mum and I will be able to pack everything up in no time.

GARDNER: God . . .

MAGS: It won't be so bad . . .

GARDNER: I'm just not up to it.

MAGS: We'll all pitch in . . .

GARDNER *sighs, speechless. A silence as* FANNY *comes staggering in with an armload of books, which she drops to the floor with a crash.*

GARDNER: WHAT WAS THAT?!   MAGS: GOOD GRIEF!

FANNY *(Sheepish)*: Sorry, sorry . . . *(She exits for more)*

GARDNER: I don't know if I can take this . . .

MAGS: Moving is awful . . . I know . . .

GARDNER *(Settling back into his pose)*:   Ever since Mum began tearing the house apart, I've been having these dreams. . . . I'm a child again back at 16 Louisberg Square . . . and this stream of moving men is carrying furniture into our house . . . van after van of tables and chairs, sofas and love seats, desks and bureaus . . . rugs, bathtubs, mirrors, chiming clocks, pianos, iceboxes, china cabinets . . . but what's amazing is that all of it is familiar . . .

FANNY comes in with another load, which she drops on the floor. She exits for more.

GARDNER: No matter how many items appear, I've seen every one of them before. Since my mother is standing in the midst of it directing traffic, I ask her where it's all coming from, but she doesn't hear me because of the racket . . . so finally I just scream out . . . "WHERE IS ALL THIS FURNITURE COMING FROM?" . . . Just as a moving man is carrying Toots into the room, she looks at me and says, "Why, from the land of Skye!" . . . The next thing I know, *people* are being carried in along with it . . .

FANNY enters with her next load; drops it and exits.

GARDNER: People I've never seen before are sitting around our dining-room table. A group of foreigners is going through my books, chattering in a language I've never heard before. A man is playing a Chopin polonaise on Aunt Alice's piano. Several children are taking baths in our tubs from Cotuit . . .

MAGS: It sounds marvelous.

GARDNER: Well, it isn't marvelous at all because all of these perfect strangers have taken over our things . . .

FANNY enters, hurls down another load and exits.

MAGS: How odd . . .

GARDNER: Well, it *is* odd, but then something even odder happens . . .

MAGS *(Sketching away)*:   Tell me, tell me!

GARDNER: Well, our beds are carried in. They're all made up with sheets and everything, but instead of all these strange people in them, *we're* in them . . . !

MAGS: What's so odd about that?

GARDNER: Well, you and Mum are brought in, both sleeping like angels . . . Mum snoring away to beat the band . . .

MAGS: Yes . . .

FANNY enters with another load lets it fall.

GARDNER: But there's no one in mine. It's completely empty, never even been slept in! It's as if I were dead or had never even existed . . .

FANNY exits.

GARDNER: "HEY . . . WAIT UP!" I yell to the moving men . . . "THAT'S MY BED YOU'VE GOT THERE!" But they don't stop; they don't even acknowledge me. . . . "HEY, COME BACK HERE . . . I WANT TO GET INTO MY BED!" I cry again and I start running after them . . . down the hall, through the dining room, past the library. . . . Finally I catch up to them and hurl myself right into the center of the pillow. Just as I'm about to land, the bed suddenly vanishes and I go crashing down to the floor like some insect that's been hit by a fly swatter!

FANNY *staggers in with her final load; she drops it with a crash and then collapses in her posing chair.*

FANNY: THAT'S IT FOR ME! I'M DEAD!

Silence.

FANNY: Come on, Mags, how about you doing a little work around here.

MAGS: That's all I've been doing! This is the first free moment you've given me!

FANNY: You should see all the books in there . . . and papers! There are enough loose papers to sink a ship!

GARDNER: Why is it we're moving, again . . . ?

FANNY: Because life is getting too complicated here.

GARDNER *(Remembering)*:   Oh, yes . . .

FANNY: And we can't afford it anymore.

GARDNER: That's right, that's right . . .

FANNY: We don't have the . . . *income* we used to!

GARDNER: Oh, yes . . . *income!*

FANNY *(Assuming her pose again)*:   Of course, we have our savings and various trust funds, but I wouldn't dream of touching those!

GARDNER: No, no, you must never dip into capital!

FANNY: I told Daddy I'd be perfectly happy to buy a gun and put a bullet through our heads so we could avoid all this, but he wouldn't hear of it!

MAGS *(Sketching away)*:   No, I shouldn't think so.

Pause.

FANNY: I've always admired people who kill themselves when they get to our stage of life. Well, no one can touch my Uncle Edmond in that department . . .

MAGS: I know, I know . . .

FANNY: The day before his seventieth birthday he climbed to the top of the Old North Church and hurled himself face down into Salem Street! They had to scrape him up with a spatula! God, he was a remarkable man . . . state senator, president of Harvard . . .

GARDNER *(Rises and wanders over to his books)*:   Well, I guess I'm going to have to do something about all of these . . .

FANNY: Come on, Mags, help Daddy! Why don't you start bringing in his papers . . .

GARDNER *sits on the floor; he picks up a book and soon is engrossed in it.* MAGS *keeps sketching, oblivious. Silence.*

FANNY *(To MAGS)*:   Darling? . . . HELLO? . . . God, you two are impossible! Just look at you . . . heads in the clouds! No one would ever know we've got to be out of here in two days. If it weren't for me, nothing would get done around here . . . *(She starts stacking* GARDNER*'s books into piles)* There! That's all the maroon ones!

GARDNER *(Looks up)*:   What do you mean, *maroon* ones?!

FANNY: All your books that are maroon are in *this* pile . . . and your books that are green in *that* pile! . . . I'm trying to bring some order into your life for once. This will make unpacking so much easier.

GARDNER: But, my dear Fanny, it's not the color of a book that distinguishes it, but what's *inside* it!

FANNY: This will be a great help, you'll see. Now what about this awful striped thing? *(She picks up a slim, aged volume)* Can't it go . . . ?

GARDNER: No!

FANNY: But it's as queer as Dick's hatband! There are no others like it.

GARDNER: Open it and read. Go on . . . open it!

FANNY: We'll get nowhere at this rate.

GARDNER: I said . . . READ!

FANNY: Really, Gar, I—

GARDNER: Read the dedication!

FANNY *(Opens and reads)*:   "To Gardner Church, you led the way. With gratitude and affection, Robert Frost." *(She closes it and hands it to him)*

GARDNER: It was published the same year as my *Salem Gardens*.

FANNY *(Picking up a very worn book)*:   Well, what about this dreadful thing? It's filthy. *(She blows off a cloud of dust)*

GARDNER: Please . . . *please?!*

FANNY *(Looking through it)*:   It's all in French.

GARDNER *(Snatching it away from her)*:   André Malraux gave me that . . . !

FANNY: I'm just trying to help.

GARDNER: It's a first edition of Baudelaire's *Fleurs du mal.*

FANNY *(Giving it back)*:   Well, pardon me for living!

GARDNER: Why do you have to drag everything in here in the first place . . . ?

FANNY: Because there's no room in your study. You ought to see the mess in there! . . . WAKE UP, MAGS, ARE YOU GOING TO PITCH IN OR NOT?!

GARDNER: I'm not up to this.

FANNY: Well, you'd better be unless you want to be left behind!

MAGS *(Stops her sketching)*:   All right, all right . . . I just hope you'll give me some more time later this evening.

FANNY *(To* MAGS*)*:   Since you're young and in the best shape, why don't you bring in the books and I'll cope with the papers. *(She exits to the study)*

GARDNER: Now just a minute . . .

FANNY *(Offstage)*:   WE NEED A STEAM SHOVEL FOR THIS!

MAGS: Okay, what do you want me to do?

GARDNER: Look, I don't want you messing around with my—

FANNY *enters with an armful of papers, which she drops into an empty carton.*

GARDNER: HEY, WHAT'S GOING ON HERE?!

FANNY: I'm packing up your papers. COME ON, MAGS, LET'S GET CRACKING! *(She exits for more papers)*

GARDNER *(Plucks several papers out of the carton)*:   What is this . . . ?

MAGS *(Exits into his study)*:   GOOD LORD, WHAT HAVE YOU DONE IN HERE?!

GARDNER *(Reading)*:   This is my manuscript.

FANNY *enters with another batch, which she tosses on top of the others.*

GARDNER: What *are* you doing?!

FANNY: Packing, darling . . . PACKING! *(She exits for more)*

GARDNER: SEE HERE, YOU CAN'T MANHANDLE MY THINGS THIS WAY!

MAGS *enters, staggering under a load of books, which she sets down on the floor.*

GARDNER: *I* PACK MY MANUSCRIPT! I KNOW WHERE EVERY-THING IS!

FANNY *(Offstage)*:   IF IT WERE UP TO YOU, WE'D NEVER GET OUT OF HERE! WE'RE UNDER A TIME LIMIT, GARDNER. KITTY'S PICKING US UP IN TWO DAYS . . . TWO . . . DAYS! *(She enters with a larger batch of papers and heads for the carton)*

GARDNER *(Grabbing* FANNY*'s wrist)*:   NOW, HOLD IT! . . . JUST . . . HOLD IT RIGHT THERE!

FANNY: OOOOOWWWWWWWW!

GARDNER: *I* PACK MY THINGS!

FANNY: LET GO, YOU'RE HURTING ME!

GARDNER: THAT'S MY MANUSCRIPT! GIVE IT TO ME!

FANNY *(Lifting the papers high over her head)*:   I'M IN CHARGE OF THIS MOVE, GARDNER! WE'VE GOT TO GET CRACKING!

GARDNER: I said . . . GIVE IT TO ME!

MAGS: Come on, Mum, let him have it.

FANNY *and* GARDNER *struggle.*

GARDNER *(Finally wrenches the pages from* FANNY*)*:   LET . . . ME . . . HAVE IT! . . . THAT'S MORE LIKE IT!

FANNY *(Soft and weepy)*:   You see what he's like? . . . I try and help with his packing and what does he do . . . ?

GARDNER *(Rescues the rest of his papers from the carton)*:   YOU DON'T JUST THROW EVERYTHING INTO A BOX LIKE A PILE OF GARBAGE! THIS IS A BOOK, FANNY. SOMETHING I'VE BEEN WORKING ON FOR TWO YEARS! *(Trying to assemble his papers, but only making things worse, dropping them all over the place)* You show a little respect for my things. . . . You don't just throw them around every which way. . . . It's tricky trying to make sense of poetry; it's much easier to write the stuff . . . that is, if you've still got it in you . . .

MAGS: Here, let me help . . . . *(Taking some of the papers)*

GARDNER: Criticism is tough sledding. You can't just dash off a few images here, a few rhymes there . . .

MAGS: Do you have these pages numbered in any way?

FANNY *(Returning to her posing chair)*:   HA!

GARDNER: This is just the introduction.

MAGS: I don't see any numbers on these.

GARDNER *(Exiting to his study)*:   The important stuff is in my study . . .

FANNY *(To MAGS)*:   You don't know the half of it . . . *not the half* . . . !

GARDNER *(Offstage; thumping around)*:   HAVE YOU SEEN THOSE YEATS POEMS I JUST HAD . . . ?

MAGS *(Reading over several pages)*:   What is this? . . . It doesn't make sense. It's just fragments . . . pieces of poems.

FANNY: That's it, honey! That's his book. His great critical study! Now that he can't write his own poetry, he's trying to explain other people's. The only problem is, he can't get beyond typing them out. The poor lamb doesn't have the stamina to get beyond the opening stanzas, let alone trying to make sense of them.

GARDNER *(Thundering back with more papers, which keep falling)*:   GOD-DAMMIT, FANNY, WHAT DID YOU DO IN THERE? I CAN'T FIND ANYTHING!

FANNY: I just took the papers that were on your desk.

GARDNER: Well, the entire beginning is gone. *(He exits)*

FANNY: I'M TRYING TO HELP YOU, DARLING!

GARDNER *(Returns with another armload)*:   SEE THAT? . . . NO SIGN OF CHAPTER ONE OR TWO . . . *(He flings it all down to the floor)*

FANNY: Gardner . . . PLEASE?!

GARDNER *(Kicking through the mess)*:   I TURN MY BACK FOR ONE MINUTE AND WHAT HAPPENS? . . . MY ENTIRE STUDY IS TORN APART! *(He exits)*

MAGS: Oh, Daddy . . . don't . . . please . . . Daddy . . . *please?!*

GARDNER *(Returns with a new batch of papers, which he tosses up into the air)*: THROWN OUT! . . . THE BEST PART IS THROWN OUT! . . . LOST . . . *(He starts to exit again)*

MAGS *(Reads one of the fragments to steady herself)*:
"I have known the inexorable sadness of pencils,
Neat in their boxes, dolor of pad and paper-weight,
All the misery of manila folders and mucilage . . ."
They're beautiful . . . just beautiful.

GARDNER *(Stops)*:   Hey, what's that you've got there?

FANNY: It's your manuscript, darling. You see, it's right where you left it.

GARDNER *(To MAGS)*:   Read that again.

MAGS:
"I have known the inexorable sadness of pencils,
Neat in their boxes, dolor of pad and paper-weight,
All the misery of manila folders and mucilage . . ."

GARDNER: Well, well, what do you know . . .

FANNY *(Hands him several random papers)*:   You see . . . no one lost anything. Everything's here, still intact.

GARDNER *(Reads)*:
"I knew a woman, lovely in her bones,
When small birds sighed, she would sigh back at them;
Ah, when she moved, she moved more ways than one:
The shapes a bright container can contain! . . ."

FANNY *(Hands him another)*:   And . . .

GARDNER *(Reads)*:   Ahh . . . Frost . . .

"Some say the world will end in fire,
Some say in ice.
From what I've tasted of desire
I hold with those who favor fire."

FANNY *(Under her breath to* MAGS*)*:   He can't give up the words. It's the best he can do. *(Handing him another)* Here you go, here's more.

GARDNER:

"Farm boys wild to couple
With anything   with soft-wooded trees
With mounds of earth   mounds
Of pinestraw   will keep themselves off
Animals by legends of their own . . ."

MAGS *(Eyes shut)*:   Oh, Daddy, I can't bear it . . . I . . .

FANNY: Of course no one will ever publish this.

GARDNER: Oh, here's a marvelous one. Listen to this!

"There came a Wind like a Bugle—
It quivered through the Grass
And a Green Chill upon the Heat
So ominous did pass
We barred the Windows and the Doors
As from an Emerald Ghost—
The Doom's electric Moccasin . . ."

SHIT, WHERE DID THE REST OF IT GO . . . ?

FANNY: Well, don't ask *me*.

GARDNER: It just stopped in mid-air!

FANNY: Then go look for the original.

GARDNER: Good idea, good idea! *(He exits to his study)*

FANNY *(To* MAGS*)*:   He's incontinent now, too. He wets his pants, in case you haven't noticed. *(She starts laughing)* You're not laughing. Don't you think it's funny? Daddy needs diapers. . . . I don't know about you, but I could use a drink! GAR . . . WILL YOU GET ME A SPLASH WHILE YOU'RE OUT THERE . . . ?

MAGS: STOP IT!

FANNY: It means we can't go out anymore. I mean, what would people say . . . ?

MAGS: Stop it. Just stop it.

FANNY: My poet laureate can't hold it in! *(She laughs harder)*

MAGS: That's enough . . . STOP IT . . . Mummy . . . I beg of you . . . *please stop it!*

GARDNER *enters with a book and indeed a large stain has blossomed on his trousers. He plucks it away from his leg.*

GARDNER: Here we go . . . I found it . . .

FANNY *(Pointing at it)*:   See that? See? . . . He just did it again! *(Goes off into a shower of laughter)*

MAGS (*Looks, turns away*):   SHUT . . . UP! . . . (*Building to a howl*) WILL
YOU PLEASE JUST . . . SHUT . . . UP!

FANNY (*To* GARDNER):   Hey, what about that drink?

GARDNER: Oh, yes . . . sorry, sorry . . . (*He heads towards the bar*)

FANNY: Never mind, I'll get it, I'll get it.

FANNY *exits, convulsed. Silence.*

GARDNER: Well, where were we?

MAGS (*Near tears*):   Your poem.

GARDNER: Oh, yes . . . the Dickinson. (*He shuts his eyes, reciting from mem-
ory, holding the book against his chest*)
"There came a Wind like a Bugle—
It quivered through the Grass
And a Green Chill upon the Heat
So ominous did pass
We barred the Windows and the Doors
As from an Emerald Ghost—"
(*Opens the book and starts riffling through it*) Let's see now, where's the rest? . . .
(*He finally finds it*) Ahhh, here we go . . . !

FANNY (*Reenters, drink in hand*):   I'm back! (*Takes one look at* GARDNER *and
bursts out laughing again*)

MAGS: I don't believe you! How you can laugh at him?!

They all speak simultaneously as MAGS *gets angrier and angrier.*

FANNY: I'm sorry, I wish I could stop, but there's really nothing else to do.
Look at him . . . just . . . look at him . . . !

MAGS: It's so cruel. . . . You're so . . . incredibly cruel to him. . . . I mean,
YOUR DISDAIN REALLY TAKES MY BREATH AWAY! YOU'RE IN
A CLASS BY YOURSELF WHEN IT COMES TO HUMILIATION!

GARDNER (*Reading*):
"The Doom's electric Moccasin
That very instant passed—
On a strange Mob of panting Trees
And Fences fled away
And Rivers where the Houses ran
Those looked that lived—that Day—
The Bell within the steeple wild
The flying tidings told—
How much can come
And much can go,
And yet abide the World!"
(*He shuts the book with a bang, pauses and looks around the room, confused*) Now,
where was I . . . ?

FANNY: Safe and sound in the middle of the living room with Mags and me.

GARDNER: But I was looking for something, wasn't I . . . ?

FANNY: Your manuscript.

GARDNER: THAT'S RIGHT! MY MANUSCRIPT! My manuscript!

FANNY: And here it is all over the floor. See, you're standing on it.

GARDNER *(Picks up a few pages and looks at them)*:   Why, so I am . . .

FANNY: Now all we have to do is get it up off the floor and packed neatly into these cartons!

GARDNER: Yes, yes, that's right. Into the cartons.

FANNY *(Kicks a carton over to him)*:   Here, you use this one and I'll start over here . . . *(She starts dropping papers into a carton nearby)* BOMBS AWAY! . . . Hey . . . this is fun!

GARDNER *(Picks up his own pile, lifts it high over his head and flings it down into the carton)*:   BOMBS AWAY. . . . This *is* fun!

FANNY: I told you! The whole thing is to figure out a system!

GARDNER: I don't know what I'd do without you, Fan. I thought I'd lost everything.

FANNY *(Makes dive-bomber noises and machine-gun explosions as she wheels more and more papers into the carton)*:   TAKE THAT AND THAT AND THAT!

GARDNER *(Joins in the fun, outdoing her with dips, dives and blastings of his own)*: BLAM BLAM BLAM BLAM! . . . ZZZZZZZZ-RAAAAAA FOOM! . . . BLATTY-DE-BLATTY-DE-BLATTY-DE-KABOOOOOOOOM! . . . WHAAAAAAA . . . DA-DAT-DAT-DAT-DAT-DAT . . . WHEEEEEEEE AAAAAAAAAAAA . . . FOOOOOO . . .

They get louder and louder as papers fly every which way.

FANNY *(Mimes getting hit with a bomb)*:   AEEEEEEIIIIIIIIIIII! YOU GOT ME RIGHT IN THE GIZZARD! *(She collapses on the floor and starts going through death throes, having an absolute ball)*

GARDNER: TAKE THAT AND THAT AND THAT AND THAT . . . *(A series of explosions follow)*

MAGS *(Furious)*:   This is how you help him? . . . THIS IS HOW YOU PACK HIS THINGS?

FANNY: I keep him company. I get involved . . . which is a hell of a lot more than you do!

MAGS *(Wild with rage)*:   BUT YOU'RE MAKING A MOCKERY OF HIM. . . . YOU TREAT HIM LIKE A CHILD OR SOME DIMWITTED SERVING BOY. HE'S JUST AN AMUSEMENT TO YOU!

FANNY *(Fatigue has finally overtaken her. She's calm, almost serene)*:   And to you who see him once a year, if that . . . what is he to *you?* . . . I mean, what do you give him from yourself that costs you something? . . . Hmmmmmm? . . . *(Imitating MAGS)* "Oh, hi Daddy, it's great to see you again. How have you been? . . . Gee, I love your hair. It's gotten so . . . *white!*" . . . What color do you expect it to get when he's this age? . . . I mean, if you care so much how he looks, why don't you come and see him once in a while? . . . But oh, no . . . you have your paintings to do and your shows to put on. You just come and see us when the whim strikes. *(Imitating MAGS)* "Hey, you know what would be really great? . . . To do a portrait of you! I've always wanted to paint you, you're such great subjects!" . . . *Paint* us?! . . . What about opening your eyes and really *seeing* us? . . . Noticing what's going on around here for a change! It's all over for Daddy and me. This is it! "Finita la commedia!" . . . All I'm trying to do is exit with a little flourish; have some fun. . . . What's so terrible about that? . . . It can get pretty grim around here, in case you haven't noticed . . . Daddy, tap-tap-tapping out his nonsense all day; me traipsing around to the thrift shops trying to amuse myself. . . . He never keeps me company anymore; never takes me out anywhere. . . . I'd put a bullet through my head in a minute, but then who'd look after him? . . . What do you think we're moving to the cottage for? . . . So I can watch him like a hawk and make sure he doesn't get lost. Do you think that's anything to look forward to? . . . Being Daddy's nursemaid out in the middle of nowhere? I'd much rather stay here in Boston with the few friends I have left, but you can't always do what you want in this world! "L'homme propose, Dieu dispose!" . . . If you want to paint us so badly, you ought to paint us as we really are. There's your picture!

FANNY points to GARDNER, who's quietly playing with a paper glide.

FANNY: Daddy spread out on the floor with all his toys and me hovering over him to make sure he doesn't hurt himself! *(She goes over to him)* YOO-HOO . . . GAR? . . . HELLO?

GARDNER *(Looks up at her)*: Oh, hi there, Fan. What's up?

FANNY: How's the packing coming . . . ?

GARDNER: Packing . . . ?

FANNY: Yes, you were packing your manuscript, remember? *(She lifts up a page and lets it fall into a carton)*

GARDNER: Oh, yes . . .

FANNY: Here's your picture, Mags. Face over this way . . . turn your easel over here . . . *(She lets a few more papers fall)* Up, up . . . and away . . .

Blackout.

Scene 2

The last day. All the books and boxes are gone. The room is completely empty except for MAGS's backdrop. Late afternoon light dapples the walls; it changes from pale peach to deeper violet. The finished portrait sits on the easel, covered with a cloth. MAGS is taking down the backdrop.

FANNY *(Offstage; to GARDNER)*: DON'T FORGET TOOTS!

GARDNER *(Offstage; from another part of the house)*: WHAT'S THAT?

FANNY *(Offstage)*: I SAID: DON'T FORGET TOOTS! HIS CAGE IS SITTING IN THE MIDDLE OF YOUR STUDY!

Silence.

FANNY *(Offstage)*: HELLO? . . . ARE YOU THERE?   GARDNER *(Offstage)*: I'LL BE RIGHT WITH YOU; I'M JUST GETTING TOOTS!

GARDNER *(Offstage)*: WHAT'S THAT? I CAN'T HEAR YOU?

FANNY *(Offstage)*: I'M GOING THROUGH THE ROOMS ONE

MORE TIME TO MAKE SURE WE DIDN'T FORGET ANYTHING. . . .
KITTY'S PICKING US UP IN FIFTEEN MINUTES, SO PLEASE BE
READY. . . . SHE'S DROPPING MAGS OFF AT THE STATION AND
THEN IT'S OUT TO ROUTE 3 AND THE CAPE HIGHWAY . . .

GARDNER *(Enters, carrying Toots in his cage)*:   Well, this is it. The big moment has finally come, eh what, Toots? *(He see* MAGS*)* Oh, hi there, Mags, I
didn't see you . . .

MAGS: Oh, hi, Daddy, I'm just taking this down . . . *(She does and walks over
to Toots)* Oh, Toots, I'll miss you. *(She makes little chattering noises into his cage)*

GARDNER: Come on, recite a little Gray's *Elegy* for Mags before we go.

MAGS: Yes, Mum said he was really good at it now.

GARDNER: Well, the whole thing is to keep at it every day. *(Slowly to Toots)*
"The curfew tolls the knell of parting day,
The lowing herd wind slowly o'er the lea . . ."
Come on, show Mags your stuff! *(Slower)*
"The curfew tolls the knell of parting day,
The lowing herd wind slowly o'er the lea . . ."

Silence; GARDNER *makes little chattering sounds.*

GARDNER: Come on, Toots, old boy . . .

MAGS: How does it go?

GARDNER *(To* MAGS*)*:
"The curfew tolls the knell of parting day,
The lowing herd wind slowly o'er the lea . . ."

MAGS *(Slowly to Toots)*:
The curfew tolls for you and me,
As quietly the herd winds down . . .

GARDNER: No, no, it's "The curfew tolls the knell of parting *day* . . ."!

MAGS *(Repeating after him)*:   "The curfew tolls the knell of parting day . . ."

GARDNER: "The lowing herd wind slowly o'er the lea . . ."

MAGS *(With a deep breath)*:
The curfew tolls at parting day,
The herd low slowly down the lea . . . no, *knell!*
They come winding down the *knell!*

GARDNER: Listen, Mags . . . *listen!*

A pause.

TOOTS *(Loud and clear with* GARDNER*'s inflection)*:
"The curfew tolls the knell of parting day,
The lowing herd wind slowly o'er the lea,
The ploughman homeward plods his weary way,
And leaves the world to darkness and to me."

MAGS: HE SAID IT. . . . HE SAID IT! . . . AND IN YOUR VOICE! . . .
OH, DADDY, THAT'S AMAZING!

GARDNER: Well, Toots is very smart, which is more than I can say for a lot
of people I know . . .

MAGS *(To Toots)*:   Polly want a cracker? Polly want a cracker?

GARDNER: You can teach a parakeet to say anything; all you need is patience . . .

MAGS: But *poetry* . . . that's so hard . . .

FANNY *enters carrying a suitcase and* GARDNER*'s typewriter in its case. She's dressed in her traveling suit, wearing a hat to match.*

FANNY: WELL, THERE YOU ARE! I THOUGHT YOU'D DIED!

MAGS *(To* FANNY*)*:   HE SAID IT! I FINALLY HEARD TOOTS RECITE GRAY'S *ELEGY. (She makes silly clucking sounds into the cage)*

FANNY: Isn't it uncanny how much he sounds like Daddy? Sometimes when I'm alone here with him, I've actually thought he *was* Daddy and started talking to him. Oh, yes, Toots and I have had quite a few meaty conversations together!

FANNY *wolf-whistles into the cage; then draws back.* GARDNER *covers the cage with a traveling cloth. Silence.*

FANNY *(Looking around the room)*:   God, the place looks so bare.

MAGS: I still can't believe it . . . Cotuit, year round. I wonder if there'll be any phosphorus when you get there?

FANNY: What on earth are you talking about? *(She carries the discarded backdrop out into the hall)*

MAGS: Remember that summer when the ocean was full of phosphorus?

GARDNER *(Taking Toots out into the hall)*:   Oh, yes . . .

MAGS: It was a great mystery where it came from or why it settled in Cotuit. But one evening when Daddy and I were taking a swim, suddenly it was there!

GARDNER *(Returns)*:   I remember.

MAGS: I don't know where Mum was . . .

FANNY *(Reentering)*:   Probably doing the dishes!

MAGS *(To* GARDNER*)*:   As you dove into the water, this shower of silvery green sparks erupted all around you. It was incredible! I thought you were turning into a saint or something; but then you told me to jump in too and the same thing happened to me . . .

GARDNER: Oh, yes, I remember that . . . the water smelled all queer.

MAGS: What *is* phosphorus, anyway?

GARDNER: Chemicals, chemicals . . .

FANNY: No, it isn't. Phosphorus is a green liquid inside insects. Fireflies have it. When you see sparks in the water it means insects are swimming around . . .

GARDNER: Where on earth did you get that idea . . . ?

FANNY: If you're bitten by one of them, it's fatal!

MAGS: And the next morning it was still there . . .

GARDNER: It was the damndest stuff to get off! We'd have to stay in the shower a good ten minutes. It comes from chemical waste, you see . . .

MAGS: Our bodies looked like mercury as we swam around . . .

GARDNER: It stained all the towels a strange yellow green.

MAGS: I was in heaven, and so were you for that matter. You'd finished your day's poetry and would turn somersaults like some happy dolphin . . .

FANNY: Damned dishes . . . why didn't I see any of this?!

MAGS: I remember one night in particular. . . . We sensed the phosphorus was about to desert us; blow off to another town. We were chasing each other under water. At one point I lost you, the brilliance was so intense . . . but finally your foot appeared . . . then your leg. I grabbed it! . . . I remember wishing the moment would hold forever; that we could just be fixed there, laughing and iridescent. . . . Then I began to get panicky because I knew it would pass; it was passing already. You were slipping from my grasp. The summer was almost over. I'd be going back to art school; you'd be going back to Boston. . . . Even as I was reaching for you, you were gone. We'd never be like that again.

Silence. FANNY *spies* MAGS's *portrait covered on the easel.*

FANNY: What's that over there? Don't tell me we forgot something!

MAGS: It's your portrait. I finished it.

FANNY: You finished it? How on earth did you manage that?

MAGS: I stayed up all night.

FANNY: You did? . . . *I* didn't hear you, did you hear her, Gar . . . ?

GARDNER: Not a peep, not a peep!

MAGS: Well, I wanted to get it done before you left. You know, see what you thought. It's not bad, considering . . . I mean, I did it almost completely from memory. The light was terrible and I was trying to be quiet so I wouldn't wake you. It was hardly an ideal situation. . . . I mean, you weren't the most cooperative models . . . *(She suddenly panics and snatches the painting off the easel. She hugs it to her chest and starts dancing around the room with it)* Oh, God, you're going to hate it! You're going to hate it! How did I ever get into this? . . . Listen, you don't really want to see it . . . it's nothing . . . just a few dabs here and there. . . . It was awfully late when I finished it. The light was really impossible and my eyes were hurting like crazy. . . . Look, why don't we just go out to the sidewalk and wait for Kitty so she doesn't have to honk—

GARDNER *(Snatches the painting out from under her grasp)*:   WOULD YOU JUST SHUT UP A MINUTE AND LET US SEE IT?

MAGS *(Laughing and crying)*:   But it's nothing, Daddy . . . *really!* . . . I've done better with my eyes closed! It was so late I could hardly see anything and then I spilled a whole bottle of thinner into my palette . . .

GARDNER *(Sets the portrait down on the easel and stands back to look at it)*: THERE!

MAGS *(Dancing around them in a panic)*:   Listen, it's just a quick sketch. . . . It's still wet. . . . I didn't have enough time. . . . It takes at least forty hours to do a decent portrait . . .

Suddenly it's very quiet as FANNY *and* GARDNER *stand back to look at the painting. More and more beside herself,* MAGS *keeps leaping around the room wrapping her arms around herself, making little whimpering sounds.*

MAGS: Please don't . . . no . . . don't . . . oh, please! . . . Come on, don't look. . . . Oh, God, don't . . . please . . .

An eternity passes as FANNY *and* GARDNER *gaze at their portrait.*

GARDNER: Well . . .

FANNY: Well . . .

More silence.

FANNY: I think it's perfectly   GARDNER: Awfully clever, aw-
dreadful!   fully clever!

FANNY: What on earth did you do to my face . . . ?

GARDNER: I particularly like Mum!

FANNY: Since when do I have purple skin?!

MAGS: I told you it was nothing, just a silly—

GARDNER: She looks like a million dollars!

FANNY: AND WILL YOU LOOK AT MY HAIR . . . IT'S BRIGHT
ORANGE!

GARDNER *(Views the painting from another angle)*: It's really very good!

FANNY *(Pointing)*: That doesn't look anything like me!

GARDNER: First-rate!

FANNY: Since when do I have purple skin and bright orange hair?!

MAGS *(Trying to snatch the painting off the easel)*: Listen, you don't have to
worry about my feelings . . . really . . . I—

GARDNER *(Blocking her way)*: NOT SO FAST . . .

FANNY: And look at how I'm sitting! I've never sat like that in my life!

GARDNER *(Moving closer to the painting)*: Yes, yes, it's awfully clever . . .

FANNY: I HAVE NO FEET!

GARDNER: The whole thing is quite remarkable!

FANNY: And what happened to my legs, pray tell? . . . They just vanish
below the knees! . . . At least my dress is presentable. I've always loved that
dress.

GARDNER: It sparkles somehow . . .

FANNY *(To* GARDNER*)*: Don't you think it's becoming?

GARDNER: Yes, very becoming, awfully becoming . . .

FANNY *(Examining it at closer range)*: Yes, she got the dress very well, how
it shows off what's left of my figure. . . . My smile is nice too.

GARDNER: Good and wide . . .

FANNY: I love how the corners of my mouth turn up . . .

GARDNER: It's very clever . . .

FANNY: They're almost quivering . . .

GARDNER: Good lighting effects!

FANNY: Actually, I look quite . . . *young,* don't you think?

GARDNER *(To* MAGS*)*: You're awfully good with those highlights.

FANNY *(Looking at it from different angles)*: And *you* look darling . . . !

GARDNER: Well, I don't know about that . . .

FANNY: No, you look absolutely darling. Good enough to eat!

MAGS *(In a whisper)*: They like it. . . . They like it!

A silence as FANNY *and* GARDNER *keep gazing at their portrait.*

FANNY: You know what it is? The wispy brush strokes make us look like a couple in a French Impressionist painting.

GARDNER: Yes, I see what you mean . . .

FANNY: A Manet or Renoir . . .

GARDNER: It's very evocative.

FANNY: There's something about the light . . .

They back up to survey the picture from a distance.

FANNY: You know those Renoir café scenes . . . ?

GARDNER: She doesn't lay on the paint with a trowel; it's just touches here and there . . .

MAGS: They *like* it . . . !

FANNY: You know the one with the couple dancing? . . . Not that we're dancing. There's just something similar in the mood . . . a kind of gaiety, almost. . . . The man has his back to you and he's swinging the woman around. . . . OH, GAR, YOU'VE SEEN IT A MILLION TIMES! IT'S HANGING IN THE MUSEUM OF FINE ARTS! . . . They're dancing like this . . .

FANNY goes up to GARDNER and puts an arm on his shoulders.

MAGS: They like it. . . . They like it!

FANNY: She's got on this wonderful flowered dress with ruffles at the neck and he's holding her like this. . . . That's right . . . and she's got the most rhapsodic expression on her face . . .

Getting into the spirit of it, GARDNER takes FANNY in his arms and slowly begins to dance around the room.

GARDNER: Oh, yes . . . I know the one you mean. . . . They're in a sort of haze . . . and isn't there a little band playing off to one side . . . ?

FANNY: Yes, that's it!

KITTY'S horn honks outside. MAGS is the only one who hears it.

MAGS: There's Kitty! *(She's torn and keeps looking towards the door, but finally gives in to their stolen moment)*

FANNY: And there's a man in a dark suit playing the violin and someone's conducting, I think. . . . And aren't Japanese lanterns strung up . . . ?

FANNY and GARDNER pick up speed, dipping and whirling around the room. Strains of a faraway Chopin waltz are heard.

GARDNER: Oh, yes! There are all these little lights twinkling in the trees . . .

FANNY: And doesn't the woman have a hat on? . . . A big red hat . . . ?

GARDNER: . . . and lights all over the dancers, too. Everything shimmers with this marvelous glow. Yes, yes . . . I can see it perfectly! The whole thing is absolutely extraordinary!

The lights become dreamy and dappled as FANNY and GARDNER dance around the room. MAGS watches them, moved to tears as slowly the curtain falls.

(1983)

QUESTIONS

1. What do we learn about the characters and their world from the opening stage directions?
2. What is the situation of the Churches? How do they respond to it?
3. What do we learn about the Churches from the various poses they assume as they "practice" for their later sitting for their portrait? What kinds of poses do they strike? With what effects?
4. What are the significance and dramatic effect of the end of Act I?
5. What is the effect of Fanny's speech to her daughter at the end of Act II, scene i?
6. What is the function of memory in the play?
7. What effect is achieved through having Gardner recite poetry? How is poetry used thematically and dramatically in the play?
8. What images of and attitudes toward the aged does the play present? How are those images and attitudes dramatized?
9. Consider how you would direct the actors in staging the play's final scene.
10. What is the theme of the play?

AUGUST WILSON

[b. 1945]

August Wilson was born and raised in Pittsburgh, Pennsylvania. He quit school at sixteen and worked at various odd jobs until moving to Minneapolis–St. Paul, where he founded the Black Horizons Theatre Company. Having dropped out of school, Wilson educated himself at the public library, discovering there the work of Ralph Ellison, Richard Wright, and Langston Hughes, three modern African-American writers whose work inspired him. Wilson is the author of *Ma Rainey's Black Bottom, Fences, Joe Turner's Come and Gone, The Piano Lesson,* and *Two Trains Running,* all notable for their depiction of the urban lives of African-Americans. The recipient of many awards, including two Pulitzer Prizes, New York Drama Critics Circle Award, and Tony Award, Wilson continues to provide a window on the lives of Americans struggling for success, equality, and survival.

AUGUST WILSON

Fences

CHARACTERS

TROY MAXSON
JIM BONO, TROY'S *friend*
ROSE, TROY'S *wife*
LYONS, TROY'S *oldest son by previous marriage*
GABRIEL, TROY'S *brother*
CORY, TROY *and* ROSE'S *son*
RAYNELL, TROY'S *daughter*

Setting. *The setting is the yard which fronts the only entrance to the Maxson household, an ancient two-story brick house set back off a small alley in a big-city neighborhood. The entrance to the house is gained by two or three steps leading to a wooden porch badly in need of paint.*

A relatively recent addition to the house and running its full width, the porch lacks congruence. It is a sturdy porch with a flat roof. One or two chairs of dubious value sit at one end where the kitchen window opens onto the porch. An old-fashioned icebox stands silent guard at the opposite end.

The yard is a small dirt yard, partially fenced, except for the last scene, with a wooden sawhorse, a pile of lumber, and other fence-building equipment set off to the side. Opposite is a tree from which hangs a ball made of rags. A baseball bat leans against the tree. Two oil drums serve as garbage receptacles and sit near the house at right to complete the setting.

The Play. *Near the turn of the century, the destitute of Europe sprang on the city with tenacious claws and an honest and solid dream. The city devoured them. They swelled its belly until it burst into a thousand furnaces and sewing machines, a thousand butcher shops and bakers' ovens, a thousand churches and hospitals and funeral parlors and money-lenders. The city grew. It nourished itself and offered each man a partnership limited only by his talent, his guile, and his willingness and capacity for hard work. For the immigrants of Europe, a dream dared and won true.*

The descendants of African slaves were offered no such welcome or participation. They came from places called the Carolinas and the Virginias, Georgia, Alabama, Mississippi, and Tennessee. They came strong, eager, searching. The city rejected them and they fled and settled along the riverbanks and under bridges in shallow, ramshackle houses made of sticks and tarpaper. They collected rags and wood. They sold the use of their muscles and their bodies. They cleaned houses and washed clothes, they shined shoes, and in quiet desperation and vengeful pride, they stole, and lived in pursuit of their own dream. That they could breathe free, finally, and stand to meet life with the force of dignity and whatever eloquence the heart could call upon.

By 1957, the hard-won victories of the European immigrants had solidified the industrial might of America. War had been confronted and won with new energies that used loyalty and patriotism as its fuel. Life was rich, full, and flourishing. The Milwaukee Braves won the World Series, and the hot winds of change that would make the sixties a turbulent, racing, dangerous, and provocative decade had not yet begun to blow full.

ACT I

Scene 1

It is 1957. TROY *and* BONO *enter the yard, engaged in conversation.* TROY *is fifty-three years old, a large man with thick, heavy hands; it is this largeness that he strives to fill out and make an accommodation with. Together with his blackness, his largeness informs his sensibilities and the choices he has made in his life.*

Of the two men, BONO *is obviously the follower. His commitment to their friendship of thirty-odd years is rooted in his admiration of* TROY'S *honesty, capacity for hard work, and his strength, which* BONO *seeks to emulate.*

It is Friday night, payday, and the one night of the week the two men engage in a ritual of talk and drink. TROY *is usually the most talkative and at times he can be crude and almost vulgar, though he is capable of rising to profound heights of expression. The men carry lunch buckets and wear or carry burlap aprons and are dressed in clothes suitable to their jobs as garbage collectors.*

BONO: Troy, you ought to stop that lying!

TROY: I ain't lying! The nigger had a watermelon this big.

He indicates with his hands.

Talking about . . . "What watermelon, Mr. Rand?" I liked to fell out!
"What watermelon, Mr. Rand?" . . . And it sitting there big as life.

BONO: What did Mr. Rand say?

TROY: Ain't said nothing. Figure if the nigger too dumb to know he carrying a watermelon, he wasn't gonna get much sense out of him. Trying to hide that great big old watermelon under his coat. Afraid to let the white man see him carrying it home.

BONO: I'm like you . . . I ain't got no time for them kind of people.

TROY: Now what he looks like getting mad cause he see the man from the union talking to Mr. Rand?

BONO: He come to me talking about . . . "Maxson gonna get us fired." I told him to get away from me with that. He walked away from me calling you a troublemaker. What Mr. Rand say?

TROY: Ain't said nothing. He told me to go down the Commissioner's office next Friday. They called me down there to see them.

BONO: Well, as long as you got your complaint filed, they can't fire you. That's what one of them white fellows tell me.

TROY: I ain't worried about them firing me. They gonna fire me cause I asked a question? That's all I did. I went to Mr. Rand and asked him, "Why? Why you got the white men driving and the colored lifting?" Told him, "what's the matter, don't I count? You think only white fellows got sense enough to drive a truck. That ain't no paper job! Hell, anybody can drive a truck. How come you got all whites driving and the colored lifting?" He told me "take it to the union." Well, hell, that's what I done! Now they wanna come up with this pack of lies.

BONO: I told Brownie if the man come and ask him any questions . . . just tell the truth! It ain't nothing but something they done trumped up on you cause you filed a complaint on them.

TROY: Brownie don't understand nothing. All I want them to do is change the job description. Give everybody a chance to drive the truck. Brownie can't see that. He ain't got that much sense.

BONO: How you figure he be making out with that gal be up at Taylors' all the time . . . that Alberta gal?

TROY: Same as you and me. Getting just as much as we is. Which is to say nothing.

BONO: It is, huh? I figure you doing a little better than me . . . and I ain't saying what I'm doing.

TROY: Aw, nigger, look here . . . I know you. If you had got anywhere near that gal, twenty minutes later you be looking to tell somebody. And the first one you gonna tell . . . that you gonna want to brag to . . . is gonna be me.

BONO: I ain't saying that. I see where you be eyeing her.

TROY: I eye all the women. I don't miss nothing. Don't never let nobody tell you Troy Maxson don't eye the women.

BONO: You been doing more than eyeing her. You done bought her a drink or two.

TROY: Hell yeah, I bought her a drink! What that mean? I bought you one, too. What that mean cause I buy her a drink? I'm just being polite.

BONO: It's all right to buy her one drink. That's what you call being polite. But when you wanna be buying two or three . . . that's what you call eyeing her.

TROY: Look here, as long as you known me . . . you ever known me to chase after women?

BONO: Hell yeah! Long as I done known you. You forgetting I knew you when.

TROY: Naw, I'm talking about since I been married to Rose?

BONO: Oh, not since you been married to Rose. Now, that's the truth, there. I can say that.

TROY: All right then! Case closed.

BONO: I see you be walking up around Alberta's house. You supposed to be at Taylor's and you be walking up around there.

TROY: What are you watching where I'm walking for? I ain't watching after you.

BONO: I see you walking around there more than once.

TROY: Hell, you liable to see me walking anywhere! That don't mean nothing cause you see me walking around there.

BONO: Where she come from anyway? She just kinda showed up one day.

TROY: Tallahassee. You can look at her and tell she one of them Florida gals. They got some big healthy women down there. Grow them right up out the ground. Got a little bit of Indian in her. Most of them niggers down in Florida got some Indian in them.

BONO: I don't know about that Indian part. But she damn sure big and healthy. Woman wear some big stockings. Got them great big old legs and hips as wide as the Mississippi River.

TROY: Legs don't mean nothing. You don't do nothing but push them out of the way. But them hips cushion the ride!

BONO: Troy, you ain't got no sense.

TROY: It's the truth! Like you riding on Goodyears!

ROSE *enters from the house. She is ten years younger than* TROY, *her devotion to him stems from her recognition of the possibilities of her life without him: a succession of abusive men and their babies, a life of partying and running the streets, the Church, or aloneness with its attendant pain and frustration. She recognizes* TROY'S *spirit as a fine and illuminating one and she either ignores or forgives his faults, only some of which she recognizes. Though she doesn't drink, her presence is an integral part of the Friday night rituals. She alternates between the porch and the kitchen, where supper preparations are under way.*

ROSE: What you all out here getting into?

TROY: What you worried about what we getting into for? This is men talk, woman.

ROSE: What I care what you all talking about? Bono, you gonna stay for supper?

BONO: No, I thank you, Rose. But Lucille say she cooking up a pot of pigfeet.

TROY: Pigfeet! Hell, I'm going home with you! Might even stay the night if you got some pigfeet. You got something in there to top them pigfeet, Rose?

ROSE: I'm cooking up some chicken. I got some chicken and collard greens.

TROY: Well, go on back in the house and let me and Bono finish what we was talking about. This is men talk. I got some talk for you later. You know what kind of talk I mean. You go on and powder it up.

ROSE: Troy Maxson, don't you start that now!

TROY [*puts his arm around her*]:   Aw, woman . . . come here. Look here, Bono . . . when I met this woman . . . I got out that place, say, "Hitch up my pony, saddle up my mare . . . there's a woman out there for me somewhere. I looked here. Looked there. Saw Rose and latched on to her." I latched on to her and told her—I'm gonna tell you the truth—I told her, "Baby, I don't wanna marry, I just wanna be your man." Rose told me . . . tell him what you told me, Rose.

ROSE: I told him if he wasn't the marrying kind, then move out the way so the marrying kind could find me.

TROY: That's what she told me. "Nigger, you in my way. You blocking the view! Move out the way so I can find me a husband." I thought it over two or three days. Come back—

ROSE: Ain't no two or three days nothing. You was back the same night.

TROY: Come back, told her . . . "Okay, baby . . . but I'm gonna buy me a banty rooster and put him out there in the backyard . . . and when he see a stranger come, he'll flap his wings and crow . . ." Look here, Bono, I could watch the front door by myself . . . it was that back door I was worried about.

ROSE: Troy, you ought not talk like that. Troy ain't doing nothing but telling a lie.

TROY: Only thing is . . . when we first got married . . . forget the rooster . . . we ain't had no yard!

BONO: I hear you tell it. Me and Lucille was staying down there on Logan Street. Had two rooms with the outhouse in the back. I ain't mind the outhouse none. But when that goddamn wind blow through there in the winter . . . that's what I'm talking about! To this day I wonder why in the hell I ever stayed down there for six long years. But see, I didn't know I could do no better. I thought only white folks had inside toilets and things.

ROSE: There's a lot of people don't know they can do no better than they doing now. That's just something you got to learn. A lot of folks still shop at Bella's.

TROY: Ain't nothing wrong with shopping at Bella's. She got fresh food.

ROSE: I ain't said nothing about if she got fresh food. I'm talking about what she charge. She charge ten cents more than the A&P.

TROY: The A&P ain't never done nothing for me. I spends my money where I'm treated right. I go down to Bella, say, "I need a loaf of bread, I'll pay you Friday." She give it to me. What sense that make when I got money to go and spend it somewhere else and ignore the person who done right by me? That ain't in the Bible.

ROSE: We ain't talking about what's in the Bible. What sense it made to shop there when she overcharge?

TROY: You shop where you want to. I'll do my shopping where the people been good to me.

ROSE: Well, I don't think it's right for her to overcharge. That's all I was saying.

BONO: Look here . . . I got to get on. Lucille going be raising all kind of hell.

TROY: Where you going, nigger? We ain't finished this pint. Come here, finish this pint.

BONO: Well, hell, I am . . . if you ever turn the bottle loose.

TROY [*hands him the bottle*]:   The only thing I say about the A&P is I'm glad Cory got that job down there. Help him take care of his school clothes and things. Gabe done moved out and things getting tight around here. He got that job. . . . He can start to look out for himself.

ROSE: Cory done went and got recruited by a college football team.

TROY: I told that boy about that football stuff. The white man ain't gonna let him get nowhere with that football. I told him when he first come to me with it. Now you come telling me he done went and got more tied up in it. He ought to go and get recruited in how to fix cars or something where he can make a living.

ROSE: He ain't talking about making no living playing football. It's just something the boys in school do. They gonna send a recruiter by to talk to you. He'll tell you he ain't talking about making no living playing football. It's a honor to be recruited.

TROY: It ain't gonna get him nowhere. Bono'll tell you that.

BONO: If he be like you in the sports . . . he's gonna be all right. Ain't but two men ever played baseball as good as you. That's Babe Ruth and Josh Gibson.° Them's the only two men ever hit more home runs than you.

TROY: What it ever get me? Ain't got a pot to piss in or a window to throw it out of.

ROSE: Times have changed since you was playing baseball, Troy. That was before the war. Times have changed a lot since then.

TROY: How in hell they done changed?

ROSE: They got lots of colored boys playing ball now. Baseball and football.

BONO: You right about that, Rose. Times have changed, Troy. You just come along too early.

TROY: There ought not never have been no time called too early! Now you take that fellow . . . what's that fellow they had playing right field for the Yankees back then? You know who I'm talking about, Bono. Used to play right field for the Yankees.

ROSE: Selkirk?

TROY: Selkirk! That's it! Man batting .269, understand? .269. What kind of sense that make? I was hitting .432 with thirty-seven home runs! Man batting .269 and playing right field for the Yankees! I saw Josh Gibson's daughter yesterday. She walking around with raggedy shoes on her feet. Now I bet you Selkirk's daughter ain't walking around with raggedy shoes on her feet! I bet you that!

ROSE: They got a lot of colored baseball players now. Jackie Robinson was the first. Folks had to wait for Jackie Robinson.

TROY: I done seen a hundred niggers play baseball better than Jackie Robinson. Hell, I know some teams Jackie Robinson couldn't even make! What you talking about Jackie Robinson. Jackie Robinson wasn't nobody. I'm talking about if you could play ball then they ought to have let you play. Don't care what color you were. Come telling me I come along too early. If you could play . . . then they ought to have let you play.

TROY *takes a long drink from the bottle.*

ROSE: You gonna drink yourself to death. You don't need to be drinking like that.

TROY: Death ain't nothing. I done seen him. Done wrassled with him. You can't tell me nothing about death. Death ain't nothing but a fastball on the outside corner. And you know what I'll do to that! Lookee here, Bono . . . am I lying? You get one of them fastballs, about waist high, over the outside corner of the plate where you can get the meat of the bat on it . . . and good god! You can kiss it goodbye. Now, am I lying?

Josh Gibson   *(1911–1947) powerful, black baseball player known in the 1930s as the Babe Ruth of the Negro leagues.*

BONO: Naw, you telling the truth there. I seen you do it.

TROY: If I'm lying . . . that 450 feet worth of lying!

Pause.

That's all death is to me. A fastball on the outside corner.

ROSE: I don't know why you want to get on talking about death.

TROY: Ain't nothing wrong with talking about death. That's part of life. Everybody gonna die. You gonna die, I'm gonna die. Bono's gonna die. Hell, we all gonna die.

ROSE: But you ain't got to talk about it. I don't like to talk about it.

TROY: You the one brought it up. Me and Bono was talking about baseball . . . you tell me I'm gonna drink myself to death. Ain't that right, Bono? You know I don't drink this but one night out of the week. That's Friday night. I'm gonna drink just enough to where I can handle it. Then I cuts it loose. I leave it alone. So don't you worry about me drinking myself to death. 'Cause I ain't worried about Death. I done seen him. I done wrestled with him.

Look here, Bono . . . I looked up one day and Death was marching straight at me. Like Soldiers on Parade! The Army of Death was marching straight at me. The middle of July, 1941. It got real cold just like it be winter. It seem like Death himself reached out and touched me on the shoulder. He touch me just like I touch you. I got cold as ice and Death standing there grinning at me.

ROSE: Troy, why don't you hush that talk.

TROY: I say . . . What you want, Mr. Death? You be wanting me? You done brought your army to be getting me? I looked him dead in the eye. I wasn't fearing nothing. I was ready to tangle. Just like I'm ready to tangle now. The Bible say be ever vigilant. That's why I don't get but so drunk. I got to keep watch.

ROSE: Troy was right down there in Mercy Hospital. You remember he had pneumonia? Laying there with a fever talking plumb out of his head.

TROY: Death standing there staring at me . . . carrying that sickle in his hand. Finally he say, "You want bound over for another year?" See, just like that . . . "You want bound over for another year?" I told him, "Bound over hell! Let's settle this now!"

It seem like he kinda fell back when I said that, and all the cold went out of me. I reached down and grabbed that sickle and threw it just as far as I could throw it . . . and me and him commenced to wrestling.

We wrestled for three days and three nights. I can't say where I found the strength from. Every time it seemed like he was gonna get the best of me, I'd reach way down deep inside myself and find the strength to do him one better.

ROSE: Every time Troy tell that story he find different ways to tell it. Different things to make up about it.

TROY: I ain't making up nothing. I'm telling you the facts of what happened. I wrestled with Death for three days and three nights and I'm standing here to tell you about it.

Pause.

All right. At the end of the third night we done weakened each other to where we can't hardly move. Death stood up, throwed on his robe . . . had him a white robe with a hood on it. He throwed on that robe and went off to look for his sickle. Say, "I'll be back." Just like that. "I'll be back." I told him, say, "Yeah, but . . . you gonna have to find me!" I wasn't no fool. I wasn't going looking for him. Death ain't nothing to play with. And I know he's gonna get me. I know I got to join his army . . . his camp followers. But as long as I keep my strength and see him coming . . . as long as I keep up my vigilance . . . he's gonna have to fight to get me. I ain't going easy.

BONO:　Well, look here, since you got to keep up your vigilance . . . let me have the bottle.

TROY:　Aw hell, I shouldn't have told you that part. I should have left out that part.

ROSE:　Troy be talking that stuff and half the time don't even know what he be talking about.

TROY:　Bono know me better than that.

BONO:　That's right. I know you. I know you got some Uncle Remus° in your blood. You got more stories than the devil got sinners.

TROY:　Aw hell, I done seen him too! Done talked with the devil.

ROSE:　Troy, don't nobody wanna be hearing all that stuff.

LYONS *enters the yard from the street. Thirty-four years old,* TROY'S *son by a previous marriage, he sports a neatly trimmed goatee, sport coat, white shirt, tieless and buttoned at the collar. Though he fancies himself a musician, he is more caught up in the rituals and "idea" of being a musician than in the actual practice of the music. He has come to borrow money from* TROY, *and while he knows he will be successful, he is uncertain as to what extent his lifestyle will be held up to scrutiny and ridicule.*

LYONS:　Hey, Pop.

TROY:　What you come "Hey, Popping" me for?

LYONS:　How you doing, Rose?

He kisses her.

Mr. Bono. How you doing?

BONO:　Hey, Lyons . . . how you been?

TROY:　He must have been doing all right. I ain't seen him around here last week.

ROSE:　Troy, leave your boy alone. He come by to see you and you wanna start all that nonsense.

TROY:　I ain't bothering Lyons.

Offers him the bottle.

Here . . . get you a drink. We got an understanding. I know why he come by to see me and he know I know.

LYONS:　Come on, Pop . . . I just stopped by to say hi . . . see how you was doing.

TROY:　You ain't stopped by yesterday.

ROSE:　You gonna stay for supper, Lyons? I got some chicken cooking in the oven.

Uncle Remus　*Black storyteller who recounts traditional black tales in the book by Joel Chandler Harris.*

LYONS: No, Rose . . . thanks. I was just in the neighborhood and thought I'd stop by for a minute.

TROY: You was in the neighborhood all right, nigger. You telling the truth there. You was in the neighborhood cause it's my payday.

LYONS: Well, hell, since you mentioned it . . . let me have ten dollars.

TROY: I'll be damned! I'll die and go to hell and play blackjack with the devil before I give you ten dollars.

BONO: That's what I wanna know about . . . that devil you done seen.

LYONS: What . . . Pop done seen the devil? You too much, Pops.

TROY: Yeah, I done seen him. Talked to him too!

ROSE: You ain't seen no devil. I done told you that man ain't had nothing to do with the devil. Anything you can't understand, you want to call it the devil.

TROY: Look here, Bono . . . I went down to see Hertzberger about some furniture. Got three rooms for two-ninety-eight. That what it say on the radio. "Three rooms . . . two-ninety-eight." Even made up a little song about it. Go down there . . . man tell me I can't get no credit. I'm working every day and can't get no credit. What to do? I got an empty house with some raggedy furniture in it. Cory ain't got no bed. He's sleeping on a pile of rags on the floor. Working every day and can't get no credit. Come back here—Rose'll tell you—madder than hell. Sit down . . . try to figure what I'm gonna do. Come a knock on the door. Ain't been living here but three days. Who know I'm here? Open the door . . . devil standing there bigger than life. White fellow . . . got on good clothes and everything. Standing there with a clipboard in his hand. I ain't had to say nothing. First words come out of his mouth was . . . I understand you need some furniture and can't get no credit." I liked to fell over. He say, "I'll give you all the credit you want, but you got to pay the interest on it." I told him, "Give me three rooms worth and charge whatever you want." Next day a truck pulled up here and two men unloaded them three rooms. Man what drove the truck give me a book. Say send ten dollars, first of every month to the address in the book and everything will be all right. Say if I miss a payment the devil was coming back and it'll be hell to pay. That was fifteen years ago. To this day . . . the first of the month I send my ten dollars, Rose'll tell you.

ROSE: Troy lying.

TROY: I ain't never seen that man since. Now you tell me who else that could have been but the devil? I ain't sold my soul or nothing like that, you understand. Naw, I wouldn't have truck with the devil about nothing like that. I got my furniture and pays my ten dollars the first of the month just like clockwork.

BONO: How long you say you been paying this ten dollars a month?

TROY: Fifteen years!

BONO: Hell, ain't you finished paying for it yet? How much the man done charged you.

TROY: Ah hell, I done paid for it. I done paid for it ten times over! The fact is I'm scared to stop paying it.

ROSE: Troy lying. We got that furniture from Mr. Glickman. He ain't paying no ten dollars a month to nobody.

TROY: Aw hell, woman. Bono know I ain't that big a fool.

LYONS: I was just getting ready to say . . . I know where there's a bridge for sale.

TROY: Look here, I'll tell you this . . . it don't matter to me if he was the devil. It don't matter if the devil give credit. Somebody has got to give it.

ROSE: It ought to matter. You going around talking about having truck with the devil . . . God's the one you gonna have to answer to. He's the one gonna be at the Judgment.

LYONS: Yeah, well, look here, Pop . . . let me have that ten dollars. I'll give it back to you. Bonnie got a job working at the hospital.

TROY: What I tell you, Bono? The only time I see this nigger is when he wants something. That's the only time I see him.

LYONS: Come on, Pop, Mr. Bono don't want to hear all that. Let me have the ten dollars. I told you Bonnie working.

TROY: What that mean to me? "Bonnie working." I don't care if she working. Go ask her for the ten dollars if she working. Talking about "Bonnie working." Why ain't you working?

LYONS: Aw, Pop, you know I can't find no decent job. Where am I gonna get a job at? You know I can't get no job.

TROY: I told you I know some people down there. I can get you on the rubbish if you want to work. I told you that the last time you came by here asking me for something.

LYONS: Naw, Pop . . . thanks. That ain't for me. I don't wanna be carrying nobody's rubbish. I don't wanna be punching nobody's time clock.

TROY: What's the matter, you too good to carry people's rubbish? Where you think that ten dollars you talking about come from? I'm just supposed to haul people's rubbish and give my money to you cause you too lazy to work. You too lazy to work and wanna know why you ain't got what I got.

ROSE: What hospital Bonnie working at? Mercy?

LYONS: She's down at Passavant working in the laundry.

TROY: I ain't got nothing as it is. I give you that ten dollars and I got to eat beans the rest of the week. Naw . . . you ain't getting no ten dollars here.

LYONS: You ain't got to be eating no beans. I don't know why you wanna say that.

TROY: I ain't got no extra money. Gabe done moved over to Miss Pearl's paying her the rent and things done got tight around here. I can't afford to be giving you every payday.

LYONS: I ain't asked you to give me nothing. I asked you to loan me ten dollars. I know you got ten dollars.

TROY: Yeah, I got it. You know why I got it? Cause I don't throw my money away out there in the streets. You living the fast life . . . wanna be a musician . . . running around in them clubs and things . . . then, you learn to take care of yourself. You ain't gonna find me going and asking nobody for nothing. I done spent too many years without.

LYONS: You and me is two different people, Pop.

TROY: I done learned my mistake and learned to do what's right by it. You still trying to get something for nothing. Life don't owe you nothing. You owe it to yourself. Ask Bono. He'll tell you I'm right.

LYONS: You got your way of dealing with the world . . . I got mine. The only thing that matters to me is the music.

TROY: Yeah, I can see that! It don't matter how you gonna eat . . . where your next dollar is coming from. You telling the truth there.

LYONS: I know I got to eat. But I got to live too. I need something that gonna help me to get out of the bed in the morning. Make me feel like I belong in the world. I don't bother nobody. I just stay with my music cause that's the only way I can find to live in the world. Otherwise there ain't no telling what I might do. Now I don't come criticizing you and how you live. I just come by to ask you for ten dollars. I don't wanna hear all that about how I live.

TROY: Boy, your mamma did a hell of a job raising you.

LYONS: You can't change me, Pop. I'm thirty-four years old. If you wanted to change me, you should have been there when I was growing up. I come by to see you . . . ask for ten dollars and you want to talk about how I was raised. You don't know nothing about how I was raised.

ROSE: Let the boy have ten dollars, Troy.

TROY [*to Lyons*]:   What the hell you looking at me for? I ain't got no ten dollars. You know what I do with my money.

To ROSE.

Give him ten dollars if you want him to have it.

ROSE: I will. Just as soon as you turn it loose.

TROY [*handing Rose the money*]:   There it is. Seventy-six dollars and forty-two cents. You see this, Bono? Now, I ain't gonna get but six of that back.

ROSE: You ought to stop telling that lie. Here, Lyons. [*She hands him the money.*]

LYONS: Thanks, Rose. Look . . . I got to run . . . I'll see you later.

TROY: Wait a minute. You gonna say, "thanks, Rose" and ain't gonna look to see where she got that ten dollars from? See how they do me, Bono?

LYONS: I know she got it from you, Pop. Thanks. I'll give it back to you.

TROY: There he go telling another lie. Time I see that ten dollars . . . he'll be owing me thirty more.

LYONS: See you, Mr. Bono.

BONO: Take care, Lyons!

LYONS: Thanks, Pop. I'll see you again.

LYONS *exits the yard*.

TROY: I don't know why he doesn't go and get him a decent job and take of that woman he got.

BONO: He'll be all right, Troy. The boy is still young.

TROY: The *boy* is thirty-four years old.

ROSE: Let's not get off into all that.

BONO: Look here . . . I got to be going. I got to be getting on. Lucille gonna be waiting.

TROY [*puts his arm around* ROSE]:   See this woman, Bono? I love this woman. I love this woman so much it hurts. I love her so much . . . I done run out of ways of loving her. So I got to go back to basics. Don't you come by my house Monday morning talking about time to go to work . . . 'cause I'm still gonna be stroking!

ROSE: Troy! Stop it now!

BONO: I ain't paying him no mind, Rose. That ain't nothing but gin-talk. Go on, Troy. I'll see you Monday.

TROY: Don't you come by my house, nigger! I done told you what I'm gonna be doing.

The lights go down to black.

Scene 2

The lights come up on ROSE *hanging up clothes. She hums and sings softly to herself. It is the following morning.*

ROSE [*Sings*] Jesus, be a fence all around me every day
Jesus, I want you to protect me as I travel on my way.
Jesus, be a fence all around me every day.

TROY *enters from the house.*

Jesus, I want you to protect me
As I travel on my way.
[*To* TROY] 'Morning. You ready for breakfast? I can fix it soon as I finish hanging up these clothes?

TROY: I got the coffee on. That'll be all right. I'll just drink some of that this morning.

ROSE: That 651 hit yesterday. That's the second time this month. Miss Pearl hit for a dollar . . . seem like those that need the least always get lucky. Poor folks can't get nothing.

TROY: Them numbers don't know anybody. I don't know why you fool with them. You and Lyons both.

ROSE: It's something to do.

TROY: You ain't doing nothing but throwing your money away.

ROSE: Troy, you know I don't play foolishly. I just play a nickel here and a nickel there.

TROY: That's two nickels you done thrown away.

ROSE: Now I hit sometimes . . . that makes up for it. It always comes in handy when I do hit. I don't hear you complaining then.

TROY: I ain't complaining now. I just say it's foolish. Trying to guess out of six hundred ways which way the number gonna come. If I had all the money niggers, these Negroes, throw away on numbers for one week—just one week—I'd be a rich man.

ROSE: Well, you wishing and calling it foolish ain't gonna stop folks from playing numbers. That's one thing for sure. Besides . . . some good things come from playing numbers. Look where Pope done bought him that restaurant off of numbers.

TROY: I can't stand niggers like that. Man ain't had two dimes to rub together. He walking around with his shoes all run over bumming money for cigarettes. All right. Got lucky there and hit the numbers . . .

ROSE: Troy, I know all about it.

TROY: Had good sense, I'll say that for him. He ain't throwed his money away. I seen niggers hit the numbers and go through two thousand dollars in four days. Man bought him that restaurant down there . . . fixed it up real nice . . . and then didn't want nobody to come in it! A Negro go in there and can't get no kind of service. I seen a white fellow come in there and order a bowl of stew. Pope picked all the meat out the pot for him. Man ain't had nothing but a bowl of meat! Negro come behind him and ain't got nothing but the potatoes and carrots. Talking about what numbers do for people, you picked a wrong example. Ain't done nothing but make a worser fool out of him than he was before.

ROSE: Troy, you ought to stop worrying about what happened at work yesterday.

TROY: I ain't worried. Just told me to be down there at the Commissioner's office on Friday. Everybody think they gonna fire me. I ain't worried about them firing me. You ain't got to worry about that.

Pause.

Where's Cory? Cory in the house? [*Calls*] Cory?

ROSE: He gone out.

TROY: Out, huh? He gone out 'cause he know I want him to help me with this fence. I know how he is. That boy scared of work.

GABRIEL *enters. He comes halfway down the alley and, hearing* TROY'S *voice, stops.*

TROY [*continues*]:   He ain't done a lick of work in his life.

ROSE: He had to go to football practice. Coach wanted them to get in a little extra practice before the season start.

TROY: I got his practice . . . running out of here before he gets his chores done.

ROSE: Troy, what is wrong with you this morning? Don't nothing set right with you. Go on back in there and go to bed . . . get up on the other side.

TROY: Why something got to be wrong with me? I ain't said nothing wrong with me.

ROSE: You got something to say about everything. First it's the numbers . . . then it's the way the man runs his restaurant . . . then you done got on Cory. What's it gonna be next? Take a look up there and see if the weather suits you . . . or is it gonna be how you gonna put up the fence with the clothes hanging in the yard.

TROY: You hit the nail on the head then.

ROSE: I know you like I know the back of my hand. Go on in there and get you some coffee . . . see if that straighten you up. 'Cause you ain't right this morning.

TROY *starts into the house and sees* GABRIEL. GABRIEL *starts singing.* TROY'S *brother, he is seven years younger than* TROY. *Injured in World War II, he has a metal plate in his head. He carries an old trumpet tied around his waist and believes with every fiber of his being that he is the Archangel Gabriel. He carries a chipped basket with an assortment of discarded fruits and vegetables he has picked up in the strip district and which he attempts to sell.*

GABRIEL [*Singing*]:　Yes, ma'am, I got plums
You ask me how I sell them
Oh ten cents apiece
Three for a quarter
Come and buy now
'Cause I'm here today
And tomorrow I'll be gone

GABRIEL *enters.*

Hey, Rose!

ROSE:　How you doing, Gabe?

GABRIEL:　There's Troy . . . Hey, Troy!

TROY:　Hey, Gabe.

Exit into kitchen.

ROSE [*to* GABRIEL]:　What you got there?

GABRIEL:　You know what I got, Rose. I got fruits and vegetables.

ROSE [*looking in basket*]:　Where's all these plums you talking about?

GABRIEL:　I ain't got no plums today, Rose. I was just singing that. Have some tomorrow. Put me in a big order for plums. Have enough plums tomorrow for St. Peter and everybody.

TROY *enters from kitchen, crosses to steps.*
[*To* ROSE]

Troy's mad at me.

TROY:　I ain't mad at you. What I got to be mad at you about? You ain't done nothing to me.

GABRIEL:　I just moved over to Miss Pearl's to keep out from in your way. I ain't mean no harm by it.

TROY:　Who said anything about that? I ain't said anything about that.

GABRIEL:　You ain't mad at me, is you?

TROY:　Naw . . . I ain't mad at you, Gabe. If I was mad at you I'd tell you about it.

GABRIEL:　Got me two rooms. In the basement. Got my own door too. Wanna see my key?

He holds up a key.

That's my own key! Ain't nobody else got a key like that. That's my key! My two rooms!

TROY:　Well, that's good, Gabe. You got your own key . . . that's good.

ROSE:　You hungry, Gabe? I was just fixing to cook Troy his breakfast.

GABRIEL:　I'll take some biscuits. You got some biscuits? Did you know when I was in heaven . . . every morning me and St. Peter would sit down by the gate and eat some big fat biscuits? Oh, yeah! We had us a good time. We'd sit there and eat us them biscuits and then St. Peter would go off to sleep and tell me to wake him up when it's time to open the gates for the judgment.

ROSE: Well, come on . . . I'll make up a batch of biscuits.

ROSE *exits into the house.*

GABRIEL: Troy . . . St. Peter got your name in the book. I seen it. It say . . . Troy Maxson, I say . . . I know him! He got the same name like what I got. That's my brother!

TROY: How many times you gonna tell me that, Gabe?

GABRIEL: Ain't got my name in the book. Don't have to have my name. I done died and went to heaven. He got your name though. One morning St. Peter was looking at his book . . . marking it up for the judgment . . . and he let me see your name. Got it in there under M. Got Rose's name . . . I ain't seen it like I seen yours . . . but I know it's in there. He got a great big book. Got everybody's name what was ever been born. That's what he told me. But I seen your name. Seen it with my own eyes.

TROY: Go on in the house there. Rose going to fix you something to eat.

GABRIEL: Oh, I ain't hungry. I done had breakfast with Aunt Jemimah. She come by and cooked me up a whole mess of flapjacks. Remember how we used to eat them flapjacks?

TROY: Go on in the house and get you something to eat now.

GABRIEL: I got to go sell my plums. I done sold some tomatoes. Got me two quarters. Wanna see?

He shows TROY *his quarters.*

I'm gonna save them and buy me a new horn so St. Peter can hear me when it's time to open the gates.

GABRIEL *stops suddenly. Listens.*

Hear that? That's the hellhounds. I got to chase them out of here. Go on get out of here! Get out!

GABRIEL *exits singing.*

Better get ready for the judgment
Better get ready for the judgment
My Lord is coming down

ROSE *enters from the house.*

TROY: He gone off somewhere.

GABRIEL [*offstage*]:   Better get ready for the judgment
Better get ready for the judgment morning
Better get ready for the judgment
My God is coming down

ROSE: He ain't eating right. Miss Pearl say she can't get him to eat nothing.

TROY: What you want me to do about it, Rose? I done did everything I can for the man. I can't make him get well. Man got half his head blown away . . . what you expect?

ROSE: Seem like something ought to be done to help him.

TROY: Man don't bother nobody. He just mixed up from that metal plate he got in his head. Ain't no sense for him to go back into the hospital.

ROSE: Least he be eating right. They can help him take care of himself.

TROY: Don't nobody wanna be locked up, Rose. What you wanna lock him up for? Man go over there and fight the war . . . messin' around with them Japs, get half his head blown off . . . and they give him a lousy three thousand dollars. And I had to swoop down on that.

ROSE: Is you fixing to go into that again?

TROY: That's the only way I got a roof over my head . . . cause of that metal plate.

ROSE: Ain't no sense you blaming yourself for nothing. Gabe wasn't in no condition to manage that money. You done what was right by him. Can't nobody say you ain't done what was right by him. Look how long you took care of him . . . till he wanted to have his own place and moved over there with Miss Pearl.

TROY: That ain't what I'm saying, woman! I'm just stating the facts. If my brother didn't have that metal plate in his head . . . I wouldn't have a pot to piss in or a window to throw it out of. And I'm fifty-three years old. Now see if you can understand that!

TROY *gets up from the porch and starts to exit the yard.*

ROSE: Where you going off to? You been running out of here every Saturday for weeks. I thought you was gonna work on this fence?

TROY: I'm gonna walk down to Taylors'. Listen to the ball game. I'll be back in a bit. I'll work on it when I get back.

He exits the yard. The lights go to black.

Scene 3

The lights come up on the yard. It is four hours later. ROSE *is taking down the clothes from the line.* CORY *enters carrying his football equipment.*

ROSE: Your daddy like to had a fit with you running out of here this morning without doing your chores.

CORY: I told you I had to go to practice.

ROSE: He say you were supposed to help him with this fence.

CORY: He been saying that the last four or five Saturdays, and then he don't never do nothing, but go down to Taylors'. Did you tell him about the recruiter?

ROSE: Yeah, I told him.

CORY: What he say?

ROSE: He ain't said nothing too much. You get in there and get started on your chores before he gets back. Go on and scrub down them steps before he gets back here hollering and carrying on.

CORY: I'm hungry. What you got to eat, Mama?

ROSE: Go on and get started on your chores. I got some meat loaf in there. Go on and make you a sandwich . . . and don't leave no mess in there.

CORY *exits into the house.* ROSE *continues to take down the clothes.* TROY *enters the yard and sneaks up and grabs her from behind.*

Troy! Go on, now. You liked to scared me to death. What was the score of the game? Lucille had me on the phone and I couldn't keep up with it.

TROY: What I care about the game? Come here, woman. [*He tries to kiss her.*]

ROSE: I thought you went down Taylors' to listen to the game. Go on, Troy! You supposed to be putting up this fence.

TROY [*attempting to kiss her again*]:   I'll put it up when I finish with what is at hand.

ROSE: Go on, Troy. I ain't studying you.

TROY [*chasing after her*]:   I'm studying you . . . fixing to do my homework!

ROSE: Troy, you better leave me alone.

TROY: Where's Cory? That boy brought his butt home yet?

ROSE: He's in the house doing his chores.

TROY [*calling*]:   Cory! Get your butt out here, boy!

ROSE *exits into the house with the laundry.* TROY *goes over to the pile of wood, picks up a board, and starts sawing.* CORY *enters from the house.*

TROY: You just now coming in here from leaving this morning?

CORY: Yeah, I had to go to football practice.

TROY: Yeah, what?

CORY: Yessir.

TROY: I ain't but two seconds off you noway. The garbage sitting in there overflowing . . . you ain't done none of your chores . . . and you come in here talking about "Yeah."

CORY: I was just getting ready to do my chores, now, Pop . . .

TROY: Your first chore is to help me with this fence on Saturday. Everything else come after that. Now get that saw and cut them boards.

CORY *takes the saw and begins cutting the boards.* TROY *continues working. There is a long pause.*

CORY: Hey, Pop . . . why don't you buy a TV?

TROY: What I want with a TV? What I want one of them for?

CORY: Everybody got one. Earl, Ba Bra . . . Jesse!

TROY: I ain't asked you who had one. I say what I want with one?

CORY: So you can watch it. They got lots of things on TV. Baseball games and everything. We could watch the World Series.

TROY: Two hundred dollars, huh?

CORY: That ain't that much, Pop.

TROY: Naw, it's just two hundred dollars. See that roof you got over your head at night? Let me tell you something about that roof. It's been over ten years since that roof was last tarred. See now . . . the snow come this winter and sit up there on that roof like it is . . . and it's gonna seep inside. It's just gonna be a little bit . . . ain't gonna hardly notice it. Then the next thing you know, it's gonna be leaking all over the house. Then the wood rot from all that water and you gonna need a whole new roof. Now, how much you think it cost to get that roof tarred?

CORY: I don't know.

TROY: Two hundred and sixty-four dollars . . . cash money. While you thinking about a TV, I got to be thinking about the roof . . . and whatever else go wrong around here. Now if you had two hundred dollars, what would you do . . . fix the roof or buy a TV?

CORY: I'd buy a TV. Then when the roof started to leak . . . when it needed fixing . . . I'd fix it.

TROY: Where you gonna get the money from? You done spent it for a TV. You gonna sit up and watch the water run all over your brand new TV.

CORY: Aw, Pop. You got money, I know you do.

TROY: Where I got it at, huh?

CORY: You got it in the bank.

TROY: You wanna see my bankbook? You wanna see that seventy-three dollars and twenty-two cents I got sitting up in there.

CORY: You ain't got to pay for it all at one time. You can put a down payment on it and carry it on home with you.

TROY: Not me. I ain't gonna owe nobody nothing if I can help it. Miss a payment and they come and snatch it right out your house. Then what you got? Now, soon as I get two hundred dollars clear, then I'll buy a TV. Right now, as soon as I get two hundred and sixty-four dollars, I'm gonna have this roof tarred.

CORY: Aw . . . Pop!

TROY: You go on and get you two hundred dollars and buy one if ya want it. I got better things to do with my money.

CORY: I can't get no two hundred dollars. I ain't never seen two hundred dollars.

TROY: I'll tell you what . . . you get you a hundred dollars and I'll put the other hundred with it.

CORY: All right, I'm gonna show you.

TROY: You gonna show me how you can cut them boards right now.

CORY *begins to cut the boards. There is a long pause.*

CORY: The Pirates won today. That makes five in a row.

TROY: I ain't thinking about the Pirates. Got an all-white team. Got that boy . . . that Puerto Rican boy . . . Clemente. Don't even half-play him. That boy could be something if they give him a chance. Play him one day and sit him on the bench the next.

CORY: He gets a lot of chances to play.

TROY: I'm talking about playing regular. Playing every day so you can get your timing. That's what I'm talking about.

CORY: They got some white guys on the team that don't play every day. You can't play everybody at the same time.

TROY: If they got a white fellow sitting on the bench . . . you can bet your last dollar he can't play! The colored guy got to be twice as good before he get on the team. That's why I don't want you to get all tied up in them sports. Man on the team and what it get him? They got colored on the team and don't use them. Same as not having them. All them teams the same.

CORY: The Braves got Hank Aaron and Wes Covington. Hank Aaron hit two home runs today. That makes forty-three.

TROY: Hank Aaron ain't nobody. That's what you supposed to do. That's how you supposed to play the game. Ain't nothing to it. It's just a matter of timing . . . getting the right follow-through. Hell, I can hit forty-three home runs right now!

CORY: Not off no major-league pitching, you couldn't.

TROY: We had better pitching in the Negro leagues. I hit seven home runs off of Satchel Paige.° You can't get no better than that!

CORY: Sandy Koufax. He's leading the league in strikeouts.

TROY: I ain't thinking of no Sandy Koufax.

CORY: You got Warren Spahn and Lew Burdette. I bet you couldn't hit no home runs off of Warren Spahn.

TROY: I'm through with it now. You go on and cut them boards.

Pause.

Your mama tell me you done got recruited by a college football team? Is that right?

CORY: Yeah. Coach Zellman say the recruiter gonna be coming by to talk to you. Get you to sign the permission papers.

TROY: I thought you supposed to be working down there at the A&P. Ain't you suppose to be working down there after school?

CORY: Mr. Stawicki say he gonna hold my job for me until after the football season. Say starting next week I can work weekends.

TROY: I thought we had an understanding about this football stuff? You suppose to keep up with your chores and hold that job down at the A&P. Ain't been around here all day on a Saturday. Ain't none of your chores done . . . and now you telling me you done quit your job.

CORY: I'm gonna be working weekends.

TROY: You damn right you are! And ain't no need for nobody coming around here to talk to me about signing nothing.

CORY: Hey, Pop . . . you can't do that. He's coming all the way from North Carolina.

TROY: I don't care where he coming from. The white man ain't gonna let you get nowhere with that football noway. You go on and get your book-learning so you can work yourself up in that A&P or learn how to fix cars or build houses or something, get you a trade. That way you have something can't nobody take away from you. You go on and learn how to put your hands to some good use. Besides hauling people's garbage.

CORY: I get good grades, Pop. That's why the recruiter wants to talk with you. You got to keep your grades to get recruited. This way I'll be going to college. I'll get a chance . . .

TROY: First you gonna get your butt down there to the A&P and get your job back.

CORY: Mr. Stawicki done already hired somebody else 'cause I told him I was playing football.

TROY: You a bigger fool than I thought . . . to let somebody take away your job so you can play some football. Where you gonna get your money to take out your girlfriend and whatnot? What kind of foolishness is that to let somebody take away your job?

CORY: I'm still gonna be working weekends.

TROY: Naw . . . naw. You getting your butt out of here and finding you another job.

CORY: Come on, Pop! I got to practice. I can't work after school and play football too. The team needs me. That's what Coach Zellman say . . .

TROY: I don't care what nobody else say. I'm the boss . . . you understand? I'm the boss around here. I do the only saying what counts.

CORY: Come on, Pop!

TROY: I asked you . . . did you understand?

CORY: Yeah . . .

TROY: What?!

CORY: Yessir.

TROY: You go on down there to that A&P and see if you can get your job back. If you can't do both . . . then you quit the football team. You've got to take the crookeds with the straights.

CORY: Yessir.

Pause.

Can I ask you a question?

TROY: What the hell you wanna ask me? Mr. Stawicki the one you got the questions for.

CORY: How come you ain't never liked me?

TROY: Liked you? Who the hell say I got to like you? What law is there say I got to like you? Wanna stand up in my face and ask a damn fool-ass question like that. Talking about liking somebody. Come here, boy, when I talk to you.

CORY *comes over to where* TROY *is working. He stands slouched over and* TROY *shoves him on his shoulder.*

Straighten up, goddammit! I asked you a question . . . what law is there say I got to like you?

CORY: None.

TROY: Well, all right then! Don't you eat every day?

Pause.

Answer me when I talk to you! Don't you eat every day?

CORY: Yeah.

TROY: Nigger, as long as you in my house, you put that sir on the end of it when you talk to me!

CORY: Yes . . . sir.

TROY: You eat every day.

CORY: Yessir!

TROY: Got a roof over your head.

CORY: Yessir!

TROY: Got clothes on your back.

CORY: Yessir.

TROY: Why you think that is?

CORY: Cause of you.

TROY: Ah, hell I know it's 'cause of me . . . but why do you think that is?

CORY [*hesitant*]:   Cause you like me.

TROY: Like you? I go out of here every morning . . . bust my butt . . . putting up with them crackers° every day . . . cause I like you? You about the biggest fool I ever saw.

Pause.

It's my job. It's my responsibility! You understand that? A man got to take care of his family. You live in my house . . . sleep you behind on my bedclothes . . . fill your belly up with my food . . . cause you my son. You my flesh and blood. Not 'cause I like you! Cause it's my duty to take care of you. I owe a responsibility to you! Let's get this straight right here . . . before it go along any further . . . I ain't got to like you. Mr. Rand don't give me my money come payday cause he likes me. He gives me cause he owe me. I gave you your life! Me and your mamma worked that out between us. And liking your black ass wasn't part of the bargain. Don't you try and go through life worrying about if somebody like you or not. You best be making sure they doing right by you. You understand what I'm saying, boy?

CORY: Yessir.

TROY: Then get the hell out of my face, and get on down to that A&P.

ROSE *has been standing behind the screen door for much of the scene. She enters as* CORY *exits.*

ROSE: Why don't you let the boy go ahead and play football, Troy? Ain't no harm in that. He's just trying to be like you with the sports.

TROY: I don't want him to be like me! I want him to move as far away from my life as he can get. You the only decent thing that ever happened to me. I wish him that. But I don't wish him a thing else from my life. I decided seventeen years ago that boy wasn't getting involved in no sports. Not after what they did to me in the sports.

ROSE: Troy, why don't you admit you was too old to play in the major leagues? For once . . . why don't you admit that?

TROY: What do you mean too old? Don't come telling me I was too old. I just wasn't the right color. Hell, I'm fifty-three years old and can do better than Selkirk's .269 right now!

ROSE: How's was you gonna play ball when you were over forty? Sometimes I can't get no sense out of you.

TROY: I got good sense, woman. I got sense enough not to let my boy get hurt over playing no sports. You been mothering that boy too much. Worried about if people like him.

ROSE: Everything that boy do . . . he do for you. He wants you to say "Good job, son." That's all.

TROY: Rose, I ain't got time for that. He's alive. He's healthy. He's got to

crackers   *white people, often used to refer disparagingly to poor whites.*

make his own way. I made mine. Ain't nobody gonna hold his hand when he get out there in that world.

ROSE:　Times have changed from when you was young, Troy. People change. The world's changing around you and you can't even see it.

TROY [*slow, methodical*]:　Woman . . . I do the best I can do. I come in here every Friday. I carry a sack of potatoes and a bucket of lard. You all line up at the door with your hands out. I give you the lint from my pockets. I give you my sweat and my blood. I ain't go no tears, I done spent them. We go upstairs in that room at night . . . and I fall down on you and try to blast a hole into forever. I get up Monday morning . . . find my lunch on the table. I go out. Make my way. Find my strength to carry me through to the next Friday.

Pause.

That's all I got, Rose. That's all I got to give. I can't give nothing else.

TROY *exits into the house. The lights go down to black.*

Scene 4

It is Friday. Two weeks later. CORY *starts out of the house with his football equipment. The phone rings.*

CORY [*calling*]:　I got it!

He answers the phone and stands in the screen door talking.

Hello? Hey, Jesse. Naw . . . I was just getting ready to leave now.

ROSE [*calling*]:　Cory!

CORY:　I told you, man, them spikes is all tore up. You can use them if you want, but they ain't no good. Earl got some spikes.

ROSE [*calling*]:　Cory!

CORY [*calling to* ROSE]:　Mam? I'm talking to Jesse.

Into phone.

When she say that? [*Pause.*] Aw, you lying, man. I'm gonna tell her you said that.

ROSE [*calling*]:　Cory, don't you go nowhere!

CORY:　I got to go to the game, Ma!

Into the phone.

Yeah, hey, look, I'll talk to you later. Yeah, I'll meet you over Earl's house. Later. Bye, Ma.

CORY *exits the house and starts out the yard.*

ROSE:　Cory, where you going off to? You got that stuff all pulled out and thrown all over your room.

CORY [*in the yard*]:　I was looking for my spikes. Jesse wanted to borrow my spikes.

ROSE: Get up there and get that cleaned up before your daddy get back in here.

CORY: I got to go to the game! I'll clean it up *when I get back.*

CORY exits.

ROSE: That's all he need to do is see that room all messed up.

ROSE *exits into the house.* TROY *and* BONO *enter the yard.* TROY *is dressed in clothes other than his work clothes.*

BONO: He told them the same thing he told you. Take it to the union.

TROY: Brownie ain't got that much sense. Man wasn't thinking about nothing. He wait until I confront them on it . . . then he wanna come crying seniority.

Calls.

Hey, Rose!

BONO: I wish I could have seen Mr. Rand's face when he told you.

TROY: He couldn't get it out of his mouth! Liked to bit his tongue! When they called me down there to the Commissioner's office . . . he thought they was gonna fire me. Like everybody else.

BONO: I didn't think they was gonna fire you. I thought they was gonna put you on the warning paper.

TROY: Hey, Rose!

To BONO.

Yeah, Mr. Rand like to bit his tongue.

TROY *breaks the seal on the bottle, takes a drink, and hands it to* BONO.

BONO: I see you run right down to Taylors' and told that Alberta gal.

TROY [*calling*]:   Hey Rose! [*To* BONO] I told everybody. Hey, Rose! I went down there to cash my check.

ROSE [*entering from the house*]:   Hush all that hollering, man! I know you out here. What they say down there at the Commissioner's office?

TROY: You supposed to come when I call you, woman. Bono'll tell you that.

To BONO.

Don't Lucille come when you call her?

ROSE: Man, hush your mouth. I ain't no dog . . . talk about "come when you call me."

TROY [*puts his arm around* ROSE]:   You hear this, Bono? I had me an old dog used to get uppity like that. You say, "C'mere, Blue!" . . . and he just lay there and look at you. End up getting a stick and chasing him away trying to make him come.

ROSE: I ain't studying you and your dog. I remember you used to sing that old song.

TROY [*he sings*]:   Hear it ring! Hear it ring! I had a dog his name was Blue.

ROSE: Don't nobody wanna hear you sing that old song.

TROY [*sings*]:   You know Blue was mighty true.

ROSE: Used to have Cory running around here singing that song.

BONO: Hell, I remember that song myself.

TROY [*sings*]:   You know Blue was a good old dog.
Blue treed a possum in a hollow log.
That was my daddy's song. My daddy made up that song.

ROSE: I don't care who made it up. Don't nobody wanna hear you sing it.

TROY [*makes a song like calling a dog*]:   Come here, woman.

ROSE: You come in here carrying on, I reckon they ain't fired you. What they say down there at the Commissioner's office?

TROY: Look here, Rose . . . Mr. Rand called me into his office today when I got back from talking to them people down there . . . it come from up top . . . he called me in and told me they was making me a driver.

ROSE: Troy, you kidding!

TROY: No I ain't. Ask Bono.

ROSE: Well, that's great, Troy. Now you don't have to hassle them people no more.

LYONS *enters from the street.*

TROY: Aw hell, I wasn't looking to see you today. I thought you was in jail. Got it all over the front page of the *Courier* about them raiding Sefus' place . . . where you be hanging out with all them thugs.

LYONS: Hey, Pop . . . that ain't got nothing to do with me. I don't go down there gambling. I go down there to sit in with the band. I ain't got nothing to do with the gambling part. They got some good music down there.

TROY: They got some rogues . . . is what they got.

LYONS: How you been, Mr. Bono? Hi, Rose.

BONO: I see where you playing down at the Crawford Grill tonight.

ROSE: How come you ain't brought Bonnie like I told you. You should have brought Bonnie with you, she ain't been over in a month of Sundays.

LYONS: I was just in the neighborhood . . . thought I'd stop by.

TROY: Here he come . . .

BONO: Your daddy got a promotion on the rubbish. He's gonna be the first colored driver. Ain't got to do nothing but sit up there and read the paper like them white fellows.

LYONS: Hey, Pop . . . if you knew how to read you'd be all right.

BONO: Naw . . . naw . . . you mean if the nigger knew how to *drive* he'd be all right. Been fighting with them people about driving and ain't even got a license. Mr. Rand know you ain't got no driver's license?

TROY: Driving ain't nothing. All you do is point the truck where you want it to go. Driving ain't nothing.

BONO: Do Mr. Rand know you ain't got no driver's license? That's what I'm talking about. I ain't asked if driving was easy. I asked if Mr. Rand know you ain't got no driver's license.

TROY: He ain't got to know. The man ain't got to know my business. Time he find out, I have two or three driver's licenses.

LYONS [*going into his pocket*]:   Say, look here, Pop . . .

TROY: I knew it was coming. Didn't I tell you, Bono? I know what kind of "Look here, Pop" that was. The nigger fixing to ask me for some money. It's Friday night. It's my payday. All them rogues down there on the avenue . . . the ones that ain't in jail . . . and Lyons is hopping in his shoes to get down there with them.

LYONS: See, Pop . . . if you give somebody else a chance to talk sometime, you'd see that I was fixing to pay you back your ten dollars like I told you. Here . . . I told you I'd pay you when Bonnie got paid.

TROY: Naw . . . you go ahead and keep that ten dollars. Put in the bank. The next time you feel like you wanna come by here and ask me for something . . . you go on down there and get that.

LYONS: Here's your ten dollars, Pop. I told you I don't want you to give me nothing. I just wanted to borrow ten dollars.

TROY: Naw . . . you go on and keep that for the next time you want to ask me.

LYONS: Come on, Pop . . . here go your ten dollars.

ROSE: Why don't you go on and let the boy pay you back, Troy?

LYONS: Here you go, Rose. If you don't take it I'm gonna have to hear about it for the next six months.

He hands her the money.

ROSE: You can hand yours over here too, Troy.

TROY: You see this, Bono. You see how they do me.

BONO: Yeah, Lucille do me the same way.

GABRIEL is heard singing offstage. He enters.

GABRIEL: Better get ready for the Judgment! Better get ready for . . . Hey! . . . Hey! . . . There's Troy's boy!

LYONS: How are you doing, Uncle Gabe?

GABRIEL: Lyons . . . The King of the Jungle! Rose . . . hey, Rose. Got a flower for you.

He takes a rose from his pocket.

Picked it myself. That's the same rose like you is!

ROSE: That's right nice of you, Gabe.

LYONS: What you been doing, Uncle Gabe?

GABRIEL: Oh, I been chasing hellhounds and waiting on the time to tell St. Peter to open the gates.

LYONS: You been chasing hellhounds, huh? Well . . . you doing the right thing, Uncle Gabe. Somebody got to chase them.

GABRIEL: Oh, yeah . . . I know it. The devil's strong. The devil ain't no pushover. Hellhounds snipping at everybody's heels. But I got my trumpet waiting on the judgment time.

LYONS: Waiting on the Battle of Armageddon, huh?

GABRIEL: Ain't gonna be too much of a battle when God get to waving that Judgment sword. But the people's gonna have a hell of a time trying to get into heaven if them gates ain't open.

LYONS [*putting his arm around* GABRIEL]:   You hear this, Pop. Uncle Gabe, you all right!

GABRIEL [*laughing with* LYONS]:   Lyons! King of the Jungle.

ROSE: You gonna stay for supper, Gabe. Want me to fix you a plate?

GABRIEL: I'll take a sandwich, Rose. Don't want no plate. Just wanna eat with my hands. I'll take a sandwich.

ROSE: How about you, Lyons? You staying? Got some short ribs cooking.

LYONS: Naw, I won't eat nothing till after we finished playing.

Pause.

You ought to come down and listen to me play, Pop.

TROY: I don't like that Chinese music. All that noise.

ROSE: Go on in the house and wash up, Gabe . . . I'll fix you a sandwich.

GABRIEL [*to* LYONS, *as he exits*]:   Troy's mad at me.

LYONS: What you mad at Uncle Gabe for, Pop.

ROSE: He thinks Troy's mad at him cause he moved over to Miss Pearl's.

TROY: I ain't mad at the man. He can live where he want to live at.

LYONS: What he move over there for? Miss Pearl don't like nobody.

ROSE: She don't mind him none. She treats him real nice. She just don't allow all that singing.

TROY: She don't mind that rent he be paying . . . that's what she don't mind.

ROSE: Troy, I ain't going through that with you no more. He's over there cause he want to have his own place. He can come and go as he please.

TROY: Hell, he could come and go as he please here. I wasn't stopping him. I ain't put no rules on him.

ROSE: It ain't the same thing, Troy. And you know it.

GABRIEL *comes to the door.*

Now, that's the last I wanna hear about that. I don't wanna hear nothing else about Gabe and Miss Pearl. And next week . . .

GABRIEL: I'm ready for my sandwich, Rose.

ROSE: And next week . . . when that recruiter come from that school . . . I want you to sign that paper and go on and let Cory play football. Then that'll be the last I have to hear about that.

TROY [*to* ROSE *as she exits into the house*]:   I ain't thinking about Cory nothing.

LYONS: What . . . Cory got recruited? What school he going to?

TROY: That boy walking around here smelling his piss . . . thinking he's grown. Thinking he's gonna do what he want, irrespective of what I say. Look here, Bono . . . I left the Commissioner's office and went down to the A&P . . . that boy ain't working down there. He lying to me. Telling me he got his job back . . . telling me he working weekends . . . telling me he working after school . . . Mr. Stawicki tell me he ain't working down there at all!

LYONS: Cory just growing up. He's just busting at the seams trying to fill out your shoes.

TROY: I don't care what he's doing. When he get to the point where he wanna disobey me . . . then it's time for him to move on. Bono'll tell you that. I bet he ain't never disobeyed his daddy without paying the consequences.

BONO: I ain't never had a chance. My daddy came on through . . . but I ain't never knew him to see him . . . or what he had on his mind or where he went. Just moving on through. Searching out the New Land. That's what the old folks used to call it. See a fellow moving around from place to place . . . woman to woman . . . called it searching out the New Land. I can't say if he ever found it. I come along, didn't want no kids. Didn't know if I was gonna be in one place long enough to fix on them right as their daddy. I figured I was going searching too. As it turned out I been hooked up with Lucille near about as long as your daddy been with Rose. Going on sixteen years.

TROY: Sometimes I wish I hadn't known my daddy. He ain't cared nothing about no kids. A kid to him wasn't nothing. All he wanted was for you to learn how to walk so he could start you to working. When it come time for eating . . . he ate first. If there was anything left over, that's what you got. Man would sit down and eat two chickens and give you the wing.

LYONS: You ought to stop that, Pop. Everybody feed their kids. No matter how hard times is . . . everybody care about their kids. Make sure they have something to eat.

TROY: The only thing my daddy cared about was getting them bales of cotton in to Mr. Lubin. That's the only thing that mattered to him. Sometimes I used to wonder why he was living. Wonder why the devil hadn't come and got him. "Get them bales of cotton in to Mr. Lubin" and find out he owe him money . . .

LYONS: He should have just went on and left when he saw he couldn't get nowhere. That's what I would have done.

TROY: How he gonna leave with eleven kids? And where he gonna go? He ain't knew how to do nothing but farm. No, he was trapped and I think he knew it. But I'll say this for him . . . he felt a responsibility toward us. Maybe he ain't treated us the way I felt he should have . . . but without that responsibility he could have walked off and left us . . . made his own way.

BONO: A lot of them did. Back in those days what you talking about . . . they walk out their front door and just take on down one road or another and keep on walking.

LYONS: There you go! That's what I'm talking about.

BONO: Just keep on walking till you come to something else. Ain't you never heard of nobody having the walking blues? Well, that's what you call it when you just take off like that.

TROY: My daddy ain't had them walking blues! What you talking about? He stayed right there with his family. But he was just as evil as he could be. My mama couldn't stand him. Couldn't stand that evilness. She run off when I was about eight. She sneaked off one night after he had gone to sleep. Told me she was coming back for me. I ain't never seen her no more. All his women run off and left him. He wasn't good for nobody.

When my turn come to head out, I was fourteen and got to sniffing around Joe Canewell's daughter. Had us an old mule we called Greyboy. My daddy sent me out to do some plowing and I tied up Greyboy and went to fooling around with Joe Canewell's daughter. We done found us a nice little spot, got real cozy with each other. She about thirteen and we done figures we was grown anyway . . . so we down there enjoying ourselves . . . ain't thinking about nothing. We didn't know Greyboy had got loose and wandered back to the house and my daddy was looking for me. We down there by the creek enjoying ourselves when my daddy come up on us. Surprised us. He had them leather straps off the mule and commenced to whupping me like there was no tomorrow. I jumped up, mad and embarrassed. I was scared of my daddy. When he commenced to whupping on me . . . quite naturally I run to get out of the way.

Pause.

Now I thought he was mad cause I ain't done my work. But I see where he was chasing me off so he could have the goal for himself. When I see what the matter of it was, I lost all fear of my daddy. Right there is where I become a man . . . at fourteen years of age.

Pause.

Now it was my turn to run him off. I picked up them same reins that he had used on me. I picked up them reins and commenced to whupping on him. The gal jumped up and run off . . . and when my daddy turned to face me, I could see why the devil had never come to get him . . . cause he was the devil himself. I don't know what happened. When I woke up, I was laying right there by the creek, and Blue . . . this old dog we had . . . was licking my face. I thought I was blind. I couldn't see nothing. Both my eyes were swollen shut. I layed there and cried. I didn't know what I was gonna do. The only thing I knew was the time had come for me to leave my daddy's house. And right there the world suddenly got big. And it was a long time before I could cut it down to where I could handle it.

Part of that cutting down was when I got to the place where I could feel him kicking in my blood and knew that the only thing that separated us was the matter of a few years.

GABRIEL *enters from the house with a sandwich.*

LYONS: What you got there, Uncle Gabe?

GABRIEL: Got me a ham sandwich. Rose gave me a ham sandwich.

TROY: I don't know what happened to him. I done lost touch with everybody except Gabriel. But I hope he's dead. I hope he found some peace.

LYONS: That's a heavy story, Pop. I didn't know you left home when you was fourteen.

TROY: And didn't know nothing. The only part of the world I knew was the forty-two acres of Mr. Lubin's land. That's all I knew about life.

LYONS: Fourteen's kinda young to be out on your own. [*Phone rings.*] I don't even think I was ready to be out on my own at fourteen. I don't know what I would have done.

TROY: I got up from the creek and walked on down to Mobile. I was through with farming. Figured I could do better in the city. So I walked the two hundred miles to Mobile.

LYONS: Wait a minute . . . you ain't walked no two hundred miles, Pop. Ain't nobody gonna walk no two hundred miles. You talking about some walking there.

BONO: That's the only way you got anywhere back in them days.

LYONS:　Shhh. Damn if I wouldn't have hitched a ride with somebody!

TROY:　Who you gonna hitch it with? They ain't had no cars and things like they got now. We talking about 1918.

ROSE [*entering*]:　What you all out here getting into?

TROY [*to* ROSE]:　I'm telling Lyons how good he got it. He don't know nothing about this I'm talking.

ROSE:　Lyons, that was Bonnie on the phone. She say you supposed to pick her up.

LYONS:　Yeah, okay, Rose.

TROY:　I walked on down to Mobile and hitched up with some of them fellows that was heading this way. Got up here and found out . . . not only couldn't you get a job . . . you couldn't find no place to live. I thought I was in freedom. Shhh. Colored folks living down there on the riverbanks in whatever kind of shelter they could find for themselves. Right down there under the Brady Street Bridge. Living in shacks made of sticks and tarpaper. Messed around there and went from bad to worse. Started stealing. First it was food. Then I figured, hell, if I steal money I can buy me some food. Buy me some shoes too! One thing led to another. Met your mama. I was young and anxious to be a man. Met your mama and had you. What I do that for? Now I got to worry about feeding you and her. Got to steal three times as much. Went out one day looking for somebody to rob . . . that's what I was, a robber. I'll tell you the truth. I'm ashamed of it today. But it's the truth. Went to rob this fellow . . . pulled out my knife . . . and he pulled out a gun. Shot me in the chest. It felt just like somebody had taken a hot branding iron and laid it on me. When he shot me I jumped at him with my knife. They told me I killed him and they put me in the penitentiary and locked me up for fifteen years. That's where I met Bono. That's where I learned how to play baseball. Got out that place and your mama had taken you and went on to make life without me. Fifteen years was a long time for her to wait. But that fifteen years cured me of that robbing stuff. Rose'll tell you. She asked me when I met her if I had gotten all that foolishness out of my system. And I told her, "Baby, it's you and baseball all what count with me." You hear me, Bono? I meant it too. She say, "Which one comes first?" I told her, "Baby, ain't no doubt it's baseball . . . but you stick and get old with me and we'll both outlive this baseball." Am I right, Rose? And it's true.

ROSE:　Man, hush your mouth. You ain't said no such thing. Talking about, "Baby, you know you'll always be number one with me." That's what you was talking.

TROY:　You hear that, Bono. That's why I love her.

BONO:　Rose'll keep you straight. You get off the track, she'll straighten you up.

ROSE:　Lyons, you better get on up and get Bonnie. She waiting on you.

LYONS [*gets up to go*]:　Hey, Pop, why don't you come on down to the Grill and hear me play?

TROY:　I ain't going down there. I'm too old to be sitting around in them clubs.

BONO:　You got to be good to play down at the Grill.

LYONS:　Come on, Pop . . .

TROY:　I got to get up in the morning.

LYONS:　You ain't got to stay long.

TROY: Naw, I'm gonna get my supper and go on to bed.

LYONS: Well, I got to go. I'll see you again.

TROY: Don't you come around my house on my payday.

ROSE: Pick up the phone and let somebody know you coming. And bring Bonnie with you. You know I'm always glad to see her.

LYONS: Yeah, I'll do that, Rose. You take care now. See you, Pop. See you, Mr. Bono. See you, Uncle Gabe.

GABRIEL: Lyons! King of the Jungle!

LYONS exits.

TROY: Is supper ready, woman? Me and you got some business to take care of. I'm gonna tear it up too.

ROSE: Troy, I done told you now!

TROY [*puts his arm around* BONO]:   Aw hell, woman . . . this is Bono. Bono like family. I done known this nigger since . . . how long I done know you?

BONO: It's been a long time.

TROY: I done known this nigger since Skippy was a pup. Me and him done been through some times.

BONO: You sure right about that.

TROY: Hell, I done know him longer than I known you. And we still standing shoulder to shoulder. Hey, look here, Bono . . . a man can't ask for no more than that.

Drinks to him.

I love you, nigger.

BONO: Hell, I love you too . . . but I got to get home see my woman. You got yours in hand. I got to go get mine.

BONO *starts to exit as* CORY *enters the yard, dressed in his football uniform. He gives* TROY *a hard, uncompromising look.*

What you do that for, Pop?

He throws his helmet down in the direction of TROY.

ROSE: What's the matter? Cory . . . what's the matter?

CORY: Papa done went up to the school and told Coach Zellman I can't play football no more. Wouldn't even let me play the game. Told him to tell the recruiter not to come.

ROSE: Troy . . .

TROY: What you Troying me for. Yeah, I did it. And the boy know why I did it.

CORY: Why you wanna do that to me? That was the one chance I had.

ROSE: Ain't nothing wrong with Cory playing football, Troy.

TROY: The boy lied to me. I told the nigger if he wanna play football . . . to keep up his chores and hold down that job at the A&P. That was the conditions. Stopped down there to see Mr. Stawicki . . .

CORY: I can't work after school during the football season, Pop! I tried to tell you that Mr. Stawicki's holding my job for me. You don't never want to listen to nobody. And then you wanna go and do this to me!

TROY: I ain't done nothing to you. You done it to yourself.
CORY: Just cause you didn't have a chance! You just scared I'm gonna be better than you, that's all.
TROY: Come here.
ROSE: Troy . . .

CORY *reluctantly crosses over to* TROY.

TROY: All right! See. You done made a mistake.
CORY: I didn't even do nothing!
TROY: I'm gonna tell you what your mistake was. See . . . you swung at the ball and didn't hit it. That's strike one. See, you in the batter's box now. You swung and you missed. That's strike one. Don't you strike out!

Lights fade to black.

ACT II

Scene 1

The following morning. CORY *is at the tree hitting the ball with the bat. He tries to mimic* TROY, *but his swing is awkward, less sure.* ROSE *enters from the house.*

ROSE: Cory, I want you to help me with this cupboard.
CORY: I ain't quitting the team. I don't care what Poppa say.
ROSE: I'll talk to him when he gets back. He had to go see about your Uncle Gabe. The police done arrested him. Say he was disturbing the peace. He'll be back directly. Come on in here and help me clean out the top of this cupboard.

CORY *exits into the house.* ROSE *sees* TROY *and* BONO *coming down the alley.*

Troy . . . what they say down there?
TROY: Ain't said nothing. I give them fifty dollars and they let him go. I'll talk to you about it. Where's Cory?
ROSE: He's in there helping me clean out these cupboards.
TROY: Tell him to get his butt out here.

TROY *and* BONO *go over to the pile of wood.* BONO *picks up the saw and begins sawing.*

TROY [*to* BONO]:   All they want is the money. That makes six or seven times I done went down there and got him. See me coming they stick out their *hands*.
BONO: Yeah. I know what you mean. That's all they care about . . . that money. They don't care about what's right.

Pause.

Nigger, why you got to go and get some hard wood? You ain't doing nothing but building a little old fence. Get you some soft pine wood. That's all you need.
TROY: I know what I'm doing. This is outside wood. You put pine wood inside the house. Pine wood is inside wood. This here is outside wood. Now you tell me where the fence is gonna be?

BONO: You don't need this wood. You can put it up with pine wood and it'll stand as long as you gonna be here looking at it.

TROY: How you know how long I'm gonna be here, nigger? Hell, I might just live forever. Live longer than old man Horsely.

BONO: That's what Magee used to say.

TROY: Magee's a damn fool. Now you tell me who you ever heard of gonna pull their own teeth with a pair of rusty pliers.

BONO: The old folks . . . my granddaddy used to pull his teeth with pliers. They ain't had no dentists for the colored folks back then.

TROY: Get clean pliers! You understand? Clean pliers! Sterilize them! Besides we ain't living back then. All Magee had to do was walk over to Doc Goldblum's.

BONO: I see where you and that Tallahassee gal . . . that Alberta . . . I see where you all done got tight.

TROY: What you mean "got tight"?

BONO: I see where you be laughing and joking with her all the time.

TROY: I laughs and jokes with all of them, Bono. You know me.

BONO: That ain't the kind of laughing and joking I'm talking about.

CORY enters from the house.

CORY: How you doing, Mr. Bono?

TROY: Cory? Get that saw from Bono and cut some wood. He talking about the wood's too hard to cut. Stand back there, Jim, and let that young boy show you how it's done.

BONO: He's sure welcome to it.

CORY takes the saw and begins to cut the wood.

Whew-e-e! Look at that. Big old strong boy. Look like Joe Louis. Hell, must be getting old the way I'm watching that boy whip through that wood.

CORY: I don't see why Mama want a fence around the yard noways.

TROY: Damn if I know either. What the hell she keeping out with it? She ain't got nothing nobody want.

BONO: Some people build fences to keep people out . . . and other people build fences to keep people in. Rose wants to hold on to you all. She loves you.

TROY: Hell, nigger, I don't need nobody to tell me my wife loves me, Cory . . . go on in the house and see if you can find that other saw.

CORY: Where's it at?

TROY: I said find it! Look for it till you find it!

CORY exits into the house.

What's that supposed to mean? Wanna keep us in?

BONO: Troy . . . I done known you seem like damn near my whole life. You and Rose both. I done know both of you all for a long time. I remember when you met Rose. When you was hitting them baseball out the park. A lot of them old gals was after you then. You had the pick of the litter. When you picked Rose, I was happy for you. That was the first time I knew you had any sense. I said . . . My man Troy knows what he's doing . . . I'm gonna follow this nigger . . . he might take me somewhere. I been following you too. I done learned a whole heap of things about life watching you. I done learned how to tell where the shit lies. How to tell it from the alfalfa. You done learned me a lot of things. You showed me how to not make the same mistakes . . . to take life as it comes along and keep putting one foot in front of the other.

Pause.

Rose a good woman, Troy.

TROY: Hell, nigger, I know she a good woman. I been married to her for eighteen years. What you got on your mind, Bono?

BONO: I just say she a good woman. Just like I say anything. I ain't got to have nothing on my mind.

TROY: You just gonna say she a good woman and leave it hanging out there like that? Why you telling me she a good woman?

BONO: She loves you, Troy. Rose loves you.

TROY: You saying I don't measure up. That's what you trying to say. I don't measure up cause I'm seeing this other gal. I know what you trying to say.

BONO: I know what Rose means to you, Troy. I'm just trying to say I don't want to see you mess up.

TROY: Yeah, I appreciate that, Bono. If you was messing around on Lucille I'd be telling you the same thing.

BONO: Well, that's all I got to say. I just say that because I love you both.

TROY: Hell, you know me . . . I wasn't out there looking for nothing. You can't find a better woman than Rose. I know that. But seems like this woman just stuck onto me where I can't shake her loose. I done wrestled with it, tried to throw her off me . . . but she just stuck on tighter. Now she's stuck on for good.

BONO: You's in control . . . that's what you tell me all the time. You responsible for what you do.

TROY: I ain't ducking the responsibility of it. As long as it sets right in my heart . . . then I'm okay. Cause that's all I listen to. It'll tell me right from wrong every time. And I ain't talking about doing Rose no bad turn. I love Rose. She done carried me a long ways and I love and respect her for that.

BONO: I know you do. That's why I don't want to see you hurt her. But what you gonna do when she find out? What you got then? If you try and juggle both of them . . . sooner or later you gonna drop one of them. That's common sense.

TROY: Yeah, I hear what you saying, Bono. I been trying to figure a way to work it out.

BONO: Work it out right, Troy. I don't want to be getting all up between you and Rose's business . . . but work it so it come out right.

TROY: Ah hell, I get all up between you and Lucille's business. When you gonna get that woman that refrigerator she been wanting? Don't tell me you ain't got no money now. I know who your banker is. Mellon don't need that money bad as Lucille want that refrigerator. I'll tell you that.

BONO: Tell you what I'll do . . . when you finish building this fence for Rose . . . I'll buy Lucille that refrigerator.

TROY: You done stuck your foot in your mouth now!

TROY *grabs up a board and begins to saw.* BONO *starts to walk out the yard.*

Hey, nigger . . . where you going?

BONO: I'm going home. I know you don't expect me to help you now. I'm protecting my money. I wanna see you put that fence up by yourself. That's what I want to see. You'll be here another six months without me.

TROY: Nigger, you ain't right.

BONO: When it comes to my money . . . I'm right as fireworks on the Fourth of July.

TROY: All right, we gonna see now. You better get out your bankbook.

BONO *exits, and* TROY *continues to work.* ROSE *enters from the house.*

ROSE: What they say down there? What's happening with Gabe?

TROY: I went down there and got him out. Cost me fifty dollars. Say he was disturbing the peace. Judge set up a hearing for him in three weeks. Say to show cause why he shouldn't be recommitted.

ROSE: What was he doing that cause them to arrest him?

TROY: Some kids was teasing him and he run them off home. Say he was howling and carrying on. Some folks seen him and called the police. That's all it was.

ROSE: Well, what's you say? What'd you tell the judge?

TROY: Told him I'd look after him. It didn't make no sense to recommit the man. He stuck out his big greasy palm and told me to give him fifty dollars and take him on home.

ROSE: Where's he at now? Where'd he go off to?

TROY: He's gone on about his business. He don't need nobody to hold his hand.

ROSE: Well, I don't know. Seem like that would be the best place for him if they did put him into the hospital. I know what you're gonna say. But that's what I think would be best.

TROY: The man done had his life ruined fighting for what? And they wanna take and lock him up. Let him be free. He don't bother nobody.

ROSE: Well, everybody got their own way of looking at it I guess. Come on and get your lunch. I got a bowl of lima beans and some cornbread in the oven. Come on get something to eat. Ain't no sense you fretting over Gabe.

ROSE *turns to go into the house.*

TROY: Rose . . . got something to tell you.

ROSE: Well, come on . . . wait till I get this food on the table.

TROY: Rose!

She stops and turns around.

I don't know how to say this.

Pause.

I can't explain it none. It just sort of grows on you till it gets out of hand. It starts out like a little bush . . . and the next thing you know it's a whole forest.

ROSE: Troy . . . what is you talking about?

TROY: I'm talking, woman, let me talk. I'm trying to find a way to tell you
. . . I'm gonna be a daddy. I'm gonna be somebody's daddy.

ROSE: Troy . . . you're not telling me this? You're gonna be . . . what?

TROY: Rose . . . now . . . see . . .

ROSE: You telling me you gonna be somebody's daddy? You telling your
wife this?

GABRIEL *enters from the street. He carries a rose in his hand.*

GABRIEL: Hey, Troy! Hey, Rose!

ROSE: I have to wait eighteen years to hear something like this.

GABRIEL: Hey, Rose . . . I got a flower for you.

He hands it to her.

That's a rose. Same rose like you is.

ROSE: Thanks, Gabe.

GABRIEL: Troy, you ain't mad at me is you? Them bad mens come and put
me away. You ain't mad at me is you?

TROY: Naw, Gabe, I ain't mad at you.

ROSE: Eighteen years and you wanna come with this.

GABRIEL [*takes a quarter out of his pocket*]:   See what I got? Got a brand new
quarter.

TROY: Rose . . . it's just . . .

ROSE: Ain't nothing you can say, Troy. Ain't no way of explaining that.

GABRIEL: Fellow that give me this quarter had a whole mess of them. I'm
gonna keep this quarter till it stop shining.

ROSE: Gabe, go on in the house there. I got some watermelon in the
frigidaire. Go on and get you a piece.

GABRIEL: Say, Rose . . . you know I was chasing hellhounds and them bad
mens come and get me and take me away. Troy helped me. He come down
there and told them they better let me go before he beat them up. Yeah, he did!

ROSE: You go on and get you a piece of watermelon, Gabe. Them bad mens
is gone now.

GABRIEL: Okay, Rose . . . gonna get me some watermelon. The kind with
the stripes on it.

GABRIEL *exits into the house.*

ROSE: Why, Troy? Why? After all these years to come dragging this in to
me now. It don't make no sense at your age. I could have expected this ten or
fifteen years ago, but not now.

TROY: Age ain't got nothing to do with it, Rose.

ROSE: I done tried to be everything a wife should be. Everything a wife
could be. Been married eighteen years and I got to live to see the day you tell
me you been seeing another woman and done fathered a child by her. And you
know I ain't never wanted no half nothing in my family. My whole family is
half. Everybody got different fathers and mothers . . . my two sisters and my
brother. Can't hardly tell who's who. Can't never sit down and talk about Papa
and Mama. It's your papa and your mama and my papa and my mama . . .

TROY: Rose . . . stop it now.

ROSE: I ain't never wanted that for none of my children. And now you wanna drag your behind in here and tell me something like this.

TROY: You ought to know. It's time for you to know.

ROSE: Well, I don't want to know, goddamn it!

TROY: I can't just make it go away. It's done now. I can't wish the circumstance of the thing away.

ROSE: And you don't want to either. Maybe you want to wish me and my boy away. Maybe that's what you want? Well, you can't wish us away. I've got eighteen years of my life invested in you. You ought to have stayed upstairs in my bed where you belong.

TROY: Rose . . . now listen to me . . . we can get a handle on this thing. We can talk this out . . . come to an understanding.

ROSE: All of a sudden it's "we." Where was "we" at when you was down there rolling around with some godforsaken woman? "We" should have come to an understanding before you started making a damn fool of yourself. You're a day late and dollar short when it comes to an understanding with me.

TROY: It's just . . . She gives me a different idea . . . a different understanding about myself. I can step out of this house and get away from the pressures and problems . . . be a different man. I ain't got to wonder how I'm gonna pay the bills or get the roof fixed. I can just be a part of myself that I ain't never been.

ROSE: What I want to know . . . is do you plan to continue seeing her. That's all you can say to me.

TROY: I can sit up in her house and laugh. Do you understand what I'm saying. I can laugh out loud . . . and it feels good. It reaches all the way down to the bottom of my shoes.

Pause.

Rose, I can't give that up.

ROSE: Maybe you ought to go on and stay down there with her . . . if she's a better woman than me.

TROY: It ain't about nobody being a better woman or nothing. Rose, you ain't the blame. A man couldn't ask for no woman to be a better wife than you've been. I'm responsible for it. I done locked myself into a pattern trying to take care of you all that I forgot about myself.

ROSE: What the hell was I there for? That was my job, not somebody else's.

TROY: Rose, I done tried all my life to live decent . . . to live a clean . . . hard . . . useful life. I tried to be a good husband to you. In every way I knew how. Maybe I come into the world backwards, I don't know. But . . . you born with two strikes on you before you come to the plate. You got to guard it closely . . . always looking for the curve ball on the inside corner. You can't afford to let none get past you. You can't afford a call strike. If you going down . . . you going down swinging. Everything lined up against you. What you gonna do. I fooled them, Rose. I bunted. When I found you and Cory and a halfway decent job . . . I was safe. Couldn't nothing touch me. I wasn't going back to the penitentiary. I wasn't gonna lay in the streets with a bottle of wine. I was safe. I had me a family. A job. I wasn't gonna get that last strike. I was on first looking for one of them boys to knock me in. To get me home.

ROSE: You should have stayed in my bed, Troy.

TROY: Then when I saw that gal . . . she firmed up my backbone. And I got to thinking that if I tried . . . I just might be able to steal second. Do you understand after eighteen years I wanted to steal second.

ROSE: You should have held me tight. You should have grabbed me and held on.

TROY: I stood on first base for eighteen years and I thought . . . well, god-damn it . . . go on for it!

ROSE: We're not talking about baseball! We're talking about you going off to lay in bed with another woman . . . and then bring it home to me. That's what we're talking about. We ain't talking about no baseball.

TROY: Rose, you're not listening to me. I'm trying the best I can to ex-plain it to you. It's not easy for me to admit that I been standing in the same place for eighteen years.

ROSE: I been standing with you! I been right here with you, Troy. I got a life too. I gave eighteen years of my life to stand in the same spot with you. Don't you think I ever wanted other things? Don't you think I had dreams and hopes? What about my life? What about me. Don't you think it ever crossed my mind to want to know other men? That I wanted to lay up somewhere and forget about my responsibilities? That I wanted someone to make me laugh so I could feel good? You not the only one who's got wants and needs. But I held on to you, Troy. I took all my feelings, my wants and needs, my dreams . . . and I buried them inside you. I planted a seed and watched and prayed over it. I planted myself inside you and waited to bloom. And it didn't take me no eigh-teen years to find out the soil was hard and rocky and it wasn't never gonna bloom.

But I held on to you, Troy. I held you tighter. You was my husband. I owed you everything I had. Every part of me I could find to give you. And upstairs in that room . . . with the darkness falling in on me . . . I gave everything I had to try and erase the doubt that you wasn't the finest man in the world. And wherever you was going . . . I wanted to be there with you. Cause you was my husband. Cause that's the only way I was gonna survive as your wife. You always talking about what you give . . . and what you don't have to give. But you take too. You take . . . and don't even know nobody's giving!

ROSE *turns to exit into the house.* TROY *grabs her arm.*

TROY: You say I take and don't give!

ROSE: Troy! You're hurting me!

TROY: You say I take and don't give.

ROSE: Troy . . . you're hurting my arm! Let go!

TROY: I done give you everything I got. Don't you tell that lie on me.

ROSE: Troy!

TROY: Don't you tell that lie on me!

CORY *enters from the house.*

CORY: Mama!

ROSE: Troy. You're hurting me.

TROY: Don't you tell me about no taking and giving.

CORY *comes up behind* TROY *and grabs him.* TROY, *surprised, is thrown off balance just as* CORY *throws a glancing blow that catches him in the chest and knocks him down.* TROY *is stunned, as is* CORY.

ROSE: Troy. Troy. No!

TROY *gets to his feet and starts at* CORY.

Troy . . . no. Please! Troy!

ROSE *pulls on* TROY *to hold him back.* TROY *stops himself.*

TROY [*to* CORY]:   All right. That's strike two. You stay away from around me, boy. Don't you strike out. You living with a full count. Don't you strike out.

TROY *exits out the yard as the lights go down.*

Scene 2

It is six months later, early afternoon. TROY *enters from the house and starts to exit the yard.* ROSE *enters from the house.*

ROSE: Troy, I want to talk to you.

TROY: All of a sudden, after all this time, you want to talk to me, huh? You ain't wanted to talk to me for months. You ain't wanted to talk to me last night. You ain't wanted no part of me then. What you wanna talk to me about now?

ROSE: Tomorrow's Friday.

TROY: I know what day tomorrow is. You think I don't know tomorrow's Friday? My whole life I ain't done nothing but look to see Friday coming and you got to tell me it's Friday.

ROSE: I want to know if you're coming home.

TROY: I always come home, Rose. You know that. There ain't never been a night I ain't come home.

ROSE: That ain't what I mean . . . and you know it. I want to know if you're coming straight home after work.

TROY: I figure I'd cash my check . . . hang out at Taylors' with the boys . . . maybe play a game of checkers . . .

ROSE: Troy, I can't live like this. I won't live like this. You livin' on borrowed time with me. It's been going on six months now you ain't been coming home.

TROY: I be here every night. Every night of the year. That's 365 days.

ROSE: I want you to come home tomorrow after work.

TROY: Rose . . . I don't mess up my pay. You know that now. I take my pay and I give it to you. I don't have no money but what you give me back. I just want to have a little time to myself . . . a little time to enjoy life.

ROSE: What about me? When's my time to enjoy life?

TROY: I don't know what to tell you, Rose. I'm doing the best I can.

ROSE: You ain't been home from work but time enough to change your clothes and run out . . . and you wanna call that the best you can do?

TROY: I'm going over to the hospital to see Alberta. She went into the hospital this afternoon. Look like she might have the baby early. I won't be gone long.

ROSE: Well, you ought to know. They went over to Miss Pearl's and got Gabe today. She said you told them to go ahead and lock him up.

TROY: I ain't said no such thing. Whoever told you that is telling a lie. Pearl ain't doing nothing but telling a big fat lie.

ROSE: She ain't had to tell me. I read it on the papers.

TROY: I ain't told them nothing of the kind.

ROSE: I saw it right there on the papers.

TROY: What it say, huh?

ROSE: It said you told them to take him.

TROY: Then they screwed that up, just the way they screw up everything. I ain't worried about what they got on the paper.

ROSE: Say the government send part of his check to the hospital and the other part to you.

TROY: I ain't got nothing to do with that if that's the way it works. I ain't made up the rules about how it work.

ROSE: You did Gabe just like you did Cory. You wouldn't sign the paper for Cory . . . but you signed for Gabe. You signed that paper.

The telephone is heard ringing inside the house.

TROY: I told you I ain't signed nothing, woman! The only thing I signed was the release form. Hell, I can't read, I don't know what they had on that paper! I ain't signed nothing about sending Gabe away.

ROSE: I said send him to the hospital . . . you said let him be free . . . now you done went down there and signed him to the hospital for half his money. You went back on yourself, Troy. You gonna have to answer for that.

TROY: See now . . . you been over there talking to Miss Pearl. She done got mad cause she ain't getting Gabe's rent money. That's all it is. She's liable to say anything.

ROSE: Troy, I seen where you signed the paper.

TROY: You ain't seen nothing I signed. What she doing got papers on my brother anyway? Miss Pearl telling a big fat lie. And I'm gonna tell her about it too! You ain't seen nothing I signed. Say . . . you ain't seen nothing I signed.

ROSE *exits into the house to answer the telephone. Presently she returns.*

ROSE: Troy . . . that was the hospital. Alberta had the baby.

TROY: What she have? What is it?

ROSE: It's a girl.

TROY: I better get on down to the hospital to see her.

ROSE: Troy . . .

TROY: Rose . . . I got to go see her now. That's only right . . . what's the matter . . . the baby's all right, ain't it?

ROSE: Alberta died having the baby.

TROY: Died . . . you say she's dead? Alberta's dead?

ROSE: They said they done all they could. They couldn't do nothing for her.

TROY: The baby? How's the baby?

ROSE: They say it's healthy. I wonder who's gonna bury her.

TROY: She had family, Rose. She wasn't living in the world by herself.

ROSE: I know she wasn't living in the world by herself.

TROY: Next thing you gonna want to know if she had any insurance.

ROSE: Troy, you ain't got to talk like that.

TROY: That's the first thing that jumped out your mouth. "Who's gonna bury her?" Like I'm fixing to take on that task for myself.

ROSE: I am your wife. Don't push me away.

TROY: I ain't pushing nobody away. Just give me some space. That's all. Just give me some room to breath.

ROSE exits into the house. TROY walks about the yard.

TROY [*with a quiet rage that threatens to consume him*]: All right . . . Mr. Death. See now . . . I'm gonna tell you what I'm gonna do. I'm gonna take and build me a fence around this yard. See? I'm gonna build me a fence around what belongs to me. And then I want you to stay on the other side. See? You stay over there until you're ready for me. Then you come on. Bring your army. Bring your sickle. Bring your wrestling clothes. I ain't gonna fall down on my vigilance this time. You ain't gonna sneak up on me no more. When you ready for me . . . when the top of your list say Troy Maxson . . . that's when you come around here. You come up and knock on the front door. Ain't nobody else got nothing to do with this. This is between you and me. Man to man. You stay on the other side of that fence until you ready for me. Then you come up and knock on the front door. Anytime you want. I'll be ready for you.

The lights go down to black.

Scene 3

The lights come up on the porch. It is late evening three days later. ROSE sits listening to the ball game waiting for TROY. The final out of the game is made and ROSE switches off the radio. TROY enters the yard carrying an infant wrapped in blankets. He stands back from the house and calls.

ROSE enters and stands on the porch. There is a long, awkward silence, the weight of which grows heavier with each passing second.

TROY: Rose . . . I'm standing here with my daughter in my arms. She ain't but a wee bittie little old thing. She don't know nothing about grown-ups' business. She innocent . . . and she ain't got no mama.

ROSE: What you telling me for, Troy?

She turns and exits into the house.

TROY: Well . . . I guess we'll just sit out here on the porch.

He sits down on the porch. There is an awkward indelicateness about the way he handles the baby. His largeness engulfs and seems to swallow it. He speaks loud enough for ROSE to hear.

A man's got to do what's right for him. I ain't sorry for nothing I done. It felt right in my heart.

To the baby.

What you smiling at? Your daddy's a big man. Got these great big old hands. But sometimes he's scared. And right now your daddy's scared cause we sitting out here and ain't got no home. Oh, I been homeless before. I ain't had no little baby with me. But I been homeless. You just be out on the road by your lonesome and you see one of them trains coming and you just kinda go like this . . .

He sings as a lullaby.

Please, Mr. Engineer let a man ride the line
Please, Mr. Engineer let a man ride the line
I ain't got no ticket please let me ride the blinds

ROSE *enters from the house.* TROY *hearing her steps behind him, stands and faces her.*

She's my daughter, Rose. My own flesh and blood. I can't deny her no more than I can deny them boys.

Pause.

You and them boys is my family. You and them boys and this child is all I got in the world. So I guess what I'm saying is . . . I'd appreciate it if you'd help me take care of her.

ROSE: Okay, Troy . . . you're right. I'll take care of your baby for you . . . cause . . . like you say . . . she's innocent . . . and you can't visit the sins of the father upon the child. A motherless child has got a hard time.

She takes the baby from him.

From right now . . . this child got a mother. But you a womanless man.

ROSE *turns and exits into the house with the baby. Lights go down to black.*

Scene 4

It is two months later. LYONS *enters from the street. He knocks on the door and calls.*

LYONS: Hey, Rose! [*Pause.*] Rose!
ROSE [*from inside the house*]:   Stop that yelling. You gonna wake up Raynell. I just got her to sleep.
LYONS: I just stopped by to pay Papa this twenty dollars I owe him. Where's Papa at?
ROSE: He should be here in a minute. I'm getting ready to go down to the church. Sit down and wait on him.
LYONS: I got to go pick up Bonnie over her mother's house.
ROSE: Well, sit it down there on the table. He'll get it.
LYONS [*enters the house and sets the money on the table*]:   Tell Papa I said thanks. I'll see you again.
ROSE: All right, Lyons. We'll see you.

LYONS *starts to exit as* CORY *enters.*

CORY: Hey, Lyons.

LYONS: What's happening, Cory. Say man, I'm sorry I missed your graduation. You know I had a gig and couldn't get away. Otherwise, I would have been there, man. So what you doing?

CORY: I'm trying to find a job.

LYONS: Yeah I know how that go, man. It's rough out here. Jobs are scarce.

CORY: Yeah, I know.

LYONS: Look here, I got to run. Talk to Papa . . . he know some people. He'll be able to help get you a job. Talk to him . . . see what he say.

CORY: Yeah . . . all right, Lyons.

LYONS: You take care. I'll talk to you soon. We'll find some time to talk.

LYONS *exits the yard.* CORY *wanders over to the tree, picks up the bat, and assumes a batting stance. He studies an imaginary pitcher and swings. Dissatisfied with the result, he tries again.* TROY *enters. They eye each other for a beat.* CORY *puts the bat down and exits the yard.* TROY *starts into the house as* ROSE *exits with* RAYNELL. *She is carrying a cake.*

TROY: I'm coming in and everybody's going out.

ROSE: I'm taking the cake down to the church for the bake sale. Lyons was by to see you. He stopped by to pay you your twenty dollars. It's laying in there on the table.

TROY [*going into his pocket*]: Well . . . here go this money.

ROSE: Put it in there on the table, Troy. I'll get it.

TROY: What time you coming back?

ROSE: Ain't no use in you studying me. It don't matter what time I come back.

TROY: I just asked you a question, woman. What's the matter . . . can't I ask you a question?

ROSE: Troy, I don't want to go into it. Your dinner's in there on the stove. All you got to do is heat it up. And don't you be eating the rest of them cakes in there. I'm coming back for them. We having a bake sale at the church tomorrow.

ROSE *exits the yard.* TROY *sits down on the steps, takes a pint bottle from his pocket, opens it, and drinks. He begins to sing.*

TROY: Hear it ring! Hear it ring!
Had an old dog his name was Blue
You know Blue was a mighty true
You know Blue was a good old dog
Blue trees a possum in a hollow log
You know from that he was a good old dog

BONO *enters the yard.*

BONO: Hey, Troy.

TROY: Hey, what's happening, Bono?

BONO: I just thought I'd stop by to see you.

TROY: What you stop by and see me for? You ain't stopped by in a month of Sundays. Hell, I must owe you money or something.

BONO: Since you got your promotion I can't keep up with you. Used to see you every day. Now I don't even know what route you working.

TROY: They keep switching me around. Got me out in Greentree now . . . hauling white folks' garbage.

BONO: Greentree, hugh? You lucky, at least you ain't got to be lifting them barrels. Damn if they ain't getting heavier. I'm gonna put in my two years and call it quits.

TROY: I'm thinking about retiring myself.

BONO: You got it easy. You can *drive* for another five years.

TROY: It ain't the same, Bono. It ain't like working the back of the truck. Ain't got nobody to talk to . . . feel like you working by yourself. Naw, I'm thinking about retiring. How's Lucille?

BONO: She all right. Her arthritis get to acting up on her sometime. Saw Rose on my way in. She going down to the church, huh?

TROY: Yeah, she took up going down there. All them preachers looking for somebody to fatten their pockets.

Pause.

Got some gin here.

BONO: Naw, thanks. I just stopped by to say hello.

TROY: Hell, nigger . . . you can take a drink. I ain't never known you to say no to a drink. You ain't got to work tomorrow.

BONO: I just stopped by. I'm fixing to go over to Skinner's. We got us a domino game going over his house every Friday.

TROY: Nigger, you can't play no dominoes. I used to whup you four games out of five.

BONO: Well, that learned me. I'm getting better.

TROY: Yeah? Well, that's all right.

BONO: Look here . . . I got to be getting on. Stop by sometime, huh?

TROY: Yeah, I'll do that, Bono. Lucille told Rose you bought her a new refrigerator.

BONO: Yeah, Rose told Lucille you had finally built your fence . . . so I figured we'd call it even.

TROY: I knew you would.

BONO: Yeah . . . okay. I'll be talking to you.

TROY: Yeah, take care, Bono. Good to see you. I'm gonna stop over.

BONO: Yeah. Okay, Troy.

BONO *exits.* TROY *drinks from the bottle.*

TROY: Old Blue died and I dig his grave
Let him down with a golden chain
Every night when I hear old Blue bark
I know Blue treed a possum in Noah's Ark.
Hear it ring! Hear it ring!

CORY *enters the yard. They eye each other for a beat.* TROY *is sitting in the middle of the steps.* CORY *walks over.*

CORY: I got to get by.

TROY: Say what? What's you say?

CORY: You in my way. I got to get by.

TROY: You got to get by where? This is my house. Bought and paid for. In full. Took me fifteen years. And if you wanna go in my house and I'm sitting on the steps . . . you say excuse me. Like your mama taught you.

CORY: Come on, Pop . . . I got to get by.

CORY starts to maneuver his way past TROY. TROY *grabs his leg and shoves him back.*

TROY: You just gonna walk over top of me?

CORY: I live here, too!

TROY [*advancing toward him*]:   You just gonna walk over top of me in my own house?

CORY: I ain't scared of you.

TROY: I ain't asked if you was scared of me. I asked you if you was fixing to walk over top of me in my own house? That's the question. You ain't gonna say excuse me? You just gonna walk over top of me?

CORY: If you wanna put it like that.

TROY: How else am I gonna put it?

CORY: I was walking by you to go into the house cause you sitting on the steps drunk, singing to yourself. You can put it like that.

TROY: Without saying excuse me???

CORY doesn't respond.

I asked you a question. Without saying excuse me???

CORY: I ain't got to say excuse me to you. You don't count around here no more.

TROY: Oh, I see . . . I don't count around here no more. You ain't got to say excuse me to your daddy. All of a sudden you done got so grown that your daddy don't count around here no more . . . Around here in his own house and yard that he done paid for with the sweat of his brow. You done got so grown to where you gonna take over. You gonna take over my house. Is that right? You gonna wear my pants. You gonna go in there and stretch out on my bed. You ain't got to say excuse me cause I don't count around here no more. Is that right?

CORY: That's right. You always talking this dumb stuff. Now, why don't you just get out my way.

TROY: I guess you got someplace to sleep and something to put in your belly. You got that, huh? You got that? That's what you need. You got that, huh?

CORY: You don't know what I got. You ain't got to worry about what I got.

TROY: You right! You one hundred percent right! I done spent the last seventeen years worrying about what you got. Now it's your turn, see? I'll tell you what to do. You grown . . . we done established that. You a man. Now, let's see you act like one. Turn your behind around and walk out this yard. And when you get out there in the alley . . . you can forget about this house. See? 'Cause this is my house. You go on and be a man and get your own house.

You can forget about this. 'Cause this is mine. You go on and get yours 'cause I'm through with doing for you.

CORY: You talking about what you did for me . . . what'd you ever give me?

TROY: Them feet and bones! That pumping heart, nigger! I give you more than anybody else is ever gonna give you.

CORY: You ain't never gave me nothing! You ain't never done anything but hold me back. Afraid I was gonna be better than you. All you ever did was try and make me scared of you. I used to tremble every time you called my name. Every time I heard your footsteps in the house. Wondering all the time . . . what's Papa gonna say if I do this? . . . What's he gonna say if I do that? . . . What's Papa gonna say if I turn on the radio? And Mama, too . . . she tries . . . but she's scared of you.

TROY: You leave your mama out of this. She ain't got nothing to do with this.

CORY: I don't know how she stand you . . . after what you did to her.

TROY: I told you to leave your mama out of this!

He advances toward CORY.

CORY: What you gonna do . . . give me a whupping? You can't whip me no more. You're too old. You just an old man.

TROY [*shoves him on his shoulder*]:   Nigger! That's what you are. You just another nigger on the street to me!

CORY: You crazy! You know that?

TROY: Go on now! You got the devil in you. Get on away from me!

CORY: You just a crazy old man . . . talking about I got the devil in me.

TROY: Yeah, I'm crazy! If you don't get on the other side of that yard . . . I'm gonna show you how crazy I am! Go on . . . get the hell out of my yard.

CORY: It ain't your yard! You took Uncle Gabe's money he got from the army to buy this house and then you put him out.

TROY [TROY *advances on* CORY]:   Get your black ass out of my yard!

TROY'S *advance backs* CORY *up against the tree.* CORY *grabs up the bat.*

CORY: I ain't going nowhere! Come on . . . put me out! I ain't scared of you.

TROY: That's my bat!

CORY: Come on!

TROY: Put my bat down!

CORY: Come on, put me out.

CORY *swings at* TROY, *who backs across the yard.*

What's the matter? You so bad . . . . put me out!

TROY *advances toward* CORY.

CORY [*backing up*]:   Come on! Come on!

TROY: You're gonna have to use it! You wanna draw that bat back on me . . . you're gonna have to use it.

CORY: Come on! . . . Come on!

CORY *swings the bat at* TROY *a second time. He misses.* TROY *continues to advance toward him.*

TROY: You're gonna have to kill me! You wanna draw that bat back on me. You're gonna have to kill me.

CORY, *backed up against the tree, can go no further.* TROY *taunts him. He sticks out his head and offers him a target.*

Come on! Come on!

> CORY *is unable to swing the bat.* TROY *grabs it.*

TROY: Then I'll show you.

CORY *and* TROY *struggle over the bat. The struggle is fierce and fully engaged.* TROY *ultimately is the stronger and takes the bat from* CORY *and stands over him ready to swing. He stops himself.*

Go on and get away from around my house.

CORY, *stung by his defeat, picks himself up, walks slowly out of the yard and up the alley.*

CORY: Tell Mama I'll be back for my things.
TROY: They'll be on the other side of that fence.

> CORY *exits.*

TROY: I can't taste nothing. Helluljah! I can't taste nothing no more. [TROY *assumes a batting posture and begins to taunt Death, the fastball on the outside corner.*] Come on! It's between you and me now! Come on! Anytime you want! Come on! I be ready for you . . . but I ain't gonna be easy.

> *The lights go down on the scene.*

Scene 5

The time is 1965. The lights come up in the yard. It is the morning of TROY'S *funeral. A funeral plaque with a light hangs beside the door. There is a small garden plot off to the side. There is noise and activity in the house as* ROSE, GABRIEL, *and* BONO *have gathered. The door opens and* RAYNELL, *seven years old, enters dressed in a flannel nightgown. She crosses to the garden and pokes around with a stick.* ROSE *calls from the house.*

ROSE: Raynell!
RAYNELL: Mam?
ROSE: What you doing out there?
RAYNELL: Nothing.

> ROSE *comes to the door.*

ROSE: Girl, get in here and get dressed. What you doing?
RAYNELL: Seeing if my garden growed.
ROSE: I told you it ain't gonna grow overnight. You got to wait.
RAYNELL: It don't look like it never gonna grow. Dag!
ROSE: I told you a watched pot never boils. Get in here and get dressed.

RAYNELL:　This ain't even no pot, Mama.

ROSE:　You just have to give it a chance. It'll grow. Now you come on and do what I told you. We got to be getting ready. This ain't no morning to be playing around. You hear me?

RAYNELL:　Yes, mam.

ROSE *exits into the house.* RAYNELL *continues to poke at her garden with a stick.* CORY *enters. He is dressed in a Marine corporal's uniform, and carries a duffel bag. His posture is that of a military man, and his speech has a clipped sternness.*

CORY [*to* RAYNELL]:　Hi.

Pause.

I bet your name is Raynell.

RAYNELL:　Uh huh.

CORY:　Is your mama home?

RAYNELL *runs up on the porch and calls through the screendoor.*

RAYNELL:　Mama . . . there's some man out here. Mama?

ROSE *comes to the door.*

ROSE:　Cory? Lord have mercy! Look here, you all!

ROSE *and* CORY *embrace in a tearful reunion as* BONO *and* LYONS *enter from the house dressed in funeral clothes.*

BONO:　Aw, looka here . . .

ROSE:　Done got all grown up!

CORY:　Don't cry, Mama. What you crying about?

ROSE:　I'm just so glad you made it.

CORY:　Hey Lyons. How you doing, Mr. Bono.

LYONS *goes to embrace* CORY.

LYONS:　Look at you, man. Look at you. Don't he look good, Rose. Got them Corporal stripes.

ROSE:　What took you so long.

CORY:　You know how the Marines are, Mama. They got to get all their paperwork straight before they let you do anything.

ROSE:　Well, I'm sure glad you made it. They let Lyons come. Your Uncle Gabe's still in the hospital. They don't know if they gonna let him out or not. I just talked to them a little while ago.

LYONS:　A Corporal in the United States Marines.

BONO:　Your daddy knew you had it in you. He used to tell me all the time.

LYONS:　Don't he look good, Mr. Bono?

BONO:　Yeah, he remind me of Troy when I first met him.

Pause.

Say, Rose, Lucille's down at the church with the choir. I'm gonna go down and get the pallbearers lined up. I'll be back to get you all.

ROSE:　Thanks, Jim.

CORY: See you, Mr. Bono.

LYONS [*with his arm around* RAYNELL]:   Cory . . . look at Raynell. Ain't she precious? She gonna break a whole lot of hearts.

ROSE: Raynell, come and say hello to your brother. This is your brother, Cory. You remember Cory.

RAYNELL: No, Mam.

CORY: She don't remember me, Mama.

ROSE: Well, we talk about you. She heard us talk about you. [*To* RAYNELL.] This is your brother, Cory. Come on and say hello.

RAYNELL: Hi.

CORY: Hi. So you're Raynell. Mama told me a lot about you.

ROSE: You all come on into the house and let me fix you some breakfast. Keep up your strength.

CORY: I ain't hungry, Mama.

LYONS: You can fix me something, Rose. I'll be in there in a minute.

ROSE: Cory, you sure you don't want nothing. I know they ain't feeding you right.

CORY: No, Mama . . . thanks. I don't feel like eating. I'll get something later.

ROSE: Raynell . . . get on upstairs and get that dress on like I told you.

ROSE *and* RAYNELL *exit into the house.*

LYONS: So . . . I hear you thinking about getting married.

CORY: Yeah, I done found the right one, Lyons. It's about time.

LYONS: Me and Bonnie been split up about four years now. About the time Papa retired. I guess she just got tired of all them changes I was putting her through.

Pause.

I always knew you was gonna make something out yourself. Your head was always in the right direction. So . . . you gonna stay in . . . make it a career . . . put in your twenty years?

CORY: I don't know. I got six already, I think that's enough.

LYONS: Stick with Uncle Sam and retire early. Ain't nothing out here. I guess Rose told you what happened with me. They got me down the work-house. I thought I was being slick cashing other people's checks.

CORY: How much time you doing?

LYONS: They give me three years. I got that beat now. I ain't got but nine more months. It ain't so bad. You learn to deal with it like anything else. You got to take the crookeds with the straights. That's what Papa used to say. He used to say that when he struck out. I seen him strike out three times in a row . . . and the next time up he hit the ball over the grandstand. Right out there in Homestead Field. He wasn't satisfied hitting in the seats . . . he want to hit it over everything! After the game he had two hundred people standing around waiting to shake his hand. You got to take the crookeds with the straights. Yeah, Papa was something else.

CORY: You still playing?

LYONS: Cory . . . you know I'm gonna do that. There's some fellows down there we got us a band . . . we gonna try and stay together when we get out . . . but yeah, I'm still playing. It still helps me to get out of bed in the morning. As long as it do that I'm gonna be right there playing and trying to make some sense out of it.

ROSE [*calling*]:   Lyons, I got these eggs in the pan.

LYONS: Let me go on and get these eggs, man. Get ready to go bury Papa.

Pause.

How you doing? You doing all right?

CORY *nods.* LYONS *touches him on the shoulder and they share a moment of silent grief.* LYONS *exits into the house.* CORY *wanders about the yard.* RAYNELL *enters.*

RAYNELL: Hi.

CORY: Hi.

RAYNELL: Did you used to sleep in my room?

CORY: Yeah . . . that used to be my room.

RAYNELL: That's what Papa call it. "Cory's room." It got your football in the closet.

ROSE *comes to the door.*

ROSE: Raynell, get in there and get them good shoes on.

RAYNELL: Mama, can't I wear these? Them other one hurt my feet.

ROSE: Well, they just gonna have to hurt your feet for a while. You ain't said they hurt your feet when you went down to the store and got them.

RAYNELL: They didn't hurt then. My feet done got bigger.

ROSE: Don't you give me no backtalk now. You get in there and get them shoes on.

RAYNELL *exits into the house.*

Ain't too much changed. He still got that piece of rag tied to that tree. He was out here swinging that bat. I was just ready to go back in the house. He swung that bat and then he just fell over. Seem like he swung it and stood there with this grin on his face . . . and then he just fell over. They carried him on down to the hospital, but I knew there wasn't no need . . . why don't you come on in the house?

CORY: Mama . . . I got something to tell you. I don't know how to tell you this . . . but I've got to tell you . . . I'm not going to Papa's funeral.

ROSE: Boy, hush your mouth. That's your daddy you talking about. I don't want to hear that kind of talk this morning. I done raised you to come to this? You standing there all healthy and grown talking about you ain't going to your daddy's funeral?

CORY: Mama . . . listen . . .

ROSE: I don't want to hear it, Cory. You just get that thought out of your head.

CORY: I can't drag Papa with me everywhere I go. I've got to say no to him. One time in my life I've got to say no.

ROSE: Don't nobody have to listen to nothing like that. I know you and your daddy ain't seen eye to eye, but I ain't got to listen to that kind of talk this morning. Whatever was between you and your daddy . . . the time has come to put it aside. Just take it and set it over there on the shelf and forget about it.

Disrespecting your daddy ain't gonna make you a man, Cory. You got to find a way to come to that on your own. Not going to your daddy's funeral ain't gonna make you a man.

CORY: The whole time I was growing up . . . living in his house . . . Papa was like a shadow that followed you everywhere. It weighed on you and sunk into your flesh. It would wrap around you and lay there until you couldn't tell which one was you anymore. That shadow digging in your flesh. Trying to crawl in. Trying to live through you. Everywhere I looked, Troy Maxson was staring back at me . . . hiding under the bed . . . in the closet. I'm just saying I've got to find a way to get rid of that shadow, Mama.

ROSE: You just like him. You got him in you good.

CORY: Don't tell me that, Mama.

ROSE: You Troy Maxson all over again.

CORY: I don't want to be Troy Maxson. I want to be me.

ROSE: You can't be nobody but who you are, Cory. That shadow wasn't nothing but you growing into yourself. You either got to grow into it or cut it down to fit you. But that's all you got to make life with. That's all you got to measure yourself against that world out there. Your daddy wanted you to be everything he wasn't . . . and at the same time he tried to make you into everything he was. I don't know if he was right or wrong . . . but I do know he meant to do more good than he meant to do harm. He wasn't always right. Sometimes when he touched he bruised. And sometimes when he took me in his arms he cut.

When I first met your daddy I thought . . . Here is a man I can lay down with and make a baby. That's the first thing I thought when I seen him. I was thirty years old and had done seen my share of men. But when he walked up to me and said, "I can dance a waltz that'll make you dizzy," I thought, Rose Lee, here is a man that you can open yourself up to and be filled to bursting. Here is a man that can fill all them empty spaces you been tipping around the edges of. One of them empty spaces was being somebody's mother.

I married your daddy and settled down to cooking his supper and keeping clean sheets on the bed. When your daddy walked through the house he was so big he filled it up. That was my first mistake. Not to make him leave some room for me. For my part in the matter. But at that time I wanted that. I wanted a house that I could sing in. And that's what your daddy gave me. I didn't know to keep up his strength I had to give up little pieces of mine. I did that. I took on his life as mine and mixed up the pieces so that you couldn't hardly tell which was which anymore. It was my choice. It was my life and I didn't have to live it like that. But that's what life offered me in the way of being a woman and I took it. I grabbed hold of it with both hands.

By the time Raynell came into the house, me and your daddy had done lost touch with one another. I didn't want to make my blessing off of nobody's misfortune . . . but I took on to Raynell like she was all them babies I had wanted and never had.

The phone rings.

Like I'd been blessed to relive a part of my life. And if the Lord see fit to keep up my strength . . . I'm gonna do her just like your daddy did you . . . I'm gonna give her the best of what's in me.

RAYNELL [*entering, still with her old shoes*]:   Mama . . . Reverend Tollivier on the phone.

ROSE *exits into the house.*

RAYNELL: Hi.
CORY: Hi.
RAYNELL: You in the Army or the Marines?
CORY: Marines.
RAYNELL: Papa said it was the Army. Did you know Blue?
CORY: Blue? Who's Blue?
RAYNELL: Papa's dog what he sing about all the time.
CORY [*singing*]:   Hear it ring! Hear it ring!
I had a dog his name was Blue
You know Blue was mighty true
You know Blue was a good old dog
Blue treed a possum in a hollow log
You know from that he was a good old dog.
Hear it ring! Hear it ring!

RAYNELL *joins in singing.*

CORY and RAYNELL: Blue treed a possum out on a limb
Blue looked at me and I looked at him
Grabbed that possum and put him in a sack
Blue stayed there till I came back
Old Blue's feets was big and round
Never allowed a possum to touch the ground.

Old Blue died and I dug his grave
I dug his grave with a silver spade
Let him down with a golden chain
And every night I call his name
Go on Blue, you good dog you
Go on Blue, you good dog you
RAYNELL: Blue laid down and died like a man
Blue laid down and died . . .
BOTH: Blue laid down and died like a man
Now he's treeing possums in the Promised Land
I'm gonna tell you this to let you know
Blue's gone where the good dogs go
When I hear old Blue bark
When I hear old Blue bark
Blue treed a possum in Noah's Ark,
Blue treed a possum in Noah's Ark.

ROSE *comes to the screen door.*

ROSE: Cory, we gonna be ready to go in a minute.
CORY [*to RAYNELL*]:   You go on in the house and change them shoes like Mama told you so we can go to Papa's funeral.
RAYNELL: Okay, I'll be back.

RAYNELL *exits into the house.* CORY *gets up and crosses over to the tree.* ROSE *stands in the screen door watching him.* GABRIEL *enters from the alley.*

GABRIEL [*calling*]:   Hey, Rose!
ROSE: Gabe?
GABRIEL: I'm here, Rose. Hey Rose, I'm here!

ROSE *enters from the house.*

ROSE: Lord . . . Look here, Lyons!
LYONS: See, I told you, Rose . . . I told you they'd let him come.
CORY: How you doing, Uncle Gabe?
LYONS: How you doing, Uncle Gabe?
GABRIEL: Hey, Rose. It's time. It's time to tell St. Peter to open the gates. Troy, you ready? You ready, Troy. I'm gonna tell St. Peter to open the gates. You get ready now.

GABRIEL, *with great fanfare, braces himself to blow. The trumpet is without a mouthpiece. He puts the end of it into his mouth and blows with great force, like a man who has been waiting some twenty-odd years for this single moment. No sound comes out of the trumpet. He braces himself and blows again with the same result. A third time he blows. There is a weight of impossible description that falls away and leaves him bare and exposed to a frightful realization. It is a trauma that a sane and normal mind would be unable to withstand. He begins to dance. A slow, strange dance, eerie and life-giving. A dance of atavistic signature and ritual.* LYONS *attempts to embrace him.* GABRIEL *pushes* LYONS *away. He begins to howl in what is an attempt at song, or perhaps a song turning back into itself in an attempt at speech. He finishes his dance and the gates of heaven stand open as wide as God's closet.*

That's the way that go!

(1986)

QUESTIONS

1. How does Wilson establish the world of his play? What kinds of details help readers and viewers orient themselves?
2. Identify the play's most important references to religion, and explain their function.
3. Identify the values each of the characters lives by. Whose values does the play seem to endorse?
4. How does Wilson make his characters believable? Which of them do you understand best? Why?
5. What metaphors do Troy and Rose use to make sense of their lives? How does the playwright use these metaphors for expressive purposes?
6. Identify the various kinds of "fences" the play includes. Explain the significance of the title.
7. Select one longer speech or one important exchange of dialogue, and explain its significance to the play's theme.
8. Select one scene or part of a scene, and explain how you would stage it.

DAVID MAMET

[b. 1947]

David Mamet is one of the best known dramatists of the American theater. His plays include *American Buffalo, Sexual Perversity in Chicago,* and *Glengarry Glen Ross. Glengary Glen Ross* was made into a film starring Al Pacino and Jack Lemmon, and the 1996 movie version of *American Buffalo* starred Dustin Hoffman and Dennis Franz. Mamet has also written screenplays for such films as *Hoffa, The Untouchables,* and *The Verdict,* for which he received an Academy Award nomination. In addition, he has published five books of nonfiction, including *Writing in Restaurants, Some Freaks,* and *The Cabin.*

Oleanna, Mamet's seventeenth play, was produced in New York in 1993. Its dramatization of the twin contemporary concerns of sexual harassment and political correctness makes it especially relevant today. Its portrayal of conflicting interpretations of gestures, looks, and conversations reveals the complex and multiperspectival nature of truth.

DAVID MAMET

Oleanna

THIS PLAY IS DEDICATED TO MICHAEL MERRITT

The want of fresh air does not seem much to affect the happiness of children in a London alley: the greater part of them sing and play as though they were on a moor in Scotland. So the absence of a genial mental atmosphere is not commonly recognized by children who have never known it. Young people have a marvelous faculty of either dying or adapting themselves to circumstances. Even if they are unhappy—very unhappy—it is astonishing how easily they can be prevented from finding it out, or at any rate from attributing it to any other cause than their own sinfulness.

—SAMUEL BUTLER, THE WAY OF ALL FLESH

"Oh, to be in Oleanna,
That's where I would rather be.
Than be bound in Norway
And drag the chains of slavery."

—FOLK SONG

CHARACTERS

CAROL: A woman of twenty
JOHN: A man in his forties

The play takes place in JOHN'S *office.*

ONE

JOHN *is talking on the phone.* CAROL *is seated across the desk from him.*

JOHN (*on phone*):   And what about the land. (*Pause*) The land. And what about the land? (*Pause*) What about it? (*Pause*) No. I don't understand. Well, yes, I'm I'm . . . no, I'm *sure* it's signif . . . I'm sure it's significant. (*Pause*) Because it's significant to mmmmmm . . . did you call Jerry? (*Pause*) Because . . . no, no, no, no, no. What did they say . . . ? Did you speak to the *real* estate . . . where *is* she . . . ? Well, well, all right. Where are her notes? Where are the notes we took with her. (*Pause*) I thought you were? No. No, I'm sorry, I didn't mean that, I just thought that I saw you, when we were there . . . what . . . ? I thought I saw you with a *pencil.* WHY NOW? is what I'm say . . . well, that's why I say "call Jerry." Well, I can't right now, be . . . no, I *didn't* schedule any . . . Grace: I *didn't* . . . I'm well aware . . . Look: Look. Did you call Jerry? Will you call Jerry . . . ? Because I can't now. I'll be there, I'm sure I'll be there in fifteen, in twenty I intend to. No, we aren't *going* to lose the, we aren't *going* to lose the house. Look: Look, I'm not minimizing it. The "easement." Did she say "easement"? (*Pause*) What did she *say; is* it a "term of art," are we *bound* by it . . . I'm sorry . . . (*Pause*) are: we: yes. *Bound* by . . . Look: (*He checks his watch.*) before the other side *goes home,* all right? "a term of art." Because: that's right (*Pause*) The yard for the boy. Well, that's the whole . . . Look: I'm going to meet you there . . . (*He checks his watch.*) Is the realtor there? All right, tell her to show you the basement again. Look at the *this* because . . . Bec . . . I'm leaving in, I'm leaving in ten or fifteen . . . Yes. No, no, I'll meet you at the new . . . That's a good. If he thinks it's necc . . . you tell Jerry to meet . . . All right? We *aren't* going to lose the deposit. All right? I'm sure it's going to be . . . (*Pause*) I hope so. (*Pause*) I love you, too. (*Pause*) I love you, too. As soon as . . . I will.

(*He hangs up.*) (*He bends over the desk and makes a note.*) (*He looks up.*) (*To* CAROL:) I'm sorry . . .

CAROL: (*Pause*) What is a "term of art"?
JOHN: (*Pause*) I'm sorry . . . ?
CAROL: (*Pause*) What is a "term of art"?
JOHN: Is that what you want to talk about?
CAROL: . . . to talk about . . . ?

JOHN: Let's take the mysticism out of it, shall we? Carol? (*Pause*) Don't you think? I'll tell you: when you have some "thing." Which must be broached. (*Pause*) Don't you think . . . ? (*Pause*)

CAROL: . . . don't I think . . . ?

JOHN: Mmm?

CAROL: . . . did I . . . ?

JOHN: . . . what?

CAROL: Did . . . did I . . . did I say something wr . . .

JOHN: (*Pause*) No. I'm sorry. No. You're right. I'm very sorry. I'm somewhat rushed. As you see. I'm sorry. You're right. (*Pause*) What is a "term of art"? It seems to mean a *term,* which has come, through its use, to mean something *more specific* than the words would, to someone *not acquainted* with them . . . indicate. That, I believe, is what a "term of art," would mean. (*Pause*)

CAROL: You don't know what it means . . . ?

JOHN: I'm not sure that I know what it means. It's one of those things, perhaps you've had them, that, you look them up, or have someone explain them to you, and you say "aha," and, you immediately *forget* what . . .

CAROL: You don't do that.

JOHN: . . . I . . . ?

CAROL: You don't do . . .

JOHN: . . . I don't, what . . . ?

CAROL: . . . for . . .

JOHN: . . . I don't for . . .

CAROL: . . . no . . .

JOHN: . . . forget things? Everybody does that.

CAROL: No, they don't.

JOHN: They don't . . .

CAROL: No.

JOHN: (*Pause*) No. Everybody does that.

CAROL: Why would they do that . . . ?

JOHN: Because. I don't know. Because it doesn't interest them.

CAROL: No.

JOHN: I think so, though. (*Pause*) I'm sorry that I was distracted.

CAROL: You don't have to say that to me.

JOHN: You paid me the compliment, or the "obeisance"—all right—of coming in here . . . All right. *Carol.* I find that I am at a *standstill.* I find that I . . .

CAROL: . . . what . . .

JOHN: . . . one moment. In regard to your . . . to your . . .

CAROL: Oh, oh. You're buying a new house!

JOHN: No, let's get on with it.

CAROL: "get on"? (*Pause*)

JOHN: I know how . . . *believe* me. I know how . . . potentially *humiliating* these . . . I have no desire to . . . I have no desire other than to help you. But: (*He picks up some papers on his desk.*) I won't even say "but." I'll say that as I go back over the . . .

CAROL: I'm just, I'm just trying to . . .

JOHN: . . . no, it will not do.

CAROL: . . . what? What will . . . ?

JOHN: No. I see, I see what you, it . . . (*He gestures to the papers.*) but your work . . .

CAROL: I'm just: I sit in class I . . . (*She holds up her notebook.*) I take notes . . .

JOHN (*simultaneously with "notes"*): Yes. I understand. What I am trying to *tell* you is that some, some basic . . .

CAROL: . . . I . . .

JOHN: . . . one moment: some basic missed communi . . .

CAROL: I'm doing what I'm told. I bought your book, I read your . . .

JOHN: No, I'm sure you . . .

CAROL: No, no, no. I'm doing what I'm told. It's *difficult* for me. It's *difficult* . . .

JOHN: . . . but . . .

CAROL: I don't . . . lots of the *language* . . .

JOHN: . . . please . . .

CAROL: The *language*, the "things" that you say . . .

JOHN: I'm sorry. No. I don't think that that's true.

CAROL: It *is* true. I . . .

JOHN: I think . . .

CAROL: It *is* true.

JOHN: . . . I . . .

CAROL: Why would I . . . ?

JOHN: I'll tell you why: you're an incredibly bright girl.

CAROL: . . . I . . .

JOHN: You're an incredibly . . . you have no problem with the . . . Who's kidding who?

CAROL: . . . I . . .

JOHN: No. No. I'll tell you why. I'll tell . . . I think you're *angry*, I . . .

CAROL: . . . why would I . . .

JOHN: . . . wait one moment. I . . .

CAROL: It *is* true. I have *problems* . . .

JOHN: . . . every . . .

CAROL: . . . I come from a different *social* . . .

JOHN: . . . ev . . .

CAROL: a different economic . . . .

JOHN: . . . Look:

CAROL: No. I: when I *came* to this school:

JOHN: Yes. Quite . . . (*Pause*)

CAROL: . . . does that mean nothing . . . ?

JOHN: . . . but look: look . . .

CAROL: . . . I . . .

JOHN: (*Picks up paper.*) Here: Please: Sit down. (*Pause*) Sit down. (*Reads from her paper.*) "I think that the ideas contained in this work express the author's feelings in a way that he intended, based on his results." What can that mean? Do you see? What . . .

CAROL: I, the best that I . . .

JOHN: I'm saying, that perhaps this course . . .

CAROL: No, no, no, you can't, you can't . . . I have to . . .

JOHN: . . . how . . .

CAROL: . . . I have to pass it . . .

JOHN: Carol, I:

CAROL: I *have* to pass this course, I . . .

JOHN: Well.

CAROL: . . . don't you . . .

JOHN: Either the . . .

CAROL: . . . I . . .

JOHN: . . . either the, I . . . either the *criteria* for judging progress in the class are . . .

CAROL: No, no, no, no, I have to pass it.

JOHN: Now, look: I'm a human being, I . . .

CAROL: I did what you told me. I did, I did everything that, I read your *book,* you told me to buy your book and read it. Everything you *say* I . . . (*She gestures to her notebook.*) (*The phone rings.*) I do. . . . Ev . . .

JOHN: . . . look:

CAROL: . . . everything I'm told . . .

JOHN: Look. Look. I'm not your *father.* (*Pause*)

CAROL: What?

JOHN: I'm.

CAROL: Did I say you were my father?

JOHN: . . . no . . .

CAROL: Why did you say that . . . ?

JOHN: I . . .

CAROL: . . . why . . . ?

JOHN: . . . in class I . . . (*He picks up the phone.*) (*Into phone:*) Hello. I can't talk now. Jerry? Yes? I underst . . . I can't talk now. I know . . . I know . . . Jerry. I can't *talk* now. Yes, I. Call me back in . . . Thank you. (*He hangs up.*) (*To* CAROL:) What do you want me to do? We are two people, all right? Both of whom have subscribed to . . .

CAROL: No, no . . .

JOHN: . . . certain arbitrary . . .

CAROL: No. You have to help me.

JOHN: Certain institutional . . . you tell me what you want me to do. . . . You tell me what you want me to . . .

CAROL: How can I go back and tell them the *grades* that I . . .

JOHN: . . . what can I do . . . ?

CAROL: *Teach* me. *Teach* me.

JOHN: . . . I'm trying to teach you.

CAROL: I read your book. I read it. I don't under . . .

JOHN: . . . you don't understand it.

CAROL: No.

JOHN: Well, perhaps it's not well *written* . . .

CAROL (*simultaneously with "written"*):   No. No. No. I want to *understand* it.

JOHN: What don't you understand? (*Pause*)

CAROL: *Any* of it. What you're trying to say. When you talk about . . .

JOHN: . . . yes . . . ? (*She consults her notes.*)

CAROL: "Virtual warehousing of the young" . . .

JOHN: "Virtual warehousing of the young." If we artificially prolong adolescence . . .

CAROL: . . . and about "The Curse of Modern Education."

JOHN: . . . well . . .

CAROL: I don't . . .

JOHN: Look. It's just a *course,* it's just a *book,* it's just a . . .

CAROL: No. No. There are *people* out there. People who came *here.* To know something they didn't *know.* Who *came* here. To be *helped.* To be *helped.* So someone would *help* them. To *do* something. To *know* something. To get, what do they say? "To get on in the world." How can I do that if I don't, if I fail? But I don't *understand.* I don't *understand.* I don't understand what anything means . . . and I walk around. From morning 'til night: with this one thought in my head. I'm *stupid.*

JOHN: No one thinks you're stupid.

CAROL: No? What am I . . . ?

JOHN: I . . .

CAROL: . . . what am I, then?

JOHN: I think you're angry. Many people are. I have a *telephone* call that I have to make. And an *appointment,* which is rather *pressing;* though I sympathize with your concerns, and though I wish I had the time, this was not a previously scheduled meeting and I . . .

CAROL: . . . you think I'm nothing . . .

JOHN: . . . have an appointment with a *realtor,* and with my wife and . . .

CAROL: You think that I'm stupid.

JOHN: No. I certainly don't.

CAROL: You said it.

JOHN: No. I did not.

CAROL: You did.

JOHN: When?

CAROL: . . . you . . .

JOHN: No. I never did, or never would say that to a student, and . . .

CAROL: You said, "What can that mean?" (*Pause*) "What can that mean?" . . . (*Pause*)

JOHN: . . . and what did that mean to you . . . ?

CAROL: That meant I'm stupid. And I'll never learn. That's what that meant. And you're right.

JOHN: . . . I . . .

CAROL: But then. But then, what am I doing here . . . ?

JOHN: . . . if you thought that I . . .

CAROL: . . . when nobody wants me, and . . .

JOHN: . . . if you interpreted . . .

CAROL: Nobody *tells* me anything. And I *sit* there . . . in the *corner.* In the *back.* And everybody's talking about "this" all the time. And "concepts," and "precepts" and, and, and, and, and, WHAT IN THE WORLD ARE YOU *TALKING* ABOUT? And I read your book. And they said, "Fine, go in that class." Because you talked about responsibility to the young. I DON'T KNOW WHAT IT MEANS AND I'M *FAILING* . . .

JOHN: May . . .

CAROL: No, you're right. "Oh, hell." I failed. Flunk me out of it. It's garbage. Everything I do. "The ideas contained in this work express the author's feelings." That's right. That's right. I know I'm stupid. I know what I am. (*Pause*) I know what I am, Professor. You don't have to tell me. (*Pause*) It's pathetic. Isn't it?

JOHN: . . . Aha . . . (*Pause*) Sit down. Sit down. Please. (*Pause*) Please sit down.

CAROL: Why?

JOHN: I want to talk to you.

CAROL: Why?

JOHN: Just sit down. (*Pause*) Please. Sit down. Will you, please . . . ? (*Pause. She does so.*) Thank you.

CAROL: What?

JOHN: I want to tell you something.

CAROL: (*Pause*) What?

JOHN: Well, I know what you're talking about.

CAROL: No. You don't.

JOHN: I think I do. (*Pause*)

CAROL: How can you?

JOHN: I'll tell you a story about myself. (*Pause*) Do you mind? (*Pause*) I was raised to think myself stupid. That's what I want to tell you. (*Pause*)

CAROL: What do you mean?

JOHN: Just what I said. I was brought up, and my earliest, and most persistent memories are of being told that I was stupid. "You have such *intelligence.* Why must you behave so *stupidly?*" Or, "Can't you *understand?* Can't you *understand?*" And I could *not* understand. I could *not* understand.

CAROL: What?

JOHN: The simplest problem. Was beyond me. It was a mystery.

CAROL: What was a mystery?

JOHN: How people learn. How *I* could learn. Which is what I've been speaking of in class. And of *course* you can't hear it. Carol. Of *course* you can't. (*Pause*) I used to speak of "real people," and wonder what the *real* people did. The *real* people. Who were they? *They* were the people other than myself. The *good* people. The *capable* people. The people who could do the things, *I* could not do: learn, study, retain . . . all that *garbage*—which is what I have been talking of in class, and that's *exactly* what I have been talking of—If you are told . . . . Listen to this. If the young child is told he cannot understand. Then he takes it as a *description* of himself. What am I? I am *that which can not understand.* And I saw you out there, when we were speaking of the concepts of . . .

CAROL: I can't understand any of them.

JOHN: Well, then, that's *my* fault. That's not your fault. And that is not verbiage. That's what I firmly hold to be the truth. And I am sorry, and I owe you an apology.

CAROL: Why?

JOHN: And I suppose that I have had some *things* on my mind. . . . We're buying a *house,* and . . .

CAROL: People said that you were stupid . . . ?

JOHN: Yes.

CAROL: When?

JOHN: I'll tell you when. Through my life. In my childhood; and, perhaps, they stopped. But I heard them continue.

CAROL: And what did they say?

JOHN: They said I was incompetent. Do you see? And when I'm tested the, the, the *feelings* of my youth about the *very subject of learning* come up. And I . . . I become, I feel "unworthy," and "unprepared." . . .

CAROL: . . . yes.

JOHN: . . . eh?

CAROL: . . . yes.

JOHN: And I feel that I must fail. (*Pause*)

CAROL: . . . but then you *do* fail. (*Pause*) You have to. (*Pause*) Don't you?

JOHN: A *pilot.* Flying a plane. The pilot is flying the plane. He thinks: Oh, my *God,* my mind's been drifting! Oh, my God! What kind of a cursed imbecile am I, that I, with this so precious cargo of *Life* in my charge, would allow my attention to wander. Why was I born? How deluded are those who put their trust in me, . . . et cetera, so on, and he crashes the plane.

CAROL: (*Pause*) He could just . . .

JOHN: That's right.

CAROL: He could say:

JOHN: My attention *wandered* for a moment . . .

CAROL: . . . uh huh . . .

JOHN: I had a *thought* I did not like . . . but now:

CAROL: . . . but now it's . . .

JOHN: That's what I'm telling you. It's time to put my attention . . . see: it is not: this is what I learned. It is Not Magic. Yes. Yes. *You.* You are going to be frightened. When faced with what may or may not be but which you are going to perceive as a test. You will become frightened. And you will say: "I am incapable of . . ." and everything *in* you will think these two things. "I must. But I can't." And you will think: Why was I born to be the laughingstock of a world in which everyone is better than I? In which I am entitled to nothing. Where I can not learn.

(*Pause*)

CAROL: Is that . . . (*Pause*) Is that what I have . . . ?

JOHN: Well. I don't know if I'd put it that way. Listen: I'm talking to you as I'd talk to my son. Because that's what I'd like him to have that I never had. I'm talking to you the way I wish that someone had talked to me. I don't know how to do it, other than to be *personal,* . . . but . . .

CAROL: Why would you want to be personal with me?

JOHN: Well, you see? That's what I'm saying. We can only interpret the behavior of others through the screen we . . . (*The phone rings.*) Through . . . (*To phone:*) Hello . . . ? (*To* CAROL:) Through the screen we create. (*To phone:*) Hello. (*To* CAROL:) Excuse me a moment. (*To phone:*) Hello? No, I can't talk nnn . . . I know I did. In a few . . . I'm . . . is he coming to the . . . yes. I talked to him. We'll meet you at the No, because I'm with a *student*. It's going to be fff . . . This is important, too. I'm with a *student,* Jerry's going to . . . Listen: the sooner I get off, the sooner I'll be down, all right. I love you. Listen, listen, I said "I love you," it's going to work *out* with the, because I feel that it is, I'll be right down. All right? Well, then it's going to take as long as it takes. (*He hangs up.*) (*To* CAROL:) I'm sorry.

CAROL:　What was that?

JOHN:　There are some problems, as there usually are, about the final agreements for the new house.

CAROL:　You're buying a new house.

JOHN:　That's right.

CAROL:　Because of your promotion.

JOHN:　Well, I suppose that that's right.

CAROL:　Why did you stay here with me?

JOHN:　Stay here.

CAROL:　Yes. When you should have gone.

JOHN:　Because I like you.

CAROL:　You like me.

JOHN:　Yes.

CAROL:　Why?

JOHN:　Why? Well? Perhaps we're similar. (*Pause*) Yes. (*Pause*)

CAROL:　You said "everyone has problems."

JOHN:　Everyone has problems.

CAROL:　Do they?

JOHN:　Certainly.

CAROL:　You do?

JOHN:　Yes.

CAROL:　What are they?

JOHN:　Well. (*Pause*) Well, you're perfectly right. (*Pause*) If we're going to take off the Artificial *Stricture,* of "Teacher," and "Student," why should *my* problems be any more a mystery than your own? Of *course* I have problems. As you saw.

CAROL:　. . . with what?

JOHN:　With my *wife* . . . with *work* . . .

CAROL:　With work?

JOHN:　Yes. And, and, perhaps my problems are, do you see? *Similar* to yours.

CAROL:　Would you tell me?

JOHN:　All right. (*Pause*) I came *late* to teaching. And I found it Artificial. The notion of "I know and you do not"; and I saw an *exploitation* in the education process. I told you. I hated school, I hated teachers. I hated everyone who was in the position of a "boss" because I *knew*—I didn't *think,* mind you, I *knew* I was going to fail. Because I was a fuckup. I was just no goddamned good. When I . . . late in life . . . (*Pause*) When I *got out from under* . . . when I worked my way out of the need to fail. When I . . .

CAROL:　How do you do that? (*Pause*)

JOHN:　You have to look at what you are, and what you feel, and how you act. And, finally, you have to look at how you act. And say: If that's what I *did,* that must be how I think of myself.

CAROL: I don't understand.

JOHN: If I fail all the time, it must be that I think of myself as a failure. If I do not want to think of myself as a failure, perhaps I should begin by *succeeding* now and again. Look. The tests, you see, which you encounter, in school, in college, in life, were designed, in the most part, for idiots. *By* idiots. There is no need to fail at them. They are not a test of your worth. They are a test of your ability to retain and spout back misinformation. Of *course* you fail them. They're *nonsense*. And I . . .

CAROL: . . . no . . .

JOHN: Yes. They're *garbage*. They're a *joke*. Look at me. Look at me. The Tenure Committee. The Tenure Committee. Come to judge me. The Bad Tenure Committee.
The "Test." Do you see? They put me to the test. Why, they had people voting on me I wouldn't employ to wax my car. And yet, I go before the Great Tenure Committee, and I have an urge, to *vomit*, to, to, to puke my *badness* on the table, to show them: "I'm no good. Why would you pick *me*?"

CAROL: They granted you tenure.

JOHN: Oh no, they announced it, but they haven't *signed*. Do you see? "At any moment . . ."

CAROL: . . . mmm . . .

JOHN: "They might not *sign*" . . . I might not . . . the *house* might not go through . . . Eh? Eh? They'll find out my "dark secret." (*Pause*)

CAROL: . . . what is it . . . ?

JOHN: There *isn't* one. But *they* will find an index of my badness . . .

CAROL: Index?

JOHN: A ". . . pointer." A "Pointer." You see? Do you see? I *understand* you. I. Know. That. Feeling. Am I entitled to my job, and my nice *home*, and my *wife*, and my *family*, and so on. This is what I'm saying: That theory of education which, that *theory*:

CAROL: I . . . I . . . (*Pause*)

JOHN: What?

CAROL: I . . .

JOHN: What?

CAROL: I want to know about my grade. (*Long pause*)

JOHN: Of course you do.

CAROL: Is that bad?

JOHN: No.

CAROL: Is it bad that I asked you that?

JOHN: No.

CAROL: Did I upset you?

JOHN: No. And I apologize. Of *course* you want to know about your grade. And, of course, you can't concentrate on anyth . . . (*The telephone starts to ring.*) Wait a moment.

CAROL: I should go.

JOHN: I'll make you a deal.

CAROL: No, you have to . . .

JOHN: Let it ring. I'll make you a deal. You stay here. We'll start the whole course over. I'm going to say it was not you, it was I who was not paying attention. We'll start the whole course over. Your grade is an "A." Your final grade is an "A." (*The phone stops ringing.*)

CAROL: But the class is only half over . . .

JOHN (*simultaneously with* "over"):   Your grade for the whole term is an "A." If you will come back and meet with me. A few more times. Your grade's an "A." Forget about the paper. You didn't like it, you didn't like writing it. It's not important. What's important is that I awake your interest, if I can, and that I answer your questions. Let's start over. (*Pause*)

CAROL: Over. With what?

JOHN: Say this is the beginning.

CAROL: The beginning.

JOHN: Yes.

CAROL: Of what?

JOHN: Of the class.

CAROL: But we can't start over.

JOHN: I say we can. (*Pause*) I say we can.

CAROL: But I don't believe it.

JOHN: Yes, I know that. But it's true. What is The Class but you and me? (*Pause*)

CAROL: There are rules.

JOHN: Well. We'll break them.

CAROL: How can we?

JOHN: We won't tell anybody.

CAROL: Is that all right?

JOHN: I say that it's fine.

CAROL: Why would you do this for me?

JOHN: I like you. Is that so difficult for you to . . .

CAROL: Um . . .

JOHN: There's no one here but you and me. (*Pause*)

CAROL: All right. I did not understand. When you referred . . .

JOHN: All right, yes?

CAROL: When you referred to hazing.

JOHN: Hazing.

CAROL: You wrote, in your book. About the comparative . . . the comparative . . . (*She checks her notes.*)

JOHN: Are you checking your notes . . . ?

CAROL: Yes.

JOHN: Tell me in your own . . .

CAROL: I want to make sure that I have it right.

JOHN: No. Of course. You want to be exact.

CAROL: I want to know everything that went on.

JOHN: . . . that's good.

CAROL: . . . so I . . .

JOHN: That's very good. But I was suggesting, many times, that that which we wish to retain is retained oftentimes, I think, *better* with less expenditure of effort.

CAROL: (*Of notes*) Here it is: you wrote of *hazing*.

JOHN: . . . that's correct. Now: I said "hazing." It means ritualized annoyance. We shove this book at you, we say read it. Now, you say you've read it? I think that you're *lying*. I'll *grill* you, and when I find you've lied, you'll be disgraced, and your life will be ruined. It's a sick game. Why do we do it? Does it educate? In no sense. Well, then, what is higher education? It is something-other-than-useful.

CAROL: What is "something-other-than-useful?"

JOHN: It has become a ritual, it has become an article of faith. That all must be subjected to, or to put it differently, that all are entitled to Higher Education. And my point . . .

CAROL: You disagree with that?

JOHN: Well, let's address that. What do you think?

CAROL: I don't know.

JOHN: What do you think, though? (*Pause*)

CAROL: I don't know.

JOHN: I spoke of it in class. Do you remember my example?

CAROL: Justice.

JOHN: Yes. Can you repeat it to me? (*She looks down at her notebook.*) Without your notes? I ask you as a favor to me, so that I can see if my idea was interesting.

CAROL: You said "justice" . . .

JOHN: Yes?

CAROL: . . . that all are entitled . . . (*Pause*) I . . . I . . . I . . .

JOHN: Yes. To a speedy trial. To a fair trial. But they needn't be given a trial *at all* unless they stand accused. Eh? Justice is their right, should they choose to avail themselves of it, they should have a fair trial. It does not follow, of necessity, a person's life is incomplete without a trial in it. Do you see?

My point is a confusion between equity and *utility* arose. So we confound the *usefulness* of higher education with our, granted, right to equal access to the same. We, in effect, create a *prejudice* toward it, completely independent of . . .

CAROL: . . . that it is prejudice that we should go to school?

JOHN: Exactly. (*Pause*)

CAROL: How can you say that? How . . .

JOHN: Good. Good. *Good.* That's right! Speak up! What is a prejudice? An unreasoned belief. We are all subject to it. None of us is not. When it is threatened, or opposed, we feel anger, and feel, do we not? As you do now. Do you not? Good.

CAROL: . . . but how can you . . .

JOHN: . . . let us examine. Good.

CAROL: How . . .

JOHN: Good. Good. When . . .

CAROL: I'M SPEAKING . . . (*Pause*)

JOHN: I'm sorry.

CAROL: How can you . . .

JOHN: . . . I beg your pardon.

CAROL: That's all right.

JOHN: I beg your pardon.

CAROL: That's all right.

JOHN: I'm sorry I interrupted you.

CAROL: That's all right.

JOHN: You were saying?

CAROL: I was saying . . . I was saying . . . (*She checks her notes.*) How can you say in a class. Say in a college class, that college education is prejudice?

JOHN: I said that our predilection for it . . .

CAROL: Predilection . . .

JOHN: . . . you know what that means.

CAROL: Does it mean "liking"?

JOHN: Yes.

CAROL: But how can you say that? That College . . .

JOHN: . . . that's my *job,* don't you know.

CAROL: What is?

JOHN: To provoke you.

CAROL: No.

JOHN: Oh. Yes, though.

CAROL: To provoke me?

JOHN: That's right.

CAROL: To make me mad?

JOHN: That's right. To force you . . .

CAROL: . . . to make me mad is your job?

JOHN: To force you to . . . listen: (*Pause*) Ah. (*Pause*) When I was young somebody told me, are you ready, the rich copulate less often than the poor. But when they do, they take more of their clothes off. Years. Years, mind you, I would compare experiences of my own to this dictum, saying, aha, this fits the norm, or ah, this is a variation from it. What did it mean? Nothing. It was some jerk thing, some school kid told me that took up room inside my head. (*Pause*)

Somebody told *you,* and you hold it as an article of faith, that higher education is an unassailable good. This notion is so dear to you that when I question it you become angry. Good. Good, I say. Are not those the very things which we should question? I say college education, since the war, has become so a matter of course, and such a fashionable necessity, for those either of or aspiring *to* to the new vast middle class, that we *espouse* it, as a matter of right, and have ceased to ask, "What is it good for?" (*Pause*)

What might be some reasons for pursuit of higher education?

One: A love of learning.

Two: The wish for mastery of a skill.

Three: For economic betterment.

(*Stops. Makes a note.*)

CAROL: I'm keeping you.

JOHN: One moment. I have to make a note . . .

CAROL: It's something that I said?

JOHN: No, we're buying a house.

CAROL: You're buying the new house.

JOHN: To go with the tenure. That's right. Nice *house,* close to the *private* school . . . (*He continues making his note.*) . . . We were talking of economic betterment (CAROL *writes in her notebook.*) . . . I was thinking of the School Tax. (*He continues writing.*) (*To himself:*) . . . *where is it written* that I have to send my child to public school. . . . Is it a law that I have to improve the City Schools at the expense of my own interest? And, is this not simply *The White Man's Burden?* Good. And (*Looks up to* CAROL) . . . does this interest you?

CAROL: No. I'm taking notes . . .

JOHN: You don't have to take notes, you know, you can just listen.

CAROL: I want to make sure I remember it. (*Pause*)

JOHN: I'm not lecturing you, I'm just trying to tell you some things I think.

CAROL: What do you think?

JOHN: Should all kids go to college? *Why* . . .

CAROL: (*Pause*) To learn.

JOHN: But if he does not learn.

CAROL: If the child does not learn?

JOHN: Then why is he in college? Because he was told it was his "right"?

CAROL: Some might find college instructive.

JOHN: I would hope so.

CAROL: But how do they feel? Being told they are wasting their time?

JOHN: I don't think I'm telling them that.

CAROL: You said that education was "prolonged and systematic hazing."

JOHN: Yes. It can be so.

CAROL: . . . if education is so *bad*, why do you do it?

JOHN: I do it because I love it. (*Pause*) Let's. . . . I suggest you look at the demographics, wage-earning capacity, college- and non-college-educated men and women, 1855 to 1980, and let's see if we can wring some worth from the statistics. Eh? And . . .

CAROL: No.

JOHN: What?

CAROL: I can't understand them.

JOHN: . . . you . . . ?

CAROL: . . . the "charts." The *Concepts,* the . . .

JOHN: "Charts" are simply . . .

CAROL: When I leave here . . .

JOHN: Charts, do you see . . .

CAROL: No, I can't . . .

JOHN: You can, though.

CAROL: NO, NO—I DON'T UNDERSTAND. DO YOU SEE??? I DON'T *UNDERSTAND* . . .

JOHN: What?

CAROL: *Any* of it. *Any* of it. I'm *smiling* in class, I'm *smiling,* the whole time. What are you *talking* about? What is everyone *talking* about? I don't *understand.* I don't know what it *means.* I don't know what it means to *be* here . . . you tell me I'm intelligent, and then you tell me I should not be *here,* what do you *want* with me? What does it *mean?* Who should I *listen* to . . . I . . .

(*He goes over to her and puts his arm around her shoulder.*)

NO! (*She walks away from him.*)

JOHN: Sshhhh.

CAROL: No, I don't under . . .

JOHN: Sshhhhh.

CAROL: I don't know what you're *saying* . . .

JOHN: Sshhhhh. It's all right.

CAROL: . . . I have no . . .

JOHN: Sshhhhh. Sshhhhh. Let it go a moment. (*Pause*) Sshhhhh . . . let it go. (*Pause*) Just let it go. (*Pause*) Just let it go. It's all right. (*Pause*) Sshhhhh. (*Pause*) I understand . . . (*Pause*) What do you feel?

CAROL: I feel bad.

JOHN: I know. It's all right.

CAROL: I . . . (*Pause*)

JOHN: What?

CAROL: I . . .

JOHN: What? Tell me.

CAROL: I don't understand you.

JOHN: I know. It's all right.

CAROL: I . . .

JOHN: What? (*Pause*) What? *Tell* me.

CAROL: I can't tell you.

JOHN: No, you must.

CAROL: I can't.

JOHN: No. Tell me. (*Pause*)

CAROL: I'm bad. (*Pause*) Oh, God. (*Pause*)

JOHN: It's all right.

CAROL: I'm . . .

JOHN: It's all right.

CAROL: I can't talk about this.

JOHN: It's all right. Tell me.

CAROL: Why do you want to know this?

JOHN: I don't want to know. I want to know whatever you . . .

CAROL: I always . . .

JOHN: . . . good . . .

CAROL: I always . . . all my life . . . I have never told anyone this . . .

JOHN: Yes. Go on. (*Pause*) Go on.

CAROL: All of my life . . . (*The phone rings.*) (*Pause.* JOHN *goes to the phone and picks it up.*)

JOHN (*into phone*):   I can't talk now. (*Pause*) What? (*Pause*) Hmm. (*Pause*) All right, I . . . I. Can't. Talk. Now. No, no, no, I *Know* I did, but. . . . What? Hello. What? She *what?* She *can't,* she said the agreement is void? How, how is the agreement *void? That's Our House.*

I have the *paper;* when we come down, next week, with the payment, and the paper, that house is . . . wait, wait, wait, wait, wait, wait, wait: Did Jerry . . . is Jerry there? (*Pause*) Is *she* there . . .? Does she have a *lawyer* . . .? How the *hell,* how the *Hell.* That is . . . it's a question, you said, of the *easement.* I don't underst . . . it's not the *whole agreement.* It's just the *easement,* why would she? Put, put, put, *Jerry* on. (*Pause*) Jer, *Jerry:* What the *Hell* . . . that's my *house.* That's . . . Well, I'm, no, no, no, I'm *not* coming ddd . . . List, *Listen, screw* her. You *tell* her. You, listen: I want you to take *Grace,* you take Grace, and get out of that house. You *leave* her there. Her and her lawyer, and you *tell* them, we'll see them in court next . . . no. No. Leave her there, leave her to *stew* in it: You tell her, we're *getting* that house, and we are going to . . . No. I'm *not* coming down. I'll be damned if I'll sit in the same rrr . . . the next, you tell her the next time I *see* her is in court . . . I . . . (*Pause*) What? (*Pause*) What? I don't understand. (*Pause*) Well, what about the house? (*Pause*) There isn't any problem with the hhh . . . (*Pause*) No, no, no, that's all right. All ri . . . All right . . . (*Pause*) Of course. Tha . . . Thank you. No, I will. Right away. (*He hangs up.*) (*Pause*)

CAROL: (*Pause*) They're proud of you.
JOHN: Well, there are those who would say it's a form of aggression.
CAROL: What is?
JOHN: A surprise.
CAROL: What is it? (*Pause*)
JOHN: It's a surprise party.
CAROL: It is.
JOHN: Yes.
CAROL: A party for you.
JOHN: Yes.
CAROL: Is it your birthday?
JOHN: No.
CAROL: What is it?
JOHN: The tenure announcement.
CAROL: The tenure announcement.
JOHN: They're throwing a party for us in our new house.
CAROL: Your new house.
JOHN: The house that we're buying.
CAROL: You have to go.
JOHN: It seems that I do.

TWO

JOHN *and* CAROL *seated across the desk from each other.*

JOHN: You see, (*pause*) I love to teach. And flatter myself I am *skilled* at it. And I love the, the aspect of *performance.* I think I must confess that.

When I found I loved to teach I swore that I would not become that cold, rigid automaton of an instructor which I had encountered as a child.

Now, I was not unconscious that it was given me to err upon the other side. And, so, I asked and *ask* myself if I engaged in heterodoxy, I will not say "gratuitously" for I do not care to posit orthodoxy as a given good—but, "to the detriment of, of my students." (*Pause*)

As I said. When the possibility of tenure opened, and, of course, I'd long pursued it, I was, of course *happy,* and *covetous* of it.

I asked myself if I was wrong to covet it. And thought about it long, and, I hope, truthfully, and saw in myself several things in, I think, no particular order. (*Pause*)

That I *would* pursue it. That I *desired* it, that I was not pure of longing for security, and that that, perhaps, was not reprehensible in me. That I had duties
beyond the school, and that my duty to my home, for instance, was, or should
be, if it were not, of an equal weight. That tenure, and security, and yes, and
comfort, were not, of themselves, to be scorned; and were even worthy of honorable pursuit. And that it was given me. Here, in this place, which I enjoy,
and in which I find comfort, to assure myself of—as far as it rests in The Material—a continuation of that joy and comfort. In exchange for what? Teaching. Which I love.

What was the price of this security? To obtain *tenure.* Which tenure the committee is in the process of granting me. And on the basis of which I contracted
to purchase a house. Now, as you don't have your own family, at this point,
you may not know what that means. But to me it is important. A home. A
Good Home. To raise my family. Now: The Tenure Committee will meet.
This is the process, and a *good* process. Under which the school has functioned
for quite a long time. They will meet, and hear your complaint—which you
have the right to make; and they will dismiss it. They will *dismiss* your complaint; and, in the intervening period, I will lose my house. I will not be able
to close on my house. I will lose my *deposit,* and the home I'd picked out for
my wife and son will go by the boards. Now: I see I have angered you. I understand your anger at teachers. I was angry with mine. I felt hurt and humiliated by them. Which is one of the reasons that I went into education.

CAROL: What do you want of me?

JOHN: (*Pause*) I was hurt. When I received the report. Of the tenure committee. I was shocked. And I was hurt. No, I don't mean to subject you to my
weak sensibilities. All right. Finally, I didn't understand. Then I thought: is it
not always at those points at which we reckon ourselves unassailable that we
are most vulnerable and . . . (*Pause*) Yes. All right. You find me pedantic. Yes.
I am. By nature, by *birth,* by profession, I don't know . . . I'm always looking
for a *paradigm* for . . .

CAROL: I don't know what a paradigm is.

JOHN: It's a model.

CAROL: Then why can't you use that word? (*Pause*)

JOHN: If it is important to you. Yes, all right. I was looking for a model.
To continue: I feel that one point . . .

CAROL: I . . .

JOHN: One second . . . upon which I am unassailable is my unflinching concern for my students' dignity. I asked you here to . . . in the spirit of *investigation,* to ask you . . . to ask . . . (*Pause*) What have I done to you? (*Pause*) And,
and, I suppose, now I can make amends. Can we not settle this now? It's pointless, really, and I want to know.

CAROL: What you can do to force me to retract?

JOHN: That is not what I meant at all.

CAROL: To bribe me, to convince me . . .

JOHN: . . . No.

CAROL: To retract . . .

JOHN: That is not what I meant at all. I think that you know it is not.

CAROL: That is not what I know. I *wish* I . . .

JOHN: I do not want to . . . you wish what?

CAROL: No, you said what amends can you make. To force me to retract.

JOHN: That is not what I said.

CAROL: I have my notes.

JOHN: Look. Look. The Stoics say . . .

CAROL: The Stoics?

JOHN: The Stoical Philosophers say if you remove the phrase "I have been injured," you have removed the injury. Now: Think: I know that you're upset. Just tell me. Literally. Literally: what wrong have I done you?

CAROL: Whatever you have done to me—to the extent that you've done it to *me,* do you know, rather than to me as a *student,* and, so, to the student body, is contained in my report. To the tenure committee.

JOHN: Well, all right. (*Pause*) Let's see. (*He reads.*) I find that I am sexist. That I am *elitist.* I'm not not sure I know what that means, other than it's a derogatory word, meaning "bad." That I . . . That I insist on wasting time, in nonprescribed, in self-aggrandizing and theatrical *diversions* from the prescribed *text* . . . that these have taken both sexist and pornographic forms . . . here we find listed . . . (*Pause*) Here we find listed . . . instances " . . . closeted with a student" . . . "Told a rambling, sexually explicit story, in which the frequency and attitudes of fornication of the poor and rich are, it would seem, the central point . . . moved to *embrace* said student and . . . all part of a pattern . . ." (*Pause*)

(*He reads.*) That I used the phrase "The White Man's Burden" . . . that I told you how I'd asked you to my room because I quote like you. (*Pause*)

(*He reads.*) "He said he 'liked' me. That he 'liked being with me.' He'd let me write my examination paper over, if I could come back oftener to see him in his office." (*Pause*) (*To* CAROL:) It's *ludicrous.* Don't you know that? It's not *necessary.* It's going to *humiliate* you, and it's going to cost me my *house,* and . . .

CAROL: It's *"ludicrous . . ."*?

(JOHN *picks up the report and reads again.*)

JOHN: "He told me he had problems with his wife; and that he wanted to take off the artificial stricture of Teacher and Student. He put his arm around me . . ."

CAROL: Do you deny it? Can you deny it . . .? Do you see? (*Pause*) Don't you see? You don't see, do you?

JOHN: I don't see . . .

CAROL: You think, you think you can deny that these things happened; or, if they *did,* if they *did,* that they meant what you *said* they meant. Don't you see? You drag me in here, you drag us, to listen to you "go on"; and "go on" about this, or that, or we don't "express" ourselves very well. We don't say what we mean. Don't we? Don't we? We *do* say what we mean. And you say that "I don't understand you . . .": Then *you* . . . (*Points.*)

JOHN: "Consult the Report"?

CAROL: . . . that's right.

JOHN: You see. You see. Can't you. . . . You see what I'm saying? Can't you tell me in your own words?

CAROL: Those are my own words. (*Pause*)

JOHN: (*He reads.*) "He told me that if I would stay alone with him in his office, he would change my grade to an A." (*To* CAROL:) What have I done to you? Oh. My God, are you so hurt?

CAROL: What I "feel" is irrelevant. (*Pause*)

JOHN: Do you know that I tried to help you?

CAROL: What I know I have reported.

JOHN: I would like to help you now. I would. Before this escalates.

CAROL (*simultaneously with* "escalates"):   You see. I don't think that I need your help. I don't think I need anything you have.

JOHN: I feel . . .

CAROL: I don't *care* what you feel. Do you see? DO YOU SEE? You can't *do* that anymore. You. Do. Not. Have. The. Power. Did you misuse it? Some-one did. Are you part of that group? *Yes. Yes.* You Are. You've *done* these things. And to say, and to say, "Oh. Let me help you with your problem . . ."

JOHN: Yes. I understand. I understand. You're *hurt*. You're *angry*. Yes. I think your *anger* is *betraying* you. Down a path which helps no one.

CAROL: I don't *care* what you think.

JOHN: You don't? (*Pause*) But you talk of *rights*. Don't you see? *I* have rights too. Do you see? I have a *house* . . . part of the *real* world; and The Tenure Committee, Good Men and True . . .

CAROL: . . . Professor . . .

JOHN: . . . Please: *Also* part of that world: you understand? This is my *life*. I'm not a *bogeyman*. I don't "stand" for something, I . . .

CAROL: . . . Professor . . .

JOHN: . . . I . . .

CAROL: Professor. I came here as a *favor*. At your personal request. Perhaps I should not have done so. But I did. On my behalf, and on behalf of my group. And you speak of the tenure committee, one of whose members is a woman, as you know. And though you might call it Good Fun, or An Historical Phrase, or An Oversight, or, All of the Above, to refer to the committee as Good Men and True, it is a demeaning remark. It is a sexist remark, and to overlook it is to countenance continuation of that method of thought. It's a remark . . .

JOHN: OH COME ON. Come on. . . . Sufficient to deprive a family of . . .

CAROL: Sufficient? Sufficient? Sufficient? Yes. It is a *fact* . . . and that story, which I quote, is *vile* and *classist,* and *manipulative* and *pornographic*. It . . .

JOHN: . . . it's pornographic . . . ?

CAROL: What gives you the *right*. Yes. To speak to a *woman* in your pri-vate . . . Yes. Yes. I'm sorry. I'm sorry. You feel yourself empowered . . . you say so yourself. To *strut*. To *posture*. To "perform." To "Call me in here . . ." Eh? You say that higher education is a joke. And treat it as such, you *treat* it as such. And *confess* to a taste to play the *Patriarch* in your class. To grant *this*. To deny *that*. To embrace your students.

JOHN: How can you assert. How can you stand there and . . .

CAROL: How can you *deny* it. You did it to me. *Here*. You *did*. . . . You *confess*. You love the Power. To *deviate*. To *invent,* to transgress . . . to *transgress* whatever norms have been established for us. And you think it's charming to "question" in yourself this taste to mock and destroy. But you should question it. Professor. And you pick those things which you feel *advance* you: publication, *tenure,* and the steps to get them you call "harmless rituals." And you perform those steps. Although you say it is hypocrisy. But to the aspirations of your students. Of *hardworking students,* who come here, who *slave* to come here—you have no idea what it cost me to come to this school—you *mock* us. You call education "hazing," and from your so-protected, so-elitist seat you hold our confusion as a *joke,* and our hopes and efforts with it. Then you sit there and say "what have I done?" And ask me to understand that *you* have aspirations too. But I tell you. I tell you. That you are vile. And that you are exploitative. And if you possess one ounce of that inner honesty you describe in your book, you can look in yourself and see those things that I see. And you can find revulsion equal to my own. Good day. (*She prepares to leave the room.*)

JOHN: Wait a second, will you, just one moment. (*Pause*) Nice day today.

CAROL: What?

JOHN: You said "Good day." I think that it is a nice day today.

CAROL: *Is* it?

JOHN: Yes, I think it is.

CAROL: And why is that important?

JOHN: Because it is the essence of all human communication. I say something conventional, you respond, and the information we exchange is not about the "weather," but that we both agree to converse. In effect, we agree that we are both human. (*Pause*)

I'm not a . . . "exploiter," and you're not a . . . "deranged," what? *Revolutionary* . . . that we may, that we may have . . . positions, and that we may have . . . desires, which are in *conflict,* but that we're just human. (*Pause*) That means that sometimes we're *imperfect.* (*Pause*) Often we're in conflict . . . (*Pause*) *Much* of what we do, you're right, in the name of "principles" is *self-serving* . . . much of what we do is *conventional.* (*Pause*) You're right. (*Pause*) You said you came in the class because you wanted to learn about *education.* I don't know that I can teach you about education. But I know that I can tell you what I *think* about education, and then *you* decide. And you don't have to fight with me. *I'm* not the subject. (*Pause*) And where I'm *wrong* . . . perhaps it's not your job to "fix" me. I don't want to fix *you.* I would like to tell you what I *think,* because that *is* my job, conventional as it is, and flawed as I may be. And then, if you can show me some better *form,* then we can proceed from there. But, just like "nice day, isn't it . . . ?" I don't think we can proceed until we accept that each of us is human. (*Pause*) And we still can have difficulties. We *will* have them . . . that's all right too. (*Pause*) Now:

CAROL: . . . wait . . .

JOHN: Yes. I want to hear it.

CAROL: . . . the . . .

JOHN: Yes. Tell me frankly.

CAROL: . . . my position . . .

JOHN: I want to hear it. In your own words. What you want. And what you feel.

CAROL: . . . I . . .

JOHN: . . . yes . . .

CAROL: My Group.

JOHN: Your "Group" . . . ? (*Pause*)

CAROL: The people I've been talking to . . .

JOHN: There's no shame in that. Everybody needs advisers. Everyone needs to expose themselves. To various points of view. It's not wrong. It's essential. Good. Good. Now: You and I . . . (*The phone rings.*)

You and I . . .

(*He hesitates for a moment, and then picks it up.*) (*Into phone*) Hello. (*Pause*) Um . . . no, I know they do. (*Pause*) I know she does. Tell her that I . . . can I call you back? . . . Then tell her that I think it's going to be fine. (*Pause*) Tell her just, just hold on, I'll . . . can I get back to you? . . . Well . . . no, no, no, we're *taking* the house . . . we're . . . no, no, nn . . . no, she will nnn, it's not a *question* of refunding the dep . . . no . . . it's not a *question* of the deposit . . . will you call Jerry? Babe, baby, will you just call Jerry? Tell him, nnn . . . tell him they, well, they're to keep the deposit, because the deal, be . . . because the deal is going to go *through* . . . because I know . . . be . . . will you please? Just *trust* me. Be . . . well, I'm dealing with the complaint. Yes. Right *Now*. Which is why I . . . yes, no, no, it's really, I can't *talk* about it now. Call Jerry, and I can't talk now. Ff . . . fine. Gg . . . good-bye. (*Hangs up.*) (*Pause*) I'm sorry we were interrupted.

CAROL: No . . .

JOHN: I . . . I was saying:

CAROL: You said that we should agree to talk about my complaint.

JOHN: That's correct.

CAROL: But we *are* talking about it.

JOHN: Well, that's correct too. You see? This is the *gist* of education.

CAROL: No, no. I mean, we're talking about it at the Tenure Committee Hearing. (*Pause*)

JOHN: Yes, but I'm saying: we can talk about it *now,* as easily as . . .

CAROL: No. I think that we should stick to the process . . .

JOHN: . . . wait a . . .

CAROL: . . . the "conventional" process. As you said. (*She gets up.*) And you're right, I'm sorry if I was, um, if I was "discourteous" to you. You're right.

JOHN: Wait, wait a . . .

CAROL: I really should go.

JOHN: Now, look, granted. I have an interest. In the status quo. All right? Everyone does. But what I'm saying is that the *committee* . . .

CAROL: Professor, you're right. Just don't impinge on me. We'll take our differences, and . . .

JOHN: You're going to make a . . . look, look, look, you're going to . . .

CAROL: I shouldn't have come here. They told me . . .

JOHN: One moment. No. No. There are *norms,* here, and there's no reason. Look: I'm trying to *save* you . . .

CAROL: No one *asked* you to . . . you're trying to save *me?* Do me the courtesy to . . .

JOHN: I *am* doing you the courtesy. I'm talking *straight* to you. We can settle this *now.* And I want you to sit *down* and . . .

CAROL: You must excuse me . . . (*She starts to leave the room.*)

JOHN: Sit down, it seems we each have a. . . . Wait one moment. Wait one moment . . . just do me the courtesy to . . .

(*He restrains her from leaving.*)

CAROL: LET ME GO.

JOHN: I have no desire to *hold* you, I just want to *talk* to you . . .

CAROL: LET ME GO. LET ME GO. WOULD SOMEBODY *HELP* ME? WOULD SOMEBODY *HELP* ME PLEASE . . . ?

THREE

(*At rise,* CAROL *and* JOHN *are seated.*)

JOHN: I have asked you here. (*Pause*) I have asked you here against, against my . . .

CAROL: I was most surprised you asked me.

JOHN: . . . against my better *judgment,* against . . .

CAROL: I was most surprised . . .

JOHN: . . . against the . . . yes. I'm sure.

CAROL: . . . If you would like me to leave, I'll leave. I'll go right now . . . (*She rises.*)

JOHN: Let us begin *correctly,* may we? I feel . . .

CAROL: That is what I wished to do. That's why I came here, but now . . .

JOHN: . . . I feel . . .

CAROL: But now perhaps you'd like me to leave . . .

JOHN: I don't want you to leave. I asked you to come . . .

CAROL: I didn't have to come here.

JOHN: No. (*Pause*) Thank you.

CAROL: All right. (*Pause*) (*She sits down.*)

JOHN: Although I feel that it *profits,* it would *profit* you something, to . . .

CAROL: . . . what I . . .

JOHN: If you would hear me out, if you would hear me out.

CAROL: I came here to, the court officers told me not to come.

JOHN: . . . the "court" officers . . . ?

CAROL: I was shocked that you asked.

JOHN: . . . wait . . .

CAROL: Yes. But I did *not* come here to hear what it "profits" me.

JOHN: The "court" officers . . .

CAROL: . . . no, no, perhaps I should leave . . . (*She gets up.*)

JOHN: Wait.

CAROL: No. I shouldn't have . . .

JOHN: . . . wait. Wait. Wait a moment.

CAROL: Yes? What is it you want? (*Pause*) What is it you want?

JOHN: I'd like you to stay.

CAROL: You want me to stay.

JOHN: Yes.

CAROL: You do.

JOHN: Yes. (*Pause*) Yes. I would like to have you hear me out. If you would. (*Pause*) Would you please? If you would do that I would be in your debt. (*Pause*) (*She sits.*) Thank You. (*Pause*)

CAROL: What is it you wish to tell me?

JOHN: All right. I cannot . . . (*Pause*) I cannot help but feel you are owed an apology. (*Pause*) (*Of papers in his hands*) I have read. (*Pause*) And reread these accusations.

CAROL: What "accusations"?

JOHN: The, the tenure comm . . . what other accusations . . . ?

CAROL: The tenure committee . . . ?

JOHN: Yes.

CAROL: Excuse me, but those are not accusations. They have been *proved.* They are facts.

JOHN: . . . I . . .

CAROL: No. Those are not "accusations."

JOHN: . . . those?

CAROL: . . . the committee (*The phone starts to ring.*) the committee has . . .

JOHN: . . . All right . . .

CAROL: . . . those are not accusations. The Tenure Committee.

JOHN: ALL RIGHT. ALL RIGHT. ALL RIGHT. (*He picks up the phone.*) Hello. Yes. No. I'm here. Tell Mister . . . No, I can't talk to him now . . . I'm sure he has, but I'm fff . . . I know . . . No, I have no time t . . . tell Mister . . . tell Mist . . . tell Jerry that I'm *fine* and that I'll call him right aw . . . (*Pause*) My wife . . . Yes. I'm sure she has. Yes, thank you. Yes, I'll call her too. I cannot talk to you now. (*He hangs up.*) (*Pause*) All right. It was good of you to come. Thank you. I have studied. I have spent some time studying the indictment.

CAROL: You will have to explain that word to me.

JOHN: An "indictment". . .

CAROL: Yes.

JOHN: Is a "bill of particulars." A . . .

CAROL: All right. Yes.

JOHN: In which is alleged . . .

CAROL: No. I cannot allow that. I cannot allow that. Nothing is alleged. Everything is proved . . .

JOHN: Please, wait a sec . . .

CAROL: I cannot *come* to allow . . .

JOHN: If I may . . . If I may, from whatever you feel is "established," by . . .

CAROL: The issue here is not what I "feel." It is not my "feelings," but the feelings of women. And men. Your superiors, who've been "polled." do you see? To whom *evidence* has been presented, who have *ruled,* do you see? Who have weighed the testimony and the evidence, and have *ruled,* do you see? That you are *negligent.* That you are *guilty,* that you are found *wanting,* and in *error;* and are *not,* for the reasons so–told, to be given tenure. That you are to be disciplined. For facts. For *facts.* Not "alleged," what is the word? But *proved.* Do you see? *By your own actions.*

That is what the tenure committee has said. That is what my lawyer said. For what you did in class. For what you did *in this office*.

JOHN: They're going to discharge me.

CAROL: As full well they should. You don't understand? You're angry? What has *led* you to this place? Not your sex. Not your race. Not your class. YOUR OWN ACTIONS. And you're *angry*. You *ask* me here. What *do* you want? You want to "charm" me. You want to "convince" me. You want me to recant. I will *not* recant. Why should I . . . ? What I say is right. You tell me, you are going to tell me that you have a wife and child. You are going to say that you have a career and that you've worked for twenty years for this. Do you know what you've *worked* for? *Power*. For *power*. Do you understand? And you sit there, and you tell me *stories*. About your *house*, about all the private *schools*, and about *privilege*, and how you are entitled. To *buy*, to *spend*, to *mock*, to *summon*. All your stories. All your silly weak *guilt*, it's all about *privilege;* and you won't know it. Don't you see? You worked twenty years for the right to *insult* me. And you feel entitled to be *paid* for it. Your Home. Your Wife . . . Your sweet "deposit" on your house . . .

JOHN: Don't you have feelings?

CAROL: That's my point. You see? Don't you have feelings? Your final argument. What is it that has no feelings. *Animals*. I don't take your side, you question if I'm Human.

JOHN: Don't you have feelings?

CAROL: I have a responsibility. I . . .

JOHN: . . . to . . . ?

CAROL: To? This institution. To the *students*. To my *group*.

JOHN: . . . your "group." . . .

CAROL: Because I speak, yes, not for myself. But for the group; for those who suffer what I suffer. On behalf of whom, even if I, were, inclined, to what, forgive? Forget? What? Overlook your . . .

JOHN: . . . my behavior?

CAROL: . . . it would be wrong.

JOHN: Even if you were inclined to "forgive" me.

CAROL: It would be wrong.

JOHN: And what would transpire.

CAROL: Transpire?

JOHN: Yes.

CAROL: "Happen?"

JOHN: Yes.

CAROL: Then *say* it. For Christ's sake. Who the *hell* do you think that you are? You want a post. You want unlimited power. To do and to say what you want. As it pleases you—Testing, Questioning, Flirting . . .

JOHN: I never . . .

CAROL: Excuse me, one moment, will you?

(She reads from her notes.)

The twelfth: "Have a good day, dear."
The fifteenth: "Now, don't *you* look fetching . . ."

April seventeenth: "If you girls would come over here . . ." I saw you. I saw you, Professor. For two semesters sit there, stand there and exploit our, as you thought, "paternal prerogative," and what is that but rape; I swear to God. You asked me in here to explain something to me, as a child, that I did not understand. But I came to explain something to you. You Are Not God. You ask me why I came? I came here to instruct you.

(She produces his book.)

And your book? You think you're going to show me some "light"? You *"maverick."* Outside of tradition. No, no, *(She reads from the book's liner notes.) "of* that fine tradition of *inquiry.* Of Polite *skepticism"* . . . and you say you believe in free intellectual discourse. YOU BELIEVE IN NOTHING. YOU BELIEVE IN NOTHING AT ALL.

JOHN: I believe in freedom of thought.

CAROL: Isn't that fine. *Do* you?

JOHN: Yes. I do.

CAROL: Then why do you question, for one moment, the committee's decision refusing your tenure? Why do you question your suspension? You believe in what *you call* freedom of thought. Then, fine. *You* believe in freedom-of-thought *and* a home, and, *and* prerogatives for your kid, *and* tenure. And I'm going to tell you. You believe *not* in "freedom of thought," but in an elitist, in, in a protected hierarchy which rewards you. And for whom you are the clown. And you mock and exploit the system which pays your rent. You're wrong. I'm not wrong. You're wrong. You think that I'm full of hatred. I know what you think I am.

JOHN: Do you?

CAROL: You think I'm a, of course I do. You think I am a frightened, repressed, confused, I don't know, abandoned young thing of some doubtful sexuality, who wants, power and revenge. *(Pause) Don't* you? *(Pause)*

JOHN: Yes. I do. *(Pause)*

CAROL: Isn't that better? And I feel that that is the first moment which you've treated me with respect. For you told me the truth. *(Pause)* I did not come here, as you are assured, to gloat. Why would I want to gloat? I've profited nothing from your, your, as you say, your "misfortune." I came here, as you did me the honor to *ask* me here, I came here to *tell* you something.

(Pause) That I think . . . that I think you've been wrong. That I think you've been terribly wrong. Do you hate me now? *(Pause)*

JOHN: Yes.

CAROL: Why do you hate me? Because you think me wrong? No. Because I have, you think, *power* over you. Listen to me. Listen to me, Professor. *(Pause)* It is the power that you hate. So deeply that, that any atmosphere of free discussion is impossible. It's not "unlikely." It's *impossible.* Isn't it?

JOHN: Yes.

CAROL: *Isn't* it . . . ?

JOHN: Yes. I suppose.

CAROL: Now. The thing which you find so cruel is the selfsame process of selection I, and my group, go through *every day of our lives.* In admittance to school. In our tests, in our class rankings. . . . Is it unfair? I can't tell you. But, if it is fair. Or even if it is "unfortunate but necessary" for us, then, by God, so must it be for you. (*Pause*) You write of your "responsibility to the young." Treat us with respect, and that will *show* you your responsibility. You write that education is just hazing. (*Pause*) But we worked to get to this school. (*Pause*) And some of us. (*Pause*) Overcame prejudices. Economic, sexual, you cannot begin to imagine. And endured humiliations I *pray* that you and those you love never will encounter. (*Pause*) To gain admittance here. To pursue that same dream of security *you* pursue. We, who, who are, at any moment, in danger of being deprived of it. By . . .

JOHN: . . . by . . . ?

CAROL: By the administration. By the teachers. By *you*. By, say, one low grade, that keeps us out of graduate school; by one, say, one capricious or inventive answer on our parts, which, perhaps, you don't find amusing. Now you *know*, do you see? What it is to be subject to that power. (*Pause*)

JOHN: I don't understand. (*Pause*)

CAROL: My charges are not trivial. You see that in the haste, I think, with which they were accepted. A *joke* you have told, with a sexist tinge. The language you use, a verbal or physical caress, yes, yes, I know, you say that it is meaningless. I understand. I differ from you. To lay a hand on someone's shoulder.

JOHN: It was devoid of sexual content.

CAROL: I say it was not. I SAY IT WAS NOT. Don't you begin to *see* . . . ? Don't you begin to understand? IT'S NOT FOR YOU TO SAY.

JOHN: I take your point, and I see there is much good in what you refer to.

CAROL: . . . do you think so . . . ?

JOHN: . . . but, and this is not to say that I cannot change, in those things in which I am deficient . . . But, the . . .

CAROL: Do you hold yourself harmless from the charge of sexual exploitativeness . . . ? (*Pause*)

JOHN: Well, I . . . I . . . I . . . You know I, as I said. I . . . think I am not too old to *learn*, and I *can* learn, I . . .

CAROL: Do you hold yourself innocent of the charge of . . .

JOHN: . . . wait, wait, wait . . . All right, let's go back to . . .

CAROL: YOU FOOL. Who do you think I am? To come here and be taken in by a *smile*. You little yapping fool. You think I want "revenge." I don't want revenge. I WANT UNDERSTANDING.

JOHN: . . . *do* you?

CAROL: I do. (*Pause*)

JOHN: What's the use. It's over.

CAROL: Is it? What is?

JOHN: My job.

CAROL: Oh. Your job. That's what you want to talk about. (*Pause*) (*She starts to leave the room. She steps and turns back to him.*) All right. (*Pause*) What if it were possible that my Group withdraws its complaint. (*Pause*)

JOHN: What?

CAROL: That's right. (*Pause*)

JOHN: Why.

CAROL: Well, let's say as an act of friendship.

JOHN: An act of friendship.

CAROL: Yes. (*Pause*)

JOHN: In exchange for what.

CAROL: Yes. But I don't think, "exchange." Not "in exchange." For what do we derive from it? (*Pause*)

JOHN: "Derive."

CAROL: Yes.

JOHN: (*Pause*) Nothing. (*Pause*)

CAROL: That's right. We derive nothing. (*Pause*) Do you see that?

JOHN: Yes.

CAROL: That is a little word, Professor. "Yes." "I see that." But you will.

JOHN: And you might speak to the committee . . . ?

CAROL: To the committee?

JOHN: Yes.

CAROL: Well. Of course. That's on your mind. We might.

JOHN: "If" what?

CAROL: "Given" what. Perhaps. I think that that is more friendly.

JOHN: GIVEN WHAT?

CAROL: And, believe me, I understand your rage. It is not that I don't feel it. But I do not see that it is deserved, so I do not resent it. . . . All right. I have a list.

JOHN: . . . a list.

CAROL: Here is a list of books, which we . . .

JOHN: . . . a list of books . . . ?

CAROL: That's right. Which we find questionable.

JOHN: What?

CAROL: Is this so bizarre . . . ?

JOHN: I can't believe . . .

CAROL: It's not necessary you believe it.

JOHN: Academic freedom . . .

CAROL: Someone chooses the books. If you can choose them, others can. What are you, "God"?

JOHN: . . . no, no, the "dangerous." . . .

CAROL: You have an agenda, we have an agenda. I am not interested in your feelings or your motivation, but your actions. If you would like me to speak to the Tenure Committee, here is my list. You are a Free Person, you decide. (*Pause*)

JOHN: Give me the list. (*She does so. He reads.*)

CAROL: I think you'll find . . .

JOHN: I'm capable of reading it. Thank you.

CAROL: We have a number of *texts* we need re . . .

JOHN: I see that.

CAROL: We're amenable to . . .

JOHN: Aha. Well, let me look over the . . . (*He reads.*)

CAROL: I think that . . .

JOHN: LOOK. I'm reading your demands. All right?! (*He reads*) (*Pause*) You want to ban my book?

CAROL: We do not . . .

JOHN (*Of list*):   It says here . . .

CAROL: . . . We want it removed from inclusion as a representative example of the university.

JOHN: Get out of here.

CAROL: If you put aside the issues of personalities.

JOHN: Get the fuck out of my office.

CAROL: No, I think I would reconsider.

JOHN: . . . you think you can.

CAROL: We can and we *will*. Do you want our support? That is the only quest . . .

JOHN: . . . to ban my *book* . . . ?

CAROL: . . . that is correct . . .

JOHN: . . . this . . . this is a *university* . . . we . . .

CAROL: . . . and we have a statement . . . which we need you to . . . (*She hands him a sheet of paper.*)

JOHN: No, no. It's out of the question. I'm sorry. I don't know what I was thinking of. I want to tell you something. I'm a teacher. I am a teacher. Eh? It's my *name* on the door, and *I* teach the class, and that's what I do. I've got a book with my name on it. And my son will *see* that *book* someday. And I have a respon . . . No, I'm sorry I have a *responsibility* . . . to *myself,* to my *son,* to my *profession.* . . . I haven't been *home* for two days, do you know that? Thinking this out.

CAROL: . . . you haven't?

JOHN: I've been, no. If it's of interest to you. I've been in a *hotel. Thinking.* (*The phone starts ringing.*) *Thinking* . . .

CAROL: . . . you haven't been home?

JOHN: . . . *thinking,* do you see.

CAROL: Oh.

JOHN: And, and, I owe you a debt, I see that now. (*Pause*) You're *dangerous,* you're *wrong* and it's my *job* . . . to say no to you. That's my job. You are absolutely right. You want to ban my book? Go to *hell,* and they can do whatever they want to me.

CAROL: . . . you haven't been home in two days . . .

JOHN: I think I told you that.

CAROL: . . . you'd better get that phone. (*Pause*) I think that you should pick up the phone. (*Pause*)

(JOHN *picks up the phone.*)

JOHN (*on phone*):   Yes. (*Pause*) Yes. Wh . . . I. I. I had to be away. All ri . . . did they wor . . . did they worry ab . . . No. I'm all right, now, Jerry. I'm f . . . I got a little turned *around,* but I'm *sitting* here and . . . I've got it figured out. I'm fine. I'm fine don't worry about me. I got a little bit mixed up. But I am not sure that it's not a blessing. It cost me my job? Fine. Then the job was not worth having. Tell Grace that I'm coming home and everything is fff . . . (*Pause*) What? (*Pause*) *What?* (*Pause*) What do you *mean?* WHAT? Jerry . . . Jerry. They . . . Who, who, what can they do . . . ? (*Pause*) NO. (*Pause*) NO. They can't do th . . . What do you mean? (*Pause*) But how . . . (*Pause*) She's, she's, she's *here* with me. To . . . Jerry. I don't underst . . . (*Pause*) (*He hangs up.*) (*To* CAROL:) What does this mean?

CAROL: I thought you knew.

JOHN: What. (*Pause*) What does it mean. (*Pause*)

CAROL: You tried to rape me. (*Pause*) According to the law. (*Pause*)

JOHN: . . . what . . . ?

CAROL: You tried to rape me. I was leaving this office, you "pressed" yourself into me. You "pressed" your body into me.

JOHN: . . . I . . .

CAROL: My Group has told your lawyer that we may pursue criminal charges.

JOHN: . . . no . . .

CAROL: . . . under the statute. I am told. It was battery.

JOHN: . . . no . . .

CAROL: Yes. And attempted rape. That's right. (*Pause*)

JOHN: I think that you should go.

CAROL: Of course. I thought you knew.

JOHN: I have to talk to my lawyer.

CAROL: Yes. Perhaps you should. (*The phone rings again.*) (*Pause*)

JOHN: (*Picks up phone. Into phone:*) Hello? I . . . Hello . . . ? I . . . Yes, he just called. No . . . I. I can't talk to you now, Baby. (*To* CAROL:) Get out.

CAROL: . . . your wife . . . ?

JOHN: . . . who it is is no concern of yours. Get out. (*To phone:*) No, no, it's going to be all right. I. I can't talk now, Baby. (*To* CAROL:) Get out of here.

CAROL: I'm going.

JOHN: Good.

CAROL (*exiting*):   . . . and don't call your wife "baby."

JOHN: What?

CAROL: Don't call your wife baby. You heard what I said.

(CAROL *starts to leave the room.* JOHN *grabs her and begins to beat her.*)

JOHN: You vicious little bitch. You think you can come in here with your political correctness and destroy my life?

(*He knocks her to the floor.*)

After how I treated you . . . ? You should be . . . *Rape you* . . . ? Are you kidding me . . . ?

(*He picks up a chair, raises it above his head, and advances on her.*)

I wouldn't touch you with a ten-foot pole. You little *cunt* . . .

(*She cowers on the floor below him. Pause. He looks down at her. He lowers the chair. He moves to his desk, and arranges the papers on it. Pause. He looks over at her.*)

. . . well . . .

(*Pause. She looks at him.*)

CAROL: Yes. That's right.

(*She looks away from him, and lowers her head. To herself:*) . . . yes. That's right.

(1992)

QUESTIONS

1. What is the dramatic effect of the telephone conversations that punctuate the discussions between Carol and John?
2. What differences between John and Carol are highlighted in the first act? Why are those differences significant?
3. To what extent are Carol and John similar? What concerns do they share? Who makes the claim for their shared commonalities? How convincing is that claim?
4. At what point does the professor's response to his student change in Act I? In Act II? In each case, what prompts his different behavior?
5. What ideas about education emerge during the course of the play? What is the teacher's attitude toward education? Toward teaching?
6. What was the teacher's offense? Do you find him guilty of serious infractions? Why or why not?
7. Is the student justified in her accusations? Is her report accurate, fair, reasonable?
8. Contrast Carol's and John's manner and language in Act II with their manner and way of speaking in Act I. What is the significance of the differences?
9. Whose views does Carol represent? Why is it important that she express the views of "the Group"?
10. What is the significance of the play's ending? How do you respond to it? Why?

WENDY WASSERSTEIN

[b. 1950]

Wendy Wasserstein was born and raised in New York City. She was educated at Smith College and at Mount Holyoke College, from which she graduated with a B.A. in 1971. Two years later she earned a master's degree in playwriting from City College of New York. From 1973 until 1976 she studied at the Yale School of Drama, from which she received a master of fine arts. In 1989 she won the Pulitzer Prize and a Tony Award for Best Play for *The Heidi Chronicles,* and in 1993 she won a Outer Circle Critics Award and a Tony nomination for *The Sisters Rosenzweig.* In addition to plays, she has written for public television and film.

Tender Offer, which was written and produced in 1977, is a one-act play that captures the relationship between a father and his teen-age daughter. The play's economy and its humor belie its underlying seriousness.

WENDY WASSERSTEIN

Tender Offer

A girl of around nine is alone in a dance studio. She is dressed in traditional leotards and tights. She begins singing to herself, "Nothing Could Be Finer Than to Be in Carolina." She maps out a dance routine, including parts for the chorus. She builds to a finale. A man, PAUL, *around thirty-five, walks in. He has a sweet, though distant, demeanor. As he walks in,* LISA *notices him and stops.*

PAUL: You don't have to stop, sweetheart.

LISA: That's okay.

PAUL: Looked very good.

LISA: Thanks.

PAUL: Don't I get a kiss hello?

LISA: Sure.

PAUL: [*Embraces her.*] Hi, Tiger.

LISA: Hi, Dad.

PAUL: I'm sorry I'm late.

LISA: That's okay.

PAUL: How'd it go?

LISA: Good.

PAUL: Just good?

LISA: Pretty good.

PAUL: "Pretty good." You mean you got a lot of applause or "pretty good" you could have done better.

LISA: Well, Courtney Palumbo's mother thought I was pretty good. But you know the part in the middle when everybody's supposed to freeze and the big girl comes out. Well, I think I moved a little bit.

PAUL: I thought what you were doing looked very good.

LISA: Daddy, that's not what I was doing. That was tap-dancing. I made that up.

PAUL: Oh. Well it looked good. Kind of sexy.

LISA: Yuch!

PAUL: What do you mean "yuch"?

LISA: Just yuch!

PAUL: You don't want to be sexy?

LISA: I don't care.

PAUL: Let's go, Tiger. I promised your mother I'd get you home in time for dinner.

LISA: I can't find my leg warmers.

PAUL: You can't find your what?

LISA: Leg warmers. I can't go home till I find my leg warmers.

PAUL: I don't see you looking for them.

LISA: I was waiting for you.

PAUL: Oh.

LISA: Daddy.

PAUL: What?

LISA: Nothing.

PAUL: Where do you think you left them?

LISA: Somewhere around here. I can't remember.

PAUL: Well, try to remember, Lisa. We don't have all night.

LISA: I told you. I think somewhere around here.

PAUL: I don't see them. Let's go home now. You'll call the dancing school tomorrow.

LISA: Daddy, I can't go home till I find them. Miss Judy says it's not professional to leave things.

PAUL: Who's Miss Judy?

LISA: She's my ballet teacher. She once danced the lead in *Swan Lake,* and she was a June Taylor dancer.

PAUL: Well, then, I'm sure she'll understand about the leg warmers.

LISA: Daddy, Miss Judy wanted to know why you were late today.

PAUL: Hmmmmmmmm?

LISA: Why were you late?

PAUL: I was in a meeting. Business. I'm sorry.

LISA: Why did you tell Mommy you'd come instead of her if you knew you had business?

PAUL: Honey, something just came up. I thought I'd be able to be here. I was looking forward to it.

LISA: I wish you wouldn't make appointments to see me.

PAUL: Hmmmmmmm.

LISA: You shouldn't make appointments to see me unless you know you're going to come.

PAUL: Of course I'm going to come.

LISA: No, you're not. Talia Robbins told me she's much happier living without her father in the house. Her father used to come home late and go to sleep early.

PAUL: Lisa, stop it. Let's go.

LISA: I can't find my leg warmers.

PAUL: Forget your leg warmers.

LISA: Daddy.

PAUL: What is it?

LISA: I saw this show on television, I think it was WPIX Channel 11. Well, the father was crying about his daughter.

PAUL: Why was he crying? Was she sick?

LISA: No. She was at school. And he was at business. And he just missed her, so he started to cry.

PAUL: What was the name of this show?

LISA: I don't know. I came in in the middle.

PAUL: Well, Lisa, I certainly would cry if you were sick or far away, but I know that you're well and you're home. So no reason to get maudlin.

LISA: What's maudlin?

PAUL: Sentimental, soppy. Frequently used by children who make things up to get attention.

LISA: I am sick! I am sick! I have Hodgkin's disease and a bad itch on my leg.

PAUL: What do you mean you have Hodgkin's disease? Don't say things like that.

LISA: Swoosie Kurtz, she had Hodgkin's disease on a TV movie last year, but she got better and now she's on *Love Sidney*.

PAUL: Who is Swoosie Kurtz?

LISA: She's an actress named after an airplane. I saw her on *Live at Five*.

PAUL: You watch too much television; you should do your homework. Now, put your coat on.

LISA: Daddy, I really do have a bad itch on my leg. Would you scratch it?

PAUL: Lisa, you're procrastinating.

LISA: Why do you use words I don't understand? I hate it. You're like Daria Feldman's mother. She always talks in Yiddish to her husband so Daria won't understand.

PAUL: Procrastinating is not Yiddish.

LISA: Well, I don't know what it is.

PAUL: Procrastinating means you don't want to go about your business.

LISA: I don't go to business. I go to school.

PAUL: What I mean is you want to hang around here until you and I are late for dinner and your mother's angry and it's too late for you to do your homework.

LISA: I do not.

PAUL: Well, it sure looks that way. Now put your coat on and let's go.

LISA: Daddy.

PAUL: Honey, I'm tired. Really, later.

LISA: Why don't you want to talk to me?

PAUL: I do want to talk to you. I promise when we get home we'll have a nice talk.

LISA: No, we won't. You'll read the paper and fall asleep in front of the news.

PAUL: Honey, we'll talk on the weekend, I promise. Aren't I taking you to the theater this weekend? Let me look. [*He takes out appointment book.*] Yes. Sunday. *Joseph and the Amazing Technicolor Raincoat* with Lisa. Okay, Tiger?

LISA: Sure. It's Dreamcoat.

PAUL: What?

LISA: Nothing. I think I see my leg warmers. [*She goes to pick them up, and an odd-looking trophy.*]

PAUL: What's that?

LISA: It's stupid. I was second best at the dance recital, so they gave me this thing. It's stupid.

PAUL: Lisa.

LISA: What?

PAUL: What did you want to talk about?

LISA: Nothing.

PAUL: Was it about my missing your recital? I'm really sorry, Tiger, I would have liked to have been here.

LISA: That's okay.

PAUL: Honest?

LISA: Daddy, you're prostrastinating.

PAUL: I'm procrastinating. Sit down. Let's talk. So. How's school?

LISA: Fine.

PAUL: You like it?

LISA: Yup.

PAUL: You looking forward to camp this summer?

LISA: Yup.

PAUL: Is Daria Feldman going back?

LISA: Nope.

PAUL: Why not?

LISA: I don't know. We can go home now. Honest, my foot doesn't itch anymore.

PAUL: Lisa, you know what you do in business when it seems like there's nothing left to say? That's when you really start talking. Put a bid on the table.

LISA: What's a bid?

PAUL: You tell me what you want and I'll tell you what I've got to offer. Like Monopoly. You want Boardwalk, but I'm only willing to give you the Railroads. Now, because you are my daughter I'd throw in Water Works and Electricity. Understand, Tiger?

LISA: No. I don't like board games. You know, Daddy, we could get Space Invaders for our home for thirty-five dollars. In fact, we could get an Osborne System for two thousand. Daria Feldman's parents . . .

PAUL: Daria Feldman's parents refuse to talk to Daria, so they bought a computer to keep Daria busy so they won't have to speak in Yiddish. Daria will probably grow up to be a homicidal maniac lesbian prostitute.

LISA: I know what that word prostitute means.

PAUL: Good. [*Pause.*] You still haven't told me about school. Do you still like your teacher?

LISA: She's okay.

PAUL: Lisa, if we're talking try to answer me.

LISA: I am answering you. Can we go home now, please?

PAUL: Damn it, Lisa, if you want to talk to me . . . Talk to me!

LISA: I can't wait till I'm old enough so I can make my own money and never have to see you again. Maybe I'll become a prostitute.

PAUL: Young lady, that's enough.

LISA: I hate you, Daddy! I hate you! [*She throws her trophy into the trash bin.*]

PAUL: What'd you do that for?

LISA: It's stupid.

PAUL: Maybe I wanted it.

LISA: What for?

PAUL: Maybe I wanted to put it where I keep your dinosaur and the picture you made of Mrs. Kimbel with the chicken pox.

LISA: You got mad at me when I made that picture. You told me I had to respect Mrs. Kimbel because she was my teacher.

PAUL: That's true. But she wasn't my teacher. I liked her better with the chicken pox. [*Pause.*] Lisa, I'm sorry. I was very wrong to miss your recital, and you don't have to become a prostitute. That's not the type of profession Miss Judy has in mind for you.

LISA: [*Mumbles.*] No.

PAUL: No. [*Pause.*] So Talia Robbins is really happy her father moved out?

LISA: Talia Robbins picks open the eighth-grade lockers during gym period. But she did that before her father moved out.

PAUL: You can't always judge someone by what they do or what they don't do. Sometimes you come home from dancing school and run upstairs and shut the door, and when I finally get to talk to you, everything is "okay" or "fine." Yup or nope?

LISA: Yup.

PAUL: Sometimes, a lot of times, I come home and fall asleep in front of the television. So you and I spend a lot of time being a little scared of each other. Maybe?

LISA: Maybe.

PAUL: Tell you what. I'll make you a tender offer.

LISA: What?

PAUL: I'll make you a tender offer. That's when one company publishes in the newspaper that they want to buy another company. And the company that publishes is called the Black Knight because they want to gobble up the poor little company. So the poor little company needs to be rescued. And then a White Knight comes along and makes a bigger and better offer so the shareholders won't have to tender shares to the Big Black Knight. You with me?

LISA: Sort of.

PAUL: I'll make you a tender offer like the White Knight. But I don't want to own you. I just want to make a much better offer. Okay?

LISA: [*Sort of understanding.*] Okay. [*Pause. They sit for a moment.*] Sort of, Daddy, what do you think about? I mean, like when you're quiet what do you think about?

PAUL: Oh, business usually. If I think I made a mistake or if I think I'm doing okay. Sometimes I think about what I'll be doing five years from now and if it's what I hoped it would be five years ago. Sometimes I think about what your life will be like, if Mount Saint Helen's will erupt again. What you'll become if you'll study penmanship or word processing. If you'll speak kindly of me to your psychiatrist when you are in graduate school. And how the hell I'll pay for your graduate school. And sometimes I try and think what it was I thought about when I was your age.

LISA: Do you ever look out your window at the clouds and try to see which kinds of shapes they are? Like one time, honest, I saw the head of Walter Cronkite in a flower vase. Really! Like look don't those kinda look like if you turn it upside down, two big elbows or two elephant trunks dancing?

PAUL: Actually still looks like Walter Cronkite in a flower vase to me. But look up a little. See the one that's still moving? That sorta looks like a whale on a thimble.

LISA: Where?

PAUL: Look up. To your right.

LISA: I don't see it. Where?

PAUL: The other way.

LISA: Oh, yeah! There's the head and there's the stomach. Yeah! [LISA *picks up her trophy*.] Hey, Daddy.

PAUL: Hey, Lisa.

LISA: You can have this thing if you want it. But you have to put it like this, because if you put it like that it is gross.

PAUL: You know what I'd like? So I can tell people who come into my office why I have this gross stupid thing on my shelf, I'd like it if you could show me your dance recital.

LISA: Now?

PAUL: We've got time. Mother said she won't be home till late.

LISA: Well, Daddy, during a lot of it I freeze and the big girl in front dances.

PAUL: Well, how 'bout the number you were doing when I walked in?

LISA: Well, see, I have parts for a lot of people in that one, too.

PAUL: I'll dance the other parts.

LISA: You can't dance.

PAUL: Young lady, I played Yvette Mimieux in a *Hasty Pudding Show*.

LISA: Who's Yvette Mimieux?

PAUL: Watch more television. You'll find out. [PAUL *stands up*.] So I'm ready. [*He begins singing*.] "Nothing could be finer than to be in Carolina."

LISA: Now I go. In the morning. And now you go. Dum-da.

PAUL: [*Obviously not a tap dancer*.] Da-da-dum.

LISA: [*Whines*.] Daddy!

PAUL: [*Mimics her*.] Lisa! Nothing could be finer . . .

LISA: That looks dumb.

PAUL: Oh, yeah? You think they do this better in *The Amazing Minkcoat?* No way! Now you go—da da da dum.

LISA: Da da da dum.

PAUL: If I had Aladdin's lamp for only a day, I'd make a wish. . . .

LISA: Daddy, that's maudlin!

PAUL: I know it's maudlin. And here's what I'd say:

LISA and PAUL: I'd say that "nothing could be finer than to be in Carolina in the moooooooooooornin'."

(1977)

QUESTIONS

1. How would you characterize the relationship between Lisa and Paul?
2. Examine the play's dialogue for shifts of direction. Account for the conversational logic of these shifts and explain their dramatic effects.
3. Explain the significance of Paul and Lisa's discussion of the meaning of "procrastination" and "maudlin."
4. What is the function of Paul's inaccuracy in naming the title of the Broadway play *Joseph and the Amazing Technicolor Dreamcoat*?
5. Explain the various meanings of the "tender offer" Paul makes Lisa.

6. Consider how you would direct the actors in staging the play's final scene—the father/daughter dance routine.
7. What is the theme of the play?

MARTIN DOCKERY

[b. 1968]

Martin Dockery began writing plays when he was eight years old. Every New Year's Eve he and a group of friends would write a play they would perform at midnight. After graduating from Kenyon College with a BA in English, he received an MFA in playwriting from Columbia University in 1994.

Oh That Wily Snake! was written in 1993 and produced in 1996 off Broadway in New York City. Beneath its comic surface run mythic echoes and references to issues of contemporary social and sexual conduct.

MARTIN DOCKERY

Oh, That Wily Snake!

CHARACTERS

MAN
WOMAN

Upstage and off to the side, there is a twin-sized bed with a simple frame, sheets, a blanket and a pillow. The characters never actually change out of their clothes and they mime all of the props. Marcel is not physically represented. A MAN *is sitting in a simple chair downstage to one side. A* WOMAN *is sitting in a simple chair downstage to the other side. They are facing the audience.*

Lights up quickly.

WOMAN: I can't wake up.
MAN: I have this dream.
WOMAN: It's not a dream.
MAN: It's something.
WOMAN: I can't forget.
MAN: Just need to sleep again.

WOMAN: I can't sleep.

MAN: This isn't happening.

WOMAN: This can't happen.

MAN: This isn't what was supposed to happen.

WOMAN: This is not what I wanted.

MAN: This is not what it can be like.

WOMAN: This is not what I'd fantasized.

MAN: This is not what I'd fantasized.

WOMAN: I don't understand, then.

MAN: My fantasy is very different than this.

WOMAN: So is mine.

MAN: Though ours are not so different from each other.

WOMAN: I want to be married: clean, pure and unstained.

MAN: And then?

WOMAN: That's it.

MAN: That's all . . . ?

WOMAN: I want to be married.

MAN: But you're not just fantasizing about marriage . . .

WOMAN: I am.

MAN: You're fantasizing about sex.

WOMAN: I'm not.

MAN: Marriage is just some sort of framework for that. It's not your FANTASY.

WOMAN: I fantasize about love.

MAN: Oh. That's easy to say.

WOMAN: Marriage is the consummation of love.

MAN: Sex is the consummation of marriage.

WOMAN: I fantasize about marriage.

MAN: You fantasize about sex.

WOMAN: Look, you don't know me. You don't know what I want.

MAN: The only difference between you and me is that you're afraid to say what you want. You've been taught that it's wrong, taught that it makes you a bad person, taught to be scared of it.

WOMAN: I'm not scared of it.

MAN: Then, what are you?

WOMAN: I imagine a husband. A union. Something spiritual. Two souls becoming one. Something consummated in a holy way. Something right and good. Something good.

MAN: Fine, but when you're alone and away from your family and church and whatever, do you ever wonder if sex can just be about two people who want to get closer, who are attracted to each other, who just want to BE closer—who just want to—because they like each other . . . . You ever have thoughts like this at all?

WOMAN: No.

MAN: Are thoughts like this wrong?

WOMAN: I don't have thoughts like that.

MAN: At all.

WOMAN: No.
MAN: You think you would tell me if you did?
WOMAN: Yes.
MAN: You think so . . . ?
WOMAN: Yes.
MAN: Even if it made you scared to tell me?
WOMAN: Yes, why do you keep asking me?
MAN: Because I think you're scared to tell me.
WOMAN: Well, that's because you don't know me.
MAN: There's a whole 'nother world out there. A whole other land about which you know nothing.
WOMAN: What you fantasize about . . .
MAN: You want to know what I fantasize about exactly?
WOMAN: I think I know.
MAN: But you just don't, you see?
WOMAN: Then what?
MAN: Well, I was thinking that maybe we could talk about it over a few drinks.

He produces a bottle of champagne.

WOMAN: Champagne?!
MAN: A little bubbly, I thought—just to loosen things up!
WOMAN: What are you doing with champagne?!
MAN: Oh, me? Champagne? I always carry champagne around!
WOMAN: Oh! And I see you brought your bed, too!
MAN: My bed? Oh now, would you look at that? I thought I'd left that thing in the car!
WOMAN: If you leave it out there in the hallway, you know, someone might steal it.
MAN: Should I bring it in, then?
WOMAN: Of course! Better safe than sorry
MAN: That's good thinking.

He drags the bed to the center of the stage so that it is parallel to the proscenium.

WOMAN: What do you have your bed up here for?
MAN: Honestly, I thought I'd left it strapped to the roof!
WOMAN: No, I mean, why do you have your bed on this side of town at all?
MAN: Oh, why? Why? Well . . . You want to know why?
WOMAN: Why?
MAN: Well . . . Hey, you'd like a drink first, maybe? You don't mind if I open up the champagne, do you?
WOMAN: Actually, we have some wine already opened in the other room.
MAN: Oh, yes? But it's not the bubbly, is it?
WOMAN: Oh! Marcel doesn't recommend drinking champagne. He says it could give you the bends.
MAN: What?
WOMAN: The bends.

MAN: Marcel?

WOMAN: The bends.

MAN: Who's Marcel?

WOMAN: You've never met Marcel?

MAN: No.

WOMAN: My love Marcel?

MAN: Your love Marcel?

WOMAN: We're fiancé and fiancie.

MAN: You've never mentioned being a fiancie . . .

WOMAN: Never mentioned being a fiancie?

MAN: You've never mentioned Marcel.

WOMAN: I never mentioned him?

MAN: You've never mentioned him!

WOMAN: Well, you've just got to meet him!

MAN: I don't want to meet Marcel.

WOMAN: Trust me, Edmund, you'll love him.

MAN: Marcel? Marcel??

WOMAN: He's from Belgium.

MAN: Great. Belgium.

WOMAN: Very romantic.

MAN: They are.

WOMAN: Speaks a foreign language.

MAN: They do.

WOMAN: Kind. Good looking. Strong.

MAN: Great.

WOMAN: You'll like him.

MAN: How strong?

WOMAN: He's strong.

MAN: I mean, is he big?

WOMAN: He's big.

MAN: Like, how tall, for instance?

WOMAN: Ten feet.

MAN: Oh, that's tall.

WOMAN: He's big.

MAN: That's great.

WOMAN: Come on, I'll introduce you.

MAN: Are you sure? Maybe I should just—

WOMAN: Not at all! Marcel will be absolutely delighted to have another guest for dinner.

MAN: Oh, I shouldn't stay for dinner—you two are having a romantic dinner—

WOMAN: You'll never get home in this traffic anyway.

MAN: No, that's all right, I've got my bed—I can always pull over—take a nap—

WOMAN: Nonsense! Come on . . . Marcel? Honey, this is Edmund. Edmund, Marcel.

MAN: Hi!

He forces a cordial chuckle and holds out his hand, but MARCEL *does not respond. He turns the shake into a short wave.*

MAN: Great, uh . . .

MARCEL stares at him.

MAN: Place! Belgium. Not that I've been there before. I haven't, actually!
. . . No, but, Marcel, tell me, uh, you'd speak a foreign language, then, hm?
Tell me about that—It's, uh, good? Language? Is it?

Silence.

MAN: Yeah, well, I'm sure it's, uh, it's good. Look, Edith, I should really go—
WOMAN: Edmund! You can't go, I need your bed for dinner.
MAN: But—but—Can I just show you something over here for a second?
WOMAN: What?
MAN: Just this—this piece of wall—just come here!
WOMAN: What piece of wall?

He pulls her away from MARCEL.

MAN: Look, Edith, I really don't think your boyfriend—
WOMAN: Fiancé—
MAN: I don't think he likes me. I just get that feeling. I don't know.
WOMAN: Oh, he's just like that. But trust me, inside he's all giggles and
love.
MAN: But he's just staring at me! I think he's mad I brought my bed.
WOMAN: Why would that make him mad?
MAN: I don't know, he's just giving me that look.
WOMAN: What look?
MAN: That MAD look—
WOMAN: Believe me, ever since I moved in Marcel's been sleeping on the
dining room table so—
MAN: You LIVE here together?
WOMAN: That's why Marcel's been sleeping on the dining room table—
He INSISTED that I take the bed, you understand!
MAN: Well, good for him.
WOMAN: Good for his back!
MAN: Well, good for his back!
WOMAN: So I'm certain—I know he'll be very happy to have something
to eat on again—if you don't mind us using your bed as a table.
MAN: This is his apartment . . .
WOMAN: Oh, but he shares it. He shares everything. He's very spiritual
that way!

She turns back to MARCEL.

WOMAN: Oh, Marcel! Sorry to keep you waiting—Come on—let's all
dig in!

She pulls up her chair to an end of the bed.

WOMAN: Please, Edmund. Pull up a chair—

He gets his chair and seats himself at the other end of the table.

WOMAN: And would you look at all these greens! Edmund, you have just got to see Marcel's little garden in the backyard!
MAN: It's green, huh.
WOMAN: Oh, it's so green it looks blue!
MAN: Well, I guess that must be pretty green.
WOMAN: You can even grow Brussels sprouts there!
MAN: Really—Is that good?
WOMAN: Good? Brussels sprouts?
MAN: I mean, can't you just get them in a store?
WOMAN: And where do you think THOSE come from?
MAN: Um, Brussels?
WOMAN: Exactly! While these come from Marcel's garden. They're special. The others lose their aroma in transit, but these—THESE! Here smell one.

She offers one.

MAN: Smell it?
WOMAN: Just smell it.
MAN: I can smell it.
WOMAN: Would you lean forward and smell it?!

He smells it.

MAN: Whoa! Wow! That'll clear your sinuses!
WOMAN: You like it?
MAN: Well, I don't know—Let me taste it—
WOMAN: No, no! Marcel's gone to great lengths to warn that what it just did to your nose is only a fraction of what it would do to your head if you age it—It clears everything out like a tag sale and leaves behind only the things you don't want to see—At least that's what he says, though I sometimes wonder if he's exaggerating just a bit—Hm, cutey-pie? Mmm? Are you, you Belgian waffle?

The MAN gets up and walks away from the bed.

WOMAN: Edmund? What's wrong?
MAN: Nothing.
WOMAN: Marcel, if you'd just excuse me one moment.

She walks over to the MAN.

WOMAN: Is everything all right?
MAN: Please—please—go back to your dinner. I just need to—stand up.
WOMAN: You don't look well.
MAN: I didn't come here for dinner, Edith.

WOMAN: Dessert, then?

MAN: No! Please, we're keeping Marceau—

WOMAN: Marcel—

MAN: Waiting. You don't want to do that.

WOMAN: Is it the sprouts?

MAN: No, they smell great—

WOMAN: Then what is it?

MAN: I don't know.

WOMAN: You want to talk to Marcel? He's very good to talk to—

MAN: What do you mean? He hasn't said a word!

WOMAN: I mean, spiritually good—

MAN: Yes—I know—spiritual! But Edith, has he ever taken you . . .

WOMAN: Yes?

MAN: No, no, never mind.

WOMAN: What?

MAN: I was just wondering if you'd ever . . .

WOMAN: What?

MAN: No! No! Nothing.

WOMAN: What?

MAN: Nothing!

WOMAN: If I'd ever . . .

MAN: Been to Aruba.

WOMAN: What . . . ?!

MAN: Never mind.

WOMAN: What do you mean?

MAN: Never mind, never mind!

WOMAN: No, no—

MAN: Forget it.

WOMAN: . . . I've never been.

MAN: Okay—

WOMAN: Ooh.

MAN: Forget it.

WOMAN: We really shouldn't be talking about this!

MAN: Let's not talk about it.

WOMAN: I mean that place is like some exotic tropical resort! It's so—eee! We shouldn't be talking about this!

MAN: I agree—

WOMAN: I had a friend who tried to bring me there once. What a disaster!

MAN: Okay. Never mind.

WOMAN: The plane crashed.

MAN: It did?

WOMAN: Upon take-off—the wheels, I think, just collapsed as we were going to taxi.

MAN: And you crashed . . .

WOMAN: Well CRASHED—You know CRASHED is a big word—I mean, we weren't actually moving yet, so—I don't know.

MAN: But you didn't get hurt?

WOMAN: Oh no, we were more embarrassed than anything, really. Especially him. It was his plane. Oh, but to think what could have happened if we had gone!

MAN: Oh yeah?

WOMAN: I've been told if you go there your ears fall off!

MAN: In Aruba?

WOMAN: No, don't say that word! Even if you just talk about it—if you hear someone talking about it—your ears'll just shrivel up and blow away in the next big wind!

MAN: Oh, no, no.

WOMAN: I wouldn't want to chance that!

MAN: That doesn't happen.

WOMAN: You've been there?

MAN: Uh-huh.

WOMAN: You have—?! But—But I wouldn't want to go. It's such a foreign place—You know, it's another country—vaccinations—

MAN: You should, at least, just see it.

WOMAN: No, no.

MAN: You should.

WOMAN: I don't think so. Tropical climates are not really my, you know. . . . Marcel, he, he's warned me, he's told me that—I don't even want to chance getting cauliflower ear—you know, it's—Hey, Marcel, you don't need to clear! Let me do that . . . . Oh, Marcel. Marcel! Now I feel bad having left him all alone like that. Look at him off stacking all those dishes in the kitchen.

MAN: Look, Edith, it's really starting to get late. I should be heading home.

WOMAN: At this hour? I'll hear nothing of it! Sleep here.

MAN: Here?

WOMAN: Exactly.

She pulls back the covers.

WOMAN: As Marcel would say—Voilá! Go on, get in.

MAN: Edith . . .

WOMAN: Come on.

MAN: I can't. You see . . . I came here tonight . . .

WOMAN: Yes?

MAN: I came here thinking . . .

WOMAN: Yes?

MAN: But I can see it's not going to work.

WOMAN: What?

MAN: I . . . didn't know you had a Marceau—

WOMAN: Marcel—!

MAN: And so I thought you'd be free . . .

WOMAN: And . . .

MAN: And so . . .

WOMAN: Yes?

MAN: So . . .

WOMAN: So . . .

MAN: So would you like to go for a little spin?

WOMAN: A little spin?

MAN: Just a little one—

WOMAN: What do you mean?

MAN: Around the block—!

WOMAN: This block?

MAN: I know a great block—

WOMAN: Now?

MAN: Right now! It's a beautiful night! And I was just thinking, what a wonderful night for a spin!

WOMAN: A spin . . .

MAN: That's why I brought my bed! What a wonderful night for a spin on my bed!

WOMAN: But—

MAN: We can take off right away—on my bed—it flies! Through the air! It picks up a wonderful breeze!

WOMAN: But Marcel—

MAN: Marcel? You mean him? He's cleaning up! Let him clean up, we'll go for a spin! I have to admit, I've been waiting for the perfect night, just to ask you—You, and only you—I know you and you'll love it! Doesn't it sound kind of great? Doesn't it?

WOMAN: It does kind of sound, well . . .

MAN: Picture it! What a view! The air! And it's perfect now! The planets are in alignment, the tectonic plates are fitting together like a puzzle—this bed will handle like a greased pig! Smooth, easy, riding, nothing holding it back! But we have to go now—quick—while we can still catch an air current!

WOMAN: It sounds . . . I should tell Marcel.

MAN: No—He won't understand—He'll want to come and it's just a twin size bed. He'll be fine!

WOMAN: I can't just leave him to do all the stacking—

MAN: He won't mind! He'll be happy for you being happy. Your relationship's spiritual that way, right? Let's just go—for the night—for right now! We'll be back before you know it—before anyone knows it—It'll be beautiful there—you can't imagine—Oh, please say yes! We can go right now!

He turns the bed ninety degrees so that its head is pointing directly downstage. He also returns the chairs to their original positions.

MAN: Let's hop on!

WOMAN: But—

MAN: Don't you want to?

WOMAN: I don't know—

MAN: Don't you feel excited?

WOMAN: I shouldn't go—

MAN: Just a quick spin . . .

WOMAN: Can't we wait?

MAN: A jaunt!

WOMAN: In the air?

MAN: Flying!
WOMAN: You think?
MAN: It'll be wonderful!
WOMAN: Wonderful—?
MAN: Wonderful!
WOMAN: Oh!
MAN: Are you ready?
WOMAN: Am I?

She sits on the bed.

MAN: Hold on!
WOMAN: Hold on?
MAN: To the bed! Pull your legs up! Grab hold!

She pulls herself up onto the bed and holds on.

WOMAN: What are we doing?
MAN: We're going! Taking off! We're just going!
WOMAN: Oh my!
MAN: Watch it now—Duck!
WOMAN: Ah!
MAN: We're up! We're airborne!
WOMAN: Oh my!
MAN: Just hold on tight and enjoy the ride. You don't want to fall off now!
WOMAN: No, I should say not!
MAN: You see? Isn't it wonderful up here? Isn't it magnificent?
WOMAN: Oh my, I've never been up this high.
MAN: Do you see how high up we are? How far away everything is?
WOMAN: It's so far!
MAN: How little everything and everyone is from up here?
WOMAN: They all look like ants!
MAN: I know! That's exactly what I thought!
WOMAN: Wow.
MAN: This is where I've wanted to take you—I couldn't eat—At dinner.
I wanted to show this all to you—
WOMAN: And the clouds?! The clouds? Are we going to go through them?!
MAN: Just watch . . .
WOMAN: Ohhhh!
MAN: Breathe them in—
WOMAN: They're just wind!
MAN: But warm wind. It's getting warmer already—
WOMAN: My head's getting tingly!
MAN: The air's thinner—
WOMAN: It is thinner! We're moving right through it like a greased pig!
MAN: Can't you feel it?
WOMAN: Oh, Marcel would just love this—
MAN: What? No—No, breath in the clouds again—
WOMAN: Poor Marcel, left to stack all those dishes . . .

MAN: Edith, don't think about him.

WOMAN: But I feel so guilty leaving him just standing there by the sink like that.

MAN: Don't feel guilty. He's fine—fine.

WOMAN: He'll worry. He'll get so mad.

MAN: No, come on, now, look at all you can see from up here—

WOMAN: I should have told him—I wish I could tell him—

MAN: Edith—

WOMAN: Do you have a phone?

MAN: A phone?

WOMAN: You have to have a phone—somewhere—Don't you—?

MAN: I left it on the night stand—

WOMAN: Oh, look! A phone!

MAN: A phone?!

WOMAN: Is it cellular, I hope?

MAN: I left that on the nightstand!

WOMAN: It is!

MAN: Don't call anyone, Edith. Please, don't.

WOMAN: I've just got to make one call, Edmund. Just one.

MAN: No, don't—trust me—please—

WOMAN: I've never made a call from the air!

MAN: It'll whip up turbulence—It'll disrupt the air flow—the current—We're on a very delicate flight path!

WOMAN: Marcel? Hi! Yeah, hi! Oh Marcel! Listen, guess where I am right now? . . . No, guess! . . . Guess! . . . Nope! . . . Aw, come on, just try! . . . Nope!

MAN: Edith . . . !

WOMAN: Nope . . . Noooope . . . Nope . . .

MAN: You're going to seriously disturb our flight pattern!

WOMAN: [Chuckles] Nooooo . . . No . . . Getting warmer! . . . No . . .

MAN: Edith!

WOMAN: Noooo . . .

MAN: We're going to smack into an air pocket!

WOMAN: Nooo . . . Come on, think! . . . Nope . . . No . . .

MAN: Are you listening to me?!

WOMAN: Nohoho . . .

MAN: The phone line's going to stir up an electrical storm!

WOMAN: Now you're getting colder! . . . Nooo . . . No . . . No . . . Yes! I can't believe you guessed!

MAN: I see trouble ahead!

WOMAN: How did you know?!

MAN: I see trouble!

WOMAN: Well, I don't know exactly where, but isn't it exciting?!

MAN: Hang up, Edith!

WOMAN: Isn't it exciting?

MAN: Hang up, Edith!

WOMAN: I said I don't know where.
MAN: Hang up!
WOMAN: Well, I see some tree tops and hills and swamps—
MAN: Edith!
WOMAN: And, and lots of swamps!
MAN: Oh!

They react to the bed hitting an air pocket.

WOMAN: Oh!—A lot of swamps! I don't know! Where are we, Edmund?
MAN: Hold on!
WOMAN: Where are we going?
MAN: We're going down!
WOMAN: Down?! Where?
MAN: Down!!
WOMAN: But—
MAN: Hang up the phone, Edith!
WOMAN: I can't! I have to tell him where we're going!
MAN: Hang it up!
WOMAN: He wants to know where we're going!
MAN: It's going to be too late!
WOMAN: He wants to know!
MAN: Aruba! Tell him Aruba!
WOMAN: Aruba?!
MAN: Hang up!
WOMAN: I hung up!
MAN: It's too late!

They yell and crash and roll off the bed. They face each other.

WOMAN: What are you doing?! Just what do you think you're doing?!
MAN: What are YOU doing?!

She looks at herself. Immediately she grabs a sheet from the bed and pulls it around her. He then looks at himself and covers his genitalia with his hands.

WOMAN: Don't look at me!
MAN: I'm not!
WOMAN: Don't look at me!!

He turns around.

WOMAN: Where did you say we were going?!
MAN: I told you!
WOMAN: Where!
MAN: Aruba!
WOMAN: Don't say that word!
MAN: What were you doing up there?
WOMAN: Me?! What about you!
MAN: I was trying to fly this thing!

WOMAN: To there?! To there?! Since when were we going there?!

MAN: Look, it's a nice island—

WOMAN: I don't want to hear about it!

MAN: You asked!

WOMAN: I didn't! I had no idea!

MAN: I just thought it'd be nice.

WOMAN: I don't want to talk about it!

MAN: Fine! Let's not talk about it!

WOMAN: Well, where are we?

MAN: I don't know.

WOMAN: We're not THERE, are we?

MAN: No. I don't think so.

WOMAN: You don't THINK so? Where are we?!

MAN: Not there.

WOMAN: Where are we?

MAN: I don't know.

WOMAN: Where are we?!

MAN: I don't know!

WOMAN: Where are we?!

The MAN *grabs the blanket and wraps it around himself.*

WOMAN: Did you hear me?

MAN: Yes! And I don't know! We crashed somewhere. You shouldn't have made that call.

WOMAN: That call . . .

MAN: I told you.

WOMAN: I hung up on Marcel.

MAN: You shouldn't have called him.

WOMAN: I just hung up on him. He's going to be so worried. So mad. I shouldn't have left him!

MAN: Look at this thing. Look at it.

The MAN *looks at the bed.*

WOMAN: Just standing there—stacking the dishes—It was so wrong of me—to just leave him—like that—to stack all the dishes—

MAN: It's so wrecked.

WOMAN: I feel so guilty! And the last thing I said to him on the phone was that I was—He thinks I'm there!

MAN: Well, we're not, so calm down!

Silence.

MAN: Are you all right?

WOMAN: No.

MAN: You hurt yourself?

WOMAN: Yes. I want to go back.

MAN: We can't. Look at the bed.

WOMAN: I want to go back!

MAN: Well, you can't. We won't make it. We'll be lucky to even get this thing to Aruba—

WOMAN: Hey!

She covers her ears.

MAN: Where we can get a normal flight—a shuttle home—

WOMAN: No!

MAN: Where it'll be much easier to get—

WOMAN: I'm not going there! We must still be close to home. We didn't go all the way, right? I mean, THERE'S not that close, right?

MAN: What do you want me to say? We're in a jungle, okay? Look around you—You see that—you see this? These trees and leaves and things? That's all I know. As much as you.

WOMAN: Well, I'm sorry, but that's NOT enough. You said everything would be okay. Just a spin—you said that. All right? A SPIN. So—so—so you said that, you did!

MAN: We'll get out of here, okay?

WOMAN: That's right we will! We better—We—I'm walking.

MAN: What? Where? Like that?

WOMAN: I can't just stand here! Marcel is worried sick out there. Wondering what's happened to me—

MAN: Would you stop thinking about him. That's what got us into this whole mess. Just stop. It doesn't help.

WOMAN: Well, I want my clothes back!

MAN: There's obviously nothing I can do about that. I'd like mine too.

WOMAN: It's ridiculous. This is ridiculous. I feel ridiculous. Standing here. No clothes.

MAN: I don't know why they got all ripped away.

WOMAN: Because you crashed, that's why! That's what happens! Your shoes pop off and everything! If you hadn't crashed us, if you knew how to fly this thing, if—

MAN: Hey—I said I'd get us out of here, so just keep—don't get excited.

WOMAN: How are you going to get us out of here?

MAN: I can fix it.

WOMAN: How?

MAN: Just trust me.

WOMAN: How?

MAN: Would you give me a chance, okay?

WOMAN: Okay. Then, do it.

MAN: I'll do it.

WOMAN: Go ahead.

MAN: I am.

He looks at the bed intently. He makes some slight adjustment with the mattress. He looks again.

MAN: Well . . .

WOMAN: What?

MAN: Well, I need, uh . . .

WOMAN: What?

MAN: I need that.

WOMAN: What? This?

MAN: Your sheet.

WOMAN: This?! I can't give this to you!

MAN: Do you want to get out of here?

WOMAN: Give me your blanket.

MAN: We need this, too.

WOMAN: Well, use yours first.

MAN: We need them both. Look, I don't want to, but I'm going to have to drop this, you know, too. So . . .

He takes the blanket off from his body. She looks away.

MAN: Fine, I'm embarrassed. I'm standing here and I'm embarrassed. What do you want? You're just going to have to do it, too. Okay? We have to . . . Edith?

After a moment, she slowly, without looking, hands him the sheet off her body.

WOMAN: Don't call me Edith. Don't call me anything.

As she stands physically trying to figure out how to conduct herself while naked, he drops the sheet with the blanket in a lump on the bed. He stands back and looks at it intently.

MAN: Fine . . . When I grunt, then, that means I'm talking to you.

WOMAN: Are you doing whatever it is you're supposed to be doing there?

MAN: I'm doing it.

WOMAN: Are you doing it quickly?

MAN: Could you maybe help?

WOMAN: "Could I maybe!" Oh, "Could I maybe." Just what exactly is "Could I maybe" supposed to mean?

MAN: You don't have to help if you don't want to.

WOMAN: Well, whether I want to or not, I don't really have a choice, do I? If I want to get out of here—You obviously can't do it yourself, even though you just said you could. What do you want me to do?

MAN: You know, there are worse places to be in on this planet, there are worse situations, there are worse people to be stuck with.

WOMAN: Like who?

MAN: Oh-hoh . . . Maybe you're right. Maybe I don't know you. I guess I was absolutely crazy to think you'd ever want to go with me to ARUBA or anywhere . . . Hm?

WOMAN: I told you, I'm not going to talk about that.

MAN: Oh, come on, enough with being ridiculous!

WOMAN: Would you stop?

MAN: I can say Aruba!

She covers her ears.

WOMAN: Stop it!

MAN: Aruba!

WOMAN: Stop it!

MAN: Aruba!
WOMAN: Haven't you done enough?!
MAN: Your ears are not going to fall off!
WOMAN: Leave me alone!
MAN: Who told you all this?
WOMAN: I can't hear you!
MAN: Was it that flying Dutchman?
WOMAN: Belgian!
MAN: You know that it's not true. You know that this is crazy—My whole head would have caved in and blown away by now!
WOMAN: Please—stop talking . . . !
MAN: What are you so afraid of?

Silence.

MAN: Fine . . . Be that way. I could care less.

After a beat he throws the blankets down upon the bed.

MAN: Forget it.

He goes and lies down upon the ground. She notices, takes her hands from her ears and becomes hesitantly worried.

WOMAN: What are you doing?
MAN: I don't know . . .
WOMAN: What do you mean?
MAN: You wouldn't understand.
WOMAN: Yes, I would.
MAN: No, you wouldn't—you've got your hands over your ears.
WOMAN: No, no, I . . . took them down.
MAN: Well, watch that a sudden gust of wind doesn't . . . you know . . . Hold onto them.

Pause.

WOMAN: How's the bed coming?
MAN: How does it look?
WOMAN: It looks like it's . . . coming along . . .
MAN: So then why did you ask?

Silence.

WOMAN: Look, I said I would help.
MAN: That's not the problem.
WOMAN: What is the problem, then?

Silence.

WOMAN: All right, I'm sorry. Now, I'M apologizing. I'm sorry for being so . . . Look, I'm going to get in a lot of trouble for being here. I should have told him before I left, but I didn't, and it's my fault, really. I'm mad at myself. So, I'm sorry. Okay?
MAN: Okay.

WOMAN: So . . .

MAN: What?

WOMAN: Can I help you finish fixing the bed?

MAN: Edith! Look, I like you, Edith, and I'm . . . It makes me so mad to see what you put up with—The things he tells you—And you believe them! I tell you—right now—I'm falling asleep from exasperation!

WOMAN: Well, wake up!

MAN: I can't.

WOMAN: That's not fair! I'm exasperated and I'm not falling asleep!

MAN: Just a quick nap . . .

WOMAN: But you have to do the bed, you have to!

MAN: And what's the point? You think I'm an idiot, you think he's great, I might as well just wait for him to find us.

WOMAN: He'll never find us down here!

MAN: Well . . . maybe, then, someone who's crop dusting or something will fly low overhead and see us, I don't know, I doubt it, but . . .

WOMAN: Or we could call him! We could use the cellular phone and have him trace our call to right here! We could do that!

MAN: What? Wait—

He springs up.

MAN: Call him again? Bring him here? What are you saying?

WOMAN: Just that.

MAN: That? Just that? That? Now?

WOMAN: We shouldn't waste a moment—

MAN: Wait—Yes, we should—Hold on—

WOMAN: Why?

MAN: That's my phone.

WOMAN: What do you mean?

MAN: I mean—You're going to make another long distance call? On my phone?

WOMAN: Just one.

MAN: You know how long it takes to trace a call? They charge double for that.

WOMAN: I'll pay you back.

MAN: Oh yeah, sure. And crows fly backwards, I bet.

WOMAN: What's the problem?

MAN: The problem? You want to know the problem? I'll tell you what the problem is—He's the problem! He's the reason we're right here. And he doesn't treat you right. Not how I would treat a fiancée! He's spouting to you all these lies—to control your life, and you accept it all completely—And this is the guy you expect me to let you call and be all friendly with and come save us?

WOMAN: I want to get out of here.

MAN: I'll get us out of here!

WOMAN: Let me call him.

MAN: He's no good, Edith!

WOMAN: Maybe so, but still—

MAN: Aha! You say maybe! You see that I could be right!

WOMAN: No—

MAN: Yes! I'll prove it to you!

WOMAN: Prove what?

MAN: . . . That he's a liar! . . . Dishonest! . . . You can't trust him!

WOMAN: Don't say that!

MAN: The champagne! He said that stuff'll give you the bends? That's preposterous! He just knows you're going to like it and doesn't want to have to start stocking any in the pantry!

WOMAN: We don't have a pantry!

MAN: I'm talking about the bends, Edith! The bends!

WOMAN: You don't know what you're talking about!

MAN: Oh, if I had my champagne here, I'd show you!

WOMAN: Well, you don't, so you can't.

MAN: Then has he told you anything crazy about trees, grass, photosynthesis—something I could show you?

WOMAN: Of course not!

MAN: Oh! He's tricky, this one! He's very tricky . . .

WOMAN: Would you let me call him now?

The MAN *sees something on the ground.*

MAN: Aha! Ah-hah!

WOMAN: What?

He picks it up.

MAN: This is it!

WOMAN: Oh my! That was right there?

MAN: All those shameful lies he doled out to you like so much soup . . .

WOMAN: Put that down . . . !

MAN: This, Edith, is a harmless vegetable, an innocent nugget of goodness.

WOMAN: The things that can do to your head!

MAN: It'll do nothing to your head.

WOMAN: It can tear through it like a tornado!

MAN: It'll do no such thing. And that's what we're going to see right now.

WOMAN: What do you mean?

MAN: Eat this, Edith.

WOMAN: Eat it?!

MAN: And see what you've been missing.

WOMAN: I can't eat that!

MAN: Eat this and then you can use the phone—I'll even let you make some other calls—whatever calls—very, very long distance ones—Just go ahead and try it.

WOMAN: No—I can't!

MAN: Because you know that I'm right! Which would mean Marcel's not only been lying to you about this—but about a whole lot of other things—namely the country of you know what, I won't say!

WOMAN: I won't eat that—

MAN: You're afraid of the truth.

WOMAN: I am not! Find something else to test it on—but that, I just—

MAN: There IS nothing else—There are no excuses. This is the truth right here.

WOMAN: It would be a breach of trust to eat that. He made me promise I wouldn't.

MAN: Your trust has already been breached, Edith. I don't know what I have to tell you to make you believe that.

WOMAN: Nothing—There IS nothing you could tell me.

MAN: It's just that these things he's told you—you've never heard them from anyone else. I never have. How would HE only know them?

WOMAN: Marcel knows everything.

MAN: So I guess he's figured it all out for himself, then. He's just tried it all and knows.

WOMAN: Hey! What are you saying? Don't say that! Marcel would not try any one of those things!

MAN: Oh? It would be bad if he did?

WOMAN: Bad? Bite your tongue! Bad! I can't believe you. What sort of person do you think he is?

MAN: Well, I don't know. If he says one thing and does another.

WOMAN: He says and does the same thing! Would you bite your tongue?

MAN: Just give me a second—

WOMAN: Bite it!

MAN: I will. Give me a second. I want to know what you would think if, say, you found out that this character Marcel had, without your knowledge, been sneaking champagne for years, now?

WOMAN: I would quickly say that that's not true!

MAN: Or if, say, between meals he'd been popping a few of these sprouts you think he keeps around for purely aromatic reasons?

WOMAN: He would never—!

MAN: Or if, supposing—let me cut to the chase—you found out that on a regular basis, he'd been making the trip down to the country of Aruba?

WOMAN: . . . How could you say that?

MAN: That would be bad . . .

WOMAN: How could you think that?

MAN: I can see it would be bad. Maybe I shouldn't tell you.

WOMAN: Tell me what?

MAN: No, I can sense that this isn't a good time.

WOMAN: What isn't a good time?!

MAN: Edith, just say the word and I won't tell you.

WOMAN: Tell me what?!

MAN: Well . . . Well. That Marcel has, in fact, been going to Aruba for several years now, whooping it up, having a great time, and having very little intention as to asking you how that makes you feel.

WOMAN: No—No, that can't be true . . .

MAN: It is true.

WOMAN: It can't be—it can't—!

MAN: It can, Edith.

WOMAN: No, I don't believe you—I won't believe you!

MAN: But you have to, it's the truth.

WOMAN: Prove it! You're such a prover, prove it! It's not true!

MAN: It doesn't have to be proven—it's obvious! He smells like Aruba. Smell him; he's like a coconut. People from Belgium do not naturally smell so much like coconuts!

WOMAN: That's his moisterizer! He has very dry skin! He uses a lot!

MAN: And that windswept hair? Tell me the guy has not been windsurfing in one of the prime windsurfing locales this side of the Prime Meridian!

WOMAN: The apartment has a very strong draft! It just catches his hair sometimes!

MAN: And that towel he was carrying around? People from Belgium do not naturally carry towels around unless they're going to lie on them!

WOMAN: He was doing the dishes! These are accusations—they're all assumptions, is what they are! You could assume differently, but you're assuming not differently, instead!

MAN: Oh, Edith—

WOMAN: You are!

MAN: Edith—

WOMAN: He hasn't been there!

MAN: Edith—

WOMAN: You don't know what you're talking about!

MAN: I do. I've seen him there. That's how I know. I've seen him. Me. I didn't want to have to tell you, but the lies. All the lies. To someone who's so good. Who deserves so much more. You're so good, Edith. The truth shouldn't be hidden from you. Not from you.

WOMAN: . . . You've really seen him there?

MAN: Playing golf.

WOMAN: He doesn't like golf . . . !

MAN: Oh, the lies, Edith, the lies . . .

WOMAN: No . . . Oh no . . . No . . .

MAN: I'm sorry.

WOMAN: Oh . . . I feel so scared, suddenly . . .

MAN: No—No—I'm here. You're safe with me.

WOMAN: Could he really have been going all this time?

MAN: If he's lying about this Brussels sprout, then he's lying about everything. It's right here. Your answer's right here.

He places the Brussels sprout in her hand.

WOMAN: It's so . . . bitesize.

MAN: It's inviting you to take a bite. Take one.

WOMAN: Oh . . .

MAN: It's all going to be okay.

WOMAN: Okay . . .

She takes a bite.

WOMAN: Oh!

MAN: What?

WOMAN: Mm!

MAN: What?

WOMAN: Ee! Hah!

MAN: What is it?

WOMAN: Oh my! I feel very—Whooh!

MAN: What!

WOMAN: Funny!

MAN: You do?

WOMAN: Do I look funny? I must look funny!

MAN: I don't know—

WOMAN: My head's tingling. My hair feels very, very—help me, what's the word!

MAN: Funny?

WOMAN: Upright! Is my hair standing on end?!

MAN: I can't tell quite—

WOMAN: My ears aren't spinning, are they? They feel like they're spinning! I'm a helicopter!

MAN: They're just—They're fine—

WOMAN: My eyes! They seem very wide!

MAN: Wide—

WOMAN: Like they're being opened!

MAN: They are open—

WOMAN: Everything's pouring in—or pouring out—I can't tell. It's sifting, sieving, straining. I'm a colander! Look at me—Wow!

MAN: But you're okay?

WOMAN: Would you have the rest of it, already? I don't want to be alone anymore—I don't want to be afraid anymore—I want someone to be with me—

MAN: I'm with you, I'm with you! This is what I've been saying, trying to get you to—

WOMAN: Eat it!

MAN: I'm eating it, I'm eating it.

He eats it.

WOMAN: There's so much out there to know . . .

MAN: Whoa!

WOMAN: Don't you feel like a cyclops!

MAN: Mmm!

WOMAN: It's so—

MAN: Whee—

WOMAN: Penetrating . . .

MAN: I guess I've never had a sprout right off the ground!

WOMAN: I feel like everything's getting clearer by the second! Everything's being revealed!

MAN: What did I tell you?

WOMAN: Imagine this with melted butter!

MAN: That's how it's served half the time!

WOMAN: Oh—I want to know everything!

MAN: I know you do! I know that. I've known that. I know!

WOMAN: Tell me about, you know . . .

MAN: What?

WOMAN: Aruba. Oh! I said it! Don't tell me—I take it back!

MAN: It's okay. Hey—Feel your ears—Can you still hear through them?

WOMAN: Yes . . .

MAN: That's because it's okay to talk about it.

WOMAN: Well, sure it is, because he's been there, of all things! I should at least be able to talk about it—To know what it's like, right? Shouldn't I?

MAN: You'd like it there, Edith.

WOMAN: Why? Why do you say that?

MAN: Do you like it here?

WOMAN: Well, it's nice.

MAN: It's nicer there.

WOMAN: It is?

MAN: It's softer. Feel this mattress, sit on it.

She sits on it.

WOMAN: Yeah?

MAN: Aruba's softer than that.

WOMAN: Really?

MAN: It's more comfortable.

WOMAN: This is pretty comfortable.

MAN: It's more comfortable. Here there's only this much room . . .

He sits next to her on the mattress.

MAN: In Aruba, there's much more room.

WOMAN: Yeah . . . ?

MAN: It's warmer, too.

WOMAN: It's warm here . . .

MAN: That's because we're sitting so close to each other . . .

WOMAN: Yeah . . . ?

MAN: Uh-huh.

WOMAN: But there they don't sit this close together . . .

MAN: Sure they do.

WOMAN: They do?

MAN: When they're feeling friendly.

WOMAN: And in Aruba they feel . . .

MAN: It's a friendly nation.

WOMAN: I'm shaking . . . !

MAN: Why? Are you nervous?

WOMAN: Nervous about what?

MAN: Why are you shaking?

WOMAN: I think the bed's moving—Is the bed moving?

MAN: Whup—It is. Lift your legs up—

WOMAN: What's happening?

MAN: It seems that we've caught a sudden breeze—Hold on—

WOMAN: What am I holding on to?

MAN: Grab my arm—I'm going to try and steer this—

WOMAN: But the bed's not ready, is it? What are we doing?

MAN: It's going to be difficult, but, when the opportunity arrives—You never know when the last breeze of the season's going to come.

WOMAN: We're up! We're going up!

MAN: That's right, Edith! Here we go! Let's fly away!

WOMAN: But—But I thought the bed COULDN'T fly.

MAN: Couldn't fly? Well, how about 'can barely' fly, huh? Because this is barely flying! It's very, very treacherous. Feel it. Treacherous.

WOMAN: But I don't understand how a bed can suddenly fly that couldn't fly before—Does that make sense?

MAN: Well, it barely makes sense. I can't explain it, But here we are in the sky. Oh, Edith! Look at the birds!

WOMAN: They're all seagulls. Seagulls fly over water—

She looks down.

WOMAN: WE'RE flying over water! What are we doing over water?

MAN: It is so incredibly wet down there . . .

WOMAN: I don't understand what we were waiting for all this time if the bed could always fly?

MAN: Edith, you really need to get past this thing you have about the bed flying. It's just a miracle, okay? Are you tense? I think you need to relax. There you go. Now, why don't we get back to Aruba.

WOMAN: What do you mean, get back to Aruba? Where are we going?

MAN: We were just talking about Aruba.

WOMAN: Where are we going?

MAN: I want to tell you about the coral.

WOMAN: Where are we going?

MAN: Edith—

WOMAN: Don't forget—Things are very clear to me now!

MAN: Would you just sit back and enjoy this?

WOMAN: Why do you need me to enjoy this? Would the bed stop flying if I didn't, is that it?

MAN: Look, you don't have to enjoy it if you don't want to, just don't get so—

WOMAN: What?

MAN: Worked up! You get so worked up! You don't have to be so scared all the time.

WOMAN: Scared of what?!

MAN: Flying!

WOMAN: I'm not scared of flying!

MAN: I understand this thing is lilting, it's rickety, sure, but it's—

WOMAN: I don't want to go to Aruba!

MAN: Can I just first say that ever since I first brought it up, you've been very excited by the idea—talking—wanting to know all about it.

WOMAN: I haven't!

MAN: You see? You can't deny that! You can't be scared to talk about it.

WOMAN: I don't want to go—

MAN: You can't be scared of it.

WOMAN: Let me off this—Let me off!

MAN: Hey—Hey! What are you doing? You're going to tip this thing!

WOMAN: I want to get off!

MAN: You can't—

WOMAN: I want to land!

MAN: There is no land to land on.

WOMAN: Turn this around!

MAN: We'll never make it back—It's too far—

WOMAN: You're a liar! I can see the truth! YOU'RE the liar! Let me go!

MAN: Hey, stop it! Now you just stop it! I've been putting up with you and all your whatever without complaining even once! And all for what? For this? For you yelling at me over and over again? I could be here with anyone but I wanted to be here with you—to show you—because I know you'd like it—I've been trying and trying to keep my patience and deal with you—But you refuse to be fair with me!

WOMAN: Are you saying that I owe you? Is that what you're saying—that I owe you?

MAN: Why don't you give me some credit? I'm out here, traipsing around the jungle, ruining my bed—and for what? Because I thought it'd be fun to go to Aruba!

WOMAN: We are going to Aruba, then!

MAN: Because I think it's high time you stopped living by other people's rules—

WOMAN: We're going to Aruba . . . !

MAN: Because you want to go!

WOMAN: Oh, Marcel, help me!

MAN: Edith, don't do that!

WOMAN: Marcel!

MAN: Edith!

WOMAN: Yes! I'm going to crash us!

MAN: What are you saying?

WOMAN: When I yell for him, it brings us down! Marcel!

MAN: Don't!

WOMAN: Marcel!

MAN: Stop moving around like that!

WOMAN: Marcel is going to save me!

MAN: Stop it!

WOMAN: Don't touch me!

MAN: You're going to spill us over! We'll fall!

WOMAN: You can't fly this if I yell for Marcel!

MAN: I can't fly this if you keep jumping around the bed like that!

WOMAN: Marcel, please!

MAN: Stop moving!

WOMAN: Ow!

MAN: Get down! Get your weight down centered in the bed! You're throwing off the balance!

WOMAN: Get off me!

MAN: I'm serious! Lie down!

He forces her down.

WOMAN: No! Ow! You can't do this!

He gets on top of her.

MAN: We have to!

WOMAN: No!

MAN: Stop it!

WOMAN: You're hurting me!

MAN: If you would just stop it!

WOMAN: Marcel!

MAN: You're going to kill us!

WOMAN: No!

MAN: We're going to crash!

WOMAN: Marcel!

MAN: The island's right there—Stop it!

WOMAN: No!

MAN: We're going to make it!

WOMAN: Please!

MAN: We're going to make it!

WOMAN: No!

MAN: We're making it!

WOMAN: No!

MAN: We're making it!

WOMAN: No!

MAN: We're making it!

WOMAN: No!

They both scream. The WOMAN has wrestled herself free and falls off the bed. There is a long pause during which the MAN, on the bed, catches his breath while the WOMAN, on the ground, lies motionless.

MAN: We made it . . . This is . . . We're here . . .

Pause.

MAN: Edith?

He climbs off the bed.

MAN: We landed just in time . . . Your fall wasn't that bad . . . We were close to the ground . . .

Pause.

MAN: It wasn't that bad.

Pause.

MAN: Edith?

Pause.

MAN: Edith?

Pause.

MAN: Are you okay? Edith? Please, are you okay?
WOMAN: . . . Don't say my name . . .
MAN: But are you okay?
WOMAN: And don't look at me . . .
MAN: But—
WOMAN: And don't talk to me.

Silence.

WOMAN: Oh . . . !
MAN: What?
WOMAN: Marcel . . . ?
MAN: Oh . . . What's he doing underneath the bed . . . ?
WOMAN: You landed on Marcel . . .
MAN: I what?
WOMAN: You killed Marcel . . . !
MAN: I didn't do anything!
WOMAN: Oh, Marcel!
MAN: You're the one that called him here!
WOMAN: He came looking for me . . .
MAN: If you hadn't made that call . . . !
WOMAN: No, please, no . . .
MAN: I mean . . .
WOMAN: No . . .
MAN: He'll be okay . . .
WOMAN: What have I done . . . ?
MAN: Look, let's get some help—We'll find a doctor, then a shuttle home—
WOMAN: I can't go home!
MAN: Look—look, don't worry—
WOMAN: It was his home! His apartment . . . I don't have the keys. I'm locked out . . .
MAN: We'll get you back in—I'm sure he had a spare somewhere.
WOMAN: No, no, this isn't happening . . . !
MAN: I mean—HAS a spare somewhere . . . .
WOMAN: I want to wake up . . .
MAN: I mean, I'm sure he'll let you in himself . . .
WOMAN: I want . . .

MAN: I mean, I'm sure . . .
WOMAN: Marcel . . .
MAN: I mean . . .
WOMAN: Help me . . .

She returns to her chair, which is in its original position. He soon does the same.

MAN: Hey, look . . . Why don't you just stay here for a little while. You're shaken up and the sun and air would be probably good for you. You know? And the people here are very friendly and . . . Well, it's usually sunny here . . . the sun mainly shines and . . . it's usually very sunny, here. This is not what it's normally like.
WOMAN: This is not what I wanted.
MAN: This is not what I wanted.
WOMAN: This is not what I'd imagined.
MAN: This is not what it can be like.
WOMAN: This is not what I'd fantasized.
MAN: This is not what I'D fantasized.
WOMAN: This is a nightmare.
MAN: Just need to wake up, then.
WOMAN: I need to sleep.
MAN: I can't sleep.
WOMAN: I can't forget.
MAN: I can't think.
WOMAN: I can't do anything.
MAN: Just need to do something.
WOMAN: I'm going to wake up.
MAN: Then, wake up.
WOMAN: I'm going to sleep.
MAN: Then, sleep.
WOMAN: Either, please.
MAN: It'll come, it has to come.
WOMAN: Just something.
MAN: Anything.
WOMAN: To make this all go away.

Lights out quickly.

QUESTIONS

1. *Oh, That Wily Snake!* makes do with a minimum of setting and props. Explain the implications of the play's minimalist setting for the actors and for the audience.
2. What does the opening dialogue reveal about the characters' views of sex and marriage? How does each understand the notion of "fantasy"?
3. What is Marcel's dramatic function in the play? Can he be considered Edmund's foil? Why or why not? What is the effect of his being a silent rather than a speaking character?

4. About a third of the way through the play the dialogue becomes more elaborate; its texture thickens. Explain the effects of this shift in dialogue.

5. Explain the symbolic significance of the flying bed, the "spin around the block," and the trip to Aruba. Consider comments such as Edith's "We didn't go all the way, right?" and Edmund's "You're just going to have to do it, too. Okay? We have to . . ."

6. How does the playwright create the illusion that the bed flies? What is the dramatic effect of watching and listening to two characters on a bed discussing their flight? Of the characters discussing their nakedness while remaining clothed?

7. Explain the significance of the play's title. Why a wily snake? Who is the liar, and why does the liar deceive?

8. Why is Edith upset at the end of the play? What has happened to upset her? How does Edmund respond? And what is the effect of the repetition of lines from the beginning of the play at the end?

JOSEFINA LÓPEZ

Josefina López wrote her first play at the age of seventeen. *Simply María* was produced in San Diego and later aired on PBS. A surreal exploration of the development of a Mexican woman growing up in the United States, the play's action occurs mostly as a dream sequence. In exploring social and gender values, *Simply María* uses irony and satire to illuminate cultural differences and evaluate cultural mythologies.

JOSEFINA LÓPEZ

Simply María
or
The American Dream

CHARACTERS

Principals:

MARÍA: daughter of Carmen and Ricardo.
CARMEN: mother of María.
RICARDO: father of María.
JOSÉ: María's husband.
PRIEST

In order of appearance:

GIRL 1

GIRL 2

GIRL 3

MOTHER: Carmen's mother.

WOMAN

NARRATOR

IMMIGRANT 1

IMMIGRANT 2

IMMIGRANT 3

IMMIGRANT 4

STATUE OF LIBERTY

MEXICAN MAN

MEXICAN WOMAN

POSTMAN

PERSON 1

VENDOR 1

VENDOR 2

BAG LADY

PROTESTOR

MAN 1

DIRTY OLD MAN

CHOLO 2

VALLEY GIRL 1

VALLEY GIRL 2

CHOLO 1

PERSON 2

PERSON 3

PERSON 4

ANGLO BUYER

MYTH

MARY

MARÍA 2

REFEREE

ANNOUNCER

FLOOR MANAGER

HUSBAND

WIFE

SALESMAN

HEAD NURSE

NURSE 2

NURSE 3

NURSE 4

BAILIFF

JUDGE

PROSECUTOR

JUROR 1

JUROR 2

Note: Many of the above characters can be played by the same actor/actress.

Place. The play begins in an unspecified town in Mexico and moves to downtown Los Angeles.

Time. Over a period of years chronicling the growth of María from birth to her womanhood.

SCENE ONE

There is a long thin movie screen on the top and across the stage that will be used to display slides of titles for a couple of seconds each. Lights rise. MARÍA, *a young woman with a suitcase, enters. She goes to the center and remains still.* THREE GIRLS *enter and stand behind her.*

GIRL 3:   (*Loud introduction.*) Romeo and Juliet elope. Or, where's the wedding dress?

(*Lights slowly fade. Then dim lights slowly rise.* RICARDO, *a tall, dark and handsome young Mexican man enters. He tries to hide in the darkness of the night. He whistles carefully, blending the sound with the noises of the night.*)

CARMEN: (*From her balcony.*) Ricardo, ¿eres tú?
RICARDO: Yes! Ready?
CARMEN: Sí. (*She climbs down from her balcony, then runs to* RICARDO, *kissing and consuming him in her embrace.*) Where's the horse?
RICARDO: What horse?
CARMEN: The one we are going to elope on.
RICARDO: You didn't say to bring one. All we agreed on was that I would be here at midnight.
CARMEN: I would have thought that you would have thought to . . .
RICARDO: Shhhh!!! ¡Mira! (*Points to* CARMEN*'s room.*)
CARMEN: ¡Mi madre! Let's go! And on what are we going?
RICARDO: On this. (*Brings an old bike.*)
CARMEN: ¡Qué! On that? No! How could . . . Everyone knows that when you elope, you elope on a horse, not on a . . . Ricardo, you promised!
MOTHER: (*Discovering* CARMEN *gone.*) ¡Carmencita! Carmen! She's gone!
CARMEN: Oh, no! Hurry! Let's go!
RICARDO: (*Hops on the bike.*) Carmen, hurry! Get on!
CARMEN: We won't fit!
MOTHER: ¡M'ija! Where are you?
CARMEN: We better fit! (*Jumps on, and they take off. She falls and then quickly hops back on.*) Ricardo, marry me! (*Crickets are heard, lights dim. Fade out.*)

SCENE TWO

THREE WOMEN *enter a church with candles. A fourth, much older, enters with a lighted candle and lights the other candles. The* THREE WOMEN *then transform into statues of the saints in the church.* PRIEST *comes downstage, waiting for a wedding to begin.* CARMEN *enters, pregnant.*

PRIEST: Will he be here soon?
CARMEN: Soon. He promised.
PRIEST: I was supposed to start half an hour ago.
WOMAN: (*Enters with a note.*) Is there anyone here named Carmen?
CARMEN: Yes . . . Is it from Ricardo? (*Reading the note.*) "I haven't been able to get a divorce. It will be some time soon, believe me . . . Just wait. I'm working hard so that I can save money to buy a little house or a ranch for the three of us. If you wait, good things will come." (*To* PRIEST.) There won't be a wedding today.

(*Exits crying with* PRIEST. *The statues become* WOMEN *and they all ad lib malicious gossip about the pregnant bride.* CARMEN *enters again, holding baby.* PRIEST *enters.* WOMEN *become statues again.*)

PRIEST: Will he be here? (RICARDO *enters.*)
CARMEN: He is here.
PRIEST: Good. Now we can start.
CARMEN: (*To* RICARDO.) I thought you wouldn't show up.
PRIEST: (*Begins his speech, which is more or less mumbled and not heard except for:*) Do you, Carmen, accept Ricardo as your lawfully wedded husband?
CARMEN: I do.
PRIEST: Do you, Ricardo, accept Carmen as your lawfully wedded wife?
RICARDO: I do.
PRIEST: Under the Catholic Church, in the holy House of God, I pronounce you husband and wife. (*Takes baby from* CARMEN, *and sprinkles holy water on baby.*) Under the Catholic Church, in the holy House of God, this child shall be known as María.

The PRIEST *puts the baby on the center of the stage.* CARMEN, RICARDO *and* PRIEST *exit. On the screen the following title is displayed:* **The Making of a Mexican Girl.**

NARRATOR: The making of a Mexican girl.

(*The statues now transform into* THREE ANGELIC GIRLS *who begin to hum, then sing beautifully with only the word "María." They come center stage and deliver the following, facing the audience:*)

ALL: María.
GIRL 1:   As a girl you are to be
GIRL 2:   Nice,
GIRL 3:   forgiving,
GIRL 1:   considerate,
GIRL 2:   obedient,
GIRL 3:   gentle,
GIRL 1:   hard-working,
GIRL 2:   gracious.
GIRL 3:   You are to like:
GIRL 1:   Dolls,
GIRL 2:   kitchens,
GIRL 3:   houses,
GIRL 1:   cleaning,

GIRL 2:　caring for children,

GIRL 3:　cooking,

GIRL 1:　laundry,

GIRL 2:　dishes.

GIRL 3:　You are not to:

GIRL 1:　Be independent,

GIRL 2:　enjoy sex,

GIRL 3:　but must endure it as your duty to your husband,

GIRL 1:　and bear his children.

GIRL 2:　Do not shame your society!

GIRL 3:　Never,

GIRL 1:　never,

GIRL 2:　never,

ALL:　Never!!!!

GIRL 1:　Your goal is to reproduce.

GIRL 2:　And your only purpose in life is to serve three men:

GIRL 3:　Your father,

GIRL 1:　your husband,

GIRL 2:　and your son.

GIRL 3:　Your father. (RICARDO *enters.*)

RICARDO:　Carmen, I must go.

CARMEN:　Ricardo, don't go. Not after all the time I've waited.

RICARDO:　I don't want to leave you, but we need the money. There's no work here. I must go to el norte, so I can find work and send for you.

CARMEN:　I don't want to be alone.

RICARDO:　You have María. I'm going so that we can have the things we don't have.

CARMEN:　I would prefer to have you and not the things I don't have.

RICARDO:　I want something else besides a life on this farm.

CARMEN:　María will not see you.

RICARDO:　She will. When I am on the other side, I will send for you. She will be very proud of me.

CARMEN:　You promise?

RICARDO:　I promise.

CARMEN:　Well, then I will wait; we will wait.

RICARDO:　I will write. (*Kisses* CARMEN *on the forehead.*)

CARMEN:　Ricardo, remember that I love you. (RICARDO *leaves.*) Don't forget to write.

(*Fade out.*)

SCENE THREE

NARRATOR:　Yes, write a lot; they will miss you. All who are in search of opportunity go to the same place: America. And America belongs to those who are willing to risk.

(A giant sail enters the stage brought on by FOUR EUROPEAN IMMIGRANTS.*)*

IMMIGRANT 1:   All for a dream.
IMMIGRANT 2:   Ciao, mia Italia!
IMMIGRANT 3:   Auf Wiedersehen, mein Deutschland!
IMMIGRANT 4:   Au revoir, mon France!
IMMIGRANT 2:   Hello, America!

(In the background "America the Beautiful" plays, the music growing louder. The STATUE OF LIBERTY *enters.)*

IMMIGRANT 3:   The Lady!
IMMIGRANT 4:   Up high in the sky, incapable of being brought down.
IMMIGRANT 2:   And like her . . .
IMMIGRANT 3:   . . . we carry . . .
IMMIGRANTS 2 & 4:   . . . a similar torch.
ALL: A torch of hope.
STATUE OF LIBERTY: Give me your tired, your poor, your huddled masses yearning to breathe free . . .

(At the bottom of the STATUE OF LIBERTY *are* THREE MEXICAN PEOPLE *[*RICARDO *is one of them] trying to go across the stage as if it is the border. They run around hiding, sneaking, and crawling, trying not to get spotted by the border patrol.)*

RICARDO: ¡Vénganse! ¡Por aquí!
MEXICAN MAN: ¿Y ahora qué hacemos?
MEXICAN WOMAN: What do we do now?
MEXICAN MAN: ¡Vámonos! ¡Por allá!
MEXICAN WOMAN: ¡Nos nortearon!
RICARDO: Let's go back.

(They go to hide behind the EUROPEAN IMMIGRANTS. *The* STATUE OF LIBERTY *composes herself and continues.)*

STATUE OF LIBERTY: I give you life, liberty and the pursuit of happiness for the price of your heritage, your roots, your history, your relatives, your language . . . Conform, adapt, bury your past, give up what is yours and I'll give you the opportunity to have what is mine.
MEXICAN MAN: Pues bueno, if we have to.
MEXICAN WOMAN: Sounds good.
IMMIGRANT 4:   Look, fireworks!
RICARDO: ¡Nos hicimos!

("America the Beautiful" becomes overwhelming; lights flash, representing the fireworks. A few seconds later the same lights that adorn the celebration for EUROPEAN IMMIGRANTS *become the lights from the helicopters hunting after the* MEXICAN PEOPLE. *Hound dogs are also heard barking, and the* MEXICAN PEOPLE *scatter and try to hide.)*

RICARDO: ¡La migra!
MEXICAN MAN: The immigration!
MEXICAN WOMAN: ¡Córranle!

(*The* EUROPEAN IMMIGRANTS *and the* STATUE OF LIBERTY *all keep pointing at the* MEXI-CAN PEOPLE *so that they can be caught. The* MEXICAN PEOPLE *run offstage, and with the sail tilted down, they charge after them. Fade out.*)

SCENE FOUR

POSTMAN: (*Throwing in paper airplane.*) Air mail for Carmen García.

CARMEN: (CARMEN *enters and reads letter.*) "Mi querida Carmen, how are you? How is María? I've sent you some more money. This is the last letter I write to you because I am now sending for you. I fixed my papers with the help of a friend, and I got an apartment where we can live. Tell María I love her, and to you I send all my love . . ." María! . . ."Leave as soon as possible . . ." Leave as soon as possible . . . María, ¡ven acá!

MARÍA: (MARÍA *enters.*) Yes, Mami.

CARMEN: María get ready; we're going.

MARÍA: Going where?

CARMEN: To join your father in the city of the angels.

MARÍA: Angels?

(MARÍA *puts on her coat for the journey. Fade out.*)

SCENE FIVE

On the screen the following title is displayed: **Los Angelitos Del Norte.** *The following is the making of a city. Actors will take on many roles. It will be organized chaos. Noises of police and firetruck sirens, along with other common city noises are heard. The lights rise on* VENDORS *selling on the streets, and all sorts of unusual and not so unusual* PEOPLE *found in downtown L.A. on Broadway.* CARMEN *and* MARÍA *are engulfed in the scene, appalled to see what they have come to.*

PERSON 1:   Broadway! Downtown L.A.!

VENDOR 1:   Cassettes, ¡cartuchos, dos dólares!

VENDOR 2:   Anillos de oro sólido. Solid gold. Not plated.

CARMEN: Perdone, señora, could you tell me . . .

BAG LADY: Get out of my way!

PROTESTOR: Homosexuality is wrong! No sex! No sex! ¡Se va a acabar el mundo! The world is coming to an end!

(*Separates* CARMEN *from* MARÍA.)

CARMEN: María! María, where are you?! (*Searches frantically.*)

MARÍA: Mami! Mami! (*Cries for* CARMEN.)

WOMAN 1:   Buy this! ¿Sombras para verte como estrella de cine?

WOMAN 2:   Hair brushes, all kinds, a dollar!

WOMAN 3:   You want to buy handbags?

WOMAN 4:   ¡Vámonos! Here comes the police.

(*All the* VENDORS *on the street run away.*)

MAN 1:   Jesus loves you! (*Hands* CARMEN *a pamphlet.*) He died for our sins!

CARMEN: ¿Qué?

WOMAN 1:   That RTD bus is late again!

DIRTY OLD MAN: Hey! Little girl! You want to get married? The world is coming to an end and you don't want to die without having experienced it.

CARMEN: María! María! ¿Dónde estás, hija mia?

CHOLO 2:   East L.A.!

TWO VALLEY GIRLS: We love it!

CHOLO 1:   Hey, bato!

TWO VALLEY GIRLS: Party and let party!

CHOLO 2:   ¡Oye, mi carnal!

PERSON 2:   ¡Viva la huelga! Boycott grapes!

PERSON 3:   Chicano Power!

TWO VALLEY GIRLS: We love it.

PERSON 3:   Chicano Power!

TWO VALLEY GIRLS: We love it.

PERSON 4:   A little culture for the gringuitos. ¡Tostadas, frijoles!

ANGLO BUYER: How much? ¿Cuánto? ¿Salsa? ¿Cerveza?

CARMEN: María!

(MARÍA *runs scared and bumps into* CARMEN. *They hug each other.* RICARDO, *dressed in a charro outfit enters and gives some yells as if ready to sing a corrido. All the chaos of the city stops, and all the city people recoil in fear.* RICARDO *becomes the hero rescuing* CARMEN *and* MARÍA *from their nightmare.*)

TWO VALLEY GIRLS: We love it!

CARMEN: ¡Ayyy! What a crazy city! It's so awful! People here are crazy! (*Almost about to cry, she embraces* RICARDO.) But Ricardo, I'm so happy to be here.

MARÍA: (*Trying to get attention.*) An ugly man chased me!

RICARDO: But you are all right?

MARÍA: Sí. Now that you are here.

RICARDO: Carmen, we are finally together like I promised.

CARMEN: Ricardo, where's our home?

RICARDO: Follow me.

(*They leave the stage. Fade out. Props for next scene are set up quickly.*)

SCENE SIX

NARRATOR: They are going to the housing projects; Pico Aliso, Ramona Gardens, Estrada Courts. No one likes it there, but it's cheap. Es Barato. (*On the screen the following title is displayed:* **Little House in The Ghetto.**) Little house in the ghetto.

RICARDO: Here we are.

CARMEN: ¿Aquí?

RICARDO: Yes, I hope it's all right. It's only for now.

MARÍA: (*Smiling.*) I like it! Look, Mami! There are swings and grass.

RICARDO: There are a lot of kids in the neighborhood you can play with.

MARÍA: Really, Papi? Would they want to play with me?

RICARDO: Sure. (*Noticing* CARMEN's *displeasure.*) What's wrong? You don't like it?

CARMEN: Oh. No, I'm just tired from the trip.

RICARDO: How was the trip?

MARÍA: (*Cutting in.*) It was great!

CARMEN: Great? You threw up on me the whole way here.

MARÍA: Except, I don't understand why the bus never got off the ground. Where are the angels? And where are the clouds? And the gate? And the music . . . Like in the stories Mami used to tell me. I thought we were going to heaven. I thought you had been called to heaven because you are an angel. Are you an angel?

RICARDO: Yes, I'm your angel always.

MARÍA: So if this isn't heaven and you're an angel, what are we doing here?

RICARDO: María, I brought you to America so that you can have a better life. It wasn't easy for me. I was hiding in a truck with a lot of other people for hours. It was so hot and humid that people preferred to get caught by the migra than die of suffocation. But I was going to make it because I knew that I had a daughter to live for. I did it for you. In America, the education is great! You can take advantage of all the opportunities offered to you. You can work hard to be just as good as anybody. You can be anything you want to be! (*Pause.*) Carmen, let me show you the kitchen. (CARMEN *and* RICARDO *exit.*)

MARÍA: America, I don't even know you yet and I already love you! You're too generous. Thank you. I'll work hard. I can be anything I want to be! (*Starts changing clothes to end up wearing a casual shirt and pants when she finishes the following:*) America, I'm ready to play the game. I'm gonna show those boys in this neighborhood how to really play football!

(*She makes some football moves. Then she runs out.* CARMEN *enters.*)

CARMEN: María, ¡ven aquí! (MARÍA *enters.*)

MARÍA: Yes, Mami.

CARMEN: La señora Martínez told me you were playing football with the boys.

MARÍA: Yes, Mami; I was.

CARMEN: I don't want you playing football with the boys. It's not proper for a lady.

MARÍA: But I'm good at sports. I'm better than some of the boys.

CARMEN: It doesn't look right. ¿Qué van a decir?

(*In the background appear the* THREE GIRLS *who are only seen and heard by* MARÍA. *They whisper to her.*)

GIRL 1:   Never shame your society.

GIRL 2:   Never,

GIRL 3:   never,

GIRL 1:   never,

ALL: NEVER!!!

MARÍA: But my Papi said . . .

CARMEN: You are not going to play with boys! (CARMEN *exits.*)

MARÍA: I don't understand. Papi tells me to compete, Mami tells me it doesn't look right. I like to compete, too. (MARÍA *exits to her room.*)

RICARDO: (*To* MARÍA.) María, ¡ven aquí! Who were you walking home with today?

MARÍA: A friend.

RICARDO: A boyfriend?

MARÍA: No, just a friend I have in my last class. He lives close by.

RICARDO: I don't want you walking home with or talking to boys. Study!

MARÍA: (*Dares to ask.*) Papi, why?

RICARDO: You're thirteen and you are very naïve about boys. The only thing on their minds is of no good for a proper girl. They tell girls that they are "special," sweet things, knowing that girls are stupid enough to believe it. They make pendejas out of them. They get them pregnant, and shame their parents . . . Go to your room!

(*The* THREE GIRLS *appear again and whisper to* MARÍA.)

GIRL 1:   Never shame your society!

GIRL 2:   Never,

GIRL 3:   (*Does not continue, but slowly walks away from the two girls.*)

GIRL 1:   Never,

GIRL 1 AND 2:   Never!!

(*Spotlight on* MARÍA. MARÍA *goes to the mirror,* GIRL 3 *appears in the mirror.* MARÍA *brushes her hair and so does* GIRL 3. *Then* GIRL 3 *begins to touch herself in intimate ways, discovering the changes through puberty, while* MARÍA *remains still, not daring to touch herself. Finally, when* MARÍA *does dare to touch herself,* CARMEN *comes into the room and discovers her. Lights quickly come back on.*)

CARMEN: María, what are you doing?

MARÍA: Nothing.

CARMEN: María, were you . . . (*Before* MARÍA *can answer.*) It is a sin to do that. Good girls don't do that. (GIRL 3 *goes behind* MARÍA.)

GIRL 3:   (*Whispering.*) Why? Why? Why?

MARÍA: Why?

CARMEN: (*Somewhat shocked.*) Because it is dirty! Sex is dirty.

GIRL 3:   Why is it dirty? What makes it dirty?

MARÍA: (*Suppresses and ignores* GIRL 3.) I'm sorry, I didn't know what I was doing.

CARMEN: María, I'm telling you for your own good. Women should be pure. Men don't marry women who are not unless they have to. Quieren vírgenes. It's best that way, if you save yourself for your wedding night. Be submissive.

GIRL 3:   Why? Why? Why?

MARÍA: Yes, but . . . Why?

CARMEN: That's the way it is. I know it's not fair, but women will always be different from men. Ni modo.

MARÍA AND GIRL 3:   I don't understand. Why must a woman be submissive? Why is sex dirty? (GIRL 1 *appears.*)

GIRL 1:   María, stop questioning and just accept.

GIRL 3:   No, María! God gave you a brain to think and question. Use it!

GIRL 1:   But it is not up to us to decide what is right and what is wrong. Your parents know best, María. They love you and do things for you.

GIRL 3:   María, they are not always right . . .

RICARDO: (*Interrupting the argument.*) María! Come and help your mother with dinner right now!

MARÍA: All right! (*She goes to the table and chairs.*)

RICARDO: What do you do in your room? You spend so much time in there.

MARÍA: I was doing my homework.

RICARDO: It takes you all that time? (RICARDO *has the mail and pulls out a letter from the pile.*)

MARÍA: Yes, I want my work to be perfect so that I can win an award . . .

RICARDO: All for an award? How about if I give you a trophy for washing the dishes when you are supposed to, and for doing the laundry right?

(*He begins to read the letter.* MARÍA *searches through the pile. She finds a letter, reads it and becomes excited.*)

CARMEN: (*To* RICARDO.) Who's the letter from?

RICARDO: My cousin, Pedro.

CARMEN: What are you going to tell him?

RICARDO: The truth. I'm going to tell him his Martita did pendejadita and is due in three months. (*To* MARÍA.) What do I tell you?

CARMEN: Ayy, ¡qué vergüenza!

RICARDO: ¡Tanto estudio y para nada! It's such a waste to educate women. How is all that education helping her now. She's pregnant and on welfare . . . What's that smell? The tortillas are burning!

MARÍA: Ayyy!!!! (MARÍA *runs to the kitchen.*)

CARMEN: When you get married, what is your husband going to say?

MARÍA: I'm sorry; I completely forgot.

CARMEN: You can't cook, you can't clean . . .

MARÍA: I try to do all the chores you ask.

CARMEN: You can't do anything right. Not even the tortillas.

MARÍA: I really try . . .

RICARDO: No Mexican man is going to marry a woman who can't cook.

CARMEN: You're almost eighteen! (*Looks to* RICARDO.) I married your father when I was eighteen and I already knew how to do everything.

MARÍA: Mamá, papá, there are other more important things . . . (*She holds the letter, but decides not to say anything.*) I just don't care for housework.

(MARÍA *goes to her room. Spotlight on* MARÍA. *She looks at the letter and* GIRL 3 *appears. They look at the letter and* GIRL 3 *reads.*)

GIRL 3:   "Congratulations! You are eligible for a four-year scholarship . . . Please respond as soon as possible . . ."

(MARÍA *jumps up in excitement. She then gets a typewriter and begins to type her response. The typewriter is not working. She goes outside to look for her father. Fade out.*)

SCENE SEVEN

RICARDO *and* MARÍA *enter.*

MARÍA: Papá . . . ¿Está ocupado?

RICARDO: I'm reading the paper.

MARÍA: Do you think . . . well . . . maybe when you have finished reading you can fix this for me? Here is the manual.

> (*She shows it to him. He pretends to look, but cannot understand it.*)

RICARDO: Go get my tool box. I'll do it my way.

(RICARDO *begins to check the typewriter carefully.* MARÍA *looks attentively and also tries to think of a way to introduce the subject of college.* GIRL 1 *appears.*)

GIRL 1:   There is no one who can take the place of my father, who loves me but cannot show it any other way. If I wasn't scared, I would hold you. I love you.

> (RICARDO *finishes fixing the typewriter and hands it to* MARÍA.)

CARMEN: ¡Ayy! ¡Qué huebona! Where is María?

RICARDO: She's in her room typing. I fixed her typewriter.

CARMEN: What is she typing?

RICARDO: I don't know. Ask her.

CARMEN: (*She goes to* MARÍA'*s room.*) María, come help me fold the clothes.

MARÍA: I'm busy!

CARMEN: Busy? Busy! Can't it wait? I have things to do, too.

MARÍA: All right. (*They start folding the clothes.* RICARDO *enters.*)

CARMEN: María, your birthday is almost here. Do you want me to make you a beautiful dress for your birthday? Maybe you can wear it for your graduation? Oh, our neighbor, la señora Martínez, told me today her daughter Rosario is graduating from a good business school. She says she already has a good job as a secretary.

MARÍA: Mamá, Papá, I don't want to be a secretary. (*Pause.*) I want to go to college.

RICARDO: What?

CARMEN: It's too expensive.

MARÍA: (*Quickly.*) I was awarded a big, four-year scholarship!

RICARDO: ¿Que? College? Scholarship?

CARMEN: ¿Para qué?

MARÍA: I want to be educated . . . (*Courageously.*) I want to be an actress.

RICARDO: You want to go to college to study to be an actress? ¿Estás loca?

CARMEN: Ayyy, María, you are crazy! You don't know what you want.

RICARDO: I didn't know you had to study to be a whore.

CARMEN: What have we done to make you want to leave us? We've tried to be good . . .

MARÍA: Nothing. It's not you. I want to be something.

RICARDO: Why don't you just get married like most decent women and be a housewife?

CARMEN: That's something.

RICARDO: That's respectable.

MARÍA: I don't understand what you are so afraid of . . .

RICARDO: I don't want you to forget that you are a Mexican. There are so many people where I work who deny they are Mexican. When their life gets better they stop being Mexican! To deny one's country is to deny one's past, one's parents. How ungrateful!

MARÍA: Papi, I won't. But you said that with an education I could be just as good as anybody. And that's why you brought me to America.

RICARDO: No. Get married!

MARÍA: I will. But I want a career as well. Women can now do both.

RICARDO: Don't tell me about modern women. What kind of wife would that woman make if she's busy with her career and can't tend to her house, children and husband.

MARÍA: And that's all a woman is for? To have children? Clean a house? Tend to her husband like a slave? And heat his tortillas?

RICARDO: ¡Qué atrevida! Why do you make it seem as if it would be some sort of nightmare? (*Sarcastically.*) Women have always gotten married and they have survived.

MARÍA: But surviving is not living.

CARMEN: María, listen to your father.

MARÍA: Papi, I listened to you. That's why! You encouraged me when I was young, but now you tell me I can't. Why?

RICARDO: (*Trying to find an answer.*) Because . . . you are a woman.

MARÍA: Papi, you're not being fair.

RICARDO: (*Trying to keep face and control.*) You ungrateful daughter! I don't want to see you. Get out of my face! (MARÍA *runs to her room, crying.*)

CARMEN: Ricardo, why don't you even let her try, ¿por favor? (*She goes to* MARÍA*'s room.* RICARDO *stands, and then exits. Lights change to* MARÍA*'s room.*) María, don't cry. Don't be angry at us either, and try to understand us. ¡M'ija! We are doing this for you. We don't want you to get hurt. You want too much; that's not realistic. You are a Mexican woman, and that's that. You can't change that. You are different from other women. Try to accept that. Women need to get married, they are no good without men.

MARÍA: Mami, I consider myself intelligent and ambitious, and what is that worth if I am a woman? Nothing?

CARMEN: You are worth a lot to me. I can't wait for the day when I will see you in a beautiful white wedding dress walking down the aisle with a church full of people. This is the most important event in a woman's life.

MARÍA: Mother, we are in America. Don't you realize you expect me to live in two worlds? How is it done? Can't things be different?

CARMEN: No sé. That's the way your father is. Ni modo.

MARÍA: Ni modo? Ni modo! Is that all you can say? Can't you do anything? (*Gives up on her and just explodes.*) ¡¡Ayy!! Get out! Get out!

(CARMEN *leaves and* MARÍA *continues to pound on her pillow with rage.* MARÍA *slowly begins to fall asleep. Fade out.*)

SCENE EIGHT

On the screen the following title is displayed: **The Dream.** GIRL 2, *who will now portray* MYTH, *appears. She wears a spring dress and looks virginal. She goes to* MARÍA.

MYTH: (*Shaking* MARÍA *lightly.*) María, get up and come see.

MARÍA: Who are you?

MYTH: I'm Myth. María, come see what can be.

MARÍA: What do you mean? What's going on?

MYTH: María, you are dreaming the American Dream. You can be anything you want to be. Follow me.

(*The sound of a horse is heard.*)

MARÍA: Is that a horse I'm hearing?

MYTH: See . . .

(*A* PRINCE *appears and he and* MYTH *begin to dance to a sweet melody. Just as they are about to kiss, the fierce sound of a whip accompanied by loud and wild cries of the horse running off are heard.*)

PRINCE: (*In a very wimpy voice.*) My horse! My horse!

(*Runs off to catch his horse.*)

MARÍA: What happened?

MYTH: I don't know.

(*Another crack of the whip is heard, but now* GIRL 3, *who will portray* "MARY," *appears with the whip.*)

MARY: Sorry to spoil the fairy tale, but Prince Charming was expected at the castle by Cinderella . . . Hello, María.

MARÍA: And who are you?

MARY: My name is Mary. It's my turn now, so get lost Myth!

(*She snaps her finger and a large hook pulls* MYTH *offstage.*)

MYTH: You're such a meanie!

MARY: Control, that's the thing to have. So come along and follow me!

MARÍA: Where are you taking me?

MARY: To liberation! Self independence, economic independence, sexual independence. We are free! María, in America, you can be anything you want to be. A lawyer. A doctor. An astronaut. An actress!!! The Mayor. Maybe even the President . . . of a company. You don't have to be obedient, submissive, gracious. You don't have to like dolls, dishes, cooking, children and laundry. Enjoy life! Enjoy liberation! Enjoy sex! Be free!

(GIRL 1, *who will portray* "MARÍA 2," *appears brandishing a broom.*)

MARÍA 2:   You bad woman! You bitch!

MARY: I'm not!

MARÍA 2:   You American demon. You are. You are. You just want to tempt her, then hurt her.

MARÍA: (*Throwing* MARY *her whip.*) Mary, catch!

MARY: Thanks! Now we will see!

(MARÍA 2 *and* MARY *have a mock sword combat, until a man blows a whistle and becomes a referee for a wrestling match.*)

REFEREE: (*Taking away the broom and the whip.*) All right, c'mon girls. I don't want weapons. Give them. (*The women push him away and charge at each other.* MARY *tries some dirty tricks.*) I told you I wanted this to be a clean fight. What were you using?

MARY: Nothing! I'm so innocent.

REFEREE: Now come over here and shake hands.

MARÍA 2:   (*Asking the audience.*) Should I? Should I?

(*Gets* MARY's *hand and twists it. They wrestle wildly, with* MARY *winning, then* MARÍA 2. *The* REFEREE *finally steps in.*)

REFEREE: Break! Break! (*He holds* MARY *and pulls her out.*)

MARY: (*Barely able to speak.*) María, before you are a wife, before you are a mother, first you are a woman! I'll be back.

(*She's dragged out.* MARÍA 2, *who won the fight, acknowledges the cheers of the crowd, then gestures for* MARÍA *to kneel and pray.* MARÍA 2 *puts a wedding veil on* MARÍA.)

MARÍA 2:   A woman's only purpose in life is to serve three men. Her father, her husband and her son. Her father.

(RICARDO *appears. He picks up* MARÍA *and escorts her to the church. The bells and the wedding march are heard. The following title is displayed:* **White Wedding.** MARÍA *walks down the aisle; the groom enters.*)

MARÍA 2:   Her husband.

(*The couple kneels and a wedding lasso is put around them.*)

PRIEST: (*Same as first* PRIEST.) Dearly beloved, we are gathered here, under the Catholic Church, in the holy House of God, to unite these two people in holy matrimony. Marriage is sacred. It is the unification of a man and a woman, their love and commitment, forever, and ever, and ever; no matter what! Well, then, let's begin . . . María, do you accept José Juan González García López as your lawfully wedded husband to love, cherish, serve, cook for, clean for, sacrifice for, have his children, keep his house, love him even if he beats you, commits adultery, gets drunk, rapes you lawfully, denies you your identity, money, love his family, serve his family, and in return ask for nothing?

MARÍA: (*Thinks about it and turns to her parents.*) I do.

PRIEST: Very good. Now, José. Do you accept María García González López as your lawfully wedded wife to support?

JOSÉ: I do.

PRIEST: Good. Well, if there is anyone present who is opposed to the union of these two people, speak now, or forever hold your truth. (RICARDO *stands up, takes out a gun and shows it to the audience.*) Do you have the ring? (JOSÉ *takes out a golden dog collar. The* PRIEST *gives it his blessings.*) Five, six, seven, eight. By the power vested in me, under the Catholic Church, in the holy House of God, I pronounce you husband and wife.

(*The* THREE GIRLS *take away* MARÍA*'s veil and bouquet. They place the dog collar around* MARÍA*'s neck. Then they get the lasso and tie it around her to make the collar work like a leash. To* JOSÉ.) You may pet the bride. (*The lasso is given to* JOSÉ. *He pulls* MARÍA, *who gets on her hands and knees. They walk down the aisle like dog and master. The wedding march plays, people begin to leave. Fade out.*)

SCENE NINE

A table and two chairs are placed in the center of the stage. MARÍA, *pregnant, walks in uncomfortably. She turns on the television, then the ensemble creates the television setting, playing roles of T.V. producer, director, make-up people, technicians, as if the actual studio is there. Brief dialogue is improvised to establish on-set frenzy.*

ANNOUNCER: And here is another chapter of your afternoon soap opera, "HAPPILY EVERAFTER." Our sultry Eliza Vázquez decides to leave Devero in search of freedom!

FLOOR MAN: Okay everyone, tape rolling, standby in ten seconds. Five, four, three, two . . .

(*He cues.*)

ACTRESS: Devero, I'm leaving you.
ACTOR: Eliza, why?
ACTRESS: I don't love you anymore. Actually, I never did.
ACTOR: Eliza, but I love you.
ACTRESS: I faked it, all of it. I did it because I had to. But now I must go and be free!

(MARÍA *claps loudly in excitement for her.*)

FLOOR MANAGER: Cut! (*To* MARÍA.) What are you doing here?
MARÍA: This is my living room.
FLOOR MANAGER: Oh, sure it is. Well go into the kitchen, make yourself a snack; we'll have the carpet cleaned in an hour. (*Pushes her aside.*) I know, I'm sorry . . . Standby. Five, four, three, two, one.
ACTRESS: . . . But now I must go and be free!
ACTOR: You can't do this to me!
ACTRESS: Oh, yes I can!
ACTOR: But I've given you everything!
ACTRESS: Everything but an identity! Well, Devero, Devero, Devero, I've discovered I no longer need you. There are unfulfilled dreams I must pursue. I want adventure.

FLOOR MANAGER: And . . . cut! That's a take. Roll commercial. Five seconds. Four, three, two, one.

(*The soap opera ends.* MARÍA *claps approvingly. A commercial quickly begins, with the ensemble creating a similar on-set frenzy. In the commercial a man comes home with a bottle of Ajax as a gift for his wife.*)

HUSBAND: Honey, I'm home! I brought you something. (*Hides the can treating it as if he had flowers.*)
WIFE: Hi, darling! (*They give each other a peck on the mouth from a distance.*) How was work?
HUSBAND: Fine . . . Ta–Dah! (*Presents the can.*)
WIFE: You shouldn't have. Oh, thank you! I need all the cleaning power I can get!
HUSBAND: I can smell you've been cleaning.
WIFE: Yes! I've mopped the floors, done the dishes, the laundry; this house is spotless.
HUSBAND: What a wife! (*They give each other another peck on the mouth from a distance.*) You're a good wife!

(MARÍA *goes to turn off the television. The doorbell rings. She goes to answer the door. It's her husband who grunts at her and comes in, asks for his dinner and sits at the table.*)

JOSÉ: María! María! I'm home. I'm hungry.
MARÍA: José, how was work? Dinner is ready. I made your favorite dish. Do you want to eat now? (JOSÉ *doesn't answer.*) Well, I'll serve you then. (MARÍA *places a plate on the table.*) My mother came to visit today and she asked me what we are going to name the baby. She thought it would be nice to call her Esperanza. (JOSÉ *grunts.*) Of course it isn't going to be a girl. It's going to be a boy, and we'll name him after you. That would be nice, wouldn't it? (MARÍA *feels pains.*) Ayyy! How it hurts. I hope after the baby is born, I will be better. I've been getting so many pains, and I have a lot of stretchmarks . . . I know you don't like me to ask for money, but I need the money to buy a dress that fits. I have nothing I can wear anymore.
JOSÉ: (*After a spoonful.*) My dinner is cold.
MARÍA: Oh, is it cold? Well, I'll heat it up right now. It will only take a minute.

(MARÍA *runs to the kitchen.* JOSÉ *leaves the table and stares at the bed. The following title is displayed:* **The Sex Object.**

JOSÉ: María! ¡Mi amor! Come here, baby! . . . Come on, m'ijita. I won't hurt you . . .

(*He continues to try to persuade her. Eventually he gets his way. There are sounds of lust and pain. Finally,* MARÍA *gives out a loud scream of pain.*)

JOSÉ: What is it?
MARÍA: The baby!

(*Fade out.*)

SCENE TEN

The lights rise after the scream. MARÍA *spreads her legs wide open, covering herself with a white sheet.* THREE NURSES *run in. On the screen the following title is displayed:* **The Reproducing Machine or Be Fruitful.** *Dolls will be used as babies.*)

SALESMAN: Here we have it. Direct from Mexico. The Reproducing Machine. You can have one by calling our toll-free number. Get your pencil.

HEAD NURSE: Now, relax. Just breathe like this. (*Example.*) Ahhh!! All in good rhythm. Good! Don't worry, millions of women have children, especially Mexican women, they have millions. But you'll get used to it. After your fourth child, they'll just slide right on out.

MARÍA: 'Amá! Mamá!

HEAD NURSE: There's nothing I can do. I went through it myself. Now, isn't the pain great? You're giving birth! Why, it's the most satisfying feeling a woman can feel. Okay, I think it's coming! Push, Push, Push.

(*A baby pops up, flying into the air. It is caught by one of the nurses. She presents the baby to the* HEAD NURSE.)

HEAD NURSE: Oh, it's a girl.

NURSE 2:   (*Presenting the baby to* JOSÉ.) Here's your baby daughter.

JOSÉ: A daughter? How could you do this to me? Well, I'll have to call her Sacrifice.

(MARÍA *screams again.*)

HEAD NURSE: What is it?

MARÍA: There's another one inside; I can feel it!

HEAD NURSE: Nahhh! Well, I'll check just in case. (*She peeps under the sheet.*) Well, I'll be! Yeah, there's another one. Push! Push! Push!

(*Another baby pops into the air.* NURSE 3 *catches the baby.*)

NURSE 2:   (*Presenting it to* JOSÉ.) Here's another lovely daughter.

JOSÉ: Another daughter? I'll have to call her Abnegation.

SALESMAN: (*Appearing from nowhere.*) Here we have this amazing machine. The world renowned Reproducing Machine!

(MARÍA *screams again.*)

HEAD NURSE: What is it?

MARÍA: There's another one!

SALESMAN: Ahh, but if you were watching earlier, you saw the other amazing function. It can also be used as a sex object.

HEAD NURSE: Push! Push! Push!

(*Another baby pops up.*)

NURSE 4:   (*Catching baby.*) I got it.

SALESMAN: Yes siree! You can be the boss. It's at your disposal. Hours of pleasure. And if it ever does go out of control, a kick and a few punches will do the job and it will be back to normal.

NURSE 2: Here's another one.

JOSÉ: Another girl? Why are you doing this to me? I'll call her Obligation.

SALESMAN: It's made in Mexico. It's cheap! It cooks! It cleans!

(MARÍA *screams again.*)

HEAD NURSE: Push! Push! Push!

(THREE BABIES *pop up into the air. Some land in the audience. All the nurses are busy collecting them.*)

SALESMAN: Its stretchmarks can stretch all the way from here to Tijuana. Not even a Japanese model can beat this one.

NURSE 2: (*To* JOSÉ.) Guess what?

JOSÉ: No, don't tell me; another girl?

NURSE 2: Surprise!

JOSÉ: (*See babies.*) Three girls! I'll call them Frustration, Regret and Disappointment.

SALESMAN: It delivers up to twenty-one children. It feeds on beans, chile and lies.

HEAD NURSE: Are there any more babies in that Mexican oven of yours?

MARÍA: I don't think so.

HEAD NURSE: See you in nine months for your next Mexican litter.

SALESMAN: You can have your own reproducing machine! Call the number on your screen now!

(*Fade out.*)

SCENE ELEVEN

Lights rise after a brief pause. On the stage is a table which serves as a crib for the six crying babies. On the screen the following title is displayed: **The Nightmare.** MARÍA *tries to quiet the babies by holding each one at a time, then by the bunch.* CARMEN, RICARDO *and* JOSÉ *enter. They stand behind her like demons.*

JOSÉ: Shut those babies up!

CARMEN: You're a bad wife!

RICARDO: This house is a mess!

CARMEN: You can't cook, you can't clean!

JOSÉ: Where's my dinner?

RICARDO: The dishes?

JOSÉ: My tortillas?

RICARDO: You're a bad wife!

CARMEN: I did it all my life!

JOSÉ: Bad wife!

MARÍA: No! I'm not! I'm a good wife! I try. I really do!

(MARÍA *goes to get the laundry and begins to fold it quickly, but nicely and carefully. Suddenly, the clothes begin to take on a life of their own. There is a giant coat, and a pair of pants surrounding* MARÍA. *They start pushing her around, then her wedding dress appears and heads towards* MARÍA'*s neck. They wrestle on the ground.*)

CARMEN: Martyr!

(MARÍA *manages to get away, and runs upstage. As she is running, a giant tortilla with the Aztec Calendar emblem falls on her, smashing her to the ground.*)

MARÍA: Help!
RICARDO: Martyr!

(MARÍA *manages to get out from under the tortilla; as she escapes, she is attacked by a storm of plates.*)

MARÍA: Help!
RICARDO, CARMEN AND JOSÉ: Martyr!!! Martyr!!! Martyr!!!
MARÍA: (*Becomes uncontrollably mad.*) Enough! Do you want your dishes cleaned? I've got the perfect solution for them. (MARÍA *gestures. Sounds of dishes being smashed are heard.*) Now you don't have to worry. I'll buy you a million paper plates! Ohhhh! And the tortillas. Mamá! I'm going to show you how they should be done. (*She gets a bag of tortillas and begins tossing them into the audience like frisbees.*) Are these good enough? I hope so! I tried to get the top side cooked first . . . or was it last? Anyway, who cares! Here are the tortillas! (*Attacks her mother with a couple of tortillas.*) I hate doing the dishes! I hate doing the laundry! I hate cooking and cleaning! And I hate all housework because it offends me as a woman! (*There is a piercing moment of silence.*) That's right. I am a woman . . . a real woman of flesh and blood. This is not the life I want to live; I want more! And from now on I am directing my own life! Action!

(*Lights come fully on.* TWO GIRLS *grab and pull* MARÍA *harshly to take her to another place. The stage now becomes a courtroom.* MARÍA *is sat next to the* JUDGE. *The following title is displayed:* **The Trial.** *The courtroom is filled with people who create a lot of commotion. The* JUDGE, *the* BAILIFF *and the* PROSECUTOR *enter.*)

BAILIFF: Please rise, the honorable hang-judge presiding.
JUDGE: (*Bangs his gavel until everyone quiets down.* JUDGE *will be done by same actor who does* PRIEST.) Quiet in my courtroom! I am warning you, anyone who causes any such commotion like this again will be thrown out! Is that understood! Let's begin!
BAILIFF: We are here today to give trial to María who is being accused by her husband of rebellion toward her implied duties of marriage.
JUDGE: How do you plead?
MARÍA: Plead? Innocent! Guilty! I don't know!
JUDGE: Are you making a joke out of my question?
MARÍA: No . . . Sir.
JUDGE: It sounds to me like you wish to challenge these laws.
MARÍA: I don't understand why I am on trial. What real laws have I broken?
JUROR 1: She knows what she's guilty of.

JUROR 2:　She knows what laws not to break!

MARÍA:　Who are they?

BAILIFF:　Your jury.

MARÍA:　But they are women, Mexican, traditional . . . They can't possibly be objective.

BAILIFF:　They are a good jury.

MARÍA:　This is unjust! I must speak up to this . . .

BAILIFF:　You have no voice.

MARÍA:　Where's my lawyer? I do get one, don't I?

(*The courtroom fills with cruel laughter, which quickly stops.*)

JUDGE:　No, you defend yourself.

MARÍA:　How do I defend myself when I can't speak?

PROSECUTOR:　(*To* MARÍA.) You're dead meat, shrimp. (*To audience.*) This trial is meant to help preserve the institution of marriage. Ladies and gentlemen of the jury . . . in this case, ladies of the jury. A man's home is his castle. Where he has his foundation. It is the place where he comes home to his family, and he becomes the king of his castle. But this poor man comes home one evening and finds his children unattended, his house a mess, his dinner unprepared and his wife sitting back, watching soap operas!

MARÍA:　I object!

JUDGE:　You have no voice.

MARÍA:　You said I was to defend myself.

JUDGE:　Not now!

PROSECUTOR:　What we are going to try to do is prove the guilt of this woman . . .

MARÍA:　I object!

JUDGE:　Shut up!

MARÍA:　I won't!

JUDGE:　Mister Prosecutor, call your first witness!

PROSECUTOR:　I call Ricardo García to the witness stand. (RICARDO *takes the stand.*) Tell us about your daughter.

RICARDO:　She was very obedient when she was young, but when she came to the United States she began to think of herself as "American" . . . She studied a lot, which is good, but she almost refused to do her chores because she thought herself above them.

PROSECUTOR:　Could you tell us what happened that evening your daughter rebelled?

RICARDO:　I'd rather not . . . That evening María was hysterical. She threw dishes, tortillas . . .

PROSECUTOR:　Thank you, that will be all. My next witness will be Carmen García. (CARMEN *takes the stand.*) Tell us about your daughter.

CARMEN:　She's really a good girl. She's just too dramatic sometimes. She's such a dreamer, forgive her.

PROSECUTOR:　Could you tell us what you saw that evening?

CARMEN:　Well, she was a little upset, so she did a few things she didn't mean to do.

MARÍA: No, Mamá! I meant it!
JUROR 1:   She admits it!
JUROR 2:   She's guilty!
ALL: Guilty!
CARMEN: No, she's just unrealistic.
MARÍA: I'm guilty then!

(*The whole courtroom becomes chaotic. Everyone yells out "guilty."* CARMEN *becomes so sad she begins to cry.*)

MARÍA: Mami, don't cry!

(*The lights go on and off and everyone disappears. Fade out.*)

SCENE TWELVE

MARÍA *begins to regain consciousness and wakes up from her dream. She is awakened by* CARMEN*'s actual crying, which continues and grows.* MARÍA *gets up and listens to* CARMEN *and* RICARDO *arguing in the kitchen.*

RICARDO: ¡Cállate! Don't yell or María will hear you.
CARMEN: Then tell me, is it true what I am saying?
RICARDO: You're crazy! It wasn't me.
CARMEN: Con mis propios ojos I saw you and la señora Martínez meet in the morning by the park. You have been taking her to work and who knows what! Tell me, is it true? If you don't, I'm going to yell as loud as I can and let this whole neighborhood know what's going on.
RICARDO: Okay. It was me! ¿Estás contenta?
CARMEN: ¿Por qué? Why do you do this to me? And with our neighbor? She lives right in front of us.
RICARDO: Look, every man sooner or later does it.
CARMEN: Do you think I don't know about all of your affairs before la señora Martínez? She is not your first! I never said anything before because I was afraid you would send us back to Mexico. But now I don't care! You break it with that bitch or . . . I'll kill her and you. ¡Ayyy! Ricardo, I've endured so much for you. I knew you were no angel when we ran off together, but I thought you would change. You would change, because you loved me. I love you, Ricardo! But I can no longer go on living like this or I'll be betraying myself and I'll be betraying María.
RICARDO: Carmen, ¡ven aquí! Carmen, wait!

(CARMEN *and* RICARDO *exit. The* THREE GIRLS *enter.* GIRL 3 *hands* MARÍA *a piece of paper and a pen.*)

MARÍA: "Dear Mamá and Papá. Last night I heard everything. Now I know that your idea of life is not for me—so I am leaving. I want to create a world of my own. One that combines the best of me. I won't forget the values of my roots, but I want to get the best from this land of opportunities. I am going to college and I will struggle to do something with my life. You taught me everything I needed to know. Goodbye."

GIRL 1: Los quiero mucho. Nunca los olvidaré.
GIRL 2: Mexico is in my blood . . .
GIRL 3: And America is in my heart.
MARÍA: "Adiós."

(Fade out.)

(1994)

QUESTIONS

1. Explain how López distinguishes among her two groups or types of characters.
2. Explain the effect of the play's opening scene. What does the allusion to Shakespeare's *Romeo and Juliet* accomplish?
3. What stereotypes about Mexican men and women does López present in Scene 2? What is her attitude toward these cultural stereotypes?
4. What political ideas emerge from Scene 3? What distinction is made between European and Mexican immigrants in America?
5. What images of America does the play present? How does María see America and her place in it?
6. What conflicting values does the play describe? What perspective is offered on the conflict between Mexican and American cultural attitudes toward sex, for example, toward gender roles, and toward self-fulfillment?
7. Identify and explain the function of three types of sound effects included in the play.
8. Explain the relevance of Scene 8—the "dream scene." Comment on the names of the characters who appear in this scene. Compare the marriage vows and ceremony in Scene 8 with those of Scene 2.
9. Explain the function of the screen and the titles projected on it throughout the play.
10. What images of marriage and motherhood does the play present? What perspectives are offered on them?

The Essay

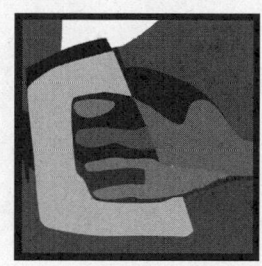

PART FOUR

The Essay

PART FOUR

CHAPTER TWENTY-NINE

Reading Essays

THE EXPERIENCE OF THE ESSAY

Our experience reading essays may differ somewhat from our experience reading fiction, poetry, and drama. In contrast to the imaginative representations of reality that are depicted in the other genres, the essay is typically factual. Thus in essays we expect to find information, data, facts rather than fictional plots, poetic speakers, or dramatic characters. The primary purpose of essays is not to delight or move us (though essays may accomplish both of these things), but to instruct and persuade us. Their usual purpose is to explain a set of circumstances and persuade us to view them in a particular way. Many of the essays we have read, in fact, and very likely those we have written, either explain ideas or present arguments.

Due to the primacy and explicitness of ideas in the essay, the genre has long had an uncertain status as literature. Instead of the suggestiveness of language and concern with symbolic form associated with the other genres, the essay is typically more direct and explicit. It usually subordinates narrative incident and figurative language to the exposition of ideas. To emphasize the primacy of ideas in the essay, however, is not to deny that essays can be imaginative, dramatic, or poetic. In fact, reading essays only for ideas and information while ignoring style and language is to miss much of the pleasure they afford. We will therefore read the essay as literature, in the same way we read the other genres. And in doing so, we will attempt to discover its distinctive literary pleasures. We can begin by considering the opening paragraphs of the following essays:

MARK TWAIN

[1835–1910]

"Cub" Wants to Be a Pilot

When I was a boy there was but one permanent ambition among my comrades in our village on the west bank of the Mississippi River. That was to be a steamboatman. We had transient ambitions of other sorts but they were only transient. When a circus came and went, it left us all burning to become clowns; the first Negro minstrel show that ever came to our section left us all suffering to try that kind of life; now and then we had a hope that, if we lived and were good, God would permit us to be pirates. These ambitions faded out, each in its turn; but the ambition to be a steamboatman always remained.

LOREN EISELEY

[1907–1977]

The Judgment of the Birds

It is a commonplace of all religious thought, even the most primitive, that the man seeking visions and insight must go apart from his fellows and live for a time in the wilderness. If he is of the proper sort, he will return with a message. It may not be a message from the god he set out to seek, but even if he has failed in that particular, he will have had a vision or seen a marvel, and these are always worth listening to and thinking about.

Each of these writers invites us to respond in a different way. Each invites us to enter a world of thought and experience—the world as the writer knows and experiences it. Twain evokes the world of nineteenth-century America when the Mississippi was alive with cargo and passengers. The focus in his opening paragraph, however, is less on the life of the river than on the ambitions of boys. As we read such a passage, we bring to it our own experience, our own goals and ambitions and dreams. We may remember when we were young, how we thought we might "grow up to be" whatever we dreamed about becoming. And we also realize that, like the young boy narrator, many of our ambitions simply faded. Some perhaps have remained, and we are now pursuing them.

Our sense of Twain's essay, then, is influenced by our ability to remember a similar experience from our younger years. We may see the humor in the young boy's enthusiastic response to circuses and minstrel shows, a response that seems natural, suitably unrealistic, and overly romantic, given the realities of growing out of impossible dreams. (Though perhaps we don't see it that way at all since we once wished—and still do—to become something fabulous or important: a circus performer, a wandering minstrel, or a world leader.) We may also see and respond favorably to the way one such dream takes hold. This dream affects a person so strongly that he or she won't give up on it—ever. We ourselves may have such dreams. And whether or not we have pursued them with the tenacity Twain implies in his opening paragraph, such dreams are relevant to our experience of reading his essay.

Loren Eiseley's introductory paragraph invites us to consider a different possibility: that anyone seeking mystical visions and deep understanding must isolate himself from the social world, presumably to tune in either to his spiritual self or to nature. Eiseley at this point doesn't say which. He does insist that when such people do not find the answers or explanations they are looking for, they do nonetheless experience something extraordinary, something that less mystical and less adventurous types should find instructive and thought-provoking.

We experience Eiseley's writing differently from the way we experience Twain's. Eiseley sounds more serious, more academic, more philosophical. His style is less conversational; his voice is less personal, less immediately engaging. However, he too invites us to bring our experience to bear on what he is saying. To follow his thoughts, we need to consider what we know about mystics and visionaries, whether they indeed somehow receive "messages" that are otherworldly, yet relevant, to our lives, or whether they have wild imaginations that enable them to believe in such happenings. We may wonder what Eiseley can possibly mean by these suggestions. We may or may not have any real knowledge of what he is talking about. And that may influence us to become skeptical of his assertions or perhaps to become curious about where his essay will lead us.

The point is that in both instances, that of Twain's boy with his ambitions and Eiseley's mystical adult, we respond largely at first by considering our own experience, by seeing what the writers say in relation to what we have previously encountered or imagined. Something similar happens, but with a slightly altered perspective, when we read the opening of the following essay by Alice Walker.

ALICE WALKER

[b. 1944]

In Search of Our Mothers' Gardens

When the poet Jean Toomer walked through the South in the early twenties, he discovered a curious thing: black women whose spirituality was so intense, so deep, so *unconscious,* they were themselves unaware of the richness they held. They stumbled blindly through their lives: creatures so abused and mutilated in body, so dimmed and confused by pain, that they considered themselves unworthy even of hope. In the selfless abstractions their bodies became to the men who used them, they became more than "sexual objects," more even than mere women: they became "Saints." Instead of being perceived as whole persons, their bodies became shrines: what was thought to be their minds became temples suitable for worship. These crazy Saints stared out at the world, wildly, like lunatics—or quietly, like suicides; and the "God" that was in their gaze was as mute as a great stone.

Walker invites us into yet another world. We may or may not understand from this single paragraph what she is suggesting, but our response to what she describes will certainly be affected by what we know either directly or indirectly of being used as a sexual object; of what we know about suffering, prejudice, and sanity; of what we know about our mothers and grandmothers. Our experience as males or females will affect our reading of this essay, as will the color of our skin or the direction of our lives. We may respond with confusion, shock, amazement, outrage, pity—but we do respond somehow emotionally. Walker clearly invites more than an intellectual response. Before she is through with us, she will ask some frightening questions, questions that are certainly disheartening for women, particularly if they are black women. "What did it mean," Walker asks, "for a black woman to be an artist in our grandmothers' time?" And again: "Did you have a genius of a great-great-grandmother who died under some ignorant and depraved white overseer's lash?" And once again: "Or was her body broken and forced to bear children (who were more often than not sold away from her)—eight, ten, fifteen, twenty children—when her one joy was the thought of modeling heroic figures of rebellion, in stone or clay?"

What kind of questions are these? Questions certainly to which we are invited to respond with feeling. We may agree or disagree with the picture Walker conjures up. We may see it as a wildly lunatic fantasy or as gripping human history. But see it we do, and react to it we must. Nor do we have to have seen or experienced directly what Walker describes to respond to her depiction of nineteenth-century black women. All we have to do is imagine it. Our capacity to imagine introduces one additional way in which we bring experience to bear on our reading of literature. For experience does not mean only what we ourselves have actually lived through; it also includes what we have seen, heard, read about, learned, and are capable of imagining.

With these thoughts in mind, we turn now to a short essay, "The Ring of Time," by E. B. White. As you read, keep track of your responses. Consider, for example, whether White provokes your thinking, stirs your feelings, triggers your memories, engages your imagination.

E. B. WHITE

[1889–1985]

The Ring of Time

After the lions had returned to their cages, creeping angrily through the chutes, a little bunch of us drifted away and into an open doorway nearby, where we stood for a while in semidarkness, watching a big brown circus horse go harumphing around the practice ring. His trainer was a woman of about forty, and the two of them, horse and woman, seemed caught up in one of those desultory treadmills of afternoon from which there is no apparent escape. The day was hot, and we kibitzers were grateful to be briefly out of the sun's glare. The long rein, or tape, by which the woman guided her charge counterclockwise in his dull career formed the radius of their private circle, of which she was the revolving center; and she, too, stepped a tiny circumference of her own, in order to accommodate the horse and allow him his maximum scope. She had on a short-skirted costume and a conical straw hat. Her legs were bare and she wore high heels, which probed deep into the loose tanbark and kept her ankles in a state of constant turmoil. The great size and meekness of the horse, the repetitious exercise, the heat of the afternoon, all exerted a hypnotic charm that invited boredom; we spectators were experiencing a languor—we neither expected relief nor felt entitled to any. We had paid a dollar to get into the grounds, to be sure, but we had got our dollar's worth a few minutes before, when the lion trainer's whiplash had got caught around a toe of one of the lions. What more did we want for a dollar?

Behind me I heard someone say, "Excuse me, please," in a low voice. She was halfway into the building when I turned and saw her—a girl of sixteen or seventeen, politely threading her way through us onlookers who blocked the entrance. As she emerged in front of us, I saw that she was barefoot, her dirty little feet fighting the uneven ground. In most respects she was like any of two or three dozen showgirls you encounter if you wander about the winter quarters of Mr. John Ringling North's circus, in Sarasota—cleverly proportioned, deeply browned by the sun, dusty, eager, and almost naked. But her grave face and the naturalness of her manner gave her a sort of quick distinction and brought a new note into the gloomy octagonal building where we had all cast our lot for a few moments. As soon as she had squeezed through the crowd, she spoke a word or two to the older woman, whom I took to be her mother, stepped to the ring, and waited while the horse coasted to a stop in front of her. She gave the animal a couple of affectionate swipes on his enormous neck and then swung herself aboard. The horse immediately resumed his rocking canter, the woman goading him on, chanting something that sounded like "Hop! Hop!"

In attempting to recapture this mild spectacle, I am merely acting as recording secretary for one of the oldest of societies—the society of those who, at one time or another, have surrendered, without even a show of resistance, to the bedazzlement of a circus rider. As a writing man, or secretary, I have always felt charged with the safe-keeping of all unexpected items of worldly or unworldly enchantment, as though I might be held personally responsible if even a small one were to be lost. But it is not easy to communicate anything of this nature. The circus comes as close to being the world in microcosm as anything I know; in a way, it puts all the rest of show business in the shade. Its magic is universal and complex. Out of its wild disorder comes order; from its rank smell rises the good aroma of courage and daring; out of its preliminary shabbiness comes the final splendor. And buried in the familiar boasts of its advance agents lies the modesty of most of its people. For me the circus is at its best before it has been put together. It is at its best at certain moments when it comes to a point, as through a burning glass, in the activity and destiny of a single performer out of so many. One ring is always bigger than three. One rider, one aerialist, is always greater than six. In short, a man has to catch the circus unawares to experience its full impact and share its gaudy dream.

The ten-minute ride the girl took achieved—as far as I was concerned, who wasn't looking for it, and quite unbeknownst to her, who wasn't even striving for it—the thing that is sought by performers everywhere, on whatever stage, whether struggling in the tidal currents of Shakespeare or bucking the difficult motion of a horse. I somehow got the idea she was just cadging a ride, improving a shining ten minutes in the diligent way all serious artists seize free moments to hone the blade of their talent and keep themselves in trim. Her brief tour included only elementary postures and tricks, perhaps because they were all she was capable of, perhaps because her warmup at this hour was unscheduled and the ring was not rigged for a real practice session. She swung herself off and on the horse several times, gripping his mane. She did a few knee-stands—or whatever they are called—dropping to her knees and quickly bouncing back up on her feet again. Most of the time she simply rode in a standing position, well aft on the beast, her hands hanging easily at her sides, her head erect, her straw-colored ponytail lightly brushing her shoulders, the blood of exertion showing faintly through the tan of her skin. Twice she managed a one-foot stance—a sort of ballet pose, with arms outstretched. At one point the neck strap of her bathing suit broke and she went twice around the ring in the classic attitude of a woman making minor repairs to a garment. The fact that she was standing on the back of a moving horse while doing this invested the matter with a clownish significance that perfectly fitted the spirit of the circus—jocund, yet charming. She just rolled the strap into a neat ball and stowed it inside her bodice while the horse rocked and rolled beneath her in dutiful innocence. The bathing suit proved as self-reliant as its owner and stood up well enough without benefit of strap.

The richness of the scene was in its plainness, its natural condition—of horse, of ring, of girl, even to the girl's bare feet that gripped the bare back of her proud and ridiculous mount. The enchantment grew not out of anything that happened or was performed but out of something that seemed to go round and around and around with the girl, attending her, a steady gleam in the shape of a circle—a ring of ambition, of happiness, of youth. (And the positive pleasures of equilibrium under difficulties.) In a week or two, all would be changed, all (or almost all) lost: the girl would wear makeup, the horse would wear gold, the ring would be painted, the bark would be clean for the feet of the horse, the girl's feet would be clean for the slippers that she'd wear. All, all would be lost.

As I watched with the others, our jaws adroop, our eyes alight, I became painfully conscious of the element of time. Everything in the hideous old building seemed to take the shape of a circle, conforming to the course of the horse. The rider's gaze, as she peered straight ahead, seemed to be circular, as though bent by force of circumstance; then time itself began running in circles, and so the beginning was where the end was, and the two were the same, and one thing ran into the next and time went round and around and got nowhere. The girl wasn't so young that she did not know the delicious satisfaction of having a perfectly behaved body and the fun of using it to do a trick most people can't do, but she was too young to know that time does not really move in a circle at all. I thought: "She will never be as beautiful as this again"— a thought that made me acutely unhappy—and in a flash my mind (which is too much of a busybody to suit me) had projected her twenty-five years ahead, and she was now in the center of the ring, on foot, wearing a conical hat and high-heeled shoes, the image of the older woman, holding the long rein, caught in the treadmill of an afternoon long in the future. "She is at that enviable moment in life [I thought] when she believes she can go once around the ring, make one complete circuit, and at the end be exactly the same age as at the start." Everything in her movements, her expression, told you that for her the ring of time was perfectly formed, changeless, predictable, without beginning or end, like the ring in which she was traveling at this moment with the horse that wallowed under her. And then I slipped back into my trance, and time was circular again—time, pausing quietly with the rest of us, so as not to disturb the balance of a performer.

Her ride ended as casually as it had begun. The older woman stopped the horse, and the girl slid to the ground. As she walked toward us to leave, there was a quick, small burst of applause. She smiled broadly, in surprise and pleasure; then her face suddenly regained its gravity and she disappeared through the door.

It has been ambitious and plucky of me to attempt to describe what is indescribable, and I have failed, as I knew I would. But I have discharged my duty to my society; and besides, a writer, like an acrobat, must occasionally try a stunt that is too much for him. At any rate, it is worth reporting that long before the circus comes to town, its most notable performances have already been given. Under the bright lights of the finished show, a performer need only reflect the electric candle power that is directed upon him; but in the dark and dirty old training rings and in the makeshift cages, whatever light is generated, whatever excitement, whatever beauty, must come from original sources—from internal fires of professional hunger and delight, from the exuberance and gravity of youth. It is the difference between planetary light and the combustion of stars.

(1956)

When we read such an essay as "The Ring of Time," we do more than look for the writer's point, though we do that as well. Before we consider what the writer is saying we can consider our responses to what he describes. Did some parts of the essay engage you more than others? Did you relate E. B. White's experience and feelings to your own? Did you find yourself agreeing or disagreeing with something he said?

As with any work of literature, we often derive more from reading an essay after sharing our responses with others. If possible, talk about "The Ring of Time" with your classmates and teacher. See how their responses amplify your own. Most literary works trigger different associations and reactions in their readers. Gaining a sense of the variety of readers' responses and seeing also what is common among them can provide both assurance that others see the work as we do and alternative perspectives from which to understand it.

Such discussions prepare us to reread the essay. This second reading differs from the first because our knowledge of the work is greater and our sense of how it might be approached is augmented. Now we can turn from the subjectivity of our first responses to a more objective consideration of the writer's point. We may, in fact, often begin doing this during our first reading, but we do it more consciously and thoroughly during the second, in which our goal is interpretation.

THE INTERPRETATION OF THE ESSAY

Our experience of reading an essay is enhanced by thinking about its ideas as we interpret it. Interpretation involves four interrelated acts: observing details, connecting or relating them, developing inferences on the basis of these connections, and forming a conclusion in light of the inferences we draw. In reading White's "The Ring of Time" we focus on its subject and theme. We begin with a few questions.

What is the subject of "The Ring of Time"? What does White seem most concerned with—the circus, performance, practice, writing, time? Something else? What ideas about these subjects surface in the essay? What is the author's attitude toward them?

Let's consider just one of the subjects of White's essay—his reflections on time. One thing White suggests is that time is circular—a ring—that it goes around and around, seeming endlessly to repeat itself. The image of the ring of time, called to our attention by the title, suggests that things don't change, that they remain essentially the same. Details supporting this cyclical view of time include the description of the mother holding the rein as her feet make small circles on the ground while she leads the horse around the ring. (Notice the many words that describe *circle* in the first paragraph.)

The circularity of time is further accented and clarified in this sentence from the sixth paragraph: "The rider's gaze, as she peered straight ahead, seemed to be circular, as though bent by force of circumstance; then time itself began running in circles, and so the beginning was where the end was, and the two were the same, and one thing ran into the next and time went round and around and got nowhere." But almost as soon as White says this, he contradicts himself by saying that although the girl "believes she can go once around the ring . . . and at the end be exactly the same age as at the start," she was really "too young to know that time does not really move in a circle at all." With this counterview, White provokes us to think about time, to decide whether it is circular or linear, to consider, in part, whether things change or remain the same. Of course, we may conclude that time can be experienced both ways, that the two views White presents are complementary rather than contradictory. We can make such a compromise if we think of the seventeen-year-old girl growing up and losing her beauty and agility—if we recognize time's linearity, its inevitable sequence of changes. We can recognize that on the other hand, even though the girl moves through time in a linear fashion, she is also part of a larger family unit, which itself is part of a still larger social context—the circus and its performers. And these larger units don't change. One day she will replace her mother at the center of the practice ring. One day she will hold the reins for another young performer, her daughter perhaps, who will practice and perform as she does now. Time, White seems to say, forms both a line and a circle.

Next we provide in more detail an interpretation of George Orwell's "Marrakech." The essay has been printed in sections with intervening comments to illustrate the four aspects of the interpretive process.

GEORGE ORWELL
[1903–1950]

Marrakech

As the corpse went past the flies left the restaurant table in a cloud and rushed after it, but they came back a few minutes later.

The little crowd of mourners—all men and boys, no women—threaded their way across the market-place between the piles of pomegranates and the taxis and the camels, wailing a short chant over and over again. What really appeals to the flies is that the corpses here are never put into coffins, they are merely wrapped in a piece of rag and carried on a rough wooden bier on the shoulders of four friends. When the friends get to the burying-ground they hack an oblong hole a foot or two deep, dump the body in it and fling over it a little of the dried-up, lumpy earth, which is like broken brick. No gravestone, no name, no identifying mark of any kind. The burying-ground is merely a huge waste of hummocky earth, like a derelict building-lot. After a month or two no one can even be certain where his own relatives are buried.

When you walk through a town like this—two hundred thousand inhabitants, of whom at least twenty thousand own literally nothing except the rags they stand up in—when you see how the people live, and still more how easily they die, it is always difficult to believe that you are walking among human beings. All colonial empires are in reality founded upon that fact. The people have brown faces—besides, there are so many of them! Are they really the same flesh as yourself? Do they even have names? Or are they merely a kind of undifferentiated brown stuff, about as individual as bees or coral insects? They rise out of the earth, they sweat and starve for a few years, and then they sink back into the nameless mounds of the graveyard and nobody notices that they are gone. And even the graves themselves soon fade back into the soil. Sometimes, out for a walk, as you break your way through the prickly pear, you notice that it is rather bumpy underfoot, and only a certain regularity in the bumps tells you that you are walking over skeletons.

Comment   Orwell's description accentuates the extreme poverty of Marrakech and the little regard in which human life is held. The gravediggers, for example, "hack" and "fling" the dirt, then "dump" the body in the ground. Moreover the dead individual is seen not as a person (is it man, woman, or child?) but as a "corpse," an inert object. Additional details reinforce the lack of dignity in death and the lack of value accorded human life. Orwell compares the burial ground to an abandoned building lot, run down and neglected. The grave plots are unmarked, which suggests that the people of Marrakech are as anonymous in death as they were in life.

The third paragraph reinforces the poverty of Marrakech's people. Many have only the rags that they will buried in. Besides accentuating their poverty and anonymity, Orwell goes further by questioning whether they are really human beings at all. They live in squalor; they die easily, readily, more like insects than people. Orwell compares them to insects by highlighting their vast number and lack of individuality. Our question here may be: Does Orwell not value them as human beings? Or is he pointing out how they live in hopelessness, poverty, and futility to awaken his readers to these facts?

Notice too that Orwell slips in a sentence of generalization, suggesting that colonial empires are built on the kinds of attitudes and conditions he describes. This comment can be taken as an indictment of colonialism or as a simple assertion of fact, of how things are, with such suffering a necessary evil that colonialism nust accommodate. This political question is crucial: our sense of Orwell's point and purpose in "Marrakech" hinge on our response to it.

The first part of the essay ends with a description of the makeshift cemetery. Here is the second section:

I was feeding one of the gazelles in the public gardens.

Gazelles are almost the only animals that look good to eat when they are still alive, in fact, one can hardly look at their hindquarters without thinking of mint sauce. The gazelle I was feeding seemed to know that this thought was in my mind, for though it took the piece of bread I was holding out it obviously did not like me. It nibbled rapidly at the bread, then lowered its head and tried to butt me, then took another nibble and then butted again. Probably its idea was that if it could drive me away the bread would somehow remain hanging in mid-air.

An Arab navvy working on the path nearby lowered his heavy hoe and sidled slowly towards us. He looked from the gazelle to the bread and from the bread to the gazelle, with a sort of quiet amazement, as though he had never seen anything quite like this before. Finally he said shyly in French:

"*I* could eat some of that bread."

I tore off a piece and he stowed it gratefully in some secret place under his rags. This man is an employee of the Municipality.

Comment   As we read this vignette about the gazelle, we look for some connection to what went before. Not until the Arab navvy (a manual laborer who excavates roads, canals) makes his appearance does the connection become apparent: he's hungry and poor. His shy, indirect request for food suggests that he wants to preserve his self-respect and dignity. There seems to be some tension between this desire and the urgency of his need. What makes the situation more poignant is that the man does not devour the bread but instead hides it under his rags. Presumably he is saving it, which implies that for him bread is a precious commodity. The final detail of the section is important: this man has a job. With this detail Orwell implies how extreme the poverty of Marrakech is.

Having read the two sections, what connections do you see? How does your sense of the first two parts prepare you to read the third?

When you go through the Jewish quarters you gather some idea of what the medieval ghettoes were probably like. Under their Moorish rulers the Jews were only allowed to own land in certain restricted areas, and after centuries of this kind of treatment they have ceased to bother about overcrowding. Many of the streets are a good deal less than six feet wide, the houses are completely windowless, and sore-eyed children cluster everywhere in unbelievable numbers, like clouds of flies. Down the centre of the street there is generally running a little river of urine.

In the bazaar huge families of Jews, all dressed in the long black robe and little black skull-cap, are working in dark fly-infested booths that look like caves. A carpenter sits crosslegged at a prehistoric lathe, turning chair-legs at lightning speed. He works the lathe with a bow in his right hand and guides the chisel with his left foot, and thanks to a lifetime of sitting in this position his left leg is warped out of shape. At his side his grandson, aged six, is already starting on the simpler parts of the job.

I was just passing the coppersmiths' booths when somebody noticed that I was lighting a cigarette. Instantly, from the dark holes all around, there was a frenzied rush of Jews, many of them old grandfathers with flowing grey beards, all clamouring for a cigarette. Even a blind man somewhere at the back of one of the booths heard a rumour of cigarettes and came crawling out, groping in the air with his hand. In about a minute I had used up the whole packet. None of these people, I suppose, works less than twelve hours a day, and every one of them looks on a cigarette as a more or less impossible luxury.

As the Jews live in self-contained communities they follow the same trades as the

Arabs, except for agriculture. Fruitsellers, potters, silversmiths, blacksmiths, butchers, leatherworkers, tailors, water-carriers, beggars, porters—whichever way you look you see nothing but Jews. As a matter of fact there are thirteen thousand of them, all living in the space of a few acres. A good job Hitler wasn't here. Perhaps he was on his way, however. You hear the usual dark rumours about the Jews, not only from the Arabs but from the poorer Europeans.

"Yes, mon vieux, they took my job away from me and gave it to a Jew. The Jews! They're the real rulers of this country, you know. They've got all the money. They control the banks, finance—everything."

"But," I said, "isn't it a fact that the average Jew is a labourer working for about a penny an hour?"

"Ah, that's only for show! They're all moneylenders really. They're cunning, the Jews."

In just the same way, a couple of hundred years ago, poor old women used to be burned for witchcraft when they could not even work enough magic to get themselves a square meal.

Comment   In the third section Orwell takes us into the Jewish ghetto. By now we realize that the essay is largely descriptive and that its descriptive details are tied together by two issues: poverty and anonymity.

We can divide this vignette into two parts. First, Orwell indicates the crowded and filthy conditions in which the Jews live. He compares the children to clouds of flies, primarily to indicate their vast numbers and insignificance. Details about the working conditions reveal their destructive consequences. Orwell doesn't spell out what the future of the six-year-old grandson who works beside his physically deformed grandfather will be. Instead, he accentuates the injustice by describing the fracas over a few cigarettes, which are beyond the purchasing power of people who work "only" twelve hours a day.

The second section of the this vignette depicts the severe prejudice Jews suffer from. The dialogue reveals Orwell's attempt to undermine the unfair caricature of the Jews as rich moneylenders. Prejudice, fear, and hatred run so deep, however, that the Jewish poverty and powerlessness described by Orwell are explained away by a poor European as a "trick." Against this kind of closed-mindedness what can be said? The analogy Orwell draws with witch hunters of an earlier time testifies to the power of prejudice, and it evokes our sympathy for those who suffer unjustly. Orwell's implied criticism of such attitudes transcends the Jewish quarter of Marrakech to all places where human dignity is violated by hatred and prejudice.

This next section is the longest of the essay.

All people who work with their hands are partly invisible, and the more important the work they do, the less visible they are. Still, a white skin is always fairly conspicuous. In northern Europe, when you see a labourer ploughing a field, you probably give him a second glance. In a hot country, anywhere south of Gibraltar or east of Suez, the chances are that you don't even see him. I have noticed this again and again. In a tropical landscape one's eye takes in everything except the human beings. It takes in the dried-up soil, the prickly pear, the palm tree and the distant mountain, but it always misses the peasant hoeing at his patch. He is the same colour as the earth, and a great deal less interesting to look at.

It is only because of this that the starved countries of Asia and Africa are accepted as tourist resorts. No one would think of running cheap trips to the Distressed Areas. But where the human beings have brown skins their poverty is simply not noticed. What does Morocco mean to a Frenchman? An orange-grove or a job in Government service. Or to an Englishman? Camels, castles, palm trees, Foreign Legionnaires, brass trays, and bandits. One could probably live there for years without noticing that for nine-tenths of the people the reality of life is an endless, back-breaking struggle to wring a little food out of an eroded soil.

Most of Morocco is so desolate that no wild animal bigger than a hare can live on it. Huge areas which were once covered with forest have turned into a treeless waste where the soil is exactly like broken-up brick. Nevertheless a good deal of it is cultivated, with frightful labour. Everything is done by hand. Long lines of women, bent double like inverted capital L's, work their way slowly across the fields, tearing up the prickly weeds with their hands, and the peasant gathering lucerne for fodder pulls it up stalk by stalk instead of reaping it, thus saving an inch or two on each stalk. The plough is a wretched wooden thing, so frail that one can easily carry it on one's shoulder, and fitted underneath with a rough iron spike which stirs the soil to a depth of about four inches. This is as much as the strength of the animals is equal to. It is usual to plough with a cow and a donkey yoked together. Two donkeys would not be quite strong enough, but on the other hand two cows would cost a little more to feed. The peasants possess no harrows, they merely plough the soil several times over in different directions, finally leaving it in rough furrows, after which the whole field has to be shaped with hoes into small oblong patches to conserve water. Except for a day or two after the rare rainstorms there is never enough water. Along the edges of the fields channels are hacked out to a depth of thirty or forty feet to get at the tiny trickles which run through the subsoil.

Every afternoon a file of very old women passes down the road outside my house, each carrying a load of firewood. All of them are mummified with age and the sun, and all of them are tiny. It seems to be generally the case in primitive communities that the women, when they get beyond a certain age, shrink to the size of children. One day a poor old creature who could not have been more than four feet tall crept past me under a vast load of wood. I stopped her and put a five-sou piece (a little more than a farthing) into her hand. She answered with a shrill wail, almost a scream, which was partly gratitude but mainly surprise. I suppose that from her point of view, by taking any notice of her, I seemed almost to be violating a law of nature. She accepted her status as an old woman, that is to say as a beast of burden. When a family is travelling it is quite usual to see a father and a grown-up son riding ahead on donkeys, and an old woman following on foot, carrying the baggage.

But what is strange about these people is their invisibility. For several weeks, always at about the same time of day, the file of old women had hobbled past the house with their firewood, and though they had registered themselves on my eyeballs I cannot truly say that I had seen them. Firewood was passing—that was how I saw it. It was only that one day I happened to be walking behind them, and the curious up-and-down motion of a load of wood drew my attention to the human being beneath it. Then for the first time I noticed the poor old earth-coloured bodies, bodies reduced to bones and leathery skin, bent double under the crushing weight. Yet I suppose I had not been five minutes on Moroccan soil before I noticed the overloading of the donkeys and was infuriated by it. There is no question that the donkeys are damnably treated. The Moroccan donkey is hardly bigger than a St. Bernard dog, it carries a load which in the British Army would be considered too much for a fifteen-hands mule, and very often its pack-saddle is not taken off its back for weeks together. But what is peculiarly pitiful is that it is the most willing creature on earth, it follows its master like a dog and does not need either bridle or halter. After a dozen years of devoted work it suddenly drops dead, whereupon its master tips it into the ditch and the village dogs have torn its guts out before it is cold.

This kind of thing makes one's blood boil, whereas—on the whole—the plight of the human beings does not. I am not commenting, merely pointing to a fact. People with brown skins are next door to invisible. Anyone can be sorry for the donkey with its galled back, but it is generally owing to some kind of accident if one even notices the old woman under her load of sticks.

Comment   This section centers on the invisibility of the natives. They are not noticed, presumably because they are not important. They become part of the landscape, a fact which further suggests their lack of distinction, and which also recalls the burial scene of section one. Their dark skins render them invisible.

The information Orwell provides about the land's aridity and the primitive farming tools and methods shows the futility and harshness of their lives. People, especially old women, are reduced to the status of beasts of burden. Orwell acknowledges his acquiescence in the *status quo:* he admits to seeing "firewood" passing rather than the human beings carrying that firewood. It is the abusive treatment of the donkeys, however, not the wretchedness of the women, that initially angers him. Perhaps Orwell suggests here how easy it is to become accustomed to such conditions—as long as one is not subject to them oneself. Perhaps he confesses his guilt, recognizing his deficiencies of perception and sensitivity.

We might note also that the language Orwell uses to describe the dead donkey echoes his description of the human burial in the first vignette. In both instances, the burial reveals a complete disregard for life. Both man and beast serve their purposes, and when they are no longer useful, are unceremoniously disposed of.

The essay concludes with a shift of focus:

As the storks flew northward the Negroes were marching southward—a long, dusty column, infantry, screw-gun batteries, and then more infantry, four or five thousand men in all, winding up the road with a clumping of boots and a clatter of iron wheels.

They were Senegalese, the blackest Negroes in Africa, so black that sometimes it is difficult to see whereabouts on their necks the hair begins. Their splendid bodies were hidden in reach-me-down khaki uniforms, their feet squashed into boots that looked like blocks of wood, and every tin hat seemed to be a couple of sizes too small. It was very hot and the men had marched a long way. They slumped under the weight of their packs and the curiously sensitive black faces were glistening with sweat.

As they went past a tall, very young Negro turned and caught my eye. But the look he gave me was not in the least the kind of look you might expect. Not hostile, not contemptuous, not sullen, not even inquisitive. It was the shy, wide-eyed Negro look, which actually is a look of profound respect. I saw how it was. This wretched boy, who is a French citizen and has therefore been dragged from the forest to scrub floors and catch syphilis in garrison towns, actually has feelings of reverence before a white skin. He has been taught that the white race are his masters, and he still believes it.

But there is one thought which every white man (and in this connection it doesn't matter twopence if he calls himself a socialist) thinks when he sees a black army marching past. "How much longer can we go on kidding these people? How long before they turn their guns in the other direction?"

It was curious, really. Every white man there had this thought stowed somewhere or other in his mind. I had it, so had the other onlookers, so had the officers on their sweating chargers and the white N.C.O.'s marching in the ranks. It was a kind of secret which we all knew and were too clever to tell; only the Negroes didn't know it. And really it was like watching a flock of cattle to see the long column, a mile or two miles of armed men, flowing peacefully up the road, while the great white birds drifted over them in the opposite direction, glittering like scraps of paper.

(1936)

Comment   The description of the Senegalese troops is charged with tension. With his description of the blackness of the troops and their servility, Orwell calls attention to a racial inequality he had implied earlier. Orwell's imagery in the final paragraphs suggests that colonial oppression cannot last forever, that when the oppressed realize their strength and numbers, they will overthrow their imperialist subjugators. It's only a matter of time.

THE EVALUATION OF THE ESSAY

To evaluate an essay means to consider its value for us as readers. Evaluation consists essentially of two different kinds of assessment: (1) a judgment about the work's aesthetic merit; (2) a judgment about the power and validity of its ideas. We will speak briefly about the aesthetic valuation of essays in a moment. First, however, we need to explain what we mean by evaluating an essay's ideas.

When we evaluate an idea, we consider its accuracy as a description, its persuasiveness as an argument, or its suggestiveness as an act of imaginative thinking. In order to evaluate any idea, we first have to abstract it from the discourse of which it is a part. We have to identify it, isolate it, and restate it as a generalization. Evaluation, in short, depends on interpretation. How we understand the point or thesis of an essay (whether this point is explicitly stated or implicitly suggested) will strongly influence how we evaluate that essay.

Once we have a clear understanding of what an essay says, we can assess the values it expresses. Usually these values are those of the writer, since the voice we hear in an essay is typically an author's own rather than that of an imagined character or persona. Our goal in evaluating any essay is to consider how an author's social attitudes, moral convictions, or cultural dispositions affect his or her argument. In making such analyses we bring to bear our own attitudes, beliefs, convictions, and dispositions.

But this kind of thinking about essays represents only one facet of our evaluation of them. Another is our consideration of their aesthetic merit, their success as works of literature. In the same way that we assess the beauty of a poem or the greatness of a play, we can evaluate the aesthetic achievement of an essay. We consider the essay's language or style and its form or structure. We also consider its power to persuade us, move us, or entertain us. To do this we analyze the work, studying how well the writer employs words to create meaning and how well he or she structures and dramatizes ideas. In the first two sections of this introduction, you read E. B. White's "The Ring of Time" and George Orwell's "Marrakech." Although you will be in a better position to evaluate their aesthetic merit after reading Chapter 31, "Elements of the Essay," it should still be useful for you to consider these works from an aesthetic standpoint. You might consider, for example, what aspects of Orwell's or White's language, selection of detail, and organization make them more than mere statements of fact, more than simple descriptions of events. (The commentary provides some implicit direction on this kind of analysis.)

The literary value of an essay also includes its ability to move us, to provide us with a unique experience of intellectual and emotional stimulation. By identifying an essay's effect on us, we acknowledge one of its sources of value.

The other kinds of values we are concerned with as we read essays are the social attitudes, moral beliefs, and cultural dispositions we see as animating the work. How we respond to any essay is determined in part by our understanding of such values and our sense of how they mesh with or collide against our own. Many of the essays in Chapter 35, "A Collection of Essays," reflect strongly held convictions based on particular social, moral, and cultural values. Jonathan Swift's "A Modest Proposal," for example, considers the problem of the Irish poor and what to do about it. E. M. Forster's "Our Graves in Gallipoli" focuses on the problem of war. James Baldwin's "Notes of a Native Son" deals with race relations and family dynamics. In these essays arguments are developed, positions taken, and experience and evidence presented, all based on explicitly delineated social, moral, and cultural values.

Consider the aesthetic value of the following essay from the standpoint of its power to affect you, and from the standpoint of its language and structure. Identify its cultural values and comment on their significance for an understanding of the essay and for an assessment of its meaning to you as a thinking reader. Consider especially the values of the central figures: the wrestler, the doctor, the boy, and the uncle. And consider, finally, how other readers with different racial, cultural, and gender characteristics might respond to the points raised here and to the essay itself.

R I C H A R D   S E L Z E R

[*b. 1928*]

The Masked Marvel's Last Toehold

MORNING ROUNDS.

On the fifth floor of the hospital, in the west wing, I know that a man is sitting up in his bed, waiting for me. Elihu Koontz is seventy-five, and he is diabetic. It is two weeks since I amputated his left leg just below the knee. I walk down the corridor, but I do not go straight into his room. Instead, I pause in the doorway. He is not yet aware of my presence, but gazes down at the place in the bed where his leg used to be, and where now there is the collapsed leg of his pajamas. He is totally absorbed, like an athlete appraising the details of his body. What is he thinking, I wonder. Is he dreaming the outline of his toes. Does he see there his foot's incandescent ghost? Could he be angry? Feel that I have taken from him something for which he yearns now with all his heart? Has he forgotten so soon the pain? It was a pain so great as to set him apart from all other men, in a red-hot place where he had no kith or kin. What of those black gorilla toes and the soupy mess that was his heel? I watch him from the doorway. It is a kind of spying, I know.

Save for a white fringe open at the front, Elihu Koontz is bald. The hair has grown too long and is wilted. He wears it as one would wear a day-old laurel wreath. He is naked to the waist, so that I can see his breasts. They are the breasts of Buddha, inverted triangles from which the nipples swing, dark as garnets.

I have seen enough. I step into the room, and he sees that I am there.

"How did the night go, Elihu?"

He looks at me for a long moment. "Shut the door," he says.

I do, and move to the side of the bed. He takes my left hand in both of his, gazes at it, turns it over, then back, fondling, at last holding it up to his cheek. I do not withdraw from this loving. After a while he relinquishes my hand, and looks up at me.

"How is the pain?" I ask.

He does not answer, but continues to look at me in silence. I know at once that he has made a decision.

"Ever hear of The Masked Marvel?" He says this in a low voice, almost a whisper.

"What?"

"The Masked Marvel," he says. "You never heard of him?"

"No."

He clucks his tongue. He is exasperated.

All at once there is a recollection. It is dim, distant, but coming near.

"Do you mean the wrestler?"

Eagerly, he nods, and the breasts bob. How gnomish he looks, oval as the huge helpless egg of some outlandish lizard. He has very long arms, which, now and then, he unfurls to reach for things—a carafe of water, a get-well card. He gazes up at me, urging. He *wants* me to remember.

"Well . . . yes," I say. I am straining backward in time. "I saw him wrestle in Toronto long ago."

"Ha!" He smiles. "You saw *me*." And his index finger, held rigid and upright, bounces in the air.

The man has said something shocking, unacceptable. It must be challenged.

"You?" I am trying to smile.

Again that jab of the finger. "You saw *me*."

"No," I say. But even then, something about Elihu Koontz, those prolonged arms, the shape of his head, the sudden agility with which he leans from his bed to get a large brown envelope from his nightstand, something is forcing me toward a memory. He rummages through his papers, old newspaper clippings, photographs, and I remember . . .

It is almost forty years ago. I am ten years old. I have been sent to Toronto to spend the summer with relatives. Uncle Max has bought two tickets to the wrestling match. He is taking me that night.

"He isn't allowed," says Aunt Sarah to me. Uncle Max has angina.

"He gets too excited," she says.

"I wish you wouldn't go, Max," she says.

"You mind your own business," he says.

And we go. Out into the warm Canadian evening. I am not only abroad, I am abroad in the *evening!* I have never been taken out in the evening. I am terribly excited. The trolleys, the lights, the horns. It is a bazaar. At the Maple Leaf Gardens, we sit high and near the center. The vast arena is dark except for the brilliance of the ring at the bottom.

It begins.

The wrestlers circle. They grapple. They are all haunch and paunch. I am shocked by their ugliness, but I do not show it. Uncle Max is exhilarated. He leans forward, his eyes unblinking, on his face a look of enormous happiness. One after the other, a pair of wrestlers enter the ring. The two men join, twist, jerk, tug, bend, yank, and throw. Then they leave and are replaced by another pair. At last it is the main event. "The Angel vs. The Masked Marvel."

On the cover of the program notes, there is a picture of The Angel hanging from the limb of a tree, a noose of thick rope around his neck. The Angel hangs just so for an hour every day, it is explained, to strengthen his neck. The Masked Marvel's trademark is a black stocking cap with holes for the eyes and mouth. He is never seen without it, states the program. No one knows who The Masked Marvel really is!

"Good," says Uncle Max. "Now you'll see something." He is fidgeting, waiting for them to appear. They come down separate aisles, climb into the ring from opposite sides. I have never seen anything like them. It is The Angel's neck that first captures the eye. The shaved nape rises in twin columns to puff into the white hood of a sloped and bosselated skull that is too small. As though, strangled by the sinews of that neck, the skull had long since withered and shrunk. The thing about The Angel is the absence of any mystery in his body. It is simply *there*. A monosyllabic announcement. A grunt. One looks and knows everything at once, the fat thighs, the gigantic buttocks,

the great spine from which hang knotted ropes and pale aprons of beef. And that prehistoric head. He is all of a single hideous piece, The Angel is. No detachables.

The Masked Marvel seems dwarfish. His fingers dangle kneeward. His short legs are
slightly bowed as if under the weight of the cask they are forced to heft about. He has
breasts that swing when he moves! I have never seen such breasts on a man before.

There is a sudden ungraceful movement, and they close upon one another. The
Angel stoops and hugs The Marvel about the waist, locking his hands behind The Marvel's back. Now he straightens and lifts The Marvel as though he were uprooting a
tree. Thus he holds him, then stoops again, thrusts one hand through The Marvel's
crotch, and with the other grabs him by the neck. He rears and . . . The Marvel is aloft!
For a long moment, The Angel stands as though deciding where to make the toss. Then
throws. Was that board or bone that splintered there? Again and again, The Angel hurls
himself upon the body of The Masked Marvel.

Now The Angel rises over the fallen Marvel, picks up one foot in both of his hands,
and twists the toes downward. It is far beyond the tensile strength of mere ligament,
mere cartilage. The Masked Marvel does not hide his agony, but pounds and slaps the
floor with his hand, now and then reaching up toward The Angel in an attitude of supplication. I have never seen such suffering. And all the while his black mask rolls from
side to side, the mouth pulled to a tight slit through which issues an endless hiss that I
can hear from where I sit. All at once, I hear a shouting close by.

"Break it off! Tear off a leg and throw it up here!"

It is Uncle Max. Even in the darkness I can see that he is gray. A band of sweat stands
upon his upper lip. He is on his feet now, panting, one fist pressed at his chest, the
other raised warlike toward the ring. For the first time I begin to think that something
terrible might happen here. Aunt Sarah was right.

"Sit down, Uncle Max," I say. "Take a pill, please."

He reaches for the pillbox, gropes, and swallows without taking his gaze from the
wrestlers. I wait for him to sit down.

"That's not fair," I say, "twisting his toes like that."

"It's the toehold," he explains.

"But it's not *fair,*" I say again. The whole of the evil is laid open for me to perceive.
I am trembling.

And now The Angel does something unspeakable. Holding the foot of The Marvel
at full twist with one hand, he bends and grasps the mask where it clings to the back
of The Marvel's head. And he pulls. He is going to strip it off! Lay bare an ultimate
carnal mystery! Suddenly it is beyond mere physical violence. Now I am on my feet,
shouting into the Maple Leaf Gardens.

"Watch out," I scream. "Stop him. Please, somebody, stop him."

Next to me, Uncle Max is chuckling.

Yet The Masked Marvel hears me, I know it. And rallies from his bed of pain. Thrusting with his free heel, he strikes The Angel at the back of the knee. The Angel falls.
The Masked Marvel is on top of him, pinning his shoulders to the mat. One! Two!
Three! And it is over. Uncle Max is strangely still. I am gasping for breath. All this I
remember as I stand at the bedside of Elihu Koontz.

Once again, I am in the operating room. It is two years since I amputated the left leg
of Elihu Koontz. Now it is his right leg which is gangrenous. I have already scrubbed.

I stand to one side wearing my gown and gloves. And . . . *I am masked.* Upon the table lies Elihu Koontz, pinned in a fierce white light. Spinal anesthesia has been administered. One of his arms is taped to a board placed at a right angle to his body. Into this arm, a needle has been placed. Fluid drips here from a bottle overhead. With his other hand, Elihu Koontz beats feebly at the side of the operating table. His head rolls from side to side. His mouth is pulled into weeping. It seems to me that I have never seen such misery.

An orderly stands at the foot of the table, holding Elihu Koontz's leg aloft by the toes so that the intern can scrub the limb with antiseptic solutions. The intern paints the foot, ankle, leg, and thigh, both front and back, three times. From a corner of the room where I wait, I look down as from an amphitheater. Then I think of Uncle Max yelling, "Tear off a leg. Throw it up here." And I think that forty years later I am making the catch.

"It's not fair," I say aloud. But no one hears me. I step forward to break The Masked Marvel's last toehold.

(1979)

QUESTIONS

1. Compare the reactions of the boy and his uncle to the wrestling match they jointly watch. How do you respond to their reactions?
2. Consider the effectiveness of the comparisons employed in paragraphs 1 and 32. What do they contribute to your understanding of the essay? To your evaluation of it?
3. Comment on Selzer's handling of time in the essay. What does he gain by breaking chronology in telling the story of the wrestler?
4. Identify parallel details between the first and second parts of the essay and between its second and third parts as well. What does this use of parallelism contribute to the effectiveness of the essay?
5. Much of the essay is given over to dialogue. To what extent does dialogue generate the emotional power of the essay?
6. In what ways does the surgeon break The Masked Marvel's last toehold? Consider the various meanings of "break."
7. In considering the aesthetic value of an essay, we measure it against others of its type or genre. How would you characterize this essay? How does it measure up against others you have read?
8. What cultural and social values do you find in the essay? What assumptions about men and boys, about doctors and patients underlie its action and meaning?
9. If you value the essay, why do you value it? If you don't, why don't you?
10. If you could ask the author one question, what would it be?

THE ACT OF READING THE ESSAY

There are many ways we can actively engage a literary work. Most require some form of writing as we read; questioning, annotating, and providing an interpolated commentary are techniques used earlier in this book. Here we will try something different: an imaginary dialogue with the author. This approach to a text is perhaps best suited to the essay, since the genre typically invites agreement with an explicitly stated idea. In choosing the essay form, in fact, writers signal their intention to persuade us of their views. One way of accepting the invitation is to enter into a kind of imaginary conversation with them.

We illustrate by reading an essay, Gretel Ehrlich's "About Men," then conducting an imaginary interview with Ehrlich.

GRETEL EHRLICH

[b. 1946]

About Men

When I'm in New York but feeling lonely for Wyoming I look for the Marlboro ads in the subway. What I'm aching to see is horseflesh, the glint of a spur, a line of distant mountains, brimming creeks, and a reminder of the ranchers and cowboys I've ridden with for the last eight years. But the men I see in those posters with their stern, humorless looks remind me of no one I know here. In our hellbent earnestness to romanticize the cowboy we've ironically disesteemed his true character. If he's "strong and silent" it's because there's probably no one to talk to. If he "rides away into the sunset" it's because he's been on horseback since four in the morning moving cattle and he's trying, fifteen hours later, to get home to his family. If he's "a rugged individualist" he's also part of a team: ranch work is teamwork and even the glorified open-range cowboys of the 1880s rode up and down the Chisholm Trail in the company of twenty or thirty other riders. Instead of the macho, trigger-happy man our culture has perversely wanted him to be, the cowboy is more apt to be convivial, quirky, and softhearted. To be "tough" on a ranch has nothing to do with conquests and displays of power. More often than not, circumstances—like the colt he's riding or an unexpected blizzard—are overpowering him. It's not toughness but "toughing it out" that counts. In other words, this macho, cultural artifact the cowboy has become is simply a man who possesses resilience, patience, and an instinct for survival. "Cowboys are just like a pile of rocks—everything happens to them. They get climbed on, kicked, rained and snowed on, scuffed up by wind. Their job is 'just to take it,'" one oldtimer told me.

A cowboy is someone who loves his work. Since the hours are long—ten to fifteen hours a day—and the pay is $30 he has to. What's required of him is an odd mixture of physical vigor and maternalism. His part of the beef-raising industry is to birth and nurture calves and take care of their mothers. For the most part his work is done on horseback and in a lifetime he sees and comes to know more animals than people. The iconic myth surrounding him is built on American notions of heroism: the index of a man's value as measured in physical courage. Such ideas have perverted manliness into a self-absorbed race for cheap thrills. In a rancher's world, courage has less to do with facing danger than with acting spontaneously—usually on behalf of an animal or another rider. If a cow is stuck in a boghole he throws a loop around her neck, takes his dally (a half hitch around the saddle horn), and pulls her out with horsepower. If a calf is born sick, he may take her home, warm her in front of the kitchen fire, and massage her legs until dawn. One friend, whose favorite horse was trying to swim a lake with hobbles on, dove under water and cut her legs loose with a knife, then swam her to shore, his arm around her neck lifeguard-style, and saved her from drowning. Because these incidents are usually linked to someone or something outside himself, the westerner's courage is selfless, a form of compassion.

The physical punishment that goes with cowboying is greatly underplayed. Once fear is dispensed with, the threshold of pain rises to meet the demands of the job. When Jane Fonda asked Robert Redford (in the film *Electric Horseman*) if he was sick as he struggled to his feet one morning, he replied, "No, just bent." For once the movies had it right. The cowboys I was sitting with laughed in agreement. Cowboys are rarely complainers; they show their stoicism by laughing at themselves.

If a rancher or cowboy has been thought of as a "man's man"—laconic, hard-drinking, inscrutable—there's almost no place in which the balancing act between male and female, manliness and femininity, can be more natural. If he's gruff, handsome, and physically fit on the outside, he's androgynous at the core. Ranchers are midwives, hunters, nurturers, providers, and conservationists all at once. What we've interpreted as toughness—weathered skin, calloused hands, a squint in the eye and a growl in the voice—only masks the tenderness inside. "Now don't go telling me these lambs are cute," one rancher warned me the first day I walked into the football-field-sized lambing sheds. The next thing I knew he was holding a black lamb. "Ain't this little rat good-lookin'?"

So many of the men who came to the West were southerners—men looking for work and a new life after the Civil War—that chivalrousness and strict codes of honor were soon thought of as western traits. There were very few women in Wyoming during territorial days, so when they did arrive (some as mail-order brides from places like Philadelphia) there was a stand-offishness between the sexes and a formality that persists now. Ranchers still tip their hats and say, "Howdy, ma'am" instead of shaking hands with me.

Even young cowboys are often evasive with women. It's not that they're Jekyll and Hyde creatures—gentle with animals and rough on women—but rather, that they don't know how to bring their tenderness into the house and lack the vocabulary to express the complexity of what they feel. Dancing wildly all night becomes a metaphor for the explosive emotions pent up inside, and when these are, on occasion, released, they're so battery-charged and potent that one caress of the face or one "I love you" will peal for a long while.

The geographical vastness and the social isolation here make emotional evolution seem impossible. Those contradictions of the heart between respectability, logic, and convention on the one hand, and impulse, passion, and intuition on the other, played out wordlessly against the paradisical beauty of the West, give cowboys a wide-eyed but drawn look. Their lips pucker up, not with kisses but with immutability. They may want to break out, staying up all night with a lover just to talk, but they don't know how and can't imagine what the consequences will be. Those rare occasions when they do bare themselves result in confusion. "I feel as if I'd sprained my heart," one friend told me a month after such a meeting.

My friend Ted Hoagland wrote, "No one is as fragile as a woman but no one is as fragile as a man." For all the women here who use "fragileness" to avoid work or as a sexual ploy, there are men who try to hide theirs, all the while clinging to an adolescent dependency on women to cook their meals, wash their clothes, and keep the ranch house warm in winter. But there is true vulnerability in evidence here. Because these men work with animals, not machines or numbers, because they live outside in landscapes of torrential beauty, because they are confined to a place and a routine embellished with awesome variables, because calves die in the arms that pulled others into life, because they go to the mountains as if on a pilgrimage to find out what makes a herd of elk tick, their strength is also a softness, their toughness, a rare delicacy.

(1985)

Interview

QUESTION: I understand that you published this essay in 1985. I wonder whether you think the cowboy continues to be as romanticized now as he was five or ten years ago. I'm also curious about your sense of where the romanticized stereotype of the cowboy derives from.

RESPONSE: [Here as readers we might imaginatively create the author's responses. And of course we can follow up our train of thought with some of our own speculations. If we are lucky we might, at least occasionally, get the author's actual responses.]

QUESTION: I hadn't really thought before of the maternal side of cowboy life. You are serious, I presume. But now that you bring up the idea, it makes me wonder about the cowboy as a parent generally. Given the long hours and the time away from home, how do these men handle their parental responsibilities?

RESPONSE:

QUESTION: In fact, I wonder if you haven't romanticized the cowboy's image yourself in this essay by suggesting that cowboys are typically "strong silent types." You know, they don't talk much about their feelings; perhaps they don't talk much about anything. And I also wonder how far you mean to suggest that this image of the man who says little is characteristic of American males generally.

RESPONSE:

QUESTION: I'm curious too about why you retitled the essay "About Men" rather than staying with its former title, "Revisionist Cowboy," which *Time* magazine used when it was first published. Which title do you actually prefer? Have you considered any others?

RESPONSE:

QUESTION: How do you respond when ranchers tip their hats and treat you according to the code of western chivalry? Do you think you should be treated like "one of the the guys"?

RESPONSE:

QUESTION: You attribute much of the character of the cowboy to his close relationship with nature. His life, as you intimate, is governed and his character formed by his direct and lasting contact with landscape, animals, weather. Is there a place for a life of the mind, for culture as well as nature in the cowboy's existence?

RESPONSE:

QUESTION: One last question: You seem concerned with debunking certain myths about the cowboy largely by complicating the stereotype. Why do you think such an image came into existence in the first place? And do you think there is a parallel stereotype of the western woman?

RESPONSE:

Imagining a conversation with the writer (or half a dialogue as we have here) promotes thought about the implications of the essay. It also stimulates a consideration of dimensions of the subject the writer has not included. And, of course, it encourages us to reread the essay and reconsider its ideas.

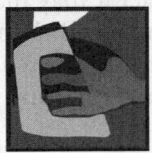

CHAPTER THIRTY

Types of Essays

We can classify essays in a rough way as speculative, argumentative, narrative, and expository. Narrative essays tell stories and chronicle events; expository essays explain ideas and attitudes; speculative essays explore ideas and feelings; argumentative essays make claims and present evidence to support them. Nearly all essays are persuasive to one degree or another. Whatever their dominant mode and form, most essays attempt to convince readers about something.

SPECULATIVE ESSAYS

Let us glance first at what we have called the *speculative essay*. *To speculate* means to contemplate, conjecture, or surmise. A *speculative essay* is concerned less with making a point overtly and decisively than with exploring an idea, perception, or feeling. The tone of a speculative essay is typically less authoritative and less insistent than the tone of expository or argumentative essays. Speculative essays frequently take their form from the way thought flows in the mind of the writer. Rather than employing a conventional pattern of organization such as comparison and contrast, a speculative essayist will find a looser, less immediately recognizable organization. John Donne's "Meditation XVII: For Whom the Bell Tolls" (page 1820), for example, is primarily associative in structure. As Donne's title indicates, his essay is more a meditation than an argument.

Writers of speculative (or meditative) essays seem less interested in advancing arguments than in exploring them. They prefer thinking around ideas rather than thinking through them. Rather than take readers on a clearly marked journey from point A through point B to point C, they often invite readers to accompany them on an excursion into thought. This is not to suggest that a speculative essay makes no point. In fact it may make multiple points as the essayist plays with ideas and explores them. E. B. White's "The Ring of Time" (page 1715) is one speculative essay that makes any number of points. But it does not have a single, clear-cut thesis as narrative and expository essays often do.

ARGUMENTATIVE ESSAYS

Unlike speculative essays, which are loose in structure and informal in tone, *argumentative essays* make their claims directly and explicitly. Though argumentative essays assume various patterns of organization, they share a basic concern: to establish a point by providing evidence to support it. The support may take the form of examples, analogies, facts, statistics, anecdote, and evidence. In addition, argumentative essayists may present counterviews and counterarguments either to dismiss or demolish them. Counter positions in an essay may include the competing claims of a pro and con structure such as the one Francis Bacon employs in "Of Love" (page 1819). Or it may take the form of debate as in E. M. Forster's "Our Graves in Gallipoli" (page 1832). Whatever structure argumentative essayists employ and whatever methods they use to discredit opposing viewpoints, their intentions are clearly and consistently persuasive.

NARRATIVE ESSAYS

Midway between the formality of the argumentative essay and the informality of the speculative essay are narrative and expository essays. *Narrative essays* include stories, sometimes a single incident, as in George Orwell's "Shooting an Elephant" (page 1835). The stories in narrative essays are almost always autobiographical: they form a part of the writer's experience. But even in cases where the story in such an essay is fictional rather than factual, it is used to make a point. Idea is primary. This distinguishes a narrative essay from a short story in which an idea may be inherent in the work, but where the fictional story *per se* takes precedence over any idea we may derive from it. Orwell's "Shooting an Elephant," for example, consists largely of the story of how Orwell (or a fictional narrator) shot an elephant. Although the incident possesses considerable interest as a story, its primary purpose is to advance an idea about imperialism, an idea which is presented explicitly midway through the essay and is referred to again at the end.

EXPOSITORY ESSAYS

Expository essays also advance ideas, but with less insistence than argumentative essays. Although expository writing may contain narrative elements (anecdote for instance), these elements are usually less developed and less central than in narrative writing. The purpose of most expository essays is explanation, to make something clear for readers. They put forth some idea or insight, some fact or experience so readers can better understand it. And although it is important to remember that nearly all essays contain some element of persuasion, their argumentative edge may be dull or sharp. In some expository prose, moreover, the persuasive dimension nearly disappears.

We have suggested that essays can be categorized with respect to their differing purposes, tones, and patterns of organization. But we should also note that essays rarely appear in such pure forms. More often than not, essayists mix modes, combining narration with exposition, or using exposition and narration in the service of argument. Knowing this will help us read essays more confidently, particularly when we confront experiments in nonfictional prose.

One such development has been the marriage of fact and fiction pioneered by writers dubbed "new journalists." One of the most widely read of the new journalists is Tom Wolfe, who has experimented more fully perhaps than anyone else with the possibilities of the form. Wolfe himself singled out four techniques that have special importance for the new essay style. These include scene-by-scene construction, with a consequent reduction of straight narrative and explanation; a heavy reliance on dialogue, for as Wolfe has noted, "realistic dialogue involves the reader more completely than any other single device"; a manipulation of point of view to "give the reader the feeling of being inside a character's mind and experiencing the emotional reality of the scene as he experiences it"; and the use of symbolic details derived from everyday experience such as gestures, habits, manners, glances, poses, and styles of dress.* Wolfe has deployed all of these techniques in his first novel, *The Bonfire of the Vanities*.

This brief overview of different types of essays is not meant to be an exhaustive catalogue of essay forms. Essayists don't choose a form from a menu. Rather, they design their essays and discover their form, making use of whatever strategies of organization suit their various purposes, audiences, and occasions. It is the sense the essay makes, the ideas it advances that matter in the end. Whatever our experience of an essay, and whatever its purpose, ultimately an essay attempts to formulate a thought, explore it, work out its implications, and communicate them to readers.

*Tom Wolfe, ed., *The New Journalism* (New York: Harper and Row, 1973), 31–32.

CHAPTER THIRTY-ONE

Elements of the Essay

An essay, like a poem, play, or story, can be studied from a number of perspectives: we can consider voice, style, structure, and thought—the elements of the essay as a literary form. To clarify our understanding of how essayists say what they mean, we begin by analyzing the essay's voice.

VOICE

When we read an essay we hear a writer's voice, someone speaking to us person to person. The essayist's voice may be commanding or cajoling, intimate or reserved, urgent and insistent, witty and charming—to suggest a few possibilities. The writer's voice is our key to his *tone,* his attitude toward his subject. Consider George Orwell's voice in the third paragraph of "Marrakech," reprinted here for convenience:

When you walk through a town like this—two hundred thousand inhabitants, of whom at least twenty thousand own literally nothing except the rags they stand up in—when you see how the people live, and still more how easily they die, it is always difficult to believe that you are walking among human beings. All colonial empires are in reality founded upon that fact. The people have brown faces—besides, there are so many of them! Are they really the same flesh as yourself? Do they even have names? Or are they merely a kind of undifferentiated brown stuff, about as individual as bees or coral insects? They rise out of the earth, they sweat and starve for a few years, and

then they sink back into the nameless mounds of the graveyard and nobody notices
that they are gone. And even the graves themselves soon fade back into the soil. Sometimes, out for a walk, as you break your way through the prickly pear, you notice that
it is rather bumpy underfoot, and only a certain regularity in the bumps tells you that
you are walking over skeletons.

Perhaps the first thing we hear is the writer speaking directly to us, calling
us "you." As our eyes and ears, the narrator shares with us what he sees, hears,
and more importantly, what he thinks and feels about these things. He also invites our response. When he asks, for example, whether the Moroccans even
have names, our response is complex. On the one hand, we may answer "no,"
for they are unknown, obscure, anonymous; on the other hand, we might answer "yes, of course they have names." And when he asks "are they merely an
undifferentiated brown stuff, about as individual as bees or coral insects," our
answer is more complex still. From one perspective the implied argument is
that they are no more individual than bees or "brown stuff." But clearly this is
not Orwell's view. In fact, it is this inhuman, exploitative view that his essay
criticizes. Orwell attacks a viewpoint that many of his readers would subscribe
to. They, of course, would not see imperialism as responsible for causing or even
contributing to the problems he describes. Orwell, however, aims to make clear
that colonialism, founded on a view of human beings as material to be exploited,
perpetuates the misery he describes.

Another thing to note about the voice of this passage is its tone at the end
and how it is achieved. The final sentence of this paragraph is a statement rather
than a question. Like the first sentence, it conveys a sense of the starkness of life
for the poor. They "rise" and "sink," "sweat" and "starve." That's it; it can
hardly be called *living* in the sense that Orwell's readers would think of life. Balancing the phrases to create a rising and falling rhythm, Orwell communicates
the heaviness of life for these people. The tone is compassionate rather than
angry. The voice is quiet and controlled with emotion held in check.

To develop your ability to hear an essayist's voice, read the following essay
by Joan Didion.

JOAN DIDION

[b. 1934]

Los Angeles Notebook

There is something uneasy in the Los Angeles air this afternoon, some unnatural stillness, some tension. What it means is that tonight a Santa Ana will begin to blow, a hot
wind from the northeast whining down through the Cajon and San Gorgonio Passes,
blowing up sandstorms out along Route 66, drying the hills and the nerves to the flash

point. For a few days now we will see smoke back in the canyons, and hear sirens in the night. I have neither heard nor read that a Santa Ana is due, but I know it, and almost everyone I have seen today knows it too. We know it because we feel it. The baby frets. The maid sulks. I rekindle a waning argument with the telephone company, then cut my losses and lie down, given over to whatever it is in the air. To live with the Santa Ana is to accept, consciously or unconsciously, a deeply mechanistic view of human behavior.

I recall being told, when I first moved to Los Angeles and was living on an isolated beach, that the Indians would throw themselves into the sea when the bad wind blew. I could see why. The Pacific turned ominously glossy during a Santa Ana period, and one woke in the night troubled not only by the peacocks screaming in the olive trees but by the eerie absence of surf. The heat was surreal. The sky had a yellow cast, the kind of light sometimes called "earthquake weather." My only neighbor would not come out of her house for days, and there were no lights at night, and her husband roamed the place with a machete. One day he would tell me that he had heard a trespasser, the next a rattlesnake.

"On nights like that," Raymond Chandler once wrote about the Santa Ana, "every booze party ends in a fight. Meek little wives feel the edge of the carving knife and study their husbands' necks. Anything can happen." That was the kind of wind it was. I did not know then that there was any basis for the effect it had on all of us, but it turns out to be another of those cases in which science bears out folk wisdom. The Santa Ana, which is named for one of the canyons it rushes through, is a *foehn* wind, like the *foehn* of Austria and Switzerland and the *hamsin* of Israel. There are a number of persistent malevolent winds, perhaps the best known of which are the mistral of France and the Mediterranean sirocco, but a *foehn* wind has distinct characteristics: it occurs on the leeward slope of a mountain range and, although the air begins as a cold mass, it is warmed as it comes down the mountain and appears finally as a hot dry wind. Whenever and wherever a *foehn* blows, doctors hear about headaches and nausea and allergies, about "nervousness," about "depression." In Los Angeles some teachers do not attempt to conduct formal classes during a Santa Ana, because the children become unmanageable. In Switzerland the suicide rate goes up during the *foehn,* and in the courts of some Swiss cantons the wind is considered a mitigating circumstance for crime. Surgeons are said to watch the wind, because blood does not clot normally during a *foehn*. A few years ago an Israeli physicist discovered that not only during such winds, but for the ten or twelve hours which precede them, the air carries an unusually high ratio of positive to negative ions. No one seems to know exactly why that should be; some talk about friction and others suggest solar disturbances. In any case the positive ions are there, and what an excess of positive ions does, in the simplest terms, is make people unhappy. One cannot get much more mechanistic than that.

Easterners commonly complain that there is no "weather" at all in Southern California, that the days and the seasons slip by relentlessly, numbingly bland. That is quite misleading. In fact the climate is characterized by infrequent but violent extremes: two periods of torrential subtropical rains which continue for weeks and wash out the hills and send subdivisions sliding toward the sea; about twenty scattered days a year of the Santa Ana, which, with its incendiary dryness, invariably means fire. At the first prediction of a Santa Ana, the Forest Service flies men and equipment from northern California into the southern forests, and the Los Angeles Fire Department cancels its ordinary non-firefighting routines. The Santa Ana caused Malibu to burn the way it did in 1956, and Bel Air in 1961, and Santa Barbara in 1964. In the winter of 1966–67 eleven men were killed fighting a Santa Ana fire that spread through the San Gabriel Mountains.

Just to watch the front-page news out of Los Angeles during a Santa Ana is to get very close to what it is about the place. The longest single Santa Ana period in recent years was in 1957, and it lasted not the usual three or four days but fourteen days, from November 21 until December 4. On the first day 25,000 acres of the San Gabriel Mountains were burning, with gusts reaching 100 miles an hour. In town, the wind reached Force 12, or hurricane force, on the Beaufort Scale; oil derricks were toppled and people ordered off the downtown streets to avoid injury from flying objects. On November 22 the fire in the San Gabriels was out of control. On November 24 six people were killed in automobile accidents, and by the end of the week the Los Angeles *Times* was keeping a box score of traffic deaths. On November 26 a prominent Pasadena attorney, depressed about money, shot and killed his wife, their two sons, and himself. On November 27 a South Gate divorcée, twenty-two, was murdered and thrown from a moving car. On November 30 the San Gabriel fire was still out of control, and the wind in town was blowing eighty miles an hour. On the first day of December four people died violently, and on the third the wind began to break.

It is hard for people who have not lived in Los Angeles to realize how radically the Santa Ana figures in the local imagination. The city burning is Los Angeles's deepest image of itself: Nathanael West perceived that, in *The Day of the Locust;* and at the time of the 1965 Watts riots what struck the imagination most indelibly were the fires. For days one could drive the Harbor Freeway and see the city on fire, just as we had always known it would be in the end. Los Angeles weather is the weather of catastrophe, of apocalypse, and, just as the reliably long and bitter winters of New England determine the way life is lived there, so the violence and the unpredictability of the Santa Ana affect the entire quality of life in Los Angeles, accentuate its impermanence, its unreliability. The wind shows us how close to the edge we are.

(1967)

QUESTIONS

1. How urgent is Didion's tone? How insistent is she about what she is saying? How personal is her voice?
2. What does her relentless accumulation of facts contribute to the essay's tone?

STYLE

A writer's style in an essay derives from choices he or she makes in diction, syntax, and figurative language. Notice how James Baldwin uses these aspects of style in this passage from "Notes of a Native Son" (page 1846) in which he describes his father:

He was, I think, very handsome. I gather this from photographs and from my own memories of him, dressed in his Sunday best and on his way to preach a sermon somewhere, when I was little. Handsome, proud, and ingrown, "like a toe-nail," somebody said. But he looked to me, as I grew older, like pictures I had seen of African tribal chieftains: he really should have been naked, with war-paint on and barbaric mementos, standing among spears. He could be chilling in the pulpit and indescribably cruel in his personal life and he was certainly the most bitter man I have ever met; yet it must be said that there was something else in him, buried in him, which lent him his tremendous power and, even, a rather crushing charm. It had something to do with his blackness, I think—he was very black—with his blackness and his beauty, and with the fact that he knew that he was black but did not know that he was beautiful. He claimed to be proud of his blackness but it had also been the cause of much humiliation and it had fixed bleak boundaries to his life. He was not a young man when we were growing up and he had already suffered many kinds of ruin; in his outrageously demanding and protective way he loved his children, who were black like him and menaced, like him; and all these things sometimes showed in his face when he tried, never to my knowledge with any success, to establish contact with any of us. When he took one of his children on his knee to play, the child always became fretful and began to cry; when he tried to help one of us with our homework the absolutely unabating tension which emanated from him caused our minds and our tongues to become paralyzed, so that he, scarcely knowing why, flew into a rage and the child, not knowing why, was punished. If it ever entered his head to bring a surprise home for his children, it was, almost unfailingly, the wrong surprise and even the big watermelons he often brought home on his back in the summertime led to the most appalling scenes. I do not remember, in all those years, that one of his children was ever glad to see him come home. From what I was able to gather of his early life, it seemed that this inability to establish contact with other people had always marked him and had been one of the things which had driven him out of New Orleans. There was something in him, therefore, groping and tentative, which was never expressed and which was buried with him. One saw it most clearly when he was facing new people and hoping to impress them. But he never did, not for long.

The style here is formal, dignified, elegant, allusive. Baldwin writes about his father, about their relationship, and about the environment in which they lived. He writes personally but not informally. Even though he writes in the first person, using *I* and *we, me* and *mine,* he treats his subject with a solemnity achieved by careful control of diction. Baldwin consistently elevates his diction: "contemptuous," "apprehensive," "unabating," "emanated," and he includes abstractions: "injustice," "hatred," "bitterness," "pride." Such elevated diction contributes to the serious tone of the essay.

Another element that contributes to the solemnity of Baldwin's style is its rhythm. Baldwin tends to interrupt the linear movement of his sentences by embedding or interpolating words and phrases that create a stop-and-go movement, a rising and falling sound. The rise and fall of the rhythm adds to the dignity of Baldwin's style. Consider the following pair of sentences and the alternative versions.

He was, I think, very handsome. (Baldwin)
I think he was very handsome. (alternate)

I do not remember, in all those years, that one of his children
was ever glad to see him come home. (Baldwin)
In all those years, I do not remember that one of his children
was ever glad to see him come home. (alternate)

Baldwin's repeated use of balance and parallelism contributes to his formal style: "He loved his children, who were black like him and menaced like him. . . . When he took one of his children on his knee to play, the child always became fretful and began to cry; when he tried to help one of us with our homework the absolutely unabating tension which emanated from him caused our minds and our tongues to become paralyzed, so that he, scarcely knowing why, flew into a rage and the child, not knowing why, was punished." Baldwin also employs parallel sentences: "It seemed to me that. . . . And it seemed to me, too, that. . . ." Again: "When he was dead I. . . . When he had been dead a long time I. . . ." Such repetitions of sentence structure and repetitions of words ("black," "blackness," and "beauty"; "bitter," "bitterness," and "pride") reinforce Baldwin's formal and solemn tone.

We hear a different tone as Alice Walker describes her mother in this passage from her essay "In Search of Our Mothers' Gardens" (page 1714).

Five children later, I was born. And this is how I came to know my mother: she seemed a large, soft, loving-eyed woman who was rarely impatient in our home. Her quick, violent temper was on view only a few times a year, when she battled with the white landlord who had the misfortune to suggest to her that her children did not need to go to school.

She made all the clothes we wore, even my brothers' overalls. She made all the towels and sheets we used. She spent the summers canning vegetables and fruits. She spent the winter evenings making quilts enough to cover all our beds.

During the "working" day, she labored beside—not behind—my father in the fields. Her day began before sunup, and did not end until late at night. There was never a moment for her to sit down, undisturbed, to unravel her own private thoughts; never a time free from interruption—by work or the noisy inquiries of her many children. And yet, it is to my mother—and all our mothers who were not famous—that I went in search of the secret of what has fed that muzzled and often mutilated, but vibrant, creative spirit that the black woman has inherited, and that pops out in wild and unlikely places to this day.

Like Mem, a character in *The Third Life of Grange Copeland*, my mother adorned with flowers whatever shabby house we were forced to live in. And not just your typical straggly country stand of zinnias, either. She planted ambitious gardens—and still does—with over fifty different varieties of plants that bloom profusely from early March until late November. Before she left home for the fields, she watered her flowers, chopped up the grass, and laid out new beds. When she returned from the fields she might divide clumps of bulbs, dig a cold pit, uproot and replant roses, or prune branches from her taller bushes or trees—until night came and it was too dark to see.

Whatever she planted grew as if by magic, and her fame as a grower of flowers spread over three counties. Because of her creativity with her flowers, even my memories of poverty are seen through a screen of blooms—sunflowers, petunias, roses, dahlias, forsythia, spirea, delphiniums, verbena . . . and on and on.

And I remember people coming to my mother's yard to be given cuttings from her flowers; I hear again the praise showered on her because whatever rocky soil she landed on, she turned into a garden. A garden so brilliant with colors, so original in its design, so magnificent with life and creativity, that to this day people drive by our house in Georgia—perfect strangers and imperfect strangers—and ask to stand or walk among my mother's art.

I notice that it is only when my mother is working in her flowers that she is radiant, almost to the point of being invisible—except as Creator: hand and eye. She is involved in work her soul must have. Ordering the universe in the image of her personal conception of Beauty.

Walker, like Baldwin, writes in the first person and about a parent. Her tone differs from his largely because her subject and attitude differ. Walker's appreciation of her mother shines through her prose and is evident in her selection of details. (Compare the details Baldwin includes to describe his father.) Walker's style is lighter, more informal than Baldwin's. Describing her mother's temper as being "on view" and saying that she "battled" with the landlord, Walker uses everyday speech rather than formal diction. Her sentences are simple and short as in the second paragraph, which begins "She made all the clothes we wore, even my brothers' overalls." . . . Walker comments on her mother's skill with flowers in an informal and directly personal way: "and not just your typical straggly country stand of zinnias either." Further accentuating her informal tone is the way she breaks into sentences with off-hand interruptions, highlighting their casualness by punctuating them with dashes: "—and still does"; "—and all our mothers who were not farmers." She even trails off at one point: ". . . and on and on."

One additional stylistic feature distinguishes Walker's style from Baldwin's and contributes to her informal tone: her sentence fragments. Twice in the passage quoted above Walker employs sentence fragments, both times at the end of a paragraph: "A garden so brilliant . . . my mother's art"; "Ordering the universe . . . conception of beauty." As a rhetorical strategy for achieving emphasis, the fragment can drive a fact or feeling across with intensity and power. Such features of Walker's prose make her writing more casual and intimate than Baldwin's. Although Walker, like Baldwin, is capable of writing long, intricate sentences, her eloquence is achieved with different stylistic techniques.

Like poets, dramatists, and fiction writers, essayists use language in literal and nonliteral ways. The kinds of figurative language most prevalent in essays are those that involve comparison, particularly in the forms of *simile* and *metaphor*. Essayists employ simile and metaphor to clarify their thought and their feeling. They use these forms of comparison to make one thing clear in terms of another. Sometimes the writer's intention in using the comparison is clear and explicit, as in the following examples. In pointing out young men's faults, Bacon notes that they "will not acknowledge or retract them, like an unready horse that will neither stop nor turn." Orwell compares the Marrakech burial ground to a derelict building lot and its lumpy earth to broken brick. Orwell's comparisons communicate an image and impression of the place that is sharper and clearer with the comparison. Bacon communicates the idea that young men can be stubborn and recalcitrant by illustrating their stubbornness with an example.

These examples, all similes, are relatively simple. Both Bacon and Orwell use other less explicit and more complex comparisons when they speak metaphorically of one thing in terms of another. Bacon does this when he suggests that some men are not "ripe for action" until they reach middle age. The implicit comparison is between men and plants, specifically fruit. Like fruit, men come to maturity over time. In the same way that not all fruit ripens at the same time, men do not all become ready for action based on mature decisions at the same time. Some men, like some fruit, ripen faster than others.

Another example of an implicit comparison occurs in Joan Didion's "Los Angeles Notebook" when she talks about *rekindling* an argument with the telephone company. The comparison is carried in her verb, "rekindle," an image of conflagration appropriate to an essay that describes the fiery consequences of the Santa Ana. Moreover, Didion develops the fire imagery much more fully in the final paragraph where she alludes to Nathanael West's novel *The Day of the Locust,* which ends with a vivid depiction of Los Angeles burning. Throughout her essay Didion refers both literally and figuratively to fire.

We can note also in this brief discussion of comparative images that the passages quoted above from Baldwin and Walker also employ comparison in various ways. Walker uses the garden as an image or symbol of her mother's creativity. Elsewhere in her essay, Walker extends the symbolic implications of the garden image to include the creativity of all women, particularly those whose creativity could not find expression in ways available to women today.

In using figurative language, expecially images of comparison, essayists ally themselves with literary artists working in other genres. In fact we might say that the essay's use of figurative language is one element that invites our consideration of it as literature rather than simply as information. Stripped of its comparative figures, of its imagery, the essay becomes less engaging as literature and more strictly a matter of factual reporting. And even though literary essayists like Orwell and Didion do a good deal of reporting in their essays, they do it by means of linguistic and rhetorical strategies and of formal patterns common to the other literary genres. By designing their essays to move us as well as instruct us, writers like Orwell, Didion, Walker, and Baldwin elevate the factuality of their essays to the status of imaginative literature.

As an exercise in examining aspects of an essayist's style, consider the following selection from Henry David Thoreau's *Walden*.

HENRY DAVID THOREAU

[1817–1862]

The Battle of the Ants

One day when I went out to my wood-pile, or rather my pile of stumps, I observed two large ants, the one red, the other much larger, nearly half an inch long, and black, fiercely contending with one another. Having once got hold they never let go, but struggled and wrestled and rolled on the chips incessantly. Looking farther, I was surprised to find that the chips were covered with such combatants, that it was not a *duellum,* but a *bellum,*° a war between two races of ants, the red always pitted against the black, and frequently two red ones to one black. The legions of these Myrmidons° covered all the hills and vales in my woodyard, and the ground was already strewn with the dead and dying, both red and black. It was the only battle which I have ever witnessed, the only battle-field I ever trod while the battle was raging; internecine war; the red republicans on the one hand, the black imperialists on the other. On every side they were engaged in deadly combat, yet without any noise that I could hear, and human soldiers never fought so resolutely. I watched a couple that were fast locked in each other's embraces, in a little sunny valley amid the chips, now at noonday prepared to fight till the sun went down, or life went out. The smaller red champion had fastened himself like a vise to his adversary's front, and through all the tumblings on that field never for an instant ceased to gnaw at one of his feelers near the root, having already caused the other to go by the board; while the stronger black one dashed him from side to side, and, as I saw on looking nearer, had already divested him of several of his members. They fought with more pertinacity than bulldogs. Neither manifested the least disposition to retreat. It was evident that their battle-cry was "Conquer or die." In the meanwhile there came along a single red ant on the hillside of this valley, evidently full of excitement, who either had dispatched his foe, or had not yet taken part in the battle; probably the latter, for he had lost none of his limbs; whose mother had charged him to return with his shield or upon it.° Or perchance he was some Achilles, who had nourished his wrath apart, and had now come to avenge or rescue his Patroclus.° He saw this unequal combat from afar,—for the blacks were nearly twice the size of the red,—he drew near with rapid pace till he stood on his guard within half an inch of the combatants; then, watching his opportunity, he sprang upon the black warrior, and commenced his operations near the root of his right fore leg, leaving the foe to select among his own members; and so there were three united for life, as if a new kind of attraction had been invented which put all other locks and cements to shame. I should not have wondered by this

---

not a duellum . . . bellum   *not a duel but a war.*   **Myrmidons**   *soldiers who followed the Greek warrior Achilles. Myrmes is the Greek word for ant.*   **to return with his shield . . . upon it**   *Spartan mothers told their sons this as they departed for war.*   **Patroclus**   *Achilles' close friend. When Patroclus was killed, Achilles, who had not been fighting because of wounded pride, returned to battle the Trojans, especially to avenge the death of his friend by killing the Trojan hero, Hector.*

time to find that they had their respective musical bands stationed on some eminent chip, and playing their national airs the while, to excite the slow and cheer the dying combatants. I was myself excited somewhat even as if they had been men. The more you think of it, the less the difference. And certainly there is not the fight recorded in Concord history, at least, if in the history of America, that will bear a moment's comparison with this, whether for the numbers engaged in it, or for the patriotism and heroism displayed. For numbers and for carnage it was an Austerlitz or Dresden.° Concord fight! Two killed on the patriot's side, and Luther Blanchard wounded! Why here every ant was a Buttrick,—"Fire, for God's sake fire!"—and thousands shared the fate of Davis and Hosmer.° There was not one hireling there. I have no doubt that it was a principle they fought for, as much as our ancestors, and not to avoid a three-penny tax on their tea; and the results of this battle will be as important and memorable to those whom it concerns as those of the battle of Bunker Hill, at least.

I took up the chip on which the three I have particularly described were struggling, carried it into my house, and placed it under a tumbler on my window-sill, in order to see the issue. Holding a microscope to the first-mentioned red ant, I saw that, though he was assiduously gnawing at the near fore leg of his enemy, having severed his remaining feeler, his own breast was all torn away, exposing what vitals he had there to the jaws of the black warrior, whose breastplate was apparently too thick for him to pierce; and the dark carbuncles of the sufferer's eyes shone with ferocity such as war only could excite. They struggled half an hour longer under the tumbler, and when I looked again the black soldier had severed the heads of his foes from their bodies, and the still living heads were hanging on either side of him like ghastly trophies at his saddle-bow, still apparently as firmly fastened as ever, and he was endeavoring with feeble struggles, being without feelers and with only the remnant of a leg, and I know not how many other wounds, to divest himself of them; which at length, after half an hour more, he accomplished. I raised the glass, and he went off over the window-sill in that crippled state. Whether he finally survived that combat, and spent the remainder of his days in some Hôtel des Invalides,° I do not know; but I thought that his industry would not be worth much thereafter. I never learned which party was victorious, nor the cause of the war; but I felt for the rest of that day as if I had had my feelings excited and harrowed by witnessing the struggle, the ferocity and carnage of a human battle before my door.

(1854)

QUESTIONS

1. Identify and comment on the effectiveness of Thoreau's comparisons. Consider the small-scale brief similes and the overall analogy between the ant war and the Trojan War.

Austerlitz or Dresden   *two fierce battles of the Napoleonic wars.*   **Concord fight . . . Hosmer**   *The first battle of the American Revolution was fought at Concord Bridge. In that famous fight, Major John Buttrick and his militiamen repelled the British regular army and hired soldiers. Davis and Hosmer were Americans killed, Blanchard an American wounded.*   **Hôtel des Invalides**   *a veteran's hospital in Paris.*

2. What does Thoreau gain by including the quoted phrases "Conquer or die" and "Fire, for God's sake fire!"?
3. What does Thoreau's Latinate diction contribute to the effects of his prose? Consider especially the following words: *incessantly, internecine, resolutely, divested, pertinacity, dispatched, eminent, carnage, assiduously, industry,* and *ferocity.*

STRUCTURE

The structural features of an essay are not as visible as the stanzas of poems or the acts and scenes of plays. We can gain some sense of the essay's structural variety by considering a few of the essays in this book.

George Orwell's "Shooting an Elephant" (page 1835) is largely a chronological account that describes the shooting of an elephant. The sequence of actions, however, is preceded by a two-paragraph introduction, which sets the scene, establishes the tone, and announces the subject. The chronological narrative is then followed by a coda in which Orwell comments on what happened. The narrative portion is thus framed by brief explanations, each of which helps us understand its significance. Moreover, Orwell breaks into the narrative section with an important explanatory paragraph, in which he comments extensively on the meaning the event had for him and on its larger, more generalized political significance.

E. B. White uses an alternating structure in "The Ring of Time" (page 1715). He presents a picture of what he sees and then raises questions about it; then he presents more description and again speculates about it. This pattern continues throughout the essay until the final paragraph, which echoes the essay's opening. This gives the essay an alternating structure and a circular one. And that, in part, is an aspect of the the essay's theme—the circular, repetitive ring of time itself.

Some clues for relating the structure of an essay to its meaning include being alert for shifts of focus such as Orwell's shifting scenes in "Marrakech" and Didion's shifts from one type of information to another in "Los Angeles Notebook." In addition, we can look for connections between one part of an essay and another, once we decide what those parts are. Orwell helps us see the parts of "Marrakech" by dividing the five parts with blank space. Didion gives us neither such visual nor such explicit verbal markers; she does, however, shift attention to different kinds of information—historical, literary, scientific, and personal.

Perhaps the most important thing to remember about the structure of essays is this: structure reflects thought and is inextricably connected with it. The form of an essay, its structure of thought, is a clue to how we should read it; its form is an aspect of its meaning. When writers alter the structure of essays, they alter both the meaning of their works and their readers' experience of them. Rearranging the paragraphs of E. B. White's "The Ring of Time," for example, to cluster descriptive paragraphs together and separate them from speculative ones alters our experience of the essay. Rewriting Orwell's "Shooting an Elephant" to keep the entire story together without the intrusion of narrative comment alters the effects the essay now creates. In short, if we change the form of a literary work, we change its meaning and effect.

Consider the structure of the following brief essay by Virginia Woolf.

VIRGINIA WOOLF

[1882–1941]

The Death of the Moth

Moths that fly by day are not properly to be called moths; they do not excite that pleasant sense of dark autumn nights and ivy-blossom which the commonest yellow-underwing asleep in the shadow of the curtain never fails to rouse in us. They are hybrid creatures, neither gay like butterflies nor sombre like their own species. Nevertheless the present specimen, with his narrow hay-coloured wings, fringed with a tassel of the same colour, seemed to be content with life. It was a pleasant morning, mid-September, mild, benignant, yet with a keener breath than that of the summer months. The plough was already scoring the field opposite the window, and where the share had been, the earth was pressed flat and gleamed with moisture. Such vigour came rolling in from the fields and the down beyond that it was difficult to keep the eyes strictly turned upon the book. The rooks too were keeping one of their annual festivities; soaring round the tree tops until it looked as if a vast net with thousands of black knots in it had been cast up into the air; which, after a few moments, sank slowly down upon the trees until every twig seemed to have a knot at the end of it. Then, suddenly, the net would be thrown into the air again in a wider circle this time, with the utmost clamour and vociferation, as though to be thrown into the air and settle slowly down upon the tree tops were a tremendously exciting experience.

The same energy which inspired the rooks, the ploughmen, the horses, and even, it seemed, the lean bare-backed downs, sent the moth fluttering from side to side of his square of the window-pane. One could not help watching him. One was, indeed, conscious of a queer feeling of pity for him. The possibilities of pleasure seemed that morning so enormous and so various that to have only a moth's part in life, and a day moth's at that, appeared a hard fate, and his zest in enjoying his meagre opportunities to the full, pathetic. He flew vigorously to one corner of his compartment, and, after waiting there a second, flew across to the other. What remained for him but to fly to a third corner and then to a fourth? That was all he could do, in spite of the size of the downs, the width of the sky, the far-off smoke of houses, and the romantic voice, now and then, of a steamer out at sea. What he could do he did. Watching him, it seemed as if a fibre, very thin but pure, of the enormous energy of the world had been thrust into his frail and diminutive body. As often as he crossed the pane, I could fancy that a thread of vital light became visible. He was little or nothing but life.

Yet, because he was so small, and so simple a form of the energy that was rolling in at the open window and driving its way through so many narrow and intricate corridors in my own brain and in those of other human beings, there was something marvelous as well as pathetic about him. It was as if someone had taken a tiny bead of pure life and decking it as lightly as possible with down and feathers, had set it dancing and zigzagging to show us the true nature of life. Thus displayed one could not get over the strangeness of it. One is apt to forget all about life, seeing it humped and bossed and garnished and cumbered so that it has to move with the greatest circumspection and dignity. Again, the thought of all that life might have been had he been born in any other shape caused one to view his simple activities with a kind of pity.

After a time, tired by his dancing apparently, he settled on the window ledge in the sun, and, the queer spectacle being at an end, I forgot about him. Then, looking up, my eye was caught by him. He was trying to resume his dancing, but seemed either so stiff or so awkward that he could only flutter to the bottom of the window-pane; and when he tried to fly across it he failed. Being intent on other matters I watched these futile attempts for a time without thinking, unconsciously waiting for him to resume his flight, as one waits for a machine, that has stopped momentarily, to start again without considering the reason of its failure. After perhaps a seventh attempt he slipped from the wooden ledge and fell, fluttering his wings, onto his back on the window sill. The helplessness of his attitude roused me. It flashed upon me he was in difficulties; he could no longer raise himself; his legs struggled vainly. But, as I stretched out a pencil, meaning to help him to right himself, it came over me that the failure and awkwardness were the approach of death. I laid the pencil down again.

The legs agitated themselves once more. I looked as if for the enemy against which he struggled. I looked out of doors. What had happened there? Presumably it was midday, and work in the fields had stopped. Stillness and quiet had replaced the previous animation. The birds had taken themselves off to feed in the brooks. The horses stood still. Yet the power was there all the same, massed outside indifferent, impersonal, not attending to anything in particular. Somehow it was opposed to the little hay-coloured moth. It was useless to try to do anything. One could only watch the extraordinary efforts made by those tiny legs against an oncoming doom which could, had it chosen, have submerged an entire city, not merely a city, but masses of human beings; nothing, I knew, had any chance against death. Nevertheless after a pause of exhaustion the legs fluttered again. It was superb this last protest, and so frantic that he succeeded at last in righting himself. One's sympathies, of course, were all on the side of life. Also, when there was nobody to care or to know, this gigantic effort on the part of an insignificant little moth, against a power of such magnitude, to retain what no one else valued or desired to keep, moved one strangely. Again, somehow, one saw life a pure bead. I lifted the pencil again, useless though I knew it to be. But even as I did so, the unmistakable tokens of death showed themselves. The body relaxed, and instantly grew stiff. The struggle was over. The insignificant little creature now knew death. As I looked at the dead moth, this minute wayside triumph of so great a force over so mean an antagonist filled me with wonder. Just as life had been strange a few minutes before, so death was now as strange. The moth having righted himself now lay most decently and uncomplainingly composed. O yes, he seemed to say, death is stronger than I am.

(1942)

QUESTIONS

1. The essay is divided into five paragraphs. What is the focus of each? How is each paragraph related to the one that precedes and follows it?
2. Woolf gives the essay a narrative structure: it recounts an incident—the death of the moth. How, where, and why does she modify the linear chronology of the narrative?
3. What details recur in the essay? What does Woolf accomplish by including them?

THOUGHT

Edward Hoagland, a contemporary American essayist, has described the essay as a work that "hangs somewhere on a line between two sturdy poles: this is what I think, and this is what I am."★ The sense of self and selves provided by essayists is manifested in their styles and voices—Hoagland's "what I am." This we have discussed in the sections on voice and style above. Here we will consider the essayist's "what I think," the way he or she speaks to us, as Hoagland says, "mind to mind."

When writers choose to write an essay rather than a poem, play, or story, it is because, presumably, they have something on their minds. The very choice of factual rather than fictional discourse testifies to the essayist's concern for expressing an idea. Even when essayists rely heavily on narrative to tell stories or description to convey feelings and attitudes, their emphasis ultimately is most often on an idea. It is this primacy of idea, in fact, that makes an essay what it is.

Let us consider the way idea is explored and illustrated in Joan Didion's "Los Angeles Notebook." Although Didion uses many concrete details in building up an impression of Los Angeles, her primary concern is to clarify the nature and effects of the Santa Ana wind. Allied with this is a persuasive intention: to argue for a causal connection between climate and human behavior. Didion enforces a proposition—that climate strongly influences people's behavior, that it determines how they act and react. How far she pushes this idea is a matter for discussion; so is our own sense of how far the idea should be taken. But propose it Didion certainly does. In fact, everything about her six-paragraph discourse is directed toward this single idea.

In a similar way we can see that George Orwell has an idea to advance in "Shooting an Elephant" (page 1835). Like the descriptive details of "Marrakech," those of "Shooting an Elephant" illustrate a point. That point surfaces most clearly in the following paragraph—the seventh of the essay.

But at that moment I glanced round at the crowd that had followed me. It was an immense crowd, two thousand at the least and growing every minute. It blocked the road for a long distance on either side. I looked at the sea of yellow faces above the garish clothes—faces all happy and excited over this bit of fun, all certain that the elephant was going to be shot. They were watching me as they would watch a conjurer

★*The Tugman's Passage* (New York: Random House, 1982), 25.

about to perform a trick. They did not like me, but with the magical rifle in my hands I was momentarily worth watching. And suddenly I realized that I should have to shoot the elephant after all. The people expected it of me and I had got to do it; I could feel their two thousand wills pressing me forward, irresistibly. And it was at this moment, as I stood there with the rifle in my hands, that I first grasped the hollowness, the futility of the white man's dominion in the East. Here was I, the white man with his gun, standing in front of the unarmed native crowd—seemingly the leading actor of the piece; but in reality I was only an absurd puppet pushed to and fro by the will of those yellow faces behind. I perceived in this moment that when the white man turns tyrant it is his own freedom that he destroys. He becomes a sort of hollow, posing dummy, the conventionalized figure of a sahib. For it is the condition of his rule that he shall spend his life in trying to impress the "natives," and so in every crisis he has got to do what the "natives" expect of him. He wears a mask, and his face grows to fit it. I had got to shoot the elephant. I had committed myself to doing it when I sent for the rifle. A sahib has got to act like a sahib; he has got to appear resolute, to know his own mind and do definite things. To come all that way, rifle in hand, with two thousand people marching at my heels, and then to trail feebly away, having done nothing—no, that was impossible. The crowd would laugh at me. And my whole life, every white man's life in the East, was one long struggle not to be laughed at.

In this paragraph, Orwell interrupts his story about the elephant to specify the significance of the experience. His political point is clear: imperialism is evil; it is destructive of both the oppressed and the oppressors. Orwell does not make this point abstractly or generally. Instead, he presents it within a specific context of time, place, and action: the shooting of an elephant in Burma in the 1930s by a British colonial. To increase the impact of his idea, Orwell uses irony and imagery. The discrepancy between appearances (that the narrator, an authority figure, is in charge) and reality (that he is at the mercy of the unarmed natives, whose will he is following) is ironic. This ironic contrast is underscored by the images of the narrator as the "leading actor" and as an "absurd puppet," with *actor* indicating his role playing and *puppet* his lack of control. Orwell further establishes his point with the image of the mask, which extends the theatrical imagery prevalent in this passage and in the essay overall. This image suggests that although a person may originally keep himself distinct from a role he performs, at some point he may actually become what he initially pretends to be. Orwell suggests that what was initially a part in a drama can become an aspect of an identity.

This complex idea leads forcefully into his statement that "when the white man turns tyrant it is his own freedom that he destroys." The last section of the paragraph explains this point. It is, of course, ironic that in gaining control over others, in assuming power, one loses one's freedom. That paradoxical idea is the heart of both this central explanatory paragraph and the essay overall. It is emphasized, moreover, in the last paragraph, where Orwell confesses that he shot the elephant "to avoid looking the fool."

A final point about idea in essays: thought does not exist independently of feeling. The ideas we discover in essays are felt, not merely thought out. They derive from the writer's emotions; they have their basis in feeling. Feeling, in fact, is mixed with all thought given expression in language. So much so that we might say there is no thinking without feeling. In essays like Alice Walker's and James Baldwin's, especially, we can discover powerful examples of thought felt with passion, of feeling conveyed with incisive intelligence.

The essay that follows expresses some thoughts about revenge. Consider both what these thoughts are and how strongly they are felt.

FRANCIS BACON

[1561–1626]

Of Revenge

Revenge is a kind of wild justice, which the more man's nature runs to, the more ought law to weed it out. For as for the first wrong, it doth but offend the law, but the revenge of that wrong putteth the law out of office. Certainly in taking revenge, a man is but even with his enemy, but in passing it over, he is superior, for it is a prince's part to pardon. And Solomon, I am sure, saith, "It is the glory of a man to pass by an offense." That which is past is gone and irrevocable, and wise men have enough to do with things present and to come; therefore they do but trifle with themselves that labor in past matters. There is no man doth a wrong for the wrong's sake, but thereby to purchase himself profit, or pleasure, or honor, or the like. Therefore why should I be angry with a man for loving himself better than me? And if any man should do wrong merely out of ill nature, why, yet it is but like the thorn or briar, which prick and scratch because they can do no other. The most tolerable sort of revenge is for those wrongs which there is no law to remedy, but then let a man take heed the revenge be such as there is no law to punish; else a man's enemy is still beforehand, and it is two for one. Some, when they take revenge, are desirous the party should know whence it cometh. This the more generous. For the delight seemeth to not be so much in doing the hurt as in making the party repent. But base and crafty cowards are like the arrow that flieth in the dark. Cosmus, duke of Florence, had a desperate saying against perfidious or neglecting friends, as if those wrongs were unpardonable: "You shall read," saith he, "that we are commanded to forgive our enemies; but you never read that we are commanded to forgive our friends." But yet the spirit of Job was in better tune: "Shall we," saith he, "take good at God's hands, and not be content to take evil also?" And so of friends in a proportion. This is certain, that a man that studieth revenge keeps his own wounds green, which otherwise would heal and do well. Public revenges are for the most part fortunate, as that for the death of Caesar, for the death of Pertinax, for the death of Henry the Third of France, and many more. But in private revenges it is not so. Nay rather, vindictive persons live the life of witches, who, as they are mischievous, so end they unfortunate.

(1612)

QUESTIONS

1. Why can revenge be defined as "a kind of wild justice"? What is wild about revenge? What about it is just?
2. What arguments does Bacon make against revenge? Are his objections primarily moral or practical?
3. What do Bacon's historical and biblical allusions contribute to his ideas about revenge? Why do you think he includes these allusions?

CHAPTER THIRTY-TWO

Approaching an Essay: Guides for Reading and Writing

The guidelines that follow summarize our discussion of reading essays; we will use them to guide our analysis of an essay by Annie Dillard.

Guidelines for Reading

1. Read through the entire essay to get a feel for what it is about. Center on subject and idea. During this initial reading, be alert to your responses to the work. Jot down your thoughts and feelings in the margins or at the end of the piece. Consider the essay in light of your own experience.
2. Make your second reading more analytical. Zero in on the structure and the development of the argument. Consider how the structure orders the ideas. Be alert for shifts of direction, for changes of language and tone, example and image, scene and point of view. Determine your sense of the writer's tone.
3. During your second reading—or possibly a third—concentrate on language and style. Notice diction and syntax; be alert for imagery and figurative

language. Consider what the style reveals about the writer's purpose and
the audience for which the essay seems to be intended.

4. Be alert for connections both within the essay and beyond it. Single out
passages that highlight the central idea.

5. Consider, in addition, whether the essay shares features with one or more
of the other literary genres, and what use the author makes of techniques
associated with those genres.

6. Consider the values the author expresses in the essay, as well as the essay's
main assumptions.

ANNIE DILLARD

[b. 1945]

Living Like Weasels

A weasel is wild. Who knows what he thinks? He sleeps in his underground den, his
tail draped over his nose. Sometimes he lives in his den for two days without leaving.
Outside, he stalks rabbits, mice, muskrats, and birds, killing more bodies than he can
eat warm, and often dragging the carcasses home. Obedient to instinct, he bites his prey
at the neck, either splitting the jugular vein at the throat or crunching the brain at the
base of the skull, and he does not let go. One naturalist refused to kill a weasel who
was socketed into his hand deeply as a rattlesnake. The man could in no way pry the
tiny weasel off, and he had to walk half a mile to water, the weasel dangling from his
palm, and soak him off like a stubborn label.

And once, says Ernest Thompson Seton—once, a man shot an eagle out of the sky.
He examined the eagle and found the dry skull of a weasel fixed by the jaws to his
throat. The supposition is that the eagle had pounced on the weasel and the weasel
swiveled and bit as instinct taught him, tooth to neck, and nearly won. I would like to
have seen that eagle from the air a few weeks or months before he was shot: was the
whole weasel still attached to his feathered throat, a fur pendant? Or did the eagle eat
what he could reach, gutting the living weasel with his talons before his breast, bending his beak, cleaning the beautiful airborne bones?

I have been reading about weasels because I saw one last week. I startled a weasel who
startled me, and we exchanged a long glance.

Twenty minutes from my house, through the woods by the quarry and across the
highway, is Hollins Pond, a remarkable piece of shallowness, where I like to go at sunset and sit on a tree trunk. Hollins Pond is also called Murray's Pond; it covers two
acres of bottomland near Tinker Creek with six inches of water and six thousand lily
pads. In winter, brown-and-white steers stand in the middle of it, merely dampening
their hooves; from the distant shore they look like miracle itself, complete with mira-

cle's nonchalance. Now, in summer, the steers are gone. The water lilies have blossomed and spread to a green horizontal plane that is terra firma to plodding blackbirds, and tremulous ceiling to black leeches, crayfish, and carp.

This is, mind you, suburbia. It is a five-minute walk in three directions to rows of houses, though none is visible here. There's a 55 mph highway at one end of the pond, and a nesting pair of wood ducks at the other. Under every bush is a muskrat hole or a beer can. The far end is an alternating series of fields and woods, fields and woods, threaded everywhere with motorcycle tracks—in whose bare clay wild turtles lay eggs.

So. I had crossed the highway, stepped over two low barbed-wire fences, and traced the motorcycle path in all gratitude through the wild rose and poison ivy of the pond's shoreline up into high grassy fields. Then I cut down through the woods to the mossy fallen tree where I sit. This tree is excellent. It makes a dry, upholstered bench at the upper, marshy end of the pond, a plush jetty raised from the thorny shore between a shallow blue body of water and a deep blue body of sky.

The sun had just set. I was relaxed on the tree trunk, ensconced in the lap of lichen, watching the lily pads at my feet tremble and part dreamily over the thrusting path of a carp. A yellow bird appeared to my right and flew behind me. It caught my eye; I swiveled around—and the next instant, inexplicably, I was looking down at a weasel, who was looking up at me.

Weasel! I'd never seen one wild before. He was ten inches long, thin as a curve, a muscled ribbon, brown as fruitwood, soft-furred, alert. His face was fierce, small and pointed as a lizard's; he would have made a good arrowhead. There was just a dot of chin, maybe two brown hairs' worth, and then the pure white fur began that spread down his underside. He had two black eyes I didn't see, any more than you see a window.

The weasel was stunned into stillness as he was emerging from beneath an enormous shaggy wild rose bush four feet away. I was stunned into stillness twisted backward on the tree trunk. Our eyes locked, and someone threw away the key.

Our look was as if two lovers, or deadly enemies, met unexpectedly on an overgrown path when each had been thinking of something else: a clearing blow to the gut. It was also a bright blow to the brain, or a sudden beating of brains, with all the charge and intimate grate of rubbed balloons. It emptied our lungs. It felled the forest, moved the fields, and drained the pond; the world dismantled and tumbled into that black hole of eyes. If you and I looked at each other that way, our skulls would split and drop to our shoulders. But we don't. We keep our skulls. So.

He disappeared. This was only last week, and already I don't remember what shattered the enchantment. I think I blinked, I think I retrieved my brain from the weasel's brain, and tried to memorize what I was seeing, and the weasel felt the yank of separation, the careening splashdown into real life and the urgent current of instinct. He vanished under the wild rose. I waited motionless, my mind suddenly full of data and my spirit with pleadings, but he didn't return.

Please do not tell me about "approach-avoidance conflicts." I tell you I've been in that weasel's brain for sixty seconds, and he was in mine. Brains are private places, muttering through unique and secret tapes—but the weasel and I both plugged into another tape simultaneously, for a sweet and shocking time. Can I help it if it was a blank?

What goes on in his brain the rest of the time? What does a weasel think about? He won't say. His journal is tracks in clay, a spray of feathers, mouse blood and bone: uncollected, unconnected, loose-leaf, and blown.

I would like to learn, or remember, how to live. I come to Hollins Pond not so much to learn how to live as, frankly, to forget about it. That is, I don't think I can learn from a wild animal how to live in particular—shall I suck warm blood, hold my tail high, walk with my footprints precisely over the prints of my hands?—but I might learn something of mindlessness, something of the purity of living in the physical senses and the dignity of living without bias or motive. The weasel lives in necessity and we live in choice, hating necessity and dying at the last ignobly in its talons. I would like to live as I should, as the weasel lives as he should. And I suspect that for me the way is like the weasel's: open to time and death painlessly, noticing everything, remembering nothing, choosing the given with a fierce and pointed will.

I missed my chance. I should have gone for the throat. I should have lunged for that streak of white under the weasel's chin and held on, held on through mud and into the wild rose, held on for a dearer life. We could live under the wild rose wild as weasels, mute and uncomprehending. I could very calmly go wild. I could live two days in the den, curled, leaning on mouse fur, sniffing bird bones, blinking, licking, breathing musk, my hair tangled in the roots of grasses. Down is a good place to go, where the mind is single. Down is out, out of your ever-loving mind and back to your careless senses. I remember muteness as a prolonged and giddy fast, where every moment is a feast of utterance received. Time and events are merely poured, unremarked, and ingested directly, like blood pulsed into my gut through a jugular vein. Could two live that way? Could two live under the wild rose, and explore by the pond, so that the smooth mind of each is as everywhere present to the other, and as received and as unchallenged, as falling snow?

We could, you know. We can live any way we want. People take vows of poverty, chastity, and obedience—even of silence—by choice. The thing is to stalk your calling in a certain skilled and supple way, to locate the most tender and live spot and plug into that pulse. This is yielding, not fighting. A weasel doesn't "attack" anything; a weasel lives as he's meant to, yielding at every moment to the perfect freedom of single necessity.

I think it would be well, and proper, and obedient, and pure, to grasp your one necessity and not let it go, to dangle from it limp wherever it takes you. Then even death, where you're going no matter how you live, cannot you part. Seize it and let it seize you up aloft even, till your eyes burn out and drop; let your musky flesh fall off in shreds, and let your very bones unhinge and scatter, loosened over fields, over fields and woods, lightly, thoughtless, from any height at all, from as high as eagles.

(1982)

Voice   Dillard's voice is informal. She speaks to us in the first person, casually, directly: "I tell you I've been in that weasel's brain for sixty seconds. . . ." In advancing the proposition that we live like weasels, Dillard reassures us with "we could, you know." She is thus both confident and authoritative while being personal, even informal. As a result we feel obliged to hear her out, to respond to her passionate insistence; we feel obliged to try to understand even when her explanation grazes mystery.

Style   Dillard's voice is part of her style. Her sentences are short—they speak to the point whether that point is factual or mystical. There are few connectives, almost no coordinative *ands, buts,* and *fors;* and there is no subordination through the use of *because, although, if,* and *whenever.* The lack of formal syntactic links contributes to the force and authority of Dillard's style. "A weasel is wild," she tells us, announcing her theme. Before long we learn just how wild. Later she notes that "a weasel lives as he's meant to," concisely summing up both the weasel and the essay.

Dillard seems fond of questions. Her questions engage us, stimulate our responses, spur our thinking: "What goes on in his brain the rest of the time? What does a weasel think about?" Like her assertions, Dillard's questions are clear and direct. Some of her questions are simultaneously speculative and provocative as when she writes, "Could two live that way? Could two live under the wild rose, and explore by the pond?" These questions she answers: "We could, you know," a somewhat frightening kind of assurance. Beyond her authoritative declarations and her frequent startling questions is a single exclamation: "Weasel!" which catches us by surprise and captures Dillard's surprise in encountering it. We shouldn't miss the imperative of her final sentence, which startles as much by its commanding tone as by its startling advice.

A further stylistic observation: Dillard leans heavily on verbs, especially verbs of action, often violent action. She stacks verbs up, which results in a driving, relentless prose. Here are two examples:

> Obedient to instinct, he bites his prey at the neck, either split
> ting the jugular vein at the throat or crunching the brain at the
> base of the skull, and he does not let go.

> It emptied our lungs. It felled the forest, moved the fields, and
> drained the pond; the world dismantled and tumbled into that
> black hole of eyes.

We should also note her fondness for and skill in using figures of comparison. Describing the weasel, Dillard compares him to "a muscled ribbon," and an "arrowhead" with a color "brown as fruitwood." Describing the impact of her encounter she reaches even further into analogy: "Our look was as if two lovers, or deadly enemies, met unexpectedly." The effect of this look, which she describes in another place as eyes locked together, is "a clearing blow to the gut." The energy of her style, moreover, is captured in the physical imagery and the taut syntax of this phrase.

Structure   The structure of the essay can be mapped like this:

1. Paragraphs 1–2: facts about weasels, especially their wildness and their ability to hang on and not let go; two stunning examples (the naturalist and the eagle) one for each of the first two paragraphs.

2. Paragraphs 3–7: This second, longer chunk of the essay depicts Dillard encountering the weasel, exchanging glances with it. The middle paragraphs (4–6) set the scene, with paragraphs 3 and 7 framing the section with the repeated mention of Dillard and the weasel's locked glances. Paragraph 5 mixes details as it contrasts wilderness and civilization. The two exist side-by-side, one within the other: beer cans coexist with muskrat holes; turtle eggs sit in motorcycle tracks; a highway runs alongside a duck pond.

3. Paragraphs 8–13: The crescendo and climax of the essay. Here Dillard describes in detail the weasel (paragraph 8); the shock of their locked looks (9 and 10); and the shattering of the spell (11). She also laments her unsuccessful attempt to reforge the link with the weasel after it had been snapped. The section ends with Dillard (and us) pondering the mystery she has experienced.

4. Paragraphs 14–17: Dillard speculates about the meaning of the encounter with the weasel. She contemplates living like a weasel—what it means, why it appeals (to her) and perhaps appalls (us). She explores the implications of what a weasel's life is like—how it relates to human life, especially her own. She concludes with an image from the opening: an eagle carrying something that is clinging fiercely to it, not letting go, holding on into and beyond death. The image brings the essay full circle—but with one significant difference: we have taken the weasel's place.

Thought   What begins as an expository essay detailing facts about weasels, especially their wildness and tenacity, turns into a meditation on the value and necessity of wildness, instinct, and tenacity in human life. By the end of the essay Dillard has made the weasel a symbol, a model of how we should live. Her tone changes from the factual declaration of the opening into speculative wonder and then into admonition.

But what does she mean? How can we live like weasels? How can we imitate and appropriate the weasel's wildness and tenacity? Dillard doesn't say, exactly. She only exhorts us to seize necessity, to lock on to what is essential and not let go for anything. She seems to invite us to decide for ourselves what our necessity is and then relentlessly catch and hold it.

Another idea surfaces in the essay: that man and animal can indeed communicate and understand one another. Dillard opts for a mystical communion between man and beast, by necessity a brief communion, one beyond the power of words to describe (though Dillard seems to have pulled it off). The experience for woman and weasel "stuns into stillness," stops time, empties one consciousness into another. In linking her mind even momentarily with the weasel, Dillard undergoes an extraordinary experience, a transforming one. It's something she would like to repeat, to get more of, find out more about. The experience prompts her to read up on weasels, reading she turns to good account in using memorable details to launch her essay. She wants not just to learn more about weasels but to know a weasel in this mystical way again. But she can't because her own consciousness, the distinctive human quality of her thinking mind, prevents her from being at one and staying at one with an animal.

There seems to be, thus, in Dillard's essay, a pull in two directions. On one hand, there is the suggestion that we can link ourselves with the weasel and like him live in necessity instinctively, opening ourselves to time and death, noticing everything and remembering nothing. On the other hand sits a counter idea: that we cannot stay linked with the weasel or with any animal, primarily because our minds prohibit it. We are creatures for whom remembering is necessary, vital. Dillard, in fact, could never have savored her experience and shared it with us without the capacity of remembering. The weasel's mindlessness, its purity of living, cannot be wholly hers or ours, for we are mindful creatures, not mindless ones. Our living as we should is necessarily different from the weasel's living as it should. Although we can learn from the weasel's instinct, its pure living, its tenacity, we can follow it only so far on the way to wildness.

Our consideration of the thought of "Living Like Weasels" brings us to its values. Dillard privileges wildness over civilization, mystical communion over separateness, instinct and tenacity over intellectuality. She prizes the majesty and mystery of nature, and she values the weasel's relentlessness, along with its consistency, predictability, and reliance on instinct. She implies that the simplicity, purity, and elementary fierceness of nature have been lost to man with the advent and development of civilization. We might agree, or we might not, choosing instead to value civilization's laws and directives over the instincts and appetites of the natural world. Whereas Dillard seems to lament her and our inability to keep ourselves joined to nature/weasel in the intense manner of her encounter, some readers may find such a disjunction not only necessary but far happier for human beings. Those readers might see Dillard's mystical union as a dangerous drifting away from human responsibility and obligation. Our reactions both to what Dillard describes directly—the weasel's and eagle's instinct to kill for survival—and what she implies about the relationship between the human and natural worlds will differ markedly depending on our own moral and cultural attitudes. Dillard's essay opens up questions about our relationship to nature, and it leads to questions about our own nature. It strikes to the heart of our values, inviting us by implication to consider what, for us, is necessary and essential. What we decide about this may be very different from what Dillard has decided for herself. And the attitude we take toward our "necessity," as she calls it, may also differ. We may believe, for example, that nothing has to be held with the weasel's tenaciousness, that it is better sometimes to let go rather than hang on.

In raising such questions, we move beyond interpreting Dillard's essay to evaluating it. Our evaluation of its implied and expressed values is an act of judgment or criticism. This judgment extends beyond the moral and cultural values of the essay to our appraisal of it as a literary work. To make such an appraisal, we rely on our experience of the work, on its power to move us. We judge it also according to its power to make us think, to instruct us. And finally, we consider whether or not it pleases us. But all of these considerations cause us to bring our minds to bear on Dillard's essay: on its images, on her style and her literary techniques, on her voice, her values and her attitudes, on the essay's subtle, internal connections, on meaning. Finally, we must consider our own ideas and values against Dillard's. We must make our own judgments, formulate our own beliefs.

Suggestions for Writing
The Experience of Essays

1. Write a paper in which you recount your experience reading a particular essay or series of essays by the same author. You may want to compare your initial experience with your experience in subsequent readings.
2. Compare reading a narrative essay with reading a fictional story. Consider how the experience is different; consider how it is similar.
3. Discuss how any essay can be related to your personal experience. Consider how the ideas of the essay can be linked with your life.

The Interpretation of Essays

4. Explicate the opening paragraph or sentences of any essay. Explain the significance of this opening.
5. Explicate the closing sentences or paragraph of an essay. Explain its success or lack thereof as an ending to the work.
6. Select two or three brief passages from an essay, passages that are significant in both what they say outright and what they implicitly suggest. Explain how the passages are related in thought and style.
7. Analyze the figurative language of an essay. Consider how particular linguistic choices enable the essayist to express an idea more effectively and memorably than could be done without figurative language. Some possibilities: Jonathan Swift's "A Modest Proposal"; Henry David Thoreau's "Battle of the Ants"; Virginia Woolf's "Death of the Moth"; John Donne's "Meditation XVII"; James Baldwin's "Notes of a Native Son."
8. Analyze the ironic dimensions of any essay. Consider why the writer may have used irony in the first place. Consider how effective the irony is and what would be gained or lost without it. Some possibilities: Jonathan Swift's "A Modest Proposal"; E. M. Forster's "Our Graves in Gallipoli"; Mark Twain's "Cub Wants to Be a Pilot."
9. Analyze the symbolism of any essay. Identify the symbols included in the essay, and explain their significance. White's "Ring of Time" and his lake in "Once More to the Lake"; Donne's tolling bell in "Meditation XVII"; Orwell's elephant in "Shooting an Elephant."
10. Analyze the structure of any essay. Consider its major parts or sections and explain what each part contributes to the essay overall and how the parts are related.
11. Discuss the thesis or main idea of any essay. Consider how well the writer presents the main idea and why you are or are not persuaded by it.

The Evaluation of Essays

12. Discuss the values the author expresses in any essay. Identify those values, measure them against your own, and comment on their significance.
13. Write a paper in which you discuss the same subject as the author of an essay. In your discussion of the topic, include references to and direct quotations from the essay.
14. Write a paper in which you explain how a writer's essays relate to the cultural, social, or moral environment of his or her time.

To Research or Imagine

15. Develop an alternate ending for an essay. Change its conclusion in any way you see fit. Be prepared to explain the rationale of your conclusion.
16. Write a paper in which you consider how the essay might be rewritten as a poem, play, or short story. Consider the advantages or disadvantages of such a transformation.
17. Read some letters by an essayist. Consider how the writer appears in the letters compared with the sense of the writer you obtain from reading his or her essays.
18. Read a full-length biography of an essayist. Write a paper explaining how reading the writer's life story increases your understanding or appreciation of the essays.
19. Read a critical study of an essayist or a general critical study of the essay as a literary form. Write a paper explaining how the book aids your understanding or increases your appreciation of what any particular essayist has accomplished with the form.
20. Compare two essayists who write largely or frequently about the same subjects (women's issues or nature, for example). Discuss what the essayists have in common and how they differ.

CHAPTER THIRTY-THREE

Writing About Essays

REASONS FOR WRITING ABOUT ESSAYS

Why write about essays? One reason is to find out what you think about an essay. Another is to induce yourself to read it more carefully. You may write about a work of nonfiction because it engages you, and you may wish to celebrate it or to argue with its implied ideas and values. Still another reason is that you may simply be required to do so as a course assignment.

Whatever your reasons for writing about essays, a number of things happen when you do. First, in writing about an essay you tend to read it more attentively, noticing things you might overlook in a more casual reading. Second, since writing stimulates thinking, when you write about essays you find yourself thinking more about what a particular work means and why you respond to it as you do. And third, you begin to acquire power over the works you write about, making them more meaningful to you.

INFORMAL WAYS OF WRITING ABOUT ESSAYS

When you write about an essay, you may write for yourself or you may write for others. Writing for yourself, often to discover what you think, often takes casual forms such as annotation and freewriting. These less formal kinds of writing are useful for helping you focus on your reading of essays. They are helpful in studying for tests. They can also serve as preliminary forms of writing when you write more formal papers.

When you annotate a text, you make notes about it, usually in the margins or at the top and bottom of pages—or both. Annotations can also be made within the text, as underlined words, circled phrases, and bracketed sentences or paragraphs. Annotations may also assume the form of arrows, question marks, and various other marks.

Annotating a literary work offers a convenient and relatively painless way to begin writing about it. Annotating can get you started zeroing on what you think interesting or important. You can also annotate to signal details that puzzle or disconcert you.

Your markings serve to focus your attention and clarify your understanding of an essay or extended work of nonfiction. Your annotations can save you time when you reread or study a work, and they can also be used when you write a more formal paper.

For examples of annotation see pages 119 (fiction), 618 (poetry), and 864 (drama).

FORMAL WAYS OF WRITING ABOUT ESSAYS

Among the more common ways of writing about essays is analysis. In writing an analytical essay about an essay or section of an essay, your goal is to explain how one or more particular aspects or issues in the work contributes to its overall meaning. You might analyze the dialogue in a scene from an essay such as "Our Graves in Gallipoli." Your goal would be to explain what the verbal exchanges between characters contribute to the essay's meaning. You might analyze the imagery of Walker's "In Search of Our Mother's Gardens" or the diction of Didion's "Los Angeles Notebook" to see what that imagery and diction suggest about the author's attitude toward the characters or the action described. Or you might analyze how Woolf's style in "The Death of the Moth" or Thoreau's allusions in "Battle of the Ants" convey attitudes toward their respective subjects that enhance their themes and enrich the meanings of their works overall.

In addition to analyzing these and other literary elements in an essay, you might also compare two essays or passages, perhaps by focusing on two writers' presentations of the same or similar subjects. Or, instead of focusing on literary elements per se, you might write to see how a particular critical perspective (see Chapter 36) illuminates an essay. For example, you might consider the ways reader response criticism or new historicism contributes to your understanding of Kingston's "No Name Woman" or Orwell's "Shooting an Elephant."

WRITING TO INTERPRET AN ESSAY

When we write to explain a literary work our concern is largely to make our understanding of it clear to others. Such writing is based not only on our impressions of the work, but on our interpretation or considered understanding of it. In this section we explore ways to write about literature that are less personal, less informal, and less subjective than those described in the previous section. We describe ways to develop your responses into interpretations. And we illustrate some forms of explanation that your writing about literary works may assume. Our purpose is to show how ideas about literary works can be developed into thoughtful interpretations.

Because the art of interpretation is crucial for literary study and essential for persuasive writing about literature, we illustrate the process more extensively now with a step-by-step explanation of the interpretive process as it leads through a series of notes to an interpretive summary. Exactly how do we arrive at an interpretation of this or any literary text? How do we go about the process of interpretation and analysis? We can outline the steps to forming an interpretation as follows:

1. We *make observations* about textual details—of information, action, and language.
2. We *establish connections* among our observations, looking for patterns and relationships among them.
3. We *develop inferences* (informed interpretive guesses) based on the connections we make.
4. We *formulate a conclusion* or interpretation, however tentative or provisional, from our inferences.

So that you can participate fully in the interpretive process from beginning to end, we provide you with a fresh text, one that does not appear elsewhere in this book. We invite you to begin by annotating Zora Neale Hurston's essay, "How It Feels to Be Colored Me."

ZORA NEALE HURSTON

[1903–1960]

How It Feels to Be Colored Me

I

I am colored but I offer nothing in the way of extenuating circumstances except the fact that I am the only Negro in the United States whose grandfather on the mother's side was *not* an Indian chief.

2   I remember the very day that I became colored. Up to my thirteenth year I lived in the little Negro town of Eatonville, Florida. It is exclusively a colored town. The only white people I knew passed through the town going to or coming from Orlando. The native whites rode dusty horses, the Northern tourists chugged down the sandy village road in automobiles. The town knew the Southerners and never stopped cane chewing when they passed. But the Northerners were something else again. They were

peered at cautiously from behind curtains by the timid. The more venturesome would come out on the porch to watch them go past and got just as much pleasure out of the tourists as the tourists got out of the village.

3   The front porch might seem a daring place for the rest of the town, but it was a gallery seat for me. My favorite place was atop the gate-post. Proscenium box for a born first-nighter. Not only did I enjoy the show, but I didn't mind the actors knowing that I liked it. I usually spoke to them in passing. I'd wave at them and when they returned my salute, I would say something like this: "Howdy-do-well-I-thank-you-where-you-goin'?" Usually the automobile or the horse paused at this, and after a queer exchange of compliments, I would probably "go a piece of the way" with them, as we say in farthest Florida. If one of my family happened to come to the front in time to see me, of course negotiations would be rudely broken off. But even so, it is clear that I was the first "welcome-to-our-state" Floridian, and I hope the Miami Chamber of Commerce will please take notice.

4   During this period, white people differed from colored to me only in that they rode through town and never lived there. They liked to hear me "speak pieces" and sing and wanted to see me dance the parse-me-la, and gave me generously of their small silver for doing these things, which seemed strange to me for I wanted to do them so much that I needed bribing to stop. Only they didn't know it. The colored people gave no dimes. They deplored any joyful tendencies in me, but I was their Zora nevertheless. I belonged to them, to the nearby hotels, to the county—everybody's Zora.

5   But changes came in the family when I was thirteen, and I was sent to school in Jacksonville. I left Eatonville, the town of the oleanders, as Zora. When I disembarked from the river-boat at Jacksonville, she was no more. It seemed that I had suffered a sea change. I was not Zora of Orange County any more. I was now a little colored girl. I found it out in certain ways. In my heart as well as in the mirror. I became a fast brown—warranted not to rub nor run.

II

6   But I am not tragically colored. There is no great sorrow dammed up in my soul, nor lurking behind my eyes. I do not mind at all. I do not belong to the sobbing school of Negrohood who hold that nature somehow has given them a lowdown dirty deal and whose feelings are all hurt about it. Even in the helter-skelter skirmish that is my life, I have seen that the world is to the strong regardless of a little pigmentation more or less. No, I do not weep at the world—I am too busy sharpening my oyster knife.

7   Someone is always at my elbow reminding me that I am the granddaughter of slaves. It fails to register depression with me. Slavery is sixty years in the past. The operation was successful and the patient is doing well, thank you. The terrible struggle that made me an American out of a potential slave said "On the line!" The Reconstruction said "Get set!": and the generation before said "Go!" I am off to a flying start and I must not halt in the stretch to look behind and weep. Slavery is the price I paid for civilization, and the choice was not with me. It is a bully adventure and worth all that I have paid through any ancestors for it. No one on earth ever had a greater chance for glory. The world to be won and nothing to be lost. It is thrilling to think—to know that for any act of mine, I shall get twice as much praise or twice as much blame. It is

quite exciting to hold the center of the national stage, with the spectators not know-ing whether to laugh or to weep.

[8]   The position of my white neighbors is much more difficult. No brown specter pulls up a chair beside me when I am down to eat. No dark ghost thrusts its leg against mine in bed. The game of keeping what one has is never so exciting as the game of getting.

III

[9]   Sometimes it is the other way around. A white person is set down in our midst, but the contrast is just as sharp for me. For instance, when I sit in the drafty basement that is The New World Cabaret with a white person, my color comes. We enter chat-ting about any little nothing that we have in common and are seated by the jazz wait-ers. In the abrupt way that jazz orchestras have, this one plunges into a number. It loses no time in circumlocutions, but gets right down to business. It constricts the tho-rax and splits the heart with its tempo and narcotic harmonies. This orchestra grows rambunctious, rears on its hind legs and attacks the tonal veil with primitive fury, rend-ing it, clawing it until it breaks through to the jungle beyond. I follow those hea-then—follow them exultingly. I dance wildly inside myself; I yell within, I whoop; I shake my assegai above my head. I hurl it true to the mark *yeeeeooww!* I am in the jungle and living in the jungle way. My face is painted red and yellow and my body is painted blue. My pulse is throbbing like a war drum. I want to slaughter something— give pain, give death to what, I do not know. But the piece ends. The men of the or-chestra wipe their lips and rest their fingers. I creep back slowly to the veneer we call civilization with the last tone and find the white friend sitting motionless in his seat, smoking calmly.

[10]   "Good music they have here," he remarks, drumming the table with his fingertips.

[11]   Music. The great blobs of purple and red emotions have not touched him. He has only heard what I felt. He is far away and I see him but dimly across the ocean and the continent that have fallen between us. He is so pale with his whiteness then and I am *so* colored.

[12]   I do not always feel colored. Even now I often achieve the unconscious Zora of Eatonville before the Hegira. I feel most colored when I am thrown against a sharp white background.

[13]   For instance at Barnard. "Beside the waters of the Hudson" I feel my race. Among the thousand white persons, I am a dark rock surged upon, and overswept, but through it all, I remain myself. When covered by the waters, I am; and the ebb but reveals me again.

IV

[14]   At certain times I have no race, I am *me*. When I set my hat at a certain angle and saunter down Seventh Avenue, Harlem City, feeling as snooty as the lions in front of the Forty-Second Street Library, for instance. So far as my feelings are concerned, Peggy Hopkins Joyce on the Boule Mich with her gorgeous raiment, stately carriage, knees knocking together in a most aristocratic manner, has nothing on me. The cosmic Zora emerges. I belong to no race nor time. I am the eternal feminine with its string of beads.

¹⁵ I have no separate feeling about being an American citizen and colored. I am merely a fragment of the Great Soul that surges within the boundaries. My country, right or wrong.

¹⁶ Sometimes, I feel discriminated against, but it does not make me angry. It merely astonishes me. How *can* any deny themselves the pleasure of my company? It's beyond me.

¹⁷ But in the main, I feel like a brown bag of miscellany propped against a wall. Against a wall in company with other bags, white, red and yellow. Pour out the contents, and there is discovered a jumble of small things priceless and worthless. A first-water diamond, an empty spool, bits of broken glass, lengths of string, a key to a door long since crumbled away, a rusty knife-blade, old shoes saved for a road that never was and never will be, a nail bent under the weight of things too heavy for any nail, a dried flower or two still a little fragrant. In your hand is the brown bag. On the ground before you is the jumble it held—so much like the jumble in the bags, could they be emptied, that all might be dumped in a single heap and the bags refilled without altering the content of any greatly. A bit of colored glass more or less would not matter. Perhaps that is how the Great Stuffer of Bags filled them in the first place—who knows?

(1928)

1. Make Observations

The first thing we do in interpreting Hurston's essay is to record our observations about it. The following list provides a sampling of such observations.

- Hurston writes as an adult looking back on her childhood and adolescence as well as at her adult experiences.
- She describes her experience of living in two places—Eatonville and Jacksonville.
- She refers to the historical past, particularly to slavery and Reconstruction.
- She describes scenes that include white and black people together: welcoming visitors to Eatonville; the jazz club.
- She uses comparisons in describing how she thinks about herself:
    as a patient after an operation (7)
    as an actress on center stage (7)
    as a player in a game of "getting" (8)
    as a "dark rock surged upon and covered by waters" (13)
    as a stone statue of a lion (14)
    as a fragment of the Great Soul (15)
    as a brown bag of miscellany containing both priceless and worthless things (17).
- She divides the essay into four sections.
- She mentions changes and contrasting states of affairs:
    the day she "became colored" (2)
    her "sea change" (5)
    different responses to cabaret music (9)
    the priceless and worthless stuff she is made of (17).

- She chronicles her feelings:
    she does not always feel colored (12)
    she feels most colored against a white background (12)
    she sometimes feels astonished (16)
    she doesn't feel angry about her situation (16)
    she has no separate feeling about being American and colored (15)
    she feels discriminated against (somehow) (16).

2. Establish Connections

Once we have recorded these and similar observations—or as we do so—we begin making connections between them. The business of making connections is a very personal one. There is no one way of making an interpretation and no predictable conclusion which you must reach. Consequently, we present the interpretive process as a series of questions. The questions are meant to stimulate your thinking and to suggest that the connections you form are only part of the interpretive process.

- What is the relationship between the two scenes Hurston describes? How, for example, does she feel serving as an unofficial welcoming committee of one for Eatonville? How does she feel while listening to music in the cabaret? What, in each case, is her relationship to the white people she is with?
- What significant differences exist for her between Eatonville and Jacksonville? How do you account for her differences in feeling about the two places?
- What common features do her comparisons about herself suggest? How are these comparisons related to the feeling she describes elsewhere?
- What is the focus of each of the four parts of the essay, and how are the parts related?

3. Develop Inferences

On the basis of connections you form, you can make inferences. When we infer something, we reasonably conclude that something is the case based on evidence, on what we know. But be careful, for your inferences are not necessarily true. In the process of drawing inferences, we refer to our own experiences and to what we know about a writer and his or her subject, and we react emotionally as well as rationally. Furthermore, we might see connections between events that other readers do not. Let's say, for example, that we make the following inferences from the information we have.

- Hurston writes about her blackness without bitterness.
- Seeing benefits in being black, possibilities unavailable to whites, she seems to prefer her color.
- She seems proud of her race.
- She values herself, is confident in her abilities, and secure in her sense of selfhood.

- She sees herself as a performer, on center stage, with an opportunity to make a strong impression as a woman, as a black, and as an artist.
- She experiences pain in discovering that she was black ("I found it out . . . in my heart as well as in the mirror.")
- She possesses an irrepressible gaiety, refusing to be depressed about the fact that she is the granddaughter of slaves.
- She is patient, tolerant, and understanding.
- She sees white people as bearing the weight of the race problem in America.

4. Draw Conclusions

As we think about these and other inferences, we might develop a short interpretation or set of conclusions based on our inferences, such as this one:

> In "How It Feels to Be Colored Me," Zora Neale Hurston reveals a black woman's confidence in her color, her talent, and her femininity. She sees the issue of color as intrinsically skin-deep and primarily a white problem, which need not result in tragic consequences for blacks. In the first part of the essay, Hurston indicates the significant change that took place in her self-perception when she moved from Eatonville to Jacksonville. She learned there what it meant to be "a little colored girl." In the second part she makes clear that although she felt the sting of discrimination, she doesn't wallow in self-pity, but instead looks hopefully to her opportunities as a human being and as an artist, seeing the world as her oyster. Part three reveals the differences she feels between herself and her white friend. It also includes her important revelation that she feels most black when she is with white people. In the fourth and final section, Hurston describes her paradoxical sense of being a small part of a complex and multifaceted cosmic whole, all the while retaining a distinctive and significant sense of selfhood. In exploring the implied question in Hurston's title (How does it feel to be Black?) Hurston provides an answer: that for her, at least, it feels fine.

If you write a still more elaborate interpretation of Hurston's essay, you would provide evidence in the form of textual detail to support your thinking. You would return to the observations and questions that led you to your interpretation. One way to do this is simply to explain in greater detail what Hurston accomplishes in each of her four sections. The first part, for example, concerns Hurston's growing perception of herself as "colored," while the second focuses on her optimism. You could devote one paragraph to each of these topics, exploring in more depth and detail your understanding of why these are important. You could then do the same for Hurston's third and fourth concerns: her sense of being different from white people, and her sense of individuality. Your expanded essay would have five paragraphs: an introductory paragraph, which appears above as our interpretation, and four additional paragraphs, each of which explains one aspect of Hurston's argument. Then you could decide whether or not you need to add a concluding paragraph.

Another way to expand on your opening paragraph would be to consider what you think of Hurston's ideas and argument. You might ask yourself, for example, whether Hurston's description is accurate or persuasive, or whether it reflects the views of contemporary blacks generally. You might also consider whether Hurston convinces you that her experience illustrates any truths about racial prejudice or about the resilience and resources of human character. You need to decide whether you believe Hurston, and then whether you agree with her—and why.

THREE STUDENT ESSAYS

The following essays analyze the writing of Maxine Hong Kingston, E. B. White, and Virginia Woolf. In the first essay, Suyin So analyzes Kingston's "No Name Woman," the opening segment of her book *The Woman Warrior*. One of the notable features of Ms. So's analysis is the way she begins—with personal experience, which she then relates to a central concern of Kingston's piece.

In the second essay, Betsy Gates analyzes one of White's most famous and popular essays, "Once More to the Lake." Her focus is on White's response to time and change. In the last essay included here Ruth Chung analyzes Virginia Woolf's sketch "Old Mrs. Grey," largely by focusing on its imagery. Toward the end of her essay, Ms. Chung makes a judgment about what Woolf implies about the title character, Old Mrs. Grey, and about humanity's responsibility for her.

Suyin So

On Kingston's "No Name Woman"

In fifth grade, the object of my affections reacted with scornful laughter when informed of my romantic interests in him. Mortified, I ran home to what I considered my source of comfort and advice, my mother. She too was mortified, but more out of rage than sympathy. Her "advice" was a command. She told me, "You're only ten. Don't like anyone." I protested, asking her how I could just "not like anyone." Her wrath grew exponentially, and I realized I was touching on an exceedingly hot subject. The question lingers with me, though. I wonder that a woman could expect a human being to put a cap on her affection, to tell themselves "No, don't like anyone."

This Victorian attitude toward male-female relations is detectable in Maxine Hong Kingston's "No Name Woman," where we are presented with the image of her long-dead, long-forgotten aunt, who throws herself and her illegitimate child into a well the same night her entire village raids their home to terrorize her family. Kingston also introduces us to her Chinese family, who buries the aunt deep in an unmarked grave and even deeper in their memory, denying she ever existed. Kingston herself is included in the introductions, as a girl, watching her father count his remaining change after she and her siblings are indulged in the extravagance of a single carnival ride. This tapestry of life, so heavily dyed with the color of the Chinese heritage and culture, is woven with many threads, each an entire tale in itself. Yet the primary image is that of the cheating aunt, the adulterer, whose story is artfully recounted by her niece, Kingston.

In this sole character of the aunt, too, there are countless facets, many of them products of Kingston's imagination and curiosity. She wonders what this formerly unknown aunt was like, what clothes she wore. Yet she is refused any answers to her questions, for, as her mother tells her, "She has never been born." Her father has no sisters, only brothers. There was never a bastard child in the family, only the legitimate products of safe, regulated, dowried, planned marriages. This denial, however, does not stop Kingston from thinking about this woman, from hazarding guesses about her nature and her ordeal. The aunt, then becomes the central point of the story, the focus of Kingston's account.

The first part of the essay is the aunt's tale as told by Kingston's mother. In a typically Chinese fashion, the mother coldly, almost scientifically, recounts the discovery of her husband's sister, the demented attack of the village on their child, "plugging up the well." The mother ends the story with a warning: "what happened to her could happen to you. Don't humiliate us." No sympathy is shown for the woman; but to them she was evil defined, a harlot who caused the honor of her family to be tainted, her family harassed and humiliated.

Kingston, her curiosity piqued, is both awed and impressed by her aunt. She wonders about her aunt, painting her in various lights. At one point, she is the victim of rape, forced to have sex with some man, for "women in the old China did not choose." At another, she is portrayed as a woman in control of herself, making herself pretty so as to lure a lover. There is a similarity between Kingston's musings and her mother's account of the story in that Kingston rather imitates her mother's concise manner of speaking. She allows no romantic conjecture to enter her thoughts. There is no mention of unrequited love or lustful fantasies. She prefers only to theorize on the nature of her aunt, the circumstances surrounding the situation. She does, however, allow a small amount of romanticization into her descriptions of the woman, placing her in a most feminine light, examining her face for sunspots, in the market hoping for a second glance from the man. It is also of value to note that Kingston rejects her earlier image of her aunt as a rape victim in favor of a less helpless, stronger idea of the woman as one making her own decisions. We see the aunt as a normal woman with normal wants and desires. Kingston uses this image of her aunt as the oppressed romantic to make clear her sympathy to her. It is, albeit, only a limited sympathy, but it is the most the aunt will receive.

Here more than anywhere, the essence of Kingston's piece emerges, in the way that mother and daughter treat the same subject. One, the product of no-nonsense Chinese tradition, uses the tale as a warning to her just-pubescent daughter. The daughter, still somewhat no-nonsense yet imbued with America's culture, dreamily wonders what her aunt was like, how she wore her hair. The "culture shock" of the first generation, the clash between old and new, tradition and change is exemplified here, as Kingston and her mother are at ideological odds about the treatment of this subject.

"Chinese-Americans, . . . how do you separate what is peculiar to childhood, to poverty, insanities, one family, your mother who marked your growing with stories, from what is Chinese?" Kingston demands an answer to her question, one asked out of confusion and bewilderment. She echoes a generation of children of immigrants, one that wonders aloud the same question. She is unable to answer herself directly. Yet in her own work, she draws lines that define what is Chinese and what is not. To her mother, who emphatically states, "She could not have been pregnant, you see, because her husband had been gone for years," adultery is distinctly *not Chinese.* To the women of the village, who looked like "great sea snails," paying too much attention to your looks was distinctly *not Chinese.* Sex, as the author maintains, was distinctly *not Chinese.*

At the heart of the essay, underneath the tale of the unfortunate aunt, is the answer to her question, an exploration of Chinese culture. Kingston mixes story with explanation, interspersing her aunt's tale with broader details about the Chinese. It is subtle but effective in educating the reader about her culture. Rather than including an outright definition of all things Chinese, she illustrates certain aspects of the culture's characteristics. The almost practical sexism—the "waste" of having a daughter in starvation time, the bartering of a woman as an object only slightly more valuable than a rooster, the slavish obeisance expected from every woman—all this is inherent in understanding Kingston. Without this foregone conclusion, one cannot comprehend the drastic double standard placed upon women, where men were allowed to wander off and abandon their traditions and women were expected to uphold them. One cannot comprehend how an entire village could destroy a home, slaughter livestock, torture the woman and her family until she kills herself, yet not even attempt to seek and punish the man who certainly played his role in the drama.

Also paramount to understanding this essay is the extreme Victorian attitude so pervasive in the Chinese. Like my mother, who expected me to control my immature affections as though emotion were an on/off switch, society in China expected women to live without passion or desire. Sex was not a pleasure, but rather a duty, a responsibility to produce someone to take care of you in old age, to fold paper into houses and clothing after your death. To indulge in anything more than the absolutely vital was a sin, to indulge in something as volatile as sex was considered a double sin.

Yet even these seemingly despicable traits are born out of Necessity, something so important to Kingston's mother it is capitalized. If a girl baby is less worthy than a boy baby, it is only because the boy will work longer and harder, will carry on the family name and produce heirs. If sex is a vile activity, it is only because a population of such huge proportions is fragile, starvation all too frequent, and food too scarce for a couple to entertain hopes of a very large family. Necessity was omnipotent, truly the river that guided their lives as it did with Kingston's mother. I do not excuse boorish behavior, but I must find and explain the practical reasons for it.

Kingston's aunt, the no name woman, without identity or persona, was unfortunate in that she was discovered violating these traditions. She dared to step out from the safe, secure confines of society's rules, to venture out into the vague unknown. In doing so, she risked persecution from society, being shoved into non-existence forever, haunting her family as a ghost, not as a spirit. She serves as a reminder to young women of the terrible consequences of hasty decisions, as a tragic character in a compelling and dramatic tale and, finally, as an illustration that teaches reader and author alike what it truly means to be Chinese.

Betsy Gates
Essay #3
Expos-17
R. DiYanni

An Analysis of White's "Once More to the Lake"

In his essay "Once More to the Lake," E. B. White tells the
story of summer as he has known it. He went to a lake in Maine
as a boy each August and now, having a son of his own, he
compares his present experience there to his experiences in
the past. Seemingly unchanging, the lake appears a constant
place that shows no years and holds all life to be the same.
White believes that his visit to the lake will make him the
boy that he was. However, nothing can stop living things from
aging and eventually passing away. Time and change serve to
link White's life to his son's as well as to confirm his role
as the father in the chain of youth and old age.

Almost immediately, White shows the lake as a haven from the
"restlessness of the tides" in his adult life. Despite having
become a "salt-water man" since his boyhood summers, he once
again seeks the "placidity of a lake in the woods." In this
first section before White actually arrives at the lake, he
speculates about how it will be different from his past
vacations. He wonders how "time would have marred this unique,
this holy spot." He speaks of time as the enemy, remembering
how the lake was so pleasant, containing the stillness of a
cathedral. While preparing himself for the desolation, he
marvels at how strange it is that "you remember one thing, and
that suddenly reminds you of another."

Once he settles in with his boy at a camp and into the kind
of summertime he had known, White could tell "that it was
going to be pretty much the same as it had been before." He
describes hearing his boy quietly sneak out to the lake in
early morning as he once did. The sensation that his boy was
he and he was his father persists. White seems to be confused
in his role with his son. The memories and his present actions
are alike and thus reverse his place in his own mind. He would
say something and suddenly it would be not he but his father
who was saying the words or making the gesture. It gave White
"a creepy sensation."

The lake represents youth and leads White to the conclusion
that "there had been no years." The arrival of a dragonfly at
his end of the fishing rod convinces him that "everything was
as it always had been." The small waves were the same, the

boat was the same boat, and under the floorboards were the same fresh-water leavings and debris. Watching his dragonfly, "there had been no years between the ducking of this dragonfly and the other one," the one that was part of his memory. He looked at the boy, who was silently watching his fly, and it was White's hands that held the boy's rod, White's eyes watching. This scenario further convinces White and the reader that the lake keeps everything the same. So far, the descriptions of White's feeling that he is his son keeps the reader content. Like White, one finds it encouraging that a place such as the lake can be found as a respite from change and time.

Nothing can change the lake. They caught two bass and killed them swiftly. Later, as they returned for a swim, the lake was exactly as they had left it. It "seemed an utterly enchanted sea, this lake you could leave to its own devices for a few hours and come back to, and find that it had not stirred, this constant and trustworthy body of water." The stillness of the lake is something for White to hold on to, and to prove to himself that there "had been no years." White wants to believe that he can leave the lake again and upon his return he will be the same. The lake makes him the same by haunting him with the memories of the past.

White, however, is fooling himself. Things change, like the middle path that he describes as having "the marks of the hooves, and the splotches of dried, flaky manure." That path is gone, and an old way of doing things with it. Although White mentions these changes nonchalantly because the lake still functions in the same way, the reader remembers that these changes signify something more. The waitresses are different in that they wash their hair, caring more about appearance in a visual world. Values are changing, but this seems insignificant compared to the fact that the same diner is still standing and its waitresses, though different, are still fifteen. The reader begins to feel sorry for White as he is still under the illusion that time has stopped at the lake. He is merely an aging father who continues to believe that he can experience youth once again.

White finally begins to show his unhappiness at some changes as he describes the arrival at the lake. The summers had "been infinitely precious and worth saving." The ritual of a big arrival, "a business in itself," was of great importance. "There had been jollity and peace and goodness." "Arrival was less exciting nowadays, when you sneaked up in your car and parked it under a tree near the camp and took out the bags and in five minutes it was all over, no fuss, no loud wonderful fuss about trunks."

White's perception has changed dramatically. As a boy, the times did not need to be saved. They were the present. The most important thing was fun. Now, to White, the important things are "peace and goodness and jollity." Another thing that was wrong was the sound of outboard motors. It jarred, unlike the peaceful hum of the inboard motors he had used as a boy. The most disturbing fact about these motors was that his son enjoyed them. The change was not missed a bit on his part. The differences between White and his son are slowly creeping in.

White says that they "had a good week at the camp. The bass were biting well and the sun shone endlessly, day after day." However, this description has none of the zest that his childhood memories do. White talks about the sweet mornings lying in bed and the girls singing and the boys playing their mandolins. While the store is in the same place, there is a tar road and cars in front of it. Yet White still says that everywhere he went he had trouble making out which was him, the one walking by his side or the one walking in his pants.

In the last section of his essay, White describes a thunderstorm as it occurs at the lake. He describes it as a revival of an old melodrama that he had seen long ago with childish awe. "The whole thing was so familiar," and all of the stages of the storm were the same. However, his feelings were not. White lacks the enthusiasm that he had as a boy. As the calm sets in, he watches all of the children run out and cry with joy and relief at the prospect of going swimming in the rain.

White is reduced to a mere observer, and the realization that he is no longer the boy that he once was begins to present itself. White describes this feeling as he languidly watches his son, who says he's going swimming without any thought of going in himself. He saw "his hard little body, skinny and bare, . . . wince slightly as he pulled up around his vitals the small, soggy, icy garment." Suddenly, his own groin felt the chill of death.

The ending is effective as it sums up the point that the essay leans toward. Nothing can stop time: everything must change. White's reaction to the thunderstorm brings to mind the title of the essay. "Once More to the Lake" suggests a finality that this "chill of death" has a strong connection to. Where is White's father during this visit with his son? Inevitably, he has passed away. It seemed as if White had found the cure for middle age, but the lake only served to remind him what had once been. White has finally realized that his fate is to be the same as his father's. He cannot change the reality of life and death.

Ruth Chung

Woolf's Old Mrs. Grey

In her essay "Old Mrs. Grey," Virginia Woolf paints a picture of a ninety-two-year old woman whose supreme desire is to die. There is no action or movement in this portrait; Mrs. Grey merely sits alone in a corner of her house. Woolf's page-long description of her not only depicts the sufferings of a single individual but of the old and the grey in general. And yet it is clear that the purpose of this piece is more than the extraction of sympathy. Woolf's purpose is to express her view that a life of such suffering is not worth living. She asserts that the physical and mental agonies of old age should not be prolonged on humanitarian grounds.

Throughout the essay, Woolf uses Mrs. Grey's house and the landscape outside to metaphorically describe her mental state. Woolf's description of the house and the rolling fields and hills seems to be just another picturesque view of England's countryside. From the context of Mrs. Grey's pain and her desire to die, however, the house, with its door wide open, may represent her body on the verge of death. The metaphor may run still deeper, describing her mind, open and ready to be enveloped and swallowed by death's rays. It also follows that the image of the fields and hills, described as places of "stainless and boundless rest; space unlimited; untrodden grass; wild birds flying" comes to represent the pure, unblemished paradise, the haven from pain for which Mrs. Grey yearns. It could also simply be a representation of death, a state of being (or of not being) that everyone must eventually face, a time when "even the busiest, most contented suddenly let fall what they hold."

Woolf further describes Mrs. Grey's longing for death using light as a symbol to enhance her metaphor. Through the seven foot by four opening of Mrs. Grey's front door, sunshine pours in from outside, putting "embarrassing pressure" on the fire burning in the grate, which appears only as "a small spot of dusty light feebly trying to escape. . . ." Here, the fire burning in the grate may represent the appeals and delights of life, which have become dreary to Mrs. Grey when compared to the lure of the after-life, the sweet respite of death, as represented by the streaming sunshine from outside. Mrs. Grey is so enamored by the prospect of going to such a paradise of rest and relief, that living for the present becomes pointless; it seems silly to do the week's wash "when

out there over the fields over the hills, there is no
washing; no pinning of clotheslines; mangling and ironing; no
work at all."

The idea of a new life dawning is also represented by
"morning spreading seven foot by four green and sunny," which
tries to infiltrate the house and beckons to Mrs. Grey through
the front door. Mrs. Grey welcomes this light as much as she
welcomes death, but the light has not yet been able to
permeate the whole house. She has put so much hope into this
state of rest, that "when the colour went out of the doorway,
she could not see the other page which is then lit up." This
"other page," represents Mrs. Grey's present chapter of life,
which has potential, even in her pain, to be enjoyable and
fulfilling. But Mrs. Grey can only see this life as she sees
the fire burning in the grate, which becomes dim in the light
of her suffering and pain. She is so weary of her life that
"her eyes had ceased to focus themselves . . . they could see
but without looking." It isn't that she is physically blind,
but that her pain is so great that it is all she can see. It
could also be that nothing in her present life seems to be
worth looking at because she cannot appreciate the little
pleasures of life: "She had never used her eyes on anything
minute and difficult; merely upon faces, and dishes and
fields."

However, it is not fair to take Mrs. Grey's suffering
lightly either, for she suffers excruciating pain. Woolf
compares her pain to a sadistic snake: "a zigzag of pain,
wriggling across the door, pain that twisted her legs as it
wriggled; jerked her body to and fro like a marionette." Woolf
also speaks of a sharp, cutting pain by describing Mrs. Grey's
body as being "wrapped around the pain as a damp sheet is
folded over a wire . . . spasmodically jerked by a cruel
invisible hand." The startling image of Mrs. Grey that these
comparisons create, of her body writhing, twisting like a live
wire shows the sufferings the elderly must endure and explains
Mrs. Grey's state of mind, her abnormal eagerness for death.

Woolf gives the reader further insight into Mrs. Grey's
mental state by taking us into her mind as well as allowing us
to hear what she has to say. She looks back to her active
childhood, her entrance into the adult world, and the time
spent with her eleven brothers and sisters. But these memories
can only bring her sorrow and loneliness when she compares
those times to the present. She is literally jerked back to
its reality by a convulsion: "The line jerked. She was thrown
forward in her chair." Her old body is sick and deteriorating
and all of her siblings have died; she has even survived her
husband and her children.

The tone of Mrs. Grey's voice as she mumbles is not bitter, for she has no energy in her weary body or soul to complain. Woolf's fragmented sentences also reflect Mrs. Grey's tiredness as though she doesn't have even enough energy to speak: " 'All dead. All dead . . . My brothers and sisters. And my husband gone. My daughter too. But I go on.' ". Her words also have an almost Mother Goose-rhyme quality to them: " 'I'm an ignorant old woman. I can't read or write and every morning when I crawls downstairs, I say I wish it were night. . . .' " This suggests a regression into a childish state, into senility, but the words are coherent, expressing her feelings of debilitation and inadequacy. While her words have no hint of bitterness in them they serve to evoke pity. Her daily supplications to God: "O let me pass" show how desperately she yearns to be relieved of her suffering. The thought of Mrs. Grey crawling downstairs and crawling into bed by herself every day is especially poignant and helps the reader to understand her fatigue and loneliness.

In the last paragraph, Woolf concludes by seeming to lay the blame for Mrs. Grey's suffering on humanity, again using metaphor. She asserts that it is the hand of humanity that jerks so cruelly on the wire of pain, that "puts out the eyes and the ears," that "pinions" the bodies of the elderly on those wires of pain by trying to keep them alive. They are like tortured birds, pinned to a barn door, like "a rook that still lives, even with a nail through it." Woolf suggests that we, humanity, are responsible for prolonging their sufferings by caring for them and by trying to ameliorate their lives "with a bottle of medicine, a cup of tea, a dying fire." In a way, it seems as if Woolf is not really blaming humanity for the sufferings of the elderly but merely reprimanding us for not being aware of them. Or perhaps she is merely voicing her own ambivalence about the issue of euthanasia. And yet her strong language in the last paragraph and in other parts of the essay accuses us of being the active perpetrators of a crime, a crime that we could not help. If Woolf's intention for this essay was, indeed, to lay the blame on us for Mrs. Grey's pain, it is an invalid and unfair indictment, for Woolf demands that we be selfish and inhumane in order to be humane, to help the elderly by turning our backs on them. Woolf does not realize that even we, who accept the suffering of our parents and grandparents, accept it for our own futures as well as an immutable fact of life.

QUESTIONS FOR WRITING ABOUT ESSAYS

In writing about the elements of essays, the following questions can help you focus your thinking and prepare yourself for writing analytical papers. Use the questions as a checklist to guide you to important aspects of any essay or extended work of nonfiction you read.

Voice and Tone

1. How would you characterize the voice of the essayist? Does the essayist speak in his or her own voice? To what extent does the essayist create imaginary voices in the piece?
2. What is the essayist's attitude toward his or her subject? What is the essayist's tone? What details of language—diction, syntax, imagery, rhythm—convey the writer's tone?

Style

3. Is the writer's style direct or indirect? Formal or informal? High or low? Familiar or detached? Easy or hard to read? Something in between each of these opposite pairs?
4. What is the effect of the writer's stylistic choices—of the degree of formality of the prose, of its directness or obliqueness?
5. What kinds of diction does the writer employ? What kinds of sentences does he or she write? How reliant upon image and metaphor is the essayist? With what effects?

Structure

6. How is the essay organized? Where are its introduction, body, and conclusion?
7. How are the parts of the essay related? To what extent does the writer make use of comparison and contrast? Of classification and causal analysis?
8. How do the individual paragraphs of the essay follow from and relate to one another?

Thought

9. What is the essayist's central idea? Where is that idea most evident? Is the idea directly implied or directly stated?
10. What kinds of evidence does the essayist use to support the central idea? Are you persuaded by the arguments? Why or why not?

Critical Perspectives

11. Which of the critical perspectives seems most useful in analyzing and interpreting the essay? Why?
12. To what extent does the essay confirm or contradict your personal beliefs and values? To what extent do your beliefs and values affect your interpretation and evaluation of the essay?

CHAPTER THIRTY-FOUR

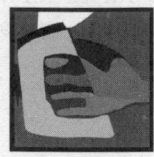

Two Essayists in Context

READING E. B. WHITE AND MAXINE HONG KINGSTON IN DEPTH

Reading the essays of E. B. White in the context of other essays is a somewhat different experience from reading the nonfiction of Maxine Hong Kingston. This is due not only to the writers' different backgrounds and generations, White as an east coast born and bred white male who came into adulthood between the First and Second World Wars, Kingston as a Chinese-American west coast woman who grew up in California in the 1950s and 1960s. It is also due in part to the fact that Kingston's work mixes fact and fiction in a unique blend of quasi-autobiographical writing. It also derives from the fact that the Kingston essays included in this chapter form parts of two books that possess an artistic unity and integrity. White's essays, on the other hand, were written at different times, in different places, for different audiences of readers, reflected in their varied places of original publication. The essays gathered here, thus, were originally published as just that—as essays rather than as parts of a larger artistic whole.

These contextual differences are accentuated by others. White's thematic interests differ dramatically from Kingston's. White writes about vacation trips to a New England lake, about visits to the circus, about raising geese—and about sailing, Model-T cars, the moon landing, and a widely ranging host of topics not reflected in the three selections included here. Kingston mines a more narrow vein, focusing almost exclusively on facets of her Chinese ancestry, dramatizing thereby ways her Chinese-American cultural context is at odds with the Chinese cultural context of previous generations.

White and Kingston offer readers additional contexts for reading their nonfiction. Both have also written fiction, though the most extensive and best known of White's fiction was written explicitly for children. Both have also written about writing. And both have attracted sufficient critical attention for there to be some disagreement about the nature and quality of their work—though this is more an issue for Kingston's prose than for White's.

It is one of the wonderful paradoxes of literary experience, however, that as much as the works of White and Kingston differ, both writers, in their highly individualistic particularity, nonetheless transcend their local selves in reflecting universal needs and concerns. One doesn't have to be a white eastern male to appreciate White's essays any more than one has to be a contemporary Asian-American woman to understand and value Kingston's prose. While reflecting the local particulars of their experience, White and Kingston speak to the broadest of human concerns—of living through time and change, of balancing conflicting cultural loyalties, of relating to the larger social and natural worlds of which we are all a part.

The essays and materials collected in this chapter provide a hint of this compelling unity and rich diversity.

QUESTIONS FOR IN-DEPTH READING

1. What general or overall thematic connections can you make between different works?
2. What stylistic similarities do you notice between and among different works?
3. How do the works differ in emphasis, tone, and style?
4. Once you have identified a writer's major preoccupations, place each work on a spectrum or a grid that represents the range of the writer's concerns.
5. What connections and disjunctions do you find between the following literary elements as they are embodied in different essays by the same writer?
   a. voice and tone
   b. language and style
   c. structure and organization
   d. theme and thought
6. To what extent are your responses to and perceptions of different works by the same writer shared by others—by critics, by classmates, and by the writers themselves?
7. What relationships and differences do you see between the work of one writer and that of another who shares similar thematic interests, stylistic proclivities, or cultural, religious, or social values?
8. Which of the critical perspectives (pages 1889–1926) seem most useful as analytical tools for approaching the body of work of particular writers?

INTRODUCTION TO E. B. WHITE

[1899–1985]

E.B. White is generally recognized as one of America's finest writers. Long associated with *The New Yorker,* for which he wrote stories, sketches, essays, and editorials, White also contributed to another prominent magazine, *Harper's,* writing a monthly column, "One Man's Meat," from 1938 to 1943. These columns were collected and published with a few additional pieces from *The New Yorker* as *One Man's Meat* (1944). This book was followed by two other collections of miscellany, *The Second Tree from the Corner* (1954) and *The Points of My Compass* (1962). Besides these collections, White published, over a slightly longer span of years, three children's books: *Stuart Little* (1945), *Charlotte's Web* (1952), and *The Trumpet of the Swan* (1970). In 1976, White published a selection of his best essays, those, as he says, which had "an odor of durability clinging to them." *The Essays of E. B. White* was followed a year later by a selection of White's letters, titled simply enough, *Letters of E. B. White. Poems and Sketches of E. B. White* appeared in 1981.

Although not a complete bibliography of White's published work, this list does suggest something of White's range and versatility, as well as something about the way writing has been for him steady work over a long stretch of time. And the steadiest of White's work, in both senses of the word, has been his essays. In fact, it is as an essayist that White is best known and most highly acclaimed. It is as an essayist that he identifies himself, defining an essayist as "a self-liberated man sustained by the childish belief that everything he thinks about, everything that happens to him, is of general interest." And again, as one who is "content with living a free life and enjoying the satisfactions of a somewhat undisciplined existence."

Edward Hoagland has noted that White's name has become almost synonymous with *essay.* And for good reason, since it is the form most congenial to his temperament, a form that allows him the latitude he needs to roam freely in thought, a form that he has been able to stamp with his own imprint. This imprint is reflected in the following elements: a scrupulous respect for his readers; an uncanny accuracy in the use of language; and an uncommon delight in common, everyday things. White sees the extraordinary in the ordinary, noticing and valuing what most of us either overlook or take for granted. And from his repeated and respectful acts of attention flow reminiscences, speculations, explorations, and questions about our common humanity, about our relationships with one another, with the past, with the worlds of technology and nature.

White is a writer whose insights derive directly from his literal observations, from what he sees. Thoreau, one of White's favorite writers—and one with whom White has much in common—once remarked that "you can't say more than you can see." White's writing bears this out. The relationship between sight and insight, between observation and speculation, is evident in essays such as "The Ring of Time," which begins with a description of a circus act and ends with speculations about time and change, and "Once More to the Lake," in which White reminisces about his boyhood summer holidays in Maine, both describing the place with startling vividness and offering unsettling speculations about the meaning of his memories. In these and other essays, White's writing is rooted in the crucial act of vision, a vision which sees into and beyond the surface of his subjects.

White's best writing, however, is more than a record of what he has seen and thought. It is also art, literature. His best work is crafted, shaped, formed with the same attention to details of structure, texture, image, and tone that poets or painters, sculptors or novelists give their work. In "The Ring of Time," "Once More to the Lake," and "The Geese," matters of fact, details of time, place, and circumstance give way to larger concerns. The circus is more than a circus ring: it becomes an emblem of time and change; the lake is more than a summer vacation place: it becomes an image of serenity and a reminder of time, change, even death; the old gander's plight becomes White's. The images of light and water, the symbolism of circus ring and lake, along with a concern for understanding the present in relation to the past and the future, the emblematic nature of the geese—these emphases lift their respective essays beyond the merely personal and reminiscent, beyond the ordinary and the everyday into the extraordinary universality of art.

About writing itself, White has said a good deal, and said it well. In the chapter he contributed to the now famous *Elements of Style,* White notes that when we speak of a writer's style we mean "the sound his words make on paper." The voice that we hear is what distinguishes one writer from another; and it is one good reason why, to get a good sense of a writer's style, we should read his or her work aloud. Beyond this concern for hearing what language can do, White notes that a writer's style "reveals something of his spirit, his habits, his capacities, his bias . . . it is the Self escaping into the open." And, as White suggests, this Self cannot be hidden, for a writer's style "reveals his identity as surely as would his fingerprints."

Recognizing that writing is hard work requiring endurance, thought, and revision ("revising is part of writing"), White advises that beginning writers let their ears be their guide, that they avoid all tricks and mannerisms, that they see writing as "one way to go about thinking," and, finally, that they achieve style both by affecting none and by believing "in the truth and worth of the scrawl."

Throughout his years as a writer, White has often been asked for advice about writing. To one seeker he wrote: "Remember that writing is translation, and the opus to be translated is yourself." On another occasion he responded to a seventeen-year-old girl this way:

> You asked me about writing—how I did it. There is no trick to
> it. If you like to write and want to write, you write, no matter
> where you are or what else you are doing or whether anyone pays
> any heed. . . . If you want to write about feelings, about the end
> of summer, about growing, write about it. A great deal of writ-
> ing is not "plotted"—most of my essays have no plot structure,
> they are a ramble in the woods, or a ramble in the basement of
> my mind.

There is a naturalness, an ease about White's writing, both in these offhand remarks from his letters and in his more elaborately plotted essays. It is an ease that derives in part from a refusal to be either pompous or pedantic; it is an ease that derives also from a consistent attempt to be honest, to achieve the candor he admires in Montaigne; and it is a naturalness that is reflected in his style, a style that mingles the high subject and the low, the big word and the small, without flamboyance or ostentation. White's style, in short, is a badge of his character—intelligent, honest, witty, exact, and fundamentally endearing.

WHITE ON WRITING

E. B. WHITE

The Essayist

The essayist is a self-liberated man, sustained by the childish belief that everything he thinks about, everything that happens to him, is of general interest. He is a fellow who thoroughly enjoys his work, just as people who take bird walks enjoy theirs. Each new excursion of the essayist, each new "attempt," differs from the last and takes him into new country. This delights him. Only a person who is congenitally self-centered has the effrontery and the stamina to write essays.

There are as many kinds of essays as there are human attitudes or poses, as many essay flavors as there are Howard Johnson ice creams. The essayist arises in the morning and, if he has work to do, selects his garb from an unusually extensive wardrobe: he can pull on any sort of shirt, be any sort of person, according to his mood or his subject matter—philosopher, scold, jester, raconteur, confidant, pundit, devil's advocate, enthusiast. I like the essay, have always liked it, and even as a child was at work, attempting to inflict my young thoughts and experiences on others by putting them on paper. I early broke into print in the pages of *St. Nicholas*. I tend still to fall back on the essay form (or lack of form) when an idea strikes me, but I am not fooled about the place of the essay in twentieth-century American letters—it stands a short distance down the line. The essayist, unlike the novelist, the poet, and the playwright, must be content in his self-imposed role of second-class citizen. A writer who has his sights trained on the Nobel Prize or other earthly triumphs had best write a novel, a poem, or a play, and leave the essayist to ramble about, content with living a free life and enjoying the satisfactions of a somewhat undisciplined existence. (Dr. Johnson called the essay "an irregular, undigested piece"; this happy practitioner has no wish to quarrel with the good doctor's characterization.)

There is one thing the essayist cannot do, though—he cannot indulge himself in deceit or in concealment, for he will be found out in no time. Desmond MacCarthy, in his introductory remarks to the 1928 E. P. Dutton & Company edition of Montaigne, observes that Montaigne "had the gift of natural candour. . . ." It is the basic ingredient. And even the essayist's escape from discipline is only a partial escape: the essay, although a relaxed form, imposes its own disciplines, raises its own problems, and these disciplines and problems soon become apparent and (we all hope) act as a deterrent to anyone wielding a pen merely because he entertains random thoughts or is in a happy or wandering mood.

I think some people find the essay the last resort of the egoist, a much too self-conscious and self-serving form for their taste; they feel that it is presumptuous of a writer to assume that his little excursions or his small observations will interest the reader. There is some justice in their complaint. I have always been aware that I am by nature self-absorbed and egotistical; to write of myself to the extent I have done indicates a too great attention to my own life, not enough to the lives of others. I have worn many shirts, and not all of them have been a good fit. But when I am discouraged or downcast I need only fling open the door of my closet, and there, hidden behind everything else, hangs the mantle of Michel de Montaigne, smelling slightly of camphor.

from Essays of E. B. White

CRITICS ON WHITE

KEN SMITH

On "The Ring of Time"

In this essay White describes a chance encounter at the circus. When he visited the winter training headquarters of the Ringling circus, in Sarasota, Florida, he and other paying spectators came upon a practice session of a young, bareback rider. In this session an enchanting incident took place, and in the first half of the essay White struggles to describe it. In drawing our attention to his struggle as a writer, White sympathizes with the bareback rider's own struggle for artistry. He argues that the richest moments of life, the grace notes of its daily melodies, are personal and elusive, and he sketches some of the ensuing concerns of the artist. He tries to show, by analogy at least, what (he believes) the rider's efforts must mean to her. But he also tries to evoke two very different senses of time, one that White argues is common to the young and one that he holds in his later years. The first of these White believes the bareback rider feels as she takes her practice ride, since she is "too young to know that time does not really move in a circle at all. . . . She is at that enviable moment in life when she believes that she can go once around the ring, make one complete circuit, and at the end be exactly the same age as at the start." In her bodily grace and ease White feels her confidence in time's enduring circuits.

This illusion is sustained by several things: the girl's youthfulness, her common sentiment of youthful immortality, the light generated by her own graceful and casual artistry, which creates the lovely circuit that time follows here; White's own artistry in recreating the circuit; and additionally, the fact that many human experiences are circular rather than linear, or at least they feel that way to us as we experience them in our bodies. As in "Once More to the Lake," the richness of physical experience as the seasons circle and move us through their displays is very seductive. This sense of time is made up of circuits that return each day and year, enveloping the body and teaching the mind what the body has known. But we commonly know time in another way as well, as a linear progression leading us into age. The first half of "The Ring of Time" evokes the charm of the first of these two senses of time and sustains it as long as possible, only to withdraw in the end and admit that the enchanting ride, the seemingly timeless event, has ended and the rider has left the arena. While the artist seeks to make something of her own artistry, to improve the golden moment, the present, and occasionally succeeds, time marches on relentlessly and sweeps away the youth's faith in the ring of time, the protected circle.

from Critical Essays on E. B. White, *Robert L. Rout, Jr., ed.*

EDWARD SAMPSON

On "Once More to the Lake"

Then, as the rhythm of the essay asserts itself, the blend again of past and present, and again White's sense of duality with his son. The unity, the circularity, of time is epitomized by the thunderstorm that comes up over the lake: the same rumbles, the same rain afterwards, the same swimmers in the rain, and the same jokes about getting wet, "linking the generations in a strong indestructible chain."

But at the end, beautifully worked out, the tone suddenly shifts. White's son, going in swimming during the rain, gets his dripping trunks from the line and puts them on: "I watched him, his hard little body, skinny and bare, saw him wince slightly as he pulled up around his vitals the small, soggy, icy garment. As he buckled the swollen belt suddenly my groin felt the chill of death." Age and death are present with frightening vividness, and time suddenly seems to reverse itself, for White is no longer young and in the past. Because the aura of death surrounds his son as well as himself, the generations are linked again, but in mortality, not in life.

We find in this essay much of the credo of E. B. White. Here is his simple love of nature; his nostalgia for the past, and along with that his inclination (never quite given in to) to reject the present (the tarred road, the outboard motors) in favor of the past; his preference for doing rather than thinking (the walking, the fishing, the boating); his feeling for the mystery outside the church, not inside it ("this holy spot," "cathedral stillness"); his vivid language, with his liking for the simple, natural figures of speech ("the boat would leap ahead, charging bullfashion at the dock"); his love for people, for his son, and his sense of identity with the young (which made him such a good writer, later on, of children's stories); and the everpresent sense of death that with White was sometimes whimsical—Thurber said, "He expects every day of his life that something will kill him: a bit of mold, a small bug, a piece of huckleberry pie" and sometimes intensely serious: his poem "The Cornfield" ends with these lines:

> And being present at the birth
> Of my child's wonderment at earth,
> I felt my own life stir again
> By the still graveyard of the grain.

Above all, we find here White's sense of reality, a sense so deceptively off-hand at times that many readers could be misled and think of White as a pale modern Thoreau who is revisiting Walden, echoing his master, and escaping from the world with a happy phrase or two.

from E. B. White

E. B. WHITE: ESSAYS

Once More to the Lake

One summer, along about 1904, my father rented a camp on a lake in Maine and took us all there for the month of August. We all got ringworm from some kittens and had to rub Pond's Extract on our arms and legs night and morning, and my father rolled over in a canoe with all his clothes on; but outside of that the vacation was a success and from then on none of us ever thought there was any place in the world like that lake in Maine. We returned summer after summer—always on August 1 for one month. I have since become a salt-water man, but sometimes in summer there are days when the restlessness of the tides and the fearful cold of the sea water and the incessant wind that blows across the afternoon and into the evening make me wish for the placidity of a lake in the woods. A few weeks ago this feeling got so strong I bought myself a couple of bass hooks and a spinner and returned to the lake where we used to go, for a week's fishing and to revisit old haunts.

I took along my son, who had never had any fresh water up his nose and who had seen lily pads only from train windows. On the journey over to the lake I began to wonder what it would be like. I wondered how time would have marred this unique, this holy spot—the coves and streams, the hills that the sun set behind, the camps and the paths behind the camps. I was sure that the tarred road would have found it out, and I wondered in what other ways it would be desolated. It is strange how much you can remember about places like that once you allow your mind to return into the grooves that lead back. You remember one thing, and that suddenly reminds you of another thing. I guess I remembered clearest of all the early mornings, when the lake was cool and motionless, remembered how the bedroom smelled of the lumber it was made of and of the wet woods whose scent entered through the screen. The partitions in the camp were thin and did not extend clear to the top of the rooms, and as I was always the first up I would dress softly so as not to wake the others, and sneak out into the sweet outdoors and start out in the canoe, keeping close along the shore in the long shadows of the pines. I remembered being very careful never to rub my paddle against the gunwale for fear of disturbing the stillness of the cathedral.

The lake had never been what you would call a wild lake. There were cottages sprinkled around the shores, and it was in farming country although the shores of the lake were quite heavily wooded. Some of the cottages were owned by nearby farmers, and you would live at the shore and eat your meals at the farmhouse. That's what our family did. But although it wasn't wild, it was a fairly large and undisturbed lake and there were places in it that, to a child at least, seemed infinitely remote and primeval.

I was right about the tar: it led to within half a mile of the shore. But when I got back there, with my boy, and we settled into a camp near a farmhouse and into the kind of summertime I had known, I could tell that it was going to be pretty much the same as it had been before—I knew it, lying in bed the first morning, smelling the bedroom and hearing the boy sneak quietly out and go off along the shore in a boat. I began to sustain the illusion that he was I, and therefore, by simple transposition, that I was my father. This sensation persisted, kept cropping up all the time we were there. It was not an entirely new feeling, but in this setting it grew much stronger. I seemed to be living a dual existence. I would be in the middle of some simple act, I would be picking up a bait box or laying down a table fork, or I would be saying something, and suddenly it would be not I but my father who was saying the words or making the gesture. It gave me a creepy sensation.

We went fishing the first morning. I felt the same damp moss covering the worms in the bait can, and saw the dragonfly alight on the the tip of my rod as it hovered a few inches from the surface of the water. It was the arrival of this fly that convinced me beyond any doubt that everything was as it always had been, that the years were a mirage and that there had been no years. The small waves were the same, chucking the rowboat under the chin as we fished at anchor, and the boat was the same boat, the same color green and the ribs broken in the same places, and under the floorboards the same fresh-water leavings and débris—the dead helgramite, the wisps of moss, the rusty discarded fishhook, the dried blood from yesterday's catch. We stared silently at the tips of our rods, at the dragonflies that came and went. I lowered the tip of mine into the water, tentatively, pensively dislodging the fly, which darted two feet away, poised, darted two feet back, and came to rest again a little farther up the rod. There had been no years between the ducking of this dragonfly and the other one—the one that was part of memory. I looked at the boy, who was silently watching his fly, and it was my hands that held his rod, my eyes watching. I felt dizzy and didn't know which rod I was at the end of.

We caught two bass, hauling them in briskly as though they were mackerel, pulling them over the side of the boat in a businesslike manner without any landing net, and stunning them with a blow on the back of the head. When we got back for a swim before lunch, the lake was exactly where we had left it, the same number of inches from the dock, and there was only the merest suggestion of a breeze. This seemed an utterly enchanted sea, this lake you could leave to its own devices for a few hours and come back to, and find that it had not stirred, this constant and trustworthy body of water. In the shallows, the dark, water-soaked sticks and twigs, smooth and old, were undulating in clusters on the bottom against the clean ribbed sand, and the track of the mussel was plain. A school of minnows swam by, each minnow with its small individual shadow, doubling the attendance, so clear and sharp in the sunlight. Some of the other campers were in swimming, along the shore, one of them with a cake of soap, and the water felt thin and clear and unsubstantial. Over the years there had been this person with the cake of soap, this cultist, and here he was. There had been no years.

Up to the farmhouse to dinner through the teeming, dusty field, the road under our sneakers was only a two-track road. The middle track was missing, the one with the marks of the hooves and the splotches of dried, flaky manure. There had always been three tracks to choose from in choosing which track to walk in; now the choice was narrowed down to two. For a moment I missed terribly the middle alternative. But the way led past the tennis court, and something about the way it lay there in the sun reassured me; the tape had loosened along the backline, the alleys were green with plantains and other weeds, and the net (installed in June and removed in September) sagged in the dry noon, and the whole place steamed with midday heat and hunger and emptiness. There was a choice of pie for dessert, and one was blueberry and one was apple, and the waitresses were the same country girls, there having been no passage of time, only the illusion of it as in a dropped curtain—the waitresses were still fifteen; their hair had been washed, that was the only difference—they had been to the movies and seen the pretty girls with the clean hair.

Summertime, oh, summertime, pattern of life indelible, the fadeproof lake, the woods unshatterable, the pasture with the sweetfern and the juniper forever and ever, summer without end; this was the background, and the life along the shore was the design, the cottagers with their innocent and tranquil design, their tiny docks with the flagpole and the American flag floating against the white clouds in the blue sky, the little paths over the roots of the trees leading from camp to camp and the paths leading back to the outhouses and the can of lime for sprinkling, and at the souvenir counters at the store the miniature birchbark canoes and the postcards that showed things looking a little better than they looked. This was the American family at play, escaping the city heat, wondering whether the newcomers in the camp at the head of the cove were "common" or "nice," wondering whether it was true that the people who drove up for Sunday dinner at the farmhouse were turned away because there wasn't enough chicken.

It seemed to me, as I kept remembering all this, that those times and those summers had been infinitely precious and worth saving. There had been jollity and peace and goodness. The arriving (at the beginning of August) had been so big a business in itself, at the railway station the farm wagon drawn up, the first smell of the pine-laden air, the first glimpse of the smiling farmer, and the great importance of the trunks and your father's enormous authority in such matters, and the feel of the wagon under you for the long ten-mile haul, and at the top of the last long hill catching the first view of the lake after eleven months of not seeing this cherished body of water. The shouts and cries of the other campers when they saw you, and the trunks to be unpacked, to give up their rich burden. (Arriving was less exciting nowadays, when you sneaked up in your car and parked it under a tree near the camp and took out the bags and in five minutes it was all over, no fuss, no loud wonderful fuss about trunks.)

Peace and goodness and jollity. The only thing that was wrong now, really, was the sound of the place, an unfamiliar nervous sound of the outboard motors. This was the note that jarred, the one thing that would sometimes break the illusion and set the years moving. In those other summertimes all motors were inboard; and when they were at a little distance, the noise they made was a sedative, an ingredient of summer sleep. They were one-cylinder and two-cylinder engines, and some were make-and-break and some were jump-spark, but they all made a sleepy sound across the lake. The one-lungers throbbed and fluttered, and the twin-cylinder ones purred and purred, and that was a quiet sound, too. But now the campers all had outboards. In the daytime, in the hot mornings, these motors made a petulant, irritable sound; at night, in the still evening when the afterglow lit the water, they whined about one's ears like mosquitoes. My boy loved our rented outboard, and his great desire was to achieve single-handed mastery over it, and authority, and he soon learned the trick of choking it a little (but not too much), and the adjustment of the needle valve. Watching him I would remember the things you could do with the old one-cylinder engine with the heavy flywheel, how you could have it eating out of your hand if you got really close to it spiritually. Motorboats in those days didn't have clutches, and you would make a landing by shutting off the motor at the proper time and coasting in with a dead rudder. But there was a way of reversing them, if you learned the trick, by cutting the switch and putting it on again exactly on the final dying revolution of the flywheel, so that it would kick back against compression and begin reversing. Approaching a dock in a strong following breeze, it was difficult to slow up sufficiently by the ordinary coasting method, and if a boy felt he had complete mastery over his motor, he was tempted to keep it running beyond its time and then reverse it a few feet from the dock. It took a cool nerve, because if you threw the switch a twentieth of a second too soon you would catch the flywheel when it still had speed enough to go up past center, and the boat would leap ahead, charging bull-fashion at the dock.

We had a good week at the camp. The bass were biting well and the sun shone endlessly, day after day. We would be tired at night and lie down in the accumulated heat of the little bedrooms after the long hot day and the breeze would stir almost imperceptibly outside and the smell of the swamp drift in through the rusty screens. Sleep would come easily and in the morning the red squirrel would be on the roof, tapping out his gay routine. I kept remembering everything, lying in bed in the mornings—the small steamboat that had a long rounded stern like the lip of a Ubangi, and how quietly she ran on the moonlight sails, when the older boys played their mandolins and the girls sang and we ate doughnuts dipped in sugar, and how sweet the music was on the water in the shining night, and what it had felt like to think about girls then. After breakfast we would go up to the store and the things were in the same place—the minnows in a bottle, the plugs and spinners disarranged and pawed over by the youngsters from the boys' camp, the Fig Newtons and the Beeman's gum. Outside, the road was tarred and cars stood in front of the store. Inside, all was just as it had always been, except there was more Coca-Cola and not so much Moxie and root beer and birch beer and sarsaparilla. We would walk out with the bottle of pop apiece and sometimes the pop would backfire up our noses and hurt. We explored the streams, quietly, where the turtles slid off the sunny logs and dug their way into the soft bottom; and we lay on the town wharf and fed worms to the tame bass. Everywhere we went I had trouble making out which was I, the one walking at my side, the one walking in my pants.

One afternoon while we were there at that lake a thunderstorm came up. It was like the revival of an old melodrama that I had seen long ago with childish awe. The second-act climax of the drama of the electrical disturbance over a lake in America had not changed in any important respect. This was the big scene, still the big scene. The whole thing was so familiar, the first feeling of oppression and heat and a general air around camp of not wanting to go very far away. In mid-afternoon (it was all the same) a curious darkening of the sky, and a lull in everything that had made life tick; and then the way the boats suddenly swung the other way at their moorings with the coming of a breeze out of the new quarter, and the premonitory rumble. Then the kettle drum, then the snare, then the bass drum and cymbals, then crackling light against the dark, and the gods grinning and licking their chops in the hills. Afterward the calm, the rain steadily rustling in the calm lake, the return of light and hope and spirits, and the campers running out in joy and relief to go swimming in the rain, their bright cries perpetuating the deathless joke about how they were getting simply drenched, and the children screaming with delight at the new sensation of bathing in the rain, and the joke about getting drenched linking the generations in a strong indestructible chain. And the comedian who waded in carrying an umbrella.

When the others went swimming, my son said he was going in, too. He pulled his dripping trunks from the line where they had hung all through the shower and wrung them out. Languidly, and with no thought of going in, I watched him, his hard little body, skinny and bare, saw him wince slightly as he pulled up around his vitals the small, soggy, icy garment. As he buckled the swollen belt, suddenly my groin felt the chill of death.

(1941)

The Geese

Allen Cove, July 9, 1971

To give a clear account of what took place in the barnyard early in the morning on that last Sunday in June, I will have to go back more than a year in time, but a year is nothing to me these days. Besides, I intend to be quick about it, and not dawdle.

I have had a pair of elderly gray geese—a goose and a gander—living on this place for a number of years, and they have been my friends. "Companions" would be a better word; geese are friends with no one, they badmouth everybody and everything. But they are companionable once you get used to their ingratitude and their false accusations. Early in the spring, a year ago, as soon as the ice went out of the pond, my goose started to lay. She laid three eggs in about a week's time and then died. I found her halfway down the lane that connects the barnyard with the pasture. There were no marks on her—she lay with wings partly outspread, and with her neck forward in the grass, pointing downhill. Geese are rarely sick, and I think this goose's time had come and she had simply died of old age. I had noticed that her step had slowed on her trips back from the pond to the barn where her nest was. I had never known her age, and so had nothing else to go on. We buried her in our private graveyard, and I felt sad at losing an acquaintance of such long standing—long standing and loud shouting.

Her legacy, of course, was the three eggs. I knew they were good eggs and did not like to pitch them out. It seemed to me that the least I could do for my departed companion was to see that the eggs she had left in my care were hatched. I checked my hen pen to find out whether we had a broody, but there was none. During the next few days, I scoured the neighborhood for a broody hen, with no success. Years ago, if you needed a broody hen, almost any barn or henhouse would yield one. But today broodiness is considered unacceptable in a hen; the modern hen is an egg-laying machine, and her natural tendency to sit on eggs in springtime has been bred out of her. Besides, not many people keep hens anymore—when they want a dozen eggs, they don't go to the barn, they go to the First National.

Days went by. My gander, the widower, lived a solitary life—nobody to swap gossip with, nobody to protect. He seemed dazed. The three eggs were not getting any younger, and I myself felt dazed—restless and unfulfilled. I had stored the eggs down cellar in the arch where it is cool, and every time I went down there for something they seemed silently to reproach me. My plight had become known around town, and one day a friend phoned and said he would lend me an incubator designed for hatching the eggs of waterfowl. I brought the thing home, cleaned it up, plugged it in, and sat down to read the directions. After studying them, I realized that if I were to tend eggs in that incubator, I would have to withdraw from the world for thirty days—give up everything, just as a broody goose does. Obsessed though I was with the notion of bringing life into three eggs, I wasn't quite prepared to pay the price.

Instead, I abandoned the idea of incubation and decided to settle the matter by acquiring three ready-made goslings, as a memorial to the goose and a gift for the lonely gander. I drove up the road about five miles and dropped in on Irving Closson. I knew Irving had geese; he has everything—even a sawmill. I found him shoeing a very old horse in the doorway of his barn, and I stood and watched for a while. Hens and geese wandered about the yard, and a turkey tom circled me, wings adroop, strutting. The horse, with one forefoot between the man's knees, seemed to have difficulty balancing himself on three legs but was quiet and sober, almost asleep. When I asked Irving if he planned to put shoes on the horse's hind feet, too, he said, "No, it's hard work for me, and he doesn't use those hind legs much anyway." Then I brought up the question of goslings, and he took me into the barn and showed me a sitting goose. He said he thought she was covering more than twenty eggs and should bring off her goslings in a couple of weeks and I could buy a few if I wanted. I said I would like three.

I took to calling at Irving's every few days—it is about the pleasantest place to visit anywhere around. At last, I was rewarded: I pulled into the driveway one morning and saw a goose surrounded by green goslings. She had been staked out like a cow. Irving had simply tied a piece of string to one leg and fastened the other end to a peg in the ground. She was a pretty goose—not as large as my old one had been, and with a more slender neck. She appeared to be a cross-bred bird, two-toned gray, with white markings—a sort of particolored goose. The goslings had the cheerful, bright, innocent look that all baby geese have. We scooped up three and tossed them into a box, and I paid Irving and carried them home.

My next concern was how to introduce these small creatures to their foster father, my old gander. I thought about this all the way home. I've had just enough experience with domesticated animals and birds to know that they are a bundle of eccentricities and crotchets, and I was not at all sure what sort of reception three strange youngsters would get from a gander who was full of sorrows and suspicions. (I once saw a gander, taken by surprise, seize a newly hatched gosling and hurl it the length of the barn floor.) I had an uneasy feeling that my three little charges might be dead within the hour, victims of a grief-crazed old fool. I decided to go slow. I fixed a makeshift pen for the goslings in the barn, arranged so that they would be separated from the gander but visible to him, and he would be visible to them. The old fellow, when he heard youthful voices, hustled right in to find out what was going on. He studied the scene in silence and with the greatest attention. I could not tell whether the look in his eye was one of malice or affection—a goose's eye is a small round enigma. After observing this introductory scene for a while, I left and went into the house.

Half an hour later, I heard a commotion in the barnyard: the gander was in full cry. I hustled out. The goslings, impatient with life indoors, had escaped from their hastily constructed enclosure in the barn and had joined their foster father in the barnyard. The cries I had heard were his screams of welcome—the old bird was delighted with the turn that events had taken. His period of mourning was over, he now had interesting and useful work to do, and he threw himself into the role of father with immense satisfaction and zeal, hissing at me with renewed malevolence, shepherding the three children here and there, and running interference against real and imaginary enemies. My fears were laid to rest. In the rush of emotion that seized him at finding himself the head of a family, his thoughts turned immediately to the pond, and I watched admiringly as he guided the goslings down the long, tortuous course through the weedy land and on down across the rough pasture between blueberry knolls and granite boulders. It was a sight to see him hold the heifers at bay so the procession could pass safely. Summer was upon us, the pond was alive again. I brought the three eggs up from the cellar and dispatched them to the town dump.

At first, I did not know the sex of my three goslings. But nothing on two legs grows any faster than a young goose, and by early fall it was obvious that I had drawn one male and two females. You tell the sex of a goose by its demeanor and its stance—the way it holds itself, its general approach to life. A gander carries his head high and affects a threatening attitude. Females go about with necks in a graceful arch and are less aggressive. My two young females looked like their mother, particolored. The young male was quite different. He feathered out white all over except for his wings, which were a very light, pearly gray. Afloat on the pond, he looked almost like a swan, with his tall, thin white neck and his cocked-up white tail—a real dandy, full of pompous thoughts and surly gestures.

Winter is a time of waiting, for man and goose. Last winter was a long wait, the pasture deep in drifts, the lane barricaded, the pond inaccessible and frozen. Life centered in the barn and the barnyard. When the time for mating came, conditions were unfavorable, and this was upsetting to the old gander. Geese like a body of water for their coupling; it doesn't have to be a large body of water—just any wet place in which a goose can become partly submerged. My old gander, studying the calendar, inflamed by passion, unable to get to the pond, showed signs of desperation. On several occasions, he tried to manage with a ten-quart pail of water that stood in the barnyard. He would chivvy one of his young foster daughters over to the pail, seize her by the nape, and hold her head under water while he made his attempt. It was never a success and usually ended up looking more like a comedy tumbling act than like coitus. One got the feeling during the water-pail routine that the gander had been consulting one of the modern sex manuals describing peculiar positions. Anyway, I noticed two things: the old fellow confined his attentions to one of the two young geese and let the other alone, and he never allowed his foster son to approach either of the girls—he was very strict about that, and the handsome young male lived all spring in a state of ostracism.

Eventually, the pond opened up, the happy band wended its way down across the melting snows, and the breeding season was officially opened. My pond is visible from the house, but it is at quite a distance. I am not a voyeur and do not spend my time watching the sex antics of geese or anything else. But I try to keep reasonably well posted on all the creatures around the place, and it was apparent that the young gander was not allowed by his foster father to enjoy the privileges of the pond and that the old gander's attentions continued to be directed to just one of the young geese. I shall call her Liz to make this tale easier to tell.

Both geese were soon laying. Liz made her nest in the barn cellar; her sister, Apathy, made hers in the tie-ups on the main floor of the barn. It was the end of April or the beginning of May. Still awfully cold—a reluctant spring.

Apathy laid three eggs, then quit. I marked them with a pencil and left them for the time being in the nest she had constructed. I made a mental note that they were infertile. Liz, unlike her sister, went right on laying, and became a laying fool. She dallied each morning at the pond with her foster father, and she laid and laid and laid, like a commercial hen. I dutifully marked the eggs as they arrived—1, 2, 3, and so on. When she had accumulated a clutch of fifteen, I decided she had all she could cover. From then on, I took to removing the oldest egg from the nest each time a new egg was deposited. I also removed Apathy's three eggs from *her* next, discarded them, and began substituting the purloined eggs from the barn cellar—the ones that rightfully belonged to Liz. Thus I gradually contrived to assemble a nest of fertile eggs for each bird, all of them laid by the fanatical Liz.

During the last week in May, Apathy, having produced only three eggs of her own but having acquired ten through the kind offices of her sister and me, became broody and began to sit. Liz, with a tally of twenty-five eggs, ten of them stolen, showed not the slightest desire to sit. Laying was her thing. She laid and laid, while the other goose sat and sat. The old gander, marveling at what he had wrought, showed a great deal of interest in both nests. The young gander was impressed but subdued. I continued to remove the early eggs from Liz's nest, holding her to a clutch of fifteen and discarding the extras. In late June, having produced forty-one eggs, ten of which were under Apathy, she at last sat down.

I had marked Apathy's hatching date on my desk calendar. On the night before the goslings were due to arrive, when I made my rounds before going to bed, I looked in on her. She hissed, as usual, and ran her neck out. When I shone my light at her, two tiny green heads were visible, thrusting their way through her feathers. The goslings were here—a few hours ahead of schedule. My heart leapt up. Outside, in the barnyard, both ganders stood vigil. They knew very well what was up: ganders take an enormous interest in family affairs and are deeply impressed by the miracle of the egg-that-becomes-goose. I shut the door against them and went to bed.

Next morning, Sunday, I rose early and went straight to the barn to see what the night had brought. Apathy was sitting quietly while five goslings teetered about on the slopes of the nest. One of them, as I watched, strayed from the others, and, not being able to find his way back, began sending out cries for help. They were the kind of distress signal any anxious father would instantly respond to. Suddenly, I heard sounds of a rumble outside in the barnyard where the ganders were—loud sounds of scuffling. I ran out. A fierce fight was in progress—it was no mere skirmish, it was the real thing. The young gander had grabbed the old one by the stern, his white head buried in feathers right where it would hurt the most, and was running him around the yard, punishing him at every turn—thrusting him on ahead and beating him unmercifully with his wings. It was an awesome sight, these two great male birds locked in combat, slugging it out—not for the favors of a female but for the dubious privilege of assuming the responsibilities of parenthood. The young male had suffered all spring the indignities of a restricted life at the pond; now he had turned, at last, against the old one, as though to get even. Round and round, over rocks and through weeds, they raced, struggling and tripping, the old one in full retreat and in apparent pain. It was a beautiful late-June morning, with fair-weather clouds and a light wind going, the grasses long in the orchard—the kind of morning that always carries for me overtones of summer sadness, I don't know why. Overhead, three swallows circled at low altitude, pursuing one white feather, the coveted trophy of nesting time. They were like three tiny fighter planes giving air support to the battle that raged below. For a moment, I thought of climbing the fence and trying to separate the combatants, but instead I just watched. The engagement was soon over. Plunging desperately down the lane, the old gander sank to the ground. The young one let go, turned, and walked back, screaming in triumph, to the door behind which his newly won family were waiting: a strange family indeed—the sister who was not even the mother of the babies, and the babies who were not even his own get.

When I was sure the fight was over, I climbed the fence and closed the barnyard gate, effectively separating victor from vanquished. The old gander had risen to his feet. He was in almost the same spot in the lane where his first wife had died mysteriously more than a year ago. I watched as he threaded his way slowly down the narrow path between clumps of thistles and daisies. His head was barely visible above the grasses, but his broken spirit was plain to any eye. When he reached the pasture bars, he hesitated, then painfully squatted and eased himself under the bottom bar and into the pasture, where he sat down on the cropped sward in the bright sun. I felt very deeply his sorrow and his defeat. As things go in the animal kingdom, he is about my age, and when he lowered himself to creep under the bar, I could feel in my own bones his pain at bending down so far. Two hours later, he was still sitting there, the sun by this time quite hot. I had seen his likes often enough on the benches of the treeless main street of a Florida city—spent old males, motionless in the glare of the day.

Toward the end of the morning, he walked back up the lane as far as the gate, and there he stood all afternoon, his head and orange bill looking like the head of a great snake. The goose and her goslings had emerged into the barnyard. Through the space between the boards of the gate, the old fellow watched the enchanting scene: the goslings taking their frequent drinks of water, climbing in and out of the shallow pan for their first swim, closely guarded by the handsome young gander, shepherded by the pretty young goose.

After supper, I went into the tie-ups and pulled the five remaining, unhatched eggs from the nest and thought about the five lifeless chicks inside the eggs—the unlucky ones, the ones that lacked what it takes to break out of an egg into the light of a fine June morning. I put the eggs in a basket and set the basket with some other miscellany consigned to the dump. I don't know anything sadder than a summer's day.

(1971)

INTRODUCTION TO MAXINE HONG KINGSTON

[b. 1940]

Although she had a novel published in 1989 *(Tripmaster Monkey: His Fake Book),* Maxine Hong Kingston is best known for her earlier mixed-genre works, *The Woman Warrior* (1976) and *China Men* (1980), winner of the American Book Award. Kingston has described the earlier work as the book of her mother since it is filled with stories her mother told her, stories about Chinese women, her Asian ancestors whom Kingston describes as the ghosts of her girlhood. *China Men,* by contrast, is her father book since it tells the stories of her male ancestors, including her father and grandfathers—though she learned these male stories too from women, especially from her mother. Both books are filled with stories. Both mix fact and fiction, autobiography and legend, combining in imaginative ways family history with fictional invention.

Kingston's books are, thus, difficult to classify. They refuse to sit still and accept the tidy categories we devise for prose narrative. The selections excerpted here from these two family chronicles reflect the curious and striking effects Kingston achieves throughout them with her blending of myth and legend with autobiography and family history. Moreover, in addition to their provocative combinations of fact and fiction, the two books possess another striking quality: their compelling voices. Kingston's narratives retell heard stories, stories told *by* her and stories told *to* her. Her stories derive from an oral tradition—the "talk story"—sustained largely by Chinese women. Kingston thus simultaneously inherits this oral narrative tradition and participates in it. Perhaps even more importantly, however, by inscribing her mother's stories and imagining her own variants of them, Kingston marks that tradition with her own distinctive imaginative imprint. In doing so, she demonstrates the power of these stories to enthrall readers outside the Chinese cultural tradition.

Maxine Hong Kingston was born and raised in Stockton, California, where her immigrant parents operated a laundry. She graduated from the University of California at Berkeley in 1962, and she has taught high school and college English, primarily in Hawaii, where she lived for seventeen years before moving to Oakland, California.

Kingston's autobiographical impulse appears strongly in "Silence," an excerpt from *The Woman Warrior.* In "Silence," we see Kingston begin to negotiate the struggle between the Chinese culture she inherited and the American culture she was born into. Her silence powerfully illustrates her uncertainty about how to invoke one cultural perspective without revoking or violating the other.

Kingston's versatility in letting the voices of others speak through her is powerfully manifested in "No Name Woman," the opening section of *The Woman Warrior*. As Esther Schor has pointed out in *Women's Voices*, the first voice we hear in "No Name Woman" is the voice of her mother, who "ironically . . . admonishes the daughter to silence even as she nourishes her with stories." Kingston's instincts as a writer are revealed not only in the stories she chooses to tell, but in the voices she creates to tell them. This is as true for the multiple voices we hear in "No Name Woman" as for the singularly different voices that sound in the other tales Kingston narrates in both books, including the brief parable, "On Discovery," which turns gender role and power inside out.

To some extent, Kingston is a woman's writer precisely because she gives public voice to what women had spoken only in private or what they had to keep silent. To some extent, she is also an ethnic writer, one who transmits stories of her Cantonese heritage. Her artistry and imaginative sympathy, however, transcend the limits of both gender and culture, as Kingston invents a world and constructs a self that appear both strange and familiar, at once "other" and recognizably our own.

KINGSTON ON WRITING

MAXINE HONG KINGSTON

Excerpts from "Imagined Life"

All right. To make your mother and your scandalous friends read about themselves and still like you, you have to be very cunning, very crafty. Don't commit yourself. Don't be pinned down. Give many versions of events. Tell the most flattering motives. Say: "Of course, it couldn't have been money that she was after." In *The Woman Warrior*, my mother-book, the No Name Woman might have been raped; she might have had a love affair; she might have been "a wild woman, and kept rollicking company. Imagining her free with sex . . ." Imagining many lives for her made me feel free. I have so much freedom in telling about her, I'm almost free even from writing itself, and therefore obeying my mother, who said, "Don't tell."

My father doesn't say, "Don't tell." He doesn't say much at all. The way to end the silence he gave me was to write this sentence: "I'll tell you what I suppose from your silences and few words, and you can tell me that I'm mistaken." You may use that sentence yourself if you like. Copy it down and see what comes next.

My father is answering me by writing poems and commentary in the margins of my books. The pirated translations have wide margins. Writing commentary is a traditional Chinese literary form. You can break reader's block by writing well.

Yes, the imagined life is so exhilarating that householders go in quest of new lands— the Gold Mountain and China. The Gold Mountain is a land of gold-cobbled streets, and it is also a country with no war and no taxes; it is governed by women. Most of us are here in America today because somebody in our families imagined the Gold Mountain vividly enough to come looking for it. I guess most people think they've found it, and "Gold Mountain" is synonymous with "United States of America." But we aren't peaceful; taxes are due the day after tomorrow; and women aren't in charge. You see how much work we have ahead of us—we still have that country to find, and we still have its stories to tell.

I haven't seen China yet. I didn't want to go there before finishing my two books because I was describing the place that we Americans imagine to be China. The mythic China has its own history, smells, flowers, one hundred birds, long-lived people, dialects, music. We can taste its sweetness when our grandmother sends us invisible candy. The place is so real that we talk about it in common, and we get mail from there. As real as the Brontës' childhood cities. As real as Dungeons and Dragons. If I had gotten on a plane and flown to the China that's over there, I might have lost the imagined land.

(1983)

CRITICS ON KINGSTON

ESTHER H. SCHOR

On Maxine Hong Kingston

The first voice we hear in Maxine Hong Kingston's *Woman Warrior* is her mother's: " 'You must not tell anyone,' my mother said, 'what I am about to tell you.' " Ironically, the mother admonishes her daughter to silence even as she nourishes her with stories of her Chinese forebears. This memorable opening signals both the complexity of Kingston's identity as a Chinese-American woman writer and the complexity of the writing itself, a stunning blend of autobiography, history, myth, folklore, and legend.

One cannot read very far in either of Kingston's books without confronting the difficulty of telling fact from fiction. In "No Name Woman," for example, she supposes that her pregnant aunt had been raped, then considers who the rapist might have been. Finally, she wonders "whether he masked himself when he joined the raid on her family." Similarly, in "The Father from China," in *China Men,* Kingston narrates five different versions of her father's entry into the United States. We cannot be sure whether he entered at New York or at San Francisco, as a stowaway or through immigration at Angel Island, illegally or legally. Instead of facts about her family, Kingston recreates for us the spell of the "talk-story," a Cantonese tradition kept alive mainly by women. (Even the stories told in *China Men,* Kingston claims, were told to her by women.) The story-talkers of Kingston's childhood tell stories in multiple versions, sometimes with graphic, startling details, sometimes in whispers. Like the powerful account of her aunt's pregnancy, childbirth, and suicide, the stories contain silences that compel the listener to venture imaginatively into the dangerous world of the story. Kingston's suppositions—"I wonder," "perhaps," "may have"—enable us to witness the writer taking up her voice among the story-talkers of her childhood. . . .

While Kingston has insisted that her two books were written "more or less simultaneously," *China Men* reveals several developments in Kingston's autobiographical art. First, Kingston intersperses brief, stark Chinese legends among lengthy narratives about her father, grandfather, great-grandfather, and brother. In "On Discovery" Kingston renders legendary material in an attenuated, suggestive, parabolic style. We sense an odd kinship between Kingston's impulse to concentrate a story and her impulse to vary a story. She is out to convince us that memorable stories owe as great a debt to the imagination and skill of the teller as they do to experience. "On Discovery" assaults the reader with the knowledge that beautiful women, like beautiful writing, arise by dint of pain and effort. In the extreme world of the parable, even a man can become a woman; Tang Ao, having submitted to the rigors of femininity, becomes disarmingly beautiful. But unlike texts, women suffer when they submit to rigorous standards that are not of their making. While "On Discovery" fantasizes a female revenge, it also probes the irony of using power to recapitulate one's own oppression.

from Women's Voices

KING-KOK CHEUNG

On *The Woman Warrior*

In *The Woman Warrior* we find it in the hushed disappointment attendant upon the birth of girls, in the expunging of the narrator's wayward aunt from family history, in the narrator's inability to speak a second language, in her choked-back anger at sexist maxims, in her impotent words against white bosses, and in her drawn-out illness incurred by self-hatred at being an inarticulate Chinese American. In *China Men* it extends beyond the exclusion of women to signify both the literal silencing of Chinese male laborers in Hawaii and the symbolic erasure of men of Chinese descent from mainstream American history . . . muffled. In fact, her works have all too often been read as factual testimony. As a result, the slippery and variable subject positions that underlie her polyphonic texts often escape the eyes of critics. Leslie W. Rabine and Stephen H. Sumida are notable exceptions. Rabine notes that *The Woman Warrior* is structured in a double and simultaneous movement, containing "the voice of a writer who in a certain sense has already returned to write about her people . . . but who writes as the girl who cannot return." Sumida suggests that Kingston's autobiography is perhaps "a work of 'fiction' in which the author uses a 'naive' if not 'unreliable' narrator . . . whose very misunderstandings or misappropriations . . . of 'Chinese' history and culture are part of the author's critical characterization of her and of a narrow 'American' society which alienates her from seeing truly." We shall see that there is more than one reason for what Sumida calls "misappropriations," and that the narrative strategies themselves contradict the narrator's explicit assertions. . . .

Asian American intellectuals have endlessly debated the "authenticity" of *The Woman Warrior*. Those who attack Kingston for blurring the line between reality and fantasy seem unmindful of the narrator's insistent admissions of her own penchant for fabrication and her inability to discern fact from fiction. Even those on the author's side tend to defend her autobiography on the ethnographic ground that the narrator's experience accords well with their own. Kingston, vexed by the anthropological approach to the book, protests: "After all, I am not writing history or sociology but a 'memoir' like Proust." Subtitled *Memoirs of a Girlhood among Ghosts*, *The Woman Warrior* is told mostly though not exclusively from the point of view of a confused female adolescent. I believe that the work, insofar as it can be construed as mimetic, mirrors not objective truth but the subjective experience of an imaginative girl growing up as a member of a racial minority amid conflicting imperatives.

from "Provocative Silence," in Articulate Silences

Feminism and History in "On Discovery"

The story of Tang Ao can be read from several feminist angles. As with Maxine's fantasy about Fa Mu Lan and the witch amazons, a first glance yields yet another instance of women's "counterinvestment," their strategy of reversing oppression by aping the oppressors. But the depiction of Tang Ao's excruciating pain—felt, I believe, by male and female readers alike—suggests not so much vindictiveness on the author's part as her attempt to foreground the asymmetrical construction of gender. Whereas Fa Mu Lan ventures into the male arena voluntarily, Tang Ao's crossover, as Donald C. Goellnicht observes, represents a "demotion": "no one, it seems, wants to fill the 'feminine' gender role." In making women the captors of Tang Ao and in inverting masculine and feminine roles, Kingston defamiliarizes patriarchal practices. Like the author of *Flowers in the Mirror*, Kingston contravenes the commonplace acceptance of Chinese women as sex objects by subjecting a man to the tortures suffered for centuries by Chinese women.

To read this fable in a feminist register alone is to obscure its significance as "metahistory." The story concludes as follows: "Some scholars say that that country [the Land of Women] was discovered during the reign of Empress Wu (A.D. 694–705), and some say earlier than that, A.D. 441, and it was in North America." Although others have speculated about a Chinese discovery of America around the fifth century, the association of the Land of Women with North America is to my knowledge purely Kingston's invention. Kingston's reference to invented sources—a ploy she shares with George Eliot, who provides many of the epigraphs that open the chapters of her later novels— is at once a parody of the patriarchal tradition of authorities and a form of self-authorization. In presenting obvious fiction as though it were history, Kingston lays bare the method she is to use throughout the book. She not only challenges the "historical" construction of China Men but presents alternative accounts as "counter-memory."

from "Provocative Silence," in Articulate Silences

MAXINE HONG KINGSTON: PROSE

No Name Woman

"You must not tell anyone," my mother said, "what I am about to tell you. In China your father had a sister who killed herself. She jumped into the family well. We say that your father has all brothers because it is as if she had never been born.

"In 1924 just a few days after our village celebrated seventeen hurry-up weddings— to make sure that every young man who went 'out on the road' would responsibly come home—your father and his brothers and your grandfather and his brothers and your aunt's new husband sailed for America, the Gold Mountain. It was your grandfather's last trip. Those lucky enough to get contracts waved good-bye from the decks. They fed and guarded the stowaways and helped them off in Cuba, New York, Bali, Hawaii. 'We'll meet in California next year,' they said. All of them sent money home.

"I remember looking at your aunt one day when she and I were dressing; I had not noticed before that she had such a protruding melon of a stomach. But I did not think, 'She's pregnant,' until she began to look like other pregnant women, her shirt pulling and the white tops of her black pants showing. She could not have been pregnant, you see, because her husband had been gone for years. No one said anything. We did not discuss it. In early summer she was ready to have the child, long after the time when it could have been possible.

"The village had also been counting. On the night the baby was to be born the villagers raided our house. Some were crying. Like a great saw, teeth strung with lights, files of people walked zigzag across our land, tearing the rice. Their lanterns doubled in the disturbed black water, which drained away through the broken bunds. As the villagers closed in, we could see that some of them, probably men and women we knew well, wore white masks. The people with long hair hung it over their faces. Women with short hair made it stand up on end. Some had tied white bands around their foreheads, arms, and legs.

"At first they threw mud and rocks at the house. Then they threw eggs and began slaughtering our stock. We could hear the animals scream their deaths—the roosters, the pigs, a last great roar from the ox. Familiar wild heads flared in our night windows; the villagers encircled us. Some of the faces stopped to peer at us, their eyes rushing like searchlights. The hands flattened against the panes, framed heads, and left red prints.

"The villagers broke in the front and the back doors at the same time, even though we had not locked the doors against them. Their knives dripped with the blood of our animals. They smeared blood on the doors and walls. One woman swung a chicken, whose throat she had slit, splattering blood in red arcs about her. We stood together in the middle of our house, in the family hall with the pictures and tables of the ancestors around us, and looked straight ahead.

"At that time the house had only two wings. When the men came back, we would build two more to enclose our courtyard and a third one to begin a second courtyard. The villagers pushed through both wings, even your grandparents' rooms, to find your aunt's, which was also mine until the men returned. From this room a new wing for one of the younger families would grow. They ripped up her clothes and shoes and broke her combs, grinding them underfoot. They tore her work from the loom. They scattered the cooking fire and rolled the new weaving in it. We could hear them in the kitchen breaking our bowls and banging the pots. They overturned the great waist-high earthenware jugs; duck eggs, pickled fruits, vegetables burst out and mixed in acrid torrents. The old woman from the next field swept a broom through the air and loosed the spirits-of-the-broom over our heads. 'Pig.' 'Ghost.' 'Pig,' they sobbed and scolded while they ruined our house.

"When they left, they took sugar and oranges to bless themselves. They cut pieces from the dead animals. Some of them took bowls that were not broken and clothes that were not torn. Afterward we swept up the rice and sewed it back up into sacks. But the smells from the spilled preserves lasted. Your aunt gave birth in the pigsty that night. The next morning when I went for the water, I found her and the baby plugging up the family well.

"Don't let your father know that I told you. He denies her. Now that you have started to menstruate, what happened to her could happen to you. Don't humiliate us. You wouldn't like to be forgotten as if you had never been born. The villagers are watchful."

Whenever she had to warn us about life, my mother told stories that ran like this one, a story to grow up on. She tested our strength to establish realities. Those in the emigrant generations who could not reassert brute survival died young and far from home. Those of us in the first American generations have had to figure out how the invisible world the emigrants built around our childhoods fits in solid America.

The emigrants confused the gods by diverting their curses, misleading them with crooked streets and false names. They must try to confuse their offspring as well, who, I suppose, threaten them in similar ways—always trying to get things straight, always trying to name the unspeakable. The Chinese I know hide their names; sojourners take new names when their lives change and guard their real names with silence.

Chinese-Americans, when you try to understand what things in you are Chinese, how do you separate what is peculiar to childhood, to poverty, insanities, one family, your mother who marked your growing with stories, from what is Chinese? What is Chinese tradition and what is the movies?

If I want to learn what clothes my aunt wore, whether flashy or ordinary, I would have to begin, "Remember Father's drowned-in-the-well sister?" I cannot ask that. My mother has told me once and for all the useful parts. She will add nothing unless powered by Necessity, a riverbank that guides her life. She plants vegetable gardens rather than lawns; she carries the odd-shaped tomatoes home from the fields and eats food left for the gods.

Whenever we did frivolous things, we used up energy; we flew high kites. We children came up off the ground over the melting cones our parents brought home from work and the American movie on New Year's Day—*Oh, You Beautiful Doll* with Betty Grable one year, and *She Wore a Yellow Ribbon* with John Wayne another year. After the one carnival ride each, we paid in guilt; our tired father counted his change on the dark walk home.

Adultery is extravagance. Could people who hatch their own chicks and eat the embryos and the heads for delicacies and boil the feet in vinegar for party food, leaving only the gravel, eating even the gizzard lining—could such people engender a prodigal aunt? To be a woman, to have a daughter in starvation time was a waste enough. My aunt could not have been the lone romantic who gave up everything for sex. Women in the old China did not choose. Some man had commanded her to lie with him and be his secret evil. I wonder whether he masked himself when he joined the raid on her family.

Perhaps she had encountered him in the fields or on the mountain where the daughters-in-law collected fuel. Or perhaps he first noticed her in the marketplace. He was not a stranger because the village housed no strangers. She had to have dealings with him other than sex. Perhaps he worked an adjoining field, or he sold her the cloth for the dress she sewed and wore. His demand must have surprised, then terrified her. She obeyed him; she always did as she was told.

When the family found a young man in the next village to be her husband, she had stood tractably beside the best rooster, his proxy, and promised before they met that she would be his forever. She was lucky that he was her age and she would be the first wife, an advantage secure now. The night she first saw him, he had sex with her. Then he left for America. She had almost forgotten what he looked like. When she tried to envision him, she only saw the black and white face in the group photograph the men had had taken before leaving.

The other man was not, after all, much different from her husband. They both gave orders: she followed. "If you tell your family, I'll beat you. I'll kill you. Be here again next week." No one talked sex, ever. And she might have separated the rapes from the rest of living if only she did not have to buy her oil from him or gather wood in the same forest. I want her fear to have lasted just as long as rape lasted so that the fear could have been contained. No drawn-out fear. But women at sex hazarded birth and hence lifetimes. The fear did not stop but permeated everywhere. She told the man, "I think I'm pregnant." He organized the raid against her.

On nights when my mother and father talked about their life back home, sometimes they mentioned an "outcast table" whose business they still seemed to be settling, their voices tight. In a commensal tradition, where food is precious, the powerful older people made wrongdoers eat alone. Instead of letting them start separate new lives like the Japanese, who could become samurais and geishas, the Chinese family, faces averted but eyes glowering sideways, hung on to the offenders and fed them leftovers. My aunt must have lived in the same house as my parents and eaten at an outcast table. My mother spoke about the raid as if she had seen it, when she and my aunt, a daughter-in-law to a different household, should not have been living together at all. Daughters-in-law lived with their husbands' parents, not their own; a synonym for marriage in Chinese is "taking a daughter-in-law." Her husband's parents could have sold her, mortgaged her, stoned her. But they had sent her back to her own mother and father, a mysterious act hinting at disgraces not told me. Perhaps they had thrown her out to deflect the avengers.

She was the only daughter; her four brothers went with her father, husband, and uncles "out on the road" and for some years became western men. When the goods were divided among the family, three of the brothers took land, and the youngest, my father, chose an education. After my grandparents gave their daughter away to her husband's family, they had dispensed all the adventure and all the property. They expected her alone to keep the traditional ways, which her brothers, now among the barbarians, could fumble without detection. The heavy, deep-rooted women were to maintain the past against the flood, safe for returning. But the rare urge west had fixed upon our family, and so my aunt crossed boundaries not delineated in space.

The work of preservation demands that the feelings playing about in one's guts not be turned into action. Just watch their passing like cherry blossoms. But perhaps my aunt, my forerunner, caught in a slow life, let dreams grow and fade and after some months or years went toward what persisted. Fear at the enormities of the forbidden kept her desires delicate, wire and bone. She looked at a man because she liked the way the hair was tucked behind his ears, or she liked the question-mark line of a long torso curving at the shoulder and straight at the hip. For warm eyes or a soft voice or a slow walk—that's all—a few hairs, a line, a brightness, a sound, a pace, she gave up family. She offered us up for a charm that vanished with tiredness, a pigtail that didn't toss when the wind died. Why, the wrong lighting could erase the dearest thing about him.

It could very well have been, however, that my aunt did not take subtle enjoyment of her friend, but, a wild woman, kept rollicking company. Imagining her free with sex doesn't fit, though. I don't know any women like that, or men either. Unless I see her life branching into mine, she gives me no ancestral help.

To sustain her being in love, she often worked at herself in the mirror, guessing at the colors and shapes that would interest him, changing them frequently in order to hit on the right combination. She wanted him to look back.

On a farm near the sea, a woman who tended her appearance reaped a reputation for eccentricity. All the married women blunt-cut their hair in flaps about their ears or pulled it back in tight buns. No nonsense. Neither style blew easily into heart-catching tangles. And at their weddings they displayed themselves in their long hair for the last time. "It brushed the backs of my knees," my mother tells me. "It was braided, and even so, it brushed the backs of my knees."

At the mirror my aunt combed individuality into her bob. A bun could have been contrived to escape into black streamers blowing in the wind or in quiet wisps about her face, but only the older women in our picture album wear buns. She brushed her hair back from her forehead, tucking the flaps behind her ears. She looped a piece of thread, knotted into a circle between her index fingers and thumbs, and ran the double strand across her forehead. When she closed her fingers as if she were making a pair of shadow geese bite, the string twisted together catching the little hairs. Then she pulled the thread away from her skin, ripping the hairs out neatly, her eyes watering from the needles of pain. Opening her fingers, she cleaned the thread, then rolled it along her hairline and the tops of her eyebrows. My mother did the same to me and my sisters and herself. I used to believe that the expression "caught by the short hairs" meant a captive held with a depilatory string. It especially hurt at the temples, but my mother said we were lucky we didn't have to have our feet bound when we were seven. Sisters used to sit on their beds and cry together, she said, as their mothers or their slave removed the bandages for a few minutes each night and let the blood gush back into their veins. I hope that the man my aunt loved appreciated a smooth brow, that he wasn't just a tits-and-ass man.

Once my aunt found a freckle on her chin, at a spot that the almanac said predestined her for unhappiness. She dug it out with a hot needle and washed her wound with peroxide.

More attention to her looks than these pullings of hairs and pickings at spots would have caused gossip among the villagers. They owned work clothes and good clothes, and they wore good clothes for feasting the new seasons. But since a woman combing her hair hexes beginnings, my aunt rarely found an occasion to look her best. Women looked like great sea snails—the corded wood, babies, and laundry they carried were the whorls on their backs. The Chinese did not admire a bent back; goddesses and warriors stood straight. Still there must have been a marvelous freeing of beauty when a worker laid down her burden and stretched and arched.

Such commonplace loveliness, however, was not enough for my aunt. She dreamed of a lover for the fifteen days of New Year's, the time for families to exchange visits, money, and food. She plied her secret comb. And sure enough she cursed the year, the family, the village, and herself.

Even as her hair lured her imminent lover, many other men looked at her. Uncles, cousins, nephews, brothers would have looked, too, had they been home between journeys. Perhaps they had already been restraining their curiosity, and they left, fearful that their glances, like a field of nesting birds, might be startled and caught. Poverty hurt, and that was their first reason for leaving. But another, final reason for leaving the crowded house was the never-said.

She may have been unusually beloved, the precious only daughter, spoiled and mirror gazing because of the affection the family lavished on her. When her husband left, they welcomed the chance to take her back from the in-laws; she could live like the little daughter for just a while longer. There are stories that my grandfather was different from other people, "crazy ever since the little Jap bayoneted him in the head." He used to put his naked penis on the dinner table, laughing. And one day he brought home a baby girl, wrapped up inside his brown western-style greatcoat. He had traded one of his sons, probably my father, the youngest, for her. My grandmother made him trade back. When he finally got a daughter of his own, he doted on her. They must have all loved her, except perhaps my father, the only brother who never went back to China, having once been traded for a girl.

Brothers and sisters, newly men and women, had to efface their sexual color and present plain miens. Disturbing hair and eyes, a smile like no other, threatened the ideal of five generations living under one roof. To focus blurs, people shouted face to face and yelled from room to room. The immigrants I know have loud voices, unmodulated to American tones even after years away from the village where they called their friendships out across the fields. I have not been able to stop my mother's screams in public libraries or over telephones. Walking erect (knees straight, toes pointed forward, not pigeon-toed, which is Chinese-feminine) and speaking in an inaudible voice, I have tried to turn myself American-feminine. Chinese communication was loud, public. Only sick people had to whisper. But at the dinner table, where the family members came nearest one another, no one could talk, not the outcasts nor any eaters. Every word that falls from the mouth is a coin lost. Silently they gave and accepted food with both hands. A preoccupied child who took his bowl with one hand got a sideways glare. A complete moment of total attention is due everyone alike. Children and lovers have no singularity here, but my aunt used a secret voice, a separate attentiveness.

She kept the man's name to herself throughout her labor and dying; she did not accuse him that he be punished with her. To save her inseminator's name she gave silent birth.

He may have been somebody in her own household, but intercourse with a man outside the family would have been no less abhorrent. All the village were kinsmen, and the titles shouted in loud country voices never let kinship be forgotten. Any man within visiting distance would have been neutralized as a lover—"brother," "younger brother," "older brother"—one hundred and fifteen relationship titles. Parents researched birth charts probably not so much to assure good fortune as to circumvent incest in a population that has but one hundred surnames. Everybody has eight million relatives. How useless then sexual mannerisms, how dangerous.

As if it came from an atavism deeper than fear, I used to add "brother" silently to boys' names. It hexed the boys, who would or would not ask me to dance, and made them less scary and as familiar and deserving of benevolence as girls.

But, of course, I hexed myself also—no dates. I should have stood up, both arms waving, and shouted out across libraries, "Hey, you! Love me back." I had no idea, though, how to make attraction selective, how to control its direction and magnitude. If I made myself American-pretty so that the five or six Chinese boys in the class fell in love with me, everyone else—the Caucasian, Negro, and Japanese boys—would too. Sisterliness, dignified and honorable, made much more sense.

Attraction eludes control so stubbornly that whole societies designed to organize relationships among people cannot keep order, not even when they bind people to one another from childhood and raise them together. Among the very poor and the wealthy, brothers married their adopted sisters, like doves. Our family allowed some romance, paying adult brides' prices and providing dowries so that their sons and daughters could marry strangers. Marriage promises to turn strangers into friendly relatives—a nation of siblings.

In the village structure, spirits shimmered among the live creatures, balanced and held in equilibrium by time and land. But one human being flaring up into violence could open up a black hole, a maelstrom that pulled in the sky. The frightened villagers, who depended on one another to maintain the real, went to my aunt to show her a personal, physical representation of the break she had made in the "roundness." Misallying couples snapped off the future, which was to be embodied in true offspring. The villagers punished her for acting as if she could have a private life, secret and apart from them.

If my aunt had betrayed the family at a time of large grain yields and peace, when many boys were born, and wings were being built on many houses, perhaps she might have escaped such severe punishment. But the men—hungry, greedy, tired of planting in dry soil—and had been forced to leave the village in order to send food-money home. There were ghost plagues, bandit plagues, wars with the Japanese, floods. My Chinese brother and sister had died of an unknown sickness. Adultery, perhaps only a mistake during good times, became a crime when the village needed food.

The round moon cakes and round doorways, the round tables of graduated size that fit one roundness inside another, round windows and rice bowls—these talismans had lost their power to warn this family of the law: a family must be whole, faithfully keeping the descent line by having sons to feed the old and the dead, who in turn look after the family. The villagers came to show my aunt and her lover-in-hiding a broken house. The villagers were speeding up the circling of events because she was too shortsighted to see that her infidelity had already harmed the village, that waves of consequences would return unpredictably, sometimes in disguise, as now, to hurt her. This roundness had to be made coin-sized so that she would see its circumference: punish her at the birth of her baby. Awaken her to the inexorable. People who refused fatalism because they could invent small resources insisted on culpability. Deny accidents and wrest fault from the stars.

After the villagers left, their lanterns now scattering in various directions toward home, the family broke their silence and cursed her. "Aiaa, we're going to die. Death is coming. Death is coming. Look what you've done. You've killed us. Ghost! Dead ghost! Ghost! You've never been born." She ran out into the fields, far enough from the house so that she could no longer hear their voices, and pressed herself against the earth, her own land no more. When she felt the birth coming, she thought that she had been hurt. Her body seized together. "They've hurt me too much," she thought. "This is gall, and it will kill me." With forehead and knees against the earth, her body convulsed and then relaxed. She turned on her back, lay on the ground. The black well of sky and stars went out and out and out forever; her body and her complexity seemed to disappear. She was one of the stars, a bright dot in blackness, without home, without a companion, in eternal cold and silence. An agoraphobia rose in her, speeding higher and higher, bigger and bigger; she would not be able to contain it; there would be no end to fear.

Flayed, unprotected against space, she felt pain return, focusing her body. This pain chilled her—a cold, steady kind of surface pain. Inside, spasmodically, the other pain, the pain of the child, heated her. For hours she lay on the ground, alternately body and space. Sometimes a vision of normal comfort obliterated reality: she saw the family in the evening gambling at the dinner table, the young people massaging their elders' backs. She saw them congratulating one another, high joy on the mornings the rice shoots came up. When these pictures burst, the stars drew yet further apart. Black space opened.

She got to her feet to fight better and remembered that old-fashioned women gave birth in their pigsties to fool the jealous, pain-dealing gods, who do not snatch piglets. Before the next spasms could stop her, she ran to the pigsty, each step a rushing out into emptiness. She climbed over the fence and knelt in the dirt. It was good to have a fence enclosing her, a tribal person alone.

Laboring, this woman who had carried her child as a foreign growth that sickened her every day, expelled it at last. She reached down to touch the hot, wet, moving mass, surely smaller than anything human, and could feel that it was human after all—fingers, toes, nails, nose. She pulled it up on to her belly, and it lay curled there, butt in the air, feet precisely tucked one under the other. She opened her loose shirt and buttoned the child inside. After resting, it squirmed and thrashed and she pushed it up to her breast. It turned its head this way and that until it found her nipple. There, it made little snuffling noises. She clenched her teeth at its preciousness, lovely as a young calf, a piglet, a little dog.

She may have gone to the pigsty as a last act of responsibility: she would protect this child as she had protected its father. It would look after her soul, leaving supplies on her grave. But how would this tiny child without family find her grave when there would be no marker for her anywhere, neither in the earth nor the family hall? No one would give her a family hall name. She had taken the child with her into the wastes. At its birth the two of them had felt the same raw pain of separation, a wound that only the family pressing tight could close. A child with no descent line would not soften her life but only trail after her, ghostlike, begging her to give it purpose. At dawn the villagers on their way to the fields would stand around the fence and look.

Full of milk, the little ghost slept. When it awoke, she hardened her breasts against the milk that crying loosens. Toward morning she picked up the baby and walked to the well.

Carrying the baby to the well shows loving. Otherwise abandon it. Turn its face into the mud. Mothers who love their children take them along. It was probably a girl; there is some hope of forgiveness for boys.

"Don't tell anyone you had an aunt. Your father does not want to hear her name. She has never been born." I have believed that sex was unspeakable and words so strong and fathers so frail that "aunt" would do my father mysterious harm. I have thought that my family, having settled among immigrants who had also been their neighbors in the ancestral land, needed to clean their name, and a wrong word would incite the kinspeople even here. But there is more to this silence: they want me to participate in her punishment. And I have.

In the twenty years since I heard this story I have not asked for details nor said my aunt's name; I do not know it. People who can comfort the dead can also chase after them to hurt them further—a reverse ancestor worship. The real punishment was not the raid swiftly inflicted by the villagers, but the family's deliberately forgetting her. Her betrayal so maddened them, they saw to it that she would suffer forever, even after death. Always hungry, always needing, she would have to beg food from other ghosts, snatch and steal it from those whose living descendants give them gifts. She would have to fight the ghosts massed at crossroads for the buns a few thoughtful citizens leave to decoy her away from village and home so that the ancestral spirits could feast unharassed. At peace, they could act like gods, not ghosts, their descent lines providing them with paper suits and dresses, spirit money, paper houses, paper automobiles, chicken, meat, and rice into eternity—essences delivered up in smoke and flames, steam and incense rising from each rice bowl. In an attempt to make the Chinese care for people outside the family, Chairman Mao encourages us now to give our paper replicas to the spirits of outstanding soldiers and workers, no matter whose ancestors they may be. My aunt remains forever hungry. Goods are not distributed evenly among the dead.

My aunt haunts me—her ghost drawn to me because now, after fifty years of neglect, I alone devote pages of paper to her, though not origamied into houses and clothes. I do not think she always means me well. I am telling on her, and she was a spite suicide, drowning herself in the drinking water. The Chinese are always very frightened of the drowned one, whose weeping ghost, wet hair hanging and skin bloated, waits silently by the water to pull down a substitute.

(1976)

Silence

When I went to kindergarten and had to speak English for the first time, I became silent. A dumbness—a shame—still cracks my voice in two, even when I want to say "hello" casually, or ask an easy question in front of the check-out counter, or ask directions of a bus driver. I stand frozen, or I hold up the line with the complete, grammatical sentence that comes squeaking out at impossible length. "What did you say?" says the cab driver, or "Speak up," so I have to perform again, only weaker the second time. A telephone call makes my throat bleed and takes up that day's courage. It spoils my day with self-disgust when I hear my broken voice come skittering out into the open. It makes people wince to hear it. I'm getting better, though. Recently I asked the postman for special-issue stamps; I've waited since childhood for postmen to give me some of their own accord. I am making progress, a little every day.

My silence was thickest—total—during the three years that I covered my school paintings with black paint. I painted layers of black over houses and flowers and suns, and when I drew on the blackboard, I put a layer of chalk on top. I was making a stage curtain, and it was the moment before the curtain parted or rose. The teachers called my parents to school, and I saw they had been saving my pictures, curling and cracking, all alike and black. The teachers pointed to the pictures and looked serious, talked seriously too, but my parents did not understand English. ("The parents and teachers of criminals were executed," said my father.) My parents took the pictures home. I spread them out (so black and full of possibilities) and pretended the curtains were swinging open, flying up, one after another, sunlight underneath, mighty operas.

During the first silent year I spoke to no one at school, did not ask before going to the lavatory, and flunked kindergarten. My sister also said nothing for three years, silent in the playground and silent at lunch. There were other quiet Chinese girls not of our family, but most of them got over it sooner than we did. I enjoyed the silence. At first it did not occur to me I was supposed to talk or to pass kindergarten. I talked at home and to one or two of the Chinese kids in class. I made motions and even made some jokes. I drank out of a toy saucer when the water spilled out of the cup, and everybody laughed, pointing at me, so I did it some more. I didn't know that Americans don't drink out of saucers.

I liked the Negro students (Black Ghosts) best because they laughed the loudest and talked to me as if I were a daring talker too. One of the Negro girls had her mother coil braids over her ears Shanghai-style like mine; we were Shanghai twins except that she was covered with black like my paintings. Two Negro kids enrolled in Chinese school, and the teachers gave them Chinese names. Some Negro kids walked me to school and home, protecting me from the Japanese kids, who hit me and chased me and stuck gum in my ears. The Japanese kids were noisy and tough. They appeared one day in kindergarten, released from concentration camp, which was a tic-tac-toe mark, like barbed wire, on the map.

It was when I found out I had to talk that school become a misery, that the silence became a misery. I did not speak and felt bad each time that I did not speak. I read aloud in first grade, though, and heard the barest whisper with little squeaks come out of my throat. "Louder," said the teacher, who scared the voice away again. The other Chinese girls did not talk either, so I knew the silence had to do with being a Chinese girl.

Reading out loud was easier than speaking because we did not have to make up what to say, but I stopped often, and the teacher would think I'd gone quiet again. I could not understand "I." The Chinese "I" has seven strokes, intricacies. How could the American "I," assuredly wearing a hat like the Chinese, have only three strokes, the middle so straight? Was it out of politeness that this writer left off the strokes the way a Chinese has to write her own name small and crooked? No, it was not politeness; "I" is a capital and "you" is lower-case. I stared at that middle line and waited so long for its black center to resolve into tight strokes and dots that I forgot to pronounce it. The other troublesome word was "here," no strong consonant to hang on to, and so flat, when "here" is two mountainous ideographs. The teacher, who had already told me every day how to read "I" and "here," put me in the low corner under the stairs again, where the noisy boys usually sat.

When my second grade class did a play, the whole class went to the auditorium except the Chinese girls. The teacher, lovely and Hawaiian, should have understood about us, but instead left us behind in the classroom. Our voices were too soft or nonexistent, and our parents never signed the permission slips anyway. They never signed anything unnecessary. We opened the door a crack and peeked out, but closed it again quickly. One of us (not me) won every spelling bee, though.

I remember telling the Hawaiian teacher, "We Chinese can't sing 'land where our fathers died.' " She argued with me about politics, while I meant because of curses. But how can I have that memory when I couldn't talk? My mother says that we, like the ghosts, have no memories.

After American school, we picked up our cigar boxes, in which we had arranged books, brushes, and an inkbox neatly, and went to Chinese school, from 5:00 to 7:30 P.M. There we chanted together, voices rising and falling, loud and soft, some boys shouting, everybody reading together, reciting together and not alone with one voice. When we had a memorization test, the teacher let each of us come to his desk and say the lesson to him privately, while the rest of the class practiced copying or tracing. Most of the teachers were men. The boys who were so well behaved in the American school played tricks on them and talked back to them. The girls were not mute. They screamed and yelled during recess, when there were no rules; they had fistfights. Nobody was afraid of children hurting themselves or of children hurting school property. The glass doors to the red and green balconies with the gold joy symbols were left wide open so that we could run out and climb the fire escapes. We played capture-the-flag in the auditorium, where Sun Yat-sen and Chiang Kai-shek's pictures hung at the back of the stage, the Chinese flag on their left and the American flag on their right. We climbed the teak ceremonial chairs and made flying leaps off the stage. One flag headquarters was behind the glass door and the other on stage right. Our feet drummed on the hollow stage. During recess the teachers locked themselves up in their office with the shelves of books, copybooks, inks from China. They drank tea and warmed their hands at a stove. There was no play supervision. At recess we had the school to ourselves, and also we could roam as far as we could go—downtown, Chinatown stores, home— as long as we returned before the bell rang.

At exactly 7:30 the teacher again picked up the brass bell that sat on his desk and swung it over our heads, while we charged down the stairs, our cheering magnified in the stairwell. Nobody had to line up.

Not all of the children who were silent at American school found voice at Chinese school. One new teacher said each of us had to get up and recite in front of the class, who was to listen. My sister and I had memorized the lesson perfectly. We said it to each other at home, one chanting, one listening. The teacher called on my sister to recite first. It was the first time a teacher had called on the second-born to go first. My sister was scared. She glanced at me and looked away; I looked down at my desk. I hoped that she could do it because if she could, then I would have to. She opened her mouth and a voice came out that wasn't a whisper, but it wasn't a proper voice either. I hoped that she would not cry, fear breaking up her voice like twigs underfoot. She sounded as if she were trying to sing through weeping and strangling. She did not pause or stop to end the embarrassment. She kept going until she said the last word, and then she sat down. When it was my turn, the same voice came out, a cripple animal running on broken legs. You could hear splinters in my voice, bones rubbing jagged against one another. I was loud, though. I was glad I didn't whisper.

How strange that the emigrant villagers are shouters, hollering face to face. My father asks, "Why is it I can hear Chinese from blocks away? Is it that I understand the language? Or is it they talk loud?" They turn the radio up full blast to hear the operas, which do not seem to hurt their ears. And they yell over the singers that wail over the drums, everybody talking at once, big arm gestures, spit flying. You can see the disgust on American faces looking at women like that. It isn't just the loudness. It is the way Chinese sounds, ching-chong ugly, to American ears, not beautiful like Japanese sayonara words with the consonants and vowels as regular as Italian. We make guttural peasant noise and have Ton Duc Thang names you can't remember. And the Chinese can't hear Americans at all; the language is too soft and western music unhearable. I've watched a Chinese audience laugh, visit, talk-story, and holler during a piano recital, as if the musician could not hear them. A Chinese-American, somebody's son, was playing Chopin, which has no punctuation, no cymbals, no gongs. Chinese piano music is five black keys. Normal Chinese women's voices are strong and bossy. We American-Chinese girls had to whisper to make ourselves American-feminine. Apparently we whispered even more softly than the Americans. Once a year the teachers referred my sister and me to speech therapy, but our voices would straighten out, unpredictably normal, for the therapists. Some of us gave up, shook our heads, and said nothing, not one word. Some of us could not even shake our heads. At times shaking my head no is more self-assertion than I can manage. Most of us eventually found some voice, however faltering. We invented an American-feminine speaking personality.

(1976)

On Discovery

Once upon a time, a man, named Tang Ao, looking for the Gold Mountain, crossed an ocean, and came upon the Land of Women. The women immediately captured him, not on guard against ladies. When they asked Tang Ao to come along, he followed; if he had had male companions, he would've winked over his shoulder.

"We have to prepare you to meet the queen," the women said. They locked him in a canopied apartment equipped with pots of makeup, mirrors, and a woman's clothes. "Let us help you off with your armor and boots," said the women. They slipped his coat off his shoulders, pulled it down his arms, and shackled his wrists behind him. The women who kneeled to take off his shoes chained his ankles together.

A door opened, and he expected to meet his match, but it was only two old women with sewing boxes in their hands. "The less you struggle, the less it'll hurt," one said, squinting a bright eye as she threaded her needle. Two captors sat on him while another held his head. He felt an old woman's dry fingers trace his ear; the long nail on her little finger scraped his neck. "What are you doing?" he asked. "Sewing your lips together," she joked, blackening needles in a candle flame. The ones who sat on him bounced with laughter. But the old woman did not sew his lips together. They pulled his earlobes taut and jabbed a needle through each of them. They had to poke and probe before puncturing the layers of skin correctly, the hole in the front of the lobe in line with the one in back, the layers of skin sliding about so. They worked the needle through—a last jerk for the needle's wide eye ("needle's nose" in Chinese). They strung his raw flesh with silk threads; he could feel the fibers.

The women who sat on him turned to direct their attention to his feet. They bent his toes so far backward that his arched foot cracked. The old ladies squeezed each foot and broke many tiny bones along the sides. They gathered his toes, toes over and under one another like a knot of ginger root. Tang Ao wept with pain. As they wound the bandages tight and tighter around his feet, the women sang footbinding songs to distract him: "Use aloe for binding feet and not for scholars."

During the months of a season, they fed him on women's food: the tea was thick with white chrysanthemums and stirred the cool female winds inside his body; chicken wings made his hair shine; vinegar soup improved his womb. They drew the loops of thread through the scabs that grew daily over the holes in his earlobes. One day they inserted gold hoops. Every night they unbound his feet, but his veins had shrunk, and the blood pumping through them hurt so much, he begged to have his feet rewrapped tight. They forced him to wash his used bandages, which were embroidered with flowers and smelled of rot and cheese. He hung the bandages up to dry, streamers that drooped and draped wall to wall. He felt embarrassed; the wrappings were like underwear, and they were his.

One day his attendants changed his gold hoops to jade studs and strapped his feet to shoes that curved like bridges. They plucked out each hair on his face, powdered him white, painted his eyebrows like a moth's wings, painted his cheeks and lips red. He served a meal at the queen's court. His hips swayed and his shoulders swiveled because of his shaped feet. "She's pretty, don't you agree?" the diners said, smacking their lips at his dainty feet as he bent to put dishes before them.

In the Women's Land there are no taxes and no wars. Some scholars say that that country was discovered during the reign of Empress Wu (A.D. 694–705), and some say earlier than that, A.D. 441, and it was in North America.

(1980)

CHAPTER THIRTY-FIVE

A Collection of Essays

There are as many kinds of essays as there are human attitudes or poses. . . . The essay, although a relaxed form, imposes its own disciplines, raises its own problems.

E. B. WHITE

The essay can do everything a poem can do, and everything a short story can do— everything but fake it. . . . There's nothing you cannot do with it; no subject matter is forbidden, no structure is proscribed. . . . The material is the world itself, which, so far, keeps on keeping on.

ANNIE DILLARD

MICHEL DE MONTAIGNE

[1533–1592]

Of smells

TRANSLATED BY DONALD FRAME

[A]It is said of some, as of Alexander the Great, that their sweat emitted a sweet odor, owing to some rare and extraordinary constitution of theirs, of which Plutarch and

*The superscript letters distinguish the three strata of the essay: A is for material published before 1588, B for writing in 1588, and C for material published after 1588

others seek the cause. But the common make-up of bodies is the opposite, and the best condition they may have is to be free of smell. The sweetness even of the purest breath has nothing more excellent about it than to be without any odor that offends us, as is that of very healthy children. That is why, says Plautus,

> A woman smells good when she does not smell.

The most perfect smell for a woman is to smell of nothing, [B]as they say that her actions smell best when they are imperceptible and mute. [A]And perfumes are rightly considered suspicious in those who use them, and thought to be used to cover up some natural defect in that quarter. Whence arise these nice sayings of the ancient poets: To smell good is to stink:

> You laugh at us because we do not smell.
> I'd rather smell of nothing than smell sweet.
>
> MARTIAL

And elsewhere:

> Men who smell always sweet, Posthumus, don't smell good.
>
> MARTIAL

[B]However, I like very much to be surrounded with good smells, and I hate bad ones beyond measure, and detect them from further off than anyone else:

> My scent will sooner be aware
> Where goat-smells, Polypus, in hairy arm-pits lurk,
> Than keen hounds scent a wild boar's lair.
>
> HORACE

[C]The simplest and most natural smells seem to me the most agreeable. And this concern chiefly affects the ladies. Amid the densest barbarism, the Scythian women, after washing, powder and plaster their whole body and face with a certain odoriferous drug that is native to their soil; and having removed this paint to approach the men, they find themselves both sleek and perfumed.

[B]Whatever the odor is, it is a marvel how it clings to me and how apt my skin is to imbibe it. He who complains of nature that she has left man without an instrument to convey smells to his nose is wrong, for they convey themselves. But in my particular case my mustache, which is thick, performs that service. If I bring my gloves or my handkerchief near it, the smell will stay there a whole day. It betrays the place I come from. The close kisses of youth, savory, greedy, and sticky, once used to adhere to it and stay there for several hours after. And yet, for all that, I find myself little subject to epidemics, which are caught by communication and bred by the contagion of the air; and I have escaped those of my time, of which there have been many sorts in our cities and our armies. [C]We read of Socrates that though he never left Athens during many recurrences of the plague which so many times tormented that city, he alone never found himself the worse for it.

^BThe doctors might, I believe, derive more use from odors than they do; for I have often noticed that they make a change in me and work upon my spirits according to their properties; which makes me approve of the idea that the use of incense and perfumes in churches, so ancient and widespread in all nations and religions, was intended to delight us and arouse and purify our senses to make us more fit for contemplation.

^CI should like, in order to judge of it, to have shared the art of those cooks who know how to add a seasoning of foreign odors to the savor of foods, as was particularly remarked in the service of the king of Tunis, who in our time landed at Naples to confer with the Emperor Charles. They stuffed his foods with aromatic substances, so sumptuously that one peacock and two pheasants came to a hundred ducats to dress them in that manner; and when they were carved, they filled not only the dining hall but all the rooms in his palace, and even the neighboring houses, with sweet fumes which did not vanish for some time.

^BThe principal care I take in my lodgings is to avoid heavy, stinking air. Those beautiful cities Venice and Paris weaken my fondness for them by the acrid smell of the marshes of the one and of the mud of the other.

(1580)

FRANCIS BACON
[1561–1626]

Of Love

The stage is more beholding to Love than the life of man. For as to the stage, love is ever matter of comedies, and now and then of tragedies, but in life it doth much mischief, sometimes like a syren, sometimes like a fury. You may observe that amongst all the great and worthy persons (whereof the memory remaineth, either ancient or recent) there is not one that hath been transported to the mad degree of love, which shows that great spirits and great business do keep out this weak passion. You must except nevertheless Marcus Antonius, the half partner of the empire of Rome, and Appius Claudius, the decemvir and lawgiver; whereof the former was indeed a voluptuous man, and inordinate, but the latter was an austere and wise man; and therefore it seems (though rarely) that love can find entrance not only into an open heart, but also into a heart well fortified, if watch be not well kept. It is a poor saying of Epicurus, *Satis magnum alter alteri theatrum sumus,*° as if man, made for the contemplation of heaven and all noble objects, should do nothing but kneel before a little idol, and make himself a subject, though not of the mouth (as beasts are), yet of the eye, which was given him for higher purposes. It is a strange thing to note the excess of this passion, and how it braves the nature and value of things, by this: that the speaking in a perpetual

Satis . . . sumus *Each of us is a great enough audience for the other.*

hyperbole is comely in nothing but in love. Neither is it merely in the phrase, for whereas it hath been well said that the arch–flatterer, with whom all the petty flatterers have intelligence, is a man's self, certainly the lover is more. For there was never proud man thought so absurdly well of himself as the lover doth of the person loved; and therefore it was well said, *That it is impossible to love and to be wise*. Neither doth this weakness appear to others only, and not to the party loved, but to the loved most of all, except the love be reciproque. For it is a true rule that love is ever rewarded either with the reciproque or with an inward and secret contempt. By how much the more men ought to beware of this passion, which loseth not only other things but itself. As for the other losses, the poet's relation doth well figure them: that he that preferred Helena quitted the gifts of Juno and Pallas.° For whosoever esteemeth too much of amorous affection quitteth both riches and wisdom. This passion hath his floods in the very times of weakness, which are great prosperity and great adversity, though this latter hath been less observed, both which times kindle love, and make it more fervent, and therefore show it to be the child of folly. They do best who, if they cannot but admit love, yet make it keep quarter and sever it wholly from their serious affairs and actions of life, for if it check once with business, it troubleth men's fortunes, and maketh men that they can no ways be true to their own ends. I know not how, but martial men are given to love; I think it is but as they are given to wine, for perils commonly ask to be paid in pleasures. There is in man's nature a secret inclination and motion towards love of others, which if it be not spent upon some one or a few, doth naturally spread itself towards many, and maketh men become humane and charitable, as it is seen sometime in friars. Nuptial love maketh mankind; friendly love perfecteth it; but wanton love corrupteth and embaseth it.

(1612)

JOHN DONNE

[1572–1631]

Meditation XVII: For Whom the Bell Tolls

Perchance he for whom this bell tolls may be so ill, as that he knows not it tolls for him; and perchance I may think myself so much better than I am, as that they who are about me, and see my state, may have caused it to toll for me, and I know not that. The church is Catholic, universal, so are all her actions; all that she does belongs to all. When she baptizes a child, that action concerns me; for that child is thereby connected to that body which is my head too, and ingrafted into that body whereof I am a mem-

---

Helena . . . Juno . . . Pallas   *The Greek goddesses Juno (war), Venus (love), and Pallas Athena (wisdom) asked Paris, prince of Troy, to decide which was most beautiful. Paris chose Venus. She rewarded him with Helen, the most beautiful woman in the world, whose abduction by Paris precipitated the Greek and Trojan war.*

ber. And when she buries a man, that action concerns me: all mankind is of one author, and is one volume; when one man dies, one chapter is not torn out of the book,
but translated into a better language; and every chapter must be so translated; God employs several translators; some pieces are translated by age, some by sickness, some by
war, some by justice; but God's hand is in every translation, and his hand shall bind up
all our scattered leaves again for that library where every book shall lie open to one another. As therefore the bell that rings to a sermon calls not upon the preacher only, but
upon the congregation to come, so this bell calls us all; but how much more me, who
am brought so near the door by this sickness. There was a contention as far as a suit
(in which both piety and dignity, religion and estimation, were mingled), which of the
religious orders should ring to prayers first in the morning; and it was determined, that
they should ring first that rose earliest. If we understand aright the dignity of this bell
that tolls for our evening prayer, we would be glad to make it ours by rising early, in
that application, that it might be ours as well as his, whose indeed it is. The bell doth
toll for him that thinks it doth; and though it intermit again, yet from that minute that
that occasion wrought upon him, he is united to God. Who casts not up his eye to the
sun when it rises? but who takes off his eye from a comet when that breaks out? Who
bends not his ear to any bell which upon any occasion rings? but who can remove it
from that bell which is passing a piece of himself out of this world? No man is an island, entire of itself; every man is a piece of the continent, a part of the main. If a clod
be washed away by the sea, Europe is the less, as well as if a promontory were, as well
as if a manor of thy friend's or of thine own were: any man's death diminishes me, because I am involved in mankind, and therefore never send to know for whom the bells
tolls; it tolls for thee. Neither can we call this a begging of misery, or a borrowing of
misery, as though we were not miserable enough of ourselves, but must fetch in more
from the next house, in taking upon us the misery of our neighbours. Truly it were
an excusable covetousness if we did, for affliction is a treasure, and scarce any man hath
enough of it. No man hath affliction enough that is not matured and ripened by it, and
made fit for God by that affliction. If a man carry treasure in bullion, or in a wedge of
gold, and have none coined into current money, his treasure will not defray him as he
travels. Tribulation is treasure in the nature of it, but it is not current money in the use
of it, except we get nearer and nearer our home, heaven, by it. Another man may be
sick too, and sick to death, and this affliction may lie in his bowels, as gold in a mine,
and be of no use to him; but this bell, that tells me of his affliction, digs out and applies that gold to me: if by this consideration of another's danger I take mine own into
contemplation, and so secure myself, by making my recourse to my God, who is our
only security.

(1624)

JONATHAN SWIFT

[1667–1745]

A Modest Proposal

FOR PREVENTING THE CHILDREN OF POOR PEOPLE
IN IRELAND FROM BEING A BURDEN TO THEIR
PARENTS OR COUNTRY, AND FOR MAKING THEM
BENEFICIAL TO THE PUBLIC

It is a melancholy object to those who walk through this great town or travel in the country, when they see the streets, the roads, and cabin doors crowded with beggars of the female sex, followed by three, four, or six children, all in rags and importuning every passenger for an alms. These mothers, instead of being able to work for their honest livelihood, are forced to employ all their time in strolling to beg sustenance for their helpless infants, who, as they grow up, either turn thieves for want of work, or leave their dear native country to fight for the Pretender in Spain, or sell themselves to the Barbadoes.

I think it is agreed by all parties that this prodigious number of children in the arms, or on the backs, or at the heels of their mothers, and frequently of their fathers, is in the present deplorable state of the kingdom a very great additional grievance; and therefore whoever could find out a fair, cheap, and easy method of making these children sound and useful members of the commonwealth would deserve so well of the public as to have his statue set up for a preserver of the nation.

But my intention is very far from being confined to provide only for the children of professed beggars; it is of a much greater extent, and shall take in the whole number of infants at a certain age who are born of parents in effect as little able to support them as those who demand our charity in the streets.

As to my own part, having turned my thoughts for many years upon this important subject, and maturely weighed the several schemes of other projectors, I have always found them grossly mistaken in their computation. It is true a child just dropped from its dam may be supported by her milk for a solar year with little other nourishment, at most not above the value of two shillings, which the mother may certainly get, or the value in scraps, by her lawful occupation of begging; and it is exactly at one year old that I propose to provide for them in such a manner as instead of being a charge upon their parents or the parish, or wanting food and raiment for the rest of their lives, they shall, on the contrary, contribute to the feeding and partly to the clothing of many thousands.

There is likewise another great advantage in my scheme, that it will prevent those voluntary abortions, and that horrid practice of women murdering their bastard children, alas! too frequent among us, sacrificing the poor innocent babes, I doubt, more to avoid the expense than the shame, which would move tears and pity in the most savage and inhuman breast.

The number of souls in this kingdom being usually reckoned one million and a half, of these I calculate there may be about two hundred thousand couples whose wives are breeders; from which number I subtract thirty thousand couples who are able to maintain their own children, although I apprehend there cannot be so many, under the present distress of the kingdom; but this being granted, there will remain an hundred and seventy thousand breeders. I again subtract fifty thousand for those women who miscarry, or whose children die by accident or disease within the year. There only remain an hundred and twenty thousand children of poor parents annually born. The question therefore is, how this number shall be reared and provided for, which, as I have already said, under the present situation of affairs is utterly impossible by all the methods hitherto proposed. For we can neither employ them in handicraft or agriculture; we neither build houses (I mean in the country) nor cultivate land: they can very seldom pick up a livelihood by stealing till they arrive at six years old, except where they are of towardly parts; although I confess they learn the rudiments much earlier, during which time they can, however, be properly looked upon only as probationers, as I have been informed by a principal gentleman in the county of Cavan, who protested to me that he never knew above one or two instances under the age of six, even in a part of the kingdom so renowned for the quickest proficiency in that art.

I am assured by our merchants that a boy or girl before twelve years old is no salable commodity; and even when they come to this age they will not yield above three pounds or three pounds and half-a-crown at most on the Exchange; which cannot turn to account either to the parents or the kingdom, the charge of nutriment and rags having been at least four times that value.

I shall now therefore humbly propose my own thoughts, which I hope will not be liable to the least objection.

I have been assured by a very knowing American of my acquaintance in London that a young healthy child well nursed is at a year old a most delicious, nourishing, and wholesome food, whether stewed, roasted, baked, or boiled; and I make no doubt that it will equally serve in a fricassee or a ragout.

I do therefore humbly offer it to public consideration that of the hundred and twenty thousand children already computed, twenty thousand may be reserved for breed, whereof only one-fourth part to be males, which is more than we allow to sheep, black cattle or swine; and my reason is that these children are seldom the fruits of marriage, a circumstance not much regarded by our savages; therefore one male will be sufficient to serve four females. That the remaining hundred thousand may at a year old be offered in sale to the persons of quality and fortune through the kingdom, always advising the mother to let them suck plentifully in the last month, so as to render them plump and fat for a good table. A child will make two dishes at an entertainment for friends; and when the family dines alone, the fore or hind quarter will make a reasonable dish, and seasoned with a little pepper or salt will be very good boiled on the fourth day, especially in winter.

I have reckoned upon a medium that a child just born will weigh twelve pounds, and in a solar year if tolerably nursed increaseth to twenty-eight pounds.

I grant this food will be somewhat dear, and therefore very proper for landlords, who, as they have already devoured most of the parents, seem to have the best title to the children.

Infants' flesh will be in season throughout the year, but more plentiful in March, and a little before and after; for we are told by a grave author, an eminent French physician, that fish being a prolific diet, there are more children born in Roman Catholic countries about nine months after Lent than at any other season; therefore reckoning a year after Lent, the markets will be more glutted than usual, because the number of popish infants is at least three to one in this kingdom; and therefore it will have one other collateral advantage, by lessening the number of Papists among us.

I have already computed the charge of nursing a beggar's child (in which list I reckon all cottagers, laborers, and four-fifths of the farmers) to be about two shillings per annum, rags included; and I believe no gentleman would repine to give ten shillings for the carcass of a good fat child, which, as I have said, will make four dishes of excellent nutritive meat, when he hath only some particular friend or his own family to dine with him. Thus the squire will learn to be a good landlord, and grow popular among his tenants; the mother will have eight shillings net profit, and be fit for work till she produces another child.

Those who are more thrifty (as I must confess the times require) may flay the carcass; the skin of which artificially dressed will make admirable gloves for ladies, and summer boots for fine gentlemen.

As to our city of Dublin, shambles may be appointed for this purpose in the most convenient parts of it, and butchers we may be assured will not be wanting; although I rather recommend buying the children alive, and dressing them hot from the knife, as we do roasting pigs.

A very worthy person, a true lover of his country, and whose virtues I highly esteem, was lately pleased, in discoursing on this matter, to offer a refinement upon my scheme. He said that many gentlemen of this kingdom, having of late destroyed their deer, he conceived that the want of venison might be well supplied by the bodies of young lads and maidens, not exceeding fourteen years of age nor under twelve, so great a number of both sexes in every country being now ready to starve for want of work and service: and these to be disposed of by their parents, if alive, or otherwise by their nearest relations. But with due deference to so excellent a friend and so deserving a patriot, I cannot be altogether in his sentiments. For as to the males, my American acquaintance assured me from frequent experience that their flesh was generally tough and lean, like that of our schoolboys, by continual exercise, and their taste disagreeable; and to fatten them would not answer the charge. Then as to the females, it would, I think, with humble submission, be a loss to the public, because they soon would become breeders themselves: and besides, it is not improbable that some scrupulous people might be apt to censure such a practice (although indeed very unjustly) as a little bordering upon cruelty; which, I confess, hath always been with me the strongest objection against any project, how well soever intended.

But in order to justify my friend, he confessed that this expedient was put into his head by the famous Psalmanazar, a native of the island Formosa, who came from thence to London above twenty years ago, and in conversation told my friend that in his country when any young person happened to be put to death, the executioner sold the carcass to persons of quality as a prime dainty, and that in his time the body of a plump girl of fifteen, who was crucified for an attempt to poison the emperor, was sold to his Imperial Majesty's prime minister of state, and other great mandarins of the court, in joints from the gibbet, at four hundred crowns. Neither indeed can I deny that if the same use were made of several plump young girls in this town, who, without one single groat to their fortunes, cannot stir abroad without a chair, and appear at the playhouse and assemblies in foreign fineries, which they never will pay for, the kingdom would not be the worse.

Some persons of a desponding spirit are in great concern about that vast number of poor people, who are aged, diseased, or maimed, and I have been desired to employ my thoughts what course may be taken to ease the nation of so grievous an encumbrance. But I am not in the least pain upon that matter, because it is very well known that they are every day dying and rotting, by cold and famine, and filth and vermin, as fast as can be reasonably expected. And as to the younger laborers, they are now in almost as hopeful a condition. They cannot get work, and consequently pine away for want of nourishment, to a degree that if at any time they are accidentally hired to common labor, they have not strength to perform it; and thus the country and themselves are happily delivered from the evils to come.

I have too long digressed, and therefore shall return to my subject. I think the advantages by the proposal which I have made are obvious and many, as well as of the highest importance.

For first, as I have already observed, it would greatly lessen the number of Papists, with whom we are yearly overrun, being the principal breeders of the nation as well as our most dangerous enemies; and who stay at home on purpose with a design to deliver the kingdom to the Pretender, hoping to take their advantage by the absence of so many good Protestants, who have chosen rather to leave their country than stay at home and pay tithes against their conscience to an Episcopal curate.

Secondly, the poorer tenants will have something valuable of their own, which by law may be made liable to distress, and help to pay their landlord's rent; their corn and cattle being already seized, and money a thing unknown.

Thirdly, whereas the maintenance of an hundred thousand children, from two years old and upwards, cannot be computed at less than ten shillings apiece per annum, the nation's stock will be thereby increased fifty thousand pounds per annum, besides the profit of a new dish introduced to the tables of all gentlemen of fortune in the kingdom who have any refinement in taste. And the money will circulate among ourselves, the goods being entirely of our own growth and manufacture.

Fourthly, the constant breeders, besides the gain of eight shillings sterling per annum by the sale of their children, will be rid of the charge of maintaining them after the first year.

Fifthly, this food would likewise bring great custom to taverns, where the vintners will certainly be so prudent as to procure the best receipts for dressing it to perfection, and consequently have their houses frequented by all the fine gentlemen, who justly value themselves upon their knowledge in good eating; and a skillful cook, who understands how to oblige his guests, will contrive to make it as expensive as they please.

Sixthly, this would be a great inducement to marriage, which all wise nations have either encouraged by rewards or enforced by laws and penalties. It would increase the care and tenderness of mothers toward their children, when they were sure of a settlement for life to the poor babes, provided in some sort by the public, to their annual profit instead of expense. We should see an honest emulation among the married women, which of them could bring the fattest child to the market. Men would become as fond of their wives during the time of their pregnancy as they are now of their mares in foal, their cows in calf, or sows when they are ready to farrow; nor offer to beat or kick them (as is too frequent a practice) for fear of miscarriage.

Many other advantages might be enumerated. For instance, the addition of some thousand carcasses in our exportation of barreled beef, the propagation of swine's flesh, and improvement in the art of making good bacon, so much wanted among us by the great destruction of pigs, too frequent at our tables, and are no way comparable in taste or magnificence to a well-grown, fat yearling child, which roasted whole will make a considerable figure at a lord mayor's feast, or any other public entertainment. But this and many others I omit, being studious of brevity.

Supposing that one thousand families in this city would be constant customers for infants' flesh, besides others who might have it at merry meetings, particularly weddings and christenings, I compute that Dublin would take off annually about twenty thousand carcasses, and the rest of the kingdom (where probably they will be sold somewhat cheaper) the remaining eighty thousand.

I can think of no one objection that will possibly be raised against this proposal, unless it should be urged that the number of people will be thereby much lessened in the kingdom. This I freely own, and it was indeed one principal design in offering it to the world. I desire the reader will observe that I calculate my remedy for this one individual kingdom of Ireland, and for no other that ever was, is, or, I think, ever can be upon earth. Therefore let no man talk to me of other expedients: of taxing our absentees at five shillings a pound; of using neither clothes nor household furniture except what is of our own growth and manufacture; of utterly rejecting the materials and instruments that promote foreign luxury; of curing the expensiveness of pride, vanity, idleness, and gaming in our women; of introducing a vein of parsimony, prudence, and temperance; of learning to love our country, in the want of which we differ even from Laplanders and the inhabitants of Topinamboo; of quitting our animosities and factions, nor act any longer like the Jews, who were murdering one another at the very moment their city was taken; of being a little cautious not to sell our country and consciences for nothing; of teaching landlords to have at least one degree of mercy toward their tenants; lastly, of putting a spirit of honesty, industry, and skill into our shopkeepers, who, if a resolution could now be taken to buy only our native goods, would immediately unite to cheat and exact upon us in the price, the measure, and the goodness, nor could ever yet be brought to make one fair proposal of just dealing, though often and earnestly invited to it.

Therefore I repeat, let no man talk to me of these and the like expedients, till he has at least some glimpse of hope that there will be ever some hearty and sincere attempt to put them in practice.

But as to myself, having been wearied out for many years with offering vain, idle, visionary thoughts, and at length utterly despairing of success, I fortunately fell upon this proposal, which, as it is wholly new, so it has something solid and real, of no expense and little trouble, full in our own power, and whereby we can incur no danger in disobliging England. For this kind of commodity will not bear exportation, the flesh being of too tender a consistence to admit a long continuance in salt, although perhaps I could name a country which would be glad to eat up our whole nation without it.

After all, I am not so violently bent upon my own opinion as to reject any offer proposed by wise men, which shall be found equally innocent, cheap, easy, and effectual. But before something of that kind shall be advanced in contradiction to my scheme, and offering a better, I desire the author or authors will be pleased maturely to consider two points. First, as things now stand, how they will be able to find food and raiment for an hundred thousand useless mouths and backs. And secondly, there being a round million of creatures in human figure throughout this kingdom, whose whole subsistence put into a common stock would leave them in debt two millions of pounds sterling, adding those who are beggars by profession to the bulk of farmers, cottagers, and laborers, with their wives and children, who are beggars in effect; I desire those politicians who dislike my overture, and may perhaps be so bold as to attempt an answer, that they will first ask the parents of these mortals whether they would not at this day think it a great happiness to have been sold for food at a year old in the manner I prescribe, and thereby have avoided such a perpetual scene of misfortunes as they have since gone through by the oppression of landlords, the impossibility of paying rent without money or trade, the want of common sustenance, with neither house nor clothes to cover them from the inclemencies of the weather, and the most inevitable prospect of entailing the like or greater miseries upon their breed for ever.

I profess, in the sincerity of my heart, that I have not the least personal interest in endeavoring to promote this necessary work, having no other motive than the public good of my country, by advancing our trade, providing for infants, relieving the poor, and giving some pleasure to the rich. I have no children by which I can propose to get a single penny; the youngest being nine years old, and my wife past child-bearing.

(1729)

MARK TWAIN
[1835–1910]

"Cub" Wants to Be a Pilot

When I was a boy there was but one permanent ambition among my comrades in our village on the west bank of the Mississippi River. That was to be a steamboatman. We had transient ambitions of other sorts but they were only transient. When a circus came and went, it left us all burning to become clowns; the first Negro minstrel show that ever came to our section left us all suffering to try that kind of life; now and then we had a hope that, if we lived and were good, God would permit us to be pirates. These ambitions faded out, each in its turn; but the ambition to be a steamboatman always remained.

Once a day a cheap, gaudy packet arrived upward from St. Louis, and another downward from Keokuk. Before these events, the day was glorious with expectancy; after them, the day was a dead and empty thing. Not only the boys but the whole village felt this. After all these years I can picture that old time to myself now, just as it was then: the white town drowsing in the sunshine of a summer's morning; the streets empty or pretty nearly so; one or two clerks sitting in front of the Water Street stores, with their splint-bottomed chairs tilted back against the walls, chins on breasts, hats slouched over their faces, asleep—with shingle-shavings enough around to show what broke them down; a sow and a litter of pigs loafing along the sidewalk, doing a good business in watermelon rinds and seeds; two or three lonely little freight piles scattered about the "levee"; a pile of "skids" on the slope of the stone-paved wharf, and the fragrant town drunkard asleep in the shadow of them; two or three wood flats at the head of the wharf but nobody to listen to the peaceful lapping of the wavelets against them; the great Mississippi, the majestic, the magnificent Mississippi, rolling its mile-wide tide along, shining in the sun; the dense forest away on the other side; the "point" above the town, and the "point" below, bounding the river-glimpse and turning it into a sort of sea, and withal a very still and brilliant and lonely one. Presently a film of dark smoke appears above one of those remote "points"; instantly a Negro drayman, famous for his quick eye and prodigious voice, lifts up the cry, "S-t-e-a-m-boat a-comin'!" and the scene changes! The town drunkard stirs, the clerks wake up, a furious clatter of drays follows, every house and store pours out a human contribution, and all in a twinkling the dead town is alive and moving. Drays, carts, men, boys, all go hurrying from many quarters to a common center, the wharf. Assembled there, the people fasten their eyes upon the coming boat as upon a wonder they are seeing for the first time. And the boat *is* rather a handsome sight, too. She is long and sharp and trim and pretty; she has two tall, fancy-topped chimneys, with a gilded device of some kind swung between them; a fanciful pilot-house, all glass and "gingerbread," perched on top of the "texas" deck behind them; the paddle-boxes are gorgeous with a picture or with gilded rays above the boat's name; the boiler-deck, the hurricane-deck, and the texas deck are fenced and ornamented with clean white railings; there is a flag gallantly flying from the jack-staff; the furnace doors are open and the fires glaring bravely; the upper decks are black with passengers; the captain stands by the big bell, calm, imposing, the envy of all; great volumes of the blackest smoke are rolling and tumbling out of the chimneys—a husbanded grandeur created with a bit of pitch-pine just before arriving at a town; the crew are grouped on the forecastle; the broad stage is run far out over the port bow and an envied deck-hand stands picturesquely on the end of it with a coil of rope in his hand; the pent steam is screaming through the gauge-cocks; the captain lifts his hand, a bell rings, the wheels stop; then they turn back, churning the water to foam, and the steamer is at rest. Then such a scramble as there is to get aboard and to get ashore, and to take in freight and to discharge freight, all at one and the same time; and such a yelling and cursing as the mates facilitate it all with! Ten minutes later the steamer is under way again, with no flag on the jack-staff and no black smoke issuing from the chimneys. After ten more minutes the town is dead again and the town drunkard asleep by the skids once more.

My father was a justice of the peace and I supposed he possessed the power of life and death over all men and could hang anybody that offended him. This was distinction enough for me as a general thing, but the desire to be a steamboatman kept intruding nevertheless. I first wanted to be a cabin-boy, so that I could come out with a white apron on and shake a table-cloth over the side, where all my old comrades could see me; later I thought I would rather be the deck-hand who stood on the end of the stage-plank with the coil of rope in his hand, because he was particularly conspicuous. But these were only day-dreams—they were too heavenly to be contemplated as real possibilities. By and by one of our boys went away. He was not heard of for a long time. At last he turned up as apprentice engineer or "striker" on a steamboat. This thing shook the bottom out of all my Sunday-school teachings. That boy had been notoriously worldly and I just the reverse; yet he was exalted to this eminence and I left in obscurity and misery. There was nothing generous about this fellow in his greatness. He would always manage to have a rusty bolt to scrub while his boat tarried at our town, and he would sit on the inside guard and scrub it, where we all could see him and envy him and loathe him. And whenever his boat was laid up he would come home and swell around the town in his blackest and greasiest clothes, so that nobody could help remembering that he was a steamboatman; and he used all sorts of steamboat technicalities in his talk, as if he were so used to them that he forgot common people could not understand them. He would speak of the "labboard" side of a horse in an easy, natural way that would make one wish he was dead. And he was always talking about "St. Looy" like an old citizen; he would refer casually to occasions when he was "coming down Fourth Street," or when he was "passing by the Planter's House," or when there was a fire and he took a turn on the brakes of "the old Big Missouri"; and then he would go on and lie about how many towns the size of ours were burned down there that day. Two or three of the boys had long been persons of consideration among us because they had been to St. Louis once and had a vague general knowledge of its wonders, but the day of their glory was over now. They lapsed into a humble silence and learned to disappear when the ruthless "cub"-engineer approached. This fellow had money, too, and hair-oil. Also an ignorant silver watch and a showy brass watch-chain. He wore a leather belt and used no suspenders. If ever a youth was cordially admired and hated by his comrades, this one was. No girl could withstand his charms. He "cut out" every boy in the village. When his boat blew up at last, it diffused a tranquil contentment among us such as we had not known for months. But when he came home the next week, alive, renowned, and appeared in church all battered up and bandaged, a shining hero, stared at and wondered over by everybody, it seemed to us that the partiality of Providence for an undeserving reptile had reached a point where it was open to criticism.

This creature's career could produce but one result, and it speedily followed. Boy after boy managed to get on the river. The minister's son became an engineer. The doctor's and the postmaster's sons became "mud clerks"; the wholesale liquor dealer's son became a barkeeper on a boat; four sons of the chief merchant and two sons of the county judge became pilots. Pilot was the grandest position of all. The pilot, even in those days of trivial wages, had a princely salary—from a hundred and fifty to two hundred and fifty dollars a month, and no board to pay. Two months of his wages would pay a preacher's salary for a year. Now some of us were left disconsolate. We could not get on the river—at least our parents would not let us.

So, by and by, I ran away. I said I would never come home again till I was a pilot and could come in glory. But somehow I could not manage it. I went meekly aboard a few of the boats that lay packed together like sardines at the long St. Louis wharf, and humbly inquired for the pilots, but got only a cold shoulder and short words from mates and clerks. I had to make the best of this sort of treatment for the time being, but I had comforting day-dreams of a future when I should be a great and honored pilot, with plenty of money, and could kill some of these mates and clerks and pay for them.

Months afterward the hope within me struggled to a reluctant death, and I found myself without an ambition. But I was ashamed to go home. I was in Cincinnati, and I set to work to map out a new career. I had been reading about the recent exploration of the river Amazon by an expedition sent out by our government. It was said that the expedition, owing to difficulties, had not thoroughly explored a part of the country lying about the headwaters, some four thousand miles from the mouth of the river. It was only about fifteen hundred miles from Cincinnati to New Orleans, where I could doubtless get a ship. I had thirty dollars left; I would go and complete the exploration of the Amazon. This was all the thought I gave to the subject. I never was great in matters of detail. I packed my valise, and took passage on an ancient tub called the *Paul Jones,* for New Orleans. For the sum of sixteen dollars I had the scarred and tarnished splendors of "her" main saloon principally to myself, for she was not a creature to attract the eye of wiser travelers.

When we presently got under way and went poking down the broad Ohio, I became a new being and the subject of my own admiration. I was a traveler! A word never had tasted so good in my mouth before. I had an exultant sense of being bound for mysterious lands and distant climes which I never have felt in so uplifting a degree since. I was in such a glorified condition that all ignoble feelings departed out of me, and I was able to look down and pity the untraveled with a compassion that had hardly a trace of contempt in it. Still, when we stopped at villages and wood-yards, I could not help lolling carelessly upon the railings of the boiler-deck to enjoy the envy of the country boys on the bank. If they did not seem to discover me, I presently sneezed to attract their attention, or moved to a position where they could not help seeing me. And as soon as I knew they saw me I gaped and stretched, and gave other signs of being mightily bored with traveling.

I kept my hat off all the time, and stayed where the wind and the sun could strike me, because I wanted to get the bronzed and weather-beaten look of an old traveler. Before the second day was half gone I experienced a joy which filled me with the purest gratitude, for I saw that the skin had begun to blister and peel off my face and neck. I wished that the boys and girls at home could see me now.

We reached Louisville in time—at least the neighborhood of it. We stuck hard and fast on the rocks in the middle of the river and lay there four days. I was now beginning to feel a strong sense of being a part of the boat's family, a sort of infant son to the captain and younger brother to the officers. There is no estimating the pride I took in this grandeur or the affection that began to swell and grow in me for those people. I could not know how the lordly steamboatman scorns that sort of presumption in a mere landsman. I particularly longed to acquire the least trifle of notice from the big stormy mate, and I was on the alert for an opportunity to do him a service to that end. It came at last. The riotous pow-wow of setting a spar was going on down on the forecastle, and I went down there and stood around in the way—or mostly skipping out of it—till the mate suddenly roared a general order for somebody to bring him a capstan bar. I sprang to his side and said: "Tell me where it is—I'll fetch it!"

If a rag-picker had offered to do a diplomatic service for the Emperor of Russia, the monarch could not have been more astounded than the mate was. He even stopped swearing. He stood and stared down at me. It took him ten seconds to scrape his disjointed remains together again. Then he said impressively, "Well, if this don't beat h——l!," and turned to his work with the air of a man who had been confronted with a problem too abstruse for solution.

I crept away and courted solitude for the rest of the day. I did not go to dinner, I stayed away from supper until everybody else had finished. I did not feel so much like a member of the boat's family now as before. However, my spirits returned, in instalments, as we pursued our way down the river. I was sorry I hated the mate so, because it was not in (young) human nature not to admire him. He was huge and muscular, his face was bearded and whiskered all over, he had a red woman and a blue woman tattooed on his right arm—one on each side of a blue anchor with a red rope to it—and in the matter of profanity he was sublime. When he was getting out cargo at a landing, I was always where I could see and hear. He felt all the majesty of his great position and made the world feel it too. When he gave even the simplest order, he discharged it like a blast of lightning and sent a long, reverberating peal of profanity thundering after it. I could not help contrasting the way in which the average landsman would give an order with the mate's way of doing it. If the landsman should wish the gang-plank moved a foot farther forward, he would probably say, "James, or William, one of you push that plank forward, please," but put the mate in his place, and he would roar out, "Here, now, start that gang-plank for'ard! Lively, now! *What*'re you about! Snatch it! *snatch* it! There! there! aft again! aft again! Don't you hear me? Dash it to dash! are you going to *sleep* over it! '*Vast* heaving. 'Vast heaving, I tell you! Going to heave it clear astern? WHERE're you going with that barrel! *for'ard* with it 'fore I make you swallow it, you dash-dash-dash-*dashed* split between a tired mud-turtle and a crippled hearse-horse!"

I wished I could talk like that.

When the soreness of my adventure with the mate had somewhat worn off, I began timidly to make up to the humblest official connected with the boat—the night watchman. He snubbed my advances at first, but I presently ventured to offer him a new chalk pipe, and that softened him. So he allowed me to sit with him by the big bell on the hurricane-deck, and in time he melted into conversation. He could not well have helped it, I hung with such homage on his words and so plainly showed that I felt honored by his notice. He told me the names of dim capes and shadowy islands as we glided by them in the solemnity of the night under the winking stars, and by and by got to talking about himself. He seemed over-sentimental for a man whose salary was six dollars a week—or rather he might have seemed so to an older person than I. But I drank in his words hungrily and with a faith that might have moved mountains if it had been applied judiciously. What was it to me that he was soiled and seedy and fragrant with gin? What was it to me that his grammar was bad, his construction worse, and his profanity so void of art that it was an element of weakness rather than strength in his conversation? He was a wronged man, a man who had seen trouble, and that was enough for me. As he mellowed into his plaintive history his tears dripped upon the lantern in his lap, and I cried too from sympathy. He said he was the son of an English nobleman, either an earl or an alderman, he could not remember which, but believed was both; his father, the nobleman, loved him but his mother hated him from the cradle; and so while he was still a little boy he was sent to "one of them old, ancient colleges," he couldn't remember which; and by and by his father died and his mother seized the property and "shook" him, as he phrased it. After his mother shook him, members of the nobility with whom he was acquainted used their influence to get him the position of "loblolly-boy in a ship," and from that point my watchman threw off all trammels of date and locality and branched out into a narrative that bristled all along with incredible adventures, a narrative that was so reeking with bloodshed and so crammed with hair-breadth escapes and the most engaging and unconscious personal villainies that I sat speechless, enjoying, shuddering, wondering, worshiping.

It was a sore blight to find out afterward that he was a low, vulgar, ignorant, sentimental, half-witted humbug, an untraveled native of the wilds of Illinois, who had absorbed wildcat literature and appropriated its marvels, until in time he had woven odds and ends of the mess into this yarn and then gone on telling it to fledglings like me until he had come to believe it himself.

(1883)

E. M. FORSTER

[1879–1970]

Our Graves in Gallipoli°

FIRST GRAVE We are important again upon earth. Each morning men mention us.

SECOND GRAVE Yes, after seven years' silence.

FIRST GRAVE Every day some eminent public man now refers to the "sanctity of our graves in Gallipoli."

SECOND GRAVE Why do the eminent men speak of "our" graves, as if they were themselves dead? It is we, not they, who lie on Achi Baba.

FIRST GRAVE They say "our" out of geniality and in order to touch the great heart of the nation more quickly. *Punch,* the great-hearted jester, showed a picture lately in which the Prime Minister of England, Lloyd George, fertile in counsels, is urged to go to war to protect "the sanctity of our graves in Gallipoli." The elderly artist who designed that picture is not dead and does not mean to die. He hopes to illustrate this war as he did the last, for a sufficient salary. Nevertheless he writes "our" graves, as if he was inside one, and all persons of position now say the same.

SECOND GRAVE If they go to war, there will be more graves.

FIRST GRAVE That is what they desire. That is what Lloyd George, prudent in counsels, and lion-hearted Churchill, intend.

SECOND GRAVE But where will they dig them?

FIRST GRAVE There is still room over in Chanak. Also, it is well for a nation that would be great to scatter its graves all over the world. Graves in Ireland, graves in Irak, Russia, Persia, India, each with its inscription from the Bible or Rupert Brooke. When England thinks fit, she can launch an expedition to protect the sanctity of her graves, and can follow that by another expedition to protect the sanctity of the additional graves. That is what Lloyd George, prudent in counsels, and lion-hearted Churchill, have planned. Churchill planned this expedition to Gallipoli, where I was killed. He planned the expedition to Antwerp, where my brother was killed. Then he said that Labour is

---

Gallipoli *During World War I the British army, and especially its Australian contingent, suffered a terrible defeat at Gallipoli in Turkey.*

not fit to govern. Rolling his eyes for fresh worlds, he saw Egypt, and fearing that peace might be established there, he intervened and prevented it. Whatever he undertakes is a success. He is Churchill the Fortunate, ever in office, and clouds of dead heroes attend him. Nothing for schools, nothing for houses, nothing for the life of the body, nothing for the spirit. England cannot spare a penny for anything except for her heroes' graves.

SECOND GRAVE   Is she really putting herself to so much expense on our account?

FIRST GRAVE   For us, and for the Freedom of the Straits. That water flowing below us now—it must be thoroughly free. What freedom is, great men are uncertain, but all agree that the water must be free for all nations; if in peace, then for all nations in peace; if in war, then for all nations in war.

SECOND GRAVE   So all nations now support England.

FIRST GRAVE   It is almost inexplicable. England stands alone. Of the dozens of nations into which the globe is divided, not a single one follows her banner, and even her own colonies hang back.

SECOND GRAVE   Yes . . . inexplicable. Perhaps she fights for some other reason.

FIRST GRAVE   Ah, the true reason of a war is never known until all who have fought in it are dead. In a hundred years' time we shall be told. Meanwhile seek not to inquire. There are rumours that rich men desire to be richer, but we cannot know.

SECOND GRAVE   If rich men desire more riches, let them fight. It is reasonable to fight for our desires.

FIRST GRAVE   But they cannot fight. They must not fight. There are too few of them. They would be killed. If a rich man went into the interior of Asia and tried to take more gold or more oil, he might be seriously injured at once. He must persuade poor men, who are numerous, to go there for him. And perhaps this is what Lloyd George, fertile in counsels, has decreed. He has tried to enter Asia by means of the Greeks. It was the Greeks who, seven years ago, failed to join England after they had promised to do so, and our graves in Gallipoli are the result of this. But Churchill the Fortunate, ever in office, ever magnanimous, bore the Greeks no grudge, and he and Lloyd George persuaded their young men to enter Asia. They have mostly been killed there, so English young men must be persuaded instead. A phrase must be thought of, and "the Gallipoli graves" is the handiest. The clergy must wave their Bibles, the old men their newspapers, the old women their knitting, the unmarried girls must wave white feathers, and all must shout, "Gallipoli graves, Gallipoli graves, Gallipoli, Gally Polly, Gally Polly," until the young men are ashamed and think, What sound can that be but my country's call? and Chanak receives them.

SECOND GRAVE   Chanak is to sanctify Gallipoli.

FIRST GRAVE   It will make our heap of stones for ever England, apparently.

SECOND GRAVE   It can scarcely do that to my portion of it. I was a Turk.

FIRST GRAVE   What! a Turk! You a Turk? And I have lain beside you for seven years and never known!

SECOND GRAVE   How should you have known? What is there to know except that I am your brother?

FIRST GRAVE   I am yours . . .

SECOND GRAVE   All is dead except that. All graves are one. It is their unity that sanctifies them, and some day even the living will learn this.

FIRST GRAVE   Ah, but why can they not learn it while they are still alive?

(1936)

VIRGINIA WOOLF

[1882–1941]

Old Mrs. Grey

There are moments even in England, now, when even the busiest, most contented suddenly let fall what they hold—it may be the week's washing. Sheets and pyjamas crumble and dissolve in their hands, because, though they do not state this in so many words, it seems silly to take the washing round to Mrs. Peel when out there over the fields over the hills, there is no washing; no pinning of clotheslines; mangling and ironing; no work at all, but boundless rest. Stainless and boundless rest; space unlimited; untrodden grass; wild birds flying; hills whose smooth uprise continues that wild flight.

Of all this however only seven foot by four could be seen from Mrs. Grey's corner. That was the size of her front door which stood wide open, though there was a fire burning in the grate. The fire looked like a small spot of dusty light feebly trying to escape from the embarrassing pressure of the pouring sunshine.

Mrs. Grey sat on a hard chair in the corner looking—but at what? Apparently at nothing. She did not change the focus of her eyes when visitors came in. Her eyes had ceased to focus themselves; it may be that they had lost the power. They were aged eyes, blue, unspectacled. They could see, but without looking. She had never used her eyes on anything minute and difficult; merely upon faces, and dishes and fields. And now at the age of ninety-two they saw nothing but a zigzag of pain wriggling across the door, pain that twisted her legs as it wriggled; jerked her body to and fro like a marionette. Her body was wrapped round the pain as a damp sheet is folded over a wire. The wire was spasmodically jerked by a cruel invisible hand. She flung out a foot, a hand. Then it stopped. She sat still for a moment.

In that pause she saw herself in the past at ten, at twenty, at twenty-five. She was running in and out of a cottage with eleven brothers and sisters. The line jerked. She was thrown forward in her chair.

'All dead. All dead,' she mumbled. 'My brothers and sisters. And my husband gone. My daughter too. But I go on. Every morning I pray God to let me pass.'

The morning spread seven foot by four green and sunny. Like a fling of grain the birds settled on the land. She was jerked again by another tweak of the tormenting hand.

'I'm an ignorant old woman. I can't read or write, and every morning when I crawls downstairs, I say I wish it were night; and every night, when I crawls up to bed, I say I wish it were day. I'm only an ignorant old woman. But I prays to God: O let me pass. I'm an ignorant old woman—I can't read or write.'

So when the colour went out of the doorway, she could not see the other page which is then lit up; or hear the voices that have argued, sung, talked for hundreds of years.

The jerked limbs were still again.

'The doctor comes every week. The parish doctor now. Since my daughter went, we can't afford Dr. Nicholls. But he's a good man. He says he wonders I don't go. He says my heart's nothing but wind and water. Yet I don't seem able to die.'

So we—humanity—insist that the body shall still cling to the wirer. We put out the eyes and the ears; but we pinion it there, with a bottle of medicine, a cup of tea, a dying fire, like a rook on a barn door; but a rook that still lives, even with a nail through it.

(1942)

GEORGE ORWELL
[1903–1950]

Shooting an Elephant

In Moulmein, in lower Burma, I was hated by large numbers of people—the only time in my life that I have been important enough for this to happen to me. I was subdivisional police officer of the town, and in an aimless, petty kind of way anti-European feeling was very bitter. No one had the guts to raise a riot, but if a European woman went through the bazaars alone somebody would probably spit betel juice over her dress. As a police officer I was an obvious target and was baited whenever it seemed safe to do so. When a nimble Burman tripped me up on the football field and the referee (another Burman) looked the other way, the crowd yelled with hideous laughter. This happened more than once. In the end the sneering yellow faces of young men that met me everywhere, the insults hooted after me when I was at a safe distance, got badly on my nerves. The young Buddhist priests were the worst of all. There were several thousands of them in the town and none of them seemed to have anything to do except stand on street corners and jeer at Europeans.

All this was perplexing and upsetting. For at that time I had already made up my mind that imperialism was an evil thing and the sooner I chucked up my job and got out of it the better. Theoretically—and secretly, of course—I was all for the Burmese and all against their oppressors, the British. As for the job I was doing, I hated it more bitterly than I can perhaps make clear. In a job like that you see the dirty work of Empire at close quarters. The wretched prisoners huddling in the stinking cages of the lock-ups, the gray, cowed faces of the long-term convicts, the scarred buttocks of the men who had been flogged with bamboos—all these oppressed me with an intolerable sense of guilt. But I could get nothing into perspective. I was young and ill educated and I had had to think out my problems in the utter silence that is imposed on every Englishman in the East. I did not even know that the British Empire is dying, still less did I know that it is a great deal better than the younger empires that are going to supplant it. All I knew was that I was stuck between my hatred of the empire I served and my rage against the evil-spirited little beasts who tried to make my job impossible. With one part of my mind I thought of the British Raj as an unbreakable tyranny, as something clamped down, in *saecula saeculorum,* upon the will of prostrate peoples; with another part I thought that the greatest joy in the world would be to drive a bayonet into a Buddhist priest's guts. Feelings like these are the normal by-products of imperialism; ask any Anglo-Indian official, if you can catch him off duty.

One day something happened which in a roundabout way was enlightening. It was a tiny incident in itself, but it gave me a better glimpse than I had had before of the real nature of imperialism—the real motives for which despotic governments act. Early one morning the sub-inspector at a police station the other end of the town rang me up on the 'phone and said that an elephant was ravaging the bazaar. Would I please come and do something about it? I did not know what I could do, but I wanted to see what was happening and I got on to a pony and started out. I took my rifle, an old .44 Winchester and much too small to kill an elephant, but I thought the noise might be useful *in terrorem*. Various Burmans stopped me on the way and told me about the elephant's doings. It was not, of course, a wild elephant, but a tame one which had gone "must." It had been chained up, as tame elephants always are when their attack of "must" is due, but on the previous night it had broken its chain and escaped. Its mahout, the only person who could manage it when it was in that state, had set out in pursuit, but had taken the wrong direction and was now twelve hours' journey away, and in the morning the elephant had suddenly reappeared in the town. The Burmese population had no weapons and were quite helpless against it. It had already destroyed somebody's bamboo hut, killed a cow and raided some fruit-stalls and devoured the stock; also it had met the municipal rubbish van and, when the driver jumped out and took to his heels, had turned the van over and inflicted violences upon it.

The Burmese sub-inspector and some Indian constables were waiting for me in the quarter where the elephant had been seen. It was a very poor quarter, a labyrinth of squalid bamboo huts, thatched with palm-leaf, winding all over a steep hillside. I remember that it was a cloudy, stuffy morning at the beginning of the rains. We began questioning the people as to where the elephant had gone and, as usual, failed to get any definite information. That is invariably the case in the East; a story always sounds clear enough at a distance, but the nearer you get to the scene of events the vaguer it becomes. Some of the people said that the elephant had gone in one direction, some said that he had gone in another, some professed not even to have heard of any elephant. I had almost made up my mind that the whole story was a pack of lies, when we heard yells a little distance away. There was a loud, scandalized cry of "Go away, child! Go away this instant!" and an old woman with a switch in her hand came round the corner of a hut, violently shooing away a crowd of naked children. Some more women followed, clicking their tongues and exclaiming; evidently there was something that the children ought not to have seen. I rounded the hut and saw a man's dead body sprawling in the mud. He was an Indian, a black Dravidian coolie, almost naked, and he could not have been dead many minutes. The people said that the elephant had come suddenly upon him round the corner of the hut, caught him with its trunk, put its foot on his back and ground him into the earth. This was the rainy season and the ground was soft, and his face had scored a trench a foot deep and a couple of yards long. He was lying on his belly with arms crucified and head sharply twisted to one side. His face was coated with mud, the eyes wide open, the teeth bared and grinning with an expression of unendurable agony. (Never tell me, by the way, that the dead look peaceful. Most of the corpses I have seen looked devilish.) The friction of the great beast's foot had stripped the skin from his back as neatly as one skins a rabbit. As soon as I saw the dead man I sent an orderly to a friend's house nearby to borrow an elephant rifle. I had already sent back the pony, not wanting it to go mad with fright and throw me if it smelt the elephant.

The orderly came back in a few minutes with a rifle and five cartridges, and meanwhile some Burmans had arrived and told us that the elephant was in the paddy fields below, only a few hundred yards away. As I started forward practically the whole population of the quarter flocked out of the houses and followed me. They had seen the rifle and were all shouting excitedly that I was going to shoot the elephant. They had not shown much interest in the elephant when he was merely ravaging their homes, but it was different now that he was going to be shot. It was a bit of fun to them, as it would be to an English crowd; besides they wanted the meat. It made me vaguely uneasy. I had no intention of shooting the elephant—I had merely sent for the rifle to defend myself if necessary—and it is always unnerving to have a crowd following you. I marched down the hill, looking and feeling a fool, with the rifle over my shoulder and an ever-growing army of people jostling at my heels. At the bottom, when you got away from the huts, there was a metalled road and beyond that a miry waste of paddy fields a thousand yards across, not yet ploughed but soggy from the first rains and dotted with coarse grass. The elephant was standing eight yards from the road, his left side toward us. He took not the slightest notice of the crowd's approach. He was tearing up bunches of grass, beating them against his knees to clean them, and stuffing them into his mouth.

I had halted on the road. As soon as I saw the elephant I knew with perfect certainty that I ought not to shoot him. It is a serious matter to shoot a working elephant—it is comparable to destroying a huge and costly piece of machinery—and obviously one ought not to do it if it can possibly be avoided. And at that distance, peacefully eating, the elephant looked no more dangerous than a cow. I thought then and I think now that his attack of "must" was already passing off; in which case he would merely wander harmlessly about until the mahout came back and caught him. Moreover, I did not in the least want to shoot him. I decided that I would watch him for a little while to make sure that he did not turn savage again, and then go home.

But at that moment I glanced round at the crowd that had followed me. It was an immense crowd, two thousand at the least and growing every minute. It blocked the road for a long distance on either side. I looked at the sea of yellow faces above the garish clothes—faces all happy and excited over this bit of fun, all certain that the elephant was going to be shot. They were watching me as they would watch a conjurer about to perform a trick. They did not like me, but with the magical rifle in my hands I was momentarily worth watching. And suddenly I realized that I should have to shoot the elephant after all. The people expected it of me and I had got to do it; I could feel their two thousand wills pressing me forward, irresistibly. And it was at this moment, as I stood there with the rifle in my hands, that I first grasped the hollowness, the futility of the white man's dominion in the East. Here was I, the white man with his gun, standing in front of the unarmed native crowd—seemingly the leading actor of the piece; but in reality I was only an absurd puppet pushed to and fro by the will of those yellow faces behind. I perceived in this moment that when the white man turns tyrant it is his own freedom that he destroys. He becomes a sort of hollow, posing dummy, the conventionalized figure of a sahib. For it is the condition of his rule that he shall spend his life in trying to impress the "natives," and so in every crisis he has got to do what the "natives" expect of him. He wears a mask, and his face grows to fit it. I had got to shoot the elephant. I had committed myself to doing it when I sent for the rifle. A sahib has got to act like a sahib; he has got to appear resolute, to know his own mind and do definite things. To come all that way, rifle in hand, with two thousand people marching at my heels, and then to trail feebly away, having done nothing—no, that was impossible. The crowd would laugh at me. And my whole life, every white man's life in the East, was one long struggle not to be laughed at.

But I did not want to shoot the elephant. I watched him beating his bunch of grass against his knees with that preoccupied grandmotherly air that elephants have. It seemed to me that it would be murder to shoot him. At that age I was not squeamish about killing animals, but I had never shot an elephant and never wanted to. (Somehow it always seems worse to kill a *large* animal.) Besides, there was the beast's owner to be considered. Alive, the elephant was worth at least a hundred pounds; dead, he would only be worth the value of his tusks, five pounds, possibly. But I had got to act quickly. I turned to some experienced-looking Burmans who had been there when we arrived, and asked them how the elephant had been behaving. They all said the same thing: he took no notice of you if you left him alone, but he might charge if you went too close to him.

It was perfectly clear to me what I ought to do. I ought to walk up to within, say, twenty-five yards of the elephant and test his behavior. If he charged, I could shoot; if he took no notice of me, it would be safe to leave him until the mahout came back. But also I knew that I was going to do no such thing. I was a poor shot with a rifle and the ground was soft mud into which one would sink at every step. If the elephant charged and I missed him, I should have about as much chance as a toad under a steamroller. But even then I was not thinking particularly of my own skin, only of the watchful yellow faces behind. For at that moment, with the crowd watching me, I was not afraid in the ordinary sense, as I would have been if I had been alone. A white man mustn't be frightened in front of "natives"; and so, in general, he isn't frightened. The sole thought in my mind was that if anything went wrong those two thousand Burmans would see me pursued, caught, trampled on, and reduced to a grinning corpse like that Indian up the hill. And if that happened it was quite probable that some of them would laugh. That would never do. There was only one alternative. I shoved the cartridges into the magazine and lay down on the road to get a better aim.

The crowd grew very still, and a deep, low, happy sigh, as of people who see the theater curtain go up at last, breathed from innumerable throats. They were going to have their bit of fun after all. The rifle was a beautiful German thing with cross-hair sights. I did not then know that in shooting an elephant one would shoot to cut an imaginary bar running from ear-hole to ear-hole. I ought, therefore, as the elephant was sideways on, to have aimed straight at his ear-hole; actually I aimed several inches in front of this, thinking the brain would be further forward.

When I pulled the trigger I did not hear the bang or feel the kick—one never does when a shot goes home—but I heard the devilish roar of glee that went up from the crowd. In that instant, in too short a time, one would have thought, even for the bullet to get there, a mysterious, terrible change had come over the elephant. He neither stirred nor fell, but every line of his body had altered. He looked suddenly stricken, shrunken, immensely old, as though the frightful impact of the bullet had paralyzed him without knocking him down. At last, after what seemed a long time—it might have been five seconds, I dare say—he sagged flabbily to his knees. His mouth slobbered. An enormous senility seemed to have settled upon him. One could have imagined him thousands of years old. I fired again into the same spot. At the second shot he did not collapse but climbed with desperate slowness to his feet and stood weakly upright, with legs sagging and head drooping. I fired a third time. That was the shot that did for him. You could see the agony of it jolt his whole body and knock the last remnant of strength from his legs. But in falling he seemed for a moment to rise, for as his hind legs collapsed beneath him he seemed to tower upward like a huge rock toppling, his trunk reaching skyward like a tree. He trumpeted, for the first and only time. And then down he came, his belly toward me, with a crash that seemed to shake the ground even where I lay.

I got up. The Burmans were already racing past me across the mud. It was obvious that the elephant would never rise again, but he was not dead. He was breathing very rhythmically with long rattling gasps, his great mound of a side painfully rising and falling. His mouth was wide open—I could see far down into caverns of pale pink throat. I waited a long time for him to die, but his breathing did not weaken. Finally I fired my two remaining shots into the spot where I thought his heart must be. The thick blood welled out of him like red velvet, but still he did not die. His body did not even jerk when the shots hit him, the tortured breathing continued without a pause. He was dying, very slowly and in great agony, but in some world remote from me where not even a bullet could damage him further. I felt that I had got to put an end to that dreadful noise. It seemed dreadful to see the great beast lying there, powerless to move and yet powerless to die, and not even to be able to finish him. I sent back for my small rifle and poured shot after shot into his heart and down his throat. They seemed to make no impression. The tortured gasps continued as steadily as the ticking of a clock.

In the end I could not stand it any longer and went away. I heard later that it took him half an hour to die. Burmans were bringing dahs and baskets even before I left, and I was told they had stripped his body almost to the bones by the afternoon.

Afterward, of course, there were endless discussions about the shooting of the elephant. The owner was furious, but he was only an Indian and could do nothing. Besides, legally I had done the right thing, for a mad elephant has to be killed, like a mad dog, if its owner fails to control it. Among the Europeans opinion was divided. The older men said I was right, the younger men said it was a damn shame to shoot an elephant for killing a coolie, because an elephant was worth more than any damn Coringhee coolie. And afterward I was very glad that the coolie had been killed; it put me legally in the right and it gave me a sufficient pretext for shooting the elephant. I often wondered whether any of the others grasped that I had done it solely to avoid looking a fool.

Orwell compares the death of the Elephant to the death of his country (1936)

LOREN EISELEY

[1907–1977]

The Judgment of the Birds

It is a commonplace of all religious thought, even the most primitive, that the man seeking visions and insight must go apart from his fellows and live for a time in the wilderness. If he is of the proper sort, he will return with a message. It may not be a message from the god he set out to seek, but even if he has failed in that particular, he will have had a vision or seen a marvel, and these are always worth listening to and thinking about.

The world, I have come to believe, is a very queer place, but we have been part of this queerness for so long that we tend to take it for granted. We rush to and fro like Mad Hatters upon our peculiar errands, all the time imagining our surroundings to be dull and ourselves quite ordinary creatures. Actually, there is nothing in the world to encourage this idea, but such is the mind of man, and this is why he finds it necessary from time to time to send emissaries into the wilderness in the hope of learning of great events, or plans in store for him, that will resuscitate his waning taste for life. His great news services, his worldwide radio network, he knows with a last remnant of healthy distrust will be of no use to him in this matter. No miracle can withstand a radio broadcast, and it is certain that it would be no miracle if it could. One must seek, then, what only the solitary approach can give—a natural revelation.

Let it be understood that I am not the sort of man to whom is entrusted direct knowledge of great events or prophecies. A naturalist, however, spends much of his life alone, and my life is no exception. Even in New York City there are patches of wilderness, and a man by himself is bound to undergo certain experiences falling into the class of which I speak. I set mine down, therefore: a matter of pigeons, a flight of chemicals, and a judgment of birds, in the hope that they will come to the eye of those who have retained a true taste for the marvelous, and who are capable of discerning in the flow of ordinary events the point at which the mundane world gives way to quite another dimension.

New York is not, on the whole, the best place to enjoy the downright miraculous nature of the planet. There are, I do not doubt, many remarkable stories to be heard there and many strange sights to be seen, but to grasp a marvel fully it must be savored from all aspects. This cannot be done while one is being jostled and hustled along a crowded street. Nevertheless, in any city there are true wildernesses where a man can be alone. It can happen in a hotel room, or on the high roofs at dawn.

One night on the twentieth floor of a midtown hotel I awoke in the dark and grew restless. On an impulse I climbed upon the broad old-fashioned window sill, opened the curtains, and peered out. It was the hour just before dawn, the hour when men sigh in their sleep or, if awake, strive to focus their wavering eyesight upon a world emerging from the shadows. I leaned out sleepily through the open window. I had expected depths, but not the sight I saw.

I found I was looking down from that great height into a series of curious cupolas or lofts that I could just barely make out in the darkness. As I looked, the outlines of these lofts became more distinct because the light was being reflected from the wings of pigeons who, in utter silence, were beginning to float outward upon the city. In and out through the open slits in the cupolas passed the white-winged birds on their mysterious errands. At this hour the city was theirs, and quietly, without the brush of a single wing tip against stone in that high, eerie place, they were taking over the spires of Manhattan. They were pouring upward in a light that was not yet perceptible to human eyes, while far down in the black darkness of the alleys it was still midnight.

As I crouched half-asleep across the sill, I had a moment's illusion that the world had changed in the night, as in some immense snowfall, and that, if I were to leave, it would have to be as these other inhabitants were doing, by the window. I should have to launch out into that great bottomless void with the simple confidence of young birds reared high up there among the familiar chimney pots and interposed horrors of the abyss.

I leaned farther out. To and fro went the white wings, to and fro. There were no sounds from any of them. They knew man was asleep and this light for a little while was theirs. Or perhaps I had only dreamed about man in this city of wings—which he could surely never have built. Perhaps I, myself, was one of these birds dreaming unpleasantly a moment of old dangers far below as I teetered on a window ledge.

Around and around went the wings. It needed only a little courage, only a little shove from the window ledge, to enter that city of light. The muscles of my hands were already making little premonitory lunges. I wanted to enter that city and go away over the roofs in the first dawn. I wanted to enter it so badly that I drew back carefully into the room and opened the hall door. I found my coat on the chair, and it slowly became clear to me that there was a way down through the floors, that I was, after all, only a man.

I dressed then and went back to my own kind, and I have been rather more than usually careful ever since not to look into the city of light. I had seen, just once, man's greatest creation from a strange inverted angle, and it was not really his at all. I will never forget how those wings went round and round, and how, by the merest pressure of the fingers and a feeling for air, one might go away over the roofs. It is a knowledge, however, that is better kept to oneself. I think of it sometimes in such a way that the wings, beginning far down in the black depths of the mind, begin to rise and whirl till all the mind is lit by their spinning, and there is a sense of things passing away, but lightly, as a wing might veer over an obstacle.

To see from an inverted angle, however, is not a gift allotted merely to the human imagination. I have come to suspect that within their degree it is sensed by animals, though perhaps as rarely as among men. The time has to be right; one has to be, by chance or intention, upon the border of two worlds. And sometimes these two borders may shift or interpenetrate and one sees the miraculous.

I once saw this happen to a crow.

This crow lives near my house, and though I have never injured him, he takes good care to stay up in the very highest trees and, in general, to avoid humanity. His world begins at about the limit of my eyesight.

On the particular morning when this episode occurred, the whole countryside was buried in one of the thickest fogs in years. The ceiling was absolutely zero. All planes were grounded, and even a pedestrian could hardly see his outstretched hand before him.

I was groping across a field in the general direction of the railroad station, following a dimly outlined path. Suddenly out of the fog, at about the level of my eyes, and so closely that I flinched, there flashed a pair of immense black wings and a huge beak. The whole bird rushed over my head with a frantic cawing outcry of such hideous terror as I have never heard in a crow's voice before and never expect to hear again.

He was lost and startled, I thought, as I recovered my poise. He ought not to have flown out in this fog. He'd knock his silly brains out.

All afternoon that great awkward cry rang in my head. Merely being lost in a fog seemed scarcely to account for it—especially in a tough, intelligent old bandit such as I knew that particular crow to be. I even looked once in the mirror to see what it might be about me that had so revolted him that he had cried out in protest to the very stones.

Finally, as I worked my way homeward along the path, the solution came to me. It should have been clear before. The borders of our worlds had shifted. It was the fog that had done it. That crow, and I knew him well, never under normal circumstances flew low near men. He had been lost all right, but it was more than that. He had thought he was high up, and when he encountered me looming gigantically through the fog, he had perceived a ghastly and, to the crow mind, unnatural sight. He had seen a man walking on air, desecrating the very heart of the crow kingdom, a harbinger of the most profound evil a crow mind could conceive of—air-walking men. The encounter, he must have thought, had taken place a hundred feet over the roofs.

He caws now when he sees me leaving for the station in the morning, and I fancy that in that note I catch the uncertainty of a mind that has come to know things are not always what they seem. He has seen a marvel in his heights of air and is no longer as other crows. He has experienced the human world from an unlikely perspective. He and I share a viewpoint in common: our worlds have interpenetrated, and we both have faith in the miraculous.

It is a faith that in my own case has been augmented by two remarkable sights. I once saw some very odd chemicals fly across a waste so dead it might have been upon the moon, and once, by an even more fantastic piece of luck, I was present when a group of birds passed a judgment upon life.

On the maps of the old voyagers it is called *Mauvaises Terres,* the evil lands, and, slurred a little with the passage through many minds, it has come down to us anglicized as the badlands. The soft shuffle of moccasins has passed through its canyons on the grim business of war and flight, but the last of those slight disturbances of immemorial silences died out almost a century ago. The land, if one can call it a land, is a waste as lifeless as that valley in which lie the kings of Egypt. Like the Valley of the Kings, it is a mausoleum, a place of dry bones in what once was a place of life. Now it has silences as deep as those in the moon's airless chasms.

Nothing grows among its pinnacles; there is no shade except under great toadstools of sandstone whose bases have been eaten to the shape of wine glasses by the wind. Everything is flaking, cracking, disintegrating, wearing away in the long, imperceptible weather of time. The ash of ancient volcanic outbursts still sterilizes its soil, and its colors in that waste are the colors that flame in the lonely sunsets on dead planets. Men come there but rarely, and for one purpose only, the collection of bones.

It was a late hour on a cold, wind-bitten autumn day when I climbed a great hill spined like a dinosaur's back and tried to take my bearings. The tumbled waste fell away in waves in all directions. Blue air was darkening into purple along the bases of the hills. I shifted my knapsack, heavy with the petrified bones of long-vanished creatures, and studied my compass. I wanted to be out of there by nightfall, and already the sun was going sullenly down in the west.

It was then that I saw the flight coming on. It was moving like a little close-knit body of black specks that danced and darted and closed again. It was pouring from the north and heading toward me with the undeviating relentlessness of a compass needle. It streamed through the shadows rising out of monstrous gorges. It rushed over towering pinnacles in the red light of the sun or momentarily sank from sight within their shade. Across that desert of eroding clay and wind-worn stone they came with a faint wild twittering that filled all the air about me as those tiny living bullets hurtled past into the night.

It may not strike you as a marvel. It would not, perhaps, unless you stood in the middle of a dead world at sunset, but that was where I stood. Fifty million years lay under my feet, fifty million years of bellowing monsters moving in a green world now gone so utterly that its very light was traveling on the farther edge of space. The chemicals of all that vanished age lay about me in the ground. Around me still lay the shearing molars of dead titanotheres, the delicate sabers of soft-stepping cats, the hollow sockets that had held the eyes of many a strange, outmoded beast. Those eyes had looked out upon a world as real as ours; dark, savage brains had roamed and roared their challenges into the steaming night.

Now they were still here, or, put it as you will, the chemicals that made them were here about me in the ground. The carbon that had driven them ran blackly in the eroding stone. The stain of iron was in the clays. The iron did not remember the blood it had once moved within, the phosphorus had forgot the savage brain. The little individual moment had ebbed from all those strange combinations of chemicals as it would ebb from our living bodies into the sinks and runnels of oncoming time.

I had lifted up a fistful of that ground. I held it while that wild flight of south-bound warblers hurtled over me into the oncoming dark. There went phosphorus, there went iron, there went carbon, there beat the calcium in those hurrying wings. Alone on a dead planet I watched that incredible miracle speeding past. It ran by some true compass over field and waste land. It cried its individual ecstasies into the air until the gullies rang. It swerved like a single body, it knew itself, and, lonely, it bunched close in the racing darkness, its individual entities feeling about them the rising night. And so, crying to each other their identity, they passed away out of my view.

I dropped my fistful of earth. I heard it roll inanimate back into the gully at the base of the hill: iron, carbon, the chemicals of life. Like men from those wild tribes who had haunted these hills before me seeking visions, I made my sign to the great darkness. It was not a mocking sign, and I was not mocked. As I walked into my camp late that night, one man, rousing from his blankets beside the fire, asked sleepily, "What did you see?"

"I think, a miracle," I said softly, but I said it to myself. Behind me that vast waste began to glow under the rising moon.

I have said that I saw a judgment upon life, and that it was not passed by men. Those who stare at birds in cages or who test minds by their closeness to our own may not care for it. It comes from far away out of my past, in a place of pouring waters and green leaves. I shall never see an episode like it again if I live to be a hundred, nor do I think that one man in a million has ever seen it, because man is an intruder into such silences. The light must be right, and the observer must remain unseen. No man sets up such an experiment. What he sees, he sees by chance.

You may put it that I had come over a mountain, that I had slogged through fern and pine needles for half a long day, and that on the edge of a little glade with one long, crooked branch extending across it, I had sat down to rest with my back against a stump. Through accident I was concealed from the glade, although I could see into it perfectly.

The sun was warm there, and the murmurs of forest life blurred softly away into my sleep. When I awoke, dimly aware of some commotion and outcry in the clearing, the light was slanting down through the pines in such a way that the glade was lit like some vast cathedral. I could see the dust motes of wood pollen in the long shaft of light, and there on the extended branch sat an enormous raven with a red and squirming nestling in his beak.

The sound that awoke me was the outraged cries of the nestling's parents, who flew helplessly in circles about the clearing. The sleek black monster was indifferent to them. He gulped, whetted his beak on the dead branch a moment, and sat still. Up to that point the little tragedy had followed the usual pattern. But suddenly, out of all that area of woodland, a soft sound of complaint began to rise. Into the glade fluttered small birds of half a dozen varieties drawn by the anguished outcries of the tiny parents.

No one dared to attack the raven. But they cried there in some instinctive common misery, the bereaved and the unbereaved. The glade filled with their soft rustling and their cries. They fluttered as though to point their wings at the murderer. There was a dim intangible ethic he had violated, that they knew. He was a bird of death.

And he, the murderer, the black bird at the heart of life, sat on there glistening in the common light, formidable, unmoving, unperturbed, untouchable.

The sighing died. It was then I saw the judgment. It was the judgment of life against death. I will never see it again so forcefully presented. I will never hear it again in notes so tragically prolonged. For in the midst of protest, they forgot the violence. There, in that clearing, the crystal note of a song sparrow lifted hesitantly in the hush. And finally, after painful fluttering, another took the song, and then another, the song passing from one bird to another, doubtfully at first, as though some evil thing were being slowly forgotten. Till suddenly they took heart and sang from many throats joyously together as birds are known to sing. They sang because life is sweet and sunlight beautiful. They sang under the brooding shadow of the raven. In simple truth they had forgotten the raven, for they were the singers of life, and not of death.

I was not of that airy company. My limbs were the heavy limbs of an earthbound creature who could climb mountains, even the mountains of the mind, only by a great effort of will. I knew I had seen a marvel and observed a judgment, but the mind which was my human endowment was sure to question it and to be at me day by day with its heresies until I grew to doubt the meaning of what I had seen. Eventually darkness and subtleties would ring me round once more.

And so it proved until, on the top of a stepladder, I made one more observation upon life. It was cold that autumn evening, and, standing under a suburban street light in a spate of leaves and beginning snow, I was suddenly conscious of some huge and hairy shadows dancing over the pavement. They seemed attached to an odd, globular shape that was magnified above me. There was no mistaking it. I was standing under the shadow of an orb-weaving spider. Gigantically projected against the street, she was about her spinning when everything was going underground. Even her cables were magnified upon the sidewalk and already I was half-entangled in their shadows.

"Good Lord," I thought, "she has found herself a kind of minor sun and is going to upset the course of nature."

I procured a ladder from my yard and climbed up to inspect the situation. There she was, the universe running down around her, warmly arranged among her guy ropes attached to the lamp supports—a great black and yellow embodiment of the life force, not giving up to either frost or stepladders. She ignored me and went on tightening and improving her web.

I stood over her on the ladder, a faint snow touching my cheeks, and surveyed her universe. There were a couple of iridescent green beetle cases turning slowly on a loose strand of web, a fragment of luminescent eye from a moth's wing and a large indeterminable object, perhaps a cicada, that had struggled and been wrapped in silk. There were also little bits and slivers, little red and blue flashes from the scales of anonymous wings that had crashed there.

Some days, I thought, they will be dull and gray and the shine will be out of them; then the dew will polish them again and drops hang on the silk until everything is gleaming and turning in the light. It is like a mind, really, where everything changes but remains, and in the end you have these eaten-out bits of experience like beetle wings.

I stood over her a moment longer, comprehending somewhat reluctantly that her adventure against the great blind forces of winter, her seizure of this warming globe of light, would come to nothing and was hopeless. Nevertheless it brought the birds back into my mind, and that faraway song which had traveled with growing strength around a forest clearing years ago—a kind of heroism, a world where even a spider refuses to lie down and die if a rope can still be spun on to a star. Maybe man himself will fight like this in the end, I thought, slowly realizing that the web and its threatening yellow occupant had been added to some luminous store of experience, shining for a moment in the fogbound reaches of my brain.

The mind, it came to me as I slowly descended the ladder, is a very remarkable thing; it has gotten itself a kind of courage by looking at a spider in a street lamp. Here was something that ought to be passed on to those who will fight our final freezing battle with the void. I thought of setting it down carefully as a message to the future: *In the days of the frost seek a minor sun.*

But as I hesitated, it became plain that something was wrong. The marvel was escaping—a sense of bigness beyond man's power to grasp, the essence of life in its great dealings with the universe. It was better, I decided, for the emissaries returning from the wilderness, even if they were merely descending from a stepladder, to record their marvel, not to define its meaning. In that way it would go echoing on through the minds of men, each grasping at that beyond out of which the miracles emerge, and which, once defined, ceases to satisfy the human need for symbols.

In the end I merely made a mental note: One specimen of Epeira observed building a web in a street light. Late autumn and cold for spiders. Cold for men, too. I shivered and left the lamp glowing there in my mind. The last I saw of Epeira she was hauling steadily on a cable. I stepped carefully over her shadow as I walked away.

(1956)

JAMES BALDWIN

[1924–1989]

Notes of a Native Son

I

On the 29th of July, in 1943, my father died. On the same day, a few hours later, his last child was born. Over a month before this, while all our energies were concentrated in waiting for these events, there had been, in Detroit, one of the bloodiest race riots of the century. A few hours after my father's funeral, while he lay in state in the undertaker's chapel, a race riot broke out in Harlem. On the morning of the 3rd of August, we drove my father to the graveyard through a wilderness of smashed plate glass.

The day of my father's funeral had also been my nineteenth birthday. As we drove him to the graveyard, the spoils of injustice, anarchy, discontent, and hatred were all around us. It seemed to me that God himself had devised, to mark my father's end, the most sustained and brutally dissonant of codas. And it seemed to me, too, that the violence which rose all about us as my father left the world had been devised as a corrective for the pride of his eldest son. I had declined to believe in that apocalypse which had been central to my father's vision; very well, life seemed to be saying, here is something that will certainly pass for an apocalypse until the real thing comes along. I had inclined to be contemptuous of my father for the conditions of his life, for the conditions of our lives. When his life had ended I began to wonder about that life and also, in a new way, to be apprehensive about my own.

I had not known my father very well. We had got on badly, partly because we shared, in our different fashions, the vice of stubborn pride. When he was dead I realized that I had hardly ever spoken to him. When he had been dead a long time I began to wish I had. It seems to be typical of life in America, where opportunities, real and fancied, are thicker than anywhere else on the globe, that the second generation has no time to talk to the first. No one, including my father, seems to have known exactly how old he was, but his mother had been born during slavery. He was of the first generation of free men. He, along with thousands of other Negroes, came North after 1919 and I was part of that generation which had never seen the landscape of what Negroes sometimes call the Old Country.

He had been born in New Orleans and had been a quite young man there during the time that Louis Armstrong, a boy, was running errands for the dives and honky-tonks of what was always presented to me as one of the most wicked of cities—to this day, whenever I think of New Orleans, I also helplessly think of Sodom and Gomorrah. My father never mentioned Louis Armstrong, except to forbid us to play his records; but there was a picture of him on our wall for a long time. One of my father's strong-willed female relatives had placed it there and forbade my father to take it down. He never did, but he eventually maneuvered her out of the house and when, some years later, she was in trouble and near death, he refused to do anything to help her.

He was, I think, very handsome. I gather this from photographs and from my own memories of him, dressed in his Sunday best and on his way to preach a sermon some-where, when I was little. Handsome, proud, and ingrown, "like a toe-nail," somebody said. But he looked to me, as I grew older, like pictures I had seen of African tribal chieftains: he really should have been naked, with war-paint on and barbaric memen-tos, standing among spears. He could be chilling in the pulpit and indescribably cruel in his personal life and he was certainly the most bitter man I have ever met; yet it must be said that there was something else in him, buried in him, which lent him his tremen-dous power and, even, a rather crushing charm. It had something to do with his black-ness, I think—he was very black—with his blackness and his beauty, and with the fact that he knew that he was black but did not know that he was beautiful. He claimed to be proud of his blackness but it had also been the cause of much humiliation and it had fixed bleak boundaries to his life. He was not a young man when we were growing up and he had already suffered many kinds of ruin; in his outrageously demanding and protective way he loved his children, who were black like him and menaced, like him; and all these things sometimes showed in his face when he tried, never to my knowl-edge with any success, to establish contact with any of us. When he took one of his children on his knee to play, the child always became fretful and began to cry; when he tried to help one of us with our homework the absolutely unabating tension which emanated from him caused our minds and our tongues to become paralyzed, so that he, scarcely knowing why, flew into a rage and the child, not knowing why, was pun-ished. If it ever entered his head to bring a surprise home for his children, it was, al-most unfailingly, the wrong surprise and even the big watermelons he often brought home on his back in the summertime led to the most appalling scenes. I do not re-member, in all those years, that one of his children was ever glad to see him come home. From what I was able to gather of his early life, it seemed that this inability to estab-lish contact with other people had always marked him and had been one of the things which had driven him out of New Orleans. There was something in him, therefore, groping and tentative, which was never expressed and which was buried with him. One saw it most clearly when he was facing new people and hoping to impress them. But he never did, not for long. We went from church to smaller and more improbable church, he found himself in less and less demand as a minister, and by the time he died none of his friends had come to see him for a long time. He had lived and died in an intolerable bitterness of spirit and it frightened me, as we drove him to the graveyard through those unquiet, ruined streets, to see how powerful and overflowing this bit-terness could be and to realize that this bitterness now was mine.

When he died I had been away from home for a little over a year. In that year I had had time to become aware of the meaning of all my father's bitter warnings, had dis-covered the secret of his proudly pursed lips and rigid carriage: I had discovered the weight of white people in the world. I saw that this had been for my ancestors and now would be for me an awful thing to live with and that the bitterness which had helped to kill my father could also kill me.

He had been ill a long time—in the mind, as we now realized, reliving instances of his fantastic intransigence in the new light of his affliction and endeavoring to feel a sorrow for him which never, quite, came true. We had not known that he was being eaten up by paranoia, and the discovery that his cruelty, to our bodies and our minds, had been one of the symptoms of his illness was not, then, enough to enable us to forgive him. The younger children felt, quite simply, relief that he would not be coming home anymore. My mother's observation that it was he, after all, who had kept them alive all these years meant nothing because the problems of keeping children alive are not real for children. The older children felt, with my father gone, that they could invite their friends to the house without fear that their friends would be insulted or, as had sometimes happened with me, being told that their friends were in league with the devil and intended to rob our family of everything we owned. (I didn't fail to wonder, and it made me hate him, what on earth we owned that anybody else would want.)

His illness was beyond all hope of healing before anyone realized that he was ill. He had always been so strange and had lived, like a prophet, in such unimaginably close communion with the Lord that his long silences which were punctuated by moans and hallelujahs and snatches of old songs while he sat at the living-room window never seemed odd to us. It was not until he refused to eat because, he said, his family was trying to poison him that my mother was forced to accept as a fact what had, until then, been only an unwilling suspicion. When he was committed, it was discovered that he had tuberculosis and, as it turned out, the disease of his mind allowed the disease of his body to destroy him. For the doctors could not force him to eat, either, and, though he was fed intravenously, it was clear from the beginning that there was no hope for him.

In my mind's eye I could see him, sitting at the window, locked up in his terrors; hating and fearing every living soul including his children who had betrayed him, too, by reaching towards the world which had despised him. There were nine of us. I began to wonder what it could have felt like for such a man to have had nine children whom he could barely feed. He used to make little jokes about our poverty, which never, of course, seemed very funny to us; they could not have seemed very funny to him, either, or else our all too feeble response to them would never have caused such rages. He spent great energy and achieved, to our chagrin, no small amount of success in keeping us away from the people who surrounded us, people who had all-night rent parties to which we listened when we should have been sleeping, people who cursed and drank and flashed razor blades on Lenox Avenue. He could not understand why, if they had so much energy to spare, they could not use it to make their lives better. He treated almost everybody on our block with a most uncharitable asperity and neither they, nor, of course, their children were slow to reciprocate.

The only white people who came to our house were welfare workers and bill collectors. It was almost always my mother who dealt with them, for my father's temper, which was at the mercy of his pride, was never to be trusted. It was clear that he felt their very presence in his home to be a violation: this was conveyed by his carriage, almost ludicrously stiff, and by his voice, harsh and vindictively polite. When I was around nine or ten I wrote a play which was directed by a young, white schoolteacher, a woman, who then took an interest in me, and gave me books to read and, in order to corroborate my theatrical bent, decided to take me to see what she somewhat tactlessly referred to as "real" plays. Theatergoing was forbidden in our house, but, with the really cruel intuitiveness of a child, I suspected that the color of this woman's skin would carry the day for me. When, at school, she suggested taking me to the theater, I did not, as I might have done if she had been a Negro, find a way of discouraging her, but agreed that she should pick me up at my house one evening. I then, very cleverly, left all the rest to my mother, who suggested to my father, as I knew she would, that it would not be very nice to let such a kind woman make the trip for nothing. Also, since it was a schoolteacher, I imagine that my mother countered the idea of sin with the idea of "education," which word, even with my father, carried a kind of bitter weight.

Before the teacher came my father took me aside to ask *why* she was coming, what *interest* she could possibly have in our house, in a boy like me. I said I didn't know but I, too, suggested that it had something to do with education. And I understood that my father was waiting for me to say something—I didn't quite know what; perhaps that I wanted his protection against this teacher and her "education." I said none of these things and the teacher came and we went out. It was clear, during the brief interview in our living room, that my father was agreeing very much against his will and that he would have refused permission if he had dared. The fact that he did not dare caused me to despise him: I had no way of knowing that he was facing in that living room a wholly unprecedented and frightening situation.

Later, when my father had been laid off from his job, this woman became very important to us. She was really a very sweet and generous woman and went to a great deal of trouble to be of help to us, particularly during one awful winter. My mother called her by the highest name she knew. She said she was a "christian." My father could scarcely disagree but during the four or five years of our relatively close association he never trusted her and was always trying to surprise in her open, Midwestern face the genuine, cunningly hidden, and hideous motivation. In later years, particularly when it began to be clear that this "education" of mine was going to lead me to perdition, he became more explicit and warned me that my white friends in high school were not really my friends and that I would see, when I was older, how white people would do anything to keep a Negro down. Some of them could be nice, he admitted, but none of them were to be trusted and most of them were not even nice. The best thing was to have as little to do with them as possible. I did not feel this way and I was certain, in my innocence, that I never would.

But the year which preceded my father's death had made a great change in my life. I had been living in New Jersey, working in defense plants, working and living among southerners, white and black. I knew about the south, of course, and about how southerners treated Negroes and how they expected them to behave, but it had never entered my mind that anyone would look at me and expect *me* to behave that way. I learned in New Jersey that to be a Negro meant, precisely, that one was never looked at but was simply at the mercy of the reflexes the color of one's skin caused in other people. I acted in New Jersey as I had always acted, that is as though I thought a great deal of myself—I had to *act* that way—with results that were, simply, unbelievable. I had scarcely arrived before I had earned the enmity, which was extraordinarily ingenious, of all my superiors and nearly all my co-workers. In the beginning, to make matters worse, I simply did not know what was happening. I did not know what I had done, and I shortly began to wonder what *anyone* could possibly do, to bring about such unanimous, active, and unbearably vocal hostility. I knew about jim-crow but I had never experienced it. I went to the same self-service restaurant three times and stood with all the Princeton boys before the counter, waiting for a hamburger and coffee; it was always an extraordinarily long time before anything was set before me; but it was not until the fourth visit that I learned that, in fact, nothing had ever been set before me: I had simply picked something up. Negroes were not served there, I was told, and they had been waiting for me to realize that I was always the only Negro present. Once I was told this, I determined to go there all the time. But now they were ready for me and, though some dreadful scenes were subsequently enacted in that restaurant, I never ate there again.

It was the same story all over New Jersey, in bars, bowling alleys, diners, places to live. I was always being forced to leave, silently, or with mutual imprecations. I very shortly became notorious and children giggled behind me when I passed and their elders whispered or shouted—they really believed that I was mad. And it did begin to work on my mind, of course; I began to be afraid to go anywhere and to compensate for this I went places to which I really should not have gone and where, God knows, I had no desire to be. My reputation in town naturally enhanced my reputation at work and my working day became one long series of acrobatics designed to keep me out of trouble. I cannot say that these acrobatics succeeded. It began to seem that the machinery of the organization I worked for was turning over, day and night, with but one aim: to eject me. I was fired once, and contrived, with the aid of a friend from New York, to get back on the payroll; was fired again, and bounced back again. It took a while to fire me for the third time, but the third time took. There were no loopholes anywhere. There was not even any way of getting back inside the gates.

That year in New Jersey lives in my mind as though it were the year during which, having an unsuspected predilection for it, I first contracted some dread, chronic disease, the unfailing symptom of which is a kind of blind fever, a pounding in the skull and fire in the bowels. Once this disease is contracted, one can never be really carefree again, for the fever, without an instant's warning, can recur at any moment. It can wreck more important things than race relations. There is not a Negro alive who does not have this rage in his blood—one has the choice, merely, of living with it consciously or surrendering to it. As for me, this fever has recurred in me, and does, and will until the day I die.

My last night in New Jersey, a white friend from New York took me to the nearest big town, Trenton, to go to the movies and have a few drinks. As it turned out, he also saved me from, at the very least, a violent whipping. Almost every detail of that night stands out very clearly in my memory. I even remember the name of the movie we saw because its title impressed me as being so patly ironical. It was a movie about the German occupation of France, starring Maureen O'Hara and Charles Laughton and called *This Land Is Mine*. I remember the name of the diner we walked into when the movie ended: it was the "American Diner." When we walked in the counterman asked what we wanted and I remember answering with the casual sharpness which had become my habit: "We want a hamburger and a cup of coffee, what do you think we want?" I do not know why, after a year of such rebuffs, I so completely failed to anticipate his answer, which was, of course, "We don't serve Negroes here." This reply failed to discompose me, at least for the moment. I made some sardonic comment about the name of the diner and we walked out into the streets.

This was the time of what was called the "brown-out," when the lights in all American cities were very dim. When we re-entered the streets something happened to me which had the force of an optical illusion, or a nightmare. The streets were very crowded and I was facing north. People were moving in every direction but it seemed to me, in that instant, that all of the people I could see, and many more than that, were moving toward me, against me, and that everyone was white. I remember how their faces gleamed. And I felt, like a physical sensation, a *click* at the nape of my neck as though some interior string connecting my head to my body had been cut. I began to walk. I heard my friend call after me, but I ignored him. Heaven only knows what was going on in his mind, but he had the good sense not to touch me—I don't know what would have happened if he had—and to keep me in sight. I don't know what was going on in my mind, either; I certainly had no conscious plan. I wanted to do something to crush these white faces, which were crushing me. I walked for perhaps a block or two until I came to an enormous, glittering, and fashionable restaurant in which I knew not even the intercession of the Virgin would cause me to be served. I pushed through the doors and took the first vacant seat I saw, at a table for two, and waited.

I do not know how long I waited and I rather wonder, until today, what I could possibly have looked like. Whatever I looked like, I frightened the waitress who shortly appeared, and the moment she appeared all of my fury flowed towards her. I hated her for her white face, and for her great, astounded, frightened eyes. I felt that if she found a black man so frightening I would make her fright worth-while.

She did not ask me what I wanted, but repeated, as though she had learned it somewhere, "We don't serve Negroes here." She did not say it with the blunt, decisive hostility to which I had grown so accustomed, but, rather, with a note of apology in her voice, and fear. This made me colder and more murderous than ever. I felt I had to do something with my hands. I wanted her to come close enough for me to get her neck between my hands.

So I pretended not to have understood her, hoping to draw her closer. And she did step a very short step closer, with her pencil poised incongruously over her pad, and repeated the formula: ". . . don't serve Negroes here."

Somehow, with the repetition of that phrase, which was already ringing in my head like a thousand bells of a nightmare, I realized that she would never come any closer and that I would have to strike from a distance. There was nothing on the table but an ordinary water-mug half full of water, and I picked this up and hurled it with all my strength at her. She ducked and it missed her and shattered against the mirror behind the bar. And, with that sound, my frozen blood abruptly thawed, I returned from wherever I had been, I *saw,* for the first time, the restaurant, the people with their mouths open, already, as it seemed to me, rising as one man, and I realized what I had done, and where I was, and I was frightened. I rose and began running for the door. A round, potbellied man grabbed me by the nape of the neck just as I reached the doors and began to beat me about the face. I kicked him and got loose and ran into the streets. My friend whispered, *"Run!"* and I ran.

My friend stayed outside the restaurant long enough to misdirect my pursuers and the police, who arrived, he told me, at once. I do not know what I said to him when he came to my room that night. I could not have said much. I felt, in the oddest, most awful way, that I had somehow betrayed him. I lived it over and over and over again, the way one relives an automobile accident after it has happened and one finds oneself alone and safe. I could not get over two facts, both equally difficult for the imagination to grasp, and one was that I could have been murdered. But the other was that I had been ready to commit murder. I saw nothing very clearly but I did see this: that my life, my *real* life, was in danger, and not from anything other people might do but from the hatred I carried in my own heart.

2

I had returned home around the second week in June—in great haste because it seemed that my father's death and my mother's confinement were both but a matter of hours. In the case of my mother, it soon became clear that she had simply made a miscalculation. This had always been her tendency and I don't believe that a single one of us arrived in the world, or has since arrived anywhere else, on time. But none of us dawdled so intolerably about the business of being born as did my baby sister. We sometimes amused ourselves, during those endless, stifling weeks, by picturing the baby sitting within in the safe, warm dark, bitterly regretting the necessity of becoming a part of our chaos and stubbornly putting it off as long as possible. I understood her perfectly and congratulated her on showing such good sense so soon. Death, however, sat as purposefully at my father's bedside as life stirred within my mother's womb and it was harder to understand why he so lingered in that long shadow. It seemed that he had bent, and for a long time, too, all of his energies towards dying. Now death was ready for him but my father held back.

All of Harlem, indeed, seemed to be infected by waiting. I had never before known it to be so violently still. Racial tensions throughout this country were exacerbated during the early years of the war, partly because the labor market brought together hundreds of thousands of ill-prepared people and partly because Negro soldiers, regardless of where they were born, received their military training in the south. What happened in defense plants and army camps had repercussions, naturally, in every Negro ghetto. The situation in Harlem had grown bad enough for clergymen, policemen, educators, politicians, and social workers to assert in one breath that there was no "crime wave" and to offer, in the very next breath, suggestions as to how to combat it. These suggestions always seemed to involve playgrounds, too. Playground or not, crime wave or not, the Harlem police force had been augmented in March, and the unrest grew—perhaps, in fact, partly as a result of the ghetto's instinctive hatred of policemen. Perhaps the most revealing news item, out of the steady parade of reports of muggings, stabbings, shootings, assaults, gang wars, and accusations of police brutality is the item concerning six Negro girls who set upon a white girl in the subway because, as they all too accurately put it, she was stepping on their toes. Indeed she was, all over the nation.

I had never before been so aware of policemen, on foot, on horseback, on corners, everywhere, always two by two. Nor had I ever been so aware of small knots of people. They were on stoops and on corners and in doorways, and what was striking about them, I think, was that they did not seem to be talking. Never, when I passed these groups, did the usual sound of a curse or a laugh ring out and neither did there seem to be any hum of gossip. There was certainly, on the other hand, occurring between them communication extraordinarily intense. Another thing that was striking was the unexpected diversity of the people who made up these groups. Usually, for example, one would see a group of sharpies standing on the street corner, jiving the passing chicks; or a group of older men, usually, for some reason, in the vicinity of a barber shop, discussing baseball scores, or the numbers, or making rather chilling observations about women they had known. Women, in a general way, tended to be seen less often together—unless they were church women, or very young girls, or prostitutes met together for an unprofessional instant. But that summer I saw the strangest combinations:

large, respectable, churchly matrons standing on the stoops or the corners with their hair tied up, together with a girl in sleazy satin whose face bore the marks of gin and the razor, or heavyset, abrupt, no-nonsense older men, in company with the most disreputable and fanatical "race" men, or these same "race" men with the sharpies, or these sharpies with the churchly women. Seventh Day Adventists and Methodists and Spiritualists seemed to be hobnobbing with Holyrollers and they were all, alike, entangled with the most flagrant disbelievers; something heavy in their stance seemed to indicate that they had all, incredibly, seen a common vision, and on each face there seemed to be the same strange, bitter shadow.

The churchly women and the matter-of-fact, no-nonsense men had children in the Army. The sleazy girls they talked to had lovers there, the sharpies and the "race" men had friends and brothers there. It would have demanded an unquestioning patriotism, happily as uncommon in this country as it is undesirable, for these people not to have been disturbed by the bitter letters they received, by the newspaper stories they read, not to have been enraged by the posters, then to be found all over New York, which described the Japanese as "yellowbellied Japs." It was only the "race" men, to be sure, who spoke ceaselessly of being revenged—how this vengeance was to be exacted was not clear—for the indignities and dangers suffered by Negro boys in uniform; but everybody felt a directionless, hopeless bitterness, as well as that panic which can scarcely be suppressed when one knows that a human being one loves is beyond one's reach, and in danger. This helplessness and this gnawing uneasiness does something, at length, to even the toughest mind. Perhaps the best way to sum all this up is to say that the people I knew felt, mainly, a peculiar kind of relief when they knew that their boys were being shipped out of the south, to do battle overseas. It was, perhaps, like feeling that the most dangerous part of a dangerous journey had been passed and that now, even if death should come, it would come with honor and without the complicity of their countrymen. Such a death would be, in short, a fact with which one could hope to live.

It was on the 28th of July, which I believe was a Wednesday, that I visited my father for the first time during his illness and for the last time in his life. The moment I saw him I knew why I had put off this visit so long. I had told my mother that I did not want to see him because I hated him. But this was not true. It was only that I *had* hated him and I wanted to hold on to this hatred. I did not want to look on him as a ruin: it was not a ruin I had hated. I imagine that one of the reasons people cling to their hates so stubbornly is because they sense, once hate is gone, that they will be forced to deal with pain.

We traveled out to him, his older sister and myself, to what seemed to be the very end of a very Long Island. It was hot and dusty and we wrangled, my aunt and I, all the way out, over the fact that I had recently begun to smoke and, as she said, to give myself airs. But I knew that she wrangled with me because she could not bear to face the fact of her brother's dying. Neither could I endure the reality of her despair, her unstated bafflement as to what had happened to her brother's life, and her own. So we wrangled and I smoked and from time to time she fell into a heavy reverie. Covertly, I watched her face, which was the face of an old woman; it had fallen in, the eyes were sunken and lightless; soon she would be dying, too.

In my childhood—it had not been so long ago—I had thought her beautiful. She had been quick-witted and quick-moving and very generous with all the children and each of her visits had been an event. At one time one of my brothers and myself had thought of running away to live with her. Now she could no longer produce out of her handbag some unexpected and yet familiar delight. She made me feel pity and revulsion and fear. It was awful to realize that she no longer caused me to feel affection. The closer we came to the hospital the more querulous she became and at the same time, naturally, grew more dependent on me. Between pity and guilt and fear I began to feel that there was another me trapped in my skull like a jack-in-the-box who might escape my control at any moment and fill the air with screaming.

She began to cry the moment we entered the room and she saw him lying there, all shriveled and still, like a little black monkey. The great, gleaming apparatus which fed him and would have compelled him to be still even if he had been able to move brought to mind, not beneficence, but torture; the tubes entering his arm made me think of pictures I had seen when a child, of Gulliver, tied down by the pygmies on that island. My aunt wept and wept, there was a whistling sound in my father's throat; nothing was said; he could not speak. I wanted to take his hand, to say something. But I do not know what I could have said, even if he could have heard me. He was not really in that room with us, he had at last really embarked on his journey; and though my aunt told me that he said he was going to meet Jesus, I did not hear anything except that whistling in his throat. The doctor came back and we left, into that unbearable train again, and home. In the morning came the telegram saying that he was dead. Then the house was suddenly full of relatives, friends, hysteria, and confusion and I quickly left my mother and the children to the care of those impressive women, who, in Negro communities at least, automatically appear at times of bereavement armed with lotions, proverbs, and patience, and an ability to cook. I went downtown. By the time I returned, later the same day, my mother had been carried to the hospital and the baby had been born.

3

For my father's funeral I had nothing black to wear and this posed a nagging problem all day long. It was one of those problems, simple, or impossible of solution, to which the mind insanely clings in order to avoid the mind's real trouble. I spent most of that day at the downtown apartment of a girl I knew, celebrating my birthday with whiskey and wondering what to wear that night. When planning a birthday celebration one naturally does not expect that it will be up against competition from a funeral and this girl had anticipated taking me out that night, for a big dinner and a night club afterwards. Sometime during the course of that long day we decided that we would go out anyway, when my father's funeral service was over. I imagine I decided it, since, as the funeral hour approached, it became clearer and clearer to me that I would not know what to do with myself when it was over. The girl, stifling her very lively concern as to the possible effects of the whiskey on one of my father's chief mourners, concentrated on being conciliatory and practically helpful. She found a black shirt for me somewhere and ironed it and, dressed in the darkest pants and jacket I owned, and slightly drunk, I made my way to my father's funeral.

The chapel was full, but not packed, and very quiet. There were, mainly, my father's relatives, and his children, and here and there I saw faces I had not seen since childhood, the faces of my father's one-time friends. They were very dark and solemn now, seeming somehow to suggest that they had known all along that something like this would happen. Chief among the mourners was my aunt, who had quarreled with my father all his life; by which I do not mean to suggest that her mourning was insincere or that she had not loved him. I suppose that she was one of the few people in the world who had, and their incessant quarreling proved precisely the strength of the tie that bound them. The only other person in the world, as far as I knew, whose relationship to my father rivaled my aunt's in depth was my mother, who was not there.

It seemed to me, of course, that it was a very long funeral. But it was, if anything, a rather shorter funeral than most, nor, since there were no overwhelming, uncontrollable expressions of grief, could it be called—if I dare to use the word—successful. The minister who preached my father's funeral sermon was one of the few my father had still been seeing as he neared his end. He presented to us in his sermon a man whom none of us had ever seen—a man thoughtful, patient, and forbearing, a Christian inspiration to all who knew him, and a model for his children. And no doubt the children, in their disturbed and guilty state, were almost ready to believe this; he had been remote enough to be anything and, anyway, the shock of the incontrovertible, that it was really our father lying up there in that casket, prepared the mind for anything. His sister moaned and this grief-stricken moaning was taken as corroboration. The other faces held a dark, non-committal thoughtfulness. This was not the man they had known, but they had scarcely expected to be confronted with *him;* this was, in a sense deeper than questions of fact, the man they had not known, and the man they had not known may have been the real one. The real man, whoever he had been, had suffered and now he was dead: this was all that was sure and all that mattered now. Every man in the chapel hoped that when his hour came he, too, would be eulogized, which is to say forgiven, and that all of his lapses, greeds, errors, and strayings from the truth would be invested with coherence and looked upon with charity. This was perhaps the last thing human beings could give each other and it was what they demanded, after all, of the Lord. Only the Lord saw the midnight tears, only He was present when one of His children, moaning and wringing hands, paced up and down the room. When one slapped one's child in anger the recoil in the heart reverberated through heaven and became part of the pain of the universe. And when the children were hungry and sullen and distrustful and one watched them, daily, growing wilder, and further away, and running headlong into danger, it was the Lord who knew what the charged heart endured as the strap was laid to the backside; the Lord alone who knew what one *would* have said if one had had, like the Lord, the gift of the living word. It was the Lord who knew of the impossibility every parent in that room faced: how to prepare the child for the day when the child would be despised and how to *create* in the child—by what means?—a stronger antidote to this poison than one had found for oneself. The avenues, side streets, bars, billiard halls, hospitals, police stations, and even the playgrounds of Harlem—not to mention the houses of correction, the jails, and the morgue—testified to the potency of the poison while remaining silent as to the efficacy of whatever antidote, irresistibly raising the question of whether or not such an antidote existed; raising, which was worse, the question of whether or not an antidote was desirable; perhaps poison should be fought with poison. With these several schisms in the mind and with more terrors in the heart than could be named, it was better not to judge the man who had gone down under an impossible burden. It was better to remember: *Thou knowest this man's fall; but thou knowest not his wrassling.*

While the preacher talked and I watched the children—years of changing their diapers, scrubbing them, slapping them, taking them to school, and scolding them had had the perhaps inevitable result of making me love them, though I am not sure I knew this then—my mind was busily breaking out with a rash of disconnected impressions. Snatches of popular songs, indecent jokes, bits of books I had read, movie sequences, faces, voices, political issues—I thought I was going mad; all these impressions suspended, as it were, in the solution of the faint nausea produced in me by the heat and liquor. For a moment I had the impression that my alcoholic breath, inefficiently disguised with chewing gum, filled the entire chapel. Then someone began singing one of my father's favorite songs and, abruptly, I was with him, sitting on his knee, in the hot, enormous, crowded church which was the first church we attended. It was the Abyssinia Baptist Church on 138th Street. We had not gone there long. With this image, a host of others came. I had forgotten, in the rage of my growing up, how proud my father had been of me when I was little. Apparently, I had had a voice and my father had liked to show me off before the members of the church. I had forgotten what he had looked like when he was pleased but now I remembered that he had always been grinning with pleasure when my solos ended. I even remembered certain expressions on his face when he teased my mother—had he loved her? I would never know. And when had it all begun to change? For now it seemed that he had not always been cruel. I remembered being taken for a haircut and scraping my knee on the footrest of the barber's chair and I remembered my father's face as he soothed my crying and applied the stinging iodine. Then I remembered our fights, fights which had been of the worst possible kind because my technique had been silence.

I remembered the one time in all our life together when we had really spoken to each other.

It was on a Sunday and it must have been shortly before I left home. We were walking, just the two of us, in our usual silence, to or from church. I was in high school and had been doing a lot of writing and I was, at about this time, the editor of the high school magazine. But I had also been a Young Minister and had been preaching from the pulpit. Lately, I had been taking fewer engagements and preached as rarely as possible. It was said in the church, quite truthfully, that I was "cooling off."

My father asked me abruptly, "You'd rather write than preach, wouldn't you?"

I was astonished at his question—because it was a real question. I answered, "Yes."

That was all we said. It was awful to remember that that was all we had *ever* said.

The casket now was opened and the mourners were being led up the aisle to look for the last time on the deceased. The assumption was that the family was too overcome with grief to be allowed to make this journey alone and I watched while my aunt was led to the casket and, muffled in black, and shaking, led back to her seat. I disapproved of forcing the children to look on their dead father, considering that the shock of his death, or, more truthfully, the shock of death as a reality, was already a little more than a child could bear, but my judgment in this matter had been overruled and there they were, bewildered and frightened and very small, being led, one by one, to the casket. But there is also something very gallant about children at such moments. It has something to do with their silence and gravity and with the fact that one cannot help them. Their legs, somehow, seem *exposed,* so that it is at once incredible and terribly clear that their legs are all they have to hold them up.

I had not wanted to go to the casket myself and I certainly had not wished to be led there, but there was no way of avoiding either of these forms. One of the deacons led me up and I looked on my father's face. I cannot say that it looked like him at all. His blackness had been equivocated by powder and there was no suggestion in that casket of what his power had or could have been. He was simply an old man dead, and it was hard to believe that he had ever given anyone either joy or pain. Yet, his life filled that room. Further up the avenue his wife was holding his newborn child. Life and death so close together, and love and hatred, and right and wrong, said something to me which I did not want to hear concerning man, concerning the life of man.

After the funeral, while I was downtown desperately celebrating my birthday, a Negro soldier, in the lobby of the Hotel Braddock, got into a fight with a white policeman over a Negro girl. Negro girls, white policemen, in or out of uniform, and Negro males—in or out of uniform—were part of the furniture of the lobby of the Hotel Braddock and this was certainly not the first time such an incident had occurred. It was destined, however, to receive an unprecedented publicity, for the fight between the policeman and the soldier ended with the shooting of the soldier. Rumor, flowing immediately to the streets outside, stated that the soldier had been shot in the back, an instantaneous and revealing invention, and that the soldier had died protecting a Negro woman. The facts were somewhat different—for example, the soldier had not been shot in the back, and was not dead, and the girl seems to have been as dubious a symbol of womanhood as her white counterpart in Georgia usually is, but no one was interested in the facts. They preferred the invention because this invention expressed and corroborated their hates and fears so perfectly. It is just as well to remember that people are always doing this. Perhaps many of those legends, including Christianity, to which the world clings began their conquest of the world with just some such concerted surrender to distortion. The effect, in Harlem, of this particular legend was like the effect of a lit match in a tin of gasoline. The mob gathered before the doors of the Hotel Braddock simply began to swell and to spread in every direction, and Harlem exploded.

The mob did not cross the ghetto lines. It would have been easy, for example, to have gone over to Morningside Park on the west side or to have crossed the Grand Central railroad tracks at 125th Street on the east side, to wreak havoc in white neighborhoods. The mob seems to have been mainly interested in something more potent and real than the white face, that is, in white power, and the principal damage done during the riot of the summer of 1943 was to white business establishments in Harlem. It might have been a far bloodier story, of course, if, at the hour the riot began, these establishments had still been open. From the Hotel Braddock the mob fanned out, east and west along 125th Street, and for the entire length of Lenox, Seventh, and Eighth avenues. Along each of these avenues, and along each major side street—116th, 125th, 135th, and so on—bars, stores, pawnshops, restaurants, even little luncheonettes had been smashed open and entered and looted—looted, it might be added, with more haste than efficiency. The shelves really looked as though a bomb had struck them. Cans of beans and soup and dog food, along with toilet paper, corn flakes, sardines and milk tumbled every which way, and abandoned cash registers and cases of beer leaned crazily out of the splintered windows and were strewn along the avenues. Sheets, blankets, and clothing of every description formed a kind of path, as though people had dropped them while running. I truly had not realized that Harlem *had* so many stores until I saw them all smashed open; the first time the word *wealth* ever entered my mind in relation to Harlem was when I saw it scattered in the streets. But one's first, incongruous impression of plenty was countered immediately by an impression of waste. None of this was doing anybody any good. It would have been better to have left the plate glass as it had been and the goods lying in the stores.

It would have been better, but it would also have been intolerable, for Harlem had needed something to smash. To smash something is the ghetto's chronic need. Most of the time it is the members of the ghetto who smash each other, and themselves. But as long as the ghetto walls are standing there will always come a moment when these outlets do not work. That summer, for example, it was not enough to get into a fight on Lenox Avenue, or curse out one's cronies in the barber shops. If ever, indeed, the violence which fills Harlem's churches, pool halls, and bars erupts outward in a more direct fashion, Harlem and its citizens are likely to vanish in an apocalyptic flood. That this is not likely to happen is due to a great many reasons, most hidden and powerful among them the Negro's real relation to the white American. This relation prohibits, simply, anything as uncomplicated and satisfactory as pure hatred. In order really to hate white people, one has to blot so much out of the mind—and the heart—that this hatred itself becomes an exhausting and self-destructive pose. But this does not mean, on the other hand, that love comes easily: the white world is too powerful, too complacent, too ready with gratuitous humiliation, and, above all, too ignorant and too innocent for that. One is absolutely forced to make perpetual qualifications and one's own reactions are always canceling each other out. It is this, really, which has driven so many people mad, both white and black. One is always in the position of having to decide between amputation and gangrene. Amputation is swift but time may prove that the amputation was not necessary—or one may delay the amputation too long. Gangrene is slow, but it is impossible to be sure that one is reading one's symptoms right. The idea of going through life as a cripple is more than one can bear, and equally unbearable is the risk of swelling up slowly, in agony, with poison. And the trouble, finally, is that the risks are real even if the choices do not exist.

"But as for me and my house," my father had said, "we will serve the Lord." I wondered, as we drove him to a resting place, what this line had meant for him. I had heard him preach it many times. I had preached it once myself, proudly giving it an interpretation different from my father's. Now the whole thing came back to me, as though my father and I were on our way to Sunday school and I were memorizing the golden text: *And if it seem evil unto you to serve the Lord, choose you this day whom you will serve; whether the gods which your fathers served that were on the other side of the flood, or the gods of the Amorites, in whose land ye dwell: but as for me and my house, we will serve the Lord.* I suspected in these familiar lines a meaning which had never been there for me before. All of my father's texts and songs, which I had decided were meaningless, were arranged before me at his death like empty bottles, waiting to hold the meaning which life would give them for me. This was his legacy: nothing is ever escaped. That bleakly memorable morning I hated the unbelievable streets and the Negroes and whites who had, equally, made them that way. But I knew that it was folly, as my father would have said, this bitterness was folly. It was necessary to hold on to the things that mattered. The dead man mattered, the new life mattered; blackness and whiteness did not matter; to believe that they did was to acquiesce in one's own destruction. Hatred, which could destroy so much, never failed to destroy the man who hated and this was an immutable law.

It began to seem that one would have to hold in the mind forever two ideas which seemed to be in opposition. The first idea was acceptance, the acceptance, totally without rancor, of life as it is, and men as they are: in the light of this idea, it goes without saying that injustice is a commonplace. But this did not mean that one could be complacent, for the second idea was of equal power: that one must never, in one's own life, accept these injustices as commonplace but must fight them with all one's strength. This fight begins, however, in the heart and it now had been laid to my charge to keep my own heart free of hatred and despair. This intimation made my heart heavy and, now that my father was irrecoverable, I wished that he had been beside me so that I could have searched his face for the answers which only the future would give me now.

(1955)

A SAMPLING OF CONTEMPORARY ESSAYS

TOM WOLFE

[b. 1931]

The Right Stuff

What an extraordinary grim stretch that had been . . . and yet thereafter Pete and Jane would keep running into pilots from other Navy bases, from the Air Force, from the Marines, who had been through their own extraordinary grim stretches. There was an Air Force pilot named Mike Collins, a nephew of former Army Chief of Staff J. Lawton Collins. Mike Collins had undergone eleven weeks of combat training at Nellis Air Force Base, near Las Vegas, and in that eleven weeks twenty-two of his fellow trainees had died in accidents, which was an extraordinary rate of two per week. Then there was a test pilot, Bill Bridgeman. In 1952, when Bridgeman was flying at Edwards Air Force Base, sixty-two Air Force pilots died in the course of thirty-six weeks of training, an extraordinary rate of 1.7 per week. Those figures were for fighter-pilot trainees only; they did not include the test pilots, Bridgeman's own confreres, who were dying quite regularly enough.

Extraordinary, to be sure; except that every veteran of flying small high-performance jets seemed to have experienced these bad strings.

In time, the Navy would compile statistics showing that for a career Navy pilot, i.e., one who intended to keep flying for twenty years as Conrad did, there was a 23 percent probability that he would die in an aircraft accident. This did not even include combat deaths, since the military did not classify death in combat as accidental. Furthermore, there was a better than even chance, a 56 percent probability, to be exact, that at some point a career Navy pilot would have to eject from his aircraft and attempt to come down by parachute. In the era of jet fighters, ejection meant being exploded out of the cockpit by a nitroglycerine charge, like a human cannonball. The ejection itself was so hazardous—men lost knees, arms, and their lives on the rim of the cockpit or had the skin torn off their faces when they hit the "wall" of air outside—that many pilots chose to wrestle their aircraft to the ground rather than try it . . . and died that way instead.

The statistics were not secret, but neither were they widely known, having been eased into print rather obliquely in a medical journal. No pilot, and certainly no pilot's wife, had any need of the statistics in order to know the truth, however. The funerals took care of that in the most dramatic way possible. Sometimes, when the young wife of a fighter pilot would have a little reunion with the girls she went to school with, an odd fact would dawn on her: *they* have not been going to funerals. And then Jane Conrad would look at Pete . . . Princeton, Class of 1953 . . . Pete had already worn his great dark sepulchral bridge coat more than most boys of the Class of '53 had worn their tuxedos. How many of those happy young men had buried more than a dozen friends, comrades, and co-workers? (Lost through violent death in the execution of everyday duties.) At the time, the 1950's, students from Princeton took great pride in going into what they considered highly competitive, aggressive pursuits, jobs on Wall Street, on Madison Avenue, and at magazines such as *Time* and *Newsweek*. There was much fashionably brutish talk of what "dog-eat-dog" and "cutthroat" competition they found there; but in the rare instances when one of these young men died on the job, it was likely to be from choking on a chunk of Chateaubriand, while otherwise blissfully boiled, in an expense-account restaurant in Manhattan. How many would have gone to work, or stayed at work, on cutthroat Madison Avenue if there had been a 23 percent chance, nearly one chance in four, of dying from it? Gentlemen, we're having this little problem with chronic violent death . . .

And yet was there any basic way in which Pete (or Wally Schirra or Jim Lovell or any of the rest of them) was different from other college boys his age? There didn't seem to be, other than his love of flying. Pete's father was a Philadelphia stockbroker who in Pete's earliest years had a house in the Main Line suburbs, a limousine, and a chauffeur. The Depression eliminated the terrific brokerage business, the house, the car, and the servants; and by and by his parents were divorced and his father moved to Florida. Perhaps because his father had been an observation balloonist in the First World War—an adventurous business, since the balloons were prized targets of enemy aircraft—Pete was fascinated by flying. He went to Princeton on the Holloway Plan, a scholarship program left over from the Second World War in which a student trained with midshipmen from the Naval Academy during the summers and graduated with a commission in the Regular Navy. So Pete graduated, received his commission, married Jane, and headed off to Pensacola, Florida, for flight training.

Then came the difference, looking back on it.

A young man might go into military flight training believing that he was entering some sort of technical school in which he was simply going to acquire a certain set of skills. Instead, he found himself all at once enclosed in a fraternity. And in this fraternity, even though it was military, men were not rated by their outward rank as ensigns, lieutenants, commanders, or whatever. No, herein the world was divided into those who had it and those who did not. This quality, that *it,* was never named, however, nor was it talked about in any way.

As to just what this ineffable quality was . . . well, it obviously involved bravery. But it was not bravery in the simple sense of being willing to risk your life. The idea seemed to be that any fool could do that, if that was all that was required, just as any fool could throw away his life in the process. No, the idea here (in the all-enclosing fraternity) seemed to be that a man should have the ability to go up in a hurtling piece of machinery and put his hide on the line and then have the moxie, the reflexes, the experience, the coolness, to pull it back in the last yawning moment—and then to go up again *the next day,* and the next day, and every next day, even if the series should prove infinite—and, ultimately, in its best expression, do so in a cause that means something to thousands, to a people, a nation, to humanity, to God. Nor was there *a test* to show whether or not a pilot had this righteous quality. There was, instead, a seemingly infinite series of tests. A career in flying was like climbing one of those ancient Babylonian pyramids made up of a dizzy progression of steps and ledges, a ziggurat, a pyramid extraordinarily high and steep; and the idea was to prove at every foot of the way up that pyramid that you were one of the elected and anointed ones who had *the right stuff* and could move higher and higher and even—ultimately, God willing, one day— that you might be able to join that special few at the very top, that elite who had the capacity to bring tears to men's eyes, the very Brotherhood of the Right Stuff itself.

None of this was to be mentioned, and yet it was acted out in a way that a young man could not fail to understand. When a new flight (i.e., a class) of trainees arrived at Pensacola, they were brought into an auditorium for a little lecture. An officer would tell them: "Take a look at the man on either side of you." Quite a few actually swiveled their heads this way and that, in the interest of appearing diligent. Then the officer would say: "One of the three of you is not going to make it!"—meaning, not get his wings. That was the opening theme, the *motif* of primary training. We already know that one-third of you do not have the right stuff—it only remains to find out who.

Furthermore, that was the way it turned out. At every level in one's progress up that staggeringly high pyramid, the world was once more divided into those men who had the right stuff to continue the climb and those who had to be *left behind* in the most obvious way. Some were eliminated in the course of the opening classroom work, as either not smart enough or not hardworking enough, and were left behind. Then came the basic flight instruction, in single-engine, propeller-driven trainers, and a few more— even though the military tried to make this stage easy—were washed out and left behind. Then came more demanding levels, one after the other, formation flying, instrument flying, jet training, all-weather flying, gunnery, and at each level more were washed out and left behind. By this point easily a third of the original candidates had been, indeed, eliminated . . . from the ranks of those who might prove to have the right stuff.

In the Navy, in addition to the stages that Air Force trainees went through, the neophyte always had waiting for him, out in the ocean, a certain grim gray slab; namely, the deck of an aircraft carrier; and with it perhaps the most difficult routine in military flying, carrier landings. He was shown films about it, he heard lectures about it, and he knew that carrier landings were hazardous. He first practiced touching down on the shape of a flight deck painted on an airfield. He was instructed to touch down and gun right off. This was safe enough—the shape didn't move, at least—but it could do terrible things to, let us say, the gyroscope of the soul. *That shape!—it's so damned small!* And more candidates were washed out and left behind. Then came the day, without warning, when those who remained were sent out over the ocean for the first of many days of reckoning with the slab. The first day was always a clear day with little wind and a calm sea. The carrier was so steady that it seemed, from up there in the air, to be resting on pilings, and the candidate usually made his first carrier landing success-fully, with relief and even *élan*. Many young candidates looked like terrific aviators up to that very point—and it was not until they were actually standing on the carrier deck that they first began to wonder if they had the proper stuff, after all. In the training film the flight deck was a grand piece of gray geometry, perilous, to be sure, but an amaz-ing abstract shape as one looks down upon it on the screen. And yet once the new-comer's two feet were on it . . . *Geometry*—my God, man, this is a . . . skillet! It *heaved,* it moved up and down underneath his feet, it pitched up, it pitched down, it rolled to port (this great beast *rolled!*) and it rolled to starboard, as the ship moved into the wind and, therefore, into the waves, and the wind kept sweeping across, sixty feet up in the air out in the open sea, and there were no railings whatsoever. This was a *skillet!*—a frying pan!—a short-order grill!—not gray but black, smeared with skid marks from one end to the other and glistening with pools of hydraulic fluid and the occasional jet-fuel slick, all of it still hot, sticky, greasy, runny, virulent from God knows what traumas—still ablaze!—consumed in detonations, explosions, flames, combustion, roars, shrieks, whines, blasts, horrible shudders, fracturing impacts, as little men in screaming red and yellow and purple and green shirts with black Mickey Mouse hel-mets over their ears skittered about on the surface as if for their very lives (you've said it now!), hooking fighter planes onto the catapult shuttles so that they can explode their afterburners and be slung off the deck in a red-mad fury with a *kaboom!* that pounds through the entire deck—a procedure that seems absolutely controlled, orderly, sub-lime, however, compared to what he is about to watch as aircraft return to the ship for what is known in the engineering stoicisms of the military as "recovery and arrest." To say that an F-4 was coming back onto this heaving barbecue from out of the sky at a speed of 135 knots . . . that might have been the truth in the training lecture, but it did not begin to get across the idea of what the newcomer saw from the deck itself, because it created the notion that perhaps the plane was gliding in. On the deck one knew differently! As the aircraft came closer and the carrier heaved on into the waves and the plane's speed did not diminish and the deck did not grow steady—indeed, it pitched up and down five or ten feet per greasy heave—one experienced a neural alarm that no lecture could have prepared him for: This is not an *airplane* coming toward me, it is a brick with some poor sonofabitch riding it *(someone much like myself!),* and it is not *gliding,* it is *falling,* a fifty-thousand-pound brick, headed not for a stripe on the deck but for *me*—and with a horrible *smash!* it hits the skillet, and with a blur of momen-tum as big as a freight train's it hurtles toward the far end of the deck—another blind-ing storm!—another roar as the pilot pushes the throttle up to full military power and another smear of rubber screams out over the skillet—and this is nominal!—quite okay!—for a wire stretched across the deck has grabbed the hook on the end of the plane as it hit the deck tail down, and the smash was the rest of the fifteen-ton brute slamming onto the deck, as it tripped up, so that it is now straining against the wire at full throttle, in case it hadn't held and the plane had "boltered" off the end of the deck and had to struggle up into the air again. And already the Mickey Mouse helmets are running toward the fiery monster . . .

And the candidate, looking on, begins to *feel* that great heaving sun-blazing death-board of a deck wallowing in his own vestibular system—and suddenly he finds him-self backed up against his own limits. He ends up going to the flight surgeon with so-called conversion symptoms. Overnight he develops blurred vision or numbness in his hands and feet or sinusitis so severe that he cannot tolerate changes in altitude. On one level the symptom is real. He really cannot see too well or use his fingers or stand the pain. But somewhere in his subconscious he knows it is a plea and a beg-off; he shows not the slightest concern (the flight surgeon notes) that the condition might be permanent and affect him in whatever life awaits him outside the arena of the right stuff.

Those who remained, those who qualified for carrier duty—and even more so those who later on qualified for *night* carrier duty—began to feel a bit like Gideon's warriors. *So many have been left behind!* The young warriors were now treated to a deathly sweet and quite unmentionable sight. They could gaze at length upon the crushed and wilted pariahs who had washed out. They could inspect those who did not have that righteous stuff.

The military did not have very merciful instincts. Rather than packing up these poor souls and sending them home, the Navy, like the Air Force and the Marines, would try to make use of them in some other role, such as flight controller. So the washout has to keep taking classes with the rest of his group, even though he can no longer touch an airplane. He sits there in the classes staring at sheets of paper with cataracts of sheer human mortification over his eyes while the rest steal looks at him . . . this man reduced to an ant, this untouchable, this poor sonofabitch. And in what test had he been found wanting? Why, it seemed to be nothing less than *manhood* itself. Naturally, this was never mentioned, either. Yet there it was. *Manliness, manhood, manly courage* . . . there was something ancient, primordial, irresistible about the challenge of this stuff, no matter what a sophisticated and rational age one might think he lived in.

Perhaps because it could not be talked about, the subject began to take on superstitious and even mystical outlines. A man either had it or he didn't! There was no such thing as having *most* of it. Moreover, it could blow at any seam. One day a man would be ascending the pyramid at a terrific clip, and the next—bingo!—he would reach his own limits in the most unexpected way. Conrad and Schirra met an Air Force pilot who had had a great pal at Tyndall Air Force Base in Florida. This man had been the budding ace of the training class; he had flown the hottest fighter-style trainer, the T-38, like a dream; and then he began the routine step of being checked out in the T-33. The T-33 was not nearly as hot an aircraft as the T-38; it was essentially the old P-80 jet fighter. It had an exceedingly small cockpit. The pilot could barely move his shoulders. It was the sort of airplane of which everybody said, "You don't get into it, you *wear* it." Once inside a T-33 cockpit this man, this budding ace, developed claustrophobia of the most paralyzing sort. He tried everything to overcome it. He even went to a psychiatrist, which was a serious mistake for a military officer if his superiors learned of it. But nothing worked. He was shifted over to flying jet transports, such as the C-135. Very demanding and necessary aircraft they were, too, and he was still spoken of as an excellent pilot. But as everyone knew—and, again, it was never explained in so many words—only those who were assigned to fighter squadrons, the "fighter jocks," as they called each other with a self-satisfied irony, remained in the true fraternity. Those assigned to transports were not humiliated like washouts—*somebody* had to fly those planes—nevertheless, they, too, had been *left behind* for lack of the right stuff.

Or a man could go for a routine physical one fine day, feeling like a million dollars, and be grounded for *fallen arches*. It happened!—just like that! (And try raising them.) Or for breaking his wrist and losing only *part* of its mobility. Or for a minor deterioration of eyesight, or for any of hundreds of reasons that would make no difference to a man in an ordinary occupation. As a result all fighter jocks began looking upon doctors as their natural enemies. Going to see a flight surgeon was a no-gain proposition; a pilot could only hold his own or lose in the doctor's office. To be grounded for a medical reason was no humiliation, looked at objectively. But it was a humiliation, nonetheless!—for it meant you no longer had that indefinable, unutterable, integral stuff. (It could blow at *any* seam.)

All the hot young fighter jocks began trying to test the limits themselves in a superstitious way. They were like believing Presbyterians of a century before who used to probe their own experience to see if they were truly among *the elect*. When a fighter pilot was in training, whether in the Navy or the Air Force, his superiors were continually spelling out strict rules for him, about the use of the aircraft and conduct in the sky. They repeatedly forbade so-called hot-dog stunts, such as outside loops, buzzing, flat-hatting, hedgehopping and flying under bridges. But somehow one got the message that the man who truly *had* it could ignore those rules—not that he should make a point of it, but that he *could*—and that after all there was only one way to find out—and that in some strange unofficial way, peeking through his fingers, his instructor halfway expected him to challenge all the limits. They would give a lecture about how a pilot should never fly without a good solid breakfast—eggs, bacon, toast, and so forth—because if he tried to fly with his blood-sugar level too low, it could impair his alertness. Naturally, the next day every hot dog in the unit would get up and have a breakfast consisting of one cup of black coffee and take off and go up into a vertical climb until the weight of the ship exactly canceled out the upward pull of the engine and his air speed was zero, and he would hang there for one thick adrenal instant—and then fall like a rock, until one of three things happened: he keeled over nose first and regained his aerodynamics and all was well, he went into a spin and fought his way out of it, or he went into a spin and had to eject or crunch it, which was always supremely possible.

Likewise, "hassling"—mock dogfighting—was strictly forbidden, and so naturally young fighter jocks could hardly wait to go up in, say, a pair of F-100s and start the duel by making a pass at each other at 800 miles an hour, the winner being the pilot who could slip in behind the other one and get locked in on his tail ("wax his tail"), and it was not uncommon for some eager jock to try too tight an outside turn and have his engine flame out, whereupon, unable to restart it, he has to eject . . . and he shakes his fist at the victor as he floats down by parachute and his half-a-million-dollar aircraft goes *kaboom!* on the palmetto grass or the desert floor, and he starts thinking about how he can get together with the other guy back at the base in time for the two of them to get their stories straight before the investigation: "I don't know what happened, sir. I was pulling up after a target run, and it just flamed out on me." Hassling was forbidden, and hassling that led to the destruction of an aircraft was a serious court-martial offense, and the man's superiors knew that the engine hadn't *just flamed out,* but every unofficial impulse on the base seemed to be saying: "Hell, we wouldn't give you a nickel for a pilot who hasn't done some crazy rat-racing like that. It's all part of the right stuff."

The other side of this impulse showed up in the reluctance of the young jocks to admit it when they had maneuvered themselves into a bad corner they couldn't get out of. There were two reasons why a fighter pilot hated to declare an emergency. First, it triggered a complex and very public chain of events at the field: all other incoming flights were held up, including many of one's comrades who were probably low on fuel; the fire trucks came trundling out to the runway like yellow toys (as seen from way up there), the better to illustrate one's hapless state; and the bureaucracy began to crank up the paper monster for the investigation that always followed. And second, to declare an emergency, one first had to reach that conclusion in his own mind, which to the young pilot was the same as saying: "A minute ago I still *had it*—now I need your help!" To have a bunch of young fighter pilots up in the air thinking this way used to drive flight controllers crazy. They would see a ship beginning to drift off the radar, and they couldn't rouse the pilot on the microphone for anything other than a few meaningless mumbles, and they would know he was probably out there with engine failure at a low altitude, trying to reignite by lowering his auxiliary generator rig, which had a little propeller that was supposed to spin in the slipstream like a child's pinwheel.

"Whiskey Kilo Two Eight, do you want to declare an emergency?"

This would rouse him!—to say: "Negative, negative, Whiskey Kilo Two Eight is not declaring an emergency."

Kaboom. Believers in the right stuff would rather crash and burn.

One fine day, after he had joined a fighter squadron, it would dawn on the young pilot exactly how the losers in the great fraternal competition were now being left behind. Which is to say, not by instructors or other superiors or by failures at prescribed levels of competence, but by death. At this point the essence of the enterprise would begin to dawn on him. Slowly, step by step, the ante had been raised until he was now involved in what was surely the grimmest and grandest gamble of manhood. Being a fighter pilot—for that matter, simply taking off in a single-engine jet fighter of the Century series, such as an F-102, or any of the military's other marvelous bricks with fins on them—presented a man, on a perfectly sunny day, with more ways to get himself killed than his wife and children could imagine in their wildest fears. If he was barreling down the runway at two hundred miles an hour, completing the takeoff run, and the board started lighting up red, should he (a) abort the takeoff (and try to wrestle with the monster, which was gorged with jet fuel, out in the sand beyond the end of the runway) or (b) eject (and hope that the goddamned human cannonball trick works at zero altitude and he doesn't shatter an elbow or a kneecap on the way out) or (c) continue the takeoff and deal with the problem aloft (knowing full well that the ship may be on fire and therefore seconds away from exploding)? He would have one second to sort out the options and act, and this kind of little workaday decision came up all the time. Occasionally a man would look coldly at the binary problem he was now confronting every day—Right Stuff/Death—and decide it wasn't worth it and voluntarily shift over to transports or reconnaissance or whatever. And his comrades would wonder, for a day or so, what evil virus had invaded his soul . . . as they left him behind. More often, however, the reverse would happen. Some college graduate would enter Navy aviation through the Reserves, simply as an alternative to the Army draft, fully intending to return to civilian life, to some waiting profession or family business; would become involved in the obsessive business of ascending the ziggurat pyramid of flying; and, at the end of his enlistment, would astound everyone back home and very likely himself as well by signing up for another one. What on earth got into him? He couldn't explain it. After all, the very words for it had been amputated. A Navy study showed that two-thirds of the fighter pilots who were rated in the top rungs of their groups—i.e., the hottest young pilots—reenlisted when the time came, and practically all were college graduates. By this point, a young fighter jock was like the preacher in *Moby Dick* who climbs up into the pulpit on a rope ladder and then pulls the ladder up behind him; except the pilot could not use the words necessary to express the vital lessons. Civilian life, and even home and hearth, now seemed not only far away but far *below,* back down many levels of the pyramid of the right stuff.

A fighter pilot soon found he wanted to associate only with other fighter pilots. Who else could understand the nature of the little proposition (right stuff/death) they were all dealing with? And what other subject could compare with it? It was riveting! To talk about it in so many words was forbidden, of course. The very words *death, danger, bravery, fear* were not to be uttered except in the occasional specific instance or for ironic effect. Nevertheless, the subject could be adumbrated in *code* or *by example.* Hence the endless evenings of pilots huddled together talking about flying. On these long and drunken evenings (the band of their family life) certain theorems would be propounded and demonstrated—and all by *code* and *example.* One theorem was: There are no *accidents* and no fatal flaws in the machines; there are only pilots with the wrong stuff. (I.e., blind Fate can't kill me.) When Bud Jennings crashed and burned in the swamps at Jacksonville, the other pilots in Pete Conrad's squadron said: *How could he have been so stupid?* It turned out that Jennings had gone up in the SNJ with his cockpit canopy opened in a way that was expressly forbidden in the manual, and carbon monoxide had been sucked in from the exhaust, and he passed out and crashed. All agreed that Bud Jennings was a good guy and a good pilot, but his epitaph on the ziggurat was: *How could he have been so stupid?* This seemed shocking at first, but by the time Conrad had reached the end of that bad string at Pax River, he was capable of his own corollary to the theorem: viz., no single factor ever killed a pilot; there was always a chain of mistakes. But what about Ted Whelan, who fell like a rock from 8,100 feet when his parachute failed? Well, the parachute was merely part of the chain: first, someone should have caught the structural defect that resulted in the hydraulic leak that triggered the emergency; second, Whelan did not check out his seat-parachute rig, and the drogue failed to separate the main parachute from the seat; but even after those two mistakes, Whelan had fifteen or twenty seconds, as he fell, to disengage himself from the seat and open the parachute manually. Why just stare at the scenery coming up to smack you in the face! And everyone nodded. (He failed—but I wouldn't have!) Once the theorem and the corollary were understood, the Navy's statistics about one in every four Navy aviators dying meant nothing. The figures were averages, and averages applied to those with average stuff.

A riveting subject, especially if it were one's own hide that was on the line. Every evening at bases all over America, there were military pilots huddled in officers clubs eagerly cutting the right stuff up in coded slices so they could talk about it. What more compelling topic of conversation was there in the world? In the Air Force there were even pilots who would ask the tower for priority landing clearance so that they could make the beer call on time, at 4 p.m. sharp, at the Officers Club. They would come right out and state the reason. The drunken rambles began at four and sometimes went on for ten or twelve hours. Such conversations! They diced that righteous stuff up into little bits, bowed ironically to it, stumbled blindfolded around it, groped, lurched, belched, staggered, bawled, sang, roared, and feinted at it with self-deprecating humor. Nevertheless!—they never mentioned it by name. No, they used the approved codes, such as: "Like a jerk I got myself into a hell of a corner today." They told of how they "lucked out of it." To get across the extreme peril of his exploit, one would use certain oblique cues. He would say, "I looked over at Robinson"—who would be known to the listeners as a non-com who sometimes rode backseat to read radar—"and he wasn't talking any more, he was just staring at the radar, like this, giving it that *zombie* look. Then I *knew* I was in trouble!" Beautiful! Just right! For it would also be known to the listeners that the non-coms advised one another: "*Never* fly with a lieutenant. *Avoid* captains and majors. Hell, man, do yourself a favor: don't fly with anybody below colonel." Which in turn said: "Those young bucks shoot dice with death!" And yet once in the air the non-com had his own standards. He was determined to remain as outwardly cool as the pilot, so that when the pilot did something that truly petrified him, he would say nothing; instead, he would turn silent, catatonic, like a zombie. Perfect! *Zombie.* There you had it, compressed into a single word all of the foregoing. I'm a hell of a pilot! I shoot dice with death! And now all you fellows know it! And I haven't spoken of that unspoken stuff even once!

The talking and drinking began at the beer call, and then the boys would break for dinner and come back afterward and get more wasted and more garrulous or else more quietly fried, drinking good cheap PX booze until 2 A.M. The night was young! Why not get the cars and go out for a little proficiency run? It seemed that every fighter jock thought himself an ace driver, and he would do anything to obtain a hot car, especially a sports car, and the drunker he was, the more convinced he would be about his driving skills, as if the right stuff, being indivisible, carried over into any enterprise whatsoever, under any conditions. A little proficiency run, boys! (There's only one way to find out!) And they would roar off in close formation from, say, Nellis Air Force Base, down Route 15, into Las Vegas, barreling down the highway, rat-racing, sometimes four abreast, jockeying for position, piling into the most listless curve in the desert flats as if they were trying to root each other out of the groove at the Rebel 500—and then bursting into downtown Las Vegas with a rude fraternal roar like the Hell's Angels— and the natives chalked it up to youth and drink and the bad element that the Air Force attracted. They knew nothing about the right stuff, of course.

More fighter pilots died in automobiles than in airplanes. Fortunately, there was always some kindly soul up the chain to certify the papers "line of duty," so that the widow could get a better break on the insurance. That was okay and only proper because somehow the system itself had long ago said *Skol!* and *Quite right!* to the military cycle of Flying & Drinking and Drinking & Driving, as if there were no other way. Every young fighter jock knew the feeling of getting two or three hours' sleep and then waking up at 5:30 A.M. and having a few cups of coffee, a few cigarettes, and then carting his poor quivering liver out to the field for another day of flying. There were those who arrived not merely hungover but still drunk, slapping oxygen tank cones over their faces and trying to burn the alcohol out of their systems, and then going up, remarking later: "I don't *advise* it, you understand, but it *can* be done." (Provided you have the right stuff, you miserable pudknocker.)

Air Force and Navy airfields were usually on barren or marginal stretches of land and would have looked especially bleak and Low Rent to an ordinary individual in the chilly light of dawn. But to a young pilot there was an inexplicable bliss to coming out to the flight line while the sun was just beginning to cook up behind the rim of the horizon, so that the whole field was still in shadow and the ridges in the distance were in silhouette and the flight line was a monochrome of Exhaust Fume Blue, and every little red light on top of the water towers or power stanchions looked dull, shriveled, congealed, and the runway lights, which were still on, looked faded, and even the land-ing lights on a fighter that had just landed and was taxiing in were no longer dazzling, as they would be at night, and looked instead like shriveled gobs of candlepower out there—and yet it was beautiful, exhilarating!—for he was revved up with adrenalin, anxious to take off before the day broke, to burst up into the sunlight over the ridges before all those thousands of comatose souls down there, still dead to the world, snug in home and hearth, even came to their senses. To take off in an F-100F at dawn and cut on the afterburner and hurtle twenty-five thousand feet up into the sky in thirty seconds, so suddenly that you felt not like a bird but like a trajectory, yet with full con-trol, full control of *four tons* of thrust, all of which flowed from your will and through your fingertips, with the huge engine right beneath you, so close that it was as if you were riding it bareback, until all at once you were supersonic, an event registered on earth by a tremendous cracking boom that shook windows, but up here only by the fact that you now felt utterly free of the earth—to describe it, even to wife, child, near ones and dear ones, seemed impossible. So the pilot kept it to himself, along with an even more indescribable . . . an even more sinfully inconfessable . . . feeling of supe-riority, appropriate to him and to his kind, lone bearers of the right stuff.

From *up here* at dawn the pilot looked down upon poor hopeless Las Vegas (or Yuma, Corpus Christi, Meridian, San Bernardino, or Dayton) and began to wonder: How can all of them down there, those poor souls who will soon be waking up and trudg-ing out of their minute rectangles and inching along their little noodle highways to-ward whatever slots and grooves make up their everyday lives—how could they live like that, with such earnestness, if they had the faintest idea of what it was like up here in this righteous zone?

But of course! Not only the washed-out, grounded, and dead pilots had been left behind—but also all of those millions of sleepwalking souls who never even attempted the great gamble. The entire world below . . . *left behind*. Only at this point can one begin to understand just how big, how titanic, the ego of the military pilot could be. The world was used to enormous egos in artists, actors, entertainers of all sorts, in politi-cians, sports figures, and even journalists, because they had such familiar and conve-nient ways to show them off. But that slim young man over there in uniform, with the enormous watch on his wrist and the withdrawn look on his face, that young of-ficer who is so shy that he can't even open his mouth unless the subject is flying—that young pilot—well, my friends, his ego is even *bigger!*—so big, it's *breathtaking!* Even in the 1950's it was difficult for civilians to comprehend such a thing, but *all* military officers and many enlisted men tended to feel superior to civilians. It was really quite ironic, given the fact that for a good thirty years the rising business classes in the cities had been steering their sons away from the military, as if from a bad smell, and the of-ficer corps had never been held in lower esteem. Well, career officers returned the con-tempt in trumps. They looked upon themselves as men who lived by higher standards of behavior than civilians, as men who were the bearers and protectors of the most im-portant values of American life, who maintained a sense of discipline while civilians abandoned themselves to hedonism, who maintained a sense of honor while civilians lived by opportunism and greed. Opportunism and greed: there you had your much-vaunted corporate business world. Khrushchev was right about one thing: when it came time to hang the capitalist West, an American businessman would sell him the rope. When the showdown came—and the showdowns always came—not all the wealth in the world or all the sophisticated nuclear weapons and radar and missile systems it could buy would take the place of those who had the uncritical willingness to face danger, those who, in short, had the right stuff.

In fact, the feeling was so righteous, so exalted, it could become religious. Civilians seldom understood this, either. There was no one to teach them. It was no longer the fashion for serious writers to describe the glories of war. Instead, they dwelt upon its horrors, often with cynicism or disgust. It was left to the occasional pilot with a literary flair to provide a glimpse of the pilot's self-conception in its heavenly or spiritual aspect. When a pilot named Robert Scott flew his P-43 over Mount Everest, quite a feat at the time, he brought his hand up and snapped a salute to his fallen adversary. He thought he had *defeated* the mountain, surmounting all the forces of nature that had made it formidable. And why not? "God is my co-pilot," he said—that became the title of his book—and he meant it. So did the most gifted of all the pilot authors, the Frenchman Antoine de Saint-Exupéry. As he gazed down upon the world . . . from up there . . . during transcontinental flights, the good Saint-Ex saw civilization as a series of tiny fragile patches clinging to the otherwise barren rock of Earth. He felt like a lonely sentinel, a protector of those vulnerable little oases, ready to lay down his life in their behalf, if necessary; a saint, in short, true to his name, flying up here at the right hand of God. The good Saint-Ex! And he was not the only one. He was merely the one who put it into words most beautifully and anointed himself before the altar of the right stuff.

(1979)

A L I C E   W A L K E R

[*b. 1944*]

In Search of Our Mothers' Gardens

> *I described her own nature and temperament. Told how they needed a larger life*
> *for their expression. . . . I pointed out that in lieu of proper channels, her emotions*
> *had overflowed into paths that dissipated them. I talked, beautifully I thought,*
> *about an art that would be born, an art that would open the way for women the*
> *likes of her. I asked her to hope, and build up an inner life against the coming of*
> *that day. . . . I sang, with a strange quiver in my voice, a promise song.*
>
> —"AVEY," JEAN TOOMER, *CANE*
> *The poet speaking to a prostitute who falls*
> *asleep while he's talking*

When the poet Jean Toomer walked through the South in the early twenties, he discovered a curious thing: black women whose spirituality was so intense, so deep, so *unconscious,* they were themselves unaware of the richness they held. They stumbled blindly through their lives: creatures so abused and mutilated in body, so dimmed and confused by pain, that they considered themselves unworthy even of hope. In the self-less abstractions their bodies became to the men who used them, they became more than "sexual objects," more even than mere women: they became "Saints." Instead of being perceived as whole persons, their bodies became shrines: what was thought to be their minds became temples suitable for worship. These crazy Saints stared out at the world, wildly, like lunatics—or quietly, like suicides; and the "God" that was in their gaze was as mute as a great stone.

Who were these Saints? These crazy, loony, pitiful women?

Some of them, without a doubt, were our mothers and grandmothers.

In the still heat of the post-Reconstruction South, this is how they seemed to Jean Toomer: exquisite butterflies trapped in an evil honey, toiling away their lives in an era, a century, that did not acknowledge them, except as "the *mule* of the world." They dreamed dreams that no one knew—not even themselves, in any coherent fashion—and saw visions no one could understand. They wandered or sat about the country-side crooning lullabies to ghosts, and drawing the mother of Christ in charcoal on court-house walls.

They forced their minds to desert their bodies and their striving spirits sought to rise, like frail whirlwinds from the hard red clay. And when those frail whirlwinds fell, in scattered particles, upon the ground, no one mourned. Instead, men lit candles to cel-ebrate the emptiness that remained, as people do who enter a beautiful but vacant space to resurrect a God.

Our mothers and grandmothers, some of them: moving to music not yet written. And they waited.

They waited for a day when the unknown thing that was in them would be made known; but guessed, somehow in their darkness, that on the day of their revelation they would be long dead. Therefore to Toomer they walked, and even ran, in slow motion. For they were going nowhere immediate, and the future was not yet within their grasp. And men took our mothers and grandmothers, "but got no pleasure from it." So complex was their passion and their calm.

To Toomer, they lay vacant and fallow as autumn fields, with harvest time never in sight: and he saw them enter loveless marriages, without joy; and become prostitutes, without resistance; and become mothers of children, without fulfillment.

For these grandmothers and mothers of ours were not Saints, but Artists; driven to a numb and bleeding madness by the springs of creativity in them for which there was no release. They were Creators, who lived lives of spiritual waste, because they were so rich in spirituality—which is the basis of Art—that the strain of enduring their un-used and unwanted talent drove them insane. Throwing away this spirituality was their pathetic attempt to lighten the soul to a weight their work-worn, sexually abused bod-ies could bear.

What did it mean for a black woman to be an artist in our grandmothers' time? In our great-grandmothers' day? It is a question with an answer cruel enough to stop the blood.

Did you have a genius of a great-great-grandmother who died under some ignorant and depraved white overseer's lash? Or was she required to bake biscuits for a lazy back-water tramp, when she cried out in her soul to paint watercolors of sunsets, or the rain falling on the green and peaceful pasturelands? Or was her body broken and forced to bear children (who were more often than not sold away from her)—eight, ten, fifteen, twenty children—when her one joy was the thought of modeling heroic figures of rebellion, in stone or clay?

How was the creativity of the black woman kept alive, year after year and century after century, when for most of the years black people have been in America, it was a punishable crime for a black person to read or write? And the freedom to paint, to sculpt, to expand the mind with action did not exist. Consider, if you can bear to imagine it, what might have been the result if singing, too, had been forbidden by law. Listen to the voices of Bessie Smith, Billie Holiday, Nina Simone, Roberta Flack, and Aretha Franklin, among others, and imagine those voices muzzled for life. Then you may begin to comprehend the lives of our "crazy," "Sainted" mothers and grandmothers. The agony of the lives of women who might have been Poets, Novelists, Essayists, and Short-Story Writers (over a period of centuries), who died with their real gifts stifled within them.

And, if this were the end of the story, we would have cause to cry out in my paraphrase of Okot p'Bitek's great poem:

> O, my clanswomen
> Let us all cry together!
> Come,
> Let us mourn the death of our mother,
> The death of a Queen
> The ash that was produced
> By a great fire!
> O, this homestead is utterly dead
> Close the gates
> With *lacari* thorns,
> For our mother
> The creator of the Stool is lost!
> And all the young men
> Have perished in the wilderness!

But this is not the end of the story, for all the young women—our mothers and grandmothers, *ourselves*—have not perished in the wilderness. And if we ask ourselves why, and search for and find the answer, we will know beyond all efforts to erase it from our minds, just exactly who, and of what, we black American women are.

One example, perhaps the most pathetic, most misunderstood one, can provide a backdrop for our mothers' work: Phillis Wheatley, a slave in the 1700s.

Virginia Woolf, in her book *A Room of One's Own,* wrote that in order for a woman to write fiction she must have two things, certainly: a room of her own (with key and lock) and enough money to support herself.

What then are we to make of Phillis Wheatley, a slave, who owned not even herself? This sickly, frail black girl who required a servant of her own at times—her health was so precarious—and who, had she been white, would have been easily considered the intellectual superior of all the women and most of the men in the society of her day.

Virginia Woolf wrote further, speaking of course not of our Phillis, that "any woman born with a great gift in the sixteenth century [insert "eighteenth century," insert "black woman," insert "born or made a slave"] would certainly have gone crazed, shot herself, or ended her days in some lonely cottage outside the village, half witch, half wizard [insert "Saint"], feared and mocked at. For it needs little skill and psychology to be sure that a highly gifted girl who had tried to use her gift of poetry would have been so thwarted and hindered by contrary instincts [add "chains, guns, the lash, the ownership of one's body by someone else, submission to an alien religion"], that she must have lost her health and sanity to a certainty."

The key words, as they relate to Phillis, are "contrary instincts." For when we read the poetry of Phillis Wheatley—as when we read the novels of Nella Larsen or the oddly false-sounding autobiography of that freest of all black women writers, Zora Hurston—evidence of "contrary instincts" is everywhere. Her loyalties were completely divided, as was, without question, her mind.

But how could this be otherwise? Captured at seven, a slave of wealthy, doting whites who instilled in her the "savagery" of the Africa they "rescued" her from . . . one wonders if she was even able to remember her homeland as she had known it, or as it really was.

Yet, because she did try to use her gift for poetry in a world that made her a slave, she was "so thwarted and hindered by . . . contrary instincts, that she . . . lost her health. . . ." In the last years of her brief life, burdened not only with the need to express her gift but also with a penniless, friendless "freedom" and several small children for whom she was forced to do strenuous work to feed, she lost her health, certainly. Suffering from malnutrition and neglect and who knows what mental agonies, Phillis Wheatley died.

So torn by "contrary instincts" was black, kidnapped, enslaved Phillis that her description of "the Goddess"—as she poetically called the Liberty she did not have—is ironically, cruelly humorous. And, in fact, has held Phillis up to ridicule for more than a century. It is usually read prior to hanging Phillis's memory as that of a fool. She wrote:

> The Goddess comes, she moves divinely fair,
> Olive and laurel binds her *golden* hair.
> Wherever shines this native of the skies,
> Unnumber'd charms and recent graces rise. [My italics]

It is obvious that Phillis, the slave, combed the "Goddess's" hair every morning; prior, perhaps, to bringing in the milk, or fixing her mistress's lunch. She took her imagery from the one thing she saw elevated above all others.

With the benefit of hindsight we ask, "How could she?"

But at last, Phillis, we understand. No more snickering when your stiff, struggling, ambivalent lines are forced on us. We know now that you were not an idiot or a traitor; only a sickly little black girl, snatched from your home and country and made a slave; a woman who still struggled to sing the song that was your gift, although in a land of barbarians who praised you for your bewildered tongue. It is not so much what you sang, as that you kept alive, in so many of our ancestors, *the notion of song*.

Black women are called, in the folklore that so aptly identifies one's status in society, "the *mule* of the world," because we have been handed the burdens that everyone else— *everyone* else—refused to carry. We have also been called "Matriarchs," "Superwomen," and "Mean and Evil Bitches." Not to mention "Castraters" and "Sapphire's Mama." When we have pleaded for understanding, our character has been distorted; when we have asked for simple caring, we have been handed empty inspirational appellations, then stuck in the farthest corner. When we have asked for love, we have been given children. In short, even our plainer gifts, our labors of fidelity and love, have been knocked down our throats. To be an artist and a black woman, even today, lowers our status in many respects, rather than raises it: and yet, artists we will be.

Therefore we must fearlessly pull out of ourselves and look at and identify with our lives the living creativity some of our great-grandmothers were not allowed to know. I stress *some* of them because it is well known that the majority of our great-grandmothers knew, even without "knowing" it, the reality of their spirituality, even if they didn't recognize it beyond what happened in the singing at church—and they never had any intention of giving it up.

How they did it—those millions of black women who were not Phillis Wheatley, or Lucy Terry or Frances Harper or Zora Hurston or Nella Larsen or Bessie Smith; or Elizabeth Catlett, or Katherine Dunham, either—brings me to the title of this essay, "In Search of Our Mothers' Gardens," which is a personal account that is yet shared, in its theme and its meaning, by all of us. I found, while thinking about the far-reaching world of the creative black woman, that often the truest answer to a question that really matters can be found very close.

In the late 1920s my mother ran away from home to marry my father. Marriage, if not running away, was expected of seventeen-year-old girls. By the time she was twenty, she had two children and was pregnant with a third. Five children later, I was born. And this is how I came to know my mother: she seemed a large, soft, loving-eyed woman who was rarely impatient in our home. Her quick, violent temper was on view only a few times a year, when she battled with the white landlord who had the misfortune to suggest to her that her children did not need to go to school.

She made all the clothes we wore, even my brothers' overalls. She made all the towels and sheets we used. She spent the summers canning vegetables and fruits. She spent the winter evenings making quilts enough to cover all our beds.

During the "working" day, she labored beside—not behind—my father in the fields. Her day began before sunup, and did not end until late at night. There was never a moment for her to sit down, undisturbed, to unravel her own private thoughts; never a time free from interruption—by work or the noisy inquiries of her many children. And yet, it is to my mother—and all our mothers who were not famous—that I went in search of the secret of what has fed that muzzled and often mutilated, but vibrant, creative spirit that the black woman has inherited, and that pops out in wild and unlikely places to this day.

But when, you will ask, did my overworked mother have time to know or care about feeding the creative spirit?

The answer is so simple that many of us have spent years discovering it. We have constantly looked high, when we should have looked high—and low.

For example: in the Smithsonian Institution in Washington, D.C., there hangs a quilt unlike any other in the world. In fanciful, inspired, and yet simple and identifiable figures, it portrays the story of the Crucifixion. It is considered rare, beyond price. Though it follows no known pattern of quiltmaking, and though it is made of bits and pieces of worthless rags, it is obviously the work of a person of powerful imagination and deep spiritual feeling. Below this quilt I saw a note that says it was made by "an anonymous Black woman in Alabama, a hundred years ago."

If we could locate this "anonymous" black woman from Alabama, she would turn out to be one of our grandmothers—an artist who left her mark in the only materials she could afford, and in the only medium her position in society allowed her to use.

As Virginia Woolf wrote further, in *A Room of One's Own:*

> Yet genius of a sort must have existed among women as it must have existed among the working class. [Change this to "slaves" and "the wives and daughters of sharecroppers."] Now and again an Emily Brontë or a Robert Burns [change this to "a Zora Hurston or a Richard Wright"] blazes out and proves its presence. But certainly it never got itself on to paper. When, however, one reads of a witch being ducked, of a woman possessed by devils [or "Sainthood"], of a wise woman selling herbs [our root workers], or even a very remarkable man who had a mother, then I think we are on the track of a lost novelist, a suppressed poet, or some mute and inglorious Jane Austen. . . . Indeed, I would venture to guess that Anon, who wrote so many poems without signing them, was often a woman. . . .

And so our mothers and grandmothers have, more often than not anonymously, handed on the creative spark, the seed of the flower they themselves never hoped to see: or like a sealed letter they could not plainly read.

And so it is, certainly, with my own mother. Unlike "Ma" Rainey's songs, which retained their creator's name even while blasting forth from Bessie Smith's mouth, no song or poem will bear my mother's name. Yet so many of the stories that I write, that we all write, are my mother's stories. Only recently did I fully realize this: that through years of listening to my mother's stories of her life, I have absorbed not only the stories themselves, but something of the manner in which she spoke, something of the urgency that involves the knowledge that her stories—like her life—must be recorded. It is probably for this reason that so much of what I have written is about characters whose counterparts in real life are so much older than I am.

But the telling of these stories, which came from my mother's lips as naturally as breathing, was not the only way my mother showed herself as an artist. For stories, too, were subject to being distracted, to dying without conclusion. Dinners must be started, and cotton must be gathered before the big rains. The artist that was and is my mother showed itself to me only after many years. This is what I finally noticed:

Like Mem, a character in *The Third Life of Grange Copeland,* my mother adorned with flowers whatever shabby house we were forced to live in. And not just your typical straggly country stand of zinnias, either. She planted ambitious gardens—and still does—with over fifty different varieties of plants that bloom profusely from early March until late November. Before she left home for the fields, she watered her flowers, chopped up the grass, and laid out new beds. When she returned from the fields she might divide clumps of bulbs, dig a cold pit, uproot and replant roses, or prune branches from her taller bushes or trees—until night came and it was too dark to see.

Whatever she planted grew as if by magic, and her fame as a grower of flowers spread over three counties. Because of her creativity with her flowers, even my memories of poverty are seen through a screen of blooms—sunflowers, petunias, roses, dahlias, forsythia, spirea, delphiniums, verbena . . . and on and on.

And I remember people coming to my mother's yard to be given cuttings from her flowers; I hear again the praise showered on her because whatever rocky soil she landed on, she turned into a garden. A garden so brilliant with colors, so original in its design, so magnificent with life and creativity, that to this day people drive by our house in Georgia—perfect strangers and imperfect strangers—and ask to stand or walk among my mother's art.

I notice that it is only when my mother is working in her flowers that she is radiant, almost to the point of being invisible—except as Creator: hand and eye. She is involved in work her soul must have. Ordering the universe in the image of her personal conception of Beauty.

Her face, as she prepares the Art that is her gift, is a legacy of respect she leaves to me, for all that illuminates and cherishes life. She has handed down respect for the possibilities—and the will to grasp them.

For her, so hindered and intruded upon in so many ways, being an artist has still been a daily part of her life. This ability to hold on, even in very simple ways, is work black women have done for a very long time.

This poem is not enough, but it is something, for the woman who literally covered the holes in our walls with sunflowers:

> They were women then
> My mama's generation
> Husky of voice—Stout of
> Step
> With fists as well as
> Hands
> How they battered down
> Doors
> And ironed
> Starched white
> Shirts
> How they led
> Armies
> Headragged Generals
> Across mined
> Fields
> Booby-trapped
> Kitchens
> To discover books
> Desks
> A place for us
> How they knew what we
> *Must* know
> Without knowing a page
> Of it
> Themselves.

Guided by my heritage of a love of beauty and a respect for strength—in search of my mother's garden, I found my own.

And perhaps in Africa over two hundred years ago, there was just such a mother; perhaps she painted vivid and daring decorations in oranges and yellows and greens on the walls of her hut; perhaps she sang—in a voice like Roberta Flack's—*sweetly* over the compounds of her village; perhaps she wove the most stunning mats or told the most ingenious stories of all the village storytellers. Perhaps she was herself a poet—though only her daughter's name is signed to the poems that we know.

Perhaps Phillis Wheatley's mother was also an artist.

Perhaps in more than Phillis Wheatley's biological life is her mother's signature made clear.

(1983)

BERNARD COOPER

[1951]

Burl's

FROM THE LOS ANGELES TIMES MAGAZINE

I loved the restaurant's name, a compact curve of a word. Its sign, five big letters rimmed in neon, hovered above the roof. I almost never saw the sign with its neon lit; my parents took me there for early summer dinners, and even by the time we left—father cleaning his teeth with a toothpick, mother carrying steak bones in a doggie bag—the sky was still bright. Heat rippled off the cars parked along Hollywood Boulevard, the asphalt gummy from hours of sun.

With its sleek architecture, chrome appliances, and arctic temperature, Burl's offered a refuge from the street. We usually sat at one of the booths in front of the plate-glass windows. During our dinner, people came to a halt before the news-vending machine on the corner and burrowed in their pockets and purses for change.

The waitresses at Burl's wore brown uniforms edged in checked gingham. From their breast pockets frothed white lace handkerchiefs. In between reconnaissance missions to the table, they busied themselves behind the counter and shouted "Tuna to travel" or "Scorch that patty" to a harried short-order cook who manned the grill. Miniature pitchers of cream and individual pats of butter were extracted from an industrial refrigerator. Coca-Cola shot from a glinting spigot. Waitresses dodged and bumped one another, frantic as atoms.

My parents usually lingered after the meal, nursing cups of coffee while I played with the beads of condensation on my glass of ice water, tasted Tabasco sauce, or twisted pieces of my paper napkin into mangled animals. One evening, annoyed with my restlessness, my father gave me a dime and asked me to buy him a *Herald Examiner* from the vending machine in front of the restaurant.

Shouldering open the heavy glass door, I was seared by a sudden gust of heat. Traffic roared past me and stirred the air. Walking toward the newspaper machine, I held the dime so tightly it seemed to melt in my palm. Duty made me feel large and important. I inserted the dime and opened the box, yanking a *Herald* from the spring contraption that held it as tight as a mousetrap. When I turned around, paper in hand, I saw two women walking toward me.

Their high heels clicked on the sun-baked pavement. They were tall, broad-shouldered women who moved with a mixture of haste and defiance. They'd teased their hair into nearly identical black beehives. Dangling earrings flashed in the sun, brilliant as prisms. Each of them wore the kind of clinging, strapless outfit my mother referred to as a cocktail dress. The silky fabric—one dress was purple, the other pink—accentuated their breasts and hips and rippled with insolent highlights. The dresses exposed their bare arms, the slope of their shoulders, and the smooth, powdered plane of flesh where their cleavage began.

I owned at the time a book called *Things for Boys and Girls to Do*. There were pages to color, intricate mazes, and connect-the-dots. But another type of puzzle came to mind as I watched those women walking toward me: What's Wrong With This Picture? Say the drawing of a dining room looked normal at first glance; on closer inspection, a chair was missing its leg and the man who sat atop it wore half a pair of glasses.

The women had Adam's apples.

The closer they came, the shallower my breathing was. I blocked the sidewalk, an incredulous child stalled in their path. When they saw me staring, they shifted their purses and linked their arms. There was something sisterly and conspiratorial about their sudden closeness. Though their mouths didn't move, I thought they might have been communicating without moving their lips, so telepathic did they seem as they joined arms and pressed together, synchronizing their heavy steps. The pages of the *Herald* fluttered in the wind. I felt them against my arm, light as batted lashes.

The woman in pink shot me a haughty glance and yet she seemed pleased that I'd taken notice, hungry to be admired by a man, or even an awestruck eight-year-old boy. She tried to stifle a grin, her red lipstick more voluptuous than the lips it painted. Rouge deepened her cheekbones. Eye shadow dusted her lips, a clumsy abundance of blue. Her face was like a page in *Things for Boys and Girls to Do,* colored by a kid who went outside the lines.

At close range, I saw that her wig was slightly askew. I was certain it was a wig because my mother owned several; three Styrofoam heads lined a shelf in my mother's closet; upon them were perched a Page-Boy, an Empress, and a Baby-Doll, all in shades of auburn. The woman in the pink dress wore her wig like a crown of glory.

But it was the woman in the purple dress who passed nearest me, and I saw that her jaw was heavily powdered, a half-successful attempt to disguise the telltale shadow of a beard. Just as I noticed this, her heel caught on a crack in the pavement and she reeled on her stilettos. It was then that I witnessed a rift in her composure, a window through which I could glimpse the shades of maleness that her dress and wig and makeup obscured. She shifted her shoulders and threw out her hands like a surfer riding a curl. The instant she regained her balance, she smoothed her dress, patted her hair, and sauntered onward.

Any woman might be a man. The fact of it clanged through the chambers of my brain. In broad day, in the midst of traffic, with my parents drinking coffee a few feet away, I felt as if everything I understood, everything I had taken for granted up to that moment—the curve of the earth, the heat of the sun, the reliability of my own eyes—had been squeezed out of me. Who were those men? Did they help each other get inside those dresses? How many other people and things were not what they seemed? From the back, the impostors looked like women once again, slinky and curvaceous, purple and pink. I watched them disappear into the distance, their disguises so convincing that other people on the street seemed to take no notice, and for a moment I wondered if I had imagined the whole encounter, a visitation by two unlikely muses.

Frozen in the middle of the sidewalk, I caught my reflection in the window of Burl's, a silhouette floating between his parents. They faced one another across a table. Once the solid embodiments of woman and man, pedestrians and traffic appeared to pass through them.

*

There were some mornings, seconds before my eyes opened and my senses gathered into consciousness, that the child I was seemed to hover above the bed, and I couldn't tell what form my waking would take—the body of a boy or the body of a girl. Finally stirring, I'd blink against the early light and greet each incarnation as a male with mild surprise. My sex, in other words, didn't seem to be an absolute fact so much as a pleasant, recurring accident.

By the age of eight, I'd experienced this groggy phenomenon several times. Those ethereal moments above my bed made waking up in the tangled blankets, a boy steeped in body heat, all the more astonishing. That this might be an unusual experience never occurred to me; it was one among a flood of sensations I could neither name nor ignore.

And so, shocked as I was when those transvestites passed me in front of Burl's, they confirmed something about which I already had an inkling: the hazy border between the sexes. My father, after all, raised his pinky when he drank from a teacup, and my mother looked as faded and plain as my father until she fixed her hair and painted her face.

Like most children, I once thought it possible to divide the world into male and female columns. Blue/Pink. Rooster/Hens. Trousers/Skirts. Such divisions were easy, not to mention comforting, for they simplified matter into compatible pairs. But there also existed a vast range of things that didn't fit neatly into either camp: clocks, milk, telephones, grass. There were nights I fell into a fitful sleep while trying to sex the world correctly.

Nothing typified the realms of male and female as clearly as my parents' walk-in closets. Home alone for any length of time, I always found my way inside them. I could stare at my parents' clothes for hours, grateful for the stillness and silence, haunting the very heart of their privacy.

The overhead light in my father's closet was a bare bulb. Whenever I groped for the chain in the dark, it wagged back and forth and resisted my grasp. Once the light clicked on, I saw dozens of ties hanging like stalactites. A monogrammed silk bathrobe sagged from a hook, a gift my father had received on a long-ago birthday and, thinking it fussy, rarely wore. Shirts were cramped together along the length of an aluminum pole, their starched sleeves sticking out as if in a halfhearted gesture of greeting. The medicinal odor of mothballs permeated the boxer shorts that were folded and stacked in a built-in drawer. Immaculate underwear was proof of a tenderness my mother couldn't otherwise express; she may not have touched my father often, but she laundered his boxers with infinite care. Even back then, I suspected that a sense of duty was the final erotic link between them.

Sitting in a neat row on the closet floor were my father's boots and slippers and dress shoes. I'd try on his wingtips and clomp around, slipping out of them with every step. My wary, unnatural stride made me all the more desperate to effect some authority. I'd whisper orders to imagined lackeys and take my invisible wife in my arms. But no matter how much I wanted them to fit, those shoes were as cold and hard as marble.

My mother's shoes were just as uncomfortable, but a lot more fun. From a brightly colored array of pumps and slingbacks, I'd pick a pair with the glee and deliberation of someone choosing a chocolate. Whatever embarrassment I felt was overwhelmed by the exhilaration of being taller in a pair of high heels. Things will look like this someday, I said to myself, gazing out from my new and improved vantage point as if from a crow's nest. Calves elongated, arms akimbo, I gauged each step so that I didn't fall over and moved with what might have passed for grace had someone seen me, a possibility I scrupulously avoided by locking the door.

Back and forth I went. The longer I wore a pair of heels, the better my balance. In the periphery of my vision, the shelf of wigs looked like a throng of kindly bystanders. Light streamed down from a high window, causing crystal bottles to glitter, the air ripe with perfume. A makeup mirror above the dressing table invited my self-absorption. Sound was muffled. Time slowed. It seemed as if nothing bad could happen as long as I stayed within those walls.

Though I'd never been discovered in my mother's closet, my parents knew that I was drawn toward girlish things—dolls and jump rope and jewelry—as well as to the games and preoccupations that were expected of a boy. I'm not sure now if it was my effeminacy itself that bothered them as much as my ability to slide back and forth, without the slightest warning, between male and female mannerisms. After I'd finished building the model of an F-17 bomber, say, I'd sit back to examine my handiwork, pursing my lips in concentration and crossing my legs at the knee.

One day my mother caught me standing in the middle of my bedroom doing an imitation of Mary Injijikian, a dark, overeager Armenian girl with whom I believed myself to be in love, not only because she was pretty but because I wanted to be like her. Collector of effortless A's, Mary seemed to know all the answers in class. Before the teacher had even finished asking a question, Mary would let out a little grunt and practically levitate out of her seat, as if her hand were filled with helium. "Could we please hear from someone else today besides Miss Injijikian," the teacher would say. *Miss Injijikian.* Those were the words I was repeating over and over to myself when my mother caught me. To utter them was rhythmic, delicious, and under their spell I raised my hand and wiggled like Mary. I heard a cough and spun around. My mother froze in the doorway. She clutched the folded sheets to her stomach and turned without saying a word. My sudden flush of shame confused me. Weren't boys supposed to swoon over girls? Hadn't I seen babbling, heartsick men in a dozen movies?

Shortly after the Injijikian incident, my parents decided to send me to gymnastics class at the Los Angeles Athletic Club, a brick relic of a building on Olive Street. One of the oldest establishments of its kind in Los Angeles, the club prohibited women from the premises. My parents didn't have to say it aloud: they hoped a fraternal atmosphere would toughen me up and tilt me toward the male side of my nature.

My father drove me downtown so I could sign up for the class, meet the instructor, and get a tour of the place. On the way there, he reminisced about sports. Since he'd grown up in a rough Philadelphia neighborhood, sports consisted of kick-the-can or rolling a hoop down the street with a stick. The more he talked about his physical prowess, the more convinced I became that my daydreams and shyness were a disappointment to him.

The hushed lobby of the athletic club was paneled in dark wood. A few solitary figures were hidden in wing chairs. My father and I introduced ourselves to a man at the front desk who seemed unimpressed by our presence. His aloofness unnerved me, which wasn't hard considering that no matter how my parents put it, I knew their sending me here was a form of disapproval, a way of banishing the part of me they didn't care to know.

A call went out over the intercom for someone to show us around. While we waited, I noticed that the sand in the standing ashtrays had been raked into perfect furrows. The glossy leaves of the potted plants looked as if they'd been polished by hand. The place seemed more like a well-tended hotel than an athletic club. Finally, a stoop-shouldered old man hobbled toward us, his head shrouded in a cloud of white hair. He wore a T-shirt that said "Instructor"; his arms were so wrinkled and anemic, I thought I might have misread it. While we followed him to the elevator, I readjusted my expectations, which had involved fantasies of a hulking drill sergeant barking orders at a flock of scrawny boys.

The instructor, mumbling to himself and never turning around to see if we were behind him, showed us where the gymnastics class took place. I'm certain the building was big, but the size of the room must be exaggerated by a trick of memory, because when I envision it, I picture a vast and windowless warehouse. Mats covered the wooden floor. Here and there, in remote and lonely pools of light, stood a pommel horse, a balance beam, and parallel bars. Tiers of bleachers rose into darkness. Unlike the cloistered air of a closet, the room seemed incomplete without a crowd.

Next we visited the dressing room, empty except for a naked middle-aged man. He sat on a narrow bench and clipped his formidable toenails. Moles dotted his back. He glistened like a fish.

We continued to follow the instructor down an aisle lined with numbered lockers. At the far end, steam billowed from the doorway that led to the showers. Fresh towels stacked on a nearby table made me think of my mother; I knew she liked to have me at home with her—I was often her only companion—and I resented her complicity in the plan to send me here.

The tour ended when the instructor gave me a sign-up sheet. Only a few names preceded mine. They were signatures, or so I imagined, of other soft and wayward sons.

When the day of the first gymnastics class arrived, my mother gave me money and a gym bag and sent me to the corner of Hollywood and Western to wait for a bus. The sun was bright, the traffic heavy. While I sat there, an argument raged inside my head, the familiar, battering debate between the wish to be like other boys and the wish to be like myself. Why shouldn't I simply get up and go back home, where I'd be left alone to read and think? On the other hand, wouldn't life be easier if I liked athletics, or learned to like them?

No sooner did I steel my resolve to get on the bus than I thought of something better: I could spend the morning wandering through Woolworth's, then tell my parents

I'd gone to the class. But would my lie stand up to scrutiny? As I practiced describing phantom gymnastics, I became aware of a car circling the block. It was a large car in whose shaded interior I could barely make out the driver, but I thought it might be the man who owned the local pet store. I'd often gone there on the pretext of looking at the cocker spaniel puppies huddled together in their pen, but I really went to gawk at the owner, whose tan chest, in the V of his shirt, was the place I most wanted to rest my head. Every time the man moved, counting stock or writing a receipt, his shirt parted, my mouth went dry, and I smelled the musk of sawdust and dogs.

I found myself hoping that the driver was the man who ran the pet store. I was thrilled by the unlikely possibility that the sight of me, slumped on a bus bench in my T-shirt and shorts, had caused such a man to circle the block. Up to that point in my life, lovemaking hovered somewhere in the future, an impulse a boy might aspire to but didn't indulge. And there I was, sitting on a bus bench in the middle of the city, dreaming I could seduce an adult. I showered the owner of the pet store with kisses and, as aquariums bubbled, birds sang, and mice raced in a wire wheel, slipped my hand beneath his shirt. The roar of traffic brought me to my senses. I breathed deeply and blinked against the sun. I crossed my legs at the knee in order to hide an erection. My fantasy left me both drained and changed. The continent of sex had drifted closer.

The car made another round. This time the driver leaned across the passenger seat and peered at me through the window. He was a complete stranger, whose gaze filled me with fear. It wasn't the surprise of not recognizing him that frightened me, it was what I did recognize—the unmistakable shame in his expression, and the weary temptation that drove him in circles. Before the car behind him honked, he mouthed "hello" and cocked his head. What now, he seemed to be asking. A bold, unbearable question.

I bolted to my feet, slung the gym bag over my shoulder, and hurried toward home. Now and then I turned around to make sure he wasn't trailing me, both relieved and disappointed when I didn't see his car. Even after I became convinced that he wasn't at my back—my sudden flight had scared him off—I kept turning around to see what was making me so nervous, as if I might spot the source of my discomfort somewhere on the street. I walked faster and faster, trying to outrace myself. Eventually, the bus I was supposed to have taken roared past. Turning the corner, I watched it bob eastward.

Closing the kitchen door behind me, I vowed never to leave home again. I was resolute in this decision without fully understanding why, or what it was I hoped to avoid; I was only aware of the need to hide and a vague notion, fading fast, that my trouble had something to do with sex. Already the mechanism of self-deception was at work. By the time my mother rushed into the kitchen to see why I'd returned so early, the thrill I'd felt while waiting for the bus had given way to indignation.

I poured out the story of the man circling the block and protested, with perhaps too great a passion, my own innocence. "I was just sitting there," I said again and again. I was so determined to deflect suspicion away from myself, and to justify my missing the class, that I portrayed the man as a grizzled pervert who drunkenly veered from lane to lane as he followed me halfway home.

My mother cinched her housecoat. She seemed moved and shocked by what I told her, if a bit incredulous, which prompted me to be more dramatic. "It wouldn't be safe," I insisted, "for me to wait at the bus stop again."

No matter how overwrought my story, I knew my mother wouldn't question it, wouldn't bring the subject up again; sex of any kind, especially sex between a man and a boy, was simply not discussed in our house. The gymnastics class, my parents agreed, was something I could do another time.

And so I spent the remainder of that summer at home with my mother, stirring cake batter, holding the dustpan, helping her fold the sheets. For a while I was proud of myself for engineering a reprieve from the athletic club. But as the days wore on, I began to see that my mother had wanted me with her all along, and forcing that to happen wasn't such a feat. Soon a sense of compromise set in; by expressing disgust for the man in the car, I'd expressed disgust for an aspect of myself. Now I had all the time in the world to sit around and contemplate my desire for men. The days grew long and stifling and hot, an endless sentence of self-examination.

Only trips to the pet store offered any respite. Every time I went there, I was too electrified with longing to think about longing in the abstract. The bell tinkled above the door, animals stirred within their cages, and the handsome owner glanced up from his work.

I handed my father the *Herald*. He opened the paper and disappeared behind it. My mother stirred her coffee and sighed. She gazed at the sweltering passersby and probably thought herself lucky. I slid into the vinyl booth and took my place beside my parents.

For a moment, I considered asking them about what had happened on the street, but they would have reacted with censure and alarm, and I sensed there was more to the story than they'd ever be willing to tell me. Men in dresses were only the tip of the iceberg. Who knew what other wonders existed—a boy, for example, who wanted to kiss a man—exceptions the world did its best to keep hidden.

It would be years before I heard the word "transvestite," so I struggled to find a word for what I'd seen. "He-she" came to mind, as lilting as "Injijikian." "Burl's" would have been perfect, like "boys" and "girls" spliced together, but I can't claim to have thought of this back then.

I must have looked stricken as I tried to figure it all out, because my mother put down her coffee cup and asked if I was O.K. She stopped just short of feeling my forehead. I assured her I was fine, but something within me had shifted, had given way to a heady doubt. When the waitress came and slapped down our check—"Thank You," it read, "Dine out more often"—I wondered if her lofty hairdo or the breasts on which her nametag quaked were real. Wax carnations bloomed at every table. Phony wood paneled the walls. Plastic food sat in a display case: fried eggs, a hamburger sandwich, a sundae topped with a garish cherry.

(1995)

Critical Perspectives and Research

PART FIVE

Critical Perspectives and Research

CHAPTER THIRTY-SIX

Critical Theory: Approaches to the Analysis and Interpretation of Literature

READINGS FOR ANALYSIS

WILLIAM CARLOS WILLIAMS

[1883–1963]

The Use of Force

They were new patients to me, all I had was the name, Olson. Please come down as soon as you can, my daughter is very sick.

When I arrived I was met by the mother, a big startled looking woman, very clean and apologetic who merely said, Is this the doctor? and let me in. In the back, she added. You must excuse us, doctor, we have her in the kitchen where it is warm. It is very damp here sometimes.

The child was fully dressed and sitting on her father's lap near the kitchen table. He tried to get up, but I motioned for him not to bother, took off my overcoat and started to look things over. I could see that they were all very nervous, eyeing me up and down distrustfully. As often, in such cases, they weren't telling me more than they had to, it was up to me to tell them; that's why they were spending three dollars on me.

The child was fairly eating me up with her cold, steady eyes, and no expression to her face whatever. She did not move and seemed, inwardly, quiet; an unusually attractive little thing, and as strong as a heifer in appearance. But her face was flushed, she was breathing rapidly, and I realized that she had a high fever. She had magnificent blonde hair, in profusion. One of those picture children often reproduced in advertising leaflets and the photogravure sections of the Sunday papers.

She's had a fever for three days, began the father, and we don't know what it comes from. My wife has given her thing, you know, like people do, but it don't do no good. And there's been a lot of sickness around. So we tho't you'd better look her over and tell us what is the matter.

As doctors often do I took a trial shot at it as a point of departure. Has she had a sore throat?

Both parents answered me together, No . . . No, she says her throat don't hurt her.

Does your throat hurt you? added the mother to the child. But the little girl's expression didn't change, nor did she move her eyes from my face.

Have you looked?

I tried to, said the mother, but I couldn't see.

As it happens, we had been having a number of cases of diphtheria in the school to which this child went during that month and we were all, quite apparently, thinking of that, though no one had as yet spoken of the thing.

Well, I said, suppose we take a look at the throat first. I smiled in my best professional manner and asking for the child's first name I said, come on, Mathilda, open you mouth and let's take a look at your throat.

Nothing doing.

Aw, come on, I coaxed, just open your mouth wide and let me take a look. Look, I said opening both hands wide. I haven't anything in my hands. Just open up and let me see.

Such a nice man, put in the mother. Look how kind he is to you. Come on, do what he tells you to. He won't hurt you.

At that I ground my teeth in disgust. If only they wouldn't use the word "hurt" I might be able to get somewhere. But I did not allow myself to be hurried or disturbed, but speaking quietly and slowly I approached the child again.

As I moved my chair a little nearer, suddenly with one catlike movement both her hands clawed instinctively for my eyes and she almost reached them too. In fact she knocked my glasses flying and they fell, though unbroken, several feet away from me on the kitchen floor.

Both the mother and father almost turned themselves inside out in embarrassment and apology. You bad girl, said the mother, taking her and shaking her by one arm. Look what you've done. The nice man. . . .

For heaven's sake, I broke in. Don't call me a nice man to her. I'm here to look at her throat on the chance that she might have diphtheria and possibly die of it. But that's nothing to her. Look here, I said to the child, we're going to look at your throat. You're old enough to understand what I'm saying. Will you open it now by yourself or shall we have to open it for you?

Not a move. Even her expression hadn't changed. Her breaths however were coming faster and faster. Then the battle began. I had to do it. I had to have a throat culture for her own protection. But first I told the parents that it was entirely up to them. I explained the danger but said that I would not insist on a throat examination so long as they would take the responsibility.

If you don't do what the doctor says you'll have to go to the hospital, the mother admonished her severely.

Oh yeah? I had to smile to myself. After all, I had already fallen in love with the savage brat, the parents were contemptible to me. In the ensuing struggle they grew more and more abject, crushed, exhausted while she surely rose to magnificent heights of insane fury of effort bred of her terror of me.

The father tried his best, and he was a big man but the fact that she was his daughter, his shame at her behavior and his dread of hurting her made him release her just at the critical moment several times when I had almost achieved success, till I wanted to kill him. But his dread also that she might have diphtheria made him tell me to go on, go on though he himself was almost fainting, while the mother moved back and forth behind us raising and lowering her hands in an agony of apprehension.

Put her in front of you on your lap, I ordered, and hold both her wrists.

But as soon as he did the child let out a scream. Don't, you're hurting me. Let go of my hands. Let them go I tell you. The she shrieked terrifyingly, hysterically. Stop it! Stop it! You're killing me!

Do you think she can stand it, doctor! said the mother.

You get out, said the husband to his wife. Do you want her to die of diphtheria?

Come on now, hold her, I said.

Then I grasped the child's head with my left hand and tried to get the wooden tongue depressor between her teeth. She fought, with clenched teeth, desperately! But now I also had grown furious—at a child. I tried to hold myself down but I couldn't. I know how to expose a throat for inspection. And I did my best. When finally I got the wooden spatula behind the last teeth and just the point of it into the mouth cavity, she opened up for an instant but before I could see anything she came down again and gripping the wooden blade between her molars she reduced it to splinters before I could get it out again.

Aren't you ashamed, the mother yelled at her. Aren't you ashamed to act like that in front of the doctor?

Get me a smooth-handled spoon of some sort, I told the mother. We're going through with this. The child's mouth was already bleeding. Her tongue was cut and she was screaming in wild hysterical shrieks. Perhaps I should have desisted and come back in an hour or more. No doubt it would have been better. But I have seen at least two children lying dead in bed of neglect in such cases, and feeling that I must get a diagnosis now or never I went at it again. But the worst of it was that I too had got beyond reason. I could have torn the child apart in my own fury and enjoyed it. It was a pleasure to attack her. My face was burning with it.

The damned little brat must be protected against her own idiocy, one says to one's self at such times. Others must be protected against her. It is social necessity. And all these things are true. But a blind fury, a feeling of adult shame, bred of a longing for muscular release are the operatives. One goes to the end.

In a final unreasoning assault I overpowered the child's neck and jaws. I forced the heavy silver spoon back of her teeth and down her throat till she gagged. And there it was—both tonsils covered with membrane. She had fought valiantly to keep me from knowing her secret. She had been hiding that sore throat for three days at least and lying to her parents in order to escape just such an outcome as this.

Now truly she was furious. She had been on the defensive before but now she attacked. Tried to get off her father's lap and fly at me while tears of defeat blinded her eyes.

EMILY DICKINSON

[1830–1886]

I'm "wife"—I've finished that—
That other state—
I'm Czar—I'm "Woman" now—
It's safer so—

How odd the Girl's life looks
Behind this soft Eclipse—
I think that Earth feels so
To folks in Heaven—now—

This being comfort—then
That other kind—was pain—
But why compare?
I'm "Wife"! Stop there!

THE CANON AND THE CURRICULUM

Interpreting literature is an art and a skill that readers develop with experience and practice. Regular reading of stories, poems, plays, and essays will give you opportunities to become a skillful interpreter. Simply reading the literary works, however, is not enough, not if you wish to participate in the invigorating critical conversations teachers and other experienced readers bring to their discussion of literature. To develop a sense of the interpretive possibilities of literary works, you will need to know something of the various critical perspectives that literary critics use to analyze and interpret literature. This chapter introduces you to a number of major critical perspectives, including historical, biographical, psychological, and sociological approaches (among others), each of which approaches the study of literature a different way.

This discussion of critical perspectives aims to provide you with a set of ideas about how literature can be analyzed and interpreted. It is not designed to explain the history of literary criticism. Nor is its goal to convert you to a particular critical approach. Neither has any attempt been made to present the intricacies and variations in interpretive analysis developed by proponents of the various critical perspectives. And although you will find in this chapter discussions of ten critical perspectives, still other approaches to literary interpretation are available, both older ones that have currently declined in use and newer approaches that are still emerging.

Before considering the first of our critical perspectives, that of formalist criticism, we should review some basic questions currently being debated, sometimes heatedly, throughout the educational establishment. You may have already heard about the controversy surrounding the literary "canon" or list of works considered suitable for study in a university curriculum. There is now considerable disagreement about just what books should be read in college courses, why they should be read, and how they should be read. As a way of putting the ten critical perspectives in context, we will take up each of these questions in a brief overview of the current debate about the university literature curriculum.

What We Read

The notion of a literary canon or collection of accepted books derives from the idea of a biblical canon—those books accepted as official scriptures. A scriptural canon contains those works deemed to represent the moral standards and religious beliefs of a particular group, Jews for example, or Muslims, Hindus, or Christians. A canon of accepted works also contains, by implication, its obverse or flip side—that some works are excluded from the canon. Just as certain works, such as the Book of Maccabees, were not accepted into the Hebrew Scriptures and the Gospel of Thomas was denied entry into the Christian New Testament, not every book or literary work written can become part of an officially sanctioned literary canon or a university curriculum. Certain works inevitably will be omitted while others just as necessarily are selected for inclusion. The central question revolves around which works should be included in the canon, and why.

As you may know, certain "classics" for a long time have dominated the canon of literature for study in university courses—epic poems by Homer and Dante, for example, plays by Ibsen and Shakespeare, poems by writers from many countries, but especially those from Europe and America, novels such as Charles Dickens's *Great Expectations,* Jane Austen's *Pride and Prejudice,* Mark Twain's *The Adventures of Huckleberry Finn*, Emily Bronte's *Wuthering Heights,* and many others. In the last two decades, however, there has been a movement to alter the canon of classical works, most of which have been written by white males of European ancestry, in the more or less distant past. Some of the changes in what we read have come from adding works by writers long omitted, such as those by minority writers—African Americans, Native Americans, Asian Americans, and other writers from around the world beyond Europe, those from Australia, India, and Africa, for example. The works added by minority writers have been largely, though not exclusively, modern and contemporary ones.

Still other changes in the literary canon have come from the rediscovery or recovery of older works, many from the Renaissance and the nineteenth century, especially works by women, which had for a long time been considered unworthy of serious study and of inclusion in college literature curricula. Such works were considered not to have withstood the test of time, lasting decades or centuries, as have the classics. What needs to be remembered, however, is that "time" is an abstraction that itself accomplishes nothing. It is, rather, individuals throughout time who make the choices about which books are to be taught in schools and universities. And it is people today of both genders and of various cultures, races, ethnicities, and sexual dispositions who are debating not only what works should be part of the canon of literature but whether the very idea of a canon is viable at all. In other words, what is a canon for? Is a literary canon inevitable? Is it even necessary?

Why We Read

These changes in what we read are related to a debate about why we read. Classic novels and plays, stories and poems have long been read because the lessons they are presumed to teach are considered valuable. The meanings of certain American canonical works, for example, have been viewed as educationally and morally good for readers to assimilate, largely because the works are believed to reflect values central to the American way of life. They reflect values relating to the importance of friendship, responsible behavior, and hard work, for example, or values relating to decency, justice, and fair play. Of course, other works accepted into the literary canon taught in American colleges and universities do not reflect such views, both works written by American writers and works by writers of other nationalities and literary traditions, many of which are included in this book.

It is certainly the case that regardless of the language(s) and tradition(s) represented by a canon of literary works, those works are often canonized because they are believed to perpetuate a tradition of moral beliefs, cultural attitudes, and social dispositions. What is interesting to note, however, is that canonical literary works of many traditions and genres—Henrik Ibsen's *A Doll House,* for example, or Emily Dickinson's lyric poems—disrupt and run counter to many traditional literary, social, religious, and cultural values. And works such as Shakespeare's tragedies and Keats's and Wordsworth's poetry harbor ideas and attitudes about which common readers and professional critics have long disagreed, a disagreement that derives partly from varying critical perspectives used to interpret the works and partly from their richness and complexity, which makes it impossible to say once and for all just what those enticing and intellectually provocative works mean.

Another reason for the continuity of the traditional canon is that it is easier to preserve the status quo than to initiate change. Change is neither welcomed nor embraced, even when it is inevitable. Moreover, later generations read the books of former ones because earlier generations want their descendants to read and value what they read and valued. Those earlier generations have the power to enforce such a decision since they hold the positions of authority in schools and on councils that design curricula and create reading lists for school program and university courses.

Today, however, many of these assumptions have been reevaluated by teachers and critics from a wide range of political persuasions. With the demographic changes that have been occurring in educational institutions in the past quarter century have come additional reasons for reading. Minority groups that now form a significant population in university classrooms, minority teachers, younger faculty raised in a much altered political environment, large numbers of women faculty—all insist on the need for multiple perspectives, varying voices, different visions of experience. They argue that literary works should be read to challenge conventional ways of behaving and orthodox ways of thinking. (Some educators say that there is nothing new in this, and that, in fact, traditional canonical works have long been read this way.) For some of these other readers, however, literature exists less for moral instruction or cultural education than to help inaugurate political and social change, a view that is less widely endorsed than the view that literary works should invite critical scrutiny and stimulate questioning and debate.

How We Read

That brings us to the important question of how we read. Just how do we read? Do we simply "just read"? And if we do, then what do we mean by "just reading"? Most often just reading means something on the order of reading for pleasure, without worrying about analysis and interpretation. From the standpoint of more analytical reading, "just reading" refers to interpreting the words on the page, making sense of them in a way that seems reasonable.

But a number of assumptions lie behind this notion. One such assumption is that the meaning of a literary work is available to anyone willing to read it carefully. Another is that literary works contain layers or levels of meaning, that they have to be analyzed to understand their complex meanings. Still another is that although different readers all bring their unique experience as members of particular genders, races, religions, and nationalities to their interpretation of literary works, they finally understand the meaning of those works in the same way. In this view, literary works such as *Hamlet* or *The Scarlet Letter* mean the same thing to every reader.

Each of these assumptions, however, has been challenged by literary theorists in the past two decades, to the extent that many serious readers find them untenable. It doesn't take long, for example, to realize that though we share some understanding of Shakespeare's play or Hawthorne's novel, we invariably see different things in them and see them differently. The differences we make of literary works and the different ways we understand them are related to the varying assumptions about literature and life that we bring to our reading. The different ways these assumptions have been modified and the different emphases and focuses serious readers and literary critics bring to bear on literary works can be categorized according to various approaches or critical perspectives. Ten critical perspectives are presented, though others could be added. These ten, however, reflect critical positions that many academic readers find useful, whether they are reading works new to the canon or older established ones.

For each critical perspective you will find an overview that introduces the critical approach, an application of the critical perspective to a short story and a poem, both reprinted at the beginning of this chapter, and a list of questions you can use to apply the critical perspective to other literary works. A set of selected readings concludes each section.

Think of these ten critical perspectives as a kind of critical smorgasbord, a set of intellectual dishes you can sample and taste. Those you find most appealing you may wish to partake of more heartily, partly by applying them in your own analytical writing, partly by reading from the list of selected books. Or your instructor may encourage you to work with ones he or she believes are especially valuable. The important thing to realize, however, is that you always interpret a literary work from a theoretical standpoint, however hidden or implicit it may be. Understanding the assumptions and procedures of the various theoretical perspectives is crucial for understanding what you are doing when you interpret literature, how you do it, and why you do it that way.

In his lively book introducing college students to literary theory, *Falling Into Theory* (1994), David H. Richter of Queens College CUNY summarizes the important issues concerning literary studies today in a series of provocative questions. Richter organizes his questions according to the categories I have borrowed from him for this introductory overview: *why we read, what we read, how we read.* Keep Richter's guiding questions in mind as you read the discussion of the various critical perspectives.

> *Why we read.* What is the place of the humanities and literary studies in society? Why should we study literature? Why do we read?
> *What we read.* What is literature and who determines what counts as literature? Is there a core of "great books" that every student should read? What is the relationship of literature by women and minority groups to the canon? Are criteria of quality universal, or are literary values essentially political?
> *How we read.* How do we and how should we read texts? Does meaning reside in the author, the text, or the reader? To what degree is the meaning of a text fixed? What ethical concerns do we bring to texts as readers, and how do these concerns reshape the

texts we read? What do we owe the text and what does it owe us?
How do the politics of race and gender shape our reading of texts?
Do political approaches to literature betray or shed light on them?

Canon and Curriculum: Selected Readings

To learn more about the controversy surrounding the literary canon and the college English curriculum, the following books provide a variety of perspectives on the issues.

Alter, Robert. *The Pleasures of Reading in an Ideological Age.* 1989.
Atlas, James. *The Battle of the Books.* 1990.
D'Souza, Dinesh. *Illiberal Education: The Politics of Sex and Race on Campus.* 1991.
Eagleton, Terry. *Literary Theory: An Introduction.* 1983.
Graff, Gerald. *Beyond the Culture Wars.* 1992.
Greenblatt, Stephen and Giles Gunn. *Redrawing the Boundaries: The Transformation of English and American Literary Studies.* 1992.
Kimball, Roger. *Tenured Radicals: How Politics Has Corrupted Higher Education.* 1990.
Lauter, Paul. *Canons and Contexts.* 1991.
Lentricchia, Frank. *Criticism and Social Change.* 1983.
Levine, George et al. *Speaking for the Humanities.* 1989.
Scholes, Robert. *Textual Power.* 1985.

FORMALIST PERSPECTIVES

An Overview of Formalist Criticism

Formalist critics view literature as a distinctive art, one that uses the resources of language to shape experience, communicate meaning, and express emotion. Formalists emphasize the form of a literary work to determine its meaning, focusing on literary elements such as plot, character, setting, diction, imagery, structure, and point of view. Approaching literary works as independent systems with interdependent parts, formalists typically subordinate biographical information or historical data in their interpretations. Underlying formalist critical perspectives is the belief that literary works are unified artistic wholes that can be understood by analyzing their parts.

According to the formalist view, the proper concern of literary criticism is with the work itself rather than with literary history, the life of the author, or a work's social and historical contexts. For a formalist, the central meaning of a literary work is discovered through a detailed analysis of the work's formal elements rather than by going outside the work to consider other issues, whether biographical, historical, psychological, social, political, or ideological. Such additional considerations, from the formalist perspective, are extrinsic, or external, and are of secondary importance. What matters most to the formalist critic is how the work comes to mean what it does—how its resources of language are deployed by the writer to convey meaning. Implicit in the formalist perspective, moreover, is that readers can indeed determine the meanings of literary works—that literature can be understood and its meanings clarified.

Two other tenets of formalist criticism deserve mention: (1) that a literary work exists independent of any particular reader—that is, that a literary work exists outside of any reader's recreation of it in the act of reading; (2) that the greatest literary works are "universal," their wholeness and aesthetic harmony transcending the specific particularities they describe.

The primary method of formalism is a close reading of the literary text, with an emphasis, for example, on a work's use of metaphor or symbol, its deployment of irony, its patterns of image or action. Lyric poetry lends itself especially well to the kinds of close reading favored by formalist critics because its language tends to be more compressed and metaphorical than the language of prose—at least as a general rule. Nonetheless, formal analysis of novels and plays can also focus on close reading of key passages (the opening and closing chapters of a novel, for example, or the first and last scenes of a play, or a climactic moment in the action of drama, poetry, or fiction). In addition, formalist critics analyze the large-scale structures of longer works, looking for patterns and relationships among scenes, actions, and characters.

One consistent feature of formalist criticism is an emphasis on tension and ambiguity. Tension refers to the way elements of a text's language reflect conflict and opposition. Ambiguity refers to the ways texts remain open to more than a single, unified, definitive interpretation. Both tension and ambiguity as elements of formalist critical approaches were picked up and elaborated to serve different interpretive arguments by critics employing the methodologies of structuralism and deconstruction.

The sections of *Literature* headed "Elements" illustrate and apply techniques of formal analysis. In Chapter 3, "The Elements of Fiction," for example, a paragraph from William Faulkner's short story "A Rose for Emily" is analyzed to show how one literary element—setting—functions in the story as a whole. On the same page the setting of Kate Chopin's "The Story of an Hour" is described in symbolic terms. Analogously, for poetry, the connotation of Wordsworth's diction in "I Wandered Lonely as a Cloud" is analyzed to show how Wordsworth's language relates to the image patterns he creates and how diction and imagery contribute to the poem's meaning. Throughout *Literature,* you will find numerous examples of formal analysis applied to fiction (Chapter 3); poetry (Chapter 9); drama (Chapter 17); and essay (Chapter 33). You can use these many focused brief analyses to model your own close readings on works in each of the four literary genres.

Thinking from a Formalist Perspective

A formalist critic reading William Carlos Williams's "The Use of Force" might consider how the story begins and ends, contrasting its opening matter-of-fact objective description with its concluding shift of perspective and heightening of language. A formalist perspective would typically include observations about the relations among the characters, particularly the doctor, who is clearly an outsider among the poor parents, and who is invited in among them only because they are desperate to help their sick daughter. Character relations are of paramount interest in Williams's story since a conflict occurs between the doctor and his patient, one that is resolved only through the use of force. The relations between the doctor and the parents are equally interesting, since their surface behavior contrasts with their feelings about each other.

Other aspects of the story of interest from a formalist perspective would include the writer's use of first-person narration, especially the way the narrator's thoughts are made known to readers (less through dialogue than through a kind of interior monologue that readers "overhear"). A formalist critic might ask what difference it would make if the story were told in the third person, or if the narrator's ideas were to be voiced in direct dialogue. At a key moment—a climactic one, in fact—the story shifts from internal report of the doctor's thoughts to direct dialogue. A formalist would be interested in the effects of this shift, especially in its artistic effectiveness.

A formalist critic reading Emily Dickinson's "I'm 'wife' " would note its neat division into three stanzas and consider the focus of each. A formalist perspective would consider why, in fact, the poem is cast in three stanzas and not one or two, four, or six. A consideration of the relationship between form and meaning might help readers notice how the poem's rhyme scheme and its sentence patterns reinforce or subvert its stanza organization.

Other considerations formalist critics would be likely to raise about the poem might include the connotations of "Czar" for the speaker. Of particular importance in this regard would be the language used to describe the "Girl's life" in the second stanza, especially how it is described as existing behind a "soft Eclipse." Readers following a formalist agenda might also question how the slant rhymes of the poem contribute to its idea and its effect.

Such questions, however, are only a starting point toward a formal analysis of Williams's story and Dickinson's poem.

A CHECKLIST OF FORMALIST CRITICAL QUESTIONS

1. How is the work structured or organized? How does it begin? Where does it go next? How does it end? What is the work's plot? How is its plot related to its structure?
2. What is the relationship of each part of the work to the work as a whole? How are the parts related to one another?
3. Who is narrating or telling what happens in the work? How is the narrator, speaker, or character revealed to readers? How do we come to know and understand this figure?
4. Who are the major and minor characters, what do they represent, and how do they relate to one another?
5. What are the time and place of the work—its setting? How is the setting related to what we know of the characters and their actions? To what extent is the setting symbolic?
6. What kind of language does the author use to describe, narrate, explain, or otherwise

create the world of the literary work? More specifically, what images, similes, metaphors, symbols appear in the work? What is their function? What meanings do they convey?

Formalist Criticism: Selected Readings

Burke, Kenneth. *Counterstatement*. 1930.
Brooks, Cleanth. *The Well Wrought Urn: Studies in the Structure of Poetry*. 1947.
Eliot, T. S. *Selected Essays*. 1932.
Empson, William. *Seven Types of Ambiguity*. 1930.
Ransom, John Crowe. *The New Criticism*. 1941.
Wellek, Rene, and Austin Warren. *Theory of Literature*. 1949, 1973.
Wimsatt, W.K. *The Verbal Icon*. 1954.

BIOGRAPHICAL PERSPECTIVES

Overview of Biographical Criticism

To what extent a writer's life should be brought to bear on an interpretation of his or her work has long been a matter of controversy. Some critics insist that biographical information at best distracts from and at worst distorts the process of analyzing, appreciating, and understanding literary works. These critics believe that literary works must stand on their own, stripped of the facts of their writers' lives.

Against this view, however, can be placed one that values the information readers gain from knowing about writers' lives. Biographical critics argue that there are essentially three kinds of benefits readers acquire from using biographical evidence for literary interpretation: (1) readers understand literary works better since the facts about authors' experiences can help readers decide how to interpret those works; (2) readers can better appreciate a literary work for knowing the writer's struggles or difficulties in creating it; and (3) readers can better assess writers' preoccupations by studying the ways they modify and adjust their actual experience in their literary works.

Knowing, for example, that Shakespeare and Molière were actors who performed in the plays they wrote provides an added dimension to our appreciation of their genius. It also might invite us to look at their plays from the practical standpoint of a performer rather than merely from the perspective of an armchair reader, a classroom student, or a theatergoer. Or to realize that Ernest Hemingway's story "The Short Happy Life of Francis Macomber" (pages 337–357) derives from experiences he had in Africa hunting big game and from one of his numerous marriages may lead readers to his biography to see just how the life and work are related, especially to see how Hemingway selected from and shaped his actual experience to create this short story. In addition, readers may be interested in knowing that in original drafts of the "The Short Happy Life of Francis Macomber," the names of the characters and certain of their defining characteristics as presented in the published story were different, and that Hemingway chose his published title after rejecting more than a dozen other possibilities, including "The New Man," "The End of the Marriage," "The Cult of Violence," "The Master Passion," and "The Struggle for Power." Considering such biographical information and using it to analyze the finished literary work can be illuminating rather than distracting or distorting. Thinking about these different alternative titles can lead readers to focus on different aspects of the story, especially to emphasize different incidents and to value the viewpoints of different characters. As with any critical approach, however, a biographical perspective should be used judiciously, keeping the focus on the literary work and using the biographical information to clarify understanding and to develop an interpretation.

A biographical critic can focus on a writer's works not only to enhance understanding of them individually but also to enrich a reader's understanding of the artist. In an essay on the relations between literature and biography, Leon Edel, author of an outstanding biography of Henry James, suggests that what the literary biographer seeks to discover about the subject are his or her characteristic ways of thinking, perceiving, and feeling that may be revealed more honestly and thoroughly in the writer's work than in his or her conscious nonliterary statements. In addition, what we learn about writers from a judicious study of their work can also be linked with an understanding of the writer's world, and thus serve as a bridge to an appreciation of the social and cultural contexts in which the writer lived.

Thinking from a Biographical Perspective

Whether one focuses on formalist questions to analyze "The Use of Force" or on other issues such as the doctor's psychological impulses or the power struggles among doctor, patient, and parents, biographical information can add to a reader's appreciation of the story. In addition to being a writer, William Carlos Williams was a doctor, a pediatrician with a practice in Rutherford, New Jersey. Williams never gave up medicine for literature, as some other writers did. Instead he continued to treat patients all his life. In fact, he acquired some of the raw material for his poetry, fiction, and essays directly from his practice of medicine.

Another biographical fact of interest is that Williams did some of his writing between seeing patients. He would typically jot notes, write lines of poems, sketch outlines for stories, record dialogue, and otherwise fill the gaps in his time with his writing. Some have suggested that Williams's many short sketches, brief stories, and short poems result directly from this method of composing. Of course, Williams did not do all of his writing in the short bursts of time between seeing his patients. He also wrote during vacations and more extended blocks of time. And, Williams did, in fact, write one of the longest American poems of the century, *Paterson,* a book-length poem in five long sections, written and published over a period of more than twenty years.

Of biographical interest regarding Dickinson's "I'm 'wife' " is the fact that Dickinson never married. A critic with a biographical bent might see in this early poem themes and concerns that became important preoccupations for the poet, issues of gender and power, concerns about the relationship between men and women in marriage, both a marriage she may have wanted for herself and the marriage of her brother, a marriage that some biographers argue was a disappointment to her, though one she initially encouraged. Biographical questions of interest would focus on whether Dickinson's poem was based on her own experience, perhaps on frustrated hopes, or whether it was simply a metaphor she played with poetically to deflect the circumstances of everyday reality.

A CHECKLIST OF BIOGRAPHICAL CRITICAL QUESTIONS

1. What influences—persons, ideas, movements, events—evident in the writer's life does the work reflect?
2. To what extent are the events described in the work a direct transfer of what happened in the writer's actual life?
3. What modifications of the actual events has the writer made in the literary work? For what possible purposes?
4. Why might the writer have altered his or her actual experience in the literary work?
5. What are the effects of the differences between actual events and their literary transformation in the poem, story, play, or essay?
6. What has the author revealed in the work about his or her characteristic modes of thought, perception, or emotion? What place does this work have in the artist's literary development and career?

Biographical Criticism: Selected Readings

Edel, Leon. *Henry James,* 5 vols. 1953–1972.
Farr, Judith. *The Passion of Emily Dickinson.* 1992.
Mariani, Paul. *William Carlos Williams: A New World Naked.* 1981.
Sewall, Richard, B. *The Life of Emily Dickinson,* 2 vols. 1974.
Williams, William Carlos. *Autobiography.* 1951, 1967.
Wolff, Cynthia Griffin. *Emily Dickinson.* 1986.

HISTORICAL PERSPECTIVES

An Overview of Historical Criticism

Historical critics approach literature in two ways: (1) they provide a context of background information necessary for understanding how literary works were perceived in their time; (2) they show how literary works reflect ideas and attitudes of the time in which they were written. These two general approaches to historical criticism represent methods and approaches that might be termed "old historicism" and "new historicism" respectively.

The older form of historical criticism, still in use today, insists that a literary work be read with a sense of the time and place of its creation. This is necessary, insist historical critics, because every literary work is a product of its time and its world. Understanding the social background and the intellectual currents of that time and that world illuminate literary works for later generations of readers.

Knowing something about the London of William Blake's time, for example, helps readers better appreciate and understand the power of Blake's protest against horrific social conditions and the institutions of church and state Blake held responsible for permitting such conditions to exist. In his poem "London" (page 562), Blake refers to chimney sweepers, who were usually young children small enough to fit inside a chimney, and whose parents sent them to a kind of work that drastically curtailed not only their childhood but also their lives. Or, to take another example, understanding something about the role and position of women in late nineteenth-century America helps readers of the late twentieth century better understand the protagonist of Kate Chopin's "The Story of an Hour" (page 38). Readers might appreciate why, for example, Mrs. Mallard feels the need to escape from her marriage and why her feelings are described by turns as exhilarating and "monstrous."

Thinking from a New Historicist Perspective

Like earlier historical approaches, a more contemporary approach identified as "new historicism" considers historical contexts of literary works essential for understanding them. A significant difference, however, between earlier historical criticism and new historicism is the newer variety's emphasis on analyzing historical documents with the same intensity and scrutiny given foregrounded passages in the literary works to be interpreted. In reading Williams's "The Use of Force," for example, a new historicist might pay as much attention to Williams's and other doctors' medical records of the 1920s and 1930s as to the details of incident and language in the story itself. Similarly, in interpreting Dickinson's "I'm 'wife' " new historicist critics would concern themselves with diaries of women written during the early 1860s, when the poem was written. In both instances the records and diaries would be read to ascertain prevailing cultural attitudes about doctor-patient relationships and middle-class marriage respectively. In addition, new historicist critics might also typically compare prevailing cultural attitudes about these issues today with those of the times in which the story and poem were written. In fact, one common strategy of new historicist critics is to compare and contrast the language of contemporaraneous documents and literary works to reveal hidden assumptions, biases, and cultural attitudes that relate the two kinds of texts, literary and documentary, usually to demonstrate how the literary work shares the cultural assumptions of the document.

An important feature of new historicist criticism is its concern with examining the power relations of rulers and subjects. A guiding assumption among many new historicist critics is that texts, not only literary works but also documents, diaries, records, even institutions such as hospitals and prisons, are ideological products culturally constructed from the prevailing power structures that dominate particular societies. Reading a literary work from a new historicist perspective thus becomes an exercise in uncovering the conflicting and subversive perspectives of the marginalized and suppressed, as, for example, the perspective and voice of the young patient in "The Use of Force," and the vision and values of the speaker in Dickinson's "I'm 'wife'," whose perspectives tend to be undervalued because they are females.

While appropriating some of the methods of formalist and deconstructive critics, new historicists differ from them in a number of important ways. Most importantly, unlike critics who limit their analysis of a literary work to its language and structure, new historicists spend more time analyzing nonliterary texts from the same time in which the literary work was written. New historicists, however, do apply the close reading strategies of formalist and deconstructive perspectives, but their goal is not, like the formalists, to show how the literary work manifests universal values or how it is unified. Nor is the new historicist goal to show how the text undermines and contradicts itself, an emphasis of deconstructive perspectives. Instead, new historicists analyze the cultural context embedded in the literary work and explain its relationship with the network of the assumptions and beliefs that inform social institutions and cultural practices prevalent in the historical period when the literary work was written. Finally, it is important to note that for new historicist critics, history does not provide mere "background" against which to study literary works, but is, rather, an equally important "text," one that is ultimately inseparable from the literary work, which inevitably reveals the conflicting power relations that underlie all human interaction, from the small-scale interactions with families to the large-scale interactions of social institutions.

One potential danger of applying historical perspectives to literature is that historical information and documents may be foregrounded and emphasized so heavily that readers lose sight of the literary work the historical approach is designed to illuminate. When the prism of history is used to clarify and explain elements of the literary work, however, whether in examining intellectual currents, describing social conditions, or presenting cultural attitudes, readers' understanding of literary works can be immeasurably enriched. The challenge for historical understanding, whether one uses the tools of the older historicist tradition or the methods of the new historicism, is to ascertain what the past was truly like, how its values are inscribed in its cultural artifacts, including its literature. Equally challenging is an exploration of the question, What was it possible to think or do at a particular moment of the past, including possibilities that may no longer be available to those living today?

A CHECKLIST OF HISTORICAL AND NEW HISTORICIST CRITICAL QUESTIONS

1. When was the work written? When was it published? How was it received by the critics and the public? Why?
2. What does the work's reception reveal about the standards of taste and value during the time it was published and reviewed?
3. What social attitudes and cultural practices related to the action of the work were prevalent during the time the work was written and published?

4. What kinds of power relations does the work describe, reflect, or embody?
5. How do the power relations reflected in the literary work manifest themselves in the cultural practices and social institutions prevalent during the time the work was written and published?
6. What other types of historical documents, cultural artifacts, or social institutions might be analyzed in conjunction with particular literary works? How might a close reading of such a nonliterary "text" illuminate those literary works?
7. To what extent can we understand the past as it is reflected in the literary work? To what extent does the work reflect differences from the ideas and values of its time?

Historical and New Historicist Criticism: Selected Readings

Armstrong, Nancy. *Desire and Domestic Fiction*. 1987.
Dollmore, Jonathan and Alan Sinfield. *Political Shakespeare*. 1985.
Geertz, Clifford. *The Interpretation of Cultures*. 1973.
Greenblatt, Stephen. *Learning to Curse: Essays in Early Modern Culture*. 1990.
Greenblatt, Stephen. *Marvellous Possessions*. 1991.
Kenner, Hugh. *The Pound Era*. 1971.
Lindenberger, Herbert. *Historical Drama*. 1975.
Levinson, Marjorie, et al. *Rethinking Historicism*. 1989.
Veeser, H. Aram. *The New Historicism*. 1989.
Veeser, H. Aram. *The New Historicism: A Reader*. 1994.

PSYCHOLOGICAL PERSPECTIVES

An Overview of Psychological Criticism

Psychological criticism approaches a work of literature as the revelation of its author's mind and personality. Psychological critics see literary works as intimately linked with their author's mental and emotional characteristics. Critics who employ a psychological perspective do so to explain how a literary work reflects its writer's consciousness and mental world, and they use what they know of writers' lives to explain features of their work. Some psychological critics are more interested in the creative processes of writers than in their literary works; these critics look into literary works for clues to a writer's creative imagination. Other psychological critics wish to study less a writer's creative process than his or her motivations and behavior; these critics may study a writer's works along with letters and diaries to better understand not just what a writer has done in life but why the writer behaved in a particular manner. Still other critics employ methods of Freudian psychoanalysis to understand not only writers such as Shakespeare or Kafka but the literary characters they create, Iago, for example, or Gregor Samsa.

Psychoanalytic criticism derives from Freud's revolutionary psychology in which he developed the notion of the "unconscious" along with the psychological mechanisms of "displacement," "condensation," "fixation," and "manifest and latent" dream content. Freud posited an unconscious element of the mind below consciousness, just beneath awareness. According to Freud, the unconscious harbors forbidden wishes and desires, often sexual, that are in conflict with an individual's or society's moral standards. Freud explains that although the individual represses or "censors" these unconscious fantasies and desires, they become "displaced" or distorted in dreams and other forms of fantasy, which serve to disguise their real meaning.

The disguised versions that appear in a person's conscious life are considered to be the "manifest" content of the unconscious wishes that are their "latent" content, which psychoanalytic critics attempt to discover and explain. Psychoanalytic critics rely heavily on symbolism to identify and explain the meaning of repressed desires, interpreting ordinary objects such as clocks and towers and natural elements such as fire and water in ways that reveal aspects of a literary character's sexuality. These critics also make use of other psychoanalytic concepts and terms such as "fixation," or "obsessive compulsion," attaching to feelings, behaviors, and fantasies that individuals presumably outgrow yet retain in the form of unconscious attractions.

Among the most important of the categories derived from Freud that psychoanalytic critics employ are those Freud used to describe mental structures and dynamics. Freud recognized three types of mental functions, which he designated the "id," the "ego," and the "superego." Freud saw the id as the storehouse of desires, primarily libidinal or sexual, but also aggressive and possessive. He saw the superego as the representative of societal and parental standards of ethics and morality. And he saw the ego as the negotiator between the desires and demands of the id and the controlling and constraining force of the superego, all influenced further by an individual's relationship with other people in the contexts of actual life. These few but important psychoanalytic concepts have been put to varied uses by critics with a wide range of psychological approaches. Freud himself analyzed Sophocles' tragic drama *Oedipus the King* (page 880) to explain how Oedipus harbored an unconscious desire to kill his father and marry his mother, events the play accounts for. Other critics have used Freud's insights—which, by the way, Freud himself says he derived from studying literary masters such as Sophocles, Shakespeare, and Kafka—to analyze the hidden motivations of literary characters. One of the most famous of all literary characters, Hamlet, has stimulated psychological critics of all persuasions to explain why he delays killing King Claudius. In his book *Hamlet and Oedipus,* Ernest Jones uses Freud's theory of the "Oedipus complex" to explain Hamlet's delay, which Jones sees, essentially, as Hamlet's inability to punish Claudius for what he, Hamlet, unconsciously wanted to do himself.

Thinking from a Psychoanalytic Perspective

We can use a psychoanalytic perspective to make a few observations about the behavior of the characters in Williams's "The Use of Force" and the marital situation described in Dickinson's "I'm 'wife'."

The doctor in "The Use of Force," for example can be seen as repressing his real desire to humiliate his young female patient under the guise of inspecting her throat for signs of illness. The girl's refusal can be seen as an unwillingness to expose herself to this strange overbearing man, who is forcing himself upon her. Her mouth can be interpreted as a displacement for her vagina, and the doctor's attempt to open it by force as a kind of rape. Even the parents' actions might be explained in psychoanalytic terms in that they act as voyeurs, alternately frightened and sexually excited by what they are witnessing.

Dickinson's speaker experiences no such overt violation. Her subjugation is more acceptable because she seems to fulfill a socially sanctioned role as "wife." What is interesting from a psychoanalytic standpoint, however, is the way she subverts that role by comparing herself to a "Czar," a powerful emperor, which seems to conflict with her role as "wife" and "Woman." Moreover, the speaker's comparison between the "Girl's life" and the wife's, which is elaborated with the analogy of differences experienced between those on Earth and in Heaven, can be seen as a displacement of her poetic ambition onto the image of a wife, which the speaker endows with spiritual and temporal powers.

A CHECKLIST OF PSYCHOLOGICAL CRITICAL QUESTIONS

1. What connections can you make between your knowledge of an author's life and the behavior and motivations of characters in his or her work?
2. How does your understanding of the characters, their relationships, their actions, and their motivations in a literary work help you better understand the mental world and imaginative life, or the actions and motivations, of the author?
3. How does a particular literary work—its images, metaphors, and other linguistic elements—reveal the psychological motivations of its characters or the psychological mindset of its author?
4. To what extent can you employ the concepts of Freudian psychoanalysis to understand the motivations of literary characters?
5. What kinds of literary works and what types of literary characters seem best suited to a critical approach that employs a psychological or psychoanalytical perspective? Why?
6. How can a psychological or psychoanalytic approach to a particular work be combined with an approach from another critical perspective—for example, that of biographical or formalist criticism, or that of feminist or deconstructionist criticism?

Psychological and Psychoanalytic Criticism: Selected Readings

Bloom, Harold. *The Anxiety of Influence*. 1973.
Chodorow, Nancy. *Feminism and Psychoanalytic Theory*. 1990.
Crews, Frederick. *The Sins of the Fathers: Hawthorne's Psychological Themes*. 1966.
Crews, Frederick. *Skeptical Engagements*. 1986.
Felman, Soshana. *Jacques Lacan and the Adventure of Insight*. 1987.
Freud, Sigmund. *The Interpretation of Dreams*. 1900.
Freud, Sigmund. *Introductory Lectures on Psychoanalysis*. 1917–1918.
Freud, Sigmund. *New Introductory Lectures on Psychoanalysis*. 1933.

Hoffman, Frederick J. *Freudianism and the Literary Mind.* 1957.

Holland, Norman. *The Dynamics of Literary Response.* 1968.

Jones, Ernest. *Hamlet and Oedipus.* 1949.

Manheim, Leonard, and Eleanor Manheim, eds. *Hidden Patterns: Studies in Psychoanalytic Literary Criticism.* 1966.

Mitchell, Juliet. *Psychoanalysis and Feminism.* 1975.

Nelson, Benjamin, ed. *Sigmund Freud on Creativity and the Unconscious.* 1958.

Skura, Meredith. *The Literary Use of the Psychoanalytic Process.* 1981.

Trilling, Lionel. *The Opposing Self.* 1955.

Wilson, Edmund. *The Wound and the Bow.* 1941.

Wright, Elizabeth, ed. *Psychoanalytic Criticism.* 1984.

SOCIOLOGICAL PERSPECTIVES

An Overview of Sociological Criticism

Like historical and biographical critics, sociological critics argue that literary works should not be isolated from the social contexts in which they are embedded. And also like historical critics, especially those who espouse new historicist perspectives, sociological critics emphasize the ways power relations are played out by varying social forces and institutions. Sociological critics focus on the values of a society and how those values are reflected in literary works. At one end of the sociological critical spectrum, literary works are treated simply as documents that either embody social conditions or are a product of those conditions. Critics employing a sociological perspective study the economic, political, and cultural issues expressed in literary works as those issues are reflected in the societies in which the works were produced.

A sociological approach to the study of Shakespeare's *Othello* (page 985) could focus on the political organization of the Venetian state as depicted in the play and its relation to the play's depiction of authority, perhaps considering as well the breakdown of authority in the scenes set in Cyprus. Another sociological perspective might focus on the play's economic aspects, particularly how money and influence are used to manipulate others. Still other sociological issues that could be addressed include the role of women in the play and the issue of Othello's race. How, for example, does Shakespeare portray the power relations between Othello and Desdemona, Iago and Emilia, Cassio and Bianca? To what extent is each of these women's relationship with men considered from an economic standpoint? Or, to what extent is Othello's blackness a factor in his demise, or is his race a defining characteristic in other characters' perceptions of him?

Two significant trends in sociological criticism have had a decisive impact on critical theory: Marxist criticism and feminist criticism. Proponents of each of these critical perspectives have used some of the tools of other critical approaches such as the close reading of the formalists and deconstructionists and the symbolic analysis of the psychoanalytic critics to espouse their respective ideologies in interpreting literature.

Marxist Critical Perspectives

In the same way that many psychoanalytic critics base their approach to literature on the theoretical works of Sigmund Freud, Marxist critics are indebted to the political theory of Karl Marx and Friedrich Engels. Marxist critics examine literature for its reflection of how dominant elite and middle-class/bourgeois values lead to the control and suppression of the working classes. Marxist critics see literature's value in promoting social and economic revolution, with works that espouse Marxist ideology serving to prompt the kinds of economic and political changes that conform to Marxist principles. Such changes would include the overthrow of the dominant capitalist ideology and the loss of power by those with money and privilege. Marxist criticism is concerned both with understanding the role of politics, money, and power in literary works, and with redefining and reforming the way society distributes its resources among the classes. Fundamentally, the Marxist ideology looks toward a vision of a world not so much where class conflict has been minimized but one in which classes have disappeared altogether.

Marxist critics generally approach literary works as products of their era, especially as influenced, even determined by the economic and political ideologies that prevail at the time of their composition. The literary work is considered a "product" in relation to the actual economic and social conditions that exist at either the time of the work's composition or the time and place of the action it describes.

Marxist analyses of novels focus on the relations among classes. In British and European novels of the nineteenth century, for example, class is a significant factor in the rise and fall of the characters' fortunes. Novels such as Charles Dickens's *Little Dorritt, Dombey and Son,* and *Oliver Twist,* George Eliot's *Middlemarch,* Anthony Trollope's *The Eustace Diamonds,* and William Makepiece Thackery's *Vanity Fair* portray a panoramic vision of society with characters pressing to move up in social rank and status. These and numerous other novels from the eighteenth through the twentieth century provide abundant territory for Marxist perspectives to investigate the ways political and economic forces conspire to keep some social, ethnic, and racial groups in power and others out. In fact, the Marxist critical perspective has been brought to bear most often on the novel, next most often on drama, and least often on poetry, where issues of power, money, and political influence are not nearly as pervasive.

Thinking from a Marxist Perspective

In applying a Marxist critical perspective to a work like Williams's "The Use of Force," one would consider the ways in which power relations are played out in the story. It seems clear that the doctor is the privileged individual who wields the power over both the girl and her family. Since he can refuse to treat the girl, insist on being paid more for his services, or berate the parents for their ineptitude (though he actually does none of these things), the parents are cowed by his presence. The girl, though defiant, is at his mercy since he is physically stronger and psychologically more powerful than she is. In addition to such observations, a Marxist critic might consider the story's action from an economic standpoint, in which the doctor performs a service for a fee, with the entire situation viewed strictly as an economic transaction. Moreover, the parents are apparently poor, and one could surmise that they and their daughter might not receive the quality of medical service or the courteous delivery of medical care they would get were they more economically prosperous.

A CHECKLIST OF MARXIST CRITICAL QUESTIONS

1. What social forces and institutions are represented in the work? How are these forces portrayed? What is the author's attitude toward them?
2. What political economic elements appear in the work? How important are they in determining or influencing the lives of the characters?
3. What economic issues appear in the course of the work? How important are economic facts in influencing the motivation and behavior of the characters?
4. To what extent are the lives of the characters influenced or determined by social, political, and economic forces? To what extent are the characters aware of these forces?

Marxist Criticism: Selected Readings

Baxandall, Lee, and Stefan Morawski, eds. *Marx and Engels on Literature and Art*. 1973.
Benjamin, Walter. *Illuminations*. 1968.
Eagleton, Terry. *Marxism and Literary Criticism*. 1976.
Jameson, Fredric. *Marxism and Form*. 1971.
Lukacs, George. *Realism in Our Time*. 1972.
Trotsky, Leon. *Literature and the Revolution*. 1924.
Williams, Raymond. *Marxism and Literature*. 1977.

Feminist Critical Perspectives

Feminist criticism, like Marxist and new historicist criticism, examines the social and cultural aspects of literary works, especially for what those works reveal about the role, position, and influence of women. Like other socially minded critics, feminist critics consider literature in relation to its social, economic, and political contexts, and indeed look to analyze its social, economic, and political content. Feminist critics also typically see literature as an arena to contest for power and control, since as sociological critics, feminist critics also see literature as an agent for social transformation.

Moreover, feminist critics seek to redress the imbalance of literary study in which all important books are written by men or the only characters of real interest are male protagonists. Feminist critics have thus begun to study women writers whose works have been previously neglected. They have begun to look at the way feminine consciousness has been portrayed in literature written by both women and men. And they have begun to change the nature of the questions asked about literature that reflect predominantly male experience. In these and other ways feminist critical perspectives have begun to undermine the patriarchal or masculinist assumptions that have dominated critical approaches to literature until relatively recently. For although feminist critics can trace their origins back to nineteenth-century politics and cite as formative influences the works of Margaret Fuller, Mary Wollstonecraft Godwin, John Stuart Mill, and Elizabeth Cady Stanton, feminist perspectives only began to be raised in literary circles with Virginia Woolf's *A Room of One's Own* (1929), which describes the difficult conditions under which women writers of the past had to work, and with Simone de Beauvoir's *The Second Sex* (1949), which analyzes the biology, psychology, and sociology of women and their place, role, and influence in western culture. It is only in the late 1960s and early 1970s, however, that feminist criticism *per se* began to emerge with the publication of Mary Ellman's *Thinking About Women* (1968), Kate Millet's *Sexual Politics* (1970), and a host of other works that have followed for more than a quarter century and show no signs of abating.

In his influential and widely used *Glossary of Literary Terms,* M. H. Abrams identifies four central tenets of much feminist criticism, summarized in the following list.

1. Western civilization is pervasively patriarchal (ruled by the father)—that is, it is male-centered and controlled, and is organized and conducted in such a way as to subordinate women to men in all cultural domains: familial, religious, political, economic, social, legal, and artistic.
2. The prevailing concepts of *gender*—of the traits that constitute what is masculine and what is feminine—are largely, if not entirely, cultural constructs that were generated by the omnipresent patriarchal biases of our civilization.
3. This patriarchal (or "masculinist," or "androcentric") ideology pervades those writings which have been considered great literature, and which until recently have been written almost entirely by men for men.
4. The traditional aesthetic categories and criteria for analyzing and appraising literary works . . . are in fact infused with masculine assumptions, interests, and ways of reasoning, so that the standard rankings, and also the critical treatments, of literary works have in fact been tacitly but thoroughly gender-biased.*

It should be noted, however, that Abrams's list, though helpful, tends to blur distinctions among the many different varieties of feminist criticism as currently practiced. Thus the ways these assumptions are reflected in feminist criticism vary enormously from the reader-response approaches used by feminist critics, such as Judith Fetterley and Elizabeth Flynn, to the cultural studies approaches

*M. H. Abrams. *A Glossary of Literary Terms,* 6th ed., 1993. pp. 234–235.

used by Jane Tompkins and Eve Kosovsky Sedgwick, to the Lacanian psycho-analytic approaches employed by Helene Cixous and Julia Kristeva. It would be better to think of feminist criticism in the plural as the criticism of feminists rather than to envision it as a singular monolithic entity.

Thinking from a Feminist Perspective

In applying the perspective of feminist criticism to "I'm 'wife'," we might consider the way the roles of woman and wife are suggested in the poem. A feminist reading would be alert for other signs of power contestation in the poem, why for example the speaker compares herself to a "Czar," and what that means in terms of her ability to exert her will and control her destiny. Feminist readers would also ask what the masculine term "Czar" signifies in the poem, and whether there is a feminine counterpart.

Feminist readers might also interrogate the poem to ask why the state of wifehood brings "comfort" and "That other" state—of girlhood—"was pain." They would probe beyond the text of the poem to consider the extent to which such differences in experience and feeling obtained in marriages during Dickinson's lifetime, thus sharing an interest with new historicist critics. Moreover, they might also wonder whether the poem's abrupt ending "I'm 'Wife'! Stop there!" with its insistent tone might not mask an undercurrent of fear or powerlessness.

A CHECKLIST OF FEMINIST CRITICAL QUESTIONS

1. To what extent does the representation of women (and men) in the work reflect the place and time in which the work was written?
2. How are the relations between men and women, or those between members of the same sex, presented in the work? What roles do men and women assume and perform and with what consequences?
3. Does the author present the work from within a predominantly male or female sensibility? Why might this have been done, and with what effects?
4. How do the facts of the author's life relate to the presentation of men and women in the work? To their relative degrees of power?
5. How do other works by the author correspond to this one in their depiction of the power relationships between men and women?

Feminist Criticism: Selected Readings

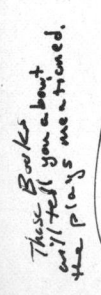

Baym, Nina. *Woman's Fiction*. 1978.
Buck, Claire. *The Bloomsbury Guide to Women's Literature*. 1992.
Cixous, Helene. *The Laugh of the Medusa*. 1976.
Fetterley, Judith. *The Resisting Reader*. 1978.
Gallop, Jane. *The Daughter's Seduction: Feminism and Psychoanalysis*. 1982.
Gates, Henry L., Jr. *Reading Black, Reading Feminist*. 1990.

Gilbert, Sandra, and Susan Gubar. *The Madwoman in the Attic*. 1979.
Heilbrun, Carolyn. *Toward a Recognition of Adrogyny*. 1973.
Moers, Ellen. *Literary Women*. 1976.
Rich, Adrienne. *On Lies, Secrets, and Silence*. 1980.
Ruthven, K. K. *Feminist Literary Studies: An Introduction*. 1984.
Schweickart, Patricinio, and Elizabeth Flynn. *Gender and Reading*. 1986.
Showalter, Elaine. *A Literature of Their Own*. 1977.
Showalter, Elaine. *The New Feminist Criticism*. 1986.
Smith, Barbara. *Toward a Black Feminist Criticism*. 1977.

READER-RESPONSE PERSPECTIVES

An Overview of Reader-Response Criticism

Reader-response criticism raises the question of where literary meaning resides—in the literary text, in the reader, or in the interactive space between text and reader. Reader-response critics differ in the varying degrees of subjectivity they allow into their theories of interpretation. Some, like David Bleich, see the literary text as a kind of mirror in which readers see themselves. In making sense of literature, readers recreate themselves. Other reader-response critics, like Wolfgang Iser, focus on the text rather than on the feelings and reactions of the reader. Text-centered reader-response critics emphasize the temporal aspect of reading, suggesting that readers make sense of texts over time, moving through a text sentence by sentence, line by line, word by word, filling in gaps and making inferences about what is being implied by textual details as they read.

Still other reader-response critics like Norman Holland focus on the psychological dynamics of reading. Holland argues that every reader creates a specific identity theme unique to him or her self in reading any literary work. He suggests that to make sense of a literary work readers must find in it, or create through the process of reading it, their identity themes.

One of the earliest and most influential reader-response critics, Louise Rosenblatt, argues against placing too much emphasis on the reader's imagination, identity, or feelings in literary interpretation. Like Iser, Rosenblatt keeps the focus on the text, though she is more concerned than is Iser with the dynamic relationship between reader and text, since it is in that interrelationship that Rosenblatt believes literary meanings are made.

For Rosenblatt, as for other reader-response critics, the meaning of a literary work cannot exist until it is "performed" by the reader. Until then literary meaning is only potential. It becomes actual when readers realize its potential through their acts of reading, responding, and interpreting.

As you might expect, reader-response critics respect not only the intellectual acts of analysis and comprehension that readers perform but also their subjective responses and their emotional apprehension of literary works. This distinction between intellectual comprehension and emotional apprehension of literature is explored earlier in this book for each of the four literary genres—fiction, poetry, drama, and essay.

One benefit of using reader-response perspectives to interpret literary works is that you begin with what is primary and basic—your initial reactions, your primary responses. Of course, as you read, you may change your mind about your reaction to a work. You may experience opposite or different feelings. Or you may make sense of the work differently because of discoveries you make later in the process of reading. What you read in the last chapter of a novel, for example, may change your understanding of what you read in the first chapter or in a middle chapter, which you had interpreted one way until you reached the end. What's important for reader-response critics is just this kind of active reading dynamic, in which a reader's changing ideas and feelings are fore-grounded. These critics describe the recursiveness of the reading process, the way in which our minds anticipate what is coming in the text based on what we have already read and, simultaneously, the way we loop back retrospectively to reconsider earlier passages in light of later ones that we read. The literary text does not disappear for reader-response critics. Instead it becomes part of read-ers' experience as they make their way through it.

Reader-response criticism thus emphasizes process rather than product, an experience rather than an object, a shifting subjectivity rather than a static and objective text and meaning. For reader-response critics the text is not a "thing"; it does not stand still, for it lives only in its readers' imaginations. For these crit-ics, then, literary works do not have an independent objective meaning that is true once and for all and that is identical for all readers. Instead, they argue that readers *make* meaning through their encounters with literary texts. And the meanings they make may be as varied as the individuals who read them.

Reader-response critics emphasize two additional points about the range and variety of readers' interpretations. First, an individual reader's interpretation of a work may change, in fact, probably will change over time. Reading Shake-speare's *Julius Caesar* in high school can be a very different experience from reading it in college or later as an adult. Second, historically, readers from dif-ferent generations and different centuries interpret books differently. The works say different things to readers of different historical eras based on their particular needs, concerns, and historical circumstances. In both the individ-ual cases and the larger historical occasions, changes occur, changes that affect how individuals perceive, absorb, and understand what they read at different times of their lives.

The crucial thing for readers is to acknowledge their own subjectivity in the act of reading and to be aware that they come to literary works with a set of beliefs, ideas, attitudes, values—with all that makes them who and what they are. Being aware of our predispositions when we read can prevent our biases and prejudices from skewing our interpretations of literary works. At the same time, we need to pay attention to the details of the text. We cannot make words and sentences mean anything at all. There are limits and boundaries to what is acceptable, limits and boundaries that are subject to negotiation and debate. For most reader-response theorists, interpretation has both latitude and limits. Ne-gotiating between them in a delicate balancing act allows readers to exercise their subjectivity while recognizing the significance of the words on the page.

Perhaps an analogy will clarify the double-sided nature of literary interpre-tation from a reader-response perspective, one that recognizes both the reader's freedom and the text's limits. You might think of a text as a musical score, one that is brought to life in performance. Readers make the potential meanings of a text come to life in much the same way that a musician brings a piece of music to life in performance. When musicians play a score or readers read a literary work, they cannot change the notes of the score or the words of the text. Both readers and musicians are limited by what is on the page. Yet there is room for differing interpretations and varied responses. Two interpretations of a literary work, like two musical performances, are likely to differ, sometimes in significant ways. The varying interpretations will be valid insofar as they respect the words or notes on the page, and insofar as they represent a reasonable and logically defensible approach to the work.

Thinking from a Reader-Response Perspective

In reading "The Use of Force," reader-response critics would consider a reader's emotional reactions to the story's action. They might ask how a reader responds to the doctor, how he or she reacts to the doctor's acknowledgment of his feelings about the parents and the child, how readers respond to the way he opens the girl's mouth. Like feminist critics, they would consider the extent to which female readers might respond differently than males, though the important thing for a reader-response perspective would be the intensity and nature of a particular reader's response.

Some reader-response critics would also examine the reader's responses at different points in the text, focusing on particular words and phrases that might signal a shift in the story's tone and hence a change in the reader's response. The doctor's response to the parents calling him a "nice man" is to grind his teeth in disgust. His remark to the girl after she knocks his glasses off is "Will you open it now by yourself or shall we have to open it for you?" And his reference to his contempt for the parents and to the child as a "little brat" are places for readers to consider their responses.

In reading Dickinson's "I'm 'wife'," reader-response critics might point to the way the poem's language associates "wife" with "Woman" and with "Czar" and invite readers to consider the extent to which these terms reflect their experience or understanding of marriage. They might ask whether the idea of marriage reflected in the poem reminds you of your own relatives' marriages, of the marriage of your parents. If so, why, a reader-response critic might ask, and, if not, why not?

Reader-response critics would also ask about readers' responses to the men who are implied but not explicitly named in the poem, and to the analogy made in the second stanza, which uses the contrast between Earth and Heaven to suggest a difference between the speaker's life before and after marriage. These critics might ask readers to explore their feelings about such an analogy and invite them to consider ways in which their own lives involve a difference such as that describing the speaker's before and after states. The emphases of reader-response critics essentially, then, would be two: (1) the reader's direct experience of the language and details of the poem in the process of reading it; (2) the reader's actual experience outside the poem which he or she brings to the reading and which is used to interpret it. Where formalist critics would play down this experiential connection to the poem and encourage readers to focus solely on the words on the page, reader-response critics want to extend the readers' perceptions about the poem and deepen their response to it by deliberately evoking actual experiences of readers that they can bring to bear on both their apprehension and their comprehension of the poem.

A CHECKLIST OF READER-RESPONSE CRITICAL QUESTIONS

1. What is your initial emotional response to the work? How did you feel upon first reading it?
2. Did you find yourself responding to it or reacting differently at any point? If so, why? If not, why not?
3. At what places in the text did you have to make inferences, fill in gaps, make interpretive decisions? On what bases did you make these inferential guesses?
4. How do you respond to the characters, the speaker, or the narrator? How do you feel about them? Why?
5. What places in the text caused you to do the most serious thinking? How did you put the pieces, sections, parts of the work together to make sense of it?
6. If you have read a work more than once, how has your second and subsequent readings differed from earlier ones? How do you account for those differences, or for the fact that there are no differences in either your thoughts or your feelings about the work?

Reader-Response Criticism: Selected Readings

Bleich, David. *Readings and Feelings.* 1975.
Bleich, David. *Subjective Criticism.* 1968.
Clifford, John, ed. *The Experience of Reading.* 1991.
Eco, Umberto. *The Open Work.* 1989.
Fish, Stanley. *Is There a Text in This Class?* 1980.
Freund, Elizabeth. *The Return of the Reader.* 1987.
Holland, Norman. *The Dynamics of Literary Response.* 1968.
Holland, Norman. *Poems in Persons.* 1973.
Iser, Wolfgang. *The Act of Reading.* 1978.
Mailloux, Steven. *Interpretive Conventions.* 1982.
Rabinowitz, Peter. *Before Reading.* 1987.
Rosenblatt, Louise. *Literature as Exploration.* 1939, 1975.
Rosenblatt, Louise. *The Reader, The Text, The Poem: A Transactional Theory of the Literary Work.* 1978.
Steig, Michael. *Stories of Reading.* 1989.
Suleiman, Susan R., and Inge Crosman, eds. *The Reader in the Text.* 1980.
Tompkins, Jane, ed. *Reader-Response Criticism.* 1980.
Wimmers, Inge Crosman. *Poetics of Reading.* 1988.

MYTHOLOGICAL PERSPECTIVES

An Overview of Mythological Criticism

In general terms a "myth" is a story that explains how something came to be. Every culture creates stories to explain what it considers important, valuable, and true. Thus the Greek myth of Persephone, who was kidnapped by Pluto, the god of the underworld, and allowed to return to her mother Demeter every year, explains the changes of the seasons. Or the Biblical story of Eve's temptation by the serpent in the book of Genesis, which concludes with God's curse of the serpent, explains, among other things, why snakes crawl on their bellies.

Myth criticism, however, is not concerned with stories that explain origins so much as those that provide universal story patterns that recur with regularity among many cultures and in many different times and places. The patterns myth critics typically identify and analyze are those that represent common, familiar, even universal human experiences, such as being born and dying, growing up and crossing the threshold into adulthood, going on a journey, engaging in sexual activity. These familiar patterns of human action and experience, however, are of interest to myth critics not primarily in and of themselves, but rather for how they represent religious beliefs, social customs, and cultural attitudes.

Birth, for example, is of interest as a symbolic beginning and death as a symbolic ending. A journey is a symbolic venturing out into the world to explore and experience what it has in store for the traveler. Sleeping and dreaming are not simply states of ordinary experience but symbolic modes of entrance into another realm and an envisioning of unusual and perhaps strange possibilities unimagined in waking life. So too with physical contests, sexual encounters, and other forms of experience, which many times are occasions for individuals to be tested, challenged, and perhaps initiated into an advanced or superior state of being—becoming a warrior, for example, a mother, a prophet, or a king.

Myth critics discover in literature of all times and places stories with basic patterns that can be explained in terms of *archetypes,* or universal symbols, which some mythological critics believe are part of every person's unconscious mind, a kind of a collective unconscious that each of us inherits by virtue of our common humanity. Besides the fundamental facts of human existence, other archetypes include typical literary characters such as the Don Juan or womanizer, the *femme fatale* or dangerous female, the trickster or con artist, the damsel in distress, the rebel, the tyrant, the hero, the betrayer. Creatures real and imaginary can also be archetypal symbols. The lion, for example, can represent strength, the eagle independence, the fox cunning, the unicorn innocence, the dragon destruction, the centaur the union of matter and spirit, animality and humanity, or even humanity and divinity.

It is on plot or the sequence of causally related incidents and actions, however, that myth criticism focuses most heavily. The archetypal images, creatures, and characters exist within stories that themselves exhibit patterns of recurrence. So, for example, there are stories of the arduous quest fraught with perils which a protagonist must survive, perhaps to rescue an innocent victim, perhaps to prove superior courage or morality, perhaps to save others from destruction. There are stories of vengeance, of death and rebirth, of resurrection, of transformation from one state of being into another, stories of enlightenment, of devastation, of lost paradises. Many such stories can be found in the religious literature of cultures around the world. The Bible, for example, contains stories of creation (Adam and Eve), fraternal rivalry and murder (Cain and Abel), destruction (Noah) and forgiveness (the ark and the covenant), wandering and enslavement (the exodus), death and resurrection (Jesus' life and ministry)—and so on. This list can be multiplied by consulting, for example, the Taoist and Confucian religious traditions of China, the Hindu traditions of India, the Buddhist traditions of Japan, and the Islamic tradition of the Middle East.

Myth critics approach the study of literary works and the study of a culture's myths in many ways. The Canadian critic Northrop Frye, for example, explains the traditional literary genres, including the novel, the drama, and epic, with reference to the recurrence in them of mythic patterns such as death and rebirth, departure and return, ignorance and insight. Frye, in fact, associates the genres of comedy, romance, tragedy, and irony or satire with the cycle of the seasons, each genre representing the natural events associated with a particular season (comedy with the fertility of spring, for example, and tragedy with the decline of the year in autumn). The French critic, Claude Lévi-Strauss, who employs the strategies of structuralist and semiotic analysis, treats cultural myths as signs whose meanings are not understood by the cultures that create those myths. His work is grounded in structural anthropology and owes much to the linguistic theory of Ferdinand de Saussure, who had a profound effect on the development of French and American structuralist perspectives on literary analysis and interpretation. And the American critic of popular culture, John Cawelti, to cite still another approach, analyzes the mythic impulse and mythic elements in forms of popular literature such as the western.

Thinking from a Mythological Perspective

What a mythological critic does with archetypal characters, stories, creatures, and even natural elements such as sun and moon, darkness and light, fire and water, is to link them up with one another, to see one literary work in relation to others of a similar type. Thus, for example, Hamlet's revenge of his father's death can be linked with myths from other cultures that include a son's avenging his father. Or the story of Hamlet can be linked with others in which the corruption poisoning a country has been eliminated through some action taken by the hero. Or, to take a different example, the story of the prodigal son (page 27), could be linked with other stories of sons wasting their inheritance, of fathers forgiving their children, or of one brother envying another.

In considering Williams's "The Use of Force" from a mythological perspective, a myth critic might consider the doctor as an intruder who comes to menace a helpless and innocent family. Or he might be seen as a hero who battles against the odds to save the life of a helpless victim. A myth critic might consider the role of Dickinson's "wife" and her rank as "Czar" in the poem "I'm 'wife' " in relation to prominent female characters from myth and legend, whether human or divine. Myth critics would probably take note too of the references to Heaven and Earth in developing an explanation of the transformation undergone by the speaker of the poem.

A CHECKLIST OF MYTHOLOGICAL CRITICAL QUESTIONS

1. What incidents in the work seem common or familiar enough as actions that they might be considered symbolic or archetypal? Are there any journeys, battles, falls, reversals of fortune?
2. What kinds of character types appear in the work? How might they be typed or classified?
3. What creatures, elements of nature, or man-made objects play a role in the work? To what extent might they be considered symbolic?
4. What changes do the characters undergo? How can those changes be characterized or named? To what might they be related or compared?
5. What religious or quasi-religious traditions with which you are familiar might the work's story, characters, elements, or objects be compared to or affiliated with? Why?

Mythological Criticism: Selected Readings

Bodkin, Maud. *Archetypal Patterns in Poetry*. 1934.
Campbell, Joseph. *The Hero with a Thousand Faces*. 1949.
Cawelti, John. *Adventure, Mystery, Romance*. 1976.
Chase, Richard. *Quest for Myth*. 1949.
Fiedler, Leslie. *Love and Death in the American Novel*. 1964.
Frazer, James G. *The Golden Bough*, rev. 1911.
Frye, Northrop. *Anatomy of Criticism*. 1957.
Graves, Robert. *The White Goddess*. 1948.
Jung, Carl Gustav. *Modern Man in Search of a Soul*. 1933.
Lévi-Strauss, Claude. *Structural Anthropology*. 1968.
Vickery, John B., ed. *Myth and Literature*, 1966.

STRUCTURALIST PERSPECTIVES

An Overview of Structuralist Criticism

It is important to distinguish the general meaning of "structure" as used by critics of varying persuasions from its use by adherents of structuralist criticism. In the traditional and most general sense, the word "structure" refers to the organization of a literary work—to its arrangement of incident and action (plot);

its division into sections, chapters, parts, stanzas, and other literary units; its employment of repetition and contrast; its patterns of imagery (light and dark images, for example) and sound (its patterns of rhythm and rhyme).

For structuralist critics, however, the notion of "structure" has another meaning, one which derives from linguistics and anthropology and which refers to the systems of signs that designate meaning. To understand the structuralist perspective one needs to understand what structuralists mean by "signs" and how language is an arbitrary system of such signs. We can illustrate with a familiar example—the word "dog," which represents the four-legged animal many of us have as a pet. Why do the letters D-O-G, when put together, signify the creature who barks at the mail carrier and wags its tail while running off with our sneakers? The answer, of course, is because of a particular set of linguistic conventions that operate due to common usage and agreement. Such use and agreement, such a convention, however, is arbitrary. That is, it could have been otherwise. In fact, in languages such as French and Italian, the word "dog" means nothing. In those languages the furry four-footed barker is respectively *chien* (pronounced sheYEN) and *cane* (pronounced CAHnay), a word that looks like the English "cane," or walking stick, but which is a sign, in Italian, for what we call a dog.

But there is one additional linguistic element of importance—that of difference. We have just seen how the English word "cane" differs from the Italian *cane* and the French *chien* and how the two languages designate the faithful canine companion, perhaps named "Fido," in different ways. In both languages (as in all languages) words are differentiated from one another by sound and by spelling. Thus, in English C-A-N-E refers to a walking stick, but C-O-N-E and C-A-P-E to entirely different things. The same is true in Italian, where *cane,* our equivalent of dog, differs from *cani* (CAHknee), the Italian plural, meaning "dogs." This notion of difference is critical to the way structuralism analyzes systems of signs, for it is through differences that languages, literatures, and other social systems convey meaning.

One technique structuralist critics rely on heavily in analyzing difference is "binary opposition," in which a text's contrasting elements are identified and examined. In employing binary opposition as an analytical instrument, structuralist literary critics imitate what structural anthropologists do when they analyze societies to determine which of their social habits and customs are meaningful. The founder of structuralist anthropology, Claude Lévi-Strauss, an important influence on literary structuralism, has explained how a society's most important values can be deciphered by analyzing such binary oppositions as the distinction between "the raw and the cooked," which became a title for one of his books.

Structuralist critics find all kinds of opposition in literature, from small-scale elements, such as letters and syllables; through symbols, such as light and dark; to motions or directions (up and down), times (before and after), places (inside and outside), distances (far and near); to elements of plot and character, such as changes of feeling and reversals of fortune. Such differences are significant structural elements requiring interpretation, whether the differences are explicit or implicit, described or only hinted at.

Semiotics

Semiotics is the study of signs and sign systems; it is, more importantly, the study of codes, or the systems we use to understand the meaning of events and entities, including institutions and cultural happenings as well as verbal and visual texts—from poems to songs to advertisements, and more. Situated on the border between the humanities and the social and behavioral sciences, semiotics is concerned with how the workings of sign systems in various disciplines such as literature and psychology enable us to understand the richly textured significations of all kinds of cultural texts, from action films and television game shows and situation comedies to professional football games to parades and fourth of July celebrations; from religious rituals such as bar mitzvahs and marriage ceremonies to social occasions such as annual company picnics and New Year's parties.

Although semiotic perspectives derive from the theoretical foundations of structuralist and poststructuralist thought, semiotics does not limit itself to the goals and methods of those critical approaches. And though semiotic analysis is sometimes presented in logical symbols and mathematical terminology, it is not restricted to those forms of language. In fact, one of the strengths of a semiotic perspective is its ability to analyze the ways various discourses convey meaning, whether these discourses employ words or communicate, as does fashion, for example, by means of other signs and symbols.

Thinking from a Structuralist Perspective

We can analyze virtually anything from a structuralist perspective—a baseball or football game, an aerobics class, a restaurant menu or a three-course dinner, fashion shows, movies, MTV videos, newspaper cartoons. The possibilities are endless, and, in fact, one critic, Roland Barthes in his book *Mythologies,* has provided a series of brilliant structuralist analyses of foods, fashions, and sports, including wrestling.

Fairy tales and folktales have been a popular source of interpretations for structuralist critics, for such basic stories contain plots and character elements that lend themselves well to binary analysis, and they often reveal much about the values of the cultures that created them. Think of Cinderella, for example, and how she exists in opposition to her stepsisters (she is beautiful while they are ugly; she is poor while they are rich; she is a servant, they her masters). Remember how she loses one slipper while retaining the other, how her coach turns into a pumpkin and her footmen into mice (or is it the other way around)? Difference functions throughout the story on many levels, including the all-important one of the reversal of her fortune with that of her stepsisters and of a prince replacing her nasty stepmother as her future companion. You may also wish to consider books and movies that make use of the "Cinderella plot," where a metaphorical Prince Charming rescues a poor common girl from an oppressive and unhappy life. The films *An Officer and a Gentleman* and *Pretty Woman* provide two examples.

Structuralist analysis is used at a number of places in *Literature*. Look, for example, in Chapter 3 at the discussion of setting in Kate Chopin's "The Story of an Hour" and William Faulkner's "A Rose for Emily." Chopin's story is seen as having a number of meaningful oppositions, including that between the enclosed inner space of Mrs. Mallard's bedroom and the open free space outside her home, an opposition that reflects the tension between her present marital subjugation and her yearning to be "free," as well as a difference between the natural world of birds and trees and her human world bound by ties of obligation. Faulkner's story, on the other hand, posits an opposition between the story's past and present, a time before the significant changes brought by twentieth-century modern ways, when Miss Emily Grierson could live according to a different code of values represented by an earlier time.

A structuralist perspective of "The Use of Force" would consider the difference between the doctor's initial thoughts as he enters the house and his later feelings as the parents call him a "nice" man—including the fact that he sees himself as different from their view of him. It would attend to the difference between the doctor's inner thoughts and his spoken dialogue, as well as to differences between how the doctor had hoped to attend to his patient and what he actually does to get her to open her mouth. It would also analyze the binary oppositions that exist in the story, including doctor/patient, adult/child, sickness/health, helping/hurting, and so on.

Dickinson's "I'm 'wife' " invites structuralist analysis as well. Not only do the poem's first and last lines begin with the words "I'm 'wife'," which gives the poem something of a circular movement, but the term "Girl's life" is contrasted with the words "wife" and "Woman," and the state of being "wife" is set off against "That other state," which is unnamed but implied. In addition there is a contrast between "comfort" and "pain" and another posited between "Earth" and "Heaven." All these oppositions would be viewed by structuralist critics as key elements of signification.

A CHECKLIST OF STRUCTURALIST CRITICAL QUESTIONS

1. What are the elements of the work—words, stanzas, chapters, parts, for example—and how can these be seen as revealing "difference"?
2. How do the characters, narrators, speakers, or other voices heard in the work reveal difference?
3. How do the elements of the work's plot or overall action suggest a meaningful pattern? What changes, adjustments, transformations, shifts of tone, attitude, behavior, or feeling do you find?
4. How are the work's primary images and events related to one another? What elements of differentiation exist, and what do they signify?
5. What system of relationships governs the work as a whole?
6. What system of relations could be used to link this work with others of its kind? With different kinds of things with which it shares some similarities?

Structuralist Criticism: Selected Readings

Barthes, Roland. *Elements of Semiology*. 1967.
Culler, Jonathan. *Structuralist Poetics*. 1975.
Genette, Gerard. *Figures*. 1966.
Hawkes, Terence. *Structuralism and Semiotics*. 1977.
Lévi-Strauss, Claude. *The Raw and the Cooked*. 1966.
Macksey, Richard, and Eugenio Donato, eds. *The Structuralist Controversy*. 1970.
Scholes, Robert. *Semiotics and Interpretation*. 1982.
Scholes, Robert. *Structuralism in Literature: An Introduction*. 1974.
Smith, Barbara Herrnstein. *On the Margins of Discourse*. 1978.
Todorov, Tzvetan. *The Poetics of Prose*, trans. 1977.

DECONSTRUCTIVE PERSPECTIVES

An Overview of Deconstructive Criticism

Deconstruction arose as a further development of structuralism. Like structuralist critics, deconstructive critics look for opposition in literary works (and in other kinds of "texts" such as films, advertisements, and social institutions, including schools and hospitals). Like structuralism, deconstruction emphasizes difference, or the structure of constituent opposition in a text or any signifying system (for example, male/female, black/white, animate/inanimate). For deconstructionist critics, any meaning is constructed as the result of an opposition, which can be read as ideologically grounded. This is the case with the use of language itself, which creates meaning by opposition (the difference in meaning between the English words "cap" and "cup," for example, is based on a difference between their middle letters). The difference is significant as the words refer to different things.

Deconstruction differs from structuralism, however, in describing at once both a pair of equally valid conflicting oppositions, and in identifying a prevailing ideology that needs to be subverted, undermined, challenged, or otherwise called into question—an ideological view, for example, that suggests that one race or gender is superior to another, or a conviction that the poor are happy with their lot. We can distinguish the more explicitly politicized type of deconstruction, "deconstructionist criticism," from a less politically animated type, "deconstructive criticism," in which the ideological impulse is implicit rather than explicit, latent rather than overtly expressed.

Through a careful analysis of a text's language, deconstructive critics unravel the text by pointing to places where it is ambivalent, contradictory, or otherwise ambiguous. Critics who employ deconstruction as a critical method actually would say that the text deconstructs itself, and that critics do not deconstruct the text so much as show how the text contradicts itself and thereby dismantles itself. They would argue that the contradictions found in any verbal text are inherent in the nature of language, which functions as a system of op-position or differences. And since language itself is radically oppositional and thereby inherently ideological, then all discourse is, first, oppositional and hence subject to deconstruction, and, second, ideological, and indicative of power dif-ferentiation. In addition, deconstructionist critics also posit the existence of ab-sent textual qualities or characteristics by suggesting that these absent elements have been suppressed by the dominant ideology that controls the apparent meaning of the work.

Deconstructionist critics operate on the premise that language is irretrievably self-contradictory and self-destroying. They argue that since language is unsta-ble, it cannot be controlled by writers. As a result, literary works mean more than their authors are aware of, and their meanings are as unstable as the lan-guage of which they are constructed. The aim of deconstructive analysis is to demonstrate the instability of language in texts, thereby revealing how a text's conflicting forces inevitably destroy its apparently logical or meaningful struc-ture and how its apparently clear meaning splits into contradictory, incompat-ible, and ultimately undecidable possibilities.

Deconstructionist criticism favors terms like "unmasking," "unraveling," "recovering," "suppression," and "contradiction." Unlike formalist criticism, which it resembles in its scrupulous attention to textual detail and its insistence on analyzing the text as a self-contained world, deconstructionist criticism at-tempts to dismantle the literary work and show that it does not mean what it appears to mean. Deconstructionist criticism includes a penchant for showing how literary texts "subvert" and "betray" themselves, an elevation of criticism to an equal stature with literary creation (so that a deconstructive critical essay on "The Use of Force," for example, is as valuable an artistic production as the original story), and its radical skepticism about the ability of language to com-municate anything except contradictions.

A crucial notion for deconstructionist criticism is that of difference, or "dif-férence," as the seminal deconstructionist philosopher and critic Jacques Der-rida spells it. By différence, Derrida means to suggest both the usual meaning of difference (dissimilarity) and the additional idea of deferral, both derived from the two meanings of the French verb "différer," which means "to differ" and "to defer" or "postpone." The kind of difference meant by Derrida is, specif-ically, a deferral of meaning that is never completed or finished because a spo-ken utterance or a written text means whatever it means as a function of dif-ferences among its elements. The result is that its meaning cannot be established as single or determinate. Meaning, thus, is indefinitely postponed, endlessly de-ferred.

This kind of playing with language is further exemplified by Derrida's ex-planation of the "self-effacing trace," his notion that a network of differences of meaning is implied even though those differences are not actually present in an utterance or a text. The explicit meaning, which is present, carries with it "traces" of the absent implied meanings, which for ideological reasons are sup-pressed, though other implications are "there" as inescapable alternative possi-bilities because they can be construed or imagined.

Thinking from a Deconstructive Perspective

"The Use of Force" yields a number of oppositions that deconstructionist critics would describe to unmask a prevailing ideology in need of subversion. Primary in importance among them is the conflict between doctor and patient, in which "doctor" is the privileged term and "patient" the submissive and submerged one. The doctor is the agent who acts upon the passive patient. In this story, however, we find that the patient is neither patient nor submissive. She is impatient with her parents and with the doctor. She actively knocks his glasses off and splinters the wooden tongue depressor he puts in her mouth by crushing it with her teeth. In this and other ways, the story reflects a tissue of contradictory attitudes and impulses, including the doctor's ambivalent feelings for the girl, whom he both hates and admires, his conflicted feelings toward her parents, whom he pities yet can barely tolerate, and his ambivalence about his own actions, which he both wants and does not want to perform. Other oppositions include those between male and female, older and younger, privileged and unprivileged, all located in the same doctor/patient relationship.

A deconstructive analysis of Dickinson's "I'm 'wife' " would include consideration of the binary oppositions noted in the discussion of "Thinking from a Structuralist Perspective" mentioned earlier. The deconstructive strategy would be to show how the terms "wife," "Woman," "Czar," and "Girl's life" cancel each other out so that a single determinate meaning of the poem is impossible to establish. Deconstructionist critics would, in addition, attempt to show how the poem's inherent contradictions privilege one pair of terms, "wife" for example, over "Girl['s]," while undermining the apparent authority and privileged status of "wife" and the state to which it refers. They would also consider absent terms suggested but not stated directly, such as "Husband."

A CHECKLIST OF DECONSTRUCTIVE CRITICAL QUESTIONS

1. What oppositions exist in the work? Which of the two opposing terms of each pair is the privileged or more powerful term? How is this shown in the work?
2. What textual elements (descriptive details, images, incidents, passages) suggest a contradiction or alternative to the privileged or more powerful term?
3. What is the prevailing ideology or set of cultural assumptions in the work? Where are these assumptions most evident?
4. What passages of the work most reveal gaps, inconsistencies, or contradictions?
5. How stable is the text? How decidable is its meaning?

Deconstructive Criticism: Selected Readings

Attridge, Derek, ed. *Acts of Literature.* 1992.
Bloom, Harold, ed. *Deconstruction and Criticism.* 1979.

Culler, Jonathan. *On Deconstruction*. 1982.
de Man, Paul. *Allegories of Reading*. 1979.
Derrida, Jacques. *Writing and Difference*. 1978.
Johnson, Barbara. *A World of Difference*. 1987.
Miller, J. Hillis. *Fiction and Repetition*. 1982.
Norris, Christopher. *Deconstruction: Theory and Practice*. 1982.
Scholes, Robert. *Protocols of Reading*. 1989.
Taylor, Mark C., ed. *Deconstruction in Context*. 1986.

CULTURAL STUDIES PERSPECTIVES

An Overview of Cultural Studies

The term "cultural studies" indicates a wide range of critical approaches to the study of literature and society. It is a kind of umbrella term that not only includes approaches to the critical analysis of society such as Marxism, feminism, structuralism, deconstruction, and new historicism, but also refers to a wide range of interdisciplinary studies, including women's studies, African-American studies, Asian, Native American, Latino studies, and other types of area studies.

Like deconstruction, feminism, and new historicism, cultural studies perspectives are multidisciplinary. These and other forms of cultural criticism typically include the perspectives of both humanistic disciplines, such as literature and art, and the social and behavioral sciences, such as anthropology, economics, and psychology. The idea of cultural studies, however, is broader than any of the particular critical perspectives described in this chapter. Cultural studies are not restricted, for example, to structuralist or deconstructionist critical procedures, nor are they solely concerned with feminist issues or Marxist causes.

As a critical perspective in the late twentieth century, cultural studies employs a definition of culture that differs from two other common ways of considering it. Traditionally, and especially from the perspective of anthropology, culture has been considered as the way of life of a people, including its customs, beliefs, and attitudes, all of which cohere in a unified and organic way of life. This traditional anthropological notion has coexisted with another idea, one of culture as representing the best that a civilization has produced—in its institutions, its political and philosophical thought, its art, literature, music, architecture and other lasting achievements.

Both of these ways of viewing culture are contested by the newer forms of cultural studies, which look not at the stable coherences of a society or a civilization's history, but at its dissensions and conflicts. For the newer versions of cultural criticism, the unifying concerns and values of older forms of cultural study are suspect, largely because they avoid issues of political and social inequality. In fact, one way of viewing the current debate over the humanities described in an earlier section of this chapter, "The Canon and the Curriculum," is as a conflict between the older view of cultural studies that emphasizes a kind of normative national cultural consensus, and newer versions, which challenge such norms and values and question the very idea of cultural consensus.

Moreover, the different goals and procedures of these contrasting cultural studies perspectives, along with the differences among the critical perspectives described earlier, powerfully illustrate how nearly everything now associated with literate culture has become contested. These areas of contestation include not only the meaning of "culture," but the meaning of teaching, learning, reading, and writing, along with notions of text, author, meaning, criticism, discipline, and department. Cultural studies perspectives breach the traditional understanding of these terms, in the process redrawing the boundaries that formerly separated them.

The notion of boundaries, in fact, is one of the more helpful metaphors for thinking about the new cultural studies. That some new emergent critical schools overlap or that critical perspectives may combine forces suggests how disciplinary borders are being crossed and their boundaries reconfigured. In addition to crossing geographical and intellectual boundaries (as well as those between high and popular culture), the new cultural studies also envision a plurality of cultures rather than seeing "Culture" with a capital "C" as singular, monolithic, or universal.

Thinking from a Cultural Studies Perspective

In considering literary works and other kinds of canonical and noncanonical texts from the various standpoints of cultural studies, it is important to note that no single approach, method, or procedure prevails. There is, then, no single "cultural studies" perspective on Williams's "The Use of Force" or Dickinson's "I'm 'wife'." Rather there are various ways of thinking about the cultural and social issues embedded in these works. Some of these issues have been raised in the explanations of feminist, Marxist, new historicist, structuralist, and deconstructionist critical perspectives.

One additional cultural studies perspective that has recently gained prominence is that of *gender criticism,* more specifically gay and lesbian studies. Gender criticism and studies overlap, to some extent, with feminist critical perspectives. In addition to studying the relations between and among men, gender criticism also explores such intra-gender issues of women as lesbian sexuality and female power relations.

One of the central problems of gender studies is the way gender is defined. To what extent, for example, does gender overlap with sex? To what extent is gender a cultural category and sex a biological one? To what extent do the language of sexuality used in the past and the current uses of both "sex" and "gender" as categories reflect biological, psychological, and socially constructed elements of sexual difference? Related to these overlapping questions are others, especially considerations of what some gender critics see as heterosocial or heterosexist bias in the very concept of gender and gender relations.

Gender critics share with adherents of other socially oriented perspectives a concern for analyzing power relations and for discerning ways in which homophobic discourse and attitudes prevail in society at large. Through analysis of various forms of historical evidence and through acts of political agency, gender critics have challenged perspectives that view homosexual acts and unions as "sinful" or "diseased." They have questioned the way AIDS has been represented in the mainstream media and have opened up discussion about what constitutes such apparently familiar notions as "family," "love," and "sexual identity."

A CHECKLIST OF GENDER STUDIES CRITICAL QUESTIONS

1. What kinds of sexual identity, behavior, and attitudes are reflected in the work? Is there any overtly or covertly expressed view of homosexuality or lesbianism?
2. To what extent does the work accommodate, describe, or exemplify same-sex relationships? To what extent are same-sex sexual relationships either in the foreground or background of the work?
3. With what kinds of social, economic, and cultural privileges (or lack thereof) are same-sex unions or relationships depicted? With what effects and consequences?

Cultural Studies: Selected Readings

Butler, Judith. *Gender Trouble*. 1989.
Comley, Nancy, and Robert Scholes. *Hemingway's Genders*. 1994.
Giroux, Henry. *Border Crossings*. 1992.
Gunn, Giles. *The Culture of Criticism and the Criticism of Culture*. 1987.
Sedgwick, Eve Kosofsky. *Between Men: English Literature and Male Homosexual Desire*. 1985.
Sedgwick, Eve Kosofsky. *Epistemology of the Closet*. 1990.
Tompkins, Jane. *Sensational Designs: The Cultural Work of American Fiction 1790–1860*. 1985.
Torgovnick, Marianna DeMarco. *Crossing Ocean Parkway*. 1994.

USING CRITICAL PERSPECTIVES AS HEURISTICS

One of your more difficult decisions regarding critical theory will be in choosing a critical perspective that is suitable and effective in analyzing a particular literary work. You might be able to offer, for example, a Marxist, deconstructionist, or feminist reading of "Humpty Dumpty" or "Little Bo Peep," even though these nursery rhymes may not be conventionally approached from any of those critical perspectives. You will need to decide whether one of those approaches offers a richer yield than a more traditional approach, such as formalism or myth criticism. The same is true of your approach to Williams's "The Use of Force" and Dickinson's "I'm 'wife'." Although both works have been analyzed in this chapter from ten critical perspectives, you probably found that certain critical perspectives made a better interpretive fit than others for Williams's story or Dickinson's poem.

Another thing to remember is that you can combine critical perspectives. There is no rule of interpretation that says you must limit yourself to the language and method of a single critical approach or method. You may wish, for example, to combine formalist and structural perspectives in analyzing "I'm 'wife',", while also raising feminist critical questions in your interpretation. Or in interpreting "The Use of Force," you may wish to combine new historicist critical concerns with those of a biographical, psychological, or structuralist approach. In some ways, in fact, various concerns of the critical perspectives explained in this chapter overlap. Feminists raise historical questions as well as psychological and biographical ones. Reader-response critics attend to structuralist and formalist issues. And new historicist critics may employ formalist or deconstructionist methods of close reading.

A danger in using any critical approach to literature is that literary texts are read with an eye toward making them conform to a particular critical theory rather than using that critical theory to illuminate the text. In the process, critics may distort the text of a literary work by quoting from it selectively or by ignoring aspects of it that do not fit their theoretical approach or conform to their interpretive perspective. Some critics, moreover, apply their favorite critical perspective in a mechanical way, so that every work of literature is read with an eye toward proving the same ideological point, regardless of how important the issue is in one work as compared with another. Or critics may put all works of literature through an identical ideological meat grinder with every work emerging ground into the same kind of critical hamburger.

The various critical perspectives you have been learning about should be used as ways to think about literary works rather than as formulas for grinding out a particular kind of interpretation. Try to see the various critical perspectives as interpretive possibilities, as intellectual vistas that open up the literary work rather than as stultifying formulas that limit what can be seen in them. Try, as well, to experience the element of intellectual playfulness, the imaginative energy and resourcefulness used in thinking with and through these critical perspectives.

Perhaps the best way to consider these and other critical perspectives is as *heuristics,* or methods for generating ideas, in this case, ideas about literature. A heuristic often takes the form of a set of questions. Writers and speakers use a sequence of questions to think through a topic in preparation for writing or speaking about it. Greek and Roman rhetoricians developed heuristics for generating ideas and for developing and organizing their thinking by using sets of questions that would enable them to think through a subject from a variety of perspectives. They used questions that invited comparison and contrast, definition and classification, analysis and division of a topic.

You can do the same with the critical perspectives described in this chapter. Instead of the classical questions that encourage comparison or causal analysis, use the questions that accompany each of the critical perspectives. Rather than deciding at first just which critical perspective is best suited to your chosen literary work, jot down answers to the questions for each of the approaches. As you think and write, you will begin to see which critical perspectives yield the most helpful ideas, which, that is, prompt your best thinking. In the course of using the critical questions to stimulate your thinking, you will also decide whether to use one critical perspective or to combine a few. You will also decide what you wish to say about the work. And you will begin to discover why you see it as you do, what you value in it, and how you can substantiate your way of seeing and experiencing it.

In addition, try to consider these critical perspectives as opportunities to engage in a play of mind. Viewing a literary work (or other cultural artifact) from a variety of critical perspectives will enable you to see more of its possibilities of signification. It will also give you a chance to live inside a variety of critical methods, to put on a number of different critical hats. Try to enjoy the experience.

CHAPTER THIRTY-SEVEN

Writing with Sources

WHY DO RESEARCH ABOUT LITERATURE?

One reason to do research about the literary works you read and study is to understand them better. Another is to see how they have been interpreted over the years, perhaps even centuries, since they were written. Moreover, scholars who have devoted their lives to the study of particular authors, periods, and genres can provide insights that can enrich your understanding and deepen your appreciation of literature.

Reading and studying literature in an academic environment also often requires research. You may be required to read books and articles about an author or a work, using your research in an essay on a literary topic. This is a fairly standard requirement in both general introductory literature courses and in more specialized courses for literature majors.

Even if research on the literature you read is not a requirement, you may find that what others who have read the same works have to say provides a stimulus for your own ideas. For example, you can use *The Humanities Index,* the *MLA Bibliography,* or your library's computerized catalog (see page 1930) to find articles about many of the selections in this book. You can also use *The New York Times Index* and *Book Review Digest* to find reviews of collections of short stories, essays, poems, or plays.

Locate several articles or reviews on a work you have read and, as you read them, notice when you have a particularly strong reaction. You may disagree with what you read, you may be surprised by a new point of view, or you may find your own opinions reinforced in a way you had not expected. You may find that one or more of the works consulted provides the spark for a fully developed essay of your own.

Research materials consist of two general kinds: primary sources and secondary sources. *Primary sources* are firsthand accounts, such as historical documents, diaries, journals, letters, and original literary works, including novels, stories, poems, plays, and essays. Primary sources constitute raw evidence you can use for your research paper. *Secondary sources* are materials written about primary sources. Secondary sources include critical writing that expresses opinions, draws conclusions, or explains an issue. Secondary sources include books, articles, pamphlets, and reviews.

CLARIFYING THE ASSIGNMENT

It is critical that you understand thoroughly the requirements of the assignment. Does your instructor expect you to write a three-page paper or a twenty-page paper—or, as is more likely, something in between? Are you expected to type your paper double-spaced? Are you required to use primary sources, secondary sources, or both? How many words, how many pages, and how many sources are required?

Are you expected to focus on a single work using only one or two sources, on a single work using multiple sources, on multiple works by an author—or something else? Are you expected to document your sources and to provide a list of works you cite in the paper? Be sure that you clarify the specific requirements of the assignment.

SELECTING A TOPIC

Instructors sometimes provide topics, either by assigning everyone the same topic (or some variation of it) or by giving individual students assigned topics of their own. If that is your situation, you can skip down to the next section on finding and using sources. Most often, however, you will need to choose your own topic for a paper utilizing literary research.

You can do a number of things to simplify the task of finding a topic. First, ask your instructor for suggestions. Second, look over your class notes and your reading notes for key points of emphasis, repeating concerns, and interesting questions and ideas. Third, talk with other students, both with your classmates and with students who have already written papers for the course you are taking. Fourth, you can consult other sources with information about the author and work (or works) you will be writing about. Any or all of these can provide guidance and suggestions about viable topics for your paper.

A *viable topic* is one you can manage in the allotted number of pages required for the assignment. It should also be a topic you can say something about in detail and with specificity. Once you have settled on a topic, it's a good idea to clear it with your instructor. Once your instructor sees what you're interested in, he or she can help you shape the topic, perhaps by narrowing or broadening it in ways that might make it more manageable or potentially more interesting, or both.

You can also get ideas for topics by consulting the ideas for writing suggestions in Chapters 4, 12, 20, and 31. In those chapters on fiction, poetry, drama, and essay, you will find additional guidelines for writing about literary works. As a general guideline for all literary papers, however, try to turn your topic into a question that your research paper answers. This question need not be explicit in your topic, but it should emerge in the opening paragraphs of your paper, either explicitly or implicitly, as you present your thesis. When you read the student papers in this chapter, notice how the focused topics lead naturally into a manageable thesis, allowing for specific observations to be developed into a cogent argument.

FINDING AND USING SOURCES

Researchers have a number of tools available for finding secondary sources—critical studies of authors, analyses of their works, and relevant biographical, social, and historical background material. Your school library's computer databases of books and articles provide comprehensive listings of such sources. But even before tapping into those databases you can consult books in the library reference room as a preliminary step. General reference works about literature can give you an overview of an author's life and work, an introduction to a genre, such as tragedy or epic, or an understanding of a critical approach, such as new historicism, or provide some other kind of generalized prelude to the more focused search you will undertake once you have refined your topic and decided how to proceed with your research.

Works you may find helpful as preliminary guides to literary research include the following:

Baker, Nancy L. *A Research Guide for Undergraduate Students: English and American Literature.* 2nd ed. MLA, 1985.

Beacham, Walton, ed. *Research Guide to Biography and Criticism: Literature.* 2 vols. Beacham, 1985.

Elliot, Emory, et al. *Columbia Literary History of the United States.* Columbia University Press, 1988.

Klein, Leonard S., ed. *Encyclopedia of World Literature in the Twentieth Century.* 5 vols. Rev. ed. Continuum, 1983–1984.

MLA International Bibliography of Books and Articles on Modern Language and Literature. MLA, 1921–.

The New Cambridge Bibliography of English Literature. 5 vols. Cambridge University Press, 1967–1977.

The Oxford History of English Literature. 13 vols. Oxford University Press, 1945–.

Preminger, Alex, and T. V. F. Brogan, eds. *The New Princeton Encyclopedia of Poetry and Poetics.* Princeton University Press, 1983.

Seymour-Smith, Martin. *The New Guide to Modern World Literature.* 4 vols. P. Bedrick Books, 1970.

Stade, George, and William T. Jackson, eds. *European Writers.* 7 vols. Macmillan, 1983–1985.

Ward, A. C., ed. *Longman Companion to Twentieth-Century Literature.* 3rd ed. Longman, 1981.

Wilson, Katharina, ed. *An Encyclopedia of Continental Women Writers.* 2 vols. Garland, 1991.

You can find some or all of these sources in the reference sections of many college libraries.

USING COMPUTERIZED DATABASES

You may have access to your university library with a link from your room, your home, your residence hall, or your school's computer center. You may also be able to access the library's holdings through computer terminals located in the library proper. One of the first things you should do is learn how to use the library's computerized catalog to access bibliographic information. You can get a friend to help you. You can get assistance from the library staff. Your school may even provide formal instructions in use of their on-line services.

All on-line catalogs are organized in a similar way. The information that is retrieved and displayed on the computer screen depends on the format you use in making your request. Most programs offer at least three search options: author, title, and subject. For example, suppose you know that you want to write about Ernest Hemingway. You don't have a precise topic in mind, and want to consult some books *about* Ernest Hemingway. To find out what books the library has about Hemingway, you would search for "Hemingway, Ernest," as subject. (The program will give you on-screen instructions on how to start the search.) Following is what one university library's on-line catalog lists for Hemingway as subject:

1. Hemingway, Ernest 1898			1 entry
2. Hemingway, Ernest 1899–1961			52 entries
3. Hemingway, Ernest 1899–1961	Appreciation		1 entry
4. Hemingway, Ernest 1899–1961	Appreciation—Germany		1 entry
5. Hemingway, Ernest 1899–1961	Bibliography		10 entries
6. Hemingway, Ernest 1899–1961	Biography		12 entries
7. Hemingway, Ernest 1899–1961	Juvenile letters		1 entry
8. Hemingway, Ernest 1899–1961	Biography—Marriage		4 entries

Notice that category 2 includes fifty-two items. Since the category has no heading, to determine the kinds of books included within it, you would press 2 and scan the listings. If you press 8, Biography—Marriage, four listings appear:

1. Along with Youth   Griffin, Peter
2. Hadley   Diliberto, Gioia
3. The Hemingway Women   Kert, Bernice
4. How It Was   Hemingway, Mary Welsh

If you want more data on one of these books, press the appropriate number. You will be provided with information about the length and size of the book, its publication date, and location. Most systems also provide information about the book's availability.

In browsing in one of these books about Hemingway's marriages, you might get an idea for a research paper that focuses on the marriage depicted in "The Short Happy Life of Francis Macomber" (page 357). Reading that story in the context of secondary biographical sources such as those listed above would be one way to gain added insight into the story. Another would be to consult critical secondary sources that are less biographical than analytical and interpretive. Here you would return to that large category of 52 items and begin scanning for titles that appeared promising. One such recent title is Paul Smith's, *A Reader's Guide to the Short Stories of Ernest Hemingway* (Boston: G. K. Hall, 1989). After locating a few such sources, you are ready to read and take notes as you work toward refining your topic and developing a thesis for your paper. To do that you should use the techniques of note taking described earlier—especially annotation (page 119) and the double-entry notebook to develop a critical perspective.

DEVELOPING A CRITICAL PERSPECTIVE

How can you use outside critical sources to develop a critical perspective? Let us say, for example, that you are required to write a five- or six-page paper analyzing and interpreting a particular literary work. Let us speculate further that you are required to read and cite in your paper two or three outside sources. And let us also imagine that you have been asked to select critical sources that provide different interpretive perspectives on the work you will be writing about. What will you do? How will you go about writing this paper?

Here is where annotation and the double-entry notebook are particularly helpful. Let's assume that you have found the relevant articles or sections of books you need. If you can photocopy the appropriate pages, do that. Then annotate those pages the same way you annotated the literary work itself. (Before you actually read any criticism, however, do some preliminary writing—annotating, listing, journal keeping.) In your journal or notebook summarize in a few sentences the thesis or main idea of each source. Opposite your summaries, jot down a set of responses. When you record your summaries of the articles and your responses leave plenty of room, as you will want to add other things that you notice on rereading them.

Still another technique useful for writing critical papers is quoting key passages and commenting on their significance or validity. In writing a paper about Hemingway's "The Short Happy Life of Francis Macomber," for example, you could (and perhaps should) quote a bit of the story directly. You might select a descriptive passage about the lion or a snatch of dialogue between Francis and Margot Macomber. Or you might select a few such passages for direct quotation. Of more importance than your apt selection of such passages, however, is the way you relate them in your comments explaining their significance. The place to get a start on this crucial process is in your reading journal or double-entry notebook, where you can record the relevant passages verbatim and practice commenting on their significance. These comments will provide the germ from which your paper will grow.

In using outside critical sources you will find yourself usually doing one of two things. Either you will agree with the critic and use his or her comments to bolster your interpretation. Or you will disagree and take exception to the critic's ideas by arguing against them in your paper. Both are acceptable ways to proceed. In fact, given a requirement to include more than two sources, it is highly unlikely that you will agree entirely with the positions taken in all of them. Thus even if you agree in part, you will need to make distinctions and to express qualified approval as you modify their viewpoints and express the reservations necessary to make them congruent with your own ideas.

DEVELOPING A THESIS

You should be able to state your thesis in a single direct sentence. Your thesis concentrates in a sentence nutshell what you wish to emphasize—your central idea, the point you wish to make about your topic. Your essay overall elaborates your thesis, providing evidence in the form of textual support.

In general, when you develop your thesis, try to make it as specific as you can. At the same time, try to avoid oversimplifying your idea by setting up mutually exclusive "black and white" categories. Introduce qualifying terms as necessary. Words such as "although," "however," "but," and "rather" suggest an approach that reflects thoughtful consideration of the issues.

Consider the theses of two of the three student papers in this chapter. In one paper, Lucienne Retelle analyzes Alice Walker's story "Everyday Use" in the context of a critical article she read about the work. Here is her thesis:

> In relating the story ["Everyday Use"] to the Biblical Prodigal
> Son, Patricia Kane shows thoughtfulness and insight; however,
> in her eagerness to expose what she sees as differences in male/female
> values, she demonstrates a superficial understanding of the
> Gospel parable and misses the central message: one of repentance
> and forgiveness.

Notice how Ms. Retelle takes issue with the critical perspective offered by Patricia Kane. She uses the critic's view as a springboard from which to launch her own analysis of the story as one whose central concerns are the prodigal son's repentance and his father's forgiveness. Her thesis is clear, direct, and specific. We know what she thinks. It remains for her to flesh out her interpretation and to refute Patricia Kane's argument.

In a second paper, Michelle Carerra discusses James Joyce's short novel, "The Dead." Her topic is the "awakening" or enlightenment of its main character, Gabriel Conroy. Here is her thesis:

> Like the stories in <u>Dubliners</u> that lead up to it, "The Dead" dramatizes a moment of self-realization. The story portrays the gradual awakening of Gabriel Conroy, whose vision of his wife, Gretta, at the end of the story, is at once a frustrating disappointment and a touching movement toward understanding and love.

Notice how Ms. Carerra's thesis is elaborated over two sentences. The first generalized sentence links "The Dead" with the stories that precede it in Joyce's linked collection of short stories, *Dubliners*. Her second sentence elaborates the thesis in more detail, specifying what she believes happens to Joyce's protagonist. Such detail is necessary in a thesis. Without detail, readers can have only a vague sense of the writer's idea.

DRAFTING AND REVISING

In writing your research paper, follow the guidelines for drafting and revising your paper just as you would for an interpretive paper in which you do not use secondary sources. Set aside sufficient time to work out the basic argument of your research paper. This will involve the extra time necessary for tracking down sources, taking notes, and reflecting on their significance for your overall argument.

In your preliminary draft you should try to articulate your argument without your sources. Get your ideas down as clearly as you can. Provide the textual support you need as evidence from the work(s) you are analyzing or otherwise discussing. Then write a second draft in which you incorporate the relevant sources either to support your idea or as representing antithetical views that you attempt to refute.

Leave time for a third draft in which you further refine your thinking, taking into consideration additional evidence you find in the text or in the secondary sources. Use this third draft also to provide precise documentation for your sources—accurate parenthetical citations and precise page references.

In general, approach the drafting of a research essay or paper as you would any other essay or assignment. Make sure you get your own ideas into the initial draft before you begin relying on your secondary sources. This is critical if you want to avoid letting your sources take over the voice and content of your research essay.

CONVENTIONS

In writing about literary works you need to observe a number of conventions, including those regarding quotations, verb tenses, manuscript form, and the strict avoidance of plagiarism.

Using Quotations

In writing about literature you will need to quote lines from poems, dialogue from plays and stories, and descriptive and explanatory passages from prose fiction and nonfiction. For quoted prose passages that exceed four typed lines in your paper, begin a new line and indent ten spaces from the left margin for each line of the quotation. This format, called block quotation, does not require quotation marks because the blocked passage is set off visually from the rest of your text.

Michelle Carerra uses two block quotations in her research paper on Joyce's "The Dead" (page 1947), both from the text of the short novel. In her research essay on E. B. White (page 1952), Radhika A. Jones uses three block quotations, two from White's works—an essay and a novel—and one from a secondary source.

When quoting poetry, separate the lines of poetry with slashes. Include a space before and after each slash.

> Lorraine Hansberry derived the title of her best-known play,
> *A Raisin in the Sun,* from a poem by Langston Hughes. In "Dream
> Deferred," the speaker asks, "What happens to a dream de-
> ferred? / Does it dry up / like a raisin in the sun?"

Chapter 14 contains example of student writers quoting from the poems they write about. For additional examples of students introducing quotations from literature into their analytical essays, see Chapters 5 (on fiction), 21 (on Drama), and 32 (on the essay).

Verb Tense Conventions in Literary Papers

In writing about literature, you will often need to describe a story, novel, poem, play, or essay. In doing so you will use present tense, past tense, or both. In most instances, it is conventional to use present tense when describing what happens in a literary work. Consider the following examples:

> In Robert Hayden's "Those Winter Sundays," the speaker <u>reflects</u>
> on his father and <u>realizes</u> how much his father <u>loved</u> the family.

The present tense is used to describe the speaker's actions of reflecting and realizing. The past tense is used to describe the father's action, which occurred in the past, well before the speaker's present acts of reflecting and realizing.

> Ibsen's <u>A Doll House</u> <u>portrays</u> a conventional middle-class envi-
> ronment and a conventional middle-class family. In displaying a
> strong concern for money and for authority, Ibsen's characters <u>re-
> veal</u> their middle-class values. Ibsen often <u>portrayed</u> characters
> with everyday problems of the middle class.

The verbs describing what the play does are in the present tense. Those describing what the dramatist did are in past tense.

Manuscript Form

In preparing your paper for submission, observe the following guidelines:

1. Type your essay double-spaced on 8 1/2-inch by 11-inch paper.
2. Leave 1-inch margins at the top and bottom, and on both sides.
3. Beginning in the upper left corner 1 inch below the top and 1 inch from the
   left side, type the following on separate lines:
     (a) your name
     (b) your instructor's name
     (c) course title, number, and section
     (d) date
4. Double-space below the date and center your title. It is not necessary to put
   quotation marks around your title or to underline or italicize it. It is necessary
   to underline titles of books and plays used in your title. And it is necessary to
   put quotation marks around the titles of short stories, poems, and essays.
5. Be sure your printer's ink supply or your typewriter ribbon is adequate for
   clear, readable copy.
6. If your printer feeds connected sheets of paper, be sure to separate them before submitting your essay.
7. Number each page consecutively beginning with the second page, 1/2 inch
   from the upper-right corner.
8. Clip or staple the paper, making sure the pages are right side up and in the
   correct numerical order.

Plagiarism

Plagiarism is the act of using someone else's words, ideas, or organizational patterns without crediting the source. Plagiarism may be the result of careless note
taking, or may be deliberate. To avoid plagiarism, it is necessary to clearly indicate what you have borrowed so your reader can distinguish your own language and ideas from those of your sources.

Research essays and papers written with little original thought and containing many long passages of quoted and summarized material strung together may
include plagiarized words and ideas. Be sure to credit each source you use at
the point of borrowing, even in the midst of a paragraph or the middle of a

sentence. Be sure not only to acknowledge using the source but also, if you have used exact language from the source, to put quotation marks around the borrowed words and phrases—even if you have separated some of the borrowed material and interspersed your own language.

Plagiarism is a serious offense. A form of academic theft, plagiarism is not tolerated in colleges and universities. Some have stringent policies, including failure for the course in which the plagiarism occurs and even expulsion from school.

To avoid plagiarism observe the following guidelines in writing your research essays and papers.

- Develop your own ideas about the works you read. Keep notes of your ideas separate from the notes you take from sources.
- Jot the title, author, and page number of a source on the page or notecard you use for your notes pertaining to material from that source.
- Put quotation marks around quoted material you copy from sources into your notes.
- When you summarize and paraphrase a source, be sure to use your own words. Avoid having the source open before you when you summarize and paraphrase.
- If you introduce any quotations from a source into your summaries and paraphrases of them, put quotation marks around the quoted words and phrases.
- Make sure that your own ideas and your own voice are the controlling centers in your research essays and papers. Use your sources to support, illustrate, and amplify your own thinking presented in your own words.
- Observe the conventions for documentation provided in the following section, in your college handbook, and in the *MLA Handbook for Writers of Research Papers,* 4th ed. (1995).

DOCUMENTING SOURCES

If you incorporate the work of others into your paper, it will be necessary to credit your sources through documentation. You should always provide source credit when quoting directly, paraphrasing (rewriting a passage in your own words), borrowing ideas, or picking up facts that aren't general knowledge.

By crediting your sources, you are participating honestly and correctly in shared intellectual activity. You are showing your reader that your knowledge of a text includes some insights into what others have thought and said about it. And you are assisting your reader, who may want to consult the sources that you found valuable.

Established conventions for documenting sources vary from one academic discipline to another. For research essays and papers in literature and language the preferred style is that of the Modern Language Association (MLA). MLA documentation style has established conventions for citing sources within the text of research essays, papers, and articles. It also has established conventions for the list of works you use in preparing your research writing—usually called "List of Works Cited" or "Works Cited."

In the current MLA style, parenthetical citations within the text indicate that a source has been used. These citations refer the reader to a reference list, which should start on a new page at the end of the paper. In the "alternate" or "old" MLA style, references are marked by raised numbers in the text that correspond to numbered notes either at the foot of the page (footnotes) or the end of the paper (endnotes). Both the reference list and the endnotes and footnotes contain bibliographic information about the sources; however, the arrangement, punctuation, and capitalization of the sources differs between the two reference styles.

New MLA Style: Parenthetical Citations Paired with a Reference List

When you refer to a specific section of a work in the body of your paper, provide your reader with the author and page numbers of your source. Place the page numbers in parentheses, and add the author's name if it isn't contained in your sentence.

> According to Lawrence Lipking (30–39), a poet's life involves much more than his or her literal biography.

> A recent critic argues that a poet's life involves much more than his or her literal biography (Lipking 30–39).

If your paper includes two or more works by the same author, add the title of the work before the page number(s). The following are examples of other kinds of citations commonly found in literature papers.

A work in an anthology:

> Bacon's "Of Revenge" affords us a glimpse at his view of human nature: "There is no man doth a wrong for the wrong's sake, but thereby to purchase himself profit, or pleasure, or honor, or the like" (DiYanni, Literature 2nd ed. 1565–1566).

(The editor's name and the page number of the quotation appear in parentheses.)

A classic verse play or poem:

> "She loved me for the dangers I had passed," recounts Othello, "And I loved her that she did pity them" (I.iii.166–167).

(Act, scene, and line numbers are used instead of page numbers. Arabic numbers may also be used for the act and scene.)

> Tennyson's Ulysses compares a dull existence to a dull sword when he says: "How dull it is to pause, to make an end, / To rust unburnished, not to shine in use!" (22–23).

(Line numbers are used instead of page numbers. Note the use of a slash [/] to indicate the end of a line.)

Styling a Reference List

The items in a reference list should be alphabetically arranged. The following are typical kinds of entries for a literature paper.

A book by a single author:

> Lipking, Lawrence. *The Life of the Poet: Beginning and Ending Poetic Careers*. Chicago: U of Chicago P, 1981.

(The second line is indented five spaces.)

An article in a book:

> Williams, Sherley Anne. "The Black Musician: The Black Hero as Light Bearer." *James Baldwin: A Collection of Critical Essays*. Ed. Kenneth Kinnamon. Englewood Cliffs, NJ: Prentice-Hall, 1974. 147–154.

(The page numbers "147–154" refer to the entire article. References to specific pages would appear in parenthetical citations.)

A journal article:

> Walker, Janet. "Hardy's Somber Lyrics." *Poetry* 17 (1976): 25–39.

(The article appeared in issue 17 of the journal *Poetry*. The page numbers refer to the entire article.)

A work in an anthology:

> Bacon, Francis. "Of Revenge." *Literature: Reading Fiction, Poetry, Drama, and the Essay*. 2nd ed. Ed. Robert DiYanni. New York: McGraw-Hill, 1990. 1565–1655.

(The page numbers refer to the entire essay.)

Cite the anthology itself if you are using more than one selection from it. The selections can simply be cited without repeating the anthology title and publication data.

> DiYanni, Robert, ed. *Literature: Reading Fiction, Poetry, Drama, and the Essay*. 2nd ed. New York: McGraw-Hill, 1990.
> Tennyson, Alfred, Lord. "Ulysses." DiYanni. 649–650.

A multivolume work; a second edition:

> Daiches, David. *A Critical History of English Literature*. 2nd ed. 2 vols. New York: Ronald, 1970.

A translation:

> Auerbach, Erich. *Mimesis: The Representation of Reality in Western Literature*. Trans. Willard Trask. Princeton: Princeton UP, 1953.

Alternate MLA Style: Note Numbers Paired with Endnotes/Footnotes

Using Note Numbers

Raised note numbers, in consecutive order, follow the quotation or information being cited. They belong *after* all punctuation, except a dash.

> "She loved me for the dangers I had passed," recounts Othello, "And I loved her that she did pity them."¹

If you include several quotations from the same text in your paper, you may switch to parenthetical citations after the first note. This will reduce the number of footnotes or endnotes.

> Emilia tells Desdemona that jealousy is "a monster begot upon itself, born on itself" (III.iv.155–156).

Using Endnotes/Footnotes

Each raised note number corresponds to a footnote or endnote. The only difference between footnotes and endnotes is their placement in the paper. Footnotes appear at the bottom of the page on which the reference occurs: quadruple-space between the last line of text and the first note. Endnotes are grouped together on a separate page immediately following the last page of text.

The following are the same sources given on pages 1938–1939, now in endnote form. Note that specific page references are given for each entry; these page references would be contained in parentheses in new MLA style.

¹Lawrence Lipking, *The Life of the Poet: Beginning and Ending Poetic Careers* (Chicago: U of Chicago P, 1981) 30–39.

²Sherley Anne Williams, "The Black Musician: The Black Hero as Light Bearer," in *James Baldwin: A Collection of Critical Essays,* ed. Kenneth Kinnamon (Englewood Cliffs, N.J.: Prentice-Hall, 1974) 147.

³Janet Walker, "Hardy's Somber Lyrics," *Poetry* 17 (1976): 35.

⁴Francis Bacon, "Of Revenge," *Literature: Reading Fiction, Poetry, Drama, and the Essay,* 2nd ed., ed. Robert DiYanni (New York: McGraw-Hill, 1990) 1565–1566.

⁵David Daiches, *A Critical History of English Literature,* 2nd ed., 2 vols. (New York: Ronald, 1970) 2:530.

[6]Erich Auerbach, *Mimesis: The Representation of Reality in Western Literature,* trans. Willard Trask (Princeton: Princeton UP, 1953) 77.

Noting Subsequent References

It is usually enough simply to list the author's name and the appropriate page(s) in subsequent references to a source.

[7]Lipking 98.

THREE STUDENT ESSAYS INCORPORATING RESEARCH

A Student Essay Using One Source As a Stimulus

The following essay, "The Prodigal Daughter in Alice Walker's 'Everyday Use,'" was discovered by Lucienne Retelle, a student who wanted to read what others had to say about Walker's story. When Lucienne found this article, she remembered reading "The Prodigal Son" in Chapter 2 of this text and became intrigued with the idea of relationships between "Everyday Use" and the biblical parable. You may want to reread Walker's story (page 408) as well as "The Prodigal Son" (page 27). Then read Patricia Kane's article and finally Lucienne Retelle's evaluation of that article. How convincing do you find Kane's argument? Retelle's responding argument? How do you think Kane might answer Retelle?

PATRICIA KANE

The Prodigal Daughter in Alice Walker's "Everyday Use"

"Everyday Use," Alice Walker's variation on the archetypal prodigal child story not only amuses with its deft humor, it also pleases by ending with the equivalent of the fatted calf remaining with the stay-at-home. Walker's tale, one of those collected in *In Love and Trouble,* displays a world in which a mother comes to see both the humbug in the returning daughter's new appreciation of the mother's realm and the everyday worth of her younger daughter. The reversals and variations from the Biblical prodigal son story suggest that when women make the choices, the tale expresses different values.

The story, narrated by the mother, begins as she awaits a visit from her older daughter, Dee. Immediately her tone establishes the values of her realm as she declares that the swept yard in which she sits is "more comfortable than most people know" (47). As she sits comfortably in her yard, she muses on her daughters. Dee, older, better looking, and brighter than Maggie, scorned the everyday world of rural blacks and went away to school. Maggie, scarred in a fire Dee may have set to destroy a house she hated, will marry a local man and remain in the familiar life. When the mother describes her life and work, including killing hogs and calves, she pictures a realm in which any special meals to mark reconciliation will be more personal than those provided through the orders of the Biblical father.

Prodigal children value what they once rejected, and the returned Dee now finds her scorned past to be fashionable. Her mother, though bemused by her exclaiming over chitlins and other familiar food, agrees to let her take the butter churn to use for a centerpiece. She humors her wish to be known as Wangero although she reminds Dee that she was named for her aunt and grandmother, not any oppressor. The elements of the familiar story seem to be in place. Although chitlins have replaced the calf at the meal, the butter churn evokes calves, and Dee/Wangero seems to now appreciate her mother's world. The matter of the name, however, which shows the mother confident of who she is while Wangero/Dee takes her sense of style from others, provides a variation in the theme and foreshadows the central scene.

Wangero/Dee claims two quilts handmade by her grandmother and earmarked for Maggie on her marriage. Wangero/Dee, who refused a quilt when she went away to college because they were out of style, proclaims these to be priceless. She will value them, she says, by hanging them whereas Maggie would "be backward enough to put them to everyday use" (57). Maggie, although this was "her portion," responds by agreeing to let her sister have the quilts because such "was the way she knew God to work" (58).

God, however, in the person of the mother, suddenly feels something like she does when the spirit of God touches her in church. She hugs Maggie for the first time and returns her portion to her. Realizing not only the worth of her daughter of everyday use, but also that even if her use of the quilts will wear them out, their value lies in use not display, she bestows the riches of her domestic kingdom not on the prodigal but on the familiar daughter. Maggie is the now-embraced lost child of this tale.

After the prodigal child leaves, the mother and Maggie sit in the yard "just enjoying" (59) in the realm of everyday use.

Work cited:
  Walker, Alice. "Everyday Use." In *In Love & Trouble,* New York: HBJ, 1973, 47–59.

Has the Prodigal Daughter Really Returned?

Reference Sources:

Kane, Patricia. "The Prodigal Daughter in Alice Walker's "Everyday Use." *Notes on Contemporary Literature*. March, 1985, 15(2): 7.

New American Bible

Lucienne Retelle
Introduction to Fiction
Prof. Judith Stanford

Patricia Kane, in her response to Alice Walker's "Everyday Use," states that this story is a variation on the theme of the Biblical story, "The Prodigal Son." She proposes that the mother in Alice Walker's story is the feminine equivalent to the father of the Prodigal Son, and as such, they both represent God. Kane suggests, however, that the male and female express different values, and that when God is represented as female, he/she makes different choices. Kane concludes that Walker exemplifies this through Mama who ultimately "bestows the riches of her domestic kingdom not on the prodigal but on the familiar daughter," and Maggie becomes the embraced lost child.

In relating the story to the Biblical Prodigal Son, Patricia Kane shows thoughtfulness and insight; however, in her eagerness to expose what she sees as differences in male/female values, she demonstrates a superficial understanding of the Gospel parable and misses the central message: one of repentance and forgiveness.

At first glance Kane's thesis is appealing and perhaps convincing; but when you compare the two stories carefully, the actions and responses of both parents have basic similarities. In both stories, the mother and father freely give their children their "portion" as they need and/or request it. The Biblical father gives his younger son his portion of property which enables him to go off to a distant place to live as he wishes. Mama, in "Everyday Use" works hard to raise money from her church which enables her daughter, Dee, to go away to school; and she offers her a quilt as well. The father is rich and the mother is poor, but the portions they give are relatively equal based upon their means.

The Prodigal Son rejects his inheritance, just as Dee rejects part of her portion, the quilt, because at the time it held no value for her. Both the Prodigal Son and Dee, the prodigal daughter, repudiate the values of their parents, and they leave home to pursue their own way of life.

The mother's and father's responses to their children when they come back are different in character: the father is fully open and receiving, while the mother is somewhat reticent. This is *not,* as Kane suggests, because they have different values, but because the children come back for different reasons and under different circumstances. The prodigal son has not been successful in his worldly life, and comes back weary and destitute, longing for the comforts of his father's

home. In contrast, Dee comes back flaunting her success and
new worldly values. She is elaborately dressed while the son
is probably in rags. He comes back humbly, hoping to be
received; she comes back confidently, intending to take.

While their actual responses may be different in character,
Mama and Biblical father both demonstrate similar parental
desires and feelings for their "lost" children. The father
waits for his son, sees him a long way off and is deeply moved
at his return. They greet warmly and the father has no words
of reproach. He immediately orders the cooking of a fatted
calf by way of celebration. Similarly, Mama also "waits." She
has a recurring dream in which she and Dee publicly reunite
with arms around each other, Dee with tears in her eyes,
grateful to her mother saying she couldn't have done anything
without her mother's help. But their reunion doesn't happen as
it does in Mama's dream. Dee arrives with haughty airs, gives
her mother a perfunctory greeting, and immediately busies
herself with her camera. Nevertheless, Mama has prepared to
celebrate. She has made her yard clean and wavy and prepares
the "fatted calf" represented by pork, collards, chitlins, and
corn bread.

Kane observes that because the biblical father "orders"
others to do the cooking while Mama prepares her own, the
mother's feast is more personal, suggesting that a woman's
mark of reconciliation is "better" or has a higher value than
the male's. This judgment is irrelevant to the message: both
parents demonstrate acceptance and desire for reconciliation
through their welcome and through offering the celebration
meal. Their different styles of doing so, whether due to
male/femaleness, lifestyles, or personal habits, do not alter
the quality of the reconciliation. Their messages are the
same; the setting and cultures are different.

A secondary theme of the Prodigal Son parable is the
attitude of the older brother who stayed at home with his
father. Kane does not address this theme, nor does she make a
comparison between this brother and Maggie, which is critical
if we are to understand more fully Mama's behavior.

In the Biblical story, the older brother is angry and
resentful at his father's lavish display of welcome for his
returning brother. The father pleads with him to join in the
celebration and reassures his son by saying the older son is
always with him and everything the father has is also the
son's.

In contrast, Maggie is shy and cowers in the presence of
her returning sister. No anger or resentfulness is implied on
her part. In her own way she is present and participates in

the celebration. Moreover, she does *not* show resentfulness, and when Dee demands the quilts, Maggie tells her she can have them. The quality of Maggie's generosity is great, considering her comparative lack of life's gifts. She is neither as intelligent, nor as attractive, nor as well educated as Dee.

Just as the biblical father reassured his older son, Mama has a protective attitude toward Maggie; she takes back the quilts from Dee, and hugs Maggie to her. Mama has already given Dee the butter churner, which in its own way is just as important and symbolic a portion. It too has intrinsic, sentimental and "everyday use" value.

Both parents demonstrate love for their "lost" children, both waited for their return, and both celebrated. The fact that Mama gives Maggie the quilts does not take away from Dee: Dee long ago rejected this portion, so it became Maggie's.

Finally, to approach the two stories as an in toto variation on the theme of the biblical story, based on differences in male/female values as Kane has done, is inappropriate, for two reasons: first, as previously described, the stay-at-home children are very different from one another, and Mama's attitude is clearly related to the kind of person Maggie is. Second, and more significant, Dee has not truly "returned" as the prodigal son has, and therefore a direct comparison cannot be made. Dee does not come back seeking forgiveness and does not indicate she has anything to repent. She is still "out there" in the world, breaking away, and the story ends with her leaving again.

I suggest, however, that if Alice Walker had written her story differently—according to Mama's dream—Mama's attitude and response assuredly would have been akin to the biblical father's. She would have been tearfully and overwhelmingly joyful at Dee's return. In addition, she would have had no need to protect Maggie from her sister's demand for her "portion"—because, most likely, Dee wouldn't have demanded it in the first place.

A RESEARCH PAPER ON A SINGLE WORK USING MULTIPLE SOURCES

The following paper was prepared for a writing and literature course in which students were given a choice of works to research and write about. They were asked to focus on an issue in the work or an aspect of it and to develop a research essay that explained their idea, using at least three secondary sources in addition to the text of the work itself.

The writer focuses on one character, the protagonist of James Joyce's short novel, "The Dead" the culminating work in a collection of short stories entitled *Dubliners*. She directs her attention to the central concern of the work, which she identifies as the "awakening" of Gabriel Conroy. Her paper explains what this awakening is, what it means for the protagonist, and why it is important.

In the course of her research essay, the writer summarizes her sources, quotes directly from them, and quotes from the story, sometimes briefly and occasionally more extensively in block form. She summarizes scenes from the work and explains their significance for her topic. Essentially an analysis of character, the paper contrasts the character of the protagonist with two other characters to better illuminate his. In the conclusion the writer broadens the scope of her analysis to implicate the reader by suggesting ways that the protagonist's experience may correspond to our own.

Michelle Carerra
Prof. Krickstein
October 15, 1994
English 120

The Awakening of Gabriel Conroy

Like the stories in <u>Dubliners</u> that lead up to it, "The Dead"
dramatizes a moment of self-realization. The story portrays
the gradual awakening of Gabriel Conroy, whose vision of his
wife, Gretta, at the end of the story is at once a frustrating
disappointment and a touching movement toward understanding
and love. Robert Adams voices the view of more than one critic
when he writes of "The Dead" that this "greatest of the
stories in <u>Dubliners</u> stands apart from the rest, being warmer
in tonality, richer in the writing, and more intimate in its
subject matter" (83). Florence Walzl concurs when she writes
that "The Dead is markedly different from the earlier stories.
. . . It is not only a longer, more fully developed narrative,
but it presents a more kindly view of Ireland" (428).

In one sense the "dead" of the title are all those who have
lived and died, those who have gone before the festive
inhabitants of Dublin who celebrate the Christmas season,
Gabriel Conroy and Gretta among them. In another sense the
dead are all those who, though alive and breathing, have lost
their naturalness, their spontaneity, and most importantly,
their passion. Gabriel, one of these, has lost touch with his
past and with traditional Irish values. He looks instead
toward continental Europe, toward the future, and toward
change for an escape from the outmoded and restrictive
attitudes of the past (Ellmann 395).

We glimpse Gabriel arriving at the party as a man coming in
from the dark, here the symbolic darkness of Gabriel's
ignorance (Walzl 433). Gabriel appears to be something of a
generous gentleman, as he slips a coin into the hand of the
servant Lily. With this gesture of holiday good will, Gabriel
attempts to buy his way out of further conversation with Lily,
but she makes him uncomfortable by commenting that "The men
that is now is only all palaver and what they can get out of
you." It is a remark, Joyce's narrator notes, that Lily
delivers "with great bitterness" (178).

Gabriel deflects further discussion by attending to his coat
and scarf and shoes. He then presses the tip into the girl's
hand and disappears up the stairs. Our first impression of
Gabriel is of someone who though cultivated and cultured, is

nonetheless naive. This small scene sets the tone for
Gabriel's more serious errors in understanding, which Joyce
saves for a later revelation.

Early in the story, Gabriel is distinguished from his wife,
Gretta, his emotional opposite. Gabriel describes Gretta as
someone who would walk home in the snow if she were allowed.
Gabriel, on the other hand, will not go out in snow or rain
without his galoshes. Unlike her more cultured husband, Gretta
is without pretention, and she is more spontaneous. She
retains the youthful romantic nature she possessed when a
young man named Michael Furey died, according to her version
of the event, for love of her. Even in middle age, Gretta
appears more comfortable with the memory of the boy from her
past than with the presence of her more cultivated husband.

Gabriel's difference from the others at the party is
revealed during a conversation with Miss Ivors. When Miss
Ivors suggests that Gabriel and Gretta accompany her and some
friends on a vacation to the primitive Irish-speaking Aran
islands off the western coast of Ireland, Gabriel does not
accept. He tells her that he has already planned to travel in
the other direction—east to France and Belgium. These
countries represent for Gabriel the world of culture and
civilization. The Irish islands, by contrast, represent what
he considers uncivilized and repugnant. Ironically, however,
his wife's family come from one of those islands—a fact that
Gabriel prefers to ignore.

During his conversation with Miss Ivors, Gabriel confesses
his disgust with Ireland this way: "O, to tell you the truth
. . . I'm sick of my own country, sick of it" (189). When
pressed for an explanation, however, Gabriel declines to
provide one. He feels superior to his ignorant countrymen, and
is out of sympathy with their restrictive political, religious
and cultural values. To say so, however, would be distasteful
and uncomfortable. It would also be discourteous. And so
Gabriel is silent.

Other important scenes put Gabriel on display, increasing
our perception of him as more concerned with surface than with
substance, more impressed by the sound of his voice than the
truth of his words or the value of his actions. Gabriel's
clichéd after-dinner speech, for example, is filled with
outlandish praise of his old aunts, whom he flatters beyond
their comprehension. Gabriel sees the old Irish past as dead,
paying it only a token and insincere tribute. His thoughts and
energies are directed elsewhere—to the future and to the
Continent. Yet Gabriel points ironically toward what seems
most true—the power of the past to continue living into the
future; the inability of individuals to completely escape

their past and their cultural roots. In rejecting those
things, Gabriel is rejecting the essential part of himself. It
is unclear how much of this he understands. At the time he
gives his speech, however, it seems clear that he believes
none of his lofty sentiments.

We begin to see just how much Gabriel is shut out of his
wife's inner life in still another scene at the party. After
dinner there is singing by Mr. Darcy. When he sings an Irish
ballad called "The Lass of Aughrim," Gretta listens
enraptured, lost in memory:

> She was standing right under the dusty
> fanlight and the flame of the gas lit up
> the rich bronze of her hair which he had
> seen her drying at the fire a few days
> before. She was in the same attitude and
> seemed unaware of the talk about her. At
> last she turned towards them and Gabriel
> saw that there was colour on her cheeks
> and that her eyes were shining (212).

At this moment Gabriel feels an immense tenderness towards
his wife and also a strong sexual desire for her. Both his
tenderness and his desire grow as the party winds down and
Gabriel accompanies Gretta to the hotel. Gabriel's desire
increases further as he rehearses mentally how he will
approach Gretta and how he will express his feelings.

The critical point of this scene concerns the thoughts
Gretta has as Gabriel watches her. He expects her to tell him
that she has been thinking of him and of their life together.
Instead, she tells Gabriel about Michael Furey, whose image
she had conjured up when Mr. Darcy sang "The Lass of Aughrim,"
a song Michael Furey himself sang before he died. As Gabriel
listens to Gretta reminisce about the poor delicate boy with
the big sad eyes, he experiences with a shock a moment of
self-realization:

> Gabriel felt humiliated by the failure of
> his irony and by the evocation of this
> figure from the dead, a boy in the
> gasworks. While he had been full of
> memories of their secret life together,
> full of tenderness and joy and desire, she
> had been comparing him in her mind with
> another. A shameful consciousness of his
> own person assailed him. He saw himself as
> a ludicrous figure, acting as a pennyboy
> for his aunts, a nervous well-meaning

> sentimentalist, orating to vulgarians and
> idealising his own clownish lusts, the
> pitiable fatuous fellow he had caught a
> glimpse of in the mirror. Instinctively he
> turned his back more to the light lest she
> might see the shame that burned upon his
> forehead (219-220).

Gabriel's humiliation is increased further when he learns
the circumstances of Michael Furey's death. With that
knowledge comes a second revelation accompanied by Joyce's
description of the snow falling over all of Ireland. The
beauty of the language, which matches the beauty of the snow-
filled scene, also suggests the beauty of Gabriel's perception
that all people share life and death, that the dead live and
the living shall join the dead in a shared humanity. "The time
had come," as the narrator puts it, "for Gabriel to set out on
his journey westward" (223), a statement that has been
characterized as "an enigmatic sentence that has bothered many
readers of "The Dead" (Benstock 167).

But as Joyce's biographer Richard Ellmann has explained
(396), it is not really so puzzling. According to Ellmann,
this westward journey is the journey back to Gabriel's past,
to his cultural roots. The tone of Joyce's sentence suggests
resignation and relinquishment, as Gabriel gives up his "sense
of the importance of civilized thinking, of Continental
tastes" (Ellmann 397) and other nice distinctions he prides
himself in making. Moreover, this journey westward is also the
ultimate journey toward the setting sun, toward the closing of
life. For Gabriel, the journey toward what he previously saw
as death is really a journey into life, the real life of
feeling as experienced by those more sincere and authentic
than he has ever been. For although Gabriel Conroy had indeed
been sick of his country, as he had told Miss Ivors, he
nevertheless finds himself drawn to it. The story, ultimately,
turns on a paradox: that to go forward one has to go back.
Gabriel's soul swoons as he hears the snow "falling faintly
through the universe and faintly falling, like the descent of
their last end, upon all the living and the dead" (224).

During Gabriel's vision, Joyce slows down the narrative pace
(Loomis 150). Time slows as we are presented a vision of
humanity's common fate. It is a vision that we share rather
than one we merely analyze. For we too know that like Gabriel
and Gretta and Michael Furey, everyone is subject to the
experiences of love and sorrow, pain and joy, passion and
tenderness, living and dying. And, like Gabriel, in realizing
and reminding ourselves of the inevitability of this simple
truth, our sympathies are enlarged and deepened for Gabriel,
for Gretta, for Michael Furey, and for one another as well.

Works Cited

Adams, Robert. <u>James Joyce</u>. New York: Octagon Books, 1980.

Benstock, Bernard. "The Dead." In <u>"Dubliners": Critical Essays</u>. Ed. Clive Hart. London: Faber and Faber, 1969. 156–69.

Ellmann, Richard. "The Backgrounds of 'The Dead.'" In <u>Dubliners: Text, Criticism, and Notes</u>. Eds. Robert Scholes and A. Walton Litz. New York: Viking, 1969. 388–403.

Joyce, James. "The Dead." In <u>Dubliners: Text, Criticism, and Notes</u>. Eds. Robert Scholes and A. Walton Litz. New York: Viking, 1969. 175–224.

Loomis, C. C. "Structure and Sympathy in Joyce's 'The Dead.'" <u>PMLA</u>, 75 (1960): 149–151.

Walzl, Florence. "Gabriel and Michael: The Conclusion of 'The Dead.'" In <u>Dubliners: Text, Criticism, and Notes</u>. Eds. Robert Scholes and A. Walton Litz. New York: Viking, 1969. 423–479.

A RESEARCH PAPER USING MULTIPLE WORKS AND MULTIPLE SOURCES

In her essay on E. B. White Radhika A. Jones presents a view of the writer's work that focuses on the way the egg functions as image and symbol of White's central themes. The writer announces her focus in the opening paragraph and highlights the way eggs pervade White's work signifying "the sanctity, the beauty, and the fragility of life." This idea the writer complicates and enriches as she develops her essay, as for example in the final sentence of paragraph 4 where she remarks that eggs are "at once sources of stability and continuity; they are links in a natural chain"; and again near the end of paragraph 8 where she sees White's recognition of eggs as sources not only of continuity but also of "subtle change." The writer also links the symbolism of the egg to White's concern with time and change and with his irrepressible idealism.

One of the more impressive aspects of Ms. Jones's essay is the way she moves back and forth among White's works she cites as evidence. Instead of treating each work once and then moving on to another, she weaves two, three, sometimes four different works into a single paragraph, showing how each illustrates or enforces the point she is making at the time. In her third paragraph, for example, she refers to two novels and two essays to explain her point. Although other features of the essay might be held up as exemplary, we might mention the writer's aptly chosen epigraph, which points toward the idea she develops in the essay. In addition, mention might be made of the way her conclusion brings the essay full circle in a return to its title.

Radhika A. Jones

Essentially Egg-Shaped

> I don't know of anything in the entire
> world more wonderful to look at than a
> nest with eggs in it. An egg, because it
> contains life, is the most perfect thing
> there is. It is beautiful and mysterious.
> An egg is a far finer thing than a tennis
> ball or a cake of soap. A tennis ball will
> always be just a tennis ball. A cake of
> soap will always be just a cake of soap—
> until it gets so small nobody wants it and
> they throw it away. But an egg will
> someday be a living creature.
>   (White, _Trumpet_ 23)

The reverent admiration that Sam Beaver, young hero of _The Trumpet of the Swan_, has for eggs can only be rivalled by that of his creator. E. B. White's work, from his essays to his children's literature, is replete with eggs—as objects of natural beauty and as sources of life. A relatively small and simple object with an infinite number of thematic associations, the egg as subject matter perfectly reflects White's ability to transform concrete observations into clear, universal conclusions. White's eggs are rich with meaning; they are links in a never-ending cycle of life; they are sources of continuity in a world fragmented by passing time. And even in those essays that do not figure literal eggs, the sanctity, the beauty, and the fragility of life that they represent pervades White's work.

Perhaps only a writer so attuned to simplicity and detail could write an essay that is just about brown and white eggs, as is White's "Riposte." In this essay he takes issue with an Englishman who believes that Americans prefer white eggs to brown because white eggs seem more hygienic and brown eggs more countrified. "My goodness" is White's comment (_Essays_ 60): "there is no such thing as an _unnatural_ egg" (_Essays_ 61). Mr. Priestley (the Englishman) has missed the point altogether—an egg is an egg; its color is irrelevant to its identity. That White would devote an entire essay to discussing this topic is a testimonial to his interest in the egg. He would not have it misjudged.

In and of themselves eggs—oval shells of calcium carbonate—

are not terribly exciting, but as sources of new life they
hold magical and exhilarating properties. In the spectrum of
White's work, eggs hatch right and left and White revels in
each birth. One pictures White as his own character Sam
Beaver, sitting awed and motionless as he witnesses the
miracle of the cygnets' birth (<u>Trumpet</u> 29-30). Or as
Charlotte the spider, offering her "sincere congratulations"
on the occasion of the newly-hatched barnyard goslings (<u>Web</u>
44). In "The Geese" White appoints himself caretaker of three
goslings and meticulously looks after their eggs as a tribute
to a goose acquaintance who had died of old age (<u>Prose</u>
145-49). "Spring" finds him caring for "254 little
innocents"—chicks for whom he and his stove act as mother-hen
(<u>Meat</u> 234-37). In short, White hails eggs as producers of
life; in his writing and in his life they are objects to be
revered and tended appropriately.

It would not be enough, however, simply to say that White is
a writer with a healthy respect for the wonder of an egg: to
do so would be to take the egg out of context. White's eggs
are very much in context; they are part of the natural cycle
of life, of development. The hatching of eggs is not a once-
in-a-lifetime occurrence. It happens every spring and every
spring it brings the renewal of youth and hope. "Each spring,"
writes White in <u>Charlotte's Web</u>, "there were new little
spiders hatching out to take the place of the old" (183).
Likewise, the three new goslings and their offspring in "The
Geese" continue the tradition of the original pair of geese
with whom White had "an acquaintance of such long standing—
long standing and loud shouting" (<u>Prose</u> 145). Eggs come as
dependably as the seasons; they are at once sources of
stability and continuity; they are links in a natural chain.

Indeed, if White can be said to have a central
preoccupation, then it is certainly the mystery of time's
cyclic nature, and the precarious yet precious relationships
that ensue. His literal tales of hatching eggs are only a few
of his many essays and stories that address the topic of
passing time and chronicle the natural cycles of life. Such
is clearly the case in <u>Charlotte's Web</u>, which begins with the
birth of Wilbur the pig and follows him into old age, while
also telling the story of his spider friend Charlotte and her
descendants. Wilbur is saved from an untimely, unnatural
death by the resourceful and clever Charlotte; he lives out
his life as Nature intended, as does she (White, <u>Web</u>). But
<u>Charlotte's Web</u> is more than a story of animal progeny; it is
a tale of how the love between two friends enriched both of
their lives. White has taken us beyond the simple hatching of
eggs to life outside the egg-shell, where we can see his joy

for life reflected in the relationships he creates among
living things.

"Once More to the Lake" and "The Ring of Time" move to the
realm of human relationships and life cycles, away from
literal eggs. "Once More to the Lake" involves the time lapse
between being a son and then becoming a father of one's own
son, and depicts the change in temperament that naturally
accompanies those passing years. White so vividly remembers
the summers when he was a boy that he is lulled into thinking
"there had been no years," but as he gradually notices subtle
changes in the lake and in himself—the cacaphonous sounds of
the new outboard motors, his reluctance to swim in the rain as
he would have done long ago—he realizes that life may be
cyclic but it spirals ever forward. He has aged and there have
undeniably been years (Essays 191-202).

"The Ring of Time" addresses the illusion of the young that
time has no ramifications. "She is at that enviable moment in
life," White writes of a young circus performer who is riding
her horse around the ring, "when she believes she can go once
around the ring, make one complete circuit, and at the end be
exactly the same age as at the start" (Essays 145). Later in
the essay he refers to this feeling as "true seduction" and a
"delusion," for "time has not stood still for anybody but the
dead, and even the dead must be able to hear the acceleration
of little sports cars and know that things have changed"
(Essays 148-49).

Eggs may come every spring, in other words, but they are not
the same eggs. Charlotte's children and grand-children cannot
really replace Charlotte in Wilbur's eyes. White recognizes
the new eggs each spring for what they are worth—sources of
continuity yet also subtle change. Life is not merely seasonal
repetition, even though this spring may be reminiscent of the
last.

The egg is a tiny microcosm of life, and as such it is a
perfect example of White's tendency to look to the smaller
things in order to facilitate a better understanding of the
larger issues of his day. "Who has the longer view of things,
anyway, a prime minister in a closet or a man on a barn roof?"
he asks in "Clear Days" (Meat 20), written slightly before the
outbreak of World War II. Later, in 1941, he writes, "I
sometimes think I am crazy—everybody else fighting and dying
or working for a cause or writing to his senator, and me
looking after some Barred Rock chickens" (Meat 236). White is
clearly concerned with the topic of war, but he continues to
write about it in the context of his experiences on his farm.

In his review of One Man's Meat, Benjamin DeMott dismisses
White's subjects because they are so ordinary. He lists them

as "Maine, progress as disaster, frustrations of urban life, and so on" (63) as if it bores him to include them at all. But I am more inclined to agree with the reviewer who wrote, "It is the gift of the poetic imagination to shape commonplace things into conclusions of considerable weight" (DeVane 164). To the attentive artist no place does not lend itself to observation, no topic is too mundane. White commits himself to reporting what he sees and thinking about what meaning he can derive from his observations, not to merely musing on grandiose abstractions. Likewise, he commits himself to preserving and protecting what life there is around him, instead of lamenting the lives he cannot save in Europe.

> I soon knew that the remaining warmth in
> this stubborn stove was all I had to pit
> against the Nazi idea of *Frühling*. . . .
> Countries are ransacked, valleys drenched
> with blood. Though it seems untimely I
> still publish my belief in the egg, the
> contents of the egg, the warm coal, and
> the necessity for pursuing whatever fire
> delights and sustains you.
>
> (Meat 237)

White invests in the egg the ultimate sanctity of human life, and he will go to great lengths to uphold it. He works within his sphere of influence to comment on more universal themes; his sight and his actions lead to insight and speculation (Hoy and DiYanni, Prose 144).

> "Look," he [Templeton] began in his
> sharp voice, "you say you have seven
> goslings. There were eight eggs. What
> happened to the other egg? Why didn't it
> hatch?"
> "It's a dud, I guess," said the goose.
> (White, Web 45)

E. B. White does not write fairy-tales; not all of his eggs hatch. White's world has a dual nature, where happiness and sorrow co-exist peacefully, naturally. Perhaps this co-existence is the reason children recognize him as a wonderful writer for he does not hide from them what well-meaning adults would. White has the ability to gently exploit the contradictions in life; his essays and stories probe the reality of not-so-happy endings.

When I was eight I cried for Charlotte, who died alone at the Fair Grounds (White, Web 171). I felt that it was grossly

unfair that she who had worked so hard should perish so soon
after her triumph—felt that she should at least be able to
return home with Wilbur. Now I realize that White has too much
respect for Nature to have permitted me that miracle.
Charlotte was a spider with a spider's life span; such things
cannot be altered, and certainly not by a writer as familiar
with and respectful of life cycles as E. B. White.

   However much White might want to promote life among his
fellow creatures, he is not idealistic enough to suppose that
he can always be successful. In "The Geese" he expresses a
desire to hatch the old goose's three eggs as a tribute to
her, but he finds himself not obsessed enough to devote
himself to an incubator for the necessary thirty days.
Instead, he purchases three new-born goslings from a neighbor
(Prose 145-46). Where there is life, there is also, so to
speak, non-life, and White presents this contrast directly:
"Summer was upon us, the pond was alive again. I brought the
three eggs up from the cellar and dispatched them to the town
dump" (Prose 147). We are not told what to make of this
incongruence, we are merely given it, and we know by the
startling juxtaposition of those two sentences that White is
thinking about it himself. His closing sentence is along
similar lines: "I don't know anything sadder than a summer's
day" (Prose 149). Summer days in "Once More to the Lake" are
tinged with sadness as well, as the son prepares to bathe in
the rain, the father feels "the chill of death" (Essays 202).
But on the other hand, those same summer days are also replete
with the joy of new life—the three goslings nurtured by
White, the son who feels no chill of death. White's world is
by no means pessimistic, nor is it idealistically optimistic.
It is a depiction of reality as seen through the eyes of a man
who acknowledges the unfortunate, yet is always willing to
"publish his belief in the egg" (White, Meat 237).

> The world White loves is more than a
> collection of things, natural and man-
> made, or a fascinating organization of
> reassuring cyclical, ongoing processes: it
> is a world in which the motive for
> creating, nurturing, teaching,
> encouraging, singing, and celebrating is
> love.
>
>   (Elledge 303)

   This love pervades White's works: it is implicit in all of
his essays, of his children's stories. It motivates him to
take his son to visit his old haunt in "Once More to the
Lake"; it motivates him to keep a vigil by the stove that

warms the chicks in "Spring"; it motivates him to raise three goslings in memory of the old goose in "The Geese." In short, it motivates him to cherish life, and to cherish the eggs, symbolic and literal, that bring life into the world. In White's world, life is nothing short of a miracle, and "to him a miracle was essentially egg-shaped" (qtd. in Elledge 25).

Works Cited

DeMott, Benjamin. "Books: Pick of the List." Rev. of <u>Essays of E. B. White</u>, by E. B. White. <u>Saturday Review</u> 20 Aug. 1977: 63.

DeVane, William C. "A Celebration of Life." Rev. of <u>One Man's Meat</u>, by E. B. White. <u>The Yale Review</u> 1942: 163–165.

Elledge, Scott. <u>E. B. White: A Biography</u>. New York: Norton, 1984.

Hoy, Pat C. II and Robert DiYanni. Headnote: "E. B. White." <u>Prose Pieces: Essays and Stories, Sixteen Modern Writers</u>. New York: Random House, 1988. 143–45.

White, E. B. <u>Charlotte's Web</u>. New York: Harper & Brothers, 1952.

------. <u>Essays of E. B. White</u>. New York: Harper & Row, 1977.

------. "The Geese." <u>Prose Pieces: Essays and Stories, Sixteen Modern Writers</u>. Ed. Pat C. Hoy II and Robert DiYanni. New York: Random House, 1988. 145–149.

------. <u>One Man's Meat</u>. 2nd ed. New York: Harper & Row, 1944.

------. <u>The Trumpet of the Swan</u>. New York: Harper & Row, 1970.

CHAPTER THIRTY-EIGHT

Critical Comments About Literature

In this section you will find comments about literature from ancient times to the present. Although many of the comments are directed toward a particular genre, such as drama or the short story, what their authors say can sometimes be applied to other genres as well.

You will find in this section philosophical observations on the nature of poetry and drama (Plato and Aristotle) along with brief discussions of technical matters, such as Gerard Manley Hopkins's observations about rhythm and Anton Chekhov's ideas about the short story.

One way to use these critical comments is to relate what is said here to what a particular writer does in his or her work. You can relate Arthur Miller's comments on tragedy, for example, to his play *Death of a Salesman;* you can use Annie Dillard's observations about what essays do as a gloss on her essay "Living Like Weasels."

For critics whose literary works do not appear in this book, you can consider their comments in relation to other works. Brecht's "Theater Notes" and Esslin's "The Theater of the Absurd," for example, can be used to think about plays by modernist playwrights whose works appear in the drama anthology.

PLATO

[*428–348 B.C.*]

Poetry and Inspiration

TRANSLATED BY BENJAMIN JOWETT

For all good poets, epic as well as lyric, compose their beautiful poems not by art, but because they are inspired and possessed. And as the Corybantian revellers when they dance are not in their right mind, so the lyric poets are not in their right mind when they are composing their beautiful strains: but when falling under the power of music and metre they are inspired and possessed; like Bacchic maidens who draw milk and honey from the rivers when they are under the influence of Dionysus but not when they are in their right mind. And the soul of the lyric poet does the same, as they themselves say; for they tell us that they bring songs from honeyed fountains, culling them out of the gardens and dells of the Muses; they, like the bees, winging their way from flower to flower. And this is true. For the poet is a light and winged and holy thing, and there is no invention in him until he has been inspired and is out of his senses, and reason is no longer in him: no man, while he retains that faculty, has the oracular gift of poetry.

Many are the noble words in which poets speak concerning the actions of men; but like yourself when speaking about Homer, they do not speak of them by any rules of art: they are simply inspired to utter that to which the Muse impels them, and that only; and when inspired, one of them will make dithyrambs, another hymns of praise, another choral strains, another epic or iambic verses, but not one of them is of any account in the other kinds. For not by art does the poet sing, but by power divine; had he learned by rules of art, he would have known how to speak not of one theme only, but of all; and therefore God takes away reason from poets, and uses them as his ministers, as he also uses the pronouncers of oracles and holy prophets, in order that we who hear them may know them to be speaking not of themselves, who utter these priceless words while bereft of reason, but that God himself is the speaker, and that through them he is addressing us. And Tynnichus the Chalcidian affords a striking instance of what I am saying: he wrote no poem that anyone would care to remember but the famous paean which is in everyone's mouth, one of the finest lyric poems ever written, simply an invention of the Muses, as he himself says. For in this way God would seem to demonstrate to us and not to allow us to doubt that these beautiful poems are not human, nor the work of man, but divine and the work of God; and that the poets are only the interpreters of the gods by whom they are severally possessed.

ARISTOTLE

[*384–322 B.C.*]

On Tragedy

TRANSLATED BY GERALD F. ELSE

At present let us deal with tragedy, recovering from what has been said so far the definition of its essential nature, as it was in development. Tragedy, then, is a process of imitating an action which has serious implications, is complete, and possesses magnitude; by means of language which has been made sensuously attractive, with each of its varieties found separately in the parts; enacted by the persons themselves and not presented through narrative; through a course of pity and fear completing the purification of tragic acts which have those emotional characteristics. By "language made sensuously attractive" I mean language that has rhythm and melody, and by "its varieties found separately" I mean the fact that certain parts of the play are carried on through spoken verses alone and others the other way around, through song.

Now first of all, since they perform the imitation through action (by acting it), the adornment of their visual appearance will perforce constitute some part of the making of tragedy; and song-composition and verbal expression also, for those are the media in which they perform the imitation. By "verbal expression" I mean the actual composition of the verses, and by "song-composition" something whose meaning is entirely clear.

Next, since it is an imitation of an action and is enacted by certain people who are performing the action, and since those people must necessarily have certain traits both of character and thought (for it is thanks to these two factors that we speak of people's actions also as having a defined character, and it is in accordance with their actions that all either succeed or fail); and since the imitation of the action is the plot, for by "plot" I mean here the structuring of the events, and by the "characters" that in accordance with which we say that the persons who are acting have a defined moral character, and by "thought" all the passages in which they attempt to prove some thesis or set forth an opinion—it follows of necessity, then, that tragedy as a whole has just six constituent elements, in relation to the essence that makes it a distinct species; and they are plot, character, verbal expression, thought, visual adornment, and song-composition. For the elements by which they imitate are two (i.e., verbal expression and song-composition), the manner in which they imitate is one (visual adornment), the things they imitate are three (plot, characters, thought), and there is nothing more beyond these. These then are the constituent forms they use.

The greatest of these elements is the structuring of the incidents. For tragedy is an imitation not of men but of a life, an action, and they have moral quality in accordance with their characters but are happy or unhappy in accordance with their actions; hence they are not active in order to imitate their characters, but they include the characters along with the actions for the sake of the latter. Thus the structure of events, the plot, is the goal of tragedy, and the goal is the greatest thing of all.

Again: a tragedy cannot exist without a plot, but it can without characters: thus the tragedies of most of our modern poets are devoid of character, and in general many poets are like that; so also with the relationship between Zeuxis and Polygnotus,° among the painters: Polygnotus is a good portrayer of character, while Zeuxis's painting has no dimension of character at all.

Again: if one strings end to end speeches that are expressive of character and carefully worked in thought and expression, he still will not achieve the result which we said was the aim of tragedy; the job will be done much better by a tragedy that is more deficient in these other respects but has a plot, a structure of events. It is much the same case as with painting: the most beautiful pigments smeared on at random will not give as much pleasure as a black-and-white outline picture. Besides, the most powerful means tragedy has for swaying our feelings, namely the peripeties and recognitions,° are elements of plot. . . .

Some plots are simple, others are complex; indeed the actions of which the plots are imitations already fall into these two categories. By "simple" action I mean one the development of which being continuous and unified in the manner stated above, the reversal comes without peripety or recognition, and by "complex" action one in which the reversal is continuous but with recognition or peripety or both. And these developments must grow out of the very structure of the plot itself, in such a way that on the basis of what has happened previously this particular outcome follows either by necessity or in accordance with probability; for there is a great difference in whether these events happen because of those or merely after them.

"Peripety" is a shift of what is being undertaken to the opposite in the way previously stated, and that in accordance with probability or necessity as we have just been saying; as for example in the *Oedipus* the man who has come, thinking that he will reassure Oedipus, that is, relieve him of his fear with respect to his mother, by revealing who he once was, brings about the opposite; and in the *Lynceus,* as he (Lynceus) is being led away with every prospect of being executed, and Danaus pursuing him with every prospect of doing the executing, it comes about as a result of the other things that have happened in the play that *he* is executed and Lynceus is saved. And "recognition" is, as indeed the name indicates, a shift from ignorance to awareness, pointing in the direction either of close blood ties or of hostility, of people who have previously been in a clearly marked state of happiness or unhappiness.

The finest recognition is one that happens at the same time as a peripety, as is the case with the one in the *Oedipus*. Naturally, there are also other kinds of recognition: it is possible for one to take place in the prescribed manner in relation to inanimate objects and chance occurrences, and it is possible to recognize whether a person has acted or not acted. But the form that is most integrally a part of the plot, the action, is the one aforesaid; for that kind of recognition combined with peripety will excite either pity or fear (and these are the kinds of action of which tragedy is an imitation according to our definition), because both good and bad fortune will also be most likely

---

Zeuxis (*fl. 420–390 B.C.*) and Polygnotus (*c. 470–440 B.C.*) *Zeuxis developed a method of painting in which the figures were rounded and apparently three-dimensional. Thus, he was an illusionistic painter, imitating life in a realistic style. Polygnotus was famous as a painter, and his works were on the Akropolis as well as at Delphi. His draftsmanship was especially praised.* **peripeties and recognitions** *The turning-about of fortune and the recognition on the part of the tragic hero of the truth. This is, for Aristotle, a critical moment in the drama, especially if both events happen simultaneously, as they do in* Oedipus Rex. *It is quite possible for these moments to happen apart from one another.*

to follow that kind of event. Since, further, the recognition is a recognition of persons, some are of one person by the other one only (when it is already known who the "other one" is), but sometimes it is necessary for both persons to go through a recognition, as for example Iphigenia is recognized by her brother through the sending of the letter, but of him by Iphigenia another recognition is required.

These then are two elements of plot: peripety and recognition; third is the *pathos*. Of these, peripety and recognition have been discussed; a *pathos* is a destructive or painful act, such as deaths on stage, paroxysms of pain, woundings, and all that sort of thing.

SIR PHILIP SIDNEY

[1554–1586]

An Apology for Poetry

But now, let us see how the Greeks named it, and how they deemed of it. The Greeks called him "a poet," which name hath, as the most excellent, gone through other languages. It cometh of this word *Poiein,* which is "to make": wherein, I know not whether by luck or wisdom, we Englishmen have met with the Greeks in calling him "a maker": which name, how high and incomparable a title it is, I had rather were known by marking the scope of other sciences than by my partial allegation.

There is no art delivered to mankind that hath not the works of Nature for his principal object, without which they could not consist, and on which they so depend, as they become actors and players, as it were, of what Nature will have set forth. So doth the astronomer look upon the stars, and, by that he seeth, setteth down what order Nature hath taken therein. So do the geometrician and arithmetician in their diverse sorts of quantities. So doth the musician in times tell you which by nature agree, which not. The natural philosopher thereon hath his name, and the moral philosopher standeth upon the natural virtues, vices, and passions of man; and "follow Nature" (saith he) "therein, and thou shalt not err." The lawyer saith what men have determined; the historian what men have done. The grammarian speaketh only of the rules of speech; and the rhetorician and logician, considering what in Nature will soonest prove and persuade, thereon give artificial rules, which still are compassed within the circle of a question according to the proposed matter. The physician weigheth the nature of a man's body, and the nature of things helpful or hurtful unto it. And the metaphysic, though it be in the second and abstract notions, and therefore be counted supernatural, yet doth he indeed build upon the depth of Nature. Only the poet, disdaining to be tied to any such subjection, lifted up with the vigour of his own invention, doth grow in effect another nature, in making things either better than Nature bringeth forth, or, quite anew, forms such as never were in Nature, as the Heroes, Demigods, Cyclopes, Chimeras, Furies, and such like: so as he goeth hand in hand with Nature, not enclosed within the narrow warrant of her gifts, but freely ranging only within the zodiac of his own wit.

SAMUEL JOHNSON

[1709–1784]

The Metaphysical Poets

The metaphysical poets were men of learning, and to show their learning was their whole endeavor; but, unluckily resolving to show it in rhyme, instead of writing poetry they only wrote verses, and very often such verses as stood the trial of the finger better than of the ear; for the modulation was so imperfect, that they were only found to be verses by counting the syllables.

If the father of criticism° has rightly denominated poetry τέχνη μιμητικὴ, *an imitative art,* these writers will, without great wrong, lose their right to the name of poets, for they cannot be said to have imitated anything; they neither copied nature for life, neither painted the forms of matter, nor represented the operations of intellect.

Those, however, who deny them to be poets, allow them to be wits. Dryden confesses of himself and his contemporaries, that they fall below Donne in wit, but maintains that they surpass him in poetry.

If wit be well described by Pope, as being "that which has been often thought, but was never before so well expressed," they certainly never attained, nor ever sought it; for they endeavored to be singular in their thoughts, and were careless of their diction. But Pope's account of wit is undoubtedly erroneous: he depresses it below its natural dignity, and reduces it from strength of thought to happiness of language.

If by a more noble and more adequate conception that be considered as wit which is at once natural and new, that which, though not obvious, is, upon its first production, acknowledged to be just; if it be that which he that never found it wonders how he missed, to wit of this kind the metaphysical poets have seldom risen. Their thoughts are often new, but seldom natural; they are not obvious, but neither are they just; and the reader, far from wondering that he missed them, wonders more frequently by what perverseness of industry they were ever found.

But wit, abstracted from its effects upon the hearer, may be more rigorously and philosophically considered as a kind of *discordia concors;* a combination of dissimilar images, or discovery of occult resemblances in things apparently unlike. Of wit, thus defined, they have more than enough. The most heterogeneous ideas are yoked by violence together; nature and art are ransacked for illustrations, comparisons, and allusions; their learning instructs, and their subtlety surprises; but the reader commonly thinks his improvement dearly bought, and, though he sometimes admires, is seldom pleased.

°*the father of criticism . . .*   Aristotle.

WILLIAM BLAKE
[1757–1827]

Art and Imagination

I know that This World Is a World of imagination & Vision. I see Every thing I paint
In This World, but Every body does not see alike. To the Eyes of a Miser a Guinea is
more beautiful than the Sun, & a bag worn with the use of Money has more beautiful proportions than a Vine filled with Grapes. The tree which moves some to tears of
joy is in the Eyes of others only a Green thing that stands in the way. Some See Nature all Ridicule & Deformity, & by these I shall not regulate my proportions; & Some
Scarce see Nature at all. But to the Eyes of the Man of Imagination, Nature is Imagination itself. As a man is, So he Sees. As the Eye is formed, such are its Powers. You
certainly Mistake, when you say that the Visions of Fancy are not to be found in This
World. To Me This World is all One continued Vision of Fancy or Imagination, & I
feel Flatter'd when I am told so. What is it sets Homer, Virgil & Milton in so high a
rank of Art? Why is the Bible more Entertaining & Instructive than any other book?
Is it not because they are addressed to the Imagination, which is Spiritual Sensation, &
but mediately to the Understanding or Reason? Such is True Painting, and such was
alone valued by the Greeks & the best modern Artists. Consider what Lord Bacon says:
"Sense sends over to Imagination before Reason have judged, & Reason sends over
to Imagination before the Decree can be acted."*

WILLIAM WORDSWORTH
[1770–1850]

Poetry and Feeling

I have said that poetry is the spontaneous overflow of powerful feelings: it takes its origin from emotion recollected in tranquillity: the emotion is contemplated till, by a
species of reaction, the tranquillity gradually disappears, and an emotion, kindred to
that which was before the subject of contemplation, is gradually produced, and does
itself actually exist in the mind. In this mood successful composition generally begins,

---

*William Blake, in a letter to Dr. Trusler on August 23, 1799, in his The Letters of William Blake, edited by
Geoffrey Keynes, The Macmillan Company, 1956, pp. 34–7.

and in a mood similar to this it is carried on; but the emotion, of whatever kind, and in whatever degree, from various causes, is qualified by various pleasures, so that in describing any passions whatsoever, which are voluntarily described, the mind will, upon the whole, be in a state of enjoyment. If Nature be thus cautious to preserve in a state of enjoyment a being so employed, the Poet ought to profit by the lesson held forth to him, and ought especially to take care, that, whatever passions he communicates to his Reader, those passions, if his Reader's mind be sound and vigorous, should always be accompanied with an overbalance of pleasure. Now the music of harmonious metrical language, the sense of difficulty overcome, and the blind association of pleasure which has been previously received from works of rhyme or metre of the same or similar construction, an indistinct perception perpetually renewed of language closely resembling that of real life, and yet, in the circumstance of metre, differing from it so widely—all these imperceptibly make up a complex feeling of delight, which is of the most important use in tempering the painful feeling always found intermingled with powerful descriptions of the deeper passions. This effect is always produced in pathetic and impassioned poetry; while, in lighter compositions, the ease and gracefulness with which the Poet manages his numbers are themselves confessedly a principal source of the gratification of the Reader. All that it is *necessary* to say, however, upon this subject, may be effected by affirming, what few persons will deny, that, of two descriptions, either of passions, manners, or characters, each of them equally well executed, the one in prose and the other in verse, the verse will be read a hundred times where the prose is read once.

from Preface to the Lyrical Ballads

JOHN KEATS

[1795–1821]

The Authenticity of the Imagination

November 22, 1817

My dear Bailey,

　★ ★ ★ O I wish I was as certain of the end of all your troubles as that of your momentary start about the authenticity of the Imagination. I am certain of nothing but of the holiness of the Heart's affections and the truth of Imagination—What the imagination seizes as Beauty must be truth—whether it existed before or not—for I have the same Idea or all our Passions as of Love they are all in their sublime, creative of essential Beauty—In a Word, you may know my favorite Speculation by my first Book and the little song I sent in my last—which is a representation from the fancy of the probable mode of operating in these Matters—The Imagination may be compared to Adam's dream—he awoke and found it truth. I am the more zealous in this affair, because I have never yet been able to perceive how any thing can be known for truth by consequitive reasoning—and yet it must be—Can it be that even the greatest Philosopher ever arrived at his goal without putting aside numerous objections—However it may be, O for a Life of Sensations rather than of Thoughts! It is "a Vision in the form of Youth" a Shadow of reality to come—and this consideration has further conv[i]nced me for it has come as auxiliary to another favorite Speculation of mine, that we shall enjoy ourselves here after by having what we called happiness on Earth repeated in a finer tone and so repeated—And yet such a fate can only befall those who delight in sensation rather than hunger as you do after Truth—Adam's dream will do here and seems to be a conviction that Imagination and its empyreal reflection is the same as human Life and its spiritual repetition. But as I was saying— the simple imaginative Mind may have its rewards in the repeti[ti]on of its own silent Working coming continually on the spirit with a fine suddenness—to compare great things with small—have you never by being surprised with an old Melody—in a delicious place—by a delicious voice, fe[l]t over again your very speculations and surmises at the time it first operated on your soul—do you not remember forming to yourself the singer's face more beautiful that it was possible and yet with the elevation of the Moment you did not think so—even then you were mounted on the Wings of Imagination so high—that the Prototype must be here after—that delicious face you will see—What a time! I am continually running away from the subject—sure this cannot be exactly the case with a complex Mind—one that is imaginative and at the same time careful of its fruits—who would exist partly on sensation partly on thought—to whom it is necessary that years should bring the philosophic Mind— such an one I consider your's and therefore it is necessary to your eternal Happiness that you not only drink this old Wine of Heaven which I shall call the redigestion of our most ethereal Musings on Earth; but also increase in knowledge and know all things. I am glad to hear you are in a fair Way for Easter—you will soon get through your unpleasant reading and then!—but the world is full of troubles and I have not much reason to think myself pestered with many—I think Jane or Marianne has a better opinion of me than I deserve—for really and truly I do not think my Brothers illness connected with mine—you know more of the real Cause than they do— nor have I any chance of being rack'd as you have been—you perhaps at one time thought there was such a thing as Worldly Happiness to be arrived at, at certain periods of time marked out—you have of necessity from your disposition been thus led away—I scarcely remember counting upon any Happiness—I look not for it if it be not in the present hour—nothing startles me beyond the Moment. The setting sun will always set me to rights—or if a Sparrow come before my Window I take part in its existence and pick about the Gravel. The first thing that strikes me on hea[r]ing a Misfortune having befalled another is this. "Well it cannot be helped.—he will have the pleasure of trying the resources of his spirit, and I beg now my dear Bailey that hereafter should you observe any thing cold in me not to but it to the account of heartlessness but abstraction—for I assure you I sometimes feel not the influence of a Passion or Affection during a whole week—and so long this sometimes continues I begin to suspect myself and the genuiness of my feelings at other times—thinking them a few barren Tragedy-tears. ★ ★ ★

Your affectionate friend
John Keats—

PERCY BYSSHE SHELLEY

[1792–1822]

Poets and Language

Poets, according to the circumstances of the age and nation in which they appeared, were called, in the earlier epochs of the world, legislators, or prophets: a poet essentially comprises and unites both these characters. For he not only beholds intensely the present as it is, and discovers those laws according to which present things ought to be ordered, but he beholds the future in the present, and his thoughts are the germs of the flower and the fruit of latest time. Not that I assert poets to be prophets in the gross sense of the word, or that they can foretell the form as surely as they foreknow the spirit of events: such is the pretence of superstition, which would make poetry an attribute of prophecy, rather than prophecy an attribute of poetry. A poet participates in the eternal, the infinite, and the one; as far as relates to his conceptions, time and place and number are not. The grammatical forms which express the moods of time, and the difference of persons, and the distinction of place, are convertible with respect to the highest poetry without injuring it as poetry; and the choruses of Aeschylus, and the book of *Job,* and Dante's *Paradise,* would afford, more than any other writings, examples of this fact, if the limits of this essay did not forbid citation. The creations of sculpture, painting, and music, are illustrations still more decisive.

Language, colour, form, and religious and civil habits of action, are all the instruments and materials of poetry; they may be called poetry by that figure of speech which considers the effect as a synonym of the cause. But poetry in a more restricted sense expresses those arrangements of language, and especially metrical language, which are created by that imperial faculty, whose throne is curtained within the invisible nature of man. And this springs from the nature itself of language, which is a more direct representation of the actions and passions of our internal being, and is susceptible of more various and delicate combinations, than colour, form, or motion, and is more plastic and obedient to the control of that faculty of which it is the creation. For language is arbitrarily produced by the imagination, and has relation to thoughts alone; but all other materials, instruments, and conditions of art, have relations among each other, which limit and interpose between conception and expression. The former is as a mirror which reflects, the latter as a cloud which enfeebles, the light of which both are mediums of communication. . . .

Poets are the hierophants of an unapprehended inspiration; the mirrors of the gigantic shadows which futurity casts upon the present; the words which express what they understand not; the trumpets which sing to battle, and feel not what they inspire; the influence which is moved not, but moves. Poets are the unacknowledged legislators of the world.

from "A Defence of Poetry"

EDGAR ALLAN POE

[1809–1849]

True Poetry

I hold that a long poem does not exist. I maintain that the phrase, "a long poem," is simply a flat contradiction in terms.

I need scarcely observe that a poem deserves its title only inasmuch as it excites, by elevating the soul. The value of the poem is in the ratio of this elevating excitement. But all excitements are, through a psychal necessity, transient. That degree of excitement which would entitle a poem to be so called at all, cannot be sustained throughout a composition of any great length. After the lapse of half an hour, at the very utmost, it flags—fails—a revulsion ensues—and then the poem is, in effect, and in fact, no longer such.

There are, no doubt, many who have found difficulty in reconciling the critical dictum that the "Paradise Lost" is to be devoutly admired throughout, with the absolute impossibility of maintaining for it, during perusal, the amount of enthusiasm which that critical dictum would demand. This great work, in fact, is to be regarded as poetical, only when, losing sight of that vital requisite in all works of Art, Unity, we view it merely as a series of minor poems. If, to preserve its Unity—its totality of effect or impression—we read it (as would be necessary) at a single sitting, the result is but a constant alternation of excitement and depression. After a passage of what we feel to be true poetry, there follows, inevitably, a passage of platitude which no critical prejudgment can force us to admire; but if, upon completing the work, we read it again; omitting the first book—that is to say, commencing with the second—we shall be surprised at now finding that admirable which we before condemned—that damnable which we had previously so much admired. It follows from all this that the ultimate, aggregate, or absolute effect of even the best epic under the sun, is a nullity:—and this is precisely the fact. . . .

On the other hand, it is clear that a poem may be improperly brief. Undue brevity degenerates into mere epigrammatism. A *very* short poem, while now and then producing a brilliant or vivid, never produces a profound or enduring effect. There must be the steady pressing down of the stamp upon the wax.

from "The Poetic Principle"

The Single Effect

The tale proper, in our opinion, affords unquestionably the fairest field for the exercise of the loftiest talent, which can be afforded by the wide domains of mere prose. Were we bidden to say how the highest genius could be most advantageously employed for the best display of its own powers, we should answer, without hesitation—in the composition of a rhymed poem, not to exceed in length what might be perused in an hour. Within this limit alone can the highest order of true poetry exist. We need only here say, upon this topic, that, in almost all classes of composition, the unity of effect or impression is a point of the greatest importance. It is clear, moreover, that this unity cannot be thoroughly preserved in productions whose perusal cannot be completed at one sitting. We may continue the reading of a prose composition, from the very nature of prose itself, much longer than we can persevere, to any good purpose, in the perusal of a poem. This latter, if truly fulfilling the demands of the poetic sentiment, induces an exaltation of the soul which cannot be long sustained. All high excitements are necessarily transient. Thus a long poem is a paradox. And, without unity of impression, the deepest effects cannot be brought about. Epics were the offspring of an imperfect sense of Art, and their reign is no more. A poem *too* brief may produce a vivid, but never an intense or enduring impression. Without a certain continuity of effort—without a certain duration or repetition of purpose—the soul is never deeply moved. There must be the dropping of the water upon the rock. . . .

Were we called upon, however, to designate that class of composition which, next to such a poem as we have suggested, should best fulfill the demands of high genius—should offer it the most advantageous field of exertion—we should unhesitatingly speak of the prose tale, as Mr. Hawthorne has here exemplified it. We allude to the short prose narrative, requiring from a half-hour to one or two hours in its perusal. The ordinary novel is objectionable, from its length, for reasons already stated in substance. As it cannot be read at one sitting, it deprives itself, of course, of the immense force derivable from *totality*. Worldly interests intervening during the pauses of perusal, modify, annul, or counteract, in a greater or less degree, the impressions of the book. But simple cessation in reading would, of itself, be sufficient to destroy the true unity. In the brief tale, however, the author is enabled to carry out the fullness of his intention, be it what it may. During the hour of perusal the soul of the reader is at the writer's control. There are no external or extrinsic influences—resulting from weariness or interruption.

A skillful literary artist has constructed a tale. If wise, he has not fashioned his thoughts to accommodate his incidents; but having conceived, with deliberate care, a certain unique or single *effect* to be wrought out, he then invents such incidents—he then combines such events as may best aid him in establishing this preconceived effect. If his very initial sentence tends not to the outbringing of this effect, then he has failed in his first step. In the whole composition there should be no word written, of which the tendency, direct or indirect, is not to the one pre-established design. And by such means, with such care and skill, a picture is at length painted which leaves in the mind of him who contemplates it with a kindred art, a sense of the fullest satisfaction. The idea of the tale has been presented unblemished, because undisturbed; and this is an end unattainable by the novel. Undue brevity is just as exceptionable here as in the poem; but undue length is yet more to be avoided.

We have said that the tale has a point of superiority even over the poem. In fact, while the *rhythm* of this latter is an essential aid in the development of the poem's highest idea—the idea of the Beautiful—the artificialities of this rhythm are an inseparable bar to the development of all points of thought or expression which have their basis in *Truth*. But Truth is often, and in very great degree, the aim of the tale. Some of the finest tales are tales of ratiocination. Thus the field of this species of composition, if not in so elevated a region of the mountain of Mind, is a tableland of far vaster extent than the domain of the mere poem. Its products are never so rich, but infinitely more numerous, and more appreciable by the mass of mankind. The writer of the prose tale, in short, may bring to his theme a vast variety of modes or reflections of thought and expression—(the ratiocinative, for example, the sarcastic, or the humorous) which are not only antagonistical to the nature of the poem, but absolutely forbidden by one of its most peculiar and indispensable adjuncts; we allude, of course, to rhythm. It may be added, here, *par parenthèse,* that the author who aims at the purely beautiful in a prose tale is laboring at a great disadvantage. For Beauty can be better treated in the poem. Not so with terror, or passion, or horror, or a multitude of such other points.

from a review of Hawthorne's *Twice-Told Tales*

ANTON CHEKHOV

[*1860–1904*]

Technique in Writing the Short Story

TRANSLATED BY CONSTANCE GARNETT

In my opinion a true description of Nature should be very brief and have a character of relevance. Commonplaces such as, "the setting sun bathing in the waves of the darkening sea, poured its purple gold, etc."—"the swallows flying over the surface of the water twittered merrily"—such commonplaces one ought to abandon. In descriptions of Nature one ought to seize upon the little particulars, grouping them in such a way that, in reading, when you shut your eyes, you get a picture.

For instance, you will get the full effect of a moonlight night if you write that on the mill-dam a little glowing star-point flashed from the neck of a broken bottle, and the round, black shadow of a dog, or a wolf, emerged and ran, etc. Nature becomes animated if you are not squeamish about employing comparisons of her phenomena with ordinary human activities, etc.

In the sphere of psychology, details are also the thing. God preserve us from commonplaces. Best of all is it to avoid depicting the hero's state of mind; you ought to try to make it clear from the hero's actions. It is not necessary to portray many characters. The center of gravity should be in two persons: him and her.   (1886)

from a Letter to Alexander P. Chekhov

You abuse me for objectivity, calling it indifference to good and evil, lack of ideals and ideas, and so on. You would have me, when I describe horse-thieves, say: "Stealing horses is an evil." But that has been known for ages without my saying so. Let the jury judge them; it's my job simply to show what sort of people they are. I write: You are dealing with horse-thieves, so let me tell you that they are not beggars but well-fed people, that they are people of a special cult, and that horse-stealing is not simply theft but a passion. Of course it would be pleasant to combine art with a sermon, but for me personally it is extremely difficult and almost impossible, owing to the conditions of technique. You see, to depict horse-thieves in seven hundred lines I must all the time speak and think in their tone and feel in their spirit, otherwise, if I introduce subjectivity, the image becomes blurred and the story will not be as compact as all short stories ought to be. When I write, I reckon entirely upon the reader to add for himself the subjective elements that are lacking in the story. (1890)

from a Letter to Aleksey S. Suvorin

HENRIK IBSEN
[1828–1906]

Notes for the Modern Tragedy

TRANSLATED BY A. G. CHATER

There are two kinds of spiritual law, two kinds of conscience, one in man and another, altogether different, in woman. They do not understand each other; but in practical life the woman is judged by man's law, as though she were not a woman but a man.

The wife in the play ends by having no idea of what is right or wrong; natural feeling on the one hand and belief in authority on the other have altogether bewildered her.

A woman cannot be herself in the society of the present day, which is an exclusively masculine society, with laws framed by men and with a judicial system that judges feminine conduct from a masculine point of view.

She has committed forgery, and she is proud of it; for she did it out of love for her husband, to save his life. But this husband with his commonplace principles of honor is on the side of the law and looks at the question from the masculine point of view.

Spiritual conflicts. Oppressed and bewildered by the belief in authority, she loses faith in her moral right and ability to bring up her children. Bitterness. A mother in modern society, like certain insects who go away and die when she has done her duty in the propagation of the race. Love of life, of home, of husband and children and family. Now and then a womanly shaking off of her thoughts. Sudden return of anxiety and terror. She must bear it all alone. The catastrophe approaches, inexorably, inevitably. Despair, conflict, and destruction.

GERARD MANLEY HOPKINS

[1844–1889]

Sprung Rhythm

I had long had haunting my ear the echo of a new rhythm which now I realised on paper. To speak shortly, it consists in scanning by accents or stresses alone, without any account of the number of syllables, so that a foot may be one strong syllable or it may be many light and one strong. I do not say the idea is altogether new; there are hints of it in music, in nursery rhymes and popular jingles, in the poets themselves, and, since then, I have seen it talked about as a thing possible in critics. Here are instances— *"Díng, dóng, béll; Pússy's ín the wéll; Whó pút her ín? Líttle Jóhnny Thín. Whó púlled her óut? Líttle Jóhnny Stóut."* For if each line has three stresses or three feet it follows that some of the feet are of one syllable only. So too *'Óne, twó,* Búckle my shóe' *passim.* In Campbell you have "Ánd their fléet alóng the *déep próudly* shóne"—"Ít was tén of Ápril *mórn bý* the chíme" etc; in Shakspere "Whý shd. *thís* désert bé?" corrected wrongly by the editors; in Moore a little melody I cannot quote; etc. But no one has professedly used it and made it the principle throughout, that I know of. Nevertheless to me it appears, I own, to be a better and more natural principle than the ordinary system, much more flexible, and capable of much greater effects. However I had to mark the stresses in blue chalk, and this and my rhymes carried on from one line into another and certain chimes suggested by the Welsh poetry I had been reading (what they call *cynghanedd*) and a great many more oddnesses could not but dismay an editor's eye, so that when I offered it to our magazine the *Month,* though at first they accepted it, after a time they withdrew and dared not print it. After writing this I held myself free to compose, but cannot find it in my conscience to spend time upon it; so I have done little and shall do less. But I wrote a shorter piece on the Eurydice, also in "sprung rhythm," as I call it, but simpler, shorter, and without marks, and offered the *Month* that too, but they did not like it either. Also I have written some sonnets and a few other little things; some in sprung rhythm, with various other experiments—as "outriding feet," that is parts of which do not count in the scanning (such as you find in Shakespere's later plays, but as a licence, whereas mine are rather calculated effects); others in the ordinary scanning *counterpointed* (this is counterpoint: *"Hóme to* his móther's hóuse *prívate* retúrned" and *"Bút to vánquish* by wísdom héllish wíles"* etc); others, one or two, in common uncounterpointed rhythm.

AUGUST STRINDBERG

[1849–1912]

The Scene

TRANSLATED BY BORGE GEDSO MADSEN

A scene, a *quart d'heure,* seems to be the type of play preferred by modern theatregoers, and it has an old history. For it can name as its origin (yes, why not?) the Greek tragedy which contains a concentrated event in a single act, if we regard the trilogy as three separate plays. But if we do not want to go way back to Paradise, we have in the eighteenth century a gentleman called Carmontelle, who was the first to cultivate on a large scale the genre he named *Proverbes Dramatiques,* of which he published ten volumes and is supposed to have left a hundred more in manuscript. The genre was later developed by Leclerq, attained its highest perfection in Musset's and Feuillet's well-known masterpieces—and more recently in Henry Becque's *La Navette* to form the transition to the fully executed one-act play which may become the formula for the drama to come.

In the proverb one got the gist of the matter, the whole dénoucment, the battle of the souls, sometimes approaching tragedy in Musset, without having to be bothered by the clanging of arms or processions of supernumeraries. By means of a table and two chairs one could present the most powerful conflicts life has to offer; and in this type of art all the discoveries of modern psychology could, for the first time, be applied in popularized form.

BERNARD SHAW

[1856–1950]

The Interpreter of Life

The great dramatist has something better to do than to amuse either himself or his audience. He has to interpret life. This sounds a mere pious phrase of literary criticism; but a moment's consideration will discover its meaning and its exactitude. Life as it appears to us in our daily experience is an unintelligible chaos of happenings. You pass Othello in the bazaar in Aleppo, Iago on the jetty in Cyprus, and Desdemona in the nave of St. Mark's in Venice without the slightest clue to their relations to one another. The man you see stepping into a chemist's shop to buy the means of committing murder or suicide, may, for all you know, want nothing but a liver pill or a toothbrush. The statesman who has no other object than to make you vote for his party at the next election, may be starting you on an incline at the foot of which lies war, or revolution, or a smallpox epidemic or five years off your lifetime. The horrible murder of a whole family by the father who finishes by killing himself, or the driving of a young girl on to the streets, may be the result of your discharging an employee in a fit of temper a month before. To attempt to understand life from merely looking on at it as it happens in the streets is as hopeless as trying to understand public questions by studying snapshots of public demonstrations. If we possessed a series of cinematographs of all the executions during the Reign of Terror, they might be exhibited a thousand times without enlightening the audiences in the least as to the meaning of the Revolution: Robespierre would perish as "un monsieur" and Marie Antoinette as "une femme." Life as it occurs is senseless: a policeman may watch it and work in it for thirty years in the streets and courts of Paris without learning as much of it or from it as a child or a nun may learn from a single play by Brieux. For it is the business of Brieux to pick out the significant incidents from the chaos of daily happenings, and arrange them so that their relation to one another becomes significant, thus changing us from bewildered spectators of a monstrous confusion to men intelligently conscious of the world and its destinies. This is the highest function that man can perform—the greatest work he can set his hand to; and this is why the great dramatists of the world, from Euripides and Aristophanes to Shakespear and Molière, and from them to Ibsen and Brieux, take that majestic and pontifical rank which seems so strangely above all the reasonable pretensions of mere strolling actors and theatrical authors.

ROBERT FROST

[1874–1963]

Poetry, Delight, and Wisdom

It should be of the pleasure of a poem itself to tell how it can. The figure a poem makes. It begins in delight and ends in wisdom. The figure is the same as for love. No one can really hold that the ecstasy should be static and stand still in one place. It begins in delight, it inclines to the impulse, it assumes direction with the first line laid down, it runs a course of lucky events, and ends in a clarification of life—not necessarily a great clarification, such as sects and cults are founded on, but in a momentary stay against confusion. It has denouement. It has an outcome that though unforeseen was predestined from the first image of the original mood—and indeed from the very mood. It is but a trick poem and no poem at all if the best of it was thought of first and saved for the last. It finds its own name as it goes and discovers the best waiting for it in some final phrase at once wise and sad—the happy-sad blend of the drinking song.

No tears in the writer, no tears in the reader. No surprise for the writer, no surprise for the reader. For me the initial delight is in the surprise of remembering something I didn't know I knew. I am in a place, in a situation, as if I had materialized from cloud or risen out of the ground. There is a glad recognition of the long lost and the rest follows. Step by step the wonder of unexpected supply keeps growing. The impressions most useful to my purpose seem always those I was unaware of and so made no note of at the time when taken, and the conclusion is come to that like giants we are always hurling experience ahead of us to pave the future with against the day when we may want to strike a line of purpose across it for somewhere. The line will have the more charm for not being mechanically straight. We enjoy the straight crookedness of a good walking stick. Modern instruments of precision are being used to make things crooked as if by eye and hand in the old days. . . .

More than once I should have lost my soul to radicalism if it had been the originality it was mistaken for by its young converts. Originality and initiative are what I ask for my country. For myself the originality need be no more than the freshness of a poem run in the way I have described: from delight to wisdom. The figure is the same as for love. Like a piece of ice on a hot stove the poem must ride on its own melting. A poem may be worked over once it is in being, but may not be worried into being. Its most previous quality will remain its having run itself and carried away the poet with it. Read it a hundred times: it will forever keep its freshness as a metal keeps its fragrance. It can never lose its sense of a meaning that once unfolded by surprise as it went.

from "The Figure a Poem Makes"

WALLACE STEVENS
[1879–1955]

Observations on Poetry

Literature is the better part of life. To this it seems inevitably necessary to add, provided life is the better part of literature.

•

After one has abandoned a belief in God, poetry is that essence which takes its place as life's redemption.

•

Accuracy of observation is the equivalent of accuracy of thinking.

•

The relation of art to life is of the first importance especially in a skeptical age since, in the absence of a belief in God, the mind turns to its own creations and examines them, not alone from the aesthetic point of view, but for what they reveal, for what they validate and invalidate, for the support that they give.

What we see in the mind is as real to us as what we see by the eye.

One reads poetry with one's nerves.

Every poem is a poem within a poem: the poem of the idea within the poem of the words.

Poetry is the gaiety (joy) of language.

To be at the end of fact is not to be at the beginning of imagination but it is to be at the end of both.

There is a nature that absorbs the mixedness of metaphors.

Imagination applied to the whole world is vapid in comparison to imagination applied to a detail.

Poetry is a response to the daily necessity of getting the world right.

from "Adagia"

T. S. ELIOT

[1888–1965]

The Poet and the Tradition

Tradition is a matter of much wider significance. It cannot be inherited, and if you want it you must obtain it by great labour. It involves, in the first place, the historical sense, which we may call nearly indispensable to anyone who would continue to be a poet beyond his twenty-fifth year; and the historical sense involves a perception, not only of the pastness of the past, but of its presence; the historical sense compels a man to write not merely with his own generation in his bones, but with a feeling that the whole of the literature of Europe from Homer and within it the whole of the literature of his own country has a simultaneous existence and composes a simultaneous order. This historical sense, which is a sense of the timeless as well as of the temporal and of the timeless and of the temporal together, is what makes a writer traditional. And it is at the same time what makes a writer most acutely conscious of his place in time, of his contemporaneity.

No poet, no artist of any art, has his complete meaning alone. His significance, his appreciation is the appreciation of his relation to the dead poets and artists. You cannot value him alone; you must set him, for contrast and comparison, among the dead. I mean this as a principle of aelsthetic, not merely historical, criticism. The necessity that he shall conform, that he shall cohere, is not one-sided; what happens when a new work of art is created is something that happens simultaneously to all the works of art which preceded it. The existing monuments form an ideal order among themselves, which is modified by the introduction of the new (the really new) work of art among them. The existing order is complete before the new work arrives; for order to persist after the supervention of novelty, the *whole* existing order must be, if ever so slightly, altered; and so the relations, proportions, values of each work of art toward the whole are readjusted; and this is conformity between the old and the new. Whoever has approved this idea of order, of the form of European, of English literature, will not find it preposterous that the past should be altered by the present as much as the present is directed by the past. And the poet who is aware of this will be aware of great difficulties and responsibilities.

   In a peculiar sense he will be aware also that he must inevitably be judged by the standards of the past. I say judged, not amputated, by them; not judged to be as good as, or worse or better than, the dead; and certainly not judged by the canons of dead critics. It is a judgment, a comparison, in which two things are measured by each other. To conform merely would be for the new work not really to conform at all; it would not be new, and would therefore not be a work of art.

from "Tradition and the Individual Talent"

BERTOLT BRECHT

[1898–1956]

Brecht on Theatre

TRANSLATED BY JOHN WILLETT

(1)

"Theatre" consists in this: in making live representations of reported or invented happenings between human beings and doing so with a view to entertainment. At any rate that is what we shall mean when we speak of theatre, whether old or new.

(2)

To extend this definition we might add happenings between humans and gods, but as we are only seeking to establish the minimum we can set such matters aside. Even if we did accept such an extension we should still have to say that the "theatre" setup's broadest function was to give pleasure. It is the noblest function that we have found for "theatre."

(3)

From the first it has been the theatre's business to entertain people, as it also has of all the other arts. It is this business which always gives it its particular dignity; it needs no other passport than fun, but this it has got to have. We should not by any means be giving it a higher status if we were to turn it, e.g., into a purveyor of morality; it would on the contrary run the risk of being debased, and this would occur at once if it failed to make its moral lesson enjoyable, and enjoyable to the senses at that: a principle, admittedly, by which morality can only gain. Not even instruction can be demanded of it: at any rate, no more utilitarian lesson than how to move pleasurably, whether in the physical or in the spiritual sphere. The theatre must in fact remain something entirely superfluous, though this indeed means that it is the superfluous for which we live. Nothing needs less justification than pleasure.

(4)

Thus what the ancients, following Aristotle, demanded of tragedy is nothing higher or lower than that it should entertain people. Theatre may be said to be derived from ritual, but that is only to say that it becomes theatre once the two have separated; what it brought over from the mysteries was not its former ritual function, but purely and simply the pleasure which accompanied this. And the catharsis of which Aristotle writes—cleansing by fear and pity, or from fear and pity—is a purification which is performed not only in a pleasurable way, but precisely for the purpose of pleasure. To ask or to accept more of the theatre is to set one's own mark too low.

GEORGE SEFERIS

[1900–1971]

Poetry and Human Living

TRANSLATED BY A. GAGNOSTOPOULOS

Among the many ways that there are to study poets, the simplest, it seems to me, is the best: to look at what their works show us. And it is not improbable that they show things which we were looking for; "which we would not have sought if we had not found them already," as someone else says; or, to remember the ancient sage, "knowledge is memory." Thus, poets complement us and we complement them. I do not intend to advise arbitrariness when we read poems. A poem is not reason enough for us to unleash our imagination in reckless wanderings. Rather, what I want to say is this: that poets, if their poetry is good, draw on a deep-rooted experience of life, which all of us, young and old, have within ourselves; how much we feel this, I don't know. These are the roots through which they communicate with us. What forms, what vestments this common experience, this common feeling of life, will take in a historical moment no one can tell. It depends, I think, not only upon the idiosyncrasy of the individual who expresses himself but also upon many intellectual, social, and political mores of the time. A poem written from a purely erotic impulse may become in another era the expression of the feeling of human humiliation, of deceit, of degradation, because the era in some way has brought such sentiments to the surface; it has made them, let's say, public. And the praise of a rose or a ray of sunlight may convey the impression of human grandeur at moments when human grandeur flashes like lightning, as Solomos would say. These variations, as time passes, indicate that poems are alive and are nourished; they have the power to complement us and they ask us to complement them. If poetry were not sustained by this kind of human solidarity, in this human community, it wouldn't have lived very long. Poetry does not express truths in the scientific meaning of the word, nor does it discover philosophies and life theories. It uses science *and* the philosophy of others, if it needs them. Poetry is not for personal confessions; if it makes them, it is not they that save it. It does not try to express the personality of the poets, but, as Eliot has written, tries rather to abolish it. But in doing this, it expresses another personality that belongs to everyone; whosoever loses his life will find it, the Gospel says. Thus, let us not ask from the poet, in order to understand him, the petty, everyday details of his life which we think he is expressing. These petty events, if they have become poetry, are events belonging to you and me, and to those who have gone before, and to those who will come after us. If it were not so, poetry would not exist. You can make the experiment yourselves. Read a rhapsody of Homer and see if whether, at the parts that move you, what you feel is merely an archaeological reference alone, or if perhaps it is a sentiment nurtured by all the human experience that has occurred from that ancient era down to your present moment.

from A Poet's Journal

FRANK O'CONNOR
[1903–1966]

Lyric Poetry and the Short Story

INTERVIEWER: Why do you prefer the short story for your medium?

O'CONNOR: Because it's the nearest thing I know to lyric poetry—I wrote lyric poetry for a long time, then discovered that God had not intended me to be a lyric poet, and the nearest thing to that is the short story. A novel actually requires far more logic and far more knowledge of circumstances, whereas a short story can have the sort of detachment from circumstances that lyric poetry has. . . .

INTERVIEWER: What about working habits? How do you start a story?

O'CONNOR: "Get black on white" used to be Maupassant's advice—that's what I always do. I don't give a hoot what the writing's like, I write any sort of rubbish which will cover the main outlines of the story, then I can begin to see it. When I write, when I draft a story, I never think of writing nice sentences about, "It was a nice August evening when Elizabeth Jane Moriarty was coming down the road." I just write roughly what happened, and then I'm able to see what the construction looks like. It's the design of the story which to me is most important, the thing that tells you there's a bad gap in the narrative here and you really ought to fill that up in some way or another. I'm always looking at the design of the story, not the treatment. Yesterday I was finishing off a piece about my friend A. E. Coppard, the greatest of all the English storytellers, who died about a fortnight ago. I was describing the way Coppard must have written these stories, going around with a notebook, recording what the lighting looked like, what that house looked like, and all the time using metaphor to suggest it to himself, "The road looked like a mad serpent going up the hill," or something of the kind, and "She said so-and-so, and the man in the pub said something else." After he had written them all out, he must have got the outline of his story, and he'd start working in all the details. Now, I could never do that at all. I've got to see what these people did, first of all, and *then* I start thinking of whether it was a nice August evening or a spring evening. I have to wait for the theme before I can do anything.

PABLO NERUDA

[b. 1904]

"The Word"

TRANSLATED BY HARDI ST. MARTIN

. . . You can say anything you want, yessir, but it's the words that sing, they soar and descend . . . I bow to them . . . I love them, I cling to them, I run them down, I bite into them, I melt them down . . . I love words so much . . . The unexpected ones . . . The ones I wait for greedily or stalk until, suddenly, they drop . . . Vowels I love . . . They glitter like colored stones, they leap like silver fish, they are foam, thread, metal, dew . . . I run after certain words . . . They are so beautiful that I want to fit them all into my poem . . . I catch them in mid-flight, as they buzz past, I trap them, clean them, peel them, I set myself in front of the dish, they have a crystalline texture to me, vibrant, ivory, vegetable, oily, like fruit, like algae, like agates, like olives . . . And then I stir them, I shake them, I drink them, I gulp them down, I mash them, I garnish them, I let them go . . . I leave them in my poem like stalactites, like slivers of polished wood, like coals, pickings from a shipwreck, gifts from the waves . . . Everything exists in the word . . . An idea goes through a complete change because one word shifted its place, or because another settled down like a spoiled little thing inside a phrase that was not expecting her but obeys her . . . They have shadow, transparence, weight, feathers, hair, and everything they gathered

from so much rolling down the river, from so much wandering from country to country, from being roots so long . . . They are very ancient and very new . . . They live in the bier, hidden away, and in the budding flower . . . What a great language I have, it's a fine language we inherited from the fierce conquistadors . . . They strode over the giant cordilleras, over the rugged Americas, hunting for potatoes, sausages, beans, black tobacco, gold, corn, fried eggs, with a voracious appetite not found in the world since then . . . They swallowed up everything, religions, pyramids, tribes, idolatries just like the ones they brought along in their huge sacks . . . Wherever they went, they razed the land . . . But words fell like pebbles out of the boots of the barbarians, out of their beards, their helmets, their horseshoes, luminous words that were left glittering here . . . our language. We came up losers . . . We came up winners . . . They carried off the gold and left us the gold . . . They carried everything off and left us everything . . . They left us the words.

EUDORA WELTY
[b. 1909]
The Origin of a Story

The origin of a story is sometimes a trustworthy clue to the author—or can provide him with the clue—to its key image; maybe in this case it will do the same for the reader. One day I saw a solitary old woman like Phoenix. She was walking; I saw her, at middle distance, in a winter country landscape, and watched her slowly make her way across my line of vision. That sight of her made me write the story. I invented an errand for her, but that only seemed a living part of the figure she was herself: What errand other than for someone else could be making her go? And her going was the first thing, her persisting in her landscape was the real thing, and the first and the real were what I wanted and worked to keep. I brought her up close enough, by imagination, to describe her face, make her present to the eyes, but the full-length figure moving across the winter fields was the indelible one and the image to keep, and the perspective extending into the vanishing distance the true one to hold in mind.

I invented for my character, as I wrote, some passing adventures—some dreams and harassments and a small triumph or two, some jolts to her pride, some flights of fancy to console her, one or two encounters to scare her, a moment that gave her cause to feel ashamed, a moment to dance and preen—for it had to be a *journey*, and all these things belonged to that, parts of life's uncertainty.

A narrative line is in its deeper sense, of course, the tracing out of a meaning, and the real continuity of a story lies in this probing forward. The real dramatic force of a story depends on the strength of the emotion that has set it going. The emotional value is the measure of the reach of the story. What gives any such content to "A Worn Path" is not its circumstances but its *subject:* the deep-grained habit of love.

What I hoped would come clear was that in the whole surround of this story, the world it threads through, the only certain thing at all is the worn path. The habit of love cuts through confusion and stumbles or contrives its way out of difficulty, it remembers the way even when it forgets, for a dumfounded moment, its reason for being. The path is the thing that matters.

RALPH ELLISON

[b. 1914]

Folklore and Fiction

INTERVIEWER: Can you give us an example of the use of folklore in your own novel?

ELLISON: Well, there are certain themes, symbols, and images which are based on folk material. For example, there is the old saying amongst Negroes: If you're black, stay back; if you're brown, stick around; if you're white, you're right. And there is the joke Negroes tell on themselves about their being so black they can't be seen in the dark. In my book this sort of thing was merged with the meanings which blackness and light have long had in Western mythology: evil and goodness, ignorance and knowledge, and so on. In my novel the narrator's development is one through blackness to light; that is, from ignorance to enlightenment: invisibility to visibility. He leaves the South and goes North; this, as you will notice in reading Negro folktales, is always the road to freedom—the movement upward. You have the same thing again when he leaves his underground cave for the open.

It took me a long time to learn how to adapt such examples of myth into my work—also ritual. The use of ritual is equally a vital part of the creative process. I learned a few things from Eliot, Joyce, and Hemingway, but not how to adapt them. When I started writing, I knew that in both *The Waste Land*° and *Ulysses*° ancient myth and ritual were used to give form and significance to the material; but it took me a few years to realize that the myths and rites which we find functioning in our everyday lives could be used in the same way. In my first attempt at a novel—which I was unable to complete—I began by trying to manipulate the simple structural unities of *beginning, middle,* and *end,* but when I attempted to deal with the psychological strata—the images, symbols, and emotional configurations—of the experience at hand, I discovered that the unities were simply cool points of stability on which one could suspend the narrative line—but beneath the surface of apparently rational human relationships there seethed a chaos before which I was helpless. People rationalize what they shun or are incapable of dealing with; these superstitions and their rationalizations become ritual as they govern behavior. The rituals become so-

---

The Waste Land   *Long, extremely influential poem (1922) by T. S. Eliot (1888–1965).*   **Ulysses**   *Experimental novel (1922) by James Joyce (1882–1941).*

cial forms, and it is one of the functions of the artist to recognize them and raise them to the level of art.

I don't know whether I'm getting this over or not. Let's put it this way: Take the "Battle Royal" passage in my novel, where the boys are blindfolded and forced to fight each other for the amusement of the white observers. This is a vital part of behavior pattern in the South, which both Negroes and whites thoughtlessly accept. It is a ritual in preservation of caste lines, a keeping of taboo to appease the gods and ward off bad luck. It is also the initiation ritual to which all greenhorns are subjected. This passage which states what Negroes will see I did not have to invent; the patterns were already there in society, so that all I had to do was present them in a broader context of meaning. In any society there are many rituals of situation which, for the most part, go unquestioned. They can be simple or elaborate, but they are the connective tissue between the work of art and the audience.

OCTAVIO PAZ

[b. 1914]

The Power of Poetry

TRANSLATED BY HELEN LANE

The operative mode of poetic thought is imagining, and imagination consists, essentially, of the ability to place contrary or divergent realities in relationship. All poetic forms and all linguistic figures have one thing in common: They seek, and often find, hidden resemblances. In the most extreme cases, they unite opposites. Comparisons, analogies, metaphors, metonymies and the other devices of poetry—all tend to produce images in which this and that, the one and the other, the one and the many are joined. The poetic process conceives of language as an animated universe traversed by a dual current of attraction and repulsion. In language, the unions and the divisions, the love affairs and the separations of stars, cells, atoms and men are reproduced. Each poem, whatever its subject and form and the ideas that shape it, is first and foremost a miniature animated cosmos. The poem unites the "ten thousand things that make up the universe," as the ancient Chinese put it. . . .

The relationship between man and poetry is as old as our history: it began when human beings began to be human. The first hunters and gatherers looked at themselves in astonishment one day, for an interminable instant, in the still waters of a poem. Since that moment, people have not stopped looking at themselves in this mirror. And they have seen themselves, at one and the same time, as creators of images and as images of their creations. For that reason I can say, with a modicum of certainty, that as long as there are people there will be poetry. The relationship, however, may be broken. Born of the human imagination, it may die if imagination dies or is corrupted. If human beings forget poetry, they will forget themselves. And return to original chaos.

ARTHUR MILLER

[b. 1915]

Tragedy and the Common Man

In this age few tragedies are written. It has often been held that the lack is due to a paucity of heroes among us, or else that modern man has had the blood drawn out of his organs of belief by the skepticism of science, and the heroic attack on life cannot feed on an attitude of reserve and circumspection. For one reason or another, we are often held to be below tragedy—or tragedy above us. The inevitable conclusion is, of course, that the tragic mode is archaic, fit only for the very highly placed, the kings or the kingly, and where this admission is not made in so many words it is most often implied.

I believe that the common man is as apt a subject for tragedy in its highest sense as kings were. On the face of it this ought to be obvious in the light of modern psychiatry, which bases its analysis upon classic formulations, such as the Oedipus and Orestes complexes, for instance, which were enacted by royal beings, but which apply to everyone in similar emotional situations.

More simply, when the question of tragedy in art is not at issue, we never hesitate to attribute to the well-placed and the exalted the very same mental processes as the lowly. And finally, if the exaltation of tragic action were truly a property of the high-bred character alone, it is inconceivable that the mass of mankind should cherish tragedy above all other forms, let alone be capable of understanding it.

As a general rule, to which there may be exceptions unknown to me, I think the tragic feeling is evoked in us when we are in the presence of a character who is ready to lay down his life, if need be, to secure one thing—his sense of personal dignity. From Orestes to Hamlet, Medea to Macbeth, the underlying struggle is that of the individual attempting to gain his "rightful" position in his society.

Sometimes he is one who has been displaced from it, sometimes one who seeks to attain it for the first time, but the fateful wound from which the inevitable events spiral is the wound of indignity, and its dominant force is indignation. Tragedy, then, is the consequence of a man's total compulsion to evaluate himself justly.

In the sense of having been initiated by the hero himself, the tale always reveals what has been called his "tragic flaw," a failing that is not peculiar to grand or elevated characters. Nor is it necessarily a weakness. The flaw, or crack in the character, is really nothing—and need be nothing—but his inherent unwillingness to remain passive in the face of what he conceives to be a challenge to his dignity, his image of his rightful status. Only the passive, only those who accept their lot without active retaliation, are "flawless." Most of us are in that category.

But there are among us today, as there always have been, those who act against the scheme of things that degrades them, and in the process of action, everything we have accepted out of fear or insensitivity or ignorance is shaken before us and examined, and from this total onslaught by an individual against the seemingly stable cosmos surrounding us—from this total examination of the "unchangeable" environment—comes the terror and the fear that is classically associated with tragedy.

More important, from this total questioning of what has been previously unquestioned, we learn. And such a process is not beyond the common man. In revolutions around the world, these past thirty years, he has demonstrated again and again this inner dynamic of all tragedy.

Insistence upon the rank of the tragic hero, or the so-called nobility of his character, is really but a clinging to the outward forms of tragedy. If rank or nobility of character was indispensable, then it would follow that the problems of those with rank were the particular problems of tragedy. But surely the right of one monarch to capture the domain from another no longer raises our passions, nor are our concepts of justice what they were to the mind of an Elizabethan king.

The quality in such plays that does shake us, however, derives from the underlying fear of being displaced, the disaster inherent in being torn away from our chosen image of what and who we are in this world. Among us today this fear is as strong, and perhaps stronger, than it ever was. In fact, it is the common man who knows this fear best.

Now, if it is true that tragedy is the consequence of a man's total compulsion to evaluate himself justly, his destruction in the attempt posits a wrong or an evil in his environment. And this is precisely the morality of tragedy and its lesson. The discovery of the moral law, which is what the enlightenment of tragedy consists of, is not the discovery of some abstract or metaphysical quantity.

The tragic right is a condition of life, a condition in which the human personality is able to flower and realize itself. The wrong is the condition which suppresses man, perverts the flowing out of his love and creative instinct. Tragedy enlightens—and it must, in that it points the heroic finger at the enemy of man's freedom. The thrust for freedom is the quality in tragedy which exalts. The revolutionary questioning of the stable environment is what terrifies. In no way is the common man debarred from such thoughts or such actions.

Seen in this light, our lack of tragedy may be partially accounted for by the turn which modern literature has taken toward the purely psychiatric view of life, or the purely sociological. If all our miseries, our indignities, are born and bred within our minds, then all action, let alone the heroic action, is obviously impossible.

And if society alone is responsible for the cramping of our lives, then the protagonist must needs be so pure and faultless as to force us to deny his validity as a character. From neither of these views can tragedy derive, simply because neither represents a balanced concept of life. Above all else, tragedy requires the finest appreciation by the writer of cause and effect.

No tragedy can therefore come about when its author fears to question absolutely everything, when he regards any institution, habit, or custom as being either everlasting, immutable, or inevitable. In the tragic view the need of man to wholly realize himself is the only fixed star, and whatever it is that hedges his nature and lowers it is ripe for attack and examination. Which is not to say that tragedy must preach revolution.

The Greeks could probe the very heavenly origin of their ways and return to confirm the rightness of laws. And Job could face God in anger, demanding his right, and end in submission. But for a moment everything is in suspension, nothing is accepted, and in this stretching and tearing apart of the cosmos, in the very action of so doing, the character gains "size," the tragic stature which is spuriously attached to the royal or the high born in our minds. The commonest of men may take on that stature to the extent of his willingness to throw all he has into the contest, the battle to secure his rightful place in his world.

There is a misconception of tragedy with which I have been struck in review after review, and in many conversations with writers and readers alike. It is the idea that tragedy is of necessity allied to pessimism. Even the dictionary says nothing more about the word than that it means a story with a sad or unhappy ending. This impression is so firmly fixed that I almost hesitate to claim that in truth tragedy implies more optimism in its author than does comedy, and that its final result ought to be the reinforcement of the onlooker's brightest opinions of the human animal.

For, if it is true to say that in essence the tragic hero is intent upon claiming his whole due as a personality, and if this struggle must be total and without reservation, then it automatically demonstrates the indestructible will of man to achieve his humanity.

The possibility of victory must be there in tragedy. Where pathos rules, where pathos is finally derived, a character has fought a battle he could not possibly have won. The pathetic is achieved when the protagonist is, by virtue of his witlessness, his insensitivity, or the very air he gives off, incapable of grappling with a much superior force.

Pathos truly is the mode for the pessimist. But tragedy requires a nicer balance between what is possible and what is impossible. And it is curious, although edifying, that the plays we revere, century after century, are the tragedies. In them, and in them alone, lies the belief—optimistic, if you will—in the perfectibility of man.

It is time, I think, that we who are without kings, took up this bright thread of our history and followed it to the only place it can possibly lead in our time—the heart and spirit of the average man.

ERIC BENTLEY

[b. 1916]

On Drama as Literature and Performance

Is a play complete without performance? The question has been answered with equal vehemence in both the affirmative and the negative. The choice goes by temperamental preference: "literary" persons believe in the unaided script; "theatrical" persons believe in performance. Both are right. A good play leads a double existence, and is a complete "personality" in both its lives. When a theatrical person says a play has been misinterpreted in performance, he is certainly implying that a play is *there* and has its integrity before the interpreters touch it. As for literary persons, their conces-sion that a play does have another life as well as that of the book is to be found, if nowhere else, in their dismissal of bits they don't like as "merely theatrical." In other words, their position really is not that the theatrical dimension doesn't exist but that they wish it didn't.

Each group is trying to make a virtue of its own *déformation professionelle.* Theatrical people have their limitations as interpreters of literature. Literary people have theirs as interpreters of theater. If we can avoid the blindnesses of both parties, the only real problem lies in understanding the *difference* between script-alone and script-as-performed, for any given passage may have a different import in the two different con-texts. Finally, one is not forced into any choice between literature and theater, and to know *Hamlet,* or any great play, should be to know it from stage and study, both. A fine performance will never fail to throw light on at least an aspect of the play, while even the best reading in the study will fall far short of embracing all its aspects.

The question whether one should prefer to read or to see a play is best answered pragmatically. If one can read well to oneself, one will hardly prefer to go and see a mediocre performance. But, for anyone capable of relishing theater—and that includes more people than know it—even though the written script has its own completeness, there is no pleasure to top that of seeing a dramatic masterpiece masterfully performed. What is added means so much in such an immediate, sensuous way. If plot, character-ization, and dialogue give body to the theme, and transform thought into wisdom, and a view into a vision, adequate performance helps them to do so in various ways but above all by adding that final and conclusive concretion, the living actor.

from "Enactment" in The Life of the Drama

MARTIN ESSLIN

[*b. 1918*]

The Theater of the Absurd

The Theater of the Absurd shows the world as an incomprehensible place. The spec-tators see the happenings on the stage entirely from the outside, without ever un-derstanding the full meaning of these strange patterns of events, as newly arrived vis-itors might watch life in a country of which they have not yet mastered the language. The confrontation of the audience with characters and happenings which they are not quite able to comprehend makes it impossible for them to share the aspirations and emotions depicted in the play. Brecht's famous "Verfremdungseffekt" (alienation effect), the inhibition of any identification between spectator and actor, which Brecht could never successfully achieve in his own highly rational theater, really comes into its own in the Theater of the Absurd. It is impossible to identify oneself with characters one does not understand or whose motives remain a closed book, and so the distance between the public and the happenings on the stage can be maintained. Emotional identification with the characters is replaced by a puzzled, critical attention. For while the happenings on the stage are absurd, they yet remain recognizable as somehow related to real life with *its* absurdity, so that eventually the spectators are brought face to face with the irrational side of their existence. Thus, the absurd and fantastic goings-on of the Theater of the Absurd will, in the end, be found to reveal the irrationality of the human condition and the illusion of what we thought was its apparent logical structure.

If the dialogue in these plays consists of meaningless clichés and the mechanical, circular repetition of stereotyped phrases—how many meaningless clichés and stereotyped phrases do we use in our day-to-day conversation? If the characters change their personality halfway through the action, how consistent and truly integrated are the people we meet in our real life? And if people in these plays appear as mere marionettes, helpless puppets without any will of their own, passively at the mercy of blind fate and meaningless circumstance, do we, in fact, in our overorganized world, still possess any genuine initiative or power to decide our own destiny? The spectators of the Theater of the Absurd are thus confronted with a grotesquely heightened picture of their own world: a world without faith, meaning, and genuine freedom of will. In this sense, the Theater of the Absurd is the true theater of our time.

WENDELL BERRY

[b. 1934]

Poetry and Song

Song is natural; we have it in common with animals. For humans, it is also artificial and traditional; it has to be made by someone who knows how to make it and sung to someone who will recognize it as song. Rhythm, fundamental to it, is its profoundest *reference*. The rhythm of a song or a poem rises, no doubt, in reference to the pulse and breath of the poet, as is often said, but that is still too specialized an accounting; it rises also in reference to daily and seasonal—and surely even longer—rhythms in the life of the poet and in the life that surrounds him. The rhythm of a poem resonates with these larger rhythms that surround it; it fills its environment with sympathetic vibrations. Rhyme, which is a function of rhythm, may suggest this sort of resonance; it marks the coincidences of smaller structures with larger ones, as when the day, the month, and the year all end at the same moment. Song, then, is a force opposed to specialty and to isolation. It is the testimony of the singer's inescapable relation to the world, to the human community, and also to tradition.

AUDRE LORDE

[*b. 1934*]

Poems Are Not Luxuries

For women, then, poetry is not a luxury. It is a vital necessity of our existence. It forms the quality of the light within which we predicate our hopes and dreams toward survival and change, first made into language, then into idea, then into more tangible action. Poetry is the way we help give name to the nameless so it can be thought. The farthest external horizons of our hopes and fears are cobbled by our poems, carved from the rock experiences of our daily lives.

As they become known and accepted to ourselves, our feelings, and the honest exploration of them, become sanctuaries and fortresses and spawning grounds for the most radical and daring of ideas, the house of difference so necessary to change and the conceptualization of any meaningful action. Right now, I could name at least ten ideas I would once have found intolerable or incomprehensible and frightening, except as they came after dreams and poems. This is not idle fantasy, but the true meaning of "It feels right to me." We can train ourselves to respect our feelings and to discipline (transpose) them into a language that catches those feelings so they can be shared. And where that language does not yet exist, it is our poetry which helps to fashion it. Poetry is not only dream or vision, it is the skeleton architecture of our lives.

MARK STRAND

[*b. 1934*]

Poetry, Language, and Meaning

What is known in a poem is its language, that is, the words it uses. Yet those words seem different in a poem. Even the most familiar will seem strange. In a poem, each word, being equally important, exists in absolute focus, having a weight it rarely achieves in fiction. (Some notable exceptions can be found in the works of Joyce, Beckett, and Virginia Woolf.) Words in a novel are subordinate to broad slices of action or characterization that push the plot forward. In a poem, they *are* the action. That is why poems establish themselves right away—in a line or two—and why experienced readers of poetry can tell immediately if the poem they are reading possesses any authority. On the other hand, it would be hard to know much about a novel on the basis of its first sentence. We usually give it a dozen or so pages to earn its right to our attention.

And, paradoxically, it has our attention when its language has all but disappeared into the events it generated. We are much more comfortable reading a novel when we don't feel distracted by its language. What we want while reading a novel is to get on with it. A poem works the opposite way. It encourages slowness, urges us to savor each word. It is in poetry that the power of language is most palpably felt. . . . Poetry is language performing at its most beguiling and seductive while being, at the same time, elusive, even seeming to mock one's desire for reduction, for plain and available order. It is not just that various meanings are preferable to a single dominant meaning; it may be that something beyond "meaning" is being communicated, something that originated not with the poet but in the first dim light of language, in some period of "beforeness." It may be, therefore, that reading poetry is often a search for the unknown, something that lies at the heart of experience but cannot be pointed out or described without being altered or diminished—something that nevertheless can be contained so that is it not so terrifying. It is not knowledge, at least not as I conceive knowledge, but rather some occasion for belief, some reason for assent, some avowal of being. It is not knowledge because it is never revealed. It is mysterious or opaque, and even as it invites the reader, it wards him off. This unknown can make him uncomfortable, force him to do things that would make it seem less strange; and this usually means inventing a context in which to set it, something that counteracts the disembodiedness of the poem. As I have suggested, it may have to do with the origin of the poem—out of what dark habitation it emerged. The contexts we construct in our own defense may shed some light, may even explain parts or features of the poem, but they will never replace it in the wholeness of its utterance. Despite its power to enchant, the poem will always resist all but partial meanings.

MARGARET ATWOOD

[b. 1939]

Our First Stories

Our first stories come to us through the air. We hear voices.

Children in oral societies grow up within a web of stories; but so do all children. We listen before we can read. Some of our listening is more like listening in, to the calamitous or seductive voices of the adult world, on the radio or the television or in our daily lives. Often it's an overhearing of things we aren't supposed to hear, eavesdropping on scandalous gossip or family secrets. From all these scraps of voices, from the whispers and shouts that surround us, even from the ominous silences, the unfilled gaps in meaning, we patch together for ourselves an order of events, a plot or plots; these, then, are the things that happen, these are the people they happen to, this is the forbidden knowledge.

We have all been little pitchers with big ears, shooed out of the kitchen when the unspoken is being spoken, and we have probably all been tale-bearers, blurters at the dinner table, unwitting violators of adult rules of censorship. Perhaps this is what writers are: those who never kicked the habit. We remained tale-bearers. We learned to keep our eyes open, but not to keep our mouths shut.

If we're lucky, we may also be given stories meant for our ears, stories intended for us. These may be children's Bible stories, tidied up and simplified and with the vicious bits left out. They may be fairy tales, similarly sugared, although if we are very lucky it will be the straight stuff in both instances, with the slaughters, thunderbolts, and red-hot shoes left in. In any case, these tales will have deliberate, molded shapes, unlike the stories we have patched together for ourselves. They will contain mountains, deserts, talking donkeys, dragons; and, unlike the kitchen stories, they will have definite endings. We are likely to accept these stories as being on the same level of reality as the kitchen stories. It's only when we are older that we are taught to regard one kind of story as real and the other kind as mere invention. This is about the same time we're taught to believe that dentists are useful, and writers are not.

Traditionally, both the kitchen gossips and the readers-out-loud have been mothers or grandmothers, native languages have been mother tongues, and the kinds of stories that are told to children have been called nursery tales or old wives' tales. It struck me as no great coincidence when I learned recently that, when a great number of prominent writers were asked to write about the family member who had had the greatest influence on their literary careers, almost all of them, male as well as female, had picked their mothers. Perhaps this reflects the extent to which North American children have been deprived of their grandfathers, those other great repositories of story; perhaps it will come to change if men come to share in early child care, and we will have old husbands' tales. But as things are, language, including the language of our earliest-learned stories, is a verbal matrix, not a verbal patrix. . . .

SEAMUS HEANEY

[b. 1939]

Feelings into Words

"Digging," in fact, was the name of the first poem I wrote where I thought my feelings got into words, or, to put it more accurately, where I thought my *feel* had got into words. Its rhythms and noises still please me, although there are a couple of lines in it that have the theatricality of the gunslinger rather than the self-absorption of the digger. I wrote it in the summer of 1964, almost two years after I had begun to dabble in verses, and as Patrick Kavanagh said, a man dabbles in verses and finds they are his life. This was the first place where I felt I had done more than make an arrangement of words: I felt that I had let down a shaft into real life. The facts and surfaces of the thing were true, but more important, the excitement that came from naming them gave me a kind of insouciance and a kind of confidence. I didn't care who thought what about it: somehow, it had surprised me by coming out with a stance and an idea that I would stand over:

> The cold smell of potato mould, the squelch and slap
> Of soggy peat, the curt cuts of an edge
> Through living roots awaken in my head.
> But I've no spade to follow men like them.
>
> Between my finger and my thumb
> The squat pen rests.
> I'll dig with it.

As I say, I wrote it down ten years ago; yet perhaps I should say that I dug it up, because I have come to realize that it was laid down in me years before that even. The pen/spade analogy was the simple heart of the matter, and *that* was simply a matter of almost proverbial common sense. People used to ask a child on the road to and from school what class you were in and how many slaps you'd got that day, and invariably they ended up with an exhortation to keep studying because "learning's easy carried" and "the pen's lighter than the spade." And the poem does no more than allow that bud of wisdom to exfoliate, although the significant point in this context is that at the time of writing I was not aware of the proverbial structure at the back of my mind. Nor was I aware that the poem was an enactment of yet another digging metaphor that came back to me years later. This was a rhyme that also had a currency on the road to school, though again we were not fully aware of what we were dealing with:

> "Are your praties dry
> And are they fit for digging?"
> "Put in your spade and try,"
> Says Dirty-Face McGuigan

Well, digging there becomes a sexual metaphor, an emblem of initiation, like putting your hand into the bush or robbing the nest, one of the various natural analogies for uncovering and touching the hidden thing. I now believe that the "Digging" poem had for me the force of an initiation: the confidence I mentioned arose from a sense that perhaps I could work this poetry thing, too, and having experienced the excitement and release of it once, I was doomed to look for it again and again.

JOHN EDGAR WIDEMAN

[b. 1941]

Stories Are Letters

TO ROBBY

Stories are letters. Letters sent to anybody or everybody. But the best kind are meant to be read by a specific somebody. When you read that kind you know you are eavesdropping. You know a real person somewhere will read the same words you are reading and the story is that person's business and you are a ghost listening in.

Remember. I think it was Geral I first heard call a watermelon a letter from home. After all these years I understand a little better what she meant. She was saying the melon is a letter addressed to us. A story for us from down home. Down Home being everywhere we've never been, the rural South, the old days, slavery, Africa. That juicy, striped message with red meat and seeds, which always looked like roaches to me, was blackness as cross and celebration, a history we could taste and chew. And it was meant for us. Addressed to us. We were meant to slit it open and take care of business.

Consider all these stories as letters from home. I never liked watermelon as a kid. I think I remember you did. You weren't afraid of becoming instant nigger, of sitting barefoot and goggle-eyed and Day-Glo black and drippy-lipped on massa's fence if you took one bit of the forbidden fruit. I was too scared to enjoy watermelon. Too self-conscious. I let people rob me of a simple pleasure. Watermelon's still tainted for me. But I know better now. I can play with the idea even if I can't get down and have a natural ball eating a real one.

Anyway . . . these stories are letters. Long overdue letters from me to you. I wish they could tear down the walls. I wish they could snatch you away from where you are.

DIANE ACKERMAN

[b. 1943]

What a Poem Knows

A poem tells us about the subtleties of mood for which we have no labels. The voluptuousness of waiting, for instance: how one's whole body can rock from the heavy pounding of the heart. It knows extremes of consciousness, knows what the landscape of imagination looks like when the mind is at full-throttle, or beclouded, or cyclone-torn.

Especially it tells us about our human need to make treaties. Often a poem is where an emotional or metaphysical truce takes place. Time slow-gaits enough in the hewing of the poem to make a treaty that will endure, in print, until the poet disowns it, perhaps in a second treaty called a "palinode." A poem knows about illusion and magic, how to glorify what is not glorious, how to bankrupt what is. It displays, in its alchemy of mind, the transmuting of the commonplace into golden saliences. It takes two pedestrian items, claps them together, and comes out with something finer than either one, makes them unite in a metaphor's common cause. . . . It *accretes* life, which is why different people can read different things in the same poem. It freezes life, too, yanks a bit out of life's turbulent stream, and holds it up squirming for view, framed by the white margins of the page. Poetry is an act of distillation. It takes contingency samples, is selective. It telescopes time. It focuses what most often floods past us in a polite blur.

ANNIE DILLARD

[b. 1945]

What Essays Can Do

In some ways the essay can deal in both events and ideas better than the short story can, because the essayist—unlike the poet—may introduce the plain, unadorned thought without the contrived entrances of long-winded characters who mouth discourses. This sort of awful device killed "the novel of idea." (But eschewing it served to limit fiction's materials a little further, and likely contributed to our being left with the short story of scant idea.) The essayist may reason; he may treat of historical, cultural, or natural events, as well as personal events, for their interest and meaning alone, without resort to fabricated dramatic occasions. So the essay's materials are larger than the story's.

The essay may deal in metaphor better than the poem can, in some ways, because prose may expand what the lyric poem must compress. Instead of confining a metaphor to half a line, the essayist can devote to it a narrative, descriptive, or reflective couple of pages, and bring forth vividly its meanings. Prose welcomes all sorts of figurative language, of course, as well as alliteration, and even rhyme. The range of rhythms in prose is larger and grander than that of poetry. And it can handle discursive idea, and plain fact, as well as character and story.

The essay can do everything a poem can do, and everything a short story can do—everything but fake it. The elements in any nonfiction should be true not only artistically—the connections must hold at base and must be veracious, for that is the convention and the covenant between the nonfiction writer and his reader. Veracity isn't much of a drawback to the writer; there's a lot of truth out there to work with. And veracity isn't much of a drawback to the reader. The real world arguably exerts a greater fascination on people than any fictional one; many people, at least, spend their whole lives there, apparently by choice. The essayist does what we do with our lives; the essayist thinks about actual things. He can make sense of them analytically or artistically. In either case he renders the real world coherent and meaningful, even if only bits of it, and even if that coherence and meaning reside only inside small texts.

TIM O'BRIEN
[b. 1946]

On the Importance of Mystery in Plot

[I]t is my view that good storytelling involves, in a substantive sense, a plunge into mystery of the grandest order. Briefly, almost in summary form, I want to examine this notion through . . . plot. . . .

It is my belief that plot revolves around certain mysteries of fact, or what a story represents as fact. What happened? What will happen? Huck and Jim hop on a raft (fact) and embark on a journey (fact) and numerous events occur along the way (facts). On the level of plot, this narrative appeals to our curiosity about where the various facts will lead. As readers, we wonder and worry about what may befall these two human beings as they float down a river in violation of the ordinary social conventions. We are curious about facts still to come. In this sense, plot involves the inherent and riveting mystery of the *future*. What next? What are the coming facts? By its very nature, the future compels and intrigues us—it holds promise, it holds terror—and plot relies for its power on the essential cloudiness of things to come. We don't know. We want to know.

In a magic act, as in a story, there is the reporting (or purporting) of certain facts. The guillotine *is* sharp, it *does* cut the carrot, the man's hand *does* enter the guillotine's hole, the blade *does* slam down. For an audience, the mystery has entirely to do with future facts. What will become of this poor man? Will he lose his hand? Will he weep? Will the stump bleed as stumps tend to do?

Without some concept of the future, these questions would be both impossible and irrelevant. It is the mystery of the future, at least in part, that compels us to turn the pages of a novel, or of a story, or of our own lives. Unlike the animals, we conceive of tomorrow. And tomorrow fascinates us. Tomorrow matters—maybe too much—and we spend a great portion of our lives adjusting the present in hope of shaping the future. In any case, we are driven to care and to be curious about questions of fate and destiny: we can't help it, we're human.

On one level, then, I am arguing in defense of old-fashioned plot—or in defense of plot in general—which is so often discredited as a sop to some unsophisticated and base human instinct. But I see nothing base in the question, "What will happen next?" I'm suggesting that plot is grounded in a high—even noble—human craving to *know,* a craving to push into the mystery of tomorrow.

This is not to argue, however, that plot need give an impression of finality. A good plot does not tie up the loose ends of the future in a tidy little knot. The plot of my own life has not often, so far as I can tell, resolved itself in any neat and final way. Death itself, when it comes, dissolves into enigma. Maybe this, maybe that. But who knows? Who really *knows?* The plot mystery of life—what will happen to us, to all of us, to the human race—is unresolved and must remain that way if it is to endure as a compelling story. As a species, I believe, we are beguiled by uncertainty. It is both a gift and a burden. We crave knowledge, yes, but we also crave its absence, for the absence alone makes possible the joy of discovery. Once the factual curtain falls—for instance, if we were to know beyond doubt that Lee Harvey Oswald acted on his own to assassinate President Kennedy—that ticklish sense of uncertainty vanishes and the puzzle no longer puzzles and the story is both finished and boring. Nothing remains to ignite curiosity. Nothing beckons, nothing tantalizes.

from "The Magic Show," in A Bread Loaf Anthology: Writers on Writing, *Robert Pack and Jay Parini, eds.*

ALICE FULTON

[b. 1952]

On the Validity of Free Verse

Until recently, I believed that Pound (along with Blake and Whitman, among others) had managed to establish beyond all argument the value of *vers libre* as a poetic medium. I thought that questions concerning the validity of free verse could be filed along with such antique quarrels as "Is photography Art?" and "Is abstract art Art?" In the past few years, however, I've heard many people—professors, poets, readers—speak of free verse as a failed experiment. To these disgruntled souls, free verse apparently describes an amorphous prosaic spouting, distinguished chiefly by its neglect of meter or rhyme, pattern or plan. Perhaps the word *free* contributes to the misconception. It's easy to interpret *free* as "free from all constraints of form," which leads to "free-for-all." However, any poet struggling with the obdurate qualities of language can testify that the above connotations of "free" do not apply to verse.

Since it's impossible to write unaccented English, free verse has meter. Of course, rather than striving for regularity, the measure of free verse may change from line to line, just as the tempo of twentieth-century music may change from bar to bar. As for allegations about formlessness, it seems to me that only an irregular structure with no beginning or end could be described as formless. (If the structure were regular, we could deduce the whole from a part. If irregular and therefore unpredictable, we'd need to see the whole in order to grasp its shape.) By this definition, there are fairly few examples of formless phenomena: certain concepts of God or of the expanding universe come to mind. However, unlike the accidental forms of nature, free verse is characterized by the poet's conscious shaping of content and language: the poet's choices at each step of the creative process give rise to form. Rather than relying on regular meter or rhyme as a means of ordering, the structures of free verse may be based upon registers of diction, irregular meter, sound as analogue for content, syllabics, accentuals, the interplay of chance with chosen elements, theories of lineation, recurring words, or whatever design delights the imagination and intellect. I suspect that the relation between content and form can be important or arbitrary in both metered and free verse. In regard to conventional forms, it's often assumed that decisions concerning content follow decisions concerning form (the add-subject-and-stir approach). However, poets consciously choose different subjects for sonnets than for ballads, thus exemplifying the interdependency of content and form. The reverse assumption is made about free verse: that the subject supersedes or, at best, dictates the form. But this is not necessarily the case. The poet can decide to utilize a structural device, such as the ones suggested previously, and then proceed to devise the content.

When we read a sestina, the form is clearly discernible. This is partly because we've read so many sestinas (familiarity breeds recognition) and partly because it's easy to perceive a highly repetitive pattern. More complex designs, however, often appear to be random until scrutinized closely. Much of what we call free verse tries to create a structure suitable only to itself—a pattern that has never appeared before, perhaps. As in serious modern music or jazz, the repetitions, if they do exist, may be so widely spaced that it takes several readings to discern them. Or the poems' unifying elements may be new to the reader, who must become a creative and active participant in order to appreciate the overall scheme. This is not meant to be a dismissal of the time-honored poetic forms. I admire and enjoy poets who breathe new life into seemingly dead conventions or structures. And I'm intrigued by poetry that borrows its shape from the models around us: poems in the form of TV listings, letters, recipes, and so forth. But I also value the analysis required and the discovery inherent in reading work that invents a form peculiar to itself. I like the idea of varying the meter from line to line so that nuances of tone can find their rhythmic correlative (or antithesis).

from Ecstatic Occasions, Expedient Forms, *David Lehman, ed.*

Glossary

Allegory A symbolic narrative in which the surface details imply a secondary meaning. Allegory often takes the form of a story in which the characters represent moral qualities.

Alliteration The repetition of consonant sounds, especially at the beginning of words.

Anapest Two unaccented syllables followed by an accented one, as in cŏmprĕheńd or ĭntĕrveńe.

Antagonist A character or force against which a main character struggles.

Argumentative essay An essay that puts forth a claim directly and explicitly supports it with evidence.

Aside Words spoken by an actor directly to the audience, which are not "heard" by the other actors on stage.

Assonance The repetition of similar vowel sounds in a sentence or a line of poetry as in "I rose and told him of my woe."

Aubade A love lyric in which the speaker complains about the arrival of the dawn, when he must part from his lover.

Ballad A narrative poem written in four-line stanzas, characterized by swift action and narrated in a direct style.

Blank verse A line of poetry or prose in unrhymed iambic pentameter.

Caesura A strong pause within a line of verse.

Catastrophe The action at the end of a tragedy that initiates the denouement.

Catharsis The purging of the feelings of pity and fear that, according to Aristotle, occur in the audience of tragic drama.

Character   An imaginary person that lives in a literary work. Literary characters may be major or minor, static or dynamic.

Characterization   The means by which writers present and reveal character.

Chorus   A group of characters in Greek tragedy who comment on the action of a play without participating in it. Their leader is the choragos.

Climax   The turning point of the action in the plot of a play or story. The climax represents the point of greatest tension in the work.

Closed form   A type of form or structure in poetry characterized by regularity and consistency in such elements as rhyme, line length, and metrical pattern.

Comedy   A type of drama in which the characters experience reversals of fortune, usually for the better. In comedy things work out happily in the end. Comic drama may be either romantic—characterized by a tone of tolerance and geniality—or satiric. Satiric plays offer a darker vision of human nature, one that ridicules human folly.

Comic relief   The use of a comic scene to interrupt a succession of intensely tragic dramatic moments. The comedy of scenes offering comic relief typically parallels the tragic action the scenes interrupt.

Complication   An intensification of the conflict in a story or play.

Conflict   A struggle between opposing forces in a story or play, usually resolved by the end of the work.

Connotation   The personal and emotional associations called up by a word that go beyond its dictionary meaning.

Convention   A customary feature of a literary work such as the use of a chorus in Greek tragedy or an explicit moral in a fable.

Couplet   A pair of rhymed lines that may or may not constitute a separate stanza in a poem.

Dactyl   A stressed syllable followed by two unstressed ones, as in flút-tĕr-ĭng or blúe-bĕr-r̆y.

Denotation   The dictionary meaning of a word.

Denouement   The resolution of the plot of a literary work.

Deus ex machina   A god who resolves the entanglements of a play by supernatural intervention (literally, a god from the machine) or any artificial device used to resolve a plot.

Dialogue   The conversation of characters in a literary work.

Diction   The selection of words in a literary work.

Dramatic monologue   A type of poem in which a speaker addresses a silent listener.

Dramatis Personae   The characters or persons of the play.

Elegy   A lyric poem that laments the dead.

Elision   The omission of an unstressed vowel or syllable to preserve the meter of a line of poetry.

Enjambment   A run-on line of poetry in which logical and grammatical sense carries over from one line into the next. An enjambed line differs from an end-stopped line in which the grammatical and logical sense is completed within the line. In the opening lines of Robert Browning's "My Last Duchess," for example, the first line is end-stopped and the second enjambed:

> That's my last Duchess painted on the wall,
> Looking as if she were alive. I call
> That piece a wonder, now. . . .

Epic   A long narrative poem that records the adventures of a hero. Epics typically chronicle the origins of a civilization and embody its central values.

Epigram   A brief witty poem, often satirical.

Exposition   The first stage of a fictional or dramatic plot in which necessary background information is provided.

Expository essay   An essay that advances an idea in a direct manner. Its primary purpose is to provide information.

Fable   A brief story with an explicit moral, often including animals as characters.

Falling action   In the plot of a story or play the action following the climax of the work that moves it towards resolution.

Falling meter   Poetic meters such as trochaic and dactylic that move or fall from a stressed to an unstressed syllable.

Fiction   An imagined story.

Figurative language   A form of language use in which writers and speakers convey something other than the literal meaning of their words. See *hyperbole, metaphor, metonymy, simile, synecdoche,* and *understatement.*

Flashback   An interruption of a work's chronology to describe or present an incident that occurred prior to the main time frame of the action.

Foil   A character who contrasts and parallels the main character in a play or story.

Foot   A metrical unit composed of stressed and unstressed syllables. For example, an *iamb* or *iambic foot* is represented by ˘ ´, that is, an unaccented syllable followed by an accented one. See the chart on pages 000–000.

Foreshadowing   Hints of what is to come in the action of a play or story.

Fourth wall   The imaginary wall of the box theater setting, supposedly removed to allow the audience to see the action.

Free verse   Poetry without a regular pattern of meter or rhyme.

Gesture   The physical movement of a character during a play.

Hyperbole   A figure of speech involving exaggeration.

Iamb   An unstressed syllable followed by a stressed one, as in tŏdáy.

Image   A concrete representation of a sense impression, a feeling, or an idea. Imagery refers to the pattern of related details in a work.

Imagery   The pattern of related comparative aspects of language in a literary work.

Irony   A contrast or discrepancy between what is said and what is meant or between what happens and what is expected to happen. In verbal irony characters say the opposite of what they mean. In irony of circumstance or situation the opposite of what is expected happens. In dramatic irony a character speaks in ignorance of a situation or event known to the audience or to other characters.

Literal language   A form of language in which writers and speakers mean exactly what their words denote.

Lyric poem   A type of poem characterized by brevity, compression, and the expression of feeling.

Metaphor   A comparison between essentially unlike things without a word such as *like* or *as*. An example: "My love is a red, red rose."

Meter   The measured pattern of rhythmic accents in poems.

Metonymy   A figure of speech in which a closely related term is substituted for an object or idea. An example: "We have always remained loyal to the crown."

Monologue   A speech by one character.

Narrative essay   A type of essay in which an idea is illustrated by means of a story or a series of incidents.

Narrative poem   A poem that tells a story.

Narrator   The voice and implied speaker of a fictional work, to be distinguished from the actual living author.

Octave   An eight-line unit, which may constitute a stanza or a section of a poem, as in the octave of a sonnet.

Ode   A long, stately poem in stanzas of varied length, meter, and form. Usually a serious poem on an exalted subject.

Onomatopoeia   The use of words to imitate the sounds they describe. Words such as *buzz* and *crack* are onomatopoetic.

Open form   A type of structure or form in poetry characterized by freedom from regularity and consistency in such elements as rhyme, line length, and metrical pattern.

Parable   A brief story that teaches a lesson often ethical or spiritual.

Parody   A humorous, mocking imitation of a literary work.

Pathos   A quality of a play's action that stimulates the audience to feel pity for a character.

Personification   The endowment of inanimate objects or abstract concepts with animate or living qualities. An example: "The yellow leaves flaunted their color gaily in the wind."

Plot   The unified structure of incidents in a literary work.

Point of view   The angle of vision from which a story is narrated.

Props   Articles or objects that appear on stage during a play.

Protagonist   The main character of a literary work.

Quatrain   A four-line stanza in a poem.

Recognition   The point at which a character understands his or her situation as it really is.

Reversal   The point at which the action of the plot turns in an unexpected direction for the protagonist.

Resolution   The sorting out or unraveling of a plot at the end of a drama or narrative.

Rhetorical question   A question to which an overt answer is not expected. Writers use rhetorical questions to set up an explanation they are about to provide and to trigger a reader's mental response.

Rising action   A set of conflicts and crises that constitute that part of a play's plot leading up to the climax.

Rising meter   Poetic meters such as iambic and anapestic that move or ascend from an unstressed to a stressed syllable.

Rhyme   The matching of final vowel or consonant sounds in two or more words.

Rhythm   The recurrence of accent or stress in lines of verse.

Romance A type of narrative fiction or poem in which adventure is a central feature and in which an idealized vision of reality is presented.

Satire A literary work that criticizes human misconduct and ridicules vices, stupidities, and follies.

Sestet A six-line unit of verse constituting a stanza or section of a poem; the last six lines of an Italian sonnet.

Sestina A poem of thirty-nine lines written in iambic pentameter. Its six-line stanzas repeat in an intricate and prescribed order the six last words of each line in the opening stanza. After the sixth stanza there is a three-line *envoi* (or envoy) which uses the six repeating words, two to a line.

Setting The time and place of a literary work that establish its context.

Simile A figure of speech involving a comparison between unlike things using *like, as,* or *as though*. An example: "My love is like a red, red rose."

Soliloquy A speech in a play which is meant to be heard by the audience but not by other characters on the stage. If there are no other characters present the soliloquy represents the character's thinking aloud.

Sonnet A fourteen-line poem in iambic pentameter. The *Shakespearean* or *English sonnet* is arranged as three quatrains and a couplet, rhyming *abab cdcd efef gg*. The *Petrarchan* or *Italian sonnet* divides into two parts: an eight-line octave and a six-line sestet, rhyming *abba abba cde cde* or *abba abba cd cd cd*.

Speculative essay A meditative essay generally loose in structure concerned with exploring an idea, a perception, or a feeling.

Spondee A metrical foot represented by two stressed syllables such as kníck-knáck.

Stage direction A playwright's descriptive or interpretive comments that provide readers (and actors) with information about the dialogue, setting, and action of a play.

Staging The spectacle a play presents in performance, including the positions of actors on stage, the scenic background, the props and costumes, and the lighting and sound effects.

Stanza A division or unit of a poem that is repeated in the same form—with similar or identical patterns of rhyme and meter.

Structure The design or form of a literary work.

Style The way an author chooses words, arranges them in sentences or in lines of dialogue or verse, and develops ideas and actions *with* description, imagery, and other literary techniques.

Subject What a story or play is about; to be distinguished from plot and theme.

Subplot A subsidiary or subordinate or parallel plot in a play or story that coexists with the main plot.

Symbol An object or action in a literary work that means more than itself, that stands for something beyond itself.

Synecdoche A figure of speech in which a part is substituted for the whole. An example: "Lend me a hand."

Syntax The grammatical order of words in a sentence or line of verse or dialogue.

Tale A story that narrates strange happenings in a direct manner, without detailed descriptions of character.

Tempo The variation in pace in which a scene is acted.

Tercet A three-line stanza.

Theme   The idea of a literary work abstracted from its details of language, character, and action, and cast in the form of a generalization.

Tone   The implied attitude of a writer toward the subject and characters of a work.

Tragedy   A type of drama in which the characters experience reversals of fortune, usually for the worse. In tragedy catastrophe and suffering await many of the characters, especially the hero.

Tragic flaw   A weakness or limitation of character resulting in the fall of the tragic hero.

Tragic hero   A privileged, exalted character of high repute, who by virtue of a tragic flaw and fate suffers a fall from glory into suffering.

Tragicomedy   A type of play that contains elements of both tragedy and comedy.

Understatement   A figure of speech in which a writer or speaker says less than what he or she means; the converse of exaggeration.

Unities   The idea established by Aristotle that a play should be limited to a specific time, place, and story. The events of the plot should occur within a twenty-four-hour period, should occur within a given geographic locale, and should tell a single story.

Villanelle   A nineteen-line lyric poem that relies heavily on repetition. The first and third lines alternate throughout the poem, which is structured in six stanzas—five tercets and a final quatrain.

Acknowledgments

Fiction

LEE K. ABBOTT   "The View of Me From Mars" reprinted by permission of The Putnam Publishing Group from *Dreams of Distant Lives* by Lee K. Abbott. Copyright © 1989 by Lee K. Abbott.

MARGARET ATWOOD   "Rape Fantasies" © 1977, 1982 by O. W. Toad Ltd. Reprinted by
permission of the author.

JORGE LUIS BORGES   "The Garden of Forking Paths" from *Labyrinths* by Jorge Luis Borges,
translated by Donald A. Yates, from *Labyrinths*. Copyright © 1962, 1964 by New Directions
Publishing Corp. Reprinted by permission of the publisher.

KAY BOYLE   "Astronomer's Wife" from *The White Horses of Vienna and Other Stories* by Kay Boyle.
Copyright © 1936, © 1965 by Kay Boyle. Reprinted by permission of the Watkins/Loomis
Agency, Inc.

RAYMOND CARVER   "Cathedral" from *Cathedral* by Raymond Carver. Copyright © 1981 by
Raymond Carver. Reprinted by permission of Alfred A. Knopf, Inc.

RALPH ELLISON   "Battle Royal" from *Invisible Man* by Ralph Ellison. Copyright 1948 by Ralph
Ellison. Reprinted by permission of Random House, Inc.

LOUISE ERDRICH   "American Horse" from *The Bingo Palace* by Louise Erdrich. Copyright ©
1994 by Louise Erdrich. Reprinted by permission of HarperCollins Publishers, Inc.

WILLIAM FAULKNER   "A Rose for Emily" from *Collected Stories of William Faulkner* by William
Faulkner. Copyright 1930 and renewed 1958 by William Faulkner. Reprinted by permission
of Random House, Inc.

EDWARD M. FORSTER   "Our Graves in Gallipoli" from *Abinger Harvest,* copyright 1936 and
renewed 1964 by Edward M. Forster, reprinted by permission of Harcourt Brace & Company
and Edward Arnold.

CAROLYN G. HEILBRUN   From *Hamlet's Mother And Other Women* by Carolyn G. Heilbrun.
Copyright © 1990 by Columbia University Press. Reprinted by permission of the publisher.

ERNEST HEMINGWAY   "The Short Happy Life of Francis Macomber by Ernest Hemingway."
Reprinted with permission of Scribner, a Division of Simon & Schuster, from *The Short Stories*

W.D. SNODGRASS "A Rocking Horse: Symbol, Pattern, Way to Live" by W.D. Snodgrass, *The Hudson Review,* Summer 1958. Reprinted by permission of the author.

AMY TAN Reprinted by permission of G.P. Putnam's Sons from "Rules of the Game" from *The Joy Luck Club* by Amy Tan. Copyright © 1989 by Amy Tan.

JOHN UPDIKE "A & P" from *Pigeon Feathers and Other Stories* by John Updike. Copyright © 1962 by John Updike. Reprinted by permission of Alfred A. Knopf, Inc. Originally appeared in "The New Yorker."

ALICE WALKER "Everyday Use" from *In Love & Trouble: Stories of Black Women,* copyright © 1973 by Alice Walker, reprinted by permission of Harcourt Brace & Company.

EUDORA WELTY "A Worn Path" from *A Curtain of Green and Other Stories,* copyright 1941 and renewed 1969 by Eudora Welty, reprinted by permission of Harcourt Brace & Company.

WILLIAM CARLOS WILLIAMS "The Use of Force" from *The Collected Stories of William Carlos Williams* by William Carlos Williams. Copyright © 1938 by William Carlos Williams. Reprinted by permission of New Directions Publishing Corp.

JUDITH WRIGHT "Woman to Child" by Judith Wright from her *Collected Poems.* Reprinted by permission of Angus and Robertson Publishers.

Poetry

BELLA AKHMADULINA "The Bride" by Bella Akhmadulina, translated by Stephen Stepanchev. Copyright © 1966 by *Harper's* Magazine. Reprinted by permission of Stephen Stepanchev.

MARGARET ATWOOD "This is a Photograph of me," © Margaret Atwood, 1966, from *The Circle Game.* Reprinted with the permission of Stoddart Publishing, 34 Lesmill Rd., Don Mills, Ontario, Canada.

W. H. AUDEN "Musee des Beaux Arts," "The Unknown Citizen," and "In Memory of W. B. Yeats" from *W. H. Auden: Collected Poems* by W. H. Auden, edited by Edward Mendelson. Copyright 1940 and renewed 1968 by W. H. Auden. Reprinted by permission of Random House.

JIMMY SANTIAGO BACA "Meditations from the South Valley" from *Martin and Meditations from the South Valley* by Jimmy Santiago Baca. Copyright © 1987 by Jimmy Santiago Baca. Reprinted by permission of New Directions Publishing Corp.

ELIZABETH BISHOP "First Death in Nova Scotia," "The Fish," and "Sestina" from *The Complete Poems 1927–1979* by Elizabeth Bishop. Copyright © 1979, 1983 by Alice Helen Methfessel. Reprinted by permission of Farrar, Straus & Giroux, Inc.

NEAL BOWERS "Driving Lessons," in *Shenandoah,* 42:2 (Summer 1992), pp. 42–43. Reprinted by permission of the author.

GWENDOLYN BROOKS "the Mother" and "First fight, Then fiddle . . ." from *Blacks* by Gwendolyn Brooks. Published by The David Company, Chicago. Copyright 1987.

RAYMOND CARVER "Photograph of My Father in His Twenty-Second Year" from *Fires: Essays, Poems and Stories.* Copyright 1983 by Raymond Carver. Reprinted by permission of Capra Press, Santa Barbara.

ROSARIO CASTELLANOS "Chess" as translated by Maureen Ahern from *A Rosario Castellanos Reader,* by Rosario Castellanos, edited by Maureen Ahern, trans. by Maureen Ahern and others. Copyright © 1988 Fondo de Cultural Economica. By permission of Maureen Ahern, Fondo de Cultural Economica, and the University of Texas Press.

C.P. CAVAFY trans. by Keeley and Sherrard. "The City" by C.P. Cavafy from *Collected Poems, Revised Edition,* translated by Edmund Keeley and Philip Sherrard. Copyright © 1975, 1992 by Edmund Keeley and Philip Sherrard, translators. Reprinted by permission of Princeton University Press.

HELEN CHASIN "The Word *Plum*" from *Coming Close and Other Poems* by Helen Chasin. Copyright © 1986. Reprinted by permission of Yale University Press.

LUCILE CLIFTON "Homage to My Hips" from *Two-Headed Woman* by Lucile Clifton. Reprinted by permission of Curtis Brown, Ltd. Copyright © 1980 by Lucille Clifton. "The Lost Baby Poem" copyright © 1987 by Lucille Clifton. Reprinted from *Good Woman: Poems and a Memoir 1969–1980* by Lucille Clifton with the permission of BOA Editions, Ltd., 260 East Ave., Rochester, NY 14604.

JUDITH ORTIZ COFER   "The Idea of Islands" by Judith Ortiz Cofer is reprinted with permission from the publisher of *Terms of Survival*. (Arte Publico Press-University of Houston, 1987).

ANNE C. COON   "Queen-Ann's-Lace" Reprinted by permission of the author.

CHRISTOPHER JANE CORKERY   "Divorce" from *Blessing* by Christopher Jane Corkery. © 1985 by Princeton University Press. Reprinted by permission of Princeton University Press.

GREGORY CORSO   "Marriage" from *The Happy Birthday of Death* by Gregory Corso. Copyright © 1960 by Gregory Corso. Reprinted by permission of New Directions Publishing Corp.

COUNTEE CULLEN   "Incident" reprinted by permission of GRM Associates, Inc., Agents for the Estate of Ida M. Cullen. From the book *Color* by Countee Cullen. Copyright © 1925 by Harper & Brothers; copyright renewed 1953 by Ida M. Cullen.

E. E. CUMMINGS   "Me up at does," "1(a," "anyone lived in a pretty how town," reprinted from *Complete Poems, 1913–1962,* by E. E. Cummings, by permission of Liveright Publishing Corporation. Copyright © 1923, 1925, 1931, 1935, 1938, 1939, 1940, 1944, 1945, 1946, 1947, 1948, 1949, 1950, 1951, 1952, 1953, 1954, 1955, 1956, 1957, 1958, 1959, 1960, 1961, 1962, by the Trustees for the E. E. Cummings Trust. Copyright © 1961, 1963, 1968 by Marion Morehouse Cummings. "Buffalo Bill's" is reprinted from *Tulips & Chimneys* by E. E. Cummings, Edited by George James Firmage, by permission of Liveright Publishing Corporation. Copyright 1923, 1925 and renewed 1951, 1953 by E. E. Cummings. Copyright © 1973, 1976 by the Trustees for the E. E. Cummings Trust. Copyright © 1973, 1976 by George James Firmage. "i thank You God for most this amazing" is reprinted from *Xaipe* by E. E. Cummings, Edited by George James Firmage, by permission of Liveright Publishing Corporation. Copyright 1950 by E. E. Cummings. Copyright © 1979, 1978, 1973 by Nancy T. Andrews. Copyright © 1979, 1973 by George James Firmage.

EMILY DICKINSON   "Because I could not stop for Death," "Crumbling is not an instant's Act," "The Wind begun to knead the Grass," "I like a look of Agony," "Some keep the Sabbath going to Church," "Wild Nights-Wild Nights," "After great pain, a formal feeling comes," "Much Madness is divinest Sense," "I died for Beauty—but was scarce," "I heard a Fly Buzz—when I died," "The Bustle in a House," "Tell all the Truth but tell it slant," "Pain—has an Element of Blank," "A narrow Fellow in the Grass," "I taste a liquor never brewed," "I dreaded that first Robin, so," "I like to see it lap the Miles," "Further in Summer than the Birds," "A Route of Evanescence," "Apparently with no surprise," "I cannot dance upon my Toes," "The Soul selects her own Society," "I'm 'wife'—I've finished that," "There's a certain Slant of light," "I felt a Funeral, in my Brain," "We grow accustomed to the Dark," "The Heart asks Pleasure—first," "There is a pain—so utter," "Remorse—is Memory—awake," "My Life had stood—a Loaded Gun," "The Last Night that She lived," and "My life closed twice before its close" reprinted by permission of the publishers and the Trustees of Amherst College from *The Poems of Emily Dickinson,* Thomas H. Johnson, ed., Cambridge, Mass.: The Belknap Press of Harvard University Press. Copyright © 1951, 1955, 1983 by the President and Fellows of Harvard College.

H. D. (HILDA DOOLITTLE)   "Heat" from *Collected Poems 1912–1944* by H. D. Copyright © 1982 by The Estate of Hilda Doolittle. Reprinted by permission of New Directions Publishing Corp.

RITA DOVE   "Conary" from *Grace Notes* by Rita Dove. Copyright © 1989 by Rita Dove. Reprinted by permission of the author and W. W. Norton & Company, Inc.

RUTH EISENBERG   "Jocasta," reprinted by permission of the author.

T. S. ELIOT   "Journey of the Magi" and "The Love Song of J. Alfred Prufrock" from *Collected Poems 1909–1962* by T. S. Eliot, copyright 1936 by Harcourt Brace & Company, copyright © 1964, 1963 by T. S. Eliot, reprinted by permission of the publisher, and Faber and Faber Ltd.

LOUISE ERDRICH   "Indian Boarding School: The Runaways" from *Jacklight*. Henry Holt and Company.

ROBERT FAGLES   "The Starry Night" from *I, Vincent: Poems from the Pictures of Van Gogh* by Robert Fagles. Copyright © 1978 by Robert Fagles. Reprinted by permission of Robert Fagles.

LAWRENCE FERLINGHETTI   "In Goya's Greatest Scenes" and "Constantly Risking Absurdity" from *A Coney Island of the Mind* by Lawrence Ferlinghetti. Copyright © 1958 by Lawrence Ferlinghetti. "Short Story on a Painting of Gustav Klimt" from *Endless Life* by Lawrence

University Press. Reprinted by permission of the publisher. "Dream Nocturne," translated by Thomas McGreevy. Reprinted by permission.

LONNELL JOHNSON   "No Mo Blues" is reprinted from *Sacred Jazz: Music, Mood and Mind* by Lonnell Johnson published by Persephone Press. Copyright © 1994 by Lonnell E. Johnson. Reprinted by permission of the author.

X. J. KENNEDY   "In a prominent bar in Secaucus one day" from *Cross Ties,* copyright 1985 by X. J. Kennedy, by permission of the University of Georgia Press.

JANE KENYON   "The Other Side" and "Otherwise" from *Otherwise.* Graywolf Press.

GALWAY KINNELL   "Saint Francis and the Sow" from *Mortal Acts, Mortal Words* by Galway Kinnell. Copyright 1980 by Galway Kinnell. Reprinted by permission of Houghton Mifflin Company. All rights reserved.

KENNETH KOCH   "Variations on a Theme by William Carlos Williams" copyright © by Kenneth Koch, 1962, 1985. Reprinted by permission of the author.

YUSEF KOMUNYAKAA   "Facing It" from *Dien Kai Dau* by Yusef Komunyakaa. © 1988 by Yusef Komunyakaa, Wesleyan UP by permission of UP of New England.

JOSEPH LANGLAND   "Hunters in the Snow: Breughel," © Joseph Langland, from *The Greed Town* (poems), Scribners, 1956. Reprinted by permission of the author.

PHILIP LARKIN   "A Study of Reading Habits" from *The Whitsun Weddings* by Philip Larkin. Reprinted by permission of Faber and Faber Ltd.

D. H. LAWRENCE   "The Piano" from *The Complete Poems of D. H. Lawrence* by D. H. Lawrence. Copyright © 1964 by Angelo Ravagli and C. M. Weekley, Executors of the Estate of Frieda Lawrence Ravagli. Used by permission of Viking Penguin, a division of Penguin Books USA Inc.

JOHN LENNON AND PAUL MCCARTNEY   "Yesterday." Words and Music by John Lennon and Paul McCartney. © Copyright 1965 by Northern Songs Limited. All Rights Controlled and Administered by MCA Music Publishing, a Division of MCA Inc., New York, NY 10019. Under license from ATV Music. Used by Permission. All Rights Reserved.

DENISE LEVERTOV   "O Taste and See" from *Poems 1960–1967* by Denise Levertov. Copyright © 1964 by Denise Levertov Goodman. Reprinted by permission of New Directions Publishing Corp.

AUDRE LORDE   "Hanging Fire" from *The Black Unicorn* by Audre Lorde. Copyright © 1978 by Audre Lorde. Reprinted by permission of W. W. Norton & Company, Inc.

DON MACLEAN   "Vincent." Words and Music by Don Maclean. © Copyright 1971, 1972 by Music Corporation of America, Inc. and Benny Bird Music. All Rights Administered by MCA Music Publishing, a Division of MCA Inc., New York, NY 10019. Used by Permission. All Rights Reserved.

ARCHIBALD MACLEISH   "Not Marble Nor the Gilded Monuments" and "Ars Poetica" from *Collected Poems 1917–1982* by Archibald MacLeish. Copyright © 1982 by The Estate of Archibald MacLeish. Reprinted by permission of Houghton Mifflin Company. All rights reserved.

BOB MCKENTY   "Snow on Frost" and "Adams's Song" © 1993, by Bob McKenty.

PETER MEINKE   "Advice to My Son" from *Trying to Surprise God* by Peter Meinke. Copyright © 1981 by Peter Meinke. Reprinted by permission of the author.

TOM MOLITO   "Cosmic Simplicities" Reprinted by permission of the author.

MARIANNE MOORE   "Poetry" reprinted with permission of Macmillan Publishing Company from *Collected Poems of Marianne Moore.* Copyright 1935 by Marianne Moore, renewed 1963 by Marianne Moore and T. S. Eliot.

HOWARD MOSS   "Shall I Compare Thee to a Summer's Day?" from "Modified Sonnets" from *A Swim Off The Rocks,* Atheneum Publishers. Copyright © 1976 by Howard Moss.

PABLO NERUDA   "The Word" from *Fully Empowered* by Pablo Neruda, translated by Alastair Reid. Translation copyright © 1975 by Alastair Reid. Reprinted by permission of Farrar, Straus & Giroux, Inc.

SHARON OLDS   "Size and Sheer Will" from *The Dead and the Living* by Sharon Olds. Copyright © 1975, 1978, 1979, 1980, 1981, 1982, 1983 by Sharon Olds. Reprinted by permission of Alfred A. Knopf, Inc.

WILFRED OWEN   "Dulce et Decorum Est" from *Collected Poems of Wilfred Owen* by Wilfred

Owen. Copyright © 1963 by Chatto & Windus Ltd. Reprinted by permission of New Directions Publishing Corp.

LINDA PASTAN   "Ethics" is reprinted from *Waiting for My Life, Poems by Linda Pastan,* by permission of W. W. Norton & Company, Inc., Copyright © 1981 by Linda Pastan.

MARGE PIERCY   "A Work of Artifice" and "To Be of Use" from *Circles on the Water* by Marge Piercy. Copyright © 1969, 1971, 1973 by Marge Piercy. Reprinted by permission of Alfred A. Knopf, Inc.

SYLVIA PLATH   "Mirror" by Sylvia Plath. Copyright © 1963 by Ted Hughes. "The Applicant" by Sylvia Plath. Copyright © 1963 by Ted Hughes. From *The Collected Poems of Sylvia Plath,* edited by Ted Hughes. Reprinted by permission of HarperCollins Publishers, and Faber and Faber Ltd.

EZRA POUND   "The River Merchant's Wife: A Letter" from *Personae* by Ezra Pound. Copyright 1926 by Ezra Pound. Reprinted by permission of New Directions Publishing Corp.

JACQUES PREVERT   "Family Portrait," translated by Harriet Zinnes. Reprinted by permission of Harriet Zinnes.

JOHN CROWE RANSOM   "Piazza Piece," from *Selected Poems* by John Crowe Ransom. Copyright 1927 by Alfred A. Knopf, Inc. and renewed 1955 by John Crowe Ransom. Reprinted by permission of Random House, Inc.

HENRY REED   "Naming of Parts" from *A Map of Verona* by Henry Reed. Reprinted by permission of John Tydeman, BBC Radio and Drama.

ADRIENNE RICH   "Aunt Jennifer's Tigers," "Rape," and "Diving into the Wreck" reprinted from *The Fact of a Doorframe, Poems Selected and New, 1950–1984,* by Adrienne Rich, by permission of W. W. Norton & Company, Inc. Copyright © 1984 by Adrienne Rich. Copyright © 1975, 1978 by W. W. Norton & Company, Inc. Copyright © 1981 by Adrienne Rich.

RAINER MARIA RILKE   "The Panther" and from *The Selected Poetry of Rainer Maria Rilke* by Rainer Maria Rilke, translated by Stephen Mitchell. Copyright © 1982 by Stephen Mitchell. Reprinted by permission of Random House, Inc.

ALBERTO RIOS   "A Dream of Husbands" by Alberto Rios. © 1985 by Alberto Rios. First published in *Five Indiscretions* (Sheep Meadow). Reprinted by permission of the author.

THEODORE ROETHKE   "Elegy for Jane," copyright 1950 by Theodore Roethke. "My Papa's Waltz," copyright 1942 by Hearst Magazines, Inc. "Waking," copyright 1948 by Theodore Roethke, from *The Collected Poems of Theodore Roethke* by Theodore Roethke. Used by permission of Doubleday, a division of Bantam Doubleday Dell Publishing Group, Inc.

KRAFT ROMPF   "Waiting Table," reprinted by permission of the author.

MURIEL RUKEYSER   "Myth" from *Breaking Away* by Muriel Rukeyser. Reprinted by permission of International Creative Management, Inc. Copyright © 1973 by Muriel Rukeyser.

NATALIE SAFIR   "Matisse's Dance," reprinted by permission of the author.

GJERTRUD SCHNACKENBERG   "Signs" from *The Lamplit Answer* by Gjertrud Schnackenberg. Copyright © 1985 by Gjertrud Schnackenberg. Reprinted by permission of Farrar, Straus & Giroux, Inc.

PETE SEEGER   "Turn! Turn! Turn! (To Everything There Is A Season)." Words from the Book of Ecclesiastes. Adaptation and Music by Pete Seeger. TRO—© Copyright 1962 (renewed) Melody Trails, Inc., New York, NY. Used by Permission.

ANNE SEXTON   "Her Kind" from *To Bedlam and Part Way Back* by Anne Sexton. Copyright © 1960 by Anne Sexton, © renewed 1988 by Linda G. Sexton. Reprinted by permission of Houghton Mifflin Co. All rights reserved. "The Starry Night" from *All My Pretty Ones* by Anne Sexton. Copyright © 1962 by Anne Sexton, © renewed 1990 by Linda G. Sexton. Reprinted by permission of Houghton Mifflin Co. All rights reserved. "Two Hands," from *The Awful Rowing Toward God* by Anne Sexton. Copyright © 1975 by Loring Conant, Jr., Executor of the Estate of Anne Sexton. Reprinted by permission of Houghton Mifflin Company. All rights reserved.

PAUL SIMON   "Richard Cory," copyright © 1966 by Paul Simon. Reprinted by permission.

LOUIS SIMPSON   "The Battle" from *Good News of Death and Other Poems.* Reprinted by permission of Louis Simpson.

STEVIE SMITH   "Mother Among the Dustbins" from *Collected Poems of Stevie Smith* by Stevie Smith. Copyright © 1972 by Stevie Smith. Reprinted by permission of New Directions Publishing Corp.

GARY SOTO "Behind Grandma's House" from *Gary Soto: New and Selected Poems*. Chronicle Books, San Francisco. Reprinted by permission.

WILLIAM STAFFORD "Traveling through the Dark" copyright © 1960 by William Stafford. From *Stories That Could Be True* by William Stafford. Copyright © 1977 by William Stafford. Reprinted by permission of HarperCollins Publishers.

WALLACE STEVENS "Thirteen Ways of Looking at a Blackbird," from *The Collected Poems of Wallace Stevens* by Wallace Stevens. Copyright 1923 renewed 1951 by Wallace Stevens. Reprinted by permission of Alfred A. Knopf, Inc.

MURIAL STUART "In the Orchard" from *Selected Poems* by Muriel Stuart. Reprinted by permission of the Estate of the author and Jonathan Cape, Publisher.

MAY SWENSON "The Universe" by May Swenson. Used with the permission of The Literary Estate of May Swenson.

WISLAWA SZYMBORSKA "Cat in an Empty Apartment" and "Nothing Twice" from *View with a Grain of Sand,* copyright © 1993 by Wislawa Szymborska, English translation by Stanislaw Baranczak and Clare Cavanagh, copyright © 1995 by Harcourt Brace & Company, reprinted by permission of the publisher.

DYLAN THOMAS "Fern Hill" and "Do not go gentle into that good night" from *Poems of Dylan Thomas* by Dylan Thomas. Copyright 1945 by The Trustees for the Copyrights of Dylan Thomas, 1952 by Dylan Thomas. Reprinted by permission of New Directions Publishing Corp., and David Higham Ltd.

JEAN TOOMER "Reapers" from *Cane* by Jean Toomer. Copyright 1923 by Boni & Liveright, renewed 1951 by Jean Toomer. Reprinted by permission of Liveright Publishing Corporation.

ROBERT WALLACE "The Double-Play" from *Views of a Ferris Wheel* by Robert Wallace. © 1961, 1965 by Robert Wallace. Reprinted by permission of the author.

RICHARD WILBUR "Junk" from *Advice to a Prophet and Other Poems,* copyright © 1961 and renewed 1989 by Richard Wilbur, reprinted by permission of Harcourt Brace & Company, and "Death of a Toad" from *Ceremony.* Harcourt.

WILLIAM CARLOS WILLIAMS "Queen-Ann's-Lace," "The Red Wheelbarrow," "Spring and All," "The Young Housewife," "Danse Russe," and "This is Just to Say" from *The Collected Poems of William Carlos Williams, 1909–1939, Vol. I.* by William Carlos Williams. Copyright 1938 by New Directions Publishing Corp. "The Danse" and "Landscape with the Fall of Icarus" from *The Collected Poems of William Carlos Williams, 1939–1962, Vol. II.* by William Carlos Williams. Copyright © 1948, 1960 by William Carlos Williams. Reprinted by permission of New Directions Publishing Corp.

JAMES WRIGHT "A Blessing," copyright 1961 by James Wright from *The Branch Will Not Break.* Reprinted by permission of the University Press of New England.

JUDITH WRIGHT "Woman to Child" by Judith Wright from her *Collected Poems.* Reprinted by permission of Angus and Robertson Publishers.

W. B. YEATS "Leda and the Swan" and "Sailing to Byzantium," copyright 1928 by Macmillan Publishing Company, renewed 1956 by Georgie Yeats. copyright 1924 by Macmillan Publishing Company, renewed 1952 by Bertha Georgie Yeats. "The Wild Swans at Coole" and "An Irish Airman Foresees His Death," copyright 1919 by Macmillan Publishing Company, renewed 1947 by Bertha Georgie Yeats. "The Second Coming," copyright 1924 by Macmillan Publishing Company, renewed 1952 by Bertha Georgie Yeats. Reprinted with permission of Macmillan Publishing Company from *The Poems of W. B. Yeats: A New Edition,* edited by Richard J. Finneran. "The Lake Isle of Innisfree," "A Dream of Death," "The Magi," "Adam's Curse" reprinted with permission of Macmillan Publishing Company from *The Poems of W. B. Yeats: A New Edition,* edited by Richard J. Finneran (New York: Macmillan, 1983).

Drama

DAVID BEVINGTON and CRAIG HARDIN "Hamlet, Prince of Denmark" by William Shakespeare, from *Introduction to Shakespeare* edited by Hardin Craig and David Bevington. Reprinted by permission of David M. Bevington.

MARTIN DOCKERY *Oh, That Wily Snake!* by Martin Dockery. Copyright © 1993 by Martin

Essays

MAXINE HONG KINGSTON "No Name Woman," and "Silence" from *The Woman Warrior* by Maxine Hong Kingston. Copyright © 1975, 1976 by Maxine Hong Kingston. Reprinted by permission of Alfred A. Knopf, Inc. and "On Discovery" from *China Men.* Knopf.

MICHELE DE MONTAIGNE "Of Smells" reprinted from *The Complete Essays of Montaigne,* translated by Donald M. Frame, with the permission of the publishers, Stanford University Press. © 1958 by the Board of Trustees of the Leland Stanford Junior University.

GEORGE ORWELL "Shooting an Elephant" from *Shooting an Elephant and Other Essays* by George Orwell, copyright 1950 by Sonia Brownell Orwell and renewed 1978 by Sonia Pitt-Rivers; and "Marrakech" from *Such, Such Were the Joys* by George Orwell, copyright 1953 by Sonia Michael Dickons, Executors of the Estate of Sonia Brownell Orwell, reprinted by permission of Harcourt Brace & Company, and A. M. Heath Ltd.

KATHERINE ANNE PORTER Excerpt from "St. Augustine and the Bullfight" from *Collected Essays and Occasional Writings,* reprinted by permission of Isabel Bayley, Literary Trustee for the Estate of Katherine Anne Porter.

RICHARD SELZER "The Masked Marvel's Last Toehold" from *Confessions of a Knife* by Richard Selzer. Copyright © 1979 by David Goldman and Janet Selzer, Trustees. By permission of William Morrow & Company, Inc.

ALLEN TATE From "Emily Dickinson" in *Collected Essays* by Allen Tate. Reprinted by permission of Helen H. Tate.

ALICE WALKER "In Search of Our Mothers' Gardens" from *In Search of Our Mothers' Gardens,* copyright © 1974 by Alice Walker, and "Women" from *Revolutionary Petunias & Other Poems,* copyright © 1970 by Alice Walker, reprinted by permission of Harcourt Brace & Company.

E. B. WHITE "Once More to the Lake" by E. B. White. Copyright 1941 by E. B. White. "The Ring of Time" by E. B. White. Copyright © 1956 by E. B. White. "The Geese" from *Essays of E. B. White.* Reprinted by permission of HarperCollins Publishers.

YVOR WINTERS "Robert Frost: or, the Spiritual Drifter as Poet" by Yvor Winters from *The Function of Criticism.* Reprinted with the permission of Ohio University Press/Swallow Press, Athens.

TOM WOLFE Excerpts from *The Right Stuff* by Tom Wolfe. Copyright © 1979 by Tom Wolfe. Reprinted by permission of Farrar, Straus & Giroux, Inc.

VIRGINIA WOOLF "Old Mrs. Grey" and "The Death of the Moth" from *The Death of the Moth and Other Essays* by Virginia Woolf, copyright 1942 by Harcourt Brace & Company and renewed 1970 by Marjorie T. Parsons, reprinted by permission of the publisher.

Example of double-entry notebook from *The Act of Writing* by Eric Gould, Robert DiYanni, and William Smith. Reprinted by permission of The McGraw-Hill Companies, Inc.

Critical Perspectives

DIANE ACKERMAN The excerpt from "What a Poem Knows" by Diane Ackerman is reprinted from *The Writer on Her Work,* edited by Janet Sternberg, by permission of W. W. Norton & Company, Inc. Copyright © 1980 by W.W. Norton & Company, Inc.

ARISTOTLE "On Tragedy" and "Poetics: Tragedy," from *Poetics* by Aristotle. Translated with an introduction by Gerald F. Else. Copyright © by the University of Michigan 1967. Published by the University of Michigan Press. Used by permission.

FREDERICK ASALS *Flannery O'Connor.* University of Georgia Press.

MARGARET ATWOOD "Our First Stories," reprinted by permission of the author. © Margaret Atwood, 1989. From *Best American Stories* published by Houghton Mifflin.

ERIC BENTLEY "On Drama as Literature and Performance" from The *Life of the Drama.* Applause Books.

WENDELL BERRY Excerpt from "The Specialization of Poetry" from *Standing by Words* by Wendell Berry. Copyright © 1983 by Wendell Berry. Reprinted by permission of North Point Press, a division of Farrar, Straus & Giroux, Inc.

BERTHOLT BRECHT Excerpt from "A Short Organum for the Theatre" from *Brecht on Theatre* edited and translated by John Willett. Translation copyright © 1964 by John Willett. Reprinted by permission of Hill and Wang, a division of Farrar, Straux & Giroux, Inc., and The Joan Daves Agency.

MAURICE CHARNEY   "Shakespeare's Villains," from *How to Read Shakespeare* by Maurice Charney. Reprinted by permission of the author.

ANTON CHEKOV   Excerpt of letter to Alexander P. Chekov and excerpt of letter to Aleksey S. Suvorin from *Letters on the Short Story* by Anton Chekhov, translated by Constance Garnett. Reprinted by permission of A. P. Watt Ltd. on behalf of The Literary Executors of the Estate of Constance Garnett.

KING-KOK CHEUNG   "Provocative Silences" from *Articulate Silences.* Cornell University Press.

EMILY DICKINSON   "On Herself and Her First Poems" from *Letters of Emily Dickinson.* Little, Brown.

ANNIE DILLARD   Excerpt from Introduction by Annie Dillard to *Best American Essays 1988,* edited by Annie Dillard and Series Editor Robert Atwan. Copyright © 1988 by Ticknor & Fields. Reprinted by permission of Annie Dillard.

LOREN EISELEY   "The Judgment of the Birds" by Loren Eiseley. From *The Immense Journey* by Loren Eiseley. Copyright © 1956 by Loren Eiseley. Reprinted by permission of Random House, Inc.

T. S. ELIOT   Excerpt from "Tradition and the Individual Talent" in *Selected Essays* by T. S. Eliot, copyright 1950 by Harcourt Brace & Company and renewed 1978 by Esme Valerie Eliot, reprinted by permission of the publisher, and Faber and Faber Ltd.

RALPH ELLISON   From "The Influence of Folklore on *Battle Royal,*" from *Invisible Man* by Ralph Ellison. Copyright © 1952 by Ralph Ellison. Reprinted by permission of Random House, Inc.

MARTIN ESSLIN   From "The Theater of the Absurd" from *The Theatre of the Absurd* by Martin Esslin. Copyright © 1961 by Martin Esslin. Used by permission of Doubleday, a division of Bantam Doubleday Dell Publishing Group, Inc.

JUDITH FARR   "On 'Wild Nights'" from *The Passion of Emily Dickinson.* Reprinted by permission of the publishers, Harvard University Press, Cambridge, Mass. Copyright © 1992 by the President and Fellows of Harvard College.

KATHLEEN FEELEY   From "On 'Good Country People'" by Kathleen Feeley from *Flannery O'Connor: Voice of the Peacock* by Kathleen Feeley. Reprinted by permission of Kathleen Feeley, S.S.N.D.

ROBERT FROST   From "Poetry, Delight, and Wisdom," from "The Figure a Poem Makes" from *Selected Prose of Robert Frost,* edited by Hyde Cox and Edward Connery Lathem. Copyright 1939, © 1967 by Henry Holt and Company, Inc. Reprinted by permission of Henry Holt and Company, Inc. "Sentence Sounds," "The Figure a Poem Makes," "Metaphor," "Spoken and Written Language," from "The Unmade World" All from *Collected Poems, Prose, and Plays.* Library of America.

ALICE FULTON   "On the Validity of Free Verse" excerpted from *Ecstatic Occasions, Expedient Forms,* David Lehman, ed. (University of Michigan Press 1996). Copyright © 1987, 1993, 1995, 1996, 1997 by Alice Fulton. Reprinted by permission of the author.

SEAMUS HEANEY   Excerpt from "Feelings into Words" from *Preoccupations* by Seamus Heaney. Copyright © 1980 by Seamus Heaney. Reprinted by permission of Farrar, Straus & Giroux, Inc. and Faber and Faber, Ltd.

CAROLYN HEILBRUN   "The Character of Hamlet's Mother" from *Hamlet's Mother and Other Women.* Columbia UP.

NORMAN HOLLAND   "Reading Frost" from *The Brain of Robert Frost* by Norman Holland (1988). Reprinted by permission of the publisher. Routledge: New York and London.

HENRIK IBSEN   "Notes for the Modern Tragedy" from *Playwrights on Playwrighting,* edited by Toby Cole, published by Hill and Wang, a division of Farrar, Straus, & Giroux, Inc.

MAXINE HONG KINGSTON   "Imagined Life" from *Michigan Quarterly Review,* 1983, by permission of the author.

BERNARD KNOX   "Sophocles' Oedipus" from *Word and Action.* Johns Hopkins University Press.

AUDRE LORDE   "Poems are Not Luxuries," from *Claims for Poetry* edited by Donald Hall. Copyright © by Audre Lorde 1978. Reprinted by permission of Charlotte Sheedy Literary Agency, Inc.

MAYNARD MACK   "The Readiness Is All" from *Everybody's Shakespeare.* University of Nebraska Press. © 1993 by Maynard Mack.

DOROTHY TUCK McFARLAND   Excerpt from "On Everything That Rises Must Converge" from *Flannery O'Connor* by Dorothy Tuck McFarland. (Frederick Ungar, 1976). Reprinted by permission of The Continuum Publishing Company.

HELEN McNEIL "Dickinson's Method" from *Emily Dickinson*. Virago Press.

ARTHUR MILLER Tragedy and the Common Man," copyright 1949, renewed © 1977 by Arthur Miller, from *The Theater Essays of Arthur Miller* by Arthur Miller, edited by Robert A. Martin. Used by permission of Viking Penguin, a division of Penguin Books USA Inc.

PABLO NERUDA "The Word" from *Memoirs* by Pablo Neruda, translated by Hardie St. Martin. Translation copyright © 1976, 1977 by Farrar, Straus & Giroux, Inc. Reprinted by permission of Farrar, Straus & Giroux, Inc.

A. D. NUTTAL "Othello" from *A New Mimesis*. Methuen.

TIM O'BRIEN "On the Importance of Mystery in Plot" from "The Magic Show" in *A Bread Loaf Anthology,* edited by Robert Pack and Jay Pereni.

FLANNERY O'CONNOR *The Habit of Being* edited by Sally Fitzgerald. Farrar, Straus & Giroux, Inc.

FRANK O'CONNOR "Frank O'Connor" by Malcolm Cowley, from *Writers at Work, First Series,* by Malcolm Cowley, Editor. Copyright © 1957, 1958 by The Paris Review, renewed © 1985 by Malcolm Cowley, © 1986 by The Paris Review. Used by permission of Viking Penguin, a division of Penguin Books USA Inc. and *Mystery and Manners*. Harcourt.

OCTAVIO PAZ Excerpt from "The Power of Poetry" from *The Other Voice* by Octavio Paz, copyright © 1991 by Octavio Paz, reprinted by permission of Harcourt Brace & Company.

PLATO "Poetry and Inspiration" from "The Ion" in *The Dialogues of Plato,* translated by Benjamin Jowett, 4th Edition revised. Reprinted by permission of Oxford University Press.

RICHARD POIRIER "On 'Stopping By Woods'," "On 'Mending Wall' " from *Robert Frost: The Work of Knowing*. Oxford University Press.

ADRIAN POOLE "Sophocles and Athens," "Hamlet and Oedipus" from *Tragedy: Shakespeare and the Greek Example*. Blackwell.

WILLIAM PRITCHARD "On 'Stopping By Woods' " from *Robert Frost: A Literary Life Reconsidered*. Oxford University Press.

EDWARD SAMPSON On "Once More to the Lake." Reprinted with permission of Twayne Publishers, an imprint of Simon & Schuster Macmillan, from *E.B. White* by Edward C. Sampson. Copyright © 1974 by Twayne Publishers, Inc.

GEORGE SEFERIS "Poetry and Human Living" reprinted by permission of the publishers from *A Poet's Journal* by George Seferis, translated by Athan Anagnostopoulos, Cambridge, Mass.: Harvard University Press, Copyright © 1974 by the President and Fellows of Harvard College.

ESTHER SCHOR "Maxine Hong Kingston" from *Women's Voices*. Ed. Pat C. Hoy II, Esther H. Schor, and Robert DiYanni. McGraw-Hill.

BERNARD SHAW "The Interpreter of Life," from *Playwrights on Playwriting,* edited by Toby Cole, published by Hill and Wang, a division of Farrar, Straus & Giroux, Inc.

KEN SMITH "On 'The Ring of Time.' " From *Critical Essays on E. B. White,* ed. Robert L. Root, Jr. G. K. Hall.

W. D. SNODGRASS "A Rocking-Horse: The Symbol, the Pattern, the Way to Live" *The Hudson Review,* XI (Summer, 1958).

MARK SPILKA "Ritual Form in the Blind Man" from *The Love Ethic of D.H. Lawrence*. Indiana University Press.

GEORGE STEINER "Principal Constants of Conflict in *Antigone*" from *Antigones*. Oxford UP.

WALLACE STEVENS Excerpt from *Opus Posthumous* by Wallace Stevens, edited by Samuel French Morse. Copyright © 1957 by Elise Stevens and Holly Stevens. Reprinted by permission of Alfred A. Knopf, Inc.

MARK STRAND "Poetry, Language, Meaning" from Introduction to *The Best American Poetry*. Reprinted by permission of the author.

ALLEN TATE "Dickinson and Knowledge," "On 'Because I Could Not Stop for Death' " from "Emily Dickinson" in *Collected Essays*. Swallo.

EUDORA WELTY "Is Phoenix Jackson's Grandson Really Dead," from *The Eye of the Story* by Eudora Welty. Copyright © 1978 by Eudora Welty. Reprinted by permission of Random House, Inc.

E. B. WHITE Specified selection from pages vii–ix of "Foreword" to *Essays of E. B. White* and

"The Essayist," Copyright © 1977 by E. B. White. Reprinted by permission of HarperCollins, Publishers, Inc.

JOHN EDGAR WIDEMAN "To Robby" from *The Stories of John Edgar Wideman* by John Edgar Wideman. Copyright © 1992 by John Edgar Wideman. Reprinted by permission of Pantheon Books, a division of Random House, Inc.

KINGSLEY WIDMER *The Art of Perversity.* University of Washington Press.

YVOR WINTERS "Robert Frost: or, the Spiritual Drifter as Poet" from *The Function of Criticism.* Swallow.

Poems and Paintings

VINCENT VAN GOGH *The Starry Night,* photograph © 1997 the Museum of Modern Art, New York.

EDWARD HOPPER *Sunday,* photograph © 1997 the Museum of Modern Art, New York.

HENRI MATISSE *Dance (First Version),* © 1998 Succession H. Matisse, Paris/Artists Rights Society (ARS), New York. Photograph © 1997 the Museum of Modern Art, New York.

PABLO PICASSO *Girl with a Mandolin (Fanny Tellier),* © 1998 Estate of Pablo Picasso/Artists Rights Society (ARS). New York. Photograph © 1997 the Museum of Modern Art, New York.

PABLO PICASSO *Still Life with Pitcher, Bowl, & Fruit,* © 1998 Estate of Pablo Picasso/Artists Rights Society (ARS), New York.

Index

of Authors, Titles, and First Lines

Selection titles appear in italics, and first lines of poems appear in roman type. Page numbers in roman type indicate the opening page of a selection; italic numbers indicate discussion. Bold page numbers indicate complete sections on specific authors.

Abbott, Lee K., *The View of Me from Mars*, 414

Abortions will not let you forget, 774

About Men, 1731

About suffering they were never wrong, 587

A break in the circle dance of naked women, 594

A broken altar, Lord, Thy servant rears, 696

Ackerman, Diane, *What a Poem Knows*, 1993

'A cold coming we had of it, 592

Acquainted with the night, 478, 677

Adam's Song, 529

Adventures of Huckleberry Finn, The, 125–128

Advice to My Son, 510, 510–511

Aeneid, 475–476

Aesop, *The Wolf and the Mastiff*, 44

After great pain, a formal feeling comes, 645

Afterwards, 736

Akhmadulina, Bella, *The Bride*, 793

...A line will take us hours maybe, 561

All the new thinking is about loss, 798

Altar, The, 696

American Horse, 445

Among twenty snowy mountains, 744

An ant on the tablecloth, 678

A narrow Fellow in the Grass, 650

An axe angles from my neighbor's ashcan, 540

Andre's Mother, 1523

A noiseless patient spider, 729

Anonymous:

    Barbara Allan, 683

    Edward, Edward, 684

    Western Wind, 486

Antigonê, 829–834, 847–848, 864–867, 871–874, 878, 922, 960–961

anyone lived in a pretty how town, 756

A & P, 32–33, 33

A poem should be palpable and mute, 754

Apollinaire, Guillaume, *Le Pont Mirabeau (Mirabeau Bridge)*, 576

Apology for Poetry, An, 1962

Apparently with no surprise, 653

Araby, 88

Aristotle:
  Simple and Complex Plots, 953
  The Six Elements of Tragedy, 952
  On Tragedy, 1960

Arms and the Man, 823–829, 839–840, 842, 846–847, 1291, 1292

Arnold, Matthew, *Dover Beach*, 612

A Route of Evanescence, 653

Ars Poetica (Huidobro), 753

Ars Poetica (MacLeish), 754

Art and Imagination, 1964

Asals, Frederick, *On "A Good Man Is Hard to Find,"* 177–178

A small girl on a porch, 801

Aspects of the Novel, 49–50

Assonance is the spirit of a rhyme, *525*

Astronomer's Wife, 62

A sudden blow: the great wings beating still, 741

As virtuous men pass mildly away, 691

A sweet disorder in the dress, 494

A toad the power mower caught, 776

At ten I wanted fame, 811

Atwood, Margaret:
  Our First Stories, 1990
  Rape Fantasies, 392
  This Is a Photograph of Me, 794

Auden, W. H.:
  In Memory of W. B. Yeats, 764
  Musée des Beaux Arts, 587
  The Unknown Citizen, 763

Aunt Jennifer's Tigers, 471

Aunt Jennifer's tigers prance across a screen, 471

Austen, Jane, *Pride and Prejudice*, 100–101

Authenticity of the Imagination, The, 1965

Avenge, O Lord, thy slaughtered saints, 697

A wayward crow, 574

Baca, Jimmy Santiago, from *Meditations on the South Valley*, 807

Bacon, Francis:
  Of Love, 1819
  Of Revenge, 1753

Baldwin, James, *Notes of a Native Son*, 1741–1743, 1846

Ballet Class at the Hotel Ansonia: For Vera Nemtchinova, 797

Barbara Allan, 683

Batter my heart, three-personed God, 694

Battle, The, 507

Battle of the Ants, The, 1746

Battle Royal, 378

Because I could not stop for Death, 515, 638–639

Because we were friends and sometimes loved each other, 777

Behind Grandma's House, 811

Behold her, single in the field, 704

Belle Dame sans Merci, La, 715

Bent double, like old beggars under sacks, 755

Bentley, Eric, *On Drama as Literature and Performance*, 1986

Berry, Wendell, *Poetry and Song*, 1988

Between my finger and my thumb, 796

Billie Holiday's burned voice, 808

Birches, 669

Bishop, Elizabeth:
  First Death in Nova Scotia, 497, 498–499
  The Fish, 767
  Sestina, 768

Black Cat, The, 102

Black reapers with the sound of steel on stones, 758

Blake, William:
  Art and Imagination, 1964
  The Clod & the Pebble, 700
  The Garden of Love, 702
  The Lamb, 701
  London, 562, 564–565, 623–627, 1899
  A Poison Tree, 512
  The Sick Rose, 591
  The Sick Rose (painting), 582
  The Tyger, 701

Blessing, A, 779

Blind Man, The, 133, 135–136, 139

Bliss, 78–79, 322

Boarding House, The, 61–62, 79, 318

Borges, Jorge Luis:
  The Garden of Forking Paths, 48, 357

Botticelli, Sandro, Giotto di Bondone, *The Adoration of the Magi* (painting), 582

Bowers, Neal, *Driving Lessons*, 805

Boyle, Kay, *Astronomer's Wife*, 62

Bradstreet, Anne, *To My Dear and Loving Husband*, 698

Brecht, Bertolt, *Theatre Notes*, 1977

Breughel the Elder, Peter:
  Hunters in the Snow (painting), 582
  Landscape with the Fall of Icarus (painting), 581

Bride, The, 793

Bright Book of Life, The, 134

Brooks, Gwendolyn:
  First fight. Then fiddle, 775
  the mother, 774

Browning, Elizabeth Barrett, *How do I love thee? Let me count the ways*, 720

Browning, Robert:
  Meeting at Night, 500
  My Last Duchess, 481, *483*
  Soliloquy of the Spanish Cloister, 726

Buffalo Bill's, 547, *547–548*

Burl's, 1876

Burns, Robert, *A Red, Red Rose*, 703

Busy old fool, unruly sun, 517, *518–519*, *532–533*

By June our brook's run out of song and speed, 673

Byron, Lord (George Gordon):
  The Destruction of Sennacherib, 538
  She walks in beauty, 711

By the road to the contagious hospital, 746

Canary, 808

Canonization, The, 690

Carrion Comfort, 571

Carroll, Lewis (Charles Lutwidge Dodgson), *Jabberwocky*, 733

Carver, Raymond:
  Cathedral, 398
  Photograph of My Father in His Twenty-second Year, 795

Castellanos, Rosario, *Chess*, 777

Cathedral, 398

Cat in an Empty Apartment, 760

Cavafy, C. P., *The City*, 551

Channel Firing, 735

Character of Hamlet's Mother, The, 1177

Charney, Maurice, *Shakespeare's Villains*, 1180

Chasin, Helen, *The Word Plum*, 531

Chekhov, Anton:
  The Lady with the Dog, 281
  Technique in Writing the Short Story, 1970

Chess, 777

Cheung, King-Kok:
  Feminism and History in "On Discovery," 1804
  On The Woman Warrior, 1803

Chopin, Kate, *The Story of an Hour*, 38, *38–42*, 51, 67, 77, *100, 101*, *122–123, 1918*

City, The, 551

Clifton, Lucille:
  Homage to My Hips, 790
  The Lost Baby Poem, 790

Clod & the Pebble, The, 700

Coleridge, Samuel Taylor, *Kubla Khan*, 709

Come live with me and be my love, 529, 609

Composed upon Westminster Bridge, September 3, 1802, 705

Constantly risking absurdity and death, 775

Coon, Anne C., *Queen-Ann's-Lace*, 615

Cooper, Bernard, *Burl's*, 1876

Corkery, Christopher Jane, *Divorce*, 801

Corso, Gregory, *Marriage*, 785

Cosmic Simplicities, 801

Crane, Stephen:
  The Open Boat, 302
  War Is Kind, 480, *481*

Crossing Brooklyn Ferry, 729

Crumbling is not an instant's Act, 552, *553*

"Cub" Wants to Be a Pilot, 1712, 1827

Cullen, Countee, *Incident*, 758

cummings, e. e.:
  anyone lived in a pretty how town, 756
  Buffalo Bill's, 547, *547–548*
  i thank You God for most this amazing, 757
  Me up at does, 522
  1 (a), 546, *546–547*

D'Ambrosio, Vinnie-Marie, *If I Were a Maker I'd*, 595
Dance, The, 548
Danse Russe, 746
Dead, The, 245, *1933, 1946–1951*
Death, be not proud, 693
Death, be not proud, though some have callèd thee, 693
Death of a Salesman, *1384*, 1385
Death of the Moth, The, 1749
Death of Toad, The, 776
Delight in Disorder, 494
Departmental, 678
Desert Places, 679
Design, 657, 679
Destruction of Sennacherib, The, 538
Dickinson, Emily, **629–654**
   After great pain, a formal feeling comes, 645
   Apparently with no surprise, 653
   Because I could not stop for Death, 515, *638–639*
   The brain is wider than the sky, 640
   The Bustle in a House, 652
   Crumbling is not an instant's Act, 552, *553*
   Further in Summer than the Birds, 651
   The Heart asks Pleasure—first—, 648
   I cannot dance upon my Toes—, 633
   I died for Beauty—but was scarce, 647
   I dreaded that first Robin, so, 645
   I felt a Funeral, in my Brain, 644
   I heard a Fly buzz—when I died—, 647
   I like a look of Agony, 642
   I like to see it lap the Miles, 648
   I'm "wife"— I've finished that, 641, 1888, *1895, 1897–1900, 1902–1903, 1908, 1911, 1914–1915, 1918, 1921, 1924–1925*
   I taste a liquor never brewed, 642
   The last Night that She lived, 652
   Much Madness is divinest Sense—, 646
   My life closed twice before its close, 654
   My Life has stood—a Loaded Gun—, 650
   A narrow Fellow in the Grass, 650
   Our God, our help in ages past, *631–632*

Dickinson (*Cont.*):
   Pain—has an Element of Blank—, *640*, 649
   Remorse—is Memory—awake, 649
   A Route of Evanescence, 653
   Some keep the Sabbath going to Church, 644
   The soul selects her own society, *634*, 641
   Tell all the Truth but tell it slant, 653
   There is a pain—so utter, 649
   There's a certain Slant of light, 643
   We grow accustomed to the Dark, 646
   Wild Nights—Wild Nights!, *637–638*, 643
   The Wind begun to rock (knead) the Grass—, 566
Dickinson and Knowledge, 635
Dickinson's Method, 639
Didion, Joan, *Los Angeles Notebook*, 1739, *1745, 1748, 1751*
Die—you can't do that to a cat, 760
Digging, 796
Dillard, Annie:
   Living Like Weasels, 1756, *1758–1761*
   What Essays Can Do, 1994
Diving into the Wreck, 783
Divorce, 801
Dockery, Martin, *Oh, That Wily Snake!*, 1658
Dodgson, Charles Lutwidge (*see* Carroll, Lewis)
Does the road wind up-hill all the way?, 511
Doll House, A, *816–823, 827–829, 842, 846–847*, 1239
Donne, John:
   Batter my heart, three-personed God, 694
   The Canonization, 690
   Death, be not proud, 693
   The Flea, 692
   Hymn to God the Father, 505
   Meditation XVII: For Whom the Bell Tolls, 1820
   Song, 689
   The Sun Rising, 517, *518–519, 532–533*
   A Valediction: Forbidding Mourning, 691
Do not go gentle into that good night, 773
Do not weep, maiden, for war is kind, 480, *481*

Doolittle, Hilda (*see* H.D.)
Double-Play, The, 506
Dove, Rita, *Canary*, 808
Dover Beach, 612
Dover Bitch, The: A Criticism of Life, 613
Dream Deferred, 602
Dream Nocturne (Nocturno Soñado), 579
Dream of Death, A, 565
Dream of Husbands, A, 810
Drink to me only with thine eyes, 695
Driving Lessons, 805
Dulce et Decorum Est, 755
Dunbar, Paul Lawrence, *We wear the mask*, 743
During Wind and Rain, 527
Dust of Snow, 573

Eagle, The, 726
Earth has not anything to show more fair, 705
Ecclesiastes: 3.1–8, 599
Edward, Edward, 684
Ego Tripping, 799
Ehrlich, Gretel, *About Men*, 1731
Eiseley, Loren, from *The Judgment of the Birds, 1712–1713*, 1840
Eisenberg, Ruth F., *Jocasta*, 962, *970–975*
Elegy for Jane, 766
Eliot, T. S.:
    Journey of the Magi, 592
    The Love Song of J. Alfred Prufrock, 749
    The Poet and the Tradition, 1976
Ellison, Ralph:
    Battle Royal, 378
    Folklore and Fiction, 1982
Erdrich, Louise:
    American Horse, 445
    Indian Boarding School: The Runaways, 812
Essayist, The, 1788
Essay on Man, An, 700
Esslin, Martin, *The Theater of the Absurd*, 1987
Ethics, 788
Eve of St. Agnes, The, 561–562
Everyday Use, 408, *1932–1933, 1940–1945*

Everything That Rises Must Converge, *173–174, 179–180*, 203
Excerpts from "Imagined Life," 1801

Facing It, 804
Fagles, Robert, *The Starry Night*, 585
Falling Into Theory, 1892–1893
Family Portrait, 487
Farewell, thou child of my right hand, and joy, 694
Farr, Judith, *On "Wild Nights,"* 637
Faulkner, William, *A Rose for Emily, 66–67*, 80, *86–87, 1918*
Feeley, Kathleen, *On "Good Country People,"* 178
Feelings into Words, 1991
Feminism and History in "On Discovery," 1804
Fences, 1570
Ferlinghetti, Lawrence:
    Constantly Risking Absurdity, 775
    Short Story on a Painting of Gustav Klimt, 597
Fern Hill, 771
Figure a Poem Makes, The, 658
Fire and Ice, 674
First Death in Nova Scotia, 497, *498–499*
First fight. Then fiddle, 775
First fight. Then fiddle. Ply the slipping string, 775
First having read the book of myths, 783
Fish, The, 767
Five years have passed, 705
Flea, The, 692
Flood-tide below me! I see you face to face!, 729
Folklore and Fiction, 1982
For God's sake hold your tongue, and let me love, 690
For Once, Then, Something, 675
Forster, E. M.:
    Aspects of the Novel, 49–50
    Our Graves in Gallipoli, 1832
Freud, Sigmund, *The Oedipus Complex*, 954, *1902*
From the sea came a hand, 780

Frost, Robert, **629–630, 654–681**
  Acquainted with the night, 478, 677
  Birches, 669
  Departmental, 678
  Desert Places, 679
  Design, 657, 679
  Dust of Snow, 573
  Fire and Ice, 674
  Home Burial, 670
  Hyla Brook, 673
  Mending Wall, *664–665*, 668
  The Most of It, 680
  Mowing, *657*, 666
  For Once, Then, Something, 675
  Once by the Pacific, 676
  Provide, Provide, 680
  Putting in the Seed, *657*, 674
  The Road Not Taken, 513
  The Silken Tent, 521
  The Span of Life, *533*
  Stopping by Woods on a Snowy
    Evening, 466, *466–468*, 516–517,
    524, 525, 534, 535–537,
    662–664
  Tree at my window, *657*, 677
  The Tuft of Flowers, 667
  Two Look at Two, 675
Fulton, Alice, *On the Validity of Free Verse*,
  1996
Further in Summer than the Birds, 651

Garcia Marquez, Gabriel, *A Very Old*
  Man with Enormous Wings,
  388
Garden of Forking Paths, The, *48*, 357
Garden of Love, The, 702
Gather ye rosebuds while ye may, 695
Geese, The, 1795
Gewanter, David, *Goya's "The Third of May,*
  1808," 586
Gilman, Charlotte Perkins, *The Yellow*
  Wallpaper, 291
Gimpel the Fool, 363
Giovanni, Nikki, *Ego Tripping*, 799
Girl, 430

Glaspell, Susan, *Trifles*, 1373
Glory be to God for dappled things—,
  738
Go, and catch a falling star, 689
God's Grandeur, 737
Gogh, Vincent van, *The Starry Night*
  (painting), 581
Good Country People, 100, 176–177,
  178–179, 180
Good Man Is Hard to Find, A, 175–176,
  177–178, 193
Gordon, George (*see* Byron, Lord)
Goya's "The Third of May, 1808," 586
Goya y Lucientes, Francesco:
  The Third of May (painting), 588
Graves, Robert, *Symptoms of Love*, 619,
  619–620
Gregory, Lady (Isabella August a Persse), *The*
  Rising of the Moon, 834–835, 849–850,
  850, *857–859*
Gr-r-r—there go, my heart's abhorrence!,
  726
Guests of the Nation, *51*, 52
Guthrie, Woody, *This Land is Your Land*,
  604

H.D. (Hilda Doolittle), *Heat*, 501
"Had he and I but met, 519
Had we but world enough, and time,
  698
Hall, Donald, *My son, my executioner*, 781
Hamlet, Prince of Denmark, 868–870,
  983–984, 1071–1072, 1072,
  1174–1178
Hamlet and Oedipus, 1174
Hanging Fire, 789
Hansberry, Lorraine, *A Raisin in the Sun*,
  1455
Hardy, Thomas:
  Afterwards, 736
  Channel Firing, 735
  The Man He Killed, 519
  Neutral Tones, 501
  The Ruined Maid, 734
  During Wind and Rain, 527

Hass, Robert, *Meditation at Lagunitas*, 798

Hatch, Gary Layne, *Terrier Torment; or, Mr. Hopkins and his Dog*, 571

Hawthorne, Nathaniel, *Young Goodman Brown*, 272

Hayden, Robert, *Those Winter Sundays*, 462, *463–465*, *469–470*, *479–480*, *516*, *618*

Heaney, Seamus:
  Digging, 796
  Feelings into Words, 1991
  Mid-Term Break, 795

Heat, 501

Hecht, Anthony, *The Dover Bitch: A Criticism of Life*, 613

He clasps the crag with crooked hands, 726

He disappeared in the dead of winter, 764

Heilbrun, Carolyn, *The Character of Hamlet's Mother*, 1177

Helen, thy beauty is to me, 721

Helmet and rifle, pack and overcoat, 507

Hemingway, Ernest, *The Short Happy Life of Francis Macomber*, 87–88, 337, *1896–1897*, *1931–1932*

Herbert, George:
  The Altar, 696
  Virtue, 514

Her body is not so white as anemone petals nor so smooth, 614

Her Kind, 539

Herlands, E. Ward, *When Edward Hopper Was Painting*, 590

Herrick, Robert:
  Delight in Disorder, 494
  Upon Julia's Clothes, 695
  To the Virgins, to Make Much of Time, 695

. . . her vespers done, *561–562*

He saw her from the bottom of the stairs, 670

He thought he kept the universe alone, 680

He was found by the Bureau of Statistics to be, 763

His sight from ever gazing through the bars, 576

His vision, from the constantly passing bars, 575

Holder, Barbara, *Ballet Class at the Hotel Ansonia: For Vera Nemtchinova*, 797

Holland, Norman, *Reading Frost*, 661

Hollander, John, *Rhyme's Reason*, *525*

Homage to My Hips, 790

Home Burial, 670

Home's the place we head for in our sleep, 812

Hood, Mary, *How Far She Went*, 453

Hopkins, Gerard Manley:
  Carrion Comfort, 571
  God's Grandeur, 737
  Pied Beauty, 738
  Spring and Fall: to a Young Child, 555, *555–558*
  Sprung Rhythm, 1972
  Thou art indeed just, Lord, 485
  In the Valley of the Elwy, 526, *526–527*, *535*
  The Windhover, 737

Hopper, Edward, *Sunday* (painting), 583

Horse Dealer's Daughter, The, *133*, *138–139*, 151

Housman, A. E.:
  To an Athlete Dying Young, 739
  When I was one-and-twenty, 738

How do I love thee? Let me count the ways, 720

Howe, Tina, *Painting Churches*, 1526

How Far She Went, 453

How It Feels to Be Colored Me, 1766, *1769–1772*

Hughes, Langston, *Dream Deferred*, 602

Huidobro, Vicente, *Ars Poetica*, 753

Hunters in the Snow: Breughel, 588

Hurston, Zora Neale, *How It Feels to Be Colored Me*, 1766, *1769–1772*

Hyla Brook, 673

Hymn to God the Father, 505

I. Know then thyself, presume not God to scan, 700

I, too, dislike it: there are things that are important beyond all this fiddle, 748

I am a gentleman in a dustcoat trying, 753

I am fourteen and my skin has betrayed me, 789

Ibsen, Henrik:
  A Doll House, 816–823, 827–829, 842, 846–847, 1239
  Notes for the Modern Tragedy, 1971
I cannot dance upon my Toes—, 633
I caught a tremendous fish, 767
I caught this morning morning's minion, 737
I chopped down the house that you had been saving to live in next summer, 570
Idea of Islands, The, 809
I died for Beauty—but was scarce, 647
I divested myself of despair, 803
I dreaded that first Robin, so, 645
I dreamed that one had died in a strange place, 565
If all the world and love were young, 610
I felt a Funeral, in my Brain, 644
If ever two were one, then surely we, 698
If I Were a Maker I'd make a melon, 595
I found a dimpled spider, fat and white, 657, 679
If when my wife is sleeping, 746
I got out of bed, 803
I have been one acquainted with the night, 478, 677
I have eaten the plums, 569
I have gone out, a possessed witch, 539
I heard a Fly buzz—when I died—, 647
I know that I shall meet my fate, 520
I learned to drive in a parking lot, 805
I like a look of Agony, 642
I like to see it lap the Miles, 648
I like to think that on a Sunday afternoon when Edward Hopper, 590
I'll show you, 586
I love the wind, 807
I met a traveler from an antique land, 711
I'm "wife"— I've finished that, 641, 1888, *1895, 1897–1900, 1902–1903, 1908, 1911, 1914–1915, 1918, 1921, 1924–1925*
In a prominent bar in Secaucus one day, 781
In Breughel's great picture, The Kermess, 548
Incident, 758
Indian Boarding School: The Runaways, 812

In ethics class so many years ago, 788
In his sea lit, 506
In Memory of W. B. Yeats, 764
In Search of Our Mothers' Gardens, 1714–1715, 1743–1745, 1869
Interpreter of Life, The, 1973
Interview with David Henry Hwang, An, 1996
In the cold, cold parlor, 497, *498–499*
In the Orchard, 484
In the Valley of the Elwy, 526, *526–527, 535*
In Xanadu did Kubla Khan, 709
Ionesco, Eugène, *The Lesson*, *1339*, 1340
I remember a house where all were good, 526, *526–527, 535*
I remember the neckcurls, limp and damp as tendrils, 766
Irish Airman Foresees His Death, An, 520
I said to my baby, 603
I sat all morning in the college sick bay, 795
I sing of warfare and a man at war, *476*
I Stand Here Ironing, 373
I taste a liquor never brewed, 642
i thank You God for most this amazing, 757
'I thought you loved me.' 'No, it was only fun.' 484
It is a beauteous evening, 493
It is a beauteous evening, calm and free, 493
It little profits that an idle king, 724
It was in and about the Martinmas time, 683
It was taken some time ago, 794
I use to be a big-time blues singer, 607
I wake to sleep, and take my waking slow, 550
I wandered lonely as a cloud, 490, *490–492, 503, 517, 537*
I wander thro' each charter'd (dirty) street, 562, *564–565, 623–627, 1899*
I was angry with my friend, 512
I was born in the congo, 799
I went to the Garden of Love, 702
I went to turn the grass once after one, 667
I will arise and go now, and go to Innisfree, 499

Jabberwocky, 733
Jilting of Granny Weatherall, The, 331

Jiménez, Juan Ramón, *Nocturno Soñado (Dream Nocturne)*, 579
Jocasta, 962, *970–975*
Johnson, Lonnelle, *No Mo Blues*, 607
Johnson, Samuel, *The Metaphysical Poets*, 1963
Jonson, Ben:
  On My First Son, 694
  Song: To Celia, 695
Journey of the Magi, 592
Joyce, James:
  Araby, 88
  The Boarding House, *61–62*, 79, 318
  The Dead, 245, *1933*, *1946–1951*
Judgment of the Birds, The, *1712–1713*, 1840
Junk, 540
Just off the highway to Rochester,
  Minnesota, 779

Kafka, Franz, *The Metamorphosis*, 215
Kane, Patricia, *The Prodigal Daughter in Alice Walker's "Everyday Use,"* 1940
Keats, John:
  The Authenticity of the Imagination, 1965
  La Belle Dame sans Merci, 715
  The Eve of St. Agnes, *561–562*
  On First Looking into Chapman's Homer, 544, *544–545*
  Ode on a Grecian Urn, 719
  Ode to a Nightingale, 716
  When I have fears, 714
Kennedy, X. J., *In a prominent bar in Secaucus one day*, 781
Kenyon, Jane:
  Notes from the Other Side, 803
  Otherwise, 803
Kincaid, Jamaica, *Girl*, 430
Kingston, Maxine Hong, **1800–1816**
  On Discovery, *1804*, 1815
  Excerpts from "Imagined Life," 1801
  No Name Woman, *1773–1776*, *1784–1785*, 1805
  Silence, 1813
  Woman Warrior, *1803–1804*
Kinnell, Galway, *Saint Francis and the Sow*, 778
Klimt, Gustav, *The Kiss* (painting), 583

Knox, Bernard, *Sophocles'* Oedipus, 956
Koch, Kenneth, *Variations on a Theme by William Carlos Williams*, 570
Komunyakaa, Yusef, *Facing It*, 804
Kubla Khan, 709

Lady with the Dog, The, 281
Laius was never any good after that, 970
Lake Isle of Innisfree, The, 499
Lamb, The, 701
Langland, Joseph, *Hunters in the Snow: Breughel*, 588
Larkin, Philip, *A Study of Reading Habits*, 777
La tierra lleva por la tierra, 579
Lawrence, D. H., **130–172**
  The Blind Man, *133*, *135–136*, 139
  The Bright Book of Life, 134
  The Horse Dealer's Daughter, *133*, *138–139*, 151
  Man and Woman, 135
  The Piano, 568
  The Rocking-Horse Winner, *133*, *136–138*, 162
Leda and the Swan, 741
Lennon, John, *Yesterday*, 607
Lesson, The, *1339*, 1340
Let me not to the marriage of true minds, 688
Let poetry be like a key, 753
Let us go then, you and I, 749
Levertov, Denise, *O Taste and See*, 549
Lines, 705
Little Lamb, who made thee?, 701
Living Like Weasels, 1756, *1758–1761*
London, 562, *564–565*, *623–627*, *1899*
Long afterward, Oedipus, old and blinded, walked the roads, 961
Long as I paint, 585
López, Josefina, *Simply María or The American Dream*, 1685
Lorde, Audre:
  Hanging Fire, 789
  Poems Are Not Luxuries, 1989
Los Angeles Notebook, 1739, *1745*, *1748*, *1751*
Lost Baby Poem, The, 790

Love and forgetting might have carried them, 675

Love is a universal migraine, 619, *619–620*

"Love seeketh not Itself to please, 700

Love Song of J. Alfred Prufrock, The, 749

Lying in a Hammock at William Duffy's Farm in Pine Island, Minnesota, 779

Lyric Poetry and the Short Story, 1979

Mack, Maynard, *The Readiness Is All: Hamlet,* 1175

Maclean, Don, *Vincent,* 605

MacLeish, Archibald:
 Ars Poetica, 754
 "Not Marble Nor the Gilded Monuments," 611

Magi, The, 593

Magic, 119

Mamet, David, *Oleanna,* 1622

Man and Woman, 135

Man He Killed, The, 519

Mansfield, Katherine, *Bliss,* 78–79, 322

Márgarét, áre you grieving, 555, *555–558*

Mark but this flea, and mark in this, 692

Marlowe, Christopher, *The Passionate Shepherd to His Love,* 609

Marrakech, 1719, *1720–1725, 1738–1739*

Marriage, 785

Marvell, Andrew, *To His Coy Mistress,* 698

Masked Marvel's Last Toehold, The, 1727

Mason, Bobbie Ann, *Shiloh,* 68

Matisse, Henri, *Dance* (painting), 583

Matisse's Dance, 594

McCartney, Paul, *Yesterday,* 607

McFarland, Dorothy Tuck, *On "Everything That Rises Must Converge,"* 179

McKenty, Bob:
 Adam's Song, 529
 Snow on Frost, 574

McNally, Terrence, *Andre's Mother,* 1523

McNeil, Helen, *Dickinson's Method,* 639

Meditation at Lagunitas, 798

Meditations on the South Valley, 807

Meditation XVII: For Whom the Bell Tolls, 1820

Meeting at Night, 500

Meinke, Peter, *Advice to My Son,* 510, *510–511*

Mending Wall, 664–665, 668

Metamorphosis, The, 215

Metaphysical Poets, The, 1963

Me up at does, 522

Mid-Term Break, 795

Miller, Arthur:
 Death of a Salesman, 1384, 1385
 Tragedy and the Common Man, 1984

Milton, John:
 On the Late Massacre in Piedmont, 697
 Paradise Lost, 476
 When I consider how my light is spent, 697

Miniver Cheevy, 492

Miniver Cheevy, child of scorn, 492

Mirabeau Bridge (Le Pont Mirabeau), 576

Mirror, The, 621–623

Modest Proposal, A, 1822

Molière (Jean-Baptiste Poquelin), *Tartuffe,* 839–840, 1182–1183, 1184

Molito, Tom, *Cosmic Simplicities,* 801

Montaigne Michel de, *Of smells,* 1817

Moore, Marianne, *Poetry,* 748

Moss, Howard, *Shall I Compare Thee to a Summer's Day?,* 573

Most of It, The, 680

Mother, Among the Dustbins, 522

Mother, among the dustbins and the manure, 522

mother, the, 774

Mowing, 657, 666

Much have I traveled in the realms of gold, 544, *544–545*

Much Madness is divinest Sense—, 646

Musée des Beaux Arts, 587

My black face fades, 804

My heart aches, and a drowsy numbness pains, 716

My Last Duchess, 481, *483*

My life closed twice before its close, 654

My Life has stood—a Loaded Gun—, 650

My mistress' eyes are nothing like the sun, 689

My Papa's Waltz, 472–474, 473, *479–480, 488–489*

My son, my executioner, 781

Myth, 961

Naming of Parts, 486

Neruda, Pablo:

"The Word," 1980

The Word, 761

Neutral Tones, 501

Nocturno Soñado (Dream Nocturne), 579

No Mo Blues, 607

No Name Woman, 1773–1776, 1784–1785, 1805

Not, I'll not, carrion comfort, Despair, not feast on thee, 571

Notes for the Modern Tragedy, 1971

Notes from the Other Side, 803

Notes of a Native Son, 1741–1743, 1846

Nothing can ever happen twice, 759

Nothing Twice, 759

Not marble, nor the gilded monuments (Shakespeare), 611

"Not Marble Nor the Gilded Monuments" (MacLeish), 611

Now as at all times I can see in the mind's eye, 593

Now as I was young and easy under the apple boughs, 771

Nuttal, A. D., Othello, 1178

Nymph's Reply to the Shepherd, The, 610

O'Brien, Tim:

On the Importance of Mystery in Plot, 1995

The Things They Carried, 418

Observations on Poetry, 1975

O'Connor, Flannery, **131, 172–213**

On "A Good Man Is Hard to Find," 175

Everything That Rises Must Converge, 173–174, 179–180, 203

Good Country People, 100, 176–177, 178–179, 180

On "Good Country People," 176

A Good Man Is Hard to Find, 175–176, 177–178, 193

On Symbol and Theme, 175

O'Connor, Frank:

Guests of the Nation, 51, 52

Lyric Poetry and the Short Story, 1979

October. Here in this dank, unfamiliar kitchen, 795

Ode on a Grecian Urn, 719

Ode to a Nightingale, 716

Ode to the West Wind, 712

Oedipus and Athens, 958

Oedipus Complex, The, 954, 1902

Oedipus Rex, 838, 878–879, 880, 954–959, 1174–1175, 1902

Of Love, 1819

Of man's first disobedience, and the fruit, 476

Of Revenge, 1753

Of smells, 1817

Oh, That Wily Snake!, 1658

Oh to be a bride, 793

Old Mrs. Grey, 1780–1782, 1834

Olds, Sharon, Size and Sheer Will, 800

Oleanna, 1622

Olsen, Tillie, I Stand Here Ironing, 373

"O'Melia, my dear, this does everything crown!, 734

O my luve's like a red, red rose, 703

On "A Good Man Is Hard to Find" (Asals), 177

On "A Good Man Is Hard to Find" (O'Connor), 175

On "Because I Could Not Stop for Death," 638

Once by the Pacific, 676

Once More to the Lake, 1777–1779, 1790–1791, 1791

Once riding in old Baltimore, 758

Once upon a midnight dreary, while I pondered weak and weary, 523, 721

On Discovery, 1804, 1815

On Drama as Literature and Performance, 1986

1 (a), 546, 546–547

One day I wrote her name upon the strand, 687

On "Everything That Rises Must Converge," 179

On First Looking into Chapman's Homer, 544, 544–545

On "Good Country People" (Feeley), 178

On "Good Country People" (O'Connor), 176

On Maxine Hong Kingston, 1802

On "Mending Wall," 664

On Metaphor, 660

On My First Son, 694

On "Once More to the Lake," 1790

On Sentence Sounds, 659

On Spoken and Written Language, 660

On "Stopping By Woods," 662

On "Stopping by Woods on a Snowy Evening," 663

On Symbol and Theme, 175

On "The Horse Dealer's Daughter," 138

On the Importance of Mystery in Plot, 1995

On the Late Massacre in Piedmont, 697

On "The Ring of Time," 1789

On the Validity of Free Verse, 1997

On The Woman Warrior, 1803

On Tragedy, 1960

On "Wild Nights," 637

Open Boat, The, 302

Origin of a Story, The, 1981

O Rose, thou art sick!, 591

Ortiz Cofer, Judith, The Idea of Islands, 809

Orwell, George:
    Marrakech, 1719, 1720–1725, 1738–1739
    Shooting an Elephant, 1736, 1748, 1751–1752, 1835

O Taste and See, 549

Othello (Nuttall), 1178

Othello (Shakespeare) (see Tragedy of Othello, The)

Others taunt me with having knelt at well-curbs, 675

Otherwise, 803

Our First Stories, 1990

Our God, our help in ages past, 631–632

Our Graves in Gallipoli, 1832

Over my head, I see the bronze butterfly, 779

Owen, Wilfred, Dulce et Decorum Est, 755

O what can ail thee, Knight at arms, 715

O wild West Wind, thou breath of Autumn's being, 712

O wind, rend open the heat, 501

Ozymandias, 711

Pain—has an Element of Blank—, 640, 649

Painting Churches, 1526

Panther, Der (The Panther), 575

Paradise Lost, 476

Passionate Shepherd to His Love, The, 609

Pastan, Linda, Ethics, 788

Paz, Octavio, The Power of Poetry, 1983

Persse, Isabella Augusta (see Gregory, Lady)

Petronius, The Widow of Ephesus, 45, 47

Photograph of My Father in His Twenty-second Year, 795

Piano, The, 568

Piazza Piece, 753

Pied Beauty, 738

Piercy, Marge:
    To Be of Use, 792
    A Work of Artifice, 791

Pirandello, War, 110, 123–125

Plath, Sylvia, The Mirror, 621–623

Plato, Poetry and Inspiration, 1959

Poe, Edgar Allan:
    The Black Cat, 102
    To Helen, 721
    The Raven, 523, 721
    The Single Effect, 1968
    True Poetry, 1968

Poems Are Not Luxuries, 1989

Poet and the Tradition, The, 1976

Poetry, 748

Poetry, Delight, and Wisdom, 1974

Poetry, Language, and Meaning, 1989

Poetry and Feeling, 1964

Poetry and Human Living, 1978

Poetry and Inspiration, 1959

Poetry and Song, 1988

Poets and Language, 1967

Poirier, Richard:
    On "Mending Wall," 664
    On "Stopping by Woods on a Snowy Evening," 663

Poison Tree, A, 512

Pont Mirabeau, Le (Mirabeau Bridge), 576

Poole, Adrian:
    Hamlet and Oedipus, 1174
    Oedipus and Athens, 958

Pope, Alexander:
    from An Essay on Man, 700
    Sound and Sense, 528

Poquelin, Jean-Baptiste (*see* Molière)

Porter, Katherine Anne:
  The Jilting of Granny Weatherall, 331
  Magic, 119

Pound, Ezra, *The River-Merchant's Wife: A Letter*, 747

Power of Poetry, The, 1983

Prévert, Jacques, *Family Portrait*, 487

Pride and Prejudice, 100–101

Principal Constants of Conflict in Antigonê, 960

Pritchard, William, *On "Stopping By Woods,"* 662

The Prodigal Daughter in Alice Walker's "Everyday Use," 1940

Prodigal Son, The, 27, 28–32, 43, 51

Provide, Provide, 680

Purgatory, 976

Put, stay put, Terrier Torment, Heel! I'll put on thee—, 571

Putting in the Seed, 657, 674

Quail and rabbit hunters with tawny hounds, 588

Queen-Ann's-Lace (Coon), 615

Queen-Ann's-Lace (Williams), 614

A Raisin in the Sun, 1455

Raleigh, Sir Walter, *The Nymph's Reply to the Shepherd*, 610

Ransom, John Crowe, *Piazza Piece*, 753

Rape, 495

Rape Fantasies, 392

The Raven, 523

Raven, The, 721

Readiness Is All, The: Hamlet, 1175

Reading Frost, 661

Reapers, 758

Red, Red Rose, A, 703

Red Wheelbarrow, The, 542

Reed, Henry, *Naming of Parts*, 486

Remorse—is Memory—awake, 649

Rhyme's Reason, 525

Rich, Adrienne:
  Aunt Jennifer's Tigers, 471
  Diving into the Wreck, 783
  Rape, 495

Richard Cory (Robinson), 601

Richard Cory (Simon), 601

Richter, David H., *Falling Into Theory, 1892–1893*

Riders to the Sea, 1364

Right Stuff, The, 1859

Rilke, Rainer Maria, *Der Panther (The Panther)*, 575

Ring of Time, The, 1715, *1718–1719*, 1748, *1789–1790*

Rios, Alberto, *A Dream of Husbands*, 810

Rising of the Moon, The, 834–835, 849–850, 850, 857–859

Ritual Form in "The Blind Man," 135

River-Merchant's Wife, The: A Letter, 747

Road Not Taken, The, 513

Robert Frost: Or, the Spiritual Drifter as Poet, 665

Robinson, Edwin Arlington:
  Miniver Cheevy, 492
  Richard Cory, 601

Rocking-Horse, A: Symbol, Pattern, Way to Live, 136

Rocking-Horse Winner, The, 133, 136–138, 162

Roethke, Theodore:
  Elegy for Jane, 766
  My Papa's Waltz, 472–474, 473, 479–480, 488–489
  The Waking, 550

Rompf, Kraft, *Waiting Table*, 806

Rose for Emily, A, 66–67, 80, 86–87, 1918

Rossetti, Christina, *Up-Hill*, 511

Ruined Maid, The, 734

Rukeyser, Muriel, *Myth*, 961

Rules of the Game, 438

Safir, Natalie, *Matisse's Dance*, 594

Sailing to Byzantium, 742

Saint Francis and the Sow, 778

Sampson, Edward, *On "Once More to the Lake,"* 1790

Sappho, To me he seems like a god, 682

Scene, The, 1973

Schnackenberg, Gertrude, *Signs*, 811

Schor, Esther, *On Maxine Hong Kingston*, 1802

Second Coming, The, 740

Seeger, Pete, *Turn! Turn! Turn!*, 599

Seferis, George, *Poetry and Human Living*, 1978

Sein Blick ist vom Vorübergehn der Stäbe, 575

Selzer, Richard, *The Masked Marvel's Last Toehold*, 1727

September rain falls on the house, 768

Sestina, 768

Sexton, Anne:
   Her Kind, 539
   The Starry Night, 584
   Two Hands, 780

Shakespeare, William, **983–1181**
   Hamlet, Prince of Denmark, 868–870, *983–984*, *1071–1072*, 1072, *1174–1178*
   Let me not to the marriage of true minds, 688
   My mistress' eyes are nothing like the sun, 689
   Not marble, nor the gilded monuments, 611
   Shall I compare thee to a summer's day?, 572
   That time of year thou may'st in me behold, 503, *504–505, 542–543*
   The' expense of spirit in a waste of shame, 688
   The Tragedy of Othello, 838, *843–846*, 984, 985, *1178–1181, 1904*
   When in disgrace with fortune and men's eyes, 687

Shakespeare's Villains, 1180

Shall I Compare Thee to a Summer's Day? (Moss), 573

Shall I compare thee to a summer's day? (Shakespeare), 572

Shaw, Bernard:
   Arms and the Man, 823–829, *839–840*, 842, *846–847, 1291, 1292*
   The Interpreter of Life, 1973

She is as in a field a silken tent, 521

Shelley, Percy Bysshe:
   Ode to the West Wind, 712

Shakespeare (*Cont.*):
   Ozymandias, 711
   Poets and Language, 1967

She walks in beauty, 711

She walks in beauty, like the night, 711

Shiloh, 68

Shooting an Elephant, *1736*, *1748*, *1751–1752, 1835*

Short Happy Life of Francis Macomber, The, 87–88, 337, *1896–1897, 1931–1932*

Short Story on a Painting of Gustav Klimt, 597

Should I get married? Should I be good?, 785

Sick Rose, The, 591

Sidney, Sir Philip, *An Apology for Poetry*, 1962

Signs, 811

Silence, 1813

Silken Tent, The, 521

Silko, Leslie, *Yellow Woman*, 431

Simon, Paul, *Richard Cory*, 601

Simple and Complex Plots, 953

Simply María or *The American Dream*, 1685

Simpson, Louis, *The Battle*, 507

Singer, Isaac Bashevis, *Gimpel the Fool*, 363

Single Effect, The, 1968

Six Elements of Tragedy, The, 952

Size and Sheer Will, 800

Smith, Ken, *On "The Ring of Time,"* 1789

Smith, Stevie, *Mother, Among the Dustbins*, 522

Snodgrass, W. D., *A Rocking-Horse: Symbol, Pattern, Way to Live*, 136

Snow falling and night falling fast, oh, fast, 679

Snow on Frost, 574

Softly, in the dusk, a woman is singing to me, 568

Soliloquy of the Spanish Cloister, 726

Solitary Reaper, The, 704

Some keep the Sabbath going to Church, 644

Some say the world will end in fire, 674

Something there is that doesn't love a wall, 664–665, 668

Somewhere beneath that piano's superb sleek black, 568

so much depends, 542

Song, 689

Song: To Celia, 695
Sophocles, **880–981**
    Antigonê, *829–834*, *847–848*, *864–867*,
        871–874, 878, 922, *960–961*
    Oedipus Rex, 838, *878–879*, 880,
        954–959, *1174–1175*, *1902*
Sophocles' Oedipus, 956
So there stood Matthew Arnold and this girl,
    613
Soto, Gary, *Behind Grandma's House*, 811
Sound and Sense, 528
Sous le pont Mirabeau coule la Seine, 576
The Span of Life, *533*
Spenser, Edmund, One day I wrote her
    name upon the strand, 687
Spilka, Mark, *Ritual Form in "The Blind
    Man,"* 135
Spring and All, 746
Spring and Fall: to a Young Child, 555,
    555–558
Sprung Rhythm, 1972
Stafford, William, *Traveling Through the dark*,
    771
Starry, starry night, 605
Starry Night, The (Fagler), 585
Starry Night, The (Sexton), 584
Steiner, George, *Principal Constants of Conflict
    in* Antigonê, 960
Stevens, Wallace:
    Observations on Poetry, 1975
    Thirteen Ways of Looking at a Blackbird,
        744
Stopping by Woods on a Snowy Evening, 466,
    466–468, *516–517*, 524, 525, 534,
    535–537, *662–664*
Stories Are Letters, 1993
Story of an Hour, The, 38, *38–42*, 51, 67, 77,
    100, 101, *122–123*, *1918*
Strand, Mark, *Poetry, Language, and Meaning*,
    1989
Strindberg, August, *The Scene*, 1973
Stuart, Muriel, *In the Orchard*, 484
Study of Reading Habits, A, 777
Sundays too my father got up early, 462,
    463–465, *469–470*, *479–480*, 516,
    618
The Sun Rising, 517, *518–519*, *532–533*
Sweet day, so cool, so calm, so bright, 514

Swenson, May:
    The Universe, 530
    Women, 770
Swift, Jonathan, *A Modest Proposal*, 1822
Symptoms of Love, 619, *619–620*
Synge, John Millington, *Riders to the Sea*,
    1364
Szymborska, Wislawa:
    Cat in an Empty Apartment, 760
    Nothing Twice, 759

Tan, Amy, *Rules of the Game*, 438
Tartuffe, *839–840*, *1182–1183*, 1184
Tate, Allen:
    On "Because I Could Not Stop for Death,"
        638
    Dickinson and Knowledge, 635
Technique in Writing the Short Story, 1970
Tell all the Truth but tell it slant, 653
Tender Offer, 1652
Tennyson, Alfred, Lord:
    The Eagle, 726
    Ulysses, 724
Terrier Torment; or, Mr. Hopkins and his Dog,
    571
That is no country for old men, 742
That night your great guns, unawares, 735
That's my last Duchess painted on the wall,
    481, *483*
That time of year thou may'st in me behold,
    503, *504–505*, *542–543*
The Assyrian came down like the wolf on
    the fold, 538
Theater of the Absurd, The, 1987
Theatre Notes, 1977
The bonsai tree, 791
The brain is wider than the sky, 640
The bud stands for all things, 778
The Bustle in a House, 652
The earth leads by the earth, 580
The earth leads through the earth, 579
The' expense of spirit in a waste of shame,
    688
The fine, green pajama cotton, 800
The gray sea and the long black land, 500
The Heart asks Pleasure—first—, 648
The last Night that She lived, 652

The mother knits, 487

The old dog barks backward without getting up, 533

The people I love the best, 792

The place where I was born, 809

The praisers of women in their proud and beautiful poems, 611

There is a cop who is both prowler and father, 495

There is a pain—so utter, 649

There's a certain Slant of light, 643

There was never a sound beside the wood but one, *657, 666*

The sea is calm tonight, 612

these hips are big hips, 790

The shattered water made a misty din, 676

The soul selects her own society, *634*, 641

the time i dropped your almost body down, 790

The time you won your town the race, 739

The town does not exist, 584

The trees are in their autumn beauty, 741

The trick is, to live your days, 510, *510–511*

The way a crow, 573

The whiskey on your breath, *472–474, 473, 479–480, 488–489*

The Wind begun to rock (knead) the Grass—, 566

The witch that came (the withered hag), 680

The Word Plum, 531

The word *plum* is delicious, 531

The word was born in the blood, 761

The world is charged with the grandeur of God, 737

The world is not with us enough, 549

The world is too much with us, 703

They are kneeling upright on a flowered bed, 597

They flee from me, 686

They flee from me, that sometime did me seek, 686

They say that Richard Cory owns one-half of this whole town, 601

They sing their dearest songs, 527

Things They Carried, The, 418

Thirteen Ways of Looking at a Blackbird, 744

This Is a Photograph of Me, 794

This Is Just to Say, 569

This Land is Your Land, 604

This land is your land, this land is my land, 604

Thomas, Dylan:
    Do not go gentle into that good night, 773
    Fern Hill, 771

Thoreau, Henry David, *The Battle of the Ants*, 1746

Those Winter Sundays, 462, *463–465, 469–470, 479–480, 516, 618*

Thou are indeed just, Lord, 485

Thou art indeed just, Lord, if I contend, 485

Though we thought it, Doña Carolina did not die, 810

Thou still unravished bride of quietness, 719

Threading the palm, a web of little lines, 811

Through rear windows, the dark slit, 797

To an Athlete Dying Young, 739

To Be of Use, 792

Today we have naming of parts, 486

To everything, 599

To every thing there is a season, 599

To Helen, 721

To His Coy Mistress, 698

To me he seems like a god, 682

To My Dear and Loving Husband, 698

Toomer, Jean, *Reapers*, 758

To serve, I wait and pluck, 806

To the Virgins, to Make Much of Time, 695

Tragedy and the Common Man, 1984

Tragedy of Othello, The, 838, *843–846, 984, 985, 1178–1181, 1904*

Traveling Through the dark, 771

Traveling through the dark I found a deer, 771

Tree at my window, *657, 677*

Tree at my window, window tree, *657, 677*

Trifles, 1373

True ease in writing comes from art, not chance, 528

True Poetry, 1968

Tuft of Flowers, The, 667

Turning and turning in the widening gyre, 740

Turn! Turn! Turn!, 599

Twain, Mark:
  from *The Adventures of Huckleberry Finn*,
    125–128
  from *"Cub" Wants to Be a Pilot*, 1712,
    1827
'Twas brillig, and the slithy toves, 733
Two Hands, 780
Two Look at Two, 675
Two roads diverged in a yellow wood, 513
Tyger, The, 701
Tyger! Tyger! burning bright, 701

Ulysses, 724
Under the Mirabeau Bridge there flows the
    Seine, 577
Under the Mirabeau Bridge the Seine, 578
Universe, The, 530
Unknown Citizen, The, 763
Updike, John, *A & P*, *32–33*, 33
Up-Hill, 511
Upon Julia's Clothes, 695
Use of Force, The, 1886, *1894–1895*, *1897*,
    1899, *1902–1903*, *1905–1906*, *1911*,
    1914–1915, *1918*, *1921*, *1924–1925*

Valediction, A: Forbidding Mourning, 691
*Variations on a Theme by William Carlos
    Williams*, 570
Very Old Man with Enormous Wings, A, 388
View of Me from Mars, The, 414
Vincent, 605
Virgil, *Aeneid*, *475–476*
Virtue, 514

Waiting Table, 806
Waking, The, 550
Walker, Alice:
  Everyday Use, 408, *1932–1933*,
    1940–1945
  from *In Search of Our Mothers' Gardens*,
    1714–1715, *1743–1745*, 1869
Wallace, Robert, *The Double-Play*, 506
War, 110, *123–125*
War Is Kind, 480, *481*

Wasserstein, Wendy, *Tender Offer*, 1652
We argued about the dot, 615
We basically don't know where we came
    from before birth, 801
We grow accustomed to the Dark, 646
Welty, Eudora, 67
  The Origin of a Story, 1981
  A Worn Path, 93
Western Wind, 486
Western wind, when will thou blow, 486
We stood by a pond that winter day, 501
We wear the mask, 743
We wear the mask that grins and lies, 743
What a Poem Knows, 1993
What Essays Can Do, 1994
What happens to a dream deferred, 602
What is it about, 530
Whenas in silks my Julia goes, 695
When Edward Hopper Was Painting, 590
Whenever Richard Cory went down town,
    601
When getting my nose in a book, 777
When I consider how my light is spent, 697
When I have fears, 714
When I have fears that I may cease to be, 714
When I heard the learn'd astronomer, *517*,
    525, *536–537*, *545*, *545*
When in disgrace with fortune and men's
    eyes, 687
When I see birches bend to left and right,
    669
When I was one-and-twenty, 738
When she learned the king's power, 962
When the Present has latched its postern
    behind my tremulous stay, 736
While my hair was still cut straight across my
    forehead, 747
White, E. B., **1786–1800**, *1951–1957*
  The Essayist, 1788
  The Geese, 1795
  Once More to the Lake, *1777–1779*,
    1790–1791, 1791
  The Ring of Time, 1715, *1718–1719*,
    1748, *1789–1790*
Whitman, Walt:
  Crossing Brooklyn Ferry, 729
  A noiseless patient spider, 729

Whitman (*Cont.*):
  When I heard the learn'd astronomer, 517,
    525, 536–537, 545, *545*
Who says you're like one of the dog days?,
  573
Whose woods these are I think I know, 466,
  466–468, 516–517, 524, 525, 534,
  535–537, 662–664
"Why does your brand sae drap wi' bluid, 684
Wideman, John Edgar, *Stories Are Letters*,
  1993
Widmer, Kingsley, *On "The Horse Dealer's
  Daughter*," 138
Widow of Ephesus, The, 45, 47
Wilbur, Richard:
  The Death of a Toad, 776
  Junk, 540
Wild Nights—Wild Nights!, *637–638*, 643
Wild Swans at Coole, The, 741
Williams, William Carlos:
  The Dance, 548
  Danse Russe, 746
  Queen-Ann's-Lace, 614
  The Red Wheelbarrow, 542
  Spring and All, 746
  This Is Just to Say, 569
  The Use of Force, 1886, *1894–1895*, 1897,
    1899, *1902–1903*, *1905–1906*, 1911,
    1914–1915, 1918, 1921, *1924–1925*
Wilson, August, *Fences*, 1570
Wilt thou forgive that sin where I begun,
  505
Windhover, The, 737
Winters, Yvor, *Robert Frost: Or, the Spiritual
  Drifter as Poet*, 665
Wolf and the Mastiff, The, 44
Wolfe, Tom, *1737*
  The Right Stuff, 1859
Woman Or they, 770
Woman to Child, 508
Woman Warrior, 1803–1804
Women, 770
Woolf, Virginia:
  The Death of the Moth, 1749
  Old Mrs. Grey, 1780–1782, 1834

Word, The, 761
"*Word, The*," 1980
Wordsworth, William:
  *Composed upon Westminster Bridge,
    September 3, 1802*, 705
  It is a beauteous evening, 493
  I wandered lonely as a cloud, 490, *490–492*,
    503, 517, 537
  Lines, 705
  Poetry and Feeling, 1964
  The Solitary Reaper, 704
  The world is too much with us, 703
Work of Artifice, A, 791
Worn Path, A, 93
Wright, James:
  A Blessing, 779
  *Lying in a Hammock at William Duffy's
    Farm in Pine Island, Minnesota*, 779
Wright, Judith, *Woman to Child*, 508
Wyatt, Thomas, *They flee from me*, 686

Yeats, William Butler, *561*
  Adam's Curse, *561*
  A Dream of Death, 565
  An Irish Airman Foresees His Death, 520
  The Lake Isle of Innisfree, 499
  Leda and the Swan, 741
  The Magi, 593
  Purgatory, 976
  Sailing to Byzantium, 742
  The Second Coming, 740
  The Wild Swans at Coole, 741
Yellow Wallpaper, The, 291
Yellow Woman, 431
Yesterday, 607
Yesterday, all my troubles seemed so far
  away, 607
You come to fetch me from my work
  tonight, *657*, 674
Young Goodman Brown, 272
You said: "I'll go to another country, go to
  another shore, 551
You who were darkness warmed my flesh,
  508

Assignment

D. Ynnni - Plot

Guest of the Nation

Journal: Exposition
complication
climax
Falling Action
Resolution
Apply Each
to Guest
of the
Nation.